DUE DATE

THIS BOOK MAY BE
RECALLED BEFORE
ITS DUE DATE

The Catholic Encyclopedia

VOLUME FOURTEEN
Simony—Tournély

THE CATHOLIC ENCYCLOPEDIA

AN INTERNATIONAL WORK OF REFERENCE
ON THE CONSTITUTION, DOCTRINE,
DISCIPLINE, AND HISTORY OF THE
CATHOLIC CHURCH

EDITED BY
CHARLES G. HERBERMANN, Ph.D., LL.D.
EDWARD A. PACE, Ph.D., D.D.   CONDÉ B. PALLEN, Ph.D., LL.D.
THOMAS J. SHAHAN, D.D.   JOHN J. WYNNE, S.J.
ASSISTED BY NUMEROUS COLLABORATORS

IN FIFTEEN VOLUMES
VOLUME XIV

New York
ROBERT APPLETON COMPANY

Nihil Obstat, July 1, 1912

REMY LAFORT, S.T.D.
CENSOR

Imprimatur

✠ JOHN CARDINAL FARLEY
ARCHBISHOP OF NEW YORK

Copyright, 1912
BY ROBERT APPLETON COMPANY

The articles in this work have been written specially for The Catholic Encyclopedia and are protected by copyright. All rights, including the right of translation and reproduction, are reserved.

Contributors to the Fourteenth Volume

AHERNE, CORNELIUS, Rector, Professor of New Testament Exegesis, St. Joseph's College, Mill Hill, London: Son of God; Son of Man; Timothy and Titus, Epistles to.

ALBERS, P., S.J., Maastricht, Holland: Thijm, Joseph Albert Alberdingk; Thijm, Peter Paul Maria Alberdingk.

ÁLDÁSY, ANTAL, Ph.D., Archivist of the Library of the National Museum, Budapest: Sirmium, Diocese of; Steinamanger, Diocese of; Stuhlweissenburg, Diocese of; Szántó, Stephan; Szatmár, Diocese of; Szentiványi, Martin.

ALLARD, PAUL, Editor, "Revue des Questions Historiques", Paris: Slavery.

ALSTON, G. CYPRIAN, O.S.B., London: Solesmes, Abbey of.

AMADO, RAMÓN RUIZ, S.J., LL.D., Ph.L., College of St. Ignatius, Sarria, Barcelona: Spain; Tarazona, Diocese of; Tarragona, Archdiocese of; Teruel, Diocese of.

ARMFELT, CARL GUSTAF BARON, Stockholm, Sweden: Stockholm.

AYME, EDWARD L., M.D., New York: Toribio, Alfonso Mogrovejo, St.

BACCHUS, FRANCIS JOSEPH, B.A., The Oratory, Birmingham, England: Sophronius; Symmachus the Ebionite; Synesius of Cyrene; Theodoric Lector; Theonas; Theophilus, Bishop of Antioch; Three Chapters; Titus, Bishop of Bostra.

BAUMGARTEN, MGR. PAUL MARIA, J.U.D., S.T.D., Rome: Statistics, Ecclesiastical.

BAUR, CHRYSOSTOM, O.S.B., Ph.D. (Louvain), Collegio di San Anselmo, Rome: Theodore, Bishop of Mopsuestia; Theodoret; Theophilus, Patriarch of Alexandria.

BECHTEL, FLORENTINE, S.J., Professor of Hebrew and Sacred Scripture, St. Louis University, St. Louis: Susa; Tostado, Alonso.

BENIGNI, MGR. UMBERTO, Prothonotary Apostolic Participante, Professor of Ecclesiastical History, Pontificia Accademia dei Nobili Ecclesiastici, Rome: Sinigaglia, Diocese of; Solimôes Superiore; Sorrento, Archdiocese of; Sovana and Pitigliano, Diocese of; Spedalieri, Nicola; Spoleto, Archdiocese of; Squillace, Diocese of; Suburbicarian Dioceses; Susa, Diocese of; Syracuse, Archdiocese of; Tanucci, Bernardo; Taranto, Diocese of; Telese, Diocese of; Teramo, Diocese of; Termoli, Diocese of; Terracina, Sezze, and Piperno, Diocese of; Tivoli, Diocese of; Todi, Diocese of; Tortona, Diocese of.

BERTREUX, EPHREM M., S.M., Prefect Apostolic of the South Solomon Islands: Solomon Islands, Prefecture Apostolic of the Southern.

BERTRIN, GEORGES, Litt.D., Fellow of the University, Professor of French Literature, Institut Catholique, Paris: Swetchine, Sophie-Jeanne-Soymonof; Tassin, René-Prosper; Tillemont, Louis-Sébastian Le Nain de.

BESSE, J. M., O.S.B., Director, "Revue Mabillon", Chevetogne, Belgium: Thebaid.

BOLLAND, JOSEPH, S.J., Stonyhurst College, Blackburn, England: Soul; Spirit; Spiritualism.

BOSMANS, H., S.J., Collège Saint Michel, Brussels: Stevin, Simon.

BOUDINHON, AUGUSTE–MARIE, S.T.D., D.C.L., Director, "Canoniste Contemporain", Professor of Canon Law, Institut Catholique, Paris: Synods, National.

BRANTS, VICTOR, J.C.D., Member of the Royal Academy of Belgium, Louvain: Thonissen, Jean Joseph.

BRAUN, JOSEPH, S.J., St. Ignatius College, Valkenburg, Holland: Stole; Surplice; Tabernacle; Throne; Tiara.

BRÉHIER, EMILE, Litt.D., Rennes, France: Stoics and Stoic Philosophy; Tancred.

BROWN, CHARLES FRANCIS WEMYSS, Lochton Castle, Perthshire, Scotland: Thomas Abel, Blessed (sub-title Blessed Edward Powell).

BURTON, EDWIN, S.T.D., F.R. Hist. Soc., Vice-President, St. Edmund's College, Ware, England: Simpson, Richard; Smith, Richard, Bishop of Chalcedon; Smith, Richard; Sodor and Man, Ancient Diocese of; Spencer, The Hon. George; Stanyhurst, Richard; Stapleton, Theobald; Stapleton, Thomas; Stuart, Henry Benedict Maria Clement; Sutton, Sir Richard; Tatwin, Saint; Taxster, John de; Theobald, Archbishop of Canterbury; Thomas of Beckington; Thomas of Bradwardine; Thomas of Hereford, Saint; Thomas Percy, Blessed; Thompson, Edward Healy; Thompson, Harriet Diana; Tichborne, Thomas, Venerable; Tierney, Mark Aloysius; Tootell, Hugh; Touchet, George Anselm.

BUTLER, RICHARD URBAN, O.S.B., Downside Abbey, Bath, England: Sixtus IV, Pope.

CABROL, FERNAND, O.S.B., Abbot of St. Michael's, Farnborough, England: Terce.

CALLAN, CHARLES J., O.P., S.T.L., Professor of Philosophy, Dominican House of Studies, Washington: Slotanus, John; Soto, Dominic; Spina, Bartolommeo; Stephen of Bourbon.

CAMPBELL, WILLIAM EDWARD, Stratton-on-the-Fosse, Bath, England: Socialism.

CARDAUNS, HERMANN, Bonn: Spee, Friedrich von.

CONTRIBUTORS TO THE FOURTEENTH VOLUME

CASANOVA, GERTRUDE, O.S.B., Stanbrook Abbey, Worcester, England: Thecla, Saint.

CEDILLO, THE CONDE DE, Madrid: Toledo, Archdiocese of.

CHABOT, JEAN-BAPTISTE, S.T.D., Director of the "Corpus Scriptorum Christianorum Orientalium", Paris: Syriac Hymnody; Syriac Language and Literature.

CHAPMAN, JOHN, O.S.B., B.A. (Oxon.), Abbaye de St. Benoît, Maredsous, Namur, Belgium: Tertullian.

CHILTON, CARROLL B., London: Thompson, Francis.

CHISHOLM, JOSEPH ANDREW, K.C., M.A., LL.B., Halifax: Thompson, Right Honourable Sir John Sparrow David.

CLEARY, GREGORY, O.F.M., J.C.D., J. Civ.D., S.T.L., sometime Professor of Canon Law and Moral Theology, St. Isidore's College, Rome: Syndic, Apostolic.

COLEMAN, CARYL, B.A., Pelham Manor, New York: Spire; Stained Glass; Tapestry.

CORDIER, HENRI, Professor at the School for Oriental Living Languages, Paris: Taoism; Tibet.

COSSIO, ALUIGI, S.T.D., S.S.D., J.U.D., Baccalaureus and Licentiatus of the University of Padua, Rome: Titulus.

COTTER, A. C., S.J., Woodstock College, Maryland: Stattler, Benedict; Tamburini, Michelangelo; Tanner, Adam; Tanner, Matthias.

COYLE, MOIRA K., New York: Streber, Hermann.

CRIVELLI, CAMILLUS, S.J., Professor of Philosophy and History, Instituto Cientifico de San José, Guadalajara, Mexico: Sinaloa, Diocese of; Sonora, Diocese of; Tabasco, Diocese of; Tamaulipas, Diocese of; Tehuantepec, Diocese of; Tepic, Diocese of; Tlaxcala.

CUMMINGS, THOMAS F., S.T.D., Holyoke, Massachusetts: Springfield, Diocese of.

CUNNINGHAM, WILLIAM M., Chancellor of the Diocese of Southwark, England: Southwark, Diocese of.

CUTHBERT, FATHER, O.S.F.C., St. Anselm's House, Oxford: Theodosius Florentini; Third Order of St. Francis in Great Britain and Ireland.

DEBUCHY, PAUL, S.J., Litt.L., Enghien, Belgium: Spiritual Exercises of Saint Ignatius.

DEGERT, ANTOINE, Litt.D., Editor of "La Revue de la Gascoigne", Professor of Latin Literature, Institut Catholique, Toulouse: Sulpitius; Sylvius, Francis; Terrasson, André; Tournély, Honoré.

DELAMARRE, LOUIS N., Ph.D., Instructor in French, College of the City of New York: Thibaut de Champagne.

DELANY, JOSEPH F., S.T.D., New York: Slander, Sloth; Temperance; Temptation; Theft.

DELAUNAY, JOHN B., C.S.C., Rome: Syntagma Canonum.

DESMOND, DANIEL F., Huron, South Dakota: Sioux Falls, Diocese of.

DEVINE, ARTHUR, C.P., St. Saviour's Retreat, Worcestershire, England: State or Way, Purgative, Illuminative, Unitive.

DOHAN, EDWARD GEORGE, O.S.A., M.A., S.T.D., President of Villanova College, Villanova, Pennsylvania: Thomas of Villanova, Saint.

DOYLE, JOHN P. M., T.O.R., M.A., S.T.D., Rector of St. Francis College, Professor of Moral Theology, Loretto, Pennsylvania: Third Order of St. Francis, Province of the Sacred Heart of Jesus.

DRISCOLL, JAMES F., S.T.D., New Rochelle, New York: Stoning in Scripture; Terrestrial Paradise; Theocracy.

DRISCOLL, JOHN JOSEPH, S.J., Superior, Wisconsin: Superior, Diocese of.

DRISCOLL, JOHN THOMAS, M.A., S.T.L., Fonda, New York: Summer Schools, Catholic; Theosophy; Totemism.

DRUM, WALTER, S.J., Professor of Hebrew and Sacred Scripture, Woodstock College, Maryland: Solomon, Psalms of; Synagogue; Temple, Liturgy of the; Theology, Pastoral; Thessalonians, Epistles to the; Tobias.

DUBRAY, C.A., S.M., S.T.B., Ph.D., Professor of Philosophy, Marist College, Washington: Species; Teleology; Telepathy.

DUGGAN, THOMAS, Editor, "Catholic Transcript", Hartford, Connecticut: Tabb, John Bannister.

DUHEM, PIERRE, Professor of Theoretical Physics, University of Bordeaux: Thierry de Freiburg.

DUNIN-BORKOWSKI, Stanislaus, S.J., Bonn, Germany: Spinoza, Benedict.

DURAND, ALFRED, S.J., Professor of Scripture and Eastern Languages, Ore Place, Hastings, England: Testament, The New.

ENGELHARDT, ZEPHYRIN, O.F.M., Santa Barbara, California: Sitjar, Buenaventura; Tapis, Esteban.

FANNING, WILLIAM H. W., S.J., Professor of Church History and Canon Law, St. Louis University, St. Louis: Societies, Catholic; Societies, Secret; Solicitation; Subdeacon; Suspension; Synod; Tarquini, Camillus; Tenure, Ecclesiastical; Tithes; Tonsure.

FAULHABER, MICHAEL, S.T.D., Bishop of Speyer, Germany: Sophonias.

FENLON, JOHN F., S.S., S.T.D., President, St. Austin's College, Washington; Professor of Sacred Scripture, St. Mary's Seminary, Baltimore: Sulpicians in the United States.

CONTRIBUTORS TO THE FOURTEENTH VOLUME

*FERET, P. CANON, SAINT-MAURICE, FRANCE: Sorbonne.

FLADGATE, GERALDINE, LONDON: Stone, Mary Jean.

FLAHERTY, MATTHEW J., M.A. (HARVARD), CONCORD, MASSACHUSETTS: Stoddard, Charles Warren.

FORD, JEREMIAH D. M., M.A., PH.D., PROFESSOR OF FRENCH AND SPANISH LANGUAGES, HARVARD UNIVERSITY, CAMBRIDGE, MASSACHUSETTS: Spanish Language and Literature; Spanish-American Literature; Tassoni, Alessandro; Tebaldeo, Antonio; Tiraboschi, Girolamo.

FORTESCUE, ADRIAN, PH.D., S.T.D., LETCHWORTH, HERTFORDSHIRE, ENGLAND: Suidas; Synaxarion; Synaxis; Syrian Rite, West; Theodosius I; Ticonius.

FOX, JAMES J., S.T.D., PROFESSOR OF PHILOSOPHY, ST. THOMAS'S COLLEGE, WASHINGTON: Slavery, Ethical Aspect of.

FOX, JOHN M., S.J., WOODSTOCK COLLEGE, MARYLAND: Tamburini, Thomas; Tongiorgi, Salvator.

FOX, WILLIAM, B.Sc., M.E., ASSOCIATE PROFESSOR OF PHYSICS, COLLEGE OF THE CITY OF NEW YORK: Torricelli, Evangelista.

FUENTES, VENTURA, B.A., M.D., INSTRUCTOR, COLLEGE OF THE CITY OF NEW YORK: Téllez, Gabriel; Torres Naharro, Bartolomé de.

GALLAVRESI, GIUSEPPE, PROFESSOR OF MODERN HISTORY, ROYAL ACADEMY OF MILAN, MILAN: Tasso, Torquato; Tosti, Luigi.

GANSS, HENRY G., MUS.D., LANCASTER, PENNSYLVANIA: Tetzel, Johann.

GARRIGAN, PHILIP J., S.T.D., BISHOP OF SIOUX CITY, IOWA: Sioux City, Diocese of.

GAUTHEROT, GUSTAVE, LITT.D., PARIS: Talleyrand-Périgord, Charles-Maurice de.

GEUDENS, FRANCIS MARTIN, C.R.P., ABBOT TITULAR OF BARLINGS, TONGERLOO ABBEY, WESTERLOO, BELGIUM: Tongerloo, Abbey of.

GEYER, FRANCIS XAVIER, TITULAR BISHOP OF TROCMADÆ, VICAR-APOSTOLIC OF THE SUDAN, EGYPT: Sudan, Vicariate Apostolic of.

GIETMANN, GERHARD, S.J., TEACHER OF CLASSICAL LANGUAGES AND ÆSTHETICS, ST. IGNATIUS COLLEGE, VALKENBURG, HOLLAND: Stalls; Steinle, Eduard von.

GIGOT, FRANCIS E., S.T.D., PROFESSOR OF SACRED SCRIPTURE, ST. JOSEPH'S SEMINARY, DUNWOODIE, NEW YORK: Synoptics; Temptation of Christ.

GILLET, LOUIS, PARIS: Tisio da Garafalo, Benvenuto; Titian.

GOYAU, GEORGES, ASSOCIATE EDITOR, "REVUE DES DEUX MONDES", PARIS: Soissons, Diocese of; Tarbes, Diocese of; Tarentaise, Diocese of; Tellier, Michel Le; Thiers, Louis-Adolphe; Thou,

Jacques Auguste de; Thou, Nicholas de; Tocqueville, Charles Alexis-Henri-Maurice-Clerel de; Toulouse, Archdiocese of; Tours, Archdiocese of.

GRATTAN–FLOOD, W. H., M.R.I.A., MUS.D., ROSEMOUNT, ENNISCORTHY, IRELAND: Spontini, Gasparo Luigi Pacifico; Sullivan, Alexander Martin; Tallis, Thomas; Tassach, Saint; Taverner, John; Ternan, Saint; Thomas, Charles L. A.; Tigris, Saint.

GRISON, GABRIEL EMILE, TITULAR BISHOP OF SAGALASSE, VICAR APOSTOLIC OF STANLEY FALLS, BELGIAN CONGO, AFRICA: Stanley Falls, Vicariate Apostolic of.

HAAG, ANTHONY, S.J., ST. IGNATIUS COLLEGE, VALKENBURG, HOLLAND: Syllabus.

HAGEN, JOHN G., S.J., VATICAN OBSERVATORY, ROME: Tempel, Wilhelm.

HANSEN, NIELS, M.A., CHARLOTTENLUND, DENMARK: Steno, Nicolaus.

HARTIGAN, J. A., S.J., LITT.D., ORE PLACE, HASTINGS, ENGLAND: Tiberias, See of.

HEALY, PATRICK J., S.T.D., ASSISTANT PROFESSOR OF CHURCH HISTORY, CATHOLIC UNIVERSITY OF AMERICA, WASHINGTON: Socrates; Sozomen, Salamanius Hermias; Tatian.

HECKMANN, FERDINAND, O.F.M., ST. JOSEPH'S COLLEGE, CALLICOON, NEW YORK: Tertiaries; Third Order Secular of the Order of Our Lady of Mount Carmel; Third Order Regular of St. Dominic in the United States; Third Order Regular of St. Francis in the United States; Third Order Secular of St. Francis; Thomas of Celano.

HENRY, H. T., LITT.D., LL.D., RECTOR OF ROMAN CATHOLIC HIGH SCHOOL FOR BOYS, PHILADELPHIA; PROFESSOR OF ENGLISH LITERATURE AND GREGORIAN CHANT, ST. CHARLES'S SEMINARY, OVERBROOK, PENNSYLVANIA: Stabat Mater; Tantum Ergo; Te Deum; Te Lucis ante Terminum.

HERBERMANN, CHARLES G., PH.D., LL.D., LITT. D., K.S.G., PROFESSOR OF LATIN LANGUAGE AND LITERATURE, COLLEGE OF THE CITY OF NEW YORK: Thébaud, Augustus.

HILGERS, JOSEPH, S.J., ROME: Sodality.

HOLWECK, FREDERIC G., ST. LOUIS, MISSOURI: Sorrows of the Blessed Virgin Mary, Feasts of the Seven; Thorns, Feast of the Crown of.

HUDLESTON, GILBERT ROGER, O.S.B., DOWNSIDE ABBEY, BATH, ENGLAND: Stephen Harding, Saint; Thomas More, Blessed.

HUDSON, DANIEL E., C.S.C., LL.D., EDITOR, "THE AVE MARIA," NOTRE DAME, INDIANA: Sorin, Edward.

HUNTER–BLAIR, SIR D. O., BART., O.S.B., M.A., FORT AUGUSTUS ABBEY, SCOTLAND: Smith, James; Strain, John; Syon Monastery; Tarkin, Saint; Tavistock Abbey; Tewkesbury Abbey; Theodore, seventh Archbishop of Canterbury; Thorney Abbey; Tintern Abbey.

HUONDER, ANTHONY, S.J., ST. IGNATIUS COLLEGE, VALKENBURG, HOLLAND: Tieffentaller, Joseph.

* Deceased.

CONTRIBUTORS TO THE FOURTEENTH VOLUME

HUSSLEIN, JOSEPH, S.J., Associate Editor "America", New York: Syndicalism.

INGOLD, A. M. P., Director "Revue d'Alsace", Colmar, Germany: Thomassin, Louis.

IRWIN, FRANCIS, S.J., Stonyhurst College, Blackburn, England: Stonyhurst College.

JARRETT, BEDE, O.P., B.A. (Oxon.), S.T.L., St. Dominic's Priory, London: Third Orders, General; Third Order of St. Dominic.

JENKINS, REGINA RANDOLPH, Baltimore, Maryland: Tincker, Mary Agnes.

JENNER, HENRY, F.S.A., Late of the British Museum, London; Cornwall, England: Syrian Rite, East.

JOHNSON, WILLIAM T., Kansas City, Missouri: Test-Oath, Missouri.

JOUVE, ODORIC M., O.F.M., Candiac, Canada: Third Order of St. Francis in Canada.

KAMPERS, FRANZ, Ph.D., Professor of Medieval and Modern Church History, University of Breslau: Theodoric the Great.

KEATING, JOSEPH IGNATIUS PATRICK, S.J., B.A., Assistant Editor, "The Month", London: Temperance Movements, Great Britain and Ireland.

KEILEY, JARVIS, M.A., Grantwood, New Jersey: South Carolina.

KELLEY, FRANCIS C., S.T.D., LL.D., President, The Catholic Church Extension Society, Chicago, Illinois: Society, The Catholic Church Extension, in the United States.

KELLY, BLANCHE M., New York: Tabernacle Societies; Tegakwitha, Catherine.

KELLY, EDWARD, Grimbsy, Ontario, Canada: Toronto, Archdiocese of.

KEMPF, CONSTANTINE, S.J., Professor of Philosophy and Pedagogy, St. Ignatius College, Valkenburg, Holland: Theodicy.

KENNEDY, DANIEL J., O.P., S.T.M., Professor of Sacramental Theology, Catholic University of America, Washington: Thomas Aquinas, Saint; Thomism.

KERBY, WILLIAM J., S.T.L., Ph.D., Doctor of Special and Political Sciences, Professor of Sociology, Catholic University of America, Washington: Sociology.

KIRSCH, MGR. JOHANN P., S.T.D., Professor of Patrology and Christian Archæology, University of Fribourg, Switzerland: Simplicius, Saint, Pope; Siricius, Saint, Pope; Stedingers; Surius, Laurentius; Switzerland; Sylvester I, Saint, Pope; Sylvester II, Pope; Symmachus, Saint, Pope; Tarachus, Probus, and Andronicus, Saints; Tarasius, Saint; Tarsicius, Saint; Telesphorus, Saint, Pope; Thecla, Saints; Theodorus and Theophanes.

KLEINSCHMIDT, BEDA, O.F.M., Bonn, Germany: Solari; Stoss, Veit; Temple; Tissot, James Joseph; Tomb.

KRIEHN, GEORGE, A.B., Ph.D., New York: Stanza.

KROSE, HERMANN A., S.J., Editor-in-Chief, "Stimmen aus Maria-Laach", and "Kirchliches Handbuch für das katholische Deutschland", St. Ignatius College, Valkenburg, Holland: Statistics, Ecclesiastical, in Germany; Statistics of Religions.

LAUCHERT, FRIEDRICH, Ph.D., Aachen: Stapf, Joseph Ambrose; Staudenmaier, Franz Anton; Stöckl, Albert; Stolz, Alban Isidor.

LAUNAY, ADRIEN, Archivist of the Society for Foreign Missions, Paris: Society of Foreign Missions of Paris.

LE BACHELET, XAVIER–MARIE, S.J., Ore Place, Hastings, England: Terrien, Jean-Baptiste.

LECLERCQ, HENRI, O.S.B., London: Station Days.

LEHMKUHL, AUGUSTINUS, S.J., St. Ignatius College, Valkenburg, Holland: Theology, Moral.

LÉNARD, LEOPOLD, S.T.D., Ph.D., Klagenfurt, Austria: Slavs, The.

LE ROY, ALEXANDER A., C.SS.P., Bishop of Alinda, Superior-General of the Congregation of the Holy Ghost, Paris: Somaliland.

LETELLIER, A., S.S.S., Superior, Fathers of the Blessed Sacrament, New York: Society of the Blessed Sacrament, The.

LIESE, WILHELM ANTON, S.T.D., Paderborn, Germany: Temperance Movements.

LINDSAY, LIONEL ST. GEORGE, B.Sc., Ph.D., Editor-in-Chief, "La Nouvelle France", Quebec: Taché, Etienne-Pascal; Talon, Jean; Talon, Pierre; Tanguay, Cyprien; Tassé, Joseph.

LINEHAN, PAUL H., B.A., Instructor College of the City of New York: Tartaglia, Nicolò; Torrubia, José.

LINS, JOSEPH, Dorsten, Westphalia, Germany: Sion, Diocese of; Strasburg, Diocese of; Tiraspol, Diocese of.

LOEHR, AUGUST OCTAV RITTER von, Ph.D., Assistant Director of the Imperial Collection of Coins and Medals, Vienna: Streber, Franz Ignaz von; Streber, Franz Seraph.

LÖFFLER, KLEMENS, Ph.D., Librarian, University of Münster: Simplicius, Faustinus, and Beatrice; Speyer, Diocese of; Staphylus, Friedrich; Staupitz, Johann von; Stolberg, Joseph; Strossmayer, Joseph Georg; Studion; Syncretism; Tauler, John; Tepl; Tewdrig; Thalhofer, Valentin, Theiner, Augustin; Theobald, Saint; Theodard, Saint; Theodore of Studium, Saint; Theodulf; Thryäus, Hermann; Tiberius; Titus, Roman Emperor.

LORKIN, ELIZABETH MARY, L.R.A.M., Glasgow, Scotland: Stradivari, Antonio; Stradivari Family, The.

CONTRIBUTORS TO THE FOURTEENTH VOLUME

LYNCH, MGR. JAMES S.M., S.T.D., LL.D., UTICA, NEW YORK: Syracuse, Diocese of.

MAAS, A. J., S.J., RECTOR, WOODSTOCK COLLEGE, MARYLAND: Theology, Dogmatic, sub-title Christology.

MacERLEAN, ANDREW A., LL.B. (FORDHAM), NEW YORK: Societies, Catholic, American Federation of; Solsona, Diocese of; Stanislawow, Diocese of; Suitbert, Saint; Sumatra, Prefecture Apostolic of; Tinin, See of.

McGOVERN, JAMES J., LOCKPORT, ILLINOIS: Starr, Eliza Allen.

MACKSEY, CHARLES, S.J., PROFESSOR OF ETHICS AND NATURAL RIGHT, GREGORIAN UNIVERSITY, ROME: Society, State and Church; Taparelli, Aloysius; Tolomei, John Baptist.

McNEAL, J. PRESTON, A.B., LL.B., BALTIMORE: Taney, Roger Brooke.

McNEILL, CHARLES, DUBLIN: Tanner, Edmund.

MacPHERSON, EWAN, NEW YORK: Thalberg, Sigismond.

MAGNIER, JOHN, C.SS.R., ST. MARY'S, CLAPHAM, LONDON: Sportelli, Cæsar, Venerable.

MAHER, MICHAEL, S.J., LITT.D., M.A. (LONDON), DIRECTOR OF STUDIES AND PROFESSOR OF PEDAGOGICS, STONYHURST COLLEGE, BLACKBURN, ENGLAND: Soul; Spirit; Spiritualism.

MANN, HORACE K., HEADMASTER, ST. CUTHBERT'S GRAMMAR SCHOOL, NEWCASTLE-ON-TYNE, ENGLAND: Sisinnius, Pope; Stephen I, Saint, Pope; Stephen II, Pope; Stephen (II) III, Pope; Stephen (III) IV, Pope; Stephen (IV) V, Pope; Stephen (V) VI, Pope; Stephen (VI)VII, Pope; Stephen (VII) VIII, Pope; Stephen (VIII) IX, Pope; Stephen (IX) X, Pope; Theodore I; Theodore II.

MARCHAND, UBALD CANON, J.U.D., CHANCELLOR OF THE DIOCESE OF THREE RIVERS, PROVINCE OF QUEBEC, CANADA: Three Rivers, Diocese of.

MARY AGNES, SISTER, MOUNT ST. JOSEPH, OHIO: Sisters of Charity of Cincinnati, Ohio.

MARY PATRICK, MOTHER, CHICAGO, ILLINOIS: Sisters of the Little Company of Mary.

MEDLEYCOTT, A. E., S.T.D., TITULAR BISHOP OF TRICOMIA, CALCUTTA, INDIA: Thomas Christians, Saint.

MEEHAN, ANDREW B., S.T.D., J.U.D., PROFESSOR OF CANON LAW AND LITURGY, ST. BERNARD'S SEMINARY, ROCHESTER, NEW YORK: Stipend; Subreption; Subsidies, Episcopal; Supremi disciplinæ; Tametsi; Taxa Innocentiana.

MEEHAN, THOMAS F., NEW YORK: Sullivan, Peter John; Tenney, William Jewett; Thanksgiving Day; Thayer, John.

MEIER, GABRIEL, O.S.B., EINSIEDELN, SWITZERLAND: Tiburtius and Susanna, Sts.; Timotheus and Symphorian, Sts.

MEISTERMANN, BARNABAS, O.F.M., LECTOR. CONVENT OF S. SALVATOR, JERUSALEM: Temple of Jerusalem; Thabor, Mount; Tomb of the Blessed Virgin Mary.

MERK, AUGUST, S.J., PROFESSOR OF APOLOGETICS, ST. IGNATIUS COLLEGE, VALKENBURG, HOLLAND: Testament, The Old.

MERSHMAN, FRANCIS, O.S.B., S.T.D., PROFESSOR OF MORAL THEOLOGY, CANON LAW, AND LITURGY, ST. JOHN'S COLLEGE, COLLEGEVILLE, MINNESOTA; Solemnity; Stanislaus of Cracow, Saint; Stephen of Autun; Subiaco; Supper, The Last; Tanner, Conrad; Thais, Saint; Theodore of Amasea, Saint; Theodotus of Ancyra, Saint; Theophanes, Saint.

MOELLER, CH., PROFESSOR OF GENERAL HISTORY, UNIVERSITY OF LOUVAIN: Swan, Order of the; Templars, Knights, The; Teutonic Order.

MONTANAR, VALENTINE HILARY, MISSIONARY APOSTOLIC, NEW YORK: Sze-ch'wan, Eastern, Vicariate Apostolic of; Sze-ch'wan, Northwestern, Vicariate Apostolic of; Sze-ch'wan, Southern, Vicariate Apostolic of.

MOONEY, JAMES, UNITED STATES ETHNOLOGIST, BUREAU OF AMERICAN ETHNOLOGY, WASHINGTON: Sioux Indians; Sipibo Indians; Sobaipura Indians; Songish Indians; Spokan Indians; Squamish Indians; Swinomish Indians; Tacana Indians; Taensa Indians; Tait Indians; Tamanac Indians; Taos Pueblo; Thompson River Indians; Ticuna Indians; Timucua Indians; Toba Indians; Tonica Indians; Tonkawa Indians; Totonac Indians.

*MORAN, PATRICK FRANCIS CARDINAL, ARCHBISHOP OF SYDNEY, PRIMATE OF AUSTRALIA: Talbot, Peter.

MORENO-LACALLE, JULIAN, B.A., EDITOR, "PAN-AMERICAN UNION", WASHINGTON: Socorro, Diocese of; Spirito Santo, Diocese of; Taubaté, Diocese of.

MORICE, A. G., B.A., O.M.I., LECTURER IN ANTHROPOLOGY, UNIVERSITY OF SASKATCHEWAN, WINNIPEG, MANITOBA, CANADA: Slaves; Taché, Alexandre-Antonin; Takkali.

MULLALY, CHARLES, S.J., TORTOSA, SPAIN: Tortosa, Diocese of.

MUNNYNCK, MARK P. DE, S.T.D., PROFESSOR OF PHILOSOPHY, UNIVERSITY OF FRIBOURG: Space; Substance.

MUTZ, FRANZ XAVIER, S.T.D., ST. PETER'S SEMINARY, FREIBURG, BADEN, GERMANY: Theology, Ascetical.

NYS, DÉSIRÉ, S.T.B., PH.D., PRESIDENT SÉMINAIRE LÉON XIII, UNIVERSITY OF LOUVAIN, BELGIUM: Time.

O'CONNELL, JOHN T., LL.D., TOLEDO, OHIO: Toledo, Diocese of.

O'CONNOR, JOHN B., O.P., ST. LOUIS BERTRAND'S CONVENT, LOUISVILLE, KENTUCKY: Thomas of Cantimpré.

O'DONOVAN, LOUIS, S.T.L., BALTIMORE: Spalding, Martin John.

*Deceased.

CONTRIBUTORS TO THE FOURTEENTH VOLUME

O'GORMAN, JOHN R., S.T.L., J.C.D., Haileybury, Ontario, Canada: Temiskaming, Vicariate Apostolic of.

O'HARAN, MGR. DENIS F., S.T.D., Sydney, Australia: Sydney, Archdiocese of.

OLIGER, LIVARIUS, O.F.M., St. Bonaventure's College, Rome: Somaschi; Spirituals; Sporer, Patritius; Taigi, Anna Maria Gesualda Antonia; Tarabotti, Helena; Third Order of St. Francis (Regular and Secular; Male and Female).

O'NEILL, ARTHUR CHARLES, O.P., S.T.L., Professor of Theology, Dominican House of Studies, Washington: Sin.

O'SHEA, JOHN FRANCIS, Taylor, Texas: Texas, State of.

OTT, MICHAEL, O.S.B., Ph.D., Professor of the History of Philosophy, St. John's College, Collegeville, Minnesota: Sixtus I, Saint, Pope; Sixtus II, Saint, Pope; Sixtus V, Pope; Smaragdus, Ardo; Spinola, Christopher Royas de; Spondanus, Henri; Stadler, John Evangelist; Stefaneschi, Giacomo Gaetani; Stephen, Saint; Stephen of Tournai; Steuco, Agostino; Symphorosa, Saint; Syncelli; Telesphorus of Cosenza; Tencin, Pierre-Guérin de; Theophanes, Kerameus; Thundering Legion; Torquemada, Tomás de.

OTTEN, JOSEPH, Pittsburgh, Pennsylvania: Sistine Choir; Song, Religious; Tartini, Giuseppe.

OUSSANI, GABRIEL, Ph.D., Professor, Ecclesiastical History, Early Christian Literature, and Biblical Archæology, St. Joseph's Seminary, Dunwoodie, New York: Solomon; Syria.

PACE, EDWARD A., Ph.D., S.T.D., Professor of Philosophy, Catholic University of America, Washington: Spiritism.

PALLEN, CONDÉ BENOIST, A.M., Ph.D., LL.D., New Rochelle, New York: Testem Benevolentiæ.

PEREZ GOYENA, ANTONIO, S.J., Editor, "Razón y Fe", Madrid: Suarez, Francisco, Doctor Eximius; Toledo, Francisco; Torres, Francisco.

*PÉTRIDÈS, SOPHRONE, A.A., Professor, Greek Catholic Seminary of Kadi-Keui, Constantinople: Sinis; Sion; Sitifis; Soli; Sora; Sozopolis; Stratonicea; Sufetula; Sura; Syene; Synaus; Synnada; Tabæ; Tabbora; Tacapæ; Tadama; Tænarum; Tamassus; Tanagra; Tavium; Telmessus; Temnus; Teuchira; Thabraca; Thacia Montana; Thænæ; Thagaste; Thagora; Thapsus; Thaumaci; Themisonium; Thermæ Basilicæ; Thibaris; Thignica; Thmuis; Thuburbo; Tiberiopolis; Timbrias; Tingis; Tlos; Torone.

PHILLIPS, EDWARD C., S.J., Ph.D., Woodstock College, Maryland: Spagni, Andrea; Stansel, Valentin; Stephens, Henry Robert; Terill, Anthony.

POHLE, JOSEPH, S.T.D., Ph.D., J.C.L., Professor of Dogmatic Theology, University of Breslau: Theology, Dogmatic; Toleration, Religious.

POLLEN, JOHN HUNGERFORD, S.J., London: Society of Jesus; Spenser, John; Stevenson, Joseph; Stone, Marmaduke.

POPE, HUGH, O.P., S.T.L., Doctor of Sacred Scripture, Professor of New Testament Exegesis, Collegio Angelico, Rome: Socinianism.

POTAMIAN, BROTHER, F.S.C., D.Sc. (Lond.), Professor of Physics, Manhattan College, New York: Toaldo, Giuseppe.

POULAIN, AUGUSTIN, S.J., Paris: Stigmata, Mystical; Surin, Jean-Joseph; Theology, Mystical.

RAGONESI, FRANCESCO DI PAOLA, O.T., Superior-General of the Theatine Order, Rome: Theatines; Theatine Nuns.

RANDOLPH, BARTHOLOMEW, C.M., M.A., Teacher of Philosophy and Church History, St. John's College, Brooklyn, New York: Tamisier, Marie-Marthe-Baptistine.

REAGAN, P. NICHOLAS, O.F.M., Collegio S. Antonio, Rome: Sinai; Sodom and Gomorrha.

REILLY, THOMAS à K., O.P., S.T.D., S.S.L., Professor of Sacred Scripture, Dominican House of Studies, Washington: Tongues, Gift of.

REVILLE, JOHN CLEMENT, S.J., Professor of Rhetoric and Sacred Eloquence, St. Stanislaus College, Macon, Georgia: Taïon, Nicolas; Tornielli, Girolamo Francesco.

ROBINSON, DOANE, Secretary, South Dakota Department of History, Pierre, South Dakota: South Dakota.

ROBINSON, PASCHAL, O.F.M., New York: Spina, Alfonso de.

RODRIGUEZ MOURE, JOSE, LL.D., J.U.D., Teneriffe, Canary Islands: Teneriffe, Diocese of.

ROMPEL, JOSEF HEINRICH, S.J., Ph.D., Stella Matutina College, Feldkirch, Austria: Tournefort, Joseph Pitton de.

RYAN, JOHN A., S.T.D., Professor of Moral Theology, St. Paul Seminary, St. Paul, Minnesota: Socialistic Communities.

RYAN, PATRICK, S.J., London: Thomas Alfield, Venerable; Thomas Cottam, Blessed.

SACHER, HERMANN, Ph.D., Editor of the "Konversationslexikon", Assistant Editor, "Staatslexikon" of the Görresgesellschaft, Freiburg-im-Breisgau, Germany: Styria; Thuringia.

SALDANHA, JOSEPH LOUIS, B.A., Editor, "The Christian Puranna"; Professor of English, St. Aloysius College, Mangalore, India: Stephens, Thomas.

SANDS, HON. WILLIAM FRANKLIN, Chevalier of the Legion of Honour; Ex-Envoy Extraordinary and Minister Plenipotentiary of the United States to Guatemala; Member:

* Deceased.

CONTRIBUTORS TO THE FOURTEENTH VOLUME

OF THE AM. SOC. INTERNATIONAL LAW; AM. ACADEMY POLITICAL AND SOCIAL SCIENCE AND THE MEXICAN SOC. OF GEOGRAPHY AND STATISTICS, NEW YORK: Tahiti, Vicariate Apostolic of.

SCHEID, N., S.J., STELLA MATUTINA COLLEGE, FELDKIRCH, AUSTRIA: Spillmann, Joseph; Stifter, Adalbert.

SCHLAGER, HEINRICH PATRICIUS, O.F.M., ST. LUDWIG'S COLLEGE, DALHEIM, GERMANY: Sonnius, Franciscus; Thangmar; Thegan of Treves; Thurmayr, Johannes.

SCHMID, ULRICH, PH.D., EDITOR, "WALHALLA", MUNICH: Tegernsee.

SCHNÜRER, GUSTAV, PH.D., PROFESSOR OF MEDIEVAL AND MODERN HISTORY, UNIVERSITY OF FRIBOURG: States of the Church.

SCHÜHLEIN, FRANZ X., PROFESSOR IN THE GYMNASIUM OF FREISING, BAVARIA, GERMANY: Talmud; Targum; Torah; Tosephta.

SCHUYLER, HENRY C., S.T.L., VICE-RECTOR, CATHOLIC HIGH SCHOOL, PHILADELPHIA, PENNSYLVANIA: Steinmeyer, Ferdinand.

SCULLY, JOHN, S.J., NEW YORK: Squiers, Herbert Goldsmith.

SCULLY, VINCENT JOSEPH, C.R.L., ST. IVES, CORNWALL, ENGLAND: Thomas à Kempis; Thomas of Jesus.

SENFELDER, LEOPOLD, M.D., TEACHER OF THE HISTORY OF MEDICINE, UNIVERSITY OF VIENNA: Skoda, Josef; Sorbait, Paul de.

SHAHAN, MGR. THOMAS J., S.T.D., J.U.D., RECTOR OF THE CATHOLIC UNIVERSITY OF AMERICA, WASHINGTON: Thomas Abel, Blessed.

SHANLEY, WALTER J., LL.D., DANBURY, CONNECTICUT: Temperance Movements in the United States and Canada.

SHIPMAN, ANDREW J., M.A., LL.M., NEW YORK: Slavonic Language and Liturgy; Slavs in America.

SILVA COTAPOS, CARLOS, CANON OF THE CATHEDRAL OF SANTIAGO, CHILE: Tarapacá, Vicariate Apostolic of.

SINKMAJER, JOS., EAST ISLIP, NEW YORK: Strahov, Abbey of.

SLATER, T., S.J., ST. FRANCIS XAVIER'S COLLEGE, LIVERPOOL, ENGLAND: Speculation; Sunday; Synderesis.

SLOANE, THOMAS O'CONOR, M.A., E.M., PH.D., NEW YORK: Thénard, Louis-Jacques, Baron.

SMITH, IGNATIUS, O.P., DOMINICAN HOUSE OF STUDIES, WASHINGTON: Thomas of Jorz.

SMITH, WALTER GEORGE, M.A., LL.B., (U. OF P.), PHILADELPHIA, PENNSYLVANIA: Smith, Thomas Kilby.

SOLLIER, JOSEPH FRANCIS, S.M., S.T.D., PROVINCIAL OF THE AMERICAN PROVINCE OF THE SOCIETY OF MARY, WASHINGTON: Supernatural Order; Theophilanthropists.

SORTAIS, GASTON, S.J., ASSOCIATE EDITOR, "ETUDES", PARIS: Tintoretto, Il.

SOUVAY, CHARLES L., C.M., S.T.D., PH.D., S.S.D., PROFESSOR, SACRED SCRIPTURE, HEBREW AND LITURGY, KENRICK SEMINARY, ST. LOUIS: Stephen, Saint; Stones, Precious, in the Bible; Tabernacle in Scripture; Tabernacles, Feast of.

SPAHN, MARTIN, PH.D., PROFESSOR OF MODERN HISTORY, UNIVERSITY OF STRASBURG: Thirty Years War, The; Tilly, Johannes Tserclæs, Count of.

SPILLANE, EDWARD P., S.J., ASSOCIATE EDITOR, "AMERICA", NEW YORK: Thimelby, Richard.

STEELE, FRANCESCA M., STROUD, GLOUCESTERSHIRE, ENGLAND: Taylor, Frances Margaret; Temple, Sisters of the.

STEICHEN, MICHAEL, MISSIONARY APOSTOLIC, TOKIO, JAPAN: Tokio, Archdiocese of.

STREICHER, FRIEDRICH, S.J., STELLA MATUTINA COLLEGE, FELDKIRCH, AUSTRIA: Toscanelli, Paolo dal Pozzo.

STUART, JANET, R.S.H., SUPERIOR VICAR, CONVENT OF THE SACRED HEART, ROEHAMPTON, LONDON: Society of the Sacred Heart of Jesus, The.

TARNOWSKI, COUNT STANISLAUS, PRESIDENT, IMPERIAL ACADEMY OF SCIENCES, PROFESSOR, POLISH LITERATURE, UNIVERSITY OF CRACOW: Skarga, Peter; Sobieski, John; Starowolski, Simon; Szujski, Joseph; Szymonowicz, Simon.

TAVERNIER, EUGENE, PARIS: Soloviev, Vladimir.

TETU, MGR HENRI, QUEBEC, CANADA: Taschereau, Elzéar-Alexandre.

THURSTON, HERBERT, S.J., LONDON: Southwell, Robert, Venerable; Stone, Corner or Foundation; Stylites; Symbolism; Tenebræ; Thanksgiving before and after Meals; Theatre, The; Thomas, Saint, the Apostle; Thomas Becket, Saint; Toleration, History of.

TOKE, LESLIE ALEXANDER ST. LAURENCE, B.A., STRATTON-ON-THE-FOSSE, BATH, ENGLAND: Socialism.

TURNER, MGR. JAMES P., S.T.D., PHILADELPHIA, PENNSYLVANIA: Tabernacle Society.

TURNER, WILLIAM, B.A., S.T.D., PROFESSOR OF LOGIC AND THE HISTORY OF PHILOSOPHY, CATHOLIC UNIVERSITY OF AMERICA, WASHINGTON: Socrates; Sophists; Summæ; Sylvester, Bernard; Telesio, Bernardino; Theodore of Gaza; Theodoric of Chartres; Thomas of Strasburg.

TYNE, THOMAS JAMES, NASHVILLE, TENNESSEE: Tennessee.

VACCON, A., AMIENS, FRANCE: Tarisel, Pierre.

VAILHÉ, SIMÉON, A.A., MEMBER OF THE RUSSIAN ARCHÆOLOGICAL INSTITUTE OF CONSTANTINOPLE, ROME: Sinope; Siunia; Smyrna, Latin Archdiocese of; Sophene; Sozusa; Sparta; Stauropolis; Syra, Diocese of; Tanis; Tarsus; Tenedos; Tentyris; Teos; Terenuthis; Termessus; Thasos; Thebes (Achaia Secunda); Thebes (Thebais Secunda); Thelepte; Themiscyra; Thennesus; Theodosiopolis; Thera, Diocese of; Thermopylæ; Thessalonica; Theveste; Thugga; Thyatira; Thynias; Tiberias; Ticelia; Tinos and Mykonos; Tipasa; Titopolis; Tius; Tomi.

VAN DER HEEREN, ACHILLE, S.T.L. (LOUVAIN), PROFESSOR OF MORAL THEOLOGY AND LIBRARIAN, GRANDE SÉMINAIRE, BRUGES, BELGIUM: Suicide.

VAN ORTROY, FRANCIS, S.J., BRUSSELS: Stanislas Kostka, Saint.

VASCHALDE, A.A., C.S.B., CATHOLIC UNIVERSITY OF AMERICA, WASHINGTON: Tell el-Amarna Tablets, The.

WAINEWRIGHT, JOHN BANNERMAN, B.A. (OXON.), LONDON: Slythurst, Thomas; Snow, Peter, Venerable; Somerset, Thomas; Southerne, William, Venerable; Southworth, John, Venerable; Speed, John, Venerable; Spenser, William, Venerable; Sprott, Thomas, Venerable; Stonnes, James; Stransham, Edward, Venerable; Sugar, John, Venerable; Sutton, Robert, Venerable; Talbot, John; Taylor, Hugh, Venerable; Teilo, Saint; Teresian Martyrs of Compiègne, The Sixteen Blessed; Thomas Ford, Blessed; Thomas Johnson, Blessed; Thomas of Dover; Thomas Woodhouse, Blessed; Thorpe, Robert, Venerable; Thulis, John, Venerable; Tichborne, Nicholas, Venerable.

WALLAU, HEINRICH WILHELM, MAINZ, GERMANY: Speyer, Johann and Wendelin von; Sweynheim, Konrad.

WALSH, JAMES A., MISSIONARY APOSTOLIC, DIRECTOR OF THE CATHOLIC FOREIGN MISSIONARY SOCIETY OF AMERICA, HAWTHORNE, NEW YORK: Théophane Vénard, Blessed.

WALSH, JAMES J., M.D., PH.D., LL.D., D.SC., DEAN OF THE MEDICAL SCHOOL, FORDHAM UNIVERSITY, NEW YORK: Spallanzani, Lazzaro.

WALTER, ALOYSIUS, C.SS.R., ROME: Steffani, Agostino.

WARD, MGR. BERNARD, CANON OF WESTMINSTER, F. R. HIST. SOC., PRESIDENT, ST. EDMUND'S COLLEGE, WARE, ENGLAND: Talbot, James; Taunton, Ethelred.

WARICHEZ, JOSEPH, DOCTEUR EN SCIENCES MORALES ET HISTORIQUES, ARCHIVIST OF THE DIOCESE OF TOURNAI, BELGIUM: Tournai, Diocese of.

WEBER, N. A., S.M., S.T.D., PROFESSOR OF CHURCH HISTORY, MARIST COLLEGE, WASHINGTON: Simony; Sirleto, Guglielmo; Sirmond, Jacques; Sixtus III, Saint, Pope; Smalkaldic League; Sophronius, Saint; Suger, Abbot of St. Denis; Sully, Maurice de; Sulpicius Severus; Swedenborgians.

WEBSTER, D. RAYMOND, O.S.B., M.A. (OXON.), DOWNSIDE ABBEY, BATH, ENGLAND: Stephen of Muret, Saint; Swithin, Saint; Sylvester Gozzolini, Saint; Sylvestrines.

WELD–BLUNDELL, EDWARD BENEDICT, O.S.B., STANBROOK, ENGLAND: Stanbrook Abbey.

WHITFIELD, JOSEPH LOUIS, M.A. (CANTAB.), OSCOTT COLLEGE, BIRMINGHAM, ENGLAND: Sykes, Edmund; Talbot, Thomas Joseph; Thomas Sherwood, Blessed; Thwing, Thomas, Venerable.

WILHELM, JOSEPH, S.T.D., PH.D., AACHEN, GERMANY: Superstition.

WILLIAMSON, GEORGE CHARLES, LITT.D., LONDON: Sodoma; Stanfield, William Clarkson; Teniers, David; Theotocopuli, Domenico; Tibaldi, Pellegrino; Tiepolo, Giovanni Battista; Torbido, Francesco.

WITTMANN, PIUS, ARCHIVIST FOR THE PRINCES AND COUNTS OF THE HOUSE OF YSENBURG-BÜDINGEN; ROYAL BAVARIAN ARCHIVIST, BÜDINGEN, GERMANY: Snorri Sturluson; Stolberg, Friedrich Leopold, Count zu; Sweden.

WOLFSGRUBER, COELESTINE, O.S.B., VIENNA: Spalato-Macarsca, Diocese of; Tarnow, Diocese of; Thugut, Johann Amadeus; Franz de Paula; Thun Hohenstein, Count Leo.

WÖRNDLE VON ADELSFRIED, HEINRICH, INNSBRUCK, AUSTRIA: Speckbacher, Josef.

ZIMMERMAN, BENEDICT, O.D.C., ST. LUKE'S PRIORY, WINCANTON, SOMERSETSHIRE, ENGLAND: Teresa of Jesus, Saint; Third Order of Our Lady of Mount Carmel; Thomas à Jesu.

ZUPAN, CYRIL, O.S.B., PUEBLO, COLORADO: Slomsek, Anton Martin.

Tables of Abbreviations

The following tables and notes are intended to guide readers of THE CATHOLIC ENCYCLOPEDIA in interpreting those abbreviations, signs, or technical phrases which, for economy of space, will be most frequently used in the work. For more general information see the article ABBREVIATIONS, ECCLESIASTICAL.

I.—GENERAL ABBREVIATIONS.

a. . . . . article.
ad an. . . . . at the year (Lat. *ad annum*).
an., ann. . . . . the year, the years (Lat. *annus, anni*).
ap. . . . . in (Lat. *apud*).
art. . . . . article.
Assyr. . . . . Assyrian.
A. S. . . . . Anglo-Saxon.
A. V. . . . . Authorized Version (i.e. tr. of the Bible authorized for use in the Anglican Church—the so-called "King James", *or* "Protestant Bible").
b. . . . . born.
Bk. . . . . Book.
Bl. . . . . Blessed.
C., c. . . . . about (Lat. *circa*); canon; chapter; *compagnie*.
can. . . . . canon.
cap. . . . . chapter (Lat. *caput*—used only in Latin context).
cf. . . . . compare (Lat. *confer*).
cod. . . . . codex.
col. . . . . column.
concl. . . . . conclusion.
const., constit. . . . Lat. *constitutio*.
curâ. . . . . by the industry of.
d. . . . . died.
dict. . . . . dictionary (Fr. *dictionnaire*).
disp. . . . . Lat. *disputatio*.
diss. . . . . Lat. *dissertatio*.
dist. . . . . Lat. *distinctio*.
D. V. . . . . Douay Version.
ed., edit. . . . . edited, edition, editor.
Ep., Epp. . . . . letter, letters (Lat. *epistola*).
Fr. . . . . French.
gen. . . . . genus.
Gr. . . . . Greek.
H. E., Hist. Eccl. . . Ecclesiastical History.
Heb., Hebr. . . . . . . Hebrew.
ib., ibid. . . . . in the same place (Lat. *ibidem*).
Id. . . . . the same person, *or* author (Lat *idem*).
inf. . . . . below (Lat. *infra*).
It. . . . . Italian.
l. c., loc. cit. . . . . . at the place quoted (Lat. *loco citato*).
Lat. . . . . Latin.
lat. . . . . latitude.
lib. . . . . book (Lat. *liber*).
long. . . . . longitude.
Mon. . . . . Lat. *Monumenta*.
MS., MSS. . . . . manuscript, manuscripts.
n., no. . . . . number.
N. T. . . . . New Testament.
Nat. . . . . National.
Old Fr., O. Fr. . . . Old Frencl.
op. cit. . . . . in the work quoted (Lat. *opere citato*).
Ord. . . . . Order.
O. T. . . . . Old Testament.
p., pp. . . . . page, pages, *or* (in Latin references) *pars* (part).
par. . . . . paragraph.
passim. . . . . in various places.
pt. . . . . part.
Q. . . . . Quarterly (a periodical), e.g. "Church Quarterly".
Q., QQ., quæst. . . . question, questions (Lat. *quæstio*).
q. v. . . . . which [title] see (Lat. *quod vide*).
Rev. . . . . Review (a periodical).
R. S. . . . . Rolls Series.
R. V. . . . . Revised Version.
S., SS. . . . . Lat. *Sanctus, Sancti*, "Saint", "Saints"—used in this Encyclopedia only in Latin context.
Sept. . . . . Septuagint.
Sess. . . . . Session.
Skt. . . . . Sanskrit.
Sp. . . . . Spanish.
sq., sqq. . . . . following page, *or* pages (Lat. *sequens*).
St., Sts. . . . . Saint, Saints.
sup. . . . . Above (Lat. *supra*).
s. v. . . . . Under the corresponding title (Lat. *sub voce*).
tom. . . . . volume (Lat. *tomus*).

xiii

TABLES OF ABBREVIATIONS.

tr. . . . . translation *or* translated. By itself it means "English translation", *or* "translated into English by". Where a translation is into any other language, the language is stated.
tr., tract. . . . . tractate.
v. . . . . see (Lat. *vide*).
Ven. . . . . Venerable.
Vol. . . . . Volume.

II.—Abbreviations of Titles.

Acta SS. . . . . *Acta Sanctorum* (Bollandists).
Ann. pont. cath. . . . . Battandier, *Annuaire pontifical catholique*.
Bibl. Dict. Eng. Cath. Gillow, Bibliographical Dictionary of the English Catholics.
Dict. Christ. Antiq. . . Smith and Cheetham (ed.), Dictionary of Christian Antiquities.
Dict. Christ. Biog. . . Smith and Wace (ed.), Dictionary of Christian Biography.
Dict. d'arch. chrét. . . Cabrol (ed.), *Dictionnaire d'archéologie chrétienne et de liturgie*.
Dict. de théol. cath. . Vacant and Mangenot (ed.), *Dictionnaire de théologie catholique*.
Dict. Nat. Biog. . . . . Stephen and Lee (ed.), Dictionary of National Biography.
Hast., Dict. of the Bible . . . . Hastings (ed.), A Dictionary of the Bible.
Kirchenlex. . . . . Wetzer and Welte, *Kirchenlexicon*.
P. G. . . . . Migne (ed.), *Patres Græci*.
P. L. . . . . Migne (ed.), *Patres Latini*.
Vig., Dict. de la Bible. Vigouroux (ed.), *Dictionnaire de la Bible*.

Note I.—Large Roman numerals standing alone indicate volumes. Small Roman numerals standing alone indicate chapters. Arabic numerals standing alone indicate pages. In other cases the divisions are explicitly stated. Thus "Rashdall, Universities of Europe, I, ix" refers the reader to the ninth chapter of the first volume of that work; "I, p. ix" would indicate the ninth page of the preface of the same volume.

Note II.—Where St. Thomas (Aquinas) is cited without the name of any particular work the reference is always to "Summa Theologica" (not to "Summa Philosophiæ"). The divisions of the "Summa Theol." are indicated by a system which may best be understood by the following example: "I-II, Q. vi, a. 7, ad 2 um" refers the reader to the *seventh* article of the *sixth* question in the *first* part of the *second* part, in the response to the *second* objection.

Note III.—The abbreviations employed for the various books of the Bible are obvious. Ecclesiasticus is indicated by *Ecclus.*, to distinguish it from Ecclesiastes (*Eccles.*). It should also be noted that I and II Kings in D. V. correspond to I and II Samuel in A. V.; and I and II Par. to I and II Chronicles. Where, in the spelling of a proper name, there is a marked difference between the D. V. and the A. V., the form found in the latter is added, in parentheses.

Full Page Illustrations in Volume XIV

	PAGE
Interior of the Church of the Gesù, Rome	84
Sorrento—Road from Sorrento to Positano, etc.	150
Spain—A Chapel in the Cathedral of Sigüenza, etc.	170
East End of the Cathedral, Segovia	176
Spain—The Alcalá Gate, Madrid, etc.	190
Spalato—Interior of the Cathedral, etc.	206
The Cathedral of Notre-Dame, Chartres	220
Stalls—Church of the Frari, Venice, etc.	242
Stonyhurst College	308
Subiaco—Church of St. Scholastica, etc.	322
The Last Supper—E. von Gebhardt	340
The Cathedral of San Lorenzo, Lugano	360
Constantine holding the Bridle of St. Sylvester's Horse	370
Tasso's Cell in the Convent of S. Onofrio, Rome	464
Theodoric's Tomb, Ravenna	576
Burial of the Conde D'Orgaz—Theotocopuli	628
St. Thomas Aquinas among the Doctors of the Church—Zurbaran	670
Blessed Thomas More—Rubens	692
Episcopal Throne, Church of SS. Nereo ed Achilleo, Rome	708
Tintern Abbey, Monmouth	736
Titian—A Knight of Malta, etc.	744
Tivoli—Medieval Castle, etc.	746
Alcantara Bridge, Toledo	758
Altar-tomb of the Emperor Maximilian I	772

Coloured Plates

Sixtus IV giving audience to the Historian Platina—M. da Forli	32
The Surrender of Breda—Velasquez	180
The Repose in Egypt—Flemish Wool and Gold Tapestry	448
The Kitchen—Teniers the Younger	508

Maps

Spain and Portugal	200
States of the Church	266
Switzerland and Liechtenstein	364

THE CATHOLIC ENCYCLOPEDIA

S

Simony (from Simon Magus; Acts, viii, 18-24) is usually defined "a deliberate intention of buying or selling for a temporal price such things as are spiritual or annexed unto spirituals". While this definition only speaks of purchase and sale, any exchange of spiritual for temporal things is simoniacal. Nor is the giving of the temporal as the price of the spiritual required for the existence of simony; according to a proposition condemned by Innocent XI (Denzinger-Bannwart, no. 1195) it suffices that the determining motive of the action of one party be the obtaining of compensation from the other. The various temporal advantages which may be offered for a spiritual favour are, after Gregory the Great, usually divided into three classes. These are: (1) the *munus a manu* (material advantage), which comprises money, all movable and immovable property, and all rights appreciable in pecuniary value; (2) the *munus a lingua* (oral advantage) which includes oral commendation, public expressions of approval, moral support in high places; (3) the *munus ab obsequio* (homage) which consists in subserviency, the rendering of undue services, etc. The spiritual object includes whatever is conducive to the eternal welfare of the soul, i. e. all supernatural things: sanctifying grace, the sacraments, sacramentals, etc. While according to the natural and Divine laws the term simony is applicable only to the exchange of supernatural treasures for temporal advantages, its meaning has been further extended through ecclesiastical legislation. In order to preclude all danger of simony the Church has forbidden certain dealings which did not fall under Divine prohibition. It is thus unlawful to exchange ecclesiastical benefices by private authority, to accept any payment whatever for holy oils, to sell blessed rosaries or crucifixes. Such objects lose, if sold, all the indulgences previously attached to them (S. Cong. of Indulg., 12 July, 1847). Simony of ecclesiastical law is, of course, a variable element, since the prohibitions of the Church may be abrogated or fall into disuse. Simony whether it be of ecclesiastical or Divine law, may be divided into mental, conventional, and real (*simonia mentalis, conventionalis, et realis*). In mental simony there is lacking the outward manifestation, or, according to others, the approval on the part of the person to whom a proposal is made. In conventional simony an expressed or tacit agreement is entered upon. It is subdivided into merely conventional, when neither party has fulfilled any of the terms of the agreement, and mixed conventional, when one of the parties has at least partly complied with the assumed obligations. To the latter subdivision may be referred what has been aptly termed "confidential simony", in which an ecclesiastical benefice is procured for a certain person with the understanding that later he will either resign in favour of the one through whom he obtained the position or divide with him the revenues. Simony is called real when the stipulations of the mutual agreement have been either partly or completely carried out by both parties.

To estimate accurately the gravity of simony, which some medieval ecclesiastical writers denounced as the most abominable of crimes, a distinction must be made between the violations of the Divine law, and the dealings contrary to ecclesiastical legislation. Any transgression of the law of God in this matter is, objectively considered, grievous in every instance (*mortalis ex toto genere suo*). For this kind of simony places on a par things supernatural and things natural, things eternal and things temporal, and constitutes a sacrilegious depreciation of Divine treasures. The sin can become venial only through the absence of the subjective dispositions required for the commission of a grievous offense. The merely ecclesiastical prohibitions, however, do not all and under all circumstances impose a grave obligation. The presumption is that the church authority, which, in this connexion, sometimes prohibits actions in themselves indifferent, did not intend the law to be grievously binding in minor details. As he who preaches the gospel "should live by the gospel" (I Cor., ix, 14) but should also avoid even the appearance of receiving temporal payment for spiritual services, difficulties may arise concerning the propriety or sinfulness of remuneration in certain circumstances. The ecclesiastic may certainly receive what is offered to him on the occasion of spiritual ministrations, but he cannot accept any payment for the same. The celebration of Mass for money would, consequently, be sinful; but it is perfectly legitimate to accept a stipend offered on such occasion for the support of the celebrant. The amount of the stipend, varying for different times and countries, is usually fixed by ecclesiastical authority (see STIPEND). It is allowed to accept it even should the priest be otherwise well-to-do; for he has a right to live from the altar and should avoid becoming obnoxious to other members of the clergy. It is simoniacal to accept payment for the exercise of ecclesiastical jurisdiction, e. g., the granting of dispensations; but there is nothing improper in demanding from the applicants for matrimonial dispensations a contribution intended partly as a chancery fee and partly as a salutary fine calculated to prevent the too frequent recurrence of such requests. It is likewise simony to accept temporal compensation for admission into a religious order; but contributions made by candidates to defray the expenses of their novitiate as well as the dowry required by some female orders are not included in this prohibition.

In regard to the parish clergy, the poorer the church, the more urgent is the obligation incumbent upon the faithful to support them. In the fulfilment of this duty local law and custom ought to be observed. The Second Plenary Council of Baltimore has framed the following decrees for the United

States: (1) The priest may accept what is freely offered after the administration of baptism or matrimony, but should refrain from asking anything (no. 221). (2) The confessor is never allowed to apply to his own use pecuniary penances, nor may he ask or accept anything from the penitent in compensation of his services. Even voluntary gifts must be refused, and the offering of Mass stipends in the sacred tribunal cannot be permitted (no. 289). (3) The poor who cannot be buried at their own expense should receive free burial (no. 393). The Second and Third Plenary Councils of Baltimore also prohibited the exaction of a compulsory contribution at the church entrance from the faithful who wish to hear Mass on Sundays and Holy Days (Conc. Plen. Balt. II, no. 397; Conc. Plen. Balt. III, no. 288). As this practice continued in existence in many churches until very recently, a circular letter addressed 29 Sept., 1911, by the Apostolic Delegate to the archbishops and bishops of the United States, again condemns the custom and requests the ordinaries to suppress it wherever found in existence.

To uproot the evil of simony so prevalent during the Middle Ages, the Church decreed the severest penalties against its perpetrators. Pope Julius II declared simoniacal papal elections invalid, an enactment which has since been rescinded, however, by Pope Pius X (Constitution "Vacante Sede", 25 Dec., 1904, tit. II, cap. vi, in "Canoniste Contemp.", XXXII, 1909, 291). The collation of a benefice is void if, in obtaining it, the appointee either committed simony himself, or at least tacitly approved of its commission by a third party. Should he have taken possession, he is bound to resign and restore all the revenues received during his tenure. Excommunication simply reserved to the Apostolic See is pronounced in the Constitution "Apostolicæ Sedis" (12 Oct., 1869): (1) against persons guilty of real simony in any benefices and against their accomplices; (2) against any persons, whatsoever their dignity, guilty of confidential simony in any benefices; (3) against such as are guilty of simony by purchasing or selling admission into a religious order; (4) against all persons inferior to the bishops, who derive gain (*quæstum facientes*) from indulgences and other spiritual graces; (5) against those who, collecting stipends for Masses, realize a profit on them by having the Masses celebrated in places where smaller stipends are usually given. The last-mentioned provision was supplemented by subsequent decrees of the Sacred Congregation of the Council. The Decree "Vigilanti" (25 May, 1893) forbade the practice indulged in by some booksellers of receiving stipends and offering exclusively books and subscriptions to periodicals to the celebrant of the Masses. The Decree "Ut Debita" (11 May, 1904) condemned the arrangements according to which the guardians of shrines sometimes devoted the offerings originally intended for Masses partly to other pious purposes. The offenders against the two decrees just mentioned incur suspension *ipso facto* from their functions if they are in sacred orders; inability to receive higher orders if they are clerics inferior to the priests; excommunication of pronounced sentence (*latæ sententiæ*) if they belong to the laity.

BALLERINI-PALMIERI, *Opus Theologicum Morale*, II (Prato, 1890), 306–74; LEHMKUHL, *Theologia Moralis* (11th ed., Freiburg, 1910), I, 297–308; II, 707–09; GÉNICOT-SALSMANS (6th ed., Brussels, 1909), 237–44; SLATER, *Manual of Moral Theology*, I (3rd ed., New York, 1909), 231–35; *Corpus Juris Canonici Decreti Gratiani*, pars IIa, causa I; *Decret. Greg.*, lib. V, tit. 3, De Simonia; *Extrav. commun.*, lib. V, tit. 1, De Simonia; SANTI-LEITNER, *Prælectiones Juris Canonici* (4th ed., Ratisbon, 1905). lib. V, 10–49; CRAISSON, *Manuale Totius Juris Canonici*, IV (8th ed., Paris, 1894), 230–52; LEINZ, *Die Simonie* (Freiburg, 1902); BARRY, *Spiritual Ministrations as an Occasion of Emolument* in *Ecclesiastical Review*, XXXIX (1908), 234–45; WEBER, *A History of Simony in the Christian Church* (Baltimore, 1909).

N. A. WEBER.

Simple (SIMPLEX). See FEASTS, ECCLESIASTICAL.

Simplicius, SAINT, POPE (468–483), date of birth unknown; d. 10 March, 483. According to the "Liber Pontificalis" (ed. Duchesne, I, 249) Simplicius was the son of a citizen of Tivoli named Castinus; and after the death of Pope Hilarius in 468 was elected to succeed the latter. The elevation of the new pope was not attended with any difficulties. During his pontificate the Western Empire came to an end. Since the murder of Valentinian III (455) there had been a rapid succession of insignificant emperors in the Western Roman Empire, who were constantly threatened by war and revolution. Following other German tribes the Heruli entered Italy, and their ruler Odoacer put an end to the Western Empire by deposing the last emperor, Romulus Augustulus, and assuming himself the title of King of Italy. Although an Arian, Odoacer treated the Catholic Church with much respect; he also retained the greater part of the former administrative organization, so that the change produced no great differences at Rome. During the Monophysite controversy, that was still carried on in the Eastern Empire, Simplicius vigorously defended the independence of the Church against the Cæsaropapism of the Byzantine rulers and the authority of the Apostolic See in questions of faith. The twenty-eighth canon of the Council of Chalcedon (451) granted the See of Constantinople the same privileges of honour that were enjoyed by the Bishop of Old Rome, although the primacy and the highest rank of honour were due to the latter. The papal legates protested against this elevation of the Byzantine Patriarch, and Pope Leo confirmed only the dogmatic decrees of the council. However, the Patriarch of Constantinople sought to bring the canon into force, and the Emperor Leo II desired to obtain its confirmation by Simplicius. The latter, however, rejected the request of the emperor and opposed the carrying out of the canon, that moreover limited the rights of the old Oriental patriarchates.

The rebellion of Basiliscus, who in 476 drove the Emperor Zeno into exile and seized the Byzantine throne, intensified the Monophysite dispute. Basiliscus looked for support to the Monophysites, and he granted permission to the deposed Monophysite patriarchs, Timotheus Ailurus of Alexandria and Peter Fullo of Antioch, to return to their sees. At the same time he issued a religious edict (*Enkyklikon*) addressed to Ailurus, which commanded that only the first three œcumenical synods were to be accepted, and rejected the Synod of Chalcedon and the Letter of Pope Leo. All bishops were to sign the edict. The Bishop of Constantinople, Acacius (from 471), wavered and was about to proclaim this edict. But the firm stand taken by the populace, influenced by the monks who were rigidly Catholic in their opinions, moved the bishop to oppose the emperor and to defend the threatened faith. The abbots and priests of Constantinople united with Pope Simplicius, who made every effort to maintain the Catholic dogma and the definitions of the Council of Chalcedon. The pope exhorted to loyal adherence to the true faith in letters to Acacius, to the priests and abbots, as well as to the usurper Basiliscus himself. In a letter to Basiliscus of 10 Jan., 476, Simplicius says of the See of Peter at Rome: "This same norm of Apostolic doctrine is firmly maintained by his [Peter's] successors, of him to whom the Lord entrusted the care of the entire flock of sheep, to whom He promised not to leave him until the end of time" (Thiel, "Rom. Pont.", 182). In the same way he took up with the emperor the cause of the Catholic Patriarch of Alexandria, Timotheus Salophakiolus, who had been superseded by Ailurus. When the Emperor Zeno in 477 drove away the usurper and again gained the supremacy, he sent the pope a completely Catholic confession of faith, whereupon Simplicius (9 Oct., 477) congratulated him on his restoration to power and exhorted him to ascribe the victory to God, who wished in this way to restore liberty to the Church.

Zeno recalled the edicts of Basiliscus, banished Peter Fullo from Antioch, and reinstated Timotheus Salophakiolus at Alexandria. He did not disturb Ailurus on account of the latter's great age, and as a matter of fact the latter soon died. The Monophysites of Alexandria now put forward Peter Mongus, the former archdeacon of Ailurus, as his successor. Urged by the pope and the Eastern Catholics, Zeno commanded the banishment of Peter Mongus, but the latter was able to hide in Alexandria, and fear of the Monophysites prevented the use of force. In a moment of weakness Salophakiolus himself had permitted the placing of the name of the Monophysite patriarch Dioscurus in the diptychs to be read at the church services. On 13 March, 478, Simplicius wrote to Acacius of Constantinople that Salophakiolus should be urged to wipe out the disgrace that he had brought upon himself. The latter sent legates and letters to Rome to give satisfaction to the pope. At the request of Acacius, who was still active against the Monophysites, the pope condemned by name the heretics Mongus, Fullo, Paul of Epheseus, and John of Apamea, and delegated the Patriarch of Constantinople to be in this his representative. When the Monophysites at Antioch raised a revolt in 497 against the patriarch Stephen II, and killed him, Acacius consecrated Stephen III, and afterwards Kalendion as Stephen's successors. Simplicius made an energetic demand upon the emperor to punish the murderers of the patriarch, and also reproved Acacius for exceeding his competence in performing this consecration; at the same time, though, the pope granted him the necessary dispensation. After the death of Salophakiolus, the Monophysites of Alexandria again elected Peter Mongus patriarch, while the Catholics chose Johannes Talaia. Both Acacius and the emperor, whom he influenced, were opposed to Talaia, and sided with Mongus. Mongus went to Constantinople to advance his cause. Acacius and he agreed upon a formula of union between the Catholics and the Monophysites that was approved by the Emperor Zeno in 482 (*Henotikon*). Talaia had sent ambassadors to Pope Simplicius to notify the pope of his election. However, at the same time, the pope received a letter from the emperor in which Talaia was accused of perjury and bribery and a demand was made for the recognition of Mongus. Simplicius, therefore, delayed to recognize Talaia, but protested energetically against the elevation of Mongus to the Patriarchate of Alexandria. Acacius, however, maintained his alliance with Mongus and sought to prevail upon the Eastern bishops to enter into Church communion with him. For a long time Acacius sent no information of any kind to the pope, so that the latter in a letter blamed him severely for this. When finally Talaia came to Rome in 483 Simplicius was already dead.

Simplicius exercised a zealous pastoral care in western Europe also notwithstanding the trying circumstances of the Church during the disorders of the Migrations. He issued decisions in ecclesiastical questions, appointed Bishop Zeno of Seville papal vicar in Spain, so that the prerogatives of the papal see could be exercised in the country itself for the benefit of the ecclesiastical administration. When Bishop John of Ravenna in 482 claimed Mutina as a suffragan diocese of his metropolitan see, and without more ado consecrated Bishop George for this diocese, Simplicius vigorously opposed him and defended the rights of the papal see. Simplicius established four new churches in Rome itself. A large hall built in the form of a rotunda on the Cælian Hill was turned into a church and dedicated to St. Stephen; the main part of this building still exists as the Church of San Stefano Rotondo. A fine hall near the Church of Santa Maria Maggiore was given by Simplicius to the Roman Church and turned by Simplicius into a church dedicated to St. Andrew by the addition of an apse adorned with mosaics; it is no longer in existence (cf. de Rossi, "Bull. di archeol. crist.", 1871, 1–64). The pope built a church dedicated to the first martyr, St. Stephen, behind the memorial church of San Lorenzo in Agro Verano; this church is no longer standing. He had a fourth church built in the city in honour of St. Balbina, "juxta palatium Licinianum", where her grave was; this church still remains. In order to make sure of the regular holding of church services, of the administration of baptism, and of the discipline of penance in the great churches of the catacombs outside the city walls, namely the church of St. Peter (in the Vatican), of St. Paul on the Via Ostiensis, and of St. Lawrence on the Via Tiburtina, Simplicius ordained that the clergy of three designated sections of the city should, in an established order, have charge of the religious functions at these churches of the catacombs. Simplicius was buried in St. Peter's on the Vatican. The "Liber Pontificalis" gives 2 March as the day of burial (VI non.); probably 10 March (VI id.) should be read. After his death King Odoacer desired to influence the filling of the papal see. The prefect of the city, Basilius, asserted that before death Pope Simplicius had begged to issue the order that no one should be consecrated Roman bishop without his consent (cf. concerning the regulation Thiel, "Epist. Rom. Pont.", 686–88). The Roman clergy opposed this edict that limited their right of election. They maintained the force of the edict, issued by the Emperor Honorius at the instance of Pope Boniface I, that only that person should be regarded as the rightful Bishop of Rome who was elected according to canonical form with Divine approval and universal consent. Simplicius was venerated as a saint; his feast is on 2 or 3 March.

Liber pontificalis, ed. DUCHESNE, I, 249–251; JAFFÉ, *Regesta Pont. Rom.*, 2nd ed., I, 77–80; THIEL, *Epist. Rom. Pontif.*, I (Brunswick, 1868), 174 sq.; LIBERATUS, *Breviar. causæ Nestor.*, xvi sq.; EVAGRIUS, *Hist. eccl.*, III, 4 sq.; HERGENRÖTHER, *Photius*, I, 111–22; GRISAR, *Geschichte Roms und der Päpste*, I, 153 sq., 324 sq.; LANGEN, *Geschichte der römischen Kirche*, II (Bonn, 1885), 126 sqq.; WURM, *Die Papstwahl* (Cologne, 1902).

J. P. KIRSCH.

Simplicius, FAUSTINUS, AND BEATRICE, martyrs at Rome during the Diocletian persecution (302 or 303). The brothers Simplicius and Faustinus were cruelly tortured on account of their Christian faith, beaten with clubs, and finally beheaded; their bodies were thrown into the Tiber. According to another version of the legend a stone was tied to them and they were drowned. Their sister Beatrice had the bodies drawn out of the water and buried. Then for seven months she lived with a pious matron named Lucina, and with her aid Beatrice succoured the persecuted Christians by day and night. Finally she was discovered and arrested. Her accuser was her neighbour Lucretius who desired to obtain possession of her lands. She courageously asserted before the judge that she would never sacrifice to demons, because she was a Christian. As punishment she was strangled in prison. Her friend Lucina buried her by her brothers in the cemetery *ad Ursum Pileatum* on the road to Porto. Soon after this Divine punishment overtook the accuser Lucretius. When Lucretius at a feast was making merry over the folly of the martyrs, an infant who had been brought to the entertainment by his mother, cried out, "Thou hast committed murder and hast taken unjust possession of land. Thou art a slave of the devil". And the devil at once took possession of him and tortured him three hours and drew him down into the bottomless pit. The terror of those present was so great that they became Christians. This is the story of the legend. Trustworthy Acts concerning the history of the two brothers and sister are no longer in existence. Pope Leo II (682–683) translated their relics to a church which he had built at Rome in honour of St. Paul. Later the greater part of the relics of the martyrs were taken to the Church of Santa Maria Maggiore. St. Simplicius is represented with a pennant, on the shield of which are three lilies called the crest of Simplicius; the lilies are a symbol of purity of heart. St. Beatrice has a cord in her hand, because she was strangled. The feast of the three saints is on 29 July.

Acta SS., July, VII, 34–37; *Bibliotheca hagiographica latina* (Brussels, 1898–1900), 1127–28.

KLEMENS LÖFFLER.

Simpson, RICHARD, b. 1820; d. near Rome, 5 April, 1876. He was educated at Oriel College, Oxford, and took his B.A. degree, 9 Feb., 1843. Being ordained an Anglican clergyman, he was appointed vicar of Mitcham in Surrey, but resigned this in 1845 to become a Catholic. After some years spent on the continent, during which time he became remarkably proficient as a linguist, he returned to England and became editor of "The Rambler". When this ceased in 1862 he, with Sir John Acton, began the "Home and Foreign Review", which was opposed by ecclesiastical authority as unsound and was discontinued in 1864. Afterwards Simpson devoted himself to the study of Shakespeare and to music. His works are: "Invocation of Saints proved from the Bible alone" (1849); "The Lady Falkland: her life" (1861); "Edmund Campion" (1867), the most valuable of his works; "Introduction to the Philosophy of Shakespeare's Sonnets" (1868); "The School of Shakespeare" (1872); and "Sonnets of Shakespeare selected from a complete setting, and miscellaneous songs" (1878). Though he remained a practical Catholic his opinions were very liberal and he assisted Mr. Gladstone in writing his pamphlet on "Vaticanism". His papers in "The Rambler" on the English martyrs deserve attention.

COOPER in *Dict. Nat. Biog.*, s. v.; GILLOW, *Bibl. Dict. Eng. Cath.*, s. v.; WARD, *Life and Times of Cardinal Wiseman* (London, 1897); GASQUET, *Lord Acton and His Circle* (London, 1906).

EDWIN BURTON.

Sin.—The subject is treated under these heads: I. Nature of Sin; II. Division; III. Mortal Sin; IV. Venial Sin; V. Permission and Remedies; VI. The Sense of Sin.

I. NATURE OF SIN.—Since sin is a moral evil, it is necessary in the first place to determine what is meant by evil, and in particular by moral evil. Evil is defined by St. Thomas (De malo, Q. ii, a. 2) as a privation of form or order or due measure. In the physical order a thing is good in proportion as it possesses being. God alone is essentially being, and He alone is essentially and perfectly good. Everything else possesses but a limited being, and, in so far as it possesses being, it is good. When it has its due proportion of form and order and measure it is, in its own order and degree, good. (See GOOD.) Evil implies a deficiency in perfection, hence it cannot exist in God who is essentially and by nature good; it is found only in finite beings which, because of their origin from nothing, are subject to the privation of form or order or measure due them, and, through the opposition they encounter, are liable to an increase or decrease of the perfection they have: "for evil, in a large sense, may be described as the sum of opposition, which experience shows to exist in the universe, to the desires and needs of individuals; whence arises, among human beings at least, the suffering in which life abounds" (see EVIL).

According to the nature of the perfection which it limits, evil is metaphysical, physical, or moral. Metaphysical evil is not evil properly so called; it is but the negation of a greater good, or the limitation of finite beings by other finite beings. Physical evil deprives the subject affected by it of some natural good, and is adverse to the well-being of the subject, as pain and suffering. Moral evil is found only in intelligent beings; it deprives them of some moral good. Here we have to deal with moral evil only. This may be defined as a privation of conformity to right reason and to the law of God. Since the morality of a human act consists in its agreement or non-agreement with right reason and the eternal law, an act is good or evil in the moral order according as it involves this agreement or non-agreement. When the intelligent creature, knowing God and His law, deliberately refuses to obey, moral evil results.

Sin is nothing else than a morally bad act (St. Thomas, "De malo", Q. vii, a. 3), an act not in accord with reason informed by the Divine law. God has endowed us with reason and free-will, and a sense of responsibility; He has made us subject to His law, which is known to us by the dictates of conscience, and our acts must conform with these dictates, otherwise we sin (Rom., xiv, 23). In every sinful act two things must be considered, the substance of the act and the want of rectitude or conformity (St. Thomas, I–II, Q. lxxii, a. 1). The act is something positive. The sinner intends here and now to act in some determined matter, inordinately electing that particular good in defiance of God's law and the dictates of right reason. The deformity is not directly intended, nor is it involved in the act so far as this is physical, but in the act as coming from the will which has power over its acts and is capable of choosing this or that particular good contained within the scope of its adequate object, i. e. universal good (St. Thomas, "De malo", Q. iii, a. 2, ad 2um). God, the first cause of all reality, is the cause of the physical act as such, the free-will of the deformity (St. Thomas, I–II, Q. lxxxix, a. 2; "De malo", Q. iii, a. 2). The evil act adequately considered has for its cause the free-will defectively electing some mutable good in place of the eternal good, God, and thus deviating from its true last end.

In every sin a privation of due order or conformity to the moral law is found, but sin is not a pure, or entire privation of all moral good (St. Thomas, "De malo", Q. ii, a. 9; I–II, Q. lxxiii, a. 2). There is a twofold privation; one entire which leaves nothing of its opposite, as for instance, darkness which leaves no light; another, not entire, which leaves something of the good to which it is opposed, as for instance, disease which does not entirely destroy the even balance of the bodily functions necessary for health. A pure or entire privation of good could occur in a moral act only on the supposition that the will could incline to evil as such for an object. This is impossible because evil as such is not contained within the scope of the adequate object of the will, which is good. The sinner's intention terminates at some object in which there is a participation of God's goodness, and this object is directly intended by him. The privation of due order, or the deformity, is not directly intended, but is accepted in as much as the sinner's desire tends to an object in which this want of conformity is involved, so that sin is not a pure privation, but a human act deprived of its due rectitude. From the defect arises the evil of the act, from the fact that it is voluntary, its imputability.

II. DIVISION OF SIN.—As regards the principle from which it proceeds sin is original or actual. The will of Adam acting as head of the human race for the conservation or loss of original justice is the cause and source of original sin (q. v.). Actual sin is committed by a free personal act of the individual will. It is divided into sins of commission and omission. A sin of commission is a positive act contrary to some prohibitory precept; a sin of omission is a failure to do what is commanded. A sin of omission, however, requires a positive act whereby one wills to omit the fulfilling of a precept, or at least wills something incompatible with its fulfillment (I–II, Q. lxxii, a. 5). As regards their malice, sins are distinguished into sins of ignorance, passion or infirmity, and malice; as regards the activities involved, into sins of thought, word, or deed (*cordis, oris, operis*); as regards their gravity, into mortal and venial. This last named division is indeed the most important of all and it calls for special treatment. But before taking up the details, it will be useful to indicate some further distinctions which occur in theology or in general usage.

Material and Formal Sin.—This distinction is based upon the difference between the objective elements (object itself, circumstances) and the subjective (advertence to the sinfulness of the act). An action which, as a matter of fact, is contrary to the Divine law but is not known to be such by the agent constitutes a material sin; whereas formal sin is committed when the agent freely transgresses the law as shown him by his conscience, whether such law really exists or is only thought to exist by him who acts. Thus, a person who takes the property of another while believing it to be his own commits a material sin; but the sin would be formal if he took the property in the belief that it belonged to another, whether his belief were correct or not.

Internal Sins.—That sin may be committed not only by outward deeds but also by the inner activity of the mind apart from any external manifestation, is plain from the precept of the Decalogue: "Thou shalt not covet", and from Christ's rebuke of the scribes and pharisees whom he likens to "whited sepulchres . . . full of all filthiness" (Matt., xxiii, 27). Hence the Council of Trent (Sess. XIV, c. v), in declaring that all mortal sins must be confessed, makes special mention of those that are most secret and that violate only the last two precepts of the Decalogue, adding that they "sometimes more grievously wound the soul and are more dangerous than sins which are openly committed". Three kinds of internal sin are usually distinguished: *delectatio morosa*, i. e. the pleasure taken in a sinful thought or imagination even without desiring it; *gaudium*, i. e. dwelling with complacency on sins already committed; and *desiderium*, i. e. the desire for what is sinful. An *efficacious* desire, i. e. one that includes the deliberate intention to realize or gratify the desire, has the same malice, mortal or venial, as the action which it has in view. An inefficacious desire is one that carries a condition, in such a way that the will is prepared to perform the action in case the condition were verified. When the condition is such as to eliminate all sinfulness from the action, the desire involves no sin: e. g. I would gladly eat meat on Friday, if I had a dispensation; and in general this is the case whenever the action is forbidden by positive law only. When the action is contrary to natural law and yet is permissible in given circumstances or in a particular state of life, the desire, if it include those circumstances or that state as conditions, is not in itself sinful: e. g. I would kill so-and-so if I had to do it in self-defence. Usually, however, such desires are dangerous and therefore to be repressed. If, on the other hand, the condition does not remove the sinfulness of the action, the desire is also sinful. This is clearly the case where the action is intrinsically and absolutely evil, e. g. blasphemy: one cannot without committing sin, have the desire—I would blaspheme God if it were not wrong; the condition is an impossible one and therefore does not affect the desire itself. The pleasure taken in a sinful thought (*delectatio, gaudium*) is, generally speaking, a sin of the same kind and gravity as the action which is thought of. Much, however, depends on the motive for which one thinks of sinful actions. The pleasure, e. g. which one may experience in studying the nature of murder or any other crime, in getting clear ideas on the subject, tracing its causes, determining the guilt etc., is not a sin; on the contrary, it is often both necessary and useful. The case is different of course where the pleasure means gratification in the sinful object or action itself. And it is evidently a sin when one boasts of his evil deeds, the more so because of the scandal that is given.

The Capital Sins or Vices.—According to St. Thomas (II–II, Q. cliii, a. 4) "a capital vice is that which has an exceedingly desirable end so that in his desire for it a man goes on to the commission of many sins all of which are said to originate in that vice as their chief source". It is not then the gravity of the vice in itself that makes it capital but rather the fact that it gives rise to many other sins. These are enumerated by St. Thomas (I–II, Q. lxxxiv, a. 4) as vainglory (pride), avarice, gluttony, lust, sloth, envy, anger. St. Bonaventure (Brevil., III, ix) gives the same enumeration. Earlier writers had distinguished eight capital sins: so St. Cyprian (De mort., iv); Cassian (De instit. cœnob., v, coll. 5, de octo principalibus vitiis); Columbanus ("Instr. de octo vitiis princip." in "Bibl. max. vet. patr.", XII, 23); Alcuin (De virtut. et vitiis, xxvii sqq.). The number seven, however, had been given by St. Gregory the Great (Lib. mor. in Job. XXXI, xvii), and it was retained by the foremost theologians of the Middle Ages.

It is to be noted that "sin" is not predicated univocally of all kinds of sin. "The division of sin into venial and mortal is not a division of genus into species which participate equally the nature of the genus, but the division of an analogue into things of which it is predicated primarily and secondarily" (St. Thomas, I–II, Q. lxxxviii, a. 1, ad 1um). "Sin is not predicated univocally of all kinds of sin, but primarily of actual mortal sin . . . and therefore it is not necessary that the definition of sin in general should be verified except in that sin in which the nature of the genus is found perfectly. The definition of sin may be verified in other sins in a certain sense" (St. Thomas, II, d. 33, Q. i, a. 2, ad 2um). Actual sin primarily consists in a voluntary act repugnant to the order of right reason. The act passes, but the soul of the sinner remains stained, deprived of grace, in a state of sin, until the disturbance of order has been restored by penance. This state is called habitual sin, *macula peccati. reatus culpæ* (I–II, Q. lxxxvii, a. 6).

The division of sin into original and actual, mortal and venial, is not a division of genus into species because sin has not the same signification when applied to original and personal sin, mortal and venial. Mortal sin cuts us off entirely from our true last end; venial sin only impedes us in its attainment. Actual personal sin is voluntary by a proper act of the will. Original sin is voluntary not by a personal voluntary act of ours, but by an act of the will of Adam. Original and actual sin are distinguished by the manner in which they are voluntary (*ex parte actus*); mortal and venial sin by the way in which they affect our relation to God (*ex parte deordinationis*). Since a voluntary act and its disorder are of the essence of sin, it is impossible that sin should be a generic term in respect to original and actual, mortal and venial sin. The true nature of sin is found perfectly only in a personal mortal sin, in other sins imperfectly, so that sin is predicated primarily of actual sin, only secondarily of the others. Therefore we shall consider: first, personal mortal sin; second, venial sin.

III. MORTAL SIN.—Mortal sin is defined by St. Augustine (Contra Faustum, XXII, xxvii) as "Dictum vel factum vel concupitum contra legem æternam", i. e. something said, done or desired contrary to the eternal law, or a thought, word, or deed contrary to the eternal law. This is a definition of sin as it is a voluntary act. As it is a defect or privation it may be defined as an aversion from God, our true last end, by reason of the preference given to some mutable good. The definition of St. Augustine is accepted generally by theologians and is primarily a definition of actual mortal sin. It explains well the material and formal elements of sin. The words "dictum vel factum vel concupitum" denote the material element of sin, a human act: "contra legem æternam", the formal element. The act is bad because it transgresses the Divine law. St. Ambrose (De paradiso, viii) defines sin as a "prevarication of the Divine law". The definition of St. Augustine strictly considered, i. e. as sin averts us from our true ultimate end, does not comprehend venial sin, but in as much as venial sin is in a manner contrary to the Divine law, although not averting us from our last end, it may be said to be included in the definition as it stands. While primarily a definition of sins of commission, sins of omission may be included in the definition because they presuppose some positive act (St. Thomas, I–II, Q. lxxi, a. 5) and negation and affirmation are reduced to the same genus. Sins that violate the human or the natural law are also included, for what is contrary to the human or natural law is also contrary to the Divine law, in as much as every just human law is derived from the Divine law, and is not just unless it is in conformity with the Divine law.

Biblical Description of Sin.—In the Old Testament sin is set forth as an act of disobedience (Gen., ii, 16–17; iii, 11; Is., i, 2–4; Jer., ii, 32); as an insult to God (Num., xxvii, 14); as something detested and punished by God (Gen., iii, 14–19, Gen., iv, 9–16); as injurious to the sinner (Tob., xii, 10); to be expiated by penance (Ps. l, 19). In the New Testament it is clearly taught in St. Paul that sin is a transgression of the law (Rom., ii, 23; v, 12–20); a servitude from which we are liberated by grace (Rom., vi, 16–18); a disobedience (Heb., ii, 2) punished by God (Heb., x, 26–31). St. John describes sin as an offence to God, a disorder of the will (John, xii, 43), an iniquity (I John, iii, 4–10). Christ in many of his utterances teaches the nature and extent of sin. He came to promulgate a new law more perfect than the old, which would extend to the ordering not only of external but also of internal acts to a degree unknown before, and, in His Sermon on the Mount, he condemns as sinful many acts which were judged honest and righteous by the doctors and teachers of the Old Law. He denounces in a special manner hypocrisy and scandal, infidelity and the sin against the Holy Ghost. In particular he teaches that sins come from the heart (Matt., xv, 19–20).

Systems which Deny Sin or Distort its True Notion.— All systems, religious and ethical, which either deny, on the one hand, the existence of a personal creator and lawgiver distinct from and superior to his creation, or, on the other, the existence of free will and responsibility in man, distort or destroy the true biblico-theological notion of sin. In the beginning of the Christian era the Gnostics, although their doctrines varied in details, denied the existence of a personal creator. The idea of sin in the Catholic sense is not contained in their system. There is no sin for them, unless it be the sin of ignorance, no necessity for an atonement; Jesus is not God (see GNOSTICISM). Manichæism (q. v.) with its two eternal principles, good and evil, at perpetual war with each other, is also destructive of the true notion of sin. All evil, and consequently sin, is from the principle of evil. The Christian concept of God as a lawgiver is destroyed. Sin is not a conscious voluntary act of disobedience to the Divine will. Pantheistic systems which deny the distinction between God and His creation make sin impossible. If man and God are one, man is not responsible to anyone for his acts, morality is destroyed. If he is his own rule of action, he cannot deviate from right as St. Thomas teaches (I, Q. lxiii, a. 1). The identification of God and the world by Pantheism (q. v.) leaves no place for sin.

There must be some law to which man is subject, superior to and distinct from him, which can be obeyed and transgressed, before sin can enter into his acts. This law must be the mandate of a superior, because the notions of superiority and subjection are correlative. This superior can be only God, who alone is the author and lord of man. Materialism, denying as it does the spirituality and the immortality of the soul, the existence of any spirit whatsoever, and consequently of God, does not admit sin. There is no free will, everything is determined by the inflexible laws of motion. "Virtue" and "vice" are meaningless qualifications of action. Positivism places man's last end in some sensible good. His supreme law of action is to seek the maximum of pleasure. Egotism or altruism is the supreme norm and criterion of the Positivistic systems, not the eternal law of God as revealed by Him, and dictated by conscience. For the materialistic evolutionists man is but a highly-developed animal, conscience a product of evolution. Evolution has revolutionized morality, sin is no more.

Kant in his "Critique of Pure Reason" having rejected all the essential notions of true morality, namely, liberty, the soul, God and a future life, attempted in his "Critique of the Practical Reason" to restore them in the measure in which they are necessary for morality. The practical reason, he tells us, imposes on us the idea of law and duty. The fundamental principle of the morality of Kant is "duty for duty's sake", not God and His law. Duty cannot be conceived of alone as an independent thing. It carries with it certain postulates, the first of which is liberty. "I ought, therefore I can", is his doctrine. Man by virtue of his practical reason has a consciousness of moral obligation (categorical imperative). This consciousness supposes three things: free will, the immortality of the soul, the existence of God, otherwise man would not be capable of fulfilling his obligations, there would be no sufficient sanction for the Divine law, no reward or punishment in a future life. Kant's moral system labours in obscurities and contradictions and is destructive of much that pertains to the teaching of Christ. Personal dignity is the supreme rule of man's actions. The notion of sin as opposed to God is suppressed. According to the teaching of materialistic Monism, now so widespread, there is, and can be, no free will. According to this doctrine but one thing exists and this one being produces all phenomena, thought included; we are but puppets in its hands, carried hither and thither as it wills, and finally are cast back into nothingness. There is no place for good and evil, a free observance or a wilful transgression of law, in such a system. Sin in the true sense is impossible. Without law and liberty and a personal God there is no sin.

That God exists and can be known from His visible creation, that He has revealed the decrees of His eternal will to man, and is distinct from His creation (Denzinger-Bannwart, "Enchiridion", nn. 1782, 1785, 1701), are matters of Catholic faith and teaching. Man is a created being endowed with free will (ibid, 793), which fact can be proved from Scripture and reason (ibid., 1041–1650). The Council of Trent declares in Sess. VI, c. i (ibid., 793) that man by reason of the prevarication of Adam has lost his primeval innocence, and that while free will remains, its powers are lessened (see ORIGINAL SIN).

Protestant Errors.—Luther and Calvin taught as their fundamental error that no free will properly so called remained in man after the fall of our first parents; that the fulfillment of God's precepts is impossible even with the assistance of grace, and that man in all his actions sins. Grace is not an interior gift, but something external. To some sin is not imputed, because they are covered as with a cloak by the merits of Christ. Faith alone saves, there is no necessity for good works. Sin in Luther's doctrine cannot be a deliberate transgression of the Divine law. Jansenius, in his "Augustinus", taught that according to the present powers of man some of God's precepts are impossible of fulfilment, even to the just who strive to fulfil them, and he further taught that grace by means of which the fulfilment becomes possible is wanting even to the just. His fundamental error consists in teaching that the will is not free but is necessarily drawn either by concupiscence or grace. Internal liberty is not required for merit or demerit. Liberty from coercion suffices. Christ did not die for all men. Baius taught a semi-Lutheran doctrine. Liberty is not entirely destroyed, but is so weakened that without grace it can do nothing but sin. True liberty is not required for sin. A bad act committed involuntarily renders man responsible (propositions 50–51 in Denzinger-Bannwart, "Enchiridion", nn. 1050–1). All acts done without charity are mortal sins and merit damnation because they proceed from concupiscence. This doctrine denies that sin is a voluntary transgression of Divine law. If man is not free, a precept is meaningless as far as he is concerned.

Philosophical Sin.—Those who would construct a moral system independent of God and his law distinguish between theological and philosophical sin. Philosophical sin is a morally bad act which violates the natural order of reason, not the Divine law. Theological sin is a transgression of the eternal law. Those who are of atheistic tendencies and contend for this distinction, either deny the existence of God or maintain that He exercises no providence in regard to human acts. This position is destructive of sin in the theological sense, as God and His law, reward and punishment, are done away with. Those who admit the existence of God, His law, human liberty and responsibility, and still contend for a distinction between philosophical and theological sin, maintain that in the present order of God's providence there are morally bad acts, which, while violating the order of reason, are not offensive to God, and they base their contention on this that the sinner can be ignorant of the existence of God, or not actually think of Him and His law when he acts. Without the knowledge of God and consideration of Him, it is impossible to offend Him. This doctrine was censured as scandalous, temerarious, and erroneous by Alexander VIII (24 Aug., 1690) in his condemnation of the following proposition: "Philosophical or moral sin is a human act not in agreement with rational nature and right reason, theological and mortal sin is a free transgression of the Divine law. However grievous it may be, philosophical sin in one who is either ignorant of God or does not actually think of God, is indeed a grievous sin, but not an offense to God, nor a mortal sin dissolving friendship with God, nor worthy of eternal punishment" (Denzinger-Bannwart, 1290).

This proposition is condemned because it does not distinguish between vincible and invincible ignorance, and further supposes invincible ignorance of God to be sufficiently common, instead of only metaphysically possible, and because in the present dispensation of God's providence we are clearly taught in Scripture that God will punish all evil coming from the free will of man (Rom., ii, 5–11). There is no morally bad act that does not include a transgression of Divine law. From the fact that an action is conceived of as morally evil it is conceived of as prohibited. A prohibition is unintelligible without the notion of some one prohibiting. The one prohibiting in this case and binding the conscience of man can be only God, Who alone has power over man's free will and actions, so that from the fact that any act is perceived to be morally bad and prohibited by conscience, God and His law are perceived at least confusedly, and a wilful transgression of the dictate of conscience is necessarily also a transgression of God's law. Cardinal de Lugo (De incarnat., disp. 5, lect. 3) admits the possibility of philosophical sin in those who are inculpably ignorant of God, but he holds that it does not actually occur, because in the present order of God's providence there cannot be invincible ignorance of God and His law. This teaching does not necessarily fall under the condemnation of Alexander VIII, but it is commonly rejected by theologians for the reason that a dictate of conscience necessarily involves a knowledge of the Divine law as a principle of morality.

Conditions of Mortal Sin: Knowledge, Free Will, Grave Matter.—Contrary to the teaching of Baius (prop. 46, Denzinger-Bannwart, 1046) and the Reformers, a sin must be a voluntary act. Those actions alone are properly called human or moral actions which proceed from the human will deliberately acting with knowledge of the end for which it acts. Man differs from all irrational creatures in this precisely that he is master of his actions by virtue of his reason and free will (I–II, Q. i, a. 1). Since sin is a human act wanting in due rectitude, it must have, in so far as it is a human act, the essential constituents of a human act. The intellect must perceive and judge of the morality of the act, and the will must freely elect. For a deliberate mortal sin there must be full advertence on the part of the intellect and full consent on the part of the will in a grave matter. An involuntary transgression of the law even in a grave matter is not a formal but a material sin. The gravity of the matter is judged from the teaching of Scripture, the definitions of councils and popes, and also from reason. Those sins are judged to be mortal which contain in themselves some grave disorder in regard to God, our neighbour, ourselves, or society. Some sins admit of no lightness of matter, as for example, blasphemy, hatred of God; they are always mortal (*ex toto genere suo*), unless rendered venial by want of full advertence on the part of the intellect or full consent on the part of the will. Other sins admit lightness of matter: they are grave sins (*ex genero suo*) in as much as their matter in itself is sufficient to constitute a grave sin without the addition of any other matter, but is of such a nature that in a given case, owing to its smallness, the sin may be venial, e. g. theft.

Imputability.—That the act of the sinner may be imputed to him it is not necessary that the object which terminates and specifies his act should be directly willed as an end or means. It suffices that it be willed indirectly or in its cause, i. e. if the sinner foresees, at least confusedly, that it will follow from the act which he freely performs or from his omission of an act. When the cause produces a twofold effect, one of which is directly willed, the other indirectly, the effect which follows indirectly is morally imputable to the sinner when these three conditions are verified: first, the sinner must foresee at least confusedly the evil effects which follow on the cause he places; second, he must be able to refrain from placing the cause; third, he must be under the obligation of preventing the evil effect. Error and ignorance in regard to the object or circumstances of the act to be placed, affect the judgment of the intellect and consequently the morality and imputability of the act. Invincible ignorance excuses entirely from sin. Vincible ignorance does not, although it renders the act less free (see IGNORANCE). The passions, while they disturb the judgment of the intellect, more directly affect the will. Antecedent passion increases the intensity of the act, the object is more intensely desired, although less freely, and the disturbance caused by the passions may be so great as to render a free judgment impossible, the agent being for the moment beside himself (I–II, Q. vi, a. 7, ad 3um). Consequent passion, which arises from a command of the will, does not lessen liberty, but is rather a sign of an intense act of volition. Fear, violence, heredity, temperament and pathological states, in so far as they affect free volition, affect the malice and imputability of sin. From the condemnation of the errors of Baius and Jansenius (Denz.-Bann., 1046, 1066, 1094, 1291–2) it is clear that for an actual personal sin a knowledge of the law and a personal voluntary act, free from coercion and necessity, are required. No mortal sin is committed in a state of invincible ignorance or in a half-conscious state. Actual advertence to the sinfulness of the act is not required, virtual advertence suffices. It is not necessary that the explicit intention to offend God and break his law be present, the full and free consent of the will to an evil act suffices.

Malice.—The true malice of mortal sin consists in a conscious and voluntary transgression of the eternal law, and implies a contempt of the Divine will, a complete turning away from God, our true last end, and a preferring of some created thing to which we subject ourselves. It is an offence offered to God, and an injury done Him; not that it effects any change in God, who is immutable by nature, but that the sinner by his act deprives God of the reverence and honor due Him: it is not any lack of malice on the sinner's part, but God's immutability that prevents Him from suffering. As an offence offered to God mortal sin is in a way infinite in its malice, since it is directed against an infinite being, and the gravity of the offence is measured by the dignity of the one offended (St. Thomas, III, Q. i, a. 2, ad 2um). As an act sin is finite, the will of man not being capable of infinite malice. Sin is an offence against Christ Who has redeemed man (Phil., iii, 18); against the Holy Ghost Who sanctifies us (Heb., x, 29), an injury to man himself, causing the spiritual death of the soul, and making man the servant of the devil. The first and primary malice of sin is derived from the object to which the will inordinately tends, and from the object considered morally, not physically. The end for which the sinner acts and the circumstances which surround the act are also determining factors of its morality. An act which, objectively considered, is morally indifferent, may be rendered good or evil by circumstances, or by the intention of the sinner. An act that is good objectively may be rendered bad, or a new species of good or evil may be added, or a new degree. Circumstances can change the character of a sin to such a degree that it becomes specifically different from what it is objectively considered; or they may merely aggravate the sin while not changing its specific character; or they may lessen its gravity. That they may exercise this determining influence two things are necessary: they must contain in themselves some good or evil, and must be apprehended, at least confusedly, in their moral aspect. The external act, in so far as it is a mere execution of a voluntary efficacious internal act, does not, according to the common Thomistic opinion, add any essential goodness or malice to the internal sin.

Gravity.—While every mortal sin averts us from out true last end, all mortal sins are not equally grave, as is clear from Scripture (John, xix, 11; Matt., xi, 22; Luke, vi), and also from reason. Sins are specifically distinguished by their objects, which do not all equally avert man from his last end. Then again, since sin is not a pure privation, but a mixed one, all sins do not equally destroy the order of reason Spiritual sins, other things being equal, are graver than carnal sins (St. Thomas, "De malo", Q. ii, a. 9; I–II, Q. lxxiii, a. 5).

Specific and numeric distinction of Sin.—Sins are distinguished specifically by their formally diverse objects; or from their opposition to different virtues, or to morally different precepts of the same virtue. Sins that are specifically distinct are also numerically distinct. Sins within the same species are distinguished numerically according to the number of complete acts of the will in regard to total objects. A total object is one which, either in itself or by the intention of the sinner, forms a complete whole and is not referred to another action as a part of the whole. When the completed acts of the will relate to the same object there are as many sins as there are morally interrupted acts.

Subject causes of Sin.—Since sin is a voluntary act lacking in due rectitude, sin is found, as in a subject, principally in the will. But, since not only acts elicited by the will are voluntary, but also those that are elicited by other faculties at the command of the will, sin may be found in these faculties in so far as they are subject in their actions to the command of the will, and are instruments of the will, and move under its guidance (I–II, Q. lxxiv).

The external members of the body cannot be effective principles of sin (I–II, Q. lxxiv, a. 2 ad 3um). They are mere organs which are set in activity by the soul; they do not initiate action. The appetitive powers on the contrary can be effective principles of sin, for they possess, through their immediate conjunction with the will and their subordination to it, a certain though imperfect liberty (I–II, Q. lvi, a. 4, ad 3um). The sensual appetites have their own proper sensible objects to which they naturally incline, and since original sin has broken the bond which held them in complete subjection to the will, they may antecede the will in their actions and tend to their own proper objects inordinately. Hence they may be proximate principles of sin when they move inordinately contrary to the dictates of right reason.

It is the right of reason to rule the lower faculties, and when the disturbance arises in the sensual part the reason may do one of two things: it may either consent to the sensible delectation or it may repress and reject it. If it consents, the sin is no longer one of the sensual part of man, but of the intellect and will, and consequently, if the matter is grave, mortal. If rejected, no sin can be imputed. There can be no sin in the sensual part of man independently of the will. The inordinate motions of the sensual appetite which precede the advertence of reason, or which are suffered unwillingly, are not even venial sins. The temptations of the flesh not consented to are not sins. Concupiscence, which remains after the guilt of original sin is remitted in baptism, is not sinful so long as consent is not given to it (Coun. of Trent., sess. V, can. v). The sensual appetite of itself cannot be the subject of mortal sin, for the reason that it can neither grasp the notion of God as an ultimate end, nor avert us from Him, without which aversion there cannot be mortal sin. The superior reason, whose office it is to occupy itself with Divine things, may be the proximate principle of sin both in regard to its own proper act, to know truth, and as it is directive of the inferior faculties: in regard to its own proper act, in so far as it voluntarily neglects to know what it can and ought to know; in regard to the act by which it directs the inferior faculties, to the extent that it commands inordinate acts or fails to repress them (I–II, Q. lxxiv, a. 7, ad 2um).

The will never consents to a sin that is not at the same time a sin of the superior reason as directing badly, by either actually deliberating and commanding the consent, or by failing to deliberate and impede the consent of the will when it could and should do so. The superior reason is the ultimate judge of human acts and has an obligation of deliberating and deciding whether the act to be performed is according to the law of God. Venial sin may also be found in the superior reason when it deliberately consents to sins that are venial in their nature, or when there is not a full consent in the case of a sin that is mortal considered objectively.

Causes of Sin.—Under this head, it is needful to distinguish between the efficient cause, i.e. the agent performing the sinful action, and those other agencies, influences or circumstances, which incite to sin and consequently involve a danger, more or less grave, for one who is exposed to them. These inciting causes are explained in special articles on OCCASIONS OF SIN and TEMPTATION. Here we have to consider only the efficient cause or causes of sin. These are interior and exterior. The complete and sufficient cause of sin is the will, which is regulated in its actions by the reason, and acted upon by the sensitive appetites. The principal interior causes of sin are ignorance, infirmity or passion, and malice. Ignorance on the part of the reason, infirmity and passion on the part of the sensitive appetite, and malice on the part of the will. A sin is from certain malice when the will sins of its own accord and not under the influence of ignorance or passion.

The exterior causes of sin are the devil and man, who move to sin by means of suggestion, persuasion, temptation, and bad example. God is not the cause of sin (Counc. of Trent., sess. VI, can. vi, in Denz.-Bann., 816). He directs all things to Himself and is the end of all His actions, and could not be the cause of evil without self-contradiction. Of whatever entity there is in sin as an action, He is the cause. The evil will is the cause of the disorder (I–II, Q. lxxix, a. 2). One sin may be the cause of another inasmuch as one sin may be ordained to another as an end. The seven capital sins, so called, may be considered as the source from which other sins proceed. They are sinful propensities which reveal themselves in particular sinful acts. Original sin by reason of its dire effects is the cause and source of sin in so far as by reason of it our natures are left wounded and inclined to evil. Ignorance, infirmity, malice, and concupiscence are the consequences of original sin.

Effects of Sin.—The first effect of mortal sin in man is to avert him from his true last end, and deprive his soul of sanctifying grace. The sinful act passes, and the sinner is left in a state of habitual aversion from God. The sinful state is voluntary and imputable to the sinner, because it necessarily follows from the act of sin he freely placed, and it remains until satisfaction is made (see PENANCE). This state of sin is called by theologians habitual sin, not in the sense that habitual sin implies a vicious habit, but in the sense that it signifies a state of aversion from God depending on the preceding actual sin, consequently voluntary and imputable. This state of aversion carries with it necessarily in the present order of God's providence the privation of grace and charity by means of which man is ordered to his supernatural end. The privation of grace is the "macula peccati" (St. Thomas I–II, Q. lxxxvi), the stain of sin spoken of in Scripture (Jos., xxii, 17; Isaias, iv, 4; 1 Cor., vi, 11). It is not anything positive, a quality or disposition, an obligation to suffer, an extrinsic denomination coming from sin, but is solely the privation of sanctifying grace. There is not a real but only a conceptual distinction between habitual sin (*reatus culpæ*) and the stain of sin (*macula peccati*). One and the same privation considered as destroying the due order of man to God is habitual sin, considered as depriving the soul of the beauty of grace is the stain or "macula" of sin.

The second effect of sin is to entail the penalty of undergoing suffering (*reatus pœnæ*). Sin (*reatus culpæ*) is the cause of this obligation (*reatus pœnæ*). The suffering may be inflicted in this life through the medium of medicinal punishments, calamities, sickness, temporal evils, which tend to withdraw from sin; or it may be inflicted in the life to come by the justice of God as vindictive punishment. The punishments of the future life are proportioned to the sin committed, and it is the obligation of undergoing this punishment for unrepented sin that is signified by the "reatus pœnæ" of the theologians. The penalty to be undergone in the future life is divided into the pain of loss (*pœna damni*) and the pain of sense (*pœna sensus*). The pain of loss is the privation of the beatific vision of God in punishment of turning away from Him. The pain of sense is suffering in punishment of the conversion to some created thing in place of God. This two-fold pain in punishment of mortal sin is eternal (I Cor., vi, 9; Matt., xxv, 41; Mark, ix, 45). One mortal sin suffices to incur punishment. (See HELL.) Other effects of sins are: remorse of conscience (Wisdom, v, 2–13); an inclination towards evil, as habits are formed by a repetition of similar acts; a darkening of the intelligence, a hardening of the will (Matt., xiii, 14–15; Rom., xi, 8); a general vitiating of nature, which does not however totally destroy the substance and faculties of the soul but merely weakens the right exercise of its faculties.

IV. VENIAL SIN.—Venial sin is essentially different from mortal sin. It does not avert us from our true last end, it does not destroy charity, the principle of union with God, nor deprive the soul of sanctifying grace, and it is intrinsically reparable. It is called venial precisely because, considered in its own proper nature, it is pardonable; in itself meriting, not eternal, but temporal punishment. It is distinguished from mortal sin on the part of the disorder. By mortal sin man is entirely averted from God, his true last end, and, at least implicitly, he places his last end in some created thing. By venial sin he is not averted from God, neither does he place his last end in creatures. He remains united with God by charity, but does not tend towards Him as he ought. The true nature of sin as it is contrary to the eternal law, repugnant namely to the primary end of the law, is found only in mortal sin. Venial sin is only in an imperfect way contrary to the law, since it is not contrary to the primary end of the law, nor does it avert man from the end intended by the law (St. Thomas, I–II, Q. lxxxviii, a. 1; and Cajetan, I–II, Q. lxxxviii, a. 1, for the sense of the *præter legem* and *contra legem* of St. Thomas).

Definition.—Since a voluntary act and its disorder are of the essence of sin, venial sin as it is a voluntary act may be defined as a thought, word, or deed at variance with the law of God. It retards man in the attainment of his last end while not averting him from it. Its disorder consists either in the not fully deliberate choosing of some object prohibited by the law of God, or in the deliberate adhesion to some created object not as an ultimate end but as a medium, which object does not avert the sinner from God, but is not, however, referable to Him as an end. Man cannot be averted from God except by deliberately placing his last end in some created thing, and in venial sin he does not adhere to any temporal good, enjoying it as a last end, but as a medium referring it to God not actually but habitually inasmuch as he himself is ordered to God by charity. "Ille qui peccat venialiter, inhæret bono temporali non ut fruens, quia non constituit in eo finem, sed ut utens, referens in Deum non actu sed habitu" (I–II, Q. lxxxviii, a. 1, ad 3). For a mortal sin, some created good must be adhered to as a last end at least implicitly. This adherence cannot be accomplished by a semi-deliberate act. By adhering to an object that is at variance with the law of God and yet not destructive of the primary end of the Divine law, a true opposition is not set up between God and that object. The created good is not desired as an end. The sinner is not placed in the position of choosing between God and creature as ultimate ends that are opposed, but is in such a condition of mind that if the object to which he adheres were prohibited as contrary to his true last end he would not adhere to it, but would prefer to keep friendship with God. An example may be had in human friendship. A friend will refrain from doing anything that of itself will tend directly to dissolve friendship while allowing himself at times to do what is displeasing to his friends without destroying friendship.

The distinction between mortal and venial sin is set forth in Scripture. From St. John (I John, v, 16–17) it is clear there are some sins "unto death" and some sins not "unto death", i. e. mortal and venial. The classic text for the distinction of mortal and venial sin is that of St. Paul (I Cor., iii, 8–15), where he explains in detail the distinction between mortal and venial sin. "For other foundation no man can lay, but that which is laid; which is Christ Jesus. Now if any man build upon this foundation gold, silver, precious stones, wood, hay, stubble: every man's work shall be manifest; for the day of the Lord shall declare it; because it shall be revealed in fire; and the fire shall try every man's work, of what sort it is. If any man's work abide, which he hath built thereupon, he shall receive a reward. If any man's work burn, he shall suffer loss; but he himself shall be saved, yet so as by fire." By wood, hay, and stubble are signified venial sins (St. Thomas, I–II, Q. lxxxix, a. 2) which, built on the foundation of a living faith in Christ, do not destroy charity, and from their very nature do not merit eternal but temporal punishment. "Just as", says St. Thomas, [wood, hay, and stubble] "are gathered together in a house and do not pertain to the substance of the edifice, so also venial sins are multiplied in man, the spiritual edifice remaining, and for these he suffers either the fire of temporal tribulations in this life, or of purgatory after this life and nevertheless obtains eternal salvation." (ibid.)

The suitableness of the division into wood, hay, and stubble is explained by St. Thomas (iv, dist. 21, Q. i, a. 2). Some venial sins are graver than others and less pardonable, and this difference is well signified by the difference in the inflammability of wood, hay, and stubble. That there is a distinction between mortal and venial sins is of faith (Counc. of Trent, sess. VI, c. xi and canons 23–25; sess. XIV, de pœnit., c. v). This distinction is commonly rejected by all heretics ancient and modern. In the fourth century Jovinian asserted that all sins are equal in guilt and deserving of the same punishment (St. Aug., "Ep. 167", ii, n. 4); Pelagius (q. v.), that every sin deprives man of justice and therefore is mortal; Wyclif, that there is no warrant in Scripture for differentiating mortal from venial sin, and that the gravity of sin depends not on the quality of the action but on the decree of predestination or reprobation so that the worst crime of the predestined is infinitely less than the slightest fault of the reprobate; Hus, that all the actions of the vicious are mortal sins, while all the acts of the good are virtuous (Denz.-Bann., 642); Luther, that all sins of unbelievers are mortal and all sins of the regenerate, with the exception of infidelity, are venial; Calvin, like Wyclif, bases the difference between mortal sin and venial sin on predestination, but adds that a sin is venial because of the faith of the sinner. The twentieth among the condemned propositions of Baius reads: "There is no sin venial in its nature, but every sin merits eternal punishment" (Denz.-Bann., 1020). Hirscher in more recent times taught that all sins which are fully deliberate are mortal, thus denying the distinction of sins by reason of their objects and making the distinction rest on the imperfection of the act (Kleutgen, 2nd ed., II, 284, etc.).

Malice of Venial Sin.—The difference in the malice of mortal and venial sin consists in this: that mortal sin is contrary to the primary end of the eternal law, that it attacks the very substance of the law which commands that no created thing should be preferred to God as an end, or equalled to Him, while venial sin is only at variance with the law, not in contrary opposition to it, not attacking its substance. The substance of the law remaining, its perfect accomplishment is prevented by venial sin.

Conditions.—Venial sin is committed when the matter of the sin is light, even though the advertence of the intellect and consent of the will are full and deliberate, and when, even though the matter of the sin be grave, there is not full advertence on the part of the intellect and full consent on the part of the will. A precept obliges *sub gravi* when it has for its object an important end to be attained, and its transgression is prohibited under penalty of losing God's friendship. A precept obliges *sub levi* when it is not so directly imposed.

Effects.—Venial sin does not deprive the soul of sanctifying grace, or diminish it. It does not produce a *macula*, or stain, as does mortal sin, but it lessens the lustre of virtue—"In anima duplex est nitor, unus quiden habitualis, ex gratia sanctificante, alter actualis ex actibus virtutum, jamvero peccatum veniale impedit quidem fulgorem qui ex actibus virtutum oritur, non autem habitualem nitorem, quia non excludit nec minuit habitum charitatis" (I–II, Q. lxxxix, a. 1). Frequent and deliberate venial sin lessens the fervour of charity, disposes to mortal sin (I–II, Q. lxxxviii, a. 3), and hinders the reception of graces God would otherwise give. It displeases God (Apoc., ii, 4–5) and obliges the sinner to temporal punishment either in this life or in Purgatory. We cannot avoid all venial sin in this life. "Although the most just and holy occasionally during this life fall into some slight and daily sins, known as venial, they cease not on that account to be just" (Counc. of Trent, sess. VI, c. xi). And canon xxiii says: "If any one declare that a man once justified cannot sin again, or that he can avoid for the rest of his life every sin, even venial, let him be anathema", but according to the common opinion we can avoid all such as are fully deliberate. Venial sin may coexist with mortal sin in those who are averted from God by mortal sin. This fact does not change its nature or intrinsic reparability, and the fact that it is not coexistent with charity is not the result of venial sin, but of mortal sin. It is *per accidens*, for an extrinsic reason, that venial sin in this case is irreparable, and is punished in hell. That venial sin may appear in its true nature as essentially different from mortal sin it is considered as *de facto* coexisting with charity (I Cor., iii, 8–15). Venial sins do not need the grace of absolution. They can be remitted by prayer, contrition, fervent communion, and other pious works. Nevertheless it is laudable to confess them (Denn.-Bann., 1539).

V. PERMISSION OF SIN AND REMEDIES.—Since it is of faith that God is omnipotent, omniscient, and all good it is difficult to account for sin in His creation. The existence of evil is the underlying problem in all theology. Various explanations to account for its existence have been offered, differing according to the philosophical principles and religious tenets of their authors. Any Catholic explanation must take into account the defined truths of the omnipotence, omniscience, and goodness of God; free will on the part of man; and the fact that suffering is the penalty of sin. Of metaphysical evil, the negation of a greater good, God is the cause inasmuch as he has created beings with limited forms. Of physical evil (*malum pœnæ*) He is also the cause. Physical evil, considered as it proceeds from God and is inflicted in punishment of sin in accordance with the decrees of Divine justice, is good, compensating for the violation of order by sin. It is only in the subject affected by it that it is evil.

Of moral evil (*malum culpæ*) God is not the cause (Counc. of Trent, sess. VI, can. vi), either directly or indirectly. Sin is a violation of order, and God orders all things to Himself, as an ultimate end, consequently He cannot be the direct cause of sin. God's withdrawal of grace which would prevent the sin does not make Him the indirect cause of sin inasmuch as this withdrawal is affected according to the decrees of His Divine wisdom and justice in punishment of previous sin. He is under no obligation of impeding the sin, consequently it cannot be imputed to Him as a cause (I–II, Q. lxxix, a. 1). When we read in Scripture and the Fathers that God inclines men to sin the sense is, either that in His just judgment He permits men to fall into sin by a punitive permission, exercising His justice in punishment of past sin; or that He directly causes, not sin, but certain exterior works, good in themselves, which are so abused by the evil wills of men that here and now they commit evil; or that He gives them the power of accomplishing their evil designs. Of the physical act in sin God is the cause inasmuch as it is an entity and good. Of the malice of sin man's evil will is the sufficient cause. God could not be impeded in the creation of man by the fact that He foresaw his fall. This would mean the limiting of His omnipotence by a creature, and would be destructive of Him. He was free to create man even though He foresaw his fall, and He created him, endowed him with free will, and gave him sufficient means of persevering in good had he so willed. We must sum up our ignorance of the permission of evil by saying in the words of St. Augustine, that God would not have permitted evil had He not been powerful enough to bring good out of evil. God's end in creating this universe is Himself, not the good of man, and somehow or other good and evil serve His ends, and there shall finally be a restoration of violated order by Divine justice. No sin shall be without its punishment. The evil men do must be atoned for either in this world by penance (see PENANCE) or in the world to come in purgatory or hell, according as the sin that stains the soul, and is not repented of, is mortal or venial, and merits eternal or temporal punishment. (See EVIL.) God has provided a remedy for sin and manifested His love and goodness in the face of man's ingratitude by the Incarnation of His Divine Son (see INCARNATION); by the institution of His Church to guide men and interpret to them His law, and administer to them the sacraments, seven channels of grace, which, rightly used, furnish an adequate remedy for sin and a means to union with God in heaven, which is the end of His law.

Sense of Sin.—The understanding of sin, as far as it can be understood by our finite intelligence, serves to unite man more closely to God. It impresses him with a salutary fear, a fear of his own powers, a fear, if left to himself, of falling from grace; with the necessity he lies under of seeking God's help and grace to stand firm in the fear and love of God, and make progress in the spiritual life. Without the acknowledgment that the present moral state of man is not that in which God created him, that his powers are weakened; that he has a supernatural end to attain, which is impossible of attainment by his own unaided efforts, without grace there being no proportion between the end and the means; that the world, the flesh, and the devil are in reality active agents fighting against him and leading him to serve them instead of God, sin cannot be understood. The evolutionary hypothesis would have it that physical evolution accounts for the physical origin of man, that science knows no condition of man in which man exhibited the characteristics of the state of original justice, no state of sinlessness. The fall of man in this hypothesis is in reality a rise to a higher grade of being. "A fall it might seem, just as a vicious man sometimes seems degraded below the beasts, but in promise and potency, a rise it really was" (Sir O. Lodge, "Life and Matter", p. 79). This teaching is destructive of the notion of sin as taught by the Catholic Church. Sin is not a phase of an upward struggle, it is rather a deliberate, wilful refusal to struggle. If there has been no fall from a higher to a lower state, then the teaching of Scripture in regard to Redemption and the necessity of a baptismal regeneration is unintelligible. The Catholic teaching is the one that places sin in its true light, that justifies the condemnation of sin we find in Scripture.

The Church strives continually to impress her children with a sense of the awfulness of sin that they may fear it and avoid it. We are fallen creatures, and our spiritual life on earth is a warfare. Sin is our enemy, and while of our own strength we cannot avoid sin, with God's grace we can. If we but place no obstacle to the workings of grace we can avoid all deliberate sin. If we have the misfortune to sin, and seek God's grace and pardon with a contrite and humble heart, He will not repel us. Sin has its remedy in grace, which is given us by God, through the merits of His only-begotten Son, Who has redeemed us, restoring by His passion and death the order violated by the sin of our first parents, and making us once again children of God and heirs of heaven. Where sin is looked on as a necessary and unavoidable condition of things human, where inability to avoid sin is conceived as necessary, discouragement naturally follows. Where the Catholic doctrine of the creation of man in a superior state, his fall by a wilful transgression, the effects of which fall are by Divine decree transmitted to his posterity, destroying the balance of the human faculties and leaving man inclined to evil; where the dogmas of redemption and grace in reparation of sin are kept in mind, there is no discouragement. Left to ourselves we fall, by keeping close to God and continually seeking His help we can stand and struggle against sin, and if faithful in the battle we must wage shall be crowned by God in heaven. (See CONSCIENCE; JUSTIFICATION; SCANDAL.)

DOGMATIC WORKS: ST. THOMAS, *Summa theol.*, I–II, QQ. lxxi–lxxxix; IDEM, *Contra gentes*, tr. RICKABY, *Of God and His Creatures* (London, 1905); IDEM, *Quæst. disputatæ: De malo* in *Opera omnia* (Paris, 1875); BILLUART, *De peccatis* (Paris, 1867–72); SUAREZ, *De pecc.* in *Opera omnia* (Paris, 1878); SALMANTICENSES, *De pecc.* in *Curs. theol.* (Paris, 1877); GONET, *Clypeus theol. thom.* (Venice, 1772); JOHN OF ST. THOMAS, *De pecc.* in *Curs. theol.* (Paris, 1886); SYLVIUS,*De pecc.*(Antwerp, 1698); *Catechismus Romanus*, tr.DONOVAN, *Catechism of the Council of Trent* (Dublin, 1829); SCHEEBEN, *Handbuch d. kath. Dogmatik* (Freiburg, 1873–87); WILHELM AND SCANNELL, *Manual of Catholic Theology*, II (London, 1908); MANNING, *Sin and its Consequences* (New York, 1904); SHARPE, *Principles of Christianity* (London, 1904); IDEM, *Evil, its Nature and Cause* (London, 1906); BILLOT, *De nat. et rat. peccati personalis* (Rome, 1900); TANQUEREY, *Synopsis theol.*, I (New York, 1907).

Cf. following on moral theology:—LEHMKUHL, *Theol. moralis* (Freiburg, 1910); GÖPFERT, *Moraltheologie*, I (Paderborn, 1899); MARC, *Inst. mor. alphonsin* (Rome, 1902); NOLDIN, *Summa theol. mor.* (Innsbruck, 1906); GENICOT, *Theol. mor. inst.*, I (Louvain, 1905); SABETTI-BARRETT, *Compend. theol. mor.* (Ratisbon, 1906); SCHIELER-HEUSER, *Theory and Practice of the Confessional* (New York, 1906); SLATER, *Manual of Moral Theology* (New York, 1908); KOCH, *Moraltheologie* (3rd ed., Freiburg, 1910).

A. C. O'NEIL.

Sinai (סִינַי, Σινᾶ, *Sinai* and *Sina*), the mountain on which the Mosaic Law was given. Horeb and Sinai were thought synonymous by St. Jerome ("De situ et nom. Hebr.", in P. L., XXIII, 889), W. Gesenius (חרב סיני), and, more recently, G. Ebers (p. 381). Ewald, Delitzsch, Ed. Robinson, E. H. Palmer, and others think Horeb denoted the whole mountainous region about Sinai (Ex., xvii, 6). The origin of the name *Sinai* is disputed. It seems to be an adjective from צין, "the desert" (Ewald and Ebers) or "the moon-god" (E. Schrader and others). The mount was called Sinai, or "the mount of God" probably before the time of Moses (Josephus, "Antiq. Jud.", II, xii.) The name is now given to the triangular peninsula lying between the desert of Southern Palestine, the Red Sea, and the gulfs of Akabah and Suez, with an area of about 10,000 sq. miles, which was the scene of the forty years' wandering of the Israelites after the Exodus from Egypt.

The principal topographical features are two. North of the Jabal et-Tih (3200 to 3950 feet) stretches an arid plateau, the desert of Tih, marked by numerous Wadis, notably El-Arish, the "River of Egypt", which formed the southern boundary of the Promised Land (Gen., xv, 18; Num., xxxiv, 5). South of Jabal et-Tih rises a mountainous mass of granite streaked with porphyry, dividing into three principal groups: the western, Jabal Serbal (6750 feet); the central, Jabal Mûsa (7380 feet), Jabal Catherine (8560 feet), and Jabal Um Schomer (8470 feet); the eastern, Jabal Thebt (7906 feet) and Jabal Tarfa, which terminates in Ras Mohammed. It is among these mountains that Jewish and Christian tradition places the Sinai of the Bible, but the precise location is uncertain. It is Jabal Mûsa, according to a tradition traceable back to the fourth century, when St. Silvia of Aquitaine was there. Jabal Mûsa is defended by E. H. and H. S. Palmer, Vigouroux, Lagrange, and others. However, the difficulty of applying Ex., xix, 12, to Jabal Mûsa and the inscriptions found near Jabal Serbal have led some to favour Serbal. This was the opinion of St. Jerome (P. L., XXIII, 916, 933) and Cosmas (P. G., LXXXVIII, 217), and more recently of Burkhard and Lepsius, and it has of late been very strongly defended by G. Ebers, not to mention Beke, Gressmann, and others, who consider the whole story about Sinai (Ex., xix) only a mythical interpretation of some volcanic eruption. The more liberal critics, while agreeing generally that the Jewish traditions represented by the "Priest-codex" and "Elohistic documents" place Sinai among the mountains in the south-central part of the peninsula, yet disagree as to its location by the older "Jahvistic" tradition (Ex., ii, 15, 16, 21; xviii, 1, 5). A. von Gall, whose opinion Welhausen thinks the best sustained, contends that Meribar (D. V. Temptation.—Ex., xvii, 7) is identical with Cades (Num., xxxiii, 36; xxvii, 14), that the Israelites never went so far south as Jabal Mûsa, and hence that Sinai must be looked for in Madian, on the east coast of Akabar. Others (cf. Winckler, II, p. 29; Smend, p. 35, n. 2; and Weill, opp. cit. infra in bibliography) look for Sinai in the near neighbourhood of Cades (Ayn Qâdis) in Southern Palestine.

Sinai was the refuge of many Christian anchorites during the third-century persecutions of the Church. There are traces of a fourth-century monastery near Mount Serbal. In 527 the Emperor Justinian built the famous convent of Mt. Sinai on the north foot of Jabal Mûsa, which has been known since the ninth century as St. Catherine's. Its small library contains about 500 volumes of valuable manuscripts in Greek, Arabic, Syriac, Ethiopic, etc. It was here that Tischendorf, during his researches in 1844, 1853, and 1859, found a very ancient Greek MS. (since known as the "Codex Sinaiticus") containing most of the Septuagint, all the new Testament, the "Epistle of Barnabas", and the first part of the "Shepherd" of Hermas. Forty-three MS. pages found by him are preserved at the University of Leipzig and known as the "Codex Friderico-Augustanus". In 1892 Mrs. Smith Lewis found at Sinai a fourth-century palimpsest Syriac text of St. Luke's Gospel. Sinai is rich in valuable inscriptions. M. de Vogüé gives 3200 Egyptian and Semitic inscriptions found in the Wâdi Mukatteb, the ruins of the temple of Ischta, or Astaroth-Carmain, and the iron and turquoise mines and granite and marble quarries, which were extensively worked under the twelfth and eighteenth Egyptian dynasties.

The present population of Sinai is 4000 to 6000 semi-nomadic Arabs, Mohammedans, governed by their tribal sheikhs and immediately subject to the commandant of the garrison at Qal' at un-Nakhl, under the Intelligence Department of the Egyptian War Office at Cairo.

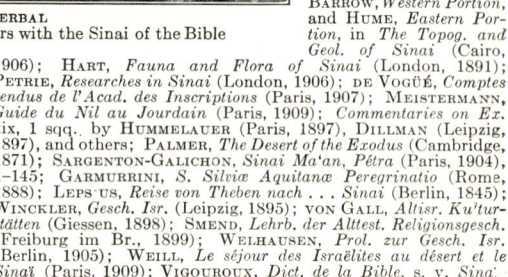

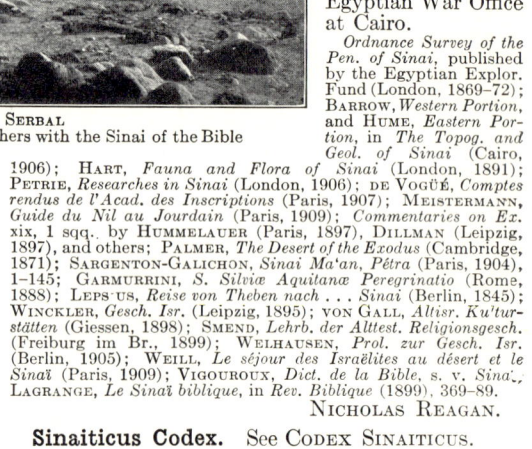

Ordnance Survey of the Pen. of Sinai, published by the Egyptian Explor. Fund (London, 1869–72); BARROW, *Western Portion*, and HUME, *Eastern Portion*, in *The Topog. and Geol. of Sinai* (Cairo, 1906); HART, *Fauna and Flora of Sinai* (London, 1891); PETRIE, *Researches in Sinai* (London, 1906); DE VOGÜÉ, *Comptes rendus de l'Acad. des Inscriptions* (Paris, 1907); MEISTERMANN, *Guide du Nil au Jourdain* (Paris, 1909); *Commentaries on Ex.* xix, 1 sqq., by HUMMELAUER (Paris, 1897), DILLMAN (Leipzig, 1897), and others; PALMER, *The Desert of the Exodus* (Cambridge, 1871); SARGENTON-GALICHON, *Sinai Ma'an, Pétra* (Paris, 1904), 1–145; GARMURRINI, *S. Silviæ Aquitanæ Peregrinatio* (Rome, 1888); LEPSIUS, *Reise von Theben nach . . . Sinai* (Berlin, 1845); WINCKLER, *Gesch. Isr.* (Leipzig, 1895); VON GALL, *Altisr. Kulturstätten* (Giessen, 1898); SMEND, *Lehrb. der Alttest. Religionsgesch.* (Freiburg im Br., 1899); WELHAUSEN, *Prol. zur Gesch. Isr.* (Berlin, 1905); WEILL, *Le séjour des Israélites au désert et le Sinaï* (Paris, 1909); VIGOUROUX, *Dict. de la Bible*, s. v. *Sinaï*; LAGRANGE, *Le Sinaï biblique*, in *Rev. Biblique* (1899), 369–89.

NICHOLAS REAGAN.

Sinaiticus Codex. See CODEX SINAITICUS.

Sinaloa, DIOCESE OF (SINALOENSIS), in the Republic of Mexico, suffragan of the Archdiocese of Durango. Its area is that of the State of Sinaloa, 27,552 sq. miles, and its population (1910) 323,499. Culiacan, the capital of the state and residence of the bishop and governor, counts a population (1910) of 13,578. The present territory of Sinaloa was discovered in 1530 by the ill-reputed D. Nuño de Guzman who founded the city of San Miguel de Culiacan. A few Spaniards established a colony there. The province of Culiacan was soon obliged to face the terrors of war brought upon it by the barbarous cruelties of Nuño and his favourite, Diego Hernandez de Proaño. So frightened was Nuño by the terrible insurrection that he removed Proaño, placing in his stead Cristóbal de Tapia, whose humanitarian measures slowly restored confidence. Although colonized from the beginning of the sixteenth century, most of the territory, excepting a few strong places, was inhabited by fierce pagan tribes, for whose conversion the Jesuits laboured early in the seventeenth century. After having subdued and evangelized the Indians of the mission of Piaxtla in a comparatively short time, and after having turned over to the Bishop of Durango the settlements under their control, the Jesuits extended their domination over the Indians living in the northern part of the actual state and at the time of their expulsion (by decree of Charles III) they fruitfully administered the missions of Chinipas and Sinaloa. In Chinipas they had residences at Guasarapes, Santa Ana, Secora, Moris, Barbaroco, Santa Ines, Serocagui, Tubares, Satebó, Baborigame, Nabogame, and San Andres; in Sinaloa (misión del Fuerte) they had residences at Mocorito, Nio, Guazave, Chicorato, Mochicave, Batacosa, Conicari, Tehueco, Ocoroni, and Bacubirito. It is notable that the towns of the misión del Rio Yaqui, which now belong to the Diocese of Sonora, were then included in the mission of Sinaloa. When the See of Durango was founded in 1620, Sinaloa, which until then had belonged to the Diocese of Guadalajara, became part of it; on the foundation (1780) of the Diocese of Sonora, it became a part of the latter. However, the residence of the bishop, after having been successively at Arispe and Alamo, passed to Culiacan, capital of Sinaloa until 1883, when Leo XIII founded the Diocese of Sinaloa, which had formed part of the ecclesiastical province of Guadalajara, and the Bishop of Sonora removed to Hermosillo. In 1891, when the new archiepiscopal See of Durango was created, Sinaloa became one of its suffragans.

The diocese has 1 seminary with 18 students; 10 parochial schools; 3 colleges with 677 students.

México á través de los siglos, II (Barcelona); DAVILA, Continuación de la historia de la C. de J. en Nueva España (Puebla, 1889).

CAMILLUS CRIVELLI.

Singleton, HUGH. See SHREWSBURY, DIOCESE OF.

Sinigaglia (SENIGALLIA), DIOCESE OF (SENOGALLIENSIS), in the Province of Ancona in the Marches (Central Italy). The city is situated on the Adriatic at the mouth of the Misa, which divides it into two parts. Maritime commerce, the cultivation and manufacture of silk, agriculture, and cattle-raising form the means of support of the population. The fortifications constructed by the dukes of Urbino and by the popes still remain in part. Among the churches, besides the cathedral, that of Santa Maria delle Grazie (1491) without the city walls deserves mention; it possesses a Madonna with six saints by Perugino, and another Madonna by Piero della Francesca. The name Senigallia records the Senones, a tribe of Gauls who possessed this city before its conquest by the Romans. The latter founded a colony here called Sena Hadria, but later the name most commonly used was Senogallia or Senigallia. In the Civil War (B.C. 82) it was sacked by Pompey, then one of Sulla's generals. It was pillaged a second time by Alaric, A.D. 408. Under the Byzantine rule it belonged to the so-called Pentapolis. Several times in the sixth and eighth centuries the Lombards attempted to capture it, and, in fact, shortly before the city was bestowed upon the Holy See it was the seat of a Duke Arioldo, who in 772 owed allegiance to King Desiderius. It afterwards shared the vicissitudes of the March of Ancona, and at the end of the twelfth century was the seat of a count. In the wars between the popes and Frederick II it belonged for the most part to the party of the Guelphs, for which reason it sustained many sieges, and was in 1264 sacked by Percivale Doria, captain of King Manfred. Hardly recovered from this calamity, it fell into the power of Guido di Montefeltro (1280). In 1306 it was captured by Pandolfo Malatesta of Pesaro and remained in his family, notwithstanding that they were expelled by Cardinal Bertrando du Poyet and later by Cardinal Albornoz (1355). In 1416 Ludovico Migliorati of Fermo and the cities of Ancona and Camerino formed a league against Galeotto Malatesta, and captured Sinigaglia, but they afterwards restored it. In 1445 it was taken by Sigismondo Malatesta of Rimini, who also secured the investiture from Eugenius IV and fortified the city.

After various vicissitudes Sinigaglia was (1474) given in fief to Giovanni della Rovere, a nephew of Sixtus IV. He married the last heiress of the duchy of Urbino, of which the city thus became a part (1508). In December, 1502, Sinigaglia, which had thrown open its gates to Cæsar Borgia, was the scene of the celebrated treachery by which Borgia rid himself of his enemies, the petty lords of the Romagna. In 1624 it came under the immediate suzerainty of the popes. In 1683 Turkish pirates disembarked and plundered the city. Sinigaglia was the birthplace of Pius IX and B. Gherardo di Serra (fourteenth century). The patron saint of Sinigaglia is St. Paulinus, whose body is preserved in the cathedral (as is attested for the first time in 1397). He is, therefore, not identical with St. Paulinus of Nola, nor is it known to what epoch he belongs. The first bishop of certain date was Venantius (502). About 562 the bishop was St. Bonifacius, who at the time of the Lombard invasion was martyred by the Arians. Under Bishop Sigismundus (c. 590) the relics of St. Gaudentius, Bishop of Rimini and martyr, were transported to Sinigaglia. Other bishops of the diocese are: Robertus and Theodosius (1057), friends of St. Peter Damianus; Jacopo (1232–1270), who rebuilt the cathedral which had been destroyed in 1264 by the Saracen troops of King Manfred; Francesco Mellini (1428), an Augustinian, who died at Rome, suffocated by the crowd at a consistory of Egenius IV. Under Bishop Antonio Colombella (1438), an Augustinian, Sigismondo Malatesta, lord of Sinigaglia, angered by his resistance to the destruction of certain houses, caused the cathedral and the episcopal palace to be demolished. The precious materials were transported to Rimini and were used in the construction of S. Francesco (*tempio Malatestiano*). Under Bishop Marco Vigerio della Rovere (1513) the new cathedral was begun in 1540; it was consecrated in 1595 by Pietro Ridolfi (1591), a learned

The Castle, Sinigaglia

writer. Other bishops were Cardinal Antonio Barberini, a Capuchin brother of Urban VIII; Cardinal Domenico Poracciani (1714); Annibale della Genga (1816), who afterwards became Pope Leo XII. The diocese is suffragan of Urbino; it has 48 parishes with 114 secular and 78 regular clergy; 92,000 souls; 15 monasteries for men; 19 convents for women; and 3 institutes for female education.

CAPPELLETTI, *Le chiese d'Italia* (Venice, 1857); COSTELLI, *Il passato e l'avvenire di Senigallia* (Ascoli, 1890); MARGUTTI, *Escursione artistica per Senigallia* (Florence, 1886).

U. BENIGNI.

Sinis, a titular see in Armenia Secunda, suffragan of Melitene. The catalogue of titular bishoprics of the Roman Curia formerly contained a see of Sinita, in Armenia. When the list was revised in 1884, this name was replaced by Sinis, mentioned as belonging to Armenia Secunda, with Melitene, now Malatia, as its metropolis. Ptolemy, V. 7, 5, mentions a town called Siniscolon in Cappadocia at Melitene, near the Euphrates. Müller in his "Notes à Ptolemy" ed. Didot, I (Paris, 1901), 887, identifies this with Sinekli, a village near the Euphrates, "ab Argovan versus ortum hibernum", about nineteen miles north of Malatia in the vilayet of Mamouret ul-Aziz. But it seems certain that Siniscolon is a mis-reading for "Sinis Colonia", a form found in several MSS. Ramsay, "Asia Minor", 71, 272, 314, reads Sinis for Pisonos in "Itinerar. Anton." and especially for Sinispora in the "Tabula Peutingeriana" (Sinis, Erpa), and places Sinis Colonia twenty-two Roman miles west of Melitene, on the road to Cæsarea. There is no mention of this town in the Greek "Notitiæ episcopatuum" among the suffragans of Melitene, and none of its bishops is known, so it seems never to have been a bishopric.

S. PÉTRIDÈS.

Sinna. See SEHNA, DIOCESE OF.

Sinope, a titular see in Asia minor, suffragan of Amasea in Helenopontus. It is a Greek colony, situated on a peninsula on the coast of Paphlagonia, of very early origin, some attributing its foundation to the Argonaut Autolycus, a companion of Hercules. Later it received a colony from Miletus which seems to have been expelled or conquered by the Cimmerians (Herodotus, IV, 12); but in 632 B.C. the Greeks succeeded again in capturing it. Henceforth Sinope enjoyed great prosperity and founded several colonies, among them being Cerasus, Cotyora, and Trapezus. The town took part in the Peloponnesian War, supporting Athens. Xenophon stopped there with his forces on the retreat of the Ten Thousand (Anab. V, v, 3; Diodor. Sicul., XIV, 30, 32; Ammien Marcel., XXII, 8). Fruitlessly besieged in 220 B.C. by Mithridates IV, King of Pontus, Sinope was taken by Pharnaces in 183 B.C., and became the capital and residence of the kings of Pontus. It was the birthplace of Mithridates the Great, who adorned it with magnificent monuments and constructed large arsenals there for his fleet. Lucullus captured it and gave it back its autonomy. Cæsar also established the Colonia Julia Cæsarea there in 45 B.C. when his supremacy began. Sinope was also the birthplace of the cynic philosopher, Diogenes, Diphilus, the comic poet, and Aquila, the Jew, who translated the Old Testament into Greek in the second century A.D. A Christian community existed there in the first half of the second century, with a bishop, the father of the celebrated heretic Marcion, whom he expelled from his diocese. Among its other bishops may be mentioned St. Phocas, venerated on 22 September, with St. Phocas, the gardener of the same town, who is possibly to be identified with him; Prohæresios, present at the Councils of Gangres and Philippopolis in 343 and 344; Antiochus at the Council of Chalcedon, 451; Sergius at the Sixth Œcumenical Council, 681; Zeno, who was exiled in 712 for opposing Monothelitism; Gregory, present at the Seventh Council in 787, beheaded in 793 for revolting against the emperor, etc. A little before 1315 the Bishop of Sinope, driven out of his see by the Turks, received in compensation the metropoles of Sida and Sylæos (Miklosich and Müller, "Acta patriarchatus Constantinopolitani", I, 34); the diocese must have been suppressed upon his death, as it is not mentioned in the "Notitiæ episcopatuum" of the fifteenth century. In 1401 a Greek merchant who visited Sinope found everything in disorder as a result of the Turkish inroads (Wächter, "Der Verfall des Griechentums in Kleinasien im XIV. Jahrhundert", 20); however, the town, which had belonged to the Empire of Trapezus from 1204 was not captured till 1470 by Mahomet II. In November, 1853, the Turkish fleet was destroyed by the Russians in the port of Sinope. Sinope is now the chief town of a sanjak of the vilayet of Castamouni, containing 15,000 inhabitants, about one half of whom are Greek schismatics.

SMITH, *Dict. of Greek and Roman Geog.* (London, 1870), s. v.; ROBINSON, *Ancient Sinope* (Baltimore, 1906); LE QUIEN, *Oriens christianus* (Paris, 1740), I, 537-40; VAILHÉ, *Les évêques de Sinope* in *Echos d'Orient*, XI, 210-12; CUINET, *La Turquie d'Asie* (Paris, 1891), IV. 574-82.

S. VAILHÉ.

Sins against the Holy Ghost. See HOLY GHOST, subtitle VIII.

Sinuessa, SYNOD OF. See MARCELLINUS, SAINT, POPE.

Sion. See JERUSALEM.

Sion, a titular see in Asia Minor, suffragan of Ephesus. No civil document mentions it. It is numbered among the suffragans of Ephesus in the Greek "Notitiæ episcopatuum", from the seventh to the thirteenth century. [See Gelzer in "Abhandlungen der k. bayer. Akademie der Wiss.", I. Cl. XXI Bd. III Abth. (Munich, 1900), 536, 552; Idem, "Georgii Cyprii descriptio orbis romani" (Leipzig, 1890), 8, 62; Parthey, "Hierocles Synecdemus e Notit. gr. episcopat. (Berlin, 1866), 61, 103, 155, 167, 203, 245.] The names of only three bishops of Sion are known: Nestorius, present at the Council of Ephesus, 431; John, at the Council in Trullo, 692; Philip, represented at Nicæa, 787, by the priest Theognis (Le Quien, "Oriens christianus", I, 721). This author asks if Basil, Bishop πόλεως Ἀσαίων represented at Chalcedon, 451, by his metropolitan does not belong to Sion; it is more likely that he was Bishop of Assus. Ramsay ("Asia Minor", 105) thinks that Sion is probably the same town as Tianae, or Tiarae mentioned by Pliny, V, 33, 3, and Hierocles, 661, 8, and Attaca, mentioned by Strabo, XIII, 607; but this is very doubtful. In any case the site of Sion is unknown.

S. PÉTRIDÈS.

Sion, DIOCESE OF (SEDUNENSIS), a Swiss bishopric depending directly on the Holy See.

History.—The Diocese of Sion is the oldest in Switzerland and one of the oldest north of the Alps. At first its see was at Octodorum, now called Martinach, or Martigny. According to tradition there was a Bishop of Octodorum, named Oggerius, as early as A. D. 300. However, the first authenticated bishop is St. Theodore (d. 391), who was present at the Council of Aquileia in 381. On the spot where the Abbey of Saint-Maurice now stands he built a church in honour of St. Mauritius, martyred here about 300. He also induced the hermits of the vicinity to unite in a common life, thus beginning the Abbey of Saint-Maurice, the oldest north of the Alps. Theodore rebuilt the church at Sion, which had been destroyed by Emperor Maximianus at the beginning of the fourth century. At first the diocese was a suffragan of Vienne; later it became suffragan of Tarentaise. In 580 the bishop, St. Heliodorus, transferred the see to Sion, as Octodorum was frequently endangered by the inundations of the Rhone and the Drance. There were frequent disputes with the monks of the Abbey of Saint-Maurice, who were jealously watchful that the bishops should not extend their jurisdiction over the abbey. Several of the bishops united both offices, as: Wilcharius (764–80), previously Archbishop of Vienne, from which he had been driven by the Saracens; St. Alteus, who received from the pope a Bull of exemption in favour of the monastery (780); Aimo II, son of Count Hubert of Savoy, who entertained Leo IX at Saint-Maurice in 1049.

The last king of Upper Burgundy, Rudolph III, granted the Countship of Valais to Bishop Hugo (998–1017); this union of the spiritual and secular powers made the bishop the most powerful ruler in the valley of the Upper Rhone. Taking this donation as a basis, the bishops of Sion extended their secular power, and the religious metropolis of the valley became also the political centre. However, the union of the two powers was the cause of violent disputes in the following centuries. For, while the spiritual jurisdiction of the bishop extended over the whole valley of the Rhone above Lake Geneva, the Countship of Valais included only the upper part of the valley, reaching to the confluence of the Trient and the Rhone. The attempts of the bishops of Sion to carry their secular power farther down the Rhone were bitterly and successfully opposed by the abbots of Saint-Maurice, who had obtained large possessions in Lower Valais. The bishops were also opposed by the patrons of the abbey, the counts of Savoy, who used this position to increase their suzerainty over Lower Valais. The medieval bishops of Sion belonged generally to noble families of Savoy and Valais and were often drawn into the feuds of these families. Moreover the bishops were vigorously opposed by the petty feudal nobles of Valais, who, trusting to their fortified castles on rocky heights, sought to evade the supremacy of the bishop who was at the same time count and prefect of the Holy Roman Empire. Other opponents of the bishops were the flourishing peasant communities of Upper Valais, which were called later the *sieben Zehnten* (seven-tenths). Their struggles with Savoy forced the bishops to grant continually increasing political rights to the peasant communities. Thus Bishop William IV of Raron (1437–57) was obliged to relinquish civil and criminal jurisdiction over the *sieben Zehnten* by the Treaty of Naters in 1446, while a revolt of his subjects compelled Bishop Jost of Silinen (1482–96) to flee from the diocese. Walter II of Supersax (1457–82) took part in the battles of the Swiss against Charles the Bold of Burgundy and his confederate, the Duke of Savoy, and in 1475 drove the House of Savoy from Lower Valais. The most important bishop of this era was Matthew Schinner (1499–1522), a highly cultivated Humanist. Bishop Schinner, fearing that French supremacy would endanger the freedom of the Swiss, placed the military force of the diocese at the disposal of the pope and in 1510 brought about an alliance for five years between the Swiss Confederacy and the Roman Church. In return for this Julius II made the bishop a cardinal. In 1513 the bishop had succeeded in having his diocese separated from the Archdiocese of Tarentaise and placed directly under the control of the pope. The defeat of the Swiss in 1515 at the battle of Marignano, at which Schinner himself fought, weakened his position in the diocese, and the arbitrary rule of his brothers led to a revolt of his subjects; in 1518 he was obliged to leave the diocese.

The new doctrines of the Reformation found little acceptance in Valais, although preachers were sent into the canton from Berne, Zurich, and Basle. In 1529 Bishop Adrian I of Riedmatten (1529–48), the cathedral chapter, and the *sieben Zehnten* formed an alliance with the Catholic cantons of the Confederation, the purpose of which was to maintain and protect the Catholic Faith in all the territories of the allied cantons against the efforts of the Reformed cantons. On account of this alliance Valais aided in gaining the victory of the Catholics over the followers of Zwingli at Cappel in 1531; this victory saved the possessions of the Catholic Church in Switzerland. The abbots of Saint-Maurice opposed all religious innovations as energetically as did Bishops Adrian I of Riedmatten, Hildebrand of Riedmatten (1565–1604), and Adrian II of Riedmatten (1604–13), so that the whole of Valais remained Catholic. Both Adrian II and his successor Hildebrand Jost (1613–38) were again involved in disputes with the *sieben Zehnten* in regard to the exercise of the rights of secular supremacy. In order to put an end to these quarrels and not to endanger the Catholic Faith he relinquished in 1630 the greater part of his rights as secular suzerain, and the power of the bishop was thereafter limited almost entirely to the spiritual sphere.

The secular power of the bishops was brought to an end by the French Revolution. In 1798 Valais, after an heroic struggle against the supremacy of France, was incorporated into the Helvetian Republic, and Bishop John Anthony Blatter (1790–1817) retired to Novara. During the sway of Napoleon Valais was separated from Switzerland in 1802 as the Rhodanic Republic, and in 1810 was united with France. Most of the monasteries were suppressed. In 1814 Valais threw off French supremacy, when the Allies entered the territory; in 1815 it joined Switzerland as one of the cantons. As partial compensation for the loss of his secular power the bishop received a post of honour in the Diet of the canton and the right to four votes. Disputes often arose as the Constitution of 1815 of the canton gave Upper Valais political predominance in the cantonal government, notwithstanding the fact that its population was smaller than that of Lower Valais. This led in 1840 to a civil war with Lower Valais, where the "Young Swiss" party, hostile to the Church, were in control. The party friendly to the Church conquered, it is true, and the influence of the Church over teaching was, at first, preserved, but on account of the defeat of the *Sonderbund*, with which Valais had united, a radical Government gained control in 1847. The new administration at once showed itself unfriendly to the Church, secularized many church landed properties, and wrung large sums of money from the bishop and monasteries. When in 1856 the moderate party gained the cantonal election, negotiations were begun with Bishop Peter Joseph von Preux (1843–75), and friendly relations were restored between the diocese and the canton. In 1880 the two powers came to an agreement as to the lands taken from the Church in 1848; these, so far as they had not been sold, were given back for their original uses. Since then the bishop and the Government have been on friendly terms. The new Constitution of 1907 declares the Catholic religion to be the religion of the canton, and forbids any union of spiritual and secular functions. The ordinances regulating the election of a bishop which have been in existence from early times, at least, contradict this (see below). The present bishop is Julius Mauritius Abbet, b. 12 Sept., 1845, appointed auxiliary bishop *cum jure successionis* 1 Oct., 1895, succeeded to the see 26 Feb., 1901.

Statistics.—The boundaries of the Diocese of Valais have hardly been changed since it was founded; the diocese includes the Upper Rhone Valley, that is, the Canton of Valais, with exception of the exempt Abbey of Saint-Maurice, and of the Catholic inhabitants of Saint-Gingolph, who belong to the French Diocese of Annecy; it also includes the parishes of Bex and

Aigle that belong to the Canton of Vaud. In 1911 the diocese had 11 deaneries, 125 parishes, 70 chaplaincies, 208 secular priests, 135 regular priests and professed, about 120,000 Catholics. Nearly 30 per cent of the population of the diocese speak German, and nearly 65 per cent French; the language of the rest of the population is Italian. The bishop is elected by the denominationally mixed Great Council from a list of four candidates presented by the cathedral chapter, and the election is laid before the pope for confirmation. The cathedral chapter consists of ten canons; in addition five rectors are included among the cathedral clergy. The clergy are trained at a seminary for priests at Sion that has six ecclesiastical professors and twelve resident students; there are also six theological students studying at the University of Innsbruck. The religious orders of men in the diocese are: Augustinian Canons, with houses on the Great St. Bernard, the Simplon, and at Martigny, containing altogether 45 priests, 6 professed and 7 lay-brothers; Capuchins, at Sion and Saint-Maurice, numbering 22 priests, 6 students of theology, and 9 lay-brothers. The exempt abbey of Augustinian Canons at Saint-Maurice contains 46 priests, 9 professed and lay-brothers. The orders and congregations of nuns in the diocese are: Bernardines at Colombay; Hospital Sisters at Sion; Sisters of St. Vincent de Paul at Saint-Maurice; Franciscan Nuns, at the same place; Sisters of Charity of the Holy Cross at Sion, Leuk, and Leukerbad; Ursuline Nuns at Sion and Brieg.

BRIGUET, *Vallesia christ. seu diœc. Sedunensis hist. sacra* (Sion, 1744); BOCCARD, *Hist. du Valais* (Geneva, 1844); BURGENER, *Die Heiligen des walliser Landes* (Einsiedeln, 1857); GREMAUD, *Catalogue des évêques de Sion* (Lausanne, 1864); IDEM, *Doc. relatifs à l'hist. du Valais* (Lausanne, 1875–84); GAY, *Hist. du Valais* (Geneva, 1888–89); IDEM, *Mélanges d'hist. valaisanne* (Geneva, 1891); RAMEAU, *Le Valais hist.* (Sion, 1891); BÜCHI, *Die kath. Kirche der Schweiz* (Munich, 1902); BOURBON, *L'archevêque s. Vultchaire* (Fribourg, 1900); *Mélanges d'hist. et d'archéol. de la soc. helvétique de Saint-Maurice* (1901); GRENAT, *Hist. moderne du Valais 1536–1815* (Geneva, 1904); BESSON, *Recherches sur les orig. des évêchés de Genève, Lausanne, Sion, etc.* (Paris, 1906); *Status venerabilis cleri diœc. Sedunen.* (Sion, 1911); *Blätter aus der walliser Gesch.* (Sion, 1899—).

JOSEPH LINS.

Sionita. See GABRIEL SIONITA.

Sioux City, DIOCESE OF (SIOPOLITAN.), erected 15 Jan., 1902, by Leo XIII. The establishment of this diocese was provided for in the Bull appointing Most Rev. John J. Keane, D.D., to the Archbishopric of Dubuque on 24 July, 1900. This provision was made on the occasion of that appointment for the reason that the new diocese was taken entirely from the Archdiocese of Dubuque. It comprises twenty-four counties in north-western Iowa, including a territory of 14,518 square miles. Sioux City is on the extreme limit of the western boundary of Iowa, situated on the east bank of the Missouri River, about one hundred miles north of Omaha. With the exception of Des Moines, the capital, it is the largest and most enterprising municipality in the State of Iowa, containing a population of between fifty and sixty thousand. It is in the midst of a large and rich agricultural country, and relies chiefly on the products of the soil, of which the staple article is corn; consequently grain-packing is the chief industry of Sioux City. The Catholic population of the diocese is almost sixty thousand. It has 138 churches, including missions, 122 priests, of whom 6 are religious (4 Friars Minor and 2 Fathers of the Sacred Heart); 53 parochial schools, with 4 hospitals; 4 academies; 2 schools of domestic science; an orphanage, a Good Shepherd home, an infant asylum, a home for the aged, and a working girls' home. There are 7327 children in the parish schools, and nearly 8000 under Catholic care. The composition of the Catholic population of the diocese is English-speaking and German. These form the principal elements of the Church's membership here, and are almost equally divided in numbers. A characteristic feature of western Catholicism is manifest here as in other western dioceses, that is the ardent desire of the people for parochial schools wherever it is possible. Out of the 10,000 children of school age (i. e. under seventeen years) in the diocese, three-fourths are in parochial schools. The following orders conduct schools and charitable institutions in the diocese: Sisters of Charity B.V.M., Sisters of Christian Charity, Sisters of St. Dominic, Sisters of St. Francis (Dubuque, Iowa), Franciscan Sisters (Clinton, Iowa), Franciscan Sisters of Perpetual Adoration, School Sisters of St. Francis, Presentation Nuns, Servants of Mary, Sisters of St. Benedict, Sisters of Mercy, Sisters of the Good Shepherd.

Since its establishment nine years ago, the diocese is thoroughly organized and has been constantly expanding by the erection of churches, schools, and other institutions. The present bishop, the Right Reverend Philip J. Garrigan, D.D., first bishop of the diocese, was born in Ireland in the early forties, came to this country with his parents, and received his elementary education in the public schools of Lowell, Mass. He pursued his classical course at St. Charles's College, Ellicott City, Maryland, and courses of philosophy and theology at the Provincial Seminary of New York at Troy, where he was ordained on 11 June, 1870. After a short term as curate of St. John's Church, Worcester, Massachusetts, he was appointed director of the Troy seminary for three years; and was for fourteen years afterwards pastor of St. Bernard's Church, Fitchburg, Massachusetts. In the fall of 1888 he was appointed first vice-rector of the Catholic University at Washington, D. C., which position he also held for fourteen years. He was named Bishop of Sioux City on 21 March, 1902, and consecrated at the see of his home diocese, Springfield, Massachusetts, on 25 May of the same year, by the Right Rev. T. D. Beaven, and on 18 June following took possession of his see.

PHILIP J. GARRIGAN.

Sioux Falls, DIOCESE OF (SIOUXORMENSIS), suffragan of St. Paul, comprises all that part of the State of South Dakota east of the Missouri River, an area of 34,861 square miles. The western portion of the state, forming the present Diocese of Lead, was detached from the Diocese of Sioux Falls, 8 August, 1902. The early history of religion in South Dakota (until 1879) must be sought for in the histories respectively of St. Paul, Dubuque, and Nebraska. The first Mass celebrated in South Dakota was in 1842, in Brown County, by the late Monsignor Ravoux of St. Paul on his first visit to the Sioux Indians; and the first church erected was in 1867, by the late Father Pierre Boucher, who was sent by Bishop Grace of St. Paul to Jefferson, Union County, to attend the Catholics scattered about that centre. In August, 1879, the Vicariate Apostolic of Dakota, whose boundaries corresponded with the then existing civil boundaries of the newly formed Territory of Dakota, was established, and the Right Reverend Martin Marty, Abbot of St. Meinrad's Benedictine Abbey, Indiana, nominated Bishop of Tiberias and vicar Apostolic of the new district. Bishop Marty was consecrated in the Church of St. Ferdinand, Ferdinand, Indiana, 1 Feb., 1880, by the Right Reverend Francis Silas Chatard, the present Bishop of Indianapolis. The vicariate was an immense district to govern (149,112 square miles) with scarcely any mode of travelling, except by the primitive ox or mule teams. A few miles of railroad existed from Sioux City to Yankton. The new vicar Apostolic went directly to Yankton, where he took up his residence. He found 12 priests administering to a scattered Catholic population of less than 14,000 souls and 20 churches. Many and heroic were the hardships endured by both bishop and priests. At the close of 1881 the number of priests increased to 37, the number of churches to 43 with 33 stations. There were 3 convents, 2 academies for young ladies, 4 parochial schools for the white and 4 schools for the Indian children, while the Catholic population, including 700 Indians, numbered 15,800 souls. The decade beginning with 1880, witnessed a wonderful development and the population increased from 135,180 to 250,000. The statistics at the end of 1883 show 45 priests, 82 churches, 67 stations, 4 convents, 4 academies, 12 parochial schools, 6 Indian schools and a Catholic population, including 1,600 Indians, of 25,600 souls. The Territory of Dakota was divided by Act of Congress, 22 February, 1889, and the two states, North and South Dakota, were admitted to the Union, 2 November, 1889. The same month witnessed the ecclesiastical division of the vicariate, and two new dioceses were formed, Sioux Falls (South Dakota) with Bishop Marty its first bishop; and Jamestown (North Dakota), now Fargo, with Bishop Shanley (d. July, 1909) its first incumbent. In 1894 Bishop Marty was transferred to the Diocese of St. Cloud, Minnesota, where he died 19 September, 1896.

The efforts of Bishop Marty were crowned with marvellous success. He devoted himself especially to the Indian race. He spoke their language and translated hymns and prayers into their tongue. The second and present (1911) Bishop of Sioux Falls, the Right Rev. Thomas O'Gorman, was born at Boston, Massachusetts, 1 May, 1843, he moved with his parents to St. Paul, and was one of the first two students selected for the priesthood by Bishop Cretin, the other was Archbishop Ireland. Having pursued his ecclesiastical studies in France, he returned to St. Paul, where he was ordained priest, 5 November, 1865. He was pastor in turn of Rochester and Faribault, Minn., and first president and professor of dogmatic theology at St. Thomas' College, St. Paul. In 1890 he was appointed Professor of Church History in the Catholic University, Washington, D. C., was consecrated in St. Patrick's Church, Washington, D. C. (19 April, 1896) by Cardinal Satolli, then Apostolic delegate to this country, and on 2 May, 1896, was installed in the pro-cathedral of his episcopal see. The statistics of the diocese then showed 51 secular and 14 regular priests, 50 churches with resident priests, 61 missions with churches, 100 stations, 10 chapels, 14 parochial schools, 61 Indian schools, 2 orphanages, and 1 hospital. There were 3 communities of men and 6 of women, while the Catholic population, white and Indian, was estimated at 30,000 souls. Bishop O'Gorman infused new life into the diocese. The population increased so rapidly that in 1902 the Diocese of Lead was erected. The statistics of the diocese (1911) are in priests, secular 102, regular 13; students 10; churches with resident priests, 91; missions with churches, 70; stations, 23; chapels, 13; parochial schools, 23 with 2,500 children in attendance; hospitals, 4. There are 3 communities of men: Benedictines, Eudists, and the Clerics of St. Viateur. The communities of women are: Dominican Sisters; Presentation Nuns; Benedictine Sisters; Sisters of the Third Order of St. Francis; School Sisters of St. Francis, and the Sisters of Charity of St. Louis. Columbus College at Chamberlain, in charge of the Clerics of St. Viateur is an institution of great promise. The Catholic population, including 500 Indians, is 50,000. In the vicariate Apostolic of thirty-one years ago, where there were only 1 bishop and 12 priests, there are now (1911) 4 bishops and 284 priests.

Diocesan Archives; Catholic Directories; personal recollections.
DANIEL F. DESMOND.

Sioux Indians, the largest and most important Indian tribe north of Mexico, with the single exception of the Ojibwa (Chippewa), who, however, lack the solidarity of the Sioux, being widely scattered on both sides of the international boundary, while the Sioux are virtually all within the United States and up to a comparatively recent period kept up close connexion among the various bands.

NAME AND AFFILIATION.—The name Sioux (pronounced Su) is an abbreviation of the French spelling of the name by which they were anciently known to their eastern Algonquian neighbours and enemies, viz. *Nadouessioux*, signifying "little snakes", i. e. little, or secondary enemies, as distinguished from the eastern Nadowe, or enemies, the Iroquois. This ancient name is now obsolete, having been superseded by the modern Ojibwa term *Buanag*, of uncertain etymology. They call themselves Dakota, Nakota, or Lakota, according to dialect, meaning "allies". From the forms Dakota, Lakota, and Sioux are derived numerous place-names within their ancient area, including those of two great states. Linguistically the Sioux are of the great Siouan stock, to which they have given name and of which they themselves now constitute nearly three-fourths. Other cognate tribes are the Assiniboin, Crow, Hidatsa, or Minitarí, Mandan, Winnebago, Iowa, Omaha, Ponca, Oto, Missouri, Kaw, Osage, and Quapaw, all excepting the Winnebago living west of the Mississippi; together with a number of tribes formerly occupying territories in Mississippi and the central regions of the Carolinas and Virginia, all now virtually extinct, excepting a handful of Catawba in South Carolina. Linguistic and traditionary evidence indicate this eastern region as the original home of the stock, although the period and causes of the westward migration remain a matter of conjecture. The Sioux language is spoken in three principal dialects, viz. Santee (pronounced Sahntee), or eastern; Yankton, or middle; and Teton, or western, differing chiefly in the interchange of *d*, *n*, and *l*, as indicated in the various forms of the tribal name. The Assiniboin are a seceded branch of the Yankton division, having separated from the parent tribe at some time earlier than 1640.

HISTORY.—When and why the Sioux removed from their original home in the East, or by what route they reached the upper Mississippi country, are unknown. When first noticed in history, about 1650, they centered about Mille Lac and Leech Lake, toward the heads of the Mississippi, in central Minnesota, having their eastern frontier within a day's march of Lake Superior. From this position they were gradually driven by the pressure, from the east, of the advancing Ojibwa, who were earlier in obtaining firearms, until nearly the whole nation had removed to the Minnesota and upper Red River, in turn driving before them the Cheyenne, Omaha, and other tribes. On reaching the buffalo plains and procuring horses, supplemented soon thereafter by firearms, they rapidly overran the county to the west and south-west, crossing the Missouri perhaps about 1750, and continuing on to the Black Hills and the Platte until checked by the Pawnee, Crow, and other tribes. At the beginning of treaty relations in 1805 they were the acknowledged owners of most of the territory extending from central Wisconsin, across

SITTING BULL
From a Photograph

the Mississippi and Missouri, to beyond the Black Hills, and from the Canada boundary to the North Platte, including all of Southern Minnesota, with considerable portions of Wisconsin and Iowa, most of both Dakotas, Northern Nebraska, and much of Montana and Wyoming. The boundaries of all that portion lying east of the Dakotas were defined by the great inter-tribal treaty of Prairie du Chien in 1825 and a supplemental treaty at the same place in 1830. At this period the Minnesota region was held by the various Santee bands; Eastern Dakota and a small part of Iowa were claimed by the Yankton and their cousins the Yanktonai; while all the Sioux territory west of the Missouri was held by bands of the great Teton division, constituting three-fifths of the whole nation.

Under the name of *Naduesiu* the Sioux are first mentioned by Father Paul le Jeune in the Jesuit Relation of 1640, apparently on the information of that pioneer western explorer, Jean Nicolet, the first white man known to have set foot in Wisconsin, probably in 1634–5. In 1655–6 two other famous French explorers, Radisson and Groseilliers, spent some time with them in their own country, about the western border of Wisconsin. At that time the Sioux were giving shelter to a band of refugee Hurons fleeing before the Iroquois. They were rated as possessing thirty villages, and were the terror of all the surrounding tribes by reason of their number and prowess, although admittedly less cruel. Fathers Allouez and Marquette, from their mission of St. Esprit, established at Lapointe (now Bayfield, Wis.) on Lake Superior in 1665, entered into friendly relations with the Sioux, which continued until 1671, when the latter, provoked by insults from the eastern tribes, returned Marquette's presents, declared war against their hereditary foes, and compelled the abandonment of the mission. In 1674 they sent a delegation to Sault Ste. Marie to arrange peace through the good offices of the resident Jesuit missionary, Father Gabriel Druillettes, who already had several of the tribe under instruction in his house, but the negotiations were brought to an abrupt end by a treacherous attack made upon the Sioux while seated in council in the mission church, resulting in the massacre of the ambassadors after a desperate encounter, and the burning of the church, which was fired over their heads by the Ojibwa to dislodge them.

The tribal war went on, but the Sioux kept friendship with the French traders, who by this time had reached the Mississippi. In 1680 one of their war parties, descending the Mississippi against the Illinois, captured the Recollect Father Louis Hennepin with two companions and brought them to their villages at the head of the river, where they held them, more as guests than prisoners, until released on the arrival of the trader, Du Luth, in the fall. While thus in custody Father Hennepin observed their customs, made some study of the language, baptized a child and attempted some religious instruction, explored a part of Minnesota, and discovered and named St. Anthony's Falls. In 1683 Nicholas Perrot established a post at the mouth of the Wisconsin. In 1689 he established Fort Perrot near the lower end of Lake Pepin, on the Minnesota side, the first post within the Sioux territory, and took formal possession of their country for France. The Jesuit Father Joseph Marest, officially designated "Missionary to the Nadouesioux", was one of the witnesses at the ceremony and was again with the tribe some twelve years later. Another post was built by Pierre LeSueur, near the present Red Wing about 1693, and in 1695 a principal chief of the tribe accompanied him to Montreal to meet the governor, Frontenac. By this time the Sioux had a number of guns and were beginning to wage aggressive warfare toward the west, driving the Cheyenne, Omaha, and Oto down upon the Missouri and pushing out into the buffalo plains. During Frontenac's administration mission work languished owing to his bitter hostility to missionaries, especially the Jesuits.

About the year 1698, through injudiciously assisting the Sioux against the Foxes, the French became involved in a tedious forty-years' war with the latter tribe which completely paralyzed trade on the upper Mississippi and ultimately ruined the Foxes. Before its end the Sioux themselves turned against the French and gave refuge to the defeated Foxes. In 1700 LeSueur had built Fort L'Huillier on the Blue Earth River near the present Mankato, Minn. In 1727, an ineffective peace having been made, the Jesuit Fathers, Ignatius Guignas and Nicolas de Gonnor, again took up work among the Sioux at the new Fort Beauharnais on Lake Pepin. Although driven out for a time by the Foxes, they returned and continued with the work some ten years, until the Sioux themselves became hostile. In 1736 the Sioux massacred an entire exploring party of twenty-one persons under command of the younger Verendrye at the Lake of the Woods, just beyond the northern (international) Minnesota boundary. Among those killed was the Jesuit father, Jean-Pierre Aulneau. In 1745–6, the Foxes having been finally crushed, De Lusignan again arranged peace with the Sioux, and between them and the Ojibwa, and four Sioux chiefs returned with him to Montreal. On the fall of Canada the Sioux, in 1763, sent delegates to the English post at Green Bay with proffers of friendship and a request for traders. They were described as "certainly the greatest nation of Indians ever yet found", holding all other Indians as "their slaves or dogs". Two thousand of their warriors now had guns, while the other and larger portion still depended upon the bow, in the use of which, and in dancing, they excelled the other tribes.

In the winter of 1766–7 the American traveller, Jonathan Carver, spent several months with the Santee visiting their burial-ground and sacred cave near the present St. Paul, and witnessing men and women gashing themselves in frenzied grief at their bereavement. Soon after this period the eastern Sioux definitively abandoned the Mille Lac and Leech Lake country to their enemies the Ojibwa, with whom the hereditary war still kept up. The final engagement in this upper region occurred in 1768 when a great canoe fleet of Sioux, numbering perhaps five hundred warriors, while descending the Mississippi from a successful raid upon the Ojibwa, was ambushed near the junction of Crow Wing River and entirely defeated by a much smaller force of the latter tribe. In 1775 peace was again made between the two tribes through the efforts of the English officials in order to secure their alliance in the coming Revolutionary struggle. The peace lasted until the close of the Revolutionary War, in which both tribes furnished contingents against the American frontier, after which the warriors returned to their homes, and the old feud was resumed. In the meantime the Teton Sioux, pressing westward, were gradually pushing the Arikara (Ree) up the Missouri, and by acquiring horses from the plains tribes had become metamorphosed from canoe men and gatherers of wild rice into an equestrian race of nomad buffalo hunters.

Some years after the close of the Revolution, perhaps about 1796, French traders in the American interest ascended the Missouri from St. Louis and established posts among the Yankton and Teton. In 1804 the first American exploring expedition, under Captains Lewis and Clark, ascended the river, holding councils and securing the allegiance of the Sioux and other tribes, and then crossing the mountains and descending the Columbia to the Pacific, returning over nearly the same route in 1806. As a result of this acquaintance the first Sioux (Yankton) delegation visited Washington in the latter year. At the same time, 1805-6, Lieutenant Zebulon Pike ascended the Mississippi on a similar errand to the Santee Sioux and other tribes of that region. In this he was successful and on 23 September, 1805, negotiated the first treaty of the Sioux with the United States, by which they ceded lands in the vicinity of the present St. Paul for the establishment of military posts, at the same time giving up their English flags and medals and accepting American ones. Up to this period and for some years later the rapidly diverging bands of the east and west still held an annual reunion east of the lower James River in eastern South Dakota. In 1807 Manuel Lisa, founder of the American Fur Company, "the most active and indefatigable trader that St. Louis ever produced" (Chittenden), established headquarters among the Sioux, at Cedar Island, below the present Pierre, S. D., later moving down to about the present Chamberlain. Lisa was a Spaniard, and like his French associates, Chouteau, Ménard, and Trudeau, was a Catholic. At his several trading posts among the Teton and Yankton Sioux, and the Omaha lower down the river, he showed the Indians how to plant gardens and care for cattle and hogs, besides setting up blacksmith shops for their benefit, without charge, and caring for their aged and helpless, so that it was said that he was better loved by the Sioux than any other white man of his time. Being intensely American in feeling, he was appointed first government agent for the upper Missouri River tribes, and by his great influence with them held them steady for the United States throughout the War of 1812, notwithstanding that most of the eastern, or Santee, Sioux, through the efforts of Tecumtha and a resident British trader, Robert Dickson, declared for England and furnished a contingent against Fort Meigs. Lisa died in 1820. At the close of the war, by a series of five similar treaties made 15 July, 1815, at Portage des Sioux, above St. Louis, the various Sioux bands made their peace with the United States and finally acknowledged its sovereignty. Other late hostile tribes made peace at the same time. This great treaty gathering, the most important ever held with the tribes of the Middle West, marks the beginning of their modern history. In 1820 Fort Snelling was built at the present Minneapolis to control the Santee Sioux and Ojibwa, an agency being also established at the same time. In 1825 another great treaty gathering was convened at Prairie du Chien for the delimitation of tribal boundaries to put an end to inter-tribal wars, and clear the way for future land cessions. At this period, and for years after, the Sioux led all other tribes in the volume of their fur trade, consisting chiefly of buffalo robes and beaver skins.

With the establishment of permanent government relations regular mission work began. In 1834 the brothers Samuel and Gideon Pond, for the Congregationalists, located among the Santee at Lake Calhoun, near the present St. Paul, Minn. In 1835 the same denomination established other missions at Lake Harriet and Lac-qui-Parle, Minn., under Rev. J. D. Stevens and Thomas Williamson respectively. In 1837 Williamson was joined by Rev. Stephen Riggs and his son Alfred. In 1852 the two last-named missions were removed to the upper Minnesota in consequence of a treaty cession. All of these workers are known for their linguistic contributions as well as for their missionary service. In 1837 a Lutheran mission was established at Red Wing and continued for some years. The successful establishment of these missions was due chiefly to the encouragement and active aid afforded by Joseph Renville, a remarkable half-breed, who stood high in the respect and affection of the eastern Sioux. Born in the wilderness in 1779 of an Indian mother, he had been taken to Canada, when a small boy, by his French father, a noted trader, and placed under the care of a Catholic priest, from whom he acquired some knowledge of French and of the Christian religion. The death of his father a few years later and his consequent return to the Sioux country put an end to his educational opportunity, but the early impression thus made was never effaced. On coming to manhood and succeeding to his father's business he sent across the ocean, probably through Dickson, the British trader, for a French Bible (which, when it came, was Protestant) and then hired a clerk who could read it to him. On the establishment of the post at Prairie du Chien he brought down his Indian wife and had her regularly married to him by a Catholic priest, he himself having previously instructed her in religion as well as he could. When the Congregationalists arrived he welcomed them as bringing Christianity, even though not of the form of his childhood teacher. He died in 1846.

RED CLOUD, A FAMOUS CHIEF OF THE OGALALA SIOUX
From a Photograph

In 1841 Father Augustine Ravoux began work among the Santee in the neighbourhood of Fort Snelling, near which Father Galtier had just built a log chapel of St. Paul, around which grew the modern city. Applying himself to the study of the language, in which he soon became proficient, Father Ravoux in 1843 repaired to Prairie du Chien, and there with his own hands printed a small devotional work, "Katolik Wocekiye Wowapi Kin", which is still used as a mission manual. He continued with the tribe for several years, extending his ministrations also to the Yankton, until recalled to parish work. As early at least as 1840 the great Jesuit apostle of the North-West, Father P. J. De Smet, had visited the bands along the Missouri River, where Father Christian Hoecken had preceded him in 1837, instructing adults and baptizing children. Father De Smet made several other brief stops later on his way to and from the Rocky Mountain missions, and in the summer of 1848 spent several months in the camps of the Brulé and Ogalala, whom he found well disposed to Christianity. In 1850 Father Hoecken was again with the Yankton and Teton, but the design to establish a permanent mission was frustrated by his untimely death from cholera, 19 June, 1851. In the same summer Father De Smet attended the great inter-tribal gathering at Fort Laramie, where for several weeks he preached daily to the Sioux and other tribes, baptizing over fifteen hundred children. From that period until his death in 1872 a large portion of his time was given to the western Sioux, among whom his influence was so great that he was several times called in by the Government to assist in treaty negotiations, notably in the great peace treaty of 1868.

In 1837 the Sioux sold all of their remaining territory east of the Mississippi. In the winter of 1837-8 smallpox, introduced from a passing steamer, swept over all the tribes of the upper Missouri River, killing perhaps 30,000 Indians, of whom a large proportion were Sioux. About the same time the war with the

Ojibwa on the eastern frontier broke out again with greater fury than ever. In a battle near the present Stillwater, Minn., in June, 1839, some 50 Ojibwa were slain and shortly afterward a Sioux raiding party surprised an Ojibwa camp in the absence of the warriors and brought away 91 scalps. In 1851 the various Santee bands sold all their remaining lands in Minnesota and Iowa, excepting a twenty-mile strip along the upper Minnesota River. Although there were then four missions among the Santee, the majority of the Indians were reported to have "an inveterate hatred" of Christianity. In March, 1857, on some trifling provocation, a small band of renegade Santee, under an outlawed chief, Inkpaduta, "Scarlet Point," attacked the scattered settlements about Spirit Lake, on the Iowa-Minnesota border, burning houses, massacring about fifty persons, and carrying off several women, two of whom were killed later, the others being rescued by the Christian Indians. Inkpaduta escaped to take an active part in all the Sioux troubles for twenty years thereafter. In 1858 the Yankton Sioux sold all their lands in South Dakota, excepting the present Yankton reservation. The famous pipestone quarry in south-western Minnesota, whence the Sioux for ages had procured the red stone from which their pipes were carved, was also permanently reserved to this Indian purpose. In 1860 the first Episcopalian work was begun among the (Santee) Sioux by Rev. Samuel D. Hinman.

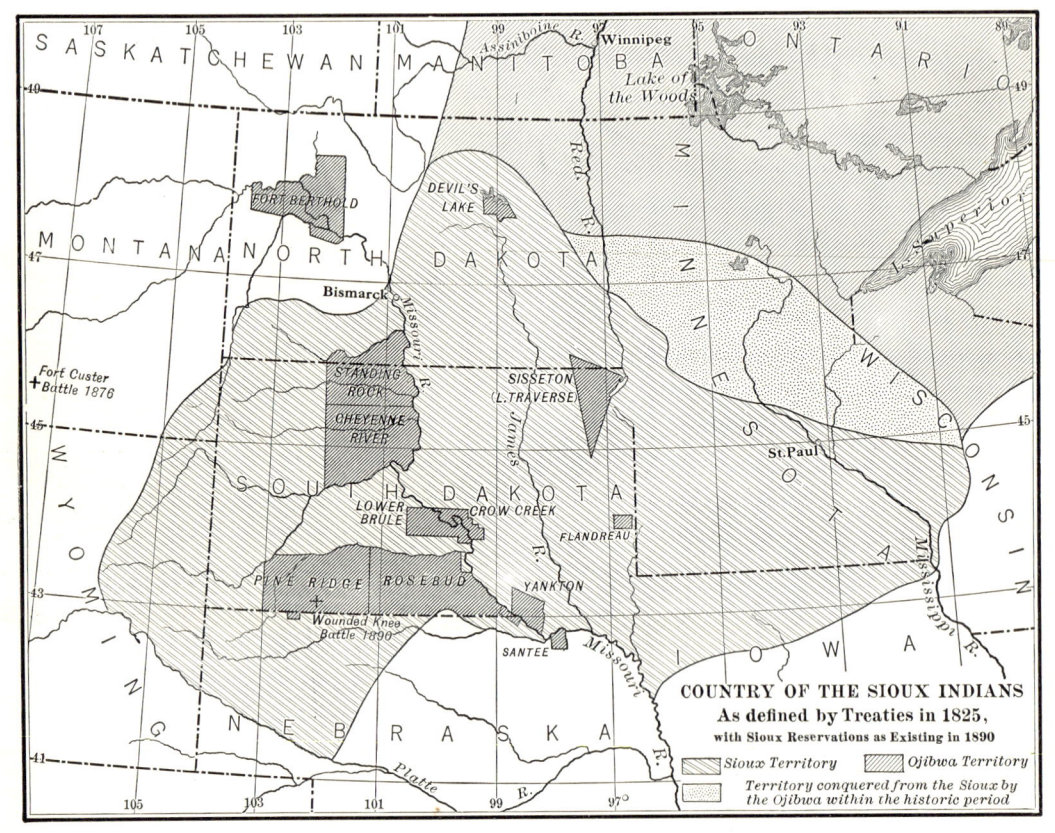

In 1862 occurred the great "Minnesota outbreak" and massacre, involving nearly all the Santee bands, brought about by dissatisfaction at the confiscation of a large proportion of the treaty funds to satisfy traders' claims, and aggravated by a long delay in the annuity issue. The weakening of the local garrisons and the general unrest consequent upon the Civil War also encouraged to revolt. The trouble began 2 August with an attack upon the agency storehouse at Redwood, where five thousand Indians were awaiting the distribution of the delayed annuity supplies. The troops were overpowered and the commissary goods seized, but no other damage attempted. On 17 Aug. a small party of hunters, being refused food at a settler's cabin, massacred the family and fled with the news to the camp of Little Crow, where a general massacre of all the whites and Christian Indians was at once resolved upon. Within a week almost every farm cabin and small settlement in Southern Minnesota and along the adjoining border was wiped out of existence and most of the inhabitants massacred, in many cases with devilish barbarities, excepting such as could escape to Fort Ridgely at the lower end of the reservation. The missionaries were saved by the faithful heroism of the Christian Indians, who, as in 1857, stood loyally by the Government. Determined attacks were made under Little Crow upon Fort Ridgely (20–21 August) and New Ulm (22 August), the latter defended by a strong volunteer force under Judge Charles Flandrau. Both attacks were finally repulsed. On 2 Sept. a force of 1500 regulars and volunteers under Colonel (afterwards General) H. H. Sibley defeated the hostiles at Birch Coulee and again on 23 September at Wood Lake. Most of the hostiles now surrendered, the rest fleeing in small bands beyond the reach of pursuit. Three hundred prisoners were condemned to death by court martial, but the number was cut down by President Lincoln to thirty-eight, who were hanged at Mankato, 26 December, 1862. They were attended by Revs. Riggs and Williamson and by Father Ravoux, but although the other missionaries had been twenty-five years stationed with the tribe and spoke the language fluently, thirty-three of the whole number elected to die in the Catholic Church, two of the remaining five rejecting all Christian ministration. Three years later Father Ravoux again stood on the scaffold with two condemned warriors of the tribe.

Two months after the outbreak Congress declared the Santee treaties abrogated and the Minnesota reservations forfeited. One part of the fugitives trying to escape to the Yanktonai was overtaken and defeated with great loss by Sibley near Big Mound, North Dakota, 24 July, 1863. The survivors fled to the Teton beyond the Missouri or took refuge in Canada, where they are still domiciled. On 3 Sept. General Sully struck the main hostile camp under Inkpaduta at Whitestone Hill, west of Ellendale, N. D., killing 300 and capturing nearly as many more. On 28 July, 1864, General Sully delivered the final blow to the combined hostile force, consisting of Santee, Yanktonai, and some northern Teton, at Kildeer Mountain on the Little Missouri. The prisoners and others of the late hostile bands were finally settled on two reservations established for the purpose, viz. the (Lower) Yanktonai at Crow Creek, S. D., and the Santee at Santee, north-eastern Nebraska. Here they still remain, being now well advanced in civilization and Christianity, and fairly prosperous. The outbreak had cost the lives of nearly 1000 whites, of whom nearly 700 perished in the first few days of the massacre. The Indian loss was about double, falling almost entirely upon the Santee. Pananapapi (Strike-the-Ree), head chief of the 3000 Yankton, and a Catholic, had steadily held his people loyal and the great Brulé and Ogalala bands of the Teton, 13,000 strong, had remained neutral. In October, 1865, at old Fort Sully (near Pierre), S. D., a general treaty of peace was made with the Sioux, and one Teton band, the Lower Brulé, agreed to come upon a reservation. The majority of the great Teton division, however, comprising the whole strength of the nation west of the Missouri, refused to take part.

In the meantime serious trouble had been brewing in the West. With the discovery of gold in California in 1849 and the consequent opening of an emigrant trail along the North Platte and across the Rocky Mountains, the Indians became alarmed at the disturbance to their buffalo herds, upon which they depended for their entire subsistence. The principal complainants were the Brulé and Ogalala Sioux. For the protection of the emigrants in 1849 the Government bought and garrisoned the American Fur Company post of Fort Laramie on the upper North Platte, in Wyoming, later making it also an agency headquarters. In September, 1851, a great gathering of nearly all the tribes and bands of the Northern Plains was held at Fort Laramie, and a treaty was negotiated by which they came to an agreement in regard to their rival territorial claims, pledged peace among themselves and with the whites, and promised not to disturb the trail on consideration of a certain annual payment. Father De Smet attended throughout the council, teaching and baptizing, and gives an interesting account of the gathering, the largest ever held with the Plains Indians. The treaty was not ratified and had no permanent effect. On 17 August, 1854, while the Indians were camped about the post awaiting the distribution of the annuity goods, occurred the "Fort Laramie Massacre", by which Lieutenant Grattan and an entire detachment of 29 soldiers lost their lives while trying to arrest some Brulés who had killed and eaten an emigrant's cow. From all the evidence the conflict was provoked by the officer's own indiscretion. The Indians then took forcible possession of the annuity goods and left without making any attempt upon the fort or garrison. The Brulé Sioux were now declared hostile, and Gen. W. S. Harney was sent against them. On 3 September, with 1200 men, he came upon their camp at Ash Hollow, Western Nebraska, and, while pretending to parley on their proffer of surrender, suddenly attacked them, killing 136 Indians and destroying the entire camp outfit.

Late in 1863 the Ogalala and Brulé under their chiefs, Red Cloud (*Makhpiya-luta*) and Spotted Tail (*Shinté-galeshka*) respectively, became actively hostile, inflamed by reports of the Santee outbreak and the Civil War in the South. They were joined by the Cheyenne and for two years all travel across the

GROUP OF SIOUX
Weasel Bear and Family, Pine Ridge, S. D.

plains was virtually suspended. In March, 1865, they were roused to desperation by the proclamation of two new roads to be opened through their best hunting grounds to reach the new gold fields of Montana. Under Red Cloud's leadership they notified the Government that they would allow no new roads or garrison posts to be established in their country, and carried on the war on this basis with such determination that by treaty at Fort Laramie through a peace commission in April–May, 1868, the Government actually agreed to close the "Montana road" that had been opened north from Laramie, and to abandon the three posts that had been established to protect it. Red Cloud himself refused to sign until after the troops had been withdrawn. The treaty left the territory south of the North Platte open to road building, recognized all north of the North Platte and east of the Bighorn Mountains as unceded Indian territory, and established the "Great Sioux Reservation", nearly equivalent to all of South Dakota west of the Missouri. Provision was made for an agency on the Missouri River and the inauguration of regular governmental civilizing work. In consideration of thus giving up their old freedom the Indians were promised, besides the free aid of blacksmiths, doctors, a saw mill, etc., a complete suit of clothing yearly for thirty years to every individual of the bands concerned, based on the actual yearly census. Among the official witnesses were Rev. Hinman, the Episcopalian missionary, and Father De Smet. This treaty brought the whole of the Sioux nation under agency restriction, and with its ratification in February, 1869, the five years' war came to a close.

In this war Red Cloud had been the principal leader, Spotted Tail having been won to friendship earlier through the kindness extended by the officers at Fort Laramie on the occasion of the death of his daughter, who was buried there with Christian rites at her own request. The Cheyenne and Northern Arapaho also acted with the Sioux. The chief fighting centered around Fort Kearney, Wyoming, which Red Cloud himself held under repeated siege, and near which on 21 December, 1866, occurred the "Fetterman Massacre", when an entire detachment of 80 men under Captain Fetterman was exterminated by an overwhelming force of Indians. By treaties in 1867 reservations had been established at Lake Traverse, S. D. and at Fort Totten, N. D., for the Sisseton and Wahpeton Santee and the Cuthead Yanktonai, most of whom had been concerned in the Minnesota outbreak. In 1870 a part of the Christian Santee separated from their kinsmen in Nebraska and removed to Flandreau, S. D., and became citizens. In 1871, despite the protest of Red Cloud and other leading chiefs, the Northern Pacific railway was constructed along the south bank of the Yellowstone and several new posts built for its protection, and war was on again with the Teton Sioux, Cheyenne, and part of the Arapaho. Several skirmishes occurred, and in 1873 General G. A. Custer was ordered to Dakota. In the next year, while hostilities were still in progress, Custer made an exploration of the Black Hills, S. D., and reported gold. Despite the treaty and the military, there was at once a great rush of miners and others into the Hills. The Indians refusing to sell on any terms offered, the military patrol was withdrawn, and mining towns at once sprang up all through the mountains. Indians hunting by agents' permission in the disputed territory were ordered to report at their agencies by 31 January, 1876, or be considered hostile, but even the runners who carried the message were unable to return, by reason of the severity of the winter, until after war had been actually declared. This is commonly known as the "Custer War" from its central event, 25 June, 1876, the massacre of General Custer and every man of a detachment of the Seventh Cavalry, numbering 204 in all, in an attack upon the main camp of the hostile Sioux and Cheyenne, on the Little Bighorn River in south-eastern Montana. On that day and the next, in the same vicinity, other detachments under Reno and Benteen sustained desperate conflicts with the Indians, with the loss of some sixty more killed. The Indians, probably numbering at least 2500 warriors with their families, finally withdrew on the approach of Generals Terry and Gibbons from the north. The principal Sioux commanders were Crazy Horse and Gall, although Sitting Bull was also present. Red Cloud and Spotted Tail had remained at their agencies.

Several minor engagements later in the year resulted in the surrender and return of most of the hostiles to the reservation, while Sitting Bull and Gall and their immediate following escaped into Canada (June, 1877). By a series of treaties negotiated 23 Sept.-27 Oct., 1876, the Sioux surrendered the whole of the Black Hills country and the western outlet. On 7 Sept, 1877, Crazy Horse, who had come in with his band some months before, was killed in a conflict with the guard at Fort Robinson, Neb. In the same month the last hostiles surrendered. Soon after the treaty a large delegation visited Washington, following which event the Red Cloud (Ogalala) and Spotted Tail (Brulé) agencies were permanently established in 1878 at Pine Ridge and Rosebud, S. D., respectively. This date may be considered to mark the beginning of civilization in these two powerful bands. In 1881 all the late hostiles in Canada came in and surrendered. Sitting Bull and his immediate followers, after being held in confinement for two years, were allowed to return to their homes on Standing Rock reservation. On 5 August, 1881, Spotted Tail was killed by a rival chief. On 29 July, 1888, Strike-the-Ree, the famous Catholic chief of the Yankton, died at the age of 84.

In the allotment of Indian agencies to the management of the various religious denominations, in accord with President Grant's "peace policy" in 1870, only two of the eleven Sioux agencies were assigned to the Catholics, namely, Standing Rock and Devil's Lake, notwithstanding that, with the exception of a portion of the Santee and a few of the Yankton, the only missionaries the tribe had ever known from Allouez to De Smet had been Catholic, and most of the resident whites and mixed-bloods were of Catholic ancestry. Santee, Flandreau, and Sisseton (Lake Traverse) agencies of the Santee division were assigned to the Presbyterians, who had already been continuously at work among them for more than a generation. Yankton reservation had been occupied jointly by Presbyterians and Episcopalians in 1869, as was Cheyenne River reservation in 1873. Pine Ridge, Rosebud, Lower Brulé and Crow Creek reservations, comprising nearly one-half the tribe, were given to the Episcopalians, who erected buildings between 1872 (Crow Creek) and 1877 (Pine Ridge). At Devil's Lake an industrial boarding school was completed and opened in 1874 in charge of Benedictine Fathers and Grey Nun Sisters of Charity. At Standing Rock a similar school was opened in 1877 in charge of Benedictine priests and Sisters. Thus by 1878 regular mission plants were in operation on every Sioux reservation. Other Catholic foundations were begun at Crow Creek and Rosebud in 1886, at Pine Ridge in 1887, and at Cheyenne River in 1892. In 1887 the noted secular missionary priest, Father Francis M. J. Craft, opened school at Standing Rock and later succeeded in organizing in the tribe an Indian sisterhood which, however, was refused full ecclesiastical recognition. In 1891 he removed with his community to the Fort Berthold reservation, N. D., where for some years the Sioux Indian Sisters proved valuable auxiliaries, particularly in instructing the women and nursing the sick of the confederated Grosventres, Arikara, and Mandan. Later on several of them won commendation as volunteer nurses in Cuba during the Spanish War. This zealous sisterhood is no longer in existence. In 1889, after long and persistent opposition by the older chiefs, the "Great Sioux Reservation" was cut in two and reduced by about one half by a treaty cession which included almost all territory between White and Cheyenne Rivers, S. D., and all north of Cheyenne River west of 102°. The ceded lands were thrown open to settlement by proclamation in the next spring, and were at once occupied by the whites. In the meantime payment for the lands was delayed, the annuity goods failed to arrive until the winter was nearly over, the crops had failed through attendance of the Indians at the treaty councils in the preceding spring, epidemic diseases were raging in the camps, and as the final straw Congress, despite previous promise, cut down the beef ration by over four million pounds on the ground of the stipulated money payment, which, however, had not arrived.

A year before rumours had come to the Sioux of a new Indian Messiah arisen beyond the mountains to restore the old-time Indian life, together with their departed friends, in a new earth from which the whites should be excluded. Several tribes, including the Sioux, sent delegates to the home of the Messiah, in Western Nevada, to investigate the rumour. The first delegation, as well as a second, confirmed the truth of the report, and in the spring of 1890 the ceremonial "Ghost Dance," intended to hasten the fulfilment of the prophecy, was inaugurated at Pine Ridge. Because of its strong appeal to the Indians under the existing conditions, the Dance soon spread among other Teton reservations until the Indians were in a frenzy of religious excitement. The newly-appointed agent at Pine Ridge became frightened and called for troops, thus precipitating the outbreak of 1890. By 1 December 3000 troops were disposed in the neighbourhood of the western Sioux reservations the under orders of General Nelson Miles. Leading events of the outbreak were: the killing of Sitting Bull, his son, and six others on 15 December, at his camp on Grand River, Standing Rock reservation, while resisting arrest by the Indian police, six of whom were killed in the encounter; the flight of Sitting Bull's followers and others of Standing Rock and Cheyenne River reservations into the Bad Lands of western South Dakota where they joined other refugee "hostiles" from Pine Ridge and Rosebud; the fight at Wounded Knee Creek, twenty miles north-east of Pine Ridge agency, 29 December, 1890, between a band of surrendered hostiles under Big Foot and a detachment of the Seventh Cavalry under Colonel Forsyth. On 16 Jan.,1891, the hostiles surrendered to General Miles at Pine Ridge, and the outbreak was at an end. With the restoration of peace, grievances were adjusted and the work of civilization resumed. Under provision of the general allotment law of 1887 negotiations were concluded from time to time with the various bands by which the size of the reservations was still further curtailed, and lands allotted in severalty, until now almost all of the Sioux Indians are individual owners and well on the way to full citizenship. Indian dress and adornment are nearly obsolete, together with the tipi and aboriginal ceremonial, and the great majority are clothed in citizen's dress, living in comfortable small houses with modern furniture, and engaged in farming and stock raising. The death of the old chief, Red Cloud, at Pine Ridge in 1909, removed almost the last link binding the Sioux to their Indian past.

RELIGIOUS STATUS.—in 1909 nearly 10,000 of the 25,000 Sioux within the United States were officially reported as Christians. The proportion is now probably at least one-half, of whom about half are Catholic, the others being chiefly Episcopalian and Presbyterian. The Catholic missions are: Our Lady of Sorrows, Fort Totten, N. D. (Devil's Lake Res.), Benedictine; St. Elizabeth, Cannonball, N. D. (Standing Rock Res.), Benedictine; St. Peter, Fort Yates, N. D. (Standing Rock Res.), Benedictine; St. James, Porcupine (Shields P. O.), N. D. (Standing Rock Res.), Benedictine; St. Benedict, Standing Rock Agency, S. D. (Standing Rock Res.), Benedictine; St. Aloysius, Standing Rock Agency, S. D., (Standing Rock Res.), Benedictine; St. Edward, Standing Rock Agency, S. D., (Standing Rock Res.), Benedictine; St. Bede, Standing Rock Agency, S. D. (Standing Rock Res.), Benedictine; Immaculate Conception, Stephan, S. D. (Crow Creek Res.), Benedictine; St. Matthew, Veblen Co. (Britton P. O.) S. D. (former Sisseton Res.), secular; Corpus Christi, Cheyenne River Agency, S. D. (Chey. R. Res.), secular; St. Francis, Rosebud, S. D. (Rosebud Res.), Jesuit; Holy Rosary, Pine Ridge, S. D. (Pine Ridge Res.), Jesuit. The two Jesuit missions maintain boarding-schools, and are assisted by Franciscan Sisters. The Immaculate Conception mission also maintains a boarding-school, with Benedictine Sisters. At the Fort Totten mission a monthly paper, "Sina Sapa Wocekiye Taeyanpaha" (Black-gown Prayer Herald), entirely in the Sioux language, is published under the editorship of Father Jerome Hunt, who has been with the mission from its foundation. Notable events in the religious life of the tribe are the Catholic Sioux congresses held in the summer of each year, one in North and one in South Dakota, which are attended by many high church dignitaries and mission workers and several thousands of Catholic Indians. Of some 470 Christian Sioux in Canada about one-fourth are Catholic, chiefly at Standing Buffalo Reservation, Sask., where they are served from the Oblate mission school at Qu'Appelle.

ORGANIZATION AND CULTURE.—The Sioux were not a compact nation with centralized government and supreme head chief, but were a confederacy of seven allied sub-tribes speaking a common language, each with a recognized head chief and each subdivided into bands or villages governed by subordinate chiefs. The seven sub-tribes, from east to west, were: (1) Mdewakantonwan (Mde-wakanton) Village (people) of the Spirit Lake (i.e. Mille Lac); (2) Wakhpekute "Leaf Shooters"; (3) Wakhpetonwan (Wahpeton), "Village in the Leaves"; (4) Sisitonwan (Sisseton), "Village of the Marsh"; (5) Ihanktonwan (Yankton), "Village at the End"; (6) Ihanktonwanna (Yanktonai), "Little Yankton"; (7) Titonwan (Teton), "Village of the Prairie". Of these, the first four, originally holding the heads of the Mississippi, constitute the Isanti (Santee) or eastern, dialectic group; The Yankton and Yanktonai, about the lower and upper courses of the James River respectively, together with the Assiniboin tribe constitute the central dialectic group. The great Teton division, west of the Missouri and comprising three-fifths of the whole nation, constitutes a third dialectic group. The Teton are divided into seven principal bands, commonly known as Ogalala (at Pine Ridge); Brulé (at Rosebud and Lower Brulé); Hunkpapa (at Standing Rock); Blackfoot (at Standing Rock and Cheyenne River); Miniconju, Sans-Arc, and Two Kettle (Cheyenne River). Among the more sedentary eastern bands chiefship seems to have been hereditary in the male line, but with the roving western bands it depended usually upon pre-eminent ability. In their original home about the heads of the Mississippi the Sioux subsisted chiefly upon wild rice, fish, and small game, and were expert canoe men, but as they drifted west into the plains and obtained possession of the horse their whole manner of life was changed, and they became a race of equestrian nomads, subsisting almost entirely upon the buffalo. They seem never to have been agricultural to any great extent. Their dwelling was the birch-bark lodge in the east and the buffalo-skin tipi on the plain. Their dead were sometimes deposited in a coffin upon the surface of the ground, but more often laid upon a scaffolding or in the tree-tops. Food and valuables were left with the corpse, and relatives gashed their bodies with knives and cut off their hair in token of grief. Besides the knife, bow, and hatchet of the forest warrior, they carried also on the plains the lance and shield of the horseman. Polygamy was recognized. There was no clan system.

To the Sioux the earth was a great island plain surrounded by an ocean far to the west of which was the spirit world. There were two souls—some said four—one of which remained near the grave after death, while the other travelled on to the spirit world, or in certain cases became a wandering and dangerous ghost. In the west also, in a magic house upon the top of a high mountain and guarded by four sentinel animals at the four doorways, lived the *Wakinyan*, or thunders, the greatest of the gods, and mortal enemies of the subterranean earth spirits and the water spirits. The sun also was a great god. There was no supreme "Great Spirit", as supposed by the whites, no ethical code to their supernaturalism, and no heaven or hell in their spirit world. Among animals the buffalo was naturally held in highest veneration. Fairies and strange monsters, both good and bad, were everywhere, usually invisible, but sometimes revealing themselves in warning portent. Dreams were held as direct revelations of the supernatural. Taboos, fasting, and sacrifices, including voluntary torture, were frequent. Among the great ceremonials the annual sun dance was the most important, on which occasion the principal performers danced at short intervals for four days and nights, without food, drink, or sleep, undergoing at the same time painful bodily laceration, either as a propitiation or in fulfilment of a thanksgiving vow. The several warrior orders and various secret societies each had their special dance, and for young girls there was a puberty ceremony. (For cults and home life see works of Dorsey and Eastman quoted in bibliography below.) In physique, intellect, morality, and general manliness the Sioux rated among the finest of the Plains tribes. Under the newer conditions the majority are now fairly industrious and successful farmers and stock-raisers.

LANGUAGE AND LITERATURE.—The Sioux language is euphonious, sonorous, and flexible, and possesses a more abundant native literature than that of any other tribe within the United States, with the possible exception of the Cherokee. By means of an alphabet system devised by the early Presbyterian missionaries, nearly all of the men can read and write their own language. The printed literature includes religious works, school textbooks, grammars, and dictionaries, miscellaneous publications, and three current mission journals, Catholic, as already noted, Presbyterian, and Episcopal, all three entirely in Sioux. The earliest publication was a spelling-book by Rev. J. D. Stevens in 1836. In linguistics the principal is the "Grammar and Dictionary of the Dakota Language", by Rev. S. R. Riggs, published by the Smithsonian Institution, Washington, in 1852, and republished in part, with editing by Dorsey, by the Bureau of Am. Ethnology, Washington, in 1892-4.

POPULATION.—Contrary to the usual rule with Indian tribes, the Sioux have not only held their own since the advent of the whites, but have apparently slightly increased. This increase, however, is due largely to incorporation of captives and intermarriage of whites. We have no reliable estimates for the whole tribe before 1849, when Governor Ramsey gave them "not over 20,000", while admitting that some resident authorities gave them 40,000 or more. Riggs in 1851 gives them about 25,000, but underestimates the western (Teton) bands. By official census of 1910 they number altogether 28,618 souls, including all mixed-bloods, distributed as follows: Minnesota, scattered, about 929; Nebraska, Santee agency, 1155; North Dakota, Devil's Lake (Fort Totten) agency, 986; Standing Rock agency, 3454; South Dakota, Flandreau agency, 275, Lower Brulé, 469, Crow Creek, 997, Yankton, 1753, Sisseton, 1994, Cheyenne River, 2590, Rosebud, 5096, Pine Ridge, 6758. Canada: Birdtail, Oak Lake, Oak River, Turtle Mountain, Portage La Prairie (Manitoba), 613; Wahspaton, Standing Buffalo, Moosejaw, Moose Woods (Sask.), 455. Those in Canada are chiefly descendants of refugees from the United States in 1862 and 1876.

BRYANT AND MURCH, *Hist. of the Great Massacre by the Sioux Indians* (St. Peter, 1872); BUREAU CATH. IND. MISSIONS, *Annual Reports of the Director* (Washington); *Annual Reports of the Dept. of Ind. Affairs* (Ottawa, Canada); CARVER, *Travels through the Interior Parts of N. Am.* (1766-8) (London, 1778, and later editions); CATLIN, *Manners, Customs and Condition of the N. Am. Inds.* (London, 1841, and later editions); CHITTENDEN, *Am. Fur Trade* (New York, 1902); CHITTENDEN AND RICHARDSON, *Life, Letters and Travels of Fr. Pierre-Jean De Smet*, (New York, 1905); COMMISSIONER OF IND. AFFAIRS, *Annual Reports* (Washington); *Condition of the Indian Tribes, Report of Joint Special Committee* (Washington, 1867); DORSEY, *Study of Siouan Cults*, in *11th Rept. Bur. Am. Eth.* (Washington, 1894); EASTMAN, *Indian Boyhood* (New York, 1902); IDEM, *Wigwam Evenings* (Boston, 1909); FINERTY, *Warpath and Bivouac* (Chicago, 1890); HAYDEN, *Conts. to the Ethnography and Philology of the Ind. Tribes of the Missouri Valley* in *Trans. Am. Philos. Soc.*, n. s., XII (Philadelphia, 1862); HENNEPIN, *Description de la Louisiane* (Paris, 1683), tr. SHEA (New York, 1880); HINMAN AND WELSH, *Journal of the Rev. S. D. Hinman* (Philadelphia, 1869); *Jesuit Relations*, ed. Thwaites, 73 vols., especially *Ottawa and Illinois*, L—LXXI (Cleveland, 1896-1901); *Indian Affairs: Laws and Treaties*, ed. KAPPLER, (Washington, 1903-4); KEATING, *Expedition (Long's) to the Sources of St. Peter's River* (Philadelphia, 1824 and later editions); LEWIS AND CLARK, *Original Journals of the Expedition of 1804-6*, ed. THWAITES, 8 vols. (New York, 1904-5, numerous other editions more or less complete, the first official report being contained in the *Message from the President*, Washington, 1806); McGEE, *Siouan Indians* in *15th Rept. Bur. Am. Ethnology* (Washington, 1897); McKENNEY AND HALL, *Hist. Ind. Tribes of North Am.* (Philadelphia, 1854, and other editions); McLAUGHLIN, *My Friend the Indian* (Boston, 1910); MALLERY, *Pictographs of the N. Am. Indians* in *4th Rept. Bur. Am. Ethnology* (Washington, 1886); IDEM, *Picture Writing of the Am. Inds.* in *10th Rept. Bur. Am. Ethnology* (Washington, 1893); MARGRY, *Découvertes et établissements des Français* (6 vols., Paris, 1879-86); MAXIMILIAN, PRINCE OF WIED, *Travels in the Interior of N. Am.* (London, 1843; original German ed. 2 vols., Coblenz, 1839-41); MILES, *Personal Recollections* (Chicago, 1896); *Minnesota Hist. Soc. Colls.* (1872-1905); MOONEY, *Siouan Tribes of the East*, Bull. 22, Bureau Am. Ethnology (Washington, 1895); IDEM, *The Ghost Dance Religion and Sioux Outbreak of 1890* in *14th Rept. Bur. Am. Ethnology*, II (Washington, 1896); NEILL, *Hist. of Minnesota* (Philadelphia, 1858); *New York, Documents Relating to the Colonial Hist. of* (15 vols., Albany, 1853-87) NICOLLET, *Report on . . . Upper Mississippi* (Senate Doc.) (Washington, 1843); *North Dakota Hist. Soc. Colls.* (2 vols., Bismarck, 1906-8); PARKMAN, *Oregon Trail* (New York, 1849, and later editions); PERRIN DU LAC, *Voyages dans les deux Louisianes, 1801-3* (Paris and Lyons, 1805); PIKE, *Expedition to the Sources of the Mississippi* (Philadelphia, 1810); PILLING, *Bibl. of the Siouan Languages*, Bull. 5, Bur. Am. Ethnology (Washington, 1887); POOLE, *Among the Sioux of Dakota* (New York, 1881); RAMSEY, *Report on Sioux* in *Rept. Comsner. Ind. Affairs for 1849* (Washington, 1850); RAVOUX, *Reminiscences, Memoirs and Lectures* (St. Paul, 1890); RIGGS, *The Dakota Language* in *Colls. Minn. Hist. Soc.*, I (St. Paul, 1851, reprint St. Paul, 1872); IDEM, *Grammar and Dict. of the Dakota Language: Smithsonian Contributions*, IV (Washington, 1852); IDEM, *Tahkoo Wahkan, or the Gospel among the Dakotas* (Boston, 1869); IDEM, *Mary and I: Forty Years with the Sioux* (Chicago, 1880); ROBINSON, *Hist. of the Sioux Indians* in *Colls. South Dakota Hist. Soc.*, II (Aberdeen, S.D., 1904); ROYCE AND THOMAS, *Indian Land Cessions* in *18th Rept. Bur. Am. Ethnology*, II (Washington, 1899); SCHOOLCRAFT, *Travels . . . to the Sources of the Mississippi* (Albany, 1821); IDEM, *Hist. Condition and Prospects of the Indian Tribes of the U. S.* (6 vols., Philadelphia, 1851-7); SHERIDAN (in charge), *Record of Engagements with Hostile Indians, etc., 1868-1882* (Washington, 1882); SHEA, *Hist. of the Catholic Missions among the Indian Tribes of the U. S.* (New York, 1855); IDEM, *Disc. and Expl. of the Mississippi Valley* (New York, 1852; and Albany, 1903); DE SMET, *Oregon Missions* (New York, 1847; Fr. edition, Ghent, 1848); IDEM, *Western Missions and Missionaries* (New York, 1863); (see also CHITTENDEN AND RICHARDSON), *South Dakota Hist. Soc. Colls.* (3 vols., Aberdeen, S. D., 1902-6); WALL, *Recollections of the Sioux Massacre (1862)* (Lake City, Minn., 1909); WARREN, *Explorations in the Dakota Country, 1855*, Senate Doc. (Washington, 1856); WARREN, *Hist. of the Ojibways* in *Minn. Hist. Soc. Colls.*, V (St. Paul, 1885); WHIPPLE, *Lights and Shadows of a Long Episcopate* (New York, 1899); *Wisconsin Hist. Soc. Colls.* (16 vols., Madison, 1855-1902).

JAMES MOONEY.

Sipibo Indians, a numerous tribe of Panoan linguistic stock, formerly centring about the Pisqui and Aguaitia tributaries of the upper Ucayali River, Province of Loreto, north-eastern Peru, and now found as boatmen or labourers along the whole course of that stream. They speak the same language as the Conibo, Pano, and Setebo, whom they resemble in habit and ceremonial.

The Sipibo became known about the same time as their cognate tribes early in the seventeenth century, but opposed a determined resistance to the entrance of both gold-hunters and missionaries (1657), for a long time frustrating all Christianizing efforts in the Ucayali region by their constant raids upon the mission settlements, particularly of the Setebo. In 1670, in common with other tribes of that region, they were greatly wasted by smallpox. In 1736 they broke the power of the Setebo in a bloody battle, but in 1764 the Franciscan Father Juan de Frezneda entered their country and so far won their good will that he succeeded in making peace between the two tribes and in the next year (1765) established the first mission among the Sipibo under the title of Santo Domingo de Pisqui. This was shortly followed by the founding of Santa Barbara de Archani and Santa Cruz de Aguaitia in the same tribe, together with a resumption of work among the Conibo, first undertaken in 1685. Among other labourers in the Sipibo field at

ABORIGINAL VILLAGE ON THE PACHYTEA RIVER, PERU

this period was Father José Amich, author of a history of the Ucayali missions. Suddenly and without warning in the summer of 1766 all the river tribes attacked the missions simultaneously, slaughtered nine of the missionaries together with their neophytes, and completely destroyed all that had been accomplished by years of persevering sacrifice. Rungato, a Setebo chief, who had professed the greatest friendship for the missionaries, appears to have been the leader. The reason of the outbreak was never known. It may have been jealousy of authority, impatience of restraint, covetousness of the mission property, some unrecorded outrage by the Spaniards on the frontier, some dream, or superstitious panic such as are of so frequent occurrence among savages. A small relief expedition sent out in charge of three Franciscans the next year learned the details of the massacre, and was forced to turn back, but was permitted to retire without molestation.

This last rising of the wild tribes of the middle Ucayali was in some measure an echo of a similar

ABORIGINAL HOUSE ON THE UCAYALI RIVER
The hanging bags contain pounded manioc root from which the poisonous juice is being pressed out.

rising of the wild Campa tribes on the upper branches of the same stream in 1742, led by Juan Santos, an apostate Quichua Indian, who assumed the title of the Inca Atahualpa (see QUICHUA), and resulting in the destruction of all the missions of that region and the slaughter of nearly eighty Franciscan missionaries. Of this rising of the Campa, Herndon says: "It is quite evident that no distaste for the Catholic religion induced this rebellion; for in the year 1750, eight years afterward, the Marquis of Mina-hermosa, marching into this country for the punishment of the rebels, found the church at Quimisi in perfect order, with candles burning before the images. He burned the town and church, and six years after this, when another entrance into this country was made by General Bustamente, he found the town rebuilt and a large cross erected in the middle of the plaza. I have had occasion myself to notice the respect and reverence of these Indians for their pastors, and their delight in participating in the ceremonial and sense-striking worship of the Roman Church." A similar instance is recorded of the revolted Pueblos (q. v.), as also of the unconverted Setebo. Following close upon the massacre of 1766 came the expulsion of the Jesuits by royal decree in the following year, and the Ucayali region was given over to barbarism until 1791, when by direction of the superior of the Franciscan college of Ocopa, Father Narciso Girbal with two companions once more braved the wilderness dangers and made successful foundation at Sarayacu (q. v.) into which mission and its branches most of the wandering river Indians were finally gathered.

A description of the Sipibo will answer in most of its details for all the tribes of the Ucayali and Huallaga region, within the former sphere of influence of the Franciscan missionaries, with the addition that certain tribes, particularly the Cashibo, were

A SIPIBO TYPE

noted for their cannibalism. There was very little tribal solidarity, each so-called tribe being broken up into petty bands ruled by local chiefs, and seldom acting together even against a common enemy. They subsisted chiefly on fish, game, turtle eggs, bananas, yuccas, and a little corn, agriculture, however, being but feebly developed. The root of the yucca was roasted as bread, ground between stones for flour, boiled or fried, while from the juice, fermented with saliva, was prepared the intoxicating *masato* or *chicha*, which was in requisition at all family or tribal festivals. Salt was seldom used, but clay-eating was common and sometimes of fatal consequence. Their houses, scattered simply at intervals along the streams, were of open framework thatched with palm leaves. The arrow poison, usually known as *curari*, was prepared from the juice of certain lianas or tree vines and was an article of intertribal trade over a great extent of territory. They either went entirely naked or wore a short skirt or sleeveless shirt woven of cotton or bark fibre. Head flattening and the wearing of nose and ear pendants and labrets were common. They blackened their teeth with a vegetable dye. The modern civilized Indians dress in light peon fashion.

Although most of the tribes could count no higher than five, their general mentality was high, and they progressed rapidly in civilized arts. Their religion was animism, dominated by the *yutumi* or priests, but with few great ceremonies. As among all savages, disease and death were commonly ascribed to evil spirits or witchcraft. Polygamy was universal, the women being frequently obtained by raids upon other tribes. Among their barbarous customs were the eating of prisoners of war, and sometimes of deceased parents, the killing of the helpless and of deformed children and twins, and a sort of circumcision of young girls at about the age of twelve years. A part of the Sipibo still roam the forests, but the majority are now civilized and employed as boatmen, rubber-gatherers, or labourers along the river. In common with all the tribes of the region their numbers are steadily decreasing. See also SETEBO INDIANS.

Consult particularly: RAIMONDI, *El Perú*, II and III, *Hist. de la Geografía del Perú*, bks. i and ii (Lima, 1876–79), Raimondi derives much of his information from a MS. history of the Franciscan missions, by Fernando Rodriguez, 1774, preserved in the convent at Lima; IDEM, *Provincia Litoral de Loreto* (Lima, 1862), condensed tr. by BOLLÆRT in *Anthropological Review* (London, May, 1863); BRINTON, *American Race* (New York, 1891); CASTELNAU, *Expédition dans les parties centrales de l'Amérique du Sud*, IV (Paris, 1891); EBERHARDT, *Indians of Peru in Smithson. Miscel. Colls.*, quarterly issue, V (Washington, 1909), 2; HERNDON, *Exploration of the Amazon* (Washington, 1854); ORDINAIRE, *Les Sauvages du Pérou* in *Revue d'Ethnographie*, VI (Paris, 1887); SMYTH and LOWE, *Journey from Lima to Pará* (London, 1836).

JAMES MOONEY.

Sirach. See ECCLESIASTICUS.

Siricius, SAINT, POPE (384–99), b. about 334; d. 26 November, 399. Siricius was a native of Rome; his father's name was Tiburtius. Siricius entered the service of the Church at an early age and, according to the testimony of the inscription on his grave, was lector and then deacon of the Roman Church during the pontificate of Liberius (352–66). After the death of Damasus, Siricius was unanimously elected his successor (December, 384) and consecrated bishop probably on 17 December. Ursinus, who had been a rival to Damasus (366), was alive and still maintained his claims. However, the Emperor Valentinian III, in a letter to Pinian (23 Feb., 385), gave his consent to the election that had been held and praised the piety of the newly-elected bishop; consequently no difficulties arose. Immediately upon his elevation Siricius had occasion to assert his primacy over the universal Church. A letter, in which questions were asked on fifteen different points concerning baptism, penance, church discipline, and the celibacy of the clergy, came to Rome addressed to Pope Damasus by Bishop Himerius of Tarragona, Spain. Siricius answered this letter on 10 February, 385, and gave the decisions as to the matters in question, exercising with full consciousness his supreme power of authority in the Church (Coustant, "Epist. Rom. Pont.", 625 sq.). This letter of Siricius is of special importance because it is the oldest completely preserved papal decretal (edict for the authoritative decision of questions of discipline and canon law). It is, however, certain that before this earlier popes had also issued such decretals, for Siricius himself in his letter mentions "general decrees" of Liberius that the latter had sent to the provinces; but these earlier ones have not been preserved. At the same time the pope directed Himerius to make known his decrees to the neighbouring provinces, so that they should also be observed there. This pope had very much at heart the maintenance of Church discipline and the observance of canons by the clergy and laity. A Roman synod of 6 January, 386, at which eighty bishops were present, reaffirmed in nine canons the laws of the Church on various points of discipline (consecration of bishops, celibacy, etc.). The decisions of the council were communicated by the pope to the bishops of North Africa and probably in the same manner to others who had not attended the synod, with the command to act in accordance with them. Another letter which was sent to various churches dealt with the election of worthy bishops and priests. A synodal letter to the Gallican bishops, ascribed by Coustant and others to Siricius, is assigned to Pope Innocent I by other historians (P. L., XIII, 1179 sq.). In all his decrees the pope speaks with the consciousness of his supreme ecclesiastical authority and of his pastoral care over all the churches.

Siricius was also obliged to take a stand against heretical movements. A Roman monk Jovinian came forward as an opponent of fasts, good works, and the higher merit of celibate life. He found some adherents among the monks and nuns of Rome. About 390–392 the pope held a synod at Rome, at which Jovinian and eight of his followers were condemned and excluded from communion with the Church. The decision was sent to St. Ambrose, the great Bishop of Milan and a friend of Siricius. Ambrose now held a synod of the bishops of upper Italy which, as the letter says, in agreement with his decision also condemned the heretics. Other heretics including Bishop Bonosus of Sardica (390), who was also accused of errors in the dogma of the Trinity, maintained the false doctrine that Mary was not always a virgin. Siricius and Ambrose opposed Bonosus and his adherents and refuted their false views. The pope then left further proceedings against Bonosus to the Bishop of Thessalonica and the other Illyrian bishops. Like his predecessor Damasus, Siricius also took part in the Priscillian controversy; he sharply condemned the episcopal accusers of Priscillian, who had brought the matter before the secular court and had prevailed upon the usurper Maximus to condemn to death and execute Priscillian and some of his followers. Maximus sought to justify his action by sending to the pope the proceedings in the case. Siricius, however, excommunicated Bishop Felix of Trier who supported Ithacius, the accuser of Priscillian, and in whose city the execution had taken place. The pope addressed a letter to the Spanish bishops in which he stated the conditions under which the converted Priscillians were to be restored to communion with the Church.

According to the life in the "Liber Pontificalis" (ed. Duchesne, I, 216), Siricius also took severe measures against the Manichæans at Rome. However, as Duchesne remarks (loc. cit., notes) it cannot be assumed from the writings of the converted Augustine, who was a Manichæan when he went to Rome (383), that Siricius took any particular steps against them, yet Augustine would certainly have commented on this if such had been the case. The mention in the "Liber Pontificalis" belongs properly to the life of Pope Leo I. Neither is it probable, as Langen thinks (Gesch. der röm. Kirche, I, 633), that Priscillians are to be understood by this mention of Manichæans, although probably Priscillians were at times called Manichæans in the writings of that age. The western emperors, including Honorius and Valentinian III, issued laws against the Manichæans, whom they declared to be political offenders, and took severe action against the members of this sect (Codex Theodosian, XVI, V, various laws). In the East Siricius interposed to settle the Meletian schism at Antioch; this schism had continued notwithstanding the death in 381 of Meletius at the Council of Constantinople. The followers of Meletius elected Flavian as his successor, while the adherents of Bishop Paulinus, after the death of this bishop (388), elected Evagrius. Evagrius died in 392 and through Flavian's management no successor was elected. By the mediation of St. John Chrysostom and Theophilus of Alexandria an embassy, led by Bishop Acacius of Berœa, was sent to Rome to persuade Siricius to recognize Flavian and to readmit him to communion with the Church.

At Rome the name of Siricius is particularly connected with the basilica over the grave of St. Paul on the Via Ostiensis which was rebuilt by the emperor as a basilica of five aisles during the pontificate of Siricius and was dedicated by the pope in 390. The name of Siricius is still to be found on one of the pillars that was not destroyed in the fire of 1823, and which now stands in the vestibule of the side entrance to the transept. Two of his contemporaries describe the character of Siricius disparagingly. Paulinus of Nola, who on his visit to Rome in 395 was treated in a guarded manner by the pope, speaks of the *urbici papæ superba discretio*, the haughty policy of the Roman bishop (Epist., V, 14). This action of the pope is, however, explained by the fact that there had been irregularities in the election and consecration of Paulinus (Buse, "Paulin von Nola", I, 193). Jerome, for his part, speaks of the "lack of judgment" of Siricius (Epist., cxxvii, 9) on account of the latter's treatment of Rufinus of Aquileia, to whom the pope had given a letter when Rufinus left Rome in 398, which showed that he was in communion with the Church. The reason, however, does not justify the judgment which Jerome expressed against the pope; moreover, Jerome in his polemical writings often exceeds the limits of propriety. All that is known of the labours of Siricius refutes the criticism of the caustic hermit of Bethlehem. The "Liber Pontificalis" gives an incorrect date for his death; he was buried in the *cœmeterium* of Priscilla on the Via Salaria. The text of the inscription on his grave is known (De Rossi, "Inscriptiones christ. urbis Romæ", II, 102, 138). His feast is celebrated on 26 November. His name was inserted in the Roman Martyrology by Benedict XIV.

Liber Pontif., ed. DUCHESNE, I, 216–17; COUSTANT, *Epist. Roman. Pont.*, I; JAFFÉ, *Reg. Pont. Rom.*, I, 2nd ed., 40–42; BABUT, *La plus ancienne Décrétale* (Paris, 1904); LANGEN, *Gesch. der röm. Kirche*, I (Bonn, 1881), 611 sqq.; RAUSCHEN, *Jahrb. der christl. Kirche* (Freiburg, 1897); GRISAR, *Gesch. Roms u. der Päpste*, I, passim; HEFELE, *Konziliengesch.*, II, 2nd ed., 45–48, 51.

J. P. KIRSCH.

Sirleto, GUGLIELMO, cardinal and scholar, b. at Guardavalle near Stilo in Calabria, 1514; d. at Rome, 6 October, 1585. The son of a physician, he received an excellent education, made the acquaintance of distinguished scholars at Rome, and became an intimate friend of Cardinal Marcello Cervino, later Pope Marcellus II. He prepared for Cervino, who was President of the Council of Trent in its initial period, extensive reports on all the important questions presented for discussion. After his appointment as custodian of the Vatican Library, Sirleto drew up a complete descriptive catalogue of its Greek manuscripts and prepared a new edition of the Vulgate. Paul IV named him prothonotary and tutor to two of his nephews. After this pope's death he taught Greek and Hebrew at Rome, numbering St. Charles Borromeo among his students. During the concluding period of the Council of Trent he was, although he continued to reside at Rome, the constant and most heeded adviser of the cardinal-legates. He was himself created cardinal in 1565, became Bishop of San Marco in Calabria in 1566, and of Squillace in 1568. An order of the papal secretary of state, however, enjoined his residence at Rome, where he was named, in 1570, librarian of the Vatican Library. His influence was paramount in the execution of the scientific undertakings decreed by the Council of Trent. He collaborated in the publication of the Roman Catechism, presided over the Commissions for the reform of the Roman Breviary and Missal, and directed the work of the new edition of the Roman Martyrology. Highly appreciative of Greek culture, he entertained very friendly relations with the East and encouraged all efforts tending to ecclesiastical reunion. He was attended in his last illness by St. Philip Neri and was buried in the presence of Sixtus V.

HURTER, *Nomenclator Lit.*, I (2d ed., Innsbruck, 1892), 95–6; BÄUMER-BIRON, *Hist. du bréviaire*, II (Paris, 1905), 169–71, passim.

N. A. WEBER.

Sirmium (SZERÉM), DIOCESE OF (SIRMIENSIS), situated near the modern town of Mitrovitz in Slavonia; its church is said to have been founded by St. Peter. The district of Szerém was subject to the Archbishop of Kalocsa after the Christianization of Hungary. In 1228, the archbishop petitioned the Holy See, in consideration of the large extent of his diocese, to found a new bishopric, and in 1229 Gregory IX established the See of Szerém, the jurisdiction of which covered almost exclusively the country on the right bank of the Sava River. The see was under the Turkish Government in 1526. It had no bishop from 1537 to 1578, and was held by a titular bishop after 1624. In 1709 the see was re-established with some changes in its territory. Clement XIV united it with Bosnia and Diakovár in 1773.

SZÖRÉNYI, *Vindiciæ Sirmienses* (Buda, 1746); FARLATI, *Illyricum sacrum*, VII, 449–811; PRAY, *Specimen Hierarchiæ Hungariæ*, II, 362–95; *A katolikus Magyarország* (Budapest, 1902).

A. ÁLDÁSY.

Sirmond, JACQUES, one of the greatest scholars of the seventeenth century, b. at Riom in the Department of Puy-de-Dôme, France, Oct., 1559; d. in Paris, 7 Oct., 1651. He entered the Society of Jesus in 1576 and was appointed in 1581 professor of classical languages in Paris, where he numbered St. Francis de Sales among his pupils. Called to Rome in 1590, he was for sixteen years private secretary to the Jesuit superior general, Aquaviva, devoting his leisure moments during the same period to the study of the literary and historical treasures of antiquity. He entertained intimate relations with several learned men then present at Rome, among them Bellarmine and particularly Baronius, to whom he was helpful in the composition of the "Annales". In 1608 he returned to Paris, and in 1637 became confessor to King Louis XIII. His first literary production appeared in 1610, and from that date until the end of his life almost every year witnessed the publication of some new work. The results of his literary labours are chiefly represented by editions of Greek and Latin Christian writings. Theodoret of Cyrus, Ennodius, Idatius of Gallicia, Sidonius Apollinaris, Theodulph of Orleans, Paschasius Radbertus, Flodoard, and Hincmar of Rheims are among the writers whose works he edited, either completely or in part. Of great importance were his editions of the capitularies of Charles the Bald and successors and of the ancient councils of France: "Karoli Calvi et successorum aliquot Franciæ regum Capitula" (Paris, 1623); "Concilia antiqua Galliæ" (Paris, 1629). His collected works, a complete list of which will be found in de Backer-Sommervogel (VII, 1237–60), were published in Paris in 1696 and again at Venice in 1728.

DE BACKER-SOMMERVOGEL, *Bibl. de la comp. de Jésus*, VII (Brussels, 1896), 1237–61; COLOMIÈS, *Vie du Père Sirmond* (La Rochelle, 1671); CHALMERS, *Biog. Dict.* (London, 1816), s. v.

N. A. WEBER.

Sis. See FLAVIAS.

Sisinnius, POPE, date of birth unknown; d. 4 Feb., 708. Successor of John VII, he was consecrated probably 15 Jan., 708, and died after a brief pontificate of about three weeks; he was buried in St. Peter's. He was a Syrian by birth and the son of one John. Although he was so afflicted with gout that he was unable even to feed himself, he is nevertheless said to have been a man of strong character, and to have been able to take thought for the good of the city. He gave orders to prepare lime to repair the walls of Rome, and before he died consecrated a bishop for Corsica.

Liber Pontificalis, I, 338; MANN, *The Lives of the Popes in the Early Middle Ages*, I, pt. ii (St. Louis and London, 1902), 124.

HORACE K. MANN.

Sisters of Charity of Cincinnati, Ohio.—On 27 October, 1829, at the request of Bishop Fenwick of Cincinnati, several sisters from Mother Seton's community at Emmitsburg, Maryland, opened an orphanage, parochial school, and academy on Sycamore Street opposite the old cathedral, then occupying the present site of St. Xavier's Church and college. When Bishop Purcell built the new cathedral on Eighth and Plum Sts., the sisters moved to Third and Plum Sts., and later the academy was transferred to George St., near John. When Father Etienne, superior of the Daughters of Charity of France, in December, 1850, effected the affiliation of the sisterhood at Emmitsburg with the Daughters of Charity of France, Sister Margaret George was superior in Cincinnati. She had entered the community at Emmitsburg early in 1812, and had filled the office of treasurer and secretary of the community, teaching in the academy during most of Mother Seton's life. She wrote the early records of the American Daughters of Charity, heard all the discussions regarding rules and constitutions, and left to her community in Cincinnati letters from the first bishops and clergy of the United States, Mother Seton's original Journal written in 1803 and some of her letters, and valuable writings of her own. She upheld Mother Seton's rules, constitutions, traditions, and costume, confirmed by Archbishop Carroll 17 Jan., 1812, objecting with Archbishop Carroll and Mother Seton to the French rule in its fullness, in that it limited the exercise of charity to females in the orphanages and did not permit the teaching of boys in the schools. The sisters in New York had separated from Emmitsburg in December, 1846, because they were to be withdrawn from the boys' orphanage. When it was finally decided that the community at Emmitsburg was to affiliate with the French Daughters of Charity, the sisters in Cincinnati laid before Archbishop Purcell their desire to preserve the original rule of Mother Seton's foundation. He confirmed the sisters in their desire and notified the superior of the French Daughters of Charity that he would take under his protection the followers of Mother Seton. Archbishop Purcell became ecclesiastical superior and was succeeded by Archbishop Elder and Archbishop Moeller.

The novitiate in Cincinnati was opened in 1852. During that year twenty postulants were received. The first Catholic hospital was opened by the sisters in November, 1852. In February, 1853, the sisters took charge of the Mary and Martha Society, a charitable organization established for the benefit of the poor of the city. On 15 August, 1853, the sisters purchased their first property on the corner of Sixth and Parks Sts., and opened there in September a boarding and select day-school. The following July they bought a stone house on Mt. Harrison near Mt. St. Mary Seminary of the West, and called it Mt. St. Vincent. The community was incorporated under the laws of Ohio in 1854 as "The Sisters of Charity of Cincinnati, Ohio". Mother Margaret George, Sister Sophia Gillmeyer, Mother Josephine Harvey, Sister Anthony O'Connell, Mother Regina Mattingly, Sister Antonio McCaffrey, and Sister Gonzalva Dougherty were the incorporators. In 1856 Mt. St. Vincent Academy was transferred to the "Cedars", the former home of Judge Alderson. It remained the mother-house until 29 Sept., 1869, and the boarding-school until July, 1906. It is now a day academy and a residence for the sisters teaching adjacent parochial schools. In 1857 Bishop Bayley of New Jersey sent five postulants to Mt. St. Vincent, Cedar Grove, Cincinnati, to be trained by Mother Margaret George. At the conclusion of their novitiate, Mother Margaret and Sister Anthony were to have gone with them to Newark, New Jersey, to remain until the little community would be well established. but affairs proving too urgent, Mother Margaret interceded with the New York community, and Sisters Xavier and Catherine were appointed superiors over the little band. In July, 1859, Mother Margaret George having held the office of mother for the two terms allowed by the constitution, was succeeded by Mother Josephine Harvey. During the Civil War many of the sisters served in the hospitals. Between 1852 and 1865 the sisters had taken charge of ten parochial schools. Archbishop Lamy of New Mexico, and Bishop Machebreuf of Colorado, both pioneer priests of Ohio, in 1865 petitioned Archbishop Purcell for a colony of Sisters of Charity to open a hospital and orphanage in the West. Accordingly four sisters left Cincinnati 21 August, 1865, arriving at Santa Fé, 13 Sept., 1865. The archbishop gave them his own residence which had been used also as a seminary. There were twenty-five orphans to be cared for and some sick to be nursed. On 15 August, 1866, Joseph C. Butler and Lewis Worthington presented Sister Anthony O'Connell with the Good Samaritan Hospital, a building erected by the Government for a Marine Hospital at a cost of $300,000. Deeply impressed by the charity done in "old St. John's" during the war, these non-Catholic gentlemen bought the Government hospital for $90,000 and placed the deeds in the hands of Sister Anthony, Butler suggesting the name "Good Samaritan". Early in 1870 Bishop Domenec of Pittsburg, desiring a diocesan branch of Mother Seton's community, sent four postulants to be trained in the Cincinnati novitiate. On their return they were accompanied by five of the Cincinnati sisters who were to remain with them for a limited time, and to be withdrawn one by one. Finally all were recalled but Mother Aloysia Lowe and Sister Ann Regina Ennis, the former being superior and the latter mistress of novices. Mother Aloysia governed the community firmly but tenderly, and before her death (1889) had the satisfaction of seeing the sisters in their new mother-house at Seton Hill, Greensburg, Pa., the academy having been blessed, and the chapel dedicated, 3 May, 1889.

Mother Aloysia's term of office had expired 19 July, 1889, and she was succeeded by Sister Ann Regina (d. 16 May, 1894). The community at Greensburg, Pa., at present number more than three hundred. Their St. Joseph Academy at the mother-house is flourishing; they teach about thirty parochial schools in the Dioceses of Altoona and Pittsburg and conduct the Pittsburg Hospital and Roselia Foundling Asylum in Pittsburg.

From 1865 to 1880 the sisters in Cincinnati opened thirty-three branch houses, one of these being the St. Joseph Foundling and Maternity Hospital, a gift to Sister Anthony from Joseph Butler. In 1869 a site for a mother-house, five miles from Cedar Grove, was purchased. The first Mass was offered in the novitiate chapel, 24 October, 1869, by Rev. Thos. S. Byrne, the chaplain, the present Bishop of Nashville, Tennessee. In 1882 the building of the new mother-house began under his direction. Before its completion Mother Regina Mattingly died (4 June, 1883). Mother Josephine Harvey again assumed the office. In 1885 the new St. Joseph was burned to the ground. The present mother-house was begun at once under the superintendence of Rev. T. S. Byrne. Mt. St. Mary Seminary, closed since the financial troubles, was now used for the sisters' novitiate. In July, 1886, the sisters took possession of the west wing of the mother-house, and the following year the seminary reopened. Mother Josephine Harvey resigned the office of mother in 1888, and was succeeded by Mother Mary Paul Hayes, who filled Mother Josephine's unexpired term and was re-elected in July, 1890, dying the following April. Mother Mary Blanche Davis was appointed to the office of mother, and held it until July, 1899. During her incumbency the Seton Hospital, the Glockner Sanitarium at Colorado Springs, St. Joseph Sanitarium, Mt. Clemens, Mich., and Santa Maria Institute for Italians were begun; additions were made to the mother-house. During the administration of Mother Sebastian Shea were built: the St. Joseph Sanitarium, Pueblo; the San Rafael Hospital, Trinidad; the St. Vincent Hospital, Santa Fé, New Mexico; the St. Vincent Academy, Albuquerque; and the Good Samaritan Annex in Clifton. Mother Mary Blanche resumed the duties of office in 1905, and was re-elected in 1908. During these terms a very large addition was built to the Glockner Sanitarium and to the St. Mary Sanitarium, Pueblo; the Hospital Antonio in Kenton, Ohio; a large boarding school for boys at Fayetteville, Ohio; the new Seton Hospital was bought; the new Good Samaritan Hospital was begun. Many parochial schools were opened, among them a school for coloured children in Memphis, Tennessee.

The community numbers: about 800 members; 74 branch houses; 5 academies; 2 orphan asylums; 1 foundling asylum; 1 Italian institute; 11 hospitals or sanitariums; 1 Old Ladies' Home; 53 parochial schools throughout Michigan, Ohio, Tennessee, Colorado, and New Mexico.

SISTER MARY AGNES.

Sisters of the Little Company of Mary, a congregation founded in 1877 in England to honour in a particular manner the maternal Heart of the Blessed Virgin, especially in the mystery of Calvary. The sisters make an entire consecration of themselves to her, and aim at imitating her virtues. They devote themselves to the sick and dying, which is their principal exterior work. They nurse the sick in their own homes, and also receive them in the hospitals and nursing-homes attached to their convents. They make no distinction of class, nationality, or creed, and exact no charge for their services, but accept any offering which may be made them. Besides the personal attendance on the sick, they are bound to pray continually for the dying, and in the novitiate watch before the Blessed Sacrament, both by day and night, praying for the dying. When circumstances require it, the sisters may engage in various forms of mission work, especially in poor districts. The rules received final approbation from Leo XIII in 1893. The order conducts houses in: Italy (1 in Rome, 1 at Florence, 1 at Fiesole); England (3 in London, 1 at Nottingham); Ireland (1 at Limerick, 1 in Fermoy); Malta (1); United States (Chicago); Australia (2 at Sydney, 1 at Adelaide); South Africa (Port Elizabeth). The sisters when in the convent wear a black habit and blue veil, with a white cloak in the chapel; when nursing, the habit is of white linen, with a blue veil.

An association of pious women, known as "Pie Donne" or "Affiliated", are aggregated to the order, and share in its prayers and good works, some residing in their own homes, others living in the convent, though in part separated from the community. A confraternity is attached to the order, called the Calvary Confraternity, the members of which assist those in their last agony by their prayers and, if possible, by personal attendance.

MOTHER M. PATRICK.

Sistine Choir.—Although it is known that the Church, from her earliest days, employed music in her cult, it was not until the time of her emergence from the catacombs that she began freely to display her beauty and splendour in sacred song. As early as in the pontificate of Sylvester I (314–35) we find a regularly-constituted company of singers, under the name of *schola cantorum*, living together in a building devoted to their exclusive use. The word *schola* was in those days the legal designation of an association of equals in any calling or profession and did not primarily denote, as in our time, a school. It had more the nature of a guild, a characteristic which clung to the papal choir for many centuries. Hilary II (461–8) ordained that the pontifical singers live in community, while Gregory the Great (590–604) not only made permanent the existing institution attached to St. John Lateran and including at that time in its membership monks, secular clergy, and boys, but established a second and similar one in connexion with the Basilica of St. Peter. The latter is supposed to have served as a sort of preparatory school for the former. For several centuries the papal *schola cantorum* retained the same general character. Its head, *archicantor* or *primicerius*, was always a clergyman of high rank and often a bishop. While it was his duty to intone the various chants to be followed by the rest of the singers, he was by no means their master in the modern technical sense.

It is at the time of the transfer of the papal see from Rome to Avignon in the thirteenth century that a marked change takes place in the institution. Innocent IV did not take his *schola cantorum* with him to his new abode, but provided for its continuance in Rome by turning over to it properties, tithes, and other revenues. Community life among the singers seems to have come to an end at this period. Clement V (1305–14) formed a new choir at Avignon, consisting for the most part of French singers, who showed a decided preference for the new developments in church music—the *déchant* and *falsibordoni*, which had in the meantime gained great vogue in France. When Gregory XI (1370–8) returned to Rome, he took his singers with him and amalgamated them with the still-existing, at least in name, ancient *schola cantorum*. Before the sojourn of the papal Court at Avignon, it had been the duty of the *schola* to accompany the pope to the church where he held station, but after the return to Rome, the custom established at Avignon of celebrating all pontifical functions in the papal church or chapel was continued and has existed ever since. The *primicerius* of former times is now no longer mentioned but is replaced by the *magister capellæ*, which title, however, continues to be more an honorary one held by a bishop or prelate than an indication of technical leadership, as may be gathered from the relative positions assigned to various dignitaries, their prerogatives, etc. Thus the *magister capellæ* came immediately after the cardinals, followed, in the order given, by the *sacrista, cantores, capellani,* and *clerici*.

With the building by Sixtus IV (1471–84) of the church for the celebration of all papal functions since known as the Sistine Chapel, the original *schola cantorum* and subsequent *capella pontificia* or *capella papale*, which still retains more or less of the guild character, becomes the *capella sistina*, or Sistine Choir, whose golden era takes its beginning. Up to this time the number of singers had varied considerably, there being sometimes as few as nine men and six boys. By a Bull dated November, 1483, Sixtus IV fixed the number at twenty-four, six for each part. After the year 1441 the records no longer mention the presence of boys in the choir, the high voices, soprano and alto, being thenceforth sung by natural (and occasionally unnatural) *soprani falsetti* and high tenors respectively. Membership in the papal choir became the great desideratum of singers, contrapuntists, and composers of every land, which accounts for the presence in Rome, at least for a time, of most of the great names of that period. The desire to re-establish a sort of preparatory school for the papal choir, on the plan of the ancient *schola*, and incidentally to become independent of the ultramontane, or foreign, singers, led Julius II (1503–13) to issue, on 19 February, 1512, a Bull founding the *capella Julia*, which to this day performs all the choir duties at St. Peter's. It became indeed, and has ever since been, a nursery for, and stepping-stone to, membership in the Sistine Choir. The high artistic aims of its founder have, however, but rarely been attained, owing to the rarity of truly great choirmasters. Leo X (1513–21), himself a musician, by choosing as head of the organization a real musician, irrespective of his clerical rank, took a step which was of the greatest importance for the future. It had the effect of transforming a group of vocal *virtuosi* on equal footing into a compact vocal body, whose interpretation of the greatest works of polyphony which we possess, and which were then coming into existence, became the model for the rest of the world, not only then but for all time. Leo's step was somewhat counteracted by Sixtus V (1585–90), who ordered the singers to elect their leader annually from their own number. Paul II (1534–49) on 17 November, 1545, published a Bull approving a new constitution of the choir, which has been in force ever since, and according to which the choir-master proposes the candidates for membership, who are then examined by the whole company of singers. Since that time the state of life of the candidate has not been a factor.

While the Sistine Choir has, since its incipiency, undergone many vicissitudes, its artistic and moral level fluctuating, like all things human, with the mutations of the times, it has ever had for its purpose and object to hold up, at the seat of ecclesiastical authority, the highest model of liturgical music as well as of its performance. When the Gregorian melodies were still the sole music of the Church, it was the papal choir that set the standard for the rest of Christendom, both as regards the purity of the melodies and their rendition. After these melodies had blossomed into polyphony, it was in the Sistine Chapel that it received adequate interpretation. Here the artistic degeneration, which church music suffered in different periods in many countries, never took hold for any length of time. The use of instruments, even of the organ, has ever been excluded. The choir's ideal has always been the purely vocal style. Since the accession of the present pope, and under its present conductor, the falsetto voices have been succeeded by boys' voices, and the artistic level of the institute has been raised to a higher point than it had occupied for the previous thirty or forty years.

HABERL, *Bausteine für Musikgeschichte*, III, *Die römische Schola Cantorum und die päpstlichen Kapellsänger bis zur Mitte des 16. Jahrhunderts* (Leipzig, 1888); SCHELLE, *Die päpstliche Sängerschule in Rom* (Leipzig, 1872); KIENLE, *Choralschule* (Freiburg, 1899); BAINI, *Memorie storico-critiche della vita e delle opere di Giovanni Pierluigi da Palestrina* (Rome, 1828).

JOSEPH OTTEN.

Sitifis, TITULAR SEE OF (SITIFENSIS), in Mauretania Sitifensis. Sitifis, situated in Mauretania Cæsarensis, on the road from Carthage to Cirta, was of no importance under the Numidian kings and became prominent only when Nerva established a colony of veterans there. When Mauretania Sitifensis was created, at the close of the third century, Sitifis became its capital. Under the Vandals it was the chief town of a district called Zaba. It was still the capital of a province under Byzantine rule and was then a place of strategic importance. Captured by the Arabs in the seventh century, it was almost ruined at the time of the French occupation (1838). It is now Setif, the chief town of an *arrondissement* in the Department of Constantine, Algeria. It contains 15,000 inhabitants, of whom 3700 are Europeans and 1600 Jews; it has a trade in cattle, cereals, leather, and cloths. Interesting Christian inscriptions are to be found there, one of 452 mentioning the relics of St. Lawrence, another naming two martyrs of Sitifis, Justus and Decurius; there are a museum and the ruins of a Byzantine fortress. St. Augustine, who had frequent relations with Sitifis, informs us that in his time it contained a monastery and an episcopal school, and that it suffered from a violent earthquake, on which occasion 2000 persons, through fear of death, received baptism (Ep., lxxxiv; Serm., xix). Five bishops of this see are known: Severus, in 409, mentioned in a letter of St. Augustine; Novatus, present at the Council of Carthage (411), where he opposed the Donatist Marcian, present at the Council of Carthage (419), dying in 440, mentioned in St. Augustine's letters; Lawrence, in 452; Donatus, present at the Council of Carthage (484), and exiled by Huneric; Optatus, at the Council of Carthage (525).

SMITH, *Dict. of Greek and Roman Geog.*, s. v. *Sitifi*; MÜLLER, *Notes à Ptolemy*, ed. DIDOT, I, 612; TOULOTTE, *Géog. de l'Afrique chrétienne: Maurétanie* (Montreuil, 1894), 185–9; DIEHL, *L'Afrique byzantine* (Paris, 1896), passim.

S. PÉTRIDÈS.

Sitjar, BUENAVENTURA, b. at Porrera, Island of Majorca, 9 Dec., 1739; d. at San Antonio, Cal., 3 Sept., 1808. In April, 1758, he received the habit of St. Francis. After his ordination he joined the College of San Fernando, Mexico. In 1770 he was assigned to California, arriving at San Diego, 21 May, 1771. He was present at the founding of the Mission of San Antonio, and was appointed first missionary by Father Junipero Serra. He toiled there until his death, up to which time 3400 Indians had been baptized. Father Sitjar mastered the Telame language, spoken at the Mission of San Antonio, and compiled a vocabulary with Spanish explanations, published at New York in 1861. Though the list of words is not as long as Arroyo de la Cuesta's dictionary of 2884 words and sentences in the Mutsun idiom of Mission San Juan Bautista, Sitjar's gives the pronunciation and fuller explanations. He also left a journal of an exploring expedition which he accompanied in 1795. His body was interred in the sanctuary of the church.

Archives of Mission of Santa Barbara; Records of Mission San Antonio; SITJAR, *Vocabulary,* in SHEA'S *Library of American Linguistics* (New York, 1861); ENGELHARDT, *The Franciscans in California* (Harbor Springs, 1897); BANCROFT, *California,* II (San Francisco, 1886).

ZEPHYRIN ENGELHARDT.

Sitten. See SION, DIOCESE OF.

Siunia, a titular see, suffragan of Sebastia in Armenia Prima. Siunia is not a town, but a province situated between Goghtcha, Araxa, and Aghovania, in the present Russian districts of Chamakha, or Baku, and Elisavetpol. The real name should be Sisacan, the Persian form, for Siunia got its name from Sisac, the son of Gegham, the fifth Armenian sovereign. Its first rulers, vassals of the kings of Armenia or the shahs of Persia, date back to the fourth century of our era; about 1046 it became an independent kingdom, but only till 1166. The Church of Siunia was established in the fifth century or perhaps a little earlier. It soon became a metropolis subject to the Catholicos of Armenia, and, as we see in a letter of the patriarch Ter Sargis in 1006, it counted twelve crosiers, which must signify twelve suffragan sees. The archdiocese contained 1400 villages and 28 monasteries. In the ninth century the metropolitan see was fixed in the convent of Tatheo, situated between Ouronta and Migri, sixty-two miles south-east of Lake Gokcha. Separated for a brief interval from Noravank, the See of Siunia was reunited to it, but was definitively separated again in the thirteenth century. In 1837 the Diocese of Siunia was, by order of the Synod of Etchmiadzin, suppressed and subjected directly to the catholicos under the supervision of the Bishop of Erivan, who had a vicar at Tatheo. The complete list of the bishops and metropolitans of Siunia, from the fifth century till the nineteenth century, is known; amongst them we may mention Petros, a writer at the beginning of the sixth century, and Stephanos Orbelian, the historian of his Church. It is not known why the Roman Curia introduced this episcopal title, which does not appear in any Greek or Latin "Notitia episcopatuum", and was never a suffragan of Sebastia.

LE QUIEN, *Oriens christianus,* I (Paris, 1740), 1443; BROSSET, *Listes chronologiques des princes et des métropolites de Siounie* in *Bulletin de l'Académie des Sciences de Saint-Pétersbourg,* IV (1862), 497–562; STEPHANOS ORBELIAN, *Histoire de la Siounie,* tr. BROSSET (Saint-Petersburg, 1864).

S. VAILHÉ.

Sivas. See SEBASTIA, ARMENIAN CATHOLIC DIOCESE OF.

Six Days' Work, THE. See HEXAEMERON.

Sixtus I, SAINT, POPE (in the oldest documents, XYSTUS is the spelling used for the first three popes of that name), succeeded St. Alexander and was followed by St. Telesphorus. According to the "Liberian Catalogue" of popes, he ruled the Church during the reign of Adrian "a consulatu Nigri et Aproniani usque Vero III et Ambibulo", that is, from 117 to 126. Eusebius, who in his "Chronicon" made use of a catalogue of popes different from the one he used in his "Historia Ecclesiastica", states in his "Chronicon" that Sixtus I was pope from 114 to 124, while in his "History" he makes him rule from 119 to 128. All authorities agree that he reigned about ten years. He was a Roman by birth, and his father's name was Pastor. According to the "Liber Pontificalis" (ed. Duchesne, I, 128), he passed the following three ordinances: (1) that none but sacred ministers are allowed to touch the sacred vessels; (2) that bishops who have been summoned to the Holy See shall, upon their return, not be received by their diocese except on presenting Apostolic letters; (3) that after the Preface in the Mass the priest shall recite the Sanctus with the people. The "Felician Catalogue" of popes and the various martyrologies give him the title of martyr. His feast is celebrated on 6 April. He was buried in the Vatican, beside the tomb of St. Peter. His relics are said to have been transferred to Alatri in 1132, though O. Jozzi ("Il corpo di S. Sisto I., papa e martire rivendicato alla basilica Vaticana", Rome, 1900) contends that they are still in the Vatican Basilica. Butler (Lives of the Saints, 6 April) states that Clement X gave some of his relics to Cardinal de Retz, who placed them in the Abbey of St. Michael in Lorraine. The Xystus who is commemorated in the Canon of the Mass is Xystus II, not Xystus I.

Acta SS., April, I, 531–4; *Liber Pontificalis,* ed. DUCHESNE, I (Paris, 1886), 128; MARINI, *Cenni storici popolari sopra S. Sisto I, papa e martire, e suo culto in Alatri* (Foligno, 1884); DE PERSIIS, *Del pontificato di S. Sisto I, papa e martire, della traslazione delle sue reliquie da Roma ecc., memorie* (Alatri, 1884); BARMBY in *Dict. Christ. Biog.,* s. v. *Sixtus* (2) I.

MICHAEL OTT.

Sixtus II (XYSTUS), SAINT, POPE, elected 31 Aug., 257, martyred at Rome, 6 Aug., 258. His origin is unknown. The "Liber Pontificalis" says that he was a Greek by birth, but this is probably a mistake, originating from the false assumption that he was identical with a Greek philosopher of the same name, who was the author of the so-called "Sentences" of Xystus. During the pontificate of his predecessor, St. Stephen, a sharp dispute had arisen between Rome and the African and Asiatic Churches, concerning the rebaptism of heretics, which had threatened to end in a complete rupture between Rome and the Churches of Africa and Asia Minor (see CYPRIAN OF CARTHAGE, SAINT).

HEAD OF ST. SIXTUS II
Detail from the Sistine Madonna, Raphael

Sixtus II, whom Pontius (Vita Cypriani, cap. xiv) styles a good and peaceful priest (*bonus et pacificus sacerdos*), was more conciliatory than St. Stephen and restored friendly relations with these Churches, though, like his predecessor, he upheld the Roman usage of not rebaptizing heretics.

Shortly before the pontificate of Sixtus II the Emperor Valerian issued his first edict of persecution, which made it binding upon the Christians to participate in the national cult of the pagan gods and forbade them to assemble in the cemeteries, threatening with exile or death whomsoever was found to disobey the order. In some way or other, Sixtus II managed to perform his functions as chief pastor of the Christians without being molested by those who were charged with the execution of the imperial edict. But during the first days of August, 258, the emperor issued a new and far more cruel edict against the Christians, the import of which has been preserved in a letter of St. Cyprian to Successus, the Bishop of Abbir Germaniciana (Ep. lxxx). It ordered bishops, priests, and deacons to be summarily put to death ("episcopi et presbyteri et diacones incontinenti animadvertantur"). Sixtus II was one of the first to fall a victim to this imperial enactment ("Xistum in cimiterio animadversum sciatis VIII. id. Augusti et cum eo diacones quattuor"—Cyprian, Ep. lxxx). In order to escape the vigilance of the imperial officers he assembled his flock on 6 August at one of the less-known cemeteries, that of Prætextatus, on the left side of the Appian Way, nearly opposite the cemetery of St. Callistus. While seated on his chair in the act of addressing his flock he was suddenly apprehended by a band of soldiers. There is some doubt whether he was beheaded forthwith, or was first brought before a tribunal to receive his sentence and then led back to the cemetery for execution. The latter opinion seems to be the more probable.

The inscription which Pope Damasus (366–84) placed on his tomb in the cemetery of St. Callistus may be interpreted in either sense. The entire inscription is to be found in the works of St. Damasus (P. L., XIII, 383–4, where it is wrongly supposed to be an epitaph for Pope Stephen I), and a few fragments of it were discovered at the tomb itself by de Rossi (Inscr. Christ., II, 108). The "Liber Pontificalis" mentions that he was led away to offer sacrifice to the gods ("ductus ut sacrificaret demoniis"—I, 155). St. Cyprian states in the above-named letter, which was written at the latest one month after the martyrdom of Sixtus, that "the prefects of the City were daily urging the persecution in order that, if any were brought before them, they might be punished and their property confiscated". The pathetic meeting between St. Sixtus II and St. Lawrence, as the former was being led to execution, of which mention is made in the unauthentic "Acts of St. Lawrence" as well as by St. Ambrose (Officiorum, lib. I, c. xli, and lib. II, c. xxviii) and the poet Prudentius (Peristephanon, II), is probably a mere legend. Entirely contrary to truth is the statement of Prudentius (ibid., lines 23–26) that Sixtus II suffered martyrdom on the cross, unless by an unnatural trope the poet uses the specific word cross ("Jam Xystus adfixus cruci") for martyrdom in general, as Duchesne and Allard (see below) suggest. Four deacons, Januarius, Vincentius, Magnus, and Stephanus, were apprehended with Sixtus and beheaded with him at the same cemetery. Two other deacons, Felicissimus and Agapitus, suffered martyrdom on the same day. The feast of St. Sixtus II and these six deacons is celebrated on 6 August, the day of their martyrdom. The remains of Sixtus were transferred by the Christians to the papal crypt in the neighbouring cemetery of St. Callistus. Behind his tomb was enshrined the bloodstained chair on which he had been beheaded. An oratory (*Oratorium Xysti*) was erected above the cemetery of St. Prætextatus, at the spot where he was martyred, and was still visited by pilgrims of the seventh and the eighth century.

For some time Sixtus II was believed to be the author of the so-called "Sentences", or "Ring of Sixtus", originally written by a Pythagorean philosopher and in the second century revised by a Christian. This error arose because in his introduction to a Latin translation of these "Sentences" Rufinus ascribes them to Sixtus of Rome, bishop and martyr. It is certain that Pope Sixtus II is not their author (see Conybeare, "The Ring of Pope Xystus now first rendered into English, with an historical and critical commentary", London, 1910). Harnack (Texte und Untersuchungen zur altchrist. Literatur, XIII, XX) ascribes to him the treatise "Ad Novatianum", but his opinion has been generally rejected (see Rombold in "Theol. Quartalschrift", LXXII, Tübingen, 1900). Some of his letters are printed in P. L., V, 79–100. A newly discovered letter was published by Conybeare in "English Hist. Review", London, 1910.

Acta SS., Aug., II, 124–42; Duchesne, *Liber Pontificalis*, I, 155–6; Barmby in *Dict. Christ. Biog.*, s. v. *Xystus*; Rohault de Fleury, *Les Saints de la messe*, III (Paris, 1893); Healy, *The Valerian Persecution* (Boston and New York, 1905), 176–9; Allard, *Les dernières persécutions du troisième siècle* (Paris, 1907), 80–92, 343–349; de Rossi, *Roma Sotteranea*, II (Rome, 1864–77), 87–97; Wilpert, *Die Papstgräber und die Cäciliengruft in der Katakombe des hl. Callistus*, supplement to de Rossi's *Roma Sotteranea* (Freiburg im Br., 1909).

MICHAEL OTT.

Sixtus III (Xystus), Saint, Pope, consecrated 31 July, 432; d. 440. Previous to his accession he was prominent among the Roman clergy and in correspondence with St. Augustine. He reigned during the Nestorian and Pelagian controversies, and it was probably owing to his conciliatory disposition that he was falsely accused of leanings towards these heresies. As pope he approved the Acts of the Council of Ephesus and endeavoured to restore peace between Cyril of Alexandria and John of Antioch. In the Pelagian controversy he frustrated the attempt of Julian of Eclanum to be readmitted to communion with the Catholic Church. He defended the pope's right of supremacy over Illyricum against the local bishops and the ambitious designs of Proclus of Constantinople. At Rome he restored the Basilica of Liberius, now known as St. Mary Major, enlarged the Basilica of St. Lawrence-Without-the-Walls, and obtained precious gifts from the Emperor Valentinian III for St. Peter's and the Lateran Basilica. The work which asserts that the consul Bassus accused him of crime is a forgery. He is the author of eight letters (in P. L., L, 583 sqq.), but he did not write the works "On Riches", "On False Teachers", and "On Chastity" ("De divitiis", "De malis doctoribus", "De castitate") attributed to him. His feast is kept on 28 March.

Duchesne (ed.), *Lib. Pont.*, I (Paris, 1886), 126–27, 232–37; Barmby in *Dict. Christ. Biog.*, s. v. *Sixtus* (3); Grisar, *History of Rome and the Popes*, tr. Cappadelta, I (St. Louis, 1911), nos. 54, 135, 140, 144, 154.

N. A. WEBER.

Sixtus IV (Francesco della Rovere), Pope, b. near Abisola, 21 July, 1414; d. 12 Aug., 1484. His parents were poor, and while still a child he was destined for the Franciscan Order. Later he studied philosophy and theology with great success at the University of Pavia, and lectured at Padua, Bologna, Pavia, Siena, and Florence, having amongst other eminent disciples the famous Cardinal Bessarion. After filling the post of procurator of his order in Rome and Provincial of Liguria, he was in 1467 created Cardinal of S. Pietro in Vincoli by Paul II. Whatever leisure he now had was devoted to theology, and in 1470 he published a treatise on the Precious Blood and a work on the Immaculate Conception, in which latter he endeavoured to prove that Aquinas and Scotus, though differing in words, were really of one mind upon the question. The conclave which assembled on the death of Paul II elected him pope, and he ascended the chair of St. Peter as Sixtus IV.

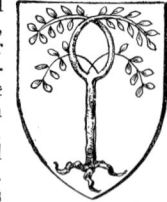

ARMS OF SIXTUS IV

His first thought was the prosecution of the war against the Turks, and legates were appointed for France, Spain, Germany, Hungary, and Poland, with the hope of enkindling enthusiasm in these countries. The crusade, however, achieved little beyond the bringing back to Rome of twenty-five Turkish prisoners, who were paraded in triumph through the streets of the city. Sixtus continued the policy of his predecessor Paul II with regard to France, and denounced Louis XI for insisting on the royal consent being given before papal decrees could be published in his kingdom. He also made an effort like his predecessor for the reunion of the Russian Church with Rome, but his negotiations were without result. He now turned his attention almost exclusively to Italian politics, and fell more and more under his dominating passion of nepotism, heaping riches and favours on his unworthy relations. In 1478 took place the famous conspiracy of the Pazzi, planned by the pope's nephew—Cardinal Rafael Riario—to overthrow the Medici and bring Florence under the Riarii. The pope was cognizant of the plot, though

SIXTUS IV GIVING AUDIENCE TO THE HISTORIAN PLATINA
MELOZZO DA FORLÌ, VATICAN

READING FROM THE RIGHT: POPE SIXTUS IV (FRANCESCO DELLA ROVERE), CARDINAL PIETRO RIARIO (NEPHEW OF THE POPE), CARDINAL GIULIANO DELLA ROVERE (AFTERWARDS POPE JULIUS II), PLATINA (LIBRARIAN OF THE VATICAN AND HISTORIAN OF THE POPES), GIROLAMO RIARIO (BROTHER OF CARDINAL PIETRO), GIOVANNI DELLA ROVERE (BROTHER OF CARDINAL GIULIANO)

probably not of the intention to assassinate, and even laid Florence under interdict because it rose in fury against the conspirators and brutal murderers of Giuliano de' Medici. He now entered upon a two years' war with Florence, and encouraged the Venetians to attack Ferrara, which he wished to obtain for his nephew Girolamo Riario. Ercole d'Este, attacked by Venice, found allies in almost every Italian state, and Ludovico Sforza, upon whom the pope relied for support, did nothing to help him. The allied princes forced Sixtus to make peace, and the chagrin which this caused him is said to have hastened his death.

Henceforth, until the Reformation, the secular interests of the papacy were of paramount importance. The attitude of Sixtus towards the conspiracy of the Pazzi, his wars and treachery, his promotion to the highest offices in the Church of such men as Pietro and Girolamo Riario are blots upon his career. Nevertheless, there is a praiseworthy side to his pontificate. He took measures to suppress abuses in the Inquisition, vigorously opposed the Waldenses, and annulled the decrees of the Council of Constance. He was a patron of arts and letters, building the famous Sistine Chapel, the Sistine Bridge across the Tiber, and becoming the second founder of the Vatican Library. Under him Rome once more became habitable, and he did much to improve the sanitary conditions of the city. He brought down water from the Quirinal to the Fountain of Trevi, and began a transformation of the city which death alone hindered him from completing. In his private life Sixtus IV was blameless. The gross accusations brought against him by his enemy Infessura have no foundation; his worst vice was nepotism, and his greatest misfortune was that he was destined to be placed at the head of the States of the Church at a time when Italy was emerging from the era of the republics, and territorial princes like the pope were forced to do battle with the great despots.

MEDAL TO COMMEMORATE THE DEFEAT OF THE TURKS AT OTRANTO, 1481
Obverse: Portrait of Sixtus IV. Reverse: Allegorical figure of Constancy, with the line from Virgil, Æneid, VI, 853: "To spare the submissive and crush the proud", with the added words: "Thou art able, O Sixtus."

PASTOR, *History of the Popes*, IV (London, 1894); GREGOROVIUS, *Rome in the Middle Ages*, VII (London, 1902); CREIGHTON, *Hist. of the Papacy*, IV (London, 1901); BURKHARDT, *Geschichte der Renaissance in Italien* (1904); FRANTZ, *Sixtus IV und die Republik Florenz* (Ratisbon, 1880).

R. URBAN BUTLER.

Sixtus V, POPE (FELICE PERETTI), b. at Grottamare near Montalto, 13 December, 1521; elected 24 April, 1585; crowned 1 May, 1585; d. in the Quirinal, 27 August, 1590. He belonged to a Dalmatian family which in the middle of the preceding century had fled to Italy from the Turks who were devastating Illyria and threatened to invade Dalmatia. His father was a gardener and it is said of Felice that, when a boy, he was a swineherd. At the age of nine he came to the Minorite convent at Montalto, where his uncle, Frà Salvatore, was a friar. Here he became a novice at the age of twelve. He was educated at Montalto, Ferrara, and Bologna and was ordained at Siena in 1547. The talented young priest gained a high reputation as a preacher. At Rome, where in 1552 he preached the Lenten sermons in the Church of Santi Apostoli, his successful preaching gained for him the friendship of very influential men, such as Cardinal Carpi, the protector of his order; the Cardinals Caraffa and Ghislieri, both of whom became popes; St. Philip Neri and St. Ignatius. He was successively appointed rector of his convent at Siena in 1550, of San Lorenzo at Naples in 1553, and of the convent of the Frari at Venice in 1556. A year later Pius IV appointed him also counsellor to the Inquisition at Venice. His zeal and severity in the capacity of inquisitor displeased the Venetian Government, which demanded and obtained his recall in 1560. Having returned to Rome he was made counsellor to the Holy Office, professor at the Sapienza, and general procurator and vicar Apostolic of his order. In 1565 Pius IV designated him to accompany to Spain Cardinal Buoncompagni (afterwards Gregory XIII), who was to investigate a charge of heresy against Archbishop Carranza of Toledo. From this time dates the antipathy between Peretti and Buoncompagni, which declared itself more openly during the latter's pontificate (1572-85). Upon his return to Rome in 1566 Pius V created him Bishop of Sant' Agata dei Goti in the Kingdom of Naples and later chose him as his confessor. On 17 May, 1570, the same pope created him cardinal-priest with the titular Church of S. Simeone, which he afterwards exchanged for that of S. Girolamo dei Schiavoni. In 1571 he was transferred to the See of Fermo. He was popularly known as the Cardinal di Montalto. During the pontificate of Gregory XIII he withdrew from public affairs, devoting himself to study and to the collection of works of art, as far as his scanty means permitted. During this time he edited the works of St. Ambrose (Rome, 1579-1585) and erected a villa (now Villa Massimi) on the Esquiline.

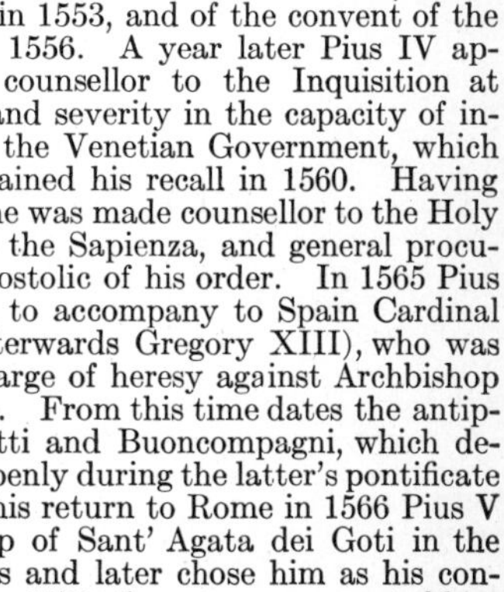

Gregory XIII died on 10 April, 1585, and after a conclave of four days Peretti was elected pope by "adoration" on 24 April, 1585.

MONUMENT OF SIXTUS V—FONTANA
Basilica of St. Mary Major

He took the name Sixtus V in memory of Sixtus IV, who had also been a Minorite. The legend that he entered the conclave on crutches, feigning the infirmities of old age, and upon his election exultantly thrust aside his crutches and appeared full of life and vigour has long been exploded; it may, however, have been invented as a symbol of his forced inactivity during the reign of Gregory XIII and the remarkable energy which he displayed during the five years of his pontificate. He was a born ruler and especially suited to stem the tide of disorder and lawlessness which had broken out towards the end of the reign of Gregory XIII. Having obtained the co-operation of the neighbouring states, he exterminated, often with excessive cruelty, the system of brigandage which had reached immense proportions and terrorized the whole of Italy. The number of bandits in and about Rome at the death of Gregory XIII has been variously estimated at from twelve to twenty-seven thousand, and in little more than two years after the accession of Sixtus V the Papal States had become the most secure country in Europe.

Of almost equal importance with the extermination of the bandits was, in the opinion of Sixtus V, the rearrangement of the papal finances. At his accession the papal exchequer was empty. Acting on his favourite principle that riches as well as severity are necessary for good government, he used every available means to replenish the state treasury. So successful was he in the accumulation of money that, despite his enormous expenditures for public buildings, he had shortly before his death deposited in the Castello di Sant' Angelo three million *scudi* in gold and one million six hundred thousand in silver. He did not consider that in the long run so much dead capital withdrawn from circulation was certain to impoverish the country and deal the death-blow to commerce and industry. To obtain such vast sums he economized everywhere, except in works of architecture; increased the number of salable public offices; imposed more taxes and extended the *monti*, or public loans, that had been instituted by Clement VII. Though extremely economical in other ways, Sixtus V spent immense sums in erection of public works. He built the Lateran Palace; completed the Quirinal; restored the Church of Santa Sabina on the Aventine; rebuilt the Church and Hospice of San Girolamo dei Schiavoni; enlarged and improved the Sapienza; founded the hospice for the poor near the Ponte Sisto; built and richly ornamented the Chapel of the Cradle in the Basilica of Santa Maria Maggiore; completed the cupola of St. Peter's; raised the obelisks of the Vatican, of Santa Maria Maggiore, of the Lateran, and of Santa Maria del Popolo; restored the columns of Trajan and of Antoninus Pius, placing the statue of St. Peter on the former and that of St. Paul on the latter; erected the Vatican Library with its adjoining printing-office and that wing of the Vatican Palace which is inhabited by the pope; built many magnificent streets; erected various monasteries; and supplied Rome with water, the "Acqua Felice", which he brought to the city over a distance of twenty miles, partly underground, partly on elevated aqueducts. At Bologna he founded the Collegio Montalto for fifty students from the March of Ancona.

Far-reaching were the reforms which Sixtus V introduced in the management of ecclesiastical affairs. On 3 Dec., 1586, he issued the Bull "Postquam verus", fixing the number of cardinals at seventy, namely, six cardinal-bishops, fifty cardinal-priests, and fourteen cardinal-deacons. Before his pontificate, ecclesiastical business was generally discharged by the pope in consistory with the cardinals. There were, indeed, a few permanent cardinalitial congregations, but the sphere of their competency was very limited. In his Bull "Immensa æterni Dei", of 11 February, 1588, he established fifteen permanent congregations, some of which were concerned with spiritual, others with temporal affairs. They were the Congregations: (1) of the Inquisition; (2) of the Segnatura; (3) for the Establishment of Churches; (4) of Rites and Ceremonies; (5) of the Index of Forbidden Books; (6) of the Council of Trent; (7) of the Regulars; (8) of the Bishops; (9) of the Vatican Press; (10) of the Annona, for the provisioning of Rome and the provinces; (11) of the Navy; (12) of the Public Welfare; (13) of the Sapienza; (14) of Roads, Bridges, and Waters; (15) of State Consultations. These congregations lessened the work of the pope, without in any way limiting his authority. The final decision belonged to the pope. In the creation of cardinals Sixtus V was, as a rule, guided by their good qualities. The only suspicion of nepotism with which he might be reproached was giving the purple to his fourteen-year-old grand-nephew Alessandro, who, however, did honour to the Sacred College and never wielded an undue influence.

In 1588 he issued from the Vatican Press an edition of the Septuagint revised according to a Vatican MS. His edition of the Vulgate, printed shortly before his death, was withdrawn from circulation on account of its many errors, corrected, and reissued in 1592 (see BELLARMINE, ROBERT FRANCIS ROMULUS, VENERABLE). Though a friend of the Jesuits, he objected to some of their rules and especially to the title "Society of Jesus". He was on the point of changing these when death overtook him. A statue which had been erected in his honour on the Capitol during his lifetime was torn down by the rabble immediately upon his death. (For his relations with the various temporal rulers and his attempts to stem the tide of Protestantism, see COUNTER-REFORMATION, THE.)

VON HÜBNER, *Sixte-Quint* (Paris, 1870), tr. JERNINGHAM (London, 1872); BALZANI, *Rome under Sixtus V* in *Cambridge Modern History*, III (London, 1905), 422–55; ROBARDI, *Sixti V gesta quinquennalia* (Rome, 1590); LETI, *Vita di Sisto V* (Losanna, 1669), tr. FARNEWORTH (London, 1754), unreliable; TEMPESTI, *Storia della vita e geste di Sisto V* (Rome, 1755); CESARE, *Vita di Sisto V* (Naples, 1755); LORENTZ, *Sixtus V und seine Zeit* (Mainz, 1852); DUMESNIL, *Hist. de Sixte-Quint* (Paris, 1869); CAPRANICA, *Papa Sisto, storia del s. XVI* (Milan, 1884); GRAZIANI, *Sisto V e la riorganizzazione della s. Sede* (Rome, 1910); GOZZADINI, *Giovanni Pepoli e Sisto V* (Bologna, 1879); SEGRETAIN, *Sixte-Quint et Henri IV* (Paris, 1861); CUGNONI, *Memorie autografe di Papa Sisto V* in *Archivio della Soc. Romana di storia patria* (Rome, 1882); BENADUCI, *Sisto V. Dodici lettere inedite* (Tolentino, 1888); DALLA SANTA, *Un documento inedito per la storia di Sisto V* (Venice, 1896); ROSSI-SCOTTI, *Pompilio Eusebi da Perugia e Sisto papa V* (Perugia, 1893); PAOLI, *Sisto V e i banditi* (Sassari, 1902); HARPER in *Amer. Cath. Quarterly Review*, III (Philadelphia, 1878), 498–521.

MICHAEL OTT.

Skarga, PETER, theologian and missionary, b. at Grojec, 1536; d. at Cracow, 27 Sept., 1612. He began his education in his native town in 1552; he went to study in Cracow and afterwards in Warsaw. In 1557 he was in Vienna as tutor to the young Castellan, Teczynski; returning thence in 1564, he received Holy orders, and later was nominated canon of Lemberg Cathedral. Here he began to preach his famous sermons, and to convert Protestants. In 1568 he entered the Society of Jesus and went to Rome, where he became penitentiary for the Polish language at St. Peter's. Returning to Poland, he worked in the Jesuit colleges of Pultusk and Wilna, where he converted a multitude of Protestants, Calvinism being at the time prevalent in those parts. To this end he first published some works of controversy; and in 1576, in order to convince the numerous schismatics in Poland, he issued his great treatise "On the Unity of the Church of God", which did much good then, and is even now held in great esteem. It powerfully promoted the cause of the Union. King Stephen Báthori prized Skarga greatly, often profited by his aid and advice, took him on one of his expeditions, and made him rector of the Academy of Wilna, founded in 1578. In 1584 he was sent to Cracow as superior, and founded there the Brotherhood of Mercy and the "Mons pietatis", meanwhile effecting numerous conversions. He was appointed court preacher by Sigismund III in 1588, and for twenty-four years filled this post to the great advantage of the Church and the nation. In 1596 the Ruthenian Church was united with Rome, largely through his efforts. When the nobles, headed by Zebrzydowski, revolted against Sigismund III,

Skarga was sent on a mission of conciliation to the rebels, which, however, proved fruitless. Besides the controversial works mentioned, Skarga published a "History of the Church", and "Lives of the Saints" (Wilna, 1579; 25th ed., Lemberg, 1883–84), possibly the most widely read book in Poland. But most important of all are his "Sermons for Sundays and Holidays" (Cracow, 1595) and "Sermons on the Seven Sacraments" (Cracow, 1600), which, besides their glowing eloquence, are profound and instructive. In addition to these are "Sermons on Various Occasions" and the "Sermons Preached to the Diet". These last for inspiration and feeling are the finest productions in the literature of Poland before the Partitions. Nowhere are there found such style, eloquence, and patriotism, with the deepest religious conviction. Skarga occupies a high place in the literature and the history of Poland. His efforts to convert heretics, to restore schismatics to unity, to prevent corruption, and to stem the tide of public and political license, tending even then towards anarchy, were indeed as to this last point unsuccessful; but that was the nation's fault, not his.

RYCHCICKI, *Peter Skarga and his age* (Lemberg, 1852); POLKOWSKI, *Life of Peter Skarga* (Cracow, 1884); BOBRSYRISKI, *Sermons to the Diet* (Cracow, 1876); CHRSANOWSKI, *Preface to Sermons to the Diet* (2nd ed., Warsaw, 1897); TARNOWSKI, *Schoolbook of Polish Literature* (Lemberg, 1999); IDEM, *History of Polish Literature*, I (Cracow, 1903)—all in Polish.

S. TARNOWSKI.

Skoda (SCHKODA), JOSEF, celebrated clinical lecturer and diagnostician and, with Rokitansky, founder of the modern medical school of Vienna, b. at Pilsen in Bohemia, 10 December, 1805; d. at Vienna, 13 June, 1881. Skoda was the son of a locksmith. He attended the gymnasium at Pilsen, entered the University of Vienna in 1825, and received the degree of Doctor of Medicine on 10 July, 1831. He first served in Bohemia as physician during the outbreak of cholera, was assistant physician in the general hospital of Vienna, 1832–38, in 1839 city physician of Vienna for the poor, and on 13 February, 1840, on the recommendation of Dr. Ludwig, Freiherr von Türkheim, chairman of the imperial committee of education, was appointed to the unpaid position of chief physician of the department for consumptives just opened in the general hospital. In 1846, thanks to the energetic measures of Karl Rokitansky, professor of pathological anatomy, he was appointed professor of the medical clinic against the wishes of the rest of the medical faculty. In 1848 he began to lecture in German instead of Latin, being the first professor to adopt this course. On 17 July, 1848, he was elected an active member of the mathematico-physical section of the Academy of Sciences. Early in 1871 he retired from his professorship, and the occasion was celebrated by the students and the population of Vienna by a great torchlight procession in his honour. Rokitansky calls him "a light for those who study, a model for those who strive, and a rock for those who despair". Skoda's benevolent disposition is best shown by the fact that, notwithstanding his large income and known simplicity of life, he left a comparatively small fortune, and in his will bequeathed legacies to a number of benevolent institutions.

Skoda's great merit lies in his development of the methods of physical investigation. The discovery of the method of percussion diagnosis made in 1761 by the Viennese physician, Leopold Auenbrugger (1722–1809), had been forgotten, and the knowledge of it was first revived in 1808 by Corvisart (1755–1821), court-physician to Napoleon I. Laennec (1787–1826) and his pupils Piorry and Bouillaud added auscultation to this method. Skoda began his clinical studies in close connexion with pathological anatomy while assistant physician of the hospital, but his superiors failed to understand his course, and in 1837, by way of punishment, transferred him to the ward for the insane, as it was claimed that the patients were annoyed by his investigations, especially by the method of percussion. His first publication, "Über die Perkussion" in the "Medizinische Jahrbücher des k.k. österreichen Kaiserstaates", IX (1836), attracted but little attention. This paper was followed by: "Über den Herzstoss und die durch die Herzbewegungen verursachten Töne und über die Anwendung der Perkussion bei Untersuchung der Organe des Unterleibes", in the same periodical, vols. XIII, XIV (1837); "Über Abdominaltyphus und dessen Behandlung mit Alumen crudum", also in the same periodical, vol. XV (1838); "Untersuchungsmethode zur Bestimmung des Zustandes des Herzens", vol. XVIII (1839); "Über Pericarditis in pathologisch-anatomischer und diagnostischer Beziehung", XIX (1839); "Über Piorrys Semiotik und Diagnostik", vol. XVIII (1839); "Über die Diagnose der Herzklappenfehler", vol. XXI (1840). His small but up to now unsurpassed chief work, "Abhandlung über die Perkussion und Auskultation" (Vienna, 1839), has been repeatedly published and translated into foreign languages. It established his universal renown as a diagnostician. In 1841, after a journey for research to Paris, he made a separate division in his department for skin diseases and thus gave the first impulse towards the reorganization of dermatology by Ferdinand Hebra. In 1848 at the request of the ministry of education he drew up a memorial on the reorganization of the study of medicine, and encouraged later by his advice the founding of the present higher administration of the medical school of Vienna. As regards therapeutics the accusation was often made against him that he held to the "Nihilism" of the Vienna School. As a matter of fact his therapeutics were exceedingly simple in contrast to the great variety of remedial agents used at that time, which he regarded as useless, as in his experience many ailments were cured without medicines, merely by suitable medical supervision and proper diet. His high sense of duty as a teacher, the large amount of work he performed as a physician, and the early appearance of organic heart-trouble are probably the reasons that from 1848 he published less and less. The few papers which he wrote from 1850 are to be found in the transactions of the Academy of Sciences and the periodical of the Society of Physicians of Vienna of which he was the honorary president.

DRASCHE, *Skoda* (Vienna, 1881).

LEOPOLD SENFELDER.

Slade, JOHN, VENERABLE See BODEY, JOHN, VENERABLE.

Slander is the attributing to another of a fault of which one knows him to be innocent. It contains a twofold malice, that which grows out of damage unjustly done to our neighbour's good name and that of lying as well. Theologians say that this latter guilt considered in itself, in so far as it is an offence against veracity, may not be grievous, but that nevertheless it will frequently be advisable to mention it in confession, in order that the extent and method of reparation may be settled. The important thing to note of slander is that it is a lesion of our neighbour's right to his reputation. Hence moralists hold that it is not specifically distinct from mere detraction. For the purpose of determining the species of this sin, the manner in which the injury is done is negligible. There is, however, this difference between slander and detraction: that, whereas there are circumstances in which we may lawfully expose the misdeeds which another has actually committed, we are never allowed to blacken his name by charging him with what he has not done. A lie is intrinsically evil and can never be justified by any cause or in any circumstances. Slander involves a violation of commutative justice and therefore imposes on its perpetrator the obligation of restitution. First of all, he must undo the injury of the defamation itself. There seems in general to be only one adequate way to do this: he must simply retract his false statement. Moralists say that if he can make full atonement by declaring that he has made a mistake, this will be sufficient; otherwise he must unequivocally take back his untruth, even at the expense of exhibiting himself a liar. In addition he is bound to make compensation to his victim for whatever losses may have been sustained as a result of his malicious imputation. It is supposed that the damage which ensues has been in some measure foreseen by the slanderer.

SLATER, *Manual of Moral Theology* (New York, 1908); BALLERINI, *Op. theol. mor.* (Prato, 1899); D'ANNIBALE, *Summula theol. mor.* (Rome, 1908); GENICOT, *Théol. moral. instit.* (Louvain, 1898).

JOSEPH F. DELANY.

Slavery.—How numerous the slaves were in Roman society when Christianity made its appearance, how hard was their lot, and how the competition of slave labour crushed free labour is notorious. It is the scope of this article to show what Christianity has done for slaves and against slavery, first in the Roman world, next in that society which was the result of the barbarian invasions, and lastly in the modern world.

I. THE CHURCH AND ROMAN SLAVERY.—The first missionaries of the Gospel, men of Jewish origin, came from a country where slavery existed. But it existed in Judea under a form very different from the Roman form. The Mosaic Law was merciful to the slave (Ex., xxi; Lev., xxv; Deut., xv, xvi, xxi) and carefully secured his fair wage to the labourer (Deut., xxiv, 15). In Jewish society the slave was not an object of contempt, because labour was not despised as it was elsewhere. No man thought it beneath him to ply a manual trade. These ideas and habits of life the Apostles brought into the new society which so rapidly grew up as the effect of their preaching. As this society included, from the first, faithful of all conditions—rich and poor, slaves and freemen—the Apostles were obliged to utter their beliefs as to the social inequalities which so profoundly divided the Roman world. "For as many of you as have been baptized in Christ, have put on Christ. There is neither Jew nor Greek: there is neither bond nor free: there is neither male nor female. For you are all one in Christ Jesus" (Gal., iii, 27–28; cf. I Cor., xii, 13). From this principle St. Paul draws no political conclusions. It was not his wish, as it was not in his power, to realize Christian equality either by force or by revolt. Such revolutions are not effected of a sudden. Christianity accepts society as it is, influencing it for its transformation through, and only through, individual souls. What it demands in the first place from masters and from slaves is, to live as brethren—commanding with equity, without threatening, remembering that God is the master of all—obeying with fear, but without servile flattery, in simplicity of heart, as they would obey Christ (cf. Eph., vi, 9; Col., iii, 22–4; iv, 1).

This language was understood by masters and by slaves who became converts to Christianity. But many slaves who were Christians had pagan masters to whom this sentiment of fraternity was unknown, and who sometimes exhibited that cruelty of which moralists and poets so often speak. To such slaves St. Peter points out their duty: to be submissive "not only to the good and gentle, but also to the froward", not with a mere inert resignation, but to give a good example and to imitate Christ, Who also suffered unjustly (I Peter, ii, 18, 23–24). In the eyes of the Apostles, the slave's condition, peculiarly wretched, peculiarly exposed to temptations, bears all the more efficacious testimony to the new religion. St. Paul recommends slaves to seek in all things to please their masters, not to contradict them, to do them no wrong, to honour them, to be loyal to them, so as to make the teaching of God Our Saviour shine forth before the eyes of all, and to prevent that name and teaching from being blasphemed (cf. I Tim., vi, 1; Tit., ii, 9, 10). The Apostolic writings show how large a place slaves occupied in the Church. Nearly all the names of the Christians whom St. Paul salutes in his Epistle to the Romans are servile *cognomina:* the two groups whom he calls "those of the household of Aristobulus" and "those of the household of Narcissus" indicate Christian servitors of those two contemporaries of Nero. His Epistle, written from Rome, to the Philippians (iv, 22) bears them greeting from the saints of Cæsar's household, i. e. converted slaves of the imperial palace.

One fact which, in the Church, relieved the condition of the slave was the absence among Christians of the ancient scorn of labour (Cicero, "De off.", I, xlii; "Pro Flacco", xviii; "Pro domo", xxxiii; Suetonius, "Claudius", xxii; Seneca, "De beneficiis", xviii; Valerius Maximus, V, ii, 10). Converts to the new religion knew that Jesus had been a carpenter; they saw St. Paul exercise the occupation of a tentmaker (Acts, xviii, 3; I Cor., iv, 12). "Neither did we eat any man's bread", said the Apostle, "for nothing, but in labour and in toil we worked night and day, lest we should be chargeable to any of you" (II Thess., iii, 8; cf. Acts, xx, 33, 34). Such an example, given at a time when those who laboured were accounted "the dregs of the city", and those who did not labour lived on the public bounty, constituted a very efficacious form of preaching. A new sentiment was thereby introduced into the Roman world, while at the same time a formal discipline was being established in the Church. It would have none of those who made a parade of their leisurely curiosity in the Greek and Roman cities (II Thess., iii, 11). It declared that those who do not labour do not deserve to be fed (ibid., 10). A Christian was not permitted to live without an occupation (Didache, xii).

Religious equality was the negation of slavery as it was practised by pagan society. It must have been an exaggeration, no doubt, to say, as one author of the first century said, that "slaves had no religion, or had only foreign religions" (Tacitus, "Annals", XIV, xliv): many were members of funerary *collegia* under the invocation of Roman divinities (Statutes of the College of Lanuvium, "Corp. Inscr. lat.", XIV, 2112). But in many circumstances this haughty and formalist religion excluded slaves from its functions, which, it was held, their presence would have defiled (Cicero, "Octavius", xxiv). Absolute religious equality, as proclaimed by Christianity, was therefore a novelty. The Church made no account of the social condition of the faithful. Bond and free received the same sacraments. Clerics of servile origin were numerous (St. Jerome, Ep. lxxxii). The very Chair of St. Peter was occupied by men who had been slaves—Pius in the second century, Callistus in the third. So complete—one might almost say, so levelling—was this Christian equality that St. Paul (I Tim., vi, 2), and, later, St. Ignatius (Polyc., iv), are obliged to admonish the slave and the handmaid not to contemn their masters, "believers like them and sharing in the same benefits". In giving them a place in religious society, the Church restored to slaves the family and marriage. In Roman law, neither legitimate marriage, nor regular paternity, nor even any impediment to the most unnatural unions had existed for the slave (Digest, XXXVIII, viii, i, § 2; x, 10, § 5). That slaves often endeavoured to override this abominable position is touchingly proved by innumerable mortuary inscriptions; but the name of *uxor*, which the slave woman takes in these inscriptions, is very precarious, for no law protects her honour, and with her there is no adultery (Digest, XLVIII, v, 6; Cod. Justin., IX, ix, 23). In the Church the marriage of slaves is a sacrament; it possesses "the solidity" of one (St. Basil, Ep. cxcix, 42). The Apostolic Constitutions impose upon the master the duty of making his slave contract "a legitimate marriage" (III, iv; VIII, xxxii). St. John Chrysostom declares that slaves have the marital power over their wives and the paternal over their children ("In Ep. ad Ephes.", Hom. xxii, 2). He says that "he who has immoral relations with the wife of a slave is as culpable as he who has the like relations with the wife of the prince: both are adulterers, for it is not the condition of the parties that makes the crime" ("In I Thess.", Hom. v, 2; "In II Thess.", Hom. iii, 2).

In the Christian cemeteries there is no difference between the tombs of slaves and those of the free. The inscriptions on pagan sepulchres—whether the *columbarium* common to all the servants of one household, or the burial plot of a funerary *collegium* of slaves or freedmen, or isolated tombs—always indicate the servile condition. In Christian epitaphs it is hardly ever to be seen ("Bull. di archeol. christiana", 1866, p. 24), though slaves formed a considerable part of the Christian population. Sometimes we find a slave honoured with a more pretentious sepulchre than others of the faithful, like that of Ampliatus in the cemetery of Domitilla ("Bull. di archeol. christ.", 1881, pp. 57–74, and pl. III, IV). This is particularly so in the case of slaves who were martyrs: the ashes of two slaves, Protus and Hyacinthus, burned alive in the Valerian persecution, had been wrapped in a winding-sheet of gold tissue (ibid., 1894, p. 28). Martyrdom eloquently manifests the religious equality of the slave: he displays as much firmness before the menaces of the persecutor as does the free man. Sometimes it is not for the Faith alone that a slave woman dies, but for the faith and chastity equally threatened—"pro fide et castitate occisa est" ("Acta S. Dulæ" in Acta SS., III March, p. 552). Beautiful assertions of this moral freedom are found in the accounts of the martyrdoms of the slaves Ariadne, Blandina, Evelpistus, Potamienna, Felicitas, Sabina, Vitalis, Porphyrus, and many others (see Allard, "Dix leçons sur le martyre", 4th ed., pp. 155–64). The Church made the enfranchisement of the slave an act of disinterested charity. Pagan masters usually sold him his liberty for his market value, on receipt of his painfully amassed savings (Cicero, "Philipp. VIII", xi; Seneca, "Ep. lxxx"); true Christians gave it to him as an alms. Sometimes the Church redeemed slaves out of its common resources (St. Ignatius, "Polyc.", 4; Apos. Const., IV, iii). Heroic Christians are known to have sold themselves into slavery to deliver slaves (St. Clement, "Cor.", 4; "Vita S. Joannis Eleemosynarii" in Acta SS., Jan., II, p. 506). Many enfranchised all the slaves they had. In pagan antiquity wholesale enfranchisements are frequent, but they never include all the owner's slaves, and they are always by testamentary disposition—that is when the owner cannot be impoverished by his bounty (Justinian, "Inst.", I, vii; "Cod. Just.", VII, iii, 1). Only Christians enfranchised all their slaves in the owner's lifetime, thus effectually despoiling themselves of a considerable part of their fortune (see Allard, "Les esclaves chrétiens", 4th ed., p. 338). At the beginning of the fifth century, a Roman millionaire, St. Melania, gratuitously granted liberty to so many thousand of slaves that her biographer declares himself unable to give their exact number (Vita S. Melaniæ, xxxiv). Palladius mentions eight thousand slaves freed (Hist. Lausiaca, cxix), which, taking the average price of a slave as about $100, would represent a value of $800,-000. But Palladius wrote before 406, which was long before Melania had completely exhausted her immense fortune in acts of liberality of all kinds (Rampolla, "S. Melania Giuniore", 1905, p. 221).

Primitive Christianity did not attack slavery directly; but it acted as though slavery did not exist. By inspiring the best of its children with this heroic charity, examples of which have been given above, it remotely prepared the way for the abolition of slavery. To reproach the Church of the first ages with not having condemned slavery in principle, and with having tolerated it in fact, is to blame it for not having let loose a frightful revolution, in which, perhaps, all civilization would have perished with Roman society. But to say, with Ciccotti (Il tramonto della schiavitù, Fr. tr., 1910, pp. 18, 20), that primitive Christianity had not even "an embryonic vision" of a society in which there should be no slavery, to say that the Fathers of the Church did not feel "the horror of slavery", is to display either strange ignorance or singular unfairness. In St. Gregory of Nyssa (In Ecclesiastem, hom. iv) the most energetic and absolute reprobation of slavery may be found; and again in numerous passages of St. John Chrysostom's discourses we have the picture of a society without slaves—a society composed only of free workers, an ideal portrait of which he traces with the most eloquent insistence (see the texts cited in Allard, "Les esclaves chrétiens", pp. 416–23).

II. THE CHURCH AND SLAVERY AFTER THE BARBARIAN INVASIONS.—It is beyond the scope of this article to discuss the legislative movement which took place during the same period in regard to slaves. From Augustus to Constantine statutes and jurisprudence tended to afford them greater protection against ill-treatment and to facilitate enfranchisement. Under the Christian emperors this tendency, in spite of relapses at certain points, became daily more marked, and ended, in the sixth century, in Justinian's very liberal legislation (see Wallon, "Hist. de l'esclavage dans l'antiquité", III, ii and x). Although the civil law on slavery still lagged behind the demands of Christianity ("The laws of Cæsar are one thing, the laws of Christ another", St. Jerome writes in "Ep. lxxvii"), nevertheless very great progress had been made. It continued in the Eastern Empire (laws of Basil the Macedonian, of Leo the Wise, of Constantine Porphyrogenitus), but in the West it was abruptly checked by the barbarian invasions. Those invasions were calamitous for the slaves, increasing their numbers which had begun to diminish, and subjecting them to legislation and to customs much harder than those which obtained under the Roman law of the period (see Allard, "Les origines du servage" in "Rev. des questions historiques", April, 1911). Here again the Church intervened. It did so in three ways: redeeming slaves; legislating for their benefit in its councils; setting an example of kind treatment. Documents of the fifth to the seventh century are full of instances of captives carried off from conquered cities by the barbarians and doomed to slavery, whom bishops, priests, and monks, and pious laymen redeemed. Redeemed captives were sometimes sent back in thousands to their own country (ibid., pp. 393–7, and Lesne, "Hist. de la propriété ecclésiastique en France", 1910, pp. 357–69).

The Churches of Gaul, Spain, Britain, and Italy were incessantly busy, in numerous councils, with the affairs of the slaves; protection of the maltreated slave who has taken refuge in a church (Councils of Orléans, 511, 538, 549; Council of Epone, 517); protection of freedmen, not only those manumitted *in ecclesiis*, but also those freed by any other process (Council of Arles, 452; of Agde, 506; of Orléans, 549; of Mâcon, 585; of Toledo, 589, 633; of Paris, 615);

validity of marriages contracted with full knowledge of the circumstances between free persons and slaves (Councils of Verberie, 752; of Compiègne, 759); rest for slaves on Sundays and feast days (Council of Auxerre, 578 or 585; of Châlon-sur-Saône, middle of the seventh century; of Rouen, 650; of Wessex, 691; of Berghamsted, 697); prohibition of Jews to possess Christian slaves (Council of Orléans, 541; of Mâcon, 581; of Clichy, 625; of Toledo, 589, 633, 656); suppression of traffic in slaves by forbidding their sale outside of the kingdom (Council of Châlon-sur-Saône, between 644 and 650); prohibition against reducing a free man to slavery (Council of Clichy, 625). Less liberal in this respect than Justinian (Novella cxxiii, 17), who made tacit consent a sufficient condition, the Western discipline does not permit a slave to be raised to the priesthood without the formal consent of his master; nevertheless the councils held at Orléans in 511, 538, 549, while imposing canonical penalties upon the bishop who exceeded his authority in this matter, declare such an ordination to be valid. A council held at Rome in 595 under the presidency of St. Gregory the Great permits the slave to become a monk without any consent, express or tacit, of his master.

At this period the Church found itself becoming a great proprietor. Barbarian converts endowed it largely with real property. As these estates were furnished with serfs attached to the cultivation of the soil, the Church became by force of circumstances a proprietor of human beings, for whom, in these troublous times, the relation was a great blessing. The laws of the barbarians, amended through Christian influence, gave ecclesiastical serfs a privileged position: their rents were fixed; ordinarily, they were bound to give the proprietor half of their labour or half of its products, the remainder being left to them (Lex Alemannorum, xxii; Lex Bajuvariorum, I, xiv, 6). A council of the sixth century (Eauze, 551) enjoins upon bishops that they must exact of their serfs a lighter service than that performed by the serfs of lay proprietors, and must remit to them one-fourth of their rents. Another advantage of ecclesiastical serfs was the permanency of their position. A Roman law of the middle of the fourth century (Cod. Just., XI, xlvii, 2) had forbidden rural slaves to be removed from the lands to which they belonged: this was the origin of serfdom, a much better condition than slavery properly so called. But the barbarians virtually suppressed this beneficent law (Gregory of Tours, "Hist. Franc.", VI, 45); it was even formally abrogated among the Goths of Italy by the edict of Theodoric (§ 142). Nevertheless, as an exceptional privilege, it remained in force for the serfs of the Church, who, like the Church itself, remained under Roman law (Lex Burgondionum, LVIII, i; Louis I, "Add. ad legem Langobard.", III, i). They shared besides, the inalienability of all ecclesiastical property which had been established by councils (Rome, 502; Orléans, 511, 538; Epone, 517; Clichy, 625; Toledo, 589); they were sheltered from the exactions of the royal officers by the immunity granted to almost all church lands (Kroell, "L'immunité franque", 1910); thus their position was generally envied (Flodoard, "Hist. eccl. Remensis", I, xiv), and when the royal liberality assigned to a church a portion of land out of the state property, the serfs who cultivated were loud in their expressions of joy (Vita S. Eligii, I, xv).

It has been asserted that the ecclesiastical serfs were less fortunately situated because the inalienability of church property prevented their being enfranchised. But this is inexact. St. Gregory the Great enfranchised serfs of the Roman Church (Ep. vi, 12), and there is frequent discussion in the councils in regard to ecclesiastical freedmen. The Council of Agde (506) gives the bishop the right to enfranchise those serfs "who shall have deserved it" and to leave them a small patrimony. A Council of Orléans (541) declares that even if the bishop has dissipated the property of his church, the serfs whom he has freed in reasonable number (*numero competenti*) are to remain free. A Merovingian formula shows a bishop enfranchising one-tenth of his serfs (Formulæ Biturigenses, viii). The Spanish councils imposed greater restrictions, recognizing the right of a bishop to enfranchise the serfs of his church on condition of his indemnifying it out of his own private property (Council of Seville, 590; of Toledo, 633; of Merida, 666). But they made it obligatory to enfranchise the serf in whom a serious vocation to the priesthood was discerned (Council of Saragossa, 593). An English council (Celchyte, 816) orders that at the death of a bishop all the other bishops and all the abbots shall enfranchise three slaves each for the repose of his soul. This last clause shows again the mistake of saying that the monks had not the right of manumission. The canon of the Council of Epone (517) which forbids abbots to enfranchise their serfs was enacted in order that the monks might not be left to work without assistance and has been taken too literally. It is inspired not only by agricultural prudence, but also by the consideration that the serfs belong to the community of monks, and not to the abbot individually. Moreover, the rule of St. Ferréol (sixth century) permits the abbot to free serfs with the consent of the monks or without their consent, if, in the latter case, he replaces at his own expense those he has enfranchised. The statement that ecclesiastical freedmen were not as free as the freedmen of lay proprietors will not bear examination in the light of facts, which shows the situation of the two classes to have been identical, except that the freedman of the Church carried a higher *wergheld* than a lay freedman, and therefore his life was better protected. The "Polyptych of Irminon", a detailed description of the abbey lands of Saint-Germain-des-Prés, shows that in the ninth century the serfs of that domain were not numerous and led in every way the life of free peasants.

III. The Church and Modern Slavery.—In the Middle Ages, slavery, properly so called, no longer existed in Christian countries; it had been replaced by serfdom, an intermediate condition in which a man enjoyed all his personal rights except the right to leave the land he cultivated and the right to freely dispose of his property. Serfdom soon disappeared in Catholic countries, to last longer only where the Protestant Reformation prevailed. But while serfdom was becoming extinct, the course of events was bringing to pass a temporary revival of slavery. As a consequence of the wars against the Mussulmans and the commerce maintained with the East, the European countries bordering on the Mediterranean, particularly Spain and Italy, once more had slaves—Turkish prisoners and also, unfortunately, captives imported by conscienceless traders. Though these slaves were generally well treated, and set at liberty if they asked for baptism, this revival of slavery, lasting until the seventeenth century, is a blot on Christian civilization. But the number of these slaves was always very small in comparison with that of the Christian captives reduced to slavery in Mussulman countries, particularly in the Barbary states from Tripoli to the Atlantic coast of Morocco. These captives were cruelly treated and were in constant danger of losing their faith. Many actually did deny their faith, or, at least, were driven by despair to abandon all religion and all morality. Religious orders were founded to succour and redeem them.

The Trinitarians, founded in 1198 by St. John of Matha and St. Felix of Valois, established hospitals for slaves at Algiers and Tunis in the sixteenth and seventeenth centuries; and from its foundation until the year 1787 it redeemed 900,000 slaves. The Order of Our Lady of Ransom (Mercedarians), founded in the thirteenth century by St. Peter Nolasco, and established more especially in France and Spain, redeemed 490,736 slaves between the years 1218 and 1632. To the three regular vows its founder had added a fourth, "To become a hostage in the hands of the infidels, if that is necessary for the deliverance of Christ's faithful." Many Mercedarians kept this vow even to martyrdom. Another order undertook not only to redeem captives, but also to give them spiritual and material assistance. St. Vincent of Paul had been a slave at Algiers in 1605, and had witnessed the sufferings and perils of Christian slaves. At the request of Louis XIV, he sent them, in 1642, priests of the congregation which he had founded. Many of these priests, indeed, were invested with consular functions at Tunis and at Algiers. From 1642 to 1660 they redeemed about 1200 slaves at an expense of about 1,200,000 livres. But their greatest achievements were in teaching the Catechism and converting thousands, and in preparing many of the captives to suffer the most cruel martyrdom rather than deny the Faith. As a Protestant historian has recently said, none of the expeditions sent against the Barbary States by the Powers of Europe, or even America, equalled "the moral effect produced by the ministry of consolation, peace and abnegation, going even to the sacrifice of liberty and life, which was exercised by the humble sons of St. John of Matha, St. Peter Nolasco, and St. Vincent of Paul" (Bonet-Maury, "France, christianisme et civilisation", 1907, p. 142).

A second revival of slavery took place after the discovery of the New World by the Spaniards in 1492. To give the history of it would be to exceed the limits of this article. It will be sufficient to recall the efforts of Las Casas in behalf of the aborigines of America and the protestations of popes both against the enslavement of those aborigines and the traffic in negro slaves. England, France, Portugal, and Spain, all participated in this nefarious traffic. England only made amends for its transgressions when, in 1815, it took the initiative in the suppression of the slave-trade. In 1871 a writer had the temerity to assert that the Papacy had not yet been able "to make up its mind to condemn slavery" (Ernest Havet, "Le christianisme et ses origines", I, p. xxi). He forgot that, in 1462, Pius II declared slavery to be "a great crime" (*magnum scelus*); that, in 1537, Paul III forbade the enslavement of the Indians; that Urban VIII forbade it in 1639, and Benedict XIV in 1741; that Pius VII demanded of the Congress of Vienna, in 1815, the suppression of the slave-trade, and Gregory XVI condemned it in 1839; that, in the Bull of Canonization of the Jesuit Peter Claver, one of the most illustrious adversaries of slavery, Pius IX branded the "supreme villainy" (*summum nefas*) of the slave-traders. Everyone knows of the beautiful letter which Leo XIII, in 1888, addressed to the Brazilian bishops, exhorting them to banish from their country the remnants of slavery—a letter to which the bishops responded with their most energetic efforts, and some generous slave-owners by freeing their slaves in a body, as in the first ages of the Church.

In our own times the slave-trade still continued to devastate Africa, no longer for the profit of Christian states, from which all slavery had disappeared, but for the use of Mussulman countries. But as European penetration progresses in Africa, the missionaries, who are always its precursors— Fathers of the Holy Ghost, Oblates, White Fathers, Franciscans, Jesuits, Priests of the Mission of Lyons— labour in the Sudan, Guinea, on the Gabun, in the region of the Great Lakes, redeeming slaves and establishing "liberty villages." At the head of this movement appear two men: Cardinal Lavigerie, who in 1888 founded the *Société Antiesclavagiste* and in 1889 promoted the Brussels conference; Leo XIII, who encouraged Lavigerie in all his projects and, in 1890, by an Encyclical once more condemning the slave-traders and "the accursed pest of servitude", ordered an annual collection to be made in all Catholic churches for the benefit of the anti-slavery work. Some modern writers, mostly of the Socialist School—Karl Marx, Engel, Ciccotti, and, in a measure, Seligman—attribute the now almost complete disappearance of slavery to the evolution of interests and to economic causes only. The foregoing exposition of the subject is an answer to their materialistic conception of history, as showing that, if not the only, at least the principal, cause of that disappearance is Christianity acting through the authority of its teaching and the influence of its charity.

WALLON, *Hist. de l'esclavage dans l'antiquité* (Paris, 1879); KAHN, *L'esclavage selon la Bible et le Talmud* (Paris, 1867); PAVY, *Affranchissement des esclaves* (Paris, 1875); ALLARD, *Les esclaves chrétiens depuis les premiers temps de l'Eglise jusqu'à la fin de la domination romaine en Occident* (Paris, 1900); IDEM, *Esclaves, serfs et mainmortables* (Paris, 1884); IDEM, *La philosophie antique et l'esclavage* in *Etudes d'histoire et d'archéologie* (Paris, 1899); IDEM in *Dict. de l'apologétique*, fasc. V (Paris, 1910), s. v. *Esclavage*; HARNACK, *Mission u. Ausbreitung des Christentums in den ersten drei Jahrhunderten*, I (Leipzig, 1906); BIOT, *De l'abolition de l'esclavage ancien en Occident* (Paris, 1840); YANOSKI, *De l'abolition de l'esclavage ancien au moyen âge* (Paris, 1860); COCHIN, *L'abolition de l'esclavage* (Paris, 1861); BROWNLOW, *Lectures on Slavery and Serfdom in Europe* (London and New York, 1892); FOURNIER, *Les affranchissements du Ve au XIIIe siècle* in *Rev. Hist.*, XXXI (Paris, 1883); CIBRARIO, *Della Schiavitù e del Servaggio* (Milan, 1868); CICCOTTI, *Il tramonto della Schiavitù* (Milan, 1899); TALAMO, *Il concetto della Schiavitù da Aristotele ai dottori scolastici* (Rome, 1908); BRANDI, *Il Papato e la Schiavitù* (Rome, 1903); DESLANDRES, *L'ordre des Trinitaires pour le rachat des captifs* (Paris, 1903); ABELLY. *Vie de S. Vincent de Paul*, I, V (Paris 1836); BONET-MAURY, *France, christianisme et civilisation* (Paris, 1907); PIOLET, *Les missions cath. françaises au XIXe siècle*, V, *Afrique* (Paris, 1902); KLEIN, *Le cardinal Lavigerie et ses œuvres d'Afrique* (Paris, 1898).

PAUL ALLARD.

Slavery, ETHICAL ASPECT OF.—In Greek and Roman civilization slavery on an extensive scale formed an essential element of the social structure; and consequently the ethical speculators, no less than the practical statesmen, regarded it as a just and indispensable institution. The Greek, however, assumed that the slave population should be recruited normally only from the barbarian or lower races. The Roman laws, in the heyday of the empire, treated the slave as a mere chattel. The master possessed over him the power of life and death; the slave could not contract a legal marriage, or any other kind of contract; in fact he possessed no civil rights; in the eyes of the law he was not a "person". Nevertheless the settlement of natural justice asserted itself sufficiently to condemn, or at least to disapprove, the conduct of masters who treated their slaves with signal inhumanity.

Christianity found slavery in possession throughout the Roman world; and when Christianity obtained power it could not and did not attempt summarily to abolish the institution. From the beginning, however, as is shown elsewhere in this article, the Church exerted a steady powerful pressure for the immediate amelioration of the condition of the individual slave, and for the ultimate abolition of a system which, even in its mildest form, could with difficulty be reconciled with the spirit of the Gospel and the doctrine that all men are brothers in that Divine sonship which knows no distinction of bond and free. From the beginning the Christian moralist did not condemn slavery as *in se*, or essentially, against the natural law or natural justice. The fact that slavery, tempered with many humane restrictions, was permitted under the Mosaic law would have sufficed to prevent the institution from being condemned by

Christian teachers as absolutely immoral. They, following the example of St. Paul, implicitly accept slavery as not in itself incompatible with the Christian Law. The apostle counsels slaves to obey their masters, and to bear with their condition patiently. This estimate of slavery continued to prevail till it became fixed in the systematized ethical teaching of the schools; and so it remained without any conspicuous modification till towards the end of the eighteenth century. We may take as representative de Lugo's statement of the chief argument offered in proof of the thesis that slavery, apart from all abuses, is not in itself contrary to the natural law. "Slavery consists in this, that a man is obliged, for his whole life, to devote his labour and services to a master. Now as anybody may justly bind himself, for the sake of some anticipated reward, to give his entire services to a master for a year, and he would in justice be bound to fulfil this contract, why may not he bind himself in like manner for a longer period, even for his entire lifetime, an obligation which would constitute slavery?" (De Justitia et Jure, disp. VI, sec. 2. no. 14.)

It must be observed that the defence of what may be termed theoretical slavery was by no means intended to be a justification of slavery as it existed historically, with all its attendant, and almost inevitably attendant, abuses, disregarding the natural rights of the slave and entailing pernicious consequences on the character of the slave-holding class, as well as on society in general. Concurrently with the affirmation that slavery is not against the natural law, the moralists specify what are the natural inviolable rights of the slave, and the corresponding duties of the owner. The gist of this teaching is summarized by Cardinal Gerdil (1718–1802): "Slavery is not to be understood as conferring on one man the same power over another that men have over cattle. Wherefore they erred who in former times refused to include slaves among persons; and believed that however barbarously the master treated his slave he did not violate any right of the slave. For slavery does not abolish the natural equality of men: hence by slavery one man is understood to become subject to the dominion of another to the extent that the master has a perpetual right to all those services which one man may justly perform for another; and subject to the condition that the master shall take due care of his slave and treat him humanely" (Comp. Instit. Civil., L, vii). The master was judged to sin against justice if he treated his slave cruelly, if he overloaded him with labour, deprived him of adequate food and clothing, or if he separated husband from wife, or the mother from her young children. It may be said that the approved ethical view of slavery was that while, religiously speaking, it could not be condemned as against the natural law, and had on its side the *jus gentium*, it was looked upon with disfavour as at best merely tolerable, and when judged by its consequences, a positive evil.

The later moralists, that is to say, broadly speaking, those who have written since the end of the eighteenth century, though in fundamental agreement with their predecessors, have somewhat shifted the perspective. In possession of the bad historical record of slavery and familiar with a Christian structure of society from which slavery had been eliminated, these later moralists emphasize more than did the older ones the reasons for condemning slavery; and they lay less stress on those in its favour. While they admit that it is not, theoretically speaking at least, contrary to the natural law, they hold that it is hardly compatible with the dignity of personality, and is to be condemned as immoral on account of the evil consequences it almost inevitably leads to. It is but little in keeping with human dignity that one man should so far be deprived of his liberty as to be perpetually subject to the will of a master in everything that concerns his external life; that he should be compelled to spend his entire labour for the benefit of another and receive in return only a bare subsistence. This condition of degradation is aggravated by the fact that the slave is, generally, deprived of all means of intellectual development for himself or for his children. This life almost inevitably leads to the destruction of a proper sense of self-respect, blunts the intellectual faculties, weakens the sense of responsibility, and results in a degraded moral standard. On the other hand, the exercise of the slave-master's power, too seldom sufficiently restrained by a sense of justice or Christian feeling, tends to develop arrogance, pride, and a tyrannical disposition, which in the long run comes to treat the slave as a being with no rights at all. Besides, as history amply proves, the presence of a slave population breeds a vast amount of sexual immorality among the slave-owning class, and, to borrow a phrase of Lecky, tends to cast a stigma on all labour and to degrade and impoverish the free poor.

Even granting that slavery, when attended with a due regard for the rights of the slave, is not in itself intrinsically wrong, there still remains the important question of the titles by which a master can justly own a slave. The least debatable one, voluntary acceptance of slavery, we have already noticed. Another one that was looked upon as legitimate was purchase. Although it is against natural justice to treat a person as a mere commodity or thing of commerce, nevertheless the labour of a man for his whole lifetime is something that may be lawfully bought and sold. Owing to the exalted notion that prevailed in earlier times about the *patria potestas*, a father was granted the right to sell his son into slavery, if he could not otherwise relieve his own dire distress. But the theologians held that if he should afterwards be able to do so, the father was bound to redeem the slave, and the master was bound to set him free if anybody offered to repay him the price he had paid. To sell old or worn-out slaves to anybody who was likely to prove a cruel master, to separate by sale husband and wife, or a mother and her little children, was looked upon as wrong and forbidden. Another title was war. If a man forfeited his life so that he could be justly put to death, this punishment might be commuted into the mitigated penalty of slavery, or penal servitude for life. On the same principle that slavery is a lesser evil than death, captives taken in war, who, according to the ethical ideas of the *jus gentium*, might lawfully be put to death by the victors, were instead reduced to slavery. Whatever justification this practice may have had in the *jus gentium* of former ages, none could be found for it now.

When slavery prevailed as part of the social organization and the slaves were ranked as property, it seemed not unreasonable that the old juridical maxim, *Partus sequitur ventrem*, should be accepted as peremptorily settling the status of children born in slavery. But it would be difficult to find any justification for this title in the natural law, except on the theory that the institution of slavery was, in certain conditions, necessary to the permanence of the social organization. An insufficient reason frequently offered in defence of it was that the master acquired a right to the children as compensation for the expense he incurred in their support, which could not be provided by the mother who possessed nothing of her own. Nor is there much cogency in the other plea, *i. e.* that a person born in slavery was presumed to consent tacitly to remaining in that condition, as there was no way open to him to enter any other. It is unnecessary to observe that the practice of capturing savages or barbarians for the purpose of making slaves of them has always been condemned as a heinous offence against justice, and no just title could be created by this procedure. Was it lawful for owners to retain in slavery the descendants of those who had been made slaves in this unjust way? The last conspicuous Catholic moralist who posed this question when it was not merely a theoretical one, Kenrick, resolves it in the affirmative on the ground that lapse of time remedies the original defect in titles when the stability of society and the avoidance of grave disturbances demand it.

St. Thomas, I–II, Q. xciv, a. 5, ad 3um; II–II, Q. lvii, a. 3, ad 2um, and a. 4, ad 2um; de Lugo, *De just. et jure*, disp. 3, 5, 2; Puffendorf, *Droit de la Nature et des Gens*, l. VI, ch. iii, s. 7; Grotius, *De Jure Belli ac Pacis*, l. ii, c. v, s. 27; Kenrick, *Theologia Moralis*, tract. V, c. vi; Meyer, *Institutiones Juris Naturalis*, par. ii, s. ii, c. iii, art. 2; Cathrein, *Moralphilosophie* (4th ed., Freiburg, 1904).

James J. Fox.

Slaves (Déné "Men"), a tribe of the great Déné family of American Indians, so called apparently from the fact that the Crees drove it back to its original northern haunts. Its present habitat is the forests that lie to the west of Great Slave Lake, from Hay River inclusive. The Slaves are divided into five main bands: those of Hay River, Trout Lake, Horn Mountain, the forks of the Mackenzie, and Fort Norman. Their total population is about 1100. They are for the most part a people of unprepossessing appearance. Their morals were not formerly of the best, but since the advent of Catholic missionaries they have considerably improved. Many of them have discarded the tepees of old for more or less comfortable log houses. Yet the religious instinct is not so strongly developed in them as with most of their congeners in the North. They were not so eager to receive the Catholic missionaries, and when the first Protestant ministers arrived among them, the liberalities of the strangers had more effect on them than on the other northern Dénés. To-day perhaps one-twelfth of the whole tribe has embraced Protestantism, the remainder being Catholics. The spiritual wants of the latter are attended to from the missions of St. Joseph on Great Slave Lake, Ste. Anne, Hay River, and Providence, Mackenzie.

Mackenzie, *Voyage through the Continent of North America* (London, 1801); McLean, *Notes of a Twenty-five Years' Service in the Hudson's Bay Territory* (London, 1849); Petitot, *Monographie des Déné-Dindjié*; Idem, *Autour du Grand Lac des Esclaves* (Paris, 1891); Morice, *The Great Déné Race* (Vienna, in course of publication, 1911).

A. G. Morice.

Slavonic Language and Liturgy.—Although the Latin holds the chief place among the liturgical languages in which the Mass is celebrated and the praise of God recited in the Divine Offices, yet the Slavonic language comes next to it among the languages widely used throughout the world in the liturgy of the Church. Unlike the Greek or the Latin languages, each of which may be said to be representative of a single rite, it is dedicated to both the Greek and the Roman Rites. Its use, however, is far better known throughout Europe as an expression of the Greek Rite; for it is used amongst the various Slavic nationalities of the Byzantine Rite, whether Catholic or Orthodox, and in that form is spread among 115,000,000 people; but it is also used in the Roman Rite along the eastern shores of the Adriatic Sea in Dalmatia and in the lower part of Croatia among about 100,000 Catholics there. Whilst the Greek language is the norm and the original of the Byzantine or Greek Rite, its actual use as a church language is limited to a comparatively small number, reckoning by population. The liturgy and offices of the Byzantine Church were translated from the Greek into what is now Old Slavonic (or Church Slavonic) by Sts. Cyril and Methodius about the year 866 and the period immediately following. St. Cyril is credited with having invented or adapted a special alphabet which now bears his name (Cyrillic) in order to express the sounds of the Slavonic language, as spoken by the Bulgars and Moravians of his day. (See Cyril and Methodius, Saints.)

Later on St. Methodius translated the entire Bible into Slavonic and his disciples afterwards added other works of the Greek saints and the canon law. These two brother saints always celebrated Mass and administered the sacraments in the Slavonic language. News of their successful missionary work among the pagan Slavs was carried to Rome along with complaints against them for celebrating the rites of the Church in the heathen vernacular. In 868 Saints Cyril and Methodius were summoned to Rome by Nicholas I, but arriving there after his death they were heartily received by his successor Adrian II, who approved of their Slavonic version of the liturgy. St. Cyril died in Rome in 869 and is buried in the Church of San Clemente. St. Methodius was afterwards consecrated Archbishop of Moravia and Pannonia and returned thither to his missionary work. Later on he was again accused of using the heathen Slavonic language in the celebration of the Mass and in the sacraments. It was a popular idea then, that as there had been three languages, Hebrew, Greek, and Latin, inscribed over our Lord on the cross, it would be sacrilegious to use any other language in the service of the Church. St. Methodius appealed to the pope and in 879 he was again summoned to Rome, before John VIII, who after hearing the matter sanctioned the use of the Slavonic language in the Mass and the offices of the Church, saying among other things: "We rightly praise the Slavonic letters invented by Cyril, in which praises to God are set forth, and we order that the glories and deeds of Christ our Lord be told in that same language. Nor is it in anywise opposed to wholesome doctrine and faith to say Mass in that same Slavonic language (Nec sanæ fidei vel doctrinæ aliquid obstat missam in eadem slavonica lingua canere), or to chant the holy gospels or divine lessons from the Old and New Testaments duly translated and interpreted therein, or the other parts of the divine office: for He who created the three principal languages, Hebrew, Greek, and Latin, also made the others for His praise and glory" (Boczek, Codex, tom. I, pp. 43–44). From that time onward the Slavonic tongue was firmly fixed as a liturgical language of the Church, and was used wherever the Slavic tribes were converted to Christianity under the influence of monks and missionaries of the Greek Rite. The Cyrillic letters used in writing it are adaptations of the uncial Greek alphabet, with the addition of a number of new letters to express sounds not found in the Greek language. All Church books in Russia, Servia, Bulgaria, or Austro-Hungary (whether used in the Greek Catholic or the Greek Orthodox Churches) are printed in the old Cyrillic alphabet and in the ancient Slavonic tongue.

But even before St. Cyril invented his alphabet for the Slavonic language there existed certain runes or native characters in which the southern dialect of the language was committed to writing. There is a tradition, alluded to by Innocent XI, that they were invented by St. Jerome as early as the fourth century; Jagić however thinks that they were really the original letters invented by St. Cyril and afterwards abandoned in favour of an imitation of Greek characters by his disciples and successors. This older alphabet, which still survives, is called the Glagolitic (from *glagolati*, to speak, because the rude tribesmen imagined that the letters spoke to the reader and told him what to say), and was used by the southern Slavic tribes and now exists along the Adriatic highlands. (See Glagolitic.) The Slavonic which is written in the Glagolitic characters is also the ancient language, but it differs considerably from the Slavonic written in the Cyrillic letters. In fact it may be roughly compared to the difference between the Gaelic of Ireland and the Gaelic of Scotland. The Roman Mass was translated into this Slavonic shortly after the Greek liturgy had been translated by Sts. Cyril and Methodius, so that in the course of time among the Slavic peoples the southern Slavonic written in Glagolitic letters became the language of the Roman Rite, while the northern Slavonic written in Cyrillic letters was the language of the Greek Rite. The prevailing use of the Latin language and the adoption of the Roman alphabet by many Slavic nationalities caused the use of the Glagolitic to diminish and Latin to gradually take its place. The northern Slavic peoples, like the Bohemians, Poles, and Slovaks, who were converted by Latin missionaries, used the Latin in their rite from the very first. At present the Glagolitic is only used in Dalmatia and Croatia. Urban VIII in 1631 definitively settled the use of the Glagolitic-Slavonic missal and office-books in the Roman Rite, and laid down rules where the clergy of each language came in contact with each other in regard to church services. Leo XIII published two editions of the Glagolitic Missal, from one of which the illustration on page 45 is taken.

The liturgy used in the Slavonic language, whether of Greek or Roman Rite, offers no peculiarities differing from the original Greek or Latin sources. The Ruthenians have introduced an occasional minor modification (see RUTHENIAN RITE), but the Orthodox Russians, Bulgarians, and Servians substantially follow the Byzantine liturgy and offices in the Slavonic version. The Glagolitic Missal, Breviary, and ritual follow closely the Roman liturgical books, and the latest editions contain the new offices authorized by the Roman congregations. The casual observer could not distinguish the Slavonic priest from the Latin priest when celebrating Mass or other services, except by hearing the language as pronounced aloud.

GINZEL, *Geschichte der Slavenapostel Cyrill u. Method, u. der slavischen Liturgie* (Vienna, 1861); HARASIEWICZ, *Annales Ruthenæ* (Lemberg, 1862); GOLUBINSKY, *Istoria Russkoi Tserkvi*, I (Moscow, 1904), ii, 326–42; TAYLOR, *Ueber den Ursprung des glagolitischen Alphabets* (Berlin, 1881); ZEILLER, *Les origines chrétiennes dans la province de Dalmatie* (Paris, 1906); NILLES, *Kalendarium Manuale*, I (Innsbruck, 1896); *Echos d'Orient*, VIII (Paris, 1905).

ANDREW J. SHIPMAN.

Slavs, THE.—I. NAME.—A. *Slavs*.—At present the customary name for all the Slavonic races is *Slav*. This name did not appear in history until a late period, but it has superseded all others. The general opinion is that it appeared for the first time in written documents in the sixth century of the Christian era. However, before this the Alexandrian scholar Ptolemy (about A.D. 100–178) mentioned in his work, "Γεωγραφικὴ ὑφήγησις", a tribe called *Stavani* (Σταυανοί), which was said to live in European Sarmatia between the Lithuanian tribes of the Galindæ and the Sudeni and the Sarmatic tribe of the Alans. He also mentioned another tribe, *Soubenoi* (Σουβενοί), which he assigned to Asiatic Sarmatia on the other side of the Alani. According to Šafařík these two statements refer to the same Slavonic people. Ptolemy got his information from two sources; the orthography of the copies he had was poor and consequently he believed there were two tribes to which it was necessary to assign separate localities. In reality the second name refers very probably to the ancestors of the present Slavs, as does the first name also though with less certainty. The Slavonic combination of consonants *sl* was changed in Greek orthography into *stl*, *sthl*, or *skl*. This theory was accepted by many scholars before Šafařík, as Lomonosov, Schlözer, Tatistcheff, J. Thunmann, who in 1774 published a dissertation on the subject. It was first advanced probably in 1679 by Hartknoch who was supported in modern times by many scholars. Apart from the mention by Ptolemy, the expression Slavs is not found until the sixth century. The opinion once held by some German and many Slavonic scholars that the names *Suevi* and *Slav* were the same and that these two peoples were identical, although the Suevi were a branch of the Germans and the ancestors of the present Swabians, must be absolutely rejected. Scattered names found in old inscriptions and old charters that are similar in sound to the word *Slav* must also be excluded in this investigation.

After the reference by Ptolemy the Slavs are first spoken of by Pseudo-Cæsarios of Nazianzum, whose work appeared at the beginning of the sixth century; in the middle of the sixth century Jordanis and Procopius gave fuller accounts of them. Even in the earliest sources the name appears in two forms. The old Slavonic authorities give: *Slověne* (plural from the singular *Slověnin*), the country is called *Slověnsko*, the language *slověnesk jazyk*, the people *slověnsk narod*. The Greeks wrote *Soubenoi* (in Ptolemy Σουβενοί), but the writers of the sixth century used the terms: *Sklabenoi* (Σκλαβηνοί), *Sklauenoi* (Σκλαυηνοί), *Sklabinoi* (Σκλαβῖνοι), *Sklauinoi* (Σκλαυῖνοι). The Romans used the terms: *Sclaueni, Sclauini, Sclauenia, Sclauinia*. Later authors employ the expressions *Sthlabenoi* (Σθλαβηνοί), *Sthlabinoi* (Σθλαβῖνοι, Σθλαβινοί), while the Romans wrote: *Sthlaueni, Sthlauini*. In the "Life of St. Clement" the expression Σθλαβενοί occurs; later writers use such terms as *Esklabinoi* (Εσκλαβῖνοι), *Asklabinoi* (Ασκλαβῖνοι), *Sklabinioi* (Σκλαβίνιοι), *Sklauenioi* (Σκλαυήνιοι). The adjectives are *sclaviniscus, sclavaniscus, sclavinicus, sclauanicus*. At the same time shorter forms are also to be found, as: *sklaboi* (Σκλαβοί), *sthlaboi* (Σθλάβοι), *sclavi, schlavi, sclavania*, later also *slavi*. In addition appear as scattered forms: *Sclauani, Sclauones* (Σκλαβῶνοι, Εσθλαβησιανοί, Σθλαβογενείς). The Armenian Moises of Choren was acquainted with the term *Sklavajin*: the chronicler Michael the Syrian used the expression *Sglau* or *Sglou*; the Arabians adopted the expression *Sclav*, but because it could not be brought into harmony with their phonetical laws they changed it into *Sakláb, Sakálibe*, and later also to *Slavije, Slavijun*. The anonymous Persian geography of the tenth century uses the term *Seljabe*.

Various explanations of the name have been suggested, the theory depending upon whether the longer or shorter form has been taken as the basis and upon the acceptance of the vowel *o* or *a* as the original root vowel. From the thirteenth century until Šafařík the shorter form *Slav* was always regarded as the original expression, and the name of the Slavs was traced from the word *Slava* (honour, fame), consequently it signified the same as *gloriosi* (αίνετοί). However, as early as the fourteenth century and later the name *Slav* was at times referred to the longer form *Slověnin* with *o* as the root vowel, and this longer form was traced to the word *Slovo* (word, speech), Slavs signifying, consequently, "the talking ones", *verbosi, veraces*, ὁμόγλωττοι. Dobrowsky maintained this explanation and Šafařík inclined to it, consequently it has been the accepted theory up to the present time. Other elucidations of the name *Slav*, as *človek* (man), *skala* (rock), *seló* (colony), *slati* (to send), *solovej* (nightingale), scarcely merit mention. There is much more reason in another objection that Slavonic philologists have made to the derivation of the word *Slav* from *slovo* (word). The ending *en* or *an* of the form *Slověnin* indicates derivation from a topographical designation. Dobrowsky perceived this difficulty and therefore invented the topographical name *Slovy*, which was to be derived from *slovo*. With some reservation Šafařík also gave a geographical interpretation. He did not, however, accept the purely imaginary locality *Slovy* but connected the word *Slověnin* with the Lithuanian *Salava*, Lettish *Sala*, from which is derived the Polish *żuława*, signifying island, a dry spot in a swampy region. According to this interpretation the word Slavs would mean the inhabitants of an island, or inhabitants of a marshy region. The German scholar Grimm maintained the identity of the Slavs with the Suevi and derived the name from *sloba*, *svoba* (freedom). The most probable explanation is that deriving the name from *slovo* (word); this is supported by the Slavonic name for the Germans *Nemci* (the dumb). The Slavs called themselves *Slovani*, that is, "the speaking ones", those who know words, while they called their neighbours the Germans, "the dumb", that is, those who do not know words.

During the long period of war between the Germans and Slavs, which lasted until the tenth century, the Slavonic territories in the north and south-east furnished the Germans large numbers of slaves. The Venetian and other Italian cities on the coast took numerous Slavonic captives from the opposite side of the Adriatic whom they resold to other places. The Slavs frequently shared in the seizure and export of their countrymen as slaves. The Naretani, a piratical Slavonic tribe living in the present district of Southern Dalmatia, were especially notorious for their slave-trade. Russian princes exported large numbers of slaves from their country. The result is that the name *Slav* has given the word *slave* to the peoples of Western Europe.

The question still remains to be answered whether the expression *Slavs* indicated originally all Slavonic tribes or only one or a few of them. The reference to them in Ptolemy shows that the word then meant only a single tribe. Ptolemy called the Slavs as a whole the *Venedai* and says they are "the greatest nation" (μεγίστον ἔθνος). The Byzantines of the sixth century thought only of the southern Slavs and incidentally also of the Russians, who lived on the boundaries of the Eastern Empire. With them the expression Slavs meant only the southern Slavs; they called the Russians *Antæ*, and distinguished sharply between the two groups of tribes. In one place (Get., 34, 35) Jordanis divides all Slavs into three groups: *Veneti, Slavs,* and *Antæ;* this would correspond to the present division of western, southern, and eastern Slavs. However, this mention appears to be an arbitrary combination. In another passage he designates the eastern Slavs by the name *Veneti*. Probably he had found the expression *Veneti* in old writers and had learned personally the names *Slavs* and *Antæ;* in this way arose his triple division. All the seventh-century authorities call all Slavonic tribes, both southern Slavs and western Slavs, that belonged to the kingdom of Prince Samo, simply Slavs; Samo is called the "ruler of the Slavs", but his peoples are called "the Slavs named Vindi" (*Sclavi cognomento Winadi*). In the eighth and ninth centuries the Czechs and Slavs of the Elbe were generally called Slavs, but also at times Wends, by the German and

Roman chroniclers. In the same way all authorities of the era of the Apostles to the Slavs, Cyril and Methodius, give the name Slav without any distinction both to the southern Slavs, to which branch both missionaries belonged, and to the western Slavs, among whom they laboured. As regards the eastern Slavs or Russians, leaving out the mention of Ptolemy already referred to, Jordanis says that at the beginning of the era of the migrations the Goths had carried on war with the "nation of Slavs"; this nation must have lived in what is now Southern Russia. The earliest Russian chronicle, erroneously ascribed to the monk Nestor, always calls the Slavs as a whole "Slavs". When it begins to narrate the history of Russia it speaks indeed of the Russians to whom it never applies the designation Slav, but it also often tells of the Slavs of Northern Russia, the Slavs of Novgorod. Those tribes that were already thoroughly incorporated in the Russian kingdom are simply called Russian tribes, while the Slavs in Northern Russia, who maintained a certain independence, were designated by the general expression Slavs. Consequently, the opinion advocated by Miklošič, namely, that the name Slav was originally applied only to one Slavonic tribe, is unfounded, though it has been supported by other scholars like Krek, Potkánski, Czermak, and Pasternek.

From at least the sixth century the expression Slav was, therefore, the general designation of all Slavonic tribes. Wherever a Slavonic tribe rose to greater political importance and founded an independent kingdom of its own, the name of the tribe came to the front and pushed aside the general designation Slav. Where, however, the Slavs attained no political power but fell under the sway of foreign rulers they remained known by the general name of Slavs. Among the successful tribes who brought an entire district under their sway and gave it their name were the Russians, Poles, Czechs, Croats, and the Turanian tribe of the Bulgars. The old general name has been retained to the present time by the Slovenes of Southern Austria on the Adriatic coast, the Slovaks of Northern Hungary, the province Slavonia between Croatia and Hungary and its inhabitants the Slavonians, and the Slovinci of Prussia on the North Sea. Up to recent times the name was customary among the inhabitants of the most southern point of Dalmatia, which was formerly the celebrated Republic of Dubrovnik (Ragusa). Until late in the Middle Ages it was retained by the Slavs of Novgorod in Northern Russia and by the Slavs in Macedonia and Albania. These peoples, however, have also retained their specific national and tribal names.

B. *Wends.*—A much older designation in the historical authorities than Slav is the name Wend. It is under this designation that the Slavs first appear in history. The first certain references to the present Slavs date from the first and second centuries. They were made by the Roman writers Pliny and Tacitus and the Alexandrian already mentioned Ptolemy. Pliny (d. A.D. 79) says (Nat. hist., IV, 97) that among the peoples living on the other side of the Vistula besides the Sarmatians and others are also the Wends (*Venedi*). Tacitus (G., 46) says the same. He describes the Wends somewhat more in detail but cannot make up his mind whether he ought to include them among the Germans or the Sarmatians; still they seem to him to be more closely connected with the first named than with the latter. Ptolemy (d. about 178) in his Γεωγραφική (III, 5, 7) calls the Venedi the greatest nation living on the Wendic Gulf. However, he says later (III, 5, 8) that they live on the Vistula; he also speaks of the Venedic mountains (III, 5, 6). In the centuries immediately succeeding the Wends are mentioned very rarely. The migrations that had now begun had brought other peoples into the foreground until the Venedi again appear in the sixth century under the name of Slavs. The name Wend, however, was never completely forgotten. The German chroniclers used both names constantly without distinction, the former almost oftener than the latter. Even now the Sorbs of Lusatia are called by the Germans Wends, while the Slovenes are frequently called Winds and their language is called Windish.

Those who maintain the theory that the original home of the Slavs was in the countries along the Danube have tried to refute the opinion that these references relate to the ancestors of the present Slavs, but their arguments are inconclusive. Besides these definite notices there are several others that are neither clear nor certain. The Wends or Slavs have had connected with them as old tribal confederates of the present Slavs the *Budinoi* mentioned by Herodotus, and also the Island of Banoma mentioned by Pliny (IV, 94), further the Venetæ, the original inhabitants of the present Province of Venice, as well as the Homeric Venetoi, Cæsar's Veneti in Gaul and Anglia, etc. In all probability, the Adriatic Veneti were an Illyrian tribe related to the present Albanians, but nothing is known of them. With more reason can the old story that the Greeks obtained amber from the River Eridanos in the country of the Enetoi be applied to the Wends or Slavs; from which it may be concluded that the Slavs were already living on the shores of the Baltic in the fourth century before Christ.

Most probably the name Wend was of foreign origin and the race was known by this name only among the foreign tribes, while they called themselves Slavs. It is possible that the Slavs were originally named Wends by the early Gauls, because the root Wend, or Wind, is found especially in the districts once occupied by the Gauls. The word was apparently a designation that was first applied to various Gallic or Celtic tribes, and then given by the Celts to the Wendic tribes living north of them. The explanation of the meaning of the word is also to be sought from this point of view. The endeavour was made at one time to derive the word from the Teutonic dialects, as Danish *wand*, Old Norwegian *vatn*, Latin *unda*, meaning water. Thus Wends would signify watermen, people living about the water, people living by the sea, as proposed by Jordan, Adelung, and others. A derivation from the German *wenden* (to turn) has also been suggested, thus the Wends are the people wandering about; or from the Gothic *vinja*, related to the German *weiden*, pasture, hence Wends, those who pasture, the shepherds; finally the word has been traced to the old root *ven*, belonging together. Wends would, therefore, mean the allied. Pogodin traced the name from the Celtic, taking it from the early Celtic root *vindos*, white, by which expression the dark Celts designated the light Slavs. Naturally an explanation of the term was also sought in the Slavonic language; thus, Kollar derived it from the Old Slavonic word *Un*, Sassinek from *Slo-van*, Perwolf from the Old Slavonic root *vęd*, still retained in the O. Slav. comparative *vestij* meaning large and brought it into connexion with the Russian *Anti* and *Vjatiči*; Hilferding even derived it from the old East Indian designation of the Aryans *Vanita*, and Šafařík connected the word with the East Indians, a confusion that is also to be found in the early writers.

II. ORIGINAL HOME AND MIGRATIONS.—There are two theories in regard to the original home of the Slavs, and these theories are in sharp opposition to each other. One considers the region of the Danube as the original home of the Slavs, whence they spread north-east over the Carpathians as far as the Volga River, Lake Ilmen, and the Caspian Sea. The other theory regards the districts between the Vistula and the Dnieper as their original home, whence they spread south-west over the Carpathians to the Balkans and into the Alps, and towards the west across the Oder and the Elbe.

The ancient Kieff chronicle, erroneously ascribed to the monk Nestor, is the earliest authority quoted for the theory that the original home of the Slavs is to be sought in the region of the Danube. Here in detail is related for the first time how the Slavs spread not commit himself to this view. The southern Slavs have held this theory from the earliest period up to the present time with the evident intention to base on it their claims to the Church Slavonic in the Liturgy. At an early period, in the letter of Pope John X (914–29) to the Croatian Ban Tomislav and the Sachlumian ruler Mihael, there is a reference to the

GLAGOLITIC MISSAL OF THE ROMAN RITE
A page from the Missa pro Sponso et Sponsa, containing the Gradual, Tract, Gospel (Matt. xix), and Special Prayer over the Bride and Groom

from the lower Danube to all the countries occupied later by them. The Noricans and Illyrians are declared to be Slavs, and Andronikos and the Apostle Paul are called Apostles to the Slavs because they laboured in Illyria and Pannonia. This view was maintained by the later chroniclers and historical writers of all Slavonic peoples, as the Pole Kadlubek, "Chronika pol." (1206), Boguchwal (d. 1253), Dlugos, Matej Miechowa, Decius, and others. Among the Czechs this theory was supported by Kozmaz (d. 1125), Dalimir (d. 1324), Johann Marignola (1355–1362), Pribik Pulkava (1374), and V. Hajek (1541). The Russians also developed their theories from the statements of their first chronicler, while the Greek Laonikos Harkondilos of the fifteenth century did prevalent tradition that St. Jerome invented the Slavonic alphabet. This tradition maintained itself through the succeeding centuries, finding supporters even outside these countries, and was current at Rome itself. Consequently if we were to follow strictly the written historical authorities, of which a number are very trustworthy, we would be obliged to support the theory that the original home of the Slavs is in the countries along the Danube and on the Adriatic coast.

However, the contrary is the case; the original home of the Slavs and the region from which their migrations began is to be sought in the basin of the Dnieper and in the region extending to the Carpathians and the Vistula. It is easy to explain the origin of the above-mentioned widely believed opinion. At the beginning of the Old Slavonic literature in the ancient Kingdom of the Bulgars the Byzantine chronicles of Hamartolos and Malala, which were besides of very little value, were translated into Slavonic. These chronicles give an account of the migrations of the nations from the region of Senaar after the Deluge. According to this account the Europeans are the descendants of Japhet, who journeyed from Senaar by way of Asia Minor to the Balkans; there they divided into various nations and spread in various directions. Consequently the Slavonic reader of these chronicles would believe that the starting point of the migrations of the Slavs also was the Balkans and the region of the lower Danube. Because the historical authorities place the ancient tribe of the Illyrians in this region, it was necessary to make this tribe also Slavonic. In the later battles of the Slavs for the maintenance of their language in the Liturgy this opinion was very convenient, as appeal could be made for the Slavonic claims to the authority of St. Jerome and even of St. Paul. Opinions which are widely current yet which do not correspond to facts are often adopted in historical writings. Among the Slavonic historians and philologists supporting this theory are: Kopitar, August Schlötzer, Šafařík, N. Arcybašef, Fr. Rački, Bielowski, M. Drinov, L. Stur, Ivan P. Filevič, Dm. Samokvasov, M. Leopardov, N. Zakoski, and J. Pic. We have here an interesting proof that a tradition deeply rooted and extending over many centuries and found in nearly all of the early native historical authorities does not agree with historical fact.

At present most scholars are of the opinion that the original home of the Slavs in South-eastern Europe must be sought between the Vistula and the Dneiper. The reasons for this belief are: the testimony of the oldest accounts of the Slavs, given as already mentioned by Pliny, Tacitus, and Ptolemy; further the close relationship between the Slavs and the Lettish tribes, pointing to the fact that originally the Slavs lived close to the Letts and Lithuanians; then various indications proving that the Slavs must have been originally neighbours of the Finnish and Turanian

CYRILLIC MISSAL OF GREEK RITE
A page from the Liturgy of St. John Chrysostom, containing the Prayers of Adoration just before Communion

tribes. Historical investigation has shown that the Thraco-Illyrian tribes are not the forefathers of the Slavs, but form an independent family group between the Greeks and the Latins. There is no certain proof in the Balkan territory and in the region along the Danube of the presence of the Slavs there before the first century. On the other hand in the region of the Dneiper excavations and archæological finds show traces only of the Slavs. In addition the direction of the general march in the migrations of the nations was always from the north-east towards the south-west, but never in the opposite direction. Those who maintain the theory that the Slavs came from the region of the Danube sought to strengthen their views by the names of various places to be found in these districts that indicate Slavonic origin. The etymology of these names, however, is not entirely certain; there are other names that appear only in the later authorities of the first centuries after Christ. Some again prove nothing, as they could have arisen without the occupation of these districts by the Slavs.

It can therefore be said almost positively that the original home of the Slavs was in the territory along the Dnieper, and farther to the north-west as far as the Vistula. From these regions they spread to the west and south-west. This much only can be conceded to the other view, that the migration probably took place much earlier than is generally supposed. Probably it took place slowly and by degrees. One tribe would push another ahead of it like a wave, and they all spread out in the wide territory from the North Sea to the Adriatic and Ægean Seas. Here and there some disorder was caused in the Slavonic migration by the incursions of Asiatic peoples, as Scythians, Sarmatians, Avars, Bulgars, and Magyars, as well as by the German migration from north-west to south-east. These incursions separated kindred tribes from one another or introduced foreign elements among them. Taken altogether, however, the natural arrangement was not much disturbed, kindred tribes journeyed together and settled near one another in the new land, so that even to-day the entire Slavonic race presents a regular succession of tribes. As early as the first century of our era individual Slavonic tribes might have crossed the boundaries of the original home and have settled at times among strangers at a considerable distance from the native country. At times again these outposts would be driven back and obliged to retire to the main body, but at the first opportunity they would advance again. Central Europe must have been largely populated by Slavs as early as the era of the Hunnish ruler Attila, or of the migrations of the German tribes of the Goths, Lombards, Gepidæ, Heruli, Rugians etc. These last-mentioned peoples and tribes formed warlike castes and military organizations which became conspicuous in history by their battles and therefore have left more traces in the old historical writings. The Slavs, however, formed the lower strata of the population of Central Europe; all the migrations of the other tribes passed over them, and when the times grew more peaceful the Slavs reappeared on the surface. It is only in this way that the appearance of the Slavs in great numbers in these countries directly after the close of the migrations can be explained without there being any record in history of when and whence they came and without their original home being depopulated.

III. Classification of the Slavonic Peoples.—The question as to the classification and number of the Slavonic peoples is a complicated one. Scientific investigation does not support the common belief, and in addition scholars do not agree in their opinions on this question. In 1822 the father of Slavonic philology, Joseph Dobrovsky, recognized nine Slavonic peoples and languages: Russian, Illyrian or Serb, Croat, Slovene, Korotanish, Slovak, Bohemian, Lusatian Sorb, and Polish. In his "Slavonic Ethnology" (1842) Pavel Šafařík enumerated six languages with thirteen dialects: Russian, Bolgarish, Illyrian, Lechish, Bohemian, Lusatian. The great Russian scholar J. Sreznejevskij held that there were eight Slavonic languages: Great Russian, Little Russian, Serbo-Croat, Korotanish, Polish, Lusatian, Bohemian, Slovak. In 1865 A. Schleicher enumerated eight Slavonic languages: Polish, Lusatian, Bohemian, Great Russian, Little Russian, Serb, Bulgarian, and Slovene. Franc Miklošič counted nine: Slovene, Bulgarian, Serbo-Croat, Great Russian, Little Russian, Bohemian, Polish, Upper Lusatian, Lower Lusatian. In 1907 Dm. Florinskij enumerated nine: Russian, Bulgarian, Serbo-Croat, Slovene, Bohemian-Moravian, Slovak, Lusatian, Polish, and Kašube. In 1898 V. Jagič held that there were eight: Polish, Lusatian, Bohemian, Great Russian, Little Russian, Slovene, Serbo-Croat, Bulgarian. Thus it is seen that the greatest representatives of Slavonic linguistics are not in accord upon the question of the number of Slavonic languages. The case is the same from the purely philological point of view. Practically the matter is even more complicated because other factors, which often play an important part, have to be considered, as religion, politics etc.

At the present time some eleven to fourteen languages, not including the extinct ones, can be enumerated which lay claim to be reckoned as distinct tongues. The cause of the uncertainty is that it is impossible to state definitively of several branches of the Slavonic family whether they form an independent nation or only the dialect and subdivision of another Slavonic nation, and further because often it is impossible to draw the line between one Slavonic people and another. The Great Russians, Poles, Bohemians, and Bulgarians are universally admitted to be distinctive Slavonic peoples with distinctive languages. The Little Russians and the White Russians are trying to develop into separate nationalities, indeed the former have now to be recognized as a distinct people, at least this is true of the Ruthenians in Austria-Hungary. The Moravians must be included in the Bohemian nation, because they hold this themselves and no philological, political, or ethnographical reason opposes. The Slovaks of Moravia also consider that they are of Bohemian nationality. About sixty years ago the Slovaks of Hungary began to develop as a separate nation with a separate literary language and must now be regarded as a distinct people. The Lusatian Sorbs also are generally looked upon as a separate people with a distinct language. A division of this little nationality into Upper and Lower Lusatians has been made on account of linguistic, religious, and political differences; this distinction is also evident in the literary language, consequently some scholars regard the Lusatians as two different peoples. The remains of the languages of the former Slavonic inhabitants of Pomerania, the Sloventzi, or Kašubes, are generally regarded at present as dialects of Polish, though some distinguished Polish scholars maintain the independence of the Kašube language. The conditions in the south are even more complicated. Without doubt the Bulgarians are a separate nationality, but it is difficult to draw the line between the Bulgarian and the Servian peoples, especially in Macedonia. Philologically the Croats and Serbs must be regarded as one nation; politically, however, and ethnographically they are distinct peoples. The population of Southern Dalmatia, the Mohammedan population of Bosnia, and probably also the inhabitants of some parts of Southern Hungary, and of Croatia cannot easily be assigned to a definite group. Again, the nationality and extent of the Slovenes living in the eastern Alps and on the Adriatic coast cannot be settled without further investigation.

From a philological point of view the following fundamental principles must be taken for guidance. The Slavonic world in its entire extent presents philologically a homogeneous whole without sharply defined transitions or gradations. When the Slavs settled in the localities at present occupied by them they were a mass of tribes of closely allied tongues that changed slightly from tribe to tribe. Later historical development, the appearance of Slavonic kingdoms, the growth of literary languages, and various civilizing influences from without have aided in bringing about the result that sharper distinctions have been drawn in certain places, and that distinct nationalities have developed in different localities. Where these factors did not appear in sufficient number the boundaries are not settled even now, or have been drawn only of late. The Slavonic peoples can be separated into the following groups on the basis of philological differences: (1) The eastern or Russian group; in the south this group approaches the Bulgarian; in the north-west the White Russian dialects show an affinity to Polish. The eastern group is subdivided into Great Russian, that is, the prevailing Russian nationality, then Little Russian, and White Russian. (2) The north-western group. This is subdivided into the Lechish languages and into Slovak, Bohemian, and Sorb tongues. The first subdivision includes the Poles, Kašubes, and Slovintzi, also the extinct languages of the Slavs who formerly extended across the Oder and the Elbe throughout the present Northern Germany. The second subdivision includes the Bohemians, Slovaks, and the Lusatian Sorbs. The Slavs in the Balkans and in the southern districts of the Austro-Hungarian Monarchy are divided philologically into Bulgarians; Stokauans, who include all Serbs, the Slavonic Mohammedans of Bosnia, and also a large part of the population of Croatia; the Cakauans, who live partly in Dalmatia, Istria, and on the coast of Croatia; the Kajkauans, to whom must be assigned three Croatian countries and all Slovene districts. According to the common opinion that is based upon a combination of philological, political, and religious reasons the Slavs are divided into the following nations: Russian, Polish, Bohemian-Slovak, Slovenes, Serbs, Croats, Bulgarians.

IV. PRESENT CONDITION—A. *Russians.*—The Russians live in Russia and the north-eastern part of Austria-Hungary. They form a compact body only in the south-western part of the Russian Empire, as in the north and east they are largely mixed with Finnish and Tatar populations. In Austria the Little Russians inhabit Eastern Galicia and the northern part of Bukowina; in Hungary they live in the eastern part on the slopes of the Carpathians. Scattered colonies of Little Russians or Ruthenians are also to be found in Slavonia and Bosnia among the southern Slavs, in Bulgaria, and in the Dobrudja. In Asia Western Siberia is Russian, Central Siberia has numerous Russian colonies, while Eastern Siberia is chiefly occupied by native tribes. There are Russians, however, living in the region of the Amur River, and on the Pacific as well as on the Island of Saghalien. Turkestan and the Kirghiz steppes have native populations with Russian colonies in the cities. There are large numbers of Russian emigrants, mostly members of sects, in Canada and elsewhere in America. Brazil, Argentina, and the United States have many Little Russian immigrants. There are small Russian colonies in Asia Minor and lately the emigration has also extended to Africa. According to the Russian census of 1897 there were in the Russian Empire 83,933,567 Russians, that is, 67 per cent of the entire population of the empire. Allowing for natural increase, at the present (1911) time there are about 89 millions. In 1900 there were in Austria 3,375,576 Ruthenians, in Hungary 429,447. Consequently in 1900 the total number of Russians could be reckoned at about 93 million persons. This does not include the Russian colonists in other countries; moreover, the numbers given by the official statistics of Austria-Hungary may be far below reality. Classified by religion the Russian Slavs are divided as follows: in Russia Orthodox Greeks, 95.48 per cent; Old Believers, 2.59 per cent; Catholics, 1.78 per cent; Protestants, .05 per cent; Jews, .08 per cent; Mohammedans, .01 per cent; in Austria-Hungary Uniat Greeks, 90.6 per cent, the Orthodox Greeks, 8 per cent. In the Russian Empire, excluding Finland and Poland, 77.01 per cent are illiterates; in Poland, 69.5 per cent; Finland and the Baltic provinces with the large German cities show a higher grade of literacy.

The Russians are divided into Great Russians, Little Russians or inhabitants of the Ukraine, and White Russians. In 1900 the relative numbers of these three divisions were approximately: Great Russians, 59,000,000; White Russians, 6,200,000; Little Russians, 23,700,000. In addition there are 3,800,000 Little Russians in Austria-Hungary, and 500,000 in America. The Russian official statistics are naturally entirely too unfavourable to the White Russians and the Little Russians; private computations of Little Russian scholars give much higher results. Hrusevskij found that the Little Russians taken altogether numbered 34,000,000; Karskij calculated that the White Russians numbered 8,000,000. A thousand years of historical development, different influences of civilization, different religious confessions, and probably also the original philological differentiation have caused the Little Russians to develop as a separate nation, and to-day this fact must be taken as a fixed factor. Among the White Russians the differentiation has not developed to so advanced a stage, but the tendency exists. In classifying the Little Russians three different types can be again distinguished: the Ukrainian, the Podolian-Galician, and the Podlachian. Ethnographically interesting are the Little Russian or Ruthenian tribes in the Carpathians, the Lemci, Boici, and Huzuli (Gouzouli). The White Russians are divided into two groups; ethnographically the eastern group is related to the Great Russians; the western to the Poles.

B. *Poles.*—The Poles represent the north-western branch of the Slavonic race. From the very earliest times they have lived in their ancestral regions between the Carpathians, the Oder, and the North Sea. A thousand years ago Boleslaw the Brave united all the Slavonic tribes living in these territories into a Polish kingdom. This kingdom, which reached its highest prosperity at the close of the Middle Ages, then gradually declined and, at the close of the eighteenth century, was divided by the surrounding powers—Russia, Prussia, and Austria. In Austria the Poles form the population of Western Galicia and are in a large minority throughout Eastern Galicia; in Eastern Galicia the population of the cities particularly is preponderantly Polish, as is also a large part of the population of a section of Austrian Silesia, the district of Teschin. The Poles are largely represented in the County of Zips in Hungary and less largely in other Hungarian counties which border on Western Galicia. There is a small Polish population in Bukowina. In Prussia the Poles live in Upper Silesia, form a large majority of the inhabitants of the Province of Posen, and also inhabit the districts of Dantzic and Marienwerder in West Prussia, and the southern parts of East Prussia. In Russia the Poles form 71.95 per cent of the population in the nine provinces formed from the Polish kingdom. In addition they live in the neighbouring district of the Province of Grodno and form a relatively large minority in Lithuania and in the provinces of White and Little Russia, where they are mainly owners of large estates and residents of cities. According to the census of 1900 the Poles in Russia numbered about 8,400,000; in Austria, 4,259,150; in Germany, including the Kasubes and Mazurians, 3,450,200; in the rest of Europe about 55,000; and in America about 1,500,000; consequently altogether, 17,664,350. Czerkawski reckoned the total number of Poles to be 21,111,374; Straszewicz held that they numbered from 18 to 19,000,000. As regards religion the Poles of Russia are almost entirely Catholic; in Austria 83.4 per cent are Catholics, 14.7 per cent are Jews, and 1.8 per cent are Protestants; in Germany they are also almost entirely Catholics, only the Mazurians in East Prussia and a small portion of the Kasubes are Protestant.

Ethnographically the Polish nation is divided into three groups: the Great Poles live in Posen, Silesia, and Prussia; the Little Poles on the upper Vistula as far as the San River and in the region of the Tatra mountains; the Masovians east of the Vistula and along the Narva and the Bug. The Kasubes could be called a fourth group. All these groups can be subdivided again into a large number of branches, but the distinctions are not so striking as in Russia and historical tradition keeps all these peoples firmly united. The Kasubes live on the left bank of the Vistula from Dantzic to the boundary of Pomerania and to the sea. According to government statistics in 1900 there were in Germany 100,213 Kasubes The very exact statistics of the scholar Ramult gives 174,831 Kasubes for the territory where they live in large bodies, and 200,000 for a total including those scattered through Germany, to which should be added a further 130,000 in America. According to the latest investigation the Kasubes are what remains of the Slavs of Pomerania who are, otherwise, long extinct.

C. *Lusatian Sorbs.*—The Lusatian Sorbs are the residue of the Slavs of the Elbe who once spread across the Oder and Elbe, inhabiting the whole of the present Northern Germany. During centuries of combat with the Germans their numbers gradually decreased. They are divided into three main groups: the Obotrites who inhabited the present Mecklenburg, Lüneburg, and Holstein whence they extended into the Old Mark; the Lutici or Veltæ, who lived between the Oder and Elbe, the Baltic and the Varna; the Sorbs, who lived on the middle course of the Elbe between the Rivers Havel and Bober. The Lutici died out on the Island of Rügen at the beginning of the fifteenth century. In the middle of the sixteenth century there were still large numbers of Slavs in Lüneburg and in the northern part of the Old Mark, while their numbers were less in Mecklenburg and in Brandenburg. However, even in Lüneburg the last Slavs disappeared between 1750-60. Only the Lusatian Sorbs who lived nearer the borders of Bohemia have been able to maintain themselves in declining numbers until the present time. The reason probably is that for some time their territory belonged to Bohemia. At present the Lusatian Sorbs number about 150,000 persons on the upper course of the Spree. They are divided into two groups, which differ so decidedly from each other in speech and customs that some regard them as two peoples; they also have two separate literatures. They are rapidly becoming Germanized, especially in Lower Lusatia. The Lusatian Sorbs are Catholics with exception of 15,000 in Upper Lusatia.

D. *Bohemians and Slovaks.*—The Bohemians and Slovaks also belong to the north-western branch of the Slavonic peoples. They entered the region now constituting Bohemia from the north and then spread farther into what is now Moravia and Northern Hungary, and into the present Lower Austria as far as the Danube. The settlements of the Slovaks in Hungary must have extended far towards the south, perhaps as far as Lake Platten, where they came into contact with the Slovenes who belonged to the southern Slavonic group. Probably, however, they did not formerly extend as far towards the east as now, and the Slovaks in the eastern portion of Slovakia are really Ruthenians who were Slovakanized in the late Middle Ages. Directly after their settlement in these countries the Bohemians fell apart into a great number of tribes. One tribe, which settled in the central part of the present Bohemia, bore the name of Czechs. It gradually brought all the other tribes under its control and gave them its name, so that since then the entire people have been called Czechs. Along with this name, however, the name Bohemians has also been retained; it comes from the old Celtic people, the Boii, who once lived in these regions. Soon, however, German colonies sprang up among the Bohemians or Czechs. The colonists settled along the Danube on the southern border of Bohemia and also farther on in the Pannonian plain. However, these settlements disappeared during the storm of the Magyar incursion. The Bohemians did not suffer from it as they did from the later immigrations of German colonists who were brought into the country by the Bohemian rulers of the native Premsylidian dynasty. These colonists lived through the mountains which encircle Bohemia and large numbers of them settled also in the interior of the country. From the thirteenth century the languages of Bohemia and Moravia became distinct tongues.

The Bohemians have emigrated to various countries outside of Bohemia-Moravia. In America there are about 800,000 Bohemians; there are large Bohemian colonies in Russia in the province of Volhynia, also in the Crimea, in Poland, and in what is called New Russia, altogether numbering 50,385. In Bulgaria there are Bohemian colonies in Wojewodovo and near Plevna; there is also a Bohemian colony in New Zealand. Nearly 400,000 Bohemians live at Vienna, and there are large numbers of Bohemians in the cities of Linz, Pesth, Berlin, Dresden, Leipzig, Triest; there are smaller, well-organized Bohemian colonies in nearly all Austrian cities, besides large Bohemian colonies in Hungary and Slavonia. In the last-mentioned country there are 31,581 Bohemians. These settlements are modern. The Slovaks occupy the south-eastern part of Moravia and the north-eastern part of Hungary from the Carpathians almost to the Danube. But there are scattered settlements of Slovaks far into the Hungarian plain and even in Southern Hungary, besides colonies of Slovaks in Slavonia. On account of the barrenness of the soil of their native land many Slovaks emigrate to America. According to the Austrian census of 1900 there were 5,955,297 Bohemians in Austria. The number may be decidedly higher. In Germany there were 115,000 Bohemians; in Hungary 2,019,641 Slovaks and 50,000 Bohemians; in America there are at least 800,000 Bohemians; in Russia 55,000; in the rest of Europe 20,000. Consequently taking all Bohemians and Slovaks together there are probably over 9,000,000. If, as is justifiable, the figures for America, Vienna, Moravia, Silesia, and Hungary are considered entirely too low, a maximum of about 10,000,000 may be accepted. As to religion 96.5 per cent of the Bohemians are Catholics, and 2.4 per cent are Protestants; 70.2 per cent of the Slovaks are Catholics, 5.3 per cent are Uniat Greeks, and 23 per cent are Protestants.

E. *Slovenes.*—The Slovenes belong, together with the Croats, Serbs, and Bulgarians, to the southern group of Slavs. The Slovenes have the position farthest to the west in the Alps and on the Adriatic. They first appeared in this region after the departure of the Lombards for Italy and the first date in their history is 595, when they fought an unsuccessful battle with the Bavarian Duke Tassilo on the field of Toblach. They occupied at first a much larger

XIV.—4

territory than at present. They extended along the Drave as far as the Tyrol, reaching the valleys of the Rivers Rienz and Eisack; they also occupied the larger part of what is now Upper Austria, Lower Austria as far as the Danube, and from the district of the Lungau in Southern Salzburg through Carinthia, Carniola, Styria, the crownland of Görz-Gradiska, and a large part of Friuli. Under German supremacy the territory occupied by them has grown considerably less in the course of the centuries. They still maintain themselves only in Carniola, in the northern part of Istria, about Görz, and in the vicinity of Triest, in the mountainous districts north of Udine in Italy, in the southern part of Carinthia and Styria, and in the Hungarian countries bordering on the farther side of the Mur River. Carinthia is becoming rapidly Germanized, and the absorption of the other races in Hungary by the Magyars constantly advances. According to the census of 1900 there were then 1,192,780 Slovenes in Austria, 94,993 in Hungary, 20,987 in Croatia and Slavonia, probably 37,000 in Italy, in America 100,000, and 20,000 in other countries. There are, taking them altogether, probably about 1,500,000 Slovenes in the world; 99 per cent of them are Catholics.

F. *Croats and Serbs.*—In speech the Croats and Serbs are one people; they have the same literary language, but use different characters. The Croats write with the Latin characters and the Serbs with the Cyrillic. They have been separated into two peoples by religion, political development, and different forms of civilization; the Croats came under the influence of Latin civilization, the Serbs under that of the Byzantines. After the migrations the warlike tribe of the Croats gained the mastery over the Slavonic tribes then living in the territory between the Kulpa and the Drave, the Adriatic and the River Cetina, in Southern Dalmatia. They founded the Croat Kingdom on the remains of Latin civilization and with Roman Catholicism as their religion. Thus the Croat nation appeared. It was not until a later date that the tribes living to the south and east began to unite politically under the old Slavonic name of Serbs, and in this region the Servian nation developed. Decided movements of the population came about later, being caused especially by the Turkish wars. The Servian settlements, which originally followed only a south-eastern course, now turned in an entirely opposite direction to the northeast. The original home of the Serbs was abandoned largely to the Albanians and Turks; the Serbs emigrated to Bosnia and across Bosnia to Dalmatia and even to Italy, where Slavonic settlements still exist in Abruzzi. Others crossed the boundaries of the Croat Kingdom and settled in large numbers in Servia and Slavonia, also in Southern Hungary, where the Austrian Government granted them religious and national autonomy and a patriarch of their own. Some of the Serbs settled here went to Southern Russia and founded there what is called the New Servia in the Government of Kherson. Consequently, the difference between the Croats and the Serbs consists not in the language but mainly in the religion, also in the civilization, history, and in the form of handwriting. But all these characteristic differences are not very marked, and thus there are districts and sections of population which cannot be easily assigned to one or the other nation, and which both peoples are justified in claiming.

Taking Serbs and Croats together there are: in Austria, 711,382; in Hungary and Croatia, 2,839,016; in Bosnia and Herzegovina, probably 1,700,000; in Montenegro, 350,000; in Servia, 2,298,551; Old Servia and Macedonia, 350,000; Albania and the vilayet of Scutari, about 100,000; Italy, 5000; Russia, 2000; America and elsewhere, 300,000. In addition there are about 108,000 Schokzians, Bunjevzians, and Krashovanians, Serbo-Croatian tribes in Hungary, who were not included with these in the census. Consequently the number of this bipartite people may be reckoned approximately as 8,700,000 persons. According to Servian computation there are about 2,300,000 Croats in Austria-Hungary; the Croats reckon their number as over 2,700,000. The controversy results from the uncertainty as to the group to which the Bosnian Mohammedans and the above-mentioned Schokzians, Bunjevzians, and Krashovanians, as well as the population of Southern Dalmatia, belong. As to religion the Serbs are almost exclusively Orthodox Greek, the Croats Catholic, the great majority of the inhabitants of Southern Dalmatia are Catholic, but many consider themselves as belonging to the Servian nation. The branches in Hungary mentioned above are Catholic; it is still undecided whether to include them among the Croats or Serbs.

G. *Bulgarians.*—The Slavonic tribes living in ancient Roman Mœsia and Thrace south of the Danube and south-east of the Serbs as far as the Black Sea came under the sway of the Turanian tribe of the Bulgars, which established the old Kingdom of Bulgaria in this region as early as the second half of the seventh century. The conquerors soon began to adopt the language and customs of the subjugated people, and from this intermixture arose the Bulgarian people. The historical development was not a quiet and uniform one; there were continual migrations and remigrations, conquests and intermingling. When the Slavs first entered the Balkan peninsula they spread far beyond their present boundaries and even covered Greece and the Peloponnesus, which seemed about to become Slavonic. However, thanks to their higher civilization and superior tactics, the Greeks drove back the Slavs. Still, Slavonic settlements continued to exist in Greece and the Peloponnesus until the late Middle Ages. The Greeks were aided by the Turkish conquest, and the Slavs were forced to withdraw to the limit that is still maintained. The Turks then began to force back the Slavonic population in Macedonia and Bulgaria and to plant colonies of their own people in certain districts. The chief aim of the Turkish colonization was always to obtain strategic points and to secure the passes over the Balkans. The Slavonic population also began to withdraw from the plains along the Danube where naturally great battles were often fought, and which were often traversed by the Turkish army. A part emigrated to Hungary, where a considerable number of Bulgarian settlements still exist; others journeyed to Bessarabia and South Russia. After the liberation of Bulgaria the emigrants began to return and the population moved again from the mountains into the valleys, while large numbers of Turks and Circassians went back from liberated Bulgaria to Turkey.

On the other hand the emigration from Macedonia is still large. Owing to these uncertain conditions, and especially on account of the slight investigation of the subject in Macedonia, it is difficult to give the size of the Bulgarian population even approximately. In approximate figures the Bulgarians number: in the Kingdom of Bulgaria, 2,864,735; Macedonia, 1,200,000; Asia Minor, 600,000; Russia, 180,000; Rumania, 90,000; in other countries, 50,000, hence there are altogether perhaps over 5,000,000. In Bulgaria there are besides the Bulgarian population, 20,644 Pomaks, that is Mohammedans who speak Bulgarian, 1516 Serbs, 531,217 Turks, 9862 Gagauzi (Bulgarians who speak Turkish), 18,874 Tatars, 66,702 Greeks in cities along the coast, 89,563 Gypsies, and 71,023 Rumanians. The kingdom, therefore, is not an absolutely homogeneous nationality. In religion the Bulgarians are Orthodox Greeks with exception of the Pomaks, already mentioned, and of the Paulicians who are Catholics. The Bulgarians are divided into a number of branches and dialects; it is often doubtful whether some of these subdivisions should not be included among the Serbs. This is especially the case in Macedonia, consequently all enumerations of the population differ extremely from one another.

If, on the basis of earlier results, the natural annual growth of the Slavonic populations is taken as 1.4 per cent, it may be claimed that there were about 156-157 million Slavs in the year 1910. In 1900 all Slavs taken together numbered approximately 136,500,000 persons, divided thus: Russians, 94,000,000; Poles, 17,500,000; Lusatian Serbs, 150,000; Bohemians and Slovaks, 9,800,000; Slovenes, 1,500,000; Serbo-Croats, 8,550,000; Bulgarians, 5,000,000.

LEOPOLD LÉNARD.

Slavs in America.—The Slavic races have sent large numbers of their people to the United States and Canada, and this immigration is coming every year in increasing numbers. The earliest immigration began before the war of the States, but within the past thirty years it has become so great as quite to overshadow the Irish and German immigration of the earlier decades. For two-thirds of that period no accurate figures of tongues and nationalities were kept, the immigrants being merely credited to the political governments or countries from which they came, but within the past twelve years more accurate data have been preserved. During these years (1899-1910) the total immigration into the United States has been about 10,000,000 in round numbers, and of these the Slavs have formed about 22 per cent. (actually 2,117,240), to say nothing of the increase of native-born Slavs in this country during that period, as well as the numbers of the earlier arrivals. Reliable estimates compiled from the various racial sources show that there are from five and a half to six millions of Slavs in the United States, including the native-born of Slavic parents. We are generally unaware of these facts, because the Slavs are less conspicuous among us than the Italians, Germans, or Jews; their languages and their history are unfamiliar and remote, besides they are not so massed in the great cities of this country.

I. BOHEMIANS (*Čech;* adjective, *český*, Bohemian). These people ought really be called *Chekh* (*Czech*), but are named Bohemians after the aboriginal tribe of the Boii, who dwelt in Bohemia in Roman times. By a curious perversion of language, on account of various gypsies who about two centuries ago travelled westward across Bohemia and thereby came to be known in France as "Bohemians", the word Bohemian came into use to designate one who lived an easy, careless life, unhampered by serious responsibilities. Such a meaning is, however, the very antithesis of the serious conservative Chekh character. The names of a few Bohemians are found in the early history of the United States. Augustýn Heřman (1692) of Bohemia Manor, Maryland, and Bedřich Filip (Frederick Philipse, 1702) of Philipse Manor, Yonkers, New York, are the earliest. In 1848 the revolutionary uprisings in Austria sent many Bohemians to this country. In the eighteenth century the Moravian Brethren (Bohemian Brethren) had come in large numbers. The finding of gold in California in 1849-50 attracted many more, especially as serfdom and labour dues were abolished in Bohemia at the end of 1848, which left the peasant and workman free to travel. In 1869 and the succeeding years immigration was stimulated by the labour strikes in Bohemia, and on one occasion all the women workers of several cigar factories came over and settled in New York. About 60 per cent of the Bohemians and Moravians who have settled here are Catholics, and their churches have been fairly maintained. Their immigration during the past ten years has been 98,100, and in 1910 the number of Bohemians in the United States, immigrants and native born, was reckoned at 550,000. They have some 140 Bohemian Catholic churches and about 250 Bohemian priests; their societies, schools, and general institutions are active and flourishing.

II. BULGARIANS (*Bŭlgar;* adjective *bŭlgarski*, Bulgarian).—This part of the Slavic race inhabits the present Kingdom of Bulgaria, and the Turkish provinces of Eastern Rumelia, representing ancient Macedonia. Thus it happens that the Bulgarians are almost equally divided between Turkey and Bulgaria. Their ancestors were the Bolgars or Bulgars, a Finnish tribe, which conquered, intermarried, and coalesced with the Slav inhabitants, and eventually gave their name to them. The Bulgarian tongue is in many respects the nearest to the Church Slavonic, and it was the ancient Bulgarian which Sts. Cyril and Methodius are said to have learned in order to evangelize the pagan Slavs. The modern Bulgarian language, written with Russian characters and a few additions, differs from the other Slavic languages in that it, like English, has lost nearly every inflexion, and, like Rumanian, has the peculiarity of attaching the article to the end of the word, while the other Slavic tongues have no article at all. The Bulgarians who have gained their freedom from Turkish supremacy in the present Kingdom of Bulgaria are fairly contented; but those in Macedonia chafe bitterly against Turkish rule and form a large portion of those who emigrate to America. The Bulgarians are nearly all of the Greek Orthodox Church; there are some twenty thousand Greek Catholics, mostly in Macedonia, and about 50,000 Roman Catholics. The Greek Patriarch of Constantinople has always claimed jurisdiction over the Bulgarian Orthodox Church, and he enforced his jurisdiction until 1872, when the Bulgarian exarch was appointed to exercise supreme jurisdiction. Since that time the Bulgarians have been in a state of schism to the patriarch. They are ruled in Bulgaria by a Holy Synod of their own, whilst the Bulgarian exarch, resident in Constantinople, is the head of the entire Bulgarian Church. He is recognized by the Russian Church, but is considered excommunicate by the Greek Patriarch, who however retained his authority over the Greek-speaking churches of Macedonia and Bulgaria.

Bulgarians came to the United States as early as 1890; but there were then only a few of them as students, mostly from Macedonia, brought hither by mission bodies to study for the Protestant ministry. The real immigration began in 1905, when it seems that the Bulgarians discovered America as a land of opportunity, stimulated probably by the Turkish and Greek persecutions then raging in Macedonia against them. The railroads and steel works in the West needed men, and several enterprising steamship agents brought over Macedonians and Bulgarians in large numbers. Before 1906 there were scarcely 500 to 600 Bulgarians in the country, and these chiefly in St. Louis, Missouri. Since then they have been coming at the rate of from 8000 to 10,000 a year, until now (1911) there are from 80,000 to 90,000 Bulgarians scattered throughout the United States and Canada. The majority of them are employed in factories, railroads, mines, and sugar works. Granite City, Madison, and Chicago, Illinois; St. Louis, Missouri; Indianapolis, Indiana; Steelton, Pennsylvania; Portland, Oregon, and New York City all have a considerable Bulgarian population. They also take to farming and are scattered throughout the north-west. They now (1911) have three Greek Orthodox churches in the United States, at Granite City and Madison, Illinois, and at Steelton, Pennsylvania, as well as several mission stations. Their clergy consist of one monk and two secular priests; and they also have a church at Toronto, Canada. There are no Bulgarian Catholics, either of the Greek or Roman Rite, sufficient to form a church here. The Bulgarians, unlike the other Slavs, have no church or benefit societies or brotherhoods in America. They publish five Bulgarian papers, of which the "Naroden Glas" of Granite City is the most important.

III. CROATIANS (*Hrvat;* adjective, *hrvatski,* Croatian).—These are the inhabitants of the autonomous or home-rule province of Croatia-Slavonia, in the south-western part of the Kingdom of Hungary where it reaches down to the Adriatic Sea. It includes not only them but also the Slavic inhabitants of Istria and Dalmatia, in Austria, and those of Bosnia and Herzogovina who are Catholic and use the Roman alphabet. In blood and speech the Croatians and Servians are practically one; but religion and politics divide them. The former are Roman Catholics and use the Roman letters; the latter are Greek Orthodox and use modified Russian letters. In many of the places on the border-line school-children have to learn both alphabets. The English word "cravat" is derived from their name, it being the Croatian neckpiece which the south Austrian troops wore. Croatia-Slavonia itself has a population of nearly 2,500,000 and is about one-third the size of the State of New York. Croatia in the west is mountainous and somewhat poor, while Slavonia in the east is level, fertile, and productive. Many Dalmatian Croats from seaport towns came here from 1850 to 1870. The original emigration from Croatia-Slavonia began in 1873, upon the completion of the new railway connexions to the seaport of Fiume, when some of the more adventurous Croatians came to the United States. From the early eighties the Lipa-Krbava district furnished much of the emigration. The first Croatian settlements were made in Calumet, Michigan, while many of them became lumbermen in Michigan and stave-cutters along the Mississippi. Around Agram (Zágráb, the Croatian capital) the grape disease caused large destruction of vineyards and the consequent emigration of thousands. Later on emigration began from Varasdin and from Slavonia also, and now immigrants arrive from every county in Croatia-Slavonia. In 1899 the figures for Croatia-Slavonia were 2923, and by 1907 the annual immigration had risen to 22,828, the largest number coming from Agram and Varasdin Counties. Since then it has fallen off, and at the present time (1911) it is not quite 20,000. Unfortunately the governmental statistics do not separate the Slovenians from the Croatians in giving the arrivals of Austro-Hungarian immigrants, but the Hungarian figures of departures serve as checks.

The number of Croatians in the United States at present, including the native-born, is about 280,000, divided according to their origin as follows: from Croatia-Slavonia, 160,000; Dalmatia, 80,000; Bosnia, 20,000; Herzegovina, 15,000; and the remainder from various parts of Hungary and Servia. The largest group of them is in Pennsylvania, chiefly in the neighbourhood of Pittsburg, and they number probably from 80,000 to 100,000. Illinois has about 45,000, chiefly in Chicago. Ohio has about 35,000, principally in Cleveland and the vicinity. Other considerable colonies are in New York, San Francisco, St. Louis, Kansas City, and New Orleans. They are also in Montana, Colorado, and Michigan. The Dalmatians are chiefly engaged in business and grape culture; the other Croatians are mostly labourers employed in mining, railroad work, steel mills, stockyards, and stone quarries. Nearly all of these are Catholics, and they now have one Greek Catholic and 16 Roman Catholic churches in the United States. The Greek Catholics are almost wholly from the Diocese of Križevač (Crisium), and are chiefly settled at Chicago and Cleveland. They have some 250 societies devoted to church and patriotic purposes, and in some cases to Socialism, but as yet they have no very large central organization, the National Croatian Union with 29,247 members being the largest. They publish ten newspapers, among them two dailies, of which "Zajednicar" the organ of Narodne Hrvatske Zajednice (National Croatian Union) is the best known.

IV. POLES (*Polak,* a Pole; adjective *polski,* Polish). —The Poles came to the United States quite early in its history. Aside from some few early settlers, the American Revolution attracted such noted men as Kosciuszko and Pulaski, together with many of their fellow-countrymen. The Polish Revolution of 1830 brought numbers of Poles to the United States. In 1851 a Polish colony settled in Texas, and called their settlement Panna Marya (Our Lady Mary). In 1860 they settled at Parisville, Michigan, and Polonia, Wisconsin. Many distinguished Poles served in the Civil War (1861–65) upon both sides. After 1873 the Polish immigration began to grow apace, chiefly from Prussian Poland. Then the tide turned and came from Austria, and later from Russian Poland. In 1890 they began to come in the greatest numbers from Austrian and Russian Poland, until the flow from German Poland has largely diminished. The immigration within the past ten years has been as follows: from Russia, 53 per cent; from Austria about 43 per cent; and only a fraction over 4 per cent from the Prussian or German portion. It is estimated that there are at present about 3,000,000 Poles in the United States, counting the native-born. It may be said that they are almost solidly Catholic; the dissident and disturbing elements among them being but comparatively small, while there is no purely Protestant element at all. They have one Polish bishop, about 750 priests, and some 520 churches and chapels, besides 335 schools. There are large numbers, both men and women, who are members of the various religious communities. The Poles publish some 70 newspapers, amongst them nine dailies, 20 of which are purely Catholic publications. Their religious and national societies are large and flourishing; and altogether the Polish element is active and progressive.

V. RUSSIANS (*Rossiyanin;* adjective *rossiiski,* Russian).—The Russian Empire is the largest nation in Europe, and its Slavic inhabitants (exclusive of Poles) are composed of Great Russians or Northern Russians, White Russians or Western Russians, and the Little Russians (Ruthenians) or Southern Russians. The Great Russians dwell in the central and northern parts of the empire around Moscow and St. Petersburg, and are so called in allusion to their stature and great predominance in number, government, and language. The White Russians are so called from the prevailing colour of the clothing of the peasantry, and inhabit the provinces lying on the borders of Poland—Vitebsk, Mohileff, Minsk, Vilna, and Grodno. Their language differs but slightly from Great Russian, inclining towards Polish and Old Slavonic. The Little Russians (so called from their low stature) differ considerably from the Great Russians in language and customs, and they inhabit the Provinces of Kieff, Kharkoff, Tchernigoff, Poltava, Podolia, and Volhynia, and they are also found outside the Empire of Russia in Galicia, Bukovina, and Hungary (see below, VI. RUTHENIANS). The Great Russians may be regarded as the norm of the Russian people. Their language became the language of the court and of literature, just as High German and Tuscan Italian did, and they form the overwhelming majority of the inhabitants of the Russian Empire. They are practically all Greek Orthodox, the Catholics in Russia being Poles or Germans where they are of the Roman Rite, and Little Russians (Ruthenians) where they are of the Greek Rite.

The Russians have long been settled in America, for Alaska was Russian territory before it was purchased by the United States in 1867. The Russian Greek Orthodox church has been on American soil for over a century. The immigration from Russia is however composed of very few Russians. It is principally made up of Jews (Russian and Polish), Poles, and Lithuanians. Out of an average emigration of from 250,000 to 260,000 annually from the Russian Empire to the United States, 65 per cent have been Jews and only from three to five per cent actual Russians. Nevertheless the Russian peasant and working class are active emigrants, and the exodus from European Russia is relatively large. But it is directed eastward instead of to the west, for Russia is intent upon settling up her vast prairie lands in Siberia. Hindrances are placed in the way of those Russians (except the Jews) who would leave for America or the west of Europe, while inducements and advantages are offered for settlers in Siberia. For the past five years about 500,000 Russians have annually migrated to Siberia, a number equal to one-half the immigrants yearly received by the United States from all sources. They go in great colonies and are aided by the Russian Government by grants of land, loans of money, and low transportation. New towns and cities have sprung up all over Siberia, which are not even on our maps, thus rivalling the American settlement of the Dakotas and the North-West. Many Russian religious colonists, other than the Jews, have come to America; but often they are not wholly of Slavic blood or are Little Russians (Ruthenians). It therefore happens that there are very few Russians in the United States as compared with other nationalities. There are, according to the latest estimates, about 75,000, chiefly in Pennsylvania and the Middle West. There has been a Russian colony in San Francisco for sixty years, and they are numerous in and around New York City.

The Russian Orthodox Church is well established here. About a third of the Russians in the United States are opposed to it, being of the anti-government, semi-revolutionary type of immigrant. But the others are enthusiastic in support of their Church and their national customs, yet their Church includes not only them but the Little Russians of Bukovina and a very large number of Greek Catholics of Galicia and Hungary whom they have induced to leave the Catholic and enter the Orthodox Church. The Russian Church in the United States is endowed by the tsar and the Holy Governing Synod, besides having the support of Russian missionary societies at home, and is upon a flourishing financial basis in the United States. It now (1911) has 83 churches and chapels in the United States, 15 in Alaska, and 18 in Canada, making a total of 126 places of worship, besides a theological seminary at Minneapolis and a monastery at South Canaan, Pennsylvania. Their present clergy is composed of one archbishop, one bishop, 6 proto-priests, 89 secular priests, 2 archimandrites, 2 hegumens, and 18 monastic priests, making a total of 119, while they also exercise jurisdiction over the Servian and Syrian Orthodox clergy besides. Lately they took over a Greek Catholic sisterhood, and now have four Basilian nuns. The United States is now divided up into the following six districts of the Russian Church, intended to be the territory for future dioceses: New York and the New England States; Pennsylvania and the Atlantic states; Pittsburg and the Middle West; Western Pacific States; Canada; and Alaska. Their statistics of church population have not been published lately in their year-books, and much of their growth has been of late years by additions gained from the Greek Catholic Ruthenians of Galicia and Hungary, and is due largely to the active and energetic work and financial support of the Russian church authorities at St. Petersburg and Moscow.

They have the "Russkoye Pravoslavnoye Obshchestvo Vzaimopomoshchi" (Russian Orthodox Mutual Aid Society) for men, founded in 1895, now (1911) having 199 councils and 7072 members, and the women's division of the same, founded in 1907, with 32 councils and 690 members. They publish two church papers, "American Orthodox Messenger", and "Svit"; although there are some nine other Russian papers published by Jews and Socialists.

VI. RUTHENIANS (*Rusin*; adjective *russky*, Ruthenian).—These are the southern branch of the Russian family, extending from the middle of Austria-Hungary across the southern part of Russia. The use of the adjective *russky* by both the Ruthenians and the Russians permits it to be translated into English by the word "Ruthenian" or "Russian". They are also called Little Russians (*Malorossiani*) in the Empire of Russia, and sometimes *Russniaki* in Hungary. The appellations "Little Russians" and "Ruthenians" have come to have almost a technical meaning, the former indicating subjects of the Russian Empire who are of the Greek Orthodox Church, and the latter those who are in Austria-Hungary and are Catholics of the Greek Rite. Those who are active in the Panslavic movement and are Russophiles are very anxious to have them called "Russians", no matter whence they come. The Ruthenians are of the original Russo-Slavic race, and gave their name to the peoples making up the present Russian Empire. They are spread all over the southern part of Russia, in the provinces of Kieff, Kharkoff, Tchernigoff, Poltava, Podolia, and Volhynia (see above, V. RUSSIANS), but by force of governmental pressure and restrictive laws are being slowly made into Great Russians. Only within the past five years has the use of their own form of language and their own newspapers and press been allowed by law in Russia. Nearly every Ruthenian author in the empire has written his chief works in Great Russian, because denied the use of his own language. They are also spread throughout the Provinces of Lublin, in Poland; Galicia and Bukovina, in Austria; and the Counties of Szepes, Saros, Abauj, Zemplin, Ung, Marmos, and Bereg, in Hungary. They have had an opportunity to develop in Austria and also in Hungary. In the latter country they are closely allied with the Slovaks, and many of them speak the Slovak language. They are all of the Greek Rite, and with the exception of those in Russia and Bukovina are Catholics. They use the Russian alphabet for their language, and in Bukovina and a portion of Galicia have a phonetic spelling, thus differing largely from Great Russian, even in words that are common to both.

Their immigration to America commenced in 1880 as labourers in the coal mines of Pennsylvania and Ohio, and has steadily increased ever since. Although they were the poorest class of peasants and labourers, illiterate for the most part and unable to grasp the English language or American customs when they arrived, they have rapidly risen in the scale of prosperity and are now rivalling the other nationalities in progress. Greek Ruthenian churches and institutions are being established upon a substantial basis, and their clergy and schools are steadily advancing. They are scattered all over the United States, and there are now (1911) between 480,000 and 500,000 of them, counting immigrants and native born. Their immigration for the past five years has been as follows: 1907, 24,081; 1908, 12,361; 1909, 15,808; 1910, 27,907; 1911, 17,724; being an average of 20,000 a year. They have chiefly settled in the State of Pennsylvania, over half of them being there; but Ohio, New York, New Jersey, and Illinois have large numbers of them. The Greek Rite in the Slavonic language is firmly established through them in the United States, but they suffer greatly from Russian Orthodox endeavours to lead them from the Catholic Church, as well as from frequent internal dissensions (chiefly of an old-world political nature) among themselves. They have 152 Greek Catholic churches, with a Greek clergy consisting of a Greek Catholic bishop who has his seat at Philadelphia, but without diocesan powers as yet, and 127 priests, of whom 9 are Basilian monks. During 1911 Ruthenian Greek Catholic nuns of the Order of St. Basil were introduced. The Ruthenians have flourishing religious mutual benefit societies, which also assist in the building of Greek churches. The "Soyedineniya Greko-Katolicheskikh Bratstv" (Greek Catholic Union) in its senior division has 509 brotherhoods or councils and 30,255 members, while the junior division has 226 brotherhoods and 15,200 members; the "Russky Narodny Soyus" (Ruthenian National Union) has 301 brotherhoods and 15,200 members; while the "Obshchestvo Russkikh Bratstv" (Society of Russian Brotherhood) has 129 brotherhoods and 7350 members. There are also many Ruthenians who belong to Slovak organizations. The Ruthenians publish some ten papers, of which the "Amerikansky Russky Viestnik", "Svoboda", and "Dushpastyr" are the principal ones.

VII. SERVIANS (*Srbin*; adjective *srpski*, Servian).—This designation applies not only to the inhabitants of the Kingdom of Servia, but includes the people of the following countries forming a geographical although not a political whole: southern Hungary, the Kingdoms of Servia and Montenegro, the Turkish Provinces of Kossovo, Western Macedonia and Novi-Bazar, and the annexed Austrian provinces of Bosnia and Herzegovina. The last two provinces may be said to furnish the shadowy boundary line between the Croatians and the Servians. The two peoples are ethnologically the same, and the Servian and Croatian languages are merely two dialects of the same Slavic tongue. Servians are sometimes called the *Shtokavski*, because the Servian word for "what" is *shto*, while the Croats use the word *cha* for "what", and Croatians are called *Chakavski*. The Croatians are Roman Catholics and use the Roman alphabet (*latinica*), whilst the Servians are Greek Orthodox and use the Cyrillo-Russian alphabet (*cirilica*), with additional signs to express special sounds not found in the Russian. Servians who happen to be Roman Catholics are called *Bunjevaci* (disturbers, dissenters).

Servian immigration to the United States did not commence until about 1892, when several hundred Montenegrins and Servians came with the Dalmatians and settled in California. It began to increase largely in 1903 and was at its highest in 1907. They are largely settled in Pennsylvania, Ohio, and Illinois. There are no governmental statistics showing how many Servians come from Servia and how many from the surrounding provinces. The Servian Government has established a special consular office in New York City to look after Servian immigration. There are now (1911) about 150,000 Servians in the United States. They are located as follows: New England States, 25,000; Middle Atlantic States, 50,000; Middle Western States, 25,000; Western and Pacific States, 25,000; and the remainder throughout the Southern States and Alaska. They have brought with them their Orthodox clergy, and are at present affiliated with the Russian Orthodox Church here although they expect shortly to have their own national bishop. They now (1911) have in the United States 20 churches (of which five are in Pennsylvania) and 14 clergy, of whom 8 are monks and 6 seculars. They publish eight newspapers in Servian, of which "Amerikanski Srbobran" of Pittsburg, "Srbobran" of New York, and "Srpski Glasnik" of San Francisco are the most important. They have a large number of church and patriotic societies, of which the Serb Federation "Sloga" (Concord) with 131 *društva* or councils and over 10,000 members and "Prosvjeta" (Progress), composed of Servians from Bosnia and Herzegovina, are the most prominent.

VIII. SLOVAKS (*Slovak;* adjective *slovenský*, Slovak).—These occupy the north-western portion of the Kingdom of Hungary upon the southern slopes of the Carpathian mountains, ranging over a territory comprising the Counties of Poszony, Nyitra, Bars, Hont, Zólyom, Trencsén, Turocz, Arva, Liptó, Szepes, Sáros, Zemplin, Ung, Abauj, Gömör, and Nógrad. A well-defined ethnical line is all that divides the Slovaks from the Ruthenians and the Magyars. Their language is almost the same as the Bohemian, for they received their literature and their mode of writing it from the Bohemians, and even now nearly all the Protestant Slovak literature is from Bohemian sources. It must be remembered however that the Bohemians and Moravians dwell on the northern side of the Carpathian mountains in Austria, whilst the Slovaks are on the south of the Carpathians and are wholly in Hungary. Between the Moravians and the Slovaks, dwelling so near to one another, the relationship was especially close. The Slovak and Moravian people were among those who first heard the story of Christ from the Slavonic apostles Sts. Cyril and Methodius, and at one time their tribes must have extended down to the Danube and the southern Slavs. The Magyars (Hungarians) came in from Asia and the East, and like a wedge divided this group of northern Slavs from those on the south.

The Slovaks have had no independent history and have endured successively Polish rule, Magyar conquest, Tatar invasions, German invading colonization, Hussite raids from Bohemia, and the dynastic wars of Hungary. In 1848–49, when revolution and rebellion were in the air, the Hungarians began their war against Austria; the Slovaks in turn rose against the Hungarians for their language and national customs, but on the conclusion of peace they were again incorporated as part of Hungary without any of their rights recognized. Later they were ruthlessly put down when they refused to carry out the Hungarian decrees, particularly as they had rallied to the support of the Austrian throne. In 1861 the Slovaks presented their famous Memorandum to the Imperial Throne of Austria, praying for a bill of rights and for their autonomous nationality. Stephen Moyses, the distinguished Slovak Catholic bishop, besought the emperor to grant national and language rights to them. The whole movement awoke popular enthusiasm, Catholics and Protestants working together for the common good. In 1862 high schools were opened for Slovaks; the famous "Slovenska Matica", to publish Slovak books and works of art and to foster the study of the Slovak history and language, was founded; and in 1870 the Catholics also founded the "Society of St. Voytech", which became a powerful helper. Slovak newspapers sprang into existence and 150 reading clubs and libraries were established. After the defeat of the Austrian arms at Sadowa in 1866, pressure was resumed to split the empire into two parts, Austrian and Hungarian, each of which was practically independent. The Slovaks thenceforth came wholly under Hungarian rule. Then the Law of Nationalities was passed which recognized the predominant position of the Magyars, but gave some small recognition to the other minor nationalities, such as the Slovaks, by allowing them to have churches and schools conducted in their own language.

In 1878 the active Magyarization of Hungary was undertaken. The doctrine was mooted that a native of the Kingdom of Hungary could not be a patriot unless he spoke, thought, and felt as a Magyar. A Slovak of education who remained true to his ancestry (and it must be remembered that the Slovaks were there long before the Hungarians came) was considered deficient in patriotism. The most advanced political view was that a compromise with the Slovaks was impossible; that there was but one expedient, to wipe them out as far as possible by assimilation with the Magyars. Slovak schools and institutions were ordered to be closed, the charter of the "Matica" was annulled, and its library and rich historical and artistic collections, as well as its funds, were confiscated. Inequalities of every kind before the law were devised for the undoing of the Slovaks and turning them into Hungarians; so much so that one of their authors likened them to the Irish in their troubles. The Hungarian authorities in their endeavour to suppress the Slovak nationality went even to the extent of taking away Slovak children to be brought up as Magyars, and forbade them to use their language in school and church. The 2,000,000 Catholic Slovaks clung to their language and Slavic customs, but the clergy were educated in their seminaries through the medium of the Magyar tongue and required in their parishes to conform to the state idea. Among the 750,000 Protestant Slovaks the Government went even further by taking control of their synods and bishops. Even Slovak family names were changed to Hungarian ones, and preferment was only through Hungarian channels. Naturally, religion decayed under the stress and strain of repressed nationality. Slovak priests did not perform their duties with ardour or diligence, but confined themselves to the mere routine of canonical obligation. There are no monks or religious orders among the Slovaks and no provision is made for any kind of community life. Catechetical instruction is at a minimum and is required to be given whenever possible through the medium of the Hungarian language. There is no lack of priests in the Slovak country, yet the practice of solemnizing the reception of the first communion by the children is unknown and many other forms of Catholic devotion are omitted. Even the Holy Rosary Society was dissolved, because its devotions and proceedings were conducted in Slovak. The result of governmental restriction of any national expression has been a complete lack of initiative on the part of the Slovak priesthood, and it is needless to speak of the result upon their flocks. In the eastern part of the Slovak territory where there were Slovak-speaking Greek Catholics, they fared slightly better in regard to the attempts to make them Hungarians. There the liturgy was Slavonic and the clergy who used the Magyar tongue still were in close touch with their people through the offices of the Church. All this pressure on the part of the authorities tended to produce an active Slovak emigration to America, while bad harvests and taxation also contributed.

A few immigrants came to America in 1864 and their success brought others. In the late seventies the Slovak exodus was well marked, and by 1882 it was sufficiently important to be investigated by the Hungarian Minister of the Interior and directions given to repress it. The American immigration figures indicate the first important Slovak influx in 1873 when 1300 immigrants came from Hungary, which rose to 4000 in 1880 and to nearly 15,000 in 1884, most of them settling in the mining and industrial regions of Pennsylvania. At first they came from the Counties of Zemplin, Saros, Szepes, and Ung, where there were also many Ruthenians. They were called "Huns" or "Hunkies", and were used at first to fill the places left vacant by strikers. They were very poor and willing to work for little when they arrived, and were accordingly hated by the members of the various unions. The Slovak girls, like the Irish, mostly went into service, and because they had almost no expense for living managed to earn more than the men. To-day the Slovaks of America are beginning to possess a national culture and organization, which presents a striking contrast to the cramped development of their kinsmen in Hungary. Their immigration of late years has ranged annually from 52,368 in 1905 to 33,416 in 1910. Altogether it is estimated that there are now some 560,000 Slovaks in the United States, including the native born. They are spread throughout the country, chiefly in the following states: Pennsylvania, 270,000; Ohio, 75,000; Illinois, 50,000; New Jersey, 50,000; New York, 35,000; Connecticut, 20,000; Indiana, 15,000; Missouri, 10,000; whilst they range from 5000 to a few hundreds in the other states. About 450,000 of them are Roman Catholics, 10,000 Greek Catholics and 95,000 Protestants.

The first Slovak Catholic church in the United States was founded by Rev. Joseph Kossalko at Streator, Illinois, and was dedicated 8 Dec., 1883. Following this he also built St. Joseph's Church at Hazleton, Pennsylvania, in 1884. In 1889 Rev. Stephen Furdek founded the Church of St. Ladislas at Cleveland, Ohio, together with a fine parochial school, both of which were dedicated by Bishop Gilmour. The American bishops were anxious to get Slovak priests for the increasing immigration, and Bishop Gilmour sent Father Furdek to Hungary for that purpose. The Hungarian bishops were unwilling to send Slovak priests at first, but as immigration increased they acceded to the request. At present (1911) the Catholic Slovaks have a clergy consisting of one bishop (Rt. Rev. J. M. Koudelka) and 104 priests, and have 134 churches situated as follows: in Pennsylvania, 81 (Dioceses of Altoona, 10; Erie, 4; Harrisburg, 3; Philadelphia, 15; Pittsburg, 35; and Scranton, 14); in Ohio, 14 (in the Diocese of Cleveland, 12, and Columbus, 2); in Illinois, 10 (in the Archdiocese of Chicago, 7; and Peoria, 3); in New Jersey, 11 (in the Diocese of Newark, 7; and Trenton, 4); in New York, 6; and in the States of Connecticut, 3; Indiana, 2; Wisconsin, 2; and Minnesota, Michigan, Missouri, Alabama, and West Virginia, one each. Some of the Slovak church buildings are very fine specimens of church architecture. There are also 36 Slovak parochial schools, that of Our Lady Mary in Cleveland having 750 pupils. They have also introduced an American order of Slovak nuns, the Sisters of Saints Cyril and Methodius, who are established under the direction of Bishop Hoban in the Diocese of Scranton, where they have four schools.

The Protestant Slovaks followed the example of the Catholics and established their first church at Streator, Illinois, in 1885, and later founded a church at Minneapolis in 1888, and from 1890 to 1894 three churches in Pennsylvania. They now have in the United States 60 Slovak churches and congregations (of which 28 are in Pennsylvania), with 34 ministers (not including some 5 Presbyterian clergymen), who are organized under the name of "The Slovak Evangelical Lutheran Synod of America". The Slovaks have a large number of organizations. The principal Catholic ones are: Prva Katolícka Slovenská Jednota (First Slovak Catholic Union), for men, 33,000 members; Pennsylvánska Slovenská Rimsko a Grécko Katolícka Jednota (Pennsylvania Slovak Roman and Greek Catholic Union), 7500 members; Prva Katolícka Slovenská Ženská Jednota (First Catholic Slovak Women's Union), 12,000 members; Pennsylvánska Slovenská Ženská Jednota (Pennsylvania Slovak Women's Union), 3500 members; Živena (Women's League), 6000 members. There are also: Národný Slovenský Spolok (National Slovak Society), which takes in all Slovaks except Jews, 28,000 members; Evanjelícka Slovenská Jednota (Evangelical Lutheran Slovak Union), 8000 members; Kalvinská Slovenská Jednota (Presbyterian Slovak Union), 1000 members; Neodvislý Národny Slovenský Spolok (Independent National Slovak Society), 2000 members. They also have a large and enterprising Press, publishing some fourteen papers. The chief ones are: "Slovenský Denník" (Slovak Journal), a daily, of Pittsburg; "Slovak v Amerike" (Slovak in America), of New York; "Narodne Noviny" (National News), a weekly, of Pittsburg, Pennsylvania, with 38,000 circulation; "Jednota" (The Union), also a weekly, of Middletown, Pennsylvania, with 35,000 circulation; and "Bratstvo" (Brotherhood) of Wilkes-Barre, Pennsylvania. There are also Protestant and Socialistic Slovak journals, whose circulation is small. Among the distinguished Slovaks in the United States may be mentioned Rev. Joseph Murgas of Wilkes-Barre, who, in addition to his work among his people, has perfected several inventions in wireless telegraphy and is favourably known in other scientific matters.

IX. SLOVENES (*Slovenec;* adjective *slovenski*, Slovenian).—These come chiefly from south-western Austria, from the Provinces of Carniola (*Kranjsko;* Ger., *Krain*), Carinthia (*Koroško;* Ger., *Kärnten*), and Styria (*Štajersko;* Ger., *Steiermark*); as well as from Resia (*Resja*) and Udine (*Videm*) in north-eastern Italy, and the Coast Lands (*Primorsko*) of Austria-Hungary. Their neighbours on the south-west are Italians; on the west and north, Germans; on the east, Germans and Magyars; and towards the south, Italians and their Slavic neighbours the Croatians. Most of them are bilingual, speaking not only the Slovenian but also the German language. For this reason they are not so readily distinguishable in America as the other Slavs, and have less trouble in assimilating themselves. At home the main centres of their language and literature have been Laibach (Ljubljana), Klagenfurt (Celovec), Graz (Gradec), and Görz (Gorica), the latter city being also largely Italian. In America they are sometimes known as Austrians, but are more often known as "Krainer", that being the German adjective of *Krain* (Carniola), from whence the larger number of them come to the United States; sometimes the word has even been mispronounced and set down as "Griner". The Slovenes became known somewhat early in the history of the United States. Father Frederic Baraga was among the first of them to come here in 1830, and began his missionary work as a priest among the Indians of Michigan, Wisconsin, and Minnesota, and finally became the first Bishop of Marquette, Michigan. He studied the Indian languages and wrote their grammars and history in his various English, German, and Slovenian works. He also published several catechisms and religious works in Slovenian, and brought over several other Slovenian priests.

In Calumet, Michigan, the Slovenes settled as early as 1856; they first appeared in Chicago and in Iowa about 1863, and in 1866 they founded their chief farming colony in Brockway, Minnesota. Here they still preserve their own language and all their minute local peculiarities. They came to Omaha in 1868, and in 1873 their present large colony in Joliet, Illinois, was founded. Their earliest settlement in New York was towards the end of 1878, and gradually their numbers have increased until they have churches in Haverstraw and Rockland Lake, where their language is used. They have also established farm settlements in Iowa, South Dakota, Idaho, Washington, and in additional places in Minnesota. Their very active immigration began in 1892, and has been (1900–1910) at the rate of from 6000 to 9000 annually, but has lately fallen off. The official government statistics class them along with the Croatians. There are now (1911) in the United States a little over 120,000 Slovenes; practically all of them are Catholics, and with no great differences or factions among them. There is a leaning towards Socialism in the large mining and manufacturing centres. In Pennsylvania there are about 30,000; in Ohio, 15,000; in Illinois, 12,000; in Michigan, 8000; in Minnesota, 12,000; in Colorado, 10,000; in Washington, 10,000; in Montana, 5000; in California, 5000; and in fact there are Slovenes reported in almost every state and territory except Georgia. Their immigration was caused by the poverty of the people at home, especially as Carniola is a rocky and mountainous district without much fertility, and neglected even from the times of the Turkish wars. Latterly the institution of Raffeisen banks, debt-paying and mutual aid associations, introduced among the people by the Catholic party (Slovenska Ljudska Stranka), has diminished immigration and enabled them to live more comfortably at home.

The Slovenes are noted for their adaptability, and have given many prominent missionary leaders to the Church in the United States. Among them are Bishops Baraga, Mrak, and Vertin (of Marquette), Stariha (of Lead), and Trobec (of St. Cloud); Monsignori Stibil, Buh, and Plut; Abbot Bernard Locnika, O.S.B.; and many others. There are some 92 Slovenian priests in the United States, and twenty-five Slovenian churches. Many of their churches are quite fine, especially St. Joseph's, Joliet, Illinois; St. Joseph's, Calumet, Michigan; and Sts. Cyril and Methodius, Sheboygan, Wisconsin. There are also mixed parishes where the Slovenes are united with other nationalities, usually with Bohemians, Slovaks, or Germans. There are no exclusively Slovenian religious communities. At St. John's, Minnesota, there are six Slovenian Benedictines, and at Rockland Lake, New York, three Slovenian Franciscans, who are undertaking to establish a Slovenian and Croatian community. From them much of the information herein has been obtained. The Franciscan nuns at Joliet, Illinois, have many Slovenian sisters; at Kansas City, Kansas, there are several Slovenian sisters engaged in school work; and there are some Slovenians among the Notre Dame Sisters of Cleveland, Ohio. Archbishop Ireland of St. Paul, Minnesota, sent to Austria for Slovenian seminarians to finish their education here, and also appointed three Slovenian priests as professors in his diocesan seminary, thus providing a Slovenian-American clergy for their parishes in his province.

There are several church and benevolent organizations among the Slovenians in America. The principal ones are: Kranjsko Slovenska Katoliška Jednota (Krainer Slovenian Catholic Union), organized in April, 1894, now having 100 councils and a membership of 12,000; Jugoslovenska Katoliška Jednota (South Slovenian Catholic Union), organized in Jan., 1901, having 90 councils and 8000 members; besides these there are also Slovenska Zapadna Zveza (Slovenian Western Union), with 30 councils and about 3000 members, Društva Sv. Barbara (St. Barbara Society), with 80 councils, chiefly among miners, and the semi-socialistic Delvaska Podporna Zveza (Workingmen's Benevolent Union), with 25 councils and a considerable membership. There are also Sv. Rafaelova Družba (St. Raphael's Society), to assist Slovenian immigrants founded by Father Kasimir, O.F.M., and the Society of Sts. Cyril and Methodius to assist Slovenian schools, as well as numerous singing and gymnastic organizations. The Slovenians publish ten newspapers in the United States. The oldest is the Catholic weekly "Amerikanski Slovenec" (American Slovene), established in 1891 at Joliet, and it is the organ of the Krainer Slovenian Catholic Union. "Glas Naroda" (Voice of the People), established in 1892 in New York City, is a daily paper somewhat Liberal in its views, but it is the official organ of the South Slavonic Catholic Union and the St. Barbara Society. "Ave Maria" is a religious monthly published by the Franciscans of Rockland Lake, New York. "Glasnik" (The Herald) is a weekly of Calumet, Michigan; as are also "Edinost" (Unity), of Pittsburg, Pennsylvania; "Clevelandska Amerika", of Cleveland, Ohio; "Narodni Vestnik" (People's Messenger), of Duluth, Minnesota; and "Slovenski Narod" (Slovenian People), of Pueblo, Colorado. There are also two purely Socialistic weeklies in Chicago: "Proletarec" (Proletarian) and "Glas Svobode" (Voice of Freedom). A very fine work, "Amerika in Amerikanci" (America and the Americans), descriptive of all the United States and Slovenian life and development here, has been published by Father J. M. Trunk at Klagenfurt, Austria.

BALCH, *Our Slavic Fellow Citizens* (New York, 1910); HOUST, *Krátké Dějiny a Seznam Česko-Katolických Osad ve Spoj. Státech Amerických* (St. Louis, 1890); KOHLBECK, *The Catholic Bohemians of the United States* in *Champlain Educator*, (New York, Jan.-Mar., 1906); xxv, 36–54; KALEFF, *V Amerika* (Madison, 1911); ZORIČIČ, *Naši izseljenici u Sjedinj. Drzavami Amerikim* (Agram, 1900); RADIC, *Moderna Kolonizacija i Slaveni* (Agram, 1904); KRUSZKA, *Historya Polska w Ameryce* (Milwaukee, 1905–09); JANIK, *Ludność Polska w Ameryce* (Lemberg, 1905); KRAITSER, *The Poles in the United States of America* (Philadelphia, 1907); *Pravoslavny Kalendar* (New York, 1900–12); *Amerikanski Russki Miesiatsoslov* (Homestead, 1907–12); FURDEK, *Život Slovakov v Amerike* in *Tovaryšstvo*, III (Ruzomberok, 1890); SETON-WATSON, *Racial Problems in Hungary* (London, 1908); FURDEK, *Catholic Slovaks of Hungary* (Wilkes-Barre, 1906); ČAPEK, *The Slovaks of Hungary* (New York, 1906); STEAD, *Servia by the Servians* (London, 1909); DURHAM, *Through the Lands of the Serb* (London, 1904); *Kalendar Sloga* (New York, 1912); ŠUMAN, *Die Slovenen* (Vienna, 1881); ŠUSTERŠIČ, *Poduk Rojakom Slovencem* (Joliet, 1903); TRUNK, *Amerika in Amerikanci* (Klagenfurt, 1911–12); *Reports of the Commissioner of Immigration* (Washington, 1900–12).

ANDREW J. SHIPMAN.

Slomšek, ANTON MARTIN, Bishop of Lavant, in Maribor, Styria, Austria, noted Slovenian educator, b. 1800; d. 24 Sept., 1862. The dawn of the nineteenth century found the Slovenian schools in a precarious condition; their number was pitifully small, and the courses they offered were inadequate and unsatisfactory. This deplorable state was due to the fact that the Austrian officials endeavoured to suppress the national language, and, to compass this end, introduced foreign teachers thoroughly distasteful to the people, whom in turn they despised. Moreover, books, magazines, papers, and other educational influences were lacking, not because they would not have been gladly welcomed, but because they were forbidden by the Government in its fear of Panslavism. This situation Bishop Slomšek was compelled to face. A man of initiative and discernment, the changes he wrought in a short time were wonderful. In the Constitution of 1848, granting national rights long denied, he found his instrument. Following this measure, though only after many futile attempts, he received official sanction to undertake the reform of the schools. The first fruits of his labours were a series of excellent text-books, many from his own pen, which proved powerful factors in the growth and development of religious as well as national education. The founding of the weekly, "Drobtinice" (Crumbs), was his next step. Essays and books on a great variety of subjects, embracing practically every question on which his countrymen stood in need of enlightenment, were published in quick succession, and his vigorous and incisive style, well adapted to the intelligence of his readers, though not lacking scholarly refinement, made his works exceedingly popular. His pastorals and sermons constitute a literature of lasting value. In 1841 he sought to realize a dream of years—the establishment of a society for the spread of Catholic literature. Unfortunately, the movement was branded as Panslavistic, and failed at the time; but ten years later this organization was effected, and *Druzba sv. Mohora* began sending a few instructive books to Catholic homes. To-day, a million educational volumes have been distributed among a million and a half of people.

Although Slomšek was ardent and active in the interests of his own race, yet he was admired and loved by great men of other nations, and his kindness and tact eliminated all bitterness from the controversies in which he was forced to engage. Patriotism, the education of his people. their temporal and spiritual welfare, were his inspiring motives, as the non-Catholic Makusev remarks: "Education, based on religion and nationality, was his lofty aim". Humility and childlike simplicity marked his life. His priests, sincerely devoted to him, frequently heard him repeat the words: "When I was born, my mother laid me on a bed of straw, and I desire no better pallet when I die, asking only to be in the state of grace and worthy of salvation".

GRAFENANER, *Hist. of Slovenian Literature* (1862).

P. CYRIL ZUPAN.

Slotanus (SCHLOTTANUS, VAN DER SLOOTEN), JOHN (JOHN GEFFEN), polemical writer; b. at Geffen, Brabant; d. at Cologne, 9 July, 1560. He joined the Dominican order at Cologne about 1525. For many years he ably defended the Faith against the heretics by preaching and writing. Later he taught sacred letters at Cologne, and in 1554 was made a doctor of theology. About this same time he became prior of his convent at Cologne, and as such exercised the offices of censor of the faith and papal inquisitor throughout the Archdiocese of Cologne and the Rhine country. In the discharge of these responsible duties Slotanus came into conflict with the learned Justus Velsius, who in 1556, on account of heretical teachings, was obliged to leave Cologne. The vehement writings which Velsius afterwards published against the Cologne theologians moved Slotanus to write two works in which nearly all the heretical doctrines of his time are discussed with admirable skill.

Among his various works those most worthy of mention are: "Disputationum adversus hæreticos liber unus" (Cologne, 1558); "De retinenda fide orthodoxa et catholica adversus hæreses et sectas" (Cologne, 1560); "De barbaris nationibus convertendis ad Christum" (Cologne, 1559). In the last-named work Slotanus witnesses to the ardent missionary zeal which fired the religious men of his time.

ECHARD, *Script. Ord. Præd.*, II, 175; HURTER, *Nomenclator*; MEUSER, *Zur Geschichte der Kölner Theologen im 16. Jahrh.* in *Kath. Zeitschr. für Wissenschaft und Kunst*, II (Cologne, 1845), 79 sq.; PAULUS, *Kölner Dominicanerschriftsteller a.d. 16. Jahrh.* in *Katholik* II (1897) 238 sq.

CHAS. J. CALLAN.

Sloth, one of the seven capital sins. In general it means disinclination to labour or exertion. As a capital or deadly vice St. Thomas (II–II, Q. xxxv) calls it sadness in the face of some spiritual good which one has to achieve (*tristitia de bono spirituali*). Father Rickaby aptly translates its Latin equivalent *acedia* (Gr. ἀκηδία) by saying that it means the don't-care feeling. A man apprehends the practice of virtue to be beset with difficulties and chafes under the restraints imposed by the service of God. The narrow way stretches wearily before him and his soul grows sluggish and torpid at the thought of the painful life journey. The idea of right living inspires not joy but disgust, because of its laboriousness. This is the notion commonly obtaining, and in this sense sloth is not a specific vice according to the teaching of St. Thomas, but rather a circumstance of all vices. Ordinarily it will not have the malice of mortal sin unless, of course, we conceive it to be so utter that because of it one is willing to bid defiance to some serious obligation. St. Thomas completes his definition of sloth by saying that it is torpor in the presence of spiritual good which is Divine good. In other words, a man is then formally distressed at the prospect of what he must do for God to bring about or keep intact his friendship with God. In this sense sloth is directly opposed to charity. It is then a mortal sin unless the act be lacking in entire advertence or full consent of the will. The trouble attached to maintenance of the inhabiting of God by charity arouses tedium in such a person. He violates, therefore, expressly the first and the greatest of the commandments: "Thou shalt love the Lord thy God with thy whole heart, and with thy whole soul, and with thy whole mind, and with thy whole strength." (Mark, xii, 30).

RICKABY, *Moral Teaching of St. Thomas* (London, 1896); SLATER, *Manual of Moral Theology* (New York, 1908); ST. THOMAS, *Summa*, II-II, Q. xxxv; BALLERINI, *Opus theologicum morale* (Prato, 1898).

JOSEPH F. DELANY.

Slythurst, THOMAS, English confessor, b. in Berkshire; d. in the Tower of London, 1560. He was B.A. Oxon, 1530; M.A., 1534; B.D., 1543; and supplicated for the degree of D.D., 1554–5, but never took it. He was rector of Chalfont St. Peter, Bucks, from 1545 to 1555, canon of Windsor, 1554, rector of Chalfont St. Giles, Bucks, 1555, and first President of Trinity College, Oxford. He was deprived of these three preferments in 1559. On 11 Nov., 1556, he was appointed with others by Convocation to regulate the exercises in theology on the election of Cardinal Pole to the chancellorship.

WARTON, *Life of Sir Thomas Pope* (London, 1772), 359; *Catholic Record Society Publications*, I (London, 1905—), 118; FOX, *Acts and Monuments*, VIII (London, 1843–9), 636.

JOHN B. WAINEWRIGHT.

Smalkaldic League, a politico-religious alliance formally concluded on 27 Feb., 1531, at Smalkalden in Hesse-Nassau, among German Protestant princes and cities for their mutual defence. The compact was entered into for six years, and stipulated that any military attack made upon any one of the confederates on account of religion or under any other pretext was to be considered as directed against them all and resisted in common. The parties to it were: the Landgrave Philip of Hesse; the Elector John of Saxony and his son John Frederick; the dukes Philip of Brunswick-Grubenhagen and Otto, Ernest, and Francis of Brunswick-Lüneburg; Prince Wolfgang of Anhalt; the counts Gebhard and Albrecht of Mansfeld and the towns of Strasburg, Ulm, Constance, Reutlingen, Memmingen, Lindau, Biberach, Isny, Magdeburg, and Bremen. The city of Lübeck joined the league on 3 May, and Bavaria on 24 Oct., 1531. The accession of foreign powers, notably England and France, was solicited, and the alliance of the latter nation secured in 1532. The princes of Saxony and Hesse were appointed military commanders of the confederation, and its military strength fixed at 10,000 infantry and 2000 cavalry. At a meeting held at Smalkalden in Dec., 1535, the alliance was renewed for ten years, and the maintenance of the former military strength decreed, with the stipulation that it should be doubled in case of emergency. In April, 1536, Dukes Ulrich of Würtemberg and Barnim and Philip of Pomerania, the cities of Frankfort, Augsburg, Hamburg, and Hanover joined the league with several other new confederates. An alliance was concluded with Denmark in 1538, while the usual accession of the German Estates which accepted the Reformation continued to strengthen the organization. Confident of its support, the Protestant princes introduced the new religion in numerous districts, suppressed bishoprics, confiscated church property, resisted imperial ordinances to the extent of refusing help against the Turks, and disregarded the decisions of the Imperial Court of Justice.

In self-defence against the treasonable machinations of the confederation, a Catholic League was formed in 1538 at Nuremberg under the leadership of the emperor. Both sides now actively prepared for an armed conflict, which seemed imminent. But negotiations carried on at the Diet of Frankfort in 1539 resulted, partly owing to the illness of the Landgrave of Hesse, in the patching up of a temporary peace. The emperor during this respite renewed his earnest but fruitless efforts to effect a religious settlement, while the Smalkaldic confederates continued their violent proceedings against the Catholics, particularly in the territory of Brunswick-Wolfenbüttel, where Duke Henry was unjustly expelled, and the new religion introduced (1542). It became more and more evident as time went on that a conflict was unavoidable. When, in 1546, the emperor adopted stern measures against some of the confederates, the War of Smalkalden ensued. Although it was mainly a religious conflict between Catholics and Protestants, the denominational lines were not sharply drawn. With Pope Paul III, who promised financial and military assistance, several Protestant princes, the principal among whom was Duke Maurice of Saxony, defended the imperial and Catholic cause. The beginning of hostilities was marked nevertheless by the success of the Smalkaldic allies; but division and irresoluteness soon weakened them and caused their ruin in Southern Germany, where princes and cities submitted in rapid succession. The battle of Mühlberg (24 April, 1547) decided the issue in favour of the emperor in the north. The Elector John Frederick of Saxony was captured, and shortly after the Landgrave Philip of Hesse was also forced to submit. The conditions of peace included the transfer of the electoral dignity from the former to his cousin Maurice, the reinstatement of Duke Henry of Wolfenbüttel in his dominions, the restoration of Bishop Julius von Pflug to his See of Naumburg-Zeitz, and a promise demanded of the vanquished to recognize and attend the Council of Trent. The dissolution of the Smalkaldic League followed; the imperial success was complete, but temporary. A few years later another conflict broke out and ended with the triumph of Protestantism.

WINCKELMANN, *Der Schmalkald. Bund (1530–32) u. der Nürnberger Religionsfriede* (Strasburg, 1892); HASENCLEVER, *Die Politik der Schmalkaldener vor Ausbruch des Schmalkald. Krieges* (Berlin, 1901); IDEM, *Die Politik Kaiser Karls V u. Landgraf Philipps von Hessen vor Ausbruch des Schmalkald. Krieges* (Marburg, 1903); BERENTELG, *Der Schmalkald. Krieg in Norddeutschland* (Münster, 1908); JANSSEN, *Hist. of the German People*, tr. CHRISTIE, V (St. Louis, 1903), passim; PASTOR, *History of the Popes*, tr. KERR, X (St. Louis, 1910), 166 sqq.

N. A. WEBER.

Smaragdus, ARDO, hagiographer, d. at the Benedictine monastery of Aniane, Herault, in Southern France, March, 843. He entered this monastery when still a boy and was brought up under the direction of Abbot St. Benedict of Aniane. On account of his piety and talents he was ordained and put at the head of the school at his monastery. In 794 he accompanied his abbot to the Council of Frankfort and in 814 was made abbot in place of Benedict, who on the invitation of Louis-le-Debonnaire had taken up his abode at the imperial Court at Aix-la-Chapelle. Smaragdus was honoured as a saint in his monastery. He is the author of a life of St. Benedict of Aniane which he wrote at the request of the monks of Cornelimünster near Aix-la-Chapelle, where Abbot Benedict had died. It was written in 822, and is one of the most reliable hagiological productions of that period. Mabillon edited it in his "Acta SS. of the Benedictine Order" (sæculum IV, I, 192–217), whence it was reprinted in P. L., CIII, 353–84. It was also edited by Waitz in "Mon. Germ. Script.", XV, I, 200–29.

Histoire Lit. de la France, V, 31–5; CEILLIER, *Histoire générale des auteurs sacrés et ecclésiastiques*, XII (Paris, 1862), 394; MABILLON, *Acta SS. Ord. S. Ben.* sæc. IV, I, 589; EBERT, *Allgemeine Gesch. der Literatur des Mittelalters*, II (Leipzig, 1880), 345–8.

MICHAEL OTT.

Smith, GEORGE. See ARGYLL AND THE ISLES, DIOCESE OF.

Smith, JAMES, journalist, b. at Skolland, in the Shetland Isles, about 1790; d. Jan., 1866. He spent his boyhood at Skolland, a small place belonging to his mother, who was a member of a branch of the Bruce family which had settled in Shetland in the sixteenth century. He studied law in Edinburgh, became a solicitor to the Supreme Court there, and married a Catholic lady (a cousin of Bishop Macdonell of the Glengarry clan), the result being his own conversion to Catholicism. Naturally hampered in his career, at that period, by his profession of Catholicism, he turned his attention to literature, and became the pioneer of Catholic journalism in Scotland. In 1832 he originated and edited the "Edinburgh Catholic Magazine", which appeared somewhat intermittently in Scotland until April, 1838, at which date Mr. Smith went to reside in London, and the word "Edinburgh" was dropped from the title of the magazine, the publication of which was continued for some years in London. Mr. Smith, on settling in London, inaugurated the "Catholic Directory" for England, in succession to the old "Laity's Directory", and edited it for many years; and he was also for a short time editor of the "Dublin Review", in 1837. Possessed of considerable gifts both as a speaker and as a writer, he was always ready to put them at the service of the Catholic cause; and during the years of agitation immediately preceding Catholic Emancipation, as well as at a later period, he was one of the most active champions of the Church in England and Scotland. He made a brilliant defence in public of Catholic doctrine when it was violently attacked by certain prominent members of the Established Church of Scotland, and published in this connexion, in 1831, his "Dialogues on the Catholic and Protestant Rules of Faith", between a member of the Protestant Reformation Society and a Catholic layman. He also edited (1838) Challoner's abridgment of Gother's "Papist Misrepresented and Represented", with copious notes. Mr. Smith was father of the Most Rev. William Smith, second Archbishop of St. Andrews and Edinburgh in the restored hierarchy of Scotland, and a distinguished Biblical scholar.

GILLOW, *Bibl. Dict. Eng. Cath.*, s. v.; *Catholic Directory for Scotland* (1893), 264.

D. O. HUNTER-BLAIR.

Smith, JAMES A. See SAINT ANDREWS AND EDINBURGH, ARCHDIOCESE OF.

Smith, RICHARD, Bishop of Chalcedon, second Vicar Apostolic of England; b. at Hanworth, Lincolnshire, Nov., 1568 (not 1566 as commonly stated); d. at Paris, 18 March, 1655. He was educated at Trinity College, Oxford, where he became a Catholic. He was admitted to the English College, Rome, in 1586, studied under Bellarmine, and was ordained priest 7 May, 1592. In Feb., 1593, he arrived at Valladolid, where he took the degree of Doctor of Theology, and taught philosophy at the English College till 1598, when he went to Seville as professor of controversies. In 1603 he went on the English mission, where he made his mark as a missioner. Chosen to represent the case of the secular clergy in the archpriest controversy, he went to Rome, where he opposed Persons, who said of him: "I never dealt with any man in my life more heady and resolute in his opinions". In 1613 he became superior of the small body of English secular priests at Arras College, Paris, who devoted themselves to controversial work. In 1625 he was elected to succeed Dr. Bishop as vicar Apostolic, but the date usually assigned for his consecration as Bishop of Chalcedon (12 Jan., 1625) must be wrong, as he was not elected till 2 Jan. He arrived in England in April, of the same year, residing in Lord Montagu's house at Turvey, Bedfordshire. As vicar Apostolic he came into conflict with the regulars, claiming the rights of an ordinary, but Urban VIII decided (16 Dec., 1627) that he was not an ordinary. In 1628 the Government issued a proclamation for his arrest, and in 1631 he withdrew to Paris, where he lived with Richelieu till the cardinal's death in 1642; then he retired to the convent of the English Augustinian nuns, where he died.

He wrote: "An answer to T. Bel's late Challenge" (1605); "The Prudentiall Ballance of Religion", (1609); "Vita Dominæ Magdalenæ Montis-Acuti" i. e., Viscountess Montagu (1609); "De auctore et essentia Protestanticæ Religionis" (1619), English translation, 1621; "Collatio doctrinæ Catholicorum et Protestantium" (1622), tr. (1631); "Of the distinction of fundamental and not fundamental points of faith" (1645); "Monita quædam utilia pro Sacerdotibus, Seminaristis, Missionariis Angliæ" (1647); "A Treatise of the best kinde of Confessors" (1651); "Of the all-sufficient Eternal Proposer of Matters of Faith" (1653); "Florum Historiæ Ecclesiasticæ gentis Anglorum libri septem" (1654). Many unpublished documents relating to his troubled episcopate (an impartial history of which yet remains to be written) are preserved in the Westminster Diocesan Archives.

DODD, *Church History*, III (Brussels *vere* Wolverhampton, 1737–1742) the account from which most subsequent biographies were derived. See also Tierney's edition of Dodd for further documents; BERINGTON, *Memoirs of Panzani* (London, 1793); *Calendar State Papers: Dom., 1625–1631*; BUTLER, *Historical Memoirs of English Catholics* (London, 1819); SERGEANT, *Account of the English Chapter* (London, 1853); FULLERTON, *Life of Luisa de Carvajal* (London, 1873); FOLEY, *Records Eng. Prov. S.J.*, VI (London, 1880); BRADY, *Episcopal Succession*, III (Rome, 1877), a confused and self-contradictory account with some new facts; ALGER in *Dict. Nat. Biog.*; GILLOW, *Bibl. Dict. Eng. Cath.*; CEDOZ, *Couvent de Religieuses Anglaises à Paris* (Paris, 1891); *Third Douay Diary*, C. R. S. Publications, X (London, 1911).

EDWIN BURTON.

Smith, RICHARD, b. in Worcestershire, 1500; d. at Douai, 9 July, 1563. He was educated at Merton College, Oxford; and, having taken his M.A. degree in 1530, he became registrar of the university in 1532. In 1536 Henry VIII appointed him first Regius Professor of divinity, and he took his doctorate in that subject on 10 July in the same year. He subsequently became master of Whittington College, London; rector of St. Dunstan's-in-the-East; rector of Cuxham, Oxfordshire; principal of St. Alban's Hall; and divinity reader at Magdalen College. Under Edward VI he is said by his opponents to have abjured the pope's authority at St. Paul's Cross (15 May, 1547) and at Oxford, but the accounts of the proceedings are obscure and unreliable. If he yielded at all, he soon recovered and accordingly suffered the loss of his professorship, being succeeded by Peter Martyr, with whom he held a public disputation in 1549. Shortly afterwards he was arrested, but was soon liberated. Going to Louvain, he became professor of divinity there. During Mary's Catholic restoration he regained most of his preferments, and was made royal chaplain and canon of Christ Church. He took a prominent part in the proceedings against Cranmer, Ridley, and Latimer. He again lost all his benefices at the change of religion under Elizabeth, and after a short imprisonment in Parker's house he escaped to Douai, where he was appointed by Philip II dean of St. Peter's church. There is no foundation for the slanderous story spread by the Reformers to account for his deprivation of his Oxford professorship. When Douai University was founded on 5 Oct., 1562, he was installed as chancellor and professor of theology, but only lived a few months to fill these offices. He wrote many works, the chief of which are: "Assertion and Defence of the Sacrament of the Altar" (1546); "Defence of the Sacrifice of the Mass" (1547); "Defensio cœlibatus sacerdotum" (1550); "Diatriba de hominis justificatione" (1550); "Buckler of the Catholic Faith" (1555–56); "De Missæ Sacrificio" (1562); and several refutations of Calvin, Melanchthon, Jewell, and Beza, all published in 1562.

FOSTER, *Alumni Oxonienses*, IV (Oxford, 1891); PITS, *De illustribus Angliæ Scriptoribus* (Paris, 1619); DODD, *Church History*,

II (Brussels *vere* Wolverhampton, 1737–42); GAIRDNER, *Letters and Papers of Henry VIII*; COOPER, *Dict. Nat. Biog.*, s. v.

EDWIN BURTON.

Smith, THOMAS KILBY, b. at Boston, Mass., 23 Sept., 1820; d. at New York, 14 Dec., 1887; eldest son of Captain George Smith and Eliza Bicker Walter. Both his paternal and maternal forefathers were active and prominent in the professional life and in the government of New England. His parents moved to Cincinnati in his early childhood, where he was educated in a military school under O. M. Mitchel, the astronomer, and studied law in the office of Chief Justice Salmon P. Chase. In 1853 he was appointed special agent in the Post Office Department at Washington, and later marshal for the Southern District of Ohio and deputy clerk of Hamilton County. He entered the Union Army, 9 September, 1861, as lieutenant-colonel, and was conspicuous in the Battle of Shiloh, 6 and 7 April, 1862, assuming command of Stuart's Brigade, Sherman's Division, during the second day. As commander of brigade in the 15th and 17th Army Corps, he participated in all the campaigns of the Army of the Tennessee, being also for some months on staff duty with General Grant.

Commissioned Brigadier-General of Volunteers, 11 August, 1863, he was assigned on 7 March, 1864, to the command of the detached division of the 17th Army Corps and rendered distinguished service during the Red River Expedition, protecting Admiral Porter's fleet after the disaster of the main army. After the fall of Mobile, he assumed the command of the Department of Southern Alabama and Florida, and then of the Post and District of Maine. He was brevetted Major-General for gallant and meritorious service. In 1866 President Johnson appointed him United States Consul at Panama. After the war he removed to Torresdale, Philadelphia. At the time of his death he was engaged in journalism in New York. On 2 May, 1848, he married Elizabeth Budd, daughter of Dr. William Budd McCullough and Arabella Sanders Piatt, of Cincinnati, Ohio. She was a gifted and devout woman, and through her influence and that of the venerable Archbishop Purcell he became a Catholic some years before his death. He was remarkable for his facility of expression, distinguished personal appearance, and courtly bearing. He left five sons and three daughters.

SMITH, *Life and Letters of Thomas Kilby Smith* (New York, 1898).

WALTER GEORGE SMITH.

Smyrna, LATIN ARCHDIOCESE OF (SMYRNENSIS), in Asia Minor. The city of Smyrna rises like an amphitheatre on the gulf which bears its name. It is the capital of the vilayet of Aïdin and the starting-point of several railways; it has a population of at least 300,000, of whom 150,000 are Greeks. There are also numerous Jews and Armenians and almost 10,000 European Catholics. It was founded more than 1000 years B. C. by colonists from Lesbos who had expelled the Leleges, at a place now called Bournabat, about an hour's distance from the present Smyrna. Shortly before 688 B. C. it was captured by the Ionians, under whose rule it became a very rich and powerful city (Herodotus, I, 150). About 580 B. C. it was destroyed by Alyattes, King of Lydia. Nearly 300 years afterwards Antigonus (323–301 B. C.), and then Lysimachus, undertook to rebuild it on its present site. Subsequently comprised in the Kingdom of Pergamus, it was ceded in 133 B. C. to the Romans. These built there a judiciary *conventus* and a mint. Smyrna had a celebrated school of rhetoric, was one of the cities which had the title of metropolis, and in which the *concilium festivum* of Asia was celebrated. Demolished by an earthquake in A. D. 178 and 180, it was rebuilt by Marcus Aurelius. In 673 it was captured by a fleet of Arab Mussulmans.

Under the inspiration of Clement VI the Latins captured it from the Mussulmans in 1344 and held it until 1402, when Tamerlane destroyed it after slaying the inhabitants. In 1424 the Turks captured it and, save for a brief occupation by the Venetians in 1472, it has since belonged to them.

Christianity was preached to the inhabitants at an early date. As early as the year 93, there existed a Christian community directed by a bishop for whom St. John in the Apocalypse (i, 11; ii, 8–11) has only words of praise. There are extant two letters written early in the second century from Troas by St. Ignatius of Antioch to those of Smyrna and to Polycarp, their bishop. Through these letters and those of the Christians of Smyrna to the city of Philomelium, we know of two ladies of high rank who belonged to the Church of Smyrna. There were other Christians in the vicinity of the city and dependent on it to whom St. Polycarp wrote letters (Eusebius, "Hist. eccl.", V, xxiv). When Polycarp was martyred (23 Feb.), the Church of Smyrna sent an encyclical concerning his death to the Church of Philomelium and others. The "Vita Polycarpi" attributed to St. Pionius, a priest of Smyrna martyred in 250, contains a list of the first bishops: Stratæs; Bucolus; Polycarp; Papirius; Camerius; Eudæmon (250), who apostatized during the persecution of Decius; Thraseas of Eumenia, martyr, who was buried at Smyrna. Noctos, a Modalist heretic of the second century, was a native of the city as were also Sts. Pothinus and Irenæus of Lyons. Mention should also be made of another martyr, St. Dioscorides, venerated on 21 May. Among the Greek bishops, a list of whom appears in Le Quien, (Oriens Christ., I, 737–46), was Metrophanes, the great opponent of Photius, who laboured in the revision of the "Octoekos", a Greek liturgical book.

The Latin See of Smyrna was created by Clement VI in 1346 and had an uninterrupted succession of titulars until the seventeenth century. This was the beginning of the Vicariate Apostolic of Asia Minor, or of Smyrna, of vast extent. In 1818 Pius VII established the Archdiocese of Smyrna, at the same time retaining the vicariate Apostolic, the jurisdiction of which was wider. Its limits were those of the vicariates Apostolic of Mesopotamia, Syria, and Constantinople. The archdiocese had 17,000 Latin Catholics, some Greek Melchites, called Alepi, and Armenians under special organization. There are: 19 secular priests; 55 regulars; 8 parishes, of which 4 are in Smyrna; 14 churches with resident priests and 12 without priests; 25 primary schools with 2500 pupils, 8 colleges or academies with 800 pupils; 2 hospitals; and 4 orphanages. The religious men in the archdiocese or the vicariate Apostolic are Franciscans, Capuchins, Lazarists, Dominicans, Salesians of Don Bosco, Assumptionists (at Koniah), Brothers of the Christian Schools, and Marist Brothers (at Metellin). Religious communities of women are the Carmelites, Sisters of Charity (13 houses with more than 100 sisters), Sisters of Sion, Dominicans of Ivrée, Sisters of St. Joseph, and Oblates of the Assumption.

SMITH, *Dict. of Greek and Roman Geogr.*, s. v.; HAMILTON, *Researches in Asia Minor*, I (London, 1842), 44–95; TEXIER, *Asie Mineure* (Paris, 1862), 302–08; SCHERZER, *Smyrna* (Vienna, 1873); RAMSAY, *The Letters to the Seven Churches of Asia* (London, 1904), 251–57; GEORGIADÈS, *Smyrne* (Paris, 1885); ROUGON, *Smyrne* (Paris, 1892); LE CAMUS, *Les sept églises de l'Apocalypse* (Paris, 1896); FILLION in VIG., *Dict. de la Bible*, s. v.; *Missiones Catholicæ* (Rome, 1907), 155–57; LAMPAKÈS, *The Seven Stars of the Apocalypse* (Athens, 1909), in Greek; JEAN-BAPTISTE DE SAINT-LORENZO, *Saint Polycarpe et son tombeau sur le Pagus. Notice sur le ville de Smyrne* (Constantinople, 1911).

S. VAILHÉ.

Snorri Sturluson, historian, b. at Hvammr, 1178; d. 1241. Snorri, who was the son of Sturla Thortsson (d. 1182), was the most important Icelandic historian of the Middle Ages. In him were united the experienced statesman and the many-sided scholar. As a child he went to the school of Saemund the Wise at Oddi, of which, at that time, Saemund's grandson Jón Loptsson was the head. On his father's side Jón was related to the most distinguished families of Iceland, while by his mother Thora he was connected with the royal family of Norway. Under this skilful teacher Snorri was thoroughly trained in many branches of knowledge, but he learned especially the old northern belief in the gods, the saga concerning Odin, and Scandinavian history. By a rich alliance Snorri obtained the money to take a leading part in politics, but his political course brought him many dangerous enemies, among whom King Haakon of Norway was the most powerful, and he was finally murdered at the king's instigation. Snorri's importance rests on his literary works of which "Heimskringla" (the world) is the most important, since it is the chief authority for the early history of Iceland and Scandinavia. However, it does not contain reliable statements until the history, which extends to 1177, reaches a late period, while the descriptions of the primitive era are largely vague narrations of sagas. The Sturlunga-Saga, which shows more of the local colouring of Iceland, was probably only partly the work of Snorri. On the other hand he is probably the author of the Younger Edda called "Snorra-Edda", which was intended as a textbook of the art of poetry. Its first part "Gylfaginning" relates the mythology of the North in an interesting, pictorial manner, and is a compilation of the songs of the early scalds, the songs of the common people, sagas, and probably his own poetic ideas.

STORM, *Snorra Sturlassons Historiæskrivning* (Copenhagen, 1873); BAUMGARTNER, *Nordische Fahrten*, I (Freiburg, 1889), 302 sqq.; SCHÜCK, *Svensk Literaturhistoria*, I (Stockholm, 1890); LUNDBORG, *Islands staatsrechtliche Stellung von der Freistaatszeit bis in unsere Tage* (Berlin, 1908), 17–18; OBRIK, *Nordisches Geistesleben*, tr. RANISCH (Heidelberg, 1908), 116, 145–50.

PIUS WITTMANN.

Snow, PETER, VENERABLE, English martyr, suffered at York, 15 June, 1598. He was born at or near Ripon, and arrived at the English College, Reims, 17 April, 1589, receiving the first tonsure and minor orders 18 August, 1590, the subdiaconate at Laon on 22 Sept., and the diaconate and priesthood at Soissons on 30 and 31 March, 1591. He left for England on the following 15 May. He was arrested about 1 May, 1598, when on his way to York with Venerable Ralph Grimston of Nidd. Both were shortly after condemned, Snow of treason as being a priest and Grimston of felony, for having aided and assisted him, and, it is said, having attempted to prevent his apprehension.

CHALLONER, *Missionary Priests*, I, no. 112; KNOX, *Douay Diaries* (London, 1878).

JOHN B. WAINEWRIGHT.

Sobaipura Indians, once an important tribe of the Piman branch of the great Shoshonean linguistic stock, occupying the territory of the Santa Cruz and San Pedro Rivers, in south-eastern Arizona and adjacent portion of Sonora, Mexico. In dialect and general custom they seem to have closely resembled the Pápago, by whom and by the closely cognate Pima most of them were finally absorbed. Their principal centre was Bac or Vaaki, later San Xavier del Bac, on Santa Cruz River, nine miles south from the present Tucson, Arizona. Here they were visited in 1692 by the pioneer Jesuit explorer of the south-west, Father Eusebio Kino, who in 1699 began the church from which the mission took its name. Other Jesuit mission foundations in the same tribe were (Santa Maria de) Suamca, just inside the Sonora line, established also by Kino about the same time, and San Miguel de Guevavi, founded in 1732 near the present Nogales, Arizona, all three missions being upon the Santa Cruz River. There were also several visiting stations. The missions shared the misfortunes attending those of the Pima and Pápago, but continued to exist until a few years after the expulsion of the Jesuits in 1767. Before the end of the century the tribe itself had disappeared, and in later years San Xavier appears as a Pápago settlement. According to tradition the tribe was destroyed about the year 1790 by the attacks of the wild Apache, by whom a part were carried off, while the others were forced to incorporate with the Pápago and Pima (q. v.).

BANCROFT, *Hist. North Mexican States and Texas* (2 vols., San Francisco, 1886–9); IDEM, *Hist. Arizona and New Mexico* (San Francisco, 1889); *Diary of Francisco Garcés, 1775–6*, ed. COUES (2 vols., New York, 1900); HODGE, *Handbook of American Indians* (2 parts, Washington, 1907–10); *Rudo ensayo . . . descripcion geographica de la provincia de Sonora* (1762) (St. Augustine, 1863), tr. GUITÉRAS in *Rec. Am. Cath. Hist. Soc.* (Philadelphia, 1894).

JAMES MOONEY.

Sobieski, JOHN, b. at Olesko in 1629; d. at Wilanow, 1696; son of James, Castellan of Cracow and descended by his mother from the heroic Zołkiewski, who died in battle at Cecora. His elder brother Mark was his companion in arms from the time of the great Cossack rebellion (1648), and fought at Zbaraż, Beresteczko, and lastly at Batoh where, after being taken prisoner, he was murdered by the Tatars. John, the last of all the family, accompanied Czarniecki in the expedition to Denmark; then, under George Lubomirski, he fought the Muscovites at Cudnow. Lubomirski revolting, he remained faithful to the king (John Casimir), became successively Field Hetman, Grand Marshal, and—after Revera Potocki's death—Grand Hetman, or Commander-in-chief. His first exploit as Hetman was in Podhajce, where, besieged by an army of Cossacks and Tatars, he at his own expense raised 8000 men and stored the place with wheat, baffling the foe so completely that they retired with great loss. When, in 1672, under Michael Wiśniowiecki's reign, the Turks seized Kamieniec, Sobieski beat them again and again, till at the crowning victory of Chocim they lost 20,000 men and a great many guns. This gave Poland breathing-space, and Sobieski became the national hero, so that, King Michael dying at that time, he was unanimously elected king in 1674. Before his coronation he was forced to drive back the Turkish hordes, that had once more invaded the country; he beat them at Lemberg in 1675, arriving in time to raise the siege of Trembowla, and to save Chrzanowski and his heroic wife, its defenders. Scarcely crowned, he hastened to fight in the Ruthenian provinces. Having too few soldiers (20,000) to attack the Turks, who were ten to one, he wore them out, entrenching himself at Zurawno, letting the enemy hem him in for a fortnight, extricating himself with marvellous skill and courage, and finally regaining by treaty a good part of the Ukraine.

For some time there was peace: the Turks had learned to dread the "Unvanquished Northern

JOHN SOBIESKI
From an unsigned portrait in the Louvre

Lion", and Poland, too, was exhausted. But soon the Sultan turned his arms against Austria. Passing through Hungary, a great part of which had for one hundred and fifty years been in Turkish hands, an enormous army, reckoned at from 210,000 to 300,000 men (the latter figures are Sobieski's) marched forward. The Emperor Leopold fled from Vienna, and begged Sobieski's aid, which the papal nuncio also implored. Though dissuaded by Louis XIV, whose policy was always hostile to Austria, Sobieski hesitated not an instant. Meanwhile (July, 1683) the Grand Vizier Kara Mustapha, had arrived before Vienna, and laid siege to the city, defended by the valiant Imperial General Count Stahremberg, with a garrison of only 15,000 men, exposed to the horrors of disease and fire, as well as to hostile attacks. Sobieski started to the rescue in August, taking his son James with him; passing by Our Lady's sanctuary at Czeństochowa, the troops prayed for a blessing on their arms; and in the beginning of September, having crossed the Danube and joined forces with the German armies under John George, Elector of Saxony, and Prince Charles of Lorraine, they approached Vienna. On 11 Sept., Sobieski was on the heights of Kahlenberg, near the city, and the next day he gave battle in the plain below, with an army of not more than 76,000 men, the Germans forming the left wing and the Poles under Hetmans Jahonowski and Sieniawski, with General Katski in command of the artillery, forming the right. The hussars charged with their usual impetuosity, but the dense masses of the foe were impenetrable. Their retreat was taken for flight by the Turks, who rushed forward in pursuit; the hussars turned upon them with reinforcements and charged again, when their shouts made known that the "Northern Lion" was on the field and the Turks fled, panic-stricken, with Sobieski's horsemen still in pursuit. Still the battle raged for a time along all the line; both sides fought bravely, and the king was everywhere commanding, fighting, encouraging his men and urging them forward. He was the first to storm the camp: Kara Mustapha had escaped with his life, but he received the bow-string in Belgrade some months later. The Turks were routed, Vienna and Christendom saved, and the news sent to the pope along with the Standard of the Prophet, taken by Sobieski, who himself had heard Mass in the morning.

Prostrate with outstretched arms, he declared that it was God's cause he was fighting for, and ascribed the victory (Veni, vidi, Deus vicit—his letter to Innocent XI) to Him alone. Next day he entered Vienna, acclaimed by the people as their saviour. Leopold, displeased that the Polish king should have all the glory, condescended to visit and thank him, but treated his son James and the Polish hetmans with extreme and haughty coldness. Sobieski, though deeply offended, pursued the Turks into Hungary, attacked and took Ostrzyhom after a second battle, and returned to winter in Poland, with immense spoils taken in the Turkish camp. These and the glory shed upon the nation were all the immediate advantages of the great victory. The Ottoman danger had vanished forever. The war still went on: step by step the foe was driven back, and sixteen years later Kamieniec and the whole of Podolia were restored to Poland. But Sobieski did not live to see this triumph. In vain had he again and again attempted to retake Kamieniec, and even had built a stronghold to destroy its strategic value; this fortress enabled the Tatars to raid the Ruthenian provinces upon several occasions, even to the gates of Lemberg. He was also forced by treaty to give up Kieff to Russia in 1686; nor did he succeed in securing the crown for his son James. His last days were spent in the bosom of his family, at his castle of Wilanow, where he died in 1696, broken down by political strife as much as by illness. His wife, a Frenchwoman, the widow of John Zamoyski, Marie-Casimire, though not worthy of so great a hero, was tenderly beloved by him, as his letters show: she influenced him greatly and not always wisely. His family is now extinct. Charles Edward, the Young Pretender, was his great-grandson—his son James' daughter, Clementine, having married James Stuart in 1719.

Listy Jana III, Króla polskiego, do krolowej Kazimierzy (Sobieski's letters to his wife), published by A. L. HELSEL, 1857. Two volumes of "*Acta Historica*", published by the Academie der Wissenschaften. TATHAM, *John Sobieski* (Oxford, 1881); DUPONT, *Mémoirs pour servir à l'histoire de Sobieski* (Warsaw, 1885); RIEDER, *Johann III, König von Polen* (Vienna, 1883).

S. TARNOWSKI.

Socialism, a system of social and economic organization that would substitute state monopoly for private ownership of the sources of production and means of distribution, and would concentrate under the control of the secular governing authority the chief activities of human life. The term is often used vaguely to indicate any increase of collective control over individual action, or even any revolt of the dispossessed against the rule of the possessing classes. But these are undue extensions of the term, leading to much confusion of thought. State control and even state ownership are not necessarily Socialism: they become so only when they result in or tend towards the prohibition of private ownership not only of "natural monopolies", but also of all the sources of wealth. Nor is mere revolt against economic inequality Socialism: it may be Anarchism (see ANARCHY); it may be mere Utopianism (see COMMUNISM); it may be a just resistance to oppression. Nor is it merely a proposal to make such economic changes in the social structure as would banish poverty. Socialism is this (see COLLECTIVISM) and much more. It is also a philosophy of social life and action, regarding all human activities from a definite economic standpoint. Moreover modern Socialism is not a mere arbitrary exercise at state-building, but a deliberate attempt to relieve, on explicit principles, the existing social conditions, which are regarded as intolerable. The great inequalities of human life and opportunity, produced by the excessive concentration of wealth in the hands of a comparatively small section of the community, have been the cause and still are the stimulus of what is called the Socialistic movement. But, in order to understand fully what Socialism is and what it implies, it is necessary first to glance at the history of the movement, then to examine its philosophical and religious tendencies, and finally to consider how far these may be, and actually have proved to be, incompatible with Christian thought and life. The first requirement is to understand the origin and growth of the movement.

It has been customary among writers of the Socialist movement to begin with references to Utopian theories of the classical and Renaissance periods, to Plato's "Republic", Plutarch's "Life of Lycurgus", More's "Utopia", Campanella's "City of the Sun", Hall's "Mundus alter et idem", and the like. Thence the line of thought is traced through the French writers of the eighteenth century, Meslier, Montesquieu, d'Argenson, Morelly, Rousseau, Mably, till, with Linguet and Necker, the eve of the Revolution is reached. In a sense, the modern movement has its roots in the ideas of these creators of ideal commonwealths. Yet there is a gulf fixed between the modern Socialists and the older Utopists. Their schemes were mainly directed towards the establishment of Communism, or rather, Communism was the idea that gave life to their fancied states (see COMMUNISM). But the Collectivist idea, which is the economic basis of modern Socialism (see COLLECTIVISM), really emerges only with "Gracchus" Babeuf and his paper, "The Tribune of the People", in 1794. In the manifesto issued by him and his fellow-conspirators, "Les Egaux", is to be found a clear vision of the collective organization of society, such as would be largely accepted by most modern Socialists. Babeuf was guillotined by the Directory, and his party suppressed. Meanwhile, in 1793, Godwin in England had published his "Enquiry Concerning Political Justice", a work which, though inculcating Anarchist-Communism (see ANARCHY) rather than Collectivism, had much influence on Robert Owen and the school of Determinist Socialists who succeeded him. But a small group of English writers in the early years of the nineteenth century had really more to do with the development of Socialist thought than had either Owen's attempts to found ideal communities, at New Lanark and elsewhere, or the contemporary theories and practice of Saint-Simon and Fourier in France.

These English writers, the earliest of whom, Dr. Charles Hall, first put forward that idea of a dominant industrial and social "system", which is the pervading conception of modern Socialism, worked out the various basic principles of Socialism, which Marx afterwards appropriated and combined. Robert Thompson, Ogilvie, Hodgkin, Gray, above all William Carpenter, elaborated the theories of "surplus value", of "production for profit", of "class-war", of the ever-increasing exploitation of the poor by the rich, which are the stuff of Marx's "Das Kapital", that "old clothes-shop of ideas culled from Berlin, Paris, and London". For indeed, this famous work is really nothing more than a dexterous combination of Hegelian Evolutionism, of French Revolutionism, and of the economic theories elaborated by Ricardo, on the one hand, and this group of English theorists on the other. Yet the services of Karl Marx and of his friend and brother-Hebrew, Friedrich Engels, to the cause of Socialism must not be underrated. These two writers came upon the scene just when the Socialist movement was at its lowest ebb. In England the work of Robert Owen had been overlaid by the Chartist movement and its apparent failure, while the writings of the economists mentioned above had had but little immediate influence. In France the Saint-Simonians and the Fourierists had disgusted everyone by the moral collapse of their systems. In Germany Lassalle had so far devoted his brilliant energies merely to Republicanism and philosophy. But in 1848 Marx and Engels published the "Communist Manifesto", and, mere rhetoric as it was, this document was the beginning of modern "scientific Socialism". The influence of Proudhon and of the Revolutionary spirit of the times pervades the whole manifesto: the economic analysis of society was to be grafted on later. But already there appear the ideas of "the materialistic conception of history", of "the bourgeoisie" and "the proletariat", and of "class-war".

After 1848, in his exile in London, Marx studied, and wrote, and organized with two results: first, the foundation of "The International Workingmen's Association", in 1864; second, the publication of the first volume of "Das Kapital", in 1867. It is not easy to judge which has had the more lasting effect upon the Socialist movement. "The International" gave to the movement its world-wide character; "Das Kapital" elaborated and systematized the philosophic and economic doctrine which is still the creed of the immense majority of Socialists. "Proletarians of all lands, unite!" the sentence with which the Communist Manifesto of 1848 concludes, became a reality with the foundation of the International. For the first time since the disruption of Christendom an organization took shape which had for its object the union of the major portion of all nations upon a common basis. It was not so widely supported as both its upholders believed and the frightened moneyed interests imagined. Nor had this first organization any promise of stability. From the outset the influence of Marx steadily grew, but it was confronted by the opposition of Bakunin and the Anarchist school. By 1876 the International was even formally at an end. But it had done its work: the organized working classes of all Europe had realized the international nature both of their own grievances and of capitalism, and when, in 1889, the first International Congress of Socialist and Trade-Union delegates met at Paris, a "New International" came into being which exists with unimpaired or, rather, with enhanced energy to the present day. Since that first meeting seven others have been held at intervals of three or four years, at which there has been a steady growth in the number of delegates present, the variety of nationalities represented, and the extent of the Socialistic influence over its deliberations.

In 1900, an International Socialist Bureau was established at Brussels, with the purpose of solidifying and strengthening the international character of the movement. Since 1904, an Inter-Parliamentary Socialist Committee has given further support to the work of the bureau. To-day the international nature of the Socialistic movement is an axiom both within and without its ranks; an axiom that must not be forgotten in the estimation both of the strength and of the trend of the movement. To the International, then, modern Socialism owes much of its present power. To "Das Kapital" it owes such intellectual coherence as it still possesses. The success of this book was immediate and considerable. It has been translated into many languages, epitomized by many hands, criticized, discussed, and eulogized. Thousands who would style themselves Marxians and would refer to "Das Kapital" as "the Bible of Socialism", and the irrefragable basis of their creed, have very probably never seen the original work, nor have even read it in translation. Marx himself published only the first volume; the second was published under Engels' editorship in 1885, two years after the death of Marx; a third was elaborated by Engels from Marx's notes in 1895; a fourth was projected but never accomplished. But the influence of this torso has been immense. With consummate skill Marx gathered together and worked up the ideas and evidence that had originated with others, or were the floating notions of the movement; with the result that the new international organization had ready to hand a body of doctrine to promulgate, the various national Socialist parties a common theory and programme for which to work. And promulgated it was, with a devotion and at times a childlike faith that had no slight resemblance to religious propaganda. It has been severely and destructively criticized by economists of many schools, many of its leading doctrines have been explicitly abandoned by the Socialist leaders in different countries, some are now hardly defended even by those leaders who label themselves "Marxian". Yet the influence of the book persists. The main doctrines of Marxism are still the stuff of popular Socialist belief in all countries, are still put forward in scarcely modified form in the copious literature produced for popular consumption, are still enunciated or implied in popular addresses even by some of the very leaders who have abandoned them in serious controversy. In spite of the growth of Revisionism in Germany, of Syndicalism in France, and of Fabian Expertism in England, it is still accurate to maintain that the vast majority of Socialists, the rank and file of the movement in all countries, are adherents of the Marxian doctrine, with all its materialistic philosophy, its evolutionary immorality, its disruptive political and social analysis, its class-conscious economics.

In Socialism, to-day, as in most departments of human thought, the leading writers display a marked shyness of fundamental analysis: "The domain of Socialist thought", says Lagardelle, has become "an intellectual desert." Its protagonists are largely occupied, either in elaborating schemes of social reform, which not infrequently present no exclusively socialist characteristics, or else in apologizing for and disavowing inconvenient applications by earlier leaders, of socialist philosophy to the domain of religion and ethics. Nevertheless, in so far as the International movement remains definitely Socialist at all, the formulæ of its propaganda and the creed of its popular adherents are predominantly the reflection of those put forward in "Das Kapital" in 1867. Moreover, during all this period of growth of the modern Socialist movement, two other parallel movements in all countries have at once supplemented and counterpoised it. These are trade-unionism and co-operation. There is no inherent reason why either of these movements should lead towards Socialism: properly conducted and developed, both should render unnecessary anything that can correctly be styled "Socialism". But, as a matter of fact, both these excellent movements, owing to unwise opposition by the dominant capitalism, on the one hand, and indifference in the Churches on the other, are menaced by Socialism, and may eventually be captured by the more intelligent and energetic Socialists and turned to serve the ends of Socialism. The training in mutual aid and interdependence, as well as in self-government and business habits, which the leaders of the wage-earners have received in both trade-unionism and the co-operative movements, while it might be of incalculable benefit in the formation of the needed Christian democracy, has so far been effective largely in demonstrating the power that is given by organization and numbers. And the leaders of Socialism have not been slow to emphasize the lesson and to extend the argument, with sufficient plausibility, towards state monopoly and the absolutism of the majority. The logic of their argument has, it is true, been challenged, in recent years, in Europe by the rise of the great Catholic trade-union and co-operative organizations. But in English-speaking nations this is yet to come, and both co-operation and trade-unionism are allowed to drift into the grip of the Socialist movement, with the result that what might become a most effective alternative for Collectivism remains to-day its nursery and its support.

Parallel with the International movement has run the local propaganda in various countries, in each of which the movement has taken its colour from the national characteristics; a process which has continued, until to-day it is sometimes difficult to realize that the different bodies who are represented in the International Congresses form part of the same agitation. In Germany, the fatherland of dogmatic Socialism, the movement first took shape in 1862. In that year Ferdinand Lassalle, the brilliant and wealthy young Jewish lawyer, delivered a lecture to an artisans' association at Berlin. Lassalle was fined by the authorities for his temerity, but "The Working Men's Programme", as the lecture was styled, resulted in The Universal German Working Men's Association, which was founded at Leipzig under his influence the following year. Lassalle commenced a stormy progress throughout Germany, lecturing, organizing, writing. The movement did not grow at first with the rapidity he had expected, and he himself was killed in a duel in 1864. But his tragic death aroused interest, and The Working Men's Association grew steadily till, in 1869, reinforced by the adhesion of the various organizations which had grown out of Marx's propaganda, it became, at Eisenach, the Socialist Democratic Working Men's Party. Liebknecht, Bebel, and Singer, all Marxians, were its chief leaders. The two former were imprisoned for treason in 1870; but in 1874 ten members of the party, including the two leaders, were returned to the Reichstag by 450,000 votes. The Government attempted repression, with the usual result of consolidating and strengthening the movement. In 1875 was held the celebrated congress at Gotha, at which was drawn up the programme that formed the basis of the party. Three years later an attempt upon the emperor's life was made the excuse for renewed repression. But it was in vain. In spite of alternate persecution and essays in state Socialism, on the part of Bismarck, the movement progressed steadily. Bismarck fell from power in 1890 and since then the party has grown rapidly, and is now the strongest political body in Germany. In 1899 Edward Bernstein, who had come under the influence of the Fabians in England since 1888, started the "Revisionist" movement, which, while attempting to concentrate the energies of the party more definitely upon specific reforms and "revising" to extinction many of the most cherished doctrines of Marxism, has yet been subordinated to the practical exigencies of politics. To all appearance the Socialist Party is stronger to-day than ever. The elections of 1907 brought out 3,258,968 votes in its favour; those of January, 1912, gave it 110 seats out of a total of 397 in the Reichstag—a gain of more than 100 per cent over its last previous representation (53 seats). The Marxian "Erfurt Programme", adopted in 1891, is still the official creed of the Party. But the "Revisionist" policy is obviously gaining ground and, if the Stuttgart Congress of 1907 be any indication, is rapidly transforming the revolutionary Marxist party into an opportunist body devoted to specific social reforms.

In France the progress of Socialism has been upon different lines. After the collapse of Saint-Simonism and Fourierism, came the agitation of Louis Blanc in 1848, with his doctrine of "The Right to Work". But this was side-tracked by the triumphant politicians into the scandalous "National Workshops", which were probably deliberately established on wrong lines in order to bring ridicule upon the agitation. Blanc was driven into exile, and French Socialism lay dormant till the ruin of Imperialism in 1870 and the outbreak of the Commune in 1871. This rising was suppressed with a ferocity that far surpassed the wildest excesses of the Communards; 20,000 men are said to have been shot in cold blood, many of whom were certainly innocent, while not a few were thrown alive into the common burial pits. But this savagery, though it temporarily quelled the revolution, did nothing to obviate the Socialist movement. At first many of the scattered leaders declared for Anarchism, but soon most of them abandoned it as impracticable and threw their energies into the propagation of Marxian Socialism. In 1879 the amnesty permitted Jules Guesde, Brousse, Malon, and other leaders to return. In 1881, after the Anarchist-Communist group under Kropotkin and Réclus had seceded, two parties came into existence, the opportunist Alliance Socialiste Républicaine, and the Marxian Parti Ouvrier Socialiste Révolutionaire de France. But these parties soon split up into others. Guesde led, and still leads, the Irreconcilables; Jaurès and Millerand have been the leaders of the Parliamentarians; Brousse, Blanqui, and others have formed their several communistic groups. In 1906, however, largely owing to the influence of Jaurès, the less extreme parties united again to form Le Parti Socialiste Unifié. This body is but loosely formed of various irreconcilable groups and includes Anarchists like Hervé, Marxists like Guesde, Syndicalists like Lagardelle, Opportunists like Millerand, all of whom Jaurès endeavours, with but slight success, to maintain in harmony. For right across the Marxian doctrinairianism and the opportunism of the parliamentary group has driven the recent Revolutionary Syndicalist movement. This, which is really Anarchist-Communism working through trade-unionism, is a movement distrustful of parliamentary systems, favourable to violence, tending towards destructive revolution. The Confédération Générale du Travail is rapidly absorbing the Socialist movement in France, or at least robbing it of the ardent element that gives it life.

In the British Isles the Socialist movement has had a less stormy career. After the collapse of Owenism and the Chartist movement, the practical genius of the nation directed its chief reform energies towards the consolidation of the trade unions and the building up of the great co-operative enterprise. Steadily, for some forty years, the trade-union leaders worked at the strengthening of their respective organizations, which, with their dual character of friendly societies and professional associations, had no small part in training the working classes in habits of combination for common ends. And this lesson was emphasized and enlarged by the Co-operative movement, which, springing from the tiny efforts of the Rochdale Pioneers, spread throughout the country, till it is now one of the mightiest business organizations in the world. In this movement many a labour leader learnt habits of business and of successful committee work that enabled him later on to deal on equal, or even on advantageous, terms with the representatives of the owning classes. But during all this period of training the Socialist movement proper lay dormant. It was not until 1884, with the foundation of the strictly Marxian Social Democratic Federation by H. M. Hyndman, that the Socialist propaganda took active form in England. It did not achieve any great immediate success, nor has it ever since shown signs of appealing widely to the English temperament. But it was a beginning, and it was followed by other, more inclusive, organizations. A few months after its foundation the Socialist League, led by William Morris, seceded from it and had a brief and stormy existence. In 1893, at Bradford, the "Independent Labour Party" was formed under the leadership of J. Keir Hardie, with the direct purpose of carrying Socialism into politics. Attached to it were two weekly papers, "The Clarion" and "The Labour Leader"; the former of which, by its sale of over a million copies of an able little manual, "Merrie England", had no small part in the diffusion of popular Socialism. All these three bodies were Marxian in doctrine and largely working class in membership.

But, as early as 1883, a group of middle-class students had joined together as The Fabian Society. This body, while calling itself Socialist, rejected the Marxian in favour of Jevonsian economics, and devoted itself to the social education of the public by means of lectures, pamphlets and books, and to the spread of Collectivist ideas by the "permeation" of public bodies and political parties. Immense as have been its achievements in this direction, its constant preoccupation with practical measures of reform and its contact with organized party politics have led it rather in the direction of the "Servile State" than of the Socialist Commonwealth. But the united efforts of the various Socialist bodies, in concert with trade unionism, resulted, in 1899, in the formation of the Labour Representation Committee which, seven years later, had developed into the Labour Party, with about thirty representatives in the House of Commons. Already, however, a few years' practical acquaintance with party politics has diminished the Socialist orthodoxy of the Labour Party, and it shows signs of becoming absorbed in the details of party contention. Significant commentaries appeared in the summer of 1911 and in the spring of 1912; industrial disturbances, singularly resembling French Syndicalism, occurred spontaneously in most commercial and mining centres, and the whole Labour movement in the British Isles has reverted to the Revolutionary type that last appeared in 1889.

XIV.—5

In every European nation the Socialist movement has followed, more or less faithfully, one of the three preceding types. In Belgium, Switzerland, Denmark, and Italy it is predominantly parliamentary: in Russia, Spain, and Portugal it displays a more bitterly revolutionary character. But everywhere the two tendencies, parliamentary and revolutionary, struggle for the upper hand; now one, now the other becoming predominant. Nor is the movement in the United States any exception to the rule. It began about 1849, purely as a movement among the German and other immigrants and, in spite of the migration of the old International to New York in 1872, had but little effect upon the native population till the Henry George movement of 1886. Even then jealousies and divisions restricted its action, till the reorganization of the Socialist Labour Party at Chicago in 1889. Since then the movement has spread rapidly. In 1897 appeared the Social Democracy of America, which, uniting with the majority of the Socialist Labour Party in 1901, formed the present rapidly growing Socialist Party. In the United States the movement is still strongly Marxian in character, though a Revisionist school is growing up, somewhat on the lines of the English Fabian movement, under the influence of writers like Edmond Kelly, Morris Hillquit, and Professors Ely and Zueblin. But the main body is still crudely Revolutionary, and is likely to remain so until the political democracy of the nation is more perfectly reflected in its economic conditions.

These main points in the history of Socialism lead up to an examination of its spirit and intention. The best idealism of earlier times was fixed upon the soul rather than upon the body: exactly the opposite is the case with Socialism. Social questions are almost entirely questions of the body—public health, sanitation, housing, factory conditions, infant mortality, employment of women, hours of work, rates of wages, accidents, unemployment, pauperism, old-age pensions, sickness, infirmity, lunacy, feeble-mindedness, intemperance, prostitution, physical deterioration. All these are excellent ends for activity in themselves, but all of them are mainly concerned with the care or cure of the body. To use a Catholic phrase, they are opportunities for corporal works of mercy, which may lack the spiritual intention that would make them Christian. The material may be made a means to the spiritual, but is not to be considered an end in itself. This world is a place of probation, and the time is short. Man is here for a definite purpose, a purpose which transcends the limits of this mortal life, and his first business is to realize this purpose and carry it out with whatever help and guidance he may find. The purpose is a spiritual one, but he is free to choose or refuse the end for which he was created; he is free to neglect or to co-operate with the Divine assistance, which will give his life the stability and perfection of a spiritual rather than of a material nature. This being so, there must be a certain order in the nature of his development. He is not wholly spiritual nor wholly material; he has a soul, a mind, and a body; but the interests of the soul must be supreme, and the interests of mind and body must be brought into proper subservience to it. His movement towards perfection is by way of ascent; it is not easy; it requires continual exercise of the will, continual discipline, continual training—it is a warfare and a pilgrimage, and in it are two elements, the spiritual and the material, which are one in the unity of his daily life. As St. Paul pointed out, there must be a continual struggle between these two elements. If the individual life is to be a success, the spiritual desire must triumph, the material one must be subordinate, and when this is so the whole individual life is lived with proper economy, spiritual things being sought after as an end, while material things are used merely as a means to that end.

The point, then, to be observed is that the spiritual life is really the economic life. From the Christian point of view material necessities are to be kept at a minimum, and material superfluities as far as possible to be dispensed with altogether. The Christian is a soldier and a pilgrim who requires material things only as a means to fitness and nothing more. In this he has the example of Christ Himself, Who came to earth with a minimum of material advantages and persisted thus even to the Cross. The Christian, then, not only from the individual but also from the social standpoint, has chosen the better part. He does not despise this life, but, just because his material desires are subordinate to his spiritual ones, he lives it much more reasonably, much more unselfishly, much more beneficially to his neighbours. The point, too, which he makes against the Socialist is this. The Socialist wishes to distribute material goods in such a way as to establish a substantial equality, and in order to do this he requires the State to make and keep this distribution compulsory. The Christian replies to him: "You cannot maintain this widespread distribution, for the simple reason that you have no machinery for inducing men to desire it. On the contrary, you do all you can to increase the selfish and accumulative desires of men: you centre and concentrate all their interest on material accumulation, and then expect them to distribute their goods." This ultimate difference between Christian and Socialist teaching must be clearly understood. Socialism appropriates all human desires and centres them on the here-and-now, on material benefit and material prosperity. But material goods are so limited in quality, in quantity, and in duration that they are incapable of satisfying human desires, which will ever covet more and more and never feel satisfaction. In this Socialism and Capitalism are at one, for their only quarrel is over the bone upon which is the meat that perisheth. Socialism, of itself and by itself, can do nothing to diminish or discipline the immediate and materialistic lust of men, because Socialism is itself the most exaggerated and universalized expression of this lust yet known to history. Christianity, on the other hand, teaches and practises unselfish distribution of material goods, both according to the law of justice and according to the law of charity.

Again, ethically speaking, Socialism is committed to the doctrine of determinism. Holding that society makes the individuals of which it is composed, and not vice versa, it has quite lost touch with the invigorating Christian doctrine of free will. This fact may be illustrated by its attitude towards the three great institutions which have hitherto most strongly exemplified and protected that doctrine—the Church, the Family, and private ownership. Socialism, with its essentially materialistic nature, can admit no *raison d'être* for a spiritual power, as complementary and superior to the secular power of the State. Man, as the creature of a material environment, and as the subject of a material State, has no moral responsibilities and can yield to no allegiance beyond that of the State. Any power which claims to appropriate and discipline his interior life, and which affords him sanctions that transcend all evolutionary and scientific determinism, must necessarily incur Socialist opposition. So, too, with the Family. According to the prevalent Socialist teaching, the child stands between two authorities, that of its parents and that of the State, and of these the State is certainly the higher. The State therefore is endowed with the higher authority and with all powers of interference to be used at its own discretion. Contrast this with the Christian notion of the Family —an organic thing with an organic life of its own. The State, it is true, must ensure a proper basis for its economic life, but beyond that it should not interfere: its business is not to detach the members of the family from their body in order to make them separately and selfishly efficient; a member is cut off from its body only as a last resource to prevent organic poisoning. The business of the State is rather that of helping the Family to a healthy, co-operative, and productive unity. The State was never meant to appropriate to itself the main parental duties, it was rather meant to provide the parents, especially poor parents, with a wider, freer, healthier family sphere in which to be properly parental. Socialism, then, both in Church and Family, is impersonal and deterministic: it deprives the individual of both his religious and his domestic freedom. And it is exactly the same with the institution of private property.

The Christian doctrine of property can best be stated in the words of St. Thomas Aquinas: "In regard to an external thing man has two powers: one is the power of managing and controlling it, and as to this it is lawful for a man to possess private property. It is, moreover, necessary for human life for three reasons. First, because everyone is more zealous in looking after a thing that belongs to him than a thing that is the common property of all or of many; because each person, trying to escape labour, leaves to another what is everybody's business, as happens where there are many servants. Secondly, because there is more order in the management of men's affairs if each has his own work of looking after definite things; whereas there would be confusion if everyone managed everything indiscriminately. Thirdly, because in this way the relations of men are kept more peaceful, since everyone is satisfied with his own possession, whence we see that quarrels are commoner between those who jointly own a thing as a whole. The other power which man has over external things is the using of them; and as to this man must not hold external things as his own property, but as everyone's; so as to make no difficulty, I mean, in sharing when others are in need" (Summa theologica, II-II, Q. lxvi, a. 2). If man, then, has the right to own, control, and use private property, the State cannot give him this right or take it away; it can only protect it. Here, of course, we are at issue with Socialism, for, according to it, the State is the supreme power from which all human rights are derived; it acknowledges no independent spiritual, domestic, or individual power whatever. In nothing is the bad economy of Socialism more evident than in its derogation or denial of all the truly personal and self-directive powers of human nature, and its misuse of such human qualities as it does not despise or deny is a plain confession of its material and deterministic limitations. It is true that the institutions of religion, of the family, and of private ownership are liable to great abuses, but the perfection of human effort and character demands a freedom of choice between good and evil as their first necessary condition. This area of free choice is provided, on the material side, by private ownership; on the spiritual and material, by the Christian Family; and on the purely spiritual by religion. The State, then, instead of depriving men of these opportunities of free and fine production, not only of material but also of intellectual values, should rather constitute itself as their defender.

In apparent contradiction, however, to much of the foregoing argument are the considerations put forward by numerous schools of "Christian Socialism", both Catholic and non-Catholic. It will be urged that there cannot really be the opposition between Socialism and Christianity that is here suggested, for, as a matter of fact, many excellent and intelligent persons in all countries are at once convinced Christians and ardent Socialists. Now, before it is possible to estimate correctly how far this undoubted fact can alter the conclusions arrived at above, certain premises must be noted. First, it is not practically possible to consider Socialism solely as an economic or social doctrine. It has long passed the stage of pure theory and attained the proportions of a movement: it is to-day a doctrine embodied in programmes, a system of thought and belief that is put forward as the vivifying principle of an active propaganda, a thing organically connected with the intellectual and moral activities of the millions who are its adherents. Next, the views of small and scattered bodies of men and women, who profess to reconcile the two doctrines, must be allowed no more than their due weight when contrasted with the expressed beliefs of not only the majority of the leading exponents of Socialism, past and present, but also of the immense majority of the rank and file in all nations. Thirdly, for Catholics, the declarations of supreme pontiffs, of the Catholic hierarchy, and of the leading Catholic sociologists and economists have an important bearing on the question, an evidential force not to be lightly dismissed. Lastly, the real meaning attached to the terms "Christianity" and "Socialism", by those who profess to reconcile these doctrines, must always be elicited before it is possible to estimate either what doctrines are being reconciled or how far that reconciliation is of any practical adequacy.

If it be found on examination that the general trend of the Socialist movement, the predominant opinion of the Socialists, the authoritative pronouncements of ecclesiastical and expert Catholic authority all tend to emphasize the philosophical cleavage indicated above, it is probably safe to conclude that those who profess to reconcile the two doctrines are mistaken: either their grasp of the doctrines of Christianity or of Socialism will be found to be imperfect, or else their mental habits will appear to be so lacking in discipline that they are content with the profession of a belief in incompatible principles. Now, if Socialism be first considered as embodied in the Socialist movement and Socialist activity, it is notorious that everywhere it is antagonistic to Christianity. This is above all clear in Catholic countries, where the Socialist organizations are markedly anti-Christian both in profession and practice. It is true that of late years there has appeared among Socialists some impatience of remaining mere catspaws of the powerful Masonic anti-clerical societies, but this is rather because these secret societies are largely engineered by the wealthy in the interests of capitalism than from any affection for Catholicism. The European Socialist remains anti-clerical, even when he revolts against Masonic manipulation. Nor is this really less true of non-Catholic countries. In Germany, in Holland, in Denmark, in the United States, even in Great Britain, organized Socialism is ever prompt to express (in its practical programme, if not in its formulated creed) its contempt for and inherent antagonism to revealed Christianity. What, in public, is not infrequently deprecated is clearly enough implied in projects of legislation, as well as in the mental attitude that is usual in Socialist circles.

Nor are the published views of the Socialist leaders and writers less explicit. "Scientific Socialism" began as an economic exposition of evolutionary materialism; it never lost that character. Its German founders, Marx, Engels, Lassalle, were notoriously anti-Christian both in temper and in acquired philosophy. So have been its more modern exponents in Germany, Bebel, Liebknecht, Kautsky, Dietzgen, Bernstein, Singer, as well as the popular papers—the "Sozial Demokrat", the "Vorwärts", the "Zimmerer", the "Neue Zeit"—which reflect, while expounding, the view of the rank and file; and the Gotha and Erfurt programmes, which express the practical aims of the movement. In France and the Netherlands the former and present leaders of the various Socialist sections are at one on the question of Christianity—Lafargue, Hervé, Boudin, Guesde, Jaurès, Viviani, Sorel, Briand, Griffuelhes, Largardelle, Téry, Renard, Nieuwenhuis, Vandervelde—all are anti-Christian, as are the popular newspapers, like "La Guerre Sociale", "L'Humanité", "Le Socialiste", the "Petite République", the "Recht voor Allen", "Le Peuple". In Italy, Austria, Spain, Russia, and Switzerland it is the same: Socialism goes hand in hand with the attack on Christianity. Only in the English-speaking countries is the rule apparently void. Yet, even there, but slight acquaintance with the leading personalities of the Socialist movement and the habits of thought current among them, is sufficient to dispel the illusion. In Great Britain certain prominent names at once occur as plainly anti-Christian—Aveling, Hyndman, Pearson, Blatchford, Bax, Quelch, Leatham, Morris, Standring—many of them pioneers and prophets of the movement in England. The Fabians, Shaw, Pease, Webb, Guest; independents, like Wells, or Orage, or Carpenter; popular periodicals like "The Clarion", "The Socialist Review", "Justice" are all markedly non-Christian in spirit, though some of them do protest against any necessary incompatibility between their doctrines and the Christian. It is true that the political leaders, like Macdonald and Hardie, and a fair proportion of the present Labour Party might insist that "Socialism is only Christianity in terms of modern economics", but the very measures they advocate or support not unfrequently are anti-Christian in principle or tendency. And in the United States it is the same. Those who have studied the writings or speeches of well-known Socialists, such as Bellamy, Gronlund, Spargo, Hunter, Debs, Herron, Abbott, Brown, Del Mar, Hillquit, Kerr, or Simmons, or periodicals like the "New York Volkszeitung", "The People", "The Comrade", or "The Worker", are aware of the bitterly anti-Christian tone that pervades them and is inherent in their propaganda.

The trend of the Socialist movement, then, and the deliberate pronouncements and habitual thought of leaders and followers alike, are almost universally found to be antagonistic to Christianity. Moreover, the other side of the question is but a confirmation of this antagonism. For all three popes who have come into contact with modern Socialism, Pius IX, Leo XIII, and Pius X, have formally condemned it, both as a general doctrine and with regard to specific points. The bishops and clergy, the lay experts on social and economic questions, the philosophers, the theologians, and practically the whole body of the faithful are unanimous in their acceptance of the condemnation. It is of little purpose to point out that the Socialism condemned is Marxism, and not Fabianism or its analogues in various countries. For, in the first place, the main principles common to all schools of Socialism have been explicitly condemned in Encyclicals like the "Rerum novarum" or the "Graves de communi"; and, in addition, as has been shown above, the main current of Socialism is still Marxist, and no adhesion to a movement professedly international can be acquitted of the guilt of lending support to the condemned doctrines. The Church, the Socialists, the very tendency of the movement do but confirm the antagonism of principle, indicated above, between Socialism and Christianity. The "Christian Socialists" of all countries, indeed, fall readily, upon examination, into one of three categories. Either they are very imperfectly Christian, as the Lutheran followers of Stöcker and Naumann in Germany, or the Calvinist Socialists in France, or the numerous vaguely-doctrinal "Free-Church" Socialists in England and America; or, secondly, they are but very inaccurately styled "Socialist"; as were the group led by Kingsley, Maurice and Hughes in England, or "Catholic Democrats" like Ketteler, Manning, Descurtins, the "Sillonists"; or, thirdly, where there is an acceptance of the main Christian doctrine, side by side with the advocacy of Revolutionary Socialism, as is the case with the English "Guild of St.

Matthew" or the New York Church Association for the Advancement of the Interests of Labour, it can only be ascribed to that mental facility in holding at the same time incompatible doctrines, which is everywhere the mark of the "Catholic but not Roman" school. Christianity and Socialism are hopelessly incompatible, and the logic of events makes this ever clearer. It is true that, before the publication of the Encyclical "Rerum novarum", it was not unusual to apply the term "Christian Socialism" to the social reforms put forward throughout Europe by those Catholics who are earnestly endeavouring to restore the social philosophy of Catholicism to the position it occupied in the ages of Faith. But, under the guidance of Pope Leo XIII, that crusade against the social and economic iniquities of the present age is now more correctly styled "Christian Democracy", and no really instructed, loyal, and clear-thinking Catholic would now claim or accept the style of Christian Socialist.

To sum up, in the words of a capable anonymous writer in "The Quarterly Review", Socialism has for "its philosophical basis, pure materialism; its religious basis is pure negation; its ethical basis the theory that society makes the individuals of which it is composed, not the individuals society, and that therefore the structure of society determines individual conduct, which involves moral irresponsibility; its economic basis is the theory that labour is the sole producer, and that capital is the surplus value over bare subsistence produced by labour and stolen by capitalists; its juristic basis is the right of labour to the whole product; its historical basis is the industrial revolution, that is the change from small and handicraft methods of production to large and mechanical ones, and the warfare of classes; its political basis is democracy. . . . It may be noted that some of these [bases] have already been abandoned and are in ruins, others are beginning to shake; and as this process advances the defenders are compelled to retreat and take up fresh positions. Thus the form of the doctrine changes and undergoes modification, though all cling still to the central principle, which is the substitution of public for private ownership."

I. History of the Socialist Movement: (1) General:—CETTY, *Les socialistes allemands* (Paris, 1907); DE SEILHAC, *Les congrès ouvriers en France* (Reims, 1908); HILLQUIT, *History of Socialism in the United States* (New York, 1902); KIRKUP, *History of Socialism* (London, 1909); LECOCQ, *La question sociale au xviii siècle* (Paris, 1909); LOUIS, *Histoire du mouvement syndical en France* (Paris, 1907); PELLOUTIER, *Histoire des Bourses de Travail* (Paris, 1902); RAE, *Contemporary Socialism* (London, 1908); SOMBART, *Socialism and the Socialist Movement* (London, 1909); STODDART, *The New Socialism* (London, 1909); TUGAN-BARONOWSKY, *Modern Socialism in its Historical Development* (London, 1910); VILLIERS, *The socialist Movement in England* (London, 1910); WINTERER, *Le socialisme contemporain* (Paris, 1895). (2) Utopian and Revolutionary Attempts.—BUONAROTTI, *Babeuf's Conspiracy for Equality* (London, 1836); CULLEN, *Adventures in Socialism* (London, 1910); HINDS, *American Communities* (Chicago, 1902); LISSAGARAY, *History of the Commune of 1871* (London, 1886); MALLOCK, *A Century of Socialistic Experiments* in *The Dublin Review* (July, 1909); MARCH, *History of the Paris Commune* (London, 1895); NORDHOFF, *Communistic Societies in the United States* (London, 1875); NOYES, *History of American Socialisms* (Philadelphia, 1870). (3) Biographies of Socialist Leaders.—BERNSTEIN, *Ferdinand Lassalle as a Social Reformer* (London, 1893); BOOTH, *Saint-Simon and Saint-Simonism* (London, 1871); GEORGE, *Life of Henry George* (London, 1900); GIBBINS, *English Social Reformers* (London, 1907); JACKSON, *Bernard Shaw, a monograph* (London, 1909); JONES, *The Life, Times and Labours of Robert Owen* (London, 1900); MACKAIL, *Life of William Morris* (2 vols., London, 1899); SPARGO, *Karl Marx, his Life and Work* (New York, 1910); TAYLOR, *Leaders of Socialism* (London, 1908).

II. History of Movements Influencing Socialism: (1) Co-operation.—FAY, *Co-operation at Home and Abroad* (London, 1908); HOLYOAKE, *History of Co-operation* (2 vols., London, 1908); LAVERGNE, *Le régime coopératif* (Paris, 1910); POTTER, *Co-operative movement in Great Britain* (London, 1899). (2) Combinations of Labour and Capital.—DE SEILHAC, *Les grèves* (Paris, 1909); DILIGENT, *Les orientations syndicales* (Paris, 1909); ELY, *Monopolies and Trusts* (New York, 1900); HIRST, *Monopolies, Trusts, and Kartells* (London, 1905); HOWELL, *Trade Unionism Old and New* (London, 1907); KIRKBRIDE AND STERRETT, *The Modern Trust Company* (New York, 1906); MACROSTY, *The Trust Movement in British Industry* (London, 1907); WEBB, *History of Trade-Unionism* (London, 1901); IDEM, *Industrial Democracy* (London, 1901). (3) Legislation.—CUNNINGHAM AND MACARTHUR, *Outlines of English Industrial History* (Cambridge, 1894); HUTCHINS AND HARRISON, *History of Factory Legislation* (London, 1910); NICHOLLS AND MACKAY, *History of the English Poor Law* (3 vols., London, 1910); WEBB, *English Poor Law Policy* (London, 1909); IDEM, *Grants in Aid* (London, 1911); IDEM, *The State and the Doctor* (London, 1910). (4) Municipal and Administrative Activities.—DARWIN, *Municipal Ownership* (London, 1907); JOLY, *La Suisse politique et sociale* (Paris, 1909); IDEM, *L'Italie contemporaine* (Paris, 1911); MEYER, *Municipal Ownership in Great Britain* (London, 1906); REEVES, *State Experiments in Australia and New Zealand* (2 vols., London, 1902); SHAW, *Municipal Government in Great Britain* (London, 1895); IDEM, *Municipal Government in Continental Europe* (London, 1896); WEBBER, *The Growth of Cities in the Nineteenth Century* (London, 1899); ZUEBLIN, *American Municipal Enterprise* (New York, 1902).

III. Socialism as Expounded by Socialists. (1) Marxism.—BAX, *Essays in Socialism New and Old* (London, 1905); BLATCHFORD, *Merrie England* (London, 1895); ENGELS, *Socialism Utopian and Scientific* (London, 1892); FERRI, *Socialism and Positive Science* (London, 1905); GRONLUND, *The Co-operative Commonwealth* (London, 1896); HUNTER, *Socialists at Work* (New York, 1908); HYNDMAN, *The Economics of Socialism* (London, 1896); JAURÈS, *Studies in Socialism* (London, 1906); MARX, *Capital* (3 vols., London, 1888, 1907, 1909); MORRIS AND BAX, *Socialism its Growth and Outcome* (London, 1897); SPARGO, *Socialism, a Summary and Interpretation* (New York, 1906); IDEM, *The Substance of Socialism* (New York, 1910). (2) Revisionism, Revolutionary Syndicalism, Fabian Expertism.—BERNSTEIN, *Evolutionary Socialism* (London, 1909); CLAY, *Syndicalism and Labour* (London, 1911); ENSOR, *Modern Socialism as Set Forth by Socialists* (New York, 1910); *Fabian Essays in Socialism* (London, 1909); *Fabian Tracts, Nos. 1–160* (London, 1884–1911); GRIFFUELHES, *L'action syndicaliste* (Paris, 1908); IDEM, *Voyages révolutionaires* (Paris, 1910); HILLQUIT, *Socialism in Theory and Practice* (New York, 1909); KELLY, *Twentieth Century Socialism* (London, 1910); LAGARDELLE. *Le socialisme ouvrier* (Paris, 1911); MACDONALD, *Socialism and Society* (London, 1905); IDEM, *The Socialist Movement* (London, 1911); MERMEIX, *Le socialisme* (Paris, 1907); IDEM, *Le syndicalisme contre le socialisme* (Paris, 1908); PATAUD AND POUGET, *Comment nous ferons la révolution* (Paris, 1909); PREZZOLINI, *La teoria sindicalista* (Naples, 1909); VANDERVELDE, *Collectivism and Industrial Revolution* (London, 1907); WEBB, *The Prevention of Destitution* (London, 1911); WELLS, *New Worlds for Old* (London, 1908).

IV. Catholic Criticism of Socialism.—ANTOINE, *Cours d'économie sociale* (Paris, 1988), 523–68; ARDANT, *Le socialisme contemporain et la propriété* (Paris, 1905); *Brochures jaunes de l'Action Populaire, Nos. 26, 28, 49, 97, 100, 163, 174, 199* (Reims, 1904–11); CASTELEIN, *Le socialisme et le droit de propriété* (Brussels); CATHREIN, *Socialism, its theoretical basis and practical application* (New York, 1904); COUSIN, *Catéchisme d'économie soc. et polit.* (Paris, 1907); DE SEILHAC, *L'utopie social.* (Paris, 1907); DEVAS, *Political Economy* (London, 1907), 514–26; KELLEHER, *Private ownership: its basis and equitable conditions* (Dublin, 1911); LEROY-BEAULIEU, *Collectivism, a Study of Some of the Leading Questions of the Day* (London, 1908); PESCH, *Liberalismus, Socialismus Christl. Gesellschaftsord.* (Freiburg, 1896); PREUSS, *The Fundamental Fallacy of Socialism* (St. Louis, 1908); SAVATIER, *Les variations du socialisme* in *Le mouvement soc.* (Paris, May, 1911); SCHRIJVERS, *Handbook of Practical Economics* (London, 1910), 25–48; TOUSSAINT, *Collectivisme et communisme* (Paris, 1907); WINTERER, *Le socialisme allemand et ses dernières évolutions* (Paris, 1907).

V. Non-Catholic Criticism of Socialism.—GUYOT, *Socialistic Fallacies* (London, 1910); FLINT, *Socialism* (London, 1908); HOBSON, *The Industrial System* (London, 1909); IDEM, *The Science of wealth* (London, 1911); KIRKUP, *An Enquiry Into Socialism* (London, 1908); MALLOCK, *A Critical Examination of Socialism* (London, 1908); NICHOLSON, *Historical Progress and Ideal Socialism* (London, 1894); SCHAEFFLE, *The Quintessence of Socialism* (London, 1899); SKELTON, *Socialism, a critical analysis* (London, 1911); *Socialism, Its Meaning and Origin; its Present Position and Future Prospects* in *Quarterly Review* (April, July, London, 1910); *The Case Against Socialism* (London, 1909).

VI. "Christian Socialism".—*Catholicism and Socialism* in *Catholic Truth Society Pamphlets* (2 vols., London, 1908, 1910); CUNNINGHAM, *Socialism and Christianity* (London, 1909); GAYRAUD, *Un Catholique peut-il être socialiste?* (Paris, 1907); GOLDSTEIN, *Socialism, the Nation of Fatherless Children* (New York, 1908); HEADLAM, DEARMER, CLIFFORD, AND WOOLMAN, *Socialism and Religion* in Fabian Socialist Series, no. 1 (London, 1908); LAMY, *Catholiques et Socialistes* (Paris, 1910); MING, *The Characteristics and the Religion of Modern Socialism* (New York, 1908); IDEM, *The Morality of Modern Socialism* (New York, 1909); NITTI, *Catholic Socialism* (London, 1895); NOEL, *Socialism in Church History* (London, 1910); SERTILLANGES, *Socialisme et Christianisme* (Paris, 1909); SODERINI, *Socialism and Catholicism* (London, 1896); STANG, *Socialism and Christianity* (New York, 1905); WORDSWORTH, *Christian Socialism in England* (London, 1903).

VII. Christian Democracy.—*Année sociale internationale, I–III* (Reims, 1910–12); CALIPPE, *L'attitude sociale des catholiques Français au XIXe siècle* (Paris, 1910); IDEM, *Les tendences sociales des catholiques libéraux* (Paris, 1911); *Catholic Social Guild Pamphlets* (2 vols., London, 1910–12); CRAWFORD, *Switzerland To-day* (London, 1911); DEVAS, *Social Questions and the Duty of Catholics* (London, 1907); IDEM, *The Key to the World's Progress* (London, 1906); GARRIGUET, *The Social Value of the Gospel* (London, 1911); *Guide Social, I–VI* (Reims, 1904–09); LUGAN, *L'enseignement social de Jésus* (Paris, 1907); NAUDET, *Le christianisme Social* (Paris, 1908); PARKINSON (ed.), *Destitution and Suggested Remedies* (London, 1911); PLATER, *Catholic Social Work* *in Germany* (St. Louis, 1910); RYAN, *A Living Wage, its Ethical and Economic Aspects* (New York, 1910); *The Catholic Church and Labour* in *Catholic Truth Society Pamphlets* (London, 1908); *The Pope and the People* (New York, 1909); TURMANN, *Le développement du catholicisme social depuis l'encyclique Rerum Novarum* (Paris, 1909); WRIGHT (ed.), *Sweated Labour and the Trade Boards Act* (London, 1911).

LESLIE A. ST. L. TOKE.
W. E. CAMPBELL.

Socialistic Communities.—This title comprehends those societies which maintain common ownership of the means of production and distribution, e. g., land, factories, and stores, and also those which further extend the practice of common ownership to consumable goods, e. g., houses and food. While the majority of the groups treated in the present article are, strictly speaking, communistic rather than socialistic, they are frequently designated by the latter term. The most important of them have already been described under COMMUNISM. Below a more nearly complete list is given, together with brief notices of those societies that have not been discussed in the former articles. At the time of the Protestant Reformation certain socialistic experiments were made by several heretical sects, including the Anabaptists, the Libertines, and the Familists; but these sects did not convert their beliefs along this line into practice with sufficient thoroughness or for a sufficient length of time to give their attempts any considerable value or interest (see Kautsky, "Communism in Central Europe at the Time of the Reformation", London, 1897).

The Labadists, a religious sect with communistic features, founded a community in Westphalia, in 1672, under the leadership of Jean de la Badie, an apostate priest. A few years later about one hundred members of the sect established a colony in Northern Maryland, but within half a century both communities ceased to exist.

The Ephrata (Pennsylvania) Community was founded in 1732, and contained at one time 300 members, but in 1900 numbered only 17.

The Shakers adopted a socialistic form of organization at Watervliet, New York, in 1776. At their most prosperous period their various societies comprised about 5000 persons; to-day (1911) they do not exceed 1000.

The Harmonists, or Rappists, were established in Pennsylvania in 1805. Their maximum membership was 1000; in 1900 they numbered 9. Connected with this society is the Bethel Community, which was founded (1844) in Missouri by a group which included some seceders from Harmony. In 1855 the Bethel leader, Dr. Keil, organized another community at Aurora, Oregon. The combined membership of the two settlements never exceeded 1000 persons. Bethel dissolved in 1880 and Aurora in 1881.

The Separatists of Zoar (Ohio) were organized as a socialistic community in 1818, and dissolved in 1898. At one time they had 500 members.

The New Harmony Community, the greatest attempt ever made in this form of social organization, was founded in Indiana in 1824 by Robert Owen. Its maximum number of members was 900 and its length of life two years. Eighteen other communities formed by seceders from the New Harmony society were about equally short-lived. Other socialistic settlements that owed their foundation to the teachings of Owen were set up at Yellow Springs, Ohio; Nashoba, Tennessee (composed mostly of negroes); Haverstraw, New York; and Kendal, Oregon. None of them lasted more than two years.

The Hopedale (Massachusetts) Community was organized in 1842 by the Rev. Adin Ballou; it never had more than 175 members, and it came to an end in 1857.

The Brook Farm (Massachusetts) Community was established in 1842 by the Transcendentalist group of scholars and writers. In 1844 it was converted into a Fourierist phalanx; this, however, was dissolved in 1846.

Of the Fourieristic phalanges two had a very brief existence in France, and about thirty were organized in the United States between 1840 and 1850. Their aggregate membership was about 4500, and their longevity varied from a few months to twelve years. Aside from the one at Brook Farm, the most noteworthy were: the North American phalanx, founded in 1843 in New Jersey under the direction of Greeley, Brisbane, Channing, and other gifted men, and dissolved in 1855; the Wisconsin, or Cresco, phalanx, organized in 1844, and dispersed in 1850; and the Sylvania Association of Pennsylvania, which has the distinction of being the earliest Fourieristic experiment in the United States, though it lasted only eighteen months.

The Oneida (New York) Community, the members of which called themselves Perfectionists because they believed that all who followed their way of life could become perfect, became a communistic organization in 1848, and was converted into a joint-stock corporation in 1881. Its largest number of members was 300.

The first Icarian community was set up in Texas in 1848, and the last came to an end in 1895 in Iowa. Their most prosperous settlement, at Nauvoo, numbered more than 500 souls.

The Amana Community was organized on socialistic lines in 1843 near Buffalo, New York, but moved to Amana, Iowa, in 1845. It is the one communistic settlement that has increased steadily, though not rapidly, in wealth and numbers. Its members rightly attribute this fact to its religious character and motive. The community embraces about 1800 persons.

A unique community is the Woman's Commonwealth, established about 1875 near Belton, Texas, and transferred to Mount Pleasant, D. C., in 1898. It was organized by women who from motives of religion and conscience had separated themselves from their husbands. As the members number less than thirty and are mostly those who instituted the community more than thirty-five years ago, the experiment cannot last many years longer.

The most important of recently founded communities was the Ruskin Co-operative Colony, organized in 1894 in Tennessee by J. A. Wayland, editor of the socialist paper, "The Coming Nation". While the capital of the community was collectively owned, its products were distributed among the members in the form of wages. Owing to dissensions and withdrawals, the colony was reorganized on a new site in 1896, but it also was soon dissolved. About 250 of the colonists moved to Georgia, and set up another community, but this in a few years ceased to exist.

A number of other communities have been formed within recent years, most of which permit private ownership of consumption-goods and private family life. As none of them has become strong either in numbers or in wealth, and as all of them seem destined to an early death, they will receive only the briefest mention here. Those worthy of any notice are: The Christian Commonwealth of Georgia, organized in 1896, and dissolved in 1900; the Co-operative Brotherhood, of Burley, Washington; the Straight Edge Industrial Settlement, of New York City; the Home Colony in the State of Washington, which has the distinction of being the only anarchist colony; the Mutual Home Association, located in the same state; the Topolambo Colony in Mexico, which lasted but a few months; and the Fairhope (Alabama) Single-Tax Corporation, which has had a fair measure of success, but which is neither socialistic nor communistic in the proper sense.

Reviewing the history of socialistic experiments, we perceive that only those that were avowedly and strongly religious, adopting a socialistic organization as incidental to their religious purposes, have achieved even temporary and partial success. Practically speaking, only two of these religious communities remain; of these the Shakers are growing steadily weaker, while the Amana Society is almost stationary, and, besides, is obliged to carry on some of its industries with the aid of outside hired labor.

See bibliography under COMMUNISM. HILQUIT, *History of Socialism in the United States* (New York, 1903); KENT in *Bulletin No. 35 of the Department of Labor*; MALLOCK, *A Century of Socialistic Experiments* in *The Dublin Review*, July, 1909; WOLFF, *Socialistic Communism in the United States* in *The American Catholic Quarterly Review*, III (Philadelphia, 1878), 522; *Socialist Colony in Mexico* in *Dublin Review*, CXIV (London, 1894), 180.

JOHN A. RYAN.

Societies, CATHOLIC.—Catholic societies are very numerous throughout the world; some are international in scope, some are national; some diocesan and others parochial. These are treated in particular under their respective titles throughout the Encyclopedia, or else under the countries or the dioceses in which they exist. This article is concerned only with Catholic societies in general. The right of association is one of the natural rights of man. It is not surprising, therefore, that from earliest antiquity societies of the most diverse kinds should have been formed. In pagan Rome the Church was able to carry on its work and elude the persecuting laws, only under the guise of a private corporation or society. When it became free it encouraged the association of its children in various guilds and fraternities, that they might more easily, while remaining subject to the general supervision of ecclesiastical authority, obtain some special good for their souls or bodies or both simultaneously. By a society we understand the voluntary and durable association of a number of persons who pledge themselves to work together to obtain some special end. Of such societies there is a great variety in the Church both for laymen and clerics, the most perfect species of the latter being the regular orders and religious congregations bound by perpetual vows. As to societies of laymen, we may distinguish broadly three classes: (a) confraternities, which are associations of the faithful canonically erected by the proper ecclesiastical superior to promote a Christian method of life by special works of piety towards God, e. g. the splendour of divine worship, or towards one's neighbour, e. g. the spiritual or corporal works of mercy (see CONFRATERNITY); (b) pious associations, whose objects are generally the same as those of confraternities, but which are not canonically erected (see ASSOCIATIONS, PIOUS); and (c) societies whose members are Catholics, but which are not in the strict sense of the word religious societies. Some of these associations are ecclesiastical corporations in the strict acceptation of the term, while others are merely subordinate and dependent parts of the parish or diocesan organization, or only remotely connected with it. Church corporations, inasmuch as they are moral or legal persons, have the right, according to canon law, of making by-laws for their association by the suffrage of the members, of electing their own officers, of controlling their property within the limits of the canons, and of making provision, according to their own judgment, for their preservation and growth. They have, consequently, certain defined rights, both original or those derived from their constitution, and adventitious or what they have acquired by privilege or concession. Among original rights of all ecclesiastical corporations are the right of exclusion or the expelling of members; of selection or the adoption of new members; of convention or meeting for debate and counsel; of assistance or aiding their associates who suffer from a violation of their corporate rights. Societies of this nature have an existence independent of the individual members and can be dissolved only by ecclesiastical decree. Catholic societies which are not church corporations may be founded and dissolved at the will of their members. Sometimes they are approved, or technically praised, by ecclesiastical authority, but they are also frequently formed without any intervention of the hierarchy. In general, it may be said that Catholic societies of any description are very desirable.

The Church has always watched with singular care over the various organizations formed by the faithful for the promotion of any good work, and the popes have enriched them with indulgences. No hard and fast rules have been made, however, as to the method of government. Some societies, e. g. the Propagation of the Faith and the Holy Childhood, are general in their scope; others, e. g. the Church Extension Society of the United States, are peculiar to one country. It sometimes happens that an association formed for one country penetrates into another, e. g. the Piusverein, the Society of Christian Mothers, etc. There are also societies instituted to provide for some special need, as an altar or tabernacle society, or for the furthering of some special devotion, as the Holy Name Society. For societies which are general in their scope, the Holy See frequently appoints a cardinal protector and reserves the choice of the president to itself. This is likewise done as a mark of special favour to some societies which are only national, as the Church Extension Society of the United States (Brief of Pius X, 9 June, 1910). In general, it may be affirmed that it is the special duty of the bishop and the parish priest to found or promote such societies as the faithful of their districts may be in need of. Utility and necessity often vary with the circumstances of time and country. In some lands it has been found possible and advisable for the Church authorities to form Catholic societies of workingmen. These are trades-unions under ecclesiastical auspices and recall the old Catholic guilds of the Middle Ages. Zealous bishops and priests have made the promotion of such societies, as in Germany and Belgium, a special work, in the hope of preventing Catholic workingmen from being allured by temporal gain into atheistic societies in which the foundations of civil and religious institutions are attacked. In these unions a priest appointed by the bishop gives religious instructions which are particularly directed against the impious arguments of those who seek to destroy the morals and faith of the workingman. Methods are pointed out for regulating the family life according to the laws of God; temperance, frugality, and submission to lawful authority are urged, and frequentation of the sacraments insisted on. These unions also provide innocent amusements for their members. Such societies at times add confraternity and sodality features to their organization.

There are a number of societies formed by Catholics which are not in a strict sense Catholic societies. Nevertheless, as the individual faithful are subject to the authority of the bishop they remain subject to the same authority even as members of an organization. It is true that the bishop may not, in consequence of his ecclesiastical jurisdiction, rule such societies in the same sense as he does confraternities and pious associations, yet he retains the inalienable right and even the obligation of preventing the faithful from being led into spiritual ruin through societies of whatsoever name or purpose. He can, therefore, if convinced that an organization is harmful, forbid it to assist at church services in its regalia, and, when no emendation results, warn individuals against entering it or remaining members of it. Finally, there are societies which are entirely secular, whose sole purpose is to promote or obtain some commercial, domestic, or political advantage, such as the ordinary trades-unions. In such organizations men of every variety of religious belief combine together, and many Catholics are found among the members. There can be no objection to such societies as long as the end intended and the means employed are licit and honourable. It remains, however, the duty of the bishops to see that members of their flock suffer no diminution of faith or contamination of morals from such organizations. Experience has proved that secular societies, while perfectly unobjectionable in their avowed ends, may cause grave spiritual danger to their members. Bishops and parish priests can not be blamed, therefore, if they display some anxiety as to membership in societies which are not avowedly Catholic. If they did otherwise, they would be false to their duty towards their flock. It may be well to quote here the weighty words of an Instruction of the Holy Office (10 May, 1884): "Concerning artisans and labourers, among whom various societies are especially desirous of securing members that they may destroy the very foundations of religion and society, let the bishops place before their eyes the ancient guilds of workingmen, which, under the protection of some patron saint, were an ornament of the commonwealth and an aid to the higher and lower arts. They will again found such societies for men of commercial and literary pursuits, in which the exercises of religion will go hand in hand with the benevolent aims that seek to assuage the ills of sickness, old age, or poverty. Those who preside over such societies should see that the members commend themselves by the probity of their morals, the excellence of their work, the docility and assiduity of their labours, so that they may more securely provide for their sustenance. Let the bishops themselves not refuse to watch over such societies, suggest or approve by-laws, conciliate employers, and give every assistance and patronage that lie in their power."

There are many societies of Catholics or societies of which Catholics are members that employ methods which seem imitations derived from various organizations prohibited by the Church. It may be well, therefore, to state that no Catholic is allowed, as a member of any society whatever, to take an oath of blind and unlimited obedience; or promise secrecy of such a nature that, if circumstances require it, he may not reveal certain things to the lawful ecclesiastical or civil authorities; or join in a ritual which would be equivalent to sectarian worship (see SOCIETIES, SECRET). Even when a society is founded by Catholics or is constituted principally of Catholics, it is possible for it to degenerate into a harmful organization and call for the intervention of the authority of the Church. Such was the fate of the once brilliant and meritorious French society "Le Sillon", which was condemned by Pius X (25 Aug., 1910). It is often expedient for Catholic societies to be incorporated by the civil authority as private corporations. In fact, this is necessary if they wish to possess property or receive bequests in their own name. In some countries, as Russia, such incorporation is almost impossible; in others, as Germany and France, the Government makes many restrictions; but in English-speaking countries there is no difficulty. In England societies may be incorporated not only by special legal act, but also by common law or by prescription. In the United States a body corporate may be formed only by following the plan proposed by a law of Congress or a statute of a state legislature. The procedure varies slightly in different states, but as a rule incorporation is effected by filing a paper in the office of the secretary of state or with a circuit judge, stating the object and methods of the society. Three incorporators are sufficient, and the petition will always be granted if the purposes of the association are not inconsistent with the laws of the United States or of the particular state in question.

LAURENTIUS, *Institutiones juris ecclesiastici* (Fribourg, 1905); WERNZ, *Jus decretalium*, III (Rome, 1901); AICHNER, *Compendium juris ecclesiastici* (Brixen, 1895); BERINGER, *Die Ablässe* (13th ed., Paderborn, 1911; French tr., 1905); TAYLOR, *The Law of Private Corporations* (New York, 1902); *Handbook of Catholic Charitable and Social Works* (London, 1912).

WILLIAM H. W. FANNING.

Societies, CATHOLIC, AMERICAN FEDERATION OF, an organization of the Catholic laity, parishes, and societies under the guidance of the hierarchy, to protect and advance their religious, civil, and social interests. It does not destroy the autonomy of any society or interfere with its activities, but seeks to unite all of them for purposes of co-operation and economy of forces. It is not a political organization, neither does it ask any privileges or favours for Catholics. The principal object of the Federation is to encourage (1) the Christian education of youth; (2) the correction of error and exposure of falsehood and injustice; the destruction of bigotry; the placing of Catholics and the Church in their true light, thus removing the obstacles that have hitherto impeded their progress; (3) the infusion of Christian principles into public and social life, by combatting the errors threatening to undermine the foundations of civil society, notably socialism, divorce, dishonesty in business, and corruption in politics and positions of public trust. The first organization to inaugurate the movement for a concerted action of the societies of Catholic laymen was the Knights of St. John. At their annual meeting held at Cleveland in 1899 they resolved to unite the efforts of their local commanderies. In 1900 at Philadelphia they discussed the question of a federation of all the Catholic societies. As a result a convention was held on 10 Dec., 1901, at Cincinnati, under the presidency of Mr. H. J. Fries. Two hundred and fifty delegates were present under the guidance of Bishop McFaul of Trenton, Bishop Messmer of Green Bay, now Archbishop of Milwaukee, the principal factors in the organization of the movement, Archbishop Elder of Cincinnati, Bishop Horstmann of Cleveland, and Bishop Maes of Covington. A charter bond was framed and the Federation formally established, with Mr. T. B. Minahan as its first president. Since then annual conventions have been held. The Federation represents close to two million Catholics. It has been approved by Popes Leo XIII and Pius X, and practically all the hierarchy of the country. The fruits of the labours of the organization have been manifold; among other things it has helped to obtain a fair settlement of the disputes concerning the church property in the Philippines, permission for the celebration of Mass in the navy-yards, prisons, reform schools; assistance for the Catholic Indian schools and negro missions; the withdrawal and prohibition of indecent plays and post-cards. It has prevented the enactment of laws inimical to Catholic interests in several state legislatures. One of its chief works has been the uniting of the Catholics of different nationalities, and harmonizing their efforts for self-protection and improvement. It publishes a monthly Bulletin, which contains valuable social studies. The national secretary is Mr. Anthony Matré, Victoria Building, St. Louis, Missouri.

MATRÉ, *Hist. of the Feder. of Cath. Soc.* in *The Catholic Columbian* (Columbus, Ohio, 18 Aug., 1911); MCFAUL, *The Amer. Feder. of Cath. Soc.* (Cincinnati, 1911).

A. A. MACERLEAN.

Societies, SECRET, a designation of which the exact meaning has varied at different times. I. DEFINITION.—"By a secret society was formerly meant a society which was known to exist, but whose members and places of meetings were not publicly known. To-day, we understand by a secret society, a society with secrets, having a ritual demanding an oath of allegiance and secrecy, prescribing ceremonies of a religious character, such as the use of the Bible, either by extracts therefrom, or by its being placed on an altar within a lodge-room, by the use of prayers, of hymns, of religious signs and symbols, special funeral services, etc." (Rosen, "The Catholic Church and Secret Societies", p. 2). Raich gives a more elaborate description: "Secret societies are those organizations which completely conceal their rules, corporate activity, the names of their members, their signs, passwords and usages from outsiders or the 'profane'. As a rule, the members of these societies are bound to the strictest secrecy concerning all the business of the association by oath or promise or word of honour, and often under the threat of severe punishment in case of its violation. If such secret society has higher and lower degrees, the members of the higher degree must be equally careful to conceal their secrets from their brethren of a lower degree. In certain secret societies, the members are not allowed to know even the names of their highest officers. Secret societies were founded to promote certain ideal aims, to be obtained not by violent but by moral measures. By this, they are distinguished from conspiracies and secret plots which are formed to attain a particular object through violent means. Secret societies may be religious, scientific, political or social" (Kirchenlex., V, p. 519). Narrowing the definition still more to the technical meaning of secret societies (*societates clandestinæ*) in ecclesiastical documents, Archbishop Katzer in a Pastoral (20 Jan., 1895) says: "The Catholic Church has declared that she considers those societies illicit and forbidden which (1) unite their members for the purpose of conspiring against the State or Church; (2) demand the observance of secrecy to such an extent that it must be maintained even before the rightful ecclesiastical authority; (3) exact an oath from their members or a promise of blind and absolute obedience; (4) make use of a ritual and ceremonies that constitute them sects."

II. ORIGIN.—Though secret societies, in the modern and technical sense, did not exist in antiquity, yet there were various organizations which boasted an esoteric doctrine known only to their members, and carefully concealed from the profane. Some date societies of this kind back to Pythagoras (582–507 B. C.). The Eleusinian Mysteries, the secret teachings of Egyptian and Druid hierarchies, the esoteric doctrines of the Magian and Mithraic worshippers furnished material for such secret organizations. In Christian times, such heresies as the Gnostic and Manichæan also claimed to possess a knowledge known only to the illuminated and not to be shared with the vulgar. Likewise, the enemies of the religious order of Knights Templars maintained that the brothers of the Temple, while externally professing Christianity, were in reality pagans who veiled their impiety under orthodox terms to which an entirely different meaning was given by the initiated. Originally, the various guilds of the Middle Ages were in no sense secret societies in the modern acceptation of the term, though some have supposed that symbolic Freemasonry was gradually developed in those organizations. The fantastic Rosicrucians are credited with something of the nature of a modern secret society, but the association, if such it was, can scarcely be said to have emerged into the clear light of history.

III. MODERN ORGANIZATIONS.—Secret societies in the true sense began with symbolic Freemasonry about the year 1717 in London (see MASONRY). This widespread oath-bound association soon became the exemplar or the parent of numerous other fraternities, nearly all of which have some connexion with Freemasonry, and in almost every instance were founded by Masons. Among these may be mentioned the Illuminati, the Carbonari, the Odd-Fellows, the Knights of Pythias, the Sons of Temperance and similar societies whose number is legion. Based on the same principles as the secret order to which they are affiliated are the women-auxiliary lodges, of which almost every secret society has at least one. These secret societies for women have also their rituals, their oaths, and their degrees. Institutions of learning are also infected with the glamour of secret organizations and the "Eleusis" of Chi Omega (Fayetteville, Ark.) of 1 June, 1900, states that there are twenty-four Greek letter societies with seven hundred and sixty-eight branches for male students, and eight similar societies with one hundred and twenty branches for female students, and a total membership of 142,456 in the higher institutions of learning in the United States.

IV. ATTITUDE OF ECCLESIASTICAL AUTHORITIES.— The judgment of the Church on secret oath-bound associations has been made abundantly clear by papal documents. Freemasonry was condemned by Clement XII in a Constitution, dated 28 April, 1738. The pope insists on the objectionable character of societies that commit men of all or no religion to a system of mere natural righteousness, that seek their end by binding their votaries to secret pacts by strict oaths, often under penalties of the severest character, and that plot against the tranquillity of the State. Benedict XIV renewed the condemnation of his predecessor on 18 May, 1751. The Carbonari were declared a prohibited society by Pius VII in a Constitution dated 13 Sept., 1821, and he made it manifest that organizations similar to Freemasonry involve an equal condemnation. The Apostolic Constitution "Quo Graviora" of Leo XII (18 March, 1825) put together the acts and decrees of former pontiffs on the subject of secret societies and ratified and confirmed them. The dangerous character and tendencies of secret organizations among students did not escape the vigilance of the Holy See, and Pius VIII (24 May, 1829) raised his warning voice concerning those in colleges and academies, as his predecessor, Leo XII, had done in the matter of universities. The succeeding popes, Gregory XVI (15 Aug., 1832) and Pius IX (9 Nov., 1846; 20 Apr., 1849; 9 Dec., 1854; 8 Dec., 1864; 25 Sept., 1865), continued to warn the faithful against secret societies and to renew the ban of the Church on their designs and members. On 20 Apr., 1884, appeared the famous Encyclical of Leo XIII, "Humanum Genus". In it the pontiff says: "As soon as the constitution and spirit of the masonic sect were clearly discovered by manifest signs of its action, by cases investigated, by the publication of its laws and of its rites and commentaries, with the addition often of the personal testimony of those who were in the secret, the Apostolic See denounced the sect of the Freemasons and publicly declared its constitution, as contrary to law and right, to be pernicious no less to Christendom than to the State; and it forbade anyone to enter the society, under the penalties which the Church is wont to inflict upon exceptionally guilty persons. The sectaries, indignant at this, thinking to elude or to weaken the force of these decrees, partly by contempt of them and partly by calumny, accused the Sovereign Pontiffs who had uttered them, either of exceeding the bounds of moderation or of decreeing what was not just. This was the manner in which they endeavoured to elude the authority and weight of the Apostolic Constitutions of Clement XII and Benedict XIV, as well as of Pius VIII and Pius IX. Yet in the very society itself, there were found men who unwillingly acknowledged that the Roman Pontiffs had acted within their right, according to the Catholic doctrine and discipline. The pontiffs received the same assent, and in strong terms, from many princes and heads of governments, who made it their business either to delate the masonic society to the Holy See, or of their own accord by special enactments to brand it as pernicious, as for example in Holland, Austria, Switzerland, Spain, Bavaria, Savoy and other parts of Italy. But, what is of the highest importance, the course of events has demonstrated the prudence of our predecessors". Leo XIII makes it clear that it is not only the society explicitly called Masonic that is objectionable: "There are several organized bodies which, though they differ in name, in ceremonial, in form and origin, are nevertheless so bound together by community of purpose and by the similarity of their main opinions as to make in fact one thing with the sect of the Freemasons, which is a kind of centre whence they all go forth and whither they all return. Now, these no longer show a desire to remain concealed; for they hold their meetings in the daylight and before the public eye, and publish their own newspaper organs; and yet, when thoroughly understood, they are found still to retain the nature and the habits of secret societies." The pope is not unmindful of the professed benevolent aims of these societies: "They speak of their zeal for a more cultured refinement and of their love of the poor; and they declare their one wish to be the amelioration of the condition of the masses, and to share with the largest possible number all the benefits of civil life. Even were these purposes aimed at in real truth, yet they are by no means the whole of their object. Moreover, to be enrolled, it is necessary that candidates promise and undertake to be thenceforward strictly obedient to their leaders and masters with the utmost submission and fidelity, and to be in readiness to do their bidding upon the slightest expression of their will." The pontiff then points out the dire consequences which result from the fact that these societies substitute Naturalism for the Church of Christ and inculcate, at the very least, indifferentism in matters of religion. Other papal utterances on secret societies are: "Ad Apostolici", 15 Oct., 1890; "Præclara", 20 June, 1894; "Annum Ingressi", 18 Mar., 1902.

V. THE SOCIETIES FORBIDDEN.—The extension of the decrees of the Apostolic See in regard to societies hitherto forbidden under censure is summed up in the well-known Constitution "Apostolicæ Sedis" of Pius IX, where excommunication is pronounced against those "who give their names to the sect of the Masons or Carbonari or any other sects of the same nature, which conspire against the Church or lawfully constituted Governments, either openly or covertly, as well as those who favor in any manner these sects or who do not denounce their leaders and chiefs". The condemned societies here described are associations formed to antagonize the Church or the lawful civil power. A society to be of the same kind as the Masonic, must also be a secret organization. It is of no consequence whether the society demand an oath to observe its secrets or not. It is plain also that public and avowed attacks on Church or State are quite compatible with a secret organization. It must not be supposed, however, that only societies which fall directly under the formal censure of the Church are prohibited. The Congregation of the Holy Office issued an instruction on 10 May, 1884, in which it says: "That there may be no possibility of error when there is question of judging which of these pernicious societies fall under censure or mere prohibition, it is certain, in the first place, that the Masonic and other sects of the same nature are excommunicated, whether they exact or do not exact an oath from their members to observe secrecy. Besides these, there are other prohibited societies, to be avoided under grave sin, among which are especially to be noted those which under oath, communicate a secret to their members to be concealed from everybody else, and which demand absolute obedience to unknown leaders". To the secret societies condemned by name, the Congregation of the Holy Office, on 20 Aug., 1894, in a Decree addressed to the hierarchy of the United States, added the Odd-Fellows, the Sons of Temperance, and the Knights of Pythias.

VI. RECENTLY CONDEMNED SOCIETIES.—The order of Odd-Fellows was formed in England in 1812 as a completed organization, though some lodges date back to 1745; and it was introduced into America in 1819. In the "Odd-Fellows' Improved Pocket Manual" the author writes: "Our institution has instinctively, as it were, copied after all secret associations of religious and moral character". The "North-West Odd-Fellow Review" (May, 1895) declares: "No home can be an ideal one unless the principles of our good and glorious Order are represented therein, and its teachings made the rule of life". In the "New Odd-Fellows' Manual" (N. Y., 1895) the author says: "The written as well as the unwritten secret work of the Order, I have sacredly kept unrevealed", though the book is dedicated "to all inquirers who desire to know what Odd-Fellowship really is". This book tells us "Odd-Fellowship was founded on great religious principles" (p. 348); "we use forms of worship" (p. 364); "Judaism, Christianity, Mohammedanism recognize the only living and true God" (p. 297). The Odd-Fellows have chaplains, altars, high-priests, ritual, order of worship, and funeral ceremonies. The order of the Sons of Temperance was founded in New York in 1842 and introduced into England in 1846. The "Cyclopædia of Fraternities" says (p. 409): "The Sons of Temperance took the lead in England in demonstrating the propriety and practicability of both men and women mingling in secret society lodges". That the object of this order and its kindred societies is not confined to temperance "is evidenced by its mode of initiation, the form of the obligation and the manner of religious worship" (Rosen, p. 162). The order of the Knights of Pythias was founded in 1864 by prominent Freemasons (Cyclop. of Fraternities, p. 263). In number, its membership is second only to that of the Odd-Fellows. Rosen (The Catholic Church and Secret Societies) says: "The principal objectionable features, on account of which the Catholic Church has forbidden its members to join the Knights of Pythias, and demanded a withdrawal of those who joined it, are: First, the oath of secrecy by which the member binds himself to keep secret whatever concerns the doings of the Order, even from those in Church and State who have a right to know, under certain conditions, what their subjects are doing. Secondly, this oath binds the member to blind obedience, which is symbolized by a test. Such an obedience is against the law of man's nature, and against all divine and human law. Thirdly, Christ is not the teacher and model in the rule of life, but the pagan Pythagoras and the pagans Damon, Pythias and Dionysius" (p. 160). The "Ritual for the subordinate Lodges of the Knights of Pythias" (Chicago, 1906) shows that this organization has oaths, degrees, prelates, and a ritual that contains religious worship. The decree of the Holy Office concerning the Odd-Fellows, Sons of Temperance, and Knights of Pythias, though not declaring them to be condemned under censure, says: "The bishops must endeavour by all means to keep the faithful from joining all and each of the three aforesaid societies; and warn the faithful against them, and if, after proper monition, they still determine to be members of these societies, or do not effectually separate themselves from them, they are to be forbidden the reception of the sacraments." A decree of 18 Jan., 1896, allows a nominal membership in these three societies, if in the judgment of the Apostolic delegate, four conditions are fulfilled: that the society was entered in good faith, that there be no scandal, that grave temporal injury would result from withdrawal, and that there be no danger of perversion. The delegate, in granting a dispensation, usually requires a promise that the person will not attend any meetings or frequent the lodge-rooms, that the dues be sent in by mail or by a third party, and that in case of death the society will have nothing to do with the funeral.

VII. ORDERS OF WOMEN.—In regard to female secret societies, the Apostolic delegation at Washington, 2 Aug., 1907, declared (Ans. no. 15,352-C): "If these societies are affiliated to societies already nominally condemned by the Church, they fall under the same condemnation, for they form, as it were, a branch of such societies. As regards other female secret societies which may not be affiliated with societies condemned expressly by the Church, the confessor must, in cases of members belonging to such societies, apply the principles of moral theology which treat of secret societies in general." The document adds that members of female secret societies affiliated to the three societies condemned in 1894 will be dealt with by the Apostolic delegate in the same manner as male members when the necessary conditions are fulfilled.

VIII. TRADES UNIONS.—The Third Council of Baltimore (no. 253) declares: "We see no reason why the prohibition of the Church against the Masonic and other secret societies should be extended to organizations of workingmen, which have no other object in view than mutual protection and aid for their members in the practice of their trades. Care must be taken, however, that nothing be admitted under any pretext which favors condemned societies; or that the workingmen who belong to these organizations be induced, by the cunning arts of wicked men, to withhold, contrary to the laws of justice, the labor due from them, or in any other manner violate the rights of their employers. Those associations are also entirely illicit, in which the members are so bound for mutual defense that danger of riots and murders is the outcome."

IX. METHOD OF CONDEMNATION.—Finally, in regard to the condemnation of individual societies in the United States, the council says (no. 255): "To avoid confusion of discipline which ensues, to the great scandal of the faithful and the detriment of ecclesiastical authority, when the same society is condemned in one diocese and tolerated in another, we desire that no society be condemned by name as falling under one of the classes [of forbidden societies] before the Ordinary has brought the matter before a commission which we now constitute for judging such cases, and which will consist of all the archbishops of these provinces. If it be not plain to all that a society is to be condemned, recourse must be had to the Holy See in order that a definite judgment be obtained and that uniform discipline may be preserved in these provinces".

STEVENS, *The Cyclopædia of Fraternities* (New York, 1907); COOK, *Revised Knights of Pythias Illustrated—Ritual for Subordinate Lodges of the Knights of Pythias Adopted by the Supreme Lodge* (Chicago, 1906); IDEM, *Revised Odd-Fellowship Illustrated—The Complete Revised Ritual* (Chicago, 1906); CARNAHAN, *Pythian Knighthood* (Cincinnati, 1888); F. J. L., *The Order of the Knights of Pythias in the Light of God's Word* (Lutheran Tract) (New Orleans, 1899); DALLMAN, *Odd-Fellowship Weighed—Wanting* (Pittsburgh, 1906); GERBER, *Der Odd-Fellow Orden. u. Das Decret vom 1894* (Berlin, 1896); MACDILL AND BLANCHARD, *Secret Societies* (Chicago, 1891); DALLMANN, *Opinions on Secret Societies* (Pittsburgh, 1906); H. C. S., *Two Discourses Against Secret Oath-Bound Societies or Lodges* (Columbus, O., s. d.); KELLOGG, *College Secret Societies* (Chicago, 1894); ROSEN, *The Catholic Church and Secret Societies* (Hollendale, Wis., 1902); IDEM, *Reply to my Critics of the Cath. Church and Secret Societies* (Dubuque, 1903). See also the extended bibliography appended to article MASONRY.

WILLIAM H. W. FANNING.

Society implies fellowship, company, and has always been conceived as signifying a human relation, and not a herding of sheep, a hiving of bees, or a mating of wild animals. The accepted definition of a society is a stable union of a plurality of persons co-operating for a common purpose of benefit to all. The fulness of co-operation involved naturally extends to all the activities of the mind, will, and external faculties, commensurate with the common purpose and the bond of union: this alone presents an adequate, human working-together.

This definition is as old as the Schoolmen, and embodies the historical concept as definitized by cogent reasoning. Under such reasoning it has become the essential idea of society and remains so still, notwithstanding the perversion of philosophical terms consequent upon later confusion of man with beast, stock, and stone. It is a priori only as far as chastened by restrictions put upon it by the necessities of known truth, and is a departure from the inductive method in vogue to-day only so far as to exclude rigidly the aberrations of uncivilized tribes and degenerate races from the requirements of reason and basic truth. Historical induction taken alone, while investigating efficient causes of society, may yet miss its essential idea, and is in peril of including irrational abuse with rational action and development.

The first obvious requisite in all society is authority. Without this there can be no secure co-ordination of effort nor permanency of co-operation. No secure co-ordination, for men's judgment will differ on the relative value of means for the common purpose, men's choice will vary on means of like value; and unless there is some headship, confusion will result. No permanence of co-operation, for the best of men relax in their initial resolutions, and to hold them at a co-ordinate task, a tight rein and a steady spur is needed. In fact, reluctant though man is to surrender the smallest tittle of independence and submit in the slightest his freedom to the bidding of another, there never has been in the history of the world a successful, nor even a serious attempt at co-operative effort without authoritative guidance (see AUTHORITY, CIVIL). Starting with this definition and requirement, philosophy finds itself confronted with two kinds of society, the artificial or conventional, and the natural; and on pursuing the subject, finds the latter differentiating itself into domestic society, or the family, civil society, or the State, and religious society, or the Church. Each of these has a special treatment under other headings (see FAMILY; STATE AND CHURCH). Here, however, we shall state the philosophic basis of each, and add thereto the theories which have had a vogue for the last three centuries, though breaking down now under the strain of modern problems before the bar of calm judgment.

CONVENTIONAL SOCIETIES.—The plurality of persons, the community of aim, the stability of bond, authority, and some co-operation of effort being elements common to every form of society, the differentiation must come from differences in the character of the purpose, in the nature of the bond. Qualifications of authority as well as modifications in details of requisite co-operation will follow on changes in the purpose and the extent of the bond. As many, then, as there are objects of human desire attainable by common effort (and their name is legion, from the making of money, which is perhaps the commonest to-day, to the rendering of public worship to our Maker which is surely the most sacred), so manifold are the co-operative associations of men. The character, as well as the existence of most of them, is left in full freedom to human choice. These may be denominated conventional societies. Man is under no precept to establish th m, nor in universal need of them. He makes or unmakes them at his pleasure. They serve a passing purpose, and in setting them up men give them the exact character which they judge at present suitable for their purpose, determining as they see fit the limits of authority, the choice of means, the extent of the bond holding them together, as well as their own individual reservations. Everything about such a society is of free election, barring the fact that the essential requisites of a society must be there. We find this type exemplified in a reading circle, a business partnership, or a private charitable organization. Of course, in establishing such a society men are under the Natural Law of right and wrong, and there can be no moral bond, for example, where the common purpose is immoral. They also fall under the restrictions of the civil law, when the existence or action of such an organization comes to have a bearing, whether of promise or of menace, upon the common weal. In such case the State lays down its essential requirements for the formation of such bodies, and so we come to have what is known as a legal society, a society, namely, freely established under the sanction and according to the requirements of the civil law. Such are mercantile corporations and beneficial organizations with civil charter.

NATURAL SOCIETIES.—Standing apart from the foregoing in a class by themselves are the family, the State, and the Church. That these differ from all other societies in purpose and means, is clear and universally admitted. That they have a general application to the whole human race, history declares. That there is a difference between the bond holding them in existence and the bond of union in every other society, has been disputed—with more enthusiasm and imagination, however, than logical force. The logical view of the matter brings us to the concept of a natural society, a society, that is to say, which men are in general under a mandate of the natural law to establish, a society by consequence whose essential requisites are firmly fixed by the same natural law. To get at this is simple enough, if the philosophical problems are taken up in due order. Ethics may not be divided from psychology and theodicy, any more than from deductive logic. With the proper premisals then from one and the other here assumed, we say that the Creator could not have given man a fixed nature, as He has, without willing man to work out the purpose for which that nature is framed. He cannot act idly and without purpose, cannot form His creature discordantly with the purpose of His will. He cannot multiply men on the face of the earth without a plan for working out the destiny of mankind at large. This plan must contain all the elements necessary to His purpose, and these necessary details He must have willed man freely to accomplish, that is to say, He must have put upon man a strict obligation thereunto. Other details may be alternatives, or helpful but not necessary, and these He has left to man's free choice; though where one of these elements would of its nature be far more helpful than another, God's counsel to man will be in favour of the former. God's will directing man through his nature to his share in the full purpose of the cosmic plan, we know as the natural law, containing precept, permission, and counsel, according to the necessity, helpfulness, or extraordinary value of an action to the achievement of the Divine purpose. We recognize these in the concrete by a rational study of the essential characteristics of human nature and its relations with the rest of the universe. If we find a natural aptitude in man for an action, not at variance with the general purpose of things, we recognize also the licence of the natural law to that action. If we find a more urgent natural propensity to it, we recognize further the counsel of the law. If we find the use of a natural faculty, the following up of a natural propensity, inseparable from the rational fulfilment of the ultimate destiny of the individual or of the human race, we know that thereon lies a mandate of the natural law, obliging the conscience of man. We must not, however, miss the difference, that if the need of the action or effort is for the individual natural destiny, the mandate lies on each human being severally: but if the need be for the natural destiny of the race, the precept does not descend to this or that particular individual, so long as the necessary bulk of men accomplish the detail so intended in the plan for the natural destiny of the race. This is abstract reasoning, but necessary for the understanding of a natural society in the fulness of its idea.

A SOCIETY NATURAL BY MANDATE.—A society, then, is natural by mandate, when the law of nature sets the precept upon mankind to establish that society. The precept is recognized by the natural aptitude, propensity, and need in men for the establishment of such a union. From this point of view the gift of speech alone is sufficient to show man's aptitude for fellowship with his kind. It is emphasized by his manifold perfectibility through contact with others and through their permanent companionship. Furthermore his normal shrinking from solitude, from working out the problems of life alone, is evidence of a social propensity to which mankind has always yielded. If again we consider his dependence for existence and comfort on the multiplied products of co-ordinate human effort; and his dependence for the development of his physical, intellectual, and moral perfectibility on complex intercourse with others, we see a need, in view of man's ultimate destiny, that makes the actualization of man's capacity of organized social co-operation a stringent law upon mankind. Taking then the kinds of social organization universally existent among men, it is plain not only that they are the result of natural propensities, but that, as analysis shows, they are a human need and hence are prescribed in the code of the Natural Law.

A SOCIETY NATURAL IN ESSENTIALS.—Furthermore, as we understand a legal contract to be one which, because of its abutment on common interests, the civil law hedges round with restrictions and reservations for their protection, similarly on examination we shall find that all agreements by which men enter into stable social union are fenced in with limitations set by the natural law guarding the essential interests of the good of mankind. When, moreover, we come to social unions prescribed for mankind by mandate of that law, we expect to find the purpose of the union set by the law (otherwise the law would not have prescribed the union), all the details morally necessary for the rational attainment of that purpose fixed by the law, and all obstacles threatening sure defeat to that purpose, proscribed by the same. A natural society, then, besides being natural by mandate, will also be natural in all its essentials, for as much as these too shall be determined and ordained by the law.

THE FAMILY A NATURAL SOCIETY.—Working along these lines upon the data given by experience, personal as well as through the proxy of history, the philosopher finds in man's nature, considered physiologically and psychologically, the aptitude, propensity, and, both as a general thing and for mankind at large, the need of the matrimonial relation. Seeing the natural and needful purpose to which this relation shapes itself to be in full the mutually perfecting compensation of common life between man and woman, as well as the procreation and education of the child, and keeping in mind that Nature's Lawgiver has in view the rational development of the race (or human nature at large) as well as of the individual, we conclude not only to abiding rational love as its distinguishing characteristic, but to monogamy and a stability that is exclusive of absolute divorce. This gives us the essential requisites of domestic society, a stable union of man and wife bound together to work for a fixed common good to themselves and humanity. When this company is filled out with children and its incidental complement of household servants, we have domestic society in its fullness. It is created under mandate of the natural law, for though this or that individual may safely eschew matrimony for some good purpose, mankind may not. The individual in exception need not be concerned about the purpose of the Lawgiver, as human nature is so constituted that mankind will not fail of its fulfilment. The efficient cause of this domestic union in the concrete instance is the free consent of the initial couple, but the character of the juridical bond which they thus freely accept is determined for them by the natural law according to Nature's full purpose. Husband and wife may see to their personal benefit in choosing to establish a domestic community, but the interests of the child and of the future race are safeguarded by the law. The essential purpose of this society we have stated above. The essential requisite of authority takes on a divided character of partnership, because of the separate functions of husband and wife requiring authority as well as calling for harmonious agreement upon details of common interest: but the headship of final decision is put by the law, as a matter of ordinary course, in the man, as is shown by his natural characteristics marking him for the preference. The essential limitations forbid plural marriage, race-suicide, sexual excess, unnecessary separation, and absolute divorce.

The State a Natural Society.—On the same principle of human aptitude, propensity, and need for the individual and the race, we find the larger social unit of civil society manifested to us as part of the Divine set purpose with regard to human nature, and so under precept of the natural law. Again, the exceptional individual may take to solitude for some ennobling purpose; but he is an exception, and the bulk of mankind will not hesitate to fulfil Nature's bidding and accomplish Nature's purpose. In the concrete instance civil society, though morally incumbent on man to establish, still comes into existence by the exercise of his free activity. We have seen the same of domestic society, which begins by the mutual free consent of man and woman to the acceptance of the bond involving all the natural rights and duties of the permanent matrimonial relation. The beginning of civil society as an historical fact has taken on divers colours, far different at different times and places. It has arisen by peaceful expansion of a family into a widespread kindred eventually linked together in a civil union. It has sprung from the multiplication of independent families in the colonizing of undeveloped lands. It has come into being under the strong hand of conquest enforcing law, order, and civil organization, not always justly, upon a people. There have been rare instances of its birth through the tutoring efforts of the gentler type of civilizers, who came to spread the Gospel. But the juridical origin is not obviously identical with this. History alone exhibits only the manifold confluent causes which moved men into an organized civil unit. The juridical cause is quite another matter. This is the cause which of its character under the natural law puts the actual moral bond of civil union upon the many in the concrete, imposes the concrete obligation involving all the rights, duties, and powers native to a State, even as the mutual consent of the contracting parties creates the mutual bond of initial domestic society. This determinant has been under dispute among Catholic teachers.

The common view of Scholastic philosophy, so ably developed by Francis Suarez, S.J., sets it in the consent of the constituent members, whether given explicitly in the acceptance of a constitution, or tacitly by submitting to an organization of another's making, even if this consent be not given by immediate surrender, but by gradual process of slow and often reluctant acquiescence in the stability of a common union for the essential civil purpose. In the early fifties of the nineteenth century Luigi Taparelli, S.J., borrowing an idea from C. de Haller of Berne, brilliantly developed a theory of the juridical origin of civil government, which has dominated in the Italian Catholic schools even to the present day, as well as in Catholic schools in Europe, whose professors of ethics have been of Italian training. In this theory civil society has grown into being from the natural multiplication of cognate families, and the gradual extension of parental power. The patriarchal State is the primitive form, the normal type, though by accident of circumstance States may begin here or there from occupation of the same wide territory under feudal ownership; by organization consequent upon conquest; or in rarer instances by the common consent of independent colonial freeholders. These two Catholic views part company also in declaring the primitive juridical determinant of the concrete subject of supreme authority (see Authority, Civil). To-day the Catholic schools are divided between these two positions. We shall subjoin below other theories of the juridical origin of the State, which have no place in Catholic thought for the simple reason that they exclude the natural character of civil society and throw to the winds the principles logically inseparable from the existing natural law.

With regard to the essential elements in civil society fixed by the natural law, it is first to be noted that the normal unit is the family: for not only has the family come historically before the commonwealth, but the natural needs of man lead him first to that social combination, in pursuit of a natural result only to be obtained thereby; and it is logically only subsequent that the purpose of civil society comes into human life. Of course this does not mean that individuals actually outside of the surroundings of family life cannot be constituent members of civil society with full civic rights and duties, but they are not the primary unit; they are in the nature of things the exception, however numerous they may be, and beyond the family limit of perfectibility it is in the interest of complementary development that civil activity is exercised. The State cannot eliminate the family; neither can it rob it of its inalienable rights, nor bar the fulfilment of its inseparable duties, though it may restrict the exercise of certain family activities so as to co-ordinate them to the benefit of the body politic.

Secondly, the natural object pursued by man in his ultimate social activity is perfect temporal happiness, the satisfacton, to wit, of his natural faculties to the full power of their development within his capacity, on his way, of course, to eternal felicity beyond earth. Man's happiness cannot be handed over to him, or thrust upon him by another here on earth; for his nature supposes that his possession of it, and so too in large measure his achievement of it, shall be by the exercise of his native faculties. Hence, civil society is destined by the natural law to give him his opportunity, i. e. to give it to all who share its citizenship. This shows the proximate natural purpose of the State to be: first, to establish and preserve social order, a condition, namely, wherein every man, as far as may be, is secured in the possession and free exercise of all his rights, natural and legal, and is held up to the fulfilment of his duties as far as they bear upon the common weal; secondly, to put within reasonable reach of all citizens a fair allowance of the means of temporal happiness. This is what is known as external peace and prosperity, prosperity being also denominated the relatively perfect sufficiency of life. There are misconceptions enough about the generic purpose native to all civil society. De Haller thought that there is none such; that civil purposes are all specific, peculiar to each specific State. Kant limited it to external peace. The Manchester School did the same, leaving the citizen to work out his subsistence and development as best he may. The Evolutionist consistently makes it the survival of the fittest, on the way to developing a better type. The modern peril is to treat the citizen merely as an industrial unit, mistaking national material progress for the goal of civic energy; or as a military unit, looking to self-preservation as the nation's first if not only aim. Neither material progress nor martial power, nor merely intellectual civilization, can fill the requirements of existing and expanding human nature. The State, while protecting a man's rights, must put him in the way of opportunity for developing his entire nature, physical, mental, and moral.

Thirdly, the accomplishment of this calls for an authority which the Lawgiver of Nature, because he has ordained this society, has put within the competency of the State, and which, because of its reach, extending as it does to life and death, to reluctant subjects and to the posterity of its citizenship, surpasses the capacity of its citizenship to create out of any mere conventional surrender of natural rights. The question of the origin of civil power and its concentration in this or that subject is like the origin of society itself, a topic of debate. Catholic philosophy is agreed that it is conferred by Nature's Lawgiver directly upon the social depositary thereof, as parental supremacy is upon the father of a family. But the determination of the depositary is another matter. The doctrine of Suarez makes the community itself the depositary, immediately and naturally consequent upon its establishment of civil society, to be disposed of then by their consent, overt or tacit, at once or by degrees, according as they determine for themselves a form of government. This is the only true philosophical sense of the dictum that "governments derive their just powers from the consent of the governed". The Taparelli school makes the primitive determinant out of an existing prior right of another character, which passes naturally into this power. Primitively this is parental supremacy grown to patriarchal dimensions and resulting at the last in supreme civil power. Secondarily, it may arise from other rights, showing natural aptitude preferentially in one subject or another, as that of feudal ownership of the territory of the community, capacity to extricate order out of chaos in moments of civic confusion, military ability and success in case of just conquest, and, finally, in remote instances by the consent of the governed.

Finally, the means by which the commonwealth will work toward its ideal condition of the largest measure of peace and prosperity attainable are embraced in the just exercise, under direction of civil authority, of the physical, mental, and moral activities of the members of the community: and here the field of human endeavour is wide and expansive. However, the calls upon the individual by the governmental power are necessarily limited by the scope of the natural purpose of the State and by the inalienable prior rights and inseparable duties conferred or imposed upon the individual by the Natural Law.

RELIGIOUS SOCIETY *de facto* A SUPERNATURAL SOCIETY.—If we analyze the moral development of man, we find looming large his obligation to worship his Creator, not only privately, but publicly, not only as an individual, but in social union. This opens up another kind of society ordered by the natural law, to wit, religious society. An examination of this in the natural order and by force of reason alone would seem to show that man, though morally obliged to social worship, was morally free to establish a parallel organization for such worship or to merge its functions with those of the State, giving a double character to the enlarged society, namely, civil and religious. Historically, among those who knew not Divine revelation, men would seem to have been inclined more to the latter; but not always so. Of course, the purpose and means of this religious social duty are so related to those of a merely civil society that considerable care would have to be exercised in adjusting the balance of intersecting rights and duties, to define the relative domains of religious and civil authority, and, finally, to adjudicate supremacy in case of direct apparent conflict. The development of all this has been given an entirely different turn through the intervention of the Creator in His creation by positive law revealed to man, changing the natural status into a higher one, eliminating natural religious society, and at the last establishing through the mission of our Lord Jesus Christ an universal and unfailing religious society in the Church. This is a supernatural religious society. (See CHURCH.)

NON-CATHOLIC THEORIES.—Thomas Hobbes, starting from the assumption which Calvin had propagated that human nature is itself perverse and man essentially inept for consorting with his fellows, made the natural state of man to be one of universal and continuous warfare. This, of course, excludes the Maker of man from having destined him originally to society, since he would in Hobbes's view have given him a nature exactly the reverse of a proportioned means. Hobbes thought that he found in man such selfish rivalry, weak cowardice, and greed of self-glorification as to make him naturally prey upon his fellows and subdue them, if he could, to his wants, making might to be the only source of right. However, finding life intolerable (if not impossible) under such conditions, he resorted to a social pact with other men for the establishment of peace, and, as that was a prudent thing to do, man, adds Hobbes, was thus following the dictates of reason and in that sense the law of nature. On this basis Hobbes could and did make civil authority consist in nothing more than the sum of the physical might of the people massed in a chosen centre of force. This theory was developed in the "Leviathan" of Hobbes to account for the existence of civil authority and civil society, but its author left his reader to apply the same perversity of nature and exercise of physical force for the taking of a wife or wives and establishing domestic society.

Jean-Jacques Rousseau, though borrowing largely from Hobbes and fearlessly carrying some of his principles to their most extreme issue, had a view in part his own. As for the family, he was content to leave it as a natural institution, with a stability, however, commensurate only with the need of putting the offspring within reach of self-preservation. Not so for the State. Man naturally, he contended, was sylvan and solitary, a fine type of indolent animal, mating with his like and living in the pleasant ease of shady retreats by running waters. He was virtuous, sufficient to himself for his own needs, essentially free, leaving others alone in their freedom, and desirous of being left alone in his. His life was not to be disturbed by the fever of ambitious desires, the burden of ideas, or the restriction of moral laws. Unfortunately, he had a capacity and an itch for self-improvement, and his inventive genius, creating new conveniences, started new deeds, and, to meet these more readily, he entered into transitory agreements with other men. Then came differences, fraud, and quarrels, and so ended the tranquil ease and innocence of his native condition. Through sheer necessity of self-defence, as in the theory of Hobbes, he took to the establishment of civil society. To do so without loss of personal freedom, there was but one way, namely, that all the members should agree to merge all their rights, wills, and personalities in a unit moral person and will, leaving the subject member the satisfaction that he was obeying but his own will thus merged, and so in possession still of full liberty in every act. Thus civil authority was but the merger of all rights and wills in the one supreme right and will of the community. The merging agreement was Rousseau's "Social Contract". Unfortunately for its author, as he himself confessed, the condition of perfect, self-sufficient, lawless man was never seen on land or sea; and his social contract had no precedent in all the centuries of the history of man. His dream ignored man's inalienable rights, took no account of coercing wills that would not agree, nor of the unauthorized merging of the wills of posterity, and drained all the vitality as well out of authority as out of obedience. He left authority a power shorn of the requisites essential for the purpose of civil security.

The evolutionist, who has left the twisted turn of all his theories in much of the common language of the day, even after the theories themselves have died to all serious scientific acceptance, wished to make ethics a department of materialistic biology, and have the aggregate of human entities assemble by the same physical laws that mass cells into a living being. Man's native tendency to persist, pure egoism, made him shrink from the danger of destruction or injury at the hands of other individuals, and this timidity became a moving force driving him to compound with his peers into a unit source of strength without which he could not persist. From common life in this unit man's egoism began to take on a bit of altruism, and men acquired at the last a sense of the common good, which replaced their original timidity as the spring of merging activity. Later mutual sympathy put forth its tendrils, a sense of unity sprang up, and man had a civil society. Herein was latent the capacity for expressing the general will, which when developed became civil authority. This evolutionary process is still in motion toward the last stand foreseen by the theorist, a universal democracy clad in a federation of the world. All this has been seriously and solemnly presented to our consideration with a naïve absence of all sense of humour, with no suspicion that the human mind naturally refuses to confound the unchanging action of material attraction and repulsion with human choice; or to mistake the fruit of intellectual planning and execution for the fortuitous results of blind force. We are not cowards all, and have not fled to society from the sole promptings of fear, but from the natural desire we have of human development. Authority for mankind is not viewed as the necessary resultant of the necessary influx of all men's wills to one goal, but is recognized to be a power to loose and to bind in a moral sense the wills of innumerable freemen.

The neo-pagan theory, renewing the error of Plato and in a measure of Aristotle also, has made the individual and the family mere creatures and chattels of the State, and, pushing the error further, wishes to orientate all moral good and evil, all right and duty from the authority of the State, whose good as a national unit is paramount. This theory sets up the State as an idol for human worship and eventually, if the theory were acted upon, though its authors dream it not, for human destruction.

The historical school, mistaking what men have done for what men should do and, while often missing the full induction of the past, scornfully rejecting as empty apriorism deductive reasoning from the nature of man, presents a materialistic, evolutionary, and positivistic view of human society, which in no way appeals to sane reason. No more does the theory of Kant, as applied to society in the Hegelian development of it; though, owing to its intellectual character and appearance of ultimate analysis, it has found favour with those who seek philosophic principles from sources of so-called pure metaphysics. It would be idle to present here with Kant an analysis of the assumption of the development of all human right from the conditions of the use of liberty consistent with the general law of universal liberty, and the creation of civil government as an embodiment of universal liberty in the unified will of all the constituents of the State.

SUAREZ, *De Opere Sex Dierum*, V, vii; IDEM, *Defensio Fidei*, III, ii, iii; IDEM, *De Legibus*, III, ii, iii, iv; COSTA-ROSETTI, *Philosophia Moralis* (Innsbruck, 1886); DE HALLER, *Restauration de la Science Politique*; TAPARELLI, *Dritto Naturale* (Rome, 1855); MEYER, *Institutiones Juris Naturalis* (Freiburg, 1900); HOBBES, *Leviathan* (Cambridge University Press); ROUSSEAU, *Du Contrat Social* (Paris, 1896), *The Social Contract*, tr. TOZER (London, 1909); SPENCER, *The Study of Sociology* (London); COMTE, *Les Principes du Positivisme*; SCHAFFLE, *Structure et La Vie du Corps Social*; BLUNTSCHLI, *The Theory of the State* (Oxford translation, Clarendon Press, 1901); STERRETT, *The Ethics of Hegel* (Boston, 1893); WOODROW WILSON, *The State* (Boston, 1909).

CHARLES MACKSEY.

Society, THE CATHOLIC CHURCH EXTENSION.— IN THE UNITED STATES.—The first active agitation for a church extension or home mission society for the Catholic Church in North America was begun in 1904 by an article of the present writer, published in the "American Ecclesiastical Review" (Philadelphia). This article was followed by a discussion in the same review, participated in by several priests, and then by a second article of the writer's. On 18 October, 1905, the discussion which these articles aroused took form, and, under the leadership of the Most Reverend James Edward Quigley, Archbishop of Chicago, a new society, called The Catholic Church Extension Society of the United States of America, was organized at a meeting held in the archbishop's residence at Chicago. The following were present at that meeting and became the first board of governors of the society: The Archbishops of Chicago and Santa Fe, the Bishop of Wichita, the present Bishop of Rockford, Reverends Francis C. Kelley, G. P. Jennings, E. P. Graham, E. A. Kelly, J. T. Roche, B. X. O'Reilly, F. J. Van Antwerp, F. A. O'Brien; Messrs. M. A. Fanning, Anthony A. Hirst, William P. Breen, C. A. Plamondon, J. A. Roe, and S. A. Baldus. All these are still (1911) connected with the church extension movement, except Archbishop Bourgade of Santa Fé, who has since died, Reverends E. P. Graham and F. A. O'Brien, and Mr. C. A. Plamondon, who for one reason or another have found it impossible to continue in the work. The Archbishop of Chicago was made chairman of the board, the present writer was elected president, and Mr. William P. Breen, LL.D., of Fort Wayne, Indiana, treasurer. Temporary headquarters were established at Lapeer, Michigan. The second meeting was held in December of the same year, when the constitution was adopted and the work formally launched. A charter was granted on 25 December, 1905, by the State of Michigan to the new society, whose objects were set forth as follows: "To develop the missionary spirit in the clergy and people of the Catholic Church in the United States. To assist in the erection of parish buildings for poor and needy places. To support priests for neglected or proverty-stricken districts. To send the comfort of religion to pioneer localities. In a word, to preserve the faith of Jesus Christ to thousands of scattered Catholics in every portion of our own land, especially in the country districts and among immigrants." In January, 1907, the headquarters of the society were moved to Chicago, and the president was transferred to that archdiocese. In April, 1906, the society began the publication of a quarterly bulletin called "Extension". In May, 1907, this quarterly was enlarged and changed into a monthly; its circulation has steadily increased, and at the present time (1911) it has over one hundred thousand paid subscribers. On 7 June, 1907, the society received its first papal approval by an Apostolic Letter of Pius X addressed to the Archbishop of Chicago. In this letter His Holiness gave unqualified praise to the young organization and bestowed on its supporters and members many spiritual favours. On 9 June, 1910, the pope issued a special Brief by which the society was raised to the dignity of a canonical institution, directly under his own guidance and protection. By the terms of this Brief, the Archbishop of Chicago is always to be chancellor of the Society. The president must be appointed by the Holy Father himself. His term of office is not more than five years. The board of governors has the right to propose three names to the Holy See for this office, and to elect, according to their laws, all other officers of the society. The Brief also provided for a cardinal protector, living in Rome. His Holiness named Cardinal Sebastian Martinelli for this office, and later on appointed the present writer the first president under the new regulations. The Brief limits the society's activities to the United States and its possessions. A similiar Brief was issued to the Church Extension Society in Canada.

Since the organization of the church extension movement, the American society has expended over half a million dollars in missionary work. It has made about seven hundred gifts and loans to poor missions, and has had about five hundred and fifty chapels built in places where no Catholic Church or chapel existed previously and the scattered people could attend Mass only with great difficulty. Both societies have been educating many students for the missions, and both have circulated much good Catholic literature. The American society operates a "chapel car" (donated by one of its members, Ambrose Petry, K. C. S. G.), which carries a missionary into the remote districts along railroad lines, preaching missions and encouraging scattered Catholics to form centres with their own little chapels as beginnings of future parishes. The Holy Father has particularly blessed this chapel car work, and has given a gold medal to the donor of the car and to the society in recognition of its usefulness. Another chapel car, much larger and better equipped, is now about to be built. The society has interested itself very greatly in the missionary work of Porto Rico and the Philippine Islands, and has achieved substantial results. The Canadian society has been very active in saving the Ruthenian Catholics of the Canadian North-West to the Faith, against which an active war has been waged, especially by the Presbyterians. It was principally through the publicity given to this activity by the Canadian Society that the situation was brought to the attention of the bishops in Canada, who at the first Plenary Council decided to raise $100,000 for this work. The American society's first quinquennial report shows splendid progress, and the present situation of both societies gives promise of great things to come. A remarkable thing about the church extension movement is the ready response of the wealthier class of Catholics in the United States to its appeals. Some very large donations have been given. The Ancient Order of Hibernians is raising a fund of $50,000 for chapel building, and the Women's Catholic Order of Foresters $25,000. The directors intend to erect a college for the American mission.

The church extension movement, as it exists in the United States and Canada, has no close parallels in other countries, but is not unlike the Boniface Association in Germany or the Œuvre of St. Francis de Sales in France. Membership is divided into founders ($5000), life members ($1000), fifteen-year members ($100), and Annual Members ($10). There is a Women's Auxiliary in both societies which now begins to flourish. The American society has also a branch for children called the "Child Apostles". From the pennies of the children, chapels are to be built and each one called the "Holy Innocents"; the children have just completed (1911) the amount needed for their first chapel. The present officers of the American society are: His Eminence, Sebastian Cardinal Martinelli, Cardinal Protector; Most Rev. James E. Quigley, D.D., Chancellor; Most Rev. S. G. Messmer, D.D., Vice-Chancellor; Very Rev. Francis C. Kelley, D.D., LL.D., President; Rev. E. B. Ledvina, Vice-President and General Secretary; Rev. E. L. Roe, Director of the Women's Auxiliary and Vice-President; Rev. W. D. O'Brien, Director of the Child Apostles and Vice-President; Mr. Leo Doyle, General Counsel and Vice-President; Mr. John A. Lynch, Treasurer. The members of the executive committee are: Most Rev. James E. Quigley, D.D.; Very Rev. Francis C. Kelley, D.D., LL.D., Rev. Edward A. Kelly, LL.D.; Messrs. Ambrose Petry, K. C. S. G., Richmond Dean, Warren A. Cartier, and Edward F. Carry. On the board of governors are the Archbishops of Chicago, San Francisco, Milwaukee, Boston, New Orleans, Santa Fé, Oregon City, with the bishops of Covington, Detroit, Wichita, Duluth, Brooklyn, Trenton, Mobile, Rockford, Kansas City, Pittsburgh and Helena, and distinguished priests and laymen.

IN CANADA.—The church extension movement was organized in Canada as an independent society (bearing the name of "The Catholic Church Extension Society of Canada") by the Most Reverend Donatus Sbarretti, Delegate Apostolic of that country, Most Rev. Fergus Patrick McEvay, D.D., Archbishop of Toronto, Rev. Dr. A. E. Burke of the Diocese of Charlottetown, Very Rev. Monsignor A. A. Sinnott, secretary of the Apostolic Delegation, the Rev. Dr. J. T. Kidd, chancellor of Toronto, the Right Honourable Sir Charles Fitzpatrick, K. C. M. G., Chief Justice of Canada, and the present writer. The Canadian society at once purchased the "Catholic Register", a weekly paper, enlarged it, and turned it into the official organ of the work. The circulation of this paper has increased marvellously. The new society in Canada received a Brief, similar to that granted the American society, establishing it canonically. The same cardinal protector was appointed for both organizations. The Archbishop of Toronto was made chancellor of the Canadian society, and Very Rev. Dr. A. E. Burke was appointed president for the full term of five years. The officers of the Canadian society are: His Eminence Cardinal Martinelli, Protector; The Archbishop of Toronto (see vacant), Chancellor; Very Rev. A. E. Burke, D.D., LL.D., President; Rev. J. T. Kidd, D.D., Secretary; Rev. Hugh J. Canning, Diocesan Director; The Archbishop of Toronto; Right Hon. Sir Charles Fitzpatrick, K. C. M. G., and the President, Executive Committee.

FRANCIS C. KELLEY.

Society for Promoting Christian Knowledge. See CHRISTIAN KNOWLEDGE, SOCIETY FOR PROMOTING.

Society of Foreign Missions of Paris.—The Society of Foreign Missions was established 1658–63, its chief founders being Mgr Pallu, Bishop of Heliopolis, Vicar Apostolic of Tonking, and Mgr Lambert de la Motte, Bishop of Bertyus, Vicar Apostolic of Cochin-China. Both bishops left France (1660–62) to go to their respective missions and as true travellers of Christ they crossed Persia and India on foot. The object of the new society was and still is the evangelization of infidel countries, by founding churches and training up a native clergy under the jurisdiction of the bishops. In order that the society might recruit members and administer its property, a house was established in 1663 by the priests whom the vicars Apostolic had appointed their agents. This house, whose directors were to form young priests to the apostolic life and transmit to the bishops the offerings made by charity, was and is still situated at Paris in the Rue du Bac. Known from the beginning as the Seminary of Foreign Missions, it secured the approval of Alexander VII, and the legal recognition, still in force, of the French Government.

The nature and organization of the society deserve special mention. It is not a religious order but a congregation, a society of secular priests, united as members of the same body, not by vows but by the rule approved by the Holy See, by community of object, and the Seminary of Foreign Missions, which is the centre of the society and the common basis which sustains the other parts. On entering the society the missionaries promise to devote themselves until death to the service of the missions, while the society assures them in return, besides the means of sanctification and perseverance, all necessary temporal support and assistance. There is no superior general; the bishops, vicars Apostolic, superiors of missions, and board of directors of the seminary are the superiors of the society. The directors of the seminary are chosen from among the missionaries and each group of missions is represented by a director. The bishops and vicars Apostolic are appointed by the pope, after nomination by the missionaries, and presentation by the directors of the seminary. In their missions they depend only on Propaganda and through it on the pope. No subject aged more than thirty-five may be admitted to the seminary nor may anyone become a member of the society before having spent three years in the mission field. Several points of this rule were determined from the earliest years of the society's existence, others were established by degrees and as experience pointed out their usefulness. By this rule the society has lived and according to it its history has been outlined.

This history is difficult, for owing to the length of the journeys, the infrequent communications, and the poverty of resources the missions have developed with difficulty. The chief events of the first period (1658-1700) are: the publication of the book "Institutions apostoliques", which contains the germ of the principles of the rule, the foundation of the general seminary at Juthia (Siam), the evangelization of Tonking, Cochin China, Cambodia, and Siam, where more than 40,000 Christians were baptized, the creation of an institute of Annamite nuns known as "Lovers of the Cross", the establishment of rules among catechists, the ordination of thirty native priests. Beside these events of purely religious interest there were others in the political order which emphasized the patriotism of these evangelical labourers: through their initiative a more active trade was established between Indo-China, the Indies, and France; embassies were sent from place to place; treaties were signed; a French expedition to Siam took possession of Bangkok, Mergin, and Jonselang, and France was on the verge of possessing an Indo-Chinese empire when the blundering of subalterns ruined an undertaking the failure of which had an unfortunate influence on the missions. But the most important work of the vicars Apostolic and the society is the application of the fruitful principle of the organization of churches by native priests and bishops. Thenceforth the apostolate in its progress has followed this plan in every part of the world with scrupulous fidelity and increasing success. In the second half of the eighteenth century it was charged with the missions which the Jesuits had possessed in India prior to their suppression in Portugal. Many of the Jesuits remained there. The missions thereupon assumed new life, especially at Se-tchoan, where remarkable bishops, Mgr Pottier and Mgr Dufresse, gave a strong impulse to evangelical work; and in Cochin China, where Mgr Pigneau de Behaine performed signal service for the king of that country as his agent in making with France a treaty, which was the first step towards the present splendid situation of France in Indo-China. At the end of the eighteenth century the French Revolution halted the growth of the society, which had previously been very rapid. At that time it had six bishops, a score of missionaries, assisted by 135 native priests; in the various missions there were nine seminaries with 250 students, and 300,000 Christians. Each year the number of adult baptisms rose on an average of 3000 to 3500; that of infant baptisms *in articulo mortis* was more than 100,000.

In the nineteenth century the development of the society and its missions was rapid and considerable. Several causes contributed to this; chiefly the charity of the Propagation of the Faith and the Society of the Holy Childhood; each bishop receives annually 1200 francs, each missionary 660 francs, each mission has its general needs and works allowance, which varies according to its importance and may amount to from 10,000 to 30,000 francs. The second cause was persecution. Fifteen missionaries died in prison or were beheaded during the seventeenth and eighteenth centuries and the beginning of the nineteenth century, but after that the martyrs among the missionaries were very numerous. The best known are Mgr Dufresse, Vicar Apostolic of Se-tchoan, beheaded in 1815; Gagelin, Marchand, Jaccard, Cornay, and Dumoulin-Borie from 1833 to 1838; and from 1850 to 1862 Schoeffler, Vénard, Bonnard, Néron, Chapdelaine, Néel, Cuenot, Vicar Apostolic of Eastern Cochin China. If, besides these, mention were made of the native priests, catechists, and nuns, in short of all who died for Christ, we should have a record of one of the bloodiest holocausts in history. These persecutions were described in Europe by books, pamphlets, annals, and journals, arousing the pity of some and the anger of others and inspiring numerous young men either with the desire of martyrdom or that of evangelization. They moved European nations, especially France and England, to intervene in Indo-China and China and open up in these countries an era of liberty and protection till then unknown. Another cause of the progress of the missionaries was the ease and frequency of communication in consequence of the invention of steam and the opening of the Suez Canal. A voyage could be made safely in one month which had formerly required from eight to ten months amid many dangers.

The following statistics of the missions confided to the Society will show this development at a glance: *Missions of Japan and Korea*.—Tokio, Nagasaki, Osaka, Hakodate, Korea, total number of Catholics, 138,624; churches or chapels, 238; bishops and missionaries, 166; native priests, 48; catechists, 517; seminaries, 4; seminarists, 81; communities of men and women, 44, containing 399 persons; schools, 161, with 9024 pupils; orphanages and work-rooms 38, with 988 children; pharmacies, dispensaries, and hospitals, 19. *Missions of China and Tibet*.—Western, Eastern, and Southern Se-tchoan, Yun-nan, Kouy-tcheou, Kouang-ton, Kouang-si, Southern Manchuria, Northern Manchuria.—Catholics, 272,792; churches or chapels, 1392; bishops and missionaries, 408; native priests, 191; catechists, 998; seminaries, 19; seminarists, 661; communities of men and women, 23, with 222 members; schools, 1879, with 31,971 pupils; orphanages and work-rooms, 132, with 4134 children; pharmacies, dispensaries, and hospitals, 364. *Missions of Eastern Indo-China*.—Tongking, Cochin China, Cambodia.—Catholic population, 632,830; churches or chapels, 2609; bishops and missionaries, 365; native priests, 491; catechists, 1153; seminaries, 14; seminarists, 1271; communities of men and women, 91, with 2583 persons; schools, 1859, with 58,434 pupils; orphanages and work-rooms, 106, with 7217 children; pharmacies, dispensaries, hospitals, 107. *Missions of Western Indo-China*.—Siam, Malacca, Laos, Southern Burma, Northern Burma.—Catholics, 132,226; churches or chapels, 451; bishops and missionaries, 199; native priests, 42; catechists, 242; seminaries, 3; seminarists, 81; communities of men and women, 47, with 529 members; schools, 320, with 21,306 pupils; orphanages and work-rooms, 132, with 3757 children; pharmacies, dispensaries, hospitals, 86. *Missions of India*.—Pondicherry, Mysore, Coimbatore, Kumbakonam.—Catholics, 324,050; churches or chapels, 1048; bishops and missionaries, 207; native priests, 67; catechists, 274; seminaries, 4; seminarists, 80; communities of men and women, 54, with 787 members; schools, 315, with 18,693 pupils; orphanages and work-rooms, 57, with 2046 children; pharmacies, dispensaries, and hospitals, 41.

In addition to these missionaries actively engaged in mission work, there are some occupied in the establishments called common, because they are used by the whole society. Indeed the development of the society necessitated undertakings which were not needed in the past. Hence a sanatorium for sick missionaries has been established at Hong-Kong on the coast of China; another in India among the Nilgiri mountains, of radiant appearance and invigorating climate, and a third in France. In thinking of the welfare of the body, that of the soul was not lost sight of, and a house of spiritual retreat was founded at Hong-Kong, whither all the priests of the society may repair to renew their priestly and apostolic fervour. To this house was added a printing establishment, whence issue the most beautiful works of the Far East, dictionaries, grammars, books of theology, piety, Christian doctrine, and pedagogy. Houses of correspondence, or agencies, were established in the Far East at Shanghai, Hong-Kong, Saigon, Singapore, and one at Marseilles, France. The Seminary of the Foreign Missions which long had only one section, has for twenty years had two.

LUQUET, Lettres à l'évêque de Langres sur la cong. des Missions-Etrangères (Paris, 1842); LAUNAY, Hist. générale de la Société des Missions-Etrangères (Paris, 1894); Docum. hist. sur la Soci. des Missions-Etrangères (Paris, 1904); Hist. des missions de l'Inde (Paris, 1898); Hist. de la mission du Thibet (Paris, 1903); Hist. des missions de Chine 8 (Paris, 1903–8); LOUVET, La Cochinchine religieuse (Paris, 1885); DALLET, Hist. de l'église de Corée (Paris, 1874); MARNAS, La religion de Jésus ressuscité au Japon (Paris, 1896).

A. LAUNAY.

Society of Jesus (COMPANY OF JESUS, JESUITS), a religious order founded by Saint Ignatius Loyola (q. v.). Designated by him "The Company of Jesus" to indicate its true leader and its soldier spirit, the title was latinized into "Societas Jesu" in the Bull of Paul III approving its formation and the first formula of its Institute ("Regimini militantis ecclesiæ", 27 Sept., 1540). The term "Jesuit" (of fifteenth-century origin, meaning one who used too freely or appropriated the name of Jesus), was first applied to the Society in reproach (1544–52), and was never employed by its founder, though members and friends of the Society in time accepted the name in its good sense. The Society ranks among religious institutes as a mendicant order of clerks regular, that is, a body of priests organized for apostolic work, following a religious rule, and relying on alms for their support [Bulls of Pius V, "Dum indefessæ", 7 July, 1571; Gregory XIII, "Ascendente Domino" (q. v.), 25 May, 1584].

As has been explained under the title "Ignatius Loyola", the founder began his self-reform, and the enlistment of followers, entirely prepossessed with the idea of the imitation of Christ, and without any plan for a religious order or purpose of attending to the needs of the days. Unexpectedly prevented from carrying out this original idea, he offered his services and those of his followers to the pope, "Christ upon Earth", who at once employed them in such works as were most pressing at the moment. It was only after this and just before the first companions broke up to go at the pope's command to various countries, that the resolution to found an order was taken, and that Ignatius was commissioned to draw up Constitutions. This he did slowly and methodically; first introducing rules and customs, and seeing how they worked. He did not codify them for the first six years. Then three years were given to formulating laws, the wisdom of which had been proved by experiment. In the last six years of the saint's life the Constitutions so composed were finally revised and put into practice everywhere. This sequence of events explains at once how the Society, though devoted to the following of Christ, as though there were nothing else in the world to care for, is also so excellently adapted to the needs of the day. It began to attend to them before it began to legislate; and its legislation was the codification of those measures which had been proved by experience to be apt to preserve its preliminary religious principle among men actually devoted to the requirements of the Church in days not unlike our own.

The Society was not founded with the avowed intention of opposing Protestantism. Neither the papal letters of approbation, nor the Constitutions of the order mention this as the object of the new foundation. When Ignatius began to devote himself to the service of the Church, he had probably not heard even the names of the Protestant Reformers. His early plan was rather the conversion of Mohammedans, an idea which, a few decades after the final triumph of the Christians over the Moors in Spain, must have strongly appealed to the chivalrous Spaniard. The name "Societas Jesu" had been borne by a military order approved and recommended by Pius II in 1459, the purpose of which was to fight against the Turks and aid in spreading the Christian faith. The early Jesuits were sent by Ignatius first to pagan lands or to Catholic countries; to Protestant countries only at the special request of the pope, and to Germany, the cradle-land of the Reformation, at the urgent solicitation of the imperial ambassador. From the very beginning the missionary labours of Jesuits among the pagans of India, Japan, China, Canada, Central and South America were as important as their activity in Christian countries. As the object of the Society was the propagation and strengthening of the Catholic Faith everywhere, the Jesuits naturally endeavoured to counteract the spread of Protestantism. They became the main instruments of the Counter-Reformation; the reconquest of southern and western Germany and Austria for the Church, and the preservation of the Catholic faith in France and other countries were due chiefly to their exertions.

INSTITUTE, CONSTITUTIONS, LEGISLATION.—The official publication which comprises all the regulations of the Society, its *codex legum*, is entitled "Institutum Societatis Jesu", of which the latest edition was issued at Rome and Florence, 1869–91 (for full bibliography see Sommervogel, V, 75–115; IX, 609–611; for commentators see X, 705–710). The Institute contains: (1) The special Bulls and other pontifical documents approving the Society and canonically determining or regulating its various works, and its ecclesiastical standing and relations.—Besides those already mentioned, other important Bulls are those of: Paul III, "Injunctum nobis", 14 March, 1543; Julius III, "Exposcit debitum", 21 July, 1550; Pius V, "Æquum reputamus", 17 January, 1565; Pius VII, "Sollicitudo omnium ecclesiarum", 7 August, 1814; Leo XIII, "Dolemus inter alia", 13 July, 1880. (2) The Examen Generale and Constitutions.—The Examen contains subjects to be explained to postulants and points on which they are to be examined. The Constitutions are divided into ten parts: (a) admission; (b) dismissal; (c) novitiate; (d) scholastic training; (e) profession and other grades of membership; (f) religious vows and other obligations as observed in the Society; (g) missions and other ministries; (h) congregations, local and general assemblies as a means of union and uniformity; (i) the general and chief superiors; (j) preservation of the spirit of the Society. Thus far in the Institute all is by St. Ignatius, who has also added "Declarations" of various obscure parts. Then come: (3) Decrees of General Congregations, which have equal authority with the Constitutions; (4) Rules, general and particular, etc.; (5) Formulæ or order of business for the congregations; (6) Ordinations of generals, which have the same authority as the rules; (7) Instructions, some for superiors, others for those engaged in the missions or other works of the Society; (8) Industriæ, or special counsels for superiors; (9) The Book of the Spiritual Exercises; and (10) the Ratio Studiorum (q. v.), which have directive force only.

The Constitutions as drafted by Ignatius and adopted finally by the first congregation of the Society, 1558, have never been altered. Ill-informed writers have stated that Lainez, the second general, made considerable changes in the saint's conception of the order; but Ignatius's own last recension of the Constitutions, lately reproduced in facsimile (Rome, 1908), exactly agrees with the text of the Constitutions now in force, and contains no word by Lainez, not even in the Declarations, or glosses added to the text, which are all the work of Ignatius. The text in use in the Society is a Latin version prepared under the direction of the third congregation, and subjected to a minute comparison with the Spanish original preserved in the Society's archives, during the fourth congregation (1581).

These Constitutions were written after long deliberation between Ignatius and his companions in founding the Society, as at first it seemed to them that they might continue their work without the aid of a special Rule. They were the fruit of long experience and of serious meditation and prayer. Throughout they are inspired by an exalted spirit of charity and of zeal for souls. They contain nothing unreasonable. To appreciate them, however, requires a knowledge of canon law as applied to monastic life and also of their history in the light of the times for which they were framed. Usually those who find fault with them either have never read them or else have misinterpreted them. Monod, for instance, in his introduction to Böhmer's essay on the Jesuits ("Les jésuites", Paris, 1910, pp. 13, 14) recalls how Michelet mistranslated the words of the Constitutions, p. VI, c. 5, *obligationem ad peccatum*, and made it appear that they require obedience even to the commission of sin, as if the text were *obligatio ad peccandum*, whereas the obvious meaning and purpose of the text is precisely to show that the transgression of the rules is not in itself sinful. Monod enumerates such men as Arnauld, Wolf, Lange, Ranke in the first edition of his "History", Häusser and Droysen, Philippson and Charbonnel, as having repeated the same error, although it had been refuted frequently since 1824, particularly by Gieseler, and corrected by Ranke in his second edition. Whenever the Constitutions enjoin what is already a serious moral obligation, or superiors, by virtue of their authority, impose a grave obligation, transgression is sinful; but this is true of such transgressions not only in the Society but out of it. Moreover such commands are rarely given by the superiors and only when the good of the individual member or the common good imperatively demands it. The rule throughout is one of love inspired by wisdom, and it must be interpreted in the spirit of charity which animates it. This is especially true of its provisions for the affectionate relations of members with superiors and with one another, by the manifestation of conscience, more or less practised in every religious order, and by mutual correction when this may be necessary. It also applies to the methods employed to ascertain the qualifications of members for various offices or ministries.

The chief authority is vested in the general congregation, which elects the general, and could, for certain grave causes, depose him. This body could also (though there has never yet been an occasion for so doing) add new Constitutions, and abrogate old ones. Usually this congregation is convened on the occasion of the death of a general, in order to elect his successor, and to make provisions for the government and welfare of the Society. It may also be called at other times for grave reasons. It consists of the general, when alive, and his assistants, the provincials, and two deputies from each province or territorial division of the society elected by the superiors and older professed members. Thus authority in the Society eventually rests on a democratic basis. But as there is no definite time for calling the general congregation, which in fact rarely occurs except to elect a new general, the exercise of authority is usually in the hands of the general, in whom is vested the fullness of administrative power, and of spiritual authority. He can do anything within the scope of the Constitutions, and can even dispense with them for good causes, though he cannot change them. He resides at Rome, and has a council of assistants, five in number at present, one each for Italy, France, Spain and countries of Spanish origin, one for Germany, Austria, Poland, Belgium, Hungary, Holland, and one for English-speaking countries—England, Ireland, United States, Canada, and British colonies (except India). These usually hold office until the death of the general. Should the general through age or infirmity become incapacitated for governing the Society, a vicar is chosen by a general congregation to act for him. At his death he names one so to act until the congregation can meet and elect his successor.

Next to him in order of authority come the provincials, the heads of the Society, whether for an entire country, as England, Ireland, Canada, Belgium, Mexico, or, where these units are too large or too small to make convenient provinces, they may be subdivided or joined together. Thus there are now four provinces in the United States: California, Maryland-New York, Missouri, New Orleans. In all there are now twenty-seven provinces. The provincial is appointed by the general, with ample

REDUCED FACSIMILE OF SPANISH MS. OF THE CONSTITUTIONS WITH AUTOGRAPH CORRECTIONS BY ST. IGNATIUS administrative faculties. He too has a council of "consultors" and an "admonitor", appointed by the general. Under the provincial come the local superiors. Of these, rectors of colleges, provosts of professed houses, and masters of novices are appointed by the general; the rest by the provincial. To enable the general to make and control so many appointments, a free and ample correspondence is kept up, and everyone has the right of private communication with him. No superior, except the general, is named for life. Usually provincials and rectors of colleges hold office for three years.

Members of the Society fall into four classes: (1) *Novices* (whether received as lay brothers for the domestic and temporal services of the order, or as aspirants to the priesthood), who are trained in the spirit and discipline of the order, prior to making the religious vows. (2) At the end of two years the novices make simple but perpetual vows, and, if aspirants to the priesthood, become *formed scholastics;* they remain in this grade as a rule from two to fifteen years, in which time they will have completed all their studies, pass (generally) a certain period in teaching, receive the priesthood, and go through a third year of novitiate or probation (the tertianship). According to the degree of discipline and virtue, and to the talents they display (the latter are normally tested by the examination for the Degree of Doctor of Theology), they may now become formed coadjutors or professed members of the order. (3) *Formed coadjutors,* whether formed lay brothers or priests, make vows, which, though not solemn, are perpetual on their part; while the Society, on its side, binds itself to them, unless they should commit some grave offence. (4) The *professed* are all priests, who make, besides the three usual solemn vows of religion, a fourth, of special obedience to the pope in the matter of missions, undertaking to go wherever they are sent, without even requiring money for the journey. They also make certain additional, but non-essential, simple vows, in the matter of poverty, and the refusal of external honours. The professed of the four vows constitute the kernel of the Society; the other grades are regarded as preparatory or as subsidiary to this. The chief offices can be held by the professed alone; and though they may be dismissed, yet they must be received back, if willing to comply with the conditions that may be prescribed. Otherwise they enjoy no privileges, and many posts of importance, such as the government of colleges, may be held by members of other grades. For special reasons some are occasionally professed of three vows and they have certain but not all the privileges of the other professed. All live in community alike as regards food, apparel, lodging, recreation, and all are alike bound by the rules of the Society.

There are no secret Jesuits. Like other orders the Society can, if it will, make its friends participators in its prayers and in the merits of its good works; but it cannot make them members of the order, unless they live the life of the order. There is indeed the case of St. Francis Borgia, who made some of the probations in an unusual way, outside the houses of the order. But this was in order that he might be free to conclude certain business matters and other affairs of state, and thus appear the sooner in public as a Jesuit, not that he might remain permanently outside the common life.

Novitiate and Training.—Candidates for admission come not only from the colleges conducted by the Society, but from other schools. Frequently postgraduate or professional students, and those who have already begun their career in business or professional life, or even in the priesthood, apply for admission. Usually the candidate applies in person to the provincial, and if he considers him a likely subject he refers him for examination to four of the more experienced fathers. They question him about the age, health, position, occupation of his parents, their religion and good character, their dependence on his services; about his own health, obligations, such as debts, or other contractual relations; his studies, qualifications, moral character, personal motives as well as the external influences that may have led him to seek admission. The results of their questioning and of their own observation they report severally to the provincial, who weighs their opinions carefully before deciding for or against the applicant. Any notable bodily or mental defect in the candidate, serious indebtedness or other obligation, previous membership in another religious order even for a day, indicating instability of vocation, unqualifies for admission. Undue influence, particularly if exercised by members of the order, would occasion stricter scrutiny than usual into the personal motives of the applicant.

Candidates may enter at any time, but usually there is a fixed day each year for their admission, towards the close of the summer holidays, in order that all may begin their training, or probation, together. They spend the first ten days considering the manner of life they are to adopt and its difficulties, the rules of the order, the obedience required of its members. They then make a brief retreat, meditating on what they have learned about the Society and examining closely their own motives and hopes of perseverance in the new mode of life. If all be satisfactory to them and the superior or director who has charge of them, they are admitted as novices, wear the clerical costume (as there is no special Jesuit habit), and begin in earnest the life of members of the Society. They rise early, make a brief visit to the chapel, a meditation on some subject selected the night before, assist at Mass, review their meditation, breakfast, and then prepare for the day's routine. This consists of manual labour, in or out of doors, reading books on spiritual topics, ecclesiastical history, biography, particularly of men or women distinguished for zeal and enterprise in missionary or educational fields. There is a daily conference by the master of novices on some detail of the Institute, notes of which all are required to make, so as to be ready, when asked, to repeat the salient points.

Wherever it is possible some are submitted to certain tests of their vocation and usefulness: to teaching catechism in the village churches; to attendance on the sick in hospitals; to going about on a pilgrimage or missionary journey without money or other provision. As soon as possible all make the spiritual exercises for thirty days. This is really the chief test of a vocation, as it is also in epitome the main work of the two years of the novitiate and for that matter of the entire life of a Jesuit. On these exercises the Constitutions, the life, and activity of the Society are based, so that they are really the chief factor in forming the character of a Jesuit. In accordance with the ideals set forth in these exercises, of disinterested conformity with God's will, and of personal love of Jesus Christ, the novice is trained diligently in a meditative study of the truths of religion, in the habit of self-knowledge, in a constant scrutiny of his motives and of the actions inspired by them, in the correction of every form of self-deceit, illusion, plausible pretext, and in the education of his will, particularly in making choice of what seems best after careful deliberation and without self-seeking. Deeds, not words, are insisted upon as proof of genuine service, and a mechanical, emotional, or fanciful piety is not tolerated. As the novice gradually thus becomes master of his judgment and will, he grows more and more capable of offering to God the reasonable service enjoined by St. Paul, and seeks to follow the Divine will, as manifested by Jesus Christ, by His vicar on earth, by the bishops appointed to rule His Church, by his more immediate or religious superiors, and by the civil powers rightfully exercising authority. This is what is meant by Jesuit obedience, the characteristic virtue of the order, such a sincere respect for authority as to accept its decisions and comply with them, not merely by outward performance but in all sincerity with the conviction that compliance is best, and that the command expresses for the time the will of God, as nearly as it can be ascertained.

The noviceship lasts two years. On its completion the novice makes the usual vows of religion, the simple vow of chastity in the Society having the force of a diriment impediment to matrimony. During the noviceship but a brief time daily is devoted to reviewing previous studies. The noviceship over, the scholastic members, i. e. those who are to become priests in the Society, follow a special course in classics and mathematics lasting two years, usually in the same house with the novices. Then, in another house and neighbourhood, three years are given to the study of philosophy, about five years to teaching in one or other of the public colleges of the Society, four years to the study of theology, priestly orders being conferred after the third, and, finally, one year more to another probation or noviceship, intended to help the young priest to renew his spirit of piety and to learn how to utilize to the best of his ability all the learning and experience he has acquired. In exceptional cases, as in that of a priest who has finished his studies before entering the order, allowance is made, and the training period need not last over ten years, a good part of which is spent in active ministry.

The object of the order is not limited to practising any one class of good works, however laudable (as preaching, chanting office, doing penance, etc.) but to study, in the manner of the Spiritual Exercises, what Christ would have done, if He were living in our circumstances, and to carry out that ideal. Hence elevation and largeness of aim. Hence the motto of the Society: "Ad Majorem Dei Gloriam". Hence the selection of the virtue of obedience as the characteristic of the order, to be ready for any call and to keep unity in every variety of work. Hence, by easy sequence, the omission of office in choir, of a specially distinctive habit, of unusual penances. Where the Protestant Reformers aimed at reorganizing the Church at large according to their particular conceptions, Ignatius began with interior self-reform; and after that had been thoroughly established, then the earnest preaching of self-reform to others. That done, the Church would not, and did not, fail to reform herself. Many religious distinguished themselves as educators before the Jesuits; but the Society was the first order which enjoined by its very Constitutions devotion to the cause of education. It was, in this sense, the first "teaching order".

The ministry of the Society consists chiefly in preaching; teaching catechism, especially to children; administering the sacraments, especially penance and the Eucharist; conducting missions in parishes on the lines of the Spiritual Exercises; directing those who wish to follow these exercises in houses of retreat, seminaries, or convents; taking care of parishes or of collegiate churches; organizing pious confraternities, sodalities, unions of prayer, Bona Mors associations in their own and in other parishes; teaching in schools of every grade—academic, seminary, university; writing books, pamphlets, periodical articles; going on foreign missions among uncivilized peoples. In liturgical functions the Roman Rite is followed. The proper exercise of all these functions is provided for by rules carefully framed by the general congregations or the generals. All these regulations command the greatest respect on the part of every member. In practice the superior for the time being is the living rule—not that he can alter or abrogate any rule, but because he must interpret and determine its application. In this fact and in its consequences, the Society differs from every religious order antecedent to its foundation; to this principally it owes its life, activity, and power to adapt its Institute to modern conditions without need of change in that instrument or of reform in the body itself.

The story of the foundation of the Society is told in the article IGNATIUS LOYOLA. Briefly, after having inspired his companions Peter Faber, Francis Xavier, James Lainez, Alonso Salmerón, Nicolas Bobadilla, Simon Rodriguez, Claude Le Jay, Jean Codure, and Paschase Brouet with a desire to dwell in the Holy Land imitating the life of Christ, they first made vows of poverty and chastity at Montmartre, Paris, on 15 August, 1534, adding a vow to go to the Holy Land after two years. When this was found to be impracticable, after waiting another year, they offered their services to the pope, Paul III. Fully another year was passed by some in university towns in Italy, by the others at Rome, where, after encountering much opposition and slander, all met together to agree on a mode of life by which they might advance in evangelical perfection and help others in the same task. The first formula of the Institute was submitted to the pope and approved of viva voce, 3 September, 1539, and formally, 27 September, 1540.

CONSTITUTIONS.—*Corpus institutorum Societatis Jesu* (Antwerp, Prague, Rome, 1635, 1702, 1705, 1707, 1709, 1869–70; Paris, partial edition, 1827–38); GAGLIARDI, *De cognitione instituti* (1841); LANCICIUS, *De præstantia instit. Soc. Jesu* (1644); NADAL, *Scholia in constitutiones* (1883); SUAREZ, *Tract. de religione Soc. Jesu* (1625); HUMPHREY, *The Religious State* (London, 1889), a digest of the treatise of Suarez; OSWALD, *Comment. in decem partes constit. Soc. Jesu* (3rd ed., Brussels, 1901); *Rules of the Society of Jesus* (Washington, 1839; London, 1863).

GENERALS PRIOR TO THE SUPPRESSION OF THE SOCIETY.—(1) St. Ignatius Loyola (q. v.), 19 April, 1541–31 July, 1556. The Society spread rapidly and at the time of St. Ignatius's death had twelve provinces: Italy, Sicily, Portugal, Aragon, Castile, Andalusia, Upper Germany, Lower Germany, France, India (including Japan), Brazil, and Ethiopia, the last-mentioned province lasting but a short time. It met with opposition at the University of Paris; while in Spain it was severely attacked by Melchior Cano.

(2) *James Lainez* (q. v.), 2 July, 1558–19 January, 1565. Lainez served two years as vicar-general, and was chosen general in the first general congregation, retarded till 1558 (19 June–10 Sept.), owing to the unfortunate war between Paul IV and Philip II. Paul IV gave orders that the Divine Office should be recited in choir, and also that the generalate should only last for three years. The pope died on 18 August, 1559, and his orders were not renewed by his successor, Pius IV; indeed he refused Father Lainez leave to resign when his first triennium closed. Through Pius's nephew, St. Charles Borromeo, the Society now received many privileges and openings, and progress was rapid. Father Lainez himself was sent to the "Colloquy of Poissy", and to the Council of Trent (1563–4), Saint Francis Borgia being left in Rome as his vicar-general. At the death of Lainez the Society numbered 3500 members in 18 provinces and 130 houses.

(3) *St. Francis Borgia* (q. v.), 2 July, 1565–1 October, 1572. One of the most delicate tasks of his government was to negotiate with Pope St. Pius V, who desired to reintroduce the singing of Office. This was in fact begun in May, 1569, but only in professed houses, and it was not to interfere with other work. Pius also ordained (Christmas, 1566) that no candidate of any religious order for the priesthood should be ordained until after his profession; and this indirectly caused much trouble to the Society, with its distinct grades of professed and non-pro-

INTERIOR OF THE CHURCH OF THE GESÙ, ROME

fessed priests. All had therefore to be professed of three vows, until Gregory XIII (December, 1572) allowed the original practice to be restored. Under his administration the foreign missionary work of the order greatly increased and prospered. New missions were opened by the Society in Florida, Mexico, and Peru.

(4) *Everard Mercurian*, Belgian, 23 April, 1573–1 August, 1580. Fr. Mercurian was born in 1514 in the village of Marcour (Luxemburg) whence his name, which he signed Everard de Marcour. He became the first non-Spanish general of the Society. Pope Gregory XIII, without commanding, had expressed his desire for this change. This, however, caused great dissatisfaction and opposition among a number of Spanish and Portuguese members, which came to a crisis during the generalate of Father Mercurian's successor, Father Claudius Acquaviva. Father Tolet was entrusted with the task of obtaining the submission of Michael Baius to the decision of the Holy See; he succeeded, but his success served later to draw on the Society the hatred of the Jansenists. Father Mercurian, when general, brought the Rules to their final form, compiling the "Summary of the Constitutions" from the manuscripts of St. Ignatius, and drawing up the "Common Rules" of the Society, and the particular rules for each office. He was greatly interested in the foreign missions and established the Maronite and English missions, and sent to the latter Blessed Edmund Campion and Father Robert Persons. Father Everard Mercurian passed thirty-two years in the Society, and died at the age of sixty-six. At that time the Society numbered 5000 members in eighteen provinces.

(5) *Claudius Acquaviva*, or Aquaviva (q. v.), Neapolitan, 19 February, 1581–31 January, 1615 (for the disputations on grace, see CONGREGATIO DE AUXILIIS). After Ignatius, Acquaviva was perhaps the ablest ruler of the Society. As a legislator he reduced to its present form the final parts of the Institute, and the Ratio Studiorum (q. v.). He had also to contend with extraordinary obstacles both from without and within. The Society was banished from France and from Venice; there were grave differences with the King of Spain, with Sixtus V, with the Dominican theologians; and within the Society the rivalry between Spaniard and Italian led to unusual complications and to the calling of two extraordinary general congregations (fifth and sixth). The origin of these troubles is perhaps eventually to be sought in the long wars of religion, which gradually died down after the canonical absolution of Henry IV, 1595 (in which Fathers Georges, Toledo, and Possevinus played important parts). The fifth congregation in 1593 supported Acquaviva steadily against the opposing parties, and the sixth, in 1608, completed the union of opinions. Paul V had in 1606 re-confirmed the Institute, which from now onwards may be considered to have won a stable position in the Church at large, until the epoch of the Suppression and the Revolution. Missions were established in Canada, Chile, Paraguay, the Philippine Islands, and China. At Father Acquaviva's death the Society numbered 13,112 members in 32 provinces and 559 houses.

(6) *Mutius Vitelleschi* (q. v.), Roman, 15 November, 1615–9 February, 1645. His generalate was one of the most pacific and progressive, especially in France and Spain; but the Thirty Years' War worked havoc in Germany. The canonization of Sts. Ignatius and Francis Xavier (1622) and the first centenary of the Society (1640) were celebrated with great rejoicings. The great mission of Paraguay began, that of Japan was stamped out in blood. England was raised in 1619 to the rank of a province of the order, having been a mission until then. Missions were established in Tibet (1624), Tonkin (1627), and the Maranhão (1640).

(7) *Vincent Caraffa* (q. v.), Neapolitan, 7 January, 1646–8 June, 1649. A few days before Father Caraffa's election as general, Pope Innocent X published a brief "Prospero felicique statui", in which he ordered a general congregation of the Society to be held every nine years; it was ordained also that no office in the Society except the position of master of novices should be held for more than three years. The latter regulation was revoked by Innocent's successor, Alexander VII, on 1 January, 1658; and the former by Benedict XIV in 1746 by the Bull "Devotam", many dispensations having been granted in the meantime.

(8) *Francis Piccolomini*, of Siena, 21 December, 1649–17 June, 1651; before his election as general he had been professor of philosophy at the Roman College; he died at the age of sixty-nine, having passed fifty-three years in the Society.

(9) *Aloysius Gottifredi*, Roman, 21 January, 1652–12 March, 1652; Father Gottifredi died at the house of the professed Fathers, Rome, within two months after his election, and before the Fathers assembled for the election and congregation had concluded their labour. He had been a professor of theology and rector of the Roman College, and later secretary of the Society under Father Mutius Vitelleschi.

(10) *Goswin Nickel*, German, b. at Jülich in 1582; 17 March, 1652–31 July, 1664. During these years the struggle with Jansenism was growing more and more heated. The great controversy on the Chinese Rites (1645) was continued (see RICCI, MATTEO). Owing to his great age Father Nickel obtained from the eleventh congregation the appointment of Father John Paul Oliva as vicar-general (on 7 June, 1661), with the approval of Alexander VII.

(11) *John Paul Oliva*, Genoese (elected vicar *cum jure successionis* on 7 June, 1661), 31 July, 1664–26 November, 1681. During his generalate the Society established a mission in Persia, which at first met with great success, four hundred thousand converts being made within twenty-five years; in 1736, however, the mission was destroyed by violent persecution. Father Oliva's generalate occurred during one of the most difficult periods in the history of the Society, as the controversies on Jansenism, the *droit de régale*, and moral theology were being carried on by the opponents of the Society with the greatest acrimony and violence. Father John Paul Oliva laboured earnestly to keep up the Society's high reputation for learning, and in a circular letter sent to all the houses of study urged the cultivation of the oriental languages.

(12) *Charles de Noyelle*, Belgian, 5 July, 1682–12 December, 1686. Father de Noyelle was born at Brussels on 28 July, 1615; so great was his reputation for virtue and prudence that at his election he received unanimous vote of the congregation. He had been assistant for the Germanic provinces during more than twenty years; he died at the age of seventy, after fifty years spent in the Society. Just about the time of his election, the dispute between Louis XIV of France and Pope Innocent XI had culminated in the publication of the "Déclaration du clergé de France" (19 March, 1682). This placed the Society in a difficult position in France, as its spirit of devotion to the papacy was not in harmony with the spirit of the "Déclaration". It required all the ingenuity and ability of Père La Chaise and Father de Noyelle to avert a disaster. Innocent XI was dissatisfied with the position the Society adopted, and threatened to suppress the order, proceeding even so far as to forbid the reception of novices.

(13) *Thyrsus González* (q. v.), Spaniard, 6 July, 1687–27 Oct., 1705. He interfered in the controversy between Probabilism (q. v.) and Probabiliorism, attacking the former doctrine with energy in a book published at Dillingen in 1691. As Probabilism

was on the whole in favour in the Society, this caused discussions, which were not quieted until the fourteenth congregation, 1696, when, with the pope's approval, liberty was left to both sides. Father González in his earlier days had laboured with great fruit as a missionary, and after his election as general encouraged the work of popular home missions. His treatise "De infallibilitate Romani pontificis in definiendis fidei et morum controversiis", which was a vigorous attack on the doctrines laid down in the "Déclaration du clergé de France", was published at Rome in 1689 by order of Pope Innocent XI; however, Innocent's successor, Alexander VII, caused the work to be withdrawn, as its effect had been to render the relations between France and the Holy See more difficult. Father González laboured earnestly to spread devotion to the saints of the Society; he died at the age of eighty-four, having passed sixty-three years in the order, during nineteen of which he was general.

(14) *Michelangelo Tamburini*, of Modena, 31 January, 1706–28 February, 1730. The long reign of Louis XIV, so favourable to the Jesuits in many respects, saw the beginning of those hostile movements which were to lead to the Suppression. The king's autocratic powers, his Gallicanism, his insistence on the repression of the Jansenists by force, the way he compelled the Society to take his part in the quarrel with Rome about the *régale* (1684–8), led to a false situation in which the parts might be reversed, when the all-powerful sovereign might turn against them, or by standing neutral leave them the prey of others. This was seen at his death, 1715, when the regent banished the once influential father confessor Le Tellier, while the gallicanizing Archbishop of Paris, Cardinal de Noailles, laid them under an interdict (1716–29). Father Tamburini before his election as general had taught philosophy and theology for twelve years and had been chosen by Cardinal Renaud d'Este as his theologian; he had also been provincial of Venice, secretary-general of the Society, and vicar-general. During the disputes concerning the Chinese Rites (q. v.), the Society was accused of resisting the orders of the Holy See. Father Tamburini protested energetically against this calumny, and when in 1711 the procurators of all the provinces of the Society were assembled at Rome, he had them sign a protest which he dedicated to Pope Clement XI. The destruction of Port-Royal and the condemnation of the errors of Quesnel by the Bull "Unigenitus" (1711) testified to the accuracy of the opinions adopted by the Society in these disputes. Father Tamburini procured the canonization of Saints Aloysius Gonzaga and Stanislaus Kostka, and the beatification of St. John Francis Régis. During his generalate the mission of Paraguay reached its highest degree of success; in one year no fewer than seventy-seven missionaries left for it; the missionary labours of St. Francis de Geronimo and Blessed Anthony Baldinucci in Italy, and Venerable Manuel Padial in Spain, enhanced the reputation of the Society. Father Tamburini died at the age of eighty-two, having spent sixty-five years in religion. At the time of his death the Society contained 37 provinces, 24 houses of professed Fathers, 612 colleges, 59 novitiates, 340 residences, 200 mission stations; in addition one hundred and fifty-seven seminaries were directed by the Jesuits.

(15) *Francis Retz*, Austrian (born at Prague, in 1673), 7 March, 1730–19 November, 1750. Father Retz was elected general unanimously, his able administration contributed much to the welfare of the Society; he obtained the canonization of St. John Francis Régis. Father Retz's generalate was perhaps the quietest in the history of the order. At the time of his death the Society contained 39 provinces, 24 houses of professed Fathers, 669 colleges, 61 novitiates, 335 residences, 273 mission stations, 176 seminaries, and 22,589 members, of whom 11,293 were priests.

(16) *Ignatius Visconti*, Milanese, 4 July, 1751–4 May, 1755. It was during this generalate that the accusations of trading were first made against Father Antoine de La Valette, who was recalled from Martinique in 1753 to justify his conduct. Shortly before dying, Father Visconti allowed him to return to his mission, where the failure of his commercial operations, somewhat later, gave an opportunity to the enemies of the Society in France to begin a warfare that ended only with the Suppression (see below). Trouble with Pombal also began at this time. Father Visconti died at the age of seventy-three.

(17) *Aloysius Centurioni*, Genoese, 30 November, 1755–2 October, 1757. During his brief generalate the most noteworthy facts were the persecution by Pombal of the Portuguese Jesuits and the troubles caused by Father de La Valette's commercial activities and disasters. Father Centurioni died at Castel Gandolfo, at the age of seventy-two.

(18) *Lorenzo Ricci* (q. v.), Florentine, 21 May, 1758, till the Suppression in 1773. In 1759 the Society contained 41 provinces, 270 mission posts, and 171 seminaries. Father Ricci founded the Bavarian province of the order in 1770. His generalate saw the slow death agony of the Society; within two years the Portuguese, Brazilian, and East Indian provinces and missions were destroyed by Pombal; close to two thousand members of the Society were cast destitute on the shores of Italy and imprisoned in fetid dungeons in Portugal. France, Spain, and the Two Sicilies followed in the footsteps of Pombal. The Bull "Apostolicum" of Clement XIII in favour of the Society produced no fruit. Clement XIV at last yielded to the demand for the extinction of the Society. Father Ricci was seized, and cast a prisoner into the Castel San Angelo, where he was treated as a criminal till death ended his sufferings on 24 November, 1775. In 1770 the Society contained 42 provinces, 24 houses of professed Fathers, 669 colleges, 61 novitiates, 335 residences, 273 mission stations, and about 23,000 members.

HISTORY. *Italy*.—The history of the Jesuits in Italy was in general very peaceful. The only serious disturbances were those arising from the occasional quarrels of the civil governments with the ecclesiastical powers. Ignatius's first followers were immediately in great request to instruct the faithful, and to reform the clergy, monasteries, and convents. Though there was little organized or deep-seated mischief, the amount of lesser evils was immense; the possibility here and there of a catastrophe was evident. While the preachers and missionaries evangelized the country, colleges were established at Padua, Venice, Naples, Bologna, Florence, Parma, and other cities. On 20 April, 1555, the University of Ferrara addressed to the Sorbonne a most remarkable testimony in favour of the order. St. Charles Borromeo was, after the popes, perhaps the most generous of all their patrons, and they freely put their best talents at his disposal. (For the difficulties about his seminary and with Fr. Guilio Mazarino, see Sylvain, "Hist. de S. Charles", iii, 53.) Juan de Vega, ambassador of Charles V at Rome, had learnt to know and esteem Ignatius there, and when he was appointed Viceroy of Sicily he brought Jesuits with him. A college was opened at Messina; success was marked, and its rules and methods were afterwards copied in other colleges. After fifty years the Society counted in Italy 86 houses and 2550 members. The chief trouble in Italy occurred at Venice in 1606, when Paul V laid the city under interdict for serious breaches of ecclesiastical immunities. The Jesuits and some other religious retired from the city, and the Senate, inspired by Paolo Sarpi, the disaffected friar, passed a decree of perpetual banishment against them. In effect, though peace was made ere long with the pope, it was fifty years before the Society could return. Italy during the first two centuries of the Society was still the most cultured country of Europe, and the Italian Jesuits enjoyed a high reputation for learning and letters. The elder Segneri is considered the first of Italian preachers, and there are a number of others of the first class. Maffei, Torsellino, Strada, Pallavicino, and Bartoli (q.v.) have left historical works which are still highly prized. Between Bellarmine (d. 1621) and Zaccharia (d. 1795) Italian Jesuits of note in theology, controversy, and subsidiary sciences are reckoned by the score. They also claim a large proportion of the saints, martyrs, generals, and missionaries. (See also BELLECIUS; BOLGENI; BOSCOVICH; POSSEVINUS; SCARAMELLI; VIVA.) Italy was divided into five provinces, with the following figures for the year 1749 (shortly before the beginning of the movement for the Suppression of the Society): Rome, 848; Naples, 667; Sicily, 775; Venice, 707; Milan, 625; total, 3622 members, about one-half of whom were priests, with 178 houses.

Spain.—Though the majority of Ignatius's companions were Spaniards, he did not gather them together in Spain, and the first Jesuits paid only passing visits there. In 1544, however, Father Araoz, cousin of St. Ignatius and a very eloquent preacher, came with six companions, and then their success was rapid. On 1 September, 1547, Ignatius established the province of Spain with seven houses and about forty religious; St. Francis Borgia joined in 1548; in 1550 Lainez accompanied the Spanish troops in their African campaign. With rapid success came unexpected opposition. Melchoir Cano, O.P., a theologian of European reputation, attacked the young order, which could make no effective reply, nor could anyone get the professor to keep the peace. But, very unpleasant as the trial was, it eventually brought advantage to the order, as it advertized it well in university circles, and moreover drew out defenders of unexpected efficiency, as Juan de la Peña of the Dominicans, and even their general, Fra Francisco Romeo. The Jesuits continued to prosper, and Ignatius subdivided (29 September, 1554) the existing province into three, containing twelve houses and 139 religious. Yet there were internal troubles both here and in Portugal under Simon Rodriguez, which gave the founder anxieties. In both countries the first houses had been established before the Constitutions and rules were committed to writing. It was inevitable therefore that the discipline introduced by Araoz and Rodriguez should have differed somewhat from that which was being introduced by Ignatius at Rome. In Spain, the good offices of Borgia and the visits of Father Nadal did much to effect a gradual unification of system, though not without difficulty. These troubles, however, affected the higher officials of the order rather than the rank and file, who were animated by the highest motives. The great preacher Ramírez is said to have attracted 500 vocations to religious orders at Salamanca in the year 1564, about fifty of them to the Society. There were 300 Spanish Jesuits at the death of Ignatius in 1556; and 1200 at the close of Borgia's generalate in 1572. Under the non-Spanish generals who followed there was an unpleasant recrudescence of the nationalistic spirit. Considering the quarrels which daily arose between Spain and other nations, there can be no wonder at such ebullitions. As has been explained under ACQUAVIVA, Philip of Spain lent his aid to the discontented parties, of whom the virtuous José de Acosta was the spokesman, Fathers Hernández, Dionysius Vásquez, Henríquez, and Mariana the real leaders. Their ulterior object was to procure a separate commissary-general for Spain. This trouble was not quieted till the fifth congregation, 1593, after which ensued the great debates *de auxiliis* with the Dominicans, the protagonists on both sides being Spaniards. (See CONGREGATIO DE AUXILIIS; GRACE, CONTROVERSIES ON.)

Serious as these troubles were in their own sphere, they must not be allowed to obscure the fact that in the Society, as in all Catholic organizations of that day, Spaniards played the greatest rôles. When we enumerate their great men and their great works, they defy all comparison. This consideration gains further force when we remember that the success of the Jesuits in Flanders and in the parts of Italy then united with the Spanish crown was largely due to Spanish Jesuits; and the same is true of the Jesuits in Portugal, which country with its far-stretching colonies was also under the Spanish Crown from 1581 to 1640, though neither the organization of the Portuguese Jesuits nor the civil government of the country itself was amalgamated with those of Spain. But it was in the more abstract sciences that the Spanish genius shone with its greatest lustre; Toledo (d. 1596), Molina (1600), de Valentia (1603), Vásquez (1604), Suárez (1617), Ripalda (1648), de Lugo (1660) (qq.v.)—these form a group of unsurpassed brilliance, and there are quite a number of others almost equally remarkable. In moral theology, Sánchez (1610), Azor (1603), Salas (1612), Castro Palao (1633), Torres (Turrianus, 1635), Escobar (1669). In Scripture, Maldonado (1583), Salmerón (1585), Francisco Ribera (1591), Prado (1595), Pereira (1610), Sancio (1628), Pineda (1637). In secular literature mention may be made especially of de Isla (q.v.), and Baltasar Gracián (1584–1658), author of the "Art of Worldly Wisdom" (El oráculo) and "El criticon", which seems to have suggested the idea of "Robinson Crusoe" to Defoe.

Following the almost universal custom of the later seventeenth century, the kings of Spain generally had Jesuit confessors; but their attempts at reform were too often rendered ineffective by court intrigues. This was especially the case with the Austrian, Father, later Cardinal, Everard Nidhard (confessor of Maria Anna of Austria), and Père Daubenton, confessor of Philip V. After the era of the great writers, the chief glory of the Spanish

THE GESÙ, ROME

Jesuits is to be found in their large and flourishing foreign missions in Peru, Chile, New Granada, the Philippines, Paraguay, Quito, which will be noticed under "Missions", below. They were served by 2171 Jesuits at the time of the Suppression. Spain itself in 1749 was divided into five provinces: Toledo with 659 members, Castile, 718; Aragon, 604; Seville, 662; Sardinia, 300; total, 2943 members (1342 priests) in 158 houses.

Portugal.—At the time when Ignatius founded his order Portugal was in her heroic age. Her rulers were men of enterprise, her universities were full of life, her trade routes extended over the then known world. The Jesuits were welcomed with enthusiasm and made good use of their opportunities. St. Francis Xavier, traversing Portuguese colonies and settlements, proceeded to make his splendid missionary conquests. These were continued by his confrères in such distant lands as Abyssinia, the Congo, South Africa, China, and Japan, by Fathers Nunhes, Silveira, Acosta, Fernandes, and others. At Coimbra, and afterwards at Evora, the Society made the most surprising progress under such professors as Pedro de Fonseca (d. 1599), Luis Molina (d. 1600), Christovão Gil, Sebastião de Abreu, etc., and from here also comes the first comprehensive series of philosophical and theological textbooks for students (see CONIMBRICENSES). With the advent of Spanish monarchy, 1581, the Portuguese Jesuits suffered no less than the rest of their country. Luis Carvalho joined the Spanish opponents of Father Acquaviva, and when the Apostolic collector, Ottavio Accoramboni, launched an interdict against the Government of Lisbon, the Jesuits, especially Diego de Areda, became involved in the undignified strife. On the other hand they played an honourable part in the restoration of Portugal's liberty in 1640; and on its success the difficulty was to restrain King João IV from giving Father Manuel Fernandes a seat in the Cortes, and employing others in diplomatic missions. Amongst these Fathers was Antonio Vieira, one of Portugal's most eloquent orators. Up to the Suppression Portugal and her colonists supported the following missions, of which further notices will be found elsewhere, Goa (originally India), Malabar, Japan, China, Brazil, Maranhão. The Portuguese province in 1749 numbered 861 members (384 priests) in 49 houses. (See also VIEIRA. ANTONIO; MALAGRIDA, GABRIEL.)

France.—The first Jesuits, though almost all Spaniards, were trained and made their first vows in France, and the fortunes of the Society in France have always been of exceptional importance for the body at large. In early years its young men were sent to Paris to be educated there as Ignatius had been. They were hospitably received by Guillaume du Prat, Bishop of Clermont, whose *hôtel* grew into the Collège de Clermont (1550), afterwards known as Louis-le-Grand. Padre Viola was the first rector, but the public classes did not begin till 1564. The *Parlement* of Paris and the Sorbonne resisted vehemently the letters patent, which Henry II and, after him, Francis II and Charles IX, had granted with little difficulty. Meantime the same Bishop of Clermont had founded a second college at Billom in his own diocese, which was opened on 26 July, 1556, before the first general congregation. Colleges at Mauriac and Pamiers soon followed, and between 1565 and 1575 others at Avignon, Chambéry, Toulouse, Rodez, Verdun, Nevers, Bordeaux, Pont-à-Mousson; while Fathers Coudret, Auger, Roger, and Pelletier distinguished themselves by their apostolic labours. The utility of the order was also shown in the Colloquies at Poissy (1561) and St-Germain-en-Laye by Fathers Lainez and Possevinus, and again by Father Brouet, who, with two companions, gave his life in the service of the plague-stricken at Paris in 1562; while Father Maldonado lectured with striking effect both at Paris and Bourges.

Meantime serious trouble was growing up with the University of Paris due to a number of petty causes, jealousy of the new teachers, rivalry with Spain, Gallican resentment at the enthusiastic devotion of the Jesuits to Rome, with perhaps a spice of Calvinism. A lawsuit for the closing of Clermont College was instituted before the *Parlement*, and Estienne Pasquier, counsel for the university, delivered a celebrated *plaidoyer* against the Jesuits. The *Parlement*, though then favourable to the order, was anxious not to irritate the university, and came to an indecisive settlement (5 April, 1565). The Jesuits, in spite of the royal license, were not to be incorporated in the university, but they might continue their lectures. Unsatisfied with this, the university retaliated by preventing the Jesuit scholars from obtaining degrees; and later (1573–6), a feud was maintained against Father Maldonado (q. v.), which was eventually closed by the intervention of Gregory XIII, who had also in 1572 raised the College of Pont-à-Mousson to the dignity of a university. But meantime the more or less incessant wars of religion were devastating the land, and from time to time several Jesuits, especially Auger and Manare, were acting as army chaplains. They had no connexion with the Massacre of St. Bartholomew (1572); but Maldonado was afterwards deputed to receive Henry of Navarre (afterwards Henry IV) into the Church, and in many places the Fathers were able to shelter fugitives in their houses; and by remonstrance and intercession they saved many lives.

FAÇADE OF THE ROMAN COLLEGE

Immediately after his coronation (1575) Henry III chose Father Auger for his confessor, and for exactly two hundred years the Jesuit court confessor became an institution in France; and, as French fashions were then influential, every Catholic Court in time followed the precedent. Considering the difficulty of any sort of control over autocratic sovereigns, the institution of a court confessor was well adapted to the circumstances. The occasional abuses of the office which occurred are chiefly to be attributed to the exorbitant powers vested in the autocrat, which no human guidance could save from periods of decline and degradation. But this was more clearly seen later on. A crisis for French Catholicism was near when, after the death of François, Duke of Anjou, 1584, Henri de Navarre, now an apostate, stood heir to the throne, which the feeble Henry III could not possibly retain for long. Sides were taken with enthusiasm, and *La sainte ligue* was formed for the defence of the Church (see LEAGUE, THE; GUISE, HOUSE OF; FRANCE). It was hardly to be expected that the Jesuits to a man should have remained cool, when the whole populace was in a ferment of excitement. It was morally impossible to keep the Jesuit friends of the *exaltés* on both sides from participating in their extreme measures. Auger and Claude Matthieu were respectively in the confidence of the two contending parties, the Court and the League. Father Acquaviva succeeded in withdrawing both from France, though with great difficulty and considerable loss of favour on either side. One or two he could not control for some time, and of these the most remarkable was Henri Samerie, who had been chaplain to Mary Stuart, and became later army chaplain in Flanders. For a year he passed as diplomatic agent from one prince of the League to another, evading, by their means and the favour of Sixtus V, all Acquaviva's efforts to get him back to regular life. But in the end discipline prevailed; and Acquaviva's orders to respect the consciences of both sides enabled the Society to keep friends with all.

JOHN PAUL OLIVA, ELEVENTH GENERAL OF THE SOCIETY OF JESUS, D. 1681

Henry IV made much use of the Jesuits (especially Toledo, Possevinus, and Commolet), although they had favoured the League, to obtain canonical absolution and the conclusion of peace; and in time (1604) took Père Coton (q. v.) as his confessor. This, however, is an anticipation. After the attempt on Henry's life by Jean Chastel (27 December, 1594), the *Parlement* of Paris took the opportunity of attacking the Society with fury, perhaps in order to disguise the fact that they had been among the most extreme of the Leaguers, while the Society was among the more moderate. It was pretended that the Society was responsible for Chastel's crime, because he had once been their student: though in truth he was then at the university. The librarian of the Jesuit College, Jean Guignard, was hanged, 7 January, 1595, because an old book against the king was found in a cupboard of his room. Antoine Arnauld, the elder, brought into his *plaidoyer* before the *Parlement* every possible calumny against the Society, and the Jesuits were ordered to leave Paris in three days and France in a fortnight. The decree was executed in the districts subject to the *Parlement* of Paris, but not elsewhere. The king, not being yet canonically absolved, did not then interfere. But the pope, and many others, pleaded earnestly for the revocation of the decree against the order. The matter was warmly debated, and eventually Henry himself gave the permission for its readmission, on 1 Sept., 1603. He now made great use of the Society, founded for it the great College of La Flèche, encouraged its missions at home, in Normandy and Béarn, and the commencement of the foreign missions in Canada and the Levant.

The Society immediately began to increase rapidly, and counted thirty-nine colleges, besides other houses, and 1135 religious before the king fell under Ravaillac's dagger (1610). This was made the occasion for new assaults by the *Parlement*, who availed themselves of Mariana's book "De rege" to attack the Society as defenders of tyrannicide. Suarez's "Defensio fidei" was burnt in 1614. The young king, Louis XIII, was too weak to curb the *parlementaires*, but both he and the people of France favoured the Society so effectively that at the time of his death in 1643 their numbers had trebled. They now had five provinces, and that of Paris alone counted over 13,000 scholars in its colleges. The confessors during this reign were changed not unfrequently by the manœuvres of Richelieu, and include Pères Arnoux de Séguiron, Suffren, Caussin (q. v.), Sirmond, Dinet. Richelieu's policy of supporting the German Protestants against Catholic Austria (which Caussin resisted) proved the occasion for angry polemics. The German Jesuit Jacob Keller was believed (though proof of authorship is altogether wanting) to have written two strong pamphlets, "Mysteria politica" and "Admonitio ad Ludovicum XIII", against France. The books were burned by the hangman, as in 1626 was a work of Father Santarelli, which touched awkwardly on the pope's power to pronounce against princes.

The politico-religious history of the Society under Louis XIV centres round Jansenism (see JANSENIUS AND JANSENISM) and the lives of the king's confessors, especially Pères Annat (1645–60), Ferrier (1660–74), La Chaise (q. v.) (1674–1709), and Michel Le Tellier, (q. v.), (1709–15).

On 24 May, 1656, Blaise Pascal (q.v.) published the first of his "Provinciales". The five propositions of Jansenius having been condemned by papal authority, Pascal could no longer defend them openly, and found the most effective method of retaliation was satire, raillery, and countercharge against the Society. He concluded with the usual evasion that Jansenius did not write in the sense attributed to him by the pope. The "Provinciales" were the first noteworthy example in the French language of satire written in studiously polite and moderate terms; and their great literary merit appealed powerfully to the French love of cleverness. Too light to be effectively answered by refutation, they were at the same time sufficiently envenomed to do great and lasting harm; although they have frequently been proved to misrepresent the teaching of the Jesuits by omissions, alterations, interpolations, and false contexts, notably by Dr. Karl Weiss, of Gratz, "P. Antonio de Escobar y Mendoza als Moraltheologe in Pascals Beleuchtung und im Lichte der Wahrheit".

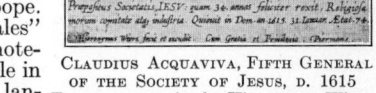

CLAUDIUS ACQUAVIVA, FIFTH GENERAL OF THE SOCIETY OF JESUS, D. 1615
From an engraving by Hieronymus Wierx

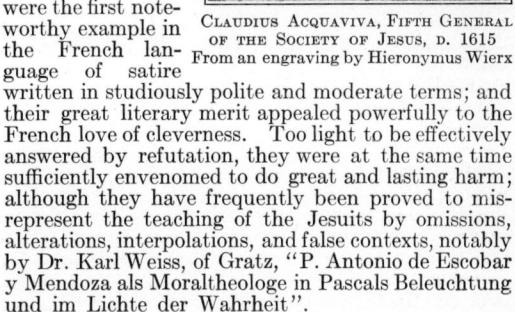

The cause of the Jesuits was also compromised by the various quarrels of Louis XIV with Innocent XI, especially concerning the *régale* and the Gallican articles of 1682. (See LOUIS XIV and INNOCENT XI. The different standpoints of these articles may help to illustrate the differences of view prevalent within the order on this subject.) At first there was a tendency on both sides to spare the French Jesuits. They were not at that time asked to subscribe to the Gallican articles, while Innocent overlooked their adherence to the king, in hopes that their moderation might bring about peace. But it was hardly possible that they should escape all troubles under a domination so pressing. Louis conceived the idea of uniting all the French Jesuits under a vicar, independent of the general in Rome. Before making this known, he recalled all his Jesuit subjects, and all, even the assistant, Père Fontaine, returned to France. Then he proposed the separation, which Thyrsus González firmly refused. The provincials of the five French Jesuit provinces implored the king to desist, which he eventually did. It has been alleged that a papal decree forbidding the reception of novices between 1684–6 was issued in punishment of the French Jesuits giving support to Louis (Crétineau-Joly). The matter is alluded to in the Brief of Suppression; but it is still obscure, and would seem rather to be connected with the Chinese rites than with the difficulties in France. Except for the interdict on their schools in Paris, 1716–29, by Cardinal de Noailles, the fortunes of the order were very calm and prosperous during the ensuing generation. In 1749 the French Jesuits were divided into five provinces with members as follows: France, 891; Aquitaine, 437; Lyons, 773; Toulouse, 655; Champagne, 594; total, 3350 (1763 priests) in 158 houses.

Germany.—The first Jesuit to labour here was Bl. Peter Faber (q. v.), who won to their ranks Bl. Peter Canisius (q. v.), to whose lifelong diligence and eminent holiness the rise and prosperity of the German provinces are especially due. In 1556 there were two provinces, South Germany (*Germania Superior*, up to and including Mainz) and North Germany (*Rhenana*, or *Germania Inferior*, including Flanders). The first residence of the Society was at Cologne (1544), the first college at Vienna (1552). The Jesuit colleges were soon so popular that they were demanded on every side, faster than they could be supplied, and the greater groups of these became fresh provinces. Austria branched off in 1563, Bohemia in 1623, Flanders had become two separate provinces by 1612, and Rhineland also two provinces in 1626. At that time the five German-speaking provinces numbered over 100 colleges and academies. But meanwhile all Germany was in turmoil with the Thirty Years War, which had so far gone, generally, in favour of the Catholic powers. In 1629 came the *Restitutionsedikt* (see COUNTER-REFORMATION), by which the emperor redistributed with papal sanction the old church property, which had been recovered from the usurpation of the Protestants. The Society received large grants, but was not much benefited thereby. Some bitter controversies ensued with the ancient holders of the properties, who were often Benedictines; and many of the acquisitions were lost again during the next period of the war.

The sufferings of the order during the second period were grievous. Even before the war they had been systematically persecuted and driven into exile by the Protestant princes, whenever these had the opportunity. In 1618 they were banished from Bohemia, Moravia, and Silesia; and after the advent of Gustavus Adolphus the violence to which they were liable was increased. The fanatical proposal of banishing them for ever from Germany was made by him in 1631, and again at Frankfort in 1633; and this counsel of hatred acquired a hold which it still exercises over the German Protestant mind. The initial successes of the Catholics of course excited further antipathies, especially as the great generals Tilly, Wallenstein, and Piccolomini had been Jesuit pupils. During the siege of Prague, 1648, Father Plachy successfully trained a corps of students for the defence of the town, and was awarded the mural crown for his services. The province of Upper Rhine alone lost seventy-seven Fathers in the field-hospitals or during the fighting. After the Peace of Westphalia, 1648, the tide of the Counter-Reformation had more or less spent itself. The foundation period had passed, and there are few external events to chronicle. The last notable conversion was that of Prince Frederick Augustus of Saxony (1697), afterwards King of Poland. Fathers Vota and Salerno (afterwards a cardinal) were intimately connected with his conversion. Within the walls of their colleges and in the churches throughout the country the work of teaching, writing, and preaching continued unabated, while the storms of controversy rose and fell, and the distant missions, especially China and the Spanish missions of South America, claimed scores of the noblest and most high-spirited. To this period belong Philipp Jenigen (d. 1704) and Franz Hunolt (d. 1740), perhaps the greatest German Jesuit preachers; Tschupick, Joseph Schneller, and Ignatius Wurz acquired an almost equally great reputation in Austria. In 1749 the German provinces counted as follows: *Germania Superior*, 1060; Lower Rhine, 772; Upper Rhine, 497; Austria, 1772; Bohemia, 1239; total, 5340 members (2558 priests) in 307 houses. (See also the Index volume under title "Society of Jesus", and such names as Becan, Byssen, Brouwer, Drechsel, Lohner, etc.)

Hungary was included in the province of Austria. The chief patron of the order was Cardinal Pázmány (q. v.). The conversion of Sweden was several times attempted by German Jesuits, but they were not allowed to stay in the country. King John III, however, who had married a Polish princess, was actually converted (1578) through various missions by Fathers Warsiewicz and Possevinus, the latter accompanied by the English Father William Good; but the king had not the courage to persevere. Queen Christina (q. v.) in 1654 was brought into the Church, largely through the ministration of Fathers Macedo and Casati, having given up her throne for this purpose. The Austrian Fathers maintained a small residence at Moscow from 1684 to 1718, which had been opened by Father Vota. (See POSSEVINUS.)

Poland.—Bl. Peter Canisius, who visited Poland in the train of the legate Mantuato in 1558, succeeded in animating King Sigismund to energetic defence of Catholicism, and Bishop Hosius of Ermland founded the college of Braunsberg in 1584, which with that of Vilna (1569) became centres of Catholic activity in north-eastern Europe. King Stephen Bathory, an earnest patron of the order, founded a Ruthenian College at Vilna in 1575. From 1588 Father Peter Skarga (d. 1612) made a great impression by his preaching. There were violent attacks against the Society in the revolution of 1607, but after the victory of Sigismund III the Jesuits more than recovered the ground lost; and in 1608 the province could be subdivided into Lithuania and Poland. The animus against the Jesuits however vented itself at Cracow in 1612, through the scurrilous satire entitled "Monita secreta" (q. v.). King Casimir, who had once been a Jesuit, favoured the Society not a little; so too did Sobieski, and his campaign to relieve Vienna from the Turks (1683) was due in part to the exhortations of Father Vota, his confessor. Among the great Polish missionaries are numbered Benedict Herbst (d. 1593) and Bl. Andrew Bobola (q. v.). In 1756 the Polish provinces were readjusted into four:— Greater Poland; Lesser Poland; Lithuania; Massovia, counting in all 2359 religious. The Polish Jesuits, besides their own missions, had others in Stockholm, Russia, the Crimea, Constantinople, and Persia. (See CRACOW, UNIVERSITY OF.)

Belgium.—The first settlement was at Louvain in 1542, whither the students in Paris retired on the declaration of war between France and Spain. In 1556 Ribadeneira obtained legal authorization for the Society from Philip II, and in 1564 Flanders became a separate province. Its beginnings, however, were by no means uniformly prosperous. The Duke of Alva was cold and suspicious, while the wars of the revolting provinces told heavily against it. At the Pacification of Ghent (1576) the Jesuits were offered an oath against the rulers of the Netherlands, which they firmly refused, and were driven from their houses. But this at last won for them Philip's favour, and under Alexander Farnese fortune turned completely in their favour. Father Oliver Manare became a leader fitted for the occasion, whom Acquiviva himself greeted as "Pater Provinciæ". In a few years a number of well-established colleges had been founded, and in 1612 the province had to be subdivided. The *Flandro-Belgica* counted sixteen colleges and the *Gallo-Belgica* eighteen. All but two were day-schools, with no preparatory classes for small boys. They were worked with comparatively small staffs of five or six, sometimes only three professors, though their scholars might count as many hundreds. Teaching was gratuitous, but a sufficient foundation for the support of the teachers was a necessary preliminary. Though preparatory and elementary education was not yet in fashion, the care taken in teaching catechism was most elaborate. The classes were regular, and at intervals enlivened with music, ceremonies, mystery-plays, and processions. These were often attended by the whole magistracy in robes of state, while the bishop himself would attend at the distribution of honours. A special congregation was formed at Antwerp in 1628, to organize ladies and gentlemen, nobles and bourgeois, into Sunday-school teachers, and in that year their classes counted in all 3000 children. Similar organizations existed all over the country. The first communion classes formed an extension of the catechisms. In Bruges, Brussels, and Antwerp between 600 and 1600 attended the communion classes.

Jesuit congregations of the Blessed Virgin were first instituted at Rome by a Belgian Jesuit, Jean Leunis, in 1563. His native country soon took them up with enthusiasm. Each college had normally four:—(1) for scholars (more often two, one for older, one for younger); (2) for young men on leaving; (3) for grown-up men (more often several)—for working-men, for tradesmen, professional classes, nobles, priests, doctors, etc., etc.; (4) for small boys. In days before hospitals, workhouses, and elementary education were regularly organized, and supported by the State; before burial-clubs, trade-unions, and the like provided special help for the working-man, these sodalities discharged the functions of such institutions, in homely fashion perhaps, but gratuitously, bringing together all ranks for the relief of indigence. Some of these congregations were exceedingly popular, and their registers still show the names of the first artists and savants of the time (Teniers, Van Dyck, Rubens, Lipsius, etc.). Archdukes and kings and even four emperors are found among the sodalists of Louvain. Probably the first permanent corps of army chaplains was that established by Farnese in 1587. It consisted of ten to twenty-five chaplains, and was styled the "Missio castrensis," and lasted as an institution till 1660. The "Missio navalis" was a kindred institution for the navy. The Flandro-Belgian province numbered 542 in 1749 (232 priests) in 30 houses: Gallo-Belgian, 471 (266 priests) in 25 houses.

England.—Founded at Rome after the English Schism had commenced, the Society had great difficulty in finding an entrance into England, though Ignatius and Ribadeneira visited the country in 1531 and 1558, and prayers for its conversion have been recited throughout the order from 1553 to the present day (now under the common designation of "Northern Nations"). Other early Jesuits exerted themselves on behalf of the English seminary at Douai and of the refugees at Louvain. The effect of Elizabeth's expulsion of Catholics from Oxford, 1562–75, was that many took refuge abroad. Some

A PUBLIC CATECHISM AT VIENNA, 1599
From a contemporary print

scores of young men entered the Society, several of these volunteered for foreign missions, and thus it came about that the forerunner of those legions of Englishmen who go into India to carve out careers was the English Jesuit missionary, Thomas Stephens. John Yate (*alias* Vincent, b. 1550; d. after 1603) and John Meade (see ALMEIDA) were pioneers of the mission to Brazil. The most noteworthy of the first recruits were Thomas Darbishire and William Good, followed in time by Blessed Edmund Campion (q.v.) and Robert Persons. The latter was the first to conceive and elaborate the idea of the English mission, which, at Dr. Allen's request, was undertaken in December, 1578.

Before this the Society had undertaken the care of the English College, Rome (see ENGLISH COLLEGE), by the pope's command, 19 March, 1578. But difficulties ensued, owing to the miseries inherent in the estate of the religious refugees. Many came all the way to Rome expecting pensions, or scholarships from the rector, who at first became, in spite of himself, the dispenser of Pope Gregory's alms. But the alms soon failed, and several scholars had to be dismissed as unworthy. Hence disappointments and storms of grumbling, the records of which read sadly by the side of the consoling accounts of the martyrdoms of men like Campion, Cottam, Southwell, Walpole, Page, and others, and the labours of a Heywood, Weston, or Gerard. Persons and Crichton too, falling in with the idea, so common abroad, that a counter-revolution in favour of Mary Stuart would not be difficult, made two or three political missions to Rome and Madrid (1582-84) before realizing that their schemes were not feasible (see PERSONS). After the Armada (q. v.), Persons induced Philip to establish more seminaries, and hence the foundations at Valladolid, St-Omer, and Seville (1589, 1592, 1593), all put in charge of the English Jesuits. On the other hand they suffered a setback in the so-called Appellant controversy (1598-1602), which French diplomacy in Rome eventually made into an opportunity for operating against Spain. (See BLACKWELL; GARNET.) The assistance of France and the influence of the French Counter-Reformation were now on the whole highly beneficial. But many who took refuge at Paris became accustomed to a Gallican atmosphere, and hence perhaps some of the regalist views about the Oath of Allegiance and some of the excitement in the debate over the jurisdiction of the Bishops of Chalcedon, of which more below. The feeling of tension continued until the missions of Pazani, Conn, and Rosetti, 1635-41. Though the first of these was somewhat hostile, he was recalled in 1637, and his successors brought about a peace, too soon to be interrupted by the Civil War, 1641-60.

Before 1606 the English Jesuits had founded houses for others, but neither they nor any other English order had yet erected houses for themselves. But during the so-called "Foundation Movement", due to many causes but especially perhaps to the stimulus of the Counter-Reformation (q. v.) in France, a full equipment of institutions was established in Flanders. The novitiate, begun at Louvain in 1606, was moved to Liège in 1614, and in 1622 to Watten. The house at Liège was continued as the scholasticate, and the house of third probation was at Ghent 1620. The "mission" was made in 1619 a vice-province, and on 21 January, 1623, a province, with Fr. Richard Blount as first provincial; and in 1634 it was able to undertake the foreign mission of Maryland (see below) in the old Society. The English Jesuits at this period also reached their greatest numbers. In 1621 they were 211, in 1636, 374. In the latter year their total revenue amounted to 45,086 *scudi* (almost £11,000). After the Civil War both members and revenue fell off very considerably. In 1649 there were only 264 members, and 23,055 *scudi* revenue (about £5760); in 1645 the revenue was only 17,405 *scudi* (about £4350).

Since Elizabeth's time the martyrs had been few— one only, the Ven. Edmund Arrowsmith (q. v.), in the reign of Charles I. On 26 October, 1623, had occurred "the Doleful Even-song". A congregation had gathered for vespers in the garrets of the French embassy in Blackfriars, when the floor gave way. Fathers Drury and Rediate with 61 (perhaps 100) of the congregation were killed. On 14 March, 1628, seven Jesuits were seized at St. John's, Clerkenwell, with a large number of papers. These troubles, however, were light, compared with the sufferings during the Commonwealth, when the list of martyrs and confessors went up to ten. As the Jesuits depended so much on the country families, they were sure to suffer severely by the war, and the college at St-Omer was nearly beggared. The old trouble about the Oath of Allegiance was revived by the Oath of Abjuration, and "the three questions" proposed by Fairfax, 1 August, 1647 (see WHITE, THOMAS). The representatives of the secular and regular clergy, amongst them Father Henry More, were called upon at short notice to subscribe to them. They did so, More thinking he might, "considering the reasons of the preamble", which qualified the words of the oath considerably. But the provincial, Fr. Silesdon, recalled him from England, and he was kept out of office for over a year; a punishment which, even if drastic for his offence, cannot be regretted, as it providentially led to his writing the history of the English Jesuits down to the year 1635 ("Hist. missionis anglicanæ Soc. Jesu, ab anno salutis MDLXXX", St-Omer, 1660).

With the Restoration, 1660, came a period of greater calm, followed by the worst tempest of all, Oates's plot (q. v.), when the Jesuits lost eight on the scaffold and thirteen in prison in five years, 1678-83. Then the period of greatest prosperity under King James II (1685-8). He gave them a college, and a public chapel in Somerset House, made Father Petre his almoner, and on 11 November, 1687, a member of his Privy Council. He also chose Father Warner as his confessor, and encouraged the preaching and controversies which were carried on with no little fruit. But this spell of prosperity lasted only a few months; with the Revolution of 1688 the Fathers regained their patrimony of persecution. The last Jesuits to die in prison were Fathers Poulton and Aylworth (1690-1692). William III's repressive legislation did not have the intended effect of exterminating the Catholics, but it did reduce them to a proscribed and ostracized body. Thenceforward the annals of the English Jesuits show little that is new or striking, though their number and works of charity were well maintained. Most of the Fathers in England were chaplains to gentlemen's families, of which posts they held nearly a hundred during the eighteenth century.

The church law under which the English Jesuits worked was to some extent special. At first indeed all was undefined, seculars and regulars living in true happy-family style. As, however, organization developed, friction between parts could not always be avoided, and legislation became necessary. By the institution of the archpriest (7 March, 1598), and by the subsequent modifications of that institution (6 April, 1599; 17 August, 1601; and 5 October, 1602), various occasions for friction were removed, and principles of stable government were introduced. As soon as Queen Henrietta Maria seemed able to protect a bishop in England, bishops of Chalcedon *in partibus infidelium* were sent, in 1623 and 1625. The second of these, Dr. Richard Smith, endeavoured, without having the necessary faculty from Rome, to introduce the episcopal approbation of confessors. This led to the Brief "Britannia", 9 May, 1631, which left the faculties of regular missionaries in their previous immediate dependence on the Holy See. But after the institution of vicars Apostolic in 1685, by a Decree of 9 October, 1695, regulars were obliged to obtain approbation from the bishop. There were of course many other matters that needed settlement, but the difficulties of the position in England and the distance from Rome made legislation slow and difficult. In 1745 and 1748 Decrees were obtained, against which appeals were lodged; and it was not till 31 May, 1753, that the "Regulæ missionis" were laid down by Benedict XIV in the Constitution "Apostolicum ministerium", which regulated ecclesiastical administration until the issue of the Constitution "Romanos Pontifices" in 1881. In the year of the Suppression, 1773, the English Jesuits numbered 274. (See COFFIN, EDWARD; CRESWELL; ENGLISH CONFESSORS AND MARTYRS; MORE, HENRY; PENAL LAWS; PERSONS, ROBERT; PETRE, SIR EDWARD; PLOWDEN; SABRAN, LOUIS DE; SOUTHWELL; SPENSER, JOHN; STEPHENS, THOMAS; REDFORD.)

Ireland.—One of the first commissions which the popes entrusted to the Society was that of acting as envoys to Ireland. Fathers Salmerón and Brouet managed to reach Ulster during the Lent of 1542; but the immense difficulties of the situation after Henry VIII's successes of 1541 made it impossible for them to live there in safety, much less to discharge the functions or to commence the reforms which the pope had entrusted to them. Under Queen Mary the Jesuits would have returned had there been men ready. There were indeed already a few Irish novices, and of these David Woulfe returned to Ireland on 20 January, 1561, with ample Apostolic faculties. He procured candidates for the sees emptied by Elizabeth, kept open a grammar school for some years, and sent several novices to the order; but he was finally imprisoned, and had to withdraw to the Continent. A little later the "Irish mission" was regularly organized under Irish superiors, beginning with Fr. Richard Fleming (d. 1590), professor at Clermont College, and then Chancellor of the University of Pont-à-Mousson. In 1609 the mission numbered seventy-two, forty of whom were priests, and eighteen were at work in Ireland. By 1617 this latter number had increased to thirty-eight; the rest were for the most part in training among their French and Spanish confrères. The foundation of colleges abroad, at Salamanca, Santiago, Seville, and Lisbon, for the education of the clergy, was chiefly due to Father Thomas White (d. 1622). They were consolidated and long managed by Fr. James Archer of Kilkenny, afterwards missionary in Ulster and chaplain to Hugh O'Neill. The Irish College at Poitiers was also under Irish Jesuit direction, as was that of Rome for some time (see IRISH COLLEGE, IN ROME).

The greatest extension in Ireland was naturally during the dominance of the Confederation (1642–54), with which Father Matthew O'Hartigan was in great favour. Jesuit colleges, schools, and residences then amounted to thirteen, with a novitiate at Kilkenny. During the Puritan domination the number of Jesuits fell again to eighteen; but in 1685, under James II, there were twenty-eight with seven residences. After the Revolution their numbers fell again to six, then rose to seventeen in 1717, and to twenty-eight in 1755. The Fathers sprang mostly from the old Anglo-Norman families, but almost all the missionaries spoke Irish, and missionary labour was the chief occupation of the Irish Jesuits. Fr. Robert Rochford set up a school at Youghal as early as 1575; university education was given in Dublin in the reign of Charles I, until the buildings were seized and handed over to Trinity College; and Father John Austin kept a flourishing school in Dublin for twenty-two years before the Suppression.

Some account of the work of Jesuits in Ireland will be found in the articles on Fathers Christopher Holywood and Henry Fitzsimon; but it was abroad, from the nature of the case, that Irish genius of that day found its widest recognition. Stephen White, Luke Wadding, cousin of his famous Franciscan namesake, at Madrid; Ambrose and Peter Wadding at Dillingen and Gratz respectively; J. B. Duiggin and John Lombard at Ypres and Antwerp; Thomas Comerford at Compostella; Paul Sherlock at Salamanca; Richard Lynch (1611–76) at Valladolid and Salamanca; James Kelly at Poitiers and Paris; Peter Plunkett at Leghorn. Among the distinguished writers were William Bathe, whose "Janua linguarum" (Salamanca, 1611) was the basis of the work of Commenius. Bernard Routh (b. at Kilkenny, 1695) was a writer in the "Mémoires de Trévoux" (1734–43), and assisted Montesquieu on his death-bed. In the field of foreign missions O'Fihily was one of the first apostles of Paraguay, and Thomas Lynch was provincial of Brazil at the time of the Suppression. At this time also Roger Magloire was working in Martinique, and Philip O'Reilly in Guiana. But it was the mission-field in Ireland itself of which the Irish Jesuits thought most, to which all else in one way or other led up. Their labours were principally spent in the walled cities of the old English Pale. Here they kept the faith vigorous, in spite of persecutions, which, if sometimes intermitted, were nevertheless long and severe. The first Irish Jesuit martyr was Edmund O'Donnell, who suffered at Cork in 1575. Others on that list of honour are: Dominic Collins, a lay brother, Youghal, 1602; William Boyton, Cashel, 1647; Fathers Netterville and Bathe, at the fall of Drogheda, 1649. Fr. David Galway worked among the scattered and persecuted Gaels of the Scottish Isles and Highlands, until his death in 1643. (See also FITZSIMON; MALONE; O'DONNELL; TALBOT, PETER; IRISH CONFESSORS AND MARTYRS.)

Scotland.—Father Nicholas de Gouda was sent to visit Mary Queen of Scots in 1562 to invite her to send bishops to the Council of Trent. The power of the Protestants made it impossible to achieve this object, but de Gouda conferred with the queen and brought back with him six young Scots, who were to prove the founders of the mission. Of these Edmund Hay soon rose to prominence and was rector of Clermont College, Paris. In 1584 Crichton returned with Father James Gordon, uncle to the Earl of Huntly, to Scotland; the former was captured, but the latter was extraordinarily successful, and the Scottish mission proper may be said to have begun with him, and Father Edmund Hay and John Drury, who came in 1585. The Earl of Huntly became the Catholic leader, and the fortunes of his party passed through many a strange turn. But the Catholic victory of Glenlivet, in 1594, aroused the temper of the Kirk to such a pitch that James, though averse to severity, was forced to advance against the Catholic lords and eventually Huntly was constrained to leave the country and, then returning, he submitted to the Kirk in 1597. This put a term to the spread of Catholicism; Father James Gordon had to leave in 1595, but Father Abercromby succeeded in reconciling Anne of Denmark, who, however, did not prove a very courageous convert. Meantime the Jesuits had been given the management of the Scots College founded by Mary Stuart in Paris, which was successively removed to Pont-à-Moussón and to Douai. In 1600 another college was founded at Rome and put under them, and there was also a small one at Madrid.

CHARLES DE NOYELLE, TWELFTH GENERAL OF THE SOCIETY OF JESUS, D. 1686

After reaching the English throne James was bent on introducing episcopacy into Scotland, and to reconcile the Presbyterians to this he allowed them to persecute the Catholics to their hearts' content. By their barbarous "excommunication", the suffering they inflicted was incredible. The soul of the resistance to this cruelty was Father James Anderson, who, however, becoming the object of special searches, had to be withdrawn in 1611. In 1614 Fathers John Ogilvie (q.v.) and James Moffat were sent in, the former suffering martyrdom at Glasgow, 10 March, 1615. In 1620 Father Patrick Anderson (q.v.) was tried, but eventually banished. After this, a short period of peace, 1625–7, ensued, followed by another persecution 1629–30, and another period of peace before the rising of the Covenanters and the civil wars, 1638–45. There were about six Fathers in the mission at this time, some chaplains with the Catholic gentry, some living the then wild life of the Highlanders, especially during Montrose's campaigns. But after Philiphaugh (1645) the fortunes of the royalists and the Catholics underwent a sad change. Among those who fell into the hands of the enemy was Father Andrew Leslie, who has left a lively account of his prolonged sufferings in various prisons. After the Restoration (1660) there was a new period of peace in which the Jesuit missionaries reaped a considerable harvest, but during the disturbances caused by the Covenanters (q.v.) the persecution of Catholics was renewed. James II favoured them as far as he could, appointing Fathers James Forbes and Thomas Patterson chaplains at Holyrood, where a school was also opened. After the Revolution the Fathers were scattered, but returned, though with diminishing numbers.

HISTORY.—A. General.—*Mon. historica Soc. Jesu*, ed. RODELES (Madrid, 1894, in progress); ORLANDINI (continued in turn by SACCHINI, JOUVANCY, and CORDARA), *Hist. Soc. Jesu, 1540–1632* (8 vols. fol., Rome and Antwerp, 1615–1750), and *Supplement* (Rome, 1859); BARTOLI, *Dell' istoria della comp. di Gesù* (6 vols. fol., Rome, 1663–73); CRÉTINEAU-JOLY, *Hist. de la comp. de Jésus* (3rd ed., 3 vols., Paris, 1859); B. N., *The Jesuits; their Foundation and History* (London, 1879); [WERNZ], *Abriss der Gesch. der Gesellschaft Jesu* (Münster, 1876); CARREZ, *Atlas geographicus Soc. Jesu* (Paris, 1900); HEIMBUCHER, *Die Orden und Kongregationen der katholischen Kirche*, III (Paderborn, 1908), 2–258, contains an excellent bibliography; [QUESNEL], *Hist. des religieux de la comp. de Jésus* (Utrecht, 1741). Non-Catholic:— STEIZ-ZÖCKLER in *Realencycl. für prot. Theol.*, s. v. *Jesuitenorden;* HASENMÜLLER, *Hist. jesuitici ordinis* (Frankfort, 1593); HOSPINIANUS, *Hist. jesuitica* (Zurich, 1619).

B. Particular Countries.—Italy.—TACCHI-VENTURI, *Storia della comp. di G. in Italia* (Rome, 1910, in progress); SCHINOSI AND SANTAGATA, *Istoria della comp. di G. appartenente al regno di Napoli* (Naples, 1706–57); ALBERTI, *La Sicilia* (Palermo, 1702); AGUILERA, *Provinciæ Siculæ Soc. Jesu res gestæ* (Palermo, 1737–40); CAPPELLETTI, *I gesuiti e la republica di Venezia* (Venice, 1873); FAVARO, *Lo studio di Padora e la comp. de G.* (Venice, 1877).

Spain.—ASTRAIN, *Hist. de la comp. de J. en la asistencia de España* (Madrid, 1902, 3 vols., in progress); ALCAZAR, *Chronohistoria de la comp. de J. en la provincia de Toledo* (Madrid, 1710); PRAT, *Hist. du P. Ribadeneyra* (Paris, 1862).

Portugal.—TELLEZ, *Chronica de la comp. de J. na provincia de Portugal* (Coimbra, 1645–7); FRANCO, *Synop. annal. Soc. Jesu in Lusitania ab anno 1 40 ad 172 ì* (Augsburg, 1726); TEIXEIRA, *Docum. para a hist. dos Jesuitas em Portugal* (Coimbra, 1899).

France.—FOUQUERAY, *Hist. de la comp. de J. en France* (Paris, 1910); CARAYON, *Docum. inéd. concernant la comp. de J.* (23 vols., Paris, 1863–86); IDEM, *Les parlements et les jésuites* (Paris, 1867); PRAT, *Mém. pour servir à l'hist. du P. Brouet* (Puy, 1885); IDEM, *Recherches hist. sur la comp. de J. en France du temps du P. Coton, 1564–1 2 ì* (Lyons, 1876); IDEM, *Maldonat et l'université de Paris* (Paris, 1856); DONARCHE, *L'univ. de Paris et les jésuites* (Paris, 1888); PIAGET, *L'établissement des jésuites en France 1540–1660* (Leyden, 1893); CHOSSAT, *Les jésuites et leurs œuvres à Avignon* (Avignon, 1896).

Germany, etc.—AGRICOLA (continued by FLOTTO, KROPF), *Hist. prov. Soc. Jesu Germaniæ superioris (1540–1641)* (5 vols., Augsburg and Munich, 1727–54); HANSEN, *Rhein. Akten zur Gesch. des Jesuitenordens 1542–82* (1896); JANSSEN, *Hist. of the German People*, tr. CHRISTIE (London, 1905–10); DUHR, *Gesch. der Jesuiten in den Ländern deutscher Zunge* (Freiburg, 1907); KROESS, *Gesch. der böhmischen Prov. der G. J.* (Vienna, 1910); MEDERER, *Annal. Ingolstadiensis academ.* (Ingolstadt, 1782); REIFFENBERG, *Hist. Soc. Jesu ad Rhenum inferiorem* (Cologne, 1764); ARGENTO, *De rebus Soc. Jesu in regno Poloniæ* (Cracow, 1620); POLLARD, *The Jesuits in Poland* (Oxford, 1882); ZALENSKI, *Hist. of the Soc. of Jesus in Poland* (in Polish, 1896–1906); IDEM, *The Jesuits in White Russia* (in Polish, 1874; Fr. tr., Paris, 1886); PIERLING, *Antonii Possevini missio moscovitica* (1883); ROSTOWSKI, *Hist. Soc. Jesu Lithuanicarum provincialium* (Wilna, 1765); SCHMIDL, *Hist. Soc. Jesu prov. Bohemiæ, 1555–1653* (Prague, 1747–59); SOCHER, *Hist. prov. Austriæ Soc. Jesu, 1540–1590* (Vienna, 1740); STEINHUBER, *Gesch. des Coll. Germanicum-Hungaricum* (Freiburg, 1895).

Belgium.—MANARE, *De rebus Soc. Jesu commentarius*, ed. DELPLACE (Florence, 1886); WALDACK, *Hist. prov. Flandro-belgicæ Soc. Jesu anni 1 38* (Ghent, 1867).

England, Ireland, Scotland.—FOLEY, *Records of the English Prov. of the Soc. Jesus*—includes Irish and Scotch Jesuits (London, 1877); SPILLMANN, *Die englischen Märtyrer unter Elizabeth bis 1583* (Freiburg, 1888); FORBES-LEITH, *Narr. of Scottish Catholics* (Edinburgh, 1885); IDEM, *Mem. of Scot. Cath.* (London, 1909); HOGAN, *Ibernia Ignatiana* (Dublin, 1880); IDEM, *Distinguished Irishmen of the XVI century* (London, 1894); MEYER, *England und die kath. Kirche unter Elisabeth* (Rome, 1910); MORE, *Hist. prov. Anglicanæ* (St-Omer, 1660); PERSONS, *Memoirs*, ed. POLLEN in *Cath. Record Society*, II (London, 1896, 1897), ii; POLLEN, *Politics of the Eng. Cath. under Elizabeth* in *The Month* (London, 1902–3); TAUNTON, *The Jesuits in England* (London, 1901).

MISSIONS.—No sphere of religious activity is held in greater esteem among the Jesuits than that of the foreign missions; and from the beginning men of the highest gifts, like St. Francis Xavier, have been devoted to this work. Hence perhaps it is that a better idea may be formed of the Jesuit missions by reading the lives of its great missionaries, which will be found under their respective names (see Index vol.), than from the following notice, in which attention has to be confined to general topics.

India.—When the Society began, the great colonizing powers were Portugal and Spain. The career of St. Francis Xavier (q. v.), so far as its geographical direction and limits were concerned, was largely determined by the Portuguese settlements in the East and the trade routes followed by Portuguese merchants. Arriving at Goa in 1542, he evangelized first the western coast and Ceylon, in 1545 he was in Malacca, in 1549 in Japan. At the same time he pushed forward his few assistants and catechists into other centres; and in 1552 set out for China, but died at the year's end on an island off the coast. Xavier's work was carried on, with Goa as headquarters, and Father Barzæus as successor. Father Antonio Criminali, the first martyr of the Society, had suffered in 1549, and Father Mendez followed in 1552. In 1579 Blessed Rudolph Acquaviva visited the Court of Akbar the Great, but without permanent effect. The great impulse of conversions came after Ven. Robert de Nobili (q. v.) declared himself a Brahmin *Sannjâsî*, and lived the life of the Brahmins (1606). At Tanjore and elsewhere he now made immense numbers of converts, who were allowed to keep the distinctions of their castes, with many religious customs; which, however, were eventually (after much controversy) condemned by Benedict XIV in 1744. This condemnation produced a depressing effect on the mission, though at the very time Fathers Lopez and Acosta with singular heroism devoted themselves for life to the service of the Pariahs. The Suppression of the Society, which followed soon after, completed the desolation of a once prolific missionary field. (See MALABAR RITES.) From Goa too were organized missions on the east coast of Africa. The Abyssinian mission under Fathers Nunhes, Oviedo, and Paes lasted with varied fortunes for over a century, 1555–1690 (see ABYSSINIA, I, 76). The mission on the Zambesi under Fathers Silveira, Acosta, and Fernandez was but short-lived; so too was the work of Father Govea in Angola. In the seventeenth century the missionaries penetrated into Tibet, Fathers Desideri and Freyre reaching Lhasa. Others pushed out in the Persian mission from Ormus as far as Ispahan. About 1700 the Persian missions counted 400,000 Catholics. The southern and eastern coasts of India, with Ceylon, were comprised after 1610 in the separate province of Malabar, with an independent French mission at Pondicherry. Malabar numbered forty-seven missionaries (Portuguese) before the Suppression, while the French missions counted 22. (See HANXLEDEN.)

Japan.—The Japanese mission (see JAPAN, VIII, 306) gradually developed into a province, but the seminary and seat of government remained at Macao. By 1582 the number of Christians was estimated at 200,000 with 250 churches and 59 missionaries, of whom 23 were priests, and 26 Japanese had been admitted to the Society. But 1587 saw the beginnings of persecution, and about the same period began the rivalries of nations and of competing orders. The Portuguese crown had been assumed by Spain, and Spanish merchants introduced Spanish Dominicans and Franciscans. Gregory XIII at first forbade this (28 Jan., 1585), but Clement VIII and Paul V (12 December, 1600; 11 June, 1608) relaxed and repealed the prohibition; and the persecution of Taïco-sama quenched in blood whatever discontent might have arisen in consequence. The first great slaughter of 26 missionaries at Nagasaki took place on 5 Feb., 1597. Then came fifteen years of comparative peace, and gradually the number of Christians rose to about 1,800,000 and the Jesuit missionaries to 140 (63 priests). In 1612 the persecution broke out again, increasing in severity till 1622, when over 120 martyrs suffered. The "great martyrdom" took place on 20 September, when Blessed Charles Spinola (q. v.) suffered with representatives of the Dominicans and the Franciscans. For the twenty ensuing years the massacre continued without mercy, all Jesuits who landed being at once executed. In 1644 Father Gaspar de Amaral was drowned in attempting to land, and his death brought to a close the century of missionary efforts which the Jesuits had made to bring the Faith to Japan. The name of the Japanese province was retained, and it counted 57 subjects in 1760; but the mission was really confined to Tonkin and Cochin-China, whence stations were established in Annam, Siam, etc. (see INDO-CHINA, VII, 774–5; MARTYRS, JAPANESE).

China.—A detailed account of this mission from 1552 to 1773 will be found under CHINA (III, 672–4) and MARTYRS IN CHINA, and in lives of the missionaries Bouvet, Brancati, Carneiro, Cibot, Fridelli, Gaubil, Gerbillon, Herdtrich, Hinderer, Mailla, Martini, Matteo Ricci, Schall von Bell, and Verbiest (qq. v.). From 1581, when the mission was organized, it consisted of Portuguese Fathers. They established four colleges, one seminary, and some forty stations under a vice-provincial, who resided frequently in Pekin; at the suppression there were 54 Fathers. From 1687 there was a special mission of the French Jesuits to Pekin, under their own superior; at the Suppression they numbered 23.

Central and South America.—The missions of Central and Southern America were divided between Portugal and Spain (see AMERICA, I, 414). In 1549 Father Nombrega and five companions, Portuguese, went to Brazil. Progress was slow at first, but when the languages had been learnt, and the confidence of the natives acquired, progress became rapid. Blessed Ignacio de Azevedo and his thirty-nine companions were martyred on their way thither in 1570. The missions, however, prospered steadily under such leaders as José Anchieta and John Almeida (qq. v.) (Meade). In 1630 there were 70,000 converts. Before the Suppression the whole country had been divided into missions, served by 445 Jesuits in Brazil, and 146 in the vice-province of Maranhão.

Paraguay.—Of the Spanish missions, the most noteworthy is Paraguay (see GUARANÍ INDIANS; ABIPONES; ARGENTINE REPUBLIC; REDUCTIONS OF PARAGUAY). The province contained 564 members (of whom 385 were priests) before the Suppression, with 113,716 Indians under their charge.

Mexico.—Even larger than Paraguay was the missionary province of Mexico, which included California, with 572 Jesuits and 122,000 Indians. (See also CALIFORNIA MISSIONS; MEXICO, pp. 258, 266, etc; AÑAZCO; CLAVIGERO; DÍAZ; DUCRUE; etc.) The conflict as to jurisdiction (1647) with Juan de Palafox y Mendoza (q.v.), Bishop of La Puebla, led to an appeal to Rome which was decided by Innocent X in 1648, but afterwards became a *cause célèbre*. The other Spanish missions, New Granada (Colombia), Chile, Peru, Quito (Ecuador), were administered by 193, 242, 526, and 209 Jesuits respectively (see ALEGRE; ARAUCANIANS; ARAWAKS; BARRASA; MOXOS INDIANS).

United States.—Father Andrew White (q.v.) and four other Jesuits from the English mission arrived in territory now comprised in the State of Maryland, 25 March, 1634, with the expedition of Cecil Calvert (q. v.) For ten years they ministered to the Catholics of the colony, converted many of its Protestant pioneers, and conducted missions among the Indians along Chesapeake Bay and the Potomac River, the Patuxents, Anacostans, and Piscataways, which last were especially friendly. In 1644 the colony was invaded by the Puritans from the neighbouring settlement of Virginia, and Father White was sent in chains to England, tried for being a Catholic, and on his release took refuge in Belgium. Although the Catholic colonists soon regained control, they were constantly menaced by their Puritan neighbours and by malcontents in the colony itself, who finally in 1692 succeeded in seizing the government, and in enacting penal laws against the Catholics, and particularly against their Jesuit priests, which kept growing more and more intolerable until the colony became the State of Maryland in November, 1776. During the 140 years between their arrival in Maryland and the Suppression of the Society, the missionaries, averaging four in number the first forty years and then gradually increasing to twelve and finally to about twenty, continued to work among the Indians and the settlers in spite of every vexation and disability, though prevented from increasing in number and extending their labours during the dispute with Cecil Calvert over retaining the tract of land, Mattapany, given to them by the Indians, relief from taxation on lands devoted to religious or charitable purposes, and the usual ecclesiastical immunity for themselves and their households. The controversy ended in the cession of the Mattapany tract, the missionaries retaining the land they had acquired by the conditions of plantation. Prior to the Suppression they had established missions in Maryland, at St. Thomas, White Marsh, St. Inigoes, Leonardtown, still (1912) under the care of Jesuits, and also at Deer Creek, Frederick, and St. Joseph's Bohemia Manor, besides the many less permanent stations among the Indians in Pennsylvania, Philadelphia, Conewago, Lancaster, Goshenhoppen, and excursion stations as far as New York where two of their number, Fathers Harvey and Harrison, assisted for a time by Father Gage, had, under Governor Dongan, ministered as chaplains in the forts and among the white settlers, and attempted unsuccessfully to establish a school, between 1683–89, when they were forced to retire by an anti-Catholic administration.

MATTEO RICCI
From a Chinese portrait preserved in the College of Propaganda

The Suppression of the Society altered but little the status of the Jesuits in Maryland. As they were the only priests in the mission, they still remained at their posts, most of them, the nine English members, until death, all continuing to labour under Father John Lewis, who after the Suppression had received the powers of vicar-general from Bishop Challoner of the London District. Only two of them survived until the restoration of the Society—Robert Molyneux and John Bolton. Many of those who were abroad, labouring in England or studying in Belgium, returned to work in the mission. As a corporate body they still retained the properties from which they derived support for their religious ministrations. As their numbers decreased some of the missions were abandoned, or served for a time by other priests but maintained by the revenues of the Jesuit properties even after the Restoration of the Society. Though these properties were regarded as reverting to it through its former members organized as the Corporation of Roman Catholic Clergymen, a yearly allowance from the revenues made over to Archbishop Carroll became during Bishop Maréchal's administration (1817–34) the basis of a claim for such a payment in perpetuity and the dispute thus occasioned was not settled until 1838, under Archbishop Eccleston.

French Missions.—The French missions had as bases the French colonies in Canada, the Antilles, Guiana, and India; while French influence in the Mediterranean led to the missions of the Levant, in Syria, among the Maronites (q. v.), etc. (See also GUIANA; HAITI; MARTINIQUE; CHINA, III, 673.) The Canadian mission is described under CANADA, and MISSIONS, CATHOLIC INDIAN, OF CANADA. (See also the accounts of the mission given in the articles on Indian tribes like the Abenakis, Apaches, Cree, Hurons, Iroquois, Ottawas; and in the biographies of the missionaries Bailloquet, Brébeuf, Casot, Chabanel, Chastellain, Chaumonot, Cholonec, Crépieul, Dablon, Druillettes, Garnier, Goupil, Jogues, Lafitau, Lagrené, Jacques- P. Lallemant, Lamberville, Lauzon, Le Moyne, Râle, etc.) In 1611 Fathers Biard and Massé arrived as missionaries at Port Royal, Acadia. Taken prisoners by the English from Virginia, they were sent back to France in 1614. In 1625 Fathers Massé, Brébeuf, and Charles Lalemant came to work in and about Quebec, until 1629, when they were forced to return to France after the English captured Quebec. Back again in 1632 they began the most heroic missionary period in the annals of America. They opened a college at Quebec in 1635, with a staff of most accomplished professors from France. For forty years men quite as accomplished, labouring under incredible hardships, opened missions among the Indians on the coast, along the St. Lawrence and the Saguenay, and on Hudson Bay; among the Iroquois, Neutral Nation, Petuns, Hurons, Ottawas, and later among the Miamis, Illinois, and among the tribes east of the Mississippi as far south as the Gulf of Mexico. When Canada became a British possession in 1763, these missions could no longer be sustained, though many of them, especially those that formed part of parochial settlements, had gradually been taken over by secular priests. The college at Quebec was closed in 1768. At the time of the Suppression there were but twenty-one Jesuits in Canada, the last of whom, Rev. John J. Casot, died in 1800. The mission has become famous for its martyrs, eight of whom, Brébeuf, Gabriel Lalemant, Daniel, Garnier, Chabanel, Jogues, Goupil and his lay companions Goupil and Lalande, were declared venerable on 27 Feb., 1912. It has also become noted for its literary remains, especially for the works of the missionaries in the Indian tongues, for their explorations, especially that of Marquette, and for its "Relations".

Jesuit Relations.—The collections known as the "Jesuit Relations" consist of letters written from members of the Society in the foreign mission fields to their superiors and brethren in Europe, and contain accounts of the development of the missions, the labours of the missionaries, and the obstacles which they encountered in their work. In March, 1549, when St. Francis Xavier confided the mission of Ormus to Father Gaspar Barzæus, he included among his instructions the commission to write from time to time to the college at Goa, giving an account of what was being done in Ormus. His letter to Joam Beira (Malacca, 20 June, 1549) recommends similar accounts being sent to St. Ignatius at Rome and to Father Simon Rodriguez at Lisbon and is very explicit concerning both the contents and the tone of these accounts. These instructions were the guide for the future "Relations" sent from all the foreign missions of the order. The "Relations" were of three kinds: Intimate and personal accounts sent to the father-general, to a relative, a friend, or a superior, which were not meant for publication at that time, if ever. There were also annual letters, intended only for members of the order, manuscript copies of which were sent from house to house. Extracts and analyses of these letters were compiled in a volume entitled:

"Litteræ annuæ Societatis Jesu ad patres et fratres ejusdem Societatis". The rule forbade the communication of these letters to persons not members of the order, as is indicated by the title. The publication of the annual letters began in 1581, was interrupted from 1614 to 1649, and came to an end in 1654, though the provinces and missions continued to send such letters to the father-general. The third class of letters, or "Relations" properly so called, were written for the public and intended for printing. Of this class were the famous "Relations de la Nouvelle-France", begun in 1616 by Father Biard. The series for 1626 was written by Father Charles Lalemant. Forty-one volumes constitute the series of 1632-72, thirty-nine of which bear the title "Relations", and two (1645-55 and 1658-59) "Lettres de la Nouvelle-France". The cessation of these publications was the indirect outcome of the controversy concerning Chinese Rites, as Clement X forbade (16 April, 1673) missionaries to publish books or writings concerning the missions without the written consent of Propaganda.

Letters from the missions were instituted by Saint Ignatius. At first they circulated in MS. and contained home as well as foreign news; e. g. *Litteræ quadrimestres* (5 vols.), lately printed in the *Monumenta* series, mentioned above. Later on *Litteræ annuæ*, in yearly or triennial volumes (1581 to 1614) at Rome, Florence, etc., index with last vol. Second Series (1650–54) at Dillingen and Prague. The *Annual Letters* were continued, and still continue, in MS., but very irregularly. The tendency was to leave home news in MS. for the future historian, and to publish the more interesting reports from abroad. Hence many early issues of *Avvisi* and *Litteræ*, etc., from India, China, Japan, and later on the celebrated *Relations* of the French Canadian missions (Paris, 1634 —). From these ever-growing printed and MS. sources were drawn up the collections—*Lettres édifiantes et curieuses écrites par quelques missionaires de la comp. de Jésus* (Paris, 1702; frequently reprinted with different matter, in 4 to 34 volumes. The original title was *Lettres de quelques missionaires*); *Der Neue-Weltbott mit allerhand Nachrichten deren Missionar. Soc. Jesu*, ed. STOCKLEIN and others (36 vols., Augsburg, Gratz, 1728—); HUONDER, *Deutsche jesuiten Missionäre* (Freiburg, 1899). For literature of particular missions see those titles. LECLERCQ, *Premier établissement de la foy dans la Nouvelle-France* (Paris, 1619), tr. SHEA (New York, 1881); CAMPBELL, *Pioneer Priests of North America* (New York, 1908–11); BOURNE, *Spain in America* (New York, 1904); PARKMAN, *The Jesuits in North America* (Boston, 1868); ROCHEMONTEIX, *Les jésuites et la Nouvelle-France au xviie siècle* (Paris, 1896); CHARLEVOIX, *Hist. de la Nouvelle-France* (Paris, 1744); CAMPBELL (B.U.), *Biog. Sketch of Father Andrew White and his Companions, the first Missionaries of Maryland* in the *Metropolitan Catholic Almanac* (Baltimore, 1841); IDEM, *Hist. Sketch of the Early Christian Missions among the Indians of Maryland* (Maryland Hist. Soc., 8 Jan., 1846); JOHNSON, *The Foundation of Maryland* in *Maryland Hist. Soc., Fund Publications*, no. 18; KIP, *Early Jesuit Missions in North America* (New York, 1882); IDEM, *Hist. Scenes from the Old Jesuit Missions* (New York, 1875); *The Jesuit Relations*, ed. THWAITES (73 vols., Cleveland, 1896–1901); SHEA, *Jesuits, Recollects, and Indians* in WINSOR, *Narrative and critical Hist. of America* (Boston, 1889); HUGHES, *Hist. of the Soc. of Jesus in North America, Colonial and Federal* (Cleveland, 1908—); SHEA, *Hist. of the Cath. Church within the limits of the United States* (New York, 1886–92); SCHALL, *Hist. relatio de ortu et progressu fidei orthod. in regno Chinesi 1581–1669* (Ratisbon, 1672); RICCI, *Opere storiche*, ed. VENTURI (Macerata, 1911).

SUPPRESSION. 1750–73.—We now approach the most difficult part of the history of the Society. Having enjoyed very high favour among Catholic peoples, kings, prelates, and popes for two and a half centuries, it suddenly becomes an object of frenzied hostility, is overwhelmed with obloquy, and overthrown with dramatic rapidity. Every work of the Jesuits—their vast missions, their noble colleges, their churches—all is taken from them or destroyed. They are banished, and their order suppressed, with harsh and denunciatory words even from the pope. What makes the contrast more striking is that their protectors for the moment are former enemies—the Russians and Frederick of Prussia. Like many intricate problems, its solution is best found by beginning with what is easy to understand. We look forward a generation and we see that every one of the thrones, the pope's not excluded, which had been active in the Suppression, is overwhelmed. France, Spain, Portugal, and Italy become, indeed still are, a prey to the extravagances of the Revolutionary movement. The Suppression of the Society was due to the same causes which in further development brought about the French Revolution. These causes varied somewhat in different countries. In France many influences combined, as we shall see, from Jansenism and Free-thought to the then prevalent impatience with the old order of things (see FRANCE, VI, 172). Some have thought that the Suppression was primarily due to these currents of thought. Others attribute it chiefly to the absolutism of the Bourbons. For, though in France the king was averse to the Suppression, the destructive forces acquired their power because he was too indolent to exercise control, which at that time he alone possessed. Outside France it is plain that autocracy, acting through high-handed ministers, was the determining cause.

Portugal.—In 1750 Joseph I of Portugal appointed Sebastian Joseph Carvalho, afterwards Marquis of Pombal (q. v.), as his first minister. Carvalho's quarrel with the Jesuits began over an exchange of territory with Spain. San Sacramento was exchanged for the seven Reductions of Paraguay, which were under Spain. The Society's wonderful missions there were coveted by the Portuguese, who believed that the Jesuits were mining gold. So the Indians were ordered to quit their country, and the Jesuits endeavoured to lead them quietly to the distant land allotted to them. But owing to the harsh conditions imposed, the Indians rose in arms against the transfer, and the so-called war of Paraguay ensued, which, of course, was disastrous to the Indians. Then step by step the quarrel with the Jesuits was pushed to extremities. The weak king was persuaded to remove them from Court; a war of pamphlets against him was commenced; the Fathers were first forbidden to undertake the temporal administration of the missions, and then they were deported from America.

On 1 April, 1758, a Brief was obtained from the aged pope, Benedict XIV (q. v.), appointing Cardinal Saldanha to investigate the allegations against the Jesuits, which had been raised in the King of Portugal's name. But it does not follow that the pope had forejudged the case against the order. On the contrary, if we take into view all the letters and instructions sent to the cardinal, we see that the pope was distinctly sceptical as to the gravity of the alleged abuses. He ordered a minute inquiry, but one conducted so as to safeguard the reputation of the Society. All matters of serious importance were to be referred back to himself. The pope died five weeks later on 3 May. On 15 May, Saldanha, having received the Brief only a fortnight before, omitting the thorough, house-to-house visitation which had been ordered, and pronouncing on the issues which the pope had reserved to himself, declared that the Jesuits were guilty of having exercised illicit, public, and scandalous commerce both in Portugal and in its colonies. Three weeks later, at Pombal's instigation, all faculties were withdrawn from the Jesuits throughout the Patriarchate of Lisbon. Before Clement XIII (q v.) had become pope (6 July, 1758) the work of the Society had been destroyed, and in 1759 it was civilly suppressed. The last step was taken in consequence of a plot against the chamberlain Texeiras, but suspected to have been aimed at the king, and of this the Jesuits were supposed to have approved. But the grounds of suspicion were never clearly stated, much less proved. The height of Pombal's persecution was reached with the burning (1761) of the saintly Father Malagrida (q. v.) ostensibly for heresy; while the other Fathers, who had been crowded into prisons, were left to perish by the score. Intercourse between the Church of Portugal and Rome was broken off till 1770.

France.—The suppression in France was occasioned by the injuries inflicted by the English navy on French commerce in 1755. The Jesuit missionaries held a heavy stake in Martinique. They did not and could not trade, that is, buy cheap to sell dear, any more than any other religious. But they did sell the products of their great mission farms, in which many natives were employed, and this was allowed, partly to provide for the current expenses of the mission, partly in order to protect the simple, childlike natives from the common plague of dishonest intermediaries. Père Antoine La Valette, superior of the Martinique mission, managed these transactions with no little success, and success encouraged him to go too far. He began to borrow money in order to work the large undeveloped resources of the colony, and a strong letter from the governor of the island dated 1753 is extant in praise of his enterprise. But on the outbreak of war, ships conveying goods of the estimated value of 2,000,000 *livres* were captured and he suddenly became a bankrupt for a very large sum. His creditors were egged on to demand payment from the procurator of the Paris province: but he, relying on what certainly was the letter of the law, refused responsibility for the debts of an independent mission, though offering to negotiate for a settlement, of which he held out assured hopes. The creditors went to the courts, and an order was made (1760) obliging the Society to pay, and giving leave to distrain in case of non-payment.

The Fathers, on the advice of their lawyers, appealed to the *Grand'chambre* of the *Parlement* of Paris. This turned out to be an imprudent step. For not only did the *Parlement* support the lower court, 8 May, 1761, but, having once got the case into its hands, the Society's enemies in that assembly determined to strike a great blow at the order. Enemies of every sort combined. The Jansenists were numerous among the *gens-de-robe*, and at that moment were especially keen to be revenged on the orthodox party. The Sorbonnists, too, the university rivals of the great teaching order, joined in the attack. So did the Gallicans, the *Philosophes*, and *Encyclopédistes*. Louis XV was weak, and the influence of his Court divided; while his wife and children were earnestly in favour of the Jesuits, his able first minister, the Duc de Choiseul (q. v.), played into the hands of the *Parlement*, and the royal mistress, Madame de Pompadour, to whom the Jesuits had refused absolution, was a bitter opponent. The determination of the *Parlement* of Paris in time bore down all opposition. The attack on the Jesuits, as such, was opened by the Jansenistic Abbé Chauvelin, 17 April, 1762, who denounced the Constitutions of the Jesuits as the cause of the alleged defalcations of the mission. This was followed by the *compte-rendu* on the Constitutions, 3–7 July, 1762, full of misconceptions, but not yet extravagant in hostility. Next day Chauvelin descended to a vulgar but efficacious means of exciting odium by denouncing the Jesuits' teaching and morals, especially on the matter of tyrannicide.

In the *Parlement* the Jesuits' case was now desperate. After a long conflict with the Crown, in which the indolent minister-ridden sovereign failed to assert his will to any purpose, the *Parlement* issued its well-known "*Extraits des assertions*", a blue-book, as we might say, containing a congeries of passages from Jesuit theologians and canonists, in which they were alleged to teach every sort of immorality and error, from tyrannicide, magic, and Arianism to treason, Socinianism, and Lutheranism. On 6 August, 1762, the final *arrêt* was issued condemning the Society to extinction, but the king's intervention brought eight months' delay. In favour of the Jesuits there had been some striking testimonies, especially from the French clergy in the two convocations summoned on 30 November, 1761, and 1 May, 1762. But the series of letters and addresses published by Clement XIII afford a truly irrefragable attestation in favour of the order. Nothing, however, availed to stay the *Parlement*. The king's counter-edict delayed indeed the execution of its *arrêt*, and meantime a compromise was suggested by the Court. If the French Jesuits would stand apart from the order, under a French vicar, with French customs, the Crown would still protect them. In spite of the dangers of refusal, the Jesuits would not consent; and upon consulting the pope, he (not Ricci) used the since famous phrase, *Sint ut sunt, aut non sint* (de Ravignan, "Clément XIII", I, 105, the words are attributed to Ricci also). Louis's intervention hindered the execution of the *arrêt* against the Jesuits until 1 April, 1763. The colleges were then closed, and by a further *arrêt* of 9 March, 1764, the Jesuits were required to renounce their vows under pain of banishment. Only three priests and a few scholastics accepted the conditions. At the end of November, 1764, the king unwillingly signed an edict dissolving the Society throughout his dominions, for they were still protected by some provincial *parlements*, as Franche-Comté, Alsace, and Artois. But in the draft of the edict he cancelled numerous clauses, which implied that the Society was guilty; and, writing to Choiseul, he concluded with the weak but significant words: "If I adopt the advice of others for the peace of my realm, you must make the changes I propose, or I will do nothing. I say no more, lest I should say too much".

Spain, Naples, and Parma.—The Suppression in Spain and its quasi-dependencies, Naples and Parma, and in the Spanish colonies was carried through by autocratic kings and ministers. Their deliberations were conducted in secrecy, and they purposely kept their reasons to themselves. It is only of late years that a clue has been traced back to Bernardo Tanucci, the anti-clerical minister of Naples, who acquired a great influence over Charles III before that king passed from the throne of Naples to that of Spain. In this minister's correspondence are found all the ideas which from time to time guided the Spanish policy. Charles, a man of good moral character, had entrusted his Government to the Count Aranda and other followers of Voltaire; and he had brought from Italy a finance minister, whose nationality made the government unpopular, while his exactions led in 1766 to rioting and to the publication of various squibs, lampoons, and attacks upon the administration. An extraordinary council was appointed to investigate the matter, as it was declared that people so simple as the rioters could never have produced the political pamphlets. They proceeded to take secret informations, the tenor of which is no longer known; but records remain to show that in September the council had resolved to incriminate the Society, and that by 29 January, 1767, its expulsion was settled. Secret orders, which were to be opened at midnight between the first and second of April, 1767, were sent to the magistrates of every town where a Jesuit resided. The plan worked smoothly. That morning 6000 Jesuits were marching like convicts to the coast, where they were deported first to the Papal States, and ultimately to Corsica.

Tanucci pursued a similar policy in Naples. On 3 November the religious, again without trial, and this time without even an accusation, were marched across the frontier into the Papal States, and threatened with death if they returned. It will be noticed that in these expulsions the smaller the state the greater the contempt of the ministers for any forms of law. The Duchy of Parma was the smallest of the so-called Bourbon Courts, and so aggressive in its anti-clericalism that Clement XIII addressed to it (30 January, 1768) a *monitorium*, or warning, that its excesses were punishable with ecclesiastical censures. At this all parties to the Bourbon "Family Compact" turned in fury against the Holy See, and demanded the entire destruction of the Society. As a preliminary Parma at once drove the Jesuits out of its territories, confiscating as usual all their possessions.

Clement XIV.—From this time till his death (2 February, 1769) Clement XIII was harassed with the utmost rudeness and violence. Portions of his States were seized by force, he was insulted to his face by the Bourbon representatives, and it was made clear that, unless he gave way, a great schism would ensue, such as Portugal had already commenced. The conclave which followed lasted from 15 Feb. to May, 1769. The Bourbon Courts, through the so-called "crown cardinals", succeeded in excluding any of the party, nicknamed *Zelanti*, who would have taken a firm position in defence of the order, and finally elected Lorenzo Ganganelli, who took the name of Clement XIV. It has been stated by Crétineau-Joly (Clement XIV, p. 260) that Ganganelli, before his election, engaged himself to the crown cardinals by some sort of stipulation that he would suppress the Society, which would have involved an infraction of the conclave oath. This is now disproved by the statement of the Spanish agent Azpuru, who was specially deputed to act with the crown cardinals. He wrote on 18 May, just before the election, "None of the cardinals has gone so far as to propose to anyone that the Suppression should be secured by a written or spoken promise"; and just after 25 May he wrote, "Ganganelli neither made a promise, nor refused it". On the other hand it seems he did write words, which were taken by the crown cardinals as an indication that the Bourbons would get their way with him (de Bernis's letters of 28 July and 20 November, 1769).

No sooner was Clement on the throne than the Spanish Court, backed by the other members of the "Family Compact", renewed their overpowering pressure. On 2 August, 1769, Choiseul wrote a strong letter demanding the Suppression within two months; and the pope now made his first written promise that he would grant the measure, but he declared that he must have more time. Then began a series of transactions, which some have not unnaturally interpreted as devices to escape by delays from the terrible act of destruction, towards which Clement was being pushed. He passed more than two years in treating with the Courts of Turin, Tuscany, Milan, Genoa, Bavaria, etc., which would not easily consent to the Bourbon projects. The same ulterior object may perhaps be detected in some of the minor annoyances now inflicted on the Society. From several colleges, as those of Frascati, Ferrara, Bologna, and the Irish College at Rome, the Jesuits were, after a prolonged examination, ejected with much show of hostility. And there were moments, as for instance after the fall of Choiseul, when it really seemed as though the Society might have escaped; but eventually the obstinacy of Charles III always prevailed.

In the middle of 1772 Charles sent a new ambassador to Rome, Don Joseph Moñino, afterwards Count Florida Blanca, a strong, hard man, "full of artifice, sagacity, and dissimulation, and no one more set on the suppression of the Jesuits". Heretofore the negotiations had been in the hands of the clever, diplomatic Cardinal de Bernis, French ambassador to the pope. Moñino now took the lead, de Bernis coming in afterwards as a friend to urge the acceptance of his advice. At last, on 6 Sept., Moñino gave in a paper suggesting a line for the pope to follow, which he did in part adopt, in drawing up the Brief of Suppression. By November the end was coming in sight, and in December Clement put Moñino into communication with a secretary; and they drafted the instrument together, the minute being ready by 4 January, 1773. By 6 February Moñino had got it back from the pope in a form to be conveyed to the Bourbon Courts, and by 8 June, their modifications having been taken account of, the minute was thrown into its final form and signed. Still the pope delayed, until Moñino constrained him to get copies printed; and as these were dated, no delay was possible beyond that date, which was 16 August, 1773. A second Brief was issued to determine the manner in which the Suppression was to be carried out. To secure secrecy one regulation was introduced which led, in foreign countries, to some unexpected results. The Brief was not to be published *Urbi et Orbi*, but only to each college or place by the local bishop. At Rome, the father-general was confined first in the English College, then in Castel S. Angelo, with his assistants. The papers of the Society were handed over to a special commission, together with its title deeds and store of money, 40,000 *scudi* (about $50,000), which belonged almost entirely to definite charities. An investigation of the papers was begun, but never brought to any issue.

In the Brief of Suppression the most striking feature is the long list of allegations against the Society, with no mention of what is favourable; the tone of the Brief is very adverse. On the other hand the charges are recited categorically; they are not definitely stated to have been proved. The object is to represent the order as having occasioned perpetual strife, contradiction, and trouble. For the sake of peace the Society must be suppressed. A full explanation of these and other anomalous features cannot yet be given with certainty. The chief reason for them no doubt is that the Suppression was an administrative measure, not a judicial sentence based on judicial inquiry. We see that the course chosen avoided many difficulties, especially the open contradiction of preceding popes, who had so often praised or confirmed the Society. Again, such statements were less liable to be controverted; and there were different ways of interpreting the Brief, which commended themselves to *Zelanti* and *Borbonici* respectively. The last word on the subject is doubtless that of St. Alphonsus di Liguori—"Poor Pope! What could he do in the circumstances in which he was placed, with all the sovereigns conspiring to demand this Suppression? As for ourselves, we must keep silence, respect the secret judgment of God, and hold ourselves in peace".

CRÉTINEAU-JOLY, *Clément XIV et les jésuites* (Paris, 1847); DANVILLA Y COLLADO, *Reinado de Carlos III* (Madrid, 1893); DELPLACE, *La suppression des jésuites* in *Etudes* (Paris, 5–20 July, 1908); FERRER DEL RIO, *Hist. del reinado de Carlos III* (Madrid, 1856); DE RAVIGNAN, *Clément XIII et Clément XIV* (Paris, 1854); ROSSEAU, *Règne de Charles III d'Espagne* (Paris, 1907); SMITH, *Suppression of the Soc. of Jesus* in *The Month* (London, 1902–3); THEINER, *Gesch. des Pontificats Clement XIV* (Paris, 1853; French tr., Brussels, 1853); KOBLER, *Die Aufhebung der Gesellschaft Jesu* (Linz, 1873); WELD, *Suppression of the Soc. of Jesus in the Portuguese Dominions* (London, 1877); ZALENSKI, *The Jesuits in White Russia* (in Polish, 1874; Fr. tr., Paris, 1886); CARAYON, *Le père Ricci et la suppression de la comp. de Jésus* (Poitiers, 1869); SAINT-PRIEST, *Chute des jésuites* (Paris, 1846); NIPPOLD, *Jesuitenorden von seiner Wiederherstellung* (Mannheim, 1867).

THE INTERIM (1773–1814).—The execution of the Brief of Suppression having been largely left to the local bishops, there was room for a good deal of variety in the treatment which the Jesuits might receive in different places. In Austria and Germany they were generally allowed to teach (but with secular clergy as superiors); often they became men of mark as preachers, like Beauregard, Muzzarelli, and Alexandre Lanfant (b. at Lyons, 6 Sept., 1726, and massacred in Paris, 3 Sept., 1793) and writers like François-X. de Feller (q. v.), Zaccharia, Ximenes. The first to receive open official approbation of their new works were probably the English Jesuits, who in 1778 obtained a Brief approving their well-known Academy of Liège (now at Stonyhurst). But in Russia, and until 1780 in Prussia, the Empress Catherine and King Frederick II desired to maintain the Society as a teaching body. They forbade the local bishops to promulgate the Brief until their *placet* was obtained.

Bishop Massalski in White Russia, 19 September, 1773, therefore ordered the Jesuit superiors to continue to exercise jurisdiction till further notice. On 2 February, 1780, with the approbation of Bishop Siestrzencewicz's Apostolic visitor, a novitiate was opened. To obtain higher sanction for what had been done, the envoy Benislaski was sent by Catherine to Rome. But it must be remembered that the animus of the Bourbon Courts against the Society was still unchecked; and in some countries, as in Austria under Joseph II, the situation was worse than before. There were many in the Roman Curia who had worked their way up by their activity against the order, or held pensions created out of former Jesuit property. Pius VI declined to meet Catherine's requests. All he could do was to express an indefinite assent by word of mouth, without issuing any written documents, or observing the usual formalities; and he ordered that strict secrecy should be observed about the whole mission. Benislaski received these messages on 12 March, 1783, and later gave the Russian Jesuits an attestation of them (24 July, 1785).

On the other hand, it can cause no wonder that the enemies of the Jesuits should from the first have watched the survival in White Russia with jealousy, and have brought pressure to bear upon the pope to ensure their suppression. He was constrained to declare that he had not revoked the Brief of Suppression, and that he regarded as an abuse anything done against it, but that the Empress Catherine would not allow him to act freely (29 June, 1783). These utterances were not in real conflict with the answer given to Benislaski, which only amounted to the assertion that the escape from the Brief by the Jesuits in Russia was not schismatical, and that the pope approved of their continuing as they were doing. Their existence therefore was legitimate, or at least not illegitimate, though positive approval in legal form did not come till Pius VII's Brief "Catholicæ Fidei" (7 March, 1801). Meantime the same or similar causes to those which brought about the Suppression of the Society were leading to the disruption of the whole civil order. The French Revolution (1789) was overthrowing every throne that had combined against the Jesuits, and in the anguish of that trial many were the cries for the re-establishment of the order. But amid the turmoil of the Napoleonic wars, during the prolonged captivities of Pius VI (1798–1800) and of Pius VII (1809–14), such a consummation was impossible. The English Jesuits, however (whose academy at Liège, driven over to England by the French invasion of 1794, had been approved by a Brief in 1796), succeeded in obtaining oral permission from Pius VII for their aggregation to the Russian Jesuits, 27 May, 1803. The permission was to be kept secret, and was not even communicated by the pope to Propaganda. Next winter, its prefect, Cardinal Borgia, wrote a hostile letter, not indeed cancelling the vows taken, or blaming what had been done, but forbidding the bishops "to recognize the Jesuits", or "to admit their privileges", until they obtained permission from the Congregation of Propaganda.

Considering the extreme difficulties of the times, we cannot wonder at orders being given from Rome which were not always quite consistent. Broadly speaking, however, we see that the popes worked their way towards a restoration of the order by degrees. First, by approving community life, which had been specifically forbidden by the Brief of Suppression (this was done for England in 1778). Second, by permitting vows (for England in 1803). Third, by restoring the full privileges of a religious order (these were not recognized in England until 1829). The Society was extended by Brief from Russia to the Kingdom of Naples, 30 July, 1804; but on the invasion of the

French in 1806, all houses were dissolved, except those in Sicily. The superior in Italy during these changes was the Venerable Giuseppe M. Pignatelli (q. v.). In their zeal for the re-establishment of the Society some of the ex-Jesuits united themselves into congregations, which might, while avoiding the now unpopular name of Jesuits, preserve some of its essential features. Thus arose the Fathers of the Faith (Pères de la Foi), founded with papal sanction by Nicolas Paccanari in 1797. A somewhat similar congregation, called the "Fathers of the Sacred Heart", had been commenced in 1794 in Belgium, under Père Charles de Broglie, who was succeeded by Père Joseph Varin as superior. By wish of Pius VI, the two congregations amalgamated, and were generally known as the Paccanarists. They soon spread into many lands; Paccanari, however, did not prove a good superior, and seemed to be working against a reunion with the Jesuits still existing in Russia; this caused Père Varin and others to leave him. Some of them entered the Society in Russia at once; and at the Restoration the others joined *en masse*. (See SACRED HEART OF JESUS, SOCIETY OF THE.)

THE RESTORED SOCIETY.—Pius VII had resolved to restore the Society during his captivity in France; and after his return to Rome did so with little delay, 7 August, 1814, by the Bull "Sollicitudo omnium ecclesiarum," and therewith the general in Russia, Thaddæus Brzozowski, acquired universal jurisdiction. After the permission to continue given by Pius VI, the first Russian congregation had elected as vicar-general Stanislaus Czerniewicz (17 Oct., 1782-7 July, 1785), who was succeeded by Gabriel Lenkiewicz (27 Sept., 1785-10 Nov., 1798) and Francis Kareu (1 Feb., 1799-20 July, 1802). On the receipt of the Brief "Catholicæ Fidei", of 7 March, 1801, his title was changed from vicar-general to general. Gabriel Gruber succeeded (10 Oct., 1802-26 March, 1805), and was followed by Thaddæus Brzozowski (2 Sept., 1805). Almost simultaneously with the death of the latter, 5 Feb., 1820, the Russians, who had banished the Jesuits from St. Petersburg in 1815, expelled them from the whole country. It seems a remarkable providence that Russia, contrary to all precedent, should have protected the Jesuits just at the time when all other nations turned against them, and reverted to her normal hostility when the Jesuits began to find toleration elsewhere. Upon the decease of Brzozowski, Father Petrucci, the vicar, fell under the influence of the still powerful anti-Jesuit party at Rome, and proposed to alter some points in the Institute. The twentieth general congregation took a severe view of his proposals, expelled him from the order, and elected Father Aloysius Fortis (18 Oct., 1820-27 Jan., 1829) (q. v.); John Roothaan succeeded (9 July, 1829-8 May, 1853); and was followed by Peter Beckx (q. v.) (2 July, 1853-4 March, 1887). Anton Maria Anderledy, vicar-general on 11 May, 1884, became general on Fr. Beckx's death and died on 18 Jan., 1892; Luis Martin (2 Oct., 1892-18 Apr., 1906). Father Martin commenced a new series of histories of the Society, to be based on the increased materials now available, and to deal with many problems about which older annalists, Orlandini and his successors, were not curious. Volumes by Astrain, Duhr, Fouqueray, Hughes, Kroess, Tacchi-Venturi have appeared. The present general, Francis Xavier Wernz, was elected on 8 Sept., 1906.

Though the Jesuits of the nineteenth century cannot show a martyr-roll as brilliant as that of their predecessors, the persecuting laws passed against them surpass in number, extent, and continuance those endured by previous generations. The practical exclusion from university teaching, the obligation of military service in many countries, the wholesale confiscations of religious property, and the dispersion of twelve of its oldest and once most flourishing provinces are very serious hindrances to religious vocations. On a teaching order such blows fall very heavily. The cause of trouble has generally been due to that propaganda of irreligion which was developed during the Revolution and is still active through Freemasonry in those lands in which the Revolution took root.

France.—This is plainly seen in France. In that country the Society began after 1815 with the direction of some *petits séminaires* and congregations, and by giving missions. They were attacked by the Liberals, especially by the Comte de Montlosier in 1823 and their schools, one of which, St-Acheul, already contained 800 students, were closed in 1829. The Revolution of July (1830) brought them no immediate relief; but in the visitation of cholera in 1832 the Fathers pressed to the fore, and so began to recover influence. In 1845 there was another attack by Thiers, which drew out the answer of de Ravignan (q. v.). The Revolution of 1848 at first sent them again into exile, but the liberal measures which succeeded, especially the freedom of teaching, enabled them to return and to open many schools (1850). In the later days of the Empire greater difficulties were raised, but with the advent of the Third Republic (1870) these restrictions were removed and progress continued, until, after threatening measures in 1878, came the decree of 29 March, 1880, issued by M. Jules Ferry. This brought about a new dispersion and the substitution of staffs of non-religious teachers in the Jesuit colleges. But the French Government did not press their enactments, and the Fathers returned by degrees; and before the end of the century their houses and schools in France were as prosperous as ever. Then came the overwhelming Associations laws of M. Waldeck-Rousseau, leading to renewed though not complete dispersions and to the reintroduction of non-religious staffs in the colleges. The right of the order to hold property was also violently suppressed; and, by a refinement of cruelty, any property suspected of being held by a congregation may now be confiscated, unless it is proved *not* to be so held. Other clauses of this law penalize any meeting of the members of a congregation. The order is under an iron hand from which no escape is, humanly speaking, possible. For the moment nevertheless public opinion disapproves of its rigid execution, and thus far, in spite of all sufferings, of the dispersal of all houses, the confiscation of churches, and the loss of practically all property and schools, the numbers of the order have been maintained, nay slightly increased, and so too have the opportunities for work, especially in literature and theology, etc. (See also CARAYON; DESCHAMPS; DU LAC; OLIVAINT; RAVIGNAN.)

Spain.—In Spain the course of events has been similar. Recalled by Ferdinand VII in 1815, the Society was attacked by the Revolution of 1820; and twenty-five Jesuits were slain at Madrid in 1822. The Fathers, however, returned after 1823 and took part in the management of the military school and the College of Nobles at Madrid (1827). But in 1834 they were again attacked at Madrid, fourteen were killed, and the whole order was banished on 4 July, 1835, by a Liberal ministry. After 1848 they began to return and were re-settled after the Concordat, 26 Nov., 1852. At the Revolution of 1868 they were again banished (12 Oct.), but after a few years they were allowed to come back, and have since made great progress. At the present time, however, another expulsion is threatened (1912). In Portugal the Jesuits were recalled in 1829, dispersed again in 1834; but afterwards returned. Though they were not formally sanctioned by law they had a large college and several churches, from which, however, they were driven out in October, 1910, with great violence and cruelty.

Italy.—In Italy they were expelled from Naples (1820-21); but in 1836 they were admitted to Lombardy. Driven out by the Revolution of 1848 from almost the whole peninsula, they were able to return when peace was restored, except to Turin. Then with the gradual growth of United Italy they were step by step suppressed again by law everywhere, and finally at Rome after 1871. But though formally suppressed and unable to keep schools, except on a very small scale, the law is so worded that it does not press at every point, nor is it often enforced with acrimony. Numbers do not fall off, and activities increase. In Rome they have charge *inter alia* of the Gregorian University, the "Institutum Biblicum", and the German and Latin-American Colleges.

Germanic Provinces.—Of the Germanic Provinces, that of Austria may be said to have been recommenced by the immigration of many Polish Fathers from Russia to Galicia in 1820; and colleges were founded at Tarnopol, Lemberg, Linz (1837), and Innsbruck in 1838, in which they were assigned the theological faculty in 1856. The German province properly so called could at first make foundations only in Switzerland at Brieg (1814) and Freiburg (1818). But after the *Sonderbund* they were obliged to leave, being then 264 in number (111 priests). They were now able to open several houses in the Rhine provinces, etc., making steady progress till they were ejected during Bismarck's *Kulturkampf* (1872), when they numbered 755 members (351 priests). They now count 1150 (with 574 priests) and are known throughout the world by their many excellent publications. (See ANTONIEWICZ; DEHARBE; HASSLACHER; PESCH; ROH; SPILLMANN.)

Belgium.—The Belgian Jesuits were unable to return to their country till Belgium was separated from Holland in 1830. Since then they have prospered exceedingly. In 1832, when they became a separate province, they numbered 105; at their seventy-five years' jubilee, in 1907, they numbered 1168. In 1832, two colleges with 167 students: in 1907, 15 colleges with 7465 students. Congregations of the Blessed Virgin, originally founded by a Belgian Jesuit, still flourish. In Belgium 2529 such congregations have been aggregated to the *Prima Primaria* at Rome, and of these 156 are under Jesuit direction. To say nothing of missions and of retreats to convents, dioceses, etc., the province had six houses of retreats, in which 245 retreats were given to 9840 persons. Belgium supplies the foreign mission of Eastern Bengal and the Diocese of Galle in Ceylon. In the bush-country of Chota Nagpur there began, in 1887, a wonderful movement of the aborigines (Kôles and Ouraons) towards the Church, and the Catholics in 1907 numbered 137,120 (i. e. 62,385 baptized and 74,735 catechumens). Over 35,000 conversions had been made in 1906, owing to the penetration of Christianity into the district of Jashpur. Besides this there are excellent colleges at Darjeeling and at Kurseong; at Kandy in Ceylon the Jesuits have charge of the great pontifical seminary for educating native clergy for the whole of India. In all they have 442 churches, chapels, or stations, 479 schools, 14,467 scholars, with about 167,000 Catholics, and 262 Jesuits, of whom 150 are priests. The Belgian Fathers have also a flourishing mission on the Congo, in the districts of Kwango and Stanley Pool, which was begun in 1893; in 1907 the converts already numbered 31,402.

England.—Nowhere did the Jesuits get through the troubles inevitable to the Interim more easily than in conservative England. The college at Liège continued to train their students in the old traditions, while the English bishops permitted the ex-Jesuits to maintain their missions and a sort of corporate discipline. But there were difficulties in recognizing the restored order, lest this should impede emancipation (see ROMAN CATHOLIC RELIEF BILL), which remained in doubt for so many years. Eventually Leo XII on 1 Jan., 1829, declared the Bull of restoration to have force in England. After this the Society grew, slowly at first, but more rapidly afterwards. It had 73 members in 1815, 729 in 1910. The principal colleges are Stonyhurst (St. Omers, 1592, migrated to Bruges, 1762, to Liège, 1773, to Stonyhurst, 1794); Mount St. Mary's (1842); Liverpool (1842); Beaumont (1861); Glasgow (1870); Wimbledon, London (1887); Stamford Hill, London (1894); Leeds (1905). In 1910 the province had in England and Scotland, besides the usual novitiate and houses of study, two houses for retreats, 50 churches or chapels, attended by 148 priests. The congregations amounted to 97,641; baptisms, 3746; confessions, 844,079; Easter confessions, 81,065; Communions, 1,303,591; converts, 725; extreme unctions, 1698; marriages, 782; children in elementary schools, 18,328. The Guiana mission (19 priests) has charge of about 45,000 souls; the Zambesi mission (35 priests), 4679 souls. (See also the articles MORRIS; PLOWDEN; PORTER; STEVENSON; COLERIDGE; HARPER.)

LUIS MARTIN
Twenty-eighth General of the Society of Jesus

Ireland.—There were 24 ex-Jesuits in Ireland in 1776, but by 1803 only two. Of these Father O'Callaghan renewed his vows at Stonyhurst in 1803, and he and Father Betagh, who was eventually the last survivor, succeeded in finding some excellent postulants who made their novitiate in Stonyhurst, their studies at Palermo, and returned between 1812 and 1814, Father Betagh, who had become Vicar-General of Dublin, having survived to the year 1811. Father Peter Kenny (d. 1841) was the first superior of the new mission, a man of remarkable eloquence, who when visitor of the Society in America (1830-1833) preached by invitation before Congress. From 1812-13 he was vice-president of Maynooth College under Dr. Murray, then coadjutor Bishop of Dublin. The College of Clongowes Wood was begun in 1813; Tullabeg in 1818 (now a house of both probations); Dublin (1841); Mungret (Apostolic School, 1883). In 1883, too, the Irish bishops entrusted to the Society the University College, Dublin, in connexion with the late Royal University of Ireland. The marked superiority of this college to the richly endowed Queen's Colleges of Belfast, Cork, and Galway contributed much to establish the claim of the Irish Catholics to adequate university education. When this claim had been met by the present National University, the University College was returned to the Bishops. Five Fathers now hold teaching posts in the new university, and a hostel for students is being provided. Under the Act of Catholic Emancipation (q. v.) 58 Jesuits were registered in Ireland in 1830. In 1910 there were 367 in the province, of whom 100 are in Australia, where they have 4 colleges at and near Melbourne and Sydney, and missions in South Australia.

United States of America.—Under the direction of Bishop Carroll the members of the Corporation of Roman Catholic Clergymen in Maryland were the chief factors in founding and maintaining Georgetown College (q. v.) from 1791 to 1805, when they resumed their relations with the Society still existing in Russia, and were so strongly reinforced by other members of the order from Europe that they could assume full charge of the institution, which they have since retained. On the Restoration of the Society in 1814 these nineteen fathers constituted the mission of the United States. For a time (1808 to 1817) some of them were employed in the Diocese of New York just erected, Father Anthony Kohlmann (q. v.) administering the diocese temporarily, the others engaging in school and parish work. In 1816 Gonzaga College, Washington, D. C., was founded. In 1833 the mission of the United States became a province under the title of Maryland. Since then the history of the province is a record of development proportionate with the growth of Catholicity in the various fields specially cultivated by the Society. The colleges of the Holy Cross, Worcester (founded in 1843), Loyola College, Baltimore (1852), Boston College (1863) have educated great numbers of young men for the ministry and liberal professions. Up to 1879 members of the Society had been labouring in New York as part of the New York-Canada mission. In that year they became affiliated with the first American province under the title of Maryland-New York. This was added to the old province, besides several residences and parishes, the colleges of St. Francis Xavier and St. John (now Fordham University), New York City, and St. Peter's College, Jersey City, New Jersey. St. Joseph's College, Philadelphia, was chartered in 1852 and the Brooklyn College opened in 1908. In the same year Canisius College, and two parishes in Buffalo, and one parish in Boston for German Catholics, with 88 members of the German province were affiliated with this province, which has now (1912) 863 members with 12 colleges and 13 parishes, 1 house of higher studies for the members of the Society, 1 novitiate, in the New England and Middle States, and in the Virginias, with the Mission of Jamaica, British West Indies.

The Missouri province began as a mission from Maryland in 1823. Father Charles Van Quickenborne, a Belgian, led several young men of his own nationality who were eager to work among the Indians, among them De Smet (q. v.), Van Assche, and Verhaegen. As a rule the tribes were too nomadic to evangelize, and the Indian schools attracted only a very small number of pupils. The missions among the Osage and Pottawatomie were more permanent and fruitful. It was with experience gathered in these fields that Father De Smet started his mission in the Rocky Mountains in 1840. A college, now St. Louis University, was opened in 1829. For ten years, 1838–48, a college was maintained at Grand Coteau, Louisiana; in 1840 St. Xavier's was opened at Cincinnati. With the aid of seventy-eight Jesuits, who came from Italy and Switzerland in the years of revolution 1847–8, two colleges were maintained, St. Joseph's, Bardstown, 1848 until 1861, another at Louisville, Kentucky, 1849–57. In this last year a college was opened at Chicago. The mission became a province in 1863, and since then colleges have been opened at Detroit, Omaha, Milwaukee, St. Mary's (Kansas). By the accession of part of the Buffalo mission when it was separated from the German province in 1907, the Missouri province acquired an additional 180 members, and colleges at Cleveland, Toledo, and Prairie du Chien, besides several residences and missions. Its members work in the territory west of the Alleghanies as far as Kansas and Omaha, and from the Lakes to the northern line of Tennessee and Oklahoma, and also in the Mission of British Honduras (q. v.).

New Orleans.—For five years, 1566–1571, members of the Peruvian province laboured among the Indians along the coast of Florida, where Father Martínez was massacred near St. Augustine in 1566. They penetrated into Virginia, where eight of their number were massacred by Indians at a station named Axaca, supposed to be on the Rappahannock River. Later, Jesuits from Canada, taking as their share of the Louisiana territory the Illinois country and afterwards from the Ohio River to the gulf east of the Mississippi, worked among the Choctaw, Chickasaw, Natchez, and Yazoo. Two of their number were murdered by the Natchez and one by the Chickasaw. Their expulsion in 1763 is the subject of a monograph by Carayon, "Documents inédits", XIV. Originally evangelized by Jesuits from the Lyons province, the New Orleans mission became a province in 1907, having 7 colleges and four residences. It has now 255 members working in the territory north of the Gulf of Mexico to Missouri as far east as Virginia.

California.—In 1907 a province was formed in California comprising the missions of California, the Rocky Mountains, and Alaska (United States). The history of these missions is narrated under CALIFORNIA MISSIONS; MISSIONS, CATHOLIC INDIAN, OF THE UNITED STATES; ALASKA; IDAHO; SIOUX INDIANS.

New Mexico.—In the mission of New Mexico ninety-three Jesuits are occupied in the college at Denver, Colorado, and in various missions in that state, Arizona, and New Mexico; the mission depends on the Italian province of Naples.

In all the provinces in the United States there are 6 professional schools, with 4363 students; 26 colleges with full courses, with 2417, and 34 preparatory and high schools with 8735 pupils.

Canada.—Jesuits returned to Canada from St. Mary's College, Kentucky, which had been taken over, in 1834, by members of the province of France. When St. Mary's was given up in 1846 the staff came to take charge of St. John's College, Fordham, New York, thus forming with their fellows in Montreal the New York-Canada mission. This mission lasted until 1879, the Canadian division having by that year 1 college, 2 residences, 1 novitiate, 3 Indian missions with 131 members. In 1888 the mission received $160,000 as its part of the sum paid by the Province of Quebec in compensation for the Jesuit estates appropriated under George III by imperial authority, and transferred to the authorities of the former Province of Canada, all parties agreeing that the full amount, $400,000, thus allowed was far short of the value of the estates, estimated at $2,000,000. The settlement was ratified by the pope and the Legislature of the Province of Quebec, and the balance was divided among the archdioceses of Quebec, Montreal, and other dioceses, the Laval University besides receiving, in Montreal, $40,000 and, in Quebec, $100,000.

In 1907 the mission was constituted a province. It has now 2 colleges in Montreal, one at St. Boniface with 263 students in the collegiate and 722 in the preparatory classes, 2 residences and churches in Quebec, one at Guelph, Indian missions, and missions in Alaska, and 309 members.

Mexico.—In Mexico (New Spain) Jesuit missionaries began their work in 1571 and prior to their expulsion, in 1767, they numbered 678 members, of whom 468 were natives. They had over 40 colleges or seminaries, 5 residences, and 6 missionary districts, with 99 missions. The mission included Cuba, Lower California, and as far south as Nicaragua. Three members of the suppressed society who were in Mexico at the time of the Restoration formed a nucleus for its re-establishment there in 1816. In 1820 there were 32, of whom 15 were priests and 3 scholastics, in care of 4 colleges and 3 seminaries. They were dispersed in 1821. Although invited back in 1843, they could not agree to the limitations put on their activities by

General Santa Anna, nor was the prospect favourable in the revolutionary condition of the country. Four of their number returning in 1854, the mission prospered, and in spite of two dispersions, 1859 and 1873, it has continued to increase in number and activity. In August, 1907, it was reconstituted a province. It has now 326 members with 4 colleges, 12 residences, 6 mission stations among the Tarahumara, and a novitiate (see also MEXICO; PIOUS FUND OF THE CALIFORNIAS).

GERARD, *Stonyhurst Centenary Record* (Belfast, 1894); CORCORAN, *Clongowes Centenary Record* (Dublin, 1912); *Woodstock Letters* (Woodstock College, Maryland, 1872—); *Georgetown University* (Washington, 1891); *The First Half Century of St. Ignatius Church and College* (San Francisco, 1905); DUHR, *Akten zur Gesch. der Jesuit-missionen in Deutschland, 1842–72* (1903); BOËRO, *Istoria della vita del R. P. Pignatelli* (Rome, 1857); PONCELET, *La comp. de Jésus en Belgique* (Brussels, 1907); ZARADONA, *Hist. de la extinción y restablecimiento de la comp. de Jésus* (Madrid, 1890); NIPPOLD, *Jesuitenorden von seiner Wiederherstellung* (Mannheim, 1867).

GENERAL STATISTICS OF THE SOCIETY OF JESUS FOR THE BEGINNING OF 1912.

Assistancy	Province	Priests	Scholastics	Coadjutors	Total
Italian	Rome	190	103	94	387
	Naples	154	109	86	349
	Sicily	113	61	71	245
	Turin	150	62	48	260
	Venice	215	59	97	371
	Total	822	394	396	1612
German	Austria	310	108	186	604
	Belgium	586	393	221	1200
	Galicia	221	133	156	510
	Germany	595	247	344	1186
	Hungary	79	51	69	199
	Netherlands	280	135	131	546
	Total	2071	1067	1107	4245
French (dispersed)	Champagne	377	221	133	731
	France	514	139	171	824
	Lyons	449	168	176	793
	Toulouse	417	167	139	723
	Total	1757	695	619	3071
Spanish	Aragon	537	264	435	1236
	Castile	563	361	410	1334
	Portugal (dispersed)	159	91	109	359
	Mexico	128	118	87	333
	Toledo	278	123	196	597
	Total	1665	957	1237	3859
English	England	391	201	124	716
	California	151	136	107	394
	Canada	153	120	100	373
	Ireland	196	116	55	367
	Maryland-New York	354	353	156	863
	Missouri	356	272	162	790
	New Orleans	132	82	41	255
	Total	1733	1280	745	3758
Grand Total					16,545

but fallible men. Sweeping denials here and an injured tone would be misplaced and liable to misconception. As an instance of Jesuit fallibility, one may mention that writings of nearly one hundred Jesuits have been placed on the Roman "Index". Since this involves a reflection upon the Jesuit book-censors as well, it might appear to be an instance of failure in an important matter. But when we remember that the number of Jesuit writers exceeds 120,000, the proportion of those who have missed

MISSIONS OF THE SOCIETY OF JESUS IN 1912.

Mission	Province	Priests	Schol.	Coadj.	Total
Europe					
Albania	Venice	5	—	4	9
Croatia	Austria	41	11	30	82
Denmark	Germany	29	12	32	73[1]
Sweden	Germany	5	—	2	7[1]
Syra and Tinos (Greece)	Sicily	8	—	7	15
Africa					
Egypt	Lyons	55	7	16	78
Belgian Congo	Belgium	17	7	14	38
Upper Zambeze	England	47	—	33	80
Lower Zambeze	Portugal	17	1	18	36[1]
Madagascar, Reunion, and Mauritius	Toulouse	60	5	18	83
Betsileo (Madagascar)	Champagne	39	—	12	51
Asia					
Armenia	Lyons	39	1	15	55
Syria	Lyons	85	10	54	149
Bombay (India)	Germany	88	16	21	125[1]
Mangalore (India)	Venice	43	6	11	60
Bengal (India)	Belgium	136	88	32	256
Galle (Ceylon)	Belgium	16	6	3	25
Trincomalee (Ceylon)	Champagne	14	1	3	18
Madura (India)	Toulouse	105	69	24	198
Goa (India)	Portugal	20	—	9	29
Nankin (China)	France	148	12	28	188
S. E. Tcheu-li (China)	Champagne	64	—	15	79
Japan		4	—	—	4[1]
Philippine Islands	Aragon	90	4	62	156
Flores, Java, and Sumatra	Netherlands	61	6	10	77
S. and E. Australia	Ireland	68	17	17	102
North America					
Indian Missions (Canada)	Canada	11	3	16	30
North Alaska (U. S. A.)	Canada	15	2	9	26
South Alaska (U. S. A.)	California	6	—	—	6
New Mexico, Colorado, and Texas	Naples	62	6	26	94
Tarahumara (Mex.)	Mexico	11	—	12	23
Cuba	Castile	49	13	37	99
Jamaica	Maryland-New York	18	—	2	20
South America					
Colombia	Castile	93	51	58	202[1]
Brit. Guiana	England	21	—	1	22
N. and Cent. Brazil	Rome	76	26	51	153
S. Brazil	Germany	111	27	66	204[1]
S. Brazil	Portugal	50	2	39	91
Ecuador	Toledo	53	10	27	90
Peru	Toledo	50	—	26	76
Chile and Argentina	Aragon	172	23	127	322
Total					3531

[1] Note.—Figures for 1911—those for 1912 not available.

APOLOGETIC.—The accusations brought against the Society have been exceptional for their frequency and fierceness. Many indeed would be too absurd to deserve mention, were they not credited even by cultured and literary people. Such for instance are the charges that the Society was responsible for the Franco-Prussian war, the *affaire* Dreyfus, the Panama scandal, the assassination of popes, kings, princes, etc.—statements found in books and periodicals of some pretence. Such likewise is the so-called Jesuit Oath, the clumsy fabrication of the forger Robert Ware, exposed by Bridgett in "Blunders and Forgeries". The fallacy of such accusations may often be detected by general principles. A. *Jesuits are fallible*, and may have given some occasion to the accuser. The charges laid against them would never have been brought against angels, but they are not in the least inconsistent with the Society being a body of good the mark cannot be considered extraordinary; the censure inflicted moreover has never been of the graver kind. Many critics of the order, who do not consider the Index censures discreditable, cannot pardon so readily the exaggerated *esprit de corps* in which Jesuits of limited experience occasionally indulge, especially in controversies or while eulogizing their own confrères; nor can they overlook the narrowness or bias with which some Jesuit writers have criticized men of other lands, institutions, education, though it is unfair to hold up the faults of a few as characteristic of the entire body.

B. *The Accusers*.—(1) In an oft-recited passage about the martyrs St. Ambrose tells us: "Vere frustra impugnatur qui apud impios et infidos impietatis arcessitur cum fidei sit magister" (He in truth, is impugned in vain who is accused of impiety by the impious and the faithless, though he is a teacher of the faith). The personal equation of the accuser is a correction of great moment; nevertheless it is to be applied with equally great caution; on no other point is an accused person so liable to make mistakes. Undoubtedly, however, when we find a learned man like Harnack declaring roundly (but without proofs) that Jesuits are not historians, we may place this statement of his beside another of his professorial dicta, that the Bible is not history. If the same principles underlie both propositions, the accusation against the order will carry little weight. When an infidel government, about to assail the liberties of the Church, begins by expelling the Jesuits, on the allegation that they destroy the love of freedom in their scholars, we can only say that no words of theirs can counterbalance the logic of their acts. Early in this century the French Government urged as one of their reasons for suppressing all the religious orders in France, among them the Society, that the regulars were crowding the secular clergy out of their proper spheres of activity and influence. No sooner were the religious suppressed than the law separating Church and State was passed to cripple and enslave the bishops and secular clergy.

(2) Again it is perhaps little wonder that heretics in general, and those in particular who impugn church liberties and the authority of the Holy See, should be ever ready to assail the Jesuits, who are especially bound to the defence of that see. It seems stranger that the opponents of the Society should sometimes be within the Church. Yet it is almost inevitable that such opposition should at times occur. No matter how adequately the canon law regulating the relations of regulars with the hierarchy and clergy generally may provide for their peaceful co-operation in missionary, educational, and charitable enterprises, there will necessarily be occasion for differences of opinion, disputes over jurisdiction, methods, and similar vital points, which in the heat of controversy often embitter and even estrange the parties at variance. Such unfortunate controversies arise between other religious orders and the hierarchy and secular clergy; they are neither common nor permanent, not the rule but the exception, so that they do not warrant the sinister judgment that is sometimes formed of the Society in particular as unable or unwilling to work with others, jealous of its own influence. Sometimes, especially when troubles of this kind have affected broad questions of doctrine and discipline, the agitation has reached immense proportions and bitterness has remained for years. The controversies *De auxiliis* led to violent explosions of temper, to intrigue, and to furious language which was simply astonishing; and there were others, in England for instance about the faculties of the archpriest, in France about Gallicanism, which were almost equally memorable for fire and fury. *Odium theologicum* is sure at all times to call forth excitement of unusual keenness; but we may make allowance for the early disputants, because of the pugnacious character of the times. When the age quite approved of gentlemen killing each other in duels on very slight provocation, there can be little wonder that clerics, when aroused, should forget propriety and self-restraint, sharpen their pens like daggers, and, dipping them in gall, strike at any sensitive point of their adversaries which they could injure. Charges put about by such excited advocates must be received with the greatest caution.

(3) The most embittered and the most untrustworthy enemies of the Society (they are fortunately not very numerous) have ever been deserters from its own ranks. We know with what malice and venom some unfaithful priests are wont to assail the Church, which they once believed to be Divine, and not dissimilar has been the hatred of some Jesuits who have been untrue to their calling.

C. *What is to be expected?* The Society has certainly had some share in the beatitude of suffering for persecution's sake; though it is not true, however, to say that the Society is the object of *universal detestation*. Prominent politicians, whose acts affect the interests of millions, are much more hotly and violently criticized, more freely denounced, caricatured, and condemned in the course of a month than the Jesuits singly or collectively in a year. When once the politician is overthrown, the world turns its fire upon the new holder of power, and it forgets the man that is fallen. But the light attacks against the Society never cease for long, and their cumulative effect appears more serious than it should, because people overlook the long spans of years which in its case intervene between the different signal assaults; Another principle to remember is that the enemies of the Church would never assail the Society at all, were it not that it is conspicuously popular with large classes of the Catholic community. Neither universal odium therefore nor freedom from all assault should be expected, but charges which, by exaggeration, inversion, satire, or irony, somehow correspond with the place of the Society in the Church.

Not being contemplatives like the monks of old, Jesuits are not decried as lazy and useless. Not being called to fill posts of high authority or to rule, like popes and bishops, Jesuits are not seriously denounced as tyrants, or maligned for nepotism and similar misdeeds. Ignatius described his order as a flying squadron ready for service anywhere, especially as educators and missionaries. The principal charges against the Society are misrepresentations of these qualities. If they are ready for service in any part of the world, they are called busybodies, mischief-makers, politicians with no attachment to country. If they do not rule, at least they must be grasping, ambitious, scheming, and wont to lower standards of morality, in order to gain control of consciences. If they are good disciplinarians, it will be said it is by espionage and suppression of individuality and independence. If they are popular schoolmasters, the adversary will say they are good for children, good perhaps as crammers, but bad educators, without influence. If they are favourite confessors, their success is ascribed to their lax moral doctrines, to their casuistry, and above all to their use of the maxim which is supposed to justify any and every evil act: "the end justifies the means". This perhaps is the most salient instance of the ignorance or ill-will of their accusers. Their books are open to all the world. Time and again those who impute to them as a body, or to any of their publications, the use of this maxim to justify evil of any sort have been asked to cite one instance of such usage, but all to no purpose. The signal failure of Hoensbroech to establish before the civil courts of Trier and Cologne (30 July, 1905) any such example of Jesuit teaching should silence this and similar accusations forever.

D. *The Jesuit Legend.*—It is curious that at the present day even literary men have next to no interest in the objective facts concerning the Society, not even in those supposed to be to its disadvantage. All attention is fixed on the Jesuit legend; encyclopedia articles and general histories hardly concern themselves with anything else. The legend, though it reached its present form in the middle of the nineteenth century, began at a much earlier period. The early persecutions of the Society (which counted some 100 martyrs in Europe during its first century) were backed up by fiery, loud, unscrupulous writers such as Hasenmüller and Hospinian, who diligently collected and defended all the charges brought against the Jesuits. The rude, criminous ideal which these writers set forth received subtler traits of deceitfulness and double-dealing through Zahorowski's "Monita secreta Societatis Jesu" (Cracow, 1614), a satire misrepresenting the rules of the order, which is freely believed to be genuine by credulous adversaries (see MONITA SECRETA). The current version of the legend is late French, evolved during the long revolutionary ferment which preceded the Third Empire. It began with the denunciations of Montlosier (1824–27), and grew strong (1833–45) in the University of Paris, which affected to consider itself as the representative of the Gallican Sorbonne, of Port-Royal, and of the *Encyclopédie*. The occasion for literary hostilities was offered by attempts at university reform, which, so the Liberals affected to believe, were instigated by Jesuits. Hereupon the "Provinciales" were given a place in the university curriculum, and Villemain, Thiers, Cousin, Michelet, Quinet, Libri, Mignet, and other respectable scholars succeeded by their writings and denunciations in giving to anti-Jesuitism a sort of literary vogue, not always with scrupulous observance of accuracy or fairness. More harmful still to the order were the plays, the songs, the popular novels against them. Of these the most celebrated was Eugène Sue's "Juif errant" (Wandering Jew) (1844), which soon became the most popular anti-Jesuit book ever printed, and has done more than any thing else to give final form to the Jesuit legend.

The special character of this fable is that it has hardly anything to do with the order at all, its traits being simply copied from masonry. The previous Jesuit bogey was at least one which haunted churches and colleges, and worked through the confessional and the pulpit. But this creation of modern fiction has lost all connexion with reality. He (or even she) is a person, not necessarily a priest, under the command of a black pope, who lives in an imaginary world of back stairs, closets, and dark passages. He is busy with plotting and scheming, mesmerizing the weak and corrupting the honest, occupations diversified by secret crimes or melodramatic attempts at crime of every sort. This ideal we see is taken over bodily from the real, or rather the supposed, method of life of the Continental mason. Yet this is the sort of nonsense about which special correspondents send telegrams to their papers, about which revolutionary agitators and crafty politicians make long inflammatory speeches, which standard works of reference discuss quite gravely, which none of our popular writers dares to expose as an imposture (see Brou, op. cit. infra, II, 199–247).

E. *Some Modern Objections.*—(1) Without having given up the old historical objections (for the study of which the historical sections of this article may be consulted), the anti-Jesuits of to-day arraign the Society as out of touch with the modern *Zeitgeist*, as hostile to liberty and culture, and as being a failure. Liberty, next to intelligence (and some people put it before), is the noblest of man's endowments. Its enemies are the enemies of the human race. Yet it is said that Ignatius's system, by aiming at "blind" obedience, paralyses the judgment and by consequence scoops out the will, inserting the will of the superior in its place, as a watchmaker might replace one mainspring by another (cf. Encyc. Brit., 1911, XV, 342); *perinde ac cadaver*, "like a corpse", again "similar to an old man's staff"—therefore dead and listless, mere machines, incapable of individual distinction (Böhmer-Monod, op. cit. infra, p. lxxvi).

The cleverness of this objection lies in its bold inversion of certain plain truths. In reality no one loved liberty better or provided for it more carefully than Ignatius. But he upheld the deeper principle that true freedom lies in obeying reason, all other choice being licence. Those who hold themselves free to disobey even the laws of God, who declare all rule in the Church a tyranny, and who aim at so-called free-love, free divorce, and free thought—they, of course, reject his theory. In practice his custom was to train the will so thoroughly that his men might after a short time be able to "level up" others (a most difficult thing) from laxity to thoroughness, without themselves being drawn down (a most easy thing), even though they lived outside cloisters, with no external support for their discipline. The wonderful achievement of staying and rolling back the tide of the Reformation, in so far as it was due to the Jesuits, was the result of the increased will-power given to previously irresolute Catholics by the Ignatian methods.

As to "blind" obedience, we should note that all obedience must be blind to some extent—"Theirs not to reason why, Theirs but to do and die." Ignatius borrowed from earlier ascetic writers the strong metaphors of the "blind man", "the corpse", "the old man's staff", to illustrate the nature of obedience in a vivid way; but he does not want those metaphors to be run to death. Not only does he want the subject to bring both head and heart to the execution of the command, but, knowing human nature and its foibles, he recognizes that cases will arise when the superior's order may appear impracticable, unreasonable, or unrighteous to a free subject and may possibly really be so. In such cases it is the acknowledged duty of the subject to appeal, and his judgment as well as his conscience, even when it may happen to be ill-formed, is to be respected; provision is made in the Constitutions for the clearing up of such troubles by discussion and arbitration, a provision which would be inconceivable, unless a mind and a free will, independent of and possibly opposed to that of the superior, were recognized and respected. Ignatius wishes his subjects to be "dead" or "blind" only in respect of sloth, of passion, of self-interest, and self-indulgence, which would impede the ready execution of orders. So far is he from desiring a mechanical performance that he explicitly disparages "obedience, which executes in work only", as "unworthy of the name of virtue" and warmly urges that "bending to, with all forces of head and heart, we should carry out the commands quickly and completely" (Letter on Obedience, § 5, 14).

GABRIEL GRUBER
Twenty-second General of the Society of Jesus

Further illustrations of Ignatian love of liberty may be found in the Spiritual Exercises and in the character of certain theological doctrines, as Probabilism and Molinism (with its subsequent modifications) which are commonly taught in the Society's schools. Thus, Molinism "is above all determined to throw a wall of security round free will" (see GRACE, CONTROVERSIES ON), and Probabilism (q. v.) teaches that liberty may not be restrained unless the restraining force rests on a basis of certainty. The characteristic of both theories is to emphasize the sacredness of free will somewhat more than is done in other systems. The Spiritual Exercises, the secret of Ignatius's success, are a series of considerations arranged, as he tells the exercitant from the first, to enable him to make a choice or election on the highest principles and without fear of consequences. Again the priest, who explains the meditations, is warned to be most careful not to incline the exercitant more to one object of choice than to another (Annot. 15).

It is notoriously impossible to expect that anti-Jesuit writers of our day should face their subject in a common-sense or scientific manner. If they did, one would point out that the only rational manner of inquiring into the subject would be to approach the persons under discussion (who are after all very approachable) and to see whether they are characterless, as they are reported to be. Another easy test would be to turn to the lives of their great missionaries Brébeuf, Marquette, Silveira, etc. Any men more unlike "mere machines" it would be impossible to conceive. The Society's successes in education confirm the same conclusion. It is true that lately, as a preparatory measure to closing its schools by violence, the French anti-Jesuits asserted both in print and in the Chamber that Jesuit education produced mere pawns, spiritless, unenterprising nonentities. But the real reason was notoriously that the pupils of the Jesuit schools were exceptionally successful at the examinations for entrance as officers into the army, and proved themselves the bravest and most vigorous men of the nation. In a controverted matter like this, the most obvious proof that the Society's education fits its pupils for the battle of life is found in the constant readiness of parents to entrust their children to the Jesuits even when, from a merely worldly point of view, there seemed to be many reasons for holding back. (A discussion of this matter, from a French standpoint, will be found in Brou, op. cit. infra, II, 409; Tampe in "Etudes", Paris, 1900, pp. 77, 749.) It is hardly necessary to add that methods of school discipline will naturally differ greatly in different countries. The Society would certainly prefer to observe *mutatis mutandis* its well-tried "Ratio Studiorum"; but it is far from thinking that local customs (as for instance those which regard surveillance) and external discipline should everywhere be uniform.

(2) Another objection akin to the supposed hostility to freedom is the alleged *Kulturfeindlichkeit*, hostility to what is cultured and intellectual. This cry has been chiefly raised by those who scornfully reject Catholic theology as dogmatism, who scoff at Catholic philosophy as Scholastic, and at the Church's insistence on Biblical inspiration as retrograde and unscholarly. Such men make little account of work for the ignorant and the poor, whether at home or on the missions, they speak of evangelical poverty, of practices of penance and of mortification, as if they were debasing and retrograde. They compare their numerous and richly endowed universities with the few and relatively poor seminaries of the Catholic and the Jesuit, and their advances in a multitude of physical sciences with the intellectual timidity (as they think it) of those whose highest ambition it is not to go beyond the limits of theological orthodoxy. The Jesuits, they say, are the leaders of the *Kulturfeindliche;* their great object is to bolster up antiquated traditions. They have produced no geniuses, while men whom they trained, and who broke loose from their teaching, Pascal, Descartes, Voltaire, have powerfully affected the philosophical and religious beliefs of large masses of mankind; but respectable mediocrity is the brand on the long lists of the Jesuit names in the catalogues of Alegambe and de Backer. Under Bismarck and M. Waldeck-Rousseau arguments of this sort were accompanied by decrees of banishment and confiscation of goods.

This objection springs chiefly from prejudice—religious, worldly, or national. The Catholic will think rather better than worse of men who are decried and persecuted on grounds which apply to the whole Church. It is true the modern Jesuit's school is often smaller and poorer than the establishment of his rival, who at times is ensconced in the academy which the Jesuits of previous times succeeded in founding and endowing. It is not to be questioned that the sum total of learned institutions in the hands of non-Catholics is now greater than those in the hands of our co-religionists, but the love of culture surely is not extinguished in the exiled French, German, or Portuguese Jesuit, who, robbed perhaps of all he possesses, at once settles down again to his task of study, of writing, or of education. Very rare are the cases where Jesuits, living among enterprising people, have acquiesced in educational inferiority. For superiority to others, even in sacred learning, the Society does not and should not contend. In their own line, that is in Catholic theology, philosophy, and exegesis, they would hope that they are not inferior to the level of their generation, and that, far from acquiescing in intellectual inferiority, they aim at making their schools as good as circumstances allow them. They may also claim to have trained many good scholars in almost every science.

The objection that Jesuit teachers do not influence masses of mankind, while men like Descartes and Voltaire, after breaking with Jesuit education, have done so, derives its force from passing over the main work of the Jesuits, which is the salvation of souls, and any lawful means that helps to this end, as, for instance, the maintenance of orthodoxy. It is easy to overlook this, and those who object will perhaps despise it, even if they recognize it. The work is not showy, whereas that of the satirist, the iconoclast, and free-lance compels attention. Avoiding comparisons, it is safe to say that the Jesuits have done much to maintain the teaching of orthodoxy, and that the orthodox far outnumber the followers of men like Voltaire and Descartes.

It would be impossible, from the nature of the case, to devise any satisfactory test to show what love of culture, especially of intellectual culture, there was in a body so diversified and scattered as the Society. Many might be applied, and one of the most telling is the regularity with which every test reveals refinement and studiousness somewhere in its ranks, even in poor and distant foreign missions. To some it will seem significant that the pope, when searching for theologians and consultors for various Roman colleges and congregations, should so frequently select Jesuits, a relatively small body, some thirty or forty per cent of whose members are employed in foreign missions or among the poor of our great towns. The periodicals edited by the Jesuits, of which a list is given below, afford another indication of culture, and a favourable one, though it is to be remembered that these publications are written chiefly with a view of popularizing knowledge. The more serious and learned books must be studied separately. The most striking test of all is that offered by the great Jesuit bibliography of Father Sommervogel, showing over 120,000 writers, and an almost endless list of books, pamphlets, and editions. There is no other body in the world which can point to such a monument. Cavillers may say that the brand-mark is "respectable mediocrity"; even so, the value of the whole will be very remarkable, and we may be sure that less prejudiced and therefore better judges will form a higher appreciation. Masterpieces, too, in every field of ecclesiastical learning and in several secular branches are not rare.

The statement that the Society has produced few geniuses is not impressive in the mouths of those who have not studied, or are unable to study or to judge, the writers under discussion. Again the objection, whatever its worth, confuses two ideals. Educational bodies must necessarily train by classes and schools and produce men formed on definite lines. Genius on the other hand is independent of training and does not conform to type. It is unreasonable to reproach a missionary or educational system for not possessing advantages which no system can offer. Then it is well to bear in mind that genius is not restricted to writers or scholars alone. There is a genius of organization, exploration, enterprise, diplomacy, evangelization, and instances of it, in one or other of these directions, are common enough in the Society.

Men will vary of course in their estimates as to whether the amount of Jesuit genius is great or not according to the esteem they make of those studies in which the Society is strongest. But whether the amount is great or little, it is not stunted by Ignatius's strivings for uniformity. The objection taken to the words of the rule "Let all say the same thing as much as possible" is not convincing. This is a clipped quotation, for Ignatius goes on to add "juxta Apostolum", an evident reference to St. Paul to the Philippians, iii, 15, 16, beyond whom he does not go. In truth Ignatius's object is the practical one of preventing zealous professors from wasting their lecture time in disputing small points on which they may differ from their colleagues. The Society's writers and teachers are surely never compelled to the same rigid acceptation of the views of another as is often the case elsewhere, e. g. in politics, diplomacy, or journalism. Members of a staff of leader-writers have constantly to personate convictions not really their own, at the bidding of the editor; whereas Jesuit writers and teachers write and speak almost invariably in their own names, and with a variety of treatment and a freedom of mind which compare not unfavourably with other exponents of the same subjects.

(3) Failure.—The Society never became "relaxed" or needed a "reform" in the technical sense in which these terms are applied to religious orders. The constant intercourse which is maintained between all parts enables the general to find out very soon when anything goes wrong, and his large power of appointing new officials has always sufficed to maintain a high standard both of discipline and of religious virtue. Of course there have arisen critics, who have inverted this generally acknowledged fact. It has been said that: (a) failure has become a note of Jesuit enterprises. Other religious and learned institutions endure for century after century. The Society has hardly a house that is a hundred years old, very few that are not quite modern. Its great missionary glories, Japan, Paraguay, China, etc., passed like smoke and even now, in countries predominantly Catholic, it is banished and its works ruined, while other Catholics escape and endure. Again, that (b), after Acquaviva's time, a period of decay ensued; (c) disputes about Probabilism, tyrannicide, equivocation, etc., caused a strong and steady decline in the order; (d) the Society after Acquaviva's time began to acquire enormous wealth, and the professed lived in luxury; (e) religious energy was enervated by political scheming and by internal dissensions.

(a) The word "failure" is here taken in two different ways—failure from internal decay and failure from external violence. The former is discreditable, the latter may be glorious, if the cause is good. Whether the failures of the Society, at its Suppression and in the violent ejections from various lands even in our own time, were discreditable failures is a historical question treated elsewhere. If they were, then we must say that such failures tend to the credit of the order, that they are rather apparent than real, and God's Providence will, in His own way, make good the loss. In effect we see the Society frequently suffering, but as frequently recovering and renewing her youth. It would be inexact to say that the persecutions which the Society has suffered have been so great and continuous as to be irreconcilable with the usual course of Providence, which is wont to temper trial with relief, to make endurance possible (I Cor., x, 13). Thus, while it may be truly said that many Jesuit communities have been forced to break up within the last thirty years, others have had a corporate existence of two or three centuries. Stonyhurst College, for instance, has been only 116 years in its present site, but its corporate life is 202 years older still; yet the most glorious pages of its history are those of its persecutions, when it lost, three times over, everything it possessed and, barely escaping by flight, renewed a life even more honourable and distinguished than that which preceded, a fortune probably without its equal in the history of pedagogy. Again the Bollandists (q. v.) and the Collegio Romano may be cited as well-known examples of institutions which, though once smitten to the ground, have afterwards revived and flourished as much as before if not more. One might instance, too, the German province, which, though driven into exile by Bismarck, has there more than doubled its previous numbers. The Christianity which the Jesuits planted in Paraguay survived in a wonderful way, after they were gone, and the rediscovery of the Church in Japan affords a glorious testimony to the thoroughness of the old missionary methods.

(b) Turning to the point of decadence after Acquaviva's time, we may freely concede that no subsequent generation contained so many great personalities as the first. The first fifty years saw nearly all the Society's saints and a large proportion of its great writers and missionaries. But the same phenomenon is to be observed in almost all orders, indeed in most other human institutions whether sacred or profane. As for internal dissensions after Acquaviva's death, the truth is that the severe troubles occurred before, not after, it. The reason for this is easily understood. Internal troubles came chiefly with that conflict of views which was inevitable while the Constitutions, the rules, and general traditions of the body were being moulded. This took till near the end of Acquaviva's generalate. The worst troubles came first, under Ignatius himself in regard to Portugal, as has been explained elsewhere (see IGNATIUS LOYOLA). The troubles of Acquaviva with Spain come next in seriousness.

(c) After Acquaviva's time we find indeed some warm theological disputations on Probabilism and other points; but in truth this trouble and the debates on tyrannicide and equivocation had much more to do with outside controversies than with internal division. After they had been fully argued and resolved by papal authority, the settlement was accepted throughout the Society without any trouble.

(d) The allegation that the Jesuits were ever immensely rich is demonstrably a fable. It would seem to have arisen from the vulgar prepossession that all those who live in great houses or churches must be very rich. The allegation was exploited as early as 1594 by Antoine Arnauld, who declared that the French Jesuits had a revenue of 200,000 *livres* (£50,000, which might be multiplied by six to get the relative buying power of that day). The Jesuits answered that their twenty-five churches and colleges, having a staff of 500 to 600 persons, had in all only 60,000 *livres* (£15,000). The exact annual revenues of the English province for some 120 years are published by Foley (Records S. J., VII, Introd., 139). Duhr (Jesuitenfabeln, 1904, 606, etc.) gives many figures of the same kind. We can, therefore, tell now that the college revenues were, for their purposes, very moderate. The rumours of immense wealth acquired still further vogue through two occurrences, the *Restitutionsedikt* of 1629 and the licence, sometimes given by papal authority, for the procurators of the foreign missions to include in the sale of the produce of their own mission farms the produce of their native converts, who were generally still too rude and childish to make bargains for themselves. The *Restitutionsedikt*, as has been already explained (see above: *Germany*), led to no permanent results, but the sale of the mission produce came conspicuously before the notice of the public at the time of the Suppression, by the failure of Father La Valette (see, in article above, SUPPRESSION, *France*). In neither case did the money transactions, such as they were, affect the standard of living in the Society itself, which always remained that of the *honesti sacerdotes* of their time (see Duhr, op. cit. infra, pp. 582-652).

During the closing months of 1761 many other prelates wrote to the king, to the chancellor, M. de Lamoignon, protesting against the *arrêt* of the *Parlement* of 6 August, 1761, and testifying to their sense of the injustice of the accusations made against the Jesuits and of the loss which their dioceses would sustain by their suppression. De Ravignan gives the names of twenty-seven such bishops. Of the minority five out of the six rendered a collective answer, approving of the conduct and teaching of the Jesuits. These five bishops, the Cardinal de Choiseul, brother of the statesman, Mgr de La Rochefoucauld, Archbishop of Rouen, and Mgrs Quiseau of Nevers, Choiseul-Beaupré of Châlons, and Champion de Cice of Auxerre, declared that "the confidence reposed in the Jesuits by the bishops of the kingdom, all of whom approve them in their diocese, is evidence that they are found useful in France", and that in consequence they, the writers, "supplicate the king to grant his royal protection, and keep for the Church of France a society commendable for the service it renders to the Church and State and which the vigilance of the bishops may be trusted to preserve free from the evils which it is feared might come to affect it". To the second and third of the king's questions they answer that occasionally individual Jesuits have taught blameworthy doctrines or invaded the jurisdiction of the bishops, but that neither fault has been general enough to affect the body as a whole. To the fourth question they answer that "the authority of the general, as it is wont to be and should be exercised in France, appears to need no modification; nor do they see anything objectionable in the Jesuit vows". In fact, the only point on which they differ from the majority is in the suggestion that "to take away all difficulties for the future it would be well to solicit the Holy See to issue a Brief fixing precisely those limits to the exercise of the general's authority in France which the maxims of the kingdom require".

Testimonies like these might be multiplied indefinitely. Among them one of the most significant is that of Clement XIII, dated 7 January, 1765, which specially mentions the cordial relations of the Society with bishops throughout the world, precisely when enemies were plotting for the suppression of the order. In his books on Clement XIII and Clement XIV de Ravignan records the acts and letters of many bishops in favour of the Jesuits, enumerating the names of nearly 200 bishops in every part of the world. From a secular source the most noteworthy testimony is that of the French bishops when hostility to the Society was rampant in high places. On 15 November, 1761, the Comte de Florentin, the minister of the royal household, bade Cardinal de Luynes, the Archbishop of Sens, convoke the bishops then at Paris to investigate the following points: (1) The use which the Jesuits can be in France, and the advantages or evils which may be expected to attend their discharge of the different functions committed to them. (2) The manner in which in their teaching and practice the Jesuits conduct themselves in regard to opinions dangerous to the personal safety of sovereigns, to the doctrine of the French clergy contained in the Declaration of 1782, and in regard to the Ultramontane opinions generally. (3) The conduct of the Jesuits in regard to the subordination due to bishops and ecclesiastical superiors, and as to whether they do not infringe on the rights and functions of the parish priests. (4) What restriction can be placed on the authority of the General of the Jesuits, so far as it is exercised in France. For eliciting the judgment of the ecclesiastics of the kingdom on the action of the *Parlement*, no questions could be more suitable, and the bishops convoked (three cardinals, nine archbishops, and thirty-nine bishops, that is fifty-one in all) met together to consider them on 30 November. They appointed a commission consisting of twelve of their number, who were given a month for their task and reported duly on 30 December. Of these fifty-one bishops, forty-four addressed a letter to the king, dated 30 December, 1761, answering all the four questions in a sense favourable to the Society and giving under each head a clear statement of their reasons.

To the first question the bishops reply that the "Institute of the Jesuits . . . is conspicuously consecrated to the good of religion and the profit of the State". They begin by noting how a succession of popes, St. Charles Borromeo, and the ambassadors of princes, who with him were present at the Council of Trent, together with the Fathers of that Council in their collective capacity, had pronounced in favour of the Society after an experience of the services it could render; how, though in the first instance there was a prejudice against it in France, on account of certain novelties in its constitutions, the sovereign, bishops, clergy, and people had, on coming to know it, become firmly attached to it, as was witnessed by the demand of the States-General in 1614 and 1615 and of the Assembly of the Clergy in 1617, both of which bodies wished for Jesuit colleges in Paris and the provinces as "the best means adapted to plant religion and faith in the hearts of the people". They refer also to the language of many letters-patent by which the kings of France had authorized the various Jesuit colleges, in particular that of Clermont, at Paris, which Louis XIV had wished should bear his own name, and which had come to be known as the College of Louis-le-Grand. Then, coming to their own personal experience, they bear witness that "the Jesuits are very useful for our dioceses, for preaching, for the guidance of souls, for implanting, preserving, and renewing faith and piety, by their missions, congregations, retreats, which they carry on with our approbation, and under our authority". Whence they conclude that "it would be difficult to replace them without a loss, especially in the provincial towns, where there is no university".

To the second question the bishops reply that, if there were any reality in the accusation that the Jesuit teaching was a menace to the lives of sovereigns, the bishops would long since have taken measures to restrain it, instead of entrusting the Society with the most important functions of the sacred ministry. They also indicate the source from which this and similar accusations against the Society had their origin. "The Calvinists", they say, "tried their utmost to destroy in its cradle a Society whose principal object was to combat their errors . . . and disseminated many publications in which they singled out the Jesuits as professing a doctrine which menaced the lives of sovereigns, because to accuse them of a crime so capital was the surest means to destroy them; and the prejudices against them thus aroused had ever since been seized upon greedily by all who had had any interested motives for objecting to the Society's existence (in the country)." The bishops add that the charges against the Jesuits which were being made at that time in so many writings with which the country was flooded were but rehashes of what had been spoken and written against them throughout the preceding century and a half.

To the third question they reply that the Jesuits have no doubt received numerous privileges from the

Holy See, many of which, however, and those the most extensive, have accrued to them by communication with the other orders to which they had been primarily granted: but that the Society has been accustomed to use its privileges with moderation and prudence.

The fourth and last of the questions is not pertinent here, and we omit the answer. The Archbishop of Paris, who was one of the assembled bishops, but on some ground of precedent preferred not to sign the majority statement, endorsed it in a separate letter which he addressed to the king.

(e) It is not to be denied that, as the Society acquired reputation and influence even in the Courts of powerful kings, certain domestic troubles arose, which had not been heard of before. Some jealousies were inevitable, and some losses of friendship; there was danger too of the faults of the Court communicating themselves to those who frequented it. But it is equally clear that the Society was keenly on its guard in this matter, and it would seem that its precautions were successful. Religious observance did not suffer to any appreciable extent. But few people of the seventeenth century, if any, noticed the grave dangers which were coming from absolute government, the decay of energy, the diminished desire for progress. The Society like the rest of Europe suffered under these influences, but they were plainly external, not internal. In France the injurious influence of Gallicanism must also be admitted (see above, *France*). But even in this dull period we find the French Jesuits in the new mission-field of Canada showing a fervour worthy of the highest traditions of the order. The final and most convincing proof that there was nothing seriously wrong in the poverty or in the discipline of the Society up to the time of its Suppression is offered by the inability of its enemies to substantiate their charges, when, after the Suppression, all the accounts and the papers of the Society passed bodily into the adversaries' possession. What an unrivalled opportunity for proving to the world those allegations which were hitherto unsupported! Yet, after a careful scrutiny of the papers, no such attempt was made. The conclusion is evident. No serious fault could be proved.

Neither at the middle of the eighteenth century nor at any previous time was there any internal decline of the Society; there was no loss of numbers, but on the contrary a steady growth; there was no falling off in learning, morality, or zeal. From 1000 members in 12 provinces in 1556, it had grown to 13,112 in 27 provinces in 1615; to 17,665 in 1680, 7890 of whom were priests, in 35 provinces with 48 novitiates, 28 professed houses, 88 seminaries, 578 colleges, 160 residences, and 106 foreign missions; and, in spite of every obstacle, persecution, expulsion, and suppression during the seventeenth and eighteenth centuries, in 1749 it numbered 22,589 members, of whom 11,293 were priests, in 41 provinces, with 61 novitiates, 24 professed houses, 176 seminaries, 669 colleges, 335 residences, 1542 churches, and 273 foreign missions. That there was no falling off in learning, morality, or zeal historians generally, whether hostile or friendly to the Society, attest (see Maynard, "The Jesuits, their Studies and their Teaching").

On this point the testimony of Benedict XIV will surely be accepted as incontrovertible. In a letter dated 24 April, 1748, he says that the Society is one "whose religious are everywhere reputed to be in the good odour of Christ, chiefly because, in order to advance the young men who frequent their churches and schools in the pursuit of liberal knowledge, learning, and culture, as well as in deeds and habits of the Christian religion and piety, they zealously exert every effort greatly to the advantage of the young".

In another bearing the same date he says: "It is a universal conviction confirmed by pontifical declaration [Urban VIII, 6 August, 1623] that as Almighty God raised up other holy men for other times, so He has raised up St. Ignatius and the Society established by him to oppose Luther and the heretics of his day: and the religious sons of this Society, following the luminous way of so great a parent, continue to give an unfailing example of the religious virtues and a distinguished proficiency in every kind of learning, more especially in sacred, so that, as their co-operation is a great service in the successful conduct of the most important affairs of the Catholic Church, in the restoration of morality, and in the liberal culture of young men, they merit new proofs of Apostolic favour." In the paragraph following he speaks of the Society as "most deserving of the orthodox religion", and further on he says: "It abounds in men skilled in every branch of learning." On 27 September, 1748, he commended the General of the Society and its members for their "strenuous and faithful labours in sowing and propagating throughout the whole world Catholic faith and unity, as well as Christian doctrine and piety, in all their integrity and sanctity". On 15 July, 1749, he speaks of the members of the Society as "men who by their assiduous labour strive to instruct and form all the faithful of both sexes in every virtue, and in zeal for Christian piety and doctrine". "The Society of Jesus", he wrote on 29 March, 1753, "adhering closely to the splendid lessons and examples set them by their founder, St. Ignatius, devote themselves to this pious work [spiritual exercises] with so much ardour, zeal, charity, attention, vigilance, labour . . .", etc.

For the early controversies see the articles *Annat, Cerrutti, Forer, Gretser, Grou,* and *Reiffenberg* in SOMMERVOGEL and the full list of Jesuit apologies, *ibid.*, X, 1501.

BÖHMER-MONOD, *Les jésuites* (Paris, 1910); GIOBERTI, *Il gesuita moderno* (Lausanne, 1846); GRIESINGER, *Hist. of the Jesuits* (London, 1872); HOENSBROECH, *Vierzehn Jahre Jesuit* (Leipzig, 1910); HUBER, *Der Jesuiten-Orden* (Berlin, 1873); MICHELET-QUINET, *Des jésuites* (Paris, 1843); MULLER, *Les origines de la comp. de Jésus* (Paris, 1898); REUSCH, *Beiträge zur Gesch. der Jesuiten* (Munich, 1894); TAUNTON, *Hist. of the Jesuits in England* (London, 1901); THEINER, *Hist. des institutions chrét. d'éducation ecclés.* (Fr. tr., COHAN, Paris, 1840). Discussions of the above and of other hostile writers will be found in the Jesuit periodicals cited above; see also PILATUS (VIKTOR NAUMANN), *Der Jesuitismus* (Ratisbon, 1905), 352–569, a fine criticism, by a Protestant writer, of anti-Jesuitical literature; BRIÈRE, *L'apologétique de Pascal et la mort de Pascal* (Paris, 1911), BROU, *Les jésuites de la légende* (Paris, 1906); *Concerning Jesuits* (London, 1902); DUHR, *Jesuiten-Fabeln* (Freiburg, 1904); DU LAC, *Jésuites* (Paris, 1901); MAYNARD, *The Studies and Teaching of the Society of Jesus* (London, 1855); *Les Provinciales et leur réfutation* (Paris, 1851–2); DE RAVIGNAN, *De l'existence et de l'institut des jésuites* (Paris, 1844), tr. SEAGER (London, 1844); WEISS, *Antonio de Escobar y Mendoza* (Freiburg, 1911); REUSCH, *Der Index der verbotenen Bücher*; DÖLLINGER AND REUSCH, *Gesch. der Moralstreitigkeiten*; DARREL, *A Vindication of St. Ignatius from Phanaticism, and of the Jesuites from the Calumnies laid to their charge* (London, 1688); HUGHES, *Loyola and the Educat. System of the Jesuits* (New York, 1892); PACHTLER-DUHR, *Ratio Studiorum in Mon. Germ. pædagogica* (Berlin, 1887); SWICKERATH, *Jesuit Education, Its History and Principles in the Light of Modern Educational Problems* (St. Louis, 1905).

DISTINGUISHED MEMBERS.—Saints: Ignatius Loyola; Francis Xavier; Francis Borgia; Stanislaus Kostka; Aloysius Gonzaga; Alphonsus Rodriguez; John Berchmans; John Francis Regis; Peter Claver; Francis de Geronimo, and Paul Miki, John Goto, James Kisai, Japanese martyrs (1597).

Blessed.—The blessed number 91; among them are Peter Faber; Peter Canisius; Anthony Baldinucci; the martyrs Andrew Bobola; John de Britto (qq. v.); Bernardino Realini; Ignatius de Azevedo (q. v.) and companions (known as the Forty Martyrs of Brazil), viz. Didacus de Andrada (priest); Antonio Suares; Benedictus a Castro; Francisco Magalhães; João Fernandes; Luiz Correa; Manoel Rodrigues; Simon Lopes; Manoel Fernandes; Alvaro Mendes; Pedro Nunhes; Andreas Gonçalves; Juan a S. Martino (scholastics); Gonzalvo Henriques; Didaco Pires; Ferdinand Sancies; Francisco Pérez Godoi; Antonio Correa; Manoel Pacheco; Nicolas Diniz; Alexius Delgado; Marco Caldeira; Sanjoannes (scholastic novices); Manoel Alvares; Francisco Alvares; Domingos Fernandes; Gaspar

Alvares; Amarus Vaz; Juan de Majorga; Alfonso de Vaena; Antonio Fernandes; Stefano Zuriare; Pedro Fontoura; Gregorio Scrivano; Juan de Zafra; Juan de Baeza; Blasio Ribeiro; João Fernandes; Simon Acosta (lay brothers); the Japanese martyrs: John Baptist Machado, 1617; Sebastian Chimura, 1622; Camillo Costanzo, 1622; Charles Spinola, 1622; Paul Navarro, 1622; Jerome de Angelis, 1623; Didacus Carvalho, 1624; Michael Carvalho, 1624; Francisco Pacheco and his companions Baltasar de Torres and Giovanni Battista Zola, 1626; Thomas Tzugi, 1627; Anthony Ixida, 1632 (priests); Augustine Ota, 1622; Gonzalvus Fusai and his companions, Anthony Chiuni, Peter Sampò, Michael Xumpò, Louis Cavara, John Chingocu, Thomas Acafoxi, 1622; Denis Fugixima and Peter Onizuchi (companions of Bl. Paul Navarro), 1622; Simon Jempo (companion of Bl. Jerome de Angelis), 1623; Vincent Caun and his companions: Peter Rinxei, Paul Chinsuche, John Chinsaco; Michael Tozò, 1626; Michael Nacaxima, 1628 (scholastics); Leonard Chimura, 1619; Ambrosio Fernandes, 1620; Gaspar Sandamatzu (companion of Bl. Francis Pacheco, 1626), lay brothers; the English martyrs: Thomas Woodhouse, 1573; and John Nelson, Edmund Campion, Alexander Briant (qq. v.); Thomas Cottam, 1582 (priests); the martyrs of Cuncolim (q. v.): Rudolph Acquaviva; Alfonso Pacheco; Pietro Berno; Antonio Francisco (priests); and Francisco Aranha, 1583 (lay brother); the Hungarian martyrs: Melchior Grodecz and Stephen Pongracz, 7 Sept., 1619.

Venerables.—The venerables number fifty and include, besides those whose biographies have been given separately (see Index vol.), Claude de La Colombière (1641–82), Apostle of the devotion to the Sacred Heart; Nicholas Lancicius (1574–1653), author of "Gloria Ignatiana" and many spiritual works, and, with Orlandini, of "Historia Societatis Jesu"; Julien Maunoir (1606–83), Apostle of Brittany.

Though the Jesuits, in accordance with their rules, do not accept ecclesiastical dignities, the popes at times have raised some of their numbers to the rank of cardinal, as Cardinals Bellarmine, Franzelin, de Lugo, Mai, Mazzella, Odescalchi, Pallavicino, Pázmány, Tarquini, Toledo, Tolomei (qq. v.); also Cardinals Casimir V, King of Poland, created 1647; Alvaro Cienfuegos (1657–1739), created 1720; Johann Eberhard Nidhard (1607–81), created 1675; Giambattista Salerno (1670–1729), created 1709; Andreas Steinhuber (1825–1907), created 1893; and Louis Billot (b. 1846), created 27 Nov., 1911.

As reference is made in most of the articles on members of the Society to Sommervogel's monumental "Bibliothèque de la Compagnie de Jésus" a brief account of its author is given here. Carlos, fourth son of Marie-Maximilien-Joseph Sommervogel and Hortense Blanchard, was born on 8 Jan., 1834, at Strasburg, Alsace, and died in Paris on 4 May, 1902. After studying at the *lycée* of Strasburg, Carlos entered the Jesuit novitiate at Issenheim, Alsace, 2 Feb., 1853, and was sent later to Saint-Acheul, Amiens, to complete his literary studies. In 1856 he was appointed assistant prefect of discipline and sub-librarian in the College of the Immaculate Conception, Rue Vaugirard, Paris. Here he discovered his literary vocation. The "Bibliothèque" of PP. Augustin and Aloys de Backer was then in course of publication, and Sommervogel, noting in it occasional errors and omissions, made a systematic examination of the whole work. Four years later P. Aug. de Backer, seeing his list of addenda and errata, a MS. of 800 pages containing over 10,000 entries, obtained leave to make use of it. Sommervogel continued at Rue Vaugirard till 1865, reviewing his course of philosophy meanwhile. He then studied theology at Amiens, where he was ordained in Sept., 1866. From 1867 till 1879 he was on the staff of the "Etudes", being managing editor from 1871 till 1879. During the Franco-German War he served as chaplain in Faidherbe's army, and was decorated in 1871 with a bronze medal for his self-sacrifice.

P. de Backer in the revised edition of his "Bibliothèque" (1869–76) gave Sommervogel's name as co-author, and deservedly, for the vast improvement in the work was in no small measure due to the latter's contributions. From 1880 till 1882 P. Sommervogel was assistant to his father provincial. Before 1882 he had never had any special opportunity of pursuing his favourite study; all his bibliographical work had been done in his spare moments. In 1884 he published his "Dictionnaire des ouvrages anonymes et pseudonymes publiés par des religieux de la Compagnie de Jésus". In 1885 he was appointed successor to the PP. de Backer and went to Louvain. He determined to recast and enlarge their work and after five years issued the first volume of the first part (Brussels and Paris, 1890); by 1900 the ninth volume had appeared; the tenth, an index of the first nine, which comprised the bibliographical part of the "Bibliothèque" was unfinished at the time of his death but has since been completed by P. Bliard, with a biographical notice by P. Brucker, from which these details had been drawn. P. Sommervogel had intended to compile a second, or historical, part of his work, which was to be a revision of Carayon's "Bibliographie historique". He was a man of exemplary virtue, giving freely to all the fruit of his devoted labours and content to lead for years a busy obscure life to which duty called him, until his superiors directed him to devote himself to his favourite study during the last fifteen years of his life. He re-edited a number of works by old writers of the Society and, in addition to his articles in the "Etudes", wrote: "Table méthodique des Mémoires de Trévoux" (3 vols., Paris, 1864–5); "Bibliotheca Mariana de la Comp. de Jésus" (Paris, 1885); "Moniteur bibliographique de la Comp. de Jésus" (Paris, 1894–1901).

MENOLOGIES, BIOGRAPHIES.—ALEGAMBE, *Mortes illustres et gesta eorum de Soc. Jesu qui in odium fidei necati sunt* (Rome, 1657); IDEM, *Heroes et victimæ charitatis* (Rome, 1658); DREWS, *Fasti Soc. Jesu* (Braunsberg, 1728); CHANDLERY, *Fasti breviores Soc. Jesu* (London, 1910); GUILHERMY, *Ménologe de la comp. de J.: Portugal* (Paris, 1867); *France* (Paris, 1892); *Italie* (Paris, 1893); *Germanie* (Paris, 1898); MACLEOD, *Menol. for the English Assistancy* (London); BOËRO, *Menologio* (Rome, 1859); STÖGER, *Historiographie Soc. Jesu* (Ratisbon, 1851); NIEREMBERG, *Claros varones de la comp. de J.* (Madrid, 1643); PATRIGNANI, *Menol. d'alcuni religiosi della comp. di G.* (Venice, 1730); TANNER, *Soc. Jesu apostolorum imitatrix* (Prague, 1694); IDEM, *Soc. Jesu usque ad mortem militans* (Prague, 1675); THOELEN, *Menol. der deutschen Ordensprovinz* (Roermond, 1901). Bibliographies of particular persons, on a larger scale than can be given here, will be found under the separate articles devoted to them. (See also Index volume.) The best-arranged historical bibliography is that of CARAYON, *Bibliographie de la compagnie de Jésus* (Paris, 1864). See also SOUTHWELL, *Bibl. scriptorum Soc. Jesus* (Rome, 1676); DE BACKER, *Bibliothèque des écriv. de la comp. de Jésus* (Liège, 1853); SOMMERVOGEL, *Bibl. des écriv. de la comp. de Jésus* (10 vols., Brussels, 1890–1910); HURTER, *Nomenclator literarius* (Innsbruck, 1892–9); DELPLACE, *Acta S. Sedis in causa Soc. Jesu* (Florence, 1887–95); HAMY, *Iconographie de la comp. de Jesus* (Paris, 1875); IDEM, *Galerie illustrée de la comp. de J.* (8 vols., Paris, 1893); DE URIARTE, *Catál. razonado de obras . . . de autores de la comp. de Jesús* (Madrid, 1904).

JESUIT PERIODICALS.—*Mémoires de Trévoux* (Trevoux and Paris, 1701–67, 265 vols.), *Table méthodique*, by SOMMERVOGEL (3 vols., Paris, 1864–65); *Civiltà cattolica* (Rome, 1850); *Etudes hist., litt., et relig.* (Paris, 1854);—began as *Etudes de théol., intermittent*, 1880–8; *Table générale, 1888–1900* (Paris, 1901); *Précis historiques* (Brussels, 1852), *Tables, 1862–72* (Brussels, 1894), in 1899 it became the *Missions belges*; *The Month* (London, 1864), *Index (1864–1908); Stimmen aus Maria-Laach* (Freiburg, 1871), began as *Die Encyclika* (1864). In connexion with this is issued a series of *Ergänzungshefte*. Also *Register I, 1871–86; Register II, 1886–99; Studien* (Utrecht, 1868); *Rev. des questions historiques* (Brussels, 1877); *Przeglad powszechny* (General Review, Cracow); *Zeitsch. für kath. Theol.* (Innsbruck, 1876); *Razón y Fe* (Madrid, 1901). Besides the above, which deal with topics of all sorts, there are a host of minor periodicals devoted to special subjects; scientific, liturgical, social, college, mission, and parochial magazines are more numerous still. The *Messenger of the Sacred Heart* has editions for many countries and in numerous languages. It is the organ of the Apostleship of Prayer; most of these editions are edited by members of the Society; *America* (New York, 1909). (See also BOLLANDISTS; RATIO STUDIORUM; RETREATS; SPIRITUAL EXERCISES OF SAINT IGNATIUS; THEATRE.)

J. H. POLLEN.

Society of the Blessed Sacrament, THE, a congregation of priests founded by Venerable Pierre-Julien Eymard (q. v.) in Paris, 1 June, 1856. His aim was to create a society whose members should devote themselves exclusively to the worship of the Holy Eucharist. Pius IX approved the society by Briefs of 1856 and 1858 and by a Decree of 3 June, 1863, approved the rule *ad decennium*. On 8 May, 1895, Leo XIII approved it *in perpetuum*. The first to join the founder was Père de Cuers, whose example was soon followed by Père Champion. The community prospered, and in 1862 Père Eymard opened a novitiate, which was to consist of priests and lay brothers. The former recite the Divine Office in choir and perform all the other duties of the clergy; the latter share in the principal end of the society—perpetual adoration, and attend to the various household employments peculiar to their state. The Blessed Sacrament is always exposed for adoration, and the sanctuary never without adorers in surplice, and if a priest, the stole. Every hour at the sound of the signal bell, all the religious kneel and recite a prayer in honour of the Blessed Sacrament and of Our Lady. Since 1856, the following houses have been established: France—Paris (1856), Marseilles (1859), Angers, (1861), Saint Maurice (1866), Trevoux (1895), Sarcelles (1898); Belgium—Brussels (1866), Ormeignies (1898), Oostduinkerke (1902), Bassenge (1902), Baronville (1910), Baelen Post Eupen on the Belgian frontier for Germans (1909); Italy—Rome (1882), Turin (1901), Castel-Vecchio (1905); Austria—Botzen (1896); Holland—Baarle-Nassau, now Nijmegen (1902); Spain—Tolosa (1907); Argentina—Buenos-Ayres (1903); Chile—Santiago (1908); Canada—Montreal (1890), Terrebonne (1902); United States—New York (1900); Suffern, N. Y. (1907). All the houses in France were closed by the Government in 1900, but Perpetual Adoration is still held in their chapel in Paris, which is in charge of the secular clergy, by the members of "The People's Eucharistic League". The first foundation in the United States took place in 1900, under the leadership of Père Estevenon, the present superior-general, in New York City, where the Fathers were received in the Canadian parish of Saint-Jean-Baptiste, 185 East 76th Street. A new church is under construction. In September, 1904, the Fathers of the Blessed Sacrament opened a preparatory seminary at Suffern, Rockland Co., N. Y. Here young boys who give evidence of a vocation are trained to the religious life, while pursuing a course of secular study. From the seminary the youths pass to the novitiate, where, after two years, they make the three vows of religion, and then enter upon their first theological course preparatory to ordination.

From every house of the Fathers of the Blessed Sacrament emanates a series of Eucharistic works, all instituted by their founder. They are: "The Eucharistic Weeks, or, Lights and Flowers", a society whose members devote themselves to the proper adornment of the altar; "The People's Eucharistic League", which numbers over 500,000; "The Priests' Eucharistic League", with a membership of 100,000; "The Priests' Communion League", an association of priests under the title of "Sacerdotal Eucharistic League", established at Rome in the church of San Claudio, July, 1906, and at once raised by Pius X to the dignity of an archconfraternity. Its object is to spread the practice of frequent and daily Communion, in conformity with the Decree of the Sacred Congregation of the Council, "De quotidiana SS. Eucharistiæ sumptione" (20 December, 1905). The means there highly recommended refer to the following points: (1) To instruct, refute objections, spread writings favouring daily Communion; (2) To encourage assistance at Holy Mass; (3) To promote Eucharistic triduums; (4) To induce children especially to approach the Holy Table frequently. "The Society of Nocturnal Adoration", the members of which for an entire night keep watch before the Host, reciting the Office of the Blessed Sacrament, and offering various acts of reparative homage; "The Work of First Communion for Adults". The apostolate of the press is a prominent feature in the labours of these religious. In the United States, they publish "Emmanuel", the organ of "The Priests' Eucharistic League", and "The Sentinel of the Blessed Sacrament".

For bibliography see EYMARD, PIERRE-JULIEN, VENERABLE.

A. LETELLIER.

Society of the Sacred Heart of Jesus, THE, an institution of religious women, taking perpetual vows and devoted to the work of education, founded 21 Nov., 1800, by Madeleine-Sophie Barat (q. v.). One of the signs of returning vigour in the Church in France after 1792 was the revival of the religious life. Religious orders had been suppressed by the laws of 18 August, 1792, but within a few years a reaction set in; the restoration of some orders and the foundations of new congregations ushered in "the second spring". One of the first was the Society of Jesus. Under the provisional title of "Fathers of the Sacred Heart" and "Fathers of the Faith", some devoted priests banded themselves together and in due time returned from their exile or emigration to devote themselves to the spiritual welfare of their country. Father Léonor De Tournély was among the founders of the Fathers of the Sacred Heart, and the first to whom it occurred that an institute of women bearing the same name and devoting themselves to the education of girls, would be one of the most efficacious means of restoring the practice of religion in France. Though many difficulties intervened, two attempts were made. Princess Louise de Bourbon Condé, before the Revolution a Benedictine abbess, and the Archduchess Mary Anne of Austria both tried to form an institute according to his idea; but neither succeeded, and he died before anything could be accomplished. He had confided his views to Father Varin who succeeded him as superior of the Fathers of the Sacred Heart. A short time afterwards Father Varin found in Madeleine-Sophie Barat, sister of Father Louis Barat, the instrument to execute his plans. The first members of the new society began their community life in Paris, under the guidance of Father Varin. The first convent was opened at Amiens in 1801, under Mademoiselle Loquet. A school which had already existed there was made over to the new institute, and some who had worked in it offered themselves as postulants for the "Dames de la Foi" or "De L'Instruction Chrétienne", the name which the new society had assumed, as that of the "Society of the Sacred Heart" might be supposed to indicate a connexion with the royalist party of La Vendée. As Mlle. Loquet, who had been acting as superior, lacked the requisite qualities, by the advice of Father Varin and with the assent of the community Sophie Barat was named superior. By education and temperament, the new superior was especially fitted for the work of foundation. In 1804 a second house was opened and a new member, Philippine Duchesne, received, who was destined to carry the work of the society beyond the limits of France. Formerly a novice of the Visitation convent at Ste. Marie d'en Haut, near Grenoble, Mlle. Duchesne found it impossible to reconstruct the religious life of the Visitation in the convent which she purchased after the Revolution. Father Varin made her acquaintance and reported to Mother Barat that the house was offered to her, and that she could find there some who wished to join her.

The first plan of the institute was drawn up by

Fathers Roger and Varin, and with a memorial composed by Mothers Barat and Duchesne was presented to the Bishop of Grenoble and approved by him. This plan and memorial set forth the end of the association, which was the perfection of its members and the salvation of souls; the spirit aimed at detachment from the world, purity of intention for the glory of the Sacred Heart, gentleness, zeal, and obedience; the means, for the religious, the training of the novitiate, and spiritual exercises, for others, boarding schools for the upper classes, free schools for the poor, and spiritual retreats. The rule in this preliminary stage was simple; the houses were to be under one superior-general, everything was to be in common, the office of the Blessed Virgin was to be recited, the time appointed for mental prayer was specified. The manner of life was to be simple without the prescribed austerities of the older orders, which would be incompatible with the work of education. On Mother Barat's return to Amiens in 1806 the first general congregation was assembled for the election of the superior-general, and she was chosen for the office. Father Varin then withdrew from the position he had held as superior of the new institute which was now regularly constituted, but he continued for years to help the young superior-general with his advice and support. The first serious trouble which arose nearly wrecked the whole undertaking. At the end of 1808 the "Dames de la Foi" had six houses; Amiens, Grenoble, Poitiers, Niort, Ghent, and Cuigniers. The first house at Amiens was governed at this time by Mother Baudemont, who fell under the influence of a priest of the Diocese of Amiens, Abbé de St-Estève, who took that house under his control and even drew up a set of rules drawn from those of the monastic orders and entirely foreign to the spirit of Father Varin and the foundress. The devotion to the Sacred Heart which was to be its very life scarcely appeared in the new rules and they were in consequence not acceptable to any of the houses outside Amiens. Abbé de St-Estève was determined to force the matter. He went to Rome and from thence sent orders, ostensibly from the Holy See. The name of the Society of the Sacred Heart was to be abandoned for that of "Apostolines", and he wrote vehement letters condemning Father Varin and the superior-general and her work. The most important letter in the case proved to be a forgery. The institute recovered its balance, but the house at Ghent had been already lost to the society.

The second general congregation (1815) examined the constitutions which had been elaborated by Father Varin and Mother Barat (they were an expansion of the first plan presented to the Bishop of Grenoble) and they were accepted by all the houses of the society. It was decided to have a general novitiate in Paris. The third general congregation (1820) drew up the first uniform plan of studies which has been developed and modified from time to time to bring it into harmony with present needs, without losing the features which have characterized it from the beginning. In 1826 the society obtained the formal approbation of Leo XII and the first cardinal protector was appointed, in place of an ecclesiastical superior whose authority would have depended too much upon local conditions. The sixth general congregation was anxious to bring the constitutions into closer conformity with those of the Society of Jesus. Mother Barat foresaw that the proposed changes were unsuitable for a congregation of women, but permitted an experimental trial of them for three years. Finally the whole affair was submitted to Gregory XVI, who decided that the society should return in all points to the constitution approved by Leo XII. The last changes in the constitutions were made in 1851 with the sanction of the Holy See. Superiors-vicar were named to help the superior-general in the government of the society by taking the immediate supervision of a certain number of houses forming a vicariate. The superiors-vicar assembled with the mother general and the assistants general, form the general congregation of the society. In 1818 Mother Philippine Duchesne introduced the society into the United States and the first houses were founded in Missouri and Louisiana. The society under the guidance of Mother Mary Aloysia Hardey (q. v.) spread rapidly, and in 1910 counted twenty-seven houses and more than eleven hundred members The extension in Europe was confined to France until 1827 when a school was opened at the Trinità dei Monti, Rome. Houses were founded in Belgium (Jette), 1836; England (Berrymead, now Roehampton) and Ireland (Roscrea), both in 1841; Canada (Montreal), 1842; Austria (Lemberg), 1843; Spain (Sarria, near Barcelona), 1846. Mother du Rousier was the pioneer in South America (Santiago de Chile in 1854). Other foundations were made in the West Indies (1858); New Zealand (1880); Australia (1882); Egypt (1903); Japan (1908). The Revolution of 1830 disturbed the house in Paris but did not destroy it; the novitiate was removed elsewhere. In 1848 the house in Switzerland had to be abandoned; the religious were expelled from Genoa, Turin, Saluzzo, and Pignerol while the houses in Rome were searched and pillaged. In 1860 Loreto, St. Elpidio, and Perugia were suppressed. The German houses were closed by the May Laws of 1873. Between 1903 and 1909 forty-seven houses in France were closed and many of them confiscated by the French Government. The mother-house was transferred to Brussels in 1909. This wholesale destruction increased the extension in foreign countries; for almost every house that has been closed another has been opened elsewhere. At present the society counts 139 houses and about 6500 religious.

The society aims at a twofold spirit—contemplative and active. It is composed of choir religious and lay sisters. Enclosure is observed in a manner adapted to the works; the Office of the Blessed Virgin is recited in choir. The choice of subjects is guided by the qualifications laid down in the constitutions. In addition to the indication of a true religious vocation there is required respectable parentage, unblemished reputation, a good or at least sufficient education with some aptitude for completing it, a sound judgment, and above all a generous determination to make an entire surrender of self to the service of God through the hands of superiors. The candidate is not allowed to make any conditions as to place of residence or employment, but must be ready to be sent by obedience to any part of the world, even the privilege of going on foreign missions is not definitely promised in the beginning to those who aspire to it. Postulants are admitted to a preliminary probation of three months, at the end of which they may take the religious habit and begin their novitiate of two years, which are spent in studying the spirit and the rules of the society, exercising themselves in its manner of living, and in the virtues which they will be called upon to practice; the second year is devoted to a course of study which is to prepare them for their educational work. To each novitiate there is attached a teaching and training department where the first course of studies may be taken, and when it is possible the young religious pass a year in this, after their vows, before they are sent to teach in the schools. The first vows, simple perpetual vows of poverty, chastity and obedience, are taken at the end of two years of noviceship, after which follow five years spent in study, teaching, or other duties. At the end of this period follows for those who have special aptitude for the work of teaching, another short course of study, and for all a period of second noviateate or probation lasting six months, at the end of which, that is to say, seven years after their admission to the society, the aspirants take their final vows and are received as professed religious. The vow of stability, that is, of perseverance in the society, is then added, and for the choir religious a vow to consecrate themselves to education of youth; provision is made, however, that this vow may be accomplished even if obedience should prescribe other duties than those of direct teaching, and may be fulfilled by concurrence in any way in the work of the society. The vow of stability binds the society to the professed until death, as well as the professed to the society; this bond can only be broken by the Holy See. The society is governed by a superior general, elected for life by the assistants general and superiors vicar. The assistants general are elected for six years, the superiors vicar and local superiors are nominated by the mother general, and may be changed at her discretion; their usual period of government is three years, but it may be prolonged or shortened according to circumstances. The superior general assembles the superiors vicar in a general congregation every six years, and with the help of the assistants general transacts with them all business connected with the general government of the society. These periodical assemblies, the occasional visits of the superior general to the houses in different countries, the regular reports and accounts sent in from every vicariate, the free access of all to the mother general by writing, and in particular the organization of the house of last probation, which as far as possible brings the young religious for six months into touch with the first superiors of the society—all tend to unity. Its union is what is most valued, and if it had been possible to define it sufficiently it is said that a fourth vow of charity would have been added to the obligations of the members.

Four principal works give scope to the activities of the society. (1) Education of the upper classes in the boarding schools and of late years in day schools. Originally the plan of studies was more or less uniform in all the houses, but it has become necessary to modify it according to the needs and educational ideals of different countries and the kind of life for which the pupils have to be prepared. The character of the education of the Sacred Heart, however, remains the same, based on the study of religion and of Christian philosophy and laying particular stress on history, literature, essay-writing, modern languages, and such knowledge of household management as can be taught at school. (2) Free or parochial schools. In some countries, as in England, these are aided by the State, and follow the regulations laid down for other public elementary schools; in others they are voluntary and adapt their teaching to the needs and circumstances of the children. Between these two classes of schools have arisen in England secondary schools, aided by the State, which are principally feeding schools for the two training colleges in London and Newcastle, where Catholic teachers are prepared for the certificates entitling them to teach in elementary state-supported schools. This work is of wider importance than the teaching of single elementary schools, and is valued as a means of reaching indirectly a far greater number of children than those with whom the religious themselves can come into contact. It likewise leavens the teaching profession with minds trained in Catholic doctrine and practice. This work for Catholic teachers also exists at Lima in a flourishing condition. (3) A work which is taking rapid development is that of spiritual retreats for all classes of persons. The spiritual exercises are given to considerable numbers of ladies who spend a few days within the convents of the Sacred Heart; in other cases the exercises are adapted for poor girls and peasant women. Retreats for First Communion in Rome, and retreats for Indian women in Mexico are special varieties of this work. (4) The congregations of Children of Mary living in the world which have their own rules and organization (see CHILDREN OF MARY OF THE SACRED HEART, THE).

See bibliographies to BARAT, MADELEINE-SOPHIE, BLESSED; HARDEY, MARY ALOYSIA; DUCHESNE, PHILIPPINE-ROSE.

JANET STUART.

Socinianism, the body of doctrine held by one of the numerous Antitrinitarian sects to which the Reformation gave birth. The Socinians derive their name from two natives of Siena, Lelio Sozzini (1525–62) and his nephew Fausto Sozzini (1539–1604). The surname is variously given, but its Latin form, Socinus, is that currently used. It is to Fausto, or Faustus Socinus, that the sect owes its individuality, but it arose before he came into contact with it. In 1546 a secret society held meetings at Vicenza in the Diocese of Venice to discuss, among other points, the doctrine of the Trinity. Among the members of this society were Blandrata, a well-known physician, Alciatus, Gentilis, and Lelio, or Lælius Socinus. The last-named, a priest of Siena, was the intimate friend of Bullinger, Calvin, and Melanchthon. The object of the society was the advocacy not precisely of what were afterwards known as Socinian principles, but of Antitrinitarianism. The Nominalists, represented by Abelard, were the real progenitors of the Antitrinitarians of the Reformation period, but while many of the Nominalists ultimately became Tritheists, the term *Antitrinitarian* means expressly one who denies the distinction of persons in the Godhead. The Antitrinitarians are thus the later representatives of the Sabellians, Macedonians, and Arians of an earlier period. The secret society which met at Vicenza was broken up, and most of its members fled to Poland. Lælius, indeed, seems to have lived most at Zurich, but he was the mainspring of the society, which continued to hold meetings at Cracow for the discussion of religious questions. He died in 1562 and a stormy period began for the members of the party.

The inevitable effect of the principles of the Reformation was soon felt, and schism made its appearance in the ranks of the Antitrinitarians—for so we must call them all indiscriminately at this time. In 1570 the Socinians separated, and, through the influence of the Antitrinitarian John Sigismund, established themselves at Racow. Meanwhile Faustus Socinus had obtained possession of his uncle's papers and in 1579 came to Poland. He found the various bodies of the sect divided, and he was at first refused admission because he refused to submit to a second baptism. In 1574 the Socinians had issued a "Catechism of the Unitarians", in which, while much was said about the nature and perfections of the Godhead, silence was observed regarding those Divine attributes which are mysterious. Christ was the Promised Man; He was the Mediator of Creation, i. e. of Regeneration. It was shortly after the appearance of this catechism that Faustus arrived on the scene and, in spite of initial opposition, he succeeded in attaching all parties to himself and thus securing for them a degree of unity which they had not hitherto enjoyed. Once in possession of power, his action was high-handed. He had been invited to Siebenburg in order to counteract the influence of the Antitrinitarian bishop Francis David (1510–79). David, having refused to accept the peculiarly Socinian tenet that Christ, though not God, is to be adored, was thrown into prison, where he died. Budnæus, who adhered to David's views, was degraded and excommunicated in 1584. The old catechism was now suppressed and a new one published under the title of the "Catechism of Racow". Though drawn up by Socinus, it was not published

XIV.—8

until 1605, a year after his death; it first appeared in Polish, then in Latin in 1609.

Meanwhile the Socinians had flourished; they had established colleges, they held synods, and they had a printing press whence they issued an immense amount of religious literature in support of their views; this was collected, under the title "Bibliotheca Antitrinitarianorum", by Sandius. In 1638 the Catholics in Poland insisted on the banishment of the Socinians, who were in consequence dispersed. It is evident from the pages of Bayle that the sect was dreaded in Europe; many of the princes were said to favour it secretly, and it was predicted that Socinianism would overrun Europe. Bayle, however, endeavours to dispel these fears by dwelling upon the vigorous measures taken to prevent its spread in Holland. Thus, in 1639, at the suggestion of the British Ambassador, all the states of Holland were advised of the probable arrival of the Socinians after their expulsion from Poland; while in 1653 very stringent decrees were passed against them. The sect never had a great vogue in England; it was distasteful to Protestants who, less logical, perhaps, but more conservative in their views, were not prepared to go to the lengths of the Continental Reformers. In 1612 we find the names of Leggatt and Wightman mentioned as condemned to death for denying the Divinity of Christ. Under the Commonwealth, John Biddle was prominent as an upholder of Socinian principles; Cromwell banished him to the Scilly Isles, but he returned under a writ of habeas corpus and became minister of an Independent church in London. After the Restoration, however, Biddle was cast again into prison, where he died in 1662. The Unitarians are frequently identified with the Socinians, but there are fundamental differences between their doctrines (for which see next section).

FUNDAMENTAL DOCTRINES.—These may be gathered from the "Catechism of Racow", mentioned above and from the writings of Socinus himself, which are collected in the "Bibliotheca Fratrum Polonorum". The basis was, of course, private judgment; the Socinians rejected authority and insisted on the free use of reason, but they did not reject revelation. Socinus, in his work "De Auctoritate Scripturæ Sacræ", went so far as to reject all purely natural religion. Thus for him the Bible was everything, but it had to be interpreted by the light of reason. Hence he and his followers thrust aside all mysteries; as the Socinian John Crell (d. 1633) says in his "De Deo et ejus Attributis", "Mysteries are indeed exalted above reason, but they do not overturn it; they by no means extinguish its light, but only perfect it". This would be quite true for a Catholic, but in the mouth of Socinian it meant that only those mysteries which reason can grasp are to be accepted. Thus both in the Racovian Catechism and in Socinus's "Institutiones Religionis Christianæ", only the unity, eternity, omnipotence, justice, and wisdom of God are insisted on, since we could be convinced of these; His immensity, infinity, and omnipresence are regarded as beyond human comprehension, and therefore unnecessary for salvation. Original justice meant for Socinus merely that Adam was free from sin as a fact, not that he was endowed with peculiar gifts; hence Socinus denied the doctrine of original sin entirely. Since, too, faith was for him but trust in God, he was obliged to deny the doctrine of justification in the Catholic sense; it was nothing but a judicial act on the part of God. There were only two sacraments, and, as these were held to be mere incentives to faith, they had no intrinsic efficacy. Infant baptism was of course rejected. There was no hell; the wicked were annihilated.

CHRISTOLOGY.—This point was particularly interesting, as on it the whole of Socinianism turns. God, the Socinians maintained, and rightly, is absolutely simple; but distinction of persons is destructive of such simplicity, therefore, they concluded, the doctrine of the Trinity is unsound. Further, there can be no proportion between the finite and the infinite, hence there can be no incarnation of the Deity, since that would demand some such proportion. But if, by an impossibility, there were distinction of persons in the Deity, no Divine person could be united to a human person, since there can be no unity between two individualities. These arguments are of course puerile and nothing but ignorance of Catholic teaching can explain the hold which such views obtained in the sixteenth and seventeenth centuries. As against the first argument, see St. Thomas, Summa, I, Q. xii, a. 1, ad 4^{am}; for the solution of the others see Petavius. But the Socinians did not become Arians, as did Campanus and Gentilis. The latter was one of the original society which held its meetings at Vicenza; he was beheaded at Berne in 1566. They did not become Tritheists, as Gentilis himself was supposed by some to be (cf. "A Short History of Valentius Gentilis the Tritheist", London, 1696). Nor did they become Unitarians, as might have been expected. Socinus had indeed many affinities with Paul of Samosata and Sabellius; with them he regarded the Holy Spirit as merely an operation of God, a power for sanctification. But his teaching concerning the person of Christ differed in some respects from theirs. For Socinus, Christ was the Logos, but he denied His pre-existence; He was the Word of God as being His Interpreter (*interpres divinæ voluntatis*). The passages from St. John which present the Word as the medium of creation were explained by Socinus of regeneration only. At the same time Christ was miraculously begotten: He was a perfect man, He was the appointed mediator; but He was not God, only deified man. In this sense He was to be adored; and it is here precisely that we have the dividing line between Socinianism and Unitarianism, for the latter system denied the miraculous birth of Christ and refused Him adoration. It must be confessed that, on their principles, the Unitarians were much more logical.

REDEMPTION AND SACRAMENTS.—Socinus's views regarding the person of Christ necessarily affected his teaching on the office of Christ as Redeemer, and consequently on the efficacy of the sacraments. Being purely man, Christ did not work out our redemption in the sense of satisfying for our sins; and consequently we cannot regard the sacraments as instruments whereby the fruits of that redemption are applied to man. Hence Socinus taught that the Passion of Christ was merely an example to us and a pledge of our forgiveness. All this teaching is syncretized in the Socinian doctrine regarding the Last Supper; it was not even commemorative of Christ's Passion, it was rather an act of thanksgiving for it.

THE CHURCH AND SOCINIANISM.—Needless to say, the tenets of the Socinians have been repeatedly condemned by the Church. As Antitrinitarianists, they are opposed to the express teaching of the first six councils; their view of the person of Christ is in contradiction to the same councils, especially that of Chalcedon and the famous "Tome" (Ep. xxviii) of St. Leo the Great (cf. Denzinger, no. 143). For its peculiar views regarding the adoration of Christ, cf. can. ix. of the fifth Œcumenical Synod (Denz., 221). It is opposed, too, to the various creeds, more especially to that of St. Athanasius. It has also many affinities with the Adoptionist heresy condemned in the Plenary Council of Frankfort, in 794, and in the second letter of Pope Hadrian I to the bishops of Spain (cf. Denz., 309–314). Its denial of the Atonement is in opposition to the decrees against Gotteschalk promulgated in 849 (cf. Denz., 319), and also to the definition of the Fourth Lateran Council against the Albigensians (Denz., 428; cf. also Conc. Trid.,

Sess. xxii., cap. i. de Sacrificio Missæ, in Denz., 938). The condemned propositions of Abelard (1140) might equally well stand for those of the Socinians (cf. Denz., 368 sqq.). The same must be said of the Waldensian heresy: the Profession of Faith drawn up against them by Innocent III might be taken as a summary of Socinian errors. The formal condemnation of Socinianism appeared first in the Constitution of Paul IV, "Cum quorundam", 1555 (Denz., 993); this was confirmed in 1603 by Clement VIII, or "Dominici gregis", but it is to be noted that both of these condemnations appeared before the publication of the "Catechism of Racow" in 1605, hence they do not adequately reflect the formal doctrines of Socinianism. At the same time it is to be remarked, that according to many, this catechism itself does not reflect the doctrines really held by the leaders of the party; it was intended for the laity alone. From the decree it would appear that in 1555 and again in 1603 the Socinians held (a) that there was no Trinity, (b) that Christ was not consubstantial with the Father and the Holy Spirit, (c) that He was not conceived of the Holy Spirit, but begotten by St. Joseph, (d) that His Death and Passion were not undergone to bring about our redemption, (e) that finally the Blessed Virgin was not the Mother of God, neither did she retain her virginity. It would seem from the Catechism that the Socinians of 1605 held that Christ was at least miraculously conceived, though in what sense they held this is not clear.

Bibliotheca Fratrum Polonorum (Amsterdam, 1656); Bock, Hist. Antitrinitariorum, Maxime Socinianismi (Königsberg, 1774–84); Dorner, Lehre v. Person Christi, ii, 751; Fock, Der Socinianismus in der Gesammtentwicklung des Christ. (Kiel, 1845); Bonet-Maury, Early Sources of the English Unitarian Church (1884), ix; Mosheim, Hist. Cent., XVI, lect. iii, pt. ii, 4, 7; Crell (Socinian, d. 1633), De Deo et ejus attributis; Orcipovius (or Przipcovius), Vita Fausti Socini (1643, 1636); Toulmin, Memoirs of the Life, Character and Writings of F. Socinus (London, 1777); Lecler, F. Socin (Geneva, 1884); Bayle, Dictionnaire Historique et Critique (1st. ed., 1696; 2d ed., 1701–11); Neander, History of Christian Dogmas, II, 626–700 (a very good account of the Socinian tenets); Blunt, Dictionary of Sects, Heresies, Ecclesiastical Parties and Schools of Thought, Religious Thought (1891); Petavius, De theologicis dogmatibus, Lib. XVI, cap. i. (where a full treatment of the Socinian dogmas will be found); Kirsch-Hergenröther, Handbuch der allgemeinen Kirchengeschichte, III, 333–38.

Hugh Pope.

Sociology.—The claims of sociology (*socius*, companion; λόγος, science) to a place in the hierarchy of sciences are subjected to varied controversy. It has been held that there is no distinct problem for a science of sociology, no feature of human society not already provided for in the accepted social sciences. Again it has been claimed that while the future may hold out prospects for a science such as sociology, its present condition leaves much to be desired. Furthermore, among sociologists themselves discussion and disagreement abound concerning aims, problems, and methods of the science. Beyond this confusion in scientific circles, misunderstanding results from the popular habit of confounding sociology with philanthropy, ethics, charity, and relief, social reform, statistics, municipal problems, socialism, sanitation, criminology, and politics. It is hardly to be expected that differences of opinion would not occur when scholars endeavour to describe in simple terms the complex social processes; to pack a vast array of historical and contemporaneous facts in rigid logical classes, and to mark off for research purposes sections of reality which in fact overlap at a hundred points. Nevertheless, efforts to create a science of sociology have led to notable results. Minds of a very high order have been attracted to the work; abundant literature of great excellence has been produced; neighbouring sciences have been deeply affected by the new point of view which Sociology has fostered; and the teaching of the science has attained to undisputed recognition in the universities of the world.

It is the aim of economic science to investigate the forms, relations, and processes that occur among men in their associated efforts to make immediate or mediate provision for their physical wants. The science deals with the phenomena resulting from the production, distribution, and consumption of wealth. The science of politics is concerned with the stable social relations resulting from the efforts of sovereign social units to maintain themselves in integrity in their internal and external relations and to promote human progress. The state is the institution in which these activities centre. Hence, the forms in which sovereignty is clothed, the processes of change which occur among them, and the varying functions of government are central problems in this field of investigation. The science of religions aims at describing the stable social relations which occur when men collectively endeavour to understand the law of their relation to a Supreme Being and to adjust their worship and conduct to His supreme will. The science of law is concerned with those principles, relations, and institutions through which the more important relations between the one and the many are defined, directed, and sanctioned by the sovereign state. The science of ethics aims at expounding the principles and sanctions by which all human conduct, both individual and social, is adjusted to the supreme end of man; or, in the Christian sense of the term, to the will of God. The science of history, which assumes the law of continuity in human society, endeavours to look out over its whole surface, to discover and describe in a large way the processes of change that have occurred in social relations of whatsoever kind. Each of these social sciences is analytical or descriptive, but in its complete development it should have a normative or directive side. To use the technical phrase, it is teleological. The complete function of each of them should include the setting forth of a purpose for human conduct and should offer direction towards it, which is modified by the relations in which each stands to the others.

Some sociologists endeavour to locate their science as logically antecedent to all of these. According to this view sociology should occupy itself with general phases of the processes of human association and should furnish an introduction to the special social sciences. Others endeavour to locate sociology as the philosophical synthesis of the results of the special social sciences, in which view it resembles somewhat the philosophy of history. Giddings includes both functions in his description of the science. He says in his "Principles of sociology": "While Sociology in the broadest sense of the word is the comprehensive science of society, coextensive with the entire field of the special social sciences, in a narrower sense and for the purposes of university study and of general exposition it may be defined as the science of social elements and first principles. . . . Its far-reaching principles are the postulates of special sciences and as such they co-ordinate the whole body of social generalizations and bind them together in a large scientific whole" (p. 33).

There is a general tendency towards the establishment of a single dominant interest in social groups. Periods of unstable equilibrium tend to be followed by constructive epochs in which some one social interest tends to dominate. This is the case when social groups are primitive and isolated as well as when they are highly organized and progressive. It may be the food interest, the maintenance of the group against invasion, the thirst for conquest incarnate in a leader, or the establishment of the Kingdom of God on earth that serves as the basis of social unity. In any case, the tendency of social groups towards unity is practically universal. In earlier stages of civilization the process is relatively simple, but to-day, when differences of climate, race, environment, type, and place are overcome by progress in transportation, travel, communication, and industry, the process is highly complex. Political institutions, languages, and race traditions no longer bound the horizon of the thinker. To-day all states are submerged in the larger view of humanity. All cultures, civilizations, centuries, all wars, and armaments, all nations and customs are before the social student. Origins heretofore hidden are exposed to his confused gaze. Interpretations, venerable with age and powerful from heretofore unquestioning acceptance, are swept away and those that are newer are substituted. Dozens of social sciences flow with torrential impatience, hurling their discoveries at the feet of the student. Thousands of minds are busy day and night gathering facts, offering interpretations, and seeking relations. The social sciences have become so overburdened with facts and so confused by varying interpretations that they tend to split into separate subsidiary sciences in the hope that the mind may thus escape its own limitations and find help in its power of generalization. Economic factors and processes are studied more industriously than ever before, but they are found to have in themselves vital bearings other than economic. Political, religious, educational, and social facts are found saturated with heretofore unsuspected meanings, which in each particular case the science itself is unable to handle.

In this situation three general lines of work present themselves. (1) There is the need of careful study of commonplace social facts from a point of view wider than that fostered in each particular social science. (2) The results obtained within the different social sciences and among them should be brought together in general interpretations. (3) A social philosophy is needed which will endeavour to take the established results of these sciences and put them together through the cohesive power of metaphysics and philosophy into an attempted interpretation of the whole course of human society itself. Professor Small thus describes the situation: "We need a genetic, static, and teleological account of associated human life; a statement which can be relied upon as the basis of a philosophy of conduct. In order to derive such a statement it would be necessary to complete a programme of analyzing and synthesizing the social process in all of its phases."

On the whole the sociological treatment of social facts is much wider than that found in the other social sciences and its interpretations are consequently broader. An endeavour is made in following out the social point of view to study social facts in the full complement of their organic relations. Thus, for instance, if the sociologist studies the question of woman suffrage, it appears as a phase in a world-movement. He goes back through the available history of all times and civilizations endeavouring to trace the changing place of woman in industry, in the home, education, and before the law. By looking outward to the horizon and backwards to the vanishing point of the perspective of history, the sociologist endeavours to discover all of the relations of the suffrage movement which confronts us to-day and tries to interpret its relation to the progress of the race. He will discover that the marriage rate, the birth rate, the movement for higher education, the demand for political and social equality are not unrelated facts but are organically connected in the processes that centre on woman in human society. The student of economics, politics, ethics, or law will be directly interested in particular phases of the process. But the sociologist will aim at reaching an all-inclusive view in order to interpret the entire movement in its organic relations to historical and actual social processes. Likewise, whether the problem be that of democracy, liberty, equality, war, armaments and arbitration, tariffs or inventions, the organization of labour, revolution, political parties, centralization of wealth, conflicts among social classes, the sociologist will endeavour to discover their wider bearings and their place in the social processes of which they are part.

The method employed in sociology is primarily inductive. At times ethnological and biological methods have predominated but their sway has been diminished in recent years. Sociology suffers greatly from its failure to establish as yet a satisfactory basis of classification for social phenomena. Although much attention has been given to this problem the results achieved still leave much to be desired. The general point of view held in sociology, as distinct from the particular point of view held in the special social sciences, renders this problem of classification particularly difficult and causes the science to suffer from the very mass of indiscriminate material which its scholarship has brought to view. Hence, the process of observation and interpretation has been somewhat uncertain and results have been subjected to vehement discussion. The fundamental problem for sociology is to discover and to interpret coexistences and sequences among social phenomena. In its study of origins and of historical development of social forms, sociology necessarily makes use of ethnological methods. It resorts extensively to comparative methods in its endeavour to correlate phenomena related to the same social process as they appear in different times and places. The statistical method is of the highest importance in determining quantities among social phenomena, while the prevailing tendency to look upon society from a psychological point of view has led to the general method of psychological analysis. The efforts to develop a systematic sociology deductively have not yet led to any undisputed results although the evolutionary hypothesis prevails widely. The range of methods to be found among sociologists might be fairly well illustrated among American writers by a comparison of the works of Morgan, Ward, Giddings, Baldwin, Cooley, Ross, Sumner, Mayo-Smith, and Small.

In as far as modern sociology has been developed on the philosophical side it has naturally been unable to remain free of metaphysics. It shows a marked tendency towards Agnosticism, Materialism, and Determinism. "He would be a bold man", says Professor Giddings, addressing the Amer. Economic Association in 1903, "who to-day after a thorough training in the best historical scholarship should venture to put forth a philosophy of history in terms of the divine ideas or to trace the plan of an Almighty in the sequence of human events. On the other hand, those interpretations that are characterized as materialistic . . . are daily winning serious respect." Even when the science has been confined to the humbler rôle of observation and interpretation of particular social facts and processes, its devotees have been unable to refrain from assumptions which are offensive to the Christian outlook on life. Theoretically, social facts may be observed as such, regardless of philosophy. But social observation which ignores the moral and social interpretation of social facts and processes is necessarily incomplete. One must have some principle of interpretation when one interprets, and one always tends towards interpretation. Thus it is that even descriptive sociology tends to become directive or to offer interpretations, and in so doing it often takes on a tone with which the Christian cannot agree.

If, for instance, the sociologist proposes a standard family of a limited number of children in the name of human progress, by implication he assumes an attitude towards the natural and Divine law which is quite repugnant to Catholic theology. Again, when he interprets divorce in its relation to supposed social progress alone and finds little if any fault with it, he lays aside for the moment the law of marriage given by Christ. When, too, the sociologist studies the relation of the State to the family and the individual or the relations of the Church and the State he comes into direct contact with the fundamental principles of Catholic social philosophy. When he studies the religious phenomena of history, he cannot avoid taking an attitude toward the distinctive claims of Christianity in his interpretation of the facts of its history. Thus it is that sociology, not only on its philosophical side but also on the side of observation, interpretations, and social direction, tends to take on a tone that is often foreign to and as often antagonistic to Catholic philosophy. Professor Ward would forbid pure sociology to have anything to do with the direction of human conduct. He says, for instance, in his "Pure Sociology": "All ethical considerations in however wide a sense that expression may be understood must be ignored for the time being and attention concentrated upon the effort to determine what actually is. Pure Sociology has no concern with what Sociology ought to be or with any social ideals. It confines itself strictly with the present and the past, allowing the future to take care of itself." But he would give to what he terms Applied Sociology the function of directing society toward its immediate ideals. He says: "The subject matter of Pure Sociology is achievement, that of Applied Sociology is improvement. The former relates to the past and the present, the latter to the future." Sociology can scarcely avoid interpretation and direction of human conduct and hence it can hardly be expected to avoid taking very definite attitudes towards the Christian outlook on life.

Modern sociology hopes to arrive at a metaphysics through the systematic observation and interpretation of present and past social facts and processes. In the Christian view of life, however, the social sciences are guided by a sanctioned metaphysics and philosophy. This philosophy is derived not from induction but from Revelation. This view of life accepts at the outset as Divinely warranted the moral and social precepts taught or re-enforced by Christ. Thus, it looks out upon the real largely from the standpoint of the ideal and judges the former by the latter. It does not, of course, for a moment forget that the systematic observation of life and knowledge of its processes are essential to the understanding and application of the Divine precepts and to the establishment of the sanctioned spiritual ideals which it professes. But Christian social philosophy did not, for example, derive its doctrine of human brotherhood by induction; it received it directly from the lips of Christ. And the consequences of that Christian principle in human history are beyond all calculation. The Christian view of life does not confound the absolute with the conventional in morality, although in the literature of Christianity too much emphasis may at times be placed upon what is relative. A Christian sociology, therefore, would be one that carries with it always the philosophy of Christ. It could not look with indifference on the varied and complicated social processes amid which we live and move. In all of its study and interpretation of what is going on in life—which is largely the function of sociology—it never surrenders concern for what ought to be, however clearly or dimly this "ought" is seen. While modern sociology is seeking descriptive laws of human desires and is endeavouring to classify human interests and to account for social functions, it is seeking merely for changes, uniformities, and interpretations unconcerned with any relation of these to the Divine law. Christian sociology, on the contrary, is actuated mainly by concern about the relations of social changes to the law and Revelation of God. It classifies processes, institutions, and relations as right or wrong, good or bad, and offers to men directive laws of human desire and distinctive standards of social valuations by which social conduct should be governed.

Economics as it developed under Christian influences related largely to the search for justice in property relations among men rather than to the evolution of property itself. Whatever attempts were made to correlate and interpret economic phenomena, they were inspired largely by the search for justice and by the hope of holding industrial relations true to the law of justice as it was understood. Political science as it developed under Christian influence never lost sight of the Divine sanction of civil authority. The study of the forms and changes of government, little as the underlying processes were then understood, never departed far from the thought of the state as a natural and Christian phenomenon and the exercise of its authority as a delegated power from on high. Thus, whatever there was of social science, rudimentary because of the static view of society which obtained, it grew out of the study and application of the moral and social principles derived from the Revelation of God and presented to the believer through the instrumentality of the Church. The great emphasis placed in our days of wonderful social investigation and of world-views of social processes causes those earlier attempts at social science to appear crude, yet they developed organically out of their historical surroundings, retaining, for all time, titles to no mean consideration. Scattered here and there throughout theological and moral treatises in Christian literature there is a vast amount of sociological material, which has its value in our own time. The present-day endeavours of sociology to classify human desires and fundamental interests appear to have been anticipated in a modest way in the work of the medieval Scholastics. Theological treatises on human acts and their morality reveal a very practical understanding of the influence of objective and subjective environment on character. Treatises on sin, on the virtues, on good and bad example touch constantly on social facts and processes as then understood. The mainspring of all of this work, however, was not to show forth social processes as such, not to look for theretofore unknown law, but to enable the individual to discover himself in the social process and to hold his conduct true to his ideals.

To some extent there is confusion in speaking of sociology in this way since reference appears to be made rather to moral direction than to social investigation. The relations between all of the social sciences are intimate. The results established in the fields of the social sciences will always have the greatest importance for Christian ethics. It must take up the undisputed results of sociological investigation and widen its definitions at times. It must restate rights and obligations in the terms of newer social relations and adjust its own system to much that it can welcome from the hands of the splendid scholarship now devoted to social study. Bouquillon (q. v.), who was a distinguished theologian, complained that we had not paid sufficient attention to the results of modern social research. Illustration may be found in the problem of private property, which is a storm centre in modern life and is the object of most acute study from the standpoint of the social sciences. *Suum cuique* may be called the law of justice that is back of all social changes and is sanctioned for all time. But the social processes which change from time to time the content of *suum* may not be neglected. Changes in the forms of property, varied consequences from the failure to have it at all and from the having of it in excess, are seen about us every day. It is undeniably the business of ethics to teach the sanctions of private property and defend them, but it must willingly learn the sociological meaning of property, the significance of changes in its forms, and the laws that govern these changes. This is largely the work of other social sciences. Ethics must proclaim the inviolable natural rights of the individual to private property in certain forms. It must proclaim the pernicious moral consequences that may flow from certain property conditions, but it will fail of its high mission unless in its indispensable ethical work it take account of the established results of social investigation. Economics, ethics, sociology, politics are drawn together by the complex problems of property and each has much to learn from the others. And so, whether the problem be that of the Christian family, the relations of social classes, altruism, the modification of the forms of government, the changing status of woman, the representative of the Christian outlook on life may not for a moment ignore the results of these particular social sciences.

Closer relations have been established between Christian ethics and sociology in modern days. Modern social conditions with their rapid changes, accompanied by ethical and philosophical unrest, have set up a challenge which the Christian Church must meet without hesitation. The Catholic Church has not failed to speak out definitely in the circumstances. The School of Catholic Social Reform, which has reached such splendid development on the European continent, represents the closer sympathy between the old Christian ethics and the later sociological investigation. Problems of poverty seen in its organic relations to social organization as a whole, problems and challenges raised by the modern industrial labouring class, demand for a widening of the definitions of individual and social responsibility to meet the facts of modern social power of whatsoever kind, reaffirmations of the rights of individuals have been taken account of in this whole Christian modern movement with the happiest result. There has been produced an abundant literature in which traditional Christian ethics take ample account of modern social investigations and the theories thus formulated have created a movement for social amelioration which is playing a notable part in the present-day history of Europe.

Since all of the social sciences are concerned with the same complex fact of human association, it is but to be expected that the older sciences would have contained in their literature much that in the long run is turned over to the newer ones. Sociological material is found, therefore, throughout the history of the other social sciences. The word "sociology" comes from Auguste Comte, who used it in his course of positive philosophy, to indicate one of the sections in his scheme of sciences. Spencer sanctioned the use of the word and gave it a place in permanent literature by using it unreservedly in his own system of philosophy. He undertook to explain all social changes as phases in the great inclusive process of evolution. Society was conceived of as an organism. Research and exposition were directed largely by the biological analogy. Schaeffle, Lilienfeld, and René Worms were later exponents of this same view. Later schools in sociology have emancipated themselves from the sway of the biological analogy and have turned toward ethnological, anthropological, and psychological aspects of the great problems involved. Repeated attempts have been made to discover the fundamental unifying principle by which all social processes may be classified and explained, but none of them have met general acceptance. The drift to-day is largely toward the psychological aspects of human association. Professors Giddings and Baldwin may be looked upon as its representatives in the United States. Aside from these attempts at systematic or philosophical sociology there is scarcely an aspect of human association which is not now under investigation from the sociological standpoint. That this activity in a field of such great interest to the welfare of the human race promises much for human progress is beyond question. Even now statesmen, religious teachers, educators, and leaders in movements for social amelioration do not fail to take advantage of the results of sociological research.

See ETHICS; PSYCHOLOGY; CHURCH; and articles on the other social sciences.

The following text-books summarize the field of sociology from various standpoints: WARD, *Outlines of Sociology* (New York, 1898); DEALY, *Sociology* (New York, 1909); GUMPLOWICZ, *Outlines of Soc.* (tr. MOORE), pub. by *Amer. Acad. of Soc. and Pol. Sc.* (1899); GIDDINGS, *Elem. of Soc.* (New York, 1898); BASCOM, *Sociology*; BLACKMAR, *Elem. of Soc.* (New York, 1905); STUCKENBERG, *Sociology* (New York, 1903).

The following general treatises aim to present the new sociological point of view: Ross, *Social Control* (New York, 1901); IDEM, *Soc. Psychology* (New York, 1908); COOLEY, *Soc. Organization* (New York, 1909); SMALL, *General Soc.* (Chicago, 1905); IDEM, *Meaning of Social Science* (Chicago, 1910); MCDOUGAL, *Soc. Psychology* (London); BALDWIN, *Social and Ethical Interpretations* (New York, 1902); KIDD, *Soc. Evolution* (New York, 1894).

Systematic Treatises: SPENCER, *Principles of Soc.*; SCHAEFFLE, *Bau und Leben des sozialen Korpers*; LILIENFELD, *Gedanken über die Sozialwissenschaft der Zukunft* (5 vols., Mitau, 1873); LETOURNEAU, *La sociologie*, tr. TRALLOPE (Paris, 1884); TARDE, *The Laws of Imitation*, tr. PARSONS (New York, 1903); SIMMEL, *Soziologie* (Leipzig, 1908); WARD, *Pure Soc.* (New York, 1903); IDEM, *Applied Soc.* (New York, 1906); GIDDINGS, *Principles of Soc.* (New York, 1899); IDEM, *Inductive Soc.* (New York, 1901).

Periodicals: *Annales de l'inst. interna. de soc.*; *Rev. intern. de soc.*; *American Jour. of Soc.*

Discussions of the nature and relations of sociology will be found in Reports of meetings of economic, historical, and political sciences associations and in text-books on the various social sciences. For discussion of the science from a Catholic standpoint, see SLATER, *Modern Sociology* in the *Irish Theo. Quart.*, VI, nos. 21, 22.

WILLIAM J. KERBY.

Socorro, DIOCESE OF (DE SUCCURSU), established in 1895 as a suffragan see of the Archdiocese of Bogota, in the Republic of Colombia, South America. The Catholic population in 1910 numbered 230,000. The city of Socorro arose at Chiancon, the settlement of an Indian chief of the same name, in 1540 defeated and captured by the discoverer Martin Galeano. In 1681 the village moved to its present site under the auspices of Our Lady of Succour (Socorro), with which name the rank of parish was given it in 1683, and it was definitively constructed eight years later. In 1771 it was raised to the rank of a town. This city was one of the first in starting the Colombian movement for independence, for as late as 1781 there was a revolt against the Spanish authorities. Socorro is the capital of the province of the same name, in the Department of Santander. The present bishop is the Rt. Rev. Evaristo Blanco. (See COLOMBIA, REPUBLIC OF.)

JULIAN MORENO-LACALLE.

Socrates, a historian of the Early Church, b. at Constantinople towards the end of the fourth century. Nothing is known of his parentage and his early years with the exception of a few details found in his own works. He tells us himself (Hist. eccl., V, xxiv) that he studied under the grammarians Helladius and Ammonius, and from the title of *scholasticus* which is given to him it has been concluded that he belonged to the legal profession. The greater part of his life was spent in Constantinople, for which reason, as he admits, the affairs of that city occupy such a large part in his works. From the manner in which he speaks of other cities and from his references as an eyewitness to events which happened outside Constantinople, he is credited with having visited other countries in the East. Though a layman he was excellently qualified to recount the history of ecclesiastical affairs. Love of history, especially the history of his own time, and a warm admiration for Eusebius of Cæsarea impelled him to undertake the task in which he was sustained by the urgent solicitation of a certain Theodorus to whom his work is dedicated. His purpose was to continue the work of Eusebius down to his own time; but in order to round out his narrative and to supplement and revise some statements of

Eusebius, he began at the year 306, when Constantine was declared emperor. His work ends with the seventeenth consulate of Theodosius the Younger, 439. The division of his history into seven books was based on the imperial succession in the Eastern Empire. The first book embraces events in the reign of Constantine (306-37): the second those in the reign of Constantius (337-60): the third includes the reigns of Julian and Jovian (360-4): the fourth deals with the reign of Valens (364-78): the fifth with that of Theodosius the Great (379-95): the sixth with that of Arcadius (393-408): the seventh with the first thirty-one years of the reign of Theodosius the Younger (408-39).

The general character of the work of Socrates can be judged from his attitude on doctrinal questions. Living as he did in an age of bitter polemics, he strove to avoid the animosities and hatred engendered by theological differences. He was in entire accord with the Catholic party in opposing the Arians, Eunomians, Macedonians, and other heretics. The moderate tone, however, which he used in speaking of the Novatians, and the favourable references which he makes to them, have led some authors into the belief that he belonged to this sect, but it is now generally admitted that the expressions which he used were based on his desire for impartiality and his wish to give even his enemies credit for whatever good he could find in them. His attitude towards the Church was one of unvarying respect and submission. He honoured clerics because of their sacred calling, and entertained the profoundest veneration for monks and the monastic spirit. His ardent advocacy and defence of Christianity did not, nevertheless, prevent him from using the writings of pagan authors, nor from urging Christians to study them. Though he entitled his work Ἐκκλησιαστικὴ Ἱστορία, Socrates did not confine himself merely to recounting events in the history of the Church. He paid attention to the military history of the period, because he considered it necessary to relate these facts, but principally "in order that the minds of the readers might not become satiated with the repetition of the contentious disputes of bishops, and their insidious designs against one another; but more especially that it might be made apparent that, whenever the affairs of the State were disturbed, those of the Church, as if by some vital sympathy, became disordered also" (Introd. to Book V). Though thus recognizing the intimate relation of civil and ecclesiastical affairs, Socrates had no well-defined theory of Church and State.

Socrates had a restricted idea of the scope and function of history. To his mind the task of the historian consisted in recording the troubles of mankind, for as long as peace continues, those who desire to write histories will find no materials for their purpose (VII, xlviii). As an example of historical composition the work of Socrates ranks very high. The simplicity of style which he cultivated, and for which he was reproached by Photius, is entirely in keeping with his method and spirit. Not the least among his merits is the sedulousness he exhibited in the collection of evidence. He had a truly scientific instinct for primary sources, and the number of authors he has drawn on proves the extent of his reading and the thoroughness of his investigations. In addition to using the works of such men as Athanasius, Evagrius, Talladius, Nestorius, he drew freely on public and official documents, conciliar Acts, encyclical letters, etc. As might be expected when writing of events so close to his own time, he had to depend frequently on the reports of eyewitnesses, but even then he used their evidence with prudence and caution. Notwithstanding his industry and impartiality, however, his work is not without serious defects. Though restricting himself so largely to the affairs of the Eastern Church, he is guilty of many serious omissions in regard to other parts of Christendom. Thus, when he speaks of the Church in the West, he is frequently guilty of mistakes and omissions. Nothing for instance is said in his history about St. Augustine. In questions of chronology, too, he is frequently at fault, but he is by no means a persistent sinner in this respect. The objection most frequently made in respect to Socrates as a historian is that he was too credulous and that he lent too ready an ear to stories of miracles and portents. This, however, is a fault of the time rather than of the man, and was shared by pagan as well as Christian authors. His most notable characteristic, however, is his obvious effort to be thoroughly impartial, as far as impartiality was consistent with conviction. He held the scales equitably, and even when he differed widely from men on matters of doctrine, he did not allow his dissent from their views to find expression in denunciation or abuse. His "Church History" was published by Stephen (Paris, 1544) and by Valesius (Paris, 1668, reprinted at Oxford by Parker, 1844, and in P. G., LXVII). A good translation is given in the Post-Nicene Fathers, II (New York, 1890), with an excellent memoir on Socrates by Zenos.

STÄUDLIN, *Geschichte und Literatur des Kirchengeschichte* (Hanover, 1827); GEPPERT, *Die Quellen des Kirchenhistorikers Socrates Scholasticus* (Leipzig, 1898); MILLIGAN in *Dict. Christ. Biog.*, s. v. Socrates (2).

PATRICK J. HEALY.

Socrates, Greek philosopher and educational reformer of the fifth century B. C., b. at Athens, 469 B. C.; d. there, 399 B. C. After having received the usual Athenian education in music (which included literature), geometry, and gymnastics, he practised for a time the craft of sculptor, working, we are told, in his father's workshop. Admonished, as he tells us, by a divine call, he gave up his occupation in order to devote himself to the moral and intellectual reform of his fellow-citizens. He believed himself destined to become "a sort of gadfly" to the Athenian State. He devoted himself to this mission with extraordinary zeal and singleness of purpose.

SOCRATES
Antique Fragment, Uffizi Gallery

He never left the City of Athens except on two occasions, one of which was the campaign of Potidea and Delium, and the other a public religious festival. In his work as reformer he encountered, indeed he may be said to have provoked, the opposition of the Sophists and their influential friends. He was the most unconventional of teachers and the least tactful. He delighted in assuming all sorts of rough and even vulgar mannerisms, and purposely shocked the more refined sensibilities of his fellow-citizens. The opposition to him culminated in formal accusations of impiety and subversion of the existing moral traditions. He met these accusations in a spirit of defiance and, instead of defending himself, provoked his opponents by a speech in presence of his judges in which he affirmed his innocence of all wrongdoing, and refused to retract or apologize for anything that he had said or done. He was condemned to drink the hemlock and, when the time came, met his fate with a calmness and dignity which have earned for him a high place among those who suffered unjustly for conscience sake. He was a man of great moral earnestness, and exemplified in his own life some of the noblest moral virtues. At the same time, he did not rise above the moral level of his contemporaries in every respect, and Christian apologists have no difficulty in refuting the contention that he was the equal of the Christian saints. His frequent references to a "divine voice" that inspired him at critical moments in his career are, perhaps, best explained by saying that they are simply his peculiar way of speaking about the promptings of his own conscience. They do not necessarily imply a pathological condition of his mind, nor a superstitious belief in the existence of a "familiar demon".

Socrates was, above all things, a reformer. He was alarmed at the condition of affairs in Athens, a condition which he was, perhaps, right in ascribing to the Sophists. They taught that there is no objective standard of the true and the false, that that is true which seems to be true, and that that is false which seems to be false. Socrates considered that this theoretical scepticism led inevitably to moral anarchy. If that is true which seems to be true, then that is good, he said, which seems to be good. Up to this time morality was taught not by principles scientifically determined, but by instances, proverbs, and apothegms. He undertook, therefore, first to determine the conditions of universally valid knowledge, and, secondly, to found on universally valid moral principles a science of human conduct. Self-knowledge is the starting-point, because, he believed, the greatest source of the prevalent confusion was the failure to realize how little we know about anything, in the true sense of the word know. The statesman, the orator, the poet, think they know much about courage; for they talk about it as being noble, and praiseworthy, and beautiful, etc. But they are really ignorant of it until they know what it is, in other words, until they know its definition. The definite meaning, therefore, to be attached to the maxim "Know thyself" is "Realize the extent of thine own ignorance."

Consequently, the Socratic method of teaching included two stages, the negative and the positive. In the negative stage, Socrates, approaching his intended pupil in an attitude of assumed ignorance, would begin to ask a question, apparently for his own information. He would follow this by other questions, until his interlocutor would at last be obliged to confess ignorance of the subject discussed. Because of the pretended deference which Socrates payed to the superior intelligence of his pupil, this stage of the method was called "Socratic Irony". In the positive stage of the method, once the pupil had acknowledged his ignorance, Socrates would proceed to another series of questions, each of which would bring out some phase or aspect of the subject, so that when, at the end, the answers were all summed up in a general statement, that statement expressed the concept of the subject, or the definition. Knowledge through concepts, or knowledge by definition, is the aim, therefore, of the Socratic method. The entire process was called "Heuristic", because it was a method of finding, and opposed to "Eristic", which is the method of strife, or contention. Knowledge through concepts is certain, Socrates taught, and offers a firm foundation for the structure not only of theoretical knowledge, but also of moral principles, and the science of human conduct. Carried away by his enthusiasm for conceptional knowledge as a basis of conduct, Socrates went so far as to maintain that all right conduct depends on clear knowledge, that not only does a definition of a virtue aid us in acquiring that virtue, but that the definition of the virtue is the virtue. A man who can define justice is just, and, in general, theoretical insight into the principles of conduct is identical with moral excellence in conduct; knowledge is virtue. Contrariwise, ignorance is vice, and no one can knowingly do wrong. These principles are, of course, only partly true. Their formulation, however, at this time was of tremendous importance, because it marks the beginning of an attempt to build up on general principles a science of human conduct.

Socrates devoted little attention to questions of physics and cosmogony. Indeed, he did not conceal his contempt for these questions when comparing them with questions affecting man, his nature and his destiny. He was, however, interested in the question of the existence of God and formulated an argument from design which was afterwards known as the "Teleological Argument" for the existence of God. "Whatever exists for a useful purpose must be the work of an intelligence" is the major premise of Socrates' argument, and may be said to be the major premise, explicit or implicit, of every teleological argument formulated since his time. Socrates was profoundly convinced of the immortality of the soul, although in his address to his judges he argues against the fear of death in such a way as apparently to offer two alternatives: "Either death ends all things, or it is the beginning of a happy life." His real conviction was that the soul survives the body, unless, indeed, we are misled by our authorities, Plato and Xenophon. In the absence of primary sources—Socrates, apparently, never wrote anything—we are obliged to rely on these writers and on a few references of Aristotle for our knowledge of what Socrates taught. Plato's portrayal of Socrates is idealistic; when, however, we correct it by reference to Xenophon's more practical view of Socrates' teaching, the result cannot be far from historic truth.

For Sources, RITTER and PRELLER, *Hist. Philosophiæ Græcæ* (Gotha, 1888), 192 sq.; BAKEWELL, *Source Book in Ancient Philosophy* (New York, 1907), 86 sq. Consult ZELLER, *Socrates and the Socratic Schools*, tr. REICHEL (London, 1885); PIAT, *Socrate* (Paris, 1900); TURNER, *Hist. of Philosophy* (Boston, 1903), 77 sq.

WILLIAM TURNER.

Sodality.—I. The sodalities of the Church are pious associations (see ASSOCIATIONS, PIOUS) and are included among the confraternities and archconfraternities (q. v.). It would not be possible to give a definition making a clear distinction between the sodalities and other confraternities; consequently the development and history of the sodalities are the same as those of the religious confraternities. A general sketch of these latter has been already given in the account of the medieval confraternities of prayer (see PURGATORIAL SOCIETIES). They are also mentioned in the article SCAPULAR. Confraternities and sodalities, in the present meaning of the word, the only ones which will be here mentioned, had their beginnings after the rise of the confraternities of prayer in the early Middle Ages, and developed rapidly from the end of the twelfth century, i. e. from the rise of the great ecclesiastical orders. Proofs of this are to be found in the Bullaria and annals of these orders, as those of the Dominicans, the Carmelites, and the Servites. [Cf. Armellini, "Le chiese di Roma" (2nd ed., Rome, 1891), 20 sqq.; "Historisch-politische Blätter", cxlviii (Munich, 1911), 759 sqq., 823 sqq.; Ebner, "Die acht Brüderschaften des hl. Wolfgang in Regensburg" in Mahler, "Der hl. Wolfgang" (Ratisbon, 1894), 182 sq.; Villanueva, "Viage literario a las Iglesias de España", VIII (Valencia, 1821), 258 sqq., Apéndice XXIII; ibid., XI (Madrid, 1850), 185 sq., Apéndice IV; Gallia Christ., XI, instr. 253 sq., n. XXVII; ibid., VI, instr. 366, n. XXXIV; Mabillon, "Annales Ordinis Benedicti", VI, Lucca, 1745, 361 sqq., ad an. 1145; Martène, "Thesaurus novus anecdotorum", IV (Paris, 1717), 165 sqq. "Confraternitas Massiliensis an. 1212 instituta"; "Monumenta

O. Servorum B.M.V.", I, 107, ad an. 1264; Gianius, "Annales O. Serv. B.M.V.", I (2nd ed., Lucca, 1719), 384, ad an. 1412; "Libro degli ordinamenti de la Compagnia di Santa Maria del Carmine scritto nel 1280" (Bologna, 1867)]. Pious associations of this kind, however, soon appeared, which were solely under the bishop and had no close connexion with an order. An interesting example of such an association of the year 1183 is described in the "Histoire générale du Languedoc" (VI, Toulouse, 1879, 106 sqq.), as an "association formed at Le Puy for the restoration of peace". A carpenter named Pierre (Durant) is given as the founder of this society. In regard to a "Confraternity of the Mother of God" which existed at Naupactos in Greece about 1050, see "La Confraternità di S. Maria di Naupactos 1048", in the "Bullettino dell' Istituto storico italiano", no. 31 (Rome, 1910, 73 sqq.).

From the era of the Middle Ages very many of these pious associations placed themselves under the special protection of the Blessed Virgin, and chose her for patron under the title of some sacred mystery with which she was associated. The main object and duty of these societies were, above all, the practice of piety and works of charity. The decline of ecclesiastical life at the close of the Middle Ages was naturally accompanied by a decline of religious associational life, the two being related as cause and effect. However, as soon as the Church rose to renewed prosperity in the course of the sixteenth century, by the aid of the Counter-Reformation and the appearance of the new religious congregations and associations, once more there sprang up numerous confraternities and sodalities which laboured with great success and, in many cases, are still effective.

Of the sodalities which came into existence just at this period, particular mention should be made of those called the Sodalities of the Blessed Virgin Mary (*congregationes seu sodalitates B. Mariæ Virginis*), because the name *sodality* was in a special manner peculiar to these, also because their labours for the renewal of the life of the Church were more permanent and have lasted until the present time, so that these sodalities after fully three hundred years still prosper and flourish. Even the opponents of the Catholic Church seem to recognize this. The article "Bruderschaften, kirchliche" in Herzog-Hauck, "Realencyklopädie für protestantische Theologie", discusses almost exclusively the Sodalities of the Blessed Virgin Mary as the pattern of Catholic sodalities. It cannot, indeed, be denied that these sodalities are, by their spirit and entire organization, better equipped than other confraternities to make their members not only loyal Catholics but also true lay apostles for the salvation and blessing of all around them. In the course of time other pious Church societies sprang from the Sodalities of the Blessed Virgin Mary, or were quickened by these to new zeal and fruitful labours, e. g. the work of foreign missions, the "Society of St. Vincent de Paul", the "Society of St. Francis Regis", and many others. While all other confraternities and sodalities have as their chief end a single pious devotion or exercise, a single work of love of God or of one's neighbour, the peculiar aim of the Sodalities of the Blessed Virgin Mary is, by means of the true veneration of the Blessed Virgin, to build up and renew the whole inner man in order to render him capable of and zealous for all works of spiritual love and charity. Consequently these sodalities are described below in detail separately from the others.

II. All sodalities, pious associations, and confraternities may be divided into three classes, although these classes are not absolutely distinct from one another. The first class, A, includes the confraternities which seek mainly to attain piety, devotion, and the increase of love of God by special veneration of God, of the Blessed Virgin, the angels, and the saints. The second class, B, consists of those sodalities which are founded chiefly to promote the spiritual and corporal works of mercy. The third class, C, may be considered to include those associations of the Church the main object of which is the well-being and improvement of a definite class of persons.

A.—The first class includes: (1) The "Confraternity of the Most Holy Trinity with the White Scapular" (see SCAPULAR). (2) The Confraternities of the Holy Ghost. In 1882 such a confraternity was established for Austria-Hungary in the church of the Lazarists at Vienna, and in 1887 it received the right of aggregation for the whole of Germany. Special mention should here be made of the "Archconfraternity of the Servants of the Holy Ghost". It was first established in 1877 at the Church of St. Mary of the Angels, Bayswater, London. In 1878 it received the papal confirmation and special indulgences, in the following year it was raised to an archconfraternity with unlimited power of aggregation for the whole world. The director of the archconfraternity, to whom application for admission can be made personally or by letter, is the superior of the Oblates of St. Charles Borromeo, at the Church of St. Mary of the Angels, Bayswater, London, W. A third confraternity for the glorification of the Holy Ghost, especially among the heathen, was established in the former collegiate Church of Our Lady at Knechtsteden, Germany. It is directed by the Fathers of the Holy Ghost and of the Immaculate Heart of Mary. Its organ is the missionary monthly, "Echo aus Knechtsteden". (3) There is no special confraternity in honour of the Heavenly Father. There is, however, an "Archconfraternity of the Most Holy Name of God and of the Most Holy Name of Jesus". Originally this formed two distinct confraternities, which owed their origin to the Dominicans. At a later date they combined and were united into one society, the establishment of which is under the control of the general of the Dominicans. Paul V cancelled the indulgences previously granted to the confraternity and granted new ones. It is probable that the Brief of 21 Sept., 1274, of Gregory IX, addressed to the general of the Dominicans, gave the first impulse to the founding of the above-mentioned confraternities. In this Brief the pope called upon the father-general to promote, by preaching, the veneration of the Holy Name of Jesus among the people. In America especially this society has spread widely and borne wonderful fruit. It has a periodical, "The Holy Name Journal," and has been granted new indulgences for those of its members who take part in its public processions [Analecta Ord. Fratr. Prædic., XVII (1909), 325 sq. See HOLY NAME, SOCIETY OF THE]. There are other confraternities and sodalities, especially in France, and also in Rome and Belgium, for the prevention of blasphemy against the name of God and of the desecration of Sundays and feast days (Beringer, "Les indulgences", II, 115 sqq.; cf. Act. S. Sed., I, 321).

(4) A triple series of confraternities has been formed about the Person of the Divine Saviour for the veneration of the Most Holy Sacrament, of the Sacred Heart, and of the Passion.

The confraternities of the Most Holy Sacrament were founded and developed, strictly speaking, in Italy from the end of the fifteenth century by the apostolic zeal of the Franciscans, especially by the zeal of Cherubino of Spoleto and the Blessed Bernardine of Feltre ("Acta SS.", Sept., VII, 837, 858). Yet as early as 1462 a confraternity of the Most Holy Sacrament existed in the Duchy of Jülich, in the Archdiocese of Cologne; other Confraternities of the Most Holy Sacrament were also founded in the Archdiocese of Cologne in the course of the fifteenth century (cf. "Köln. Pastoralblatt", 1900, 90). At Rome the Confraternity of the Most Holy Sacrament was founded (1501) in the Church of San Lorenzo in Damaso by the devotion and zeal of a poor priest and four plain citizens. Julius II confirmed this sodality by a Brief of 21 Aug., 1508, and wished to be entered himself as a member in the register of the confraternity. It is not, however, this sodality but another Roman confraternity that has been the fruitful parent of the countless confraternities of the Most Holy Sacrament which exist to-day everywhere in the Catholic world (cf. Quétif-Echard, I, 197 sq.). This second confraternity, due to the zeal of the Dominican Father, Thomas Stella, was erected by Paul III on 30 Nov., 1539, in the Dominican Church of Santa Maria sopra Minerva. This confraternity alone is understood when mention is simply made of the Confraternity of the Sacrament. Along with the honorary title of archconfraternity it received numerous indulgences and privileges by the Bull of 30 Nov., 1539. The indulgences were renewed by Paul V. It was made known at its inception that this confraternity could be established in parish churches, and that such confraternities should share in the indulgences of the archconfraternity without formal connexion with the Roman confraternity. This privilege was reconfirmed at various times by the popes, who expressed the wish that the bishops would establish the confraternity everywhere in all parish churches (cf. Tacchi-Venturi, "La vita religiosa in Italia durante la prima età della Compagnia di Gesù", Rome, 1910, 191 sqq.).

In the nineteenth century, however, confraternities for the adoration of the Most Holy Sacrament were also established in other countries, and these now extend all over the Catholic world. Mention is made in the article PURGATORIAL SOCIETIES of the "Archconfraternity of the Perpetual Adoration of the Blessed Sacrament under the Protection of St. Benedict." This association, that was founded in 1877 under Pius IX in Austria, was transferred to North America in 1893 during the pontificate of Leo XIII, and in 1910 received from Pius X the right of extension throughout the entire world.

In 1848 a pious woman, Anne de Meeûs, established at Brussels in Belgium a religious society which had as its object to unite the adoration of the Most Holy Sacrament with work for poor churches. In 1853 this society was raised to an archconfraternity for Belgium; soon after this separate archconfraternities of the same kind were erected for Bavaria, Austria, and Holland. At the same time there sprang from the original society a female religious congregation which, after receiving papal confirmation, established itself at Rome, and since 1879 has conducted the archconfraternity from Rome. It has authority to associate everywhere with itself confraternities of the same name and purpose, and to share with these all its indulgences. The archconfraternity has received large indulgences and privileges, and labours with much success in nearly all parts of the world. Entrance into this confraternity is especially to be recommended to all altar societies. The full title of the confraternity is "The Archconfraternity of the Perpetual Adoration of the Blessed Sacrament and Work of Poor Churches". Any information desired as to the working of the confraternity and the conditions of its establishment may be obtained from its headquarters, Casa delle Adoratrici perpetue, 4 Via Nomentana, Rome. Since 1900 the religious association of the Sisters of the Perpetual Adoration has had a house with a chapel at Washington, U. S. A., from which they extend and conduct the confraternity in America.

The "Society of the Most Holy Sacrament", founded by the Venerable Pierre-Julien Eymard (d. 1868) also sought, by means of a new confraternity established by it, to incite the faithful to adoration and zeal for the glorification of Jesus Christ in the Holy Eucharist. In 1897 this society was raised to an archconfraternity with the right of aggregation throughout the world. In 1898 its summary of indulgences was confirmed by the Congregation of Indulgences. The main condition of membership is a continuous hour of adoration of the Most Holy Sacrament once a month. The headquarters of the confraternity are at Rome, in the church of the Fathers of the Most Holy Sacrament, whence the society has the name of "The Archconfraternity of the Most Holy Sacrament in the Church of Sts. Andrew and Claudius at Rome" (San Claudio, 160 Via del Pozzetto, Rome).

"The Perpetual Adoration of Catholic Nations" was founded at Rome in 1883, its purpose being the union of the nations and peoples of the world for perpetual solemn expiatory prayer in order to avert God's just wrath and to implore His aid in the grievous troubles of the Church. The association is conducted by the Redemptorist Fathers in the Church of St. Joachim at Rome, lately built in memory of the jubilee of Leo XIII as priest and bishop. Special countries are assigned to each one the different days of the week for the adoration of reparation, e. g. Thursday, North and Central America; Friday, South America. The rector of the Church of St. Joachim (Prati di Castello, Rome) is the director-general of the association, which has the right to appoint diocesan directors in all countries, including missionary ones. In order to enter the association, application should be made to one of these directors or to the director general. Two other associations were founded in France for the purpose of expiation and atonement; these have already extended over the world. One is the "Association of the Communion of Reparation", the other the "Archconfraternity of the Holy Mass of Reparation". The "Association of the Communion of Reparation", established in 1854 by Father Drevon, S.J., was canonically erected in 1865 at Paray-le-Monial, in the monastery where the Divine Saviour had commanded Blessed Margaret Mary Alacoque to make reparation by Holy Communion for the ingratitude of men. This is also the purpose of the entire association, which can be canonically erected anywhere. The "Archconfraternity of the Holy Mass of Reparation" owes its origin to a poor widow of Paris, in June, 1862. Each member makes it his duty to attend a second Mass on Sundays and feast-days as expiation for those who sinfully fail to attend Mass on these days. In 1886 the confraternity was erected into an archconfraternity with the right of aggregation for France. At a later date other countries received in like manner a similar archconfraternity. Even in parts of the world where no such archconfraternity exists it is easy to be received into the confraternity. By a Decree of 7 Sept., 1911, of the Holy Office, all former indulgences were cancelled, and richer ones, to be shared equally by all the archconfraternities and confraternities of the Holy Mass of Reparation, were granted (Ad. Apost. Sed., III, 476 sq.). In this class belongs also the "Ingolstadt Mass Association". (See PURGATORIAL SOCIETIES.)

(5) As early as 1666 confraternities of the Blessed Jean Eudes for the united veneration of the Heart of Jesus and the Heart of Mary were established. It was not until after the death of Blessed Margaret Mary Alacoque that there arose confraternities for the promotion of the adoration of the Sacred Heart of Jesus in the manner desired by her. During the years 1697–1764 more than a thousand such confraternities were erected by papal Briefs and granted indulgences. At Rome the first "Confraternity of the Sacred Heart of Jesus" was established in 1729 by the efforts of Father Joseph Gallifet, S. J. This confraternity still exists at the Church of St. Theodore, at the foot of the Palatine. The membership of this "Confraternity of the Sacconi" has included celebrated and holy men. Only men, however, can belong to it.

Consequently it was given to another confraternity of the Sacred Heart to spread from Rome over the entire world. This is the sodality established in 1797 by Father Felici, S.J., in the little Church of Our Lady *ad Pineam*, called *in Cappella*. The sodality was raised in 1803 to an archconfraternity, and was afterward transferred by Leo XII to the Church of Santa Maria della Pace. Application to join this confraternity is made at the church. More than 10,000 confraternities have already united with it. The confraternities of the Sacred Heart erected in Belgium can unite with the archconfraternity of Paray-le-Monial, those established in France can either join this archconfraternity or that at Moulins. In addition a new confraternity of the Sacred Heart of Jesus was established in 1876 at Montmartre, Paris. In 1894 this society received the right to incorporate into itself other confraternities of the same name and object in any part of the world and to share its indulgences with these. The object of this confraternity, like that of the great church at Montmartre, is expiatory, and the society is to pray for the freedom of the pope and the salvation of human society.

The "Archconfraternity of Prayer and Penance in honour of the Heart of Jesus", founded at Dijon in 1879 with the right of aggregation for the entire world, has, since 1894, been established at the church of Montmartre. A wish expressed by the Divine Saviour long before to Blessed Margaret Mary Alacoque was fulfilled on 14 March, 1863. On this day the "Guard of Honour of the Most Sacred Heart of Jesus" was founded in the monastery of the Visitation at Bourg-en-Bresse, France. The name expresses the object of this sodality, which is to collect faithful hearts around the Saviour for constant adoration and love and to make reparation to him for the ingratitude of men. In 1864 the association at Bourg-en-Bresse was confirmed as a confraternity, and in 1878 was made an archconfraternity for France and Belgium. In 1879 the confraternity was established at Rome in the Church of Sts. Vincent and Anastasius, and defined as an archconfraternity for Italy and all countries which have no archconfraternity of their own. In 1883 the confraternity of Brooklyn, New York, conducted by the Sisters of the Visitation, was confirmed by Leo XIII as an archconfraternity, with the right of aggregation for the United States. For the "Apostleship of Prayer" see THE CATHOLIC ENCYCLOPEDIA, vol. I, 633; Hilgers, "Das Goldene Büchlein", Ratisbon, 1911. In 1903 Leo XIII established at the Church of St. Joachim at Rome a special "Archconfraternity of the Eucharistic Heart of Jesus", granting it the right to unite sodalities bearing the same name as itself. The confraternity is intended to offer in a special manner adoration, gratitude, and love to the Heart of Jesus for the institution of the Holy Eucharist. Mention should also be made of the "Archconfraternity of the Holy Agony of Our Lord Jesus Christ", conducted by the Lazarist Fathers in Paris, which was established in 1862 in the Diocese of Lyons and was defined in 1865 as an archconfraternity for this diocese. In 1873 the confraternity at Paris was declared an archconfraternity for all France, and in 1894 it received the right of aggregation for the whole world. The "Archconfraternity of the Holy Hour" is also connected with a wish expressed by the Saviour and a revelation of Himself given in 1673. At that time the Saviour demanded of Blessed Margaret Mary Alacoque an hour of union with Himself in prayer at midnight on Thursdays in memory of His Agony on the Mount of Olives. In 1829 this sodality was founded at Paray-le-Monial, and finally in 1911 it received the right of aggregation for the entire world (Acta Apost. Sed., III, 157). The members can observe the holy hour of prayer from Thursday afternoon onwards. A similar society was founded at Toulouse in 1885 and canonically erected in 1907, under the title of "The Holy Perpetual Hour of Gethsemani". In 1909 it received indulgences from Pius X (Acta. Ap. Sed., I, 483), and in 1912 new indulgences with the right of aggregation for the whole of France.

(6) The confraternities mentioned above are also in part sodalities of the Passion, particularly those which especially venerate Christ's Agony. Besides these should be mentioned particularly "The Archconfraternity of the Most Precious Blood". This society was founded on 8 Dec., 1808, in the Church of S. Nicola in Carcere at Rome by the saintly Francesco Albertini, who died in 1819 as Bishop of Terracina. The members pledge themselves to a special veneration of Christ's Passion, and in particular to offer the Precious Blood to the Heavenly Father for the expiation of sins, for the conversion of sinners, for the needs of the Church, and for the consolation of the poor souls. In 1809 the confraternity was canonically erected; in 1815 it was richly endowed with indulgences, and in the same year was raised to an archconfraternity. Applications for membership can be made to the director of the archconfraternity at S. Nicola in Carcere, or to the Missioners of the Precious Blood, 1 Via Poli Crociferi, Rome, for since 1851 the general of these missioners has had all necessary powers. Blessed Caspar of Buffalo, founder of the mission houses of the Precious Blood, did much to promote this confraternity. He was beatified in 1894. A rescript of 3 Aug., 1895, of the Congregation of Indulgences granted in perpetuity that the bishops of the United States of North America and Canada *pro suo arbitrio et prudentia* might erect the Confraternity of the Precious Blood in all parish churches without regard to their location, that these then could unite with the society at Rome, the "Unio Prima-Primaria", in the church of the Missioners of the Precious Blood, and could share in its indulgences and privileges (cf. "Amerikan Pastoralblatt", 1897,104). See PRECIOUS BLOOD, ARCHCONFRATERNITY OF THE MOST.

Religious associations have also been formed to encourage the practice of the Holy Way of the Cross, especially the "Pious Association of the Perpetual Way of the Cross", and the "Association of the Living Way of the Cross". Both societies are under the care of the Franciscans (cf. Mocchegiani, "Collectio Indulg.", no. 1264, sqq.). In 1884 the "Archconfraternity of the Holy Face" was formed at Tours as a work of expiation. It was provided with indulgences and in 1885 was erected into an archconfraternity for the whole world. The insignia of the brotherhood is the Face of the Suffering Saviour on the veil of St. Veronica. The members wear this picture on a scapular, a cross, or a medal. Lastly, there was founded in 1904 at the congress in honour of the Blessed Virgin at Rome the "Pious Union of the Crucifix of Pardon". This association has for its object the reconciliation with God of nations, families, and individuals. The headquarters of the association are in the Church of the Annunciation at Lyons. The badge of the members is a specially-consecrated crucifix (cf. Beringer, op. cit., Appendice by Hilgers, Paris, 1911).

(7) The Confraternities of the Mother of God, which have been confirmed for the entire Church, exist in such large numbers that all cannot be given here. Especially numerous are the sodalities and associations erected in honour of the Blessed Virgin in individual cities, dioceses, districts, or countries. The most important, most widely extended, and best-known of the confraternities of the Blessed Virgin are: (a) the "Confraternity of the Holy Rosary" (q. v.); in the article concerning it the "Perpetual Rosary" and the "Living Rosary" are also mentioned; (b) the "Confraternity of the Scapular of Our Lady of Mount Carmel" (see SCAPULAR); (c)

the Sodalities of the Blessed Virgin Mary (see below).

In addition, mention has already been made of: the "Confraternity of the Black Scapular of the Seven Dolours of Our Lady" (see SCAPULAR); the "Archconfraternity of the Immaculate Conception of the Blessed Virgin Mary", which is now combined with the Blue Scapular (see SCAPULAR); the "Pious Union of Our Lady of Good Counsel and the Scapular of Our Lady of Good Counsel" (see OUR LADY OF GOOD COUNSEL, FEAST OF; SCAPULAR); the "Archconfraternity of Our Lady of the German Campo Santo at Rome" (see PURGATORIAL SOCIETIES); the "Archconfraternity for the relief of the Souls in Purgatory, established under the title of the Assumption of the Blessed Virgin, in the Church of Santa Maria in Monterone, at Rome" (see PURGATORIAL SOCIETIES).

Furthermore, mention should be made of the "Archconfraternity of Our Lady of the Sacred Heart." This society was established in 1864 at Issoudun, France, by the Missioners of the Sacred Heart of Jesus. Since 1872 its headquarters as an archconfraternity have been at Rome, and in 1897 they were transferred to the newly-built Church of Our Lady of the Heart of Jesus, in the Piazza Navona. Only this confraternity at Rome has the right to incorporate in itself confraternities of the same title erected in any part of the world and to share with these its indulgences. The object of the confraternity is the veneration of the Blessed Virgin in her intimate relation to the Heart of Jesus. The "Confraternity of the Immaculate Conception of the Blessed Virgin Mary", established at Lourdes in 1872, in 1873 was raised to an archconfraternity, and in 1878 was made an archconfraternity for the entire world by Leo XIII. The head of the archconfraternity is the Bishop of Tarbes.

The "Association of the Children of Mary", under the protection of the Immaculate Virgin and St. Agnes, was established for girls alone. It was canonically erected in 1864, in the Church of S. Agnese fuori le mura, Rome; in 1866 it received its indulgences and privileges with the right of aggregation for all similar societies. Since 1870 this power of aggregation has belonged to the abbot-general of the Reformed Augustinian Canons of the Lateran, near San Pietro in Vincoli, Rome. The intention of the society is to keep Christian young women under the standard of the Blessed Virgin, and to promote the loyal fulfilment by its members of their duties. (See CHILDREN OF MARY; CHILDREN OF MARY OF THE SACRED HEART.) For the "Archconfraternity of Our Lady of Compassion for the Return of England to the Catholic Faith", see UNIONS OF PRAYER. The miraculous picture of Our Lady of Perpetual Succour, venerated at Rome in the Church of St. Alphonsus, is known everywhere. In 1871 a confraternity was erected in this church, and in 1876 was made an archconfraternity under the title of the "Archconfraternity of Our Lady of Perpetual Succour and of St. Alphonsus Liguori". The general of the Redemptorists has the power to incorporate everywhere confraternities of the same name in the archconfraternity and to grant these the same indulgences. There are also various confraternities of the Cord, whose members wear a cord as insignia just as members of other confraternities wear a scapular. The oldest and most celebrated of these Confraternities of the Cord is probably the "Archconfraternity of the Black Leathern Belt of St. Monica, St. Augustine and St. Nicholas of Tolentino", also called the "Archconfraternity of Our Lady of Consolation". This society has particularly extensive indulgences (cf. "Rescr. authent. S. Congr. Indulg.", II, no. 40, and especially the lately-issued summary of indulgences in the "Acta S. Sedis", XXXV, 630). The headquarters of the society are at Rome, in the Church of St. Augustine where the body of St. Monica lies.

(8) There are also numerous confraternities in honour of angels and saints which are dedicated to the patron saints of individual districts, countries, cities, and localities; these are consequently more local in their character, e. g. the "Boniface Association" in Germany and Austria (see BONIFACE ASSOCIATION). However, there are also such for the whole world, e. g. the "Confraternity of St. Benedict" (see SCAPULAR), the "Archconfraternity of the Girdle of St. Francis of Assisi", and the "Pious Union in honour of St. Anthony of Padua", as also the "Young Men's Sodality of St. Anthony of Padua", which, through a Brief (10 March, 1911) of Pius X (Act. Apost. Sedis, III, 128 sq.), was granted indulgences and recommended to the faithful [cf. Acta Ord. Fratr. Min., XXX (1911) 177 sqq.]. Only a few more of these confraternities can be noticed here. In 1860 the "Confraternity of St. Michael" was founded at Vienna to implore the protection of the archangel for the pope and the Church, and to collect gifts as Peterspence for the oppressed pope. There is another "Confraternity of St. Michael", with a scapular (see SCAPULAR). In 1860 the "Confraternity in honour of St. Joseph" was established at Rome in the Church of St. Roch. In 1872 it received indulgences and was raised to an archconfraternity with the right of incorporation for the whole world. The members also wear a consecrated cord in honour of St. Joseph. Special indulgences are connected with the wearing of this cord. There is also another Archconfraternity of the Cord of St. Joseph, which was erected in 1860 at Verona and to which Pius IX granted indulgences. There are besides many confraternities of St. Joseph for individual countries. Several were founded especially for France (cf. Beringer, op. cit.). In 1892 an "Archconfraternity of St. Joseph" was erected in the Church of St. Joseph, West de Père, Wisconsin, U. S. A., that is already widely spread over America. Connected with it is a children's league under the patronage of St. Joseph [cf. Seeberger, "Key to the Spiritual Treasures" (2nd ed., 1897), 20 sqq.]. In 1866 the "Confraternity of St. Peter's Chains" was canonically erected at Rome in the Basilica of San Pietro in Vincoli. In 1866 and 1867 the confraternity was granted indulgences and at the same time received as an archconfraternity the right of aggregation for the entire world. The purpose of the society is to promote loyalty to the pope, and to pray and work for the real freedom of the papacy, by the veneration of the Holy Chains of St. Peter. The "Militia Angelica", or the "Confraternity of the Cord of St. Thomas Aquinas", has been in existence a long time. It possesses indulgences granted it in 1586 by Sixtus V. Its purpose is the protection of purity by the intercession and aid of the Angelic Doctor who, according to tradition, was girt in his youth with a cord by angels after an heroic and successful struggle for purity. The father-general of the Dominicans has charge of the administration and erection of the "Militia Angelica". The members receive a consecrated cord which they wear constantly.

B.—In this second class, which contains those confraternities that have been established to promote the work of zeal for souls and Christian charity, there are a number of societies that are named after an angel or saint, and thus could also be included in the previous class. On the other hand a number of confraternities, such as the "Confraternity of St. Michael" and the "Confraternity of St. Peter's Chains", and even all confraternities of expiation that have already been described in the first class, could also quite properly be included here in the second class. Besides these, special mention should be made of the following:—

(1) All confraternities or sodalities for the relief of the poor souls (see PURGATORIAL SOCIETIES). (2) The "Bona Mors Confraternity", i. e. the Confraternity of the Agony of Christ. The object of this con-

gregation is the preparation of the faithful for a holy death. It was established in 1648 by the Jesuit general Caraffa in the Church of the Gesù, under the title of "The Congregation of the Bona Mors in honour of Jesus Dying on the Cross and His Sorrowing Mother". The contemplation of the Passion is one of the chief means of attaining the object of the sodality. In 1729 this congregation was raised to the rank of an archcongregation, with power to erect similar sodalities everywhere in Jesuit churches and to share its indulgences with these. In 1821 this privilege was reconfirmed, and in 1827 the general of the Jesuits received authority for the erection and aggregation of such sodalities in other churches also. In order to share in the indulgences of the Roman chief congregation, these sodalities must be incorporated with this congregation by the general of the Jesuits. Pius X increased the indulgences and privileges of the congregation, and confirmed anew its entire summary of indulgences on 20 March, 1911. The "Archiconfrérie du Cœur agonisant de Jésus et du Cœur compatissant de Marie pour le salut des mourants" (Archconfraternity of the Agonizing Heart of Jesus and the Compassionate Heart of Mary for the help of the Dying), erected in 1864 at the place which was the scene of the Agony in the Garden, has the same object as the above-mentioned confraternity. In 1867 it was raised to an archconfraternity and received the right to incorporate other societies with itself throughout the world. Since this date it has grown and spread steadily. In 1897, 1901, and 1907 it received new indulgences.

(3) The "Archconfraternity of the Most Holy and Immaculate Heart of Mary for the Conversion of Sinners" founded in 1836 by the parish priest of the Church of Our Lady of Victories, Paris. In 1838 it was raised to an archconfraternity with the right of aggregation throughout the world. The confraternity includes many millions of members, and has had remarkable success in the conversion of sinners. The special veneration of the Immaculate Heart of Mary, which is the first aim of the confraternity, is also the chief means of attaining the second aim, the conversion of sinners. In this class may be included the Confraternity of Our Lady of Compassion already noticed, which has as its aim the return of England and all English-speaking peoples to the Catholic Church. For the "Pious Union of Prayer to Our Lady of Compassion for the Conversion of Heretics" and the "Archconfraternity of Prayers and Good Works for the Reunion of the Eastern Schismatics with the Church, under the patronage of Our Lady of the Assumption, founded at the Church of the Anastasis at Constantinople", see UNIONS OF PRAYER.

(4) The "Pious Work of St. Francis of Sales for the Defence and Preservation of the Faith", established first at Nemours and then in 1857 at Paris. The association soon spread through other countries and other peoples, and especially in America. It aids the clergy in all possible ways in home missions. It was praised, blessed, and granted indulgences by Pius IX and Leo XIII. The society has already spent more than thirty million francs for its noble aims. The "Association of St. Francis Xavier", founded at Brussels, Belgium, in 1854, for the training of lay apostles to aid the priests in home missions. The members at first were only men and youths, but women can also enter it and give apostolic aid by their prayers, especially for the conversion of sinners. In 1855 and 1856 the association received indulgences and was made an archconfraternity for Belgium, and in 1878 was raised to the same for the entire world. It is now widespread and exerts an apostolic influence in the spirit of its great patron. Applications for membership are made to the director of the archconfraternity at Brussels (Collège Saint-Michel). (5) The "Society of St. Francis Regis for the Revalidation of Pagan Marriages", founded at Paris in 1826. It has laboured with great success in many cities, provinces, and countries for the increase of peace, morality, and sanctity in family life. At Paris the society settles nine hundred and more of such matrimonial cases annually; at the Paris Exhibition of 1900 it received a gold medal.

(6) The "Confraternity of Christian Doctrine, or Association of Jesus, Mary, and Joseph for the promotion of Instruction in the principal truths of the Faith". This is a long-established society, having been founded in the sixteenth century by the Fathers of Christian Doctrine (the Doctrinaires). In 1607 it was erected by Paul V into an archconfraternity for the entire world, with its seat at St. Peter's, and granted large indulgences. Its duty is to give religious instruction to the children of the Church, and to encourage the reception of the sacraments. Since 1610 this confraternity can be erected in all parish churches. In 1686 Innocent XI in an Encyclical urgently exhorted all bishops to establish this society as far as possible. Pius X in an Encyclical in 1905 directed that the confraternity should be established everywhere in the parish churches. To obtain the indulgences for all the confraternities of a diocese it suffices if a single canonically erected confraternity of this diocese unites with the Roman archconfraternity that is now established in the Church of Santa Maria del Pianto. New societies of Christian doctrines were formed in the second half of the nineteenth century and were granted indulgences. In particular such associations were founded after the year 1851 by the Ladies of the Perpetual Adoration of Brussels, who established there the Confraternity of the Adoration mentioned above. In these societies of Christian doctrine ladies, students, and men have taught many thousands of boys and girls, and, in particular, have prepared many for First Communion. In 1894 the "Pious Union of Christian Doctrine" of Brussels was made an archconfraternity for Belgium and in 1900 for Holland also. (7) The Society of St. Teresa, which was founded at Salamanca in 1882, as a general society of prayer, and is already widespread in Spain, Germany, and Austria. (8) The "General Association of St. Cecilia for the Promotion of Religious Music", established in 1887 in Germany for the encouragement of Catholic Church music. It flourishes chiefly in the dioceses of Germany, Austria, Switzerland, and Italy. (9) Temperance societies, for encouraging abstinence from alcoholic drinks, are treated elsewhere (see LEAGUE OF THE CROSS; TEMPERANCE; TEMPERANCE MOVEMENTS). In Germany the confraternity that has existed since 1851, in the parish of Deutsch-Pickar belonging to the Diocese of Breslau, was raised to an archconfraternity in 1901 under the name of the "Purification of Mary", and given a general right of aggregation. (10) The St. Vincent de Paul Societies; these are fully described under VINCENT DE PAUL, SAINT. See also ELIZABETH ASSOCIATIONS. (11) The confraternities founded for the aid and defence of the pope and the Church have been noticed above. Another society having the same purpose is the "Leo Association", founded at St. Louis, U. S. A. It was approved by Leo XIII and in 1891 was granted indulgences.

(12) Finally, some account should be given here of the many missionary societies, and especially of: (a) "The Society for the Propagation of the Faith", also called the "Missionary Society of Lyons", or the "Society of St. Francis Xavier". Twelve laymen, led by a priest, formed the plan of establishing a society for all the nations of the earth, and for the benefit of all the missions in the world. The society was formed at Lyons 3 May, 1822. Mademoiselle Jaricot may be called the real founder, because she organized the system of contributions. The society was formally confirmed in 1840 by Gregory XVI; each

succeeding pope has distinguished it by praise and renewed approval. Finally in 1904 Pius X made St. Francis Xavier its patron, and raised the feast of the saint to a greater double for the entire Church. The society has received many indulgences and privileges. It is directed by two general councils composed of ecclesiastics and laymen, the one council having its seat at Lyons (12 Rue Sala), the other at Paris (20 Rue Cassette). These directorates and their presidents settle together the apportionment of the funds to the various missions. In the dioceses there are diocesan or administrative councils, and in the parishes or cities directors who are at the head of each 10, 100, or 1000 members, in order to collect and remit the contributions of the respective divisions. The conditions for reception and membership are very simple, the main ones being the daily repetition of an Our Father and a Hail Mary with the addition "St. Francis Xavier, pray for us", and a monthly contribution of at least five cents paid to the director. More than 300,000 copies of the bi-monthly issued by the society are published in twelve languages. It gives regularly the most interesting and edifying news from the missions of the entire world. The annual income of the society is more than $1,200,000; in 1890 for the first time it was over $1,400,000. In 1904 the income was $1,352,017, of which sum more than half was collected in France. These figures give clear evidence of the beneficial labours of the society. (b) The "Association of the Holy Childhood", in connexion with the Guardian Angel societies. This society was established in 1843 at Paris by the Bishop of Nancy, Charles de Forbin-Janson. Its aim is to teach Christian children from earliest childhood to exercise Christian charity for the temporal and eternal salvation of poor heathen children and for the joy thereby given to the Divine Child Jesus. In 1858 the society was canonically erected by Pius IX; he, as well as Leo XIII and Pius X, praised the great services of the society and recommended it to all the faithful. In order to be a member of the society a monthly contribution of one cent for the heathen children must be paid and a Hail Mary must be said daily, with the addition "Holy Virgin Mary, pray for us, and the poor little pagan children". The constitution and organization of the society is very simple and practical. The society is widely spread over the Catholic world, and has accomplished a great work. The first year (1843) the income of the society was $4,580; the annual amount now is about $712,500. In 1900 and 1901 the income was nearly $950,000, of which amount Germany alone gave nearly one-third. In 1904 the society aided 223 missions, with 1112 orphanages, 7207 schools, 2805 industrial schools; altogether 11,134 institutions. There were 401,059 heathen children baptized, and 359,053 children were taught and cared for. In Germany since 1895 it has become customary to unite the Societies of the Holy Childhood with the Societies of the Guardian Angel, for the benefit of poor Catholic children in the mission districts of Germany. The members pay about one cent more monthly, and collect money at their own First Communion in order that the many poor children in the missions may also have the blessing of the First Communion and receive good religious instruction. About $19,000 were collected in this way in 1896, and in 1904 more than $23,750. The seat of the central committee of the Association of the Holy Childhood is at 146, Rue de Bac, Paris; there are managing committees for the different countries, each diocese having its own diocesan committee, with which the parish committees are connected. (c) The "Missionary Union of Catholic Women and Girls". This sodality was first founded in 1893 for the African missions; then in 1902 it was reorganized for the support of all missions. It has changed its headquarters from Fulda to Coblenz, in the Diocese of Trier. In 1910 it received a new summary of indulgences from Pius X, containing large indulgences and privileges especially for priests who conduct or promote the society. The whole body of sodalities of different countries, as those of Austria, Switzerland, and Rumania, have united with the main society, and this action is contemplated for the United States also. (d) In 1894, at Salzburg, Austria, the "St. Peter Claver Sodality" was founded by Countess M. Theresia Ledóchowska to aid the African missions and to foster the pious work of freeing slaves. Leo XIII favoured the organization by granting indulgences and privileges the very same year. The sodality includes: (1) the members of a female religious institute who devote themselves totally as helpers of the work of the African missions. These lead a community life in civilized countries and have their headquarters at Rome (via dell' Olmate 16); (2) laymen and women, who devote themselves, as far as their state in life permits, to the work of the sodality, especially by managing the succursals; (3) common helpers of either sex, who foster the work by contributions and other means. From the outset the work of the sodality was carried on with great zeal and has borne much fruit.

C.—The third class includes those sodalities which have for their chief aim the promotion of the prosperity of certain classes of society.

(1) There are sodalities for the benefit of the Christian family. In 1861 Father Francoz, S.J., founded such a society at Lyons. As the labours of this society proved very beneficial Leo XIII in 1892 enlarged it, with some changes, to embrace the whole world. The pope personally confirmed the new statutes, and granted new indulgences and privileges. The title of the sodality is: "The General Pious Association of Christian Families in Honour of the Holy Family of Nazareth". Another similar sodality, which existed before the founding of this one, and still exists, is the "Archconfraternity of the Holy Family of Jesus, Mary, and Joseph" (see HOLY FAMILY, ARCHCONFRATERNITY OF THE).

(2) The "Archconfraternity of Christian Mothers, under the patronage of Our Lady of the Seven Dolours, established at Notre-Dame de Sion, Paris", having for its object the development of truly Christian mothers, who will bring up their children according to the will of God and under the direction of the Church. A sodality of this kind was first formed at Lille in 1850; in 1856 this was raised to an archconfraternity. This society has now unlimited power of aggregation, and has its seat at Paris in the chapel of the Sisters of Our Lady of Sion (Notre-Dame des Champs). The Sodality of Christian Mothers, founded in 1863 at Rome in the Church of St. Augustine, has also a general power of aggregation. In 1865 this sodality was raised to the rank of a *societas primaria* Similar associations have appeared in Germany also since 1860, especially one in 1868 at Ratisbon. In 1871 this society was raised to an archconfraternity, and since 1883 it has had the right in all places where German is the most commonly-spoken language to incorporate with itself confraternities having the same name. The title of the sodality is: "The Society of Christian Mothers under the Patronage and Intercession of the Sorrowing Virgin Mary". Since 1878 there has been a confraternity of Christian mothers for the United States at Pittsburg, Pennsylvania. In 1881 it was made an archconfraternity for the whole of North America. Its headquarters are at the Church of St. Augustine at Pittsburg. A monthly periodical is published at New York, under the title "The Christian Mother".

(3) To bring the great blessing of the True Faith to poor heathen children, "The Association of the Holy Childhood" was established for Catholic children, and has richly blessed both (see above). A Confra-

ternity of the Child Jesus was also established at Bethlehem somewhat later than 1905 by the Christian Brothers. In 1908 the society received its indulgences and in 1909 Pius X made it an archconfraternity with the right of aggregation for the whole world. Since 1910 not only children but also their parents, and in general all who are interested in the training of children, can become members. The noble aim of the sodality is to implore the Divine Child to protect and bless all children, especially those in schools where religion is not taught. Applications for membership are made to the director of the Archconfraternity of the Child Jesus, Bethlehem, Palestine ("Acta Ap. Sed.", I, 757 sq.; Hilgers, "Appendice" in Beringer, op. cit.). In 1889 the Capuchin Father Cyprian founded at Ehrenbreitstein the "Seraphic Charity" for endangered youth. Its object is the rescue of religiously and morally endangered children, and their protection also in later years after the periods of school and apprenticeship are over. The members pay two and one-half cents monthly. In twenty-two years more than 10,000 poor children have been aided, and seven new institutions have been founded, at a total expenditure of $1,118,000. In Germany the society has 350,000 members; it is also established in Austria, Switzerland, Italy, and the United States, and has a total membership of over 500,000. The money is collected by 12,000 patrons and patronesses, who aid in the housing and supervision of the children. The society received its indulgences in 1902 from Leo XIII, who blessed and recommended it (cf. "Analecta Ord. Min. Cap.", 1902, 171).

(4) There are a number of sodalities very beneficial in their results for the sanctification and perfection of priests. Not only have Congregations of the Blessed Virgin Mary been formed especially for priests, but there are also other special associations of priests. Mention has already been made in the article PURGATORIAL SOCIETIES of the "Priests' Association under the Protection of St. Benedict for the Relief of the Poor Souls in Purgatory". See also PRIESTS' EUCHARISTIC LEAGUE; PRIESTS' COMMUNION LEAGUE. For the "Pious Union of St. Paul the Apostle", see PRIESTS, CONFRATERNITIES OF. See also APOSTOLIC UNION OF SECULAR PRIESTS. For "Associatio perseverantiæ sacerdotalis" see PRIESTS, CONFRATERNITIES OF, III. There are also the "Associatio sacerdotalis reparationis" and the "League for Sacerdotal Holiness", for priests who strive after higher perfection. Cf. "Acta S. Sedis", XLI, 170 sqq.; "Acta Apost. Sedis", I, 739; II, 474 sqq.; also the pamphlet "Ligue de Sainteté sacerdotale", 4th ed., 1909; and Hilgers, "Appendice" in Beringer, "Les Indulgences", 72 sqq. After the death of the founder of the league, P. Feyerstein, P. Reimsbach (28 rue Werby, Bar-le-Duc, France) became its director. Communications may be addressed to the sub-director of the League, Abbé Lachambre (101 rue du Pont à la Faulx, Peruwelz, Hainaut, Belgium). Those desiring further knowledge as to the origin and history of such confraternities of priests are referred to the article PURGATORIAL SOCIETIES, and for the history of the "Fraternitas Romana" in particular to Armellini, "Le chiese di Roma" (2nd ed., Rome, 1891), 20 sqq. (5) The "Pious Association of Mass-servers and Sacristans, under the protection of St. John Berchmans of the Society of Jesus", an association for acolytes and sacristans. This society was confirmed in 1865 by Pius IX, and, with the permission of the bishop, can be introduced anywhere without further formalities. Pius X also granted indulgences to the society (cf. "Acta S. Sed.", I, 689 sq., 699 sqq.). (6) The Catholic Journeymen's Societies, established by Adolph Kolping, the father of these associations, are well known (see GESELLENVEREINE). (7) The "Society of St. Raphael", for the protection of emigrants, established in 1871, originally for German emigrants.

In 1883 the "American Raphael Society" was founded; other countries also have their special associations of this name, as Austria, Belgium, and Italy. Since its establishment the society has proved a great blessing to many thousands of poor emigrants (see EMIGRANT AID SOCIETIES). (8) Book societies have been founded, especially in Austria and Germany, for the spread of good books (cf. Beringer, op. cit.). Concerning the "Society of St. Charles Borromeo", see BORROMEO, THE SOCIETY OF ST. CHARLES. Various other church societies of similar nature have been founded, especially in France, as societies for the sick, for labourers and mechanics, for young working-women, for country people, and even for travellers (Beringer, op. cit.).

(9) The "Confraternity of the Worthy First Communion and of Perseverance", established at Prouille, France, in 1891. In 1893 the Dominicans took charge of its direction. In 1896 the society was confirmed by Leo XIII; in 1910 Pius X transferred its headquarters to Rome, where the general of the Dominicans is entrusted with the entire guidance of this association. The object of this confraternity is to obtain for children the grace of a good First Communion and further perseverance in goodness. It can be established anywhere, and all, without exception, who desire to work for the aims of the confraternity can become members of the same and share in the indulgences and privileges. Applications for the establishment of such confraternities or for the personal right to take members into the society should be made to the general of the Dominicans at Rome (Collegio Angelico, 15 Via San Vitale). A similar confraternity was erected at Rome in the Church of San Claudio, and by Brief of Pius X (4 Jan., 1912) was raised to the Unio Primaria with the right of aggregation for the whole world (Act. Apost. Sed., IV, 49 sq.). Little requires to be said as to the value and advantages of the sodalities. Their aims are undoubtedly the highest; the means used to attain these aims are the noblest. Consequently the results are always the best, and often astonish both friends and foes; therefore the most competent judges, the popes and the saints, have repeatedly recommended these associations to Catholics. The history of the sodalities and the results of their labours, as publicly exhibited and known to all the world, loudly proclaim the usefulness of these associations for all eras. As new times bring new demands, fresh and noble branches full of strength and renewed vitality grow on the fruitful tree of the associational life of the Catholic Church. Without exaggeration it may be said that ordinarily the most zealous and active Catholics are brought together in the sodalities in order to pursue the noblest aims. It is true that the influence of the sodalities, especially of the first group, cannot be estimated by measure and weight. However, the Christian and Catholic who knows why man is upon earth, knows also that a single act of love of God is of inestimable value. He knows also what a power there is in united prayer, what miracles it can work. As proof need only be mentioned the "Apostleship of Prayer" and the "Messengers of the Heart of Jesus". Moreover, these societies of piety and prayer labour ordinarily in the most unselfish, self-sacrificing manner, and are filled with a most noble-minded zeal for souls. This is shown by the innumerable hosts of poor souls who owe their release from Purgatory to the Confraternities for Poor Souls, and by the hundreds of thousands of poor sinners who owe their eternal salvation to the sodalities. The salvation of innumerable souls of poor heathens is attributable to the single Society of St. Francis Xavier and the single Association of the Holy Childhood. The society mentioned above for the Propagation of the Faith alone has collected since its foundation $90,000,000 for heathen missions. (Beringer, op. cit.; Seeberger, "Key to the

Spiritual Treasures"; Migne, "Dictionnaire des Confrèries".)

III.—The Sodality of the Blessed Virgin Mary was founded in 1563 at Rome in the Roman College of the Society of Jesus. The actual founder was John Leunis (Lat. *Leonius* or *Leonis*), b. at Liège, Belgium; received into the Society of Jesus by St. Ignatius on 13 Jan., 1556; and died at Turin, 19 Nov., 1584, the year in which his Roman Sodality was erected into an archsodality by the Bull, "Omnipotentis Dei", of Gregory XIII. Leunis distinguished himself in the last years of his life by heroic charity towards the sick. In the afternoon, when school was over, and especially on Sundays and feast days, Leunis gathered together, while teacher of grammar at the Roman College, the most zealous of his pupils for prayer and pious exercises, especially for devotions in honour of the Blessed Virgin. Pupils of other classes soon joined the company and in this way a foundation was laid for a school of devotion and virtue, the Marian Sodalities. As in the following year the members numbered already seventy, the first rules were drawn up. The sodality was placed under the special protection of the Blessed Virgin, and the object was declared to be personal perfection in virtue and study, as well as works of charity and zeal for souls. The members generally met on Sundays and feast days, and the meetings were conducted by a Jesuit Father, who delivered an address. The council was chosen from the members, and aided the director in the administration by counsel and other help.

In 1569 a division of the sodality in the Roman College became necessary on account of the large number of members. The older pupils, those over eighteen years of age, formed a sodality for themselves, while the younger were formed into another. Soon there were three sodalities in the Roman College. The meetings of the sodality composed of the older pupils were held regularly in the college church, which bore the title of the Annunciation. From this church the sodality received the title of Primary Sodality (*Prima-Primaria*) of the Annunciation. This title was given in the Bull, "Omnipotentis Dei", of 5 Dec., 1584, issued by Gregory XIII. At the same time the pope gave the general of the order in this Bull the power to receive as members of the the Primary Sodality (*Prima-Primaria*) not only pupils of the college, but also other persons, and also the power to erect similar sodalities in the colleges and churches of the society, which were to be connected with the Primary Sodality and to share in its indulgences and privileges. Before this sodalities had also been formed in France, Germany, the Netherlands, Spain, and elsewhere. These societies did much good among students and the laity, were a protection against the new erroneous teaching, and strengthened loyal Catholics in their faith.

The permission to erect more than one sodality in each college was granted by Sixtus V and powers for Jesuit residences were added by Clement VIII and Gregory XV. The latter, moreover, declared explicitly that the sodalities of the Blessed Virgin were not to be placed under the control of the regulations for confraternities contained in the Bull of Clement VIII, "Quæcunque". Lastly, Benedict XIV confirmed all earlier indulgences and privileges, and added to these in the Golden Bull (27 Sept., 1748), which is, in a certain sense, the crowning glory of the sodalities. "It is almost incredible", says Benedict XIV, "what results have sprung from this pious and praiseworthy institution for the faithful of all classes". Finally, by a Brief of 8 Sept., 1751, he granted the Jesuit general authority to unite with the Roman main sodality other sodalities of either sex that had been canonically erected in the Jesuit churches. These sodalities were to share in all the indulgences and privileges of the *Prima-Primaria*. After the suppression of the Jesuits in 1773 the sodalities were kept in existence by the solicitude of the pope and the efforts of zealous priests. The Society of Jesus was re-established in 1814, and Leo XII restored to the Jesuit general his old rights and privileges as regards the Sodalities of the Blessed Virgin by a Brief of 17 May, 1824. In addition, by a Rescript of March, 1825, addressed to the Jesuit general, the same pope granted the right to unite all sodalities to the Roman archsodality, even if they existed outside of Jesuit houses, and to share with these subsidiary sodalities all its indulgences and privileges. Leo XIII further granted to the general of the Jesuits the authority even to erect canonically such sodalities everywhere, with the permission or consent of the diocesan bishops. He also declared all sodalities of every kind independent and exempted from the regulations of the Constitution, "Quæcunque", of Clement VIII.

Leo XIII also granted other favours to the sodalities of the Blessed Virgin, which he called "excellent schools of Christian piety and the surest protection of youthful innocence". Finally, Pius X not only gave the sodalities the highest praise, but also granted them new privileges and indulgences, and confirmed the new summary of indulgences on 21 July, 1910. On 8 Dec. of the same year the general of the Society of Jesus approved new general rules for the sodalities under Jesuit direction. These rules were intended to serve as a model for all other Sodalities of the Blessed Virgin; they give the clearest statement as to the nature and purpose, organization and working of all such bodies. These sodalities aim at making genuine Christians of their members by a profound devotion to, and childlike love of, the Blessed Virgin; the members are not merely to strive to perfect themselves, but are also, as far as their social position permits, to seek the salvation and perfection of others and to defend the Church of Jesus Christ against the attacks of godless men (cf. tit. I, reg. 1). The entire tendency of the sodalities and the councils (which are selected from the sodality), the regular meetings and lectures, the careful control and supervision of all members, in addition to all the various exercises and works prescribed or advised, and the constant close personal intercourse of the members with the director, serve to make the members noble, moral human beings, who, with the aid of the Blessed Virgin, lead others to Christ. In general the spirit and occupation of the members is not to be a vaguely enthusiastic piety and asceticism, but a sober, genuinely Catholic devotion and a joyous, zealous effectiveness for good in the sphere in which each member moves. Consequently, in separate sections the members should have all possible opportunity to develop all the capabilities of mind and heart, in order to attain as completely as possible the high aim of the society (cf. Reg., 12–14). The history of the sodalities of the Blessed Virgin gives clear proof of their great and beneficial influence in all epochs of their existence. These beneficial results have been recognized by both State and Church. The enemies of Christianity and of the Church have also shown their recognition of these results by their particular hatred and persecution of sodalities.

The sodalities developed rapidly even at the very beginning. After thirteen years of existence they included 30,000 members. Wherever the Society of Jesus went to establish colleges or missions, a sodality of the Blessed Virgin was soon erected in that place. In all the larger cities of Europe where the Jesuits established themselves firmly, they founded not merely one, but as many as seven or even twenty different sodalities. During the period that the sodalities were connected with the houses and churches of the Jesuits the membership rose to many hundred thousands. The number increased when, from 1751, married women and girls were admitted. After the restoration of the Society of Jesus the sodalities grew enormously. In the fifty years after the declaration of the dogma of the Immaculate Conception nearly 35,000 new sodalities were united with the Roman main sodality. In the year 1910, 1132 new sodalities were established, of which 178 were in North America. At various times and in various countries emperors, kings, and princes have been zealous members of sodalities, and have encouraged the growth of these bodies. In the seventeenth century alone eighty cardinals and seven popes came from them. In all Catholic countries the Sodalities of the Blessed Virgin include among their most faithful members, the greatest and noblest men of every position in life, generals and scholars of the highest rank. St. Stanislaus Kostka, St. John Berchmans, St. Francis de Sales, St. Fidelis of Sigmaringen, St. Leonard of Port Maurice, St. Peter Fourier, St. John Baptist de Rossi, the Venerable Jean Eudes, and many other saints, blesseds, and venerables, were proud to belong to the sodalities of the Blessed Virgin. For six years St. Francis de Sales worked, during his student life, in the sodality of the College of Clermont at Paris as member, assistant, and prefect. Others, like St. Alphonsus Liguori and St. Charles Borromeo, praised and recommended the Sodalities of the Blessed Virgin as nurseries for youth and for growth in perfection. Above all it has always been the teachers and shepherds of the entire Catholic Church, the popes, who have, in their words and actions, highly honoured these sodalities, and who have earnestly recommended them to all the faithful, e. g. Gregory XIII, Sixtus V, Gregory XV, Benedict XIV, Leo XIII, Pius X.

Undoubtedly a well-conducted Sodality of the Blessed Virgin is in itself the best method of spiritual development for the members and also the best aid to the priest in his anxiety for the well-being of his entire flock. In addition these sodalities are the most universally extended of all pious associations and confraternities, for they can be and are erected separately for each sex, for every age, and every station in life, so that they include in themselves the advantages of all unions for different positions in life. Moreover, as has been already clearly shown, they seek to attain as fully as possible in their members the twofold object which all other confraternities, in a certain sense, only strive for partially, namely, to attain to true love of God by the exercises of the Divine service, prayer and reception of Holy Communion, and to attain to true charity by exercising the most universal possible zeal for souls.

BERINGER, *Die Ablässe;* Fr. tr. (Paderborn, 1911); IDEM, *De Congregationibus Marianis Documenta et Leges* (Vienna, 1909); MULLAN, *The Sodality of Our Lady Studied in the Documents* (New York, 1912); DELPLACE, *Histoire des Congrégations de la Sainte Vierge* (Bruges, 1884); LÖFFLER, *Die marianischen Congregationen* (3rd ed., Freiburg); *Stimmen aus Maria-Laach,* LXXVIII, 457 sqq.

JOSEPH HILGERS.

Sodoma (GIOVANNI ANTONIO BAZZI, or DE'BAZZI, often miscalled RAZZI, more usually known by his nickname, SODOMA), Piedmontese and Florentine painter, b. at Vercelli in Piedmont, 1477; d. at Siena, 1549. His father, Giacono da Bazzi, was a shoemaker who had settled in Vercelli. The son was in 1490 apprenticed for seven years to a glass-painter from Casale, named Spanzotti, and with him the young Sodoma went to Milan, where he came under the influence of Leonardo da Vinci, although it is exceedingly doubtful whether he ever entered his studio. He executed his first important decorative work in 1503 for a small Olivetan convent near Pienza, and, two years after, he passed on to the mother-convent of the same order, known as Monte Oliveto Maggiore, to continue the work commenced by Signorelli. There he not only painted twenty-five large frescoes, but many other smaller ones; these constitute his most notable and perhaps his greatest works. Two years later he was at Rome, one of a number of artists employed by Julius II to decorate the Vatican. He then went to Siena, and, returning to Rome, executed important commissions for Agostino Chigi in the Villa Farnisena. Having completed that work he returned to Siena, where he spent a considerable time, painting some wonderful pictures, including his "Christ Bound to the Column". We do not know where he was between 1518 and 1525, but in the latter year he was at work at fresco decoration, painting a world-renowned panel, now in the Uffizi Gallery at Florence, with its almost unapproachable figure of San Sebastian; and various smaller pictures. In 1526 he was back at Siena, painting his famous frescoes in the Chapel of St. Catherine and St. Domenico, following them by other fresco works in the Palazzo Pubblico, and then by his decorations in the Chapel of San Spirito. It was these latter works which obtained honours for him from the Emperor Charles V, who created him a count palatine. He then wandered to Volterra, Pisa, Lucca, and various other places, leaving behind him traces of fine artistic work, and finally returned to Siena in his old age. He was an erratic and extraordinary man. Vasari gives various malicious reports about him, many of which are palpably untrue, and others probably exaggerated. There is little doubt, however, that his moral character was not above reproach, and at the very least coarse and lascivious. He drew perfectly, and with great ease, his colouring is delightful, sumptuous, and at times sensuous; he was greatly influenced by Leonardo, and to a certain extent by Raphael, and there is a remarkable charm and poetic feeling running through all his works, while at times the beauty of the faces of his women and children is almost irresistible. His works are scattered all over Italy, perhaps the greatest being those which are at or near Siena, the painting already alluded to in Florence, and examples of his work at Milan, Munich, London, and Rome. Every possible scrap of information respecting him has been gathered together in a memoir issued in 1906 by R. H. H. Cust. This is the standard book on Sodoma, and contains the very latest information concerning him. It is more important than his original statements, to form a proper judgment concerning the artist, because it contains all that Vasari states, together with many important documents and new pieces of information, dealing with the life of the painter, and refuting many of the statements which have been made concerning him. He must be regarded as an extraordinary genius,

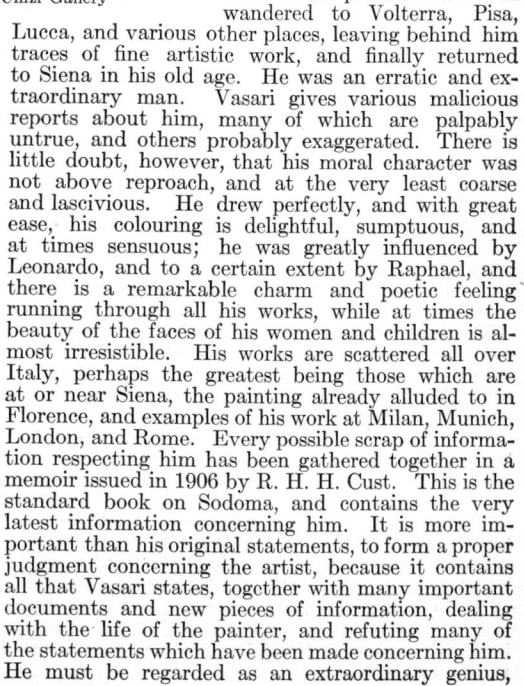

GIOVANNI ANTONIO BAZZI, CALLED SODOMA
Self-portrait, Uffizi Gallery

because at times he reached the very highest of his ideals, and then at times completely failed. He must also be regarded as a man against whom many writers have thrown mud, and who now can be safely considered as a far greater man than his contemporaries regarded him, and not so evil in disposition as many were prepared to believe him to be.

BORGHESI AND BAUCIN, *Nuovi Documenti dell' Arte Senese* (Siena, 1898); BRUZZA, *Primi Studi del Sodoma* (Turin, 1862); DELLA VALLE, *Lettere Sanesi* (Rome, 1786); MILANESI, *Documenti dell' Arte Senese* (Siena, 1856); ORLANDI, *Abecedario Pittorica* (Bologna, 1704); VASARI, *Le Vite de' Pittori* (Milan, 1811); CUST, *The Art of Bazzi* (London, 1906).

GEORGE CHARLES WILLIAMSON.

Sodom and Gomorrha.—Sodom, a city of Pentapolis (Wisd., x, 6; Gen., xiv, 2): Sodom, Gomorrha, Adama, Seboim, and Bala—later called Segor (Gen., xix, 22). They were situated in "the country about the Jordan" (Gen., xiii, 10); their exact location is unknown (cf. Gen., xiv, 3, 8, 10, 17; xix, 20–22, 30, 37; Deut., xxxiv, 3). Josephus identifies Segor with "Zoara of Arabia" at the south end of the Dead Sea ("Bel. Jud.", IV, viii, 4; cf. "Ant. Jud.", I, xi, 4; XIII, xv, 4; XIV, i, 4). Conder identifies it with Tell esh-Shaghûr, seven miles north of the Dead Sea; Burkhard, Wetstein, and others with Chirbet es-Safieh, three miles south of the Dead Sea; E. Robinson puts it on Lisan, etc. For the unnatural sins of their inhabitants Sodom, Gomorrha, Adama, and Seboin were destroyed by "brimstone and fire from the Lord out of heaven" (Gen., xiii, 13; xviii, 20; xix, 24, 29; Osee, xi, 8). Since then, their names are synonymous with impenitent sin, and their fall with a proverbial manifestation of God's just wrath (Deut., xxix, 23; xxxii, 32; Is., i, 10 sqq.; Ezech., xvi, 49; Matt., xi, 23 sq.; II Peter, ii, 6; Jude, 7). The Septuagint rendering of ויהפך by κατέστρεψε (Gen., xix, 25) probably led to the erroneous opinion that the destruction of Sodom was accompanied by great upheavals of the earth, and even to the formation of the Dead Sea (see DEAD SEA).

HUMMELAUER, *Comment. in Gen.* (Paris, 1895), 376, 416 sq.; BUHL, *Geog. des Alt. Pal.* (Leipzig, 1896), 271–74; ROBINSON, *Bibl. Researches in Palestine*, II (Boston, 1847), 480 sqq.; *Palestine Explor. Fund* (1879), 15, 99, 144 (1881), 277 (1884), 126 (1886), 19–22; BLANCHENHORN in *Zeitschr. des deutsch. Pal. Vereins* (1896); CONDER, *Handbook to the Bible* (London, 1873), 38; IDEM, *Heth and Moab* (London, 1880), 154 sq.

NICHOLAS REAGAN.

Sodor and Man, ANCIENT DIOCESE OF (SODORENSIS).—The early history of this see is extremely obscure. The Scandinavian diocese, which included Man and the western isles of Scotland (the Southern Hebrides), was called *Sodor* (*Suðr-eyjar*) in contradistinction to *Nordr* (*Norðr-eyjar*)—the Orkneys and Shetland. It is not known when Man was united with Sodor, but it may have been in the time of Magnus Barefoot (1098). Before that Man seems to have been a distinct see dependent on Dublin. When Man became the head of a separate kingdom, under the suzerainty of Norway, the joint Diocese of Sodor and Man was placed under the Archiepiscopate of Nidaros (Trondhjem) in Norway by Eugenius III (1152), an arrangement which was confirmed by Anastasius IV (1154). From then till 1458 Man remained under Drontheim, when Calixtus III transferred it to York.

The political connexion of Man with Norway had been severed in 1266, after which it depended on Scotland till 1334 and finally on England. In the reign of Henry IV the king gave the island to the Stanleys, who thus acquired the patronage of the bishoprics, but the bishops never attained the status of spiritual lords of Parliament. The last Catholic bishop was Thomas Stanley, who was appointed during the reign of Mary and was recognized as a bishop till his death in 1568. It is uncertain whether he accepted Elizabeth's changes or enjoyed immunity under the protection of the Stanleys. The cathedral, dedicated to St. Germain, was situated on St. Patrick's Isle and was built in 1245 on the site of an earlier building. It is now in a ruined state. There were only seventeen parishes in the island, all comprised in one archdeaconry. The arms of the see were: upon three ascents, the Virgin Mary standing with her arms extended between two pillars, on the dexter whereof a church, in base the ancient arms of Man.

Chronicon Manniæ, ed. MUNCH (Christiania, 1860); TRAIN, *Historical account of the Isle of Man* (2 vols., Douglas, 1845); CUMMING, *Isle of Man, Its history, physical, ecclesiastical, civil, and legendary* (London, 1848); MOORE, *Sodor and Man* (London, 1893).

EDWIN BURTON.

Sofia and Philippopolis, VICARIATE APOSTOLIC OF. See BULGARIA; SARDICA.

Soissons, DIOCESE OF (SUESSIONENSIS), includes, with the exception of two hamlets, the entire Department of Aisne. It was re-established by the Concordat of 1802 as suffragan of Paris, but in 1821 it became suffragan of Reims. It consists of (1) all the ancient Diocese of Soissons, except the civil district of Compiègne, which went to the Diocese of Beauvais; (2) all the Diocese of Laon, except two parishes, which went to Reims; (3) that portion of Vermandois which formerly belonged to the Diocese of Noyon (see BEAUVAIS); (4) a few parishes which formerly belonged to Cambrai, Meaux, Troyes, Reims.

WEST FRONT OF THE CATHEDRAL, SOISSONS

After a vain attempt made by the unexecuted Concordat of 1817 to re-establish the See of Laon, the bishops of Soissons were authorized by Leo XII (13 June, 1828) to join the title of Laon to that of their own see; by Leo XIII (11 June, 1901) they were further authorized to use the title of St-Quentin, which was formerly the residence of the bishops of Noyon. The territory of Soissons and Laon played an important political part under the Merovingians. After the death of Clovis (511), Soissons was the capital of one of the four kingdoms into which his states were divided. The kingdom of Soissons, which ceased to exist in 558, when Clotaire I reunited all the Frankish states, came into being again in 561 when the death of Clotaire led to the redivision of the territory. It finally disappeared in 613 when the Frankish lands were once more reunited under Clotaire II.

I. THE SEE OF SOISSONS.—Concerning the traditions that make St. Sixtus and St. Sinicius the earliest apostles of Soissons as envoys of St. Peter, see REIMS. Sts. Crepinus and Crepinianus martyrs (c. 288) are patrons of the diocese. According to Mgr Duchesne, the establishment of a see at Soissons dates from about 300. Among its bishops are: St. Divitianus (c. 310–20); St. Onesimus (c. 350–61); St. Edibius (c. 431–62); St. Principius (462–505), brother of St. Remi of Reims; St. Lupus (505–35); St. Baudarinus (Baudry) (535–45), whom Clotaire I exiled for seven years to England, where he served as gardener in a monastery; St. Ansericus or Anscher (623–52); St. Drausinus (657–76), founder of the monastery of

Notre Dame de Soissons and of the Abbey of Rethondes; St. Adolbertus (677–85); St. Gaudinus (685–707), assassinated by usurers; Rothadius (832–869), famous for his quarrel with Hincmar (q. v.); Riculfus (884–902), whose pastoral issued in 889 is one of the greatest extant treasures of the ecclesiastical literature of the period; St. Arnoul de Pamèle (1081–1082), elected through the efforts of Hugues de Die, legate from Gregory VII, and who was disturbed in the possession of his see by two bishops nominated successively by Philip I; Jocelyn de Vierzy (1126–52), who aided in the victory of Innocent II over the antipope Anacletus, and wrote an explanation of the Apostles' Creed and the Lord's Prayer; Hugues de Champfleury (1159–75), chancellor of Louis VII; Gui de Château Porcien (1245–50), who accompanied St. Louis on the Crusade and was killed in Palestine; Languet de Gergy (1715–30), who wrote the life of Mary Alacoque. In 1685 Louis XIV nominated the famous *littérateur* Huet Bishop of Soissons, but the strained relations existing then between France and Rome prevented him from receiving his Briefs, and he exchanged that see for Avranches in 1689.

II. The See of Laon.—The Diocese of Laon was evangelized at an uncertain date by St. Beatus; the see was founded in 497 by St. Remi who cut it off from Reims and made his nephew St. Genebaldus bishop. Among the bishops of Laon are: St. Chagnoaldus (c. 620–3), brother of St. Faro, Bishop of Meaux, and of St. Fara; Hincmar (857–76); Adalbero Ascelin (977–1030), driven from his see (981) by the Carlovingian Louis V who accused him of undue intimacy with Emma, widow of Lothaire, and who was afterwards very loyal to the interests of Hugh Capet, to whom he handed over the Carlovingian Charles of Lorraine and Arnoul, Archbishop of Reims. He was the author of a satirical poem addressed to King Robert; Gaudri (1106–12), who held out against the commune movement, and who was slain in a brawl at Laon; Barthélemy de Jura, de Vir, or de Viry (1113–51), who attracted St. Norbert to the diocese; Gautier de Mortagne (1155–74), author of six small theological treatises; Robert Le Cocq (1352–8), who in October, 1356, and March, 1357, after the imprisonment of John II by the English held an important position in the States General, took the side of Stephen Marcel, conspired with him and Charles the Bad, King of Navarre, against the dauphin, the future Charles V and then fled to Aragon, where he became Bishop of Calahorra; Pierre de Montaigut (1371–86), cardinal in 1383; the historian Jean Juvenel des Ursins (1444–9), afterwards Archbishop of Reims; Louis de Bourbon Vendôme (1510–52), cardinal in 1517; César d' Estrées (1653–81), cardinal in 1672, was elected to the French Academy, and in Rome was involved in the difficulties between Louis XIV and Innocent XI, Alexander VIII, and Innocent XII; Jean de Rochechouart de Faudoas (1741–77), cardinal in 1761. Louis Séguier, nominated by Henry IV, Bishop of Laon in 1598, refused the nomination to make room for his young nephew Peter de Bérulle, afterwards cardinal, and founder of the Oratorians; de Bérulle refused the see.

The Bishop of Soissons as senior suffragan of Reims had the privilege during a vacancy of the metropolitan see to replace the archbishop at the ceremony of anointing a King of France. The Bishop of Laon ranked as duke and peer from the twelfth century. As second ecclesiastical peer he had the privilege of holding the *ampulla* during the anointing of the king. The chapter of Laon was one of the most illustrious of the kingdom. From the twelfth century its members numbered eighty-four; it had to engage in bitter struggles with the communal regime; three popes, Urban IV, Nicholas III, and Clement VI, sixteen cardinals, and more than fifty archbishops and bishops belonged to it. Jacques Pantaléon who became pope as Urban IV was a choir boy, then canon of the cathedral of Laon. He arranged the *cartularium* of the church of Laon, and was commissioned by Gregory IX to settle the dispute between the chapter and Enguerrand de Coucy. As archdeacon of Laon he assisted, in 1245, at the Council of Lyons. Under the direction of St. Anselm of Laon (q. v.), appointed by Eugene III to restore theological studies in France, the school in connexion with the Laon cathedral drew young men from all parts of Europe.

The Abbey of St-Médard at Soissons, founded in 557 by Clotaire I to receive the body of St. Médard,

The Cathedral, Laon

was looked upon as the chief Benedictine Abbey in France; it held more than two hundred and twenty fiefs. Hilduin, abbot (822–30), in 826 obtained from Eugene II relics of St. Sebastian and St. Gregory the Great; he caused the relics of St. Godard and St. Remi to be transferred to the abbey; he rebuilt the church which was consecrated 27 Aug., 841, in the presence of Charles the Bald and seventy-two prelates. The king bore the body of St. Médard into the new basilica. The church was pulled down but rebuilt and reconsecrated in 1131 by Innocent II, who granted those visiting the church indulgences known as "St. Médard's pardons". In this abbey Louis the Pious was imprisoned in 833, and there he underwent a public penance. Among the abbots of St. Médard are: St. Arnoul, who in 1081 became Bishop of Soissons; St. Gerard (close of the eleventh century); Cardinal de Bernis, made commendatory abbot of St. Médard in 1756. The Benedictine Abbey of Notre Dame de Soissons was founded in 660 by Ebroin and his wife Leutrude. The Cistercian Abbey of Longpont, founded in 1131, counted among its monks the theologian Pierre Cantor (q. v.), who died in 1197, and Blessed John de Montmirail (1165–1217), who abandoned the court of Philippe-Auguste in order to become a monk. The abbey of St. Vincent at Laon was founded in 580 by Queen Brunehaut. Among its earlier monks were: St.

Gobain, who, through love of solitude, retired to a desert place near the Oise and was slain there; St. Chagnoaldus, afterwards Bishop of Laon, who wished to die in his monastery; St. Humbert, first abbot of Maroilles in Hainaut. The abbey adopted the Rule of St. Benedict. It was reformed in 961 by Blessed Malcaleine, a Scotchman, abbot of St. Michael at Thierache, and in 1643 by the Benedictines of St. Maur. Among the abbots of St. Vincent were: St. Gerard (close of the eleventh century), who wrote the history of St. Adelard, abbot of Corbie; Jean de Nouelles (d. 1396), who wrote a history of the world, and began the cartulary of his monastery. The Abbey of St. John at Laon was founded about 650 by St. Salaberga, who built seven churches there; she was its first abbess; St. Austruda (d. 688) succeeded her. In 1128 the abbey became a Benedictine monastery. The Abbey of Nogent sous Coucy was founded in 1076 by Albéric, lord of Coucy. Among its abbots were St. Geoffroy (end of eleventh century) and the historian Guibert de Nogent, who died in 1124 and whose autobiography "De Vita Sua" is one of the most interesting documents of the century. Under the title "Gesta Dei per Francos" he wrote an account of the First Crusade. The Abbey of Cuissy in the Diocese of Laon was founded in 1116 by Blessed Lucas de Roucy, dean of Laon, and followed the rule of Premonstratensians. In the Diocese of Soissons the Premonstratensians had the abbeys: Chartreuve, Valsery, St. Yved de Braine, Villers Cotterets, Val Secret, Vauchrétien, Lieurestauré. (See PREMONTRÉ, ABBEY OF.)

The portion of the ancient Diocese of Noyon within the jurisdiction of the present Diocese of Soissons includes the town, St-Quentin (Augusta Vermanduorum), where St-Quentin was martyred under Diocletian. It was the chief town of a diocese until 532, when St. Médard, the titular, removed the see to Noyon. Abbot Fulrade built the Church of St-Quentin in the eighth century, and Pope Stephen II blessed it (816). From the time of Charles Martel until 771, and again from 844 the abbots of St-Quentin were laymen and counts of Vermandois. During the Middle Ages a distinct type of religious architecture sprang up in the region of Soissons; Eugène Lefèvre Pontalis has recently brought out a work dealing with its artistic affiliations. After investigation Canon Bouxin concludes that the cathedral of Laon, as it exists, is not the one consecrated in 1114 and visited by Innocent II in 1132; that was the restored ancient Romanesque building; the present one was built 1150–1225. Louis d'Outremer (936), Robert the Pious (996), Philip I (1059) were anointed in Notre Dame de Laon; in the twelfth century Hermann, Abbot of St. Martin's of Tournai, wrote a volume on the miracles of Notre Dame of Laon. The Hôtel-Dieu of Laon, once known as Hôtellerie Notre Dame, was founded in 1019 by the Laon chapter. The Hôtel-Dieu of Château Thierry was founded in 1304 by Jeanne, wife of Philip the Fair.

Besides the saints already mentioned, the following are specially honoured as connected with the religious history of the diocese: St. Montanus, hermit, who foretold the birth of St. Remi (fifth century); St. Marculfus, Abbot of Nanteuil (sixth century) in the Diocese of Coutances, whose relics, transferred to Corbeny in the Diocese of Laon, were visited by the kings of France who, after their anointing at Reims, were wont to go to the tomb of St. Marculfus to cure the king's evil (see REIMS, ARCHDIOCESE OF); St. Sigrada, mother of St. Leodagarius, exiled by Ebroïn to the monastery of Notre Dame at Soissons (seventh century); St. Hunegundis, a nun from the monastery of Homblières (d. c. 690); St. Grimonia, an Irishwoman martyred at La Chapelle (date uncertain); St. Boetianus (Bosan), husband of St. Salaberga, and St. Balduinus, martyr, his son (seventh century); St. Voël, or Vodoalus, hermit (d. c. 720). Among the natives of the diocese may be mentioned: Pierre Ramus (1515–72), Racine (1639–99), La Fontaine (1621–95), Dom Luc d'Achéry (1609–85), Charlevoix (1683–1761), Camille Desmoulins (1760–1794). The chief pilgrimages are: Notre Dame de Liesse, a shrine founded in the thirteenth century, and replaced at the end of the fourteenth century by the present church; Notre Dame de Paix at Fieulaine, which dates back to 1660. Before the application of the Congregations Law (1901), there were in the Diocese of Soissons Jesuits, Trinitarians, and several teaching congregations of brothers. Some congregations of women had their origin in the diocese: the Nursing and Teaching Sisters of the Child Jesus, with mother-house at Soissons, founded in 1714 by Madame Brulard de Genlis; the Sisters of Notre Dame de Bon Secours, a nursing and teaching order, founded in 1806, with mother-house at Charly; Sisters of Notre Dame, nursing and teaching order, with mother-house at St-Erme, founded in 1820 by the Abbé Chrétien; the Franciscan nuns of the Sacred Heart, a nursing order founded in 1867, with mother-house at St-Quentin; the servants of the Heart of Jesus, of whom there are two branches, the "Marys" who lead a contemplative life and the "Marthas" who nurse the sick; they were founded at Strasburg in 1867 and brought to St-Quentin after the war of 1870–1.

At the close of the nineteenth century the religious congregations in the diocese had charge of 40 nurseries, 2 deaf and dumb schools, 1 orphanage for boys, 14 for girls, 6 work bureaus, 1 home for the poor, 29 hospitals, 10 district nursing homes, 1 retreat house, and 1 lunatic asylum. In 1905, when the Concordat was broken, there were in the Diocese of Soissons: 535,583 inhabitants, 39 parishes, 538 auxiliary parishes, and 15 curacies recognized by the State.

Gallia Christiana, nova, IX (1751), 333–88, 506–693, 978–1036; *instrum.,* 95–146, 187–202, 359–94; FISQUET, *France Pontificale: Soissons et Laon* (Paris, 1866); PÉCHEUR, *Annales du diocèse de Soissons* (10 vols., Soissons, 1863–91); LEDOUBLE, *Etat relig. ancien et moderne des pays qui forment aujourd'hui le diocèse de Soissons* (Soissons, 1880); MARTIN AND LACROIX, *Histoire de Soissons* (2 vols., Soissons, 1837–8); MALLEVILLE, *Histoire de la ville de Laon et de ses institutions* (2 vols., Laon, 1846); BROCHE, *Les rapports des évêques avec la commune de Laon* in *Nouvelle revue historique de droit français et étranger,* XXV (1901); DEMARSY, *Armorial des évêques de Laon* (Paris, 1865); POQUET, *Notre Dame de Soissons, son hist., ses églises, ses tombeaux, ses abbesses, ses reliques* (2nd ed., Paris, 1855); LEFÈVRE PONTALIS, *L'architecture religieuse dans l'ancien diocèse de Soissons au XI*e *et au XII*e *siècle* (2 vols., Paris, 1894–7); BOUXIN, *La Cathédrale de Laon* (Laon, 1892); LECOCQ, *Hist. de la Ville de Saint-Quentin* (St-Quentin, 1875).

GEORGES GOYAU.

Solari (SOLARIO), a family of Milanese artists, closely connected with the cathedral and with the Certosa near Pavia. (1) GUINIFORTE SOLARI, b. 1429; d. 1481. He was the son of Giovanni (b. c. 1400; d. 1480), superintendent of the building of the cathedral and of the Certosa. Guiniforte was one of the architects of the Certosa (1465), was employed on the Ospedale Maggiore, and was also one of the architects of the fortified castle of the Sforza family and of several of the churches of Milan. His son PIETRO ANTONIO (d. 1493) worked also for a time on the cathedral; there is proof that in 1476 he was still there. Later he was called to Moscow where he was employed on the rebuilding of the Kremlin. (2) ANDREA SOLARI, painter, b. at Milan about 1465; d. 1515. From 1490 he was a pupil of Giovanni Bellini at Venice and his early works recall this painter, as for example a Madonna with Saints, painted in 1495 for the Church of San Pietro at Murano and now in the Brera at Milan. After his return to Milan he copied the style of Leonardo da Vinci so closely that he was considered the latter's best pupil. He is very like Leonardo, especially in the treatment of the heads, plastic modelling, and colouring. A beautiful Descent from the Cross, painted in 1503, is still in existence. About this date he also painted many portraits and in this way came into connexion with Cardinal Charles d'Amboise, for whom he painted a number of pictures during the years 1507–9 at Gaillon in Normandy. These works are now in galleries in England. During the second half of his working period he changed his style to a brighter tone and his works are easily recognized by the clear, luminous colours and the manner in which they flow into and blend with one another. The School of Leonardo, however, is always perceptible. Among other paintings belonging to this time is a Madonna with a Child lying on a cushion to whom she offers the breast; the figures are surrounded by a beautiful landscape. This picture is in the Louvre and the same gallery has another of his works, a Salome receiving from the executioner the head of John the Baptist, with the delicate face turned away from the object. The Poldi-Pezzoli Gallery of Milan contains a large number of his works; among these are: "Repose on the Flight to Egypt" (1515), one of the best pictures of Leonardo's school; "St. Catherine"; "St. Anthony"; "The Crowning with Thorns". His last and most important work is the "Assumption of the Blessed Virgin", at the Certosa near Pavia, which, however, he was not able to complete.

(3) Andrea's brother CRISTOFORO SOLARI, called IL GOBBO, sculptor and architect, b. at Milan before 1475; d. in 1527. In 1490 he went with Andrea to Venice where some sculptures executed by him are still in existence. In 1498 he returned to Milan and entered the service of Ludovico Sforza at whose order he executed his chief work, the tomb of Ludovico's wife. The figures of Beatrice d'Este and Ludovico upon the tomb belong in their massive severity, individuality of treatment, and technical excellencies to the best works of the early Renaissance in Lombardy. The monument was erected in the Church of Maria delle Grazie, but was unfortunately destroyed at a later era; in 1821 the two statues were taken to the Certosa near Pavia. Besides these, a number of statues in the cathedral of Milan are ascribed to him: four doctors of the Church, Adam and Eve, Sebastian, Christ bound to the pillar. They are marked by a less vigorous naturalism, the influence of a stay at Rome, whither he went after the overthrow of the Sforza family. From 1503 he was again in Milan, where he took charge of the construction of the cathedral. He also designed the great cupola of Santa Maria della Passione at Milan. (4) ANTONIO SOLARI, b. in 1382; d. 1445. He is called IL ZINGARO (the gypsy), a nickname probably given him either because his father was apparently a Bohemian blacksmith who had emigrated to Venice, or from the wandering life he himself led until he settled permanently in Naples. He is said to have worked at his father's trade until his love for the beautiful daughter of an artist led him to turn to art. As at Naples he was very soon able to win the favour of Queen Joanna, it was not long before he became the most important painter of the capital. He founded a school which produced a number of masters of moderate ability. His most important work, which is also the best production of Neapolitan painting at that period, is a series of twenty frescoes in the court of a monastery near San Severino which show traces of the influence of the schools of Venice and Ferrara. They represent the life of St. Benedict and contain a large number of lifelike figures in dignified and graceful positions. His "Carrying of the Cross" in the Church of San Domenico Maggiore and a "Madonna" in the museum at Naples show nobility of conception combined with a vigorous realism. (5) SANTINO SOLARI, architect and sculptor, b. at Como, Upper Italy; d. 1646. He is best known by his share in the construction of the cathedral at Salzburg; he ornamented the palace and the gardens of the Bishop of Salzburg with statues.

ALOE, *Le pitture dello Zingaro nel chiostro di S. Severino in Napoli, dinotanti i fatti dellai vita di S. Benedetto* (Naples, 1836); MOSCHIMI, *Memorie della vita di Antonio Solari, detto il Zingaro, pittori Veneziano* (Venice, 1828); FRIZZONI, *Il Sodoma, Guadenzio Ferari, Andrea Solari illustrati in tre opere in Milano recentemente recuperate* in *Arch. stor. arte*, IV (Rome, 1891); VENTURI, *Eine umbekammte marmorgruppe von Cristoforo Solari* in *Mitth. Inst. österr. gesch.*, V (Innsbruck, 1884), 295–302.

BEDA KLEINSCHMIDT.

Solemnity (from Lat. *solet* and *annus*), a yearly celebration, is used to denote the amount of intrinsic or extrinsic pomp with which a feast is celebrated. Intrinsic solemnity arises from the fact that the feast is *primarium* for the entire Church, or for a special place, because in it a saint was born, lived, or died; or because his relics are honoured there. Extrinsic solemnity is added by *feriatio*, by the number of sacred ministers, decoration of the church or adjoining streets, the ringing of bells, the number of candles, costly vestments, etc. In the "Roman Martyrology" Easter Sunday is announced as the "solemnity of solemnities"; the first Sunday of October, as the solemnity of the Rosary of the Most Blessed Virgin Mary. The term "solemnity" is also used in contracts, especially matrimony, in votive Masses, in vows, and in ecclesiastical trials.

FRANCIS MERSHMAN.

Solesmes, ABBEY OF, a Benedictine monastery in Department of Sarthe, near Sablé, France. It was founded in 1010 by Geoffrey, seigneur of Sablé, as a priory dependent on the Abbey of St-Pierre de la Couture at Le Mans. During the Hundred Years' War it was twice pillaged and once almost entirely destroyed by fire. Apart from these disasters its history was uneventful for several centuries. Towards the end of the fifteenth century the rebuilding of the church was commenced, Prior Philibert de la Croix changing it from basilica form to that of a Latin cross. His successor, Jean Bougler (1505–1556), completed the restoration of the church, added the tower, and rebuilt the cloisters, sacristy, and library. Under his direction two famous groups of statuary, known as the "Saints of Solesmes", were set up in the church. It is not known for certain who the sculptors were, but the groups were probably the work of several hands. They are placed in the two transeptal chapels and form one of the chief attractions of the place. One represents the entombment of Our Lord and the other various episodes of the Dolours of Our Lady. The groups contain eight and fifteen life-size figures respectively, besides various subsidiary figures, and are adorned with bas-reliefs and other sculptural ornamentation. Some of the faces, notably that of Mary Magdalen, are wonderfully expressive; that of Joseph of Arimathea is supposed to be a portrait of King René (d. 1480). In the sixteenth century these masterpieces were in danger of being destroyed by the Huguenots and other Iconoclasts, but the monks saved them by erecting barricades. Jean Bougler was the last Regular Prior of Solesmes, a succession of commendatory priors being appointed after his death. In 1664 the monastery was absorbed by the Congregation of St. Maur, and in 1722 it was, with the exception of the church, entirely rebuilt on a larger scale. In 1791 it was suppressed and the buildings passed into private hands, so remaining for forty years. In 1831 the property was put up for sale, and Dom Prosper Guéranger, then a young priest of twenty-seven, who had been born in the neighbourhood and had long lamented its state of desecration, was inspired to acquire it and restore it to God and the Church as a home of monastic life. He set about raising the necessary funds, bought the entire property, and, with five other like-minded zealous priests, took possession in 1833. Three years later, with the full approval of the Bishop of Le Mans, they commenced the Benedictine life. In 1837 Dom Guéranger was professed at Rome and a few months later Pope Gregory XVI raised Solesmes to the rank of an abbey, naming Dom Guéranger first abbot and formally erecting at the same time the new "Congregation of France" with Solesmes as the mother-house and its abbot as superior-general. In course of time daughter-houses have been founded from Solesmes, viz: Ligugé (1853), Silos in Spain (1880), Glanfeuil (1892), and Fontanelle (1893),—these four being old monasteries restored; also new foundations at Marseilles (1865), Farnborough in England and Wisque (1895), Paris (1893), and Kergonan (1897). Since its restoration Solesmes has been dissolved by the French Government no less than four times. In 1880, 1882, and 1883 the monks were ejected by force but, receiving hospitality in the neighbourhood, succeeded each time in re-entering their abbey. At the final expulsion in 1903 they were, like all the other religious of France, obliged to leave the country. Between the years 1890 and 1900 an entirely new and imposing monastery had been added to the existing buildings, which had become too small for the growing community. Hardly, however, had the monks got settled in it when they were driven forth. They then established themselves in the Isle of Wight, where, after a few years' sojourn in a rented house at Appuldurcombe, they have now nearly completed the building of a new abbey at Quarr, on what was formerly monastic property.

The community of Solesmes has achieved a worldwide reputation for its erudition and its devotion to monastic and liturgical studies, the foundation for which was laid by Dom Guéranger himself. Amongst those who have thus brought fame to the abbey may be mentioned Dom Pitra, afterwards cardinal and Librarian at the Vatican, Dom Pothier, Dom Cabrol, Dom Férotin, Dom Mocquereau, Dom Besse, Dom Quentin, and Dom Leclercq. But the greatest work, perhaps, done by the monks of Solesmes, and that for which they are best known, has been the restoration of the true Gregorian chant of the Church. Dom Guéranger set himself the task of resuscitating sound liturgical traditions in France at a time when such were at their lowest ebb. He revived the accent and rhythm of plainsong, which had been lost, and in restoring the true text of the chant he laid down the principle, which has since been always strictly adhered to, that when various manuscripts of different periods and places agreed on a version, there existed the most correct text. He entrusted the work to Dom Jansions and Dom Pothier, the latter producing his "Les Mélodies Grégoriennes" in 1880 and the "Liber Gradualis" in 1883. These, as well as many other publications, were all printed at the Solesmes Imprimerie, which for many years was an important appanage of the abbey. Unfortunately the entire plant was confiscated by the French government at the suppression and since then the Solesmes books have been printed by Desclée of Tournai. Dom Pothier followed the Reims-Cambrai edition as far as possible, so as to shelter himself under the authority it still possessed, though the still higher authority of Ratisbon proved an obstacle in his way. Through this desire to be conciliatory, and also the insufficiency of manuscripts, the absence of any competent check, and the want of practical preparatory trial, the earlier Solesmes editions were bound to be defective. But they served their purpose in the return to antiquity and have formed the basis for further research. Dom Pothier's pioneer labours have been followed by those of Dom Mocquereau, whose great work has been the personal training of the Solesmes *Schola*, which has indirectly influenced many others, and the publication of the "Paléographie Musicale". By means of photographic reproductions of scores of manuscripts from all the principal libraries of Europe, a far greater degree of exactness has been secured than was possible with mere transcripts which might contain copyists' errors. These reproductions have been brought together and studied at Solesmes and the variants of the different melodies classified according to their school or church of origin, date, etc. Intrinsic qualities also have been carefully considered in deciding on the most correct and universal version, but when these criteria have proved insufficient preference has been given to the Roman version, when there has happened to be one. This method of selection is described in detail, with examples, in the little brochure of Dom Cagin and Dom Mocquereau referred to in the bibliography. The labours of the Solesmes fathers received the highest possible recognition in 1904, when Pope Pius X (Motu Proprio, 25 April, 1904) entrusted "particularly to the monks of the French Congregation and to the monastery of Solesmes" the work of preparing an official Vatican edition of the Church's Chant, and appointed a Commission for the purpose with Dom Pothier as its president. The Gradual has already appeared and the Antiphonal is in preparation. (See GUÉRANGER, PROSPER LOUIS PASCAL.)

PITRA, *Spicilegium Solesmense* (Paris, 1852–8); GUÉRANGER, *Essai historique sur l'abbaye de Solesmes* (Le Mans, 1846); HOUTIN, *Dom Couturier* (Angers, 1899); DAVID, *Les grandes abbayes de l'occident* (Lille, 1907); CAGIN AND MOCQUEREAU, *Plainchant and Solesmes* (tr., London, 1904).

G. CYPRIAN ALSTON.

Soli, a titular see in Cyprus, suffragan of Salamis. Soli was an important port on the Clarius, on the southern side of the western portion of Cyprus. It was an Athenian colony founded by Demophon, son of Theseus, or, according to another tradition, by Phalerus and Acamas. At first called Œpea, it was transferred to a better site by Philocyprus, King of Œpea, on the suggestion of Solon, from whom it got its new name, becoming the capital of one of the nine kingdoms in the island. It possessed temples of Aphrodite and Isis. The rest of its history is unknown, though it is mentioned by many ancient geographers. Its ruins, called *Palæa Chora*, or old town, are near the village of Karavostasi, about two miles north-west of Lefka. Its first bishop was St. Auxibius, whose name occurs in the "Roman Martyrology" on 19 February; he is said to have been baptized by John Mark, the companion of St. Barnabus, and to have had for successors another Auxibius, his disciple, and his brother Themistagoras. The feasts of two other bishops of Soli, St. Marcellus and St. Eutychius, are celebrated in the Greek Church. Another, Peter, probably a legendary character, is mentioned in the calendar of the Abyssinian Church on 2 January. We find later: Evagrius, 431; Epiphanius, 451; Stratonicus, 680; Eustathius, 787; Leontius, 1222; Nibo, 1260; Neophytus, died in 1301; Leo, his successor; Theophanes, towards the close of the Venetian occupation. During this occupation Soli was the residence of the Bishop of Leucosia. We hear also of a Benjamin, Bishop of Soli in 1660, owing doubtless to a temporary restoration of the see by the Greeks.

SMITH, *Dict. of Greek and Roman Geog.* (London, 1870), s. v.; LE QUIEN, *Oriens christianus*, II (Paris, 1740), 1071; EUBEL, *Hierarchia catholica medii ævi*, I, 481; HACKETT, *A History of the Orthodox Church of Cyprus* (London, 1901), 240 sq., 323 sq.

S. PÉTRIDÈS.

Solicitation (Lat. *sollicitare*), technically in canon law the crime of making use of the Sacrament of Penance, directly or indirectly, for the purpose of drawing others into sins of lust. The Church legislation on this point is very severe, and numerous popes have denounced this crime vehemently and decreed punishments for its commission. The principal document on the subject is that of Gregory XV, "Universi Gregis" (30 Aug., 1622), confirmed by the

Constitution of Benedict XIV, "Sacramentum pœnitentiæ" (1 June, 1721). There are, in addition, a number of other pontifical Constitutions and Decrees of the Holy Office on the same subject, notably those of 27 Sept., 1724, 20 Feb., 1867, and 20 July, 1890. The crime of *sollicitatio ad turpia* is defined as the soliciting any person to carnal sin, to be committed with himself or another, by any priest secular or regular, immediately before, during, or immediately after sacramental confession, or on the occasion of or under pretext of confession, or in the confessional itself or in any other place generally used for hearing confessions, or in a place chosen by the penitent to make a confession, and this whether a sacramental confession be actually made or not. Moreover, the crime of solicitation may be committed not merely by words, but also by signs or other expressive actions, or by a letter to be read then or afterwards. If any penitent has been thus solicited to sin, he or she cannot be absolved by any confessor until the penitent actually denounces the delinquent priest to the proper ecclesiastical authority or promises to make such denunciation as soon as possible. Even though the wicked confessor has since amended his life, or though the crime of solicitation took place many years ago, the obligation of denouncing him still remains, because the law is made, not merely to procure amendment, but also to inflict punishment. If the penitent, without sufficient cause, does not make the denunciation within a month from the time he or she has learned the obligation to do so, excommunication is incurred *ipso facto*. When the negligence has been repaired, any approved priest may absolve from the excommunication. If the penitent has reasonable ground for fearing serious damage to self or family from a formal denunciation, some other method of informing on the delinquent priest may be sought for. The denunciation is to be made to the bishop of the place where the penitent lives. If the soliciting priest be of another diocese, the ordinary of the person solicited will forward the denunciation to the bishop of the accused confessor. The denunciation must be sworn to and be made personally and by word of mouth if possible. It may also be done, in special cases, by writing or by a third party. When the denunciation is made by letter, it must be signed with full name and address, and must be a circumstantial account of the alleged crime. Whether the penitent has consented to the solicitation or not need not be expressed. Bishops are directed to pay no attention whatever to anonymous letters of denunciation. On the receipt of the accusation, the ecclesiastical authority makes inquiry as to the reputation and reliability of the accuser. If the confessor be found guilty, he is subject to suspension from the exercise of his orders, privation of his benefices, dignities, and offices with perpetual inability to receive such again. Regulars, in addition, lose the right of voting or being voted for in the chapter of their religious order. Benedict XIV added perpetual exclusion from celebrating Mass. While the Church is thus severe on delinquent confessors, she is equally careful to protect innocent priests from calumnious charges. If any one falsely denounce a confessor on the charge of solicitation, the calumniator can obtain absolution for the perjured falsehood only from the pope himself, except at the point of death.

SLATER-MARTIN, *Manual of Moral Theology*, II (New York, 1908); FERRARIS, *Bibliotheca canonica*, II (Rome, 1891), s. v. *Confessarius*, art. v; *ibid.*, VII, s. v. *Sollicitatio*, where the pontifical documents are given in full. Consult also works on moral theology in general, e. g.: SABETTI-BARRETT, *Compendium theologiæ moralis* (New York, 1902); TAUNTON, *The Law of the Church* (London, 1906), s. v. *Solicitation*.

WILLIAM H. W. FANNING.

Solimôes Superiore.—A prefecture Apostolic in the State of Amazonas, Brazil, erected by a decree of the Sacred Congregation of Consistory, 23 May, 1910. The territory of this prefecture forms a part of the extensive Diocese of Manaos or of Amazonas, from which it was separated at the same time with the territory of Toffé, which last forms another prefecture Apostolic. Solimôes is situated between the left bank of the Amazon and the River Jacura, a tributary of the former; the territory is traversed by a great number of watercourses and natural canals. The region has as yet been little explored, and little has been done in the way of preaching the Gospel, as is the case with all the regions along the tributaries of the Amazon. In recent years the Holy See has devoted its attention to the problem of evangelizing these vast but sparsely populated regions. The mission of Solimôes is intrusted to the Capuchin Fathers. (See "Acta S. Sedis", Rome, 1 July, 1910.)

U. BENIGNI.

Solomon.—Our sources for the study of the life, reign, and character of Solomon are III Kings i–xii; and II Par. i–ix. Solomon (Heb. שְׁלֹמֹה "peaceful"), also called Jedidiah, i. e., "beloved of Yahweh", was the second son of David by his wife, Bathsheba, and the acknowledged favourite of his father. This may have been due partly to the fact that he, as a late offspring, considerably younger than David's other sons, was born in his father's old age, and partly to the intense love of David for Bathsheba and the beautiful qualities of Solomon himself. Solomon was not the logical heir to the throne, but David conferred it upon him instead of his other brothers, and in doing so he committed no wrong according to Israelitish ideas. Solomon was eighteen years old when he ascended the throne, or at least no older than this, and his successful reign of forty years speaks well for his intelligence, ability, and statesmanship. His reign offers a striking contrast to that of his father. It was almost entirely devoid of incident, and was marked by none of the vicissitudes of fortune which were so notable a feature in the career of David. Enjoying for the most part peaceful relations with foreign powers, and set free from the troubles that menaced him at home, Solomon was enabled to devote himself fully to the internal organization of his kingdom and the embellishment of his Court. In particular he gave much attention to the defence of the country (including the construction of fortresses), the administration of justice, the development of trade, and the erection of a national temple to the Almighty.

The territory over which sovereignty is claimed for Solomon by the historian of III Kings extended from the Euphrates to the River of Egypt (*el Arish*), or, to name the cities at the limits of his realms, from Tiphsah (Thapsacus) to Gaza (III Kings, iv, 24). The account of his reign shows that even his father's dominions were not retained by him unimpaired. But if some of the outlying portions of David's empire, such as Damascus and Edom, were lost by Solomon, the integrity of the actual soil of Israel was secured alike by the erection of fortresses in strong positions (including Hazor, Megiddo, one or both of the Beth-horons, and Baalath) and by the maintenance of a large force of war-chariots. Of the cities selected for fortification Hazor guarded the northern frontier, Megiddo protected the plain of Esdrælon, whilst the Beth-horons, with Baalath, commanded the Valley of Aijalon, thus defending the capital against an attack from the maritime plain. Additional security in this direction was obtained by the acquisition of Gezer. This city had hitherto been left in the hand of the Canaanites, and came into Solomon's power by a marriage alliance with Egypt. Under David, Israel had become a factor to be reckoned with in Eastern politics, and the Pharaoh found it prudent to secure its friendship. The Pharaoh was probably Psieukhannit (Psebkhan) II, the last king of the 21st dynasty, who had his capital at Zoan (Tanis), and ruled over the Delta. Solomon wedded his daughter; and the Egyptian sovereign, having attacked and burnt Gezer and destroyed the Canaanite inhabitants, bestowed it as a dowry upon the princess. It was now rebuilt and made a fortified city of Solomon. In Jerusalem itself additional defences were constructed, and the capital was further adorned by the erection of the temple and the royal palaces described below. In view of the trade route to the Red Sea, which the possession of the ports of Edom gave to Israel, Tamar (perhaps Hazezon Tamar) was likewise fortified. Cities had also to be built for the reception and support of the force of chariots and cavalry which the king maintained, and which he seems to have been the first to introduce into the armies of Israel. This force is stated to have consisted of 1400 chariots and 12,000 horsemen (III Kings, x, 26). The numbers of the foot-soldiery are not given, perhaps because, being a militia and not a standing army, it was only mustered when there was occasion for its services; but the levies available were, probably, not inferior to those which the nation could raise at the close of David's reign.

Solomon's foreign policy was one of international friendship and peace. His relation with the Pharaoh of Egypt has already been alluded to, and the same may be said of his relation with his other great neighbour, Hiram, King of Tyre, and lord of the Phœnician Riviera which lies between Lebanon and the sea. To him belonged the famous cedar forests, and the no less famous artisans of Gabal were his subjects. Solomon formed with him a commercial treaty, surrendering certain towns on the northern frontier (III Kings, ix, 11) in exchange for floats of timber conveyed to Joppa and skilled workmen lent him for wood-carving, stone-fashioning, and bronze-casting. What Solomon gained by the alliance was knowledge of the Phœnician manner of trading. As ruler of Edom he had possession of the port of Eloth, at the head of the Gulf of Akaba. Here he built ships and sent his own servants, under Phœnician masters, to trade with Arabia. The profits went into the king's coffers. As Arabia was a gold-producing country, we need not suppose that South Africa was reached by these fleets. Whether the commerce of India reached him by this route is not certain. The list of products imported has sometimes been interpreted in this sense. But one or two obscure words in a comparatively late text can hardly establish the conclusion. The money value of the importations, four hundred and twenty talents in a single voyage, must be viewed with suspicion.

Solomon's internal policy was one of justice and concentration of power and authority. In the administration of justice David's policy and reign of remissness and incoherence was improved upon by Solomon's stern administration and equanimity. He also took steps to make the royal authority stronger, more efficient, and more far-reaching, chiefly, as far as our records go, with a view to the collection of revenue and the maintenance of an army, which latter, apparently, he did not know how to use. We have a longer list of ministers. David's government included a commander-in-chief, a captain of the mercenary guard, a superintendent of forced labour, a recorder, a scribe and priests, and a "king's friend". In addition to these, Solomon had a superintendent of prefects and a master of the household. A more striking innovation was the division of the country into twelve districts, each under a royal representative or prefect, charged with the duty of provisioning the Court month by month. This division largely ignored the ancient tribes, and seems to show that the tribal system was passing away. Like most powerful rulers, Solomon signalized his reign by numerous splendid buildings, and for this purpose made extensive use of the corvee or forced labour. This again led to increased exertion of authority by the central government; and, incidentally, the complete subjugation of the Canaanites was shown by the fact that they had to bear the main portion of this burden. According to our present biblical data, Solomon went beyond any ancient monarch in the luxury of the harem. The enormous number of wives (700) and concubines (300) attributed to him must be made up by counting all the female slaves of the palace among the concubines. Even then the figures must be grossly exaggerated. Klostermann has wisely remarked that the two items are not in the right proportion, and he is inclined, and we think with good reason, to suspect that 70 wives and 300 concubines was the original statement of the sacred narrator.

The building operations of Solomon were on a large scale and of a remarkable magnitude and splendour. Besides the erection of a magnificent temple he succeeded in emulating the great kings of Western Asia and Egypt by building for himself in the city of Jerusalem, palaces, houses, and gardens. (See TEMPLE OF JERUSALEM.) In the erection of these, thirteen years were spent as well as a large sum of money, while thousands of labourers and craftsmen were employed. The royal residence embraced several distinct structures: (1) The house of the forest of Lebanon (so named from the quantity of cedar-wood used in it), which measured 100x50x30 cubits, and rested upon three rows (so Sept.) of pillars (each row being composed of fifteen columns) in addition to the external walls; (2) the porch of pillars, 50x30 cubits; (3) the porch of the throne (to which the last-mentioned may have served as an ante-chamber), forming a judgment hall where the king's throne of ivory and gold (III Kings, x, 18–20) was placed when he dispensed justice; (4) the king's private palace, surrounded by a court; (5) the palace of Pharaoh's daughter, probably included within the court just named. All these were built of costly hewn stone, the wood employed being cedar. Of Solomon's closing years nothing further is recorded. His reign is stated to have lasted forty years; but it is probable that this is merely a round number employed to indicate a considerable period (perhaps a full generation) and the actual duration of his rule is unknown. The year of his death may be approximately fixed between 938 and 916 B. C., a date arrived at from a consideration of the number of years assigned by the Bible to his successors, corrected by the chronology of certain Assyrian inscriptions.

In the view of the Hebrew historian, Solomon was unsurpassed for sagacity and knowledge. On his accession to the throne, it is related that Jehovah appeared to him at Gibeon in a dream, and bade him choose a boon; and the young king, instead of asking for long life or riches or success in war, prayed to be endowed with an understanding heart that he might judge the people committed to him. His request was granted; and riches and honour were added thereto, with a promise of length of days if he kept Jehovah's commandments. In consequence of this endowment, he was reputed to be wiser than all men; people flocked from all quarters to hear his wisdom; and the Queen of Sheba, in particular, came to prove him with hard questions. He was at once a philospher and a poet. He spake 3000 proverbs; his songs were 1005; and his utterances embraced references alike to the vegetable and the animal kingdoms. So great, indeed, was his reputation for practical insight that in later times the bulk of the Hebrew Gnomic literature was ascribed to him. In the light of after-events, it is impossible fully to endorse the historian's estimate of his sagacity, or even to clear his memory from imputations of criminal folly. To his oppressive exactions, in furtherance of his schemes of luxury and magnificence, was due the discontent which in the reign of his son broke his kingdom in two, and ultimately led to the destruction in detail of the Hebrew nation by the power of Assyria and Babylon. It is clear likewise that, besides being fond of display, he was voluptuous and sensual, and that he was led by his wives and concubines to worship strange gods.

The fact that Solomon's reign was passed in tranquillity, except for the attempts of Edom and Damascus to regain their independence, testifies to the care he displayed for the defence of the realm. That he showed no ambition to undertake foreign conquests redounds to his credit; after the exhausting wars of David the nation needed repose. And if he spent his people's wealth lavishly, his commercial policy may have helped to produce that wealth, and perhaps even given to the Jewish people that impulse towards trade which has been for centuries so marked a trait in their character. Nor can the indirect effects of the commerce he fostered be overlooked, inasmuch as it brought the people into closer contact with the outside world and so enlarged their intellectual horizon. And in two other respects he profoundly influenced his nation's after-history, and thereby mankind in general. In the first place, whatever the burdens which the construction of the temple entailed upon the generation that saw it erected, it eventually became the chief glory of the Jewish race. To it, its ritual, and its associations, was largely due the stronger hold which, after the disruption, the religion of Jehovah had upon Judah as contrasted with Northern Israel; and when Judah ceased to be a nation, the reconstructed temple became in a still higher degree the guardian of the Hebrew faith and hope. And secondly, the Book of Proverbs, though parts are expressly ascribed to other authors than Solomon, and even those sections which are attributed to him may be complex of origin, is nevertheless the product of Solomon's spirit and example, and much that it contains may actually have proceeded from him. And as Proverbs served as a model for many works of a similar character in later times, some of which, as has been said, were popularly ascribed to him (Ecclesiastes, Wisdom), the debt which the world of literature indirectly owes to the Hebrew king is considerable. The works named do not exhaust the list of productions with which Solomon's name is connected. The Song of Songs is attributed to him; two of the Canonical psalms are entitled his; and a book of Psalms of quite late date also goes by his name.

Besides the *Histories of the Hebrews and of the Old Testament* by MILMAN (1866); STANLEY (1868); EWALD (1869); STADE (1884); KÖHLER (1884); KLOSTERMANN (1896); WELLHAUSEN (1897); KITTEL (1895); RENAN (1892); WADE (1910); etc., see: MACCURDY, *History, Prophecy and the Monuments* (3 vols., New York, 1894–1901), §§205 sqq.; BACON, *Solomon in tradition and in fact* in *New World*, June, 1898; WEIL, *The Bible, the Koran, and the Talmud* (London, 1846), 200–48; CONWAY, *Solomon and Solomonic Literature* (Chicago, 1899); CARDINAL MEIGNAN, *Solomon, son règne, ses écrits* (Paris, 1890); VIGOUROUX, *La Bible et les découvertes modernes*, III (Paris, 1896), 253–405; KENT, *Student's Old Testament*, II (New York, 1905), 14–16, 165–199; BEER, *Saul, David, Solomon* (Tübingen, 1906). See also the articles on Solomon in KITTO'S, SMITH'S, HASTINGS'S, CHEYNE'S, and VIGOUROUX'S dictionaries of the Bible.

GABRIEL OUSSANI.

Solomon, PSALMS OF, eighteen apocryphal psalms, extant in Greek, probably translated from a Hebrew, or an Aramaic original, commonly assigned to the first century B. C. They contain little of originality and are, for the most part, no more than *centos* drawn from the Psalms of David. In them Messianic hope is not bright; a gloom enshrouds that hope—the gloom caused by Pompey's siege of Jerusalem [see APOCRYPHA, I, (3)].

SOLOMON, ODES OF, forty-two lyric poems, an apocryphal work, recently discovered and published (1909) by J. Rendel Harris. *History.*—The existence of these apocryphal odes was known by various references. The pseudo-Athanasian Synopsis Sanctæ Scripturæ (sixth century) lists the "Antilegomena" and adds σὺν ἐκείνοις δὲ καὶ ταῦτα ἠρίμηνται . . . . . ψαλμοὶ καὶ ᾠδὴ Σολομῶντος. The "Stichometry" of Nicephorus, Patriarch of Constantinople (beginning of ninth century), in like manner includes among the "Antilegomena", "the Psalms and Odes of Solomon containing 2100 στίχοι". It may be that these odes are the new psalm-book written for Marcion and excluded from the Muratorian Canon (end of second century). The ψαλμοὶ ἰδιωτικοί, prohibited as non-canonical by the Council of Laodicea (c. A. D. 360), if taken as "psalms of personal experience", might readily be the "Odes of Solomon". Lactantius (Div. instit., IV, xii) writes: "Solomon ita dicit: Infirmatus est uterus Virginis et accepit fœtum et gravata est, et facta est in multa miseratione mater virgo". In the MSS. of Lactantius the gloss is added *in Ode undevigesimo*, or *in Psalmo undevigesimo*. Ode XIX, verse 6, of the Syriac translation (discovered by Harris) reads: "(The Spirit) opened the womb of the Virgin, and she conceived and brought forth, and the Virgin became a Mother with many mercies". Lactantius is clearly citing a Latin translation of the Odes of Solomon, done by the beginning of the fourth century A. D. The Sahidic "Pistis Sophia", a Gnostic work of the Copts of the latter part of the third century, uses the "Odes of Solomon" as canonical Scripture. Harris (p. 81) thinks he has found traces of the Odes in Saints Irenæus and Clement of Alexandria. These important apocryphal writings had been lost for centuries till they were discovered and published (1909) by J. Rendel Harris, after they had lain on his shelves two years in a heap of Syriac MSS. brought from the neighbourhood of the Tigris. The Syriac MS. of the odes is of paper probably three or four hundred years old, contains the "Psalms of Solomon", the odes (incomplete in the beginning and the end), coarsely written, pointed here and there in the Nestorian manner, and at times with the Jacobite vowels.

Original Text.— (a) The language of the odes may have been Hebrew or Aramaic. Our Syriac version is probably from a Greek text, which in turn was a translation of an original Hebrew or Aramaic text. This opinion is warranted by the continual grouping of the odes with the "Psalms of Solomon", the constant reference of them to Solomon as author, and the Semitic spirit which equally permeates both sets of lyrics. (b) The time of composition would seem to have been not later than the middle of the second century, nor earlier than the beginning thereof. The *terminus ad quem* is set by the fact that there is some doubt as to the canonicity of the odes. Such doubt is scarcely intelligible, especially in the third-century author of "Pistis Sophia", unless the odes were composed before the middle of the second century. The *terminus a quo* is set by the content of Ode XIX. The painlessness of the Virgin birth (verse 7), though a logical corollary to the dogma of the supernatural character of the Divine birth of Jesus, is an idea which we find no trace of even so late as the Johannine writings. Whereas the absence of a midwife from the Virgin birth (verse 8) is a detail which clearly parallels these odes with the apocryphal Gospels of the Infancy and prohibits us from assigning Ode XIX to a period earlier than the beginning of the second century. (c) The author is considered by Harris and Hausleiter (Theol. Litbl., XXXI, no. 12) to have been a gentile in a Palestine Judeo-Christian community. Harnack thinks that the *Grundschrift* is Jewish and all Christian sentiments are the superadded work of a Christian interpolator. Cheyne (Hibbert Journal, Oct., 1910) agrees with Harnack.

Importance.—This latest find of Mr. Harris is one of the most important contributions ever made to extant apocryphal Biblical literature. The importance has been greatly exaggerated by Harnack. With his usual keen sense of sources, the Berlin professor scents here a unique source of the Johannine tradition; in the "Odes of Solomon", he tells us, we have the very "quarry wherefrom the Johannine blocks have been hewn" (p. 111). We have already given two ideas of Ode XIX which are most decidedly post-Johannine; others still could be given. The points common to both odes and the Fourth Gospel are striking,—for instance, adopted sonship founded on love of Jesus,—"because I love Him, the Son, I shall be a son" (Ode III, 9). Odes IV and VI have much of Christian thought. An hypothesis, hitherto unsuggested, yet far likelier than Harnack's wild quarry-dream, is that the odes are a new link, long lost, of the Johannine tradition; that they draw their Christian sentiment from St. John's Gospel. The traditional view in regard to the Apostolic authority of the Gospel is strengthened by a new witness,—a Judeo-Christian genius, who perhaps works over some pre-existing and baser Jewish metal. Whoever the author is, he very likely tried to combine the ideas of the Sapiential Books with those of the Fourth Gospel.

HARRIS, *The Odes and Psalms of Solomon now first published from the Syriac version* (Cambridge, 1909); *Ein Jüdisch-christliches Psalmbuch aus dem ersten Jahrhundert*, tr. from the Syrian by FLEMMING, edited and published by HARNACK in *Texte und Untersuchungen*, XXXV (Leipzig, 1910), 4.

WALTER DRUM.

Solomon Islands, PREFECTURE APOSTOLIC OF THE NORTHERN, established on 23 May, 1898, by separation from the Vicariate Apostolic of New Pomerania (q. v.), includes the Islands of Ysabel, Choiseul, Bougainville, and all the islets under German protectorate (see SOLOMON ISLANDS, PREFECTURE APOSTOLIC OF THE SOUTHERN). In 1897 the islands were put under the jurisdiction of Mgr Broyer, Vicar Apostolic of Samoa, and in 1898 formed into a new prefecture under Mgr Joseph Forestier, who resides at Kieta, on Bougainville Island. In 1911 the mission contained: 3 churches; 3 stations; 10 Marist Fathers; 5 lay brothers; 7 Sisters of the Third Order of Mary; 2 Samoan catechists; 5 Catholic schools, with 140 pupils; 2 orphanages; and a few hundred Catholics. The Marist missionaries belong to the Province of Oceania, the superior of which resides at Sydney, New South Wales. Fever is very prevalent at the mission, and most of the fathers who went to the islands in 1898 have been carried off by disease.

PIOLET, *Les missions françaises*, IV (Paris, 1902), 343–68; *Australasian Catholic Directory* (Sydney, 1911), 165.

Solomon Islands, PREFECTURE APOSTOLIC OF THE SOUTHERN (INSULARUM SOLOMONIARUM).—The Solomon Islands are in the Pacific Ocean, lying between 154° 40′ and 162° 30′ East long., and 5° and 11° South lat. The Spanish navigator Alvaro Mendaña de Neyra discovered the Islands of Ysabel, Guadalcanar, and San Christoval in 1567. Impressed by the natural riches of the islands, he called that group after King Solomon. Mass was celebrated by the Franciscan chaplain of the expedition, but the soldiers and sailors were not in sufficient number to organize a permanent settlement. Mendaña and his expedition returned to Peru, 26 July, 1569. On 5 April, 1595, Mendaña, with three hundred and sixty-eight emigrants, men, women, and children, started for the Solomon Islands, and landed at Santa Cruz, a small archipelago between the Solomon Islands and the New Hebrides. He died two months after; his widow Dona Ysabel, and Quiros, the chief pilot, took command of the expedition, and returned to Spain with the remainder of the colony. Thereafter for two centuries, the existence of the Solomon Islands came to be doubted, although seamen spoke of them as a rich and marvellous country. In 1781 M. Buaché, a French geographer, presented a paper to the Académie des Sciences, showing that the Solomon Islands discovered by the Spaniards should be sought about 12° 30′ South latitude, between Santa Cruz and New Guinea, and that those islands discovered by Carteret in 1767, Bougainville in 1768, and by Surville in 1769 were the same. D'Entrecasteaux found later that the surmises of the French geographer were correct, and many of the names bestowed by the Spaniards were restored. The group, which is the most important of the Pacific, lies about five hundred miles east of New Guinea and covers an area of 17,000 square miles. The names of the principal islands, proceeding from the south-east in a north-westerly direction, are San Christoval, Malaita, Guadalcanar, Florida, New Georgia, Vella Lavella, Ysabel, Choiseul, and Bougainville.

A Brief dated 19 July, 1844, and signed by Gregory XVI, entrusted the Society of Mary with the evangelization of the country which extends from New Guinea to the Gilbert group. Towards the end of October, 1845, Mgr Epalle, S.M., sailed from Sydney with eighteen missionaries. The ship sighted San Christoval on 1 December at the southern extremity of the Solomon group. Thanks to the kindness of the captain, the bishop was able to survey the coast for a few days, but on discovering that the position was not a central one, the party decided to steer for Ysabel. On 12 December they were lying at anchor in the Bay of Astrolabe. The vicar Apostolic, three priests, and a handful of sailors went ashore, to be met by the aborigines, who, at a signal from their chief, mortally struck Bishop Epalle and dangerously wounded a Marist Father and a seaman. The rest of the party escaped and interred the remains of Bishop Epalle in a lonely islet, where fifty-six years after Father Rouillac, S.M. was fortunate enough to recover and identify them. Mgr Collomb, S.M., embarked on the "Arche d'Alliance", a barque which had been specially fitted out for Catholic propaganda work by a French naval officer, Commander Marceau, and joined the missionaries at San Cristoval. Three Fathers had been killed and eaten by the cannibals, another succumbed to malarial fever. Determined not to uselessly court massacre any longer on that spot, they set out for Woodlark and Rook Islands, where the new bishop and some of his followers died. Of the eighteen who had left Port Jackson, ten years before, five only now survived. On the representations of Propaganda, the Society of Mary gave up the Solomons temporarily. In 1852 Propaganda committed the care of these unhappy islands to the Fathers of the Foreign Missions of Milan; but they also were obliged to leave. In 1897 Rome asked the Marist authorites to make a new effort towards the civilization of the Solomon tribes. Mgr Vidal, S.M. (Vicar Apostolic of Fiji), on 21 May, 1898, landed with three Fathers at Rua-Sura, near Guadalcanar. On 22 August, 1903, the mission was made a prefecture Apostolic, comprising the Islands of New Georgia, Florida, Guadalcanar, Malaita, San Christoval, the Santa Cruz archipelago, and all the islets under British protectorate. Rev. E. M. Bertreux, S.M., was appointed prefect Apostolic, and at the present time (1912) seventeen priests, ten sisters, and a lay brother labour with him in that portion of the Solomon group. They attend to nine principal churches, forty-eight chapels, nine schools, numbering each from twenty to seventy pupils. Several hundred natives have been baptized, and a fair proportion are sufficiently prepared to be admitted to the sacraments every month. The nuns teach eighty girls in three schools. About three hundred women are regular catechumens, and assemble every Sunday for instruction in Christian doctrine. There are about three thousand neophytes.

GUPPY, *The Solomon Islands and their Natives* (London, 1887); WOODFORD, *A Naturalist among the Head-hunters* (Melbourne and Sydney, 1890); MONFAT, *Dix années en Mélanésie* (Lyons, 1891); *The Discovery of the Solomon Islands*, tr. AMHERST AND THOMSON, from original Spanish manuscripts (London, 1901); *Les Missions Catholiques Françaises au XIXe siècle* (Paris, 1900).

E. M. BERTREUX.

Solsona, DIOCESE OF (CELSONENSIS), in Lerida, Spain, suffragan of Tarragona, erected by Clement VIII, 19 July, 1593, from the Dioceses of Urgel and Vich, suppressed in 1851, by virtue of the Concordat, after a vacancy of eleven years (the last bishop being

Mgr. de Tessada). It was to have been joined to Vich, but the union was not effected, and it has been governed since by an administrator Apostolic. It is bounded on the north and west by the See of Urgel, on the south by those of Lérida and Tarragona, and on the east by the Diocese of Vich. It contains 152 parishes, 330 priests and clerics, 259 churches, 16 chapels, and about 120,000 inhabitants. There are many religious communities—men: Religious of the Immaculate Heart of Mary (Solsona); Misioneros Paules (Bellpuig, Cervera); Cistercians of Senanque (Casserras, Tarrega); Mercedarians (Portell); Benedictines (Riner); Piarists (Tárrega)—nuns: Carmelites of Charity, 11 houses; Discalced Carmelite Tertiaries, 2 houses; Dominican Tertiaries, 6 houses; Sisters of the Holy Family of Urgel, Hermanitas de Ancianos desamparados, Sisters of the Holy Family, 1 house each. The cathedral of Solsona is dedicated to the Assumption of the Blessed Virgin; the apse, in Roman style, dates probably from the twelfth century, the façade is Baroque, and the nave and transept Gothic; the church contains the highly venerated Virgen de Solsona, an excellent specimen of Byzantine work. The present ordinary, Mgr. Amigo y Ferrer, titular Bishop of Thagaste, succeeded Mgr. Benlloch y Vivó, transferred on 6 Dec., 1906, to the See of Urgel. Solsona, the Xelsa of the Lacetani, Setelsis of the Romans, and later Selsona, lies about fifty miles from Lérida and Barcelona on the Rio Negro and Rio Cardoner. It was a military post of strategic importance and was frequently besieged. In 819 it was captured by the Moors; in 1520, a university, transferred later to Cervera, was established there. On 30 July, 1590, Solsona was made a city by Philip II. In the following century it rebelled against the Madrid Government and was captured, 7 Dec., 1655. In the War of Succession it sided with the archduke. The Carlists attacked it unsuccessfully in 1835 and 1837. Solsona has important manufactures of thread, lace, gloves, and hardware.

BATTANDIER, *Annuaire pontifical catholique.*

A. A. MACERLEAN.

Somaliland, a triangular-shaped territory in the north-eastern extremity of Africa, projecting into the ocean towards the Island of Socotra; its apex is Cape Guardafui. It is bounded on the north by the Gulf of Aden, on the east by the Indian Ocean, on the west by the hills of Harrar and Shoa. It has an area of about 356,000 square miles, and a population of 1,000,000. The Greek navigators called it the "Country of aromatic gums"; at the present time it is called Somaliland from the name of the people who inhabit it. Its exploration was begun in the sixteenth century by Portuguese employed in the service of Ethiopia, was interrupted for a long time, and was recommenced in the nineteenth century by Burton, von der Decken, Brenner, Menges, Georges Révoil, etc. Our knowledge of it is still imperfect: the severity of the climate, aridity of the soil, lack of means of transportation, and above all the fanatical, treacherous, and thieving character of the natives have always made Somaliland one of the most inhospitable places of residence in the world. The country has more or less the appearance of a desert. The lower section bordering on the sea is naturally dry and barren and barely supports a poor and scanty flora. The mountain slopes have a fine vegetation, which includes the coffee-tree. The central region, called Ogaden, has an average elevation of 3000 feet and is a large plateau covered with steppes and affording pasturage. The chief rivers are the Daror, which empties into the Indian Ocean between Cape Guardafui and Ras Hafun, Webi, which, descending from the Harrar district, flows along the coast and loses itself in the ground, and Juba, which was explored in 1873 by the American Chaillé-Long who was in the service of the Khedive of Egypt.

The people called Somali, who have remained untouched by exterior influences, are remarkably homogeneous. Ethnographers connect them with the Ethiopic, Cushitic, or Hamitic group represented by the Ethiopians, or Abyssinians, Bedjas or Nubians, the Danakil, the Oromo or Gallas. Taken generally the Somali type is very interesting: slight in figure, with limbs well-proportioned, regular and remarkably delicate features, wavy hair, a fine black skin. They dress elegantly in the classic manner; the poorest know how to carry themselves with a naturalness, ease, and pride that are not lacking in dignity. They are intelligent, but fickle, and their industries are rudimentary; they disdain tilling the soil. They work chiefly as herdsmen, fishers, boatmen, traders; above all they prefer travel, adventure, and robbing strangers. They are, moreover, divided into a great number of clans forming three or four main groups which unite and separate according to the vicissitudes of the alliance and of war and have no national cohesion. Their language, which has been made known by the Capuchin missionaries, is related to that of the Gallas; it has incorporated a large number of Arabic idioms.

However, European influence has made itself felt in Somaliland since 1829 when the Red Sea was first used as a route to India; but it is only of late years that France, England, and Italy have taken actual possession of the Somali coast. France acquired Obok in 1882, then took the entire Bay of Tajurrah, and finished by taking Jibuti as the chief town of the "Protectorate of the French Coast of Somali", which contains an area of about 80 square miles. Jibuti has been united by a railway with the fertile districts of the Harrar and of Abyssinia. England is established to the east on the entire coast facing Arabia as far as Cape Guardafui; its principal towns are Zeila and Berbera. Lastly, Italy, called by England to these latitudes in 1894, occupies the principal towns of the eastern coast known under the name of Benadir (Arabic *Al Banader*, the gateways), where the Sultan of Zanzibar formerly maintained small garrisons: Obbia, Warsheik, Mogdishu, Merka, Barawa, Kisima-yu (the last name is of Swahilic origin, *Kisima* meaning wells, *yu* meaning upper). The Somali are all Mohammedans. Those of the north and of the towns on the coast are rigorous and fanatical observers of the principles of Islam and despise "the infidels" whether white or black. The Somali of the interior unite some of the beliefs and practices of ancient fetishism with their Mohammedan faith. There are, however, few populations of the world that are more difficult to bring to the Gospel. Properly speaking there is no Christianity in Somaliland. The few Christians, perhaps one or two hundred, that can actually be counted, have come from the schools and orphanages of the Catholic missions of Aden, Jibuti, and of Berbera. As Somaliland is divided into three zones of influence, French, English, and Italian, there are three distinct mission centres: the French Somali coast is under the care of the Vicariate Apostolic of the Gallas, which is entrusted to the French Capuchins of the Province of Lyons; English Somaliland is under the care of the Vicariate Apostolic of Arabia, also confided to the Capuchins; Italian Somaliland was detached in 1904 from the Vicariate Apostolic of Zanzibar, erected into the Prefecture Apostolic of Benadir, and confided to the ancient Order of the Holy Trinity or Trinitarians.

RÉVOIL, *La Vallée de Darror* (Paris, 1882); IDEM, *Dix mois à la côte orientale d'Afrique* (Paris, 1888); SMITH, *Through Unknown African Countries* (London, 1897); PEEL, *Somaliland* (London, 1899); SWAYNE, *Seventeen Trips through Somaliland* (London, 1900); HENDEBERT, *Au pays des Somalis et des Comoriens* (Paris, 1901); FERRAND, *Les Çomâlis* (Paris, 1903).

A. LE ROY.

Somaschi, name of a charitable religious congregation of regular clerics, founded in the sixteenth century by St. Jerome Emiliani with the motherhouse at Somasca (Venice), whence the name. For all particulars on development and history of the order see JEROME EMILIANI, SAINT. Following are the latest statistics, obtained from F. Gius. Landini of the Somaschi at the Curia Generalitia at Rome. The order counts in three provinces (Rome, Lombardy, and Liguria) 16 houses, all but one (in Bellinzona, Switzerland) in Italy, and about 180 members, of whom 100 are priests, 50 clerics, and 30 lay brothers. At Rome they have three houses: San Girolamo della Carità, residence of the general and one of the three novitiates (the other two being in Genoa and Somasca); Santa Maria in Aquiro with a parish and orphanage; San Alessio on the Aventine for blind boys. The congregation manages three colleges with classical and technical studies at Spello, Como, Nervi, and finally, including those already mentioned, three orphanages and five parishes.

LIVARIUS OLIGER.

Somerset, THOMAS, confessor, b. about 1530; d. in the Tower of London, 27 May, 1587; second son of Henry, second Earl of Worcester. He was committed to the Fleet, 10 June, 1562, "for translating an oratyon out of Frenche, made by the Cardinall of Lorraine", Charles de Guise, Archbishop of Reims, "and putting the same without authority in prynte". On 27 June, 1562, he was summoned before the Lords of the Council at Greenwich, who expected "an humble submission, for wante whereof, and for that he seamed to go about to justifye his cause, he was returned to the Flete, there to remaine untill he" should "have better considered of himself". After an imprisonment of close on twenty years he was released on bail, 28 Feb., 1581-82, to attend to legal business in Monmouthshire. On 2 May, 1582, he was too ill to travel, and was permitted to remain at liberty till he should recover. By 22 October, 1585, he was in the Tower on a charge of high treason. Being possessed of properties in Gloucestershire and Monmouthshire, he paid the costs of his imprisonment, and his name therefore is not to be found in the Tower Bills.

Catholic Record Society's Publications, I (London, 1905, etc.), 49; DASENT, *Acts of the Privy Council* (London, 1890–1907), VII, 108; XIII, 336, 407; *Calendar State Papers Domestic 1581–90* (London, 1865), 249, 278, 305; COLLINS, *Peerage,* I (London, 1779), 201

JOHN B. WAINEWRIGHT.

Sommervogel, CARLOS. See SOCIETY OF JESUS.

Sonderbund. See SWITZERLAND.

Song, RELIGIOUS (or SACRED), is the general designation given to the numerous poetical and musical creations which have come into existence in the course of time and are used in connexion with public Divine worship, but which are not included in the official liturgy on account of their more free and subjective character. It has its origin in the desire on the part of the faithful, a desire ever encouraged but always guided and controlled by the Church, to participate actively in the public religious ceremonies of the Church. While the psalms were sung in traditional fashion during the early Eucharistic celebrations at the public meetings, and the love-feasts, or agapæ, of the early Christians, there soon sprang up the custom of improvising songs, participated in by the whole assembly, which, though religious in burden, by their spontaneity and freedom stood in contrast to the psalms and other lyric parts of the Holy Scripture in use at the Eucharistic celebration. These creations in course of time lost their spiritual character, dignity, and fervour as the institution which gave them birth and of which they formed an important part degenerated in character, departed from its original purpose, and became an occasion for pleasure and dissipation. The songs thus originated continued in use long after the institution had lost official sanction, and have become known in history by the name of the institution which gave rise to them.

As Christianity spread, there was an ever greater increase of spontaneous creations of this kind originating in the desire on the part of their authors to get nearer to the people and to convey to them by this means instruction as well as edification. As early as the fourth century there had come into use so many chants, hymns, and songs, in various parts of the Christian world, and abuses and aberrations had become so general, that the Council of Laodicea (360–381) forbade the singing of any text not taken from Holy Scripture. The hymns by St. Hilary and St. Ambrose of Milan (especially the latter)—which now form a part of the liturgy—had for their original purpose the instruction of the people by having them sing in striking metrical form and to vigorous melodies the fundamental truths of religion. The sequences and tropes which came into existence with such exuberance in the early Middle Ages, while popular in form, sprang directly from the liturgy and always partook of its character. In those regions where the liturgical language remained at the same time the tongue of the people, at least in a modified form, participation in the official chant of the Church on the part of all was general for many centuries, and in consequence the influence of the spirit of the liturgy and its music prevented the early development of a more subjective religious poetry and music than was to be the case in later times in other regions. This is probably the reason why in Italy, Spain, and the other Latin countries the religious song in the vernacular has never taken root.

While this was also true of France, for a considerable time, we find there an early and rapid growth of songs of every kind, bearing a strong national character. Every important event in the domestic and religious life of the people soon found expression in song. The festivals of the Church inspired them and became by these means in turn impressed upon the popular imagination. One of these characteristically French songs is the *noël,* or Christmas song, which had great vogue in the eleventh century, a vogue which reached its height in the seventeenth century and has survived in a certain form, even to our day. The *noël,* the words of which were often paraphrases of liturgical texts, set to melodies naïve and pastoral in character, was popular in every section of the kingdom and sung in every dialect in use. Processions, pilgrimages, and especially the mystery and miracle plays gave rise to many forms of songs. The troubadours in the south and trouvères in the north exerted great influence on the development and propagation not only of secular but of religious songs as well. Among the many forms in use was the complaint, a song in narrative form of which the "Story of the Resurrection" (O filii et filiæ) is a prominent type. The pastorale was another form which flourished from the twelfth to the sixteenth century, sometimes having religious texts and then again voicing secular sentiments. With the sixteenth century began the custom of substituting secular airs in use at the time for the melodies to which the sacred texts of the *noëls,* complaints, etc., had thus far been sung; they were not only modelled on the Gregorian chant but had a distinctively nïave simple character. This substitution sometimes involved even the partial taking over of the profane text as well. This was the beginning of the decadence which finally, in some places, reached the point where *chansons de galanterie,* or love songs, were completely transformed into *cantiques,* or religious songs, by merely substituting the name of the Blessed Virgin or that of Jesus Christ, for the name of the beloved one mentioned in the original. The modern French *cantique*, which has taken the place of the traditional religious songs, is sentimental, quasi-military, and savours of the world, plainly showing the influence of the favourite French musical form, the opera.

On account of their total unfamiliarity with the Latin language, the Germanic races were prevented from participating in the liturgical chant introduced with Christianity itself by their first missionaries. At most they joined in singing the Kyrie Eleison, and that in the form of a refrain. This primitive practice became so general that it survived long after songs in the vernacular had come into universal use. The latter would frequently end with the above invocation, which was gradually abbreviated into "Kyrieleis". The songs or hymns in the vernacular were themselves called later on "Kyrieleis" and "Leisen". The word "lay", which designates a vast song literature of a whole subsequent period, is derived from "Leisen". To wean their neophytes from pagan beliefs and practices, the early missionaries were wont to make use of melodies familiar to the people, apply Christian texts to them, and turn them into effective means of instruction. This practice soon led the naturally emotional and subjective race to give vent to their growing religious feelings in words and melodies of their own invention, so that as early as the latter part of the ninth century words in the vernacular were mixed with those of liturgical chants, the former forming a sort of glossary to the latter. From this time on there is a constant growth in songs of all kinds in honour of Jesus Christ, the Blessed Virgin, the saints, inspired by the great feasts; songs called forth by national events, the Crusades, and, as elsewhere, processions and pilgrimages, many of them created and all of them fostered by the minnesingers and poets of the day. The texts in the vernacular and the melodies originated from the earliest days of Christianity up to the Reformation in Germanic countries; they were usually sung by the whole congregation, and belong to what is most sturdy and profound in sentiment and expression in this field. The fact that some 1500 melodies, antedating the Reformation, have come down to us gives us some idea of the hold the religious song had upon the people. The Reformers, like the Arians of the fourth century, availed themselves of the love for song on the part of the people, and converted it into an insidious and powerful means for the dissemination of their erroneous doctrines. The impetus thus given to singing exclusively in the vernacular by the leaders of Protestantism was so widespread and powerful that it soon reacted upon those who remained loyal to the faith of their fathers. It resulted not only in the creation of a large number of new hymn books but also in the custom, which has not yet been rooted up in all places. of singing in German during liturgical services.

A number of influences have contributed to the degeneration of the hymn in the vernacular which reached its limit in the eighteenth century. The most potent factors in its decay were the growth of Rationalism affecting even those within the fold and the ever-increasing ascendancy of secular music, resulting in the seventeenth century in the abandonment of the Gregorian modes, upon which practically all hymn melodies had been modelled, and the substitution of the modern keys. With the revival of the Catholic spirit at the beginning of the nineteenth century came a return to early ideals. Poets and musicians of the right stamp, both clerical and lay, inspired by the spirit of the Church and later fostered by the powerful agency of the Saint Cecilia Society, have restored to the Catholic people of German-speaking countries a song literature in the vernacular tongue, which is as rich in variety as it is sturdy in its expression of faith. In France a vigorous effort is being made, as part of the Gregorian restoration, to reconstruct a sound and wholesome taste among the people by the republication and propagation of proses, *rhythmes*, sequences, and other chants in honour of Jesus Christ, the Blessed Virgin, the saints, or the church festivals, written in one or other of the Gregorian modes, and in vogue during the ages of simple and lively faith. Competent church musicians and Gregorianists are successfully creating similar new melodies to standard texts. Their use is becoming widespread.

There is very little trace of the existence in early times in most English-speaking countries of religious songs in the vernacular. The missionaries sent from Rome in the sixth century introduced the liturgical chant into the British Isles and seem to have made but little effort to utilize any characteristically national melodies already existing. Unlike their colleagues in regions across the Channel, the gleemen, harpers, and bards of old continued to cultivate chiefly the secular field, and their productions and activity had not much influence on the creation and development of a national religious song literature, nor does Celtic musical and poetical culture seem to have been directed into that channel. While polyphonic music had attained a highly flourishing state before the sixteenth century, it was only at the time of the Reformation that singing in the vernacular assumed greater importance in England. As in the other Protestant countries the song in the vernacular became a great factor in British national worship. On account of most unpropitious conditions during several hundred years English-speaking Catholics had created but very little of any permanent value until, about the middle of the last century, a new era was inaugurated by religious poets like Faber and Newman. Unfortunately their lyrics have as yet seldom found adequate musical interpretation. What is true of transatlantic English-speaking Catholics holds good in a greater degree in the United States of America. Partly on account of the scarcity of suitable and worthy hymns in the English vernacular and partly on account of incompetency on the part of those who undertake to supply the deficiency, the taste of the people has been formed by trivial and superficial tunes, generally echoes of the opera, the shallow popular air, and even the drinking-song set to sentimental and often trivial texts. Of late years, however, several collections of hymns in the vernacular, indicating a return to what is best in religious poetry and in popular sacred song, have come into existence and are gradually making their way into general use.

WEINMANN, *History of Church Music* (New York, 1910); BAÜMKER, *Das deutsche Kirchenlied in seinen Singweisen* (Freiburg, 1901); WAGNER, *Einführung in die gregorianischen Melodien* (Fribourg, 1901); TIERSOT, *Melodies populaires des provinces de France, noëls français, etc.* (Paris, 1894); DUCHESNE, *Christian Worship* (London, 1903).

JOSEPH OTTEN.

Songish Indians.—A tribe of some importance formerly holding the south coast of Vancouver Island, B. C., in the immediate vicinity of the present Victoria and now gathered upon small reservations at Songhees, Cheerno (Beecher Island), Discovery Island, and Esquimalt, within their former territory, and under the Cowichan agency. Their proper name is Lkungen, the other being a corruption of Stsangés, the name of a former principal division. They are of Salishan linguistic stock and speak the same language as the Sanetch and Sooke of Vancouver Island and the Czalam and Lummi of Washington. From 1000 souls they have wasted away from small-pox and diseases induced by dissipation on the first advent of the whites about fifty years ago. In 1895 they still numbered 215, but by 1910 had decreased to 171, and within another generation will probably cease to exist. Although visited by several of the early voyagers their first regular communication with the whites dates from the establishment of Fort Camosum by the Hudson's Bay Company in 1843 at the present site of Victoria and close to the village of the principal Songish chief. The secular priest, Father John B. Bolduc (d. 1889), already known for his missionary work among the tribes of Puget Sound, had been requested to accompany the expedition, and through his good offices a friendly meeting was arranged with the Indians. On Sunday, 19 March, the whole tribe thronged to attend Mass and a sermon, which was held in a temporary chapel, after which over one hundred children were baptized. No continuous work was undertaken until the arrival of the Oblate vicar, Father L. J. d'Herbomez, who established a residence at Esquimalt in 1857 and was joined two years later by several Sisters of Saint Ann. In 1859 the distinguished Oblate missionary Father Casimir Chirouse, beloved by all the tribes of Puget Sound, arrived from the Columbia Country, and was soon joined by two younger workers of the same order, almost equally noted later, Fathers Pierre P. Durieu and Léon Fouquet. Protestant work was begun by the Episcopalian Rev. John B. Good in 1861. In the meantime the discovery of gold on the mainland had resulted in an influx of miners and dissolute adventurers, which made Victoria a centre of dissipation and for a long time virtually nullified missionary effort. In 1862 a small-pox epidemic swept over the whole region and terribly wasted all the tribes. Of the whole number two-thirds are now Catholic, most of the others being Methodists. They are reported as industrious and prosperous farmers, fishermen, and labourers, moral and fairly temperate.

In their primitive condition the Songish had the clan system, with twelve clans, each of which had its own fishing and hunting territory. Chiefship was hereditary in the male line and they had the three castes of nobles, commons, and slaves. Salmon-fishing and berry-picking were the chief dependence for subsistence. They lived in large rectangular communal houses of cedar planks, adorned with carved and jointed totem posts. They had large dug-out canoes of cedar, and wove blankets from dogs' hair, duck down, and the wool of the mountain goat. They had the potlatch or ceremonial gift distribution, common to all the tribes of the north-west coast. Head flattening was also practised. There were many curious customs, beliefs, and taboos concerning births, puberty, marriage, and death. The dead were buried in canoes or boxes upon the surface of the ground, or laid away in trees. Slaves were frequently sacrificed at the grave. The names of the dead were never mentioned. As with other tribes of the region their culture hero was the Great Transformer. The religion was animism, each man having his protecting dream spirit, and the tribal life and ceremonial were dominated by two secret societies.

BANCROFT, *Hist. of British Columbia* (San Francisco, 1887); MAYNE, *Four Years in British Columbia and Vancouver Island* (London, 1862); BOAS, *Sixth Report on North-western Tribes of Canada*, Brit. Assn. for Advancement of Science (London, 1890); CANADA, Dept. of Indian Affairs, Annual Reports (Ottawa); MORICE, *Catholic Church in Western Canada* (Toronto, 1910).

JAMES MOONEY.

Song of Solomon. See CANTICLE OF CANTICLES.

Sonnius, FRANCISCUS, theologian, b. at Zon in Brabant, 12 August, 1506; d. at Antwerp, 30 June, 1576, His real name was Van de Velde, but in later years he called himself after his native place. He went to school at Bois-le-Duc and Louvain, and afterwards studied medicine for a time, then theology; in 1536 he received the licentiate and in 1539 the doctorate in theology. After labouring for a short time as a parish priest at Meerbeek and Louvain he became professor of theology at Louvain in 1544, and attended the Council of Trent in 1546, 1547, and 1551. He was sent to the council first by Bishop Karl de Croy van Doornik, then by Maria of Hungary, the regent of the Netherlands. In 1557 he also took an active part in the religious disputation of Worms. Not long after this Philip II sent him to Rome to negotiate with Paul IV in regard to ecclesiastical matters in the Netherlands, especially as to increasing the number of dioceses and separating the Belgian monasteries from the German, as in the latter heresy was rapidly spreading. In acknowledgment of his successful labours he was appointed Bishop of Bois-le-Duc in 1566, but he was not consecrated until two years later, by Cardinal Granvella. In 1569 he was appointed the first Bishop of Antwerp and in the following year came into possession of his diocese. He did much to strengthen the Church, founding an ecclesiastical court and personally visiting all the parishes of his diocese. He proclaimed at once the decisions of the Council of Trent and established regular meetings of the deaneries. As Bishop of Antwerp, he held two diocesan synods, setting an example that exerted influence far beyond the boundaries of the Archbishopric of Mechlin. He showed particular zeal in combatting the errors of Calvinism and wrote for this purpose a clear summary of its teachings for the use of the clergy, under the title "Succincta demonstratio errorum confessionis Calvinistæ recenter per has regiones sparsæ" (Louvain, 1567). He also wrote a textbook of dogmatics: "Demonstrationum religionis christianæ libri tres" (Antwerp, 1564), to which in 1577, after his death, a fourth book was added, "De sacramentis". In 1616 the cathedral chapter and the city erected a monument to him.

GILS AND COPPENS, *Nieuwe beschrijving van het bisdom van 's Bosch*, I (Bois-le-Duc, 1840), 218; *Allge. deutsche Biog.*, XXXIV.

PATRICIUS SCHLAGER.

Son of God. IN THE OLD TESTAMENT.—The title "son of God" is frequent in the Old Testament. The word "son" was employed among the Semites to signify not only filiation, but other close connexion or intimate relationship. Thus, "a son of strength" was a hero, a warrior, "son of wickedness" a wicked man, "sons of pride" wild beasts, "son of possession" a possessor, "son of pledging" a hostage, "son of lightning" a swift bird, "son of death" one doomed to death, "son of a bow" an arrow, "son of Belial" a wicked man, "sons of prophets" disciples of prophets, etc. The title "son of God" was applied in the Old Testament to persons having any special relationship with God. Angels, just and pious men, the descendants of Seth, were called "sons of God" (Job, i, 6; ii, 1; Ps. lxxxviii, 7; Wisd., ii, 13; etc.). In a similar manner it was given to Israelites (Deut., xiv, 1); and of Israel, as a nation, we read: "And thou shalt say to him: Thus saith the Lord: Israel is my son, my firstborn. I have said to thee: Let my son go, that he may serve me" (Ex., iv, 22 sq.).

The leaders of the people, kings, princes, judges, as holding authority from God, were called sons of God. The theocratic king as lieutenant of God, and especially when he was providentially selected to be a type of the Messias, was honoured with the title "son of God". But the Messias, the Chosen One, the Elect of God, was *par excellence* called the Son of God (Ps. ii, 7). Even Wellhausen admits that Ps. ii is Messianic (see Hast., "Dict. of the Bible", IV, 571). The prophecies regarding the Messias became clearer as time went on, and the result is ably summed up by Sanday (*ibid.*): "The Scriptures of which we have been speaking mark so many different contributions to the total result, but the result, when it is attained, has the completeness of an organic whole. A Figure was created—projected as it were upon the clouds—which was invested with all the attributes of a person. And the minds of men were turned towards it in an attitude of expectation. It makes no matter that the lines of the Figure are drawn from different originals. They meet at last in a single portraiture. And we should never have known how perfectly they meet if we had not the New Testament picture to compare with that of the Old Testament. The most literal fulfilment of prediction would not be more conclusive proof that all the course of the world and all the threads of history are in one guiding Hand." The Messias besides being the Son of God was to be called Emmanuel (God with us), Wonderful, Counsellor, God the Mighty, the Father of the world to come, Prince of Peace (Is., viii, 8; ix, 6) (see MESSIAS).

IN THE NEW TESTAMENT.—The title "the Son of God" is frequently applied to Jesus Christ in the Gospels and Epistles. In the latter it is everywhere employed as a short formula for expressing His Divinity (Sanday); and this usage throws light on the meaning to be attached to it in many passages of the Gospels. The angel announced: "He shall be great, and shall be called the Son of the most High . . . the Holy which shall be born of thee shall be called the Son of God" (Luke, i, 32, 35). Nathaniel, at his first meeting, called Him the Son of God (John, i, 49). The devils called Him by the same name, the Jews ironically, and the Apostles after He quelled the storm. In all these cases its meaning was equivalent to the Messias, at least. But much more is implied in the confession of St. Peter, the testimony of the Father, and the words of Jesus Christ.

Confession of St. Peter.—We read in Matt., xvi, 15, 16: "Simon Peter answered and said: Thou art Christ, the Son of the living God. And Jesus answering, said to him: Blessed art thou, Simon Bar-Jona: because flesh and blood hath not revealed it to thee, but my Father who is in heaven." The parallel passages have: "Thou art the Christ" (Mark, viii, 29), "The Christ of God" (Luke, ix, 20). There can be no doubt that St. Matthew gives the original form of the expression, and that St. Mark and St. Luke in giving "the Christ" (the Messias), instead, used it in the sense in which they understood it when they wrote, viz. as equivalent to "the incarnate Son of God" (see Rose, VI). Sanday, writing of St. Peter's confession, says: "the context clearly proves that Matthew had before him some further tradition, possibly that of the Logia, but in any case a tradition that has the look of being original" (Hastings, "Dict. of the Bible"). As Rose well points out, in the minds of the Evangelists Jesus Christ was the Messias because He was the Son of God, and not the Son of God because He was the Messias.

Testimony of the Father.—(1) At the Baptism.— "And Jesus being baptized, forthwith came out of the water: and lo, the heavens were opened to him: and he saw the Spirit of God descending as a dove, and coming upon him. And behold a voice from heaven, saying: This is my beloved Son, in whom I am well pleased" (Matt., iii, 16, 17). "And there came a voice from heaven: Thou art my beloved Son; in thee I am well pleased" (Mark, i, 11; Luke, iii, 22).

(2) At the Transfiguration.—"And lo, a voice out of the cloud, saying: This is my beloved Son, in whom I am well pleased: hear ye him" (Matt., xvii, 5; Mark, ix, 6; Luke, ix, 35). Though Rose admits that the words spoken at the Baptism need not necessarily mean more than what was suggested by the Old Testament, viz. Son of God is equal to the Messias, still, as the same words were used on both occasions, it is likely they had the same meaning in both cases. The Transfiguration took place within a week after St. Peter's confession, and the words were used in the meaning in which the three disciples would then understand them; and at the Baptism it is probable that only Christ, and perhaps the Baptist, heard them, so that it is not necessary to interpret them according to the current opinions of the crowd. Even so cautious a critic as the Anglican Professor Sanday writes on these passages: "And if, on the occasions in question, the Spirit of God did intimate prophetically to chosen witnesses, more or fewer, a revelation couched partly in the language of the ancient Scriptures, it would by no means follow that the meaning of the revelation was limited to the meaning of the older Scriptures. On the contrary, it would be likely enough that the old words would be charged with new meaning—that, indeed the revelation . . . would yet be in substance a new revelation. . . . And we may assume that to His (Christ's) mind the announcement 'Thou art my Son' meant not only all that it ever meant to the most enlightened seers of the past, but, yet more, all that the response of His own heart told Him that it meant in the present. . . . But it is possible, and we should be justified in supposing—not by way of dogmatic assertion but by way of pious belief—in view of the later history and the progress of subsequent revelation, that the words were intended to suggest a new truth, not hitherto made known, viz. that the Son was Son not only in the sense of the Messianic King, or of an Ideal People, but that the idea of sonship was fulfilled in Him in a way yet more mysterious and yet more essential; in other words, that He was Son, not merely in prophetic revelation, but in actual transcendent fact before the foundation of the world" (Hastings, "Dict. of the Bible").

Testimony of Jesus Christ.—(1) The Synoptics.— The key to this is contained in His words, after the Resurrection: "I ascend to my Father and to your Father" (John, xx, 17). He always spoke of *my* Father, never of *our* Father. He said to the disciples: "Thus then shall *you* pray: Our Father", etc. He everywhere draws the clearest possible distinction between the way in which God was His Father and in which He was the Father of all creatures. His expressions clearly prove that He claimed to be of the same nature with God; and His claims to Divine Sonship are contained very clearly in the Synoptic Gospels, though not as frequently as in St. John.

"Did you not know, that I must be about my father's business?" (Luke, ii, 49); "Not every one that saith to me, Lord, Lord, shall enter into the kingdom of heaven: but he that doth the will of my Father who is in heaven, he shall enter into the kingdom of heaven. Many will say to me in that day: Lord, Lord, have not we prophesied in thy name, and cast out devils in thy name, and done many miracles in thy name? And then will I profess unto them, I never knew you: depart from me you, that work iniquity" (Matt., vii, 21–23). "Everyone therefore that shall confess me before men, I will also confess him before my Father who is in heaven" (Matt., x, 32). "At that time Jesus answered and said: I confess to thee, O Father, Lord of heaven and earth, because thou hast hid these things from the wise and prudent, and hast revealed them to little ones. Yea, Father; for so hath it seemed good in thy sight. All things are delivered to me by my Father. And no one knoweth the Son, but the Father: neither doth any one know the Father, but the Son, and he to whom it shall please the Son to reveal *him*. Come to me, all you that labour, and are burdened, and I will refresh you" (Matt., xi, 25–30; Luke, x, 21, 22). In the parable of the wicked husbandmen the son is distinguished from all other messengers: "Therefore having yet one son, most dear to him; he also sent him unto them last of all, saying: They will reverence my son. But the husbandmen said one to another: This is the heir; come let us kill him" (Mark, xii, 6). Compare Matt., xxii, 2, "The kingdom of heaven is likened to a king, who made a marriage for his son." In Matt., xvii, 25, He states that as Son of God He is free from the temple tax. "David therefore himself calleth him Lord, and whence is he then his son?" (Mark, xii, 37). He is Lord of the angels. He shall come "in the clouds of heaven with much power and majesty. And he shall send his angels" (Matt., xxiv, 30, 31). He confessed before Caiphas that he was the Son of the blessed God (Mark, xiv, 61–2). "Going therefore, teach ye all nations, baptizing them in the name of the Father, and of the Son, and of the Holy Ghost . . . and behold I am with you all days, even to the consummation of the world" (Matt., xxviii, 19, 20).

The claims of Jesus Christ, as set forth in the Synoptic Gospels, are so great that Salmon is justified in writing (Introd. to New Test., p. 197): "We deny that they [Christ's utterances in the Fourth Gospel] are at all inconsistent with what is attributed to Him in the Synoptic Gospels. On the contrary, the dignity of our Saviour's person, and the duty of adhering to Him, are as strongly stated in the discourses which St. Matthew puts into His mouth as in any later Gospel. . . . The Synoptic Evangelists all agree in representing Jesus as persisting in this claim [of Supreme Judge] to the end, and finally incurring condemnation for blasphemy from the high-priest and the Jewish Council. . . . It follows that the claims which the Synoptic Gospels represent our Lord as making for Himself are so high . . . that, if we accept the Synoptic Gospels as truly representing the character of our Lord's language about Himself, we certainly have no right to reject St. John's account, on the score that he puts too exalted language about Himself into the mouth of our Lord."

(2) *St. John's Gospel.*—It will not be necessary to give more than a few passages from St. John's Gospel. "My Father worketh until now; and I work. . . . For the Father loveth the Son, and sheweth him all things which he himself doth: and greater works than these will he shew him, that you may wonder. For as the Father raiseth up the dead, and giveth life: so the Son also giveth life to whom he will. For neither doth the Father judge any man, but hath given all judgment to the Son. That all may honour the Son, as they honour the Father" (v, 17, 20–23). "And this is the will of my Father that sent me: that everyone who seeth the Son, and believeth in him, may have life everlasting, and I will raise him up in the last day" (vi, 40). "Father, the hour is come, glorify thy Son, that thy Son may glorify thee. . . . And now glorify thou me, O Father, with thyself, with the glory which I had, before the world was, with thee" (xvii, 1, 5).

(3) *St. Paul.*—St. Paul in the Epistles, which were written much earlier than most of our Gospels, clearly teaches the Divinity of Jesus Christ, and that He was the true Son of God; and it is important to remember that his enemies the Judaizers never dared to attack this teaching, a fact which proves that they could not find the smallest semblance of a discrepancy between his doctrines on this point and that of the other Apostles.

LEPIN, *Jésus Messie et Fils de Dieu* (Paris, 1906); also Eng. tr. (Philadelphia); ROSE, *Studies on the Gospels* (London, 1903); SANDAY, *Hist. Dict. Bible.*

C. AHERNE.

Son of Man.—In the Old Testament "son of man" is always translated in the Septuagint without the article as υἱὸς ἀνθρώπου. It is employed (1) as a poetical synonym for man, or for the ideal man, e. g. "God is not as a man, that he should lie, nor as a son of man, that he should be changed" (Num., xxiii, 19). "Blessed is the man that doth this and the son of man that shall lay hold on this" (Is., lvi, 2). "Let thy hand be upon the man of thy right hand: and upon the son of man whom thou hast confirmed for thyself" (Ps. lxxix, 18). (2) The Prophet Ezechiel is addressed by God as "son of man" more than ninety times, e. g. "Son of man, stand upon thy feet, and I will speak to thee" (Ezech., ii, 1). This usage is confined to Ezechiel except one passage in Daniel, where Gabriel said: "Understand, O son of man, for in the time of the end the vision shall be fulfilled" (Dan., viii, 17).

(3) In the great vision of Daniel, after the appearance of the four beasts, we read: "I beheld therefore in the vision of the night, and lo, one like a son of man came with the clouds of heaven, and he came even to the Ancient of days: and they presented him before him. And he gave him power, and glory, and a kingdom: and all peoples, tribes, and tongues shall serve him: his power is an everlasting power that shall not be taken away: and his kingdom shall not be destroyed" (vii, 13 sq.). The person who appears here as son of man is interpreted by many non-Catholics as representing the Messianic kingdom, but there is nothing to prevent the passage from being taken to represent not only the Messianic kingdom, but *par excellence* the Messianic king. In the explanation, verse 17, the four beasts are "four kings" R.V., not "four kingdoms" as translated by D. V., though they appear to signify four kingdoms as well, for the characteristics of oriental kingdoms were identified with the characters of their kings. So when it is said in verse 18: "But the saints of the most high God shall take the kingdom: and they shall possess the kingdom for ever and ever", the king is no more excluded here than in the case of the four beasts. The "son of man" here was early interpreted of the Messias, in the Book of Henoch, where the expression is used almost as a Messianic title, though there is a good deal in Drummond's argument that even here it was not used as a Messianic title notwithstanding the fact that it was understood of the Messias. It has to be added that in the time of Christ it was not very widely, if at all, known as a Messianic title.

The employment of the expression in the Gospels is very remarkable. It is used to designate Jesus Christ no fewer than eighty-one times—thirty times in St. Matthew, fourteen times in St. Mark, twenty-five times in St. Luke, and twelve times in St. John. Contrary to what obtains in the Septuagint, it appears everywhere with the article, as ὁ υἱὸς τοῦ ἀνθρώπου. Greek scholars are agreed that the correct translation of this is "the son of man", not "the son of the man". The possible ambiguity may be one of the reasons why it is seldom or never found in the early Greek Fathers as a title for Christ. But the most remarkable thing connected with "the Son of Man" is that it is found only in the mouth of Christ. It is never employed by the disciples or Evangelists, nor by the early Christian writers. It is found once only in Acts, where St. Stephen exclaims: "Behold, I see the heavens opened, and the Son of Man standing on the right hand of God" (vii, 55). The whole incident proves that it was a well-known expression of Christ's. Though the saying was so frequently employed by Christ, the disciples preferred some more honorific title and we do not find it at all in St. Paul nor in the other Epistles. St. Paul perhaps uses something like an equivalent when he calls Christ the second or last Adam. The writers of the Epistles, moreover, probably wished to avoid the Greek ambiguity just alluded to.

The expression is Christ's, in spite of the futile attempts of some German Rationalists and others to show that He could not have used it. It was not invented by the writers of the Gospels to whom it did not appear to be a favourite title, as they never use it of Christ themselves. It was not derived by them from what is asserted was a false interpretation of Daniel, because it appears in the early portions of the public ministry where there is no reference to Daniel. The objection that Christ could not have used it in Aramaic because the only similar expression was *bar-nasha*, which then meant only "man", *bar* having by that time lost its meaning of "son", is not of much weight. Only little is known of the Aramaic spoken in Palestine in the time of Christ; and as Drummond points out special meaning could be given to the word by the emphasis with which it was pronounced, even if *bar-nasha* had lost its primary meaning in Palestine, which is not at all proved. As the same writer shows, there were other expressions in Aramaic which Christ could have employed for the purpose, and Sanday suggests that He may have occasionally spoken in Greek.

The early Fathers were of the opinion that the expression was used out of humility and to show Christ's human nature, and this is very probable considering the early rise of Docetism. This is also the opinion of Cornelius a Lapide. Others, such as Knabenbauer, think that He adopted a title which would not give umbrage to His enemies, and which, as time went on, was capable of being applied so as to cover His Messianic claims—to include everything that had been foretold of the representative man, the second Adam, the suffering servant of Jehovah, the Messianic king.

Jésus Messie et Fils de Dieu (Paris, 1906); ROSE, *Studies on the Gospels* (London, 1903); DRUMMOND, *The Jour. of Theol. Studies*, II (1901), 350, 539; HARTL, *Anfang und Ende des Titels "Menchensohn"* in *Bibl. Zeitschrift* (Freiburg, 1909), 342.

C. AHERNE.

Sonora, DIOCESE OF (DE SONORA), in the Republic of Mexico, suffragan of the Archdiocese of Durango. Its area is that of the state of the same name, 76,619 sq. miles, and its population (1910) 262,545. The bishop and the governor of the state reside at Hermosillo, a city situated 681 ft. above sea level, containing (1910) about 14,518 inhabitants. The Gospel was first preached in the territory of the Diocese of Sonora by the celebrated Father Niza, who accompanied the daring expeditions of the first explorers and conquerors of Mexico. The Spaniards settled at different places in this section; they evangelized the numerous tribes who lived in that region in the beginning of the seventeenth century, after having established the new See of Durango, to which all these lands were given. The Jesuits, who were assigned the task of converting to Christianity the people of these lands, founded the famous missions of Rio Yaqui, Rio Mayo, and Upper and Lower Pimeria. Notable among these priests was the celebrated Father Kino (q. v.). When the Jesuits were expelled from all the Spanish colonies (1767) they had the following residences: Mission of the Upper and Lower Pimeria (Guazaves, Aconche, Mátape, Oposura, Movas, S. Ignacio, Arizpe, Aribechi, Batuco, Onavas, Cucurupe, Cumuripa, Saguaripa, Sta Maria Soanca, Tubutama, Odope, Saric, Tecoripa, Ures, Caborca, Babispe, Baca de Guachi, Cuquiarachi, Onapa, Banamichi); S. Javier del Bac, Santa Maria Basoraca, and Guebabi, which were then in the territory now belonging to the United States; Mission del Rio Yaqui (Huirivis, Belem, Rahum, Torim, Bacum); Mission del Rio Mayo (Santa Cruz, Caamoa, Nabojoa, Conicari, Batacosa).

On 7 May, 1779, Pius VI established the Diocese of Sonora, to which belonged at that time the present states of Sinaloa and Sonora and the two Californias (Upper and Lower). It was suffragan of the then immense Archdiocese of Mexico. This territory was divided in 1840 when the See of S. Francisco de California was founded. In 1863 it ceased to be a suffragan of Mexico and became suffragan of the new metropolitan see established at Guadalajara. In 1873 it was separated from Lower California, which became a vicariate Apostolic, and in 1883, when the See of Sinaloa was created, the See of Sonora was reduced to its present limits. In 1891 Leo XIII, by the Bull *Illud in Primis*, separated this See from the ecclesiastical Province of Guadalajara and made it a suffragan of the new Archdiocese of Durango. The bishop's residence was first situated in the city of Arizpe, but owing to the uprising of the Indians it was removed to Alamos and later to Culiacan, the present capital of the State of Sinaloa. When the new See of Sinaloa was created the Bishop of Sonora made his residence at Hermosillo.

This diocese has 1 seminary with 10 students, 17 parochial schools, 2 Catholic colleges with about 700 students. Protestants have founded 11 churches. Among the 221,000 inhabitants a great number of Indians from the Seris, Yaquis, Apaches, Papagos, and other tribes are to be found; these have unfortunately returned in large numbers to barbarism since the missionaries abandoned them. Few Apaches and Papagos Indians remain in the Sonora territory. The Seris Indians are more numerous and live in the large island of Tiburon in the Gulf of California and in a large part of the territory along the banks of the Rio Sonora. Those who live on the island are savage and opposed to civilization, while those on the continent have formed agricultural colonies and are quite subdued since the last uprising. As to the Yaqui Indians, the Federal Government of Mexico has had some serious trouble with them. It appears, however, that had they not been deprived of their lands a more peaceful people could hardly be found.

VERA, *Catecismo geográfico histórico de la Iglesia Mexicana* (Amecameca, 1881); DÁVILA, *Continuación de la historia de la C. de J. en Nueva España* (Puebla, 1889); CARREZ, *Atlas geographicus Societatis Jesu* (Paris, 1900); DOMENECH, *Guia general descriptiva de la Republica Mexicana* (Mexico, 1899).

CAMILLUS CRIVELLI.

Soothsaying. See DIVINATION.

Sophene, a titular see, suffragan of Melitene in Armenia Secunda. In the sixth century "Notitiæ episcopatuum" of Antioch, Sophene is a suffragan of Amida in Mesopotamia ("Echos d'Orient", X, 145). Justinian in a letter to Zetas, "magister militum" of Armenia and Pontus Polemoniacus, grants him jurisdiction over various provinces, among them Sophene and Sophenene, "in qua est Martyropolis" ("Codex. Just.", I, 29, 5). At the beginning of the seventh century George of Cyprus ("Descriptio orbis romani", ed. Gelzer, 49) mentions Sophene in Armenia Quarta, and we know elsewhere that Arsamosata was the capital of the latter province. From these texts we conclude, first, that there were two distinct districts, Sophene situated more to the north and very well known to the classical writers as an Armenian province, subject to the Roman Empire, and, second, Sophenene, situated near Martyropolis and Amida. The latter is probably the titular see. Le Quien ("Oriens christianus", II, 1001), mentions two bishops of Sophene: Arsaphus, present at the Council of Constantinople in 381; Euphemius, at Chalcedon, 451. The exact situation of this bishopric is unknown.

SMITH, *Dict. of Greek and Roman Geog.* (London, 1870), s. v.; GELZER, *Georgii Cyprii Descriptio orbis romani*, LXI; CHAPOT, *La frontière de l'Euphrate* (Paris, 1907), 168-70.

S. VAILHÉ.

Sophists, a group of Greek teachers who flourished at the end of the fifth century B. C. They claimed to be purveyors of wisdom—hence the name σοφισταί, which originally meant one who possesses wisdom—but in reality undertook to show that all true certitude is unattainable, and that culture and preparation for the business of public life are to be acquired, not by profound thinking, but by discussion and debate. In accordance with this principle, they gathered around them the young men of Athens, and professed to prepare them for their career as citizens and as men by teaching them the art of public speaking and the theory and practice of argumentation. They did not pretend to teach how the truth is to be attained. They did not care whether it could be attained or not. They aimed to impart to their pupils the ability to make the better cause seem the worse, and the worse the better. If we are to believe their opponents, Plato and Aristotle, they affected all kinds of refinement, in dress, speech, gesture, etc., and carried their love of argumentation to the point where all seriousness of purpose ceased and quibbling and sophistry began.

The principal Sophists were: Protagoras of Abdera, called the Individualist; Gorgias of Leontini, surnamed the Nihilist; Hippias of Elis, the Polymathist; and Prodicus of Ceos, the Moralist. Gorgias was called the Nihilist because of his doctrine "nothing exists: even if anything existed, we could know nothing about it, and, even if we knew anything about anything, we could not communicate our knowledge". Hippias was called the Polymathist because he laid claim to knowledge of many out-of-the-way subjects, such as archæology, and used this knowledge for the sophistical purpose of dazzling and embarrassing his opponent in argument. Prodicus, called the Moralist because in his discourses, especially in that which he entitled "Hercules at the Cross-roads", he strove to inculcate moral lessons, although he did not attempt to reduce conduct to principles, but taught rather by proverb, epigram, and illustration. The most important of all the Sophists was Protagoras, the Individualist, so called because he held that the individual is the test of all truth. "Man is the measure of all things" is a saying attributed to him by Plato, which sums up the Sophists' doctrine in regard to the value of knowledge.

The Sophists may be said to be the first Greek sceptics. The materialism of the Atomists, the idealism of the Eleatics, and the doctrine of universal change which was a tenet of the School of Heraclitus —all these tendencies resulted in a condition of unrest, out of which philosophy could not advance to a more satisfactory state until an enquiry was made into the problem of the value of knowledge. The Sophists did not undertake that enquiry—a task reserved for Socrates (q. v.)—however, they called attention to the existence of the problem, and in that way, and in that way only, they contributed to the progress of philosophy in Greece. The absurdities to which the Sophistic method was carried by the later Sophists was due in part to the Megarians, who made common cause with them, and substituted the method of strife (Eristic method) for the Socratic method of discovery (Heuristic method). It was inevitable, therefore, that the name Sophist should lose its primitive meaning, and come to designate, not a man of wisdom, but a quibbler, and one who uses fallacious arguments. The Sophists represent a phase of Greek thought which, while it had no constructive value, and is, indeed, a step backward and not forward, in the course of Greek speculation is nevertheless of great importance historically, because it was the evil influence of the Sophists that inspired Socrates with the idea of refuting them by showing the conditions of true knowledge. It was, no doubt, their methods, too, that Aristotle had in mind when he wrote his treatise of the fallacies, and entitled it "De Sophisticis Elenchis".

For texts see RITTER AND PRELLER, *Historia Phil. Græcæ* (Gotha, 1888), 181 sq.; BAKEWELL, *Source Book in Ancient Philosophy* (New York, 1907), 67 sq.; ZELLER, *Pre-Socratic Philosophers*, tr. ALLEYNE (London, 1881); II, 304 sq.; TURNER, *History of Philosophy* (Boston, 1903), 70 sq.

WILLIAM TURNER.

Sophonias, the ninth of the twelve Minor Prophets of the Canon of the Old Testament, preached and wrote in the second half of the seventh century B. C. He was a contemporary and supporter of the great Prophet Jeremias. His name (Heb. *Zephanja*, that is "the Lord conceals", "the Lord protects") might, on the analogy of Gottfried, be most briefly translated by the words God protect. The only primary source from which we obtain our scanty knowledge of the personality and the rhetorical and literary qualities of Sophonias, is the short book of the Old Testament (containing only three chapters), which bears his name. The scene of his activity was the city of Jerusalem (i, 4–10; iii, 1 sqq.; 14 sqq.).

I. DATE.—The date of the Prophet's activity fell in the reign of King Josias (641–11). Sophonias is one of the few Prophets whose chronology is fixed by a precise date in the introductory verse of the book. Under the two preceding kings, Amon and Manasse, idolatry had been introduced in the most shameful forms (especially the cult of Baal and Astarte) into the Holy City, and with this foreign cult came a foreign culture and a great corruption of morals. Josias, the king with the anointed sceptre, wished to put an end to the horrible devastation in the holy places. One of the most zealous champions and advisers of this reform was Sophonias, and his writing remains one of the most important documents for the understanding of the era of Josias. The Prophet laid the axe at the root of the religious and moral corruption, when, in view of the idolatry which had penetrated even into the sanctuary, he threatened to "destroy out of this place the remnant of Baal, and the names of the . . . priests" (i, 4), and pleaded for a return to the simplicity of their fathers instead of the luxurious foreign clothing which was worn especially in aristocratic circles (i, 8). The age of Sophonias was also a most serious and decisive period, because the lands of Anterior Asia were overrun by foreigners owing to the migration of the Scythians in the last decades of the seventh century, and because Jerusalem, the city of the Prophets, was only a few decades before its downfall (586). The far-seeing watchman on Sion's battlements saw this catastrophe draw near: "for the day of the Lord is near" is the burden of his preaching (i, 7). "The great day of the Lord is near, it is near and exceeding swift: . . . That day *is* a day of wrath, a day of tribulation and distress, a day of calamity and misery, a day of darkness and obscurity, a day of clouds and whirlwinds" (i, 14–15).

II. CONTENTS.—The book of the Prophet naturally contains in its three chapters only a sketch of the fundamental ideas of the preaching of Sophonias. The scheme of the book in its present form is as follows:

(a) i, 2–ii, 3.—The threatening of the "day of the Lord", a *Dies iræ dies illa* of the Old Testament. The judgment of the Lord will descend on Juda and Jerusalem as a punishment for the awful degeneracy in religious life (i, 4–7a); it will extend to all classes of the people (i, 7b–13), and will be attended with all the horrors of a frightful catastrophe (i, 14–18); therefore, do penance and seek the Lord (ii, 1–3).

(b) ii, 4–15.—Not only over Jerusalem, but over the whole world (*urbi et orbi*), over the peoples in all the four regions of the heavens, will the hand of the Lord be stretched—westwards over the Philistines (4–7), eastwards over the Moabites and Ammonites (8–11), southwards over the Ethiopians (12), and northwards over the Assyrians and Ninivites (13–15).

(c) With a special threat (iii, 1–8), the Prophet then turns again to Jerusalem: "Woe to the provoking, and redeemed city. . . . She hath not hearkened to the voice, neither hath she received discipline"; the severest reckoning will be required of the aristocrats and the administrators of the law (as the leading classes of the civil community), and of the Prophets and priests, as the directors of public worship.

(d) iii, 9–20.—A consolatory prophecy, or prophetic glance at the Kingdom of God of the future, in which all the world, united in one faith and one worship, will turn to one God, and the goods of the Messianic Kingdom, whose capital is the daughter of Sion, will be enjoyed. The universality of the judgment as well as of the redemption is so forcibly expressed in Sophonias that his book may be regarded as the "Catholic Epistle" of the Old Testament.

(e) The last exhortation of Sophonias (iii, 9–20) also has a Messianic colouring, although not to an extent comparable with Isaias.

III. CHARACTER OF THE PROPHET.—Sophonias' prophecy is not strongly differentiated from other prophecies like that of Amos or Habacuc, it is confined to the range of thought common to all prophetic exhortations: threats of judgment, exhortation to penance, promise of Messianic salvation. For this reason Sophonias might be regarded as the type of Hebrew Prophets and as the final example of the prophetic terminology. He does not seek the glory of an original writer, but borrows freely both ideas and style from the older Prophets (especially Isaias and Jeremias). The resemblances to the Book of Deuteronomy may be explained by the fact that this book, found in the Josian reform, was then the centre of religious interest. The language of Sophonias is vigorous and earnest, as became the seriousness of the period, but is free from the gloomy elegiac tone of Jeremias. In some passages it becomes pathetic and poetic, without however attaining the classical diction or poetical flight of a Nahum or Deutero-Isaias. There is something solemn in the manner in which the Lord is so frequently introduced as the speaker, and the sentence of judgment falls on the silent earth (i, 7). Apart from the few plays on words (cf. especially ii, 4), Sophonias eschews all rhetorical and poetical ornamentation of language. As to the logical and rhythmical build of the various exhortations, he has two strophes of the first sketch (i, 7 and 14) with the same opening ("the day of the Lord is near"), and closes the second sketch with a hymn (ii, 15)—a favourite practice of his prototype, Jeremias. A graduated development of the sentiment to a climax in the scheme is expressed by the fact that the last sketch contains an animated and longer lyrical hymn to Jerusalem (iii, 14 sqq.). In Christian painting Sophonias is represented in two ways; either with the lantern (referring to i, 12: "I will search Jerusalem with lamps") or clad in a toga and bearing a scroll bearing as text the beginning of the hymn "Give praise, O daughter of Sion" (iii 14).

IV. CRITICAL PROBLEMS OFFERED BY SOPHONIAS.—The question of authorship is authoritatively answered by the introductory verse of the book. Even radical higher critics like Marti acknowledge that no reason exists for doubting that the author of this prophecy is the Sophonias (Zephaniah) mentioned in the title ("Das Dodekapropheton", Tübingen, 1904, 359). The fact that this Prophet's name is mentioned nowhere else in the Old Testament does not affect the conclusive force of the first verse of the prophecy. Sophonias is the only Prophet whose genealogy is traced back into the fourth generation. From this has been inferred that the fourth and last ancestor mentioned Ezechias (Hizkiah) is identical with the king of the same name (727–698). In this case, however, the explanatory phrase "King of Judah" would undoubtedly have been put in apposition to the name. Consequently the statement concerning the author of the book in the first part of the introductory verse appears entirely worthy of belief, because the statement concerning the chronology of the book given in the second half of the same verse is confirmed by internal criteria. The descriptions of customs, especially in the first chapter, showing the state of religion and morals at Jerusalem are, in point of fact, a true presentation of conditions during the first years of the reign of King Josias. The worship of the stars upon the flat roofs, mentioned in i, 5, an imitation of the Babylonian worship of the heavens that had become the fashion in Palestine from the reign of Manasses is also mentioned by the contemporary Prophet, Jeremias (xix, 13; xxxii, 29), as a religious disorder of the Josianic era. All this confirms the credibility of the witness of i, 1, concerning the authorship of Sophonias.

Critical investigations, as to where the original texts in the Book of Sophonias end and the glosses, revisions of the text, and still later revisions begin, have resulted in a unanimous declaration that the first chapter of the book is the work of Sophonias; the second chapter is regarded as not so genuine, and the third still less so. In separating what are called the secondary layers of the second chapter nearly all the higher critics have come to different conclusions,—*quot capita, tot sensus*. Each individual verse cannot be investigated here as in the detailed analysis of a commentator. However, it may be pointed out in general that the technical plan in the literary construction of the speeches, especially the symmetrical arrangement of the speeches mentioned in section II, and the responses spoken of in section III, forbid any large excisions. The artistic form used in the construction of the prophetic addresses is recognized more and more as an aid to literary criticism.

The passage most frequently considered an addition of a later date is iii, 14–20, because the tone of a herald of salvation here adopted does not agree with that of the prophecies of the threatening judgment of the two earlier chapters. It is, however, the custom of the Prophets after a terrifying warning of the judgments of Jahve to close with a glimpse of the brilliant future of the Kingdom of God, to permit, as it were, the rainbow to follow the thunder-storm. Joel first utters prophetic denunciations which are followed by prophetic consolations (Joel in Vulgate, i–ii, 17; ii, 18–iii); Isaias in ch. i calls Jerusalem a city like Sodom and directly afterwards a city of justice, and Micheas, whose similarity to Sophonias is remarked upon by critics, also allows his threats of judgment to die away in an announcement of salvation. One of the guiding eschatological thoughts of all the Prophets is this: The judgment is only the way of transition to salvation and the consummation of the history of the world will be the salvation of what is left of the seed. For this reason, therefore, Sophonias, iii, 14–20 cannot be rejected. The entire plan of the book seems to be indicated in a small scale in the first address, which closes ii, 1–3, with an exhortation to seek the Lord that is with a consolatory theme directly after the terrible proclamation of the Day of the Lord.

The queries raised by the textual criticism of the Book of Sophonias are far simpler and nearer solution than those connected with the higher criticism. The condition of the text, with exception of a few doubtful passages, is good and there are few books of the Biblical canon which offer so few points of attack to Biblical hypercriticism as the Book of Sophonias.

REINKE, *Der Prophet Zephanja* (Münster, 1868); KNABENBAUER, *Comment. in proph. min.* (Paris, 1886); VAN HOONACKER, *Les douze pet. proph.* (Paris, 1908); LIPPL, *Das Buch des Proph. Sophon.* (Freiburg, 1910), containing (pp. ix–xvi) an excellent bibliography; SCHWALLY, *Das Buch Zephanja* (Giessen, 1890); SCHULZ, *Comment. über den Proph. Zephanja* (Hanover, 1892); ADAMS, *The Minor Proph.* (New York, 1902); DRIVER, *The Min. Proph.* (*Nahum, Habakkuk, Zephaniah*) (Edinburgh, 1907); the compete commentaries of STRACK-ZÖCKLER; NOWACK; MARTI; and G. A. SMITH.

M. FAULHABER.

Sophronius, SAINT, Patriarch of Jerusalem and Greek ecclesiastical writer, b. about 560 at Damascus of noble parentage; d. probably 11 March, 638, at

Jerusalem. In company with John Moschus he travelled extensively through the East and also went to Rome. He probably became a monk in Egypt about 580 and later removed to Palestine. From the year 633 until his death he was the principal opponent of Monothelitism. Conspicuous for his learning and piety he became in 634 Patriarch of Jerusalem, and sorrowfully witnessed during his reign the conquest of Palestine by the Arabs and their capture of Jerusalem. He must very probably be identified with the Sophronius known as the rhetorician (σοφιστής), and was the author of biographies, homilies, and hymns. Among the first named are: his Life of John the Almoner, written in collaboration with J. Moschus and only partly preserved in Symeon Metaphrastes; the lives of Sts. Cyrus and John; and probably a Life of St. Mary of Egypt. Ten homilies which have been preserved deal chiefly with ecclesiastical festivals, and are remarkable for their dogmatic contents and oratorical style. Numerous anacreontic odes entitle him to a place among Greek ecclesiastical poets. A large work in which he collected 600 testimonies of the Fathers in favour of the two wills of Christ has perished.

The most comprehensive collection of the works of Sophronius is found in *P. G.*, LXXXVII, iii, 3147–4014; VENABLES in *Dict. Christ. Biog.*, s. v. *Sophronius (12)*; VAILHÉ, *Sophrone le sophiste et Sophrone le patriarche* in *Revue de l'Orient Chrétien*, VII (1902), 360–85; VIII (1903), 32–69, 356–87; BARDENHEWER-SHAHAN, *Patrology* (St. Louis, 1908), 559–61, 564–66.

N. A. WEBER.

Sophronius, Bishop of Constantina or Tella in Osrhoene, was a relative of Ibas, Bishop of Edessa, and apparently of the same theological tendency, i. e. strongly anti-Monophysite and liable to be suspected of Nestorianism. He was present at a synod held at Antioch in 445 at which Athanasius, Bishop of Perrha, was deposed on charges of misconduct, the chief among which was that he had purloined some silver pillars belonging to the church. We have no means of judging whether these charges were true; very possibly, if not trumped up, they were too easily credited from partisan motives. Four years later at the Robber Council of Ephesus (q. v.) most extraordinary charges of magic and sorcery were brought against Bishop Sophronius. For some reason or other, perhaps because it was foreseen that the charges would break down, perhaps because he was not worth crushing in view of the more important personages being pursued, Sophronius's case was referred to the new Bishop of Edessa, when one should be appointed in place of Ibas whom the Conciliabulum had deposed. Sophronius is next heard of at the Council of Chalcedon. At the eighth session, after Theodoret had anathematized Nestorius, "the most reverend bishops cried out 'Let Sophronius also anathematize'. Sophronius, the most reverend bishop of Constantina, said 'anathema to Nestorius and Eutyches'".

The charges against Sophronius have only been brought to light in recent years by the discovery of a Syriac version of the Acts of the Robber Council. They were made by a priest and two deacons of Tella (Constantina), who claimed to represent the rest of the clergy of that city. The bishop, they declared, practised astrology and other vaticinative arts of the pagans. The miserable heresy of Nestorius which he had learnt from Ibas was not enough for him, so he threw himself into those other abominations. He once lost some money, and not content with making the suspected persons swear on the Gospels, "he, further testing them by the ordeal of bread and cheese, compelled them to eat". This not succeeding, he had recourse to the divining cup. He used the son of one of his servants as a medium, and with two others, after some incantations, placed the youth before a vessel containing oil and water. In this mixture the youth first saw flames of fire, then "a man sitting on a throne of gold, and clad in purple and a crown upon his head". After this they put the oil and water in a hole near the door, and the medium saw the bishop's son Habib who was returning home from Constantinople "seated on a black mare-mule that is blind-folded; and behind him two men on foot". The lad confessed these and other like things on oath. He was haunted by seven men dressed in white and lost his reason, and was with difficulty cured by being brought into holy places and anointed with oil. Many persons, among others the copyists, could testify to Sophronius's astrological writings. A deacon who came to him, to have a ticket of alms signed, found him inspecting a brass sphere. His son Habib introduced a Jew into his father's house and ate with him after the manner of the Jews. "During the week of Lent, when we fast, he feasted with this Jew, and kept him at table till ten o'clock; and even carried his audacity (so far as) to bring him into the Sanctuary of the Apostles, at the time that Service was being held. The city and the clergy, shocked by this conduct, chased both the Jew and Habib, who sought refuge in the Prætorium of the Commandant (Duke) Florus. The impious and pagan Florus rushed upon the city, where (his people) laid violent hands on a great number of men and children—certainly more than a hundred. In despair, these took refuge near the Tabernacle; but the arrows reached their bodies, their blood was shed before the Altar, and many died in the act of embracing it."

The Second Synod of Ephesus, from Syriac MSS., ed. PERRY (Dartford, 1881), pp. 189–199; see art. *Sophron. of Constantine* in *Dict. of Christ. Biog.*

FRANCIS J. BACCHUS.

Sora. See AQUINO, SORA, AND PONTECORVO, DIOCESE OF.

Sora, a titular see in Paphlagonia, suffragan of Gangra. Sora must have been an insignificant town; an inscription discovered at Zorah, a village in the vilayet of Castamouni, in which a local era and the worship of Zeus Epicarpios are mentioned, has enabled its exact position to be fixed. (Doublet in "Bull. de correspondance hellénique", 1889, p. 310.) It was placed later under the government of the Prætor of Paphlagonia (Novel., 29, 1; Hierocles, 695, 7). It is spoken of by Constantine Porphyrogenitus, "De themat.", I, 7. Le Quien ("Oriens christ.", I, 557), mentions six of its bishops: Theodore, represented by his metropolitan at the Council of Chalcedon (451); Olympius, who signed the letter of the bishops of the province to Emperor Leo in 458; John, present at the Council of Constantinople (692); Theophanes, at the Seventh Œcumenical Council of Nicæa (787); Phocas, at the eighth general Council at Constantinople (869); Constantine, at the Photian Council of Constantinople (879). The Greek "Notitiæ episcopatuum" mentions the see till the thirteenth century.

SMITH, *Dict. of Greek and Roman Geog.*, s. v.; RAMSAY, *Asia Minor* (London, 1890), passim.

S. PÉTRIDÈS.

Sorbait, PAUL DE, physician, b. in Hainault, 1624; d. at Vienna, 19 April, 1691. He went to school at Paderborn, then attended the University of Padua, where apparently he obtained his degree of Doctor of Philosophy and Medicine. He practised as a physician at Rome, Cologne, and Arnheim, and in August, 1652, was made a member of the medical faculty of the University of Vienna. In 1655 he became professor of theoretical medicine at the same university, and in 1666 professor of practical medicine. In 1658 he was appointed court-physician to the Empress-Dowager Eleonora. In 1676 he rebuilt at his own expense the students' hall "Goldberg" and added a chapel to it. During the year of the pest (1679), the

Emperor Leopold I appointed him official councillor and chief supervisor of sanitary conditions in Vienna. Soon after this he was ennobled. In 1681 he resigned his professorship and founded a scholarship for medical students. During the siege of Vienna by the Turks in 1683 he commanded the company formed of students as chief sergeant-major. His tomb is in the Cathedral of St. Stephen at Vienna. In 1909 the national association of the official doctors of Austria selected Sorbait's portrait as the insignia of the association. He gained a high reputation as a teacher at Vienna by zealous encouragement of anatomy and botany, as well as by firm adherence to the Hippocratic school. His prominent position in the year 1679 gave him the opportunity to organize sanitary conditions in Vienna. His writings show a harmonious mixture of profound thinking, strong piety, and a merry wit. His style frequently recalls that of the Augustinian monk and Viennese preacher Abraham a Santa Clara, but Sorbait was not an imitator of the latter, as the orations delivered upon receiving a higher position were delivered in part before 1666, consequently before Father Abraham's appearance as a speaker at Vienna.

Sorbait's works are the following: "Universa medicina tam theorica quam practica" etc. (Nuremberg, 1672, 1675); this is his chief work. It was issued in a revised and enlarged form under the title: "Praxios medicæ tractatus VII" (Vienna, 1680 and 1701); "Commentaria et controversiæ in omnes libros aphorismorum Hippocratis" (Vienna, 1660); "Nova et aucta institutionum isagoge" (Vienna, 1678); "Modus promovendi doctores in archilycæo Viennensi" (Vienna, 1667), in "Praxios medicæ tract.", 553–577; "Encomiastica neoprofessuræ prolegomena", oration delivered on entrance to his professorship, 31 January, 1655; "Discursus academicus in renovatione magistratus civici", 7 Jan., 1669, in German; "Resignatio rectoratus", 25 Nov., 1669; "Exhortatio in honorem St. Barbaræ", 25 Jan., 1664; all these are to be found in the "Prax. med. tract.", 578–90; "Die Johann Wilhelm Mannagellasche Pestordnung im Auftrag der Regierung von P. Sorbait herausgegeben und vermehrt" (1679); "Consilium medicum seu dialogus loimicus de peste Viennensi" (Vienna, 1679; also in German, 1679; 1713; Berlin, 1681), Sorbait's most popular book; "Catalogus rectorum" (Vienna, 1669 and 1670). He also wrote short articles which are to be found in the "Miscellanea curiosa academiæ cæsareæ Leopoldinæ II, III".

Oesterreichischer Galenus, dass ist Lob- Leich- und Ehrenpredig Thro Magnificenz dess Wohl-Edel Gebohrnen und hochgelehrten Pauli de Sorbait von P. Emericus Pfendtner O.F.M., 10 Mai, 1691 (Vienna); SENFELDER, *Paul de Sorbait* in *Wiener klinische Rundschau* (1906), nos. 21–27, 29–30.

LEOPOLD SENFELDER.

Sorbonne.—This name is frequently used in ordinary parlance as synonymous with the faculty of theology of Paris. Strictly speaking it means, as in this article, the celebrated theological college of the French capital. The title was adopted from the name of the university institute founded by Robert de Sorbon, a native of Le Réthelois, a distinguished professor and famous preacher who lived from 1201 till 1274. Sorbon found that there was a defect in the primitive organization of the University of Paris. The two principal mendicant orders—the Dominicans and the Franciscans—had each at Paris a college and delivered lectures at which extern students might attend without fee. In order that the university, which was already engaged in a struggle with the religious, might offer the same advantages, Robert de Sorbon decided that it also should provide gratuitous instruction and that this should be given by a society of professors following, except as regards the matter of vows, the rules of the cenobitic life. This important work was rendered possible by the high esteem in which Robert was held at Paris, together with his brilliant parts, his great generosity, and the assistance of his friends. The foundation dates from the year 1257 or the beginning of 1258. Nor was the aid he received merely pecuniary; Guillaume de Saint-Amour, Gérard d'Abbeville, Henry of Ghent, Guillaume des Grez, Odo or Eudes of Douai, Chrétien de Beauvais, Gérard de Reims, Nicolas de Bar are but a few of the most illustrious names inseparably connected either with the first chairs in the Sorbonne, or with the first association that constituted it. These savants were already attached to the university staff.

The constitution of the society as conceived by Robert was quite simple: an administrator (*provisor*), associates (*socii*), and guests (*hospites*). The pro-

CHAPEL OF THE SORBONNE

visor was the head; nothing could be done without consulting him; he installed the members selected by the society, and confirmed the statutes drawn up by it; in a word, as his title signifies, he had to provide for everything. The associates formed the body of the society. To be admitted to it, the candidate was required to have taught a course of philosophy. There were two kinds of associates, the *bursaires* and the *pensionnaires*. The latter paid forty (Paris) pounds a year, the former were provided for by the house, which expended a like sum from its revenues. The burse could be granted only to persons not having an income of forty (Paris) pounds. There was a *primus inter pares*, the prior, who presided over all internal affairs of the house. Doctors and bachelors were alike eligible, but, owing to the number of the latter, the custom rapidly grew up of selecting only bachelors. Other persons were candidates for admission to the society rather than members of it. From the material and intellectual point of view they enjoyed the same privileges as the members: board, lodging, books, spiritual and scholastic exercises; but they had no votes. When they had fulfilled the condition of teaching philosophy, they were admissible as members. The course of studies lasted ten years, during which time their burses continued; but, if at the end of ten years, they had not given proof of their ability, either as teachers or as preachers, their burse was vacated. The ordinary lectures were public, and consequently were attended by students who belonged to neither of the divisions of the society. The doctors and bachelors were authorized to give shelter to other poor pupils. Besides the work of the classroom, there was the duty of preaching or labouring in the parishes. In preparation for this, the associates, on certain days, had to deliver sermons or conferences (*collationes*) in presence of the community. The purely spiritual side was not forgotten. Conferences, usually delivered by the prior, on this important part of the Christian and priestly life were given, if not exclusively, at least specially, to the interns. For twenty years the ability of the administrator, or provisor, corresponded to the foreseeing devotedness of the founder. This lapse of time showed the wisdom of the regulations and administrative measures, which Robert had adopted, after taking the best possible advice, and which he laid down in thirty-eight articles. This rule was directed towards the maintaining of common life, from silence in the refectory, which was not very strict, to simplicity of the authorized dress. As soon as circumstances permitted, Robert (about 1271) added to the theological college a literary college: this was the Collège de Calvi or the "little Sorbonne".

Fruit of deep thought and personal experience, the constitution given by Robert de Sorbon to his college received the consecration of time, for it lasted throughout centuries. If Héméré saw in the project the conception of a powerful intellect, "Hoc primus in lyeaco Parisiensi vidit Robertus", its realization was surely a work of genius. That this was so appears from the fact that, while Robert united in his work whatever good he found in the university, his college when completed served as a model to the others. It is unnecessary to dwell on each word of the original title, for some persons rather enigmatical, of the society. The expression "Pauvres maîtres étudiants en théologie" seems to emphasize the two primary or essential characteristics of the society: equality in poverty, an equality so perfect between masters and pupils that it designated them by a common name; the poverty of the pupils, since most of them were *bursaires;* the poverty of the masters, since, content with what was strictly necessary, they renounced all other professional remuneration. This equality was always maintained with scrupulous care; the Sorbonnists repeated as an axiom, "Omnes nos sumus socii et æquales", and referred to the college as "pauperem nostram Sorbonem".

From the outset the college enjoyed the favour of the Holy See. Alexander IV (1259) urged the French bishops to support it, Urban IV (1262) recommended it to the goodwill of the whole Christian world, and Clement IV (1268) granted it papal approbation. Wealthy benefactors provided it with ample endowment. A high standard of scholarship was maintained and the severity of the "actus Sorbonnicus", or examination for degrees, including the defence of the "thesis Robertina", became proverbial. The professorial corps was highly respected, and from all parts of Europe different theological and even political questions were sent to it for solution. As the other teachers of theology in the university became members of the Sorbonne, its staff, at the beginning of the sixteenth century, was practically identical with the university faculty. Robert de Sorbon had realized the necessity of a library and had taken measures to supply one. This increased rapidly, owing chiefly to numerous gifts. In 1470 the Sorbonne introduced the art of printing into France by calling to Paris three of Gutenberg's associates, Gering, Friburger, and Crantz. Among its principal patrons and benefactors was Cardinal Richelieu, who held for a time the office of provisor and who, in 1635, laid the cornerstone of an edifice to be built at his expense for the use of the college. He was buried in the church of the Sorbonne, where his tomb is still preserved. The doctors of the college were loyal defenders of the Catholic faith against the inroads of Protestantism and against the so-called Enlightenment. On the other hand, they gave their support to Gallicanism and obliged their members to subscribe the "four articles". This attitude naturally weakened the prestige of the Sorbonne as a theological school, and obliged ecclesiastical students to seek their education in the seminaries. The Sorbonne itself was suppressed by decree of 5 April, 1792, but was restored by Napoleon in 1808 as the theological faculty of the newly organized university. It did not, however, regain its former standing or influence, though it continued in existence until 1882, when it was finally suppressed. In 1884 the construction of the present building was begun and it was completed in 1889. It is now occupied by the various departments of letters and science which form the "École des Hautes Etudes".

De Boulay, *Hist. Univers. Paris.* (Paris, 1665-73); Crevier, *Hist. de l' Univ. de Paris* (Paris, 1761); Jourdain, *Hist. de l'univer. de Paris au XVIIe et au XVIIIe siècle;* (Paris, 1866); Denifle, *Chartularium Univers. Paris.* (Paris, 1889-97); Jadard, *Robert de Sorbon* (Reims, 1877); Méric, *La Sorbonne et son fondateur* (Paris, 1888); Raleigh, *Univ. of Paris;* Feret, *La faculté de théologie de Paris et ses docteurs les plus célèbres* (Paris, 1894-1909); Idem, *Sorbonæ origines, disciplina et viri illustres,* and other manuscripts; Franklin, *La Sorbonne, ses origines, sa bibliothèque* (Paris, 1875); Randolph, *History of the Sorbonne;* Rashdall, *The Universities of Europe in the Middle Ages* (Oxford, 1893).

P. Feret.

Sorin, Edward, the founder of Notre Dame, Indiana; b. 6 Feb., 1814, at Ahuillé, near Laval, France; d. 31 Oct., 1893, at Notre Dame, U. S. A. His early education was directed by his mother, a woman remarkable for intelligence as well as virtue. After completing his classical studies, his vocation for the priesthood being marked, M. Sorin at once entered the diocesan seminary, where he was distinguished for superior ability and exemplary life. Among his fellow students were Cardinal Langénieux and others who shed lustre on the Church.

Father Sorin
From a Photograph

At the time of Father Sorin's ordination, glowing reports of missionary enterprise in foreign lands had fired afresh the hearts of the French clergy, and inspired numerous vocations, not a few of which were those of future martyrs, particularly in China and Japan. It was to the first of these countries that the Abbé Sorin felt attracted; and to the end of his long life accounts of the trials and triumphs of Chinese missionaries had for him a singular fascination. He was influenced by circumstances to enroll himself in the Congregation of the Holy Cross, a community of priests, brothers, and sisters lately founded at Le Mans by the Abbé Moreau. The need of missionaries in the United States, so earnestly represented in letters from bishops in this country and in addresses by others who had occasion to visit Europe, was not to be disregarded by the heads of religious orders; and although France had not as yet recovered from the effects of the Revolution, she generously contributed men and means for the support and spread of American missions. Father Sorin, but recently

SORRENTO

ROAD FROM SORRENTO TO POSITANO
PANTANELLO BRIDGE ON THE ROAD TO POSITANO
MONASTERY OF IL DESERTO, NEAR SORRENTO

VIEW ON THE SHORE OF THE BAY
CAMPANILE OF THE CATHEDRAL
ROAD LEADING TO MONASTERY OF IL DESERTO

ordained, was selected by his superiors to establish the Congregation of the Holy Cross in what was then considered a remote district of the United States.

Accompanied by six brothers, he arrived in New York in the autumn of 1841, and immediately set out for Indiana, which was destined to be the field, the centre rather, of his apostolate for upwards of half a century. After a short stay at St. Peter's, in the Diocese of Vincennes, he proceeded northward with five of his confrères. In the beginning of an exceptionally rigorous winter, in poverty and privation he began the foundation of Notre Dame, which, under his fostering care, from an Indian missionary station, developed into one of the largest religious and educational institutions in the New World, the centre of far-reaching activities for the work of the Church. Several colleges which Father Sorin founded elsewhere are also in a flourishing condition.

It is a far cry from Indiana to India; but the flourishing mission in Eastern Bengal, in charge of the Congregation of the Holy Cross, owes much of its success to Father Sorin's ardent zeal and active co-operation. Thither he sent its former bishop and other priests whose services could ill be spared, together with a band of sisters, the superior of whom, a native of New York, died at her distant post, a victim of her self-sacrifice. The founding of the Congregation of the Sisters of the Holy Cross in the United States is rightly regarded as one of Father Sorin's most important services to religion. Under his administration and care, this community, at first a handful, has become a host, with flourishing establishments in a dozen states. During the Civil War, thanks to Father Sorin's forethought, this sisterhood was able to furnish nearly fourscore nurses for sick and wounded soldiers on transports and in hospitals. A number of priests of the Congregation of the Holy Cross served as chaplains at the front. Another of Father Sorin's many claims to the grateful remembrance of English-speaking Catholics is the "Ave Maria", which he founded in 1865.

Father Sorin was elected superior-general of his order in 1868, and held this important office during the rest of his life. In recognition of his work in educational lines, the French Government conferred upon him the insignia of an Officer of Public Instruction (1888). Soon after the celebration of his sacerdotal golden jubilee (the same year), the venerable founder of Notre Dame entered upon a long period of mental and physical suffering, which closed with a peaceful and painless death on the eve of All Saints', 1893.

MOREAU, *Le Très Révérend Père Basil-Antoine Moreau* (Paris, 1900); *A Story of Fifty Years* (Notre Dame, 1905); *Circular Letters of the Very Rev. Edward Sorin, C. S. C.*, privately printed.
DANIEL E. HUDSON.

Sorrento, ARCHDIOCESE OF, in the Province of Naples, with one suffragan, Castellamare. The city is situated on the southern arm of the Gulf of Naples and is protected towards the south by Mount Sant' Angelo, which makes Sorrento a popular summer resort. The peninsula is bounded on the one side by the Gulf of Naples, on the other side by the Gulf of Amalfi, and was in Roman antiquity dotted with villas. Sorrento is situated at a considerable altitude above the sea, as it were on a peak. The churches are more ornate than beautiful. There are also ruins of certain temples: of Ceres, described by Vitruvius (a few columns and mosaics); of Venus, near the Marina grande; of Sirena; and of Minerva, the latter said to have been built by Ulysses, the reputed founder of the city, which in ancient times had its own coins and was autonomous. In 312 B. C. it became the ally of Rome; but Hannibal captured it in the Second Punic War. Augustus sent a colony thither. In A. D. 645 Radolfo, Duke of Beneventum, besieged it in vain; it remained Byzantine, and as late as the eighth century had probably a *dux* (chief magistrate) of its own, and was almost completely independent of Constantinople. In 890 the Sorrentines won a naval victory over the inhabitants of Amalfi. In 1035 it was conquered by Guaimario IV, Duke of Salerno, who made his brother Guido Duke of Sorrento; but forty years afterwards it fell with Salerno under Norman domination. Sorrento is the birthplace of Torquato Tasso. The Gospel was preached at Sorrento probably as early as the first century; the martyrs Quartus, Quartillus, and their companions are venerated there. Among the known bishops the first is St. Renatus, a native of Angers, at the beginning of the fifth century. His successor was St. Valerius, who died in 453; Rosarius was present at Rome in 499. The Sorrentines venerate other bishops of the see: St. Athanasius, St. Johannes (about 594), St. Amandus (d. 617), St. Baculus (seventh century), St. Hyacinthus (679). In the tenth century it became a metropolitan see, the first archbishop being Leo Parus. Among its bishops were Francesco Remolino (1501), who was made a prisoner by the Turks and ransomed with the treasures of the church (in part his own donations), and Filippo Strozzi (1525), said to have been three times rescued from prison in the sack of Rome in 1527. In 1558 the Turks under Pialy Pasha effected a landing at Salerno, and plundered and burned the city, on which occasion the archives perished. The new bishop, Giulio Pavesi, sought to repair the damages. Diego Pietra (1680) founded the seminary, afterwards enlarged by Filippo Anastasi (1699); the latter defended the immunities of the Church and was forcibly exiled to Terracina. In 1861 Francesco Apuzzo was, by order of the new Government, exiled to France. In 1818 the Dioceses of Massa Lubrense, Vico Equense, a suffragan of Amalfi, and Capri were united with Sorrento. Massa is an ancient city, the fame of whose celebrated temple (*delubrum*) of Juno Argiva is still preserved in the title of the church known as the Madonna della Lobra. It became an episcopal see probably when Sorrento was made metropolitan; the first known bishop was Pietro Orsi, in 1289 delivered from prison in Sicily. Vico Equense, the ancient Æqua, destroyed in the Social War, probably had a bishop at the same time as Massa Lubrense; the first known was Bartolomeo (1294). Paolo Regi (1582), a renowned legist, compiled the lives of the Neapolitan saints, and was a prolific writer. The last bishop was Michele Natali (1797), condemned to death in 1799 for having taken part in the revolution of that year.

The Island of Capri was even in antiquity celebrated for its climate. Augustus acquired it from the Neapolitans, and Tiberius built there his famous villa. Commodus banished thither his wife Crispina. Justinian gave the island to the Benedictines. In 868 it was captured by the inhabitants of Amalfi; from 1806–1808 it was in possession of the English. The Archbishop of Amalfi named its first bishop (987), a certain Johannes. Sorrento has thirty-six parishes, 267 secular and 34 regular clergy, and 56,900 souls; 8 monasteries for men and 21 convents for women, 3 institutes for boys and 10 for girls.

CAPPELLETTI, *Le chiese d'Italia*, XX; ANASTASIO, *Lucubrationes in Sorrentinorum ecclesiasticas civilesque antiquitates* (Rome, 1731); CAPASSO, *Topografia storico-archeologica della penisola sorrentina* (Naples, 1846); FASULO, *La penisola sorrentina* (Naples, 1900).
U. BENIGNI.

Sorrows of the Blessed Virgin Mary, FEASTS OF THE SEVEN.—(1) Friday before Palm Sunday, major double; (2) third Sunday in September, double of the second class. The object of these feasts is the spiritual martyrdom of the Mother of God and her compassion with the sufferings of her Divine Son. (1) The seven founders of the Servite Order, in 1239, five years after they established themselves on Monte Senario, took up the sorrows of Mary, standing under the Cross, as the principal devotion of their order. The corresponding feast, however, did not originate with them; its celebration was enacted by a provincial synod of Cologne (1413) to expiate the crimes of the iconoclast Hussites; it was to be kept on the Friday after the third Sunday after Easter under the title: "Commemoratio angustiæ et doloris B. Mariæ V.". Its object was exclusively the sorrow of Mary during the Crucifixion and Death of Christ. Before the sixteenth century this feast was limited to the dioceses of North Germany, Scandinavia, and Scotland. Being termed "Compassio" or "Transfixio", "Commendatio, Lamentatio B. M. V.", it was kept at a great variety of dates, mostly during Eastertide or shortly after Pentecost, or on some fixed day of a month (18 July, Merseburg; 19 July, Halberstadt, Lübeck, Meissen; 20 July, Naumburg; cf. Grotefend, "Zeitrechnung", II, 2, 166). Dreves and Blume (Analecta hymnica) have published a large number of rhythmical offices, sequences, and hymns for the feast of the Compassion, which show that from the end of the fifteenth century in several dioceses the scope of this feast was widened to commemorate either five dolours, from the imprisonment to the burial of Christ, or seven dolours, extending over the entire life of Mary (cf. XXIV, 122-53; VIII, 51 sq.; X, 79 sq., etc.). Towards the end of the sixteenth century the feast spread over part of the south of Europe; in 1506 it was granted to the nuns of the Annunciation under the title "Spasmi B. M. V.", Monday after Passion Sunday; in 1600 to the Servite nuns of Valencia, "B. M. V. sub pede Crucis", Friday before Palm Sunday. After 1600 it became popular in France and was termed "Dominæ N. de Pietate", Friday before Palm Sunday. To this latter date the feast was assigned for the whole German Empire (1674). By a Decree of 22 April, 1727, Benedict XIII extended it to the entire Latin Church, under the title "Septem dolorum B. M. V.", although the Office and Mass retain the original character of the feast, the Compassion of Mary at the foot of the Cross. At both Mass and Office the "Stabat Mater" of Giacopone da Todi (1306) is sung.

(2) The second feast was granted to the Servites, 9 June and 15 September, 1668, double with an octave for the third Sunday in September. Its object from the beginning has been the popular devotion of the seven dolours of Mary (according to the responsories of Matins: the sorrow (a) at the prophecy of Simeon; (b) at the flight into Egypt; (c) having lost the Holy Child at Jerusalem; (d) meeting Jesus on his way to Calvary; (e) standing at the foot of the Cross; (f) Jesus being taken from the Cross; (g) at the burial of Christ). This feast was extended to Spain (1735); to Tuscany (double of the second class with an octave, 1807). After his return from his exile in France Pius VII extended the feast to the Latin Church (18 September, 1814, major double); it was raised to the rank of a double of the second class, 13 May, 1908. The Servites celebrate it as a double of the first class with an octave and a vigil. Also in the Passionist Order, at Florence and Granada (N. S. de las Angustias), its rank is double of the first class with an octave. The hymns which are now used in the Office of this feast were probably composed by the Servite Callisto Palumbella (eighteenth century). On the devotion, cf. Kellner, "Heortology", p. 271. The old title of the "Compassio" is preserved by the Diocese of Hildesheim in a simple feast, Saturday after the octave of Corpus Christi. A feast, "B. M. V. de pietate", with a beautiful medieval office, is kept in honour of the sorrowful mother at Goa in India and Braga in Portugal, on the third Sunday of October; in the ecclesiastical province of Rio de Janeiro in Brazil, last Sunday of May, etc. (cf. the corresponding calendars). A special form of devotion is practised in Spanish-speaking countries under the term of "N. S. de la Soledad", to commemorate the solitude of Mary on Holy Saturday. Its origin goes back to Queen Juana, lamenting the early death of her husband Philip I, King of Spain (1506).

To the oriental churches these feasts are unknown; the Catholic Ruthenians keep a feast of the sorrowful Mother on Friday after the octave of Corpus Christi.

NILLES, *Kalendarium man.* (Innsbruck, 1896); HOLWECK, *Fasti Mariani* (Freiburg, 1892); CALVENERIUS, *Kal. Marianum*, 17 March in *Summa Aurea*, III, 590 sq.; ALBERS, *Blüthenkränze*, V (Paderborn, 1894), 40-190.

F. G. HOLWECK.

Soter, SAINT, POPE. See CAIUS AND SOTER, SAINTS.

Soto, DOMINIC, Dominican, renowned theologian, b. at Segovia, 1494; d. at Salamanca, 15 Nov., 1560. His first studies were made in his native city. He next studied at the University of Alcalá under St. Thomas of Villanova, and later went to Paris, where he obtained his baccalaureate in philosophy. Having studied theology for a time at Paris, he returned to Alcalá about 1520, and was made professor of philosophy in the College of San Ildefonso. In this capacity he distinguished himself by securing a complete triumph of moderate Realism over the errors of Nominalism. Already enjoying a wide reputation as a professor, and apparently destined for higher honours, he was suddenly moved in 1524 to abandon his chair as teacher and join a religious order. Straightway he made a retreat at the Benedictine monastery of Montserrat, and then sought admission into the Order of Preachers at Burgos, where he was received and entered upon his novitiate in the Convent of St. Paul. The following year (23 July, 1525) he was admitted to profession, and was made at once professor of dialectics in his convent. In 1529 appeared his first work called "Summulæ", which in simplicity, precision, and clearness was a decided improvement on the manuals of logic then in use. After teaching in his convent for seven years, he was called to a chair of theology in the University of Salamanca on 27 Nov., 1532, and continued to teach there till 1545, when he was chosen by Charles V imperial theologian at the Council of Trent. During his labours at the council he rendered great service in helping to formulate dogmatic decrees and in solving theological difficulties. The general of his order, Albertus Casaus, having died just before the opening of the council, it fell to Soto to represent his order during the first four sessions. In the following sessions he represented the newly-elected general, Franciscus Romæus. It was at Trent that Soto wrote and dedicated to the fathers of the council his treatise "De natura et gratia", in which he clearly and ably expounds the Thomistic teaching on original sin and grace. When the council was interrupted in 1547, Soto was summoned by Charles V to Germany as his confessor and spiritual director. He refused the Bishopric of Segovia offered him by the emperor, and in 1550 was permitted to return to his convent at Salamanca, where he was elected prior the same year. Two years later he succeeded Melchior Cano in the principal chair of theology at the University of Salamanca, at that time the metropolis of the intellectual world. In 1556 Soto resigned his professorial chair. Chief among his philosophical works, besides the "Summulæ", are: "In dialecticam Aristotelis commentarii" (Salamanca, 1544); "In VIII libros physicorum" (Salamanca, 1545). The following are his best-known theological works: "De natura et gratia libri III (Venice, 1547); "De ratione tegendi et detegendi secretum" (Salamanca, 1541); "De justitia et jure libri X" (Salamanca, 1556); "Comment. in Ep. ad Romanos" (Antwerp, 1550); "In IV sent. libros comment." (Salamanca, 1555-56).

Echard, *Script. ord. præd.*, II, 171 sq.; Hurter, *Nomenclator*, II (Innsbruck, 1906), 1373 sq.; Veil in *Revue thomiste* (May, June, 1904), 151 sqq.; (May, June, 1905), 174 sqq.

Charles J. Callan.

Soto, Hernando de. See De Soto, Hernando.

Soul (Gr. ψυχή; Lat. *anima;* Fr. *âme;* Ger. *Seele*).
—The question of the reality of the soul and its distinction from the body is among the most important problems of philosophy, for with it is bound up the doctrine of a future life. Various theories as to the nature of the soul have claimed to be reconcilable with the tenet of immortality, but it is a sure instinct that leads us to suspect every attack on the substantiality or spirituality of the soul as an assault on the belief in existence after death. The soul may be defined as the ultimate internal principle by which we think, feel, and will, and by which our bodies are animated. The term "mind" usually denotes this principle as the subject of our conscious states, while "soul" denotes the source of our vegetative activities as well. That our vital activities proceed from a principle capable of subsisting in itself, is the thesis of the substantiality of the soul: that this principle is not itself composite, extended, corporeal, or essentially and intrinsically dependent on the body, is the doctrine of spirituality. If there be a life after death, clearly the agent or subject of our vital activities must be capable of an existence separate from the body. The belief in an animating principle in some sense distinct from the body is an almost inevitable inference from the observed facts of life. The lowest savages arrive at the concept of the soul almost without reflection, certainly without any severe mental effort. The mysteries of birth and death, the lapse of conscious life during sleep and in swooning, even the commonest operations of imagination and memory, which abstract a man from his bodily presence even while awake—all such facts invincibly suggest the existence of something besides the visible organism, internal to it, but to a large extent independent of it, and leading a life of its own. In the rude psychology of the savage, the soul is often represented as actually migrating to and fro during dreams and trances, and after death haunting the neighbourhood of its body. Nearly always it is figured as something extremely volatile, a perfume or a breath. Often, as among the Fijians, it is represented as a miniature replica of the body, so small as to be invisible. The Samoans have a name for the soul which means "that which comes and goes". Many savage peoples, such as the Dyaks and Sumatrans, bind various parts of the body with cords during sickness to prevent the escape of the soul. In short, all the evidence goes to show that Dualism, however uncritical and inconsistent, is the instinctive creed of "primitive man" (see Animism).

The Soul in Ancient Philosophy.—Early literature bears the same stamp of Dualism. In the "Rig-Veda" and other liturgical books of India, we find frequent references to the coming and going of *manas* (mind or soul). Indian philosophy, whether Brahminic or Buddhistic, with its various systems of metempsychosis, accentuated the distinction of soul and body, making the bodily life a mere transitory episode in the existence of the soul. They all taught the doctrine of *limited immortality*, ending either with the periodic world-destruction (Brahminism) or with attainment of Nirvana (Buddhism). The doctrine of a world-soul in a highly abstract form is met with as early as the eighth century before Christ, when we find it described as "the unseen seer, the unheard hearer, the unthought thinker, the unknown knower, the Eternal in which space is woven and which is woven in it".

In Greece, on the other hand, the first essays of philosophy took a positive and somewhat materialistic direction, inherited from the pre-philosophic age, from Homer and the early Greek religion. In Homer, while the distinction of soul and body is recognized, the soul is hardly conceived as possessing a substantial existence of its own. Severed from the body, it is a mere shadow, incapable of energetic life. The philosophers did something to correct such views. The earliest school was that of the Hylozoists; these conceived the soul as a kind of cosmic force, and attributed animation to the whole of nature. Any natural force might be designated ψυχή: thus Thales uses this term for the attractive force of the magnet, and similar language is quoted even from Anaxagoras and Democritus. With this we may compare the "mind-stuff" theory and Pan-psychism of certain modern scientists. Other philosophers again described the soul's nature in terms of substance. Anaximander gives it an aeriform constitution; Heraclitus describes it as a fire. The fundamental thought is the same. The cosmic ether or fire is the subtlest of the elements, the nourishing flame which imparts heat, life, sense, and intelligence to all things in their several degrees and kinds. The Pythagoreans taught that the soul is a harmony, its essence consisting in those perfect mathematical ratios which are the law of the universe and the music of the heavenly spheres. With this doctrine was combined, according to Cicero, the belief in a universal world-spirit, from which all particular souls are derived.

All these early theories were cosmological rather than psychological in character. Theology, physics, and mental science were not as yet distinguished. It is only with the rise of dialectic and the growing recognition of the problem of knowledge that a genuinely psychological theory became possible. In Plato the two standpoints, the cosmological and the epistemological, are found combined. Thus in the "Timæus" (p. 30) we find an account derived from Pythagorean sources of the origin of the soul. First the world-soul is created according to the laws of mathematical symmetry and musical concord. It is composed of two elements, one an element of "sameness" (ταὐτόν), corresponding to the universal and intelligible order of truth, and the other an element of distinction or "otherness" (θάτερον), corresponding to the world of sensible and particular existences. The individual human soul is constructed on the same plan. Sometimes, as in the "Phædrus", Plato teaches the doctrine of plurality of souls (cf. the well-known allegory of the charioteer and the two steeds in that dialogue). The rational soul was located in the head, the passionate or spirited soul in the breast, the appetitive soul in the abdomen. In the "Republic", instead of the triple soul, we find the doctrine of three elements within the complex unity of the single soul. The question of immortality was a principal subject of Plato's speculations. His account of the origin of the soul in the "Timæus" leads him to deny the *intrinsic* immortality even of the world-soul, and to admit only an immortality conditional on the good pleasure of God. In the "Phædo" the chief argument for the immortality of the soul is based on the nature of intellectual knowledge interpreted on the theory of reminiscence; this of course implies the pre-existence of the soul, and perhaps in strict logic its eternal pre-existence. There is also an argument from the soul's necessary participation in the idea of life, which, it is argued, makes the idea of its extinction impossible. These various lines of argument are nowhere harmonized in Plato (see Immortality). The Platonic doctrine tended to an extreme Transcendentalism. Soul and body are distinct orders of reality, and bodily existence involves a kind of violence to the higher part of our composite nature. The body is the "prison", the "tomb", or even, as some later Platonists expressed it, the "hell" of the soul. In Aristotle this error is avoided. His definition of the soul as "the first entelechy of a physical organized body potentially possessing life" emphasizes the closeness of the union of soul and body. The difficulty in his theory is to determine what degree of distinctness or separateness from the matter of the body is to be conceded to the human soul. He fully recognizes the spiritual element in thought and describes the "active intellect" (νοῦς ποιητικός) as "separate and impassible", but the precise relation of this active intellect to the individual mind is a hopelessly obscure question in Aristotle's psychology. (See INTELLECT; MIND.)

The Stoics taught that all existence is material, and described the soul as a breath pervading the body. They also called it Divine, a particle of God (ἀπόσπασμα τοῦ θεοῦ); it was composed of the most refined and ethereal matter. Eight distinct parts of the soul were recognized by them: (a) the ruling reason (τὸ ἡγεμονικόν); (b) the five senses; (c) the procreative powers. Absolute immortality they denied; relative immortality, terminating with the universal conflagration and destruction of all things, some of them (e. g. Cleanthes and Chrysippus) admitted in the case of the wise man; others, such as Panætius and Posidonius, denied even this, arguing that, as the soul began with the body, so it must end with it.

Epicureanism accepted the Atomist theory of Leucippus and Democritus. Soul consists of the finest grained atoms in the universe, finer even than those of wind and heat which they resemble: hence the exquisite fluency of the soul's movements in thought and sensation. The soul-atoms themselves, however, could not exercise their functions if they were not kept together by the body. It is this which gives shape and consistency to the group. If this is destroyed, the atoms escape and life is dissolved; if it is injured, part of the soul is lost, but enough may be left to maintain life. The Lucretian version of Epicureanism distinguishes between *animus* and *anima:* the latter only is soul in the biological sense; the former is the higher, directing principle (τὸ ἡγεμονικόν) in the Stoic terminology, whose seat is the heart, the centre of the cognitive and emotional life.

THE SOUL IN CHRISTIAN THOUGHT.—Græco-Roman philosophy made no further progress in the doctrine of the soul in the age immediately preceding the Christian era. None of the existing theories had found general acceptance, and in the literature of the period an eclectic spirit nearly akin to Scepticism predominated. Of the strife and fusion of systems at this time the works of Cicero are the best example. On the question of the soul he is by turns Platonic and Pythagorean, while he confesses that the Stoic and Epicurean systems have each an attraction for him. Such was the state of the question in the West at the dawn of Christianity. In Jewish circles a like uncertainty prevailed. The Sadducees were Materialists, denying immortality and all spiritual existence. The Pharisees maintained these doctrines, adding belief in pre-existence and transmigration. The psychology of the Rabbins is founded on the Sacred Books, particularly the account of the creation of man in Genesis. Three terms are used for the soul, *nephesh, nuah,* and *neshamah;* the first was taken to refer to the animal and vegetative nature, the second to the ethical principle, the third to the purely spiritual intelligence. At all events, it is evident that the Old Testament throughout either asserts or implies the distinct reality of the soul. An important contribution to later Jewish thought was the infusion of Platonism into it by Philo of Alexandria. He taught the immediately Divine origin of the soul, its pre-existence and transmigration; he contrasts the *pneuma*, or spiritual essence, with the soul proper, the source of vital phenomena, whose seat is the blood; finally he revived the old Platonic Dualism, attributing the origin of sin and evil to the union of spirit with matter.

It was Christianity that, after many centuries of struggle, applied the final criticisms to the various psychologies of antiquity, and brought their scattered elements of truth to full focus. The tendency of Christ's teaching was to centre all interest in the spiritual side of man's nature; the salvation or loss of the soul is the great issue of existence. The Gospel language is popular, not technical. Ψυχή and πνεῦμα are used indifferently either for the principle of natural life or for spirit in the strict sense. Body and soul are recognized as a dualism and their values contrasted: "Fear ye not them that kill the body . . . but rather fear him that can destroy both soul and body in hell."

In St. Paul we find a more technical phraseology employed with great consistency. Ψυχή is now appropriated to the purely natural life; πνεῦμα to the life of supernatural religion, the principle of which is the Holy Spirit, dwelling and operating in the heart. The opposition of flesh and spirit is accentuated afresh (Rom., i, 18 etc.). This Pauline system, presented to a world already prepossessed in favour of a quasi-Platonic Dualism, occasioned one of the earliest widespread forms of error among Christian writers —the doctrine of the Trichotomy. According to this, man, perfect man (τέλειος), consists of three parts: body, soul, spirit (σῶμα, ψυχή, πνεῦμα). Body and soul come by natural generation; spirit is given to the regenerate Christian alone. Thus, the "newness of life", of which St. Paul speaks, was conceived by some as a superadded entity, a kind of oversoul sublimating the "natural man" into a higher species. This doctrine was variously distorted in the different Gnostic systems. The Gnostics divided man into three classes (a) *pneumatici* or spiritual, (b) *psychici* or animal, (c) *choici* or earthy, ascribing to each class a different origin and destiny. The spiritual were of the seed of Achemoth, and were destined to return in time whence they had sprung, viz. into the *pleroma*. Even in this life they are exempted from the possibility of a fall from their high calling; they therefore stand in no need of good works, and have nothing to fear from the contaminations of the world and the flesh. This class consists of course of the Gnostics themselves. The *psychici* are in a lower position: they have capacities for spiritual life which they must cultivate by good works. They stand in a middle place, and may either rise to the spiritual or sink to the *hylic* level. In this category stands the Christian Church at large. Lastly, the earthy souls are a mere material emanation, destined to perish: the matter of which they are composed being incapable of salvation (μὴ γὰρ εἶναι τὴν ὕλην δεκτικὴν σωτηρίας). This class contains the multitudes of the merely natural man.

Two features claim attention in this the earliest essay towards a complete anthropology within the Christian Church: (1) an extreme spirituality is attributed to "the perfect"; (2) immortality is *conditional* for the second class of souls, not an intrinsic attribute of all souls. It is probable that originally the terms *pneumatici, psychici,* and *choici* denoted at first elements which were observed to exist in all souls, and that it was only by an afterthought that they were employed, according to the respective predominance of these elements in different cases, to represent supposed real classes of men. The doctrine of the four temperaments and the Stoic ideal of the Wise Man afford a parallel for the personification of abstract qualities. The true genius of Christianity, expressed by the Fathers of the early centuries, rejected Gnosticism. The ascription to a creature of an absolutely spiritual nature, and the claim to endless existence asserted as a strictly *de jure* privilege in the case of the "perfect", seemed to them an encroachment on the incommunicable attributes of God. The theory of Emanation too was seen to be a derogation from the dignity of the Divine nature. For this reason, St. Justin, supposing that the doctrine of natural immortality logically implies eternal existence, rejects it, making this attribute (like Plato in the "Timæus") dependent on the free will of God; at the same time he plainly asserts the *de facto* immortality of every human soul. The doctrine of *conservation*, as the necessary complement of creation, was not yet elaborated. Even in Scholastic philosophy, which asserts natural immortality, the abstract possibility of annihilation through an act of God's absolute power is also admitted. Similarly, Tatian denies the simplicity of the soul, claiming that absolute simplicity belongs to God alone. All other beings, he held, are composed of matter and spirit. Here again it would be rash to urge a charge of Materialism. Many of these writers failed to distinguish between corporeity in strict essence and corporeity as a necessary or natural concomitant. Thus the soul may itself be incorporeal and yet require a body as a condition of its existence. In this sense St. Irenæus attributes a certain "corporeal character" to the soul; he represents it as possessing the form of its body, as water possesses the form of its containing vessel. At the same time, he teaches fairly explicitly the incorporeal nature of the soul. He also sometimes uses what seems to be the language of the Trichotomists, as when he says that in the Resurrection men shall have each their own body, soul, and spirit. But such an interpretation is impossible in view of his whole position in regard to the Gnostic controversy.

The dubious language of these writers can only be understood in relation to the system they were opposing. By assigning a literal divinity to a certain small aristocracy of souls, Gnosticism set aside the doctrine of Creation and the whole Christian idea of God's relation to man. On the other side, by its extreme dualism of matter and spirit, and its denial to matter (i. e. the flesh) of all capacity for spiritual influences, it involved the rejection of cardinal doctrines like the Resurrection of the Body and even of the Incarnation itself in any proper sense. The orthodox teacher had to emphasize: (1) the soul's distinction from God and subjection to Him; (2) its affinities with matter. The two converse truths, viz. those of the soul's affinity with the Divine nature and its radical distinction from matter, were apt to be obscured in comparison. It was only afterwards and very gradually, with the development of the doctrine of grace, with the fuller recognition of the supernatural order as such, and the realization of the Person and Office of the Holy Spirit, that the various errors connected with the *pneuma* ceased to be a stumbling-block to Christian psychology. Indeed, similar errors have accompanied almost every subsequent form of heterodox Illuminism and Mysticism.

Tertullian's treatise "De Anima" has been called the first Christian classic on psychology proper. The author aims to show the failure of all philosophies to elucidate the nature of the soul, and argues eloquently that Christ alone can teach mankind the truth on such subjeects. His own doctrine, however, is simply the refined Materialism of the Stoics, supported by arguments from medicine and physiology and by ingenious interpretations of Scripture, in which the unavoidable materialism of language is made to establish a metaphysical Materialism. Tertullian is the founder of the theory of Traducianism, which derives the rational soul *ex traduce*, i. e. by procreation from the soul of the parent. For Tertullian this was a necessary consequence of Materialism. Later writers found in the doctrine a convenient explanation of the transmission of original sin. St. Jerome says that in his day it was the common theory in the West. Theologians have long abandoned it, however, in favour of Creationism, as it seems to compromise the spirituality of the soul (cf. TRADUCIANISM). Origen taught the pre-existence of the soul. Terrestrial life is a punishment and a remedy for pre-natal sin. "Soul" is properly degraded spirit: flesh is a condition of alienation and bondage (cf. Comment. ad Rom., i, 18). Spirit, however, finite spirit, can exist only in a body, albeit of a glorious and ethereal nature.

Neo-Platonism, which through St. Augustine contributed so much to spiritual philosophy, belongs to this period. Like Gnosticism, it uses emanations. The primeval and eternal One begets by emanation *nous* (intelligence); and from *nous* in turn springs *psyche* (soul), which is the image of *nous*, but distinct from it. Matter is a still later emanation. Soul has relations to both ends of the scale of reality, and its perfection lies in turning towards the Divine Unity from which it came. In everything, the neo-Platonist recognized the absolute primacy of the soul with respect to the body. Thus, the mind is always active, even in sense-perception; it is only the body that is passively affected by external stimuli. Similarly, Plotinus prefers to say that the body is in the soul rather than vice versa: and he seems to have been the first to conceive the peculiar manner of the soul's location as an undivided and universal presence pervading the organism (*tota in toto et tota in singulis partibus*). It is impossible to give more than a very brief notice of the psychology of St. Augustine. His contributions to every branch of the science were immense; the senses, the emotions, imagination, memory, the will, and the intellect—he explored them all, and there is scarcely any subsequent development of importance that he did not forestall. He is the founder of the introspective method. *Noverim Te, noverim me* was an intellectual no less than a devotional aspiration with him. The following are perhaps the chief points for our present purpose: (1) he opposes body and soul on the ground of the irreducible distinction of thought and extension (cf. DESCARTES). St. Augustine, however, lays more stress on the volitional activities than did the French Idealists. (2) As against the Manichæans he always asserts the worth and dignity of the body. Like Aristotle he makes the soul the final cause of the body. As God is the Good or *Summum Bonum* of the soul, so is the soul the good of the body. (3) The origin of the soul is perhaps beyond our ken. He never definitely decided between Traducianism and Creationism. (5) As regards spirituality, he is everywhere most explicit, but it is interesting as an indication of the futile subtleties current at the time to find him warning a friend against the controversy on the corporeality of the soul, seeing that the term "corpus" was used in so many different senses. "Corpus, non caro" is his own description of the angelic body.

Medieval psychology prior to the Aristotelean revival was affected by neo-Platonism, Augustinianism, and mystical influences derived from the works of pseudo-Dionysius. This fusion produced sometimes, notably in Scotus Eriugena, a pantheistic theory of the soul. All individual existence is but the development of the Divine life, in which all things are destined to be resumed. The Arabian commentators, Averroës and Avicenna, had interpreted Aristotle's psychology in a pantheistic sense. St. Thomas, with the rest of the Schoolmen, amends this portion of the Aristotelean tradition, accepting the rest with no important modifications. St. Thomas's doctrine is briefly as follows: (1) the rational soul, which is one with the sensitive and vegetative principle, is the form of the body. This was defined as of faith by the Council of Vienne of 1311; (2)

the soul is a substance, but an incomplete substance, i. e. it has a natural aptitude and exigency for existence in the body, in conjunction with which it makes up the substantial unity of human nature; (3) though connaturally related to the body, it is itself absolutely simple, i. e. of an unextended and spiritual nature. It is not wholly immersed in matter, its higher operations being intrinsically independent of the organism; (4) the rational soul is produced by special creation, at the moment when the organism is sufficiently developed to receive it. In the first stage of embryonic development, the vital principle has merely vegetative powers; then a sensitive soul comes into being, educed from the evolving potencies of the organism; later yet, this is replaced by the perfect rational soul, which is essentially immaterial and so postulates a special creative act. Many modern theologians have abandoned this last point of St. Thomas's teaching, and maintain that a fully rational soul is infused into the embryo at the first moment of its existence.

THE SOUL IN MODERN THOUGHT.—Modern speculations respecting the soul have taken two main directions, Idealism and Materialism. Agnosticism need not be reckoned as a third and distinct answer to the problem, since, as a matter of fact, all actual agnosticisms have an easily recognized bias towards one or other of the two solutions aforesaid. Both Idealism and Materialism in present-day philosophy merge into Monism, which is probably the most influential system outside the Catholic Church.

History.—Descartes conceived the soul as essentially thinking (i. e. conscious) substance, and body as essentially extended substance. The two are thus simply disparate realities, with no vital connexion between them. This is significantly marked by his theory of the soul's location in the body. Unlike the Scholastics he confines it to a single point—the pineal gland—from which it is supposed to control the various organs and muscles through the medium of the "animal spirits", a kind of fluid circulating through the body. Thus, to say the least, the soul's biological functions are made very remote and indirect, and were in fact later on reduced almost to a nullity: the lower life was violently severed from the higher, and regarded as a simple mechanism. In the Cartesian theory animals are mere automata. It is only by the Divine assistance that action between soul and body is possible. The Occasionalists went further, denying all interaction whatever, and making the correspondence of the two sets of facts a pure result of the action of God. The Leibnizian theory of Pre-established Harmony similarly refuses to admit any inter-causal relation. The superior monad (soul) and the aggregate of inferior monads which go to make up the body are like two clocks constructed with perfect art so as always to agree. They register alike, but independently: they are still two clocks, not one. This awkward Dualism was entirely got rid of by Spinoza. For him there is but one, infinite substance, of which thought and extension are only attributes. Thought comprehends extension, and by that very fact shows that it is at root one with that which it comprehends. The alleged irreducible distinction is transcended: soul and body are neither of them substances, but each is a property of the one substance. Each in its sphere is the counterpart of the other. This is the meaning of the definition, "Soul is the Idea of Body". Soul is the counterpart within the sphere of the attribute of thought of that particular mode of the attribute of extension which we call the body. Such was the fate of Cartesianism.

English Idealism had a different course. Berkeley had begun by denying the existence of material substance, which he reduced merely to a series of impressions in the sentient mind. Mind is the only substance. Hume finished the argument by dissolving mind itself into its phenomena, a loose collection of "impressions and ideas". The Sensist school (Condillac etc.) and the Associationists (Hartley, the Mills, and Bain) continued in similar fashion to regard the mind as constituted by its phenomena or "states", and the growth of modern positive psychology has tended to encourage this attitude. But to rest in Phenomenalism as a theory is impossible, as its ablest advocates themselves have seen. Thus, J. S. Mill, while describing the mind as merely "a series [i. e. of conscious phenomena] aware of itself as a series", is forced to admit that such a conception involves an unresolved paradox. Again, W. James's assertion that "the passing thought is itself the Thinker", which "appropriates" all past thoughts in the "stream of consciousness", simply blinks the question. For surely there is something which in its turn "appropriates" the passing thought itself and the entire stream of past and future thoughts as well, viz. the self-conscious, self-asserting "I", the substantial ultimate of our mental life. To be in this sense "monarch of all it surveys" in introspective observation and reflective self-consciousness, to appropriate without itself being appropriated by anything else, to be the genuine owner of a certain limited section of reality (the stream of consciousness), this is to be a free and sovereign (though finite) personality, a self-conscious, spiritual substance in the language of Catholic metaphysics.

Criticism.—The foregoing discussion partly anticipates our criticism of Materialism (q. v.). The father of modern Materialism is Hobbes, who accepted the theory of Epicurus, and reduced all spirits either to phantoms of the imagination or to matter in a highly rarefied state. This theory need not detain us here. Later Materialism has three main sources: (1) Newtonian physics, which taught men to regard matter, not as inert and passive, but as instinct with force. Why should not life and consciousness be among its unexplored potencies? (Priestley, Tyndall, etc.) Tyndall himself provides the answer admitting that the chasm that separates psychical facts from material phenomena is "intellectually impassable". Writers, therefore, who make thought a mere "secretion of the brain" or a "phosphorescence" of its substance (Vogt, Moleschott) may be simply ignored. In reply to the more serious Materialism, spiritualist philosophers need only re-assert the admissions of the Materialists themselves, that there is an impassable chasm between the two classes of facts. (2) Psychophysics, it is alleged, shows the most minute dependence of mind-functions upon brain-states. The two orders of facts are therefore perfectly continuous, and, though they may be superficially different, yet they must be after all radically one. Mental phenomena may be styled an epiphenomenon or by-product of material force (Huxley). The answer is the same as before. There is no analogy for an epiphenomenon being separated by an "impassable chasm" from the causal series to which it belongs. The term is, in fact, a mere verbal subterfuge. The only sound principle in such arguments is the principle that essential or "impassable" distinctions in the effect can be explained only by similar distinctions in the cause. This is the principle on which Dualism, as we have explained it, rests. Merely to find relations, however close, between mental and physiological facts does not advance us an inch towards transcending this Dualism. It only enriches and fills out our concept of it. The mutual compenetration of soul and body in their activities is just what Catholic philosophy (anticipating positive science) had taught for centuries. Man is two and one, a divisible but a vital unity. (3) Evolutionism endeavours to explain the origin of the soul from merely material forces. Spirit is not the basis and principle; rather it is the ultimate efflorescence of the Cosmos,

If we ask then "what *was* the original basis out of which spirit and all things arose?" we are told it was the Unknowable (Spencer). This system must be treated as Materialistic Monism. The answer to it is that, as the outcome of the Unknowable has a spiritual character, the Unknowable itself (assuming its reality) must be spiritual.

As regards monistic systems generally, it belongs rather to cosmology to discuss them. We take our stand on the consciousness of individual personality, which consciousness is a distinct deliverance of our very highest faculties, growing more and more explicit with the strengthening of our moral and intellectual being. This consciousness is emphatic, as against the figments of a fallaciously abstract reason, in asserting the self-subsistence (and at the same time the finitude) of our being, i. e. it declares that we are *independent* inasmuch as we are truly *persons* or *selves*, not mere attributes or adjectives, while at the same time, by exhibiting our manifold limitations, it directs us to a higher Cause on which our being depends.

Such is the Catholic doctrine on the nature, unity, substantiality, spirituality, and origin of the soul. It is the only system consistent with Christian faith, and, we may add, morals, for both Materialism and Monism logically cut away the foundations of these. The foregoing historical sketch will have served also to show another advantage it possesses, viz. that it is by far the most comprehensive, and at the same time discriminating, synthesis of whatever is best in rival systems. It recognizes the physical conditions of the soul's activity with the Materialist, and its spiritual aspect with the Idealist, while with the Monist it insists on the vital unity of human life. It enshrines the principles of ancient speculation, and is ready to receive and assimilate the fruits of modern research. See ANIMISM; CONSCIOUSNESS; ENERGY, THE LAW OF THE CONSERVATION OF; FACULTIES OF THE SOUL; FORM; FREE WILL; IDEA; IMMORTALITY; INTELLECT; LIFE; MIND; METEMPSYCHOSIS; PSYCHOLOGY; SPIRITUALISM.

The following works may be consulted: LADD, *Philosophy of Mind* (New York and London, 1895); IDEM, *Elements of Physiological Psychology* (New York, 1887); JAMES, *Principles of Psychology* (2 vols., New York, 1898); DRISCOLL, *The Soul* (New York, 1898); MAHER, *Psychology* (6th ed., London, 1909); McDOUGALL, *Body and Mind: A Defence of Animism* (London, 1911); COCONNIER, *L'âme humaine* (Paris, 1890); MERCIER, *Psychologie* (Louvain, 1904); IDEM, *Les origines de la psychologie contemporaine* (Louvain, 1908); FARGES, *Le cerveau, l'âme et les facultés* (Paris, 1888); GARDAIR, *Philosophie de S. Thomas: la nature humaine* (Paris, 1896); GUTBERLET, *Die Psychologie* (Münster, 1896); BOUILLIER, *Le principe vital et l'âme pensante* (Paris, 1873); LEBRETON, *Les origines de la doctrine de la Trinité* (Paris, 1910); LE ROY, *La religion des primitifs* (Paris, 1908); TYLOR, *Anthropology* (London, 1904); IDEM, *Primitive Culture* (London, 1903); DE WULF, *Scholastic Philosophy*, tr. COFFEY (Dublin and London, 1907); ESSER, *Die Seelenlehre Tertullians* (Würzburg, 1893); BRÉHIER, *Philon d'Alexandrie* (Paris, 1908); LAGRANGE, *Etudes sur les réligions sémitiques* (Paris, 1903). For the references to ST. THOMAS and ST. AUGUSTINE see the articles in the CATHOLIC ENCYCLOPEDIA. See also *Dict. de théol. cathol.* (Paris, 1909), s. v. Ame.

MICHAEL MAHER.
JOSEPH BOLAND.

South Carolina, one of the thirteen original colonies of the United States, has an area of 30,570 square miles throughout its 35 counties, with an extreme breadth of 235 miles and an extreme width of 215. It is bounded eastward by North Carolina and the Atlantic, with a coast line of 200 miles; Georgia lies to the west and North Carolina bounds it on the north. Columbia is the capital.

PHYSICAL CHARACTERISTICS.—South Carolina rises from marshland in its eastern tidewater section to a mountainous region in the extreme western portion of the state. The Pedee and the Santee are navigable rivers flowing into the Atlantic and reaching the sea through deltas in the marsh regions. It is probable that more than half of the state was at one time in dense timber.

POPULATION.—The state is twenty-sixth in rank of population according to the census of 1910. The population in 1820 was 502,741; in 1840, 594,398; in 1860, 703,708; in 1880, 995,577; in 1900, 1,340,316; in 1910, 1,515,400. Beaufort County is the fifth county in the United States in point of density of negro population, having a percentage of 90.5. In 1790 South Carolina was second only to Virginia in the number of its slaves, having 107,097. The largest cities with their respective populations are as follows: Charleston, 58,833; Columbia, 26,319; Spartanburg, 17,517; Greenville, 15,741.

RESOURCES.—More than one-third of the cultivated land is devoted to cotton. It is the fourth cotton state in the Union, producing in 1910, 1,116,000 bales. The islands along the coast and the swampy tidewater region from the very beginning yielded much rice, the state ranking second in the Union in this product. Much attention is given to the production of early fruit and vegetables for northern markets and a more recent industry is the planting and shipping of tea. From the pine forests lumber and naval supplies are obtained, and a great deal of phosphate rock is dug in the southern tidewater region, yielding a rich supply of fertilizer for export. The chief manufacturing industries are cotton weaving, lumber milling, turpentine distilling, rice cleaning, and fertilizer. According to the state census of 1905 the capital invested in its manufacturing industries was $113,422,224, employing 59,441 wage earners who were paid $13,868,950. The value of the product totalled $79,376,262. The cereal crop of 1910 was oats, 4,599,000 bushels; corn, 44,733,000; wheat, 4,983,000; rye, 40,000. The railway mileage of the state in 1907 was 3,324.41. Charleston has long been one of the leading cities of the South, owing its prosperity largely to its fine harbour. Its imports in 1907 were $3,528,553; in 1908, $3,375,997; its exports in 1907, $1,082,466, and in 1908, $2,510,965. Columbia, the capital, is on the Congaree River, and its fine water power is used for several large cotton factories. Greenville and Spartanburg manufacture cotton cloth. The banks of the state are in a prosperous condition, and scarcely a town of any consequence is without its banks, either national, state, or private. There is a State Bank Examiner, who regularly watches the operations of all these institutions, and a bank failure is rarely chronicled. There are 19 national banks with a capital of $2,713,000; 143 state banks with a capital of $6,332,871, and 9 private banks with a capital of $106,000.

SEAL OF SOUTH CAROLINA

EDUCATION.—The supervision of public instruction is vested in a state superintendent of education, elected for two years; a state board of education, composed of the governor, the state superintendent of education, and not above seven persons appointed by the governor; a county superintendent, elected for four years, and, in each county, a county board of education of three members, one of whom shall be the county superintendent and the other two appointees of the state board, whose terms of office are two years. The General Assembly makes provision for the election or appointment of all other necessary school officers, provides a system of free public schools for all children between the ages of six and twenty-one, and divides the county into school districts. The main school fund derives from a three-mill tax on all taxable property, an annual dog tax of fifty cents, and the poll tax assessed and collected in the various school districts. In addition to these sources the school fund drew, up to 1907, the state dispensary tax, the most unique feature of the law. School districts are allowed to vote for special taxation. No public money from whatever source derived shall be used, either directly or indirectly, in aid or maintenance "of any college, school, hospital, orphan house or other institution, society or organization of whatever kind which is wholly or in part under the direction or control of any church or of any religious or sectarian denomination, society or organization". Separate schools are provided for children of the white and coloured races, and no child of either race is ever permitted to attend the school provided for children of the other race.

Section 1201a of the General Code reads: "That the nature of alcoholic drinks and narcotics and special instruction as to their effect upon the human system, in connection with the several divisions of the subject of Physiology and Hygiene, shall be included in the branches of study taught in the common or public schools in the State of South Carolina and shall be studied and taught as thoroughly and in the same manner as other like required branches are in said schools, by the use of text books in the hands of pupils where other branches are thus studied in said schools, and orally in the case of pupils unable to read, and shall be taught by all teachers and studied by all pupils in all said schools supported wholly or in part by public money . . . and any officer, school director, committee, superintendent or teacher who shall refuse or neglect to comply with the requirements of this Act, or shall neglect or fail to make proper provisions for the instruction required and in the manner specified by the first section of this Act, for all pupils in each and every school under his jurisdiction shall be removed from office and the vacancy filled as in other cases." Schools must be kept open and the exercises continued in each school district for a period of at least three months in each year. "Arbour Day", the third Friday in November, and Calhoun's Birthday, 18 March, "South Carolina Day", are observed in an appropriate manner. The age limit of pupils—between the ages of six and twenty-one—has been ruled under an opinion of the attorney-general as prohibiting the establishing of free kindergartens.

For white children there are 2712 public schools in the state (1909), employing 933 men teachers and 3247 women, and reaching 153,807 pupils with an average attendance of 107,368. For negro children there are 2354 public schools, employing 894 men teachers and 1802 women, and teaching 181,095 pupils, with an average attendance of 123,481. The total revenue for both white and negroes was $2,345,647.72; out of which there was expended $1,590,732.51 for whites and $308,153.16 for negroes. The state's *per capita* expenditure, according to enrolment, was in 1899, $4.90 for white, $1.42 for negro, $2.69 average for both; in 1904, $6.88 for white, $1.47 for negro, $4.08 for both; in 1909, $10.34 for white, $1.70 for negro, $5.67 for both. There are 27 institutions of higher education for whites and 11 for negroes. Of the 27 institutions for whites, 5, non-sectarian, receive a total state support of $355,994.88; 5 are Presbyterian, 3 Methodist, 3 Baptist, and 2 Lutheran. The remainder are non-sectarian seminaries or technical colleges. The University of South Carolina, chartered in 1801, is located at Columbia, has 29 officers and members of faculty, 298 students and a total income of $97,385.18. Clemson Agricultural College, chartered in 1889, located at Clemson, has 47 officers and members of the faculty, 665 students, and a total income of $201,477.28. The Winthrop Normal and Industrial College, chartered in 1891, located at Rock Hill, has 45 officers and members of faculty, and a total income of $94,685.37.

History.—A. *Civil.*—Owing in part to presumably unfavourable climatic conditions, in part to the fact that the land lay in the disputed zone between the English and Spanish settlements, colonization in the Carolinas was tardy and spasmodic. In 1629, a patent to the territory had been granted by Charles I and forfeited through inaction on the part of the patentees. Virginia assumed to make grants without any permanent results, though a small company of dissenters, in 1653, migrated from that colony and began the Albemarle settlement, with a considerable number of Quakers; while New Englanders, a few years later, purchased land from the Indians on Cape Fear River, but abandoned the settlement with disgust. At last, in 1663, Charles II granted to the Earl of Clarendon and seven other of his favourites all Carolina from the 36° to 31° north, and Cape Fear was settled under this grant by colonists from Barbadoes. The proprietors were nearly absolute in their power, though the "advice, consent, and approbation" of the freemen were necessary before laws could become valid and there was to be freedom of religious worship. The colony, however, did not prosper, and the relations between proprietors and colonists were further strained by an attempt to govern the colony under a constitution framed by the Earl of Shaftesbury, with more or less assistance from the philosopher Locke. This document was a remarkably impractical product, based, quaintly, upon medieval and aristocratic ideas with one of its principal and avowed motives—"to avoid erecting a numerous democracy". Its model was the independent Palatinate of Durham; officials were called palatines, chancellors, high stewards, and admirals. Two-fifths of the land was to belong to the nobility. There was to be a Parliament, which was to consider nothing but what was referred to it by the Proprietory Council. Freedom of worship was granted, but citizens must profess their belief in God and the obligation to worship, and, contrary to the wish of Locke, the Church of England was to be an Established Church. Dissatisfaction with this Constitution, which was never enforced, and with the Navigation Acts, kept the Carolinas in a perpetual ferment.

In 1670 the foundation of South Carolina was laid in the settlement of the Ashley River and an independent governor was appointed. Locke's Constitution was abandoned, and a mode of government was adopted limiting the powers of the executive and outlining a legislature of elected delegates. In 1672 Charleston was fixed as the permanent site for the settlement, a number of Dutch immigrants from New York having arrived the year before, as well as a shipload of slaves, the latter only too soon to outnumber the whites. The colony was further augmented by Presbyterian Scotch-Irish in 1683, but the most important addition to the little colony was the coming of the French Huguenots, upon the revocation of the Edict of Nantes, who settled on the Cooper River, and were later admitted to the political rights of the colony. But worthless settlers, selfish and unenlightened proprietors, tactless governors, religious dissent with the party of the Church and the king, and the uneasy proximity of the Spanish settlements, led to open revolt, the banishment of a governor, and, in 1689, the declaration of martial law. Trouble was averted by the appointment of Archdale, one of the proprietors and a Quaker, as governor, who made many important concessions, as did his successor, Blake. In 1697 religious liberty was accorded to all "except Papists". An attempt was made in 1704 to exclude Dissenters from the Assembly, but the law was annulled by Queen Anne. From now on until the Revolution the course of South Carolina was a succession of cumulatively forcible resistances to interference on the part of the proprietors, and, after 1721, when the Crown assumed control, on the part of the sovereign and the royal governors, interspersed with the dissolving of popular assemblies, the annulment of governmental decrees, and a series of bloody campaigns against the Indians, with the gradual formation of two distinct social classes, the rise of Charleston as a mart of trade, a seat of wealth and fashion, and a virile and cosmopolitan community. The colony warmly sympathized with the northern colonies, the royal governor being forced to abdicate, taking refuge on a British man-of-war in September, 1775. A State Constitution was first adopted on 26 March, 1776, and, by a vote of 149 to 73, the national Constitution was ratified on 23 May, 1788.

Early in its state history South Carolina evinced a feeling for States' Rights, which made it the leader in the southern agitation that led up to the Civil War. A Nullification Act was passed in 1832 in opposition to the high tariff upon importations passed by the Federal Government; but the trouble was temporarily relieved by the passing of a compromise tariff in the succeeding session of Congress. Serious difficulties arose upon the election of Lincoln to the presidency. On the day of his election both Houses of the State Legislature in joint session passed a resolution providing for a state convention to consider the withdrawal of the state from the Union. In November the Legislature passed an act authorizing such a convention, declaring that "a sovereign State of the Union had a right to secede from it; that the States of the Union are not subordinate to the national government, were not created by it, and do not belong to it; that *they* created the national government; that from them it derives its power; that to them it is responsible; and that when it abuses the trust reposed in it they, as equal sovereigns, have a right to resume the powers respectively delegated to it by them." Orators now stumped the state, vigilance committees were organized, assemblages of negroes were dispersed, and the delegates chosen on 3 December, 1860, met at Columbia on the 17th, adjourning to Charleston, owing to the prevalence of smallpox. On 20 December an ordinance declaring that "the union now subsisting between South Carolina and other States under the name of the United States of America is hereby dissolved" was unanimously adopted forty-five minutes after it was submitted. A proclamation to this effect was read and adopted amid scenes of the wildest enthusiasm. All federal office-holders at once resigned. A new banner was adopted for "The Independent Commonwealth". A committee was appointed to wait on the president and treat for the possession of public lands within the state. They urged the president to immediately withdraw all national troops from Charleston harbour and presented him with a resolution of secession. Lincoln was courteous but firm. He replied that he would present their demands to Congress, but gave them to understand that he should defend Fort Sumter. A taunting reply was forthcoming from the commissioners which the president declined to answer. The commissioners returned and, on 12 April, 1861, South Carolinians attacked Fort Sumter, compelled its evacuation by federal troops, and the state for four years became one of the most energetic and zealous defenders of the Confederacy.

At the close of the war a provisional government was set up by the president on 30 June, 1865, and a state convention, in the fall of the same year, repealed the ordinance of secession and declared slavery abolished. An election was held in November and a state government was elected which continued in office until superseded by the military government in 1867—South and North Carolina being included in one military district. The state passed safely through the terrors of the Reconstruction Period. On 14 January, 1868, at a convention composed of 34 whites and 63 blacks the Constitution was adopted and ratified at an election the following year, which chose 85 negroes and 72 white men for the State Legislature. On 13 July, 1868, the Fourteenth Amendment was ratified and the military authorities were withdrawn. The Fifteenth Amendment was ratified by the State Legislature, 11 March, 1869.

In the city of Charleston, from 1 December, 1901, to 1 May, 1902, a "South Carolina Interstate and West Indian Exposition" was held, which eloquently demonstrated the development of the Southern states since the Civil War and the industries and resources of Cuba, Porto Rico, Mexico, and South America.

B. *Ecclesiastical*.—In the stormy period of religious dissent that characterized the early colonial years of the Carolinas, Catholics bore no part; nor indeed does there appear any evidence of the presence of a single active Catholic in South Carolina until after the Revolution. This religious dissent came from the Quakers and a growing class of colonists, indifferent to religious ideals, who objected to the enforced establishment of the Church of England, involving on their part the payment of three-fourths share for the maintenance of a religious establishment representing a minority. But the hypothetical presence of Catholics was duly provided for in the Acts of 1696 renewing toleration, by the usual parenthetical intrusion of the phrase—"Papists only excepted". Indeed it was not until a generation after the Revolution, with its disestablishment of the Anglican Church in the states of North and South Carolina, that the Metropolitan of the United States solicited the pope to erect a southern diocese for the bands of Catholics scattered through Georgia and the Carolinas who were already becoming indifferent and malcontent, if not actually heretical. To include these states in its territory, the See of Charleston was erected by Pius VII, 11 July, 1820, and the Rev. John England, the parish priest of Killorgan and Ballymoodan, Ireland, was consecrated its bishop at the Cathedral of St. Finnbar, refusing at the same time to take a special oath of allegiance to the King of England. The bishop embarked for the United States on 22 October; set about his onerous duties with indefatigable assiduity; founded the first Catholic newspaper of America, "The United States' Catholic Miscellany", which, with a slight intermission, endured up to the Civil War; established The Philosophical and Classical Seminary of Charleston for Catholics and non-Catholics alike; organized, in 1830, the Sisters of Our Lady of Mercy; drew up a model Constitution for the Church, and incorporated its trustees. Bishop England combined in a remarkable degree practical insight, indomitable energy, and wide culture, while struggling against baffling difficulties.

In 1850, during the episcopate of Bishop Reynolds, the See of Savannah was erected with jurisdiction over Georgia and Eastern Florida, and the Diocese of Charleston henceforth comprised the Carolinas with a Catholic population estimated at 8000. The Civil War wrought terrible havoc with Catholic lives and Church property, culminating in the horrors of Sherman's march to the sea, and Bishop Lynch displayed remarkable energy in building up again his ruined and penniless diocese. The Vicariate Apostolic of North Carolina was erected by a Papal Bull, 3 March, 1868, so that under the present episcopate of Bishop Henry P. Northrop, the Diocese of Charleston comprises simply the State of South Carolina. There are in the diocese 108 religious women, novices and postulants, 19 secular priests, 12 churches with resident priests, 17 missions with churches, 75 stations and 8 chapels; 5 academies for young ladies with 395 pupils; 9 parishes with parochial schools providing for 859 pupils; one hospital, the Infirmary and Sanitarium of St. Francis Xavier, under the Sisters of Mercy, at Charleston. The diocese supports and cares for 72 orphans and the estimated Catholic population of the state is 9650.

DENOMINATIONAL STATISTICS (1908)

Denominations	No. Churches	No. Ministers	Membership
Baptist	1,003	410	118,217
M. E. Church, South	798	357	85,441
Presbyterian	275	121	23,442
Lutheran	85	34	13,993
Episcopal	94	47	7,620
Unitarian	1	1	117
Congregational	1	1	71
A. R. Presbyterian	45	36	4,227
Catholic	30	19	9,650

LEGISLATION AFFECTING RELIGION.—The State allows a rectory and two acres of land with building to be exempt from taxation. Nor are religious houses taxed. Teaching orders have special privileges exempting their schools, as the parochial schools, from taxation.

Full liberty of conscience is granted in South Carolina, but it has been held that this does not legalize wilful or profane swearing or scoffing or prevent legislation prohibiting the conduct of secular business, not of an imperative nature, on Sunday. South Carolina recognizes as legal holidays 1 January, 19 January, Lee's Birthday, 11 May, Confederate Memorial Day, 3 June, Jefferson Davis' Birthday, 4 July, Labour Day, Election Day, Christmas, and Thursday of Fair Week, but no Church holy days, as such, are recognized as holidays. The law allows the same privileges to communications made to a priest under the seal of a confession as it does to confidential communications made by a client to his counsel or by a patient to his physician. The statutes contain no provisions making any exception between the rights and privileges of civil or ecclesiastical corporations. The property of the Church in the diocese is held by the bishop and his successors in office. The sessions of the Legislature are opened with prayer; those of the Courts are not.

Marriage and Divorce.—The marriage laws of South Carolina prohibit all marriages within the Levitical degree, of white with negro, or white with Indian. It is one of the few states in the Union that does not require the taking out of marriage licenses. A startling feature of the South Carolina law is the fact that no divorces are granted. All laws permitting divorce were repealed in 1878 and have never been re-enacted. From 1867 to the repeal of the Divorce Law South Carolina had granted but 163 divorces, which was at the rate of 1 per 100,000 of population.

EXCISE AND DISPENSARY ACT.—Quite the most unique feature of the prohibition legislation of South Carolina—indeed one of the most unique excise features of any state legislation—was the passing of the Dispensary Act which placed the entire control of the liquor traffic in the hands of the Government, the profits from which accrued to the state school fund. This Act was abolished in 1907 under the pressure of a temperance movement that was sweeping through the Southern states and local option was adopted with the result that in 1909 eighteen counties had voted prohibition. The Dispensary Law had scarcely been enacted in 1892 when it met with fierce opposition, receiving, however, hearty official support from Governor Tillman. In 1894 the Supreme Court of the State decided that it was unconstitutional, but successive Legislatures modified the original act in conformity to the ruling of the Court. In 1897, the United States Supreme Court decided that the section forbidding the importation of liquor into the state by private persons violated the inter-state commerce laws of Congress.

WILLS.—Every person is entitled to make a will unless insane, under age, or labouring under some disability of law arising from want of capacity or want of perfect liberty of action. Married women deal, in every respect, as though they were single, and have the same power to make contracts with regard to their separate property as do their husbands. All wills shall be in writing and signed by the party devising, or by some other person in his presence and by his express direction, and shall be attested and subscribed, in the presence of said devisor, by three or more credible witnesses, each in the presence of the other. No noncupative will shall be good, where the estate exceeds fifty dollars, unless the same is provided by the oaths of three witnesses who were present at the making thereof and bid by the testator to bear witness that such was his will, or words to that effect; nor unless such will was made during the last sickness of the deceased, in the house or place where he shall have died. No testimony shall be admitted to prove such a will, if six months shall have elapsed after speaking the testamentary words, except such testimony, or the substance thereof, was committed to writing within six days after the making of said will, and not then, unless such will shall be presented for probate within twelve months. The assets which come into the hands of the executors or administrators shall be applied to the payment of the debts of the estate in the following order: (1) Funeral and other expenses of last sickness, charges of probate or letters of administration; (2) Debts due to public; (3) Judgments, mortgages, and executions—the oldest first; (4) Rent; (5) Bonds, debts by speciality and debts by simple contract.

Colonial Records North Carolina (1886-90); South Carolina Hist. Society's *Collections;* RIVERS, *Sketch of the Hist. of South Carolina to 1719* (Charleston, 1856); MCGRADY, *South Carolina under Royal Government* (New York, 1899); ELIZA LUCAS, *Journal and Letters* (Holbrook's ed. 1850); O'CONNELL, *Catholicity in the Carolinas and Georgia* (New York, 1879); SHEA, *Hist. of the Catholic Church in the U. S* (New York, 1886); BISHOP ENGLAND'S *Works.*

JARVIS KEILEY.

Southcote, JOANNA. See SABBATARIANS, SABBATARIANISM.

South Dakota, the thirty-ninth state, admitted to the Union on 2 November, 1889, is officially bounded as follows: "Beginning at the point of intersection of the western boundary of Minnesota with the northern boundary of Iowa and running thence northerly along the western boundary of Minnesota to its intersection with the 7th standard parallel, thence west on the line of the 7th standard parallel produced due west to the intersection with the 27th meridian of longitude west of Washington (Approx. 104 W. Greenwich) thence south on the 27th meridian of longitude to its intersection with the northern boundary line of Nebraska, thence easterly along said northern boundary line of Nebraska to its intersection with the western boundary line of Iowa, thence north along the western boundary line of State of Iowa to the north-west corner of said State of Iowa, thence east along the northern boundary line of Iowa to the place of beginning."

The state contains 76,850 square miles. Generally the surface is undulating prairie lands, except in the south-western portion which is occupied by the Black Hills. The general altitude is about fifteen hundred feet above sea level. The lowest point, Bigstone Lake on the eastern boundary, is 962 feet, and Harney's Peak in the Black Hills rises to 7216 feet. The Missouri River divides the state into nearly equal portions having quite distinct soil characteristics; the portion east of the river being glacial clay, and the portion west being in part covered with a tenacious clay formed by the disintegration of Fort Pierre Shales, and the remainder with Laramie loam eroded from the western mountains. The population numbers 583,888 (1910) and is chiefly of American origin. The chief foreign elements are German and Scandinavian. There are about 18,000 Sioux Indians residing upon lands in severalty in the state.

RESOURCES.—Agriculture is the chief resource and the main products for 1910 were:

Corn	54,050,000	bushels—	$21,620,000
Wheat	46,720,000	" —	41,581,000
Oats	35,075,000	" —	10,522,000
Barley	18,655,000	" —	10,633,000
Rye	595,000	" —	363,000
Flaxseed	3,300,000	" —	7,557,000
Potatoes	2,420,000	" —	2,057,000
Hay	2,750,000	tons —	19,000,000

The Black Hills region is rich in minerals and gold mining is an important industry. There are extensive lime and cement works in the state and considerable stone quarries. The mineral product of 1909 was as follows: gold, $6,447,093; mica, $1,-000,000; lime, cement and other minerals, and stone, $2,552,917. In 1910 the value of gold produced fell to $5,187,070. Manufacturing is but little developed. Flour milling and the manufacture of butter in creameries are the leading industries. The last figures are for 1905 when the total product of manufactories was $13,085,333, of which $2,182,653 was produced by creameries and $6,519,354 by flour mills. A considerable wholesaling is done from Aberdeen, Sioux Falls, Watertown, and other points. Agricultural products in 1909 shipped to markets outside the state returned $123,706,000. South Dakota is well provided with railroad communication for intra state and interstate transportation, the total mileage (1910) being 3953 miles.

EDUCATION.—The public education system is correlated from the common schools through the high schools to the state university. For the maintenance of public education in the state, Congress granted a total of 3,531,174 acres of land. About one-eighth of this has been sold for the sum of $7,725,637, which returns an annual revenue of interest and rentals of a half million dollars. The school fund is most carefully guarded by the constitution and laws. It is believed the ultimate school fund will maintain public education without taxation. The total expenditure for public school purposes (1909) was $3,152,000.09. There were 169,706 persons of school age (between 6 and 21 years), of whom 121,165 attended school in 1909. There were then 4358 schoolhouses and 5555 teachers. The state university, located at Vermilion, was first opened and endowed by the territory in 1882. It has colleges of letters, arts and sciences, law, medicine, engineering, and music, each presided over by a dean under the general direction of the president. There are 48 members of the faculty and 445 students. The State College of Agriculture and Mechanic Arts, located at Brookings, is supported jointly by the State and Federal governments. It was opened in the autumn of 1884. There were forty-three members of the faculty and 525 students (1909).

The State maintains four normal schools, located respectively at Madison, Spearfish, Springfield, and Aberdeen; the latter institution has industrial features. The State likewise maintains a school for the deaf at Sioux Falls, for the blind at Gary, and for the feeble-minded at Redfield; the training school for incorrigible boys and girls is at Plankinton. The schools for the deaf, blind, feeble-minded, and incorrigibles are under the supervision of the State Board of Charities, but the university and other schools of higher education are under the State Regents of Education. Several religious denominations maintain colleges in the state; the Baptists at Sioux Falls, the Catholics at Chamberlain, the Congregationalists at Yankton and Redfield, the Scandinavian Lutherans at Canton and German Lutherans at Eureka, the Mennonites at Freeman, the Methodist Episcopals at Mitchell, the Presbyterians at Huron. The Episcopalians maintain a seminary for young ladies at Sioux Falls, and the Free Methodists have a seminary at Wessington Springs. The Catholic Church has academies at Aberdeen, Bridgewater, Bristol, Dell Rapids, Elkton, Epiphany, Farmer, Turton, Hoven, Howard, Jefferson, Kranzburg, Marion, Milbank, Mitchell, Parkston, Salem, Sioux Falls, Sturgis, Tabor, Vermilion, Webster, Woonsocket, Watertown, Yankton, and Zell. The Scandinavian Lutherans have a normal school at Sioux Falls. Columbus College, the Catholic institution at Chamberlain, was founded in 1909, when Bishop O'Gorman purchased from the Federal Government the plant of the Government Indian School, but very shortly after the establishment of the college the main building was burned. A reorganization was effected in time to reopen with the regular college year for 1910–11.

SEAL OF SOUTH DAKOTA

HISTORY.—*Civil.*—The first settlers within the present boundaries of South Dakota were French fur traders, who established a fur post on Cedar Island in the Missouri River thirty miles below the present capital in 1796. The next year a second post was established at a point near the present Greenwood post office in Charles Mix County. These posts were discontinued after several years, but in 1817 Joseph La Frambois established Ft. Teton on the present site of Ft. Pierre and the settlement at that place has been continuous since. The first agricultural settlement was made at Sioux Falls in 1857. Owing to the hostility of the Indians, settlement was slow until the discovery of gold in the Black Hills in 1874, and until that time was confined to narrow strips along the Missouri and the Lower Big Sioux. About 1877 began a great influx of homesteaders, and within five years most of the land east of the Missouri had been settled upon, and all of the chief towns date from that period. The Constitution of South Dakota was made by a convention authorized by the territorial Legislature, which met in Sioux Falls in September, 1885. This Constitution was revised to meet certain requirements of the Enabling Act of 1889 and adopted by the people on 1 October, 1889.

Ecclesiastical.—The first Catholics to come into South Dakota were probably the men of Charles Pierre Le Sueur, who visited the Sioux Valley in 1800. The Verendrye brothers were here in 1745 on an exploration trip and were accompanied by a priest. In June, 1842, Father Ravoux of St. Paul made a trip to the Missouri River to baptize the families of French Catholics living at Fort Pierre. In 1845 Father Ravoux visited Vermilion for the same purpose. In 1848 Father DeSmet came among the Indians of the Dakota country and laboured with them until his death, about 1866. Father DeSmet was assisted in his work among the Dakotas by

XIV.—11

Fathers Christian and Adrian Hoecken. The first permanent mission plant in South Dakota was made at Jefferson in 1867. A considerable number of French Catholic families had settled in that neighbourhood, and Bishop Grace sent Father Pierre Boucher among them as Apostolic missionary, and he organized and built St. Peter's Church at Jefferson, the first Catholic church building in the state. From that time there had been a steady growth in Catholic population, distributed among the Germans, Irish, and French, with a few Italians and other South Europe immigrants. The original Vicariate Apostolic of Dakota was established with the episcopal seat at Yankton, but upon the division of the territory and the admission of South Dakota in 1889, the Diocese of Sioux Falls was established to embrace the entire state. Rt. Rev. Martin Marty was the first bishop and he was succeeded, after an interval during which the diocese was administered by Rt. Rev. Henry Wensing, by Rt. Rev. Thomas O'Gorman, the present incumbent. In 1902 the diocese was divided, and that portion of the state west of the Missouri River became the Diocese of Lead with Rt. Rev. John Stariha as bishop; in 1909 Bishop Stariha resigned and was succeeded by Bishop Busch. There are in the two dioceses, 150 priests, 208 churches, 13 chapels, 71 stations, 28 parochial schools, with 3530 pupils, and a Catholic population of about 68,000. While Catholics have been largely represented in the Legislature and county offices, not many, in proportion to their numerical strength have held state office. Peter C. Shannon was chief justice of the territory (1873-81); John E. Kelley represented the state in Congress (1896-98); Beotius H. Sullivan was surveyor general (1889-93); Patrick F. Wickham, internal revenue collector (1893); and John A. Bowler, warden of the penitentiary (1897-1901).

The latest religious census of South Dakota, taken in 1906, is as follows:

Denomination	No. Churches	No. Members
Adventists	40	1,042
Baptists	92	6,198
Brethren (Plymouth)	1	3
Christian Science	8	237
Congregationalists	168	8,599
Disciples	21	1,478
Dunkers	2	155
Eastern (Greek)	4	230
Evangelical	59	1,797
Friends	5	103
German Evangelical	6	325
Independent	8	334
Latter Day Saints	1	85
Lutheran	505	45,018
Mennonites	15	995
Methodists	322	16,143
Presbyterians	125	6,990
Protestant Episcopal	126	7,055
Reform Bodies	55	2,711
Roman Catholic	199	61,014
Salvation Army	7	109
Swedish Evangelical	22	1,042
Theosophists	1	7
Unitarians	1	21
United Brethren	7	257
Universalists	1	13
Total	1,798	161,961

MATTERS AFFECTING RELIGION.—The Constitution guarantees complete freedom of worship. A chapter of the penal code defines crimes against religion and conscience, especially making blasphemy, profane swearing, and desecration of the Sabbath, misdemeanors. No religious holidays are observed by law as such, except Thanksgiving Day. Christmas is a holiday. Every session of the Legislature is opened with prayer. One of the chaplains in sessions of 1907 and 1909 was a Catholic priest. Church societies may incorporate under a simple and inexpensive statutory provision. All property used for religious and educational purposes is exempt from taxation; clergymen are exempt from jury and military duty and poll taxes; marriages may be celebrated by any regular minister of the Gospel, or before justices of the peace and the judges of the courts; a rigid marriage license law is enforced; and consanguineous marriages are forbidden; all marriages are finally recorded in the State Vital Statistics Division at Pierre. Divorces are allowed for adultery, extreme cruelty, wilful desertion, wilful neglect, habitual intemperance, or conviction of felony. The plaintiff must have been in good faith a resident of the state one year and of the county three months before bringing action for divorce. Free education is offered every person and elementary education is compulsory; training in parochial schools may be substituted for compulsory training in public schools. The Bible may be read in the public schools but all sectarian teaching is forbidden. All state-supported charitable institutions, prisons, and reformatories are under the control of the State Board of Charities and Corrections. These institutions are the Hospital for the Insane at Yankton, the School for Feebleminded at Redfield, the School for the Deaf, Sioux Falls, the School for the Blind at Gary, the Training School for Incorrigibles at Plankinton, the penitentiary at Sioux Falls, and sanatorium for tuberculous patients at Custer. The Catholic Church maintains fine hospitals at Aberdeen, Cascade Springs, Deadwood, Pierre, Mitchell, Sioux Falls, Webster, and Yankton. The Scandinavian Lutherans maintain an orphanage at Beresford, and the State Children's Home at Sioux Falls is maintained as a public benevolence. The last-named is not a church institution, though Bishop O'Gorman of the Catholic Diocese of Sioux Falls is a member of its board of control.

The sale of liquor is strictly regulated by law; a high license system prevails; $1000 per year is the minimum license fee. Every person of sound mind may dispose of all his property by will, but a corporation cannot make a will; there is no provision of law regulating or affecting charitable bequests. Cemetery corporations or individuals may provide cemeteries; burial upon a cemetery lot renders the title thereto inalienable; no corpse may be buried within the state without a permit from a justice of the peace.

Brief History of South Dakota (New York, 1905); ROBINSON, *History of South Dakota* (Indianapolis, 1904); *Journals of Lewis and Clarke*; *South Dakota Historical Collections* I, II (Pierre, 1902, 1904); *Annual Review of the Progress of South Dakota* (Pierre, 1909); *Revised Statutes of South Dakota* (Pierre, 1909).

DOANE ROBINSON.

Southerne, WILLIAM, VENERABLE, English martyr, suffered at Newcastle-under-Lyme, 30 April, 1618. An alumnus and priest of the English College at Douai, he laboured mainly at Baswich, near Stafford, which then belonged to a branch of the Fowler family. He was arrested while saying Mass, and committed by a neighbouring justice to Stafford gaol. He was immediately sentenced to death for being a priest and refusing to take the oath of allegiance; he remained in prison for six days after condemnation, no hangman being forthcoming.

CHALLONER, *Missionary Priests*, II, no. 159.

JOHN B. WAINEWRIGHT.

Southwark, DIOCESE OF (SOUTHWARCENSIS), suffragan of Westminster, England, comprises the south-eastern counties of Kent, Surrey, and Sussex south of the Thames, including the southern half of the administrative County of London. Southwark, the principal borough in South London, is the episcopal city. This diocese was founded on the restoration of the hierarchy in England in 1851, and when first erected included Berkshire, Hampshire, and the Channel Islands in addition to Surrey, Kent and Sussex. Previous to this these five counties formed part of the London District, which district was governed by a vicar Apostolic, to whom also was committed episcopal jurisdiction over North America and the Bahama Islands. In 1850 London, even at that time a comparatively small city, which, owing to the exigencies of the times, had previously been under the jurisdiction of a single bishop, was now divided between the two new Dioceses of Westminster (north of the Thames) and Southwark (south of the Thames), the newly-erected Church of St. George, Southwark, a stately and magnificent structure in the Gothic style designed by the elder Pugin, being designated as the cathedral of the newly-erected see. On 6 July, 1851, Right Rev. Thomas Grant, D.D., vice-rector of the English College, Rome, was consecrated as first bishop at the early age of thirty-five. He was succeeded 25 March, 1871, by Right Rev. James Danell, formerly his vicar-general. The next occupant of the see was Bishop Robert Coffin, who at the time of his appointment in 1882 was Provincial of the Redemptorists in Great Britain and Ireland. On his demise in 1885 the choice of the Holy See fell upon his auxiliary, Bishop John Butt, who governed the diocese for twelve years until his resignation in 1897, when he was succeeded by his coadjutor, Bishop Francis Bourne, who became Archbishop of Westminster in 1903.

The present bishop, Right Rev. Peter Emmanuel Amigo, was born at Gibraltar, 26 May, 1864. He studied at St. Edmund's, Ware, and St. Thomas's, Hammersmith: was ordained priest, 25 Feb., 1888; was for a short time at Stoke Newington, then professor at St. Edmund's from Sept., 1888, to July, 1892. He was then appointed assistant priest at Hammersmith from Sept., 1892, to June, 1896. He was afterwards at St. Mary's and St. Michael's, Commercial Road, first as assistant priest, then as rector from June, 1896, to April, 1901. He was then appointed rector of the mission at Walworth in the Diocese of Southwark, and remained there until his consecration as Bishop of Southwark, 25 March, 1904. He is strenuously engaged in carrying on to their fullness the various important works initiated by his predecessors by multiplying much-needed churches and schools in all parts of this important diocese, as well as endeavouring to pay off the enormous liabilities that in past years have had to be incurred in emergencies when there would have been the gravest danger of loss of faith, especially to the destitute little ones of the diocese, if the large and magnificently-equipped orphanages and poor-law schools of the diocese had not been promptly erected. In addition to the debts on the institutions there are also enormous debts incurred in the building of new churches and schools in new and rapidly-growing centres of population, which were necessary if work for the good of souls was to be adequately carried on in the midst of the huge population of South London and its environs. There is every prospect that the efforts of the present bishop in this direction will be crowned with complete success, as he has already succeeded in securing for the important work of safeguarding the poorer children of the diocese from loss of faith the united and cordial co-operation of not only the whole of the clergy, but also of every class of the laity, which is eloquently attested by the totals of the subscriptions and collections for this purpose, which go on steadily increasing from year to year. As a consequence of this united support of clergy and laity, joined with the establishment of a sinking fund for the gradual extinction of mission debts, Bishop Amigo looks forward to handing over to his successor at the close of his life a splendid array of churches, schools, and institutions, all entirely free from debt.

Southwark in many ways occupies a notable position amongst the dioceses of England. First of all, South London, with its enormous population of close on two million inhabitants (census of 1911, 1,844,310) is one of the largest cities in the world as well as one of the poorest. Being for the most part a place of residence for the salaried workers of London north of the Thames, where all trade and business is concentrated, South London, with its immense population, has scarcely a single hotel above the level of the third class to be found within its area. Outside the boundaries of South London proper there stretches towards the south a fringe of more sparsely populated residential districts, inhabited chiefly by the well-to-do professional and business people of the City of London, amongst whom there are very few Catholics. Between this residential zone and the English Channel lies, still further to the south, a pleasant well-wooded agricultural district that is also day by day becoming more residential in character, until the sea-coast is reached with its chain of watering places, girdling the coast line of Kent and Sussex from the mouth of the Thames on the north to beyond Selsey Bill on the south. These resorts are really suburbs of London by the sea, and in the summer months especially are filled by visitors drawn from all parts of London.

The County of Kent, one of the most important of the rural divisions of this diocese, will always have an interest for English-speaking Catholics of all times, as the district in which Christianity was first preached in the Saxon tongue by St. Augustine and his followers, who landed near Richborough on the coast of Kent in 597. The actual church in which the Apostle of England offered up the Holy Sacrifice is still to be seen to this very day at Canterbury, which, once the Primatial See of England, is now an unimportant and dwindling country town of this large diocese. The Diocese of Southwark, it may be noted, includes within its present boundaries not only the whole of the territories formerly belonging to the former Dioceses of Canterbury, Rochester,

INTERIOR OF ST. GEORGE'S CATHEDRAL, SOUTHWARK

and Chichester, but also a large portion of the former Diocese of Winchester. The Church may also be said to owe the world-wide devotion of the Brown Scapular to this diocese, as St. Simon Stock, its propagator, was born in the Weald of Kent towards the end of the twelfth century.

Another striking characteristic of this diocese is the very marked increase shown in the numbers of churches, clergy, and Catholic population. Thus in 1882 the Diocese of Southwark comprised South London, the five counties of Kent, Surrey, Sussex, Berkshire, and Hampshire, and the Channel Islands. On the appointment of Bishop Coffin in 1882 the diocese was divided, and the Counties of Berkshire and Hampshire, together with the Isle of Wight and the Channel Islands, were separated from the diocese and erected into the new Diocese of Portsmouth. Before the division Southwark had 148 public churches, chapels, and stations, with 247 priests. After the division the present diocese started afresh with only 93 public churches, chapels, and stations, served by 198 priests. The diocese now has 218 public churches, chapels, and stations, with a population of almost 120,000 Catholics, whilst the number of priests attached to or working in the diocese amounts to 591, a higher total than any other English diocese. Besides the above-mentioned public places of worship, there are also 160 private chapels, either belonging to religious communities or in private houses, where Mass is as a rule celebrated daily.

As might be expected from the foregoing facts, the clergy of this diocese, owing to the encouragement they have always received from a succession of broad-minded and progressive bishops with high ideals and exceptional gifts of organization, have always been noted for their zeal, initiative, and gift of combination amongst themselves for the furtherance of every good work. It has always been their pride to have the most up-to-date and best-equipped schools in the country, and they led the way in the foundation of voluntary pupil-teachers' centres, for the training of the coming generation of teachers, before the work was made a public charge. The clergy of South London especially have also distinguished themselves by the active share they have always taken, with their bishop's hearty approval, in the great work of local government and administration, many of them having done splendid work for religion on public bodies such as the former London School Board, as well as upon the Boards of Guardians and the local councils. The South London League, a non-political body for the protection of Catholic interests in South London, with the bishop as president, bears witness to the very successful way in which the clergy as well as the laity of all parties have discovered the secret of successful organization on a purely Catholic platform, to the exclusion of party or national politics.

Ever since 1891, when it was first started, "Pastoralia", the popular little clergy review for the discussion of pastoral topics, has been edited by a committee mainly of South London clergy, and has a large circulation amongst the clergy of English-speaking lands. Its pages are full of interest as giving an insight into problems and difficulties the Church has to face in great cities, as well as the practical means by which new methods are evolved to meet present-day exigencies.

Synodi Diœcesis Southwarcensis, 1850–1868 (London, 1868); *The Catholic Directory* (London, 1850–1911), passim; *Pastoralia* (London, 1891–1911), passim.

W. M. CUNNINGHAM.

Southwell (SOTWEL), NATHAN. See BACON, NATHANIEL.

Southwell, ROBERT, VENERABLE, poet, Jesuit, martyr, b. at Horsham St. Faith's, Norfolk, England, in 1561; hanged at Tyburn, 21 Feb., 1595. His grandfather, Sir Richard Southwell, had been a wealthy man and a prominent courtier in the reign of Henry VIII. It was Richard Southwell who in 1547 had brought the poet Henry Howard, Earl of Surrey, to the block, and Surrey had vainly begged to be allowed to "fight him in his shirt". Curiously enough their respective grandsons, Father Southwell and Philip, Earl of Arundel, were to be the most devoted of friends and fellow-prisoners for the Faith. On his mother's side the Jesuit was descended from the Copley and Shelley families, whence a remote connexion may be established between him and the poet Percy Bysshe Shelley. Robert Southwell was brought up a Catholic, and at a very early age was sent to be educated at Douai, where he was the pupil in philosophy of a Jesuit of extraordinary austerity of life, the famous Leonard Lessius. After spending a short time in Paris he begged for admission into the Society of Jesus—a boon at first denied. This disappointment elicited from the boy of seventeen some passionate laments, the first of his verses of which we have record. On 17 Oct., 1578, however, he was admitted at Rome, and made his simple vows in 1580. Shortly after his noviceship, during which he was sent to Tournai, he returned to Rome to finish his studies, was ordained priest in 1584, and became prefect of studies in the English College. In 1586 he was sent on the English mission with Father Henry Garnett, found his first refuge with Lord Vaux of Harrowden, and was known under the name of Cotton.

Two years afterwards he became chaplain to the Countess of Arundel and thus established relations with her imprisoned husband, Philip, Earl of Arundel, the ancestor of the present ducal house of Norfolk, as well as with Lady Margaret Sackville, the earl's half-sister. Father Southwell's prose elegy, "Triumphs over Death", was addressed to the earl to console him for this sister's premature death, and his "Hundred Meditations on the Love of God", originally written for her use, were ultimately transcribed by another hand, to present to her daughter Lady Beauchamp ("The Month", June, 1900, p. 600). Some six years were spent in zealous and successful missionary work, during which Father Southwell lay hidden in London, or passed under various disguises from one Catholic house to another. For his better protection he affected an interest in the pursuits of the country gentlemen of his day (metaphors taken from hawking are common in his writings), but his attire was always sober and his tastes simple. His character was singularly gentle, and he has never been accused of taking any part either in political intrigues or in religious disputes of a more domestic kind. In 1592 Father Southwell was arrested at Uxenden Hall, Harrow, through the treachery of an unfortunate Catholic girl, Anne Bellamy, daughter of the owner of the house. The notorious Topcliffe, who effected the capture, wrote exultingly to the queen: "I never did take so weighty a man, if he be rightly used." But the atrocious cruelties to which Southwell was subjected did not shake his fortitude. He was examined thirteen times under torture by members of the Council, and was long confined in a dungeon swarming with vermin. After nearly three years in prison he was brought to trial and the usual punishment of hanging and quartering was inflicted.

Father Southwell's writings, both in prose and verse, were extremely popular with his contemporaries, and his religious pieces were sold openly by the booksellers though their authorship was known. Imitations abounded, and Ben Jonson declared of one of Southwell's pieces, "The Burning Babe", that to have written it he would readily forfeit many of his own poems. "Mary Magdalen's Tears", the Jesuit's earliest printed work, licensed in 1591, probably represents a deliberate attempt to employ in the cause of piety the euphuistic prose style, then so popular. "Triumphs over Death", also in prose, exhibits the same characteristics; but this artificiality of structure is not so marked in the "Short Rule of Good Life", the "Letter to His Father", the "Humble Supplication to Her Majesty", the "Epistle of Comfort" and the "Hundred Meditations". Southwell's longest poem, "St. Peter's Complaint" (132 six-line stanzas), is imitated, though not closely, from the Italian "Lagrime di S. Pietro" of Luigi Tansillo. This with some other smaller pieces was first printed, with license, in 1595, the year of his death. Another volume of short poems appeared later in the same year under the title of "Mæoniæ". The early editions of these are scarce, and some of them command high prices. A poem called "A Foure-fold Meditation", which was printed as Southwell's in 1606, is not his, but was written by his friend the Earl of Arundel (see "The Month", Jan., 1896). Perhaps no higher testimony can be found of the esteem in which Southwell's verse was held by his contemporaries than the fact that, while it is probable that Southwell had read Shakespeare, it is practically certain that Shakespeare had read Southwell and imitated him (Camb. Hist. Eng. Lit., IV, 129).

LEE in *Dict. Nat. Biog.*, s. v.; FOLEY, *Records of the English Province*, I; TAYLOR, *Robert Southwell, Poet and Martyr* (St. Louis, 1910); THURSTON in *The Month* (Feb.–March, 1895; Jan., 1896; June, 1900; Sept., 1905); NOLAN in *American Cath. Quar. Rev.* (1882), 426; EGAN in *Catholic World*, XVII, 40; XXXII, 121; *Catholic Record Society Publications*, vol. V (London, 1908); CHILD in *Cambridge History of English Literature*, IV (Cambridge, 1909), 127–40; POLLEN, *Father Robert Southwell and the Babington Plot* in *The Month* (London, March, 1912), 302–05. The best edition of Southwell's poems still remains that of GROSART in the *Fuller Worthies Library* (London, 1872).

HERBERT THURSTON.

Southworth, JOHN, VENERABLE, English martyr, b. in Lancashire, 1592, martyred at Tyburn, 28 June, 1654. A member of a junior branch of the Southworths of Samlesbury Hall, Blackburn, he was ordained priest at the English College, Douai, and was sent on the mission, 13 October, 1619. He was arrested and condemned to death in Lancashire in 1627, and imprisoned first in Lancaster Castle, and afterwards in the Clink, London, whence he and fifteen other priests were, on 11 April, 1630, delivered to the French Ambassador for transportation abroad. In 1636 he had been released from the Gatehouse, Westminster, and was living at Clerkenwell, but frequently visited the plague-stricken dwellings of Westminster to convert the dying. In 1637 he seems to have taken up his abode in Westminster, where he was arrested, 28 November, and again sent to the Gatehouse. Thence he was again transferred to the Clink and in 1640 was brought before the Commissioners for Causes Ecclesiastical, who sent him back there 24 June. On 16 July he was again liberated, but by 2 December he was again in the Gatehouse. After his final apprehension he was tried at the Old Bailey, and as he insisted on pleading "guilty" to being a priest, he was reluctantly condemned by the Recorder of London, Serjeant Steel. He was allowed to make a long speech at the gallows, and his remains were permitted to pass into the possession of the Duke of Norfolk's family, who had them sent to the English College at Douai. The wonderful recovery in 1656 of Francis Howard, seventh son of Henry Frederick, Earl of Arundel, was attributed to these relics, which were secreted during the French Revolution, and the present location of which is now unknown.

CHALLONER, *Memoirs of Missionary Priests*, II, no. 190; BRUCE, *Calendar State Papers Domestic 1629–31* (London, 1860), 233; *Calendar*, etc., *1637* (London, 1868), 572; HAMILTON, *Calendar* etc., *1640* (London, 1880), 341, 482; *Calendar*, etc., *1640–1* (London, 1882), 294.

JOHN B. WAINEWRIGHT.

Sovana and Pitigliano, DIOCESE OF (SUANENSIS ET PITILIANENSIS).—The two towns, Sovana and Pitigliano, are situated in the Province of Grosseto, Central Italy. Sovana was an ancient Etruscan city, and preserved a certain importance till the end of the thirteenth century, having been from the days of Charlemagne the capital of the counts of Aldobrandeschi, lords of Southern Tuscany. In 1240 the city withstood a siege by Frederick II. Later it passed under the sway of the Orsini, who transferred their residence to Pitigliano, a more salubrious locality, mentioned for the first time in 1081. In 1401 it fell into the power of the Republic of Siena. In 1434 Count Gentile Orsini having been killed at Sovana, the people of Pitigliano put the town to fire and sword, and brought about its complete decay, so that in 1833 it contained only 64 inhabitants. The territory of this diocese includes the celebrated Vallombrosan Abbey of Monte Calvello, which was transferred in 1496 to within the city limits. St. Gregory VII was born at Sovana. Its first known bishop is Mauritius (680); other bishops were: Raineri (963), who re-introduced common life among the canons; Pier Nicolò Blandinelli (1380), who had the doors of the cathedral made; Apollonio Massaini (1439), under whom the relics of S. Mamiliano, Bishop of Palermo, were translated from the Island of Giglio; Alfonso Petrucci (1498), son of the Tyrant of Siena, later a cardinal, condemned to death by Leo X in 1537; his successor, Lattanzio Petrucci, was accused of high treason and forced to flee, but he was acquitted by Adrian VI; Carvajal Simoncelli (1535) ruled the diocese for sixty-one years; Francesco Pio Santi (1776) resisted the innovations of Leopold and the Synod of Pistoia. For a long time the bishops of Sovana have resided at Pitigliano. In 1844 that city was made an episcopal see and united *æque principaliter* to that of Sovana. The diocese is suffragan of Siena, and contains 47 parishes, with 90 secular and 8 regular priests; 2 Franciscan convents, 4 convents of nuns, and 38,500 inhabitants.

CAPPELLETTI, *Le Chiese d'Italia* (Venice, 1857).

U. BENIGNI.

Sozomen, SALAMINIUS HERMIAS, one of the famous historians of the early Church, b. at Bethelia, a small town near Gaza in Palestine, in the last quarter of the fourth century; d. probably in 447 or 448. What the epithet Salaminius means cannot be determined. The supposition that it had some connexion with Salamis in Cyprus has no foundation. On the authority of Sozomen himself ("Hist. eccl.", V, xv) we learn that his grandfather became a Christian through witnessing a miracle wrought by St. Hilarion. Through many years of persecution the family remained faithful, and Sozomen thus enjoyed the advantage of being trained in a Christian household. His early education was directed by the monks in his native place. It is impossible to ascertain what curriculum he followed in these monastic schools, but his writings give clear evidence of the thoroughness with which he was grounded in Greek studies. A reference to Berytos has led to the mistaken supposition that he pursued legal studies in the famous law school of that place. Wherever his professional training was acquired, he settled in Constantinople, probably about the beginning of the fifth century, to commence his career as a lawyer. While thus engaged he conceived the project of writing a history of the Church. A preliminary study containing a summary of the history of Christianity from the Ascension to 323 has been lost. He purposed to continue the history of Eusebius, and to deal with the period between 323 and 439. The period actually covered in his work ends at 425. Sozomen dedicated his work (Historia ecclesiastica) to Theodosius the Younger. It is divided into nine books, distributed according to the reigns of the emperors. Books I and II embrace the reign of Constantine (323–37); III and IV the reigns of his sons (337–61); books V and VI the reigns of Julian, Jovian, Valentinian I, and Valens (361–75);

books VII and VIII the reigns of Gratian, Valentinian II, Theodosius I, and Arcadius (375–408). Book IX deals with the reign of Theodosius the Younger (408–39). As the work of Socrates appeared at the same time as that of Sozomen and dealt with the same subject and the same period, an important question arises as to the relation, if any, which existed between the two authors. There can be no doubt that the work of Socrates antedated that of Sozomen, and that the latter made use of the work of his predecessor. The extent of this dependence cannot be accurately determined. At most it would appear that, while Sozomen used the work of Socrates as a guide, as well in regard to materials as to order, and while at times he did not hesitate to use it as a secondary source, he was, nevertheless, neither an indiscriminate borrower nor a plagiarist. In some matters, however, as in regard to the Novatians, Sozomen is entirely dependent on Socrates. The ninth book, which Sozomen expressly declared would terminate at the year 439, is manifestly incomplete. There is no reason to think that portion of it has been lost. It is more likely that, because of advancing age or some other cause, he was unable to carry the work to the date he had set before himself. Internal evidence points to the fact that Sozomen undertook to write his history about 443, and that what he succeeded in doing was accomplished in a comparatively short time

The work of Sozomen suffers in many ways by comparison with that of Socrates. Though the style is reputed to be better, the construction of the work is inferior, and the author's grasp of the significance of historical movements is less sure. Nevertheless, Sozomen made a painstaking effort to be acquainted with all the sources of information on the subjects which he touched, and he had a passionate desire for the truth. He was filled with a profound conviction of the Providential purpose of Christianity, and of its mission, under Divine guidance, for the regulation of the affairs of mankind. In doctrinal matters he aimed constantly at being in thorough accord with the Catholic party, and was a consistent opponent of heresy in all its forms. But, while he maintained a constant attitude of hostility to Arianism, Gnosticism, Montanism, Apollinarianism, etc., he never assailed the leaders of these heresies or allowed himself to indulge in bitter personal attacks. "Let it not be accounted strange", he says, "if I have bestowed commendations upon the leaders or enthusiasts of the above-mentioned heresies. I admire their eloquence and their impressiveness in discourse. I leave their doctrines to be judged by those whose right it is" (III, xv).

The work of Sozomen is interesting and valuable for many reasons. In the first place he pays more attention than any of the older historians to the missionary activity of the Christians, and to him we are indebted for much precious information about the introduction of Christianity among the Armenians, the Saracens, the Goths, and other peoples. The history is especially rich in information regarding the rise and spread of monasticism. His account of the labours of the early founders of monasteries and monastic communities, though sympathetic, cannot be said to be overdrawn. The history as a whole is fairly comprehensive, and though his treatment of affairs in the Western Church is not full, his pages abound in facts not available elsewhere and in documentary references of the highest importance. In his attitude towards the Church, in his treatment of the Scriptures, and in his views of the hierarchy and ecclesiastical order and dignity, he is always animated by feelings of submission and respect. There are many faults and shortcomings in his work. Of many of these he himself was conscious, but it was not in his power to correct them. Frequently it was hard for him to know the truth because of the mass of divergent evidence with which he had to deal, frequently there was not enough evidence, but in every case he aimed at expressing the truth and at making his work serve some useful purpose in the defence or elucidation of Christian ideas. The work of Sozomen was printed at Paris in 1544. There are later editions by Christophorson and Ictrus (Cologne, 1612) and by Valesius (Paris. 1668). The text of Valesius was reprinted by Hussey (Oxford, 1860), and by Migne (P. G., LXVII). There is an excellent English translation by Hartranft, with a learned though somewhat diffuse introduction, in the "Nicene and Post-Nicene Fathers", II (New York, 1890).

JEEP, *Quellenuntersuchungen z. d. griech. Kirchenhistorikern* (1884); BATIFFOL, *Sozomene et Sabinos* in *Byzantinische Zeitschr.*, VII (1898), 265 sqq.

PATRICK J. HEALY.

Sozopolis, titular see in the Balkans, suffragan of Adrianopolis. The town, at first called Antheia, was founded in Thrace on the shore of the Pontus Euxinus, principally on a little island, by Anaximander (b. 610–609 B.C.) at the head of Milesian colonists. The name was soon changed to Apollonia, on account of a temple to Apollo in the town, containing a statue of the god 30 cubits high, transported later to Rome by Lucullus and placed in the Capitol. The coins, which begin in the fourth century B.C., bear the name Apollonia and the image of Apollo; the imperial coins, which continue to the first half of the third century A.D., and the "Tabula Peutinger" also contain the name Apollonia; but the "Periplus Ponti Euxini", 85, and the "Notitiæ episcopatuum" have only the new name Sozopolis. In 1328 Cantacuzene (ed. Bonn, I, 326) speaks of it as a large and populous town. The islet on which it stood is now connected with the mainland by a narrow tongue of land. Sozopolis, in Turkish Sizebolou, in Bulgarian Sozopol, is in the Department of Bourgas, Bulgaria. Its 3000 inhabitants, almost exclusively Greeks, lived by fishing and agriculture. Le Quien (Oriens christianus, I, 1181) knows only eight of its bishops: Athanasius (431); Peter (680); Euthymius (787); Ignatius (869); Theodosius (1357); Joannicius, who became Patriarch of Constantinople (1524); Philotheus (1564); Joasaph (1721). This list might be easily lengthened, the see still existing among the Greeks. From being suffragan to Adrianopolis it became in the fourteenth century a metropolis without suffragan sees; it disappeared perhaps temporarily with the Turkish conquest, but reappeared later; in 1808 it was united to the See of Agathopolis and has remained so. The titular resides at Agathopolis, now Akhtébolou, in the vilayet of Adrianopolis, in Turkey. Its relations to the new Bulgarian kingdom are not yet settled. Eubel (Hierarchia catholica medii ævi, I, 194) mentions four Latin bishops of the fourteenth century.

SMITH, *Dict. of Greek and Roman Geog.*, s. v. *Apollonia*; PAULY AND WISSOWA, *Real-Encyclopädie*, s. v. *Apollonia*; TOMASCHEK, *Zur Kunde der Hämus-Halbinsel* (Vienna, 1887), 23; BOUTYRAS, *Dict. of Hist. and Geog.* (Greek), VII, 1148.

S. PÉTRIDÈS.

Sozusa, a titular see of Palestina Prima, suffragan of Cæsarea. The town, at first called Apollonia, is mentioned by Pliny, "Hist. nat.", V, 14, and Ptolemy, V, xv, 2, between Cæsarea and Joppa, and by other geographers. According to Josephus, "Ant. jud.", XIII, xv, 4, it belonged at first to the Phœnicians. From Appianus, "Hist. rom. Syr.", 57, it seems to have been founded by a King Seleucus, whose name it was given, but the history of this maritime city and the date of its establishment, are entirely unknown. The Roman proconsul, Gabinius, found it ruined in 57 B.C. and had it rebuilt (Josephus, "Bel. jud.", I, viii, 4). On the arrival of the Crusaders it was called Arsur or Azuffium, and was protected by strong walls; Godfrey de Bouillon attempted to capture it, but failed for want of ships (William of Tyre, IX, x). King Baldwin I took it in 1102, after a siege by land

and sea, allowing the inhabitants to withdraw to Ascalon. Occupied in 1191 by Saladin, the town was captured by Richard Cœur de Lion after his victory at Rochetaillée. In 1251 St. Louis re-erected its ramparts, and fourteen years later, in 1265, after a siege of forty days, it was stormed by the sultan Bibars; the inhabitants were killed or sold as slaves and the town completely razed. It never recovered, and in the fourteenth century the geographer Abulfeda said it contained no inhabitants ("Tabula Syriæ", 82). Its name Apollonia was replaced by Sozusa at an early period; in 449 at the Robber Council of Ephesus Baruchius signs with this title; its bishops, Leontius in 518, and Damianus in 553, are also known (Le Quien, "Oriens christianus", III, 595). Under the name of Sozusa it occurs in the Byzantine geographers Hierocles and George of Cyprus. In the Middle Ages it was confused with Antipatris, situated more inland, and it is under this name that some of its titular bishops are to be sought. To-day its ruins may be seen at Arsûf, north of Jaffa.

SMITH, *Dict. of Greek and Roman Geog.*, s. v. *Apollonia*; RELAND, *Palæstina ex monumentis veteribus illustrata*, II (Utrecht, 1714), 1023; GUÉRIN, *Description de la Palestine, Samarie*, II (Paris, 1875), 375–82; PAULY AND WISSOWA, *Real-Encyclopädie der classischen Altertumswissenschaft*, s. v. *Apollonia*.

S. VAILHÉ.

Space (Lat. *spatium*).—The idea of space is one of the most important in the philosophy of the material world; for centuries it has preoccupied and puzzled philosophers and psychologists, and even to-day the views as to its nature are far from being harmonious.

It is important first to ascertain the exact meaning of the term. In ordinary language space means empty extension occupied by bodies, and in which local motion takes place. This notion of emptiness is so closely connected with it, that the word is often used to mean the distance between bodies. Space is thus put in contrast with bodies, and we imply, more or less unconsciously, that space by itself contains no body—in a word, that it is empty. Evidently space in this popular sense is the extension of the world. It surpasses in magnitude all that the strongest imagination can picture, and consequently it is assigned no limits. Not indeed that space, in the popular sense, is considered strictly infinite; but rather it is conceived as something "indefinite". Again, space, in the popular mind, is clearly conceived as being tri-dimensional, that is, we can draw in it three straight lines each of which is perpendicular to both of the others, and which exhaust all its dimensional possibilities.

The concept which mathematicians form of space does not correspond in every respect with the popular notion. The geometrician is concerned only accidentally with the space of the world. From it he derives his idea of mathematical space; but he eliminates from it all predicates which are not absolutely necessary to establish his geometrical relations. Mathematical space therefore abstracts from all existence. It is conceived as an extensive, continuous, abstract quantity, in which geometrical points and places can be determined. Mathematical space is said to be infinite—not a metaphysical infinity, which affirms the positive absence of all limits, and with which the mathematician has no concern, but that mathematical infinity, which signifies that the nature of a reality is such that no limit can be assigned to it. The distinction beween mathematical and metaphysical infinity is somewhat subtle, but it is real; it prevents much confusion and facilitates the solution of difficult problems. It may be remarked here that mathematical space is not necessarily tri-dimensional or homogeneous, matters to which we shall refer presently.

Philosophers cannot be satisfied with mathematical space, an abstract construction useful for theoretical purposes, for they wish to arrive at the real space of nature. Nor can they restrict themselves to the popular notion, for their task is precisely to purify the data of common sense from all the extraneous factors modifying them and giving rise to latent contradictions. But in their efforts to discover pure and real space, they have sometimes arrived at the most perplexing results; so that many philosophers, while not subscribing to the doctrines of Kantian criticism, consider the idea of space as hopelessly contradictory, as a purely illusory fancy. To recall all the successive explanations of the nature of real space given by the great philosophers it would be necessary to go through the history of philosophy; but, leaving aside the complete negation of extension, all the doctrines, from Hesiod (cf. Aristotle, IV Phys., vi, 213b) to our day, fluctuate between the idea of absolute space, a real substance independent of the bodies it contains, and purely relative space, a mental fiction based on the real extension of material bodies. The most radical expressions of these two conflicting views are those of Newton and Clarke, on the one hand, who consider space as the *sensorium* of God, and on the other, of Leibniz, who asserts that there is no space independent of extended bodies, and reduces it to "the order of co-existing things".

The traditional philosophy of the Catholic schools rejects absolute space. Newton's idea is incompatible with the concept which the great doctors of the school, following Aristotle, formed of quantity. Suarez declares that space is only "a conceptual entity [*ens rationis*], not, however, formed at will like chimeras, but extracted from bodies, which by their extension are capable of constituting real spaces" (Met. disp., 51). The expression *ens rationis* may be equivocal, but it expresses somewhat exaggeratedly the very active part played by the human intellect in the construction of space. Space is not material bodies themselves, since it appears to be rather a receptacle containing them. From this point of view it must be pure extension, an unqualified quantity. In the strict sense of the terms a quantity without quality is contradictory; for quantity is only the multiplicity of the homogeneous parts in the unity of a body; it is the distribution of an essence, simple in its formal determination. Multiplicity implies a thing that is multiplied, and distribution something that is distributed. Every quantity is the quantity of something; all extension is therefore, in itself, the extension of an extended substance. Yet quantity is something more than a modal accident; it is in truth the absolute accident *par excellence* (see ACCIDENT); it confers on a substance a perfection such that, granted the existence of a substance, the corporeal body is measured by its quantity. It is none the less true that quantity postulates a quantitative substance; and, in a sense, entirely different however from the fancies of ancient physics, it may always be said that an empty quantity is a contradiction in terms. From this we must conclude that extension is only a derivative of quantity; a non-qualified extension, pure extension, pure space in the reality of the corporeal world is contradictory. We conceive it, however, and what is, properly speaking, contradictory is inconceivable. The contradiction arises when we add the condition of existence to pure space. Space is not contradictory in the mind, though it would be contradictory in the real world, because space is an abstraction. Extension is always the extension of something; but it is not the thing extended. Mentally we can separate extension from the substances from which we distinguish it; and it is extension thus separated, conceived apart, which constitutes the space of the universe. Space is therefore as real, as objective, as the corporeal world itself, but in itself it exists apart only in the human mind, seeing that in the reality of existing things it is only the extension of bodies themselves.

Space thus conceived avoids many of the difficulties raised against its reality. But there still remain questions that have taxed the ingenuity of philosophers. What is to be thought of the infinity of space, which to many philosophers seems to be an indisputable postulate? Here we must carefully distinguish the two ideas to which we alluded above. Mathematicians do not understand infinity in the same sense as philosophers. The latter consider absolute infinity as the plenitude of being, being itself; spatial infinity for them can signify only plenitude of extension. There are no limits to an infinite space, nowhere can there exist a definite relation to its extremities or even to itself. It is impossible to add even mentally anything to such extension, for it would be an absurdity to conceive anything greater than infinite extension. Mathematical infinity is something quite different. It is not considered solely in relation to the being to which it is attributed, but in relation to this being and to the determinations of limits possible to the intellect. Whatever by its nature surpasses all the limits we can assign it, that is mathematically infinite. It must be carefully noted that these two ideas in no way coincide, since it is possible that the intellect may not grasp the nature of a being fully enough to determine its limits: the possibility that this nature may surpass all assignable limits does not involve the conclusion that the being is in itself unlimited. Mathematical infinity introduces into the problem a factor extrinsic to the nature of the being: the relative perfection, or rather the imperfection, of the human idea; and it is noteworthy that in all problems concerning quantity our intellect is, to a very great extent, dependent on our senses and our imagination. This distinction being established, we may remark that real space evidently surpasses all that experience can teach us. We are forced, consequently, to solve the problem by analysis.

Mathematical space is abstract and mathematically infinite; but we are dealing here with the real universe. The notion of mathematical infinity may be applied to it in a secondary sense. The nature of real space is such as not to demand any definite dimensions. No part of space in itself needs be the last. For all we know, or do not know, about it, space may be greater than any limits whatsoever we might assign. But space cannot be metaphysically infinite. It is impossible to have an actual quantitive infinite being composed of finite parts. To infinite extension nothing can be added, and from it nothing can be taken away, even mentally. For if, by hypothesis, infinite extension is divided in two, neither of the parts is infinite since neither by itself contains the plenitude of extension. Both therefore are finite; by their union they would form the original whole, but it is absurd to imagine that an infinite whole is formed by the union of two finite parts. It is clear that we can mentally take way a portion of space. Hence it is clear that space cannot be metaphysically infinite. An actually infinite quantity is a contradiction in terms. Here of course our imagination cannot follow our intellect. We cannot represent exactly to ourselves what may be the limits of the world; and it is clear that in this case certain physical laws, those of motion, for instance, cannot be fully applied. It is useless to discuss the subject further because, owing to the limitations of our experience, we are apt to indulge in mere fantastic and arbitrary speculations.

A still more abstruse subject is reached when we come to deal with the number of dimensions of space and its homogeneity. Our imagination always represents real space as having but three dimensions. We reach this intuitive space (see below) spontaneously; it seems to us so natural, so inevitable, that we have great difficulty in freeing ourselves from the domination of this image, and in conceiving (to imagine it is impossible) a space with more than three dimensions. However, the question has been raised; for geometricians reason frequently about a space of four, of five, or of n dimensions. The problem is not of the experimental order. Our sensory experiences and everything in practical life reveal only three dimensions. But does experience exhaust the possibilities of real space? and can this space have no more than three dimensions? Nothing obliges us to believe that such is the case. The material world requires essentially only quantity, and this is not identical with extension. Quantity confers on substance a multiplicity of parts; extension supposes this multiplicity and gives a relative position to the parts. Quantity implies a distinction of parts, extension adds extraposition, i. e. the placing of part outside of part; hence it will be seen that, in a strict sense, material beings do not necessarily postulate extension. It would then be quite arbitrary to declare a priori that they must have extension according to three mutually perpendicular directions, and that they cannot have any more. The word *dimensions* is here used, of course, only by analogy with the three dimensions perceived by experience; we can get at pure quantity only through extension. But the intellect in its analysis goes beyond the data offered to it by sense, and it is forced to conclude that space of more than three dimensions implies no contradiction.

By a very similar process we can solve the problem, so perplexing for the average mind, of the homogeneity of space. The essential properties of quantity require no definite number of dimensions. The same may be said of the quality, or rather intensity, of extension: the parts may be more or less extraposed. The parts, remaining the same, may give a greater or a less extension in the ordinary sense of the word. There is nothing contradictory, therefore, in all the parts of space being everywhere equally extraposed, in which case space would be homogeneous. But, on the other hand, there is no reason why space should not be differently extraposed in different parts, and if this be so, space would be heterogeneous; and if the variation be simple and constant, we can formulate the laws of these spaces and determine the properties of the figures formed therein. This explains why geometry, so rigorous in its methods and simple in its postulates, is not necessarily one. The ancient geometry of Euclid takes for granted the homogeneity of space; but it is well known that non-Euclidian geometries have been constructed, notably those of Riemann and of Lobatchewski, differing from Euclid's and yet free from all incoherency.

These speculations on the nature of space cannot, however, do away with the fundamental fact that the human mind is dominated by an image, imposing irresistibly on it a homogeneous tri-dimensional space. One of the central questions of classic psychology concerns the origin of this representation. We dismiss Kant's well-known view, that space is an a priori form of sensory activity. But psychologists fluctuate between two extremes: on the one hand, nativism, represented by Johann Müller, Fichte, Sigwart, Mach, and many others; and on the other hand, empiricism. followed by Locke, Hume, Condillac, Maine de Biran, John Stuart Mill, Bain, Spencer, and others. The former hold that we obtain the image of space from the primordial subjective dispositions of our mentality; and many of them see therein a condition precedent of all experience. The second class, on the contrary, believe that this image is acquired, that it results from visual and tactile impressions and is only a result of association. Many authorities hesitate and try to discover an intermediate position. From the facts adduced and the analysis to which they have been subjected it seems clear that the image of space is in reality acquired like all other images: in very young children we see it, so to say, in process of formation. It is the result of the spontaneous interpretation of all the extensive sensations; and it is because this interpretation takes place in the simplest manner that our intuitive space is homogeneous and tri-dimensional. Evidently this elaboration supposes a special nature in the subject, the faculty of receiving extensive impressions, and that of combining them by synthesis. But this is natural to man, and there is nothing to justify us in speaking of an innate image of space.

Every philosopher and psychologist has treated the question of space; here merely a few important works are cited to help towards a deeper study of the question.—FARGES, *L'idée du continu dans l'espace et le temps* (Paris, 1892); HODGSON, *Time and Space* (London, 1865); JAMES, *Perception of Space* in *Mind*, XII (1887); FULLERTON, *The Doctrine of Space and Time* in *Philos. Rev.*, X (1901); GUTBERLET, *Die neue Raumtheorie* (Mainz, 1882); WILLEMS, *Institutiones philosophicæ*, II (Trier, 1906); NYS, *La notion d'espace au point de vue cosmologique et psychologique* (Louvain, 1901); WUNDT, *Grundriss der Psychologie* (Leipzig, 1907); IDEM, *Grundzüge der physiol. Psychologie*, II (Leipzig, 1903); HÖFFDING, *Esquisse d'une psychologie basée sur l'expérience* (Paris, 1906); EBBINGHAUS-DURR, *Grundzüge der Psychologie* (Leipzig, 1911); ZIEHEN, *Physiologische Psychologie* (Jena, 1911); EISLER, *Wörterbuch der philosophischen Begriffe* (Berlin, 1910); BERGSON, *Essai sur les données immédiates de la conscience* (Paris, 1908).

M. P. DE MUNNYNCK.

Spagni, ANDREA, educator and author, b. at Florence, 8 Aug., 1716; d. at Rome, 16 Sept., 1788. He entered the Society of Jesus, 22 Oct., 1731, and was employed chiefly in teaching philosophy and theology, though for a time he professed mathematics at the Roman College, and assisted Father Asclepi in his astronomical observations. The most noted of his writings is the work "De Miraculis" (Rome, 1777), which he carefully revised in two succeeding editions (Rome, 1779 and 1785). In this work, besides giving the positive doctrine on the nature and reality of miracles, he has marshalled together with great thoroughness the objections brought forward by the rationalists of his own and preceding times against the chief miracles of the Old and the New Testament, so that the work may be considered as a compendium of the literature of the subject, up to the last quarter of the eighteenth century. His other chief works are: "De Causa efficiente" (Rome, 1764); "De Bono, Malo et Pulchro" (Rome, 1766); "De Mundo" (Rome, 1770); "De Ideis Mentis humanæ" (Rome, 1772); "De Motu" (Rome, 1774); "De Anima Brutorum" (Rome, 1775); "De Signis Idearum" (Rome, 1781).

SOMMERVOGEL, *Bibl. de la C. de J.*, VII (Brussels, 1896).

EDWARD C. PHILLIPS.

Spagnoli. See BAPTISTA MANTUANUS, BLESSED.

Spain.—This name properly signifies the whole peninsula which forms the south-eastern extremity of Europe. Since the political separation of Portugal, however, the name has gradually come to be restricted to the largest of the four political divisions of the Peninsula: (1) Spain; (2) Portugal; (3) the Republic of Andorra; (4) the British possession of Gibraltar, at the southern extremity. The etymology of the name *Spain (España)* is uncertain. Some derive it from the Punic word *tsepan*, "rabbit", basing the opinion on the evidence of a coin of Galba, on which Spain is represented with a rabbit at her feet, and on Strabo, who calls Spain "the land of rabbits". It is said that the Phœnicians and Carthaginians found the country overrun with these rodents, and so named it after them. Another derivation is from *sphan*, "north", from the circumstance that the country was north of Carthage, just as the Greeks called Italy *Hesperia*, because it was their western boundary, or the land of sunset (ἐσπέρα). Again, some Bascophiles would assert a Basque origin for the name of Spain: *Espania*, "Land of the Shoulder", because it formed the western shoulder of ancient Europe. Padre Larramendi has remarked that, in the Basque language, *ezpaña* means "tongue", "lip", or "extremity", and might thus have been applied to the extreme south-western region of Europe. The Spanish Peninsula has also been called the Iberian, from its original inhabitants, and (by synecdoche) the Pyrenean, from the mountains which bound it on the north. As the Spaniards named one part of America—Mexico—*Nueva España* (New Spain), we speak of "the Spains", in the plural, to signify the Spanish possessions.

I. PHYSICAL CHARACTERISTICS AND STATISTICS.—The geographical boundaries of Spain are: on the north, the Pyrenees, the Republic of Andorra, and the Bay of Biscay (known in Spain as *Mar Cantabrico*, or "Cantabrian Sea"); on the east, the Mediterranean; on the south, the Mediterranean, the Straits of Gibraltar, and the Atlantic; on the west, Portugal and the Atlantic. Its four extreme points are: on the north, the Estaca de Vares, in N. lat. 43° 47′ 32″; on the south, the southern extremity of the Island of Tarifa, in S. lat. 35° 59′ 49″; on the east, Cape Creus, in longitude 3° 20′ 16″ E. of Greenwich, on the west, Cape Torinana, in longitude 9° 17′ 33″ W. of Greenwich. The total area of the Spanish territory in the Peninsula is 194,563 square miles, with a coast line of 2060 miles in length. The combined French and Portuguese frontiers measure 3094 miles.

The surface of Spain presents the most varied geological features. In the seas of the Cambrian epoch the first elements of the Peninsula appeared as a multitude of islands. The most important of these islands formed what is now Galicia and the North of Portugal, with parts of the Provinces of Caceres, Salamanca, and Zamora. To the south-east of this was another island, where is now Bejar and the Sierra de Gredos, comprising part of the Provinces of Avila, Segovia, and Toledo. To the north-east, the Pyrenees and the Catalonian coast took the form of islets, while in other directions other islets occupied the sites of Lisbon, Evora, Cáceres, Badajoz, Seville, Cordova, and Jaen. The upheaval of the land went on during the Devonian and Silurian epochs until it formed what is now the whole of Galicia, part of the Asturias, Leon, and Zamora, and as far down as Toledo, Ciudad Real, Cordova, Huelvas, and the Algarves, while, to the east and north, were formed the Catalonian coast and a great part of the Pyrenees. Large islands arose in the neighbourhoods of Burgos, Soria, Daroca, Granada, Malaga, and Gibraltar. No Permian formation is to be found in Spain, nor does there appear any Triassic worth mentioning, the formations of these two periods having been submerged during later periods. During the Jurassic period long parallel tracts were formed along the present courses of the Ebro and the Turia, as well as a great mass between Jaen, Granada, Malaga, Osuna, and Montilla. The eastern portions of the Peninsula were built up during the Cretacean period, while, between these formations and the Granitic and Silurian, extensive lakes were left which have since disappeared but which may still be traced in the level steppes of Aragon and the two Castiles. What is now the Ebro was then a vast lake extending through the Eocene and Pliocene formations of Lérida, Saragossa, and Logroño, and joining, in the regions of Sto. Domingo de la Calzada, Haro, and Briviesca, another lake which then covered the sites of Burgos, Valladolid, Leon, Zamora, and Salamanca. Another extension of the Eocene formation was from the region where Madrid now stands to that of Albacete and Murcia. The Quaternary formations are found chiefly on the east coast and the Provinces of Madrid (northwest), Segovia, Valladolid, Palencia, and Asturias, and the basins of the principal rivers. Down to this last period Spain does not seem to have been definitively separated from Africa, its formations—Eocene and Miocene, as well as Silurian—being continued in that region.

Owing to the diversity of formations described above, and the elevation of the central portions, the surface of the Peninsula is, in general, of an uneven character with a very unequally distributed irrigation, some regions enjoying a wonderful fertility, while others are nothing but steppes. In other parts, again, the abrupt slope of the ground is such that the rains produce torrential floods in the rivers and thus negative their beneficial action. The unevenness of the country at the same time results in great differences of climate. The arid prairies of certain parts of the Castiles and Estremadura are in as striking contrast with the fertile, though monotonous, plains of the Campos district and Lower Aragon, and the extremely rich arable lands and meadows of Andalusia and the eastern provinces, as are the perpetual snows of the Pyrenees, the Cantabrian Range, and the Sierra Nevada with the parched lowlands of Estremadura, Andalusia, Murcia, and Alicante. No less uneven is the distribution of rainfall—from the northern provinces, with their ever-clouded skies, to the almost invariably dry and transparent atmosphere of the south. The contrast extends even to the seas surrounding Spain—the tranquil Mediterranean, the stormy Bay of Biscay, and the Atlantic with a character midway between.

The general structural form of the Peninsula is somewhat that of a truncated pyramid, sloping abruptly towards the west, but gently towards the east. The elevated plains of the centre are intersected by mountain ranges. The mountain masses may be divided into six groups: (1) the northern, consisting of the Pyrenees on the east and the Cantabrian Range on the west, and terminated by Capes Creus and Finisterre; (2) the Iberic, or eastern, comprising the mountains which bound the basin of the Ebro and extend as far as Cape Gata; (3) the central system, the Carpetan, or Carpeto-Vetonic, Range, so called from the Carpetani and Vetones who inhabited its slopes in ancient times; (4) the Mountains of Toledo, or Cordillera Oretana; (5) the Betic system, or Cordillera Mariánica, forming the right-hand side of the basin of the Betis, or Guadalquivir, and the chief part of which is the Sierra Morena; (6) the Penibetic system, extending from the Sierra Nevada to Cape Tarifa. The highest elevations are: Maladeta (11,004 ft.) and Pico de Nethou (11,168 ft.), in the Pyrenees; Peña de Cerredo (8784 ft.), and Moncayo (7593 ft.), in the Cantabrian Range; Plaza del Moro Almanzor (8692 ft.), in the Carpetan Range; the plateau of Corocho de Rocigalgo (4750 ft.), in the Toledo Mountains; Estrella (4260 ft.), in the Betic Range; Mulhacen (11,417 ft.) and Veleta (11,382 ft.) in the Penibetic.

For hydrographic purposes the surface of Spain is divided by the Instituto Geográfico into the following ten basins: (1) the Eastern Pyrenees, basin of the Rivers Muga, Fluvía, Ter, Tordeva, Besós, Llobregat, Foix, and Francolí; (2) the basin of the Ebro, to the south and west of the preceding, containing the Nela, Zadorra, Ega, Arga, Aragón, Arba, Gallego, Cinea, and Segre, affluents of the Ebro, on its right side, and the Oca, Tiron, Oja, Najerilla, Iregua, Alhama, Jalón, Huerva, Aguas, Martin, Guadalope, Matarrana, and other smaller affluents on its left; the south-eastern region, watered by the Cenia, Migares, Palancia, Turia (or Guadalaviar), Jucar, Serpis, Vinalopó, Segura, and Almanzora; (4) the southern region, intersected by small streams, the most important rivers being the Almería, Adra, Guadalfeo, Guadalhorce, Guadiaro, and Guadalete; (5) the basin of the Guadalquivir, the affluents of which are, on the right, the Rivers Borosa, Guadalimar, Rumblar, Jándula, Yeguas, Guadamellato, Guadiato, the Brook of Huesna, the River Viar, and the Brooks of Cala, Huelva, and Guadiamar, and on the left, the Guadiana Menor, Genil, Guadabullón, Guadajoz, Corbones, Guadaira, and Salado de Morón; (6) the basin of the Guadiana, with its tributaries, the Záncara, or Cigüela, Bullaque,
and Gévora, on the right, and the Javalón, Zujar, Ardila, and Chanza, on the left; (7) the basin of the Tagus, which river rises in the Province of Teruel, in the Sierra de Molina, and receives, on the right, the Gallo, Jarama, Guadarrama, Alberche, Tiétar, Alagón and Eljas, and, on the left, besides other streams of slight importance, the Guadiela and the Almonte. The Jarama, in its turn, receives the Lozoya, Guadalix, Manzanares (which flows by Madrid), Henares, and Tajuña; (8) the basin of the Douro, which rises in the Peña (Rock) Urbión, in the Province of Logroño, 7216 feet above the sea level. The chief affluents of the Douro are, on the right, the Pisuerga and the Esla, and on the left, the Eresma and the Tormes. The Pisuerga, again, receives, on the right, the Burejo, Vallarna, Astudillo, and Carrión, and on the left, the Camesa, Odra, Arlanzón, Baltanás, and Esguera. Affluents of the Esla, on the right, are the Curueño, Bernesga, Orbigo, Tera, and Aliste, and on the left, the Cea. (9) The western region of Galicia, the chief rivers of which are the Miño, Oitaben, Lerez, Umia, Ulla, Tambre, Jallas, Castro, Rio del Puerto, Allones, Mero, Mandeo, Lume, Jubia, Rio de Porto do Cabo, Mera, and Sor. (10) The northern basin, containing the Eo, Navia Nalón, and Sella, in the Asturias; the Deba, Nansa, Besaya, Mas, and Miera, in Santander; the Nervión, Oria, and Bidasoa, in the Basque country. The only important lakes in Spain are the lagoons: those of Gallocanta, in Aragon; the Alfaques, in Catalonia; the Albufera, in Valencia, and, in Cadiz, that of Janda, the scene of the battle which has been generally known as the battle of Guadalete, which put an end to the power of the Goths.

Silver, lead, and iron are abundant, the last especially in Biscay. Veins of quicksilver are found in Almadén, besides others of less importance elsewhere. There are also copper, tin, zinc, gold, cobalt, nickel, antimony, bismuth, and molybdenum. Spain is not rich in coal, which, however, is found in the Provinces of Gerona, Lérida, Santander, Asturias, León, Palencia, Burgos, Guadalajara, Cuenca, Ciudad Real, Badajoz, Cordova, and Seville. The most important carboniferous deposits are those of S. Juan de las Abadesas (Gerona), Mieres (Asturias), Barruelo and Orbó (Palencia), Puertollano (Ciudad Real), Bélmez and Espiel (Cordova), and Villanueva del Rio (Seville). There are also deposits of anthracite, lignite, asphalt, and turf, while springs of petroleum, though not of any importance, exist in Barcelona, Burgos, Cadiz, and Guadalajara. On the other hand, sulphur is abundant, as well as common salt, and waters impregnated with sulphates and with sulphur.

The botanical resources are abundant and various —the chestnut, the oak, the cork tree, the pine, and a number of other conifers. Castile produces a great quantity of cereals; Valencia, rice, oranges, lemons, *chufas* (the tuber of a variety of sedge), melons, and other fruits in immense variety; Catalonia, potatoes, oil, figs, filberts, carobs, pomegranates, alfalfa; Murcia, peppers, dates, saffron etc.; Andalusia, oil; Estremadura, pasturage etc. Excellent wines are produced in nearly all the provinces, the most highly esteemed being those of Jerez, Malaga, Montilla (Andalusia), Cariñena (Aragon), Valdepeñas, Rioja etc. The soil of Spain is apportioned agriculturally as follows:

	Acres.
Market gardens	391,128
Orchards	704,522
Grain	32,014,934
Vineyards	3,480,816
Olive groves	2,001,705
Meadows	1,803,809
Pasturage	6,307,100
Highways and woods	207,767
Mountain	11,608,197
Untilled, but fit for grazing	8,264,063
Waste	4,024,770
Total	70,808,811

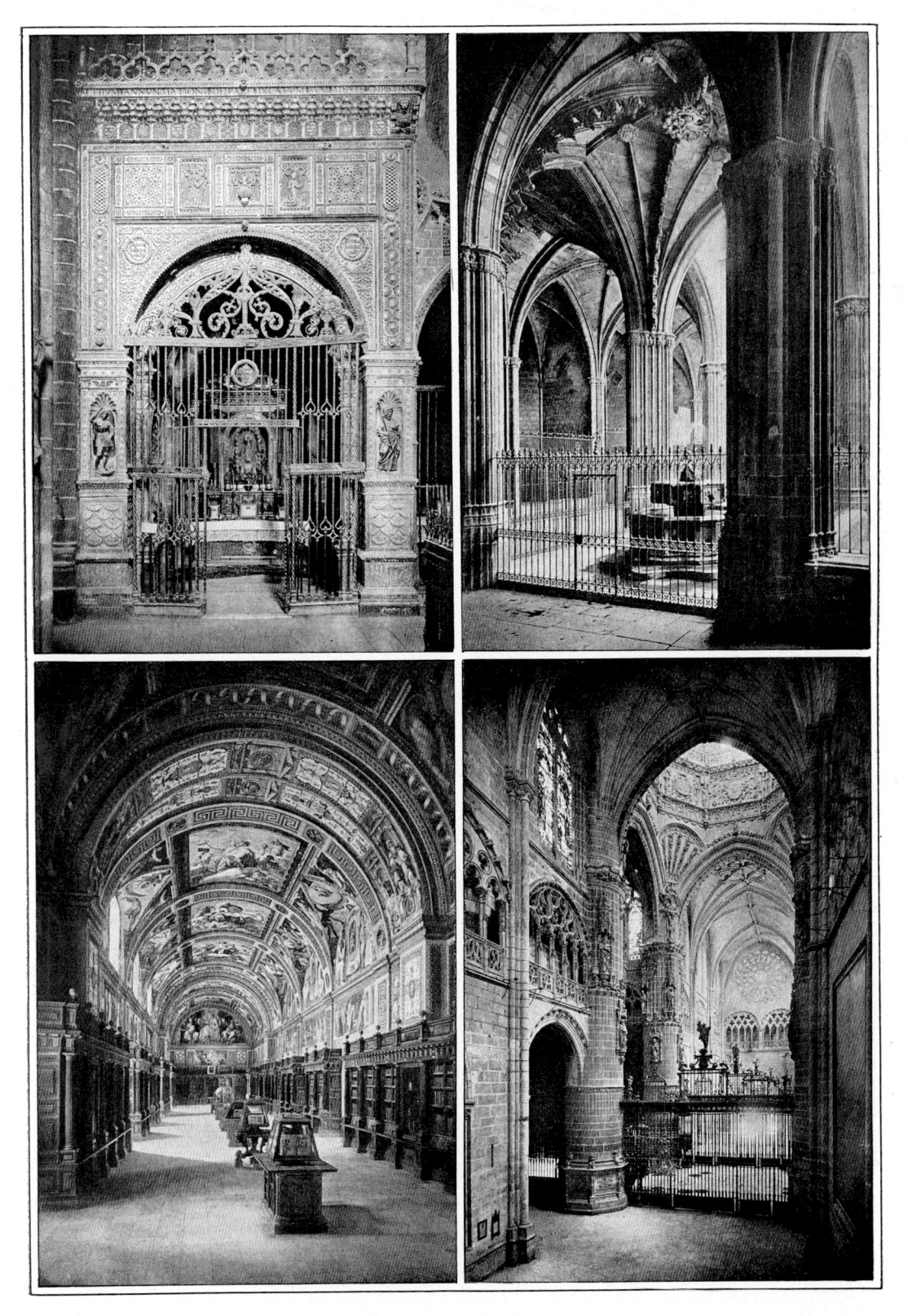

SPAIN

A CHAPEL IN THE CATHEDRAL OF SIGÜENZA, 1520   FOUNTAIN IN THE CATHEDRAL CLOISTER, BARCELONA
THE LIBRARY OF THE ESCORIAL, 1563–84   INTERIOR OF THE TRANSEPT, CATHEDRAL OF BURGOS

The normal agricultural production is:

	English bushels.		English gallons.
Wheat	90,167,965	Oil	73,947,467
Barley	47,895,912	Wine	509,712,819
Rye	20,337,766		
Maize	21,425,538		
Oats	7,245,315		
Total production of grain	187,072,496		

It is not easy to ascertain the number of head of stock bred in Spain; great pains are taken to conceal the statistics, owing to the increase of taxation. The following statement, may be taken as approximately correct: horses, 500,000; mules, 900,000; asses, 950,000; cattle, 2,500,000; sheep, 18,000,000; goats, 3,000,000; hogs, 3,000,000. At the end of the eighteenth century there were 19,000,000 head of sheep. One of the chief causes of the decline in this respect was the laicization of religious houses, which eventually resulted in the mountain slopes being denuded. It is estimated that 68,000,000 kilogrammes (66,830 English tons, or 74,849 American tons) of fish are caught annually on the sea coasts of Spain. Of this quantity 24,000,000 kilogrammes are salted, and 8,000,000 pickled. The quantity exported is 26,000,000 kilogrammes (25,590 English tons, or 28,660 American tons).

While Spain does not rank as a manufacturing nation, it has important manufactures of woollen, cotton, silk, linen, and hempen textiles; of paper, leather, porcelain, earthenware, and glass; of chocolate, soap, and chemicals. Weapons are manufactured at Toledo, Oviedo, Seville, Trubia (ordnance), Eibar, Plasencia, Saragossa, and Albacete (the famous Albacete *navajas*, or knives). There are also notable manufactures of bricks, glazed tiles (*azulejos*), and other ceramic products. The principal articles of importation are cotton, wheat, coal, timber, sugar, salted codfish, woollen fabrics, and machinery; of exportation, wine, oil, metals, and other mineral products, cork, and fruit, both dried and fresh. The principal banks are the Bank of Spain; the Bank of Barcelona, the Banco Hipotecario, the Sociedad Tabacalera de Filipinas, etc. The first-class maritime customhouses are those of Aguilas, Alicante, Almería, Barcelona, Bilbao, Cadiz, Carril, Cartagena, Corunna, Gijon, Grao de Valencia, Huelva, Mahón, Malaga, Palamós, Palma in Majorca, Pasajes, Ribadeo, San Sebastián, Santander, Seville, Tarragona, Vigo, and Vinaroz. The first-class inland custom-houses are those of Junquera, Portbou, Irún, Canfranc, Benasque, Palau, Sallent, Torla, Les, Alós, Bosost, Farga de Moles, Dancharinea, and Valcarlos, on the French frontier, and, on the Portuguese frontier, those of Albuquerque, Badajo, Olivenza, San Vicente, Alcántara, Herrera de Alcántara, Valencia de Alcántara, Paimogo, Verín, Cadovos, Puente Barjas, La Guardia, Salvatierra, Tuy, Fregeneda, Albergueria, Aldea del Obispo, Barba del Puerco, Alcañices, Fermoselle and Pedralva.

According to the census for those years respectively, the population of Spain was: 15,464,340 in 1857; 15,673,481 in 1860; 16,634,345 in 1877; 17,565,632 in 1887; 18,132,475 in 1897; 18,618,086 in 1900. The last of these census shows a distribution according to sex of 9,087,821 males and 9,530,265 females, an excess of 442,444 females; there were 5,200,816 unmarried men, and 5,109,609 unmarried women; 7,021,512 married men and women; 391,452 widowers and 888,629 widows (excess of widows 497,177); condition not ascertained, 3615 men and 2453 women. In regard to age the married persons were divided as follows:

	Males.	Females.
Between 11 and 15 years of age	11	324
Between 16 and 20 years of age	3,700	55,296
Between 21 and 25 years of age	136,903	350,957
Between 26 and 30 years of age	461,439	557,630

Unmarried persons were divided as follows:

	Males.	Females.
Between 41 and 45 years of age	35,291	50,617
Between 46 and 50 years of age	32,549	59,067
Between 51 and 60 years of age	45,255	78,037

As to longevity, the figures were:

	Males.	Females.
Persons living between 71 and 80 years of age	174,815	184,504
Persons living between 81 and 90 years of age	28,075	35,948
Persons living between 91 and 100 years of age	1,656	3,048
Persons living over 100 years of age	28	124

II. GOVERNMENT.—A. *Civil and Military Organization*.—Spain was formed by the coalition of various states, which for many centuries had kept their own names and boundaries, and had differed considerably in laws (the *fueros*), customs, characteristics, and methods of government. These states were: The Kingdoms of Galicia, León, Old and New Castile, Estremadura, Andalusia, Murcia, Valencia, the Balearic Isles, Aragon, and Navarre, the two principalities of Asturias and Catalonia, and the Basque Provinces. The Bourbons, with their French propensity to centralize, made the government uniform, converting the ancient states into so many *intendencias*, or departments. In 1809, Joseph Bonaparte, the intruded occupant of the Throne, divided Spain into 38 departments, and the present division, into 49 provinces, was legally enacted in 1834. The ancient Kingdom of Galicia makes four provinces: Corunna (or Coruña), Lugo, Orense, and Pontevedra. The Principality of Asturias is the Province of Oviedo. Old Castile forms the eight provinces of Avila, Segovia, Soria, Valladolid, Palencia, Burgos, Logroño, and Santander; New Castile, those of Madrid, Toledo, Ciudad Real, Cuenca, and Guadalajara. The three Basque Provinces are: Alava, Guipuzcoa, and Vizcaya, their respective capitals being Vitoria, S. Sebastian, and Bilbao. Navarre forms a single province, with Pamplona for its capital. Aragon is divided into the three Provinces of Saragossa, Huesca, and Teruel; Catalonia forms those of Barcelona, Tarragona, Lérida, and Gerona; León, those of León, Zamora, and Salamanca; Estremadura, those of Cáceres and Badajoz; Valencia, those of Alicante and Castellón de la Plana; Murcia, those of Murcia and Albacete. Andalusia forms the eight Provinces of Cordova, Almería, Granada, Malaga, Jaen, Cadiz, Huelva and Seville. The Balearic Isles form one province, with Palma for its capital; the Canaries, another, with Las Palmas for its capital. This division has many inconveniences: it is ill-adapted to historical analysis; it is extremely unequal, some provinces being three times as large as others. Moreover, it does not fit in with the ecclesiastical organization of the country.

At the head of each province is a civil governor, the office being both administrative and political in character, and one of the few the incumbents of which change with the changes of political parties in power. Subject to the civil governor are all the departments of the provincial administration; the Exchequer, presided over by a delegate, the Police, etc. The civil governor also wields authority over the civil "facultative corps", as they are called—the engineers of highways, forests, and mines, and the agricultural experts—as well as over public instruction, charities, and so on. Each province is divided into municipalities, which are governed by municipal councils (*ayuntamientos*), with an *alcalde*, or mayor, at the head of each *ayuntamiento*. Each alcalde is dependent on the governor of the province, and in his turn controls the officials of his own municipal government. The total number of municipalities and *ayuntamientos* in Spain is 9290. Every village not large enough to form a municipality has a sub-mayor (*alcalde pedaneo*), governing the village in dependence upon the *ayuntamiento* of the municipality of which it forms a part. The theories of Centralism have made the municipal *ayuntamientos* organs of the central political power; but in practice these bodies aspire to be really representative, each of its own community, in relation to the Government, and this forms the programme of the Municipal Autonomy movement.

The central Government is administered by the various ministerial offices and the bureaux dependent upon them. These ministerial offices are: the Presidency of the Council of Ministers, with its administrative corps; the Ministry of State, with the diplomatic and consular corps, the corps of interpreters, and the auxiliary administrative corps; the Ministry of Grace and Justice, which has charge of ecclesiastical relations, of the judges, notaries, registrars of property, clerks (*escribanos*), and relators, and the direction of prisons and penal establishments; the Ministry of Finance, or the Exchequer (*Hacienda*), which controls the administration of the customs, the advocates of the State, and the examiners of accounts, besides its own special administrative bureau. The Ministerio de Gobernación (equivalent to Home Office or Department of the Interior) has charge of public health and the Police, as well as the Postal and Telegraph Services, and public charities. The Ministry of Public Instruction and Fine Arts has charge of the archives, libraries, copyright (*propiedad literaria*), geographical, topographical, and astronomical workers, independent industrial enterprises, and state professors and teachers. The Ministry of Public Works controls the state engineers and exercises supervision over highways, mines, agriculture, manufactures and commerce, and forests, besides special administration. The Ministry of War has charge of all that relates to national defence; the Ministry of Marine, of the whole administration of the Navy, both as to material and men. The Ministerio de Ultramar (Ministry of the Colonies) has ceased to exist since the loss of the colonies.

The ordinary administration of justice in Spain is carried on by judges of first instance, territorial courts (*audiencias*) of second instance, and the Supreme Court, sitting at Madrid, to which causes of great importance are taken in the last instance. There are fifteen territorial courts, or jurisdictions (*audiencias*): (1) at Albacete; (2) Barcelona; (3) Burgos; (4) Cáceres; (5) Corunna; (6) Granada; (7) Madrid; (8) Oviedo; (9) Palma (Majorca); (10) Las Palmas (Canary Islands); (11) Pamplona; (12) Seville; (13) Valencia; (14) Valladolid; and (15) Saragossa. Of these jurisdictions (1) comprises the Provinces of Albacete (eight judicial districts, eighty-five *ayuntamientos*), Ciudad Real (ten judicial districts), Cuenca (eight districts), and Murcia (ten districts); (2) of Barcelona (seventeen districts), Gerona (six districts), Lérida (eight districts), and Tarragona (eight districts); (3) of Alava (three districts), Burgos (twelve districts), Logroño (nine districts), Santander (eleven districts), Soria (five districts), and Biscay (five districts); (4) of Badajoz (fifteen districts), and Cáceres (thirteen districts); (5) of Corunna (fourteen districts), Lugo (eleven districts), Orense (eleven districts), and Pontevedra (eleven districts); (6) of Almería (ten districts), Granada (fifteen districts), Jaén (thirteen districts), and Malaga (fifteen districts); (7) of Avila (six districts), Guadalajara (nine districts), Madrid (seventeen districts), Segovia (five districts), and Toledo (twelve districts); (8) comprises the single province of Oviedo, divided into fifteen districts; (9) comprises the Balearic Isles, with six districts; (10) the seven districts of the Canary Islands; (11) the Provinces of Guipuzcoa (four districts), and Navarre (five districts); (12) of Cadiz (fourteen districts), Cordova (seventeen districts), Huelva (six districts), and Seville (fourteen districts); (13) of Alicante (fourteen districts), Castellon (nine districts), and Valencia (twenty-one districts); (14) of Leon (ten districts), Palencia (seven districts), Salamanca (eight districts), Valladolid (eleven districts), and Zamora (eight districts); (15) of Huesca (eight districts), Teruel (ten districts), and Saragossa (thirteen districts).

The Peninsula and its adjacent islands are divided into fourteen military districts, or captaincies-general (*capitanias generales*): New Castile, Catalonia, Andalusia, Valencia, Galicia, Aragon, Granada, Old Castile, Estremadura, Navarre, Burgos, the Basque District, the Balearic, and the Canary Islands. Each district is commanded by a lieutenant-general with the title of captain-general, to whom all the troops in the district, and all persons connected with the army, are subject. A general of division, called the *segundo cabo* (second chief), takes his place in case of absence or illness, and is also the military governor of the chief province of the district. There is also a commander-in-chief at Ceuta, who is not dependent upon any district commander. Each civil province also forms a military government, usually commanded by a general of brigade or, in the case of the principal ones, by a general of division. Every fortress or place of high strategic importance constitutes a special military government under a *comandante de plaza*.

B. *Ecclesiastical Organization.*—Spain is divided into the following ecclesiastical provinces: I. Burgos; II. Granada; III. Santiago; IV. Saragossa; V. Seville; VI. Tarragona; VII. Toledo; VIII. Valencia; IX. Valladolid. By the Concordat of 1851 it was agreed that eight sees should be suppressed. These eight were: Albarracín, Barbastro, Ceuta, Ciudad Rodrigo, Iviza, Solsoña, Tenerife, and Tudela. (See map.)

I. (1) The Archdiocese of Burgos (*Burgensis*), erected in 988, made metropolitan by Alfonso VI, numbers 1220 parishes, 47 rural deaneries, in the Provinces of Burgos, Santander, Palencia, and Soria. (2) The Diocese of Calahorra and La Calzada (*Calagurritana*) is of Apostolic origin. It has 266 parishes, 47 rural deaneries, in the Provinces of Logroño and Navarre. By the provisions of the Concordat its capital should have been transferred to Logroño, but, owing to difficulties which arose, it is at present (1910) administered by the Archbishop of Burgos. (3) The Diocese of León (*Legionensis*), founded in the third century, has 345 parishes, 37 rural deaneries, in the Provinces of León, Valladolid, and Oviedo. (4) The Diocese of Osma (*Oxomensis*) is of Apostolic origin. It was suppressed on account of the Arab invasion, and restored in the ninth century. It numbers 349 parishes, 28 rural deaneries, in the Provinces of Soria and Burgos. (5) The Diocese of Palencia (*Palentina*), founded in the third century, has 345 parishes, 24 rural deaneries, in the Provinces of Palencia, Valladolid, and Burgos. (6) The Diocese of Santander (*Santanderiensis*), erected in the year 1354, has 425 parishes, 26 rural deaneries, nearly all in the same province. (7) The Diocese of Vitoria (*Victoriensis*), erected in 1862, pursuant to the Concordat of 1851, has 930 parishes, 36 rural deaneries, in the three Basque provinces.

II. (1) The Archdiocese of Granada (*Gramatensis*), of very ancient origin, was restored and made metropolitan by the Catholic sovereigns in 1492. It numbers 182 parishes, 13 rural deaneries, nearly all in the Provinces of Granada and Almería. (2) The Diocese of Almería (*Almeriensis*), of very ancient origin, was restored by the Catholic sovereigns. It has 66 parishes, 7 rural deaneries, in the province of the same name. (3) The Diocese of Cartagena-Murcia (*Cartaginiensis*) is of unknown origin. Urban IV restored it and fixed its see in Murcia. It has 134 parishes, 17 rural deaneries, in the Provinces of Murcia, Alicante, Almería, and Albacete. (4) The Diocese of Guadix (*Accitana*) founded by St. Torquatus in the first century, restored at the end of the fifteenth century, has 61 parishes, 5 rural deaneries, in the Provinces of Almería and Granada. (5) The Diocese of Jaén (*Gienensis*), of very ancient origin, was restored by Innocent IV in 1249. It numbers 119 parishes, 12 rural deaneries, in its own province. (6) The Diocese of Malaga (*Malacitana*) dates from the Apostolic period and was restored by the Catholic Sovereigns. It has 131 parishes, 17 rural deaneries, in the Provinces of Malaga, Cádiz, and Seville, and the African possessions of Spain (Melilla).

III. (1) The Archdiocese of Santiago, or of Compostela (*Compostellana*) is of Apostolic origin. It has 788 parishes, 36 rural deaneries, in the Provinces of Corunna and Pontevedra. (See COMPOSTELA.) (2) The Diocese of Lugo (*Lucensis*), founded in the third century and restored by Alfonso I in 739, numbers 647 parishes, 40 rural deaneries, in the Provinces of Lugo and Pontevedra. (3) The Diocese of Mondoñedo (*Mindonensis*), of which nothing is known earlier than the sixth century, its see having been established at Mondoñedo by Doña Urraca, has 277 parishes, 18 rural deaneries, in the Provinces of Lugo and Coruña. (4) The Diocese of Orense (*Auriensis*), of very ancient, some say Apostolic, origin, has 519 parishes, 30 rural deaneries, nearly all in its own province. (5) The Diocese of Oviedo (*Ovetensis*) appears to have had its origin in the ninth century, although some attribute to it a higher antiquity. It numbers 969 parishes, 78 rural deaneries, in its own province and a part of León. (6) The Diocese of Tuy (*Tudensis*) is of Apostolic origin. It has 276 parishes, 14 rural deaneries, in the Provinces of Orense and Pontevedra.

IV. (1) The Archdiocese of Saragossa (*Cæsaraugustana*), founded in the first century, restored in 1117, made metropolitan in 1138, has 370 parishes, 15 rural deaneries, in its own province and that of Teruel. (2) The Diocese of Barbastro (*Barbastrensis*), erected in the reign of Pedro I of Aragon (1094–1104), is to be reunited, in pursuance of the Concordat, with the Diocese of Huesca, from which it was separated in the time of Philip II. It numbers 154 parishes, 10 rural deaneries, in the Province of Huesca. (3) The Diocese of Huesca (*Oscensis*) dates from the first century and was restored in 1086. It has 167 parishes, 9 rural deaneries, in the Provinces of Huesca and Saragossa. (4) The Diocese of Jaca (*Jacensis*), erected by Don Ramiro of Aragon (eleventh century) and separated in 1575, has 70 parishes, 8 rural deaneries, in the Provinces of Huesca, Saragossa, and Navarre. (5) The Diocese of Pamplona (*Pampilonensis*) is of Apostolic origin, its first bishop having been St. Ferminus. It has 567 parishes, 21 rural deaneries, in the Province of Navarre. (6) The Diocese of Tarazona (*Turiasonensis*) dates from the Gothic period and was restored in 1115. It has 138 parishes, 9 rural deaneries, in the Provinces of Logroño, Navarre, and Saragossa. (7) The Diocese of Teruel (*Turulensis*), founded in 1577 at the petition of Philip II, has 96 parishes, 5 rural deaneries, in the province of the same name. Its jurisdiction now includes that of Albarracin. (8) The Diocese of Tudela (*Tutelensis*) has had but four bishops, the last consecrated in 1819. It was suppressed by the Concordat, and its jurisdiction given to the Bishop of Tarazona. It has a collegiate church and 26 parishes in the Province of Navarre.

V. (1) The Archdiocese of Seville (*Hispalensis*) dates from the third century, and was restored by St. Ferdinand in 1248. It has 270 parishes, 21 rural deaneries, in the Provinces of Seville, Huelva, Cadiz, and Malaga. (2) The Diocese of Badajoz (*Pacensis*) is supposed to be of Apostolic origin, although there is no documentary proof of its existence earlier than the seventh century. It has 136 parishes, 13 rural deaneries, in the province of the same name. (3) The Diocese of Cadiz-Ceuta (*Gaditana*) founded by Alfonso X in 1263, has 32 parishes, 6 rural deaneries, in its own province and Ceuta. (4) The Diocese of the Canaries (*Canariensis*) erected by Innocent VII in 1406, has 42 parishes, 5 rural deaneries, in the Canary Islands. (See CANARY ISLANDS.) (5) The Diocese of Cordova (*Cordubensis*), dating from the first century, has 124 parishes, 17 rural deaneries, in the Provinces of Cordova and Badajoz. (6) The Diocese of Tenerife (*Nivariensis*), erected in 1819 by Pius VIII, is to be incorporated, according to the Concordat, with that of the Canaries. Its see is at La Laguna (Palma) and it numbers 62 parishes, 10 rural deaneries.

VI. (1) The Archdiocese of Tarragona (*Tarraconensis*) was erected in the first century, and disputes with Toledo the right of primacy. It was restored by Ramón Berenguer, Count of Barcelona, in 1088, and numbers 150 parishes, 6 rural deaneries, in the Provinces of Tarragona and Lérida. (2) The Diocese of Barcelona (*Barcinonensis*) is believed to be of Apostolic origin, and was restored in the twelfth century by Ramón Berenguer. By a recent concession of the Holy See, its bishop wears the pallium, like a metropolitan. It has 231 parishes, 10 rural deaneries, in the Provinces of Barcelona, Tarragona, Lérida, and Gerona. (3) The Diocese of Gerona (*Gerundensis*) dates from the third century, and was restored in the eighth. It has 363 parishes in the Provinces of Gerona and Barcelona. (4) The Diocese of Lérida (*Ilerdensis*) is one of the most ancient in Spain. It numbers 249 parishes, 12 rural deaneries, in the Provinces of Lérida and Huesca. (5) The Diocese of Solsona (*Excelsonensis*) was erected in 1593, suppressed by the Concordat, and again constituted as an Apostolic administration with a titular bishop. It has 152 parishes, 11 rural deaneries, in the Provinces of Barcelona, Lérida, and Gerona. (6) The Diocese of Tortosa (*Dertusensis*), believed to be of Apostolic origin, restored in 1141, has 159 parishes, 12 rural deaneries, in the Provinces of Tarragona, Teruel, and Castellón. The Concordat provides for the transfer of its capital to Castellón de la Plana. (7) The Diocese of Urgel (*Urgellensis*) is very ancient, and its bishop is the sovereign of the Valleys of Andorra. It has 395 parishes, 19 rural deaneries, in the

ALMINAR, OR TOWER OF THE CATHEDRAL, CORDOVA

Provinces of Lérida and Gerona and in the Republic of Andorra. (8) The Diocese of Vich (*Vicensis*), in the ancient Ausona, was erected in 713, and restored by Ludovico Pio, and, later, by Vifredo the Hairy, Count of Barcelona. It has 248 parishes, 11 rural deaneries, in the Provinces of Barcelona, Gerona, and Tarragona.

VII. (1) The Archdiocese of Toledo (*Toletana*), erected in the first century, had for its first bishop St. Eugenius. In the fifth century the see was made metropolitan, and after the Reconquest it became the principal see of the Spains. The archdiocese contains 442 parishes divided into 20 rural deaneries, and covers the Province of Toledo and part of those of Jaén, Guadalajara, and Cáceres. (2) The Diocese of Coria (*Cauriensis*) existed as early as the year 589 and was restored in 1142 by Alfonso VIII. It comprises 124 parishes, divided into 11 rural deaneries, in the Provinces of Cáceres, Salamanca, and Badajoz. (3) The Diocese of Cuenca (*Conquensis*) was erected in 1179 by Pope Lucius III. It has 326 parishes, in 12 rural deaneries, in the Provinces of Cuenca and Guadalajara. (4) The Diocese of Madrid-Alcalá (*Matritensis-Complutensis*) was erected by the Bull of 7 March, 1885, in pursuance of the Concordat of 1851. It has 232 parishes, divided into 18 rural deaneries, in the Province of Madrid. (5) The Diocese of Plasencia (*Placentina*), erected in 1190 by Alfonso VIII, has 260 parishes, divided into 14 rural deaneries, in the Province of Cáceres, Salamanca, Badajoz, and Avila. (6) The Diocese of Sigüenza (*Saguntina*) existed in the time of the Goths, and was restored by Alfonso VIII. It has 350 parishes, 18 rural deaneries, in the Provinces of Guadalajara, Saragossa, and Soria.

VIII. (1) The Archdiocese of Valencia (*Valentina*) erected in the third century, and restored by Jaime I, the Conqueror, in 1238, has 313 parishes, 25 rural deaneries, in the Provinces of Alicante, Valencia, and Castellón. (2) The Diocese of Iviza (*Ebusensis*) is to be merged in that of Majorca, pursuant to the Concordat. It has 37 parishes. (3) The Diocese of Majorca (*Majoricensis*) was erected by Jaime, the Conqueror, in 1229. The see is at Palma, and its incorporation with the Diocese of Iviza is provided for by the Concordat. It has 59 parishes, 7 rural deaneries, in the Balearic Isles. (4) The Diocese of Minorca (*Minoricensis*), erected in 1795, has its see at Ciudadela and numbers 14 parishes. (5) The Diocese of Orihuela (*Oriolensis*) was erected in 1564. Its see should, by the terms of the Concordat, be transferred to Alicante. It has 60 parishes, 11 rural deaneries, in the Provinces of Alicante, Valencia, and Almeria. (6) The Diocese of Segorbe (*Segobricensis*) founded in the time of the Goths, restored in 1171, and again in 1245, has 65 parishes, 7 rural deaneries, in the Provinces of Castellón, Valencia, and Teruel.

IX. (1) The Archdiocese of Valladolid (*Vallisoletana*) was founded in 1595 and became metropolitan in 1859. It has 93 parishes, 9 rural deaneries, in the province of the same name. (2) The Diocese of Astorga (*Asturicensis*) is of Apostolic origin, and was restored by Alfonso I in 747. It has 582 parishes and 18 rural deaneries in the Provinces of León, Zamora, and Orense. (3) The Diocese of Avila (*Abulensis*) was erected by St. Secundus in Apostolic times, and restored after the Arab invasion, by Alfonso VI. It has 339 parishes, divided into 20 rural deaneries, in the Provinces of Avila, Toledo, and Valladolid. (4) The Diocese of Ciudad Rodrigo (*Civitatensis*), founded by Alexander III, in 1175, is one of those suppressed under the Concordat, its territory having been added to that of Salamanca since 1884 under an Apostolic administrator with episcopal character. It has 150 parishes, 11 rural deaneries, in the Province of Salamanca. (5) The Diocese of Salamanca (*Salmanticensis*) dates from the first century, and was restored by Alfonso I, the Great, in 901. It numbers 286 parishes, 19 rural deaneries, in the province of the same name. (6) The Diocese of Segovia (*Segoviensis*) was erected in the time of the Goths and restored by Alfonso VI. It has 276 parishes, 15 rural deaneries, in the Provinces of Segovia, Avila, and Valladolid. (7) The Diocese of Zamora (*Zamorensis*) was founded in the year 905. It has 265 parishes, 13 rural deaneries, in the Provinces of Zamora and Valladolid.

Besides these nine provinces, there is the Diocese-Priorate of the four military orders, or of Ciudad-Real (*Cluniensis*), which was erected as *vere nullius* by the Bull "Ad Apostolicum", put into execution by the Decree of August, 1876. It has 115 parishes, in 11 rural deaneries.

The privileged ecclesiastical jurisdictions are the Apostolic Nunciature and the Supreme Tribunal of the Rota, both at Madrid, and the Chapel Royal (*Clero de la Real Capilla y Patrimonio*), with a grand almoner (*capellan mayor*) to His Majesty, honorary chaplains, etc. The military chaplains are under the jurisdiction of a Vicar-General of the Army and Navy. There are four deputy vicars and a proportionate number of chaplains-general, and first-class and second-class chaplains.

Notwithstanding the measures of disamortization which have deprived them of their property, and the general expulsion effected a second time by the Revolution of 1868, the religious orders of both sexes prosper and possess many establishments in Spain. Owing, however, to their anomalous legal position, it is extremely difficult to obtain statistics of them, although an approximation may be made. The Liberals assert that, since the Concordat of 1851, only three religious orders of men have any right to be admitted to the country, while the Conservatives and Catholics in general understand that the Concordat places these three orders in a privileged position, but admits all the other orders conformably with the provisions of the canon law to which its stipulations are subject. In 1903 the religious orders in Spain numbered 597 communities of men and 2463 communities of women. The number of male religious was 10,630; of female 40,030. These communities were divided, according to the chief object of their institutions, as follows:—

	Communities: Of Men.	Of Women.
The Contemplative life	75	717
Charitable works	39	1029
Teaching	294	717
The priesthood	97	....
Missions	92	....
Total	597	2463

Of late years there has been a notable increase in these figures, but statistics are not obtainable. The most numerous orders are the Jesuits, Franciscans, Capuchins, Augustinians, Piarists, Missionaries of the Heart of Mary, Brothers of the Christian Schools, Marist Brothers, and Lazarists.

C. *Education*.—Three educational grades are recognized: the higher, intermediate, and primary. Higher education is divided into academical (*facultativa*) and technical (*special*): the former of these divisions is taught in the universities, with their faculties of law, philosophy and letters, sciences, medicine, and pharmacy. Technical education is given in the special schools of engineering, architecture, veterinary surgery, and manual-training, and in the military schools. There are three schools of industrial engineering (mechanics, chemistry, and electricity), at Madrid, Barcelona, and Bilbao. At Madrid are also a school of civil engineering (*Escuela de Ingenieros de Caminos, Canales y Puertos*), a school of mines, and a school of agriculture, while at the Escorial is a school of forestry (*Escuela de Ingenieros y de Montes*). There are schools of architecture at Madrid and at Barcelona; veterinary schools at Madrid, Saragossa, Leon, Cordova, and Santiago (Corunna). There are fourteen Government schools of commerce, besides many independent ones under Brothers of the Christian Schools, Marists, Jesuits, etc. Manual-training schools (*Escuelas de artes é industrias*, or *de artes y oficios*) are of recent origin in Spain; the national government maintains thirteen of them and gives subventions to many others which are supported by the municipalities or provincial governments. There are also schools of the fine arts, conservatories of music, etc. The military schools are: at Guadalajara, for the Engineers; at Segovia, for the Artillery; at Valladolid, for the Cavalry; at Toledo, for the Infantry; at Avila, for the Army Service Corps (*Administración Militar*); at Madrid, for the Army Medical Corps; and again at Madrid, for the Staff (*Estado Mayor*). Other institutions for military education are the College of the Guardias Civiles, at Valdemoro, that of the Carabineros, at the Escorial, etc. The schools of naval engineering and of marine artillery are at S. Fernando (Cadiz). There are schools and nautical institutes for the merchant marine, the practical examinations being under the supervision of the naval authorities. Preparation for teaching in the upper branches of literature is given in the normal schools established in the provincial capitals; the degrees are *Maestro Elemental*, *Maestro Superior*, and *Maestro Normal*. A higher school of pedagogy has recently been opened at Madrid.

Ecclesiastical education, since the suppression of the theological faculties in the universities, has been given in the conciliar seminaries established in all the dioceses, as prescribed by the Council of Trent. In some dioceses there are also lesser seminaries, which prepare students for the greater. The universities now in existence are: Madrid (formerly Alcalá), Salamanca, Barcelona, Granada, Seville, Valladolid, Valencia, Saragossa, Santiago, and Oviedo. In the last-named the only faculty in operation is that of law. There are intermediate schools in all the provincial capitals, as well as others in certain other localities—Baeza, Cabra, Figueras, Gijón, Jerez, Mahon, and Reus. The number of Government primary schools is very inadequate; the deficiency, however, is compensated by the number of private and religious institutions. By the School Census of 1903, there were in Spain altogether 31,838 schools (20,324 for boys; 10,970 for girls; 544 for infants). The following statistics of pupils are taken from the Census of 1900:

	Boys.	*Girls.*
Pupils of the age of 5 years	222,619	214,573
Pupils of the age of 6 years	214,174	215,737
Pupils of the age of 7 years	215,682	211,997
Pupils of the age of 8 years	217,572	211,840
Pupils of the age of 9 years	195,675	193,188
Pupils of the age of 10 years	213,911	211,939
Pupils of the age of 11 to 15 years	934,027	923,993
Total	2,213,660	2,183,267

making a total of 4,396,927 of both sexes. As it is estimated that two-thirds of the population of school age attend private or religious schools, it follows that the dearth of educational facilities in Spain is not so great as is commonly supposed. The number of absolutely illiterate has been much exaggerated, owing to the lack of proper statistics. That that number is as large as it really is may be explained by the ineffective enforcement of the legal school-attendance.

Although the Constitution of 1876, which is still in force, grants freedom of teaching, the right has been very much curtailed by legal enactments. There are but two independent universities, that of Deusto (Bilbao), directed by the Jesuits, and that of the Escorial, under the Augustinians. There are also, at Madrid, two independent institutions of university character, the Academia Universitaria Católica, under the presidency of the Bishop of Madrid-Alcalá, and the Institución Libre de Enseñanza (Free Institution of Education), directed by the Krausists. For intermediate, or gymnasium, education the religious orders have many colleges, some of which also take charge of interne pupils. The Jesuits, of whom there are three provinces in Spain, have colleges as follows: Province of Aragon.—With boarders at Sarriá (Barcelona), Saragossa, Valencia, and Orihuela (former Dominican university); half-boarding (*medio-pensionado*) school at Barcelona. Province of Castile.—For

FAÇADE OF THE CATHEDRAL, GERONA

boarders at Gijon (Asturias), La Guardia (Pontevedra), Orduña (Vizcaya), Tudela (Navarre), and Valladolid; also day schools at Durango (Biscay), Carrión (Palencia), and Oña (Burgos). Province of Toledo.—Boarding schools at Charmarlín de la Rosa (Madrid), Seville, Malaga, Puerto de Sta. María (Cadiz), and Villafranca de los Barros (Badajoz); also a Catholic school of arts and crafts (*escuela técnica*), and a half-boarding school at Madrid. The Jesuits also conduct the following ecclesiastical colleges: For the formation of religious, houses of higher studies at Oña (Burgos), Tortosa (Tarragona), Granada, and S. Jeronimo; literary colleges at Loyola (Guipuzcoa), Veruela (Saragossa), Carrión (Palencia), Gandía (Valencia), and Burgos. The Province of Castile has a pontifical seminary at Comillas (Santander) and directs the episcopal seminary of Salamanca. It also has an Apostolic school at Xavier (Navarre).

The second religious institute in the work of teaching is that of the Piarists, or Fathers of the Pious Schools, which has been largely represented in Spain since the seventeenth century. As the Revolution has generally shown some respect for the Piarists, they have kept a larger number of their colleges than the Jesuits, who have been repeatedly expelled, and so obliged to establish their colleges over again.

There are Piarist colleges at Madrid, Barcelona, Valencia, Saragossa, etc., besides others at less important centres of population. In recent times some of the older orders which are not primarily teaching orders, such as the Augustinians, Dominicans, Franciscans, and Lazarists, have established boarding schools. In technical, commercial, and primary teaching, the Brothers of the Christian Schools of St. John Baptist de La Salle and Père Champagnat's Marist Brothers have attained a position of great importance; their establishments in Spain are numerous and have become more so since their expulsion from France. The Christian Brothers now have 53 colleges in Spain; the Marists, 67. The education of girls is to a great extent under the care of a number of congregations of religious women, who have boarding and half-boarding schools as well as day schools. The principal are: The Religious de la Enseñanza (Society of Our Lady) of Bl. Lestonac, who have 12 cloistered *pensions*. The Visitandines of St. Jeanne Françoise Frémoit de Chantal, established in Spain since 1758. The Religious of the Sacred Heart of Bl. Barat, with 15 houses, established in Spain since 1846. The Religious of Jesus and Mary, founded by M. Thévenet, entered Spain in 1850. The Ursulines have a college at Molina de Aragón (New Castile), and there are some colleges of the English Ladies and of Our Lady of Loreto. There are, in addition to these, numerous small schools for girls and many religious congregations for women—in particular, Carmelite Tertiaries, Franciscan Tertiaries, Augustinians, and Sisters of Charity.

III. History.—The old historians say that Spain was populated by the children of Tubal and of Tarsis, son and grandson of Japhet. These were the Iberians, who were divided into Iberians proper and Tartesians; the latter, in the South; the former, in the North. Some have held that the Iberians were Basques, and consequently were of the Uralo-Altaic, or Mongoloid, race, as the similarity of the Basque with the Finnish languages would seem to indicate. However this may be, the Iberians and Tartesians appear to have formed the aboriginal population, and the Celts, who occupied a great part of France, Great Britain, and Ireland, would seem to have come in upon them by way of the Bay of Biscay. The collision of the two races produced the population which later settlers and conquerors found in Spain: Celts in the North and West, Iberians in the East and South, and in the centre (Aragon and part of Castile) Celtiberians, whose very name indicates a fusion of the two races—no doubt, after a great deal of conflict.

It is very remarkable that the differences of language in the Iberian Peninsula still, partially, correspond to this first distribution of the inhabiting races. In the regions of the pure Iberians, Catalan is spoken, with its dialects, the Valencian and Balearic; in the regions conquered by the Celts, the languages are Gallego, Portuguese, and the *bable* of Asturias; in the Celtiberian and Tartesian portions, Castilian. This fact seems to support the theory of Padre Lorenzo Hervas y Panduro, that races, even when they change their grammar, never entirely change their own way of pronouncing the language which they use. Upon these first strata of population, which may be considered aboriginal, were superimposed the colonists and conquerors. The colonists were Greeks and Phœnicians; the conquerors, Carthaginians, Romans, Goths, and Arabs. Taking this as a guide, Spanish history may be divided into periods as follows: A. Colonies in Celtiberian Spain; B. Carthaginian Spain (third century B. C.); C. Roman Spain (third century B. C., to fifth century of our era); D. Visigothic Monarchy (fifth to eighth century); E. Arab Spain and Kingdoms of the Reconquest (eighth to fifteenth century); F. The Unification of Spain (fifteenth century to the present time).

A. *Colonies.*—The Phœnicians, who colonized all the Mediterranean coasts, established a great many colonies, or factories, in the South of Spain—Carteya, Calpe, Malaga, Sexi, and chief of all, Gades (Cádiz), the centre of their power in Spain and their cult of Hercules, which is symbolized on the Gaditanian coins. Soon after the Phœnicians, the Greeks began establishing their colonies, the chief colonizers being the Rhodians at Rosas, south of Cape Creus (910 B.C.), the Phocians, at Emporium (Ampurias, the present name, or Ampurdan, being derived from *Emporitanum*) and at Artemisium (Denia, from *Diana*, another name for Artemis), and the Zacynthians, who founded Saguntum and populated Iviza, giving it the name of Ophiusa.

B. *Carthaginian Spain.*—The Carthaginians settled in the Balearic Isles in the seventh century B. C. In the sixth century, having aided the Phœnicians of Cadiz against the Tartesians, they took possession of that city and began trading in Bætica. After the First Punic War they sought to indemnify themselves for their losses in Sicily by conquering Spain. The conquest was begun by Hamilcar Barca, and extended as far as the Ebro; then, too, began that struggle of the Spaniards for independence which was to last until the nineteenth century of the Christian Era. Istolacius and Indortes, the former a Celtic chieftain, the latter chief of certain Celtiberian tribes of the Ebro, raised an army, according to Diodorus Siculus, of 50,000 men; but they were defeated and condemned to death. However, Orison, another Iberian chief, achieved the rout and death of Hamilcar at Elice, or Elche (230). Hasdrubal, the founder of Cartagena, (New Carthage), was assassinated by a slave, and Hannibal, to complete the conquest of Spain, laid siege to Saguntum, which city then immortalized itself by its heroic act of self-destruction. The issue of the Second Punic War caused the Carthaginians to lose Spain, and the Romans succeeded to their mastery of the country.

C. *Roman Spain.*—But the Spaniards showed no more docility to the Romans than to the Carthaginians. Indibil and Mandonius commenced that course of resistance which ended only when Spain had been romanized—vanquished not so much by the arms as by the superior civilization of Rome, a culture which Spain assimilated to such a degree as to produce rhetoricians like Quintilian, poets like Lucan, Martial, and Silius Italicus, philosophers like Seneca, and emperors like Trajan, Hadrian, and Theodosius. Noteworthy among the wars of the Spaniards against Roman domination are those of Viriathus (150–140 B. C.), a Lusitanian chieftain; the struggle of Numantia (133), which imitated the example set by Saguntum; that of Sertorius, a partisan of Marius, who was proscribed by Sulla, fled to Spain, and there put himself at the head of the Spaniards. Sertorius did more than anyone else to romanize the country; he gave it Roman institutions, and founded at Huesca a high school with Greek and Latin teachers. After this, although the Spaniards took the side of Pompey against Cæsar, resistance to the Roman power as such was confined to the Cantabri and the Asturias, who were conquered, though not subdued, in the time of Augustus. The Romans at first divided their Spanish territories into Hither and Further Spain (*Hispania Citerior, Ulterior*), taking the Ebro as dividing line, but Augustus divided the country into *Tarraconensis, Lusitania*, and *Bætica*. Spain is covered with Roman remains, particularly aqueducts and bridges, but the most penetrating Roman influence was linguistic, giving to the inhabitants a neo-Latin tongue, which has survived in great perfection in Castile and, with greater modifications, owing to the aspirated utterance, in the East.

Under the Roman domination Spain received Christianity. There is a venerable tradition that the

EAST END OF THE CATHEDRAL, SEGOVIA

Apostles Paul and James came to the country, as well as the Seven Apostolic Men (Torquatus, Ctesiphon, Secundus, Indalecius, Cæcilius, Hesychius, and Euphrasius) to whom the foundation of various churches is attributed. Connected with the coming of St. James is the very ancient tradition of Our Lady of the Pillar (*la Virgen del Pilar*) of Saragossa. Prudentius says that there were martyrs in Spain in every one of the persecutions. Of uncertain date are the martyrdoms of Sts. Facundus and Primitius in Galicia; of St. Firminus and Sts. Marcellus and Nonia, with their twelve children, in Leon; of Sts. Acisclus and Victoria at Cordova. Sts. Hemeterius and Celedonius suffered in the Decian persecution, as did Sts. Justa and Rufina, St. Laurence, St. Fructuosus, St. Augurius, and St. Eulogius. The most famous of Spanish martyrs, however, are those who suffered in the persecution of Diocletian, when Dacian was prefect; among them were Sts. Cucufatis, Eulalia, and Severus, Bishop of Barcelona, Sts. Felix, Poncius, and Victor, Narcissus, Bishop of Gerona, Engratia, Valerius, Bishop of Saragossa, and his deacon, Vincentius, Justus and Pastor of Alcalá, Leocadia of Toledo, Eulalia of Mérida, Cyricus and Paula of Malaga, Vincentius, Sabina, and Cristeta of Talavera. During this period, too, many councils were held in Spain, the most important being those of Elvira (or Illiberis) and of Saragossa, and the First Council of Toledo. At that of Elvira (300) the Acts, which are still extant, were signed by nineteen bishops, and, among other things, the celibacy of the clergy was insisted upon. At the Council of Saragossa (380) Priscillianism was condemned. The Priscillianists abjured their heresy at the Council of Toledo (400), where, also, the symbol was pronounced with the *Filioque*. Among illustrious Spaniards of the period may be mentioned Pope St. Damasus, the great Hosius, St. Pacianus, Bishop of Barcelona, and his son, Flavius Dexter, Juvencus, and Prudentius.

D. *Visigothic Spain.*—When the Germanic peoples invaded the provinces of the Roman Empire, the hordes, urged forward by the pressure of the Huns in their rear, hurled themselves for the first time upon the Pyrenean Peninsula—the Alani, a people of Scythian, or Tatar, race; the Vandals and Suevians, Germanic races. The Alani were, for the most part, quickly brought into subjection. The Vandals, after establishing themselves in Bætica, to which they gave the name of Vandalusia (Andalusia), passed on into Africa, while the Visigoths hemmed in the Suevi in Galicia until the latter were completely brought under control. These Visigoths, or Western Goths, after sacking Rome under the leadership of Alaric (410), turned towards the Iberian Peninsula, with Ataulf for their leader, and occupied the north-eastern portion, which thereafter received the name of Gotha-landia (Catalaunia, later Catalonia). Valia extended his rule over most of the Peninsula, keeping the Suevians shut up in Galicia. Theodoret took part, with the Romans and Franks, in the battle of Châlons, where Attila was routed. Euric (466), who put an end to the last remnants of Roman power in the Peninsula, may be considered the first monarch of Spain, though the Suevians still maintained their independence in Galicia. Euric was also the first king to give written laws to the Visigoths.

In the following reigns the Catholic kings of France assumed the rôle of protectors of the Hispano-Roman Catholics against the Arianism of the Visigoths, and in the wars which ensued Alaric II and Amalric lost their lives. Atanagild, having risen against King Agilas, called in the Byzantine Greeks and, in payment for the succour they gave him, ceded to them the maritime places of the South-East (554). Leovigild restored the political unity of the Peninsula, subduing the Suevians, but the religious divisions of the country, reaching even the royal family, brought on a civil war. St. Hermengild, the king's son, putting himself at the head of the Catholics, was defeated and taken prisoner, and suffered martyrdom for rejecting communion with the Arians. Recared, son of Leovigild and brother of St. Hermengild, added religious unity to

XIV.—12

the political unity achieved by his father, accepting the Catholic Faith in the Third Council of Toledo (589). The religious unity established by this council was the basis of that fusion of Goths with Hispano-Romans which produced the Spanish Nation. Sisebut and Suintila completed the expulsion of the Byzantines from Spain. Chindasvint and Recesvint laboured for legislative unity, and legalized marriages, hitherto prohibited, between Goths and Latins. After Wamba, famous for his opposition to his own election, an unmistakable decline of the Gothic monarchy set in. Manners were relaxed, immorality increased, and Witiza has stood in Spanish history for the type of that decay which, in the next reign, that of Roderic (710–14), ended in the ruin of the kingdom.

During this period many very important councils were held in Spain. Among the most memorable were: that of Tarragona (516), at which ten bishops

TRIUMPHAL ARCH OF FERNAN GONZALEZ, BURGOS, 1539

assisted, the First Council of Barcelona (540), and those of Lérida and Valencia (546). But most important of all, and of a special character, were the Councils of Toledo and of Braga (Bracara). Eminent among the saints of the same period are the two holy brothers Leander, who presided at the Third Council of Toledo, and Isidore, who presided at the Fourth, and who wrote a celebrated encyclopedia (The Etymologies) and contributed to the upbuilding of Mozarabic literature, St. Saturius, the solitary, St. Emilian (Millán), the father of monks, St. Victorian, abbot of the monastery of Asana, St. Gaudiosus, Bishop of Tarazona, St. Toribius, St. Martin of Dumio, St. Ildefonsus, St. Braulius, St. Eugenius, and St. Tajón, Bishop of Saragossa. To this period, also, belong the poets Orentius and Dracontius, the chroniclers Idacius and John of Biclara, and the historian Paulus Orosius.

E. *Arab Spain.*—(1) The Moslem Domination.—While the Gothic kingdom was decaying through effeminacy and the discord produced by the elective system of monarchy, the fanatical sectaries of the Koran were advancing through North Africa. Legend has it that Count Julian, the governor of Ceuta, in revenge for the violation of his daughter, Florinda (also called La Cara), by King Roderic, invited the Moslems and opened to them the gates of the Peninsula. The first expedition of the Arabs was led by Tarif, who gave his name to Tarifa; the second, by Tarik, who gave his name to Gibraltar (Gebal-Tarik, "Mountain of Tarik"). Roderic went forth to meet the invaders, and, in July, 711, the terrific battle was fought which is generally called the battle of Guadalete, but which really took place near the River Barbate. This river flows into the Lagoon of Janda and was known to the Arabs as Wadi Becca. The battle appears to have been lost through the treachery of partisans of Witiza, the last king. Roderic disappeared; it is not known whether he perished in the fight. The Arabs spread rapidly through Andalusia, soon reaching Toledo, the Gothic capital, while the Jews, who were numerous in the cities, facilitated their entrance. Musa, governor of Barbary, came to share the triumphs of Tarik. In 714 he captured Saragossa and followed up his conquests as far as Lugo and Gijon, while Tarik reached Leon and Astorga. Some of the Spaniards settled down to live under Arab rule, calling themselves Mozarabs; the rest fled to the mountains of the North, where they formed the four chief rallying-points for the Reconquest: Asturias, Navarre, Aragon, and Catalonia.

Arab Spain was at first governed by emirs whose authority was derived from the Omayyad Caliphs of Damascus. The most noted of these emirs were Abdelaziz, son of Musa, who recognized the independence of the little state, defended by Todmir, with its capital at Orihuela, and Abderraman el Gafequi, who, having penetrated into Aquitaine, was vanquished by Charles Martel at Poitiers (732). Before long, divisions arose among the Spanish Mussulmans, out of the antagonisms of Arabs and Berbers, Quelvites and Mahadites. At length Abderraman I, a scion of the Omayyad stock, who had escaped the slaughter of his family by the Abassids, when the latter founded the Caliphate of Bagdad, himself became the founder of the independent Emirate of Cordova. Here the culture of the Spanish Arabs reached its greatest splendour, influenced, in great measure, by the Mozarabs, who were more advanced in the sciences and arts. In 786 Abderraman began the famous mosque of Cordova (now the cathedral), one of the largest and most magnificent edifices of the Arab style. The first caliphs treated the Mozarabic Christians with comparative leniency; Abderraman II, however, initiated a policy of persecution, and his son Mohammed I continued it. In the city of Cordova there were seven Catholic churches and a monastery connected with the Church of S. Ginés, while in the neighbourhood were the monasteries of S. Cristóbal, S. Félix, S. Martín, Stos. Justo y Pastor, S. Salvador, S. Zoilo, Cuteclara, and Los Tábanos. In 839 a council of three archbishops and five bishops was held at Cordova. The epoch of the Martyrs here began with the decollation of the priest Perfecto, in 850. In the following year the monk Isaac spontaneously offered himself for martyrdom, and six monks and several laymen, among them the celebrated Paulo Cordobés, died for the Faith. In 852 Gumersindo and Servideo, with eight other monks and seculars, were martyred. The readiness with which martyrs offered themselves to the tribunals incensed the Caliph Abderraman II, and he caused the Council of Cordova of 852 to assemble under the presidency of Recafredo, Archbishop of Seville. In this council it was proposed to deny the credit of martyrdom to those who provoked persecution. But persecution recommenced in 853, under Mohammed I, and the monks Fandila and Felix, the virgin Digna, Benildis, Columba, and Pomposa shed their blood for the Faith, as did the presbyters Abundio and Elias, the monks Pedro, Paulo, Isidoro, and Argimiro, the youth Amador, Luis of Cordova, Witesindo, Rodrigo, Solomon, and the virgin Aurea in the following year. St. Eulogius, who had encouraged the martyrs, himself suffered on 11 March, 859, and the virgin Leocridia followed him. Distinguished as writers among the Mozarabs were St. Eulogius and Alvar Cordobés, and their master, the Abbot Speraindeo; also the Abbot Samson, who combated the anthropomorphism of the perverse Bishop Hostegesis and others. But the Mozarabs gradually died out in their Mohammedan environment, so that St. Ferdinand found hardly any traces of them in the cities he conquered.

After stifling an insurrection of the national party, the Arab aristocracy, and the Berbers, and reducing Toledo to obedience, Abderraman III established an absolute monarchy, the Caliphate of Cordova (929). His son, Al Haken II, distinguished himself by fostering the arts of peace; he collected a vast number of books, and founded schools and academies. In the reign of Hixem II, both the home government and the armies were directed by his *haschib* Almanzor (the Victorious), who, by dint of almost annual incursions into the Christian kingdoms, well-nigh reduced them to the condition of the first days of the Reconquest, and indeed threatened them with total destruction. He took and burned Barcelona, mastered Leon, Zamora, and Pamplona, and razed Santiago de Compostela (997). At last the Christians, united, crushed him at Calatañazor (1002), and he went to Medina Celi to die. After its fleeting day of glory, the Caliphate fell into a rapid decay, until it was broken up into more than twenty states known as the Kingdoms of Taifas. Thus was the progress of the Reconquest favoured by circumstances; it would have been completed in the thirteenth century, had not divisions and discords among the Christians impeded it. The Spanish Mussulmans then sought aid from the Moors of Africa. This they received chiefly on three occasions; from the Almoravids, after the taking of Toledo by Alfonso VI (1085); from the Almohads, in the time of Alfonso VIII, who was defeated by them at Alarcos and defeated them at Las Navas de Tolosa (1212); from the Beni Merines, in the reign of Alfonso XI, who vanquished them in the battle of El Salado. From that time the Spanish Mussulmans were confined to the Kingdom of Granada, which had been founded by Mohammed Alhamar in 1238, and lasted until 1492, when Boabdil was conquered by Ferdinand and Isabella.

(2) The Reconquest.—All the elements of the Spanish People already existed in the kingdom of the Catholic Goths: the Latinized Celtiberian race, or Hispano-Romans, the Gothic element, and the Catholic Faith. These elements, however, were as yet uncombined, and still lacked that thorough fusion which was to make one people out of them, with a character and historical destiny of its own. The agency employed by Divine Providence to effect this fusion was the terrible force of the Mussulman invasion. Under its immense pressure the Goths and Hispano-Romans, in the mountains of the North, became one people with one religion and one national aspiration, to reconquer their Spanish fatherland and make the Cross triumph over the Crescent. Though already morally a unit, the Spanish people were still eight centuries away from political unity, and the Reconquest was begun from four distinct centres. Chief among these four centres was Asturias. The fugitive Goths found a retreat in those mountains where the Romans had never been able to effectively establish their authority; only a few years after the rout of Guadalete, they gained a victory over Alkama, the lieutenant of El Horr, in the portentous battle of Covadonga, where popular faith saw Divine aid fighting for the Christians. Here was erected a sanctuary of the Blessed Virgin which afterwards became a collegiate church and still exists. Don Pelayo, or Pelagius, the Gothic chieftain who was victor at Covadonga, was acclaimed king, and took up his residence at Cangas. His son Favila was killed while hunting, torn to pieces by a bear, and was succeeded by Alfonso I, son-in-law of Don Pelayo, who set about pushing the Reconquest as far as Galicia and Tierra de Campos (the "Gothic Fields" or *Campos Góticos*). Fruela I (727–

General View of the Bridge and City of Cordova

728) founded Oviedo. He was assassinated, and was succeeded by several insignificant kings (Aurelio, Silio, Mauregato, and Bermudo I, the Deacon) and at last by Alfonso I, the Chaste, who set up his Court at Oviedo, recommenced the great expeditions against the Arabs, and seems to have invited Charlemagne to come to Asturias, thus occasioning the Frankish monarch's expedition which ended in the disaster of Roncesvalles.

In this region occurred the discovery of the body of St. James (Santiago) at Compostela. Ramiro I repelled the Northmen who tried to effect a landing in Asturias. To him legend attributes the victory of Clavijo. According to this legend, Mauregato had promised the Moors a tribute of one hundred maidens, which Ramiro refused to pay. In the battle that ensued, the Apostle St. James, Patron of the Spaniards, was seen fighting, mounted on a white charger—"Es visus in Prælio, equoque et ense acerrimus, mauros furentes sternere" as the Spanish Breviary has it. This king is said to have made the "Vow of Santiago", by which he bound himself to pay a certain tribute to the Church of Compostela. Modern critics pronounce the document apocryphal, but the national tradition loses none of its force thereby. Ordoño I emulated the exploits of Ramiro, driving back the Northmen and defeating the Moors at Albelda; he also rebuilt Leon, Tuy, Astorga, and other cities. Alfonso III, the Great, continued the forays as far as the Sierra Morena, and founded Burgos, the future capital of Castile. His sons rebelled against him, and he abdicated the Crown, dividing his dominions among them. With him ended the Kingdom of Asturias, the territory of which soon became subject to Leon.

Another rallying-point of the Reconquest was Aragon; the other two, Navarre and Catalonia, were placed by the circumstances of their origin in peculiar relations with France. The Basques on either side of the Western Pyrenees, dissatisfied with Frankish rule, rebelled on several occasions. At Roncesvalles they annihilated the armies of Charlemagne, and in 824 another victory secured the independence of the Basques of Pamplona. The names and dates of their kings, or chieftains, are very uncertain until we come to Sancho II, Abarca. He abdicated in favour of his son Garcia III, the Trembler, in whose time the Leonese and Navarrese together were routed at Valdejunquera. Sancho III, the Great, was one of the monarchs who most influenced Spanish history; he was eventually King of Navarre, Castile, Aragon, and Sobrarbe. At his death (1035) he divided his kingdoms, giving Navarre to his eldest son Garcia, Castile, with the title of King, to Fernando, Aragon to Ramiro, and Sobrarbe to Gonzalo. This fashion of regarding the various states as patrimonial possessions—an idea borrowed from French feudalism, and previously unknown in the Spanish kingdoms—was introduced at this time; it resulted in the numerous divisions which led to so many wars and which long formed an obstacle to the unity of the Reconquest in the West. (On the origin of the Countship of Barcelona, the fourth centre of the Reconquest, see CATALONIA).

As the Reconquest advanced, the churches destroyed by the Mohammedan invasion were restored. The Reconquest went forward in the name of the Holy Faith. Alfonso I of Asturias, surnamed the Catholic, restored a great many churches; Alfonso II, the Chaste, founded the Diocese of Oviedo and built its first cathedral and the royal burial-place. The Dioceses of Pamplona and Sasave corresponded to the nascent Kingdoms of Navarre and Aragon, while in Catalonia the Diocese of Urgel seems never to have ceased to exist, and that of Gerona was soon restored. Unhappily distinguished among the bishops of Urgel is Felix, who, with Elipando of Toledo, embraced the Adoptionist heresy, asserting that Christ is the adoptive son of God. This heresy was combated by Theodulus, Bishop of Seville, by Etherius of Osma, and by St. Beatus of Liebana, and was condemned by the Council of Ratisbon. In the same period lived *el Pacense*, Isidore, Bishop of Beja, whose Chronicle, a continuation of St. Isidore's, begins at the year 610 and ends with 754.

As the year 1000 approached, it seemed that the Kingdom of Christ in Spain was about to be annihilated by the terrible and victorious expeditions of Almanzor. A second restoration began gloriously with Ferdinand (Fernando) I, who assembled the Council of Coyanza (Valencia de Don Juan), obtained from the King of Seville the relics of St. Isidore, which were translated to Leon, and fostered the Churches of Coimbra, Leon, Santiago, and Oviedo, and the monasteries of Oña, Arlanza, and Sahagún. Fernando González, Count of Castile, restored the monastery of Silos, which has now been reoccupied by French Benedictines. Sancho the Elder restored and reformed many monasteries, and brought the Cluniac monks into Spain. Alfonso VI transferred to Burgos the ancient See of Valpuesta. During the same period the Dioceses of Osma, Sigüenza (1102), Segovia (1120), Salamanca, and Zamora were restored. Ferdinand II of Leon erected the Diocese of Ciudad Rodrigo, restoring the old Diocese of Caliabria (1171), Alfonso VII re-established that of Coria, and Alfonso VIII of Castile founded that of Plasencia. St. Olegario prepared the way for the restoration of the metropolitan See of Tarragona, which had his successor, Gregorio, for its first archbishop (1137). But eminent above all the other churches of Spain was that of Santiago de Compostela, to which was united the ancient Bishopric of Iria. The famous Don Diego Gelmirez, having been elected bishop (1100), raised the number of canons from twenty-four to seventy-two, obtained from Rome the ratification of the Vow of Santiago, as well as the privilege of wearing mitres for the canons, and at last made Compostela the archiepiscopal see of the Province of Mérida, or Emérita.

As early as the eighth century there existed the monasteries of San Millán (or S. Emiliano), Sahagún (S. Facundo), S. Vicente de Oviedo, and Sta. Maria de Obona, and in Catalonia that of Sta. Maria de Lavax. In the ninth century two hundred monks of the monastery of Cardeña, near Burgos, suffered martyrdom. From the monastery of Moreruela, on the banks of the River Esla, its two founders, St. Froilan and St. Atilanus, went to occupy the Sees of Leon and Zamora. St. Eulogius has left us an account of the monasteries which he visited in the ninth century— S. Salvador of Leire, S. Zacarías, Urdax, S. Martín de Cillas, and S. Vicente de Igal. That of S. Cugat, in Catalonia, seems to date from Gothic times, while the first independent count founded those of Ripoll and Montserrat. In the eleventh century the Cluniac Reform was introduced into Spain. Bernard, formerly a monk of Saint-Orence at Aux, planted it at Sahagún, making the monastery there the mother-house of the reformed branch in Spain, as Cluny was in France. The migration of French monks into Spain made its influence felt in the famous reform of the Mozarabic Rite, for which the Roman was substituted. Known also as the Isidorean, or Spanish, Rite, the former was abolished in Aragon in 1071, through the exertions of the Cluniacs and the queen, who was a Frenchwoman, and the Roman Rite was first introduced in the Cluniac monastery of S. Juan de la Peña. The same innovation was made a little later in Catalonia, and in 1076 in Navarre. The Castilians offered a strong resistance to the supplanting of their ancient rite, and Pope John X, having sent the Legate Zanelo to examine and report on it, approved it. Fifty years later, Alexander II sent Cardinal Hugo Candido, but neither would he undertake to make any change. Gregory VII sent Cardinal Ricardo, who, together with Alfonso VI, the conqueror of Toledo, decreed the

THE SURRENDER OF BREDA, 1625
VELASQUEZ, THE PRADO, MADRID

abolition of the ancient rite, although, according to the chronicle, appeal was made to the trial by combat, and Don Juan Ruiz, the champion of the Mozarabic Rite, was victorious. It was, nevertheless, permitted in certain churches, and is even yet preserved at Toledo as an historical monument of the ancient Spanish Church.

The Cistercian Reform, too, was introduced into Spain, during the lifetime of St. Bernard, and the cathedral chapters lived by the Rule of St. Augustine. The most characteristic development of this period, however, was that of the military orders. The oldest of them seems to have been that of the Knights of La Terraza, founded by Don García de Najera, in the eleventh century; but this order, as well as those of the Palms, of the Redeemer, and of the Crusaders, established by Alfonso I of Aragon in the twelfth century, disappeared, becoming merged with the orders which came from Palestine. The Order of Calatrava was founded by St. Raymond, Abbot of Fitero, in La Rioja, who, in 1158, undertook to defend the stronghold of Calatrava, abandoned by the Templars. Its habit is white with a red cross. The Order of Alcántara was at first known as that of St. Julian of the Peartree (del Pereiro), but it soon took the name of the town of Alcántara, which was ceded to it by the Knights of Calatrava. Its habit is white with a green cross. The order of Santiago was founded to protect pilgrims to Compostela, to which service thirteen knights vowed themselves. With these knights the Augustinian Canons of S. Eloy of Leon joined to form the famous order whose badge is an elongated red cross (1170). These three orders were all approved by Alexander III.

THE ROYAL PALACE, MADRID
From the Calle Bailem

The importance to which the Spanish military orders attained may be gathered from the fact that King Alfonso the Fighter (*El Batallador*) wished to hand over the Kingdom of Aragon to them, believing that there was no better way of securing the speedy completion of the Reconquest. The Aragonese, however, would not consent to their king's testamentary disposition of them, and had recourse to Ramiro, a monk of S. Ponce de Tomeras, who wore the Crown until a successor was forthcoming.

F. *The Unification of Spain.*—Several difficulties stood in the way of the union of the various states formed in Spain by the Reconquest: the diversity of its points of departure was the principal. Navarre and Catalonia were in particularly close contact with France, and the marriage of Ramón Berenguer the Great with Dulcia, heiress of Provence, made the relations between the peoples of the *langue d'oc* so close that the subsequent development of Catalonia was connected rather with that of the South of France. In Navarre, again, when the dynasty of Sancho the Elder became extinct, the Crown passed in succession to the houses of Champagne (1234), of France, and of Evreux (1349-1441), with the result that Navarre, until the fifteenth century, lived in much closer relations with the French monarchy than with the Spanish states. On the other hand, the feudal usages introduced in the Western Kingdoms by the House of Navarre brought about repeated partitions of states. Ferdinand I divided his kingdom into five parts, Castile, Leon, Galicia, Zamora, and Toro, though, in the event, his son Sancho the Strong despoiled his brothers and restored the kingdom to unity. But Alfonso VII, the Emperor, again separated Castile and Leon, leaving the former to his son Sancho, and the latter to Ferdinand.

Another result of feudal customs introduced by the Burgundian princes was the separation of Portugal. For Alfonso VI gave his daughters Urraca and Teresa in marriage to Raymond and Henry of Burgundy, who founded two dynasties: that of Portugal, and that of Castile and Leon, which began with Alfonso VII. The Kingdoms of Asturias, Galicia, Leon, and Castile were definitively united under St. Ferdinand, heir of Leon through his father Alfonso IX, and of Castile through his mother Berenguela. In the same way Catalonia and Aragon were definitively united by the marriage of Ramón Berenguer, the Saint, with Doña Petronila, daughter of Ramiro, the Monk, of Aragon, of whom legend says that he made the famous "Bell of Huesca" out of the heads of rebellious nobles. These three principal states, to which the divisions of the Peninsula had been reduced, completed the Reconquest; they were not united, to form Iberian national unity, until three centuries later.

The kingdom formed by the union of Aragon and Catalonia was the first to complete that portion of the Reconquest which the geographical conditions assigned to it; then it directed its strength eastward. Pedro II, the Catholic, sovereign of Aragon and Catalonia, went to Rome to seek the annulment of his marriage with Marie of Montpelier, and to have himself crowned by the pope. The former purpose he failed to accomplish; the latter occasioned him a great deal of trouble, as the Aragonese nobles refused to recognize the position of vassalage to the Holy See in which Pedro had placed his kingdom. These nobles then formed for the first time that union, or confederation, which was the cause of such serious disturbances until Pedro IV with his dagger cut in pieces the document which recorded it. Pedro II, the Catholic, fell in the battle of Muret (1213), defending his Albigensian kinsmen against Simon de Montfort, whom Innocent III had sent against them. His son, Jaime I, the Conqueror, completed the Catalan-Aragonese Reconquest, winning Majorca (1228) and Valencia (1238) besides helping his son-in-law, Alfonso X, the Wise, to complete the conquest of Murcia. His son and successor gave a new direction to Catalan-Aragonese policy by enforcing the rights of his wife, Doña Costanza of Suabia, to the kingdoms of Sicily and Naples. Profiting by the rising of the Sicilian Vespers against the Angevins (1282), he possessed himself of Sicily and attacked Naples.

This conquest, however, placed the kings of Aragon in a position of antagonism with the popes, who defended the rights of the House of Anjou. Martin IV having excommunicated Pedro III, the Aragonese nobles took advantage of the fact to extend their privileges at the expense of the royal power. The demands of the nobles increased in the reign of Alfonso III, who was forced to confirm to them the famous *Privilegio de la Unión*. Jaime II became reconciled with the Holy See, accepting Corsica and Sardinia in lieu of Sicily. Pedro IV, the Ceremonious, defeated the nobles at Epila (1348) and used his dagger to cut in pieces the charter they had extorted from his predecessors. In the meantime the Catalans and Aragonese who were left in Sicily offered themselves to the Emperor Andronicus Palæologus to fight the Turks. Having conquered these, they turned their arms against the Greeks, who treacherously slew their leaders; but for this treachery the Spaniards, under Bernard of Rocafort and Berenguer of Entença, exacted the terrible penalty celebrated in history as "The Catalan Vengeance" and moreover seized the Duchies of Athens and Naupatria (1313). The royal line of Aragon became extinct with Martin the Humane, and the Compromise of Caspe gave the Crown to the dynasty of Castile, thus preparing the final union. Alfonso V, the Magnanimous, once more turned Aragonese policy in the direction of Italy, where he possessed the Kingdom of Sicily and acquired that of Naples by having himself made adoptive son of Queen Joanna. With these events began the Italian wars which were not to end until the eighteenth century.

Meanwhile the Reconquest languished in Castile; at first, because of the candidacy of Alfonso the Wise for the imperial Crown of Germany, in which candidacy he had secured a majority of the electoral princes. This was followed by a disputed succession to the Throne, the rival claimants being the Cerda heirs (sons of Fernando, the eldest son of Alfonso X) and the second son of Sancho IV. Next came the minorities of Ferdinand IV, Alfonso XI, Henry III, and John II, and fresh civil strife in the reigns of Pedro the Cruel and of Henry IV. Ferdinand IV succeeded to the Throne at the age of nine, being under the tutelage of his mother Doña María de Molina. Alfonso XI was little more than one year old when his father died (1312); and though his reign was in many respects glorious, and he overcame the Beni-Merines in the battle of El Salado (1340), still his amours with Doña Leonor de Guzmán, by whom he had several children, resulted in the wars of the following reign, that of Pedro the Cruel, who was at last slain by his bastard brother, Henry of Trastamara, and succeeded on the Throne by him under the title of Henry II. John I, who married Beatriz of Portugal (1383), sought to unite the two kingdoms on the death of Ferdinand, the last King of Portugal of the Burgundian line. The Portuguese, however, defeated John of Castile at the battle of Aljubarota, and the Portuguese Crown went to the Master of Aviz, who became John I of Portugal (1385). Henry III, who married Catherine of Lancaster, was the first to take the title of Prince of Asturias as heir to the Crown, which he inherited during his minority, as did his son, John II.

National unity was eventually attained by the most unexpected means: Isabel of Castile, who was not the heiress of Henry IV, married Fernando (Ferdinand) of Aragon, who was not the heir of John II, and the tragic death of the Prince of Viana, on the one hand, and, on the other hand, the no less tragic fate of Juana la Beltraneja contributed to a result which no doubt entered into the designs of Providence (see ISABELLA THE CATHOLIC). Portugal, which failed to be united with Castile on the extinction of the House of Burgundy, was united with it when the Aviz dynasty ended, in the time of Philip II, to be again separated, however, under Philip IV, when the House of Braganza secured the Crown. But, before reviewing the civil history of united Spain, it will be well to glance at its ecclesiastical history during this period of transition.

G. *Religious Development*.—The great monarchs of the Reconquest were distinguished by their zeal in restoring and founding churches, or converting the conquered mosques into Catholic churches. St. Ferdinand re-established the ancient churches and sees of Jaén, Cordova (where the great mosque became the cathedral), and Seville, and began the erection of the magnificent cathedrals of Burgos and Toledo. His contemporary, Jaime the Conqueror, is said to have consecrated to God no fewer than 2000 churches; he founded the Cathedral of Majorca (1229) and restored the ancient See of Valencia, making it suffragan to Tarragona, though it afterwards, in the fifteenth century, became metropolitan. Its first bishop was Ferrer of San Martin. The thirteenth century was a very prosperous epoch for the Spanish Church: it was then that the Carmelites, Dominicans, and Franciscans were established in the Peninsula, as well as the Order of the Most Holy Trinity for the redemption of captives. For this same object, also, Jaime the Conqueror, St. Peter Nolasco, and St. Raymond of Penafort founded the Mercedarians (*Orden de la Merced*), at first a military order, but afterwards monastic (1228). When Philip the Fair brought about the extinction of the Templars, Jaime II of Aragon and the Councils of Salamanca and Tarragona asserted their innocence and, when obliged to carry out the decree of suppression, divided their possessions between the Orders of St. John of Jerusalem and Montesa, the latter created to defend the frontiers of Valencia previously defended by the Templars. The Knights of Montesa took for their device the plain red cross on a white mantle.

In the Great Schism of the West Spain played a great part, chiefly through the influence of the Aragonese, Pedro de Luna (antipope Benedict XIII). As a cardinal, his influence led Henry II of Castile and Pedro IV of Aragon to recognize Clement VII, and after his own election he ended by withdrawing to Spain, where he lived in the castle of Peñíscola. In 1399 an assembly held at Alcalá resolved to obey neither pope, as it was not known which of the two was legitimate. The antipope favoured the election of Ferdinand of Antequera in the Compromise of Caspe, in which St. Vincent Ferrer, an ardent partisan of Ferdinand, was arbitrator. In this way the antipope secured recognition from the Spaniards. At last, in 1416, St. Vincent Ferrer and the kings abandoned the cause of Benedict XIII and gave their adherence to the Council of Constance. Gil Sanchez Muñoz, a native of Teruel, was, on the death of Benedict XIII, elected by the cardinals of Peñíscola, who were supported by Alfonso V of Aragon; but he soon afterwards resigned his claims, in the Council of Tarragona, recognized Martin V, and was made Bishop of Majorca.

During this period the Jews in Spain became very numerous and acquired great power; they were not only the physicians, but also the treasurers of the kings. Don Jusaph de Ecija administered the revenues of Alfonso XI, and Samuel Leví was chief favourite of Pedro the Cruel. The Jews of Toledo then set on foot their migration (*Transito*) in protest against the laws of Alfonso X (*Las Partidas*), which prohibited the building of new synagogues. After the accession of Henry of Trastamara to the Throne, the populace, exasperated by the preponderance of Jewish influence, perpetrated a massacre of Jews at Toledo; in 1391 another general massacre took place, beginning at Seville; a little later, the jewries of Toledo, Burgos, Valencia, and Cordova were attacked, and the like scenes were enacted in Aragon, especially at Barcelona. St. Vincent Ferrer converted innumerable Jews, among them the Rabbi Josuah Halorqui, who took the name of Jeronimo de Santa Fe and in his town converted many of his former coreligionists in the famous Dispute of Tortosa (1413). Oppressed by vexatious laws, and abhorred by the people, whom they ruined with their usury, perverted, and scandalized with their sacrileges, they were finally expelled from Spain by the Catholic Sovereigns, who regarded them as dangerous to the religious unity and the security of the country on account of the relations which they maintained with the Moors.

Connected with the persecutions of the Jews is the institution of the Inquisition. It was introduced into Spain by Jaime I the Conqueror, King of Aragon, to stop the invasion of the same Albigensian heretics against whom it had been established by Innocent III. The Count of Foix and the Viscount of Castellbó, with many of their subjects, embraced the Albigensian errors. Arnaldo of Vilanova and some Beghards of Aragon were punished by the Inquisition. There were also in Catalonia Fraticelli and other heretics, like Raimundo of Tárrega, as the Holy Office was informed. In 1376 Padre Nicolas Eymerich published the "Directorium Inquisitorum". But the Spanish Inquisition did not acquire its true character and importance until the Catholic Sovereigns established it in Castile under authority obtained from Pope Sixtus IV (1478). It was a mixed tribunal, in which the ecclesiastical element took cognizance of the orthodoxy or heterodoxy of doctrines and, consequently, of offences against Catholic faith or morals; after sentence was pronounced, the culprit was handed over to the secular arm to be punished according to the laws of the realm. Such a law was that of title 26 of the seven *Partidas*, which provided the punishment of death by fire for heretics who refused to be converted, and, again, those of book IV, title 1, of the *Fuero Real*, which imposed the same penalty for heresy and apostasy. The laws regulating the processes of the Inquisition, indeed, were Spanish, and not laws of the Roman Church. The Spanish Inquisition, although established by virtue of a pontifical Bull, became to some extent independent of Rome, as appeals lay to the Archbishop of Seville, who passed sentence in the pope's name. The Tribunal of the Holy Office, as it was called, was made up of thirteen —afterwards fifteen—provincial tribunals, with territorial jurisdiction, and a supreme council, which supervised them and pronounced on appeals. The procedure was minutely regulated and was far superior to the procedure of other tribunals of its time. It is not certain that anonymous accusations were considered, although the names of the accusers and witnesses were concealed from the accused. Torture was not arbitrarily employed, but only when sufficient proof already existed, and even then it was applied less barbarously than in the contemporary civil tribunals. The prisons were of the most humane kind. The sentences pronounced were: abandonment to the temporal arm (*relajacion*) for the impenitent heretic; reconciliation for the repentant; abjuration, when there was a suspicion of heresy; and absolution. Only the impenitent were condemned to the stake, and the number of condemnations has been much exaggerated.

H. *Modern Period.*—The political and religious development which we have outlined above resulted in Spanish national unity, and explains the character of Spain as a Catholic nation. The struggle of eight centuries to recover the territory wrested from them by the Mussulmans, who were enemies at once of their land and of their faith, effected in the Spanish people that intimate fusion of patriotic and religious feeling which distinguished them during many centuries. *Non sine numine*, it may be said, did a Spanish pope (Alexander VI) give the title of Catholic, by eminence, to the sovereigns who first united reconquered Spain under their sceptre, for they and their successors deemed it the first duty of the Crown to maintain the purity of the Catholic Faith in their realms, to propagate it in the vast countries which they colonized, and defend it in Europe against the assaults of heretics. The same pope, Alexander VI, issued in 1493 a Bull, in which, to prevent the disputes that might arise between Spaniards and Portuguese in regard to their discoveries in the East Indies and (as America was then called) the West Indies, he established as a line of demarcation between them the meridian running 100 leagues west of the Azores, decreeing that the newly discovered lands west of that line should belong to the Spaniards, and those east of it to the Portuguese. Afterwards, in the Treaty of Tordesillas, another line, 360 leagues west of the Cape Verde Islands, was substituted—an arrangement which gave Brazil to Portugal.

The Catholic Sovereigns, by reuniting the Crowns of Castile and Aragon, annexing Navarre, and completing the Reconquest with the reduction of Granada (1492), established the political unity of Spain; with

THE OLD CATHEDRAL, SALAMANCA, FROM THE EAST

the Inquisition and the expulsion of the Jews they achieved its religious unity; the marriages of their children with the Kings of Portugal and of England and the son of the Emperor Maximilian, secured to Spain the friendship of the leading states; by the discovery of America and the conquests in Africa a broad road was opened for Spain's colonial expansion. But the death of their son Prince John caused the Crown to pass to Charles I (the Emperor Charles V), son of Juana la Loca, and entirely changed the course which the magnanimous Isabella had traced for Spanish policy. Charles V, attracted to Italy by the ancient strife with France for the possession of the Italian states, and to Germany by his inheritance of the imperial Throne from his grandfather Maximilian, was more the Emperor of Germany than the King of Spain, and completely diverted Spanish policy from America and Africa. Philip II, though he did not succeed his father in the empire, could not extricate himself from his father's European policy, and Spain was exhausted by the wars in Flanders against France and England. Nevertheless, unlike his father, Philip II was a thoroughly Spanish king, and united the whole Iberian Peninsula under his sway by the incorporation of Portugal.

With the death of Philip II the decay of Spanish power began. The monarchy, which needed the shoulders of a giant to support it, fell upon those of the pious but feeble Philip III (1598–1621), who left the task of government to a favourite or minister—first, the Duque de Lerma and then his son the Duque de Uceda. In the Low Countries he arranged the Twelve Years' Peace. He brought aid to the Catholics of Ireland, sending an expedition under Aguilar (1602), and intervened in behalf of the German Catholics in the first period of the Thirty Years' War. While thus aiding Catholics abroad, he resolved to guard against the danger that threatened religious unity at home in the presence of the Moriscoes, or subjugated Moors, who were suspected of conspiring with the Moors of Africa; these he expelled from Spain. In this reign and the next, Castilian literature and art attained their finest flower. Philip IV (1621–65), less pious than his father, was nevertheless a better ruler. For his prime ministers and favourites he had, first, the Conde-Duque de Olivares and then Don Luis de Haro. In this reign the colossal monarchy of Philip II began to crumble. The Duke of Braganza was proclaimed King of Portugal as John IV; Catalonia rose and maintained a war lasting twelve years; Naples and Sicily also rebelled, the famous Spanish infantry regiments (*tercios españoles*) were beaten at Rocroy, and Spain, by the Peace of the Pyrenees with France, lost Roussillon and, by the Treaty of Westphalia (1648), a great part of her importance in Europe.

The weakening of Spain continued under the sickly Charles II (1665–1700), who succeeded his father at the age of four. The regency fell to the queen, Doña Mariana, who shifted the burden of government on her confessor, Padre Nithard, and, after him, on her favourite Valenzuela, the husband of one of her ladies-in-waiting. Spain, after intervening on the side of Catholicism in all the conflicts of the European states, now saw herself an object of ambition to foreigners. The failure of the king's health obliged him to leave the duties of government to ambitious ministers, while France reached her apogee in the reign of Louis XIV, and Spanish power abroad continued to decline. The king being without issue, the rivalries of France and Austria for the succession began even in his lifetime and led up to the project for the dismemberment of the Spanish monarchy. Following the advice of Cardinal Portocarrero, Charles disinherited his Austrian kindred and designated as his heir the Duke of Anjou, afterwards Philip V. Upon the death of Charles II, the reign of the House of Austria ended in Spain, and that of the House of Bourbon commenced, bringing French centralism into Spanish administration, and helping to change the national character by linking the nation more closely with France.

Philip V (1700–46) had to sustain the War of the Succession with French assistance. By the Peace of Utrecht, which terminated that war, Gibraltar and Minorca fell to the share of England; the Italian possessions and the Low Countries, to Austria. Catalonia, having vigorously defended the rights of the Archduke Charles, was despoiled of a part of her constitutional rights (*Fueros*). Philip V, who had been under French influence during the lifetime of his first wife, Maria Luisa of Savoy, gave himself up to Italian influence after his marriage with Isabel Farnese, being directed by Alberoni. To find possessions for the children of Isabel Farnese, the Italian claims of Spain were revived; Alberoni, however, fell before he succeeded in obtaining anything more than the cardinalate for himself and the Duchies of Parma and Tuscany for the Infante Don Carlos. In 1724 Philip abdicated in favour of his son Luis, but the death of the latter in the same year obliged his father to resume the Crown. By the Treaty of Vienna (1735) Naples and Sicily were given to the Infante Don Carlos. Unquestionably the most glorious reign of the Spanish Bourbons was that of Ferdinand VI, thanks to the care with which he maintained neutrality between France and England. The Peace of Aix-la-Chapelle (Aachen) ended the wars undertaken to find crowns for the children of Isabel Farnese: the Duchies of Parma, Piacenza, and Guastalla were given to Don Felipe (Philip). The king thenceforward left the task of government to his ministers, Carvajal and the Marques de la Ensenada, while he surrendered himself to the enchantment of Farinelli's music. By the concordat which he made with Benedict XIV, the *Real Patronato* (royal patronage) over all the Churches within the monarchy was recognized, as it had already been in force in the foreign possessions and the Kingdom of Granada. Although the English party, led by the ambassador, Keene, and the minister, Wall (successor to Carvajal), succeeded in overthrowing Ensenada, and although the French offered the restoration of Minorca, and the English of Gibraltar, the king persevered in his neutrality, with the result that the nation prospered, and the coffers of the treasury were filled almost to bursting.

Ferdinand died of a broken heart occasioned by the loss of his wife, Doña Barbara (1759). He was succeeded by his brother Charles III, who was already King of Naples, and whose greatest mistake was the abandonment of his predecessor's policy of neutrality by that fatal "Family Compact" (1761) which united the fortunes of Spain with those of the degenerate French Bourbons. With this began a war with England, issuing in the loss of Havana and Manila (1763). Meanwhile Spain was governed by two foreigners, Grimaldi and Esquilacce, and the people rose in the famous "Hat-and-Cloak Riots" (*motin de las capas y sombreros*), which led to the Madrileños being prohibited the use of the national dress. Pombal and Choiseul had driven the Jesuits out of Portugal and France, and their enemies in Spain exploited this tumult to persuade the king that the Society was a menace to public order. Adding other calumnies (such as the story that the Jesuits denied the king's being the legitimate son of Philip V), they succeeded in inducing Charles III to order the Jesuits out of his dominions without stating any reason, reserving "in his royal breast" the motive of their banishment. Under the ministry of Floridablanca Spain intervened in support of the independence of the United States. During this reign many public buildings were constructed—the Fine Arts Academy, the Botanical Gardens of Madrid, etc.—with money saved during the preceding reign. But the king's shortsightedness admitted to his counsels men imbued with Voltairean ideas, who, however little they may have been aware of it, were the allies of the Revolution that was to ruin the Bourbons.

Charles IV (1788–1808), even more deficient in ability and character than Charles III, had to suffer the consequences of political errors committed in the preceding reign. In his time the French Revolution broke out, and the Spanish Bourbons went so far as to ally themselves eventually with that Revolutionary France which had beheaded Louis XVI. The Aranda ministry, having overthrown that of Floridablanca, was in turn overthrown by Don Manuel Godoy, the queen's favourite no less than the king's, who made the Treaty of S. Ildefonso, allying Spain with France against England, and leading up to the disaster of Trafalgar (1805). This reign ended in a most disgraceful manner: Prince Ferdinand having rebelled against his father and the inept Godoy, the Aranjuez rising resulted in the abdication of Charles IV, when the French had already treacherously gained a footing in Spain. The king and queen having sought refuge at Bayonne, Napoleon made them surrender the Crown of Spain to him, intending it for his brother Joseph Bonaparte. But this humiliation the

Spanish people would not brook; rising, after the terrible Second of May, 1808, they fought the glorious War of Independence, in which Napoleon suffered his first reverses. The most celebrated battles of this war were those of Bruch, in the highlands of Montserrat, in which the Catalan *sometanes* (peasant soldiers) routed a French army; Bailén, where Castañes, at the head of the army of Andalusia, defeated Dupont; and the sieges of Saragossa and Gerona, which were worthy of the ancient Spaniards of Saguntum and Numantia. The British general, Wellington, gained the battles of Salamanca (1812) and Vittoria (1813), and helped to drive the French out of the Peninsula. But while the Spanish people were shedding their blood for their faith, their country, and their king, the Liberals, assembled in the Cortes of Cadiz (1812), were drafting a Constitution modelled on the French. Ferdinand VII, however, liberated by Napoleon, returned to Spain, refused to recognize this Constitution, and restored the old regime, thus initiating that struggle between Absolutists and Liberals which lasted throughout the nineteenth century. The old colonies of Spain in Mexico and South America took advantage of this conflict to make themselves independent.

That moral unity which the Catholic Sovereigns had restored in Spain by the expulsion of the Jews, the subjection of the Moors, and the establishment of Catholic unity, was broken by the influx of ideas from the French Revolution and English Liberalism. Face to face with the Spanish people, so strongly attached to their ancient traditions and forms of government, there arose the Constitutional Party, which at first proclaimed no further aim than the establishment of representative government, saving the principle of religious unity. But the Liberals, persecuted in 1812, pushed their ideas to extremes and, profiting by a military insurrection in 1820 (Don Rafael de Riego), finally proclaimed the Constitution and forced Ferdinand VII to swear to it. The Constitutionalists then split into the two parties—Extremes and Moderates (*Exaltados* and *Moderados*)—which have continued to the present time. The intervention of the Holy Alliance, however, which sent to Spain the "hundred thousand sons of St. Louis", restored the old order of things. The French soldiers, who had met with such desperate resistance at the hands of the Spaniards in the time of Napoleon, were then received as brothers and liberators, and the Constitution was abolished. But the Liberals took advantage of the dynastic question, which arose on the death of Ferdinand VII, to revive their party. The king had no male issue and only two daughters, who by the Salic Law (brought into Spain by the Bourbons), were incapable of succeeding to the Throne. The king accordingly proposed to set aside the Salic Law and re-establish the ancient Spanish law of succession, which admitted females, failing male issues. The question, whether the Salic Law was or was not legitimately abrogated, formed the legal basis of the dynastic quarrel between Don Carlos (Charles) V, brother of Ferdinand VII, and his daughter Doña Isabel II.

The true animus of the conflict, however, arose from the division of Spaniards into Traditionalists who supported the cause of Don Carlos, and Liberals, who sided with Doña Isabel and her mother, Doña Cristina. This division—the origin of all the ills which Spain suffered in the nineteenth century—led to the Seven Years' War, from 1833, when Ferdinand VII died, to 1839, when the Convention of Vergara was signed. In the meantime the Liberals ruled, except in the provinces occupied by the Carlists, and the Moderate ministry of Martínez de la Rosa, during which the horrible massacre of friars took place at Madrid (17 July, 1834), was succeeded by those of Toreno and of Mendizábal, who put up the possessions of the Church for sale (1836). The predominance of the *Exaltados* culminated with the regency of Espartero (1841), who closed the Nunciature and broke off all relations with Rome. The queen having been declared of age, the Moderate Narvaez ministry came into power, exiled Espartero, and suspended the sale of church property. Relations with Rome were resumed, and Spain intervened in behalf of Pius IX, who had been driven to take refuge at Gaeta. In 1851 the Concordat, regulating the new conditions of

VIEW OF SALAMANCA, WITH THE NEW CATHEDRAL, FROM THE RIVER TORMES

the Spanish Church, was signed. From 1854 to 1856 (the *Bienio Liberal*) the Liberals, with Espartero and O'Donnell, were again in power, and O'Donnell acquired prestige in the African war of 1859. This ministry also re-established the Constitution of 1845 and stopped the sale of church property (1856).

It was succeeded by the Narvaez ministry (1866), and after these two generals, Prim and Serrano, who had been exiled, obtained the aid of the Navy, commanded by Topete, and effected the Revolution of September, 1868, which dethroned the Bourbons and summoned to the Throne Amadeus I (Duke of Aosta), of the House of Savoy. Prim having been assassinated just as Amadeus landed in the Peninsula, the new king was left without any solid support and, in February, 1873, was obliged to abdicate. On 8 June of the same year the Cortes proclaimed the republic, which lasted but two years and had four presidents: Figueras, Pí y Margall, Salmerón, and Castelar. In the mean time the Spanish Catholics, exasperated by the excesses of the Liberals, rallied round the Duke of Madrid, Don Carlos de Borbón, in whom the Traditionalists saw the legitimate heir of Ferdinand VII and Charles V, and the Third Carlist War began—the second having been nothing more than General Ortega's attempt in behalf of the Count of Montemolín. In the existing condition of political disorganization, the Carlists were enabled to gain substantial advantages, and were on the point of making themselves masters of the Government. But the aristocracy and the financial interests, making General Martínez Campos their instrument, effected the restoration of the female branch of the Bourbons, proclaiming Alfonso XII, in whose favour Isabel II had abdicated. Don Alfonso landed at Cadiz, 9 January, 1875, and in a short time the Carlist rising was suppressed, as well as that of Cuba (October, 1877). As a result of the Bourbon Restoration, and of an agreement between Antonio Cánovas, leader of the Conservatives (successors of the Moderates), and Práxedes Mateo Sagasta, leader of the Liberals, who had inherited the aspirations of the Revolution, there was created in Spain the political situation which has lasted until now (1910), establishing the legal alternation (*turno legal*) of the Alphonsist-Monarchical parties in power. Alfonso XII died 25 November, 1885, leaving the regency to Doña Maria Cristina of Habsburg, as mother of his posthumous son, Alfonso XIII (b. 17 May, 1886). During the regency the Cuban Insurrection, and that of the Philippines, gave rise to the war with the United States, which led to the loss of the last remnants of Spain's colonial empire.

IV. ACTUAL CONDITIONS.—A. *Legislation*.—The Spanish nationality being formed out of two elements, the Gothic and the Hispano-Roman, had at the outset two different legislative systems. Euric, in the code which bears his name, collected the laws of the Goths, while the "Breviarium" of Anianus (in the time of Alaric II) sums up the provisions of the Roman law for the government of the Hispano-Latins. But when the two races had become fused, there was also a fusion of the two systems of legislation in the "Forum Judicum", or "Fuero Juzgo" (completed in the Sixteenth Council of Toledo), which is the first of the Spanish Codes, and in which the Gothic element predominates in the law of persons, the Roman in that of contracts. During the Reconquest there arose the *fueros*, special laws, or privileges, granted by the kings to certain particular cities or provinces and which were also known (as in England and France) as *cartas*, or *cartas pueblas*, i. e., charters granted to those who populated a new city. Another general code for Castile was the "Fuero Viejo" (Old Privilege), of uncertain origin, but probably commenced in the time of Alfonso VIII and completed in that of Pedro I. Alfonso IX published the "Fueros Real", which included the declarations called the "Leyes del Estilo"—rules of style, or of procedure. The legislative work undertaken in the time of St. Ferdinand ended with Alfonso X, the Wise, author of the "Siete Partidas", or "Seven Parts". This king, however, being a man of theory rather than a practical man, modified the national laws and customs to excess, allowing himself to be carried away by his admiration for the Roman Law. Hence the "Siete Partidas" have never been in legal force, except as a supplementary code and as bearing on certain particular

PRINCIPAL FAÇADE, CHURCH OF S. DOMINGO, SALAMANCA

points—the succession of the Crown, for instance, until the Bourbons grafted upon the Spanish code the Salic Law which they brought from France.

The fact that the "Siete Partidas" had not acquired legal force was the reason why Castilian legislation remained entangled with a mass of *fueros*, ordinances, and special provisions. One of these, the Ordinance of Alcalá, passed by the Cortes of Alcalá in the time of Alfonso XI, established, among other matters, the order of precedence of the Spanish codes. Others were the Laws of Toro and the Ordinances of Montalvo, made in the time of the Catholic Sovereigns. The other kingdoms of Spain continued to elaborate their own several legislations—Catalonia, with its very ancient "Usatges" and its "Consulat de Mar" (the oldest commercial code in Europe); Aragon, Navarre, and the rest, with their respective special *fueros*. Wishing to give the united monarchy a civil code, Philip II published the "Nueva Recopilación" (New Digest) of the Spanish laws, though, indeed the charter laws of the various provinces were at the same time left in full vigour. In the reign of Charles IV (1805), a "Novísima Recopilación" (Latest Digest) was published, also leaving untouched the charter laws of the provinces. Finally, in the nineteenth century, there arose the division of laws into political, civil, penal, and laws of procedure.

The Cortes of Cadiz, in 1812, formulated the first Liberal Constitution, which, however, showed some regard for Catholic unity. This Constitution was not accepted by the king, when he was released from his captivity by Napoleon, but Riego's military insurrection at Las Cabezas de S. Juan, in 1820, forced it upon him. It was overthrown by the French intervention in 1823. In 1834 the queen-regent authorized the Estatuto Real, a sort of moderate constitution. Next came the Liberal Constitution of 1837, in which Catholic unity is not stipulated for, although it is stated that the Catholic Religion is that professed by Spaniards. Again, in the Constitution of 1845 it is declared that the religion of Spain is the Catholic Apostolic, Roman. In the Constitution of 1856 toleration of other creeds is established much as it now exists. The Revolution of 1868 produced the Liberal Constitution of 1869, which established freedom of worship (art. xxi), maintaining, however, the Catholic Religion and its ministers. Finally, the Constitution of 1876, published under the Restoration, admitted religious toleration, but declared the Catholic Religion that of the State. In practice, there is in Spain a great deal of religious liberty, the only conditions being that dissenting places of worship must comply with certain outward forms—such as not having signs placed on their exteriors. This last Constitution places the legislative power in the Cortes with the king. The Cortes are composed of two chambers: the Senate and the Congress. Some of the senators sit of their own right (grandees, archbishops, etc.), others for life, others by election. The members of Congress (*diputados*) are all elected. The king can convoke or prorogue the Cortes. The executive power belongs to the king and his ministers, who are responsible for the conduct of the government. In the succession to the Throne the ancient order, superseded by the Salic Law, is followed. The heir to the Throne takes the title of Prince of Asturias. The king attains his majority at the age of sixteen and in minority is under the regency of his nearest relative: Alfonso XIII, posthumous son of Alfonso XII, was under the regency of his mother, Doña Cristina of Habsburg; on attaining his majority he was sworn king, but was not solemnly crowned. The judicial power is entrusted to tribunals which administer justice in the king's name. The latter has the prerogative of pardon.

The relations of Church and State in Spain have been regulated by various concordats. By law 13, title 1, Book I, of the "Novísima Recopilación", the Council of Trent is the law of the realm. The chief concordats with Spain are: that of 1737 (Clement XII and Philip V); 1752 (Benedict XIV and Ferdinand VI); 1851 (Pius IX and Isabel II). The last-named is still in force, although Liberal Governments violate it in various ways and pretend to modify it, invoking it, nevertheless, whenever convenient for their purposes. According to this concordat, which was intended to regulate the grave disorders consequent upon the confiscation of church property (disamortization), the Catholic is the only religion of the Spanish people. Public instruction is under the inspection of the bishops and other diocesan prelates. The number of dioceses is diminished (see above: Ecclesiastical Organization); the form of provision for bishoprics and other benefices is determined (*Patronato Real*), as also the remuneration of the clergy, maintenance of church buildings, etc. The Archbishop of Toledo receives 40,000 pesetas ($8000 or £1600); other archbishops, from 37,500 to 32,500 pesetas ($7500 to $6500); bishops, 25,000 to 20,000 pesetas ($5000 to $4000).

In the civil law of Spain the predominant tendency is to suppress the individualities of the charter law (*derecho foral*) in the various parts of the country. These local peculiarities are found especially in the law of family relations. In Catalonia the Roman Law prevailed, the father enjoyed freedom of testamentary disposition, and the right of the children was limited to the legal one-fourth; in Castile the right of testamentary disposition was limited to one-third and one-fifth of what could be disposed of for the individual advantage of one favoured child. Castile followed the Gothic custom by which the bridegroom paid *arras* to the bride at the wedding, while in Catalonia the Roman dowry system was in force. In other parts of the country other laws limited the power of testamentary disposition even more than in Castile. The unifying tendency was especially prevalent in the "Codigo Civil" published in 1888 by the minister, Alonso Martínez, and which came into force on 1 May, 1889. Although the charter law is preserved to some extent, modifications are introduced such as that bearing on the *bienes gananciales* of Castile, providing that the *gananciales*, or property acquired after marriage, must, when the estate is liquidated, be divided between husband and wife.

MAIN DOORWAY OF THE NEW CATHEDRAL, SALAMANCA

Moreover, the fact that the magistrates belong to different provinces has its influence upon the process of unification, as also the spirit of the Supreme Tribunal, the decisions of which have the force of jurisprudence, and serve as norms for the adjudication of parallel cases. In criminal law the Penal Code, published in 1870 by the minister, Laureano Figuerola, is in force. In many respects it betrays the spirit of the Revolution, during which it originated, and for this reason the Catholic and Conservative elements are demanding its reform in many points. The commercial code now in force is that of 1885, published by the minister, Fr. Silvela. Judicial procedure is governed by the Law of Civil Suits (*Enjuiciamiento Civil*) published by the minister, Alvarez Bugallal, in 1881.

Although the old privileged jurisdictions have been abolished, and all Spaniards are equal before the law, there is still the military jurisdiction (*fuero militar*), certain specified cases being reserved for the military tribunals, and the ecclesiastical jurisdiction (*fuero eclesiástico*), by which the rights of the Church to take cognizance of certain cases are safeguarded.

Canonical marriage has legal force for all Spanish Catholics, without the necessity of any civil marriage, provided the civil authorities are notified that Christian marriage has been contracted, such marriage being subject in Spain to the Decrees of the Council of Trent. Civil marriage exists only for non-Catholics, and Spaniards who wish to contract it must first make a declaration of having abandoned the Catholic Religion and Church. The Church also has jurisdiction over cemeteries, which are blessed canonically. For unbelievers, apostates, and other persons by law excluded from ecclesiastical sepulture, a separate cemetery is provided, usually near the Catholic cemetery, and under the control of the civil authority. In Spain, where feudalism took little root, the aristocracy has lost its exemptions and privileges, civil and political, but as a social distinction it still exists, together with certain titles of modern creation. The royal family consists of the king, the queen consort, and the queen-mother (collectively spoken of in Spanish as *los reyes*, literally, "the kings"), the Prince of Asturias (heir apparent), and the "infantes of Spain"—such relations of the king as may be granted that dignity. At the head of the nobility are the grandees of Spain of the first and the second class. The dukes, marquesses, counts, viscounts, and barons follow in order. The civil decorations most used are the American Order of Isabella the Catholic, and the Order of Charles III. There are grand crosses, commanderies (*encomiendas*), and simple crosses; those who wear the grand cross are given the title of *Excelentísimos Señores*. Of recent foundation is the Civil Order of Alfonso XII. The ancient military orders of Santiago, Alcántara, Montesa, and Calatrava also continue to exist as honorary distinctions.

B. *The Political Situation.*—The elements which go to make up the existing political situation in Spain are (besides the foreign influences, chiefly English Liberalism and French Jacobinism) the dynastic question, the *turno legal*, or alternation, of the two Restoration parties (see above), and the growth of Republicanism. The political parties form three groups: Dissidents of the Right, legal parties, and Dissidents of the Left. The Dissidents of the Right consist of the old Carlist party, dormant during the last years of the reign of Isabel II, but which developed extraordinary vigour under the Republic and the period of extreme Liberalism, maintaining a civil war. It is still ready and willing to defend the ideal of traditional Spain whenever the excesses of Liberalism destroy the equilibrium of Spanish society. By the death of Don Carlos de Borbón, whom the Carlists regarded as the lawful King of Spain, Don Jaime de Borbón has inherited his rights. In the summer of 1888 another division arose within the Traditionalist party, its Extreme Right being formed, owing to the approximation of Don Carlos to constitutionalist ideas. This division, not yet entirely healed, resulted in the Integrist Party, directed by Don Ramón de Nocedal and, after his death, by a *junta*, or committee.

Although all the political parties are recognized as Parliamentary minorities, only those are called *legal* which recognize the reigning dynasty and take turns in office. They are, at present, the Union Liberal-Conservatives, whose undisputed leader is Don Antonio Maura, and the Liberal Democratic Party, the leadership of which is disputed between Moret, Canalejas, and Montero Rios. The former of these two parties endeavours to find Catholic and Conservative solutions for political problems within the bounds of actually existing conditions; it is commonly charged with excessive tenderness for the accomplished facts left by the Liberals as the result of their period of supremacy. The Liberal Democratic Party, on the contrary, though unwilling to call itself anti-Catholic, calls itself anti-Clerical, and tends towards French Jacobinism. Its aims are the secularization of marriage and of burial, the laicization of education, and the repression of the natural growth of religious orders by legislative interference.

The Dissidents of the Left are the Republicans, whose numbers are increasing among the less educated, and who are divided into numberless factions, each more radical than the other. The Vandal proceedings of Barcelona, in July, 1909—when churches and sepulchres were burned and profaned, and persons consecrated to God were murdered and violated—exhibited the aspirations of these extremists. And yet their chief, Ferrer, who was shot for these crimes, has found sympathizers and defenders in Europe and America. In their general anarchy and lack of influential leaders, the Republicans are divided into Federals, Socialists, Anarchists, Acratists, etc. Besides these political parties there are the Regionalists of Catalonia and the Basque Provinces, whose aim is administrative decentralization.

Divisions among Catholics and the indifference of a great portion of the people have resulted in a feeble Catholic Press, particularly in the department of daily papers. There are three Catholic dailies at Madrid: "El Correo Español" (Carlist), "El Siglo Futuro" (Integrist), "El Universo" (Alfonsist Catholic). In the provinces there are many of similar tendencies, such as "El Correo Catalan" of Barcelona, "La Gaceta del Norte" of Bilbao, "El Noticiero" of Saragossa, "La Voz" of Valencia. Among the weeklies mention should be made of "La Lectura Dominical" (Madrid), and among scientific reviews "Razón y Fe" (Jesuit), "La Ciudad de Dios", and "España y América" (both Augustinian), "Los Estudios Franciscanos", "La Ilustración de Clero". The Moderate Liberals have good periodicals, such as "La Correspondencia de España", the "A. B. C.", "La Época", "El Diario de Barcelona"; weeklies such as "Blanco y Negro", "La Ilustración Española y Americana"; but their reviews are inferior to the Catholic, with the exception of their professional periodicals—for medicine, engineering, bulletins of scientific societies, etc. The periodicals of the Extreme Liberal Press are widely read—"El Imparcial", "El Liberal", and "El Heraldo" of Madrid (forming a newspaper trust), and many others in the provinces, "El Pais" is notable for its Atheistical impiety, and it is followed by "El Pueblo" of Valencia, "España Nueva", etc. The official organ is "La Gaceta de Madrid", while in each province there is the "Boletín Oficial", and a "Boletín" in each diocese.

C. *Educational and Social Improvement.*—Beside the educational institutions, there are various academies for the cultivation of the sciences, which are at the same time consultative adjuncts of the State. The principal of these is the Spanish Academy, or "Academia de la Lengua", founded in 1713 under the patronage of Philip V. The statutes which now govern it were approved by decree of 20 August, 1859. It is composed of 36 active academicians, who must reside at Madrid, 24 Spanish correspondents, who are honorary members, and an undetermined number of foreign correspondents. Its chief concern is the Castilian language, in which it is regarded as authoritative. It has published twelve editions of the Castilian Grammar and Dictionary, and many other important works, among the more recent being the complete Works of Lope de Vega, under the direction of Menendez Pelayo. The Academy of History was created in 1735 and approved by royal decree of 17 June, 1738, the former functions of the official chronicler of Spain and the Indies being vested in it. Its present statutes were approved by decree of May, 1856. It is charged with the preservation of national antiquities and monuments. The Academy of Fine Arts of St. Ferdinand was founded in 1752 under the name of "Real Academia de las tres nobles Artes de S. Fernando". Its present statutes were approved by the Decree of 3 December, 1873. Its function is the encouragement and direction of the study of painting, sculpture, architecture, and music, for which, at the same time, special conservatories exist. The Academy of Exact Sciences, Physical and Natural, created in 1847, has 36 academicians resident at Madrid and 36 corresponding members in Spain and abroad. The Academy of Moral and Political Sciences was established in 1857 by the Law of Public Instruction of the same year. It has 36 academicians resident at Madrid, 30 corresponding members in Spain and abroad, and 10 foreign honorary members. There are also Academies of Medicine at Madrid, Barcelona, and other leading cities, as well as Academies of Jurisprudence and Legislation, of the Fine Arts, etc. Notable among those of the provinces are the Literary Academy (Academia de Buenos Lettras) of Barcelona, dating from the end of the seventeenth century; the Literary Academy of Seville, the Academia Juridica Aragonesa, of Saragossa (1733), the Real Academia de las nobles y bellas Artes de S. Carlos, of Valencia, etc. The members of numerous American Academies are correspondents of the Spanish Academy—those of Colombia, Ecuador (Quito), Mexico, Salvador, Venezuela, Chile, Peru (Lima), Argentina, Guatemala, and the Republic of Honduras. For the study of astronomy there are several observatories, the principal being the two State observatories of S. Fernando, founded at Cadiz in 1754, by Don Jorge Juan, and transferred in 1779, and of Madrid, the project of which had already been formed in the reign of Charles III, though it was not realized until the reform of public education in 1845. Among the private observatories should be mentioned that of Tibidabo (Barcelona), that of the Ebro, and the Jesuit observatory at Tortosa, where the various branches of astro-physics, terrestrial magnetism, etc., are studied.

It is very difficult to obtain correct statistics of the works of social improvement existing in Spain, owing to the persistent tendency of officials to suppress all mention of Catholic institutions. The Institute of Social Reforms, managed chiefly by the Krausist Free-Teaching Institution, published in 1907 the following account of workingmen's associations existing in the year 1904:—

Catholic associations	67	Political	86
For the amelioration of the conditions of labour	1147	For instruction and recreation	79
Co-operative	93	Musical (including choral)	84
Mutual benefit	309		
		Total	1865

In 1908 the following figures are given:—

Savings banks	13	Mutual insurance	42
Co-operative societies	274		
Mutual benefit	1691	Total	2020

The following statistics published by "La Paz Social" (a social review of Saragossa and Madrid) give a better idea of Catholic social enterprise:

	In 1904.	1907.	1909.
Catholic rural banks	38	112	373
Catholic agricultural syndicates	..	108	450

From this it appears that the number of Catholic social enterprises is rapidly increasing, which is due to the appreciation by the clergy of the importance of combining social work with the pastoral ministry, so as to meet both the spiritual and temporal needs of the people. For the general direction of these works there has been formed at Madrid a Central Committee (*Junta*) of Catholic Action. The duties of this committee are to co-operate with the prelates of the respective dioceses in the preparation of Catholic congresses in such dioceses, to carry out the resolutions of the congresses approved by the prelates, and to direct the Catholic propaganda in all its branches. It is made up of a president [at present (1910) the Bishop of Madrid-Alcalá] and 18 members, nine of whom represent the nine ecclesiastical provinces. Up to the present (1910) six Catholic congresses have been held: at Madrid (1887), Seville, Saragossa, Tarragona, Burgos, and Santiago (1902). Eucharistic congresses have also been held at Valencia, Lugo, and Madrid, and "congresses of the good Press" at Seville and Saragossa (1908). But political dissensions among Catholics have hindered the practical results which might have been expected. The "social weeks" are also held among some communities, to bring together those who are engaged in works of this kind and to spread the knowledge of them in the various provinces. In 1907 the "Social Popular Movement" was inaugurated at Barcelona, in imitation of the *Volksverein* at Munich-Gladbach, in Germany.

D. *Charity*.—Though the charity of Catholic Spain has flourished in all ages and been manifested by the foundation of numerous benevolent institutions, it is undeniable that the second half of the nineteenth century saw a greater number of such foundations than did many of the centuries preceding it. The cause of this was partly the reaction of religious feelings after the Revolution and partly the necessity for such works resulting from the destruction, by disamortization, of those which had previously existed. Under the administration of Señor La Cierva as Director-General, there was published in folio (cii–704 pages) "Memoranda for the Study and Organization of Benevolent and Provident Institutions" (Apuntes para el estudio . . . de las Instituciones de Beneficencia) from which the following data are extracted. The benevolent institutions may be classified as general, provincial, municipal, and private. The general institutions, supported by the State, are nine in number, and may be divided into hospitals, asylums, and schools, according to the objects for which they exist. The hospitals are those of La Princesa, with 300 beds, for acute cases in medicine and surgery; the Ophthalmic Institute, with 100 beds;

THE CHURCH OF THE KNIGHTS OF CALATRAVA, MADRID

the insane asylum of Santa Isabel, at Leganés, with 130 beds for poor patients, 30 beds for paying patients of the first, and 40 for those of the second, class. The objects of these last two establishments are indicated by their names. The asylums are the Hospitals of Jesús Nazareno, the Carmen, the King's Hospital at Toledo, and that for superannuated workingmen, the first and second of these being for men and for women respectively, each with 250 beds; the third, mixed, 60 beds for either sex; the last, for men only, to the number of 80. The schools for the blind are: Santa Catalina (29 pupils); La Union, for 106 orphan girls.

The number of persons benefited in all these establishments was 30,606 during the five years from 1904 to 1908. Moreover, in the single year 1908, the public consulting-room of the Princesa Hospital prescribed for more than 8000 persons; that of the Ophthalmic Institute for more than 4000. The appropriation for charitable purposes in the general estimate of the Government amounted to 2,665,775 pesetas ($499,208), not including subventions to certain private establishments. The annual expenditure on the general establishments is 774,818 pesetas.

The charitable institutions, municipal and provincial, may be classified as follows:

Spain. Without counting the important donations with which it has contributed to more efficient service in the department of public charities, the alms given directly for the maintenance of many charitable associations, to the needy on the public highways, or privately to succour those who are ashamed to beg, it may be said that the capital expended by private charity in Spain for the relief of the physically and morally indigent is enormous. Indeed, were it not for the rapacity of many, the egoism of some, and the carelessness of all, this alone would suffice to counteract in great part the ravages of extreme poverty and to solve many of the problems of pauperism. The number of charitable institutions founded and sustained in Spain by private means is 9107. Large as this number is, it represents less than one-half the number of those that have existed and those that still exist without being known. Their capital amounts to 400,652,370.36 pesetas ($80,130,000), yielding an income of 10,405,872.18 pesetas ($2,081,000). Of this capital 152,417,413 pesetas ($30,480,000) are invested in registered bonds; 80,095,269 ($16,019,000) in certificates payable to bearer; 28,048,888 ($5,609,000) in city property; 31,951,114 ($6,390,000) in mortgages and country property; 17,753,815 ($3,550,000)

	Number.	Cases.	Beds.	Expenses.	Alms Distributed.
Hospitals { Municipal	51	3,520,975	11,558	5,927,052	22,355.07
Hospitals { Provincial	339	4,342,354	18,263	7,243,964	155,370.56
Asylums	70	3,740,431	14,322	3,113,476	296,360.00
Insane Asylums	19	1,427,349	4,236	1,133,232	
Leper Hospitals	7	10,650	104		
Homes for the Aged	8	78,485	354	24,603	13,045.00
Poor Houses	34	3,351,662	9,944	3,508,893	82,710.00
Establishments of various kinds	53	3,056,709	11,052	5,031,436	88,979.00

The figures in the fourth and fifth columns of the above table represent Spanish pesetas. The peseta is approximately equivalent to 19 cents United States currency.

Besides these charitable institutions, the dispensaries, consulting stations and clinics, noted in the "Memoranda" above referred to as a single group, must be taken into consideration. They are 113 in number and exist in all the provinces except Cáceres, Cuenca, Gerona, Guadalajara, Huesca, Lérida, Logroño, Lugo, Orense, and Toledo. Through these institutions 1,261,361 persons have received assistance, 420,397 medical prescriptions have been given, 45,893 food rations, and 4762 articles of clothing distributed, 10,565 allowances provided for nursing mothers, amounting to 37,829 pesetas ($7,500), and 608,686 quarts of milk distributed. In the statistics of provincial and municipal charities may also be included gratuitous medical attendance and attention to sanitary precautions. The first is supplied by 7769 physicians who visit 813,815 families, approximately 3,257,260 individuals, that is to say that each physician has 419 persons under his care; the second is carried on by means of establishments in 23 of the provinces. The expenditure of the provinces on charities amounts to 26,436,273 pesetas (about $5,270,000), 44.72% of their budget; and of the municipalities, 18,206,329 pesetas ($3,600,000), 6.23% of their budget. The average for each individual is 2.26 pesetas (about 42⅔ cents). The provincial and municipal revenues for charitable purposes are respectively 5,961,794 pesetas ($1,190,000), and 2,387,347 pesetas ($470,000), a total of 8,349,141 ($1,660,000), a rate of 0.44 pesetas (about 8¼ cents) per capita. These totals do not include Navarre and the Basque provinces.

In striking contrast with the insufficiency and scarcity of funds and resources which characterizes the official charities, is the enormous amount expended and the variety of institutions founded by private munificence in the endeavour to meet this need in

in loans; and 27,694,432 ($5,538,000) in shares of the Bank of Spain. All this capital, however, does not produce the results intended by the donors. In Señor La Cierva's "Memoranda" the number of the institutions which are inoperative, with their properties, are summarized under one heading (No. 4). Fortunately they are not many—4631—with a capital of 6,862,380 pesetas ($1,372,000) and an income of 378,832 pesetas ($75,700).

It is to be noted, also, that the capital for charitable purposes increases continually and in no insignificant proportion. The reports of the registrars and notaries, and the data published by the "Dirección General de lo Contencioso", show that the acquisitions to charitable institutions, official and private, from 1899 to 1908 have netted 161,330,354.38 pesetas ($32,266,000) for the State, from taxes on inheritances and transfers of real estate, which gives a total annual average of 17,925,596.04 pesetas ($3,585,000), an annual average of .96 pesetas (nearly 18 cents) for each inhabitant. Chronologically the charitable foundations may be classified as follows:

FOUNDATIONS.	CENTURY.					
	XV	XVI	XVII	XVIII	XIX	XX
Religious	5	4	5	4	2	2
For the Poor	4	5	4	5	5	6
For the Sick	6	3	2	2	4	4
Economic and Social		1	1	1	3	3
Educational	2	2	3	6	6	5
For dowries and pensions	3	6	6	3	1	1

(The figures in this table are symbolical, representing only the proportionate numbers of the respective classes.)

THE ALCALÁ GATE, MADRID FRANCESCO SABATINI, 1778   SPAIN   CHURCH OF S. PEDRO, AVILA, 1100 VIEW OF THE EASTERN
THE HUELGAS CONVENT, BURGOS   END CONVENT OF S. MARCOS, LEON, 1513-43

From the foregoing table the change in the nature of the charitable works may be noted according to the various epochs. Those of a distinctly pious nature reached the maximum point from the fifteenth to the eighteenth centuries and decreased rapidly in the following centuries; with those dealing with social-economic problems exactly the contrary was the case. This is a natural consequence of the politico-social character of the respective periods. Similar is the development of the foundations for the benefit of women and similar causes serve to explain it. On the other hand, charities having for their object the relief of the sick and poor are not subject to decided variations, doubtless because this special form of need is constant. Grouped according to their objects, the foundations established down to the present are as follows:

	Active.	Inoperative.
For the Poor	797	716
For the Sick	696	714
Social and economic	120	55
Educational	757	549
Dowries and pensions	1153	1059
Religious	592	309

Ninety-five per cent of the beneficent foundations in Spain have had their mainspring in charity, have been sustained by Christian sentiments, and have suffered from the animosity of Radicals of all stamps. The four hundred and forty-two official charitable institutions (provincial or municipal) are attended by religious communities or by associations of women. In one hundred and eleven of these institutions these services are rendered gratuitously; and in two hundred and eighty-eight they receive a peseta (about 19 cents) daily for food and ten pesetas a month for clothing. All the private institutions are attended by religious communities and many of them supported by them as well. The organizations through which charities are operated are a Protectorate and Provincial and Municipal Committees. To the Protectorate, directed by the minister of the Interior and the president of the Council, pertain the functions of classifying, creating, enlarging, or modifying the various charitable institutions, the distribution of surplus funds, the authorization of representatives of the institutions to have recourse to courts of justice and to sell property, the appointment and suspension, dissolution and reorganization of committees (*juntas*), authorization of transfers of scrip in the public debt, approval of statements and accounts, etc. The *juntas*, as subordinate organs, have only to co-operate with the protectorate, acting as agents and distributors of the property of the various institutions.

Radical and sweeping reforms were introduced and carried through by Señor La Cierva. He began by reorganizing the protectorate, giving it a more numerous and better qualified personnel, creating the "Junta Superior de Beneficencia" to assist the Protectorate, and constituting a special bureau for the management of expenditures, liquidations, and savings effected by it in favour of the charitable institutions. Another measure was the formation of archives, provincial and municipal, with corresponding indexes, giving a great deal of correct, though incomplete, statistics, to serve as a basis for the knowledge of the work done in behalf of charity, the number, capital, and patronage of the various charitable institutions. In this way the Protectorate is ably assisted in the performance of its important duties. Further measures were also prescribed which completed the reform.

Religion, Morality, Customs.—The greatest diversity in all respects exists in Spain between the inhabitants of the various regions; but certain zones may be marked off in which some characteristics in common may be observed. Some similarity may be noted between the regions which were longest under the sway of Arab influences—**Valencia, Murcia, and Andalusia**—and also between those which in more recent times have come more directly in contact with foreigners, especially the maritime regions of Galicia and Andalusia, and the most populous centres of commerce.

The Spanish people are as a rule religious, and naturally inclined to the practices of Catholic worship. In their popular festivals secular diversions hold an equal place with religious observances. The morning is devoted to magnificent church functions, and the afternoon to balls, bull-fights, and other amusements, which are carried on into the night. A great variety may be noted in the character of the popular diversions in the different sections, while the religious features are uniform and universal. In Andalusia and Murcia the bull-fight still holds first place; in Valencia the enthusiasm for it is not so great, and still less in Catalonia, Aragon, and other regions. In the Basque provinces the favourite sports are *pelota, barra*, and others. Catalonia is much addicted to dancing, and its popular dances are very various; here the ancient and extremely artificial dance of the *Sardanas*, in which a great number of persons take part, dancing in the form of a great circle, is still the fashion. The name is connected with that of *Sardos* or *Cerdanes* of Sardinia. In Aragon the *jota*, where the partners, man and woman, dance facing each other, but without taking hands, is still popular. In Andalusia and other provinces they have similar dances where the partners do not take hands. But as a rule more modern dances—the waltz, etc.—are more common. There are many regions, however, where the people scarcely dance at all.

There is also great difference in the popular songs of various sections. In the sections where Arabic influences have prevailed, singing is very general, but without chorus, sometimes accompanied by the castanets, sometimes by the guitar. Another instrument very much used is the *gaita* (bagpipe), a goatskin bag filled with air by means of which a kind of pipe is made to produce a continuous, monotonous sound. The inhabitants of the Basque provinces are noted for their good ear and the tunefulness of their songs, and of all the Spanish peoples they practice choral singing most. In Andalusia the *seguidillas*, *malagueñas*, etc. are very popular, some of them, as the *saetas* of Seville, being sung in religious processions. Religious feasts are celebrated with long church functions, solemn Mass, music, and sermons, besides processions and pilgrimages. There are processions which have become widely celebrated, to which the people of all the surrounding district flock, such as the festivities of Holy Week at Seville and of Our Lady of the Pillar in Saragossa. The most popular devotion of the Spaniards is to the Blessed Virgin, the Mother of God, particularly under her titles of the Immaculate Conception, of the Seven Dolours, of Mount Carmel, and of the Rosary. Innumerable Spanish women bear the name of Mary to which is added some distinguishing title, *de la Concepción, del Rosario, del Carmen, de los Dolores*. Commonly, however, they are addressed only by the particular invocation, hence the Carmens, Dolores, Rosarios, Conchas (Concepción), Mercedes, etc. There is scarcely a town which does not possess a chapel or sanctuary dedicated to the Blessed Virgin, to which pilgrimages are made once or more frequently during the year. Many of these images are considered miraculous and are the centres of poetic legends.

The sacraments are much frequented in Spain, especially in the more cultured sections—Catalonia, Valencia, Navarre, the Basque provinces, Old Castile, so that the Decree of Pius X with regard to daily communion was well received and the practice taken up. All kinds of pious congregations and confraternities, both ancient and modern,—such as those of Mount Carmel, the Rosary, the Third Orders, especially that of St. Francis—are very widely spread in Spain. Certain idiosyncrasies noticeable in the character of the people in some sections may easily be traced to the influence exercised by these pious practices. Nevertheless, impiety, incredulity, and indifferentism are making appreciable progress, mainly owing to the effects of pernicious journals, which are published and circulated with incredible freedom. It is difficult to determine to just what degree this propaganda has altered the traditional character of the Spanish people, and the Catholics of Spain seem not to agree in estimating the extent to which this damage has extended, some believing that it is deep and irremediable, others that it is superficial and could easily be arrested by repressive measures enacted against the agents of public immorality.

BURKE, *A History of Spain from the Earliest Times to the Death of Ferdinand the Catholic* (London, 1895); WATTS, *The Christian Recovery of Spain, 711–1492* (New York, 1894); WARD, *The Truth about Spain* (London, 1911); HERBERT, *Impressions of Spain* (New York, 1869); BOISSEL, *La question religieuse en Espagne* in *Etudes*, III (Paris, 1907), 51–57; O'REILLY, *Heroic Spain* (New York, 1910); *The Reaction in Spain* in *Dublin Rev.*, CXLII (London, 1907), 272–84; SHIPMAN, *Spain of To-Day* in *The Catholic World* (Sept., 1910), 801–16; BIDWELL, *Spain and the Church* in *Dublin Rev.*, CXLVII (1910), 376–96; BELLOC, *The International* in *Dublin Rev.*, CXLVI (1910); *Reseña Geográfica y Estadística de España, por la Dirección General del Instituto Geográfico y Estadístico* (Madrid, 1888); VILANOVA Y PIERA AND DE LA RADA Y DELGADO, *Geología y Protohistoria Ibéricas* (Madrid, 1890); LAFUENTE, *Hist. Gen. de Esp.* (Madrid, 1861); PEREZ BELLOSO, *Anuario Ecl. de Esp.* (Madrid, 1904); INSTITUTO GEOGRÁFICO Y ESTADISTICO, *Censo de Población de Esp.* (Madrid, 1907); IDEM, *Censo Escolar de Esp.* (Madrid, 1904); GEBHARDT, *Hist. Gen. de Esp.* (Barcelona, s. d.); REAL ACAD. DE LA HISTORIA, *Hist. Gen. de Esp.* (Madrid, 1890); MARIANA, *Hist. Gen. de Esp.* (Valencia, 1794); DE LA FUENTE, *Hist. Ecl. de Esp.* (Madrid, 1873); MENÉNDEZ Y PELAYO, *Historia de los Heterodoxos Españoles* (Madrid, 1881).

RAMÓN RUIZ AMADO.

SPANISH LANGUAGE AND LITERATURE.—Spanish, a Romance language, that is, one of the modern spoken forms of Latin, is the speech of the larger part of the Iberian or most westerly peninsula of Europe. It belongs to the more central part of the region: Portuguese is spoken in the western part, Basque in the Pyrenees district and adjacent territory, and Catalan in the east. By colonial operations Spanish has been carried to the Western Hemisphere, and over 40,000,000 of persons use it in South America (where Brazil and the Guianas are the most important tracts escaping its sway), in Central America, Mexico, Cuba, Porto Rico, and sporadically in southern parts of the United States, such as Texas, California, New Mexico, and places near by. As the official language it has long prevailed in the Philippines, although it has been far from supplanting the native dialects, for the reason that the Catholic missionaries, to whom the civilization of the islands is due, set themselves the task of learning the native Oriental dialects, rather than the easier one of teaching the inhabitants their own Spanish idiom. In the earliest period of Spanish geographical exploration the language was carried to the Canaries. The expulsion, from 1492 on, of the Spanish-speaking Arabs and Jews has led to the extension of Spanish dialects to various parts of Northern Africa, to Turkey, and to other places. On the whole, no fewer than 60,000,000 of persons use Spanish as their native language in widely separated parts of the universe. In the New World the Indian languages have reacted somewhat upon the Spanish vocabulary.

As a medium of literary expression Spanish asserted itself first in the twelfth century: it had been six or seven centuries in the process of evolution out of Latin. Now, while we properly call it a modern spoken form of Latin, we must recognize the fact that it does not represent the highly-refined language of such classic Latin writers as Vergil or Cicero. Quite on the contrary, it is the natural development of the common, every-day Latin of the masses in Italy and, in particular, of the speech used by the Latin soldiers and colonists who, as a result of the Roman conquest, settled in a part of the Iberian Peninsula. This Latin, generally called Vulgar Latin (and sometimes termed, less accurately, Low Latin), is no less respectable in point of antiquity than the noble Latin of our classics. Latin authors like Plautus, who introduce popular characters to our notice, make them exhibit in their diction features that the modern Romance languages have perpetuated. It was, of course, the severance of relations with Italy, incident upon the invasion of the barbarian tribes and the fall of imperial Rome, that led to the independent development of the various Romance tongues (Spanish, Portuguese, French, Provençal, etc.) out of Vulgar Latin. The more important elements of differentiation between this latter and classic Latin were these: phonologically, it made principles of vowel quality and syllabic stress superior to the classic distinction of quantitation; morphologically, it tended greatly toward simplification, since it ignored many of the classic flexional variations; syntactically, its analytical methods prevailed over the complicated system of word-order which the elaborate classic inflexions made possible. These differences are all reflected amply in Spanish. There is little need of concerning oneself with the Iberian and Celtic languages current in Spain before the time of the Roman colonization. So entire was the romanization of the land that they vanished wholly, except for some few and very doubtful survivals in the lexicon. The groundwork of the Spanish vocabulary is Vulgar Latin, with certain historical and literary additions from classic Latin, Germanic, Arabic, French, Italian, and, in a slighter degree, from the East and West Indian and other languages.

Vulgar Latin possessed these accented vowels: a (= Lat. $\bar{a}$ and $\breve{a}$); open e (= Lat. $\breve{e}$ and ae); close e (= Lat. $\bar{e}$, $\bar{\imath}$, and oe); close i (= Lat. $\bar{\imath}$); open o (= Lat. $\breve{o}$); close o (= Lat. $\bar{o}$ and $\breve{u}$); the diphthong au; and close u (= Lat. $\bar{u}$). In the transition into Spanish, the open vowels (whether in a free or a protected position) became the diphthongs ie and ue respectively (as in *piedra*, "stone"; *fuerte*, "strong"). An adjoining palatal sound could, however, prevent the diphthongization. In general a and the close vowels maintained themselves in Spanish (*padre*, "father"; *seda*, "silk" from Lat. $s\bar{e}ta$; *lid*, "contest" from Lat. *lis*, *litem*; *hora*, "hour"; *tu*, "thou"): the diphthong au became close o (*aurum*, Span. *oro*): but a neighbouring palatal could close the V. L. a to e (*leche*, "milk" from *lac*, *lacte*), the V. L. close e to i (*cirio*, "wax taper", Lat. $c\bar{e}reum$, whose e in hiatus before the u provided the modifying palatal force), and the V. L. close o to u. For the substantive (noun and adjective) it should be said that a V. L. form corresponding to the Latin accusative case was the basis of the Spanish word.

The history of the V. L. unaccented vowels passing into Spanish varied according to the position of the vowel in the word: in the initial syllable it was more likely to be preserved; in the medial position or at the end (i. e. in the last syllable of the word) it often disappeared or underwent some modification. Distinctions of quality were unimportant for the V. L. unaccented e and o in Spain, so that we are now concerned with but five vowels sounds, a, e, i, o, and u (all of which tended to be close in value) and with the V. L. diphthong au (which became close o in Spanish). At the end of a word these sounds were reduced in Spanish to three, a, e, o, in the really popular pronunciation: unaccented final i and u are found now only in Spanish words of a more or less learned type (as in *crisis* and *tribu*). Here a and o have proved to be quite tenacious; e has disappeared except after certain consonantal sounds which Spanish does not tolerate as final. In the first syllable of a word, unaccented a was treated usually as it was treated under the accent; *e* remained unless closed to *i* by a following palatal or labial element of the accented syllable (as in *simiente*, "seed", Lat. *semens, semĕntem; igual*, "equal", Lat. *æqualis-em*, V. L. *equalem*); *i* generally was preserved, but through dissimilation from accented Lat. *ī* it sometimes became *e* (*vicinus, -um,* Span. *vecino*); *o* remained and V. L. *au* became *o*, but a preceding or following palatal (Lat. *jocari*, V. L. *iocare,* Span. *jugar,* "to play"; *dormiendum,* Span. *durmiendo,* "sleeping") could close the *o* to *u* and by dissimilation from a following accented *o* the unaccented *o* could become *e* (*formōsus-um,* Span. *hermoso,* "beautiful"). In the medial position *a* as a rule remained (*anas, anătem,* Span. *ánade,* "duck"); the other vowels were lost in the popular pronunciation, but in certain cases, of doubtful popular origin, they appear to have been kept in order to present the juxtaposition of consonants not easily pronounced together (*lacrĭma,* Span. *lágrima,* "tear"). In a great variety of cases analogy has interfered with the strictly phonological development of the Latin vowels into Spanish. Later borrowings have conformed either not at all, or only in part, to the laws of popular development.

JUAN BOSCAN

For the greater part the syllable entitled to the stress in Latin has retained it in Spanish: in the verb conjugation, however, no few exceptions are encountered. These are chiefly due to the operation of analogy: hence the dislocation of the accent in the 1st and 2nd persons plural of imperative tenses (*amabāmus*, but Span. *amábamos*, to accord with *amába, amábas, amában*). For obviously convenient purposes the Spanish Academy has devised a system of written accents. Ordinarily the mere aspect of the word is a sufficient index to the place of the syllable stress, since, properly, words ending in a vowel or in *n* or *s* stress the second last syllable, while those ending in a consonant (except *n* or *s*) stress the last syllable: all words violating these two leading principles and all stressing any syllable except the last or second last require the written accent (e. g. *amigo,* "friend"; *salud,* "health"; *aman,* "they love"; *llevas,* "thou bearest": but *bajá,* "bashaw"; *huésped,* "guest"; *nación,* "nation"; *interés,* "interest"; *huérfano,* "orphan").

Excepting such notable cases as *g* (before *e* or *i*) and *c* (before *e* or *i*), the V. L. consonants were practically those of classic Latin. As for the vowels, so for the V. L. consonants, their lot in Spanish being dependent upon their being in the initial, the medial, or the final position. In the initial position they resisted change to a large degree; in the medial position they simplified, if double, and in general they displayed a tendency to adapt themselves to the surrounding vocalic conditions (e. g. single voiceless consonants voiced, certain voiced consonants were absorbed, etc.); in the final position their enunciation sometimes became so weak as to lead to their disappearance. While the modern Spanish vowels have preserved much of the sonority of their Latin originals, the consonants have greatly weakened in the force and precision of their utterance; even refined and careful speakers often fail now to pronounce the intervocalic *d* of the past participial ending in *amado*, etc., which for them become *amao* (or *amau*), etc. At the beginning of the words these V. L. consonants remain: *p, b, t, d, c* (before *a, o, u,* or *r*), *g* (before *a, o, u,* or *r*), *l, r, m, n, s, v* (as in *padre, bebe* from *bĭbit, tanto* from *tantum, dar* from *dare, cadena* from *catena,* etc). While in the Old Spanish period, i. e. down to the fifteenth century, the initial *b* remained the stop or explosive (like English *b*) that it was in Latin, it has become in more recent times a bilabial spirant and as such is now co-equal with the Spanish *v*, which early gained this value both initially and medially. Still, if pronounced with emphasis in the initial position and everywhere after *m* and *n*, the *b* and *v* both have the stop sound. The *d*, too, initially, medially, and at the end of the word, has lost much of its explosive energy and become practically a spirant; in fact in the final position it is seldom heard in popular pronunciation. The initial *r* has a well-rolled trill of the tongue and is equivalent to the intervocalic *rr,* while the final *r* like the medial single *r* or *r* after a consonant (except *n, s, l*) has a feebler sound; even this latter, however, is stronger than the ordinary English *r*. Latin initial *h* was valueless in V. L. and usually was not written in Old Spanish (Lat. *habēre,* O. Sp. *aver,* modern *haber*); its appearance in the modern speech is due to an unnecessary etymological restoration.

A characteristic change in really popular words is that of Latin initial *f* (except before *l, r* and *ue*) into a strong aspirate *h* sound, still incorrectly denoted by *f* in the Old Spanish period. Later on *h* was substituted in writing for this aspirate *f*, and still later, like the original Lat. *h*, this one lost all sound (Lat. *ferrum,* O. Sp. *fierro,* modern *hierro*). There is no real reason for supposing, as has been done, that this transformation of Lat. *f* was the result of an Iberian or Celto-Iberian inability to pronounce initial *f*. Before *r* and *ue* (from Lat. *ó*) and also, in quite a number of cases not well understood before any sound, the *f* remains, as in Latin, a labio-dental spirant (English *f*). When followed by *l* the history of *f* was like that of *c* and *g*: the result for all three was a palatalized *l* which soon began to be represented by *ll* (approximate to *li* in English "filial": *flamma,* Span. *llama, clamare,* Span. *llamar,* etc.). There are cases of the retention of the *f* and *p* (*flor, planta,* etc.). Before *e* or *i*, *g* had already in V. L., like Lat. *j* and like Lat. *d* before an *e* or an *i* in hiatus, the value of *y:* in all cases this *y* disappeared before unaccented *e* and *i* (*germanus-um,* O. Sp. *ermano,* modern *hermano* with meaningless *h*, etc.), before an accented *e* or *i* or the other unaccented or accented vowels the *y* might remain (*gener, generum,* Span. *yerno; jacet;* Span. *yace,* etc.) or become in O. Sp. a *j* (English *j* sound) which in the modern speech has developed into a velar sound (*jam, magis,* Span. *jamás*). Before *e* (Lat. *e, œ, æ*) and *i* the *c* had already begun to assibilate in Latin itself; in O. Sp. it yielded the voiceless dental sibilant

GARCILASO DE LA VEGA

c (pronounced *ts*): in modern Castilian this sound has become the lisped one *th* (as in "thin"), and is written *c* before *e* or *i* (*centum*, Span. *ciento; civitas, civitatem*, Span. *ciudad*). In Andalusia and largely in Colonial Spanish the sound is now that of a voiceless *s*. The Lat. combination *qu* ceased in Spanish to have its *u* pronounced before *e* and *i*, and the spelling with *u* is only conventional (*quem*, Span. *quien*, etc.), before unaccented *a* and *o* the *u* disappeared absolutely (*quattuordecim*, Span. *catorce; quomo[do]*, Span. *como*, treated as unaccented in the sentence); before accented *a* the *u* retains its value as a *w*, and the combination is now written *cu* (*quando*, Span. *cuando*). To every Latin word beginning with *s* + a consonant Spanish has prefixed an *e* (*scribo*, Span. *escribo*).

In the medial (intervocalic) position double *p*, *t*, and *c* (before *a, o, u,*) simplified (*cappa*, Span. *capa*, etc.); but single *p, t,* and *c* voiced to *b, d,* and *g* (*lupa*, Span. *loba*, etc.); and this voicing also occurred before *r* (*capra*, Span. *cabra*, etc.). If *i* or *u* in hiatus (i. e., a semi-consonant) followed the single *p, t, c*, the voicing did not occur (*sapiat*, Span. *sepa; sapui*, O. Sp. *sope*, modern *supe*). Between vowels *b* and *g* have usually been kept, the former as a bilabial spirant: in more popular treatment *d* has disappeared (*sedere*, O. Sp. *seer*, modern *ser*), but there are many instances of its retention (*sudare*, Span. *sudar*, etc.). After Lat. *i* the *v* disappeared (*rivus-um*, Span. *río*), but in most other cases it remained as a bilabial spirant equal in value to originally intervocalic *b* (*novus-um*, Span. *nuevo*). As in the initial position, *g* disappeared before *e* and *i* (*regina*, Span. *réina*) and remained before the other vowels (*negare*, Span. *negar*, etc.). While single *l, n,* and *r* remained unchanged, the double *r* remained as a very strongly-trilled sound (like initial single *r*) and double *n* and *l* ordinarily palatalized to the written *ñ* and *ll* (with sounds approximate to those of *ny* in English "canyon" and *li* in "filial"). In Latin the intervocalic *s* was voiceless (English *s* of "case"); in Spanish it voiced early to the sound of English *z*, but this *z* unvoiced again to the sharply hissing *s* in modern Spanish. If double, the Lat. *ss* continued to be so written in O. Sp., and remains a voiceless single *s* in modern Spanish, which tolerates no double consonantal sounds except in rare cases, those of *cc* and *nn*. Spanish (and already V. L.) developed new sibilant sounds out of intervocalic *t* and *c+y* (i. e. *e* or *i* in "hiatus"). For *ty*, O. Sp. had a voiced *dz* sound denoted by *z* (*ratio, rationem*, Span. *razon*) and for *cy* either that same sound or the corresponding voiceless one of *ts* denoted by O. Sp. *ç* (V. L. *capicia*, O. Sp. *cabeça*) and modern *z* (*cabeza*). The Lat. intervocalic *c* followed by *e* or *i*, likewise produced the voiced *dz* sound, written *z* in O. Sp. and now written *c* or *z* (in the final position) with the lisped sound *th* (*crux, crucem, cruces*, Span. *cruz, cruces*).

There are a great many other medial consonant combinations. Notable are the changes of *ct* to *ch* (pronounced as in English "church"; *nox, noctem*, Span. *noche*), of *l* + consonant to *u* + consonant (*alter*, *alterum*, Span. *otro* though × *autro* × *outro*) or to a palatalization of the consonant (*multum*, Span. *mucho*, with *ch* like that in English "church"), of *ly* to *j* (*cilia*, Span. *ceja*) of *ny* to palatalized *n* (written *ñ*; *cuneus-um*, Span. *cuño* etc.). The variations in the cases of consonant combinations containing *l* have not yet been properly studied. Of the final consonants usual in Latin *s* and *n* remain, the former especially as a sign of the plural of substantives and of verbal inflexion; *t, d,* and *c* were lost (*amat*, Span. *ama; amant, aman; est*, Span. *es; ad*, Span. *a; nec*, Span. *ni*).

It is in its phonological development that Spanish differentiates itself most from the related Romance languages: in its morphological and syntactical development it is more closely akin to them and the problems that arise belong in general to comparative Romance Philology. Therefore much less attention need be devoted to them in an individual account of Spanish. As in general Romance, so in Spanish the Latin declensions are reduced practically to three, corresponding to the Latin first, second, and third; the neuter gender disappears in the noun (the Latin neuters usually figuring in the second declension as Spanish masculines) and remains only in the demonstrative pronoun (*esto, eso, aquello*) and the article (*lo*); for nouns and adjectives the only case and number distinctions left are those corresponding to the Lat. accusative singular and accusative plural, with retentions of the nominative (vocative) and other cases in only learned formations (*Dios* from *Deus*, *Carlos* from *Carolus*) or in petrefactions [as in *jueves*, "Thursday" from *Jovis* (*dies*); *ogaño* "this year" from *hoc anno*, etc.]. The pronoun has preserved more of the Latin cases (*ego*, V. L. × *eo*, Span. *yo;* acc. *me*, Span. *me; mihi*, Span. *mi*, etc.).

The passive and deponent voices of Latin have disappeared and are usually replaced by periphrases (e. g. a reflexive formation *el libro se lee=liber legitur* or by a combination of the verb "to be" or some equivalent auxiliary with the past participle of the main verb). The four regular conjugations of Latin have been reduced to three, which parallel the Lat. first, second, and fourth, and practically to two, since the second and the fourth differ in only four forms. A peculiarity of the language is the appearance of a number of so-called radical-changing verbs, which, regular as to their tense and personal endings, show a variation between *ie* and *ue* in the accented root syllable and *e* (upon occasion *i*) and *o* (upon occasion *u*) in that same syllable unaccented (*siento, sentir, sintamos*, etc.). There are many irregular (strong) verbs. Of the indicative tenses, the present

MIGUEL DE CERVANTES SAAVEDRA

abides; while the future has been supplanted by a periphrasis consisting of the infinitive of the main verb + the present (or endings of the present) indicative of *haber* Lat. *habere* (*amar* + *he*, "to love" + "I have", whence *amaré*, "I shall love"). In like manner a conditional (past future) has been formed by adding the endings of the imperfect indicative of *haber* to the infinitive of the main verb (*amar* + [*hab*]*ia*, whence *amaría*, "I should love"). The Lat. perfect indicative has become a simple preterite in ordinary use and a new perfect has been produced by combining the present indicative of *habeo* with the past participle of the verb in question (*amé* from *amavi*, "I loved"; *he amado* from *habeo amatum*, "I have loved"). The future perfect has coalesced with the present perfect of the subjunctive to form the future (or hypothetical) subjunctive, which tense, however, is now little used in spoken language.

Of the Latin imperative only the second singular and plural present have remained (*ama*, Lat. *ama*; *amad*, Lat. *amate*), and these are of restricted service: their place is generally taken in polite usage by forms derived from the present subjunctive. To go with these latter there has been devised a new pronoun of ceremonious import, *usted*, *ustedes* (from *vuestra merced*, "Your Grace", etc.), which is frequently abridged to *Vd.*, *Vds.* or *V.,VV*. It may be said once for all that all the perfect tenses of the indicative and subjunctive both are made up of the requisite form of the auxiliary *haber* and the past participle of the principal verb. Of the Latin subjunctive tenses the present remains; the imperfect has vanished wholly; the pluperfect has become an imperfect in force (*amase*, "I should love", from *amavissem, amassem*); the perfect has been spoken of. A second subjunctive imperfect largely interchangeable in use with the other is one derived from the Latin pluperfect indicative (*amara*, "I should love", Lat. *amaveram, amaram*). This still has occasionally its original pluperfect (or even preterite) indicative force. Of the Latin non-finite forms, the infinitive, the gerund (with uninflected present participial use) and the past participle (originally passive, but in Spanish also active) alone survive. In the perfect tenses which it forms the past participle is invariable: when employed adjectively it agrees with the word to which it refers in both gender and number. The Latin present participle (in *ans, antem*, etc.) has become a mere adjective in Spanish.

A further peculiarity of Spanish is its possession of two verbs "to have", *tener* and *haber*, of which the latter can appear only as the auxiliary of perfect tenses or as the impersonal verb (*hay*, "there is", "there are", *había*, "there was", "there were", etc.) and of two verbs "to be", *ser* and *estar*, which are likewise kept apart in their uses (*ser* indicates permanency and *estar* only transiency when they predicate a quality; *estar* alone can be employed where physical situation is concerned; etc.). A striking syntactical fact in Spanish is the employment of the preposition, *á* "to", or "at", before the noun (or any pronoun except the conjunctive personal pronoun) denoting a definite personal object (*veo al hombre*, "I see the man"). The word-order is rather lax as compared with that existing in the sister-languages.

LITERATURE.—As has been stated above, Spanish literature properly so-called began in the twelfth century. Of course Latin documents written in Spain and running through the Middle Ages from the fifth century on show, here and there, words which are obviously no longer Latin and have assumed a Spanish aspect, but these charters, deeds of gift, and like documents have no literary value. None attaches either to the linguistically interesting Old Spanish glosses of the eleventh century, once preserved in the Monastery of Santo Domingo de Silos at Burgos, and now at the British Museum in London. But in the epic "Poema del Cid" and in the dramatic "Auto de los reyes magos" of the twelfth century we find Spanish appropriated to the purposes of real literature. It is not absolutely certain which of these two compositions antedates the other; each is preserved in but a single MS. and in each case the MS. is defective. The little *auto*, or play, of "The Magian Kings" seems to have been based on an earlier liturgical Latin play written in France, and is certainly not the work of an apprentice hand, for in diction and versification it shows no little skill on the part of him who wrote it. In dramatic technic it marks an improvement upon the methods discernible in the group of Franco-Latin plays to which it is related. It deals of course with the visit of the Three Wise Men to the stable of the Child Jesus at Bethlehem, but the MS. breaks off at the point where they quit Herod. Thus in Spain, as in ancient Greece and as in the other lands of Modern Europe, the drama, in its inception, has close affiliations with religious worship. Curiously enough, we have no further absolutely certain records of a written Spanish play until the fifteenth century. We are certain, nevertheless, that plays were constantly acted in Spanish during this long interval, for the law-books speak of the presence of actors on the soil and brand some of them, especially those producing *juegos de escarnio* (a kind of farce), as infamous.

All the evidence tends to place the date of composition of the "Poema del Cid" (also called "Gesta de Myo Cid" or "Cantares de Myo Cid") at about the middle of the twelfth century. The fourteenth-century MS. containing it is in a deplorably garbled condition, having folios missing here and there and showing lines of very uneven length as well as assonating rhymes frequently imperfect. The chances are that it was written at first in regularly framed assonance verses of fourteen to sixteen syllables—each breaking normally into half-lines of seven to eight syllables, such as now form the usual *romance* or ballad line—and that these verses constituted stanzas or *laisses* of irregular length, such as we find in the Old French "Chanson de Roland" and other *chansons de geste*. The hero celebrated in the poem was the doughty warrior Rodrigo (Ruy) Díaz de Bivar, who died in 1099 and whom the Arabs styled *Cidy*—"My Lord". He had been able exiled from his native Castile and, after serving now this and now that Moorish kingling in his wars against his neighbours, Rodrigo had been able to take Valencia from the infidels and establish himself there as an independent ruler. In the 3700 and more lines of the "Poema" although the historical element is large, the figure of the Cid is highly idealized; he is no longer fractious with respect to his monarch, Alfonso of Castile, as history shows him to have been, and when he has achieved independence he still avouches himself an adherent of that monarch. A great deal is made in the "Poema" of certain unhistorical marriages of the Cid's daughters to fictitious Infantes of Carrion, who desert their brides but are later degraded after being defeated in the lists by the Cid's champions. The poem breathes throughout the spirit of war; battle scenes are always described with great zest and the various conquests of the hero in his victorious progress through Moordom are enumerated fully. To the thirteenth century there may be ascribed another epic poem treating of the Cid. This, also preserved in a single late and garbled MS., is called by scholars the "Crónica rimada" or the "Rodrigo". It deals with wholly imaginary exploits of the youthful Cid. Here we find the germs of the story of Rodrigo and Ximena which grew into the plot of Guillén de Castro's Golden-Age play, "Las Mocedades del Cid", and passed thence to Pierre Corneille's famous French tragi-comedy, "Le Cid" (1636). The original metrical and rhyming scheme of the Rodrigo was probably that which we have assumed for the "Poema del Cid".

LUIS DE GRANADA

Another and earlier Castilian hero is the protagonist of a thirteenth-century epic poem, the "Poema de Fernán González", found in a defective fifteenth-century MS. As we have it, this "Poema" seems to be a redaction, made by a monk of the monastery of Arlanza, of an older popular epic. It is in the verse form called *cuaderna vía*, i. e. monorhymed quatrains of Alexandrines, a form much utilized by the didactic writers of the thirteenth century, when the Alexandrine was imported from France. The adventures of the battlesome tenth-century Count Fernán González in conflict with Moor and Christian and especially with the hated suzerain, the King of Leon, are described in detail. The latter part of the poem is missing, but we have the whole of its story narrated in an exceedingly important document, the "Crónica general" (or "Crónica de España") of Alfonso X (thirteenth century).

This ostensibly historical compilation became, in the form given to it by Alfonso and his assistants and in the later redactions made of it, a veritable storehouse of Old Spanish epic poetry. Dealing with historical or legendary figures, the "Crónica" will give what is regarded as the true record of fact in connexion with them and then proceeds to tell what the minstrels (*juglares*) sing about them, thus providing us with the matter of a number of lost poems. The "Crónica" is in prose, but in the portions concerned with the accounts attributed by it to the minstrels it has been discovered that the seeming prose will, in places, readily break up into assonanced verses of the epic type. So, while the "Poema del Cid", the "Rodrigo" and the "Fernán González" are the only monuments of Old Spanish epic verse preserved in compositions of any length, the "Crónica general" has snatches of other epic poems whose plots it has taken over into its prose. Interesting among these is the account which it contains of the fictitious Bernardo del Carpio, whose epic legend would appear to have been a Spanish re-fashioning of the story of the French epic hero, Roland. On this account some scholars have assumed that the Old Spanish epic was modelled from the inception on the French epopee; but it is probable that there were Spanish epics antedating the period of French influence (e. g. the Fernán González). French influence aided doubtless in the artistic development of the later Spanish epic legends. Elements of fact have been discovered in the *Leyenda* or "Legend of the Infantes of Lara", whose tragic deaths, as well as the revenge wrought for them by their Moorish half-brother, are described in the "Crónica general". The brilliant Spanish *savant*, Menéndez Pidal, has succeeded in re-casting in verse form an appreciable part of the "Crónica" narrative. Probably once made the subject of poetic treatment were Roderick the Goth and the foreign hero, Charlemagne, who had had much to do with Spain; the "Crónica" has no little to say of them. Before leaving this matter it is meet to advert to the theory once exploited that the Spanish epic was the outgrowth of of short epico-lyric songs of the type of certain of the extant ballads (*romances*) some of which deal with the heroes celebrated in the epics. But it has been shown that the ballads hardly go back of the fourteenth century and that the oldest among them were derived, in all likelihood, from episodes in the epic poem or were based upon the chronicle accounts.

In the thirteenth century a considerable amount of religious and didactic verse appeared. Now we meet with the first Spanish poet known to us by name, the priest Gonzalo de Bérceo, who was active during the first half of the century. Adopting the *cuaderna vía* as his verse form, he wrote several lives of Saints ("Vida de Sto. Domingo de Silos", "Estoria de S. Millán", etc.), a series of homely but interesting narrations of miracles performed by the Blessed Virgin (Milagros de Nuestra Señora), and other devout documents. In all of these he speaks in plain terms with the express purpose of reaching the common man. Of late there has been ascribed to him, but not with certainty, a lengthy poem in *cuaderna vía*, the "Libro de Alexandre", which brings together many of the ancient and medieval stories about the Macedonian warrior. A number of the writings of this period reflect, more or less faithfully, French or Provençal models. They include the "Libro de Apolonio", which may primarily have been of Byzantine origin, the "Vida de Santa María Egipciaqua" (dealing with the notorious sinner and later holy hermitess, St. Mary of Egypt), the "Book of the Three Kings of the East" (erroneously so called, and better termed the "Legend of the Good Thief": the MS. has no Castilian title), and the "Disputa del Alma y el Cuerpo" (a form of the frequent medieval debates between body and soul). Doubtless also borrowed from Gallic sources is a "Debate del Agua y el Vino", which is combined with a more lyrical composition, the "Razón feita d'Amor".

FERNANDO DE HERRERA

Prose composition on any large scale is posterior to that of verse. Apart from the "Fuero Juzgo" (1241: a Castilian version of the old Gothic laws) and some minor documents, no notable works in prose appeared before the advent of Alfonso X (1220-84), who began to reign in 1252. An unwise ruler, he was a great scholar and patron of scholarship, so much so as to be called *el Sabio* (the Learned) and he made his Court a great centre of scientific and literary activity, gathering about him scholars, Christian, Arabic, and Hebrew, of whom he made use in his vast labours. These he engaged in the compilation of his historical, legal, and astronomical works, toiling with them and taking especial pains to refine the literary forms. We have already spoken somewhat of his "Crónica de España" (more commonly known as the "Crónica general"), in which he sought, using all available earlier historical treatises, to make a record of the history of his own land down to his time. He thus inaugurated a series of Spanish chronicles which were continued uninterruptedly for several centuries after him. Another extensive historical document is the "Grande y general historia", which he seems to have intended to be a summary of the world's history; it remains unedited. In the "Siete partidas", so styled because of the seven sections into which it is divided, he codified all laws previously promulgated in the land, adding thereto philosophical disquisitions on the need of those laws and on multifarious matters of human interest. For astronomy he had a particular affection, as the extant Alphonsine Tables and other works demonstrate. Apparently he indited no verse in Castilian; he has left us some "Cantigas de Sta. Maria", written in Galician-Portuguese, in which at the time other Castilians and Leonese also composed lyric verse.

His example was followed by his son and successor Sancho IV, who had put together the didactic "Castigos de D. Sancho", as a primer of general instruction for his own son. To Sancho's reign (1284-95) or later belongs the "Gran Conquista de Ultramar", which adds to matter derived from William of Tyre's narrative of a crusade fabulous and romanesque elements of possible French and Provençal derivation. This work paved the way for narrative prose fiction in Spanish. In fact there came ere long the first original novel in Spanish, the "Caballero Cifar". Some prose Castilian versions of Oriental aphoristic and like didactic material were followed by the fruitful labours of Alfonso X's nephew, Juan Manuel (1282-1348). In spite of much time spent upon the battle-field or in administrative pursuits, Juan Manuel found the leisure to write or dictate about a dozen different treatises, whose interest is chiefly didactic, e. g. the "Libro de la caza" (on falconry), the "Libro del caballero y del escudero" (a catechism of chivalrous behaviour), etc. Some of these are not now discoverable. His masterpiece is the framework of tales, the "Conde Lucanor" (or "Libro de Patronio"). The stories told here by him are of various provenience, Oriental, and Occidental, and some reflect his own experience. Two of them contain the essentials of the plot of "The Taming of the Shrew". A collection of songs which, like Alfonso, he probably wrote in Galician, has passed from view.

Returning now to follow down the course of Spanish poetry we encounter in the fourteenth century, and in the first half of it, a real poet, Juan Ruiz, archpriest of Hita. He was a bad cleric and his bishop kept him long in prison for his misdeeds. As a poet he was the first to strike in Spanish the true lyrical and subjective note, revealing unblushingly his own inner man in his scabrous "Libro de buen amor", which is in part an account of his lubricous love adventures. He was a man of some reading, as his use of Ovidian or Pseudo-Ovidian matter and of French *fableaux*, *dits*, etc., shows. His rhymes and metres are varied according to his subject-matter and his mood. Rodrigo Yáñez's "Poema de Alfonso Onceno", a sort of chronicle of Alfonso XI's deeds, may be only a version from the Galician. The Rabbi Sem Tob's "Proverbios morales", a collection of rhymed maxims, is not devoid of grace. In the second half of the century there stands forth Pedro López de Ayala, statesman, satirical poet, and historian, who died Grand Chancellor of Castile, after serving four successive monarchs whose exploits he chronicled in his prose "Crónicas de los reyes de Castilla". His poetical work is the "Rimado de palacio", which is chiefly a satirical arraignment of the society of his time, and useful as a picture of living manners of the period. Besides his "Crónicas" he wrote other prose works and made versions of Latin compositions.

The fifteenth century is, throughout its first half, pre-eminently an age of court poetry. At the Court of Juan II of Castile (1419–54) hundreds of poetasters dabbled in verse; a few really gifted spirits succeeded occasionally in writing poetry. There was much debating on love and kindred themes, and, following up Provençal processes, the debating took often the form of versified plea, replication, rejoinder, sur-rejoinder, etc. Along with this arid, provençalizing, love speculation, we find two other factors of importance in the literature of the period: (1) an allegorizing tendency, which continued, generally in a pedestrian manner, the allegorical methods of the Italians Dante, Petrarch, and Boccaccio, and, doubtless, also of the "Roman de la Rose" and similar French works, and (2) a humanistic endeavour, which manifests itself especially by the rendering into Castilian of noted classical documents of Latin antiquity. The occasional pieces of the court poetizers will be found represented fully enough in the collection made by the king's physician, Juan Baena, in his "Cancionero". In general it is safe to say that the countless pallid, amorous effusions of the court poets transfer to the Castilian Court the earlier Galician aping of the conventionalized Provençal manner. And not only did the Castilians, gathered about their king, Juan II, trifle thus with the poetic muse: the Aragonese and the Castilian nobles who followed the Aragonese arms to the domination of Naples and Sicily engaged in the same practice, and their futilities are embalmed in the "Cancionero de Stúñiga", prepared at the Aragonese Court in Naples.

At the opening of the century, one man, Enrique de Villena, related to the royal houses of both Castile and Aragon, calls for particular attention. He did much to propagate the Provençal style of poetry, but at the same time he was a forerunner of the Spanish Humanists, for he made a version of the Æneid, and he declared his love of allegory by writing his "Doce trabajos de Hércules" and his love for the Italians by translating Dante. Francisco Imperial, a scion of a Genoese family settled in Spain, did much to spread the Dantesque evangel. A friend of Villena and, like him, a lover of Latin antiquity—though he read no Latin himself, he was a patron of those who did—and a venerator of the great Italian poets, whom he imitated, was the Marqués de Santillana, Iñigo López de Mendoza (1398–1458). He was the first to write in Spanish sonnets copying the Italian structure: in this respect his example was not followed. Not only did he allegorize in verse less tedious than that of most contemporaries, but he showed an unwonted eclecticism by imitating the popular songs of the mountains and pastoral folk. His interest in the literature of the people is avouched also by a collection of their rhymed proverbs which he made. Not the least admirable of his productions is a little prose letter, "Carta al condestable de Portugal", in which he provided the first account of the history of Spanish literature ever committed to writing. Another luminary of the age was Juan de Mena (1411–56), the royal historiographer, to whom we are indebted especially for the "Laberinto", in which he not only indulged his allegorizing propensities but also makes obvious his devotion to the ancient Spanish Latin poet Lucan. At times Mena soars to real poetic heights.

ALBERTO LISTA Y ARAGON

The inevitableness of death had engaged the attention of the plastic and pictorial artist and the *littérateur* to no slight extent during the later Middle Ages: the French "Danse Macabre" shows what a hold this melancholy idea had taken upon thinking minds. One of the most finished examples of the literary treatment of the subject is the Spanish "Danza de la muerte", which is of the early fifteenth century. It surpasses in poetic vigour the French model which it is said to have followed. A not unworthy historian is Fernán Pérez de Guzmán, author of the "Mar de historias", who evinces no mean power as a portrayer of character in his "Generaciones y semblanzas", in which he describes famous personages of his time. The prose satire in all its virulence is represented by the "Corbacho" of the archpriest of Talavera, Martínez de Toledo (died about 1470), an invective upon womankind. Two noteworthy satires of the second half of the century are the anonymous "Coplas del provincial" and "Coplas de Mingo Revulgo", setting forth administrative vices and the wrongs done to the people at large. The renascence of the Spanish drama is now foreshadowed in some pieces of Gómez Manrique, whose nephew, Jorge Manrique (1440–78), gained enduring fame by his sweet and mournful "Coplas" on the death of his father, which Longfellow has skilfully rendered into English verse. An event of transcendent importance throughout the civilized world was the establishment at this time of the printing-press; it was set up in Spain in 1474.

Of all lands Spain has the richest supply of ballads (*romances*); no fewer than 2000 are printed by Durán in his "Romancero general". We have reason to suppose that they began to be written in the fourteenth century, but the earliest extant seem to date from the fifteenth century. The great majority, however, are of the sixteenth and seventeenth centuries. While the earlier among them are anonymous, the later ones are often by well-known writers and are clearly artificial in character. Towards the end of the century there appeared in print the first great modern novel, the "Amadis de Gaula", which soon begot many other novels of chivalry like unto itself, recounting the exploits of other Amadises, of Palmerins, etc. The vogue of the progeny of the first "Amadis"—which certainly existed in a more primitive form back in the fourteenth century and has been claimed, against the greater likelihood, for Portuguese literature—became a veritable plague, reaching down into the opening of the seventeenth century, when the success of the "Don Quixote" gave it its death stroke. Over against the idealism of the novels of chivalry there stands already, at the close of the fifteenth century, the crass realism of the "Celestina" (or Tragicomedia de Calisto y Melibea), a novel of illicit love to which the author, presumably Fernando de Rojas, gave a somewhat dramatic form. The work influenced later dramatic production and has yielded graces of style. With the "Eglogas" of Juan del Encina (about 1469–1533), the old sacred drama, already timidly attempted by Gómez de Manrique, reappears without showing any clear advance over the ancient "Auto de los reyes magos". Encina also essayed the farce.

Soon after the dawn of the sixteenth century there commences the most glorious period in Spain's political history, that represented by the expansion of her foreign dominion during the reigns of Isabella and Ferdinand, Charles V, and Philip II. Wealth flowed in from the transatlantic colonies and provided the means for developing the arts on a grandiose scale. The literary art keeps pace with the others, and there now ensues what the Spaniards call the *siglo de oro*, the Golden Age of their literature, which extends even through the seventeenth century despite the political, social, and economic decay which that century so obviously shows. A dependence upon Italy and its Renaissance literary methods manifests itself in practically every form of literary composition. Italian verse-forms (the hendecasyllable, the octave, the sonnet, the *canzone*, etc.) are naturalized definitively by Juan Boscán (about 1490–1542) and Garcilaso de la Vega (1503–36), who inaugurate an Italianizing lyric movement, which triumphs over all opposition. After them the great poets use the imported Italian measures no less frequently than the native ones. Contemporary Italianates are the Portuguese Sâ de Miranda, Cetina, Acuña, and the versatile Hurtado de Mendoza; of but little effect was the reactionary movement of Castillejo and Silvestre. What the nascent drama of Spain in the sixteenth century owes to stimulus from the Italian drama has not yet been made out fully. Encina had been in Italy; Torres Naharro (died about 1530) published his "Propaladia", a collection of dramatic pieces, at Naples (then an Aragonese Court), in 1517. With him the punctilio, or point of honour, is already an important dramatic *motif*. In Lope de Rueda (about 1510–65)

MARTINEZ DE LA ROSA

we see a genuinely dramatic spirit; he was an actor, playwright, and theatrical manager and understood fully how to appeal to a popular audience, as he clearly did in his *pasos*, or comic interludes, dealing with popular types. After him the dramatists became legion in number; it would be tedious and futile to enumerate them all; only the more prominent and successful need engage our attention.

Juan de la Cueva (about 1550–1609) brings historical and legendary subjects upon the boards; Cervantes (1547–1616), contrary to the real bent of his genius, seeks dramatic laurels; Lope de Vega (1562–1635), Tirso de Molina (Gabriel Téllez, 1571–1658), Calderón (1600–81), Guillén de Castro (1569–1631), Ruiz de Alarcón (about 1581–1639), Rojas Zorrilla (about 1590–1660), and Moreto (1618–1669) bring imperishable fame to the Spanish theatre and make it one of the most marvellously original and fascinating in the history of the world. Love of the Catholic religion and glorification of its practices, blind loyalty to the monarch and exaltation of the feeling called the point of honour, are among the leading characteristics animating the thousands of plays composed by these and lesser spirits. For the individual merits and defects of the chief writers reference may be had to the separate articles dealing with them. To us not the least attractive category of the plays is that dealing with living manners of the time (*comedias de capa y espada*), in the production of which Lope de Vega was the most successful. The form of the religious play called the *auto sacramental* (Eucharistic play) was carried to the height of its perfection by Calderón. It should be said that this enormous dramatic output is almost invariably in verse, and every single play interweaves in its make-up a considerable number of the possible measures. It was in this century, too, that Francisco de Guzman wrote his "Triunfos morales" and "Flor de sentencias de sabios" (1557).

Of the prose compositions of the age, the novel and tale are the most brilliant. The novels of chivalry continue to be written down to the end of the sixteenth century, but already at the end of the first quarter of that period they encounter a formidable rival in the extremely realistic novel of roguery (*novela picaresca*) or picaroon romance, the first and greatest example of which is the "Lazarillo de Tormes" which some scholars would deny to Hurtado de Mendoza, already mentioned as an Italianate. This record of the knavish deeds and peregrinations of a social outcast is paralleled at about 1602 by the "Guzmán de Alfarache" of Mateo Alemán (about 1548–1609), after which come the account of the female rogue contained in the "Pícara Justina" (1605) of the Toledan physician López de Ubeda, the "Buscón" (also called Pablo, el Gran Tacaño, about 1608) of Quevedo—the second best of its kind— and the "Marcos de Obregón" (1618) of Vicente Espinel. As the novel of roguery continued to be written, the element of adventurous travel became more prominent in it. There were many tale-tellers dealing with a matter-of-fact world never so good as it ought to be: notable among them were Timoneda, whose anecdotes come from Italian models, Salas Barbadillo, Castillo Solórzano, and María de Zayas, all of whom are greatly surpassed by Cervantes in his "Novelas ejemplares," to say naught of the "Don Quixote" (1605-15: see CERVANTES SAAVEDRA). Even more idealistic than the novel of chivalry is the pastoral romance, which, in the wake of the Italian Sannazzaro's "Arcadia" and the Portuguese Ribeiro's imitation of it, makes its first and best appearance in Spanish in the "Diana" (about 1558) of Jorge de Montemayor (or Montemôr, since he was a Portuguese by birth). Two sequels were written, that of Gil Polo being of much merit: in general, however, the pastoral romance was a fashionable pastime and had no popular appeal. Cervantes with his "Galatea" and Lope de Vega with his "Arcadia" are two of the many attempting this ultra-conventionalized literary form. There is one worthy representative of the historical novel, the "Guerras civiles de Granada" of Pérez de Hita.

In philosophical speculation the Spaniards, though active enough, at least in the sixteenth century, have not shown great initiative in dealing with modern problems. Mysticism, nevertheless, has informed some of their best thinking spirits, several of whom used both prose and verse. Noteworthy among them are the illustrious St. Theresa (1515–82), St. John of the Cross (1542–91), Luis de Granada (c. 1504–88), and the noble poet and prose-writer, Luis de León (1527–91). Luis de León was of Salamanca, at whose university he taught: at Seville an excellent poet was Fernando de Herrera (about 1534–97), whose martial odes and sonnets, celebrating Lepanto and Don John of Austria, are illustrative of his muse. The best lyricists of this age, besides León and Herrera, are Francisco de Rioja (1583–1659), Rodrigo Caro (1573–1647), and Francisco de Aldana, called by his contemporaries *el divino*. Several efforts are made now to revive the epic: while Lope de Vega and Barahona de Soto vie with the Italians Ariosto and Tasso to but little purpose, Alonso de Ercilla (1533–94) alone, out of those celebrating recent or current heroic happenings, achieves real success. His "Araucana" turns upon the Spanish campaigns against the Araucanian Indians in South America. Besides the epic poem of Ercilla, there are three more worthy of mention: the "Bernardo" of B. de Balbuena (1568–1627), the "Monserrat" of Cristóbal de Virués (1548–1616), and the "Cristiada" of Diego de Hojeda (d. 1611), who won by his work the title of "The Spanish Klopstock". Pedro de la Cerda y Granada and Francisco de Enciso Monzón are also authors of two epic poems on the life of Christ. The series of chronicles inaugurated back in the thirteenth century continues into the Golden Age, and in the work of the Jesuit Juan de Mariana (1537–1623) the dignity of real history-writing is achieved. He wrote his "Historia de España" in Latin and then translated it into excellent Spanish. We find also excellent historians of this period in Alonso de Ovalle (1610–88), Martin de Roa (1561–1637), Luis de Guzman (1543–1605), José de Acosta (1539–1600), whose "Historia natural y moral de las Indias" has been highly praised by A. Humbolt; Antonio de Solis (1610–88), author of the famous "Historia de Nueva España", Gonzalo de Illescas (d. 1569), who wrote a "Historia Pontifical", and Pedro de Rivadeneira (1526–1611), whose "Historia del Cisma de Inglaterra" was composed from most authentic documents. Care must be taken not to regard as real history the "Marco Aurelio con el reloj de príncipes" (1529) and the "Década de los Césares" (1539) of the Bishop Antonio de Guevara (died 1545). His "Epístolas familiares" (1539) and the "Marco Aurelio" (Dial of Princes) passed through a French version into English: without good reason the rise of euphuism in England has been attributed to imitation of the style of these works of Guevara.

Vices of style were, however, to become all too prominent and general in Spanish literature of the seventeenth century and to pervade verse and prose alike. The poet Góngora (1561–1627) gave currency to the literary excesses of style (bombast, obscurity, exuberance of tropes and metaphors, etc.) which is called Culteranism, or, after him, Gongorism, and they spread to all forms of composition. To Gongorism above all other things may be ascribed the wretched decay in letters which ensued upon the end of the seventeenth century: this canker-worm ate into the heart of literature and brought about its corruption. While even the great Lope de Vega and Cervantes (the many works of both of these are treated *in extenso* in the articles dealing with them), the masters of the whole age, yielded to the blandishments of Gongorism, the sturdy spirit Quevedo fought it strenuously. His satires (Sueños, 1627) and other writings, his political treatises ("Política de Dios", 1626, "Marco Bruto", 1644; etc.), and his multitudinous brief compositions in verse are fairly free from the Culteranistic taint. On the other hand he practised conceptism, another regrettable excess resulting from overmuch playing with concepts or philosophical ideas. A regular code of the principles of conceptism was prepared by the Jesuit Gracián (1601-58) in his "Agudeza y arte de ingenio" (1648); other notable writings of his are the "Héroe" and the "Criticón". As has been intimated, Spanish literature, infected with Gongorism, fell to a very low level at the end of the Golden Age.

Early in this period the Argensola brothers, Bartolomé Juan and Lupercio, flourished. The latter (d. 1613) produced three tragedies ("Isabela", "Filis", and "Alejandra") which Cervantes makes one of his characters in "Don Quijote" commend highly; Bartolomé Juan, a priest (d. 1631), is best known by his "Historia de la conquista de las Islas Molucas" and other works of contemporary history. Jerónimo Zurita y Castro (1512-80), called "the Tacitus of Spain", spent thirty years in preparing his "Anales". During the fifteenth century, too, the religious orders in Spain produced a vast amount of devotional and ecclesiological writing which deserves, in many cases, to rank with the most enduring monuments of Spanish Literature. The list of religious writers includes José de Sigüenza, a Hieronymite (1540-1606), of whose history of his own order a French critic said it made him regret that Sigüenza had not undertaken to write the history of Spain. The Dominican Alonso de Cabrera (1545-95) is considered to be the greatest preacher of Spain, which fact is tested by his numerous sermons and by his famous funeral oration on Philip II. In oratory B. Juan de Avila (1502-69), the Augustinian Juan Marquez (1564-1621), the Franciscan Gabriel de Toro, the Jesuit Florencia and the Archbishop of Valencia Sto. Tomás de Villanueva rank very high. Also worthy of mention is the Jesuit Juan Pineda (1557-1637), who has left, besides a panegyric on Doña Luisa de Caravajal, two masterly discourses on the Immaculate Conception. Another Juan Pineda, a Friar Minor, was the author of copious commentaries and of such Spanish devotional works as "Agricultura Christiana" (1589). Two other Jesuits, Luis de la Palma and Juan Eusebio de Nieremberg, have left works in Spanish which are still esteemed as gems of spiritual literature: the former, "Historia de la Sagrada Pasión" (1624); the latter, among others, the famous treatise "De la diferencia entre lo temporal y lo eterno" (1640). The "Ejercicio de perfección y virtudes cristianas" of Alonso Rodriguez (1526-1616) and the "Conquista del reino de Dios" of Fray Juan de los Angeles (d. 1595) rank among the most classic works of Spanish literature. The writings of Ven. Luis de la Puente (1554-1624), (see Lapuente, Luis de), of Malón de Chaide (1530-1592), Domingo García, and many other ascetic authors are also of much literary value.

In the first half of the eighteenth century—a period much troubled by the political turmoil resulting upon the establishment of the Bourbons on the throne of Spain—writers still abounded, but not a genius, not even a man of average talent, was to be found among them. The æsthetic sense had been ruined by Gongorism. To reform the taste of both writers and the public was the task which Ignacio de Luzán (1702-54) set himself in his "Poética", published in 1737. Here he argued for order and restraint and, addressing himself especially to dramatic writers, urged the adoption of the laws of French classicism, the three unities, and the rest. The doctrines thus preached by him were taken up by others (Nasarre, Montiano, etc.) and, despite some objection, they eventually prevailed. While they were applied with some felicity in the plays of the elder Moratín (Nicolás Fernández de M., 1737-80) and of Jove Llanos (1744-1811), it was only in the pieces, especially the prose plays, "El café" and "El sí de las niñas" (1806), of the younger Moratín (Leandro Fernández de M., 1760-1828) that their triumph was made absolute, for he really gained popular favour. A refinement of the poetic sense and a decided partiality for classicism is apparent in the lyrics of the members of the Salamancan School, whose head was Meléndez Valdés (1754-1817); they included also Cienfuegos, Diego González, and Iglesias. French influence extends to the two verse fabulists, Iriarte (1750-91) and Samaniego (1745-1801); they were familiar with La Fontaine as well as the Phædrus and the English fabulist Gay. An admirable figure is the Benedictine Feijóo (1726-1829), who, with the essays contained in his "Teatro crítico" and "Cartas eruditas y curiosas", sought to disseminate through Spain a knowledge of the advances made in the natural sciences. The name of Feijóo suggests that of his great contemporary José Rodriguez (1777), a man of great talent and literary skill, and also that of the famous Dominican Francisco Alvarado (1756-1814), commonly called *el filósofo rancio*. The Jesuit Isla (1703-81) attracts notice by the improvement of the pulpit oratory of the time which he brought about through the medium of his satirical novel, the "Fray Gerundio" (1758). Isla made a Spanish version of the picaroon romance, "Gil Blas", of the Frenchman Le Sage. In the writings of the young officer, José de Cadalso (1741-82), there are exhibited the workings of a charming eclectic sense: his "Noches lugubres" were inspired by Young's "Night Thoughts", his "Cartas Marruecas" repeat prettily the scheme of Montesquieu's "Lettres persanes" and Goldsmith's "Citizen of the World". Alone among the dramatists of the latter half of the century Ramón de la Cruz (1731-94) shows a fondness for the older native dramatic tradition, giving new life to the old *paso* (interlude) in his "Sainetes". The last part of the eighteenth century, during which the Jesuits were exiled by Charles III, was a flourishing literary period for them. Among those who deserve mention are: Estéban de Arteaga (1747-99), who, according to Menendez y Pelayo, was the best critic of æsthetics in his time; Juan Andrés (1740-1812), who wrote the first history of universal literature, Lorenzo Hervás y Panduro (1735-1809), founder of modern philological science, Francisco Masden, author of a comprehensive "Historia crítica de España". An excellent poet was Juan Clímaco Salazar (1744-1815), whose "Mardoque" is one of the best Spanish plays of that century. The Augustinian Enrique Florez began to publish in 1747 his monumental historical work entitled "España Sagrada"; in the mean time (1768-1785) the two brothers Rafael and Pedro Rodriguez Mohedano gave to Spain a literary history in ten volumes of the first centuries of her Roman civilization. Many other capable men devoted their labours to historical research, such as Andrés Burriel, Perez Bayer, Sarmiento, Rafael Floranes, and Antonio Capmany (1742-1813).

In the early years of the nineteenth century French influence remains predominant in the world of letters. Quintana (1772-1857) and the cleric Gallego (1777-1853), even in the very heroic odes in which they voice the Spanish patriotic protest against the invasion of the Napoleonic power, remain true to French classicist principles. In his various compositions Quintana is essentially a Rationalist of the type of the French encyclopedist of the eighteenth century. A growing tendency to break through the shackles of French classicism is manifest already in the literary endeavours of the men who formed what is usually called the School

PORTUGAL
ATLANTIC OCEAN
BAY OF BISCAY
MEDITERRANEAN SEA
AZORES ISLANDS
(PORTUGUESE)
English Statute Miles
Longitude West from Greenwich
Lisbon
Oporto
Coimbra
Braga
Evora
Beja
Faro
Madrid
Toledo
Salamanca
Valladolid
Zamora
Burgos
Leon
Oviedo
Santiago de Compostela
La Coruña
Lugo
Orense
Badajoz
Caceres
Merida
Seville
Huelva
Cadiz
Cordova
Granada
Malaga
Jaén
Ciudad Real
Avila
Segovia
Palencia
Santander
Gibraltar (British)
Ceuta (Spanish)
MOROCCO
Strait of Gibraltar
Gulf of Cadiz
C. Finisterre
C. St. Vincent
C. Roca
C. Espichel
Angra
Terceira
São Jorge
Fayal
Horta
Graciosa
St. Michaels (São Miguel)
Ponta Delgada
Santa Maria
Flores
Santa Cruz
COPYRIGHT, 1912, BY ROBE
THE MATTHEWS-NORTHRUP WO

5 Diocese of Oviedo
6 Diocese of Tuy

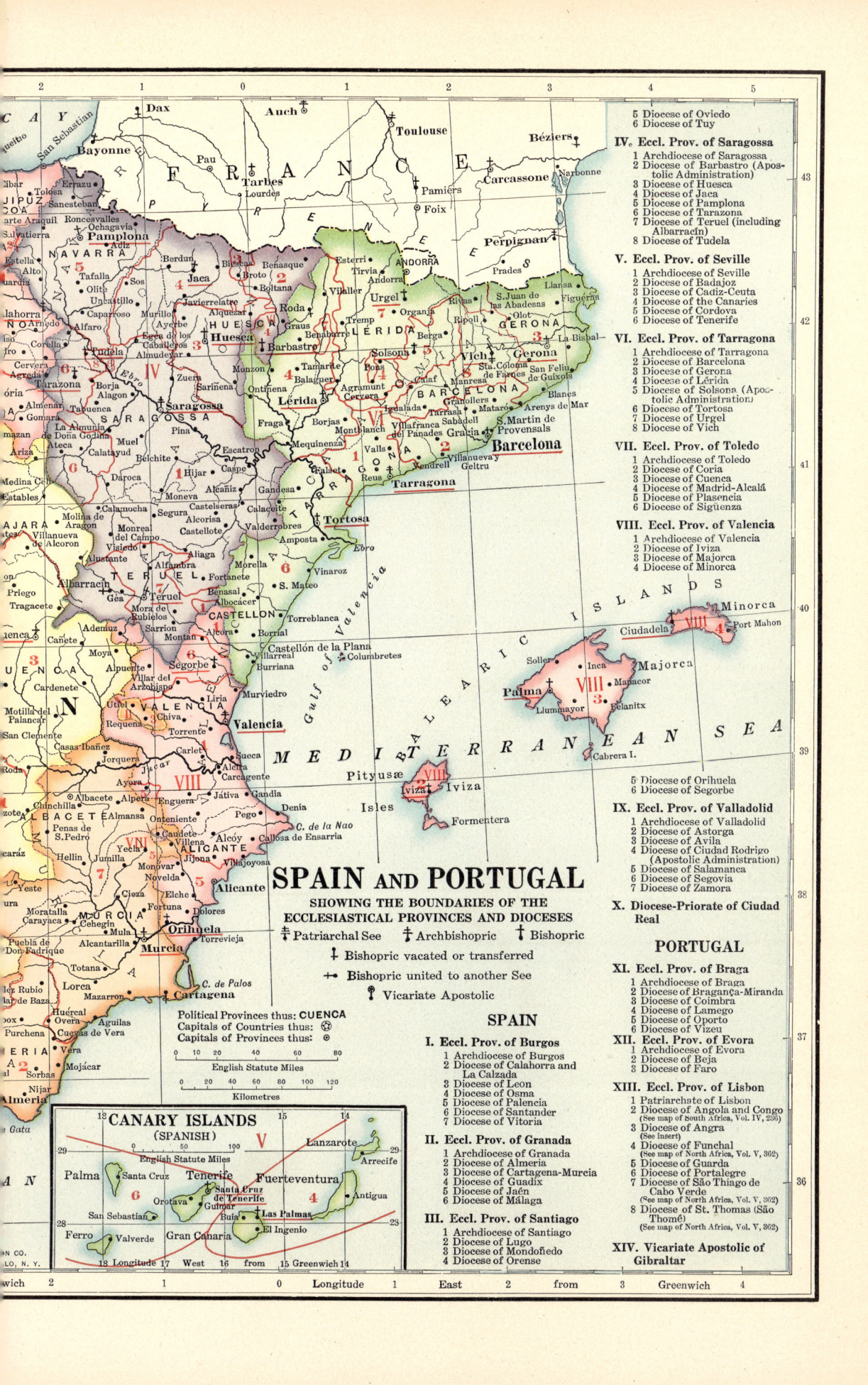

IV. Eccl. Prov. of Saragossa
 1 Archdiocese of Saragossa
 2 Diocese of Barbastro (Apostolic Administration)
 3 Diocese of Huesca
 4 Diocese of Jaca
 5 Diocese of Pamplona
 6 Diocese of Tarazona
 7 Diocese of Teruel (including Albarracin)
 8 Diocese of Tudela

V. Eccl. Prov. of Seville
 1 Archdiocese of Seville
 2 Diocese of Badajoz
 3 Diocese of Cadiz-Ceuta
 4 Diocese of the Canaries
 5 Diocese of Cordova
 6 Diocese of Tenerife

VI. Eccl. Prov. of Tarragona
 1 Archdiocese of Tarragona
 2 Diocese of Barcelona
 3 Diocese of Gerona
 4 Diocese of Lérida
 5 Diocese of Solsona (Apostolic Administration)
 6 Diocese of Tortosa
 7 Diocese of Urgel
 8 Diocese of Vich

VII. Eccl. Prov. of Toledo
 1 Archdiocese of Toledo
 2 Diocese of Coria
 3 Diocese of Cuenca
 4 Diocese of Madrid-Alcalá
 5 Diocese of Plasencia
 6 Diocese of Sigüenza

VIII. Eccl. Prov. of Valencia
 1 Archdiocese of Valencia
 2 Diocese of Iviza
 3 Diocese of Majorca
 4 Diocese of Minorca
 5 Diocese of Orihuela
 6 Diocese of Segorbe

IX. Eccl. Prov. of Valladolid
 1 Archdiocese of Valladolid
 2 Diocese of Astorga
 3 Diocese of Avila
 4 Diocese of Ciudad Rodrigo (Apostolic Administration)
 5 Diocese of Salamanca
 6 Diocese of Segovia
 7 Diocese of Zamora

X. Diocese-Priorate of Ciudad Real

PORTUGAL

XI. Eccl. Prov. of Braga
 1 Archdiocese of Braga
 2 Diocese of Bragança-Miranda
 3 Diocese of Coimbra
 4 Diocese of Lamego
 5 Diocese of Oporto
 6 Diocese of Vizeu

XII. Eccl. Prov. of Evora
 1 Archdiocese of Evora
 2 Diocese of Beja
 3 Diocese of Faro

XIII. Eccl. Prov. of Lisbon
 1 Patriarchate of Lisbon
 2 Diocese of Angola and Congo (See map of South Africa, Vol. IV, 236)
 3 Diocese of Angra (See insert)
 4 Diocese of Funchal (See map of North Africa, Vol. V, 362)
 5 Diocese of Guarda
 6 Diocese of Portalegre
 7 Diocese of São Thiago de Cabo Verde (See map of North Africa, Vol. V, 362)
 8 Diocese of St. Thomas (São Thomé) (See map of North Africa, Vol. V, 362)

XIV. Vicariate Apostolic of Gibraltar

SPAIN AND PORTUGAL
SHOWING THE BOUNDARIES OF THE ECCLESIASTICAL PROVINCES AND DIOCESES

☨ Patriarchal See   ☩ Archbishopric   ✝ Bishopric
⚰ Bishopric vacated or transferred
✠ Bishopric united to another See
♁ Vicariate Apostolic

Political Provinces thus: **CUENCA**
Capitals of Countries thus: ⊛
Capitals of Provinces thus: ⊙

English Statute Miles
Kilometres

CANARY ISLANDS (SPANISH)

SPAIN

I. Eccl. Prov. of Burgos
 1 Archdiocese of Burgos
 2 Diocese of Calahorra and La Calzada
 3 Diocese of Leon
 4 Diocese of Osma
 5 Diocese of Palencia
 6 Diocese of Santander
 7 Diocese of Vitoria

II. Eccl. Prov. of Granada
 1 Archdiocese of Granada
 2 Diocese of Almeria
 3 Diocese of Cartagena-Murcia
 4 Diocese of Guadix
 5 Diocese of Jaén
 6 Diocese of Málaga

III. Eccl. Prov. of Santiago
 1 Archdiocese of Santiago
 2 Diocese of Lugo
 3 Diocese of Mondoñedo
 4 Diocese of Orense

of Seville: the leaders among them were Lista, Arjona, Reinoso, and Blanco (known as Blanco White in England, whither he went later as an apostate priest). Under the despotic rule of Fernando VII many Liberals had fled the land. Going to England and France they had there become acquainted with the Romantic movement already on foot in those regions, and, when the death of the tyrant in 1833 permitted their return, they preached the Romantic evangel to their countrymen, some of whom, even though they had stayed at home, had already learned somewhat of the Romantic method. With his "Conjuración de Venecia" (1834) Martínez de la Rosa (1787–1862) shows Romantic tendencies already appearing upon the boards, although in most of his pieces (Edipo, etc.) he remains a classicist. Manuel Cabanyes (1808–33) and Monroy (1837–61) two of the greatest poets of this period, also remained classicists even amidst the Romantic tendencies. The Romantic triumph was really achieved by the Duque de Rivas (1791–1865), who won the victory all along the line for it, in his play, "Don Álvaro" (1835), his narrative poem, "El moro expósito" (1833) and his lyrical "Faro de Malta". The greatest poets of the Spanish Romantic movement are Espronceda (1809–42), in whom the revolt against classic tradition is complete, and Zorrilla (1817–93). The former is noted for his "Diablo mundo", a treatment of the Faust theme, his "Estudiante de Salamanca", reviving the Don Juan story, and a series of anarchical lyrics: the latter displays the Romanticist's liking for the things of the Middle Ages in his "Leyendas" and has provided one of the most famous and popular of modern Spanish plays in his "Don Juan Tenorio".

Towards the middle of the nineteenth century Romanticism began to wear away and to yield in Spain, as elsewhere, to a new movement of Realism. Even during the Romantic ferment the dramatist Bretón de los Herreros (1796–1873) had remained unaffected and sought fame simply as a painter of manners, while the Cuban playwright and poetess, Gertrudis de Avellaneda (1814–73), oscillated between Classicism and Romanticism. In the plays of Tamayo y Baus (1829-98) and Abelardo López de Ayala (1829–79) Realism and psychology take the upper hand: both assail the Positivism and Materialism of the time. In both the lyrics and the prose of Gustavo Adolfo Bécquer (1837–70) there comes to view the mournful subjectivity of the Teutonic north whence his ancestors had come. The essay, written with a particular attention to the customs and manners of the day, had flourished in the first half and about the middle of the century. Mariano José de Larra (Fígaro, 1809–37), Estébanez Calderón (1799–1867) and Mesonero Romanos (1803–82) with their character sketches and their pictures of daily happenings had paved the way for the novel of manners, which became an actuality in the stories written by Fernán Caballero (pseudonym for Cecilia Böhl de Faber; 1796–1877). Her stories ("La Gaviota"; "Clemencia"; etc.) are, so to speak, moral geographies of Southern Spain. The growth of the novel has been the particular pride of Spanish literature of the nineteenth century: it continues to be a gratifying spectacle still. The novel of manners, started by the authoress Fernán Caballero, has been treated with skill by José María de Pereda (1834–95), Luis Coloma (b. 1851), María Pardo Bazán (born 1851), Antonio de Trueba (1819–89), Pedro Antonio de Alarcón (1833–91), and the humourist Vital Aza (b. 1851). The historical novel has been cultivated with success by F. Navarro Villostada (1818–1895) in his "Amaya" and by Luis Coloma in his "Reina Martir" and "Jeromín". Amós Escalante (1831–1902) has also attempted this branch of fiction. Most of these show more or less of an inclination to indulge in naturalistic methods of the French order without, however, descending to the extremes of the Zolaesque method. While these story-tellers belong to the realistic category, Juan Valera (1824–1905) has been consistently an idealistic. However high his principles, his "Comendador Mendoza" and "Pepita Jiménez" by no means evidence high moral spirit in their author.

Not less than the development of fiction has been the advance of oratory, history, and belles-lettres in modern Spain, and to such an extent that since the Golden Age there has been neither such an abundance nor such excellence. With such men as Donoso y Cortés (1809–53), Aparisi y Guijarro (1815–72), Cándido Nocedal (1821–85), and Ramón Nocedal (1842–1907), political oratory has been raised to a high standard maintained at present by La-Cierva, Vasquez Mella, Maura, and Senante. As sacred orators those deserving mention are: José Vinuesa (1848–1903), Juan María Solá (b. 1853), and the Piarist Calasanz Rabaza. In the field of religious literature lasting fame has been acquired by Donoso Cortés, author of an "Ensayo sobre el Catolicismo, el Liberalismo y el Socialismo", Jaime Balmes (1810–48), whose "Protestantismo comparado con el Catolicismo" possesses all the charm of literary style, Francisco Mateos-Gago (1827–1890), Adolfo de Claravana, Manuel Ortí y Lara and D. F. Sardá y Salvany. Tomás Camara, Antonio Comellas y Cluet and José Mendive, in works as complete and sound in their learning and philosophy as they are cumulative in arguments, have refuted the doctrines of Mr. William Drapper introduced into Spain by the irreligious philosopher Salmerón. Historical and critical research has been carried on by such writers as Antonio Cavaniller (1805–1864), Modesto and Vicente La Fuente, who respectively have written the most comprehensive "Historia de España" and "Historia eclesiástica de España". Foremost in archæology were Aureliano Fernandez Guerra (1816–94), José María Quadrado (1819–96), Pedro de Madrazo (1816–98), Pablo Piferrer (1818–48), who have been succeeded by Eduardo de Hinojosa, Antonio Paz y Melia, Fidel Fita, and many others whose discoveries have brought light to bear on many obscure facts in the history of Spain. Literary research has been extended by the most capable men, such as by Laverde Ruiz (1840–90) to whom a great part of the present literary movement in Spain is to be attributed, J. Amador de los Rios (1818–78), author of a masterly "Historia de la literatura española", also M. Milá y Fontanals, L. A. Cueto, Gonzalez Pedroso, Alfonso Durán, and Adolfo de Castro have won a high name in criticism by their valuable works on literary investigation. Of living critics particular mention should be made of M. Menendez y Pelayo, Manuel Serrano y Sanz, and Ramón Menendez y Pidal, who combine literary graces with the methods of true scientific research. Juan Mir y Noguera (b. 1840) is one of the most prolific and remarkable writers of the present day. During the second half of the nineteenth century, high rank among the lyric poets was attained by Vicente W. Queral (1836–1889), J. Coll y Vetri (d. 1876), Federico Balart (1835–1903), Ram de Viu (d. 1907), José Selgas (1824–82), known as the poet of the flowers as J. M. Gabriel y Galán (1870–1905) is the poet of the fields. Nuñez de Arce (1834–1903) is also a lyricist of inspiration and author of the best historical drama of the period ("El Haz de leña", dealing with the Don Carlos tradition).

The literature of Spain has been greatly enriched by the modern Renaissance of the Catalan literature. The Renaissance period includes Mossen Jacinto Verdaguer (1843–1902), author of "Idilis y cants mistics", "Patria", "Canigo", and "Allantida", and perhaps the greatest poet of modern Spain; Francisco Casas y Amigó, Jaime Colell, Joan Maragall (1860–1912), Rubió y Ors, author of "Lo Gaiter del Llobregat", and M. Costa y Llobera, who has written both in Spanish and Catalan such works as "Poesías líricas" "Horacianes" and "Visions de Palestina". The inspired compositions of Teodoro Llorrente (1836–1911) are written both in Spanish and in his native Valencian dialect.

LANGUAGE.—BAIST, *Die spanische Sprache* in GRÖBER, *Grundriss der romanischen Philologie*, I (2nd ed., Strasburg), 878 sqq.; MENÉNDEZ PIDAL, *Manual elemental de Gramática histórica española* (2nd ed., Madrid, 1905); IDEM, *Gramática del Cid;* ZAUNER, *Altspanisches Elementarbuch* (Heidelberg, 1908); IDEM, *Roman. Sprachwissenschaft* (2nd ed., Leipzig, 1905); HANSSEN, *Spanische Gram.* (Halle, 1910); FORD, *Old Spanish Readings* (Boston, 1911); DIEZ, *Gram. der roman. Sprachen* (3rd ed., 1870–72: cf. the French tr.); MEYER-LUBKE, *Gram. der roman. Sprachen* (Leipzig, 1890—, cf. the French tr.); BELLO-CUERVO, *Gramática de la lengua castellana;* various articles in the *Romania,* the *Zeits. für romanischen Sprachen,* etc., the *Bull. hispanique,* the *Revue hispanique,* the *Cultura moderna, Modern Philology,* the *Modern Language Notes,* etc., the *Grammars* for English-speaking students by RAMSEY; HILLS AND FORD, GARNER, etc., some of which give extensive bibliographies.

LITERATURE.—BAIST, *Die spanische Litt.* in GRÖBER, *Grundriss der roman. Philol.,* II (Strasburg, 1897), i, 383 sqq.; TICKNOR, *Hist. of Span. Literature* (6th ed., Boston, 1888: cf. the German and Spanish tr. for corrections and additions); BEER, *Span. Literaturgesch.* (Leipzig, 1903: in the *Göschen Series*); FITZ-MAURICE-KELLY, *Hist. of Span. Literature* (London, 1898: better are the Spanish and especially the French tr.: the latter has a copious bibliography); MÉRIMÉE, *Précis d'hist. de la litt. espagn.* (Paris, 1908); and the periodicals cited above.

J. D. M. FORD.

SPANISH-AMERICAN LITERATURE, the literature produced by the Spanish-speaking peoples of Mexico, Central America, Cuba and adjacent islands, and of South America with the notable exceptions of Brazil (whose speech is Portuguese) and the Guianas. In the main the methods and the ideals of the Spanish-American writers, whether those of the colonial period or those of the period which has elapsed since the various American states achieved their independence, have not differed radically from those of Spain, the motherland. In spite of the acerbity due to political differences, the Spanish-American colonies and republics have never forgotten that they are of the same race, the same religion, and the same speech as the Spaniards. Quite unlike the settlers of North America, the colonists who came from the Latin countries of Southern Europe made no organized attempt to extirpate the aborigines, and the latter still remain to the extent of millions in number. Some of the aboriginal races still maintain their languages, more or less interlarded with Spanish words, but the intellectual development given to them has been limited. The literature of the indigenous Indian population, mixed or pure, is Spanish no less than that of the descendants of the Spanish colonists. Naturally, in the colonial period, when the work of discovery, exploration, and settlement was being carried on, the literary output was not very great; yet it compares favourably, to say the least, with the output in French and British North America.

In the early times of the colonies no few Spaniards, whom chance or an adventurous spirit brought to the new world, wrote their most notable works there. Among the number is one of considerable worth, Alonso de Ercilla (1533–94), the author of an epic poem, "La Araucana". This deals with the conflicts between the Araucanian Indians and the invading Spaniards, and has the honour of being the first distinguished piece of belles-lettres produced in the New World, antedating by far any comparable works written in North America. Just as men of Spanish birth composed their prose or verse documents in America, so, also, certain American-born colonials passed over to the motherland and, writing and publishing there, added lustre to the history of the literature of the Iberian Peninsula. A good example is Juan Ruiz de Alarcón, one of the most admired of Spanish dramatists of the *siglo de oro,* whose play, "La verdad sospechosa", furnished Corneille with the inspiration and the material for his "Menteur", which in its turn is the cornerstone of the classic comedy of France. The printing press was set up in the new regions in 1539, eighty years before the Pilgrims reached Massachusetts, and about 1550 Charles V signed the decree establishing the University of Mexico. To some among the explorers we are indebted for accounts of their journeys of discovery and conquest. These writings of scientific and historical interest were followed in later generations by others treating mainly of botanical and astronomical subjects, to the study of which the impetus was given by the labours, on the soil, of noted foreigners such as the Spanish botanist José Celestino Mutis (1732–1808), the Frenchmen La Condamine, de Jussieu etc., and, of course, the great German Alexander Humboldt.

As might be expected, Gongorism, the plague of the literature of the motherland, infected the compositions of the seventeenth and the early eighteenth centuries in America. That neo-Classicism, which Luzan and his followers established in Spain, was echoed by this or that poet of the Western world. In the revolutionary period patriotic verse flourished, being governed chiefly by the models provided by the Spaniards Quintana and Gallego, who, with their heroic odes, had voiced the peninsula protests against the Napoleonic invasion. In terms hardly less passionate than theirs the insurgent Spanish colonists celebrated their struggle against the domination from over the sea. The romantic movement, following in the wake of neo-Classicism, had owed its great success in European lands to its evocation of traditions of the medieval past. Naturally, none such existed for the colonists of the newly-found lands, and it is rather with respect to matters of external form than those of substance that romanticism found a reflex in the Spanish-American literature. In general, it may be said that, of the various genres, it is the lyric that had received the greatest development in the Spanish-American regions. The novel has been written with more or less success by an occasional gifted spirit; the drama has not fared equally well. For a more detailed consideration of the subject with which we are concerned it seems best to deal with it according to the geographical divisions marked by the existing states.

Mexico.—This was formerly the Viceroyalty of New Spain. It was the colony most favoured by the Spanish administration and in it culture struck its deepest roots. Here was set up the first printing press, and here was founded, as has been said, the first university, which, authorized by the Emperor Charles V, began its useful career in 1553. The first book was sent from the press in 1540; during the sixteenth century over a hundred works were published in Mexico. A number of Andalusian poets visited Mexico during the sixteenth and seventeenth centuries and influenced its literary productions. Among them were Diego Mejía (sixteenth century), who, shipwrecked on the coast of San Salvador, made there his Castilian version of the elegies of Ovid; Gutierre de Cetina (1520–60); Mateo Alemán, the well-known author of the picaroon novel, "Guzmán de Alfarache", who published in Mexico, in 1609, his "Ortografía castellana"; and possibly Juan de la Cueva, the first thorough-going dramatist, actor, and stage manager of the Spanish-speaking world. At Mexico City there was promoted in 1583 a poetical tournament (*certamen poético*) of the kind so much favoured in Latin Europe; about three hundred persons presented their verse compositions in this competition. Cervantes, in the "Canto de Caliope" printed with his "Galatea" in 1584, celebrates the Peruvian poet Diego Martínez de Ribera in equal terms with those in which he praises the Mexican Francisco de Terrazas, a contemporary of whom he says "tiene el nombre acá y allá tan conocido". Various occasional lyrics and an unfinished epic, "Nuevo Mundo y Conquista", constitute the known work of Terrazas. The

"Peregrino Indiano" of Antonio Saavedra Guzmán, printed at Madrid in 1599, gives in its twenty cantos a very pedestrian account of the conquest of the region. Apparently the earliest specimens of the drama actually written in Mexico are those contained in the "Coloquios espirituales y Poesías sagradas" of Hernán González de Eslava, published in 1610, years after the death of the author, who may have been an Andalusian by birth. His plays are little religious pieces of the category of the *auto* and seem to have been written between 1567 and 1600. It may be remarked that from the very beginning of the Spanish rule it had been the custom to perform the little religious pieces called *autos* (two of the *autos* of Lope de Vega had been translated into the Indian dialect called Nahuatl), and the Jesuits, who constantly fostered scenic performances in connexion with the work of higher education administered by them, did their best to develop an interest in the drama. Certainly a Spaniard by birth, but trained in Mexico and raised to the episcopacy as Bishop of Porto Rico, Bernardo de Balbuena (1568–1627) exhibits in his verse a love for both Spain and his adopted land, mingling therewith many reminiscences of his reading of classic poetry; he celebrates especially the beauty of external nature in his little poem "La Grandeza Mexicana" (Mexico, 1604 and 1860; Madrid, 1821–2; New York, 1828), which elicited praise from the Spanish poet and critic Quintana and which, in the opinion of Menéndez y Pelayo, is the poem from which we should date the birth of Spanish-American poetry properly so called. His chief work is "El Bernardo", an epic showing the influence of the Latin epic poets and also of Ariosto. A Mexican by birth, Juan Ruiz de Alarcón's (d. 1639) literary activity belongs to the history of the literature of Spain, where he passed the greater part of his life and died. His dramas are technically to be reckoned among the best in the Spanish classic répertoire.

Gongorism infected the compositions of the Jesuit Matías Bocanegra, known chiefly for his "Canción al desengaño". Carlos de Sigüenza y Góngora (1645–1700) was a scholar of importance who put forth documents dealing with matters of mathematical, philosophical, and antiquarian interest. Among his writings is his "Elogio fúnebre de sor Juana Inés de la Cruz", praising the virtues of one of the most distinguished of the authoresses in Spanish that either the Old World or the New World has produced, unequal though her genius was in its manifestations. Before becoming a nun she was Juana Inés de Asbaje (1651–91), noted for both her beauty and her learning at the viceregal Court. To her earlier career belong her love lyrics and the still popular *redondillas* championing the cause of woman against her detractor, man. Some of her verses are devout and mystical in character; an *auto sacramental* (El divino Narciso) and little comedy (Los empeños de una casa) deserve particular mention. Gongorism, which mars certain of the writings of Sor Inés de la Cruz, continued to exert its baneful influence during the first half of the eighteenth century. Some of the pedestrian poets of the period are Miguel de Reyna Zeballos, author of "La elocuencia del silencio" (Madrid, 1738), and Francisco Ruiz de León, whose "Hernandía" (1755) is hardly more than a versification of the "Conquista de México" of Solís. The "Poesías sagradas y profanas" (Puebla, 1832) of the cleric Jorge José Sartorio (1746–1828) are mostly translations. On a higher plane than any versifier since the time of Inés de la Cruz stands the Franciscan Manuel de Navarrete (1768–1809), who reflects in his "Entretenimientos poéticos" (Mexico, 1823) the manner of Cienfuegos, Diego González, and other members of the Salamancan School. The events of the revolutionary war were sung by mediocre poets, such as Andrés Quintana Roo (1787–1851), who was the President of the Congress which made the first declaration of independence; Manuel Sánches de Tagle (1782–1847); Francisco Ortega (1793–1849); and Joaquín María del Castillo (1781–1878). The priest Anastasio María Ochoa (1783–1833) translated poems from Latin, French, and Italian, and produced some original compositions of a satirical and humorous nature ("Poesías", New York, 1828; also two plays). More remarkable than for his lyrics is Manuel Eduardo de Gorostiza (1789–1851, "Teatro original", Paris, 1822; and "Teatro escogido", Brussels, 1825). His plays are chiefly comedies of manners (see especially the "Indulgencia para todos" and "Contigo pan y cebolla"), and, having been written during his sojourn in Spain, form a kind of transition between the methods of the younger Moratín and Bretón de los Herreros.

Through imitation of Espronceda, Zorilla, and other Spanish romanticists, the movement of romanticism spread from Europe to Mexico. It has its representatives already in the lyric poets and dramatists, Ignacio Rodríguez Galván (1816–42; "Obras", Mexico, 1851; his verse "Profecías de Guarimoc" is the masterpiece of Mexican romanticism), and Fernández Calderón (1809–45; "Poesías", Mexico, 1844 and 1849). Eclectic restraint, with a tendency towards classicism, as well as great Catholic fervour, actuates the works of two writers who are among the most careful in form that Mexico has had. These are José Joaquín Pesado (1801–61), who is the best known Mexican poet, and the physician Manuel Carpio (1791–1860). Pesado translated from Latin (the "Song of Songs", the "Psalms", etc., from the Vulgate), Italian, and French, succeeding best in his version of the Psalms. In his composition entitled "Las Aztecas" he is supposed to have put into Spanish certain Aztec legends; like Macpherson in his dealing with Celtic tradition, Pesado doubtless added to the native legends matter of his own invention, but he certainly showed skill in doing this ("Poesías originales y traducciones", Mexico, 1839, 1849, and 1886). In his narrative and descriptive verse Carpio treats generally of Biblical subjects. An admirer and imitator of the Spanish mystic and poet Luis de Leon was Alejandro Arango (1821–83). Materialism and so-called Liberalism inspire the verse of Ignacio Ramírez (1818–79) and Manuel Acuña (1849–73), while eroticism prevails in the effusions of Ignacio M. Altamirano (1834–93) and Manuel María Flores (1840–85). Juan de Dios Peza (1852–1910) devoted himself to the task of embalming in verse, which is not always as correct as it might be, many of the popular traditions of his country ("Poesías completas", Paris, 1891–2). He is perhaps the most read Mexican poet of the second half of the nineteenth century. Some influence of the French school of Parnassiens may be detected in the "Poesías" (Paris, 1909) of Manuel Gutiérrez Najera (d. 1888).

Peru.—The position of pre-eminence occupied by Mexico in the Spanish part of the northern continent was held by Peru in the earlier history of the civilization of South America. But a gradual loss of territory and of political importance has greatly weakened the place of Peru among the Spanish-American states; and though Peru was once the heart of a great native Inca Empire, and Spanish governors ruled the greater part of South America from within its bounds during the colonial periods, its standing in the world of American politics and letters is to-day one of no great prestige. From the earliest period of the settlement there dates little of value. In the sixteenth century there comes to view Garcilasso de la Vega (1540–1616), surnamed the Inca, as he was of native origin on the side of his mother, a princess of the Inca race. He wrote in good Spanish prose his "Florida", an account of the discovery of that region, and his "Comentarios reales", dealing with the history of Peru and blending much legendary and fictitious matter with a statement of real events. During the golden age of Spanish letters both Cervantes and Lope de Vega praise a number of Peruvian poets. An unknown poetess of Huanuco, writing under the name of Amarilis, produced in her verses, addressed to Lope de Vega and praising him, the best poetical compositions of the early colonial time in Peru. Lope responded with his epistle, "Belardo á Amarilis". Another anonymous poetess of this period wrote in terzarima a "Discurso en loor de la poesía" in which she records the names of contemporary Peruvian poets. An Andalusian colouring was given to composition in Peru during the latter part of the sixteenth century and the early years of the seventeenth by the presence on her soil of certain Spanish writers hailing especially from Seville; among these were Diego Mexía, Diego de Ojeda, and Luis de Belmonte.

Gongorism penetrated into Peru as everywhere else in the Spanish-speaking world, and found a defender there in the person of Juan de Espinosa Medrano. An impetus was given to poetical composition by a Viceroy of Peru, the Marqués de Castell-dos-Rius (d. 1710), who had gatherings at his palace every Monday evening at which the invited *littérateurs* would recite their poems. A number of these poems appeared in the volume styled "Flor de Academias". A conspicuous member of the coterie thus formed was Luis Antonio de Oviedo-Herrera, the author of two long religious poems. A poem, "Lima fundada", and several dramas, especially "Rodoguna" an adaptation of Corneille's French play, are to be put to the credit of Pedro de Peralta Barnuevo (1695–1743), who combined with his activity in the field of belles-lettres much labour in the world of scholarship, winning renown as an historian and also as a geometrician and jurisconsult. Pablo Antonio de Olavide (1725–1803) was a Peruvian who went to the motherland and played a leading part in the Court of Charles III, to whom he suggested certain agricultural reforms. To literature he contributed the prose document, "El Evangelio en triunfo", in which, as a good Catholic, he makes amends for earlier indiscretions.

As a result of later geographical divisions, Olmedo, one of the very greatest of Spanish-American writers, became eventually a citizen of Ecuador and he will therefore be considered in connexion with the literature of that state. Mariano Melgar (1719–1814; shot by the Spaniards) attracted some attention by his endeavour to reproduce in Spanish the spirit of the *yaraví*, a lyric form of the native Quichua or language of the Incas. Next in importance to Olmedo as a poet among those born in the land is Felipe Pardo y Aliaga (1806–68). Trained in Spain by Alberto Lista, he shared the conservative and classic feelings of that poet and teacher. His political satires and his comedies of manners are clever and interesting. Of the nature of the modern *género chico* are the little farces of Manuel Ascensio Segura (1805–71). With much imitation of Espronceda and Zorilla and with considerable echoing of the manner of Lamartine and of Victor Hugo, there was inaugurated about 1848 a romantic movement. The leader in this was a Spaniard from Santander, Fernando Velarde, around whom gathered a number of young enthusiasts. These copied Velarde's own method as well as those of the great foreign romanticists. Among them were: Manuel Castillo (1814–70) of Arequipa; Manuel Nicolás Corpancho (1830–63), who met an untimely fate by shipwreck; Carlos Augusto Salaverry (1830–91); Manuel Adolfo García (1829–83), the author of a noted ode to Bolívar; Clement Althaus (1835–91); and Constantino Carrasco (1841–87), who put into Spanish verse the native Quichua drama, "Ollantay". With respect to the original play in Quichua it was long thought to be entirely of native origin, but now the critics tend to believe that it is an imitation of the Spanish classical drama written in the Quichua language by a Spanish missionary in the region. In an artificial way Quichua verse is still cultivated in Peru and Ecuador. Allied in spirit to the foregoing romanticists is Ricardo Palma, who owes his fame to his prose, "Tradiciones peruanas", rather than to his verse. The more recent writers have undergone in no slight measure the influence of French decadentism and symbolism; a good example of them is José S. Chocano (1867–1900).

Ecuador.—This region belonged to the Viceroyalty of Peru until 1721. Thereafter it was governed from Bogotá until 1824, when Southern Ecuador was annexed to the first Colombia. In 1830 it became a separate state. The first colleges were established in Ecuador about the middle of the sixteenth century by the Franciscans for the natives, and by the Jesuits, as elsewhere in America, for the sons of Spaniards. Some chronicles by clerical writers and other explorers were written during the earlier colonial period, but no poetical writing appeared before the seventeenth century. The Jesuit Jacinto de Evia, a native of Guayaquil, published at Madrid in 1675 a "Ramillete de varias flores poéticas" etc., containing a number of Gongoristic compositions due to himself and to two other versifiers, a Jesuit from Seville, Antonio Bastidas, and a native of Bogotá, Hernando Domínguez Canargo. The best verses of the eighteenth century were collected by the priest Juan Velasco (b. 1727; d. in Italy, 1819) and published in six volumes with the title of "Colección de poesías hecha por un ocioso en la ciudad de Faenza". These volumes contained poems by Bautista Aguirre of Guayaquil, José Orozco (b. 1773; author of an epic, "La conquista de Menorca", which is not without its graceful passages), Ramón Viescas and others, chiefly Jesuits. The Jesuits spared no effort to promote literary culture here and elsewhere in Spanish-America during the whole period down to 1767. The expulsion of them in that year, causing as it did the closing of several colleges, impeded greatly the work of classical education. To scientific study an incentive had been given already by the advent into the land of certain French and Spanish scholars who came to measure a degree of the earth's surface at the equator. A still further impetus to inquiry and research was given by the arrival of Humboldt in 1801. By 1779 the native doctor and surgeon, Francisco Eugenio de Santa Cruz y Espejo (1740–96), had written his "Nuevo Luciano", assailing the prevailing educational and economic systems and repeating ideas which the Benedictine Feijóo had already put forth in Spain.

As has been said above, Ecuador has given to Spanish-America one of her most gifted poets, José Joaquin de Olmedo of Guayaquil (1780–1847). Out of all the Spanish-American poetical writers there can be ranked with him only two others, the Venezuelan Bello and the Cuban Heredia. Guayaquil was still part of Peru when Olmedo was born, but he identified himself rather with the fortunes of Ecuador when his native place was permanently incorporated into that state. In form and spirit, which are semi-classical, Olmedo reminds us of the Spanish poet Quintana,

JOSÉ CELESTINO MUTIS

whose artistic excellence and lyric grandiloquence he seems to parallel. The bulk of his preserved verse is not great, but it is marked by a lyric perfection hitherto unsurpassed in the New World. His masterpiece is the patriotic poem, "La victoria de Junín", which celebrates Bolívar's decisive victory over the Spaniards on 6 August, 1824. Its diction is pure, its versification harmonious, and its imagery beautiful, although at times rather forced and over-wrought. Other noteworthy poems of Olmedo are the "Canto al General Flores", praising a revolutionary general whom he later on assails in bitter terms, and "A un amigo en el nacimiento de su primogénito", in which he gives expression to his philosophical meditations. After reaching middle life he produced nothing, and when he became silent no inspired poet appeared to take his place. Gabriel García Moreno (1821–75), a sturdy Catholic, wrote some satires; Juan León Mera (1832–94), a literary historian and a critic of force as he evinces in his "Ojeada histórico-crítica sobre, la poesía ecuatoriana" (2nd ed., Barcelona, 1893), produced a popular novel, "Cumandà", besides his "Poesías" (2nd ed., Barcelona, 1893) and a volume of "Cantares del pueblo". This latter has, in addition to songs in Spanish, a few in the Quichua language. Mention may be made of a few more recent poets, such as Vicente Piedrahita, Luis Cordero, Quintiliano Sánchez, and Remigio Crespo y Toral.

Colombia.—The United States of Colombia was formerly known as New Granada. In 1819, soon after the beginning of the revolution, a state called Colombia was established, but this was later divided into three independent countries, Venezuela, New Granada, and Ecuador. In 1861 New Granada assumed the name Colombia; recently Colombia has lost the part of the territory running up on the Isthmus of Panama. It is generally admitted that the literary production of Colombia (including the older New Granada) has exceeded that of any other Spanish-American country. Menéndez y Pelayo, the Spanish critic, has called its capital, Bogotá, "the Athens of America". During the colonial period, however, New Granada produced but few literary works. The most important among them is the verse chronicle or pseudo-epic of the Spaniard Juan de Castellanos (b. 1552) which, because of its 150,000 lines, has the doubtful honour of being the longest poem in Spanish. Largely prosaic in character, it does reveal poetic flights and it is valuable for the light which it throws upon the lives of the early colonists. Its first three parts, entitled "Elegías de varones ilustres de Indias" (of these only the first was published in 1589), are to be found in the "Biblioteca de autores españoles" (vol. IV); the fourth part is published in two volumes of the "Escritores castellanos" as the "Historia del Nuevo Reino de Granada". The seventeenth century, too, was far from fertile. There appeared posthumously in 1696, at Madrid, a long epic poem, replete with Gongorism, and coming from the pen of Hernando Domínguez Camargo, already mentioned in connexion with Evia's "Ramillete". It is called the "Poema heroico de San Ignacio de Loyola" and treats, of course, of the career of the illustrious founder of the Jesuit Order.

Early in the eighteenth century a nun, Sor Francisca Josefa de la Concepción (d. 1742), wrote an account of her life and spiritual experiences reflecting the mysticism of St. Teresa. About 1738 the printing press was brought to Colombia by the Jesuits, and there ensued a great intellectual awakening. Many colleges and universities had already been founded, following the first of them established in 1554. The famous Spanish botanist José Celestino Mutis took, in 1762, the chair of mathematics and astronomy in the Colegio del Rosario, and there he trained many scientists, notably Francisco José de Caldas (1771–1816; shot by the Spaniards). An astronomical observatory was soon established and it was the first in America. As has already been said, the advent of Humboldt in 1801 fostered scientific research. In 1777 a public library was founded and in 1794 a theatre. Prominent among the works published in the second half of the eighteenth century are the "Lamentaciones de Pubén" of Canon José María Gruesso (1779–1835) and several compositions of José María Salazar (1785–1828), including his "Placer público de Santa Fé", his "Colombiada", and his Spanish verse translation of the "Art poétique" of Boileau. During the revolutionary period two poets of note made their appearance. They were José Fernández Madrid (d. 1830), whose lyrics praise Bolívar and show hate for Spain, and Luis Vargas Tejada (1802–29), whose patriotic verse was directed against Bolívar. The four most prominent poets of Colombia are J. E. Caro, Arboleda, Ortiz, and Gutiérrez González. Juan Eusebio Caro (1817–53) sang of God, love, and liberty with great fervour and his poems evince (Bogotá, 1873) no little philosophical meditation. He underwent the influence first of Quintana and then of Byron. Under the stress of romanticism and through his knowledge of English prosody he sought to introduce into Spanish verse writing certain metrical changes that have not found favour with the critics in the motherland.

Julio Arboleda (1817–61) was a friend of Caro and, like him, a representative of the most polished and aristocratic type of Colombian writers of the first half of the nineteenth century ("Poesías", New York, 1883). Assassinated before he could assume the office of President of the Republic to which he had been elected, he left in a fragmentary state his epic poem, "Gonzálo de Oyón", which, if completed, might have been the most distinguished work of its class produced in Spanish-America. Absolutely Catholic in the expression of his religious feeling, José Joaquín Ortiz (1814–92) favoured the romantic movement without ceasing to be partly neo-classic. Gregorio Gutiérrez González (1820–72), jurisconsult and poet, has no inconsiderable amount of sentimentalism in his verse of a lyric nature. His best work is the Georgic "Memoria sobre el cultivo del maíz en Antioquia", which is concerned with the rustic labours of the country-folk of his native Colombian region of Antioquia. Of lesser poets of the first half of the century there may be cited: Manuel María Madiedo (b. 1815); Germán Gutiérrez de Piñeres (1816–72); Joaquín Pablo Bosada (1825–80); Ricardo Carrasquilla (b. 1827); José Manuel Marroquín (b. 1827), notable as a humorist; José María Samper (b. 1828); José María Vergara (1831–72), noted for his Catholic devoutness; Rafael Pombo (b. 1833); Diego Fallón (b. 1834); Jorge Isaacs (1837–95), better known for his popular novel, "María". In the second half of the nineteenth century the most eminent man of letters has been Miguel Antonio Caro (b. 1834), a son of J. E. Caro. He has worked for classical ideals in literature, and his translation of Virgil ranks high among the Spanish versions. Of the many writers of the closing years of the century we may point out: Diógenes Arrieta (b. 1848), Ignacio Gutiérrez Ponce (b. 1850), José Rivas Groot (b. 1864), and the authoress Agripina Montes del Valle.

Venezuela.—This state, the old Captain-generalcy of Caracas, has the honour of having given to Spanish-America the great liberator, Simon Bolívar, and the eminent man of letters, Andrés Bello. The growth of literary culture in the region was slow, in part because politically and otherwise it was overshadowed by the neighbouring district of New Granada, to which for a while it was subject, and in part because the heterogeneous nature of its population, with a preponderance of native Indian and negro elements, largely lacking civilization, retarded the course of events. The Colegio de Santa Rosa was founded at

Caracas in 1696; it became a university in 1721. According to some accounts the printing press was not set up in Venezuela until after the beginning of the nineteenth century. But already her great man in the world of scholarship and letters had made his appearance: Andrés Bello was born at Caracas in 1781, two years before Bolivar. He early began to teach the humanities and philosophy. In 1810 he was sent to London, on a mission to the British Government, which the rebellious colonies desired to gain over to their interests. He remained there nineteen years, devoting himself in part to literary pursuits and founding two reviews, the "Biblioteca americana" and the "Repertorio americano". Then he left England to pass the rest of his life in Chile, the Government of which had called him to a post in the ministry of foreign affairs. He reorganized the University of Chile, of which he was made rector, and he did great service to the land by preparing an edition of its Civil Code. He died in 1865. In 1881 the Government began to publish his "Obras completas". His most finished literary production is the masterly "Silva á la agricultura de la Zona Tórrida", a Georgic celebrating the beauties of external nature in tropical America and urging his fellow-citizens to engage in agricultural pursuits. As a result of this work Bello ranks high among the imitators of Virgil; in the purity of its Spanish diction it has never been surpassed; in poetic force it is on the whole evenly maintained. A leading place among his other poetical compositions is occupied by the sonnet "Á la victoria de Bailén". His versions of the "Orlando innamorato" of Boiardo, and of different poems of Byron and Hugo (especially of the "Prière pour tous" of the last-named) are much admired. Not his least title to the admiration and gratitude of the Spanish-speaking peoples is his "Gramática castellana", first published at Santiago de Chile in 1847, still the most important of all Spanish grammars, especially in the revised form of it prepared by R. J. Cuervo. For his investigations into Spanish prosody and for his scholarly edition of the old Spanish "Poema del Cid" he will always be remembered favourably.

The names of the more recent Venezuelan authors pale greatly in the light of Bello's. Rafael María Baralt (1810–60), who prepared an "Historia de la República de Venezuela" and a useful "Diccionario de galicismos", passed over to Spain, where he was made a member of the Academy. Like him there also went to Spain, where he rose to the position of a general in the army, Antonio Ros de Olano (1802–87); Ros de Olano found time to produce some romantic writings, particularly his "Poesías" (Madrid, 1886) and several novels. Among the minor writers belong: José Heriberto García de Quevedo (1819–71), Abigail Lozano (1821–66), José Antonio Maitín (1804–74), Eloy Escobar (1824–89), and José Ramón Yépez (1822–81). As verse translators there have gained attention José Pérez Bonalde (1846–92), with a version of Heine, and Miguel Sánchez Pesquera, with one of part of Moore's "Lalla Rookh".

Chile.—A predominance of the practical sense over the imagination has greatly hindered the development of belles-lettres in Chile, which from first to last has been one of the least disturbed politically among the South American states and has been able to pursue rather calmly an even tenor of way. A profound respect for science and the didactic arts seems characteristic of the people of Chile. The history of real literature in the land begins with the epic, "La Araucana", of Alonso de Ercilla in the sixteenth century, but that work, since it was completed by its author in Spain, is usually treated under the head of the literature of Spain. On the model of Ercilla's poem a Chilian, Pedro de Oña, began, but did not finish, although it has 16,000 lines, his "Arauco domado" (Lima, 1596), in virtue of which he is the first native author in Chile. To the life and customs of the Araucanian Indians, already treated by Ercilla and Oña, Francisco Núñez de Pineda (1607–82) devoted himself in his poems and above all in his "Cautiverio feliz".

Much history writing of a serious nature followed these early attempts at an epic rendering of actual historical happenings, and no poets of greater importance than Oña and Núñez de Pineda appeared during colonial times. On the other hand, periodical literature flourished. In 1820 a theatre was set up for the purpose of providing an *espejo de virtud y vicio*, i. e. for purely didactic ends. The dramatic literature provided therefore was of slight account. Among the dramatists was Camilo Henríquez (1769–1825), whose pieces represent the pedantic tendencies. Some stimulus to general culture and to the study of the humanities, philosophy, and law was given by the coming to Santiago in 1828 of the Spanish *littérateur* José Joaquín de Mora, and of the Venezuelan Andrés Bello in 1829. In 1824 there was started the periodical "El Semanario de Santiago", in the management of which there collaborated many young men of letters; it led to the establishment of other literary journals. In 1843 the University of Santiago de Chile was inaugurated officially with Bello as its rector. In the fifth decade of the nineteenth century the French and Spanish dramas of romantic import invaded the theatre. The writers of the middle and second half of the century have not been pre-eminent in ability as regards literary creation. These may be listed, however: Doña Mercedes Marín del Solar (1810–66); Hermógenes de Irisarri, for his verse translations of French and Italian poets; Eusebio Lillo; Guillermo Blest Gana; Eduardo de la Barra, both poet and prosodist; etc. Among those cultivating the novel is Alberto Blest Gana. Of the scholars engaged in historical study and publication during the nineteenth century the more notable are: José Victoriana Lastarria (1817–88); Miguel Luis de Amunátegui (1828–88); Benjamín Vicuña Mackenna (1831–86); and José Toribio Medina.

Argentine Republic.—Literary culture developed later in Argentina than in most of the other states for the obvious reason that it was colonized later than the others. From the colonial period there comes but one work deserving of mention, and its literary value is scant; it is the "Argentina y conquista de la Plata" (1602) of the Spaniard Martín del Barco Centenera. Much patriotic verse of mediocre value was called forth by the British attack upon Buenos Aires in the first decade of the nineteenth century. During the revolutionary period there came to the fore a number of neo-classicists such as: Vicente López Planes (1784–1856), who wrote the Argentina national hymn; Esteban Luca (1786–1824); and Juan Cruz Varela (1794–1839), who was both a lyric poet and a dramatist. The first great poet of the Argentine Republic was Esteban Echeverría (1805–81), who was educated at the University of Paris and, returning thence in 1830, introduced romanticism directly from France. Of his various compositions "La cautiva" is full of local colour and distinctively American. Ventura de la Vega (1807–65) was born in Buenos Aires, but he spent most of his life in Spain and his admirable dramas are claimed by the mother country. To the authors of the earlier period of independence there belong: Juan María Gutiérrez (1809–78), a good literary critic; Claudio Mamerto Cuenca (1812–66); and José Marmol (1818–71), who produced some verse and also the best of Argentine novels, his "Amalia". In the language of the *gauchos* or cow-boys of the Rio de la Plata district, there has been published by José Fernández a collection of songs in "romances", entitled "Martín Fierro" (1872). These are very popular. In the second half of the nineteenth century the poets of prime importance have been Andrade and Obligado. Olegario Víctor Andrade (1838–82), the

SPALATO

1. INTERIOR OF THE CATHEDRAL.   2. THE BAPTISTERY.   3. THE CAMPANILE, RESTORED XV CENTURY.
4. DIOCLETIAN'S PALACE

author of "Prometeo" and "Atlantida", is one of the foremost of the recent poets of South America and probably the best poet that the Argentine Republic has yet produced. For poetic technic he harks back to Victor Hugo; his philosophy is that of modern progress; everywhere his verse is redolent of patriotic fervency. The "Atlántida" is a hymn to the future of the Latin race in America. Occasional incorrectness of diction mars his works. Rafael Obligado (1852——) is more correct and elegant than Andrade, but he is not equal to him in inspiration. He delights in poetical descriptions of the beauties of nature and in the legendary tales of his native land.

To the literary activity of Uruguay it is hardly necessary to devote a separate section, since geographical contiguity and other circumstances have bound up the history of the two lands. However, mention should be made of several writers as peculiarly Uruguayan. Bartolomé Hidalgo with his "Dialogos entre Chano y Contreras" (1822) really began the popular *gaucho* literature of the region of the Rio de la Plata. Francisco Acuña Figueroa (1790–1862) wrote in pure Spanish and, though his original lyrics do not soar to any poetical heights, he had some success in his versions of Biblical songs and odes of Horace. Many poets of modest power were prompted to indite poems when the romantic wave struck the land. A celebrity of recent times is Juan Zorrilla San Martín, the author of the epic poem "Tabaré" (Montevideo, 1888), which in certain respects has been compared to the famous Brazilian epic composition of Araujo Porto-Alegre. A novelist of the more immediate period is Carlos María Ramírez, the author of "Los amores de Marta".

Central America.—Scant is the output of the territory called Central America, and for this climatic and political considerations may easily be alleged. The Republic of Guatemala has surpassed the other Central American states in literary energy. The literary pioneer here is the Jesuit Rafael Landívar, who, expelled from Spain by the cruel edict of 1767, came to the New World and there anticipated Bello's Georgic composition with his Latin "Rusticatio Mexicana" which in diction and terms of description presents praiseworthy pictures of Central-American rustic life as he saw it. The Guatemalan José Batres y Montúfar (1809–44) tried his hand at narrative verse, emulating both the Italian Casti and the Englishman Byron. Romantic sentimentalism prevails in the lyrics of Juan Diéguez. The most interesting figure among the Central-American men of letters is Rubén Darío (b. 1864), a Nicaraguan who has lived much abroad and has cosmopolite and eclectic principles. He is an artist both in prose and in verse and has already his disciples among the Spanish-American writers of the present generation.

Cuba.—In the Island of Cuba the development given to literature in Spanish has been late but brilliant. Nothing cultural of real importance and deserving record occurred before the eighteenth century when, by a Bull of Innocent XIII, the University of Havana was established in 1721. A printing-press had been set up at Santiago de Cuba as early as 1698, but its activity was short-lived; it was re-established by 1792. At about this latter date periodical literature began. Properly speaking, the two first poets in Cuba are Manuel de Zequeira y Arango (1760–1846), who cultivated both the bucolic and the heroic ode, and Manuel Justo de Rubalcava (1769–1805), whose lyric worth was proclaimed in Spain by Lista and in France and England by several critics. Cuba's greatest poet and the peer of Bello and Olmedo is José María Heredia (1803–39). Exiled because of his association with the party hostile to the Spanish rule, he spent a brief period in the United States and went to Mexico, where he rose to a place of great importance in the judiciary. Despite the brevity of his life his verse is imperishable. A gentle melancholy pervades his lyrics, which are full of love for his native isle, forbidden to him. A keen sympathy with the moods of external nature is clear in some of his writings, e. g. his poems "En una tempestad", "Niágara", and "Al Sol", and makes him akin to the romanticists. The American landscape inspires also his beautiful "En el Teocalli de Cholula", which records as well the perishability of all the handiwork of man. His language and verse, although not at all impeccable, are in general satisfactory; the expression of his thought, free as it is from turgidity, appeals inevitably.

After Heredia six other Cuban poets of decided worth require notice; they are Avellaneda, Plácido, Milanés, Mendive, Luaces, and Zenea. Gertrudis Gómez de Avellaneda (1814–73) went to Spain about her twentieth year and there produced the lyrics, dramas, and novels that have made her justly famous throughout the Spanish-speaking territory. So great was her vogue in Spain that she was elected to membership in the Spanish Academy in which, however, she was prevented from taking her seat because it was discovered that the regulations forbade her entrance. Her career belongs to the history of Spanish literature. Plácido is the pseudonym of Gabriel de la Concepción Valdés (1809–44), a mulatto who triumphed over the rigours of fate, which deprived his youth of most of the advantages of education, and succeeded in composing verse which, if often incorrect in the preserved form, still bears the impress of genius. His best remembered lyric is the "Plegaria á Dios", written while he was under sentence of death for complicity in a conspiracy against the Spanish government in which he really had no part. Soft, melancholy strains or stirring patriotic notes resound throughout the verse of the other four poets mentioned: José Jacinto Milanés (1814–63); Rafael María Mendive (1847–86); Joaquín Lorenzo Luaces (1826–67); and Juan Clemente Zenea (1832–71). Milanés attempted the drama with some degree of good fortune. The novel has been cultivated more or less felicitously by Cirilo Villaverde ("Cecilia Valdés", 1838–1882) and Ramón Meza. A literary critic of undoubted distinction is Enrique Piñeyro, whose essays are received with acclaim in Europe and everywhere. By way of record it may be said that Porto Rico and Santo Domingo have not yet produced writers comparable to those listed for the other lands. In our own days, however, José Gautier Benítez of Porto Rico and Fabio Fialloa of Santo Domingo have met with praise for their verse.

MENENDEZ Y PELAYO, *Antología de Poetas Hispano-Americanos* (Madrid, 1893–95), selections with critical introductions; BLANCO GARCÍA, *La literatura española en el siglo, XIX*, pt. iii (Madrid, 1894); VALERA, *Cartas americanas* (1889–90); HILLS, *Bardos cubanos* (Boston, 1901); *Diccionario enciclopédico hispano-americano*; MENDIBURU, *Diccionario histórico y biográfico del Perú* (Lima, 1874); GUTIÉRREZ, *America poética* (Valparaiso, 1846); HERRERA, *Literatura ecuatoriana* (1860); MERA, *Ojeada histórico-crítica sobre la poesía ecuatoriana* (2nd ed., Barcelona, 1893); CAÑETE, *Escritores españoles é hispano-americanos* (Madrid, 1884); VARGARE, *Historia de la literatura en Nueva Granada* (Bogotá, 1867); ÁÑEZ, *Parnaso colombiano* (Bogotá, 1886–87); ISAZA, *Antología colombiana* (Paris, 1895); DE SOUZA, *Biblioteca hispano-americana setentrional* (Santiago, 1897); LAGOMAGGIORE, *America literaria* (Buenos Aires, 1883); CURRIER, *Spanish-American Literature* in *Catholic University Bulletin* (May, 1911), 411–17.

J. D. M. FORD.

Spalato-Macarsca (SALONA), DIOCESE OF (SPALATENSIS ET MACARSCENSIS), suffragan of Zara. Salona is the most sacred ground in the Austrian monarchy, where Titus the pupil of St. Paul preached, where the followers of Jesus Christ first shed their blood as martyrs, and where beautiful examples of basilicas and other early Christian sculpture have been discovered. Byzantine art spread under Justinian I to the shores of the Adriatic Gulf, the baptistery in Salona dating from this period. Forty-seven bishops of Salona are known: Hesychius III is mentioned in the twentieth book of St. Augustine's "De Civitate Dei"; an epistle from Gelasius I is addressed to Honorius; Honorius III conducted a synod in 530; Natalis at a Council in 590, unjustly deposed his archdeacon Honoratus, but Gregory the Great took the latter's part. In 639 Salona was destroyed by the Slavs. In 647 the city of Spalato began to arise from the ruin of Salona, and after an interregnum of eleven years its archbishops took over the territory of the archbishops of Salona. Out of the long series of its seventy-nine archbishops may be mentioned St. Rayner (d. 1180), and the unfortunate Marcus Antonius de Dominis, who was deprived of his office after having filled it for fourteen years and died an apostate at Rome in 1624; Thomas, who resigned his office voluntarily (thirteenth century), is the author of a history of the bishops of Salona and Spalato.

The Gregorian reform decrees were discussed at synods in Dalmatia as early as 1075 and executed in 1111 by Archbishop Ascentius. At the great provincial synod in St. Andrew's Church in 1185, Archbishop Petrus VII excommunicated the heretics and all who had taken possession of church property. He also prescribed the daily chanting of the Office of the Blessed Virgin. In the Council of 1292, John VII, Primate of Dalmatia, threatened to punish all bishops who interfered with other dioceses. With the death of Archbishop Lælius Cippico (1807) began another interregnum which lasted twenty-three years. The Church in Dalmatia was then reorganized, Macarsca united with Spalato, and the latter as a simple bishopric made subject to Zara. Paul Miossich was appointed first bishop of the new diocese in 1830.

The See of Spalato-Macarsca numbers 199,800 Catholics; 231 secular priests; 91 male religious in 15 stations; and 125 nuns in 9 stations.

THE PIAZZA DEL DUOMO, SPALATO
The Great Court of the Palace of Diocletian, built A. D. 300. The Arcade shows the earliest ascertained example of arches springing directly from column without entablature

FARLATI, *Illyricum sacrum*, I–III (Venice, 1751); THEINER, *Monum. slav. merid.*, 4, 13, 15, 72, 113, 115, 161, 224 sq., 354, 358, 377, 419, 442, 495, 546–48, 638 sq., 651; *Monum. Hungariæ*, I, 496, 521, 762; II, 374; GAMS, *Series Epp.*, 419–21.

CÖLESTIN WOLFSGRUBER.

Spalding, MARTIN JOHN, seventh Archbishop of Baltimore, b. Bardstown, Kentucky, 23 May, 1810; d., at Baltimore, 7 Feb., 1872. His forbears came from England and settled in Maryland about the middle of the seventeenth century; his grandfather removed to Kentucky in 1790. Martin Spalding entered St. Mary's College, Lebanon, Kentucky, in 1821, taught mathematics there at the age of fourteen, was graduated in 1826, and studied philosophy and theology during four years in the seminary at Bardstown. In 1830 he entered the Propaganda, Rome, where after a brilliant course he was ordained 13 Aug., 1834, and received the doctorate in theology at the close of a public defence of 256 theses. Upon his return to Bardstown, he became pastor of the cathedral and editor of the "Catholic Advocate", founded in 1835. After the transfer of the see to Louisville, he was appointed vicar-general (1844), coadjutor *cum jure* to Bishop Flaget (1848), and Bishop of Louisville (1850). The diocese, which then numbered over 30,000 Catholics, was well provided with schools for girls, but there were comparatively few schools for boys. To supply this need and to recruit the clergy, Bishop Spalding, shortly after the dedication of the cathedral in 1852, went to Europe and secured the services of the Xaverian Brothers who came to Louisville in 1854. During his visit to Belgium, the bishop conceived the idea of founding the American College at Louvain which, mainly through his efforts, was opened in 1857. Much of his time was devoted to lectures and controversial writings in defence of the Church, especially against the Know-Nothing movement and the common school system from which religious instruction was excluded. He had already published "Evidences of Catholicity", a series of lectures delivered in 1844–5, and the "Life, Times and Character of Benedict Joseph Flaget" (Louisville, 1852); these were followed by his "Miscellanea" (1853) and his "History of the Protestant Reformation" (1860) in which he enlarged his "Review of D'Aubigné's 'History of the Reformation'", published in 1840. He also lectured at the Smithsonian Institute, Washington, and in Baltimore, New York, Brooklyn, and other cities. In 1864, on the death of Archbishop Kenrick, Bishop Spalding succeeded him in the See of Baltimore. Here he organized the St. Vincent de Paul Society, founded the House of the Good Shepherd and St. Mary's Industrial School, and completed the cathedral. In October, 1866, the Second Plenary Council assembled at Baltimore; Archbishop Spalding arranged the details and presided over the deliberations. He had previously suggested the idea of a Catholic university, and it was chiefly due to his efforts that the project was endorsed by the council. In 1867 he again visited Rome and took part in the celebration of the centenary of St. Peter's martyrdom. As the American College in Rome was in need of funds, Archbishop Spalding issued an appeal, which resulted in placing the college on a sound financial basis. His labours in behalf of religion and the spreading of Catholic truth were incessant. In 1868 he consecrated Bishop Becker for the See of Wilmington and Bishop Gibbons for the Vicariate Apostolic of North Carolina. Within one year (1868–9) he administered confirmation a hundred times, one eighth of the recipients being converts. He welcomed the Little Sisters of the Poor to Baltimore (1869), invited Father Herbert Vaughan to evangelize the negroes (1871), and aided Father Hecker in establishing the Catholic Publication Society of New York. At the Vatican Council he was a member of the Commission on Faith and of the Commission on "Postulata" which had to examine all the matters proposed for deliberation before they were presented to the council. He was a strong supporter of the doctrine of papal infallibility and he drew up a *postulatum* in which he favoured a definition by implication in preference to an explicit affirmation of the dogma. Immediately after the final vote on infallibility, Archbishop Spalding addressed a pastoral letter to the clergy and laity of his archdiocese, in which he set the action of the council in the proper light and cleared away numerous misrepresentations. Shortly after his return to America he spoke at Philadelphia in defence of the temporal power of the pope, and on 18 June, 1871, he commemorated with fitting observance the jubilee of the elevation of Pius IX to the papal chair, the last notable celebration in which he took part. Archbishop Spalding was a fine representative of the type of men who organized and developed the Church in the United States. To a strong faith he added sincere piety and tender devotion, to scholarship a high degree of administrative ability, and to his zeal for Catholicism a loyal interest in the welfare of his country. He enjoyed the esteem of those who were foremost in Church and State, and his death was the occasion of tributes from all classes of his fellow-citizens. His complete works were published at Baltimore in several editions.

MARTIN JOHN SPALDING
Archbishop of Baltimore

J. L. SPALDING, *The Life of the Most Rev. M. J. Spalding, D.D.* (New York and Baltimore, 1873); CLARKE, *Lives of the Deceased Bishops*, III (New York, 1888); *Archives of the Cathedral* (Baltimore).

LOUIS O'DONOVAN.

Spallanzani, LAZZARO, a distinguished eighteenth-century scientist, b. at Scandiano in Modena, Italy, 10 January, 1729; d. at Pavia, 12 February, 1799. His early education was received at the Jesuit College of Reggio. His scientific career began at the University of Bologna under the inspiration of his cousin, Laura Bassi, the famous woman professor of natural philosophy and mathematics. He gave up the study of law and was ordained a priest; at twenty-five he became professor of logic, metaphysics, and Greek in the University of Reggio. His favourite authors were Homer, Demosthenes, and St. Basil, and his work attracted so much attention that he was offered chairs at Coimbra (Portugal), Parma, and Cesena (Italy). He preferred a chair at Modena (1760) and devoted all his spare time to natural science. His work here brought offers of professorships at other Italian universities and from the Academy of St. Petersburg. In 1768, at the personal solicitation of the Empress Maria Theresa, he accepted the chair of natural history in the University of Pavia which was then being reorganized. He greatly enriched the museum here by collections made in journeys in Switzerland and along the Mediterranean. After the death of Vallisneri, whose chair at Padua had been the centre of interest in the natural sciences, Spallanzani was invited to take it, but the Austrian authorities doubled his salary and gave him a long leave of absence for a scientific expedition in Turkey to retain him. His home-coming was an ovation. He continued to make scientific journeys and special studies of Vesuvius and the volcanoes of Sicily and of the Lipari Islands. His contributions to every phase of physical science are valuable, but it was in biology that his work counted for most; his studies in regeneration are still classic. He showed experimentally that many animals like the lizard and the snail, if accidentally injured, regenerate important parts of their bodies; the land snail regenerates even

XIV.—14

its head. It was afterwards shown that this does not contain the brain, but it does contain eyes, mouth, tongue, and teeth, and these are all regenerated. Spallanzani made a long series of interesting experiments on artificial fecundation. His most important work is "Dissertazioni di fisica animale e vegetale" (Modena, 1780). His researches were so much appreciated that he was made a member of academies and learned societies in London, Madrid, Stockholm, Upsala, Göttingen, Holland, Lyons, Bologna, Milan, Siena, Turin, Padua, Mantua, Geneva, and Berlin. The University of Paris, then the most important of universities for the sciences, tempted him to come as a professor. His personal character was charming and he made many friends. His biological work brought him into controversies with Needham and Buffon over spontaneous generation, and with John Hunter over digestion. He came off victorious in both contests but with such gentle courtesy as not to offend, though his opponents in the taste of the time indulged in personalities. His family were devoted to him, and his sister Marianne herself became a distinguished naturalist while helping him. He was devoutly religious, and as Senebier says, "he perceived with firmness his end approaching and endeavoured by his piety and his faith to edify those who surrounded him."

LAZZARO SPALLANZANI
From a Portrait by G. B. Busani

SENEBIER in *Memoirs on Respiration* (London, 1804); *Edinburgh Medical Journal*, 1807; TOURDES in *Experiments on the Circulation of the Blood* (London, 1801).

JAMES J. WALSH.

Sparta, a celebrated town of the Peloponnesus, mentioned several times under this name or under that of Lacedæmon in the Bible (I Mach., xii, 2–23; xiv, 16–23; xv, 23; II Mach., v, 9). Letters were exchanged between Onias I, high priest of the Jews, and Arius I, King of Sparta, about the years 309 or 300 B. C. (I Mach., xii, 7–8, 19–23; Josephus, "Ant. Jud.", XII, iv, 10). Arius, who sought to maintain the independence of his country against the Syrian successors of Alexander by creating a diversion against them in Palestine, pretended to have found a writing relative to the Spartans, showing that they themselves and the Jews were two peoples—brothers both descending from Abraham. This assertion has little foundation, although perhaps there had been such a tradition. Later Jonathan wished to renew this friendship with the Spartans and sent them a letter by the delegates Numenius, son of Antiochus, and Antipater, son of Jason, recalling to them that "we therefore at all times without ceasing, both in our festivals, and other days, wherein it is convenient, remember you in the sacrifices that we offer" (I Mach., xii, 2, 5–18; Josephus, "Ant. Jud.", XIII, v, 8). After Jonathan's death the Spartans renewed with his brother Simon the friendship and alliance which they had concluded previously and sent him a letter on this subject by the same Numenius and Antipater who had undertaken the first embassy (I Mach., xiv, 16–23).

Although the relationship of the two peoples may well be called in question, there is no proof that the documents are not authentic—everything indicates the contrary, as the coexistence of the King Arius and the high-priest Onias, and the fact that under Jonathan the Bible does not speak of kings of Sparta, as in fact the last tyrant Nabis died in 192 B. C. We see again towards the year 170 B. C. the high priest Jason took advantage of the bonds of relationship of the Jews with Sparta to take refuge there— where he died (II Mach., v, 9). In 139 B. C. the Romans addressed to Sparta, and likewise to other kingdoms and cities a circular in favour of the Jews (I Mach., xv, 23); this would seem to prove that there was already a Jewish community established in this city. The belief in the consanguinity of the two peoples existed even in the time of Josephus (Bel. Jud., I, xxvi, 1), and Sparta participated in the generosities of Herod the Great (Bel. Jud., I, xxi, 11), perhaps because he had there a Jewish community.

Christianity was introduced into Sparta at an early date. Eusebius (Hist. eccl., IV, xxiii) reports that under Marcus Aurelius, the Bishop of Corinth, Denis, wrote to the Lacedemonians a letter which is "a catechism of orthodoxy and which has peace and unity for its object". Le Quien (Oriens christ., II, 189–92) mentions fifteen bishops, among them Hosius in 458, Theodosius in 681, Theocletus in 898, finally the metropolitan Chrysanthus, who must have become a Catholic in the seventeenth century. In the beginning suffragan of Corinth, then of Patras, the see was made a metropolis in 1082 and numbered several suffragan bishoprics, of which there were three in the fifteenth century (Gelzer, "Ungedruckte . . . Texte der Notitiæ episcopatuum", 635). In 1833, after the Peloponnesus had been included in the Kingdom of Greece, Sparta was reduced to the rank of a simple bishopric; it remains the same to-day, but the see is called Monembasia and Sparta. The bishop resides at Sparta and exercises his jurisdiction over all the district of this name. When the region fell into the power of the Franks, Honorius III established there in 1217 a Latin see which by degrees became a titular and finally disappeared (Eubel, "Hier. cath. med. ævi", I, 302; II, 188; III, 234). The city numbers to-day 5000 inhabitants.

PALMER, *De epistolarum quas Spartiani atque Judæi invicem sibi misisse dicuntur veritate* (Darmstadt, 1828).

S. VAILHÉ.

Spear, THE HOLY. See LANCE, THE HOLY.

Spear and Nails, FEAST OF THE. See PASSION OFFICES.

Species, in scholastic terminology, the necessary determinant of every cognitive process. Few scholastic doctrines have been more frequently misunderstood, misrepresented, and ridiculed than that of the *species intentionales*. And yet few are more obvious and unobjectionable, although we are no longer accustomed to them. While using different terms, modern psychology offers an explanation of knowledge which, in its essential features, is identical with that which was proposed by the great thinkers of the Middle Ages.

Knowledge is essentially the union of an object with the mind. As the cognitive process takes place in the mind, it follows that the known object must in some manner be present in the mind. "Cognitio contingit secundum quod cognitum est in cognoscente" (St. Thomas, "Contra gentiles", II, c. lxxvii and xcviii). Any cognitive faculty is indetermined, or *in potentia* in two ways: (1) as we have no innate ideas, it is at first a mere aptitude to acquire knowledge, a power which is not always exercised; (2) the same faculty is capable of knowing many things. Thus the eye can perceive any colour; the ear, any sound; the intellect, any conceptual relation, etc. To pass from this state of twofold indetermination to a concrete and determined act of knowledge, the faculty needs a complement, a determining principle, or *actus* (see ACTUS ET POTENTIA). It must be "informed", or acted upon, by its object. For this reason all faculties of knowledge were called passive, not in the sense that the mind is merely passive in its cognitive process, but in the sense that it must first be acted upon, and thence be enabled to exercise its own cognitive activity. In other words, knowledge is not a spontaneous activity springing from the mind alone, but a reaction in response to an external stimulation.

The "species", frequently also called *forma*, is the determinant of the mind in the process of knowledge. It partakes of the nature both of the object from which it proceeds, and of the faculty in which it is received, for, as the scholastic axiom expresses is: "Quidquid recipitur per modum recipientis recipitur." And more specifically: "Cognitum est in cognoscente secundum modum cognoscentis" (St. Thomas, "Summa theol.", I, Q. xii, art. 4). Hence the *species impressa* is the modification of the faculty by the action of the object. The *species expressa* is the reaction of the mind as a cognitive process. The former is impressed in the faculty which it determines, and corresponds to the passive phase of knowledge which is a necessary condition but is not yet actual knowledge. The latter is the active response of the faculty, the cognitive process itself by which the mind reaches the object. The species must not be conceived as a substitute for the object, but as a mere medium of knowledge. The mind reaches the object directly and immediately, not the species. The species is not that which is known, "id quod cognoscitur", but that by which the object is known, "id quo objectum cognoscitur" (St. Thomas, "Summa theol.", I, Q. xii, art. 9; Q. xiv, art. 5; Q. lxxxv, art. 2; "De Veritate", Q. x, art. 8, ad 2um, etc.). The object as acting on the faculty, and the faculty as acted on by the object, are one and the same reality. *Actio* and *passio* are the same thing with two aspects or phases. Hence there is no need of a bridge to pass from the subject to the object. The question: how can the mind know extramental objects? has no meaning when knowledge is conceived as the vital union of the known object with the knowing mind.

This general function of the species applies to both sensitive or organic and intellectual or spiritual faculties of knowledge. The *species sensibilis* is not an efflux from the object, not a physical miniature of it—a view which was accepted by some interpreters of Aristotle, but which the great scholastics, with St. Thomas, reject. It is a modification of the sense organ by the action of the object. It is sometimes called material because it results from the activity of material objects, and is a modification of a material organ. Sometimes also it is called intentional, or even spiritual, because it is not in itself a material representation, and is not received in physical matter, but in an organ which is animated by the soul. In other words, it is psychophysical. The *species intelligibilis* is the determinant of the intellectual act of knowledge. It is elaborated from the data of the senses by a special activity of the intellect (*intellectus agens*), and received in the *intellectus patiens* or *possibilis* which elicits the act itself of knowledge (see INTELLECT).

BOURQUARD, *Doctrine de la connaissance d'après St. Thomas d'Aquin* (Paris, 1877); KLEUTGEN, *Die Philosophie der Vorzeit* (Münster, 1867); LIBERATORE, *Della conoscenza intellettuale* (Rome, 1873); MAHER, *Psychology* (New York and London, 1910); PESCH, *Institutiones psychologicæ* (Freiburg, 1897); TURNER, *History of Philosophy* (Boston, 1903), 363.

C. A. DUBRAY.

Speckbacher, JOSEF, a Tyrolean patriot of 1809, b. at Gnadenwald, near Hall, in the Tyrol, 13 July, 1767; d. at Hall, 28 March, 1820. Speckbacher was the son of a peasant and spent his youth in roaming, and he did not learn to read and write until later in life. At the age of twelve he was a poacher and was often involved in fights with the customs officers. When a little older, he worked in the imperial salt-mines at Hall. On 10 Feb., 1794, he married Maria Schmiederer of Judenstein, and in this way came into possession of her farm and house. At the beginning of the war with France he became one of the volunteers who sought to defend the fatherland; his first encounter with the enemy took place at the bloody skirmish near Spinges on 2 April, 1797. He was a fine sharp-shooter and one of the most zealous of the Tyrolean patriots. In 1805 he fought under Lieutenant-Colonel Swinburne against Marshal Ney, but was obliged like the other patriots to accept the cession of the Tyrol to Bavaria in 1806. When in 1808 the Archduke John entered into negotiations with Andreas Hofer for regaining the Tyrol, Speckbacher soon became one of the most trusted friends of Hofer and courageously supported the latter in preparing for the struggle for liberty. With the entrance of the Austrian army into the Pustertal in the month of April, 1809, began the heroic struggle of the Tyrolese. Speckbacher took a prominent part in the three efforts to free the country from the yoke of Napoleon. He showed himself to be not only a daring fighter, but above all a cautious, unterrified strategist. In this year, according to his own diary, he took part in thirty-six battles and skirmishes. On 12 April, 1809, he surprised the city of Hall early in the morning, made the garrison prisoners, and prevented the flight of the French into the valley of the lower Inn. On 31 May he commanded the left wing of the battle of Mount Isel, and fought victoriously near Hall and Volders. He conducted the siege of the castle of Kufstein (23 June–16 July). Here he gave countless proofs of personal courage, built batteries, destroyed the mills and boats, burnt the city, captured the train of provisions, and made his way as a spy into the castle. From 4 Aug. to 11 Aug. he was most of the time the commander in the battles between Sterzing and Franzensfeste against Marshal Lefebvre. He forced the marshal to retire and with Hofer and Haspinger commanded at the famous third battle of Mount Isel (13 and 15 August). After the enemy had been driven away, he and his men forced their way into the mountains of Salzburg, and stimulated there the defence of the country; on 25 Sept. he defeated the allied French and Bavarians at Lofer and with great loss fell back on Reichenhall. On 16 Oct. he was surprised at Melleck by a superior force of the enemy and was obliged to retire; his young son Andreas was taken prisoner, and he himself was severely wounded. At Waidring on 17 Oct. and at Volders on 23 Oct. he was able to maintain himself against the foe, escaped capture once more in a skirmish on 28 Oct., and captured a battalion of the enemy. After the last and unsuccessful fight on Mount Isel on 1 Nov., he wished to continue the struggle, but was obliged to abandon the unequal contest. He was proscribed, and a reward of five hundred florins was offered to anyone who would deliver him alive or dead.

Speckbacher spent the entire winter in the Tyrolese mountains, sometimes hid among friends at lonely farms, sometimes hid in Alpine huts and always hunted by enemies. He was betrayed only once, but he saved himself this time by a daring flight and hid himself until Jan., 1810, in the clefts of the rocks, being often near death from hunger. His wife and four children were also obliged to seek safety by flight and to hide in the mountains. Speckbacher's last hiding-place was near the summit of a high mountain in the Voldertal, where the only person who came to him was his faithful servant George Zoppel, who brought him food. On 14 March he was severely injured by an avalanche which overwhelmed him. He was brought by friends to his farm at Judenstein, where Zoppel hid him in the stable under the floor until 2 May.

When scarcely well Speckbacher fled amid great dangers through the Pinzgau and Styria to Vienna, where he was warmly received by the Emperor Francis I. The emperor presented him with a chain of honour and a pension. The emperor's plan to settle the Tyrolean refugees in Hungary could not be carried out and in 1811 Speckbacher was made the superintendent of an estate near Linz given by the ruler to Hofer's son. Speckbacher's wife, who had been imprisoned thirteen weeks at Munich, however, remained on the farm in the Tyrol. In the autumn of 1813 Speckbacher returned to the Tyrol as a major of the Tyrolese volunteers in the imperial army under General Fenner. He shared with these troops in the garrisoning of Southern Tyrol against the French and in maintaining these garrisons against the enemy. On 12 Sept., however, the Bavarian government at Innsbruck once more set a price, 1000 florins, on his head, and it was not until the summer of 1814 that Speckbacher was able to return home unmolested. A year later he received a second gold chain of honour, and in 1816 at the time of the national demonstration he received the personal notice of the emperor. He joyfully met his son, who had been well educated at Munich, and looked forward to a peaceful old age, but the hardships he had undergone forced him to sell his farm and move to Hall, where he died after a short illness.

He was first buried at Hall, but in the summer of 1852, at the command of the Emperor Francis Joseph I, his remains were transferred to the Court church at Innsbruck, where they were placed by those of Hofer and Haspinger. In 1908 a bronze statue was erected to him at Hall. His widow received a pension from the emperor of 500 florins and a supplementary sum for the education of her children. She died in 1846. Speckbacher's eldest son Andreas only lived to the age of thirty-seven years. After conpleting his studies as a mining engineer he went to the iron works at Mariazell and Eisenerz in Styria, received positions at Pillersee, Brixlegg, and Jenbach in the Tyrol, where he did much to improve the methods of mining ore. He married Aloisia Mayr and died in 1834. His sons and his brother died at an early age, and the family is extinct in the male line. Speckbacher was one of the most striking of the men who shared in the struggle for freedom in the Tyrol. His character is well expressed in his epitaph: "In war wild but also human, in peace quiet and faithful to the laws, he was as soldier, subject, and man worthy of honour and love".

HIRN, *Tirols Erhebung 1809* (Innsbruck, 1910); MAIR, *Speckbacher, eine Tiroler Heldengeschichte* (Innsbruck, 1904); DOMANIG, *Speckbacher, der Mann von Rinn. Schauspiel in fünf Akten* (Kempten, 1909), from the dramatic trilogy *Der Tyroler Freiheitskampf*); VON SCALA, *Josef Speckbacher, der Mann von Rinn. Volksschauspiel in vier Aufzügen* (Brixen, 1905).

HEINRICH VON WÖRNDLE.

Speculation, a term used with reference to business transactions to signify the investing of money at a risk of loss on the chance of unusual gain. The word is commonly used only when the risk of loss is greater than ordinary business methods and prudence warrant. A coal merchant who sees grounds for thinking that the coming winter will be severe, and that there will be a general strike among coal miners, shows enterprise if he lays in a large stock of coal with the expectation of reaping more than usual profit from its sale. He incurs the ordinary risks of business, he does not speculate. But if a man thinks, on trivial indications, that there is going to be a great development in the opening up of a new country, and buys large tracts of prairie land in the district on the chance of its rising rapidly in value, he would be said to speculate in land. More specifically, speculation is used to designate dealings in futures and options on the Exchanges, especially when the parties to the transaction do not intend any effective transference of commodities or securities, but only the payment of differences between making-up prices and those agreed on. Such time-bargains are universally practised nowadays on the world's Exchanges, and the volume of business done in them vastly surpasses that where effective transfer of securities or commodities is contemplated. The transactions may vary indefinitely in character between *bona fide* and perfectly lawful buying and selling, on the one hand, and the merest gambling or betting on future prices, on the other.

Some of the ordinary types of such operations are the following. A speculator buys at the current rate a thousand dollars' worth of stock for the account at the end of the month. When the day for settlement arrives, if the price has risen, he is paid the difference between the price at which he bought and the making-up price. If the price is lower, the speculator loses and pays the difference to the broker. In the slang of the Exchange, this is a "future", or "time-bargain", or a deal in "differences"; and one who speculates for the rise of prices is called a "bull", while one who speculates for the fall is called a "bear". When the operator loses, he may prefer to extend the time of settling the account to the next settling day. This may be done by arrangement with the broker, and the transaction is known as "carrying over". A speculator may purchase at a fixed rate the right to receive or to refuse a certain amount of a certain stock or commodity at a future date. This is called an "option". If he purchases the right either to sell or to buy, it is a "put and call", or a "double option". Of course no objection can be raised against such contracts as these when they are entered into by merchants or others with a view to the effective transfer of what is bought and sold. A merchant or manufacturer requires a constant and steady supply of what he deals in so as to be able to conduct his business. Effective dealings in "futures" and "options" guarantee the steady supply which is needed, and that at fixed rates settled beforehand. Such business methods benefit the dealer and the public as well. They ensure a constant supply of commodities at medium rates. But the speculator does not intend effective transfer. His buying and selling are fictitious; he only pockets his differences if he wins, and pays them if he loses. His methods give rise to serious moral, economic, and political questions, which have been the subject of much discussion.

There is no great moral harm in the practices which have been mentioned if they are considered singly by themselves and in the abstract. Without incurring the reproach of great moral obliquity I may buy a thousand dollars' worth of stock at the current rate from a broker when neither buyer nor seller intends effective transfer of the stock, but merely the payment of differences when the settling day arrives. In essentials the transaction is a bet as to what the price of the stock will be on settling day. And if the buyer and the seller have the free disposal of the money which is staked on the bet, and there is no fraud, unfair dealing, or other evil adjuncts or effects of the transaction, the *bet* will not be morally wrong. (See BETTING; GAMBLING.) However, betting and gambling are almost always dangerous pastimes and often morally wrong. Just in the same way speculation tends to develop a passion which frequently leads to the ruin of a speculator and his family. The hope of becoming rich quickly and without the drudgery of labour distracts a man from pursuing the path of honest work. The speculator, even if he succeeds, produces nothing; he reaps the fruit of the toil of others, he is a parasite who lives by preying on the community. Moreover, in practice, the event on which the bet is laid by one who speculates in futures is seldom left to the operation of natural causes. When large sums of money are at stake the temptation to influence the course of prices becomes almost irresistible. Hence the fierce and frequent contests between "bulls" and "bears" on the Exchanges. Cliques of one party, interested to bring about a rise in prices, buy the stock in order that the increased demand may produce the effect desired. Often the buying is merely fictitious, but this fact is not known to the outside world. The purchases are published, industriously commented upon by the venal financial press, puffs and mendacious reports are inserted in the papers in order to raise the price of the stock and attract moneyed investors. The opposite party adopts the contrary, but equally immoral, tactics. They indulge in real or fictitious sales and do all they can to depreciate the stock in their favour by fair or foul means. Great financiers with command of large sums of money can and do influence the markets almost as they please, and the small speculator is usually swallowed up by them. Wealthy financiers and gigantic syndicates can often buy or obtain effective control over all the available supply of some stock or commodity and then charge monopoly prices. Such "rings", or "corners", even when they do not succeed entirely according to the intention of the operator, produce widespread inconvenience, hardship, and ruin. The result is that in practice speculation deserves all the evil reputation which attaches to the word.

Speculation indeed has its defenders and advocates, especially among brokers and jobbers, who claim that it equalizes prices and prevents the fluctuations which would otherwise be inevitable. Some affirm that speculative dealings have little appreciable effect on buying and selling for transfer. In volume and number speculative transactions are very much larger than those for effective transfer, but the two are conducted separately and to a great extent between different parties. It is asserted that the speculative market is to a large extent separate and distinct from the real market. These two arguments in favour of speculative dealings mutually destroy each other. If speculative dealings equalize prices, it cannot be true that they have little appreciable effect on the markets. As the result of the speculation depends on the actual market price of the security or commodity in question at the time agreed upon, it cannot be said that speculative transactions are independent of effective buying and selling for transfer. It is patent that the various devices to which "bulls" and "bears" have recourse do produce some effect. The acute and experienced men who devote themselves to speculative business, and who frequently have recourse to the methods described above in order to influence the market in their favour, would be the last people in the world to expend uselessly time, effort, and money. The contention, then, of producers and consumers that speculation has a disastrous effect on real business transactions seems to be well grounded. They maintain that speculators denaturalize prices. These should be regulated, and are naturally regulated, by the varying costs of production and by the mutual interaction of supply and demand; but the artificial dealings of speculators tend to fix prices without reference to those natural factors. Hence, producers and consumers are robbed by clever men, who manipulate the markets in their own interests, produce nothing, perform no useful social service, and are parasites on commerce. In Germany the Exchange Law of June, 1896, forbade gambling in options and futures in agricultural produce, and after a severe struggle with the Berlin Exchange the Government succeeded in maintaining the law. A similar law was passed in Austria in January, 1903. America and Great Britain as yet have no special laws on the matter, though more measures than one have been proposed to Congress. The great difficulty of distinguishing between transactions for effective delivery and mere time-bargains, and the ease with which positive laws on the matter could be evaded, have checked the tendency to positive legislation. In England the existing laws against gambling and fraud have been found sufficiently effective to provide a remedy for cases of special importance.

ANTOINE in *Dictionnaire de Théologie Catholique* (Paris, 1905), s. v. *Bourse (Jeux de)*; BRANTS, *Les grandes lignes de l'Economie Politique* (Louvain, 1908); *Ecclesiastical Review*, XXXII (New York, 1905), 2; INGALL AND WITHERS, *The Stock Exchange* (London, 1904).

T. SLATER.

Spedalieri, NICOLA, priest, theologian, and philosopher, b. at Bronte in the Province of Catania, Sicily, 6 December, 1740; d. at Rome, 26 November, 1795. He studied in the seminary of Monreale, then the most flourishing in Sicily, was ordained priest, and appointed professor of philosophy and mathematics, and later of theology. At the same time he cultivated the arts of poetry, music, and painting. Disgusted at the opposition stirred up by certain theological theses, which were branded as heretical at Palermo but approved at Rome, he withdrew from Monreale to Rome (1773 or 1774), where for ten years he led a life of penury but of fruitful study and labour. However, he always retained his affection for the seminary of Monreale. In 1784 he obtained from Pius VI a benefice in the Vatican Basilica, and then ceased the efforts he had made for years to obtain a chair in the Universities of Pisa, Pavia, and Turin. His first published work was "Analisi dell' Esame critico di Fréret" ("Examen critique des apologies de la religion chrétienne", a work wrongly attributed to Fréret, really written by Naigeon), Rome, 1778. In 1779 he published "Ragionamento sopra l'arte di governare" and "Ragionamento sull' influenza della religione cristiana sulla società civile". In 1784 he issued, also at Rome, his "Confutazione di Gibbon" in which he combats the thesis of the English historian who blames Christianity for the downfall of the Roman Empire. In it, as in the Apology against Fréret, he shows especially the benefits conferred by the Christian religion on the social and political order, inasmuch as Christianity is the most powerful bulwark against despotism.

In 1791 appeared his principal work, "I diritti dell' uomo", also at Rome; this was evidently intended as a Catholic answer to the proclamation of the "Rights of Man", made in France in 1789, which was the signal for the French Revolution. Notwithstanding the hearty reception given to this work by Pius VI who said, "For a long while rulers have been asking *quid est papa*. Your book will teach them *quid est populus*", a storm of criticism and refutation burst on the head of its author. Governments took notice of it and (e. g. Piedmont) forbade its circulation. The controversy continued even after Spedalieri's death. In his book, except in certain details, the writer only expressed in the language of the eighteenth century the teaching of the scholastic doctors on the popular origin of political sovereignty, a doctrine commonly taught from St. Thomas to Suarez and Bellarmine, which does not exclude the Divine origin of the same sovereignty. Spedalieri's thesis could not prove acceptable to the absolutism of princes and the Cartesian doctrines then in vogue, which did not admit the existence of a natural moral law but made all depend on the arbitrary Will of God; much less could it please the regalists. On the other hand, it is easy to understand how his theory might give rise to a fear that it was too favourable to the ideas of the revolutionaries. Spedalieri was wrongly claimed by the Liberals as one of theirs, and if some of them accuse him of a want of loyalty when he wishes to conciliate democracy and a Divine sanction of the social order, it is because they do not understand the true nature of democracy or of the saying that all authority comes from God. The controversies about Spedalieri were renewed on the occasion of the centenary of his death. Shortly before his decease he completed a "Storia delle Paludi Pontine", a book Pius VI ordered him to write and which was published by his intimate friend Nicolai, in the work "De bonificamenti delle terre pontine" (Rome, 1800). His death was attributed to poison; a modern writer has not hesitated to lay the blame on the Jesuits, forgetting that Spedalieri's enemies were the bitterest adversaries of the Jesuits.

NICOLAI, *Laudatio Nicolai Spedalieri* (Rome, 1795); CIMBALI, *Nicola Spedalieri, Pubblicista e riformatore del sec. XVIII* (Castello, 1905); IDEM, *L'Anti-Spedalieri* (Turin, 1909); IDEM, *Nel primo centenario della morte di N. Spedalieri* (Rome, 1899).

U. BENIGNI.

Spee, FRIEDRICH VON, poet, opponent of trials for witchcraft, b. at Kaiserswerth on the Rhine, 25 February, 1591; d. at Trier, 7 August, 1635. On finishing his early education at Cologne, he entered the Society of Jesus in 1610, and, after prolonged studies and activity as a teacher at Trier, Fulda, Würzburg, Speyer, Worms, and Mainz, was ordained priest in 1622. He became professor at the University of Paderborn in 1624; from 1626 he taught at Speyer, Wesel, Trier, and Cologne, and was preacher at Paderborn, Cologne, and Hildesheim. An attempt to assassinate him was made at Peine in 1629. He resumed his activity as professor and priest at Paderborn and later at Cologne, and in 1633 removed to Trier. During the storming of Trier by the imperial forces in March, 1635, he distinguished himself in the care of the suffering, and died soon afterwards from the results of an infection contracted in a hospital. He was one of the noblest and most attractive figures of the awful era of the Thirty Years' War. His literary activity belongs to the last years of his life, the details of which are little known. Two of his works were not published until after his death: "Goldenes Tugendbuch" (Golden Book of Virtues), a book of devotion highly prized by Leibniz, and the "Trutznachtigall", a collection of fifty to sixty sacred songs, which, though not free from the weaknesses of the day, take a prominent place among religious lyrics of the seventeenth century, and have been in recent times repeatedly printed and revised. But the assumption that the author in this work applied the metrical principle independent of Opitz, is at least doubtful. His principal work, through which he obtained a well-deserved and world-wide reputation, is the "Cautio Criminalis", written in admirable Latin. It is an arraignment of trial for witchcraft, based upon his own awful experiences probably principally in Westphalia, for the traditional assumption that he acted for a long time as "witch confessor" in Würzburg has no documentary authority. This work was printed in 1631 at Rinteln without Spee's name or permission, although he was doubtlessly widely known as its author. He does not advocate the immediate abolition of trials for witchcraft, but describes in thrilling language and with cutting sarcasm the horrible abuses in the prevailing legal proceedings, particularly the inhuman use of the rack. He demands measures of reform, such as a new German imperial law on the subject, liability to damages on the part of the judges, etc., which, if they had been conscientiously carried out, would have quickly put an end to the persecution of witches. Many a generation passed before witch burning ceased in Germany, the classic land of these outrages; but at all events the "Cautio Criminalis" brought about its abolition in a number of places, especially at Mainz, and led the way to its gradual suppression. The moral impression created by its publication was very great. Even in the seventeenth century a number of new editions and German translations appeared, Protestants also eagerly assisting in promoting its circulation. Among the members of Spee's order his treatise seems to have usually found a favourable reception, although it was published without official sanction, and its publication led to a correspondence between the general of the Jesuits, the provincial of the order on the Lower Rhine, and Spee himself. The general wished more exact information as to how the printing took place and expressed the suspicion that Spee, even if he, perhaps, did not directly cause it, at least allowed it, and wrote him a mild rebuke.

The earlier literature is enumerated by CARDAUNS, *Friedrich Spee* in *Frankfurter zeitgemässe Broschüren*, V, pt. 4 (1884), where the first exact analysis of the *Cautio* is given. Since then much new material has appeared in the publications of DUHR, *Die Stellung der Jesuiten in den deutschen Hexenprocessen*, published by the Görresgesellschaft (1900); DIEL, *Friedrich Spee in Sammlung historischer Bildnisse*, second edition revised by DUHR (1901). Valuable articles by DUHR have appeared in the *Historisches Jahrbuch der Görresgesellschaft* (1900), 328 sqq.; (1905), 327 sqq. For a good bibliography see the introduction to the latest edition of the *Trutznachtigall* by WEINRICH (1907), xxxvii sqq.

HERMANN CARDAUNS.

Speed, JOHN, VENERABLE, English martyr, executed at Durham, 4 Feb., 1593–4, for assisting the venerable martyr John Boste (q. v.), whom he used to escort from one Catholic house to another. He died with constancy, despising the inducements offered to bring him to conformity. With him was condemned Mrs. Grace Claxton, wife of William Claxton, of the Waterhouse, in the parish of Brancepeth, Durham, at whose house Boste was taken and probably Speed also. She was, however, reprieved on being found to be with child.

CHALLONER, *Missionary Priests*, I, no. 100, ad finem; POLLEN, *English Martyrs 1584–1603* (London, 1908), 239.

JOHN B. WAINEWRIGHT.

Spells. See SUPERSTITION.

Spencer, THE HON. GEORGE (in religion, IGNATIUS OF ST. PAUL), Passionist, b. at the Admiralty, London, 21 Dec., 1799; d. at Carstairs, Scotland, 1 Oct., 1864. He was the youngest son of the second Earl Spencer and Lavinia, daughter of Sir Charles Bingham. From Eton he went to Trinity College, Cambridge, received Anglican orders, 13 June, 1824, and became chaplain to Bishop Blomfield of Chester, and shortly afterwards rector of Brington, Northamptonshire. In 1830 he became a Catholic and went to Rome for his ecclesiastical studies, being ordained priest there, 26 May, 1832. He returned to England fired with zeal for its conversion and laboured incessantly to procure the prayers of Catholics on the Continent for that intention. From 1832 to 1839 he worked as priest at West Bromwich, building the church at his own cost; then he was professor at Oscott till 1846, when he entered the Passionist novitiate. He was professed at Aston Hall in January, 1848. He spent the rest of his life in arduous missionary labours as a true apostle for the conversion of England. He translated the life of Blessed Paul of the Cross (London, 1860) and published many sermons.

A Short Account of the Conversion of the Hon. and Rev. G. Spencer, written by himself (Cath. Inst. Tracts, London, no date); DEVINE, *Life of Father Ignatius of St. Paul, Passionist* (Dublin, 1866); GILLOW, *Bibl. Dict. Eng. Cath.*; PURCELL, *Ambrose Phillipps de Lisle*.

EDWIN BURTON.

Spenser, JOHN (*alias* HATCLIFFE and TYRRWHIT), b. in Lincolnshire, 1601; d. at Grafton, 1671. He was converted while a student at Cambridge, and entered the Society of Jesus in 1627. After having professed moral theology at Liège, 1642, and also having served the arduous "Camp Mission", he returned to England and partook, Whitsuntide, 1657, in a conference, much spoken of at the time, with two Anglican divines, Dr. Peter Gunning and Dr. John Pearson, afterward Bishops of Ely and Chester. All the disputants, including Spenser's Catholic colleague, Dr. John Lenthall, M.D., were Cambridge men, and may have known one another. An account of the conference was published in Paris, 1658, under the title, "Schism Unmasked", probably by Spenser. He also wrote: "[Thirty-Six] Questions propounded to the Doctors of the Reformed Religion" (Paris, 1657); "Scripture Mistaken" (London, 1660); and other books which won him a high name as a controversialist. At the time of his death he was chaplain to the Earl of Shrewsbury.

FOLEY, *Records of the English Province*, S.J. (1884), II, 194; GILLOW, *Bibl. Dict. Eng. Cath.*, s. v.

J. H. POLLEN.

Spenser, WILLIAM, VENERABLE, English martyr, b. at Ghisburn, Yorkshire; executed at York, 24 September, 1589. His maternal uncle, William Horn, who signed for the Rectory of Cornwell, Oxfordshire, in 1559, sent him in 1573 to Trinity College, Oxford, where he became Fellow in 1579 and M.A. in 1580. There, convinced of the truth of Catholicism, he used his position to influence his pupils in that direction; but he delayed his reconciliation till 1582, when, with four other Trinity men (John Appletree, B.A., already a priest; William Warford, M.A. and Fellow, afterwards a Jesuit; Anthony Shirley, M.A. and Fellow, afterwards a priest; and John Fixer, B.A., afterwards a priest), he embarked from the Isle of Wight, and landed near Cherbourg, arriving at Reims, 2 November. Received into the Church five days later, he was ordained sub-deacon and deacon at Laon by the bishop, Valentine Douglas, 7 April, 1583, and priest at Reims by the Cardinal Archbishop de Guise, 24 September, and was sent on the mission 29 August, 1584. He effected the reconciliation of his parents and his uncle (the latter was living as a Catholic priest in 1593), and afterwards voluntarily immured himself in York Castle to help the prisoners there. He was condemned under 27 Elizabeth, c. 2, merely for being a priest. With him suffered a layman, Robert Hardesty, who had given him shelter.

POLLEN, *Acts of the English Martyrs* (London, 1891), 273–8; *English Martyrs 1584–1603* (London, 1908), 34, 35; KNOX, *Douay Diaries* (London, 1878); and, for William Horn, see GEE, *Elizabethan Clergy* (Oxford, 1898), 119; and Public Record Office, *S. P. Dom. Add. Eliz.*, XXXII, 64.

JOHN B. WAINEWRIGHT.

Speyer, DIOCESE OF (SPIRA), in Bavaria. The city dates back to the stronghold of Noviomagus, in the territory of the German tribe of the Nemetes, on the left bank of the Rhine. In the course of time a Roman municipality (*Colonia Nemetum*) developed out of this stronghold; in 451 the municipality was entirely destroyed by Attila. From its ashes arose a new city, Spira or Speyer. Christianity found entrance into the city in the time of the Romans. The first bishop, Jesse (Jessius), is mentioned in the Acts of the Synods of Sardica (343) and of

SEAL OF THE CITY OF SPEYER

Cologne (346), but his historicity is not quite certain. On the other hand there is positive proof of Bishop Hilderich who attended the Synod of Paris held in 614. Since his episcopate the succession of bishops has been unbroken. In 748 Speyer was made suffragan of Mainz; and in 1030 the first stone of the present Romanesque Cathedral of Our Lady was laid; it was intended to be the mausoleum of the Salian emperors. In the struggle over investitures, Bishops Huzmann (1073–90) and Johann I (1090–1104) upheld the Emperor Henry IV and died under the ban of the Church. In 1146 St. Bernard preached the

Crusade at Speyer and won King Conrad III to the cause. Besides the four Salian emperors, Philip of Swabia, Rudolph of Habsburg, and the rival kings, Adolph of Nassau and Albert of Austria, are also buried in the cathedral. A lay brotherhood, the Twelve Brothers of Prayer, prayed without intermission in the cathedral, for the repose of the souls of these kings. Among the later bishops Matthias of Ramung (1464–78) should be especially mentioned for his reforming the clergy and people, and bringing new life into the diocese.

At the time of the Reformation several Diets were held at Speyer, the most important being in 1526 and 1529. In 1526 the condition of political affairs enabled the Protestants to secure the relatively favourable decision that each constituent state should act in reference to the matters contained in the Edict of Worms (1521) as it could answer to God and the emperor. But the action taken in 1529 was more decided: the Edict of Worms was to be executed, and the ecclesiastical innovations were to be abolished. Against this the Evangelical constituents protested. By the Reformation the diocese lost two thirds of its churches and benefices. Bishop Eberhard von Dienheim (1581–1610) sought to introduce the reforms ordered by the Council of Trent in the remaining territory. The gains temporarily acquired during the Thirty Years' War were nearly all lost by the Treaty of Westphalia (1648). The diocese suffered greatly during the predatory wars of Louis XIV of France, and in 1689 the city and cathedral were burned. In 1794 the cathedral, which had been restored at great expense, was once more ravaged by the lawless soldiery of the French Revolution. In 1801 that part of the diocese on the left bank of the Rhine had to be ceded to Mainz; in 1815 the diocese was assigned to Bavaria; in 1817 it received new boundaries in the Bavarian Concordat and was made suffragan of the new metropolitan Bamberg. By the liberality of King Louis I of Bavaria, the cathedral was suitably decorated (1846–53), the frescoes being done by Schraudolph. The area of the diocese corresponds to that of the Bavarian Palatinate of the Rhine. Dr. Michael Faulhaber, formerly a professor at the University of Strasburg, was appointed bishop in 1910. The diocese has 12 deaneries, 235 parishes, 6 curacies, 86 chaplaincies and vicarships, 377 secular clergy, and 10 regular clergy. The Catholic population is 413,481; the Protestant population is about 500,000. The diocese has also 1 Dominican monastery (Oggersheim), 1 Capuchin monastery (St. Ingbert), and 100 houses for nuns.

REMLING, *Gesch. der Bischöfe zu Speyer nebst Urkundenbuch* (4 vols., Mainz, 1852–54); IDEM, *Neuere Gesch. der Bischöfe zu Speyer* (Speyer, 1867); GEISSEL, *Der Kaiserdom zu Speier*, I–III (Mainz, 1828; 2nd ed., Cologne, 1876).

KLEMENS LÖFFLER.

Speyer, JOHANN and WENDELIN VON, German printers in Venice from 1468 to 1477. They were among the first of those who, after 1462, left Mainz for Italy to introduce there the art of printing books. We have scant knowledge of their lives. They came originally from Speyer (capital of the Bavarian palatinate). Early in 1460–61 Johann appears in Mainz as a "goldsmith"—it was there, no doubt, that he learned the art of printing books. In 1468, with his wife, children, and brother Wendelin, he set out for Venice. The establishment of their printing house, the first in Venice, took place under the most favourable auspices. The Venetian Senate extended a cordial welcome to Johann, and granted him a full monopoly of printing for five years. His first book, Cicero's "Epistolæ ad familiares", appeared in 1469. During the printing of Augustine's "De Civitate Dei" (1470) Johann died, and Wendelin completed it. The latter assumed control of the business after the death of Johann and carried it on successfully until 1477. About 1472 he associated with him the German printer, Johann von Köln. Together they issued seven works. Besides their great skill as printers, their extraordinary industry is worthy of note. Before Johann died, four great works had been issued: two editions of Cicero; Pliny; and one volume of Livy. The "De Civitate Dei" had been begun. Within seven months eight hundred volumes were printed.

From 1470 to 1477 Wendelin issued over seventy great works (Italian and Roman classics, Fathers of the Church, jurists, etc.). Johann printed in an antique type modelled after the best Italian manuscript writing, beautiful, and carefully cut. It is decidedly superior to the later antique type, which deteriorated through desire to save space, and it is almost equal to the beautiful type of Jenson. Johann's clear type and his entire technical execution are surprisingly perfect. In addition to this first type, Wendelin used five newly cut types of exquisite workmanship, among them three slender Gothic models, probably reduced to save space. His work showed the same correctness of text, beauty of printing, and evenness that had characterized Johann's. The latter was the first printer to number the leaves with Arabic figures, and was also the first who used the colon and interrogation point. In Wendelin's books appeared for the first time the so called catch-words (*Kustoden*), that is to say he printed on the lower margin of each page the first word of the page following.

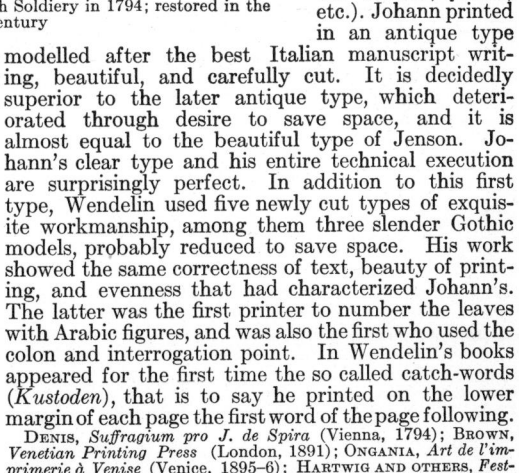

DENIS, *Suffragium pro J. de Spira* (Vienna, 1794); BROWN, *Venetian Printing Press* (London, 1891); ONGANIA, *Art de l'imprimerie à Venise* (Venice, 1895–6); HARTWIG AND OTHERS, *Festschrift zum 500 jähr. Geburtstage von Johann Gutenberg* (Mainz, 1900), 342.

HEINRICH W. WALLAU.

Spillmann, JOSEPH, author, b. at Zug, Switzerland, 22 April, 1842; d. at Luxemburg, 20 February, 1905. He attended the primary school and *gymnasium* of his native town, but feeble health necessitated his leaving his studies and devoting himself to his father's business. At the age of sixteen he resumed his interrupted studies at the Jesuit college of Feldkirch. Having entered the Jesuit novitiate at Gorheim (1862), he was sent, during the Franco-Prussian War (1870), to France, to nurse the sick. Two years later, when his order was banished from Germany, he went to England to complete his theological studies, and in 1874 was ordained priest. The life work of Spillmann, who had already shown his poetical gift in his contributions to "Der Hausfreund" (a calendar published by Father Pachtler in 1872), was clearly marked out for him. He was appointed collaborator on the "Stimmen aus Maria-Laach" (founded in 1871) and the "Katholische Missionen" (founded in 1873).

Spillmann's fruitful literary activity resulted chiefly from his connexion with these periodicals, especially the "Katholische Missionen", which he edited from 1880 to 1890. From his "Beilagen für die Jugend" grew seven portly volumes of "Reisebilder", while twenty-one booklets, "Aus fernen Landern", owe their origin to the same source; these consisted of edifying and tastefully illustrated stories for the young, with whom they have become favourites, as the numerous editions and translations prove. His comprehensive "Geschichte der Katholikenverfolgung in England von 1535–1681" began with articles in the "Stimmen aus Maria-Laach", was continued in the supplements to this periodical, and was completed in five large volumes. For the calendar, the "Hausfreund", which was given up in 1881, Spillmann wrote many stories; these were afterwards collected under the title "Wolken und Sonnenschein", eight pretty stories for the young which have been frequently republished and translated into other languages. Spillmann also wrote seven longer romances, the first (Die Wunderblume von Woxindon) appearing in 1893; and the last (Der schwarze Schumacher) ten years later; they are written in the style of his favourite authors, Sir Walter Scott and Charles Dickens. An eighth romance was sketched, but a serious illness prevented its completion. Spillmann's importance arises chiefly from his works for the young.

In addition to the necrologies in various newspapers and periodicals, see BAUMGARTNER in *Stimmen aus Maria-Laach*, LXIX, 1–22.

N. SCHEID.

Spina, ALFONSO DE, Spanish Franciscan, date of birth unknown; d. about 1491. A convert from Judaism, he was for many years superior of the house of studies of the Friars Minor at Salamanca, and in 1491 was created Bishop of Thermopylæ in Greece. He was a man of great learning and attained considerable renown as a preacher, but his chief title to fame is the work entitled "Fortalitium Fidei" which Mariana (lib. XXII "De rebus Hispan.", c. xlvi) describes as "opus eruditum, splendido titulo, voce barbara, et divinarum rerum cognitione præstanti". As appears from the text, this work was written in 1458, but it was added to by the author at different times up to the year 1485. The first edition was issued about 1464–76; the edition published at Nuremberg in 1485 begins thus: "Incipit prohemium Fortalitii Fidei conscriptum per quendam Doctorem eximium ordinis minorum anno MCCCCLIX in partibus occidentis." The fact that the "Fortalitium Fidei" appeared anonymously gave rise to some difference of opinion as to its authorship. The reason why the work is included in the "Scriptores O.P." is that one edition of it appeared under the auspices of Gulielmus Totani, O. P., for its author was undoubtedly a Franciscan, as Echard himself notes (Script. Ord. Præd., ed. 1721, II, 61), and modern scholars are practically unanimous in attributing it to Alfonso de Spina. The "Fortalitium Fidei" deals with the different kinds of armour to be used by preachers and others in their warfare against the enemies of the Christian religion. It is divided into five books, the first directed against those who deny the Divinity of Christ, the second against heretics, the third against the Jews, and the fourth against the Mohammedans, while the fifth book treats of the battle to be waged against the Gates of Hell. In this last book the author dwells at length upon the demons and their hatred of men, the powers they have over men and the diminution of these powers, owing to the victory of Christ on the Cross, the final condition of the demons, etc.

Besides the "Fortalitium", Alfonso de Spina published at least three other works: (1) Sermones de Nomine Jesu Vigintiduos, issued about 1454 (erroneously confounded with the "Fortalitium" by Oudin); (2) "Sermones plures de excellentia nostræ fidei", preached in 1459; (3) a treatise on fortune, dedicated to John, King of Castile (1404–54).

WADDING, *Annales minorum, ad an. 1452*, XXXI; IDEM, *Scriptores ord. min.* (Rome, 1906), 14; SBARALEA, *Supplementum*, pt. I (Rome, 1908), 29–30; HURTER, *Nomenclator*, II (1906), 1019.

PASCHAL ROBINSON.

Spina, BARTOLOMMEO, Scholastic theologian, b. at Pisa about 1475; d. at Rome, 1546. He joined the Dominican Order at Pisa about 1494. Having taught for many years in the schools of his order, he was appointed (1536) by the Venetian Senate to the chair of theology at Padua. He was also for a time *socius* of the master-general of his order, and prior provincial of the Holy Land. In July, 1542, he was made Master of the Sacred Palace by Paul III, and during the four years that he discharged the duties of that office he rendered great services to the Holy See and to the Fathers of the Council of Trent, regarding many difficult and mooted questions. From the year 1518 Spina was engaged in a heated controversy with his famous confrère, Cardinal Cajetan. Still more harsh was his opposition to Ambrose Catharinus, whom he denounced as guilty of heresy to Paul III about the beginning of the year 1546. The most important of Spina's works are: "Tutela Veritatis de Immortalitate Animæ contra Petrum Pomponatium" and "Flagellum in Tres Libros Apologiæ Pomponatii de Immortalitate Animæ", both published in 1518. Of special interest are also "Tractatus de Stringibus et Lamiis" (Venice, 1523), and "Apologiæ Tres adversus Joann. Franc. Ponzinibium Jurisperitum" (Venice, 1525). These last two works were also published at Rome in 1576. In his treatise "De Conceptione B. Mariæ Virg." (Venice, 1533), Spina opposed the doctrine of the Immaculate Conception.

ALVA Y ASTORGA, *Monumenta Dominicana: pro immac. concept.* (Louvain, 1666), 4 sq.; ECHARD, *Script. Ord. Præd.*, II, 126 sq.; HURTER, *Nomenclator*.

CHAS. J. CALLAN.

Spinola, CHRISTOPHER ROYAS DE, Bishop of Wiener-Neustadt, b. of a noble Spanish family, near Roermond in Gelderland in 1626; d. at Wiener-Neustadt, 12 March, 1695. Educated at Cologne, he entered the Franciscan Order at that place and for some time taught philosophy and theology. Going to Spain, he was made provincial of his order, and in 1661 accompanied Margaret Theresa, the first wife of Emperor Leopold I, to Vienna, where he became one of the emperor's influential diplomats. He was appointed titular Bishop of Knin in Dalmatia in 1668 and Bishop of Wiener-Neustadt, 19 January, 1686. In his endeavours to bring about a reunion between Protestants and the Catholic Church he had the support of Leopold I. His negotiations with well-known Protestant theologians, such as Molanus, Callistus, Leibniz, etc., and various Protestant courts, especially Hanover and Brandenburg, were encouraged by Innocent XI, and in 1683 led to a conference of Protestant theologians to whom Spinola submitted his plan of reunion. The plan was apparently approved by the Protestant theologians, but French influence and Spinola's too liberal concessions induced Innocent XI to take no action. On 20 March, 1691, the emperor appointed Spinola commissary-general of the movement for ecclesiastical reunion in Austria-Hungary. The extreme concessions which he now made to the Protestants of Austria-Hungary, such as Communion under both species, freedom for priests to marry, Mass in the German language, and suspension of the Tridentine decrees until a new council was held, were rejected by Rome.

LANDWEHR, *Spinolas Unionsbestrebungen in Brandenburg* in *Märkische Forschungen*, XX (Berlin, 1887); KIESL, *Der Friedensplan des Leibniz zur Wiedervereinigung der getrennten christlichen Kirchen* (Paderborn, 1904); KNÖPFLER in *Allg. Deutsche Biog.*, XXXV, 202–4.

MICHAEL OTT.

Spinoza (D'ESPINOSA, DESPINOZA), BENEDICT, b. at Amsterdam, 24 Nov., 1632; d. at The Hague, 21 Feb., 1677. He belonged to a family of Jewish merchants of moderate means, and was originally called Baruch, a name that he later translated into its Latin equivalent Benedict. His father's name was Michael, his mother, Michael's second wife, was called Hana Debora. In 1641 Michael married a third wife who was named Hester de Espinosa. The family probably had some connexion with the little town of Espino in Spanish Galicia, and with the celebrated Marrano family there called Espinosa. (The Marranos were Spanish Jews compelled to conform outwardly to Christianity.)

BENEDICT SPINOZA

Baruch attracted attention in the school for Portuguese Jews at Amsterdam by his talents and application to study. He made rapid progress in Hebrew and the study of the Talmud, and his teachers, especially Rabbi Saul Levi Morteira, had the greatest hopes of his future. It was intended that he should become a rabbi. The subtle methods of the teachers of the Talmud undoubtedly trained his intellect and led it particularly to reasoning by analogy. The moral teaching of the Haggada had a great and permanent influence upon his code of living. However, the difficulties in regard to the Scriptures, which he deduced from what he read, made a stronger impression upon him than their solutions. Thus he was a troublesome and critical pupil, although at the same time a modest one. He read and despised the Cabalists; yet traces of their influence are recognizable in his philosophy; mention should here be particularly made of the book called "Zohar" and of Herrera's work "Porta cœli". He studied industriously the Jewish writers on the philosophy of religion, especially Maimonides, Gersonides, Chasdai Kreskas, and Ibn Esra, and later adopted much from them. The writings of the Arabian philosopher Al Farabi and of his commentator Ismail show striking similarities, even in the smallest details, with the later system of Spinoza. There are also clear evidences of connexion between the strange work of Ibn Tofaíl, the story of "Hai Ibn Joktan", and the conceptions of Spinoza.

About 1651 Spinoza, unable to see his way clearly, seems for a short time to have abandoned metaphysical studies, and to have fought a hard battle with his passions. Even at this time he was looked upon with suspicion by orthodox Jews. He now devoted himself to the natural philosophy of Descartes. Coming back in this way to metaphysics, he completely overcame the scepticism, and, resuming his first studies, began to lay the foundation of his new system. The philosophy of Descartes aided him in recasting the notions which he had previously acquired. After the death of his father in 1654, Spinoza was almost completely cast off by his family and, having no means, taught in the private Humanistic school of the ex-Jesuit and freethinker Franz van den Enden. Here he perfected himself in Latin and continued his philosophical investigations by the study of St. Augustine, the Stoics, Scholasticism (in a somewhat superficial manner), the philosophy of the Renaissance and that of some modern writers, especially of Hobbes. His later psychology shows extraordinary similarities with the teachings of Marcus Marci and of Glisson.

Spinoza now frequented almost exclusively the society of Christians, i. e. of the free-thinking sort, and especially of Mennonites. His lifelong friendships, as known from his letters, date in part from this period. In 1656 he was formally expelled from the Jewish community and soon afterwards from Amsterdam. A somewhat legendary attack upon his life is said to have been made about this time. He never became a Christian. He now began to dictate in Latin some of the principles of his philosophy to a company of pupils at Ouderkerk near Amsterdam. A Dutch translation of this dictation exists in two manuscripts which were discovered in 1853 and 1861 by Friedrich Muller, a Dutch bookseller. The translation as found in these manuscripts had been largely revised, had notes that were traceable, however, to Spinoza himself, and had been somewhat unskilfully handled by an editor. Since the discovery the manuscripts have been published a number of times both in the original text and in translations. The characteristics of the later system of the "Ethics" are evident in this "Korte Verhandeling van God, de Mensch, en deszelos Welstand". But neither the doctrine of the one and only Divine substance, nor the higher unity of "extension" and "thought" in the infinite and the finite, nor the instinct of self-preservation, is clearly expressed in it. Spinoza, obliged to seek some other means of support, became a very skilful grinder of lenses; his work commanded good prices. About 1660 he retired to the village of Rijnsburg near Leyden. The little house in which he lived still stands, and has been bought by admirers of the philosopher; it contains a fine library. Here Spinoza devoted himself to a revision of the "Korte Verhandeling" which was never completed. The result of these labours was an important unfinished treatise "De intellectus emendatione", with preparations for his great work, the "Ethics", and the development of the "geometrical method". While at Rijnsburg he was greatly stimulated in his work by the reports of the lectures of the professors of philosophy of Leyden (among whom should be included Geulincx), which were brought to him by students of the university. While at this village he also became acquainted with the celebrated Stensen, and had here a pupil named Casearius, whom he instructed in the Cartesian philosophy. In 1663 Spinoza published a book under his own name called "Renati des Cartes principiorum philosophiæ Pars I et II, more geometrico demonstratæ", and a supplement to this under the title, "Cogitata metaphysica". The work does not give Spinoza's own philosophy, but glimpses of his views may be found in it.

While at Rijnsburg Spinoza also taught by correspondence some young friends at Amsterdam who had formed a Spinoza club. In the spring of 1663 he moved to Voorberg, near The Hague. His acquaintance with scholars and statesmen increased. He was witty, was esteemed as a great Biblical critic and mathematician, and had the reputation of possessing a fine political sense. Jan de Witt and van Beuningen held him in high regard. Huygens interested himself in Spinoza's lenses. Great expectations were expressed of his philosophy by Heinrich Oldenburg of Bremen, who had visited Spinoza at Rijnsburg and now, in connexion with Robert Boyle, was active in London as the secretary of the Royal Society, and by the learned Ludwig Meyer. While living at Voorburg Spinoza worked hard on a lengthy treatise to which he later gave the title of "Tractatus theologico-politicus". He drew largely for this work from the Arabian and Jewish philosophy of religion and from the old rabbinical exegesis. But his main sources were early, little-known Jewish heretics and obscure Christian writers of his own time, especially Peyrère's "Systema theologicum ex Præadamitarum hypothesi" (1655). Spinoza's political views were largely inspired by Jan de Witt and his friends; the same opinions are to be found in the writings of other Dutch political writers of the same period, e. g. van Hove. Spinoza, however, in publishing his treatise, had special aims in view. It was intended to establish and enlarge the ecclesiastical and political principles of Jan de Witt and at the same time to lead the way to the publication of his own philosophy. According to Spinoza the Holy Scriptures of the Old Testament are not without error and are not inspired in the strict sense. They do not teach us with certainty as to the nature of God and His characteristics, but only concerning obedience to God, piety, and love. Consequently the text of the Bible can never come into conflict with philosophy and civil law. But, according to Spinoza, the limitations of philosophy and law are also clearly defined. As it is only in the State that justice and law, injustice and transgression are conceivable, the individual, in order to be able to live according to reason, must surrender his rights to the community. Then, too, he must obey the government in everything, even against his reason and conviction, unless a command contradicts universal feeling, as the murder of parents. Freedom of thinking and speaking, however, cannot be forbidden by the State; if it has the power to do this, the right, indeed, cannot be denied it, but the prohibition would be disadvantageous to it, because its own existence would be endangered by such tyranny. No man can ever act according to his convictions, if a law of the State stands in the way. Thus Spinoza upholds only a partial freedom of conscience. On the other hand the government has the right to supervise the external practice of religion. It is easy to understand that the Church councils and synods of Holland took energetic measures against this work, which appeared anonymously in 1670. Up to 1676 at least thirty-seven decisions or edicts against the work had appeared.

From 1670 Spinoza lived at The Hague, at first in the Verkade, then not far from this spot in the Paviljoensgracht, near the monument erected in 1880. Both houses are still in existence, but the latter, in which Spinoza died, has lately been completely rebuilt. The philosopher laboured with zeal on his great work; in order to be independent and undisturbed in elaborating his system of philosophy he declined a call to a professorship at Heidelberg. His plan to publish his system of ethics in 1675 failed, owing to the opposition of his enemies. Originally Spinoza seems to have had the intention to found a kind of philosophical world-religion. He believed that the basic ideas of his view of the world were to be found among the old Hebrews, in Christ, and in St. Paul. In his opinion this philosophy, without the Holy Scriptures, sufficed for the truly wise. In order to understand his conception of the original Christianity it must be remembered that his acquaintance from the beginning had been among latitudinarian Christians, who emphasized the moral life, not dogma, that, with many of his Christian friends, he regarded the Antitrinitarians as the most genuine Christians, that he found traces of his philosophy in the writings of Christian mystics, and finally that among the first writings which had introduced him to Christianity had been Hobbes's books "De cive" and "Leviathan". Towards the end of his life Spinoza had bitter disappointments, which, however, seldom disturbed his stoical composure. He lived tranquilly at The Hague in the midst of his work, his correspondence, and his friends. He began an exceedingly interesting political treatise in which he did not change his earlier views but rather carried them further. He also wrote a short treatise on the rainbow, and a Hebrew grammar, and, as it seems, translated the Pentateuch. He was a victim to the disease from which his family suffered, consumption, and this was aggravated by his work in grinding lenses. He died peacefully, in the presence of a physician who was a friend. Even the other people in the house did not know he was dying. The little he left was, as it were, a mirror of his life. Spinoza was a very frugal and unselfish man. He declined all money and pensions that he did not absolutely require. His way of living could not be simpler; it was only for books that he spent relatively large sums. The virtues which he most highly prized and consistently practised were control of the feelings, equability of spirit, love of country, loyalty and industry, moderation and love of the truth. In society he was animated and witty; he enjoyed being alone, and yet was kindly disposed towards his fellow men. Union with God, as he conceived of the Deity, i. e. as a thinking and infinite, necessarily existing, immanent cause of all existence, and love for this Being were to him the highest of all things. He was immovably convinced that his was the true philosophy, could scarcely understand any view that deviated from his own, was hard and unjust in his judgments of other thinkers, was not easily approached with objections, and was incapable of appreciating with historical objectivity other views of the world.

In 1677 his literary remains were published under the title "B. D. S. Opera posthuma". In this publication were included his system of ethics, the unfinished political tractate, the treatise "De emendatione intellectus", letters to and from him, and lastly his compendium of Hebrew grammar. The Dutch translation of the same year has great critical value. The tractate on the rainbow was first published anonymously in Dutch at The Hague in 1687. The problems added for the calculus of probabilities are not by Spinoza. The philosopher seems to have destroyed his translation of the Pentateuch; the Spanish apology which he drew up when expelled from the synagogue has not, so far, been found.

It is impossible to describe in a short article the Spinozistic system as a whole. For it is just the rigidly unified, minute construction of that system and the labyrinth of its thought processes that are of importance for the history of philosophy as an original creation. On the other hand, the elements, bases, and individual results are neither new nor original. Spinoza's view of the world is so constructed that the final results can be reached with equal logic from its epistemological and psychological assumptions, and from its ethical and metaphysical axioms. The view of Spinozism held by the present writer, which frequently varies from the views formerly held, can merely be indicated in what follows.

According to Spinoza there are no universal notions. Only that is thinkable which actually exists or will exist at some time. Further, only the necessary is thinkable. Existence and necessity, however, cannot be deduced from the nature of finite things; we must therefore conceive of a Being (God) necessarily existing and necessarily acting, from which all else follows of necessity. This Being is not the cause but the first principle in the manner of mathematical entities; the things come from it by mathematical sequence; for only in this way, says the philosopher, can the immutability of the first principle be maintained, only thus is a relation of the infinite to the finite thinkable; and only in this way is the unity of nature preserved, without fusing the substance of God with that of finite things. Yet the axiom "God= Nature" is valid because the things necessarily following from the Being of God belong in some way to God. Only the Being of God is independent; Spinoza calls this Being alone substance. All things (*modi*) must be founded in the attributes of God. This is one approach to Spinozism.

Another is the following: Spinoza observed in nature, on the one side, only systems of motion and rest which were derived from one another in an endless series of causes and effects; on the other side, running exactly parallel to these, but not influenced by them, a series of ideas. These systems of motion and ideas cannot be understood of themselves alone, but only with the aid of the notions of extension and thought, and these two notions contain in themselves the characteristic of infinity. Thus we are brought to a necessarily existing Being on whom all other beings must depend in their existence and nature. The facts of experience, as *conditio sine qua non*, lead us to the knowledge that the change which we observe can only be explained by an instinct of self-preservation existing in all things, which constitutes their individual nature. This instinct, then, is the relative factor in the scientific construction of ethics and politics. The Absolute, which corresponds to it and establishes it, consists of the immanently working, countless attributes of the universal substance. This is the second approach to Spinozism.

We now come to a third: Scepticism is completely overcome only when the idea is nothing else than the objective side of the process of movement which is identical with it under another point of view. Only then does the succession of things fully coincide with the succession of ideas. Thus truth and certainty are the same. The fact that there are ill-defined and false ideas can, accordingly, only be explained in that these ideas, so far as they do not prove themselves to be arbitrary combinations and fictions, are merely part-knowledge. Such part-knowledge, however, signifies that the one with such knowledge is in some sense part of an absolute intelligence. Therefore the part-extension identical with and corresponding with the part-knowledge is only a part of an infinite and indivisible extension. Consequently, in the infinite also, extension and thought are, absolutely considered, identical; as relative things they are different. Applied to ethics this doctrine signifies that good and evil have meaning only from the point of view of an incomplete part-knowledge; applied to politics it sets up for the individual life the axiom right is might, and ascribes to the State the creation of right.

Lastly, ethics as a doctrine of happiness, which is really Spinoza's starting-point, leads to the same result. His main question was, how is perfect happiness possible? Now he could only conceive of perfect peace and happiness on the supposition that all earthly happenings proceed as the necessary consequence of the nature of the absolutely infinite Being; whoever recognizes this and rests lovingly in this knowledge enjoys perfect peace. The aim of life is to attain this knowledge *cognitio sub specie æternitatis*. From this opinion, however, it follows necessarily that the individual acts of knowledge proceed in some manner from God's own thought (the soul therefore is no substance), that the nature of the individual soul is an individual instinct towards perfection (*conatus in suo esse perseverandi*—in order to preserve the continuity of all self-consciousness), that evil proceeds from a lack of adequate knowledge, that the material is only another side of the spiritual, because otherwise Spinoza would have had to suppose a second source of evil besides imperfect knowledge.

These statements show also the way in which Spinoza can be refuted. It must be shown that God's unchangeableness does not involve the necessity of all Divine action; it must be proved that the dependence of the finite upon the infinite does not demand a counter-relation in the infinite, and that there is a metaphysic world of pure possibility and universal conceptions. Further, it must be shown that an objectively true knowledge is possible, even though the order of ideas does not run strictly parallel to the order of things, and though the two orders are not identical. The positive contradictions of this identity in the finite must be revealed, and it must be shown that in the Spinozistic psychology the continuity of self-consciousness, notwithstanding the instinct of self-preservation, is destroyed, and that the part-knowledge of Spinoza, with the system of happiness built upon it, involves an impenetrable mystery and therefore is untenable as a philosophical view of the world. Some friends and later admirers of Spinoza thought they could combine his philosophy with Christianity. A hopeless attempt in this direction is made in the introduction to the "Opera posthuma" written by Ludwig Meyer. Jarrig Jellis, Spinoza's friend, also exerted himself to bring Spinozism and Christianity together. More ingenious and profound but also exceedingly sophistical is the treatise issued anonymously in 1684 by Abraham Cuffeler, "Specimen artis ratiocinandi naturalis et artificialis ad pantosophiæ principia manuducens". A number of writers leave one in doubt as to whether they did not use Christianity merely as a cloak. Others, e. g. Bredenburg, and Wittich in his "Anti-Spinoza", adopted only individual principles of Spinozism. When in the second half of the eighteenth century the reputation of Spinoza was again revived both in Germany and France simultaneously, the effort was once more made to reconcile Spinozism and Christianity. Mention might here be made of Heydenreich, Herder, and Sabatier de Castres.

That in the present time Spinoza has again become very modern is traceable to nine reasons: his criticism of the Scriptures, his doctrine of free-thought, his theory of the State as the source of right, his doctrine of happiness founded on necessity, his doctrine of morals dissociated from positive religion, his axiom *Deus sive Natura* and the justification of this axiom, his conception of the identity of thought and movement in the Absolute, his distinction of absolute and relative knowledge, finally his realism in the theory of knowledge to which many modern philosophers are returning.

The bibliography prepared by van der Linde extends only to 1871. It has been partially supplemented by Grunwald, *Spinoza in Deutschland* (Berlin, 1897), by Weg, *Katalog 29* (Leipzig, 1893), which contained the collection of works on Spinoza that had been sold for America, and by the Katalog "Spinoza", No. 598 (Frankfort, 1912). The relatively best but in no way complete edition of his works is that of van Vloten and Land (2nd ed., The Hague, 1895). Of this publication the "Ethics" alone has appeared in a third edition (1905). English translations of Spinoza, omitting the defective one of Willis, are: Fullerton, *Ethics* (New York, 1894), Hale White and Hutchinson Stirling (3rd ed., London, 1899); this edition includes also the *De intellectus emendatione;* Elwes has edited the chief works (London, 1883–84), but with the letters freely abridged; Gillingham Robinson, *Korte Verhandeling* (Chicago, 1909), defective, see below Wolf. An excellent translation into Dutch of all the works of Spinoza is that of Meyer (Amsterdam, 1897–1905); the best French translation is that of Appuhn (Paris, 1907–09), the correspondence and the theologico-political and the political treatises have yet to be published. Among the German translations should be mentioned the one made for the Philosophical Library by Bänsch, Buchenau, and Gebhardt. An excellent facsimile edition of all the letters was issued by Meijer in numbered copies at The Hague. A facsimile of the notes in handwriting to the theologico-political treatise was published by Altkirch in the journal *Ost und West* (1901).

Freudenthal, *Die Lebensgeschichte Spinozas in Quellenschriften, Urkunden und nichtamtlichen Nachrichten* (Leipzig, 1899). and *Spinoza I, Das Leben Spinoza* (Stuttgart, 1904). A quantity of new material is in Meinsma, *Spinoza en zijn Kring* (The Hague).

1896). The youth and development of Spinoza is described in detail by DUNIN-BORKOWSKI, *Der junge De Spinoza, Leben u. Werdegang im Lichte der Weltphilosophie* (Münster, 1910).

Other biographies which also contain expositions of the ethical system are: POLLOCK, *Spinoza, His Life, and Philosophy* (2nd ed., London, 1899); WILLIS, *B. de Spinoza, His Life, Correspondence and Ethics* (2nd ed., London, 1870); KUNO FISCHER, *Spinozas Leben, Werke und Lehre* (5th ed., Heidelberg, 1909); COUCHOUD, *Benoît de Spinoza* (Paris, 1902); BRUNSCHVICG, *Spinoza* (2nd ed., Paris, 1906). WOLF has lately issued an English translation of the *Korte Verhandeling*, with a life of Spinoza (London, 1910).

There are innumerable presentations of Spinoza's theories; among those of earlier times the works of BOULAINVILLIERS, JACOBI, the two SIGWARTS, TRENDELENBURG, and BOEHMER are very readable. Later works are: MARTINEAU, *A Study of Spinoza* (2nd ed., London, 1899); CAIRD, *Spinoza* (cheap ed., London, 1903); JOACHIM, *A Study of the Ethics of Spinoza* (Oxford, 1901); DUFF, *Spinoza's Political and Ethical Philosophy* (Glasgow, 1903); PICTON, *Spinoza, a Handbook to the Ethics* (London, 1907); CAMERER, *Die Lehre Spinozas* (1877); *Spinoza und Schleiermacher* (Stuttgart, 1903); WINDELBAND in his history of modern philosophy. Very important for Spinoza's teaching is BRUNNER, *Die Lehre von den Geistigen und vom Volke*, I, pt. II (Berlin, 1908).

Of other important monographs there can only be mentioned: FULLERTON, *On Spinozistic Immortality* (Philadelphia, 1899); DELBOS, *Le problème moral dans la philosophie de Spinoza* (Paris, 1893); WORMS, *La morale de Spinoza* (Paris, 1891); RIVAUD, *Les notions d'essence et d'existence dans la philos. de Spinoza* (Paris, 1906); LÉON, *Les éléments Cartésiens de la doctrine Spinoziste* (Paris, 1907); FREUDENTHAL, *Spinoza und die Scholastik* (Leipzig, 1887), 83, 138, one of the philosophical essays dedicated to W. Zeller; LUDWIG STEIN, *Leibniz und Spinoza* (Berlin, 1890); JOEL, *Beiträge zur Geschichte der Philosophie* (2 vols., Breslau, 1876), important for the history of the development of Spinoza; BALTZER, *Spinozas Entwicklungsgang* (Kiel, 1888); VOLKELT, *Pantheismus und Individualismus im System Spinozas* (Leipzig, 1872); ZULAWSKI, *Das Problem der Kausalität bei Spinoza* (Berne, 1899); GEBHARDT, *Spinozas Abhandlung über die Verbesserung des Verstandes* (Heidelberg, 1905); ZEITSCHEL, *Erkenntnislehre Spinozas* (Leipzig, 1889); RICHTER, *Der Willensbegriff in der Lehre Spinozas* (Leipzig, 1898); BUSOLT, *Die Grundzüge der Erkenntnistheorie und Metaphysik Spinozas* (Berlin, 1875); BECHER, *Der Begriff des Attributs bei Spinoza* (Halle, 1905). There are also a large number of more or less valuable essays in the *Revue de Métaphysique et de Morale*, from 1900 in the *Année philosophique*; also in the *Archiv für Geschichte der Philosophie*, in *Zeitschrift für Philosophie und philosophische Kritik*, in *Vierteljahrsschrift für wissenschaftliche Philosophie*; also several in *Mind*, in *Navorscher*, in *Oud-Holland*, in *Tijdschr. voor Wijsbegeerte*, in *Revue philosophique*, in *Stimmen aus Maria-Laach*, especially vol. LXXIX, 521 sq., and in the *Studiën of Godsdienstig, wetenschappelijk en letterkundig gebied*, no. 48, 460 sqq.

STAN. DUNIN BORKOWSKI.

Spire (A. S. *spir*, "a stalk", "shoot"), a tapering construction, in plan conical, or pyramidal, or octagonal, or hexagonal, crowning a steeple or tower, or surmounting a building, and usually developed from the cornice; often pierced by ornamental openings and, where there were ribs, enriched with crockets. Sometimes an open lantern was interposed between the steeple, tower, or roof and the spire. On the Continent the architects aimed to make the steeple and spire one, merging them into each other, while in England they openly confessed it was a separate structure by masking its point of origin behind a plain or pierced parapet, or ornamental battlements. A spire properly belongs to Pointed architecture and hence has never been fully developed except in Gothic buildings. As early as the twelfth century they took on different forms, and almost everywhere, from the thirteenth to the sixteenth century, became the terminating construction of every church steeple, tower, or lantern, and also those of secular buildings, more especially in Germany and France. Their decorative value was very great, more particularly in varying and enriching the sky-line of the buildings which they crowned, and by the numerous variations of forms and variety of types employed. These forms ranged from such simple examples as that surmounting the south tower of Chartres Cathedral to that of Burgos, where the whole structure is an openwork of tracery. In England Norman churches were without spires, but with the coming in of Early English short ones were introduced; Decorated Gothic called for much higher ones, and the Perpendicular still higher. The earlier spires were generally built of timber, and they were always so when the building was roofed with wood. These early timber spires were, as a rule, not very tall, but later they reached a greater elevation; that which crowned old St. Paul's in London is said to have been 527 feet in height. The most lofty spires now in existence—such as those of Salisbury, Coventry, and Norwich—are all of stone. In Central England there are many, and in fact wherever suitable stone was easily obtainable. In the north of England, however, in Scotland, and in Wales among the mountains the bell-gable takes the place of a spire, no doubt because the large area of the thinly populated parishes made it necessary to keep the bells uncovered, so that they might be more widely heard. The most beautiful examples of existing spires are to be seen at Chartres, Reims, Laon, Freiburg, Ratisbon, Cologne, Antwerp, Vienna, Burgos, and Salisbury. On some of these buildings there are several spires, in many instances built at different periods: the south spire of Chartres, culminating in a pinnacle 350 feet above the ground, was erected in 1175, while the north spire, with its apex 380 feet above the ground, was not finished until 1513. The so-called spires of the Renaissance and those built by Sir Christopher Wren are not true spires, but merely steeples terminating in a point.

CARYL COLEMAN.

Spires. See SPEYER, DIOCESE OF.

Spirit (Lat. *spiritus*, *spirare*, "to breathe"; Gk. πνεῦμα, δαίμων; Fr. *esprit*; Ger. *Geist*.) As these names show, the principle of life was often represented under the figure of a breath or air. The breath is the most obvious symptom of life, its cessation the invariable mark of death; invisible and impalpable, it stands for the unseen mysterious force behind the vital processes. Accordingly we find the word "spirit" used in several different but allied senses: (1) as signifying a living, intelligent, incorporeal being, such as the soul; (2) as the fiery essence or breath (the Stoic *pneuma*) which was supposed to be the universal vital force; (3) as signifying some refined form of bodily substance, a fluid believed to act as a medium between mind and the grosser matter of the body. The hypothesis of "spirits" in this sense was familiar to the Scholastic physicists. Albertus Magnus distinguished corporeal and incorporeal spirits, and long after the Scholastic age, in fact, down to the end of the eighteenth century, "animal spirits", "vital spirits", "natural spirits" were acknowledged agencies in all physiological phenomena (cf. Vesalius, Descartes, Harvey, Erasmus Darwin, etc.). "Magnetic" spirits were employed by Mesmer in his theory in very much the same way as modern Spiritists invoke the "ether" of the physicists.

In Psychology, "spirit" is used (with the adjective "spiritual") to denote all that belongs to our higher life of reason, art, morality, and religion as

ONE SPIRE OF THE VOTIVKIRCHE, VIENNA
—FERSTEL

THE CATHEDRAL OF NOTRE-DAME, CHARTRES

THE SOUTH SPIRE, 350 FEET HIGH, DATES FROM 1175; THE NORTH SPIRE, 380 FEET HIGH, WAS COMPLETED IN 1513

contrasted with the life of mere sense-perception and passion. The latter is intrinsically dependent on matter and conditioned by its laws; the former is characterized by freedom or the power of self-determination; "spirit" in this sense is essentially personal. Hegelianism, indeed, in its doctrines of Subjective, Objective, and Absolute Spirit, tries to maintain the categories of spiritual philosophy (freedom, self-consciousness and the like), in a Monistic framework. But such conceptions demand the recognition of individual personality as an ultimate fact.

In Theology, the uses of the word are various. In the New Testament, it signifies sometimes the soul of man (generally its highest part, e. g., "the spirit is willing"), sometimes the supernatural action of God in man, sometimes the Holy Ghost ("the Spirit of Truth Whom the world cannot receive"). The use of this term to signify the supernatural life of grace is the explanation of St. Paul's language about the spiritual and the carnal man and his enumeration of the three elements, spirit, soul, and body, which gave occasion to the error of the Trichotomists (I Thess., v, 23, Eph., iv, 23).

Matter has generally been conceived as in one sense or another the limitation of spirit. Hence, finite spirits were thought to require a body as a principle of individuation and limitation; only God, the Infinite Spirit, was free from all admixture of matter. Thus, when we find the angels described as ἀσώματοι or ἄυλοι, in the writings of the Fathers, this properly means only that the angels do not possess a gross, fleshly body; it does not at all imply a nature absolutely immaterial. Such Scripture expressions as "bread of angels", "they shall shine as the angels", as well as the apparitions of these heavenly beings, were adduced as proofs of their corporeality. So speak Sts. Ambrose, Chrysostom, Jerome, Hilary, Origen, and many other Fathers. Even in Scholastic times, the degree of immateriality that belongs to finite spirits was disputed. St. Thomas teaches the complete simplicity of all spiritual natures, but the Scotists, by means of their famous *materia primo prima*, introduced a real composition, which they conceived to be necessary to a created nature. As regards the functions of spirits in the world, and their active relations to the visible order of things, see GUARDIAN ANGELS and DEMONOLOGY. Scripture abounds in instances of their dealings with men, chiefly in the character of intermediaries between God and His servants. They are the heralds who announce his commands, and often too the ministers who execute His justice. They take a benevolent interest in the spiritual good of men (Luke, xv, 10). For these reasons, the Church permits and encourages devotion to the angels.

BERKELEY, *Siris* in *Works*, II. See also bibliographies, SPIRITUALISM; SOUL.

MICHAEL MAHER.
JOSEPH BOLLAND.

Spiritism is the name properly given to the belief that the living can and do communicate with the spirits of the departed, and to the various practices by which such communication is attempted. It should be carefully distinguished from Spiritualism (q. v.), the philosophical doctrine which holds, in general, that there is a spiritual order of beings no less real than the material and, in particular, that the soul of man is a spiritual substance. Spiritism, moreover, has taken on a religious character. It claims to prove the preamble of all religions, i. e. the existence of a spiritual world, and to establish a world-wide religion in which the adherents of the various traditional faiths, setting their dogmas aside, can unite. If it has formulated no definite creed, and if its representatives differ in their attitudes toward the beliefs of Christianity, this is simply because Spiritism is expected to supply a new and fuller revelation which will either substantiate on a rational basis the essential Christian dogmas or show that they are utterly unfounded. The knowledge thus acquired will naturally affect conduct, the more so because it is hoped that the discarnate spirits, in making known their condition, will also indicate the means of attaining to salvation or rather of progressing, by a continuous evolution in the other world, to a higher plane of existence and happiness.

THE PHENOMENA.—These are classified as physical and psychical. The former include: production of raps and other sounds; movements of objects (tables, chairs) without contact or with contact insufficient to explain the movement: "apports", i. e. apparitions of objects (e. g. flowers) in a closed room without any visible agency to convey them; moulds, i. e. impressions made upon paraffin and similar substances; luminous appearances, i. e., vague glimmerings of light or faces more or less defined; levitation, i. e. raising of objects from the ground by supposed supernormal means; materialization or appearance of a spirit in visible human form; spirit-photography, in which the features or forms of deceased persons appear on the plate along with the likeness of a living photographed subject. The psychical, or significative, phenomena are those which express ideas or contain messages. To this class belong: table-rapping in answer to questions; automatic writing; slate-writing; trance-speaking; clairvoyance; descriptions of the spirit-world; and communications from the dead.

HISTORY.—For an account of Spiritistic practices in antiquity see NECROMANCY. The modern phase was ushered in by the exhibitions of mesmerism and clairvoyance. In its actual form, however, Spiritism dates from the year 1848 and from the experiences of the Fox family at Hydesville, and later at Rochester, in New York State. Strange "knockings" were heard in the house, pieces of furniture were moved about as though by invisible hands, and the noises became so troublesome that sleep was impossible. At length the "rapper" began to answer questions, and a code of signals was arranged to facilitate communication. It was also found that to receive messages special qualifications were needed; these were possessed by Catherine and Margaret Fox, who are therefore regarded as the first "mediums" of modern times. Similar disturbances occurred in other parts of the country, notably at Stratford, Connecticut, in the house of Rev. Dr. Phelps, a Presbyterian minister, where the manifestations (1850–51) were often violent and the spirit-answers blasphemous. In 1851 the Fox girls were visited in Buffalo by three physicians who were professors in the university of that city. As a result of their examination the doctors declared that the "raps" were simply "crackings" of the knee-joints. But this statement did not lessen either the popular enthusiasm or the interest of more serious persons. The subject was taken up by men like Horace Greeley, Wm. Lloyd Garrison, Robert Hare, professor of chemistry in the University of Pennsylvania, and John Worth Edmonds, a judge of the Supreme Court of New York State. Conspicuous among the Spiritists was Andrew Jackson Davis, whose work, "The Principles of Nature" (1847), dictated by him in trance, contained a theory of the universe, closely resembling the Swedenborgian. Spiritism also found earnest advocates among clergymen of various denominations, especially the Universalists; it appealed strongly to many people who had lost all religious belief in a future life; and it was welcomed by those who were then agitating the question of a new social organization—the pioneers of modern Socialism. So widespread was the belief in Spiritism that in 1854 Congress was petitioned to appoint a scientific commission for the investigation of the phenomena. The petition, which bore some 13,000 signatures, was laid on the table, and no action was taken.

In Europe the way had been prepared for Spiritism by the Swedenborgian movement and by an epidemic of table-turning which spread from the Continent to England and invaded all classes of society. It was still a fashionable diversion when, in 1852, two mediums, Mrs. Hayden and Mrs. Roberts, came from America to London, and held séances which attracted the attention of scientists as well as popular interest. Faraday, indeed, in 1853 showed that the table movements were due to muscular action, and Dr. Carpenter gave the same explanation; but many thoughtful persons, notably among the clergy, held to the Spiritistic interpretation. This was accepted also by Robert Owen, the socialist, while Professor De Morgan, the mathematician, in his account of a sitting with Mrs. Hayden, was satisfied that "somebody or some spirit was reading his thoughts". The later development in England was furthered by mediums who came from America: Daniel Dunglas Home (Hume) in 1855, the Davenport Brothers in 1864, and Henry Slade in 1876. Among the native mediums, Rev. William Stainton Moses became prominent in 1872, Miss Florence Cook in the same year, and William Eglinton in 1886. Spiritism was advocated by various periodical publications, and defended in numerous works some of which were said to have been dictated by the spirits themselves, e. g. the "Spirit Teachings" of Stainton Moses, which purport to give an account of conditions in the other world and form a sort of Spiritistic theology. During this period also, scientific opinion on the subject was divided. While Professors Huxley and Tyndall sharply denounced Spiritism in practice and theory, Mr. (later Sir Wm.) Crookes and Dr. Alfred Russell Wallace regarded the phenomena as worthy of serious investigation. The same view was expressed in the report which the Dialectical Society published in 1871 after an inquiry extending over eighteen months, and at the Glasgow meeting of the British Association in 1876 Professor Barrett, F.R.S., concluded his account of the phenomena he had observed by urging the appointment of a committee of scientific men for the systematic investigation of such phenomena.

The growth of Spiritism on the Continent was marked by similar transitions from popular curiosity to serious inquiry. As far back as 1787, the Exegetic and Philanthropic Society of Stockholm, adhering to the Swedenborgian view, had interpreted the utterances of "magnetized" subjects as messages from the spirit world. This interpretation gradually won favour in France and Germany; but it was not until 1848 that Cahagnet published at Paris the first volume of his "Arcanes de la vie future dévoilées", containing what purported to be communications from the dead. The excitement aroused in Paris by table-turning and rapping led to an investigation by Count Agénor de Gasparin, whose conclusion ("Des Tables tournantes", Paris, 1854) was that the phenomena originated in some physical force of the human body. Professor Thury of Geneva ("Les Tables tournantes", 1855) concurred in this explanation. Baron de Guldenstubbe ("La Réalité des Esprits", Paris, 1857), on the contrary, declared his belief in the reality of spirit intervention, and M. Rivail, known later as Allan Kardec, published the "spiritualistic philosophy" in "Le Livre des Esprits" (Paris, 1853), which became a guide-book to the whole subject.

In Germany also Spiritism was an outgrowth from "animal magnetism". J. H. Jung in his "Theorie der Geisterkunde" declared that in the state of trance the soul is freed from the body, but he regarded the trance itself as a diseased condition. Among the earliest German clairvoyants was Frau Frederica Hauffe, the "Seeress of Prevorst", whose experiences were related by Justinus Kerner in "Die Seherin von Prevorst" (Stuttgart, 1829). In its later development Spiritism was represented in scientific and philosophical circles by men of prominence, e. g. Ulrici, Fichte, Zöllner, Fechner, and Wm. Weber. The last-named three conducted (1877-8) a series of experiments with the American medium Slade at Leipzig. The results were published in Zöllner's "Wissenschaftliche Abhandlungen" (cf. Massey, "Transcendental Physics", London, 1880, in which the portions relating to spiritism are translated). Though considered important at the time, this investigation, owing to lack of caution and accuracy, cannot be regarded as a satisfactory test. (Cf. "Report of the Seybert Commission", Philadelphia, 1887—, which also contains an account of an investigation conducted at the University of Pennsylvania with Slade and other mediums.)

The foregoing outline shows that modern Spiritism within a generation had passed beyond the limits of a merely popular movement and had challenged the attention of the scientific world. It had, moreover, brought about serious divisions among men of science. For those who denied the existence of a soul distinct from the organism it was a foregone conclusion that there could be no such communications as the Spiritists claimed. This negative view, of course, is still taken by all who accept the fundamental ideas of Materialism. But apart from any such a priori considerations, the opponents of Spiritism justified their position by pointing to innumerable cases of fraud which were brought to light either through closer examination of the methods employed or through the admissions of the mediums themselves.

In spite, however, of repeated exposure, there occurred phenomena which apparently could not be ascribed to trickery of any sort. The inexplicable character of these the sceptics attributed to faulty observation. The Spiritistic practices were simply set down as a new chapter in the long history of occultism, magic, and popular superstition. On the other hand, a certain number of thinkers felt obliged to confess that, after making due allowance for the element of fraud, there remained some facts which called for a more systematic investigation. In 1869 the London Dialectical Society appointed a committee of thirty-three members "to investigate the phenomena alleged to be spiritual manifestations, and to report thereon". The committee's report (1871) declares that "motion may be produced in solid bodies without material contact, by some hitherto unrecognized force operating within an undefined distance from the human organism, and beyond the range of muscular action"; and that "this force is frequently directed by intelligence". In 1882 there was organized in London the "Society for Psychical Research" for the scientific examination of what its prospectus terms "debatable phenomena". A motive for investigation was supplied by the history of hypnotism, which had been repeatedly ascribed to quackery and deception. Nevertheless, patient research conducted by rigorous methods had shown that beneath the error and imposture there lay a real influence which was to be accounted for, and which finally was explained on the theory of suggestion. The progress of Spiritism, it was thought, might likewise yield a residuum of fact deserving scientific explanation.

The Society for Psychical Research soon counted among its members distinguished representatives of science and philosophy in England and America; numerous associations with similar aims and methods were organized in various countries. The "Proceedings" of the Society contain detailed reports of investigations in Spiritism and allied subjects, and a voluminous literature, expository and critical, has been created. Among the most notable works are: "Phantasms of the Living" by Gurney, Myers, and Podmore (London, 1886); F. W. H. Myers, "Human Personality and its Survival of Bodily Death" (London, 1903); and Sir Oliver Lodge, F. R. S., "The

Survival of Man" (New York, 1909). In recent publications prominence is given to experiments with the mediums Mrs. Piper of Boston and Eusapia Palladino of Italy; and important contributions to the literature have been made by Professor Wm. James of Harvard, Dr. Richard Hodgson of Boston, Professor Charles Richet (University of Paris), Professor Henry Sidgwick (Cambridge University), Professor Th. Flournoy (University of Geneva), Professor Morselli (University of Genoa), Professor Cesare Lombroso (University of Turin), Professor James H. Hyslop (Columbia University), Professor Wm. R. Newbold (University of Pennsylvania). While some of these writers maintain a critical attitude, others are outspoken in favour of Spiritism, and a few (Myers, James), lately deceased, arranged before death to establish communication with their surviving associates.

HYPOTHESES.—To explain the phenomena which after careful investigation and exclusion of fraud are regarded as authentic, three hypotheses have been proposed. The telepathic hypothesis takes as its starting-point the so-called subliminal consciousness. This, it is claimed, is subject to disintegration in such wise that segments of it may impress another mind (the percipient) even at a distance. The personality is liberated, so to speak, from the organism and invades the soul of another. A medium, on this hypothesis, would obtain information by thought-transference either from the minds of persons present at the séance or from other minds concerning whom the sitters know nothing. This view, it is held, would accord with the recognized facts of hypnosis and with the results of experimental telepathy; and it would explain what appear to be cases of possession. Similar to this is the hypothesis of psychical radiations which distinguishes in man the material body, the soul, and an intermediate principle, the "perispirit". This is a subtle fluid, or astral body, which in certain persons (mediums) can escape from the material organism and thus form a "double". It also accompanies the soul after death and it is the means by which communication is established with the perispirit of the mediums. The Spiritistic hypothesis maintains that the communications are received from disembodied spirits. Its advocates declare that telepathy is insufficient to account for all the facts, that its sphere of influence would have to be enlarged so as to include all the mental states and memories of living persons, and that even with such extension it would not explain the selective character of the phenomena by which facts relevant for establishing the personal identity of the departed are discriminated from those that are irrelevant. Telepathy at most may be the means by which discarnate spirits act upon the minds of living persons. For a discussion of the hypotheses see Hyslop, "Science and a Future Life" (Boston, 1905); Lodge, "The Survival of Man"; and Flournoy, "Spiritism and Psychology" (tr. Carrington, New York, 1911); Grasset, "The Marvels beyond Science" (New York, 1910).

For those who admit that the manifestations proceed from intelligences other than that of the medium, the next question in order is whether these intelligences are the spirits of the departed or beings that have never been embodied in human form. The reply has often been found difficult even by avowed believers in Spiritism, and some of these have been forced to admit the action of extraneous or non-human intelligences. This conclusion is based on several sorts of evidence: the difficulty of establishing spirit-identity, i. e. of ascertaining whether the communicator is actually the personality he or it purports to be; the love of personation on the part of the spirits which leads them to introduce themselves as celebrities who once lived on earth, although on closer questioning they show themselves quite ignorant of those whom they personate; the trivial character of the communications, so radically opposed to what would be expected from those who have passed into the other world and who naturally should be concerned to impart information on the most serious subjects; the contradictory statements which the spirits make regarding their own condition, the relations of God and man, the fundamental precepts of morality; finally the low moral tone which often pervades these messages from spirits who pretend to enlighten mankind. These deceptions and inconsistencies have been attributed by some authors to the subliminal consciousness (Flournoy), by others to spirits of a lower order, i. e. below the plane of humanity (Stainton Moses), while a third explanation refers them quite frankly to demonic intervention (Raupert, "Modern Spiritism", St. Louis, 1904; cf. Grasset, "The Marvels beyond Science," tr. Tubeuf, New York, 1910). For the Christian believer this third view acquires special significance from the fact that the alleged communications antagonize the essential truths of religion such as the Divinity of Christ, atonement and redemption, judgment and future retribution, while they encourage agnosticism, pantheism, and a belief in reincarnation.

Spiritism indeed claims that it alone furnishes an incontestable proof of immortality, a scientific demonstration of the future life that far surpasses any philosophical deduction of Spiritualism, while it gives the death-blow to Materialism. This claim, however, rests upon the validity of the hypothesis that the communications come from disembodied spirits; it gets no support from the telepathic hypothesis or from that of demonic intervention. If either of the latter should be verified the phenomena would be explained without solving or even raising the problem of human immortality. If, again, it were shown that the argument based on the data of normal consciousness and the nature of the soul cannot stand the test of criticism, the same test would certainly be fatal to a theory drawn from mediumistic utterances which are not only the outcome of abnormal conditions, but are also open to widely different interpretations. Even where all suspicion of fraud or collusion is removed—and this is seldom the case—a critical investigator will cling to the idea that phenomena which now seem inexplicable may eventually, like so many other marvels, be accounted for without having recourse to the Spiritistic hypothesis. Those who are convinced, on philosophical grounds, of the soul's immortality may say that communications from the spirit world, if any such there be, go to strengthen their conviction; but to abandon their philosophy and stake all on Spiritism would be more than hazardous; it would, indirectly at least, afford a pretext for a more complete rejection of soul and immortality. In other words, if Spiritism were the sole argument for a future life, Materialism, instead of being crushed, would triumph anew as the only possible theory for science and common sense.

DANGERS.—To this risk of philosophical error must be added the dangers, mental and moral, which Spiritistic practices involve. Whatever the explanation offered for the medium's "powers", their exercise sooner or later brings about a state of passivity which cannot but injure the mind. This is readily intelligible in the hypothesis of an invasion by extraneous spirits, since such a possession must weaken and tend to efface the normal personality. But similar results may be expected if, as the alternate hypothesis maintains, a disintegration of the one personality takes place. In either case, it is not surprising that the mental balance should be disturbed, and self-control impaired or destroyed. Recourse to Spiritism frequently produces hallucinations and other aberrations, especially in subjects who are predisposed to insanity; and even those who are otherwise normal expose themselves to severe physical and mental strain (cf.

Viollet, "Le spiritisme dans ses rapports avec la folie", Paris, 1908). More serious still is the danger of moral perversion. If to practise or encourage deception of any sort is reprehensible, the evil is certainly greater when fraud is resorted to in the inquiry concerning the future life. But apart from any intention to deceive, the methods employed would undermine the foundations of morality, either by producing a disintegration of personality or by inviting the invasion of an extraneous intelligence. It may be that the medium "yields, perhaps, innocently at first to the promptings of an impulse which may come to him as from a higher power, or that he is moved by an instinctive compulsion to aid in the development of his automatic romance—in any case, if he continues to abet and encourage this automatic prompting, it is not likely that he can long retain both honesty and sanity unimpaired. The man who looks on at his hand doing a thing, but acquits himself of responsibility for the thing done, can hardly claim to be considered as a moral agent; and the step is short to instigating and repeating a like action in the future, without the excuse of an overmastering impulse . . . To attend the séances of a professional medium is perhaps at worst to countenance a swindle; to watch the gradual development of innocent automatism into physical mediumship may be to assist at a process of moral degeneration" (Podmore, "Modern Spiritualism", II, 326 sqq.).

Action of the Church.—As Spiritism has been closely allied with the practices of "animal magnetism" and hypnotism, these several classes of phenomena have also been treated under the same general head in the discussions of theologians and in the decisions of ecclesiastical authority. The Congregation of the Inquisition, 25 June, 1840, decreed: "Where all error, sorcery and invocation of the demon, implicit or explicit, is excluded, the mere use of physical means which are otherwise lawful, is not morally forbidden, provided it does not aim at unlawful or evil results. But the application of purely physical principles and means to things or effects that are really supernatural, in order to explain these on physical grounds, is nothing else than unlawful and heretical deception". This decision was reiterated on 28 July, 1847, and a further decree was issued on 30 July, 1856, which, after mentioning discourses about religion, evocation of departed spirits and "other superstitious practices" of Spiritism, exhorts the bishops to put forth every effort for the suppression of these abuses "in order that the flock of the Lord may be protected against the enemy, the deposit of faith safeguarded, and the faithful preserved from moral corruption." The Second Plenary Council of Baltimore (1866), while making due allowance for fraudulent practice in Spiritism, declares that some at least of the manifestations are to be ascribed to Satanic intervention, and warns the faithful against lending any support to Spiritism or even, out of curiosity, attending séances (Decreta, nn. 33–41). The council points out, in particular, the anti-Christian character of Spiritistic teachings concerning religion, and characterizes them as an attempt to revive paganism and magic. A decree of the Holy Office, 30 March, 1898, condemns Spiritistic practices, even though intercourse with the demon be excluded and communication sought with good spirits only. In all these documents the distinction is clearly drawn between legitimate scientific investigation and superstitious abuses. What the Church condemns in Spiritism is superstition with its evil consequences for religion and morality. (Cf. Perrone, "De virtute religionis", Turin, 1867; Noldin, "Summa Theol. Moralis", Innsbruck, 1904, II).

Works by Catholic authors are marked with an asterisk. Capron, *Modern Spiritualism; its Facts and Fanaticisms* (Boston, 1855)—the movement in America; Podmore, *Modern Spiritualism* (London, 1902)—historical survey; Idem, *Studies in Psychical Research* (New York, 1897); Idem, *The Naturalisation of the Supernatural* (New York, 1908); * Brownson, *The Spirit-Rapper* (Boston, 1854) in IX of *Works* (Detroit, 1884); * Wieser, *Der Spiritismus u. das Christenthum* (Innsbruck, 1881); * W. Schneider, *Der neuere Geisterglaube* (Paderborn, 1885); Carpenter, *Mesmerism, Spiritualism, etc.* (New York, 1889); A. R. Wallace, *Miracles and Modern Spiritualism* (London, 1897); * Surbled, *Spiritualisme et spiritisme* (Paris, 1898); Idem, *Spirites et médiums* (Paris, 1901); Flournoy, *Des Indes à la planète Mars* (Paris, 1900); * Gutberlet, *Der Kampf um die Seele*, II (2nd ed., Mainz, 1903); Hyslop, *Enigmas of Psychical Research* (Boston, 1906); Maxwell, *Les phénomènes psychiques* (Paris, 1906); Bennett, *Spiritualism* (New York, 1907); Carrington, *The Physical Phenomena of Spiritualism* (Boston, 1907); Morselli, *Psicologia e spiritismo* (Turin, 1908); Lombroso, tr. Kennedy, *After Death—What?* (Boston, 1909); * Bessmer in *Stimmen aus Maria-Laach*, LXII (1902), LXIV (1903), LXXVII (1909).

Edward A. Pace.

Spirito Santo, Diocese of (Spiritus Sancti), suffragan of São Sebastião do Rio de Janeiro, established in 1896. Its jurisdiction comprises the State of Espirito Santo, United States of Brazil, South America, with twenty-eight municipalities and a Catholic population in 1911 of 202,000 inhabitants, 20 secular priests and 15 friars. Of Catholic educational institutions there are, in the city of Victoria, the capital of the state and seat of the bishop, a *gymnasio* or college of secondary instruction directed by secular priests and having the same privileges as a federal school; and the Collegio das Irmas de Caridade, for girls, under the direction of the Sisters of Charity. At Victoria are also located the "Hospital da Misericordia", in which five Sisters of Charity serve as nurses, and the Santa Casa de Misericordia, a charitable institution founded in 1545, and by decree of 1 June, 1606, it was accorded the same privileges of the Santa Casa de Misericordia of Lisbon; an important annex of this institution is the Orphanato Santa Luzia, an orphan asylum. There are also twelve Catholic associations in Victoria. In other cities and towns of the diocese there are also various Catholic schools, charitable institutions, etc. The present bishop is the Rt. Rev. Fernando de Sousa Monteiro, b. 22 Sept., 1866, raised to the see 1 March, 1902. (See Brazil.)

Julian Moreno-Lacalle.

Spirits, Discernment of. See Discernment of Spirits.

Spiritual Exercises of Saint Ignatius, a short work composed by St. Ignatius of Loyola and written originally in Spanish.

The Text.—The autograph MS. of this "Spiritual Exercises" has unfortunately been lost. What is at present called the "autograph" is only a quarto copy made by a secretary but containing corrections in the author's handwriting. It is now reproduced by phototypy (Rome, 1908). Two Latin translations were made during the lifetime of St. Ignatius. There now remain: (1) the ancient Latin translation, *antiqua versio latina*, a literal version probably made by the saint; (2) a free translation by Father Frusius, more elegant and more in accordance with the style of the period, and generally called the "Vulgate". The *antiqua versio* is dated by the copyist "Rome, 9 July, 1541"; the vulgate version is later than 1541, but earlier than 1548, when the two versions were together presented to Paul III for approval. The pope appointed three examiners, who praised both versions warmly. The Vulgate, more carefully executed from a literary point of view, was only chosen for printing, and was published at Rome on 11 September, 1548, under the simple title: "Exercitia spiritualia". This *princeps* edition was also multiplied by phototypy (Paris, 1910). Besides these two Latin translations there exist two others. One is the still unpublished text left by Bl. Peter Faber to the Carthusians of Cologne before 1546; it holds a middle place between the literal version and the Vulgate. The second is a new literal translation by Father Roothaan, twenty-first general of the Society of Jesus, who, on account of the differences between the Vulgate and the Spanish autograph, wished to retranslate the "Exercises" into Latin, as accurately as possible, at the same time making use of the *versio antiqua*. His intention was not to supplant the Vulgate, and he therefore published the work of Frusius along with his own in parallel columns (1835).

The Spanish autograph text was not printed until long after the Vulgate, by Bernard de Angelis, secretary of the Society of Jesus (Rome, 1615); it has often been republished. The most noteworthy English versions are: (1) "The Spiritual Exercises of St. Ignatius. With Approbation of Superiours. At Saint Omers; Printed by Nicolas Joseph Le Febvre." This translation bears no date but it can be traced back to 1736; the printer was a lay brother of the Society. (2) "The Spiritual Exercises of St. Ignatius. Translated from the Authorized Latin; with extracts from the literal version and notes of the Rev. Father Rothaan [sic] by Charles Seager, M.A., to which is prefixed a Preface by the Right Rev. Nicholas Wiseman, D.D., bishop of Melipotamus" (London, Dolman, 1847); which was republished by Murphy at Baltimore, about 1850. (3) "The Text of the Spiritual Exercises of St. Ignatius, translated from the original Spanish", by Father John Morris, S.J., published by Burns and Oates (London, 1880). The reader of the "Exercises" need not look for elegance of style. "St. Ignatius", says F. Astrain, "writes in coarse, incorrect, and laboured Castilian, which only at times arrests the attention by the energetic precision and brevity with which certain thoughts are expressed." There are outpourings of the soul in different colloquies, but their affecting interest does not lie in words; it is wholly in the keen situation, created by the author, of the sinner before the crucifix, the knight before his king, etc.

COMPOSITION OF THE EXERCISES.—The book is composed of documents or spiritual exercises, reduced to the order most fitted to move the minds of the faithful to piety, as was remarked in the Brief of approval. We find in this work documents (instructions, admonitions, warnings), exercises (prayers, meditations, examination of conscience, and other practices), and the method according to which they are arranged. The sources of the book are the Sacred Scriptures and the experiences of spiritual life. Ignatius indeed was little by little prepared by Divine Providence to write his book. From 1521 the thoughts which precede his conversion, the progress of his repentance, the pious practices which he embraces at Montserrat and at Manresa helped to give him a knowledge of asceticism. His book is a work lived by himself and later on lived by others under his eyes. But a book so lived is not composed all at once; it requires to be retouched, corrected, and added to frequently. These improvements, which neither Polanco nor Bartoli hide, are revealed by a simple examination of the Spanish text, where along with the Castilian there are found Latin or Italian expressions, together with Scholastic terms which the writer could not have used before, at least, the beginning of his later studies. Ignatius himself admitted this to Father Luis Gonzales: "I did not compose the Exercises all at once. When anything resulting from my own experience seemed to me likely to be of use to others, I took note of it". Father Nadal, Ignatius's friend and contemporary, writes of the final redaction: "After having completed his studies, the author united his first attempts of the Exercises, made many additions, put all in order, and presented his work for the examination and judgment of the Apostolic See".

It seems probable that the "Exercises" were completed while St. Ignatius was attending lectures at the University of Paris. The copy of Bl. Peter Faber, written undoubtedly about the time when he followed the Exercises under Ignatius's direction (1533), contains all the essential parts. Moreover, some parts of the book bear their date. Such are: the "Rules for the distribution of alms", intended for beneficed clergymen, masters, or laureates of the university, in which occurs a citation of the Council of Carthage, thus leading one to suppose that the writer had studied theology; the "Rules for thinking with the Church", which appear to have been suggested by the measures taken by an assembly of theologians at Valladolid in 1527 against the Erasmists of Spain, or by the Faculty of Paris in 1535, 1542, against the Protestants. The final completion of the "Exercises" may be dated from 1541, when a fair copy of the *versio antiqua*, which St. Ignatius calls "Todos exercicios breviter en latin", was made. It may be asked how far the work of composition was carried out during the residence of the saint at Manresa. This spot, where Ignatius arrived in March, 1522, must always be considered as the cradle of the "Exercises". The substance of the work dates from Manresa. Ignatius found there the precious metal which for a long time he wrought and polished. "A work," as Fr. Astrain rightly says, "which contributes throughout so admirably to realize the fundamental idea set up by the author, is evidently not an invention made by parts, or composed of passages written at various times or under varying circumstances." The "Exercises" clearly bear the mark of Manresa. The mind of Ignatius, during his retirement there, was full of military memories and of thoughts of the future; hence the double characteristic of his book, the chivalrous note and the march towards the choice of a state of life. The ideas of the knight are those of the service due to a sovereign, of the shame that clings to the treason of a vassal (first week), and in the kingdom, those of the crusade formed against the infidels, and of the confrontation of the Two Standards (second week). But during his convalescence at the castle, the reading of the lives of the saints gave a mystical turn to his chivalrous ideas; the great deeds to be imitated henceforth are no longer those of a Roland, but of a Dominic or a Francis.

To help him in his outline of evangelical perfection, Ignatius received a special assistance, which Polanco and Ribadeneira call the unction of the Holy Ghost. Without this grace, the composition of the "Exercises" remains a mystery. How could a rough and ignorant soldier conceive and develop a work so original, so useful for the salvation and the perfection of souls, a book which astonishes one by the originality of its method and the powerful efficacy of its virtue? We ought not, however, to consider this Divine assistance as a complete revelation. What St. Ignatius knew of spiritual ways, he had learned chiefly from personal experience and by the grace of God, Who treated him "as the schoolmaster does a child". It does not mean that he had not the advice of a confessor to guide him, for he was directed by John Chanones at Montserrat; nor does it mean that he had read nothing himself, as we know that he had books at hand. We must therefore consider the revelation of the "Exercises", not as a completely supernatural manifestation of all the truths contained in the work, but as a kind of inspiration, or special Divine assistance, which prevented all essential error, and suggested many thoughts useful for the salvation of the author, and of readers at all times. This inspiration is the more admissible as Ignatius was favoured with great light in Divine things. Ribadeneira, writing from Madrid, 18 April, 1607, to Fr. Girón, rector of Salamanca, dwells on the wonderful fruits of the "Exercises", fruits foreseen and willed by God. Such a result could not be the effect of merely human reading and study, and he adds: "This has been the general opinion of all the old fathers of the Society, of us all who have lived and conversed with our blessed father".

Another tradition concerns the part taken by the

Blessed Virgin in the composing of the "Exercises" at Manresa. It is not based on any written testimony of the contemporaries of St. Ignatius, though it became universal in the seventeenth century. Possibly it is founded upon earlier oral testimony, and upon a revelation made in 1600 to the Venerable Marina de Escobar, and related in the "Life of Father Balthazar Alvarez". This tradition has often been symbolized by painters, who represent Ignatius writing from the Blessed Virgin's dictation.

Although Ignatius had been educated just like the ordinary knights of his time, he was fond of caligraphy and still more of reading; his convalescence at Loyola enabled him to gratify this double inclination. We know that he wrote there, in different coloured inks, a quarto book of 300 folios in which he seems to have gathered together extracts from the only two books to be found in the castle, which were "The Flower of the Saints" in Spanish, and "The Life of Jesus Christ" by Ludolph of Saxony or the Carthusian, published in Spanish at Alcalá, 1502 to 1503. "The Flower of the Saints" has left no apparent trace in the "Exercises", except an advice to read something similar after the second week. Ludolph's influence is more noticeable in expressions, ascetic principles, and methodic details. The part of the "Exercises" treating of the life of Christ, is especially indebted to him.

Ignatius, having recovered his health and determined to lead a hermit's life, left Loyola for Montserrat and Manresa. He spent the greater part of the year 1522 in the latter town, three leagues distant from Montserrat, under the direction of his confessor, Dom John Chanones. According to a witness in the process of canonization Ignatius went to see Chanones every Saturday. He could moreover have met him or other Benedictines at the priory of Manresa, which was dependent on Montserrat. It is possible that he received from them a copy of the "Imitation of Christ" in Spanish, for he certainly had that book at Manresa; they must have given him also the "Ejercitatorio de la vida espiritual", of Dom Garcia de Cisneros, published at Montserrat in 1500. Ribadeneira in his letter to Fr. Girón thinks it very probable that St. Ignatius was acquainted with this Castilian work, that he availed himself of it for prayer and meditation, that Chanones explained different parts to him, and that the title "Exercises" was suggested to him by the "Ejercitatorio". The Benedictines made use of this book for the conversion or edification of the pilgrims of Montserrat; in fact the tradition of the monastery relates that Chanones communicated it to his penitent. The "Exercises" borrow very little expressly from the "Imitation of Christ". There is, however, to be noticed a general concordance of its doctrine and that of the "Exercises", and an invitation to read it.

Was the "Ejercitatorio" more closely followed? In trying to solve this question it is not sufficient to draw conclusions from the resemblance of the titles, or to establish a parallel with a few details; it is necessary above all to compare the plans and methods of the two works. Whilst the "Exercises" consider the word "week" in its metaphorical sense and give liberty to add or to omit days, the "Ejercitatorio" presents a triple series of seven meditations, one and not several for each day of the real week. The whole series of twenty-one meditations is exhausted in just three weeks, which answer to the three lives: the purgative, the illuminative, and the unitive. The author seeks only to raise the "exercitator" gradually to the contemplative life, whereas St. Ignatius leads the exercitant to determine for himself the choice of a state of life amongst those most pleasing to God. The "Ejercitatorio" does not mention anything of the foundation, nor of the kingdom, of the particular examination, of the election, of the discernment of spirits, nor of the rules for rightly regulating one's food and for thinking with the Orthodox Church, nor of the three methods of praying. Only a few counsels of Cisneros have been adopted by St. Ignatius in the annotations 2, 4, 13, 18, 19, 20, and the additions 2, 4. Some of Cisneros's ideas are to be found in the meditations of the first week. The other weeks of St. Ignatius are entirely different. The similarities are so reduced in fact to a very small number.

But the work of Cisneros itself is only a compilation. Cisneros admits having reproduced passages from Cassian, Bernard, Bonaventure, Gerson etc.; moreover, he does not give the names of the contemporaries from whom he copied. Amongst other books Cisneros read and copied the "De spiritualibus ascensionibus" of Gerard Zerbolt of Zutphen (1367–98) and the "Rosetum exercitiorum spiritualium" of John Mombaer, or Mauburnus (d. 1502), who was also indebted to Gerard. Almost all in Cisneros that pertains to the method of spiritual exercises is extracted from the "Rosetum". The different ways of exercising oneself in the contemplation of the life and passion of Jesus Christ are taken from the "De spiritualibus ascensionibus". All Cisneros's borrowings were disclosed by Fr. Watrigant (see bibliography). Zutphen and Mombaer, like Thomas à Kempis, belonged to the Society of the Brothers of Common Life, founded towards the end of the fourteenth century by Gerard de Groote and Florence Radewyns. This society caused a revival of spiritual life by the publication of numerous ascetic treatises, several of which appeared under the title of "Spiritual Exercises". The Brothers of Common Life, or the Devoti, devoted themselves also to the reform of the clergy and monasteries. The Benedictine Congregation of Valladolid, on which Monserrat was dependent, had been under the influence of Lewis Barbo, who was connected with the brothers. We must therefore conclude that Ignatius may have profited by the result of Zutphen's and Mauburnus's labours whilst he read Cisneros or listened to Chanones's explanations at Manresa. Later, when he understood Latin, during his studies at the Universities of Alcalá and Paris, or while travelling in Flanders he may himself have become acquainted with the works of the Devoti. A greater analogy is to be noticed between Zutphen and Ignatius, two practical minds, than between Loyola and Cisneros.

ORIGINALITY OF THE WORK.—We may therefore look upon the question of a supposed plagiarism on the part of St. Ignatius to the detriment of Cisneros, as being definitively settled. This question was raised by Dom Constantine Cajetan, or rather by some one who assumed his name, in a treatise published at Venice in 1641: "De religiosa S. Ignatii . . . per patres Benedictinos institutione . . . ". The Jesuit John Rho answered him in his "Achates" (Lyons, 1644). Both the attack and reply were put on the Index, no doubt on account of their excessive acrimony. Besides, the general assembly of the Congregation of Monte Cassino which met at Ravenna in 1644, by a decree dissociated itself from the aggressor. The quarrel was afterwards renewed on several occasions, chiefly by the heterodox, but always without success. Benedictines and Jesuits agree to acknowledge that if St. Ignatius owes anything to Montserrat, he has retained his entire originality. Whatever may be said about the works he read and what he borrowed, his book is truly his own. A writer is never blamed for having previously searched and studied, if his own work is impressed with his personality, and treats the subject from a new point of view. This has been successfully accomplished by St. Ignatius, and with all the greater merit, as he could not change anything of the traditional truths of Christianity, or pretend to invent mental prayer.

Ignatius's originality appears at first sight in the

selection and co-ordination of his material. To select some of the great truths of religion, to drive them deeply into the heart, until man thoroughly impressed falls at the Lord's feet, crying out like another Saul "Domine, quid me vis facere?", such is the genius, the ascetic character, of St. Ignatius. But to bring about this result it was necessary for the selected truths to be linked together in a logical series and animated by a progressive movement. The methodic order and irresistible deduction of the "Exercises" distinguish them from a large number of spiritual works. Above all the originality of St. Ignatius is displayed in the care with which he combines the subjects of meditation and ascetic principles, and the minute advice that guides and moderates, when necessary, the application of the "Exercises". We find in the annotations at the beginning, in the notes strewn here and there, in the rules for the discernment of spirits a real system of spiritual training, that makes adequate provision for the different states of soul of the exercitant, and warns him, or rather his director, of what is most fitting, according to the circumstances of the case. Nothing is left to chance. One sees how to adapt the general progress of the retreat to different persons, according to their occupations, the degree of their fervour, and the advantage they derive from the "Exercises". This art of proportioning spiritual instruction to the powers of the soul and to Divine grace was entirely new, at least under the precise and methodic form given to it by St. Ignatius.

DOCTRINE OF THE BOOK.—The two words that form the general title of St. Ignatius's book bespeak at once the soul's action and labour, and the interior struggle. The still more explicit title which we find immediately after the annotations leaves one no doubt: "Spiritual Exercises to conquer oneself and regulate one's life, and to avoid coming to a determination through any inordinate affection". A method is here offered, which with God's grace teaches and helps one to overcome oneself, that is to say one's unruly passions, and by gaining control over every conscious act, to acquire inward peace—a method of self-conquest and self-governent. A general idea of the "Exercises" may best be gained from Diertins's summary: After setting forth the end for which God created man and all other things, the book, ever considering this truth as the first foundation, leads us in a short time by the way known as the purgative way to acknowledge the ugliness of the sins which have caused us to stray shamefully from the end, and to cleanse our souls from sin. Setting before us the example of Christ, our King and Leader, the author then invites us, in what is termed the illuminative life, to avoid the devil's standard and to follow the standard of this very good and wise Chief, and to imitate His virtues; indeed he almost forces us to do so by the meditation of the three classes, or grades, of men (the first of which is reluctant to follow Christ, the second eager to do so, but with limitations, and the last bent on following Him at once, wholly, and always). These resolutions are strengthened more and more in the third week, at the sight of Jesus Christ walking before us with His cross. Lastly, in the unitive way, which comprises the fourth week, he enkindles in our hearts a desire for the glory of Jesus risen, and for His purest love. To this are joined annotations, additions, preludes, colloquies, examinations, modes of election, rules for rightly regulating one's food, for discerning spirits, for the scrupulous, for thinking with the Orthodox Church, etc. The whole, if applied in the prescribed order, possesses the incredible strength of leading one to solid virtue and to eternal salvation. The four weeks have been summed up still more briefly in as many sentences: (1) deformata reformare; (2) reformata conformare; (3) conformata confirmare; (4) confirmata transformare; that is: (1) to reform what has been deformed by sin; (2) to make what is thus reformed conform to the Divine model, Jesus; (3) to strengthen what thus conforms; (4) to transform by love the already strengthened resolutions.

This method of spiritual progress had already been traced by St. Paul (Hebr., xii, 1-2). It cannot be repeated too often that, if St. Ignatius displayed his originality in uniting and co-ordinating the materials of his book, he did not compose the matter itself. He derived it from the ever open treasury of the Catholic Church, from Scripture and Tradition, from the Bible and the Fathers. The Gospel is the marrow of the "Exercises". The spirituality of St. Ignatius is in constant harmony with the teachings of Christ and His Apostles. What is the "homo vincat seipsum", but an echo of the "abneget semstipsum"? And whence came Loyola's idea of giving us the soldier's theory, a warlike book which contains all the plan of a campaign of man's struggle against himself, if not from the Saviour's words, which are a declaration of war: "Do not think that I came to send peace upon earth: I came not to send peace, but the sword" (Matt., x, 34). The spirituality of the "Exercises" belongs, therefore, to the active and militant kind. We must also remark that the work is not a mere book for reading or a mere manual of devotion; it gives us in the high sense of the word a psychological and pedagogic method. Mr. Orby Shipley, a convert from Protestantism to Catholicism, judged them rightly, when he said in the preface of his edition (London, 1870): "This treatise is not so much a manual as a method—and a method the value, the extraordinary power, of which does not appear at first sight. One of its great marvels consists in the fact that it has done so very much by such very simple means . . . They are no mere theoretical compositions, but they have been framed upon the closest study of the human mind; . . . they enter into its several emotions, encounter its numberless difficulties, and probe to their very depths its several springs of thought and action".

To obtain the desired result St. Ignatius uses only a few words, but these are so selected as to make a deep impression on the mind and, if seriously meditated on by the exercitant and fostered in his soul, will soon develop into powerful thoughts and become a source of great spiritual enlightenment and consequently of earnest energetic resolutions. However, though the method of St. Ignatius leaves the exercitant to think for himself, the author does not intend that the latter should use it without guidance. He places the "Book of Exercises" in the hands of a director, and entrusts him with applying it to the exercitant. He teaches him how to guide a soul in the choice of a state of life and in the work of self-reform. The annotations, which provide a key to the "Exercises", are intended more especially for the director. The greater part of them—the second, sixth, seventh, eighth, ninth, tenth, twelfth, thirteenth, fourteenth, fifteenth, seventeenth, eighteenth, a total of twelve out of twenty—is written for "el que da los Exercicios" (the person who gives the exercises). The fifteenth advises him to proceed with great discretion, so as not to interfere between the Creator and the creature, and to abstain especially in the case of a retreat of election, from any suggestion regarding the determination to be taken, even should it be, strictly speaking, for the very best. This advice shows how falsely some critics of the Exercises represent them as bringing undue influence to bear on the will, with a view to enslaving or paralyzing it. From this also appears the absurdity of Muller's thesis in "Les origines de la Compagnie de Jésus" (Paris, 1898), in which he strives to show the Mohammedan origin of the Exercises and of the Society of Jesus. In this way, therefore, the director in compliance with the author's desire respects the soul's freedom, a freedom already regulated by the authority of the Church, of which he is the representative. He also considers the soul's capacity; the Exercises contain in themselves matters useful to all, but taken altogether they may not be suitable to every one. The eighteenth annotation forbids them to be given indiscriminately, without considering who the exercitant is. Finally to sum up, all St. Ignatius's spirituality lies in traditional Catholic instruction, in a method favourable to personal activity, and in the importance of prudent direction.

The commentators who have attempted to explain and penetrate the doctrine of the "Exercises" are theorists who consider either the entire book or certain parts of it, and show the book's order and connexion and when necessary justify the thought. Several of them, not satisfied with simply discussing the method, deal also with the practice. Those whose names we give here belong to the Society of Jesus, but they did not write solely for their order: sixteenth century—Achille Gagliardi; seventeenth century—Francisco Suarez, Antoine Le Gaudier, Luis de la Palma, Giovanni Bucellani, Tobias Lohner, Ignatius Diertins; eighteenth century—Claude Judde, Jean-Joseph Petitdidier, Baltasar de Moncada, Peter Ferrusola; nineteenth century—Johann Philipp Roothaan, Pierre Jennesseaux, Antoine Denis, Marin de Boylesve, Jaime Nonell, James Clare, Franz de Hummelauer, Jaime Gutiérrez.

CRITICISM UNFAVOURABLE AND FAVOURABLE.—We refer the reader to Diertins's narration of the "persecutions" to which the "Exercises" were subjected during the lifetime of St. Ignatius. He counts no less than twelve. The first attacks may be attributed to the surprise felt by ecclesiastics at the sight of a layman treating of spiritual matters, before having made his theological studies; the others arose from some difficulty of interpretation or from erroneous judgments as to the meaning of the text. These malevolent or over-zealous censurers were answered by Nadal and Suarez, who were justified by the approbation of the Holy See. The attacks of the present day are generally unscientific, inspired by passion, and made without any preliminary examination of the question. When the adversary's mind conceives a caricature of the "Exercises" either because he has not read them, or because before reading them he has been influenced by the erroneous statements of other hostile critics, the attack appears legitimate; in reality it will be found to refer to something that is not in the "Exercises". Besides the attacks by their mutual opposition destroy one another. The "Exercises" cannot have, simultaneously, a machiavellian and an anodyne character, or be rapt in the clouds and yet crawl upon the soil. Long ago they were, and to-day are, charged with being a clever machinery destined to strike and move the imagination, and finally through hallucination produce ecstasies. Michelet and Quinet in their too famous lectures revived this calumny, which has been answered by Fr. Cahour in his pamphlet: "Des jésuites par un jésuite". To this charge of charlatanry one reply will suffice, the answer made by a young religious, Rodrigo de Menezès, on being asked whether he had not been favoured with any kind of vision: "Yes, I witnessed a very affecting sight, the state of my soul, the nothingness of this world and the misfortune of losing God for ever".

This sight, if it can move a sinner to conversion, is not one likely to cause a steady mind to wander. And yet W. James mentions, as the culminating point of the "Exercises", "a half-hallucinated monoideism" ("L'Expérience religieuse", Paris, 1906, p. 345). Certain critics have reproached the "Exercises" with favouring private inspiration, in the Protestant sense, and with opening a path to illuminism. This criticism was emphasized in the beginning by Thomas de Pedroche, O.P., and arose from an erroneous interpretation of the fifteenth annotation, in which St. Ignatius advises the director not to substitute his own views for those God may have upon the exercitant. There is no question of leaving him an exaggerated liberty which might draw him beyond the limits laid down by the Church. We therefore see that some find in Ignatius's method illuminism, hallucination, and phantasmagoria; others see in it nothing dazzling, but rather dulness and insipidity. "There are people," said the Abbé Guetée, "who consider this book a masterpiece, and others find it but very ordinary" ("Histoire des Jésuites", Paris, 1858, I, 12). This charge appears again under a different form,—the "Exercises" afford but a scanty method, "a Japanese culture of counterfeited dwarfish trees" (Huysmans, "En Route", Paris, 1896, p. 398). Finally, some Catholics see in it only a book for beginners, a retreat for the time of conversion, and a suitable means to guide one's first steps in the way of perfection. A Protestant clergyman, Rev. Mr. Carter, observes, on the contrary, that the method is rather wide and free, since "one of the first rules laid down by St. Ignatius for the director of a retreat is, that he is to adapt the Exercises to the age, the capacity, the strength of the person about to perform them" ("Retreats with notes of addresses", London, 1893, p. xxv).

The praise bestowed on the "Exercises" far exceeds the adverse criticism. As they are considered a school of sanctity, it is interesting to know what the saints thought of them. The practice of Saints Philip Romolo Neri, Charles Borromeo, Francis de Sales, and Alphonsus Liguori is more eloquent testimony in favour of the "Exercises" than anything they have written; and it will be sufficient to recall the words of St. Leonard of Port-Maurice: "During these holy days we must exercise ourselves in the Divine art of making secure the great important affair of our salvation. As God has inspired the glorious founder of the illustrious Society of Jesus with this precious art, we have but to follow the method laid down by him in his admirable book of the Exercises." Since the approbation given by Paul III in 1548, the "Exercises" have often been favoured by the sovereign pontiffs; the praises they have bestowed on them are mingled with recommendations of retreats, the usage of which, according to St. Francis de Sales, was revived by St. Ignatius. We need mention only Alexander VII, Clement XII, Benedict XIV, Clement XIII, and Pius IX. All their eulogies have been resumed by Leo XIII in his Brief of 8 February, 1900: "The importance of St. Ignatius's book with regard to the eternal welfare of souls has been proved by an experience of three centuries and by the evidence of those remarkable men, who, during this lapse of time, have distinguished themselves in the ascetic paths of life or in the practice of sanctity."

Mgr Camus, Bishop of Belley, calls the "Exercises" a "Golden book, of pure gold, more precious than either gold or topaz" ("Direction à l'Oraison mentale", Lyons, 1623, c. xix, p. 157); Mgr Freppel, "A book that I should call the work of a man of genius, if it were not that of a saint, a wonderful book, which, with the 'Imitation of Christ', is perhaps of all books written by man the one which gains the most souls to God" ("Discours-Panégyriques", Paris, 1882, II, 36, 37); and Cardinal Wiseman: "There are many books from which the reader is taught to expect much; but which, perused, yield him but little profit. Those are few and most precious, which, at first sight, and on slender acquaintance, seem to contain but little; but the more they are studied, the more instruction, the more solid benefit they bestow; which are like a soil that looks bare and unadorned, but which contains beneath its surface rich treasures that must be digged out and drawn from a great depth. To this second class I know no book that so justly belongs as the little work here presented to the public" (Preface to Fr. ed. of the "Exercises" by Seager, London, 1847, p. xi). Janssen says: "This little book, considered by the Protestants themselves as a first class psychological masterpiece, has been for the German nation, and towards the history of its faith and civilization, one of the most important writings of modern times. . . . It has worked such extraordinary influence over souls, that no other ascetic work may be compared to it" ("L'Allemagne et la Réforme", Fr. ed., IV, 402).

Non-Catholics also praise it. "The Spiritual Exercises", according to Macaulay, "is a manual of conversion, proposing a plan of interior discipline, by means of which, in neither more nor less than four weeks, the metamorphosis of a sinner into a faithful servant of Christ is realized, step by step" ("Edinburgh Review", November, 1842, p. 29). More recently, the Canon Charles Bodington, praising the Jesuit missionaries, so lavish of their sweat and blood, really "worthy of hearty admiration and respect", added: "Probably the noble and devotional side of the lives of these remarkable men has been largely sustained by the use of the method of the spiritual exercises left to them by their founder" ("Books of Devotion", London, 1903, p. 130). Finally, a short time ago Karl Holl (see bibliography), a German, declared the "Exercises" to be a masterpiece of pedagogy, which instead of annihilating personality serves to elevate the spirit. The Positivist P. Lafitte, in the lectures delivered by him at the Collège de France, declares: "These Exercises are to my mind a real masterpiece of political and moral wisdom and merit careful study. . . . The destination of these Exercises is to so organize the moral life of the individual that by a prolonged, solitary, and personal labour he himself realizes the most perfect balance of the mind" ("Revue occidentale", 1 May, 1894, p. 309).

Monumenta historica, S. J. (Madrid, 1894); SOMMERVOGEL, Bibl. de la Compagnie de Jésus (Brussels, 1890); Acta SS., VII, July; STÖGER, Die aszetische Literatur über die geistlichen Uebungen (Ratisbon, 1850); DIERTINS, Hist. exercitiorum spiritualium (Rome, 1732); WATRIGANT, La genèse des exercices de saint Ignace (Amiens, 1897); DEBUCHY, Introduction à l'étude des exercices spirituels (Enghien, 1906); BARTOLI-MICHEL, Hist. de s. Ignace de Loyola (Bruges, 1893); ASTRAIN, Hist. de la compañia de Jesús en la asistencia de España (Madrid, 1902); JOLY, Saint Ignace de Loyola (Paris, 1899); BESSE, Une question d'histoire littéraire au XVIe siècle in Revue des quest. hist. (January, 1897); SUAREZ, De religione, IV, tr. X, IX, v; CLARE, The Science of Spiritual Life according to the Spiritual Exercises (New York, 1896); JANSSEN, L'Allemagne et la réforme, IV (Paris, 1895); HOLL, Die geistlichen Übungen des Ignatius von Loyola (Tübingen, 1905).

PAUL DEBUCHY.

Spiritualism.—The term "Spiritualism" has been frequently used during recent years to denote the belief in the possibility of communication with disembodied spirits, and the various devices employed to realize this belief in practice. The term "Spiritism" (q. v.), which obtains in Italy, France, and Germany, seems more apt to express this meaning. Spiritualism, then, suitably stands opposed to Materialism. We may say in general that Spiritualism is the doctrine which denies that the contents of the universe are limited to matter and the properties and operations of matter. It maintains the existence of real being or beings (minds, spirits) radically distinct in nature from matter. It may take the form of Spiritualistic Idealism, which denies the existence of any real material being outside of the mind; or, whilst defending the reality of spiritual being, it may also allow the separate existence of the material world. Further, Idealistic Spiritualism may either take the form of Monism (e. g. with Fichte), which teaches that there exists a single universal mind or ego of which all finite minds are but transient moods or stages: or it may adopt a pluralistic theory (e.g. with Berkeley), which resolves the universe into a Divine Mind together with a multitude of finite minds into which the former infuses all those experiences that generate the belief in an external, independent, material world. The second or moderate form of Spiritualism, whilst maintaining the existence of spirit, and in particular the human mind or soul, as a real being distinct from the body, does not deny the reality of matter. It is, in fact, the common doctrine of Dualism. However, among the systems of philosophy which adhere to Dualism, some conceive the separateness or mutual independence of soul and body to be greater and others less. With some philosophers of the former class, soul and body seem to have been looked upon as complete beings merely accidentally united. For these a main difficulty is to give a satisfactory account of the inter-action of two beings so radically opposed in nature.

Historically, we find the early Greek philosophers tending generally towards Materialism. Sense experience is more impressive than our higher, rational consciousness, and sensation is essentially bound up with the bodily organism. Anaxagoras was the first, apparently, among the Greeks to vindicate the predominance of mind or reason in the universe. It was, however, rather as a principle of order, to account for the arrangement and design evident in nature as a whole, than to vindicate the reality of individual minds distinct from the bodies which they animate. Plato was virtually the father of western spiritualistic philosophy. He emphasized the distinction between the irrational or sensuous and the rational functions of the soul. He will not allow the superior elements in knowledge or the higher "parts" of the soul to be explained away in terms of the lower. Both subsist in continuous independence and opposition. Indeed, the rational soul is related to the body merely as the pilot to the ship or the rider to his horse. Aristotle fully recognized the spirituality of the higher rational activity of thought, but his treatment of its precise relation to the individual human soul is obscure. On the other hand, his conception of the union of soul and body, and of the unity of the human person, is much superior to that of Plato. Though the future life of the human soul, and consequently its capacity for an existence separate from the body, was one of the most fundamental and important doctrines of the Christian religion, yet ideas as to the precise meaning of spirituality were not at first clear, and we find several of the earliest Christian writers (though maintaining the future existence of the soul separate from the body), yet conceiving the soul in a more or less materialistic way (cf. Justin, Irenæus, Tertullian, Clement, etc.). The Catholic philosophic doctrine of Spiritualism received much of its development from St. Augustine, the disciple of Platonic philosophy, and its completion from Albertus Magnus and St. Thomas, who perfected the Aristotelian account of the union of soul and body.

Modern Spiritualism, especially of the more extreme type, has its origin in Descartes. Malebranche, and indirectly Berkeley, who contributed so much in the sequel to Monistic Idealism, are indebted to Descartes, whilst every form of exaggerated Dualism which set mind and body in isolation and contrast traces its descent from him. In spite of serious faults and defects in their systems, it should be recognized that Descartes and Leibnitz contributed much of the most effective resistance to the wave of Materialism which acquired such strength in Europe at the end of the eighteenth and during the first half of the nineteenth centuries. In particular, Maine de Biran, who emphasized the inner activity and spirituality of the will, followed by Jouffroy and Cousin, set up so vigorous an opposition to the current Materialism as to win for their theories the distinctive title of "Spiritualism". In Germany, in addition to Kant, Fichte, and other Monistic Idealists, we find Lotze and Herbart advocating realistic forms of Spiritualism. In England, among the best-known advocates of

Dualistic Spiritualism, were, in succession to the Scottish School, Hamilton and Martineau; and of Catholic writers, Brownson in America, and W. G. Ward in England.

Evidence for the Doctrine of Spiritualism.—Whilst modern Idealists and writers advocating an extreme form of Spiritualism have frequently fallen into grievous error in their own positive systems, their criticisms of Materialism and their vindication of the reality of spiritual being seem to contain much sound argument and some valuable contributions, as was indeed to be expected, to this controversy. (1) *Epistemological Proof.*—The line of reasoning adopted by Berkeley against Materialism has never met with any real answer from the latter. If we were compelled to choose between the two, the most extreme Idealistic Spiritualism would be incomparably the more logical creed to hold. Mind is more intimately known than matter, ideas are more ultimate than molecules. External bodies are only known in terms of consciousness. To put forward as a final explanation that thought is merely a motion or property of certain bodies, when all bodies are, in the last resort, only revealed to us in terms of our thinking activity, is justly stigmatized by all classes of Spiritualists as utterly irrational. When the Materialist or Sensationist reasons out his doctrine, he is landed in hopeless absurdity. Materialism is in fact the answer of the men who do not think, who are apparently quite unaware of the presuppositions which underlie all science. (2) *Teleological Proof.*—The contention, old as Anaxagoras, that the order, adaptation, and design evidently revealed in the universe postulate a principle distinct from matter for its explanation is also a valid argument for Spiritualism. Matter cannot arrange itself. Yet that there is arrangement in the universe, and that this postulates the agency of a principle other than matter, is continually more and more forced upon us by the utter failure of natural selection to meet the demands made on it during the last half of the past century to accomplish by the blind, fortuitous action of physical agents work demanding the highest intelligence. (3) *Ethical Proof.*—The denial of spiritual beings distinct from, and in some sense independent of, matter inexorably involves the annihilation of morality. If the mechanical or materialistic theory of the universe be true, every movement and change of each particle of matter be the inevitable outcome of previous physical conditions. There is no room anywhere for effective human choice or purpose in the world. Consequently, all those notions which form the constituent elements of man's moral creed—duty, obligation, responsibility, merit, desert, and the rest—are illusions of the imagination. Virtue and vice, fraud and benevolence are alike the inevitable outcome of the individual's circumstances, and ultimately as truly beyond his control as the movement of the piston is in regard to the steam-engine. (4) *Inefficacy and Uselessness of Mind in the Materialist View.*—Again, unless the reality of spirit distinct from, and independent of, matter be admitted, the still more incredible conclusion inexorably follows that mind, thought, consciousness play no really operative part in the world's history. If mind is not a real distinct energy, capable of interfering with, guiding, and influencing the movements of matter, then clearly it has played no real part in the creations of art, literature, or science. Consciousness is merely an inefficacious by-product, an epiphenomenon which has never modified in any degree the movements of matter concerned in the history of the human race. (5) *Psychological Proof.*—The outcome of all the main theses of psychology, empirical and rational, in Catholic systems of philosophy is the establishment of a Spiritualistic Dualism, and the determination of the relations of soul and body. Analysis of the higher activities of the soul, and especially of the operations of intellectual conception, judgment, reasoning, and self-conscious reflexion, proves the faculty of intellect and the soul to which it belongs to be of a spiritual nature, distinct from matter, and not the outcome of a power inherent in a bodily organ. At the same time the Scholastic doctrine, better than any other system, furnishes a conception of the union of soul and body which accounts for the extrinsic dependence of the spiritual operations of the mind on the organism; whilst maintaining the spiritual nature of the soul, it safeguards the union of soul and body in a single person.

Ward, *Naturalism and Agnosticism* (London and New York, 1899); Ladd, *Philosophy of Mind* ((New York, 1895); Balfour, *Foundations of Belief* (London, 1895); Castelein, *Matérialisme et Spiritualisme* (Brussels, 1895); Romanes, *Fallacy of Materialism in Nineteenth Cent.* (1882), xii; Balmes, *Fundamental Philosophy* (tr., New York, 1896); Lotze, *Microcosmus*, tr. Jones (Edinburgh, 1885); Ferrier, *Lectures and Phil. Remains* (Edinburgh and London, 1866); Klimke, *Der Monismus* (Freiburg, 1911); Herbert, *Modern Realism Examined* (London and New York, 1886); Willmann, *Geschichte des Idealismus* (Brunswick, 1894).

Michael Maher.
Joseph Bolland.

Spirituals, a general term denoting several groups of Friars Minor, existing in the second half of the thirteenth and the beginning of the fourteenth centuries, who, in opposition to the main body of the order, pretended to observe the Rule of St. Francis in its primitive severity. The derivation of the name is not quite clear. *Homo spiritualis* in the Middle Ages signified a profoundly religious and ascetic man, almost in the same sense as it occurs in I Cor., ii, 15; Gal., vi, 1. In this sense the word is commonly used in the thirteenth century. See examples in "Archiv" of Ehrle-Denifle, III, 600. In its limited application to the Friars Minor, according to some it owes its origin to the Rule of St. Francis, where it is said: "Wheresoever there are brothers who see and know that they are not able to observe the rule spiritually they ought to, and can recur to their ministers". Quite recently, Father Balthasar, O.F.M., traces it with some probability to the terminology of Joachimism. Joachim in fact styles the "Evangelium æternum" as the spiritual Gospel, whose understanding is given through the spiritual intellect of spiritual men who are to preach it (Archiv, I, 53–55). To the present writer it would seem that the name was given by the people, with whom the Spirituals, on account of their austerity, were generally in favour. In fact in a document of 1316 quoted by Ehrle, "Archiv", III, 601, the Spirituals themselves deny that they have ever sought the name of Spirituals, and declare that they want no other name than that of Friars Minor imposed by St. Francis. Moreover, we have also a direct testimony, hitherto overlooked, in the "Vita prima" of Clement V, in which it is recorded that "some called them [the Spirituals] Sarabaites and excommunicated, but by the people they are called Spirituals" (Baluzius, "Vit. Pap. Aven.", Paris, 1693, I, 19). From this it is clear that the name Spirituals is taken in its general sense, when applied by the people to the above-mentioned groups of Friars Minor.

The origin of the Spirituals is not less a subject for controversy than their name. If we are to believe Angelo Clareno's "Chronicle of the seven tribulations" the spiritual tendency in opposition to the larger observance of the community is as old as the order itself. Before modern historians began the history of the Spirituals (1274), Angelo had already told of four persecutions of friars, under Elias, even in the very lifetime of St. Francis himself, and that of Bl. John of Parma under Crescentius in the lifetime of St. Bonaventure. It must be admitted that the spiritual tendency existed shortly after the death of St. Francis (1226). Nevertheless, it cannot be denied that Spiritualism appeared first in those places where the first zealous companions of St. Francis lived, such as central Italy. There is no doubt that Angelo Clareno, Ubertin of Cassale, and others who entered the order shortly after 1260 came in contact with some of those men or their disciples, for in their writings these authors constantly refer to the companions of St. Francis and especially to the works of Brother Leo. To understand and appreciate the movement of the Spirituals, we have above all to consider the Order of Friars Minor in its general aspect in the second half of the thirteenth century, and here we are for-ed to admit a certain development, perhaps not clearly foreseen by St. Francis when writing the Rule of 1223. Whilst the founder does not appear to have attached very much importance to the scientific studies of his order (see chap. x in the Rule of 1223), it was, however, impossible for such a large moral body as his order to keep aloof from the great speculative and scientific movements of the thirteenth century. Moreover, sovereign pontiffs had bestowed on the Mendicants many privileges to enable them to work with more fruit for the benefit of souls and the service of the Church. Thus, convents of larger dimensions, which in the time of St. Francis were mostly poor hermitages, were being built in the towns, and beside them sprang up churches.

Attendance at the universities and life in towns required certain modifications in the life of the friars, perhaps somewhat different from what it may have been in St. Francis's time. The doubts that arose amongst the friars about the observance of the rule were generally settled by the sovereign pontiffs with a view of meeting new conditions, and at the same time safeguarding the letter of the rule. Whilst the greater part of the order followed without reluctance this natural and logical evolution, some more zealous friars, to whom every development seemed a departure from the first ideal of St. Francis, were strongly opposed to it. A similiar movement had taken place in the Order of St. Dominic, at the same time and in the same region, i. e. that of the Roman Province, which comprised, besides Rome itself, the Marches, Umbria, and Tuscany. Here, towards the end of the thirteenth and in the beginning of the fourteenth centuries, a reform party had arisen who aimed at a return to the primitive simplicity. The point was discussed in several general and provincial chapters, at last in the provincial chapter at Todi (1319). Here (1) the innocence of the zealous friars was asserted, and the discussion of controversial points forbidden; (2) the name *Spirituals*, as a name engendering discord, was not permitted. At the general chapter of the Order of Preachers at Florence (1321), the Master-General Heroæus Natabis confirmed the decrees of Todi, and the whole question seems to have been definitively settled (see bibliography).

Before entering on the history of the different groups of the Franciscan Spirituals, we must determine the points which are characteristic of all of them: (1) Literal observance of the Rule and Testament of St. Francis. (2) An overrated appreciation of the same rule, and especially of the Franciscan poverty. Basing their interpretation on the words of their rule (chap. I), "the rule and life of the Minor brothers is this, namely, to observe the holy Gospel", they considered their rule identical with the Gospel, and as the pope, they reasoned further, cannot dispense from the Gospel, so he cannot dispense from, or even explain, the rule in any other than a literal sense. Consequently they refused the authentic papal interpretations. (3) Joachimism. It was the great error of the Spirituals to combine their arguments in favour of reform with the ideas of Joachimism. Holzapfel (Handbuch, p. 41) goes so far as to say that their poverty was only to cover Joachimism, which was the true aim of the Spirituals. This is certainly exaggerated, for Joachimism existed in the order before the spiritual movement was apparent. Perhaps it is more just to presume that the ideas of Joachimism, promising a better near future, were resorted to by the Spirituals more as a help and a consolation in their manifold hardships and persecutions. It is certain at any rate that, in the great intellectual contest between the Spirituals and the community at Avignon (1310–12), the object of the Spiritualist contention was not Joachimism, but the real observance of poverty, and of the rule in general. However Joachimism was widely spread amongst the *Zelanti*, and was most prejudicial to their cause. To their grievances with regard to the observance of the rule the community replied by accusing them of heresy, taking the proof of their assertion from the writings of the great Spiritual, Olivi.

According to the time and place of origin we have to distinguish three distinct groups of Spirituals: (1) the oldest, those of the Marches of Ancona, about 1274; (2) the Spirituals in Provence, France, under Olivi (d. 1298); (3) the Tuscan group, about 1309.

(1) *The Spirituals of the Marches* are those as to whose fate we are best informed owing to the fact that Angelo Clareno, author of "Historia septem Tribulationum" and "Epistola excusatoria", belonged to them, and after the death of Peter, *alias* Liberatus, of Macerata, 1307, became their leader. (On their history see FRATICELLI.) They were excommunicated by John XXII by the Bull "Sancta Romana et universalis Ecclesia", dated from Avignon, 30 Dec., 1317; they continued to exist, however, as the Fraticelli.

(2) *The Province of Spirituals* were led by Pierre-Jean Olivi. To this group is due the great process between the Spirituals and the Community at the Papal Court at Avignon (1310–12). There are several versions as to what constituted the exact cause. Clareno (Archiv, II, 129) tells us that Arnold of Villanueva, the remarkable lay theologian, went to Charles II of Sicily, and induced the king to write to the minister-general of the order, Gundisalvus of Valleboa, requesting him to desist from interference with the Spirituals of Provence. Meanwhile, Arnold saw Clement V personally, and, on the general's advice, the pope summoned the heads of the Spirituals in Provence: Raymond Ganfredi, Guido of Mirepoix, Bartholomew Sicardi, and others, as also Ubertin of Casale from Italy, commanding them to report upon all observances which were not in accordance with the rule. Another version is given by Raymond of Fronsac, procurator-general of the order (Archiv, III, 18), and by Bonagratia of Bergamo (Archiv, III, 36). They relate that the citizens of Narbonne (1309) appealed publicly in favour of the Spirituals, and particularly the memory of Olivi. The two versions can very well be combined as they do not exclude each other, and are both in themselves very probable. Ehrle (Archiv, II, 360) and Balthasar (Armutstreit, 264), however, are inclined to believe that King Robert, who succeeded to his father, Charles II, in May, 1309, was the one to whom Arnold applied for protection of the Spirituals. Be this as it may, Clement V on 14 April, 1310, promulgated the Bull "Dudum ad apostolatus" (Bull. Franc., V, 65) which was very favourable to the Spirituals convoked to the Papal Court. They obtained full immunity for the time of the process between them and the community, and through the same Bull was instituted a commission of cardinals and theologians to hear and examine both parties. It is unnecessary to go into the details of this discussion, which lasted three years, and in which bitter words were said on both sides; it will suffice to point out the result.

The great aim of the Spirituals had been to obtain authorized separation from the order; for, said Ubertin (Archiv, III, 87), "there will never be peace in the Order until leave is given to those who want it, to observe the Rule literally". The Community on the contrary was opposed to that plan, and continued to discredit their opponents by insisting on the real or pretended errors in the doctrine of Olivi. In 1312 two papal decretals put a term to the *magna disceptatio*: "Fidei catholicæ fundamento" (Bull. Franc., V) and "Exivi de Paradiso" (Bull. Franc., V, I) condemning some errors of Olivi. The second enjoined stricter observance of the rule. Clement V exhorted the French Spirituals, who during the process had withdrawn from the community, to return to their convents, and even went so far as to depose some superiors, who had treated them unfairly (Archiv, II, 140; IV, 34). The Spirituals went to the convents of Beziers, Narbonne, and Carcassonne. But when Clement and the minister general, Alexander of Alexandria, had died (1314), the former harsh superiors were restored (1315). The Spirituals now took a desperate step, in possessing themselves by force of the convents of Beziers and Narbonne, from which they ejected the *Relaxati*. Thereupon they were excommunicated by William of Astre, *custos* of Narbonne (Archiv, I, 544; II, 140). The Spirituals appealed to the General Chapter of Naples in 1316 (Archiv, II, 159). John XXII, who was less favourable to the *Zelanti* than his predecessor, cited them to his court (Bull. Franc., V, 118; 120) in 1317 and had them examined before a commission, with the result that their leaders were imprisoned, and the others detained in convents. The Bull "Quorumdam exigit", 1317 (Bull. Franc., V, 128), was intended to put an end to the question. After some explanations of the rule the pope enjoined them under obedience and pain of excommunication to give up all particularities and to submit to the orders of the minister general, and concluded by saying "great is poverty, but greater is obedience". Twenty-five of the detained Spirituals utterly refused to accept the Bull and were therefore put before the inquisitor, who succeeded in converting twenty-one of them, whilst the four others, refusing to obey and to recognize the principle of papal authority on the Franciscan Rule, were handed over to the civil power, 7 May, 1318, and burned as heretics at Marseilles (see sentence of the inquisitor Michael Monachi in "Miscellanea" of Baluzius-Mansi, Lucca, 1761, II, 248).

(3) *The Spirituals of Tuscany*, appear in 1309 (see Fraticelli). After their flight to Sicily, John XXII directed against them, 23 Jan., 1318, the Bull "Gloriosam Ecclesiam" (Bull. Franc., V, 137) by which they were excommunicated. The movement of the Spirituals failed to obtain its aim; it even led through the errors of its leaders, to schism and heresy. However, the zeal for stricter observance of the rule combined with full submission to authority shortly after revived in the first Observant convents and led the order to new prosperity.

For general bibliography see Friars Minor and Fraticelli. Eubel, *Bullarium Franciscanum*, V (Rome, 1898); Ehrle's fundamental works in *Archiv für Litteratur und Kirchengeschichte*, I–IV (Berlin and Freiburg, 1885–88); René de Nantes, *Histoire des Spirituels* (Paris, 1909); Balthasar, *Geschichte des Armutsstreites im Franziskanerorden bis zum Konzil von Vienne* (Münster, 1911); Holzapfel, *Handbuch der Geschichte des Franziskanerordens* (Freiburg, 1909), 50–66; Lat. ed. (Freiburg), 45–58; Bihl, *E documentis ad historiam Spiritualium nuper per cl' mum v. Dr. Prof. Hen. Finke editis* in *Archivum Franciscanum Historicum*, II (Quarracchi, 1909), 158–163; Glaser, *Die Franziskanische Bewegung, ein Beitrag zur Geschichte sozialer Reformideen im Mittelalter* (Stuttgart and Berlin, 1903); Tocco, *Studii Francescani* (Naples, 1909); Muzzey, *Were the Spiritual Franciscans Montanist Heretics?* (Chicago, 1908), reprinted from the *Journal of Theology*, XII (1908), n. 3–4; Garavani, *Gli Spirituali Francescani nelle Marche* (Urbino, 1905).

On the Dominican Spirituals see Masetti, *Monumenta et antiquitates veteris disciplinæ Ord. Præd. ab anno 1216 ad 1348 præsertim in Romana Provincia*; Quétif-Echard, *Scriptores Ordinis Prædicatorum*, I (Paris, 1719), 534; Reichert, *Monumenta Ordinis Prædicatorum*, IV (Rome, 1899), 137 sq.; Ehrle, *Archiv*, etc., III, 611.

Livarius Oliger.

Spokan Indians, an important tribe of Salishan linguistic stock, closely cognate with the Colville, Cœur d'Alêne, Kalispel, and Flathead, and formerly holding the country upon Spokane River in Eastern Washington and the adjacent portion of Idaho. They were first noted, under the name of Lartielo, by the American explorers, Lewis and Clarke, in 1805. At a later period they came into communication with the traders of the Hudson Bay Company and American Fur Company. In 1839 a Presbyterian mission was established among the Lower Spokan at Chemakane, Washington, and continued until 1849, when it was abandoned in consequence of the massacre of Rev. Marcus Whitman and his companions of the Presbyterian mission of Waiilatpu among the Cayuse. The Spokan chief, Garry, however, gave protection to those at Chemakane until the danger was past. A Spokan primer, published by the missionaries in charge in 1842, was one of the earliest books printed on the Pacific coast.

The Upper Spokan came under the influence of the Jesuit Fathers De Smet, Point, and their successors, about 1841, with the result that that portion of the tribe is Catholic. Throughout the Yakimá war of 1856–8 the Spokan remained quiet, chiefly through the effort of the Catholic missionaries. In 1872 those of Washington, constituting the larger body, were gathered with other cognate tribes upon the Colville reservation, North-eastern Washington, where they now reside. Those in Idaho are associated with the Cœur d'Alêne and are all Catholic. At Colville the Lower band is Protestant, while the Upper band, somewhat smaller in numbers, is Catholic. From perhaps 1200 souls a century ago they have declined (1911) to 600, of whom 96 are on the Cœur d'Alêne reservation. The religious centre for those of Colville is the mission of St. Francis Regis, at Ward, Washington, under Jesuit management. The centre for Cœur d'Alêne is the Jesuit mission of the Sacred Heart, at De Smet, Idaho. In language, primitive custom, and characteristics the Spokan are virtually identical with the Cœur d'Alêne and Kalispel Indians.

Bancroft, *Hist. of Oregon* (San Francisco, 1886–88); Idem, *Hist. Washington, Idaho and Montana* (San Francisco, 1890); De Smet, *Oregon Missions* (New York, 1847); *Bur. Cath. Ind. Missions: Annual Reports of Director* (Washington); *Commissioner of Ind. Affairs; Annual Reports*, especially Stevens (Washington, 1854) and Winans (Washington. 1870); Mooney, *Ghost Dance Religion* in *Fourteenth Ann. Rept. Bur. Amer. Ethnology*, pt. II (Washington, 1896).

James Mooney.

Spoleto, Archdiocese of (Spoletana), in the Province of Umbria, Italy. The city is situated on a spur of Monteluco, which belongs to the Sybilline Mountains. In the neighbourhood are marble quarries and coal mines; mineral earths are also found, and in the forests of Monteluco, truffles. The situation of the city upon a steep rock, protected by the mountain, has made it in all times an important fortress. The cathedral is an interesting Lombard building, begun in 617 by Duke Theudelapius; the campanile belongs to the tenth century, and the façade of 1207 is adorned with a large mosaic by Solsernus; the ornaments of the portal are by Gregorious Meloriantius (twelfth century). The interior, restored in 1640 by Bernini, contains frescoes by Pinturicchio and by Fra Filippo Lippi, who is buried here. Without the city, beyond the Porta della Torre (604?), is the ancient Church of San Pietro (fifth century), with interesting sculptures of the twelfth century. Not far away, on the crest of the mountain is the Church of San Giuliano, where the monastery of San Isacco (sixth century) arose. Other churches are: Il Crocifisso, built on the site and from the materials of an ancient temple; San Ansano, beneath which the foundations of another temple may be visited; San Pietro Martire, with frescoes by Spagna; San Filippo, with four columns of green porphyry taken from the temple of Clitumnus. Among the civic edifices are: Palazzo Comunale, with a collection of paintings; the castle of Cardinal Albornoz; and near the cathedral Palazzo Arroni, which is believed to have been the palace of the dukes of Spoleto. The relics of antiquity include: Porta della Fuga; the ruins of an amphitheatre, and of the Ponte Sanguinario (the bloody bridge); the arch of Drusus and Germanicus.

Spoletium, a city of the Umbrians, received a Roman colony 241 B. C. In 217 Hannibal, after his victory at Lake Trasimenus, was repulsed from the walls of Spoleto. Here, in the Civil Wars, Pompey and Crassus (82 B. C.) conquered the troops of Marius, who, however, found refuge in the city, and were thus the cause of its punishment. Here Æmilianus was proclaimed emperor (249), and killed three months later. In the Gothic war (537) the city surrendered to the Byzantine general, Constantine; but in 546 it was recovered by Totila, and it was not retaken by the Byzantines until 552, when Narses restored the fortifications. In 572 Spoleto became the seat of a Lombard duke, Faroald. He was succeeded by Ariulf, who made frequent expeditions against the Byzantine dominions (579–92 against Ravenna; 592 against Rome). Ariulf was succeeded by Theudelapius, son of Faroald, then came Atto (653), Transemund I (663), Faroald II (703), who ruled conjointly with his brother Wachilap. Faroald II had already captured Classe (the port of Ravenna), when he was obliged by Luitprand to restore it. He was deposed by his son Transemund II (724), who also rebelled against King Luitprand and formed an alliance with Gregory III, with whom he found refuge in 738. Ilderic, who had replaced him as duke, was slain by Transemund in 740, but in 742 the latter was obliged to become a cleric by King Luitprand, and the duchy was conferred upon Agiprand (742), who was succeeded by Theodicius. Under Hildebrand the Duchy of Spoleto was promised to the Holy See by the King of the Franks, and the duke himself was named by Pope Adrian (773), but the succeeding dukes were named by the Frankish emperors. Winigisus aided Pope Leo III against his enemies. Among the dukes of this epoch are the following: Sicco, who was expelled because of his hostility to the Franks, but was received and made duke at Beneventum; Guido I, who divided the duchy between his two sons Lambert and Guido II, the latter receiving the Duchy of Camerino. Lambert distinguished himself in the wars against the Saracens, but disgraced himself by massacres at Rome in 867; he was afterwards deposed (871), then restored (876), but was a second time excommunicated by Pope John VIII. In 883 Guido II united under his sway the entire dukedom, which from this time was called the Duchy of Spoleto and Camerino. After the death of Charles III the Bald (888), Guido had himself crowned Roman Emperor and King of Italy under Pope Stephen V (891); Pope Formosus in 892 also crowned his son Lambert II, who succeeded his father in the dukedom, kingdom, and empire.

THE ARCH OF DRUSUS AND GERMANICUS, SPOLETO

Alberico I, Duke of Camerino (897), and afterwards of Spoleto, married the notorious Marozia; he was killed by the Romans in 924. His son Alberico II made himself also master of Rome and remained there until the election to the papacy of his son John XII. At this time the Emperor Otto I detached from the Duchy of Spoleto the so-called Sabina Langobardica, which was bestowed upon the Holy See. In 967 Otto II united the duchy with that of Capua and Benevento, which was then ruled by Pandolfo Testa di Ferro; but after the death of the latter he detached Spoleto, which was in 989 granted to Hugo, Duke of Tuscany. The duchy was united with Tuscany a second time in 1057, when Godfrey of Lorraine espoused Beatrice, the widow of Boniface, Duke of Spoleto, and it remained so until the death of the Countess Matilda. During the conflict between the papacy and the Emperor Henry IV, the latter named other dukes of Spoleto. After this the dukedom was in the family of the Werners (Guarnieri) of Urslingen, Margraves of Ancona. In 1155 Frederick Barbarossa destroyed the city for having made a prisoner of his ambassador to Apulia. In 1158 the emperor gave the duchy to Guelf VI of Este; Henry VI invested Conrad of Urslingen with it, upon whose death in 1198 it was ceded to Pope Innocent III, the cession being confirmed by Otto of Brunswick. The latter, however, in 1209 occupied the duchy for himself, making Dipold von Vohburg duke. In like manner Frederick II in his different treaties with the Holy See acknowledged its sovereignty over the duchy, but when at war with the papacy he occupied it for the empire, and was always joyfully received by the populace (1240). His son, Manfred, on the other hand, did not succeed in winning the people. The popes maintained at Spoleto a governor, who was often a cardinal. As early as the thirteenth century, and more frequently in the fourteenth, Spoleto was involved in wars with Perugia, Terni, and other cities; in 1324 it was almost destroyed by the Perugians. In 1319 the struggle between the Guelphs and Ghibellines tore the city. Cardinal Albornoz favoured the city for the services which it rendered in the restoration of the papal power, and made it independent of Perugia. At the beginning of the Great Schism, Pietro di Prato succeeded in occupying Spoleto for the anti-pope Clement VII, but was expelled by Boniface IX. Ladislaus II, King of Naples, in 1414 endeavoured in vain to make himself master of the city. Pope Eugenius IV named as governor the Abbot of Monte Cassino, Piero Tomacelli, who was tyrannical to such an extent that the people besieged him in his castle, and in 1438 summoned the bands of Piccinino to free them. In 1480 Cardinal Vitelleschi ended the tyranny of Piero and of the Trinci of Foligno. The former perished in the Castle of Sant' Angelo. During the fifteenth century the city was often at war and in rebellion against the papal power. In the campaign of 1860 in Umbria, Spoleto was heroically defended by Colonel O'Reilly.

Spoleto venerates as its apostle St. Brictius, who is also venerated in other cities of Umbria and Tuscany. It is difficult to discuss the epoch in which he lived because the legend of his life is so full of anachronisms. The names of other martyrs are also recorded at Spoleto, like St. Gregory the Priest; indeed, the name Ponte Sanguinario is said to record a great massacre of Christians. Another martyred bishop was St. Saturnius (270), and during the persecution of Diocletian the martyrdom of St. Savinus, Bishop of Assisi, took place at Spoleto. The first bishop of certain date is Cæcilianus, to whom Pope Liberius wrote a letter in 354. There is record of Bishop Achilles, who during the conflict between Pope St. Boniface and the antipope Eulalius was a visitor of the Church of Rome (418); Bishop Spes (fifth century), who collected the relics of the martyrs and erected many churches; St. Amasius (d. 489); St. Johannes, killed by Totila (546). At the time of Bishop Petrus (573) Spoleto was under Arian rule. It is related that an Arian bishop in Spoleto wished to enter the Church of San Pietro, then the cathedral, by force, but was stricken with blindness. To Bishop Chrysanthus (591) St. Gregory the Great wrote four letters, in one of which he admonished him not to discipline fugitive monks so lightly. Other bishops were: Adeodatus (about 777); Siguald (827), formerly Abbot of Echternach; Adalbert (1015), who built the new cathedral and the episcopal residence within the city. After he had destroyed the city, Barbarossa presented to the cathedral the so-called Madonna of St. Luke, a Byzantine work with inscriptions of a dialogue between Mary and Jesus. Bishop Nicolò Porta, who became bishop in 1228, was transferred in 1236 to the Patriarchate of Constantinople. Bartolommeo de Bardi, O.Min. (1320), rendered excellent services as Governor of Terni. In 1417, on the death of Bishop Jacopo, who was a partisan of Pope John XXIII, the clergy wished to proceed to the election of a new pastor but the people prevented them, proclaiming as bishop Nicolò Vivari, the nominee of Gregory XII. Again in 1433 the clergy wished to revive their right of electing a bishop, but the intervention of Eugenius IV prevented them. Other bishops were: Berardo Erubi (1448), afterwards cardinal, who played an important part in the government of the church; Alessandro Farnese (1555); Alfonso Visconti (1601), founder of the seminary, which was enlarged by his successor Maffeo Barberini (1603), afterwards Pope Urban VIII, who ordered the restoration of the cathedral. After the death of Cardinal Locatelli (1812), Napoleon nominated Bishop Antonio de Longo, whom the canons were unwilling to obey, and were therefore nearly all exiled. In 1820 Spoleto became a metropolitan see and the ancient Diocese of Norcia was taken from its territory. Of the archbishops we should record: Mastai Ferretti (1827–32), afterwards Pius IX, whose episcopal rule was noteworthy for the manner in which (1837) he persuaded four thousand rebels to lay down their arms.

To the Diocese of Spoleto has been united that of Bevagna (*Mævania*), an ancient city, which venerates as first bishop St. Vincent the Martyr; the first bishop of certain date is Innocentius (487). In the time of St. Gregory the Great it was very difficult to provide a bishop for this see, but in 649 and in 844 bishops are again recorded. Bevagna (Mævania, where, in ancient days the white bulls destined for the sacrificial altars were pastured) is situated twenty-two miles south-east of Perugia, at the confluence of the Clitunno and Tupino, and contains 6000 inhabitants. The ancient cathedral was dedicated to St. Michael. The body of Blessed James Bianconi is preserved at Bevagna. Blessed James was born there in 1220. At sixteen he was received into the Dominican order at Spoleto. After his ordination, he devoted his energies especially to the work of extirpating the heresy of the Nicolaites from Umbria, and finally succeeded in converting its chief propagator, Ortinellus. After a life of extraordinary austerity James died on 15 August, 1301. In later times his remains were exposed on three occasions and were found to be incorrupt. Numerous miracles were attributed to his intercession and even to-day they are of not rare occurrence. Pope Boniface IX has granted indulgences to all those who visit his relics during the first three days of May; Pope Clement X extended the celebration of his feast (23 August) to the whole Dominican Order (cf. Jacobilli, "Vita del beato Giacomo da Bevagna", Foligno, 1644; Piergi, "Vita del beato Giacomo Bianconi da Bevagna", Rome, 1729). Another Blessed James, a Franciscan martyr, who died on 2 September, 1377, is honoured at Bevagna (see "Acta SS.", I Sept., 595–6; "Année dominicaine", VIII, 1898, pp. 779–94).

Another ancient diocese united with Spoleto is Trevi. The town of Trevi (in ancient days Trebia), about four leagues from Spoleto, is situated on the right bank of the River Clitunno, on a rugged slope at the extremity of Monte Petino. It is in Umbria and so is to be distinguished from the Latin town Trebia. It was founded probably as early as the fifth century B. C. Pliny speaks of it as flourishing and calls its inhabitants "Trebiates Umbriæ populi". There is evidence to show that the Faith was preached there before the end of the second century. In A. D. 296 Pope Marcellinus consecrated, as first Bishop of Trevi,

THE CATHEDRAL, SPOLETO
Begun, 617; campanile, X Century

Æmilianus, an Armenian, who, with his companions Hilarian, a monk, and Hermippus and Denis, was martyred on 28 January, 302, under Diocletian. The body of Æmilianus was brought to Spoleto and interred there. During the troubles caused by the barbarian and internal wars the relics were concealed, but in 1660 they were discovered in the cathedral. Up to the year 1050 nine other bishops of Treviare known from the lists of prelates present at synods in Rome; they include: Constantine, in 487; Laurentius, in 499; Propinquus, in 501; Grisus or Priscus, in 743; Valerimus, in 769; Paulus in 826; and Crescentius, in 853. About the middle of the eighth century Trevi came under the temporal dominion of the Church. In 840 and 881 the city suffered from the Saracen inroads, and in 915 and 924 from an Hungarian invasion. The Trevans sided with the Guelph party in their struggles with the Ghibellines. Among the natives of Trevi the following may be mentioned: Saints Vincent, Bishop of Bevagna, and Benignus, deacon, martyrs; St. Constantinus, Bishop and patron of Perugia (feast 29 January); Blessed Thomas of Naples, hermit of the Institute of Celestine V; Benedetto Valenti, the learned jurisconsult; and Virgilio Lucarini, canon of St. George's Velabro, who founded the college of Trevi, which was opened in 1674. Giotta da Vespignano painted a beautiful fresco in the Church of the Holy Cross. In the Church of San Martino was a very valuable painting, representing "The Coronation of the Blessed Virgin in Heaven", attributed by some to Giovanni Spagna, but more likely a work of Pietro Vannucci (Perugino); it is now in the Pinacoteca Vannucci, Perugia.

In the valley below the town is the celebrated church and shrine of Santa Maria delle Lagrime (Our Lady of the Tears). The story of the miraculous image is briefly this: Diotallevio d'Antonio, who lived near the road leading from Spoleto to Trevi, had painted an image of the Madonna and Child on the outside wall of his house. One day tears were noticed falling from the eyes of the Madonna. The report of this extraordinary phenomenon, which continued for some time, spread far and wide. Official records of the occurrence were made by the municipal authorities. Many graces and favours were obtained through prayer before the picture. A small chapel was erected in August, 1485, and Mass was daily offered therein. On 26 July, 1846, Santa Maria delle Lagrime was chosen patroness of the town. On 27 March, 1487, the large basilica was begun, which on its completion, 8 March, 1489, was confided to the Olivetans. A contemporary account of the miraculous origin of the shrine by Father Francesco Mugnoni, an Olivetan, who resided within a short distance of d'Antonio's house, is preserved. The basilica contains Perugino's "The Adoration of the Magi", and Giovanni Spagna's "Deposition from the Cross". The shrine has been enriched with many beautiful offerings in commemoration of the numerous benefits conferred upon the people of the neighbourhood and visiting pilgrims through the intercession of Our Lady of Tears. Notable among these is a representation, in silver relief, of the city of Ferni given by its inhabitants and neighbouring towns in remembrance of their deliverance from the plague.

The archbishop, Mgr. Domenico Serafini, a Benedictine of the Congregation of Monte Cassino, was born at Rome on 3 August, 1852; professed at Subiaco on 16 June, 1874; ordained priest on 21 October, 1877; appointed procurator-general of the congregation five years later; in June, 1892, he was elected abbot-general; on 19 April, 1900, he was named archbishop and on 6 May, 1900, consecrated, in succession to Mgr. Mariano Elzeviro Pagliari (born at Camerino, in the Marches, on 11 September, 1834, and named to the see on 28 February, 1879). Spoleto has no suffragan see; it has 172 parishes, with 170 secular and 60 regular clergy, 92,000 souls, 14 monasteries for men, and 11 convents for women, 3 colleges for boys, and 2 for girls. Its seminary serves for southern Umbria. A Catholic weekly and a religious periodical are published here.

CAPPELLETTI, *Le Chiese d' Italia*, IV (Venice, 1857); CAMPELLO, *Delle Historie di Spoleto* (Spoleto, 1672); BARBANTI, *Ristretto dell' antico e moderno stato di Spoleto* (Foligno, 1731); SANSI, *Degli edifizi e dei frammenti storici di Spoleto*; FATTESCHI, *Memorie istorico-diplomatiche riguardanti la serie dei duchi ecc. di Spoleto* (Spoleto, 1801); ANGELI-ROTA, *Spoleto e dintorni* (Spoleto, 1905); JENNY, *Geschichte des langobardischen Herzogtums Spoleto* (Bâle, 1890); MANASSEI, *Alcum documenti per la storia delle città di Terni et Spoleto trascritti ed annotati* in *Archiv stor. ital.*, XXII (1875), 367–415; SANSI, *Storia dei commune di Spoleto dal secolo XII, al XVII* in *Accad. spolet.* (1879); PILA CAROCCI, *Della zecca e delle monete di Spoleto* (Camerino, 1886); PRAMPOLINI, *La rocca di Spoleto* in *Rev. Europea, XII* (1879), 92–7; HARDOUIN, *Concilia*, VII, 239; MANSI, *Concilia*, XXIII, 344; UGHELLI, *Italia sacra*, X, 114; LODI, *Breve storia delle cose memorabili di Trevi* (Milan, 1647); BARIZZA, *Istoria della Vergine delle Lagrime di Trevi* (Milan, 1721); ALBERTI, *Notizie antiche e moderne risguardanti Bevagna città dell' Umbria, raccolte in compendio*; GIORGETTI, *Breve istorico compendio dell' imagine miracolosa di Maria detta delle Lacrime, venerato alla falde di Trevi nell' Umbria* (Todi, 1782).

U. BENIGNI.

Spondanus (DE SPONDE), HENRI, a convert from Calvinism, Bishop of Pamiers, and one of the continuators of Baronius, b. at Mauléon, in the French Department of Basses-Pyrénées, 6 January, 1568; d. at Toulouse, 18 May, 1643. After studying humanities at the Calvinist college of Orthez, he accompanied the royal ambassador to Scotland and, upon his return, took up the study of jurisprudence. In 1589 he was jurist at the Parliament of Tours. Convinced of the truth of the Catholic religion by the writings of Bellarmine and the instructions of Duperron, he became a Catholic, 21 Sept., 1595. In 1600 he accompanied Cardinal de Sourdis to Rome, where he was ordained priest on 7 March, 1606; Pope Paul V then appointed him reviser of the briefs of the Pœnitentiaria. In 1625 he was created Bishop of Pamiers, in which capacity he laboured with great zeal for the preservation of Catholicism and converted numerous Protestants. Owing to ill-health he resigned his diocese in 1639 and retired to Toulouse. His writings are: "Les cimetières sacrés" (Bordeaux, 1596); "Annales ecclesiastici Cæsaris Baronii in Epitomen redacti" (Paris, 1612); "Annales sacri a mundi creatione ad ejusdem redemptionem" (Paris, 1637), an epitome of the "Annals" of Tornielle; "Annalium Baronii continuatio ab a. 1197 quo is desinit ad a. 1622" (Paris, 1639).

FRIZON, *Vita Spondani* in later editions of the last-named work; RAESS, *Die Convertiten seit der Reformation*, III (Freiburg, 1866), 285–95.

MICHAEL OTT.

Sponsor. See BAPTISM; CONFIRMATION.

Spontini, GASPARO LUIGI PACIFICO, composer, b. at Magolati, near Jesi, Ancona, 14 Nov., 1774; d. there, 14 Jan., 1851. He was intended for the Church, but decided on a musical career. In 1791 he entered the Conservatorio de' Turchini at Naples, where he had Sala, Tritto, and Tarantino as masters, and soon displayed his skill in composition. Between the years 1796 and 1799 he had written six operas, which were duly produced in Rome and Florence, and in 1800 succeeded Cimarosa as Court composer at Palermo. In 1803 he settled in Paris, and for a time did not make any marked impression, but in 1804 his "Milton" (one-act opera) attracted considerable attention, and his triumph was assured by the production of "La Vestale" (15 Dec., 1807) and "Fernando Cortez" (28 November, 1809). He was appointed conductor of Italian Opera at the Odéon in 1810, and brought forward many notable works by various composers.

GASPARO LUIGI PACIFICO SPONTINI
From a contemporary portrait

His "Olympic" (15 Dec., 1819) he regarded as his best opera, yet it was not a success at first. At length after considerable revision he again presented it on 28 Feb., 1826, when his judgment was finally endorsed by the public.

Removing in 1820 to Berlin, where he was appointed chief *Kapellmeister* at a salary of 4000 thalers annually and a yearly benefit concert, he composed music for Moore's "Lalla Rookh", produced at the Royal Palace on 27 Jan., 1821. His "Agnes von Hohenstaufen" got its first hearing on 12 June, 1829. In 1829 he received the honorary doctorate of Halle University, and in 1834 he conducted a performance of his "Vestale" at Hamburg. He visited his native place in 1835, and journeyed to England in 1838, returning to Paris, where he was made a member of the Institute in the same year. A revised version of his "Agnes" was given in 1837, after which he ceased writing operas. In 1842 he left Berlin for good (being succeeded by Meyerbeer), and went to Rome, where many distinctions awaited him. The pope created him Count of St. Andrea in 1844, in which year he returned to Paris. That year is memorable for a visit to Dresden, on which occasion Richard Wagner got up his "Vestale" conducted by the composer. Feeling his end approaching he retired to Magolati in 1850. Although he loomed so large in the first half of the last century, Spontini's music is now almost on the top shelves. He was not a very loveable personality owing to his egotism, pride, and bad temper, but he was generous to needy musicians and at his death he bequeathed all his property for charitable purposes.

GROVE, *Dict. of Music and Musicians* (new ed., London, 1908); FETIS, *Biographie Universelle des Musiciens* (2nd ed., Paris, 1860–65); LEDEBUR, *Berliner Tonkünstler-Lexicon* (Berlin, 1861); LEE, *Story of Opera* (London, 1909).

W. H. GRATTAN-FLOOD.

Sporer, PATRITIUS, moral theologian, b. at Passau, Bavaria; d. there, 29 May, 1683. In 1637 he entered the Order of Friars Minor in the convent of his native town, which then belonged to the religious Province of Strasburg. He taught theology for many years, obtained the title of *Lector jubilatus*, and was also the theologian of the Bishop of Passau. Sporer is the author of several works: (1) "Amor Dei super omnia" (Würzburg, 1662); (2) "Actionum humanarum immediata regula Conscientia moraliter explicata atque ad disputationem publicam exposita" (Würzburg, 1660); (3) "Theologia moralis, decalogalis et sacramentalis" (3 folio vols., 1681; re-edited, Salzburg, 1692; Venice, 1724, 1726, 1755, 1756). Some editions have additional notes by K. Kazenberger and Ch. Mayr, two well-known Franciscan moralists. The latest edition with up-to-date supplements is by Irenæus Bierbaum, O. F. M. (3 vols. 8vo, Paderborn, 1897-1901; 2nd ed., 1901-5).

Sporer was one of the best moralists of his time and is much appreciated even to-day. St. Alphonsus Liguori often quotes him and Lehmkul numbers him amongst the classical authors of moral theology. For other testimonies see Preface of Bierbaum's edition. As to his moral system he follows Probabilism. In questions at issue between St. Thomas Aquinas and Duns Scotus he defends and follows the latter, as for instance in the question of indifferent human actions. Very often also Sporer lays under contribution his own large experience as director of souls, thus rendering his work all the more useful.

JOANNES A S. ANTONIO, *Bibliotheca universa Francescana*, II (Madrid, 1732), 426; MINGES, *Gesch. der Franziskaner in Bayern* (Munich, 1896), 227; HURTER, *Nomenclator*, IV (3d ed., Innsbruck, 1910), 944.

LIVARIUS OLIGER.

Sportelli, CÆSAR, VENERABLE, b. at Nola in Bari, Italy, 29 March, 1702; d. at Pagani, 19 April, 1750. His mother, who died with the reputation of a saint, brought Cæsar up with all care. He became a distinguished lawyer, uniting the perfection of a Christian life with the duties of his profession. He was thirty-three when under the guidance of Fr. Falcoia of the "Pii Operarii" he joined St. Alphonsus, and was the first clerical novice of the saint's institute. He was ordained priest by his director, now become Bishop of Castellamare. Sportelli was St. Alphonsus's first and most faithful companion. When others abandoned him, Sportelli only clung more closely to him and like himself was determined, at any cost, to devote his life to the evangelization of abandoned souls. In this he succeeded admirably, nor was he less successful in his work for priests and religious. Severe with himself, he was full of charity to others. There was nothing austere in his virtue: it drew all hearts to him. His union with God was manifest, and although he preached the great truths with vehemence he repelled no one. He was the saint's advisor and helped him more than anyone else to extend the influence of his Institute. In times of great difficulty he founded the house of Mater Domini, Caposele, and the house of Pagani in which St. Alphonsus lived and died and where his relics repose. He wore himself out working and on his way to preach a retreat he was struck by apoplexy in a lonely place. Bandits helped him to reach Pagani, where after a tedious illness he died on the day he had foretold. Three years and seven months after his interment it was decided to transfer his remains to a place in a newly built crypt. The coffin was opened in the presence of the Bishop of Nocera, Right Rev. Gerard Volpe, the Abbot of Angri, D. Thomas Cortora, and others. The vestments in which the servant of God had been clothed turned to dust, while the body was in perfect preservation, flexible and exhaling a sweet fragrance. The countenance was beautiful and when a vein was opened blood flowed just as if he were living. St. Alphonsus wished to take steps at once for his beatification, but was prevented from doing so by many difficulties. It was not till 1899 that the cause was introduced and that he was declared venerable.

LANDI, *Notizia de P. Sportelli*; A REDEMPTORIST, *Compendio della vita del Servo de Deo P. D. Cesare Sportelli* (Avellono, 1895); *Introductio Causæ*.

J. MAGNIER.

Springfield, DIOCESE OF (CAMPIFONTIS), in Massachusetts, erected in June, 1870. It comprises five counties of Central and Western Massachusetts: Worcester, Hampden, Hampshire, Franklin, and Berkshire. Its area is 4320 square miles, a little over half that of the entire state. According to the census of 1910 the population of the territory within the limits of the diocese was 843,212. Of this number 323,122 are Catholics.

Early History.—Some of the early Puritans of Central and Western Massachusetts became Catholics in a remarkable manner: children taken captive by French and Indians at Deerfield and Westboro were carried to Canada and there educated in the Catholic Faith. They married in Canada, and the descendants of some of them attained eminence. Joseph-Octave Plessis, who in 1806 became Archbishop of Quebec and in a trying time ruled the Canadian Church with firmness and prudence, was a grandson of Martha French, who a little over a century before had been carried away from the home of her father, Deacon French of Deerfield. Some Acadians were quartered at Worcester in 1755, but the last of them returned to Canada in 1767. At the time of the Revolutionary War many Irishmen lived in Central and Western Massachusetts. Some of them must have been Catholics, but there is no evidence that they contributed in any way to the upbuilding of the future Church of Springfield. The foundations of this Church were laid by Irish immigrants, who in 1826 and later came to Worcester, to Chicopee (then a part of Springfield), and to Pittsfield, to dig canals, to lay railroads, and to build and operate factories. The faith of these immigrants was nourished by apostolic men, of whom the foremost was Rev. James Fitton. He was born in Boston in 1805 and ordained priest by Bishop Fenwick (1827). After a short stay among the Indians at Eastport, Maine, he was made pastor at Hartford. His missionary zeal carried him into all parts of New England. In Massachusetts his labours extended from "Boston on the east, to Great Barrington in the Berkshires on the west". In 1830 he said Mass in Chicopee. On 7 July, 1834, he laid at Worcester the foundation of the first church which was built in the territory now ruled by the Bishop of Springfield. He became pastor of Worcester in 1836. Contemporary with the erection of the church at Worcester, Father Fitton purchased land south of the town, on which he built a school. This property he deeded (1843) to the Rt. Rev. Benedict J. Fenwick, Bishop of Boston. Bishop Fenwick erected upon it the College of the Holy Cross, which he induced the Jesuits of Maryland to assume charge of. This was the first Catholic college in New England. It began with seventeen students. It has become the largest of the Catholic colleges of the United States, whose students all follow a classical course, including Greek. Its influence is now felt in all parts of the American possessions. The parish at Worcester was composed mainly of Irish, though it included also French, English, and Americans. From Worcester Father Fitton made missionary trips to the towns along the Blackstone, and to the settlements along the Western Railroad. This work was continued and developed by the pastors who succeeded him at Worcester. Of these the most energetic, as a missionary, was Rev. Matthew W. Gibson, who in thirteen years built churches in nine places of Worcester County and in ten more established parishes.

The first resident pastor of Western Massachusetts was Rev. John D. Brady. In 1841 he assumed charge of the parish of Chicopee, which extended over four counties. For four years he shepherded this vast parish alone. In 1845 Rev. Bernard O'Cavanaugh came to him as an assistant. Rev. Jeremiah O'Callaghan, the zealous and able, if somewhat eccentric, missionary of Vermont, had said Mass at Pittsfield in 1835 and yearly thereafter till 1839. This remarkable man in his old age founded the first Catholic parish in Holyoke. In 1844 Father Brady built the first church at Pittsfield, of which Rev. Bernard O'Cavanaugh became pastor in 1848. His successor, Rev. Patrick Cudahy, the "church builder of the Berkshires", and Rev. William Blenkinsop, who continued the work of Father Brady in the Connecticut Valley, organized into new parishes and prepared for further development the Church which was now firmly established in Western Massachusetts. To this development Pius IX contributed when he made of Central and Western Massachusetts a diocese with its see at Springfield.

Bishops.—Rt. Rev. Patrick T. O'Reilly, the first Bishop of Springfield, was born in Cavan, Ireland, 24 Dec., 1833. He came to Boston in his boyhood. He studied classics at St. Charles's College, Maryland, theology at St. Mary's Seminary, Baltimore, and was ordained in Boston, 15 August, 1857, by Bishop Bacon of Portland. He served as assistant to Father Boyce at St. John's Church, Worcester, till 1862, when he was sent to organize the parish of St. Joseph's, Boston. In 1864 he returned to Worcester as pastor of St. John's. There he remained until he was appointed Bishop of Springfield (28 June, 1870), being consecrated 25 September of the same year. He ruled the Diocese of Springfield for twenty-one years and a half. During this time its population increased from 90,000 to 200,000; its priests from 43 to 196; its religious women from 12 to 321; its parishes from 43 to 96; its schools from 2 to 30. Bishop O'Reilly confirmed 77,000 persons. He dedicated 45 churches, and laid the corner-stones of nearly a hundred buildings consecrated either to religion or to education. He gave encouragement to works of charity. The hospital of the Sisters of Providence at Holyoke and the orphan asylums at Holyoke and at Worcester were begun during his administration. He died 28 May, 1892. He was succeeded by the present (1911) bishop, Rt. Rev. Thomas D. Beaven, D.D., who was born at Springfield, March, 1851. He studied at Holy Cross College and at the Grand Seminary, Montreal, and was ordained to the priesthood, 18 Dec., 1875. He laboured at Spencer for three years as assistant and for ten as pastor. In 1888 he was made pastor of the Church of the Holy Rosary, Holyoke. Four years later (31 July) he was appointed Bishop of Springfield. He was consecrated 18 Oct., 1892. Bishop Beaven is an organizer. He has applied to the temporal affairs of the Church sound business principles. He has developed the school system of the diocese and made it efficient. He has encouraged the establishment of high schools and academies, and organized and developed the charitable institutions of his diocese. Brightside, with its infants' home, its orphan asylum, its Beaven-Kelly Home for aged men, owes its existence to his inspiration and largely to his generosity. During his administration hospitals have been opened in Worcester, Springfield, Montague City, and Adams, orphan asylums at Holyoke, Worcester, and Leicester, a House of the Good Shepherd at Springfield, and homes for working girls in many places. Springfield has for years been remarkable among the dioceses of the country for the number of its vocations to the priesthood and the religious life. Four of its priests have become bishops during the present administration; Rt. Rev. Thomas J. Conaty, D.D. (Monterey and Los Angeles); Rt. Rev. Philip J. Garrigan, D.D. (Sioux City); Rt. Rev. Daniel F. Feehan, D.D. (Fall River), and Rt. Rev. Josphe J. Rice, D.D. (Burlington).

Causes of Growth.—The growth of the Diocese of Springfield is due largely to immigration. The Irish were quickly followed by Canadians, and these by Poles and Lithuanians. The Italians and the Syrians came later. These immigrants came to Massachusetts to get a market for their labour. They prospered and their descendants are among the most esteemed citizens of the commonwealth.

Religious Communities.—About 380 religious women are engaged in charitable work in the diocese. Most of these are Sisters of Providence. The Sisters of Mercy (the first religious community to enter the diocese) conduct orphan asylums at Worcester and Leicester, the Grey Nuns an orphanage at Worcester, the Little Franciscan Sisters of Mary an old people's home at Worcester; and the Sisters of the Good Shepherd have a house at Springfield. The educational work of the diocese requires the services of 750 sisters. The Sisters of St. Joseph have a normal college in Springfield, an academy at Chicopee, and high schools in many parishes. They also do a great part of the parochial school work. The Sisters of Notre Dame conduct high schools at Worcester, Springfield, Holyoke, and Chicopee. Other communities of women engaged in teaching are: the Sisters of Holy Cross and of the Seven Dolors, Sisters of St. Ann, Sisters of the Assumption, Sisters of Providence, Faithful Companions of Jesus, Sisters of St. Joseph (Hartford), Presentation Nuns (St. Hyacinth, P. Q.), Presentation Nuns (Fitchburg, Massachusetts), Felician Sisters, Franciscan Sisters (Buffalo), and Daughters of the Holy Ghost. The religious orders of men represented in the diocese are: the Jesuits, at Worcester; the Fathers of La Salette, at Fitchburg, Ware, and Westfield; the Franciscans, at Chicopee and Holyoke; the Vincentians, at Springfield; the Fathers of the Assumption, at Worcester; and the Xaverian Brothers, at Worcester and Millbury.

Statistics.—Official reports for 1911 give the following figures: 300 diocesan and 14 regular priests (not including the Jesuits at Holy Cross and the Assumptionists of the Apostolic School); 160 parishes; 28 missions with churches and 10 stations; 2 colleges attended by 600 students; 4 academies; 61 parochial schools, with 25,600 pupils; 5 orphan asylums; 1 infants' home; 27,000 young people under Catholic care; 6 hospitals; 5 homes for the aged; 3 working girls' homes; 1 industrial school; and 1 House of the Good Shepherd.

McCoy, *History of the Catholic Church in New England* (Boston, 1899); Fitton, *Sketches of the Establishment of the Catholic Church in New England* (Boston, 1872); Shea, *History of the Catholic Church in the United States* (New York, 1890); Malaney, *Catholic Pittsfield and Berkshire* (Pittsfield, 1897); *The Official Catholic Directory* (New York, 1911).

Thomas F. Cummings.

Sprott (Spratt), Thomas, Venerable, English martyr, b. at Skelsmergh, near Kendal, Westmoreland; suffered at Lincoln with Thomas Hunt, 11 July, 1600. Sprott was ordained priest from the English College, Douai, in 1596, was sent on the mission that same year, and signed the letter to the pope, dated 8 November, 1598, in favour of the institution in England of the archpriest. Hunt, a native of Norfolk, was a priest of the English College of Seville, and had been imprisoned at Wisbech, where he had escaped with five others, some months previously. They were arrested at the Saracen's Head, Lincoln, upon the discovery of the holy oils and two Breviaries in their mails. When brought to trial, though their being priests was neither proved nor confessed, nor was any evidence produced, the judge, Sir John Glanville, directed the jury to find them guilty, which was done. The judge died sixteen days afterwards under unusual circumstances, as Dr. Worthington (quoted by Bishop Challoner) records.

Challoner, *Missionary Priests*, I (Edinburgh, 1877), nos. 118 and 119; Knox, *Douay Diaries* (London, 1878), 16, 32; Pollen, *English Martyrs 1584-1683* in *Cath. Rec. Soc.* (London, 1908), 384.

John B. Wainewright.

Squamish Indians.—A considerable tribe of Salishan linguistic stock, speaking a distinct language, holding the territory about Squamish River and Howe Sound, above Fraser River in South-western British Columbia. From possibly 2000 souls a century ago they have dwindled, by smallpox visitation in 1862 and from results of earlier dissipation, to 690 in 1890, and to 396 in 1910, on six small reservations under the Fraser River agency, viz. Mission or Burrard Inlet (219), False Creek, Kapilano Island, Burrard Inlet No. 3, Squamish or Howe Sound, and Seymour Creek. The Squamish are first mentioned by the voyager, Vancouver, who met and traded with them in 1792, but regular contact with the whites dates from the establishment of the Hudson Bay Company trading posts in Lower British Columbia (1810–20). The earliest missionary worker was Father (afterwards bishop) Modeste Demers, who made a short missionary visit to the Lower Fraser in 1841. In 1857 the work of civilization and Christianization was regularly taken up by the Oblates—among them Fathers Casimir Chirouse, Léon Fouquet, and Pierre Durieu—with such success that the entire tribe is long since civilized and almost entirely Catholic. The educational work is in charge of the Sisters of the Holy Infant Jesus at the Squamish Mission, Burrard Inlet, by whom, according to the official report (1910), "every attention and care possible is being bestowed on the children". The Indians are described as subsisting by farming, fishing, hunting, lumbering, and labouring, with good dwellings and stock well cared for; very industrious and of good morals, excepting a few intemperates. In this connexion Hill-Tout says: "Many of them have to-day, I am told, snug little sums judiciously invested by their good friend and spiritual director, the late Bishop Durieu, in safe paying concerns. It is only fair to say, however, that they deserve to be prosperous. They are probably the most industrious and orderly band of Indians in the whole province, and reflect great credit upon the Roman mission established in their midst."

In their primitive condition the Squamish resembled, in their leading characteristics, the Sechelt, Songish, Lillooet, and other Salishan tribes of Southern British Columbia. They lived chiefly by fishing, their main dependence being the salmon. They also hunted the deer with dogs, driving the deer into the water and there shooting it from canoes. Roots and wild berries completed their commissary. Their ordinary houses were enormous communal structures from 20 to 40 feet in width and from 200 or 300 even to 600 feet in length, built of cedar planks, each family having its own separate fire and sleeping platform. Back from the coast they had also the communal semi-subterranean round house of the interior tribes. In household furnishing, baskets, of which they had a great variety, predominated. Their greatest skill was displayed in the shaping of their great dug-out cedar canoes, of which they had several types. Like their neighbours the tribe was divided into nobles, commons, and slaves. Chiefship was hereditary, each village being independent of the others. Polygamy was common. The dead were buried in boxes or canoes, laid upon the surface of the ground, and there were many peculiar mourning regulations, particularly as concerned the widow. Abortion was common and female infants were deliberately strangled by wholesale. A suitor signified his purpose by sitting beside the door of the girl's house for four days and nights without eating or drinking. The "potlatch", or ceremonial gift distribution, was the great intertribal festival; an instance is on record where over 2000 persons sat down to the feast and goods to the value of $5000 were given away. The puberty ordeal for girls included a four days' complete abstinence from food or drink, followed by an agonizing scratching over the whole body with thorny brambles. There were hypnotic dance performances and a barbarous dance common also to several other tribes, in which the principal dancer held in his hands a live dog which he devoured piecemeal as he danced. According to their cosmogony the human race sprang from a race of animals with semi-human characteristics, the world being afterwards made fit for human occupation by four brother culture heroes. The best summary of their mythology and analysis of the language is that given by Hill-Tout. See also Lillooet Indians, Sechelt Indians, Songish Indians.

Hill-Tout, *Notes on the Skqomic* in *Rept. Brit. Assn. Advancement Sci.* (70th meeting, London, 1900); Idem, *Cosmogony and History of the Skuamish* in *Trans. and Proc. Roy. Canada, 1897–98*, Section II, 2nd series, IV (Montreal, 1898); Bancroft, *Hist. Brit. Columbia* (San Francisco, 1887); *Canada Dept. Ind. Affairs, Annual Rept.* (Ottawa); Morice, *Catholic Church in Western Canada* (2 vols., Toronto, 1910); Vancouver, *Voyage of Discovery, etc., 1790–5* (6 vols., London, 1801).

James Mooney.

Squiers, Herbert Goldsmith, army officer and diplomatist; b. at Madoc, Canada, 20 April, 1859; d. at London, 19 Oct., 1911. The son of John I. and Elizabeth Squiers, he was educated at Canandaigua Academy, Minnesota Military Academy, Maryland Agricultural School, and Fordham University (A.M. and LL.D.); in 1877 he became second lieutenant, U. S. Army, and from 1885 to 1890 U. S. military instructor at St. John's College, Fordham; he left to join his regiment, the 7th Cavalry, at the Indian Battle of Wounded Knee, and resigned as first lieutenant, 1891. In 1894 he became second Secretary at the Legation at Berlin, and in 1898 first Secretary at the Legation at Peking, where he and his family were received into the Church by Archbishop Favier; during the siege of the Legations, 1900, he was chief of staff under Sir Claude Macdonald, the British Minister to China, who with de Giers, the Russian Minister, pronounced "Mr. Squiers's services invaluable in keeping people and things together in the midst of exaggerated racial feelings"; for his "bravery and distinguished services" he was formally thanked by the British Government and by President McKinley. In 1902 he was appointed Minister to Cuba; he resigned in 1905 but was the next year appointed Minister to Panama, in both of which offices his tact and firmness and his Catholic faith were of immense service to all in solving many complicated questions of these early days. He was devoted to his Church, and was very charitable but unostentatiously so. He helped many deserving students to a Catholic education. One of his last acts was to establish at the Catholic University two burses of $250 each for ten years. Broken in health by eight years in the tropics, he spent the last two years of his life cruising in European waters. His last words after receiving the last rites were: "I am alone with God". His wonderful collection of antique Chinese porcelain was purchased for him by Mr. Pethick, the famous connoisseur. Many were bought to assist Chinese friends. His first wife, Helen L. Fargo (m. 1881, d. 1886), left him four children, Gladys (Mrs. Rousseau), Georgia (Mrs. H. Whitman), Fargo (d. 1906), and Helen. In 1889 he married Harriette Bard Woodcock, who survives him, with their sons Herbert G., Bard, and John Astor Squiers.

HOOKER, *Behind the Scenes in Peking* (New York); MARTIN, *Siege of Peking* (1900); SMITH, *China in Convulsions* (1901).

JOHN SCULLY.

Squillace, DIOCESE OF (SQUILLACENSIS), suffragan of Reggio, in Calabria, Southern Italy. The city of Squillace, in the civil Province of Catanzaro, stands near the Ionian Sea at the base of a hill between the two branches of the River Alessi, and is a centre of the wine, olive, and silk industries; it also possesses lead and iron mines, and earthenware works. The ancient Scyllaceum, or Scylletium, had a harbour, which is now a marsh. According to Cassiodorus, who was born there and died in a monastery founded there by him, the city was established by an Athenian colony. Invasions of Saracens in the ninth and tenth centuries, a landing of the Turks in 1595, and the earthquake of 1783 caused its ruin. The diocese possesses the bodies of many saints, including: St. Achatius, martyr, in the cathedral; St. John Terrestre, abbot, a contemporary of St. Nilus in the (then Basilian) monastery of Stilo; and the holy monks Bartolomew, Nicholas, and Basil. St. Bruno established two Carthusian monasteries within the limits of the diocese, S. Maria dell' Eremo and S. Stefano in Nemore, the latter having the less rigorous discipline.

The first known Bishop of Squillace is Gaudentius (465); Zachæus accompanied Pope Vigilius to Constantinople (551); John, previously Bishop of Lissa, in Dalmatia, having been driven out by the barbarians, was transferred hither by St. Gregory the Great. After Bishop Demetrius (870), no bishops are mentioned until the Norman conquest, after which Count Roger erected the cathedral, into which the Latin Rite was introduced, while the Greek Rite continued much longer in the diocese. The series of bishops commences again with Theodore Mismer (1094). Other bishops were: Francesco degli Arcesi (1418–76); Cardinal Enrigo Borgia (1539); Cardinal Guglielmo Sirleto (1568), who resigned in favour of his nephew, Marcello (1573), the founder of a monastery for penitent women, and famous for his erudition; Tommaso (1594) and Fabrizio Sirleto (1693); Nicolò Micheli, who enlarged the seminary. The territory of Squillace contains Stilo, the ancient Consilinum, three bishops of which are known, Sabinus (495) being the earliest. The diocese contains 59 parishes, with 198 secular and 24 regular priests, 130,000 inhabitants, 5 convents of men and 1 of nuns.

CAPPELLETTI, *Le chiese d'Italia*, XXI.

U. BENIGNI.

Stabat Mater, the opening words of two companion hymns, one of which (Stabat Mater Dolorosa) is in liturgical use, while the other (Stabat Mater Speciosa) is not. They celebrate the emotions of Our Lady at the Cross and at the Manger—Calvary and Bethlehem—respectively, and may conveniently be differentiated here by the third word (*Dolorosa, Speciosa*). The Speciosa contains thirteen (double) stanzas of six lines; the Dolorosa, ten. In other respects the two hymns are in quite perfect parallelism of phrase throughout, as the first stanza may serve to illustrate:

$$\text{Stabat mater} \begin{cases} \text{dolorosa} \\ \text{speciosa} \end{cases}$$

$$\text{Juxta} \begin{cases} \text{crucem lacrimosa} \\ \text{fœnum gaudiosa} \end{cases}$$

$$\text{Dum} \begin{cases} \text{pendebat} \\ \text{jacebat} \end{cases} \text{filius}$$

The question, which is the original, which the imitation, will be discussed under II. THE SPECIOSA.

I. THE DOLOROSA.—The hymn was well known to all classes by the end of the fourteenth century. Georgius Stella, Chancellor of Genoa (d. 1420), in his "Annales Genuenses", speaks of it as in use by the Flagellants in 1388, and other historians note its use later in the same century. In Provence, about 1399, the "Albati", or "Bianchi", sang it during their nine days' processions. "The Church did not receive the hymn from the heretics, but the heretics despoiled the Church of the Sequence" (Daniel, "Thesaurus Hymnologicus", II, 140). If the very questionable ascription to Jacopone da Todi be correct, the hymn probably found its way from Franciscan houses into those of other religious bodies and into popular use. It is found in several European (but not English) Missals of the fifteenth century, but was not introduced into the Roman Breviary and Missal until 1727 (Feast of the Seven Dolours B. V. M., assigned to Friday after Passion Sunday. The September feast of the same name employs other hymns in the Breviary Office). In the Breviary it is divided into three parts: at Vespers, "Stabat Mater dolorosa"; at Matins, "Sancta Mater, istud agas"; at Lauds, "Virgo virginum præclara".

The authorship of the hymn has been ascribed to St. Gregory the Great (d. 604), St. Bernard of Clairvaux (d. 1153), Innocent III (d. 1216), St. Bonaventure (d. 1274), Jacopone (d. 1306), Pope John XXII (d. 1334), Gregory XI (d. 1378). Of these ascriptions, the only probable ones are those to Innocent III and Jacopone. Benedict XIV gives it without question to Innocent, and quotes three authorities; Mone, in his notes, and Hurter, in his "Life", give it to the same great pontiff. Duffield, in his "Latin Hymn Writers and their Hymns", rejects with much positiveness, and Mearns, in Julian, "Dictionary of Hymnology", questions, the ascription. Gregorovius also denies it to the pope of "the great and cold intellect"; but for a similar reason he might question the ascription of the Corpus Christi hymns, redolent of devotional warmth and sweetness, to the rigorously scholastic mind of St. Thomas Aquinas; he adds, however, a reference to a fourteenth-century manuscript containing poems by Jacopone with an ascription to him of the Stabat. The argument for Jacopone is not satisfactory. While his hymns written in the Umbrian dialect commanded popularity and deserved respect, some of the Latin hymns ascribed to him are certainly not his, and it is doubtful if he ever wrote any—or at all events anything better than imitations of—Latin hymns.

A large literature has grown about the hymns, Protestants sharing with Catholics a deep, and often glowingly expressed, admiration for its pathos, its vividness of description, its devotional sweetness and unction, its combination of easy rhythmic flow with exquisite double rhyming and finished stanzaic form. Daniel styles it "the queen of sequences" (op. cit., V, 59) and devotes much space to its praise (II, 136–138). Dr. Philip Schaff (in "Literature and Poetry", 191) says: "The secret of the power of the 'Mater Dolorosa' lies in the intensity of feeling with which the poet identifies himself with his theme, and in the soft, plaintive melody of its Latin rhythm and rhyme, which cannot be transferred to any other language." Dr. Coles, a physician, devotes a long "Proem" to his own translation, to an estimate of the hymn, and thinks the hymn "powerful in its pathos beyond almost anything that has ever been written". Mingled with his praise is much very strong denunciation of its "Mariolatry." Schaff also notes the usual Protestant objection, but gently answers his co-religionists, concluding with the reminder that Catholics "do not pray to Mary as the giver of the mercies desired, but only as the interceder, thinking that she is more likely to prevail with her Son than any poor unaided sinner on earth". This affection of Protestants for the hymn has resulted in manifold translation. Dean Trench, however, excluded the hymn from his "Sacred Latin Poetry", and Saintsbury, in "The Flourishing of Romance" (p. 77, footnote), characterizes the exclusion as "a little touch of orthodox prudery". There are over sixty translations into English (in whole or in part), Caswall's being the most extensively used in hymnals. Amongst the translations are those of D. F. McCarthy, Aubrey de Vere, and Father Tabb.

Because of its vividly epic and lyric character, the hymn has received multiform musical setting. There are four well-known plainsong settings, the authentic form being found in the Vatican Gradual (1908). Josquin des Prés (fifteenth century) wrote a Stabat as elaborate as any of his "most highly developed Masses" (Rockstro). His great effort was distanced by the immortalizing twain of settings by Palestrina. Of Pergolesi's Stabat the German poet Tieck confesses: "I had to turn away to hide my tears, especially at the place, 'Vidit suum dulcem natum'". Haydn's Stabat is considered "a treasury of refined and graceful melody". Some less familiar names in the long list are Steffani, Clari, Astorga, Winter, Raimondi, Vito, Lanza, Neukomm. Rossini had written his "William Tell" before he essayed his much-abused Stabat. While it is not indeed fitted for liturgical use, Father Taunton (History and Growth of Church Music, 78-9) defends it; and Rockstro, refusing to discuss the question whether its sensuous beauty befits the theme, thinks that "critics who judge it harshly, and dilettanti who can listen to it unmoved. . . . must either be case-hardened by pedantry, or destitute of all 'ear for music'". The long list may close with Dvořák, who, in his original musical phrases, illustrated anew the perennial freshness of the theme.

II. The Speciosa.—An edition of the Italian poems of Jacopone published at Brescia in 1495 contained both Stabats; but the Speciosa fell into almost complete oblivion until A. F. Ozanam transcribed it from a fifteenth-century manuscript in the Bibliothèque Nationale for his "Poètes Franciscains en Italie au Treizième siècle", Paris, 1852. He thought Jacopone had composed both Stabats at the same time; and, remarking of the Dolorosa that "this incomparable work would have sufficed for the glory of Jacopone", he confesses that he gave up the attempt to translate the Speciosa in verse, and concluded to present both hymns in simple prose, because "the untranslatable charm of the language, of the melody, and of the old quaintness, I feel are escaping me". The Anglican hymnologist, Dr. J. M. Neale, introduced the Speciosa to the English-speaking world in 1866, and ascribed it to Jacopone. Dr. Schaff dissents: "This is improbable. A poet would hardly write a parody on a poem of his own." Noting the unfinished style and the imperfect rhyme of the Speciosa, Neale thought it indicated the work of an apprentice shaping his hand to the work of Latin verse—in which case it must have preceded the Dolorosa, which is a perfect piece of work. Schaff, however, points out that the opening words of the Dolorosa were borrowed from the Vulgate Latin (John, xix, 25) "with reference to Mary at the Cross, but not at the Cradle", and also that the sixth line, "Pertransivit gladius", might have suggested the similar line of the Speciosa, "Pertransivit jubilus", but not vice versa. Coles doubts "a simultaneous birth, or even a common parentage". In his "Essay on Minor Rites and Ceremonies" Cardinal Wiseman seized on the parallelism of contrast in the two poems—similarity of form and phrase, and complete antithesis of theme and thought. Finally, it should be said that the great ruggedness of the Speciosa may be due to the carelessness of copyists.

Kayser, *Beiträge zur Geschichte und Erklärung der ältesten Kirchenhymnen*, II (Paderborn, 1886), 110–192, gives text of both *Stabats* with variants and much comment. Henry, *The Two Stabats*, in *Amer. Cath. Quarterly Rev.* (January, 1903), 68–89 and (Apr., 1903), 291–309, texts and translations, comment on authorship and "Mariolatry", and comparison of trs.; Coles, *Stabat Mater (Dolorosa)* (2nd ed., New York, 1868); Idem, *Stabat Mater (Speciosa)* (New York, 1868); Julian, *Dict. of Hymnology* (2nd ed., London, 1907), 1081–84, 1590, 1706. To his entries must be added Henry (as above); Tabb in *Catholic News* (New York, Apr. 7, 1906); *In the Shadow of the Rood*; McKenzie in *The Beacon* (Boston, May 7, 1887); *Stood the Virgin Mother Weeping*, and others noted in Henry, loc. cit.; Bagshawe, *Breviary Hymns and Missal Sequences* (London, 1900), 109, *The Mother in deep sorrow stood*; Donahoe in *Early Christian Hymns* (New York, 1908), 197, *Waiting by the cross atoning*; a good version, perhaps by a Catholic, reprinted in *The Catholic World* (April, 1870) from *The Democratic Magazine* of thirty years previously: *Brokenhearted, lo, and tearful*. The same issue of *The Catholic World* has a tr. into Greek by Mayer. Victori in *Cæcilia* (Strasburg, Dec., 1909) analyzes the *Christus* of Franz Liszt (the *Speciosa*, 182–5; the *Dolorosa*, 196–200); Shipley adds others in *Amer. Eccl. Review*, XII (1895), 453. Pacheu, *L'Auteur du 'Stabat'* in *Revue du Clergé Français* (Mar., 1904), 163–75, thinks the author is, in all probability, Jacopone, and that the *Speciosa* is not his, but probably the work of some humanist of the fifteenth century. D'Udenhout, *Le 'Stabat Mater Speciosa' de Jacopone da Todi*, in *Etudes Franciscaines* (Aug., 1909), 140–8. Shipley, *Annus Sanctus* (London, 1884), gives the trs. of McCarthy, de Vere, and Aylward. There is an anonymous tr. of the *Speciosa* (*Joy her tender breast expanding*), quoted from *The Catholic Magazine* in *The Rosary of the Blessed Virgin Mary* (London, s. d.), 62. Dreves, *Analecta hymnica* (Leipzig, 1888—), gives many poems founded on the *Dolorosa*, e. g. XXIV, 127; 150; 122 (from a Dominican Breviary, fifteenth century); see also II, 53, and VIII, 55–56, for illustrations of the fourteenth to the fifteenth century. Husenbeth, *Missal for the Use of the Laity* (new ed., London, 1906), 234–6, gives Latin text and new translation. The Latin text is in many places different from that of the *Roman Missal* (although the preface declares that the book "will be found strictly conformable to the *Roman Missal*, as used by authority in this country"—sc. England). The Latin text includes the line, "Inflammatus et accensus", which is not in the *Roman Missal* text, but is found in Rossini's, and even in Liszt's *Stabat Mater*. For information concerning the line, cf. Kayser, Henry, opp. cit., or Mone, *Lateinische Hymnen des Mittelalters*, II, 148, at end. The typical and official text of the *Vatican Graduale* (1908) is the same as that of the *Roman Missal*.

H. T. Henry.

Stadion, Christopher von. See Augsburg, Diocese of.

Stadler, John Evangelist, a Bavarian hagiographer, b. at Parkstetten, in the Diocese of Ratisbon, 24 Dec., 1804; d. at Augsburg, 30 Dec., 1868. After completing the humanities in the *gymnasium* of Straubing in 1821, he entered the University of Landshut, where, in addition to the philosophical and theological studies prescribed for candidates to the priesthood, he devoted much of his time to the study of Oriental and modern languages. The year preceding his ordination to the priesthood he spent at the diocesan seminary of Ratisbon, where under the direction of the learned and saintly Michael Wittmann, the future auxiliary Bishop of Ratisbon, he prepared himself for the priesthood. After being ordained priest by Bishop Sailer at Ratisbon 22 June, 1827, he was occupied a few months in parochial work at the little village of Otzing in Lower Bavaria, whereupon he continued his theological studies at the Georgianum in Munich in November, 1828, and obtained the doctorate in theology in 1829. In 1830 he was "co-operator" at the Hospital of the Holy Ghost at Munich, in 1831 *Privatdocent* for Old Testament exegesis at the University of Munich, and in 1832 he succeeded Pruggmeyr as *subregens* of the Georgianum. In addition he was in 1833 appointed professor-extraordinary and in 1837 professor-ordinary of exegesis at the university. In 1838 he became canon and in 1858 dean at the Cathedral of Augsburg. Stadler was well versed in all the branches of theology, but he was especially fond of linguistic studies. Besides having a perfect mastery of German, French, Italian, and English among the modern languages, he knew Latin, Greek, Hebrew, Syriac, Arabian, Persian, Sanskrit, and in his later years he studied also Spanish and Polish. He is best known as the author of "Vollständiges Heiligen-Lexikon oder Lebensgeschichten aller Heiligen, Seligen u. a. aller Orte und aller Jahrhunderte, deren Andenken in der kath. Kirche gefeiert oder sonst geehrt wird" (Augsburg, 1858-82). The work is alphabetically arranged and contains more lives than any other work of its kind. The "Acta Sanctorum" of the Bollandists, as far as they were finished, that is, to the end of October, were condensed into short sketches, but many new lives were introduced and newly discovered data were added to the lives contained in the "Acta". The work is rather popular than scientific and from a critical point of view leaves much to be desired. In the preparation of the first volume Stadler was assisted by Rev. Fr. J. Heim, while the second and the third volume contain contributions from several priests of the Diocese of Augsburg. Stadler died before the third volume was finished, leaving the writing of the last two volumes to Rev. J. R. Ginal, pastor of Zusmarshausen. Other works of Stadler are: a Hebrew-Latin lexicon (1831); "De identitate Sapientiæ Veteris Testamenti et Verbi Novi Testamenti", which served as his thesis for the doctorate (1829); and "Dissertatio super Joannem VIII, 25" (Munich, 1832).

HÖRMANN in STADLER's *Heiligen-Lexikon*, III, 6-10; SCHMID, *Geschichte des Georgianums* (Munich, 1894), 306, 309; PRANTL, *Geschichte der Ludwig-Maximilians-Universität*, II (Munich, 1872), 525.

MICHAEL OTT.

Stagefyr. See FERBER, NICHOLAS.

Stained Glass, the popular name for the glass used in the making of coloured windows. The term is a misnomer, as stained glass is only one of the glasses so employed. It is more the result of a process than a glass *per se*, as it is produced by painting upon any glass, clear or coloured, with the oxide of silver, which penetrates the glass when subjected to heat and gives a yellow reaction. In building a coloured window a variety of glass can be used, but usually there is only one kind employed, viz.; pot-metal, a glass that is coloured throughout its substance while in a molten state. This is used either directly or after it has been toned, or ornamented, or made a background for a figure subject by painting the same upon it with vitrifiable pigments, fused to its surface or incorporated with its substance by means of heat. Nevertheless, although the word *stained-glass* is inaccurately used, usage has so fixed its erroneous meaning in the public mind that in all probability it will continue for all time to be applied in naming coloured windows and their glass.

I. Documentary, and, far more, monumental history, demonstrates that glass has been in use from the most remote ages; that the ancients were familiar with it; moreover, that its origin, or discovery, or invention is lost in the twilight of fables. In many cases where china and metal are now employed the ancients used glass: they blew, cast, and cut into it thousands of objects with which they furnished tombs and temples, palaces and private houses; and adorned their persons, their garments, and their buildings. It is indeed doubtful if there was any branch of the art of glass-making and the utilization of its products that was not known to them, a fact proved by the fragments of innumerable articles found to-day in countless numbers among the ruins of Egypt, Chaldea, Phœnicia, Greece, and Rome. It is true, however, that the glazing of window openings with glass cannot be traced back beyond the year 306 B. C. At this early date in the Far East coloured windows were made by arranging small gem-like pieces of pot-metal in perforated wooden or stone panels. This kind of window, still in use in the Orient, found its most notable development after the advent of Christianity; but it was not until the birth of Gothic architecture, with its large window-openings, that the full value of glass as a transmitter of light and a polychromatic decorative material was fully appreciated. Gothic window-openings called for a filling strong enough to keep out the weather, yet transparent enough to admit the light; on the other hand, as, in this form of architecture, the wall-spaces were necessarily small, the windows offered the only opportunity for the decorator's art in so far as it depended upon colour. As glass at that time was to be had only in small pieces, the glazier was compelled, in order to fill the window-openings, to make his lights a mosaic, that is a combination of pieces of glass of various sizes and colours worked to a given design by placing them in juxtaposition. These pieces of glass had to be kept in place by some other material, and the best medium for the purpose was found to be lead, applied in strips made with lateral grooves for the reception of the edges of the glass.

The early windows were purely ornamental transparent mosaics; later, when figure subjects were portrayed, the artist, on account of the limitations of the mosaic method, was compelled to use paint in order to get the proper effect, painting directly upon the glass with ordinary transparent pigments; but as this was not durable, when exposed to atmospheric changes, he protected the painted portion by covering it with another piece of glass which was held in place by means of leads, and thus insured its preservation, at least as long as the superimposed glass remained intact. This imperfect method was not long in use before a great discovery was made at Limoges in France, where a Venetian colony of glass-workers had settled as early as the year 979. The new process, which revolutionized the art, consisted in painting with metallic pigments which could be fused into the glass, the painting being thus made as lasting as the glass itself. Not the first, but one of the first, to employ this permanent process of painting on glass to any considerable extent was the great twelfth-century promoter of all things ecclesiological, the Abbot Suger. Recognizing the value of the invention, he caused the windows of the Church of St. Denis at Paris to be executed in this way, and they were so successful that picture-windows became thereafter a necessary constituent of every ecclesiastical edifice.

The oldest painted picture-window that has survived the action of time is one representing the Ascension in the cathedral of Le Mans, which is believed by many antiquarians to be a work of the late eleventh century. The glass composing it is very beautiful, more particularly the browns, which are rich in tone, the rubies, which are brilliant, streaked and studded with gemlike blobs of black, and the blues, which are of a greenish azure hue, while the general colour treatment is extremely oriental. The drawing of the figures is most effective, although simple in line, and Byzantine in character, differing in this point from those at St. Denis, which are Romanesque. The painting is peculiar in that the hair of the figures is rendered in solid black, and not in lines. Although Le Mans was one of the first places where windows made by the new process were used, yet it did not become the centre of work; the city of Chartres took the lead, and became the greatest of the schools of medieval glass-painting, and from it the new art slowly made its way to Germany and England, keeping always its essentially French character. Even to-day the Chartres windows are the most beautiful in existence.

At the very beginning—the eleventh and twelfth centuries—there were two methods of work: one school of artists freely employed paint in their windows, the other avoided its use, striving to obtain the result sought by a purely mosaic method, a system destined to be revived and developed in after ages; but the former school almost at once gained the mastery and held it for eight hundred years. Examples of the early work of these rival schools can best be studied by comparing the painted windows erected at Le Mans with those at Strasburg, which were built in accord with mosaic motives. In many of the first windows the figure subjects were painted upon small pieces of glass imbedded in a wide ornamental border, a large number of these medallions entering into the composition of a single window, and each section held in place by an iron armature—a constructive necessity, as the window-openings were without mullions. The medallions were all related to one another through their colour key, depicting various incidents in the same history or a number of points in a theological proposition. This form of window, peculiarly adapted to a single light, continued in fashion from the twelfth century until the introduction of tracery, and in some parts of France long after the single light had given way to the mullioned window. Contemporaneous with these medallion windows there were two other kinds: the canopy and Jesse windows. In the first there was a representation of one or two figures, executed in rich colours on a coloured or white ground within borders and under a low-crowned, rude, and simple canopy, usually out of proportion to the figure or figures it covered. The second variety, of pictorial genealogy of the Redeemer, consisted of a tree or vine springing from the recumbent form of Jesse, lying asleep at the foot of the window, the branches forming a series of panels, one above another, in which kings and patriarchs of the royal house of the Lion of Juda were pictured.

The windows of the twelfth century are admired on account of their ingenious combinations of colour, their rich rug-like effects and the brilliancy of the glass. It was reserved, however, for the thirteenth and fourteenth centuries to see the full unfolding of the possibilities and inherent beauty of coloured glass. Among the most noted of these windows are the exquisite jewel-like ones in the cathedral of Chartres, a hundred and forty-three in number, containing no less than one thousand three hundred and fifty subjects, with over three thousand figures; there are also some fine examples to be seen at Reims, Bourges, Tours, and Poitiers. These magnificent windows are only a small portion of the almost incredible number that once existed. The windows of the thirteenth century are not only more brilliant in colour, but the colours are more skilfully blended than in those of the preceding century; at the same time the drawing of the figures is better the faces are oval in form, more delicately treated, often refined and vigorous; the eyes have a natural expression, and the hair is rendered in lines of varying thickness. The compositions are simple and not over-crowded, the draperies are broader in treatment, the ornaments and architectural details, taking their motives mostly from natural objects, are well drawn. The range of subjects represented being limited by the paramount object of all ecclesiastical decorations of the Middle Ages, viz. the instruction of the illiterate and promotion of piety among the people, these windows present scenes from Biblical history and the lives of the saints, and symbolic portrayals of the dogmas of the Church. In fact they were sermons which "reached the heart through the eyes instead of entering at the ears". But their choice of subjects was not made at random; it fell under the same rule that guided the encyclopedias of the time in their classification of the universe, commencing with God and the creation of angelic beings, and so on through nature, science, ethics, and history. The windows were indeed poems in glass, "The first canto, reflecting the image of God as the Creator, the Father, and the giver of all good gifts; the second, nature, organic and inorganic; the third, science; the fourth, the moral sense; and lastly, the entire world". Where there were not enough windows in a church to carry out the complete scheme, one or more portions were represented.

The windows of the fourteenth century show a steady increase in knowledge of the art, more particularly in matters of drawing and harmonious use of colour. The later advance was brought about by the discovery of the yellow stain, which placed in the artists' hands not only various shades of yellow, but also a colour with which they could warm their white glass. It also led them to develop a style of glass window that first made its appearance in the days of St. Bernard and was used largely by the Cistercians, whose churches were a protest against the luxury, the pomp of colour and ornamentation, of those built by rival monastic bodies, particularly by the art-loving Cluniac monks. These grisaille, or stippled, windows were white and black, or gray and gray, brown and brown, warmed by the yellow stain and were painted upon white or clear glass. Towards the end of the fourteenth century the artists began to break away from the tutelage of the architect and abandoned the sound rules of the great school of the thirteenth century, ignoring the principle that "all ornament should consist of enrichment of the essential construction of a building". The sins of the glass-painters of the fifteenth century were still greater, for it mattered little to them if their windows were out of key with the architectural design of the building in which they were placed; their sole wish seemed to be to make their work do them honour. This abandonment of the fixed canons of the art, the abuse of its materials, and the exaggeration of individualism marked the beginning of the end of good glasswork, the deterioration becoming complete just as a revolution in religious thought was born into the world which destroyed in its destructive march not only the glass-painter's art, but many others, and also wrecked the art treasures of medieval culture, while it paralyzed for years, in Northern Europe, ecclesiastical art of every kind.

In the sixteenth century the windows were purely pictorial and wholly divorced from their architectural surroundings. At the end of this century and all through the next the windows rapidly degenerated, the art of making them finally passing from the hands of artists into the greedy grasp of tradesmen. The last windows made in which there was still some artistic merit are those in the Church of St. John at Gouda. In these the painters introduced landscapes, arcades, and corridors, aiming at absolute realism and startling perspectives, and treating their glass as they

STALLS

CHURCH OF THE FRARI, VENICE GOTHIC CHOIR STALLS, THE CATHEDRAL, SIENA
ARCHIEPISCOPAL STALL IN NOTRE DAME, PARIS CHURCH OF S. MARIA DELLA SALUTE, VENICE

would canvas. In the seventeenth and eighteenth centuries the use of paints and enamels became so excessive as to almost do away with pot-metal. Many of the windows were made wholly by painting and staining clear glass, and were purely articles of trade, with a very poor market, which became smaller from year to year until all demand ceased, and the noble art of placing images of beauty between earth and heaven for the edification of the people, for the glory of the art, for the love of the beautiful, and the honour of God disappeared for a time from off the face of the earth.

II. Continental Europe and Great Britain, in its recoil from the black night of unbelief, indifference, and disorder that wrecked good morals at the end of the eighteenth century and the beginning of the nineteenth, fell back upon the faith of the past as its only anchor of hope. As the Faith revived among the people it called for a material expression of its dogmas and history under forms of beauty, opening once again the field of religious art to architects, painters, and sculptors. All over Europe every branch of art found able leaders—men of enthusiasm, rare talents, and great energy. Each one, architect, painter, and sculptor, entered upon the work with the spirit of faith, love, and sacrifice, in their hearts, and tried to make their art "a frame for the sacred picture of truth". Amid this revival of the major arts, those which developed most rapidly were painting and architecture, and among the handmaidens of the latter the glazier's art almost at once took a leading position. To Germany belongs the honour of reviving coloured windows, although both France and England have a prior claim, as having produced the first picture windows subsequent to the French Revolution; but these were nothing more than isolated efforts of individuals, while in Germany associated artists of ability gave their attention to the matter and founded a school of glass-painters, and Munich became the centre of the movement. One of the greatest efforts of the Munich School is to be seen in Glasgow Cathedral, where it reached its limit of excellency. This was indeed a noble effort, but on the whole a lamentable failure, due to the nature of the glass, as well as a lack of knowledge of the requirements of the art and of its place as an adjunct to architecture. The windows are marked by thinness of colour, exaggerated diapered backgrounds, inharmonious borders, and defective blending of the colours, while there is a lack of harmony between the ornaments of the building and its architecture.

The modern French school of window-makers is very similar to the German, with even a stronger tendency to look upon coloured windows as easel pictures, with little or no leaning towards medieval processes, and without any apparent effort to attain the incomparable beauty of the windows which adorn the French cathedrals of the thirteenth and fourteenth centuries. The English school of glass-painters are by far the most successful, and all because their highest aim has been to make their windows good copies of the best glass of the Middle Ages. Much of their work is very beautiful, deeply imbued with a devotional spirit, and of high artistic merit. The American artist in glass, impatient of tradition, caring very little for either the subjects or the symbolism of the past, has attempted to do something new by using opal glass, with its limitless colour field, along the lines of the mosaic system, and build a window perfect in colour effect. In practice he separates his lights and darks from one another by carefully studied lead lines, which he endeavours to lose by making them look like a part of the glass and an essential constituent of the design. At the same time he tries to heighten the colour values of his glass by superimposing one colour upon another, seemingly always keeping in mind Ruskin's dictum: "Colour, to be perfect, must have a soft outline or a simple one; it cannot have a refined one; and you will never produce a good window with good figure drawing in it. You will lose perfection of colour as you give perfection of line. Try to put in order and form the colour of a piece of opal." So far the American artist in glass has not been successful in making good church windows, and all because he disregards their true purpose, their architectural surroundings, and because he has overestimated the value of coloured glass as a decorative material, hence sacrificing everything to his window. It is true, however, that he has made a few good windows, translucent mosaics which indeed are great works of art, with wonderful niceties of light and shade, with prismatic play of colours, and admirably harmonious.

In the future, as in the past, the proper field for this art is an ecclesiastical one. It therefore behoves the artist in glass, if he hopes to reach a high degree of perfection, to study the principles which govern Christian art, and ever to bear in mind that the glazier's art is but an auxiliary to the architect's.

HENDRE (tr.), *An Essay upon Various Arts, by Theophilus called also Rugerus, a Monk of the Eleventh Century* (London, 1847); LASTEGRIE, *Histoire de la peinture sur verre, d'après les monuments français de France* (Paris, 1843), FROMBERG; tr. CLARK, *The Art of Painting on Glass* (London, 1848); GESSERT, tr. POLE, *The Art of Glass Painting* (London, 1848); LENOIR, *Traité historique de la peinture sur verre* (Paris, 1856); LÉVY, *Histoire de la peinture sur verre en Europe* (Brussels, 1860); HUCHER, *Vitraux de la cathédrale du Mans* (Le Mans, 1864); WINSTON, *An Inquiry into the Difference of Style Observable in Ancient Glass Painting* (Oxford, 1867); VIOLLET-LE-DUC, *Vitraux*, in *Dictionnaire raisonné d'architecture* (Paris, 1875); WESTLAKE, *A History of Design in Painted Glass* (London, 1881); MAGNE, *Verriers de Montmorency d'Econem et de Chantilly* (Paris, 1885); COLEMAN, *A Sea of Glass* in *The Architectural Record*, II (1893); X (1901), *The Second Spring*; XXI (1907), *The Windows of Gouda, The Jesse Tree*; TIFFANY, *American Art Supreme in Colored Glass* in *The Forum*, XV (New York, 1893); HOLIDAY, *Stained Glass as an Art* (London, 1896); DAY, *Windows* (London, 1897); HUYSMANS, *The Cathedral: Stained Glass Tours in France* (New York, 1909).

CARYL COLEMAN.

Stalls, seats in a choir, wholly or partly enclosed on the back and sides, are mentioned from the eleventh century. In the earliest times the *subsellia*, usually of stone, of the clergy were placed to the right and left of the *cathedra* of the bishop in the apse of the basilica. After the numbers of the clergy had greatly increased they appear to have stood during choir service, as is evident from the Rule of St. Chrodegang and from the statutes of Aachen of the year 816. Even as late as the eleventh century St. Peter Damien wrote "Contra sedentes in choro". Those who were weak supported themselves on a T-shaped crutch called *reclinatorium*, which was sometimes censured, sometimes permitted, as in the second "Ordo Romanus". Soon, however, the *formæ* or *formulæ*, seats with backs, appeared (plan of St. Gall of the ninth century), as well as the actual *stalli*, connected seats in which only arms separated the individual seats, and an architectural effect was sought. The seats, which earlier were frequently movable, now became fixed; the sides and backs were made higher; the ornamentation, originally pictorial, soon became architectural and was carved. A few examples of these have been preserved in Germany from the Romanesque period. At Ratzeburg there are side-pieces, each supported by two small columns with base and capital, that are rounded above like a beam and beautifully broken in the middle by curved fluting. There are also small columns on the oldest choir-stall at Xanten; the face of the back is even more boldly curved, and fantastic heads completely in the round project from it. During the Gothic period the architectonic element was at times exaggerated; the mathematical forms of the labyrinths of lines and the scribing are too jejune, and the structure is often too high and uncomfortable. On the other hand the baldachinum over the highest row of seats was often very magnificent. Germany and France possess a large number of stalls that are masterpieces. These stalls are found on both sides of the choir in the churches of monasteries and collegiate foundations. The seats on the Epistle side are called *chorus abbatis* or *præpositi*, those on the Gospel side *chorus prioris* or *decani*. The last of the ascending rows is generally a back wall crowned with artistic decorations. The back of each preceding row serves the succeeding one as a prayer-desk; the first row has a projection built in front of it for the same purpose. On feast days, for the sake of comfort and ornament, tapestries were hung on the backs of the stalls, cushions laid on the seats, and rugs put under the feet. Ornamental designs or figures carved in the wood decorated both the front and rear faces of the high backs of all the stalls as well as the double arms that were used both when standing and sitting. On the arms as well as in subordinate parts, especially on the *misericordia* or console—against which, after the seat had been turned up, the cleric could support himself while standing—it was not unusual to carve fantastic figures of animals or grotesque devils. Choir-stalls of stone, which are always colder, occur but rarely (for example, at Kaurim in Bohemia). Among the oldest still existing examples of Gothic choir-stalls in France are those in the Church of Notre-Dame-de-la-Roche; especially rich in their ornamentation are those in the cathedrals at Amiens, Paris, Auch, and others. Viollet-le-Duc gives some beautiful examples in his "Dictionnaire de l'Architecture", s. v. *Stalles*. Among examples in Belgium the Church of St. Gertrude at Louvain shows late Gothic choir-stalls with statuettes and twenty-eight reliefs portraying the life of Christ, of St. Augustine, and of St. Gertrude. The most celebrated choir-stalls in Germany are those in the Cathedral at Ulm; these are reproduced in all their details in Egle, "Der Dom zu Ulm" (1872). There are eighty-nine seats with gable hood-mouldings and pinnacles, on each seat there are two rows of decorations, on the back and on the side, representing Christ as the anticipation of the heathen and the prediction of the prophets, and in addition there is delineated the founding of the New Covenant. The choir-stalls at Dordrecht, Holland, belong to the style of the Renaissance; they represent on the back the triumph of the Church and of the Holy Sacraments; on the opposite side, the triumphs of Charles V. There are superb creations of the same style in Italy, especially with inlaid work called *tarsia*, as at Assisi, Siena, Florence, and Venice (cf. Kraus, "Geschichte der christl. Kunst", II, 685). Modern times have made but few changes in the practical and artistic form that was fixed in an earlier era.

CHOIR STALLS IN THE CHURCH OF S. SPIRITO, FLORENCE

Besides the authors already mentioned: REITZ, *Das Chorgestühl des Domes zu Köln* (Dresden, 1847); TSCHISCHKA, *Der Stephansdom in Wien* (Vienna, 1832). A comprehensive treatise is given by RIGGENBACH, *Chorgestühl des Mittelalters* in *Zeitschr. für christl. Archäol. u. Kunst*, II; *Mitteil. der k. k. Central-Kommission zu Wien*, VIII (Vienna, 1865); GAILHABAUD, *Architecture du Ve au XVIIe siècle et des arts qui en dépendent* (Paris, 1850–8).

GERHARD GIETMANN.

Stanbrook Abbey, an abbey of Benedictine nuns, midway between Malvern and Worcester, England. The abbey and church are dedicated to Our Lady of Consolation, the title of the original foundation at Cambrai, Spanish Flanders, 1625, effected by the Benedictine Monks of the English Congregation, under whose immediate jurisdiction the community has always remained. Of the nine English ladies who began the foundation, Helen More (Dame Gertrude) was chief foundress because of the liberality of her father, Cresacre More, great-grandson of Sir Thomas More; wherefore the community has special claims on the patronage of this blessed martyr. The other ladies were: Margaret Vavasour; Anne Morgan; Catherine Gascoigne; Grace and Anne More, cousins of Helen; Frances Watson; and two lay sisters, Mary Hoskins and Jane Martin. Dame Frances Gawen, one of three nuns lent by the Benedictines of Brussels to train the postulants, governed as abbess until the infant community was in a position to choose one from its own body, Dame Catherine Gascoigne, abbess, 1629–1676. Dom Augustine Baker, to whom their spiritual formation was entrusted, wrote at the Cambrai Abbey, for their use, spiritual treatises which give him celebrity. In 1793 the French revolutionists, seizing their house and property, conveyed the nuns, twenty-two in number, to a prison in Compiègne. Here, consequent on hardship, four of them died, as also the Very Reverend Dom Augustine Walker, President of the Anglo-Benedictine Congregation, who had been arrested in their priests' quarters. Subsequently they had as fellow-prisoners the Carmelites (since beatified), who were led thence to martyrdom in Paris, July, 1794. Though a similar death awaited the Benedictines this was averted by the downfall of Robespierre, their deliverance from jail being effected only on 25 April, 1795. Clad in worn-out secular attire left in the Compiègne prison by the Carmelite martyrs, they reached England in utter destitution, but were charitably lodged in London for some days. Thence they proceeded to Lancashire, where the Very Reverend Dr. Brewer, President of the Anglo-Benedictine Congregation, made over to them the Ladies' School belonging to the Woolton mission under his care.

In 1807 the community removed to Salford Hall, near Evesham, where by the joint kindness of its owner, Mrs. Stanford, and the life-heir, Robert Berkeley, Esq., of Spetchly, they lived free of rent, till able to purchase Stanbrook Hall, to which they removed in 1838. In 1871 an entirely new monastic structure was inaugurated by the consecration of the abbey-church, designed by Edward Welby Pugin. The starting of this project was mainly attributable to the zeal and energy of the then *Vicarius monialium*, Dom James Laurence Shepherd, the well-known translator of Dom Guéranger's "Année Liturgique". The rest of the abbey building, of which Messrs. Cuthbert and Peter-Paul Pugin were the architects, was gradually erected during the abbacy of Lady Gertrude L. d'Aurillac Dubois, d. 1897. The abbey, with its extensive grounds, is enclosed by the canonical wall completed by the present abbess. As formerly at Cambrai, so at Stanbrook, the solemn celebration of the Divine Office, strictness of enclosure, and monastic observance are leading features. Though essentially devoted to the contemplative life, the nuns receive for education within the cloister a small number of alumnæ. They are girls of the upper classes of life, and are fitted for their future position in society by a strong traditional training on monastic lines according to the spirit of St. Benedict's Rule. Stanbrook Abbey has some reputation for its contributions to Catholic literature, as also to the popularization of Gregorian Chant. Lady Cecilia A. Heywood, who was blessed abbess in November, 1897, is the twentieth in succession from the year 1629. [See MORE, HELEN (DAME GERTRUDE.)]

WELDON, *Chronological Notes* (Stanbrook, 1881); WELD-BLUNDELL, *Inner Life and Writings of D. Gertrude More*, 2 vols. (London, 1910); SWEENEY, *Life and Spirit of Father Baker* (London, 1861); CODY, *Ampleforth Journal* (April, 1897); ALSTON, *Downside Review* (Christmas, 1906–7); WAUGH, *Downside Review* (July, 1909); GUÉRANGER, (*Vie de*), *par un Bénédictin de Solesmes* (Paris, 1910); BILLECOCQ, *Bulletin Trimestriel de l'Archiconfrérie de N. D. de Compassion* (September, 1907); DE TEIL, *Le Correspondant* (Paris, 1906); WILLSON, *Martyrs of Compiègne* (London, 1907); DE COURSON, *Carmelites of Compiègne*.

E. B. WELD-BLUNDEL.

Stanfield, WILLIAM CLARKSON, English painter, b. at Sunderland, 1793; d. at Hampstead, near London, 1867. He became a sailor, and on one of his journeys to New Guinea made the acquaintance of Thomas Clarkson, who was strongly interested in the abolition of the slave trade; in proof of his warm friendship with whom, he added the name of Clarkson to his own, and thereafter styled himself William Clarkson Stanfield. He was disabled in 1816, and then started as a scene-painter in a theatre, much frequented by sailors, from which he obtained engagements to the various other London theatres. Making the acquaintance of Douglas Jerrold and Captain Marryat, the novelist, he was strongly recommended to take up the painting of panel pictures, and to try his chance at an exhibition. He exhibited at the Society of British Artists in 1824, and again in 1827, gaining considerable attention and encouragement. Two years later he sent a picture to the Academy, which was favourably received, and, gaining a prize of fifty guineas from the British Institution, he relinquished scene-painting and started on a Continental tour, painting various pictures. From that time he was a steady exhibitor at the Academy, sending in nearly one hundred and forty pictures to its exhibitions. His paintings partook of the character of scene-painting in their spectacular and stagey effect, but many of them were very charming, and were greatly admired, and some of his best will hardly ever be excelled as fine representations of sea scenes. Perhaps his greatest is the one in the possession of Mrs. Burns; other works of importance are those painted for the Marquess of Lansdowne at Bowood, and the four beautiful examples in the Victoria and Albert Museum. He was a man of tremendous energy, and regarded by his friends as exceedingly charming and pleasant. A devout Catholic, he spent the latter part of his life in an old house at Hampstead, still standing, and used partly as a library and partly as a residence. His funeral took place in the Catholic cemetery at Kensal Green, and a couple of years after his death there was a memorial exhibition of his works in the Royal Academy.

WILLIAM CLARKSON STANFIELD
From a Photograph

There is no work dealing with this painter that has any claim for special recognition; consult the memoirs in the local papers of Hampstead, and in the principal journals of the day.

GEORGE CHARLES WILLIAMSON.

Stanislas Kostka, SAINT, b. at Rostkovo near Prasnysz, Poland, about 28 October, 1550; d. at Rome during the night of 14–15 August, 1568. He entered the Society of Jesus at Rome, 28 October, 1567, and is said to have foretold his death a few days before it occurred. His father, John Kostka, was a senator of the Kingdom of Poland and Lord of Zakroczym; his mother was Margaret de Drobniy Kryska, the sister and niece of the Dukes Palatine of Masovia and the aunt of the celebrated Chancellor of Poland, Felix Kryski. The marriage was blessed with seven children, of whom Stanislas was the second. His older brother Paul survived him long enough to be present at the celebration of the beatification of Stanislas in 1605. The two brothers were first taught at home, the main feature of this early education being the firmness, even severity, of their training; its results were the excellent habits of piety, modesty, temperance, and submission. After this they were sent to Vienna with their tutor to attend the Jesuit college that had been opened there four years before, reaching Vienna, 25 July, 1564. Among the students of the college Stanislas was soon conspicuous not only for his amiability and cheerfulness of expression, but also for his religious fervour and angelic piety. This spirit of devotion continued to grow during the three years he remained in Vienna. His brother Paul said of him during the process of beatification: "He devoted himself so completely to spiritual things that he frequently became unconscious, especially in the church of the Jesuit Fathers at Vienna. It is true," added the witness, "that this had happened at home to my brother at Easter when he was seated at table with our parents and other persons." Among other practices of devotion he joined while at Vienna the Congregation of St. Barbara, to which many students of the Jesuit college belonged. If the confidences he then made to his tutor and later to a fellow-member of the Society at Rome are to be believed, it was Saint Barbara who brought two angels to him during the course of a serious illness, in order to give him the Eucharist. So much piety, however, did not please the older brother Paul; his exasperation led him to treat with violence the innocent Stanislas. The latter finally lost patience, and one night after Stanislas had again suffered the harsh comments and blows of his brother he turned on Paul with the words: "Your rough treatment will end in my going away never to return, and you will have to explain my leaving to our father and mother." Paul's sole reply was to swear violently at him.

Meantime the thought of joining the Society of Jesus had already entered the mind of the saintly young man. It was six months, however, before he ventured to speak of this to the superiors of the Society. At Vienna they hesitated to receive him, fearing the tempest that would probably be raised by his father against the Society, which had just quieted a storm that had broken out on account of other admissions to the Company. Stanislas quickly grasped the situation and formed the plan of applying to the general of the Society at Rome. The distance was five hundred leagues, which had to be made on foot, without equipment, or guide, or any other resources but the precarious charity that might be received on the road. The prospective dangers and humiliations of such a journey, however, did not alarm his courage. On the morning of the day on which he was to carry out his project he called his servant to him early and told him to notify his brother Paul and his tutor in the course of the morning that he would not be back that day to dinner. Then he started, taking the first opportunity to exchange the dress of a gentleman for that of a mendicant, which was the only way to escape the curiosity of those he might meet. By nightfall Paul and the tutor comprehended that Stanislas had turned from them as he had threatened. They were seized with a fierce anger, and as the day was ended the fugitive had gained twenty-four hours over them. They started to follow him, but were not able to overtake him; either their exhausted horses refused to go farther, or a wheel of their carriage would break, or, as the tutor frankly declared, they had mistaken the route, having left the city by a different road from the one that Stanislas had taken. It is noticeable that in his testimony Paul gives no explanation of his ill-luck.

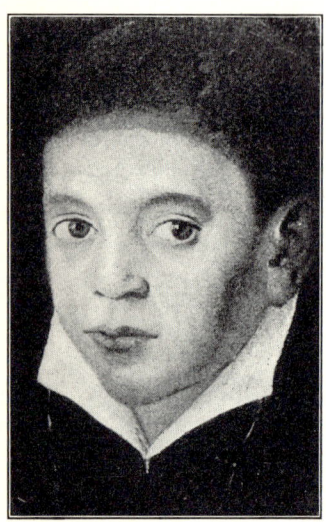

St. Stanislas Kostka
From a portrait preserved at St-Symphorien-d'Oxon, Isère, France

Stanislas stayed for a month at Dillingen, where the provincial of that time, the Blessed Peter Canisius, put the young aspirant's vocation to the test by employing him in the boarding-school. Subsequently he went on to Rome, where he arrived 25 October, 1567. As he was greatly exhausted by the journey, the general of the order, St. Francis Borgia, would not permit him to enter the novitiate of Saint Andrew until several days later. During the ten remaining months of his life, according to the testimony of the master of novices, Father Giulio Fazio, he was a model and mirror of religious perfection. Notwithstanding his very delicate constitution he did not spare himself the slightest penance ("Monumenta hist. Societatis Jesu, Sanctus Franciscus Borgia", IV, 635). He had such a burning fever in his chest that he was often obliged to apply cold compresses. On the eve of the feast of St. Lawrence, Stanislas felt a mortal weakness made worse by a high fever, and clearly saw that his last hour had come. He wrote a letter to the Blessed Virgin begging her to call him to the skies there to celebrate with her the glorious anniversary of her Assumption (ibid., 636). His confidence in the Blessed Virgin, which had already brought him many signal favours, was this time again rewarded; on 15 August, towards four in the morning, while he was wrapt in pious utterances to God, to the saints, and to the Virgin Mary, his beautiful soul passed to its Creator. His face shone with the most serene light. The entire city proclaimed him a saint and people hastened from all parts to venerate his remains and to obtain, if possible, some relics (ibid., 637). The Holy See ratified the popular verdict by his beatification in 1605; he was canonized on 31 December, 1726. St. Stanislas is one of the popular saints of Poland and many religious institutions have chosen him as the protector of their novitiates. The representations of him in art are very varied; he is sometimes depicted receiving Holy Communion from the hands of angels; sometimes receiving the Infant Jesus from the hands of the Virgin; or he is shown in the midst of a battle putting to flight the enemies of his country. At times he is depicted near a fountain putting a wet linen cloth on his breast. He is invoked for palpitations of the heart and for dangerous cases of illness (Cahier, "Caractéristiques des Saints").

This account has been drawn almost exclusively from the depositions of witnesses cited for the process of canonization of Stanislas (cf. Archivio della Postulazione generale d. C. d. G., Roma). The accompanying portrait is by Scipione Delfini and is the oldest of St. Stanislas in existence. Having probably been painted at Rome the year of his death, perhaps after death, it may be regarded as the best likeness. The face is strikingly Slavonic, a fact that is not noticeable in his other portraits.

Lives of Stanislas were written at Rome in the year of his death by Fathers Fazio and Warsevitz (Brussels, 1895). The former remained in manuscript, but the substance of both has been given in later biographies. Among these latter the most complete and most fully based on documentary evidence is that of Ubaldini in *Analecta Bollandiana*, IX–XVI (1890–1897). Equally worthy of recommendation are the works of Sacchini, Bartoli, Gruber, Goldie, and Michel.

FRANCIS VAN ORTROY.

Stanislaus of Cracow, Saint, bishop and martyr, b. at Szczepanow (hence called Szczepanowski), in the Diocese of Cracow, 26 July, 1030; d. at Cracow, 8 May, 1079; feast on 7 May in Roman Martyrology, but on 8 May at Cracow, which has a special feast of the translation of his relics on 27 September; patron of Poland and of the city and Diocese of Cracow; invoked in battle. In pictures he is given the episcopal insignia and the sword. Larger paintings represent him in a court or kneeling before the altar and receiving the fatal blow. No contemporary biography of the saint is in existence. At the time of his canonization a life appeared written by a Dominican Vincent(?) (Acta SS., May, II, 196) which contains much legendary matter. His parents, Belislaus and Bogna, pious and noble Catholics, gave him a religious education. He made his studies at Gnesen and Paris(?). After the death of his parents he distributed his ample inheritance among the poor. Lambert Zula, Bishop of Cracow, ordained him priest and made him pastor of Czembocz near Cracow, canon and preacher at the cathedral, and later, vicar-general. After the death of Lambert he was elected bishop, but accepted only on explicit command of Pope Alexander II. He worked with his wonted energy for his diocese, and inveighed against vices among high and low, regardless of consequences. Boleslaw II had become King of Poland. The renown he had gained by his successful wars he now sullied by atrocious cruelty and unbridled lust. Moreover the bishop had several serious disputes with the king about a piece of land belonging to the Church which was unjustly claimed by Boleslaw, and about some nobles, who had left the king before Kiev and returned to their homes to ward off various evils threatening their families and who were in consequence cruelly treated by the king. Stanislaus spared neither tears nor prayers and admonitions to bring the king to lead a more Christian life. All being in vain, Boleslaw was excommunicated and the canons of the cathedral were instructed to discontinue the Divine Offices in case the king should attempt to enter. Stanislaus retired to the Chapel of St. Michael in a suburb of Cracow. The king was furious and followed the bishop with his guards, some of whom he sent to kill the saint.

These dared not obey, so Boleslaw slew him during the Holy Sacrifice. The body was at first buried in the chapel, but in 1088 it was transferred to the cathedral by Bishop Lambert III. St. Stanislaus was canonized 1253 by Innocent IV at Assisi.

Bibl. hag. lat., 1134; GFRÖRER, *Papst Gregor VII* (Schaffhausen, 1851), 561; *St. Stanislaus of Cracow* in BUTLER, *Lives of the Saints*, II, May 7.

FRANCIS MERSHMAN.

Stanislawow, DIOCESE OF (STANISLAOPOLIENSIS), of the Greek-Ruthenian Rite, in Galicia, Austria, suffragan of Lemberg. The establishment of this see was decided on in May, 1850, but the plan was not carried out till the issuing of the Brief "De universo dominico grege" (26 March, 1885) and the imperial decrees of 26 December, 1885. The diocese includes most of south-eastern Galicia and all Bukovina as far as Halicz, which was reserved to the metropolitan *mensa* of Lemberg. It comprises the districts of Stanislawow, Kolomyja, and Czerniowce. There are 21 deaneries, 433 churches with, and 298 without, resident priests, 63 chapels, 579 secular, and 13 regular, priests, 4 Reformed Basilian monasteries with 22 religious, 2 Basilian convents with 11 nuns, and 10 convents of the Servants of the Blessed Virgin Mary with 37 nuns. The Greek-Ruthenian Catholics number 920,000 out of a population of 1,387,930, of whom about 5000 belong to the Armenian, and 230,000 to the Latin, Rite. An ecclesiastical seminary was established in 1907, the clergy having been trained previously at Lemberg and Vienna. The episcopal town of Stanislawow was founded by Stanislav Potocki (d. 1683), and rebuilt after a disastrous fire in 1868. It is situated on the Bisthritza, 87 miles south-east of Lemberg, and has a population of 30,410, mostly Jews; it has a beautiful parish church containing the tombs of the Potocki, a Polish and a Ruthenian *gymnasium*, a Polish-Ruthenian normal school, 3 hospitals, a Jesuit residence, and convents of the Sisters of Charity and the Servants of the Immaculate Conception. It is a busy manufacturing centre (paper, lace, tanning, milling, and engineering works).

The bishops of Stanislawow were: (1) Mgr. Julian Pelesz, author of the "Geschichte der Union der ruth. Kirche mit Rom" (Vienna, 1878–81), previously rector of the Greek-Ruthenian Seminary, Vienna, then archpriest of Lemberg cathedral, preconized on 27 March, 1885; consecrated, 1 November, 1885; enthroned, 10 January, 1886; died 1891. (2) Mgr. Julian Kujlowski, b. at Krolewski in the Diocese of Przemysl, 1 May, 1826, elected titular Bishop of Ephestum, 26 June, 1890; transferred to Stanislawow, 22 September, 1891; held a diocesan synod in 1897. (3) Mgr. Count Andrea Alexander de Szeptyce-Szeptychi, member of a distinguished ancient Ruthenian family which joined the Latin Rite in the eighteenth century, b. at Przylbice, in the Diocese of Przemysl, 15 July, 1865, embraced the Ruthenian Rite to enter the Basilian Order, laboured energetically to strengthen the spirit of reform among the monks; was ordained, 29 August, 1892; accepted the episcopal dignity only on the formal order of Leo XIII; elected to the see, 19 June, 1899; promoted to the Archdiocese of Lemberg, 17 December, 1900. (4) Mgr. Gregorius Chomyszyn, b. on 24 March, 1867–8, elected, 19 April, 1904, and still governing the diocese.

A. A. MACERLEAN.

Stanley Falls, VICARIATE APOSTOLIC OF, in the Belgian Congo. It is bounded on the east by the meridian 30° E. long.; on the south by a line running from the extreme point of Lake Albert Edward to the confluence of the Elila and the Congo, and thence to Bena-Kamba on the Lomani; on the west, by the right bank of the Lomani to its junction with the Congo, and the Congo to the watershed of the Ilimbiri; on the north by this same watershed of the Ilimbiri and the Congo and then the watershed of the Welle and the Arwimi as far as the meridian 30° E. long. The vicariate has an area of about 90,000 square miles.

The mission of Stanley Falls was established by the Fathers of the Sacred Heart in 1897. The pioneer missionaries, setting out from Antwerp on 6 July, 1897, settled definitively on Christmas Day following at a spot on the right bank of the River Congo four miles below Stanleyville, and gave to their first foundation, an orphanage, the name of St. Gabriel. The mission at that time formed part of the Vicariate of Belgian Congo. Their work was rapidly crowned with success and the mission on 3 August, 1904, was erected into a prefecture Apostolic, and on 10 March, 1908, was made a vicariate Apostolic. In 1901 the Franciscan Missionary Sisters of Mary came to assist the Fathers of the Sacred Heart and settled at St. Gabriel, taking charge of a girls' orphanage, a school, and a dispensary; since then they have given their services to the victims of sleeping-sickness in the quarantine station between the mission and Stanleyville. Four years later another band of the same Sisters arrived to take care of the hospital founded by the "Compagnie du Chemin de Fer des Grands Lacs", at Stanleyville, on the left bank of the river; they are about to establish (October, 1911) a house at Basoko at the mouth of the Arwimi. This year (1911) the Little Brothers of Mary are coming to Stanleyville to take care of the State school.

The mission has ten centres: St. Gabriel; Stanleyville, right bank; Stanleyville, left bank and railway; Lokandu; Lileke; Basoko; Banalya; Avakubi; Beni. Each centre spreads out and establishes secondary posts, with a chapel, dwelling-house for the missionary on his rounds, and house for the catechist; and posts of third rank, which have a catechist, but no chapel or house for the missionary. Each centre has its primary school, and St. Gabriel has a school for catechists. Most of the natives are fetishists or Mohammedans; the chief language spoken is Kishwali, but there are twenty-five others. The present superior is Mgr. Gabrielle-Emile Grison, titular Bishop of Sagalassus, who resides at St-Gabriel-lès-Falls, near Stanleyville. The latest annual religious statistics (1910–11) are: baptisms, 1839; confirmations, 1104; paschal communions, 5191; Christians, 7172; catechumens, 10,754; there are approximately 150 posts of second or third rank. The statistics of 1909 as given in Battandier, "Annuaire pontificale", are: Christians, 5969; catechumens, 7113; religious (men), 29, of whom 23 are priests and 6 lay brothers; churches, 9; chapels, 25; schools, 9; orphanages, 4; hospitals, 3; nuns, 11.

STANLEY, *The Congo* (London, 1895); IDEM, *In Darkest Africa* (London, 1890); JOHNSTON, *George Grenfree and the Congo* (London, 1908).

GABRIEL GRISON.

Stansel, VALENTIN, astronomer, b. at Olmütz, Moravia, 1621; d. at Bahia, Brazil, 18 Dec., 1705. He entered the Society of Jesus on 1 Oct., 1637, and taught rhetoric and mathematics at Olmütz and Prague. After his ordination he was, at his own request, appointed to work on the Jesuit mission in India, and went to Portugal to await an opportunity of taking ship for his destination. Meantime, he lectured on astronomy with considerable success at the college of Evora. While there, in order to conform to the language of the country, he changed his name to the form "Estancel", in which form it appears on the title pages of most of his published works. Obstacles having arisen which prevented his going to India, he was sent to Brazil, and was attached to the Jesuit College and Seminary of San Salvador (Bahia), where he filled the post of professor of moral theology, and later on that of superior. At the same time he continued his astronomical labours, and made extensive observations, particularly on comets, the results of which he sent to Europe for publication. His chief works are: "Dioptra geodetica" (Prague, 1652 or 1654), "Propositiones selenegraphicæ, sive de luna" (Olmütz, 1655); "Orbe Affonsino, horoscopio universal" (Evora, 1658); "Mercurius brasilicus, sive de Cœli et soli brasiliensis œconomia"; "Zodiacus Divini Doloris, sive Orationes XII" (Evora, 1675), "Legatus uranicus ex orbe novo in veterum, h. e. Observationes Americanæ cometarum factæ, conscriptæ et in Europam missæ" (Prague, 1683); "Uranophilus cœlestis peregrinus" (Ghent, 1685).

SOMMERVOGEL, *Bibl. de la C. de J.*, VII (Brussels, 1896).

EDWARD C. PHILLIPS.

Stanyhurst, RICHARD, Catholic controversialist, historian, and devotional writer, b. at Dublin, 1547; d. at Brussels, 1618. He was the son of James Stanyhurst, speaker of the Irish House of Commons and a leading Dublin Protestant. After leaving his school at Waterford he went to University College, Oxford, becoming B.A. in 1568, and then studied law in London. At Oxford he had met Bl. Edmund Campion, and he accompanied the latter on his visit to Ireland, helping him to collect material for his history of Ireland. He himself wrote the "Description of Ireland" and the "History of Ireland under Henry VIII", both published in Holinshed's "Chronicles", 1577. In several ways these works gave offence to Irish Catholics. In 1579 Stanyhurst's first wife, Janet Barnewall, died, and he left England for the Low Countries, where he became a Catholic. At Leyden he published his extraordinary translation of Virgil's Æneid into English hexameters (1582). Later he wrote "De rebus in Hibernia gestis" (1584) and "De Vita S. Patricii" (1587). In 1585 he married Helen Copley, by whom he had two sons, both afterwards Jesuits. Subsequently he spent some years in Spain as adviser to the Government on English affairs. On the death of his second wife, in 1602, he became a priest and was appointed chaplain to Archduke Albert, also assisting the English Benedictine nuns at Brussels. He published two devotional works, "Hebdomada Mariana" (1609) and "Hebdomada Eucharistica" (1614). His last work was "Brevis præmunitio pro futura concertatione cum Jacobo Usserio", in which he replied to the treatise of his Protestant nephew, James Ussher, afterwards Archbishop of Armagh.

WOOD, ed. BLISS, *Athenæ Oxonienses* (London, 1813–20); SIMPSON, *Life of Edmund Campion* (London, 1867); FOLEY, *Records Eng. Prov., S.J.*, VII (London, 1882); WRIGHT, *The Ussher Memoirs* (London, 1889); LEE in *Dict. Nat. Biog.*, s. v.; ARBER, *Introduction* to his *Reprint of Stanyhurst's Tr. of Virgil* (London, 1895).

EDWIN BURTON.

Stanza, an Italian word signifying room, chamber, apartment. In English the term is chiefly used for Raphael's celebrated *Stanze* in the Vatican Palace, four in number, the walls of which were frescoed by Raphael and his pupils. The paintings in these chambers by Raphael's own hand belong to the most sublime monuments of Italian art, and rank with Michelangelo's ceiling frescoes of the Sistine Chapel. For a description of the paintings consult the articles RAPHAEL; VATICAN.

Stapf, JOSEPH AMBROSE, theologian, b. at Fliess in the valley of the Upper Inn in the Tyrol, Austria, 15 August, 1785; d. at Brixen, 10 January, 1844. He studied at Innsbruck, and obtained the Degree of Doctor of Theology, and in 1821 became professor of moral theology at the lyceum at Innsbruck. In 1823 he was made professor of moral theology and pedagogy at the seminary of Brixen, where he was later a cathedral canon. His chief work is "Theologia moralis in compendium redacta" (4 vols., Innsbruck, 1827-30; 6th ed., 1846; 7th ed., 1855); the merits of this work consist in its strictly orthodox character, clear and precise presentation, and practical usefulness. From 1830 it was officially made a text-book for all seminaries of Austria. Much used as a text-book also was a compendium of this work: "Epitome theologiæ moralis publicis prælectionibus accommodata" [2 vols., Innsbruck, 1832; 2nd ed., 1842; 3rd ed. revised by J. V. Hofmann (volume I) and Simon Aichner (volume II), 1863-65]. At a later date Stapf made a free German revision, which showed the influence of Hirscher "Die christliche Moral. Als Antwort auf die Frage: Was wir thun müssen, um in das Reich Gottes einzugehen" [4 vols., Innsbruck, 1841-42; 2nd ed. edited after Stapf's death by J. V. Hofmann under the title: "Die christliche Sittenlehre" (3 vols., 1848-49)]. Besides these Stapf wrote: "Erziehungslehre im Geiste der katholischen Kirche" (Innsbruck, 1832; 4th ed., 1846; 5th ed. edited by J. V. Hofmann, 1854); "Expositio casuum reservatorum in diocesi Brixinensi" (Brixen, 1836); "Der hl. Vincentius von Paul, dargestellt in seinem Leben und Wirken" (anonymous, 2 vols., Vienna, 1837); "Biblische Geschichte des Alten und Neuen Bundes zum Gebrauche der Hauptschulen in den k. k. österreichischen Staaten" (1840).

WURZBACH, *Biographisches Lexikon des Kaiserthums Oesterreich*, XXXVII (Vienna, 1878), 144 sq.; HURTER, *Nomenclator*, III (2nd ed.), 1151.

FRIEDRICH LAUCHERT.

Staphylus, FRIEDRICH, theologian, b. at Osnabrück, 27 Aug., 1512; d. at Ingolstadt, 5 March, 1564. His father, Ludeke Stapellage, was an official of the Bishop of Osnabrück. Left an orphan at an early age he came under the care of an uncle at Danzig, then went to Lithuania and studied at Cracow, after which he studied theology and philosophy at Padua. About 1536 he went to Wittenberg, obtained the Degree of *magister artium* in 1541 and at Melanchthon's recommendation became a tutor in the family of the Count of Eberstein. In 1546 Duke Albert of Prussia appointed Staphylus professor of theology at the new University of Königsberg, which the duke had founded in 1544. At this time Staphylus was still under the influence of Luther's opinions, as is shown by his academic disputation upon the doctrine of justification, "De justificationis articulo". However, at his installation as professor he obtained the assurance that he need not remain if the duke tolerated errors which "might be contrary to the Holy Scriptures and the *primitivæ apostolicæ et catholicæ ecclesiæ consensum*". This shows that even then he regarded with suspicion the development of Protestantism. He had at Königsberg a violent theological dispute with William Gnapheus. In 1547-48 he was the first rector elected by the university, but in 1548 he resigned his professorship, because he met with enmity, and was dissatisfied with religious conditions in Prussia. Still he continued to be one of the councillors of the duke. In 1549 he married at Breslau the daughter of John Hess, a reformer of that place.

Returning to Königsberg, a new dispute broke out between him and Osiander. The dogmatic dissension, which seemed to him to make everything uncertain, drove him continually more and more to the Catholic idea of Tradition and to the demand for the authoritative exposition of the Scriptures by the Church. He expressed these views in the treatise "Synodus sanctorum patrum antiquorum contra nova dogmata Andreæ Osiandri", which he wrote at Danzig in 1552. A severe illness hastened his conversion, which took place at Breslau at the end of 1552. After this he first entered the service of the Bishop of Breslau, for whom he established a school at Neisse. In 1555 the Emperor Ferdinand I appointed him a member of the imperial council. At the Disputation of Worms in 1557 he opposed, as one of the Catholic collocutors, the once venerated Melanchthon. In his "Theologiæ Martini Lutheri trimembris epitome" (1558) he severely attacked the lack of union in Protestantism, the worship of Luther, and religious subjectivism. The treatise called forth a number of answers. In 1560 Duke Albert of Bavaria, at the request of Canisius, appointed Staphylus professor of theology at the Bavarian University of Ingolstadt after Staphylus had received the Degree of Doctor of Theology and Canon Law in virtue of a papal dispensation, as he was married. As superintendent (curator) he reformed the university. After this he took an active part in the Catholic restoration in Bavaria and Austria. He drew up several opinions on reform for the Council of Trent, as the "Counsel to Pius IV", while he declined to go to the council personally. In 1562 the pope sent him a gift of one hundred gulden, and the emperor raised him to the nobility. His learning and eloquence are frankly acknowledged by his Lutheran fellow-countryman Hermann Hamelmann. The attempt is now no longer made to trace his conversion to mercenary motives.

STAPHYLUS, *In causa religionis sparsim editi libri in unum volumen digesti* (Ingolstadt, 1613); TSCHACKERT, *Urkundenbuch zur Reformationsgeschichte des Herzogtums Preussen*, I and III (Leipzig, 1890), passim; SOFFNER, *Friedrich Staphylus* (Breslau, 1904).

KLEMENS LÖFFLER.

Stapleton, THEOBALD, b. in Co. Kilkenny, Ireland, but was English by descent, though not connected with the Yorkshire Stapletons. Nothing is known of his career, except that he was a priest living in Flanders, and that in 1639 he published at Brussels a book called "Catechismus seu doctrina christiana latino-hibernica", which was the first book in which Irish was printed in Roman type. His object in publishing it was to promote the use of Irish in religious literature, and to further this object he added to the book an appendix in nineteen sections giving directions for reading Irish.

MEEHAN, *Rise and Fall of the Irish Franciscan Monasteries* (Dublin, 1870); MOORE in *Dict. Nat. Biog.*, s. v.

EDWIN BURTON.

Stapleton, THOMAS, controversialist, b. at Henfield, Sussex, July, 1535; d. at Louvain, 12 Oct., 1598. He was the son of William Stapleton, one of the Stapletons of Carlton, Yorkshire. He was educated at the Free School, Canterbury, at Winchester, and at New College, Oxford, where he became a fellow, 18 Jan., 1553. On Elizabeth's accession he left England rather than conform to the new religion, going first to Louvain, and afterwards to Paris, to study theology. In 1563, being in England, he was summoned by the Anglican bishop Barlow to repudiate the pope's authority, but refused and was deprived of the prebend of Woodhorne in Chichester Cathedral, conferred on him in 1558. He then retired to Louvain with his father and other relatives. In 1568 he joined Allen at Douai and took a great part in founding the English college there, both by lecturing and by devoting to its support his salary as lecturer in theology at Anchin College.

His talents were so remarkable that he was soon appointed public professor of divinity, and canon of St. Amatus; and together with Allen he completed the degree of D.D. on 10 July, 1571. In 1584 he resigned these preferments to enter the Society of Jesus, but did not complete his novitiate, and returned to Douai. Philip II appointed him professor of Scripture at Louvain in 1590, to which office a canonry in St. Peter's Church was annexed; and soon after he was made dean of Hilverenbeeck in the Diocese of Bois-le-Duc. The emoluments of these offices were all spent in relieving necessitous English Catholics. Meanwhile his fame as a theologian had spread to Rome and Pope Clement VIII thought so much of his theological writings that he caused them to be read aloud at his table. Twice he invited Stapleton to Rome in vain, but his offer to make him prothonotary Apostolic in January, 1597, was accepted. It was generally believed that he would be created cardinal, a suggestion which was disapproved of by Father Agazzari, S. J., rector of the English College, and obstacles were put in the way of his journey to Rome (Eley, "Certaine Briefe Notes", p. 254). He accordingly remained at Louvain till his death in the following year. He left his books and manuscripts (now lost) to the English College at Douai. An original painting of Stapleton is preserved at Douai Abbey, Woolhampton, England.

His first works were translations: Ven. Bede's "History of the Church in England" (Antwerp, 1556), the "Apology of Staphylus" (Antwerp, 1565), and Hosius on "The Expresse Word of God" (1567). His original works were very numerous: "A Fortress of the Faith" (Antwerp); "A Return of Untruths" (Antwerp, 1566); "A Counterblast to M. Horne's vain blast" (Louvain, 1567); "Orationes funebres" (Antwerp, 1577); "Principiorum fidei doctrinalium demonstratio" (Paris, 1578); "Speculum pravitatis hæreticæ" (Douai, 1580); "De universa justificationis doctrina" (Paris, 1582); "Tres Thomæ" (Douai, 1588); "Promptuarium morale" in two parts (Antwerp, 1591, 1592); "Promptuarium Catholicum in Evangelia Dominicalia" (Cologne, 1592); "Promptuarium Catholicum in Evangelia Ferialia" (Cologne, 1594) and "Promptuarium Catholicum in Evangelia Festorum" (Cologne, 1592); "Relectio scholastica" (Antwerp, 1592); "Authoritatis Ecclesiasticæ circa S. Scripturarum approbationem defensio" (Antwerp, 1592); "Apologia pro rege Philippo II" (Constance, 1592), published under the punning pseudonym of Didymus Veridicus Henfildanus, i. e. Thomas the Stable-toned [truth-speaking] Henfieldite. "Antidota Evangelica", "Antidota Apostolica contra nostri Temporis Hæreses" (both at Antwerp, 1595); "Antidota Apostolica in Epistolam Pauli ad Romanos" (Antwerp, 1595); "Triplicatio inchoata" (Antwerp, 1596); "Antidota Apostolica in duas Epistolas ad Corinthios" (Antwerp, 1598); "Orationes catecheticæ" (Antwerp, 1598); "Vere admiranda, seu de Magnitudine Romanæ Ecclesiæ" (Antwerp, 1599); "Orationes academicæ miscellaneæ" (Antwerp, 1602); "Oratio academica" (Mainz, 1608). All his works were republished in four folio volumes in Paris in 1620, with an autobiography of the author in Latin verse and Henry Holland's "Vita Thomæ Stapletoni".

HOLLAND, *Vita Thomæ Stapletoni*, prefixed to the *Opera Omnia*, (Paris, 1620); PITTS, *De illustribus Angliæ scriptoribus* (Paris, 1619); DODD, *Church History*, II (Brussels *vere* Wolverhampton, 1739–42); *Laity's Directory* (London, 1812), with engraved portrait; COOPER, in *Dict. Nat. Biog.*, s. v.; GILLOW, *Bibl. Dict. Eng. Cath.*, s. v.; *Douay Diaries* (London, 1878); *Letters and Memorials of Cardinal Allen* (London, 1882); ELEY, *Certaine Briefe Notes* (Paris, 1603); DUTHILLŒUL, *Bibl. Douaisienne* (Douai, 1835–38); MOLANUS, *Histoire de Louvain* (Brussels, 1861); FOSTER, *Alumni Oxonienses* (Oxford, 1891); À WOOD, *Athenæ Oxonienses* (London, 1813–20).

EDWIN BURTON.

Starowolski, SIMON, b. at Stara Wola, near Cracow, 1585; d. at Cracow, 1656; studied at Louvain, but took his degrees in the University of Cracow, after which he travelled in various countries of Western Europe. Returning, he taught philosophy in the University of Cracow, and then became secretary to Chodkiewicz, whom he accompanied on his expedition to Chocim. For years he was a tutor to young noblemen, and again went over Europe in this capacity with the Hetman Koniecpolski's son. In 1639 he was ordained priest, and subsequently became a canon in Cracow. During the Swedish siege (1655) he administered the diocese for Bishop Gębicki, and it became his duty to show the cathedral to the Swedish king. When he pointed to the tomb of Łokietek who, he said, thrice an exile, had returned thrice, Charles Gustavus remarked that "John Casimir would never return". "Serenissime Rex", he replied, "fortuna variabilis, Deus immutabilis." He died some months later, before John Casimir's triumphant return.

Starowolski wrote most abundantly and on every possible subject—history, geography, law, strategy, theology, and politics. His province also embraced literature, for his "Scriptorum Polonicorum Hecatontas" is a short biography of Polish authors, with the titles of their works. This he wrote during his travels abroad, where he published it in Latin, to instruct foreigners in Polish matters. At the same time he wrote books in Polish, chiefly of a moral character, and many theological treatises; also two collections of sermons entitled: "The Lord's Sanctuary" and "The Ark of the Testament". His chief political works are: an exhortation to put down the Tatars; "The True Knight"; and three works intended to reform Polish morals, with different titles, and in different degrees of elaboration. Last, and shortly before his death, appeared his famous though short "Lament of the dying Mother, Poland, over her undutiful sons"; from Skarga's days to those of Mickiewicz, no equally lofty expression of patriotism appeared. Starowolski wrote more than sixty books; but those mentioned suffice to give an idea of the extent of his learning, intelligence, assiduity, and zeal for his country's welfare. In the commonwealth, tottering to its fall, he was one of the most public-spirited men; possibly there was not a single evil in Poland which he did not denounce. And thus, though no genius, he is most worthy of respect, and is the principal literary figure of those times. As a writer, perhaps on account of his numerous works, he is neither very correct nor very brilliant; yet at times (as in the Lament), under the influence of his indignation, he rises to heights of thrilling eloquence. As a political writer, he possesses the quality of sound common sense, and not unfrequently succeeds in pointing out the right means of saving the State. On the whole, he is somewhat more of a moralist than of a politician; at all events, in his writings, the reform of morals takes up a larger place than the regeneration of the commonwealth.

TYSZNSKI, *Symon Starowolski* (Warsaw, 1874); WIERSBOWSKI, *Simonis Starowolskii Elenchus operum* (Warsaw, 1854); BRÜCKNER, *Gesch. der polnischen Literatur* (Leipzig, 1901).

S. TARNOWSKI.

Starr, ELIZA ALLEN, b. at Deerfield, Massachusetts, 29 Aug., 1824; d. at Durand, Illinois, 8 Sept., 1901. She was educated at her father's home. On her father's side she was descended from Dr. Comfort Starr of Ashford, County Kent, England, who settled at Cambridge, Massachusetts, in 1633, and, on her mother's side, from the "Allans of the Bars", who came from Chelmsford, Essex, England. She inherited the love of literature from her parents, and when thirteen years of age went to Boston, where she finished her studies in 1845. In Boston she opened a studio, but, the climate proving unfavourable to her health, she moved to Brooklyn, thence to Philadelphia. She finally accepted a position as teacher in the family of a wealthy planter at Natchez, Mississippi. In 1853 she returned to Brooklyn as teacher of drawing in a boarding-school. In 1848 she returned to Philadelphia. It was during this visit to her kinsfolk she met the Rt. Rev. Francis Patrick Kenrick, afterward Archbishop of Baltimore. It was from this saintly and learned churchman that the germs of faith already in her heart received their first activities. After an incessant struggle of nine years she was received into the Catholic Church at Boston by Bishop Fitzpatrick on 23 December, 1854, and made her first Communion on the following Christmas morning in the chapel of the Sisters of Charity. In 1856 Miss Starr entered upon a larger field of labour. In Chicago she found her life work. She laboured with her pen, and with the pencil illustrated her books. She lectured throughout the United States, and in the auditorium of her home annually gave a course of ten lectures upon art and literature.

Her published works are: "Songs of a Lifetime"; "Patron Saints"; "Pilgrims and Shrines"; "Isabella of Castile"; "What we see"; "Ode to Christopher Columbus"; "Christmas-tide"; "Christian art in our own age"; "The Seven Dolours of the Virgin Mary"; "Literature of Christian Art"; "The Three Keys to the Camera della Segnatura in the Vatican"; "Art in the Chicago Churches", published in the "New World"; "Woman's work in Art"; and "The Three Archangels and the Guardian Angels in Art". In recognition of this last work Leo XIII sent to her a beautiful medallion. She was the first woman to receive the Lætare Medal, which was conferred on her in 1865 by the University of Notre Dame, Indiana.

CLARKE, *Eliza Allen Starr, Poet, Artist and Teacher of Christian Art* in *Cath. World*, LXVI (New York, 1897), 254–60: MERRILL, *Eliza Allen Starr* in *Cath. World*, LXXIV (New York, 1902), 607–13.

JAMES J. MCGOVERN.

State and Church.—The Church and the State are both perfect societies, that is to say, each essentially aiming at a common good commensurate with the need of mankind at large and ultimate in a generic kind of life, and each juridically competent to provide all the necessary and sufficient means thereto. The State is ethically demonstrated to be such, and the Church has a like demonstration from the theology of Christian Revelation. By reason of coexistence on the earth, community of subjects, and a need in common of some of the same means of activity, it is inevitable that they should have mutual relations in the juridical order. To declare these relations in brief from an ethical viewpoint, which is the scope of the present article, it will be necessary to state: I. The basis of their respective rights; II. The range of their respective jurisdictions; III. Their mutual corporate relation; IV. The union of Church and State; V. Counter theories.

I. THE BASIS OF RIGHTS.—All rights and duties on earth come ultimately from God through the Divine Law, either natural or positive. The character of our natural rights and duties is determined by the purpose to which the Creator shaped the nature of man, and natural knowledge of them is acquired by human reason from the aptitudes, tendencies, and needs of nature. Duties and rights descending from positive Divine Law are determined by some additional purpose of God, over and above the exigencies of human nature, and are to be learned only from Divine Revelation, either in its explicit declaration or its rational content. Man has one ultimate purpose of existence, eternal happiness in a future life, but a twofold proximate purpose, one to earn his title to eternal happiness, the other to attain to a measure of temporal happiness consistent with the prior proximate purpose. The State is a natural institution, whose powers, therefore, come from the natural law and are determined by the character of the natural purpose of the State *plus* whatever limitation God has, because of qualifications in the last end of man, ordained in the Divine Positive Law. The Church is a positive institution of Christ the Son of God, whose powers, therefore, are derived from the Divine Positive Law and are determined by the nature of the purpose He has assigned to it, *plus* whatever further concession He has made to facilitate the accomplishment of that purpose. In any consideration of the mutual relations of Church and State the above propositions are fundamental.

The goal of the State is the temporal happiness of man, and its proximate purpose the preservation of external juridical order and the provision of a reasonable abundance of means of human development in the interests of its citizens and their posterity. Man himself, however, as we have said, has a further goal of perfect happiness to be realized only after death, and consequently a proximate purpose to earn in this life his title to the same. In the pursuit of this latter purpose, speaking in the abstract, he had a natural right to constitute a social organization taking over the worship of God as a charge peculiarly its own. In the concrete, however, i. e. as a matter of fact, God by positive law has vacated this natural right and established a universal society (the Church) for Divine worship and the securing of perfect happiness in the hereafter. God, furthermore, has appointed for man a destiny which cannot be attained by mere natural means, and consequently God has conceded to man additional means commensurate with this ultimate purpose, putting these means at the disposal of man through the ministration of the Church. Finally, He has determined the form of external public worship to be rendered, centring it about a sacrifice, the efficacy of which is from itself, being, as it is, a repetition of the Sacrifice of Calvary. The goal, then, of the Church is the perfect supernatural happiness of man; its proximate purpose, to safeguard the internal moral order of right and wrong; and its external manifestation, to care for Divine worship and minister to man the supernatural means of grace. The State, then, exists to help man to temporal happiness, the Church, to eternal. Of these two purposes the latter is more ultimate, man's greater good, while the former is not necessary for the acquisition of the latter. The dominating proximate purpose of man must be to earn his title to eternal salvation: for that, if needs be, he must rationally sacrifice his temporal happiness. It is clear, therefore, that the purpose of the Church is higher in the order of Divine Providence and of righteous human endeavour than that of the State. Hence, in case of direct collision of the two, God's will and man's need require that the guardian of the lower purpose should yield. Likewise the argument for the extension of the powers of the higher society in a measure into the domain of the lower will not hold for such extension from the lower into the higher.

II. The Range of Jurisdiction.—As there are many distinct States of equal natural right the subjects of each are restricted in number, and its government of them is practically confined within the limits of its own territory. Within this territory it has full power to govern them, defining their rights and in some cases restricting the exercise of these rights, conferring purely civil rights and imposing civil duties, holding its citizens to a proper condition of public morality, owning property and qualifying private ownership of the same—all within the exigencies of the civic purpose of preserving external juridical order and promoting the prosperity of the citizens, and over all bound by the enactment of the Divine Law, both natural and positive. In a word, the State controls its own subjects, in the pursuit of its own natural end, in all things where a higher right does not estop it. A higher right will be a right existent because of an ulterior or a more essential destiny of man than the purpose which civil society pursues for him. The Church has the right to preach the Gospel everywhere, willing or nilling any state authority, and so to secure the rights of its members among the subjects of any civil polity whatever. The Church has the right to govern her subjects, wherever found, declaring for them moral right and wrong, restricting any such use of their rights as might jeopardize their eternal welfare, conferring purely ecclesiastical rights, acquiring and holding property herself, and empowering her subordinate associations to do the same—all within the limits of the requirements of her triple purpose, as laid down by the Divine Positive Law, of preserving the internal order of faith and morals and its external manifestation, of providing adequate means of sanctification for her members, and of caring for Divine worship, and over all bound by the eternal principles of integrity and justice declared in the natural and positive Law of God.

In all purely temporal subject-matter, so long as it remains such, the jurisdiction of the State over its own subjects stands not only supreme, but, as far as the Church is concerned, alone. Purely temporal matter is that which has a necessary relation of help or hindrance to man's temporal happiness, the ultimate end of civil society or the State, in such wise that it is at the same time indifferent in itself as a help or hindrance to man's eternal happiness. It is of two kinds: primarily it includes all human acts so related, and secondarily persons or external things as far as they are involved in such acts. In all purely spiritual subject-matter, so long as it remains such, the jurisdiction of the Church over her ecclesiastical subjects obtains to the complete exclusion of the State; nor is the Church therein juridically dependent in any way upon the State for the exercise of its legitimate powers. Purely spiritual subject-matter is primarily made up of human acts necessarily related as help or hindrance to man's eternal happiness, the last end of the Church, and at the same time indifferent in themselves as a help or hindrance to man's temporal happiness; secondarily it extends to all persons and external objects as involved in such acts. In all subject-matter not purely spiritual nor purely temporal, but at the same time both spiritual and temporal in character, both jurisdictions may enter, and so entering give occasion to collision, for which there must be a principle of solution. In case of direct contradiction, making it impossible for both jurisdictions to be exercised, the jurisdiction of the Church prevails, and that of the State is excluded. The reason of this is obvious: both authorities come from God in fulfillment of his purposes in the life of man: He cannot contradict Himself; He cannot authorize contradictory powers. His real will and concession of power is determined by the higher purpose of His Providence and man's need, which is the eternal happiness of man, the ultimate end of the Church. In view of this end God concedes to her the only authority that can exist in the case in point.

In a case where there is no direct contradiction, but a possibility of both jurisdictions being exercised without hurt to the higher, though neither jurisdiction is voided, and they both might, absolutely speaking, be exercised without mutual consultation, practically there is a clear opening for some adjustment between the two, since both jurisdictions are interested in avoiding friction. Though concordats were not devised precisely for this purpose, they have in many cases been used for such adjustment (see Concordat). Consistently with the superiority of essential purpose indicated above, the judicial decision as to when a question does or does not involve spiritual matter, either purely or in part, rests with the Church. It cannot lie with the State, whose jurisdiction, because of the inferiority of its ultimate end and proximate purpose, has not such judicial faculty in regard to the subject-matter of a jurisdiction which is as far above its own as the ultimate end and proximate purpose thereof is above that of the State. In analogous fashion every higher court is always judge of its own jurisdiction as against a lower.

All the above is matter of principle, argued out as a question of objective right, and it supposes that the jurisdiction is to be applied through the respective subjects of the same. In point of fact the duty of submission in a citizen of a State to the higher jurisdiction of the Church does not exist where the citizen is not a subject of the Church, for over such the Church claims no governing power. It may also be by accident subjectively obscured in one who, though in point of right the Church's subject, in good faith fails, through an erroneous conscience, to recognize this fact, and, by consequence, the Church's right and his own duty. The subject of the State has been made fairly clear by human law and custom; but the frequent rebellion, continued through centuries, of great numbers of the Church's subjects has confused in the mind of the non-Catholic world the notion of who is by revealed law a subject of the Church. The juridical subject of the Church is every human being that has validly received the Sacrament of Baptism. This birth into the Church by baptism is analogous to the birth within the territory of a State of the offspring of one of its citizens. However, this new-born subject of the State can, under certain circumstances, renounce his allegiance to his native State and be accepted as the subject of another. Not so one born into the Church by baptism: for baptism is a sacrament leaving an indelible character upon the soul, which man cannot remove and so escape legitimate subjection. Yet, as in a State, a man may be a subject without full rights of citizenship; may even, while remaining a subject, lose those rights by his own act or that of his parents; so, analogously, not every subject of the Church is a member thereof, and once a member, he may lose the social rights of membership in the Church without ceasing to be its subject. For full membership in the Church, besides valid baptism, one must by union of faith and allegiance be in fellowship with her, and not be deprived of the rights of membership by ecclesiastical censure. Hence, those validly baptized Christians who live in schism or, whether by reason of apostasy or of initial education, profess a faith different from that of the Church, or are excommunicated therefrom, are not members of the Church, though as a matter of objective right and duty they are still her subjects. In practice the Church, while retaining her right over all subjects, does not—except in some few matters not of moment here—insist upon exercising her jurisdiction over any but her members, as it is clear that she cannot expect obedience from those Christians who, being in faith or government separated from her, see no right in her to command, and consequently recognize no duty to obey. Over those who are not baptized she claims no right to govern, though she has the indefeasible right to preach the Gospel among them and to endeavour to win them over to become members of Christ's Church and so citizens of her ecclesiastical polity.

III. Mutual Corporate Relation of Church and State.—Every perfect society must acknowledge the rights of every other perfect society; must render to it all duties consequent upon such rights; must respect its autonomy; and may demand the recognition of its own rights and the fulfilment of obligations arising therefrom. Whether one may also command such recognition and fulfilment is another question: one does not involve the other; thus, for instance, the United States may demand its rights of England, but cannot command England to acknowledge them, as the United States has no authority over England or any other nation. Prescinding from this for the moment, the Church must respect the rights of the State to govern its subjects in all purely temporal matters, and, if the subjects of the State are likewise subjects of the Church, must hold the latter to the fulfilment of their civil duties as an obligation in conscience. On the other hand, in principle, as a matter of objective duty, the State is bound to recognize the juridical rights of the Church in all matters spiritual, whether purely so or of mixed character, and its judicial right to determine the character of matters of jurisdiction, in regard, namely, to their spiritual quality. The State, furthermore, is bound to render due worship to God, as follows from the same argument from the natural law which proves man's obligation to external worship, namely, that man must acknowledge his dependence upon God and his subjection to Him in every capacity in which he is so dependent, and therefore not only in his private capacity as an individual but also in that public, corporate capacity whereby he and his fellow citizens constitute the State. Due worship, in the present economy, is that of the religion of Christ, entrusted to the care of the Church. The State must also protect the Church in the exercise of her functions, for the reason that the State is bound to protect all the rights of its citizens, and among these their religious rights, which as a matter of fact would be insecure and fruitless were not the Church protected. The State is even under obligation to promote the spiritual interests of the Church; for the State is bound to promote whatever by reaction naturally works for the moral development of its citizens and consequently for the internal peace of the community, and in the present condition of human nature that development is necessarily dependent upon the spiritual influence of the Church.

There being, then, an obligation upon the State as such, arising out of the Natural and the Divine Positive Law, to render public Divine worship in accordance with the guidance of the Church, in whose charge Christ has placed the worship due in the present order of things, an obligation also to protect the Church and to promote her interests, the Church clearly has a perfect right to demand the fulfilment of these duties, since their neglect would infringe her right to the benefit proceeding from the fulfilment. To have the further right to command the State in their regard implies that the Church has a right to impose the obligations of her authority in their regard, to exact them authoritatively from the State. Now in purely temporal matters, while they remain such, the Church cannot command the State any more than she can command the subjects of the State, even though these are at the same time her own subjects. But in spiritual and mixed matters calling for corporate action of the State, the question depends upon whether the physical persons who make up the moral personality of the State are themselves subjects of the Church. In case they are, then the Church has in consequence jurisdiction therein over the State. The reason is that owing to the supremacy in man's life purposes of his eternal happiness, man in all his capacities, even of a civil nature, must direct his activities so that they shall not hinder this end, and where action even in his official or civil capacity is necessary for this ultimate purpose he is bound to place the action: moreover, in all these activities so bearing on this end, since they are thereby spiritual matter, every subject of the Church is under the jurisdiction of the Church. If, then, the physical persons constituting the moral person of the State are the subjects of the Church, they are still, in this joint capacity, subject to her in like matters, namely, in the fulfilment of all civil duties of the State towards religion and the Church. The Church, because of the uselessness of her insistence, or because of greater evils to be so avoided, may waive the exercise of this jurisdiction; but in principle it is hers.

In practice we distinguish, from a religious point of view, four kinds of civil authority. First, in a Catholic State, in which, namely, the physical persons constituting the moral personality of the State are Catholic, the Church's jurisdiction in matters of her competency is in every way complete. Secondly, in a non-Christian State, for instance that of the Turks, where the constituency is not even baptized, the Church claims no jurisdiction over the State as such: the foundation of such jurisdiction is lacking. Third, in a Christian but non-Catholic State, where the constituency, though by baptism subjects, are not members of the Church, *per se* the jurisdiction of the Church would stand, but *per accidens* its exercise is impossible. Fourth, a mixed State, one, namely, the constituents of whose moral personality are necessarily of diverse religions, practically lies outside the reach of ecclesiastical jurisdiction, since the affiliation of some of the constituents could not make a subject of the Church out of the moral personality constitutionally made up of elements not all of which share such affiliation. The subordination here indicated is indirect: not that the Church does not directly reach spiritual and mixed matters, but that in their regard it directly reaches only its immediate subjects and indirectly through them the State which they constitute. Again, the State as such does not in such matters directly act for the supernatural purpose of the Church (the eternal happiness of its subjects), but for its own temporal purpose inasmuch as such action will make for their temporal happiness; and so it acts for the Church by indirection.

There is no parallel argument to give the State indirectly jurisdiction over the Church in matters purely temporal, and therefore of the State's sole competency. The Church is universal and cannot be a member or subject of any particular State. Even were there but one universal State in the world, the Church would not be a member thereof, for its members are not citizens of the State to the extent that in every capacity they must submit their activities for the purpose of the State, particularly not the activities concerned directly with the higher purpose of eternal life. Moreover, the Church is not constituted merely by the exercise of the natural rights of the men who are citizens of the State, but by the supernatural endowment of the Divine Positive Law. Finally, the Church in its corporate capacity is not bound to seek the temporal happiness of her members as a means to their eternal welfare, while the State as such is bound to Divine worship and to the protection and promotion of the Church in the interests of religion, because this is a necessary element involved in the perfect temporal happiness of the Catholic citizen. The State, therefore, has not, either in temporal or in spiritual things, any authority over the Church as such, however much it may have in things purely temporal over the members of the Church, who are subjects of the State. The State can, as was said above, demand its rights of the Church: it cannot command them.

IV. UNION OF CHURCH AND STATE.—There is some confusion in the public mind about the meaning of the union of Church and State. The essential idea of such union is a condition of affairs where a State recognizes its natural and supernatural relation to the Church, professes the Faith, and practises the worship of the Church, protects it, enacts no laws to its hurt, while, in case of necessity and at its instance, taking all just and requisite civil measures to forward the Divinely appointed purpose of the Church—in so far as all these make for the State's own essential purpose, the temporal happiness of its citizens. That this is in principle the normal and ethically proper condition for a truly Catholic State should be evident from the religious obligations of the Catholic State as above declared. That in practice it has in the past sometimes worked evil to both Church and State, is an accidental effect consequent upon the frailty and passion of the human instruments then ruling in Church, or in State, or in both. As a partial attempt at security against such evil consequences, the Church has for centuries established concordats with Catholic States; but even these have not always saved the situation. For concordats, like all other agreements, however firm in principle, are in practice only as strong as the conscientiousness of those whose duty it is to observe them. The conscienceless can destroy them at pleasure. Between the Church and a non-Christian or a Christian, but non-Catholic, State a condition of separation, as meaning a condition of indifference of the State towards the Church, is to be expected, as the foundation of the specific obligations involved in union are wanting. Such a separation for a Catholic State would be criminal, as ignoring the sacred obligations of the State.

For a State once Catholic and in union with the Church to declare a separation on the ground that it has ceased to be Catholic is an action which as a matter of objective right has no standing; for in objective truth the duty of the people would be to regain their lost faith, if they had really lost it, or to live up to it, if in reality it were not lost. But on the supposition that the essential constituency of a State has been transformed from Catholics to those who, not by hypocritical pretence, but in the fulness of good faith, are not Catholics—a condition easier of supposition than of realization—the State through such mistaken conscience might seek for separation without subjective fault, provided the separation were effected without the summary dissolution of existing contracts, without the violation of vested rights of the Church or its members. It may be noted in passing that in the recent instances of separation in France and Portugal, i. e. the breaking up of an existing condition of union between Church and State, the separation has been effected where the bulk of the people is still Catholic, has been conducted in violation of rights and contracts both natural and positive, and has resulted, as it was aimed to do, in an attempt at complete subjection of the Church and of all civil subjects in the matters of religion to the tyranny of administrations which scoff at all religion. That in States whose personality is constitutionally made up of every complexion of religious faith, much of it in its diversity sincere, there should be a governmental abstention from any specific denominational worship or profession of belief, and a general protection and encouragement of the individual in the practice of religion according to his own religious principles within the limits of the Natural Law, or of a general acceptance of Christianity, seems a practical necessity of evil times, when unity of faith is so widely lacking, and a *modus vivendi* which, if sincerely carried out, seems to work as little harm to objective right as can be expected in a condition of consciences sincerely differing in the matter of right established by the Divine Positive Law.

V. COUNTER THEORIES.—The theories opposed to the Catholic position on the true relations between the Church and State are threefold, differing in latitude of negation of ecclesiastical right.

A. *Absolute Liberalism* is the most extreme. Having its source in the principles of the French Revolution and beginning with those who denied the existence of God, it naturally takes the position that the State prescinds from God: the State, it says, is atheistic. Undertaking, with the elimination of revelation and the Divine Positive Law, to get back to purely natural principles, it accepted from Rousseau and the Utilitarians the principle that all right comes from the State, all authority from the consentient wills of the people of the State. The position logically followed that the Church has no rights—not even the right to existence—save such as are conceded to it by the civil power. Hence it is not a perfect society, but a creature of the State, upon which it depends in all things, and upon which it must be directly subordinate, if it is to be allowed to exist at all. (See LIBERALISM.)

B. *Qualified Liberalism*, as formulated by Cavour and Minghetti in Italy at the close of the first half of the nineteenth century, does not go so far. While claiming to admit that the Church is more or less a perfect society with foundations in the Divine Positive Law of Christian Revelation, it contends that the Church and State are disparate in such fashion as to prosecute their respective ends independently in behalf of the individual, having no subordination whatever one to the other. Consequently, in all public affairs the State must prescind from every religious society, and deal with such either as private associations existing within the State or as foreign corporations to be treated with accordingly. The axiom of this newer Liberalism is "A free Church in a free State", which in point of fact means an emasculated Church with no more freedom than the shifting politics, internal and external, of a State chose to give, which in the event, as was to be foreseen, amounted to servitude. (See ITALY: *Political and Civil Government: (2) Church and State*.)

C. *The Theory of the Regalists* conceded to the Church a certain amount of social right from its Divine Founder, but conditioned the exercise of all social powers upon the consent of the civil government. This theory, originating with Gallicanism (q. v.), practically denied the Church to be a perfect society, inasmuch as it made its jurisdiction depend for its valid exercise upon the civil power. The theory gradually extended its contentions so far as to make the Church indirectly subordinate to the State, attributing to the State the authority to forbid the Church any juridical act that might work to the detriment of the State and to command the Church in case of necessity to put forth her full powers to promote the interests of the State.

PIUS IX, *Encyclical, Quanta Cura, and Syllabus Errorum* (Rome, 1864); LEO XIII, *Encyclicals Immortale Dei and Sapientiæ Christianæ*, tr. in *The Pope and His People* (London, 1910); COSTA-ROSSETTI, *Philosophia Moralis* (Innsbruck, 1886); PALMIERI, *De Romano Pontifice* (Rome, 1877); HAMMERSTEIN, *De Ecclesia et Statu* (Trier, 1886); CAVAGNIS, *Della Natura di Società Giuridica e Pubblica Competente alla Chiesa* (Rome, 1887); LIBERATORE, *La Chiesa e lo Stato* (Naples, 1872); LABOULAYE, *Le Parti Libéral* (Paris, 1864); MINGHETTI, *Lo Stato e la Chiesa* (Turin, 1878); MARCA, *De Concordia Sacerdotii et Imperii* (Frankfort, 1708).—The last three present non-Catholic views.

CHARLES MACKSEY.

State or Way, PURGATIVE, ILLUMINATIVE, UNITIVE.—The word *state* is used in various senses by theologians and spiritual writers. It may be taken to signify a profession or calling in life, as where St. Paul says, in I Cor., vii, 20: "Let every man abide in the same calling in which he was called". We have, in this sense, states of perfection, classified in the Church as the clerical state, the religious state, and the secular state; and among religious states, again, we have those of the contemplative, the active, and the mixed orders. The word is also used in the classification of the degrees or stages of Christian perfection, or the advancement of souls in the supernatural life of grace during their sojourn in the world. This has reference to the practice of all the virtues, both theological and moral, and to all their acts both external and internal. It includes two elements, namely our own efforts and the grace of God assisting us. This grace is never wanting for those acts which are positively commanded or inspired by God, and the work of perfection will proceed according to the energy and fidelity with which souls correspond to its aids.

DIVISION OF THE STATES OR WAYS.—It is in the latter sense we have to understand the word *state* in this article, and, according to the various classes of souls who aspire to perfection in this life, the Fathers and theologians distinguish three states or stages of perfection. These are the state of beginners, the state of progress, and the state of the perfect. These states are also designated "ways", because they are the ways of God by which souls are guided on the road to heaven according to the words of the Psalmist: "He hath made his ways known to Moses: his wills to the children of Israel" (Ps. cii, 7). Hence we have the division of the spiritual life which has been adopted since the time of the Pseudo-Dionysius, into the "purgative" way, the "illuminative" way, and the "unitive" way. (See St. Thomas, II-II, Q. clxxxiii, a. 4; Suarez, "De Religione", Tr. VIII, lib. I, c. xiii.) St. Thomas well explains the reason for this division when he says: "The first duty which is incumbent on man is to give up sin and resist concupiscence, which are opposed to charity; this belongs to beginners, in whose hearts charity is to be nursed and cherished lest it be corrupted. The second duty of man is to apply his energies chiefly to advance in virtue; this belongs to those who are making progress and who are principally concerned that charity may be increased and strengthened in them. The third endeavour and pursuit of man should be to rest in God and enjoy Him; and this belongs to the perfect who desire to be dissolved and to be with Christ." Among the condemned propositions of Miguel de Molinos, the author of "The Spiritual Guide" (in which the false mysticism known as Quietism is propounded), is the following: "These three kinds of way, the *purgative, illuminative,* and *unitive*, are the greatest absurdity in Mystical Theology" (cf. Constitution "Cœlestis Pastor" of Innocent XI, 1687). Avoiding this and other errors of false mystics, it must be borne in mind that energy and activity are required in every stage of our spiritual life, and that we have to accept the degrees of that life and to follow the kind of prayer which is proper to one or other of them according to our state, whether it be the purgative, illuminative, or unitive. Various descriptions of these three ways are given by eminent masters of the spiritual life. Substantially they may all be said to agree, though in details and manner of treatment they may differ.

The Purgative Way.—The purgative way is the way, or state, of those who are beginners, that is those who have obtained justification, but have not their passions and evil inclinations in such a state of subjugation that they can easily overcome temptations, and who, in order to preserve and exercise charity and the other virtues, have to keep up a continual warfare within themselves. It is so called because the chief concern of the soul in this state is to resist and to overcome the passions by nourishing, strengthening, and cherishing the virtue of charity. This can and ought to be done not only by keeping the Commandments, but by foreseeing the occasions in which the precepts oblige, so as to be ready by a prompt and well-disposed will to resist and avoid any sins opposed to them. This state, although in one sense it is imperfect, in another sense may be called a state of perfection, because the soul remains united to God by grace and charity so long as it is free from the stain of mortal sin. Purity of soul may be said to be the proper end of the purgative way, and the forms of prayer suitable for this way or state are meditations on sin and its consequences, and on death, judgment, hell, and heaven. The acts which aid towards uprooting the remnants and habits of former sins, and preventing one from ever returning to them, are corporal austerities, mortification of the appetite, abnegation of one's own will, and conformity to the will of God. In a word, the distinctive notes of this state are war against those temptations which entice the soul to sin by the attraction of pleasures of the senses and the natural shrinking from pain; and repugnance to acts known to be contrary to the will of God. The characteristic virtue of this state is humility, by which the soul is made sensible of its own weakness and its dependence upon the succours of the grace of God.

What mystical writers describe as the active and passive purifications of the spiritual life may be brought under, and arranged according to, their three states of perfection, though not confined to any one of them. The active purification consists in all the holy efforts, mortifications, labours, and sufferings by which the soul, aided by the grace of God, endeavours to reform the mind, heart, and the sensitive appetite. This is the characteristic work of the purgative way. The passive purifications are the means which God employs to purify the soul from its stains and vices, and to prepare it for the exceptional graces of the supernatural life. In the works of St. John of the Cross these purifications are called nights, and he divides them into two classes, the night of the senses and the night of the spirits. In the state of beginners the soul is often favoured by God with what are called "sensible consolations" because they have their beginning and are felt chiefly in the senses or sensible faculties. They consist in sensible devotion and a feeling of fervour arising from the consideration of God's goodness vividly represented to the mind and heart; or, from external aids, such as the ceremonies of the Church. These consolations are often withdrawn, and a state of desolation ensues, and then the passive purification of the senses begins.

The Illuminative Way.—The illuminative way is that of those who are in the state of progress and have their passions better under control, so that they easily keep themselves from mortal sin, but who do not so easily avoid venial sins, because they still take pleasure in earthly things and allow their minds to be distracted by various imaginations and their hearts with numberless desires, though not in matters that are strictly unlawful. It is called the illuminative way, because in it the mind becomes more and more enlightened as to spiritual things and the practice of virtue. In this grade charity is stronger and more perfect than in the state of beginners; the soul is chiefly occupied with progress in the spiritual life and in all the virtues, both theological and moral. The practice of prayer suitable for this state is meditation on the mysteries of the Incarnation, the Life of Our Saviour, and the mysteries of His Sacred Passion. "Though the mysteries of the Passion", as Ven. Luis de Lapuente says, "belong to the illuminative way, especially in its highest degree, which approaches nearest to the *unitive* way, nevertheless they are exceedingly profitable for all sorts of persons, by whatever way they walk, and in whatever degree of perfection they live; for sinners will find in them most effectual motives to purify themselves from all their sins; beginners to mortify their passions; proficients to increase in all kinds of virtue; and the perfect to obtain union with God by fervent love" (introduction to "Meditations on the Passion"). The fundamental virtue of this state is recollection, that is, a constant attention of the mind and of the affections of the heart to thoughts and sentiments which elevate the soul to God—exterior recollection which consists in the love of silence and retirement, interior recollection in simplicity of spirit and a right intention, as well as attention to God in all our actions. This does not mean that a person has to neglect the duties of his state or position in life, nor does it imply that honest and needful recreation should be avoided, because these lawful or necessary circumstances or occupations can well be reconciled with perfect recollection and the most holy union with God.

The soul in the illuminative way will have to experience periods of spiritual consolations and desolations. It does not at once enter upon the unitive way when it has passed through the aridities of the first purgation. It must spend some time, perhaps years, after quitting the state of beginners, in exercising itself in the state of proficients. St. John of the Cross tells us that in this state the soul, like one released from a rigorous imprisonment, occupies itself in Divine thoughts with much greater freedom and satisfaction, and its joy is more abundant and interior than it ever experienced before it entered the night of the senses. Its purgation is still somewhat incomplete, and the purification of the senses is not yet finished and perfect. It is not without aridities, darkness, and trials, sometimes more severe than in the past. During the period of desolation it will have to endure much suffering from temptations against the theological virtues and against the moral virtues. It will also have to endure sometimes other diabolical attacks upon its imagination and senses. Also, God will permit natural causes to combine in afflicting the soul, such as the persecutions of men, and the ingratitude of friends. Patient suffering and resignation have to be borne during all these trials, and the devout soul should remember the encouraging words of the pious and learned Blosius: "Nothing more valuable can befall a man than tribulation, when it is endured with patience for the love of God; because there is no more certain sign of the divine election. But this should be understood quite as much of internal as of external trials, which people of a certain kind of piety forget." And again he says: "It is the chain of patient suffering that forms the ring with which Christ espouses a soul to Himself" (Institutio Spiritualis, viii, §3).

The Unitive Way.—The unitive is the way of those who are in the state of the perfect, that is those who have their minds so drawn away from all temporal things that they enjoy great peace, who are neither agitated by various desires nor moved by any great extent by passion, and who have their minds chiefly fixed on God and their attention turned, either always or very frequently, to Him. It is the union with God by love and the actual experience and exercise of that love. It is called the state of "perfect charity", because souls who have reached that state are ever prompt in the exercise of charity by loving God habitually and by frequent and efficacious acts of that Divine virtue. It is called the "unitive" way, because it is by love that the soul is united to God, and the more perfect the charity, the closer and the more intimate is the union. Union with God is the principal study and endeavour of this state. It is of this union St. Paul speaks when he says: "He who is joined to the Lord, is one spirit" (I Cor., vi. 17). Souls thus united to God are penetrated by the highest motives of the theological and moral virtues. In every circumstance of their lives the supernatural motive which ought to guide their actions is ever present to their mind, and the actions are performed under its inspiration with a force of will which makes their accomplishment easy and even delightful. These perfect souls are above all familiar with the doctrine and use of consolations and desolations. They are enlightened in the mysteries of the supernatural life, and they have experience of that truth proclaimed by St. Paul when he said: "We know that to them that love God, all things work together unto good, to such as, according to his purpose, are called to be saints" (Rom., viii, 28). The form of prayer suitable to persons in the unitive way is the contemplation of the glorious mysteries of Our Lord, His Resurrection, Appearances, and Ascension, until the coming of the Holy Ghost, and the preaching of the Gospel. These mysteries may also be the subject of meditation for beginners and for those in a state of progress, but in a peculiar manner they belong to the perfect. Union with God belongs substantially to all souls in a state of grace, but it is in a special manner the distinguishing characteristic of those in the unitive way or in the state of the perfect.

It is in this state that the gift of contemplation is imparted to the soul, though this is not always the case; because many souls who are perfect in the unitive way never receive in this life the gift of contemplation and there have been numerous saints who were not mystics nor contemplatives, and who nevertheless excelled in the practice of heroic virtue. Souls, however, who have attained to the unitive state have consolations of a purer and higher order than others, and are more often favoured by extraordinary graces; and sometimes with the extraordinary phenomena of the mystical state, such as ecstasies, raptures, and what is known as the prayer of union. The soul is not, however, in this state always free from desolations and passive purgation. St. John of the Cross tells us that the purification of the spirit usually takes place after the purification of the senses. The night of the senses being over, the soul for some time enjoys, according to this eminent authority, the sweet delights of contemplation; then, perhaps when least expected, the second night comes, far darker and far more miserable than the first, and this is called by him the purification of the spirit, which means the purification of the interior faculties, the intellect and the will. The temptations which assail the soul in this state are similar in their nature to those which afflict souls in the illuminative way, only more aggravated, because felt more keenly; and the withdrawal of the consolations of the spirit which they have already experienced is their greatest affliction. To these trials are added others, peculiar to the spirit, which arise from the intensity of their love for God, for Whose possession they thirst and long. "The fire of Divine love can so dry up the spirit and enkindle its desire for satisfying its thirst that it turns upon itself a thousand times and longs for God in a thousand ways, as the Psalmist did when he said: For Thee my soul hath thirsted; for Thee my flesh, O how many ways" (St. John of the Cross, op. cit. infra, bk. II, xi). There are three degrees of this species of suffering designated by mystical writers as the "inflammation of love", the "wounds of love", and the "languor of love".

SPIRITUAL STATES OF CONSOLATION AND DESOLATION.—Consolation and desolation may be said to be phases of the various states or stages of the spiritual life, rather than distinct states in themselves. The character or permanence does not usually belong to them. They succeed each other, as a rule, and devout souls have to experience both the one and the other, but as they may have sometimes a long period of consolation or desolation the term *states* may be used in a wide sense when treating of them. Speaking in a general sense, the state of consolation is that in which the soul enjoys a spiritual sense or impression of close union and intimate converse with God. The state of desolation, on the contrary, is that in which the soul feels itself as it were abandoned by God. Consolation and desolation may be more easily understood when considered in opposition to each other.

Consolation.—In the spiritual order consolation is of three kinds. The first kind, which is known as "sensible consolation", is that which has its beginning and is felt chiefly in the senses or sensible faculties. It consists in sensible devotion and a feeling of fervour arising from the consideration of God's goodness vividly represented to the mind and heart; or from the external aids and ceremonies of the Church. It is not to be disregarded on this account because it leads us finally to good. St. Alphonsus says: "Spiritual consolations are gifts which are much more precious than all the riches and honours of the world. And if the sensibility itself is aroused, this completes our devotion, for then our whole being is united to God and tastes God" (Love for Jesus, xvii). The second kind of consolation, which is often the result of the first, and usually remains with the third, is characterized by a facility and even delight in the exercise of the virtues, especially the theological virtues. St. Ignatius says that any increase of faith, hope, and charity may be called a consolation (Rule 3 for the discernment of spirits). By this kind of consolation the soul is raised above the sensible faculties; and, in the absence of sensible consolation, truth is perceived at a glance, faith alone operating, enlightening, sustaining, and directing the soul, and fervour of the will succeeds to sensible fervour. We should be thankful to God for consolations of this kind and pray for their continuance, and it is these we ask for in the prayer "En ego" usually recited after Communion. The third kind of consolation affects the higher faculties of the soul, namely the intellect and the will, and in a more perfect way than the second. It consists in special tranquillity and peace of soul, and is the result of the firm determination of the will to live for God with entire confidence in His grace. It is present when, as St. Ignatius says, "the soul burns with the love of its Creator, and can no longer love any creature except for His sake" (Rule 3 for the discernment of spirits). The soul is conscious of its happiness, even though the inferior and sensible faculties may be depressed and afflicted. This is the most perfect kind of all, and it is not often experienced except by the perfect. As the first kind is said to belong to beginners in the way of perfection, the second to those making progress, so the third is said to belong to the perfect.

Desolation.—Spiritual desolation means the feeling of abandonment by God, and of the absence of His grace. This feeling of estrangement may arise from various causes. It may be the result of natural disposition or temperament, or of external circumstances; or it may come from the attacks of the devil; or from God Himself when for our greater good He withdraws from us spiritual consolation. In contradistinction to consolation spiritual desolation may be of three kinds. The first is called sensible desolation and is the opposite of sensible consolation. It includes aridities, dissipation of mind, weariness, and disgust in the exercises of piety; and it is often experienced by beginners in the practice of mental prayer. It may co-exist with consolation of a higher order, just as, in the natural order, we may feel pain of body and joy of soul at one and the same time. The second kind of desolation affects the intellect and will, and consists in the privation of the feeling of the presence of the supernatural virtues as described by St. Teresa in her Life (ch. xxx). This trial is extremely severe, but if generously accepted and patiently endured, it may be turned into great merit, and many fruits of sanctity will be the result. (See Letter of St. Francis of Sales to S. Jane Frances de Chantal, 28 March, 1612.) The third kind of desolation is still more severe. It is a darkening of the mind and a feeling of abandonment so great that the soul is tempted to distrust concerning salvation and is tormented by other terrible thoughts against faith, against purity, and even by blasphemous thoughts— the most painful experience which a holy soul has to endure (see St. John of the Cross, op. cit. infra, bk. I, ch. xiv). It would be a great mistake to imagine that spiritual desolation arrests progress in virtue or enfeebles the spirit of fervour. On the contrary, it affords occasion of heroic virtue and of absolute detachment from sensible pleasure, whether natural or supernatural. At the same time we may hope and wish that these interior griefs may be diminished or made to disappear, and we may pray God to deliver us from them, but if all our efforts are in vain, and God permits the desolation to continue, it only remains to resign ourselves generously to His Divine Will.

DIRECTIONS.—For the better understanding of the three states or ways in their relations to each other and their effects upon souls tending towards perfection the following directions and observations may be useful.

(1) The three states or ways are not so entirely distinct that there may not appear in any one of them something of the other two. In each and all of them is found the effort and care to preserve and guard the soul from sin, though this is said to belong (appropriately) to the purgative way; in each, virtue has to be practised, and from its practice light and progress result. Again, in each of them the soul gives itself to God to live in Him and for Him the supernatural life which He imparts to it, and this may be said to be the commencement of the unitive way. The characteristic and distinctive feature of these states is determined by the form which is dominant in the soul in its efforts towards perfection. When strife and fear predominate, the soul is said to be still in the purgative way; when the desire and fervour to advance in virtue and the attraction of hope prevail above fear, then the soul is said to be in the illuminative way. If charity is dominant above all, the soul is in the unitive way; but so long as this mortal life lasts, for the strong and the feeble there will always be the labour and activity of purgation, illumination, and of union in the work of supernatural perfection. Suarez teaches this doctrine in very distinct terms. "These three states", he says, "are never so distinct that any one of them may not participate of the other two. Each of them takes its name and character from that which predominates in it. And it is certain that no one can attain to such a state of perfection in this life that he may not or cannot make further progress" (De Orat., l. II, c. xi, n. 4).

(2) According to the usual manner of advancement, the majority of souls are gradually raised to the state of perfect union after passing through the states of purification and illumination. But this rule is by no means absolute, and a miraculous intervention or an extraordinary grace may bring a soul suddenly from the lowest depths of moral abjection to the most sublime heights of charity, as may be seen in the case of St. Mary Magdalen and other celebrated penitent saints. On the other hand we may find saints in whom the purgative state may predominate even to the end of their lives, and God sometimes withholds the favours of the unitive way from many faithful and fervent souls who have advanced generously in the degrees of the purgative and illuminative ways, and who have all along preserved the fervour of holy charity, which is the essence and crown of perfection.

(3) As a rule, supernatural phenomena of mysticism appear in the most perfect state, namely that of union; one special favour of the mystical life, namely spiritual espousals, supposes the unitive way, and cannot be ascribed to either of the inferior grades of perfection. Many of the other mystical favours, such as ecstasies, visions, locutions, etc., may be found, by way of exception, in the less advanced stages of the spiritual life. As regards the gift of contemplation, although it is proper to those who are perfect in virtue and holiness, still it is sometimes granted to the imperfect and even to beginners so that they may taste of its sweetness. Souls by the exercise of Christian asceticism can prepare themselves for this intimate communication with God, but they should await with humility and patience the time and occasion in which they are to be introduced by their heavenly Spouse into the mystical state of contemplation.

(4) In order to decide as to the dispositions required for frequent and daily communion, it is no longer necessary for a spiritual director to find out or to judge whether a soul is in one or other of these states according to the rules laid down by some modern theologians. All that is now required, as stated in the first clause of the Decree of the Sacred Congregation of the Council of 20 Dec., 1905, is that the recipient be in a state of grace and approach the Holy Table with a right intention. As already stated, these three states are not easily distinguishable, and the lines of demarcation between them cannot easily be discerned, and therefore could not have been regarded as at any time very useful as a rule of guidance for frequent Communion. Now the rule is inapplicable, for those in the purgative way may receive Holy Communion just as often as those who are in the illuminative and unitive, as is evident from the Decree referred to. We are not, however, to suppose that the rules given by theologians and ascetical writers, founded as they are on the teaching of the ancient Fathers, with regard to Holy Communion according to the three states or ways no longer serve for edification. They indicate to us what is to be expected as the fruits of frequent Communion received worthily. Frequent Communion is the chief means of preserving and perfecting in our souls the spiritual life, and of supporting them in all its ways.

BENEDICT XIV, *Heroic Virtue* (London, 1851); DE PONTE (VEN. LUIS DE LAPUENTE), *Meditations on the Mysteries of our Holy Faith* (London, 1854); DEVINE, *Manuals of Ascetical and of Mystical Theology* (London, 1901 and 1903); MOROTIO, *Cursus vitæ spiritualis* (New York, 1891); RIBET, *La mystique divine* (Paris, 1903); SMEDT, *Notre vie surnaturelle*, II (Brussels, 1911); ST. THOMAS, II–II, Q. clxxxiii; SUAREZ, *De religione*; IDEM, *De Oratione*; ST. JOHN OF THE CROSS, *The Obscure Night of the Soul*; ST. TERESA, *Life*, xi, xxix, xxx; ST. IGNATIUS LOYOLA, *Spiritual Exercises*; POULAIN, *The Graces of Interior Prayer* (London, 1910); PONTLEVOY, *Vie du P. Xavier de Ravignan* (Paris, 1862), xxv; SAUDREASE, tr. CAMM, *Degrees of the Spiritual Life* (London, 1907).

ARTHUR DEVINE.

States of the Church (Ital. *Lo Stato della Chiese*), the civil territory which for over 1000 years (754–1870) acknowledged the pope as temporal ruler. The expression "Patrimonium Sancti Petri" originally designated the landed possessions and revenues of various kinds that belonged to the Church of St. Peter at Rome. Until the middle of the eighth century this consisted wholly of private property, but the term was later applied to the States of the Church, and more particularly to the Duchy of Rome. Our subject may thus be conveniently treated under the following heads: I. Patrimony of St. Peter (tracing the origin of the States of the Church to the time of Charlemagne); II. History of the States of the Church.

I. PATRIMONY OF ST. PETER.—(1) *Patrimonial Possessions of the Church of Rome.*—The law of Constantine the Great (321), by which the Christian Church was declared qualified to hold and transmit property, first gave a legal basis to the possessions of the Church of Rome. Subsequently the possessions were rapidly augmented by donations. Constantine himself set the example, the Lateran Palace being most probably presented by him. Constantine's gifts formed the historical nucleus, which the Sylvester Legend later surrounded with that network of myth, that gave rise to the forged document known as the "Donation of Constantine". The example of Constantine was followed by wealthy families of the Roman nobility, whose memory frequently survived, after the families themselves had become extinct, in the names of the properties which they had once presented to the Roman See. The donation of large estates ceased about 600. The

Byzantine emperors subsequently were less liberal in their gifts; the wars with the Lombards likewise had an unfavourable effect, and there remained few families in a position to bequeath large estates. Apart from a number of scattered possessions in the Orient, Dalmatia, Gaul, and Africa, the patrimonies were naturally for the most part situated in Italy and on the adjacent islands. The most valuable and most extensive possessions were those in Sicily, about Syracuse and Palermo. The revenues from the properties in Sicily and Lower Italy in the eighth century, when Leo the Isaurian confiscated them, were estimated at three and one-half talents of gold. But the patrimonies in the vicinity of Rome were the most numerous and, after most of the remote patrimonies had been lost in the eighth century, were managed with especial care. Of other patrimonies may be mentioned the Neapolitan with the Island of Capri, that of Gaeta, the Tuscan, the *Patrimonium Tiburtinum* in the vicinity of Tivoli, estates about Otranto, Osimo, Ancona, Umana, estates near Ravenna and Genoa, and lastly properties in Istria, Sardinia, and Corsica.

With these landed possessions, scattered and varied as they were, the pope was the largest landowner in Italy. For this reason every ruler of Italy was compelled of necessity to reckon with him first of all; on the other hand he was also the first to feel the political and economical disturbances that distressed the country. A good insight into the problems that required the attention of the pope in the administration of his patrimonies can be obtained from the letters of Gregory the Great (Mon. Germ. Epist., I). The revenues from the patrimonies were employed, not only for administrative purposes, for the maintenance and construction of church edifices, for the equipment of convents, for the household of the pope, and the support of the clergy, but also to a great extent to relieve public and private want. Numerous poorhouses, hospitals, orphanages, and hospices for pilgrims were maintained out of the revenues of the patrimonies, many individuals were supported directly or indirectly, and slaves were ransomed from the possession of Jews and heathens. But, above all, the popes relieved the emperors of the responsibility of providing Rome with food, and later also assumed the task of warding off the Lombards, an undertaking generally involving financial obligations. The pope thus became the champion of all the oppressed, the political champion of all those who were unwilling to submit to foreign domination, who were unwilling to become Lombards or yet wholly Byzantines, preferring to remain Romans.

(2) *Political Position of the Papacy.*—This political aspect of the papacy became in time very prominent, inasmuch as Rome, after the removal of the imperial residence to the East, was no longer the seat of any of the higher political officials. Even after the partition of the empire, the Western emperors preferred to make the better-protected Ravenna their residence. Here was the centre of Odoacer's power and of the Ostrogothic rule; here also, after the fall of the Ostrogoths, the viceroy of the Byzantine emperor in Italy, the exarch, resided. In Rome, on the other hand, the pope appears with ever-increasing frequency as the advocate of the needy population; thus Leo I intercedes with Attila and Geiserich, and Gelasius with Theodoric. Cassiodorus as *præfectus prætorio* under the Ostrogothic supremacy actually entrusted the care of the temporal affairs to Pope John II. When Emperor Justinian issued the Pragmatic Sanction (554), the pope together with the Senate was entrusted with the control of weights and measures. Thenceforth for two centuries the popes were most loyal supporters of the Byzantine Government against the encroachments of the Lombards, and were all the more indispensable, because after 603 the Senate disappeared. They, too, were the only court of judicature at which the Roman population, exposed as it was to the extortion of the Byzantine functionaries and officers, could find protection and defence. No wonder then that at scarcely any other time was the papacy so popular in Central Italy, and there was no cause which the native population, who had again begun to organize themselves into bodies of militia, espoused with greater zeal then the freedom and independence of the Roman See. And naturally so, for they took part in the election of the pope as a separate electoral body.

When the Byzantine emperors, infected with cæsaro-papist tendencies, attempted to crush the papacy also, they found in the Roman militia an opposition against which they were able to accomplish nothing. The particularism of Italy awoke and concentrated itself about the pope. When Emperor Justinian II in 692 attempted to have Pope Sergius II (as formerly the unfortunate Martin I) forcibly conveyed to Constantinople to extract from him his assent to the canons of the Trullan Council, convoked by the emperor, the militia of Ravenna and of the Duchy of Pentapolis lying immediately to the south assembled, marched into Rome, and compelled the departure of the emperor's plenipotentiary. Such occurrences were repeated and acquired significance as indicating the popular feeling. When Pope Constantine, the last pope to go to Constantinople (710), rejected the confession of faith of the new emperor, Bardanas, the Romans protested, and refused to acknowledge the emperor or the *dux* (military ruler) sent by him. Not until news was brought that the heretical emperor had been replaced by one of the true Faith was the *dux* allowed to assume his office. That was in 713. Two years later the papal chair, which had last been occupied by seven Oriental popes, was filled by a Roman, Gregory II, who was destined to oppose Leo III the Isaurian in the Iconoclastic conflict. The time was ripening for Rome to abandon the East, turn toward the West, and enter into that alliance with the Germano-Romanic nations, on which is based our Western civilization, of which one consequence was the formation of the States of the Church. It would have been easy for the popes to throw off the Byzantine yoke in Central Italy as early as the time of Iconoclasm. If they resisted the impulse, it was because they correctly recognized that such an attempt would have been premature. They foresaw that the end of the Byzantine supremacy and the beginning of the Lombard power would have been encompassed at the same time. It was necessary first to establish the fact that the Byzantines could no longer protect the pope and the Romans against the Lombards, and then to find a power that could protect them. Both of these conditions were fulfilled in the middle of the eighth century.

(3) *Collapse of the Byzantine Power in Central Italy.*—The strange shape which the States of the Church were destined to assume from the beginning is explained by the fact that these were the districts in which the population of Central Italy had defended itself to the very last against the Lombards. The two chief districts were the country about Ravenna, the exarchate, where the exarch was the centre of the opposition, and the Duchy of Rome, which embraced the lands of Roman Tuscany north of the Tiber, and to the south the Campagna as far as the Garigliano, where the pope himself was the soul of the opposition. Furthermore, the greatest pains were taken, as long as it was at all possible, to retain control of the intervening districts and with them communication over the Apennines. Hence the strategic importance of the Duchy of the Pentapolis (Rimini, Pesaro, Fano, Sinigaglia, Ancona) and Perugia. If this strategic connexion were broken,

it was evident that Rome and Ravenna could not singly maintain themselves for any length of time. This was recognized by the Lombards also. The same narrow strip of land in fact broke the connexion between their Duchies of Spoleto and Benevento and the main portion of the king's territories in the north, and it was against this therefore that, from the second decade of the eighth century, they aimed their attacks with ever-increasing energy. In the beginning the popes were able repeatedly to wrest from their hands all that they had gained. In 728 the Lombard king Liutprand took the Castle of Sutri, which dominated the highway at Nepi on the road to Perugia. But Liutprand, softened by the entreaties of Pope Gregory II, restored Sutri "as a gift to the blessed Apostles Peter and Paul". This expression of the "Liber pontificalis" was erroneously interpreted to mean that in this gift the beginning of the States of the Church was to be recognized. This is incorrect inasmuch as the popes continued to acknowledge the imperial Government, and Greek officials appear in Rome for some time longer. True it is, however, that here for the first time we meet the association of ideas on which the States of the Church were to be constructed. The pope asked the Lombards for the return of Sutri for the sake of the Princes of the Apostles and threatened punishment by these sainted protectors. The pious Liutprand was undoubtedly susceptible to such pleas, but never to any consideration for the Greeks. For this reason he gave Sutri to Peter and Paul, that he might not expose himself to their punishment. What the pope then did with it would be immaterial to him.

The belief that the Roman territory (at first in the more restricted, but afterwards also in the wider sense) was defended by the Princes of the Apostles became more and more prevalent. In 738 the Lombard duke Transamund of Spoleto captured the Castle of Gallese, which protected the road to Perugia to the north of Nepi. By the payment of a large sum of money Gregory III induced the duke to restore the castle to him. The pope then sought by an alliance with Duke Transamund to protect himself against Liutprand. But Liutprand conquered Spoleto, besieged Rome, laid waste the Duchy of Rome, and seized four important frontier fortresses (Blera, Orte, Bomarzo, and Amelia), thereby cutting off the communication with Perugia and Ravenna. In this exigency the pope now (739) for the first time turned to the powerful Frankish kingdom, under the protection of which Boniface had begun his successful labours as a missionary in Germany. He sent to Charles Martel, "the powerful mayor of the palace" of the Frankish monarchy and the commander of the Franks in the famous battle at Tours, undoubtedly with the consent of the Greek *dux*, and appealed to him to protect the tomb of the Apostle. Charles Martel replied to the embassy and acknowledged the gifts, but was unwilling to offer aid against the Lombards, who were helping him against the Saracens. Accordingly the successor of Gregory III, Zacharias (the last Greek, who occupied the papal chair), changed the policy that had been previously followed toward the Lombards. He formed an alliance with Liutprand against Transamund, and received (741) in return the four castles. This Zacharias obtained as the result of a personal visit to the camp of the king at Terni. Liutprand also restored a number of patrimonies that had been seized by the Lombards, and furthermore concluded a twenty years' peace with the pope. The duchy now had a respite from Lombard attacks. The Lombards fell upon Ravenna, which they had already held from 731 to 735. The exarch had no other recourse than to seek the aid of the pope. Liutprand did in fact allow himself to be induced by Zacharias to surrender the greater part of his conquests. Nor was it unimportant that these districts too once owed their rescue to the pope. Only a short time after Liutprand's death (744) Zacharias was successful in further postponing the catastrophe. When Rachis, the Lombard king, was besieging Perugia (749), Zacharias so wrought upon his conscience that the king raised the siege. But as a result of this Rachis was overthrown, and Aistulf, who was put into his place, at once showed by his acts that no consideration could halt him in his course.

In 751 Aistulf conquered Ravenna, and thereby decided the long delayed fate of the exarchate and the Pentapolis. And when Aistulf, who held Spoleto also under his immediate sway, directed all his might against the Duchy of Rome, it seemed that this too could no longer be held. Byzantium could send no troops, and Emperor Constantine V Copronymus, in answer to the repeated requests for help of the new pope, Stephen II, could only offer him the advice to act in accordance with the ancient policy of Byzantium, to pit some other Germanic tribe against the Lombards. The Franks alone were powerful enough to compel the Lombards to maintain peace, and they alone stood in close relationship with the pope. It is true that Charles Martel had on a former occasion failed to respond to the entreaties of Gregory III. But meanwhile the relations between the Frankish rulers and the popes had become more intimate. Pope Zacharias had only recently (751), at Pepin's accession to the throne, spoken the word that removed all doubts in favour of the Carlovingian mayor of the palace. It was not unreasonable, therefore, to expect an active show of gratitude in return, when Rome was most grievously pressed by Aistulf. Accordingly Stephen II secretly sent a letter to Pepin by pilgrims, soliciting his aid against Aistulf and asking for a conference. Pepin in turn sent Abbot Droctegang of Jumièges to confer with the pope, and a little later dispatched Duke Autchar and Bishop Chrodengang of Metz to conduct the pope to the Frankish realm. Never before had a pope crossed the Alps. While Pope Stephen was preparing for the journey, a messenger arrived from Constantinople, bringing to the pope the imperial mandate to treat once more with Aistulf for the purpose of persuading him to surrender his conquests. Stephen took with him the imperial messenger and several dignitaries of the Roman Church, as well as members of the aristocracy belonging to the Roman militia, and proceeded first of all to Aistulf. In 753 the pope left Rome. Aistulf, when the pope met him at Pavia, refused to enter into negotiations or to hear of a restoration of his conquests. Only with difficulty did Stephen finally prevail upon the Lombard king not to hinder him in his journey to the Frankish kingdom.

(4) *Intervention of the Franks. Formation of the States of the Church.*—The pope thereupon crossed the Great St. Bernard into the Frankish kingdom. Pepin received his guest at Ponthion, and there promised him orally to do all in his power to recover the Exarchate of Ravenna and the other districts seized by Aistulf. The pope then went to St-Denis near Paris, where he concluded a firm alliance of friendship with the first Carlovingian king, probably in January, 754. He anointed King Pepin, his wife, and sons, and bound the Franks under the threat of excommunication never thereafter to choose their kings from any other family than the Carlovingian. At the same time he bestowed on Pepin and his sons the title of "Patrician of the Romans", which title, the highest Byzantine officials in Italy, the exarchs, had borne. Instead of the latter the King of the Franks was now to be the protector of the Romans. The pope in bestowing this title probably acted also in conformity with authority conferred on

him by the Byzantine emperor. In order, however, to fulfil the wishes of the pope Pepin had eventually to obtain the consent of his nobles to a campaign into Italy. This was rendered imperative, when several embassies, which attempted by peaceful means to induce the Lombard king to give up his conquests, returned without accomplishing their mission. At Quiercy on the Oise the Frankish nobles finally gave their consent. There Pepin executed in writing a promise to give to the Church certain territories, the first documentary record for the States of the Church. This document, it is true, has not been preserved in the authentic version, but a number of citations, quoted from it during the decades immediately following, indicate its contents, and it is likely that it was the source of the much interpolated "Fragmentum Fantuzzianum", which probably dates from 778–80. In the original document of Quiercy Pepin promised the pope the restoration of the lands of Central Italy, which had been last conquered by Aistulf, especially in the exarchate and in the Roman Duchy, and of a number of more or less clearly defined patrimonies in the Lombard Kingdom and in the Duchies of Spoleto and Benevento. The lands were not yet in Pepin's hands. They had therefore first to be conquered by Pepin, and his gift was conditioned by this event. In the summer of 754 Pepin with his army and the pope began their march into Italy, and forced King Aistulf, who had shut himself up in his capital, to sue for peace. The Lombard promised to give up the cities of the exarchate and of the Pentapolis, which had been last conquered, to make no further attacks upon or to evacuate the Duchy of Rome and the districts of Venetia and Istria, and acknowledged the sovereignty of the Franks. For the cities in the exarchate and in the Pentapolis, which Aistulf promised to return, Pepin executed a separate deed for the pope. This is the first actual "Donation of 754". But Pepin had hardly recrossed the Alps on his return home, when Aistulf not only failed to make preparations for the return of the promised cities, but again advanced against Rome, which had to endure a severe siege. The pope sent a messenger by sea, summoning Pepin to fulfil anew his pledge of loyalty. In 756 Pepin again set out with an army against Aistulf and a second time hemmed him in at Pavia. Aistulf was again compelled to promise to deliver to the pope the cities granted him after the first war and, in addition, Commachio at the mouth of the Po. But this time the mere promise was not considered sufficient. Messengers of Pepin visited the various cities of the exarchate and of the Pentapolis, demanded and received the keys to them, and brought the highest magistrates and most distinguished magnates of these cities to Rome. Pepin executed a new deed of gift for the cities thus surrendered to the pope, which together with the keys of the cities were deposited on the grave of St. Peter (Second Donation of 756).

The Byzantine Government naturally did not approve of this result of the intervention of the Franks. It had hoped through the instrumentality of the Franks to regain possession of the districts that had been wrested from it by the Lombards. But Pepin took up arms, not to render a service to the Byzantine emperor, but for the sake of St. Peter alone, from whose protection he expected earthly happiness and everlasting salvation. Just as kings at that time founded monasteries and endowed them with landed properties, that prayers might be offered for them there, so Pepin wished to provide the pope with temporal territories, that he might be certain of the prayers of the pope. Therefore Pepin answered the Byzantine ambassadors, who came to him before the second expedition of 756 and asked him to return to the emperor the cities to be taken from the Lombards, that he had undertaken the expedition for St. Peter alone and not for the emperor; that to St. Peter alone would he restore the cities. Thus did Pepin found the States of the Church. The Greeks undoubtedly had the formal right to the sovereignty, but as they had failed to meet the obligation of sovereignty to give protection against foreign enemies, their rights became illusory. If the Franks had not interfered, the territory would by right of conquest have fallen to the Lombards; Pepin by his intervention prevented Rome with the native population from falling into the hands of the foreign conquerors. The States of the Church are in a certain sense the only remnant of the Roman Empire in the West which escaped foreign conquerors. Gratefully did the Roman population acknowledge that they had escaped subjection to the Lombards only through the mediation of the pope. For it was only for the pope's sake that Pepin had resolved to interfere. The results were important, (a) chiefly because the pope through his temporal sovereignty received a guarantee of his independence, was freed from the fetters of a temporal power, and obtained that freedom from interference which is necessary for the conduct of his high office; (b) because the papacy threw off the political ties that bound it to the East and entered into new relations with the West, which made possible the development of the new Western civilization. The latter was destined to become especially prominent under Pepin's son, Charlemagne.

Under Charlemagne the relations with the Lombards soon became strained again. Adrian I complained that the Lombard king Desiderius had invaded the territories of the States of the Church, and reminded Charlemagne of the promise made at Quiercy. As Desiderius also championed the claims of Charlemagne's nephews, he endangered the unity of the Frankish kingdom, and Charlemagne's own interests therefore bade him to oppose Desiderius. In the autumn of 773 Charlemagne entered Italy and besieged Desiderius at Pavia. While the siege was in progress, Charlemagne went to Rome at Easter, 774, and at the request of the pope renewed the promises made at Quiercy. Soon after this Desiderius was forced to capitulate, and Charlemagne had himself proclaimed King of the Lombards in his place. Charlemagne's attitude toward the States of the Church now underwent a change. With the title of King of the Lombards he also assumed the title as "Patricius Romanorum", which his father had never used, and read into this title rights which under Pepin had never been associated with it. Moreover, differences of opinion arose between Adrian and Charlemagne concerning the obligations which had been assumed by Pepin and Charlemagne in the document of Quiercy. Adrian construed it to mean that Charlemagne should take an elastic concept of the "respublica Romana" to the extent of giving up not only the conquests of Aistulf in the exarchate and in the Pentapolis, but also earlier conquests of the Lombards in Central Italy, Spoleto, and Benevento. But Charles would not listen to any such interpretaion of the document. As both parties were anxious to come to an understanding, an agreement was reached in 781. Charlemagne acknowledged the sovereignty of Adrian in the Duchy of Rome and in the States of the Church founded by Pepin's donations of 754–56. He now executed a new document in which were enumerated all the districts in which the pope was recognized as ruler. The Duchy of Rome (which had not been mentioned in the earlier documents) heads the list, followed by the exarchate and the Pentapolis, augmented by the cities which Desiderius had agreed to surrender at the beginning of his reign (Imola, Bologna, Faenza, Ferrara, Ancona, Osimo, and Umana); next the patrimonies were specified in various groups: in the Sabine, in the Spoletan and Beneventan districts, in Calabria, in Tuscany, and in Corsica. Charlemagne, however, in his character as "Patricius", wanted to be considered as the highest court of appeal in criminal cases in the States of the Church. He promised on the other hand to protect freedom of choice in the election of the pope, and renewed the alliance of friendship that had been previously made between Pepin and Stephen II.

The agreement between Charlemagne and Adrian remained undisturbed. In 787 Charlemagne still further enlarged the States of the Church by new donations. Capua and a few other frontier cities of the Duchy of Benevento, besides several cities in Lombardy, Tuscany, Populonia, Roselle, Sovana, Toscanella, Viterbo, Bagnorea, Orvieto, Ferento, Orchia, Marta, and lastly Città di Castello appear to have been added at that time. All of this, of course, is based upon painstaking deductions, since no document has come down to us either from the time of Charlemagne or from that of Pepin. Adrian in these negotiations proved himself no mean politician, and is justly ranked with Stephen II as the second founder of the States of the Church. His arrangements with Charlemagne remained authoritative for the relations of the later popes with the Carlovingians and the German emperors. These relations were given a brilliant outward expression by Charlemagne's coronation as emperor in 800.

CHIEF SOURCES.—DUCHESNE, *Liber Pontificalis*, I (Paris, 1886); GUNDLACH, *Mon. Germ. Epistolæ*, III: *Codex Carolinus* (Hanover, 1892). LITERATURE.—FABRE, *De patrimoniis Romanæ ecclesiæ usque ad ætatem Carolinorum* (Lille, 1892); GRISAR, *Ein Rundgang durch die Patrimonien des hl. Stuhles um 600* and *Verwaltung u. Haushalt der päpstl. Patrimonien um 600* in *Zeitschr. für kath. Theol.*, I (1877); IDEM, *Gesch. Roms u. der Päpste im M. A.*, I (Freiburg, 1901); SCHWARZLOSE, *Die Patrimonien der röm. Kirche bis zur Entstehung des Kirchenstaates* (Berlin, 1887); IDEM, *Die Verwaltung u. finanzielle Bedeutung der Patrimonien* in *Zeitschr. für Kirchengesch.*, XI (1890); MOMMSEN, *Die Bewirtschaftung der Kirchengüter unter P. Gregor I* in *Zeitschr. für Sozial- u. Wirtschaftsgesch.*, I (1893); ARMBRUST, *Die territoriale Politik der Päpste von 500–800* (Göttingen, 1885); FICKER, *Forschungen zur Reichs- u. Rechtsgesch. Italiens*, II (Innsbruck, 1869); HAMEL, *Untersuchungen zur älteren Territorialgesch. des Kirchenstaates* (Göttingen, 1899); HARTMANN, *Gesch. Italiens*, II (Leipzig, 1900 sqq.); OELSNER, *Jahrbücher des fränkischen Reiches unter Pippin* (Leipzig, 1871); ABEL AND SIMSON, *Jahrbücher des fränkischen Reiches unter Karl. d. Gr.*, I (2nd ed., Leipzig, 1888); DIEHL, *Etudes sur l'administration byzantine dans l'exarchat de Ravenne* (Paris, 1888); DUCHESNE, *Les premiers temps de l'état pontifical* (2nd ed., Paris, 1904); SCHEFFER-BOICHORST, *Pippins u. Karls d. Gr. Schenkungsversprechen* in *Mitteil. des Instituts für österr. Geschichtsforschung*, V (1884); MARTENS, *Die römische Frage unter Pippin u. Karl d. Gr.* (Stuttgart, 1881); IDEM, *Beleuchtung der neuesten Controversen über die röm. Frage unter Pippin u. Karl d. Gr.* (Munich, 1898); BRUNENGO, *Le origini della sovranita temporale dei papi* (3rd ed., Prato, 1889); IDEM, *Il Patriziato Romano di Carlomagno* (Prato, 1893); LAMPRECHT, *Die römische Frage von König Pippin bis auf Kaiser Ludwig den Frommen* (Leipzig, 1889); LINDNER, *Die sogenannten Schenkungen Pippins, Karls d. Gr. Ottos an die Päpste* (Stuttgart, 1896); GUNDLACH, *Die Entstehung des Kirchenstaates und der kuriale Begriff der Respublica Romanorum* (Breslau, 1899); KEHR, *Die sogen. Karolingische Schenkung von 774* in *Histor. Zeitschr.*, LXX (1893); IDEM, *Ueber die Chronologie der Briefe Papst Pauls I* in *Nachrichten der Göttinger Gesellschaft* (1896); CRIVELLUCCI, *Delle origini dello stato Pontif.* in *Studi storici*, X–XII (Rome, 1901–03); SCHNÜRER, *Die Entstehung des Kirchenstaates* (Cologne, 1894); Ital. tr. by MERCATI, *L'origine dello stato della chiesa* (Siena, 1899); IDEM AND ULIVI, *Das Fragmentum Fantuzzianum* (Fribourg, 1906); IDEM, *Zum Streit um das Fragmentum Fantuzzianum* in *Histor. Jahrbuch der Görresgesellschaft*, XXIX (1908).

II. STATES OF THE CHURCH.—(1) *The Period of the Carlovingian Emperors*.—The States of the Church founded by the Carlovingians were the security for the friendly alliance between the papacy and the empire which dominated the Middle Ages. But this friendly alliance also was and remained the necessary condition for the existence of the States of the Church. Without the protection of the great power beyond the Alps the States of the Church could not have been maintained. The worst dangers threatened the States of the Church, not so much from foreign enemies, as from the factions of the nobility in the city of Rome, who were continually engaged in jealous quarrels, each striving to get control of the spiritual and temporal power attaching to the papacy. The degradation of the papacy reached its lowest point when it could obtain no protection from the empire against the lust for power of the factions of the Roman nobility or of the neighbouring patrician families. This lust for power manifested itself principally at the election of a new pope. For this reason the emperors, when they assumed the responsibility of protecting the States of the Church, also guaranteed a canonical election, and the popes laid great stress upon having this obligation renewed in writing by each new emperor in the confirmation of the old charters. Of these charters the oldest whose text is preserved is the "Hludovicianum" or *Pactum* of Louis the Pious, i. e. the instrument executed by that monarch for Paschal I in 817. With Paschal's successor, Eugene II, the friendly alliance was, by order of Louis, renewed in 824 by his eldest son and colleague in the empire, Lothair I. The pope, dependent on the protection of the emperor, then granted the emperor new rights, which mark the zenith of the imperial influence under the Carlovingians. The emperor received the right of supervising the government and the administration of justice at Rome through the instrumentality of permanent envoys, and no new pope was to be consecrated until he had, together with the Romans, taken the oath of allegiance to the emperor in the presence of imperial envoys.

In this way the empire received in the "Constitution of Lothair" an indirect influence over the election of the pope and a supervision of the papal government in the States of the Church. But soon after this the Carlovingians were so busily occupied by their dynastic quarrels that they had but little time to concern themselves about Rome. Leo IV had, in concert with some seaport towns of Italy, to take measures personally for the defence of Rome against the Saracens. The soldiers blessed by him won a brilliant victory at Ostia in 849. As the right bank of the Tiber with its Basilica of St. Peter was exposed to the pillage of the Saracens, Leo fortified it with a wall (848–52), and in his honour the part of the city so protected was called *Civitas Leonina*. In 850 Leo crowned Lothair's son, Louis II, as emperor. Although this emperor bravely opposed the Saracens in Lower Italy with all his power, this power was no longer that of Charlemagne, for Louis's rule extended only over Italy. To the papacy, then represented by Nicholas II, the regency of Louis II was at times a danger rather than a protection. His representative, Duke Lambert of Spoleto, under the pretence of superintending the election of the pope, invaded Rome in 867, and treated it as conquered territory. This was the prelude to the wretched period following the death of Louis (875), when Rome and the pope were placed at the mercy of the neighbouring feudal lords, who had come into Italy with the Carlovingians, and who now quarrelled first with the Carlovingians still ruling beyond the Alps, then among themselves for the apple of discord, the imperial crown. In vain did the able Pope John VIII hope for help and protection from the West Frankish king, Charles the Bald, who had been crowned emperor in 875. It is true Charles renewed the old charter relative to protection and donations and increased the domain of the States of the Church by new donations (Spoleto and Benevento); he also gave up the claim to have envoys present at the consecration of the pope as well as the assignment to these envoys of the administration of justice. But beyond these donations on paper he did nothing. John VIII, at the head of his fleet at Cape Circeo (877), had to defend himself unaided against the Saracens. Fleeing from the dukes Lambert of Spoleto and Adalbert of Tuscany, who bore themselves as representatives of the imperial power, he went to France, vainly imploring the Carlovingians for help. The East Frank, Charles the Fat, who received the imperial crown from John VIII in 881, likewise did nothing, and Arnulf, who was crowned emperor in 896, was compelled by illness to suspend further interference. Severely did the defenceless pope have to suffer for having summoned him. Pope Stephen V had previously (891) yielded to the urging of Duke Guido of Spoleto and bestowed on him the imperial crown. Stephen's successor, Pope Formosus, had been compelled to give the crown also to Guido's son, Lambert, as the associate of his father in the empire (892); he thus incurred the fierce hatred of Lambert, when he afterwards summoned Arnulf to Rome and crowned him emperor. When Lambert, after the death of Formosus, entered Rome in 897, he took a horrible revenge upon the corpse of the pope through the medium of Stephen VI.

The papacy was now completely at the mercy of the struggling factions of the nobility. Benedict IV in 901 crowned as emperor Louis, King of Lower Burgundy, who had been summoned by the Italian nobles. In 915 John X crowned Louis's opponent, the Marquis Berengar of Friuli. Berengar was the last to receive the imperial crown before the founding of the Roman Empire of the German Nation. At Rome itself the greatest influence was won by the family of the later Counts of Tusculum, which traced its descent to the senator and *dux*, Theophylactus, and whose power was for a time represented by the wife of Theophylactus, Theodora (called *Senatrix* or *Vesteratrix*), and her daughters Marozia and Theodora the Younger. The papacy also came under the power of these women. Alberic, the husband of Marozia, with John X, who had been raised to the papacy by the elder Theodora, defeated the Saracens on the Garigliano (916), and thereafter called himself Consul of the Romans. After his death this rank was transmitted to Marozia, and, on her fall, to his son Alberic. Marozia had John X deposed, and finally had her own son by her first husband placed upon the papal chair as John XI. John XI was entirely dominated by his mother. When Marozia's son, Alberic II, finally put an end to the despotic rule of his mother (932), the Romans proclaimed him their lord and master, conferred on him all temporal power, and restricted the pope's authority to purely spiritual matters. Alberic, who had a palace on the Aventine, refused the German king Otto I permission to enter Rome, when the latter appeared in Upper Italy in 951. But, when Otto appeared for the second time in Italy, conditions had changed.

(2) *From the Coronation of Otto I as Emperor to the end of the Hohenstaufen Line.*—Alberic II died in 954. In accordance with a promise made to him, the Romans in 955 elected to the papacy as John XII his seventeen-year-old son Octavian, who had succeeded him in the temporal power. This pontiff thus united the spiritual and temporal power, but only in the territory which had been subject to Alberic—that is substantially the old Duchy of Rome, or the "Patrimonium Petri". The Pentapolis and the exarchate were in other hands, ultimately falling to King Berengar of Ivrea. To obtain protection against Berengar, John XII called upon Otto I for help. Otto came and on 2 February, 962, received the imperial crown. On 13 February he drew up the charter (still extant in a contemporary caligraphic copy, preserved in the archives of the Vatican), in which he renewed the well-known covenants of his predecessors, increased the donations by the addition of several new ones, and undertook to secure the canonical election of the popes. The pope was not to be consecrated until imperial envoys had assured themselves of the legality of the election and obtained from the pope a sworn promise of allegiance (cf. Th. Sickel, "Das Privilegium Ottos I für die römische Kirche", Innsbruck, 1883). The necessary condition for the coöperation of emperor and pope was their common opposition to Berengar. This was removed when John XII, who not unreasonably feared Otto's power, entered into secret negotiations with Berengar. Otto thereupon again came to Rome, which the pope had left, and demanded of the Romans an oath that henceforth they would never again elect a pope without the express consent and sanction of the emperor. Therewith the papacy was declared subject to the emperor. This at once became evident, when a synod, over which Otto presided, deposed the pope. But Leo VIII, who was chosen in accordance with Otto's wishes, was unable to remain at Rome without Otto. The Romans, after the death of John XII, elected Benedict V, but Otto sent him into exile at Hamburg. Other afflictions beset John XIII, to secure whose elevation the Romans and Otto had acted in harmony in 966. John needed the protection of the emperor against a rebellious faction of the nobility, whereupon Otto appointed a prefect of Rome and enfeoffed him with drawn sword. In return the pope crowned the son of Otto I (Otto II) with the imperial crown in the next year (967), and later married him to the Greek princess Theophano. Otto II had to render the same protection to the popes of his time. John XIII's successor, Benedict VI, was imprisoned and murdered in the Castle of S. Angelo by hostile nobles. The Frank who was chosen in his place (Boniface VII) had to flee to Constantinople, but the position of Benedict VII, who was raised to the papacy with the consent of Otto II, remained uncertain until Otto in 980 came to Rome, where, after his defeat near Capo Colonne, he died (983) and was buried in St. Peter's. Boniface VII, who returned from Constantinople, had during the minority of Otto's son displaced John XIV, the successor of Benedict VII, and exposed him to death by starvation in the Castle of S. Angelo. And beside John XV, who was made pope after the fall of Boniface VII, the dux, Crescentius, under the usurped title of "Patrician", ruled over Rome, so that the times of an Alberic seemed to have returned.

John V therefore earnestly desired the arrival of a German army. It appeared in 996 under the command of the sixteen-year-old Otto III. As John had died before Otto entered Rome, the German king, whom the Romans had asked to propose a candidate, designated, on the advice of the princes, his relative, the young Bruno, who was then elected at Rome and graced the papal chair as Gregory V (996–99). Crescentius was besieged in the Castle of S. Angelo and beheaded. Gregory V, who crowned Otto III emperor, was the first German pope. His successor, the first French pope, also designated by Otto, was the learned Sylvester II, near whom on the Aventine the emperor desired permanently to make his residence, that he might govern the West as the Roman emperors had once done. The old Roman law and a ceremonial fashioned after Byzantine forms were to be put into effect. But these plans soon came to naught. Only a few years later, in 1002, the youthful and visionary emperor, bitterly disillusioned, died in his camp outside Rome, which had risen against him. And, when Sylvester II also passed away in 1003, John Crescentius, the son of the Crescentius who had been beheaded by Otto III, having possessed himself of the patriciate, seized the government at Rome. After his death the Counts of Tusculum began to contend with the Crescentians for the supremacy, and, in opposition to the pope set up by their opponents, raised one of their own followers to the papal chair as Benedict VIII; the latter was recognized as the lawful pope by Henry II, whom he crowned emperor at Rome on 14 February, 1014. An intimate friendship united Benedict and Henry. Together they planned a reform of the Church, which unfortunately was not carried out. Benedict was succeeded by his brother, John XIX, a man less worthy of the honour, who had previously held the temporal power in the city, and who as pope for the most part thought only of the interests of his family. These urged him to gain the good will of Henry's successor, Conrad II, whom he crowned emperor at Rome in 1027. The papal dignity sank to a still lower level under the nephew of John XIX, Benedict IX, whose elevation to the papal throne at the age of twenty was secured by his family through simony and violence. When the Romans set up an anti-pope, Sylvester III, in opposition, Benedict wavered for a time in doubt whether he ought not to resign; finally he relinquished the pontificate to his godfather John Gratian for 1000 pounds of silver. The purchaser had had recourse to this measure only to put an end to the abominable practices of the Tusculan. He called himself Gregory VI, and stood in friendly relations with the Cluniac monks. But as John again asserted his claims, and all three popes had evidently secured the dignity only through simony, the party of reform saw no other remedy than to induce the German king, Henry III, to intervene. Henry III, through the synods of Sutri and Rome, had all three popes deposed. Gregory VI in the capacity of secretary went into exile to Germany with Hildebrand (later Pope Gregory VII). Then, marking the zenith of the German imperial power at Rome, there followed a number of German popes: Clement II, who crowned Henry III emperor in 1046, conferring on him also the rank of Patrician, and with it the right of nomination at papal elections; Damasus II; Saint Leo IX of Alsace, with whom the drift toward ecclesiastical reform finally reached the papal chair; and Victor II.

The reaction soon set in. Under the Burgundian Nicholas II the effort to free the papacy from the commanding influence of the empire becomes clearly noticeable. At the Easter Synod of 1059 the papal election was placed under new regulations, being reposed essentially in the hands of the cardinals. The German king was no longer to have the right of designation, but at most only that of confirmation. As the German Court was unwilling to yield the right of designation without a struggle, which, according to its concept, was conferred together with the hereditary rank of Patrician, the first conflicts between empire and papacy began. In opposition to Alexander II, who was elected to succeed Nicholas II, the German Government set up Bishop Cadalus of Parma (Honorius II). Soon afterward, under Henry IV and Gregory VII, the conflicts broadened out into the conflict concerning investiture. In this contest the papacy had pressing need of a temporal power to support it against the German Empire. This support was destined to be furnished by the Normans, whose state, founded in Lower Italy, became of ever-increasing importance to the papacy.

The relations between the Holy See and the Normans were not always friendly. When these at the time of Leo IX advanced into the Lombard Duchy of Benevento, the Beneventans sought to defend themselves against them by expelling the reigning prince and electing the pope in 1051 as their sovereign. Thus was Benevento added to the States of the Church. Actually, of course, the popes had possession only of the city of Benevento with the district immediately under its jurisdiction, and that only since 1077. Through Benevento Leo IX became involved in a quarrel with the Normans and took the field against them, but was defeated and made captive near Civitate in 1053. The victors, however, did not fail to recognize and to respect in the captive the successor of Peter, and subsequently, as the result of negotiations with Nicholas II, the treaty of Melfi was made in 1059, in which the Normans acknowledged themselves vassals of the Holy See for the conquered territories—Benevento was excepted—and engaged to pay a yearly tribute. They now also took upon themselves the protection of the papacy and the States of the Church, as well as of the canonical election of the pope. A Norman army under Robert Guiscard rescued Gregory VII in the greatest distress, when Henry IV had come to Rome with his anti-pope Clement III, received the imperial crown from the latter, and imprisoned Gregory VII in the Castle of S. Angelo. Before the powerful Norman army Henry had to withdraw from Rome in 1084.

A valuable ally of the papacy in its conflict with the empire was the great Countess Matilda of Tuscany, at whose Castle of Canossa King Henry IV appeared in January, 1077, to beg Gregory VII for absolution from the ban of the Church. Matilda had by will bequeathed her freehold estates to the pope, but had also in 1111 made promises to Emperor Henry V, but probably only in such a way that the Roman Church would remain chief owner. The succession to the lands bequeathed by Matilda furnished after her death (1115) a new cause, first for strained relations, then for a quarrel between emperor and pope. This was partly due to the fact that the lands, because of their location, had a high strategic value. Whoever possessed them commanded the passage of the Apennines from the plains of the Po into Tuscany. Henry V at once took possession of the lands, and subsequent kings and emperors to Frederick II also occupied or bestowed them in spite of the repeated protests of the Curia. Amid all this we often see pope and emperor working in harmony. The anti-pope Anacletus II with his protector, King Roger II of Sicily, was attacked by Emperor Lothair, who took up the cause of Innocent II. Frederick I had Arnold of Brescia, who had openly preached against the temporal power of the popes, executed as a heretic and rebel (1155).

The various matters of dispute, which had led under Frederick I to the eighteen years' conflict with Alexander III and had been then settled in the Treaty of Venice, were again revived when Henry VI, as husband of the Norman heiress Constance, at the death of the childless King William II in 1189, laid claim to the Norman Kingdom, which embraced Sicily and Lower Italy. The pope as lord paramount wished to have the unrestricted disposal of the Norman kingdom, and first bestowed it on the illegitimate Tancred of Lecce. But Henry disregarded this action, and conquered the kingdom after Tancred's death in 1194. He desired to transform Italy and Germany into an hereditary monarchy. He also made old parts of the States of the Church subject to him, when in 1195 he placed the Margravate of Ancona, the Duchy of Ravenna, and the ancient exarchate (the Romagna) under the lord high steward of the realm, Markwald of Anweiler, as his viceroy. But with his death in 1197 all the plans for world dominion collapsed. In Italy a national movement was started, which the youthful and energetic Innocent III utilized to re-establish and extend the States of the Church. First of all he enforced the papal authority at Rome itself by exacting an oath of allegiance from the senators as well as from the prefect, previously appointed by the emperor. After this nearly all the towns and villages of the territory bequeathed by Matilda, in the March of Ancona, and in the Duchy of Spoleto, also Assisi and Perugia, submitted to him. Innocent thus became the restorer of the States of the Church. After the precedent set by Otto IV (Neuss, 8 June, 1201), the son of Henry VI, Frederick II, who had been protected by Innocent III, confirmed anew the States of the Church in their constituent parts by a golden bull executed in the name of the empire at Eger on 12 July, 1213: these parts were the old Patrimony from Ceperano to Radicofani, the March of Ancona, the Duchy of Spoleto, the territories of Matilda, the County of Bertinoro (south of Ravenna), the exarchate, and the Pentapolis. All these new acquisitions and the States of the Church in their entirety were again placed in the greatest jeopardy when the great struggle between Frederick II and the Curia broke out. With the exception of the city of Rome the emperor had brought the States of the Church into his power. Innocent IV fled to his native city Œcumenical Genoa and thence to Lyons, where at the thirteenth Œcumenical Council in 1245 he placed Frederick II under the ban of the Church and deposed him. The conflict raged for several years longer, but the star of the Hohenstaufen was rapidly setting. The emperor's son Enzio, commander-in-chief in Central and Upper Italy, was captured by the Bolognese in 1249. The emperor himself died in 1250, and his son Conrad IV died a few years later (1254). When Frederick's illegitimate son Manfred undertook the continuation of the struggle and had himself crowned at Palermo, the French pope Clement IV summoned to his aid the brother of King Louis IX of France, Charles of Anjou, who had accepted the Kingdom of Lower Italy as a fief of the pope. Charles vanquished Manfred in 1266 at Benevento, and Conradin, the youthful nephew of Frederick II, at Tagliacozzo in 1268, and had this last descendant of the Hohenstaufen house executed in the market-place of Naples. With this the danger to the papacy from the Hohenstaufen was removed, but a worse danger took its place.

(3) *From the Avignon Exile to the End of the Fifteenth Century.*—The papacy was now not only dependent upon the protection of France, but was also entirely at its mercy. This was seen in the utter disregard shown by Philip the Fair in his attitude toward Boniface VIII and his successors. Clement V, a native of Southern France, did not venture to go to Italy, after his election in 1305, but had himself crowned at Lyons, and after 1309 resided at Avignon, which now remained the residence of the popes until 1376. The country about Avignon constituted the County of Venaissin or the Margravate of Provence, which, on the ground of a former donation of the Counts of Toulouse in 1273, had been given up to the pope by the French king, Philip III the Bold. The city of Avignon itself first came into the possession of the Holy See by purchase in 1348. During the residence of the popes in Avignon the papal dominion in the States of the Church almost ceased. In Rome the Colonna and Orsini fought for the supremacy. In the other cities the French regents, who were sent from Avignon, found anything but willing obedience. Bologna revolted in 1334 against the pope's relative, Beltram. Cola di Rienzi deluded the Romans with the phantom of a republic. The state of anarchy was first ended by the Castilian Cardinal Albornoz (see GIL DE ALBORNOZ, ALVAREZ CARILLO), whom Innocent VI sent to the States of the Church as his vicar-general in 1353. Albornoz not only brought the States of the Church under subjection to the pope, but also reorganized them by means of the Ægidian Constitutions, which were in force in the States of the Church until 1816. But the successes of Albornoz were soon nullified again, when the Great Schism occurred during the residence at Avignon. After its termination Martin V (1417–31) sought to establish a centralized monarchy out of the various conflicting rights, privileges, and usurpations, and in this had much success. New afflictions were brought by the period of the Renaissance, in which visionaries of radical views loved to pose as liberators from tyranny. Thus the conspiracy of Stefano Porcaro alarmed Nicholas V in 1453, and the conspiracy of 1468 alarmed Paul II. Other dangers lay in the growth of power of certain families of the feudal nobility in the States of the Church, in the nepotism of some of the popes, who provided for their relatives at the expense of the States of the Church, or in their international policies, for which the States of the Church had to suffer.

(4) *From the Sixteenth Century to the Treaty of Vienna.*—Under Alexander VI the States of the Church disintegrated into a series of states held by papal relatives of the Borgia family. Cesare Borgia, whom Machiavelli admired, laboured earnestly from his Duchy of Romagna to transform the States of the Church into a Kingdom of Central Italy. After his fall (1504) Venice sought to bring the cities on the Adriatic Sea under its power. Julius II then in his impetuous way had recourse to force to re-establish and extend the States of the Church. He conquered Perugia and Bologna and by the League of Cambrai forced Venice to give up Ravenna, Cervia, Faenza, and Rimini. But, after he had been satisfied by the Venetians, he concluded the Holy League for the expulsion of the French from Italy. It is true that the French in 1512 were once more victorious over the troops of the League at Ravenna, but thanks chiefly to the Swiss mercenaries, whom the pope had enlisted through Cardinal Schinner, Julius attained his object. On the surrender of the Duchy of Milan to Maximilian Sforza, Julius II made a still further gain for the States of the Church, since Parma and Piacenza were taken from the duchy and incorporated in the States of the Church. Reggio and Modena, which belonged to the Duke of Ferrara, were also taken possession of by the pope, but his successor Leo X had to restore these cities to the duke in 1515. A dreadful catastrophe was brought upon Rome by the vacillating policy of Clement VII. The disorderly troops of Charles V overran and plundered the States of the Church, occupied Rome on 6 May, 1527, and for eight days rioted there frightfully (*Sacco di Roma*). In the Castle of S. Angelo the pope was held captive until 6 December. It was long before these wounds were healed, although the pope in 1529 concluded a peace with the emperor at Barcelona and received back the States of the Church. The conclusion of peace was confirmed by the Conference of Bologna, at which Charles V on 24 April, 1530, received the imperial crown from Clement VII.

During this time as well as later a number of districts were for a time separated from the States of the Church and conferred as separate principalities by popes on their relatives. The Rovere pope Sixtus IV had in 1474 made Federigo of Montefeltro Duke of Urbino, and married Federigo's daughter Giovanna to his nephew Giovanni della Rovere. The son of this Giovanni, Francesco Maria della Rovere, came into possession of the Duchy of Urbino in 1508, during the pontificate of the other Rovere pope, Julius II. In addition to this Julius II in 1512 conferred on him the Vicariate of Pesaro, which had previously been a fief in the hands of the Malatesta and since 1445 of the Sforza. Not until the male line of the Rovere became extinct in 1631 were Montefeltro and Urbino together with Pesaro restored to the States of the Church. Pope Paul III in 1545 bestowed Parma and Piacenza as a duchy on his son Pier Luigi Farnese. Even after the Farnese line had become extinct, the duchies reverted, not to the States of the Church, but to a branch of the Spanish Bourbons, and finally in 1860 to Sardinia. To make up for this Ferrara, which had once belonged to Matilda of Canossa as a papal fief, had in 1208 fallen to the Guelph family of Este, and had in 1471 been made a duchy. After the main line of the Este had become extinct in 1597, Ferrara reverted to the States of the Church, and remained part thereof (except during the Napoleonic period) until the Italian annexation in 1860. Modena and Reggio, however, fell in 1597 to a collateral line of the Este as a fief of the empire. Thus the States of the Church before the outbreak of the French Revolution embraced substantially the territory that had belonged to them at the time of Charlemagne, except that some portions of the old Duchy of Spoleto had been added in the south since the time of Innocent III.

Rapid changes came with the time of the French

Revolution and of Napoleon. In 1791 the French National Assembly announced the union of Avignon and Venaissin with France, and in the Peace of Tolentino (1797) Pius VI had to give them up, while at the same time relinquishing the legations of Ferrara, Bologna, and Romagna to the Cisalpine Republic. In February, 1798, General Berthier, who had been sent to Rome by Napoleon, formed the rest of the States of the Church into the Roman Republic. The pope, because he would not renounce his claim, was taken away as a captive and eventually confined in Valence, where death soon released him (29 August, 1799). People were already rejoicing that the papacy and the church had come to an end. Their joy was, however, premature. Under the protection of Emperor Francis II the cardinals in 1800 elected Pius VII as pope at Venice. But hard trials awaited him. It is true that in 1801 Pius VII by Napoleon's favour got back the States of the Church as bounded in the Peace of Tolentino. But the position of the States of the Church remained extremely precarious. Napoleon in 1806 conferred Benevento on Talleyrand and Pontecorvo on Bernadotte. In 1808, because Pius VII would not close his ports to the English, the States of the Church were again occupied and in 1809 completely confiscated. The Marches, Urbino, Camerino, and Macerata were annexed to the newly-created Kingdom of Italy, the rest of the States of the Church to France. Not until the Congress of Vienna, where the able Consalvi represented the pope, were the States of the Church again established (1815), almost in their old dimensions except that Avignon and Venaissin were not restored to the pope, and Austria received a narrow strip along the frontier of the Ferrara district north of the Po and the right of garrisoning Ferrara and Comachio.

(5) *From the Peace of Vienna to 1870.*—The liberal and national ideas prevalent throughout Central Europe undermined the States of the Church, just as they did the rest of Italy, and found expression in the high-sounding phrases "constitution" and "national unification". The French Revolution and Napoleon had awakened these ideas. The name of a Kingdom of Italy, whose crown Napoleon had worn, was not forgotten. With the old conditions, which the congress of Vienna had restored, the people were by no means satisfied. They lamented the division of Italy into various states, bound together by no common bond, and above all the fact that they were ruled by foreigners. The pope and the King of Sardinia alone were looked upon as really native rulers. The other rulers were regarded more or less as foreigners. Naples-Sicily was ruled by the Bourbon line, which had come there in 1738, and which was opposed particularly by Sicily. In Parma and Piacenza also the Bourbon line, first established here in 1748, ruled again from the death (1847) of Marie-Louise, wife of Napoleon I. In Modena and Tuscany collateral lines of the house of Austria ruled: in the Duchy of Modena, a line which had in 1803 become the heir of the ancient ducal house of Este; in Tuscany, which, after the Medici had become extinct, had fallen to the ducal house of Lorraine, the line sprung from Ferdinand III, brother of Emperor Francis I of Austria. Furthermore, the Austrians were the immediate rulers of the Lombard-Venetian Kingdom. The current of national feeling was directed above all against the rule of the Austrians at Milan and Venice, hated as a government by foreigners, and also against the governments which pursued the policies of and were protected by Austria. Austria's statesman Metternich had at heart the maintenance of the order established by the Congress of Vienna in 1815. As the States of the Church were included among the governments under Austria's protection, they gradually shared the hatred against Austria.

The narrow police spirit of the absolute governments, which did not distinguish between what was justifiable and what was not, promoted the growth of dissatisfaction, which first took shape in secret societies. Carbonarism and freemasonry spread rapidly. The Greek war of independence, which excited universal admiration, aroused the national spirit in Italy. The Sanfedists (*per la santa fede*), as the loyal Catholics were called, were only a weak support for the Papal Government in the States of the Church. The Carbonari, led by exiles and made fugitives in Paris and yielding to the impression made by the Revolution of July, profited by the vacancy of the papal chair after the death of Pius VIII, in 1830, to inaugurate rising in the States of the Church, especially in Bologna. Under the presidency of Mazzini, the founder of the revolutionary society of the "Giovane Italia", delegates assembled at Bologna in 1831, as a parliament of the united provinces, to establish a republican form of government, and elected a provisional government. When the new pope Gregory XVI asked for Austria's assistance, Metternich was ready to intervene without delay. The Austrians restored peace in the States of the Church, as also in Modena and Parma. But hardly had the troops departed, when new disorders broke out, and, in answer to the pope's renewed call for help, the Austrians reappeared at Bologna in 1832 under Radetsky. To neutralize the influence of the Austrians the French Government of Louis Philippe sent to Ancona troops, which remained there as long as the Austrians occupied Bologna (until 1838). In opposition to the followers of Mazzini there were not lacking for a while men who strove to bring about the unification of Italy with the co-operation of the pope. Their spokesman was at first the former chaplain of King Charles Albert of Sardinia, Vincenzo Gioberti, who in 1843, as an exile in Brussels, wrote the treatise "Il primato morale e civile degli Italiani", a publication which caused a great sensation. He desired that the pope should become the head of the national union of states in Italy, from which the foreign princes were to be excluded. Piedmont, however, was to act as regularly appointed protector of the pope and Italy. The priest, Count Antonio Rosmini, desired an Italian confederation with the pope at its head and two deliberative chambers. He published his ideas in 1848 in the treatise "Delle cinque piaghe della S. Chiesa", in which he also particularly recommended the reform of the Church. The son-in-law of Manzoni, Marchese Massimo d' Azeglio, set forth the perverse political conditions in Italy and especially in the States of the Church more unsparingly in the treatise "Gli ultimi casi di Romagna" (1846), in which he urgently advocated reform, but at the same time warned against conspiracy and revolution. The majority of those who were enthusiastic about the unification of Italy put their hope in Piedmont, "la spada d' Italia". Cesare Balbo in his book "Le speranze d' Italia", which appeared in 1844, expected first of all the founding of a union of the Lombard states.

The demand for reform in the States of the Church was in fact not unjustified. It was expected that it would be inaugurated by Gregory XVI's successor, who was hailed with extravagant hopes, when as Pius IX he ascended the papal chair on 16 June, 1846. Men saw in him the pope of whom Gioberti had dreamed. Pius IX convoked at Rome a council of state composed of representatives of the various provinces, established a formal cabinet council, and sanctioned the formation of a militia in the States of the Church. In addition he suggested to Tuscany and Sardinia the formation of an Italian customs union. But the country was wrought up too highly to continue peacefully and slowly along such a course. The Liberals at Rome were dissatisfied because the laity were excluded from participation in the government of the States of the Church. Even before the outbreak of the French Revolution of February they forced by a popular uprising the appointment in 1848 of a cabinet of laymen. On 14 March, 1848, Pius IX after long hesitation decided to proclaim the fundamental law for the temporal government of the lands of the Holy See; as in other lands two chambers were to vote upon the laws, which were to be drawn up by a council of state. But the chambers were forbidden to interfere in any way in questions purely spiritual or of a mixed character, and the College of Cardinals had the right of veto over the decision of the chambers. This proved unsatisfactory. Pius IX was also expected to accommodate himself to the national desires when Milan and Venice after the outbreak of the revolution in Vienna had risen against the Austrians and Piedmont was preparing to support the uprising. The pope too, it was thought, should draw the sword against Austria.

When Pius IX in an Encyclical announced on 29 April, 1848, that he could never persuade himself to engage in a war against a Catholic power such as Austria, and that he would never assume the headship of an Italian confederation, his popularity in Liberal-National circles was wellnigh at an end. The party of those, who with Gioberti had dreamed of a unification of Italy under the pope, crumbled away. Mazzini made the demand that Rome be erected into a republic. A portion of the civic guard surrounded the Castle of S. Angelo and compelled the pope to appoint Liberal ministers. But the revolutionary republicans would have nothing to do with such a compromise. They became bolder than ever when King Charles Albert was defeated by Radetsky at Custozza on 24–25 July, 1848, and the monarchical national party had thereby met with complete failure. When the Liberal minister Rossi sought to reorganize the States of the Church and at the same time urged on the formation of a confederation of the Italian states, he was stabbed to death on the steps of the Palace of the Cancelleria on 15 November, 1848. On the following day the pope found himself besieged in the Quirinal. Only with difficulty could the Swiss Guards protect him from the fury of the populace. On 24 November Pius IX escaped in disguise to Gaeta in the Neapolitan Kingdom, whither King Ferdinand II had returned to take command in person. After the flight of the pope an assembly was elected to administer the government, the republic was proclaimed at Rome on 9 February, 1849, and the temporal sovereignty declared abolished. Mazzini with his international following ruled at Rome. In Florence also the republic was proclaimed on 18 February. But reaction followed quickly. This was hastened when the Austrians in a new passage of arms had defeated the Piedmontese at Mortara on 21 March, 1849, and at Novara on 23 March. Charles Albert thereupon resigned in favour of his son Victor Emmanuel II. The Austrians were now more powerful in Upper Italy than ever. They brought back to Florence the Grand Duke of Tuscany. Ferdinand II suppressed the revolution in Sicily. Pius IX was readily heard when he appealed to the Catholic powers for assistance against the republic. To anticipate Austria Louis Napoleon, then president of the Second Republic, with the consent of the Constituent Assembly in Paris, sent a force under Oudinot into the States of the Church, where besides Mazzini many revolutionaries from other lands (including Garibaldi) had gathered, and a triumvirate, composed of Mazzini, Aurelio Saffi, and Carlo Armellini, was administering the government. Oudinot's small force soon after its landing at Civitavecchia was, it is true, at first defeated before Rome. But now the Austrians also entered the States of the Church in the north, in the south the Neapolitans, while in Terracina Spaniards landed. Oudinot received reinforcements and began the siege of Rome. Garibaldi with 5000 volunteers cut his way through to continue the struggle in the Apennines. On 2 July, 1849, Oudinot entered Rome and again restored the temporal power of the pope. Pius IX re-entered Rome on 12 April, 1850.

Thus not only the Piedmontese and their followers, but the Republicans also had been routed, and had shown that they were unable to bring about the unity of Italy. By the military power of Austria all of Italy's forces had been shattered. But the object was not abandoned. A different programme was now adopted: to proceed with foreign aid under Piedmont's leadership against the pope. Piedmont sought to retain the sympathies of all Liberals by keeping the constitution, while the remaining governments of Italy had returned to absolutism. Pius IX, bitterly disillusioned, declared the retention of a constitution wholly incompatible with the most vital interests and the canons of the Church, as well as with the independence and freedom of the pope. Between him, the States of the Church, and Italy no efforts could bring about an understanding that was satisfactory to all. A French garrison maintained the sovereignty of the pope at Rome, while the Austrians secured tranquillity in the legations. The question was: how long would the two foreign powers continue harmoniously side by side in Italy? It was answered when Napoleon III undertook to show Europe the splendour of his imperial power and to force Austria out of its position of military supremacy in Italy. The change of temper in those circles of Italy that were striving for national unification was shown in a new treatise of Gioberti, who in 1843 in his "Primato" had assigned the guidance to the pope. In 1851 he published his book "Rinnovamento civile d' Italia", in which he set forth that the unification could be accomplished without Rome, and even against Rome with the aid of Piedmont. To prepare Piedmont for this rôle was the task of Camillo Cavour, who was made prime minister in 1852. It was also he who found for Sardinia the ally who united with it against Austria. At Plombières, a watering-place in Lorraine, he interested Napoleon in his plans in July, 1859, and all measures down to the smallest details were here agreed upon. The Piedmontese succeeded in joining their forces with the French army, and the allies defeated the Austrians at Magenta and Solferino. Napoleon, however, then swiftly concluded with the Emperor Francis Joseph the Peace of Villafranca-Zürich, by the terms of which Austria had to give up Lombardy only, not Venetia; in it provision was also made for an Italian confederation, into which all Italian states, including Austria for Venetia, were to enter, and over which it was intended that the pope should preside. Napoleon feared the intervention of the other powers, and at the same time was eager to show consideration for the feelings of the French Catholics.

In national circles in Italy men were at first furious at the conditions of this treaty of peace. But calm soon returned when it was seen that Napoleon made no preparations to bring back the expelled petty princes, and that the pope would have nothing to do with the rôle assigned to him. Cavour was able to continue his efforts in behalf of his schemes by the secret path of conspiracy. At his instigation apparently independent governments were established at Florence, Modena, and Bologna; in reality, however, these were directed from Turin, and were supported by England, since England did not desire a Kingdom of Italy dependent on France. In Tuscany, in the district of Modena-Parma, which had formed itself into the Republic of Emilia, and in the legations a vote of the inhabitants was taken,

STATES OF THE CHURCH

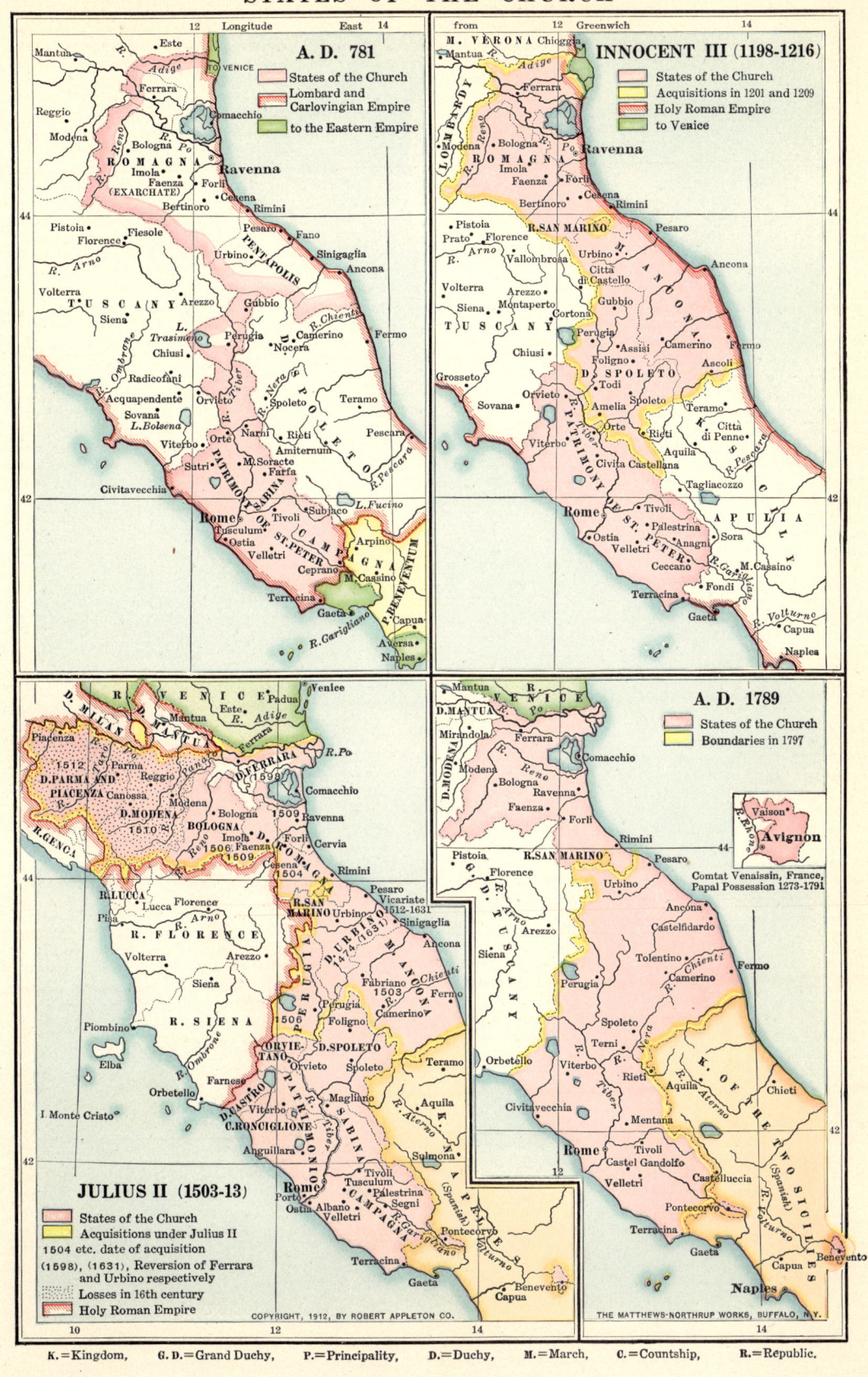

15-20 March, 1860, which resulted unanimously in favour of annexation to Sardinia. Napoleon himself had half desired this deceptive expedient, by means of which he had himself once risen to power, in order that he might have an excuse for letting matters take their own course. By the same expedient he now had voted to him the indemnity, stipulated in advance, for his interference in Italy, namely Savoy and Nice, which by a popular vote declared themselves for France. The pope did not suffer the annexation of the legations quietly. He excommunicated Victor Emmanuel and those who had assisted him. At the same time he issued a call for the formation of a volunteer army, which was joined by many of the French legitimists. The command of the army was undertaken by a bitter enemy of Napoleon, General Lamoricière, who had distinguished himself in Algeria. In a very short time the volunteer army saw active service. Garibaldi with 1000 armed insurgents had come from Genoa and landed at Marsala in May, 1860, had revolutionized Sicily, and was marching against Naples. The Government at Turin, which had at first allowed Garibaldi to do as he pleased, now saw with displeasure the progress of the Republicans, and feared that these might anticipate it at Rome and Naples. It sent an army to the south. Napoleon, whose consent Cavour had sought for the foreseen clash with the pope, sent word to Turin "Fate presto" (act quickly) and crossed to Algeria that he might not see what was going on. At Castelfidardo, not far from Ancona, the Piedmontese army met the papal forces under Lamoricière, and Lamoricière was defeated on 18 September, 1860. The Piedmontese occupied the Marches, and then advanced into the Kingdom of Naples. By a vote of the inhabitants on 21 September the population was then allowed to declare itself in favour of annexation to Sardinia. King Francis II of Naples after a brave defence was forced to capitulate at Gaeta on 13 February, 1861, and retired to Rome. All the annexed provinces sent representatives to the Turin Parliament, and Victor Emmanuel II was here proclaimed King of Italy on 13 March, 1861. Rome and Venetia alone were still to be won. Venetia was added to Italy in 1866 as the result of the victories of its ally, Prussia.

At last Rome was also to follow. Napoleon had at the end of December, 1866, withdrawn the small French garrison from Rome. It is true indeed that a foreign legion, composed for the most part of French soldiers and officers, was formed at Antibes to undertake the protection of Rome, but its position was nevertheless very critical. Garibaldi in the autumn of 1867 invaded the States of the Church with his insurgents. Then Napoleon once more sent a force from Toulon, which together with the papal army repulsed the forces of Garibaldi near Mentana, northeast of Rome on 3 November, 1867. The French garrison after this remained in Rome, since the Parisian Government had to yield to the wishes of the Catholics of France. Not until 20 July, 1870, after the Franco-German War had broken out, were the troops withdrawn. After Napoleon had been taken prisoner at Sedan, Italy, which had removed its capital to Florence in 1865, sent troops against Rome under Cadorna, and these on 20 September, 1870, entered the city through the breach at the Porta Pia. A vote, which declared in favour of annexation to Turin, was here also to give approval to the occupation. Pius IX excommunicated all participants in and authors of the occupation of the States of the Church. All Catholics condemned the action of Italy. To protect itself against the remonstrances, Italy on 13 May, 1871, issued the so-called law of the Papal Guarantees (see GUARANTEES, LAW OF), which was to secure to the pope his sovereignty, the inviolability of his person, as well as the freedom of the conclave and of the œcumenical councils. In addition to this a yearly pension of 3,225,000 francs was voted to him. The Vatican, the Lateran, and the country-seat Castel Gandolfo were declared extra-territorial. But Pius IX, to maintain his protests against the seizure of the States of the Church, refused to accept the law, and shut himself up in the Vatican.

The Roman question remains unsettled to the present day, since its solution by Italy has thus far been absolutely one-sided, besides having been brought about by violence. Without heeding the protests of the pope, Rome was declared the capital of Italy on 30 June, 1871. The radical elements, who were hostile to the Church and who had contributed so much to the unification of Italy, continued for the future also to hold the upper hand. Pope Pius IX by the Decree "Non expedit" of 29 February, 1868, had forbidden the Italian Catholics to participate in the political life and especially in the election of representatives of the Kingdom of Italy. Only in very recent years has a gradual tendency to a change of relations become noticeable. Although Pius X, because of the principle involved, adheres to the "Non expedit", he permits the participation of Catholics in administrative elections (municipal and provincial elections), and since the Encyclical "Certum Consilium" of 11 June, 1905, in certain cases on the recommendation of the bishop also participation in the parliamentary elections. Since that time the Catholics have begun to take part in the political life of Italy (1909: 22 representatives) and to exert an influence which we hope will redound to the welfare of the Church and of Italy.

GENERAL WORKS.—THEINER, *Codex diplomaticus dominii temporalis S. Sedis* (3 vols., Rome, 1861); REUMONT, *Gesch. der Stadt Rom* (3 vols., Berlin, 1867—); GREGOROVIUS, *Gesch. der Stadt Rom im Mittelalter* (8 vols., 4th ed., Stuttgart, 1886—); BROSCH, *Gesch. des Kirchenstaates*, I (Gotha, 1880), dealing with the sixteenth and seventeenth centuries, II (1882), extending from 1700 to 1870; SUGENHEIM, *Gesch. der Entstehung u. Ausbildung des Kirchenstaates* (Leipzig, 1854).

SPECIAL WORKS TO THE FIRST AND SECOND PERIODS.—HARTMANN, *Geschichte Italiens im Mittelalter*, III (Gotha, 1908-11); FICKER, *Forschungen zur Reichs- u. Rechtsgesch. Italiens* (4 vols., Innsbruck, 1868-74); NIEHUES, *Gesch. des Verhältnisses zwischen Kaisertum u. Papsttum im Mittelalter*, I (2 vols., 2nd ed., Münster, 1877), 87; GIESEBRECHT, *Gesch. der deutschen Kaiserzeit* (6 vols., Leipzig, 1881-95); SIMSON, *Jahrbücher des fränkischen Reiches unter Ludwig d. Frommen* (2 vols., Leipzig, 1874-76); DÜMMLER, *Gesch. des ostfränkischen Reiches* (2nd ed., 3 vols., Leipzig, 1887—); DOPFFEL, *Kaisertum u. Papsttum unter den Karolingern* (Freiburg, 1889); SICKEL, *Die Verträge der Päpste mit den Karolingern und das neue Kaisertum* in *Deutsche Zeitschr. für Geschichtswissenschaft* (1894-95); IDEM, *Alberich II und der Kirchenstaat* in *Mitteil. des Instituts für österreich. Geschichtsforschung*, XXIII (1902); SCHEFFER-BOICHORST, *Zu den Mathildischen Schenkungen* in *Mitt. des Instituts für österr. Geschichtsforschung*, IX (1888); OVERMANN, *Gräfin Mathilde von Tuscien, ihre Besitzungen: Gesch. ihres Gutes von 1115-1230* (Innsbruck, 1895); LUCHAIRE, *Innocent III, Rome e l' Italie* (2nd ed., Paris, 1906); WINKELMANN, *Philipp v. Schwaben u. Otto IV* (2 vols., Leipzig, 1873-78); IDEM, *Kaiser Friedrich II* (2 vols., Leipzig, 1889-97).

TO THE THIRD AND FOURTH PERIODS.—PASTOR, *Gesch. der Päpste seit dem Ausgange des Mittelalters* (5 vols., Freiburg, 1886-1909); tr. ANTROBUS, *Hist. of the Popes from the Close of the Middle Ages*, I (St. Louis, 1902—); CREIGHTON, *History of the Papacy during the Reformation* (5 vols., London, 1882-94; new ed., 1901); RANKE, *Die römischen Päpste in den letzten 4 Jahrhunderten* (3 vols., 10th ed., Leipzig, 1900); EITEL, *Der Kirchenstaat unter Klemens V* (Berlin, 1907); WURM, *Kard. Albornoz, der 2 Begründer des Kirchenstaates* (Paderborn, 1892); FILIPPINI, *La prima legazione del card. Albornoz in Italia* in *Studi storici*, V (Rome, 1896); IDEM, *La riconquista dello stato della chiesa per opera di Egidio Albornoz* in *Studi storici*, VI, VIII (Rome, 1897, 1899); CALISSE, *Costituzione del patrimonio di S. Pietro in Tuscia nel secolo XIV* in *Archivo storico della societa Romana di storia patria* (1892); BROSCH, *Papst Julius II und die Gründung des Kirchenstaates* (Gotha, 1878).

TO THE FIFTH PERIOD.—NÜRNBERGER, *Papsttum u. Kirchenstaat im 19. Jahrh.* (3 vols., Mainz, 1897-1900); HERGENRÖTHER, *Der Kirchenstaat seit der französischen Revolution* (Freiburg, 1860); RAMONDINI, *L' Italia durante la dominazione francese* (Naples, 1882); BALDI, *Storia della rivoluzione italiana della fucilazione del re Giovacchino Murat ai moti del 31 e 48* (Florence, 1908); RINIERI, *Il congresso di Vienna e la Santa Sede* (Turin, 1904); IDEM, *La sovranità del Papa e i sovrani di tutta l' Europa nel 1814* in *Civilta catt.*, 18th series, V (1902); FARGES, *Le pouvoir temporel au début du pontificat de Grégoire XVI d'après la correspondance de Stendhal* in *Revue historique*, XLII (Paris, 1890); FARINI, *Lo stato romano dal 1814 al 1840* (4 vols., 3rd ed., Florence, 1853);

Reuchlin, *Gesch. Italiens* (4 vols., Leipzig, 1859–73); van Duerm, *Rome et la francmassonerie. Vicissitudes du pouvoir temporel des papes de 1790 à nos jours* (Lille, 1890); Crétineau-Joly, *L'église romaine en face de la révolution* (2 vols., Paris, 1861); Balleydier, *Hist. de la révolution de Rome* (2 vols., Paris, 1850); Gruber, *Mazzini, Massoneria e Rivoluzione* (Rome, 1901); Bastia, *Il dominio temporale dei Papi 1815–46* (Bologna, 1890); Lyons, *Dispatches resp. the Condition of the Papal States* (London, 1860); Ballerini, *Le prime pagine del pontificato di Papa Pio IX* (Rome, 1909); Bischoffshausen, *Die ersten Regierungsjahre des Papstes Pius IX nach den amtlichen Berichten des preussischen Gesandten Guido v. Usedom* in *Kultur* (1903); Idem, *Pius IX im Revolutionsjahr. Pius IX in Gaeta. Der Kirchenstaat in den Jahren 1851–52* (1904); del Clero, *Cospirazione romane, 1817–68* (Rome, 1899); Giovagnoli, *Pellegrini Rossi e la rivoluzione romana* (Rome, 1898); de Mevius, *Hist. de l'invasion des Etats pontificaux en 1867* (Paris, 1875); Balan, *La politica italiana dal 1863 al 1870* (Rome, 1880); de Cesare, *Roma e lo stato del Papa dal ritorno di Pio IX al 20 sett.* (Rome, 1906); Durand-Morimbau, *La question romaine, depuis le traité de Paris 1856 jusqu'au 20 sept., 1870* (Paris, 1901); Gustine, *La loi des garanties et la situation internationale de la papauté* (Paris, 1901); Vergnes, *La condition internationale de la papauté* (Paris, 1905).

Gustav Schnürer.

Station Days.—Days on which in the early Church fast was observed until the Hour of None (between twelve and three o'clock), later of Sext (nine to twelve), as distinct from the strict observance of the fast day proper until Vespers (three to six). The ancient liturgical writers commonly apply the word *statio* to fast days, but a distinction must be made between *jejunium* and *statio*. Pamelius will not admit this distinction, but Cardinal Bona is less uncompromising and admits that though *statio* is sometimes identical with *jejunium* this is not an absolute rule. The *statio* came to an end at the Hour of None, but the *jejunium* was not broken till the Hour of Vespers, which is a notable difference. However, Tertullian speaks of a less rigorous fast which was broken sooner and which he calls *semi-jejunium*. In this case the faithful did as on a day of *statio*, and the fast did not differ from the one on that day. To Tertullian *solvere stationem* meant exactly the same as *solvere jejunium*. But St. Gregory the Great designated certain churches in Rome as *stationes* and recommended that on the more solemn festivals they should be made stations (*stationes fieri*) until the Hour of Sext, and at these same churches on the appointed days (*statis diebus*) the faithful should assist at the Office. The stations have long since been abandoned and have left their trace only in the Missal, but in some instances the fast lasted longer and has been preserved even to modern times. The classic text on the *stationes* is found in Tertullian's "De Oratione" (XIV): "Similiter et stationum diebus non putant plerique sacrificiorum orationibus interveniendum quod statio solvenda sit accepto corpore Domini". (In the same way many think that on Station days we must not be present at the prayers of the sacrifices because the Station should be finished when the Lord's Body is received.) Comparison of other phrases of the same author with this passage shows that the *statio* was celebrated on Wednesday and Friday, of each week, lasting until the ninth hour. The 69th Apostolic Canon enjoins the observance of a fast on these two days.

An explanation of the fast of the *stationes* has been found in the fact that the solemnity was fixed *statis diebus*, but this is a purely verbal coincidence; and it seems difficult to find in it anything else. St. Ambrose gives a reason which may have been accepted in his time: "Our fasts", he says (Sermo XXV), "are our encampments against the attacks of the devil; they are called *stationes* because we remain standing" (*stantes*). It also seems probable that these days of fasting and prayer were characterized by endless watchings, and processions either within or around the church, when the faithful were obliged to remain standing, *stantes*, as is said in modern French in exactly the same sense, *stationner*, to stand. *Statio* became the place before which or within which the faithful walked in procession and, tired out, but always standing, sometimes leaning on a stick, assisted, before separating, at the celebration of the Liturgy. The churches to which they repaired took the name of *stationes*, though incorrectly, and the route followed to reach them became *statio ad*. . . . The tomb of a martyr became the object of a kind of pilgrimage to which the faithful went in a body, and thus arose another *statio ad*. . . . But the *martyria* alone did not attract the crowds; it became the custom to go to the celebrated basilicas, and sometimes all the clergy of a large city assembled at a certain point, probably in the vicinity of the episcopal residence, to go thence with the bishop, the patriarch, or the pope himself to the place assigned for the celebration of the Eucharist. As time went on parishes or *tituli* were formed in the cities and their grouping gave rise to vexatious questions of precedence, which were solved as well as could be by "rotation". Rome has preserved the most complete accounts of its stational churches, but we know that these celebrations also took place at Jerusalem and Constantinople. The going to the *statio* was quite a ceremony; thither were carried the sacred vessels, liturgical instruments, all that was peculiar to the service of the pope, and also, doubtless, all that would supplement the insufficient liturgical furniture of the church to which they were going. The "Liber pontificalis" states that Leo III (795) had twenty silver vessels made which were borne by acolytes in the processions to the stations. There is extant a writing called "De locis sanctis martyrum quæ sunt foris civitatis Romæ", the last chapter of which contains the list of "station basilicas" of Rome. This little document, the work of a German pilgrim, dates from the pontificate of Honorius I (625–38), but seems to be based on an older compilation dating at least from Pelagius II (579–90).

The following is the list of the station churches as it was compiled in the time of St. Gregory: Patriarchal basilicas, S. Giovanni in Laterano, S. Pietro, S. Maria Maggiore, S. Paolo Fuori le Mura, S. Lorenzo Fuori le Mura; cardinalitial titles, S. Sisto, SS. Giovanni e Paolo, SS. Quattro Coronati, S. Clemente, S. Marcellino e Pietro, S. Pietro in Vincoli, S. Silvestro ai Monti, S. Prassede, S. Pudenziana, S. Eusebio, S. Vitale, S. Susanna, S. Ciriacos, S. Marcello, S. Lorenzo in Lucina, S. Lorenzo in Damaso, S. Marco, S. Anastasia, S. Nereo e Achilleo, S. Balbina, S. Sabina, S. Prisca, S. Maria in Trastevere, S. Cecilia, S. Crisogono; diaconates (those which had been stations before they were diaconates), S. Nicolo in Carcere, SS. Cosma e Damiano, S. Maria in Via Lata, S. Maria in Porticu, S. Maria in Domnica. The number of stations is eighty-six, and, that of the churches being less, some of them have the station several times in the year. S. Sabina, the station established by Urban VIII for Ash Wednesday, is the most important of all because it was long customary for the popes to repair thither on that day to distribute the ashes to the people.

Persons desirous of gaining the station indulgences first repair to a church in the vicinity of the station in imitation of the ancient collect, or gathering of the clergy and the people, preparatory to the procession. In this church prayers are recited from the Station Manual, consisting of invocations to the Blessed Virgin and the Martyrs. Then begins the journey to the station accompanied by the recitation of the Miserere, 5 Paters, the Ave and Gloria, and the steps of the Passion of Christ. On arrival at the station church the Litany of the Saints is said with versicles and prayers, ending with the "De Profundis". The pope grants dispensations to all who are unable to go in person to the stations, such as cloistered religious, prisoners, the sick, etc., who are free to visit their own church and say the prayers prescribed. Cardinals

and their attendants and prelates of the papal court may gain the station indulgence by reciting certain prayers in their oratory. These prayers are printed annually and distributed to the cardinals and prelates who assist at the first Sistine chapel of Lent.
BURNICHON in *Etudes*, CIV (Paris, 1905), 205–24.

H. LECLERCQ.

Stations. See STATION WAYS.

Stations of the Cross. See WAY OF THE CROSS.

Statistics, ECCLESIASTICAL.—In dealing with statistics, both theoretically and practically, it is unimportant whether the men, matters, or actions subject to observation are ecclesiastical or civil. Hence the methods used for the collection and tabulation of ecclesiastical statistics ought not to differ from those employed in the preparation of general statistics, if accurate results are to be attained. The concise classification tested and adopted for general statistics will therefore serve for ecclesiastical statistics: (a) personal statistics, when men are the object of observation; (b) material statistics, when things and actions are under observation.

By the study of theoretical statistics (methods, scope, limitation, etc.) practical statistics were by degrees perfected until they reached the point where it is possible to sift thoroughly the materials gathered and to discover their connecting links. Ecclesiastical statistics need no other methods or technic. The statistics of economics sift, classify, and group all possible questions concerning economic and industrial life. Ethical statistics group and collate all manifestations, whether favourable, indifferent, or unfavourable, of the free will of man in the sphere of morals, while other branches of this science investigate clearly-defined groups of interests. Similarly, ecclesiastical statistics have their own peculiar province, though the boundaries between this and other branches of statistics cannot always be sharply defined in every direction. The method of gathering statistics concerns itself with resultant totals, in order to enable us to investigate properly the most varied conditions, events, circumstances, omissions, etc. The science of statistics handles the data thus obtained in its own peculiar way, so that we may acquire a correct knowledge of the facts of governmental, ecclesiastical, and national life. For our purpose it is irrelevant whether statistics are an exact science or not.

1.—HISTORY.—From time immemorial the city, State, and Church have called for tabulation in some form, however rough and empirical, of the statistical knowledge acquired. The fixing of the relationship of family and tribe (see the statements of the Old Testament), the just division of public burdens, the preparation of lists of men able to bear arms, and many other matters gradually led the proper authorities to make the desired records. The execution of such records continually improved, though naturally dependent on the means of intercourse and administrative powers at hand. The medieval Church, through its organs and institutions, notably influenced statistical science, however unreliable in many cases the results obtained. Later the increase of general culture, the greater freedom of intercourse, and the larger claims made by the modern State upon its citizens led through the taking of a census at indefinite periods, or for casual reasons, to a regular periodical enumeration. It has not hitherto been noticed in statistical science that the earliest of these periodical enumerations are those of the inhabitants of Rome which were annually made at Easter by the parish priests. As the parish priests were supported by the civil power, all persons residing at Rome—Christians of all kinds, Jews, Mohammedans, pagans—were counted and classified under definite heads. These very exact statistical enumerations can be traced back far into the sixteenth century and ceased only with the fall of the temporal power in 1870. Rich printed material still awaits investigation. Immense manuscript records of the Roman parishes show exactly the methods used in making these enumerations. Not until the seventeenth century do secular statistics show a periodical census; it becomes more frequent in the eighteenth century. In Prussia the first periodical census was taken in 1719. In 1755 Sweden began a comprehensive agricultural census. In 1790 the United States of America took a census of its own on a large scale (census every ten years). In the nineteenth century periodical census-taking reached its acme. In the German Empire the census of 1 December, 1871, was thorough and scientific.

It was not for statistical science, but solely for purposes of discipline and administration that the Catholic Church ordained the exact keeping of registers of all kinds, first by special laws, then by the general Tridentine law. There were baptismal registers, cemetery registers, confirmation books, etc. Sixtus V (1585–90) made it the duty of all bishops to send comprehensive reports of their dioceses at stated periods. These are of great value in the administration of the Church (see Constitution "Romanus Pontifex", of 20 December, 1585). Similarly the Apostolic nuncios were commanded to send to Rome full reports of ecclesiastical conditions in their respective territories. This original material, official in character, has never been officially elaborated on its statistical side. Of late years attempts have been made, solely for the sake of its historical interest, to publish it (Schmidlin, Pasture, Friedensburg, and others); so far, however, no comprehensive statistical tabulation of the material has appeared. With episcopal reports as a basis, it would not be difficult to produce a general ecclesiastical manual of statistics; attention is particularly called to this continuous authoritative source of ecclesiastical statistics. In the "Acta Apostolicæ Sedis" (1910), pp. 1 and 17, appeared a new and exhaustive list of queries for these reports. Other Roman authorities, particularly the Congregation of Propaganda, have likewise collected valuable material, intended almost entirely for disciplinary and administrative purposes. Access to these statistical sources is rather difficult, though in course of time they may be thrown open. Mention should also be made here of the very valuable reports sent to Rome for many centuries by the heads of orders from all the respective provinces of their orders, but these reports have been made accessible to students only in a restricted way.

It is evident from these and other facts not here mentioned, that the history of ecclesiastical statistics is of great interest, even though these materials were not collected to serve the ends of scientific statistics. The missionaries were probably the first to present ecclesiastical conditions in a more or less crudely digested statistical form; it was necessary for them to show their patrons in what way the given alms had been used. The first imperfect attempts to present ecclesiastical statistics in a periodical way are found in old works containing collections of missionary reports.

Among those who contributed to develop statistics as a science special mention is due to Hermann Conring (1606–81), professor at the University of Helmstädt; Gottfried Aschenwall (1719–72), professor at Göttingen; Johann Peter Süssmilch (1707–67), superintendent and consistorial councillor in Prussia, who obtained largely from ecclesiastical registers the material for his epoch-making work: "Die göttliche Ordnung in den Veränderungen des menschlichen Geschichtes"; also Quételet (1796–1874), a Belgian, who must be regarded as the father of moral statistics, although the philosophical basis of his theory should be rejected as wrong. In the last fifty years so many distinguished writers in most civilized countries have given their attention to the establishment and maintenance of statistics that we cannot mention even the most noted of them. Readers are referred to the work of Mayr, "Statistik und Gesellschaftslehre" (1895–97).

Among the difficulties that obstruct the advantageous and exhaustive collection of statistics by private individuals are modern intercourse and industrial life, the highly specialized development of governmental, parliamentary, and municipal administration, and the military organization of most civilized countries. Statistics had first to be put under control of the State, and then to be taken up by the municipal and county authorities. Thus began the statistical bureaux aided by government authority in their investigations. On the other hand their tasks, serving purely practical ends, are exactly laid down for them, without any regard to larger scientific demands. Nevertheless the labours of the official statistical bureaux are satisfactory and valuable. Official ecclesiastical bureaux for the collection of ecclesiastical statistics are almost entirely lacking, although numerous suggestions and propositions have been made for such.

A clear distinction must be made between statistics concerning religions and ecclesiastical statistics. The classification of mankind according to religions pertains to general statistics, i. e. so far as the civilized countries of the whole world are concerned (see STATISTICS OF RELIGIONS). Hitherto only a few countries, and these for trivial reasons, have failed to ascertain exactly this important fact. The religious classification being made, then, ecclesiastical statistics are the work of those who hold the Christian faith; the first task of these statistics is to make a further classification of Christian denominations. After this each denomination makes such collections of statistics as enable the investigation (so far as possible) of all the diverse relations of the individual, the parish, and the whole body to the denominations, ecclesiastical authorities, institutions, etc. It can, therefore, be said that the statistics of religions separate mankind into groups, and that ecclesiastical statistics in the strict sense classify the great Christian group into subdivisions; that in these subdivisions religious statistics investigate methodically all religious and ecclesiastical events capable of being considered statistically, make clear their characteristic criteria, and lay bare the connexion between cause and effect. In addition to questions strictly religious and ecclesiastical, Church statistics should include all those other domains in which a Christian population and the ecclesiastical authorities should be interested, as: schools, charities, religious associational life, missions, and many other matters. Ecclesiastical geography, topography, and similar topics are naturally excluded from the survey of ecclesiastical statistics, even though they necessarily make much use of statistics.

In ecclesiastical statistics, as in every statistical collection of aggregates, the reliability of the surveys depends upon the excellence of the preparation and execution of the undertaking. The most essential preliminary conditions for a well-managed statistical survey are: determination of the period of time and extent of space to be covered; selection of the collectors of the statistics and their procedure; the preparation of clear, simple, comprehensive questions for the statistical inquiry-papers. Next come revision, supplementary additions, and expert arrangement of the original material. Third, one of the known methods of performing such work must be selected, as the system of small strokes, that of small blanks to be filled, or an electrical counting-machine, and the respective divisions of the work must be closely scrutinized. The most common way of presenting results is to exhibit the matter in the form of a table, the figures of which can have a qualified or an unconditional value. Particularly clear results are obtained by the calculation of averages and by relative numbers; their scientific valuation, however, is subject to certain precautions. It is easily understood that the full value of many results can be recognized only when they are placed in suitable relation to other results. Of late, the use of the graphical method has somewhat increased in ecclesiastical statistics, while, so far as I know, the plastic method has not yet been tried. Diagrams (geometrical figures of all kinds) have been profitably used; ecclesiastical statistics also use what are called cartograms, or coloured representations of geographical surfaces. Occasionally, use has been made of various combinations of these forms of presentation, the reading of which is easy to the practised eye. Such presentations of statistical results in popular forms were employed in secular statistics on a large scale for the first time by Hickmann of Vienna in his various pocket atlases, of which large editions were printed and sold. While it is evident that Catholics cannot concede to statistical laws the character of unchangeable natural laws, ecclesiastical statistics show that the absolutely free will of man is indeed influenced by passions, customs, environment, education, character, etc., but can never be entirely annulled.

Ecclesiastical statistics have not shared so far in the benefits of international coöperation in the treatment of statistical questions. Not even in the larger civilized countries has it been possible to introduce uniform, and universally observed principles. At the general congress of German Catholics held at Osnabrück in 1901, the present writer urged the establishment of an international bureau of ecclesiastical statistics. The proposition was received enthusiastically, but nothing further has been done. On account of the large demands now made on ecclesiastical life everywhere, it is imperatively necessary that the question then discussed and afterwards dropped should receive more practical consideration.

If the total of Protestant statistical work and that of the Catholic Church be compared, it may be said that both bodies have accomplished about the same and with the same success. If the work of the two bodies be compared in individual countries or in large sections of a country, the result is sometimes favourable to Protestant statistics, sometimes to Catholic. Differences of considerable importance are to be found in the methods of carrying on the work, so that the requirements of comparative statistics cannot, very often, be met. This is most perceptible in the views on which are based the methods of collecting aggregates in missionary statistics, e. g. what constitutes a catechumen, an ordained missionary, and similar questions. Since this article does not propose to go more fully into Protestant statistics, those desiring to learn more on that head are referred to the bibliography at the end.

Catholic Church statistics can be classified in the most varied manner. The following classification is in accordance with the most important principles:—

I. Arranged according to the source of collection: (a) official statistics, when they are classified for official purposes by the central administration of the Church, or by metropolitans, bishops, or parish priests in their official capacity; (b) associational statistics, when orders, sodalities, associations, or parts of such organizations are accustomed to gather statistics in any manner for their own needs; (c) private statistics, when individuals or groups of such collect and digest statistical data for scientific or practical ends.

II. Classified according to geographical area: (a) statistics of the world, for all or any category of church questions that can be statistically considered; (b) national statistics, when the above-mentioned statistics refer to a country or an essential part of it; (c) provincial and diocesan statistics, when the observation of aggregates is confined to a church province or diocese; (d) parish statistics, when the statistical investigations refer only to a parish; (e) associational statistics, when the geographical territory claimed by the members of a society as the field of their work is investigated.

III. Classified according to the subject-matter and extent of the inquiries: (a) general statistics for the whole world; (b) world-wide statistics for special questions; (c) partial statistics for special questions.

Without considering further classifications it may be said that by far the weakest point in the first group is official statistics.

If Catholic church statistics are to be complete, the subject-matter should include all persons, objects, and actions connected directly or indirectly with the Church, its entire organization, its authorities, and all its various regulations. Statistics of this exhaustive character do not now exist nor will it be possible in the near future to obtain such, even if it be conceded that the carrying out of such a task be possible. What exists is the tabulation of some of the most important ecclesiastical objects and persons of the Catholic world; these statements, however, are not official but solely the result of private industry. Consequently, the new statistical tables (Baumgarten and Krose) only claim to have the value of the material on which they are based. For earlier general statistical work see Streit, "Führer durch die deutsche katholische Missionsliteratur" (Freiburg, 1911), 99–102. Both authors were but seldom in a position where they could either obtain an enumeration themselves or always fill out the gaps in the available material.

Theoretically it must be conceded that the central administration of the Church has the necessary means and power to attain in time an exhaustive, absolutely correct description of all the possessions of the Church in the world. Practically no use has been made of this power, for the "Gerarchia cattolica", now the "Annuario pontificio" (1912), is not a statistical work. Leaving out scattered and unimportant statistical researches made by this or that Roman administrative board, the Congregation of Propaganda alone has given official attention to statistics. The result of the inquiries of the congregation in the regions under its care are seen in a work which appears at irregular intervals, "Missiones Catholicæ cura S. Congregationis de Propaganda Fide descriptæ". This bulky work (last edition, Rome, 1907) serves, indeed, the purposes of an historical and statistical work of modest pretensions, but it lacks that scientific exactness which the compilation of modern statistics demands. It is a striking fact that the German periodical, "Die katholische Missionen" of Freiburg is often able to make statements more really exact than this official manual of the Congregation of Propaganda. The reviews of the irregularly issued volumes of this work often point out clearly enough its very considerable defects, but no essential improvement in the collection or treatment of the matter has followed.

The English-speaking branches of the Catholic Church have the best official statistical publications for entire countries and continents. Without exception they all issue year-books which contain the most important records more or less complete. Although the statistics are seldom thoroughly worked over in these publications, yet the statistician does not lay great stress on this, because he can do it himself, and is satisfied if he can get the raw material fairly complete. The best of these annual publications is "The Official Catholic Directory and Clergy List", which was formerly published at Milwaukee, Wisconsin, now at New York. The publication of this year-book is a private undertaking, but in reality, in a certain sense, it is an official ecclesiastical work, because the publisher is almost entirely dependent on the co-operation of the episcopal authorities of the United States. It must, however, be said that the episcopal chanceries measure the very important figures of the increase of Catholics in the individual dioceses more by estimate than as a result of detailed information. Arthur Preuss, in his "Catholic Fortnightly Review", has often pointed out this unfortunate defect, without, however, any great improvement in this regard being attained. It should be said that the difficulties encountered in determining exactly the number of Catholics in a diocese are especially great in the United States. The same applies to the statistics of schools and school-children, which must be characterized as inadequate. Most excellent, on the other hand, are the carefully revised records of the number of priests and their addresses at the time of publication. The statements of this year-book concerning other American countries are also serviceable, although not quite so copious and reliable.

The second place belongs to "The Irish Catholic Directory and Almanac, with Complete Directory in English" (Dublin). This excellent year-book not only contains the usual general statistical statements, but also includes well-arranged tables hardly to be found elsewhere. Especially well presented are the losses in population so characteristic of Ireland. There is some lack of uniformity in the statements.

"The Catholic Directory, Ecclesiastical Register and Almanac" (London) is an official annual publication for the Catholic Church in England. Although it would be desirable to have a greater uniformity in the contributions of the different dioceses, yet the copious material offered is a cause of great satisfaction. In view of the difficulties attending the problem of pastoral care in the large cities of England, it is at times a cause of surprise that the statistics presented can be so exact. The fourth year-book to be noticed is described in its title as official: "The Catholic Directory for the Clergy and Laity in Scotland. By Authority of the Archbishops and Bishops of Scotland" (Aberdeen). It is a great credit to the small body of Catholics in Scotland that they have an official year-book of their own; at the same time it reflects on those countries which, with many millions of Catholics, have not yet made equal progress in this direction. Even in this carefully-prepared annual there are some records that require more careful supervision. The fifth place is to be assigned to an annual year-book, issued at Madras for the whole of south-eastern Asia, and formerly entitled "The Madras Catholic Directory and General Annual Register", but now (1912) "The Catholic Directory of India", a work of great industry. If in a number of particulars the other year-books were taken as models, this meritorious publication could be brought to a high standard of excellence. The typographical work is somewhat poor, but that matters little. The sixth place belongs to the year-book: "Australasian Catholic Directory containing the Ordo Divini Officii, the Fullest Ecclesiastical Information and an Alphabetical List of the Clergy of Australasia" (Sydney). The organization of the church provinces is well given in this work, but the accounts of the individual missionary districts, especially of those on the mainland, are not complete. The list of year-books issued in English-speaking countries may be closed with "The Catholic Directory of British South Africa" (Capetown). This offers only a limited amount of data to the statistician, still a very praiseworthy effort is evident to develop gradually the contents of the directory.

There is an evident difference in the value of the works just mentioned, but that does not detract from the fact that this group of church year-books presents as a whole a very imposing piece of work. The annual publication of such volumes is made possible by the aid of advertisements which enable the publishers not only to cover the heavy expenses, but also to obtain a moderate return for their work. This points out clearly the way in which other countries can reach the same goal.

Each year the "Annuaire pontifical catholique", edited by Battandier (Paris), offers a great variety of useful statistical information which can be found elsewhere with difficulty or not at all; it contains also many historically and otherwise instructive articles and other valuable ecclesiastical information. For a number of years there has been published in Italy the comprehensive work "Annuario ecclesiastico", which presents the conditions of the Church in Italy with great minuteness, if not always with clearness and reliability. The large amount of matter that may be drawn from its records is shown in the present writer's volume, "Kirchliche Statistik" (Wörishofen, 1905). It should be said that the editors make every effort to overcome the inequalities still to be found in the contributions. The material offered by the "Annuario" for countries outside of Italy has no claim to consideration. If it were possible to develop this second part, so that it should be unexceptionable, there would be the beginning of a statistical handbook for the entire Catholic world. In that case the Italian part would have to be somewhat abridged, and the whole work divided into two volumes. The "Annuaire complet du clergé belge et répertoire des établissements religieux" (Brussels) is well arranged and copious in matter. It would have been well to include in it also the statistics concerning the Congo. The same excellent standard is maintained by the year-book issued in Holland, the "Pius-Almanak". Besides information regarding the Church there are also literary contributions, while the Dutch colonies receive suitable mention. Up to 1904 two year-books were issued in France, of which, unfortunately, the larger and better, the "Clergé français" (Tours) ceased with the publication of 1904. The volumes of this annual still have a great and permanent value, because they have presented in a manner that is absolutely a model the life of the French orders. The second publication, "La France ecclésiastique", has existed for sixty years and meets more modest statistical demands. As to the two Spanish hand-books, "Anuario eclesiástico de España" and "Guia eclesiástica de España", no recent information is forthcoming, and it is doubtful if new editions have appeared during recent years. The Hungarian year-book and schematism "Évkönyve és Névtára" is a successful work in which much industry has been displayed, as far as the specific Hungarian records are concerned. The statistical data concerning other hierarchies have been obtained at second and third hand.

The small book, "Taschenkalender für den katholischen Klerus" seeks, more or less successfully, to collect the data for Germany, and the "Frommes Kalender für den katholischen Klerus Oesterreich-Ungarns" undertakes to do the same for the Austro-Hungarian monarchy. Neither is suited in any way to the importance of the hierarchies of both countries. The excellent "Kirchliches Handbuch", edited by Krose, issued by Herder since 1908, gives full information regarding the affairs of the Church in Germany; every effort is made to improve and develop the work. (For fuller discussion of ecclesiastical statistics in Germany, see below.)

As the majority of Catholics in Canada are of French descent and still speak French, especially in the Province of Quebec, the Canadian year-book is published in French; it is entitled "Le Canada ecclésiastique". The book is accurately and carefully prepared and does good service. However, nearly all its statistical records are to be found in the "Official Directory" of the United States, so that it is seldom necessary to consult the Canadian work. There are a few other smaller publications which need hardly be enumerated here. The foregoing description will serve as a sufficiently exhaustive summary of the statistical authorities of official or semi-official character. It should also be said that in writings on the subject reference is made to a kind of general statistical outline for the whole of Portugal, but when the statistical tables for the present writer's large work, "Die katholische Kirche unserer Zeit und ihre Diener in Wort und Bild", were being prepared it was not possible to find a copy of this Portuguese publication. Neither is it known whether any general ecclesiastico-statistical work has been published in the South American countries, except the "Guía eclesiástica de la Republica Argentina". Such compendiums would be all the more desirable, because the zealous activity of Pius X in increasing the number of ecclesiastical provinces and dividing dioceses has greatly increased the difficulties in determining from a distance the statistics of these territories. (See summaries in "Theologische Revue", 1904, Nos. 4, 5, 12, 15, 16, and in "Literarische Rundschau", Nos. 7, 8.)

After the year-books for entire countries or continents come the diocesan compendiums, so far as the contents of these exceed purely liturgical information in reference to the observances of the church year, commands or prohibitions for the clergy, and similar administrative matter. Excellent samples of general outlines, and large historical and statistical records are to be found in Bavaria, Austria, Hungary, as well as a number in Germany outside of Bavaria and in Switzerland. They are model diocesan compendiums and are of great value to the statistician. Although all are not issued regularly, yet so large a proportion are published annually that they can easily be placed among the ecclesiastical year-books. Publications of the same character containing serviceable matter also appear in some other countries, but copies are hard to find, so that it is impossible to present an exact summary. Official compendiums of this kind should be issued, if not in all dioceses, at least in all ecclesiastical provinces. The aims of the *Landesdirektorien*, or government directories, are frequently other than those of ecclesiastico-statistical compendiums, from which many more details of their subjects are expected. (See Brüning, "Bemerkungen zu den Handbüchern und Schematismen der deutschen Diözesen" in "Literarische Beilage der Kölnischen Volkszeitung", No. 42, 19 October, 1911; Liese, "Die Diözesanschematismen", ibid., No. 44, 2 Nov., 1911.) Some years ago, when, owing to the pressure of modern conditions, the former customary general parochial supervision was replaced by the supervision of the individual members of the parish, all ways and methods were sought to reach the individual in some practical way, especially in the large cities. This led to the excellent proposal to issue periodical parish papers, so as to give the members of the parish all the essential facts of the parochial life. This method has been successfully tried in a good many places in Austria, Germany, England, and, here and there, in the United States. In these papers, which appear at regular or irregular intervals, statistical records and reports collected by the parochial authorities are published with constantly increasing frequency. These statements have in all instances attracted much attention and have often developed new interest in the parish and its religious services. If this good custom were introduced everywhere, it would soon be easy to draw up a really lifelike presentation of the Church in every diocese.

After this enumeration of the various kinds of statistical works prepared by the church authorities, or at least liberally aided by them, it must be noted that in not a few countries the government authorities collect information concerning ecclesiastical matters or present, in the national statistical works, first-hand material which is exceedingly valuable to the ecclesiastical statistician. He is, indeed, frequently dependent upon them, because these figures are not to be found anywhere else. In addition the "Hofkalender" or "Almanach de Gotha", as it is called in the French edition, gives statistics of all kinds, the exactness of which may generally be relied upon. This almanac is well known throughout the world. The state directories and the "Hofkalender", which are frequently the authoritative and the only sources for the statistics of religion, are sometimes also important sources for ecclesiastical statistics. While formerly the public had but little interest in exact data concerning the great Catholic orders, there has been a change in the present era. The latest statistics collected are published more or less regularly and attract much attention. These figures are based on thorough investigations, which make it possible at regular intervals to offer an exact summary of the growth and development of the respective orders. Only a few, however, of these important statistical records are published, and only in isolated instances are they to be found by the laity in the book trade or elsewhere. Two important works belong to this class, "Schematismus totius ordinis Fratrum Minorum" (Assisi) and "SS. Patriarchæ Benedicti Familæ confœderatæ" (Rome). Along with these are excellent outlines for the congregations. General statistics are drawn from the catalogues of each Jesuit province which are at the disposal of those who desire to know, while the catalogues themselves are very seldom given to the public. It is not possible to say, from the only—and very scanty—statistics of the Dominican Order known to the present writer, whether, besides the enumeration of provinces, congregations, monasteries, and members of the order, other statistical work is also undertaken. The Capuchins publish statistical summaries in their "Analecta ordinis", of which one volume is issued annually. The further statistical summaries of other orders need not be mentioned here; for these the reader is referred to the respective articles in THE CATHOLIC ENCYCLOPEDIA. There are only a few statistical outlines of monasteries for other countries. The year-books mentioned above give copious records of the monasteries for both sexes in the territories covered at the time of publication.

A very important section of ecclesiastical statistics is that comprising the statistics of the missionary labours of the Catholic Church. As already mentioned, this branch of statistical work was the earliest undertaken and the most has been done in it. Consequently it is in this field that we have the most thorough and complete statistics. What the Propaganda has, in this respect, done officially has already been noted. The statistical labours of the missionaries have, from crude beginnings, developed in the present time to imposing performances. It is not, however, meant that there could not be improvements and additions in many particulars: above all there might be greater uniformity in the *questionnaires* and clearer, presentation of the headings to be conveyed. The immense amount of material, brought together by individual missionaries, by orders and congregations, and from other sources, has of late been critically examined and collated, largely by German and French scholars. For further particulars of this collation see MISSIONS, CATHOLIC, where a copious bibliography is given; see also the work of Streit mentioned above, on the bibliography of German Catholic missions.

Much alarm was expressed by the timid at the time when the statistics of charitable work were first demanded, when the opinion was maintained that a statistical record should be kept of needy persons and applicants for help, and a combined organization of charitable work was demanded. The fear was expressed that the noble, world-embracing conception of Christian love would suffer from the business-like

XIV.—18

treatment of it that would be necessary. Nothing of this kind has happened; the result of the new method has rather been to add new and enthusiastic members to charitable associations, because each could see clearly that the impelling force of Christian charity had really increased through the unity of organization and the labours of statisticians. The statistics which reveal a good, a merely even, or a poor ratio between relief and need, on the one hand, and between the work done and the expenditures, on the other, make possible a more exact use or a greater output of the power latent in the forces in question. Another, and very important, point is that exact statistical records covering large territories facilitate the prevention of unwise expenditures. From the present writer's experience it may be asserted that lack of knowledge of organizations still capable of doing work has led to the establishment of new ones on much the same lines for which no need existed. The fact that those desiring to inaugurate charitable work of a certain kind did not know the existence near by of organizations with the same object has, unfortunately, been at times the reason for a needless expenditure of money which was far more imperatively needed for other purposes. It may also be noted here that the statistics of the actual results are effectual to inspire to greater endeavours those who co-operate in the work.

The idea of combining all Catholic charitable organizations was first realized on a large scale in the celebrated charity organization society (*Charitasverband*) established in Germany in 1897. This was followed in Austria by an imperial organization for all the charitable societies in the monarchy. For further particulars concerning the two organizations see "Kirchliches Handlexikon", s. v. "Charitas", where a bibliography is also given. For the United States a beginning of such general organization was made in the First National Conference of Catholic Charities held at the Catholic University, Washington, in 1910. An exceedingly valuable work is done in many countries—as Belgium, Bavaria, Prussia, Austria—and in many cities and provinces by the preparation of statistical summaries of all charitable associations with which Catholics are connected. Such handbooks of Christian benevolence save much time and labour; they show exactly what exists and also make existing gaps equally plain. In addition to this is the work done by the secretaries of the charity organization, who are able from their records to distinguish between the really needy and worthy and the professional beggars. Thus it is evident that a comprehensive statistical grasp of Christian benevolence has already been exceedingly useful and beneficial, and will be still more so in the future. But, while these two facts by no means, exhaust the list of advantages. a further enumeration cannot be entered upon here.

Wherever Catholic schools are permitted in addition to state schools, the number of these schools, of their teachers and scholars, and the expenditure on the same form an important branch of ecclesiastical statistics. Figures are far more merciless than the most severe denunciation of the indolent. In addition to the importance of such statistics for the elementary schools, statistics of the middle schools and universities show whether any, and how many, Catholics receive a liberal education, or are studying for technical callings, or pursue literary courses, and also make clear whether the figures are in proportion to the Catholic population. For if a deficiency in Catholic intelligence appears, because Catholics do not send their sons in sufficient numbers to the higher schools, leaders will surely be lacking to the Catholics in the next generation.

Ecclesiastical statistics also include the statistics of Catholic associations, whether purely religious, social, political, religious-political, or of any other kind. They show whether the individual societies are sufficiently developed and whether they are working with success or not. As regards the reports of the boards of managers of these societies, it may be said that, as all societies have more or less to do with money, it is desirable that the total amount of money given for the purposes of the society from its foundation should be counted up and that this total sum should appear in the annual report together with the amounts for the year, so that the reader of the report may be able to estimate the whole work done by the society. If the society has other works besides the collection and disbursement of money, these should also be presented in condensed form from the time of the establishment of the society. Once the labour of collecting these statistics for the entire period of the existence of the society is done, it is only necessary after that to add to these totals the records of the year just closed.

The brief outline given above by no means exhausts the possible applications of ecclesiastical statistics. Each one must apply the principles here explained to spheres not yet under statistical examination in order to gain a full realization of the great usefulness and absolute necessity of thorough statistical records. When the statistical work of the State takes up ecclesiastical affairs, it is not necessary in every case to reject it at once. There are, however, undoubtedly affairs of the Church which are outside of all statistical investigation on the part of the State. The State can successfully collect statistics of the external activities of the Church in training and education, associational life, and similar branches. In my opinion the church authorities of all ranks have in such case the imperative duty of collecting for their respective departments all those statistics which are adapted to present an image of the labours of the Church in each field. The uses of the often difficult and prolonged computations are evident. The filling out of exact statistical papers is of great value for all leaders of the Catholic people, showing who are really Catholics. This applies just as much to what is purely religious as to what pertains to charitable, social, and associational life. Comparative statistics make it possible to detect failures from the figures, and also to find out what fields it is absolutely necessary to cultivate, what have not been worked at all or worked but little. In the same way the successes are as easily to be seen from the figures and greatly increase the desire to go on working and the joy in the work.

As daily experience shows, the sum total of the statistical records of the Church is of great importance for the reputation of the Church. The opponents of the Church take more interest in its statistics than many Catholics. When, therefore, from the carelessness of those whose duty it is, the statistical presentation is an imperfect one, the importance of the Church is greatly damaged, because its opponents can conclude, with apparent right, that the Church is absolutely unable to produce effects in this or that domain, or else labours with very little success. As an example of what is needed in this direction, it may be well to notice here a brochure recently published by Bishop Canevin of Pittsburgh, "An Examination, Historical and Statistical, into Losses and Gains of the Catholic Church in the United States" (1912). The frequent unedifying controversies with opponents, who fall back on our scanty statistical figures, show that every force should be strained to produce an exact, complete, satisfactory statistical survey of the Church. Father Alberts says in "Literarische Rundschau", No. 8 (1905): "Like all statistical material, the protocols of visitations are a two-edged sword in the hands of the user, according as he wishes to use them for a good or undesirable end. As a rule the latter aim is the one sought, as it is seldom or not at all customary to keep a record of good works. If, therefore, any association in State or Church is not willing to yield the records of its inner administration to unrestrained misuse, it must itself undertake the publication of such statistics themselves in order to set the user on the right road by offering the necessary explanations."

It is not necessary in an article on church statistics to give the titles of the numberless works in which the results of these computations are arranged and given. These results have been published in various articles of THE CATHOLIC ENCYCLOPEDIA treating matters in which church statistics were necessarily referred to. Chief among these are the numerous geographical, ecclesiastical, social, and historical articles, which give the bibliographies of the respective subjects. Besides the books and treatises mentioned in the course of this article, it is only necessary to mention a few publications which treat church statistics, their uses, and necessity theoretically: *Kirchliches Handlexikon*, s. v. *Statistik*; BAUMGARTEN, *Kirchliche Statistik* (Wörishofen, 1905); *Historisch-politische Blätter*, CXXXIV, 831; *Germania* (Berlin, 1905), No. 5, 6 January, in regard to the question of the establishment of a German bureau for church statistics; *Augsburger Postzeitung* (1905), No. 49, 1 March; *Zur kirchlichen Statistik* in *Kölnische Volkszeitung* (Cologne, 1905), No. 63, 22 January; *Neues vom Gebiete der kirchlichen Statistik* in No. 272 (1905), 3 April; *Berliner protestantisch-kirchliche Statistik* (1905), No. 600, 22 July.

PAUL MARIA BAUMGARTEN.

IN GERMANY, beginning with the earliest years of the twentieth century, an active movement took shape towards the creation of a general and uniform body of ecclesiastical statistics. At the Forty-eighth Congress of the Catholics of Germany at Osnabrück the erection of a German bureau for ecclesiastical statistics was warmly recommended as a preliminary step towards an international institute for ecclesiatical statistics. This resolution has, indeed, not been carried out as yet; but the endeavours of the Catholic Congresses have not remained without result. The want of universal ecclesiastical statistics was to some degree supplied by a book on general ecclesiastical statistics for Germany which appeared in 1908 under the title of "Kirchliches Handbuch"; a second volume was published in 1909 and a third in 1911. It gives statistical information from governmental and ecclesiastical official publications dealing with the movement of the Catholic population of Germany. It includes also the number of priests and of candidates for the priesthood, statistics of religious orders, ecclesiastical action, and the position of Catholics regarding national education and morality. The manual, moreover, gives information on the organization of the whole Church in general and of the Church of Germany in particular, on ecclesiastical legislation and decisions, on the social and philanthropic activity of Catholics, the position of the Church in other countries, and Catholic missions among the heathen. The church authorities, too, favoured a further development of ecclesiastical statistics, both by recommending the "Kirchliches Handbuch", and especially by drawing up a *questionnaire* satisfying every scientific requirement. Whether these efforts of the church authorities will produce the desired effect depends on the response they meet with from governmental and municipal statistical bureaus and from registrars' offices; for without such co-operation the proportion of baptisms to births, of marriages before a minister of the Church to those before a registrar, and of ecclesiastical funerals to deaths cannot be ascertained.

The Protestant State Churches of Germany followed the example of the Catholics with regard to the keeping of parish-registers. But the results were published only in the nineteenth century, especially during the last decades. This is chiefly due to the "Kirchliches Jahrbuch", edited by J. Schneuder, which has been published for thirty-eight years; statistical records of individual churches, however, and a general account published in 1862 by the statistician Zeller of Würtemberg (Zur kirchlichen Statistik des evangelischen Deutschland im Jahr 1862) preceded the publication of the "Jahrbuch". The Church Conference of Eisenbach (now "Deutsche evangelische Kirchenkonferenz"), in which all the Protestant Churches of Germany are represented, has formed a special statistical commission which, since 1880, has annually published the "Statistischen Mitteilungen aus den deutschen evangelischen Landeskirchen", a table of the baptisms, marriages, funerals, confirmations, communicants, losses, and conversions within the states of the German Empire and the provinces of Prussia. These statistics are accompanied by the corresponding figure of the movement of the Protestant population, which are for this purpose placed at disposal of the conference by the governmental statistical bureaus. An official centre for ecclesiastical statistics has, however, not yet been erected by the Protestant Churches of Germany.

GERMAN DIOCESAN FORM OF STATISTICAL TABLE.
1. Chief Churches of the Parish..........................
2. Dependent Churches................................
3. Public Chapels....................................
   Church Institutions for:—
4.   (a) Teaching...................................
5.   (b) Care of Orphans............................
6.   (c) Communicants..............................
7.   (d) Sickness, Insanity and Incurables............
8.   (e) the Care of the Poor and Old................
9.   (f) Other Purposes............................
10. Parish Priests....................................
11. Other Secular Priests.............................
12. Other Priests belonging to Orders..................
13. Houses of Male Orders............................
14. Members of Orders in them.......................
    Chief Occupation of These Regulars Consists in:—
15.   (a) Cure of Souls, at...........................
16.   (b) Contemplative Life, at......................
17.   (c) Training and Education, at..................
18.   (d) Christian Charities, at......................
19. Houses of Female Orders..........................
20. Members of Orders in them.......................
    Chief Occupation of these Orders Consists in
21.   (a) Contemplative Life, at......................
22.   (b) Training and Education, at..................
23.   (c) Christian Charities, at......................
24. Members of Parish on 1 January, 19—..............
25. Marriages of Catholic Couples....................
26. Catholic Betrothals of Catholic Couples............
    Mixed Marriages
27.   (a) Catholic Groom............................
28.   (b) Catholic Bride.............................
    Catholic Betrothals for Couples unlike in Faith
29.   (a) Catholic Groom............................
30.   (b) Catholic Bride.............................
31. Living Births from Marriages of Catholics..........
32. Baptisms from purely Catholic Marriages..........
33. Living Births from Mixed Catholic Marriages........
34. Catholic Baptisms from Mixed Catholic Marriages...
35. Living Births from unmarried Catholic Mothers.....
36. Catholic Baptisms of Children of unmarried Catholic Mothers.....................................
37. Deceased Catholics..............................
38. Burials by the Church............................
39. Conversions to the Catholic Church, Total.........
40. Conversions from Protestantism..................
41. Of these, Children under 14 Years................
42. Return of those who had withdrawn from the Church...
43. Communions....................................
44. Of these, Easter Communions are................

Valuable material for ecclesiastical statistics is also offered by many of the German diocesan year-books. They are limited, however, to statements concerning the particular diocese and have, therefore, only special interest. The directories issued in English, as Kenedy, "Official Catholic Directory", "The Catholic Directory" (London) "Australian Catholic Directory", "Madras Directory", "Catholic Directory of British South Africa", have the advantage over the German works of this class, that they give information of ecclesiastical affairs for a much larger part of a country. In particular, the "Official Catholic Directory" contains much matter and is an indispensable reference-work for anyone who wishes to gain information concerning the affairs of the Church in the United States and Canada. The statements in these directories are generally limited to the names of the dignitaries of the Church and the priests, to the church institutions, schools, and monastic houses. The statistical records in the British and American directories are scanty and are not generally collected on a uniform plan. There is an almost entire lack of statistical records as to ecclesiastical action, the receiving of the sacraments, and the proportion of Catholic baptisms to births from Catholic and mixed marriages, of religious betrothals to Catholic and mixed marriages, burials with the rites of the Church to the deaths among Catholics.

It would be a good thing if the uniform table of ecclesiastical statistics which has been introduced of late in all the German dioceses were adopted by Catholics of other countries, as it meets all scientific demands. A translation of this table is given above. In German dioceses there are two query-sheets: Sheet A, which contains the queries given above, is sent by the episcopal curia to all the parish priests of the diocese. Before a definite date Sheet A must be filled out by the parish priest and sent to the dean, who is to examine it as to completeness and correctness and is to enter and summarize by a definite date all the events of his deanery in the blank provided for the district supervised by a dean (Sheet B); it is then sent to the episcopal curia, where the statistics for the entire diocese are put together.

NEHER, *Kirchliche Geographie und Statistik*, I–II (Ratisbon, 1864 and 1865); KARL VOM HL. ALOYS, *Statistisches Jahrbuch der Kirche*, I–II (Ratisbon, 1860 and 1862); PIEPER, *Kirchliche Statistik Deutschlands* (Freiburg and Tübingen, 1899); BAUMGARTEN, *Das Wirken der katholischen Kirche auf dem Erdenrund* (Munich, 1901); IDEM, *Kirchliche Statistik: Drei Aufsätze* (Wörischofen, 1905); KROSE. *Kirchliches Handbuch*, I–III (Freiburg, 1908–1911).

H. A. KROSE.

Statistics of Religions.—I. DEFINITION.—This study concerns itself with religious bodies, the number of their members, and their distribution over various countries. In a wider sense the numerical account of the external manifestations of religious life also belongs to the same study, but of late it has been customary to comprise this latter group of facts under the designation of "Ecclesiastical Statistics" and to treat of them separately. As the whole field has only in the last decades been thoroughly worked, language has not as yet afforded a clear distinction between these terms. Practical reasons, however, speak in favour of such a distinction, and therefore we retain it in the present article, and treat ecclesiastical statistics separately (see STATISTICS, ECCLESIASTICAL).

II. HISTORICAL DEVELOPMENT.—The first attempts to determine exactly the number of members of a religious body are found in the records of the Jesuit and Franciscan missionaries of the sixteenth and seventeenth centuries. But they only give the number of the Christians, and not that of the adherents of the indigenous religions in the respective countries. Dating from the eighteenth century, some accounts indeed of the various religious systems and their spread are extant, but they only mention the countries over which the respective religions extended; as to the number of their followers we possess but scattered data even of that period, and no comprehensive and comparative records. It was only in the nineteenth century that an effort was made to distinguish statistically, according to religion, the entire population of the earth. The accounts given in Table I are the most accurate.

In all these calculations the total of the earth's population is considerably underrated. The numbers of the non-Christians are evidently only vague estimates without any solid foundation, as is clear from the round numbers and the great differences between the various estimates. Regarding Christians the computation is indeed more accurate, but very far from the exactness requisite for scientific research. Even the attempts made by geographers, such as Hübner, Peterman, Kolb, between 1850 and 1880, do not show any essential progress.

Statistics of religions that should come up to the requirements of science would be possible only if for every country the number of members of the various religious bodies were ascertained from reliable sources, and the totals arrived at from the individual results were tabulated. Average estimates that extend over entire groups of countries without definite indications of the numbers of the population and its distribution with regard to religious denominations are of little use for statistical investigations. Detailed religious statistics, dealing distinctly with all countries of the earth, were for the first time presented by Fournier de Flaix to the second congress of the International Institute of Statistics, held in Paris, in 1889. His example was followed by F. Von Juraschek (1898), H. Zeller, and H. A. Krose, S.J. (1903). The figures given by Fournier de Flaix mostly correspond to the of millions of inhabitants, Buddhism, Confucianism, and ancestor-worship cannot be sharply separated from one another; they are at times professed and practised by the same individual. It must be borne in mind, too, that the population of China has hitherto been difficult to estimate precisely—as much so, indeed, as that of the interior of Africa. Regarding the three religions of Eastern Asia, as well as the Fetishism of Africa, the statistical data necessary for a reliable calculation are wanting even now, and therefore

TABLE I.

	Malte Brun 1810	Graberg 1813	C. G. Stein 1819	Pinkerton 1827	Balbi 1844
Christians	228,000,000	236,000,000	228,000,000	235,000,000	260,000,000
Jews	5,000,000	5,000,000	6,600,000	5,000,000	4,000,000
Mohammedans	110,000,000	120,000,000	120,000,000	120,000,000	96,000,000
Brahmins	60,000,000	60,000,000		60,000,000	60,000,000
Buddhists	150,000,000	150,000,000	353,400,000	180,000,000	170,000,000
Other Heathens	100,000,000	115,000,000		100,000,000	147,000,000
Total	653,000,000	686,000,000	708,000,000	700,000,000	737,000,000

conditions at the beginning or the middle of the eighties; those of Juraschek to the period 1890–97. Zeller has in essentials taken over the statements of Juraschek and made them the basis of his own investigations; he has, however, completed and arranged them more clearly (in Warneck's "Allgemeine Missionszeitschrift," 1903), and has added exact references for the various items. The numbers as given by Krose belong to the last decade of the nineteenth century and only in a few cases to 1901. The total results of these four accounts are shown in Table II.

fluctuations of the estimates are easily understood. Again, Juraschek-Zeller did not make special categories for Taoism in Japan and ancient cults in India, but added them to the great collective groups just mentioned; and the individuals having no religious denomination seem to have been allotted by Juraschek to other groups on certain principles. Juraschek decidedly underestimated the number of Mohammedans: recent investigations have proved that Mohammedanism is far more widely extended in Africa than was believed. Otherwise the statistical accounts

TABLE II.

	Fournier de Flaix	Juraschek and Zeller	Krose
Catholics	230,866,533	254,500,000	264,505,922
Protestants	143,237,625	165,830,000	166,627,109
Greek-Orthodox	98,016,000	106,480,000	109,147,272
Other Christians	4,960,000	8,130,000	8,728,284
Total Christians	477,080,158	534,940,000	549,017,341
Jews	7,056,000	10,860,000	11,036,607
Mohammedans	176,834,372	175,290,000	202,048,240
Brahmins	190,000,000	214,570,000	210,100,000
Ancient Indian Cults			12,113,756
Buddhists	147,900,000	120,750,000	120,250,000
Adherents of Ancestor Worship and of Confucianism	256,000,000	300,630,000	235,000,000
Shintoists	14,000,000	14,000,000	17,000,000
Taoists	43,000,000		32,000,000
Other Heathens	117,681,669	173,300,000	144,700,000
Others and Undenominational		170,000	2,844,482
Total	1,429,552,199	1,544,510,000	1,536,110,426

The differences between the first and the last two accounts seem to be considerable. But we must keep in mind that Fournier's figures refer to a time about ten years previous to that of Juraschek-Zeller; and that the distance in time from Krose's record is even greater. Within a period like this an increase of from 10 to 15 per cent is by no means extraordinary. Hence, so far as regards the Christians, the statements may easily be made to agree. (The Raskolniks have apparently been counted with the "Greek Orthodox" by Fournier and with "Other Christians" by Juraschek-Zeller.) Neither is the disagreement regarding the Mohammedans and the Brahmins remarkable. The number of the Jews, however, has evidently been underrated by Fournier, and that of the Buddhists overestimated. The latter may easily be accounted for, as in the great Chinese Empire, with its hundreds

of Juraschek-Zeller and Krose show a far-reaching agreement, considering the different periods of their estimates. Their calculations having been carried out in complete independence of each other, this harmony no doubt confirms the reliability of the results.

III. PRESENT STATUS OF RELIGIOUS BODIES.—The tables of Juraschek-Zeller and Krose given in section II correspond on the whole to the last decade of the nineteenth century. At present, therefore, the first decade of the twentieth century being over, their accounts need complementing and revising. This is especially necessary with the various Christian denominations considering their steady and vigorous increase, while the estimates made ten years ago of the Asiatic and African religions may even now be to a large extent accepted in the absence of more exact computation. The great difficulties of religious statistics have been hinted at above. They are indeed greater than the difficulties of any other branch of statistics bearing on population. Even countries possessing in other respects well-grounded official statistics often lack official accounts regarding religion. The science of statistics has long since come to the conclusion that religion belongs to the essential items of every census. As early as 1872 the Eighth International Congress for Statistics at St. Petersburg expressly emphasized this, pointing out the great importance that must be attributed to a full and clear statement of the individual's religion, "one of the most essential elements of civilization". This want is less felt in countries like Belgium, Spain, Portugal, and the majority of the republics of South and Central America, whose populations generally profess one and the same religion, excepting a small minority, whose number can usually be ascertained in other ways with sufficient accuracy. But the difficulty is great with countries of mixed denominations, like Great Britain and the United States, where up to now the distribution of the various religious bodies has not been ascertained by a universal census. In such cases the defect is to some degree remedied by an ecclesiastical census; but this is the case only when all the individuals are counted; and the census is not reliable when only the communicants or those with full right of membership are counted, and a certain ratio is added for the rest, as is commonly done in the Protestant denominations of England and America. The totals arrived at in this way are vague estimates, possessing only approximate value. The same applies to Protestant missionary statistics as far as English and American missionary societies are concerned.

Another difficulty in comprehensive statistics of religions lies in the classification of the various creeds. We cannot but combine smaller communities into collective groups. This, however, is a great inconvenience; for thus denominations differing from one another must be connected, and then the large totals produce the impression that one important religion is meant, whereas in fact it is but a combination of a number of religious communities, possessing neither common organization nor identity of belief. In the first place this holds good of that great collective group comprised under the designation of "Protestantism". This term can, in the statistics of religions, be applied only in the widest and merely negative sense, i. e., as meaning all those Christians who are neither Roman Catholic nor members of a Greek or Oriental schismatical Church. As soon as we try to point out a note proper to this whole group and to it exclusively, we find ourselves at a loss. In the following list, therefore, we have reckoned the group, designated as "Other Christians" in some official statistics, under the heading "Protestants". On principle, only those are to be counted as Catholics who are in communion with the Church of Rome; it is evident that differences in rite or liturgical language, which do not constitute any diversity of creed, are to be neglected. The self-styled "Old Catholics" do not belong to the Catholic Church, even though the official statistics of some countries reckon them as Catholics; this, however, is of no importance, as their number is insignificant. The designation "Schismatic Greeks" comprises all the Russian or Greek Orthodox, whether they acknowledge the Patriarch of Constantinople as their head or belong to independent Churches. The schismatic Armenians, Syrians, Chaldeans, Copts, and Thomas Christians may be collectively grouped under "Schismatic Orientals". The Russian Raskolniks, on the contrary, must be regarded as a separate group, distinct from the Christian denominations mentioned above.

With all religious bodies only external membership comes under statistical reckoning. Thereby it is not denied that, e. g., among the 38 millions of France belonging exteriorly to the Catholic Church many, perhaps even many millions, are interiorly altogether separated from the Church, just as in Germany and other Teutonic nations we have the analogous fact regarding Protestantism. In the Christian religions which are, after all, the most important, membership, ever since the days of primitive Christianity, is founded on baptism; this membership, from the point of view of statistics, must be considered as severed only by a formal withdrawal or excommunication from the particular religious body. In official census of religions nothing but the individual's own declaration comes into consideration.

A census represents the religious status of a country at a given date. Of course, when hundreds of states are to be taken into account, there cannot be one fixed date, but at least a limited period ought to be assigned, so that the calculations for the different countries may not lie too far apart. Otherwise the general impression conveyed would not be correct.

On these principles the following tables are made up, the data being taken as a rule from the years 1905 to 1910, in most cases 1907 or 1908. The results of official census taken in 1910 and 1911 have not yet been published, and although a few more recent figures have become known since these lists were put together in 1910 for the "Staatslexikon der Görresgesellschaft", they have not been incorporated, in order not to impair the uniform character of the tables. In the first place, the official government census of religions has been followed in each case; but with regard to those countries in which since 1900–1901 no Government census of religions has been taken, though the numerical status of the population is officially ascertained every year, the ratio of the various religious bodies established by the preceding census of religions has been applied to the present number of inhabitants; for, excepting the "immigration countries", the ratio of denominational membership shows little change within ten years. Where a government census is wanting, the data of the religious bodies themselves are made use of. Our sources are given in full in the bibliography at the end of this article. In Table III (second column) the results of the government census of religions are marked C, along with the year in which the census was taken; the computations founded upon the ratio derived from previous official records, are marked R; the non-official figures and estimates are marked E. (See Table III.)

Of the nearly 430 millions living in Europe at present, almost 411 millions (95·5 per cent) are Christians. The number of Jews (2·3 per cent) may in reality be a little less than appears in the table, as the considerable emigration of Jews from Russia during the last decade could not be taken into account. On the other hand, the natural increase of the Jewish population of Russia, in contrast to that of the Jews in Germany and Western Europe, was exceptionally large within the period in question, so that the total number of Jews living at present (1911) in Europe should be at least 9 millions. Not quite so large is the number of Mohammedans (2 per cent). Finally there remain 1 million (2 per thousand) of other non-Christians, of individuals without religious denomination, etc. Among the Christians, Catholics form by far the most numerous group. They make up 43·8 per cent of the total population of Europe. Formerly the percentage was even higher. The extraordinary increase of the Slavic races, chiefly Greek Orthodox, and the great exodus of emigrants from Austria-Hungary, Italy, Spain, and Ireland are the principal causes of the relative decrease of Catholics. The Greek Orthodox have, on account of their high birth-rate, outnumbered the Protestants. The former are now 26·4 per cent of the total, the latter only 24·7 per cent, while, according to the earlier computation by Krose, the Greek Orthodox (omitting the

Schismatic Orientals added to the "Greek-Catholics" by Juraschek-Zeller and others) were a little below the Protestants. In the total of Christians are included 2,056,000 Raskolniks in Russia (the real number probably is much greater), 232,000 Gregorian Armenians in Turkey, Bulgaria, and Rumania, 24,000 Old Catholics in Austria, and about 9000 Jansenists in Holland.

In Asia (see Table IV) government censuses of religions have been taken only within Russian and British territories. Regarding the other countries only the number of Christians and Jews can be ascertained with any degree of certainty. Of the widespread religions of Eastern Asia we have nothing but estimates of very doubtful value. The Christians of the various creeds amount in all to about 32,270,000, only 3·9 per cent of the total population of Asia, which may be reckoned as 829 millions. Among the Christians the Greek Orthodox (in round numbers, 13,800,-000) are the best represented; yet the Catholics (12,660,000) come fairly close to them. The Protestants (2,350,000) are far fewer, even if the high estimates of Warneck regarding China and Korea be accepted. The remainder (3,500,000) are Armenians, Raskolniks, Thomas Christians in India, and what is still left of the old Christian communities in Japan.

Of about 6,634,000 inhabitants of Australia and Oceania (see Table V), about 5,240,000 are Christians. The Protestant denominations take the lead (almost 77 per cent of the total). The Australian continent, Tasmania, New Zealand, New Caledonia, Fiji, the Tonga and Navigator Islands are almost completely Christianized; whereas the populations of New Guinea, the Bismarck Archipelago, the Solomon Islands, and most of the smaller groups of islands are for the most part pagan. Jews are few on the Australian continent and New Zealand; Buddhists and Mohammedans are found among the immigrants in Hawaii and on the continent. An official census of religions was taken in New Zealand in 1906 and by the Commonwealth in 1900. As, however, the population has grown very considerably since the last census, we have applied to the Catholics of the Australian Commonwealth the results of the ecclesiastical census of 1909 and raised in due proportion the number of Protestants ascertained in 1900. With regard to the other countries and islands, the Catholic and Protestant missionary statistics have served as our chief sources of information. Thus a fairly high degree of accuracy is attained concerning the Christians, while for the pagans mere estimates have had to suffice.

In Africa (see Table VI) there are, in a total of about 126 millions, more than 11 millions of Christians, of whom more than half belong to the Monophysites of Abyssinia and Egypt. Catholics and Protestants are in almost equal numbers, if we add to Africa the Canary Islands and Madeira, which administratively belong to the European possessions of Spain and Portugal. The main stock of Protestants live in British South Africa, the numerous immigrants being for the most part of English and Dutch extraction; but the Protestants have won many converts among the natives. Of Catholics the greater number reside in the French, Spanish, and Portuguese colonies. With regard to the last-named, especially Angola, much higher figures were formerly given, but without sufficient foundation; hence we have inserted in our table the lowest estimate. Jews are somewhat more numerous in Abyssinia, Tunis, Algeria, and Morocco, their total being about half a million. More than one-third of Africa professes Mohammedanism, which is ever gaining ground and encroaching on

TABLE III.—EUROPE.

Countries.	Year.	Catholics.	Protestants.	Greek Russian Orthodox.	Total of Christians.	Jews.	Mohammedans.	Others and Undenominational.
Andorra	E. 1900	5,231			5,231			
Austria-Hungary	R. 1907	38,195,000	4,488,000	3,621,000	46,328,000	2,239,000		103,000
Belgium	E. 1908	7,350,000	30,000		7,380,000	4,000		3,000
Bosnia	C. 1909	413,354		808,321	1,221,675	11,481	616,628	6,051
Bulgaria	C. 1905	29,684	5,644	3,344,806	3,392,756	37,656	603,867	1,296
Denmark (1)	E. 1906	7,871	2,664,200	100	2,673,000	(2) 3,500		20,000
France	R. 1906	38,467,000	628,000		39,095,000	55,000		102,000
German Empire	C. 1905	22,094,492	(3)37,906,569	1,991	60,016,213	607,862		17,203
Great Britain and Ireland (4)	E. 1909	5,786,000	39,630,000		45,416,000	240,000		100,000
Greece	E. 1907	44,265		2,554,300	2,598,565	8,350	24,000	1,000
Italy	E. 1908	33,750,000	70,000		33,820,000	50,000		40,000
Lichtenstein	C. 1906	9,650			9,650			
Luxemburg	C. 1905	242,572	2,264		244,836	1,128		511
Monaco	E. 1909	19,000			19,000			
Montenegro	E.	12,900		201,100	214,000		13,800	
Netherlands	E. 1908	2,045,000	3,524,000		5,578,000	116,000		130,000
Norway	E. 1908	2,000	2,330,000	100	2,332,000	700		15,000
Portugal (5)	E. 1905	5,438,000	5,000		5,443,000	1,200		
Rumania	E. 1907	167,000	25,000	6,160,000	6,362,000	250,000	50,000	20,000
Russia (6)	R. 1907	13,450,000	7,458,000	91,651,000	(7)114,623,000	6,042,000	4,224,000	460,000
San Morino	C. 1906	11,439			11,439			
Servia	E. 1905	11,000	1,500	2,653,000	2,665,500	6,000	16,000	
Spain (8)	E. 1907	19,280,000	8,000		19,288,000	4,000		17,000
Sweden	E. 1907	2,600	5,370,000		5,372,600	4,000		
Switzerland	R. 1907	1,463,000	2,034,000		3,497,000	14,000		14,000
Turkey (9)	E. 1900	280,000	20,000	2,740,000	(10)3,240,000	100,000	3,100,000	
Europe		188,577,058	106,200,177	113,735,718	410,826,465	9,795,877	8,648,395	1,050,061

(1) With dependencies.
(2) This number corresponds to the ratio (14 in 10,000) deducted from the last official census of religions; according to the Jewish Year Book, London, 1910, the number of Jews in France runs up to 95,000.
(3) Inclusive of "other Christians."
(4) Together with Malta, Gibraltar and the Channel Islands.
(5) Without Madeira.
(6) Together with Finland.
(7) Inclusive of 2,056,000 Raskolniks.
(8) Without the Canary Islands.
(9) With Crete.
(10) Inclusive of 200,000 Armenians.

paganism; yet the latter remains the religion of the majority. A more accurate determination of the number of Mohammedans and pagans in Africa is not possible, as the population has not yet been ascertained in many districts of the interior.

America (see Table VII) roughly counts 169 millions of inhabitants. Of these more than half tained only the number of communicants (i. e., according to English and American usage, partakers of the Lord's Supper, or full members), not the total number of adherents to the different denominations. These data, however, do not carry us very far for the purposes of general statistics of religions. The proportion of communicants to non-communicants differs

TABLE IV.—ASIA.

Countries.	Catholics.	Protestants.	Greek Orthodox.	Total of Christians	Jews.	Mohammedans.	Brahmins.	Buddhists.	Adherents of Confucianism and Ancestor Worship.	Taoists and Shintoists.	Other Heathens.
Persia, Afghanistan, Baluchistan, and Independent States in the Himalayas	629,797	80,000	1,600,000	*3,610,000	40,000	15,000,000	2,000,000	1,000,000			
Turkish Possessions					560,000	130,00,000					
Russian Possessions and pendencies	112,000	98,000	12,000,000	†14,087,000	125,000	12,100,000					350,000
British Possessions	‡2,350,000	1,195,000	183,000	§3,982,000	18,000	64,000,000	208,000,000	13,500,000			‖12,220,000
Portuguese Possessions											
French Indo-China	931,357			931,357							
Siam (with Laos)	33,267	9,500		42,767							
China with Dependencies	1,210,054	¶285,000		1,495,000		20,000,000		110,000,000	240,000,000	32,000,000	
Korea	68,016	¶113,499		181,515	2,000						
Japan	65,741	71,818	23,000	180,000						17,000,000	
Dutch Possessions	**56,214	472,000		528,214		31,000,000		500,000			4,000,000
Philippines	7,205,052	30,000		7,235,052		?					300,000
Asia	12,661,498	2,354,817	13,806,000	32,272,905	745,000	155,100,000	210,000,000	125,000,000	240,000,000	49,000,000	16,870,000

* Inclusive of 1,300,000 Armenians and other Schismatic Orientals.
† Inclusive of 512,000 Raskolniks and 1,365,000 Armenians and other Schismatic Orientals.
‡ Inclusive of the French Possessions in India.
§ Inclusive of 254,000 schismatic Thomas-Christians.
‖ Inclusive of 12,114,000 adherents to ancient Indian Cults.
¶ These numbers are taken over from the "Abriss der Geschichte der protestantischen Missionen," by Warneck, 9th ed., and are founded on estimates which probably are much too high.
** Inclusive of North-Borneo.

(87,614,635, or 51·8 per cent) are Catholics; 70,868,923 (41·9 per cent) Protestants. In all 93·7 per cent are Christians. The number of Jews, very small up to a few decades ago, has increased considerably of late on account of the immigration from Russia. There are nearly 2 millions at present. The pagan Indians and widely in the various denominations. Calculation of membership in the denominations from these data results only in vague estimates of very doubtful value. Still, as Carroll's list is of some interest, his figures for the more important denominations are given below (table: "Number of Communicants, United States")

TABLE V.

AUSTRALIA AND OCEANIA.

Countries.	Catholics.	Protestants.	Jews.	Mohammedans.	Buddhists.	Fetich worshippers and other Heathens.	Others and undenominational.
Commonwealth of Australia	951,429	3,013,000	15,000	20,000	10,000		110,000
New Zealand	127,227	719,087	1,867			2,000	24,000
Other British Possessions (1)	35,000	147,500				650,000	
French Possessions	53,000	21,000				10,000	
New Hebrides	3,000	22,000				60,000	
German Possessions (1)	27,399	44,460				390,000	
American Possessions	47,000	30,000			60,000		40,000
Australia and Oceania	1,244,055	3,997,047	16,867	20,000	70,000	1,112,000	174,000

(1) Inclusive of British and German New Guinea.—Dutch New Guinea was included in the Dutch East Indies.

Negroes may be put down at from 2¼ to 2½ millions; in their case a more accurate estimate is out of the question. The great variety of denominations in the United States makes it very difficult to determine their creeds; an official census of religions has never yet been taken. The American statistician, Dr. Carroll, has tried to find a substitute by inquiries addressed to the church authorities, but in this way he has ascertained as they appear in "The Christian Advocate" for 26 January, 1911, omitting only the ordinal numbers indicating the relative numerical importance of each denomination. From this table it is evident that the Catholic Church is by far the largest religious denomination in the United States, and that, excepting the Mormons, no other body shows as high a rate of increase within the last twenty years, the number of communicants having almost doubled. Further, the totals of the official Catholic Directory (for 1909: 14,347,027; for 1910: 14,618,761) are by far too low. For, although the proportion of non-communicants is much smaller among Catholics than

NUMBER OF COMMUNICANTS, UNITED STATES

	In 1910.	In 1890.
Catholics	12,321,746	6,257,871
Methodists	6,596,168	4,589,284
Baptists	5,774,066	3,717,969
Lutherans	2,243,486	1,231,072
Presbyterians	1,920,765	1,278,362
Episcopalians	938,390	540,509
Reformed	448,190	309,458
Mormons	400,650	166,125
United Brethren	303,319	225,281
Jews	143,000	130,496
Friends	123,718	107,208
Dunkard Brethren	122,847	73,795
Adventists	95,646	60,491

among Protestants, yet, even with Catholics, the number of communicants was, up to 1910, hardly more than two-thirds of the total. Moreover, the statistics furnished by the parochial clergy for Wiltzius' Directory can, from the nature of the case,

estant" in the wider sense explained above (Christians who are neither Catholics nor connected with the Greek or Oriental schismatical Churches), we have put down the number as 65 millions. The number of Jews in full membership given by Carroll is evidently far too low, nor is it clear what Carroll understands by this term in the case of Jews. We have therefore given preference to the number of "The Jewish Year Book" for 1910 (1,777,000).

In Southern and Central America the determination of religious profession is easier, as the entire population may be regarded as Catholic, making allowance for the few Protestants and the uncivilized Indians not included in the census. The same may be said of Cuba, Porto Rico, Haiti, San Domingo, and the French West Indies, while in the British, Danish, and Dutch colonies there are partly official, partly ecclesiastical data. In Mexico, too, a census of religions was taken by the Government in 1901.

According to the synopsis presented in Table VIII, the entire population of the Earth at present (i. e. the average for the years 1906–08) amounts to about 1561 millions. The various figures show a notable difference when compared with the previous accounts of Krose and Zeller-Juraschek. In the first place, the latest figures are considerably higher, at least as far as the Christian denominations are con-

TABLE VI.—AFRICA.

COUNTRIES.	Catholics.	Protestants.	Oriental Christians	Jews.	Mohammedans.	Fetish-worshippers and other Heathens.
Egypt	(1)100,257	37,446	743,989	38,635	10,269,445	
Abyssinia	3,000	?	5,000,000	200,000	300,000	?
Tripoli	6,100	?		10,000	1,000,000	
Algeria and Tunis	663,000	?		125,000	5,900,000	
Morocco	10,000	1,000		150,000	7,000,000	
Liberia		22,000			500,000	1,000,000
French North and West Africa	53,898	7,000			3,000,000	10,000,000
Other French Possessions	365,000	344,000			300,000	2,000,000
Spanish Possessions (2)	434,000				280,000	?
Portuguese Possessions (3)	(4)568,000	4,000			1,500,000	5,000,000
Belgian Congo	34,475	26,000			?	19,000,000
German Possessions	55,004	47,223			1,000,000	13,000,000
British North and West Africa	21,829	133,000			7,000,000	9,000,000
British South Africa	90,587	1,911,000		50,000	50,000	6,700,000
Other British Possessions	267,689	101,991			5,000,000	5,000,000
Italian Possessions	17,000		80,000		200,000	300,000
Africa	2,689,839	2,634,660	5,823,989	573,635	43,299,445	71,000,000

(1) Inclusive of United Oriental Catholics, who were put down separately in the official census of 1907.
(2) Inclusive of Canary Islands.
(3) Inclusive of Madeira.
(4) With regard to the Catholics of Angola the data vary considerably; we have taken the lowest estimate, 250,000.

comprise only those Catholics who have for some time resided in a parish and are known to the clergy; such records, therefore, fall far short of the reality, on account of the great Catholic immigration and the great fluctuation in the population. Hence the present writer believes that, of the 5½ millions whose denomination is marked in our tables as unknown, the majority are Catholics. In those tables, however, Wiltzius' figures for 1909 have been used in default of any accurate data for another estimate.

The total number of Protestant communicants in the United States, according to Carroll, is 21,663,248. As, on the average, there is one communicant to every 2.6 inhabitants, this would mean at most 56 millions of Protestants, and it is quite clear from Carroll's statistics that there are millions in the United States unconnected with any denomination, a fact which ought to be taken into consideration in calculating the total number of adherents from the number of communicants. Taking, however, the term "Prot-

cerned. The reason of this is that more than a decade has passed since the last calculations. Considering the high birth-rate of the Christian nations, an increase of 10 to 15 per cent is not improbable. Besides, the recent and more accurate census in Southern and Central America brought in far higher figures than the older and rougher estimates. As these territories are almost exclusively Catholic, it is clear that the increase of Catholics apparently surpasses that of the Protestants. On the other hand, the column of Fetish-worshippers and other pagans of lower civilization shows a very considerable decrease, which is explained by the recent estimate of the population of Central Africa. While in 1898 Juraschek supposed the population of Africa to be 178 millions, in 1908 he reckoned the population as 129 millions. Thus in these regions religious statistics are subject to great fluctuations. The total number of Christians amount to 618 millions, or 39.6 per cent. of the entire population of the earth. Of the Christians, not quite one-half—292¾ millions, or 47.4 per cent—belong to the

Catholic Church; 186 millions, or 30.1 per cent are Protestants; 127½ millions, or 20·6 per cent, Greek Orthodox; the rest are Oriental Schismatics or belong to sects not separately mentioned in the table— ism and Mohammedanism, of all religious denominations, approach nearest to Catholicism: they each have more than 200 millions of followers. But their extension is not so universal as that of Catholicism;

TABLE VII.—AMERICA.

COUNTRIES.	Catholics.	Protestants.	Jews.	Heathens.	Others and Undenominational.
British North America	3,017,231	4,332,769	60,000	50,000	?
United States	14,347,027	65,000,000	1,777,000	500,000	5,500,000
Mexico	13,533,013	51,795	8,972		13,219
Central American Republics	4,353,000	15,000		120,000	
Cuba	1,824,897	20,000	4,000	12,000	160,000
Porto Rico	1,000,000	?			12,000
Haiti	1,488,000				300,000
San Domingo	600,000				
British West Indies (1)	303,928	986,000	2,000	600,000	80,000
French Possessions	400,000			18,000	
Dutch and Danish Possessions	77,539	63,359	2,000	12,000	12,000
Venezuela	2,640,000	4,000	400		
Colombia	4,300,000	?		30,000	
Ecuador	1,270,000			130,000	
Peru	4,500,000	10,000		300,000	
Bolivia	2,150,000			100,000	
Chile	3,800,000	30,000		50,000	
Argentine Republic	6,100,000	80,000	1,000	50,000	
Uruguay	1,080,000	25,000			
Paraguay	580,000	1,000		50,000	
Brazil	20,250,000	250,000	3,000	600,000	12,000
Total, North and South America	87,614,635	70,868,923	1,858,372	2,622,000	6,089,219

(1) Inclusive of British Honduras and British Guiana.

Raskolniks, Jansenists, Old Catholics etc. The Roman Catholic Church alone comprises almost one-fifth of mankind, and has more followers than any other form of religion. Buddhism, Ancestor-worship, locally and ethnographically they are much more limited. In Table VIII the Jews probably appear more numerous than they are in reality, as the great emigration from Russia could not be determined

TABLE VIII.—SYNOPSIS OF TABLES III TO VII.

(A) CHRISTIANS.

PARTS OF THE WORLD.	Catholics.	Protestants.	Greek Russian (Orthodox)	Oriental Schismatics.	Total of Christians.
Europe	188,577,058	106,200,177	113,735,718	232,000	410,826,865
Asia	12,661,498	2,354,817	13,806,000	2,919,000	32,272,905
Australia and Oceania	1,244,055	3,997,047			5,241,102
Africa	2,689,839	2,634,660		5,823,989	11,148,488
America	87,614,635	70,868,923			158,483,558
Totals	292,787,085	186,055,624	127,541,718	8,974,989	617,972,918

(B) NON-CHRISTIANS.

PARTS OF THE WORLD.	Jews.	Mohammedans.	Brahmins.	Buddhists.	Adherents of Ancestor-Worship and Confucianism.	Taoists and Shintoists.	Fetish-Worshippers and other Heathens.	Others and Undenominational.
Europe	9,795,877	8,648,395						1,050,061
Asia	745,000	155,100,000	210,000,000	125,000,000	240,000,000	49,000,000	16,870,000	
Australia and Oceania	16,867	20,000		70,000			1,112,000	174,000
Africa	573,635	43,299,445					71,000,000	
America	1,858,372		100,000	200,000			2,622,000	6,089,219
Totals	12,989,751	207,067,840	210,100,000	125,270,000	240,000,000	49,000,000	91,604,000	7,313,280

and Confucianism, which, taken together, would indeed possess a larger number of adherents, are not distinct religious bodies, but forms of religion and systems of religious customs all of which, as mentioned above, are at times observed by the same individual. With reference to the number of adherents, Brahmin- numerically for want of reliable official statistics, while in the most recent records from countries to which they migrate, the Jews seem to be included. Nevertheless the total number of Jews can scarcely fail to reach 12 millions. (See also MIGRATION: *Immigration to the United States*.) The remaining

7⅓ millions not classified are individuals without any religious denomination and, still more, those whose creeds could not be ascertained.

STEIN, *Handbuch der Geographie und Statistik* (4th ed., 1819); BALBI, *Abrégé de Géographie* (3rd ed., Paris, 1844); KOLB, *Handbuch der vergl. Statistik* (1857); FOURNIER DE FLAIX, *Mémoire sur la statistique des religions* in *Bulletin de l'Institut International de Statistique*, IV (Rome, 1889); PIEPER, *Kirchl. Statistik Deutschlands* (1899); ZELLER, *Vergleichende Religionsstatistik* in *Warnecks Allgemeiner Missions-Zeitschrift* (1903); KROSE, *Die Verbreitung der wichtigsten Religionsbekenntnisse zur Zeit der Jahrhundertwende* in *Stimmen aus Maria-Laach*, LXV (1903); IDEM, *Konfessionsstatistik Deutschlands* (1904); *Missiones Catholicæ* (Rome, 1907); KROSE, *Kath. Missionsstatistik* (1908); IDEM, *Kirchl. Handbuch*, I–III (1908–11); *Die Kath. Missionen* (1908–09, 1909–10); *Statesman's Year Book* (London, 1909); SCHNEIDER, *Kirchl. Jahrbuch* (36th ed., 1909); JURASCHEK, *Geogr. Statist. Tabellen* (1909); *Gothaischer Genealogischer Hofkalender* (1910), 147; *Annuario Ecclesiastico* (Rome, 1910); *Annuaire Pontifical Catholique* (Paris, 1910); HARRIS, *The Jewish Year Book* (London, 1910); WARNECK, *Abriss einer Gesch. der protestant. Missionen* (9th ed. 1910); *The Official Catholic Directory* (Milwaukee and New York, 1910).

H. A. KROSE.

Stattler, BENEDICT, Jesuit theologian, b. at Kötzting, Bavaria (Diocese of Ratisbon), 30 Jan., 1728; d. at Munich, 21 Aug., 1797. He entered the Jesuit novitiate at Landsberg in 1745 and, after the usual studies, taught philosophy and theology in Solothurn (Switzerland), Innsbruck, and Ingolstadt. In the last-named place he continued to occupy the chair of theology even after the suppression of the Society. In 1783, when all former-Jesuits were excluded from the office of teaching, he took charge of the parish of Kemnath, but soon exchanged this post for that of ecclesiastical adviser and member of the electoral committee on censures in Munich. After four years his health compelled him to resign this office, and he lived thereafter in retirement till his death. A man of keen intellectual vision and an unlimited capacity for work, Stattler was ever ready to guard and defend Catholic principles. Shortly after Adam Weishaupt had founded the secret society of the Illuminati, Stattler, in an anonymous work, laid bare the rationalistic ideas and the pernicious designs of these forerunners of freemasonry. Kant's "Critique of Pure Reason" appeared in its first edition in 1781; in 1788 Stattler launched against its subversive principles his "Anti-Kant", and skilfully parried the attack which his book provoked in the literary world of Germany. When the doctrines of the French revolutionists began to be echoed in his fatherland, he lost no time in pointing out to his compatriots the false ring which he detected in their boastful promises of liberty. The bulk of his writings, however, is devoted to Catholic philosophy and theology. It was his avowed purpose to adapt the traditional teachings of the School to the living needs of his time, "to plow anew the entire field of scholastic philosophy and theology and to fructify it with fresh seeds", as Bishop Sailer of Ratisbon, Stattler's great pupil, expressed it. With this end in view, he wrote "Philosophia methodo scientiæ propria explanata" (Augsburg, 1769–72) and "Demonstratio Evangelica" (Augsburg, 1770). Yet his attachment to the rationalistic philosophy of Wolff and the far-going concessions he made to religious toleration and Febronianism led him astray and marred the lustre of his merits. The suppression of his order and the consequent loss of wise direction by superiors proved a veritable calamity to him. His "Demonstratio Catholica" (Pappenheim, 1775) fell under the censure of the Roman authorities, and, shortly before his death, his "Loci Theologici" (Weissenburg, 1775), "Theologia Christiana Theoretica" (Ingolstadt and Munich, 1776–79) and two other works were placed on the Index.

Biography by SAILER in *Sämmtl. Werke* (Sulzbach, 1841), xxxviii, 115 sq.; HURTER, *Nomenclator*, III, 236 sqq.; SOMMERVOGEL, *Bibliothèque*, VII, 1498 sqq.; WERNER, *Gesch. d. kath. Theologie* (Munich, 1866).

A. C. COTTER.

Staudenmaier, FRANZ ANTON, theologian, b. at Donzdorf, Würtemberg, 11 Sept., 1800; d. at Freiburg im Breisgau, 19 Jan., 1856. He was a pupil at the Latin school of Gmünd in the years 1815-18, and at the Gymnasium at Ellwangen 1818-22. During the years 1822-26 he studied theology and philosophy at the University of Tübingen, where Drey, Herbst, Hirscher, and Möhler were his teachers; in the autumn of 1826 he entered the seminary at Rottenburg, where he was ordained priest on 15 Sept., 1827. After performing the duties of a parish priest for a year he became, in the autumn of 1828, a tutor in the Catholic theological seminary, "Wilhelmsstift" at Tübingen; in 1830 he was made regular professor of dogmatic theology in the newly-established Catholic theological faculty of the University of Giessen, which owed its brief period of prosperity largely to Staudenmaier and his colleague Kuhn. In the autumn of 1837 he became the regular professor of dogmatic theology at the University of Freiburg im Breisgau; from 1843 he was also a cathedral canon.

Staudenmaier was one of the most brilliant figures in the Catholic theology of Germany in the first half of the nineteenth century, and one of the most important writers on dogmatics of the Catholic Tübingen school. He was a scholar of far-reaching knowledge, of great productive energy, and at the same time a philosopher with a brilliant talent for speculation. His imperishable service consisted in securing a deep speculative foundation for Christian truth and in defending this truth against the errors of the pantheistic speculation of that era, especially of the Hegelian philosophy. The most important of his numerous literary works are the following: "Geschichte der Bischofswahlen" (Tübingen, 1830); "Johannes Scotus Erigena und die Wissenschaft seiner Zeit" (1 pt. only, Frankfort, 1834); "Encyklopädie der theologischen Wissenschaften als System der gesammten Theologie" (Mainz, 1834; 2nd ed. 1 vol. only, Mainz, 1840), at the time of its publication an epoch-making work in the domain of Catholic theology; "Der Pragmatismus der Geistesgaben oder das Wirken des göttlichen Geistes im Menschen und in der Menschheit" (Tübingen, 1835); "Der Geist des Christenthums dargestellt in den heiligen Zeiten, in den heiligen Handlungen und in der heiligen Kunst" (2 pts., Mainz, 1835; 5th ed., 1855; 8th ed., 1880), an introduction to the understanding of Catholic Christianity and its worship, based on a presentation of the Catholic Church year, and expressed in language that can be understood by all educated Christians, the most widely-circulated book of Staudenmaier; "Geist der göttlichen Offenbarung, oder Wissenschaft der Geschichtsprincipien des Christenthums" (Giessen, 1837); "Die Philosophie des Christenthums oder Metaphysik der heiligen Schrift als Lehre von den göttlichen Ideen und ihrer Entwicklung in Natur, Geist, und Geschichte: Vol. I, Die Lehre von der Idee" (Giessen, 1840); "Darstellung und Kritik des Hegel'schen Systems. Aus dem Standpunkt der christlichen Philosophie" (Mainz, 1844); "Die christliche Dogmatik" (vols. I–IV, i, Freiburg im Br., 1844-52). This is Staudenmaier's principal work; unfortunately it was never finished. He also published "Das Wesen der katholischen Kirche, mit Rücksicht auf ihre Gegner dargestellt" (Freiburg im Br., 1845); "Zum religiösen Frieden der Zukunft, mit Rücksicht auf die religiös-politische Aufgabe der Gegenwart" 3 pts., Freiburg im Br., 1846-51). In addition he did much for two theological periodicals which he aided in founding and on which he collaborated; with his colleagues at Giessen he established the "Jahrbücher für Theologie und christliche Philosophie" (three yearly series in seven vols., Frankfort-on-the-Main, 1834-35; Mainz, 1836); in conjunction with his colleagues at Freiburg he established the "Zeitschrift für Theologie" (21 vols., Freiburg im Br., 1839-49). Both periodicals came into existence chiefly through his efforts and attained high scholarly reputation largely through his contributions.

LAUCHERT, *Franz Anton Staudenmaier, 1800-1856, in seinem Leben und Wirken dargestellt* (Freiburg im Br., 1901), with portrait.

FRIEDRICH LAUCHERT.

Staupitz, JOHANN VON, Abbot, b. at Motterwitz near Leisnig (or Moderwitz near Meustadt an der Orla) about 1460; d. at Salzburg, 28 Dec., 1524. He was descended from an ancient family of Saxony, studied at Leipzig, and was matriculated in 1485. He later joined the Augustinian Order, probably at Munich, and in 1497 moved to Tübingen, where in 1498 he became prior and in 1500 Doctor of Theology. He was subsequently prior at Munich, and in 1503 was elected Vicar-General of the German Congregation of Augustinians and summoned as professor to the new University of Wittenberg, in which he was the first dean of the theological faculty. In 1512 he resigned his professorship, and moved to South Germany, where he thenceforth resided (at Munich, Nuremberg, and Salzburg), except for some journeys to the Netherlands and Belgium. He resigned the office of vicar-general in 1520, received a dispensation to join the Benedictines in 1522, and finally became Abbot of St. Peter's, Salzburg. On a tour of visitation he had become acquainted with Luther in the monastery at Erfurt, and had consoled the emaciated brother, who was torturing himself with his sinfulness, by speaking to him of the sin-remitting grace of God and man's redemption in the Blood of Christ. For this Luther remained always grateful. In 1518 he was deputed by the promagister of the order to remonstrate with the heretic Luther. Luther remained obstinate and through Staupitz sent an explanation of his theses on indulgences to Rome. This circumstance has led some to include Staupitz among Luther's followers. In reality his attitude was hesitating—being partly suspicious and anxious, and partly encouraging and confirmatory—because he still believed that it was only a question of a protest against ecclesiastical abuses. By releasing Luther from obedience to the order, he separated its fate from that of Luther, but also gave the latter freedom of action. In 1520 revocation and abjuration were demanded of Staupitz; he hesitated at first, because there was no need to revoke what he had never asserted, but finally declared that he recognized the pope as his judge. Luther saw in this declaration a defection. However, Staupitz was no Lutheran but thoroughly Catholic in matters of faith (especially as regards the freedom of the will, the meritoriousness of good works, and justification). This has been established by Paulus from the writings of Staupitz.

KOLDE, *Die deutsche Augustinerkongregation u. Staupitz* (Gotha, 1879); KELLER, *Johann v. Staupitz u. die Anfänge der Reformation* (Leipzig, 1888); PAULUS, *Johann v. Staupitz. Seine vorgeblich protestantischen Gesinnungen* in *Histor. Jahrb. der Görresgesellschaft*, XII (1891), 309-46.

KLEMENS LÖFFLER.

Stauropolis, a titular metropolitan see of the Province of Caria. The city, founded by the Leleges, was at first called Megalopolis, then Ninoe, and finally Aphrodisias. The legend which in explanation of the name Ninoe attributes its foundation to Ninus only proves that the town is very ancient. Built at the foot of Mount Cadmus and watered by numerous sources, Aphrodisias had a celebrated temple of Aphrodite which secured for it from the Roman emperors, especially from Cæsar, the privilege of a free city and the right of asylum. Apollonius, the historian of Caria, was born there, as was Alexander, the commentator of Aristotle in the second century of our era. The name Aphrodisias is still used by the "Hierocles Synecdemus", by Novel clx of Justinian, and figures in the signatures of the Fifth Œcumenical Council in 553. That of Stauropolis appears for the first time about 640 in the "Ecthesis" of pseudo-Epiphanius (Gelzer, "Ungedruckte . . . Texte der Notitiæ episcopatuum", 534). The name Tauropolis, said to have been borne by the town prior to that of Stauropolis, is an error of several scholars (Revue des études grecques, XIX, 228-30).

Le Quien (Oriens christ., I, 899-904) mentions twenty bishops of this see, among whom were Ammonius at Nicæa in 325, Eumenius at Constantinople in 381, Cyrus at Ephesus in 431, Critonianus at Chalcedon in 451, Severianus at Constantinople in 553, Ephraem of Caria, a liturgical poet, etc. Another was Theopropios, mentioned by an inscription (Revue des études grecques, XIX, 298). In the seventh century Stauropolis had twenty-eight suffragan bishops and twenty-six at the beginning of the tenth century. Between 1356 and 1361 the see must have been abandoned by the metropolitan, but the title was long retained and he was given the revenues of other churches (Waechter, "Der Verfall des Griechentums in Kleinasien im XIV. Jahrhundert", Leipzig, 1903, 34-7). Isaias of Stauropolis attended the Council of Florence (1439) and fled to avoid signing the decree of union. Excavations begun in 1904 at Ghere, the modern name of Stauropolis in the caza of Echme and the sanjak of Saroukhan, have brought to light the *thermæ*, the temple of Aphrodite dating from the second century after Christ, and the stadium   A part of the walls, which date from the fourth century of our era, is preserved.

SMITH, *Dict. of Gr. and Rom. Geog.*, s. v. *Aphrodisias*; PATON in *Journal of Hellenic Studies*, XX (London), 73 sq.; TEXIER, *Asie Mineure* (Paris, 1862), 642-7; LABORDE, *Voyage en Asie Mineure* (Paris, 1837-8), 95-100; WADDINGTON, *Voyaye archéologique: Asie Mineure*, 589-96, 1585-1650; LIERMANN, *Analecta epigraphica et agonistica* in *Dissertationes Phil. Halenses*, X (Halle); IDEM in *Bericht des deutschen Hochstiftes zu Frankfort am Main* (Frankfort, 1892), 364-91; KUBICEK in *Monatsblätter des Wissensch. Clubs in Wien*, XXI (Vienna), 2; COLLIGNON in *Revue de l'art ancien et moderne* (Paris, 10 Jan., 1906), 33-50; IDEM in *Académie des Inscriptions* (Paris, 1904), 703 sq.; MENDEL, *op. cit.* (Paris, 1906), 158-84; REINACH, *Inscriptions d'Aphrodisias* in *Revue des études grecques*, XIX (Paris), 79-150, 205-98.

S. VAILHÉ.

Stedingers (a word meaning those living along a shore), a tribe of Frisian peasants in Northern Germany who revolted against their lord, the Archbishop of Bremen, and had to be subdued by arms. The Stedingers refused to pay tithes and to perform forced labour as serfs. These duties were demanded of them with considerable severity, and Archbishop Gerhard II of Bremen (1219-58) sent troops against them. His army, however, was defeated in 1229, whereupon the Stedingers destroyed churches and monasteries, and ill-treated and killed priests. A synod held at Bremen, 17 March, 1230, accused them, in addition to the acts of violence above-mentioned, of contempt for the authority of the Church and for the sacraments, as well as of superstitious practices; it also excommunicated them. The Stedingers refused to submit, and Gregory IX commissioned the Bishop of Lübeck and the Dominicans to labour among them for the extirpation of unbelief. The Emperor Frederick II placed the rebels under the ban of the empire, and on 9 Oct., 1232, Gregory IX issued a Bull commanding the Bishops of Lübeck, Minden, and Ratzeburg to preach a crusade against them. An army was collected and advanced against the Stedingers, but it was defeated in the winter of 1232-33. A new crusading army defeated a part of the tribe, but the other part was once more victorious. The pope now issued another Bull, addressed to several bishops of Northern Germany, commanding a fresh crusade, and on 27 May, 1234, the Stedingers were completely defeated near Bremen. The majority of them now submitted; on 24 August, 1236, Gregory IX commanded that they should be relieved from excommunication after performing penance and satisfaction, and should be received again in the Church.

The Stedingers were not heretics, but rebels against lawful ecclesiastical and secular authority.

HAHN, *Geschichte der Ketzer im Mittelalter*, III (Stuttgart, 1845); SCHUMACHER, *Die Stedinger; Beitrag zur Geschichte der Wesermarschen* (Bremen, 1865); FELTEN, *Papst Gregor IX* (Freiburg im Br., 1886), 220 sq.

J. P. KIRSCH.

Stefaneschi, GIACOMO GAETANI, cardinal deacon, b. at Rome, about 1270; d. at Avignon, 23 June, 1343. He was the son of the senator Pietro Stefaneschi and his wife, Perna Orsini. He received his early education at Rome, and was sent to the University of Paris to pursue higher studies. After three years of diligent application he received the degree of Master of Arts, and intended to devote himself to the study of philosophy and Holy Scripture, having already begun to teach at the university, when his parents recalled him to Italy in order that he should study canon and civil law. He was highly esteemed by Celestine V, who made him canon of St. Peter's and auditor of the Rota; and was created cardinal-deacon of the titular Church of San Giorgio in Velabro, 17 Dec., 1295, by Boniface VIII, who also sent him as legate to Cesena, Forli, Faenza, and Bologna in 1296, to suppress civil disturbances. John XXII appointed him protector of the Minorites, 23 July, 1334. He was never ordained priest.

Stefaneschi is best known as the author of "Opus Metricum", a life of Celestine V composed in dactylic hexameter. Abstracting from a short autobiography left in his cell by Celestine when he became pope, the "Opus Metricum" of Stefaneschi is the earliest biography of the hermit-pontiff. It is composed of three parts, each complete in itself and written at a different time. In 1319 the author united these three separate poems into one work and sent it with a dedicatory epistle to the prior and the monks of San Spirito at Sulmona, the mother-house of the Celestines. The first part contains in three books an account of the election, reign, and abdication of Celestine. It was written before Stefaneschi became cardinal. The second part describes in two books the election and coronation of Boniface VIII, and was written five years later, when Stefaneschi was already cardinal. The third part is composed of three books and describes the life of Celestine after he had abdicated, his canonization, and miracles. The poem is preceded by an introduction in prose, which contains valuable data of the author's life and a synopsis of the whole work. Though of great historical value, the poem is devoid of all literary excellence, and at times is even extremely clumsy and barbarous. It was first edited by Papebroch, "Acta SS.", IV, May, 436–483. A new edition by Professor Sdralek of Breslau is in course of preparation. The other works of Stefaneschi are: "Liber de Centesimo sive Jubileo", edited by Quattrocchi in "Bessarione" (Rome, 1900, VII, 299–317), an interesting and historically important account of the first Roman Jubilee, held in 1300; "Liber ceremoniarum Curiæ Romanæ", a book of ceremonies to be observed at the Roman Court, edited according to a highly interpolated manuscript by Mabillon in "Museum Italicum" (II, 243–443), re-edited in part by Ehrle in "Archiv für Literatur und Kirchengeschichte" (V, 565–587), and by Labande in "Bibliothèque de l'école des chartes" (LIV, 45–74); "Vita S. Georgii Martyris", a eulogy on St. George, the patron of Stefaneschi's titular church; and "Historia de miraculo Mariæ facto Avinione", a short narrative of how a young man, who had been condemned to death at Avignon, was miraculously delivered by the Virgin Mary.

HOSL, *Kardinal Jacobus Gaietani Stefaneschi* (Berlin, 1908); ANGELI, *Jacopo Stefaneschi e il suo "Opus Metricum"* in ANTINORI, *Celestino V ed il VI Centenario della sua incoronazione* (Aquila, 1894), 381–486; THURSTON, *The Holy Year of Jubilee* (London and St. Louis, 1900), passim. See also QUATTROCHI, EHRLE, and LABANDE, loc. sup. cit.

MICHAEL OTT.

Stefano, CAVALIERE GIOVANNI DI. See LANFRANCO, GIOVANNI.

Steffani, AGOSTINO, titular Bishop of Spiga, diplomatist and musician, b. at Castelfranco in the Province of Treviso, in 1655; d. at Frankfort in 1728 or 1730. At the age of twelve he was brought to Munich by Count Tattenbach, who had heard him singing at St. Mark's in Venice. At the Court of the Elector of Bavaria, where he remained for twenty-one years, he soon obtained the position of court and chamber musician, and afterwards that of director and court organist. In 1673 he went for one year to Rome in order to perfect himself in his art. In 1688 he left Munich, and was attached as musician to the Court of Hanover, where resided the famous philosopher Leibniz with whom he was on intimate terms. Ten years later, in 1698, he took up his residence at the Court of the Elector Palatine, at Düsseldorf. His compositions may be ranged in three classes: (1) his religious music, for example, a "Laudate pueri" for nine voices in two choirs, a "Psalmodia Vespertina" scored for eight voices, a "Stabat Mater" for six voices and orchestral accompaniment (of which it has been said that his great contemporary Alessandro Scarlatti produced nothing finer); (2) his chamber duets, more than a hundred of which are preserved, and which were esteemed the most perfect of their kind, so that the most renowned singers delighted in them; (3) and his operas for the stage, five of which are known to have been written for the Court at Munich, nine for that of Hanover, and at least two for Düsseldorf. In later years, when his high position did not allow him to appear as composer of operas, his secretary and copyist Gregorio Piva signed these compositions for him. In 1695 he published a pamphlet, "Sui Principii della Musica", in which is shown how music is grounded on nature and science.

But this remarkable man is not only famous for his musical talents. Being ordained priest, probably about 1680, the Holy See made him Prothonotary Apostolic for North Germany, and in recognition of his services for the cause of Catholicism in Hanover, the Holy Father appointed him Bishop of Spiga (the ancient Cyzicus), in Asia Minor. When in 1712 a new church had been built at Brunswick by the Duke Anton Ulrich, who had become a Catholic, the pope sent Bishop Steffani, "Vicario Apostolico delle Missioni Settentrionali," to perform the consecration and opening service of the new building. But if he was held in such esteem by the ecclesiastical authorities, he was also the confidant and ambassador of temporal princes. A delicate mission was entrusted to him at the various German courts in 1696, and in 1698 at the court in Brussels, for which office he was singularly fitted by his gentle and prudent manners. His merits as a musician were solemnly recognized in London by the Academy of Ancient Music electing him its honorary president for life (1724).

HAWKINS, *Biography*, as introduction to the *Duets*; PIEMANN, *Musik-Lexikon* (Leipzig); CUSINS in *Grove's Dictionary of Music and Musicians* (New York, 1908), s. v.

A. WALTER.

Steinamanger (SZOMBATHELY), DIOCESE OF, in Hungary, suffragan of Gran, founded in 1777 under Queen Maria Theresa. Originally Colonia Claudia Sabaria and capital of Pannonia during the Roman era, the city was in 445 laid waste by the Huns. In the ninth century Steinamanger, an episcopal see even before the invasion of the Huns, was placed under the jurisdiction of the Archbishop of Salzburg; King St. Stephen, it is said, gave Steinamanger to the Bishop of Veszprém. In 1777 the see was reconstituted at the expense of the Dioceses of Agram and Veszprém. It includes the Counties of Vas and Zala and the territory lying on the River Mura. Its first bishop was John Szily (1777–99), who built the episcopal residence and the cathedral. His successor, Cardinal Franz Herzen (1799–1804), was envoy of Joseph II to the Holy See. Bishop Count Mikes is the present incumbent (since 1911). The Abbey of Jaák, one of the chief Romanesque edifices in Hungary, is in this diocese. The

THE CATHEDRAL, STEINAMANGER (Szombathely)

chapter of Steinamanger sprang from the chapter of Vasvár that claims as its founder King St. Stephen, though its documents are of later date. This chapter, richly endowed by the Hungarian kings, declined in the fifteenth century, and in 1578, during the invasions of the Turks, was removed to Steinamanger; on the foundation of the see it became the cathedral chapter. The number of canons was 6 with as many titular canons. The diocese has 6 archdeaneries, 189 priests, 54 parishes. A right of patronage is exercised. There are 5 abbeys and 3 titular abbots, 4 titular provosts, and 25 monasteries with 216 members. The clergy numbers 268 and the Catholic laity 463,947.

A Katolikus Magyarország (Catholic Hungary) (Budapest, 1901); *Schematismus* (1909).

A. ALDÁSY.

Steinle, EDUARD VON, historical painter, b. at Vienna, 2 July, 1810; d. at Frankfort, 19 Sept., 1886. Steinle came successively under the influence of the painters Kupelweiser, Overbeck, and Cornelius, and was thus introduced into the new and vigorous methods of the German painters who had formed themselves into a school at Rome. Steinle went himself several times to Rome, but preferred to work in Germany. He received his first large commission, the painting of the chapel of the Castle of Rheineck, while living at Frankfort-on-the-Main; a second one was for work in the Hall of the Emperors (*Kaisersaal*) at Frankfort, where he painted the pictures of Albert I and Ferdinand III. These commissions and his friendship with Philip Veit and the Brentano family decided him to take up his permanent residence at Frankfort. From 1850 he was professor of historical painting at the Städel Art Institute of Frankfort. Like his friend Schwind he was one of the last of the great painters of the Romantic School and one of those of this school who were largest in their scope. Like Schwind also he was probably more a master in the art of painting ordinary subjects. Still Constant von Wurzbach was able to write an appreciation of Steinle with the title "Ein Madonnamaler unserer Zeit" (Vienna, 1879), for Steinle left more than a hundred religious panel pictures, besides numerous cartoons for church windows. He was also regarded as the great master of monumental fresco painting in the districts of the Rhine.

Besides his work at Rheineck he painted cycles of pictures in the Castle of Klein-Heubach, in the Church of St. Ægidius at Münster, and in the Church of Our Lady at Aachen. He also painted the groups of angels in the choir of the cathedral at Cologne, and did

EDUARD VON STEINLE
From a photograph

part of the work in the apse of the choir of the Minster at Strasburg and in the imperial cathedral at Frankfort. Nevertheless, however striking these frescoes may be, too much stress is laid on detail, and the large, monumental character essential to such painting is not sufficiently apparent. This lack is still more evident in the frescoes showing the historical development of civilization on the stairway of the Wallraf-Richartz Museum at Cologne. Among Steinle's smaller religious pictures are some very fine ones, as that of the enthroned "Madonna holding the Child" while an angel plays a musical instrument in front of them, the "Visitation", the "Holy Family at the Spring", "Mary Magdalen seeking Christ", "Christ Walking with His Disciples", the "Legend of St. Euphrosyne", and the "Great Penitentiary". Steinle was not so willing to condescend to extremes in pleasing popular taste as Schwind, although he had a keen eye for ordinary life and a sense of humour. He placed the idea presented by the picture prominently in the foreground, so that at times the method of portrayal seems too artificial. Among his noblest and most universally admired paintings that are not directly religious are: the "Warder of the Tower", the "Fiddler", the "Sibyl", the "Lorelei", and the pictures of the story of Parsifal; no less remarkable are his illustrations of Shakespeare, and especially those to accompany Brentano's writings. Steinle's works show both graceful and well-defined composition, poetic conception, healthy religious feeling, and, of not less importance, pleasing colour.

ALPH. VON STEINLE published his father's correspondence (Freiburg, 1897), also his father's collected works (Kempten, 1910); VEIT, *Eduard von Steinle* (Leipzig, 1887); POPP, *Eduard von Steinle* (Mainz, 1906)

G. GIETMANN.

Steinmeyer (FARMER), FERDINAND, Jesuit missionary, b. in Swabia, Germany, 13 Oct., 1720; d. at Philadelphia, 17 Aug., 1786. He entered the Society of Jesus at Landsberg in Sept., 1743. He desired to labour on the missions in China but was sent to America instead, whither he came in 1752. His first mission was at Lancaster, where he remained until 1758, when he was transferred to St. Joseph's Church in Philadelphia, to look after the Germans in that section. His labours were not, however, limited to that city. He made numerous missionary journeys through Eastern Pennsylvania and Northern and Central New Jersey. He also crossed over into New York, but of his priestly labours in the latter state prior to the close of the Revolution we have no written record. This absence of written evidence is easily accounted for by the fact that a priest rendered himself liable to the death penalty for attempting to enter New York while it remained under British rule. There can be little doubt, however, that Father Farmer on his journeys through Northern New Jersey crossed over into New York and attended to the Catholics there, even venturing into the city itself, where he kept the faith alive and practically founded St. Peter's Church. With all his missionary work he found time to take an active interest in public and literary affairs. In 1779 he was appointed one of the first trustees of the University of Pennsylvania, while as a philosopher and astronomer his reputation had reached the learned societies of Europe with whom he corresponded. He died at Philadelphia a few months after returning from a missionary trip to New York. His funeral was held at St. Mary's Church, but the remains were interred in old St. Joseph's.

GRIFFIN, *Am. Cath. Hist. Researches* (Philadelphia, Jan., 1888; July, 1890; Jan., 1897; Jan. and July, 1900); *Records Am. Cath. Hist. Soc.*, I, II, III, IV, V and VI (Philadelphia, June, 1900; Dec., 1908; Dec., 1909), passim; SHEA, *Life and Times of Archbishop Carroll* (New York, 1888); KIRLIN, *Catholicity in Philadelphia* (Philadelphia, 1909).

H. C. SCHUYLER.

Steno, NICOLAUS (NIELS STEENSEN), an eminent Danish anatomist and geologist, convert and saintly bishop, b. at Copenhagen, 1 Jan., 1638; d. at Schwerin in Germany, 25 Nov., 1686. For many years the name of Steno was almost forgotten; in science he was centuries in advance of his time. During the last thirty years justice has been done to his merits as a scientist. When a young man of twenty-two years he went to the Netherlands to proceed with his anatomic studies; there he discovered, among other things, the excretory duct of the parotid glands (*ductus Stenonianus*) and the circulation of the blood in the human body. In spite of his achievements his countrymen failed to appoint him professor at the University of Copenhagen, in consequence of which he went to Florence, where he was cordially received by the Grand Duke of Tuscany. He was appointed anatomist at the Hospital of Santa Maria Nuova and continued his researches. Even while residing in the Netherlands he had begun to doubt the truth of the Lutheran doctrines. At Cologne he conferred with a Jesuit, and at Florence he became convinced of the truth of Catholicism. After many struggles he entered the Church on 4 November, 1667. Shortly after a royal letter came from Denmark, that called him home and offered him a high annual salary. But it was too late; as a Catholic he could not return to Denmark. He remained in Italy and made many geological discoveries, which were not appreciated until our time. He was also the first who gave a scientific explanation of the many petrifactions which are found in the earth. In Denmark men began to regret Steno's loss, and through the influence of Griffenfeldt he was nominated, not professor—for a Catholic could not hold that position —but *anatomicus regius* in his native city, but he remained there only two years, as he was exposed to narrow-minded treatment.

Feeling a higher call, he returned to Italy, where he received Holy orders in 1675, and two years after was consecrated a bishop. As such, he lived a most self-denying and mortified life, giving all he had to the poor. He was made vicar Apostolic for the northern missions and worked nine years as an apostle in the north of Germany. He died, worn out by his labours, at the early age of forty-eight. His remains were brought to Florence and deposited in a vault in the Basilica of St. Lawrence. He wrote several ascetic works. Of his sixteen theological works the more interesting are his "Epistola de propria conversione" (Florence, 1677), and "Defensio et plenior elucidatio epistolæ de propria conversione" (Hanover, 1680). His scientific writings were published recently by Maar, "Nicolai Stenonis opera philosophica" (2 vols., Copenhagen, 1910), a very fine work in quarto, containing his thirty-two anatomical dissertations, with introduction and notes in English. A facsimile edition of his "De solido intra solidum naturaliter contento dissertationis prodromus" appeared at Berlin in 1904.

MAAR, *To uudgivne Arbejder af Nicolaus Steno fra Biblioteca Laurentiana* (Copenhagen, 1910); PLENKERS, *Der Däne Niels Stensen* (Freiburg, 1884); JÖRGENSEN, *Nils Steensen* (Copenhagen, 1884); ROSE, *Nicolaus Stenos Liv og Död. Oversat af V. Maar* (Copenhagen, 1906); METZLER, *Nikolaus Steno* in *Pastor bonus*, XXIII (Trier, 1911).

NIELS HANSEN.

Stephen, SAINT, one of the first deacons and the first Christian martyr; feast on 26 December. In the Acts of the Apostles the name of St. Stephen occurs for the first time on the occasion of the appointment of the first deacons (Acts, vi, 5). Dissatisfaction concerning the distribution of alms from the community's fund having arisen in the Church, seven men were selected and specially ordained by the Apostles to take care of the temporal relief of the poorer members. Of these seven, Stephen, is the first mentioned and the best known.

Stephen's life previous to this appointment remains for us almost entirely in the dark. His name is Greek and suggests he was a Hellenist, i. e., one of those Jews who had been born in some foreign land and whose native tongue was Greek; however, according to a fifth-century tradition, the name Stephanos was only a Greek equivalent for the Aramaic Kelil (Syr. *kelilâ*, crown), which may be the protomartyr's original name and was inscribed on a slab found in his tomb. It seems that Stephen was not a proselyte, for the fact that Nicolas is the only one of the seven designated as such makes it almost certain that the others were Jews by birth. That Stephen was a pupil of Gamaliel is sometimes inferred from his able defence before the Sanhedrin; but this has not been proved. Neither do we know when and in what circumstances he became a Christian; it is doubtful whether the statement of St. Epiphanius (Hær., xx, 4) numbering Stephen among the seventy disciples is deserving of any credence. His ministry as deacon appears to have been mostly among the Hellenist converts with whom the Apostles were at first less familiar; and the fact that the opposition he met with sprang up in the synagogues of the "Libertines" (probably the children of Jews taken captive to Rome by Pompey in 63 B. C. and freed—hence the name *Libertini*), and "of the Cyrenians, and of the Alexandrians, and of them that were of Cilicia and Asia" shows that he usually preached among the Hellenist Jews. That he was pre-eminently fitted for that work, his abilities and character, which the author of the Acts dwells upon so fervently, are the best indication. The Church had, by selecting him for a deacon, publicly acknowledged him as a man "of good reputation, full of the Holy Ghost and wisdom" (Acts, vi, 3). He was "a man full of faith, and of the Holy Ghost" (vi, 5), "full of grace and fortitude" (vi, 8); his uncommon oratorical powers and unimpeachable logic no one was able to resist, so much so that to his arguments replete with the Divine energy of the Scriptural authorities God added the weight of "great wonders and signs" (vi, 8). Great as was the efficacy of "the wisdom and the spirit that spoke" (vi, 10), still it could not bend the minds of the unwilling; to these the forceful preacher was fatally soon to become an enemy.

The conflict broke out when the cavillers of the synagogues "of the Libertines, and of the Cyreneans, and of the Alexandrians, and of them that were of Cilicia and Asia", who had challenged Stephen to a dispute, came out completely discomfited (vi, 9–10); wounded pride so inflamed their hatred that they suborned false witnesses to testify that "they had heard him speak words of blasphemy against Moses and against God" (vi, 11). No charge could be more apt to rouse the mob; the anger of the ancients and the scribes had been already kindled from the first reports of the preaching of the Apostles. Stephen was arrested, not without some violence it seems (the Greek word συνήρπασαν implies so much), and dragged before the Sanhedrin, where he was accused of saying that "Jesus of Nazareth shall destroy this place [the temple], and shall change the traditions which Moses delivered unto us" (vi, 12–14). No doubt Stephen had by his language given some grounds for the accusation; his accusers apparently twisted into the offensive utterance attributed to him a declaration that "the most High dwelleth not in houses made by hands" (vii, 48), some mention of Jesus foretelling the destruction of the Temple and some inveighing against the burthensome traditions fencing about the Law, or rather the asseveration so often repeated by the Apostles that "there is no salvation in any other" (cf. iv, 12)—the Law not excluded —but Jesus. However this may be, the accusation left him unperturbed and "all that sat in the council . . . saw his face as if it had been the face of an angel" (vi, 15).

Stephen's answer (Acts, vii) was a long recital of the mercies of God towards Israel during its long history and of the ungratefulness by which, throughout, Israel repaid these mercies. This discourse contained many things unpleasant to Jewish ears; but the concluding indictment for having betrayed and murdered the Just One whose coming the Prophets had foretold, provoked the rage of an audience made up not of judges, but of foes. When Stephen "looking up steadfastly to heaven, saw the glory of God, and Jesus standing on the right hand of God", and said: "Behold, I see the heavens opened, and the Son of man standing on the right hand of God" (vii, 55), they ran violently upon him (vii, 56) and cast him out of the city to stone him to death. Stephen's stoning does not appear in the narrative of the Acts as a deed of mob violence; it must have been looked upon by those who took part in it as the carrying out of the law. According to law (Lev., xxiv, 14), or at least its usual interpretation, Stephen had been taken out of the city; custom required that the person to be stoned be placed on an elevation from whence with his hands bound he was to be thrown down. It was most likely while these preparations were going on that, "falling on his knees, he cried with a loud voice, saying: Lord, lay not this sin to their charge" (vii, 59). Meanwhile the witnesses, whose hands must be first on the person condemned by their testimony (Deut., xvii, 7), were laying down their garments at the feet of Saul, that they might be more ready for the task devolved upon them (vii, 57). The praying martyr was thrown down; and while the witnesses were thrusting upon him "a stone as much as two men could carry", he was heard to utter this supreme prayer: "Lord Jesus, receive my spirit" (vii, 58). Little did all the people present, casting stones upon him, realize that the blood they shed was the first seed of a harvest that was to cover the world.

The bodies of men stoned to death were to be buried in a place appointed by the Sanhedrin. Whether in this instance the Sanhedrin insisted on its right cannot be affirmed; at any rate, "devout men"—whether Christians or Jews, we are not told—"took order for Stephen's funeral, and made great mourning over him" (viii, 2). For centuries the location of St. Stephen's tomb was lost sight of, until (415) a certain priest named Lucian learned by revelation that the sacred body was in Caphar Gamala, some distance to the north of Jerusalem. The relics were then exhumed and carried first to the church of Mount Sion, then, in 460, to the basilica erected by Eudocia outside the Damascus Gate, on the spot where, according to tradition, the stoning had taken place (the opinion that the scene of St. Stephen's martyrdom was east of Jerusalem, near the Gate called since St. Stephen's Gate, is unheard of until the twelfth century). The site of the Eudocian basilica was identified some twenty years ago, and a new edifice has been erected on the old foundations by the Dominican Fathers.

The only first-hand source of information on the life and death of St. Stephen is the Acts of the Apostles (vi, i–viii, 2). On the question of the place of St. Stephen's stoning, see LAGRANGE, S. Étienne et son sanctuaire à Jérusalem (Paris, 1894).

CHARLES L. SOUVAY.

Stephen, SAINT, first King of Hungary, b. at Gran, 975; d. 15 August, 1038. He was a son of the Hungarian chief Géza and was baptized, together with his father, by Archbishop St. Adalbert of Prague in 985, on which occasion he changed his heathen name Vaik (Vojk) into Stephen. In 995 he married Gisela, a sister of Duke Henry of Bavaria, the future Emperor St. Henry II, and in 997 succeeded to the throne of Hungary. In order to make Hungary a Christian nation and to establish himself more firmly as ruler, he sent Abbot Astricus to Rome to petition Pope Sylvester II for the royal dignity and the power to establish episcopal sees. The pope acceded to his wishes and, in addition, presented him with a royal crown with which he was crowned at Gran on 17 August, 1001 (see HUNGARY.—*History*). He founded a monastery in Jerusalem and hospices for pilgrims at Rome, Ravenna, and Constantinople. He was a personal friend of St. Bruno of Querfurt and corresponded with Abbot St. Odilo of Cluny. The last years of his life were embittered by sickness and family troubles. When on 2 September, 1031, his only son, St. Emeric, lost his life on a bear hunt, his cherished hope of transferring the reins of government into the hands of a pious Christian prince were shattered. During his lifetime a quarrel arose among his various nephews concerning the right of succession, and some of them even took part in a conspiracy against his life. He was buried beside his son at Stuhlweissenburg, and both were canonized together in 1083. His feast is on 2 September, but in Hungary his chief festival is observed on 20 August, the day on which his

ST. STEPHEN PREACHING, BEATO ANGELICO, VATICAN

relics were transferred to Buda. His incorrupt right hand is treasured as the most sacred relic in Hungary.

Three old lives are extant: *Vita major* in *Mon. Germ. Hist., Script.*, XI, 229-39, written probably before 1083; *Cronica Ungarorum* in *Mon. Pol. hist.*, I, 495-515, written about 1086; *Vita minor* in *Mon. Germ. Hist., Script.*, XI, 226-9, written about 1100. Another Life written by Hartwig shortly after the *Vita minor* in *Script. rerum Hung.*, I, 413-28, is based on the three preceding ones. Karacsonyi, *Szent Istvan kiraly elete* (Budapest, 1904); Idem, *Szent Istvan kiraly okleveley es a Szilveszter bulla* (Budapest, 1894); Horn, *St. Etienne, roi apostolique de Hongrie* (Paris, 1899); Stilting, *Vita s. Stephani regis Hungariæ* (Raab, 1747; Kaschau, 1767); Butler, *Lives of the Saints*, 2 September; Baring-Gould, *Lives of the Saints*, 2 September.

Michael Ott.

Stephen I, Saint, Pope. Although there is some doubt as to the dates connected with the pontificate of Stephen, it is generally believed that he was consecrated 12 May, 254, and that he died 2 August, 257. According to the most ancient catalogues, he was a Roman by birth, and the son of Jovius, and there is no reason to doubt the assertion of the "Liber Pontificalis" that Lucius I, when about to be martyred, made over the care of the Church to his archdeacon Stephen (254). Most of what we know regarding Pope Stephen is connected directly or indirectly with the severe teachings of the heretic Novatus. Concerning his most important work, his defence of the validity of heretical baptism against the mistaken opinion of St. Cyprian and other bishops of Africa and Asia, there is no need to speak now, as the history of this important controversy will be found under Baptism and Cyprian of Carthage, Saint. Suffice it here to call attention to certain newly discovered letters on the subject by St. Dionysius of Alexandria ("Eng. Hist. Rev.", Jan., 1910, 111 sq.), and to note, with the late Archbishop Benson of Canterbury, that Stephen "triumphed, and in him the Church of Rome triumphed, as she deserved" [E. W. Benson, "Cyprian, His Life, His Times, His Works", VIII (London), 1897, 3]. In the early part of his pontificate Stephen was frequently urged by Faustinus, Bishop of Lyons, to take action against Marcian, Bishop of Arles, who, attaching himself to doctrines of Novatus, denied communion to the penitent *lapsi*. For some reason unknown to us Stephen did not move. The bishops of Gaul accordingly turned to Cyprian, and begged him to write to the pope. This the saint did in a letter which is our sole source of information regarding this affair (Epp. lxix, lxviii). The Bishop of Carthage entreats Stephen to imitate his martyred predecessors, and to instruct the bishops of Gaul to condemn Marcian, and to elect another bishop in his stead. As no more is said by St. Cyprian on this affair, it is supposed that the pope acted in accordance with his wishes, and that Marcian was deposed. The case of the Spanish bishops Martial and Basilides also brought Stephen in connexion with St. Cyprian. As *libellatici* they had been condemned by the bishops of their province for denying the Faith. At first they acknowledged their guilt, but afterwards appealed to Rome, and, deceived by their story, Stephen exerted himself to secure their restoration. Accordingly some of their fellow bishops took their part, but the others laid the case before St. Cyprian. An assembly of African bishops which he convoked renewed the condemnation of Basilides and Martial, and exhorted the people to enter into communion with their successors. At the same time they were at pains to point out that Stephen had acted as he had done because "situated at a distance, and ignorant of the true facts of the case" he had been deceived by Basilides. Anxious to preserve the tradition of his predecessors in matters of practical charity, as well as of faith, Stephen, we are told, relieved in their necessities "all the provinces of Syria and Arabia". In his days the vestments worn by the clergy at Mass and other church services did not differ in shape or material from those ordinarily worn by the laity. Stephen, however, is said by the "Liber Pontificalis" to have ordained that the vestments which had been used for ecclesiastical purposes were not to be employed for daily wear. The same authority adds that he finished his pontificate by martyrdom; but the evidence for this is generally regarded as doubtful. He was buried in the cemetery of St. Calixtus, whence his body was transferred by Paul I to a monastery which he had founded in his honour.

Duchesne, *Liber Pontificalis*, I (Paris, 1886) xcvii, 153-4; Eusebius, *Hist. Eccles.*, VII, 2-5; the letters of St. Cyprian, lxvii sq., in any ed. of his *Works*, or ap. Coustant, *Epp.*; *Rom. Pont.*, I (Paris, 1721), 211 sq.; Jaffé, *Regesta*, I (Leipzig, 1888), 20-1; Hefele, *Conciles*, I (Paris, 1869), 97 sq.

Horace K. Mann.

Stephen II, Pope.—On the death of Zachary, a certain priest Stephen was unanimously elected to succeed him (about 23 March, 752); but on the third day after his election, whilst transacting some domestic affairs, he was struck with apoplexy, and expired on the next day. As he died before his consecration, earlier writers do not appear to have included him in the list of the popes; but, in accordance with the long standing practice of the Roman Church, he is now generally counted among them. This divergent practice has introduced confusion into the way of counting the Popes Stephen.

Ed. Duchesne, *Liber Pontificalis*, I (Paris, 1886), 440; Mann, *Lives of the Popes*, I, pt. ii (London, 1902), 290 sq.

Horace K. Mann.

Stephen (II) III, Pope, unanimously elected in St. Mary Major's, and consecrated on 26 March (or 3 April), 752; d. 26 April, 757. He had at once to face the Lombards who were resolved to bring all Italy under their sway. With the capture of Ravenna (751), they had put an end to the power of the Byzantine exarchs and were preparing to seize the Duchy of Rome. In vain did Stephen apply for help to Constantinople and freely spent his money to induce them to keep the peace they had made with him, and to refrain from hostilities. He accordingly devoted himself to prayer and endeavoured to obtain assistance from Pepin and the Franks. As a last resource he went himself to Gaul to plead his cause before the Frankish king. Receiving a most favourable reception, he crowned Pepin as King of the Franks, and at Kiersey was solemnly assured by him that he would defend him, and would restore the exarchate to St. Peter. Failing to make any impression on Aistulf, the Lombard king, by repeated embassies, Pepin forced the passes of the Alps, and compelled him to swear to restore Ravenna and the other cities he had taken (754). But no sooner had Pepin withdrawn from Lombardy than Aistulf roused the whole Lombard nation, appeared in arms before the walls of Rome (Jan., 756), ravaged the neighbourhood, and made a desperate attempt to capture the city. After receiving one appeal for help after another from the pope, Pepin crossed the Alps a second time (756), and again forced Aistulf to submission. This time Stephen was put in possession of the cities of the exarchate and of the Pentapolis, and became practically the first pope-king. Towards the close of this same year Aistulf died amid preparations for once more violating his engagements. On his death two rivals claimed the Lombard throne, Desiderius, Duke of Istria and Ratchis, brother of Aistulf, who in 749 had resigned the Lombard crown, and had taken the monastic habit in Monte Cassino. Desiderius at once invoked the assistance of the pope, and, on condition of his help, promised to restore to Rome certain cities in the exarchate and the Pentapolis which still remained in the hands of the Lombards, and to give the pope a large sum of money. Stephen at once sent envoys to both the rivals, and, impressing on Ratchis the duty of being true to his monastic vows, succeeded in bringing about peace, and preventing civil war. Ratchis returned to his monastery and Desiderius was recognized as king (about March, 757). The latter, however, did not fulfil his promise to the pope in its entirety. He gave up Faenza, Ferrara, and two small towns, but retained Bologna, Imola, and other towns in the Pentapolis till his overthrow by Charlemagne. Stephen had scarcely established a system of government in the exarchate when he had to quell the rebellion of Sergius, Archbishop of Ravenna, whom he had made its governor. He, however, caused the rebel to be brought to Rome, and kept him there whilst he lived. Stephen corresponded with the Emperor Constantine on the subject of the restoration of the sacred images, and himself restored many of the ancient churches of the city. Remarkable for his love of the poor, Stephen built hospitals for them near St. Peter's, in which church he was buried.

Ed. DUCHESNE, *Liber Pontificalis*, I (Paris, 1886), 440 sq.; ed. JAFFÉ, *Codex Carolinus* (Berlin, 1867); *Mon. Ger. Hist.*; *Epp.*, III (Berlin, 1892); *Script.*, I; *Script. rerum Langob.* Most of these sources will be found in HALLER, *Die quellen zur Gesch. der Entstehung des Kirchenstaates* (Leipzig, 1907); HODGKIN, *Italy and her Invaders*, VII (Oxford, 1899); DUCHESNE, *The Beginning of the Temporal Sovereignty of the Popes* (London, 1908), iii, iv; MANN, *Lives of the Popes in the Early Middle Ages*, I, pt. ii (London, 1902), 289 sqq.

HORACE K. MANN.

Stephen (III) IV, POPE, b. about 720; d. 1 or 3 August, 772. Paul I was not dead when trouble began about the election of his successor. Toto of Nepi with a body of Tuscans burst into Rome, and, despite the opposition of the *primicerius* Christopher, forcibly intruded his brother Constantine, a layman, into the chair of Peter (June, 767). In the spring of 768, however, Christopher and his son Sergius contrived to escape from the city, and with the aid of the Lombards deposed the usurper. They were also able to overthrow the monk Philip, whom some of their Lombard allies had clandestinely elected pope. By their efforts Stephen, a Sicilian, the son of Olivus, was at length canonically elected and consecrated (7 August, 768). He had been a Benedictine monk, and had been ordained priest by Pope Zachary. After his consecration the antipopes were treated with the greatest cruelty which, it seems to be generally allowed, Stephen was unable to hinder. To prevent the recurrence of such an election as that of Constantine, the Lateran council forbade laymen to be elected popes or to take part in their election for the future. Only cardinals were to be chosen popes (April, 769). Through Stephen's support the archdeacon Leo was enabled to hold the See of Ravenna against a lay intruder, and in turn through the support of the brothers Charlemagne and Carloman, Kings of the Franks, Stephen was able to recover some territories from the Lombards. But their king, Desiderius, managed to strike two serious blows at Stephen. He brought about a marriage between his daughter and Charlemagne, and in some mysterious manner effected the fall of the pope's chief ministers, Christopher and Sergius. He also allied himself with Paul Afiarta, Stephen's chamberlain, who practised great cruelties when the pope lay dying. Desiderius also brought about trouble in Istria by trying to cause a schism against the Patriarch of Grado, but Stephen defended the patriarch promising him even armed support if necessary. Stephen is honoured as a saint in some Martyrologies.

For bibliography see STEPHEN (II) III, POPE.

HORACE K. MANN.

Stephen (IV) V, POPE (816–17), date of birth unknown; d. 24 Jan., 817. Stephen, the son of Marinus, was of the same noble Roman family which gave two other popes to the Church. During his youth he had been patronized by Hadrian I and Leo III, the latter of whom had ordained him deacon. His virtues were celebrated, and he was elected pope and consecrated immediately after Leo's death, about 22 June, 816. He at once caused the Romans to take an oath to the Emperor Louis the Pious as their suzerain, and he sent notice of his election to him. He then went to France and crowned Louis. From that benevolent prince he received a number of splendid presents, and with him renewed the pact or agreement that had already existed for some time between the Franks and the papacy. Whilst still in Gaul he granted the pallium to Theodulf of Orleans, one of the emperor's chief advisers. When returning to Rome he visited Ravenna, there exposing the sandals of Christ to the veneration of the faithful, and he brought back with him a number of exiles whom political reasons had sent into exile during the pontificate of Leo III. He was buried in St. Peter's.

Liber Pontificalis, ed. DUCHESNE, II, 49 sqq.; *Lives of Louis the Pious and various annals in Mon. Germ. Hist.: Script.*, II; MANN, *Lives of the Popes*, II, 111 sqq.

HORACE K. MANN.

Stephen (V) VI, POPE (885–91), date of birth unknown; d. in Sept., 891. His father, Hadrian, who belonged to the Roman aristocracy, entrusted his education to his relative, Bishop Zachary, librarian of the Holy See. Stephen was created cardinal-priest of SS. Quattro Coronati by Marinus I, and his obvious holiness was the cause of his being chosen pope. He was consecrated in September, 885, without waiting for the imperial confirmation; but when Charles the Fat found with what unanimity he had been elected he let the matter rest. Stephen was called upon to face a famine caused by a drought and by locusts, and as the papal treasury was empty he had to fall back on his father's wealth to relieve the poor, to redeem captives, and to repair churches. To promote order he adopted Guido III, Count of Spoleto, "as his son" and crowned him Emperor (891). He also recognized Louis the Blind as King of Provence. As Aurelian, Archbishop of Lyons, would not consecrate Teutbold who had been canonically elected Bishop of Langres, Stephen himself consecrated him. He had also to oppose the arbitrary proceedings of the Archbishops of Bordeaux and Ravenna, and to resist the attacks which the Patriarch Photius made on the Roman See. His resistance was successful, and the Emperor Leo sent the disturber into exile. When writing against Photius, he begged the emperor to send warships and soldiers to enable him to ward off the assaults of the Saracens. Stephen, who received many English pilgrims and envoys bringing Peterspence, was buried in the portico of the basilica of that Apostle.

Liber Pontificalis, II, 191 sqq., 226; *Letters of* STEPHEN in *P. L.*, CXXIX, and LOWENFELD, *Epp. Pont. Rom.* (Leipzig, 1885), 35 sqq.; various annals in *Mon. Germ. Hist.: Script.*, I; FRODOARD in *ibid.*, XIII; DUCHESNE, *The Beginnings of the Temporal Sovereignty of the Popes* (London, 1907), 189, 194–5; MANN, *Lives of the Popes*, III, 367 sqq.

HORACE K. MANN.

Stephen (VI) VII, POPE (896–7), date of birth unknown; d. about August, 897. Stephen was a Roman, and the son of John, a priest. He had been consecrated Bishop of Anagni, possibly against his will, by Formosus, and became pope about May, 896. Whether induced by evil passion or perhaps, more probably, compelled by the Emperor Lambert and his mother Ageltruda, he caused the body of Formosus to be exhumed, and in January, 897, to be placed before an unwilling synod of the Roman clergy. A deacon was appointed to answer for the deceased pontiff, who was condemned for performing the functions of a bishop when he had been deposed and for passing from the See of Porto to that of Rome. The corpse was then stripped of its sacred vestments, deprived of two fingers of its right hand, clad in the garb of a layman, and ultimately thrown into the Tiber. Fortunately it was not granted to Stephen to have time to do much else besides this atrocious deed. Before he was put to death by strangulation, he forced several of those who had been ordained by Formosus to resign their offices and he granted a few privileges to churches.

Liber Pontificalis, II, 229; privileges of Stephen in *P. L.*, CXXIX; DUMMLER, *Auxilius and Vulgarius* (Leipzig, 1866); DUCHESNE, *The Beginnings of the Temporal Sovereignty of the Popes*, 198 sqq.; MANN, *Lives of the Popes*, IV, 76 sqq.

HORACE K. MANN.

Stephen (VII) VIII, POPE (929–31), date of birth unknown; d. in Feb. or March, 931. He became pope either at the end of 928 or at the beginning of 929. Except that he was a Roman, the son of Teudemund, and sometime cardinal-priest of St. Anastasia, and that when pope he issued certain privileges for monasteries in France and Italy, and was buried in St. Peter's, nothing more is known of him.

Liber Pontificalis, II, 242; JAFFÉ, *Regesta* (Leipzig, 1888), 453–4; MANN, *Lives of the Popes*, IV, 189 sqq.

HORACE K. MANN.

Stephen (VIII) IX, POPE, 939–942, date of birth unknown; he became pope about 14 July, 939, and d. about the end of Oct., 942. Despite the contrary assertions of late writers, there is no doubt that Stephen was a Roman and cardinal-priest of SS. Silvester and Martin. He supported the declining Carlovingian dynasty, and by threat of excommunication forced the nobles to be faithful to the Frankish King Louis IV d'Outre-Mer. Throughout the whole of his pontificate he was subject to Alberic, Prince of the Romans, and so had little opportunity of distinguishing himself.

Liber Pontificalis, II, 244; privileges, *P. L.*, CXXXII; FRODOARD, *Annals;* MANN, *Lives of the Popes in the Early Middle Ages*, IV (London, 1910), 212 sq.

HORACE K. MANN.

Stephen (IX) X, POPE, b. probably about the beginning of the eleventh century; d. at Florence, 29 March, 1058. (Junian?) Frederick, destined to become Pope Stephen X, was the son of Gozelon, Duke of Lower Lorraine and of Junca, the daughter of Berengarius II, King of Italy. As he advanced in years he became as distinguished for character and learning as he was for his birth. It was seemingly whilst he was a canon of Liège that his cousin Leo IX met him and made him chancellor and librarian of the Roman Church (c. 1051). He accompanied Leo IX in his apostolic journeyings throughout Europe, and was sent by him on the famous embassy to Constantinople (1054) which terminated in the final separation of the Eastern and Western Churches. On his return from the East he was robbed by the Count of Teate, and, to avoid falling into the hands of the Emperor Henry III, the Black (who seems to have distrusted him as the brother of the rebellious Godfrey the Bearded, Duke of Lorraine), he became a monk at Monte Cassino (1055), and, after the death of the Emperor Henry, its abbot (1057). He was made cardinal-priest of St. Chrysogonus by Victor II, and, on the latter's death, he was freely chosen his successor, and consecrated on the following day (3 August, 1057). As pope, he carried on the work of reformation which had been inaugurated by St. Leo IX. To show how much he was in earnest, he at once made cardinals of both that zealous champion of reform, St. Peter Damian, and the quondam monk Humbert, his own uncompromising companion on the embassy to Constantinople. He also made no little use of Cardinal Hildebrand (afterwards St. Gregory VII), the soul of the reforming party. He sent him to Milan to effect an improvement in the morals of its clergy with instructions to proceed to Germany and to induce the regent, the empress-mother Agnes, to accept his election which had been made without any reference to her. It was further arranged that Hildebrand was then to go on to France. Stephen was preparing to reopen negotiations with the Greek Church, and to try to stop the advance of the Normans in southern Italy, when he died, exhorting the cardinals to await the return of Hildebrand before electing his successor. He was buried in the Church of St. Reparata.

Liber Pontificalis, II, 278, ed. DUCHESNE (Paris, 1892); *De ortu et obitu just. cænob. Cas.*, n. 58, ap. MAI, *Script. Vet.*, VI, 278; *P. L.*, CXLIII, U. ROBERT has put together all that is known of Stephen X in his *Hist. du P. Etienne X* (Brussels, 1892); MANN, *Lives of the Popes in the Middle Ages*, VI (London, 1910); 207 sq.

HORACE K. MANN.

Stephen Gobarus. See MONOPHYSITES AND MONOPHYSITISM.

Stephen Harding, SAINT, confessor, the third Abbot of Cîteaux, was born at Sherborne in Dorsetshire, England, about the middle of the eleventh century; d. 28 March, 1134. He received his early education in the monastery of Sherborne and afterwards studied in Paris and Rome. On returning from the latter city he stopped at the monastery of Molesme and, being much impressed by the holiness of St. Robert, the abbot, joined that community. Here he practised great austerities, became one of St. Robert's chief supporters and was one of the band of twenty-one monks who, by authority of Hugh, Archbishop of Lyons, retired to Cîteaux to institute a reform in the new foundation there (see CÎTEAUX, ABBEY OF). When St. Robert was recalled to Molesme (1099), Stephen became prior of Cîteaux under Alberic, the new abbot. On Alberic's death (1110) Stephen, who was absent from the monastery at the time, was elected abbot. The number of monks was now very reduced, as no new members had come to fill the places of those who had died. Stephen, however, insisted on retaining the strict observance originally instituted and, having offended the Duke of Burgundy, Cîteaux's great patron, by forbidding him or his family to enter the cloister, he was even forced to beg alms from door to door. It seemed as if the foundation were doomed to die out when (1112) St. Bernard with thirty companions joined the community. This proved the beginning of extraordinary prosperity. The next year Stephen founded his first colony at La Ferté, and before his death he had established thirteen monasteries in all. His powers as an organizer were exceptional, he instituted the system of general chapters and regular visitations and, to ensure uniformity in all his foundations, drew up the famous "Charter of Charity" or collection of statutes for the government of all monasteries united to Cîteaux, which was approved by Pope Callistus II in 1119 (see CISTERCIANS). In 1133 Stephen, being now old, infirm, and almost blind, resigned the post of abbot, designating as his successor Robert de Monte, who was accordingly elected by the monks. The saint's choice, however, proved unfortunate and the new abbot only held office for two years.

Stephen was buried in the tomb of Alberic, his predecessor, in the cloister of Cîteaux. In the Roman calendar his feast is 17 April, but the Cistercians themselves keep it on 15 July, with an octave, regarding him as the true founder of the order. Besides the "Carta Caritatis" he is commonly credited with the authorship of the "Exordium Cisterciencis cenobii", which however may not be his. Two of his sermons are preserved and also two letters (Nos. 45 and 49) in the "Epp. S. Bernardi".

WILLIAM OF MALMESBURY, *Gesta Regum*, ed. Stubbs in *Rolls Series*, IV (London, 1889), §§ 334–7; *Gallia christ.*, IV (Paris, 1728), 980–4; *Acta SS.*, II, April (Venice, 1738), 493–8; MABILLON, *Acta SS., O.S.B.*, II (Paris, 1668), 1062; HÉLYOT, *Hist. des ordres religieux*, V (Paris, 1792), 336–7; DUGDALE, *Monasticon anglicanum*, V (London, 1846), 220–6; DALGAIRNS, *Life of St. Stephen Harding* (London, 1844); new edition with notes, ed., THURSTON (London, 1898).

G. ROGER HUDLESTON.

Stephen of Autun, bishop, liturgical writer, b. at Bangé (hence surnamed Balgiacus or de Balgiaco) in Anjou; d. at the abbey of Cluny, 1139 or early in 1140. Of his younger days nothing is known except that he was the son of Gaucerannus, lord of Bangé, and the uncle of Humbert, Archbishop of Lyons. He appears in history (1112) as Bishop of Autun. As such he was present (1115) at a synod of Tournus. A letter is in existence of the year 1116, written to him from the Lateran by Pascal II in which the pope places the Diocese of Autun under his special protection and confirms to Stephen various privileges. In 1129 Stephen was among the prelates who assisted at the coronation of Philip, eldest son of Louis VI of France. He built a cathedral, beginning in 1120, which was solemnly consecrated (1131) by Pope Innocent II. He always showed a great admiration for the religious state, and in 1136 resigned his see and entered the monastery of Cluny. The abbot, Peter the Venerable, under whom he entered and died, gives great praise to his learning and piety. His "Tractatus de Sacramento Altaris", printed, together with some other documents relating to Stephen, in P. L., CLXXII, 1371, is an ascetico-liturgical treatise, consisting of twenty chapters and a preface, in which he speaks of the ordination and duties of each of the Minor and Major Orders; and of the Holy Sacrifice of the Mass and gives a literal and allegorical explanation of the Canon. He is one of the earliest writers using the term transubstantiation. This treatise, published in 1517 by Montalon, canon of Autun, was ascribed by some to Stephen II of Autun (d. 1189), but is vindicated for the earlier bishop by Mabillon, "Annales O. S. B.", VI, 270.

HURTER, *Nomencl.*, II (Innsbruck, 1906), 75; *Gallia christiana*, IV, 389; DUCHESNE, *Fastes Episc.*, I, 339; *Hist. Litt. de la France*, XI (Paris, 1759), 710; CEILLIER, *Auteurs Sacrés*, XIV (Paris, 1863), 304.

FRANCIS MERSHMAN.

Stephen of Bourbon, illustrious writer and preacher, especially noted as a historian of medieval heresies, b. at Belleville (Archdiocese of Lyons) towards the end of the twelfth century; d. in 1261. Having received his early education from the cathedral clergy of Macon, he made his higher studies in Paris, about 1220, and there shortly afterwards, as it seems, he entered the Order of Preachers. From 1230 he was very active for many years as preacher and inquisitor in the districts of Lyonnais, Burgundy, Franche-Comté, Savoy, Champagne, Lorraine, Auvergne, Languedoc, and Roussillon. In his work for preachers entitled "De septem donis Spiritus Sancti", or "Tractatus de diversis Materiis prædicabilibus", Stephen has embodied much useful matter out of the many years of his practical experience. The parts of this work more valuable at the present day were published in Paris in 1877 by A. Lecoy de la Marche under the title "Anecdotes historiques, légendes et apologues, tirés du recueil inédit d'Etienne de Bourbon dominicain du 13e siècle". Considered as a whole Stephen's work affords a clear insight into the different sects and superstitions of the age, while giving at the same time valuable information regarding the most prominent of his contemporaries. Although credulous to a marked degree, Stephen was, nevertheless, a strenuous opponent of superstition. A free use of his writings was made by a later compiler to form a "Speculum Morale", which for a long time was falsely ascribed to Vincent of Beauvais.

ECHARD, *Script. ord. præd.*, I, 184 sq.; HURTER, *Nomenclator*, II (Innsbruck, 1906), 375; LECOY DE LA MARCHE, Introd. to work cited above; HAUREAU in *Journal des savants*, 1881, 591 sq., 739 sq.; MÜLLER, *Die Waldenser* (Gotha, 1886), 166 sq.

CHARLES J. CALLAN.

Stephen of Muret, SAINT, b. 1045; d. at Muret, 8 February, 1124, founder of the Abbey and Order of Grandmont (q. v.). Serious chronological difficulties are presented by the traditional story of his early life, which runs as follows: Stephen in his twelfth year accompanied his father, the Viscount of Thiers, to Italy where he was left to be educated by Milo, Archbishop of Benevento; after passing twelve years in this prelate's household, he became the inmate of a Benedictine monastery in Calabria, but never received the habit. He then returned to France to bid farewell to his parents, having formed the design of entering religion, but, finding them dead, returned to Italy. His patron Milo having also died, he established himself at Rome, where he studied the rules of the religious houses of the city. After a four years' sojourn he obtained a Bull from Gregory VII authorizing him to found an institute resembling that of the solitaries he had frequented in Calabria, and returned to France. He is said to have settled at Muret in 1076. This story is impossible; his father visited Italy in order to make a pilgrimage to St. Nicholas at Bari; but St. Nicholas's relics were not placed there till some years later; Milo was not Archbishop of Benevento for twelve years. These are not the only difficulties, but for a discussion of these chronological questions see Martène, "Amplissima Collectio", VI, præf., viii sq. The exact truth as to St. Stephen's life cannot now be established. He went to Italy and there saw some religious whose holy life inspired him with a desire to imitate them, but who they were, Carthusians or Benedictines, we do not know. The quarrel as to what great order could claim Grandmont as its offspring, with the consequent forgeries, has done much to involve the founder's life in obscurity. Though Stephen was certainly the founder of the Order of Grandmont, he did little for his disciples except offer them the example of his holy life, and it was not till after his death that the order was firmly established. His head is preserved in the parish Church of St. Sylvestre, Canton of Laurière (Haute Vienne). He was canonized in 1189 and his feast occurs on 8 February. His works (not authentic) may be found in Migne, P. L., CCIV, 997–1162.

Acta SS., Feb., II, 199 sq.; MARTÈNE, *Amplissima Coll.*, VI (1729); CHEVALIER, *Biobibliographie*, 1378.

RAYMUND WEBSTER.

Stephen of Tournai, canonist, b. at Orléans, 1128; d. at Tournai, September, 1203. He entered the Order of the Canons Regular at Saint-Euverte in Orléans about 1150, then studied canon and Roman law at Bologna, returning to his monastery in 1160. He was elected abbot of Saint-Euverte in 1167 and of Sainte-Geneviève at Paris in 1177. The latter monastery he almost entirely rebuilt, establishing a monastic school in connexion with it. In 1192 he became Bishop of Tournai, but was greatly hampered in the exercise of his episcopal functions by the opposition of the people as well as by the interdict placed on France on account of the divorce proceedings of Philip II. He is the author of "Summa in decretum Gratiani" (1159), which is to a great extent based on the similar works of Paucapalea, Rufinus, and Rolandus (Alexander III). It was first edited by Schulte (Giessen, 1891). His letters, edited by Molinet (Paris, 1679), are printed in P. L., CXI, 309–625.

BERNOIS, *Etienne de Tournai, 1128–1203* (Orléans, 1906); SCHULTE in the introduction to his edition of the *Summa*; WAUTERS in *Biog. belgique*, VI (Brussels, 1878), 719–25.

MICHAEL OTT.

Stephens, HENRY ROBERT, Belgian theologian, b. of English parentage at Liège, 5 August, 1665; d. there, 15 June, 1623. He entered the Society of Jesus, 7 Sept., 1683, and for over twenty years was attached to the episcopal seminary of Liège, first as professor of dogmatic theology and later as its superior. During this period the Jansenists were active in Belgium, both in attacking the Jesuits and in opposing the papal Decrees condemnatory of Jansenism. All of Father Stephens's published works were occasioned by these attacks. In a libellous work entitled "Specimen doctrinæ a Jesuitis in Seminario Leodiensi traditæ" the Jesuits were accused, among other things, of corrupting faith and morals by their teaching. In answer to these accusations Father Stephens published a set of theses, "Conclusiones theologicæ miscellaneæ" (Liège, 1702) and had them publicly defended by one of his pupils. In answer to another Jansenistic work known as the "Epistola Leodiensis de formula Alexandri VII", he published his "Vera defensio authoritatis Ecclesiæ" (Liège, 1707). The Jansenist, Henry Denys, thereupon defended the "Epistola" in an anonymously published work which called forth Father Stephens's "Author epistolæ Leodiensis denuo confutatus" (Liège, 1709). His other works are the "Dissertatio theologica de Condemnatione Libri Janseniani" (Liège, 1710), and the "Consilium pacis adversariis propriis inter se disputantibus" (Liège, 1710). In all these works his name appears in the latinized form of Stephani.

SOMMERVOGEL, *Bibl. de la Comp. de J.*, VII (Brussels, 1896).

EDWARD C. PHILLIPS.

Stephens, THOMAS (also known in India as PADRE ESTEVÃO or ESTEVAM; less familiarly PADRE BUSTEN, BUSTON, or DE BUBSTON), b. about 1549 at Bulstan, Wiltshire; d. in 1619 at Goa, India. He is admittedly the first Englishman in India. His father was an influential London merchant. Little is known of his boyhood and youth. Though Hakluyt ("Voyages") and Philip Anderson ("The English in Western India") believe him to have been educated at New College, Oxford, while A. F. Pollard in the "Dictionary of National Biography" identifies him with the Thomas Stephen of Bourton, Dorset, who was elected scholar of Winchester in 1564, a careful search among the registers of Oxford students gives no evidence of his ever having been at any of the colleges of Oxford. The error of counting Stephens as an Oxonian may easily have arisen from his name having been mistaken either for that of Richard Stephens his brother, who studied at New College, or for that of another Thomas Stephens who is said to have taken his degree at St. John's College, Oxford, in 1577, when the subject of this article was already a novice at Sant' Andrea's in Rome. Though not a student at Oxford, owing to his father's influential position and to his own brilliant parts, he very probably came into familiar contact with Edmund Campion and several other Catholic Oxford students whose examples may have influenced his subsequent conversion. Soon after he had finished his scholastic career Stephens attached himself to one Thomas Pounde. The perusal of the accounts of the Indian Missions seems to have engendered in them the desire of entering the Society of Jesus. Their common aspirations and a similarity of tastes brought the two friends often together during the persecutions of the English Catholics. Finally, impatient of delay in carrying out their spiritual object, they determined to set out for Rome, but Pounde, betrayed, was doomed to pass the next thirty years in prison. Stephens travelled alone to Rome and entered the Society of Jesus. Having finished his novitiate, Stephens received permission to proceed to India. He sailed from Lisbon (4 April, 1579) and reached Goa, then the principal city of the East Indies, on 24 October of the same year. From Goa he wrote a series of letters to his father, which appear to have held out "the strongest inducements which London merchants had been offered to embark on Indian speculations", coming, as they did, from one with a thorough grasp of commercial ideas. It has been undoubtedly put forth that these communications on the mercantile chances and possibilities in the East subsequently led to the formation of the East India Company; but, unfortunately, only two of the letters have been preserved. One of them (10 November, 1579), the first he wrote to his father on reaching Goa, is included in Hakluyt's "Voyages". The other (24 October, 1583), written in Latin to his brother in Paris, is preserved in part in the National Library of Brussels, and published by Dr. Gerson da Cunha in the "Instituto Vasco da Gama", II. Fr. Stephens's first five years were spent as minister of the professed house at Goa, rector of Salsette College, and temporary *socius* to the visitor. The remaining thirty-five years of his ministry were spent among the Brahmin Catholics of Salsette. His energy and zeal won the devotion of the people and his influence often protected travellers, not only his countrymen, but other Europeans as well.

In the midst of his missionary labours he found time for considerable literary work, though few of his writings remain. The suppression of the Society of Jesus in 1773 and the checkered career of the Konkani race (the descendants of the Brahmin Catholic community of Salsette) destroyed most of his works and renders the drawing up of anything like a complete list impossible. M. Pollard states that Padre Estevão was the first to make a scientific study of Canarese, that he also learned Hindustani, and that in both these languages he published manuals of piety and grammar. Yet not a single trace of these productions is extant. His greatest surviving work, "The Christian Purânna", shows that he must have acquired a complete mastery of Marâthi and Konkani and of Sanskrit, and it is possible to suppose that he must have written more works with the help of these than are preserved to us. The following list includes all the extant writings: the two letters mentioned above; a Catechism of Christian Doctrine which first appeared under the title, "Doutrina Christã em lingua Bramana-Canarin, Ordenada a maniera de dialogo para ensinar os meninos, pelo Padre Thomas Estevão, Jesuita, no Collegio de Rachol" (1622); "Arte de lingua Canarin", a grammar of the Konkani language, the first grammar of an Indian tongue by a European, chiefly of bibliographical interest (Rachol, 1640), revised and improved by Fr. Diogo Ribiero, S. J., and bearing the *imprimatur* of the *præpositus* General of the Society, Fr. Vitelleschi. Only two copies of the first edition are known to exist; a second edition was issued in 1857; "The Christian Purânna" (1616, 1649, and 1654), but no copies of any of these editions are extant. An *editio princeps*, reproduced from authenticated MS. copies by the present writer, was issued in 1907 from the Jesuit Press at Mangalore, India. "The Christian Purânna" is a Marathi-Konkani metrical composition, consisting of 10,962 strophes, divided into two parts treating of the Old and the New Testament respectively.

HAKLUYT, *Navigation, Voyages and Discoveries of the English Nation* (Edinburgh, 1886—); DODD, *Church History*, II (Brussels, *vere* Wolverhampton, 1737–42); FOLEY, *Records of the English Province S. J.*, III (London, 1878); ANDERSON, *The English in Western India* (Bombay, 1856); DA CUNHA RIVARA, *Ensaio Historico da Lingua Concani* (New Goa, 1858); POLLARD in *Dict. Nat. Biog.*, s. v. *Stephens* or *Stevens, Thomas*, in supplement; SOMMERVOGEL, *Bibliothèque de la C. de J.* (Brussels, 1890–1900); BAUMGARTNER, *Gesch. der Weltliteratur* (Freiburg, 1900); GRIERSON, *Linguistic Survey of India*, VII, *Marâthi Language* (Calcutta, 1905); DA CUNHA in *Instituto Vasco da Gama*, II (New Goa, 1873); IDEM, *Materials for the History of Oriental Studies amongst the Portuguese* (paper read before the International Congress of Orientalists, Florence, 1878, and published in the *Atti* of that Congress, II, Florence, 1881); IDEM, *The Origin of Bombay* (Bombay, 1900); BURNELL, *Tentative list of works on the Portuguese in India* (Mangalore, 1880; only fifteen copies printed by the Board Mission Press); IDEM, *Specimens of South Indian Dialects* (Mangalore, 1872); FERNANDES in *The Mangalore Magazine*, I; SALDANHA, *The Indian Caste*, I (Bombay, 1904); IDEM, *The Christian Purânna*, an essay (Bombay, 1903); MONIERWILLIAMS, *Facts of Indian Progress* in *Contemporary Review*; MASCARENHAS in *The Indian Antiquary* (April, 1878); BHÂGAVAT in *Vividha Dnyâna Vistâra* (December, 1906).

JOSEPH L. SALDANHA.

Steuco (STEUCHUS), AGOSTINO, exegete, b. at Gubbio, Umbria, 1496; d. at Venice, 1549. At the age of seventeen he entered the order of the Canons Regular of the Lateran at Gubbio, and in 1525 he was made director of the library of Cardinal Grimani at Venice. In 1530 he became prior of the canons of Reggio and shortly after at Gubbio. Early in 1538 he was appointed Bishop of Kisamos in Crete by Paul III, who also made him director of the Vatican Library on 27 Oct. of the same year, but in the latter capacity Steuco did not accomplish much (Pastor, "Geschichte Pauls III," Freiburg, 1909, p. 738). In 1547 Paul III sent him as legate to the Tridentine Council, which had been transferred to Bologna, and he died on his way back to Rome. He was a man of varied talents, well versed in history, philosophy, and theology, and had a fair mastery of Greek and Hebrew. His works, chiefly exegetical, were edited in three volumes by Ambrogio Morando (Paris, 1578; Venice, 1591 and 1601).

TIRABOSCHI, *Storia della Letteratura Italiana*, VII, I, 396–400; WILLMANN, *Gesch. des Idealismus*, III (Brunswick, 1897), 170–77; HURTER, *Nomenclator*.

MICHAEL OTT.

Stevens, CORNEILLE. See BELGIUM.

Stevenson, JOSEPH, archivist, b. at Berwick-on-Tweed, 27 Nov., 1806; d. in London, 8 Feb., 1895. Though his parents were Presbyterians, he was educated at Durham under the historian, James Raine, and afterwards at the University of Glasgow. Coming to London he found work, first among the Government records, then in the British Museum, 1831; later he married Mary Ann Craig, and gradually gave up Presbyterianism. The death of his eldest and much-loved son so affected him that he returned to Durham and took Anglican orders. He became librarian at the cathedral (1841-48), and was afterwards instituted rector of Leighton Buzzard (1849-63). All this time he was constantly editing ancient texts: for the Maitland Club, Glasgow, eight volumes (1833-42); for the English Historical Society, five volumes (1838-41); for the Roxburghe Club, four volumes; for the Surtees Society, seven volumes, with eight volumes of "The Church Historians of England." In 1856 the English Government was making plans for dealing with the national records on a large scale. Stevenson was one of those appointed to report on the subject, and when the Public Record Office was instituted, 1857, he was one of the first editors engaged. He now edited seven volumes for the Rolls Series, seven volumes of Calendars, Foreign Series, and two of the Scottish Series. Meantime he had been received into the Church, 24 June, 1863, and after his wife died, 1869, he entered the seminary of Oscott, and was ordained priest by Bishop Ullathorne in 1872. Next year he was in Rome searching for documents concerning English history from the Vatican archives, being employed by the British Government to begin the series of "Roman Transcripts" for the Record Office; he also wrote many reports for the Historical Manuscript Commission. In 1877 he gave up these occupations to enter the Society of Jesus, though nearly seventy-two years of age, but after his novitiate he returned again to historical research, and continued his studies until the end. His chief work of this period was the discovery and publication of Claude Nau's "Life of Mary Queen of Scotts" (Edinburgh, 1883). In 1892 he received the honorary degree of Doctor of Laws from the University of St. Andrews. Prolonged literary work, instead of stiffening the mind, left Stevenson ever fresh and elastic, the friend of children and prodigal of kindness to others.

The Month (March, April, 1895); GILLOW, *Bibl. Dict. Eng. Cath.*, s. v.

J. H. POLLEN.

Stevin, SIMON, b. at Bruges in 1548; d. at Leyden in 1620. He was for some years book-keeper in a business house at Antwerp; later he secured employment in the administration of the Franc of Bruges. After visiting Prussia, Poland, Sweden, and Norway he took up his residence in the Netherlands, where he spent the rest of his life. The Stadtholder Maurice of Nassau esteemed him so highly that he studied under his direction mathematics, science, and engineering, rewarding him for his services by making him director of finances, inspector of dykes of the Low Countries, and quartermaster-general of the Government. His was an upright, modest, and inventive mind. His influence on the development of science was great and lasting. He began with the publication in 1582 of his "Tafelen van Interest" (Tables of Interest; Plantin, Antwerp), thus distributing through the business world an easy and valuable method of calculation, still carefully preserved by the wealthy merchants of the Low Countries. Then came successively: in 1583 the "Problematum geometricorum libri V", a very original work, somewhat imperfectly reproduced in subsequent editions of the author's works, the "Dialektike ofte bewysconst", a treatise on logic, re-edited at Rotterdam in 1621, but not found in the large editions of the author's works, and "De Thiende", a small pamphlet of thirty-six pages containing the oldest systematic and complete explanation of decimal calculus, both published by Plantin at Leyden in 1585. "De Thiende" has often caused its author to be regarded as the inventor of calculus; he was indisputably the first to bring to light its great advantages. Stevin translated the pamphlet into French and re-edited it the same year under the title "La Disme", with his Arithmetic published at Antwerp by Plantin. In 1586 appeared the most famous of his works, "De Beghinselen der Weeghconst, De Weeghdaet, De Beghinselen der Waterwichts" (Antwerp). This was the first edition of his mechanics, in which he sets forth for the first time several theorems since then definitely embodied in science; the hydrostatic paradox; equilibrium of bodies on inclined planes; the parallelogram of forces, formulated, it is true, under a different enunciation by constructing a triangle by means of two components and their results.

Stevin's "Vita politica, Het Burgherlick leven", a treatise on the duties of the citizen which is no longer printed in large editions of his works, was published by Raphelengen at Leyden in 1590. It gave rise during the nineteenth century to a long and violent controversy. From some pages of this volume the inference has been drawn that when entering the service of Maurice of Nassau Stevin apostatized from the Catholic Church, but this opinion is hardly tenable and has now been abandoned. In 1594 appeared the "Appendice Algebraïque", an eight-page pamphlet, the rarest of his works (there is a copy at the Catholic University of Louvain) and one of the most remarkable; in it he gave for the first time his famous solution of equations of the third degree by means of successive approximations. In the same year was published "De Sterctenbouwing", a treatise on fortifications, and in 1599, "Havenvinding", a treatise on navigation, instructing mariners how to find ports with the aid of the compass. From 1605 to 1608 Stevin re-edited his chief works in two folio volumes entitled "Wisconstige gedachtenissen" (Bouwenz, Leyden). A Latin translation of them, under the title "Hypomnemata mathematica", was confided to Willebrord Snellius; and an incomplete French translation, entitled "Mémoires mathématiques", was the work of Jean Tuning, secretary of the Stadtholder Maurice. These two versions were published at Leyden by Jean Paedts. The "Wisconstige gedachtenissen" and the "Hypomnemata mathematica" contain several treatises then published for the first time, notably the trigonometry, geography, cosmography, perspective, book-keeping, etc.

In 1617 Waesberghe published at Rotterdam Stevin's "Legermeting" and "Nieuwe maniere van Stercktebouw door spilsluysen", of which French translations were published by the same editor in the following year under the titles "Castramétation" and "Nouvelle manière de fortifications par écluses". These were the last publications made during his lifetime, but he left important MSS., the chief of which were published in 1649 by his son Henri, who composed the "Burgherlicke Stoffen" (political questions); the others were lost, but later recovered. Bierens de Haan edited two of them at Amsterdam in 1884: "Spiegeling der singconst" (mirror of the art of singing) and "Van de molens" (on mills). After Stevin's death Albert Girard translated several of his works and annotated others, thus forming a large folio volume published at Leyden in 1634 by the Elzevirs as "Œuvres mathématiques de Simon Stevin de Bruges". Abroad Stevin is often known only through this translation, but it does not convey an adequate idea of his works and should be supplemented by several of the original editions mentioned above. Unfortunately these have become bibliographical rarities almost unobtainable outside of Belgium and the Netherlands. M. Ferd. van der Haeghen has made them the subject of a masterly study in his "Bibliotheca Belgica" (1st series, XXIII, Ghent and The Hague, 1880-90), in which he notes most of the copies preserved in the libraries of both countries.

GOETHALS, *Notice hist. sur la vie et les travaux de Simon Stevin de Bruges* (Brussels, 1841); STEICHEN, *Mém. sur la vie et les travaux de Simon Stevin* (Brussels, 1846); CANTOR, *Vorlesungen über Gesch. des Mathematik*, II (2nd ed., Leipzig, 1900).

H. BOSMANS.

Stifter, ADALBERT, poet and pedagogue, b. at Oberplan in Bohemia, 23 October, 1805; d. at Linz, 28 October, 1868. His father was a linen weaver and flax dealer. In these humble surroundings the talented boy received the first intellectual stimulus from his mother and grandmother, who told him fairy-tales, stories, and legends. At school he was an apt scholar and, among other things, showed talent for music and drawing. After the sudden death of his father in 1817, his grandfather sent him to the Benedictine *gymnasium* at Kremsmünster in Upper Austria, where Father Plazidus Hall took the clever boy under his care. In 1827 Stifter went to the University of Vienna. Here, after completing the usual philosophical course, he applied himself to legal studies; but his natural bent eventually led him to attend lectures in mathematics and the natural sciences. He supported himself by giving private lessons among the leading families, and in this way formed a wide connexion among the Viennese aristocracy, his circle of acquaintances including the family of the imperial chancellor, Prince Metternich. He wished to be a teacher of natural science and passed the written examination for this with honour in 1830, without the oral examination, however. Although now thirty-two years old and still a candidate for the position of teacher, he married the penniless daughter of a retired artillery officer. It was impossible for him to find a more secure position, and he was obliged to continue earning a precarious livelihood by giving private lessons. His position, however, improved when a story, "Der Condor", published in the "Wiener Zeitschrift" in 1840, suddenly made him famous. This was soon followed by other stories, which were later collected and published under the title of "Studien".

A new era in Stifter's existence began with the year 1848. It was in that year that the revolutionary uprisings, which filled the streets of Vienna with turmoil and violence, drove him from the capital to Linz. There, after vainly trying to obtain a position as a teacher, he offered his services to the provincial government of Upper Austria, and his great pedagogical abilities were now at last recognized. Count Leo Thun, the reorganizer of the Austrian school system, appointed Stifter in 1850 a member of the school board at Linz. There was no longer any lack of honours and recognition: he received the medal for art and science and the cross of a knight of the Order of Francis Joseph, and was greatly esteemed by the Empress Elizabeth. But, in spite of all this, Stifter gradually became morose and eccentric. It became impossible for him to overcome an ever-increasing depression, the after-effect of his early disappointments. As he entered the sixties, a severe liver complaint developed which obliged him to make repeated visits to Karlsbad. In 1865 he retired with his full salary and the title of imperial councillor. He visited his home for the last time in 1867, and soon after was seized with the painful illness which, in spite of his wife's careful nursing, proved fatal. He died childless.

As a poet, Stifter belonged to the late Romantic School, like Droste-Hülshoff and Mörike. His contemplative spirit, his delicate perception of nature, the richness of his imagination, and his shrinking from the tumult of the day are all traits of true Romanticism, as is evident in his "Studien", and "Bunte Steine". As an older man, about 1850, the greater composure of his style bore a resemblance to the classicism of Goethe, as is shown in his "Nachsommer", and still more in his "Witiko". That he was also an excellent pedagogue is made evident not only in his work as a member of the school-board, but also in his writings, which bear evidence of his excellent pedagogical knowledge. His latest biographer says: "In advance of his times, he held up as the aim of the future most of the achievements which have been realized by modern pedagogy, and was thus, until death, in word and deed a model, a leader, and a discoverer of new paths for the school he loved so dearly." Several of his works were often reprinted during his lifetime. A complete edition, edited by Apprent, was issued at Pesth in 1870. A popular edition of selected works was published at Leipzig in 1887. Professor Sauer is editing a new and carefully prepared edition for the "Library of German Authors of Bohemia" ("Bibliothek deutscher Schriftsteller aus Böhmen", Prague, 1901——).

HEIN, *Adalbert Stifter, sein Leben und seine Werke* (Prague, 1904); *Adalbert Stifter, eine Selbstcharakteristik des Menschen und des Künstlers, ausgewählt und eingeleitet von P. G. Harmuth* (Munich, 1905); KOSCH, *Adalbert Stifter* (Leipzig, 1905); *Adalbert Stifter und die Romantik*, in *Prager deutsche Studien*, I (1905); HULLER, *Zu Stifters Stil*, in *Euphorion*, XVI (1909), 136-47, 460-71.

N. SCHEID.

Stigmata, MYSTICAL.—I. To describe merely the facts without deciding whether or not they may be explained by supernatural causes, history tells us that many ecstatics bear on hands, feet, side, or brow the marks of the Passion of Christ with corresponding and intense sufferings. These are called visible stigmata. Others only have the sufferings, without any outward mark, and these phenomena are called invisible stigmata. Their existence is so well established historically that, as a general thing, they are no longer disputed by unbelievers, who now seek only to explain them naturally. Thus a free-thinking physician, Dr. Dumas, professor of religious psychology at the Sorbonne, clearly admits the facts (Revue des Deux Mondes, 1 May, 1907), as does also Dr. Pierre Janet (Bulletin de l'Institut psychologique international, Paris, July, 1901).

St. Catherine of Siena at first had visible stigmata but through humility she asked that they might be made invisible, and her prayer was heard. This was also the case with St. Catherine de' Ricci, a Florentine Dominican of the sixteenth century, and with several other stigmatics. The sufferings may be considered the essential part of visible stigmata; the substance of this grace consists in pity for Christ, participation in His sufferings, sorrows, and for the same end—the expiation of the sins unceasingly committed in the world. If the sufferings were absent, the wounds would be but an empty symbol, theatrical representation, conducing to pride. If the stigmata really come from God, it would be unworthy of His wisdom to participate in such futility, and to do so by a miracle. But this trial is far from being the only one which the saints have to endure: "The life of stigmatics," says Dr. Imbert, "is but a long series of sorrows which arise from the Divine malady of the stigmata and end only in death" (op. cit. infra, II, x). It seems historically certain that ecstatics alone bear the stigmata; moreover, they have visions which correspond to their rôle of co-sufferers, beholding from time to time the blood-stained scenes of the Passion. With many stigmatics these apparitions were periodical, e. g. St. Catherine de' Ricci, whose ecstasies of the Passion began when she was twenty (1542), and the Bull of her canonization states that for twelve years they recurred with minute regularity. The ecstasy lasted exactly twenty-eight hours, from Thursday noon till Friday afternoon at four o'clock, the only interruption being for the saint to receive Holy Communion. Catherine conversed aloud, as if enacting a drama. This drama was divided into about seventeen scenes. On coming out of the ecstasy the saint's limbs were covered with wounds produced by whips, cords etc.

Dr. Imbert has attempted to count the number of stigmatics, with the following results: (1) None are known prior to the thirteenth century. The first mentioned is St. Francis of Assisi, in whom the stigmata were of a character never seen subsequently: in the wounds of feet and hands were excrescences of flesh representing nails, those on one side having round black heads, those on the other having rather long points, which bent back and grasped the skin. The saint's humility could not prevent a great many of his brethren beholding with their own eyes the existence of these wonderful wounds during his lifetime as well as after his death. The fact is attested by a number of contemporary historians, and the feast of the Stigmata of St. Francis is kept on 17 September. (2) Dr. Imbert counts 321 stigmatics in whom there is every reason to believe in a Divine action. He believes that others would be found by consulting the libraries of Germany, Spain, and Italy. (3) In this list there are 41 men. (4) There are 62 saints or blessed of both sexes, of whom the best known (numbering twenty-six) were: St. Francis of Assisi (1186–1226); St. Lutgarde (1182–1246), a Cistercian; St. Margaret of Cortona (1247–97); St. Gertrude (1256–1302), a Benedictine; St. Clare of Montefalco (1268–1308), an Augustinian; Bl. Angela of Foligno (d. 1309), Franciscan tertiary; St. Catherine of Siena (1347–80), Dominican tertiary; St. Lidwine (1380–1433); St. Frances of Rome (1384–1440); St. Colette (1380–1447), Franciscan; St. Rita of Cassia (1386–1456), Augustinian; Bl. Osanna of Mantua (1499–1505), Dominican tertiary; St. Catherine of Genoa (1447–1510), Franciscan tertiary; Bl. Baptista Varani (1458–1524), Poor Clare; Bl. Lucy of Narni (1476–1547), Dominican tertiary; Bl. Catherine of Racconigi (1486–1547), Dominican; St. John of God (1495–1550), founder of the Order of Charity; St. Catherine de' Ricci (1522–89), Dominican; St. Mary Magdalen de' Pazzi (1566–1607), Carmelite; Bl. Marie de l'Incarnation (1566–1618), Carmelite; Bl. Mary Anne of Jesus (1557–1620), Franciscan tertiary; Bl. Carlo of Sezze (d. 1670), Franciscan; Bl. Margaret Mary Alacoque (1647–90), Visitandine (who had only the crown of thorns); St. Veronica Giuliani (1600–1727), Capuchiness; St. Mary Frances of the Five Wounds (1715–91), Franciscan tertiary.

(5) There were 29 stigmatics in the nineteenth century. The most famous were: Catherine Emmerich (1774–1824), Augustinian; Elizabeth Canori Mora (1774–1825), Trinitarian tertiary; Anna Maria Taïgi (1769–1837); Maria Dominica Lazzari (1815–48); Marie de Moerl (1812–68) and Louise Lateau (1850–83), Franciscan Tertiaries. Of these, Marie de Moerl spent her life at Kaltern, Tyrol (1812–68). At the age of twenty she became an ecstatic, and ecstasy was her habitual condition for the remaining thirty-five years of her life. She emerged from it only at the command, sometimes only mental, of the Franciscan who was her director, and to attend to the affairs of her house, which sheltered a large family. Her ordinary attitude was kneeling on her bed with hands crossed on her breast, and an expression of countenance which deeply impressed spectators. At twenty-two she received the stigmata. On Thursday evening and Friday these stigmata shed very clear blood, drop by drop, becoming dry on the other days. Thousands of persons saw Marie de Moerl, among them Görres (who describes his visit in his "Mystik", II, xx), Wiseman, and Lord Shrewsbury, who wrote a defence of the ecstatic in his letters published by "The Morning Herald" and "The Tablet" (cf. Boré, op. cit. infra). Louise Lateau spent her life in the village of Bois d'Haine, Belgium (1850–83). The graces she received were disputed even by some Catholics, who as a general thing relied on incomplete or erroneous information, as has been established by Canon Thiery ("Examen de ce qui concerne Bois d'Haine", Louvain, 1907). At sixteen she devoted herself to nursing the cholera victims of her parish, who were abandoned by most of the inhabitants. Within a month she nursed ten, buried them, and in more than one instance bore them to the cemetery. At eighteen she became an ecstatic and stigmatic, which did not prevent her supporting her family by working as a seamstress. Numerous physicians witnessed her painful Friday ecstasies and established the fact that for twelve years she took no nourishment save weekly communion. For drink she was satisfied with three or four glasses of water a week. She never slept, but passed her nights in contemplation and prayer, kneeling at the foot of her bed.

II. The facts having been set forth, it remains to state the explanations that have been offered. Some physiologists, both Catholics and Free-thinkers, have maintained that the wounds might be produced in a purely natural manner by the sole action of the imagination coupled with lively emotions. The person being keenly impressed by the sufferings of the Saviour and penetrated by a great love, this preoccupation acts on her or him physically, reproducing the wounds of Christ. This would in no wise diminish his or her merit in accepting the trial, but the immediate cause of the phenomena would not be supernatural. We shall not attempt to solve this question. Physiological science does not appear to be far enough advanced to permit a definite solution, and the writer of this article adopts the intermediate position, which seems to him unassailable, that of showing that the arguments in favour of natural explanations are illusory. They are sometimes arbitrary hypotheses, being equivalent to mere assertions, sometimes arguments based on exaggerated or misinterpreted facts. But if the progress of medical sciences and psychophysiology should present serious objections, it must be remembered that neither religion nor mysticism is dependent on the solution of these questions, and that in processes of canonization stigmata do not count as incontestable miracles.

No one has ever claimed that imagination could produce wounds in a normal subject: it is true that this faculty can act slightly on the body, as Benedict XIV said, it may accelerate or retard the nerve-currents, but there is no instance of its action on the tissues (De canoniz., III, xxxiii, n. 31). But with regard to persons in an abnormal condition, such as ecstasy or hypnosis, the question is more difficult; and, despite numerous attempts, hypnotism has not produced very clear results. At most, and in exceedingly rare cases, it has induced exudations or a sweat more or less coloured, but this is a very imperfect imitation. Moreover, no explanation has been offered of three circumstances presented by the stigmata of the saints: (1) Physicians do not succeed in curing these wounds with remedies. (2) On the other hand, unlike natural wounds of a certain duration, those of stigmatics do not give forth a fetid odour. To this there is known but one exception: St. Rita of Cassia had received on her brow a supernatural wound produced by a thorn detached from the crown of the crucifix. Though this emitted an unbearable odour, there was never any suppuration or morbid alteration of the tissues. (3) Sometimes these wounds give forth perfumes, for example those of Juana of the Cross, Franciscan prioress of Toledo, and Bl. Lucy of Narni. To sum up, there is only one means of proving scientifically that the imagination, that is auto-suggestion, may produce stigmata: instead of hypotheses, analogous facts in the natural order must be produced, namely wounds produced apart from a religious idea. This has not been done.

With regard to the flow of blood it has been objected that there have been bloody sweats, but Dr. Lefebvre, professor of medicine at Louvain, has replied that such cases as have been examined by physicians were not due to a moral cause, but to a specific malady. Moreover, it has often been proved by the microscope that the red liquid which oozes forth is not blood; its colour is due to a particular substance, and it does not proceed from a wound, but is due, like sweat, to a dilatation of the pores of the skin. But it may be objected that we unduly minimize the power of the imagination, since, joined to an emotion, it can produce sweat; and as the mere idea of having an acid bon-bon in the mouth produces abundant saliva, so, too, the nerves acted upon by the imagination might produce the emission of a liquid, and this liquid might be blood. The answer is that in the instances mentioned there are glands (sudoriparous and salivary) which in the normal state emit a special liquid, and it is easy to understand that the imagination may bring about this secretion; but the nerves adjacent to the skin do not terminate in a gland emitting blood, and without such an organ they are powerless to produce the effects in question. What has been said of the stigmatic wounds applies also to the sufferings. There is not a single experimental proof that imagination could produce them, especially in violent forms.

Another explanation of these phenomena is that the patients produce the wounds either fraudulently or during attacks of somnambulism, unconsciously. But physicians have always taken measures to avoid these sources of error, proceeding with great strictness, particularly in modern times. Sometimes the patient has been watched night and day, sometimes the limbs have been enveloped in sealed bandages. M. Pierre Janet placed on one foot of a stigmatic a copper shoe with a window in it through which the development of the wound might be watched, while it was impossible for anyone to touch it (op. cit. supra).

IMBERT, *La stigmatisation* (Paris, 1894); LEFEBVRE, *Louise Lateau, étude médicale* (Louvain, 1873); RIBET, *La mystique* (Paris, 1899); POULAIN, *Des grâces d'oraison* (Paris, 1911); tr. *The Graces of Interior Prayer* (London, 1910); BORÉ, *Les stigmatisées du Tyrol* (Paris, 1846); SCHMEGER, *Vie de Catherine Emmerich* (French tr., Paris, 1868).

AUG. POULAIN.

Stipend [Lat. *stipendium*, a tax, import, tribute; in military use, pay, salary; contraction for *stipipendium*, from *stips*, a gift, donation, alms (given in small coin), and *pendere*, to weigh out], a fixed pay, salary; retribution for work done; the income of an ecclesiastical living. In canon law stipend is a general designation of means of support (*sustentatio congrua* or *congrua*) provided for the clergy. In the early ages of the Church no special provision was made for the maintenance of the clergy. St. Paul, the tent-maker, set the example (I Cor., iv, 12) of earning his own livelihood. In imitation of him many clerics worked at some craft or followed some profession, living by the labour of their own hands. Even in the fifth and sixth centuries there were bishops, priests, and deacons, who in keeping with the advice of the Fourth Council of Carthage (a. 398, cann. 52, 53) supported themselves by their own labour. Early legislation (Canon. Apost., can. 6), which forbade the clergy to take up certain occupations and professions, is an indication that clerics sought to maintain themselves. Many of the laity, however, even from the beginning, were quick to follow the instructions of Christ and his Apostles (Matt., x, 10; Luke, x, 7; I Cor., ix, 13; I Tim., v, 17–18), founded on the practice in vogue among the Jews (Lev., xxvii, 30 sq.; Num., xviii, 23 sq.; etc.), who gave tithes of all their goods and produce for the sustenance of priests and levites. Thus did the laity provide for the bodily welfare of the clergy in return for the spiritual gifts received through their ministry. Later the payment of tithes was frequently insisted on by St. Ambrose, St. Augustine, and others (Thomassin, "Vet. et nov. eccl. disc.," III, II, xii, xiv). The Synods of Tours (560) and Mâcon (586) strenuously exhorted the faithful to pay the tithes ordained by God. Charlemagne made their payment obligatory on his subjects by a royal ordinance of 779, the requirements of which he himself faithfully observed. The obligation of giving tithes has long since ceased almost universally, but the faithful, of course, must contribute to the proper support of sacred ministers.

The voluntary offerings of the people made on Sundays and other occasions were also intended in part for the maintenance of clerics, that they might not be compelled to engage in pursuits which might ill become the ecclesiastical state or withdraw the clergy from their spiritual work. In most countries the offerings of the laity still constitute the chief support of the clergy. A quasi-contract obtains between the parish on the one hand and the clergy who minister to its wants on the other. Pastor and assistants are engaged in the work of the parish and receive in return a definite salary from the income or revenues of the parish. These revenues are derived from pew-rental, offerings, collections, subscriptions, and whatever other sources of income the parish may possess. Clerics engaged in teaching or other work not parochial are supported in much the same way, obtaining a salary from the institution by which they are employed. The salary (*congrua*) of pastors and assistants should be a fixed sum, such as will suffice for their necessities. The amount paid will depend on various circumstances of time, place, persons, income of the parish, and duties of the incumbent. The Council of Trent (Sess. XXIV, c. 13, de ref.) directs bishops to arrange the *congrua* in the most convenient way. Salaries of pastors in the United States are determined in diocesan synods or otherwise with the advice of the diocesan consultors (Conc. Plen. Balt. III, n. 273). Stole fees (jura stolæ), or perquisites received on the occasion of the administration of the sacraments or sacramentals, are not in the nature of stipends. At times, nevertheless, by diocesan regulations, they form a portion of the salary of pastor and assistants.

In regard to so-called state aid of the clergy, the State began indirectly to help the clergy in the time of Constantine, who gave a legal existence to churches as corporate bodies, permitting them to receive donations and legacies and to hold the same in perpetuity (Cod. Theod., XVI, 2, 4). He ordered contributions of grain to be given annually to the clergy out of the public granaries. He contributed large sums from his own resources for the support of the clergy in Africa, and exempted the Church from imposts in an edict imposing a general tax (Cod. Theod., XI, i, 1). Direct support of the clergy by the State is of comparatively modern origin, having developed since the Reformation. It obtains particularly in Catholic countries that have entered into a concordat, or treaty, with the Holy See for the support of the clergy. This support is in recompense, far inadequate indeed, for the sequestration of ecclesiastical funds and property. Austria, Spain, Italy, and certain countries of Central and South America thus directly support the clergy, paying salaries to bishops, vicars-general, pastors, and assistants. France and Portugal, as well as Cuba, Porto Rico, and the Philippines, when under Spanish rule, did the same.

Since the time of Constantine the right of the Church to possess temporal goods has been universally acknowledged and protected by civil governments with some exceptions. These exceptions refer chiefly to bequests and legacies. The possession by the Church of temporal goods and the surrendering of the same to the clergy for their sustenance gave rise to benefices, the fruits or income of which constitute the chief provision for the maintenance of the clergy possessing them. The fruits of a benefice will maintain the incumbent, even though he have private means of support. He should have not only what is necessary for sustenance, but sufficient for fitting recreation and hospitality, and a modest portion for future contingencies: he may also assist near relatives to some extent. If anything remain, it is to be used in charitable works. Ecclesiastical goods are not to be bequeathed in any considerable quantity to profane purposes. There are other methods in vogue for the support of the clergy akin to, or divisions of, those mentioned: voluntary offerings, tithes, quasi-contracts, state aid, and benefices. Stipends for the application of Masses were originally intended for the daily maintenance of the celebrant. (For treatment of the Mass-stipend see MASS, SACRIFICE OF THE.) It is in this latter sense that the word is mostly used at present, though it occasionally designates certain allowances made from ecclesiastical foundations in favour of students seeking a more special or more profound training in the arts or sciences. (See BENEFICE; ENDOWMENT; TITHES.)

ANDREW B. MEEHAN.

Stockholm, the capital of the Kingdom of Sweden, is situated on Lake Maelar at the spot where it opens into the Saltsjö, a rocky bay of the Baltic 59° 20′ N. lat. The city, through which flows the short but fine river the Norrström, is built partly on islands, partly on heights, on both banks of the river, from which there is a view over Maelar and the Saltsjö. It is claimed that Stockholm was founded by Birger Jarl (d. 1266), and the coat of arms of the city still bears the picture of King St. Eric (d. 1160). The city has a population of 341,986 and is the court residence of the king and the seat of the government, of the diplomatic corps, and of the vicar Apostolic. The entrance to Stockholm is defended by the fortresses Oscar Fredriks Borg and Waxholm. It is the seat of the chief military authorities of the fourth and fifth military districts, including artillery, cavalry, infantry, and transport, and is a station of the fleet. As the capital it is the seat of the central administration of the kingdom, and contains the supreme court, the Svea upper court, the national royal bank, the mint, and exchange. As regards administration the city of Stockholm forms a separate district, which is ruled by a governor and is distinct from the Province of Stockholm (Stockholms län). The city has burgomasters, magistrates, and a common council of one hundred members. The importance of the city in regard to commerce, manufactures, and shipping is shown by the following statistics of the year 1908: value of imports, 157,966,681 kronen; value of exports, 45,934,890 kronen; factories, 732, with 29,948 workmen and an output of the value of 166,540,075 kronen. The shipping trade of the city is carried on by 249 ships of 124,037 tons. The vessels over ten tons which call at the port of Stockholm number 36,338.

Schools of higher learning in Stockholm are the Högskola, a free college founded in 1878, the Caroline medico-surgical institute, founded in 1815, the military academy, the academy for the artillery and engineering corps, the academy for music (1771), the academy of fine arts (1773), the technical high school, and the commercial high school. The learned societies are the Swedish Academy, with eighteen members, founded by Gustavus III in 1786; the Academy of Sciences, founded in 1739; the Nobel Institute, which has an endowment of over thirty million kronen; the Royal Library, containing over 300,000 volumes; and the observatory. The most important public buildings are the royal castle, built in the Renaissance style, one of the finest works of the celebrated Swedish architect Count Nicodemus Tessin the Younger (d. 1728); the Parliament building; the House of the Swedish Nobility, where the council of nobles formerly met, built in the Renaissance style of 1661; the royal opera house and royal theatre; the national museum, with picture and sculpture galleries; the Northern Museum, with collections to illustrate the ethnography and development in civilization of the Scandinavian peoples; the Skansen, a large open-air museum and zoölogical garden. The Northern Museum and the Skansen were founded by Dr. A. Hazelius (d. 1901). The chief public statues are those of Birger Jarl, Gustavus Vasa, Gustavus II Adolphus, Charles XII, and Charles XIII, both of these last mentioned statues being in the "Kungsträdgården", Gustavus III, Charles XIV, a statue of Linnæus in a park bearing his name, and one of Berzelius.

Stockholm has very few buildings belonging to the Middle Ages, as the finest of this era, the monasteries and churches, were either disfigured or torn down at the introduction of the Reformation. Thus, for example, Gustavus Vasa had the churches of St. Mary Magdalen, St. Clara, and St. Jacob torn down; after his death they were rebuilt in the style of a later period. This king also caused the choir of the Church of St. Nicholas (Storkyrkan) to be shortened. This church, founded about 1260, is one of the finest monuments still in existence of the Catholic period of Stockholm. The Riddarholm church, originally the church of a Franciscan monastery, is the burial place of the Swedish kings. The Protestant church buildings of Stockholm belong to a large number of different Protestant denominations. The State Church is Lutheran; among the other denominations represented are: the followers of Waldenström, Baptists, Methodists, Irvingites, Adventists, the Salvation Army, Mormons, etc. Many of the adherents of these sects have not withdrawn officially from the State Church.

There are in Stockholm about 1800 Catholics, for whom there are two Catholic churches, that of St. Eugenia, in Norra Smedjegatan, and that of St. Eric, in Götgatan. The Catholic cemetery has a chapel called St. Joseph's. The vicar Apostolic for Sweden lives at St. Eric's; the present vicar Apostolic is Dr. A. Bitter, titular Bishop of Doliche. Catholic elementary schools are connected with both churches. A higher school for girls is under the care of the French Sisters of St. Joseph. The Sisters of St. Elizabeth devote themselves to the care of the sick and have also charge of two asylums, Oscars Minne and Jozefinahemmet. It was not until recent times that the two Catholic churches of Stockholm were built, St. Eugenia in 1837 and St. Eric in 1892, and schools established. From the introduction of the Reformation to the edict of toleration issued by Gustavus III in 1781 public Catholic worship was forbidden. Mass could be said only in the private chapels of the foreign ambassadors at Stockholm, and attendance at these services was forbidden to Lutherans under severe penalties. Conversion was punished by expulsion from the country and confiscation of goods. As late as 1858 six women who had returned to the Catholic Church were expelled from the country. It was not until 1860 that a restricted religious liberty was granted in Sweden. Thus, for example, institutions and foundations of denominations not belonging to the State Church cannot hold real estate in the country without royal permission. Monasteries are forbidden. By the royal edict of 1910 the names of Catholics are to be entered in the Lutheran Church books by the Lutheran pastors of the State Church, and Catholics must apply to these pastors for their marriage certificates.

DAHLGREN, *Stockholm*, II (Stockholm, 1897), xxii, 95; NORDENSVAN, *Maelardrottningen* (Stockholm, 1896); *Boken om Stockholm* (Stockholm, 1901); *Statistisk Arsbok för Stockholms Stadår 1908* (Stockholm, 1910); *Religious Liberty in Sweden* in *America*, no. 102 (New York, 25 March, 1911).
G. ARMFELT.

Stöckl, ALBERT, neo-Scholastic philosopher and theologian, b. at Möhren, near Freuchtlingen, in Middle Franconia, Bavaria, 15 March, 1823; d. at Eichstädt, 15 November, 1895. He received his classical education at the *gymnasium* at Eichstädt, studied philosophy and theology at the episcopal lyceum in the same city (1843-48), and was ordained priest 22 April, 1848. His first position was that of curate at the pilgrimage church at Wemding. In 1850, he was made instructor of philosophy at the episcopal lyceum at Eichstädt, and two years later was appointed professor of theoretical philosophy in the same institution. He received the Degree of Doctor of Philosophy (1855) from the University of Würzburg; and was transferred (1857) to the theological section of the lyceum as professor of exegesis and Hebrew. In the autumn of 1862 he accepted a call as professor of philosophy at the academy of Münster in Westphalia. The disagreeable divisions and discord which arose in this institution at the time of the Vatican Council led Stöckl, in the summer of 1871, to resign his professorship and return to the Diocese of Eichstädt as parish priest at Gimpertshausen. On 7 March, 1872, he was installed as a cathedral canon at Eichstädt. At the same time he again became professor of practical philosophy, philosophy of religion, and pedagogy in the lyceum. In addition to his labours as a scholar Stöckl also took an active part in political life. From 1878 to 1881 he was a member of the lower house of the Reichstag. During the many years of his life spent in teaching, Stöckl wrote a large number of text-books covering the entire field of philosophy which had a large circulation not only in Germany but also in other countries, including the United States of America. As one of its most distinguished representatives, he had an important share in the revival of Thomistic philosophy. Both as teacher and as author he was noted for simplicity, logical acumen, and lucidity.

Among his numerous writings the following should be mentioned particularly: "Liturgie und dogmatische Bedeutung der alttestamentlichen Opfer" (Ratisbon, 1848); "Die speculative Lehre vom Menschen und ihre Geschichte" (Würzburg, 2 vols., 1858–59); "Die Lehre der vornicänischen Kirchenväter von der göttlichen Trinität" (Eichstädt, 1861, in the "Programm" of the lyceum); "Das Opfer nach seinem Wesen und nach seiner Geschichte" (Mainz, 1861); "Geschichte der Philosophie des Mittelalters" (3 vols., Mainz, 1864–66); "Lehrbuch der Philosophie" (Mainz, 1868; 7th ed., 3 vols., 1892; 8th ed., revised by G. Wohlmuth, 1905—); "Lehrbuch der Geschichte der Philosophie" (Mainz, 1870; 3rd ed., 2 vols., 1888; tr. "Handbook of the History of Philosophy", by T. A. Finlay, S.J., Dublin, 1887); "Die Infallibilität des Oberhauptes der Kirche und die Zustimmungsadressen an Herrn von Döllinger" (Münster, 1870; 2nd ed., 1870); "Grundriss der Aesthetik" (Mainz, 1871; 3rd ed., 1889, under the title, "Lehrbuch der Aesthetik"); "Grundriss der Religionsphilosophie" (Mainz, 1872; 2nd ed., 1878); "Lehrbuch der Pädagogik" (Mainz, 1873; 2nd ed., 1880); "Lehrbuch der Geschichte der Pädagogik" (Mainz, 1876); "Der Materialismus geprüft in seinen Lehrsätzen und deren Consequenzen" (Mainz, 1877); "Das Christenthum und die grossen Fragen der Gegenwart auf dem Gebiete des geistigen, sittlichen und socialen Lebens. Apologetisch-philosophische und socialpolitische Studien" (3 vols., Mainz, 1879-80); "Geschichte der neueren Philosophie von Baco und Cartesius bis zur Gegenwart" (2 vols., Mainz, 1883); "Das Christenthum und die modernen Irrthümer. Apologetisch-philosophische Meditationen" (Mainz, 1886); "Geschichte der christlichen Philosophie zur Zeit der Kirchenväter" (Mainz, 1891); "Grundzüge der Philosophie" (Mainz, 1892; 2nd ed., edited by Ehrenfried, 1910); "Grundriss der Geschichte der Philosophie" (Mainz, 1894); "Lehrbuch der Apologetik" (2 pts., Mainz, 1895). Stöckl contributed numerous papers on apologetic, philosophico-historical, and pedagogical subjects to the periodical press, especially to "Der Katholik". He also wrote a large number of articles for the second edition of the "Kirchenlexikon", and several of the longer articles for the "Staatslexikon der Görres-Gesellschaft".

[PEMSEL], *Dr. Albert Stöckl, Domkapitular und Lycealprofessor in Eichstätt. Eine Lebensskizze verfasst von einem seiner Schüler* (Mainz, 1896), with portrait; PRUNER, *Dr. Albert Stöckl* in *Der Katholik*, I (1896), 1–11; ROMSTÖCK, *Personalstatistik u. Bibliogr. des Lyceums in Eichstätt* (Ingolstadt, 1894), 157–62.
FRIEDRICH LAUCHERT.

Stoddard, CHARLES WARREN, American author, b. 7 August, 1843, at Rochester, N. Y.; d. 23 April, 1909, at Monterey, California. He was descended in a direct line from Anthony Stoddard of England, who settled at Boston, Mass., in 1639. While he was still a child his parents moved to New York City, where they lived till 1855, when they migrated to San Francisco, California. In 1857 he returned alone to New York, lived with his grandparents for two years, and then rejoined his family in San Francisco. In a short time he began writing verses, which he sent anonymously to a local newspaper. They met with great success and were later published with the modest title "Poems by Charles Warren Stoddard". Poor health compelled him to give up his plans for a college education. He tried the stage, but soon realized that such a life was not his calling. In 1864 he visited the South Sea Islands and from there wrote his "Idyls" —letters which he sent to a friend who had them published in book form. "They are," as Mr. Howells says, "the lightest, sweetest, wildest, freshest things that were ever written about the life of that summer ocean." He made four other trips to the South Sea Islands, and gave his impressions in "Lazy Letters from Low Latitudes" and "The Island of Tranquil Delights". Several times he visited Molokai, and became well acquainted with Father Damien, the Apostle to the Lepers, and wrote his interesting little book, "The Lepers of Molokai", which, with Stevenson's famous letter, did much to establish Father Damien's true position in public esteem. In 1867, soon after his first visit to the South Sea Islands, he was received into the Catholic Church, for which he had a most tender devotion. The story of his conversion he has told in a small book interestingly written: "A Troubled Heart and How it was Comforted". Of this book he has said: "Here you have my inner life all laid bare." To this change in his religious belief are due in great measure those genial optimistic qualities that endeared him to all who knew him.

In 1873 he started on a long tour as special correspondent of the "San Francisco Chronicle". His commission was a roving one, without restrictions of any kind. He was absent for five years, during which he travelled over Europe and went as far east as Palestine and Egypt. He sent considerable matter to his newspaper, much of which was never reprinted, though some of it was among his best work. In 1885, having decided to settle down, he accepted the chair of English literature in the University of Notre Dame, Indiana; but owing to ill-health he soon resigned. The same reason caused him to resign a corresponding position which he held in the Catholic University, Washington, D. C., from 1889 to 1902. In a short time he moved to Cambridge, Mass., intending to devote himself exclusively to literary work. A serious and almost fatal illness interfered with his plans, yet he was not idle. He put forth his "Exits and Entrances", a book of essays and sketches which he called his favourite work, probably because it told of his intimate friend Stevenson and of others among his host of literary acquaintances. At this time he also wrote his only novel, "For the Pleasure of His Company", of which he said, "Here you have my Confessions." So strictly biographical are most of his writings that Stoddard hoped by supplying a few missing links to enable the reader to trace out the whole story of his life. In 1905 he returned to California and settled in Monterey with a hope of recovering his health. He lingered on till 1909, when he died in his sixty-sixth year. To superficial observers he was a man of contradictions. He was essentially Bohemian, but of the higher type, a man who could not resist the call of the far-away land, his home, as he himself said, being always under his hat. And yet he was a mystic and a recluse even in his travels. "Imaginative and impressionable", two epithets which he applied to his South Sea friends, are particularly appropriate to Stoddard himself.

That charm of his traits which may be described as "sweetness, peacefulness, tenderness, gentleness" he imparted to his writings. Noted English authors have given the highest praise to some of his work, and have taken to task the American public for their lack of appreciation of him. Besides the books already mentioned he wrote: "Summer Cruising in the South Seas" (1874); "Marshallah, a Flight into Egypt" (1885); "A Trip to Hawaii" (1885); "In the Footprints of the Padres" (1892); "Hawaiian Life" (1894); "The Wonder Worker of Padua" (1896); "A Cruise under the Crescent" (1898); "Over the Rocky Mountains to Alaska" (1899); "Father Damien, a Sketch" (1903); "With Staff and Scrip" (1904); "Hither and Yon"; "The Confessions of a Reformed Poet" (1907); "The Dream Lady" (1907).

JAMES in *California Classics Series* (1909); *Nat. Mag.* (Aug., 1911); *Ave Maria* (June, 1909); *Overland Monthly* (Jan., June, 1909).

M. J. FLAHERTY.

Stoics and Stoic Philosophy.—The Stoic School was founded in 322 B. C. by Zeno of Cittium and existed till the closing of the Athenian schools (A. D. 429). (It took its name from the Στοὰ ποικίλη, the painted hall or colonnade in which the lectures were held.) Its history may be divided into three parts: (1) *Ancient Stoicism;* (2) *Middle Stoicism;* (3) *New Stoicism.* (1) *Ancient Stoicism (322–204).*— Zeno of Cittium (b. 366; d. in 280) was the disciple of Crates the Cynic and the Academicians Stilpo, Xenocrates, and Polemon. After his death (264), Cleanthes of Assium (b. 331; d. 232) became head of the School; Chrysippus of Soli (b. 280) succeeded and was scholarch till 204. These philosophers, all of Oriental origin, lived at Athens, where Zeno played a part in politics and were in communication with the principal men of their day. The Stoic doctrine, of which Zeno laid the foundations, was developed by Chrysippus in 705 treatises, of which only some fragments have been preserved. In addition to the principles accepted by all the thinkers of their age (the perception of the true, if it exist, can only be immediate; bodies alone exist; the wise man is self-sufficient; the political constitution is indifferent), derived from the Sophists and the Cynics, they base the entire moral attitude of the wise man (conformity to oneself and nature, indifference to external things on a comprehensive concept of nature, in part derived from Heraclitus, but inspired by an entirely new spirit. It is a belief in a universal nature which is at one and the same time Fate infallibly regulating the course of events (εἱμαρμένη, *logos*); Zeus, or providence, the external principle of finality adapting all other things to the needs of rational beings; the law determining the natural rules that govern the society of men and of the gods; the artistic fire, the expression of the active force which produced the world, one, perfect, and complete from the beginning, with which it will be reunited through the universal conflagration, following a regular and ever recurring cycle. The popular gods are different forms of this force, described allegorically in the myths. This view of nature is the basis of the optimism of the Stoic moral system: confidence in the instinctive faculties, which, in the absence of a perfect knowledge of the world, ought to guide man's actions; and again, the infallible wisdom of the sage, which Chrysippus tries to establish by means of a dialectic derived from Aristotle and the Cynics. But this optimism requires them to solve the following problems: the origin of the passions and the vices; the conciliation of fate and liberty; the origin of evil in the world. On the last two subjects they propounded all the arguments, that were advanced later up to the time of Leibniz.

(2) *Middle Stoicism (second and first centuries B. C.).* —Stoicism during this period was no longer a Greek School; it has penetrated into the Roman world, and became, under the influence of Scipio's friend, Panætius (185–112), who lived at Rome, and of Posidonius (135–40), who transferred the School to Rhodes, the quasi-official philosophy of Roman imperialism. Its doctrines were considerably modified, becoming less dogmatic in consequence of the criticism of the new Academician, Carneades (215–129). In Stoic morality Panætius develops the idea of humanity. Posidonius is at once a savant, historian, geographer, mathematician, astronomer, and a mystic who, commenting on Plato's works, revives his theories on the nature and destiny of the soul.

(3) *New Stoicism* (to A. D. 429).—The new Stoicism is more ethical and didactic. Science is no longer the knowledge of nature, but a kind of theological *summa* of moral and religious sentiments. Very little has been preserved of the short popular treatises and discourses, wherein, with a vivid style introduced under the influence of the Cynic diatribe, the philosopher endeavoured to render his ethical principles practical. The letters of Seneca (2–68) to Lucilius, the conversations of Musonius (time of Nero), and of Epictetus (age of Domitian), the fragments of Hierocles (time of Hadrian), the memoirs of Marcus Aurelius (d. 180), give but an incomplete idea. Stoicism, which gradually disappeared as the official School, was the most important of the Hellenic elements in the semi-oriental religions of vanishing paganism.

ZELLER, *Phil. d. Griechen*, III, pt. i, tr. *Stoics* by RIECHEL (London, 1892); DYROFT, *Die Ethik der Stoa* (Berlin, 1897); BROWN, *Stoics and Saints* (New York, 1893); LEONARD ALSTON, *Stoic and Christian* (London, 1906); ARNIM, *Stoicorum veterum fragmenta* (Leipzig, 1903, 1905); BAKE, *Posidonii reliquiæ* (Leyden, 1810); BONHÖFFER, *Epiktet u. die Stoa* (Stuttgart, 1890); STEIN, *Psychologie der Stoa* (Berlin, 1886); IDEM, *Die Erkenntnisselehre der Stoa* (Berlin, 1888); BARTH, *Die Stoa* (Leipzig, 1908); BRÉHIER, *Chrysippe* (Paris, 1910).

EMILE BRÉHIER.

Stolberg, FRIEDRICH LEOPOLD, COUNT ZU, b. at Brammstedt in Holstein (then a part of Denmark), 7 November, 1750; d. at Sondermühlen near Osnabrück, 5 December, 1819. He belonged to the younger branch of the Stolberg family and was the son of a Danish magistrate and owner of a manorial estate. A few years after his birth the family moved to Copenhagen and soon formed friendships with distinguished literary men, especially Klopstock. Klopstock was then at the height of his fame and the fundamental principles which he held, devotion to God and country, made a deep impression on the young Stolberg. Stolberg's religious ideas, it must be acknowledged, remained at first somewhat misty and confused, as his parents held to an eclectic form of Christianity and read for their own edification the most heterogeneous authors, as Augustine and Luther, Fénelon and Saurin, Zinzendorf and Young. Together with his brother Christian, Friedrich Leopold went to the University of Halle in 1770, in order to study law. His other studies embraced the classics and various historical courses. Two years later the two brothers went to Göttingen, where they joined the little company called the "Hainbund", a society of young men who had high aspirations for the freedom of the country, and who cultivated German poetry. Some of the poetry by the members of the "Bund", has a permanent value. However, besides Bürger, Hölty, and Voss, of all the members of the "Bund" only Stolberg has, in reality, not been forgotten, and his name continues to live less on account of his literary productions than because of his conversion to Catholicism.

After completing his studies at the university Stolberg made a journey in Switzerland with Goethe and Count von Haugwitz in 1775. Here, besides meeting other distinguished persons, he became acquainted with Lavater, with whom he formed a lasting friendship. In 1777 he entered the service of the Protestant Prince-Bishop of Lübeck, and was for a while the bishop's envoy at the Danish Court. Somewhat later, in 1781, he was chief administrator at Eutin and in 1785 magistrate at Neuenburg in the Duchy of Oldenburg. Four years after this he was the Danish ambassador at Berlin. In 1791 he was appointed president of the board of ecclesiastical administration of the Prince-Bishop of Lübeck, and in 1797 he was sent as ambassador to Russia. On 1 June, 1800, he joined the Catholic Church in the private chapel of the Princess Gallitzin at Osnabrück, and on 22 August he resigned his various positions. After this he lived first at Münster in Westphalia, then from 1812 at Tatenhausen near Bielefeld, and finally from 1816 at Sondermühle near Osnabrück, where he died after a short illness. He was buried in the cemetery at Stockkempen. Stolberg was twice married. His first wife, Agnes von Witzleben, died on 11 November, 1788, after six years of happy married life, leaving two sons and two daughters. Two years later Stolberg married Countess Sophie von Redern. After their marriage he and his wife took a long journey through Germany, Switzerland, and Italy. This tour was of great importance for his religious development, as he then made the acquaintance of the devout Catholic Freiherr von Droste-Vischering, as well as of Droste-Vischering's resident tutor, the distinguished theologian Katerkamp. By his second marriage Stolberg had a large family, and all, with the exception of the oldest daughter, followed the father's example and joined the Catholic Church in 1801. The oldest daughter, Agnes, was betrothed to the Lutheran Count Ferdinand of Stolberg-Wernigerode, but her son in 1854 became a Catholic. Four sons and two sons-in-law took part in the campaign against France in 1814; one of these sons was killed at Ligny (1815).

Stolberg's change of religion attracted great attention. Many of his numerous friends deserted and some abused him, such as Gleim, Jacobi, and others, or attacked him with bitter hatred as Voss in his pamphlet "Wie ward Fritz Stolberg ein Unfreier?" He was charged, and this charge is even now repeated, with having been a Catholic for years before he publicly left the Protestant Church. Men who judged of the facts as they were, as Freiherr von Stein, Goethe, and especially Lavater, looked on his conversion in a kindly spirit and imputed no ignoble motives to him. They were entirely justified in so doing, for even after his conversion and notwithstanding his genuine piety Stolberg was never able to rid himself altogether of the syncretism of the paternal home. Both in days of good and ill health he sought edification, after his conversion as before, from Protestant hymns and sermons. Even when dying, besides the prayers and hymns of the Church, he had read aloud to him Klopstock's poems and passages from the writings of the "Wandsbecker Boten", the well-known freemason, Claudius. He was also a warm friend of the later Bishop Sailer. Sailer's orthodoxy was doubted in his own day, but without reason; whatever be thought of his peculiar mysticism, he was a strong believer in the primacy of the pope, and a defender of the Church against State encroachments.

As regards Stolberg's literary works, there is no doubt that the quantity exceeded the quality. They may be divided thus: translations, as "Homer" (1778) "Plato" (1796); "Æschylus" (1802); poetry, as "Ballads" (1779), "Iambics" (1784), "Plays" (1787); "Travels" (1791); novels, as "The Island" (1788). After his conversion he devoted himself chiefly to the preparation of a "Geschichte der Religion Jesu Christi" (1806–), which is marked by a warmth of tone, although not without errors in investigation. He also wrote a history of Alfred the Great (1816); a life of St. Vincent de Paul; translated passages from the works of St. Augustine, and also wrote meditations on the Holy Scriptures, which, however, together with the "Büchlein der Liebe", and the polemical pamphlet "Kurze Abfertigung des langen Schmähschrifts des Hofrats Voss", did not appear until after his death. At first Stolberg's muse was entirely influenced by the ideas of Klopstock. However, the poet soon abandoned the antique poetic measures and successfully adopted German rhyme. Most of his poetry is now out of date and scarcely half-a-dozen of his "Lieder" are known to the present generation. In his own day his translations from the classics were considered well done. At times credulity and lack of critical discernment mar his descriptions of travel and historical writings. Probably his best work is contained in his devotional writings, but even these are not entirely satisfactory, especially the translation of the numerous passages from the Bible, which at times are not very correct.

See the histories of German literature, both the earlier histories and the more modern ones; of the modern ones, in particular the works of ENGEL and BARTELS; of the earlier histories: MENZEL, *Deutsche Dichtung*, III (Stuttgart, 1824), 175 sqq.; BRÜHL, *Gesch. der kath. Lit. Deutschlands vom XVII. Jahrhundert bis zur Gegenwart* (Leipzig, 1854), 73–128. Of other works: MENZEL, *Neuere Geschichte der Deutschen*, XII, pt. II (Breslau, 1848), 49; MENGE, *Friedrich Leopold von Stolberg u. seine Zeitgenossen* (2 vols., Gotha, 1862); HENNES, *Stolberg in den letzten Jahrzehnten seines Lebens* (Mainz, 1875); IDEM, *Aus Friedrich Leopold von Stolberg's Jugendjahren* (Frankfort, 1876); JANSSEN, *Friederich L. Graf zu Stolberg* (Freiburg, 1876–77); HELLINGHAUS, *Fr. L. Graf zu Stolberg u. J. H. Voss* (Münster, 1882); IDEM, *Briefe Fr. L. Graf zu Stolberg u. der Seinigen an J. H. Voss* (Münster, 1891); ROSENTHAL, *Convertitenbilder*, I (Ratisbon, 1889), 1–49.

PIUS WITTMANN.

JOSEPH, son of the poet Friedrich Leopold, b. 12 August, 1804; d. 5 April, 1859. In 1849 he was president of the general assembly of Catholic Associations held at Ratisbon (2–5 October). At this congress the St. Boniface Association was founded, and Stolberg was elected its first president. In the winter of 1849–50 he made a laborious journey to all the episcopal sees of Germany, and until his death was constantly active in the interests of the association. Since 1904 his son Hermann (b. at Westheim in Westphalia, 28 February, 1854) has been president of the St. Boniface Association.

KATHARINA, sister of Friedrich Leopold, b. at Bramstedt, 5 December, 1751; d. at Peterswaldau, 22 February, 1832. Gifted with a highly poetical nature, she was one of the most learned women of her age. As she was most devotedly attached to her brother and lived with him after the death of his wife, his conversion aroused in her an intense struggle between her love for him and her Evangelical belief. In 1802 she also joined the Catholic Church; however, new mental struggles followed, and finally she returned to Protestantism.

Gothaischer genealogischer Hofkalender, s. v.; Allgme. deutsche Biog., s. v.

KLEMENS LÖFFLER.

Stole, a liturgical vestment composed of a strip of material from two to four inches wide and about eighty inches long. It has either a uniform width throughout, or is somewhat narrower towards the middle, widening at the ends in the shape of a trapezium or spade. A small cross is generally sewed or embroidered on the stole at both ends and in the middle; the cross, however, is prescribed only for the middle, where the priest kisses the stole before putting it on. There are no express precepts concerning the material of the stole, but silk, or at least a half-silk fabric, is most appropriate. Stoles for festivals are generally ornamented with embroidery, especially what are called "vesper stoles".

PRESENT USE.—The stole is worn only by deacons, priests, and bishops. For deacons and priests it is the specific mark of office, being the badge of the diaconal and priestly orders.

STOLE FOUND IN ST. CUTHBERT'S TOMB

The wrongful use of the stole by subdeacons, therefore, would imply the usurpation of a higher order, and would constitute an irregularity. Deacons wear the stole like a sash, the vestment resting on the left shoulder and thence passing across the breast and back to the right side. The stole of the priest extends from the back of the neck across the shoulders to the breast, where the two halves either cross each other or fall down straight according as the stole is worn over the alb or the surplice. The stole is worn by a bishop in the same manner as a priest, except that it is never crossed on the breast, as a bishop wears the pectoral cross. As a mark of order the stole is used in a special ceremony, at the ordination of deacons and priests. At the ordination of deacons the bishop places it on the left shoulder of the candidate, saying: "Receive from the hand of God the white garment and fulfil thy duty, for God is mighty enough to give thee His grace in rich measure." At the ordination of priests the bishop draws the part of the stole that rests at the back of the candidate's neck forward over the breast and lays the two ends crosswise, saying: "Receive the yoke of the Lord, for His yoke is sweet and His burden is light." The Sacred Congregation of Rites has given a large number of decisions concerning the use of the stole. As a general rule it may be stated: the stole is only used, and must be used, at a function peculiar to the deacon, priest, and bishop, a function that presupposes the order (e. g., at the celebration of Mass, when the Blessed Sacrament is touched, when the sacraments are administered), but not for example, in processions or at Vespers. The wearing of the stole by the bishop at Solemn Vespers is an exception; its use by a priest while preaching depends on local custom. The stole is not a specific mark of parochial jurisdiction.

The use of the stole is also customary in the Oriental rites, in which, as in the West, it is one of the chief liturgical vestments (Greek, ὡράριον, the deacon's stole, and ἐπιτραχήλιον, the priest's stole; Armenian, urar; Syrian and Chaldaic, uroro; Coptic, batrashîl). According to present Oriental custom the stole is a strip of silk about seven or eight inches wide, having at the upper end a hole through which the head is inserted; it is either undivided (Syrian, Coptic, and Armenian custom) or opens down the front from the opening for the head (Greek custom). Among the Chaldeans (Nestorians) the stole of the priest resembles that used in the West, and is, like this, crossed over the breast. The deacon's stole generally hangs down straight from the left shoulder both in front and at the back, but in certain rites is first wound like a sash around the breast and back. Among the Syrians and Chaldeans the subdeacon also uses the stole, but he first twists it like a scarf around the neck, the ends being then let hang from the left shoulder in front and behind.

HISTORY.—We possess few references to the stole anterior to the ninth century. In the East, however, it is mentioned very early, the deacon's stole being frequently referred to even in the fourth and fifth centuries. The priest's stole is not mentioned in the East until the eighth century. The stole is first mentioned in the West in the sixth and seventh centuries (Synod of Braga, 563; Fourth Council of Toledo, 633; Gallican explanation of the Mass), but then as a thing which had long been in use. The earliest evidences of the use of the stole at Rome date from the second half of the eighth century and the beginning of the ninth. But in the ninth century, subdeacons and acolytes still wore both the planeta and the stole, although, to distinguish them from the deacons, priests, and bishops, there were definite limitations to their use of the latter vestment. After the ninth century the stole is very frequently mentioned, and even then the manner of its use was essentially the same as to-day. In the ninth and tenth centuries in the Frankish Empire the priests were commanded to wear the stole constantly as a badge of their calling, especially when on a journey. In Spain and Gaul in the pre-Carlovingian period, the deacons wore the stole over the tunic like the Greeks; in Southern Italy this practice was continued until at least the thirteenth century; at Milan the stole is still worn over the dalmatic. The custom for the priests to wear the stole crossed in front of the breast at Mass was known as early as the Synod of Braga (675), but did not become general until the late Middle Ages.

DEVELOPMENT.—Very little is known concerning the nature of the stole in the pre-Carlovingian period. Originally it was probably a cloth folded into the form of a band, and gradually developed into a simple band. In the eleventh and twelfth centuries the stole was very long, and at the same time extremely narrow. It was customary, even in the ninth century, to ornament the ends with fringe, tassels, or little bells. Towards the thirteenth century the ends came to be trapezium-shaped; in the fourteenth century this shape disappeared, and until the sixteenth century the stole was a strip of material of uniform width, and only ornamented with fringe at the ends. During the course of the sixteenth century it began again to be customary to broaden the ends of the stole; the eighteenth century produced the ugly stoles, in which the ends seemed to spread out into huge spades; these were also called "pocket stoles". It was not until the sixteenth century that it became customary to place a cross in the centre and at the ends of the stole; in the Middle Ages this practice was unusual.

ORIGIN.—Various hypotheses have been suggested concerning the origin of the stole. The theory formerly universally held, but quite wrong, that it originated in the ornamental trimming of a garment called "stole", which in the course of time disappeared leaving behind only this trimming, has been abandoned. The theory that traced the stole to the Jewish praying mantle has also been given up. At the present time the stole is either traced back to a liturgical napkin, which deacons are said to have carried, or to a neckcloth formerly peculiar to priests, or it is regarded as a liturgical badge (introduced at the latest in the fourth century) which first came into use in the East, and then in the West. It was also brought, as it would seem, to Rome, where it was not at first adopted as a badge of the higher orders of the clergy, but as a distinctive mark of the Roman clergy in general. The giving of the stole to the candidate at ordination in Rome was intended to convey a double symbolism; first, that the elevation to the clergy of the Roman Church occurred *de benedictione S. Petri*, and secondly that by ordination the candidate entered the service of St. Peter, that is of the Roman Church. It was also customary before the ordination to lay the *oraria* upon the *Confessio* of St. Peter. This liturgical badge was called *orarium* on account of its similarity to the secular *orarium* both in shape and material, and in the way it was worn. (For further details as to the various hypotheses concerning the origin of the name, cf. J. Braun, "Die liturgische Gewandung", 608–20.) The name "stole", as the designation of the *orarium*, is of Gallic origin, not Roman. As early as the ninth century the expression "stole" prevailed in the Frankish Empire; it made its entrance into Italy about the tenth century, and here also came rapidly into general use. From the thirteenth century the name *orarium* appears only in isolated instances.

BOCK, *Gesch. der liturgischen Gewänder*, II (Bonn, 1866); ROHAULT DE FLEURY, *La Messe*, VII (Paris, 1889); MARRIOTT, *Vestiarium christianum* (London, 1868); WILPERT, *Un capitolo della storia del vestiario* (Rome, 1898–99); IDEM, *Die Gewandung der ersten Christen* (Cologne, 1898); BRAUN, *Die priesterl. Gewänder des Abendlandes* (Freiburg, 1898); IDEM, *Die liturgische Gewandung im Occident u. Orient*.

JOSEPH BRAUN.

Stolz, ALBAN ISIDOR, Catholic theologian and popular author, b. at Bühl, Baden, 3 Feb., 1808; d. at Freiburg, 16 Oct., 1883. He first studied at the gymnasium at Rastatt (1818-27), and then proceeded to the University of Freiburg, where, after attending lectures in jurisprudence for a brief period, he devoted himself to the study of theology (1827-30). Owing to the unfortunate condition of the theological faculty of Freiburg, he fell into scepticism, and could not bring himself to enter the clerical seminary; but after studying philology at Heidelberg from 1830 to 1832 he regained his former faith. Having determined to embrace the clerical state, he entered the ecclesiastical seminary at Freiburg in the autumn of 1832, and in August, 1833, was ordained to the priesthood. During the following eight years he was engaged in parochial work, being curate first at Rothenfels in the Murgthal, and from June, 1835, at Neusatz, in the District of Bühl. In the autumn of 1841 he was appointed instructor in religion at the gymnasium of Bruchsal, and on 1 March, 1843, teacher of moral and pastoral theology at the theological college of Freiburg. From May, 1845 he was temporary director of this institution, but his appointment as permanent director was prevented by opponents holding Liberalistic views. In 1845 he became doctor of theology, and in the autumn of 1847, despite the opposition to his appointment, was made professor of pastoral theology and pedagogics at the university. On 13 October, 1848, he was named ordinary professor, and during 1859-60 he was rector of the university. He was made honorary doctor of the theological faculty of the University of Vienna in 1865, and in 1868 archiepiscopal spiritual counsellor. In both the charitable and social fields Stolz displayed a great and successful activity; in 1851 he founded at Freiburg the Catholic Journeymen's Association after the model of Kolping's, and conducted it as director and later as diocesan president. He likewise introduced into Freiburg the Society of St. Vincent de Paul, of which he remained director until his death. He devoted all the receipts from his writings to the assistance of the poor and charitable institutions, to the needs of the Church, and to home and foreign missions.

As a theologian Stolz was too self-opinionated, his theological teachers having failed to give him any fundamental training, and he lacked the exact knowledge of the achievements of earlier theology. Hirscher's writings, for which he had an unbounded veneration, were his chief authority. For the teaching of practical subjects, however, he was admirably qualified, and numerous theological students from foreign parts, especially Switzerland, came to Freiburg to attend his scholarly and suggestive lectures. Of his writings in the theological domain we may mention: "Katechetische Auslegung des Freiburger Diöcesan-Katechismus (Hirscher's Katechismus) für Geistliche, Lehrer und Eltern" (3 vols., Freiburg, 1844-47); "Ueber die Vererbung sittlicher Anlagen" (University Report, Freiburg, 1859); "Erziehungskunst" (Freiburg, 1873; 7th ed. by Julius Mayer, 1910); "Homiletik als Anweisung den Armen das Evangelium zu predigen", published by Jakob Schmitt after the author's death (Freiburg, 1885; 2nd ed., 1899).

In the domain of popular religious literature, Stolz acquired imperishable fame. Gifted and original, a keen observer of human nature, a master of language with every shade of expression at command, he united a broad sense of humour and an effective satire with a deep sincerity of religious feeling, a delicacy in the portrayal of conditions of the soul, and a poetical force and beauty in his descriptions of nature. Among his works, which, besides being published in Germany, have been translated into French, English, Italian, and other languages, his "Kalender für Zeit und Ewigkeit",written for the years 1843-47, 1858-59, 1864, 1873-81, and 1884, has been most widely read, these discourses were collected and issued in four volumes under the titles "Kompass für Leben und Sterben" (1861 and frequently); "Das Vaterunser und der unendliche Gruss" (1861); "Wachholder-Geist gegen die Grundübel der Welt: Dummheit, Sünde und Elend" (1879); "Die Nachtigall Gottes" (1888). Very popular also is his "Legende oder der christliche Sternhimmel" (in parts, 1851-60; 12th ed. in 1 quarto vol., 1904; 10th ed. in 4 octavo vols., 1894). With this must be associated another ascetico-religious work, "Die heilige Elisabeth" (1865; 16th ed., 1909), which many consider the ripest work of Stolz. As the fruits of his travels in Spain in 1850 he published (1853) the brilliant and highly humorous work "Spanisches für die gebildete Welt" (12th ed., 1908); his pilgrimage to the Holy Land in 1855 resulted in "Besuch bei Sem, Cham und Japhet, oder Reise in das Heilige Land" (1857; 10th ed., 1909). The works "Witterungen der Seele" (1867; 7th ed., 1910), "Wilder Honig" (1870;

4th ed., 1908), and "Dürre Kräuter" (1877; 4th ed., 1908), consist of excerpts from his diaries.

Stolz also wrote a number of pamphlets and brochures, some of polemical and some of moral and ascetical contents, collected under the title of "Kleinigkeiten" (2 collections, 1868 and 1887; 4th ed., 1909). His works were issued in nineteen volumes in Freiburg (1871-95), exclusive of the "Legende" and the explanation of the catechism; a popular edition of his works has appeared in twelve volumes (1898-1909). From his papers were edited an autobiography, "Nachtgebet meines Lebens. Nach dem Tode des Verfassers herausgegeben und durch Erinnerungen an Alban Stolz ergänzt von Jakob Schmitt" (Freiburg, 1885; 2nd ed., 1908), and "Predigten" (ed. Julius Mayer, Freiburg, 1908). Another valuable contribution is the correspondence of Stolz with the convert, Julie Meineke, edited by Mayer under the title "Fügung und Führung" (Freiburg, 1909). Extracts from the writings of Stolz are given in the works "Edelsteine aus reicher Schatzkammer. Eine Sammlung schöner Stellen aus den Schriften von Alban Stolz. Ausgewählt von Heinrich Wagner" (Freiburg, 1905; 3rd ed., 1910), and "Bilder zur christkatholischen Glaubens- und Sittenlehre, aus den Schriften von Alban Stolz. Geistlichen und Lehrern sowie dem christlichen Volke gewidmet von Karl Telch" (Freiburg, 1909).

HÄGELE, *Alban Stolz nach authentischen Quellen* (3rd ed., Freiburg, 1889), with portrait; REINFRIED in *Badische Biographieen*, IV (Karlsruhe, 1891), 454-61; HETTINGER, *Aus Welt u. Kirche*, II (4th ed., Freiburg, 1897), 396-447; SAUER, *Die neuere Alban Stolz-Literatur* in *Literar. Rundschau*, nn. 5-6 (1910), coll. 214-20, 263-70.

FRIEDRICH LAUCHERT.

Stone, CORNER OR FOUNDATION.—A rite entitled "De benedictione et impositione Primarii Lapidis pro ecclesia ædificanda" (Of the blessing and laying of the Foundation Stone for the building of a church) is provided in the Roman Pontifical. As it appears in the same form in the "Giunta Pontificale" of 1520, it is probably at least as old as the time of Patricius Piccolomini (fifteenth century), and it may in substance go back two centuries farther to the time of Durandus of Mende (see Catalani, "Pont. Rom.", II, 31). The rite itself is simple enough. Before the work of building a church is set about the rubric directs that adequate provision should be made for its maintenance, also the foundations are to be marked out subject to the approval of the bishop or his delegate, and a wooden cross set up to indicate the place where the altar is to stand. In the function which ensues the bishop first blesses holy water with the ordinary forms, then sprinkles the place where the cross stands and afterwards the foundation stone. Upon the stone itself he is directed to engrave crosses on each side with a knife, and then he pronounces the following prayer: "Bless, O Lord, this creature of stone [*creaturam istam lapidis*] and grant by the invocation of Thy holy name that all who with a pure mind shall lend aid to the building of this church may obtain soundness of body and the healing of their souls. Through Christ Our Lord, Amen." After the Litany of the Saints, followed by an appropriate antiphon and Psalm cxxvi, "Unless the Lord build the house" etc., the stone is lowered into its place with another prayer and again sprinkled with holy water. More antiphons and psalms follow, while the bishop once more visits and sprinkles the other foundations, dividing them into three sections and ending each little tour with a special prayer. Finally the "Veni Creator Spiritus" is sung, and two short prayers. Then the bishop, if he deems it opportune, sits down and exhorts the people to contribute to the fabric, after which he dismisses them with his blessing and the proclamation of an indulgence.

In the Middle Ages this or some analogous rite was not unknown, but the number of Pontificals which contain anything of the sort is comparatively small (Martène, for example, in his "De ritibus" gives no specimen of the forms used in any such function.) One of the few that provide such a rite is Archbishop Chichele's Pontifical, representing, no doubt, the use of Sarum in the early fifteenth century. The function in its details differs considerably from that just described. The only feature that is quite identical is the prayer above quoted, "Benedic, Domine, creaturam istam lapidis", for blessing the stone, but it is supplemented in the English rite by another and much longer prayer, containing many Scriptural allusions, among the rest, one to the "stone rejected by the builders". Moreover, in England the stone is anointed with chrism while a prayer is said which has reference to this ceremony. Of all this there is no trace in the Roman type of service.

It is not easy to assign a date to the beginning of this practice of blessing the foundation stone. An interesting fragment of evidence is, however, furnished by what is apparently the inscribed foundation stone of the first church of St. Mark at Venice. (See the paper of F. Douce in "Archæologia", xxvi, 217 sq.) As it is roughly circular in form, between six and seven inches in diameter, and only half an inch thick, we have probably to do with a tablet let into the foundation stone proper. It bears a rudely scratched head (of St. Mark?) and the inscription in ninth-century characters: ECCL. S. MARCI PRIMAM PETRAM POSVIT DUX IO. PARTICI [aco]; the rest is broken off. The Doge, John Particiaco, dedicated the first Church of St. Mark in A. D. 828. Of course this inscription does not make reference to any religious ceremony, but, as forms for the dedication of a church were employed much before this date, it seems unlikely that such a function should not have been accompanied by at least some simple form of ecclesiastical blessing. Moreover, the English liturgist Belethus in the twelfth century was evidently familiar with a rite of this kind. "When the foundations have been dug", he says, "it is necessary that the bishop sprinkle the place with holy water and that he himself, or some priest at his bidding, should lay the first stone of the foundation, which ought to have a cross engraved upon it. And it is absolutely necessary that the church should be built towards the east" (Belethus, ii; P. L., CCII, 10). Similar language is used by Sicardus (P. L., CCXIII, 17 and 20) and Durandus (Rationale, II, 7) less than a century later.

A question arises connected with the practice (1) of laying money upon the stone as a contribution to the fabric of the church and (2) of enclosing coins within or beneath it as evidence of the date. The former custom might not improbably be traced to the terms of the prayer quoted above, which, in blessing the foundation stone, in particular invokes special favours upon all "who with pure mind lend their aid to the building of this church". It is curious, however, that in the one detailed description which we possess of a pagan ceremony of the same sort, viz., that which preceded the restoration of the Roman Temple of Jupiter upon the Capitol in the time of Vespasian (Tacitus, "Hist.", IV, 53), we find not only that the foundations were washed with lustral water, but that attention was especially centred upon the great stone (*ingens saxum*) which was dragged into its place by magistrates and people together. Moreover, gold and silver in an unwrought and virgin state were scattered upon the foundations. Stranger still, a similar ceremony seems to have prevailed in ancient Assyria, where an inscription of Nabopolassar (604 B. C.) describes how that monarch, in building a temple to Merodach, cast gold and silver upon the foundations (Schrader, "Keilinschriftliche Bibliothek", III, ii, 5). Further, the ceremonial rite of laying a foundation stone seems to reach back to the time of Sargon, c. 3800 B. C. (ibid., pp. 85-93). The custom of placing coins in or under the foundation stone, now very general, needs further elucidation. The earliest definite instance at the moment discoverable is an entry in an account-book at Bruges, which records that, when the palace of the magistrates of the Franc was rebuilt in 1519, an angel (coin) was paid out to be placed under the foundation stone (W. H. J. Weale in "Notes and Queries", 27 Aug., 1870, p. 184). It is just conceivable that this burial of gold and silver may represent a more primitive form of sacrifice in which a human victim was immolated and buried under the masonry; but the evidence of any widespread custom of this barbarous kind is by no means so conclusive as is maintained by such writers as Tylor (Primitive Culture, 1903, I, p. 104 sq.) and Trumbull (The Threshold Covenant, pp. 45–57).

For the ecclesiastical function see CATALANI, *Commentary on the Pontificale Romanum*, II (Rome, 1739), 1–32; SAUER, *Symbolik* (Ratisbon, 1902), 114 sq. Cf. also DOUCE in *Archæologia*, XXVI (London, 1836), 217 sq.; TRUMBULL, *The Threshold Covenant* (Edinburgh, 1896), 45–57.

HERBERT THURSTON.

Stone, MARY JEAN, b. at Brighton, Sussex, in 1853; d. at Battle, Sussex, 3 May, 1908. She was educated at a Calvinist school in Paris and at Aschaffenburg in Germany, where she acquired an intimate knowledge of French, German, and Italian. In Germany Miss Stone was brought into touch with the Catholic religion, and exchanged Protestantism for the "free atmosphere", as she expressed it, of the Catholic Church. She was received into the Church by Monsignor Ketteler, then Bishop of Mainz. Her historical studies, for which, perhaps, she is best known to the public, were, on her return to England, encouraged by the fathers of the Society of Jesus. Her talent and painstaking method of research earned for her a speedy recognition in her "Mary the First, Queen of England" (1901). This is a study of the unhappy queen which takes first rank amongst historical monographs. Miss Stone also wrote "Faithful unto Death", a study of the martyrs of the Order of St. Francis during the Reformation period (1892); "Eleanor Leslie", a memoir of a notable Scottish convert to the Church (1898); "Reformation and Renaissance", a group of studies on the periods indicated (1904); "Studies from Court and Cloister", reprinted essays, of which perhaps the most interesting are those on "Margaret Tudor", "Sir Henry Bedingfeld", and a "Missing Page from the Idylls of the King" (1905); "The Church in English History", a higher textbook for teachers of history (1907). Her "Cardinal Pole", begun for the St. Nicholas Series, was interrupted by her death. She was a frequent contributor to the greater periodicals, the "Dublin Review", "Month", "Blackwood's", "Cornhill", etc., and contributed several articles to THE CATHOLIC ENCYCLOPEDIA.

G. FLADGATE.

Stone, MARMADUKE, Jesuit, b. at Draycot, 28 Nov., 1748; d. at St. Helens, 21 Aug., 1834. He was educated at St. Omers, shared in its historic exodus to Bruges, 10–17 August, 1762 (see SAINT OMER, COLLEGE OF), entered the Society of Jesus in 1767, later became a master at the Liège Academy. In 1790 he succeeded as president to Father William Strickland, who then became procurator at London; with his assistance Father Stone succeeded in peacefully guiding the English ex-Jesuits through more than a score of tempestuous years (see MILNER, JOHN; POYNTER, WILLIAM). Father Stone's confrères, though held together by a common vocation and their still uncancelled vows, were not allowed by the brief of suppression to reunite for purposes of government. He could therefore only rule by appealing to conscience; no easy task when one remembers the exterior difficulties, the adventuresome ardour that animated the young men of his college staff, and the peculiar ways into which the middle-aged missionaries were prone to subside. When dealing with the bishops, he could claim no rights, not even those essential to religious bodies. Fortunately, they were not hostile, though their views on Jesuit property and privileges caused Father Stone much trouble.

On 14 July, 1794, the College at Liège was transferred to Stonyhurst (q. v.). In spite of the magnitude of the task, it was accomplished in good order; and schools reopened 22 October following. A rescript from Propaganda (14 Feb., 1796) confirmed Stonyhurst in all the privileges of Liège. Though it was impossible to hope for a restoration of the Society during the Revolutionary and Napoleonic wars, it was not impracticable to work for a reunion with the Russian Jesuits, whose corporate existence had lately been recognized at Rome. In this Father Stone was successful. On 19 May, 1803, having made his profession, he was declared provincial, and admitted others to their vows, for England, Ireland, and Maryland; on 29 September a novitiate was opened at Hodder. Rome, however, gave no public recognition of the restored order, though the pope privately expressed his pleasure. When the Bull of Restoration finally came (7 August, 1814), the interpretation was added (2 Dec., 1816), that it was to apply only where the secular government wished: in England, therefore, the Jesuits were to be regarded as still in their old position (see SOCIETY OF JESUS). The college had grown enormously since its transfer to England and the Jesuit missions had prospered steadily. Father Stone, notwithstanding his years, continued to act as college minister till 1827, when he finally retired to St. Helens. Here the good news reached him (1829) that the English Jesuits had at last been formally recognized. Though he might not look an ideal leader, Father Stone was wonderfully adapted to his circumstances; his unfailing kindness, simplicity, sincerity, patience, and self-devotion were irresistible. If he acted slowly, he made no mistakes; he was capable of undertaking great enterprises, and of carrying them through with strong tenacity of purpose.

Correspondence at Stonyhurst and elsewhere; GERARD, *Stonyhurst College* (1894); FOLEY, *Records S.J.*, vii, 741; WARD, *The Dawn of the Catholic Revival* (London, 1909); IDEM, *The Eve of Catholic Emancipation* (London, 1912).

J. H. POLLEN.

Stones, PRECIOUS, IN BIBLE.—Precious stones are stones remarkable for their colour, brilliancy, or rarity. Such stones have at all times been held in high esteem everywhere, particularly in the East. We gather from various passages of Sacred Scripture that very early the Orientals appropriated them for divers ornamental uses: rings, bracelets, collars, necklaces; the crowns of kings as also their garments and those of their officers and of the priests were set with precious stones. The Hebrews obtained their precious stones from Arabia, India, and Egypt. At the time of the Exodus Egypt was flooded with riches, and we know how the Israelites on leaving the land possessed themselves of many precious stones, according to the commandment of God (Ex., iii, 22; xii, 35–36). Later when they were settled in Palestine they could easily obtain stones from the merchant caravans travelling from Babylonia or Persia to Egypt and those from Saba and Reema to Tyre (Ezech., xxvii, 22) Solomon even equipped a fleet which returned from Ophir laden with precious stones (III Kings, x, 11).

The precious stones of the Bible are chiefly of interest in connexion with the breastplate of the high-priest (Ex., xxviii, 17–20; xxxix, 10–13), the treasure of the King of Tyre (Ezech., xxviii, 13), and the foundations of the New Jerusalem (Tob., xiii, 16–17, in the Greek text, and more fully, Apoc., xxi, 18–21). The twelve stones of the breastplate and the two stones of the shoulder-ornaments seem to have been considered by the Jews as the most precious; they undoubtedly serve as the standard of whatever is beautiful and rich beyond measure; both Ezech., xxviii, 13, and Apoc., xxi, 18-21, are patterned after the model of the rational; no wonder therefore that the stones entering its composition should have been the objects of a considerable amount of literature from the fourth century. That such a literature should have arisen is of itself convincing proof that the identification of the stones was no easy problem to solve. It must be remembered too that at the time of the Septuagint translation the stones to which the Hebrew names apply could no longer be identified, and the translators rendered the same Hebrew name by different Greek words. So also did Josephus who, however, claimed he had seen the actual stones. This, coupled with the fact that the late Biblical lists, although visibly depending on that of Exodus, exhibit here and there notable changes, makes the task of identifying the stones a very arduous one. It should be noticed that the ancients did not classify their precious stones by analyzing their composition and crystalline forms: names were given them from their colour, their use, or the country from which they came. Thus it happens that stones of the same or nearly the same colour, but of different composition or crystalline form, bear identical names. Another difficulty is due to the names having changed in the course of time: thus the ancient chrysolite is our topaz, the sapphire is our lazuli, etc. However, we know most of the stones accounted precious in Egypt, Assyria, and Babylonia. Owing to the neighbourhood and to the influence of these countries on Palestine, it is highly probable that the score of substances called in the Bible "desirable stones" (Is., liv, 12) must be contained in the fairly long list of the precious and ornamental stones of the Assyro-Babylonians and the Egyptians.

This is not the place to enter upon a critical and exegetical discussion of the Biblical passages above referred to, where lists of precious stones are given. It will be sufficient to treat briefly of these stones according to the alphabetical order of the English names.

AGATE, Heb. שְׁבוֹ; Sept. ἀχάτης; Vulg. achates (Ex., xxviii, 19; xxxix, 12, in Heb. and Vulg.; also Ezech., xxviii, 13, in Sept.).—This is the second stone of the third row of the rational, where it very probably represented the tribe of Aser. The derivation of the Hebrew word is doubtful, but the stone has generally been acknowledged to be the agate. Fürst (Hebr. u. Chald. Wörterb.) derives שְׁבוֹ from שָׁבַב, "to flame"; it may also be related to Saba (שְׁבָא), whence caravans brought the stone to Palestine. The Greek and Latin names are taken from the river Achates, the modern Dirillo, in Sicily, where this stone was first found (Theophrastus, "De lapid.", 38; Pliny, "Hist. nat.", XXXVII, liv). The stone belongs to the silex family (chalcedony species) and is formed by deposits of siliceous beds in hollows of rocks. To this mode of formation are due the bands of various colours which it contains. Its conchoidal clevage is susceptible of a high polish. To this stone various medicinal powers were attributed until far into the Middle Ages. It was supposed to render the action of all poisons void, to counteract the infection of contagious diseases; if held in the hand or in the mouth it was believed to alleviate fever. The eagle, it was said, placed an agate in its nest to guard its young against the bite of venomous animals. The red agate was credited with the power of sharpening the vision. At present agate and onyx differ only in the manner in which the stone is cut; if it is so cut as to show the layers of colour, it is called agate; if cut parallel to the lines, onyx. Formerly an agate that was banded with well-defined colours was the onyx. The banded agate is used for the manufacture of cameos.

AMETHYST, Heb. אַחְלָמָה; Sept. ἀμέθυστος, also Apoc.,

xxi, 20, where it is the twelfth and last stone of the foundation of the New Jerusalem. It is the third stone in the third row of the rational, representing the tribe of Issachar (Ex., xxviii, 19; xxxix, 12); the Septuagint enumerates it among the riches of the King of Tyre (Ezech., xxviii, 13). The Greek name alludes to the popular belief that the amethyst was a preventive of intoxication; hence beakers were made of amethyst for carousals, and inveterate drinkers wore amulets made of it to counteract the action of wine. Abenesra and Kimchi explain the Hebrew אַחְלָמָה in an analogous manner, deriving it from חָלַם, to dream; חָלַם in its first meaning signifies "to be hard" (Fürst, Hebr. Handwörterbuch). We have no reason to doubt the accuracy of the translation since we find a general agreement among the various versions; Josephus (Ant. Jud., III, vii, 6) also has "amethyst"; the Targum of Onkelos and the Syriac Version have "calf's eye", indicating the colour. The amethyst is a brilliant transparent stone of a purple colour resembling that of diluted wine and varying in shade from the violet purple to rose. There are two kinds of amethysts: the oriental amethyst, a species of sapphire, is very hard (cf. Heb., חָלַם), and when colourless can hardly be distinguished from the diamond; the occidental amethyst is of the silex family, hence different in composition from the oriental stone. But the identity of names is accounted for by the identity of colour. The occidental amethyst is easily engraved. It is found of various sizes. Its shape is different from the round pebble to the hexagonal, pyramid-capped crystal.

BERYL, Heb. יַהֲלֹם; Sept. βήρυλλος; Vulg. beryllus.— In the breastplate this stone occupied the third place of the second row and was understood to represent Nephtali (Ex., xxviii, 19; xxxix, 13); according to the Septuagint it is the second of the fourth row, and third of the fourth according to the Vulgate; Ezech., xxviii, 13, mentions it in the third place; it is cited also in the Greek text of Tob., xiii, 17, but is wanting in the Vulgate; Apoc., xxi, 20, gives it as the eighth stone of the foundation of the New Jerusalem. There is great difference of opinion as to the exact Hebrew correlative of this word. The best supported is יַהֲלֹם, though שֹׁהַם also does not lack probability. יָשְׁפֵה has likewise been suggested, but without sufficient reason, it seems, for to this Hebrew יָשְׁפֵה must correspond jasper, Gr. ἴασπις, Lat. jaspis. This mistaken idea mo t probably arose from the supposition that the translated words must have occupied the same position as in the original. This is not the case, as a comparison of the the Greek and Latin translations shows; in the Vulgate, indeed, we find jasper in the same position as יָשְׁפֵה, whereas the Greek βήρυλλος does not correspond to the Latin beryllus; the same may have happened as regards the translation of the Hebrew into Greek, especially as in the old manner of writing the two words יַהֲלֹם and יָשְׁפֵה might be easily confused. The authority of Josephus is here of little weight, for he most likely quoted from memory, the position of the words being at variance even in his two lists (Bell. Jud., V, v, 7; Ant. Jud., III, vii). Our choice, therefore, is limited to the two words יַהֲלֹם and שֹׁהַם. By comparing various texts of the Vulgate—the Greek is very inconsistent—we find that שֹׁהַם is always translated by onyx: this alone seems sufficient to render fairly probable the opinion that beryl corresponds to Heb. יַהֲלֹם. That the beryl was among the stones of the rational appears beyond doubt since all translations mention it. The etymology giving us no special help, by elimination we come to the generally accepted conclusion that beryl and יַהֲלֹם stand for each other. The beryl is a stone composed of silica, alumina, and glucina. The beryl and the emerald are of the same species. The difference between the beryl, the aqua marine, and the emerald is determined by the colouring matter and the peculiar shade of each. The beryl, though sometimes white, is usually of a light blue verging into a yellowish green; the emerald is more transparent and of a finer hue than the beryl; as a gem, it is more beautiful and hence more costly; the aqua marine is a beautiful sea-green variety. The emerald derives its colour from a small quantity of oxide of chromium; the beryl and aqua marine from a small quantity of oxide of iron. The beryl occurs in the shape either of a pebble or of an hexagonal prism. It is found in metamorphic limestone, slate, micaschist, gneiss, and granite. In ancient times it was obtained from Upper Egypt and is still found in the mica slate of Mt. Zaborah, The largest beryls known have been found in Acworth and Grafton, New Hampshire, and in Royalston, Massachusetts, United States of America; one weighs 2900 lb., measures 51 inches in length, 32 inches through in one direction and 22 in another transverse. The beryl has been employed for cabalistic uses (Aubrey, "Miscellanies").

CARBUNCLE, Heb., נֹפֶךְ; Sept. ἄνθραξ (Ex., xxviii, 18; xxxix, 11; Ezech., xxviii, 13; omitted in Ezech., xxvii, 16); Vulg., carbunculus (Ex., xxviii, 18; xxxix, 11; Ezech., xxviii, 13), gemma (Ezech., xxvii, 16), the first stone of the second row of the rational; it represented Juda, and is also the eighth stone mentioned of the riches of the King of Tyre (Ezech., xxviii, 13), being, not a native product, but an object of importation (Ezech., xxvii, 16); it is perhaps the third stone of the foundation of the celestial city (Apoc., xxi, 19). The ancient authors are far from agreeing on the precise nature of this stone. It very probably corresponds to the ἄνθραξ of Theophrastus (De lap., 18), the carbunculus of Pliny (Hist. nat., XXXVII, xxv), the charchedonius of Petronius, and the ardjouani of the Arabs. If so it is a red glittering stone, probably the Oriental ruby, though the appellation may have been applied to various red gems. Theophrastus says of it: "Its colour is red and of such a kind that when it is held against the sun it resembles a burning coal." This description tallies fairly well with that of the Oriental ruby. He relates also that the most perfect carbuncles were brought from Carthage, Marseilles, Egypt, and the neighbourhood of Siena. Carbuncles were named differently according to the places whence they came. Pliny (Hist. nat., XXXVII, xxv) cites the lithizontes, or Indian carbuncles, the amethystizontes, the colour of which approached that of the amethyst, and the sitites. Most probably, then, the name of carbuncle applied to several stones.

CARNELIAN, Heb. אֹדֶם from אָדַם, to be red, especially "red blooded"; Sept. and Apoc. σάρδιον; Vulg. sardius; the first stone of the breastplate (Ex., xxviii, 17; xxxix, 10) representing Ruben; also the first among the stones of the King of Tyre (Ezech., xxviii, 13), the sixth foundation stone of the celestial city (Apoc., xxi, 19). The word σάρδιον has sometimes been rendered sardonyx; this is a mistake, for the same word is equivalent to carnelian in Theophrastus (De lap., 55) and Pliny (Hist. nat., XXXVII, xxxi), who derive the name from that of the city of Sardes where, they say, it was first found. The carnelian is a siliceous stone and a species of chalcedony. Its colour is a flesh-hued red, varying from the palest flesh-colour to a deep blood-red. It is of a conchoidal structure. Usually its colour is without clouds or veins; but sometimes delicate veins of extremely light red or white are found arranged much like the rings of an agate. Carnelian is used for rings and seals. The finest carnelians are found in the East Indies.

CHALCEDONY, Apoc., xxi, 19, χαλκηδών; Vulg. chalcedonius, the third foundation stone of the celestial Jerusalem. Some claim the writing χαλκηδών is erroneous, and that it should be χαρκηδών, the carbuncle. Though this view is countenanced by but few MSS., yet it is not devoid of reason; for whilst the other eleven stones correspond to a stone in the rational it is singular that this should be the only exception. Moreover the ancients very often confounded the names of these two stones. The chalcedony is a siliceous stone. Its name is supposed to be derived from Chalcedon, in Bithynia, whence the ancients obtained the stone. It is a species of agate and bears various names according to its colour. It is usually made up of concentric circles of various colours. The most valuable of these stones are found in the East Indies. Sets for rings, seals, and, in the East, cups and beakers are made of chalcedon.

CHODCHOD, כַּדְכֹּד (Is., liv, 12; Ezech., xxvii, 16); Sept. ἴασπις (Is., liv, 12), χορχόρ (Ezech., xxvii, 16); Vulg. jaspis (Is., liv, 12), chodchod (Ezech., xvii, 16).—This word is used only twice in the Bible. The chodchod is generally identified with the Oriental ruby. The translation of the word in Is. both by the Septuagint and the Vulgate is jasper; in Ezech. the word is merely transliterated; the Greek χορχόρ is explained by considering how easy it is to mistake a ר for a ד. "What chodchod signifies", says St. Jerome, "I have until now not been able to find" (Comment. in Ezech., xxvii, 16, in P. L., XXV, 255). In Is. he follows the Septuagint and translates chodchod by jaspis. The word is probably derived from כָּדַד, "to throw fire"; the stone was therefore brilliant and very likely red. This supposition is strengthened by the fact that the Arabic word kadzkadzat, evidently derived from the same stem as chodchod, designates a bright red. It was therefore a kind of ruby, likely the Oriental ruby, perhaps also the carbuncle (see above).

CHRYSOLITE, Heb. תַּרְשִׁישׁ (Ex., xxviii, 20; xxxix, 13; Ezech., i, 16; x, 9; xxviii, 13; Cant., v, 14; Dan., x, 6); Sept., χρυσόλιθος (Ex., xxviii, 20; xxxix, 13; Ezech., xxviii, 13); θαρσίς (Cant., v, 14; Dan., x, 6); θαρσείς (Ezech., 1, 16; x, 9); Vulg. chrysolithus (Ex., xxviii, 20; xxxix, 13; Ezech., x, 9; xxviii, 13; Dan., x, 6), hyacinthus (Cant., v, 14); quasi visio maris (Ezech., i, 16); Apoc., xxi, 20, χρυσόλιθος; Vulg. chrysolithus.— This is the tenth stone of the rational, representing the tribe of Zabulon; it stands fourth in the enumeration of Ezech., xxviii, 13, and is given as the seventh foundation stone of the celestial city in Apoc., xxi, 20. In none of the Hebrew texts is there any hint as to the nature of this stone; however, since the Septuagint habitually translates the Hebrew word by χρυσόλιθος, except where it merely transliterates it and in Ezech., x, 9, since, moreover, the Vulgate follows this translation with very few exceptions, and Aquila, Josephus, and St. Epiphanius agree in their rendering, we can safely accept the opinion that the chrysolite of the ancients, which is our topaz, was meant. The word tharsis very likely points to the place whence the stone was brought (Tharsis). The modern chrysolite is a green oblong hexagonal prism of unequal sides terminated by two triangular pyramids. The topaz, or ancient chrysolite, is an octangular prism of an orange-yellow colour; it is composed of alumina, silica, hydrofluoric acid, and iron. It is found in Ceylon, Arabia, and Egypt, and several species were admitted to exist (Pliny, "Hist. nat.", XXXVII, xlv). In the Middle Ages it was believed to possess the power of dispelling the fears of night and of driving away devils; it was also supposed to be an excellent cure for the diseases of the eye.

CHRYSOPRASUS, Greek χρυσόπρασος, the tenth foundation stone of the celestial Jerusalem (Apoc., xxi, 20). This is perhaps the agate of Ex., xxviii, 20, and xxxix, 13, since the chrysoprasus was not very well known among the ancients. It is a kind of green agate, composed mostly of silica and a small percentage of nickel.

CORAL, Heb. רָאמוֹת (Job, xxviii, 18; Prov., xxiv, 7; Ezech., xxvii, 16); Sept. μετέωρα, ῥαμωθ; Vulg. excelsa, sericum.—The Hebrew word seems to come from רָאָה or רוּם, "to be high", probably connoting a resemblance to a tree. It may be also that the name came from a strange country, as did the coral itself. It is obvious that the ancient versions have completely missed the sense; they even felt it so well that in one place they merely transliterated the Hebrew word. In Ezech., xxvii, 16, coral is mentioned as one of the articles brought by the Syrians to Tyre. The Phœnicians mounted beads of coral on collars and garments. These corals were obtained by Babylonian pearl-fishers in the Red Sea and the Indian Ocean. The Hebrews made apparently very little use of this substance, and hence it is seldom mentioned in their writings; this explains also the difficulty felt by the translators in rendering the word. Gesenius (Thesaurus, p. 1113) translates פנינים (Job, xxviii, 18; Prov., iii, 15; viii, 11; xx, 15; xxxi, 10; Lam., iv, 7) by "red coral"; but many maintain that the pearl is meant in these passages. The coral spoken of in the Bible is the precious coral (*corallum rubrum*), the formation of which is well known. It is a calcareous secretion of certain polyps, having a tree-like formation. At present coral is found in the Mediterranean, the northern coast of Africa furnishing the dark red, Sardinia the yellow or salmon-coloured, and the coast of Italy the rose-pink coral. One of the greatest coral-fisheries of the present day is Torre del Greco, near Naples.

CRYSTAL, Heb. גבש (Job, xxviii, 18), קרח (Ezech, i, 22): both words signify a glassy substance; Sept. γαβίς; Vulg. *eminentia* (Job, xxviii, 18); κρύσταλλος, *crystallus* (Ezech., i, 22).—This was a transparent mineral resembling glass, most probably a variety of quartz. Job places it in the same category with gold, onyx, sapphire, glass, coral, topaz, etc. The Targum renders the קרח of Ezech. by "ice"; the versions translate by "crystal". We find crystal again mentioned in Apoc., iv, 6; xxi, 11; xxii, 1. In Ps. cxlvii, 17, and Ecclus., xliii, 22, there can be no question but that ice is meant. The word זכוכית, Job, xxviii, 17, which some translate by crystal, means glass.

DIAMOND, Heb. שמיר; Sept. ἀδαμαντίνος; Vulg. *adamas, adamantinus* (Ezech., iii,9; Zach., vii, 12; Jer., xvii, 1).—Whether or not this stone is really the diamond cannot be ascertained. Many passages in Holy Writ point indeed to the qualities of the diamond, especially its hardness (Ezech., iii, 9; Zach., vii, 12; Jer., xvii, 1). In the last Jeremias informs us of a use to which this stone was put, which agrees admirably with the use to which the diamond is put at this day: "The sin of Juda is written with a pen of iron, with the point of a diamond". But although diamond is used to engrave hard substances, yet it should be remarked that other stones may serve the same purpose. The Septuagint omits the passages of Ezech. and Zach., while the first five verses of Jer., xvii, are missing in the Cod. Vaticanus and Alexandrinus, but are found in the Complutensian edition and in the Syriac and Arabic Versions. Despite the qualities mentioned in the Bible, the stone spoken of in the places referred to may be the limpid corindon, which exhibits the same qualities, and is used in India for the same purposes as we use the diamond. The diamond was not very well known among the ancients; and if we add to this reason the similarity between the words σμίρις, the Egyptian *asmir*, "emery", a species of corindon used to polish precious stones, and שמיר, the Hebrew word supposed to mean the diamond, we may conclude with probability that the limpid corindon was intended. Aben-Esra and Abarbanel translate יהלם by "diamond"; but יהלם we have shown above to be the beryl. The diamond is made up of pure carbon, mostly of a white transparent colour, but sometimes tinted. The white diamond is the most precious, owing to its beauty and rarity. South Africa contains the largest diamond fields.

EMERALD, Heb. ברקת; Sept. σμάραγδος; Vulg. *smaragdus;* the third stone of the rational (Ex., xxviii, 17; xxxix, 10), where it represents the tribe of Levi; it is the ninth stone in Ezech., xxviii, 13, and the fourth foundation stone of the celestial Jerusalem (Apoc., xxi, 19). The same precious stone is also mentioned in Tob., xiii, 16 (Vulg. 21); Jud., x, 21 (Vulg. 19); and in the Greek text of Ecclus., xxxii, 8, but there is no indication of it in the MS. B. of the Hebrew text, found in the Genizah of Cairo in 1896. That ברקת stands for "emerald" is verified by the fact that practically all versions, as well as Josephus (Ant. Jud., III, vii, 5; Bell. Jud., V, v, 7) translate it thus. The Hebrew root ברק, from which it is probably derived, signifies "to glitter", which quality agrees eminently with the emerald. The word may also come from the Sanskrit *marakata* which is certainly the emerald; the Greek form σμάραγδος is not so distant from the Hebrew that no similarity can be found between them. In Job, xiii, 21; Jud., x, 19; Ecclus., xxxii, 8; and Apoc., xxi, 19, the emerald is certainly the stone spoken of. The word נפך also has sometimes been translated by *smaragdus;* but this is a mistake, for נפך is the carbuncle. The emerald is a green variety of beryl and is composed of silicate of alumina and glucina. Its form is a hexagonal crystal; its colour is a brilliant reflecting green. The stone admits of a high polish. The emerald is found in metamorphic rocks, granites, and mica schists; the finest specimens come from Muzo, Bogotá, South America. The ancients obtained the stone from Egypt and India. It has sometimes been asserted that they knew nothing of the emerald; but this is plainly refuted by Pliny, Theophrastus, and others, though the name may have been used possibly for other stones. In the Middle Ages marvellous powers were attributed to the emerald, the most conspicuous being the power to preserve or heal the sight.

HYACINTH, Greek ὑάκινθος; Vulg. *hyacinthus* (Apoc., xxi, 20); the eleventh stone of the foundation of the heavenly city. It corresponds very probably to Heb., the ligurius of Ex., xxviii, 19; xxxix, 12 (St. Epiphan., "De duodecim gemmis" in P. G., XLIII, 300). The stone spoken of in Cant., v, 14, and called *hyacinthus* in the Vulgate is the Hebrew תרשיש, which has been shown above to be the chrysolite. The exact nature of the hyacinth cannot be determined, the name having been applied to several stones of similar colours, and most probably designating stones of the same colours as the flower hyacinth. Hyacinth is a zircon of a crimson, red, or orange hue. It is harder than quartz and its cleavage is undulating and sometimes lamellated. Its form is an oblong quadrangular prism terminated on both ends by a quadrangular pyramid. It was supposed to be a talisman against tempests.

JASPER, Heb. ישפה; Sept. ἴασπις; Vulg. *jaspis;* the twelfth stone of the breastplate (Ex., xxviii, 18; xxxix, 11), representing Benjamin. In the Greek and Latin texts it comes sixth, and so also in Ezech., xxviii, 13; in the Apocalypse it is the first (xxi, 19). Despite this difference of position *jaspis* is undoubtedly the ישפה of the Hebrew text. The jasper is an anhydrate quartz composed of silica, alumina, and iron. There are jaspers of nearly every colour. It is a completely opaque stone of a conchoidal cleavage. It seems to have been obtained by the Jews from India and Egypt.

LIGURUS, Heb. לשם; Sept. λιγύριον; Vulg. *ligurius;* the first stone of the third row of the rational (Ex., xxviii, 19; xxxix, 12), representing Gad. It is missing in the Hebrew of Ezech., xxviii, 13, but present in the Greek. This stone is probably the same as the hyacinth (St. Epiphan., loc. cit.). This identification, admitted by tradition, rests on the remark that the twelve foundation stones of the celestial city in Apoc., xxi, 19–20, correspond to the twelve stones of the rational, from which it would appear that the ligurus is the same as the hyacinth. Some have identified it with the turmaline, a view rejected by most scholars.

ONYX, Heb. שהם; Sept. ὀνύχιον; Vulg. *lapis onychinus;* the eleventh stone of the breastplate in the Hebrew and the Vulgate (Ex., xxviii, 20; xxxix, 13), representing the tribe of Joseph; in the Sept. it is the twelfth stone; it is the fifth in Ezech., xxviii, 13, in the Heb., but the twelfth in the Greek; it is called sardonyx and comes in the fifth place in Apoc., xxi, 20. The exact nature of this stone is disputed. Many think, because the Greek word βηρύλλος occurs instead of the Hebrew שׁהם that the beryl is meant; but this is not so (see BERYL above). The Vulgate indeed gives onyx as the equivalent of the Hebrew שׁהם. True, this alone would be a very weak argument; but we have other and stronger evidences in the fact that the Hebrew word occurs frequently in Holy Writ (Gen., ii, 12; Ex., xxv, 7; xxv, 9, 27; I Par., xxxix, 2; etc.) and on each occasion, save Job, xxviii, 16, it is translated in the Vulgate by *lapis onychinus* (*lapis sardonychus* in Job, xxviii, 16). The Greek is very inconsistent in its translation, rendering שׁהם differently in various texts; thus in Gen., ii, 12, it is λίθος πράσινος, σάρδιος in Ex. xxv, 7; xxxv, 9; σμάραγδος in Ex., xxviii, 9; xxxv, 27; xxxix, 6; σοάμ, a mere transcription of the Hebrew word in I Par., xxix, 2; and ὄνυξ in Job, xxviii, 16. The other Greek translators are more uniform: Aquila has σαρδόνυξ; Symmachus and Theodotion have ὄνυξ; the paraphrase of Onkelos had *būrla*, the Syriac *berūla*, both of which evidently are the Greek βηρύλλος, "beryl". Since the translations do not observe the same order as the Hebrew in enumerating the stones of the rational (see BERYL above), we are in no way bound to accept the Greek βήρυλλος as the translation of שׁהם, and relying on the testimony of the various versions we may safely hold the onyx is the stone signified by שׁהם. The onyx is a variety of quartz analogous to the agate and other crypto-crystalline species. It is composed of different layers of variously coloured carnelian much like banded agate in structure, but the layers are in even or parallel planes. Hence it is well adapted for the cutting of cameos and was much used for that purpose by the ancients. The colours of the best are perfectly well defined, and are either white and black, or white, brown, and black. The best specimens are brought from India. Sardonyx has a structure like onyx, but is composed usually of alternate layers of white chalcedony and carnelian, although the carnelian may be associated with layers of white, brown, and black chalcedony. The ancients obtained the onyx from Arabia, Egypt, and India.

PEARL.—The pearl can hardly be termed a stone; we may nevertheless, by giving the word "stone" a broad meaning, treat here of the pearl, as we have treated above of coral. It is comparatively certain that the pearl (Greek μαργαρίτη, Vulg. *margarita*) was known among the Jews, at least after the time of Solomon, as it was among the Phœnicians. What word designated it is uncertain. The following have been suggested: גביש, which, however, signified "crystal" (see above; also Furst, "Hebr. u. Chald. Wörterb."); פנינים, which Gesenius renders by "red coral"; דר, Esth.. i, 6, which is translated in the Vulg. by *lapis parius*, "marble"; the Arabic *dar*, however, means "pearl", and thus also Furst renders the Hebrew word. In the New Testament we find the pearl mentioned in Matt., xiii, 45, 46; I Tim., ii, 9; etc. The pearl is a concretion consisting chiefly of carbonate of lime found in several bivalve mollusks, but especially in the *avicula margaritifera*. It is generally of a whitish blue, sometimes showing a tinge of pink; there are also yellow pearls. This gem was considered the most precious of all among the ancients, and was obtained from the Red Sea, the Indian Ocean, and the Persian Gulf.

RUBY.—This may have been either the carbuncle or the chodchod (see above). There is, however, a choice between the oriental ruby and the spinel ruby; but the words may have been used indiscriminately for both. The former is extremely hard, almost as hard as the diamond, and is obtained from Ceylon, India, and China. It is considered a most precious gem.

SAPPHIRE, Heb. ספיר; Septuag. σάπφειρον; Vulg. *sapphirus*.—The sapphire was the fifth stone of the rational (Ex., xxviii, 19; xxxix, 13), and represented the tribe of Dan. It is the seventh stone in Ezech., xxviii, 14 (in the Hebrew text, for it occurs fifth in the Greek text); it is also the second foundation stone of the celestial Jerusalem (Apoc., xxi, 19). The genuine sapphire is a hyaline corindon of a beautiful blue colour; it is composed of nearly pure alumina, its colour being due to the presence of oxide of iron. The ancients gave the name of sapphire also to our lapis-lazuli, which is likewise a blue stone, often speckled with shining pyrites which give it the appearance of being sprinkled with gold dust. It is composed of silica, alumina, and alkali; it is an opaque substance easily engraved. Which of these two is referred to in the Bible? Both may be meant, but the lapis-lazuli seems more probable, for as often as its qualities are described, it is spoken of as being easily engraved (Lam., iv, 7; Ex., xxviii, 17; xxxix, 13). The sapphire was obtained from India.

SARDONYX; SARD.—These two words are often confounded by interpreters. The sard is the carnelian, while the sardonyx is a species of onyx.

TOPAZ, Heb. פטדה; Sept. τοπάζιον; Vulg. *topazius*, the second stone of the rational (Ex., xxviii, 17; xxxix, 19), representing Simeon; also the second stone in Ezech., xxviii, 13; the ninth foundation stone of the celestial Jerusalem (Apoc., xxi, 20); also mentioned in Job, xxviii, 19. This topaz is generally believed to have been the chrysolite rather than our topaz. The oriental topaz is composed of nearly pure alumina, silica, and fluoric acid; its shape is an orthorhombic prism with a cleavage transverse to its long axis. It is extremely hard and has a double refraction. When rubbed or heated it becomes highly electric. It varies in colour according to the country from which it comes. The Australian topaz is green or yellow; the Tasmanian clear, bright, and transparent; the Saxon pale violet; the Bohemian sea-green and the Brazilian red, varying from a pale red to a deep carmine. The ancients very probably obtained it from the East.

ST. EPIPHANIUS, *De duodecim gemmis* in P. G., XLIII, 294–304; ST. ISIDORE, *De lapidibus* in *Etymol.*, xvi, 6–15, in P. L. LXXXII, 570–580; KING, *Antique Gems* (2d ed., London, 1872); IDEM, *The Natural History of Gems or Decorative Stones* (2d ed., London, 1870); BRAUN, *Vestitus sacerdotum hebræorum* (Leyden, 1680); BABELON in DAREMBERG AND SAGLIO, *Dict. des antiquités grecques et romaines*, s. v. *Gemmæ*; LESÊTRE in VIGOUROUX, *Dict. de la Bible*, s. v. *Pierres précieuses*; ROSENMÜLLER, *Handbuch der biblischen Alterthumskunde* (Leipzig); WINER in *Biblisches Realwörterbuch* (Leipzig, 1847), s. v. *Edelsteine*.

CHARLES L. SOUVAY.

Stoning in Scripture.—Palestine being a very rocky country, the abundance of stones made it natural to use them as missiles. Stone throwing might be merely a mark of hatred and contempt (II Kings, xvi, 6–13), or the means of carrying out murderous intentions against which provision had to be made in the Law (Ex., xxi, 18; Num., xxxv, 17). Stoning to death which was at first an expression of popular fury analogous to "lynching", later came to be a natural and legally recognized method of execution. It was thus regulated by law as an appointed means of capital punishment (Deut., xvii, 5–7; Acts, vii, 58). Death by stoning is prescribed in the Pentateuch as the penalty for eighteen different crimes including Sabbath-breaking, but for one crime only—murder—is it the penalty prescribed in all the codes. The execution of the criminal usually took place outside the city walls, and according to Deut., xvii, 7, the witnesses in the case were to cast the first stone: "Thou shalt bring forth the man or the woman, who have committed that most wicked thing, to the gates of thy city, and they shall be stoned. By the mouth of two or three witnesses shall he die who is to be slain. . . . The hands of the witnesses shall be first upon him to kill him, and

STONYHURST COLLEGE, WEST FRONT
FROM THE POINT OF VIEW CHOSEN BY TURNER FOR HIS PICTURE OF STONYHURST
STONYHURST COLLEGE, FROM THE SOUTH

afterwards the hands of the rest of the people". (Deut., xvii, 5–7). Stoning is also mentioned in Acts, vii 57–58, as the means by which Stephen the first Christian martyr was put to death: "And casting him forth without the city, they stoned him."

JAMES F. DRISCOLL.

Stonnes, JAMES, English priest, b. 1513; d. after 1585. He was ordained at Durham by Bishop Tunstall in 1539. After Elizabeth's accession he never entered a church, but wandered about Durham and Yorkshire, with occasional visits to Lancashire, where he was known as Uncle James, saying Mass as often as the opportunity of time, place, and company gave leave. He was eventually arrested by the Earl of Derby about midnight 19 Nov., 1585, at the house of a very poor man, a victualler, and an under-tenant, living eight miles from the earl's seat, Newpark, in the Parish of Ormskirk, Lancashire. As he would not commit himself to the royal supremacy, though he acknowledged the queen as temporal sovereign, and wished she might have Nestor's years, and as he confessed that he regarded her ecclesiastical policy as contrary to God's law and refused to give up saying Mass, he was committed to the New Fleet, Manchester, where, as he was then aged 72, it is probable he died. At the time of his arrest he had with him, an alb, a surplice or amice, a thread girdle, a vestment, a stole, a fannel, "a Corpus and a Corpus Case", a super-altar, a tin chalice with a cover, three little pewter boxes in a leather case for oil and chrism, a crewet, two little pewter bottles for wine, three crucifixes, an Agnus Dei, "a porthouse with the pope's name in the Callender in many places", a piece of an old primer in parchment, a piece of an old book of sermons, and an old Mass-book.

GIBSON, *Lydiate Hall and its Associations* (privately printed, Edinburgh and London, 1876), 231–3.

JOHN B. WAINEWRIGHT.

Stonyhurst College.—The history of Stonyhurst as a school dates back to a period considerably prior to its foundation on English soil in 1794. Stonyhurst is the lineal descendant of the college founded by Father Robert Persons in 1592, at St. Omer in Artois, for English boys, compelled by the penal laws of Elizabethan times to seek on the continent that religious education which was denied them at home. Driven from St. Omer in 1762 by the hostility of the *Parlement* of Paris, the college was transferred to Bruges, where it remained under the protection of the Empress Maria Theresa till dispersed by the suppression of the Society in 1773. Within the same year, however, the staff and students had reassembled and continued their collegiate life at Liège under the patronage of the prince bishop of that city. The approach of the French revolutionary armies in 1794 again compelled the college to seek a new home, and this time it found one in its native land at the mansion of Stonyhurst Hall in Lancashire, which had been placed at the disposal of the community by Mr. Thomas Weld of Lulworth, heir of the Shireburns of Stonyhurst and himself a past student of the college at Bruges. By a strange coincidence Stonyhurst Hall had been rebuilt by Sir Richard Shireburn in 1592, the very year of the foundation of St. Omer; so that the scholastic life of the college, which has now been established at Stonyhurst for 117 years, but reaches back more than 200 years before that final settlement, is coeval with that of its present domicile.

The character of the education given at Stonyhurst has, needless to say, varied with the requirements of the time. The predominant position occupied by classical educational ideals in the earlier half of the nineteenth century—a predominance so congenial to the Ratio Studiorum of the Jesuits—has gradually been modified to meet the development of the study of modern languages and of science, and the demands of public examinations. Hence the curriculum of Stonyhurst at the present day differs in no essential particular from that of the leading public schools in England. It includes classical literature and the chief European languages, history, geography, mathematics, physics, chemistry, astronomy, philosophy, and law. At the Stonyhurst training college more advanced courses in these subjects are followed by students of the Society, who are engaged in such additional subjects as pedagogy, biology, anthropology, etc. The "Philosophers", numbering usually about thirty, possess the status of university students. They have private rooms and sundry privileges, and are quite separate from the rest of the school, though they may join the "Higher Line" in games. Their studies include courses of philosophy, law, and political economy, in addition to the usual literary and science classes. The rector of Stonyhurst is one of a limited number of headmasters to whom the War Office has granted the power of giving direct nominations to the Royal Military College, Sandhurst. This privilege is reserved for those schools where the officers' training corps—of which Stonyhurst has three full companies—attains a certain standard of strength. The college has also been inspected and approved by the Royal College of Physicians (London) and the Royal College of Surgeons (England) as a school for preparing candidates for medical diplomas and exempting them from part of their professional course.

The influence exerted in the course of its history on Church, State, science and art, by a college which has for so long held a prominent place in the education of English Catholics, may best be gauged by the number of distinguished *alumni* who have risen to eminence in these departments. Among the early sons of Stonyhurst, when the establishment was still at St. Omers, are eighteen martyrs now bearing the title of Venerable—fourteen Jesuits, three Franciscans, and one secular priest—besides three who died in prison for the Faith. Father Emmanuel Lobb, who received into the Church the Duke of York, afterwards James II, and Father Edward Petre, the confessor of the same king, were St. Omer men. The unspeakable Titus Oates also spent some time there as a kind of "parlour-boarder", and contemporary letters make it clear that he was intensely unpopular with the boys. The peculiar dress worn at that date by the boys of St. Omers is referred to by Massinger in his play "The Fatal Dowry". Conspicuous among the St. Omer men of a later date are the first two archbishops of Baltimore, John Carroll and Leonard Neale. In more modern times Stonyhurst counts among its pupils Cardinal Weld, Bishop Riddell (Vicar Apostolic of the Northern District), Cardinal Vaughan, Bishop William Vaughan of Plymouth, Bishop Clifford of Clifton, Archbishop Porter of Bombay, Archbishop Gillow of Puebla (Mexico), and Archbishop Maguire of Glasgow. Among distinguished laymen who received their education here may be mentioned Charles Waterton, the famous naturalist (the "W" of Thackeray's "Newcomes"); Richard Lalor Sheil, the great parliamentary orator; Sir Thomas Wyse, a well-known and successful diplomat of the last century; Chief Baron Woulfe of the Irish Court of Exchequer, the first Catholic to be elevated to the Irish Bench, and Judge Nicholas Ball, the second Catholic to enjoy that dignity; the Hon. Charles Langdale, one of the foremost Catholic leaders of Emancipation days; Dr. George Oliver, the antiquary and Church annalist; Sir Frederick Weld, successively Premier of New Zealand, Governor of Tasmania, and Governor of the Straits Settlements, in which last-named colony another Stonyhurst man, Sir Thomas Sidgreaves, was Chief Justice; Sir William Hackett, Chief Justice of the Supreme Court, Ceylon; the Rt. Hon. Sir Nicholas O'Conor, British Ambassador at St. Petersburg and at Constantinople; General Sir Montague Gerard, *doyen* of the foreign military attachés with the Russian army during the Russo-Japanese War; General Sir Charles Chichester, brigadier-general under General De Lacy Evans in the British Auxiliary Legion in Spain in 1835; Admiral Arthur Jerningham, who was attached to the personal guard of Queen Victoria during the alarms of the Chartist disturbance; the late Mr. Justice Walton; Edward de Romaña, a former president of Peru; Thomas Francis Meagher, the orator of the Young Ireland movement and subsequently a general on the Federal side during the American Civil War. To this selection may be added in the domains of literature and art Mr. Percy Fitz-Gerald, F.S.A., a personal friend of Charles Dickens, and author of many literary works; Father John Gerard, S.J., the widely known writer on scientific, historical, and controversial subjects; Bernard Partridge, the "Punch" cartoonist; Alfred Austin, the Poet Laureate.

The fame of the Stonyhurst Observatory, built in 1838, has been kept alive in scientific circles by a succession of distinguished astronomers, several of whom have been at various times selected by the British Government to take charge of important astronomical expeditions. The latest of these was the British Solar Eclipse Expedition to the Tonga Islands in 1911, which was placed under the charge of Father Cortie, one of the directors of the Stonyhurst Observatory. Perhaps the best known of the Stonyhurst astronomers is Father Stephen Perry, F. R. S., Francis Thompson's "starry amorist", who met his death in 1889 while engaged on solar observations for the Government in the West Indies. Among the contributions to Catholic literature the best known are the Stonyhurst Series of Philosophical Textbooks, written by members of the professorial staff: Father Harper's profound work, "The Metaphysics of the School"; and Father Gerard's various writings on natural science and evolution, the Gunpowder Plot, and his remarkably successful reply to Haeckel's "Riddle of the Universe": the works of Father Joseph Rickaby on philosophic and ascetical subjects and the liturgical and historical writings of Father Thurston.

Stonyhurst, which is to-day the largest of the Catholic colleges in England, is the parent of a number of other flourishing schools in Great Britain and Ireland, of which the following is a list together with the approximate number of boys in each: Beaumont College near Windsor, and Mount St. Mary's College in Derbyshire, with more than 200 boarders each; St. Francis Xavier's College, Liverpool, a day-school with nearly 400 boys; St Aloysius' College, Glasgow, with over 300 day scholars; Wimbledon College with some 150 scholars; St Ignatius' Day College, Stamford Hill, London, with about 250 boys; the day colleges at Preston and Leeds with about 150 boys each; and Clongowes Wood College, in Ireland, with 250 boarders. Including the Philosophers and the younger boys at the preparatory school, the total number of boarders at Stonyhurst to-day is 345, with a professorial staff of 40. At the training college the students number about 70, with 8 professors. The college buildings, which are very extensive, are furnished with libraries and museums, numerous lecture rooms, physical and chemical laboratories, observatories, recreation and music rooms, a theatre, swimming bath, carpenter's shops and covered drill-hall. In the large library, which contains over 40,000 volumes, there is a very valuable collection of incunabula, numbering 250, of which some are unique; a First Folio Shakespeare; some priceless manuscripts; and very complete geological, entomological, and other scientific collections. In the museums and other parts of the building are a large number of valuable engravings by Rembrandt and Dürer, together with art treasures in ivory, alabaster, and precious metals; relics of the days of persecution; paintings by some of the Old Masters; and vestments of great intrinsic and historical worth.

GERARD, *Stonyhurst College Centenary Record* (Belfast, 1894); GRUGGEN and KEATING, *History of Stonyhurst* (London, 1901); *Memorials of Stonyhurst College* (London, 1881); HEWITSON, *Stonyhurst College Past and Present* (Preston, 1878); FITZGERALD, *Saxonhurst: a Story of Schooldays* (London, 1901); *British Association Excursion to Stonyhurst and Whalley* (Southport, 1903); *The Stonyhurst Magazine* (school periodical); *Stonyhurst and its Tercentenary* (Clitheroe); three articles in *Country Life* (London, October, 1910); *Moral Instruction and Training in Schools*, ed. SADLER, I (New York and London, 1908), the articles "*Jesuit System of Education*", and "*Stonyhurst*", by MAHER in *The Teachers' Encyclopedia* (London, 1911).

FRANCIS IRWIN.

Stork, AMBROSE. See PELARGUS, AMBROSE.

Stoss, VEIT, sculptor, b. at Nuremberg in 1438; d there in 1533. In 1477 he established a large workshop at Cracow, Poland, but in 1496 he returned to

DEATH AND ASSUMPTION OF THE BLESSED VIRGIN
Veit Stoss, Church of Our Lady, Cracow, 1477-84

Nuremberg. With Adam Kraft and Peter Vischer, he is considered the most important representative of the late Gothic sculpture in Germany. A quick, skilful workman, of great technical ability, in his youth he carried naturalism to the extreme, while often there was a lack of spirituality. Perhaps this may be traced to a trait of his own character as in the documents of the same era he is spoken of as a "restless, unquiet citizen". A certain lack of repose is evident, especially in his treatment of the drapery, while in his entire handling of the figure he is very independent of the Gothic style and carries out his designs in his own manner throughout. His later works, however, show an undoubted depth of feeling. Moreover, the question as to the number of his productions is not yet satisfactorily settled; the latest investigation regards him as the creator of most of the works of the celebrated Vischer, whom it represents as merely the bronze-founder who carried out Stoss's designs. His earliest work (1477) is the celebrated altar of the Blessed Virgin in the Church of Our Lady at Cracow, which is made in three parts, as an altar with wings. In the centre is seen the almost life-size figure of the

Mother of God as she sinks dying into the arms of an Apostle. Another altar of his in this church has reliefs depicting six scenes in the life of St. Stanislaus. The fine qualities of this work, especially the animation of the portrayal and the effective composition, obtained for him in 1492 the commission of making the tomb of King Casimir IV in the Cathedral of Cracow. Probably, however, he only prepared the design of the marble sarcophagus; the king is represented in his coronation robes, while statuettes showing the people as mourners are placed on the sides. For unknown reasons Stoss returned to Nuremberg, where he accomplished a large amount of work; however, only a few of the works attributed to him are authentic, as in former times nearly every important piece of carving in southern Germany was ascribed to him. Perhaps his best work is the "Salutation of the Angel" in the Church of St. Laurence at Nuremberg (1518): the archangel, a finely conceived figure, and Mary, are surrounded by a huge wreath of roses in which are inwoven the Seven Joys of Mary; the figure of the Blessed Virgin is however somewhat commonplace. Other excellent but less celebrated productions are the memorial tablet of Konrad Imhoff, now in the national museum at Munich, and the reliefs of the Carrying of the Cross and the Burial of Christ in the Church of Our Lady at Nuremberg. Of the altars which he carved, mention should be made of those at Schwabach, Bamberg, and of that in the Church of St. Ægidius at Nuremberg.

DAUN, *Veit Stoss und seine Schule* (Leipzig, 1903); IDEM, *Veit Stoss* (Bielefeld, 1906); STASIAK, *Die Wahrheit über Peter Vischer* (Cracow, 1910).

BEDA KLEINSCHMIDT.

Stradivari, ANTONIO, the famous Cremonese violin-maker, b. in 1649 or 1650; d. at Cremona, 18 or 19 Dec., 1737. He was the son of Alessandro Stradivari and Anna Moroni. As there is no evidence of his birth and baptism in any of the parish registers of Cremona, it is supposed that he was born in some village near that town. In 1667 he began to make stringed instruments. Some violins, dated in the seventies, and signed by him, are supposed to exist, but evidences of Stradivari's workmanship are to be found in many violins of this date which are signed by Nicholas Amati. It is probable that during the years 1667–79 he worked as a pupil in Amati's workshop.

In 1680 Stradivari set up for himself in the Piazza San Domenico, and his fame as a violin-maker was soon established. He now began to show his originality, and to make alterations in Amati's model. The arching was improved, the various degrees of thickness in the wood were more exactly determined, the formation of the scroll altered, and the varnish more highly coloured. From 1698 to 1725 Stradivari produced his finest instruments, and carried his manufacture to the highest possible finish, the outlines are designed with taste and purity, the wood is rich and carefully selected, the arching falls off in gentle and regular curves, the scroll is carved with great perfection, and the varnish is fine and supple. The interior workmanship is no less perfect, the degrees of thickness are carefully adjusted, and are remarkable for a precision which could only have been attained by much study and experiment. Everything has been foreseen, calculated, and determined with certainty. The instruments produced from 1725–30 are not so fine. After 1730 many are signed "sub disciplina Stradivarii", and were probably made by his sons, Omobono and Francesco.

Stradivari fixed the exact shape and position of the sound-holes, and his model has been copied by most makers since his time. He definitively settled the shape and details of the bridge, which cannot be altered in the slightest degree without in some way injuring the tone of the instrument. The only essential part of the violin which has had to be changed since Stradivari's time is the bass-bar. On account of the gradual rise in pitch the increased pressure of the strings demands an increased power of resistance in the bar underneath the bridge, hence it has been found necessary to re-bar all the old violins and violoncellos. Stradivari was buried in the Basilica of San Domenico.

ELIZABETH LORKIN.

Stradivari Family, The.—The name Stradivari goes back to the Middle Ages; we find it spelt in various ways, Stradivare, Stradiverto, Stradivertus. Fétis professes to find it in the municipal archives of Cremona for the years 1127 and 1186. The name was certainly borne by more or less distinguished citizens of Cremona during the twelfth and thirteenth centuries. Signor Mandelli gives, as the earliest known mention of it, a document dated May 1188, in which it is recorded that certain pieces of land were leased by the canon and chief warden of the cathedral of Cremona to one Giovanni Stradiverto and his heirs. Arisi, the Cremonese monk, who wrote concerning Antonio Stradivari in 1720, mentions: Galiero Stradivari, a learned Orientalist, who lived in the thirteenth century; Alessandro Stradivari, another Orientalist, about the end of the thirteenth century; Costanzo Stradivari, of about the same period, a monk, who wrote a treatise on the natural philosophy of Aristotle. Fétis also mentions: Guglielmus Stradivertus, an excellent lawyer, who died in 1439. It is certain that the name was a common one in Cremona, but we have no exact evidence to prove that Stradivari, the violin-maker, was directly connected with the above-mentioned persons. The earliest documentary record of his ancestry is to be found in the marriage register of the cathedral of Cremona, where there is an entry, dated April, 1600, of the marriage of Giulio Cesare Stradivari, of the parish of S. Michele Vecchio, to Doralice Milani, of the parish of the cathedral. They had a son, Alessandro, christened in the church of S. Michele in January, 1602; and in the register of the parish of S. Prospero, is the entry of the marriage of this Alessandro Stradivari and Anna Moroni—the father and mother of Antonio.

Francesco Stradivari, son of Antonio, b. 1 Feb. 1671; d. 11 May, 1743. He followed his father's calling, and was the only one of Stradivari's sons to inherit any of the father's skill in making stringed instruments. He made very good violins; some are signed by himself, and others, made with the help of his brother Omobono, are signed "sotto la disciplina d'Antonio Stradivari". His work is quite distinct in character from Antonio's. Both Francesco and Omobono were overshadowed by the genius of their father; they produced good work, if not work of the highest quality.

Omobono Stradivari, son of Antonio, b. 14 Nov., 1679; d. 8 June, 1742. He also followed his father's trade, and made some violins in conjunction with his brother Francesco. His work was chiefly confined to the repair and fitting up of instruments; possibly he made bows, instrument-cases—which were specially designed for wealthy patrons, and often things of great value and beauty—and various fittings, such as bridges, pegs, tail-pieces, etc.

Paolo Stradivari, the youngest son of Antonio by a second marriage, b. 26 Jan., 1708; d. 14 Oct., 1776. He was a cloth merchant, and the only son of the great Stradivari who married. On the death of Francesco, Paolo received the collection of tools, moulds, patterns, drawings, correspondence, and memoranda left by their father, and also several instruments, including the famous "Alard" Strad of 1715, and the unrivalled "Messie" violin of 1716. In 1775 this collection of relics was sold by Paolo to the Count Cozio de Salabue, and afterwards passed into the hands of the late Marquis Alessandro Dalla Valle. Cesare

Stradivari, a grandson of Paolo, b. in 1789, was celebrated as a physician.

GROVE, *Dictionary of Music and Musicians* (London, 1898), III; FÉTIS, *Notice of Anthony Stradivari*, tr. BISHOP (London, 1864).

ELIZABETH LORKIN.

Strahov, ABBEY OF, a Premonstratensian abbey at Prague, Bohemia, founded in 1140 by Bishop Henry Zdik of Olmütz, Bishop John of Prague, and Prince

ST. MARK WRITING HIS GOSPEL
From the Strahov Manuscript

Ladislaus II. A colony of monks from Steinfeld, near Cologne, was brought here, and Gero, a canon of Cologne, became its first abbot. This new abbey in a very short time flourished to such an extent that some of its members were soon appointed bishops of Prague.

During the twelfth, thirteenth, and fourteenth centuries the abbots of Strahov took keen interest in the public affairs of the kingdom, and their names are often mentioned in public documents and grants of special privileges.

On 19 Oct., 1259, the abbey was destroyed by fire, but Abbot John I (1250–66) built a new and magnificent church. The monastery suffered greatly during the plundering reign of the king's regent, Otto of Brandenburg and that of Henry of Carinthia. It, however, again flourished under Charles IV. On 8 May, 1420, the Hussites set fire to the buildings, and looted and destroyed everything. The main cause of anger of the fanatics against the abbey was that John Zelezný, Bishop of Leitomischl, a Premonstratensian, was one of the accusers of Hus at the Council of Constance.

From this time onward Strahov continued to decline, and its lands were gradually stolen and sold, until in 1577 and 1578 not one of its members remained, and the meagre income was turned over to the chaplain of the Emperor Ferdinand I. Later a Premonstratensian, John Lohelius, who subsequently became Archbishop of Prague, gathered monks from various monasteries, colonized Strahov anew, infusing into it new physical as well as spiritual life. Lohelius rebuilt the church and a greater part of the monastery, and Abbot Caspar of Questenberg (1620–40) completed the work. During the bombardment of Prague in 1842 Strahov suffered greatly; the damage, however, was soon repaired. When the Emperor Joseph II suppressed 58 abbeys in Bohemia, Strahov was saved from a similar fate by Abbot Wenceslaus Mayer (d. 1800), who had won favour even at the hostile Court by the interest that he took in fostering schools and education. Abbot Zikmund Starý (1879–1905) built the new church and improved the old church. The present abbot, Method Zavoral, is a man of great ability as a preacher.

The monastic Church of the Assumption, built in 1601–1605 by Abbot Lohelius, is beautifully decorated by numerous frescos; the pictures on the arched ceiling symbolize some of the invocations contained in the Litany of the Blessed Virgin, and on the side walls are scenes from the life of St. Norbert. These beautiful frescos are the work of the Prague artist Georg Wilhelm Neuherz (d. 1743). The Chapel of St. Norbert has the saint's relics in a casket of copper and bronze, richly gilded. The organ is the work of the Strahov monk Lohel Oehlschlägel (d. 1774).

The monastic library contains upwards of 110,000 volumes, of which 1200 are *incunabula*. Of these there are about sixty unique volumes. Of the many rare manuscripts the most precious is the "Evangelistarium" of the sixth century, written in uncial letters and still well-preserved. Among others may be mentioned: "Gerlaci Chronicon", Codex Strahoviensis from 1220; the "Pontificale" of Bishop Albert of Sternberg, made in 1376; the "Missale" of the Premonstratensian Abbey of Louky of 1480; the miniature manuscript of the Bible of the thirteenth century, written by a nun of the cloister of Doksany; "Sich's Graduale" of 1610, weighing fifty pounds. The art

REFECTORY OF THE ABBEY OF STRAHOV

gallery has the original painting of Dürer's "Blessed Virgin of the Rosary", of 1506, with the master's own portrait; and paintings by Correggio, Van Dyck, Holbein, van Aachen, Reiner, Skréta, Brandl, etc.

MAYER, *Historische Beschreibung der vom Ant. Maulbertsch, k.k. Kammermahler, am Bibliothek-Gewölbe der königl. Præm.-Kanonie am Berge Sion zu Prag im Jahre 1794 in Fresco dargestellten Kalkmahlerei* (Prague, 1797); WEYRAUCH, *Gesch. des königl. præmonstatenser Chorherren Stiftes Strahow* (Prague, 1863); IDEM, *Geschichte und Beschreibung des königl. Stift Strahöwer Bibliothek* (Prague, 1858); BRUNNER, *Ein Chorherrenbuch* (Würzburg and Vienna, 1883), 548–88; HANTICH, *Prague* (Paris and Prague, 1905), 62, 63; ČERMÁK, *Præmonstrati v Čechách a na Moravě* (Prague, 1877); EKERT, *Postvátná mista kral. hl. města Prahy* (Prague, 1883), *dědictví sv. Jana Nep.*, 116–44.

JOS. ŠINKMAJER.

Strain, JOHN, Archbishop of St. Andrews and Edinburgh, b. at Edinburgh, 8 December, 1810; d. there, 2 July, 1883. Educated at Edinburgh High School, at Aquhorties Seminary, and at the Scots College, Rome, he was ordained priest in 1833 and, after work in Edinburgh and Dumfries, was appointed to the mission of Dalbeattie, where he laboured for twenty-three years. Transferred to Dumfries in 1857, he was appointed in the following year president of Blairs College, Aberdeen; and on the death of Bishop Gillis in 1864 he was nominated to succeed him as vicar Apostolic of the eastern district, named Bishop of Abila, and consecrated by Pius IX at the Vatican on 25 September. During his nineteen years' episcopate he saw the number of clergy and missions largely increased in his district; many new schools were opened, and several religious communities, both of men and women, introduced. The bishop laboured long and strenuously for the restoration of the regular hierarchy to Scotland; and it was greatly due to his effects that the restoration took place, under Leo XIII, in 1878. He became himself the first Archbishop of St. Andrews and Edinburgh, and held his first diocesan synod in 1881. His death occurred whilst Catholic Scotland was preparing to celebrate with befitting honour the golden jubilee of his ordination.

Catholic Directory for Scotland (1884), 169–80; *The Tablet*, LXI (7 July, 1883), 26.

D. O. HUNTER-BLAIR.

Stransham, EDWARD, VENERABLE, English martyr, b. at Oxford about 1554; suffered at Tyburn, 21 January, 1586. He was educated at St. John's College, Oxford, becoming B. A. in 1575–6; arrived at Douai in 1577, and went with the college to Reims in 1578, whence he came back to England owing to illness. In 1579, however, he returned to Reims, and was ordained priest at Soissons in Dec., 1580. He left for England, 30 June, 1581, with his fellow-martyr, Nicholas Woodfen, of London Diocese, ordained priest at Reims, 25 March, 1581. In 1583 Stransham came back to Reims with twelve Oxford converts. After five months there he went to Paris, where he remained about eighteen months at death's door from consumption. He was arrested in Bishopgate Street Without, London, 17 July, 1585, while saying Mass, and was condemned at the next assizes for being a priest. Details of his career will be found in the article mentioned below.

WAINEWRIGHT in *Downside Review* (1911) s. v., and the authorities there cited.

JOHN B. WAINEWRIGHT.

Strasburg, DIOCESE OF (ARGENTINENSIS), a German diocese immediately dependent on the Papal See. According to legend the Diocese of Strasburg was founded in the third or fourth century. St. Arbogast and Florentius were distinguished bishops of the sixth or seventh century. The first bishop known to history is Ansoald, one of the signers of the Acts of the Council of Paris of 614. His successor Eddo or Heddo, of the ducal family of Ettichos, organized his ecclesiastical diocese in conjunction with St. Boniface, aided by the Carolovingians. The boundaries then given remained essentially the same throughout the Middle Ages. On the left bank of the Rhine the diocese extended over the present Province of Alsace with exception of the south-eastern part between the Ill, Blind, and Rhine; on the right bank it extended from the Rhine to the crest of the Black Forest, and southward from the mouth of the Murg to the Elz. This territory was divided into seven archdiaconates, of which one included Strasburg, and one the region on the right bank of the Rhine. This subdivision remained substantially the same from the eleventh century to the French Revolution.

Charlemagne granted Bishop Heddo unlimited jurisdiction in the valley of the Breusch, and in 775 the bishop received freedom from customs duty throughout the empire for himself and his vassals (*homines ecclesiæ*). By the Treaty of Verdun (843) the Diocese of Strasburg fell to the empire of Lothair; in 870 it became part of the east Frankish kingdom, later the Holy Roman Empire, so that the German character of the diocese was preserved. Both Lothair and Louis the German confirmed the privileges that their forefathers had granted to the Church of Strasburg. Bishops Udo (950–65) and Erchanbald (965–91) restored Church discipline which had fallen into decay at the beginning of the tenth century. Emperor Otto I granted Udo the ownership of the royal mint at Strasburg; Otto II (974) confirmed this gift and gave the bishop the right to establish a mint in any town of the diocese he desired. In 982 Otto II granted Erchanbald absolute jurisdiction over the city of Strasburg and its environs, thus forming the main foundation of the secular supremacy of the bishop. Werner I of Habsburg (1001–29) received from emperors Henry II and Conrad II a large number of grants, including the old Abbey of St. Stephen with all its rights. A new cathedral, to replace the one destroyed in 1002 by Hermann of Swabia, was begun by Werner I in 1015 and dedicated in 1031. The bishop gave to the library of the minster numerous manuscripts which he had collected in Italy. During the conflict of investitures the bishops generally sided with the imperial party: Werner II (1065–79); Theobald (1079–82), who took part in the election of the anti-pope Clement II; and Otto of Hohenstaufen (1082–1100), who accompanied Godfrey of Bouillon on the First Crusade. Gebhard I (1131–41) and Burkhard I (1141–62) were zealous promoters of Church reform; during the episcopate of Berthold I of Teck (1223–44), about 1230, the new orders of Franciscans and Dominicans settled at Strasburg.

The city of Strasburg developed under episcopal administration, and in the twelfth century it prospered greatly. Its efforts to abolish episcopal suzerainty and to obtain new privileges were especially successful during the Conflict of Investitures. The town-council acquired great independence and the right of co-optation, although the right of the bishop to appoint the council had been reconfirmed in 1214 by charter of Emperor Frederick II. At the beginning of his episcopate Walter of Geroldseck (1260–63) wished to enforce this right, to dispose of communal property, and to regulate the taxes. The populace, siding with the council and the patricians, defeated the episcopal forces at Hausberger, 8 March, 1262, thus practically establishing the independence of the city. The succeeding bishop, Henry of Geroldseck (1263–73), made a treaty in 1263 by which at the close of the official year the council elected its own successors, and the citizens themselves had the right to settle all questions regarding communal property. The bishop retained only the right to appoint the town magistrate, the castellan of the castle, the official in charge of the collection of the customs, and the superintendent of the mint. These offices, except that of magistrate, gradually sank in importance, and the bishop no longer appointed the officials. Conrad of Lichtenberg (1273–99) completed the rebuilding in Gothic style of the nave of the minster, and began the construction of the beautiful west façade. Bishops Johannes of Dirpheim (1306–28), chancellor of King Albert II, and Berthold II of Bucheck (1328–53) were both capable administrators, appointed by the pope. Notwithstanding their share in imperial politics, these bishops found time to hold synods and labour effectually for church discipline in the diocese.

In 1359 John II of Lichtenberg (1353–65) obtained the Landgraviate of Lower Alsace from the Counts of Oettingen. A land-register, that gave exact information concerning the secular possessions of the diocese, was drawn up during his administration. The diocese included: in Lower Alsace the districts of Benfield, Markolsheim, Schirmeck, Dachstein, Kochersberg, Wanzemau, and Zabern; in Upper Alsace the stewardship of Rufach; in the present Duchy of Baden the districts of Oberjirch and Ettenheim. The episcopal possessions in Alsace were only exceeded in area by those of Hamburg. With shrewd policy the bishops had opportunely broken the power of the local governors, and had successfully opposed the restoration of imperial administrative suzerainty over diocesan territories. Under John's successors began the decline of the diocese, promoted by unhappy political conditions and by the Great Schism. This decay was especially rapid during the episcopate of William of Diest (1394–1439), who, to carry on innumerable private and public wars, frequently mortgaged and squandered the episcopal lands. His successors, who, with the aid of the cathedral chapter, finally paid off his debts, were: Rupert of the Pfalz (1440–78), who called the celebrated preacher Geiler von Kaysersberg (q. v.) to the pulpit of the minster; Albert of the Pfalz (1478–1506); and William III of Honstein (1507–41).

Soon after 1520 the Reformation gained many adherents in the city of Strasburg, owing to the labours of Luther's friends, Wolfgang Capito and Martin Bucer, the efforts of the preacher Matthias Zell and of the Humanists Sturm and Hedio. In 1529 the council abolished the Mass; in 1531 the city joined the Smalkaldic League, whereupon the bishop transferred his see to Zabern. Despite the vigorous opposition of William of Honstein and Erasmus of Limburg (1541–68), all the secular lordships of the diocese in Lower Alsace adopted the new doctrine, except the landgraviate; even part of the cathedral chapter became Protestant. John IV of Manderscheid-Blankenheim (1569–92) summoned the Jesuits to Molsheim to check the apostasy, and encouraged the Counter-Reformation. After his death there was a double election: the Protestant cathedral canons chose John George of Brandenburg as administrator; the Catholic canons, Cardinal Charles of Lorraine. The struggle between the two candidates, called the Bishops' War of Strasburg (1592–1604), caused the diocese great misery. Charles of Lorraine was victor. Catholic ownership was further secured in the successive election of two Austrian archdukes as bishop: Leopold (1607–25), a brother of Emperor Ferdinand II, and Leopold William (1625–62), one of Ferdinand's sons. During the Thirty Years' War the territory was so ravaged by Ernst of Mansfeld, the Swedes, and the French, that the population decreased 75 per cent. In 1680, during the episcopate of Charles Egon of Fürstenberg (1663–82), whose sympathies were French, Louis XIV seized all the territory of the diocese on the left bank of the Rhine under pretence of "reunion"; the city of Strasburg became a French possession in 1681. The bishop retained the internal administration of his possessions in Alsace and the title of landgrave. The districts on the right bank of the Rhine remained within the German Empire, and the bishop was still their ruler as prince of the empire. The occupation of Strasburg by the French brought the minster once more into the hands of the Catholics. William Egon of Fürstenberg (1682–1704) established the seminary for priests at Strasburg and placed the Jesuits in charge of it. The succeeding four bishops belonged to the French princely family of de Rohan; the last of these, Louis René de Rohan (1779–1802), was involved in the notorious affair of the diamond necklace. In 1790 the Constituent National Assembly secularized the Alsatian possessions of the diocese and Rohan transferred his see to the German portion of his bishopric. In Strasburg Brendel, a constitutional bishop, was elected; Eulogius Schneider, whom he appointed vicar-general, persecuted Catholic priests who refused to take the oath, until the overthrow of the Reign of Terror in Paris put an end to this injustice.

By the Concordat of 1801 the Diocese of Strasburg received new boundaries, extending the jurisdiction of the bishop over and beyond Alsace to the Lake of

View of the Cathedral, Strasburg

Bienne in Switzerland, and south-westerly as far as Montbéliard. Rohan having resigned at the request of the pope, Peter Saurine (1802–13), former constitutional bishop, became Bishop of Strasburg. The districts on the right bank of the Rhine fell to Baden on account of the secularization of the German Church in 1803. The diocese, which had been a suffragan of Mainz until 1802, became (1822) a suffragan of Besançon; it was reduced in size towards the south and south-west. Bishop Andreas Räss (1842–87) endeavoured to revive Catholicism in Germany, to promote the education of the clergy, and to establish religious associations. When Alsace became a German possession in 1871, the diocese received its present extent and was declared directly dependent on the Holy See by Decrees of 10 and 14 July, 1874, and by the Treaty of Paris of 7 October, 1874. Räss was succeeded by Peter Paul Stumpf (1887–90), and the present bishop, Adolf Fritzen, consecrated on 21 July, 1891. Bishop Fritzen has especially encouraged Catholic associations, the Catholic press, Church liturgy and psalmody. In 1902 he established a theological faculty at the University of Strasburg.

Statistics.—The Diocese of Strasburg includes the departments of Upper and Lower Alsace in the German Crown-Province of Alsace-Lorraine. In 1911 it contained 57 deaneries, 710 parishes, 283 curacies, 710 parish priests, 454 curates and ecclesiastics in other positions, 92 priests retired or on leave elsewhere, 106 regulars, and 846,100 Catholics, while 350,000 of the population belonged to other faiths. The bishop is appointed by the pope in agreement with the German Emperor, and the cathedral chapter is appointed by the bishop. In regard to educational and charitable institutions and religious houses of the diocese, see ALSACE-LORRAINE. The most important church is the minster at Strasburg, the oldest parts of which belong to the eleventh century. The crypt is Romanesque, the upper part of the choir and the transepts belong to the Transition period, the nave is Gothic. The famous façade is the chief work of Erwin of Steinbach (1284-1318). The north tower, about 465 feet high, was completed in 1429-39 by Johann Hültz of Cologne. The minster is rich in stained glass of the period from the twelfth to the fifteenth century. Other churches are: St. Martin at Colmar, St. George at Schlettstadt, St. Theobald at Thann, St. Nicholas at Hagenau, St. Leodegar and the Church of Our Lady at Gebweiler, Old and New St. Peter at Strasburg, etc. Much frequented places of pilgrimage are: Drei Aehren near Colmar, St. Odilien near Barr, Dusenbach near Rappoltsweiler, St. Morand near Altkirch, etc.

For complete bibliography see MARCKWALD, *Elsass-lothringische Bibliographie* (Strasburg, 1889); *Zeitschrift für Gesch. des Oberrheins* (Karlsruhe, 1890——). Most important works: *Gallia christiania*, V (Paris, 1725); SCHÖPFLIN, *Alsatia illustrata* (Colmar, 1751); GRANDIDIER, *Histoire de l'église et des évêques de Strasbourg*, I, II (Strasburg, 1776-78), III (Colmar, 1862); IDEM, ed. LIBLIN, *Œuvres historiques inédites* (Colmar, 1866-68); IDEM, *Alsatia sacra* (Colmar, 1898-99); RÖHRICH, *Gesch. der Reformation in Elsass* (Strasburg, 1830-32); *Chroniken der deutschen Städte*, VIII, IX (Leipzig, 1870-71); KRAUS, *Kunst u. Altertum in Elsass-Lothringen* (Strasburg, 1876-92); *Urkunden u. Akten der Stadt Strassburg*, I-X (Strasburg, 1879——); GLÖCKLER, *Gesch. des Bistums Strassburg* (Strasburg, 1880-81); GEIGEL, *Das französiche u. reichländische Staatskirchenrecht* (Strasburg, 1884, 1888); *Die alten Territorien des Elsass* (Strasburg, 1896); *Regesten der Bischöfe von Strassburg* (Innsbruck, 1908——); LANDMANN, *Das Schulwesen des Bistums Strassburg von 1802-1904* (Strasburg, 1908); VON BORRIES, *Gesch. der Stadt Strassburg* (Strasburg, 1909); DE LA HACHE, *La cathédrale de Strasbourg* (Paris, 1910); *Strassburger kathol. Jahrbuch* (Strasburg, 1908——); *Strassburger theol. Studien* (Freiburg, 1892——); *Strassburger Beiträge zur neueren Gesch.* (Strasburg, 1906); *Jahrbuch der Gesellschaft für elsass-lothringische Gesch. u. Altertumskunde* (Strasburg, 1888——).

JOSEPH LINS.

Strasburg, GOTTFRIED OF. See GOTTFRIED VON STRASSBURG.

Stratonicea, a titular see in Caria (Asia Minor) suffragan of Stauropolis. Stratoniceia or Stratonicea was founded perhaps on the site of the more ancient Idrias, in the interior of Caria, south-east of Mylassa, and south of the Marsyas, by Antiochus Soter, who named it after his wife Stratonice. His successors embellished it with magnificent monuments, and it became one of the chief towns of Caria. Later it was ceded to the Rhodians. Mithridates lived in it some time, and while there married the daughter of one of the principal citizens. Later it sustained a vigorous siege by Labienus. It is mentioned as a free town by Pliny. Some of its coins have been found. Near the city was a temple of Zeus Chrysaoreus, where the confederated Carian towns held their assemblies. To-day it is the small town of Eski Hissar, in the caza of Moughla, vilayet of Smyrna. It has extensive ruins, a theatre, tomb, columns, etc. The "Notitiæ episcopatuum" mention the see till the thirteenth century among the suffragans of Stauropolis. Only three of its bishops are known, by their signatures at councils: Eupeithus, at Chalcedon, 451; Theopemptus, at Constantinople, 692; Gregory, at Nicæa, 787.

LE QUIEN, *Oriens christ.*, I, 911; CHANDLER, *Travels in Asia Minor* (2 vols., Oxford, 1825), 240; LEAKE, *Asia Minor* (London, 1824), 229; FELLOWS, *Asia Minor* (London, 1852), 254 sqq.; IDEM, *Lycia*, 80 sqq.; SMITH, *Dict. of Greek and Roman Geog.*, s. v.

S. PÉTRIDÈS.

Streber, FRANZ IGNAZ VON, numismatist and theologian, b. at Reisbach, Lower Bavaria, 11 Feb., 1758; d. at Munich, 26 April, 1841. In 1783 he was made court chaplain, in 1821 auxiliary bishop, in 1822 cathedral provost of Munich. In 1782 he was appointed curator of the cabinet of coins of the elector. His work was to unite the Mannheim or Palatinal collection with the Munich or Bavarian collection of the Wittelsbach line, which had been in disorder since the Thirty Years' War, and to arrange the combined collection in scientific order. On account of the disturbances caused by war he was obliged to carry off and conceal the cabinet of coins five times, each time re-arranging it anew. He wrote a history of the royal Bavarian cabinet of coins, and several treatises on Bavarian and Greek numismatics, most of which appeared in the transactions of the Academy of Munich.

STREBER, *Rede zum Andenken an Ignaz von Streber*, read at the public session of the Academy, 28 March, 1843.

AUG. V. LOEHR.

Streber, FRANZ SERAPH, numismatist and nephew of the above, b. at Deutenkofen, Lower Bavaria, 26 Feb., 1805; d. at Munich, 21 Nov. 1864. He first studied theology and philosophy, then archæology and numismatics, and wrote in 1830 as his dissertation for obtaining the degree of Doctor of Philosophy at Erlangen a paper on the genealogy of the Burgraves of Nuremberg. In 1854 he became a member of the Academy of Munich. In 1835 he was made professor of archæology at the University of Munich, of which he was twice rector. In 1827 he was made clerk, in 1830 assistant, and in 1841 curator of the royal cabinet of coins. He also worked on the numismatic collection of Vienna and prepared a critical catalogue of 18,000 Greek coins and a numismatico-iconographic lexicon with drawings of about 6000 Greek coins belonging to the Viennese and Munich collections. In 1834 he published the work "Numismata nonnulla græca", which corrected false and inexact designations of coins; this was crowned with a prize by the Academy of Paris as was also his important investigation concerning what are called the rainbow patina, which he was the first to recognize as Celtic (vol. IX of the papers of the Munich Academy). Further papers on Celtic, Greek, and medieval coins, also on archæology, mythology, and the history of art, appeared chiefly in the publications of the Munich Academy. He also drew up a "Promemoria" that is preserved among the records of the royal cabinet of coins, as to the expenses and the plan of a monumental work covering the entire field of Greek numismatics that was to take the place of the old work by Eckhel and be about one-half larger. Streber was also prominent in politics as a strong supporter of the ecclesiastico-conservative party. He founded the association for a constitutional monarchy and religious freedom, and wrote many political memorials at its request.

Transactions of the Academy of Munich, I (1865), 2661 sq.; *Histor.-politische Blätter*, LV (1865), 85 sq.

AUG. V. LOEHR.

Streber, HERMANN, son of Franz Seraph Streber, b. at Munich, 27 Sept., 1839; d. at Tölz, 9 Aug., 1896. He entered the Ludwigsgymnasium in 1850, but a nervous fever prevented him from qualifying for the university through the usual final school examination. From this ailment he never completely recovered. Entering the university by a private examination in 1858, he devoted over two years to the study of philosophy and theology, attending besides historical lectures. During this period he compiled a description and catalogue of the ancient coins in the Royal Cabinet of Medals. In 1861 he entered the archiepiscopal seminary at Freising, and in 1864 was ordained priest. Owing to the death of his father he was unable to pursue his original intention of studying numismatics. In 1867 he was appointed religious teacher at the Wihelmsgymnasium. Having received six months' leave of absence in 1868, he won the doctorate in theology in Rome (Jan., 1869). He then resumed his duties as religious teacher until June, 1870, when he was dismissed for alleged "intriguing in favour of the dogma of infallibility". He was then named pastor of Wolfersdorf, near Freising. Invited by Professor Hergenröther to assist him in editing the new edition of the "Kirchenlexikon",

Streber resigned his parish, and settled in Würzburg. When Hergenröther was summoned as cardinal to Rome, Streber moved to Bonn to be near Kaulen, the new editor, and performed notable services in perfecting the "Nomenclator". He wrote many articles for the "Kirchenlexikon", the direction of which was for a time entirely in his hands. In 1892 illness forced him to withdraw to his brother's house at Tölz, where he lived in retirement until death.

BUCHBERGER, *Kirchlich. Handlexikon*, s. v.; KAULEN in *Kirchenlexikon*, s. v.

MOIRA K. COYLE.

Streicher, HENRY. See VICTORIA NYANZA, VICARIATE APOSTOLIC OF NORTHERN.

Strikes. See LABOUR UNIONS, MORAL ASPECTS OF.

Strossmayer, JOSEPH GEORG (JOSIP JURAJ), Bishop of Diakovár, b. at Essegg in Croatia-Slavonia, 4 February, 1815; d. 8 April, 1905. He came from a family of German peasants who had immigrated into Croatia. After attending the *gymnasium* of his native town, he studied theology in the seminary at Diakovár and the higher seminary at Budapest, where he obtained the degree of Doctor of Philosophy when only twenty years of age. In 1838 he was ordained priest and was for two years vicar at Peterwardein. In 1840 he went to the Augustineum at Vienna; in 1842 obtained the degree of Doctor of Theology, and was then made professor at Diakovár. In 1847 he became court chaplain, prefect in the Augustineum and professor of canon law at the University of Vienna. On 18 November, 1849, he was appointed Bishop of Diakovár, and was consecrated on 8 September, 1850. At the same time he was Apostolic Administrator of Belgrade-Semendria in Servia. In 1898 the pope conferred the pallium upon him. At the Vatican Council he was one of the most notable opponents of papal infallibility, and distinguished himself as a speaker. The pope praised Strossmayer's "remarkably good Latin". A speech in which he defended Protestantism made a great sensation. Afterwards another speech, delivered apparently on 2 June, 1870, was imputed to him. It is full of heresies and denies not only infallibility but also the primacy of the pope. The forger is said to have been a former Augustinian, a Mexican named Dr. José Agustín de Escudero. After the council Strossmayer maintained his opposition longer than all the other bishops and kept up a connexion with Döllinger and Reinkens until October, 1871. Then he notified them that he intended to yield "at least outwardly". Finally, on 26 December, 1872, he published the decrees of the council in his official paper. At a later date he repeatedly proclaimed his submission to the pope, as in his pastoral letter of 28 February, 1881, on Sts. Cyril and Methodius, expressing his devotion to the papal see at times in extravagant language.

In politics he was an active supporter of the Croatian national party and Panslavism. He exerted himself to advance his people in civilization, yet he strengthened national hatreds by his political agitation. He used the large revenues of his diocese to found primary schools, a seminary, the academy for southern Slavs at Agram (1867), the university (1874), and a picture gallery also at Agram. Under his direction Augustín Theiner edited the "Vetera monumenta Slavorum meridionalium" (1863). During 1866–82 he built a fine and splendidly ornamented cathedral. He sought to win the Servians who were not Uniats for Rome by the use of the Old Slavonic liturgy.

SMICIKLAS, *Strossmayer* (Agram, 1906); *Die kath. Kirche unserer Zeit*, ed. by the LEO SOCIETY, II (Berlin, 1900), 645–9; GRANDERATH-KIRCH, *Gesch. des vatikanischen Konzils*, II, III (Freiburg, 1903–06), passim; SCHULTE, *Der Altkatholizismus* (Giessen, 1887), 251–264.

KLEMENS LÖFFLER.

Stuart, HENRY BENEDICT MARIA CLEMENT, cardinal, Duke of York, known by the Jacobites as HENRY IX, KING OF GREAT BRITAIN, FRANCE, AND IRELAND; b. at Rome, 11 March, 1725; d. at Frascati, 13 July, 1807. He was the second son of James Francis Edward Stuart, the Chevalier de St. George, and Clementina, daughter of Prince James Sobieski. In 1745, when hopes of a Stuart restoration ran high, he visited France, hoping to embark with French troops to the assistance of his brother Charles Edward. Having spent several months at Dunkirk without effect, he returned to Rome with the intention of entering the ecclesiastical state. In 1747, at the age of twenty-two, he was created cardinal, and during the following year he received Holy orders, being ordained priest on 1 September. He was immediately made archpriest of the Vatican Basilica, and shortly afterwards cardinal camerlengo. In Nov., 1759, he was consecrated titular Archbishop of Corinth, and on 13 July, 1761, became Cardinal-Bishop of Frascati. Being sincerely pious and earnest, he proved a zealous administrator of his see, reforming the clergy, and founding a seminary which he endowed with a magnificent library. At the French Revolution he lost his French benefices, sacrificed many other resources to assist the pope, and finally was reduced to poverty by the seizure of his Frascati property by the French. Old and infirm, he fled to Padua and thence to Venice. King George III then came to his assistance, aiding him with a life-annuity till he was able to return to Frascati in 1800. In return for this kindness the cardinal bequeathed to the Prince of Wales, afterwards George IV, the crown jewels of James II. In September, 1803, he became Bishop of Ostia and Velletri, and Dean of the Sacred College, though he still resided at Frascati. At his death the Stuart papers in his possession were bought by George IV for the Royal Library, and others are now in the British Museum. There are three pictures of him in the National Portrait Gallery, London, and one at Blairs College, Aberdeen. The cardinal lies buried in St. Peter's at Rome, where Canova's monument preserves his memory.

HENRY BENEDICT STUART
Cardinal of York, Titular King of Great Britain and Ireland

VAUGHAN, *The Last of the Royal Stuarts* (London, 1906); KELLY, *Life of Henry Benedict Stuart, Cardinal Duke of York* (London, 1899); WISEMAN, *Recollections of the Last Four Popes* (London, 1858); JESSE, *The Pretenders and their Adherents* (London, 1845); MASTROFINI, *Orazione per la morte di Enrico Cardinale Duca de York* (Rome, 1807); HENDERSON in *Dict. Nat. Biog.*, s. v. *Henry Benedict Maria Clement*; GILLOW, *Bibl. Dict. Eng. Cath.*, s. v. *Stuart, Henry Benedict Maria Clement*.

EDWIN BURTON.

Stuart, MARY. See MARY QUEEN OF SCOTS.

Studion (STUDIUM), the most important monastery at Constantinople, situated not far from the Propontis in the section of the city called Psamathia. It was founded in 462 or 463 by the consul Studios (Studius), a Roman who had settled in Constantinople, and was dedicated to St. John the Baptist. Its monks came from the monastery of Accœmetæ. At a later date the laws and customs of Studion were taken as models by the monks of Mount Athos and of many other monasteries of the Byzantine Empire; even to-day they have influence. The Studites gave the first proof of their devotion to the Faith and the Church during the schism of Acacius (484–519); they also remained loyal during the storms of Iconoclastic dispute in the eighth and ninth centuries. They were driven from the monastery of Studion and the city by Emperor Constantine Copronymus; after his death (775), however, some of them returned. Abbot Sabbas zealously defended the Catholic doctrine against the Iconoclasts at the Seventh Œcumenical Council of Nicæa (787). His successor was St. Theodore of Studion to whom the monastery owes the most of its fame, and who especially fostered study. During St. Theodore's administration also the monks were harassed and driven away several times, some of them being put to death. Theodore's pupil Naucratius re-established discipline after the Iconoclastic dispute had come to an end. Abbot Nicholas (848–51 and 855–58) refused to recognize the Patriarch Photius and was on this account imprisoned in the Studion. He was succeeded by five abbots who recognized the patriarch. The brilliant period of the Studion came to an end at this time. In the middle of the eleventh century, during the administration of Abbot Simeon, a monk named Nicetas Pectoratus (Stethatos) made a violent attack on the Latins in a book which he wrote on unleavened bread, the Sabbath, and the marriage of priests. In 1054 he was obliged to recant in the presence of the emperor and of the papal legates and to throw his book into the fire, but he began the dispute again later. As regards the intellectual life of the monastery in other directions it is especially celebrated for its famous school of caligraphy which was established by St. Theodore. In the eighth and eleventh centuries the monastery was the centre of Byzantine religious poetry; a number of the hymns are still used in the Greek Church. Besides St. Theodore and Nicetas, a number of other theological writers are known. In 1204 the monastery was destroyed by the Crusaders and was not rebuilt until 1290; the greater part of it was again destroyed when the Turks captured Constantinople (1453). The only part now in existence is the Church of St. John Baptist, probably the oldest remaining church in Constantinople, a basilica which still preserves from the early period two stories of columns on the sides and a wooden ceiling, and which is now the mosque Imrachor-Dschamissi.

MÜLLER, *Studium cœnobium Constantinopolitanum* (Leipzig, 1721); SALZENBERG, *Altchristl. Baudenkmäler von Konstantinopel* (Berlin, 1854), 36–41, plates II–IV; MARIN, *De Studio cœnobio Constantinopolitano* (Paris, 1897).

KLEMENS LÖFFLER.

Stuhlweissenburg (SZÉKES-FEHÉRVÀR) DIOCESE OF (ALBÆ REGALENSIS), in Hungary, and Suffragan of Gran. It was formed in 1777 from the Dioceses of Gyor and Veszprem. In earlier times there was here a collegiate chapter of the Diocese of Veszprem, founded in 1006 by King St. Stephen; it was under a provost and was endowed with great privileges, the provost being chosen by the chapter, and the members of the chapter by the provost. Provost, chapter, and church were exempt from the jurisdiction of the bishop and directly subject to the pope. The chapter members were recruited from the chief families, and were once about forty, but in 1543, during the invasions of the Turks, the chapter became extinct, though the provosts and canons were yet nominated. The Provost of Stuhlweissenburg, according to the laws of the thirteenth century, was royal chancellor. The archives of the chapter were the most important in Hungary, and preserved a copy of the Golden Bull of 1222, the Magna Charta of Hungary. During the invasion of the Turks these archives were destroyed. The cathedral, in which the royal insignia were preserved, was later enlarged by the kings of Hungary and richly decorated. In 1601 it was destroyed by the Turks.

From 1380 to 1527 Stuhlweissenburg was both coronation and burial place for the Hungarian kings. The diocese includes the entire County of Fejér and a part of the ancient County of Pilis, also the Island of Csepel in the Danube. Budapest, the capital of Hungary, though territorially within this diocese, is subject to the Archbishop of Gran.

The first Bishop of Stuhlweissenburg was Ignatius Nagy (1777–1789). Among his successors are Joseph Kopácsy (1821–1825), afterwards Archbishop of Gran; Vincent Jekelfalussy (1866–1874), the first Hungarian bishop to promulgate the dogma of the infallibility without previously asking the royal consent (*placet regium*), and for which he was rebuked. In 1901 Bishop Julius Városy was appointed Archbishop of Kalocsa. At present the see is ruled by Ottokar Prohaszka, a famous preacher and leader of the Hungarian Catholic movement. The diocese is divided into arch-deaconries; the parish priests number 92, and the clergy 152. In the diocese are 8 abbeys and 5 provostships, 4 monasteries for men and 12 for women, in all 109 members. Right of patronage belongs to 46 persons. Since 1841 the cathedral chapter, at the head of which is a chief provost, consists of 8 canons; the Catholic faithful are 230,305.

Das katholische Ungarn (Budapest, 1902) in Hungarian; *Schematismus of the Diocese for 1910*; KÁROLY, *Hist. of the County of Fejér* (Székes-Fehérvàr, 1886–1901), in Hungarian.

A. ÁLDÁSY.

Stylites (PILLAR SAINTS) were solitaries who, taking up their abode upon the top of a pillar ($\sigma\tau\hat{v}\lambda os$), chose to spend their days amid the restraints thus entailed and in the exercise of other forms of asceticism. This practice may be regarded as the climax of a tendency which became very pronounced in Eastern lands in the latter part of the fourth century. The duration and severity of the fasts then practised almost pass belief, but the evidence is overwhelming (Butler; Palladius, I, 188, 240–1), and the general correctness of the accounts preserved to us is now hardly disputed. Besides the mortification of the appetite, submission to restraints of all kinds became at this period an end in itself. Palladius tells us (ch. xlviii) of a hermit in Palestine who dwelt in a cave on the top of a mountain and who for the space of twenty-five years never turned his face to the West. St. Gregory of Nazianzus (P. G., XXXVII, 1456) speaks of a solitary who stood upright for many years together, absorbed in contemplation, without ever lying down. Theodoret assures us that he had seen a hermit who had passed ten years in a tub suspended in mid air from poles (Philotheus, ch. xxviii).

There seems no reason to doubt that it was the ascetical spirit manifested in such examples as these which spurred men on to devise new and more ingenious forms of self-crucifixion and which in 423 led Simeon Stylites the Elder (q. v.) first of all to take up his abode upon the top of a pillar. Critics, it is true, have recalled a passage in Lucian (De Syria Dea, cc. xxviii–xxix) which speaks of a high column at Hierapolis to the top of which a man ascended twice a year and spent a week in converse with the gods, but even such an authority as Nöldeke thinks it unlikely that Simeon had derived any suggestion from this pagan custom, which certainly had died out before his time. In any case Simeon had a continuous series ot imitators, more particularly in Syria and Palestine. St. Daniel Stylites may have been the first of these, for he had been a disciple of St. Simeon and began his rigorous way of life shortly after his master died. Daniel was a Syrian by birth but he established himself near Constantinople, where he was visited by both the Emperor Leo and the Emperor Zeno. Simeon the Younger (q. v.), like his namesake, lived near Antioch; he died in 596, and had for a contemporary a hardly less famous Stylites in St. Alypius, whose pillar had been erected near Adrianople in Paphlagonia.

Saint Alypius after standing upright for fifty-three years found his feet no longer able to support him, but instead of descending from his pillar lay down on his side and spent the remaining fourteen years of his life in that position.

St. Luke the Younger, another famous pillar hermit, whose life has recently been printed for the first time in the "Analecta bollandiana" (1909, pp. 5–56), lived in the tenth century on Mount Olympus, but he also seems to have been of Asiatic parentage. There were many others besides these who were not so famous and even women Stylites were also known. One or two isolated attempts seem to have been made to introduce this form of asceticism into the West but it met with little favour. In the East cases were found down to the twelfth century; in the Orthodox Russian Church it lasted until 1461, and among the Ruthenians even later. There can be no doubt that for the majority of the pillar hermits the extreme austerity of which we read in the lives of the Simeons and of Alypius was somewhat mitigated. Upon the summit of some of the columns for example a tiny hut was erected as a shelter against sun and rain, and we hear of other hermits of the same class among the Monophysites, who lived inside a hollow pillar rather than upon it; but the life in any case must have been one of extraordinary endurance and privation. Probably the best justification of these excesses of austerity is to be found in the fact that, like the great renunciation of St. Melania the Younger (see Cardinal Rampolla's "Sta Melania Giuniore"), they did, in an age of terrible corruption and social decadence, impress the need of penance more than anything else could have done upon the minds and imagination of Oriental Christians.

Delehaye in *Congrès scientifique international des Catholiques*, II (Brussels, 1895), 191–232; *Analecta bollandiana* (1909), 5–56; Nöldeke, *Sketches from Eastern History* (tr. London, 1892), 210–25; Ehrhard in *Kirchenlexicon*, s. v. *Styliten*.

Herbert Thurston.

Styria (Ger. Steiermark), a duchy and Austrian crownland, divided by the River Mur into Upper and Lower Styria. The province is rich in minerals, as iron ore, brown coal, etc. Its area is 8980 sq. miles, and in 1910 it had 1,441,604 inhabitants. Of the population 68 per cent are Germans, and 32 per cent Slovenes. The Slovenes, who are a branch of the Slavonic race, live chiefly in the southern and southeastern portions of the province, in Lower Styria. Ninety-eight per cent of the population is Catholic; one per cent Protestant; the rest are Jews or belong to the Orthodox Greek Church. The capital of the province is Graz (152,000 inhabitants); it is the residence of the governor and the seat of the administration of the province. In the Roman era Styria was a part of Noricum. During the great migrations various German tribes traversed the region, and about A. D. 600 the Slavs took possession of it. Styria came under the supremacy of Charlemagne as a part of Karantania (Carinthia). Large numbers of Germans, especially Bavarians, came into the country, settled in colonies in it, and made it Christian. The work of conversion was carried on mainly from Salzburg; Bishop Virgilius of Salzburg (745–84), an Irishman, was largely instrumental in converting the country to Christianity, and gained for himself the name of "Apostle of Karantania". The Patriarchs of Aquileia also shared in the work. In 811 Charlemagne made the Drave River the boundary of the Dioceses of Salzburg and Aquileia. In the tenth century a part of Styria was separated from Carinthia under the name of the Carinthian Mark; it was also named the Windic March. The margaves ruling the mark took from the name of the fortified castle of Steier the title of Margraves of Steiermark, and the country received in German the name of Steiermark. During the reign of Margrave Ottokar II (1164–92) Styria was raised to a duchy by the Emperor Frederick Barbarossa in 1180. With the death of Ottokar the first line of rulers of Styria became extinct; the region fell to the Babenberg family who then ruled in Austria. In a short time this family became extinct also, and Styria then passed under the control of Hungary (1254–60), and of King Ottokar of Bohemia; finally in 1276 it came into the possession of the Habsburgs, whose property it still remains. During the years 1379–1439 and 1564–1619 it was ruled by princes of its own from a branch of the Habsburgs. At the time of the Turkish invasions in the sixteenth and seventeenth centuries the land suffered severely. The Turks made incur-

City Hall, Graz

sions into Styria nearly twenty times; churches, monasteries, cities, and villages were destroyed and plundered, while the population was either killed or carried away into slavery.

The Reformation made its way into the country about 1530. During 1564–90 the country was ruled by Duke Karl, whose wife was the Duchess Maria of Bavaria, a courageous champion of Catholicism. He introduced the Counter-Reformation into the country on the basis of the Religious Peace of Augsburg of 1555. In 1573 he summoned the Jesuits and in 1586 he founded the University of Graz. In 1598 his son and successor, Ferdinand, suppressed all Protestant schools and expelled the foreign teachers and preachers. The common people again accepted with but slight opposition the Catholic faith. The Protestant doctrines were maintained only in a few isolated mountain valleys, as in the valley of the Inn and the valley of the Mur. The nobility were not forced to return to the Church; each could have Protestant services in his own house. After Ferdinand had become Emperor of Germany (1619) and had defeated his Protestant opponents in the battle of the White Mountain near Prague (1620), he forbade in 1625 all Protestant church services. In 1628 he commanded the nobility also to return to the Catholic faith. A large number of noble families, consequently, emigrated from the country; but most of them either returned, or their descendants did so, becoming Catholics and recovering their possessions. In the second half of the seventeenth century the Protestant spirit broke out again, especially in the distant valleys in the mountains, owing to events in the Duchy of Salzburg. The agitators from the Protestant districts of Germany were expelled, and the peasants who would not give up Protestantism were condemned to compulsory emigration to Transylvania. It should be remembered that the harsh laws issued by the Catholic rulers of Styria and Austria were the application of the axiom then current in European national law: *cujus regio ejus religio*, and that the Protestant princes suppressed and persecuted Catholicism and its adherents much more severely in their territories. The

Edict of Toleration issued by the Emperor Joseph II in 1781 put an end to the religious contest of more than two hundred years. The Protestants then received the right to found parish communities and to exercise their religion there undisturbed. On account of the constitutions gained by the German people in 1848 all the provinces of the Austrian Empire received complete liberty of religion and of conscience, parity of religions, and the right to the public exercise of religion. As regards the present relation between Church and State, the Church and the schools, conditions are the same as in the other sections of Austria.

Ecclesiastically the province is divided into two prince-bishoprics, Seckau and Lavant. Ever since the time of their foundation both have been suffragans of the Archdiocese of Salzburg. The Prince-Bishopric of Sekau was established in 1218; since 1786 the see of the prince-bishop has been Graz. The Prince-Bishopric of Lavant was founded as a bishopric in 1228, and raised to a prince-bishopric in 1446; since 1847 Marburg on the Drave has been the see of the prince-bishop. There are in the entire Duchy of Styria 96 deaneries and 551 parishes, altogether 1163 parochial districts, each district containing on an average 1151 Catholics. Styria contains many old and celebrated houses of the orders, as: the collegiate foundation of the Reformed Augustinian Canons of Vorau (founded 1163); the Benedictine abbeys at Admont (1074); at St. Lambrecht (1066); at Seckau (founded as a house of the Augustinian Canons in 1140, suppressed in 1782, from 1883 a monastery, since 1887 abbey of the Beuronese Benedictines); the Cistercian abbey at Rein (1120); the Franciscan monastery at Graz (since 1515; founded in 1230 as a monastery of the Minorites), at Maria-Lankowitz (1456), at Maria-Nazareth (1632); the Minorite monasteries at Graz (1526), and of St. Peter and Paul at Pettau (1239); the Capuchin monasteries at Cilli (1611), Leibnitz (1634), Hartberg (1654), and Schwanberg (1706); the collegiate foundations of the Redemptorists at Mautern (dating from 1826; founded in 1670 as a Franciscan monastery), and at Leoben (1844); the Trappist Abbey of Maria-Erlösung at Reichenberg (1881; abbey since 1891), etc. There are also many houses of female orders and congregations. The Catholic societies and confraternities are large and numerous.

Von Muchar, *Geschichte des Herzogtums Steiermark* (8 vols., Graz, 1844–67); Gebler, *Geschichte des Herzogtums Steiermark* (Graz, 1862); Mayer, *Geschichte des Steiermark mit besonderen Rücksicht auf das Kulturleben* (Graz, 1898); Cæsar, *Staats und Kirchengeschichte Steiermarks* (7 vols., Graz, 1785–87); *Steiermark* in *Die österreich-ungarische Monarchie in Wort und Bild* (Vienna, 1890); Immendörfer, *Landeskunde von Steiermark* (Vienna, 1903).
Hermann Sacher.

Suárez, Francisco, Doctor Eximius, a pious and eminent theologian, as Paul V called him, b. at Granada, 5 Jan., 1548; d. at Lisbon, 25 Sept., 1617. He entered the Society of Jesus at Salamanca, 16 June, 1564; in that city he studied philosophy and theology from 1565 to 1570, and was ordained in 1572. He taught philosophy at Avila and at Segovia (1571), and later, theology at Avila and Segovia (1575), Valladolid (1576), Rome (1580–85), Alcalá (1585–92), Salamanca (1592–97), and Coimbra (1597–1616). All his biographers say that he was an excellent religious, practicing mortification, laborious, modest, and given to prayer. He enjoyed such fame for wisdom that Gregory XIII attended his first lecture in Rome; Paul V invited him to refute the errors of King James of England, and wished to retain him near his person, to profit by his knowledge; Philip II sent him to the University of Coimbra to give prestige to that institution, and when Suárez visited the University of Barcelona, the doctors of the university went out to meet him, with the insignia of their faculties. His writings are characterized by depth, penetration and clearness of expression, and they bear witness to their author's exceptional knowledge of the Fathers, and of heretical as well as of ecclesiastical writers. Bossuet said that the writings of Suárez contained the whole of Scholastic philosophy; Werner (*Franz Suárez*, p. 90) affirms that if Suárez be not the first theologian of his age, he is, beyond all doubt, among the first; Grotius (Ep. 154, J. Cordesio) recognizes in him one of the greatest of theologians and a profound philosopher, and Mackintosh considers him one of the founders of international law.

In Scholasticism, he founded a school of his own, "Suarism", the chief characteristic principles of which are: (1) the principle of individuation by the proper concrete entity of beings; (2) the pure potentiality of matter; (3) the singular as the object of direct intellectual cognition; (4) a conceptual distinction between the essence and the existence of created beings; (5) the possibility of spiritual substances only numerically distinct from one another; (6) ambition for the hypostatic union as the sin of the fallen angels; (7) the Incarnation of the Word, even if Adam had not sinned; (8) the solemnity of the vow only in ecclesiastical law; (9) the system of Congruism that modifies Molinism by the introduction of subjective circumstances, as well as of place and of time, propitious to the action of efficacious grace, and with predestination *ante prævisa merita;* (10) possibility of holding one and the same truth by both science and faith; (11) belief in Divine authority contained in an act of faith; (12) production of the body and blood of Christ by transubstantiation as constituting the Eucharistic sacrifice; (13) the final grace of the Blessed Virgin Mary superior to that of the angels and saints combined.

"Suárez classes" were established in several universities—Valladolid, Salamanca (1720), Alcalá (1734) —and various Scholastic authors wrote their works *ad mentem Suarezii.* Charles III suppressed those classes throughout his dominions by a royal decree of 12 August, 1768, and prohibited the use of Jesuit authors, and therefore of Suárez, in teaching. It is obvious, says Cardinal Gonzalez, that, in so many volumes written by Suárez, there are to be found some matters of little utility, or the practical or scientific importance of which are not in proportion to the time and space that Suárez devotes to them. He is also charged with being somewhat diffuse. His book "De Defensione Fidei" was burned at London by royal command, and was prohibited by the Parliament of Paris (1614) on the ground that it contained doctrines that were contrary to the power of sovereigns.

WORKS.—Suárez published his first work, "De Deo Incarnato", at Alcalá, in 1590; he published twelve other volumes, the last of which, "De Defensio Fidei," written against the King of England, was published at Coimbra, in 1613. After his death the Jesuits of Portugal published ten other volumes of his works, between 1619 and 1655. Of all of these works, two different editions were made; the first, at Venice, 23 volumes in folio (1740–1757); and the second in Paris (Vives), 28 volumes (1856–1861). In 1859 Mgr Manlou published another volume in folio, containing six short treatises that had not been previously published. Father De Scorraille (Etudes, Vol. LXIV, pp. 151–175) gave an account of the manuscripts of Suárez, noting the fact that they were numerous and that he himself possessed seventy-five of them. Many of these and others besides were found by Father Rivière. The works of Suárez were held in the highest esteem in his day, as is shown by the numerous partial editions that were made of them (Lyons, Salamanca, Madrid, Coimbra, Mayence, Cologne, Paris, Evora, Genoa), as also by the fact, related by his biographers, that one of the wings of the old college of the Jesuits at Salamanca was restored with the product of the sale of his metaphysical works. A compendium of the theology of Suárez was published by Father Noel, S.J. (Madrid, 1732); a short epitome of his theological disputes, by the Portuguese Father Francis Soárez, S.J. (Lisbon, 1626), and a compendium of the metaphysics, by Father Gregorio Iturria, S.J. (Madrid, 1901).

DESCAMPS or DESCHAMPS, *Vida del V. P. Francisco Suárez de la Compañía de Jesús* . . . (2 vols., Perpignan, 1670–1671). It is the most complete biography of Suárez; MASSEI, *Vita di Venerabili servi di Dio ed esimio teologo P. Francesco Suárez* . . . (Rome, 1687); SÁRTOLO (BERNARDO), *El eximio Doctor y Venerable Padre Francisco Suárez* . . . (Salamanca, 1693); RIBEIRO DE VASCONCELLOS, *Francisco Suárez. Colleçao de documentos*, (Coimbra, 1897); WERNER, *Franz Suárez u. die Scholastik der letzten Jahrhunderte* (Ratisbon, 1861); HURTER, *Nomenclator*, I, no. 115 (Innsbruck, 1892); SOMMERVOGEL, *Bibliothèque*, VII, 1661–87; COLERIDGE in *The Month* (1865), 53–67, 172–185.

A. PÉREZ GOYENA.

Subcinctorium. See MANIPLE.

Subdeacon.—The subdiaconate is the lowest of the sacred or major orders in the Latin Church. It is defined as the power by which one ordained as a subdeacon may carry the chalice with wine to the altar, prepare the necessaries for the Eucharist, and read the Epistles before the people (Ferraris, op. cit. *infra*, No. 40). According to the common opinion of theologians at present, the subdeaconship was not instituted by Christ, nor are there any sufficient grounds for maintaining that it had an Apostolic origin. There is no mention of the subdiaconate in Holy Scripture or in the authentic writings of the Apostolic Fathers. These authorities make reference only to bishops, priests, and deacons. At the Council of Benevento (A. D. 1091), Urban II says: "We call sacred orders the deaconship and priesthood, for we read that the primitive Church had only those orders" (Can. I). Gratian (Dist. 21) says: "In the course of time, the Church herself instituted subdeacons and acolytes". It is true that the Council of Trent (Sess. XXIII, cap. 17, de ref.) says that "the functions of Holy orders from the deaconship to the ostiariate were laudably sanctioned in the Church from the times of the Apostles"; but these words simply indicate that the "functions" were so exercised (that is as part of the diaconate); it was only in the course of time that they were separated from the office of deacon and committed to inferior ministers. This explains why some theologians (e. g. Thomassinus, p. I, lib. II, cap. xl) speak of the subdeaconate as of Divine institution, that is they look on it as made up of functions proper to deacons. Gasparri (op. cit. *infra*, I, No. 35) says: "The Church, in the institution [of the subdeaconship] proceeded thus. She wished to commit to others the inferior functions of the order of diaconate, both because the deacons, with the increase of the faithful, could not suffice for their many and grave duties, and because she wished that others, received among the clergy and marked with the clerical tonsure, should ascend through minor orders, only after trial, to major orders. Imitating the Divine Law of the first three grades (bishop, priest and deacon), she decreed that the power of performing these functions should be conferred by external rites similar to those by which major orders were bestowed."

The subdiaconate is most probably, some say certainly, not a true sacrament, but a sacramental instituted by the Church. If it can not be repeated, this is because the Church has so wished, for she could institute a sacramental similar to a sacrament externally without thereby obliging us to hold that it imprints an indelible character on the soul of the recipient. Wernz (op. cit. *infra*, No. 158) says: "Since ordinations below the deaconship are most probably not true sacraments, but rather sacramentals, they do not imprint the true sacramental character, hence, if they are conferred validly, they give a power of order instituted solely by human law and circumscribed by its limits."

Historically, the earliest mention of the subdiaconate seems to be found in the letter of Pope Cornelius (A. D. 255) to Fabius of Antioch, in which he states that there are among the Roman clergy forty-six priests, seven deacons, and seven subdeacons. There is nothing to indicate, however, that the subdiaconate is not older than the third century. That there were subdeacons in the African Church in the same century is evident from the letters of St. Cyprian (e. g. ep. 8). The fourth Council of Carthage also mentions them in 398. The Synod of Elvira (305) in Spain does the same (c. 30). Their existence in the Oriental Church is testified to by St. Athanasius in 330 (ep. 2) and by the Council of Laodicea (can. 21) in 361. At present, among the Greeks and other orientals, as also formerly in the Western Church, subdeaconship is only a minor order. It has been counted among the major orders in the Latin Church, however, for nearly seven centuries. It seems to have been elevated to the rank of a sacred order in the thirteenth century, but it is impossible to fix the precise date. Urban II, at the close of the eleventh century, expressly limited the sacred orders to priesthood and diaconate, and in the middle of the twelfth century, Hugh of St.Victor still calls the subdeaconship a minor order. But at the end of the twelfth century, Peter Cantor (De verbo mirifico) says that the subdiaconate had lately been made a sacred order. Early in the thirteenth century, Innocent III authoritatively declared that the subdeaconship was to be enumerated among the major orders and that subdeacons could be chosen to a bishopric without special dispensation (Cap. 9. x, de æt., I, 14). The reason for this change of discipline was probably not because subdeacons were bound to celibacy, for this obligation began to be imposed upon them in the Latin Church in the fifth and sixth centuries [thus Leo I in 446 (in c. 1, dist. 32) and the Council of Orleans in 538], but more likely because their functions brought them so closely into the service of the altar.

Subdeaconship is conferred when the bishop gives the empty chalice and paten to the candidate to be touched, saying: "See what kind of ministry is given to you, etc." Two ceremonies following, the presentation of the cruets by the archdeacon and the imposition of the vestments, are not essential and need not be supplied if omitted (S. R. C., 11, March, 1820). Then the bishop gives the candidate the Book of Epistles to be touched, saying: "Take the Book of Epistles and receive power to read them in the holy Church of God for the living and the dead in the name of the Lord." In case of omission, this rite must be supplied and is probably an essential part of the ordination (S. C. C., 11 Jan., 1711). In the Greek Church, there is a laying on of hands and a suitable prayer, but there is no imposition of hands in the Latin Church. It is true that a letter of Innocent III to the Bishop of Ely in England (A. D. 1204) is cited as requiring that if the laying on of hands in the subdeaconship be omitted, it must be afterwards supplied (cap. l, x, de sacr. non interand, 1. 6), but there seems no doubt that the word "deaconship" was in the original text (Correct. Rom. ad cit. cap. 1).

The duties of a subdeacon are to serve the deacon at Mass; to prepare the bread and wine and sacred vessels for the Holy Sacrifice; to present the chalice and paten at the Offertory and pour water into the wine for the Eucharist; to chant the Epistles solemnly; to wash the sacred linen. In the Greek Church, subdeacons prepare the chalice at the Prothesis and guard the gates of the sanctuary during the Holy Sacrifice. In the ancient Roman Church, the subdeacons administered in great part the temporal goods of the Holy See and were often employed on important missions by the popes. A candidate for the subdiaconate must have been confirmed and have received minor orders. He must have the knowledge befitting his grade in the Church and have entered on his twenty-second year. He must also have acquired a title to orders. After ordination, he is bound to celibacy and to the recitation of the Divine Office.

GASPARRI, *De sacra ordinatione* (Paris, 1894); WERNZ, *Jus decret.*, II (Rome, 1899); FERRARIS, *Bibl. canon.*, V (Rome, 1891), s. v. *Ordo;* TAUNTON, *The Law of the Church* (London, 1906), s. v.

WILLIAM H. W. FANNING.

Subiaco (SUBLACUM, SUBLACEUM, SUBLAQUEM), a city in the Province of Rome, twenty-five miles from Tivoli, received its name from the artificial lakes of the villa of Nero and is renowned for its sacred grotto (*Sagro Speco*), the Abbey of St. Scholastica, and the archiepiscopal residence and Church of St. Andrew, which crowns the hill. When St. Benedict, at the age of fourteen, retired from the world he lived for three years in a cave above the River Anio, supplied with the necessaries of life by a monk, St. Roman. The grotto became the cradle of the Benedictine Order. St. Benedict was able to build twelve monasteries and to place twelve monks in each. The one at the grotto seems to have had but a short existence; in 854 we find a record of its renovation. In this year Leo IV is said to have consecrated an altar to Sts. Benedict and Scholastica and another to St. Sylvester. Another renovation took place in 1053 under Abbot Humbert of St. Scholastica. Abbot John V, created cardinal by Gregory VII, made the grotto the terminus of a yearly procession, built a new road, and had the altars reconsecrated. Shortly before 1200 there existed a community of twelve, which Innocent III made a priory; John XXII in 1312 appointed a special abbot. A new road was built by the city in 1688. The sacred grotto is still a favourite pilgrimage, and on 27 October, 1909, Pius X granted a daily plenary indulgence to those who receive Holy Communion there and pray according to the intention of the Holy Father (Acta Ap. Sedis, II, 405). A short description of the grotto, the church, and chapels, is given by Chandlery, "Pilgrim Walks in Rome" (New York, 1908), p. 469. The Abbey of St. Scholastica, about a mile and a half below the grotto, was built by St. Benedict himself (about 520), and endowed by the Roman patricians, Tertullus and Æquitius. The second abbot, St. Honoratus, changed the old monastery into a chapter room and built a new one, dedicating it to Sts. Cosmas and Damian. It was destroyed by the Lombards in 601 and abandoned for a century. By order of John VII it was rebuilt by Abbot Stephen and consecrated to Sts. Benedict and Scholastica. Demolished in 840 by the Saracens and again in 981 by the Hungarians, it rose from its ruins. Benedict VII consecrated the new church, and henceforth the abbey was known by the name St. Scholastica. In 1052 Leo IX came to Subiaco to settle various disputes and to correct abuses; a similar visit was made by Gregory VII. Special favour was shown by Pascal II, who took the abbey from the jurisdiction of the Bishop of Tivoli and made it an abbacy *nullius*. Its temporal welfare was also a care of the popes. Thus, among others, Innocent III, at his visit in 1203, increased the revenues of the abbey. With the decline of religious fervour, strifes and dissensions arose to such an extent that Abbot Bartholomew in 1364, by command of the pope, had to dismiss some of the incorrigible monks and fill their places with religious from other monasteries. Numbers were brought in from Germany, and for many decades Subiaco was a centre of German thrift, science, and art. Still, it seems the discipline was not satisfactory, for Urban VI (1378-89) abolished the abbots for life, took away from the monks the right of election, and gave the administration and revenues to a member of the Curia. Callistus III, in 1455, gave the abbey *in commendam* to a cardinal. The first of these was the Spanish Cardinal Torquemada and the second Roderigo Borgia (later Alexander VI), who remodelled the Castrum Sublacence, once the summer resort of the popes, and made it the residence of the commendatory abbot.

Many of these abbots cared but little for the religious life of the monks and looked only for the revenues. As an example, Pompeo Colonna, Bishop of Rieti, commendatory abbot since 1506, squandered the goods of the abbey and gave the income to unworthy subjects. On complaint of the community, in 1510, Julius II readjusted matters and restored the monastic possessions. For spiritual benefit a union had been made between Subiaco and the Abbey of Farfa, but it lasted only a short time. In 1514 Subiaco joined the Congregation of St. Justina, whose abbot-general was titular of St. Scholastica, while a cardinal remained commendatory abbot. Even after this union there were continual quarrels between Subiaco and Farfa, Subiaco and Monte Cassino, the Germans and the Italians. After this but little is known about the abbey until the middle of the nineteenth century. In 1851 some of the monasteries of Italy, with consent of the Holy See, formed a separate province, though still belonging to the Congregation of St. Justina. Soon other monasteries in various parts of the world wished to join this union, and Pius IX, by Decree of 9 March, 1872, established the Cassinese Congregation of primitive observance. This congregation, known also as the Congregatio Sublacensis, has had a marvellous growth for, according to the "Familiæ Confœderatæ" of 1910, it embraces 35 monasteries in 5 provinces, with a total of 1050 religious. The troubles of Subiaco did not cease for by order of 19 June, 1873, the property was sequestrated by the Italian Government, the abbey declared a national monument, and the religious tolerated as custodians of the same. At first but few monks remained, but in 1897 there was again a community of 25 and the "Familiæ Confœderatæ" of

1910 notes 21 priests, 10 clerics, 8 lay brothers, and 3 novices. On 7 January, 1909, Pius X restored to the monks the right of electing their own abbot. On the 28th they elected Lawrence Salvi. The pope conferred on him the right of wearing the *cappa magna* on 17 Feb., and four days later Salvi received the abbatial benediction. In 1904 Luigi Cardinal Macchi resigned his office as commendatory abbot, and Pius X retained the position for himself, ordering the Acts of the Curia to bear the heading: "Pius X Abbas Sublacensis". The abbacy *nullius* comprises 24 parishes, 91 priests (Benedictines, Franciscans, Capuchins, and secular), and 23,000 inhabitants [Annuaire Pont. Ecclés. (1911), 339]. The episcopal functions are performed by Victor M. Corvaia, O.S.B., titular Bishop of Tripolis. The library and archives were once of great value. In Subiaco the German printers, Sweinheim and Pannartz, found a home and printed "Donatus pro parvulis", "Lactantius" (1465), and "De Civitate Dei" (1467). To-day the printing press is doing valuable work; in 1908 appeared "Petri Boherii in Regulam S. Benedicti Commentarium nunc primum editum cura et studio P. Allodi".

MANN, *Lives of the Popes* (London, 1902), passim; *I Monasteri di Subjaco* (Rome, 1904); *Annales O.S.B.* (1909), 153; LUBIN, *Abbatiæ Italiæ* (Rome, 1893); *Studien u. Mittheilungen aus dem Bened. u. Cist. Orden*, XIX, 154; XXIV, 759; XXVIII, 236; *Kunstdenkmäler von Subjaco* in *Stimmen aus Maria Laach*, XLIII, 337; *Historisches Jahrbuch*, XXIV, 20; *Consuetudines Sublacenses* in *Revue Bénédictine*, XIX, 183.

FRANCIS MERSHMAN.

Subreption (Lat. *subreptio*), in canon law the concealment or suppression of statements or facts that according to law or usage should be expressed in an application or petition for a rescript. In its effects subreption is equivalent to obreption (q. v.), which consists in a positive allegation of what is false. Subreption may be intentional and malicious, or attributable solely to ignorance or inadvertence. It may affect the primary, substantial reason or motive of the grant, or constitute merely a secondary or impellent cause of the concession. For the effect of subreption on the validity of grants see RESCRIPTS.

Decretalia, I, 3, c. 20, *De Rescriptis*, and canonists generally.

A. B. MEEHAN.

Subsidies, EPISCOPAL (Lat. *subsidia*, tribute, pecuniary aid, subvention); since the faithful are obliged to contribute to the support of religion, especially in their own diocese, a bishop may ask contributions for diocesan needs from his own subjects, and particularly from the clergy. These offerings as far as possible should be voluntary, rather than taxes or assessments strictly so called. Of the contributions given to bishops, some are ordinary, made annually or at stated times; others are extraordinary, given as special circumstances demand. Under ordinary subsidies are classed the *cathedraticum*, a fixed sum given annually to the bishop from the income of the churches of the diocese, and which in the United States constitutes the chief revenue of bishops; *census*, or pensions, which a bishop may impose at times in accordance with the law; hospitality or procuration (*procuratio, comestio, circada, albergaria*) extended to the bishop and his assistants canonically visiting the diocese; contributions (*seminaristicum, alumnaticum*) for the support of diocesan seminaries, or for the education of ecclesiastical students; fees of the chancery office (*jus sigilli:* see TAXA INNOCENTIANA). In regard to the maintenance of students for the priesthood, in some dioceses of the United States an annual collection is made of the voluntary offerings of the people; in others an assessment is imposed on each parish. Chancery fees go to meet the expenses of the office; the surplus, if any, is employed in charitable works, and not for the bishop personally. Formerly there too was a share falling to the bishop from legacies, bequests, etc. (*quarta mortuaria, quarta funerum, quarta episcopalis, portio canonica*), and likewise a portion of the tithes (*quarta decimarum, quarta decimatio*), which accrued to the churches of the diocese.

The chief extraordinary tax, which a bishop may levy, is a charitable subsidy (*subsidium caritativum*). This may be asked from all churches and benefices, secular or regular not exempt, and from clerics possessing benefices, but not from lay persons. The following conditions must be observed. There must be a reasonable and evident cause for the subsidy, as, for example, to meet the necessary expenses of the bishop's consecration, his visit *ad limina*, attendance at a general council, prosecuting the rights of the diocese, or for the general good of the diocese; this extraordinary tax, however, is permissible only when other means are wanting (S. C. C., 17 Feb., 1663); the exaction, though varying according to the need in question, must be moderate, the amount being determined chiefly by custom; the advice of the cathedral chapter or the diocesan consultors must be obtained; the poor are not to be taxed. In Italy it is only when taking formal possession of his see that a bishop is free to exact this tribute (Taxa Innocentiana, 8 Oct. 1678); on other occasions the consent of the Holy See is required. Although the subvention is asked in the name of charity, it is binding, and delinquents may be compelled by ecclesiastical punishments to meet this obligation. Such a tax, if imposed for the benefit of the pope, is called Peter's pence. Patriarchs, primates, or metropolitans are not allowed such tribute from the dioceses of their suffragan bishops. Abbots and religious superiors, through privilege or custom, may exact a similar subsidy from their monasteries or communities for the evident good of their orders. The Third Plenary Council of Baltimore (n. 20) declares that a bishop, having consulted his diocesan advisers, must have recourse to Rome, if a new tax is to be imposed for the bishop beyond what is allowed in common law.

Decretalia Greg. IX, l. III, tit. 39, *De Censibus, Exactionibus, et Procurationibus; Extravagantes Communes,* l. III, tit. 10; manuals of canon law.

A. B. MEEHAN.

Substance (Lat. *sub-stare, substantia*), the first of Aristotle's categories, signifies being as existing in and by itself, and serving as a subject or basis for accidents and accidental changes.

I.—Substance, being a *genus supremum*, cannot strictly be defined by an analysis into genus and specific difference; yet a survey of the universe at large will enable us to form without difficulty an accurate idea of substance. Nothing is more evident than that things change. It is impossible for anything to be twice in absolutely the same state; on the other hand all the changes are not equally profound. Some appear to be purely external: a piece of wood may be hot or cold, lying flat or upright, yet it is still wood; but if it be completely burnt so as to be transformed into ashes and gases, it is no longer wood; the specific, radical characteristics by which we describe wood have totally disappeared. Thus there are two kinds of changes: one affects the radical characteristics of things, and consequently determines the existence or non-existence of these things; the other in no way destroys these characteristics, and so, while modifying the thing, does not affect it fundamentally. It is necessary, therefore, to recognize in each thing certain secondary realities (see ACCIDENT) and also a permanent *fundamentum* which continues to exist notwithstanding the superficial changes, which serves as a basis or support for the secondary realities—what, in a word, we term the substance. Its fundamental characteristic is to be in itself and by itself, and not in another subject as accidents are.

The Scholastics, who accepted Aristotle's definition, also distinguished primary substance (*substantia prima*) from secondary substance (*substantia secunda*):

SUBIACO

CHURCH OF ST. SCHOLASTICA
BERNINI'S STATUE OF ST. BENEDICT

MONASTERY OF ST. BENEDICT
THE SACRED GROTTO

the former is the individual thing—substance properly so called; the latter designates the universal essence or nature as contained in genus and species. And, again, substance is either complete, e. g. man, or incomplete, e. g. the soul, which, though possessing existence in itself, is united with the body to form the specifically complete human being. The principal division, however, is that between material substance (all corporeal things) and spiritual substance, i. e. the soul and the angelic spirits. The latter are often called *substantiæ separatæ*, to signify that they are separate from matter, i. e. neither actually conjoined with a material organism nor requiring such union as the natural complement of their being (St. Thomas, "Contra Gentes", II, 91 sqq.). St. Thomas further teaches that the name *substance* cannot properly be applied to God, not only because He is not the subject of any accidents, but also because in Him essence and existence are identical, and consequently He is not included in any genus whatever. For the same reason, it is impossible that God should be the formal being of all things (*esse formale omnium*), or, in other words, that one and the same existence should be common to Him and them (op. cit., I, 25, 26).

In the visible world there is a multitude of substances numerically distinct. Each, moreover, has a specific nature which determines the mode of its activity and at the same time, through its activity, becomes, in some degree, manifest to us. Our thinking does not constitute the substance; this exists independently of us, and our thought at most acquires a knowledge of each substance by considering its manifestations. In this way we come to know both the nature of material things and the nature of the spiritual substance within us, i. e. the soul. In both cases our knowledge may be imperfect, but we are not thereby justified in concluding that only the superficial appearances or phenomena are accessible to us, and that the inner substantial being, of matter or of mind, is unknowable.

Since the close of the Scholastic period, the idea of substance and the doctrines centring about it have undergone profound modifications which in turn have led to a complete reversal of the Scholastic teaching on vital questions in philosophy. Apart from the traditional concept formulated above, we must note especially Descartes' definition that substance is "a being that so exists as to require nothing else for its existence". This formula is unfortunate: it is false, for the idea of substance determines an essence which, if it exists, has its own existence not borrowed from an ulterior basis, and which is not a modification of some being that supports it. But this idea in no way determines either the manner in which actual existence has been given to this essence or the way in which it is preserved. The Cartesian definition, moreover, is dangerous; for it suggests that substance admits of no efficient cause, but exists in virtue of its own essence. Thus Spinoza, following in the footsteps of Descartes, declared that "substance is that which is conceived in itself and by itself", and thence deduced his pantheistic system according to which there is but one substance—i. e. God—all things else being only the modes or attributes of the Divine substance (see PANTHEISM). Leibniz's definition is also worthy of note. He considers substance as "a being gifted with the power of action". Substance certainly can act, since action follows being, and substance is being *par excellence*. But this property does not go to the basis of reality. In every finite substance the power to act is distinct from the substantial essence; it is but a property of substance which can be defined only by its mode of existence.

II.—The most important question concerning substance is that of its reality. In ancient days Heraclitus, in modern times Hume, Locke, Mill, and Taine, and in our day Wundt, Mach, Paulsen, Ostwald, Ribot, Jodl, Höffding, Eisler, and several others deny the reality of substance and consider the existence of substance as an illusory postulate of naïve minds. The basis of this radical negation is an erroneous idea of substance and accident. They hold that, apart from the accidents, substance is nothing, a being without qualities, operations, or end. This is quite erroneous. The accidents cannot be separated thus from the substance; they have their being only in the substance; they are not the substance, but are by their very nature modifications of the substance. The operations which these writers would thus attribute to the accidents are really the operations of the substance, which exercises them through the accidents. Finally, in attributing an independent existence to the accidents, they simply transform them into substance, thus establishing just what they intend to deny. It can be said that whatever exists is either a substance or in a substance.

The tendency of modern philosophy has been to regard substance simply as an idea which the mind indeed is constrained to form, but which either does not exist objectively or, if it does so exist, cannot be known. According to Locke (Essay ii, 23), "Not imagining how simple ideas can subsist by themselves, we accustom ourselves to suppose some substratum wherein they do subsist and from which they do result; which therefore we call substance; so that if any one will examine himself concerning his notion of pure substance in general, he will find he has no other idea of it at all, but only a supposition of he knows not what support of such qualities, which are capable of producing simple ideas in us; which qualities are commonly called accidents." He protests, however, that this statement refers only to the idea of substance, not to its being; and he claims that "we have as clear a notion of the substance of spirit as we have of body" (ibid.). Hume held that the idea of substance "is nothing but a collection of simple ideas that are united by the imagination and have a particular name assigned to them, by which we are able to recall, either to ourselves or others, that collection" (Treatise, bk. I, pt. IV); and that the soul is "a bundle of conceptions in a perpetual flux and movement".

For Kant substance is a category of thought which applies only to phenomena, i. e. it is the idea of something that persists amid all changes. The substantiality and immortality of the soul cannot be proved by the pure reason, but are postulated by the moral law which pertains to the practical reason. J. S. Mill, after stating that "we may make propositions also respecting those hidden causes of phenomena which are named substances and attributes", goes on to say: "No assertion can be made, at least with a meaning, concerning those unknown and unknowable entities, except in virtue of the phenomena by which alone they manifest themselves to our faculties" (Logic, bk. i, I, c. v): in other words, substance manifests itself through phenomena and yet is unknowable. Mill defines matter as "a permanent possibility of sensation", so that no substantial bond is required for material objects; but for conscious states a tie is needed in which there is something "real as the sensations themselves and not a mere product of the laws of thought" ("Examination", c. xi; cf. Appendix). Wundt, on the contrary, declares that the idea (hypothetical) of substance is necessary to connect the phenomena presented in outer experience, but that it is not applicable to our inner experience except for the psycho-physical processes (Logik, I, 484 sqq.). This is the basis of Actualism, which reduces the soul to a series of conscious states. Herbert Spencer's view is thus expressed: "Existence means nothing more than persistence; and hence, in mind, that which persists in spite of all changes, and maintains the unity of the aggregate in defiance of all attempts to divide it, is that of which existence in the full sense of the word must be predicated—that which we must postulate as the substance of mind in contradistinction to the varying forms it assumes. But, if so, the impossibility of knowing the substance of mind is manifest" (Princ. of Psychol., Pt. II, c. i). Elsewhere he declares that it is the same Unknowable Power which manifests itself alike in the physical world and in consciousness—a statement wherein modern Agnosticism returns to the Pantheism of Spinoza.

This development of the concept of substance is instructive; it shows to what extremes subjectivism leads, and what inconsistencies it brings into the investigation of the most important problems of philosophy. While the inquiry has been pursued in the name of criticism, its results, so far as the soul is concerned, are distinctly in favour of Materialism; and while the aim was supposed to be a surer knowledge on a firmer basis, the outcome is Agnosticism either open or disguised. It is perhaps as a reaction against such confusion in the field of metaphysics that an attempt has recently been made by representatives of physical science to reconstruct the idea of substance by making it equivalent to "energy". The attempt so far has led to the conclusion that energy is the most universal substance and the most universal accident (Ostwald, "Vorlesungen über Naturphilosophie", 2nd ed., Leipzig, 1902, p. 146).

For the theological significance of substance see EUCHARIST. See also ACCIDENT; SOUL; SPIRITUALISM.

BALMES, *Fundamental Philosophy*, II (new ed., New York, 1903); JOHN RICKABY, *General Metaphysics* (3rd ed., New York, 1898); WALKER, *Theories of Knowledge* (New York, 1910); HARPER, *The Metaphysics of the School* (London, 1879–84); MERCIER, *Ontologie* (Louvain, 1903); LORENZELLI, *Philosophiæ theoreticæ institutiones* (Rome, 1896); WILLEMS, *Institutiones philosophicæ*, I (Trier, 1906); KLEUTGEN, *Philosophie d. Vorzeit*, II; PRAT, *De la notion de substance* (Paris, 1903).—See also the bibliographical references in EISLER, *Wörterbuch der philosophischen Begriffe*, III (Berlin, 1910).

M. P. DE MUNNYNCK.

Subtile. See TUNIC.

Subunists. See HUS AND HUSSITES.

Suburbicarian Dioceses, a name applied to the dioceses nearest Rome, viz. Albano, Frascati (Tusculum), Palestrina, Sabina, Ostia and Velletri, Porto and S. Rufina, the bishops of which form the order of cardinal bishops (see CARDINAL). The See of Albano (*Albanensis*) has its cathedral, on the site of a basilica built by Constantine, on the Appian Way, about ten miles from Rome. The name corresponds to the Latin *ager Albanus* which commemorated the ancient city of Alba Longa, famous in Roman history. The diocese now comprises twelve parishes, and has a population of 41,000. Frascati, the ancient Tusculum, is in the Alban Hills, twelve miles from Rome. The diocese (*Tusculana*) contains eight parishes and has a population of 16,000; within its limits is the famous Basilian Abbey of Grottaferrata (q. v.). The capital of the Diocese of Palestrina (*Prænestinensis*) is the ancient Præneste, on the Via Labicana. The diocese, divided into twenty-four parishes, has a population of 45,700. The Diocese of Sabina (*Sabinensis*) was formed out of three oldest dioceses: S. Maria in Vescovio, Corese, and Mentana. Corese is the ancient Cures, which was, in remote ages, the Sabina capital; hence, obviously, the name *Sabina*. This, the largest of the suburbicarian dioceses, contains some 55,000 inhabitants, in thirty-five parishes. Ostia and Velletri (*Ostiensis et Velliternensis*) was formed in the twelfth century by the union of the Diocese of Velletri (the ancient Velitræ of the Volscians) with that of Ostia. The latter place was the seaport of ancient Rome. This diocese has sixteen parishes with 34,000 inhabitants. Porto, opposite Ostia at the mouth of the Tiber, was the Roman port (*portus*) constructed by the Emperor Claudius. The Basilica of Sts. Rufina and Secundus, about fourteen miles from Rome, on the Via Aureliana, having become the see of a bishop in the fifth century, this see was eventually united with that of Ostia. The diocese (*Portuensis et S. Rufinæ*) has eighteen parishes with a population of about 5000.

The term *suburbicarius* is taken from Roman public law, the expression *regiones* or *provinciæ suburbicariæ* meaning the districts adjacent to Rome. The term *ecclesiæ suburbicariæ* occurs first in Rufinus [Hist. eccl., I (x), 6], where he refers to the sixth canon of Nicæa treating of the extension of the patriarchal power of Rome. Rufinus certainly uses the words in the sense of "all the Churches *de facto* subject to the *episcopus urbicus*, that is, of Rome", meaning all the Churches of the West. The so-called Old (*prisca*) Version of the Nicene canons says that the jurisdiction of Rome extends over "suburbicaria loca et omnem provinciam suam", where *suburbicarius* is certainly more restricted in meaning than in the passage from Rufinus, and so must have been employed as it was used in Roman public law. In fairly recent times the expression was used synonymously with *suburbanus*, that is "in the immediate vicinity of Rome", to signify the above-mentioned dioceses.

Naturally these dioceses had a certain importance in the Church of Rome. Some authorities have suggested that the bishops were merely auxiliaries of the pope with jurisdiction, subject, however, to his. Certainly they had some prerogatives. For instance, the Bishop of Ostia, in the fourth century and probably in the third, consecrated the pope; in the sixth century the Bishop of Albano recited the second prayer in the consecration ceremony, and the Bishop of Porto the third. In the eighth century we read (Vita Stephani, III) of the most ancient custom in virtue of which seven of these bishops, called *hebdomadarii*, celebrated Mass in turn in place of the pope and were called *episcopi cardinales*, from being permanently attached to the *cardo*, that is the cathedral church of Rome; but we are not told who they were. In the eleventh century there were seven (six after the union of Porto and Silva Candida). Besides the titles *episcopi hebdomadarii* (twelfth century) and *cardinales Romanæ Sedis* they were also known as *Vicarii* and *Cooperatores papæ* and *episcopi romani*. The last title must have had a wider signification, as it was used of other bishops besides the seven, like the bishops of Tivoli, Gabii (united later with Palestrina), Lavicum (united with Tusculum), Villetri, Nepi, and Segni. In addition to the districts already mentioned these bishops had others. For instance the Bishop of Porto had ordinary delegated jurisdiction in Trastevere, and the Bishop of Silva Candida in the Leonine city and also in the Basilica of St. Peter. Both had residence on the Tiber island, and the Bishop of Albano had an episcopal residence near the Lateran. Probably as early as the eleventh century these bishops had the right of participating in the election of the pope; the Constitution of Nicholas II (1059), which fixed the right of electing the pope as belonging exclusively to the bishops and cardinal clerics of Rome, supposes that the former already enjoyed the right.

As the cardinal-bishops are largely absorbed in the business of the Curia, some of them, in particular the Bishops of Sabina and Velletri, have for centuries had auxiliary bishops. Pius X, in his Constitution "Apostolicæ Romanorum" (1910), ordained that there should be suffragan bishops for all the suburbicarian dioceses. The Constitution decrees that: (1) the cardinal-bishop is always the true bishop of the suburbicarian see; (2) each cardinal-bishop shall in future have a titular bishop as suffragan, (3) who shall be nominated by the pope; to take possession of his office the nominee must present to the cardinal the document containing his nomination; (4) in virtue of the present Constitution it is presumed that the cardinal-bishop has given his suffragan all the faculties necessary for the government of his diocese, such as other resident bishops have, with the following restrictions: (5) the auxiliary governs the diocese in the name and place of the cardinal; (6) with the death or transfer of the latter the jurisdiction of the auxiliary does not cease, he continues to rule the diocese as administrator Apostolic; (7) he must make an annual report to the cardinal on the moral and economic condition of the diocese; (8) where possible, a part of the episcopal palace shall be set aside for the suffragan and the Curia; (9) the blessing of the holy oils, the pontifical celebrations on the greater feasts of the year in accordance with the "Cæremoniale" of the bishops, is reserved to the cardinal, who may, however, delegate the auxiliary; (10) the obligation of celebrating Mass for the people is imposed on the cardinal, who (11) has the right of having his coat-of-arms on the palace, the cathedral, and other customary places; (12) the episcopal throne is reserved to the cardinal whose name alone is mentioned in the canon; (13) the cardinal, even when absent from the diocese, can grant an indulgence of 200 days; (14) if the cardinal is in the diocese he alone may officiate, or grant permission to officiate, pontifically; (15) the auxiliary may not grant benefices in the chapter and parishes not reserved to the Holy See without the consent of the cardinal; (16) the cardinal may personally supervise and visit the diocese; (17) the cardinal retains the right of assisting at marriages and of administering the other sacraments. The auxiliary is charged specially with examining candidates for tonsure and the other orders; but he may not confer or authorize the conferring of orders without the permission of the cardinal; (18) the diocesan synod is to be held with the consent and in the name of the cardinal, who alone has the right of approving and promulgating its decrees; (19) uniting or dividing benefices, even parochial, requires the consent of the cardinal, who (20) is to be consulted on appointments to offices and chairs in the seminary; (21) after the death or transfer of the suffragan, the cardinal through his vicar general shall provide for the government of the diocese till the appointment of a new suffragan; (22) when a cardinal-bishop dies the same ceremonies shall take place as are customary on the deaths of resident cardinal-bishops.

ANDREUCCI, *Hierarchia eccl.*, I, tr. iii; PHILLIPS, *Kirchenrecht*, VI (Ratisbon, 1864), 145-220; FERRARIS, *Prompta bibl.*, s. v. *cardinalis; Acta Apost. Sedis* (1910), fasc. 7, 279 sqq.

U. BENIGNI.

Succession, APOSTOLIC. See APOSTOLIC SUCCESSION.

Sudan, VICARIATE APOSTOLIC OF.—The Vicariate of Sudan or Central-Africa (SUDANENSIS SEU AFRICÆ CENTRALIS), in North-Eastern Africa, includes the whole Anglo-Egyptian Sudan, the part of Egypt south of Assuan, the French territory from Fezzan to 10° N. lat., parts of Adamaua and Sokoto on Lake Tchad, and the Nile Province of Uganda Protectorate. It was erected on 3 April, 1846, by Gregory XVI. In 1851 the Emperor Francis Joseph I of Austria took the mission under his protection. From 1883 to 1898 the Sudan (then an Egyptian province) was closed by the insurrection of the Mahdi Mohammed Ahmed and his successor Khalifa Abdullahi, and the missionaries were compelled to work outside the circuit of their jurisdiction in Egypt. On 2 Sept., 1898, the Anglo-Egyptian army, which in 1896 had begun operations for the recovery of the lost provinces, completed the overthrow of the Khalifa, although he was not slain until November of the following year. The country still suffers from the effects of the Dervish oppression, during which it was largely depopulated, wide tracts having gone out of cultivation and trade having been abandoned. In 1899 mission work was recommenced. The two religious congregations, the Sons of the Sacred Heart and the Pious Mothers of Nigritia furnish missionaries and sisters to the vicariate, and the two periodical papers "La Nigrizia" (Verona) and "Stern der Neger" (Brixen) print articles about this mission. The number of inhabitants is uncertain, perhaps about eight millions. Missionary work is limited to the southern and heathen part with the Shillouki Dinka, Nuer, Jur, Golo, Nyam-Nyam, and other negro tribes. In the northern and Mohammedan part are some European and Oriental Catholic immigrants. Statistics:—stations at Assuan, Omdurman, Khartoum (central station); Lul and Atigo (White Nile); Wau, Kayango, and Cleveland (Bahrel-Ghazal); Omach and Gulu (Uganda); besides twenty-five localities provided *excurrendo*. Catholics, 3000; catechumens, 1030; priests, 35; brothers, 28; sisters, 45. Vicar Apostolic, Francis Xavier Geyer, Bishop of Trocmade.

FRANCIS XAVIER GEYER.

Sufetula, a titular see of North Africa. Sufetula seems to be Suthul where Jugurtha had deposited his treasures (Sallust, xxxvi). The Latin name is a diminutive of Sufes (Shiba), the name of a small town 25 miles further north, from which many roads branched out to neighbouring towns. It became a Roman colony. In 647 it was the capital of the Byzantine patrician, Gregory, who had declared himself independent and was killed in a great battle with the Arabs fought near the town, which was stormed, pillaged, and cruelly laid waste. The "Roman Martyrology" mentions on 30 August the martyrs of Sufetula, who seem to belong rather to Sufes (St. Augustine, "Letters", 50). At an unknown date a council was held at Sufetula, one of its canons being still preserved (Hardouin, I, 1512). Only three bishops of this see are known: Privatian, present at the Council of Carthage, 255; Jucundus, at the Councils of Carthage, 411 and 419; St. Præsidius, exiled in 484 by Huneric after having been scourged, mentioned in the "Roman Martyrology" on 6 September. Sufetula is called *Sbeitha* in Arabic; it is a village on the road from Tebessa to Kairwan about 70 miles east of Tebessa (Tunisia). It has important Roman ruins: three temples, a triumphal arch, a theatre, and an amphitheatre, etc.; worthy of note are the ruins of four three-naved churches, Byzantine fortifications, and numerous fragments of Christian sculpture.

SMITH, *Dict. of Greek and Roman Geog.*, s. v.; TOULOTTE, *Géog. de l'Afrique chrétienne: Byzacène et Tripolitaine* (Montreuil, 1894), 176–80; DIEHL, *L'Afrique byzantine* (Paris, 1896), passim.

S. PÉTRIDÈS.

Suffragan. See ARCHBISHOP.

Sugar (SUKER), JOHN, VENERABLE, b. at Wombourn, Staffordshire, 1558; suffered at Warwick, 16 July, 1604. He matriculated at Oxford from St. Mary Hall, 30 October, 1584, and is described as *clerici filius*. He left without taking a degree, it is said because he disliked the Oath of Supremacy; but it appears that he acted as a Protestant minister at Cannock, Staffordshire, for some time. He was ordained priest from the English College, Douai (1601), and sent on the mission the same year. He was arrested 8 July, 1603, at Rowington, Warwickshire, with Venerable Robert Greswold (Grissold), a native of Rowington (in the service of Mr. Sheldon of Broadway, Worcestershire), who was in attendance on him. After a year's imprisonment at Warwick they were condemned there 14 July, Sugar for being a priest, and Greswold for assisting him. Sugar was cut down before he was fully dead. Greswold was offered his life if he would promise to conform.

CHALLONER, *Missionary Priests*, II, nos. 135, 136; FOSTER, *Alumni Oxonienses* (Oxford, 1892); KNOX, *Douay Diaries* (London, 1878), 17, 32; POLLEN, *Acts of the English Martyrs* (London, 1891), 321.

JOHN B. WAINEWRIGHT.

Suger, Abbot of St-Denis, statesman and historian, b. probably at or near St-Denis, about 1081; d. there, 13 Jan., 1151. Towards 1091 he was offered to the monastery of St-Denis where he became a fellow-student of King Louis VI. From 1104 to 1106 he attended another monastic school, perhaps that of St-Benoît-sur-Loire near Orléans. He became secretary to Abbot Adam of St-Denis in 1106, was named provost of Berneval in Normandy towards 1107 and of Toury in Beauce in 1109. Louis VI sent him (1118) to the Court of Gelasius II at Maguelonne in Southern France, and later to that of Callistus II at Rome. During his stay at Rome (1121–22) he was elected Abbot of St-Denis, and ordained to the priesthood on his return. He attended the First General Council of the Lateran in 1123, and so favourably impressed Callistus II that eighteen months after his return to France this pope, desirous of conferring new honours (probably the cardinalate) upon him, invited him to Rome. Suger proceeded as far as Lucca, but retraced his steps upon receipt of the news of the pope's death. Henceforth most of his time was spent at Court until 1127, when he initiated, and subsequently successfully accomplished, the reform of his monastery. He continued to remain, however, the constant adviser of Louis VI and of his successor Louis VII. During the latter's absence on the Second Crusade he was appointed regent of the kingdom (1147–49). He had opposed the king's departure on the ground that the powerful and turbulent vassals were a danger to the royal power, but so successful was his administration that the king, upon his return, bestowed upon him the title of "Father of the Country". Although the crusade ended in failure, Suger equipped an army and was about to depart for the Holy Land when he died. As a statesman he sought to strengthen the royal power, to improve agriculture, commerce, and trade, and to reform the administration of justice. As abbot he not only introduced thorough-going reforms, but also completed in 1144 the new monastic church. He has left an account of the consecration of this edifice, "Libellus de consecratione eccl. S. Dionysii", and a memoir on his own abbatical administration, "Liber de rebus in administratione sua gestis". Of greater importance for the knowledge of the period are his "Vita Ludovici Grossi regis", a eulogistic but reliable life of Louis the Fat, and "Historia Ludovici VII", a history of Louis VII, which in its present form is the work of a Burgundian monk of St-Germain-des-Prés. We also possess of him some letters, official documents, and a will of the year 1137.

From Desrochers' "Hommes Illustres", Paris, 1760

The complete works of SUGER were published by DE LA MARCHE, Œuvres complètes de Suger (Paris, 1867); they are also in P. L., CLXXXVI, 1211–1468; HUGUENIN, Étude sur l'abbé Suger (Paris, 1855); CARTELLIERI, Abt Suger von Saint-Denis (Berlin, 1898); MASSON, Early Chroniclers of Europe: France (London, s. d.), 56–59; MOLINIER, Les Sources de l'hist. de France, I, ii, nos. 1845–50.

N. A. WEBER.

Suggestion. See PSYCHOTHERAPY.

Suicide.—This article will treat the subject under the following three heads:—I. The notions and divisions of suicide; II. The principles according to which its morality must be judged; III. Statistics and explanations of its frequency.

I. NOTION.—Suicide is the act of one who causes his own death, either by positively destroying his own life, as by inflicting on himself a mortal wound or injury, or by omitting to do what is necessary to escape death, as by refusing to leave a burning house. From a moral standpoint we must treat therefore not only the prohibition of positive suicide, but also the obligation incumbent on man to preserve his life. Suicide is direct when a man has the intention of causing his own death, whether as an end to be attained, or as a means to another end, as when a man kills himself to escape condemnation, disgrace, ruin etc. It is indirect, and not usually called by this name when a man does not desire it, either as an end or as a means, but when he nevertheless commits an act which in effect involves death, as when he devotes himself to the care of the plague-stricken knowing that he will succumb under the task.

II. MORALITY.—The teaching of the Catholic Church concerning the morality of suicide may be summarized as follows:—

A. *Positive and Direct Suicide* perpetrated without God's consent always constitutes a grave injustice towards Him. To destroy a thing is to dispose of it as an absolute master and to act as one having full and independent dominion over it; but man does not possess this full and independent dominion over his life, since to be an owner one must be superior to his property. God has reserved to himself direct dominion over life; He is the owner of its substance and He has given man only the serviceable dominion, the right of use, with the charge of protecting and preserving the substance, that is, life itself. Consequently suicide is an attempt against the dominion and right of ownership of the Creator. To this injustice is added a serious offence against the charity which man owes to himself, since by his act he deprives himself of the greatest good in his possession and the possibility of attaining his final end. Moreover, the sin may be aggravated by circumstances, such as failure in conjugal, paternal, or filial piety, failure in justice or charity, if by taking his life one eludes existing obligations of justice or acts of charity which he could and should perform. That suicide is unlawful is the teaching of Holy Scripture and of the Church, which condemns the act as a most atrocious crime and, in hatred of the sin and to arouse the horror of its children, denies the suicide Christian burial. Moreover, suicide is directly opposed to the most powerful and invincible tendency of every creature and especially of man, the preservation of life. Finally, for a sane man deliberately to take his own life he must, as a general rule, first have annihilated in himself all that he possessed of spiritual life, since suicide is in absolute contradiction to everything that the Christian religion teaches us as to the end and object of life and, except in cases of insanity, is usually the natural termination of a life of disorder, weakness, and cowardice.

The reason we have advanced to prove the malice of suicide, namely, God's right and dominion, likewise justifies the modification of the general principle: God being the master of our life He may with His own consent remove from suicide whatever constitutes its disorder. Thus do some authorities justify the conduct of certain saints, who, impelled by the desire of martyrdom and especially to protect their chastity, did not wait for their executioners to put them to death, but sought it in one manner or other themselves; nevertheless, the Divine will should be certain and clearly manifested in each particular case. The question is asked: Can one who is condemned to death kill himself if ordered to do so by the judge? Some authors answer this question in the affirmative, basing their argument on the right which society possesses to punish certain malefactors with death and to commission any executioner, hence also the malefactor himself, to carry out the sentence. We share the most widely accepted opinion, that this practice, prevalent in certain countries of the East, is not lawful. Vindictive, and for that matter all, justice requires a distinction between the subject of a right and that of a duty, hence in the present case between the one who punishes and the one who is punished. Finally, the same principle which forbids anyone to personally compass his own death also forbids him to advise, direct, or command, with the direct intention of suicide, that another should slay him.

B. *Positive but Indirect Suicide* committed without Divine consent is also unlawful unless, everything considered, there is sufficient reason for doing what will cause death to follow. Thus, it is not a sin, but an act of exalted virtue, to go into savage lands to preach the Gospel, or to the bedside of the plague-stricken, to minister to them, although they who do so have before them the prospect of inevitable and speedy death; nor is it a sin for workmen in the discharge of duties to climb on roofs and buildings, thus exposing themselves to danger of death, etc. All this is lawful precisely because the act itself is good and upright, for in theory the persons in question have not in view either as end or means the evil result, that is, death, that will follow, and, moreover, if there be an evil result it is largely compensated for by the good and useful result which they seek. On the other hand there is sin in exposing oneself to danger of death to display courage, to win a wager, etc., because in all these cases the end does not in any way compensate for the danger of death that is run. To judge whether or not there is sufficient reason for an act which will apparently be followed by death, all the circumstances must be weighed, namely, the importance of the good result, the greater or less certainty of its being attained, the greater or less danger of death, etc., all questions which may in a specific case be very difficult to solve.

C. *Negative and Direct Suicide* without the consent of God constitutes the same sin as positive suicide. In fact man has over his life only the right of use with corresponding obligations to preserve the object of God's dominion, the substance of his life. Hence, it follows obviously that he fails in this obligation of usufructuary who neglects the necessary means for the preservation of life, and this with the intention of destroying the latter, and consequently violates the rights of God.

D. *Indirect and Negative Suicide* without the consent of God is also an attempt against the rights of the Creator and an injustice towards Him whenever without sufficient cause a man neglects all the means of preservation of which he should make use. If a man as usufructuary is obliged in justice to preserve his life, it follows that he is equally bound to make use of all the ordinary means which are indicated in the usual course of things, viz.: (1) he should employ all the ordinary means which nature itself provides, such as to eat, drink, sleep, and so on; (2) moreover, he should avoid all dangers which he may easily avoid, e. g. to flee from a burning house, to escape from an infuriated animal when it may be done without difficulty. In fact to neglect the ordinary means for preserving life is equivalent to killing one's self, but the same is not true with regard to extraordinary means. Thus theologians teach that one is not bound in order to preserve life to employ remedies which, considering one's condition, are regarded as extraordinary and involving extraordinary expenditure; one is not obliged to undergo a very painful surgical operation, nor a considerable amputation, not to go into exile in order to seek a more beneficial climate, etc. To use a comparison, the lessee of a house is bound to take care of it as becomes a good father of a family, to make use of the ordinary means for the preservation of the property, for instance, to extinguish a fire which he may easily extinguish, etc., but he is not bound to employ means considered extraordinary, such as to procure the latest novelties invented by science to prevent or extinguish fire.

The principles which have been outlined in the four propositions or divisions above given should serve for the solution of particular cases; however, the application may not always be equally easy, and thus a person may by an objectively unlawful act take his life and nevertheless consider it permissible and even an act of exalted virtue. It may be asked whether by performing or omitting a certain act a person may injure his health and shorten his life. To apply the foregoing principles: it is first of all clear (1st and 3rd propositions, A and C) that one may not have in view this hastening of death, but, this hypothesis aside, it may be said on the one hand that to expose oneself without sufficient reason to a considerable shortening of life constitutes a serious injury to the rights of the Creator; but on the other hand if the danger of death be not imminent, although it is to be feared that life may be shortened even by several years, it is not a grave but only a venial sin. This is the case with the drunkard who by his intemperance causes his premature death. Again it must be borne in mind that with the addition of a reasonable motive the thing may be entirely lawful and even an act of virtue; thus the workman does not sin by devoting himself to the rough labour of the mines, glass-works, etc., and the saints performed a very meritorious and highly virtuous act when in order to overcome their passions they lacerated and tortured their flesh by penance and fasting and were thus the cause of their earlier death.

III. Frequency of Suicide; Chief Causes.—The plague of suicide belongs especially to the period of decadence of the civilized peoples of antiquity, Greeks, Romans, and Egyptians. The Christian Middle Ages were unacquainted with this morbid tendency, but it has reappeared at a more recent period, has developed constantly since the Renaissance, and at present has reached such an intensity among all civilized nations that it may be considered the special evil of our time. At present the increase in the tendency to suicide is, with that to mental alienation, the saddest and thereby the most important characteristic fact of our era (Masaryk, 140). The officially established number of suicides during the nineteenth century was a million and a half, of which 1,300,000 were in Europe. Again Father Krose estimates the real number for Europe alone at two millions. During the last ten years of the nineteenth century there were 400,000 suicides, of which France and Germany alone furnished half. The following details are given by Nieuwbarn and Jacquart. Taking the countries in the order of the frequency of the rate of suicides, and taking as a scale the number of the latter to the million of inhabitants, we have the following results for the last ten years of the nineteenth century: France, 239; Denmark, 234; Switzerland, 232; Germany, 206 (in Saxony especially the sinister rate was 308, which figure rose to 325 for 1901–05); Austria, 158; Sweden, 147; Hungary, 145; Belgium, 124; England, 84; Norway, 63; Italy, 60; Scotland, 59; Low Countries, 56; Russia, 32; Ireland, 26; Spain, 21. But, as is shown by the indications furnished by Jacquart for this period of 1901–05 (64 sqq.), this figure has risen in recent years to an alarming extent. For instance, England in 1905 had risen to 103 to the million inhabitants; Switzerland to 232; the Low Countries to 64; and Ireland to 33. In the United States the annual average of suicides from 1901–5 was 4548 or 107 per million of population; in 1908, the latest available statistics.

the number of suicides was 8332, or 116 per million of population.

In this number must obviously be included the suicides attributable to madness, but we cannot accept the opinion of a large number of physicians, moralists, and jurists who, led into error by a false philosophy, lay it down as a general rule that suicide is always due to dementia, so great is the horror which this act inspires in every man of sane mind. The Church rejects this theory and, while admitting exceptions, considers that those unfortunates who, impelled by despair or anger, attempt their life often act through malice or culpable cowardice. In fact, despair and anger are not as a general thing movements of the soul which it is impossible to resist, especially if one does not neglect the helps offered by religion, confidence in God, belief in the immortality of the soul and in a future life of rewards and punishments. Widely different reasons have been advanced to explain this frequency of suicide, but it is more correct to say that it does not depend on any one particular cause, but rather on an assemblage of factors, such as the social and economic situation, the misery of a great number, a more feverish pursuit of what is considered happiness, often ending in cruel deceptions, the ever more refined search for pleasure, a more precocious and intense stimulation of sexual life, intellectual overwork, the influence of the Press and the sensational news with which it daily provides its readers, the influences of heredity, the ravages of alcoholism, etc. But it is undeniable that the religious factor is by far the most important, as statistics prove (cf. the detailed investigations of Jacquart); the proportion of suicides in Protestant countries being as a general rule greater than that in Catholic countries, and the increase in suicides keeping step with the de-Christianization of a country. France presents a painful example parallel to the systematic de-Christianization; the number of suicides for each 100,000 of population has increased from 8.32 in 1852 to 29 in 1900. The reason is obvious. Religion alone, and especially the Catholic religion, instructs us with regard to the true destiny of life and the importance of death; it alone furnishes a solution of the enigma of suffering, inasmuch as it shows man living in a land of exile and suffering as a means of acquiring the glory and happiness of a future life. By its doctrines of the efficacy of repentance and the practice of confession it relieves the moral suffering of man; it forbids and prevents to a large extent the disorders of life; in a word it is of a nature to prevent the causes which are calculated to impel a man to the extreme act.

General works of moral theology as also of moral philosophy, especially in reference to the principles as well as the frequency and causes of suicide: WALTER in *Staatslexikon* (2nd ed., Freiburg, 1903), s. v. *Selbstmord*; MASARYK, *Der Selbstmord als sociale Massenerscheinung der modernen Civilisation* (Vienna, 1881); MORSELLI, *Suicide, International Scientific Series* (New York, 1882); BAILEY, *Modern Social Conditions* (New York, 1906); SCHNAPPER-ARNDT, *Socialstatistik* (Leipzig, 1906); KROSE, *Des Selbstmord im 19en Jahrhundert* (Freiburg, 1906); NIEUWBARN, *Beknopt kerkelyk Handwoordenboek* (Tilburg, 1910); JACQUART, *Essais de statistique morale:* I, *Le Suicide* (Brussels, 1908).

A. VANDER HEEREN.

Suidas (Σουΐδας, Σούδας), author of, perhaps, the most important Greek lexicon or encyclopedia. Nothing is known of Suidas himself except that he lived about the middle of the tenth century, apparently at Constantinople, and that he was probably an ecclesiastical person devoted to literary studies. But his lexicon is one of the most valuable documents of Greek philology, grammar, and literary history. He uses material from the classical period down to his own time; a long chain of later authors, from Eustathius of Thessalonica (c. 1192), quote from him. Suidas's lexicon is something between a grammatical dictionary and an encyclopedia in the modern sense. He explains the source, derivation, and meaning of words according to the philology of his period, using such earlier authorities as Harpokration and Hellanios. There is nothing specially important about this part of his work. It is the articles on literary history that are valuable. In these he gives a supply of details, and to some extent quotations, from authors whose works are otherwise lost. He uses older *scholia* to the classics (Homer, Thucydides, Sophocles, etc.), and for later writers, Polybius, Josephus, the "Chronicon Paschale", George Syncellus, George Hamartolus, and so on.

So his lexicon represents a convenient work of reference for persons who played a part in political, ecclesiastical, and literary history in the East down to the tenth century. His chief source for this is the encyclopedia of Constantine VII Porphyrogenitus (912-59), and for Roman history the excerpts of John of Antioch (seventh century). Krumbacher (op. cit., 566) counts two main sources of his work: Constantine VII for ancient history, Hamartolus (Georgios Monarchos) for the Byzantine age. The lexicon is arranged, not quite alphabetically, but according to a system (formerly common in many languages) called *antistoichia* (ἀντιστοιχία); namely the letters follow phonetically, in order of sound (of course in the pronunciation of Suidas's time, which is the same as modern Greek). So for instance αι comes after ε; ει, ηι come together after ζ, ω after ο, and so on. The system is not difficult to learn and remember, but in some modern editions (Bekker) the work is rearranged alphabetically. Suidas contains much material for church history among his biographical articles. But there is very little of this kind that is not also known from other sources. His lexicon still may fulfil its original purpose as a convenient work of reference.

DEMETRIOS CHALKONDYLES published the *editio princeps* at Milan in 1499. GAISFORD, *Suidæ lexicon* (3 vols., Oxford, 1834); BERNHARDY, *Suidæ lexicon* (2 vols., Halle and Brunswick); BEKKER, *Suidæ lexicon* (Berlin, 1854); FABRICIUS-HARLES, *Bibliotheca græca* (Hamburg, 1790–1809); VI, 389–595; P. G., CXVII, 1193–1424; VOLKMANN, *De Suidæ biographicis quæstiones selectæ* (Bonn, 1861). KRUMBACHER, *Byzantinische Litteratur* (Munich, 1897), 562–70.

ADRIAN FORTESCUE.

Suitbert (SUIDBERT), SAINT, Apostle of the Frisians, b. in England in the seventh century; d. at Suitberts-Insel, now Kaiserswerth, near Düsseldorf, 1 March, 713. He studied in Ireland, at Rathmelsigi, Connacht, along with St. Egbert (q. v.). The latter, filled with zeal for the conversion of the Germans, had sent St. Wihtberht, or Wigbert, to evangelize the Frisians, but owing to the opposition of the pagan ruler, Rathbod, Wihtberht was unsuccessful and returned to England. Egbert then sent St. Willibrord and his twelve companions, among whom was St. Suitbert. They landed near the mouth of the Rhine and journeyed to Utrecht, which became their headquarters. The new missionaries worked with great success under the protection of Pepin of Heristal, who, having recently conquered a portion of Frisia, compelled Rathbod to cease harassing the Christians. Suitbert laboured chiefly in North Brabant, Guelderland, and Cleves. After some years he went back to England, and in 693 was consecrated in Mercia as a missionary bishop by St. Wilfrid of York. He returned to Frisia and fixed his see at Wijkbij Duurstede on a branch of the Rhine. A little later, entrusting his flock of converts to St. Willibrord, he proceeded north of the Rhine and the Lippe, among the Bructeri, or Boructuari, in the district of Berg, Westphalia. This mission bore great fruit at first, but was eventually a failure owing to the inroads of the pagan Saxons; when the latter had conquered the territory, Suitbert withdrew to a small island in the Rhine, six miles from Düsseldorf, granted to him by Pepin of Heristal, where he built a monastery and ended his days in peace. His relics were rediscovered in 1626 at Kaiserswerth and are still venerated there. St. Suitbert of

Kaiserwerdt is to be distinguished from a holy abbot, Suitbert, who lived in a monastery near the River Dacore, Cumberland, England, about forty years later, and is mentioned by Venerable Bede.

BOUTERWEK, *Swidbert, der Apostel des bergischen Landes* (Eberfeld, 1859); HOOF in *Anal. bollandiana*, VI (1887), 73–6; SURIUS, *Vitæ sanctorum*, III (1618), 3–16; BEDE, *Hist. eccl.*, V, xi; *Acta SS.*, I March, 67–85; BUTLER, *Lives of the Saints*.

A. A. MACERLEAN.

Sullivan, ALEXANDER MARTIN, Irish politician, lawyer, and journalist, b. at Bantry in 1830; d. at Darty Lodge, Rathmines, Dublin, 17 Oct., 1884. He received his early education in his native town. Drifting into journalism in 1850, he became assistant-editor of the "Nation" in 1855, and was subsequently editor and proprietor. In 1861 he married Frances, daughter of John Donovan of New Orleans. From 1861 to 1884, in conjunction with his elder brother, T. D. Sullivan (still living), he made the "Nation" one of the most potent factors in the cause of true nationality, and also issued the "Weekly News" and "Zozimus". In 1874 he was elected M. P. for Louth, and was afterwards M. P. for Meath. Called to the Irish Bar in 1876, he was made Q. C. in 1881. As a member of the Dublin Corporation he secured a magnificent site for the Grattan Monument, towards which he generously gave £400, the amount of a subscription by his admirers while he was undergoing imprisonment for a political offence in 1868. This monument was formally unveiled, January, 1876. Between the years 1878 and 1882 he was engaged in many notable trials. His last great case was on 30 November, 1883, when he was the colleague of Lord Russell of Killowen in the defence of Patrick O'Donnell for the murder of James Carey, the Irish Informer. He was buried at Glasnevin. In addition to his labours Alexander Sullivan was a great temperance reformer. He also wrote two notable books, the "Story of Ireland" and "New Ireland", and contributed many sketches (including some verse) to "Irish Penny Readings" (1879–85).

MACDONAGH in *Dict. Nat. Biog.*, s. v.; private correspondence; family papers.

W. H. GRATTAN-FLOOD.

Sullivan, PETER JOHN, soldier, lawyer, b. at Cork, Ireland, 15 March, 1821; d. at Cincinnati, Ohio, 2 March, 1883. His parents brought him to Philadelphia when he was two years old, and he received his education at the University of Pennsylvania. He served in the Mexican War, receiving the commission of major for meritorious services. After retiring to civil life he became one of the official stenographers of the U. S. Senate and in 1848 went to live in Cincinnati, where he was admitted to the Bar. He was prominent there as an opponent of the Knownothing movement. During the Civil War he took a very active part in organizing several volunteer regiments and went to the scene of action as colonel of the 48th Ohio regiment. On 13 March, 1865, he was brevetted Brigader-General of Volunteers. Soon after he was appointed U. S. Minister to Colombia and held that office until 1869. He then returned to the practice of the law.

Catholic Telegraph (Cincinnati) files; *Appleton's Cyclop. of Am. Biog.* s. v.

THOMAS F. MEEHAN.

Sully, MAURICE DE, Bishop of Paris, b. of humble parents at Sully-sur-Loire (Soliacum), near Orléans, at the beginning of the twelfth century; d. at Paris, 11 Sept., 1196. He came to Paris towards 1140 and studied for the ecclesiastical state. He soon became known as an able professor of theology and an eloquent preacher. It has been frequently asserted, but without sufficient proof, that he was canon of Bourges. In 1159 he appears as Archdeacon of Paris and on 12 Oct., 1160, largely through the influence of Louis VII, he was elected to succeed Peter Lombard in the episcopal see of that city. The present Cathedral of Notre-Dame stands as a monument to his episcopal administration. Its construction was begun and almost entirely completed under him. Alexander III, in 1163, laid the cornerstone of the magnificent edifice, and in 1185 the Patriarch of Jerusalem, Heraclius, officiated in the completed sanctuary. Maurice de Sully also rebuilt the episcopal palace in which the nobility and clergy met in 1179 at the coronation of Philip Augustus as joint ruler with his father Louis VII. He enjoyed in a high degree the confidence of both rulers, accompanied Louis to his meeting with Frederick Barbarossa at Saint-Jean-de-Losne in 1162, and was one of the guardians of the royal treasury during the crusade (1190).

In the controversy between St. Thomas Becket and King Henry II he energetically defended the former and, in three letters still extant, pleaded his cause with Alexander III. He forbade the celebration of the feast of the Immaculate Conception in his diocese, but is said to have strongly supported by appeals to Holy Writ (Job, xix, 25–27) the doctrine of the resurrection of bodies, against some sceptical noblemen. Although he retained the administration of his diocese, he retired, late in life, to the monastery of Saint-Victor, where he died. Maurice de Sully is the author of a treatise on the Canon of the Mass, preserved in manuscript at Bourges. Numerous sermons, some in Latin, others in vernacular, are also attributed to him. Those written in the Latin tongue were not directly destined for the people, but rather for the use and study of the clergy. The French sermons do not seem to be in their present form the original work of Maurice de Sully; they are more commonly considered as reproductions made by ecclesiastics from his Latin collection. No critical edition of these sermons has yet been published; his three letters to Alexander III are printed in P. L., CC, 1419–22, as are also some of his official documents (CCV, 897–914).

BAUNARD, *Maurice de Sully* (Orleans, 1862); MORTET, *Maurice de Sully, évêque de Paris, 1160–96* (Paris, 1890); MEYER, *Les manuscrits des sermons français de Maurice de Sully in Romania*, XXIII (1894); HIATT, *Notre-Dame de Paris* (London, 1902).

N. A. WEBER.

Sulmona. See VALVA AND SULMONA, DIOCESE OF.

Sulpicians in the United States.—The Sulpicians came to the United States at the very rise of the American Hierarchy. When the French Revolution was threatening to involve them in the impending ruin of the Church the superior-general, Father Emery, looking for a place of refuge abroad, was meditating an establishment at Gallipolis, a French settlement on the Ohio; but the papal nuncio at Paris, Cardinal Dugnani, made the happier suggestion of Baltimore, which had just been erected into the first American see. An interview in London between Bishop Carroll, who had come to England (1790) for episcopal consecration, and Father Nagot resulted in the bishop gladly accepting the offer of Father Emery to found a theological seminary at Baltimore. On 10 July, 1791, four Sulpicians landed at Baltimore: Francis Charles Nagot, Superior, Anthony Garnier, Michael Levadoux, and John Tessier. They purchased the One Mile Tavern on the edge of the city, dedicated the house to the Blessed Virgin, and in October opened classes with five students whom they had brought from France. This was the beginning of St. Mary's, the first American seminary, which still stands on the same spot. The number of Sulpicians was augmented the following year by the arrival of Flaget, David, Chicoisneau, Maréchal, Richard, and Ciquard, and in 1795 by the accession of Dubourg, nearly all of whom were destined to become important figures in the history of the American Church. These ten or eleven new workers were a large accession to the small body of American priests, then only about thirty-five, who were endeavouring to serve a diocese extending from the Atlantic to the Mississippi Valley. The Church was in its infancy; there was no organized community of priests (since the suppression of the Jesuits), no teaching sisterhood, no Catholic schools. An academy for boys was about to open at Georgetown. Non-Catholic education in Maryland was almost as backward as the Catholic. In these conditions Bishop Carroll's greatest need and most difficult task, as he had long recognized, was to recruit a sufficiently numerous and fit clergy, if possible native, which he could hope for only from a seminary. Naturally, he welcomed the coming of the Sulpicians as "a great and auspicious event" for his diocese.

But the time was not ripe for a seminary as there were no students prepared to enter it. Georgetown Academy, founded chiefly to develop priestly vocations, instead of being an aid to the seminary drew on St. Mary's few students to recruit its teaching staff. The natural remedy of opening a preparatory seminary at Baltimore was forbidden (see below). The almost hopeless condition may be judged from the fact that during each of the first three years there were only five students and in the next year, 1794, only two, nearly all of whom were from Europe; from 1795 to 1797 there were none at all. So with little or no opportunity of cultivating their own field, the Sulpicians offered themselves to the bishop for any work at hand. Flaget, David, Maréchal, and Dubourg taught at the Georgetown Academy; Dubourg, an enterprising and energetic man, being made president (1796–99), greatly increased its numbers and prestige. Ciquard worked among the Indians of Maine; Levadoux, Dilhet, and Richard among the French and the Indians of Illinois and Michigan. Richard, still well remembered at Detroit, which some years ago placed his statue on the city hall, deserves special mention. He restored religion, established Catholic schools, founded a young ladies' academy and a preparatory seminary for young clerics, set up the first printing press in the West, published the first newspaper in Michigan and the first Catholic paper in the United States; was a founder, vice-president, and professor of the University of Michigan and the only Catholic priest ever elected to Congress. Gallitzin, a pioneer priest in Western Pennsylvania, converted six thousand non-Catholics. The Sulpicians at Baltimore ministered in the churches of the city and the missions of the country. They were considered as clergy of the cathedral and are credited with having introduced into the United States some of the dignity and splendour of old-world Catholic worship.

St. Mary's Seminary.—After a trial of ten or eleven years the seminary at Baltimore had no prospects of success; an academy which Dubourg had opened for foreign boys was not allowed to receive Americans (see below); the Sulpicians there had no means of support. Meanwhile, the Revolution in France had passed, religion was restored by Napoleon, and the seminaries were being reopened. In these circumstances of 1802 only one course seemed possible to the superior-general in Paris: to recall his subjects to France gradually. Bishop Carroll, who had the highest esteem for the Sulpicians and regarded them as the hope of his diocese, was very deeply afflicted by this resolution, and in many letters begged Father Emery not to carry it out. "If it be necessary for me", he wrote, "to bear the terrible trial of seeing the greater number of them depart, I implore you to leave here at least a germ which may produce fruit in the season decreed by the Lord." Nevertheless, Garnier (who afterwards became superior-general), Maréchal, and Levadoux departed for France in 1803, though with the greatest reluctance; Nagot was detained from going by ill-health. The seminary seemed doomed. It was saved by Pius VII, whom Father Emery, moved by the bishop's appeals, consulted at Paris in 1804. "My son," said the pope, "let it stand, let that seminary stand. It will bear fruit in its own time." Father Emery accepted these words as the voice of God, and the Sulpicians remained. But progress was slow; St. Mary's College, Baltimore, and Mt. St. Mary's, Emmitsburg, both founded by the Sulpicians (see below), furnished few students to the seminary. Still, Bishop Carroll had the consolation of seeing thirty priests ordained from there before his death in 1815.

Under the second superior, Father Tessier (1810–29), the seminary became solidly established, although the number of ordinations averaged only two or three a year. His chief support up to 1817 was Father Ambrose Maréchal, whose abilities raised him in that year to the Archbishopric of Baltimore. In 1822 St. Mary's Seminary was endowed by Pius VII with all the privileges of a Catholic university. The third superior, Father Louis Regis Deluol (1829–49), a man of exceptional ability and character, exerted a strong influence not only on the seminary and college over which he presided, but on the general affairs of the Church in America. St. Charles' College was founded during his administration. St. Mary's College was suppressed under his successor, Father Francis L'Homme (1849–60). The Irish immigration, the spread of Catholicism, and the foundation of St. Charles' College, contributed to render the seminary as fruitful in vocation in the one decade of Father L'Homme's administration as it had been in the preceding sixty years. Two directors at St. Mary's, Fathers Alphonse Flammant (1856–64) and Francis Paulinus Dissez (1857–1907), deserve mention here as saintly men who deeply influenced Cardinal Gibbons, the first Archbishop Keane of Dubuque, and other leaders of the American Church. A half-century of teaching at St. Mary's made Father Dissez one of the best known and most venerated priests of America.

St. Mary's prospered and grew under the fourth superior, Father Joseph Paul Dubreul (1860–78), and still more under his successor, Father Alphonse Magnien (1878–1902), who saw an enrolment of over three hundred students. Father Dubreul built the central portion of the present seminary in 1878: the building was completed by Father Magnien. All that remains from the old days is the sisters' house, in which Mother Seton began her work as a Sister of Charity, and the seminary chapel, built in 1806, which long served as a parish church and was regarded in those days as a gem of architecture. Both Dubreul and Magnien were marked types of the true ecclesiastic, and moulded the character of hundreds of priests now living. Probably no priest in our day was better known or better loved by priests than the good and genial "Abbé" Magnien. He was the close friend and trusted adviser of Cardinal Gibbons, who said of him some time after his death: "I had been so much accustomed to consult the venerable Abbé on important questions, and to lean upon him in every emergency, that . . . I feel as if I had lost my right arm. He was indeed *dimidium animæ meæ.*" The present superior, Father Edward Randall Dyer, D.D., was appointed in Aug., 1902, after Father Magnien's health had failed. St. Mary's Seminary has given over thirty bishops and eighteen hundred priests to the Church of America, of whom more than fourteen hundred are still living. The largest of our American seminaries, and national in its scope, it draws its students from every quarter of the country. It has always taken a leading part in the seminary conferences of the Catholic Educational Association. It was the scene of the Third Plenary Council and of many notable ecclesiastical gatherings. Its archives and library are rich in materials of early American Church History.

St. Mary's College, Baltimore.—The impossibility of getting students for the seminary led the fathers to teach Latin to a few boys in 1793–94, in the hope of recruiting vocations; but this was discontinued through fear of injuring the Georgetown Academy. Father Dubourg resigned the presidency of Georgetown in 1799 in order to found a college at Havana. Unsuccessful in the attempt, he returned to Baltimore in Aug., 1799, with three young Spaniards; these, with a few French boys, he lodged and instructed at the seminary. In the following year a building was erected for them alongside the seminary, and the institution was named St. Mary's College. In deference to the wishes of the bishop, no American boys were admitted, but many students came from Cuba, San Domingo, Jamaica, and Porto Rico, besides French boys from the United States. In 1803 the doors were opened to American students, without distinction of creed; and in 1805 the college was raised to the rank of a university by an act of the legislature. The students numbered then, or in the following year, 106, which was considered a remarkable success; for the history of all higher education in Maryland up to that time had been, almost without exception, a record of failures. It drew students from the whole country, but chiefly from Maryland and the neighbouring states, north and south. Many were non-Catholics. Some continued to come from the West Indies and from Central America. The college had vicissitudes, chiefly financial, but it maintained a high standard and enjoyed a high reputation, for it was conducted by able men who brought the culture of France to a country where education was still in a very crude condition. Its student roll rose at times to two hundred or over. Among its eleven presidents are numbered Archbishops Dubourg and Eccleston, and Bishops David, Bruté, and Chance; and the names of many bishops and notable priests and citizens are found on the list of its professors and students.

Despite its half-century of useful and distinguished work, it did not adequately fulfil the main purpose of its foundation; a college, frequented by sons of rich parents, and containing many non-Catholics, was found unfavourable to the fostering, and even to the preservation, of priestly vocations. Accordingly it was resolved in 1848, on the occasion of the official visit of Father Faillon from Paris, to suppress St. Mary's College and start an ecclesiastical college. In the autumn of that year, St. Charles' College was opened (see below); and in 1852 St. Mary's College by order of the superior-general, Father de Courson, was closed at the height of its prosperity. By an understanding with the Jesuits, Loyola College supplied its place.

Mount St. Mary's, Emmitsburg.—The necessity of a strictly clerical school had forced itself upon the mind of Father Nagot in the first years of St. Mary's College. In 1806 this saintly old man of over seventy gathered about a dozen boys around him at Pigeon Hill, Adams Co., Pennsylvania, in a Catholic region that had long been ministered to by the Jesuits. After two years of instruction, they were transferred to the care of the Rev. John Dubois (q. v.), pastor of Emmitsburg, Maryland, who himself was already instructing a few boys. In 1808 Father Dubois, who had become a Sulpician, acquired land and built Mount St. Mary's College, in the name of the Society of St.-Sulpice. He did heroic work, single-handed, as teacher and as pastor. In 1812 he was joined by Father Bruté. Together they were the main factors in creating a flourishing college where the spirit of Catholic piety reigned and was very fruitful in vocations. Mount St. Mary's, founded to supply vocations to St. Mary's Seminary, became a rival by force of circumstances, for it could obtain teachers only by retaining the graduates of the college who taught the younger boys at the same time they pursued their clerical studies. It also became a rival of St. Mary's College when it began to admit boys who did not aspire to the priesthood, and even non-Catholics. For these, and also for financial reasons, the Society of St.-Sulpice in 1826 made an amicable separation from Mount St. Mary's, which has continued the noble spirit of Bruté and Dubois and done invaluable services to the Church of America.

St. Charles' College, Ellicott City.—Persisting in the effort to establish a purely clerical college, according to the spirit of their vocation and the mind of the Church, the Sulpicians, in 1831, laid the cornerstone of St. Charles' College, near Ellicott City, Maryland. The ground, together with a small sum of money, had been donated by Charles Carroll of Carrollton, who survived to witness the cornerstone laying. Lack of funds long delayed the completion of the college. It was opened in 1848 with four students by the Rev. Oliver Jenkins, who became its first president. In ten or twelve years the students numbered over a hundred. Here, at last, was a strictly clerical college, firmly established, giving a solid classical education and maintaining the purest traditions of clerical discipline and spirit. St. Charles' became well known throughout the country, no section of which has not been well represented among its student body. The enrolment for years has been about two hundred. It has trained over fourteen hundred priests for the American Church and pointed the way to the clerical colleges now becoming numerous and most helpful. Father Jenkins remained president till 1869, though he had been temporarily replaced by the Revs. G. Raymond (1849–51) and S. Ferté, D.D. (1851–52). His successors have been Father Ferté (1869–76), Revs. P. P. Denis (1876–86), F. M. L. Dumont (1886–94), Charles B. Rex (1894–97), Charles B. Schrantz (1897–1906), and F. X. McKenny. To the older generations of students the best remembered of the professors is Father J. B. Menu, who for forty years (1849–88) "hammered Latin and Greek into the most stubborn heads". The best known to the outside world is Father John B. Tabb, a true poet, whose exquisite lyrics have won him a secure place in English literature. The spacious building, with its beautiful chapel, its libraries, and valuable documents, was destroyed by fire on 16 March, 1911. Classes were resumed in a few weeks in temporary quarters at Cloud Gap, near Baltimore. On that spot the fathers have now begun (1912) the construction of a new and greater St. Charles.

St. John's Seminary, Brighton, was opened in 1884 and entrusted by the Most Rev. John J. Williams, Archbishop of Boston, to the care of the Sulpicians, whose pupil he had been at Montreal and Paris. Its presidents have been the Very Revs. John Hogan (1884–89, 1894–1901), Charles B. Rex (1889–94), Daniel E. Maher (1901–06), and Francis P. Havey (1906–11). In June, 1911, at the request of the Most Rev. William H. O'Connell, Archbishop of Boston, the Sulpicians withdrew from the seminary.

St. Joseph's Seminary, Yonkers.—Archbishop Hughes, who had been their pupil at Mount St. Mary's, had desired the Sulpicians, in 1862, to assume charge of the seminary about to be opened at Troy, New York. This wish was carried out only in 1896, under Archbishop Corrigan, when St. Joseph's Seminary was transferred to Dunwoodie, Yonkers, New York. The first rector was the Very Rev. E. R. Dyer, 1896–1902. Called to the presidency of St. Mary's Seminary, Baltimore, he was succeeded by the Very Rev. James F. Driscoll. In January, 1906, Father Driscoll and four of his associates withdrew from the Society of St-Sulpice, and were accepted by Archbishop Farley into his diocese, continuing their work in the seminary, which thus passed from the charge of the Sulpicians.

St. Patrick's Seminary, Menlo Park.—The Sulpicians, whose houses had hitherto been located in the Atlantic states, accepted a call to the Far West in 1898. Most of the students for the San Francisco archdiocese had for many years been sent to St. Mary's Seminary, Baltimore. A long-cherished desire of Archbishop Riordan was realized when St. Patrick's Seminary was opened 20 Sept., 1898, under the care of the Sulpicians. The institution was to comprise a preparatory seminary or college and a seminary proper, of philosophy and theology. It began with only three classes of the college department, the succeeding classes in the college and seminary being added according as the students were prepared. Very Rev. A. J. B. Vuibert was the first president of the college department, and had under him, at the beginning, seven professors, four of whom were Sulpicians, and twenty-eight students. He was succeeded in 1911 by Rev. John J. Doran, S.S. The theological department was opened in 1904, when Very Rev. Henry A. Ayrinhac, S.S., D.D., became president of the seminary. The magnificent structure was greatly damaged in the earthquake of 1906, but was soon restored, thanks to the characteristic energy of Archbishop Riordan. There are at present over one hundred students in this flourishing and hopeful young seminary.

Catholic University. — Leo XIII, in granting a constitution to the Catholic University of America, laid upon the Sulpicians the duty of caring for the discipline and spiritual direction of the ecclesiastical students and of assisting them in the choice and pursuit of their studies. Divinity College was opened in October, 1889, under Very Rev. John B. Hogan, who remained president till 1894. His successors have been Very Revs. F. M. L. Dumont (1894–1911), and John F. Fenlon.

St. Austin's College.—The aspirants to the Society of St-Sulpice pursue their studies in the seminary, undistinguished from the other students; until recently, the American aspirants generally were sent to Rome or Paris for post-graduate studies after ordination and to the Solitude at Issy, near Paris, for their novitiate. In Oct., 1901, the American scholasticate of the Sulpicians, known as St. Austin's College, was opened near the Catholic University, Washington. The students, who are received only after having completed their seminary studies, follow courses at the university in philosophy, theology, science, or letters, to prepare themselves for work in college or seminary. It has been presided over by Very Revs. James F. Driscoll (1901–02), Daniel P. Duffy (1902–04), John F. Fenlon (1904–11), and Francis P. Havey. In 1911 the first American novitiate of the Sulpicians, known as the Solitude, was begun in this house under Father Havey as director.

The government of the Sulpician houses in the United States was, until recent years, dependent directly upon the superior-general in Paris. In 1903 the President of St. Mary's Seminary, Father Dyer, was appointed vicar-general of the Superior of St-Sulpice, an office resembling that of provincial in a religious order. He governs ordinary Sulpician affairs in the United States with the advice and assistance of his council. In the early days of the American hierarchy several Sulpicians were among its members: Maréchal (1817–28), and Eccleston (1834–51), Archbishops of Baltimore; Flaget, first Bishop of Bardstown (1810–50), with David (1819–41), and Chabrat (1834–47), as coadjutors; Dubourg, Bishop of New Orleans (1815–26), died Archbishop of Besançon in 1833; Dubois of New York (1826–42); Bruté, first Bishop of Vincennes (1834–39), who, with Flaget and David, is well remembered for great sanctity of life; Chance, first Bishop of Natchez (1841–52); Vérot, Bishop of Savannah (1859–70); afterwards first Bishop of St. Augustine (1870–76), of which he had been vicar Apostolic in 1858; and O'Farrell, Bishop of Trenton (1881–94). More than twenty American archbishops, past and present, and more than sixty bishops have received their clerical formation, at least in part, in Sulpician houses at home or abroad. All the rectors of the Catholic University have been their pupils. Father David, sent by Father Emery with Bishop Flaget to establish a seminary, founded St. Thomas's Seminary at Bardstown, and taught its students almost single-handed for many years. The diocese had only three priests when he arrived in 1810; he trained up forty-seven, mostly natives, of whom the most illustrious is Martin J. Spalding. To this little-known seminary is attributed the greatest part in the preservation and spread of Catholicism in Kentucky.

Six seminaries in all, Baltimore, Bardstown, Brighton, Emmitsburg, Dunwoodie, and Menlo Park, were founded or directed by Sulpicians, and their traditions and spirit have been carried into many new institutions by their *alumni*. Largely through their efforts, the Propagation of the Faith was established in this country and for a long time developed. The Sisters of Charity at Emmitsburg were established by their direction and co-operation, and united, through Father Deluol, to the foundation of St. Vincent de Paul at Paris. Father Joubert founded the coloured sisterhood of the Oblates at Baltimore, and Father David the Sisters of Nazareth, in Kentucky. Bishop Dubourg introduced the Vincentians into the United States, also the Religious of the Sacred Heart. He was the founder of St. Louis Latin Academy which developed, under the Jesuits, into the St. Louis University. On Flaget's invitation the Good Shepherd Sisters came to this country. In the early days the Sulpicians ministered to the coloured Catholics of Baltimore, and since the foundation of St. Joseph's Seminary for work among the negroes, its students have made their seminary studies at St. Mary's. The secretarial work of the Negro and Indian Commission has always been carried on in connexion with St. Mary's Seminary. The fathers of the seminary have acted as secretaries or theologians in the synods and in the provincial and plenary councils of Baltimore. The literary productions of the Sulpicians have, almost without exception, grown directly out of their work as educators; they have written books on Latin grammar, history, ancient and modern, English literature, liturgy, rubrics, dogmatic and moral theology, Holy Scripture, devotion, etc. They have translated many standard French works into English, and English into French. Their best-known writers are Father Hogan, whose "Clerical Studies" is the classic of its subject, and Father Adolphe Tanquerey, whose text-books on dogmatic and moral theology are used in numerous seminaries throughout the world.

SHEA, *History of the Catholic Church in the United States* (New York, 1888); O'GORMAN, *A History of the Roman Catholic Church in the United States* (New York, 1895); *St. Mary's Seminary* (Memorial Volume of the Centenary, Baltimore, 1891); *Catalogues of St. Mary's Seminary, St. Joseph's Seminary of New York, St. Patrick's Seminary of San Francisco*, and *St. Charles's College. History of Education in Maryland*, published by the United States Bureau of Education (Washington, 1894), vii, ix; *The Catholic Church in the United States*, I, published by the Catholic Editing Company (New York, 1908); *Bulletin trimestriel des anciens élèves de St. Sulpice*, containing a series of articles by ANDRÉ on the Sulpicians' history in the United States (Paris, 1908——); MCSWEENEY, *The Story of the Mountain*, I (Mount St. Mary's, Emmitsburg, 1911), i–xii; SPALDING, *Life of Bishop Flaget* (Louisville, 1852); HOWLETT, *St. Thomas, Seminary, near Bardstown* (St. Louis, 1906); SHEA, *History of Georgetown College* (Washington, 1911); MOREAU, *Les prêtres français emigrés* (Paris, 1856); FINOTTI, *Bibliographia Catholica Americana* (New York, 1872); *Catholic Educational Review*, I (Washington, 1911), 347–48.

JOHN FRANCIS FENLON.

Sulpicius Severus, an ecclesiastical writer, b. of noble parents in Aquitaine c. 360; d. about 420–25. The scanty information which we possess concerning his life is derived mainly from the writings of his friend Paulinus of Nola and Gennadius. He enjoyed excellent educational advantages, studied jurisprudence, and was renowned as an eloquent lawyer. His marriage with the daughter of a wealthy consular family seemed to seal his earthly happiness. His wife, however, was snatched away by a premature death and shortly after 390 Severus renounced his brilliant career and followed his friend Paulinus into monastic retirement. Through this sudden change of life he incurred his father's displeasure, but was encouraged in his determination by his mother-in-law. He became a personal friend and enthusiastic disciple of St. Martin and lived near Eauze, at Toulouse and Luz in Southern France. His ordination to the priesthood is vouched for by Gennadius, but no details of his priestly activity have reached us. According to the same Gennadius he was caught in the toils of Pelagianism towards the close of his life and, upon discovering his error, subjected himself to lifelong silence in expiation of his imprudence in speech.

The following works are undoubtedly genuine: (1) "The Chronicle"; (2) "Life of St. Martin"; (3) two dialogues, formerly divided into three; (4) three letters. "The Chronicle" ("Chronicorum Libri duo" or "Historia sacra") extends from the creation of the world to A. D. 400, but omits the historical events recorded in the New-Testament writings. It was published in or after 403 and has been preserved in a single eleventh-century manuscript. It is a source of primary importance for the history of Priscillianism and contains considerable information respecting the Arian controversy. More popular during the Middle Ages was his "Life of St. Martin", as were also the dialogues and letters which relate to the same subject. The biography was written during the lifetime of the saint, but was published only after his death. Like the dialogues, it abounds in miraculous events. Beside the above-mentioned three letters, seven others have been attributed to Severus. These are rejected as spurious by some critics, whilst the genuineness of the first two is admitted, rightly it would seem, by others. The "World Chronicle" of the so-called Sulpicius Severus has nothing to do with the subject of this biography; it was written in Spain in the sixth century. Sulpicius Severus has been rightly styled the Christian Sallust; his diction, notably in the "Chronicle", is elegant and reminds the reader of the classical age.

His works are to be found in *P. L.*, XX, 95–248; later edition by HALM in *Corpus script. eccl. lat.*, I (Vienna, 1866); BERNAYS, *Über die Chronik des Sulpicius Severus* (Berlin, 1861); BARDENHEWER, tr. SHAHAN, *Patrology* (St. Louis, 1908), 451–53; BENNETT in *Dict. Christ. Biog.*, s. v. *Severus* (18).   N. A. WEBER.

Sulpitius.—Two bishops of Bourges bore this name. (1) The first, St. Sulpitius the Severe, wrongly identified with Sulpicius Severus, the historian of St. Martin, was raised to the see in 584. He was, says St. Gregory of Tours, a man of high birth, one of the first senators of Gaul, of great oratorical talent, and expert in the art of poetical rhythms. The See of Bourges having become vacant with the death of Remigius, several candidates offered gifts to King Gontran to secure the assistance of his favour. But the latter rejected all these simoniacal gifts to favour the election of Sulpitius. He was elected, given Holy orders, and consecrated bishop. Shortly afterwards he held a council in Auvergne, to adjust the dispute which had arisen between two of his suffragans, Innocentius, Bishop of Rodez, and Ursicinus, Bishop of Cahors, with regard to parishes for which they contended. The council decided that the Bishop of Cahors should retain the contested parishes, which the Bishop of Rodez had not proved that he or his predecessors had long possessed. Sulpitius assisted at a Council of Mâcon in 585; he died in 591, his feast being inserted in the Roman Martyrology on 29 January.

(2) Sulpitius the Pious (or the Débonnaire), b. at Vatan (Diocese of Bourges), of noble parents, before the end of the sixth century, devoted himself from his youth to good works and the study of Holy Scripture. Austregisilus, Bishop of Bourges, ordained him cleric of his church, then deacon, and finally made him director of his episcopal school. Clotaire II, King of the Franks, who had heard his merits spoken of, summoned him and made him chaplain of his armies. But at the death of Bishop Austregisilus (c. 624) he was recalled to Bourges to take his place. Sulpitius thenceforth laboured with much zeal and success to re-establish ecclesiastical discipline, for the relief of the poor and the conversion of the Jews. In 626 he assisted at the Council of Clichy and held several others with the bishops of his province, but nothing of them remains. He intervened with King Dagobert in behalf of his flock, of whom a too heavy tax was exacted. At the request of the same king he consecrated to the See of Cahors his treasurer St. Didier, who was his personal friend, and there are extant three letters which he addressed to him. Towards the end of his life Sulpitius took a coadjutor, Vulfolnde, and retired to a monastery which he had founded near Bourges. There he died 17 Jan., 646, which day several MSS. of the Hieronymian Martyrology indicate as his feast. In his honour the church bearing his name was built in Paris, from which the Society of St. Sulpice derives its own.

(1) *Gregorii Turonensis Opera*; *Hist. Franc.*, ed. ARNDT AND KRUSCH, VI, 39; *Acta SS.*, Jan., III, 582; *Gallia Christiana* (Paris, 1873), II, xiv–xvi.
(2) KRUSCH, *Mon. Germ. Hist.: Script. rerum merov.* (Hanover, 1902), IV; *Acta SS.*, II, 529; *Catalogus codicum hagiographicorum bibliothecæ Bruxellensis* (Brussels, 1889), II, 76; MABILLON, *Acta SS. O.S.B.* (Paris, 1669), II, 168; *Gallia Christiana* (Paris, 1873), II, xvi.   ANTOINE DEGERT.

Sumatra, PREFECTURE APOSTOLIC OF, erected by a Decree of 30 June, 1911, and entrusted to the Dutch Capuchins. Previously it formed part of the Vicariate Apostolic of Batavia (q. v.), which is under the care of the Jesuits of Holland. The new prefecture comprises Sumatra and the surrounding islands, including Bangka (area, 4888 sq. miles; population, 78,000). The Island of Sumatra, referred to as Jabadin by Ptolemy, and visited by Marco Polo in 1292, was discovered by the Portuguese navigator Siqueira in 1508, and occupied by the Dutch in 1599. It extends from 95° 16' to 106° 3' E. long., and from 5° 40' N. to 5° 59' S. lat., and has an area of about 181,000 square miles. The natives, of Malayan race, number about 5,500,000, exclusive of the little known inland tribes. They are indolent and cruel; their religion is a mixture of fetishism and Mahommedanism. At the beginning of 1911 the Jesuits had four chief mission centres in Sumatra,—at Medan, Padang, Koata Radja, and Tandjeong-Sakti,—and sixteen minor stations. The Sisters of Charity of Tilburg (Holland) were established at Padang. There were two mission schools, and 4600 Catholics of whom 3200 were Europeans.

Missiones Catholicæ (Rome, 1907), 263–6; *Pius Almanak* (Amsterdam, 1912); ZONDERVAN, *Banka en zijne bewoners* (Amsterdam, 1895); YZERMAN, *Dwars door Sumatra* (Haarlem, 1896).   A. A. MACERLEAN.

Summæ (SUMMULÆ), compendiums of theology, philosophy, and canon law which were used both as textbooks in the schools and as books of reference during the Middle Ages. Some historians of theology cite Origen's περὶ ἀρχῶν as the first summary of Catholic theology. Others consider that the first in point of time is "De Trinitate" by St. Hilary of Poitiers. Quite recently the distinction has been accorded to Radulfus Ardens, an eleventh-century theologian and preacher, a native of Beaulieu, author of a comprehensive "Speculum Universale", still in MS. In this wide sense of the word, however, the encyclopedic treatises of St. Isidore, Rabanus, Maurus etc., entitled "De Etymologiis" or "De Universo" might also be considered to be summaries of theology and philosophy. In the stricter sense of the word, "Summa" is applied to the more technical systematic compendiums which began to appear in the twelfth century. An alternative title is "Sentences" (*Libri Sententiarum*), the diminutive, "Summulæ", being of later origin. What is peculiar to these "summists" or "sententiaries", as the authors of these works are called, is the adoption of the method first suggested by Gerbert in his "De Rationali et Ratione Uti", and used by Abelard in his "Sic et Non". This consisted in an exposition of contradictory views, the affirmative and negative; and progress towards the final form of the thirteenth-century "Summæ" is marked by the greater care which was taken, as time went on, to explain in a systematic manner the apparent contradiction among the conflicting opinions presented. Besides this method of exposition, the twelfth-century summists adopted dialectic definitely as a means of elucidating, not only philosophical, but also theological truth. Finally the summists adopted more or less unanimously a fixed division of the field of theology and philosophy, and adhered more or less closely to a definite order of topics. Here, of course, there was room for individual preferences in the matter of arrangement and sequence of problems, as we see when we compare with one another the "Summæ" even of the latest period of Scholasticism.

The first great summist was Peter Lombard (died 1160), author of the "Books of Sentences" and surnamed "Master of Sentences". The order of topics in the "Books of Sentences" is as follows: In the first place, the topics are divided into *res* and *signa*, or things and signs. "Things" are subdivided into I. The object of our happiness, God—to this topic Peter devotes the first book; II. Means of attaining this object, viz., creatures—the topic treated in the second book; III. Virtues, men, and angels, that is, special means of happiness and subjects of happiness—the topic of the third book. The fourth book is devoted to *signs*, namely, the sacraments. How far Peter Lombard was influenced by earlier summists, such as Robert Pullen, Hugh of St. Victor, and the author of the "Summa Sententiarum" which was immediately inspired by Abelard's work, historians have not determined. It is generally admitted that the Lombard was not entirely original. He deserves his renown as the first great summist chiefly because, in spite of the opposition which his work met during his lifetime, its influence grew greater in time, until in the thirteenth century it was universally adopted as a text. Notwithstanding all that hostile critics of Scholasticism have said about the dryness and unattractiveness of the medieval "Summæ", these works have many merits from the point of view of pedagogy, and a philosophical school which supplements, as Scholasticism did, the compendious treatment of the "Summæ" with the looser form of treatment of the "Quæstiones Disputatæ" and the "Opuscula", unites in its method of writing the advantages which modern philosophy derives from the combination of textbook and doctor's dissertation. For a description of the "Summa Theologica" of St. Thomas, the most perfect specimen of this kind of literature, see THOMAS AQUINAS, SAINT. The term "Summulæ" was used, for the most part, to designate the logical compendiums which came to be adopted as texts in the schools during the thirteenth century. The best known of these is the "Summulæ Logicales" of Peter Hispanus, afterwards Pope John XXI.

DE WULF, *History of Medieval Philosophy*, tr. COFFEY (New York, 1909); GRABMANN, *Gesch. der schol. Methode* (Freiburg, 1909).
WILLIAM TURNER.

Summer Schools, CATHOLIC.—A Catholic summer school is an assembly of Catholic clergy and laity held during the summer months to foster intellectual culture in harmony with Christian faith by means of lectures and special courses along university extension lines. It first took form in the Champlain Summer School which was founded at New London, Connecticut, 1892, and located permanently in 1893 at Cliff Haven, N. Y. The Columbian Summer School was established at Madison, Wisconsin, 1895, and is now permanently located at Milwaukee; the Winter school of New Orleans was founded in 1896, and the Maryland Summer School in 1900. This interesting feature of Catholic intellectual and sociological work in the United States is the natural development and coalescence of various tendencies previously existing in the Church, viz., reading circles, university extension, summer institutes.

(a) The reading circle has its germ in the Christian family. St. Philip Neri strongly urged the advantage of reading circles for people in the world. As a student at the Sorbonne, Frederick Ozanam organized a circle of this nature which was the origin of the Conference of St. Vincent de Paul. In the United States the reading circle appeared during the early part of the last century in the young men's lyceums where courses of lectures and literary exercises were held. In 1864 Very Rev. Isaac Hecker founded a library in connexion with the Sunday-school of St. Paul's Church, New York City, and prescribed that the reading and discussion of a book should form part of the Sunday-school class. Thus each class became a reading circle. The graduates of this Sunday-school formed in 1886 a reading circle, in the special sense of the term, called The Ozanam; its members meet weekly. In 1885 the Young Ladies' Sodality of Youngstown, Ohio, established a reading circle. In Dec., 1888, Miss Julia Perkins of Milwaukee strongly advocated through the "Catholic World" the establishment of these circles in every parish. Warren Mosher took up the work, and in April, 1889, organized the Catholic Educational Union. In June, 1889, the Paulists founded the Columbian Reading Union with Rev. Thomas McMillan as president. These unions have for their aim the propagation and unification of reading circles. The movement spread, and in Jan., 1891, the "Catholic Reading Circle Review" was established by Mr. Mosher as the organ of reading circles; it afterwards became the organ of the summer school. The Catholic Educational Union, the Columbian Reading Union, and the "Reading Circle Review" were strong advocates of a summer assembly. Thus, in germ, the Cliff Haven Summer School was an annual convention of the members of reading circles.

(b) The purpose of university extension is to bring the university into touch with the people and make its influence of wider scope. This is attained through a body of organized teachers formed from graduates of the university, who travel through the country and give series of lectures; attendance at these lectures with examination may entitle to a university degree. Thus the university is brought to people who otherwise could not have access to it. The phrase itself became current through discussion on university reform in England, begun in 1850, and resulting in the new statutes of 1880. The movement spread to America and became a part of American university life. Thus the Cliff Haven Summer School received from the Regents of the University of the State of New York, 9 Feb., 1893, a charter by virtue of which it received legal existence as a corporation under the laws of the State of New York, and was classified within the system of public instruction devoted to university extension. Under university extension should be included the Association Catholique de la Jeunesse Française organized in 1886, the School of Social Science of Munchen-Gladbach founded in 1893 under the auspices of the Catholic Volksverein, and the Institute of Social Science established by Archbishop Farley at New York in 1911.

(c) The idea of summer institutes is not new to Catholic education. It has long been a recognized feature in the religious educational bodies of the Catholic Church, each teaching congregation holding summer institutes of its own members. In more recent years these teachers' institutes became diocesan in form, e. g., in Rochester, Los Angeles, and the Archdiocese of Oregon. In 1911 the Catholic University at Washington opened a summer institute which was attended by 284 teachers from 23 religious bodies, representing 56 dioceses and 31 states with 9 from Canada and 1 from England. The same year the De Paul University of Chicago opened a summer institute for teachers with an attendance of 125.

The coalescence of these three elements in the Cliff Haven Summer School has made it a characteristic and powerful factor of intellectual and social American Catholic life. The Young Men's National Union, organized in 1875, and the first Catholic National Congress of Baltimore, in 1889, had created the desire for lay Catholic national unity. At suggestion of Mr. Mosher, Mgr. James Loughlin, President of the Y. M. N. U., published, 17 Jan., 1892, in the "Catholic Review" of New York City, a letter urging the establishment of a summer assembly. Clergy, laity, and the press endorsed the project with enthusiasm. A meeting was held at the Catholic Club, New York City, 12 May, 1892, under the auspices of Archbishop Corrigan and plans were laid for an opening session at New London, Conn., 15 July to 5 August, 1892. One thousand persons representing twenty states were in attendance. Among the promoters were Mgr. James Loughlin, Mgr. M. J. Lavelle, Mgr. D. J. McMahon, Bishop Conaty, Mgr. John Walsh, Mgr. Henry Brann, Rev. Morgan Sheedy, Rev. John F. Mullany, Rev. F. P. Siegfried, Rev. Joseph H. McMahon, Rev. P. A. Halpin, Rev. John Talbot Smith, Rev. Thomas McMillan, C.S.P., Rev. Denis O'Sullivan, S.J., Very Rev. James P. Kiernan, Rev. Thomas P. Joynt, Rev. A. P. Doyle, C.S.P., Rev. Thomas Hughes, S.J., Rev. Walter P. Gough, Brother Azarias, Charles G. Herbermann, George Parsons Lathrop, Richard Malcom Johnson, Maurice Francis Egan, Mary Elizabeth Blake, Katherine E. Conway, John A. Mooney, Richard D. Clark, Thomas B. Fitzpatrick, John D. Crimmins, Hon. John B. Riley, John A. Haaran, George E. Hardy, John P. Brophy, Wm. R. Claxton, Jacques M. Mertens, Wm. J. Moran. Permanent organization followed with president, vice-president, secretary, treasurer, and a board of twenty-four trustees.

The following year an offer, made by the Delaware and Hudson Company through its agent, of 450 acres of land on the shore of Lake Champlain, three miles south of Plattsburg, N. Y., was accepted. The sessions of 1893, 1894, and 1895, were held in Plattsburg. In 1896 the session was held on the assembly grounds, named Cliff Haven. With the approbation of Leo XIII and Pius X, of the Apostolic delegates, Cardinal Satolli, Cardinal Martinelli, and Cardinal Archbishop Falconio, and of the hierarchy of the United States, the movement has grown with each year until it now has property valued at $500,000, courses of lectures covering eleven weeks, and an attendance of about 10,000. With a daily program of lectures, concerts, dramatic recitals, and social gatherings, it brings together in social intercourse Catholics from all parts of the country and offers a stimulus and an opportunity for study along lines of advanced thought. Its main purpose is: to give from the most authoritative sources among our Catholic writers and thinkers, the Catholic point of view on all the issues of the day in history, literature, philosophy, art, political science, upon economic and social problems that are agitating the world, upon the relations between science and religion; to state in the clearest possible terms the underlying truth in each and all of these subjects; to remove false assumptions; and to correct false statements. It thus meets a recognized want of clergy and laity, is an important popular educational centre in America, and has contributed much to organize Catholic intellectual forces and to solve the problems of American life.

Catholic Reading Circle Review; Mosher's Magazine; Champlain Educator, I–XII; *Report of U. S. Commissioner of Education* (1894–95); LAVELLE in *Amer. Cath. Quart. Rev.* (Jan., 1892); SHEEDY in *Ecclesiastical Review* (Oct., 1904); EGAN in *Ave Maria* (1892); CONWAY in *Report of Columbian Catholic Congress* (Chicago, 1894); *Messenger of the Sacred Heart* (Oct., 1902); *Catholic World* (June, 1905; Feb. and Aug., 1906; March, 1909).

JOHN T. DRISCOLL.

Summons. See CITATION.

Sunday (Day of the Sun), as the name of the first day of the week, is derived from Egyptian astrology. The seven planets, known to us as Saturn, Jupiter, Mars, the Sun, Venus, Mercury, and the Moon, each had an hour of the day assigned to them, and the planet which was regent during the first hour of any day of the week gave its name to that day (see CALENDAR). During the first and second century the week of seven days was introduced into Rome from Egypt, and the Roman names of the planets were given to each successive day. The Teutonic nations seem to have adopted the week as a division of time from the Romans, but they changed the Roman names into those of corresponding Teutonic deities. Hence the *dies Solis* became Sunday (German, *Sonntag*). Sunday was the first day of the week according to the Jewish method of reckoning, but for Christians it began to take the place of the Jewish Sabbath in Apostolic times as the day set apart for the public and solemn worship of God. The practice of meeting together on the first day of the week for the celebration of the Eucharistic Sacrifice is indicated in Acts, xx, 7; I Cor., xvi, 2; in Apoc., i, 10, it is called the Lord's day. In the Didache (xiv) the injunction is given: "On the Lord's Day come together and break bread. And give thanks [offer the Eucharist], after confessing your sins that your sacrifice may be pure". St. Ignatius (Ep. ad Magnes, ix) speaks of Christians as "no longer observing the Sabbath, but living in the observance of the Lord's Day, on which also Our Life rose again". In the Epistle of Barnabas (xv) we read: "Wherefore, also, we keep the eighth day (i. e. the first of the week) with joyfulness, the day also on which Jesus rose again from the dead".

St. Justin is the first Christian writer to call the day Sunday (I Apol., lxvii) in the celebrated passage in which he describes the worship offered by the early Christians on that day to God. The fact that they met together and offered public worship on Sunday necessitated a certain rest from work on that day. However, Tertullian (202) is the first writer who expressly mentions the Sunday rest: "We, however (just as tradition has taught us), on the day of the Lord's Resurrection ought to guard not only against kneeling, but every posture and office of solicitude; deferring even our businesses lest we give any place to the devil" ("De orat.", xxiii; cf. "Ad nation.", I, xiii; "Apolog.", xvi).

These and similar indications show that during the first three centuries practice and tradition had consecrated the Sunday to the public worship of God by the hearing of Mass and resting from work. With the opening of the fourth century positive legislation, both ecclesiastical and civil, began to make these duties more definite. The Council of Elvira (300) decreed: "If anyone in the city neglects to come to church for three Sundays, let him be excommunicated for a short time so that he may be corrected" (xxi). In the Apostolic Constitutions, which belong to the end of the fourth century, both the hearing of Mass and rest from work are prescribed, and the precept is attributed to the Apostles. The express teaching of Christ and St. Paul prevented the early Christians from falling into the excesses of Jewish Sabbatarianism in the observance of the Sunday, and yet we find St. Cæsarius of Arles in the sixth century teaching that the holy Doctors of the Church had decreed that the whole glory of the Jewish Sabbath had been transferred to the Sunday, and that Christians must keep the Sunday holy in the same way as the Jews had been commanded to keep holy the Sabbath Day. He especially insisted on the people hearing the whole of the Mass and not leaving the church after the Epistle and Gospel had been read. He taught them that they should come to Vespers and spend the rest of the day in pious reading and prayer. As with the Jewish Sabbath, the observance of the Christian Sunday began with sundown on Saturday and lasted till the same time on Sunday. Until quite recent times some theologians taught that there was an obligation under pain of venial sin of assisting at Vespers as well as of hearing Mass, but the opinion rests on no certain foundation and is now commonly abandoned. The common opinion maintains that, while it is highly becoming to be present at Vespers on Sunday, there is no strict obligation to be present. The method of reckoning the Sunday from sunset to sunset continued in some places down to the seventeenth century, but in general since the Middle Ages the reckoning from midnight to midnight has been followed. When the parochial system was introduced, the laity were taught that they must hear Mass and the preaching of the Word of God on Sundays in their parish church. However, toward the end of the thirteenth century, the friars began to teach that the precept of hearing Mass might be fulfilled by hearing it in their churches, and after long and severe struggles this was expressly allowed by the Holy See. Nowadays, the precept may be fulfilled by hearing Mass in any place except a strictly private oratory, and provided Mass is not celebrated on a portable altar by a privilege which is merely personal.

The obligation of rest from work on Sunday remained somewhat indefinite for several centuries. A Council of Laodicea, held toward the end of the fourth century, was content to prescribe that on the Lord's Day the faithful were to abstain from work as far as possible. At the beginning of the sixth century St. Cæsarius, as we have seen, and others showed an inclination to apply the law of the Jewish Sabbath to the observance of the Christian Sunday. The Council held at Orleans in 538 reprobated this tendency as Jewish and non-Christian. From the eighth century the law began to be formulated as it exists at the present day, and the local councils forbade servile work, public buying and selling, pleading in the law courts, and the public and solemn taking of oaths. There is a large body of civil legislation on the Sunday rest side by side with the ecclesiastical. It begins with an Edict of Constantine, the first Christian emperor, who forbade judges to sit and townspeople to work on Sunday. He made an exception in favour of agriculture. The breaking of the law of Sunday rest was punished by the Anglo-Saxon legislation in England like other crimes and misdemeanours. After the Reformation, under Puritan influence, many laws were passed in England whose effect is still visible in the stringency of the English Sabbath. Still more is this the case in Scotland. There is no federal legislation in the United States on the observance of the Sunday, but nearly all the states of the Union have statutes tending to repress unnecessary labour and to restrain the liquor traffic. In other respects the legislation of the different states on this matter exhibits considerable variety. On the continent of Europe in recent years there have been several laws passed in the direction of enforcing the observance of Sunday rest for the benefit of workmen.

VILLIEN, *Hist. des commandements de l'Eglise* (Paris, 1909); DUBLANCHY in *Dict. de théol. cathol.*, s. v. *Dimanche* (Paris, 1911); SLATER, *Manual of Moral Theology* (New York, 1908); the moral theologians generally.   T. SLATER.

Supererogation, WORKS OF. See WORKS, GOOD.

Superior, DIOCESE OF (SUPERIORENSIS), situated in the northern part of Wisconsin, comprises the following counties: Ashland, Barron, Bayfield, Burnett, Douglas, Iron, Lincoln, Oneida, Polk, Price, Rusk, Sawyer, St. Croix, Taylor, Vilas, and Washburn. In area it covers 15,715 square miles, and has its episcopal residence in the city of Superior. On 3 May, 1905, the diocese was established, being formed from the northern part of the Diocese of La Crosse (see LA CROSSE, DIOCESE OF) and the northwestern part of the Diocese of Green Bay (see GREEN BAY, DIOCESE OF).

When Superior, which is one of the suffragans of Milwaukee, was formed, there were 39 secular and 17 regular priests attending to the needs of the people in 93 churches and 33 stations. The Catholic population at the time was about 38,000. Besides the English-speaking congregations there were then as there are at present churches in which the spiritual wants of Germans, Poles, French, Italians, Slovaks and Bohemians were looked after. The spiritual and other needs of the Indians of the district have been well taken care of. There are flourishing industrial schools at Odonah, Bayfield, and other places, that are under the charge of the Sisters of St. Francis and are attended by the Franciscan Fathers. The bishop, ably seconded by his clergy, has started throughout the diocese wherever it was possible parochial schools for the Christian education of the young. In consequence the various cities and towns have one or more such bringing excellent results, considering the meagre resources available. At Superior and Ashland especially the schools are well attended.

The first bishop of the diocese, still in office, is the Rt. Rev. Augustin Francis Schinner, D. D. He was consecrated 25 July, 1905, and appointed to the see of Superior 13 May of the same year. He came to Superior from Milwaukee, where he had held the position of administrator of the archdiocese after the death of Archbishop Katzer. Bishop Schinner was born in Milwaukee 1 May, 1863. He entered the seminary at St. Francis, Wis., and at the age of twenty-two on 7 March, 1886, was ordained priest by Archbishop Heiss of Milwaukee. For about a year he was pastor of the Church at Richfield, Wis., and was then made a professor at St. Francis Seminary, Milwaukee. In 1891 Archbishop Katzer selected him as his secretary, and in 1895 he was made vicar-general of the archdiocese, holding the same position under Archbishop Messmer, until his appointment as Bishop of Superior.

There are now in the diocese the following religious communities of men: Franciscans, Jesuits, Servites; and of women: Franciscan Sisters of the Perpetual Adoration, Sisters of St. Agnes, Sisters of St. Dominic, Poor Handmaids of Jesus Christ, Sisters of St. Francis, School-Sisters of St. Francis, Franciscan Sisters of Charity, School-Sisters of Notre Dame, Sisters of the Sorrowful Mother, Sisters of the Divine Saviour, Sisters of St. Joseph. There are (1911): secular priests, 56; priests of religious orders, 23; churches with resident priests, 55; missions with churches, 65; chapels, 8; stations, 23; high school, 1; parish schools, 23; pupils of parochial schools, 4869; industrial schools, 2; inmates, 225; orphans, 45; total number of young people under Catholic care, 5094; hospitals, 5; Catholic population (Census of 1910): White, 48,028; Indians, 3015.

Official Catholic Directory, 1905–11; *The Catholic Church in Superior, Wis.* (Superior, 1905).   JOHN J. DRISCOLL.

Supernatural Order, the ensemble of effects exceeding the powers of the created universe and gratuitously produced by God for the purpose of raising the rational creature above its native sphere to a God-like life and destiny. The meaning of the phrase fluctuates with that of its antithesis, the natural order. Those who conceive the latter as the world of material beings to the exclusion of immaterial entities, or as the necessary mechanism of cause and effect to the exclusion of the free agency of the will, or again as the inherent forces of the universe to the exclusion of the extrinsic concurrence of God, quite consistently call supernatural all spiritual facts or voluntary determinations or Divine operations. There is no objection to that way of speaking provided the assertion of the supernatural so understood be not made, by a fallacious transference of meaning, to screen the negation of the supernatural as defined above. Catholic theologians sometimes call supernatural the miraculous way in which certain effects, in themselves natural, are produced, or certain endowments (like man's immunity from death, suffering, passion, and ignorance) that bring the lower class up to the higher though always within the limits of the created, but they are careful in qualifying the former as accidentally supernatural (*supernaturale per accidens*) and the latter as relatively supernatural (*præternaturale*). For a concept of the substantially and absolutely supernatural, they start from a comprehensive view of the natural order taken, in its amplest acceptation, for the aggregate of all created entities and powers, including the highest natural endowments of which the rational creature is capable, and even such Divine operations as are demanded by the effective carrying out of the cosmic order. The supernatural order is then more than a miraculous way of producing natural effects, or a notion of relative superiority within the created world, or the necessary concurrence of God in the universe; it is an effect or series of effects substantially and absolutely above all nature and, as such, calls for an exceptional intervention and gratuitous bestowal of God and rises in a manner to the Divine order, the only one that transcends the whole created world. Although some theologians do not consider impossible the elevation of the irrational creature to the Divine order, v. g., by way of personal union, nevertheless it stands to reason that such an exalted privilege should be reserved for the rational creature capable of knowledge and love. It is obvious also that this uplifting of the rational creature to the supernatural order cannot be by way of absorption of the created into the Divine or of fusion of both into a sort of monistic identity, but only by way of union or participation, the two terms remaining perfectly distinct.

Not being an a priori conception but a positive fact, the supernatural order can only be known through Divine revelation properly supported by such Divine evidences as miracle, prophecy, etc. Revelation and its evidences are called extrinsic and auxiliary supernatural, the elevation itself retaining the name of intrinsic or, according to some, theological supernatural. There are three principal instances of such elevation: the hypostatic union or the assumption of the Sacred Humanity of Christ into the personal dignity of the Son of God; the calling of the faithful angels to the beatific vision whereby they see always the face of the Father who is in heaven (Matt., xviii, 10), and the elevation of man to the state of grace here and glory hereafter. The hypostatic union and the angelic supernatural are both closely connected with our own elevation. From St. John (i, 12-14) we know that the hypostatic union is the ideal and instrument of it, and St. Paul declares that the angels are "all ministering spirits, sent to minister for them, who shall receive the inheritance of salvation" (Heb., i, 14). Leaving for separate treatment the auxiliary supernatural (see REVELATION; MIRACLE; PROPHECY), the hypostatic union (see INCARNATION), and the angels' elevation (see ANGELS), this article deals with the supernatural order in man both in its history and analysis.

Briefly, the history is this: From the beginning, man was raised, far above the claims of his nature, to a life which made him, even here below, the adopted child of God, and to a destiny which entitled him to the beatific vision and love of God in heaven. To these strictly supernatural gifts by which man was truly made partaker of the Divine nature (II Pet., i, 4) were added preternatural endowments, that is immunity from ignorance, passion, suffering and death, which left him "little lower than the angels" (Ps. viii, 6; Hebr., ii 7). Through their own fault, our first parents forfeited for themselves and their race both the God-like life and destiny and the angel-like endowments. In His mercy God promised a Redeemer who, heralded by ages of prophecy, came in the fulness of time in the person of Jesus Christ, the incarnate Son of God. By His Incarnation, labours, passion, and death, Jesus Christ restored mankind to its former Divine sonship and heavenly inheritance, if not to its quasi-angelic prerogatives, the virtue of Redemption being applied to us through the joint ministrations of the inner Spirit and of the visible Church, in the form of actual helps, habitual sanctity, and the power of meriting Heaven.

An analysis of the supernatural order, barely inaugurated by the Fathers, but brought to a point of great perfection by the Schoolmen and post-Tridentine theologians, discloses the various elements that make up order, that is an end, means, and laws The end is man's destination to see God face to face and to love Him correspondingly. If, as will be shown, the intuitive vision of God is our true destiny and moreover transcends our highest natural powers, then we must be given means capable of attaining that end, that is supernatural. Those means can be no other than our own actions, but invested with a higher power that makes them meritorious of Heaven. Grace, both actual and habitual, is the source of that meriting power: while habitual grace, with its train of infused virtues or faculties raises our mode of being and operating to a sphere which is God's own, actual grace spurs us on to justification and, once we stand justified, sets in motion our supernatural powers causing them to yield good and meritorious works. In the supernatural order, as in all others, there are also specific laws. The work of man's sanctification depends in a manner on the general laws of the universe and most certainly upon the carrying out of all the moral precepts written in our hearts. Besides these laws, which Christ came not to abolish, there are positive or freely established enactments ranging all the way from the Divinely appointed conditions of salvation to the revealed obligations and even the rules governing our growth in holiness. Glory and grace, being the central features of the supernatural order, special reference will be made to them both in the exposition of errors and the establishment of the Catholic doctrine.

I. ERRORS.—The theories denying or belittling the supernatural order may be classified from the standpoint of both their historical appearance and logical sequence, into three groups according as they view the supernatural (1) in our present *de facto* condition, (2) in the original status of man, (3) in its possibility and evidences.

To the first group belong Pelagianism and Semi-pelagianism. Influenced, no doubt, by the Stoic ideal and their own ascetic performances, the Pelagians of the fifth century so magnified the capacity of human nature as to pronounce natural to it both the beatific vision and the human acts by which it is merited. They were condemned by the Councils of Mileve and Carthage, 418. Less daring, the Semi-pelagians, censured by the Council of Orange (529), subtracted from the supernatural only certain phases of man's life as the beginning of faith and final perseverance. To this group belong also, in a manner, the false mystics of the fourteenth century, the Beghards condemned by the Council of Vienne (1312), for claiming that the rational creature possesses beatitude in itself without the help of the *lumen gloriæ* and Eckhart, whose identification of the Creator and the creature in the act of contemplation was censured by John XXII in 1329.

To the second group belong the early Reformers and the Jansenist School, though in different degrees. Misinterpreting the still imperfect terminology of the Fathers who called natural, in the sense of original, the elevation of our first parents, the early Reformers held that, according to Patristic teaching and contrarily to the Schoolmen, that elevation was not supernatural. Their error, rejected by the Council of Trent (Sess. V, decretum de peccato originali, can. 1), was taken up again, but in a more refined form, by Baius who, indeed, designated as supernatural man's original condition but nullified the meaning of the word by stating that our first parent's elevation was demanded by and due to the normal condition of humanity. In spite of his condemnation by Pius V (Denzinger, 9th ed., nn. 901, 903, 906, 922) he was followed by the Jansenist Quesnel and the pseudo-Synod of Pistoia, the former censured by Clement XI (Denzinger, nn. 1249, 1250) and the latter by Pius VI (Denzinger, nn. 1379, 1380, 1383). A confusion between the moral and the supernatural order, frequently found in the Baianist and Jansenist writings, was reproduced more or less consciously by some German theologians like Stattler, Hermes, Günther, Hirsh, Kuhn, etc., who admitted the supernatural character of the other gifts but contended that the adoption to eternal life and the partaking of the Divine nature, being a moral necessity, could not be supernatural. That revival of an old error found a strong and successful opponent in Kleutgen in the second volume of his theology on the supernatural.

To the third group belongs the Rationalist School from Socinus to the present Modernists. While the foregoing errors proceeded less from a direct denial than from a confusion of the supernatural with the natural order, the Rationalist error rejects it in its entirety, on the plea of philosophical impossibility or critical non-existence. The Syllabus of Pius IX and the Vatican Constitution "De fide catholica" (Denzinger, n. 1655) checked for a while that radical Naturalism which, however, has reappeared lately in a still more virulent form with Modernism. While there is nothing common between Rosmini and the present Modernists, he may, all unwittingly, have paved the way for them in the following vaguely Subjectivist proposition: "The supernatural order consists in the manifestation of Being in the plenitude of its reality, and the effect of that manifestation is a God-like sentiment, inchoate in this life through the light of faith and grace, consummate in the next through the light of glory" (36th Rosminian proposition condemned by the Holy Office, 14 Dec., 1887). Preserving the dogmatic formulæ while voiding them of their contents, the Modernists constantly speak of the supernatural, but they understand thereby the advanced stages of an evolutive process of the religious sentiment There is no room in their system for the objective and revealed supernatural: their Agnosticism declares it unknowable, their Immanentism derives it from our own vitality, their symbolism explains it in term of subjective experience and their criticism declares non-authentic the documents used to prove it. "There is no question now," says Pius X, in his Encyclical "Pascendi" of 8 Sept., 1907, "of the old error by which a sort of right to the supernatural was claimed for human nature. We have gone far beyond that. We have reached the point where it is affirmed that our most holy religion, in the man Christ as in us, emanated from nature spontaneously and entirely. Than this, there is surely nothing more destructive of the whole supernatural order."

II. CATHOLIC DOCTRINE.—From the above documents, it may be summarized in three points: (1) The fact of man's elevation to grace and glory as against the Pelagian error; (2) the supernatural character of that elevation as against the Protestant and Jansenist theory; and (3) as against Rationalism, its possibility and the validity of its credentials.

(1) The fact of man's elevation, probably alluded to in the likeness of God imprinted in Adam (Gen., i, 26), in the tree of life from which he was barred in consequence of his sin (Gen., iii, 22), and in the intimate union of man with God, as described in the Sapiential and Prophetic books, has its full expression in the discourses of Jesus Christ (John, vi and xiv-xvii), in the prologue of the Fourth Gospel compared with John, ii and iii, and in the introduction to several Epistles like I Cor., Eph., and I Pet. The direct and face-to-face vision of God is our future destiny (I Cor., xiii, 12; I John, iii, 2). In this world we are not in name only but in very fact the sons of God (I John, iii, 1), being born anew (I John, iii, 7) and having the charity of God infused in our hearts by the Holy Ghost who is given to us (Rom., v, 5). The emphasis laid by the early Fathers on man's deification has been shown elsewhere (see ADOPTION). In view of all this it is not true that the Fathers had not even a name to designate the supernatural, as is often asserted by modern critics. De Broglie (Le surnaturel, p. 45) shows that there were at least four different phrases to express the supernatural gifts: ὑπὲρ φύσιν (above nature), adscititia (super-added), ἔξωθεν τῆς οὐσίας (foreign to the essence), χάρις, χαρίσματα (gratuitous).

(2) The gratuitous or supernatural character of the beatific vision was placed in bold relief by St. Paul (I Tim., vi, 15) and St. John (i, 18 and vi, 46). St. Irenæus merely paraphrases their teaching in the famous sentence: "Homo a se non videt Deum; ille autem volens videre hominibus quibus vult, quando vult, quemadmodum vult; potens est enim in omnibus Deus" (Contra hæres., v, 20). Neither can one read such passages as Eph., i, 16-19 and iii, 14-21; Col., i, 10 sq.; II Pet., i, 4; etc., without realizing that the supernatural character of the intuitive vision applies likewise to present charity "which surpasses all knowledge". The transcendence of the supernatural order, not only above our present *de facto* condition, but also above our native constitution viewed philosophically in the elements and properties and exigencies of human nature, is not emphasized in early Christian literature, which deals not with abstractions. St. Paul, however, describing the rôle of the Redeemer which is to renovate, repair, and restore, comes very near the point by hinting that our present, clearly supernatural elevation is but a return to the no less supernatural condition of the "old Adam"; and while the point is not fully discussed by the Fathers before the Pelagian controversies concerning original sin, yet some passing remarks by St. Irenæus (Contra hæres., III, xviii, l, 2) and St. John Chrysostom (X Homily on St. John, 2) show that there is no chasm between the early Fathers, St. Augustine, who presented a bold, if not finished, delineation of the supernatural as such, and the Schoolmen and post-Tridentine theologians (as Soto, "De natura et gratia"; Ripalda, "De ente supernaturali"; Suarez, "De variis statibus") who carefully distinguished the various states of human nature. Ripalda's opinion to the effect that the beatific vision which is *de facto* supernatural

to the whole actual creation might become natural to some possible higher creature, has never been formally condemned by the Church; it is however unanimously rejected by theologians, as it seems less conformable to Scriptural sayings and tends to destroy the absolute transcendence of the supernatural order.

(3) The philosophical possibility and the critical ascertainment of the supernatural order are the central point of Christian apologetics. Against the prejudicial views of the Rationalists who pronounce it inexistent, or unnecessary, or mischievous, or even impossible, Christian apologists urge, and to good purpose, the critical value of the records on which it rests, its quasi-necessity for the correct conduct of life, the profits it brings to its recipients, and the utter want of foundation of its so-called antinomies. Having thus cleared the ground, they proceed to collect and interpret and organize the various data of Revelation, the result being a harmonious and truly grandiose system of overlife. From the commonly received axiom that "grace does not destroy but only perfects nature" they establish between the two orders a parallelism that is not mutual confusion or reciprocal exclusion, but distinction and subordination. The Schoolmen spoke freely of nature's possibilities (*potentia obedientialis*) and even conations (*appetitus naturalis*) towards the supernatural. To those traditional methods and views some Christian writers have, of late, endeavoured to add and even substitute another theory which, they claim, will bring the supernatural home to the modern mind and give it unquestionable credentials. The novel theory consists in making nature postulate the supernatural. Whatever be the legitimacy of the purpose, the method is ambiguous and full of pitfalls. Between the Schoolmen's *potentia obedientialis* and *appetitus moralis* and the Modernist tenet according to which the supernatural "emanates from nature spontaneously and entirely" there is space and distance; at the same time, the Catholic apologist who would attempt to fill some of the space and cover some of the distance should keep in mind the admonition of Pius X to those "Catholics who, while rejecting immanence as a doctrine, employ it as a method of apologetics, and who do this so imprudently that they seem to admit that there is in human nature a true and rigorous necessity with regard to the supernatural order and not merely a capacity and suitability for the supernatural such as has at all times been emphasized by Catholic apologists" (Encyclical "Pascendi").

RIPALDA, *De ente supernaturali* (Paris, 1870); SCHRADER, *De triplici ordine* (Vienna, 1864); TERRIEN, *La grace et la gloire* (Paris, 1897); BAINVEL, *Nature et surnaturel* (Paris, 1903); DE BROGLIE, *Le surnaturel* (Paris, 1908); LIGEARD, *Le rapport de la nature et du surnaturel d'après les théologiens scolastiques du XIII⁵ au XVIII⁵ siècles* (Paris, 1910). A more complete bibliography is found in: WILHELM AND SCANNELL, *Manual of Cath. Theology*, I (London, 1906), 430; TANQUEREY, *Synopsis theol. dogmat.*, I (New York), 345; BAREILLES, *Le catéchisme romain*, III (Montrejeau, 1908), 352; LABAUCHE, . . . *L'homme* . . . in *Leçons de théol. dogmatique* (Paris, 1908).

J. F. SOLLIER.

Superpellicium. See SURPLICE.

Superstition [from *supersisto*, "to stand in terror of the deity" (Cicero, "De Nat. deorum", I, xlii, 117); or from *superstes*, "surviving": "Qui totos dies precabantur et immolabant, ut sibi sui liberi superstites essent, superstitiosi sunt appellati", i. e. "Those who for whole days prayed and offered sacrifice that their children might survive them, were called superstitious" (Cicero, ibid., II, xxviii, 72). Cicero also drew the distinction: "Superstitio est in qua timor inanis deorum, religio quæ deorum cultu pio continetur", i. e. "Superstition is the baseless fear of the gods, religion the pious worship." According to Isidore of Seville (Etymolog., l. 8, c. iii, sent.), the word comes from *superstatuo* or *superinstituo*: "Superstitio est superflua observantia in cultu super statuta seu instituta superiorum", i. e. "observances added on to prescribed or established worship"] is defined by St. Thomas (II-II, Q. xcii, a. 1) as "a vice opposed to religion by way of excess; not because in the worship of God it does more than true religion, but because it offers Divine worship to beings other than God or offers worship to God in an improper manner". Superstition sins by excess of religion, and this differs from the vice of irreligion, which sins by defect. The theological virtue of religion stands midway between the two. (II-II, Q. xcii, a. 1.)

DIVISION.—There are four species of superstitions: (1) improper worship of the true God (*indebitus veri Dei cultus*); (2) idolatry; (3) divination; (4) vain observances, which include magic and occult arts. This division is based upon the various ways in which religion may be vitiated by excess. Worship becomes *indebitus cultus* when incongruous, meaningless, improper elements are added to the proper and approved performance; it becomes idolatrous when it is offered to creatures set up as divinities or endowed with divine attributes. Divination (q. v.) consists in the attempt to extract from creatures, by means of religious rites, a knowledge of future events or of things known to God alone. Under the head of vain observances come all those beliefs and practices which, at least by implication, attribute supernatural or preternatural powers for good or for evil to causes evidently incapable of producing the expected effects. The number and variety of superstitions appear from the following list of those most in vogue at different periods of history: astrology, the reading of the future and of man's destiny from the stars; aeromancy, divinations by means of the air and winds; amulets, things worn as a remedy or preservative against evils or mischief, such as diseases or witchcraft; chiromancy, or palmistry, divination by the lines of the hand; capnomancy, by the ascent or motion of smoke; catroptomancy, by mirrors; alomancy, by salt; cartomancy, by playing cards; anthropomancy, by inspection of human viscera; belomancy, by the shuffling of arrows (Ezechiel, xxi, 21); geomancy, by points, lines, or figures traced on the ground; hydromancy, by water; idolatry, the worship of idols; Sabianism, the worship of the sun, moon, and stars; Zoolatry, Anthropolatry, and Fetishism, the worship of animals, man, and things without sense; Devil-worship; the worship of abstract notions personified, e. g. Victory, Peace, Fame, Concord, which had temples and a priesthood for the performance of their cult; necromancy, the evocation of the dead, as old as history and perpetuated in contemporary Spiritism; oneiromancy, the interpretation of dreams; philtres, potions, or charms intended to excite love; omens or prognostics of future events; witchcraft and magic in all their ramifications; lucky and unlucky days, numbers, persons, things, actions; the evil eye, spells, incantations, ordeals, etc.

ORIGIN.—The source of superstition is, in the first place, subjective. Ignorance of natural causes leads to the belief that certain striking phenomena express the will or the anger of some invisible overruling power, and the objects in which such phenomena appear are forthwith deified, as, e. g. in Nature-worship. Conversely, many superstitious practices are due to an exaggerated notion or a false interpretation of natural events, so that effects are sought which are beyond the efficiency of physical causes. Curiosity also with regard to things that are hidden or are still in the future plays a considerable part, e. g. in the various kinds of divination. But the chief source of superstition is pointed out in Scripture: "All men are vain, in whom there is not the knowledge of God: and who by these good things that are seen, could not understand him that is, neither by attending to the works have acknowledged who was the workman: but have imagined either the fire, or the wind, or the swift air, or the circle of the stars, or the great water, or the sun and moon, to be the gods that rule the world" (Wisdom, xiii, 1–2). It is to this ignorance of the true God, coupled with an inordinate veneration for human excellence and the love of artistic representations appealing to the senses, that St. Thomas ascribes the origin of idolatry. While these are dispositive causes, the consummative cause, he adds, was the influence of demons who offered themselves as objects of worship to erring men, giving answers through idols and doing things which to men seemed marvellous (II–II, Q. xciv, a. 4).

These causes explain the origin and spread of superstition in the pagan world. They were to a large extent eliminated by the preaching of Christianity; but so deep-rooted was the tendency to which they gave rise that many of the ancient practices survived, especially among peoples just emerging from barbarism. It was only by degrees, through the legislation of the Church and the advance of scientific knowledge, that the earlier forms of superstition were eradicated. But the tendency itself has not wholly disappeared. Side by side with the Rationalistic philosophy and the rigorous scientific methods which are characteristic of modern thought, there are still to be found various sorts of superstition. So far as this includes the worship of things other than God, it is not only an essential part, but the foundation also of the Positivistic system (Comte), which sets up humanity as the object of religious worship (see POSITIVISM). Nor can Pantheism (q. v.), which identifies God and the world, lead consistently to any but superstitious practices, however it may in theory disclaim such a purpose. The human mind, by a natural impulse, tends to worship something, and if it is convinced that Agnosticism is true and that God is unknowable, it will, sooner or later, devise other objects of worship. It is also significant that just when many scientists supposed that belief in a future life had been finally proved an illusion, Spiritism (q. v.), with its doctrines and practices, should have gained such a strong hold not only on the ignorant, but also, and in a much more serious sense, on leading representatives of science itself. This may indeed be interpreted as a reaction against Materialism; but it is none the less, at bottom, an evidence of man's restless desire to penetrate, by any and every means, the mystery that lies beyond death. While it is easy to condemn Spiritism as superstitious and vain, the condemnation does not do away with the fact that Spiritism has become widespread in this age of enlightenment. Now as in the past the rejection of Divine truth in the name of reason often opens the way to beliefs and practices which are at once unworthy of reason and dangerous to morality.

SINFULNESS OF SUPERSTITION IN GENERAL.—Superstition of any description is a transgression of the First Commandment: "I am the Lord thy God,— thou shalt not have strange gods before me. Thou shalt not make to thyself a graven thing, nor the likeness of anything that is in heaven above, or in the earth beneath . . . thou shalt not adore them nor serve them" (Exod., xx, 2–5). It is also against the positive law of the Church, which visits the worst kinds of superstition with severe punishments, and against the natural law inasmuch as it runs counter to the dictates of reason in the matter of man's relations to God. Such objective sinfulness is inherent in all superstitious practices from idolatry down to the vainest of vain observances, of course in very different degrees of gravity. With regard to the subjective guilt attaching to them it must be borne in mind that no sin is mortal unless committed with full knowledge of its grievous wickedness and with full deliberation and consent. Of these essential factors the first is often wanting entirely, and the second is only imperfectly present. The numerous cases in which the event seemed to justify the superstitious practice, and the universality of such incongruous beliefs and performances, though they may not always induce inculpable ignorance, may possibly obscure the knowledge and weaken the will to a point incompatible with mortal sin. As a matter of fact, many superstitions of our own day have been acts of genuine piety at other times, and may be so still in the hearts of simple folk.

SPECIAL SUPERSTITIONS.—The principal species of superstition, viz., idolatry, divination, occult arts, have received adequate treatment in other articles. Something remains to be said on (1) *cultus indebitus*, or the pious vagaries which people intermingle with Catholic religion; (2) vain observances in daily life.

(1) Improper worship (*cultus indebitus*) consists in introducing *false* or superfluous elements into the practice of true religion. Such false elements, be their origin culpable deceit or inculpable credulity, vitiate the virtue of religion by substituting error for truth in the service of God. A layman performing priestly functions, a pardoner selling spurious indulgences, a fanatic devotee inventing false miracles and answers to prayers in order to introduce or spread his own favourite devotion, wholesale believers in supernatural apparitions, visions, revelations, which serve no good purpose—all these are guilty of superstition, at least material. As regards formal guilt, this is often reduced to the vanishing point by the prevailing credulity and common practice of the period. The worship of imaginary saints or relics, devotion based upon false revelations, apparitions, supposed miracles, or false notions generally, is usually excusable in the worshipper on the ground of ignorance and good faith; but there is no excuse for those who use similar means to exploit popular credulity for their own pecuniary profit. The originators of such falsehoods are liars, deceivers, and not rarely thieves; but a milder judgment should be pronounced on those who, after discovering the imposture, tolerate the improper cultus. For it is no easy matter, even for the highest authorities, to eradicate beliefs or to check the growth of devotions which have taken a strong hold on the popular mind: the long struggle of the Inquisition with the Spiritual Franciscans, who, on the assumption that the rule of St. Francis was a direct revelation from heaven, attributed to the practice of poverty an exaggerated importance, and cheerfully went to the stake rather than relinquish their ways, is but one example among scores that could be cited. There is always the fear of uprooting the wheat with the tares, and the hope of seeing the improper worship die a natural death; for devotions also have their changing seasons. The pope and the bishops are the proper authorities to act in these matters, for to them belongs the regulation of worship, both public and private, and it is the duty of every Catholic to abide by their decision.

The same reflections apply to another kind of improper worship, the *cultus superfluus* which consists in expecting from certain pre-arranged circumstances a greater efficacy of the religious performance; e. g. to expect a greater benefit from Masses said before sunrise with a certain number of candles disposed in a certain order, by a priest bearing a special saint's name or being of the supposed stature of Christ. Triduums, novenas, First Friday Communions, nine consecutive First Friday Communions, Saturday fasting, though they seem to attach special importance to number and dates, are approved by the Church, because these dates and numbers are convenient for shaping and regulating certain excellent devotions. The Catholic devotions which are connected with holy places, holy shrines, holy wells, famous relics, etc. are commonly treated as superstitious by non-Catholics who either reject all worship of saints and relics or assume pious frauds on the part of the priests who benefit by the

THE LAST SUPPER

PAINTING BY E. VON GEBHARDT, BERLIN

worship. It must be admitted that these hallowed spots and things have occasioned many legends; that popular credulity was in some cases the principal cause of their celebrity; that here and there instances of fraud can be adduced; yet, for all that, the principles which guide the worshipper, and his good intentions, are not impaired by an undercurrent of error as to facts. If superstition there be, it is only material. Moreover, the Church is always careful to remove any fraud or error inconsistent with true devotion, although she is tolerant of "pious beliefs" which have helped to further Christian piety. Thus, alleged saints and relics are suppressed as soon as discovered, but belief in the private revelations to which the feast of Corpus Christi, the Rosary, the Sacred Heart and many other devotions owe their origin is neither commanded nor prohibited; here each man is his own judge.

(2) Turning now to vain observances in daily life, properly so called, we first meet with the superstitions observed in the administration of justice during many centuries of the Middle Ages, and known as ordeals or "judgments of God". Among the early Germans a man accused of a crime had to prove his innocence, no proof of his guilt being incumbent on his accusers. The oath of a free man, strengthened by the oaths of friends, sufficed to establish his innocence, but when the oath was refused or the required number of "compurgators" failed, the defendant, if he was a free man, had to fight his accuser in single combat; bondmen and women had either to find a champion to fight for them or to undergo some other form of ordeal as fixed by law, arranged by the judge, or chosen by one of the parties. Besides the judicial combat the early German laws recognized as legitimate means to discriminate between guilt and innocence the casting or drawing of lots, trial by fire in several forms—holding one's hand in fire for a determined length of time; passing between two piles of burning wood with no covering for the body except a shirt impregnated with wax; carrying with the naked hand a red-hot iron weighing from one to three pounds a distance of from nine to twelve paces; walking barefoot over nine red-hot ploughshares disposed in a line nine steps long. At the root of these and many analogous practices (see ORDEALS) lay the firm belief that God would work a miracle rather than allow the innocent to perish or the wicked to prevail. These "judgments of God" gave rise to new superstitions. Whether guilty or not, persons subjected to the trials would often put more confidence in charms, magic formulas, and ointments than in the intervention of Providence. The ordeals gradually gave way before the rationalistic temper of modern times; trials by torture, which survived the ordeals, seem to have been inspired by the same idea, that God will protect the innocent and give them superhuman endurance.

The power of the evil eye (*fascinatio*) has been believed in for a long time, and is still dreaded in many countries. The number thirteen continues to strike terror into the breasts of men who profess not to fear God. The apparent success which so often attends a superstition can mostly be accounted for by natural causes, although it would be rash to deny all supernatural intervention (e. g. in the phenomena of Spiritism). When the object is to ascertain, or to effect in a general way, one of two possible events, the law of probabilities gives an equal chance to success and failure, and success does more to support than failure would do to destroy superstition, for, on its side, there are arrayed the religious instinct, sympathy and apathy, confidence and distrust, encouragement and discouragement, self-suggestion and—perhaps strongest of all—the healing power of nature.

ST. THOMAS, *Summa*, II-II, QQ. xcii–xcvi; ST. ALPHONSUS LIGUORI, *Theol. Mor.*, IV, i, ed. LE NOIR (Lyons, 1873), contains useful notes; FERRARIS, *Prompta Bibliotheca*, s. v. *Superstitio*; SIMAR, *Der Aberglaube* (3d ed., 1894); THIERS, *Tracté des Superstitions* (2 vols., Paris, 1679; 2 more vols., Paris, 1704) (a work of immense erudition, but put on the Index by decrees of 13 Feb., 1702, and 10 May, 1757); BRAND, *Observations on Popular Antiquities* (London, 1888) (a classic on English superstition); GÖPFERT, *Moraltheologie*, I (2nd ed., Paderborn, 1899). See also bibliography under DIVINATION; NECROMANCY; ORDEALS; SPIRITISM.

J. WILHELM.

Supper, THE LAST, the meal held by Christ and His disciples on the eve of His Passion at which He instituted the Holy Eucharist.

TIME.—The Evangelists and critics generally agree that the Last Supper was on a Thursday, that Christ suffered and died on Friday, and that He arose from the dead on Sunday. As to the day of the month there seems a difference between the record of the synoptic Gospels and that of St. John. In consequence some critics have rejected the authenticity of either account or of both. Since Christians, accepting the inspiration of the Scriptures, cannot admit contradictions in the sacred writers, various attempts have been made to reconcile the statements. Matt., xxvi, 17, says, "And on the first day of the Azymes"; Mark, xiv, 12, "Now on the first day of the unleavened bread, when they sacrificed the pasch"; Luke, xxii, 7, "And the day of the unleavened bread came, on which it was necessary that the pasch should be killed". From these passages it seems to follow that Jesus and his disciples conformed to the ordinary custom, that the Last Supper took place on the 14th of Nisan, and that the Crucifixion was on the 15th, the great festival of the Jews. This opinion, held by Tolet, Cornelius a Lapide, Patrizi, Corluy, Hengstenberg, Ohlshausen, and Tholuck, is confirmed by the custom of the early Eastern Church, which, looking to the day of the month, celebrated the commemoration of the Lord's Last Supper on the 14th of Nisan, without paying any attention to the day of the week. This was done in conformity with the teaching of St. John the Evangelist. But in his Gospel, St. John seems to indicate that Friday was the 14th of Nisan, for (xviii, 28) on the morning of this day the Jews "went not into the hall, that they might not be defiled, but that they might eat the pasch". Various things were done on this Friday which could not be done on a feast, viz., Christ is arrested, tried, crucified; His body is taken down "(because it was the parasceve) that the bodies might not remain upon the cross on the sabbath day (for that was a great sabbath day)"; the shroud and ointments are bought, and so on.

The defenders of this opinion claim that there is only an apparent contradiction and that the differing statements may be reconciled. For the Jews calculated their festivals and Sabbaths from sunset to sunset: thus the Sabbath began after sunset on Friday and ended at sunset on Saturday. This style is employed by the synoptic Gospels, while St. John, writing about twenty-six years after the destruction of Jerusalem, when Jewish laws and customs no longer prevailed, may well have used the Roman method of computing time: from midnight to midnight. The word *pasch* does not exclusively apply to the paschal lamb on the eve of the feast, but is used in the Scriptures and in the Talmud in a wider sense for the entire festivity, including the *chagigah;* any legal defilement could have been removed by the evening ablutions; trials, and even executions and many servile works, though forbidden on the Sabbath, were not forbidden on feasts (Num., xxviii, 16; Deut., xvi, 23). The word *parasceve* may denote the preparation for any Sabbath and may be the common designation for any Friday, and its connexion with pasch need not mean preparation for the Passover but Friday of the Passover season, and hence this Sabbath was a great Sabbath. Moreover it seems quite certain that if St. John intended to give a different date from that given by the Synoptics and sanctioned by the custom of his own

Church at Ephesus, he would have said so expressly. Others accept the apparent statement of St. John that the Last Supper was on the 13th of Nisan and try to reconcile the account of the Synoptics. To this class belong Paul of Burgos, Maldonatus, Petau, Hardouin, Tillemont, and others. Peter of Alexandria (P. G., XCII, 78) says: "In previous years Jesus had kept the Passover and eaten the paschal lamb, but on the day before He suffered as the true Paschal Lamb He taught His disciples the mystery of the type." Others say: Since the Pasch, falling that year on a Friday, was reckoned as a Sabbath, the Jews, to avoid the inconvenience of two successive Sabbaths, had postponed the Passover for a day, and Jesus adhered to the day fixed by law; others think that Jesus anticipated the celebration, knowing that at the proper time He would be in the grave.

PLACE.—The owner of the house in which was the upper room of the Last Supper is not mentioned in Scripture; but he must have been one of the disciples, since Christ bids Peter and John say, "The Master says". Some say it was Nicodemus, or Joseph of Arimathea, or the mother of John Mark. The hall was large and furnished as a dining-room. In it Christ showed Himself after His Resurrection; here took place the election of Matthias to the Apostolate and the sending of the Holy Ghost; here the first Christians assembled for the breaking of bread; hither Peter and John came when they had given testimony after the cure of the man born lame, and Peter after his liberation from prison; here perhaps was the council of the Apostles held. It was for a while the only church in Jerusalem, the mother of all churches, known as the Church of the Apostles, or of Sion. It was visited in 404 by St. Paula of Rome. In the eleventh century it was destroyed by the Saracens, later rebuilt and given to the care of the Augustinians. Restored after a second destruction, it was placed in charge of the Franciscans, who were driven out in 1561. At present it is a Mohammedan mosque.

SEQUENCE OF EVENTS.—Some critics give the following harmonized order: washing of the feet of the Apostles, prediction of the betrayal and departure of Judas, institution of the Holy Eucharist. Others, believing that Judas made a sacrilegious communion, place the institution of the sacrament before the departure of Judas.

IN ART.—The Last Supper has been a favourite subject. In the catacombs we find representations of meals giving at least an idea of the surroundings of an ancient dining hall. Of the sixth century we have a bas-relief in the church at Monza in Italy, a picture in a Syrian codex of the Laurentian Library at Florence, and a mosaic in S. Apollinare Nuovo at Ravenna. One of the most popular pictures is that of Leonardo da Vinci in Santa Maria delle Grazie, Milan. Among the modern school of German artists, the Last Supper of Gebhardt is regarded as a masterpiece.

FOUARD, *The Christ, the Son of God*, tr. GRIFFITH, II (London, 1895), 386; MADAME CECILIA, *Cath. Scripture Manuals: St. Matthew*, II, 197; *The Expository Times*, XX (Edinburgh, 1909), 514; *Theolog. praktische Quartalschrift* (1877), 425; LANGEN, *Die letzten Lebenstage Jesu* (Freiburg, 1864), 27; KRAUS, *Gesch. der chr. Kunst*, s. v. *Abendmahl*; *Stimmen aus Maria Laach*, XLIX, 146; CHWOLSON in *Mém. de l'Acad. impér. des Sciences de St. Pétersbourg*, 7th ser., XLI, p. 37; VIGOUROUX, *Dict. de la Bible* (Paris, 1899), s. vv. *Cène; Cénacle*, where a full bibliography may be found.

FRANCIS MERSHMAN.

Suppression of Monasteries. See MONASTERIES, SUPPRESSION OF.

Supralapsarianism. See CALVINISM; INFRALAPSARIANS.

Supremacy, ACT OF. See ENGLAND; OATHS, ENGLISH POST-REFORMATION.

Supremi disciplinæ, Motu Proprio of Pius X, promulgated 2 July, 1911, relating to Holy Days of obligation. On Holy Days of precept a twofold duty is incumbent on the faithful, of hearing Mass and of abstaining from servile work. Owing particularly to the high cost of living and to the necessity of caring in due season for crops, fruits, etc., the discipline of the Church has tended to lessen the number of Holy Days in certain countries. Pius X deemed it advisable to extend this policy to the Universal Church, thus effecting greater uniformity. Aside, then, from all Sundays, the obligation of hearing Mass and abstaining from servile work is now confined to eight days: Christmas, New Year's Day or the feast of the Circumcision, Epiphany (6 Jan.), the Ascension of Our Lord, the Immaculate Conception (8 Dec.), the Assumption of the Blessed Virgin (15 Aug.), the feast of Sts. Peter and Paul (29 June), and, finally, the feast of All Saints (1 Nov.). Where, however, any of the above feasts has been abolished or transferred, the new legislation is not effective. In the United States consequently the Epiphany and the feast of Sts. Peter and Paul are not days of precept (see Third Plenary Council of Baltimore, tit. III, c. ii and p. cv). Feasts of patrons are no longer Holy Days of obligation. Bishops may, if they choose, transfer the celebration of these patronal feasts to the following Sunday in accordance with liturgical laws. If it is desired in certain countries or dioceses to retain as days of precept one or other feast abrogated by the Constitution "Supremi disciplinæ", permission must be obtained from the Holy See.

There is no longer any obligation, as formerly in many countries, of assisting at the Holy Sacrifice or abstaining from servile work on the feast of St. Joseph (19 March), the Nativity of St. John the Baptist (24 June), or Corpus Christi. According to the present Motu Proprio the feast of St. Joseph, with an octave, is to be celebrated on the Sunday following 19 March, unless that date fall on Sunday; the Nativity of St. John the Baptist on the Sunday preceding the feast of Sts. Peter and Paul (29 June); Corpus Christi on the first Sunday after Trinity Sunday. Scarcely, however, was the "Supremi disciplinæ" promulgated, when (S. R. C., 24 July) it was modified as follows: The solemn commemoration of St. Joseph without an octave remains on 19 March. The feast of the Patronage of St. Joseph, however, on the third Sunday after Easter is raised to a double of the first class, a primary feast with an octave. Likewise the feast of Corpus Christi with its privileged octave is observed as formerly on the Thursday after Trinity Sunday, but the solemnity of the feast is transferred to the following Sunday. Liturgical questions, to which the above changes gave rise, were settled by a Decree of the Sacred Congregation of Rites, 28 July, 1911.

The present Motu Proprio institutes another important change in legislation. As feasting and fasting are incompatible Pius X has abolished the obligation of fasting as well as that of abstinence for the Universal Church, should such obligation coincide with any of the eight feasts, as above. According to the "Nouvelle Revue Theologique", November, 1911, by decree of the S. Cong. of the Council, 28 August, 1911, this dispensation is not for feasts already suppressed, like the Epiphany in the United States. The same general dispensation from the laws of abstinence and fasting is granted by the Holy Father on patronal feasts, abolished by the present Constitution, should they be celebrated solemnly and with a large concourse of the faithful.

ANDREW B. MEEHAN.

Sura, titular see in Augusta Euphratensis, suffragan of Hierapolis. Sura, situated on the banks of the Euphrates, at the intersection of the roads from Palmyra and Beroea or Chalcis, was a military station, and at the beginning of the fifth century was the residence of the prefect of the *legio XVI Flavia Firma*. In his second Syrian campaign Chosroes assaulted the town; the Armenian, Arsaces, the *magister militum*, directed the defence; when he fell the inhabitants sent their bishop to Chosroes as an envoy; but the latter, incensed by the resistance he had met with, ordered the destruction of the town, which had held out only half an hour. Justinian erected powerful fortifications there. Its ruins, of little importance, are near the present military post of El Hamman, not far from Rekka in the vilayet of Aleppo. Le Quien, "Oriens christianus", II, 949, mentions three bishops of Sura: Uranius, represented by his metropolitan at Chalcedon, 451; Marion, exiled as a Monophysite in 518; and the one who was envoy to Chosroes, whose name is unknown. The see is mentioned in the "Notitiæ episcopatuum" of the Patriarchate of Antioch in the sixth and tenth centuries.

VAILHÉ in *Echos d'Orient*, X (Paris, 1907), 94, 145; SMITH, *Dict. of Greek and Roman Geog.*, s. v.; MÜLLER, *Notes à Ptolemy*, ed. Didot, I, 985; CHAPOT, *La frontière de l'Euphrate à la conquête arabe* (Paris, 1907), 285–88 and passim.

S. PÉTRIDÈS.

Surin, JEAN-JOSEPH, b. 1600; d. at Bordeaux, 1665. He belonged to the Society of Jesus, and enjoyed great celebrity for his admirable virtues, his trials, and his talents as a spiritual director. Bossuet declared him "consumed with spirituality". At the suggestion of the Fathers of the Province of Aquitaine, assembled in provincial congregation (1755), the father general ordered his name inscribed in the "Ménologe de l'assistance de France". At the age of eight he took a vow of chastity, at ten he was taught to meditate by a Carmelite. Having been sent to Loudun to exorcize certain Ursulines tormented by the evil one, he was so horrified at the terrible sacrileges intended for three desecrated hosts that he immediately made an offering of his own spirit to be possessed by demons in expiation for this frightful crime. His prayer was granted, and for more than twenty years he was harassed by evil spirits, plunged in the depths of despair over his eternal damnation. At times he was unable to use his hands, his feet, his eyes, his tongue, or was impelled to commit a thousand extravagances, which even the most charitably inclined deemed foolish. The wrong impression under which he laboured at such times caused him the greatest joy. At no time, however, did this state of obsession prevent his devoting himself to preaching. It is true he was unable to prepare himself for this by any reading or study, but on entering the pulpit and making the sign of the cross a wonderful transformation was manifest. His vigorous mind instantly gained the ascendancy; his powerful voice and facile oratory won universal attention and admiration. His physician declared it miraculous. Even in writing or dictating his works he seemed gifted with Divine inspiration. He was healed eight years before his death and was thenceforth absorbed in the abundance of Divine communications. His principal works are: "Catéchisme spirituel" (Paris, 1659), published by the Prince de Conti, anonymously; "Fondements de la vie spirituelle" (Paris, 1667); "Cantiques spirituels" (Paris, 1660); "Dialogues spirituels" (Paris, 1704); "Lettres spirituelles" (Paris, 1695). His "Catéchisme spirituel" is on the Index, but with certain modifications soon to be made, it will be taken from the list.

BOUIX, *Vie du Père Surin* (Paris, 1876), an abridgment of the life published by BOUDON (Paris, 1689); DE GUILHERMY, *Ménologe de la C. de J., Assistance de France* (Paris, 1892).

A. POULAIN.

Surius, LAURENTIUS, hagiologist, b. at the Hanseatic city of Lübeck, 1522; d. at Cologne, 23 May, 1578. It is not certain whether his parents were Catholics or Lutherans. According to a remark made by Peter Canisius ("Epistolæ", ed. Braunsberger, I, 36), he was born a heretic and was brought into the Church by Canisius. Surius studied at the universities of Frankfort-on-the-Oder and Cologne. In the latter university Peter Canisius was a fellow-student. Surius also met there Johannes Justus Lansperger, who induced him to enter the Carthusian monastery at Cologne, in 1542. The greater part of his life after this was spent in his monastery, where he was a model of piety, of rigid observance of the rules of the order, and of earnest work as a scholar; for these reasons he was held in high esteem by St. Pius V. He devoted himself chiefly to the domains of church history and hagiography, and wrote a large number of works on these subjects. He also translated into Latin many works, mainly ascetical and theological. Among these translations should be mentioned writings by Tauler, Heinrich Seuse, Ruysbroeck, Gropper's work on the reality of Christ's Flesh and Blood, the sermons of Michael Sidonius, the apologies of Friedrich Staphylus, and an oration by Martin Eisengrein. He completed the "Institutiones" of Florentius of Haarlem, prior of the Carthusians of Louvain, and edited a new edition of the "Homiliarium" of Charlemagne. He wrote against Sleidanus his "Commentarius brevis rerum in orbe gestarum ab a. 1500 ad a. 1564" (Cologne, 1566), which was continued by others. He was also the author of a collection of the Acts of the councils: "Concilia omnia tum generalia tum provincialia" (4 vols., Cologne, 1567).

His most important and still valuable work is his collection of the lives of the saints, "De probatis Sanctorum historiis ab Al. Lipomano olim conscriptis nunc primum a Laur. Surio emendatis et auctis", the first edition of which appeared in six volumes at Cologne in 1570–77. He began a second edition which was finished after his death by his colleague in the monastery, Mosander, who added a seventh volume (Cologne, 1582). A third edition with an improved text appeared at Cologne in 1618; a new and revised edition was published (1875–80) at Turin in thirteen volumes. Notwithstanding the liberties taken by Surius with the text of the manuscripts he used, his work has rendered great service and has furnished many narratives concerning the lives of the saints that have been published in various languages.

HURTER, *Nomenclator*, III (3rd ed.), 111–115; HARTZHEIM, *Bibliotheca Coloniensis* (Cologne, 1747), 218 sq.; *Allgemeine deutsche Biographie*, s. v.

J. P. KIRSCH.

Surplice, a large-sleeved tunic of half length, made of fine linen or cotton, and worn by all the clergy. The wide sleeves distinguish it from the rochet and the alb; it differs further from the alb inasmuch as it is shorter and is never girded. It is ornamented at the hem and the sleeves either with embroidery, with lace-like insertions, or with lace. The lace should never be more than fifteen inches wide, as otherwise the real vestment is necessarily too much shortened by this merely ornamental addition. The surplice belongs to the liturgical vestment in the strict sense, and is the vestment most used. It is the choir dress, the vestment for processions, the official priestly dress of the lower clergy, the vestment worn by the priest in administering the sacraments, when giving blessings, at Benediction of the Blessed Sacrament, etc.; in the last-mentioned cases it is the substitute for the alb, which, according to present custom, is worn only at Mass and a few other functions. The blessing of the surplice by the bishop or by authorized priest is proper, but not strictly prescribed. As the distinctive sacerdotal dress of the lower clergy the bishop, after giving the tonsure, places it on the candidate for orders with these words: "May the Lord clothe thee with the new man, who is created in righteousness and true holiness after the image of God."

HISTORY.—The time of the introduction of the surplice cannot be exactly determined. Without doubt it was originally merely a choir vestment and a garment to be worn at processions, burials, and on similar occasions. As a liturgical dress in this sense it is met outside of Italy (in England and France) as early as the eleventh century, but is not found in Italy until the twelfth century. The surplice may have been used in isolated cases during the twelfth century instead of the alb in administering the sacraments and at blessings, but this use did not become general until the thirteenth century; it appeared latest probably in Italy and especially at Rome, where it was hardly customary at these functions before the end of the thirteenth century. Towards the close of the twelfth century the surplice was already the distinctive dress of the lower clergy, even though this was not the case everywhere. However, the placing of the surplice on the clerics after the giving of the tonsure (cf. above), is first testified by the Pontificals of the fourteenth and fifteenth centuries.

The name of the surplice arises from the fact that it was worn by the clergy, especially in northern Europe, over (*super*) the universally customary fur clothing (*pelliceæ*). This is stated by Durandus and by the English grammarian Gerlandus, both of whom lived to the thirteenth century. The fur clothing not only led to the name of the surplice, but was probably also the cause of its appearance. For it is evident that a large-sleeved, ungirdled tunic was better suited to go over heavy fur coats than a narrow-sleeved, girded alb. It seems most probable that the surplice first appeared in France or England, whence its use gradually spread to Italy. It is possible that there is a connexion between the surplice and the Gallican alb, an ungirdled liturgical tunic of the old Gallican Rite, which was superseded during the Carlovingian era by the Roman Rite. The founding of the Augustinian Canons in the second half of the eleventh century may have had a special influence upon the spread of the surplice. Among the Augustinian Canons the surplice was not only the choir vestment, but also a part of the habit of the order. In addition to the surplice we find frequent early mention of a "cotta". It is possible that between the *superpelliceum* and the *cotta* there may have been some small difference (perhaps in length or width), but most probably these terms were only different names for the same liturgical vestment (cf. Braun, op. cit. in bibliography, p. 142).

Originally the surplice was a full-length tunic —that is, it reached to the feet. In the thirteenth century it began to be shortened, although in the fifteenth century it still reached halfway between the knee and ankle. In the sixteenth and seventeenth centuries it became steadily shorter until it fell a little above the knee; in the eighteenth century, however, it was so short that it frequently reached only just below the hips. As the length of the surplice was lessened, the length and breadth of the sleeves were naturally reduced, so that in this respect also there is a great difference between the original surplice and that of the eighteenth century. More striking than these mere alterations of size were other changes made in the surplice, some of which appeared as early as the thirteenth century, and by which its entire shape and appearance was more or less altered, various forms of the surplice being produced. Thus, surplices appeared with slit-up sleeves (thus with wings of materials rather than sleeves); then surplices which, besides being slit up on the under side of the sleeve, were also open at the sides, the surplices being thus like scapulars in form. Also surplices without sleeves, having mere slits for the arms; finally surplices resembling the medieval bell-shaped chasuble with only an opening in the middle for the head—this shape was customary in the sixteenth and seventeenth centuries, especially in Venetian territory. These variations met with the disapproval of provincial and diocesan synods, but their prohibitions had no permanent effect. The scapular-like band that took the place of the surplice among Augustinian Canons on non-liturgical occasions is not a curtailment of the surplice, but a substitute for it.

ORNAMENTATION.—In the Middle Ages the surplice apparently seldom received a rich ornamentation. In pictures and sculpture it appears as a garment hanging in many folds, but otherwise plain throughout. There is a surplice at Neustift near Brixen in the Tyrol that dates back to the twelfth (or, at least, to the thirteenth) century; it is the only medieval surplice that we possess. This surplice shows geometrical ornaments in white linen embroidery on the shoulders, breast, back, and below the shoulders, where, as in the albs of the same date, large full gores have been inserted in the body of the garment. After the lace industry developed in the sixteenth century the hem and sleeves of the surplice were often trimmed with lace—at a later period, unfortunately, too often at the expense of the vestment itself. It apparently did not become customary to lay the surplice in folds until the close of the Middle Ages. This custom had vogue especially in Italy, but it frequently degenerated into undignified straining after effect and effeminate display.

BRAUN, *Die liturg. Gewandung im Occident u. Orient* (Freiburg, 1907); ROHAULT DE FLEURY, *La Messe*, VII (Paris, 1888); BOCK, *Gesch. der liturg. Gewänder*, II (Bonn, 1866).

JOSEPH BRAUN.

Susa (Heb. שׁוּשָׁן; Gr. Σοῦσαν, Σοῦσα), the capital of the Kingdom of Elam, and from the time of Cyrus, or more probably of Darius I, the winter residence of the kings of Persia. It was situated on the River Ulai or Eulæus (Dan., viii, 2, 16; Pliny, "Hist. Nat.", VI, 27), which was probably a branch of the Choaspes, now the Kerkha, formerly connected with the Pasitigris, now the Karun. After an existence of more than fifteen centuries the city was destroyed by Assurbanipal about 647 B. C., but it rose from its ruins, and under Persian rule enjoyed great prosperity. It began to decay under the Seleucids, and after the destruction of the Sassanid monarchy by the Arabs it was gradually abandoned. The "castle" (II Esd., i, 1; Dan., viii, 2), or acropolis, was distinct and separated from the city, though in the Book of Esther the Vulgate neglects the distinction (in i, 2, 5; ii, 3, 5, 8.; iii, 15; viii, 14; ix, 6, 11, 12, the "castle", and not the city, is meant). Here Darius I built a vast palace, in which under his successor occurred the events narrated in the Book of Esther. The ruins of the acropolis, covering about 300 acres, have been explored by Williams and Loftus, and more thoroughly by Dieulafoy and de Morgan. The excavations have yielded some important finds, among others the code of Hammurabi.

LOFTUS, *Chaldæa and Susiana* (London, 1857), 344 sqq.; DIEULAFOY, *La Perse, la Chaldée, et la Susiane* (Paris, 1887); IDEM, *L'Acropole de Suse* (Paris, 1893); JANE DIEULAFOY, *A Suse: Journal des Fouilles* (Paris, 1888); DE MORGAN, *Délégation en Perse* (Paris, 1899—); BILLERBECK, *Susa* (Leipzig, 1893).

F. BECHTEL.

Susa (SEGUSIN), DIOCESE OF (SEGUSIENSIS), in the Province of Turin, Piedmont, Northern Italy. The city is situated at an elevation of about 1600 feet above sea-level, in a wide valley to the right of

CAMPANILE OF THE CATHEDRAL, SUSA

the Dora Riparia; near by are some valuable marble quarries (*verde di Susa*). The cathedral, dedicated to St. Justus and founded by Ulderico Manfredi, (1029) contains much of interest: specimens of very fine inlaid work in the choir stalls; the baptismal font and the bronze group of the "Madonna del Roccia Melone" (Madonna with the Child, St. George transfixing the dragon, and a knight on bended knee); in a chapel may be seen the tomb of the Countess Adelaide, with her statue in wood, an excellent example of eleventh-century work. In ancient times the city was called Segusio, and in the days of Augustus it still had a king, who held sway over fourteen other towns. This king submitted voluntarily to the Romans and erected, in honour of Augustus, a triumphal arch, which still exists. Under Nero the kingdom was abolished and became a municipium. In addition to the arch, there still exist the ruins of the Thermæ Gratianæ constructed by Valentinian I. Susa being situated near one of the principal Alpine valleys was always a place of great strategic importance. Constantine destroyed it while advancing against Maxentius; after the Langobard invasion, the Byzantine garrison remained there till 593. Later it came into possession of the Franks. It was captured twice by Pepin and once by Charlemagne (774), who by a skilful manœuvre compelled the Lombards to fall back on Pavia. From that time it formed part of the Kingdom of Italy. In 942 it became the residence of Ardoino Glabrio, Count of Susa and later Marquis of Turin, who was succeeded by Manfredo (975), Olderico (1001), and Adelaide (1034). The latter having married Odo of Savoy in her third marriage, Susa passed into the power of Savoy. In the twelfth century it acquired communal liberty; though destroyed (1174) by Barbarossa, it soon rose again, and in 1197 had already adopted new statutes. In the wars of the thirteenth century it sided with the Guelphs, and was a subject of dispute between the marquises of Saluzzo and the counts of Savoy; it was definitely given to the latter in 1295. Later during the wars of the sixteenth and eighteenth centuries it fell on five occasions into the hands of the French (1536–62; 1628–31; 1639–42; 1704–7; 1798–1814); in 1798 the fortifications constructed by the dukes of Savoy were dismantled.

In early days, Susa seems to have belonged to the Diocese of Maurienne. The Abbey of St. Justus having been erected in 1029, the abbot had quasi-episcopal jurisdiction. The Benedictines succeeded the Canons Regular, and under Benedict XIV were replaced by secular canons. In 1772 this prelacy *nullius* became a diocese, and the territory of the famous Abbey of Novalesa was added to that of Susa. The first bishop was Francesco M. Ferraris. Napoleon suppressed the see in 1803, but it was restored in 1817, and its territory increased by the inclusion of the Abbey S. Michele della Chiusa. The diocese, suffragan of Turin, contains 61 parishes with 75,000 inhabitants, and 130 secular and regular priests; 5 religious houses of men and 7 of women; 3 institutes for boys and 3 for girls.

CAPPELLETTI, *Le Chiese d'Italia;* SACHETTI, *Memorie della Chiesa di Susa* (Turin, 1786); GENUI, *Il marchesato di Susa* (1891); BACCO, *Cenni storici su Avigliana e Susa* (Susa, 1881).

U. BENIGNI.

Susanna, SAINT. See TIBURTIUS AND SUSANNA, SAINTS.

Susanna. See DANIEL, BOOK OF.

Suso, HENRY. See HENRY SUSO, BLESSED.

Suspension, in canon law, is usually defined as a censure by which a cleric is deprived, entirely or partially, of the use of the power of orders, office, or benefice. Although ordinarily called a censure because it is generally a medicinal punishment inflicted after admonitions and intended to amend the delinquent, yet it is not necessarily so for it is occasionally employed as a chastisement for past offences. As early as the time of St. Cyprian (d. 258), we read of clerics deprived of the income of their charges and also of suspension from the determined functions for which one had been ordained. We know also that clerics were sometimes temporarily deprived of Communion (Can. Apost., 45; Conc. Illib., c. 21). The Council of Neocæsarea (Can. 1) in 315 decrees perpetual suspension from all functions for certain misdemeanours, while the Fourth Council of Carthage (can. 68), by forbidding a delinquent bishop to ordain, gives an example of partial suspension. Again, the Third Council of Orléans (can. 19) in 538 decrees suspension from orders but not from stipend, and the Council of Narbonne (can. 11) suspends certain clerics from receiving the fruits of their benefices.

When a suspension is total, a cleric is deprived of the exercise of every function and of every ecclesiastical right. When it is partial, it may be only from the exercise of one's sacred orders, or from his office which includes deprivation of the use of orders and jurisdiction, or from his benefice which deprives him of both administration and income. When a suspension is decreed absolutely and without limitation, it is understood to be a total suspension. A partial suspension deprives a cleric of the use of that power only which is expressed in the sentence. A cleric does not incur an irregularity when he violates a suspension imposed for a former transgression, because then there is no violation of a censure. The same holds good if he has been suspended for some defect of mind or body not blameworthy. Irregularity is contracted when a cleric performs a solemn act of sacred orders, from the use of which he had been suspended. Thus, if a bishop forbidden to celebrate Mass pontifically were to perform such a function, he would not incur irregularity because he does not thereby exercise any substantial act of episcopal orders. As the Church can not deprive a suspended cleric of the power of sacred orders, but only forbids their use, it follows that acts of sacred orders remain valid after suspension. On the other hand, acts of jurisdiction become null and void after a suspended cleric has been denounced by name, because the Church has power to deprive one totally of jurisdiction. Suspension *ex informata conscientia* has the same effect as a formal suspension, but it is not inflicted by judicial sentence, but as an extraordinary remedy, without the canonical monitions being necessary, and it is imposed for occult but grave crimes.

When a cleric has been suspended from the income of his benefice, it is not the Church's desire that he be reduced to actual want. Consequently sufficient support is to be given to him, provided he have no means of his own and be willing to amend. Even when he does not turn from his evil ways, the clerical dignity requires that he be not suffered to fall into extreme want or danger of starvation. The principal grounds on which suspension is incurred *ipso facto* in the present discipline of the Church are found in the Decrees of the Council of Trent and in the Constitution "Apostolicæ Sedis Moderationi", though a few others have been added. A cleric is relieved of suspension, if it was a censure, by the absolution of him to whom it was reserved in case of reservation. When it was inflicted for a definite time or under a certain condition, it ceases of itself when the limitation is fulfilled. If the suspension was perpetual and decreed on account of a former crime, it may be removed by mere dispensation of the proper authority.

TAUNTON, *The Law of the Church* (London, 1906), s. v.; SMITH, *The New Procedure in Criminal and Disciplinary Causes* (New York, 1890); SLATER-MARTIN, *Manual of Moral Theology*, II (New York, 1908).

WILLIAM H. W. FANNING.

Sutri. See NEPI AND SUTRI.

Sutton, ROBERT, VENERABLE, priest, martyr, b. at Burton-on-Trent; quartered at Stafford, 27 July, 1587. He is not to be confused with the Venerable Robert Sutton, who was a companion of the Venerable William Hartley (q. v.). He took the degree of M. A. from Christ Church, Oxford, 9 July, 1567, and became Rector of Lutterworth, Leicestershire, in 1571, but was converted by his younger brother William, afterwards S.J. With his younger brother Abraham, who matriculated from Hart Hall in 1576, aged 25, he arrived at Douai, 23 March, 1575 (1576). They were both ordained subdeacons at Cambrai in September, deacons in December, and priests in the following February; having said their first Masses, 7 March, they left for England, 19 March, 1577 (1578). Robert was arrested at Stafford, and condemned merely for being a priest. He was cut down alive. After the lapse of a year Catholics managed to secure one of his quarters, when the thumb and index-finger were found to be intact. Abraham Sutton gave Father John Gerard the thumb, which is now at Stonyhurst College.

POLLEN, *Acts of the English Martyrs* (London, 1891), 323–6; IDEM, *English Martyrs 1584–1603* (London, 1908), 288, 291; CHALLONER, *Missionary Priests*, I (Edinburgh, 1877), no. 44; KNOX, *Douay Diaries* (London, 1878); FOSTER, *Alumni Oxonienses*, early series (Oxford, 1892).

JOHN B. WAINEWRIGHT.

Sutton, SIR RICHARD, co-founder of Brasenose College, Oxford, date of birth unknown; d. September or October, 1524. He was the younger son of Sir William Sutton, of Sutton, Leicestershire. It is not known where he was educated, but he devoted himself to the legal profession, became a member of the Inner Temple, and achieved considerable success. In 1498 he was a privy councillor and held the valuable position of steward of the monastery of Sion, near London, to which house he gave benefactions of land. The chief work of his life was the building and endowment of Brasenose College, which he carried out in conjunction with Bishop Smyth of Lincoln. Their plans were laid in 1508, and during the following years Sutton bought for its endowment estates in Middlesex, Leicestershire, Oxfordshire, and Essex. These he formally made over to Brasenose in 1519, and in May, 1523, Brasenose Hall and Little University Hall, which he had leased from the university, were conveyed to the new college. His other benefactions during life or at death included the foundation of a chantry at Macclesfield or Sutton, the making of a highway at St. Giles-in-the-Fields, London, and donations or legacies to Corpus Christi College, Oxford, the Temple (wherein he held high office) and Clement's Inn, London, the monastery of Sion, and Macclesfield Grammar School. He was knighted by Henry VIII between May, 1522, and March, 1524. From his will it would seem that in earlier life he had been of strong Yorkist sympathies.

CHURTON, *Lives of William Smyth and Sir Richard Sutton* (Oxford, 1800); INDERWICK, *Calendar of the Inner Temple Records* (London, 1896); BUCHAN, *Brasenose College* (Oxford, 1898).

EDWIN BURTON.

SIR RICHARD SUTTON
From an engraving by Johan Faber, the Elder

Swan, ORDER OF THE, a pious confraternity, indulgenced by the pope, which arose in 1440 in the Electorate of Brandenburg, originally comprising, with the Elector Frederick at their head, thirty gentlemen and seven ladies united to pay special honour to the Blessed Virgin. It spread rapidly, numbering in 1464 about 330 members, as well as branches established in the Margraviate of Anspach (1465) and in the possessions of the Teutonic Order in Prussia. But Protestantism, by suppressing devotion to Mary, abolished the confraternity's *raison d'etre*. In 1843 King Frederick William IV of Prussia, in his infatuation for the Middle Ages, thought of re-establishing this order, but this was never more than a project. The name is due to the fact that the members wore a medal of the Blessed Virgin to which was attached a swan, the symbolic meaning being variously interpreted.

Jung, *Miscellanea* (Leipzig, 1739), I, 133 sqq.; II, 46 sqq.; Stillfried-Hänle, *Das Buch von Schwanenorden* (Berlin, 1881).

Charles Moeller.

Swastika. See Cross and Crucifix, The.

Sweden, the largest of the three Scandinavian countries and the eastern half of the Scandinavian peninsula, lies between 55° and 68° north latitude and 12° and 24° east longitude. It is bounded on the west by Norway, the Skager Rack, and the Cattegat, on the east by Russian Finland and the Baltic. (For map see Denmark.) Including the Islands of Gotland and Öland, Sweden has an area of 172,876 square miles, of which 73,040 are forest land; 15,000, water; over 20,000, farming and grass land, while what is left consists of barren land, moorland, and pasture land. Although the elevation of the land is on the whole considerably higher than that of Denmark, still the country lacks the mountainous districts of Norway; it is only in the northern part that there are found some mountain peaks, as Suliteluma, which rises to a height of 6150 ft. and glaciers such as Sylfjell. The ground consists chiefly of primitive rock, granite, and gneiss, the disintegrated parts of which form the soil. In Gotland and Öland chalk also appears, and in Skåne coal is found. No country in Europe, with exception of Russia, has larger lakes than Sweden. The largest is Lake Wenern (2200 square miles), the most beautiful is the Wettern (733 square miles), the one containing the greatest number of islands and most frequented is Lake Mälar. Stockholm, the beautiful capital of Sweden, is situated on the outlet that connects Lake Mälar with the sea. The country's many, and generally swift, rivers not only form beautiful waterfalls, as Trollhættan, Tænnforsen etc., but also contain in their great abundance of water about 5,000,000 horsepower. Lakes and rivers are frequently connected with one another and with the sea by canals; one of the most important is the Göta Canal. The climate is relatively mild, especially in the southern provinces and Gotland. The rainfall is fairly regular. In summer the days are not only long and bright, but also very warm. In the northern part of Sweden the sun does not set from the end of May until the middle of July. Naturally the winter is a complete contrast to this: for months the land is covered with heavy snow, and the water has a thick covering of ice.

Sweden is very heavily wooded; in the south the forests consist chiefly of beeches and oaks; in the higher latitudes conifers take the place of these; birches are found below 69° N. lat. The forests and open country give shelter and food to large numbers of wild animals; besides hares and deer there are also reindeer and squirrels. Formerly wolves and bears were numerous, but now they are only found in the most unfrequented parts of the northern provinces and will before long disappear. In Southern and Central Sweden the same varieties of grain and vegetables are cultivated as are grown in Germany, Denmark, and Northern France. In sheltered places grapes are grown as high as 60° N. lat. and at times are sweet in this latitude, but are not suitable for wine. Much attention is given to the breeding of cattle and the making of butter and cheese. The mines, especially at Gellivare, yield a large quantity of fine iron ore. The river and high-sea fishing (salmon, cod, herring) has attained large proportions. The Scandinavian exhibition held in 1897 showed the extraordinary development of manufacture during the last hundred years. The most valuable exports are wood, either in the rough or worked, and iron in the ore or in bars; the annual value of the export of the first is 200,000,000 kronen and of the second 100,000,000 kronen. Butter and cheese to the value of about 40,000,000 kronen are exported annually; live-stock, hides, and fish, 20,000,000 kronen. The value of the most important imports is as follows: coal, 66,000,000 kronen; all kinds of groceries and manufactures, 50,000,000 kronen; grain, 52,000,000 kronen. Traffic and commerce are promoted by the numerous canals and the excellent roads; by a large number of railways, having a length altogether of 8694 miles and owned partly by the State and partly by private citizens; by an excellent postal, telegraph, and telephone system. In 1909 the Swedish merchant marine included 1800 sailing vessels with 200,000 tons, and 1200 steamships with 583,000 tons. In 1908 more than 35,000 ships entered or left Swedish ports. The unit of coinage is the krone, which equals 100 öre or 1·12 marks of the German coinage, and equals 27 cents in U. S. money. Weights and measures follow the metric system.

The great majority of the population of 5,500,000 persons consist of Swedes (*Svear* and *Götar*), and of people of Danish descent settled in the southern provinces who are now Swedish in speech and thought. In the north Finns and Lapps are found who, although they understand Swedish, still hold to their own customs and languages. Officially nearly the entire population belongs to the Lutheran State Church. Nevertheless, large numbers are indifferent or have no belief; the sects are steadily multiplying. The few thousand Catholics are scattered through the entire country and regularly organized parishes exist only at Stockholm, Gothenburg, Malmö, Norrköping, and Gefle. The number of marriages (33,000) is increasing, while the annual birth-rate changes but little. Divorce has become quite frequent. Emigration, however, has declined. As regards education and training, there are five schools of high rank, including the two well-endowed universities Upsala and Lund; a large number of technical schools, *gymnasia*, primary and itinerant schools. The national wealth is estimated at four milliards; the national debt in 1910 amounted to 527,000,000 kronen.

Sweden is a constitutional monarchy; the crown is hereditary in accordance with the law of primogeniture. The Parliament consists of two houses, and the king has the right of veto. Administration and justice in Sweden, like the same departments of government in England, have retained many German peculiarities. For administration the kingdom is divided into twenty-five districts, called *læns*, each of which is governed by a *landshoefding*. Justice is administered by district and upper courts. For ecclesiastical purposes Sweden is divided into twelve dioceses, each containing a large number of parishes; at the head of each diocese is a bishop. The primate of Sweden is the Archbishop of Upsala; the king is the *summus episcopus*. In Sweden liability to military service lasts twenty years; twelve years are spent in the first levy (Beværing), eight years in the reserve. The time of actual service is short, being barely one year in most instances. Naturally the officers receive a thorough military training. In times of peace the army numbers 66,000 men, of whom 6000 serve in the cavalry, 7000 in the artillery, 2000 in the engineer corps. In war time the army can easily be doubled. The Swedish navy is small but good; it is only used for coast defence. Its equipment consists of 1000 officers and non-commissioned officers and 4000 marines and sailors. The national colours are yellow and blue. The battleflag is blue with a yellow horizontal cross that runs out into a tongue; the two blue sections of the flag likewise end in tongues. The flag of the merchant marine is square, blue in colour with a yellow horizontal cross. There are several decorations of honour, the highest being the Order of the Seraphim. The Order of Charles XIII is only intended for Freemasons. The present King of Sweden is Gustavus V, who was born 16 July, 1858, and is a member of the Bernadotte family; in 1887 he married Princess Victoria of Baden.

Generalstabens Karta öfver Sverige, for Northern Sweden (issued by the Topographical Corps); NATHORST, *Sveriges geologi* (Stockholm, 1894), gives the geology and physical geography of the country; NYSTRÖM, *Sveriges geografi* (Stockholm, 1895); SUNDBERG, *Sveriges land och folk* (Stockholm, 1901); *Hist. statist. Handbuch; Svenska Turistföreningens Resehandböcker* (Stockholm, 1901), especially vol. IV, *Sweden; Svenska Turistföreningens Vägvisare* (Stockholm, 1895), especially vol. X, *Stockholm*, containing many illustrations; *Svenska Turistföreningens årsskrifter* (1887——); STYFFE, *Skandinavien undeunionstiden* (2nd ed., Stockholm, 1880), contribution to historical geography; *Historiskt geografiskt och statistiskt lexikon öfver Sverige* (7 vols. and index, Stockholm, 1859–69); BAUMGARTNER, *Nordische Fahrten: Durch Skandinavien nach St. Petersburg*, I (Freiburg, 1890), 275–248 treats of Sweden; WITTMANN, *Führer durch Schweden* (1893); *Stockholms Kommunalkalendar* (Stockholm, 1911), with 5 small maps.

ECCLESIASTICAL HISTORY.—Nothing positive is known as to the religious ideas of the prehistoric inhabitants of Sweden during the Stone and Bronze Ages. It is hardly possible, however, to doubt that they believed in a life after death, as they were accustomed to offer sacrifices at the graves of their dead, and to place in these graves the weapons, tools, utensils, and ornaments of those there buried. Their religion was an ancestral worship. Light or its chief repesentative, the sun, appears to have received as Ty-deus, equivalent perhaps to Zeus, the veneration of a divinity. This is shown by two symbols derived from the Stone Age, the wheel and the axe. Subordinate to this may have been a form of worship paid to individual trees, springs, rivers, and lakes, as striking natural phenomena, which is not entirely extinct even yet. For example, sacrifices are offered in "fairy-mills" (*älfkvarnar*), and despite attempts to dispel superstitions by the schools the belief in house spirits and forest spirits is still to be found here and there. Great fires are still kindled about Easter time, just as was customary thousands of years ago. At a later date than that above-mentioned the sun-god was regarded from varying points of view and received various names. This led gradually to a number of gods: Thor, Odin, and Frey, or Freyr. However, Thor, not Odin, always remained the chief god; he was the god of lightning and of strength. It is indeed asserted that the worship of Odin came from the South; this, however, is contradicted by the fact that his greatest temple stood in Upsala, and that the Scandinavians were the chief worshippers of this god. Among the Germans Wodan, as he was called by them, was treated with but little respect; this is especially true of the tribes of Southern Germany. Moreover, the Scandinavian mythology, as it has come down in the two Eddas, is totally lacking in unity and is in part influenced by Christian ideas. Bloody sacrifices, generally animals, as horses or dogs, were offered to the gods to conciliate them or to gain gifts from them. At times human beings were sacrificed, as bondsmen, freemen, and even kings, who in the literal sense of the word were killed with the sword. Those dedicated to Odin were hung in his groves. Once in nine years the feast of the equinoxes was celebrated with special and horrible pomp. On each of the nine days of sacrifice at least one human being was killed, besides large numbers of animals. Dozens of bodies often hung from the trees. A distinct sacerdotal order seems to have been unknown, and the chiefs of the tribes offered the sacrifices themselves.

The first contact with Christianity arose from the expeditions of the Vikings. In this way the Scandinavians became acquainted with, and learned to appreciate, the higher civilization of the southern races; some of the northern warriors were baptized. Thus gradually the ground was prepared for the seed of the Gospel. The first effort to convert the country to Christianity was made by the Frank, Ansgar. At the request of Swedish nobles he was commissioned by the Emperor Louis the Pious to go to Sweden and reached the commercial town of Birka in Maelarsee in 630, after a hard and dangerous journey. Here with the consent of King Björn he preached zealously for more than a year. Twenty-three years later Ansgar, who had in the meantime become Archbishop of Hamburg-Bremen, returned to Sweden, and by his shrewdness and gentleness overcame the hostile efforts of the worshippers of the heathen gods. His successor as archbishop, Rimbert, also sought to carry on the work of converting the Scandinavians. However, internal turmoils and wars soon destroyed what the two pious men had built up. It was not until the beginning of the eleventh century that the Church resumed the work. German and English missionaries competed with one another in preaching the Word, and not without results. In 1008 Olaf Skötkonung was baptized by Siegfried at Husaby in Western Gotland. But the Church made very slow progress. In the reign of King Stenkil a diocese was founded at Skara. In the reign of Ynge the Old, the new faith gained the mastery. The English missionaries David and Eskil, the German missionary Stephen, and the Swede Botvid preached chiefly in Södermanland, Vestmanland, and Norrland. The first-mentioned died a natural death, the others gained the crown of martyrdom. Still heathenism maintained itself for a long time in isolated spots in the valleys among the mountains.

Naturally the leaven of the Gospel penetrated the hearts of the battle-loving warriors very slowly, and the majority of the baptized were only half Christians. Their knowledge of religion must have remained very limited on account of the lack of printing and of schools. The secular clergy, and later the monks especially, sought with praiseworthy zeal to raise the neophytes to a higher spiritual and moral level. They opposed with growing success drunkenness, violence, polygamy, and the exposure of children. A second diocese was established at Linköping in the reign of Sverker the Old. Both here and in the monasteries (Alvastra, Nydala, Varnhem, etc.) promising youths were instructed in religion as well as in secular knowledge. The lack of the written word was supplied by zealous preaching of the doctrine of salvation. The poor and sick were tenderly cared for. Christian festivals took the place of the heathen ones, and the organization of the Church made rapid progress. The first national synod was held at Linköping in 1152 under the presidency of the papal legate, Bishop Nicholas of Albano. Soon after this Upsala was made the see of a diocese; its first bishop was an Englishman named Henrik. Before long he joined a crusade to Finland, remained in that country, and was killed for the Faith. In 1164 Pope Alexander III raised Upsala to an archdiocese and placed the Swedish Church province under it. As early as the national synod just mentioned the collection of Peterspence was sanctioned; the power of the Church was still further increased when in 1200 Sverker the Younger freed the clergy from the secular jurisdiction and made the payment of tithes obligatory. By the decisions of the national synod held at Skenninge in 1248 the influence of the bishops became greater still. At this synod the election of the bishops was transferred to the cathedral chapters, the study of canon law and the rigid observance of the law of celibacy were made obligatory, while the synod also released the entire clerical body from taking the oath of loyalty to the secular authorities. In 1281, during the reign of Magnus Ladulås, the clergy were released from the payment of taxes, and thus was laid the foundation of their too abundant possessions which were only in part applied to good purposes, such as the building and adornment of churches and the founding of schools and homes for the needy. Birgitta or Brigit, the founder of the Brigittine Order, laboured during the reign of King Magnus Eriksson; she also exerted influence as a writer on mystical subjects, and died at a great age at Rome during the latter part of the fourteenth century. At a later date she was canonized.

The civil wars which wasted the country for hundreds of years were alike injurious to faith and morals. In the course of time the possessions of both nobility and clergy became very great; consequently Margaret, queen of the united Scandinavian countries at the end of the fourteenth century, found it necessary to confiscate a part of these lands, which frequently had been gained by doubtful means. On the other hand there were also excellent princes of the Church, as for example, Archbishop James Ulfsson, for whom may be claimed the honour not only of establishing the first printing press in Sweden in 1483, but, what is more, that of founding the University of Upsala. The last Catholic Bishop of Linköping, Hans Brask, also showed much ability and was as zealous in his episcopal duties as in his promotion of learning. However, the great lack of the true Apostolic spirit among the other Church dignitaries is shown by the fact that Archbishop Bengtsson and Bishop Carlsson led troops against their kings. In addition, Bishop Hemming Gad did everything he could in 1500 and the following years to overthrow the union of the three kingdoms, and then made common cause with the Danes, while Archbishop Gustavus Trolle, who was a strong supporter of the idea of unity, was deposed on this account by the Swedish national council. This last procedure led to the interference of the pope, an act which though just was ill-timed. The victorious King Christian II was guilty of great cruelty to his former foes, largely due to the influence of Archbishop Trolle, and this made the Church very unpopular among a large portion of the population. Consequently Gustavus Eriksson (Vasa), who was elected king in 1523 on account of having incited and led a successful revolution against the domination of Denmark, found the way only too well prepared for the overthrow of all religious conditions.

The first representative of what is called the "ideas of the Reformation" was Olavus Petri, the son of a smith, who was born in 1497 at Örebro. He was a pupil of Luther at Wittenberg and returned home in 1519. As cathedral canon at Straengnaes he won over to his opinions the archdeacon Laurentius Andreas. Very soon the new ruler saw how advantageous it would be to him if he were able to crush the power of the bishops and to confiscate the lands of the Church. As early as 1524 Gustavus Vasa broke off the official connexion of the country with the Roman Curia and permitted Olavus to preach the heretical principles of his former teacher openly in the chief church of Stockholm. Prelates who held strictly to the Faith, as Bishop Peter Jakobsson (Sunnanwäder) and the cathedral provost Knut of Västerås, were accused of treason and executed without any further legal process. At a diet at Västerås three years later Gustavus Vasa was able, by skilful dissimulation, to obtain the passage of laws which made him the *summus episcopus* of the Swedish Church and brought the Church into helpless subordination to the State. In order to dupe the people the Mass, veneration of saints, and pilgrimages were not discontinued at first, ecclesiastical vestments and ceremonies were also retained almost without change. But at the same time, the king and the nobility appropriated as much of the Church lands for themselves as was possible, taking twelve thousand large peasant farms. Even the sacred utensils and bells were seized by Vasa. Many monks and nuns were driven out of their monasteries; a number, including all the members of the Franciscan monastery at Raumo, were killed under circumstances of great cruelty. In order to win over the priests they were permitted to marry, and a great effort was made to win over the common people to the new doctrine by translating the Bible into the vernacular. The attempts of the Dalecarlians and Smålanders, who held to the Church, to check the rapid advance of Protestantism was defeated with bloodshed. The most prominent leaders of the Catholic party, Bishop Brask of Linköping, Bishop Haraldsson of Skara, "Lagman" Ture Jonsson, and others, were obliged to flee. Nils Dacke, a peasant of Småland, who for some time successfully led his countrymen against the king, was finally killed in battle. At a second diet held at Västerås in 1544 nearly all the feast days were suppressed and all Catholic customs excepting a few were done away with. The declaration was also made that the country would "never again abandon the word of God and the pure Gospel".

The two chief reformers of Sweden were Olaf and his brother Lars (Laurentius). Gustavus Vasa had made the latter Archbishop of Upsala after the flight of the last lawful bishop, John Magni. Three years before the second Diet of Västerås the two brothers fell into disgrace with the king and were condemned to death; however, upon the payment of a large fine they were pardoned. They were replaced as councillors of the princely tyrant by two Germans, Konrad of Pyhy and Georg Normann, until Konrad was also sent to prison. The skill and success with which Gustavus "purified" the Church is shown by the fact that, although originally almost penniless, at his death he possessed 1,300,000 thalers in coin (about $6,250,000 at the present value of money), and 5000 large farms. This landed property was afterwards called the "Gustavian patrimony". After his death ecclesiastical matters remained for a time as he had left them. However, his son, John III, who had married a Catholic princess, Katherine Jagellon of Poland, was strongly inclined to the Catholic Church. At the diet held in Stockholm in 1577 he forced the Protestant clergy to consent to a new liturgy (*Röda Boken*) and new ecclesiastical regulations. The negotiator for the papacy, Antonio Possevino, S.J., was even able to persuade the monarch to enter the Catholic Church and to begin negotiations with the pope. As, however, the pope could not consent to the Swedish demands, no permanent agreement was made. After John's death his brother Charles called a church assembly at Upsala in 1593 which was largely composed of preachers (135) from the Diocese of Upsala, while the other dioceses were only scantily represented. The members of the assembly repudiated John's liturgy and, in order to avoid all dissension, the "unchanged Augsburg Confession" was made the religion of the State. Severe punishment was the penalty of apostasy from it, while the exercise of any other form of worship was strictly forbidden. In the Province of Finland, just as in Sweden, Protestantism was introduced by force; it was not until towards the end of the sixteenth century, however, that there were no longer nuns at Vadstena and Nådendal and that Catholicism came to an end.

In this period the intolerance of Protestantism was so great that Sigismund, son of John III, who was also King of Poland and a Catholic, was not allowed to hold Catholic services in private, and the expulsion of all non-Lutherans was decreed. After Sigismund's overthrow in 1598 and deposition in 1599 a number of the noblest men of the country were executed on account of their loyalty to their king and their Church. Draconian laws were to put an end forever to "popery". Conversion to Catholicism was punished with loss of all civil rights and perpetual banishment. Foreign ecclesiastics who remained in the country to carry on a propaganda were to be punished with severe imprisonment and heavy fines, and even to be expelled. Conditions did not become better until two hundred years later when, in 1780, King Gustavus III at the request of the Estates granted the free exercise of their religion to "Christians of other faiths" who desired to settle in Sweden for the sake of carrying on commerce or manufactures. In consequence of this, Rome in 1783 appointed a vicar Apostolic for Sweden, who, however, could effect but little, as up to the year 1860 natives of Sweden were forbidden to enter the Catholic Church under penalty of expulsion from the country. Since the year 1873 members of the national Church who are over eighteen years of age may join other religious societies. All proselytizing by the dissenters is forbidden. Moreover, there still exist a series of juggling enactments, which have lately been multiplied, so that there is very little actual religious freedom. According to the literal interpretation of the Constitution Christians of all faiths may be appointed to all offices, excepting the Council of State, but this is not carried out in practice, and in this regard no change will be made within the near future.

Those desiring the history in detail of the development of the Lutheran State Church of Sweden will find it given very exactly and with copious foot-notes in the excellent work of the Anglican Bishop of Salisbury, Dr. John Wordsworth, quoted in the bibliography. It is only necessary to remark here that gradually new life sprang up from the ruins of the Catholic Church organization. The University of Upsala was revived and another university was founded at Lund; in these schools as well as in a number of sees men excellent in their way carried on fruitful labours; missions to the heathen were begun in Sweden earlier than elsewhere—for example, the missions to the Laplanders and the Indians. However, there was no lack of strife and sectarian movements in the Church (Pietism, Moravianism, Swedenborgianism, etc.); since the middle of the eighteenth century Rationalism and Infidelity have assumed formidable proportions. Freemasonry is strong in Sweden, and among its members are many clergymen, church dignitaries, and even bishops. The majority of teachers in the higher schools and many preachers reject belief in the Trinity and regard Christ simply as a sage and philanthropist. Even the instruction for confirmation is at times made use of to sow the seeds of doubt in youthful hearts; matters have gone so far that a bishop declared, without exciting much opposition, that the Apostles' Creed was unnecessary. The number of the unbaptized is constantly increasing. Attendance at church and at the Communion service (8 per cent of the normal attendance) is rapidly declining of late years. Among many intense love of pleasure and unbridled sensuality prevail. Notwithstanding the practice of abortion in many places, every third child is illegitimate. These things lead many of the better classes to join the sects, among which the largest memberships belong to the Methodists and Baptists.

The number of clergy grows continually less, and those who still hold to the Confession of the State Church are hampered in their efforts to maintain religion by the fact that their energies are largely absorbed by matters of secular administration. Consequently the men who courageously fight for their convictions deserve all the more credit, even though they are at the present opponents of Rome. It is due to them that of late far more than formerly efforts have been made to renovate all the churches, and to build new ones, and to improve church music and religious art; as regards the liturgy, a desire to revive the old forms has of late become apparent. Much is done for missions both by the State Church and by the followers of Valdenström, who, notwithstanding their separatistic inclinations, work in union with the State Church in this matter. The various missionary associations labour among the heathen in South Africa, the Congo State, India, China, and Japan. In Palestine the effort is made, with but slight success, to bring the "pure Gospel" to Roman Catholics and Orthodox Greeks. The same effort in Abyssinia is defeated by the conservatism of the Coptic Christians. Missions are also established for converting Jews and Mohammedans although little has been accomplished. On the other hand, home missions and work among the Swedes, especially in America, have made considerable progress.

WORDSWORTH, *The National Church of Sweden* in Hale Lectures, XIX (London, Oxford, Milwaukee, 1911), 459; REUTERDAHL, *Svenska Kyrkans hist.* (5 vols., Ger. tr., Berlin, 1837), goes back to 1533; CORNELIUS, *Svenska Kyrkans hist. efter reformationen* (Upsala, 1886); THEINER, *Schweden u. seine Stellung zum H. Stuhl unter S. Johann III., Sigismund u. Karl IX.* (1838); BIAUDET, *Le st siège et la Suède*, I (Paris, 1906); ARNDT, *Bidrag till biskop Hans Brasks lefnadsteckning* (1904); HEDQUIST, *Den Kristna Kärleksverksamheten i Sverige under medeltiden* (1893); DAHLBERG, *Bidrag till Svenska fattiglagstiftningens hist.* (1893); HALL, *Bidrag till kännedomen om Cistercienserorden i Sverige* (1899); LEINBERG, *De finska klostrens historia* (1890); BERGSTRÖM *Arboga Krönika* (2 vols., 1892–95); IDEM, *Sancta Birgitta* (1895); FLAVIGNY, *Sainte Birgitte de Suède* (Paris, 1892); BINDER, *Die heil. Birgitta von Schweden* (Munich, 1891); SELLIN, *Vadstena, Omberg, Alvastra* (1890); SCHÜCK, *Olavas Petri* (Stockholm, 1900); LJUNGQUIST, *Det evangeliskt lutherska Kyrkosamfundet och sekterna i Sverige*, with the supplement, *Den kyrkliga gudotjensten und Kyrkoårct* (1890); RUNDGREN, *Statistiska studier rörande Svenska Kyrkan* (1897); NORBERG, *Svenska Kyrkans mission vid Delaware* (1893); RODHE, *De Svenska Bibelsällskapens uppkomst; Katholische Missionen* (1873—), passim; EVANGELISKA FOSTERLANDS-STIFTELSEN, *Missionstidning*, for foreign missions; IDEM, *Budbäraren*, for home missions; ANNERSTEDT, *Upsala universitets historia* (5 vols., Upsala, 1877–1910); ANDERSSON, *Uppsala Universitets matrikel* (1900—); GEYER, *Upsala universitet 1872–1897* (1897); WITTMANN, *Würzburger Bücher in der k. schwed. Universitätsbibliothek zu Upsala* (1891); WEIBULL, *Lunds universitets hist. 1668–1868* (Lund, 1868), continued by TEGNER (Lund, 1897).

POLITICAL HISTORY.—It will probably never be possible to determine when Sweden was first inhabited. However, the large number of objects found by excavating justify the belief that several thousand years before Christ there were people living along the seashore (Baltic, Cattegat) and by the lakes to whom the use of metals was unknown. With constantly increasing skill they manufactured weapons and utensils from horn, stone, and clay. Their only food was gained by hunting and fishing. The raising of cattle and agriculture seem to have become customary very slowly. The dead were buried either in a recumbent or sitting position, in curiously formed stone chambers over which at times mounds of earth of considerable size were raised. Scientific men do not agree as to the original home from which the prehistoric inhabitants of Sweden came. It seems hardly probable that they all spread from the south to the north. Still this may be true of the inhabitants of the present Provinces of Skåne, Blekinge, and Halland. The Stone Age at last gave way to the Age of Bronze. Some two thousand years before our era men learned how to fuse copper and tin, as is proved by great numbers of utensils, as knives, daggers, swords, and shields that have been preserved, which were sometimes very ingeniously made. Gold also began to be used in this period. Bronze was gradually replaced by iron. Roman traders brought into the country not only articles produced by Roman skill in art but also gold coinage. Up to this time the people had tried to preserve the memory of important events by primitive marks (*hällristningar*) scratched on rocks; they now learned from the Roman traders the use of letters, but turned these to suit their own taste into the Runic writing that was long in use. The earliest historical knowledge of Scandinavia and its inhabitants is due to Roman authors. Tacitus (Germania, c. xliv) is the first to call the people "Suiones". How closely this tribe living north of Lakes Wetter and Roxen was related to the Goths living to the south and west, and how it was able to absorb the latter and give its own name to the combined body will always remain obscure.

About the fifth century of the Christian era the civilization of the country had greatly advanced; this is proved by numerous remains of gold utensils, ornaments, runic stones with inscriptions, burial urns, and other articles. Just as in the later Bronze Age, the bodies of the dead were sometimes burned, sometimes buried; however, the latter custom had the greater prevalence. The Swedes had only a small share in the viking expeditions which, from the eighth century onward, were the terror of the peoples of Europe. Besides, in their expeditions they gained a firm foothold in Finland and also came into closer connexion with their neighbours the Russians. The first efforts of missionaries to convert the Swedes to Christianity occurred in the ninth century. It was not until about the year 1000, when Olaf Skötkonung was baptized by the Anglo-Saxon missionary Siegfried, that Christianity was fairly established. Olaf's family, of whose deeds little is known, died out with Emund the Old (1060). At that time the Kingdom of Sweden included only the present northern provinces, while Skåne, Blekinge, and Halland belonged to Denmark and remained united with this country for centuries. The vast forests were largely the cause of the individual development of the tribes, who were separated from one another by them, rendering a common administration for all much more difficult. As roads were lacking, the rivers and lakes were used to connect the different parts of the country. In regard to the government the election of the king customary in earlier times gave way to a settled succession to the throne. Naturally the machinery of government in the modern sense did not exist. Everything depended upon the initiative and force of the ruler, whose commands might, indeed, not be carried out at all or only in part by the great officials or *jarls*. The various provinces had each its own laws (*lag*), and the *lagmen*, or expounders of the law, exerted much influence. They were often able to make their office hereditary. The provinces were divided into hundreds (*härrads*) at the head of each of which was a *höfding*, whose chief duty was to maintain peace and order. For a long time the father of the family still remained the master within his house. The people were divided into the higher and lower freemen (*odalbönder* and *bönder*) and the serfs (*trälar*), and generally lived together on farms or in villages. The houses were built of wood or clay and were covered with shingles or straw. Even at this time, however, there were larger places with occasional stone buildings, as Skara, Linköping, Orebro, Straengnaes, Vesterås, Upsala, Sigtuna, and, at a little later era, Stockholm, which rose rapidly into prominence. The national character showed sharp contrasts: harshness and gentleness, loyalty and deceit, magnanimity and revengefulness. No observer doubts that the gradual improvement in public morals was due to the influence of the Church.

After the old ruling family was extinct a chief named Stenkil was chosen king. He was connected with the former rulers by his wife who was the daughter of Emund the Old, and was an ardent supporter of Christianity. During his reign the first diocese, Skara, was established in eastern Gotland. However, as the actual Sweden (*Uppsvear*) still held to heathenism, rival rulers appeared, and for more than twenty years internal strife prevailed. Finally Inge, the second son of Stenkil, was able to defeat his opponents and bring about a complete victory for Christianity. With the death of a nephew, Inge the Younger, in 1125, the family of Stenkil came to an end. The East Goth Sverker, who married Inge's widow, was able for a time to re-establish the unity that had been disturbed, but his son Charles could not maintain himself. On the other hand Erik, a Swede from the northern provinces, won universal recognition. Erik undertook a crusade in Finland and after his return was killed in a battle (1160) with a Danish pretender Magnus Henriksson. In the following year Magnus was killed by the people. Sverker's son Charles obtained the ascendency, but he had to give way in 1167 to Knut Eriksson. During Knut's administration the first Swedish money was coined and Stockholm was founded. After Knut's death Sverker Karlsson, the son-in-law of Birger Brosa, Knut's chief councillor, obtained the throne (1195), although Knut had left children. Birger owed this success to the clergy, whom he favoured on all occasions. A war broke out between Knut's sons and Sverker after Birger's death; Sverker was obliged to flee, and when he sought with Danish aid to regain the throne he suffered a decisive defeat in 1208 near Falköping. Two years later he also lost a battle near Gestitren, when he was killed. His successful rival Erik Knutsson, the first King of Sweden to be crowned, died in 1216. He was followed by John Sverkersson, at whose death in 1222 the family of Sverker became extinct. Erik, the posthumous son of Erik Knutsson, now came to the throne, but he proved an incompetent ruler and was for a time deposed. By the marriage of his sister Ingeborg with the vigorous Jarl Birger of the Folkunger family he sought to gain Birger for his cause. In 1249 Birger won Finland, which never before had been conquered, for Erik. While Birger was in Finland Erik died, and the nobles of the kingdom elected Birger's son Waldemar. During Waldemar's minority his father carried on the administration with success and skill, maintained good relations with the adjoining countries, and sought to preserve peace at home by wise laws. His son Waldemar, who ruled from 1266, was very unlike his father and had, therefore, to yield the administration to his more strenuous brother Magnus, later called Ladulås.

Magnus was the first to call himself "King of the Swedes and Goths". He continued the work of his father, was able to protect the common freemen (*allmogen*) against the encroachments of the higher nobility, and in 1285 was able to gain the valuable island of Gotland without a blow. When Magnus died in 1290 his heir Birger was a minor; the lord chamberlain, Torgil Knutsson, carried on the government excellently and without self-advantage. After Birger himself came to power Torgil continued to be his most trusted adviser. Finally the king's brothers were able to so arouse Birger's suspicions of Torgil that he seized and beheaded him without trial in 1306. Punishment for such a shameless act did not fail to follow. Left without his one true friend, Birger was made a prisoner by his intriguing brothers and lost his throne. The unfortunate quarrel between the brothers ended apparently four years later with a settlement whereby Birger received a part of the country. However, he misused the power he had regained to obtain revenge, and allowed his two brothers to die of starvation in prison. At this the indignant people drove him from the throne and elected Magnus (1319), the three-year-old son of the late Duke Erik. Shortly before this Magnus had become heir to the throne of Norway by the death of his childless relative King Hakon. When in 1332 Magnus came to power he had the opportunity for the first time to unite temporarily the Danish Provinces of Skåne and Blekinge with his kingdom. His reign was marked by many misfortunes; in particular, the pneumonic plague carried off two-thirds of his subjects. Although the king did much for Sweden by introducing common law and suppressing serfdom, yet he was hardly able to maintain himself in his own country, still less in Norway, especially as he came into disagreement with the pope. He found himself obliged to recognize his son Hakon as King of Norway (1343) and to accept his son Erik as co-regent of Sweden (1356). After Erik's death he reigned jointly with Hakon over both countries. By Hakon's marriage with Margaret, the youthful daughter of King Waldemar of Denmark, the way was prepared for the future union of the three countries.

Discontent with the growing power of the king led the Swedish nobles to revolt against Magnus and offer the crown to Duke Albert of Mecklenburg, who was able, with the aid of German ruling princes, to overthrow Magnus and Hakon (1364). However, as Duke Albert was obliged by agreements made before election to leave unpunished the greatest excesses of the nobles, while the brutality of his vassals and mercenaries aroused universal indignation, it was resolved to elect Margaret Regent of Sweden. In 1375 Margaret had followed her father in the government of the Kingdom of Denmark, and in 1387, after the death of her son Olaf, had been recognized in Norway as the fully authorized and rightful ruler. Albert was defeated by Margaret's army (1389) and was taken prisoner. For a time his adherents continued the struggle for supremacy as pirates (the Vitalians), but finally, in 1395, Queen Margaret came into possession of Stockholm. Before this event the nobles of all three kingdoms at an assembly held at Calmar, 20 July, 1397, had crowned as king of the united kingdoms a boy of seven years, Duke Erik of Pomerania, son of Margaret's niece. At the same time it was settled how the "Union" was in future to be carried on. On account of the great difference in interests and character of the three peoples it is evident that the Union could never attain real strength. As long as Margaret ruled, which was only for fifteen years, everything went smoothly. A woman of great talents and masculine energy, she personally superintended the entire government, saw to the prompt administration of justice, and sought to increase the power of the Crown at the expense of the nobility; her one mistake was that she granted the Danish element too much influence and thus estranged the Swedes. During Margaret's last years Erik began to share in the government, and it was owing to him that a long war broke out with the Counts of Holstein. His attempt to wring a tax from all vessels passing the Oresund made the Hanseatic League his enemy. Only the ability of his wife, Philippa, the daughter of an English nobleman, prevented Copenhagen from falling into the hands of the enemy. Under Erik's autocratic rule the internal government grew worse from year to year, and the growing discontent of the people found vent in bloody revolts. Under the leadership of Engelbrechtsson the Dalecarlians drove away all the Danish supervisors and chose a head of their own (until 1435). The nobles alone for the time being held to the king, but they sought to weaken his power by means of agreements, and as Erik did not keep these promises, allegiance to him was declared to be no longer necessary at the Diet of Arboga (1436) and Charles Knutsson was elected as administrator or stadtholder of the kingdom. Although the democratic Engelbrecht was murdered soon after this, yet the efforts to reconcile king and people had no lasting success, and Erik was deposed in 1439. He also lost the crowns of Norway and Denmark. Denmark elected Duke Christopher of Bavaria king; he was recognized by Sweden in 1440, and later by Norway. The chief event of his short reign (1440–48) was a famine. The condition of the peasants also grew worse. His efforts, however, to establish a settled code of law are very creditable to him.

After Christopher's death the Union fell rapidly to pieces, as the Swedes elected Charles Knutsson, who has already been mentioned, as king, and the Danes and Norwegians Christian of Oldenburg (1448). In 1457 the latter was able to obtain his election in Sweden also, but he could not make any headway against King Charles or Sten Sture the Old, the successor of Charles in the administration of the country. Christian I was followed in Denmark by his son Hans (1481), who gradually gained recognition in Norway (1483) and Sweden (1497). When, however, he was defeated in a battle with the Dithmarschen, Sweden again abandoned its allegiance to him (1501) and on the death of Sten Sture the Old in 1503 the Swedes made Svante Sture the administrator of the country (1503); after this latter's sudden death in 1512 the government passed to Sten Sture the Younger. The son of the late King Hans, Christian II, now sought by arms to force Sweden to re-enter the Union. In this policy he was supported particularly by Archbishop Gustavus Trolle of Upsala, against whom the hatred of all the friends of Sture was naturally directed. The Danish troops which landed at Stockholm in 1517 were soon defeated and driven back, and the next year Christian's troops suffered a still severer defeat at Brännkyrka. The national Swedish party deposed and imprisoned the dignitaries of the Church without any regard to canon law, consequently the pope excommunicated its leaders, placed Sweden under an interdict, and commissioned King Christian to carry out the punishment. Early in 1520 King Christian sent a large army into Western Gotland, and after successful skirmishes the Swedes were overwhelmingly defeated at Upsala. Stockholm alone held out for a time, but when Christian, approached the city with a strong fleet, it was obliged to surrender. The conqueror had been recognized by a part of the council as king before this; he entered the city in state, was able to obtain homage as hereditary ruler, and was then crowned. Unfortunately the adherents of the Union were not content with what had been attained; Archbishop Trolle demanded the punishment of his enemies, and Christian made short work of these. Bishops Matthias of Strængnæs and Vincent of Skara, and a large number of nobles, councillors, and citizens were executed as proclaimed rebels and heretics, and their property was confiscated. While on his return to Denmark the king had various persons executed, hoping in this way to suppress the spirit of insurrection forever. In this he was mistaken.

In January of the next year a peasant insurrection broke out in Dalarne, which spread rapidly. Gustavus Eriksson (Vasa) became the leader of the insurgents, who soon numbered 15,000 men. Vasa had lost his father and brother-in-law in the slaughter at Stockholm, and had been taken prisoner at Brænnkyrka as the chief standard-bearer, but had made his escape. His strength grew as leader of the rebellion through several fortunate skirmishes, and as he succeeded in winning over the influential Bishop Hans Brask to his cause, a popular assembly at Vadstena appointed him *stadtholder* of the kingdom (1521); two years later he was unanimously elected king at Strængnæs. He gained Stockholm and Calmar during the summer months of 1523, and Öland and Finland also acknowledged his sovereignty. At the same time his position was by no means a favourable one, for he lacked the money to meet the most necessary expenses, while the constant civil wars had largely destroyed the sense of order and respect for law. The bishops were powerful and wealthy lords and only partially satisfied with the new conditions; neither could much dependence be placed upon the nobility. Gustavus, however, was never at a loss for expedients. By means of clever dissimulation and deceitful promises he was able to make the citizens and peasants his adherents. The introduction of Luther's doctrines not only freed him from the tutelage of the bishops, but in particular offered him the possibility of gaining control of the Church lands and treasures. As the nobility also gained large sums by this confiscation, community of interest bound them to their princely ruler. Resistance, wherever shown, was crushed mercilessly, generally by foreign mercenaries. Gustavus repaid the loyalty of the Dalecarlians, to whom above all he owed his success, by the execution of their best men. He was an unusually powerful man of coarse instincts; in old age he married for his third wife a very young woman, and had little interest in higher moral aims when they were of no benefit to his practical schemes. For schools he did not care at all, and he allowed the one university, Upsala, to sink into decay. The preachers frequently received mere pittances, and in many cases stood on a low moral and intellectual level. On the other hand much was done to improve agriculture, mining, and commerce, as well as to strengthen the defences of the country. However, the monarch gave much more thought to his own advantage than to the well-being of the nation. When he died in (1560) he was the richest prince in Europe.

Among the later rulers of Sweden only one was a Catholic, Sigismund; two princesses of the royal family, Cecilia Vasa, daughter of Gustavus I, and Christina, daughter of Gustavus II Adolphus, became converts in their later years. The nation was permanently separated from Rome, consequently it is only necessary here to treat the later history of the country very briefly, especially as during the period of the "great powers" it is closely connected with that of Europe. The sons of Gustavus Vasa ruled Sweden from 1560 to 1611. Erik, the first to come to power, was half-crazy, was soon deposed by his brother John, and died in prison. On account of mental deficiencies Magnus never came to the throne. On the other hand Vasa's youngest son, Duke Charles, who had inherited both the good and bad qualities of his father, was able to drive his Catholic nephew Sigismund from the throne and to leave it to his son Gustavus II Adolphus, whose share in the Thirty Years War was of such far-reaching importance. The conversion to Catholicism of his daughter Christina was of as little political importance as the earlier conversion of the most beautiful of Gustavus Vasa's daughters, Cecilia. Cecilia was the ancestress of the Catholic heroes, Margrave Leopold William and Louis William of Baden; she outlived all her brothers and sisters and died at Brussels in 1627.

The guilty family of Vasa was succeeded by relatives who were descendants of the Wittelsbach Palatinate family (1654–1718). The successful warrior Charles X Gustavus reigned only six years. During the reign of Charles XI a large part of the earlier territorial possessions was lost; the imprudence and recklessness of his son Charles XII almost ruined Sweden, although at first he gained some temporary and brilliant successes. These two kings ruled as absolute monarchs and cut down greatly both the rights and possessions of the nobility. The succeeding kings, however, Frederick of Hesse and Adolphus Frederick of Holstein Gottorp, were limited in their sovereignty by political parties (Hats and Caps). Gustavus III (1771–92), son of the last-named sovereign, restored the former splendour of the monarchy, but was assassinated when barely forty-six years old. During his reign the first breach was made in the rigid system of the state Church. His son and successor Gustavus IV Adolphus (1792–1809), of honourable but obstinate character, was naturally not the one to direct state affairs skilfully in an era of universal upheaval. He was deposed by a military conspiracy (23 March, 1809). His uncle and successor, Duke Charles (King Charles XIII), sought to secure peace for the country by the surrender of territory which he could not hold. As he was childless, he first adopted Prince Christian Augustus of Augustenburg and, after the sudden death of this heir, the French marshal, Jean Bernadotte, who accepted the election as crown prince and became a Protestant to secure the succession to the throne for himself and his descendants. Even during the lifetime of his adopted father he was the real ruler. As the representative of the interests of his country he came into collision with his former protector Napoleon, joined the allied powers in 1812, and sent 30,000 men to the Army of the North. After the battle of Leipzig he led his troops (of whom he had taken great care) against the Danes. Denmark was made to sign the Treaty of Kiel (1814) in which it yielded Norway to Sweden. The unwilling Norwegians only consented under pressure of circumstances, and their differences with Sweden were never fully settled. Finally, in 1905, the Norwegian Storthing proclaimed the independence of Norway, and Sweden had to consent to the separation. Conditions in Sweden have greatly improved under the new ruling family, although friction, especially at first, arose between ruler and people. Jean Bernadotte reigned as King Charles XIV John (1818–44). Especially prosperous was the reign of Oscar I (1844–59); his wife Josephine, a Catholic princess of Bavaria, was universally beloved on account of her charitableness. During the reigns of their sons Charles XV (1859–72) and Oscar II (1872–1907) the country developed greatly in all directions, especially as regards political and religious freedom. Oscar II was also a distinguished author. The present king is Gustavus V Adolphus.

Scriptores rerum Suecicarum medii ævi (3 vols., Upsala, 1818, 1828, 1876); *Svenskt Diplomatarium*, ed. LILJEGREN and HILDEBRAND, I–VIII (Stockholm, 1829–1902); *Svenska Riksarkivets pergamentsbref från och med år 1351 förtecknade med angifvande af innehållet* (Stockholm, 1866–72); *Svenska riksdagsakter*, ed. HILDEBRAND for the years 1521–1716, continuation by WESTRIN, *Sveriges historia från äldsta tid till våra dagar*, 1st ed. MONTELIUS, WEIBULL, etc. (Stockholm, 1877–81); 2nd ed., revised, enlarged, and with more than 2000 illustrations, HILDEBRAND (Stockholm, 1900): Index, LINDSTRÖM; GEIJER AND CARLSON, *Gesch. Schwedens* in [HEEREN-UCKERT] *Gesch. der europ. Staaten* (7 vols, 1855–87); HILDEBRAND, *Sveriges medeltid* (VIII pts., 1885–1903); ODHNER, *Lärobok i fäderneslandets historia*; HILDEBRAND, revised ed. with maps: pt. I (1907) treats the heathen and Catholic periods; pt. II (1906) treats period since the introduction of Protestantism; WITTMANN, *Kurzer Abriss der schwed. Gesch.* (Breslau, 1896), STYFFE, *Skandinavien under unionstiden* (Stockholm, 1881); SJÖGREN, *Gustav Vasa* (Stockholm, 1896); IDEM, *Gust. Vasas söner* (Stockholm, 1901); ODBERG, *Om prinsessan Cecilia Wasa, markgrefvinna af Baden-Rodemachern* (Stockholm, 1896); WIESELGREN, *Markgrefvinnan Cecilia, Gustaf Wasas skönaste dotter* in *Småkrifter* (1900); *Kung Gustafs I. Registratur* (25 vols., covering the years 1521–55); BERG, *Bidrag till den inre stadförvaltningens historia under Gustaf I.* (1893); CRONHOLM, *Sveriges historia under Gustaf II. regering* (6 vols., Stockholm, 1857–72); FORSSELL, *Gustaf II. Adolf* (Stockholm, 1894); STAVENOW, *Gustaf II. Adolf. Hans personlighet och hans betydelse* (2nd ed., 1894); *Axel Oxenstjernasskrifter och brefväxling* (1888–); ANNERSTEDT, *Samhällsklasseer och lefnadssätt under förre hälften af 1600– talet in Fören. Heimdals folksskrifter*, xxxiii, xxxiv (1891); SJÖGREN, *Karl XI. och svenska folket påhans tid* (Stockholm, 1895); IDEM, *Karl XI. och hans män* (1899); CARLSON AND WESTRIN, *Sveriges historia under konungarne af Pfalziska huset* (8 vols., Stockholm, 1855–1910); STAVENOW, *Frihetstiden* (Gothenburg, 1898); IDEM, *Konung Gustaf III.* (ibid., 1901); ODHNER, *Sveriges politiska historia under konung Gustaf IIIs regering* (2 vols., Stockholm, 1885–96); DE HEIDENSTAM, *La fin d'une dynastie* (Paris, 1911); SANDEGREN, *Till historien om stadshvälfningen i Sverige 1809* (1893); ALMÉN, *Atten Bernadotte* (1893); NORDLUND, *Den svensk-norska krisen* (Upsala, 1905); SETTERWALL, *Svensk. hist. bibliografi* (1907), including the years 1875–1900; *Historisk Tidskrift* (Stockholm, 1881–), 30 vols., in no regular order, containing historical material from early times until the Bernadotte family ascended the throne, also criticisms of works on Sweden. For further bibliography see DAHLMANN-WAITZ, *Quellenkunde der deutschen Gesch.* (7th ed., Göttingen, 1906).

ART.—Even as early as the end of the ancient Stone Age, probably a thousand years before Christ, the people of Sweden showed a desire to improve the shapes of utensils in common use, as is evidenced by the discovery of numerous utensils belonging to this long past era. There was a steady improvement in the forms of tools, especially of the axes. Vessels of clay were not only adorned with graceful designs, but at times they were also ornamented with more or less skilful drawings of animals. In the Bronze Age the sense of beauty rapidly increased; weapons and ornaments (rings and diadems) reached a high degree of correctness and beauty, although in part this was plainly due to the influence of foreign skill in art. On the other hand the representations of the human form showed decided clumsiness for a long time. In this period use was also made of the higher metals, gold and silver, especially in ornamenting the weapons for defence and attack. The weapons were first made of bronze and afterwards of iron. Apparently articles made of glass were brought from other lands. The Runic alphabet was first employed in the early Iron Age; the runes were cut on

XIV.—23

memorial stones that had been formerly without inscriptions. During the era of the Migrations and of the Viking expeditions the æsthetic sense of the Swedish people developed as they became acquainted with artistic models; this is shown especially in the ornamental work. The final victory of the Romano-Christian civilization exerted a profound influence upon technical artistic skill and the tendencies of art. Although goldsmiths and armourers were still held in high repute, and the memory of unusually skilful masters was preserved in song, nevertheless from now on art was above all employed in the service of religious ideas. The royal palaces and princely dwellings, which were chiefly built of wood, have disappeared.

In Norway a number of the old wooden churches are still in existence, but in Sweden only the unassuming little chapel of Hedared, situated between Borås and Alingsås, has withstood the storms of time. On the other hand there are a number of tasteful stone churches in various architectural styles and sometimes very interesting details such as doorways, arcades, tabernacles etc. Some, as the Romanesque cathedrals of Lund and Linköping (Transition Period) and the Gothic cathedral of Upsala, fall but little below the celebrated architectural works of more southern countries in size and splendour. Among the churches worthy of notice are those at Skara, Västerås, and Strängnäs; the monastic churches at Varnhem and Sko (Cistercian), Sigtuna (Dominican), and Vadstena (Brigittine), also several churches, which are in good condition, as the Tyska Kyrkan or the Church of the Virgin at Visby, and some preserved as ruins, especially on the Island of Gotland. The majority of the country churches were built in the Romanesque period; many of them were altered later during the Gothic era. At times the churches are round in shape with remarkably heavy walls; apparently they were used when occasion required for purposes of defence. A number of churches, as those at Råda, Risinge, Arboga etc., were adorned with frescoes, which were afterwards covered with whitewash. Of later years the whitewash has at times been removed and the pictures thus exposed have been skilfully renovated. The churches were also adorned with stone and wood carvings, such as images of Christ, of the Madonna, and the saints, carved altars, baptismal fonts of stone or metal, reliquaries, hanging chandeliers and standing candelabra, chalices and patens, costly ciboriums, monstrances, and ostensories, processional crosses, censers, organs, bells, superb vestments, etc.

Fortunately, notwithstanding the thorough "purification of the Church" undertaken by Gustavus Vasa, enough remains to show that in Sweden also during the Middle Ages there was a sense of pious sacrifice and of purified art. As everywhere else the effect of what is called the "Reformation" was at first destructive, and for centuries nothing new of importance was produced in the domain of ecclesiastical art. It is only of late years that a more and more marked change for the better has appeared. Here and there altars of Catholic origin have been brought from old lumber-rooms and garrets and restored to their former places. Mosaic work is also used. A continually increasing number of orthodox pastors make use of embroidered vestments in the services of the Church and there are signs of a ritualistic movement, which, however, is energetically attacked by the Liberal and unorthodox clergy.

The development of secular art since the twelfth century does not lie within the province of the present article. Instead of building churches Protestant Sweden has very largely erected castles and citadels; these have been filled with weapons, gorgeous furniture and table equipments, ancestral portraits and pictures on panels; on sepulchres, high-sounding epitaphs were common. In isolated instances artists have ventured to represent Biblical subjects. There is no Catholic art; the poverty and small memberships of the Catholic communities forbid the encouragement of such an art. Still the Church of St. Erik in Stockholm is a well-decorated building. The other Catholic churches, as St. Eugenia at Stockholm, those at Göteborg, Malmö, etc., have been able, in the course of time, to obtain better vestments and utensils.

MONTELIUS, *Kulturgesch. Schwedens* (1908), with 540 cuts; HILDEBRAND, *Kyrkliga konsten under Sveriges medeltid* (2nd ed., Stockholm, 1907, with 300 cuts); HAZELIUS, *Bidrag till vår odlings häfder*, continuation by SALIN, *Fataburen* (1881); BERGSTRÖM, *Medeltidsmålningarna i Arboga-stadskyrka* (1898); WRANGEL, *Cisterciensernas inflytande på medeltidens byggnadskonst i Sverige* (1899); IDEM, *Tegelårkitekturen i Norra Europa och Uppsala Domkyrka* in *Antiqu. Tidskrift for Sverige* (which gives on p. 6 further authorities), del. 15, no. 1; JANSE, *Medeltidsminnen från Ostergötland* (Stockholm, 1906); *Utställning af äldre kyrklig konst från Strängnäs stift*; catalogue of the same (1906); CURMAN AND ROOSVAL, *Sveriges Kyrkor: Erlinghundra härad*, II (Upsala, 1912), fasc. i; *Templum Cathedrale Vaztenense* (1898), contains accounts of other churches—Orberg, Skenninge, etc.; RIPA, *Vadstena och dess minnesmärken* (1883); LINDSTRÖM, *Anteckningar om Gotlands medeltid*, I, II (1892, 1895); HILDEBRAND, *Visby och dess minnesmärken* (1893); STEFFEN, *Romanska småkyrkor i Österojöländerna med särskild hänsyn till svenska förhållanden* (1901); UPPMARK, *Die Architektur der Renaissance in Schweden* (1897—), includes the years 1530–1760; NYBLOM, *Upsala universitets konstsamlingar* (1902); HASSELGREN, *Utställningen i Stockholm; Beskrifvning i ord och bild öfver allmänna Konst och industriutställningen* (1897); BUMPUS, *The Cathedrals of Norway, Sweden, and Denmark* (New York, 1908).

LITERATURE.—In pre-Christian times there was no real literature in Sweden as neither written language nor runes came into use until quite a late period. The oldest known writing of a historical character, the so-called "Röksten" from East Gotland, appeared probably about the year 900. It recounts in alliterative verse the heroic deeds of a king; later inscriptions have also the same theme. It may be assumed with certainty that there were songs of gods and heroes that were orally preserved, but of which next to no traces now remain. The first to arouse the intellectual life of the nation were Catholic priests, especially monks; in doing this they both practised and taught the art of writing with intense energy. They wrote chiefly in the language of the Church; in all countries these Latin and exclusively religious works are very similar and therefore will not be considered here. Gradually, however, the language of the people came more and more into use for literary purposes. It became a serviceable instrument for the expression of higher ideals and noble sentiments. Thus the way was prepared for a literature in the Swedish language. The early writings in Swedish were very largely practical. Thus the current conceptions of law were brought together into codes of law in the twelfth and thirteenth centuries, as the "Västgötalagen" and "Ostgötalagen", the "Upplandslagen" and "Gutalagen". A treatise of the thirteenth century called "Om styrilsi Konunga och höftinga" gives rules for right living. The "Revelations" (*Uppenbarelser*) of St. Birgitta (d. 1373), which are at times very extravagant in style, have been translated into many languages. Of the writings of Magister Mathias, cathedral canon of Linköping and father-confessor of St. Birgitta, there is still in existence a translation of the Bible, besides several sermons and edifying treatises.

The first connected accounts of historical events were two chronicles in rhyme, the chronicle of Erik and that of Karl. The first relates in doggerel the quarrels of the Folkunger family up to the year 1319 and gives, in particular, a vivid description of the actions of King Magnus Ladulås. The other chronicle covers the era, 1389–1452. Poems of imaginary adventures and French metrical romances, as "Ivan and the Lion", "Fleur and Blanchefleur", were imitated in Sweden, and history in a romantic garb, as the legend of Alexander or that of Duke Frederick of Normandy etc., was also recast by Swedish writers. As one of the most important of these early poets should be mentioned Bishop Thomas Simonsson of Strängnäs (d. 1443). He wrote an account in fairly good verse of the national hero Engelbrecht, and in his songs praised the virtue of loyalty and the blessings of freedom. Jöns Budde, a Brigittine monk, who was by birth a German, prepared while living first at Vadstenn and then at Nådendal, Finland, various versions of ascetic works, lives of saints and similar treatises, and also translated several books of the Bible, as Judith, Esther, Ruth, and Machabees. Peder Månsson wrote text-books on mining. Bishop Brask of Linköping wrote two works now lost; one a chronicle of his diocese, issued in 1523, the other a genealogy of the Swedish nobility (1530). Lastly many reminiscences of the heroic and Catholic eras are still found in the *Folkvisorna* (folk-songs). Accounts of the five periods of Protestant Swedish literature may be found in works on the subject. Mention should be made here of John Messenius, author of "Scandia illustrata", the chronicle of a bishop, and various dramas. He was imprisoned for twenty years on account of Catholic tendencies and on his death-bed openly joined the Catholic Church. He left a work in manuscript called "Hertig Carls Slagtarbänk" (Duke Charles's Shambles), now in the royal library at Stockholm, which, although perhaps somewhat too severe and at times exaggerated in tone, describes the bloody persecution that Catholics who were faithful to king and Church suffered from the cruel father of Gustavus Adolphus. It should also be said that Erik John Stagnelius (d. 1823) belongs with Wallin and, in part, Tegner, to the foremost Protestant poets of Sweden; in his drama "The Martyrs" Stagnelius produced a work which is of value particularly to Catholics. Naturally there is nothing to be said of a Catholic Swedish literature of the modern era. The missionaries, however, have not been idle. Besides prayerbooks, contemplative works, and catechisms, they have issued several apologetic works, as Gibbons in his "Våra fäders tro" (Faith of our Fathers); also Hammerstein, who has written "Edgar", and devotional treatises (*philothea*), and has been a successful translator of Latin and German hymns into Swedish.

Schück–Warburg, *Illustrerad svensk Literaturhistoria* (Stockholm, 1896–97); Schück, *Svensk Literaturhistoria* (Stockholm, 1890); Bernardini, *La littérature Scandinave* (1894); Niemann, *Das Nordlandbuch* (1909), an introduction to Scandinavian natural history and civilization; Andersson, *Catalogue de l'exposition Suédoise de l'enseignment supérieure* (1900), contains many authorities; *Ordbok öfver svenska språket*, issued by the Swedish Academy; Tamm, *Etymologist svensk ordbok* (Upsala, 1890—); Söderwall, *Ordbok öfver svenska medeltidsspråket*.

P. Wittmann.

Sweden, Vicariate Apostolic of. See Sweden.

Swedenborgians, the believers in the religious doctrines taught by Emanuel Swedenborg. As an organized body they do not call themselves Swedenborgians, which seems to assert the human origin of their religion, but wish to be known as the "Church of the New Jerusalem", or "New Church", claiming for it Divine authorship and promulgation through human instrumentality.

I. Life of Swedenborg.—Emanuel Swedenborg was b. at Stockholm, 29 Jan., 1688; d. in London, 29 March, 1772. His father was Dr. Jesper Swedberg, who later became the Lutheran Bishop of Skara. Swedenborg's life falls into two very distinct periods: the first extends to the year 1745 and reveals him as an adept in the mathematical and physical sciences; in the second he appears as a writer on theological subjects. Endowed with extraordinary talents, he completed his university course at Upsala in 1710 and travelled for four years in England, Holland, France, and Germany. Shortly after his return to Sweden, he was appointed by King Charles XII to an assessorship on the Board of Mines (1716). He gave signal proof of his engineering ability during the siege of Frederickshall (1718) by inventing a means to transport boats and galleys overland for a distance of fourteen miles. His family was ennobled in 1719, a distinction indicated in the change of the name from Swedberg to Swedenborg. He declined (1724) the chair of mathematics at the University of Upsala and published at Leipzig in 1743 his important "Philosophical and Mineral Works" ("Opera philosophica et mineralia"). A year later appeared his treatise "On the Infinite and Final Cause of Creation" which includes a discussion of the relation between the soul and the body. Another scientific journey took him to Denmark, Germany, Holland, France, and Italy, and in 1740–41 appeared at Amsterdam one of his larger anatomical works ("Œconomia regni animalis"). The trend of his thoughts became distinctly religious in 1734 and exclusively so in 1745. He alleged that at the latter date Our Lord appeared to him in London, initiated him into the spiritual sense of the Scriptures, and commissioned him to expound it to his fellow men. With this vision there began, he declared, an intercourse with God, angels, and spirits which was to terminate only with his death. In 1747 he resigned his assessorship and, at his request, received as a pension the half of his salary. He now spent his time between London, Amsterdam, and Stockholm, and wrote in Latin his voluminous theological works. These soon attracted the attention of the Lutheran clergy of Sweden; a commission was instituted in 1771 to examine them, but took no action against their author. At his death Swedenborg received the Lord's Supper from a Protestant clergyman, to whom he affirmed his final attachment to his religious principles. He was never married, was simple in his habits, worked and slept without much regard to day or night, and lay at times in a trance for several consecutive days. In 1908 his remains were transferred from London to Sweden and deposited in the cathedral at Upsala.

II. Doctrinal Principles.—Swedenborg and his followers hold that as the Christian religion succeeded the Jewish so the Swedenborgian teaching supplemented the Christian. This new dispensation promulgated by Swedenborg is, according to them, based on a Divinely revealed interpretation of the Sacred Scriptures. Some of the characteristic features of this new religious system are presented in the following outline. God is Love Itself and Wisdom Itself. His Power is from and according to these as they flow forth into creative act. The Trinity does not consist of three distinct Divine persons as Catholics maintain; but is understood in the sense that in the Incarnation the Father or Jehovah is essentially the Divine Being, while the Son is the human (or sub-spiritual) element assumed by the Godhead in order to become present among men. The Holy Spirit is the Divine Presence and Power consequent upon this assumption and resultant transfiguration (glorification in Swedenborgian language) of the human element which thus became "a Divine Human" with all power in heaven and on earth. Jesus Christ is, therefore, not the Incarnation of a second Divine person, but of the Divine as a whole; he includes the Father (Godhead), the Son (assumed humanity), and the Holy Spirit (Divine-human power). Life does not exist except in Him or from Him, and cannot be created. Its presence in created forms is accounted for by continuous Divine influx.

On this earth man enjoys the highest participation of life, but he is greatly inferior, in this respect, to the races undoubtedly inhabiting other planets, e. g., Jupiter, Mercury. His three constituent elements are soul, body, and power. Originally granted full freedom in the use of his faculties, he erroneously concluded that he held them from no one but himself and fell away from God. The Lord, after the fall, did not abandon the sinner, but appeared to him in the form of an angel and gave him the law to reclaim him from his evil ways. These efforts were useless, and God clothed Himself with a human organism and redeemed man, opening anew his faculties to the influx of Divine life. Men are admitted into the New Church through baptism; they are strengthened in the spiritual life by the reception of the Eucharist. Justification cannot be obtained by faith alone; good works are likewise necessary. The seclusion of the cloister is not a help but a hindrance to spiritual growth; the healthiest condition for the latter is a life of action in the world. Miracles and visions produce no real spiritual change because they destroy the requisite liberty. The hope of reward is not to be recommended as an incentive to virtue, for good actions are vitiated when prompted by motives of self-interest. Death is the casting off by man of his material body which has no share in the resurrection. Immediately after death all human souls enter into the intermediate state known as the world of spirits, where they are instructed and prepared for their final abodes, heaven or hell. We need not expect the Last Judgment for it has already taken place; it was held in 1757 in Swedenborg's presence. No pure spirits exist; both angels and devils are former members of the human race, have organic forms, and experience sensation. The liturgy of the New Church is modelled on the Anglican service. The Church organization in Great Britain is congregational; in the United States most of the various religious societies are grouped in state associations under the charge of general pastors, while the "General Church" (see below) is avowedly episcopal in government.

III. HISTORY OF THE NEW CHURCH; STATISTICS; EDUCATIONAL AND PUBLISHING ACTIVITIES.—Swedenborg made no attempt at founding a separate Church; he presented his doctrinal works to university and seminary libraries in the hope that they might be of service; how far ahead he thought is uncertain, as he seemed to hold that his followers might be members of any Christian denomination. But his views were, in many respects, so entirely new that their adoption made the foundation of a distinct religious body inevitable. Few accepted his opinions completely during his lifetime. They found zealous advocates, however, in two Anglican clergymen, Thomas Hartley, rector of Winwick in Northamptonshire, and John Clowes, rector of St. John's at Manchester. These divines rendered his works into English and through the efforts of Clowes, who never separated from the Church of England, Lancashire became at an early date the Swedenborgian stronghold which it still remains to-day. The formal organization of the New Church took place in 1787, and James Hindmarsh, a former Methodist preacher, was chosen by lot to officiate at the inaugural meeting. The first public service was held in 1788 in a chapel at Great Eastcheap, London. Swedenborgian societies were soon formed in various English cities, and in 1789 the first general conference of the New Church met in the place of worship just mentioned. The number of adherents did not increase rapidly. The conference has held annual meetings ever since 1815. Its minutes for 1909 contain the following statistics for England: 45 ministers, 70 societies, 6665 registered members, and 7907 Sunday scholars.

In America the Swedenborgian doctrines were first introduced in 1784 at public lectures delivered in Philadelphia and Boston. The first congregation was organized at Baltimore in 1792. Since then the principles of the New Church have spread to many states of the Union. The first general convention was held in Philadelphia in 1817. It meets annually at present and is mainly composed of delegates sent by the various state organizations. In 1890 the General Church of Pennsylvania severed its connexion with the convention and assumed in 1897 the name of the General Church of the New Jerusalem. It numbered, in 1911, 24 ministers, 16 churches, and 890 communicants; whereas the main body had 107 ministers, 130 churches, and 8500 communicants (Statistics of Dr. H. K. Carroll, in "The Christian Advocate", N. Y., 25 Jan., 1912). Congregations of the New Church are to be found in all civilized countries; but their membership is small. In Germany the Protestant prelate Öttinger translated (1765–86) numerous writings of Swedenborg, but the most important name identified with the history of the denomination in that country is that of Immanuel Tafel (1796–1863), professor and librarian of Tübingen, who devoted his life to the spread of Swedenborgianism. His efforts were mainly literary; but he also organized a congregation in Southern Germany. The religion was proscribed in Sweden until 1866, when greater religious freedom was granted; the churches are still very few, and the membership insignificant. New Churchmen claim, however, that there as well as in all other countries the influence of Swedenborg cannot be gauged by the enrolled membership, because many communicants of other denominations hold Swedenborgian views.

The denomination maintains for the training of its ministry the New Church College at Islington, London, and the New Church Theological School at Cambridge, Mass. A preparatory school is located at Waltham, Mass., and an institution for collegiate and university studies at Urbana, Ohio. The General Church conducts a seminary at Bryn Athyn, Pa., and maintains several parochial schools. The denomination has displayed a remarkable publishing activity. The Swedenborg Society was founded in London in 1810 for the printing of Swedenborgian literature and in celebration of its centenary the International Swedenborg Congress met in the English metropolis in 1910. Other publishing agencies are the New Church Union of Boston, the American Swedenborg Printing and Publishing Society of New York, and a publishing house at Stuttgart, Germany. A monumental edition of Swedenborg's scientific works is in course of publication under the auspices of the Swedish Royal Academy of Sciences. His theological works are available in complete Latin and English editions and have been partly published in numerous modern languages, including Hindu, Arabic, and Japanese. The New Church publishes two quarterly reviews, some monthly magazines, and several weekly papers.

I. TAFEL, *Documents concerning the Life and Character of Swedenborg* (London, 1875–77). Numerous *Biographies of Swedenborg* have been written: in English by DOUGHTY (London, 1857); FLETCHER (ibid., 1859); HYDE (ibid., 1863); WHITE (ibid., 1867); WORCESTER (Boston, 1883); WILKINSON (London, 1886); ODHNER (Philadelphia, 1893); TROBRIDGE (London, s. d.); in French by BALLET (Paris, 1899); BYSE (Paris, 1901); in German by RANZ (Schwäbisch Hall, 1851).

II. These biographies usually contain an exposition of Swedenborg's doctrine; a more complete presentation will be found in his own works, particularly in: *The True Christian Religion; Arcana Cælestia; The Apocalypse Revealed; The Apocalypse Explained; Divine Love and Wisdom, Divine Providence; Heaven and Hell.* PARSONS, *Outlines of the Religion and Philosophy of Swedenborg* (Boston, 1894); *Transactions of the International Swedenborg Congress* (London, 1910).

III. HINDMARSH, *Rise and Progress of the New Church* (London, 1861); DOLE, *The New Church, What, How, Why?* (New York, 1906).

For further bibliographical details consult HYDE, *Bibliographical Index to the Published Writings of Emanuel Swedenborg* (London, 1897). Catholic writers on Swedenborg and his doctrine: GÖRRES, *Emanuel Swedenborg, seine Visionen u. sein Verhältniss zur Kirche* (Speyer, 1827); MÖHLER, tr. ROBERTSON, *Symbolism* (3rd ed., New York, s. d.), 353, 436–67.

N. A. WEBER.

Sweetheart Abbey. See NEW ABBEY.

Swetchine, SOPHIE-JEANNE SOYMONOF, writer, b. at Moscow, 22 Nov., 1782; d. in Paris, 10 Sept., 1857. She was a member of a noble family, and became associated with French literature through her correspondence and other writings. Impressed by her precocious intelligence, her father gave her a very careful education in everything except religion, which he ignored. At fourteen she was appointed maid of honour to the empress. At seventeen she was married to General Swetchine who was forty-two. By birth she belonged to the Greek, or Orthodox Church, but from the time that her trials, her reading, and her own reflections had made her a Christian, she felt the necessity of following to the end the path which was leading her to the truth, and she became a Catholic, despite the anguish of her heart. "My Faith," she said afterwards, "is to me what Benjamin was to Rachel, the child of my sorrow." At the time of her conversion she was thirty-three years old. She had already left the court, her husband having been disgraced, with his father, as the result of a plot of which he was the victim. Thenceforth she had to leave even her country, since as an avowed Catholic she could not remain at St. Petersburg. With her husband she went to reside at Paris at the beginning of the Restoration. She had been preceded by a letter from Joseph de Maistre, who wrote to Bonald: "In a short time you will see at Paris a Russian lady whom I especially commend to you. Never will you see such moral strength, wit, and learning joined to such goodness." In her *salon* in the Rue Saint Dominique, open from three to six, and from to nine to midnight, she saw all the most distinguished men of the period: Chateaubriand, Bonals, Cuvier, Cousin, Donoso Cortoes, and among her intimates were Augustin Cochin, Tocqueville, Falloux, who wrote her biography, Lacordaire, and Montalembert, who were like her spiritual sons. Her influence was incontestable. She died as a devout Christian in 1857 at the age of seventy-five.

She was remarkable more for the beauty of her soul than that of her countenance. Her intellect was lofty, quick, and penetrating. She read a great deal, and always with her pen in hand. She was pious to the verge of mysticism, and although constantly ill—for she was one of those who never pass a day without suffering—she was resigned to the will of Providence. While kind to all she was an incomparable friend. True modesty prevented her from publishing anything, but at her death she left enough to fill many volumes. De Falloux collected extracts from her manuscripts which were published: "Mme. Swetchine, sa vie, ses œuvres" (2 vols., 1860). There have since appeared: "Lettres de Mme. Swetchine" (1861); "Journal de sa conversion" (1863); "Correspondance du Père Lacordaire et de Mme. Swetchine" (1864); and "Nouvelles lettres de Mme. Swetchine" (1875). Although a Russian Mme. Swetchine wrote well in French; her style is delicate and original, even studied.

GEORGES BERTIN.

Sweynheim (SCHWEINHEIM), KONRAD, printer, b. at Schwanheim, Frankfort, Germany; d. in Rome, 1477. Sweynheim and Arnold Pannartz of Prague, both of whom were ecclesiastics, were the first printers in Italy. At the invitation of Cardinal John Turrecremata they established a printing-press for books in 1464 at the Abbey of Subiaco; in 1467 they removed their press to the Massimi Palace at Rome, and carried on the business jointly until 1472. The first books they printed were: "Donatus" (1464); Cicero's "De oratore" and the "Divinarum institutionum libri septem" of Lactantius (1465). During the years 1464-72 they issued over 12,000 copies of thirty-seven works, these works being chiefly the classics and the Fathers. This shows the remarkable skill of the two printers, who were entirely dependent on themselves. Being an engraver Sweynheim was probably the die-cutter, the type-founder, and the type-setter of the undertaking, while Pannartz had charge of the actual printing and of matters connected with it. The dies cut by Sweynheim deserve especial attention as they embody the preliminary steps of the present type for Latin characters. Sweynheim's typographical capitals are the first to show the forms used in the Roman inscriptions on stone, while some of his small letters repeat the characters used in manuscripts of the ninth to tenth centuries. He also cast the first Greek type; it is to be found in his third book, that of Lactantius, and the type copies the forms of Greek characters found in manuscripts of the seventh to the eighth centuries. Notwithstanding the greatest industry and technical skill the two printers had no pecuniary success. In 1472 their patron and fellow-worker as editor and proofreader, Bishop John Andreas Bussi of Aleria, secretary of the Vatican Library, asked Sixtus IV to aid them. The papal assistance was given in the form of an expectancy. Sweynheim received a canonry in the collegiate Church of St. Victor at Mainz to whose secular brotherhood the inventor Gutenberg also belonged. In 1472 Sweynheim and Pannartz dissolved partnership. Sweynheim worked until his death as engraver on the maps of the "Cosmography" of Ptolemy. He was the first to apply copper engraving to the production of maps; twenty-seven of the beautifully executed plates of the edition of the "Cosmography" of 1478 are his work. Especially characteristic of Sweynheim as a maker of matrices is the fact that the beautiful even writing of the names of places are stamped in the engraved plate by means of individual dies. It is certain that Sweynheim was in close connexion with Mainz until his death, although he did not return there to enjoy his benefice. There is no doubt that he learned the art of printing at Mainz.

HARTWIG, *Festschrift zum 500 jähr. Geburtstage von J. Gutenberg* (Mainz, 1900).

HEINRICH W. WALLAU.

Swinomish Indians.—A tribe of Salishan linguistic stock, closely connected with the Skagit. They formerly held the territory about the mouth of the river Skagit together with the adjacent portion of Whidbey Island, and are now gathered upon a reservation in the same territory, near Mount Vernon, Skagit County, north-western Washington. They were missionized about 1850, by Father Casimir Chirouse and the Oblates; Skagit the entire tribe, to the number of 267 in 1910, is now civilized and Catholic. They are one of the tribes included under the jurisdiction of Tulalip agency. For history and general description see TULALIP INDIANS.

JAMES MOONEY.

Swithin (SWITHUN), SAINT, Bishop of Winchester; d. 2 July, 862. Very little is known of this saint's life, for his biographers constructed their "Lives" long after his death and there is hardly any mention of him in contemporary documents. Swithin was one of the two trusted counsellors of Egbert, King of the West Saxons (d. 839), helping him in ecclesiastical matters, while Ealstan of Sherborne was his chief advisor in secular business. He probably entrusted Swithin with the education of his son Ethelwulf and caused the saint to be elected to the Bishopric of Winchester in succession to Helmstan. His consecration by Ceolnoth, Archbishop of Canterbury, seems to have taken place on 30 Oct., 852. On his death-bed Swithin begged that he should be buried outside the north wall of his cathedral where passers-by should pass over his grave and raindrops from the eaves drop upon it. More than a century later (931) his body was translated with great pomp to a shrine within the new church erected by Bishop Ethelwulf (d. 984). A number of miraculous cures took place and Swithin was canonized by popular acclamation. In 1093 his remains were again translated to the new church built by Bishop Walkelin. The shrine was destroyed and the relics scattered in 1538. It has often been said that the saint was a Benedictine monk and even Prior of Winchester but there is no evidence for this statement. From the first translation of his relics in

984 till the destruction of the shrine St. Swithin was the patron of Winchester Cathedral. He is best known from the popular superstition attached to his name and expressed in the following rhyme:

> St. Swithin's day if thou dost rain
> For forty days it will remain;
> St. Swithin's day if thou be fair
> For forty days 'twill rain nae mair.

There have been many attempts to explain the origin of this belief, but none have proved generally satisfactory. A similar belief attaches in France to 8 June, the feast of Sts. Gervasius and Protasius, and to other feasts in different countries (see "Notes and Queries", 1885, XII, 137, 253). St. Swithin's feast is kept on 15 July, the date of his first translation, and is retained in the Anglican Calendar.

The materials for the saint's life will be found in *Acta SS.*, July, I, 321 sqq. See also POTTHAST, *Wegweiser*, 1588; HUNT in *Dict. Nat. Biog.*, s. v. *Swithun;* HARDY, *Descriptive Catalogue*, I (1862), ii, 513 sqq.

RAYMUND WEBSTER.

Switzerland, a confederation in the central part of Western Europe, made up of twenty-two cantons, three of which are divided into half-cantons. The country lies between 45° 49′ 2″ and 47° 48′ 32″ north latitude, and 5° 57′ 26″ and 10° 29′ 40″ longitude east of Greenwich. Its area is 15,976 square miles. The name comes from the designation of one of the original cantons, Schwyz (Schwiz), which was extended in the course of time to the entire confederation.

PHYSICAL GEOGRAPHY AND ETHNOGRAPHY.—As regards its physical geography Switzerland is divided into three divisions: the Alps, the central region, and the Jura. The Swiss Alps form a part of the great curve of the Alpine chain of central Europe; they extend from Mont-Dolent in the chain of Mont Blanc in the west to Piz Mondin, in the Lower Engadine in the east, and have a length measured in a straight line of 170 miles. The smaller part of the Jura range, including, however, its highest peaks, is on Swiss soil. Between the Alps and the Jura extends the central region, which is traversed by countless valleys and includes about 30 per cent of the entire area of Switzerland. The highest peak of the Swiss Alps is Monte Rosa, 15,217 ft. The rivers which have their sources in Switzerland belong to one or another of the following four river-basins: the basin of the Rhine, the waters of which flow into the North Sea; the basin of the Rhone, which carries its waters to the western Mediterranean; the basin of the Po, which empties into the eastern Mediterranean, and the basin of the Inn, which empties into the Danube and with this into the Black Sea. The three river-basins first mentioned have a common watershed, the range of the Gothard. Switzerland also contains a large number of lakes, the largest of which are on the edges of the Alps and Jura, such as Geneva or Leman, Constance, Neuchâtel, Lucerne, Lugano, Maggiore, and Zurich. The lofty mountain chain of the Swiss Alps above a definite height is permanently covered with snow which feeds the glaciers. Switzerland contains altogether not less than 1077 glaciers, which cover an area of 709 sq. miles. Taken altogether 25.2 per cent of the area of Switzerland is completely unproductive.

The climate of Switzerland is not uniform. The differences in temperature of the various parts are conditioned by the differences in altitude, which vary from 581 feet to 15,217 feet above sea-level, and by the Alps, the southern slopes of which have a Mediterranean climate, while their northern slopes show that of central Europe. These striking differences determine the character of the flora and fauna. With the exception of the vegetation which flourishes on a seashore all European types of flora are to be found. The species of animals characteristic of the Alps are: the chamois, the ibex, the marmot, the golden eagle and several other species of birds. Of the productive area 3390 sq. miles are covered with forests, 8427 sq. miles are farm and pasture lands, and 108 sq. miles are planted with vineyards.

In 1850 the total population of Switzerland was 2,392,740 persons; the census of 1910 showed 3,753,293 inhabitants; on 1 December, 1910, the resident population (those actually present in the different localities) was altogether 3,765,002 persons. The original inhabitants of Switzerland were predominantly of Celtic race, although south of the Alps the Italian Lepontii lived in Ticino, and the Grisons was apparently inhabited by Etruscan Rhæti. A mixed population appeared in most parts of the territory owing to the Roman supremacy, the arrival of the Burgundians in the south-western district and of the Alamanni in other parts of the country. Four different languages appeared: German in the districts inhabited by the Alamanni, French in the western regions, where the scanty Burgundian population intermarried with the romanized Helvetii, Italian in Ticino, and Rhæto-Romanic in the Grisons. According to the last census the inhabitants were classified, by native tongues, as follows: Of 3,765,002 inhabitants, 2,599,154 spoke German; 796,244 French; 301,325 Italian; 39,834 Romanic; 28,445 spoke other languages.

POLITICAL HISTORY.—In the prehistoric era the territory of the present Switzerland was partly inhabited far up into the valleys of the Alps, as is evident from remains found in various caves and graves. Switzerland entered its historical era with the overthrow of the western Helvetii by Cæsar in the year 58 B. C. The entire country came under the control of the Roman Empire after the eastern districts were conquered by Drusus and Tiberius in 15 B. C. On the organization of the Roman provinces before Diocletian the north-western part of the territory of Switzerland belonged to the Province of Germania Superior, the south-western section (Geneva) to the Provincia Narbonensis, the eastern and the greater part of the south-eastern region to the Province of Rhætia. The region of the south-western Alps was divided into special administrative districts, of which the district of the "Alpes Pœninæ" included the present canton of Valais and the adjoining portions of Savoy. In the reorganization of the empire by Diocletian the Province of Rhætia and the district of the "Alpes Pœninæ" were left as they were, the north-western part of the country was included in the Province of Maxima Sequanorum, the south-western section in the Provincia Viennensis, the southern point of Ticino to Liguria, a province of Northern Italy.

During the migrations the territory of Switzerland was occupied by two German tribes. The Burgundians, who had settled in 443 south of Lake Geneva, pushed northwards and occupied the south-western and western regions of Switzerland. They mingled with the Romanic population and quickly adopted the Romanic tongue and customs, so that the language of this section remained Romanic (French). In the fifth century the Alamanni pushed forward as far as the Alps and completely destroyed Roman civilization, so that the language of this section became German. At the beginning of the sixth century all Switzerland north of the Alps fell under the supremacy of the Frankish Kingdom. At a later date, when the Lombard Kingdom was conquered by the Franks, the districts of Switzerland south of the Alps also came under the Frankish mastery. Thus Switzerland belonged to Charlemagne's great empire and shared its fortunes. In the partition of the Frankish Empire by the Treaty of Verdun in 843 the central and eastern parts of Switzerland fell to the Kingdom of Alamannia, the western to the Kingdom of Lorraine, and later to France. The power of the counts grew constantly, and in 888 Count Rudolph of the Guelphic family founded the Kingdom of Burgundy, of which western Switzerland formed a part. The German regions of Switzerland fell to the Duchy of Swabia in 917. In the ninth and tenth centuries several dynasties rose to power and importance, as: the Houses of Zähringen (extinct 1218), of Lenzburg, of Kyburg, and of Savoy. The inheritance of the Lenzburg family fell to the counts of Habsburg. In the twelfth and thirteenth centuries there were some twenty great feudal ruling families in the present Switzerland. The counts of Zähringen sought to secure their supremacy against the attacks of the rural nobility by founding cities, as Fribourg in 1178 and Berne in 1191. The dioceses and abbeys also gradually acquired secular power and rich possessions. When Duke Burkhard of Swabia died childless in 973 the duchy reverted to the German Empire. In 1033, after the death of King Rudolph III of Burgundy, his kingdom also fell to Germany, as Rudolph left it to the empire by will. Consequently the whole of present Switzerland, with the exception of Ticino, which was a part of Lombardy, belonged to the German Empire.

The inhabitants of the Alpine valleys of central Switzerland sought to protect their ancient rights against the growing power of the counts of Habsburg. In 1231 the people of Uri received from the German emperor, Henry, a charter which released them from the control of the counts of Habsburg; this is the first document by which the freedom of the early League of Switzerland was established. Schwyz received a similar charter in 1240 from Emperor Frederick II. In this way the territories of Uri and Schwyz were immediately dependent on the empire. Like the people of these two territories, the inhabitants of Unterwalden had also founded a provincial confederation. During the era of the struggle over the empire Rudolph of Habsburg strengthened his power in Switzerland; when in 1273 he became Emperor of Germany, his conquests transferred the centre of the power of the Habsburgs to Austria. Nevertheless, the emperor vigorously maintained his supremacy over his possessions in Switzerland. Directly after Rudolph's death (1291) the inhabitants of the districts combined in the original Swiss League sought to make use of the opportunity to secure their rights and privileges. On 1 August, 1291, the representatives of the provincial associations formed by Uri, Schwyz, and Unterwalden met and renewed the League that had been formed earlier. The purpose of the League was by united action to protect its members as far as possible against all attacks. The establishment of the League has been poetically embellished by the well-known story of the struggle of William Tell and his companions against the governor, Gessler, who oppressed the people.

Adolph of Nassau, who was elected King of Germany after the death of Rudolph of Habsburg, confirmed the charters of Uri and Schwyz, as did King Henry VII of Luxemburg on 3 June, 1309; at the same time Henry extended the rights and privileges contained in them to Unterwalden. After the death of Henry VII (1313) an old dispute as to the rights over the march between Schwyz and the Abbey of Einsiedeln broke out again and the confederated Swiss attacked the abbey, for which they were excommunicated by the Bishop of Constance and put under the ban of the empire at the same time. Louis of Bavaria withdrew the ban in 1315 and obliged the Archbishop of Mainz to recall the excommunication of the inhabitants of the forest districts (Uri, Schwyz, Unterwalden, and Lucerne). In the struggle for the imperial throne between Louis of Bavaria and Frederick of Austria the Swiss League, made up of these districts, held to Louis. Frederick's brother, Duke Leopold of Austria, attempted to overthrow the League and to punish its members for the attack on Einsiedeln, but his army was defeated by the Swiss at Morgarten on 15 November, 1315. On 9 December, 1315, Schwyz, Uri, and Unterwalden renewed the League and confirmed the same by additional regulations. In the truce concluded with the Duke of Austria the independence of the League was in some degree recognized. The further development of political conditions and the struggle with the Habsburgs connected with it led to the union with the forest districts of the city of Lucerne in 1332, the city of Zurich in 1351, and the district of Glarus and the city of Zug in 1352, all these new members joining the League. In 1353 the city of Berne also joined the League, so that now the old Confederation of eight cities and districts came into existence. The war with the League was renewed by Duke Leopold III of Austria, but in the battle near Sempach in 1386 his army was defeated and he himself was killed. This victory greatly strengthened the independence of the eight members of the Swiss League. The Austrians were again defeated in 1388 at Näfels, during the war with Glarus, which had declared its independence. In this way the freedom and independence of the eight communities were secured and a new compact made on 10 July, 1393.

The success of the Confederates encouraged the inhabitants of neighbouring territories in their struggles for political freedom. The city of St-Gall, which had been a free city of the empire from 1281, sought to make itself as independent as possible of the mastery of the prince-bishop. The inhabitants of Appenzell, who were subjects of the Abbot of St-Gall, also did the same; they gained their freedom and overthrew the lordship of the abbot by success in battle. In 1411 seven of the confederated communities (Berne not taking part) formed an agreement with Appenzell, by which it was taken under the protection of the League; in 1412 a similar agreement was made for ten years with the city of St-Gall, and in 1455 these treaties were changed into the "Everlasting Compact". The inhabitants of Upper Valais, who were subjects of the Bishop of Sion (Sitten), also gained for themselves a certain amount of political freedom, which they successfully defended in battle; they then formed a compact with the districts of Uri, Unterwalden, and Lucerne (1403 and 1416). The districts of Uri and Obwalden won territories south of the Alps in the Val Leventina (1403); some years later (1411) the League occupied jointly the Val d'Ossola and in 1419 bought the Countship of Bellinzona. However, in 1422, the League was defeated by the Duke of Milan and in 1426 it gave up its rights to the Val Leventina and the Val d'Ossola. During the Council of Constance Duke Frederick of Austria was declared under the ban of the empire by Emperor Sigismund. The Swiss League, by the order of the emperor, seized the Swiss lands of the duke; Berne took the cities of Aargau; Lucerne and Zurich took other cities and territories; the League conquered jointly other cities belonging to the Habsburgs. Thus the members of the League obtained subject lands, sometimes subject to the authority of an individual member of the League, sometimes ruled jointly by several members; this changed the former basis of the League, Count Frederick of Toggenburg, who had great possessions, had made various treaties with different members of the League. When he died without heirs in 1436, a dispute arose as to his domains, and Zurich became involved in a war with Schwyz. Zurich formed an alliance with the Emperor Frederick III against the other members of the League, and in the war which followed (1443) Zurich was defeated, while a general of the emperor defeated the League at Basle. In 1450 Zurich made peace by abandoning its alliance with the emperor. Various districts that had been subject to the counts of Toggenburg fell to Schwyz, Glarus, and Appenzell. In 1460 the districts of Thurgau and Sargans were occupied by the League as common property.

A new opponent of the Swiss Confederates now appeared in Duke Charles the Bold, of Burgundy. The Confederates formed an alliance with France and declared war against this powerful prince, who was allied, on his side, with the Duke of Savoy. The Swiss severely defeated Charles in the battles of Grandson and Murten in 1476. The city of Fribourg had taken part with the confederated Swiss and the two cities of Berne and Fribourg now took possession of several cities of Vaud, while the inhabitants of Upper Valais conquered Lower Valais, that belonged to Savoy. In 1841 the cities of Fribourg and Solothurn (Soleure) were taken as members into the League of the Confederates. The Burgundian War had brought the confederated districts into alliance with France, and consequently their connexion with the German Empire grew weaker and weaker. When in 1495 Emperor Maximilian sought to reorganize the empire, the Confederates were unwilling to recognize the changes. In the struggle, called the Swabian War between the Swiss Confederates and the imperial troops the Swiss were victorious. The Treaty of Basle of 1499 granted the Confederates almost complete independence from the German Empire by releasing them from the jurisdiction of the imperial chamber. Later, in the Peace of Westphalia of 1648, the political separation of Switzerland from Germany was expressly declared. On account of the Swabian War, the cities of Basle and Schaffhausen joined the Confederation in 1501, and in 1513 Appenzell also was accepted as a district belonging to it, so that the Confederation now included thirteen districts. In addition the Countship of Neuchâtel became an associate member, and the Confederation was joined as associate members by the three leagues of the Rhætian Alps: the "Grauer Bund", the "Zehngerichtenbund" (League of the Ten Jurisdictions), and the "Gotteshausbund".

Upper Valais and other spiritual and secular lordships also became associate members. There was no central organized authority over all. The individual members formed special alliances among themselves; their common affairs were discussed at the assembly of the members, which was a congress of sovereign states. In addition to the representatives of the thirteen members of the Confederation most of the associate districts of the Confederation had also the right to send representatives. Other territories were subject lands of one or several members of the Confederation, or belonged in common to the entire Confederation of the thirteen districts. Geneva had formed an alliance with Fribourg and Berne for the protection of its liberties against the bishops and dukes of Savoy; this made it an associate member. From this time on the Swiss Confederates took an important part in the general politics of Europe, especially in the wars in Italy. The Confederates acquired new possessions south of the Alps in Ticino. However, at the battle of Marignano in 1515, the Swiss troops were severely defeated, which put an end to Swiss intervention in European politics.

The inner organization of the different districts of the Confederation varied greatly. Some had a democratic organization; in others the rule of the patrician town council was aristocratic. In the course of the eighteenth century many disputes arose in the cities on account of the despotic patrician government. After the outbreak of the French Revolution this state of affairs led to the interference of France, and in 1798 the territories of the Confederation were occupied by French troops. After the dissolution of the oligarchic governments, the "indivisible Helvetic Republic" with a new Constitution was proclaimed. All the confederated districts and the former subject lands were incorporated in the Republic. The opposition of the original Swiss League was crushed by the French army, the Helvetic Republic was entirely dependent on France. New quarrels constantly arose in Switzerland over the Constitution. Napoleon, therefore, on 19 February, 1803, issued the Act of Mediation, by which Switzerland was changed into a Confederation of nineteen cantons under the protection of France. The Diocese of Basle, the city of Geneva, Ticino, and Valais were annexed by France; the Principality of Neuchâtel was given to Marshal Berthier. In 1815 the Congress of Vienna gave back to Switzerland the districts of Geneva, Valais, and Ticino. Berne was obliged to grant freedom to its former subject lands of Aargau and Vaud, and received as compensation the greater part of the territories of the Bishop of Basle in the Jura; Neuchâtel was at the same time a Prussian principality and a Swiss canton. The second Treaty of Paris gave further districts of France and Savoy to Geneva. Thus Switzerland received its present extent of territory, and formed a confederation of twenty-two cantons, united in complete equality.

The inner political development of several cantons led to disputes concerning the Constitution, especially after the outbreak of the French Revolution of July, 1830. Half the cantons received democratic constitutions; this caused a civil war in Basle that divided the canton into two half-cantons (city of Basle and rural Basle). At the same time a movement for the revision of the Treaty of Confederation of 1815 was started by seven democratic cantons which had formed an agreement among themselves. The Catholic cantons opposed a revision because they feared that it would not only result in a reduction of cantonal sovereignty, but also lead to interference with their religious freedom. The Articles of Baden, agreed to in 1834 by several cantons, introduced Josephinism into the relations between Church and State and greatly impaired ecclesiastical rights. In December, 1845, the seven Catholic cantons, namely, Uri, Schwyz, Unterwalden, Lucerne, Zug, Fribourg, and Valais, united in a league, called the "Sonderbund" (separate league), for the protection of their sovereignty and of their territories. The majority of the cantons decided at the Diets of August, 1846, and of July, 1847, that this league should be dissolved, because it was not compatible with the Treaty of Confederation of 1815. At the same time the same majority voted for a revision of the Constitution, and also voted against the continued presence of the Jesuits in Switzerland. The seven Catholic cantons made ready for war. At the Diet held in October, 1847, their representatives moved that their sovereignty and their ecclesiastical rights be recognized, and that the question as to the Jesuits be removed from the subjects for discussion. The motion was rejected, and the protesting deputies of the seven cantons left the Diet. The civil war, called the War of the Sonderbund, now broke out. The Catholic cantons were defeated, and the war ended without much bloodshed. Radical governments were now forced upon the conquered cantons, but these administrators were later set aside by the popular majorities of the Catholic Conservative party. The expenses of the war to the amount of five million francs were imposed upon the defeated cantons, the result of which was their economic impairment. The Jesuits were driven out and about fifty monasteries and religious foundations were suppressed. It was a victory of Radical Liberalism over the Conservative party. In 1848 Neuchâtel freed itself from Prussia and adopted a new republican Constitution.

On 12 September, 1848, the new Constitution of the Confederation was proclaimed and put in force. It transformed Switzerland into a Confederation similar to the United States. The individual cantons retained, indeed, their sovereignty and their separate Constitutions, but the exercise of sovereignty was

THE CATHEDRAL OF SAN LORENZO, LUGANO, 1517

limited by the federation. There was an assembly to represent the individual states called the Council of States (*Ständerat*), and one to represent the entire Swiss nation called the National Council (*Nationalrat*), which formed together the legislative body of the Confederation. The executive authority was in the hands of a body called the Federal Council. The cantons, however, still retained the right of levying taxes, of police supervision, of the administration of justice, and religious affairs, and all legislation regarding schools. The universities of Switzerland also all remained cantonal institutions; they exist at the present time in Basle, Zurich, Berne, Geneva, Lausanne, Fribourg, and Neuchâtel. Foreign affairs, the army, customs, postal administration, and coinage were transferred to the federation. The Constitution was revised in 1874, and on 9 April of this year the new Constitution was accepted; with a few partial changes it is still in existence. It rests on the principles of a decided centralization as regards the army and the judiciary, and, unfortunately, contains also severe articles directed against the Catholic Church (prohibition of houses of Jesuits, of the founding of new monasteries, etc.). A federal supreme court was established for the entire Confederation. In many of the cantons a strong movement began for making the cantonal constitutions more democratic, and during the last decades new constitutions have been introduced in a large number of them. The creation of a common code of law for civil and criminal cases was transferred to the Confederation. The railways were made state property by the purchase of the larger railways from the companies owning them, the purchase being confirmed in 1898; in this way their administration belongs to the Confederation.

THE COMMONWEALTH.—Switzerland forms a confederation made up of the following twenty-two cantons, three being divided into half-cantons. The cantons have sovereign authority in all matters which are not under the jurisdiction of the Confederation. These competencies, however, frequently conflict, as in matters respecting the army, sanitary officers, and police supervision of foreigners. The decisions of the Federal Government are generally executed by the cantonal Governments. The main matters under the jurisdiction of the Confederation are: Intercourse with other countries and the exclusive right to make treaties with them and to direct the foreign policy; since 1898 the entire domain of civil and criminal law, for the purpose of unifying these two codes, although, with the exception of the Federal Court, the organization of the courts belongs to the cantons; the army, all legislation, and the supervision of legislative work; the right to carry out public works that benefit a considerable part of the country; further, the right of general supervision over water and forest inspection. The Confederation also established a federal polytechnic high school at Zurich, the supervision of which belongs exclusively to the federal authorities, while all other schools are cantonal and receive in part subventions from the Federal Government. The Federal Government owns and has the control of the customs, post-office, telegraph and telephone, coinage (since 1905 the monopoly of the issuing of bank-notes has been given to the federal national bank), the manufacture and sale of powder, wholesale selling of alcohol. Trade inspection is also largely regulated by federal law, and the Government has the right to introduce sickness and accident insurance; a law in reference to these was accepted by the nation in 1912. Since they were made state property the larger, standard-gauge railways have been carried on by the Federal Government. The Constitution of the Confederation guarantees freedom of faith and conscience, as well as freedom of worship. Notwithstanding this, the Constitution forbids the reception of Jesuits and affilliated orders and the founding of new monasteries, while the establishment of new dioceses in Switzerland is made dependent on the consent of the Confederation. All these special ordinances refer only to the Catholic Church.

The federal authorities are: (1) legislative; (2) executive; (3) judicial. (1) The legislative authority is the Federal Assembly, composed of two concurrent chambers: the National Council and the Council of States. The National Council is elected directly by the people for three years, there being a deputy for each 20,000 inhabitants, or for a fraction over 10,000 inhabitants of a canton. For this purpose Switzerland is divided into federal electoral districts. The election is direct and the ballot secret. All Swiss citizens over twenty years of age, who are not prevented by cantonal laws from exercising political rights, are entitled to vote. All citizens entitled to vote are also entitled to hold office. The Council of States consists of 44 deputies, of whom each canton appoints two, and each half-canton one. The members of the Council of States are elected, according to the law of each canton, either by the people of the canton, or by the cantonal council, which is the cantonal legislative body. The passage of a law requires the agreement of both the States and National Councils. These two councils unite in the Federal Assembly for certain matters, especially for the election of the executive authorities and of the members of the Federal Court, for voting upon petitions for pardon, for settling disputes as to jurisdiction between federal authorities. The nation has the right of the referendum; when 30,000 citizens entitled to vote, or eight cantons of Switzerland, make the demand, any federal law and any generally binding federal ordinance, if not of a pressing nature, must be laid before the nation, so that the latter by a majority vote can accept or reject it. In 28 cases during the years 1874–1906 in which the referendum vote was taken, the law or the federal decision was rejected in 19 cases. The people also have an initiative in matters respecting the Federal Constitution, inasmuch as 50,000 citizens entitled to vote may petition for a change in the Constitution upon a definite point. The Federal Assembly also can present a similar demand for a change in the Constitution.

(2) The executive authority is the Federal Council, which is composed of seven members, elected by the joint Federal Assembly for three years. Any citizen eligible to the National Council can be elected to the Federal Council. The president of the Federal Council is elected each year by the Federal Assembly, as is also the vice-president; the president cannot be re-elected for the ensuing year. The Federal Council is responsible for the exercise of its office to the Federal Assembly, yet the rejection by the chambers of a bill offered by a member of the Federal Council does not necessitate the dismissal of the respective member. The executive administration of the Confederation is divided into seven departments, each of which is under the direction of a member of the Federal Council; the Department of Foreign Affairs, which is always under the direction of the president of the Confederation; the Department of the Interior, which controls the numerous federal subventions, supervises game and fish inspectors, weights and measures, and directs the sanitary inspectors, and the execution of the laws respecting food; the Department of Justice and Police; the Military Department; the Department of Finance and Customs; the Department of Commerce, Industry, and Agriculture; the Post-Office and Railway Department. (3) The judicial authority is the Federal Court at Lausanne. Up to 1912 the court consisted of nineteen members; when the number was raised to twenty-four, to which should be added nine substitute members. The federal judges are elected for six years by the Federal Assembly. The court is divided into three sections;

one for appeals in the domain of public law and certain matters of civil law, the second for the other appeals in civil law, the third for complaints respecting the law of bankruptcy and the law of obligation. For criminal cases there is a criminal court of three judges and twelve assessors. The federal attorney-general is appointed by the Federal Council.

The Constitutions of the Swiss cantons are in all cases democratic. However, great differences are to be found in the various cantons in regard to the cantonal Constitution, taxation, communal Government, etc. In the larger cantons the legislative body is a council elected by the people, called the Cantonal Council, or the Great Council. The members of the cantonal Governments are elected either by this council or directly by the people. The smaller cantons have as the legislative body the cantonal assembly, composed of all the active citizens of the canton, which elects the cantonal authorities. The chief political parties of Switzerland, as represented in the Federal Assembly, especially in the chamber called the National Council, are: (1) The Radical or Progressive-Democratic party that avowedly strives after greater centralization; this principle is especially advocated by the Radicals of German-Switzerland. At times this part shows anti-Catholic tendencies, as was particularly evidenced in the War of the Sonderbund, and in the turmoil caused by the Old Catholic movement; during the last twenty years, however, this hostility has not been so marked. This party is the dominating one throughout the entire Confederation. (2) The Catholic-Conservative party. (3) The Liberal-Conservative, or Protestant party. Both the Catholic- and Liberal-Conservative parties are Federalists, but lay stress upon the rights of cantonal sovereignty. (4) The Social-Democratic party.

ECCLESIASTICAL HISTORY.— There is no doubt that Christian missions were started in the territory of the present Switzerland as early as the third century, but it was not until after the Constantinian era that they made decided progress. The missionaries of Christianity entered the country by three main roads: by way of the valley of the Rhone to Geneva, from Italy over the Great St. Bernard to Valais and into western Switzerland to the Helvetii, and over the passes of the Alps by way of the Grisons into eastern Switzerland to the Rhætians. After the political repartition of the Roman Empire during the reign of Diocletian, the earliest Swiss dioceses appeared in the course of the fourth century: in Valais the Diocese of Octodurum (Martigny), the see of which was transferred in the sixth century to Sion (*Sitten*); in the south-west the Diocese of Geneva (*Genava*) was founded in the *Civitas Genavensium*, which belonged to the great territories of the Allobroges; western and central Switzerland received the Diocese of the Helvetii, that was established in the *Civitas Helvetiorum;* its bishop lived now at Aventicum (*Avenches*), now at Vindonissa (*Windisch*), until at a later date, between the years 585 and 650, the see was transferred to Lausanne, and the northern part of the region, that had been taken by the Alamanni, was assigned to the Diocese of Constance. In the north-west the Diocese of Basle, the origin of which is obscure, was established in the *Civitas Rauracorum*. A part of the present Swiss Jura belonged to the Diocese of Besançon; towards the east, in Rhætia, the Diocese of Chur (Coire) was established. The territories south of the Alps belonged in part to the Dioceses of Como and Milan. A famous shrine was the church built over the graves of the martyr St. Mauritius and his companions (St. Maurice in Valais); in 515 the Burgundian King Sigismund founded an abbey at this spot, the oldest monastery on Swiss soil.

The occupation of western Switzerland by the Burgundians, although they were Arians, led to no serious interruption of the life of the Church. At the beginning of the sixth century King Sigismund became a Catholic; this was quickly followed by the adoption of the Catholic Faith by the Burgundians. From 534 the entire territory of the Burgundians belonged to the Kingdom of the Franks, as they took part in the religious development of this kingdom. The Alamanni were still heathen and when they migrated into northern and north-eastern Switzerland they destroyed, along with the Roman civilization, almost the entire organization of the Church. After the Franks subjugated the Alamanni in 496 the Irish missionaries began to labour in their territories. In the sixth century the Diocese of Constance was founded for Alamannia; it included those parts of Switzerland occupied by this people. St. Columba and St. Gall from the Irish monastery of Bangor laboured on the shores of Lake Constance and on those of Lake Zurich. When about 612 Columba went to Italy, Gall remained behind and founded a monastery, from which developed the celebrated Abbey of St-Gall. The monastery of Reichenau was of great importance in the further spread of Christianity on Lake Constance. Other monasteries were founded in eastern Switzerland, among them Pfaefers and Dissentis, and in the tenth century Einsiedeln. In western Switzerland famous abbeys were established in the territory of the Burgundians, as St-Imier, St-Ursanne, and Romainmotier; these, however, did not appear until the Frankish era. As time went on the growth of religion and civilization brought rich possessions and large secular power to the bishops and abbeys.

The great movement for the reformation of the monasteries during the tenth century, in which Cluny led the way, reached western Switzerland and caused the founding of new and important abbeys, such as Payern in Vaux, St-Victor in Geneva, St-Alban in Basle, and others. Several more Benedictine abbeys were established in the twelfth century; among these were Muri in Schaffhausen, Fischingen at Thurgau; some Cistercian abbeys were also founded, as Hauterive in Fribourg, St-Urban in Lucerne, and Wettingen in Aargau, while the Premonstratensians and Carthusians established numerous monastic houses in various districts of Switzerland. The change in monastic life introduced in the thirteenth century by the Franciscans and Dominicans, who settled in the cities to exercise pastoral care, extended throughout Switzerland at an early date. Both Franciscan and Dominican monasteries sprang up in numerous cities, at Basle, Zurich, Berne, Schaffhausen, Solothurn, Chur, Fribourg, Lausanne, Geneva, and others. Among the knightly orders, the Knights of St. John of Jerusalem had the largest number of houses, some of which were endowed with large revenues. Other orders had a few monasteries. There were also large numbers of convents for women. Besides the monasteries there were houses of Augustinian canons in Switzerland, a few of which still exist in the Catholic cantons. Thus a rich religious life sprang up in the various districts of Switzerland around the numerous religious foundations of various kinds, the sees of the dioceses, the abbeys and other monasteries, and the religious institutions of the cities.

The Protestant schism of the sixteenth century began in German Switzerland with the position taken by Zwingli in Zurich at the same time that it appeared in Germany. At first the religious innovation met with but little success. On 8 April, 1524, the five districts of Uri, Schwyz, Unterwalden, Zug, and Lucerne decided to retain the old, true Christian Faith and to suppress the erroneous doctrine within their territories. At the Diet of the Confederation held at Lucerne on 20 April of the same year this decision was adopted by all the districts excepting Zurich and Schaffhausen. During this period Anabaptists made their appearance, especially in St-Gall and the Grisons, and Anabaptist communities were established in several districts including Schaffhausen and Appenzell. A peasant revolt broke out, partly in connexion with the Anabaptist movement; this outbreak, however, was mainly settled by negotiations after serfdom had been abolished. Notwithstanding the decisions of the Diet of 1524 and all efforts made by the Catholic districts of central Switzerland, Zwinglianism spread to other Swiss cities and territories. The heretical doctrine was introduced into the city of St-Gall by Joachim von Watt (Vadianus) and his followers; in 1528 all Catholics were excluded from the council, and only the abbey remained loyal to the Catholic Faith. Zwinglianism extended from St-Gall into Appenzell and spread among the communes of Appenzell-Ausserrhoden. Through the influence of Zurich, Protestantism was introduced into Toggenburg, which belonged to the Abbey of St-Gall, and into Thurgau, so that in 1525 the majority of the inhabitants of both these districts belonged to the new faith. Protestantism also found entrance into Glarus, Sargans, and the valley of the Rhine, as well as into the Grisons. In these districts, however, the adherents of the heretical doctrine could not attain absolute control. The cities of Basle and Schaffhausen also fell away from the Catholic Faith; much was done for the spread of Protestantism at Basle by Œcolampadius (q. v.). For a considerable time Berne wavered, but in 1528 the new doctrines urged by Francis Kolb, N. Manuel, Berchtold Haller, and Johann Haller conquered, and the heretical doctrine was introduced by force in all the territories of Berne.

The districts that had become Protestant united both with one another and with foreign Protestant cities. The five Catholic districts of Switzerland, mentioned above, had also united in defence of the old Faith in their territories, and had formed an alliance with Austria. Zwingli now sought to force them to submit to his erroneous teachings. This resulted in the two wars of Kappel (1528-31), which ended in the victory of the Catholic districts by the battle near Kappel in 1531, in which Zwingli was killed. In the second Peace of Kappel which was now signed (1531) the Catholic Faith was completely restored in the common dependencies of Baden, Freiamt, and Rapperswyl, and numerous parishes in Thurgau; the valley of the Rhine became Catholic again and the monasteries were re-established. The Protestant Faith was recognized by the Constitution; in the religiously mixed districts and in the German subject lands the individual parishes could decide to which faith to belong, but the free exercise of the religion of the minority was protected; the districts which were entirely Protestant or entirely Catholic retained their respective confessions, and the alliance of the Zwinglian districts was dissolved. In the meantime the heretical doctrine had been carried from Berne into French Switzerland. Among the lordships belonging to the Bishop of Basle in the Jura the new faith made its way into the Münsterthal, Biel, the city of Neuchâtel, and also in the district of Neuchâtel. In 1536 Berne conquered the district of Vaux and introduced Protestantism into it by force, as well as in the lands that Berne owned in common with Fribourg. Berne also supported the adherents of the new faith, which in 1535 had gained the supremacy in the possesions of its ally Geneva, where Calvin soon made his appearance and where he established a new centre of Protestantism.

In religious matters the Confederation was now divided as follows: the five districts of Uri, Schwyz, Unterwalden, Zug, and Lucerne with their dependencies (among them Ticino), also Fribourg, Solothurn, the allied Valais, the Abbot of St-Gall, and the common dependencies of Baden, Freiamt, and Rapperswyl remained Catholic; Zurich, Berne with Vaud, Basle, Schaffhausen, the city of St-Gall, and Geneva were Protestant; both confessions existed together in Appenzell, which in 1597 was divided into Catholic Innerrhoden and Protestant Ausserrhoden, Glarus, the Grisons (where only the "graue Bund" remained Catholic), and in the dependent districts of Aargau Thurgau, Werdenberg, the valley of the Rhine, and Toggenburg. True inner religious reform, based on the pure Catholic Faith, found zealous promoters in Switzerland in the era of the Council of Trent. St. Charles Borromeo (q. v.) laboured with great success, as did also Bishop Christopher Blarer of Basle. Of great value in this work was the summoning of the Jesuits, of whom the most important was Peter Canisius (q. v.); in the years succeeding 1574 they erected flourishing colleges in numerous cities, as Lucerne, Fribourg, Porrentruy, Siders, Brig, Sion, and Solothurn. The Capuchins also entered Switzerland at the same time, and erected their first monastery on Swiss soil at Altorf in 1579; this was gradually followed by the founding of nearly thirty more houses, so that their spiritual labours embraced the larger part of the Catholic districts of the Confederation. Another important factor in the revival of ecclesiastical and religious life was the establishment of a permanent papal nunciature to the Confederation with its seat at Lucerne (from 1579). The Collegium Helveticum at Milan and the Collegium Germanicarum at Rome, both of which had a number of free scholarships for Swiss theologians, did much for the thorough education and earnest religious training of the clergy. The revival of Catholic life was vigorously supported by zealous and orthodox priests, such as provost Schneuwly at Fribourg, and Catholic statesmen, such as L. Pfyffer, of Lucerne, and M. Lussy in the forest districts that had formed the original Swiss League. The internal reform of the Church based on the decrees of the Council of Trent made its way throughout Catholic Switzerland to the great benefit of the loyal Catholic population. The seven Catholic districts formed the Borromæan League in 1586 to prevent the further advance of Protestantism.

The subject lands of Bormia, Chiavenna, and Val Tellina, which had belonged to the Grisons since 1513, remained loyal to the Catholic Faith. They were hard pressed, and the attempts to spread the heretical doctrine in these regions also were supported in every possible manner by the Protestant majority in the Grisons. During the violent political disputes which raged in the Grisons during the seventeenth century a revolt broke out in Val Tellina. The knight James of Grossoto marched into the valley in 1620 and a large part of the Protestant population was killed (the Valtelline Massacre). This led to a war between the Protestant and Catholic districts and their foreign allies, the final end of which was that the Val Tellina and the other Italian subject lands were lost to the Confederates. After the Peace of Kappel of 1531 the Catholic districts had the majority in the Diet of the Confederation, a point of much importance in the garrisoning of the lands held in common that separated Berne and Zurich from each other. These two powerful Protestant members of the Diet sought an occasion to change this state of affairs. The suppression of a Protestant community in Arth, that belonged to Schwyz, gave rise to a dispute between the Catholic and Protestant districts which led to the two Villmergen wars (1656 and 1712). The Catholic districts conquered in the first war; disturbances in Toggenburg led to the second war, in which political questions were especially prominent. This latter war ended in the victory of the Protestant districts, and it was followed by a new partition of the common lordships in favour of the conquerors, as well as by the granting of complete parity to the Protestant inhabitants of the subject lands. This treaty divided the Confederation into two distinct confessional groups.

The hostility to the Church shown in the French

Revolution was also evidenced in the measures adopted by the Helvetic Republic in Switzerland. By a decree of 1798 the possessions of all Swiss monasteries were declared to be national property, and a further decree suppressed, in theory, all monasteries. The papal nuncio was expelled, and foreign bishops were permitted to exercise their ecclesiastical jurisdiction only through delegates who were nominated by the Helvetic Directory. The decree respecting the monasteries was not executed. By the Act of Mediation of 1803 the property of the monasteries was returned to them, and the monasteries could be reopened. Only the venerable Abbey of St-Gall was definitely suppressed. Part of the abbey lands were incorporated in the state property of the Canton of St-Gall, and part were reserved as a special fund for the Catholics of the canton. After the turmoil of the Napoleonic era and after the suppression of the Diocese of Constance the ecclesiastical administration was gradually reorganized during the period of the Restoration. By an agreement of 28 March, 1828, the Diocese of Basle was re-established, with the see at Solothurn (Soleure). The Swiss portion of the Diocese of Geneva was united with the Diocese of Lausanne, and the bishop, whose see was Fribourg, received the title of Bishop of Lausanne and Geneva. The Diocese of Sion (Sitten) was left essentially as before. In 1836 Pope Gregory XVI erected the Vicariate Apostolic of St-Gall, which was later changed into a bishopric. The old Diocese of Chur, which continued to exist, received new boundaries by agreements made with the cantons that had formed the original League. In 1888, after long negotiations, the Canton of Ticino was released from its diocesan connexion with Como and Milan and made a diocese which was, however, united with Basle; it is ruled by an Apostolic administrator with the rank of a bishop.

The War of the Sonderbund greatly damaged Catholic interests in Switzerland. Not only were the Jesuits driven out and their flourishing schools suppressed, but most of the monasteries in the Catholic cantons were also suppressed by the violent radical Governments that had come into power. Even at a later date the Cantons of Thurgau, Zurich, Solothurn, and Aargau secularized the monasteries in their territories and confiscated the monastic possessions. During the nineteenth century some sixty monastic institutions were suppressed throughout Switzerland. In a number of the cantons a strong spirit of Josephinism became apparent, and the free exercise of ecclesiastical authority was frequently prevented. The Catholic minority in the Protestant cantons was oppressed in various ways. This was especially the case on the appearance of Old Catholicism which caused a regular persecution of Catholic priests and people in some cantons, especially Berne and Geneva. The opposition which sprang up in various countries to the definitions of the Vatican Council also manifested itself in Switzerland, and small Old Catholic parishes were formed in various places. The Old Catholics of Switzerland united to form the "Christian Catholic National Church" which received formal recognition both from the Federal Council and from the Governments of several cantons. The Governments of the Cantons of Berne and Geneva settled renegade priests over Catholic parishes by force; churches, parsonages, and the church property were given to these priests and their few adherents by the administrative authorities. A Christian Catholic theological faculty for the training of Old Catholic priests was established at the University of Berne; this faculty still continues a languishing existence.

When Lachat was appointed Administrator Apostolic of Ticino, and Mermillod, Bishop of Lausanne and Geneva, the authorities of the Confederation and some of the cantonal Governments began to yield somewhat in the struggle with the Catholics. Many churches in the Bernese Jura and in Geneva were returned to the Catholics, frequently, though, under great material sacrifice by the latter. The Old Catholic movement in Switzerland, as everywhere else, began very soon to decline. Of late years the attempt has been made in different Swiss cantons to separate Church and State. This separation has been carried out practically in Geneva and Basle. Catholic life has greatly developed in Switzerland notwithstanding the difficulties caused by the War of the Sonderbund and the persecution caused by the Old Catholic movement. Among the larger Catholic organizations which extend over the whole of Switzerland mention should be made of the Catholic People's Union; this society unites the individual organizations into one large association, and labours with much success in the fields of religion, charity, social work, and education. The section for home missions, that aids Catholic parishes in the *diaspora*, distributed for this purpose the sum of 202,720 francs in 1910, and helped 105 mission parishes. The historical section supports the "Zeitschrift für schweizerische Kirchengeschichte". In addition to the People's Union mention should also be made of the "Association of Swiss Catholic Students", which is active in all of the Swiss universities, in several foreign ones, and in the Swiss lyceums, and which has a large membership. A matter of much importance for Catholic life was the founding of the cantonal University of Fribourg (q. v.).

RELIGIOUS STATISTICS.—Of the 3,765,002 actual inhabitants of Switzerland on 1 December, 1910, 2,108,590 were Protestants, 1,590,792 were Catholics, 19,023 Jews, and 46,597 belonged to other confessions or to none. A comparison of the number of Catholics with that of the Protestants at the census of 1900 shows that the Catholics have increased at a more rapid rate within the last ten years than the Protestants. This arises mainly from the fact that the adjacent parts of the neighbouring countries are all Catholic, so that immigration almost always increases only the Catholic population. The Catholic inhabitants of Switzerland belong to the following dioceses: (1) Basle-Lugano; in this double bishopric the Diocese of Basle includes the Cantons of Solothurn, Lucerne, Zug, Berne, Aargau, Thurgau, Basle, and Schaffhausen, while the Diocese of Lugano embraces the Canton of Ticino. (2) Chur, which includes the Cantons of the Grisons, Schwyz, Uri, Unterwalden (both Obwalden and Nidwalden), Glarus, Zurich, and, in addition, the Principality of Lichtenstein. (3) Lausanne-Geneva, which includes the Cantons of Fribourg, Vaud (with exception of a few parishes which belong to Sion), Neuchâtel and Geneva. (4) St-Gall, which includes the cantons of St-Gall, and the two half-Cantons of Appenzell. (5) Sion, which includes the Canton of Valais and the Catholic parishes of the governmental department of Aigle in the Canton of Vaud. In addition there are: the exempt episcopal Abbey of Saint-Maurice in Valais, the abbot of which is always the titular Bishop of Bethlehem, the exempt Abbey of Einsiedeln, the exempt priory of the Great St-Bernard, and two prefectures Apostolic in the Grisons, namely Misox-Calanca, and Rhætia.

With the exception of the Moravians and two Lutheran parishes in Geneva, all the Protestants of Switzerland belong to the Evangelical Reformed Church. The great majority of these belong to the "National Churches", of which there are fifteen, which are organized according to cantons. There are numerous differences in details in the constitutions of these cantonal National Churches. Besides these there are also large independent Protestant Churches and Evangelical sects of the most varied kinds. In the census the Old Catholics are not counted as independent confessions, but are enumerated among the Catholics. Altogether they number about 30,000 persons (more exact statistics are not obtainable). Four

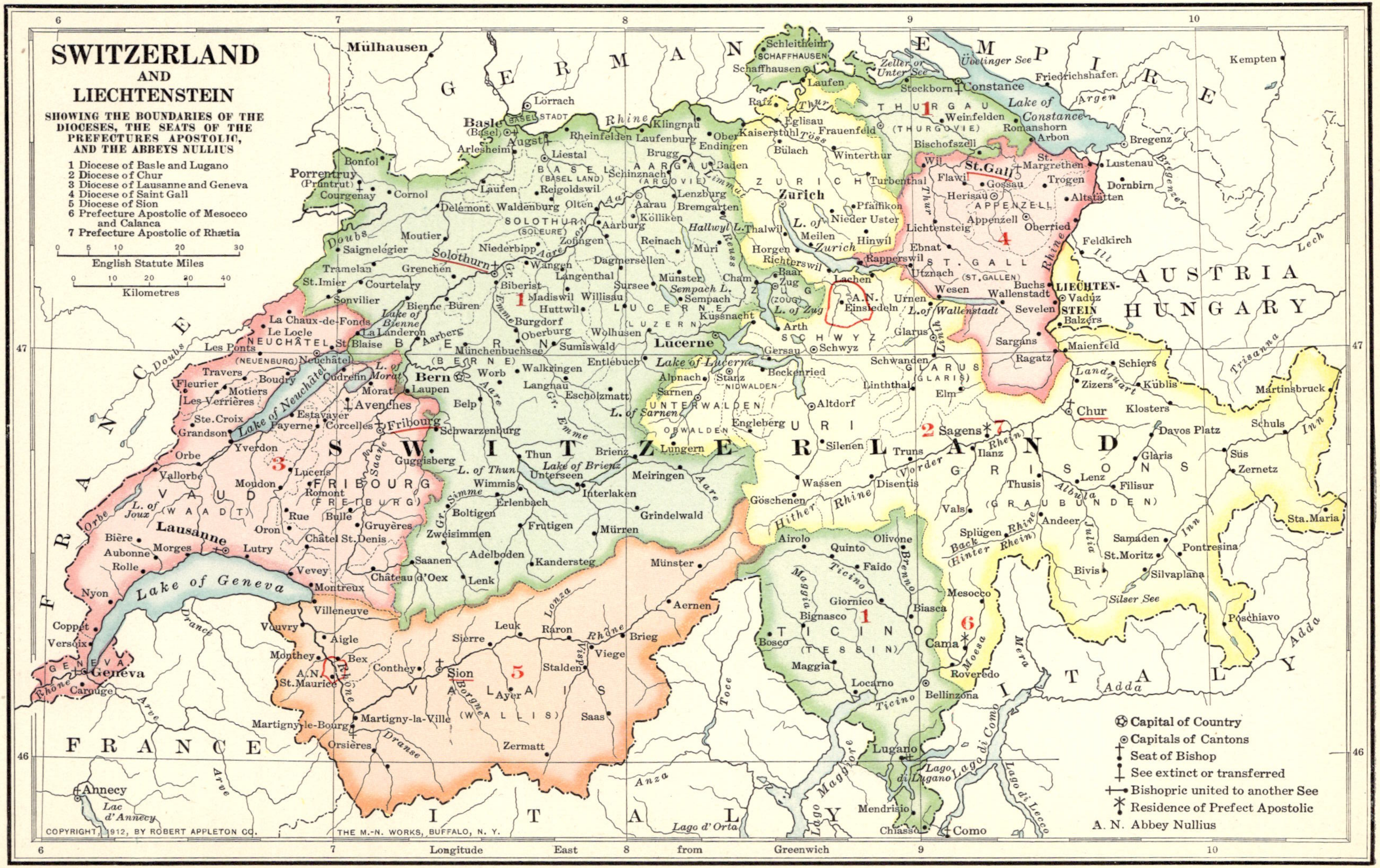

SWITZERLAND
AND
LIECHTENSTEIN
SHOWING THE BOUNDARIES OF THE DIOCESES, THE SEATS OF THE PREFECTURES APOSTOLIC, AND THE ABBEYS NULLIUS
1 Diocese of Basle and Lugano
2 Diocese of Chur
3 Diocese of Lausanne and Geneva
4 Diocese of Saint Gall
5 Diocese of Sion
6 Prefecture Apostolic of Mesocco and Calanca
7 Prefecture Apostolic of Rhætia
English Statute Miles
Kilometres
Capital of Country
Capitals of Cantons
Seat of Bishop
See extinct or transferred
Bishopric united to another See
Residence of Prefect Apostolic
A. N. Abbey Nullius
GERMAN EMPIRE
AUSTRIA HUNGARY
FRANCE
ITALY
SWITZERLAND
LIECHTENSTEIN
Basle
Bern
Zurich
Lucerne
Lausanne
Geneva
St.Gall
Chur
Sion
Fribourg
Solothurn
Lugano
Lake of Geneva
Lake of Constance
Lake of Neuchâtel
Lake of Lucerne
Longitude East from Greenwich
COPYRIGHT, 1912, BY ROBERT APPLETON CO.
THE M.-N. WORKS, BUFFALO, N. Y.

years ago the list of Old Catholic clergy gave 56 names; in the summer half-year of 1910 the Old Catholic theological department at Berne had three Swiss and six foreign students. In addition to the Old Catholic bishop, the Christian Catholic National Church is administered by a national synod which meets annually; besides the Old Catholic priests and the bishop its membership includes delegates elected by the parishes. The Swiss Jews are united for worship into twenty-two communities which are organized in accordance with the laws of the Confederation for associations.

STUDER, *Geologie der Schweiz* (Zurich, 1851–53); HEER, *Die Urwelt der Schweiz* (2nd ed., Zurich, 1879); SCHRÖTER, *Das Pflanzenleben der Alpenwelt* (Zurich, 1907); VON TSCHUDI, *Das Tierleben dor Alpenwelt* (11th ed., Leipzig, 1890); ZIMMERLI, *Die deutsch-französische Sprachgrenze in der Schweiz* (Basle, 1891–99); VON SALIS, *Bundesrecht* (5 vols., 2nd ed., Berne, 1903—); MEYER, *Gesch. des schweizerischen Bundesrecht* (Winterthur, 1875–78), supplement (1881); *Amtlicher Sammlung der älteren eidgenössichen Abscheide von 1247 bis 1798* (17 vols., Zurich and Lucerne, 1839–1886); *Amtl. Sammlung der Akten aus der Zeit der helvetischen Republik* (10 vols., Berne, 1886–1907); HIDBER, *Schweizerisches Urkundenregister* (Berne, 1863–1877); *Quellen zur Schweizergeschichte* (since 1877); HÜRBIN, *Handbuch der Schweizergesch.*(Stans, 1900–1908), with a full list of authorities and bibliography; VON MÜLLER, *Gesch. der schweiz. Eidgenossenschaft* (15 vols., Zurich, 1805–1853), continued by several writers, by DÄNLIKER (3 vols., 1900—), DIERAUER (1887–1907); GELPKE, *Kirchengesch. der Schweiz* (Berne, 1856–61); VON MÜLINEN, *Helvetia sacra* (Berne, 1858–1861); LÜTOLF, *Die Glaubensboten der Schweiz vor St. Gallus* (Lucerne, 1871); EGLI, *Kirchengesch. der Schweiz bis auf Karl d. Gr.* (Zurich, 1893); BÜCHI, *Die kathol. Kirche in der Schweiz* (Munich, 1902); HURTER, *Die Befeindung der kathol. Kirche in der Schweiz* (Schaffhausen, 1842); CRÉTINEAU-JOLY, *Hist. du Sonderbund* (Fribourg, 1850); SIEGWART-MÜLLER, *Der Kampf zwischen Recht u. Gewalt* (Altorf, 1863–1866); GAREIS AND ZORN, *Staat u. Kirche in der Schweiz* (Zurich, 1877-78); *Hist. de la persécution religieuse à Genève* (Paris, 1878); TROXLER, *Die "katholisch"-theologische Fakultät an der Hochschule Bern* (Basle, 1903); IDEM, *Die neuere Entwicklung des Altkatholizismus* (Cologne, 1908); cf. also the bibliographies to the articles on the Swiss dioceses and to the articles CALVIN and ZWINGLI.

J. P. KIRSCH.

Sword, KNIGHTS OF THE. See MILITARY ORDERS, THE.

Sydney, ARCHDIOCESE OF (SYDNEYENSIS).—The vast territories formerly known as New Holland and Van Diemen's Land and since 1900 as The Commonwealth of Australia were erected into the Vicariate Apostolic of New Holland in 1834. John Bede Polding (q. v.), a Benedictine, was appointed vicar Apostolic. He was consecrated bishop in London on 29 June, 1834. Dr. Polding visited Rome in 1841–2, and at his suggestion new sees were erected in Hobart and Adelaide. A few years later Melbourne and Brisbane were also detached from the archdiocese. In New South Wales dioceses were erected at Maitland, Goulburn, Bathurst, Armidale, Lismore, and Wilcannia; these form at present the suffragan sees of Sydney, which was erected into an archdiocese on 15 February, 1842. The archdiocese stretches along the Pacific coast from Red Head on the north to Cape Howe on the south, and inland to the Dividing Range. When Dr. Polding landed at Sydney, there were only four priests in the district; Father Ullathorne, an English Benedictine who had come to Australia in 1833, was vicar general, assisted by Fathers Therry, McEncroe, and Dowling, three Irish priests, the last named a Dominican. The official census of 1833 gave the population of the colony as 60,794, the Protestants of all denominations being 43,095 and the Catholics 17,283. The government allowance in the same year for the maintenance of the Catholic Church was $4000; whilst to the Church of England, exclusive of its rich land endowments, was assigned the sum of $95,355. There were 10 Catholic schools receiving about $2000 from the Government, whilst the Protestant schools were allowed $28,680, in addition to a grant of $16,500 for the building of the Protestant King's School at Parramatta. In 1836 Dr. Ullathorne sailed for England and Ireland to secure priests and nuns for the increasing demands of the diocese. He availed himself of this opportunity to publish a pamphlet setting forth the sad condition of the convicts, and the maladministration of affairs in official quarters. Seventy-five thousand copies of this pamphlet were circulated in England and throughout the Continent, and its effect was seen in the altered conditions of administration soon after introduced. His mission was successful, and in 1841 Dr. Polding was enabled to report to Propaganda that the diocese had 24 priests, a community of nuns, 9 churches completed and 6 others in course of erection, with several small chapels, and 31 schools.

During a visit to Rome in 1846–47 Dr. Polding secured the appointment of Dr. Davis, O.S.B., titular Bishop of Maitland, as his coadjutor bishop. He, however, died in Sydney in 1854. In 1873 Archbishop Roger Bede Vaughan was appointed coadjutor, and he succeeded Dr. Polding on 16 March, 1877. He was remarkable for his eloquence, and upheld with great vigour the Catholic cause in the matter of religious education. On 19 April, 1883, he sailed for England via San Francisco, but died two days after his arrival in Liverpool (18 August). Patrick Francis Moran (see below), Bishop of Ossory, Ireland, was appointed to the vacant see, his Brief being dated 21 March, 1884. Dr. Higgins was appointed auxiliary bishop in 1888, and in 1899 was translated to the See of Rockhampton in Queensland. Most Rev. Michael Kelly, titular Archbishop of Achrida, was appointed coadjutor in 1901. The cathedral under the invocation of Our Lady Help of Christians, begun as far back as 1820 by Father Therry and completed by Archbishop Polding, was destroyed by fire on 29 June, 1865. It was rebuilt according to plans by Wardell, and consecrated by Archbishop Vaughan on 8 September, 1882. Archbishop Moran landed at Sydney on 8 September, 1884. The following year he was summoned to Rome to be promoted to the cardinalate. He convened and presided at three plenary synods (1885, 1895, 1905), and also presided at the Catholic congresses held in 1900, 1904, and 1909. Conferences of the clergy and diocesan synods have been held every year. St. Patrick's Ecclesiastical College, for the secular clergy, was erected at Manly on a government grant of eighty acres; the foundations were blessed during the plenary synod of 1885, and dedicated in 1888. It was built and fully equipped at the sole expense of Cardinal Moran, who wished it to be his gift to the Australian Church, as it was intended not for Sydney alone but for all the Australian dioceses. It has in the present year (1911) eighty students, all Australians, and has since its opening furnished one hundred and thirty priests to the Australian mission. A preparatory ecclesiastical college at Springwood, in the Blue Mountains, was opened last year. It is erected on a site of six hundred acres, the purchase of the land and the erection of the building being a further gift of the cardinal to the diocese. There are two Catholic weekly newspapers: "The Catholic Press" and "The Freeman's Journal"; there is also the quarterly "Australasian Catholic Record", besides, some minor monthly publications. The Catholic Club, organized in 1810, has a considerable enrolment.

When the Dr. Polding was appointed vicar Apostolic, several English Benedictines volunteered for the Australian mission. Some years later, at Dr. Polding's petition, St. Mary's was declared a Benedictine cathedral, the adjoining presbytery was raised to the dignity of a Benedictine priory, and it was hoped by the archbishop that the whole diocese would be efficiently served by an Anglo-Australian Benedictine community. This, however, was soon found to be impracticable. From the first many difficulties beset the Benedictine Order in Sydney. The community was finally dissolved by Archbishop Vaughan, himself a Benedictine, and missions were assigned to its priests in the ranks of the secular clergy. The religious orders of men are at present represented by the Marist Fathers, who entered on their missionary work in 1837, the Jesuits, Franciscans, Missionaries of the Sacred Heart, Vincentians, Passionists, Missionaries of the Divine Word, and Capuchins. In 1883 the members of the religious orders numbered 41; at present they are 79. The Irish Congregation of Sisters of Charity was the first of the orders of nuns to arrive (1 January, 1839) in Australia. For some years their special care was devoted to the female convicts. Later they engaged in the work of education, took charge of St. Vincent's Hospital, the first Catholic hospital in Australia, and visited the prisons. The congregation now numbers in Australia 320 nuns (in Sydney 235). The Benedictine Nuns arrived in Sydney in 1849, and at their monastery of Subiaco devote themselves to the higher branches of education. The Good Samaritans, a purely Australian order instituted in Sydney in 1857, are spread through other dioceses, and number in Sydney 220. The Sisters of St. Joseph are also an Australian institute spread through several

THE CATHEDRAL OF ST. MARY, SYDNEY, NEW SOUTH WALES

dioceses, numbering in Sydney 255. Other religious orders of nuns are the Sisters of Mercy, Religious of the Sacred Heart of Jesus, Poor Clares, Carmelites, Nursing Sisters of the Little Company of Mary, Little Sisters of the Poor, Sisters of St. Brigid, Dominican Nuns, Institute of the Blessed Virgin of Loreto, Sisters of Our Lady of the Sacred Heart, and Marists. At the close of Archbishop Vaughan's episcopate the number of nuns in the diocese was 252; at present (1911) they number 1400. St. John's college is associated with the Sydney University. The Jesuits have the flourishing College of St. Ignatius at Riverview, and the High School of St. Aloysius at Milson's Point. The Marist Brothers have a novitiate besides the College of St. Joseph, the High School at Darlinghurst, and several parochial schools. The Christian Brothers from Ireland were the first teaching religious order to come to Australia. Three Brothers accompanied Dr. Polding to Sydney in 1843, and within a few months they had three schools; sufficient means for their support were lacking and they returned to Ireland in 1844. They returned to Sydney in 1887, and have now a novitiate, two flourishing high schools, and eight parochial schools. The Patrician Brothers have also a flourishing college and some parochial schools. The total number of teaching Brothers at the close of Dr. Vaughan's episcopate was 78; they now number 220.

In 1883 there were 10,936 children in the schools of the diocese; there are at present 25,000. Official returns published last year (1910) in connexion with the cardinal's silver jubilee set forth that during those twenty-five years of his administration 160 churches had been erected or enlarged and about as many schools; 45 presbyteries had been provided, and 34 new parochial districts organized. In 1885 there was only one Catholic orphanage and that was maintained by the Government. In 1888 the government aid was withdrawn and the orphanage suppressed. Since then 9 orphanages have been established and 2 Catholic industrial schools. In 1885 there was only one Catholic hospital, St. Vincent's; it has since then been considerably enlarged, and five other hospitals have been built. A Home for the Aged Poor has also been established, and several other charitable institutions.

In 1911 the Archdiocese of Sydney contained: 175,000 Catholics; churches, 189; districts, 75; priests, secular, 120, regular, 79; religious men, 220, women, 1374; seminaries, 3; colleges, 7; boarding schools (girls) 25; superior day schools (boys), 4; (girls), 47; primary schools, 250; poor schools, 2; night schools (girls), 2; (boys), 1; orphanages, 7; industrial schools, 3; total number of pupils in Catholic schools, 25,000; hospitals, 8; Hospice for the Dying, 1; Foundling Hospital, 1; Home for the Aged Poor, 1; Home for the Blind, 1; Magdalen Retreats, 2; Servants' Home, 1; Home for Mental Invalids, 1; St. Charles' Villa for Aged and Infirm Priests, 1.

PATRICK FRANCIS CARDINAL MORAN, third Archbishop of Sydney, b. at Leighlinbridge, Ireland, 16 Sept., 1830; d. at Manly, Sydney, 16 Aug., 1911. He was the only son of Patrick Moran and Alice Cullen, sister of Cardinal Cullen. Of his three sisters two became nuns, one of them offered her life to God for the cholera patients whom she nursed, and died the last victim of the plague in Ireland. Both his parents died before his eleventh year. He left Ireland in 1842 to pursue his studies in Rome. His "Acta Publica" in universal theology was so masterly as to gain for him the doctorate by acclamation. Among the principal objectors was Cardinal Joachim Pecci, afterwards Leo XIII, who was impressed by the genius of this Irish student. He was appointed vice-rector of the Irish College, and also filled the chair of Hebrew at Propaganda, and was some time vice-rector of the Scots College. In 1886 he was appointed secretary to Cardinal Cullen and professor of Scripture at Clonliffe College. He founded the "Irish Ecclesiastical Record". In 1869 he accompanied Cardinal Cullen to the Vatican Council, and was appointed procurator for one of the absent bishops.

Selected as coadjutor Bishop of Ossory, he was consecrated Bishop of Olba. The diocese was distracted by dissensions between the infirm bishop, Dr. Walsh, and some of his priests and people. Dr. Moran ruled with a firm yet benign hand, and his episcopate was fruitful of much spiritual and temporal advancement in the diocese. He established many religious institutions. At Callan was founded the convent of St. Brigid's Apostolic School, which has blessed with the missionary spirit so many distant lands. He introduced the Sisters of Mercy also into the Irish workhouses, and transformed those dens of misery into homes for the indigent and poor. He established industrial schools for boys and girls, under the guidance of the Sisters of Charity, and was the pioneer in that grand network of child industrial training which has since become the pride of Ireland. He completed the chancel of and adorned the Kilkenny Cathedral, added a new wing to St. Kiernan's College, and founded the public library and archæological society. He always defended the rights of the people and championed Home Rule. He knew Ireland and loved her deeply. He was consulted by W. E. Gladstone prior to the introduction of his Home Rule Bills and his knowledge of the commercial, industrial, and economic conditions of the country was a source of wonder to the prime minister, who ever afterwards cherished for him a profound respect and affection. His great diplomatic skill secured for him the confidence of the Irish hierarchy, and he represented them in many of their most delicate negotiations with the Holy See. Though the Benjamin of the episcopate, he was selected as one of the secretaries to the first National Synod of Maynooth. The Brief of Dr. Moran's translation to Sydney was issued 21 March, 1884. In the archbishop's farewell audience with Leo XIII it was made evident that the intrigues of parties, the interference of government agencies, and the influence of high ecclesiastics had made the matter almost impossible of decision by Propaganda. In the presence of others the Holy Father said clearly, "We took the selection into Our own hands. You are Our personal appointment". In his first outward journey he drew up that spiritual programme which gave such a colouring to his after life. "I must esteem nothing save the service of the Redeemer, everything else is beside my mission; *Ich dien* [I serve] in its highest meaning must be my motto . . . To do the will of my Divine Master must be my life, my light, my love, my all."

In 1886 he travelled 2500 miles over land and sea, and visited all the dioceses of New Zealand. In the following year he traversed 6000 miles to consecrate Dr. Gibney at Perth. In subsequent years he went to Ballarat, Bathurst, Bendigo, Hobart, Goulburn, Lismore, Melbourne, and Rockhampton for the consecration of their respective cathedrals. In 1908 he revisited and dedicated the cathedral of Auckland, and in the last year of his life he again covered 6000 miles to consecrate Dr. Clune Bishop of Perth. He consecrated fourteen bishops, ordained nearly five hundred priests, dedicated more than five hundred churches, and professed five thousand nuns. The thirty-two charities which he founded in the city of Sydney remain as the crowning achievement of his life. As a statesman he forecasted the necessity of Australian federation, an Australian navy, and an Australian citizen soldiery. By sheer force of character he pressed these questions on the public mind, and lived long enough to see a Federal Labour Ministry remodelling the class legislation of past centuries and equitably evolving the rights of the working classes, the first unit of an Australian navy patrolling Australian waters, and the first 100,000 Australian youths called into disciplinary camps. Rt. Rev. Dr. Hoare, Bishop of Ardagh, was first named to assist Cardinal Moran in the administration of the archdiocese. He was unable to leave Ireland, and Rt. Rev. Dr. Higgins was appointed auxiliary bishop March, 1889. He was transferred to the See of Rockhampton on 4 May, 1899, and now occupies the See of Ballarat. On 20 July, 1901, Dr. Kelly, rector of the Irish College, Rome, was appointed auxiliary, *cum jure successionis*, and succeeded the cardinal at his death. A quarter of a million people witnessed the funeral procession through the heart of the city of Sydney. By permission of the State Government and of the municipal authorities he was interred with the pioneer priests in his beloved St. Mary's Cathedral.

Among his works may be named: "Monasticon Hibernicon"; "Spicilegium Ossoriense", "Memoir of Oliver Plunkett"; "Persecutions of Irish Catholics"; "Lives of the Archbishops of Dublin"; "Life of David Roth"; essays in "Dublin Review"; "Irish Saints in Great Britain"; "Birthplace of St. Patrick"; "St. Bartholomew's Massacre"; "Father Mathew"; "Our Primates"; "Civilisation of Ireland"; "Church and Social Progress"; "Acta Sancti Brendani"; "History of the Catholic Church in Australasia"; "Reunion of Christendom"; "Capital and Labour"; "Mission Field in the Nineteenth Century"; "Patron Saints of Ireland: Patrick, Brigid, and Columbkille"; "Lives of Sts. Canice and Carthage"; "Mission of the Catholic Church"; "Divine Credentials of the Church"; "Discourses on Cardinals Newman and Manning"; "The Anglican Reformation"; "Rights and Duties of Labour"; "Blessed Thomas More"; "Catholics and Irishmen"; "Catholic Democracy"; "The Thirteenth Century"; "Infallible Authority of the Church"; "Perpetuity of the Church"; "The Apostolate of St. Patrick"; "Australian Federation"; "Heritage of Blessings in the Catholic Church"; "Christopher Columbus"; "Fruits of Redemption"; "Discovery of Australia"; etc., "The Beginnings of the Catholic Church in the United States", from unpublished documents.

DENIS F. O'HARAN.

Syene, a titular see in Thebais Secunda, suffragan of Ptolemais. Syene (Egyptian, Souanou, Coptic, Souan), was originally the market-place of the Island of Elephantine (in Egyptian, Abou). Under the Pharaohs, Abou was the capital of a principality, then the chief town of the nome. It is not known at what epoch its suburb across the Nile commenced to grow at its cost; for a long time the two cities were treated as one, Souanou being the port and city of work. Its quarries, with those of Rohannou, were the principal ones of Egypt; they supplied a certain kind of red granite called syenite, out of which were cut the obelisks, monolithic temples, the colossus, etc. From the time of the ancient empire royal Egyptian envoys went there to look for the stone destined for the sarcophagus of the king. These quarries were in full activity in the Roman epoch, and syenite was exported throughout the empire. Another celebrated place in Syene was a pit, which was incorrectly thought to have been placed exactly under the equator. For this reason it was chosen by Eratosthenes as the starting point of his measure of the surface of the earth (230 B. C.). The Syene of the Romans to the south-west of the present city, suffered much from the incursions of the Blemmyes, and from the pest; its inhabitants abandoned it to live in the higher parts built by the Saracens. This new city which was at first very prosperous suffered also from the troubles which followed the extinction of the Fatimite dynasty. Taken and retaken by the Qenous or Barabra of Lower Nubia, and by the Haouârah of Upper Egypt, it was nearly ruined and did not regain its importance until the Sultan Selim established a Turkish garrison there (1517). The Arabian name of the city is Assouan. There the French fought the Mamelukes, on 16 May, 1799. This city of about 10,000 inhabitants, and which may be reached by a railroad, as it is situated to the south of the first cataract of the Nile, is very interesting on account of its picturesque aspect and the strange character of its population composed of Arabs, Barbarins, negroes, Bisharis, and Ababdèh; curious bazaars and quays; remains of Roman quays, inscriptions on rocks, little temple of Isis, Arabian ruins and cemetery. The places of interest in the neighbourhood are the old quarries, the Island of Elephantine (to-day Geziret Assouan), an old necropolis, the beautiful Coptic convent of St. Simeon, and the famous Island of Philæ. Syene is mentioned by the Prophet Ezechiel, who threatened Egypt with devastation "from the tower of Syene, even to the borders of Ethiopia" (Ezech., xxix, 10). See St. Jerome and the modern commentators on this passage, where the Vulgate differs from the Hebrew and the Greek text. Le Quien (Oriens christ., II, 613) mentions two bishops of Syene: St. Ammonius, martyr at Antinoe where he had a church, and Befam, a Jacobite (1086). The Synaxarion of the Coptic church tells us that the city had a bishop from the time of the Patriarch Timothy, one of the successors of St. Athanasius.

AMÉLINEAU, *La géographie de L'Egypte à l'époque Copte* (Paris, 1893), 467; SMITH, *Dict. of Greek and Roman geogr.* s. v.; MÜLLER, *Notes on Ptolemy*, ed. DIDOT, I, 725; BUTCHER, *The Story of the Church of Egypt* (London, 1897), passim.

S. PÉTRIDÈS.

Sykes, EDMUND, b. at Leeds; martyred at York Tyburn 23 March, 1586-7; was a student at the College at Reims where he was ordained 21 Feb., 1581, and sent to the English Mission on 5 June following. He laboured in his native Yorkshire with such zeal and sacrifice, that his strength failed. Arthur Webster, an apostate, took advantage of his illness to betray him, and he was committed to the York Kidcot by the Council of the North. In his weakness he consented to be present at the heretical service, but he refused to repeat the act and remained a prisoner. After confinement for about six months, he was again brought before the Council and sentenced to banishment. On 23 Aug., 1585, he was transferred to the Castle of Kingston-upon-Hull, and within a week shipped beyond the seas. He made his way to Rome, where he was entertained at the English College for nine days from 15 April, 1586, his purpose being to atone for his lapse by the pilgrimage, and he also entertained some thoughts of entering religion. There he understood that it was God's will that he should return to the English mission, and reaching Reims on 10 June, he left again for England on 16. After about six months he was betrayed by his brother, to whose house in Wath he had resorted, and was sent a close prisoner to York Castle by the Council. He was arraigned at the Lent Assizes, condemned as a traitor on the score of his priesthood, and on 23 March, 1586-7 was drawn on the hurdle from the castle yard to York Tyburn, where he suffered the death penalty.

Douay Diaries, Collectanea F, in FOLEY, *Records S.J.*, III; *Diary of English College, Rome* in FOLEY, *Records S.J.*, VI; MORRIS, *Troubles of our Catholic Forefathers*, III.

J. L. WHITFIELD.

Syllabus (σύλλαβος, "collection"), the name given to two series of propostions containing modern religious errors condemned respectively by Pius IX (1864) and Pius X (1907).

I. THE SYLLABUS OF PIUS IX.—A. *History*.—The first impulse towards the drawing up of the Syllabus of Pius IX came from the Provincial Council of Spoleto in 1849. Probably on the motion of the Cardinal Archbishop of Perugia, Pecci (later on Leo XIII), a petition was laid before Pius IX to bring together under the form of a Constitution the chief errors of the time and to condemn them. The preparation began in 1852. At first Pius IX entrusted it to Cardinal Fornari, but in 1854 the Commission which had prepared the Bull on the Immaculate Conception took matters in hand. It is not known how far the preparation had advanced when Gerbet, Bishop of Perpignan, issued, in July, 1860, a "Pastoral Instruction on various errors of the present" to his clergy. With Gerbet's "Instruction" begins the second phase of the introductory history of the Syllabus. The "Instruction" had grouped the errors in eighty-five theses, and it pleased the pope so much, that he set it down as the groundwork upon which a fresh commission, under the presidency of Cardinal Caterini, was to labour. The result of their work was a specification, or cataloguing, of sixty-one errors with the theological qualifications. In 1862 the whole was laid for examination before three hundred bishops who, on the occasion of the canonization of the Japanese Martyrs, had assembled in Rome. They appear to have approved the list of theses in its essentials. Unfortunately, a weekly paper of Turin, "Il Mediatore", hostile to the Church, published the wording and qualifications of the theses, and thereby gave rise to a far-reaching agitation against the Church. The pope allowed the storm to subside; he withheld the promulgation of these theses, but kept to his plan in what was essential.

The third phase of the introductory history of the Syllabus begins with the appointment of a new commission by Pius IX; its most prominent member was the Barnabite (afterwards Cardinal) Bilio. The commission took the wording of the errors to be condemned from the official declarations of Pius IX and appended to each of the eighty theses a reference indicating its content, so as to determine the true meaning and the theological value of the subjects treated. With that the preparation for the Syllabus, having occupied twelve years, was brought to an end. Of the twenty-eight points which Cardinal Fornari had drawn up in 1852, twenty-two retained their place in the Syllabus; of the sixty-one theses which had been laid before the episcopate for examination in 1862, thirty were selected. The promulgation, according to the original plan, was to have taken place simultaneously with the proclamation of the dogma of the Immaculate Conception; in the event it was ten years later (8 December 1864) that Pius IX published the Encyclical "Quanta Cura", and on the same day, by commission of the pope, the secretary of State, Cardinal Antonelli, sent, together with an official communication, to all the bishops the list of theses condemned by the Holy See. The title of the document was: "A Syllabus containing the most important errors of our time, which have been condemned by our Holy Father Pius IX in Allocutions, at Consistories, in Encyclicals, and other Apostolic Letters".

The reception of the Syllabus among Catholics was assured through the love and obedience which the children of the Church bear towards the vicar of Christ on earth. They were, besides, prepared for its contents by the various announcements of the pope during the eighteen years of his pontificate; and, as a matter of fact, no sooner had it made its appearance than it was solemnly received in national and provincial councils by the episcopate of the whole world. Among the enemies of the Church, no papal utterance had stirred up such a commotion for many years: they saw in the Syllabus a formal rejection of modern culture, the pope's declaration of war on the modern State. In Russia, France, and also in those parts of Italy then subject to Victor Emmanuel, its publication was forbidden. Bismarck and other statesmen of Europe declared themselves against it. And to the present day, it is a stumbling-block to all who favour the licence of false Liberalism.

B. *Binding Power*.—The binding power of the Syllabus of Pius IX is differently explained by Catholic theologians. All are of the opinion that many of the propositions are condemned if not in the Syllabus, then certainly in other final decisions of the infallible teaching authority of the Church, for instance in the Encyclical "Quanta Cura". There is no agreement, however, on the question whether each thesis condemned in the Syllabus is infallibly false, merely because it is condemned in the Syllabus. Many theologians are of the opinion that to the Syllabus as such an infallible teaching authority is to be ascribed, whether due to an ex-cathedra decision by the pope or to the subsequent acceptance by the Church. Others question this. So long as Rome has not decided the question, everyone is free to follow the opinion he chooses. Even should the condemnation of many propositions not possess that unchangeableness peculiar to infallible decisions, nevertheless the binding force of the condemnation in regard to all the propositions is beyond doubt. For the Syllabus, as appears from the official communication of Cardinal Antonelli, is a decision given by the pope speaking as universal teacher and judge to

Catholics the world over. All Catholics, therefore, are bound to accept the Syllabus. Exteriorly they may neither in word nor in writing oppose its contents; they must also assent to it interiorly.

C. *Contents.*—The general contents of the Syllabus are summed up in the headings of the ten paragraphs, under which the eighty theses are grouped. They are: Pantheism, Naturalism, Absolute Rationalism (1–7); Moderate Rationalism (8–14); Indifferentism and false Tolerance in Religious matters (15–18); Socialism, Communism, Secret Societies, Bible Societies, Liberal Clerical Associations (reference is made to three Encyclicals and two Allocutions of the pope, in which these tendencies are condemned), Errors regarding the Church and its rights (19–38); Errors on the State and its Relation to the Church (39–55); Errors on Natural and Christian Ethics (56–64); Errors on Christian Marriage (65–74); Errors on the Temporal Power of the Pope (75–76); Errors in Connection with Modern Liberalism (77–80). The content of any one thesis of the Syllabus is to be determined according to the laws of scientific interpretation. First of all, one has to refer to the papal documents connected with each thesis. For, in accordance with the peculiar character of the Syllabus, the meaning of the thesis is determined by the meaning of the document it is drawn from. Thus the often-cited eightieth thesis, "The pope may and must reconcile himself with, and adapt himself to, Progress, Liberalism, and Modern Civilization", is to be explained with the help of the Allocution "Jamdudum cernimus" of 18 March, 1861. In this allocution the pope expressly distinguishes between true and false civilization, and declares that history witnesses to the fact that the Holy See has always been the protector and patron of all genuine civilization; and he affirms that, if a system designed to de-Christianize the world be called a system of progress and civilization, he can never hold out the hand of peace to such a system. According to the words of this allocution, then, it is evident that the eightieth thesis of the Syllabus applies to false progress and false Liberalism and not to honest pioneer-work seeking to open out new fields to human activity.

Moreover, should a thesis, according to the papal references, be taken from a condemned book, the meaning of the thesis is to be determined according to that which it has in the condemned book. For the thesis has been condemned in this particular meaning and not in any other which might possibly be read into its wording. For instance, the fifteenth thesis, "Everyone is free to adopt and profess that religion which he, guided by the light of reason, holds to be true", admits in itself of a right interpretation. For man can and must be led to the knowledge of the true religion through the light of reason. However, on consulting the Apostolic Letter "Multiplices inter", dated 10 June, 1851, from which this thesis is taken, it will be found that not every possible meaning is rejected, but only that particular meaning which, in 1848, Vigil, a Peruvian priest, attached to it in his "Defensa". Influenced by Indifferentism and Rationalism, Vigil maintained that man is to trust to his own human reason only and not to a Divine reason, i. e. to the truthful and omniscient God Who in supernatural revelation vouches for the truth of a religion. In the sense in which Vigil's book understands the fifteenth thesis, and in this sense alone does the Syllabus understand and condemn the proposition.

The view held by the Church in opposition to each thesis is contained in the contradictory proposition of each of the condemned theses. This opposition is formulated, in accordance with the rules of dialectics, by prefixing to each proposition the words: "It is not true that . . ." The doctrine of the Church which corresponds, for instance, to the fourteenth thesis is as follows: "It is not true, that 'philosophy must be treated independently of supernatural revelation.'" In itself no opposition is so sharply determined as by the contradictory: it is simply the negation of the foregoing statement. However, the practical use of this negation is not always easy, especially if a compound or dependent sentence is in question, or a theoretical error is concealed under the form of an historical fact. If, as for instance in thesis 42, the proposition, that in a conflict between civil and ecclesiastical laws the rights of the State should prevail, be condemned, then it does not follow from this thesis, that, in every conceivable case of conflicting laws the greater right is with the Church. If, as in thesis 45, it be denied that the entire control of the public schools belongs exclusively to the State, then it is not maintained that their control does in no way concern the State, but only the Church. If the modern claim of general separation between Church and State is rejected, as in thesis 55, it does not follow that separation is not permissible in any case. If it be false to say that matrimony by its very nature is subject to the civil power (thesis 74), it is not necessarily correct to assert that it is in no way subject to the State. While thesis 77 condemns the statement that in our time it is no longer expedient to consider the Catholic religion as the only State religion to the exclusion of all other cults, it follows merely that to-day also the exclusion of non-Catholic cults may prove expedient, if certain conditions be realized.

D. *Importance.*—The importance of the Syllabus lies in its opposition to the high tide of that intellectual movement of the nineteenth century which strove to sweep away the foundations of all human and Divine order. The Syllabus is not only the defence of the inalienable rights of God, of the Church, and of truth against the abuse of the words *freedom* and *culture* on the part of unbridled Liberalism, but it is also a protest, earnest and energetic, against the attempt to eliminate the influence of the Catholic Church on the life of nations and of individuals, on the family and the school. In its nature, it is true, the Syllabus is negative and condemnatory; but it received its complement in the decisions of the Vatican Council and in the Encyclicals of Leo XIII. It is precisely its fearless character that perhaps accounts for its influence on the life of the Church towards the end of the nineteenth century; for it threw a sharp, clear light upon reef and rock in the intellectual currents of the time.

II. THE SYLLABUS OF PIUS X.—A. *History.*—The Syllabus of Pius X is the Decree "Lamentabili sane exitu", issued on 3 July, 1907, condemning in sixty-five propositions the chief tenets of Modernism. This Decree, later on called the Syllabus of Pius X on account of its similarity with the Syllabus of Pius IX, is a doctrinal decision of the Holy Office, i. e. of that Roman Congregation which watches over the purity of Catholic doctrine concerning faith and morals. On 4 July, 1907, Pius X ratified it and ordered its publication; and on 18 November, 1907, in a Motu Proprio he prohibited the defence of the condemned propositions under the penalty of excommunication, reserved ordinarily to the pope. The Decree is supplemented by the Encyclical "Pascendi" of 8 September, 1907, and by the oath against Modernism prescribed on 1 September, 1910. Thus, the Syllabus of Pius X is the first of a series of ecclesiastical pronouncements dealing with the condemnation of Modernism, whilst the Syllabus of Pius IX sums up the condemnations previously passed by the same pope.

B. *Contents.*—By far the greater number of the theses of this Syllabus are taken from the writings of Loisy, the leader of the Modernists in France; only a few are from the works of other writers (e. g., thesis 6, Fogazzaro; 26, Le Roy). As a rule the quotation is not literal, for it would have been possible only in a few cases clearly to express the error in a short proposition. According to their contents the theses may be divided into six groups. They condemn the doctrine of the Modernists on ecclesiastical decisions (1-8), and on Holy Writ (9-19); the Modernist Philosophy of Religion (20-26) and Modernist Christology (27-38); the theory of the Modernists on the origin of the sacraments (39-51) and the evolution of the Church with regard to its constitution and doctrine (52-65). In detail the Syllabus of Pius X condemns the following assertions: ecclesiastical decisions are subject to the judgment of scientific scrutiny and do not demand interior assent (1-8); "excessive simplicity or ignorance is shown by those who believe that God is really the Author of Holy Scripture" (9); God neither inspired (in the Catholic sense of the word) the sacred writers nor guarded them from all error; the Gospels in particular are not books worthy of historic belief, as their authors have consciously, though piously, falsified facts (10-19); Revelation can be nothing else than the consciousness acquired by man of his relation to God, and does not close with the Apostles (20-21); "The Dogmas, which the Church proposes as revealed are not truths fallen from Heaven, but an interpretation of religious facts, acquired by the human mind through laborious process of thought" (this twenty-second thesis, with the somewhat crude expression, "truths fallen from Heaven", is taken from Loisy's "L'Evangile et l'Eglise"); one and the same fact can be historically false and dogmatically true; faith is based upon a number of probabilities; dogmatic definitions have only a passing practical value as norms in life (23-26); the Divinity of Christ is a dogma which the Christian consciousness deduced from its idea of the Messiah; the real, historical Christ is inferior to the Christ idealized by faith; Jesus Christ erred; His resurrection is no historical event; His vicarious death is a Pauline invention (27-38); the sacraments were not instituted by Christ, but are additions made by the Apostles and their successors, who, under the pressure of events, interpreted the idea of Christ (39-51); Jesus Christ did not think of founding a Church; the latter is a purely human society subject to all the changes of time; of the Primacy, Peter himself knew nothing; the Church is an enemy of scientific progress (5-57); "Truth is as changeable as man, because it is evolved with him, in him, and by him" (58); there are no immutable Christian dogmas, they have developed and must develop with the progress of the centuries (59-63); "Scientific progress demands a reform of the Christian dogmatic conception of God, creation, revelation, the Person of the Word Incarnate, and redemption" (64); "The Catholicism of to-day is irreconcilable with genuine scientific knowledge, unless it be transformed into a Christendom without dogmas, i. e. a broad and liberal Protestantism" (65).

C. *Binding Power*.—Many theses of the Syllabus of Pius X, as all Catholic theologians affirm, are heresies, i. e. infallibly false; for their contradictory is dogma, in many cases even fundamental dogma or an article of faith in the Catholic Church. With regard to the question, whether the Syllabus is in itself an infallible dogmatic decision, theologians hold opposite opinions. Some maintain that the Decree is infallible on account of its confirmation (4 July, 1907) or sanction (18 November, 1907) by the pope; others defend the opinion that the Decree remains nevertheless the doctrinal decision of a Roman Congregation, and is, viewed precisely as such, not absolutely immune from error. In this theological dispute, therefore, liberty of opinion, which has always been safeguarded by the Church in undecided questions, still remains to us. Yet all theologians agree that no Catholic is allowed to maintain any of the condemned theses. For in the decrees of a Roman Congregation we not only have the verdict of a scientific commission, which gives its decisions only after close investigation, but also the pronouncement of a legitimate religious authority competent to bind the whole Church in questions within its competence (cf. what has been said above regarding the Syllabus of Pius IX; under I. B.).

D. *Importance*.—The Syllabus of Pius X may be taken as an introduction to the Encyclical "Pascendi", which gives a more systematic exposition of the same subject. It may be, therefore, that later generations will not find it necessary to distinguish between the importance of the Syllabus and that of the Encyclical. Nevertheless, the Syllabus was published at the most opportune moment. The Catholics of those countries in which Modernism had worked its ill effects felt relieved. By this Decree the tenets of religious evolutionism were laid before them in short theses and condemned. Up to that time the significance and the bearing of isolated Modernist views, appearing now here, now there, had not always been fully grasped. Now, however, everyone of good will had to recognize that the Modernists, under the plea of assimilation to modern ideas of development, had tried to destroy the foundations of all natural and supernatural knowledge. Moreover, to the whole Catholic world the Decree sounded a note of warning from the supreme pastor and drew attention to the excellent principles of scholastic theology and to the growing importance of a thorough schooling in exegetical criticism and in the history of dogma, which the Modernists had abused in the most unpardonable manner.

DENZINGER, *Enchiridion*, No. 1700 sqq.; No. 2001 sqq.; *The Doctrinal Authority of the Syllabus* in *The Catholic World*, XXII (New York, 1886), 31; WARD, *The Life of John Henry Cardinal Newman*, II (London, 1912); GLADSTONE, *Rome and the Newest Fashions in Religion* (London, 1875); NEWMAN, *Letter to the Duke of Norfolk on Occasion of Mr. Gladstone's Recent Expostulation* (London, 1875); MANNING, *The Vatican Decrees in their Bearing on Civil Allegiance* (London, 1875), another reply to Gladstone; MACCAFFREY, *History of the Catholic Church in the Nineteenth Century* (St. Louis, 1910), I, 249, 438, 440, 487; II, 60, 462, 480; CHOUPIN, *Valeur des décisions* (Paris, 1907); HOURAT, *Le Syllabus* (Paris, 1904); HEINER, *Der Syllabus in ultramontaner und anti-ultramontaner Beleuchtung* (Mainz, 1905); RINALDI, *Il valore del Syllabo* (Rome, 1888); HEINER, *Der neue Syllabus* (Mainz, 1907); BESSMER, *Philosophie und Theologie des Modernismus* (Freiburg, 1912); VILLADA, *Razón y Fe*, XIX, 154; LEPIN, *Les théories de M. Loisy* (Paris, 1908).

A. HAAG.

Sylvester I, SAINT, POPE (314-335), date of birth unknown; d. 31 December, 335. According to the "Liber pontificalis" (ed. Duchesne, I, 170) he was the son of a Roman named Rufinus; the legendary "Vita beati Sylvestri" calls his mother Justa. After the death of Miltiades (Melchiades) Sylvester was made Bishop of Rome, and occupied this position twenty-one years. This was the era of Constantine the Great, when the public position of the Church so greatly improved, a change which must certainly have been very noticeable at Rome; it is consequently to be regretted that there is so little authoritative information concerning Sylvester's pontificate. At an early date legend brings him into close relationship with the first Christian emperor, but in a way that is contrary to historical fact. These legends were introduced especially into the "Vita beati Sylvestri" (Duchesne, loc. cit., Introd., cix sq.) which appeared in the East and has been preserved in Greek, Syriac, and Latin in the "Constitutum Sylvestri"—an apocryphal account of an alleged Roman council which belongs to the Symmachian forgeries and appeared between 501 and 508, and also in the "Donatio Constantini". The accounts given in all these writings concerning the persecution of Sylvester, the healing and baptism of Constantine, the emperor's gift to the pope, the rights granted to the latter, and the council

CONSTANTINE HOLDING THE BRIDLE OF ST. SYLVESTER'S HORSE

XII-CENTURY MOSAIC IN THE CHAPEL OF S. SYLVESTER, CHURCH OF THE SANTI QUATTRO CORONATI, ROME

of 275 bishops at Rome, are entirely legendary. The pope, however, took part in the negotiations concerning Arianism and the Council of Nicæa, and the expression ὁμοούσιος was probably agreed upon with him before the council. The pontiff also sent legates to the first œcumenical council. Still it is not certain whether Constantine had arranged beforehand with Sylvester concerning the actual convening of the council, nor whether there was an express papal confirmation of the decrees beyond the signatures of the papal legates (cf. Funk in "Kirchengesch. Abhandlungen und Untersuchungen", I, 95, 501 sq.).

During Sylvester's pontificate were built the great churches founded at Rome by Constantine, e.g. the basilica and baptistery of the Lateran near the former imperial palace where the pope lived, the basilica of the Sessorian palace (Santa Croce), the Church of St. Peter in the Vatican, and several cemeterial churches over the graves of martyrs. No doubt the pope helped towards the construction of these churches. Sylvester's memory is especially connected with the titular Church of Equitius, which takes its name from a Roman presbyter who is said to have erected this church on his property. It was situated near the *thermæ* of Diocletian, and still exists. Parts of the present building may date from the fourth century. No doubt the pope contributed to the development of the liturgy of the Church at Rome. During his reign, moreover, the first martyrology of Roman martyrs was probably drawn up. Sylvester is connected also with the establishment of the Roman school of singing. On the Via Salaria he built a cemeterial church over the Catacomb of Priscilla, the ruins of which have lately been brought to light. In this church he was buried. His feast is given under 31 December in the "Depositio episcoporum", or list of the burial days of the Roman bishops, which was compiled barely a year after his death; the same date is given in the "Calendar" of Philocalus. This day, therefore, is doubtless the day of his burial. For his possible relations with Armenia, see GREGORY THE ILLUMINATOR.

ST. SYLVESTER'S CHAIR, CLOISTER OF THE LATERAN

Liber pontificalis, ed. DUCHESNE, I, 170-201: introduction, cix sq.; JAFFE, *Regesta rom. pont.*, 2nd ed., I, 28-30; *Vita beati Sylvestri* in LAND, *Anecdota syriaca*, III, 46 sq. and in SURIUS, *Vitæ sanct.*, VI, 1173 sq.; LANGEN, *Gesch. der römischen Kirche*, I 395 sqq.; DÖLLINGER, *Papstfabeln* (2nd ed., 1890), 61 sqq.; MARUCCHI, *La basilica papale del cimitero di Priscilla* (Rome, 1908).

J. P. KIRSCH.

Sylvester II (GERBERT), POPE (999-1003), b. at or near Aurillac, Auvergne, France, about 940-50, of humble parents; d. at Rome, 12 May, 1003. Gerbert entered the service of the Church and received his first training in the Monastery of Aurillac. He was then taken by a Spanish count to Spain, where he studied at Barcelona and also under Arabian teachers at Cordova and Seville, giving much attention to mathematics and the natural sciences, in which he made unusual progress. From Spain he proceeded to Rome with Bishop Hatto of Vich, who had been his chief theological instructor, and John XIII recommended him to the Emperor Otto I, who sent him to Reims to the archdeacon Gerannus. There he was soon appointed a teacher in the cathedral school by Archbishop Adalbero. He undertook journeys of considerable length, e.g. to Ravenna, where he held a disputation with Ortricus of Magdeburg before Otto II. In 983 Otto II bestowed on him the Abbey of Bobbio, but the abbey was very poor and Gerbert returned to Reims. He again taught the most varied branches with great success, devoted himself zealously to study, and helped to raise Hugh Capet to the throne. Adalbero wished Gerbert to be his successor, but when the former died in 988 Arnulph, a natural son of King Lothaire, was raised to the see at the instigation of Hugh Capet. Arnulph was deposed in 991 by a synod held near Reims for alleged treason against the king, and Gerbert was elected his successor. Although Gerbert soon held a provincial synod to condemn those who had injured the property of the Church, and these decisions were confirmed at another synod held at Chela under the presidency of Robert, King of France, there was much opposition to Gerbert's elevation to the See of Reims. Consequently John XV sent Leo, Abbot of Sts. Boniface and Alexius at Rome, as legate to France. On 2 June, 995, Leo held a synod at Mouson. Gerbert appeared personally to defend himself, but was temporarily suspended from his episcopal office. He sought to show that this decree was unlawful, but a further synod (concilium Causeiense), held on 1 July, 995, at which Gerbert was present, declared Arnulph's deposition and Gerbert's elevation illegal and invalid.

Gerbert now went to the Court of the youthful Emperor Otto III, whose teacher he became and whom he accompanied to Italy for the coronation. As the Archbishopric of Reims was not restored to Gerbert, he remained in Italy, and in 998 Gregory V appointed him Archbishop of Ravenna. Gerbert attended the Roman synod before which the marital affairs of King Robert of France were laid. When Gregory V died on 18 February, 999, Gerbert was elected his successor through the influence of the emperor, and took the name of Sylvester. He was the first French pope. The new head of the Church administered his high office with great earnestness and a profound sense of responsibility. His discourse upon the episcopal office shows what his view of the chief spiritual pastors of the Church was ("Sermo de informatione episcoporum", P. L., CXXXIX, 169 sq.). He took energetic measures against the abuses in the life of the clergy caused by simony and concubinage, and was anxious that only capable men of spotless lives should receive the episcopal office. His relations with Otto III were very friendly, and he supported the emperor's political ideas. Otto gave the pope eight Italian countships, which had formerly belonged to the States of the Church, by a deed of gift the genuineness of which, however, is questioned (Wilmans, "Jahrbücher des deutschen Reiches unter den sächsischen Kaisern", II, pt. II, 233 sq.). At the same time the emperor declared the Donation of Constantine to be a forgery. During Otto's residence at Rome in the winter of 1000-1001 Sylvester held a Roman synod on 1 February, 1001, in the presence of the emperor, at which among other matters the affairs of the convent of Gandersheim were discussed. A revolt at Rome directed against the emperor forced Otto and the pope to flee. Sylvester was obliged to remain away for several months, during which the city suffered from party quarrels. On 27 December he called a second synod at Todi on account of the difficulties at Gandersheim, and shortly after was present at Otto's death.

Sylvester regulated important ecclesiastical matters in various countries. Soon after his elevation to the papacy he confirmed anew his former opponent Arnulph as Archbishop of Reims, and in the Bull which he sent to him gives clear proof that he had now abandoned his earlier position in regard to the authority of the papal decisions concerning the disputed see. The pope established an ecclesiastical metropolitan for Poland at Gnesen, and one for Hungary at Gran. On 27 March, 1000, he granted the title of king to the ruler of Hungary and appointed him papal vicar for his country. He energetically maintained church discipline in the question of the marriage of the French King Robert, and obliged the king to send Bertha away. Sylvester returned to Rome soon after Otto's death, although the leaders of the different parties of nobles still retained all their power. A little later he died. His epitaph has been preserved (cf. Forcella, "Iscrizioni delli chiese di Roma", VIII, 9). Besides a dogmatic treatise, "De corpore et sanguine Domini", Sylvester wrote a series of works principally on philosophical, mathematical, and physical subjects; they are to be found in P. L., CXXXIX; Olleris, "Œuvres de Gerbert, pape sous le nom de Sylvester II" (Paris, 1867); "Opera mathematica", ed. Bubnov (Berlin, 1891); "Lettres de Gerbert", published by Havet (Paris, 1889). He was held in high repute for his learning; the common people regarded him as a magician in league with the devil, and many legends grew up around his name. He is said to have introduced the use of Arabic figures into Western Europe, and to have invented the pendulum clock.

Liber pontificalis, ed. DUCHESNE, II, 263; JAFFÉ, Regesta rom. pont., 2nd ed., I, 469 sq.; PICAVET, Gerbert, un pape philosophe, d'après l'hist. et la légende (Paris, 1897); LAIR, Etudes crit., I, Lettres de Gerbert (Paris, 1899); HOCK, Gerbert oder Papst Sylvester II und sein Jahrh. (Vienna, 1837); BÜDINGER, Ueber Gerberts wissenschaftl. und polit. Stellung (Cassel, 1851); WERNER, Gerbert von Aurillac, die Kirche und die Wissenschaft seiner Zeit (2nd ed., Vienna, 1881); SCHULTESS, Papst Sylvester II. als Lehrer und Staatsmann (Hamburg, 1891); IDEM, Die Sagen über Sylvester II (Hamburg, 1893); LUX, Sylvesters II Einfluss auf die Politik Ottos III (Breslau, 1898); SCHLOCKWERDER, Untersuchungen zur Chron. der Briefe Gerberts (Halle, 1893); NAGL, Gerbert und die Rechenkunst des X. Jahrh. in Sitzungsbericht der Wiener Akademie, CXVI (1888), 861 sq.; WEISSENBORN, Zur Gesch. der Einführung der jetzigen Ziffern in Europa durch Gerbert (Berlin, 1892); HEFELE, Konziliengesch., IV (2nd ed.), 636, and passim; MANN, Lives of the Popes in the Early Middle Ages (London, 1910); IV, 352–67, and passim, V, 1–120; ALLEN, Gerbert, Pope Sylvester II in English Hist. Rev. (1892), 625–68; Dublin Rev., VI (1839).

J. P. KIRSCH.

Sylvester III, ANTIPOPE. See BENEDICT IX, POPE.

Sylvester IV (MAGINULF), ANTIPOPE. See PASCHAL II, POPE.

Sylvester, BERNARD, of Chartres, more properly, of Tours, a twelfth-century philosopher of Neo-Platonic tendencies. Little is known about him. Between the years 1145 and 1153 he composed a work called "De Mundi Universitate", which he dedicated to Thierry (Theodoric) of Chartres with the words "Terrico veris scientiarum titulis Doctori famosissimo Bernardus Silvestris opus suum". From this inscription it is inferred that Bernard was probably a pupil of Thierry or of some other member of the famous School of Chartres. He is not, however, to be confounded with Bernard of Chartres, who died in 1125, and is the author of a work "De Expositione Porphyri". The treatise, "De Mundi Universitate" (republished by Barach, "Bibliotheca Philosophorum Mediæ Ætatis", I, Innsbruck, 1876), is divided by its author into two books, the first of which, "Megacosmus, seu Maior Mundus", is an address of Nature to Intellect, and the second, the response of Intellect to Nature. The style and method of composition remind one of Marcianus Capella. The contents are very curious indeed. There is a good deal of Neo-Platonism and Neo-Pythagoreanism, philosophical tendencies which are very rare in the twelfth century, and practically unknown outside the School of Chartres. It is not at all improbable that Bernard, like the pantheists, Amaury and David, who were his contemporaries, was influenced by the writings of Eriugena. His philosophy is an attempt to account for the universe of nature (physics) by describing the cosmic emanations from an original *Monad*. Not the least valuable portions are those in which the author describes the mountains, rivers, animals, and plants, although the allegorical, poetical manner of the poem very often obscures the meaning. The pantheistic drift of Bernard's philosophy is clear from the expression "Deus omnia, omnia ex Deo sunt". Towards the traditional theology he seems to adopt a sceptical attitude: "Si theologis fidem præbeas argumentis". His favourite philosopher is Plato, although it is clear that he is not acquainted with any of the "Dialogues", except, perhaps, the "Timæus".

CLERVAL, Ecoles de Chartres au Moyen-Âge (Chartres, 1895); DE WULF, Hist. of Medieval Philosophy, tr. COFFEY (New York, 1909), 220 sq.; TURNER, Hist. of Philosophy (Boston, 1903), 306.

WILLIAM TURNER.

Sylvester Gozzolini, SAINT, founder of the Sylvestrines, b. of the noble family of the Gozzolini at Osimo, 1177; d. 26 Nov., 1267. He was sent to study jurisprudence at Bologna and Padua, but, feeling within himself a call to the ecclesiastical state, abandoned the study of law for that of theology and Holy Scripture, giving long hours daily to prayer. On his return home we are told that his father, angered at his change of purpose, refused to speak to him for ten years. Sylvester now accepted a canonry at Osimo and devoted himself to pastoral work with such zeal as to arouse the hostility of his bishop, whom he had respectfully rebuked for the scandals caused by the prelate's irregular life. The saint was threatened with the loss of his canonry, but decided to leave the world on seeing the decaying corpse of one who had formerly been noted for great beauty. In 1227 he retired to a desert place about thirty miles from Osimo and lived there in the utmost poverty until he was recognized by the owner of the land, a certain nobleman named Conrad, who offered him a better site for his hermitage. From this spot he was driven by damp and next established himself at Grotta Fucile, where he eventually built a monastery of his order. In this place his penances were most severe, for he lived on raw herbs and water and slept on the bare ground. Disciples flocked to him seeking his direction, and it became necessary to choose a rule. According to the legend the various founders appeared to him in a vision, each begging him to adopt his rule. St. Sylvester chose for his followers that of St. Benedict and built his first monastery on Monte Fano, where, like another St. Benedict, he had first to destroy the remains of a pagan temple. In 1247 he obtained from Innocent IV, at Lyons, a bull confirming his order, and before his death founded a number of monasteries. An account of his miracles and of the growth of his cultus will be found in Bolzonetti. His body was disinterred and placed in a shrine (1275–85) and is still honoured in the church of Monte Fano. Clement IV first recognized the title of blessed popularly bestowed on Sylvester, who was inscribed as a saint in the Roman Martyrology by order of Clement VIII (1598). His office and Mass were extended to the Universal Church by Leo XIII. His feast is kept on 26 November.

BOLZONETTI, Il Monte Fano e un Grande Anacoreta (Rome, 1906); FABRINUS, De Vita . . . b. Sylvestri (Venice, 1599).

RAYMUND WEBSTER.

Sylvestrines, a minor monastic order or, strictly speaking, congregation following in general the Rule of St. Benedict but distinct from the Black monks and not forming a part of the confederation of Benedictine congregations. The Sylvestrines were founded by St. Sylvester Gozzolini on Monte Fano near Fabriano in 1231. The Rule of St. Benedict was observed in its primitive form, but in many points the founder went considerably beyond it in point of austerity, laying special stress on the strictest observance of poverty. At the death of St. Sylvester in 1267 eleven monasteries were under his leadership of which some had been founded by him, while others, though of older foundation, had adopted his institute. The congregation had been formally sanctioned by Innocent IV twenty years before the founder's death. Except for a few houses in Portugal and Brazil and the Ceylon foundation mentioned below, there have been no Sylvestrine monasteries outside Italy. Under St. Sylvester's immediate successors in the generalship, Giuseppe della Serra San Quirico (d. 1258), Blessed Bartolomeo di Cingoli (d. 1298), and Andrea Giacomo di Fabriano, the biographer of the founder, a number of houses were founded in the March of Ancona, Tuscany, and Umbria. Since 1568 the congregation has possessed at Rome the Church of San Stefano del Cacco in the neighbourhood of the Pantheon; the first possession of the Sylvestrines in Rome was the Church of San Giacomo in Settimania (or alla Lungara), granted to St. Sylvester himself by the Chapter of St. Peter's.

At the present day, besides the Roman monastery at San Stefano, which is the residence of the abbot-general and counts as the mother-house of the order, the Sylvestrines have monasteries at Fabriano, Sasso Ferrato, Perugia, Osimo, Serra San Quirico, and Matelica. Since 1855 they have also had a large mission in Ceylon with its headquarters in the Abbey of Saint Antony at Kandy. At the present day (1911) the congregation numbers some 100 members, of whom about 70 are choir monks; of the total about 40 are in Ceylon. The chief Sylvestrine saints are: the founder, St. Bonfilius, Bl. Giovanni del Bastonne, and the Bl. Giuseppe and Ugo di Serra San Quirico. The congregation is governed by an abbot-general assisted by a vicar; the head of each monastery is a prior or titular abbot. These officials were formerly elected for life, they were made triennial by Paul II in 1543, but since 1690 have been elected every four years. The Constitutions are still those which were confirmed by Alexander VIII in 1690 after the severance of the short-lived union between the Sylvestrine and Vallumbrosan orders (1662–80). The Sylvestrine habit is similar in form to that of the Cassinese Benedictines but blue in colour; fasts are strictly observed and flesh meat is never eaten except in case of illness. A convent of Sylvestrine nuns was founded at Serra San Quirico during the lifetime of the founder, but the only convent now under Sylvestrine rule is that of San Benedetto in Perugia. The arms of the order are three green hills on a blue ground, surmounted by a golden crozier with two rose branches in flower at its side.

There is no satisfactory history of the order. The above is taken from HEIMBUCHER, *Orden u. Kongregationen*, I (2nd ed., Paderborn, 1907); HÉLYOT, *Histoire des ordres monastiques*, VI (Paris, 1859); FABRINI, *Breve Cronica della Congregazione de' Monachi Silvestrini* (Rome, 1706); *Costituzioni della Congregazione di S. Benedetto di Monte Fano* (Camerino, 1610; Rome, 1690).

RAYMUND WEBSTER.

Sylvius, FRANCIS, theologian, b. at Braine-le-Comte, Hainault, Belgium, 1581; d. at Douai, 22 Feb., 1649. He was remarkable from an early age for his love of study and his piety. After completing his humanities at Mons, he studied philosophy at Louvain and theology at Douai, in a seminary founded by the bishops of the Province of Cambrai in connexion with the faculty of theology. While studying theology he taught philosophy at the royal college. On 9 Nov., 1610, he was made doctor of theology with the highest honours. The faculty of theology wished to retain this promising scholar, but there was no chair vacant. An eminent professor, Barthélemy Pierre de Lintra, resigned his position in favour of Sylvius, but, upon the death of Estius (20 Sept., 1613), the great light of the University of Douai, Sylvius succeeded him and later was called to direct the episcopal seminary in which he had been a student. He was appointed (1 Feb., 1618) canon of the collegiate Church of St. Amat, and finally dean (28 Jan., 1622), and to this title was added that of vice-chancellor of the university. Henceforth, absorbed by study and the discharge of his duties, his life was tranquil and undisturbed for thirty years until his death. He was buried in the choir of the Church of St. Amat, and an epitaph engraved on his tomb recalled, with his titles and qualities, his attachment to St. Augustine and St. Thomas as a faithful disciple of one and a lucid interpreter of the other, also his liberality towards the poor and religious, whom he made his heirs.

To his piety and austerity, which were admirable, he united an unchangeable attachment to sound doctrines. At the commencement of his works, as at the beginning of his lectures, he never failed to profess his intention to remain always united to the Faith, and submissive to the authority of the Roman Church. When in 1648 the theologians of Louvain sought to win the University of Douai over to Jansenism, Sylvius opposed them vigorously; but throughout the controversy he preserved the moderation and sweetness of his character; always refraining from angry responses to the attacks of his opponents. He gained his reputation as a theologian chiefly through his commentary on the "Summa" of St. Thomas Aquinas. With that of Cajetan it ranks among the best, and many even prefer it on account of its clearness and fullness; besides, Sylvius wrote after the Council of Trent, and profited by its decisions. It contained four folio volumes, which he was prevailed upon to publish. He wrote also several treatises on dogmatic theology and controversy, and some on moral theology. Among his other works may be mentioned: (1) an edition with valuable notes, of Binsfeld's "Enchiridion theologiæ pastoralis", which had great success in Belgium and France, where it was the first manual of theology used by seminarians; (2) resolutions of cases of conscience, in which he showed himself a Probabilist, moderate, solid, and clear. He wrote also commentaries on Genesis, Exodus, Leviticus, and Numbers, the learning, conciseness, and penetration of which were praised by Calmet. He adapted the "Instructions" of St. Charles Borromeo for use of the Church in Belgium, and he made additions to the "Summa Conciliorum" of Carranza. His complete works were published by Père Norbert d'Elbecque at Antwerp in 1698, in six folio volumes, the first of which contains the life of Sylvius. This edition was reproduced at Venice in 1726; it is the best, though the editor omitted the works of Sylvius against Jansenism.

FOPPENS, *Bibliotheca Belgica* (Brussels, 1739), t. IV, 309, HURTER, *Nomenclator*.

ANTOINE DEGERT.

Symbolism may for our present purpose be defined to be the investing of outward things or actions with an inner meaning, more especially for the expression of religious ideas. In a greater or less degree symbolism is essential, to every kind of external worship and we need not shrink from the conclusion that in the matter of baptisms and washings, of genuflexions and other acts of reverence, of lights and sweet smelling incense, of flowers and white vestures, of unctions and the imposing of hands, of sacrifice and the rite of the communion banquet, the Church has borrowed, without hesitation, from the common stock of significant actions known to all periods and to all nations. In such matters as these Christianity claims no monopoly. Religious symbolism is effective precisely in the measure in which it is sufficiently natural and simple to appeal to the intelligence of the people. Hence the choice of suitable acts and objects for this symbolism is not so wide that it would be easy to avoid the appearance of an imitation of paganism even if one deliberately set to work to invent an entirely new ritual.

In any case the Old Testament, and more particularly the religious worship of the Old Testament, is full of symbolism. However literal may be our interpretation of the early chapters of Genesis, we cannot fail to recognize the symbolic element which pervades them. When we read for example how "God created man to his own image", or how He "formed man of the slime of the earth and breathed into his face the breath of life", we can hardly doubt that it was upon the underlying moral lesson rather than upon the material fact suggested by the words that the attention of the writer was concentrated. Still more clearly the words "sitteth at the right hand of God the Father Almighty", by which the Creed recalls the language of Psalm cix, 1, or the whole purport of such a writing as the Canticle of Canticles (q. v.), compels a symbolical interpretation. But it is in the details of worship that the tendency is most apparent. In prayer we constantly find the spreading out of the palms of the hands (see Ex., ix, 29, 33; III Kings, viii, 22, 38, 54; Job, xi, 13; etc.), clearly emphasizing the idea that the worshipper comes forward as a suppliant expectant of good gifts. In the act of blessing the hand is laid upon the head of the recipient or at least is stretched towards him (Gen., xlviii, 14; Lev., ix, 22; IV Kings, xiii, 16; etc.) with the suggestion that virtue passes out to the person so blessed. The rite of circumcision is to be performed in memory of the covenant between God and Abraham (Gen., xvii, 11), and all the Jewish festivals beginning with the Pasch are similarly commemorative of God's mercies to His people. So again of the loaves of proposition (Lev., xxiv, 5 sq.) we are told, "Thou shalt put upon them the clearest frankincense, that the bread may be for a memorial of the oblation of the Lord". Although nothing more is said as to the precise significance of this offering which was to remain from sabbath day to sabbath day in the Holy of Holies, it is clear that it could have served no utilitarian purpose and that its object was purely symbolical. Again the same may be said of the whole sacrificial ritual of the Old Testament, and in the case of the incense the words of Ps. cxl, 2, "let my prayer be directed as incense in thy sight; the lifting up of my hands, as evening sacrifice" (cf. Apoc., v, 8; viii, 3), seem sufficiently to declare what was the spiritual meaning underlying the outward sign. In any case the atmosphere of mystery which surrounded the ark of the covenant and later on the Temple and all the adjuncts of its imposing worship must have been a fertile soil for the growth of a teaching rich in symbolic interpretations. These things clearly suggested inquiry into their hidden significance and if the meaning were not in itself obvious, we may be assured from the genius of the people as manifested in the later Talmud that an explanation would readily be evolved to meet the case.

Coming now to Christian times the conditions of self-effacement and frequently recurring persecution under which the faithful lived in the first ages of the Church must have helped much to develop any tendencies towards a symbolistic treatment of religious truths which they had derived from Judaism. In point of fact the life of the Catacombs and the Discipline of the Secret (q. v.), which partly grew out of it, necessitated a veiling of Christian beliefs under types and figures. Moreover, so far as regards any graphic presentment of these mysteries in sculpture and painting, it seems intrinsically probable that the faithful deliberately availed themselves of such symbols as would not attract too much attention, and that consequently they gave the preference to representations which had some pagan analogue. In the earlier period no representations of the Crucifixion are found, and hardly one of the cross, at least in a large and conspicuous form; neither are the episodes of Christ's life commonly depicted realistically and historically, but only conventionally. But the type of the Good Shepherd carrying the sheep on his shoulders occurs frequently, and this preference may well be due to its resemblance to the pagan figures of Hermes Kriophorus or Aristæus, which at this period were much in vogue. The Christian understood clearly the reference to the loving self-sacrifice of Our Saviour, but pagan curiosity was not aroused by anything startling and unwonted. Again the banquet scenes with fish and bread (see EUCHARIST, EARLY SYMBOLS OF THE), which spoke so eloquently to the faithful of Holy Communion and the marriage supper of the blessed in heaven, seemed to the Roman of the second and third century, who paid homage to the dead with banquets as well as sacrifices, a perfectly natural decoration for a funeral chamber. Even the fable of Orpheus was borrowed pictorially and referred to Christ. Similarly the story of Eros and Psyche was revived and Christianized, serving to remind the believer of the resurrection of the body and the eternal beatitude of heaven. The group of the Twelve Apostles probably attracted the less attention because the twelve *Dii Majores* were often also grouped together. Again the figure of the *Orans* (q. v.), the woman with arms uplifted in prayer, was quite familiar to classical antiquity. Though the precise significance attached to it as it is found in the catacombs is in dispute, it was clearly designed to awaken some spiritual idea in the minds of the initiated. Similarly the fish symbol (see FISH, SYMBOLISM OF THE), representing Christ, the anchor of hope, the palm of victory, were all sufficiently familiar as emblems among pagans to excite no particular attention. Hence even in the case of an inscription which breathes so unmistakably the atmosphere of early Christian symbolism as the epitaph of Abercius (q. v.) with its allusions to the Fish (Christ) in the Eucharist, the shining seal (baptism), the chaste shepherd (Christ), etc., it has been possible for writers like Ficker to deny its Christian significance though in defiance of all probability as Zahn, Duchesne, and many other writers have shown. From whatever cause it arose the strong symbolistic colouring of religious practice during the first ages of Christianity is disputed by hardly anyone, and it was manifestly in harmony with the allegorical tone of the Apocalypse, of the Pastor of Hermas, and of other early apocryphal writings. Further it is certain that the tradition thus created only deepened and spread throughout both the early and the later Middle Ages. The tendency seems to have been particularly fostered by the allegorical exegesis of the theologians of Alexandria which the writings of St. Jerome and St. Gregory the Great helped to make familiar to western Europe. The works of Isidore of Seville and of St. Bede helped in the same direction. Neither must the so-called "Clavis" attributed to St. Melito of Sardis be left out of account. There is certainly no sufficient reason to identify it with the genuine work of St. Melito which bore a corresponding name, but the Clavis gathered up a variety of symbolical interpretations current in St. Augustine and the Fathers, and it seems to be of fairly early date (cf., however, Rotmanner in "Theol. Quartalschrift", 1896, lxxviii, 614–29).

With regard to the early ritual of the Church, the part that symbolism plays in all connected with the sacraments need not be insisted on. The outward sign of the sacrament was itself symbolical. But there was much more than this. In the case of baptism, for instance, nearly all the ceremonial is of very early date. The exorcism of Satan by blowing or breathing, the giving of salt (*sal sapientiæ*), the rite of the *Ephpheta*, and the use of spittle, imitating the action of Our Lord in some of His miracles, the ancient practice of turning to the West when renouncing

Satan but of facing eastwards in making the profession of faith, the white robe or *chrysom* bestowed as an emblem of innocence, the lighted candle typical of the illumination of faith (hence the baptized were early called φωτισθέντες, i. e. the illuminated), and finally the curious custom of giving milk and honey to the newly-baptized infant are all in the highest degree symbolical. In confirmation we have the marking of the Sign of the Cross upon the brow and the use of oil representing the fatness and abundance of grace. The blow upon the cheek, significant of the warfare in which the resolute Christian is engaged, is of much later date and probably imitated from the sword blow by which the young Teutonic warrior was dubbed a knight. The laying of the hand upon the penitent's head, which was practised almost everywhere during the Middle Ages when absolution was given, no doubt symbolized the imparting of grace, as the imposition of hands undoubtedly does in the Sacrament of Orders. Even in the ritual of matrimony such a pagan practice as the giving of the espousal ring, which was probably in the beginning part of the *arrhæ*, was invested at a later period with the mystic meanings of perpetuity and fidelity.

That much of the symbolism which is found in the medieval liturgists was invented *ex post facto* cannot be doubted. We may readily allow that the greater part of the ceremonial practices now adopted by the Church were utilitarian in their origin. For example, the priest washed his hands before the Preface because he had been using the thurible or at least taking up the offerings of the faithful; it was not until later that this act was connected by the liturgist with spiritual purification or even with the hand-washing of Pilate. At the same time it is possible to exaggerate the utilitarian explanation, and the liturgist Claude de Vert, who laid so much stress upon this aspect of the matter, in some instances went too far. For example, de Vert held that the candle given to the newly-baptized was only meant to help them to find their way back from the baptistery to the sanctuary in the darkness of the Easter vigil. But the very early use of the above-mentioned term φωτισθείς (illuminated) for a baptized person shows the extravagance of this explanation and, as Le Brun sagely pointed out, the catechumens would have needed candles as much to find their way to the baptistery as to return from it. Whether de Vert was wrong in maintaining that the extinction of the Tenebræ candles one by one had originally no symbolical reference to the abandonment of Christ by His disciples but was simply due to the fact that fewer candles were needed as dawn approached and the office drew to an end, or again in his contention that the noise made at the end of Tenebræ had no reference to the earthquake on Calvary but was simply the signal for departure given by the celebrant after an interval of silent prayer, may like many other familiar problems be left an open question.

It is perhaps most of all in the matter of liturgical vestments that the tendency to attach symbolical meanings to usages originally adopted for some simple and practical purpose shows itself most conspicuously. The prayers recited by the celebrant in assuming these attributes a mystical significance to each, thus the chasuble which covers all denotes charity, and the girdle self-restraint and continence, while medieval liturgists have devised many more; but modern authorities are agreed that in hardly any case has a vestment been adopted in the Church for mystical reasons. The amice, for example, was simply a cloth used like a modern collar to protect the rich chasuble or tunic from contact with the skin. It was only afterwards that the priest was bidden to regard it as a "helmet of salvation to overthrow the assaults of the evil one". And the same holds true of all the rest. Of the pallium, a white woollen band encircling the neck and hanging before and behind, it can at least be said that from the time of St. Gregory the Great it has been sent by the pope to archbishops with the distinctly expressed purpose of symbolizing the archiepiscopal jurisdiction conferred upon them, a purpose for which it is expressly blessed and laid "upon the body of Blessed Peter" in the "confession" of the great Roman basilica" (see TENEBRAE).

In any account of Christian symbolism an important place must always be given to the Church, and that whether the institution or the material building is regarded. It is considered by some that the veiled *Orans*, already spoken of, which appears so frequently in the catacombs represents the Church (see the Pastor of Hermas, iii, 3, 10, and compare the term Virgin Mother παρθένος μήτηρ used of the Church in the second century; Eusebius, "Hist. Eccl.", V, i, 43). This is not certain, but the Church in early mosaics is undoubtedly often personified, as indeed we should expect from the early and widely-read visions contained in the Pastor of Hermas (see HERMAS), and sometimes we find not one, but two, contrasted figures representing respectively the Church of the Gentiles and the Church of the Circumcision. The contrast is also presented to us in the form of two towns set over against each other and duly labelled Bethlehem and Jerusalem, or even more frequently in the confronting portraits of St. Paul and St. Peter. At a later date also, beginning early in the Middle Ages, we repeatedly find two contrasted types, but here representing the Church and the Synagogue. The Church is a crowned and often sceptred figure with a chalice emblematic of her sacramental system. The Synagogue, on the other hand, has lost her crown, her staff is broken, and her attitude betokens defeat. These figures are constantly to be found on either side of early medieval representations of the Crucifixion. Here there is plain opposition between the two types (see Sauer, "Symbolik", p. 247), whereas in early Christian imagery the Church of the Circumcision and the Church of the Gentiles are depicted as constitutive parts of the one Kingdom of God upon earth. This example shows that continuity between primitive and medieval symbolism must not always be assumed, though in many cases we can securely trace back a type to its origins in the earliest ages.

Another early and accepted emblem of the Church was the ship. In the Apostolic Constitutions (II, xlvii) the bishop surrounded by the assembly of the faithful is compared to the helmsman of a ship; but the idea is as old as Tertullian (De bap., xii; P. L., I, 1214) and it was varied sometimes by comparing the Church to the Ark of Noe. In any case the ship was a recognized Christian symbol and Clement of Alexandria approved it for a signet ring. "Let the dove or the fish", he says, "the vessel flying before the wind,—or the marine anchor be our signets" (Pæd. III, ii; P. G., VIII, 633), and numerous representations of ships, sometimes serving as the design for a lamp, with the figure of Christ or St. Peter as helmsman are preserved to us. The name which we still retain for the "nave" (French, *nef*) of a church bears testimony to the persistence of the same idea. Moreover, from the spiritual Church, idealized as the heavenly Jerusalem, to the material edifice the transition was very easy. As early as the Pastor of Hermas the individual members of the Church were looked upon as the stones of which the spiritual building was fashioned, the thought being perpetuated to all time in the magnificent hymn "Cœlestis urbs Jerusalem". No wonder that the liturgists of the Middle Ages found no more fruitful theme than the interpretation of every detail in the fabric and ornamentation of their great cathedrals. Moreover, in this case undoubtedly there was action and reaction. Not only did the teachers set themselves to give mystical explanations of what already existed, but their spiritual conceptions influenced the generations that came after, and architects designed and built with the conscious purpose of rendering in stone the beautiful thoughts which had become to them as a new language. To begin with the church was "oriented", i. e. its chancel (apart from the Roman basilicas where the celebrant offered Mass facing the people) pointed to the East. Whether one is to recognize here the Christianization of a form of sun-worship, which some have traced to the influence of the emperor Constantine, or whether the faithful looked eastward to greet the coming of the "Sun of Justice", the "Orient from on high", certain it is that already in the Apostolic Constitutions of the fourth century (II, xlvii) the church was built to face the East. The practice lasted on throughout the Middle Ages. From this indication of the points of the compass it followed that the deacon in reading the Gospel turned himself sideways so as to proclaim the glad tidings to the barbarous races of the north. The great porch at the western end, on the other hand, faced the setting sun and led men's thoughts to the close of life. Hence it is that this became the conventional position for those magnificent sculptures or paintings of the last judgment found in many of our old cathedrals. With regard to the door itself there is frequently some significant scheme of decoration which emphasizes the idea that the door is Christ (*Ego sum ostium*, John, x, 7) and this is alone sufficient justification for the glorification of these portals, one, two, or three in number, often encased in great arches and crowded with stone carvings of angels and saints.

In such liturgical treatises as the "Rationale" of Durandus every detail in the construction of the church has a special significance assigned to it. The roof represents charity which covers a multitude of sins; the beams which tie the building together betoken the champions of ecclesiastical right who defend it with the sword; the vaulting signifies the preachers who bear up the dead weight of man's infirmity heavenwards; the columns and piers stand for the Apostles, bishops, and doctors; the pavement symbolizes the foundation of faith or the humility of the poor; and so on. In all this the mystical interpretation of numbers holds a great place. There are twelve consecration crosses, and this, besides a reference to the Twelve Apostles (in not a few instances each consecration cross is marked upon a shield borne by one of the Apostles), symbolizes the spiritualizing of human nature and of the world by faith, or, as others put it, it betokens the universal Church. The reason is that three, the number of the Blessed Trinity, figures the Divine nature, and four, the number of the elements, typifies the number of the material world. Twelve is the product of three and four, and it consequently betokens the penetration of matter with spirit. So again eight denotes perfection and completion, for the visible world was made in seven days and the invisible kingdom of grace follows upon that. In this way the octagonal shape was judged specially appropriate for the baptistery or for the font, on the ground that this initiation into the supernatural order of grace completed the work of creation. Naturally five recalls the wounds of Christ, and five grains of incense are inserted cross-wise in the Paschal Candle, while ten, the number of the Commandments, is typical of the Old Law. Seven again has its own very special attraction as the number of the sacraments, of the gifts of the Holy Ghost, of the virtues and vices, and many other things. There can be little doubt that much of this symbolism of numbers is to be traced back to Egypt and Assyria, where the movements of the seven planets, as men then counted them, were continuously studied and where the elements of three and four into which seven was divided lent themselves to other combinations also regarded as peculiarly sacred, for example the number sixty, the product of three, four, and five.

Of isolated pieces of symbolism of various kinds medieval art and literature are full. The early monogram of Christ, sometimes spoken of as the *chirho*, as it is a combination of these two letters X P, thus ☧ or ⳩, sometimes again as the *labarum* and ☧ in ⳨ French as the *chrisme*, has been discussed under Cross (IV, 522). Another Christ emblem (besides Fish, treated in a separate article) was the lamb, often associated with a flag. This actually took the place of the figure of Our Saviour, and it was represented in combination with the cross instead of the human form, being sometimes even surrounded by a cruciform nimbus. As there seemed a danger of the Sacred Humanity being lost in allegory, the Council, "In Trullo", at Constantinople (691) decreed that the lamb in future should not be used in this way, but that the figure of Christ should be substituted. As for the first Person of the Blessed Trinity the earliest symbolical representation seems to be found in the Divine hand which is often seen extended from the clouds in early representations of the baptism of Our Saviour and of other operations of grace.

It is hardly needful to add that a vast chapter in the history of symbolism is supplied by the saints and their emblems. Almost everyone of the more familiar saints has some emblem, often more than one, by the presence of which his identity is made known. The gridiron of St. Lawrence, the scallop shell of St. James, the special cross of St. Andrew, the lion of St. Jerome etc. might be quoted in illustration, but often also there are emblems common to a whole group of saints, the palm branch, for example being in general indicative of a martyr, and the deacons being nearly always represented in their dalmatics. For the Evangelists there have been used from very early times certain conventional emblems—a winged man or an angel for St. Matthew, a winged lion for St. Mark, a winged calf for St. Luke, and an eagle for St. John. All these are taken from the description of the heavenly liturgy in Apoc., iv, v, and must have been suggested by the vision of Ezechiel (Ezech., i, 10). In the art of the early Middle Ages these emblems play a very prominent part. Other forms of symbolism are of much later development, for example the type which as been called "the Eucharistic Ecce Homo" representing Our Saviour with the sacred wounds, divested of his garments and standing in the tomb, not dead but living. In the paintings, etc., known as the Mass of St. Gregory which were popular in the fifteenth and sixteenth centuries, Our Lord is generally depicted in this way. Again Our Lady of the Seven Dolours, with the seven swords piercing her heart, is a type of comparatively late occurrence, and this of course is still more true of the pictures connected with the Sacred Heart. The monogram, I. H. S. surrounded by rays, which, from the fact that it was much used by the early Jesuits, has sometimes been supposed to be the peculiar device of the Society of Jesus, really owes its popularity to the preaching of St. Bernardine of Siena (q. v.) at the beginning of the fifteenth century. It represents the Holy Name written in a Greek abbreviated form and had originally nothing to do with *Iesus Hominum, Salvator*.

For another section of symbolism which is concerned with the mystical significance attached to the representations of animals, the reader is referred to the article Bestiaries.

An excellent compendium of the whole subject is that of Jenner, *Christian Symbolism* (London, 1910); a fuller treatise is supplied by Sauer, *Symbolik des Kirchengebaudes* (Freiburg, 1902), which concerns itself chiefly with architecture. The same is true of Kreuser, *Christliche Kirchenbau* (Brixen, 1868–9). Auber, *Hist. et théorie du symbolisme réligieux* (4 vols., Paris, 1874), is very diffuse. Nieuwbarn, *Het roomsche Kergebouw* (tr. Nymwegen, 1908), is too slight and sketchy. For the later Middle Ages and for France in particular there are the two admirable books of Male, *L'art rélig. de la fin du moyen-âge* (Paris, 1908), and *L'art religieux du XIIIe siècle en France* (3rd ed., Paris, 1910). See also Allen, *Early Christian Symbolism in Great Britain and Ireland* (London, 1887); Huysmans, *La Cathédrale*

(Paris, 1898). Regarding the liturgy see: THALHOFER, *Liturgik* (Freiburg, 1883); FRERE, *Principles of Religious Ceremonial* (London, 1906); HULME, *Symbolism in Christian Art* (London, 1899). On the emblems of the saints see: CAHIER, *Caractéristiques des saints* (Paris, 1887); DETZEL, *Christliche Ikonographie* (Freiburg, 1894); PFLEIDERER, *Die Attributen der Heiligen* (Ulm, 1898); RADOWITZ, *The Saints in Art* (Rome, 1898); JAMESON, *Sacred and Legendary Art* (London, 1848), and other works; GREENE, *Saints and Their Symbols* (London, 1904). The great storehouse of medieval symbolism is the *Rationale divinorum officiorum* of DURANDUS (modern ed., Naples, 1859), parts of which have been translated (Leeds, 1843, and London, 1899).

HERBERT THURSTON.

Symeon Metaphrastes. See METAPHRASTES, SYMEON.

Symeon Stylites, SAINT. See SIMEON.

Symmachus, SAINT, POPE (498–514), date of birth unknown; d. 19 July, 514. According to the "Liber pontificalis" (ed. Duchesne, I, 260) he was a native of Sardinia and his father was named Fortunatus. Symmachus was baptized at Rome (Thiel, "Epist. pont. rom.", I, 702), entered the ranks of the clergy of Rome, and was ordained deacon. Directly after the death of Pope Anastasius II, Symmachus was elected his successor by a majority of the Roman clergy at the Lateran Basilica on 22 November, 498. The election was approved by a part of the Roman Senate and he was at once consecrated Bishop of Rome. Later on the same day a minority of the clergy who were friendly to the Byzantines and were supported by a party in the Senate met in the Basilica of Santa Maria Maggiore and elected the Roman archpresbyter Laurentius as antipope. According to Theodorus Lector (P. G., LXXXVI, 193), the Laurentian party was aided with money supplied chiefly by the rich Senator Festus, who hoped that Laurentius would be influenced by this to sign the "Henotikon", the edict of faith of the Emperor Zeno. The other authorities do not speak of such motives, which are very probable, and the testimony of Theodorus can very readily be accepted. Both parties, however, agreed that the two candidates should appear at Ravenna before the Gothic king Theodoric, the ruler of Italy, and abide by his decision. Theodoric pronouncing in favour of Symmachus on the ground that he was elected first and by the majority of the clergy, Laurentius submitted to the decision. At a synod held at Rome on 1 March, 499, the Acts of which have been preserved, Symmachus, who was now universally acknowledged, bestowed on Laurentius the Diocese of Nocera in Campania. The synod ordained that any Roman cleric who sought to gain votes for a successor to the papacy during the lifetime of the pope, or who called conferences and held consultations for that purpose, should be deposed. King Theodoric was given a vote of thanks by acclamation for his unpartizan decision. When the king came to Rome in the following year he had a brilliant reception both from the pope and the people. However, the Byzantine party, headed by the two senators Festus and Probinus, did not abandon its hostility and hope of overthrowing the pope and gaining the papal see for Laurentius. The opportunity occurred in the following year, 501. Pope Symmachus celebrated Easter on 25 March, following the old Roman cycle, while the Byzantines and others observed the feast on 22 April, according to a new reckoning. The Laurentian party appealed to King Theodoric against the pope, making other accusations besides this digression in the celebration of Easter. Theodoric summoned the pope and Symmachus set out to meet him. At Rimini Symmachus learned the contents of the indictment and, refusing to acknowledge the king as his judge, returned home. The opposing party now accused him of squandering the property of the Church and other matters. It gained in strength and occupied the Lateran palace, so that the pope was obliged to live near the Church of St. Peter outside the city walls. His opponents requested the king to call a synod for the investigation of the accusations and to appoint a visitor for Rome. Symmachus agreed to the calling of a synod, but he and his adherents protested against the sending of a visitor. Theodoric, however, sent as visitor Bishop Peter of Altinum in upper Italy, who was to administer the Roman Church in the place of the accused pope. Peter came to Rome and, contrary to the commands of the king, allowed himself to be won over by the adherents of Laurentius, so that Theodoric at a later date dismissed him. Not long after Easter, between May and July, 502, the synod met in the basilica of Julius (Santa Maria in Trastevere). The pope declared before the synod that it had been called with his consent and that he was ready to answer the accusations before it, if the visitor were removed and he were re-established as the administrator of the Church. To this the majority of the bishops agreed and sent an embassy to the king to demand the execution of these conditions. Theodoric, however, refused, and demanded, first of all, an investigation of the accusations against the pope. A second session of the synod was held, therefore, on 1 September, 502, in the Sessorian basilica (Santa Croce in Gerusalemme), and the minority had the indictment made by the Laurentian party read aloud. Symmachus desired to go from St. Peter's to the synod in order to defend himself, but on the way there he was attacked by his opponents and maltreated, and, escaping only with great difficulty, returned to St. Peter's; several priests who were with him were killed or severely wounded. The Goths sent by Theodoric promised him a reliable escort but the pope now refused to appear before the synod, although invited three times. Consequently the assembled bishops declared at the third session, held about the middle of September, they could not pass judgment upon the pope, because he had appeared twice before his judges, and because there was no precedent showing that an occupant of the Roman See had been subjected to the judgment of other bishops. They called upon the opposing clergy to submit to the pope, and requested the king to permit the bishops to return to their dioceses. All these steps were in vain; the majority of the clergy and people sided indeed with Symmachus, but a minority of the clergy and a majority of the Senators were at that time partizans of Laurentius. A fourth session, therefore, was held on 23 October, 502, called the "Synodus Palmaris" (Palmary synod) either from the place where it was held (*ad Palmata, Palma*), or because it was the most important session (*palmaris*). At this session it was decided that on account of the reasons given earlier the decision must be left to the judgment of God; Symmachus was to be regarded as free from all the crimes of which he was accused, and therefore entitled to the full exercise of his episcopal office; the whole property of the Church was to be transferred to him; whoever returned to his obedience should escape punishment, but whoever undertook ecclesiastical functions at Rome without papal permission was to be regarded as a schismatic. The decision was signed by seventy-five bishops, among them the bishops of Milan and Ravenna. Many bishops now returned to their dioceses. The majority, however, met with the Roman priests in St. Peter's for a fifth session under the presidency of Symmachus on 6 November, 502. The edict issued by the prefect Basilius, in 483, regulating the administration of the possessions of the Church was declared invalid and Symmachus issued a new edict respecting the administration of this property, and especially in regard to its sale.

King Theodoric, not satisfied with the decision of the synod, although the great majority of the Italian episcopate was on the side of the rightful pope, did nothing to carry out the new ordinances. Consequently the opposition called its candidate Laurentius again to Rome. He resided in the Lateran palace, which was in the hands of his adherents, while Symmachus retained the house of the bishop (*episcopium*) near St. Peter's. The division continued for four years, during which both parties carried on a furious quarrel at Rome. Laurentius had his portrait added to the series of popes in the Church of Saint Paul Without the Walls. However, certain prominent persons exerted their influence in favour of Symmachus, as Bishop Avitus of Vienne, who, at the request of the Gallican bishops, addressed an urgent letter to the Senate on behalf of the rightful pope and for the restoration of unity. Symmachus gradually won over a number of the adherents of the opposition. The greatest factor in the healing of the schism was the interposition of Deacon Dioscurus of Alexandria, who had come to Rome. He was commissioned by Symmachus to go to Theodoric, and won the king over to the side of the rightful pope. Apparently political motives were involved, as the king wished to take action against the Laurentian party, which inclined to Constantinople. He commanded Senator Festus, the head of the hostile party, to return all Roman churches to Symmachus. Laurentius having lost many adherents among the senators the king's command was executed without difficulty. The antipope, obliged to leave Rome, retired to a farm belonging to his protector Festus. Only a small party still held to Laurentius and refused to recognize Symmachus as Bishop of Rome; but it was insignificant and was reconciled later to Hormisdas, the successor of Symmachus. During the schism a number of polemical writings appeared, as from the party of Laurentius the treatise "Contra Synodum absolutionis incongruæ", to which Deacon Ennodius replied in "Libellus adversus eos qui contra Synodum scribere præsumpserunt" ("Mon. Germ. Hist.: Auct. ant.", VII, 48 sq.). While the author of the life of Symmachus in the completely preserved text of the "Liber pontificalis" is very favourable to this pope, the writer of another continuation of the papal biographies supports the cause of Laurentius ("Fragment Laurentien", ed. Duchesne in ".Liber pontificalis", I, 44–46). During the dispute the adherents of Symmachus drew up four apocryphal writings called the "Symmachian Forgeries"; these were: "Gesta synodi Sinuessanæ de Marcellino"; "Constitutum Silvestri"; "Gesta Liberii"; "Gesta de purgatione Xysti et Polychronii accusatione". These four works are to be found in Coustant, "Epist. rom. pontif." (Paris, 1721), appendix, 29 sq.; cf. Duchesne, "Liber pontificalis", I, introduction, CXXXIII sq.: "Histoire littéraire des apocryphes symmachiens". The object of these forgeries was to produce alleged instances from earlier times to support the whole procedure of the adherents of Symmachus, and, in particular, the position that the Roman bishop could not be judged by any court composed of other bishops. Still these forgeries are not the first documents to maintain this latter tenet.

Symmachus zealously defended the supporters of orthodoxy during the disorders of the Acacian schism. He defends, although without success, the opponents of the "Henotikon" in a letter to Emperor Anastasius I (491–518). At a later date many of the persecuted Oriental bishops addressed themselves to the pope to whom they sent a confession of faith. Shortly after 506 the emperor sent him a letter full of invectives, to which the pope sent a firm answer, maintaining forcibly the rights and liberty of the Church (Thiel, "Epist. rom. pont.", I, 700 sq.) In a letter of 8 October, 512, addressed to the bishops of Illyria, the pope warned the clergy of that province not to hold communion with heretics. Soon after the beginning of his pontificate Symmachus interposed in the quarrel between the Archbishops of Arles and Vienne as to the boundaries of their respective territories. He annulled the edict issued by Anastasius II in favour of the Archbishop of Vienne and later (6 November, 513) confirmed the metropolitan rights of Archbishop Cæsarius of Arles, as these had been fixed by Leo I. Moreover, he granted Cæsarius the privilege of wearing the pallium, the first-known instance of such a grant by the Holy See to a bishop outside of Italy. In a letter of 11 June, 514, he appointed Cæsarius to represent the interests of the Church both in Gaul and Spain, to hold synods of the bishops in certain cases, to give letters of recommendation to clergy who journeyed to Rome. More important matters were to be laid before the Holy See. In the city of Rome, according to the "Liber pontificalis", the pope took severe measures against the Manichæans, ordered the burning of their books, and expelled them from the city. He erected or restored and adorned various churches. Thus he built a Church of St. Andrew near St. Peter's, a Basilica of St. Agnes on the Via Aurelia, adorned the Church of St. Peter's, completely rebuilt the Basilica of Sts. Sylvester and Martinus, and made improvements over the Catacomb of the Jordani on the Via Salaria. He built episcopal houses (*episcopia*) to the right and left of the parvis of St. Peter's. These buildings were evidently connected with the residence of the pope for several years near St. Peter's during the disorders of the Laurentian schism. He also built asylums for the poor near the three churches of St. Peter, St. Paul, and St. Laurence that were outside the city walls. The pope contributed large sums for the support of the Catholic bishops of Africa who were persecuted by the rulers of the Arian Vandals. He also aided the inhabitants of the provinces of upper Italy who suffered so sorely from the invasion of the barbarians. After his death he was buried at St. Peter's. Symmachus is venerated in the Roman Church as a saint.

Liber pontificalis, ed. DUCHESNE, I, 260–268; JAFFÉ, *Regesta pont. rom.* (2nd ed.), I, 96 sq.; THIEL, *Epist. rom. pontif.*, 639 sq.; *Acta synodorum Romæ habit.* a. 499, 501, 502 in *Mon. Germ. Hist.: Auct. ant.*, XII, 393 sq.; GRISAR, *Gesch. Roms und der Päpste*, I, 460 sqq.; LANGEN, *Gesch. der römischen Kirche*, II, 219 sqq.; HEFELE, *Hist. of the Councils of the Church*, tr. CLARK, IV (Edinburgh, 1895), 49 sqq., 58–75; STÖBER, *Quellenstudien zum laurentianischen Schisma* in *Sitzungsber. der Wiener Akademie*, CXII (1886), 269 sqq.; MAASSEN, *Gesch. der Quellen des Kirchenrechtes*, I, 411 sqq.; PFEILSCHIFTER, *Theoderich der Grosse* in *Weltgeschichte in Karakterbildern* (Mainz, 1910), 44 sqq.; HARTMANN, *Gesch. Italiens im Mittelalter*, I (Leipzig, 1897), 142 sqq.

J. P. KIRSCH.

Symmachus the Ebionite, author of one of the Greek versions of the Old Testament included by Origen in his Hexapla and Tetrapla. Some fragments of this version survive in what remains of the Hexapla. Symmachus also wrote "Commentaries", not extant, apparently to support the heresy of the Ebionites by attacking the Gospel of St. Matthew. "Origen states that he obtained these and other commentaries of Symmachus on the Scriptures from a certain Juliana, who, he says, inherited them from Symmachus himself" (Eusebius, "Hist. Eccl.", VI, xvii). Palladius (Hist. Laus., lxiv) found in a manuscript "very ancient and arranged in *stichoi*" the following entry made by Origen: "This book I found in the house of Juliana, the virgin in Cæsarea, when I was hiding there; who said she had received it from Symmachus himself the interpreter of the Jews". The date of Origen's stay with Juliana was probably 238–41, i. e. during the persecution of Maximin, but this tells us nothing about the date of Symmachus's version of the Scriptures which was known to Origen when he wrote (about 228) his earliest commentaries (see Swete, "Introd. to O. T. in Greek", p. 50). It used commonly to be accepted, on the supposed authority of St. Epiphanius (De mens. et pond., xvi), that Symmachus flourished in the age of Severus (193–211), but the text of Epiphanius is full of the wildest blunders. The Syriac translator who (as was first pointed out by Lagarde), had a less corrupt text before him, reads Verus not Severus, and explains a little later that by this emperor is meant Marcus Aurelius (161-80). All that can be said is that there is nothing improbable about this date. Epiphanius says further that Symmachus was a Samaritan who having quarrelled with his own people went over to Judaism, but all other ancient authorities are unanimous in making him an Ebionite. From the language of many writers who speak of Symmachus (Ambrosiaster, "Prol. in Ep. ad Galat"; Philastrius, lxiii; St. Augustine, "Contra Faust.", XIX, iv, xii), Symmachus must have been a man of great importance in his sect, if not the founder of a sect within a sect. His version of the Old Testament was largely used by St. Jerome, who twice speaks of two editions of it. As a translator he aimed at writing good Greek and not at the slavish literalness of Aquila. "Aquila et Symmachus et Theodotio . . . diversum pæne opus in eodem opere prodiderunt, alio nitente verbum de verbo exprimere, alio sensum potius sequi, tertio non multum a veteribus discrepare" (St. Jerome, "Prolog. in Euseb. Chronicon").

HARNACK, *Gesch. der altchristl. Lit. bis Eusebius* (3 vols., Leipzig, 1893–1904); *Dict. Christ. Biog.*, s. v. *Hexapla, Symmachus, Theodotion*; SWETE, *Introduct. to O. T. in Greek* (London, 1891); Mercati, *L'età di Simmaco l'Interprete e S. Epifanio* (Modena, 1892).

FRANCIS J. BACCHUS.

Symmachus Version. See VERSIONS OF THE BIBLE.

Symphorosa, SAINT, martyred with her seven sons at Tibur (Tivoli) towards the end of the reign of Emperor Hadrian (117-138). The story of their martyrdom is told in an old Passio, the reliability of which is seriously questioned by many modern hagiologists. According to this Passio, Symphorosa was a lady living at Tibur, the widow of the tribune, Getulius, who had previously been martyred by Emperor Hadrian at Gabii, now Torri, a town of the Sabines. When Hadrian had completed his costly palace at Tibur and began its dedication by offering sacrifices, he received the following response from the gods: "The widow Symphorosa and her sons torment us daily by invoking their God. If she and her sons offer sacrifice, we promise to give you all that you ask for." When all the emperor's attempts to induce Symphorosa and her sons to sacrifice to the gods were unsuccessful, he ordered her to be brought to the Temple of Hercules, where, after various tortures, she was thrown into the river (Anio), with a heavy rock fastened to her neck. Her brother Eugenius, who was a member of the council of Tibur, buried her in the outskirts of the city. The next day the emperor summoned her seven sons, and being equally unsuccessful in his attempts to make them sacrifice to the gods, he ordered them to be tied to seven stakes which had been erected for the purpose round the Temple of Hercules. Each of them suffered a different kind of martyrdom. Crescens was pierced through the throat, Julian through the breast, Nemesius through the heart, Primitivus was wounded at the navel, Justinus was pierced through the back, Stracteus (Stacteus, Estacteus) was wounded at the side, and Eugenius was cleft in two parts from top to bottom. Their bodies were thrown into a deep ditch at a place which the pagan priests afterwards called "Ad septem Biothanatos". (The Greek word βιοδάνατος, or rather βιαιοδάνατος, was employed for self-murderers and, by the pagans, applied to Christians who suffered martyrdom). Hereupon the persecution ceased for one year and six months, during which period the bodies of the martyrs were buried on the Via Tiburtina, eight or nine miles from Rome.

It is difficult to ascertain how much reliability these Acts possess. The opinion that they were written by Julius Africanus (third century) has been almost universally rejected, since neither Eusebius nor any other historian of that period makes the least allusion to any Acts of Roman or Italian martyrs composed by this African writer. The "Hieronymian Martyrology", which was compiled by an unknown author in the second half of the fifth century, commemorates St. Symphorosa and her sons on 18 July, but here the names of her sons are entirely different from those given in the Acts. One of the manuscripts (codex Bernensis) of this martyrology states that the Acts of these martyrs are extant: "quorum gesta habentur" ("Martyrologium Hieronymianum", edited by De Rossi and Duchesne in Acta SS. Novembris II, I, 93). Since here the names of Symphorosa's sons are different from those of the Acts which we possess, there must have existed some other "Gesta" to which the author of the martyrology refers. In the same martyrology, on 27 June, are commemorated seven brother-martyrs, whose names are identical with those which our Acts assign to the sons of Symphorosa. It is probable that the author of the Acts, guided by the tradition that Symphorosa had seven sons who were martyred, made her the mother of the seven martyrs, whom he found mentioned in the martyrology on 27 June. If this is the case, we may infer, provided Symphorosa had seven sons at all, that their names were not those mentioned in the Acts. Whether they were those assigned to them in the "Hieronymian Martyrology," will also remain doubtful as long as we have no certainty that the "Gesta" to which the author refers are authentic. Some hagiologists consider the seven sons of Symphorosa, like those of Felicitas (q. v.), a mere adaptation of the seven sons of the Maccabean Mother. In the seventeenth century, Bosio discovered the ruins of a basilica at the place popularly called "le sette fratte" (the seven brothers), on the Via Tiburtina, nine miles from Rome. (Bosio, "Roma Sotteranea", 105-9). The Acts and the "Hieronymian Martyrology" agree in designating this spot as the tomb of Symphorosa and her sons. Further discoveries, that leave no room for doubt that the basilica was built over their tomb, were made by Stevenson. The remains were transferred to the Church of S. Angelo is Pescaria at Rome by Stephen (II) III in 752. A sarcophagus was found here in 1610, bearing the inscription: "Hic requiescunt corpora SS. Martyrum Simforosæ, viri sui Zotici (Getulii) et Filiorum ejus a Stephano Papa translata." The Diocese of Tivoli honours them as patrons and the whole Church celebrates their feast 18 July.

ALLARD, *Hist. des Persécutions pendant les deux premiers siècles* (Paris, 1903), 276–92; ACHELIS, *Die Martyrologien, ihre Geschichte u. ihr Wert* (Berlin, 1900), 159–62; STEVENSON, *Scoperta della basilica di santa Sinforosa e dei suoi sette figli al nono miglio della via Tiburtina*, I (Rome, 1878), 502–5; BUTLER, *Lives of the Saints*, 18 July; *Acta SS. Julii IV*, 350–9.

MICHAEL OTT.

Sympson. RICHARD, VENERABLE. See GARLICK, NICHOLAS, VENERABLE.

Synagogue, the place of assemblage of the Jews. This article will treat of the name, origin, history, organization, liturgy and building of the synagogue.

I. NAME.—The Greek συναγωγή, whence the Latin *synagoga*, French *synagogue*, and English synagogue, means a meeting, an assembly; and is used by the Septuagint to translate the Hebrew עֵדָה. The Aramaic translation is כְּנִשְׁתָּא (cf. Arabic *Kanîsah*, a church) to which is akin the New Hebrew כְּנֶסֶת. The place of assemblage was termed in New Hebrew, בֵּית הַכְּנֶסֶת, meeting-house, i. e., οἶκος συναγωγῆς. In the course of time, the single word synagogue came to mean not only the meeting but the meeting-house, the teaching thereof and, in the broadest sense, the body politic of the Jews. This broad sense of the word synagogue is seen in John's use of 'ἀποσυνάγωγος, "excommunicated" or "put out of the synagogue" (cf. ix, 22; xii, 42; xvi, 2). Another Greek name for synagogue in use among Hellenistic Jews, is προσευχή shortened after the analogy of συναγωγή, from οἶκος προσευχῆς, house of prayer (cf. Philo, "In Flacc.", §§ 6.7; "Ad Gaium", §§ 20.23.43). This phrase is in the Septuagint translation of Isaias (lvi, 7): "My house shall be called the *house of prayer* [בית תפלה] for all nations." The Latinized proseucha of Juvenal (Sat., III, 296) means the Jewish house of prayer or synagogue. Josephus (Antiq., XVI, vi, 2) cites an edict of Augustus which calls the Synagogue σαββατεῖον, the *Sabbath-house*.

II. ORIGIN.—Obscurity enshrouds the first beginnings of the synagogue. The Jerusalem Talmud (in Ex., xviii, 20) dates it from the time of Moses; so, too, the tradition of the Alexandrian Jews, according to the witness of Philo, "De Vita Mosis" (III, 27) and Josephus, "Contra Apion." (II, 17).

REMAINS OF A SYNAGOGUE AT KEFR BIR'IM, PALESTINE

This rabbinical tradition is not reliable. It was probably during the Babylonian captivity that the synagogue became a national feature of Hebrew worship. Afar from their Temple, the exiled Jews gathered into local meeting-houses for public worship. Sacrifice was denied them; prayer in common was not. The longer their exile from the national altar of sacrifice, the greater became their need of houses of prayer; this need was met by an ever-increasing number of synagogues, scattered throughout the land of exile. From Babylonia this national system of synagogue worship was brought to Jerusalem. That the synagogue dates many generations earlier than Apostolic times, is clear from the authority of St. James: "For Moses of old time [ἐκ γενεῶν ἀρχαίων] hath in every city them that preach him in the synagogues, where he is read every sabbath" (Acts, xv, 21).

III. HISTORY.—From the outset of Christianity the synagogue was in full power of its various functions; the New Testament speaks thereof fifty-five times. The word is used to denote the body politic of the Jews twelve times: twice in Matthew (x, 17; xxiii, 34); once in Mark (xiii, 9); three times in Luke's Gospel (viii, 41; xii, 11; xxi, 12), and four times in his Acts (vi, 9; ix, 2; xxii, 19; xxvi, 11); and twice in the Johannine writings (Apoc., ii, 9; iii, 9). The more restricted meaning of meeting-house occurs forty-three times in the New Testament—seven in Matthew (iv, 23; vi, 2. 5; ix, 35; xii, 9; xiii, 54; xxiii, 6); seven times in Mark (i, 21, 23, 29, 39; iii, 1; vi, 2; xii, 39); twelve times in Luke's Gospel (iv, 15; 16, 20, 28, 33, 38, 44; vi, 6; vii, 5; xi, 43; xiii, 10; xx, 46), and fourteen times in his Acts (ix, 20; xiii, 5, 14, 42; xiv, 1; xv, 21; xvii, 1, 10, 17; xviii, 4, 7, 19, 26; xix, 8); twice in John (vi, 59; xviii, 20); once in James (ii, 2). Our Lord taught in the synagogues of Nazareth (Matt., xiii, 54; Mark, vi, 2; Luke, iv, 16), and Capharnaum (Mark, i, 21; Luke, vii, 5; John, vi, 59). Saint Paul preached in the synagogues of Damascus (Acts, ix, 20), Salamina in Cyprus (Acts, xiii, 5), Antioch in Pisidia (Acts, xiii 14), Iconium (xiv, 1), Philippi (xvi, 13), Thessalonica (xvii, 1), Berœa (xvii, 10), Athens (xvii, 17), Corinth (xviii, 4, 7), and Ephesus (xviii, 19). It is worthy of note that despite his frequent use of the Jewish meeting-house, St. Paul in his stern antagonism never once deigns to make mention of the synagogue. He designates Judaism by the term "circumcision", and not, as do the Evangelists, by the word "synagogue". And even in speaking of the Jews as "the circumcision", St. Paul avoids the received word περιτομή, "a cutting around", a word employed by the Alexandrian Philo for Judaism and reserved by the Apostle for Christianity. The sworn foe of the "false circumcision" takes a current word κατατομή, "a cutting down", and with the vigourous die of his fancy, stamps thereon an entirely new and exclusively Pauline meaning—the false circumcision of Judaism.

At the time of the destruction of Jerusalem (A.D. 70) there were in the city itself 394 synagogues, according to the Babylonian Talmud (Kethub. 105 a); 480, according to the Jerusalem Talmud (Megilla 73d). Besides these synagogues for the Palestinian Jews, each group of Hellenistic Jews in Jerusalem had its own synagogue—the Libertines, the Alexandrians, the Cyrenians, the Cilicians, etc. (Acts, vi, 9). Josephus speaks of the synagogue which Agrippa I erected in Dora (Antiq., XIX, vi, 3), of the Cæsarean synagogue which revolted against Rome (Bell, Jud., II, xiv, 4), of the great synagogue of Tiberias (Vita, 54), and of the synagogue of Antioch in Syria to which the sacred vessels were borne away in the time of the Seleucid War (Bell. Jud., VII, iii, 3). Philo is authority for the existence, during the first century A. D., of many synagogues in Alexandria (Leg. ad Gaium, 20), and of not a few in Rome (Ibid., 23). In Northern Galilee, are numerous ruins whose style of architecture and inscriptions are indications of synagogues of the second and, maybe, the first century A. D. The Franciscans are now engaged in the restoration of the ruined synagogue of Tel Hum, the site of ancient Capharnaum. This beautiful and colossal synagogue was probably the one in which Jesus taught (Luke, vii, 5). Of the ruined synagogues of Galilee, that of Kefr Bir'im is the most perfectly preserved. Various Greek inscriptions, recently discovered in Lower Egypt, tell of synagogues built there in the days of the Ptolemies. A marble slab, unearthed in 1902 some twelve miles from Alexandria, reads: "In honour of King Ptolemy and Queen Berenice, his sister and wife, and their children, the Jews (dedicate) this προσευχήν". Both the Jerusalem and the Babylonian Talmud make mention of numerous Galilean synagogues which were centres of rabbinical literary, and religious and political influence at Sepphoris, Tiberias, Scythopolis, etc. Every Jewish settlement was obliged by Talmudic law to have its synagogue; the members of the community could oblige one another to the building and maintaining thereof; indeed the members of the Jewish community were designated "sons of the synagogue". For further history of the synagogue, see JEWS AND JUDAISM.

The Great Synagogue is worthy of special mention, as to it is assigned, by Jewish tradition, the important rôle of forming the Canon of the Old Testament. It is said to have been founded by Esdras in the middle of the fifth century B. C., and to have been a permanent and legislative assemblage for two and a half centuries. The Mishnah (Pirke Aboth, I, 1) claims that the Prophets handed down the Torah to the men of the Great Synagogue. "Aboth Rabbi Nathan" (a post-Talmudic treatise) paraphrases this statement by including the last three Prophets in this assemblage: "Aggeus, Zacharias and Malachias received [the Torah] from the Prophets; and the men of the Great Synagogue received from Aggeus, Zacharias and Malachias". How long this supposedly authoritative body held control of the religion of Israel, it is impossible to tell. Jewish chronology from the Exile to Alexander's conquest is far from clear. Rabbi Jeremiah (Jerus. Talmud, Berakot, 4d) says that one hundred and twenty elders made up this body and instituted the prayers and benedictions of *Kiddush* and *habdalah*. The Talmud, on the contrary (Peah, II, 6), hands down Torah from the Prophets to the Zugoth (Pairs) without the intervention of the Great Synagogue. Be the Great Synagogue of Jewish tradition what it may, historical criticism has ruled it out of court. Kuenen, in his epoch-making monograph "Over die Mannen der groote synagoge" (Amsterdam, 1876), shows that a single meeting came to be looked upon as a permanent institution. The Levites and people met once and only once, probably on the occasion of the covenant described by Nehemias (II Esd., viii–x), and the important assemblage became the nucleus round which were wrapped the fables of later Jewish tradition. Such is the conclusion of W. R. Smith, "The Old Testament in the Jewish Church", p. 169; Ryle, "Canon of the Old Testament", p. 250; Buhl, "Canon and Text of the Old Testament", p. 33; Driver, "Introduction to the Literature of the Old Testament", 6th ed., p. 7.

IV. ORGANIZATION.—(1) *Judicial*.—The "sons of the synagogue" were governed by a council called *bêth dîn*, "house of justice"; or συνέδριον "council" (transliterated סנהדרין, Sanhedrin); or βουλή, "council". The members of this council were twenty-three in larger towns, seven in smaller; and were called ἄρχοντες, "rulers" (Matt., ix, 18, 23; Luke, viii, 41), or πρεσβύτεροι, "ancients" (Luke, vii, 3). The "rulers of the synagogue" had it in their power to punish by excommunication, scourging and death. (a) Excommunication from the synagogal community was termed *ḥerém*, חרם, ἀνάθεμα (see ANATHEMA). Both the Hebrew and Greek words mean that an object is "sacred" or "accursed" (cf. Arabic *ḥárîm*, the harem, a precinct sacred to the women of a household or the mosque of a community). (b) Scourging (מכות, cf. Makkoth, III, 12; μαστιγόω, cf. Matt. x, 17; xxiii, 34; δέρω, cf. Mark, xiii, 9; Acts, xxii, 19) was thirty-nine stripes (Makkoth, III, 10; II Cor., xi, 24) laid on by the "servant of the synagogue", *ḥazzan*, ὑπερέτης, for minor offences. Three elders made up a tribunal competent to inflict the penalty of scourging. It is likely to this lesser tribunal that Our Lord refers: "Whosoever is angry with his brother shall be in danger of the judgment", ἔνοχος ἔσται τῇ κρίσει (Matt., v, 22). (c) The death penalty was inflicted by the Sanhedrin in full session of twenty-three elders (cf. Sanhedrin I, 4). To this penalty or to that of excommunication should probably be referred Our Lord's words: "And whosoever shall say to his brother, Raca, shall be in danger of the council", ἔνοχος ἔσται τῷ συνεδρίῳ (Matt., v, 22).

(2) *Liturgical*.—The "ruler of the synagogue", ἀρχισυνάγωγός (Mark, v, 22, 35, 36, 38; Luke, viii, 49; xiii, 14; Acts, xiii, 15; xviii, 8, 17), *rôsh hákkenesêth* (Sota, VII, 7) presided over the synagogue and its services. This presidency did not prevent the "sons of the synagogue" from freely officiating. Witness the freedom with which Our Lord and St. Paul stood up to explain the Scriptures in the various synagogues of Palestine and the Diaspora. The *ḥazzan*, "servant", handed the scrolls to the readers and taught the children.

V. LITURGY.—There were five parts in the synagogue service: (1) the Shĕma' is made up of Deut., vi, 4–9; xi, 13–21; Num., xv, 37–41—two opening blessings for morning and evening, one closing blessing for morning and two for evening. These benedictions are named *Shĕma'* from the opening word, the imperative שְׁמַע: "Hear, O Israel; Jahweh our God is one Jahweh". The origin of the *Shĕma'*, as of other portions of Jewish liturgy, is unknown. It seems undoubtedly to be pre-Christian. For it ordains the wearing of the phylacteries or frontlets—prayer-bands borne upon the arm and between the eyes—during the recitation of the great commandment of the love of God (cf. Deut., vi, 8; xi, 18). These phylacteries (φυλακτήρια) are called in the Talmud, "the prayer which is for the hand", תפלה של יד, and "the prayer which is for the head", תפלה של ראש. The wearing of the two bands was in vogue in Christian times (Matt., xxiii, 5; Josephus, "Antiquit.", IV, viii, 13).

(2) *The Prayer* is called "the eighteenth", *Shemónéh 'esréh* (שמנה עשרה), because of its eighteen benedictions and petitions. There are two recensions—the Babylonian, which is commonly in use, and the Palestinian, which Schechter recently discovered in a Cairo *genizah* (MSS.-box). Dalman (Worte Jesu, p. 304) considers that petitions 7, 10–14, are later than the destruction of Jerusalem (A. D. 70). The twelfth petition of the Palestinian recension shows that the Christians were mentioned in this daily prayer of the synagogue:

"May the Christians and heretics perish in a moment;
May they be blotted out of the book of life;
May they not be written with the just."

The Babylonian recension omits נצרים, Christians. The Lord's prayer is made up, in like manner, out of petitions and praises, but in a very unlike and unJewish spirit of love of enemies.

(3) *Torah*.—The Jerusalem Talmud (Megilla, 75a) tells us that the reading of the Law on sabbaths, feast-days, new moons, and half feast-days is of Mosaic institution; and that Esdras inaugurated the reading of Torah on Mondays, Thursdays, and Saturdays. This Talmudic tradition, though not very reliable, points to a very ancient custom. The law is divided into fifty-four sections, *sedārîm*, which make up a pericopic sabbath reading of the Pentateuch. Special readings are assigned for special sabbaths; seven readers are called upon at random, and each reads his share.

(4) *The Prophets*.—Parallel to the pericopic reading of Torah is a pericopic reading from the Prophets, or second part of the Hebrew Canon. These sections are chosen with a view to exemplify or drive home the lesson from the Law which precedes. The name of the section from the Prophets, *haphtārā* (from Hiph'il of פטר, "to dismiss"), indicates that at first the synagogue service here came to a close.

(5) *The Scripture Lesson*.—Even by the time of Christ, the exposition of Scripture was part of the synagogal liturgy (Matt., iv, 23; Mark, i, 21; vi, 2). Any of the brethren might be called upon to give the "word of exhortation" (Acts, xiii, 15). The Talmudic statute (Megilla, IV, 4) was that the *methúrgemān*, interpreter, paraphrase the section from Torah one verse at a time and the section from the Prophets one to three verses at a time. These paraphrases are called *tárgûmîm*; a lengthy exposition of a section is a *midrāsh*. There was formerly an antiphonal chanting of one or other of Psalms cv–cvii, cxi–cxix, cxvi–cxvii, cxxxv, cxxxvi, cxxxvi–cl. The precentor chanted verse after verse and the choir repeated the first verse of the psalm. At the end, he chanted the doxology and called upon the people to answer "Amen", which they did.

VI. BUILDING.—(1) *Site*.—In Palestine, the synagogues were built within the city. In the Diaspora, a site was generally chosen outside the city gate and either by the seaside or river-side (Acts, xvi, 13). The Tosephta (Megilla, IV, 22) ordains that the synagogue be in the highest place of the city and face to the east. The ruins of Galilean synagogues show no observance of this ordinance.

(2) *Style of Architecture.*—There seems to have been no established style of synagogal architecture. Until recent years, the synagogue has been built in whatsoever style had vogue in the place and at the time of building. The ruined synagogue of Merom is in severe Doric. That of Kafr Bir'im is in a Græco-Roman modification of Corinthian. The building is quadrangular in form. On the main façade there are three doorways, each of which has a highly ornamented architrave; above the centre doorway is a carefully carved Roman arch. Later on, Russian synagogues were built in decidedly Russian style. In Strasburg, Munich, Cassel, Hanover, and elsewhere the synagogues show the influence of the different styles of the churches of those cities. The cruciform plan is naturally not followed; the transepts are omitted. Synagogues of Padua, Venice, Livorno and other Italian cities are in the Renaissance style. Since the expulsion of the Jews from Spain, Moorish forms have gradually come to be considered the distinctive trait of synagogal architecture. El Transito and Santa Maria la Blanca, both in Toledo, are two of the finest examples of this Moorish architecture under Jewish influence.

(3) *Interior Setting.*—The Ark, *arôn tēbāh*, containing the sacred scrolls, stood at the eastern end opposite the entrance to the rectangular building. In the center was a raised platform (βῆμα, בִּימָה), and thereupon the lectern (ἀναλογεῖον, אֲנָלוֹגִי). This elevated platform is also called "Almemar", a word corrupted from the Arabic *Al-minbar*, the "chair", the "pulpit". These two furnishings are the most essential interior settings of the synagogue. The Ark was originally but a niche in the wall. In time, as the most dignified feature, it received most concern in the decorative scheme. Nowadays, it is raised on high, approached by three or more steps and covered by an elaborately embellished canopy. The Almemar, too, has undergone various embellishments. It is approached by steps, sometimes has seats, is railed in and at times surrounded by a grille, round about or on both sides of it, are the seats for the congregation (κλιντήρ, קלִצֵּר). The first seats, πρωτοκαθεδρία (cf. Matt., xxiii, 6; Mark, xii, 39; Luke, xi, 43 and xx, 46) are those nearest the Ark; they are reserved for those who are highest in rank (cf. Tosephta, Megilla, IV, 21). Women, at least since the Middle Ages, sit in galleries to which they enter by stairways from the outside. These galleries were formerly set very high; but now are low enough to show both the Ark and the Almemar.

SCHÜRER, *Gesch.*, II (3rd ed., Leipzig, 1873), 427–64, tr. (Edinburgh, 1885–87); GRÄTZ, *Gesch.*, IV–XI (Leipzig, 1863–88); ZUNZ, *Gottesdienstliche Vorträge der Juden* (Berlin, 1832); DALMAN, *Synagogaler Gottesdienst*, in HERZOG'S *Real-Encyklopädie;* ABRAHAMS, *Jewish Life in the Middle Ages* (London, 1896); LÖW, *Der Synagogale Ritus in Monatsschrift*, 1884, IV, 1–71; KOHLER, *Ueber die Ursprünge u. Grundformen der synagogalen Liturgie* in *Monatsschrift*, 1893, XXXVII, 441–51.

WALTER DRUM.

Synaus (SYNAITANSIS), a titular see in Phrygia Pacatiana, suffragan of Laodicea. Nothing is known of the history of this city located by Ptolemy (V, ii, 22) in Great Phrygia, and in the sixth century by Hierocles (668, 13), in Phrygia Pacatiana, its metropolis being Laodicea. It is now Semao (or Simao), chief town of a caza in the vilayet of Broussa near the springs of Semav Sou, formerly Macestus; containing 5000 inhabitants all Mussulmans. It has a few inscriptions but no ruins. Le Quien (Oriens christianus, I, 813) mentions the following bishops: Arabius, represented by his metropolitan at Chalcedon (451); Pronimus, at Constantinople (553); Stephanus, at Nicæa (787); Constantine at Constantinople (869); Sisinnius and Eusebius, supporters respectively of St. Ignatius and Photius, at the Photian Council of Constantinople (879); Isaac, at the Council of Constantinople (1351), which approved the doctrines of Palamas. To these may be added Stephanus, whose name occurs in the inscription (eighth century?) "Corp. inser. græc.", 8666 perhaps the Stephanus mentioned in 787. In 1394 the See of Synaus was united to Philadelphia. In the seventh century it was still suffragan of Laodicea; it seems also that at this time it was united to the See of Ancyra, now Kilissé Keui. In the ninth century it was attached to the metropolis of Hierapolis and remained so till its disappearance, as appears from the Greek "Notitiæ episcopatuum"; however, the Roman Curia's official list of titular sees makes it suffragan of Laodicea.

HAMILTON, *Researches in Asia Minor*, II (London, 1842), 124; SMITH, *Dict. of Greek and Roman Geog.*, s. v.; TEXIER, *Asie mineure*, 407; CUINET, *La Turquie d'Asie*, LV, 222; WÄCHTER, *Der Verfall des Griechentums in Kleinasien im XIV. Jahrhundert* (Leipzig, 1903), 62.

S. PÉTRIDÈS.

Synaxarion (συναξάριον, collection), the name of a liturgical book of the Byzantine Church. The exact meaning of the name has changed at various times. Its first use was for the index to the Biblical and other lessons to be read in church. In this sense it corresponds to the Latin Capitulare and Comes (see LESSONS IN THE LITURGY). Then the Synaxarion was filled up with the whole text of the pericopes to be read. As far as the Holy Liturgy was concerned this meant that it was replaced by the "Gospel" and "Apostle" books. Synaxarion remained the title for the index to other lessons. Without changing its name it was filled up with complete texts of these lessons in the same way. As the lessons in the Byzantine Divine Office are always lives of saints, the Synaxarion became the collection of short lives of saints and accounts of events whose memory is kept (like the lessons of our second nocturn). It is often compared to the Roman Martyrology. The parallel would be more exact, if we imagine the second nocturn lessons arranged together in a separate book. The mere index of such lessons is generally called μηνολόγιον ἑορταστικόν, a book hardly needed or used, since the Typikon supplies all that is wanted. There are a great number of medieval Synaxaria extant in manuscript. They are important for Byzantine heortology and church history. The short lives that form the lessons were composed or collected by various writers. Of these Symeon Metaphrastes (q. v.) is the most important. The accounts are of very varying historical value. Emperor Basil II (976–1025) ordered a revision of the Synaxarion, which forms an important element of the present official edition (Analecta Bollandiana, XIV, 1895, p. 404). The Synaxarion is not now used as a separate book; it is incorporated in the Menaia. The account of the saint or feast is read in the Orthros after the sixth ode of the Canon. It is printed in its place here, and bears each time the name συναξάριον as title. Synaxarion then in modern use means, not the whole collection, but each separate lesson in the Menaia and other books. An example of such a Synaxarion (for St. Martin I, 13 April) will be found in Nilles, *op. cit.*, infra, I, xlix. Certain metrical calendars extant in the Middle Ages were also called Synaxaria. Krumbacher ("Gesch. der byzantin. Lit.", 2nd ed., Munich, 1897, pp. 738, 755) describes those composed by Christopher of Mytilene (d. about 1050) and Theodore Prodromus (twelfth century).

The *Menologion (Synaxarion) of Basil II* was edited by URBINO (3 vols., 1727), reprinted in *P. G.*, CXVII; ALLATIUS, *De libris eccles. Græcorum* (Paris, 1645), 78–93; DELEHAYE, *Le Synaxaire de Sirmond* in *Analecta Bolland.*, XIV (1895), 396–434;

GEDEON, Βυζαντινὸν ἑορτολόγιον in Σύλλογος, XXIV (1895), 121-60. See also MENAION.
ADRIAN FORTESCUE.

Synaxis (σύναξις from συνάγω) means gathering, assembly, reunion. It is exactly equivalent to the Latin *collecta* (from *colligere*), and corresponds to synagogue (συναγωγή), the place of reunion. In Christian and liturgical use the Synaxis is the assembly for any religious function, either in the abstract sense (*nomen actionis*) or concretely for the people assembled (cf. German *Sammlung* and *Versammlung*). The verb συνάγω occurs frequently in the New Testament, for gathering together a religious meeting (Acts, xi, 26; xiv, 27 etc.), as also for the Jewish services and councils (e. g. John, xi, 47). So also in the Apostolic Fathers (Didache, ix, 4; xiv, 1; I Clem., xxxiv, 7; in general for the union of the church, Ignatius, "Magn.", x, 3). We must distinguish the liturgical (eucharistic) from the aliturgical Synaxis, which consisted only of prayers, readings, psalms, out of which our Divine Office evolved. Dionysius the Pseudo-Areopagite uses the word only for the eucharistic service ("De eccles. hier.", iii, in P. G., III), and Cardinal Bona thinks that so it may have a mystic meaning, as referring to our union with God or Communion (Rerum liturg., I, iii, 3). But it occurs frequently for any religious assembly, and in this sense was adopted in the West by St. Benedict ("Regula Ben.", 17: "Vespertina Synaxis"—Vespers) and by John Cassian ("Collat.", IX, 34: "ad concludendam synaxim"; ed. Hurter, Innsbruck, 1887, p. 315) etc. In this signification the word is now archaic in Greek and Latin. It is preserved, however, in the Byzantine Calendar as the title of certain feasts on which the people assemble in some particular church for the Holy Liturgy, and therefore corresponds to the Roman *statio*. Thus 4 January is the "Synaxis of the holy Seventy", that is the feast of the seventy disciples (Luke, x, 1, where the Vulgate has seventy-two, on which day the assembly was once made in some church (at Constantinople?) dedicated to them (Nilles, "Kalendarium manuale," I, 2nd ed., Innsbruck, 1896, p. 52); 26 December is the "Synaxis of the Theotokos and of Joseph the spouse and guardian of the Virgin", a feast in memory of the flight into Egypt, on which again the station was at a special church (ibid., 366).

ADRIAN FORTESCUE.

Syncelli (σύγκελλοι, from σύν, with, and κέλλιον, the Græcized form of the Latin *cella*, cell), a name which in the early Church was given to those monks or clerics who lived in the same room with their bishops, and whose duty it was to be witnesses to the purity of their lives or to perform the daily spiritual exercises in common with them. In the Eastern Church they soon became the councillors and confessors of the patriarchs and bishops, and exerted a great influence over them. They held the first place after their masters and had a seat and vote in the councils of the Church. In the course of time the patriarchs took two or more syncelli, the most distinguished of whom was called protosyncellus (πρωτοσύγκελλος). Since the tenth century their influence began to decrease, but in the Greek Church they still exist. In the Latin Church they never became very influential, though popes and bishops had syncelli as witnesses of their mode of life (Gregory the Great, "Epistolarum libri XIV", IV, ep. xliv). They gradually developed into the *consiliarii papales et episcopales* (spiritual councillors).

PELLICCIA, *De christ. eccl. politia*, I (Cologne, 1829), 61 sq.; MORINUS, *Comment. de sacris ecclesiæ ordinationibus*, II (Paris, 1655); BINTERIM, *Die vorzüglichsten Denkwürdigkeiten der christkatholischen Kirche* (Mainz, 1825-41), I; II, 61 sq.

MICHAEL OTT.

Syncellus, GEORGE. See GEORGIUS SYNCELLUS.

Syncretism, from συγκρητίζειν (not from συγκεραννύναι). An explanation is given by Plutarch in a small work on brotherly love ("Opera Moralia", ed. Reiske, VII, 910). He there tells how the Cretans were often engaged in quarrels among themselves, but became immediately reconciled when an external enemy approached. "And that is their so-called Syncretism." In the sixteenth century the term became known through the "Adagia" of Erasmus, and came into use to designate the coherence of dissenters in spite of their difference of opinions, especially with reference to theological divisions. Later, when the term came to be referred to συγκεραννύναι, it was inaccurately employed to designate the mixture of dissimilar or incompatible things or ideas. This inexact use continues to some extent even to-day.

(1) Syncretism is sometimes used to designate the fusion of pagan religions. In the East the intermixture of the civilizations of different nations began at a very early period. When the East was hellenized under Alexander the Great and the Diadochi in the fourth century B. C., the Grecian and Oriental civilizations were brought into contact, and a compromise to a large extent effected. The foreign deities were identified with the native (e. g. Serapis = Zeus, Dionysus) and a fusion of the cults succeeded. After the Romans had conquered the Greeks, the victors, as is known, succumbed to the culture of the vanquished, and the ancient Roman religion became completely hellenized. Later the Romans gradually received all the religions of the peoples whom they subdued, so that Rome became the "temple of the whole world". Syncretism reached its culmination in the third century A. D. under the emperors Caracalla, Heliogabalus, and Alexander Severus (211-35). The countless cults of the Roman Empire were regarded as unessential forms of the same thing—a view which doubtless strengthened the tendency towards Monotheism. Heliogabalus even sought to combine Christianity and Judaism with his religion, the cult of the sun-god. Julia Mamæa, the mother of Alexander Severus, attended in Alexandria the lectures of Origen, and Alexander placed in his *lararium* the images of Abraham and Christ.

(2) A modern tendency in the history of religions sees in the Biblical revealed religion a product of syncretism, the fusion of various religious forms and views. As regards the Old Testament, the Chanaanite myth, the Egyptian, Old Babylonian, and Persian religions are regarded as the sources of Israelitic religion, the latter itself having developed from Fetichism and Animism into Henotheism and Monotheism. It is sought to explain the origin of Christianity from the continuation and development of Jewish ideas and the influx of Brahmanistic, Buddhist, Græco-Roman, and Egyptian religious notions, and from the Stoic and Philonic philosophy; it is held to have received its development and explanation especially from the neo-Platonic philosophy. That Judaism and Christianity agree with other religions in many of their external forms and ideas, is true; many religious ideas are common to all mankind. The points of agreement between the Babylonian religions and the Jewish faith, which provoked a lively discussion some years ago after the appearance of Friedrich Delitzsch's "Babel und Bibel", may be explained in so far as they exist (e. g.) as due to an original revelation, of which traces, albeit tainted with Polytheism, appear among the Babylonians. In many cases the agreement can be shown to be merely in form, not in content; in others it is doubtful which religion contained the original and which borrowed. As to the special doctrines of the Bible, search has been vainly made for sources from which they might have been derived. Catholic theology holds firmly to revelation and to the foundation of Christianity by Jesus of Nazareth.

(3) The Syncretistic Strife is the name given to the theological quarrel provoked by the efforts of Georg Calixt and his supporters to secure a basis on which

the Lutherans could make overtures to the Catholic and the Reformed Churches. It lasted from 1640 to 1686. Calixt, a professor in Helmstedt, had through his travels in England, Holland, Italy, and France, through his acquaintance with the different Churches and their representatives, and through his extensive study, acquired a more friendly attitude towards the different religious bodies than was then usual among the majority of Lutheran theologians. While the latter firmly adhered to the "pure doctrine", Calixt was not disposed to regard doctrine as the one thing necessary in order to be a Christian, while in doctrine itself he did not regard everything as equally certain and important. Consequently, he advocated unity between those who were in agreement concerning the fundamental minimum, with liberty as to all less fundamental points. In regard to Catholicism, he was prepared (as Melanchthon once was) to concede to the pope a primacy human in origin, and he also admitted that the Mass might be called a sacrifice. On the side of Calixt stood the theological faculties of Helmstedt, Rinteln, and Königsberg; opposed to him were those of Leipzig, Jena, Strasburg, Giessen, Marburg, and Greifswald. His chief opponent was Abraham Calov. The Elector of Saxony was for political reasons an opponent of the Reformed Church, because the other two secular electors (Palatine and Brandenburg) were "reformed", and were getting more and more the advantage of him. In 1649 he sent to the three dukes of Brunswick, who maintained Helmstedt as their common university, a communication in which he voices all the objections of his Lutheran professors, and complains that Calixt wished to extract the elements of truth from all religions, fuse all into an entirely new religion, and so provoke a violent schism. In 1650 Calov was called to Wittenberg as professor, and he signalized his entrance into office with a vehement attack on the Syncretists in Helmstedt. An outburst of polemical writings followed. In 1650 the dukes of Brunswick answered the Elector of Saxony that the discord should not be allowed to increase, and proposed a meeting of the political councillors. Saxony, however, did not favour this suggestion. An attempt to convene a meeting of theologians was not more successful. The theologians of Wittenberg and Leipzig now elaborated a new formula, in which ninety-eight heresies of the Helmstedt theologians were condemned. This formula (*consensus*) was to be signed by everyone who wished to remain in the Lutheran Church. Outside Wittenberg and Leipzig, however, it was not accepted, and Calixt's death in 1656 was followed by five years of almost undisturbed peace.

The strife was renewed in Hesse-Cassel, where Landgrave Wilhelm VI sought to effect a union between his Lutheran and Reformed subjects, or at least to lessen their mutual hatred. In 1661 he had a colloquy held in Cassel between the Lutheran theologians of the University of Rinteln and the Reformed theologians of the University of Marburg. Enraged at this revival of the Syncretism of Calixt, the Wittenberg theologians in vehement terms called on the Rinteln professors to make their submission, whereupon the latter answered with a detailed defence. Another long series of polemical treatises followed. In Brandenburg-Prussia the Great Elector (Frederick William I) forbade (1663) preachers to speak of the disputes between the Evangelical bodies. A long colloquy in Berlin (Sept., 1662–May, 1663) led only to fresh discord. In 1664 the elector repeated his command that preachers of both parties should abstain from mutual abuse, and should attribute to the other party no doctrine which was not actually held by such party. Whoever refused to sign the form declaring his intention to observe this regulation, was deprived of his position (e. g. Paul Gerhardt, writer of religious songs). This arrangement was later modified, in that the forms were withdrawn, and action was taken only against those who disturbed the peace. The attempts of the Wittenberg theologians to declare Calixt and his school un-Lutheran and heretical were now met by Calixt's son, Friedrich Ulrich Calixt. The latter defended the theology of his father, but also tried to show that his doctrine did not so very much differ from that of his opponents. Wittenberg found its new champion in Ægidius Strauch, who attacked Calixt with all the resources of learning, polemics, sophistry, wit, cynicism, and abuse. The Helmstedt side was defended by the celebrated scholar and statesman, Hermann Conring. The Saxon princes now recognized the danger that the attempt to carry through the "Consensus" as a formula of belief might lead to a fresh schism in the Lutheran Church, and might thus render its position difficult in the face of the Catholics. The proposals of Calov and his party to continue the refutation and to compel the Brunswick theologians to bind themselves under obligation to the old Lutheran confession, were therefore not carried into effect. On the contrary the Saxon theologians were forbidden to continue the strife in writing. Negotiations for peace then resulted, Duke Ernst the Pious of Saxe-Gotha being especially active towards this end, and the project of establishing a permanent college of theologians to decide theological disputes was entertained. However, the negotiations with the courts of Brunswick, Mecklenburg, Denmark, and Sweden were as fruitless as those with the theological faculties, except that peace was maintained until 1675. Calov then renewed hostilities. Besides Calixt, his attack was now directed particularly against the moderate John Musæus of Jena. Calov succeeded in having the whole University of Jena (and after a long resistance Musæus himself) compelled to renounce Syncretism. But this was his last victory. The elector renewed his prohibition against polemical writings. Calov seemed to give way, since in 1683 he asked whether, in the view of the danger which France then constituted for Germany, a Calixtinic Syncretism with "Papists" and the Reformed were still condemnable, and whether in deference to the Elector of Brandenburg and the dukes of Brunswick, the strife should not be buried by an amnesty, or whether, on the contrary, the war against Syncretism should be continued. He later returned to his attack on the Syncretists, but died in 1686, and with his death the strife ended. The result of the Syncretist Strife was that it lessened religious hatred and promoted mutual forbearance. Catholicism was thus benefited, as it came to be better understood and appreciated by Protestants. In Protestant theology it prepared the way for the sentimental theology of Pietism as the successor of fossilized orthodoxy.

(4) Concerning Syncretism in the doctrine of grace, see GRACE, CONTROVERSIES ON, VI, 713.

(1) FRIEDLÄNDER, *Darstellungen aus der Sittengesch. Roms*, IV (8th ed., Leipzig, 1910), 119–281; CUMONT, *Les religions orientales dans le paganisme romain* (Paris, 1907); WENDLAND, *Die hellenistisch-römische Kultur in ihren Beziehungen zu Judentum u. Christentum* (Tübingen, 1907); REVILLE, *La religion à Rome sous les Sévères* (Paris, 1886).
(2) SCHANZ, *Apologie des Christentums*, II (3rd ed., Freiburg, 1905); WEBER, *Christl. Apologetik* (Freiburg, 1907), 163–71; REISCHLE, *Theologie u. Religionsgesch.* (Tübingen, 1904).
(3) DORNER, *Gesch. der protest. Theol.* (Munich, 1867), 606–24; HENKE, *Georg. Calixtus u. seine seit*, I–II (Halle, 1853–60).

KLEMENS LÖFFLER.

Synderesis, or more correctly *synteresis*, is a term used by the Scholastic theologians to signify the habitual knowledge of the universal practical principles of moral action. The reasoning process in the field of speculative science presupposes certain fundamental axioms on which all science rests. Such are the principle of contradiction, "a thing cannot both be and not be at the same time", and self-evident truths like "the whole is greater than its part". These are the first principles of the speculative intellect. In the field of moral conduct there are similar first principles of action, such as: "evil must be avoided, good done"; "Do not to others what you do not wish to be done to yourself"; "Parents should be honoured"; "We should live temperately and act justly". Such as these are self-evident truths in the field of moral conduct which any sane person will admit if he understands them. According to the Scholastics, the readiness with which such moral truths are apprehended by the practical intellect is due to the natural habit impressed on the cognitive faculty which they call synderesis. While conscience is a dictate of the practical reason deciding that any particular action which I am contemplating is right or wrong, synderesis is a dictate of the same practical reason which has for its object the first general principles of moral action.

St. Thomas, *Summa*, I, Q. lxxix, a. 12 (Parma, 1852); Patuzzi, *De ratione humana* in Migne, *Theologiæ Cursus completus*, XI (Paris, 1841).

T. Slater.

Syndic, Apostolic.—A layman who in the name, and by the authority, of the Holy See assumes the care and civil administration of the temporalities and in particular the pecuniary alms destined for the support and benefit of Franciscan convents, and thence provides for the requirements of the brethren. To the Friars Minor corporate as well as individual ownership was forbidden by the constitution or the rule. During the first years of the order's existence, the literal observance of this precept, being feasible as well as possible, presented no difficulty; but as time went on, and the order developed as a vast organization, and spread over the whole world, countless difficulties had to be faced and fierce controversy arose, the *quæstio de paupertate* lasting for centuries. To preserve and safeguard as far as possible the letter as well as the spirit of the complete "expropriation" advocated by St. Francis, the popes adopted the *fictio juris* of assuming to themselves the ownership of all goods bestowed upon the friars. Thus the friars were legally regarded as mere users, the right of property being vested in the Roman pontiff, except in cases where the donors made explicit reservation in their own behalf. But as the civil administration of property in one's own interest is an act of ownership, and this was prohibited by the rule, such administration had to be exercised by a steward appointed, or at least authorized, by the Holy See.

According to the Decretal of Nicolas III, "Exiit qui seminat" (art. 12, n. 2), 14 August, 1279, the appointment of the syndic Apostolic rested with the sovereign pontiff or the cardinal protector,—sometimes bishops acted as their delegates in this matter; but Martin IV ("Exultantes", 18 January, 1283) empowered the superiors of the order—the general, the provincials, and the custodes—within their respective spheres of jurisdiction, to appoint and remove syndics as circumstances might require. The larger powers with which the syndic was invested by Martin IV and by his successors, Martin V ("Constitutiones Martinianæ" in Wadding, "Annales", X, 301) and Paul IV ("Ex Clementi", 1 July, 1555), gave rise to the appellation *syndicus Martinianus* in contradistinction to *syndicus communis*. This latter, as constituted by Nicholas III (Exiit) and Clement V ("Exivi de Paradiso", 6 May, 1312), could deal only with movable property (valuables excepted) and with purchase moneys. The Martinian syndic on the other hand, as trustee and agent of the Holy See on behalf of the friars, might receive and dispose of all goods movable and immovable (money offerings, legacies, and remunerations) and, in pursuance of his trust, institute proceedings in the courts and take such other steps as might be deemed necessary to protect the interests of the community in whose favour he acted. The Apostolic syndic and his wife and children were accorded the enjoyment of all and sundry indulgences, pardons, and privileges which the friars themselves have obtained, or shall obtain, from the Holy See (Clement VII, "Dum Consideramus", 16 April, 1526).

Bullarium Franciscanum (Rome, 1759–1908), passim; Wadding, *Annales*, passim; St. Bonaventure, *Opera Omn.*, VIII (Quaracchi, 1882–1902), 332; Ferraris, *Bibliotheca* (Rome, 1885), s. v. *Syndicus*; Marchant, *Relectio Theol. de Institutione et Usu Syndicorum sec. Regulam FF. Min.* (Antwerp, 1648). The expositors of the Rule (ch. iv) including the subtle and erudite, if sometimes erratic, Hilarius de Parisiis, *Regula FF. Minorum* (Paris, 1870); Brice, *The Scottish Friars*, I (London, 1909), 433–70; Holzapfel, *Manuale Hist. Ord. FF. Minorum* (Freiburg, 1909).

Gregory Cleary.

Syndicalism.—The term Syndicalism has been derived from the French *syndicats*, associations of workingmen uniting members of the same trade or industry for the furtherance of common economic interests. Syndicalism should therefore be synonymous with Industrial or Trades Unionism; but like "Socialism" the word has come to be used almost exclusively in a restricted sense and implies the principles expressed in theory and practice by French syndicates united in the Confédération Générale du Travail (General Confederation of Labour). Three influences have combined in the formation of this new system: revolutionary unionism, Anarchism, and Socialism. The theories of Proudhon together with those of Marx and Bakounine are here combined in a new form of industrial agitation which has received the name of "direct action". There has been no scientific or purposeful adaptation of the various doctrines. The mere co-operation in the same *syndicats* by followers of these often most antagonistic leaders has gradually brought about an agreement upon fundamental principles of revolutionary action to which all could subscribe, while free divergence of opinion might still find its individual expression outside the Syndicalist movement. While Syndicalism has but recently forced itself into popular notice, it is not new in its doctrines, which had almost all been accepted by the old "International" of Paepe, Marx, and Bakounine. When this was finally swept away during the revolutionary period of 1870–71, the present *syndicats* were gradually constructed, and after countless vicissitudes the Socialistic and Anarchistic elements were at last consolidated in the Confédération Générale du Travail.

The primary object of revolutionary Syndicalism is common to the various groups of which it is composed and consists in the destruction of the existing order of society, the expropriation and abolition of capital, and the elimination of the entire system of wages. Its basic doctrine is the teaching of the class struggle, while, like Socialism and Anarchism, it sees in patriotism one of its worst enemies. The State is to be violently combatted even when it enacts measures beneficial to the labourer, since all reforms are said to be deceptive unless forced from it by the syndicalist workers themselves. There are but two divisions of mankind, the employers and the employed, and anything which can foment bitterness and disagreement between these two is a triumph for the worker. All this is pure Marxian doctrine. The method by which revolutionary Syndicalism would bring about its purpose is known as direct action, i. e. the absolute rejection of all intermediary influences between the worker and his intended revolution. It disregards politics and parliamentary activity, repudiates intellectualism, and refuses to employ any agency except that of the workingman alone. Although direct action does not in itself imply violence, yet the employment of physical force is considered inseparable from its successful application. The particular form in which direct action is to find its adequate expression is the general strike. Each strike now takes on the nature of a skirmish preceding the great battle and becomes an end in itself independently of its success or failure. It calls for the support of the entire working class, and the more severe the conflict the greater the class-consciousness that is developed.

The culmination of these minor conflicts is to be the great battle which is proposed as the immediate object of Syndicalism, the general strike. This idea had already been clearly formulated by the "International". Success by the ballot is considered illusory because of its demoralizing influence upon the leaders, while street barricading and fighting seem useless against modern armaments. Nothing therefore is said to remain for the worker except the general strike of all industries at the same time. This will distribute the army over every section of the entire country and so render it helpless. The business and industrial sections of the cities will thus fall into the possession of the *syndicats*, who are at present to be prepared by education and class morality to take instant and successful control of all productive enterprises. The struggle itself is to be brief, but intense.

Two special theories are connected with the general strike. They are known as the minority and the myth theories. The syndicalists are only a small proportion of the French workingmen and without financial resources to sustain a prolonged strike. To answer the difficulties which this condition naturally suggests it is taught that their lack of resources will beget a spirit of recklessness, while their revolutionary education will infuse enthusiasm into the comrades, whose leaders they are destined to become. Thus the "conscious" or "bold" minority will suffice for the victory. The second theory was first proposed by Sorel in his "Réflexions sur la violence". Myths are defined by him as "artificial combinations invented to give the appearance of reality to hopes that inspire men in their present activity". Such a myth, he says, was for the early Christians the second coming of Christ and the Kingdom of Heaven; such for the syndicalist revolutionists is the myth of the general strike which has no objective reality in the present.

We have hitherto advisedly spoken of "revolutionary" Syndicalism, since there is likewise a "reformist" element in the Syndicalist movement, or as it is more appropriately called, a "reformist revolutionary" group. It consists of a certain portion of the socialist following, whose ultimate object is identical with that of their comrades, the general strike and the social revolution; but who are opposed to the practice of violence, as inexpedient, and for the same reason likewise exercise greater precaution in dealing with other critical questions, such as patriotism and militarism. They believe likewise in securing a safe financial status for the *syndicats* and in fighting for present reforms. These reforms, however, are to be understood in a purely Socialistic and Syndicalistic sense. Nothing that does not actually weaken the capitalistic class and prepare for its destruction is to be accounted of any value; while no concession that can ever be gained is to be considered final. It is difficult to ascertain the exact strength of this reformist element. Although it is in nowise inconsiderable; yet the Confédération Générale du Travail has hitherto sailed under exclusively revolutionary colours. The ultimate aim of Syndicalism, as far as this can be ascertained, is the establishment of an "economic federalism" in which the Bourses du Travail, or Labour Exchanges, which are affiliated with the Confédération Générale du Travail, are meant to play an important rôle. The units of society are to be the *syndicats* united in the trade federations, which in turn are to be centralized in the general confederation. The supreme thought of the present is, however, the general strike, and the *syndicats* united for this purpose are known as the *syndicats rouges* in distinction to the *syndicats jaunes*, who are opposed to Syndicalism and favour the strike only as an extreme measure.

The term Syndicalism has not as yet been officially applied to any labour association in the United States; nevertheless the movement itself exists in the organization of the "Industrial Workers of the World" and is likewise widely agitated under the form of industrial unionism by leading American socialists. In England a strong Syndicalist movement has sprung up since 1910, in which year Tom Mann issued the first number of his "Industrial Syndicalist". While radical Socialists have been obliged to construct a new labour union in the United States, their fellows in England have striven to develop the existing unions in the direction of solidarity and "direct action".

LEVINE, *The Labour Movement in France* (New York, 1912); CLAY, *Syndicalism and Labour* (New York, 1911); ACHT, *Der Moderne Französische Syndikalismus* (Jena, 1911); CORNÉLISSEN, *Ueber den internationalen Syndikalismus* (Tübingen, 1910); CHALLAYE, *Syndicalisme révolutionnaire et Syndicalisme réformiste* (Paris, 1909); SOREL, *Réflexions sur la Violence* (Paris, 1910, 2nd ed.); YVETOT, *A.B.C. Syndicaliste* (Paris), *The Times* (London), 25 March, 16 April, 1912; GRIFFUELHES AND KEUFER, *Le Mouvement Socialiste* (Jan.-April, 1905), 1.

JOSEPH HUSSLEIN.

Synedrium. See SANHEDRIN.

Synesius of Cyrene, Bishop of Ptolomais, neo-Platonist, date of birth uncertain; d. about 414. He was a younger son of an ancient family of Cyrene which traced its descent from the Heracleidæ, the mythical founders of the city. Synesius pursued his higher studies at Alexandria, where he became a devoted disciple of the famous Hypatia, to whom several of his letters are addressed and for whom he entertained a life-long devotion. After serving some time in the army he settled in his native land, "studying philosophy, mathematics, astronomy, everything; farming, hunting, having many a brush with hordes of pilfering Libyans; and every now and then upholding the cause of some one who had undeservedly fallen into difficulties". This kind of life, in every way suited to his tastes and disposition, was interrupted by a mission to Constantinople, the object of which was to present a gold crown to the new emperor, Arcadius, and obtain alleviation of the burden of taxation. Nearly three years he waited for an audience. The all-powerful Eutropius who sold the provinces to the highest bidder was not the man to allow the emperor to be troubled with complaints. Finally, Synesius obtained an audience and delivered his famous oration "On Kingship". He left Constantinople in 400. According to some authorities before, and according to others after, the mission to Constantinople, Synesius visited Athens. He has described the visit in two letters [54 and 135] to his brother, Euoptius. His reason for undertaking the voyage was, he jestingly said, that "a number of people, priests and private persons, had had revelations in dreams that, unless he did so, some great evil would befall him. Then he would escape the present evils and would no longer have to revere people who had been to Athens and regarded themselves as demigods, and those who had not as demidonkeys or mules." Athens was a disappointment. Like a beast that had been sacrificed, only the hide remained. At Alexandria, Synesius married a Christian by whom he had several children. During this period he did most of his literary work and carried on a large correspondence with his friends. Owing to the incapacity and cowardice of the military authorities, the desultory raids of the barbarians assumed almost the proportions of regular warfare. Synesius took a leading part in organizing defensive measures, levying volunteers, procuring arms, etc.

In 409 Synesius was elected Metropolitan of Ptolemais. The bishop-elect unbosomed himself in a letter [Ep. cv] to Euoptius. The duties of a bishop were uncongenial to him, fond as he was of his amusements as well as of religious study. He could not forsake the wife given him by "God, the law and the sacred hand of Theophilus". His amusements might go, much as he would hate to see his "darling dogs no longer allowed to hunt". Still, "if it is God's will, I will submit". But there was a worse obstacle.

"Philosophy is opposed to the opinions of the vulgar. I certainly shall not admit that the soul is posterior to the body . . . that the world and all its parts shall perish together. The resurrection . . . I consider something sacred and ineffable and am far from sharing the ideas of the multitude". He could keep silence but not "pretend to hold opinions which he did not hold". Theophilus, he said, must know everything and decide. Seven months elapsed between the writing of this letter and Synesius's consecration. That Synesius should yield is hardly surprising. His dogmatic perceptions were not keen enough to make him realize the falseness of his position as a bishop. Theophilus, the persecutor of the Origenists, is the difficulty. Perhaps, like many masterful men, he could put the telescope to his blind eye and refuse to see what he did not wish to see. Perhaps the negations in Synesius's letter were not his last word with regard to doctrinal questions. Baronius held that Synesius defamed himself to escape the episcopate, and this was also the opinion of Jeremy Taylor, "for all this Theophilus, Bishop of Alexandria, consecrated him, as knowing all this to be but stratagem and the arts of an odd fantastic humility" [Ductor dubitantium, iii, 2]. The "fantastic humility" solution of the problem has found very few supporters. As a bishop, Synesius devoted himself to the multiform duties of this office, without, however, concealing how uncongenial such a press of business was to him. We find him first warning and then excommunicating a bloodthirsty governor, denouncing the Eunomians, superintending the elections of bishops, etc. His latter days were embittered by the death of his three sons and the ruin of his country by the barbarians. His last letter was to Hypatia. She had been to him, "a mother, a sister, and a teacher". In his last hymn he recommends himself to Christ. It is a prayer that "his sins may be forgiven and that he may behold the glory of the Saviour".

The following are his writings: "De Providentia", first part composed while in Constantinople, second part after return to Cyrene: a political pamphlet in which Gainas and Aurelian figure as Typhon and Osiris; "De regno", in which an ideal Roman emperor is presented in an oration, delivered before Arcadius; "De dono astrolabii", a treatise accompanying the gift of a planisphere to one Paconius at Constantinople. The following were written between 400 and 409: the "Cynogetics" (not extant), a treatise on the breeding of dogs; "De insomniis", a curious treatise on dreams. Divination, according to Synesius, following Plotinus, was possible because of the unity of nature. All parts of the universe are in sympathy, so in each thing there are indications of other things. "Dion", a vindication of his manner of life against stern asceticism; "Calvitii Encomium", a facetious eulogy on baldness by a man who suffered from that complaint. The following belong to 409–14: two fragments of homilies; "Constitutio sive elogium Anysii" (Anysius was a general who had been successful against the barbarians); "Catastasis", describing the ruin of Pentapolis. There are one hundred and fifty-five epistles and ten hymns written at different periods of his life, the latter valuable because of the light which they throw on his religious and philosophical views, the former, the most precious of his writings, because of the light they throw on the writer's personality, and the picture which they give of the age in which he lived.

The only complete edition of Synesius's writings is that published by PETAVIUS (Paris, 1612); the fourth edition (1640) is the best; KRABINGER (1825–35) published the *De regno, Calvitii Encomium*, and *De providentia*, with German translations and the first volume of a complete edition, *Synesii opera omnia. I: Orationes et homiliarum fragmenta* (Landshut, 1850). This volume contains the greater works but not the hymns or epistles. A new edition of the Hymns was brought out by BOISSONADE, *Sylloge poetarum græc.*, XV (Paris, 1825); by CHRIST AND PARANIKAS in *Anthologia græca carminum christianorum* (Leipzig, 1871). There is a French translation of the Epistles by LAPATZ (Paris, 1870), very useful but not always trustworthy. See also VOLKMANN, *Synesius von Cyrene* (Berlin, 1869); CLAUSEN, *De Synesio* (Copenhagen, 1831); HALCOMB, *Dict. Christ. Biog.*; GARDNER, *Synesius of Cyrene* (London, 1886); CRAWFORD, *Synesios, the Hellene* (London, 1901); KRAUS, *Studien über Synesios von Cyrene* in *Theol. Quartalschr.* (Tübingen, 1865–66). For the religious views of Synesius when he was elected bishop see also HOLSTENIUS, *Dissertatio de Synesio et Fuga Episcopatus*, which will be found in READING's edition of *Evagrius and Theodoret* (Cambridge, 1720). Holstenius's view is opposed to that of Baronius.

F. J. BACCHUS.

Synnada, titular metropolis in Phrygia Salutaris. Synnada is said to have been founded by Acamas who went to Phrygia after the Trojan war and took some Macedonian colonists. The consul Manlius Vulso passed through that city on his expeditions against the Galatians. It was situated in the south-eastern part of Eastern Phrygia, or Parorea, thus named because it extended to the foot of the mountains of Pisidia. After having belonged to the kingdom of the Attali, it became the capital of a district of the province of Asia, except on two occasions during the last century of the Republic when it was temporarily attached to Cilicia. Under these two regimes Synnada was the centre of an important *conventus juridicus*, or judicial centre; it was to preside at this assembly that Cicero stopped at Synnada on his way from Ephesus to Cilicia and on his return. Although small, the city was celebrated throughout the empire on account of the trade in marble which came from the quarries of the neighbouring city of Dacimium. Under Diocletian at the time of the creation of Phrygia Pacatiana, Synnada, at the intersection of two great roads, became the metropolis. On its coins, which disappear after the reign of Gallienus, its inhabitants call themselves Dorians and Ionians. To-day it is the city of Schifout Kassaba, situated five hours south of Afioun Kara Hissar, vilayet of Broussa.

Christianity was introduced at an early date into Synnada. The "Martyrologium Hieronymianum" mentions several of its martyrs. For St. Trophimus, honoured by the Latin and Greek Churches on 19 Sept., see "Acta SS.", VI Sept., 9 sq. A reliquary in the form of a sarcophagus containing some of the bones of this martyr has been discovered at Schifout Kassaba and transported to the museum at Broussa; this curious monument may date back to the third century [see Mendel in "Bulletin de Correspondance Hellénique", XXXIII (1909), 342 sq.]. Eusebius (Hist. Eccl., VI, 19) speaks of its pious bishop Atticus who entrusted to the layman Theodore the duty of instructing the Christians. About 230–5 a council on the rebaptizing of heretics was held there (Euseb., Hist. Eccl., VII, 7). St. Agapetus, mentioned in the Roman Martyrology on 24 March as Bishop of Synnada, belonged to Synaus. For a list of other bishops see Le Quien, "Oriens christ.", I, 827. Mention must be made of Procopius (321); Cyriacus, friend of St. John Chrysostom; Theodosius and his competitor Agapetus, at first a Macedonian heretic; Severus (431); Marinianus (448–51); Theogenes (536); Severus (553); St. Pausicacus, during the reign of Maurice, honoured by the Greek Church on 13 May; Cosmas, 680; John, adversary of the Iconoclasts in the time of Patriarch St. Germanus; St. Michael, honoured by the Latin and Greek churches 23 May, died 23 May, 826, in exile for his zeal in defending the worship of images; Peter under Photius; John under Photius; Pantaleon under Leo the Wise; Leo under Basil II; Nicetas in 1082; Georgios at the Council of St. Sophia, about 1450, if one can believe the apocryphal Acts of this council, which perhaps never occurred. The last Bishop of Synnada spoken of in the documents, without mentioning his name, probably lived under John Cantacuzenus (see "Cantacuz. Hist.", III, 73) and probably never lived at Synnada on account of the

Turkish conquest. Several years after (1385) the see was committed to the Metropolitan of Philadelphia. In conclusion may be mentioned St. Constantine, a converted Jew of Synnada, who lived in the tenth century; he became a monk, and is honoured by the Greek Church 26 December.

SMITH, *Dict. of Greek and Roman Geog.*; TEXIER, *Asie Mineure*, 430; RAMSAY, *Asia Minor*; IDEM, *Cities and Bishoprics of Phrygia*; PERRET in *Revue archéologique*, new series, XXXI (January to June, 1876), 190–203); WÄCHTER, *Der Verfall des Griechentums in Kleinasien in XIV. Jahrhundert* (Leipzig, 1903), 37.

S. PÉTRIDÈS.

Synod (Gr. σύνοδος, an assembly), a general term for ecclesiastical gatherings under hierarchical authority, for the discussion and decision of matters relating to faith, morals, or discipline. It corresponds to the Latin word *concilium*. The word *synodus* appears probably for the first time in the so-called "Apostolic canons", while the word *concilium* was employed in the same meaning by Tertullian more than a century earlier. Synod and council are, therefore, synonymous terms. When the bishops of the whole world are congregated under the presidency of the pope, the synod is denominated œcumenical or general. It is only to such an assembly that it is lawful to apply the term *sancta synodus* (see COUNCILS, GENERAL). If the bishops of an ecclesiastical province meet under the headship of their metropolitan, the council is termed provincial. When the hierarchs of all the provinces of a nation assemble, the synod is called national, or, under certain circumstances, plenary. The regulations governing provincial and plenary councils are practically the same. In addition to those mentioned, there are other synods that are more difficult of classification, as synods of the East or the West, the *synodoi endemousai* of Constantinople, and the mixed councils of ecclesiastical and secular dignitaries who assembled together to make regulations for both spiritual and civil matters.

Different from all other councils is the diocesan synod. Other councils are assemblies of bishops who have a definitive vote in the matters under consideration, but in a diocesan synod there is only one voter and only one lawgiver, the bishop of the diocese. This article deals mainly with diocesan synods. In his book "De Synodo Diœcesana" (lib. 1, c. i) Benedict XIV thus defines a diocesan synod: "A lawful assembly convoked by the bishop, in which he gathers together the priests and clerics of his diocese and all others who are bound to attend it, for the purpose of doing and deliberating concerning what belongs to the pastoral care." The Council of Trent (Sess. XXIV, c. ii, "De ref.") requires that a diocesan synod be held once a year. This law is still in force, but a mild interpretation, introduced by custom, has been tacitly sanctioned by the Holy See. Usually, the date for holding the synod should be announced on the Feast of the Epiphany. A month before the opening the decree of convocation should be affixed to the cathedral doors, and it should be published on three successive Sundays in parish churches. When two dioceses are united under one bishop, the synod should be celebrated alternately in the cathedral of each such diocese. It belongs to the bishop to convoke the diocesan synod whether he be consecrated as yet or not. An archbishop, however, who has not yet received the pallium, has not the same right. Vicars-general can assemble a synod only in virtue of a special mandate of the bishop. When a diocese is vacant, the vicar capitular can and should hold a diocesan synod if a year has elapsed since the celebration of the last one. Ordinarily, the convocation of a synod should take place after the episcopal visitation of the diocese, as the bishop can then be better guided in forming his statutes. When, however, the visitation has been neglected for years, it is considered more advisable to hold the synod first. As the bishop is the only lawgiver at a synod, it belongs to him to draw up the various decrees which he may wish to promulgate at its sessions. While he convokes the synod by his own authority and is not required to consult his chapter concerning the convocation or its preparatory acts, yet he must ask the counsel of his chapter or diocesan consultors as to the decrees he desires to enact, though he is not bound to follow their advice. The bishop is exhorted, in the formation of his decrees, to hold private conferences with the prudent, learned, and pious clerics of his diocese, and then to consult his chapter on the proposed statutes thus formed (S. C. C., 26 Nov., 1689). Only in this way does the bishop deliberate with the clergy of his diocese at a synod, and though the finished decrees will receive all their authority from him, yet it is consonant with the mind of the Church that, in the formation of the statutes, the opinion of the clergy be heard and considered. Summonses to a diocesan synod should be given to the vicar-general, the members of the cathedral chapter, holders of benefices, and all others who have care of souls. If there is a custom to that effect, all the clergy of the diocese may be summoned. Regulars who have care of souls are obliged to attend a synod. Their superiors are not, however, obliged to attend, unless they personally act as parish priests or curates. The bishop has power to punish with censures all those legitimately summoned who fail to attend. Laymen may also be invited by the bishop to be present at a synod if there is a custom to that effect, but under no circumstances can they acquire a right to such summons.

At the synod the decrees determined on by the bishop are promulgated, and a period of two months is allowed for having recourse against them to the bishop or the Holy See. All the clergy and laity of the diocese are bound by these decrees, and it is not necessary for the bishop to send his statutes to Rome for revision before publication. Exempt regulars are bound to observe diocesan decrees in all things which concern the sacred canons, the Constitutions of popes and councils, and the decrees of the Sacred Roman Congregations. The bishop may not force his clergy to buy printed copies of the diocesan statutes (S. C. C., 14 Dec., 1658). During the synod the appointment is made of synodal examiners. To the former duties of these officials has been added by the "Maxima Cura" of Pius X (20 Aug., 1910) that of being associated with the bishop in drawing up the decree for the administrative removal of parish priests. By the same papal Constitution, parochial consultors, who are to be assessors in case of recourse against a decree of removal, are also to be chosen by the synod from among the parish priests. Synodal witnesses are likewise chosen at some synods, whose main duty it is to help in the framing of deliberative questions or to report at the following synod what has been the effect of the degrees promulgated at the last assembly, or to suggest new ones. Synodal judges are also to be chosen, though they are rarely now employed. Their office is to expedite such causes as may be committed to their judgment outside Rome by the Holy See. These judges should be at least four in number in every diocese, and their names must be forwarded to Rome as soon as selected. The subject-matter of the decrees framed at a diocesan synod should concern only the preservation of faith or discipline. Under no circumstances may such a synod define any new article of faith or decide any doctrinal point in dispute between Catholic theologians or frame statutes contrary to the common canon law of the Church.

For synods in general use see bibliography of article COUNCILS, GENERAL. The best work on diocesan synods is that of BENEDICT XIV, *De Synodo Dioecesana*. BOUIX treats of these synods in *De Episcopo*, II (3rd ed., Paris, 1883); FERRARIS, *Bibliotheca Canonica*, II (Rome, 1891), s. v. *Concilium*, art. 3; in TAUNTON, *The Law of the Church* (London, 1906), s. v.; HEFELE, *Councils of the Church*, ed. CLARK (Edinburgh, 1871—), and new French translation by LECLERCQ (Paris, 1907—).

W. H. W. FANNING.

Synods, National.—According to the recent canon law, national councils are the deliberating assemblies at which all the bishops of a nation are convoked by the patriarch or primate (Cf. Bened. XIV, "De Synodo", I, i), but, in order to include the ancient national synods, it would be more correct to say a legitimate assemblage of the episcopate of a nation, the decisions of which are valid for an entire national Church. For the classic definition is far from being applicable to all the ancient national councils, as it is difficult to apply to all recognized œcumenical councils the present classic definition and conditions for such councils.

Councils are commonly divided into general or œcumenical, or particular; the latter are subdivided into national and provincial according as they assemble the bishops of a whole nation or of an ecclesiastical province. Finally come the assemblies of the clergy of a diocese, which are called diocesan synods rather than councils. But writers point out that this classification is not and cannot be very exact. For instance, to what category belongs the Council of Arles of 314, at which Constantine in agreement with the pope convoked all the bishops, or at least a representation, of the whole episcopate of his empire at that time? So also if we agree with most authors in regarding as national councils the assemblies of African bishops, it may be objected that Africa did not form a distinct nation in the Roman Empire. On the other hand there have been councils which, while they did not assemble all the bishops of a nation, may nevertheless be regarded as real national synods; such were the reform assemblies held at the command of Charlemagne in 814 simultaneously at Arles, Reims, Mainz, Tours, and Châlons. Moreover, if in order to be national a council must be presided over by a patriarch or primate, we must remove from the list of national councils nearly all the episcopal assemblies of the Frankish Kingdom and Empire, for they were convoked at the command of kings and emperors, and the Frankish Church never had any patriarchal or primatial see whose bishop was qualified to convoke or preside over the entire national episcopate. Besides the term "national" was not very widespread in ancient times, it being the custom to speak rather of "universal" or "plenary" councils as in Africa or Spain, but this word was not used as synonymous with œcumenical. It meant plenary for all the provinces of Roman Africa or for the whole Visigothic Kingdom, in the same sense that the plenary Councils of Baltimore were meetings of the episcopate of the United States.

This being understood, the canonical prescriptions regarding national councils are the same, proportionately speaking, as for general and provincial councils. To be legitimate their convocation must proceed from the authority having competent jurisdiction over the national church, either partiarch or primate (provided that these titles be not merely honorary). In default of this authority the convocation should proceed from the Holy See, as was done for the recent national councils enumerated below. It was because the convocation was not competent that the "national council" of Paris of 1811 was not legitimate. To this convocation corresponds on the part of the bishops the obligation to appear in person at the assembly unless they have a legitimate reason. But representation of a numerous episcopate will suffice, as was the case in Africa, according to canon ix of the Plenary Council of Milevis in 402. The presidency rightfully belongs to the delegates of the Holy See, if there are any; if not, to the partiarch or primate, or to the oldest metropolitan, as was the custom in the Frankish kingdoms. A national council freely discusses the ecclesiastical or mixed matters which have been the cause of the meeting; the decisions adopted become a law for the entire nation, but like those of provincial councils, and with much more reason, they must first be submitted to the approval of the Holy See.

No historical or canonical interest of any importance determines which of the ancient councils held at Antioch, Alexandria, and Constantinople may be classed as national councils. Obviously, the presence and authority of the patriarchs of the various churches rendered this sort of meeting very easy. On several occasions the Patriarchs of Constantinople convoked the whole episcopate of the Byzantine Empire. But these councils have left no very distinct traces in the Greek canonical collections, whereas those of the Nestorian Church of the Persian Empire consist chiefly of canons of the national councils held from 410 to 775 (cf. "Synodicon Orientale", ed. Chabot, 1903). In the West also there was an important series of national councils, the most noteworthy being the assemblies of the episcopate of Christian Africa under the presidency of the Bishop of Carthage, especially the twenty-one plenary councils held during the episcopate of Aurelius (393–427), which form almost the entire canonical collection of Africa. In like manner the Spanish canonical collection is chiefly composed of the canons of the seventeen national councils which the episcopate of the Visigothic Kingdom held, nearly always at Toledo, from 589 to 694. But while the African councils consisted wholly of bishops, the kings and nobles of the kingdom assisted at those of Toledo, without, however, otherwise interfering in matters properly religious. The same was true of the Frankish national councils, where the episcopal assemblies were, as it were, duplicated by an assembly of nobles; occasionally, as at Mainz in 813, there was a third group, composed of abbots and monks. The list opens with three national councils which assembled the episcopate of the three kingdoms into which Gaul was divided at the beginning of the fifth century: Agde (506) for the Arian Visigothic Kingdom; Orléans (511), for the Kingdom of the Franks; Epaone (517), for that of the Burgundians. Most of the Frankish councils held under the Merovingians and Carlovingians assembled the episcopate of one, sometimes of several kingdoms. The king often assisted thereat and the conciliar decisions bearing on discipline were the subject of royal ordinances or capitulars. These double assemblies of bishops and *comites* (counts) were the usual method in the Frankish kingdoms, and Thomassin rightly regards them as the historical origin of parliaments. The acts of these meetings have not been gathered into a uniform complete canonical collection.

In recent centuries Catholic national councils have been resumed in the East and the West at the instance of the popes and under the presidency of their legates. Without going into details, the most noteworthy of these were: the provincial or national councils of Mount Lebanon, for the Maronites, in 1736, confirmed by Benedict XIV; those of 1803 and 1871 for the Albanians; those of Zamosk 1720 and 1891 for the Ruthenians; that of 1841 for the Melchites; that of Sciarfa in the Lebanon (1888) for the Syrians; that of Cairo in 1898 for the Copts; that of Rome in 1911 for the Armenians; in America the three plenary Councils of Baltimore (1852, 1866, 1884), and the plenary rather than national council of Latin America in 1899.

Thomassin, *Vetus et nov. disc.*, part II, III, xliii sq.; Benedict XIV, *De Synodo diœcesana*, I, i; Hefele, *Hist. des conciles*, I, introduction.

A. Boudinhon.

Synodal Examiners. See Examiners, Synodal.

Synods, Mixed. See Councils, General, sub-title II.

Synoptics, the name given since Griesbach's time (about 1790) to the first three canonical Gospels. It is derived from the fact that these Gospels admit,—differently from the evangelical narrative of St. John,—of being arranged and harmonized section by section, so as to allow the eye to realize at a glance (σύνοψις) the numerous passages which are common to them, and also the portions which are peculiar either to only two, or even to only one, of them.

I. *Differences and Resemblances.*—Turning over the pages of an ordinary harmony of the four, or of a synopsis of the first three, Gospels, which show in parallel columns the coincident parts of the evangelical narratives, the reader will at once notice the large amount of matter which is common to the Gospels of St. Matthew, St. Mark, and St. Luke. Brief as these three sketches of Christ's life actually are, they run parallel to one another in no less than 330–370 verses or about one-third of their whole account of Christ's words and deeds, while, with the exception of a few incidents (68 verses), the whole contents of St. Mark are practically found in St. Matthew and in St. Luke. This agreement in the facts related appears all the more striking, because of the great amount of historical material which must have been at the disposal of each Synoptical writer. The Synoptists are, each and all, fully aware that Jesus healed vast numbers of various diseases; they nevertheless agree in selecting the same cases of healing for fuller record; and while they distinctly speak of His unceasing and extensive teaching, yet they usually concur in reporting the same discourses. A no less wonderful similarity may be observed between the first three Gospels with regard to the general conception and the order of the whole narrative. In all three, Christ's public life is distinctly connected with the preaching of St. John the Baptist, is chiefly confined to Galilee, and is set forth in certain epochs, as the early Galilean ministry, the crisis in Galilee, the ministry in Perea and Jerusalem, and the tragic end in the Holy City followed by a glorious Resurrection. In constructing their several records, the Synoptists adopt the same general method of presentation, giving not a consecutive narrative that would result from a fusing of the material employed, but a series of little accounts which are isolated by peculiar introductory and concluding formulæ, and which repeatedly agree in details and in order even where a deviation from the chronological sequence is manifest. Together with all these resemblances, there is throughout the Synoptics a remarkable agreement in words and phrases, which can be more particularly realized by means of a Greek harmony or a close translation of the original text. This verbal agreement in the Greek Gospels is all the more surprising, as Jesus spoke in Aramaic, and as in most cases, it is plain that the verbal resemblances cannot be referred to an accidental similarity, since they are due to the common use of very peculiar terms and expressions, of identical variations from either the Hebrew or the Septuagint in quotations from the Old Testament.

The interconnexion of the Synoptics is not, however, simply one of close resemblance, it is also one of striking difference. When compared attentively, the three records appear distinct as well as similar in incidents, plan, and language. Each Synoptical writer introduces into his narrative fragments more or less extensive, at times entire episodes which are not related by the other two Evangelists. St. Mark says nothing of the infancy and the early life of Christ, while St. Matthew and St. Luke, who speak of them, do not as a rule narrate the same facts. St. Mark does not even allude to the Sermon on the Mount, and St. Luke alone narrates in detail the last journey of Jesus from Galilee to Jerusalem. On the other hand, Matt., xiv, 22—xvi, 12 and Mark, vi, 45—viii, 26, record a series of Galilean incidents which are nowhere found in the third Gospel. Despite his obvious conciseness, St. Mark has two miracles and two parables wholly peculiar to himself. St. Matthew, who apparently does not aim at brevity, makes no reference to the Ascension. Moreover, in the very passages which indicate a close relation of the three, or of at least two, Synoptics, in their sources, minor differences in the events recorded continually appear, which can be fully realized only through a diligent study of the parallel passages, or through the perusal of larger commentaries in which such constant differences are distinctly pointed out. At times the divergences are so great as to appear, at first, actual contradictions. Of this description are the differences noticeable between the genealogies of Jesus (Matt., i, 1–17; Luke, iii, 23–38), the accounts of the episode of the demoniacs of Gerasa (Matt., viii, 28–34; Mark, v, 1–20; Luke, viii, 26–39), of the miraculous healing connected with Jericho (Matt., xx, 29–34; Mark, x, 46–52; Luke, xviii, 35–43), of the petition of the mother of James and John (Matt., xx, 20–28; Mark, x, 35–45), of the incidents relative to the Resurrection, etc. The general disposition of the events narrated betrays also considerable differences. Thus while St. Matthew devotes three successive chapters to the Sermon on the Mount (v-vii) and gives together the parables of the kingdom in one chapter (xiii), St. Luke divides this twofold topic into several portions which he connects with distinct circumstances. It is well known too, that St. Matthew very often gathers together topics which are similar, while St. Mark and St. Luke follow more closely the chronological order, whence arise numerous transpositions which affect the general arrangement of the narrative.

Numerous variations can likewise be noticed in the particular arrangement of facts and words, for the elements of the one and the same episode often occupy a different place in one or other of the Synoptics, or either Evangelist suppresses or adds a detail which modifies the incident. Finally, the verbal differences between the first three Gospels are hardly less numerous and striking than their verbal resemblances. Each Synoptist has his peculiar and favourite words and expressions, which have been carefully tabulated by recent Biblical scholars (Hawkins, "Horæ synopticæ"; Allen, on St. Matthew; Swete, on St. Mark; Plummer, on St. Luke). The verbal differences appear in the very passages which abound in verbal coincidences (cf. for instance, Matt., xviii, 2, 3; Mark, ix, 47, 48), the identity of expression never extending through passages of any length, and unless in reported discourses of Christ rarely beyond a few words at a time. This is often due to the use of synonymous terms, or of different tenses, or of different propositions, or of short glosses which either Synoptist adds to the same name or detail. We find for instance, in Matt., ix, 6, κλίνη, in Mark, ii, 11, κράββατος, in Luke, v, 24, κλινίδιον; in Matt., iii, 16, "Spirit of God", in Mark, i, 10, "Spirit", in Luke, iii, 22, "the Holy Ghost"; etc. And what is of particular significance in this connexion, is the fact that the verbal differences occur when one should most naturally expect an absolute identity of expressions, as for instance, in the words of the institution of the Holy Eucharist, in the record of the title on the Cross, etc.

II. *The Synoptic Problem.*—These resemblances and differences, the extent and complexity of which grow upon the student who compares carefully the Synoptic Gospels and contrasts them with St. John's narrative, constitute a unique phenomenon in ancient and modern literature. They are facts which no one can refer either to mere chance, or to the direct influence of inspiration. On the one hand, the resemblances are too numerous and too striking to be regarded as explicable on the hypothesis that the first three Evangelists wrote independently of one another. On the other, the differences are at times so significant as to imply that they are due to the use of different documents by the Evangelists, as for example in the case of the two genealogies of Jesus Christ. The harmony and the variety, the resemblances and the differences must be both accounted for. They form together a literary problem,—the Synoptic Problem, as it is called,—the existence of which was practically unknown to the ancient ecclesiastical writers. In point of fact, St. Chrysostom and St. Augustine are the only Fathers who have formulated views concerning the mutual relation of the Synoptic Gospels, and the writers of the Middle Ages do not seem to have taken into account these patristic views which, after all, were far from affording a complete solution of that difficult question. Subsequent leading scholars, such as Grotius, Rich, Simon, Le Clerc, had little more than a suspicion of the problem, and it is only in the course of the eighteenth century that the scientific examination of the question was actually started.

Ever since the last quarter of that century, the discussion of the origin of the mutual relationship between the first three Gospels has been carried on with great ardour and ingenuity especially in Germany. As might well be expected, the supposition that these Gospels are so like one another because their respective authors made use of each other's writings was first tried, and in settling the order, that in which the Synoptic Gospels stand in the canon first found favour. As fresh investigations brought new facts to light, new forms of hypothesis sought to satisfy the facts, with the gradual result that the domain of possibility well-nigh appears to have been measured out. Numerous and conflicting as the successive attempts at solution have been, their history shows that a certain progress has been made in the discussion of the Synoptic Problem. The many relations of the question have come into clearer light, and the data for its solution have been revealing themselves while mere a priori views or unsound inferences have been discarded.

III. *Solutions of the Synoptic Problem.*—All attempts at assigning the cause of the resemblances and differences of the first three Gospels admit of being classified under three general heads, according as the relationship of the Synoptics has been explained by appealing to: A, oral tradition; B, mutual dependence; or C, earlier documents.

A. *Oral Dependence.*—The hypothesis of oral tradition implies that before our Gospels arose there were no written records of Christ's ministry, or at least none which was used by the Synoptists. It asserts that these Evangelists have drawn from narratives of sayings and deeds of Jesus which eye-witnesses of His public life handed on by word of mouth, and which gradually assumed a greater or less degree of fixity with constant repetition. According to this theory, the resemblances between the first three Gospels can be easily accounted for. The sections common to all are explained by a cycle of teaching probably formed in Jerusalem, actually made up of incidents and discourses connected with Christ's life from the baptism of John to the Ascension (cf. Acts, i, 21, 22), and faithfully preserved with regard to order and language by the trained retentiveness of Eastern memories. In like manner, the differences of the Synoptic Gospels are easily explained. Sections are found only in two, or one, of the Gospels because the bond established between the narratives was at times modified to suit the various circles of the hearers, and other differences in order or wording are due either to previous variations in oral tradition or to the personal initiative of the several Evangelists who fixed it in writing. This theory of an oral Gospel, handed on everywhere in very similar form, was enunciated by Herder, and chiefly elaborated by Gieseler and A. Wright. With differences in detail, it has been admitted by a large number of Catholic exegetes (Schegg, Haneberg, Friedlieb, Kaulen, Cornely, Knabenbauer, Meignan, Fillion, Fouard, Le Camus, Felten), and by many Protestant scholars (Credner, Guericke, De Wette, Ebrard, Lange, Hase, Wetzel, Thompson, Westcott, Godet, etc.). It undoubtedly points to a *vera causa* in the spread of the Gospel, and cannot be wholly left out of account in an endeavour to explain the origin of our written records of Christ's life. One of its claims to acceptance is that it dispenses with the unseemly supposition that any of the Evangelists made wholesale use in their own Gospels of written records composed by others, and nevertheless did not reproduce them with greater fidelity. Appeal is also made in favour of this theory, to its simplicity, and to its aptness to account for the resemblances and the differences exhibited by the Synoptics.

By itself, however, the hypothesis of oral tradition can hardly be considered as an adequate solution of the Synoptical problem. First, it does not satisfactorily explain the selection of the material included in our first three Gospels. Oral tradition had undoubtedly preserved much more than the Synoptics record, and of this the Evangelists themselves were fully aware (Matt., xi, 21; xxiii, 37; Luke, x, 13; John, xxi, 25; etc.); whence then does it come that the framework of the Synoptic narrative is practically the same in all the first three Gospels, that it consists very largely of the same events and the same discourses, and gives no account of Jesus' ministry in Jerusalem, that is, of His ministry in the very place where the oral tradition is generally supposed to have been formed?

Secondly, the hypothesis of oral tradition does not account for the general identity of order noticeable in the Synoptics. The order of St. Mark is, as it seems, the fundamental order, and it can hardly be said to have been known simply as an oral tradition to St. Matthew and St. Luke, else the sequence of its sections, when additions were made by these two Evangelists, would not have remained as little altered as it has. Again and again, the thread of the common order is resumed at the point at which it had been left. On the supposition of a written source to which St. Matthew and St. Luke had recourse, this is natural enough. But if they depended on memory, the natural effect of the working of the laws of association, would be that when some fresh incident or some part of Christ's teaching was recalled, the old order would be disturbed more or less extensively than we notice it to be.

Thirdly, the verbal relationship between the Greek Gospels is not satisfactorily explained on the hypothesis of oral tradition. This oral tradition was primitively in Aramaic, and the coincidences in the Greek with regard to rare words, irregular arrangement of the sentence, etc., cannot be explained by supposing that our Gospels are independent translations of one and the same Aramaic oral tradition. It is true that in order to account for these coincidences in the Greek, the early formation of an oral Greek tradition which would more or less be the counterpart of the Aramaic one, and which would have been directly utilized by our Evangelists, has been postulated by many advocates of the theory under review. But it remains very doubtful whether such oral Greek tradition would really explain the coincidences in question; and it is quite certain that it would not satisfactorily account for the variations in Greek wording of such important passages as the words of the institution of the Holy Eucharist, of the Lord's Prayer, of the Beatitudes, of the title on the Cross, etc. Lastly, there are historical proofs of the existence of written documents at the time when our Synoptics were written (cf. Matt., xxiv, 15, 16; Mark, xiii, 14; Luke, i, 1), and the most natural supposition is that our Evangelists availed themselves of them. In fact, many phenomena disclosed by the attentive study of the first three Gospels render the supposition so probable, not to say necessary, that several advocates of the hypothesis of oral tradition (Eckermann, Fillion, Le

Camus, etc.), have been led to admit a limited use of written helps by the Synoptists.

B. *Mutual Dependence.*—The hypothesis of mutual dependence assumes that the authors of the Synoptic Gospels used each other's writings, each successive writer availing himself of earlier contributions, so that the second Evangelist (in the order of time) borrowed from the first, and the third from both first and second. According to it, the passages which are alike reproduce those of earlier writings; those which are divergent come from the personal memory of the author or from an oral source. This, it is said, is the most natural, as it is the oldest, manner of explaining the resemblances and differences of the first three Gospels. It is the most natural, inasmuch as if three other writers exhibited such a close resemblance in their works as the Synoptists do, it would readily occur to the reader's mind that they are not independent of each other. It is the oldest also, for it goes back to St. Augustine who formulated it in a general way in his "De consensu evangelistarum" (I, ii, 4), and who in describing the order of succession of the Synoptics, naturally followed the one embodied in the canon: Matthew, Mark, Luke. This order of succession has been accepted by many scholars, Catholic (Hug, Danko, Reithmayr, Patrizi, De Valroger, Wallon, Schanz, Coleridge, Bacuez) and Protestant (Mill, Wetstein, Bengel, Credner, Hilgenfeld, etc.). But every other possible order of arrangement has found advocates, in accordance with their respective views concerning the priority and order of sequence of the Synoptics. The order: Matthew, Luke, Mark, was advanced by Griesbach and has been adopted by De Wette, Bleek, Maier, Langen, Grimm, Pasquier. The arrangement: Mark, Matthew, Luke, with various modifications as to their interdependence, is admitted by Ritschl, Reuss, Meyer, Wilke, Simons, Holtzmann, Weiss, Batiffol, Weizsäcker, etc. It is often designated under the name of the "Mark hypothesis", although in the eyes of most of its defenders, it is no longer a hypothesis, meaning thereby that it is an established fact. Besides these principal orders, others (Mark, Luke, Matthew; Luke, Matthew, Mark; Luke, Mark, Matthew) have been proposed, and more recent combinations (such as those advocated by Calmet, Zahn, Belser, and Bonaccorsi) have also been suggested. As regards the theory of Baur and his school concerning the composition of the Gospels, suffice it to say that it should not really be connected with the hypothesis of mutual dependence, inasmuch as its contention as to the origin of the canonical Gospels has nothing to do with the literary process of composition propounded by that hypothesis to explain the relationship of the Synoptics.

By itself alone, the theory of mutual dependence cannot be regarded as a full solution of the Synoptic Problem. Whichever order be adopted, there are always narratives where one of the Evangelists,—at times, St. Mark himself,—is more complete than the one who is given as his source, and consequently is independent of him, so that in all such cases appeal must needs be made either to oral tradition or to non-canonical writings. Again, in any form of the theory, the differences in form of narration, especially where one writer seems irreconcilable with the other, and the differences in arrangement, where the temporal sequence is very close, remain unaccounted for. Obviously, there is little need to criticize all the forms of this hypothesis by bringing forward special instances of the general objections just mentioned. These forms of it, however, which have found most able and numerous advocates, may be briefly considered. Against the form which asserts that St. Mark made use of St. Matthew, and St. Luke made use of both, it may more particularly be urged: (1) that St. Mark bears in the Greek too manifest a stamp of originality that it should be regarded simply as the work of an abbreviator of St. Matthew; (2) that the use of both St. Matthew and St. Mark by St. Luke, even though we should suppose it to be a fact, is insufficient for explaining by itself alone the presence in our Third Gospel of an independent genealogy of Christ, the insertion by St. Luke of an altogether new narrative of Jesus's birth and infancy, his scattering of many of Christ's sayings grouped by St. Matthew in the Sermon on the Mount, his detailed account of the Perean journey which is absent from both St. Matthew and St. Mark, etc.

The arrangement advocated by Griesbach, to wit, that St. Luke made use of St. Matthew and St. Mark utilized both, is likewise open to weighty objections. Plainly, the supposition that St. Mark followed and epitomized the other two Synoptics renders it more difficult to account for the freshness and power of his narrative; and in point of fact, it clearly appears that if a direct dependence is to be admitted at all, it is time and again not on the side of St. Mark's rugged style and shorter account of the Galilean ministry, but on the side of the smoother form and larger framework of St. Matthew and St. Luke. Again, the dependence of St. Luke on St. Matthew alone leaves unaccounted for the additions, transpositions, etc., already referred to. Finally, the following are the principal difficulties urged against the "Mark hypothesis". Its supposition that St. Mark is prior to the other two Evangelists, goes against the traditional data which describe St. Matthew's Gospel (in the Aramaic) as written first, and St. Mark's narrative as originating independently of any written Gospel. Again, the assumed priority of St. Mark to St. Matthew and St. Luke makes it hard to imagine on what principle the later two Evangelists partitioned between themselves practically all the contents of St. Mark's writing. It is also urged that in the "Mark hypothesis" neither the simple dependence of St. Matthew on St. Mark alone, nor that of St. Luke on both St. Matthew and St. Mark can account for all the phenomena (additions, inversions, verbal changes, etc.), which are disclosed by an attentive study of the Synoptics.

C. *Earlier Documents.*—The documentary hypothesis is the prevalent theory among non-Catholics. Its general principle of solution of the Synoptic Problem is that in the composition of their writings, the first three Evangelists have all made use of earlier written material. The application of this general principle has given rise to a great number of suppositions, the principal of which may be briefly considered. Since Eichhorn (close of the eighteenth century), and especially since Resch (close of the nineteenth), attempts have been made to get behind our Greek Gospels to one or more Semitic documents used in them, and thus to account for the relationship of the Synoptics. This written source, the primitive contents and wording of which might still be detected, was Hebrew according to Resch and Abbott, Aramaic according to Marshall, Hoffmann, etc. In general, the variation in the words and clauses in our Gospels is accounted for by the different translations given to the Aramaic or Hebrew words. It is undoubted that the recent advocates of the hypothesis of a Semitic source have displayed great learning and ingenuity in pointing out the Semitic expressions which might underlie the divers readings noticeable in parallel passages of the Synoptics. It is undoubted, too, that the general background of the Gospels is Semitic in thought and forms of expression, and even that Semitic documents (for instance, Christ's genealogies) have been used by their authors.

By itself alone, however, the theory of a Semitic source does not appear a satisfactory solution of the Synoptic Problem. It is not certain that the whole Semitic background of the Synoptics had assumed a written shape before it was utilized by the Evangelists, for countless instances of Semitic forms of thought and expression may equally well be accounted for through the direct use of oral tradition, to which source, as a matter of fact, Papias refers the origin of St. Mark's Gospel. Again, the differences between the parallel passages of the first three Gospels are very often such as to point directly to the use by the Synoptists of the same Greek sources, so that in large portions of their works, it is much more natural to account for such differences by the individual literary taste, general purpose, etc., of the Evangelists, than by an appeal to the collateral use of a Semitic original, or a multiplicity of versions of it, the very existence of which is doubtful, and the knowledge of which by the Synoptists is still more questionable.

A more plausible form of the documentary hypothesis goes back in substance to Schleiermacher (1817). It maintains that, at an early period, many evangelical fragments, Greek as well as Aramaic, were scattered throughout the Churches,—traditions floating about of which written accounts had been made. These the three Synoptists worked in their Gospels, together with materials which each had himself collected; and in this manner the coincidences and the differences of the Synoptics may be accounted for. This theory of a plurality of primitive documents,— which in certain of its modifications is combined with that of a dependence of later, on earlier, canonical Gospels,—is admitted by many scholars (Renan, Wrede, Schmiedel, Loisy, etc.). This form of the documentary hypothesis does not necessarily go against the inspired character of the Synoptic Gospels. The actual use of certain primitive documents, notably by St. Matthew and St. Luke, may also be readily granted. But tradition ascribes to St. Mark's Gospel a very different origin from the one supposed by this theory, and a careful study of the contents and the style of that Gospel has recently convinced several prominent scholars that the work is not a compilation from written sources. Again, it is not proved that because St. Matthew and St. Luke employed written documents, they exclusively confined themselves to the use of such sources. In their day, oral tradition was certainly much alive. At that time, the difference between oral tradition and a document was not great in many cases where it had easily become stereotyped by frequent repetition. And it is not a safe position to deny the use of this tradition by St. Luke, in particular, that is, by a writer who would naturally utilize every source of information at his disposal. Finally, a constant appeal to new documents, the contents, extent, and very existence of which cannot, many a time, be ascertained, gives to this theory an air of artificiality which recommends it little as an exact description of the actual manner in which the Synoptic Gospels were composed.

The last general form of the documentary hypothesis which remains to be examined is the "Two Document theory", according to which two large works form the main sources of the Synoptics. One work like our Gospel of St. Mark, if not identical with it, is the source of the narratives common to the first three Gospels, and the other, containing the Sayings of Jesus, is the source of the didactic matter common to St. Matthew and St. Luke. Modified in various ways, this solution of the Synoptic problem has had, and has yet, numerous advocates chiefly among Protestant scholars. In the eyes of all such critics, the theory of only two main written sources is especially commendable for its simplicity and plausibility. The contents of the Synoptics comprise two classes of parallel sections: the one consists of narratives of actions and events found in all three Gospels; the other consisting of Christ's teaching appears only in St. Matthew and St. Luke. Now, as in the selection of material, the arrangement, and the language of sections parallel in all three, St. Matthew constantly agrees with St. Mark against St. Luke, and St. Luke with St. Mark against St. Matthew, but St. Matthew and St. Luke scarcely ever agree against St. Mark, the simplest supposition is that St. Matthew and St. Luke made independent use of St. Mark as we have it, or of a Gospel like it (Ur-Marcus). The freshness and power of St. Mark's narrative go also to prove its priority to that of the other two Evangelists. Thus far of the material common to the first three Gospels. The great bulk of the additional matter found only in St. Matthew and St. Luke consists mainly of the words and discourses of Jesus, and although it is very differently given as to historic connexion and grouping, yet it is pervaded by such similarity of thought and expression as to suggest forcibly the hypothesis of a single main source as its natural explanation. The "Two Document theory" is also claimed to explain the peculiar phenomenon of "doublets" in St. Matthew and St. Luke. Finally, it is said to be supported by tradition rightly interpreted. Papias, speaking of books about Christ written by St. Matthew and St. Mark, says: "Mark, being the interpreter of Peter, wrote carefully, though not in order, as he remembered them, the things spoken and done by Christ". "Matthew wrote the *Logia* in the Hebrew language, and every one translated them as he was able". These statements seem to point to two books as the fountains of evangelical written tradition. One can be distinctly named; it is practically our second Gospel. The other, according to Harnack, Wellhausen, Stanton, can still be reconstructed; it is a record of *Logia* chiefly embodied in our first Gospel (Ur-Mattheus) and also utilized by St. Luke.

The "Two Document theory" is advocated by many prominent critics (H. Holtzmann, B. Weiss, Wendt, Wernle, Soltau, Jülicher, Hawkins, etc.). Yet, is is not an adequate solution of the Synoptic problem. It leaves its defenders hopelessly divided on points of considerable importance, such as the compilatory character of St. Mark's Gospel; the extent and exact nature of the Logian document (Q) utilized by our first and third Evangelists; the manner of its use by St. Matthew and St. Luke, respectively; the question whether it was used by St. Mark also; the number of the sources employed by St. Matthew and St. Luke besides St. Mark and Q; etc. A greater difficulty sometimes urged against this theory, regards the priority of St. Mark, which its advocates treat as a point altogether settled. Tradition has it that St. Matthew's Gospel existed in a Semitic form before it was rendered into Greek, that is before it assumed the only form now available for a comparison, with St. Mark's narrative. Hence, it is claimed that St. Matthew's dependence in the Greek on our second Gospel is one arising from the fact that its Greek translation was made with the aid of our second Gospel, and leaving intact the priority of the earlier Semitic form of St. Matthew's Gospel to the composition of St. Mark's writing. Among other difficulties against the "Two Document theory" may be mentioned: (1) its inherent tendency to appeal to subsidiary written sources, the extent and nature of which cannot be determined; (2) its general disregard of the influence of oral tradition in the composition of the Synoptics; (3) its common, but very improbable, denial of St. Luke's dependence on both St. Matthew and St. Luke.

From the foregoing rapid survey of the attempts at solving the Synoptic Problem, it is plain that none of them has been really successful. The problem is very intricate; the historical information concerning the origin of our first three Gospels, incomplete; and every theory, one-sided. The satisfactory hypothesis, yet to be formulated, must be a combination hypothesis gathering and uniting, in due proportions, all the truths presented by the various opinions, and also a more thorough theory taking fully into account both the data of Patristic tradition and those disclosed by literary analysis. Such theory, when framed, will undoubtedly supply the fullest vindication of the historical value of our Synoptic records.

THE SYNOPTIC QUESTION AND THE BIBLICAL COMMISSION.—The only decree thus far enacted by the Biblical Commission, which has a bearing on the Synoptic Question, was issued 19 June, 1911. Its direct object is to affirm the traditional authorship, date of composition, and historical character of St. Matthew's Gospel. Accordingly, it declares that the author of our first Gospel is no other than the Apostle St. Matthew, who wrote before the other Evangelists and considerably before the destruction of Jerusalem, in the language of the Palestinian Jews for whom he composed his work. It authoritatively affirms that the original work of St. Matthew was not a mere collection of the sayings and deeds of Christ, but a Gospel substantially identical with our present Greek Gospel according to St. Matthew. It finally proclaims the historical character of our first Gospel and the genuineness of some of its portions (the first two chapters; dogmatic passages concerning the primacy of Peter, the form of baptism, etc.), which has been questioned by modern critics. Hence it is plain that by this decree the Biblical Commission did not intend to deal with the Synoptic problem, to set forth an explanation of the resemblances and differences disclosed by a comparison of our first three Gospels. Yet, the Roman decree has a particular bearing on the theories of mutual dependence and earlier documents put forth as solutions of the Synoptic question. In deciding the priority of St. Matthew's Gospel in its original language and substance, to the other evangelical narratives, the Biblical Commission has solemnly disapproved of any form of those theories which maintains that St. Matthew's original work was not a complete Gospel or the first Gospel in the order of time. In fact those Catholic scholars who admit either of these theories regard our Greek Gospel according to St. Matthew as a work which goes back in its primitive Aramaic form to the Apostle of that name, and restrict its dependence on St. Mark to its extant Greek translation.

(The names of Catholic authors are marked with an asterisk.)
Synopses:—RUSHBROOKE, *Synopticon* (London, 1880); WRIGHT, *A Synopsis of the Gospels in Greek* (London, 1903); HUCK, *Synopse* (Tübingen, 1910); CAMERLYNCK* AND COPPIETERS*, *Evangeliorum sec. Matt., Marc., et Luc. synopsis* (Bruges, 1910).
Introductions to N. T.:—CORNELY* (Paris, 1897); WEISS (Berlin, 1897); GODET (Neuchatel, 1904); BELSER* (Freiburg, 1905); GUTJAHR* (Gratz, 1905); JACQUIER* (Paris, 1905); JÜLICHER (Tübingen, 1906); ZAHN (tr. Edinburgh, 1909); BRASSAC* (Paris, 1910); MOFFATT (New York, 1911).
Works on the Synoptic Problem:—CALMES*, *Comment se sont formés les évangiles* (Paris, 1899); WERNLE, *Die synoptische Frage* (Freiburg, 1900); BONACCORSI*, *I tre primi vangeli e la critica letteraria ossia la questione sinottica* (Monza, 1904); WELLHAUSEN, *Einleitung in die drei ersten Evangelien* (Berlin, 1905); WEISS, *Die Quellen der synoptischen Überlieferung* (Leipzig, 1908); NICOLARDOT, *Les procédés de rédaction des trois premiers évangélistes* (Paris, 1908); HAWKINS, *Horæ synopticæ* (Oxford, 1909); BONKAMP*, *Zur Evangelien Frage* (Münster, 1909); HARNACK, *The Sayings of Jesus* (New York, 1908); IDEM, *The Date of the Acts and Synoptic Gospels* (New York, 1911); STANTON, *The Gospels as Historical Documents*, II (Cambridge, 1909); CAMERLYNCK* AND COPPIETERS*, *Synopsis* (Bruges, 1910); BURKITT, *The Earliest Sources for the Life of Jesus* (New York, 1910); SANDAY, *Oxford Studies in the Synoptic Problem* (Oxford, 1911); PASQUIER*, *La solution du problème synoptique* (Tours, 1911).
For action of the Biblical Commission see *Acta Apostolicæ Sedis* (Rome, 1911).

FRANCIS E. GIGOT.

Syntagma Canonum, a canonical collection made in 1335 by Blastares, a Greek monk about whose life nothing certain is known. The collector aimed at reducing canon law to a handier and more accessible form than it appeared in the Nomocanon of Photius, and to give a more comprehensive presentation than the epitomes and synopses of earlier writers such as Stephen (fifth century), Aristenus (1160), Arsenius (1255), etc. The author arranged his matter in alphabetical order. He made 24 general divisions, each marked off by a letter of the Greek alphabet. These sections he subdivided into 303 titles, themselves distinguished by letters; for example, the third section contains such topics as: περὶ γάμου (about marriage), περὶ γυναικῶν (about women), etc. The titles ordinarily treat of the civil law (νόμοι πολιτικοί), as well as ecclesiastical law. Some titles however are purely ecclesiastical, others purely civil. The church ordinances are quoted from previous collections, especially from the Nomocanon (883), while the extracts from the civil law are for the most part transcribed without any reference to their origin. The compilation soon came into general use among the clergy, and preserved its authority even under Turkish rule. A translation into Servian followed close upon its first publication. It even worked its way into the political life of the Servian people through an abridgment which King Douchan appended to his code of laws (1349). From this the purely ecclesiastical enactments were excluded, but the civil law contained in the Syntagma was reproduced whenever adaptable to the social condition of the people. In the sixteenth century the Syntagma Canonum was translated into Bulgarian; in the seventeenth century into Russian.

BEVERIDGE, *Synodicon orientale*, II, 1–272; P. G., CXLIV, 959–1400; MORTREUIL, *Hist. du droit byzantin*, III, 457–64; HEIMBACH, *Griech.-Röm. Recht* in ERSCH AND GRUBER, *Encyclop.* LXXXVI, 467–70, tr. PETIT in VACANT AND MANGENOT, *Dict. de théol. cathol.*, s. v. Blastares.

JOHN DELAUNAY.

Syon Monastery, Middlesex, England, founded in 1415 by King Henry V at his manor of Isleworth. The "Monastery of St. Saviour and St. Bridget of Syon" was the only one in England belonging to the modified order of St. Augustine, as reformed by St. Bridget (see BRIGITTINES), and comprised thirteen priests, four deacons, and eight lay brethren, besides sixty nuns. The property extended for half a mile along the bank of the Thames, near Twickenham; and the chief duty of the community was to pray for the souls of the royal founder and his near relatives and for all the faithful departed. Martin V confirmed the foundation in 1418, and the first novices were professed in 1420. Six years later the Regent (John, Duke of Bedford) laid the first stone of the chapel; endowments and benefactions rapidly flowed in, and towards the close of the century and a quarter which elapsed between its foundation and dissolution, the annual income of the monastery was estimated at £1730, equal in modern money to 100,000 dollars. The good observance of Syon was maintained to the last; and even Layton and Bedell, Henry VIII's servile commissioners, could find little or nothing to bring against the community. The inmates were nevertheless expelled in 1539, and the buildings seized by Henry, who imprisoned his fifth wife, Katherine Howard, in them for some months. The nuns retired to a house of their order in Flanders, but in 1557, on the accession of Queen Mary, they returned to Syon, and the greater part of their property was restored to them. At the queen's death, however, they were once more exiled, and after various wanderings in France and Spain settled in Lisbon, where they still own property. The Lisbon community returned to England in 1861, settling at Spettisbury, Dorsetshire (transferred to Chudleigh, Devon, in 1887). The Isleworth monastery was granted by James I to the ninth Earl of Northumberland, whose descendants still hold it. The present mansion is mostly the work of Inigo Jones, the ancient mulberry-trees in the garden being, it is said, the sole relic of the conventual domain.

AUNGER, *History and Antiquities of Syon Monastery* (London, 1840); BLUNT, *The Myroure of our Ladye: offices used at Syon* (London, 1873), historical introduction; DUGDALE, *Monastic. Anglican.*, VI (London, 1825), 540, 541; WILLIS, *History of Abbies*, II (London, 1719), 136; TANNER, *Notitia monastica: Middlesex*, II (London, 1787); BAXTER, *Syon Abbey* (Chudleigh, s. d.); GASQUET, *Henry VIII and the English Monasteries*, II (London, 1889), 256, 459, 476, 483.

D. O. HUNTER-BLAIR.

Syra, Diocese of (Syrensis) a Latin diocese, suffragan of Naxos, comprising the Island of Syra of the Cyclades in the Ægean Sea. The island has an area of about thirty-one square miles and 32,000 inhabitants; it was first called Syria and also Syros, and appears to have been inhabited by the Phœnicians. It was the country of the swineherd Eumæus who described it at length (Odyssey, XV, 403 sq.); and of the philosopher Pherecydes, the teacher of Pythagoras. It possessed two leading cities, Syros (now the modern Hermupolis) and another city on the western coast where stands to-day Maria della Grazia. The island played no rôle in antiquity nor in the Christian epoch; it was not even a diocese, at a time when the smallest island possessed its bishop. Devastated several times during the Middle Ages with the other Cyclades by the Sicilians, Arabs, Turks, and Venetians, it was definitively conquered by these last in 1207. They kept it until 1522 when the corsair Barbarossa took possession of it for the Turks; after 1821 it was annexed to the Hellenic kingdom. The Venetians established there a Latin bishopric which was subject to the Archbishopric of Athens until 1525, afterwards to that of Naxos. The list of titulars may be found in Le Quien (Oriens christianus, III, 865–868) and in Eubel (Hierarchia catholica medii ævi, I, 492; II, 267; III, 324). The most celebrated among them is the Venerable John Andrew Carga, strangled by the Turks in 1617 for having refused to become a Mussulman (Pétridès in "Revue de l'Orient chrétien", V, 407–422). From the occupation of the island by the Turks in the sixteenth century, the Greeks established there a metropolitan: Joseph (Le Quien, op. cit., II, 233) is the earliest known, with Symeon who died in 1594 (Ampelas, "Histoire de Syros", 411) and Ignatius in 1596 (Miklosich and Mueller, "Acta patriarchatus constantinopolitani", V, 461). The island became for the most part Catholic (Ricaut, "Histoire de l'estat présent de l'Eglise grecque", 361; Hilaire de Barenton, "La France Catholique en Orient", 171–173).

Syra took no part in the Greek revolt of 1821; but here the refugees flocked and founded the town of Hermupolis, which rapidly became the leading port of Greece. Since 1870 the ports of Piræus and Patras have greatly injured it from a commercial standpoint. The diocese numbers 8000 Catholics, 21 secular priests and 8 regulars, 7 parishes, 7 churches with a resident priest, 3 without a priest, and 56 chapels. The Capuchins and Jesuits have each an establishment; the Sisters of Charity, 2 houses, one of which is a hospital; the Sisters of St. Joseph of the Apparition have a boarding-school.

Smith, *Dict. of Greek and Roman Geog.*, s. v.; Lacroix, *Iles de la Grèce* (Paris, 1853), 447–50; Mandat-Grancey, *Aux pays d'Homère* (Paris, 1904), 78–92; *Missiones catholicæ* (Rome, 1907), 150; Ampelas, *Hist. of Syros* (Hermupolis, 1874), in Greek.

S. Vailhé.

Syracuse, Archdiocese of (Syracusana), in Sicily. The city is situated upon a peninsula extending into the Ionian Sea, near the mouth of the River Anapus, on the banks of which the papyrus plant is still cultivated. The territory produces all varieties of grains, vegetables, and fruits. Of the two harbours of the city, the principal one is the largest in Sicily and one of the largest of the Mediterranean; two islets, San Marciano and Castelluccio, render it secure without obstructing the entrance. At present the exports exceed the imports. The cathedral is built on the ruins of an ancient temple of Minerva, which was a hexastylo-peripteros with thirty-six columns of which only twenty-two remain. In front of the cathedral are statues of St. Peter and St. Paul by Marabitti; in the interior are several pictures (Madonna of the Pillar; Birth of the Virgin) by Agostino Scilla, who also painted the frescoes of the vault of the Chapel of the Blessed Sacrament and the silver statue of St. Lucy. The baptismal font is fashioned from a large Greek crater, resting upon seven small lions of bronze, found in the catacombs of San Giovanni. Among the furniture is a storiated amber chalice. Other churches are: Santa Lucia, with a "Martyrdom" of the saint by Guinaccia; San Benedetto, containing a picture of the saint by Minniti; San Martino; San Spirito; San Domenico; Il Gesù (the church of the Jesuits), with paintings of the Venetian School and a statue of St. Ignatius by Marabitti; the Church of Santa Lucia dei Riformati without the city, possessing a painting by Caravaggio. Among the civic buildings are the fort of Giorgios Maniakes and Palazzo Montaldo, in the Gothic and Moorish styles. The museum is rich in both Greek and Latin inscriptions (among which are many Christian inscriptions from the catacombs) and fragments

The Cathedral, Syracuse, Sicily

of statues, including a Venus leaving the bath. The public library has an important collection of medals. Ancient ruins at Syracuse are much less numerous than one would expect. There are still to be seen: the amphitheatre (epoch of Augustus); the Greek theatre, excavated from the rock; sepulchres also excavated in the rock; the colossal altar of Hiero II, seven hundred and sixty feet long, upon which, after the expulsion of Thrasybulus, four hundred and fifty oxen were sacrificed; the "Latomie", i. e. caves in the rock where condemned prisoners of war and others were incarcerated, of which the most famous is the "Ear of Dionysius". The fountain of Arethusa, which issues forth in the ward of Ortygia (the present Syracuse), in antiquity was sweet but since an earthquake of the twelfth century has become salt. The Catacombs of San Giovanni, of Santa Maria del Gesù, and the catacombs Cassai, similar to those at Rome, are well known; besides these there have been discovered in the environs of Syracuse various tombs (Lentini, Valle del Molinello, Priolo, San Alfano, Palazzolo, etc.) which have rather the character of ancient tombs of the Sicelioti (aboriginal inhabitants). The present Syracuse occupies only a part of the ancient city. The latter was composed of five great quarters: (1) Ortygia, originally an island but afterwards artificially joined with the mainland, the most ancient part of the city, containing the acropolis dismantled by Timoleon, and the palace of King Hiero, where in later days the Roman govenors resided; (2) Achradine, the most sumptuous quarter, where most business was conducted, situated on the small port or the Trogilos (now the Gulf of Manghisi). It was fortified and contained the temple of Jupiter Olympicus, the prytaneion, the theatre, and the catacomb of San Giovanni; (3) Tyche, the most populous part, deriving its name from the temple of Fortune and containing the palaces of Diocles and Dionysius, the lighthouse, and the Galeagra Tower; (4) Neapolis or Temenites, containing various temples, the theatre, the amphitheatre, and the Latomie; (5) Epipolai, which arose on the heights dominating the remainder of the city, and contained the fort Euryalos. All the city was surrounded by strong walls and beyond Epipolai was the castle of Labdalon. The circumference of the city was 180 *stadia* (20 miles). The name Syracuse is derived from the swamps of the valley of the Anapus. The ancient aqueduct is still in use.

When in 734 the Corinthian Archias approached the isle of Ortygia, it was inhabited by natives whom he expelled. The colony flourished amid continual petty wars with the natives, whose greatest leader, Ducetius (450 B. C.) voluntarily surrendered to the Syracusans, who sent him to Corinth. The government was in the hands of the landowners (*geomoroi*), against whom in 484 the slaves revolted. The landowners were expelled, but were conducted back into the city by Gelon, tyrant of Gela, who in this manner became lord also of Syracuse. It being easier, as he said, to govern one hundred rich than a single poor man, the poor were sold. Otherwise Gelon was an excellent ruler. He conquered the Carthaginians at Himera, aspired to dominion over the whole island, and was an object of wonder to all the aristocrats of Syracuse. It was he who aggrandized the city by bringing in the inhabitants of Camarina, of Megara, of Euboea, and part of those of Gela. In 478 he was succeeded by his brother Hiero, who held a splendid court, favoured poets, orators, and philosophers. He contrived to avoid a war with Girgenti, aided the Cumaneans to conquer the Etruscans by sea (474), and established his dominion as far as Mt. Etna. He should have been succeeded by his son, but his brother Thrasybulus assumed the government, which he carried on with such cruelty and perfidy that he was expelled after a year. Syracuse was again free, and the government then became a democracy. Following the example of Athenian ostracism they introduced the practice of "petalism", according to which each man wrote on an olive leaf the name of the most powerful citizen; whoever obtained the greatest number of leaves was banished for five years. At first the democracy was favourable to the greatness of the city, which obtained a sort of hegemony over the Greek cities of Sicily, and also of Magna Græcia. The arts and literature flourished. The ambitious designs of the Syracusans at the expense of the Leontines (427) and of Egesta (416) caused the intervention of the Athenians, instigated especially by Alcibiades. In 415 a splendid fleet sailed for Sicily and anchored in the great harbour. The city would perhaps have fallen if the Spartans, lead by Gylippos, had not come to the rescue. Finally, in September, 413, the Athenian army and fleet were totally destroyed. The prisoners were either slain or thrown into the Latomie. Syracuse received from Diocles a new constitution and new laws which were most severe. But soon the interference of Syracuse in the quarrels of Egesta and Selinus provoked the intervention of Carthage. The victories of the Carthaginians at Himera (409) gave the opportunity to Hermocrates, then an exile, to attempt to overturn the Government, an attempt which cost him his life (407). Dionysius, proceeding more craftily, first had himself elected among the judges. By flattering the common people and discrediting his colleagues he obtained for himself the sole command of the army and succoured Gela against Hannibal the Elder (405). On his return the people gave him unlimited powers. He surrounded himself with a bodyguard, fortified and enlarged the city, combatted with varying fortunes the Carthaginians, who were conquered at Motye in 397, and obliged to retreat from Syracuse, which they had besieged by land and by sea (396). Every reverse of the tyrant was followed by revolts, which were, however, always crushed with extreme severity. Having made peace with the Carthaginians in 392, he attempted the subjection of Magna Græcia as well, until the activities of the Carthaginians called him back to Syracuse (383–68). Dionysius perfected the science and technic of war, favoured poets and philosophers, and was a wise ruler, but he was suspicious and cruel.

He was succeeded in 368 by his son Dionysius II, a vicious young man, upon whom his uncle Dion and Plato in vain attempted to exercise a beneficent influence. Dion deposed him in 356, but imprudently rendered himself unpopular and was slain (354) by the Athenian Callipus. The latter was in turn expelled by Hipparinus, another son of Dionysius I (353–51). Nysæus followed in succession (350–47), but in 346 Dionysius II, who had remained in exile at Locri, expelled Nysæus, and resumed the government with greater tyrnanny than ever. The nobility conspired against him, and summoned Hicatas, tyrant of Leontini, who succeeded in conquering and imprisoning Dionysius. Others, however, had applied for aid to Corinth, which in 345 sent Timoleon, who conquered Hicatas and the Carthaginians (340), and re-established the constitution of Diocles. In 317 Agathocles, an able general, by the slaughter of six hundred of the richest Syracusans obtained the appointment to the command of the troops and the government. A good ruler, he warred with the Carthaginians, who in 311, for the third time, entered the port of Syracuse. By an act of supreme audacity, Agathocles shifted the scene of the war into Africa, and thus liberated his country. His star afterwards declined and he was killed by his nephew Archagathus (289). The city fell into a state of anarchy, ended in 288 by Hicatas, who was in turn deposed by Tinion (280). In 271 it was found necessary to summon the aid of Pyrrhus, King of Epirus, who raised the siege of the city, but soon retired. The ravages of the Mamertines gave occasion to Hiero II to oppose them successfully, and thus to acquire the government of Syracuse (269). This war brought him into opposition with the Romans, with whom he finally concluded peace by becoming their tributary, and even aided them after their disaster at Cannæ. His nephew and successor, Hieronymus (216), changed this policy, forming an alliance with Hannibal, which policy was continued after his murder by the popular government. For this reason the city was besieged and blockaded in 214 by Claudius Marcellus, and finally taken and sacked in 212. The statues and other objects of art or of value were transported to Rome. Syracuse became the seat of the Roman government in Sicily, and remained such until the Byzantine epoch. During the Roman period the Latin language replaced the Greek, which was restored under the Byzantines. From 663 to 668 the Emperor Constantine II resided here until he was slain by his general Mezezius, who in his turn was killed by the soldiery of Italy. News of these events brought over the Saracens from Africa, who sacked the city. A century later (878) the city was taken and pillaged for forty days by the Arabs. Its decline, which began during the Roman period, progressed more and more, particularly after Palermo became the capital. In the attempted reconquest by the Byzantines, George Maniakis, after having taken Messina, captured Syracuse (1038). In 1086 it was taken by Count Ruggiero, and from this time it followed the fate of Sicily. In 1194 it was besieged and captured by the Emperor Henry VI; on the other hand, in 1298, it successfully resisted the Aragonese fleet, and in like manner the blockade by the French admiral, Vivonne (1677). In 1504 it became the residence of the Spanish viceroys, but after a century this honour was given to Palermo, whither the noble families were also transferred. In 1542 and again in 1693 it was damaged by earthquakes. In 1798 and 1805 the port of Syracuse was of great importance for the operations of the English fleet against the French.

Among the illustrious Syracusans of antiquity were: the poets Theocritus, Callimachus, and Moschus; Epicharmus, the writer of comedies; the philosopher Philolaos; the orators Ctesias, Dion, and Lysias; the historian Flavius Vopiscus, and St. Methodius, monk and Patriarch of Constantinople. (d. 1847). Syracuse claims to be the second Church founded by St. Peter, after that of Antioch. It also claims that St. Paul preached there. As the first bishop it venerates St. Marcianus, the date of whose life is not an easy matter to establish, since too little authenticity can be assigned to the list of the seventeen bishops who were predecessors of Cherstus, to whom the Emperor Constantine wrote a letter. In the times of St. Cyprian (the middle of the third century), Christianity certainly flourished at Syracuse, and the catacombs clearly show that this was the case in the second century. Besides its martyred bishops, Syracuse boasts of not a few other martyrs, such as Sts. Benignus and Eugarius (204), St. Bassianus (270); and the martyrdom of the deacon Euplius and the virgin Lucy under Diocletian are beyond doubt true. The names of the known bishops of the following century are few in number: Germanus (346); Eulalius (465); Agatho (553), during whose rule Pope Virgilius died at Syracuse; Maximianus and Joannes (586), who received letters from St. Gregory the Martyr; while another bishop was denounced by Pope Honorius for the protection which he accorded to women of the streets; St. Zozimus (640), who founded the monastery of Santa Lucia fuori-le-mura; St. Elias (d. 660). Of Marcianos II it is related that he was consecrated not at Rome, but at Syracuse, since the Emperor Leo the Isaurian (726) had removed Southern Italy from the jurisdiction of Rome, and had then elevated Syracuse to the dignity of a metropolitan see, over the thirteen other dioceses of Sicily. Stephen II (768) carried to Constantinople the relics of St. Lucy for safety against the Saracen incursions. Gregorios Asbestas (about 845) was deposed by St. Ignatius, Patriarch of Constantinople, and then became the principal abettor of the schismatic Photius. In 878 St. Sophronius, together with the monk Theodosius, was thrown into prison at Palermo where he died in a dungeon. Until the Norman Conquest the names of further bishops are not known. The series reopens in 1093 with Bishop Roger, who received the pallium from Urban II; in 1169 the Englishman Richard Palmer was also invested by papal authority. In 1188 the see became suffragan of Monreale. Among the bishops of this period are: Rinaldo de Lusio, killed in 1154; Pietro de Moncada (1313) and Ruggero Bellomo (1419), who restored the cathedral; Jacopo Venerio (1460), afterwards cardinal; Pietro de Urries (1516), ambassador of Charles V to the Lateran Council; Gerolamo Bononi (1541), a distinguished reformer at the Council of Trent; Jacopo Orozco (1562), who introduced the Roman ritual in place of the Gallican, and who founded the seminary.

During the sixteenth and seventeenth centuries, celebrated synods were frequently held at Syracuse. Bishop Annibale Termini (1695) rebuilt the church, thirty-five monasteries, and the seminary, which had been destroyed by an earthquake. In 1816 the Diocese of Caltagirone was detached from Syracuse. Piazza Armerina and Noto were made its suffragan sees, but the latter was detached in the same year.

The archdiocese has 31 parishes, 400 secular and 70 regular clergy, with 300,000 souls; six monasteries for men and eight convents for women; it publishes a Catholic weekly and "Il Foglio Ecclesiastico".

CAPPELLETTI, *Le Chiese d' Italia*, XXI (Venice, 1857); PRIVITERA, *Siracusa antica e moderna* (Naples, 1879); CAVALLARI AND HOLM, *Topografia archeologica di Siracusa* (Rome, 1884); LUPUS, *Syrakus im Altertum;* FÜHRER, *Forschungen zur Sicilia sotterranea* (Munich, 1897); STRAZZULLA, *Dei recenti scavi eseguiti nei cimiteri di Sicilia* (Palermo, 1896); *Museum epigraphicum seu inscriptionum quæ in Syracusanis catacombis repertæ sunt corpusculum* (Palermo, 1897); ORSI in *Notizie degli Scavi. Antichita* (Rome).

U. BENIGNI.

Syracuse, DIOCESE OF (SYRACUSENSIS), in the State of New York, comprises the counties of Broome, Chenango, Cortland, Madison, Oneida, Onondaga, and Oswego, and contains an area of 5626 square miles, a little more than one-ninth of the entire state. Out of a population of 609,041, about 161,000, or a little more than one-fourth, are Catholics.

MISSIONS AMONG THE INDIANS.—The Oneidas and the Onondagas occupied lands near the shores of the lakes which bear their names. The first chosen president of the Iroquois was the venerable Ato-tao-ho, a famous Onondaga chief. The Onondagas were the central nation of the League, and not far from the present episcopal city, on Indian Hill, between the ravines formed by the west and middle branches of Limestone Creek in the town of Pompey, about two miles south of Manlius, was the village of Onondaga, the seat of government for the League of the Five Nations. It is probable that some of the Franciscan Fathers of the Recollect reform, whom Champlain obtained from France in 1614 to minister to the French settlers and convert the natives, visited this territory and offered up the Holy Sacrifice of the Mass on the shores of Lakes Onondaga or Oneida, and perhaps in what is now Oswego as early as 1615. Father Le Moyne, S.J., however, must be considered the real founder of the Church in the Diocese of Syracuse. Fathers Joseph Chaumonot and Claude Dablon were selected to begin the work of evangelization. They said Mass on the chosen site Sunday, 14 November, 1654. A little bark chapel was soon constructed with the assistance of the Indians. St. John the Baptist had been adopted as the patron of the mission, and it was doubtless under his patronage that this first chapel on the soil of New York was dedicated. Another chapel was built for the French settlers, St. Mary's of Ganantaa (Lake Onondaga). But these first missions among the Onondagas and the Oneidas had but an ephemeral existence. The Iroquois were constantly incited against the French missionaries by both the Dutch and English in Albany. James II ascended the throne of England in 1685 and openly professed the Catholic Faith. While Duke of York (1682) he had appointed Colonel Thomas Dongan Governor of the Colony of New York. Dongan, an Irishman and a Catholic, presided over the first representative assembly of New York which gave us the charter of liberties. Loyal to his Faith and country alike he sought to preserve and perpetuate the Catholic missions among the Iroquois without strengthening French influence in the colony. For this purpose he brought over with him three English Jesuits: Thomas Harvey, Charles Gage, and Henry Harrison. He established a Latin school in New York and placed it in charge of these Jesuits. He planned also to establish a settlement of Irish Catholics in the interior of the colony, very likely somewhere within the limits of the present diocese. But when Dongan fell all prospect of liberty for Catholic worship in the colony of New York disappeared, and the hope was expressed at the time of his downfall "that Papists would not henceforth come so freely to settle in the colony". Governor Bellemont of New York secured the passage of a law by the colonial legislature punishing with perpetual imprisonment any priest remaining in the province or coming after 1 November, 1700, and any priest who escaped from his dungeon was liable to the penalty of death if he should be retaken. To harbour a Catholic was to incur a fine of £250 and to stand in the pillory for three days. Under these circumstances the Jesuit missions were necessarily closed among the Five Nations. The mission of Ogdensburg, established a little later for the Onondagas and the Oneidas by Abbé François Picquet, a Sulpician, was finally abandoned in 1760, and the last chapter was closed in the story of the Jesuit missions among the Iroquois.

THE CHURCH AMONG THE WHITES.—Less than a quarter of a century after the final destruction of the missions among the Iroquois the first white settler came to Oriskany. Gradually, a few Catholics followed, John Cunningham of Utica being the first Catholic of whom history makes mention. Rev. Paul McQuade who was ordained in Montreal in 1808 was the first missionary. He was pastor of St. Mary's church, Albany, from 1813 to 1815, and made frequent visitations to Utica. There is no record of where the first Mass was celebrated in Utica, but there is no doubt that it was in the home of John C. Devereux, one of the pioneer Catholics then (1813) a member of the board of trustees of St. Mary's church, Albany. Rev. Michael O'Gorman, a native of Ireland, pastor of St. Mary's church, Albany, from 1817 to 1819, was the founder of the first parish in the Diocese of Syracuse, though not the first pastor. He celebrated the first public Mass in Utica, in the Court House, 10 January, 1819. He organized the Catholics, and it was decided to erect a church for Central and Western New York, at Utica. A corporation was duly formed under the name of the "Trustees of the first Catholic Church in the Western District of New York". The first trustees were: John O'Connor of Auburn; John C. Devereux and Nicholas Devereux of Utica; Morris Hogan of New Hartford; Oliver Western of Johnstown; Thomas McCarthy of Syracuse; John McGuire of Rochester; and Charles Carroll of Genesee River. The resident congregation did not exceed thirty. Rev. John Farnan, a native of Ireland, appointed pastor, began at once the erection of St. John's church, Utica, and the little chapel was dedicated by Bishop Connoly, 19 August, 1821. While pastor of Utica, Father Farnan visited Rochester, in 1820, and celebrated the first public Mass in that city. He was also the first resident priest to attend the Catholics of Brooklyn. Among the Catholic laymen of that early period, might be mentioned James Lynch and Thomas McCarthy of Syracuse, and Dominick Lynch of Lynchville, now Rome, N. Y. Dominick Lynch was one of the first trustees of St. Peter's church, New York, and in 1790 when the Catholics of the United States presented an address of congratulation to George Washington, on his election to the presidency, he was one of the four laymen who signed it.

THE DIOCESE OF SYRACUSE.—The Diocese of Syracuse was projected by the Holy See, 12 September, 1886, and Rt. Rev. Patrick Anthony Ludden, D.D., then vicar-general of the Diocese of Albany, and rector of St. Peter's church, Troy, was nominated for the contemplated see. Father Ludden declined the honour. Thereupon, considerable correspondence passed between Archbishop Corrigan of New York and the Cardinal Prefect of the Sacred Congregation of the Propaganda in Rome. Finally, the Diocese of Syracuse was erected by Leo XIII, 20 November, 1886, and Father Ludden, in spite of his emphatic refusal, was appointed bishop of the new see, 14 December, 1886. He was born 4 February, 1836, near Castlebar, County Mayo, Ireland, and was ordained priest, 21 May, 1864, in the Grand Seminary, Montreal, by Bishop Bourget. He was rector of the Cathedral of the Immaculate Conception, Albany, under Bishop McCloskey, and vicar general under Bishops Conroy and McNeirny, and for seven years previous to his appointment as Bishop of Syracuse, he had been rector of St. Peter's church, Troy. He was consecrated at Syracuse, 1 May, 1887, by Archbishop Corrigan of New York, assisted by Bishop McQuade of Rochester, and Bishop McNeirny of Albany. When the diocese was established, there were but 64 secular, and 10 religious priests; 46 parish, and 20 mission churches; 15 chapels; 16 parochial schools; 2 academies; 5 orphan asylums; and 2 hospitals. Rt. Rev. Mgr. John Grimes, D.D., was appointed coadjutor Bishop of Syracuse, with the title of Bishop of Imeria, 9 February, 1909. He was born in Ireland, 18 December, 1852, made his ecclesiastical studies in the Grand Seminary, Montreal, and was ordained to the priesthood in Albany, 19 February, 1882, by Bishop McNeirny, of Albany. He was consecrated bishop 16 May, 1909, in the Cathedral of the Immaculate Conception, Syracuse, by Archbishop Farley of New York. St. John the Evangelist church in Syracuse was the pro-cathedral until 1903. At that time, Bishop Ludden purchased with his own money, property adjoining St. Mary's church which had been planned and constructed by Rev. James A. O'Hara, D. D., for many years one of the most prominent figures in Central New York. He died 26 Dec., 1889. Bishop Ludden, at his own expense, erected on the property a new cathedral and consecrated it 25 September, 1910.

Among the pioneer priests of the diocese may be mentioned: Right Rev. David W. Bacon and the Right Rev. Francis P. McFarland; Fathers William Beecham, Thomas Daly, Michael Hackett, Michael Heas, Bartholomew F. McLoghlin, Leopold Moczygemba, O.M.C., Walter J. Quarter. The prominent laymen include Francis Baumer, Ulric Burke, M. D., John Carton, John C. Devereux, Nicholas Devereux, Capt. David Dodge, Francis Kernan, James Lynch, John McCarthy, Thomas McCarthy, Peter McGuire, Michael McQuade, Francis Murphy, Owen O'Neil, Edward White.

There are many causes for the remarkable growth of the Catholic Church in Central New York. It was chiefly the Irish immigrants who dug the Erie Canal, which was begun 4 July, 1817, almost the exact date of the organization of the first church in the diocese. The salt springs of Syracuse discovered by Father Le Moyne, in the missionary period, added much to the wealth of these parts and attracted many. When through tariff reduction this investment became no longer profitable, extensive cotton and woolen mills, foundries and factories of all kinds, were established. Another cause which contributed to the growth as well as to the cosmopolitan character of the people, was the coming of various nationalities at different periods. The Germans began to come in small numbers, soon after the erection of the first church (1820). According to the official records, Rev. John Lewis Wariath was placed in charge of these immigrants as early as 1837. The Italian immigration began with the construction of the West Shore Railroad in the early eighties. The Poles began to locate in the diocese about a quarter of a century ago. They have now large and flourishing parishes, churches, and schools in various parts of the diocese. The Lithuanians are, as yet, comparatively few in number. They have fine property, a temporary church, a resident priest in Utica, and give evidence of rapid progress. The Syrians began to come about a decade ago. They are found chiefly in Syracuse and Utica. In the latter city, they have a handsome church, and a resident priest. They worship according to the Syro-Maronite Rite. The Slovaks began coming to the diocese only within the last few years. They are of the Latin and the Greek Rite, and are found principally in Syracuse and in Binghamton. In the latter city they have a resident priest and a flourishing parish.

RELIGIOUS COMMUNITIES.—Another important factor in the upbuilding of the diocese, was the work of the different religious communities devoted to education and charity. The Franciscan Fathers of the Order of Minor Conventuals came in 1859. The mother-house of the Order of the Minor Conventuals in the United States is located in Syracuse. The Christian Brothers have been labouring in the diocese for more than half a century. They have a large and flourishing academy in Syracuse. Assumption Academy is the academic department for boys of the Utica Catholic Academy. The Sisters of Charity of St. Vincent de Paul (Emmitsburg) for more than three-quarters of a century have laboured in Utica, and for most of that time in Syracuse, caring for the orphans and building up their schools. The Sisters of St. Joseph, from St. Louis, Mo., have an academy for young ladies in Binghamtom and have charge of many parochial schools. The Sisters of the Holy Name have an academy for young ladies at Rome. The Sisters of the Third Order of St. Francis have charge of hospitals in Syracuse and Utica.

Statistics for 1911 are: priests, regular 16, secular 115; parish churches, 75; mission churches, 34; chapels, 35; parochial schools, 25; parochial high schools, 4; academies, 4; orphan asylums, 5; maternity hospital, 1; infant asylums, 2; hospitals, 3. In the various religious orders there are: brothers, 33; sisters, 330; lay teachers, 8. The pupils in Catholic schools number 10,000. The Catholic population includes, English-speaking, 95,000; Italians, 25,000; Germans, 15,000; Poles, 120,000; Lithuanians, 1000; Slavs (Latin and Greek), 2000; Bohemians, 100; French, 2000; Syrians, 1000.

MARTIN, *Life of Father Jogues* (New York, 1896); DONGAN, *Reports* in *Documents relating to the Colonial History of New York City*, III (Albany, 1853); ed. THWAITES, *Jesuit Relations* (Cleveland, 1896–1901); O'CALLAGHAN, *Documentary History of the State of New York* (Albany, 1849–51); SHEA, *History of the Catholic Church in the United States* (New York, 1886–92); DONOHUE, *The Iroquois and the Jesuits* (Buffalo, 1895); BRUCE, *Memorial History of the City of Syracuse* (Syracuse, 1891); BANNON, *Pioneer Irish of Onondaga* (Syracuse, 1911); COOKINHAM, *History of Oneida County* (Utica, 1912); BUGG, *Memoirs of Utica* (Utica, 1884); CAMPBELL, *Pioneer Priests of North America* (New York, 1908); HEWITT, *History of the Diocese of Syracuse* (Syracuse, 1909); LYNCH, *A Page of Church History in New York* (Utica, 1903); *U. S. Cath. Hist. Society, Historical Records and Studies* (New York, April, 1909–Feb., 1911); FARLEY, *History of St. Patrick's Cathedral* (New York, 1908); ZWIERLEIN, *Religion in New Netherland* (Rochester, 1910); BAYLEY, *A Brief Sketch of the Early History of the Catholic Church in the Island of New York* (New York, 1870); GRIFFIS, *The Story of New Netherland* (New York, 1909); DIEFENDOFF, *The Historic Mohawk* (New York, 1910).

J. S. M. LYNCH.

Syria.—GEOGRAPHY AND POLITICAL DIVISIONS, ANCIENT AND MODERN.—A country in Western Asia, which in modern times comprises all that region bounded on the north by the highlands of the Taurus, on the south by Egypt, on the east by Mesopotamia and the Arabian Desert, and on the west by the Mediterranean; thus including within its area the ancient and modern countries of Aram or North Syria, a portion of the Hittite and Mitanni kingdoms, Phœnicia, the Land of Canaan or Palestine, and even a section of the Sinaitic Peninsula. Strictly speaking, however, and especially from the point of view of Biblical and classical geography, which is the one followed in this article, Syria proper comprises only that portion of the above-mentioned territories that is bounded on the north and north-west by the Taurus and Asia Minor, on the south by Palestine, on the east by the Euphrates, the Syro-Arabian desert, and Mesopotamia, and on the west by the Mediterranean. The northern portion is elevated, the eastern is level, extending to the Syro-Arabian desert; the north-western is crowned by the Amanus and Taurus mountains, while the mountains of Lebanon and Anti-Lebanon are parallel ranges on the north of Palestine or south of Syria. Between these two ranges is the long narrow valley called Cœle-Syria (Hollow Syria). Its chief rivers are the Litâny (*Leontes*), the Orontes (*Al-'Asi*), and the Barada or Abana. Cœle-Syria varies in breadth from three or four miles to fifteen miles, and is in some places broken by projecting spurs of the Lebanon ranges. At its northern end it curves round to the west and opens out to the Mediterranean. It has two slopes, a northerly and a southerly one, and both are fertile and beautiful. This valley was always an important route of travel between Mesopotamia, the Mediterranean coast, Arabia, and Egypt. The whole of Syria, however, is about 250 miles in length, and an average of 130 miles in breadth, having a total area of about 32,500 square miles. The most important towns of Syria in ancient times were Damascus, Karkamish, Hamath, Baalbec, Palmyra or Tadmur, Riblah, Antioch, Daphne, Seleucia, Abila, Chalcis, Lybo, Laodicea, Arethusa, and Apamea, whereas the famous cities of Tyre, Sidon, Berytus Byblos, and Aradus belong properly speaking to Phœnicia. The most important towns of modern Syria are Alexandretta, Antakiah, Beirut, Aleppo, Latakyah, Hamah, Homs, Tripoli, Damascus, Sayda, Akka, and Jaffa.

The name "Syria" was formerly believed to be either an abbreviation of "Assyria" or derived from Tsur (Tyre), hence Tsurya, and that it was of Greek origin. This, however, is untenable, as the name, in all probability, is derived from the old Babylonian name *Suri*, applied originally to the north-eastern region of the present Syria. Later on the name Syria was applied by the Greeks and Romans to the whole of Syria, or the country lying between the Euphrates, the Mediterranean, the Taurus, and Egypt. By the Babylonians and Assyrians it was called "Amurru" (the Land of the Amorites) and "Martu" (the West-Land). The extreme northern part of it was also known as "Khatti", or the Land of the Hittites, whilst the most southern region was known as "Kena'nu" or "Kanaan" (Palestine). In Arabic it is called either "Suriyya" (Syria), or "Al-Sham" (the country situated to the "left"), in opposition to "El-Yemen" or South Arabia, which is situated to the "right". The political and geographical divisions of Syria have been numerous and constantly varying. In the Old Testament it is generally called "Aram", and its inhabitants, "Arameans". But there were several Biblical "Arams", viz.: "Aram-naharaim", or "Aram of the two rivers", i. e. Mesopotamia; "Paddon-Aram" (the region of Harran), in the extreme north of Mesopotamia; "Aram-Ma'ak", to the north of Palestine; "Aram-beth Rehob"; "Aram-Sobah", etc. The Syrian Aram, however, which corresponds to the classical Syria is called generally in the Old Testament "Aram of Damascus", from the principal city of the country. It is of these Arameans or Syrians, who occupied Central Syria, with Damascus as the capital city, that we hear most in the Old Testament.

During the Greek and Roman dominations the political divisions of Syria were indefinite and almost unintelligible. Strabo mentions five great provinces: (1) Commagene, a small territory in the extreme north, with Samosata for capital, situated on the Euphrates; (2) Seleucia, lying south of the former, and subdivided into four districts according to the number of its chief cities, viz.: Antioch Epidaphne; Seleucia, in Pieria; Apamea, and Laodicea; (3) Cœle-Syria, comprising Laodicea ad Libanum, Chalcis, Abilene, Damascus, Ituræa, and others farther south, included in Palestine; (4) Phœnicia; (5) Judæa. Pliny's divisions are still more numerous than those of Strabo. It appears that each city on rising to importance gave its name to a surrounding territory, larger or smaller, and this in time assumed the rank of a province. Ptolemy mentions thirteen provinces: Cammagene, Pieria, Cyrrhestica, Seleucia, Casiotis, Chalibonitis, Chalcis, Apamene, Laodicea, Phœnicia, Cœle-Syria, Palmyrene, and Batanea, and he gives a long list of the cities contained in them. Under the Romans, Syria became a province of the empire. Some portions of it were permitted to remain for a time under the rule of petty princes, dependent on the imperial government. Gradually, however, all these were incorporated, and Antioch was the capital. Under Hadrian the province was divided into two parts: Syria Major, on the north, and Syria-Phœnice, on the south. Towards the close of the fourth century another partition of Syria was made, and formed the basis of its ecclesiastical government: (1) Syria Prima, with Antioch as its capital; (2) Syria Secunda, with Apamea as capital; (3) Phœnicia Prima, including the greater part of ancient Phœnicia, with Tyre as its capital; (4) Phœnicia Secunda, also called Phœnicia ad Libanum, with Damascus as its capital. During the Arabian domination, i. e. from the seventh to the fifteenth century, Syria was generally divided into six large districts (*Giunds*), viz.: (1) Filistîn (Palestine), consisting of Judæa, Samaria, and a portion of the territory east of the Jordan, its capital was Ramlah, Jerusalem ranking next; (2) Urdun (Jordan), of which the capital was Tabaria (Tiberias), roughly speaking it consisted of the rest of Palestine as far as Tyre; (3) Damascus, a district which included Baalbek, Tripoli, Beirut, and the Hauran; (4) Homs, including Hamah; (5) Qinnasrin, corresponding to Northern Syria; the capital at first was Qinnasrin, to the south of Aleppo, by which it was afterwards superseded; (6) the sixth district was the military frontier ('*awâsim*) bordering upon the Byzantine dominions in Asia Minor. Under the present Turkish rule, Syria is divided into the following six vilayets, or provinces: (1) the Vilayet of Aleppo, with the 3 *liwas* of Aleppo, Marash, and Urfa: (2) the independent *Liwa* of Zor (*Deir ez-Zor*); (3) the Vilayet of Beirut, including the coast south of the mouth of the Orontes, the mountain-district of the Nosairiyeh and Lebanon to the south of Tripoli, further the town of Beirut and the country between the sea and the Jordan from Saida to the north of Jaffa, and is divided into 5 *liwas*: Ladikiyeh, Tarabulus, Beirut, 'Akka (Acre), and Nabulus; (4) Lebanon, from the south of Tripoli to the north of Saida, exclusive of the town of Beirut, forms an independent *liwa*, administered by a governor with the rank of *mushîr;* (5) the Vilayet of Suriyya (Syria) comprises the country from Hamah to the Hijaz—the capital is Damascus—and is divided into the *liwas* of Hamah, Damascus, Hauran, and Kerak; (6) El-Quds, or Jerusalem, is an independent *liwa* under a *mutesarrif* of the first class. At the head of each vilayet is a *vali*, or governor-general, whose province is divided into departments (*sanjak, liwa*) each presided over by a *mutesarrif;* each department again contains so many divisions (*kaimmakam-lik, kada*) each under a *kaimmakam;* and these again are divided into districts (*mudiriyeh, nahiya*) under *mudirs*. The independent *liwas* of Ez-Zor and El-Quds stand in direct connexion with the central government at Constantinople.

ETHNOGRAPHY OF MODERN SYRIA —Ethnographically, the modern inhabitants of Syria consist of Syrians, Arabs, Turks, Jews, and Franks or Europeans.

(1) The Syrians are the direct descendants of the ancient Arameans who inhabited the country from about the first millennium B. C., and who spoke Aramaic. Most of these embraced Christianity and continued to speak Aramaic till about the seventh century, when the Arab invasion forced the Arabic language to become the vernacular tongue of the country. Aramaic, however, held its ground for a considerable time, and traces of it are still to be found in the liturgy of the so-called Syrian, Chaldean, and Maronite Churches, as well as in three villages of the anti-Libanus. (2) The Arabian population consists of *hadari*, or settled, and *bedawi* (pl. *bedu*) or nomadic tribes. The settled population is of very mixed origin, but the Bedouins are mostly of pure Arab blood. They are the direct descendants of the half-savage nomads who have inhabited Arabia from time immemorial. Their dwellings consist of portable tents made of black goats' hair. There are two main branches; one of these consists of the 'Ænezeh, who migrate in winter towards Central Arabia, while the other embraces those tribes which remain permanently in Syria. (3) The Turks are not a numerous class of the community of Syria. They are intellectually inferior to the Arabs, but the lower classes are generally characterized by patriarchal simplicity of manner. There are two parties of Turks, the Old, and the Young, or Liberal Party. In Northern Syria, as well as on the Great Hermon, are still several nomadic Turkish tribes, or Turcomans, whose mode of life is the same as that of the Bedouin Arabs. (4) The Jews who remained in the country are but few in number; most of those who now reside in Palestine are comparatively recent settlers from Europe. (5) The Franks (Europeans) form a very small proportion of the population. Distinct from them are the so-called "Levantines", who are either Europeans or descendants of Europeans, who have entirely adopted the manners of the country.

RELIGIONS OF MODERN SYRIA.—In regard to religion the modern inhabitants of Syria consist of Mohammedans, Christians, and Jews. The first are divided into Sunnites or orthodox Mohammedans, Metawileh, Nusairiyyeh or Ansairiyyeh, and Ismailiyyeh. To these may be added the Druzes. The Christians include Roman Catholics of the Latin Rite; Greek Orthodox; Roman Catholic Greeks or Melchites; Maronites (all Roman Catholic); Roman Catholic Syrians, Roman Catholic Chaldeans, Roman Catholic Armenians; Schismatic Syrians, i. e. Monophysites, commonly called Jacobites; Schismatic Armenians, Catholic Armenians, and Protestants.

The Mohammedans or Moslems are and have been for the last twelve centuries the lords of the land and still constitute the great majority of its inhabitants. They are generally ignorant and fanatical, although of late education has spread among the better class in the larger towns. Till a few years ago they were inclined to look with contempt on all other peoples and religions. This, however, is gradually disappearing owing mainly to the wonderful stride the Christians of Syria have been making of late in the matter of schools, universities, hospitals, seminaries, and educational and commercial institutions. The Syrian Moslems are generally noble in bearing, polite in address, and profuse in hospitality; but they are regardless of truth, dishonest in their dealings, and immoral in their conduct. In large towns the greater proportion of the upper classes are both physically and mentally feeble, owing to the effects of polygamy, early marriages, and degrading vices; but the peasantry are robust and vigorous, and much might be hoped from them if they were brought under the influence of liberal institutions, and if they had examples around them of the industry and the enterprise of Western Europe. Experience, indeed, has already shown that they are not slow to adopt the improvements of other lands. In religion the Mohammedans of Syria are Sunnites, or Traditionists—that is, in addition to the written word of the Koran, they recognize the authority of the Sunna, a collection of traditional sayings of the "Prophet", which is a kind of supplement to the Koran, directing the right observance of many things omitted in that book. They are in general exact in the observance of the outward rites of their religion.

The Metawileh (sing. Metawly) are the followers of 'Aly, the son-in-law of Mohammed. His predecessors, Abu Bekr, 'Omar, and Othman, they do not acknowledge as true khalifs. 'Aly they maintain to be the lawful Imam; and they hold that the supreme authority, both in things spiritual and temporal, belongs of right to his descendants alone. They reject the Sunna, and are therefore regarded as heretics by the orthodox. They are allied in faith to the Shi'ites of Persia. They are almost as scrupulous in their ceremonial observances as the Hindus. The districts in which they chiefly reside are Ba'albek, where their chiefs are the noted family of Harfush; Belad Besharah, on the southern part of the Lebanon range; and a district on the west bank of the Orontes, around the village of Hurmul. They also occupy several scattered villages in Lebanon.

The Nusairiyyeh.—It is not easy to tell whether these people are Mohammedans or not. Their religion still remains a secret, notwithstanding all attempts lately made to dive into their mysteries. They are represented as holding a faith half Christian and half Mohammedan. They believe in the transmigration of souls; and observe in a singular, perhaps idolatrous, manner a few of the ceremonies common in the Eastern Church. They inhabit a range of mountains extending from the great valley north of Lebanon to the gorge of the Orontes at Antioch.

The Ismailiyyeh, who inhabit a few villages on the eastern slopes of the Ansairiyeh Mountains, resemble the Nusairiyyeh in this, that their religion is a mystery. They were originally a religious-political subdivision of the Shi'ites, and are the feeble remnant of a people too well known in the time of the Crusades as the Assassins. They have still their chief seat in the Castle of Masyad, on the mountains west of Hamah.

The Druzes (The generic name in Arabic is *ed-Deruz*, sing. *Durzy*).—The peculiar doctrines of the Druzes were first propagated in Egypt by the notorious Hakim, third of the Fatimite dynasty. This khalif, who gave himself out as a prophet, though he acted more like a madman, taught a system of half-materialism, asserting that the Deity resided in 'Aly. In A. D. 1017 a Persian of the sect of Batanism, called Mohammed Ben-Ismail ed-Dorazy, settled in Egypt, and became a devoted follower and stimulator of Hakim. He not only affected to believe in and propagate the absurd pretensions of the new Egyptian prophet, but he added to his doctrines that of the transmigration of souls, which he had brought from his native country, and he carried his fanaticism to such an extent that the people at last drove him out of Egypt. He took refuge in Wady el-Teim, at the western base of Hermon; and, being secretly supplied with money by the Egyptian monarch, propagated his dogmas, and became the founder of the Druzes. His system was enlarged, and in some degree modified, by other disciples of Hakim, especially by the Persian Hamzeh, whom the Druzes still venerate as the founder of their sect and the author of their law. Hamzeh tried to gain over the Christians by representing Hakim as the Messiah whose advent they expected. For further details see DRUZES.

The Jews of Syria are of several different classes. The Sephardim are Spanish-Portuguese Jews, who immigrated after the expulsion of the Jews from Spain under Isabella I; most of them now speak Arabic, though some still speak a Spanish patois. The Ashkenazim are from Russia, Galicia, Hungary, Bohemia, Moravia, Germany, and Holland, and speak the dialect known as Yiddish. These again are subdivided into the Perushim and the Chasadim. The Jews of the East have retained their original character to a considerable extent, and are generally tall and slender in stature. They live in the towns, generally in a quarter of their own.

HISTORY OF CHRISTIANITY IN SYRIA.—The history of Christianity in Syria proper during the first three centuries and down to the Council of Nicæa (A. D. 325) centres chiefly about Antioch, while from the time of the Council of Nicæa down to the Arab invasion it is absorbed into that of the Antiochene Patriarchate (see ANTIOCH, THE CHURCH OF), just as the Christianity of Palestine is practically that of Jerusalem, of Egypt that of Alexandria, of the West that of Rome, of Mesopotamia and Persia that of Seleucia Ctesiphon, and of the Byzantine Greek Church that of Constantinople. As Jewish Christianity originated in Jerusalem, so Gentile Christianity started at Antioch, then the leading city of the Hellenistic East, with Peter and Paul as its leading Apostles. From Antioch it spread to the various cities and provinces of Syria, among the Hellenistic Syrians as well as among the Jews who, as a result of the great rebellions against the Romans in A. D. 70 and 130, were driven out from Jerusalem and Palestine into Syria. The spread of the new religion was so rapid and successful that at the time of Constantine Syria was honeycombed with Christian churches. The history of the Christian Church in Syria during the second and third centuries is rather obscure, yet sufficient data to furnish a fair idea of the rapid spread of Christianity in Syria during those two centuries have been collected by Harnack in his well-known work, "The Mission and Expansion of Christianity in the First Three Centuries" (Eng. tr., 2nd ed., London, 1908, vol. II, pp. 120 sqq.).

Outside the gates of Antioch, that "fair city of the Greeks" (see Isaac of Antioch's "Carmen", 15, ed. Bickell, i, 294), Syriac was the language of the people; in fact it was spoken by the lower classes in Antioch itself and only among the upper classes of the Greek towns was it displaced by Greek. The Syriac spirit was wedded to Greek, however, even here, and remained the predominant factor in religious and in social life, although at first and indeed for long it did not look as if it would. Yet, in this Syrian world, Christianity seems to have operated from Edessa rather than from Antioch. The wide territory lying between these cities was consequently evangelized from two centres during the third century: from Antioch in the West by means of a Greek Christian propaganda, and from Edessa in the East by means of one which was Syro-Christian. The inference is that the larger towns practically adopted the former, while the country towns and villages went over to the latter. At the same time there was also a Western Syrian movement of Christianity, though it did not amount to much, both in and after the days of Paul of Samosata and Zenobia. The work of conversion, so it would appear, made greater headway in Cœle-Syria, however, than in Phœnicia. No fewer than twenty-two bishops from Cœle-Syria attended Nicæa (two chorepiscopi), including several who had Hellenic names. Hence we may infer the existence of no inconsiderable number of national Syrian Christians. By about 325 the districts round Antioch seem to have contained a very large number of Christians, and one dated (331) Christian inscription runs as follows: "Christ, have mercy; there is but one God".

In Chrysostom's day these Syrian villages appear to have been practically Christian. Lucian, the priest of Antioch, declares in his speech before the magistrate in Nicomedia (311) that "almost the greater part of the world now adheres to this Truth, yea whole cities; even if any of this evidence seems suspect, there is no doubt regarding multitudes of country-folk, who are innocent of guile" (pars paene mundi iam maior huic veritati adstipulatur, urbes integræ, aut si in his aliquid suspectum videtur, contestatur de his etiam agrestis manus, ignara figmenti); and although this may reflect impressions which he had just received in Bithynia, there was substantial ground for the statement in the local circumstances of Syria. The number of clergy in 303 throughout Syria is evident from Eus., H. E., viii, 6: "An enormous number were put in prison at every place. The prisons, hitherto reserved for murderers and riflers of graves, were now packed everywhere with bishops, priests, deacons, lectors, and exorcists". Further data at our command are as follows: (1) Acts, xv, already mentions Churches in Syria besides Antioch. (2) Ignatius, apropos of Antioch (ad Philad., 10) mentions "Churches in the neighbourhood" which had already bishops of their own. These certainly included Seleucia, the seaport of Antioch mentioned in Acts, xiii, 4. (3) Apamæa was a centre of the Elkesaites. (4) Dionys. Alex. (in Eus., "H. E.", VII, v) observes that the Roman Church frequently sent contributions to the Syrian Churches. (5) The document of the Antiochene Synod of 268 (Eus., VII, xxx) mentions, in connexion with Antioch, "bishops of the neighbouring country and cities".

The towns in the vicinity of Antioch, far and near, must already have had bishops, in all or nearly all cases, if country bishops were in existence. From Eus., VI, xii we learn that by about A. D. 200 there was a Christian community at Rhossus which was gravitating towards Antioch. (6) Two chorepiscopi from Cœle-Syria attended the Council of Nicæa. In Martyrol. Hieron. (Achelis, "Mart. Hieron.," p. 168) a martyrdom is noted as having occurred "in Syria provincia regione Apameæ vico Aprovavictu", but both these places are unknown. (7) Bishops from the following places in Cœle-Syria were present at Nicæa: Antioch, Seleucia, Laodicea, Apamæa, Raphaneæ, Hierapolis (=Mabug, Bambyce), Germanicia, Samosata, Doliche, Balaneæ Gabula, Zeugma, Larissa, Epiphania, Arethusa, Neocæsarea, Cyrrhus, Gindron, Arbokadama, and Gabala. These towns lay in the most diverse districts of this wide country, on the seaboard, in the Valley of the Orontes, in the Euphrates Valley, between the Orontes and the Euphrates, and in the north. Their distribution shows that Christianity was fairly uniform and fairly strong in Syria about 325, as is strikingly shown by the rescript of Daza to Sabinus (Eus., "H. E.", IX, ix), for we must understand the experiences undergone by the Churches of Syrian Antioch and Asia Minor, when we read the emperor's words about almost all men abandoning the worship of the gods and attaching themselves to the Christian people. This remark is not one to be taken simply as a rhetorical flourish. For after speaking in one place about the first edict of Diocletian, Eusebius proceeds as follows: "Not long afterwards, as some people in the district called Melitene and in other districts throughout Syria attempted to usurp the kingdom, a royal decree went forth to the effect that the head officials of the churches everywhere should be put in prison and chains" (VIII, vi, 8). Eusebius does not say it in so many words, but the context makes it quite clear that the emperor held the Christians responsible for both of these outbreaks (that in Melitene being unknown to history). This proves that the Christians in Melitene and Syria must have been extremely numerous, otherwise the emperor would never have met revolutionary outbreaks (which in Syria, and, one may conjecture, in Melitene also, originated with the army) with edicts against the Christian clergy. The Bishop of Rhossus was not at Nicæa (Rhossus, however, may also be assigned to Cilicia). But, as we already know, Rhossus did possess a Christian Church about A. D. 200, which came under the supervision of the Church at Antioch. There was a Jewish Christian Church at Berœa (Aleppo) in the fourth century. The local Gentile Christian Church cannot have been important; cf. the experience of Julian there (Ep. xxvii, p. 516, ed. Hertlein).

As to Phœnicia, one of the most important provinces of Syria, the history of Christianity there is also obscure. Here again, we learn from the Acts of the Apostles that Christianity reached the Phœnician cities at a very early period. When Paul was converted, there were already Christians at Damascus (Acts ix, 2, 10 sq., 19); for Christians in Tyre see xxi, 4; for Ptolemais see xxi, 7; for Sidon xxvii, 3; and in general xi, 19. The metropolitan position of Tyre, which was the leading city in the East for manufactures and trade, made it the ecclesiastical capital of the province; but it is questionable if Tyre enjoyed this pre-eminence as early as the second century, for at the Palestinian Synod on the Eastern controversy Cassius, the Bishop of Tyre, and Clarus, the Bishop of Ptolemais, took counsel with the Bishop of Ælia and of Cæsarea (Eus., "H. E.", V, xxv) to whom they seem to have been subordinate. On the other hand, Marinus of Tyre is mentioned in a letter of Dionysius of Alexandria (ibid., VII, v, 1) in such a way as to make his metropolitan dignity extremely probable. Martyrs in or from Tyre, during the great persecution, are noted by Eusebius, VIII, vii, 1 (VIII, viii), VIII, xiii, 3. Origen died at Tyre and was buried there. It is curious also to note that the learned Antiochene priest Dorotheus, the teacher of Eusebius, was appointed by the emperor (Diocletian, or one of his immediate predecessors) to be the director of the purple-dyeing trade in Tyre (Eus., "H. E.", VII, xxxii). A particularly libellous edict issued by the Emperor Daza against the Christians is preserved by Eusebius (IX, vii) who copied it from the pillar in Tyre on which it was cut, and the historian's work reaches its climax in the great speech upon the reconstruction of the church at Tyre, "by far the most beautiful in all Phœnicia" (X, iv). This speech is dedicated to Paulinus, Bishop of Tyre, in whose honour indeed the whole of the tenth book of its history is written. Unfortunately we get no information whatever, in this long address, upon the Christian community at Tyre. We can only infer the size of the community from the size of the church building, which may have stood where the ruins of the large crusading church now astonish the traveller (cf. Baedeker's "Palestine", pp. 300 sq.). Tyre as a Christian city was to Phœnicia what Cæsarea was to Palestine. It seems to have blossomed out as a manufacturing and trading centre during the imperial age, especially in the third century. A number of passages in Jerome give characteristic estimates of its size and importance. In Sidon Origen stayed for some time (Hom. xiv, 2, in Josuam), while it was there that the presbyter Zenobius (Eus., "H. E.", VIII, xiii, 3) died during the great persecution, as did some Christians at Damascus (IX, v). Eleven bishops, but no chorepiscopi, were present at the Council of Nicæa from Phœnicia; namely the bishops of Tyre, Ptolemais, Damascus, Sidon, Tripolis, Paneas, Berytus, Palmyra, Alassus, Emesa, and Antaradus. From Eusebius we also learn that many Jewish Christians also resided in Paneas (Eus., "H. E.", VII, xvii, 18). Tripolis is mentioned even before the Council of Nicæa (in "Mart. Pal.," III, where a Christian named Dionysius comes from Tripolis); the Apostolic Constitutions (vii, 46) declare that Marthones was bishop of this town as early as the Apostolic age; while, previous to the Council of Nicæa, Hellenicus, the local bishop, opposed Arius (Theodoret, "H. E.", I, iv), though Gregory, Bishop of Berytus, sided with him (loc. cit.; for Berytus, see also

"Mart. Pal.", iv). The local church was burnt under Julian (cf. Theod., "H. E.", IV, xxii). Eusebius (VIII, xiii) calls Silvanus, at the period of the great persecution, bishop, not of Emesa but of "the churches round Emesa". Emesa thus resembled Gaza; owing to the fanaticism of the inhabitants Christians were unable to reside within the town itself, they had to quarter themselves in the adjoining villages. Anatolius, the successor of Silvanus, was the first to take up his abode within the town. Theodoret ("H. E.", III, vii), writing of the age of Julian, says that the church there was νεόδυητος (newly built). With regard to Heliopolis we have this definite information, that the town acquired its first church and bishop, thanks to Constantine, after 325 (cf. "Vita Constant.," III, lviii, and Socrat., I, xviii). The "Mart. Syriacum" mentions one martyr, Lucian, at Heliopolis. Christians also were deported ("Mart. Pal.," XIII, ii) by Daza to Lebanon for penal servitude. One martyrdom makes it plain that there were Christians at Byblus. At Choda (Kabun), north of Damascus, there were also numerous Jewish Christians in the days of Eusebius.

We have no information in detail upon the diffusion and density of the Christian population throughout Phœnicia. Rather general and satisfactory information is available for Syria, a province with which Phœnicia was at that time very closely bound up; even the Phœnician tongue had long been dislodged by Syriac. From the letters of Chrysostom and the state of matters which still obtained in the second half of the sixth century, however, it is quite clear that Christianity got a firm footing only on the seaboard, while the inland districts of Phœnicia remained pagan for the most part. Yet it was but recently, not earlier than the third century, that these Phœnician-Hellenic cults had experienced a powerful revival. The situation is quite clear: wherever Christianity went, it implied Hellenizing, and vice versa. Christianity, in the first instance, only secured a firm footing where there were Greeks. The majority of the Phœnician towns where Christian bishops can be traced lay on the coast; i. e., they were towns with a strong Greek population. In the large pagan cities, Emesa and Heliopolis, on the other hand, Christians were not tolerated. Once we leave out inland localities where "heretics", viz., Marcionites and Jewish Christians, resided, the only places in the interior where Christians can be found are Damascus, Paneas, and Palmyra. Damascus, the great trading city, was Greek (cf. Mommsen, "Rom. Gesch.", V., p. 473; Eng. trans., II, 146); so was Paneas. In Palmyra, the headquarters of the desert trade, a strong Greek element also existed (Mommsen, pp. 425 sq.; Eng. trans., II, 96 sq.). The national royal house in Palmyra, with its Greek infusion, was well disposed not towards the Greek but towards the scanty indigenous Christians of Syria, as may be inferred from the relations between Paul of Samosata and Zenobia, no less than from the policy adopted by Rome against him.

The Edict of Milan (A. D. 313) marks the beginning of a better-known period in the history of Syrian Christianity, during which the See of Antioch was filled by a succession of bishops illustrious throughout the Church, and the Church of Syria was involved in the most troublesome period of church history and theology, which marks the beginning of those fatal schisms, heresies, and Christological controversies that led to the final separation of the Syrian Church and the Churches of the East from the Church of Rome (See ARIANISM; NESTORIANISM; MONOPHYSITISM). The death of Severus (542), the deposed Monophysite Patriarch of Antioch, may be taken to mark the beginning of a new period in the history of the Syrian Church; for from this date the double succession in the See of Antioch has been maintained to the present day. The death of the Emperor Maurice (A. D. 602) and the succession of his murderer, Phocas, gave the signal for the Persians to ravage the Roman dominions. Hitherto Mesopotamia had been the arena of war between the rival powers, and Dara, Amida, and Nisibis the keys of possession. But Heraclius came to the throne in 602 to find all Syria in the hands of Chosroes. First Damascus, then the Holy City itself fell before the Persian general Shahrbarz (614), and the Patriarch Zacharias of Jerusalem was carried off with the True Cross itself, to grace the infidel's triumph. Never since Constantinople was built had there been such a disaster; and at Chalcedon itself, almost opposite the very walls of the capital, the Persians were encamped, stretching out their hands to the Slavs and Avars, who threatened the city on the north side of the isthmus, and inviting them to join in its destruction. An insulting and blasphemous letter from the Persian king aroused the emperor and all Christendom; while from Constantinople to Arabia the Church poured forth her treasures of plate and money to help in the crusade. Constantinople was fortified and with a gigantic effort, worthy of the great conquerors of the world's history, Heraclius drove back the Persians, cutting them off in Cilicia, and forcing them finally to make an abject appeal for mercy in the very royal palace of Dastagerd itself. Chosroes had been already murdered by his son, who submitted to Heraclius (A. D. 628). The emperor returned, leaving the East in peace, to restore the Cross to its place in Jerusalem.

Meanwhile in an obscure corner of the empire Mohammed had been born, and in this very year sent round a letter demanding for a new creed the submission of the kings of the earth. "The year of flight" (A. D. 622) had passed, and Mohammed was at the head of a devoted band of followers, ready to conquer Arabia and perhaps the world. It was an epoch of the world's history, and twice the patriarchs of Jerusalem saw the abomination of desolation standing in the holy place, and thought the end of all things at hand. Ten years after Shahrbarz (637), when the glories of Heraclius paled before the storm of Arab conquest, Sophronius the Patriarch and Omar the Arab stood side by side at the altar of the Church of the Holy Sepulchre in Jerusalem. East of the Mediterranean the Roman Empire had given way for ever, and the Arab arms now ruled the Churches which the councils of two centuries before had cut off from the orthodox communion. For the future it was not the Melchite or Imperialist to whom the Eastern Churches were to acknowledge an unwilling homage, but to the sword of Islam. Byzantine history now affected them little, for the successors of Heraclius had enough to do to keep the Saracen fleets away from the capital. The famous Iconoclastic controversy, begun by Leo the Isaurian, was continued for nearly a hundred years (720–802) by his successors. How little the second great controversy of the times affected the Syrians may be judged by their own language in regard to the "Procession of the Holy Ghost". The words inserted in the Creed by the Western Church were the occasion of the rupture, for which the rival claims of Gregory of Rome and John Scholasticus of Constantinople had paved the way; and the ninth century witnessed the unseemly recriminations and the final break between the two great communions

In the seventh century the Syrian Christians fade from the general history of the Church. The Arabs were inclined to favour them as rivals of the Greeks, and early in the eighth century Wâlid secured the entry of their patriarch into Antioch, whence they had been driven by the Greeks since the death of Jacobus Baradæus. But he remained there only a short time, nor were his people free from the persecutions which Abdelmalik and Yazid ordered against the Christians; while in 771 the Khalif Abdullah took a census throughout Syria and Mesopotamia, ordering all Jews and Christians, especially at Jerusalem, to be branded on the neck and forehead. A short-lived union between the Syrians and Armenians (726) was followed by persecution at the hands of the Greeks (750), who took away many Syrian and Armenian slaves from Mesopotamia to the West. Two centuries later Nicephorus Phocas, anxious to unite Christendom against the Arabs, caused John Sarighta, the Patriarch of the Syrians, to be brought to Constantinople, there to discuss with Polyeuctus, Patriarch of that city, the differences that divided them. In the letter written by John to Mennas of Alexandria we perceive how much the controversy had become a mere matter of verbal expression, and how the Syrians clung to the words which Greek tyranny had made the badge of a rival party. The imprisonment of John, added to other acts of tyranny, confirmed their hatred of the Greeks, and made them prefer even the domination of the Moslem. From the eighth and ninth centuries down to our own times the history of Christianity in Syria is the history of Nestorianism and of the Nestorian Church, of Eutychianism and the Monophysite or Jacobite Syriac Church, of the Monophysite Armenian Church of Syria, of the Greek Schism and of the Byzantine, Russian, and Greek, or the so-called Orthodox Eastern Church; the Schismatic and Melchite (Catholic) Greek Patriarchates of Antioch; the Syrian, Monophysite, and Catholic Patriarchates of Antioch, the Latin Patriarchate of Antioch, and the Maronite Church, for all which see respective articles.

STATISTICS OF THE VARIOUS CHRISTIAN SECTS AND CHURCHES.—The Christians of Modern Syria, schismatic as well as Catholic, are divided into the following sects and churches:—

Greek Orthodox, i. e. the Syrian Greek Schismatic Church.—The Greek Orthodox of Syria are under the jurisdiction of the Patriarch of the Greek Orthodox of Antioch, whose residence is at Damascus and who has under his jurisdiction 2 suffragan or auxiliary bishops attached to him personally, and 13 eparchies, or archdioceses, 50,000 families, or about 250,000 subjects, most of whom dwell in Syria proper. Of these thirteen eparchies eleven are in Syria, one in Northern Mesopotamia, one in Armenia and Asia Minor. The Greek Orthodox of Syria have 5 schools with 810 pupils in Beirut; 24 in Damascus and surrounding villages, with 2215 pupils and 60 teachers; and 12 in Northern Syria with 2400 pupils and 65 teachers. The liturgy of the Syrian Greek Orthodox is that of the Greek Church, and the liturgical language, Greek with a great deal of Arabic, which is the vernacular of all the Christians of Syria.

Greek-Melchites, i. e. Roman Catholic Syrians of the Greek Rite.—These are under the jurisdiction of the Greek-Melchite Patriarch of Antioch, whose residence is at Damascus, and who has under his patriarchal jurisdiction 4 archdioceses, 8 dioceses, 2 patriarchal vicariates (at Jerusalem and Alexandria), with a total of about 125,000 souls, divided as follows: (1) Archdiocese of Aleppo, 6 churches and chapels, 10,000 souls, 86 colleges superintended by Franciscan, Capuchin and Jesuit missionaries; (2) Archdiocese of Bostra and Hauran with 12,000 souls, 4 churches, 8 chapels, 15 priests and 4 schools; (3) Archdiocese of Homs and Hamah, with 8000 souls, 20 churches and chapels, 20 priests and 18 schools, residence at Homs; (4) Archdiocese of Tyre, with 6200 souls, 11 churches and chapels, 20 priests, of which 15 are Basilian monks, and 13 schools, residence at Sur (Tyre); (5) Diocese of Beirut and Djebail, with 15,000 souls, one seminary at Ain-Traz, 150 parishes, 195 churches and chapels, and 19 schools, residence at Beirut; (6) Diocese of Cæsarea-Philippi, or Baneas, with 4500 souls, 15 parishes, 9 churches and chapels, 17 priests, and 19 schools, residence at Gemaidat-Marjoun; (7) Diocese of Damascus, of which the patriarch himself is the ordinary, with one suffragan bishop, with 12,000 souls, 9 parishes, and 9 churches; (8) Diocese of Heliopolis or Ba'albek, with 5000 souls, 9 parishes, 10 churches, 15 priests, and 8 schools, residence at Ba'albek; (9) Diocese of Ptolemais or Saint John of Acre, with 9000 souls, 24 stations, 25 churches, 34 priests, and 8 schools, residence at Akka; (10) Diocese of Sidon, with 18,000 souls, 38 churches and chapels, 41 priests, 34 schools, residence at Sayda; (11) Diocese of Tripoli, erected in 1897; (12) Diocese of Zahle and Furzoul, with 17,000 souls, 30 churches and chapels, 35 priests, 12 schools, residence at Zahle.

The two patriarchal vicariates at Jerusalem and Alexandria have a dozen parishes in the latter and four or five parishes in the former. The Greek-Melchites have also a parish with a church in Marseilles, another in Paris (since 1889), and several in the United States. In Jerusalem they have the Seminary of St. Anne, founded in 1882 by Cardinal Lavigerie under the direction of the White Fathers. The number of these average between 125 and 150. They have also a seminary in Rome founded for them in 1577 by Gregory XIII, under the name of College of St. Athanasius; also a small seminary in Beirut, and a larger one at Ain-Traz. Three indigenous religious orders, for men and women alike, are still in existence among the Greek-Melchites in Syria, viz: The Aleppine, with 40 monks and 18 nuns; the Baladites of the Order of St. John, with 96 monks and 42 nuns; and the Mokhallasites, or Salvatorians, with 200 monks and 25 nuns. The rules followed by these three orders are either those of St. Basil or St. George. From the time of Gregory XVI (1831–46) the patriarch of the Greek-Melchites is allowed to assume the official title of "Patriarch of Antioch, Alexandria, and Jerusalem".

The Syrian Jacobites, i. e. Monophysites.—They are under the jurisdiction of the Syrian Jacobite Patriarch of Antioch, whose residence is at Der-el-Zafaran near Mardin in Northern Mesopotamia. The Syrian Jacobites were formerly very numerous and scattered all over Western Asia, Egypt, and India, having had in the twelfth and thirteenth centuries as many as 20 metropolitans and 100 bishops or dioceses. At present, they have but 8 archbishops and 3 bishops with a total of about 80,000 souls, not including those of Malabar, in India, who are not under the direct jurisdiction of the Syrian Jacobite Patriarch of Antioch. The episcopal sees of this Church, with the exception of the one of Jerusalem, whose titular bishop resides at Za'faran near Mardin, are all situated in Mesopotamia, and in the extreme northeastern section of Syria. Their liturgical language is Syriac (see MONOPHYSITES).

Catholic Syrians.—These consist mainly of those Syrian Jacobites who in the last five or six centuries have gradually given up their Monophysite heresy, and embraced the Catholic Faith, though retaining their Syrian Rite, customs, and liturgy. In course of time they have become numerous enough to have a patriarch of their own with several dioceses and bishops. They are to be found mainly in Syria, Palestine, Mesopotamia, and Babylonia. Their patriarch, whose official residence is at Mardin, but who lives sometimes in Mosul and sometimes in Aleppo or Beirut, in Syria, is officially entitled the "Syrian Patriarch of Antioch", having under his jurisdiction nine dioceses with a total of about 40,000 souls, divided as follows: (1) Archdiocese of Bagdad, with 2000 souls, 3 churches, 6 priests, and 1 school, residence Bagdad; (2) Archdiocese of Damascus, with 4000 souls, 6 parishes, 6 churches, 12 priests, and 6 schools, residence Damascus; (3) Archdiocese of Homs and Hamah, with 3000 souls, 5 parishes, and 5 churches, residence Homs; (4) Diocese of Aleppo, with 4000 souls, 3 parishes, 3 churches, and 15 priests, residence Aleppo; (5) Diocese of Beirut, with 700 souls, 1 church, and 3 priests; (6) Diocese of Diarbekir, with 1000 souls, 3 parishes, 3 churches, and 7 priests. (7) Diocese of Djezire, with 2000 souls, 7 churches, 10 priests, and 6 schools, residence Djezire; (8) Diocese of Mardin, with 5000 souls, 7 stations, 9 churches, 25 priests, and 7 schools; (9) Diocese of Mosul, with 10,000 souls, 8 parishes, 12 churches, and 25 priests, residence Mosul. The liturgical language of this Church is Syriac.

Catholics of the Latin Rite.—The Catholics of the Latin Rite in Syria are not very numerous, and are under the jurisdiction of the Apostolic Delegate of Syria, whose residence is at Beirut (formerly at Aleppo). They number about 7000, scattered all over the large towns of Syria, and are either of Italian or French descent, having settled in Syria mainly for commercial or educational purposes. The so-called Latin Patriarchate of Antioch owes its origin to the times of the Crusades of the eleventh, twelfth, and thirteenth centuries, in connexion with the establishment of the Latin Patriarchate of Jerusalem, both of which are nowadays simply titular, without any jurisdiction, and their titulars reside in Rome. The Latin Patriarch of Antioch has under his purely titular jurisdiction the following titular archbishoprics: Apamea, Adana, Tarsus, Anazarbe, Seleucia, Irenopolis, Cyr, Hierapolis, Edessa, Amida, Nisibis, Emesa, Heliopolis, Palmyra, Damascus, Philadelphia, Bostra, Almire, Derbe, Epiphania, Gabala, and Rosea. For Armenians (Catholic and Schismatic) see ARMENIA; for Chaldeans (Catholic) see CHALDEAN CHRISTIANS. The last group of Christians in Syria, and, perhaps the most important one, consists of the Maronites of Mt. Lebanon. They form by far the largest Christian community of Syria, and are all in union with the Catholic Church. (See MARONITES.)

The latest approximate statistics of the population and various denominations in Syria are—total population, 3,226,160; Mohammedans, 2,209-450; Catholic Christians, 555,949; non-Catholic Christians, 435,389; Nusairiyyeh, about 150,000; Ismailiyyeh, about 120,000; Druzes, about 70,000; Jews, 65,246.

CATHOLIC MISSIONS IN SYRIA.—The beginnings of Catholic missions in Syria may be appropriately traced back to the age of the Crusaders and the establishment of the Latin Patriarchate of Antioch in 1100, and that of the Vicariate Apostolic of Aleppo in 1762. The first Latin Patriarch of Antioch was appointed either in 1100 (according to Le Quien) or 1098 (according to Mas Latrie) by Pope Urban II. The first appointee was Bernard, Bishop of Artesia, near Antioch. He died in 1132 and was succeeded by Raoul, from Dumfront in Normandy, who, owing to flagrant acts of impertinence and insubordination to the Holy See, was forced to resign in 1142. He was succeeded by Aimeric or Amaury, of Limoges, who, having incurred the displeasure of Renaud de Chatillon, Prince of Antioch, was persecuted, tortured, and finally compelled to flee to Jerusalem. In 1160, however, he was restored to his see by Baudouin II, Prince of Aleppo. Soon, however, Bohemond III, Prince of Antioch, drove Amaury out of his see and offered it instead, in 1161, to the Greek Patriarch, Athanasius. On the death of the latter in 1170, caused by a terrific earthquake, in which most of the Greek clergy also lost their lives, the Greeks lost their influence and power with the people. In 1196 Amaury himself died and was succeeded by Pierre d'Angoulême, Bishop of Tripoli. In 1204 Pietro di Capua, known as Pietro d'Amalfi, was chosen Patriarch of Antioch. Bohemond IV, however, soon began to intrigue in order to replace him with the Greek Patriarch, Simeon III; but he was excommunicated by the patriarch and by the pope himself, Innocent III, which caused the whole Latin clergy to rebel against the king. Pietro d'Amalfi, nevertheless, was imprisoned by Bohemond and died in 1208, and was succeeded by the Latin Bishop of Jerusalem, Pietro di Capua, nephew of the deceased patriarch. Bohemond IV, however, refused to acknowledge him. In the meanwhile, after many quarrels and vicissitudes, King Bohemond and the Latin clergy agreed to the election of Rainier, in 1219, as Patriarch of Antioch, after having succeeded in inducing the pope to create the Greek occupant of the see, the Patriarch Peter, a cardinal. Rainier died in 1226 and was succeeded in 1228 by Albert Rezato, who was present at the Council of Lyons in 1245 and who died a short time afterwards.

In the thirteenth and fourteenth centuries several Latin patriarchs occupied the See of Antioch, but were constantly harassed and molested by the native Greek clergy and by the Frankish princes themselves, who for political purposes were ever ready to sacrifice religious interests in order to secure the good will of the native Greek Syrians. In the year 1348, however, the Latin Patriarchate of Antioch came to an end, as far as effective jurisdiction was concerned, although it continued to exist till our own times simply as a titular dignity. The present Latin Patriarch of Antioch resides in Rome. In the thirteenth century, however, when it was at its height, the Latin Patriarchate of Antioch had under its jurisdiction the Latin sees of Laodicea, Gabala, Antaradus or Tortosa, Tripoli, Byblos, Seleucia, Tarsus, Corycos, Mamistra, Edessa, Apamea, Balanea, Artesia, Albaria, Larissa, Mariames, Hierapolis, Cyr, Nicosia, Paphos, Famagusta, and Limassol (see Le Quien, "Oriens Christianus", III, 1165–1232). During these two centuries, the presence of so many Catholic bishops, clergy, and lay people of the Latin Rite in Palestine and Syria was productive of good Catholic missionary results, as, owing precisely to the contact of the Latins with the various Oriental Schismatic Churches of the Near East, a large number of Greeks, Nestorians, Jacobite Syrians and Monophysite Armenians, not seldom led by their own bishops and clergy, embraced the Catholic Faith.

The second centre of Catholic propaganda in Syria was the Latin Vicariate Apostolic of Aleppo. This Vicariate was first established in 1762, extending its jurisdiction and its beneficial missionary influence over all Syria, Cyprus, Egypt, and Arabia, all of which provinces were then, by a special decree of the Congregation of the Propaganda, detached from the Vicariate Apostolic of Constantinople. Its first occupant was the Lazarist Bassu. After his death, and, in fact, several decades later, in 1817, he was succeeded by Mgr. Gandolfi, of the Congregation of the Mission, who was replaced in 1827 by Mgr. Losanna, titular Bishop of Abydos. From 1827 down to 1896, owing to the special rights and privileges enjoyed by the Franciscans as the custodians of the Holy Land, all the Latin Vicars Apostolic of Aleppo were selected from the Franciscan order as follows: A. Fazio (1836–38); Father Fillardell (1839–52) who died a martyr in Constantinople in 1852; P. Brunoni (1853); S. Milani (1874–76); L. Piavi in 1877, who in 1889 was made Latin Patriarch of Jerusalem; and G. Bonfigli in 1890, who in 1896 was transferred to the Latin Vicariate Apostolic of Egypt. In the meanwhile the residence was transferred from Aleppo to Beirut, which was gradually becoming the most influential and progressive town of the Near East. In 1896 a French Dominican, Mgr Charles Duval, for nearly thirty years missionary at Mosul, succeeded Bonfigli. Duval died in 1904 and was succeeded on January 17 of the following year (1905) by Mgr. Frediano Giannini, titular Archbishop of Serra.

During the course of the nineteenth century the Vicariate Apostolic of Syria suffered several losses. In 1838 Egypt and Arabia were taken away; and in 1848 Jerusalem was elevated to the rank of Latin patriarchate with jurisdiction over Palestine, Southern

Phœnicia, and the Island of Cyprus. But on the other hand the Vicariate Apostolic of Syria obtained full jurisdiction over all the Latins of this vicariate, this prerogative being definitely withdrawn from the supervision of the Holy Land. The Vicariate Apostolic of Syria embraces at present the following territory: on the north its boundary line starts from the Gulf of Adalia, and touching the southern limits of Taurus, stretches toward the Euphrates, making a bend at Hamah. On the east is the Desert of Palmyra; on the south, Palestine; on the west the Mediterranean Sea. Since their institution the vicars of Syria have held the title of vicars Apostolic of the Holy See for the non-Latin Catholics who live within the limits of their province. Their power as delegates however has not undergone the same restrictions as their authority of Vicars Apostolic; and Catholics of the Oriental Rite in the Latin Patriarchate of Jerusalem are subject to Syria by way of delegation.

The Latin communities, especially the French, have developed very extensively, particularly in this century, under the Vicariate Apostolic of Syria. They afford at the present time the strongest bulwark against the increasing encroachments of both Protestant and Orthodox missions which are seducing with money and promises the hard-working, but poor people of Syria. The Capuchins, stationed in Syria since 1627, care for the parishes of Antioch, Baabdath, Beirut, and Mersina: they have besides houses at Aleppo, Abey, Ghazir, Koderbek, and Salima. Their religious however are but few in number. The Franciscans have twelve convents in the following places: Aintab, Aleppo, Beirut, Damascus, Harissa, Ienige-Kale, Kenaye, Latakie, Marash, Sayda, Sour, and Tripoli. They also have 10 parishes, and number about 56 religious. Their college at Aleppo is in a flourishing condition and numbers 140 pupils. The Trappists have a house at Sheikle by Akbes, near Alexandretta. The Lazarists, established in Syria since 1784, have five houses with parishes and missions at Antoura, Beirut, Damascus, and Tripoli. They number about 37 religious, and possess in the villages of Lebanon a large number of primary schools which they themselves visit and maintain. The Carmelites, stationed in Syria since 1650, have five residences: at Alexandretta, which forms a parish, in Beylan, Biscerri, Kobbayat, and Tripoli. Their religious are about 8 in number. The Brothers of the Christian Schools have 4 primary schools in Beirut, Latakie, Tripoli, and Tripoli By-the-Sea.

The Jesuits were established for the first time in 1595, and later returned to Syria at the invitation of Mgr. Mazloum and in obedience to the order of Gregory XVI. Their mission numbers 174 members, of whom 66 are priests, 47 scholastics, and 61 brother assistants. After being stationed at Zeilah, and later in Mesopotamia, the Jesuits founded at Ghazir in 1846 the Oriental Seminary which was transferred to Beirut in 1875 and has an enrollment of 50 students. This seminary has already sent forth over 130 priests. The younger religious of the Antonines, of the Maronite Rite, of the Basilian, and of the Greek Rite, follow their courses of philosophy and theology with the seminarists, all being related by similarity of rite. In 1848 the Jesuits established another college at Ghazir; this too was transferred to Beirut, and has become the celebrated College of St. Joseph. In 1883 the medical school was added, which to-day is attended by 130 students; the college has 500 students enrolled. Eighty religious professors and six French doctors take part in the instruction of the students and direct the most complete printing establishment in the Orient, publishing a weekly newspaper in Arabic, the "Beshîr", and the bi-monthly Arabic review, "Al-Mashrik". In 1896 P. Barnier founded at Sayda in the region of Akkar a normal school which is attended by 40 pupils; also an orphanage at Tanail.

During the last three centuries the Catholic missionaries of Syria have had to contend against heavy odds and difficulties occasioned by the Mohammedans, the Druzes, and the various Oriental Schismatic Churches, and, in the last century, also against many obstacles and antagonisms offered by the various Syrian Protestant Missions. But notwithstanding opposition they have forged ahead and are regenerating the Christians of Syria into a new life, mainly through the channels of religious instruction, conversion, and educational and philanthropic enterprises. The Jesuits, the Lazarists, and, of late, the Christian Brothers have achieved such progress in the line of religious and educational work that they have under their care, at present, nearly 300 schools, with 400 teachers and some 14,000 pupils. The Jesuits alone have under their care 155 elementary schools scattered all over Syria: 5 in Beirut with 16 teachers and 900 pupils; 5 in Damascus with 6 teachers and 250 pupils; 19 in Bikfaya with 29 teachers and 1300 pupils; 29 in Ghazir with 27 teachers and nearly 2000 pupils; 21 at Homs with 30 teachers and 1000 students; 37 at Sayda with 55 teachers and 1500 pupils; 18 at Tanial with 22 teachers and 900 students; and 21 at Zahle with 30 teachers and nearly 1300 students. The Lazarists, established in Syria in 1784, have under their care 110 elementary schools with 130 teachers and nearly 6000 pupils. Their high school and college at Antoura and Damascus have 300 and 200 students respectively. The Sisters of St. Vincent de Paul have charge of some 80 female schools and 4000 girls. The Sisters of Nazareth of Lyons, established since 1871, have schools and *pensionnats* at Beirut, St. John of Acre, Shefamar, Haiffa, and Nazareth, with about 2000 pupils. The Sisters of St. Joseph of Marseilles, established in Syria in 1846, have several schools in Beirut, Sayda, Nazareth, Tyre, and Deir-el-Qamar, with about 1500 pupils. The Sisters of the Holy Family have a large school at Beirut, with over 250 pupils. The Sisters of the Good Shepherd of Angers, have an orphanage at Hammana with 150 inmates. Finally, the Mariamettes, an order of native nuns, established in 1860, have under their care not less than 41 schools, 85 teachers, and some 3500 pupils, scattered all over Syria; 1 at Beirut, 2 at Celip, 9 at Bikfaya, 1 in Damascus, 6 in Ghazir, 2 at Homs, 6 at Sayda, 6 at Tanail, and 8 at Zahle.

BURCKHARDT, *Travels in Syria and the Holy Land* (1822), 1–309; WORTABET, *The Syrians* (London, 1856); CHESNEY, *Euphrates Expedition* (London, 1838); RITTER, *Erdkunde von Asien*, XVII, pts. 1 and 2 (Berlin, 1854–55); VON KREMER, *Mittelsyrien und Damascus* (Vienna, 1872); BURTON AND DRAKE, *Unexplored Syria* (London, 1872); RECLUS, *Nouv. géog. univers. d'Asie Antérieure* (1884); PORTER, *Five Years in Damascus* (London, 1855); BLUNT, *Bedouins of the Euphrates* (London, 1870); DE VOGÜÉ, *Syrie Centrale* (Paris, 1865–77); IDEM, *Syrie, Palestine, Mont Athos* (Paris, 1879); SACHAU, *Reise in Syrien u. Mesopotamien* (Leipzig, 1883); MILLER, *Alone through Syria* (London, 1891); CHARMES, *Voyage en Syrie* (Paris, 1891); LADY BURTON, *Inner Life of Syria* (London, 1875); POST, *Flora of Syria, Palestine and Sinai* (Beirut, 1896); HUMANN AND PUCHSTEIN, *Reisen in Nord-Syrien* (1890); POST, *Essays on the Sects and Nationalities of Syria*, etc. (London, 1890); GOODRICH-FREER, *In a Syrian Saddle* (London, 1905); BELL, *The Desert and the Sown* (London, 1907); LORTET, *La Syrie d'aujourd'hui* (Paris, 1884); CURTIS, *To-day in Syria and Palestine* (New York, 1903); LIBBEY AND HOSKINS, *The Jordan Valley and Petra* (New York, 1905); INCHBOLD, *Under the Syrian Sun* (Philadelphia, 1907); KELMAN AND THOMAZ, *From Damascus to Palmyra* (London, 1908); MARGOLIOUTH, *Cairo, Jerusalem and Damascus* (London, 1907); QUINET, *Syrie, Liban et Palestine* (Paris, 1896); BAEDEKER, *Palestine and Syria* (Leipsic, 1906); DUPONT, *Cours Géographique de l'Empire Ottoman* (Paris, 1907); G. SMITH, *Historical Geography of the Holy Land* (London, 1900).

For the religious history of Christian Syria see the bibliographies appended to articles on the various Oriental schisms, Churches, rites, etc.; also BURKITT, *Early Eastern Christianity* (London, 1904); HARNACK, *Mission and Expansion of Christianity*, etc. (2 vols., 2nd ed., 1908); ADENEY, *The Greek and the Eastern Churches* (Edinburgh, 1908); FORTESCUE, *The Orthodox Eastern Church* (London, 1907); STANLEY, *The Eastern Church* (London, 1876); PARRY, *Six Months in a Syrian Monastery* (1895); BADGER, *The Nestorians and their Rituals* (London, 1852); NEALE, *Hist. of the Holy Eastern Church* (5 vols., London, 1850–61); IDEM, *Hist. of the Patriarchate of Antioch* (London,

1873); ASSEMANI, *Bibliotheca Orientalis* (4 vols., Rome, 1719–28); LE QUIEN, *Oriens Christianus* (Paris, 1740); SIDAROUSS, *Des Patriarchats*, etc. (1906); DE JEHAY, *De la Situation des sujets Ottomans non-Musulmans* (Brussels, 1906); O'LEARY, *The Syrian Church and Fathers* (London, 1909); RABBATH, *Documents pour servir à l'histoire du Christianisme en Orient*, I (Paris, 1905); CHARON, *Hist. des Patriarcats Melkites*, etc. (Rome, 1909——); AVRIL, *Les Eglises autonomes et autocéphales* (1895); IDEM, *Les Grecs Melkites* (1899); IDEM, *Une Mission religieuse en Orient au XVI*e *siècle* (1866); BETH, *Die orientalisch Christenheit der Mittelmeerländer* (Berlin, 1902); BRÉHIER, *Le schisme Orientale du XI*e *siècle* (1899); BRIGHTMAN, *Liturgies, Eastern and Western*, I (Oxford, 1896); DUCHESNE, *The Churches Separated from Rome* (New York, 1907); HEFELE-LE CLERCQ, *Hist. des Conciles* (Paris, 1907 sqq.); NILLES, *Kalendarium Manuale utriusque Ecclesiæ Orientalis et Occidentalis*, (Innsbruck, 1896–97); PISANI, *Etudes d'histoire religieuse, à travers l'Orient* (Paris, 1897); PITZIPIOS, *L'Eglise Orientale* (1855); SCHOPOFF, *Les Réformes et la Protection des Chrétiens en Turquie* (1673–1904) (Paris, 1904); VERNAY AND DAMBMANN, *Les Puissances étrangères dans le Levant, en Syrie et en Palestine* (1900); See also the general histories of the Church by SCHAFF, HERGENRÖTHER, ALZOG, DUCHESNE, etc., and in particular the two French periodicals, devoted mainly to the study of the Oriental Churches, viz.: *Revue de l'Orient Chrétien*, and *L'Echos d'Orient*, Paris; also the full bibliography in Chevalier's *Répertoire des sources historiques du Moyen Age*, under the articles *Syrie* and *Antioche*.
Catholic Missions.—WADDING, *Annales Minorum* (10 vols., 1731–45); MARCELLINO DA CIVEZZO, *Storia Universale delle Missioni francescane* (4 vols., 1859); LE QUIEN, *Oriens Christ.* (Paris, 1740); *Missiones Catholicæ descriptæ* (Rome, 1901); PIOLET, *Les Missions Cath. Françaises au XIX*e *siècle*, I (Paris, 1901), 295–360; LOUVET, *Les Missions Cath. au XIX*e *siècle* (Lille, 1895); LAUNAY, *Hist. des Missions Etrangères* (3 vols., Paris, 1894); HENRION, *Hist. des Missions Cath.*. (Paris, 1847); PISANI, op. cit.; WERNER, *Atlas des Missions Cath.* (Freiburg, 1886); *Annales de la Propagation de la foi* (Lyons), passim; *Bulletin des Œuvres d'Orient*, passim; SILBERNAGL, *Verfassung der Kirchen des Orients* (Ratisbon, 1865); KOEHLER, *Die katholischen Kirchen des Morgenlandes* (Darmstadt, 1906); WERNER, *Orbis terrarum catholicus* (Freiburg, 1890); FRANCO, *L'Eglise Grecque Melchite*, etc. (1898); JULLIEN, *La nouvelle mission de la compagnie de Jésus en Syrie* (Tours, 1899); W. M. MARSHALL, *Christian Missions* (London, 1888); HAHN, *Gesch. der katho. Missionen* (5 vols., Cologne, 1857–65); DJUNKOVSKY, *Dict. des Missions Cath.* (Paris, 1864); BERNARDIN DE ROUEN, *Hist. universelle des missions franciscaines* (Paris, 1898); and the two reviews mentioned above. viz.: *Revue de l'Orient Chrétien*, passim, and *Echos d'Orient*.

GABRIEL OUSSANI.

Syriac Hymnody.—To the general consideration set forth in the article HYMNODY AND HYMNOLOGY must be added some bearing particularly on the structure and liturgical use of hymns (*madrashê*), exclusive of poetical homilies or discourses (*mimrê*), which belong to the narrative and epic class, while the hymns are lyrical. The chief basis of Syriac metre is the fixed number of syllables of the verses, without distinction of *long* and *short* syllables, as in several modern languages. Verses of all lengths from two to twelve syllables are known, but the metres most used in hymnody are verses of twelve syllables formed of three equal measures (4+4+4), verses of seven syllables formed of two measures (4+3 or 3+4), and verses of five syllables also formed of two measures (2+3 or 3+2). These verses may be employed alone or grouped in strophes, the latter form being most frequent in hymns composed of verses of five and seven syllables. A strophe is generally composed of equal verses, but it sometimes happens that the first or the last verse is in a different measure from the other verses of the strophe. All the strophes of a hymn are usually of the same construction.

Besides variety of metre and division into strophes the Syrians prior to the ninth century knew no other artifice than the arrangement of acrostic poems. The acrostic played an important part in Syriac hymnody and its use, especially the alphabetic acrostic, seems to have been introduced in imitation of the Psalms and the Lamentations of Jeremias. Sometimes the acrostic is linear, simple when each verse begins successively with one of the twenty-two letters of the Syriac alphabet, multiple, when two, three, or more verses begin with the same letter without forming strophes; sometimes it is strophic, when each strophe is marked by a letter of the alphabet. This letter may be only at the beginning of the first verse or it may be repeated at the beginning of each verse of the strophe. There may be two or more successive strophes beginning with the same letter, each letter regularly marking the same number of strophes throughout the poem which thus consists of forty-four strophes, of sixty-six, or of any other multiple of twenty-two. The verbal acrostic is more rare. The name of Jesus Christ, of Mary, or of the saint in whose honour the hymn is composed serves to form linear or strophic acrostics. St. Ephraem signed some of his poems with his acrostic.

From the ninth century the influence of Arabic poetry made itself felt in Syriac hymnody, especially by the introduction of rhyme; this manner of marking the final stroke of a verse had been hitherto unknown, the rare examples held to have been discovered among older authors being merely voluntary or fortuitous assonances. But the Syrians made varied use of rhyme. There are poems in which all the verses have the same rhyme as in the "Kasida" of the Arabs; in others, and these are the more numerous, the verses of each strophe have a single rhyme which is not the same for all the strophes. In others the verses of a strophe rhyme among themselves, with the exception of the last, which repeats the rhyme of the first strophe like a refrain. In acrostic poems the rhyme is sometimes supplied by the corresponding letter of the alphabet; thus the first strophe rhymes with *a*, the second with *b*, etc. In verses of twelve syllables formed of three tetrasyllabic measures the rhyme is at the end of each verse or at each measure, so that it is repeated three times in each verse. There may also be a different rhyme for the first two measures and for the last. These are the most frequent combinations, but there are others.

Most ancient hymns, e. g. those of St. Ephraem, Narses, and Balai, although composed for one or two choirs, were not originally intended for liturgical use properly so called. They were addressed as much to the laity as to clerics, and date from a period when the codification of harmony, if we may so speak, was not yet regularly established. The result of adapting these hymns to liturgical offices was that they underwent various modifications: (1) in the assignment of authorship—the Syrian Jacobites and the Maronites in adopting those of Nestorian origin either suppressed the name of the author or substituted the name of one whom they considered orthodox, most frequently St. Ephraem; (2) in revision, those which were too long were shortened and heterodox expressions were modified—thus the term "Mother of Christ" was replaced by "Mother of God", etc.; (3) in general arrangement, especially by the addition of a refrain when there was none in the original. Thus a hymn by St. Ephraem the acrostic of which forms the name "Jesus Christ", begins with the strophe:—

Jesus Our Lord the Christ [Father;
Has appeared to us from the bosom of His
He has come to deliver us from darkness,
And to illumine us with his resplendent light.

It was preceded by the following distich which forms the refrain:

Light is arisen upon the just
And joy for those who are broken-hearted.

Likewise a hymn of Narses on the Epiphany begins:—

Error like darkness,
Was stretched over creatures;
The light of Christ is risen
And the world possesses knowledge.

Its refrain is the following distich:—

The light of the appearing of Christ
Has rejoiced the earth and the heavens.

Hymns do not occur only in the Office which corresponds to the Roman Breviary; the Syrians also made use of them in various liturgical functions, such as funerals and marriage celebrations.

Simple hymns without refrain are called *teshbuhtê* (glorifications); the name *cala* (voice) is given to the hymns in which each strophe is preceded by a sentence (metrical or not) expressing a thought in conformity with that of the strophe. It is in a manner an invitation from the first choir to which the second replies by strophe, e. g.:—

First choir: Open to me the gates of justice.
Second choir: Open to us, Lord, the great treasure, (strophe of four verses).
First choir: And I will enter to praise the Lord.
Second choir: At the gate of thy mercies (etc., strophe of four verses).

Sometimes the strophes are interspersed with versicles from the Psalms.

The hymns in the Jacobite Office which conclude the part known as *sedra* and replace the short prayers of the Nestorian Office are called *ba'utha* (prayer, request). Most hymns of this class are in pentasyllabic verses and are the work of the poet Balai (d. about 450). They show great simplicity of thought tand language and consist of two strophes, generally of six verses each, sometimes of four, as for example:—

During forty days
Moses fasted on the mountain:
And with the splendour of its light
His countenance shone.

During forty days
Ninive fasted:
And the Lord was appeased,
And annulled the sentence.

Instead of the *ba'utha* occasionally occurs a metrical composition called *seblata* (stairs), which are factitious arrangements of verses borrowed from various sources and arbitrarily arranged by those who co-ordinated or revised the Offices, and are of no assistance in the study of Syriac hymnody. The *sagithâ* is less frequently replaced by the *augîtha*, a canticle in the form of a dialogue which recalls the "Victimæ paschali" of the Roman Missal. All the poems of this kind known to us are of Nestorian origin, and are probably the work of Narses. They are uniformly constructed with an introduction and a dialogue; the introduction is composed of from five to ten strophes of four heptasyllabic verses; the dialogue between two persons or two groups of persons contains forty-four strophes (twenty-two for each interlocutor) similar to those in the prologue and forming an alphabetic acrostic. These compositions of rather lively measure are stamped by a certain grace. The subject is adapted to the feast of the day; thus in the canticle for Christmas the dialogue is between the Blessed Virgin and the Magi; for the Annunciation, between Gabriel and Mary; for the feast of the Syrian Doctors, between Cyril and Nestorius, etc. These three kinds of hymns correspond to the three subjects which form their usual theme, praise, prayer, and instruction, but as has been said the last-named was chiefly imparted by the *mimrê*.

Extensive study of Syriac hymnody would show whether there is any relationship between it and Byzantine hymnody, an hypothesis which has had as many opponents as defenders; but this study has not yet been attempted, and it is an undertaking fraught with difficulties, owing to the small number of documents published in satisfactory condition. Indeed the knowledge of hymns supplied by editions of the liturgical books of Uniat Chaldeans, Syrians, or Maronites is inadequate for the reasons indicated above. The works of St. Ephraem which contain a large number of them (authentic or apocryphal) have not been critically edited. The Nestorian Breviaries which have most faithfully preserved the ancient texts have never been printed and MSS. are rare, while the collections of hymns apart from liturgical books are few and have not been sufficiently studied.

(a) Studies.—CARDAHI, *Liber thesauri de arte poetica Syrorum* (Rome, 1875); MARTIN, *De la métrique chez les Syriens* (Leipzig, 1879); LAMY, *On Syriac Prosody* (London, 1891); MAYER, *Anfang und Ursprung der lateinischen und griech. rythmischen Dichtung* (Munich, 1885); GRIMME, *Der Strophenbau in den Gedichten Ephraems* (Fribourg, 1893); refuted by BROCKELMANN in *Zeitsch. der deutsch morg. Gesellschaft*, LII, 402; DUVAL, *Notes sur la poésie syriaque* in *Journ. asiat.*, II (1897), 57; ZINGERLE, *Harfenklänge von Libanon* (Innsbruck, 1840); IDEM, *Das syrische Festbrevier aus Libanons Gärten* (Villengen, 1846); DENZINGER, *Ritus orientalium* (Würzburg, 1863); BICKELL, *Ausgewählte gedichte der syrischen Kirchenväter* (Kempten, 1872); MACLEAN, *East Syrian Daily Offices* (London, 1894).

(b) Editions.—For the liturgical books of the Syrians see BICKELL, *Conspectus rei Syrorum litterariæ* (Munich, 1871); NESTLE, *Litteratura syriaca* (Berlin, 1888), §3; for the works of St. Ephraem see EPHRAEM, bibliography; other editions; ASSEMANI, *Codex liturgicus* (Rome, 1749–66); ZINGERLE, *Zeitschr. d. morg. Geselsch.* (1865), 730; SPLIETH in DANIEL, *Thesaurus hymnologicus*, III (Halle, 1856); OVERBECK, S. *Ephraemi syri . . . Balaci aliorumque opera selecta* (Oxford, 1865); DEUTSCH, *Edition dreier syrischen Lieder* (Berlin, 1895); SACHAU, *Uber die Poesie in der Volksprache der Nestorianer* (Berlin, 1896); FOLKMANN, *Ausgewählte nestorianische Gedichte von Giwargîs Warda* (Kirchain, 1896); FELDMANN, *Syrische Wechsellieder von Narses* (Leipzig, 1896); ZETTERSTEIN, *Beiträge zur Kenntnis der religiösen Dichtung Balai's* (Leipzig, 1902); HILGENFELD, *Ausgewählte Gesänge des G. Warda* (Leipzig, 1904). Some hymns by various authors are in MANNA, *Morceaux choisis de littérature araméenne* (Mosul, 1901), and in *Ktabuna dpartutê* (Ourmia, 1898).

J. B. CHABOT.

Syriac Language and Literature.—Syriac is the most important branch of the group of Semitic languages known as Aramaic. In the time of Alexander the Great, Aramaic was the official language of all the nations from Asia Minor to Persia, from Armenia to the Arabian Peninsula. It was divided into two dialects: the western, used in Palestine and Syria by the Jews, Palmyrans, and Nabateans; the eastern, spoken in Babylonia by Jews, Mandeans, Manichæans, and the peoples of Upper Mesopotamia. The Syriac language, as we know it from its literature, did not spring from the dialect spoken in Syria, but from the eastern Mesopotamian dialect. When the weakened Seleucides ceased to defend the Euphrates, small independent principalities were formed in that region. The most famous was the little Kingdom of Edessa whose capital Osrhoene was the religious centre of the country (cf. R. Duval, "Hist. d'Edesse", Paris, 1893). This city also became an intellectual centre, and even then the language of its people attained great perfection. A little later under the influence of Christianity it developed considerably, and eventually became the liturgical and literary language of all the Churches from the shores of the Mediterranean to the centre of Persia. The suppleness and flexibility of this dialect and its loose and variable syntax readily lent itself to the most different constructions, and offered to Christianity a more appropriate instrument than Greek for the expression and spread of new ideas. In Syria proper and western Mesopotamia Syriac was first used simultaneously with Greek, but after the Monophysite schism Greek gradually fell into disuse. The period from the middle of the fifth century to the end of the seventh was the most brilliant period of Syriac literature. The Mussulman invasion brought about the decadence by imposing Arabic as the official language; the latter rapidly came into general use, and Syriac was no longer spoken or understood by the people, although it was upheld as a literary language for four centuries longer, and until the present time as a liturgical language. Nevertheless, the destruction was not complete; Syriac, or rather Aramaic, modified according to the laws of evolution common to all languages, is still spoken in three villages in the neighbourhood of Damascus, in Tour Abdin (Mesopotamia, between

Nisibis and the Tigris), and in Kurdistan, especially in the neighbourhood of Ourmiah. The language of this city is even in process of becoming a literary tongue, through the efforts of the missionaries (American Protestants and French Lazarists), who print numerous works in this dialect, Bibles, text-books, prayer-books, and even reviews.

The works transmitted to us in the Syriac language form an essentially and almost exclusively Christian religious literature. After Latin and Greek there is none more useful to the exegete, the theologian, and the ecclesiastical historian. We know of more than 150 authors who enriched it from the fourth to the thirteenth century. The libraries of Europe and those of some eastern monasteries which are of easy access possess nearly 3000 MSS., containing the greater part of these works. Our short list will take only the best-known authors and the most important works. Of pagan literature there remain only a few short inscriptions, most of them funereal, and a letter from Mara bar Serapion, Stoic philosopher of Samosata, to his son, written probably in the course of the third century (ed. Cureton, "Spicelegium Syr.", London, 1855). The writings of the Gnostic Bardesanes of the same period, with a Gnostic hymn inserted in the Acts of St. Thomas, form a sort of transition between Pagan and Christian literature. The earliest monument of the latter is the version of the Bible called the Peschitta (simple), which is treated elsewhere (see VERSIONS OF THE BIBLE). It suffices to mention also the two oldest orthodox writers, Aphraates the Persian Sage (d. 350), and St. Ephraem, the most brilliant of the Fathers of the Syrian Church (d. 373). Among the disciples of Ephraem was Mar Aba, the author of commentaries on the Gospels and of a homily on Job; Zenobius, deacon of Edessa, who wrote treatises against Marcion and Pamphylus and a "Life of St. Ephraem"; Paulinus, who possibly fell into heresy after having written against Marcion and the sceptics. Abamya, a nephew of Ephraem, has been wrongly identified with Cyrillona, an unknown author who wrote in 397 a poem on the two plagues of that period, the locusts and the Huns.

At the beginning of the fifth century there flourished at Edessa the famous school of the Persians, in which the doctrines of Theodore of Mopsuestia and Nestorius found fervent adherents. The bishop then was Rabbula, son of a pagan priest of Kennesrin (Chalcis). He was converted by Eusebius, bishop of that city, distributed his goods to the poor, and embraced the ascetic life. In 412 Acacius of Aleppo appointed him Bishop of Edessa; he died in 435. After inclining to Nestorianism he became an ardent partisan of St. Cyril of Alexandria. His severity made him formidable to his clergy, and won for him the title "tyrant of Edessa". At Constantinople he delivered a discourse against Nestorius, which was translated into Syriac, as well as several of his letters. He himself translated the treatise "Of the Orthodox Faith" which Cyril addressed to him. His extant works were translated by Overbeck (Oxford, 1865). His successor was the famous Ibas, or Hiba, who favoured the Nestorians. Mari the Persian of Rewardashir, to whom the celebrated letter of Ibas was addressed, wrote a commentary on Daniel and a controversial treatise against the Magians. He also commentated the (lost) letters of Acacius of Amida (Diarbekir), an avowed Nestorian, less noted for his writings than for his charity, which won him a place in the Roman Martyrology (9 April). He must not be confounded with Acacius of Melytene who joined Rabbula in his warfare against Nestorianism, nor with Acacius of Seleucia, patriarch of the Nestorians (484–96), author of homilies on fasting and of treatises against the Monophysites; he also translated into Persian the treatise on faith of Osee, Bishop of Nisibis, who in 496 promulgated the statutes of the school of that city (ed. Guidi). About the middle of the century lived Isaac of Antioch, called the Great and regarded as a saint. His history is unknown. The Syrians have attached his name to a considerable collection of metrical homilies (partly edited by Bickell, Giessen, 1873–77, and by Bedyan, Paris, 1903), but it is certain that the works of several authors of the same name have been attributed to him.

Among these are Isaac of Edessa, a Monophysite of the end of the sixth century, and Isaac of Amida. The last-named is the author of a poem on secular games (414) and on the taking of Rome (410). In the first half of the century lived Balai, chorepiscopus of Aleppo, the author of numerous poems which have been preserved in part. At the death of Ibas the doctors of the school of Edessa were expelled, and withdrew to the Persian Empire. Among them were Barsauma, who became Bishop of Nisibis and was noted for his despotism; we have six of his letters addressed to the Patriarch Acacius. He also wrote exhortations, funeral orations, and hymns; Narsai joined him and was the real founder of the School of Nisibis which continued the tradition of that of Edessa; he taught there for more than forty years. He was praised in most exalted terms by his co-religionists, who called him "the Tongue of the East", "the Poet of Religion", "the Harp of the Holy Ghost". The Monophysites nicknamed him "the Leper". He died about 502. He is said to have composed commentaries on most of the books of the Old Testament, and 360 metrical discourses. Many of them have been edited by Mingana (Mossoul, 1905). Mana, who became a bishop in Persia, was distinguished at Edessa for his translation of the works of Theodore of Mopsuestia.

Eliseus bar Kozbaye and Abraham of Beit Rabban, the successors of Narsai in the direction of the school, wrote Biblical commentaries and numerous treatises against the Magians. Most of the Nestorian authors of the sixth century proceeded from this school. One of the most famous was the Patriarch Mar Aba I (540–52), a convert from Zoroastrianism; he studied at Nisibis, learned Greek at Edessa, and went to Constantinople; later he founded the School of Seleucia. He preached boldly against the Magi; Khusrau I exiled him; on his return to Seleucia he was thrown into prison, where he died. He is credited with a translation of the Scriptures, but there is no trace of it; he wrote Biblical commentaries, homilies, and synodal letters. He also translated into Syriac the liturgy of Nestorius. Paul the Persian, very learned in profane philosophy, composed a treatise on the "Logic" of Aristotle, dedicated to King Khusrau (ed. Land), and several other didactic works, preserved in part. His namesake, Paul of Nisibis, a disciple of Mar Aba, was the author of Biblical commentaries. Theodore, made Bishop of Merw in 540, wrote a commentary on the Psalms and a reply to ten questions of Sergius of Reshayna. His brother Gabriel, Bishop of Hormisdardashir, wrote controversial books against the Manichæans, and the solution of difficult Scriptural questions. To Abraham bar Kardahe, of Nisibis, are attributed homilies, funeral orations, sermons, and a letter against Shisban, probably a Magian. Another Abraham, of Kashkar, founded and governed on Mount Izla near Nisibis a famous monastery called the Great Convent. The rules he established in 571 were published (Chabot, Rome, 1898) with those of Dadisko, his successor (588–604).

The physician Joseph, the successor of Mar Aba (552–67), is spoken of as the author of an apocryphal correspondence attributed to the Patriarch Papa (fourth century). Joseph Houzaya of Al-Ahwaz was then teaching at Nisibis; he is credited with the oldest grammatical treatise known to Syriac literature, and is regarded as the inventor of the system of punctuation in use among the Nestorians, compiled in imitation of the Massoretic signs, perhaps with the assistance of the Jews of Nisibis. Henana of Adiabene at the end of the sixth century drew to Nisibis a large number of disciples; his teaching caused serious dissensions in the Nestorian Church, for he abandoned the doctrines of Theodore of Mopsuestia to attach himself to St. John Chrysostom. His doctrine, censured by Ishoyahb I, was condemned by the Synod of Sabrisho (596). Most of his literary work consists of Biblical commentaries. They are lost, but extensive fragments are inserted in the "Garden of Delights", a twelfth-century compilation, which has preserved numerous extracts from the oldest Nestorian exegetes. Under the patriarchate of Ezechiel (570–81) Barhadbeshabba, who became Bishop of Holwan, a partisan of Henana, wrote numerous controversial and exegetical works and a treatise "On the Reason of the Schools" (ed. Scher, Paris, 1909), which throws light on the history of Nisibis. We have the synodal letters, and twenty-two questions on the sacraments of the Patriarch Ishoyahb I of Arzon (582–95).

At the end of this century the Syrians had a copious hagiographical literature, of which the oldest and most authentic portion consists of the Acts of the Martyrs of the persecution of Sapor II (see Persecution). To these were added numerous passions, lives of saints, and biographies translated from the Greek, the whole forming a rich mine for the historian and the hagiographer. In this century also there were translated and were often re-written the Greek apocrypha of the Old and New Testament which have come down to us in Syriac, together with some native productions, such as the teaching of Addai. The curious romance of Julian the Apostate (ed. Hoffmann) dates from the sixth century as well as the valuable chronicle of Edessa and the large historical compilation (ed. Land) ascribed to Zacharias the Rhetorician; it consists in part of original documents and partly of Greek sources, and is of Monophysite origin.

While Mesopotamia and especially Persia was attached to Nestorianism, the western Syrians embraced the Monophysite doctrines of Eutyches, propagated by the monk Barsauma, condemned as a heretic by the Council of Chalcedon (451), and in this they claimed to remain faithful to the traditions of St. Cyril of Alexandria (see Monophysites and Monophysitism). All their theological and polemical literature was inspired by this doctrine, which was defended by talented writers. The foremost were James of Sarugh and Philoxenes of Mabboug. The latter was born at Tabal in Mesopotamia, studied at Edessa in the time of Ibas, and later ardently embraced the Monophysite cause. Appointed Bishop of Mabboug (Hierapolis) in 485, he went twice to Constantinople and was much esteemed by the Emperor Anastasius. He presided at the council which made the famous Severus Patriarch of Antioch (512). He was exiled by Justin and died at Gangres about 523. Despite his eventful life he was one of the most prolific and elegant of Syriac writers. Of his writings we possess liturgies and prayers, thirteen homilies (ed. Budge, London, 1894) which constitute a treatise of Christian ethics, a commentary on the Gospels (preserved only in part), a treatise on the Trinity and the Incarnation (ed. Vaschalde, Paris, 1907), some discourses, professions of faith, several short polemical treatises against the Catholics and the Nestorians, and numerous letters.

James and Philoxenes wrote against Stephen bar Sudailê, a pious monk, born at Edessa; on his return from a journey to Egypt he preached pantheistic doctrines. Driven from Edessa he withdrew to Palestine, where among the Origenistic monks he found a fertile field for his ideas (cf. Frothingham, "Stephen bar Sudaili", Leyden, 1886). None of his letters or mystical commentaries on the Bible remain, but he is the author of a book, "The Hidden Mysteries of the House of God", which he issued under the name of Hierotheus, the pretended master of Dionysius the Areopagite. This extensive treatise was very influential in the development in Syria of pseudo-Dionysian literature; it was afterwards forgotten, and in the thirteenth century Barhebræus had great difficulty in securing a copy; this copy is now in the British Museum.

Among the other Monophysite writers of the sixth century were: Simeon of Beit Arsham, a skilful dialectician who combatted the Nestorians. He died at Constantinople in the reign of Justinian. His letters on the propagation of Nestorianism and on the Christian martyrs of Yemen (Himyarites) are famous. John bar Cursus, Bishop of Tella, expelled from his see in 521, died at Antioch in 538. He is the author of exhortations to the clergy and disciplinary questions, a profession of faith, and a commentary on the Trisagion. Paul, Bishop of Callinicus, deposed in 519, translated into Syriac the works of Severus of Antioch. Jacob Barbuadæus, the real founder of the Monophysite Church, from whom it derived its name of Jacobite, died in 578. His letters and profession of faith are preserved in Syriac translations. The lives of all these men are more or less well-known through numerous monographs which cannot be enumerated here, and through the valuable historical works of John of Ephesus.

Sergius of Reshaina was a physician and a distinguished scholar; his friendship with the Nestorians and the part he played at the end of his life caused him to be suspected of having abandoned Monophysite doctrines. He studied at Alexandria, where he learned Greek. In 535 he was sent to Rome by Ephrem, Orthodox Patriarch of Antioch, and escorted Pope Agapetus to Constantinople. Here Sergius sought to expel the patriarchs Severus of Antioch, Theodosius of Alexandria, and Anthinus, who had met there. He died there in 536. His considerable literary work consists almost entirely of Greek translations remarkable for their fidelity; his version of the works of the pseudo-Areopagite greatly influenced the theology of the western Syrians, and his translations of profane authors (Porphyry, Aristotle, Galen, etc.) hold a special place in the body of Syriac translations. A number of the works of Sergius have reached us; they have been published in part; mention must also be made of Rhoudemeh of Tagrit (d. 575), who left philosophical and grammatical works; Moses of Aghel, translator of the works of Cyril of Alexandria; and the Patriarch Peter of Callinicus (578–91), whose theological writings against Damian of Alexandria and the Tritheists have reached us, together with some letters.

Among the Nestorians the literature of the seventh century begins with Babai the Great, Abbot of Mount Izla, who governed the Church of Persia during the vacancy of the patriarchal see (608–29) brought about by the hostility of Khusrau II. He composed many works; his treatise on the union of the two natures of Christ which we possess is one of the most important works of Nestorian theology. There are extant a hymn and a dogmatic letter by the Patriarch Ishoyahb II of Gedala (628–43). Ishoyahb III of Adiabene (648–60) was a prolific writer, and remarkable for his studied style; he composed controversial treatises, funeral orations, hymns, numerous liturgical works, and the history of the martyr Ishosabran. We have also a collection of 104 of his letters (ed. Duval, Paris, 1904), which is important for the religious history of this period. Ishoyahb energetically opposed Sahdona (Martyrius), Bishop of Mahoze, his former friend and his companion in the embassy from Boran to the Emperor Heraclius in 630. Sahdona became converted to Catholicism. The extant portion of his numerous writings has been edited by Bedjan (Leipzig, 1902); it consists mainly of the end of a treatise in moral and dogmatic theology of which the first seventeen chapters were assailed by Ishoyahb. To this period belong the two most original ascetic writers, Isaac of Nineveh and John of Phanek (often called John Saba); the works of the latter, many of which have been preserved, embrace all subjects relating to religious perfection. Under the patriarchate of George (661–80) the monk Enanisho composed the work entitled "Paradise"; it consists of two parts, the first a translation of the "Lausiac History" of Palladius and the "Monastic History" of Rufinus, the second a collection of apothegms from the Fathers, and questions concerning the ascetic life (ed. Bedjan, Leipzig, 1897). This work must not be confounded with the "Paradise of Orientals", which contains the lives of Eastern ascetics and was compiled by Joseph Hazaya (the Seer), an austere monk, the author of numerous ascetical treatises, and the warm partisan of Henana, with whom he was condemned; he lived at the beginning of the seventh century.

The Jacobite writers of this period are less numerous: John I, Patriarch of Antioch 631–48, is the author of numerous liturgical prayers; Maranta of Tagrit (d. 649) left a liturgy, hymns, and commentaries; Severus Sebokt, his contemporary, devoted himself in the celebrated convent of Kenneshrê on the banks of the Euphrates to philosophical and scientific studies; his works, which are partly preserved, exercised great influence on the following centuries. His letters deal with theological subjects. His disciple Athanasius of Balad, who became patriarch (634–88), likewise devoted himself to Greek philosophy. All these names were eclipsed by another of his disciples, James of Edessa, a writer as distinguished for the extent and variety of his knowledge as for his literary talent.

During the seventh century public events had created new conditions in the lands where Syriac was spoken. The end of the Roman domination in Syria almost coincided with the fall of the Persian dynasty of the Sassanides, and the Mussulman rule enforced the use of the Arabic tongue. These new conditions introduced a new character in literature, among Nestorians as well as Jacobites. Theological treatises were thenceforth more didactic than polemic, and Biblical exegesis became chiefly grammatical and philological. The eighth century began a period of decadence. Among Nestorian writers were Babai of Gebilta, a reformer of religious music in the time of the Patriarch Salibazekha (714–28); he was the author of funeral orations, hymns, and letters, preserved in part; Bar Sahdê, of Karka of Beit Slok, the author of an ecclesiastical history and of a treatise against Zoroastrianism, both lost; he lived in the time of the Patriarch Pethion (731–40). About the same time David of Beit Rabban wrote "The Little Paradise", a kind of monastic history from which Thomas of Marga borrowed. Abraham bar Daschandad, a disciple of Babai, was the author of a book of exhortations, homilies, letters, "The Book of the Royal Way", and a commentary on the writings of the monk Marcus. Mar Aba II, who became patriarch at the age of 100 (741–51), wrote a commentary on the works of St. Gregory of Nazianzus, and another on the Dialectics of Aristotle, a "Book of Military Governors", demonstrations, and letters. His compatriot, Simeon bar Tabbakhê, treasurer of the Caliph al-Mansur, was the author of an ecclesiastical history.

Surinus, Bishop of Nisibis and later of Holwan, elected patriarch in 754 and immediately deposed, is regarded as the author of a treatise against the heretics. Cyprian, Bishop of Nisibis (741–67), composed a commentary on the theological discourses of St. Gregory of Nazianzus and a treatise on ordination. Abu Noah of Anbar, secretary of the Governor of Mosul at the end of this century, wrote a refutation of the Koran, a refutation of heretics, and a life of John of Dailam. The Patriarch Henanisho II (775–79) is the author of letters, hymns for the dead, metrical homilies, and canonical questions. He was succeeded by Timotheus, whose literary work excels that of all his contemporaries.

Timotheus I, a native of Hazza (near Arbelles), a disciple of Abraham bar Daschandad, became Bishop of Beit Bagash; at the death of Henanisho he was elected patriarch by intrigue and the favour of the Governor of Mosul; he quieted the rivalry and was installed in 780, dying in 823. During his patriarchate the Nestorian missions in Central Asia received powerful encouragement, and he introduced important disciplinary reforms into his church (cf. Labourt, "De Timotheo patriarcha", Paris, 1904). His literary work comprises an astronomical treatise entitled "Book of the Stars" (lost), two volumes of canonical questions, a controversy concerning the Christian faith maintained before the Caliph Al-Mahidi, a commentary on the works of St. Gregory of Nazianzus, and about 200 letters. Sixty of these letters, the controversy, and a large proportion of the questions are extant in various MSS. Through him was made the first collection of the Nestorian councils, which under the name "Synodicon Orientale" (ed. Charbot, Paris, 1903) comprises the acts of thirteen synods convened by his predecessors from 410 to 775. It is the basis of the Nestorian canon law and the official exposition of its creed. About this time lived Theodorus bar Kônî, the author of a book of *scholia* (ed. Scher, Paris, 1908–11), which contains *scholia* on the Old and New Testament, a treatise against the Monophysites, one against the Arians, a colloquy between a pagan and a Christian, and a treatise on heresies. Ishodenah (or Denahisho), Bishop of Bassorah, composed an ecclesiastical history (lost), and the "Book of Chastity" (ed. Chabot, Rome, 1898), which contains 150 notices of the founders of Oriental convents.

The share of the Jacobites in the literary work of this period is far inferior to that of the Nestorians. With the exception of George, Bishop of the Arabs, a disciple of James of Edessa who is treated elsewhere (see MONOPHYSITES AND MONOPHYSITISM), the writers are of only secondary interest. Of Elias, Patriarch of Antioch (709–24), we have an apology explaining why he abandoned the Diophysite doctrine; it is addressed to Leo, Diophysite Bishop of Harran and author of controversial writings. Daniel of Salah wrote an extensive commentary on the Psalms, in three volumes; the first to have reached us in the original text and the third in an Arabic version. David bar Paulos left a grammatical work, letters, a commentary on chap. x of Genesis, a dialogue on the addition of the words "who was crucified for us" to the Sanctus. To him are also ascribed poems which seem to belong to a later period. A celebrated author was Theophilus of Edessa, called Maronite by Bar-Hebræus, and Chalcedonian by Michael the Syrian; this distinguished astronomer, who was much esteemed by the Caliph al-Mahdi, died in 785. His works include astronomical treatises, a history, and a Syriac version of Homer, several quotations from which have been found. About 775 Lazarus of Beit Kandasa compiled a commentary on the New Testament, a portion of which (St. Mark, St. John, and ten Epistles of St. Paul) is extant. George of Beelthan, a monk of Kenneshrê who became patriarch (758–90), is the author of a discourse and of some homilies (lost) and of a commentary on the Gospel of St. Matthew (partly preserved). His successor Syriacus (793–817) left a liturgy, canons, some homilies, and letters.

The ninth century witnessed a renaissance in scientific and historical studies. Among the Nestorians there was a series of Christian physicians who enjoyed the favour of the caliphs of Bagdad; Gabriel Boktisho (d. 828), John bar Maswai (d. 857), Honein (d. 873), and at the end of the century John bar Serapion were famous among Christians and Mussulmans for their medical works and their translations into Syriac and Arabic of the works of Dioscorides, Hippocrates, Galen, and Paul of Agima. Honein was at once physician, philosopher, historian, grammarian, and lexicographer. His disciple Isho bar Ali is the author of a voluminous lexicon (ed. Hoffmann, Kiel, 1874; Gottheil, Rome, 1910). The patriarch, Isho bar Noun (823–27), was esteemed as a theologian and canonist; of his numerous works there remain juridical questions, questions of Scripture, funeral orations, and letters. Ishodad of Merw, Bishop of Haditha, about the middle of the century composed commentaries on the Old and New Testaments, which are of great interest in the history of exegesis. In 840 Thomas, Bishop of Marga, a former monk of Beit Abê, wrote the history of that famous convent which was located in his diocese, and fortunately he inserted therein numerous documents which would not otherwise be known to us; hence his work sheds much light on the history of the whole Nestorian Church during a period of three centuries. It has been edited by Budge (London, 1893) and by Bedjan (Leipzig, 1901).

The less numerous list of Jacobite writers of the ninth century opens with the name of Dionysius of Tell Mahre, who was elected patriarch in 815 and died in 845. He wrote an ecclesiastical history in two parts, each consisting of eight books divided into chapters. It extended from 581 to 833; unfortunately it is lost but is made known to us by the copious extracts which Michael inserted in his own chronicle (see below). This work is quite different from the chronicle which Assemani incorrectly ascribes to Dionysius. The latter, which stops at the year 775, is divided into four parts. The first (ed. Eulberg, Upsala, 1851) goes as far as Constantine, and relies chiefly on Eusebius; the second, as far as Theodosius the Younger, mainly follows Socrates; the third reproduces the second part (lost) of the history of John of Asia and the chronicle of Josue the Stylite (ed. Wright, London, 1882); the fourth (ed. Chabot, Paris, 1895) is the personal work of the author, probably a monk at the convent of Touknin in Tour Abdin. The work of Dionysius was dedicated to Iwannis (John), Bishop of Dara, one of the most esteemed Monophysite theologians, of whom we possess a treatise on the priesthood, one of the Resurrection, one of the soul, and a commentary on the books of the Pseudo-Areopagite. Theodosius of Edessa, brother of the Patriarch Dionysius, executed a version of the poems of St. Gregory of Nazianzus. He was the close friend of a monk of Tagrit, Antonius, surnamed the Rhetorician, author of a treatise on rhetoric, a treatise on Providence, of panegyrics, letters, hymns, and prayers. Lazarus bar Sabtha, Bishop of Bagdad, deposed in 828, was the author of a liturgy and an explanation of the offices of the church. Nonnius, Archdeacon of Nisibis, about the middle of the century wrote a controversy against Thomas of Marga and some polemical letters. The monk Romanus, who took the name of Theodosius when he became patriarch (887–96), compiled a medical collection (lost), a copious commentary on the book of Hierotheus, and a collection of Pythagorean maxims (ed. Zotenberg, Paris, 1876). No writer of this century was so prolific as Moses bar Cephas (q. v.) who took the name Severus when he became bishop.

The next two centuries mark the lowest point of the period of decadence. Most of the ecclesiastical dignitaries and the rare authors who concerned themselves with learning wrote chiefly in Arabic. There was not a single Jacobite writer during the whole of the tenth century; among the Nestorians those worthy of mention were Henanisho bar Seroshwa, Bishop of Hira at the beginning of the century; he composed Scriptural disquisitions, and a lexicon, now lost, but included almost in its entirety in that of Bar Bahlul; Elias, Bishop of Perozshabur (c. 920), wrote letters, homilies, an apology, and a collection of maxims known as "Centuries"; George, Metropolitan of Arbella (d. 987), is the author of a canonical collection and some hymns. To him is also attributed an interesting "Explanation of the liturgical offices". Emmanuel bar Shahharé (d. 980) wrote a treatise "On the six days of creation and Providence", divided into four parts and twenty-eight books; the second book is missing in all known MSS. Towards the end of the century Andrew, a grammarian, composed a treatise on punctuation and some hymns. At the same period at Bagdad where he taught, Abu' l' Hassan, known as Bar Bahlul, compiled his famous "Lexicon", a small encyclopedia in which he collected, together with the lexicographical works of his predecessors, numerous notices on the natural sciences, philosophy, theology, and Biblical exegesis (ed. Duval, Paris, 1888–1901). At the end of the century John Bar Khaldon wrote the life of the monk Joseph Bosnaya, in which he inserted a curious treatise on mystical theology. The following are the foremost Nestorian writers of the eleventh century. Elias of Tirhan, who became patriarch (1028–49), is famous for his treatise on grammar; he completed the canonical collection made by Timotheus, adding later decisions, and wrote legal treatises. Elias bar Shinaya, Metropolitan of Nisibis, is the most remarkable writer of this century. Appointed Bishop of Beit Nouhadrê in 1002, and of Nisibis in 1008, he occupied the see more than forty years and survived the Patriarch Elias. He is the author of a Syriac grammar, an Arabic-Syriac grammar, hymns, metrical homilies, letters, and a collection of canonical decisions. His most important work is his "Chronography", written in 1019; it includes a chronicle and a treatise on the calendar (ed. Brooks-Chabot, Paris, 1909–10). Elias also wrote in Arabic several dogmatic and moral treatises. Abdisho bar Bahriz, who became Bishop of Arbela and Mosul in 1030, is the author of a collection of "Laws and Judicial Sentences". Among the Jacobites were: John of Maroun (d. 1003), the author of a commentary on the Book of Wisdom; and Isho bar Shoushan, Patriarch of Antioch under the name of John (1064–73). He composed a liturgy, canons, a treatise in defence of the Syrian custom of mixing salt and oil in the Eucharistic bread, four poems on the pillage of Nelitene by the Turks (1058), and several letters in Syriac or Arabic. At the time of his death he was engaged in collecting the works of St. Ephrem and Isaac of Antioch.

In the thirteenth century the Nestorians also began to write in Arabic. Elias III Abuhalim, Metropolitan of Nisibis and afterwards patriarch (1176–90), composed prayers and wrote letters. John bar Malkon, who took the name of Ishoyahb when he became Bishop of Nisibis (1190), is the author of a grammatical treatise. The monk Simeon of Shanklawa about the same period wrote a chronological treatise and poem in enigmatic style. He is probably the author of the "Book of the Fathers", which has been ascribed to Simeon bar Sabbaê (fourth century). His disciple John bar Zoubi is chiefly known for his grammatical works.

The Jacobites had able writers. John, Bishop of Harran and Mardin, wrote on the capture of Edessa by Zangui (1144). James bar Salibi is the most prolific writer of the century. He took the name of Dionysius when he became Bishop of Marash in 1154; in 1166 Michael transferred him to Amida, where he died in 1171. His most important work is his commentary on the Old and New Testament, a vast compilation in which he cites or recapitulates the whole exegesis of the Western Syrians. Among his other writings were: a commentary on the "Centuries" of

Evagrius, a commentary on dialectics, letters, an abridgment of the histories of the Fathers, saints, and martyrs, a collection of canons, several theological treatises, two liturgies, an explanation of the Mass (ed. Labourt, Paris, 1903), a voluminous treatise against the heresies, a treatise on Providence, homilies, and occasional verses. His commentaries and most of his other works are extant. Michael the Syrian (Michael the Great), the son of a priest of Nelitene, was Abbot of Barasuma when he was elected patriarch (1166–99). He is the author of several liturgical works, but his chief work is his "Chronicle" (ed. Chabot, Paris, 1898–1911). It is the most voluminous historical compilation transmitted to us by the Syrians; that of Bar Hebræus is generally only a faithful abridgment of it. Many earlier documents are inserted or summarized in it; the author furnishes valuable information concerning the historians who preceded him, and for his own period furnishes interesting details concerning the occupation of Edessa by the Crusaders, and the wars of the Mussulman princes who occupied Asia Minor, especially Cappadocia. Michael's "Chronicle" begins with the Creation and stops with the death of Saladin (1196). Theodore bar Wahboun, a disciple of Michael, who rebelled against him and had himself named patriarch by the dissatisfied bishops, is the author of a liturgy.

The thirteenth century marks the end of Syriac literature. Among the Jacobites were: James (Severus) bar Shakako, Bishop of Mosul (d. 1241), whose "Dialogues" are a philosophical course, and his "Book of Treasures" a course in theology; Aharon (John) bar Madani, who was Bishop of Mardin, Maphrian (1232), later patriarch (1252–61), and the author of numerous poems; and Maphrian Gregory bar Hebræus, a man of encyclopedic learning, whose name worthily terminates this list (see BAR HEBRÆUS). Mention must be made of the book of the "Knowledge of Truth" (ed. Kayser, Leipzig, 1889), the author of which plans to assemble in one religious community Christians, Jews, and Mussulmans; also of the chronicle, likewise anonymous, recently discovered by Mgr Rahmani. Among the Nestorians were Solomon, Bishop of Bassora (c. 1222) whose chief work is the "Book of the Bee", an historico-theological compilation in which he inserted numerous legends (ed. Budge, Oxford, 1886); George Warda and Khamis bar Kardahe, authors of numerous hymns in the Nestorian office. Gabriel Kamsa, author of a theological poem, and John of Mosul, who wrote edifying poems, belong to the second half of the century. The history of the Patriarch Yaballaha III (1281–1318) is a very curious document; his successor Timotheus II is the author of a book on the Sacraments. Addisho bar Brika is the last writer deserving of mention. He was Bishop of Nisibis and died in 1318. His most useful work is his "Catalogue of writers", a sort of literary history of the East Syrians (ed. Assemani, "Bibl. Orientalis", III); he concludes with a list of his own numerous and various works: commentaries on the Old and New Testaments, a work on the Life of Christ, one against heresies, one on the mysteries of the Greek philosophers, twelve treatises on the sciences. These works of his have been lost, but we possess his "Nomocanon", or methodical collection of canon law, and his theological treatise called "The Pearl" (both edited by Mai, Rome, 1838), his "Rule of Ecclesiastical Judgments", a kind of code of procedure, fifty metrical homilies which form the "Book of the Paradise of Eden", and twenty-two poems on love and wisdom. From the fourteenth century Syriac literature produced no works of value. The few authors who cultivated it showed neither talent nor originality; nevertheless useful indications concerning local history may be found in their occasional writings.

The great services rendered to scholarship by translations which form a large part of Syriac literature should not be lost sight of; they include both profane and Christian works. The former were chiefly Greek scientific and theological works, principally those of Aristotle and his school. It was through this intermediary that the Arabs became acquainted with scientific culture, and came into contact with Hellenic philosophy, so that the important part they played in the propagation of the sciences during the Middle Ages had its origin in Syriac literature. The "Romance of Alexander" and that of "Kalila and Dimna" were both translated from the Pahlowi about the sixth century. A portion of the works of the most celebrated of the Greek fathers of the fourth and fifth centuries were translated into Syriac; they possess only a secondary importance where we have the original texts, but are of the greatest value when they represent lost works, as is the case with regard to the "Apology of Aristides", the festal letters of St. Athanasius, the treatise of Titus of Bosra against the Manichæans, the Theophany of Eusebius, the commentaries of Cyril of Alexandria on St. Luke, the works of Severus of Antioch, the commentary of Theodore of Mopsuestia on St. John and his treatise on the Incarnation, the Apology of Nestorius, etc.

Powla Language: CHABOT, *Les langues et les littératures araméennes* (Paris, 1910); NÖLDEKE, *Kurzgefasste syrische Grammatik* (2nd ed., Leipzig, 1898); DUVAL, *Traité de grammaire syriaque* (Paris, 1881); PAYNE-SMITH, *Thesaurus syriacus* (Oxford, 1868–1901).

Literature: ASSEMANI, *Bibliotheca orientalis* (Rome, 1719–28); BICKELL, *Conspectus rei Syrorum litterariæ* (Münster, 1871); NESTLE, *Litteratura Syriaca* (Berlin, 1888); WRIGHT, *Syriac Literature* (2nd ed., London, 1894); DUVAL, *La Littérature syriaque* (3rd ed., Paris, 1907); BROCKELMANN, *Die Syrische und die christlich-arabische Litteratur* (Leipzig, 1907).

A complete and detailed bibliography will be found in NESTLE, WRIGHT, and DUVAL, op. cit.

J. B. CHABOT.

Syriac Versions of the Bible. See VERSIONS OF THE BIBLE.

Syrian Rite, EAST, also known as the CHALDEAN, ASSYRIAN, or PERSIAN RITE.

HISTORY AND ORIGIN.—This rite is used by the Nestorians and also by the Uniat bodies in Syria, Mesopotamia, Persia, and Malabar, who have separated from them. The Syrian and Mesopotamian Uniats are now commonly called Chaldeans, or Syro-Chaldeans; the term Chaldean, which in Syriac generally meant magician or astrologer, denoted in Latin and other European languages Syrian nationality and the Syriac or Aramaic language (especially that form of the latter which is found in certain chapters of Daniel), until the Latin missionaries at Mosul in the seventeenth century adopted it to distinguish the Catholics of the East Syrian Rite from the West Syrian Uniats, whom they call "Syrians", and from the Nestorians. The last call themselves "Syrians" (Surayi), and even "Christians" only, though they do not all repudiate the name "Nestorayi", and distinguish themselves from the rest of Christendom as the "Church of the East" or "Easterns", as opposed to "Westerns", by which they denote Latin Catholics, Orthodox, Monophysites, and Protestants. In recent times they have been called, chiefly by Anglicans, the "Assyrian Church", a name which can be defended on archæological grounds. Brightman, in his "Liturgies Eastern and Western", includes Chaldean and Malabar Uniats and Nestorians under "Persian Rite", and Bishop Arthur Maclean of Moray and Ross (Anglican) who is probably the best living authority on the existing Nestorians, calls them "East Syrians", which is perhaps the most satisfactory term. The catalogue of liturgies in the British Museum has adopted the usual Catholic nomenclature, calling the rite of the East Syrian Uniats and Nestorians the "Chaldean Rite", that of the South Indian Uniats and schismatics the "Malabar Rite", and that of the West Syrian Monophysites and Uniats the "Syrian Rite", a convenient arrangement in view of the fact that most printed liturgies of these rites are Uniat. The language of all three forms of the East Syrian Rite is Syriac, a modern form of which is still spoken by the Nestorians and some of the Uniats. The origin of the rite is unknown. The tradition—resting on the legend of Abgar and of his correspondence with Christ, which has been shown to be apocryphal (see ABGAR, THE LEGEND OF)—is to the effect that St. Thomas the Apostle, on his way to India, established Christianity in Mesopotamia, Assyria, and Persia, and left Adæus (or Thaddeus), "one of the Seventy", and Maris in charge. To these the normal liturgy is attributed, but it is said to have been revised by the Patriarch Yeshuyab III in about 650. Some, however, consider this liturgy to be a development of the Antiochene.

After the Council of Ephesus (431), the Church of Seleucia-Ctesiphon, which had hitherto been governed by a catholicos under Antioch, refused to accept the condemnation of Nestorius, and cut itself and the Church to the East of it off from the Catholic Church. In 498 the catholicos assumed the title of "Patriarch of the East", and for many centuries this most successful missionary Church continued to spread throughout Persia, Tartary, Mongolia, China, and India, developing on lines of its own, very little influenced by the rest of Christendom. At the end of the fourteenth century the conquests of Tamerlane all but destroyed this flourishing Church at one blow, and reduced it to a few small communities in Persia, Turkey in Asia, Cyprus, South India, and the Island of Socotra. The Cypriote Nestorians united themselves to Rome in 1445; in the sixteenth century there was a schism in the patriarchate between the rival lines of Mar Shimun and Mar Elia; the Christianity of Socotra, such as it was, died out about the seventeenth century; the Malabarese Church divided into Uniats and Schismatics in 1599, the latter deserting Nestorianism for Monophysitism and adopting the West Syrian Rite about fifty years later; in 1681 the Chaldean Unia, which had been struggling for existence since 1552, was finally established, and in 1778 received a great accession of strength in the adhesion of the whole Mar Elia patriarchate, and all that was left of the original Nestorian Church consisted of the inhabitants of a district between the Lakes of Van and Urmi and the Tigris, and an outlying colony in Palestine. These have been further reduced by a great massacre by the Kurds in 1843, and by the secession of a large number to the Russian Church within the last few years. About twenty years ago there was an attempt to form an "Independent Catholic Chaldean Church", on the model of the "Old Catholics". This resulted in separating a few from the Uniats.

MSS. AND EDITIONS.—The authorities for this rite are chiefly in manuscript, the printed editions being very few. Few of the manuscripts, except some lectionaries in the British Museum, were written before the fifteenth century, and most, whether Chaldean or Nestorian, are of the seventeenth and eighteenth. The books in use are: (1) *Takhsa*, a priest's book, containing the Eucharistic service (*Qurbana* or *Qudasha*) in its three forms, with the administration of other sacraments, and various occasional prayers and blessings. It is nearly the *Euchologion* of the Greeks (see CONSTANTINOPLE, RITE OF). (2) *Kthawa dhaqdham wadhwathar* or *Qdhamuwathar*, "Before and After", contains the Ordinary of the Divine Office, except the Psalter, arranged for two weeks. (3) *Dawidha* (David), the Psalter, divided into *hulali*, which answer more or less to the καθίσματα of the Greeks. It includes the collects of the *hulali*. (4) *Qiryana, Shlika w'Iwangaliyuna*, lections, epistles, and gospels, sometimes together, sometimes in separate books. (5) *Turgama*, explanatory hymns sung before the Epistle and Gospel. (6) *Khudra*, containing the variables for Sundays, Lent and the Fast of the Ninevites, and other holy days. (7) *Kashkul*, a selection from the *Khudra* for weekdays. (8) *Geza*, containing variables for festivals except Sundays. (9) *Abukhalima*, a collectary, so called from its compiler, Elias III, Abu Khalim ibn al-Khaditha, Metropolitan of Nisibis, and patriarch (1175–99). (10) *Ba'utha d'Ninwayi*, rhythmical prayers attributed to St. Ephraem, used during the Fast of the Ninevites. (11) *Takhsa d'amadha*, the office of baptism. (12) *Burakha*, the marriage service. (13) *Kahnita*, the burial service for priests. (14) *Anidha*, the burial service for lay people. (15) *Takhsa d'siamidha*, the ordination services. (16) *Takhsa d'khusaya*, the "Office of Pardon", or the reconciliation of penitents. These last (11 to 16) are excerpts from the *Takhsa*. Of the above the following have been printed in Syriac:

For the Nestorians.—The *Takhsa*, in two parts, by the Archbishop of Canterbury's Assyrian Mission (Urmi, 1890–92). The Society for Promoting Christian Knowledge has published an English translation of the first part of the *Takhsa*, both parts "unmodified except by the omission of the heretical names" (Brightman); *Dhaqdham wadhwathar*, by the same (Urmi, 1894); *Dawidha*, by the same (Urmi, 1891).

For the Chaldean Uniats: "Missale Chaldaicum", containing the Liturgy of the Apostles in Syriac and the Epistles and Gospels in Syriac with an Arabic translation, in Carshuni (Propaganda Press fol., Rome, 1767). A new and revised edition, containing the three liturgies and the lections, epistles and gospels, was published by the Dominicans at Mosul in 1901. The Order of the Church Services of Common Days, etc., from *Kthawa dhaqdham wadhwathar* (8vo, Mosul, 1866). "Breviarium Chaldaicum in usum Nationis Chaldaicæ a Josepho Guriel secundo editum" (16mo, Propaganda Press, Rome, 1865). "Breviarium Chaldaicum", etc. [8vo, Paris (printed at Leipzig), 1886].

For the Malabar Uniats: "Ordo Chaldaicus Missæ Beatorum Apostolorum, juxta ritum Ecclesiæ Malabaricæ" (fol., Propaganda Press, Rome, 1774). "Ordo Chaldaicus Rituum et Lectionum", etc., (fol., Rome, 1775). "Ordo Chaldaicus ministerii Sacramentorum Sanctorum", etc. (fol., Rome, 1775). These three, which together form a *Takhsa* and Lectionary, are commonly found bound together. The Propaganda reprinted the third part in 1845. "Ordo Baptismi adultorum juxta ritum Ecclesiæ Malabaricæ Chaldæorum" (8vo, Propaganda Press, Rome, 1859), a Syriac translation of the Roman Order.

The Malabar Rite was revised in a Catholic direction by Aleixo de Menezes, Archbishop of Goa, and the revision was authorized by the Synod of Diamper in 1599. So effectively was the original Malabar Rite abolished by the Catholics in favour of this revision, and by the schismatics (when in 1649, being cut off from their own patriarch by the Spaniards and Portuguese, they put themselves under the Jacobite patriarch) in favour of the West Syrian Liturgy, that no copy is known to exist, but it is evident from the revised form that it could not have differed materially from the existing Nestorian Rite.

THE EUCHARISTIC SERVICE, *Qurbana*, "the Offering", *udasha*, "the Hallowing".—There are three Anaphoræ; that of the Apostles (Sts. Adæus and Maris), that of Nestorius, and that of Theodore (of Mopsuestia) the Interpreter. The first is the normal form, and from it the Malabar revision was derived. The second is used by the Chaldeans and Nestorians on the Epiphany and the feasts of St. John the Baptist and of the Greek Doctors, both of which occur in Epiphany-tide on the Wednesday of the Fast of the Ninevites, and on Maundy Thursday.

The third is used by the same (except when the second is ordered) from Advent Sunday to Palm Sunday. The same pro-anaphoral part serves for all three. Three other Anaphoræ are mentioned by Ebedyeshu (Metropolitan of Nisibis, 1298) in his catalogue, those of Barsuma, Narses, and Diodorus of Tarsus; but they are not known now, unless Dr. Wright is correct in calling the fragment in Brit. Mus. Add. 14669, "Diodore of Tarsus".

The Mass is preceded by a preparation, or "Office of the Prothesis", which includes the solemn kneading and baking of the loaves. These among the Nestorians are leavened, the flour being mixed with a little oil and the holy leaven (*malka*), which, according to the legend, "was given and handed down to us by our holy fathers Mar Addai and Mar Mari and Mar Tuma", and of which and of the holy oil a very strange story is told. The real leavening, however, is done by means of fermented dough (*khmira*) from the preparation of the last Mass. The Chaldean Uniats now use unleavened bread.

The Mass itself is introduced by the first verse of the *Gloria in Excelsis* and the Lord's Prayer, with "farcings" (*giyura*), consisting of a form of the *Sanctus*. Then follow:

(1) The Introit Psalm (variable), called *Marmitha*, with a preliminary prayer, varying for Sundays and greater feasts and for "Memorials" and ferias. In the Malabar Rite, Pss. xiv, cl, and cxvi are said in alternate verses by priests and deacons.

(2) The "Antiphon of the Sanctuary" (*Unitha d'qanki*), variable, with a similarly varying prayer.

(3) The Lakhumara, an antiphon beginning "To Thee, Lord", which occurs in other services also preceded by a similarly varying prayer.

(4) The Trisagion. Incense is used before this. In the Uniat Rite at low Mass the elements are put on the altar before the incensing.

(5) The Lections. These are four or five: (a) the Law and (b) the Prophecy, from the Old Testament, (c) the Lection from the Acts, (d) the Epistle, always from St. Paul, (e) the Gospel. Some days have all five lections, some four, some only three. All have an Epistle and a Gospel, but, generally, when there is a Lection from the Law there is none from the Acts, and vice versa. Sometimes there is none from either Law or Acts. The first three are called *Qiryani* (Lections), the third *Shlikha* (Apostle). Before the Epistle and Gospel, hymns called *Turgama* (interpretation) are, or should be, said; that before the Epistle is invariable, that of the Gospel varies with the day. They answer to the Greek προκείμενα. The *Turgama* of the Epistle is preceded by proper psalm verses called *Shuraya* (beginning), and that of the Gospel by other proper psalm verses called *Zumara* (song). The latter includes Alleluia between the verses.

(6) The Deacon's Litany, or *Ektene*, called *Karazutha* (proclamation). This resembles the "Great Synapte" of the Greeks. During it the proper "Antiphon [*Unitha*] of the Gospel" is sung by the people.

(7) The Offertory. The deacons proclaim the expulsion of the unbaptized, and set the "hearers" to watch the doors. The priest places the bread and wine on the altar, with words (in the Nestorian, but not in the Chaldean Uniat Rite) which seem as if they were already consecrated. He sets aside a "memorial of the Virgin Mary, Mother of Christ" (Chaldean; usual Malabar Rite, "Mother of God"; but according to Raulin's Latin of the Malabar Rite, "Mother of God Himself and of the Lord Jesus Christ"), and of the patron of the Church (in the Malabar Rite, "of St. Thomas"). Then follows the proper "Antiphon of the Mysteries" (*Unitha d'razi*), answering to the Offertory.

(8) The Creed. This is a variant of the Nicene Creed. It is possible that the order or words "and was incarnate by the Holy Ghost and was made man, and was conceived and born of the Virgin Mary", may enshrine a Nestorian idea, but the Chaldean Uniats do not seem to have noticed it, their only alteration being the addition of the *Filioque*. The Malabar Book has an exact translation of the Latin. In Neale's translation of the Malabar Rite the *Karazutha*, the Offertory, and the Expulsion of the Unbaptized come before the Lections, and the Creed follows immediately on the Gospel, but in the Propaganda edition of 1774 the Offertory follows the Creed, which follows the Gospel.

(9) The first Lavabo, followed by a *Kushapa* ("beseeching", i. e., prayer said kneeling) and a form of the "Orate fratres", with its response. It is now that the variations of the three Anaphora begin.

(10) The Kiss of Peace, preceded by a *G'hantha*, i. e., a prayer said with bowed head.

(11) The prayer of Memorial (*Dukhrana*) of the Living and the Dead, and the Diptychs; the latter is now obsolete among the Nestorians.

(12) The Anaphora. As in all liturgies this begins with a form of the Sursum corda, but the East Syrian form is more elaborate than any other, especially in the Anaphora of Theodore. Then follows the Preface of the usual type ending with the Sanctus.

(13) The Post-Sanctus (to use the Hispano-Gallican term). This is an amplification (similar in idea and often in phraseology to those in all liturgies except the Roman) of the idea of the Sanctus into a recital of the work of Redemption, extending to some length and ending, in the Anaphoræ of Nestorius and Theodore, with the recital of the Institution. In the Anaphora of the Apostles the recital of the Institution is wanting, though it has been supplied in the Chaldean and Malabar Uniat liturgies and in the Anglican edition of the Nestorian book. Hammond (Liturgies Eastern and Western, p. lix) and most other writers hold that the Words of Institution belong to this Liturgy and should be supplied somewhere; Hammond (loc. cit.) suggests many arguments for their former presence. The reason of their absence is uncertain. While some hold that this essential passage dropped out in times of ignorance, others say it never was there at all, being unnecessary, since the consecration was held to be effected by the subsequent Epiklesis alone. Another theory, evidently of Western origin and not quite consistent with the general Eastern theory of consecration by an Epiklesis following Christ's words, is that, being the formula of consecration, it was held too sacred to be written down. It does not seem to be quite certain whether Nestorian priests did or did not insert the Words of Institution in old times, but it seems that many of them do not do so now.

(14) The Prayer of the Great Oblation with a second memorial of the Living and the Dead, a *Kushapa*.

(15) The *G'hantha* of the Epiklesis, or Invocation of the Holy Spirit. The Epiklesis formula itself is called *Nithi Mar* (May He come, O Lord) from its opening words. The Liturgy of the Apostles is so vague as to the purpose of the Invocation that, when the Words of Institution are not said, it would be difficult to imagine this formula to be sufficient on any hypothesis, Eastern or Western. The Anaphoræ of Nestorius and Theodore, besides having the Words of Institution, have definite Invocations, evidently copied from Antiochene or Byzantine forms. The older Chaldean and the Malabar Uniat books have inserted the Words of Institution with an Elevation, *after* the Epiklesis. But the 1901 Mosul edition puts the Words of Institution first.

(16) Here follow a Prayer for Peace, a second Lavabo and a censing.

(17) The Fraction, Consignation, Conjunction, and Commixture. The Host is broken in two, and the sign of the Cross is made in the Chalice with one

half, after which the other half is signed with the half that has been dipped in the Chalice. The two halves are then reunited on the Paten. Then a cleft is made in the Host "qua parte intincta est in Sanguine" (Renaudot's tr.), and a particle is put in the chalice, after some intricate arranging on the paten.

(18) The Communion. The veil is thrown open, the deacon exhorts the communicants to draw near, the priest breaks up the Host for distribution. Then follows the Lord's Prayer, with Introduction and Embolism, and the *Sancta Sanctis*, and then the "Antiphon of the Bema" (Communion) is sung. The Communion is in both species separately, the priest giving the Host and the deacon the Chalice. Then follows a variable antiphon of thanksgiving, a post-communion, and a dismissal. Afterwards the *Mkaprana*, an unconsecrated portion of the holy loaf, is distributed to the communicants, but not, as in the case of the Greek ἀντίδωρον, and as the name of the latter implies, to non-communicants. The Chaldean Uniats are communicated with the Host dipped in the Chalice. They reserve what is left of the Holy Gifts, while the Nestorian priests consume all before leaving the church.

Properly, and according to their own canons, the Nestorians ought to say Mass on every Sunday and Friday, on every festival, and daily during the first, middle, and last week of Lent and the octave of Easter. In practice it is only said on Sundays and greater festivals, at the best, and in many churches not so often, a sort of "dry Mass" being used instead. The Chaldean Uniat priests say Mass daily, and where there are many priests there will be many Masses in the same Church in one day, which is contrary to the Nestorian canons. The Anglican editions of the liturgies omit the names of heretics and call the Anaphoræ of Nestorius and Theodore the "Second Hallowing" and "Third Hallowing". Otherwise there are no alterations except the addition of Words of Institution to the first Anaphoræ. The recent Uniat edition has made the same alterations and substituted "Mother of God" for "Mother of Christ". In each edition the added Words of Institution follow the form of the rite of the edition. The prayers of the Mass, like those of the Orthodox Eastern Church, are generally long and diffuse. Frequently they end with a sort of doxology called *Qanuna*, which is said aloud, the rest being recited in a low tone. The *Qanuna* in form and usage resembles the Greek ἐκφώνησις.

The vestments used by the priest at Mass are the *Sudhra*, a girded alb with three crosses in red or black on the shoulder, the *Urara* (ὠράριον) or stole worn crossed by priests, but not by bishops (as in the West), and the *Ma'apra*, a sort of linen cope. The deacon wears the *Sudhra*, with an *Urara* over the left shoulder.

THE DIVINE OFFICE.—The nucleus of this is, as is usual, the recitation of the Psalter. There are only three regular hours of service (Evening, Midnight, and Morning) with a rarely used Compline. In practice only Morning and Evening are commonly used, but these are extremely well attended daily by laity as well as clergy. When Nestorian monasteries existed (which is no longer the case) seven hours of prayer were the custom in them, and three *hulali* of the Psalter were recited at each. This would mean a daily recitation of the whole Psalter. The present arrangement provides for seven *hulali* at each ferial night service, ten on Sundays, three on "Memorials", and the whole Psalter on feasts of Our Lord. At the evening service there is a selection of from four to seven psalms, varying with the day of the week, and also a *Shuraya*, or short psalm, with generally a portion of Ps. cxviii, varying with the day of the fortnight. At the morning service the invariable psalms are cix, xc, ciii (1–6), cxii, xcii, cxlviii, cl, cxvi. On ferias and "Memorials" Ps. cxlvi is said after Ps. cxlviii, and on ferias Ps. l, 1–18, comes at the end of the psalms. The rest of the services consist of prayers, antiphons, litanies, and verses (*giyura*) inserted, like the Greek στιχηρά, but more extensively, between verses of psalms. On Sundays the *Gloria in Excelsis* and *Benedicite* are said instead of Ps. cxlvi. Both morning and evening services end with several prayers, a blessing, (*Khuthama*, "Sealing"), the kiss of peace, and the Creed. The variables, besides the psalms, are those of the feast or day, which are very few, and those of the day of the fortnight. These fortnights consist of weeks called "Before" (*Qdham*) and "After" (*Wathar*), according to which of the two choirs begins the service. Hence the book of the Divine Office is called *Qdham u wathar*, or at full length *Kthawa daqdham wadhwathar*, the "Book of Before and After".

THE CALENDAR.—The Calendar is very peculiar. The year is divided into periods of about seven weeks each, called *Shawu'i*; these are Advent (called *Subara*, "Annunciation"), Epiphany, Lent, Easter, the Apostles, Summer, "Elias and the Cross", "Moses", and the "Dedication" (*Qudash idta*). "Moses" and the "Dedication" have only four weeks each. The Sundays are generally named after the *Shawu'a* in which they occur, "Fourth Sunday of Epiphany", "Second Sunday of the Annunciation," etc., though sometimes the name changes in the middle of a *Shawu'a*. Most of the "Memorials" (*dukhrani*), or saints' days, which have special lections, occur on the Fridays between Christmas and Lent, and are therefore movable feasts, but some, such as Christmas, Epiphany, the Assumption, and about thirty smaller days without proper lections are on fixed days. There are four shorter fasting periods besides the Great Fast (Lent); these are: (1) the Fast of Mar Zaya, the three days after the second Sunday of the Nativity; (2) the Fast of the Virgins, after the first Sunday of the Epiphany; (3) the Rogation of the Ninevites, seventy days before Easter; (4) the Fast of Mart Mariam (Our Lady), from the first to the fourteenth of August. The Fast of the Ninevites commemorates the repentance of Nineveh at the preaching of Jonas, and is carefully kept. Those of Mar Zaya and the Virgins are nearly obsolete. As compared with the Latin and Greek Calendars, that of the Chaldeans, whether Uniat or Nestorian, is very meagre. The Malabar Rite has largely adopted the Roman Calendar, and several Roman days have been added to that of the Chaldean Uniats. The Chaldean Easter coincides with that of the Orthodox Eastern Church, as the Julian Calendar is used, but the years are numbered, not from the birth of Christ, but from the Seleucid era, 311 B.C.

THE OTHER SACRAMENTS AND OCCASIONAL SERVICES.—The other Sacraments in use among the Nestorians are Baptism, with which is always associated an anointing, which as in other eastern rites answers to Confirmation, Holy Order and Matrimony, but not Penance or Unction of the Sick. The latter appears to be unknown to the Nestorians, though Assemani ("Bibliotheca Orientalis", pt. II, p. cclxxii) considers it might be shown from their books that its omission was a modern error. The Chaldean Uniats now have a form not unlike the Byzantine and West Syrian. The nearest approach to Penance among the Nestorians is a form, counted as a sacrament, for the reconciliation of apostates and excommunicated persons, prayers from which are occasionally used in cases of other penitents. Assemani's arguments (ibid., cclxxxvi–viii) for a belief in Penance as a Sacrament among the ancient Nestorians or for the practice of auricular confession among the Malabar Nestorians are not conclusive. The Chaldeans have a similar form to that of the Latin Rite. The Nestorians omit Matrimony from the list, and according to Ebedyeshu make up the number of the mysteries to seven by including the Holy Leaven and the Sign of the Cross, but they are now rather vague about the definition or numeration. The only other rite of any interest is the consecration of churches. Oil, but not chrism, plays a considerable part in these rites, being used in Baptism, possibly in Confirmation, in the reconciliation of apostates, etc., in the consecration of churches, and the making of bread for the Eucharist. It is not used in ordination or for the sick. There are two sorts of oil; the one is ordinary olive oil, blessed or not blessed for the occasion, the other is the oil of the Holy Horn. The last, which, though really only plain oil, represents the chrism (or μύρον) of other rites, is believed to have been handed down from the Apostles with the Holy Leaven. The legend is that the Baptist caught the water which fell from the Body of Christ at His baptism and preserved it. He gave it to St. John the Evangelist, who added to it some of the water which fell from the pierced Side. At the Last Supper Jesus gave two loaves to St. John, bidding him keep one for the Holy Leaven. With this St. John mingled some of the Blood from the Side of Christ. After Pentecost the Apostles mixed oil with the sacred water, and each took a horn of it, and the loaf they ground to pieces and mixed it with flour and salt to be the Holy Leaven. The Holy Horn is constantly renewed by the addition of oil blessed by a bishop on Maundy Thursday.

The baptismal service is modelled on the Eucharistic. The Mass of the Catechumens is almost identical, with of course appropriate Collects, psalms, Litanies, and Lections. After the introductory *Gloria*, Lord's Prayer, *Marmitha* (in this case Ps. lxxxiii) and its Collect, follow the imposition of hands and the signing with oil, after which follow an Antiphon of the Sanctuary and Ps. xliv, cix, cxxxi, with *giyuri*, Litanies, and Collects, then the *Lakhumara*, Trisagion, and Lections (Epistle and Gospel), and the *Karazutha*, after which the priest says the prayer of the imposition of hands, and the unbaptized are dismissed. An antiphon answering to that "of the mysteries" follows, and then the Creed is said. The bringing forward of the Holy Horn and the blessing of the oil take the place of the Offertory. The Anaphora is paralleled by Sursum corda, Preface, and Sanctus, a *Nithi Mar*, or Epiklesis, upon the oil, a commixture of the new oil with that of the Holy Horn, and the Lord's Prayer. Then the font is blessed and signed with the holy oil, and in the place of the Communion comes the Baptism itself. The children are signed with the oil on the breast and then anointed all over, and are dipped thrice in the font. The formula is: "N., be thou baptized in the name of the Father, in the name of the Son, in the name of the Holy Ghost. Amen." Then follows the post-baptismal thanksgiving. Confirmation follows immediately. There are two prayers of confirmation and a signing between the eyes with the formula: "N. is baptized and perfected in the name, etc." It is not quite clear whether oil should be used with this signing or not. Then any oil that remains over is poured into the Holy Horn, held over the font, and the water in the font is loosed from its former consecration with rather curious ceremonies. The Chaldean Uniats have added the renunciations, profession of faith, and answers of the sponsors from the Roman Ritual, and anoint with chrism.

The marriage service (*Burakha*, "Blessing") has nothing very distinctive about it, and resembles closely the Byzantine, and to some extent the Jewish rite.

The orders of the Nestorians are those of reader (*Qaruya*), subdeacon (*Hiupathiaqna*), deacon (*Shamasha*), priest (*Qashisha*), archdeadon (*Arkidhyaquna*) and bishop (*Apisqupa*). The degree of archdeacon, though it has an ordination service of its own, is only counted as a degree of the presbyterate, and is by some held to be the same as that of *chorepiscopus* (*Kurapisqupa*), which never involved episcopal ordination among the Nestorians. When a priest is engaged in sacerdotal functions, he is called *Kahna* (i. e., ἱερεύς; sacerdos, cf. Hebrew כֹּהֵן) and a bishop is similarly *Rab Kahni* (Chief of the Priests, ἀρχιερεύς, pontifex). *Quashisha* and *Apisqupa* only denote the degree. *Kahnutha*, priesthood, is used of the three degrees of deacon, priest, and bishop. The ordination formula is: "N. has been set apart, consecrated, and perfected to the work of the diaconate [or of the presbyterate] and to the Levitical and Stephanite Office [or for the Office of the Aaronic priesthood], in the Name, etc. In the case of a bishop it is: "to the great work of the episcopate of the city of——". A similar formula is used for archdeacons and metropolitans.

The Consecration of churches (*Siamidha* or *Qudash Madhbkha*) consists largely of unctions. The altar is anointed all over, and there are four consecration crosses on the four interior walls of the sanctuary, and these and the lintel of the door and various other places are anointed. The oil is not that of the Holy Horn, but fresh olive oil consecrated by the bishop.

BADGER, *The Nestorians and their Ritual* (London, 1852); IDEM, *The Syriac Liturgies of the Apostles, of Theodorus and of Nestorius* (Eastern Church Assoc., London, 1875); ETHERIDGE, *The Syrian Churches* (London, 1846); MACLEAN AND BROWNE, *The Catholicos of the East and His People* (London, 1892); MACLEAN, *East Syrian Daily Offices* (London, 1894), a translation of the *Kthawa dhaqdham wadhwathar*, with introduction and notes; IDEM, *The East Syrian Epiphany Rites* in CONYBEARE, *Rituale Armenorum* (Oxford, 1905); S.P.C.K., *The Liturgy of the Holy Apostles, etc.* (London, 1893); RILEY, *The Archbishop of Canterbury's Mission to the Assyrian Christians. Narrative of a visit, 1884. Report of the foundation of the Mission in 1886* (London, 1891); IRVING, *The ceremonial use of oil among the East Syrians* (Eastern Church Assoc., Oxford, 1902); RENAUDOT *Liturgiarum Orientalium Collectio* (Frankfort, 1847); LA BIGNE, *Magna Bibliotheca veterum Patrum* (Paris, 1654); RAULIN, *Historia Ecclesiæ Malabaricæ cum Diamperitana Synodo* (Rome, 1745); BICKELL, *Der katholische Orient* (Münster, 1874); IDEM, *Conspectus rei Syrorum literariæ* (Münster, 1871); BRIGHTMAN, *Liturgies Eastern and Western* (Oxford, 1896); NEALE AND LITTLEDALE, *The Liturgies of SS. Mark, James, Clement, Chrysostom and Basil and of the Church of Malabar* (London, 1859); PRINCE MAX OF SAXONY, *Missa chaldaica* (Ratisbon, 1907), a Latin translation of the second Liturgy; NEALE, *History of the Holy Eastern Church. General Introduction* (London, 1850); MORINUS, *Commentarius de sacris Ecclesiæ ordinationibus* (Antwerp, 1695), including the Nestorian; DIETTRICH, *Die nestorianische Taufliturgie* (Giessen, 1903); D'AVRIL, *La Chaldée chrétienne* (Paris, 1892); GIAMIL, *Genuinæ Relationes inter Sedem Apostolicam et Assyriorum Orientalium seu Chaldæorum Ecclesiam* (Rome, 1902); BRAUN, *Das Buch der Synhados* (Stuttgart and Vienna, 1900); ASSYRIAN MISSION, *Letters from Assyria* (London, 1887–89); IDEM, *Quarterly Paper* (London, 1890——). Besides the Syriac editions of the service books mentioned above.

HENRY JENNER.

Syrian Rite, WEST.—The rite used by the Jacobite sect in Syria and by the Catholic Syrians is in its origin simply the old rite of Antioch in the Syriac language. Into this framework the Jacobites have fitted a great number of other Anaphoras, so that now their Liturgy has more variant forms than any other. The oldest form of the Antiochene Rite that we know is in Greek (see ANTIOCHENE LITURGY). It was apparently composed in that language. The many Greek terms that remain in the Syriac form show that this is derived from Greek. The version must have been made very early, evidently before the Monophysite schism, before the influence of Constantinople and Byzantine infiltrations had begun. No doubt as soon as Christian communities arose in the country parts of Syria the prayers which in the cities (Antioch, Jerusalem, etc.) were said in Greek, were, as a matter of course, translated into the peasants' language (Syriac) for their use. The "Peregrinatio Silviæ" describes the services at Jerusalem as being Greek; but the lessons, first read in Greek, are then translated into Syriac *propter populum* (ed. Geyer, p. 99). As long as all Western Syria was one communion, the country dioceses followed the rite of their patriarch at Antioch, only changing the language. Modifications adopted at Antioch in

Greek were copied in Syriac by those who said their prayers in the national tongue. This point is important because the Syriac Liturgy (in its fundamental form) already contains all the changes brought to Antioch from Jerusalem. It is not the older pure Antiochene Rite, but the later Rite of Jerusalem-Antioch. The Syriac Liturgy in its Intercession, like the Greek "St. James", prays first not for the Church of Antioch, but "for the holy Sion, the mother of all churches" (Brightman, pp. 89–90). The fact that the Jacobites as well as the Orthodox have the Jerusalem-Antiochene Liturgy is the chief proof that this had supplanted the older Antiochene Use before the schism of the fifth century.

Our first Syriac documents come from about the end of the fifth century ("Testamentum Domini," ed. by Ignatius Rahmani II, Life of Severus of Antioch, sixth century). They give us valuable information about local forms of the Rite of Antioch-Jerusalem. The Jacobite sect kept a version of this rite which is obviously a local variant. Its scheme and most of its prayers correspond to those of the Greek St. James; but it has amplifications and omissions, such as we find in all local forms of early rites. It seems too that the Jacobites after the schism made some modifications. We know this for certain in one point (the Trisagion). The first Jacobite writer on their rite is James of Edessa (d. 708), who wrote a letter to a priest Thomas comparing the Syrian Liturgy with that of Egypt. This letter is an exceedingly valuable and really critical discussion of the rite. A number of later Jacobite writers followed James of Edessa. On the whole this sect produced the first scientific students of liturgy. Benjamin of Edessa (period unknown), Lazarus bar Sabhetha of Bagdad (ninth century), Moses bar Kephas of Mosul (d. 903), Dionysius bar Salibhi of Amida (d. 1171) wrote valuable commentaries on the Jacobite Rite. In the eighth and ninth centuries a controversy concerning the prayer at the Fraction produced much liturgical literature. The chronicle of their Patriarch Michael the Great (d. 1199) discusses the question and supplies valuable contemporary documents.

The oldest Jacobite Liturgy extant is the one ascribed (as in its Greek form) to St. James. It is in the dialect of Edessa. The pro-anaphoral part of this is the *Ordo communis* to which the other later Anaphoras are joined. It is printed in Latin by Renaudot (II, 1–44) and in English by Brightman (pp. 69–110). This follows the Greek St. James (see Antiochene Liturgy) with these differences. All the vesting prayer and preparation of the offering (*Proskomide*) are considerably expanded, and the prayers differ. This part of the Liturgy is always most subject to modification; it began as private prayer only. The *Monogenes* comes later; the litany before the lessons is missing; the incensing is expanded into a more elaborate rite. The *Trisagion* comes after the lessons from the Old Testament; it contains the addition: "who wast crucified for us". This is the most famous characteristic of the Jacobite Rite. The clause was added by Peter the Dyer (Fullo), Monophysite Patriarch of Antioch (d. 488), was believed to imply Monophysism and caused much controversy during those times, eventually becoming a kind of watchword to the Jacobites (see Zacharias Rhetor, "Hist. eccl.", P. G., LXXXV, 1165). The litany between the lessons is represented by the word *Kurillison* said thrice. There is no chant at the Great Entrance (a Byzantine addition in the Greek Rite). The long Offertory prayers of the Greek Rite do not occur. The Epiklesis and Intercession are much the same as in Greek. The Lord's Prayer follows the Fraction. At the Communion-litany the answer is *Halleluiah* instead of *Kyrie eleison*.

In this Syriac Liturgy many Greek forms remain: *Stomen kalos, Kurillison, Sophia, Proschomen*, etc.

Renaudot gives also a second form of the *Ordo communis* (II, 12–28) with many variants. To the *Ordo communis* the Jacobites have added a very great number of alternative Anaphoras, many of which have not yet been published. These Anaphoras are ascribed to all manner of people; they were composed at very different periods. One explanation of their attribution to various saints is that they were originally used on their feasts. Renaudot translated and published thirty-nine of these. After that of St. James follows (in his work) a shortened form of the same. This is the one commonly used to-day. Then: (3) Liturgy of St. Xystus, which is placed first in the Maronite books; (4) of St. Peter; (5) another of St. Peter; (6) of St. John; (7) of the Twelve Apostles; (8) of St. Mark; (9) of St. Clement of Rome; (10) of St. Dionysius; (11) of St. Ignatius; (12) of St. Julius of Rome; (13) of St. Eustathius; (14) of St. John Chrysostom; (15) of St. John Chrysostom (from Chaldæan sources); (16) of St. Maruta; (17) of St. Cyril; (18) of Dioscor; (19) of Philoxenus of Hierapolis; (20) a second Liturgy also ascribed to him; (21) of Serverus of Antioch; (22) of James Baradæus; (23) of Matthew the Shepherd; (24) of St. James of Botnan and Serug; (25) of James of Edessa, the Interpreter; (26) of Thomas of Heraclea; (27) of Moses bar Kephas; (28) of Philoxenus of Bagdad; (29) of the Doctors, arranged by John the Great, Patriarch; (30) of John of Basora; (31) of Michael of Antioch; (32) of Dionysius Bar-Salibhi; (33) of Gregory Bar-Hebræus; (34) of St. John the Patriarch, called Accemetus ($Ἀκοίμητος$); (35) of St. Dioscor of Kardu; (36) John, Patriarch of Antioch; (37) of Ignatius of Antioch (Joseph Ibn Wahib); (39) of St. Basil (another version, by Masius).

Brightman (pp. lviii-lix) mentions sixty-four Liturgies as known, at least by name. Notes of this bewildering number of Anaphoras will be found after each in Renaudot. In most cases all he can say is that he knows nothing of the real author; often the names affixed are otherwise unknown. Many Anaphoras are obviously quite late, inflated with long prayers and rhetorical expressions, many contain Monophysite ideas, some are insufficient at the consecration so as to be invalid. Baumstark (Die Messe im Morgenland, 44–46) thinks the Anaphora of St. Ignatius most important, as containing parts of the old pure Antiochene Rite. He considers that many attributions to later Jacobite authors may be correct, that the Liturgy of Ignatius of Antioch (Joseph Ibn Wahib; d. 1304) is the latest. Most of these Anaphoras have now fallen into disuse. The Jacobite celebrant generally uses the shortened form of St. James. There is an ancient Armenian version (shortened) of the Syriac St. James. The Liturgy is said in Syriac with (since the fifteenth century) many Arabic substitutions in the lessons and proanaphoral prayers. The Lectionary and Diaconicum have not been published and are hardly known. The vestments correspond almost exactly to those of the Orthodox, except that the bishop wears a latinized mitre. The Calendar has few feasts. It follows in its main lines the old order of Antioch, observed also by the Nestorians, which is the basis of the Byzantine Calendar. Feasts are divided into three classes of dignity. Wednesday and Friday are fast-days. There are also the four great fasts, as with the Orthodox. The Divine Office consists of Vespers, Compline, Nocturns, Lauds, Terce, Sext, and None, or rather of hours that correspond to these among Latins. Vespers always belongs to the following day. The great part of this office (known in the West chiefly by the Uniat books and now by Dr. Baumstark's "Festbrevier u. Kirchenjahr der syrischen Jakobiten") consists of long poems composed for the purpose, like the Byzantine odes. Baptism is performed by immersion; the priest confirms at once with chrism blessed by the patriarch. Confession is not much used; it has fallen into the same decay as in most Eastern Churches. Communion is administered under both kinds; the sick are anointed with oil blessed by a priest—the ideal is to have seven priests to administer it. The orders are bishop, priest, deacon, subdeacon, lector, and singer. There are many chorepiscopi, not ordained bishop. It will be seen, then, that one little Jabobite Church has followed much the same line of development in its rites as its powerful Orthodox neighbour.

The Syrian Uniats use the same rite as the Jacobites. But (as is the case with most Uniat Churches) it is better organized with them. There is not much that can be called Romanizing in their books; but they have the advantage of well-arranged, well-edited, and well-printed books. All the great students of the West-Syrian Rite (the Assemani, Renaudot, etc.) have been Catholics. Their knowledge and the higher Western standard of scholarship in general are advantages of which the Uniats rather than the Jacobites profit. Of the manifold Syrian Anaphoras the Uniats use seven only—those of St. James, St. John, St. Peter, St. Chrysostom, St. Xystus, St. Matthew, and St. Basil. That of St. Xystus is attached to the *Ordo communis* in their official book; that of St. John is said on the chief feasts. The lessons only are in Arabic. It was inevitable that the Syrian Liturgies, coming from Monophysite sources, should be examined at Rome before they were allowed to Uniats. But the revisers made very few changes. Out of the mass of Anaphoras they chose the oldest and purest, leaving out the long series of later ones that were unorthodox, or even invalid. In the seven kept for Uniat use what alterations have been made are chiefly the omission of redundant prayers, simplification of confused parts in which the Diaconicum and the Euchologion had become mixed together. The only important correction is the omission of the fatal clause: "Who was crucified for us" in the Trisagion. There is no suspicion of modifying in the direction of the Roman Rite. The other books of the Uniats, the Diaconicum, officebook, and ritual are edited at Rome, Beirut, and the Uniat Patriarchal press at Sharfé; they are considerably the most accessible, the best-arranged books in which to study this rite.

The West-Syrian Rite has also been used at intervals by sections of the (schismatical) Malabar Church. Namely, as the Malabar Christians at various times made approaches to the Jacobite Patriarch or received bishops from him, so did they at such times use his Liturgy. Most of Malabar has now returned to the Nestorian communion; but there are still Jacobite communities using this rite among them.

The Maronite Rite is merely a Romanized adaptation of that of the West Syrians.

I. Texts.—A. Jacobite editions: BODERIANUS, *D. Severus alexandrinus de ritibus baptismi et sacræ synaxis* (Antwerp, 1572), Syriac and Latin; RENAUDOT, *Liturgiarum orientalium collectio*, II (2nd ed., Frankfort, 1847), II, 1–560, Latin; BRIGHTMAN, *Eastern Liturgies* (Oxford, 1896), 69–110, using BODERIANUS for the *Ordo communis*, with the Anaphora of St. James.
B. Uniat editions: *Missale Syriacum iuxta ritum ecclesiæ antiochenæ syrorum* (Rome, 1843), Syriac; *Diakonikon* in Syriac only (Beirut, 1888); PRINCE MAX OF SAXONY, *Missa Syro-Antiochena* (Ratisbon, 1908), with the Anaphora of St. John, Latin only.
C. Malabar editions: HOUGH, *Christianity in India*, II (London, 1845), 623–45; HOWARD, *The Christians of St. Thomas* (Oxford, 1864), 199–219.
II. Commentaries:— *Vie de Sévère par Zacharie le Scholastique* in *Patrologia Orientalis*, II (Paris, 1903), 1; LABOURT, *Dionysios Bar Salibi, Expositio liturgiæ* in *Corp. Script. Orient.: Script. Syri*, II (Paris, 1903), 93; ASSEMANI, *Bibliotheca orientalis*, II (Rome, 1719–28), §10; RENAUDOT, *op. cit.*; BAUMSTARK, *Die Messe im Morgenland* in KÖSEL, *Collection* (Kempten and Munich, 1906); *Festbrevier u. Kirchenjahr der syrischen Jakobiten* (Paderborn, 1910).

ADRIAN FORTESCUE.

Syro-Chaldaic Rite. See SYRIAN RITE, EAST.

Syro-Jacobite Liturgy. See SYRIAN RITE, WEST.

Syro-Malabar Church. See THOMAS CHRISTIANS.

Syro-Malabar Rite. See SYRIAN RITE, EAST.

Syro-Maronite Rite. See MARONITES; SYRIAN RITE, WEST.

Szamos-Ujvar. See ARMENIERSTADT.

Szántó (ARATOR), STEPHAN, b. in the Diocese of Raab, Hungary, 1541; d. at Olmütz, 1612. On finishing his studies in Vienna, he attached himself to the Diocese of Raab, and in 1560 was sent by his bishop to the German College at Rome. Here he joined the Jesuit Order, and after his novitiate was ordained priest. In 1566 he returned to Vienna, and thence went as professor to Nagy-Szombát. The succeeding years were spent at the universities of Vienna and Graz, where he lectured on philosophy. From 1568 Szántó strove to found a Catholic mission for Transylvania, where Protestantism was making great headway; this project he continued in Rome, whither he was summoned in 1579 as Hungarian penitentiary. This last position he held until 1579. His endeavours to found a Hungarian college in Rome after the model of the German College met with but temporary success. The monastery of the Hermits of St. Paul near St. Stephen's on the Cœlian was to serve for this purpose; the deed of foundation was approved by Gregory XIII and the college was opened on 28 May, 1579. The pope, however, soon united the college with the German College. At the end of 1579 Szántó left Rome, and proceeded to Transylvania, where he displayed great activity in the work of Catholic missions at Klausenburg (Kolozsvár) and later at Várad. At this time occurred his literary polemics with the Reform preacher, Peter Beregszászi, against whom he wrote his "Epistola apologetica". In 1585 Szántó proceeded to Gyula-Fehérvár and thence, on the expulsion of the Jesuit Order from Transylvania, to Séllye. In 1600 he went to Znióváralja, and in 1605, on the destruction of this place by the troops of Bocskay, to Olmütz, where he remained until his death. During the siege of Znióváralja his books and manuscripts, including the Hungarian catechism which he composed in Rome, were lost; until his death he was working on a translation of the New Testament, which was later used by Georg Káldy. Szántó must also be credited, as has been recently proved, with the Hungarian portion of the great dictionary of Calepino.

FRAKNÓI, *Egy magyar jezsuita a XVI. században* (*A Hungarian Jesuit in the Sixteenth Century*) in *Katolikus Szemle* (Budapest, 1888); SZINNYEI, *Magyar irók* (Hungarian Authors), I; STEINHUBER, *Gesch. des Collegium Germanicum-Hungaricum*, I (Freiburg, 1895).

A. ÁLDÁSY.

Szatmár, DIOCESE OF (SZATMARIENSIS), in Hungary, suffragan of Eger, from which it was formed, by King Francis I, at the same time as the See of Kassa. The diocese includes the counties (*Komitate*) of Szatmár, Bereg, Mármaros, Ugocsa, Ungvar, and a small part of the district of Szabolcs. The first bishop was Stephen Fischer (1804–7), later Archbishop of Eger. Of his successors may be mentioned: Peter Klobusiczky (1807–21), who rendered great service in the organization of the diocese; John Hám (1827–57), who gave great attention to education. Under them the cathedral was enlarged and renewed, and several other churches were built. Many of the charitable institutions of the diocese owe their foundation to Hám, whose beatification is under consideration. Tiburtius Boromisza (1906) is the present bishop. His residence is at Szatmár-Németi. The diocese is divided into 5 archdeaneries, and consists of 95 parishes. The clergy number 177. There are: 1 titular abbey, 2 titular provostships, and 15 monasteries with 703 members. The chapter consists of 6 members and 6 titular canons. Roman Catholics number 149,807; and Greek Catholics, 625,627.

A' *Katolikus Magyarország*, Catholic Hungary (Budapest, 1901); *Schematismus* (1864, 1910).

A. ÁLDÁSY.

Sze-ch'wan, EASTERN, VICARIATE APOSTOLIC OF.—The mission of Eastern Sze-ch'wan was separated from North-western Sze-ch'wan and erected in a vicariate Apostolic in 1856. Its first name was South-eastern Sze-ch'wan. There were nine European and ten native priests. The Right Rev. Mgr Desflèches (1844–87), titular Bishop of Sinita, was elected first vicar Apostolic. Missionaries and Christians had at first to undergo many persecutions. At last after the Franco-Chinese war, in 1860, they obtained entire freedom to preach the Christian doctrine. In 1860 the mission was divided in two vicariates Apostolic: Eastern and Southern Sze-ch'wan. The missionaries got from Chinese officials a piece of ground in the city of Ch'ung-k'ing, as compensation for the losses undergone by the mission. New persecutions broke out. At Yu-yang Father Eyraud was put in jail, Fathers Mabileau and Rigaud were murdered. At Kien-Kiang Fathers Hue and Tay were killed in 1873. On 8 March, 1876, the settlements of the Christians were pillaged at Kiang-pe. Father Coupat was elected coadjutor in 1882, and in 1883 succeeded Bishop Desflèches, appointed Archbishop of Mandianopolis. In 1886 the buildings of the mission at Ch'ung-k'ing were pillaged and destroyed. The bishop and missionaries had to retire into the Chinese tribunal. In 1891 the Right Rev. Mgr Chouvellon, titular Bishop of Dansara, succeeded Bishop Coupat. In 1898 Father Fleury was captured by Yu-man-tse and kept as prisoner for several months. The mission is confided to the Society of the Foreign Missions of Paris. The present vicar Apostolic is the Right Rev. Celestin-Felix-Joseph Chouvellon, consecrated titular Bishop of Dansara in 1891. He resides at Ch'ung-k'ing. In 1889 the mission numbered: 1 bishop, 32 missionaries, 33 native priests, 2 seminaries with 74 students, 151 schools with 1963 pupils, 105 churches or chapels, 31,539 Catholics. In 1910, there were: 1 bishop, 51 missionaries, 46 native priests, 3 seminaries with 130 students, 341 schools with 5365 pupils, 175 churches or chapels, 3 orphanages with 327 orphans, 40,587 Catholics.

LAUNAY, *Atlas de la société des missions-étrangères* (1890).

V. H. MONTANAR.

Sze-ch'wan, NORTH-WESTERN, VICARIATE APOSTOLIC OF.—The mission of North-western Sze-ch'wan includes the territories known as Ch'wan-si and Ch'wan-pe, the cities of Kiong-chu, Ta-y-hien, the Principality of Mu-pin, and a part of the civil prefecture of Tsechu. There are 25,000,000 inhabitants, 23,500,000 are Chinese and 1,500,000 are Barbarian Man-tse. On 17 August, 1658, the Holy See entrusted the mission of Sze-ch'wan to Bishop Pallu, of the Society of the Foreign Missions of Paris, Vicar Apostolic of Tong-king. But neither Bishop Pallu nor his successor, Bishop de Lyonne (1699–1713) who was the first Vicar Apostolic of Sze-ch'wan, could get into the province. In 1707 Fathers de la Balluère and Basset, of the Society of the Foreign Missions of Paris, and Fathers Mullener and Appiani, priests of the Congregation of St. Vincent de Paul, got into Sze-ch'wan where they found some Christians who had emigrated from other provinces. Father de la Balluère, elected vicar Apostolic in 1713, died in 1715 before being consecrated bishop. Father Mullener was consecrated titular Bishop of Myriopolis in 1717. Bishop Enjobert de Martillat succeeded him. He established the Institute of the Christian Virgins. The following four missionaries were elected as vicars Apostolic, but were not consecrated bishops: Fathers Lacerre, Maigrot (1752), de Raymond (1756), Kerhervé (1756). It is only from the year 1765 and the consecration of Bishop Pottier (1769–92) that really dates the existence of this mission. It numbered then about 4000 Christians, including those of Yun-nan and Kwei-chou. Fathers Delpont and Devaux died in the jails of Pekin; Bishop de Saint-Martin (1784–1801), coadjutor and successor to Bishop Pottier, was banished with Father Dufresse. 40,000 pagans were christened. Bishop Dufresse (1801–15) succeeded Bishop de Saint-Martin, with Bishop Frenchant as coadjutor (1802–06). The Synod of Sze-ch'wan took place and completed the organization of the mission. On 14 September, 1815, Blessed Gabriel Taurin-Dufresse, titular Bishop of Tabraca, was sentenced to death and executed. He was beatified in 1900. At the death of the bishop, Sze-ch'wan had only two missionaries, and the Christians were everywhere persecuted. This awful persecution came to an end only in 1840, two years after the death of Bishop Fontana (1820–38), whom Bishop Perocheau (1838–61) succeeded. In 1840 Yun-nan was separated from Sze-ch'wan; Kwei-chou was separated in 1846, South-eastern Sze-ch'wan in 1856, and Southern Sze-ch'wan in 1861. Bishop Pinchon, coadjutor in 1858, succeeded Bishop Perocheau in 1861. In 1864 the seminary of Mu-pin was burned and many Christians killed. On 28 May, 1895, the buildings of the Protestants at Chen-tu were destroyed and the following day the Catholic settlements had a similar fate. The mission of North-western Sze-ch'wan is entrusted to the Society of the Foreign Missions of Paris. The present vicar Apostolic is the Right Rev. Marie-Julien Dunand, consecrated in 1893 titular Bishop of Caloe. He resides at Chen-tu. In 1890 the mission numbered: 1 bishop, 27 missionaries, 39 native priests, 2 seminaries with 87 students, 413 schools with 3023 pupils, 43 churches or chapels, 38,800 Catholics. In 1910 there were: 1 bishop, 39 missionaries, 49 native priests, 2 seminaries with 110 seminarians, 340 schools with 5322 pupils, 5 orphanages with 962 orphans, 105 churches or chapels, 45,000 Catholics.

LAUNAY, *Atlas des missions de la société des missions-étrangères* (1890).

V. H. MONTANAR.

Sze-ch'wan, SOUTHERN, VICARIATE APOSTOLIC OF.—On 24 January, 1860, the mission of Southern Sze-ch'wan was separated from Eastern Sze-ch'wan and erected into a vicariate Apostolic by a Decree of Pius IX. The Right Rev. Mgr Pichon, titular Bishop of Helenopolis, was the first vicar Apostolic. The mission numbered 12,000 Catholics and the bishop there was the only European missionary with three native priests and four chapels. Bishop Desflèches gave him one missionary, Father Larcher, and one Chinese priest. In 1862 Bishop Pichon established a seminary at Ho-ti-keou. In 1871 he died in France, and Bishop Lepley succeeded him. Bishop Chatagnon succeeded Bishop Lepley in 1887. On 28 May, 1895, the buildings of the Protestants at Chen-tu were destroyed. The following day the settlements of Bishop Dunand were also ruined. About half of the Catholic settlements in the Southern Sze-ch'wan missions were destroyed. Bishop Chatagnon escaped into the tribunal of Mei-chou. In July, 1898, a new persecution broke out. In 1900 the mission did not suffer much from the Boxers. In 1902 there was an awful persecution. Many Christians were killed. From 1895 till 1904 there were about thirty Christians murdered on account of their Faith. The mission is entrusted to the Society of the Foreign Missons of Paris. The present vicar Apostolic is Right Rev. Marc Chatagnon, titular Bishop of Chersonesus, who resides at Sui-fu, and has as his

Coadjutor Right Rev. Pierre-Marie Fayolle, consecrated titular Bishop of Lampas in 1909. In 1910 the mission of Kien-Chang was separated from Southern Sze-ch'wan and Father J.-B.-Marie de Guébriant elected bishop and first vicar Apostolic. As this mission has been newly formed, it has been impossible to get any information about the number of the Christians. In 1889 the mission numbered: 1 bishop, 26 missionaries, 9 native priests, 50 catechists, 38 churches and chapels, 1 seminary with 31 students, 68 schools with 1265 pupils, 18,000 Catholics. In 1910 there were 2 bishops, 40 missionaries, 15 native priests, 98 catechists, 2 seminaries with 115 students, 284 schools with 5765 pupils, 6 orphanages with 153 orphans, 104 churches or chapels, 30,618 Catholics.

Compte rendu de la société des missions-étrangères, 1910.

V. H. MONTANAR.

Székes-Fehérvár. See STUHLWEISSENBURG, DIOCESE OF.

Szentiványi, MARTIN, b. at Szentiván, Hungary, 20 October, 1633; d. at Nagy-Szombát (Tyrnau), 5 March, 1708. He entered the Society of Jesus in 1653, and was professor of Scripture for five years at Vienna and Nagy-Szombát, professor of mathematics and philosophy for nine years, and professor of canon law and theology for seven years. For twelve years he filled the office of chancellor of the University of Nagy-Szombát, and in addition was for nine successive years governor of the Pasmaneum in Vienna and of the academy at Nagy-Szombát. His numerous writings appeared in Hungarian, Latin, German, and Slovak, and some were translated into French. The most important are: "Curiosiora et selectiora variarum scientiarum miscellanea in tres partes divisa" (Tyrnau, 1689); "Dissertationes septem, etc." (Tyrnau, 1689); "Rectus modus interpretandi scripturam sacram" (Tyrnau, 1696); "Summarium chronologiæ Hungariæ" (Tyrnau, 1697); "Hungaria in immaculatam conceptionem b. Mariæ virginis magnæ dominæ suæ credens et iuvans" (Tyrnau, 1701); "Doctrina fidei christianæ" (Louvain, 1708); "Lutheranicum nunquam et nusquam" (Tyrnau, 1702); "Relatio status futuræ vitæ" (Tyrnau, 1699); "Dissertationes hæresiologico-polemicæ de hæresiarchis, hæresibus, et erroribus in fide, dogmatibus, hoc sæculo nostro (Tyrnau, 1701); "Solutiones catholicæ, etc." (Tyrnau, 1701); "Quinquaginta rationes et motiva cur in tanta varietate religionum et confessionum fidei in christianitate moderno tempore vigentium, sola religio Romano-catholica sit eligenda et omnibus aliis preferenda" (Tyrnau, 1701; German and Hungarian, Tyrnau, 1702).

SZINNYEI, *Magyar Írók* (Hungarian Authors), XIII, 741–45, contains a complete list of his works and bibliography.

A. ALDÁSY.

Szeny. See ZENGG-MODRUS, DIOCESE OF.

Szepes. See ZIPS, DIOCESE OF.

Szerem. See SIRMIUM, DIOCESE OF.

Szombathely. See STEINAMANGER, DIOCESE OF.

Szujski, JOSEPH, b. at Tarnow, 1835; d. at Cracow, 1883. He studied at Tarnow, then at Cracow (1854) and at Vienna (1858–9). He began his career as a poet, and continued to write verses till the end of his brief and fruitful life. Apart from many short lyrical poems, his first attempts were dramatic: "Samuel Zborowski", "Halszka of Ostrog", and a translation of the "Agamemnon" of Æschylus. Before his marriage (1861) he had also published his "Portraits, not by Van Dyck", in which various types of Poles are characterized perhaps too roughly, but with acumen, often with accuracy. He began working at a manual of Polish history, publishing two volumes in 1862, but was presently convinced of the necessity of independent research, of which volumes three and four (1864–6) give good evidence. The calamitous insurrection of 1863 was a terrible blow to Szujski's buoyant hopes for Poland's future, and he resolved to devote his whole life to seeking the causes of his beloved country's misfortunes, with a view to her regeneration. At the time that he was publishing the poems: "The Servant of the Tombs", "The Defence of Czestochowa", and the dramas, "George Lubomirski" and "Wallas", he placed himself in the front rank of Polish historians by his work, "Some Truths of our History" (1865). "No nation", he said, "can fall save through her own fault, nor rise again, save by her own intelligent labour and spiritual activity"; and he most courageously indicated all Poland's faults, not however omitting the means of reformation. He founded the "Polish Review" (1866), and the next year brought out "Hedwige" and "Twardowski", both dramas. When the use of the national language was restored in Cracow University, Szujski was named (1869) professor of Polish history; later, he was chosen rector. As early as 1872, he was the life and the moving spirit of the Academy of Sciences at Cracow in his capacity of secretary. About that time, for his researches were not confined to Poland, he published a sketch of the literary history of the non-Christian world; studies on Marcus Aurelius and on Lucian; translations from Æschylus and Aristophanes; "Maryna Mnischowna", and "The Death of Ladislaus IV", dramas of his own, together with several other works. After his rectorate (1879) Szujski was made a peer. But his health, which had always been precarious, now failed completely, and consumption set in. He continued to work, however, till he could work no more.

As a historian, Szujski ranks with Kalinka. He united the most ardent patriotism with a supreme love for truth and a remarkable comprehension of political situations and the characters of those who played their parts in them; consequently no one could explain so well as he the sequence of events and the causes which, for good or evil, influenced the nation. His history, first sketched in four volumes, from the sixteenth century on, was supplemented by three other volumes, entitled "Relations and Researches"; the most admirable parts being those dealing with the Renaissance and the Reformation. It has been said of him that "the historian killed the poet"; and indeed his attempts to force into his historical dramas every incident relative to their times in many cases impede their proper development; but he allowed history to dominate his art through a feeling of duty to his country. The lessons which he found in the annals of the nation he sought to reproduce upon the stage. He was himself well aware of his shortcomings, and believed his plays destined merely to pave the way for a simpler expression of patriotic feeling, without morbid sentimentality. Though sometimes lacking in style, due to the great amount of work which he undertook, Szujski was a great historian, a poet of high ideals and aspirations, and one to whom the Polish nation of the present day owes much.

SMOLKA, *Joseph Szujski* (Cracow, 1883); GERMAN, *O dramatach Szujskiego* (Cracow, 1887); TARNOWSKI, *Szujski jako poeta* (Cracow, 1901). Also the histories of Polish literature by BRÜCKNER, TARNOWSKI, and others.

ST. TARNOWSKI.

Szymonowicz, SIMON, known also by the Latin name of Simonides, b. at Lemberg, 1558; d. 1629. He studied first at Lemberg, afterwards in the Cracow Academy, and then abroad in the Netherlands and in France. On his return, he became a private tutor; among other young men, he taught Sobieski's father and the son of John Zolkiewski, who took Moscow. He enjoyed intimate relations with the famous John Zamoyski, whose son he also educated; after which (1614) he retired to the country, where he remained until his death. He was never married. Szymonowicz may be styled the last of the Polish Humanists, to whom indeed he belongs both by his erudition and by the character of his creations. He spent the greater part of his life writing Latin poems, once much appreciated throughout Europe. The best of these are: "Flagellum Livoris", a collection of odes dedicated to Zamoyski; "Ælinopæan", in honour of one of Zamoyski's victories; "Joel Propheta", a paraphrase of the Book of Joel, inscribed to Clement VIII, whom our poet had known personally as a legate in Poland; "Hercules Prodiceus", written for his pupil, the young Thomas Zamoyski; and two dramas: "Penthesilea" and "Castus Joseph".

His first Polish verses were written in 1606, in favour of the rebellion of Zebrzydowski. He also wrote a few fugitive poems, but his fame mainly rests on his "Idyls", which appeared in 1614. They were the first and still remain the best poems of the kind in the Polish language. They faithfully follow the old classical type, so often imitated by French and Italian Humanists in the fifteenth and sixteenth centuries; but under this form there is a true national element, and the Polish landscape and peasantry are gracefully described. Like Virgil's "Eclogues", all are short; several were composed on special occasions. Not all are uniformly beautiful, indeed the finest are often marred by weak passages. But they have the merit of simplicity, not unfrequent depth of feeling or pleasant wit and humour, profound political allusions, clarity of thought and a noble diction. His influence is visible in the writings of both the Zimorowicz, and also in Gavinski's "Idyls". More recently he has been imitated by Naruszewicz, and at times by Kniaznin and Karpinski. In the nineteenth century Mickiewicz appreciated him admirably in his course of lectures on Slavic literature, and, we may say, rediscovered him.

BIELOWSKI, *Szymon Szymonowicz* (Cracow, 1875); TYSZYNSKI, *Szymonowicz i jegosielanki* (Warsaw, 1875); WEILEWSKI, *Sielanki Szymona Szymonowicza* (Kutno, 1864); KALLENBACH, *Szymonowicza Dramat Castus Joseph* (Warsaw, 1892); URANOWICZ, *Zywot S. Szymonowiera* (Zloczow, 1894); CHRZANOWSKI, *Tragedya S. Szymonowicza Castus Joseph* (Warsaw, 1892); HAHN, *Szymonowicz jakz filo of* (Lemberg, 1897).

ST. TARNOWSKI.

T

Tabæ, titular see in Caria, suffragan of Stauropolis; according to Strabo (XII, 570, 576) it was located in a plain in Phrygia on the boundaries of Caria. Stephanus Byzantius (s.v.) mentions two cities of this name, one in Lydia, the other in Caria. Livy (XXXVIII, 13) says that it was on the frontier of Pisidia towards the coast of the Gulf of Pamphylia. The town in question, however, some coins of which are extant, was one which claimed to have been founded by one Tabus. Others derive its name from *tabi*, which in Semitic languages means "good", and others from a native word *taba*, meaning "rock", which seems a probable derivation. In 189 B. C. the consul Gneius Malius Vulso, having defeated the natives who blocked his passage, exacted from Tabæ a fine of 25 talents and 10,000 *medimni* of wheat. Three bishops of Tabæ are known: Rufinus, present at the Council of Ephesus (431); Severus, at Constantinople (553); Basilius, at Nicæa (787) (Le Quien, "Oriens christ.", I, 905). The "Notitiæ Episcopatuum" continue to mention the see among the suffragans of Stauropolis until the thirteenth century. Tabæ is now the village of Davas which gives its name to a caza of the vilayet of Smyrna; some inscriptions and numerous ancient remains are found.

SMITH, *Dict. of Greek and Roman Geogr.*, s. v.; PAPE-BENSELER, *Wörterbuch der griechischen Eigennamen*, s. v.; TEXIER, *Asie mineure* (Paris, 1862), 466.

S. PÉTRIDÈS.

Tabasco, DIOCESE OF (TABASQUENSIS), in the Republic of Mexico, suffragan of the Archbishopric of Yucatán. It comprises the States of Tabasco, having an area of 10,872 sq. miles and a population (in 1910) of 183,805. The bishop and the governor reside at San Juan Bautista, founded in 1598 under the name of Villa de Felipe II, known as Villa Hermosa till 1826, when it got its present name. The city has at present (1910) a population of 12,084 inhabitants. In the decree of Charles V, 19 September, 1525, we read:—"At the request and with the express assent of the said Bishop Don Fray Julián Garcés, we declare, make known, and appoint as the boundaries of the said Bishopric of Yucatán and Santa María de los Remedios the following provinces and territories: First, the entire Province of Tlaxcaltechle, and San Juan de Ullua, ...; the Villa de Medellín and the territory of Tabasco", etc. The Gospel was preached here in the early period of the Spanish conquest. In 1545 the Dominican Fathers going to Chiapas passed through Tabasco and in 1578 organized the house of Oxolotlán, the first vicar of which was Padre Tomás Aguilar. Christianity in Tabasco must already have made considerable progress, for Philip II during the time of the Viceroy Velasco planned the erection of a see there. Philip III also intended to do so, in 1609, but was unsuccessful. Another futile attempt was made in 1680. Finally, in 1864, Mgr. Rodríguez de la Gala, Apostolic administrator, later Bishop, of Yucatán, promoted the establishment of a see which was created by Leo XIII on the petition of Mgr. Labastida, Archbishop of Mexico. The new diocese was established in 1880 from parishes taken from the Sees of Chiapas, Oaxaca, and Yucatán. It was suffragan to the Archdiocese of Mexico until 1891; to the See of Oaxaca from 1891 till 1906; and finally in 1906 to the See of Yucatán. The diocese contains: an ecclesiastical seminary with 6 students; 7 parochial schools; 4 Catholic colleges, and about 600 *alumni;* a Protestant college with 25 pupils; and 3 churches.

VERA, *Catecismo geográfico-histórico-estadístico de la Iglesia mexicana* (Amecameca, 1881); CARILLO, *El Obispado de Yukatán* (Mérida, 1895).

CAMILLUS CRIVELLI.

Tabb, JOHN BANNISTER, an American poet and educator, b. at "The Forest" near Richmond, 1845; d. at Ellicott City, Md., 1909. Descended from one of the oldest and wealthiest Virginian families, he was carefully trained by private tutors. At the age of fourteen his sight was so poor that he had to give up his books, and for three years spent much time at the piano, becoming proficient in music. On the breaking out of the Civil War he enlisted under the Confederacy and served in the navy till taken captive, 4 June, 1864. He was sent to the "Bull-Pen" at Point Lookout, where he formed an enduring friendship with Sidney Lanier. Released from prison the following February, he was penniless. He undertook to fit himself for a musical career and to that end practised seven hours a day. His patron failing, he was obliged to maintain himself as a teacher, securing a position at St. Paul's School, Baltimore. While there he fell under the influence of the Rev. Alfred Curtis, who later on was converted from Episcopalianism to the Catholic Church. Tabb followed his master into the fold in 1872. A few years later he entered St. Charles's College to prepare for the priesthood. On completing his classical studies he was retained by the faculty as teacher of English. Thus interrupted, his theological studies were not completed till the Christmas of 1884, when he was ordained. He continued to teach English Grammar at St. Charles's till a short time before his death and till he had become totally blind. His "Bone Rules" is counted a valuable contribution to his art. It is his only prose work. Father Tabb consecrated all his energies to the vocation of teacher. His poems were written here, there, and everywhere; but every one of them bears the stamp of a highly cultivated and gifted mind. They were contributed to the foremost magazines and were read with avidity. Concise and suggestive, these literary gems cling to the fancy and thus realize the modest ambition of their author as expressed in the opening poem of his "Later Lyrics":

"O little bird, I'd be
A poet like to thee
Singing my native song,
Brief to the ear, but long
To love and memory."

In the lyric field he was greatly admired. Under his muse inanimate things took on life and beauty and the abstract became concrete and personal. His poems are collected in five volumes which were published in the following order: "Poems"; "Lyrics"; "Child Verse"; "Later Lyrics"; "Sonnets".

MEYNELL, *Father Tabb* in *The Catholic World* (Feb., 1910); DUGGAN, *Father Tabb* in *America* (5, 12, 19 Feb., 1910).

T. S. DUGGAN.

Tabbora, a titular see in Africa Proconsularis, suffragan of Carthage. Tabbora or Talbora has been identified with two groups of ruins rather close to each other, now called Tembra, west of Bijga (ancient Bisica) in the valley of Wady Siliana, Tunis. Two bishops are known: Marinus, present at the Conference of Carthage (411), where his rival was Victor, also rival of the Bishop of Bisica; and Constantine, who signed the letter from the bishops of the province to Paul, Patriarch of Constantinople, against the Monothelites (646).

TOULOTTE, *Géog. de l'Afrique Chrétienne: Proconsulaire* (Paris, 1892), 257.

S. PÉTRIDÈS.

Tabernacle (TABERNACULUM) signified in the Middle Ages sometimes a ciborium-altar, a structure resting on pillars and covered with a baldachino that was set over an altar, sometimes an ostensory or monstrance, a tower-shaped vessel for preserving and exhibiting relics and the Blessed Sacrament, sometimes, lastly, like to-day, it was the name of the vessel holding the pyx. That is, at the present time in ecclesiastical usage it is only the name for the receptacle or case placed upon the table of the high altar or of another altar in which the vessels containing the Blessed Sacrament, as the ciborium, monstrance, custodia, are kept. As a rule, in cathedrals and monastic churches it is not set upon the high altar but upon a side altar, or the altar of a special sacramentary chapel; this is to be done both on account of the reverence due the Holy Sacrament and to avoid impeding the course of the ceremonies in solemn functions at the high altar. On the other hand it is generally to be placed upon the high altar in parish churches as the most befitting position ("Cærem. ep.", I, xii, No. 8; "Rit. rom.", tit. IV, i, no. 6; S. C. Episc., 10 February, 1579). A number of decisions have been given by the Sacred Congregation of Rites regarding the tabernacle. According to these, to mention the more important decisions, relics and pictures are not to be displayed for veneration either on or before the tabernacle ("Decreta auth.", nos. 2613, 2906). Neither is it permissible to place a vase of flowers in such manner before the door of the tabernacle as to conceal it (no. 2067). The interior of the tabernacle must either be gilded or covered with white silk (no. 4035, ad 4); but the exterior is to be equipped with a mantle-like hanging, that must be either always white or is to be changed according to the colour of the day; this hanging is called the *canopeum* (no. 3520; cf. "Rit. rom., loc. cit.). A benediction of the tabernacle is customary but is not prescribed.

HISTORY.—In the Middle Ages there was no uniform custom in regard to the place where the Blessed Sacrament was kept. The Fourth Lateran Council and many provincial and diocesan synods held in the Middle Ages require only that the Host be kept in a secure, well-fastened receptacle. At the most they demand that it be put in a clean, conspicuous place. Only a few synods designate the spot more closely, as the Synods of Cologne (1281) and of Münster (1279), which commanded that it was to be kept above the altar and protected by locking with a key. In general, four main methods of preserving the Blessed Sacrament may be distinguished in medieval times: (1) in a cabinet in the sacristy, a custom that is connected with early Christian usage; (2) in a cupboard in the wall of the choir or in a projection from one of the walls which was constructed like a tower, was called Sacrament-House, and sometimes reached up to the vaulting; (3) in a dove or pyx, surrounded by a cover or receptacle and generally surmounted by a small baldachino, which hung over the altar by a chain or cord; (4) lastly, upon the altar table, either in the pyx alone or in a receptacle similar to a tabernacle, or in a small cupboard arranged in the reredos or predella of the altar. This last method is mentioned in the "Admonitio synodalis" of the ninth century by Regino of Prüm (d. 915), later by Durandus, and in the regulations issued by the Synods of Trier and Münster already mentioned. Reredoses containing cupboards to hold the Blessed Sacrament can be proved to have existed as early as the fourteenth century, as, for instance, the altar of St. Clara in the Cologne cathedral, although they were not numerous until the end of the medieval period. The high altar dating from 1424 in the Church of St. Martin at Landshut, Bavaria, is an example of the combination of reredos and Sacrament-House. From the sixteenth century it became gradually, although slowly, more customary to preserve the Blessed Sacrament in a receptacle that rose above the altar table. This was the case above all at Rome, where the custom first came into use, and in Italy in general, influenced largely by the good example set by St. Charles Borromeo. The change came very slowly in France, where even in the eighteenth century it was still customary in many cathedrals to suspend the Blessed Sacrament over the altar, and also in Belgium and Germany, where the custom of using the Sacrament-House was maintained in many places until after the middle of the nineteenth century, when the decision of the Sacred Congregation of Rites of 21 August, 1863, put an end to the employment of such receptacles.

THIERS, *Traité de l'exposition du St-Sacrement de l'autel* (Paris, 1673); CORBLET, *Hist. du Sacrement de l'Eucharistie*, I (Paris, 1885); ROHAULT DE FLEURY, *La Messe*, II (Paris, 1883); LAIB AND SCHWARZ, *Studien über die Geschichte des christl. Altars* (Stuttgart, 1857); SCHMID, *Der christl. Altar* (Ratisbon, 1871); RAIBLE, *Tabernakel Einst u. Jetzt* (Freiburg, 1908).

JOSEPH BRAUN.

Tabernacle (Latin *tabernaculum*, tent) in Biblical parlance usually designates the movable tent-like sanctuary of the Hebrews before the erection of Solomon's Temple. The various expressions in the Hebrew text in reference to the Tabernacle (*'ohel*, tent; *'ohel mo'ed*, tent of meeting; *'ohel ha-'eduth*, tent of the testimony; *mishkan*, dwelling; *mishkan ha- 'eduth*, dwelling of the testimony; *mishkan 'ohel*, dwelling of the tent; *beth Yahweh*, house of Yahweh; *qodesh*, holy; *miqdash*, sanctuary; *hekal*, temple), while enabling us to form a fair idea of this construction, raise, by the seeming consistency of the passages in which they severally occur, many problems with which all modern commentators of the Scriptures have to grapple. Thus, Exodus describes the ark as sheltered in a tent (xxxiii, 7; Hebr. *'ohel mo'ed*), whose position was "without the camp afar off" (Cf. Num., xi, 16 sqq.; 24–30; xii; Deut., xxxi, 14 sqq.), guarded by "Josue the son of Nun" (11), and at the door of which Yahweh was wont to manifest himself to Moses (9–11; cf. Num., xii, 5; Deut., xxxi, 15). That this "tent of tryst" (or better, perhaps, "tent of the oracle") was not identical with the tabernacle modern independent critics urge from the fact that this *'ohel mo'ed* was in existence before Beseleel and Ooliab commenced the construction of the Tabernacle (Ex., xxxv–xxxvi) and that the customary place of the latter was in the very midst of the encampment (Num., ii, 1 sqq.; x, 15 sqq.). Much stress is laid upon this and other seeming discrepancies to conclude that the description of the tabernacle found in Ex., xxv–xxxi, xxxix–xl, is the work of the post-exilian authors of the Priestly Code.

Assuming, however, the historical accuracy of the Biblical narratives, we shall limit ourselves here to a brief description of that "portable sanctuary" of the Hebrews. In this sanctuary we should distinguish the tent or tabernacle proper from the sacred enclosure in which the tent stood. The "court of the tabernacle" (Ex., xxvii, 9) was a rectangular space, measuring 100 by 50 cubits (probably the Egyptian cubit, 20¾ ins.), screened off by curtains of "fine twisted linen" (xxvii, 9), 5 cubits high, 100 cubits long on the north and south sides, 50 on the east and 15 on the west, and 20 cubits on either side of the entrance. The entrance was closed by a hanging of fine twisted linen, embroidered in violet, purple, and scarlet and "twice dyed" on a white ground (probable meaning of Ex., xxvii, 16). All these curtains were suspended from sixty pillars, but not in a "loose and flowing manner", as Josephus wrongly states, since the total length of the curtains is exactly the same as the perimeter of the court, one pillar being assigned to every five cubits of curtain. These pillars of setimwood, five cubits high, stood on bases ("sockets", Ex., xxxix, 39) of brass and were held in position by means of cords (ibid., xxxix, 40) fastened to brass pegs ("pins", ibid., xxxv, 18) which were stuck in the ground; the pillars ended in a capital ("head", Exod., xxxix, 17, etc.; we must believe that the height given above includes both the base and capital of the pillar) with a band or necking (to hang the curtain) overlaid with silver. East of the entrance were found successively: the altar of holocausts (Ex., xxvii, 1–8, etc.), the brazen layer (xxx, 18–21; xxxviii, 8, etc.), and the tabernacle proper. The latter was conceived to be the dwelling-tent of God; hence it consisted essentially of curtains, the wooden framework, though indispensable, being only of secondary importance. The whole structure measured 30 by 10 cubits, and was divided into two sections; the one to the west, the "Holy Place", containing the altar of incense, the golden candlestick, and the table of shewbreads; and the other, the "Holy of Holies", containing the Ark of the Covenant with the propitiatory and the cherubim. These sections were respectively 20 and 10 cubits long.

Jewish exegetical tradition, followed by almost every Christian exponent of the Bible, understood the wooden framework to be made up of 48 massive boards (rather beams) of setim wood, measuring 10 by 1½ by 1 cubit, placed side by side. This means a weight (about fifty tons) out of proportion with what these beams would have to bear and very difficult of transportation. Some modern scholars having studied more closely the technical terms used in the original adopt another view. According to them the "boards" of the tabernacle must be understood as light frames consisting of two uprights joined (probably at the top, middle, and bottom) by ties or cross-rails (the "mortises" in Ex., xxvi, 17). Of these frames, overlaid with gold (xxvi, 29), there were 20 on the north side of the tabernacle, 20 on the south, and 6 on the east. To provide solidity and rigidity, a slanting frame was put at the north-east and south-east corners to buttress the structure (xxvi, 23); the lower part of the uprights was sunk deep into silver sockets or bases, probably to be understood as square blocks (about 1 cubit high and ¾ cubit square); finally, five wooden bars, passing through rings attached to the frames, ran along the sides (xxvi, 26–28). On the west the frames were to be replaced by five pillars of setim-wood overlaid with gold, sunk in brass bases, and crowned with golden capitals (xxvi, 37). Four pillars of the same workmanship, with silver bases, separated the Holy Place from the Holy of Holies.

A curtain, two pieces of fine tapestry joined by golden rings, was spread over the whole framework; each piece of tapestry consisted of five strips, 28 by 4 cubits, fitted together by loops. The total dimension of this being 20 by 40 cubits, it must have reached on the north and south the top of the bases, against which it was possibly fixed (there were loops at the top of the curtains likely for this purpose), whereas on the east it reached to the ground. Covering this curtain was another, woven of goats' hair (the ordinary tent material), fitted in somewhat similarly; its dimensions, 11 (6+5)×4=44 by 30 cubits, were so calculated as to cover entirely the inside curtain on the north, east, and south sides and to hang down doubled on the west side, thus covering the tops and capitals of the pillars (Ex., xxvi, 7–13). Two outer coverings (no dimensions are given), one of dyed rams' skin and one of dugongs' skin, protected the whole structure. A hanging, of apparently the same workmanship as that closing the entrance of the court, screened the entrance of the tabernacle (ibid., 36); finally, a veil of the same tapestry as the inner curtain, hooked from the four pillars mentioned above, completed the separation of the Holy of Holies from the Holy Place.

History.—Delayed by the people's outburst of idolatrous worship pending the long intercourse of Moses with God on Mount Sinai, the construction was achieved by the skilful workmen selected by God, and was dedicated on the first day of the second year after the flight from Egypt. Henceforth the tabernacle, under the special care of the Levites of the family of Gerson, accompanied the Israelites through their wanderings in the wilderness; during marches, it came after the first six tribes and before the other six (Num., ii, 3–34); in encampments, it occupied the middle of the camp, three tribes being on each side. After the crossing of the Jordan, it remained very likely at Galgala until its removal to Silo (Jos., xviii, 1), where it remained many years. In Saul's time we hear of the tabernacle at Nobe (I Kings, xxi, 1–6), and later at Gabaon (I Par., xvi, 39), until Solomon had it removed to his new Temple (III Kings, viii, 4; II Par., v, 5). It disappeared in the first years of the sixth century B. C., being either taken away by the Babylonian army in 588, or, if credence be given the letter prefacing II Mach., hidden by Jeremias in an unknown and secure place.

JOSEPHUS, *Jewish Antiquities*, III, vi; PHILO, *De Vita Moysis*. Talmud Babyl.: Tract. *Middoth*, a baraitha gives the opinions of the ancient doctors on the subject. BROWN, *The Tabernacle* (6th ed., 1899); ORR, *The Problem of the O. T.* (New York, 1906); OTTLEY, *Aspects of the O. T.* (Oxford, 1897); WELLHAUSEN, *Prolegomena* (Edinburgh, 1885); WESTCOTT, *Essay on the General Significance of the Tabernacle* in *The Epistle to the Hebrews* (New York, 1889), 233 sqq.; BÄHR, *Symbolik des mosaisch. Kultus* (1837–39); FRIEDRICH, *Symbolik der mos. Stiftshütte* (Leipzig, 1841); GRAF, *Die geschichtl. Bücher des A. T.* (Leipzig, 1866), 51 sqq.; NEUMANN, *Die Stiftshütte* (Gotha, 1861); POPPER, *Der bibl. Bericht über die Stiftshütte* (Leipzig, 1862); RIGGENBACH, *Die mosaisch. Stiftshütte* (1861); SCHICK, *Stiftshütte u. Tempel* (1898).

CHARLES L. SOUVAY.

Tabernacles, FEAST OF, one of the three great feasts of the Hebrew liturgical calendar, even the greatest, according to Philo (ἑορτῶν μεγίστη) and Josephus (ἑορτὴ ἁγιωτάτη καὶ μεγίστη). The common name, feast of Tabernacles—among Greek-speaking Jews σκηνοπηγία, that is, "the pitching of the tent" (John, vii, 2)—recalls to mind the custom established by the law of Lev., xxiii, 40, of erecting on the roofs of houses, and even in streets and public squares, booths of branches and foliage, wherein all who were not exempted through illness or weakness were obliged to live during the entire celebration. It is sometimes asserted that the origin of the feast was similar to our "harvest-home" festivities.

This naturalistic view, based on the assumption that the religious enactments of the Law are of relatively recent date and mere sacerdotal ordinances, takes no account of the significance which at all times attached to the feast. True it is that one of the features of the celebrations was to be, after a fashion, a harvest-home, and to offer thanksgiving for the crops of the year (Deut., xvi, 13; Ex., xxiii, 16); and it is perhaps owing to this special feature that the character of the feast was one of joy and merriment (cf. Ps. iv, 7–8, in Heb.; Joseph., Ant., VIII, iv, 1), and that numerous sacrifices were then offered (Num., xxix, 12–39); yet to the Jews the feast of Tabernacles was always and primarily in commemoration of their forefathers' indwelling in tents in the wilderness (Lev., xxiii, 43) and in thanksgiving for the permanent abode given them in the Promised Land, and, later on, after the erection of the Temple, for a permanent place of worship (cf. III Kings, viii, 2; xii, 32). The feast began on the fifteenth day of the seventh month, Ethanim of Tishri (about our September), and lasted seven days (Lev., xxiii, 34–36). Every male Israelite was, according to law, obliged to go to Jerusalem, and "every one who was of the people of Israel" was bound to live in booths, which, though involving some discomfort, at the same time contributed much to the merriment attending the celebration. The distinctions between rich and poor were then somewhat obliterated in the general encampment, and thus the feast had a most beneficial social influence. The first day was held most solemn and considered a sabbath, all servile work being forbidden on that day (Lev., xxiii, 39; Num., xxix, 35); during the whole octave numerous sacrifices were offered (Num., xxix, 12–39) and on the eighth day [styled the great(est) day of the feast in John, vii, 37], was held a sabbath like the first and marked by special sacrifices of its own, the booths were broken up and the people returned home.

After the Exile, the feast was protracted to the twenty-fifth of the month, and two new rites were added to the old ceremonial. Every morning of the celebration a priest went down to the Siloe Fountain, whence he brought in a golden ewer water which was poured on the altar of holocausts amidst the singing of the Hallel (Pss. cxii–cxvii) and the joyful sound of musical instruments. It was possibly the performance of this ceremony (the institution of which may have been suggested by Is., xii, 3) which afforded to Our Lord the occasion to compare the action of the Holy Ghost in the faithful to a spring of living water (John, vii, 37–39). The other new feature added to the ritual of the feast was the illuminations of the women's court, together with the singing of the Psalms of the Degrees (Pss. cxix–cxxxiii) and the performance of dances or processions in the sacred precincts. On the eighth day a procession went seven times around the altar, the people carrying myrtle-boughs and palms and shouting: "Hosannah!" in memory of the fall of Jericho.

Every seven years, that is in the year of release, during the feast of Tabernacles, the Law was to be read before all the people according to the command found in Deut., xxxi, 10. But this enactment was probably soon found to be impracticable; and thus the Jewish authorities arranged to read on every sabbath, commencing with the sabbath after the feast of Tabernacles in one year of release and ending with the feast of Tabernacles in the next year of release, a portion of the Law so calculated that the whole Pentateuch would be read through in seven years. Thus would in some way the commandment be fulfilled. Some time later, the Jews of Palestine lengthened the sections for each sabbath in such a manner that the entire Law could be read in three years (Talm. Babyl. Megillah, 29b). At present (and this custom seems to go back to the first century B. C.) the Jews have the Pentateuch so divided that they read it through every year, the first *Parashah* (division) being appointed for the sabbath after the feast of Tabernacles, and the last chapters for the last day of the feast in the next year, this being the day of "rejoicing in the Law".

GREEN, *The Hebrew Feasts* (Cincinnati, 1886); IKEN, *Antiquitates Hebraicæ* (Bremen, 1741); RELAND, *Antiquitates sacræ* (Utrecht, 1741); BAHR, *Symbolik des mosaischen Cultus* (Heidelberg, 1839); BENZIGER, *Herbräische Archäologie* (Frieburg im Br., 1894); SCHEGG, *Biblische Archäologie* (Freiburg im Br., 1894), 591 sq.; WELLHAUSEN, *Prolegomena zur geschichte Israels* (4th ed., Berlin, 1895); EDERSHEIM, *The Life and Times of Jesus the Messiah* (New York, 1897), II, 149, 156–160, 165; IDEM, *The Temple, Its Ministry and Services* (London, 1874), 232–49; *Talmud*, ROOKINSON (Boston, s. d.), IV, Tract. Succah; KORTLEITNER, *Archæol. Bibl.* (Innsbruck, 1906), 99–101; LESÊTRE in VIG., *Dict. de la Bible*, V, 1961–66.

CHARLES L. SOUVAY.

Tabernacle Societies.—The Association of Perpetual Adoration of the Blessed Sacrament and of work for poor churches was founded at Brussels in 1848 by Anne de Meeûs. By 1851 it had the approval of the bishops of Belgium. Within a few years a number of its members formed themselves into a religious congregation, that of the Sisters of Perpetual Adoration (q. v.), Mdlle de Meeûs becoming the first superior general. In 1853 the society became an archconfraternity for Belgium, but quickly spread to the nearby countries where it met similar needs and received similar privileges, and in 1863 Pius IX granted the mother-society at Brussels the right to affiliate confraternities throughout the world, except in the city of Rome. This last restriction was removed when the mother-house of the Sisters of Perpetual Adoration was transferred to Rome, which then became the centre of the association. An archconfraternity with the same name and purpose already existing at Rome, but founded subsequent to that of Brussels, was merged with the latter. The statutes of the archconfraternity were approved by the Congregation of Bishops and Regulars, 12 January, 1880, and Leo XIII by a Brief of 21 June, 1881, approved its transfer to Rome and right to affiliate; and by a Brief of 30 July, 1895, granted it the title of *Prima Primaria*.

The members pledge themselves to spend an hour each month in adoration before the Blessed Sacrament and to pay yearly dues into a fund for the benefit of poor churches. The contributions are used to purchase materials for vestments which are made by women members of the society and given to poor churches. A great work is thus done and many churches have been benefited in Belgium, Germany, Austria, England, the United States, and the mission fields. The eleventh Eucharistic Congress was held in Brussels in 1898 in the church in which the society was founded, and on that occasion a glowing tribute was paid to its work. In Belgium alone it has nearly 200,000 members. Special mention should be made of the association as it is maintained in convents of Religious of the Sacred Heart. It was founded in the houses of the United States by Rev. Mother Hardey, then assistant superior general of the Society, on the occasion of her visit in 1874. She established it in connexion with the Sodality of the Children of Mary, and its marvellous growth and work for poor churches are attested by the annual reports issued by each house. Paris is the centre of the Archconfraternity of Perpetual Adoration and work for Tabernacles, founded there in the Church of St. Thomas Aquinas in 1846 and with affiliations in the dioceses of France and Algiers. It was approved by Pius IX in 1856 and made a confraternity in 1858.

BERINGER, *Les Indulgences*, II (Paris, 1905), 130, 133; RUGGIERI, *L'œuvre de l' Adoration perpetuelle et des églises pauvres* (Brussels, 1881); MARY ALOYSIA HARDEY, *Religious of the Sacred Heart* (New York, 1910).

BLANCHE M. KELLY.

Tabernacle Society, Notre Dame Convent, Philadelphia, a society of persons affiliated with the Association of Perpetual Adoration and Work for Churches in Rome. The Philadelphia organization was begun by five graduates of the convent in 1866, who formed the first Sodality of the Children of Mary in that city, affiliated with the Roman Sodality, who resolved to do some work for the altar. On 1 Oct., 1878, Archbishop Wood had the society affiliated to the Association of Perpetual Adoration and Work for Poor Churches in Brussels. This association was transferred to Rome in 1879, and the Philadelphia organization was aggregated to it 8 Oct., 1881. There are now 22 societies in the United States thus aggregated with the arch-association. The Philadelphia Association is authorized to affiliate parishes, and these share in all the benefits. From the beginning until the present the Philadelphia Society has enrolled over 10,000 members. It now has 1800 active members in and around the city, and many more throughout the country in affiliated parishes. It has the approbation of 92 archbishops and bishops. It has helped about 4600 parishes and missions in every part of the United

States, and many foreign countries. It expends about $4000 a year for materials which are made up by the members without compensation. About 100 sacred vessels are given away each year, and these are all donated, generally as memorials of the dead or for some favour received. The association publishes its "Annals" three times a year: the January number contains the report for the previous year.

Manual of Tabernacle Soc., and *Annals of Association of Perpetual Adoration and Work for Poor Churches* (Notre Dame Convent, Philadelphia).

JAMES P. TURNER.

Tabor. See THABOR.

Tacana Indians, the collective designation for a group of tribes constituting the Tacanan linguistic stock in different dialects, occupying the upper valleys of the Beni and Madre de Dios Rivers, on the eastern slope of the Andes, Department of Beni, northwestern Bolivia. The group includes: the Tacana proper, the Isiamo, the Cavina, and the Aten or Leco, all missionized by the Franciscan Fathers of the College of Ocopa, Peru, about the end of the eighteenth century; the still uncivilized Toromona and Araume and several others; and the more remote Sapibocona of the Moxos mission farther to the south. In 1832 the five Tacana missions contained 5304 Christian Indians, while the wild Toromona were estimated at 1000 more. In 1852 the traveller Weddell spent some time at the mission of Guanay and has given us a good description of the Indians as he found them. In 1883 Heath reports them as greatly reduced, the 1000 Cavina of 1832 having dwindled to 70 souls. Like their neighbours, the Mozetena and Yurucare, the Tacana are noted for their light complexion, fine features, and tall stature, averaging over five and a half feet. Of their language, which is extremely guttural and jerky in pronunciation, we have vocabularies by Heath and Weddell, besides a small devotional publication. In their primitive condition they subsisted, and still do, by agriculture, hunting, and fishing, went naked except for feather decorations on dance occasions, and lived in small communities subject to petty chiefs. Some of their tribes were reputed cannibals. The civilized Tacana wear as their principal garment a sleeveless shirt or chemise, keeping the head and feet bare. They are expert at weaving and the making of straw hats, but are not industrious beyond their immediate needs.

ARMENTIA, *Diario del Viaje al Madre de Dios* (La Paz, 1890); BRINTON, *American Race* (New York, 1891); HEATH in *Kansas City Review of Science*, VI (Kansas City, 1883); MARKHAM, *Tribes in the Valley of the Amazon* in *Jour. Anthrop. Institute*, XXIV (London, 1895); D'ORBIGNY, *L'Homme Américain* (2 vols., Paris, 1839); WEDDELL, *Voyage dans le Nord de la Bolivie* (Paris and London, 1853).

JAMES MOONEY.

Tacapæ, titular see of Tripolitana in northern Africa. The official list of titular sees of the Roman Curia calls this see Tacapæ; the ancient milestones bear the name Tacapas, Tacapa, Tacapes; the Greek name was probably Tacape. It is mentioned in numerous ancient geographical documents, but nothing is known of its history. It was located in the interior of Syrtis Minor in a fertile country, was provided with several roads, and was the commercial centre of the region. At first attached to Byzantium, in the third century it became a Roman colony and formed part of Tripolitana. It is now Gabes, chief town of a civil control and the seat of a military commandery which comprises all the southern part of Tunis. It has 1200 inhabitants of whom 400 are French and live in an oasis due to the waters of Wady Gabes, with the two neighbouring villages of Djara (3000 inhabitants) and Menzel (300 inhabitants). Three of its bishops are known: Dulcitius, legate of the bishops of Tripolitana to the Council of Carthage (403) and present at the Conference of Carthage in 411; Servilius, exiled by Huneric in 484; Caius or Gallus, legate of the bishops of his province to the Council of Carthage in 525. The see still survived under Justinian who fortified the town.

SMITH, *Dict. of Greek and Roman Geogr.*, s. v.; MÜLLER, *Notes to Ptolemy*, ed. DIDOT, I, 626; TOULOTTE, *Géographie de l'Afrique chrétienne: Byzacène et Tripolitaine* (Montreuil, 1894), 261; DIEHL, *L'Afrique byzantine* (Paris, 1896), passim.

S. PÉTRIDÈS.

Taché, ALEXANDRE-ANTONIN, first Archbishop of St. Boniface, Manitoba, missionary, prelate, statesman, and writer of Western Canada, b. at Fraserville, Province of Quebec, 23 July, 1823; d. at St. Boniface, 22 June, 1894. By his father, Charles Taché, he belonged to one of the principal French Canadian families, and through his mother, Louise Henriette de La Broquerie, he was a descendant of Lavérendrye (q. v.), the discoverer of the country in which he was to pass forty-nine years of his life. His classical studies were made at the College of St. Hyacinthe, whence he went (1 Sept., 1841) to the seminary of Montreal to study for the priesthood. Thence he passed to the novitiate of the recently-arrived Oblates of Mary Immaculate, and when Bishop Provencher obtained the co-operation of this Institute for his distant missions of the Red River, Brother Taché, though still a novice, was chosen to accompany thither Father Pierre Aubert, O.M.I. After a two months' journey through Canadian territory, Taché arrived at St. Boniface on 25 August, 1845. On the first Sunday following he was ordained deacon by Bishop Provencher, and, on 12 October of the same year, was promoted to the priesthood, pronouncing the final vows of an Oblate on the next day. For nine months he studied the Saulteux language; this knowledge, however, was not to be of assistance to him until years later, for in July, 1846, he was sent to Ile-à-la-Crosse. There he spent four years, learning the language of the Chippewayans, his new flock, among whom he laboured, literally changing the morals, no less than the creed, of the northern aborigines. On snow-shoes and by canoe he made long journeys for the benefit of the Crees, Chippeways, Athabaskans, and Caribou-Eaters, until, at the age of twenty-seven he was chosen as the coadjutor and future successor of Mgr. Provencher. In obedience to the founder of his congregation, Bishop de Mazenod, he crossed over to Marseilles, and was consecrated (23 November, 1851) titular Bishop of Arath. On 27 June, 1852, he was back at St. Boniface, and on 10 September, 1852, he arrived at Ile-à-la-Crosse. He then continued his missionary life, which was rendered locally all the more useful as the Indians had resented his departure and the presence of priests not familiar with their language.

ALEXANDRE-ANTONIN TACHÉ
First Archbishop of St. Boniface

So absorbed was Taché in his apostolic labours that on the death of Bishop Provencher (7 June, 1853) he did not deem it incumbent upon himself to immediately return to St. Boniface. He went on with his peregrinations among Indians and halfbreeds until in the course of 1854 he proceeded south to officially take possession of his see. On 5 June, 1855, he returned north, going as far as Great Slave Lake, where he established a mission for the benefit of another Déné tribe. Then, as his diocese was becoming too large for one man to administer, he had one of his priests, Father Vital J. Grandin, O.M.I., appointed his coadjutor. Between 1860 and 1861 Mgr. Taché resumed his journeyings among the natives, and, nine miles from Edmonton, decided upon the site of a new mission which Father Lacombe was to establish under the name of St. Albert. Returning to St. Boniface, he learned of the destruction by fire (14 December, 1860) of his residence and the cathedral, the latter, whose bells have been sung of by the Quaker poet Whittier, was the pride of the settlement. He then passed into Canada, as the East of the present Dominion was called, and, by his appeals, secured the means of commencing a new and more modest cathedral. He even went as far as Europe, and procured the erection, in the most northern part of his immense diocese, of a new vicariate Apostolic which was entrusted to the care of Bishop Faraud.

This division enabled Mgr. Taché to give more attention to the home, or southern, missions and the embryonic parishes of what is to-day Manitoba. This territory, then called Assiniboia, was peopled by a mixed population under the paternal rule of the Hudson Bay Company, assisted by a legislative body of which the Bishop of St. Boniface was a member. A restless alien element, hailing mostly from Ontario, was at that time striving to change a political regime which was satisfactory to all classes of the local society, French and English, Catholic and Protestant. When the provinces of the east had been united into a confederation, one of the first cares of the new power resulting from the 1867 Act was to obtain from the Imperial Government the transfer, in consideration of £300,000, of Assiniboia and surrounding regions which had previously belonged to the Hudson Bay Company. Not only were the inhabitants of those territories not consulted as to the advisability of this transaction, but the emissaries of Ottawa in the valley of the Red River acted so rashly and in such a domineering way towards the French and Catholic part of the population, at a time when the Federal authorities whom they represented had not as yet any jurisdiction over the country, that the discontent they caused culminated (11 October, 1869) in open revolt under Louis Riel.

The Federal authorities begged Taché, who was then attending the Œcumenical Council of the Vatican, to come and intervene in the interest of peace. On his way home the prelate had interviews with the governor-general and his ministers, and was assured by them of a full amnesty for the *métis* in arms if the latter would only send delegates to Ottawa to treat of the matters in dispute and would not oppose the coming of the military expedition that was dispatched to Red River under Wolseley. In the meantime the Provisional Government, regularly formed there by the properly elected representatives of both portions of the population, had found it necessary to execute a troublesome character named Thomas Scott. The bishop's arrival (9 March, 1870), five days after the execution, was timely, inasmuch as Riel had manifested his intention of resisting the progress of the Anglo-Canadian troops. After Taché's intervention, which was based on the promise of an amnesty received at Ottawa, the métis could no longer be relied on to pursue an aggressive policy. Delegates were sent to the Federal capital, their efforts resulting in the Manitoba Act.

Unfortunately, the authorities took the execution of Scott, a rabid Orangeman, as an excuse for refusing the amnesty to which they had solemnly pledged themselves. This was a great blow to Mgr. Taché's prestige among his people. For years he laboured to secure for the leaders in the movement of resistance against the unwarranted aggression of the representatives of Ottawa that meed of justice to which he thought they had a right. He would probably have been more successful had he shown himself less confident in their honesty in his dealings with politicians, and required written assurances when it was scarcely possible to refuse them. It was not till the end of October, 1874, that a partial amnesty was proclaimed, but not before one of Riel's lieutenants, A. D. Lépine, had been condemned to death, a sentence which Mgr. Taché had had commuted into eighteen months' imprisonment. Taché had been appointed Archbishop of St. Boniface on 22 September, 1871. Thenceforth his efforts were mostly directed towards bringing in Catholic immigrants to the new ecclesiastical province and founding new parishes within his own archdiocese. In the midst of these labours the Saskatchewan Rebellion of 1885, under the same L. Riel who had directed the legitimate rising of 1869 (see SASKATCHEWAN AND ALBERTA), took place. Taché wrote (7 Dec., 1885) a little pamphlet, "La Situation", a masterpiece of its kind, in which he deplored the rebellion, yet remained to the end sympathetic to his former protégé. The latter had paid with his life (16 Nov., 1885) for excesses that were due to good intentions rendered ineffective by the failure of an overworked brain. From 13 to 24 July, 1889, were held at St. Boniface the sessions of its First Provincial Council. But soon after this joyful event the separate schools which were guaranteed by the provincial Constitution were ruthlessly abolished. The archbishop made numerous attempts to obtain redress, publishing several letters and pamphlets to show the injustice done his people; he also had appeals taken to the various courts, but the findings were contradictory, and therefore futile, until the Privy Council of the Empire acknowledged the reality of the grievances and pointed out the Federal Parliament as the party which had power to redress them (29 Jan., 1895). Taché did not live to see this tardy justice. The anxieties of the last few years had accentuated the ravages of a malady which carried him off, to the regret of friends and foes alike. Apart from the respectful tributes of the press, some 15,000 Protestants publicly testified after his death their recognition of his worth.

Archbishop Taché had to a considerable extent shaped the destinies of the Canadian West. He was a writer of no mean order. His literary productions have a special aroma of delicacy and, at times, quiet wit, which denote the well-bred gentleman, and his French is remarkably pure and free from foreign elements. Of his first book, "Vingt Années de Missions" (Montreal, 1866), 15,000 copies were sold, and it is now very rare. A short time later he published his "Esquisse sur le Nord-Ouest de l'Amérique", almost a classic on the subject; besides a second edition, it had the honour of an English translation. The harassing school persecution which began in the year 1890 was responsible for several public documents of Archbishop Taché's, prominent among which is "A Page of the History of the Schools in Manitoba"; this document was published in English and French, and is regarded as a model of close dialectics and irrefutable logic.

DAVID, *Monseigneur Alexandre-Antonin Taché* (Montreal, 1883); HARGRAVE, *Red River* (Montreal, 1871); HILL, *Manitoba* (Toronto, s. d.); HULOT, *De l'Atlantique au Pacifique* (Paris, 1888); JONQUET, *Monseigneur Grandin* (Montreal, 1903); BENOIT, *Vie de Mgr Taché* (2 vols., Montreal, 1904); MORICE, *Dict. historique des Canadiens et des Métis Français de l'Ouest* (Quebec, 1908); IDEM, *Hist. of the Catholic Church in Western Canada* (2 vols., Toronto, 1910); SAVAÈTE, *Vers l'Abîme*, VII (Paris, 1910); ROUTHIER, *De Québec à Victoria* (Quebec, 1893); LAMOTHE, *Cinq mois chez les Français d'Amérique* (Paris, 1879).

A. G. MORICE.

Taché, ETIENNE-PASCAL, statesman, b. at St. Thomas (Montmagny, Province of Quebec), 5 Sept., 1795, son of Charles, and Geneviève Michon; d. 30 July, 1865. Through his grandmother, he was a descendant of Joliet, the discoverer of the Mississippi. He served in the war of 1812 as lieutenant of the "Chasseurs canadiens". He was a self-made man, who after a mere elementary course succeeded in graduating at Philadelphia as a physician, and later in taking the foremost rank among Canadian statesmen. After twenty-two years of successful medical practice, he entered politics as member of the Legislative Assembly at the first election following the Union (1841), which he had strenuously opposed. Re-elected in 1844, he accepted (1846) the post of adjutant-general of militia. In 1848 he became chief commissioner of public works in the Lafontaine-Baldwin ministry, and helped to save the former's life during the violent sessions of 1849. M. Taché was a member of each successive Cabinet from 1848 to 1856. In 1858 he was knighted by Queen Victoria, and in 1860 appointed aide-de-camp to Her Majesty, with the rank of colonel in the regular army. In 1862 Pius IX bestowed on him the title of Commander of the Order of St. Gregory. He aided in reorganizing the militia at the time of the Trent affair. In 1864 he formed the Taché-MacDonald administration, and presided over the conference of the delegates of the British North American provinces preparatory to confederation. Taché was ever a loyal Catholic.

TURCOTTE, *Le Canada sous l' Union* (Quebec, 1872); MORGAN, *Bibliotheca canadensis* (Ottawa, 1867); ROY, *La famille Taché* (Lévis, 1904).

LIONEL LINDSAY.

Tadama, a titular see in Mauretania Cæsariensis, of which nothing is known. Its bishop David is mentioned among the bishops of Mauretania Cæsariensis in the "Notitiæ episcopatuum" of 482. He is also the hundredth and fifth on the list of the bishops of that province who went in 484 to the Conference of Carthage and were subsequently exiled by Huneric. His name is followed by the word *probatus*, showing that he died in exile for the Faith.

TOULOTTE, *Géographie de l'Afrique chrétienne: Maurétanies* (Montreuil, 1894), 149.

S. PÉTRIDÈS.

Tænarum, a titular see in Greece, suffragan of Corinth. Tænarum, or Tænarus, was situated five English miles north of Cape Tænarum, now Cape Matapan. It contained a temple of Demeter, also one of Aphrodite. It is to-day the village of Kyparrisos. After their freedom from the Spartan yoke, the maritime Laconians formed a confederation, and founded a capital, called Cænepolis, i. e. new town. From inscriptions we learn that this new city was really Tænarum, which still preserved its old name. However, there may have been two distinct cities, in close proximity; but there is no mention of Tænarum in the "Notitiæ episcopatuum", or of any of its bishops.

SMITH, *Dict. of Greek and Roman Geog.*, s. v.; MÜLLER, *Notes to Ptolemy*, ed. DIDOT, I, 551.

S. PÉTRIDÈS.

Taensa Indians, a tribe of Muskhogean stock and somewhat superior culture, living when first known on the west bank of the Mississippi, within the present limits of Tensas parish, Louisiana, and numbering perhaps 1200 souls, in several villages. The meaning of the name is unknown. In language, religion, and custom they were nearly identical with the celebrated Natchez, their near neighbours on the opposite bank of the Mississippi, a little lower down. The Taensa were sedentary and agricultural and expert canoe men, living in large houses described as having walls of earth, but more probably of logs plastered with clay, and roofed with mats of woven cane splits. Their chiefs exercised despotic power and were treated with great respect, in marked contrast to the custom among the northern tribes. On one occasion of a ceremonial visit to La Salle the chief was accompanied by attendants who, with their hands, swept the road in front of him as he advanced. Towards the French they manifested from the first a warm friendship, but although described by the early explorers as dignified, polished, docile, and even "humane", their religion, like that of the Natchez, was notable for its bloody rites. Their chief deities seem to have been the sun and the serpent. Their dome-shaped temple was surmounted by the figures of three eagles facing the rising sun, the outer walls and the roof being of cane mats painted entirely red, and the whole was surrounded with a palisade of stakes, on each of which was set a human skull, the remains of a former sacrifice. Inside was an altar, with a rope of human scalp locks, and a perpetual fire guarded day and night by two old priests. When a chief died his wives and personal attendants were killed that their spirits might accompany him to the other world. At one chief's funeral thirteen victims were thus slaughtered. On another occasion Father Montigny, being present, interposed and prevented the sacrifice. Shortly afterwards, during a thunder storm, the temple was struck by lightning and entirely consumed. The high priest interpreted this as a sign of the anger of the god at the neglect of the ancient custom, and for reparation called upon the women to throw their children into the fire. In response five mothers rushed forward and cast their infants into the flames and others were about to follow when the soldiers of Iberville's party interfered. The five mothers who had thus given their children to death were afterwards led in procession, clad in white robes woven from the fiber of the inner bark of the mulberry.

The Taensa may have been visited by De Soto's expedition in 1540, but their definite history dates from 1682, when the French commander La Salle, accompanied by Tonti and the Recollect Father Zenobius Membré, stopped at their villages for a day or two while descending the Mississippi and met a friendly reception. In 1686 Tonti again visited them, and in 1690 he made their villages the starting-point for his expedition to the west in search of La Salle. In 1698 they were terribly wasted by a smallpox epidemic which ravaged all the tribes of the lower Mississippi, but were still estimated at about 800. In the same year, Fathers F. J. de Montigny, Antoine Davion, and Thaumur de la Source were sent out from Quebec by the Seminary of Foreign Missions (Missions Étrangères) which had undertaken work among the southern tribes. After a preliminary reconnaissance, Father Montigny, with powers of vicar-general from the Bishop of Quebec, went in 1699 to the Taensa, assigning Davion to the Tonica. Later on Father Buisson de St. Cosme, of the same seminary, arrived and was assigned to the Natchez. Father Montigny was well received, and, as has been stated, was able at the time to prevent the funeral slaughter on the death of the chief, as also to make peace between the Taensa and the Natchez. In 1700 they were visited by Iberville, governor of the Louisiana colony. The missions, however, did not prosper. Iberville himself was unfriendly to the Quebec order, and the Taensa and Tonica, while apparently kindly, were too much attached to their own ritual and custom to be moved. The murder of Father Foucault by a neighbouring hostile tribe, the Koroa, in 1702, led to the withdrawal of the seminary priests and the abandonment of the missions.

In 1706 the hostility of the Chickasaw and Yazoo compelled the Taensa to abandon their villages and retire lower down the river. In consequence of their treacherous attack upon a tribe which had given them shelter, they were again forced to become refugees and finally, about 1740, removed to Tensas river near Mobile, Alabama, under the protection of the French. They were still mainly heathen. On the cession of Mobile to the English in 1763 they, with several other small tribes, again moved over into Louisiana, settling on Red River, where they still resided in 1805, reduced then to 25 men or perhaps 100 souls. Some years later they removed south to Bayou Bœuf and thence to Grand Lake, after which the remnant disappears from history.

In 1880–2 considerable interest was aroused among philologists by the publication in Paris of what purported to be important material of the Taensa language, including papers, songs, a grammar and vocabulary, but which proved to be the fraudulent invention of a young clerical student named Parisot, or of some one else from whom the manuscripts had originally come. The deception was exposed by Brinton in 1885 and has been more recently pointed out by Swanton.

BRINTON, *Essays of an Americanist* (Philadelphia, 1890); FRENCH, *Hist. Colls. of Louisiana*, I (New York, 1846); HAMILTON, *Colonial Mobile* (Boston and New York, 1897); LE PAGE DU PRATZ, *Hist. de la Louisane* (3 vols., Paris, 1758, tr. London, 1763, 1774); MARGRY, *Découvertes et établissements des Français* (6 vols., Paris, 1879, 1886); SHEA, *Discovery and Exploration of the Mississippi Valley* (New York, 1852; Albany, 1903); IDEM, *Hist. Catholic Ind. Missions* (New York, 1855 and 1870); SWANTON, *Ind. Tribes of the Lower Miss.* in Bulletin 43 of *Bur. Am. Ethnology* (Washington, 1911).

JAMES MOONEY.

Tahiti, VICARIATE APOSTOLIC OF.—Tahiti, the most important of the Society Islands, has an area of 600 square miles and a population of 11,691 inhabitants, and lies between 17° 29′ 30″ and 17° 47′ S. lat. and 151° 29′ 53″ and 151° 56′ W. long. It was discovered by Wallis in 1757. This honour is also claimed for Fernández Quiros, the pilot of the Mendana expedition from Peru to the Philippines, about 1600. Bougainville, Cook, and other explorers made Tahiti famous in Paris as "La Nouvelle Cythère", and in London aroused an enthusiasm for "the lovely isle", which led to the formation, by Dr. Haweis and others, of the London Missionary Society in 1794–95, and the despatch of the "Duff" in 1796 with some 60 persons, missionaries and teachers of trades and crafts, for the conversion of the island and its neighbours. The representatives of the society made little progress until Pomaré II, King of Tahiti, accepted Protestantism in 1815. Under his successors they gained great influence in the island government. In 1836 two priests of the Congregation of the Sacred Hearts of Jesus and Mary of Picpus arrived in Tahiti from the Gambier Islands, where Catholicism had gained a foothold. They were twice expelled by Queen Pomaré IV, with the support and approbation of the English Protestant missionaries, and took their cause to Paris. In 1838 a French naval expedition exacted from Queen Pomaré an indemnity and guarantees for the future for French residents in the island. In 1841 a mission was established by the Congregation of Picpus. In 1842 Pomaré IV signed a convention with Admiral Dupetit-Thouars, establishing a French protectorate and guaranteeing full religious liberty in Tahiti, which was ratified by Louis-Philippe in 1843. An uprising of the natives against the protectorate resulted in a punitive expedition by the French admiral, the flight of Queen Pomaré, and the forcible expulsion from the island of Rev. W. T. Pritchard of the London Missionary Society, whom the admiral held responsible for the revolt. This act was disavowed by the French Government and an indemnity paid to Great Britain based upon the claim that Pritchard, at the time of his expulsion, had been appointed British consul.

In 1848 Tahiti with its dependent islands was detached from the Vicariate of the Marquesas, and placed under the able and scholarly Mgr Jaussen. In 1880 King Pomaré, with the consent of the French Chambers, proclaimed Tahiti an integral part of the French Republic. In 1887 the French Government secularized the schools. Upon the death of Mgr Jaussen in 1891 Mgr Verdier, his assistant since 1884, succeeded to his labours, made doubly difficult by the sectarian missions and the attitude of French officials. Since 1903 the various groups of French islands in Oceania, exclusive of New Caledonia and its dependencies, have been united in one homogeneous colonial establishment, administered from Tahiti by a governor and privy council, with an administrative council. The present Vicariate of Tahiti covers the Society group, the Leeward and Gambier Islands, the Tuamotu group, Tubuai and Rapa, all belonging to France; the Cook and Penrhyn Islands, annexed to New Zealand in 1902; Pitcairn (unattached) and Easter Island, belonging to Chile. The Mission consists of: 1 bishop (Mgr Hermel, whose residence is at Papeete, the chief town of Tahiti), 1 coadjutor with right of succession, 30 priests and several brothers of the Congregation of Picpus; 6 brothers of Ploërmel; 12 churches with resident pastors; 50 other churches and chapels; 24 Sisters of St. Joseph of Cluny; 1 boys' school; 1 girls' school; 20 parochial schools; 2 hospitals. The total population of the vicariate is estimated at 31,000 inhabitants, with 7700 Catholics.

RAMBAUD, *La France coloniale* (Paris, 1895); GAFFAREL, *Les colonies françaises* (Paris, 1893); DE LANESSAN, *L'expansion coloniale de la France* (Paris, 1886); LEROY-BEAULIEU, *Colonisation chez les peuples modernes* (Paris, 1908); PIOLET, *Les missions catholiques françaises au XIX*^{e} *siècle* (Paris, 1902); BATTANDIER, *Annuaire pontifical catholique* (Rome, 1911); VIEILLEMARD, *Missions catholiques de la Mélanésie, Micronesie et Polynésie* (Paris, 1896); *Missiones catholicæ* (Rome, 1907); HAWEIS, *Travel and Talk, 1885–93–95* (London and New York, 1896); LOVETT, *Hist. of the London Missionary Society 1795–1895* (London, 1899); WILKS, *Tahiti, a Review of the Origin, Character and Progress of French Roman Catholic Efforts for the Destruction of English Protestant Missions in the South Sea* (London, 1844); PRITCHARD, *Polynesian Reminiscences* (London, 1866); NORMAN, *Colonial France* (London, 1886).

W. F. SANDS.

Taigi, ANNA MARIA GESUALDA ANTONIA (maiden name GIANNETTI), Venerable Servant of God, b. at Siena, Italy, 29 May, 1769; d. at Rome, 9 June, 1837. Her parents, Luigi Giannetti and Maria Masi, kept an apothecary shop at Siena, but lost all their fortune and were obliged to go to Rome in search of a livelihood. Anna Maria was then five years old. Having been educated in all the domestic virtues, she was married in course of time, 7 Jan., 1789, to Dominico Taigi, a retainer of the noble family of Chigi, with whom she lived happily for forty-eight years. Hitherto nothing extraordinary had happened in her life. But one day while she knelt with her husband at the *Confessio* in St. Peter's she felt a strong inspiration to renounce such little vanities of the world as she had allowed herself. She began to pay little attention to dress and to listen to the inner voice of grace. Soon afterwards she was received publicly in the Third Order of Trinitarians in the Church of S. Carlo alle Quatro Fontane, and having found holy spiritual directors, she made rapid progress in the way of perfection. All the money she could spare she devoted to the poor and miserable, and though not rich she was very charitable. Of the hospitals she regularly visited, the preferred one was S. Giacomo of the Incurables. Despite her love for the poor, she never neglected her own family. Of her children two died young, the others grew up in piety under the surveillance of the mother. But she never availed herself of her connexions with persons of good position to take her children out of their humble social environment. The whole family were wont to assemble for prayers in a small private chapel, and here, later on, Mass was celebrated by a priest who dwelt with the family. The great virtues of Anna Maria were rewarded by extraordinary gifts of God's grace. During many years, when praying in her chapel she had ecstasies and frequent visions, in which she foresaw the future. She exercised a peculiar influence over individuals and converted many a sinner to God. During her life she suffered much both corporally and spiritually, and was at times meanly calumniated. But after death her name soon became venerated in Rome. Her body was several times transferred, and rests finally at S. Crisogono in Trastevere. The process of her beatification was begun in 1863, but has not yet been finished.

SILVESTRO DELL' ADDOLORATA, *Vita de la ven. serva di Dio Anna-Maria Taigi* (Rome, 1901); CALIXTE DE LA PROVIDENCE, *Vie de la vén. Anna-Maria Taïgi* (4th ed., Tournai, 1877), tr. SMITH SLIGO (London, 1873); LUQUET, *Abrégé de la vie d'Anna Maria-Taïgi* (Paris, 1854); BALSOFIORE, *Della ven. serva di Dio, Anna Maria Taigi* (Rome, 1865); BOUFFIER, *La vén. servante de Dieu, Anna-Maria Taïgi* (5th ed., Paris, 1901).

G. LIVARIUS OLIGER.

Tait Indians (*Te-it*, "Those up river"), a collective term for those members of the Cowichan tribe, of Salishan linguistic stock, occupying the Lower Fraser River, Yale District, British Columbia (Canada), between Nicomen and Yale, where they border upon the Thompson River Indians. They have several small reserves within the jurisdiction of Fraser River agency, of which the principal are Chehalis (116), Cheam (95), Hope (79), and Yale (76). From perhaps 3000 souls a century ago they have decreased, through smallpox, disease, and former dissipation, since the occupation of the country by the whites, to 932 in 1890 and 578 in 1910. The gospel was preached to them by the Oblates, beginning with Fr. Charles Grandidier in 1869, at which time the whole Cowichan tribe was sunk in the lowest stage of degradation from drunkenness and association with depraved whites, drunken murders being of almost nightly occurrence. Within two years they were completely reclaimed, all Christians, sober and law-abiding; all due, according to Protestant testimony, "To the honest and persevering labours of a poor Catholic priest who receives no salary, and is fed by the Indians" ("The British Colonist", Victoria, B. C., 26 March, 1861, quoted in Morice, "History of the Catholic Church in Western Canada", II, 312). Of the whole number all but seventy-five are now Catholic, the others being Anglican or Methodist, and are officially reported as law-abiding, industrious, strictly moral, and generally temperate. Their principal educational centre is St. Mary's Mission, on the Fraser River, established in 1861 under the management of the Oblates assisted by the Sisters of St. Ann, besides a smaller and more recent mission school at Yale. Of the Cowichan language, which is spoken by a number of bands about Lower Fraser and on the opposite coast of Vancouver Island, very little has been recorded beyond some vocabularies by Tolmie and Dawson. A brief sketch of the ethnology of the tribe group is given by Boas in "Reports to the British Association for the Advancement of Science". In their primitive customs and characteristics they resembled the cognate Songish, Squamish, Shuswap, and Lillooet.

BOAS, *First General Report on Indians of British Columbia* in *Reports to the British Association for the Advancement of Science* (London, 1889); IDEM, *Indian Tribes of the Lower Fraser River* (loc. cit., 1890); *Annual Reports of the Department of Indian Affairs of Canada* (Ottawa); MORICE, *History of the Catholic Church in Western Canada* (2 vols., Toronto, 1910); TOLMIE AND DAWSON, *Comparative Vocabularies . . . of British Columbia* in *Geological and Natural History Survey of Canada* (Montreal, 1884).

JAMES MOONEY.

Takkali (more properly TAKHEHL, plural TAK-HEHLNE), the hybrid name by which the Carrier Indians of the northern interior of British Columbia were originally made known by the fur traders, who sometimes comprised under that denomination the Chilcotin and the Babine tribes as well. The Carriers proper inhabit more or less permanent villages disseminated from the forks of Lake Tatla in the north to Alexandria in the south, or from 55° 15' to 52° 30' N. lat. They are subdivided into a number of septs, based mostly on differences in speech, all of which can be reduced to two main branches: the Lower and the Upper Carriers, the line of demarcation running between Stuart and Fraser Lakes. They number to-day some 1614 individuals, distributed in twelve villages. We may remark that under the fostering care of the missionaries, the population of some of those villages has of late years been constantly on the increase. This cannot be said of their southern neighbours, the Chilcotins, a rather restless horde now temporarily settled along the Chilcotin valley. As late as 1864 they still numbered fully 1500 souls; but attacks of small-pox and other causes have reduced their population to some 450. When the Babines in the north were first visited by the whites, those amongst them who claimed as their home the valley of the lake called after them boasted alone a population of at least 2000. Together with their congeners on the Bulkley River they do not now number more than 530 souls.

Socially speaking, the Carriers and the Babines follow matriarchy, succession to titles and property being among them along the female line. They are in a way ruled over by a number of hereditary petty chiefs, who alone own the land on which their co-clansmen hunt for the benefit of their respective headmen. A number of clans divide the tribes, which in the eyes of the natives are the source of a relationship at least as binding as regular consanguinity is with us. Before the advent of the missionaries the main duty of these chiefs, or noblemen, was the giving of noisy feasts called "potlatches" on the North Pacific coast, which consisted in the public distribution, to the members of clans different from that of the donors, of eatables, dressed skins, blankets, and other pieces of wearing apparel. These bounties usually celebrated the demise of some individual. They had to be scrupulously reciprocated as soon as a similar occasion presented itself to the recipients of the same. The Chilcotins knew also of those "potlatches", but among them inheritance followed patrilineal principles, and their chiefs had more power because less numerous and unconnected with the clan system. With them the son of a chief succeeded his father, instead of a nephew taking the place of his maternal uncle as among the Carriers and Babines. Likewise, while the two last-named tribes cremated their dead, the Chilcotins buried them, generally on hills or knolls. The members of the three tribes believed in the immortality of the soul and followed the religious system outlined in the article DÉNÉS, where the reason for the names Carrier and Babine will also be found.

The first contact of the Carriers with the whites dates from 1793; the Chilcotins first met them in 1808, and the Babines in 1812, while the first notions they obtained of the religion of the newcomers were derived from the Catholic servants of the traders among them. In 1842 the Carriers received their first missionary in the person of Rev. M. Demers (q. v.), and four years later Father J. Nobili not only retraced his itinerary but also evangelized the Babines. The good seed distributed by these apostolic men could not, however, come to full germination before the spring of 1873, when a permanent mission was established by Father J.-M. Le Jacq, O.M.I., on the banks of Lake Stuart, whence the Carrier and Babine villages were periodically visited. The less sedentary Chilcotins had already received a few visits from this priest since 1867, the date of the foundation of St. Joseph's Mission, some distance from their lands. The Carriers, especially, proved easily amenable to Catholic ways of thinking, and in the course of years all of them were fully converted to the Catholic religion. Such was the state of affairs among them when A. G. Morice left the north after a residence of nineteen years among the Carriers. Though as religiously inclined, the Babines took more time to fully attain the moral standard presented to their appreciation. To-day all those aborigines are Catholics, and the conduct of most of them is an honour to the Faith they profess.

MACKENZIE, *Voyages from Montreal to the Frozen Pacific Ocean* (2 vols., London, 1801); HARMON, *A Journal of Voyages* (Andover, 1820); ROSS, *Adventures on the Columbia River* (New York, 1832); MACLEAN, *Notes of a Twenty-Five Years' Service in the Hudson's Bay Territory* (London, 1849); MORICE, *The Western Dénés* (Toronto, 1889); IDEM, *Carrier Sociology and Mythology* (Ottawa, 1892); IDEM, *Notes on the Western Dénés* (Toronto, 1894); IDEM, *Three Carrier Myths* (Toronto, 1896); IDEM, *Au pays de l'ours noir* (Paris, 1897); IDEM, *History of the Northern Interior of British Columbia* (Toronto, 1904); IDEM, *Hist. of the Catholic Church in Western Canada* (Toronto, 1910); IDEM, *The Great Déné Race* (in course of publication at Vienna, Austria).

A. G. MORICE.

Talbot, JAMES, fourth son of George Talbot and brother of the fourteenth Earl of Shrewsbury (b. 1726; d. 1790), is chiefly known for having been the last priest to be indicted in the public courts for saying Mass. He was educated at Douai, to which college he was a great benefactor. In 1759, at the age of thirty-three, he was consecrated coadjutor bishop to Dr. Challoner. During his episcopate he was twice brought to trial, on the information lodged by the well-known "Informer" Payne, in 1769 and 1771 respectively. In each case he was acquitted for want of evidence, but the judge, Lord Mansfield, was plainly on his side, in consequence of which, though he was no friend to Catholics as such, his house was sacked during the Gordon Riots in 1780. On the death of Bishop Challoner in 1781, Bishop James Talbot became Vicar Apostolic of the London District, which he ruled for nine years. He lived a retired life at Hammersmith, his unbounded charity gaining for him the title of "the Good Bishop Talbot". His chief work during these years was the completion of the purchase of the property at Old Hall, Herts, where he had a preparatory academy which afterwards developed into St. Edmund's College. The penal law against Catholic schools still existed, and Bishop Talbot was again threatened with imprisonment; but he contrived to evade punishment. During the last years of his life the Catholic Committee was already threatening trouble. In order to control it, Bishop Talbot allowed himself to be elected a member; but it was soon evident that the laymen were beyond control. The crisis however had not yet arrived when Bishop Talbot died at his house at Hammersmith.

The only connected account of his episcopate is in WARD, *Dawn of Catholic Revival* (London, 1909). For details of his trials, see BARNARD, *Life of Challoner* (London, 1784); BURTON, *The Life and Times of Bishop Challoner* (London, 1910); further allusions in HUSENBETH, *Life of Milner* (Dublin, 1862); BRADY, *Catholic Hierarchy* (London, 1877); AMHERST, *History of Catholic Emancipation* (London, 1886); WARD, *History of St. Edmund's College* (London, 1893); HAILE AND BONNEY, *Life of Lingard* (London, 1911). See also MILNER'S *Obituary Sermon* (MS. in Westminster Archives).

BERNARD WARD.

Talbot, JOHN, English Catholic layman, b. 1535(?); d. 1607(?). Only son and heir of Sir John Talbot, of Grafton, Worcestershire, he was the father, by Katharine, d. of Sir William Petre, of the Rev. George Talbot, Catholic priest, and ninth Earl of Shrewsbury. He became a member of Lincoln's Inn, 10 February, 1555–6. It was when passing through Smithfield, London, in July, 1580, with Mr. and Mrs. Talbot, that Bl. Robert Johnson, the martyr, was recognized by Sledd, the informer. Indeed, Fr. Persons, S.J., calls Bl. Robert "Mr. Talbot's priest" (Cath. Rec. Soc., II, 27), though, as it appears, he was, rather, Lady Petre's. Talbot was committed to the custody of the Dean of Westminster, 24 August, 1580, and afterwards removed to the house of his brother-in-law, Sir John Petre, in Aldersgate Street. On 1 October, 1581, the plague being then rife in the City, he was moved to some other house within ten or twelve miles of London. In 1583 the priest, Hugh Hall, confessed that he had in past years been entertained by him. Later Talbot was restricted to the house of one Henry Whitney, at Mitcham, Surrey, and two miles round it. In 1588 he was imprisoned in Wisbech Castle for having heard Mass contrary to the provisions of the statute 23 Eliz. c. i. From 9 Dec., 1588, to about 13 May, 1589, he was liberated on bail, owing to his own and his wife's bad health. He then seems to have been restricted to his house in Clerkenwell. On 12 March, 1589–90, he was ordered into confinement at the house of Richard Fiennes at Broughton in Oxfordshire, whence he was released on bail for a fortnight on 24 May, 1590. He was again allowed out on bail on 20 December, 1590, and 22 July, 1591. In 1592 he was at "Bickslie" (Bexley or Bickley?) Kent. On 27 August, 1592, the recusants formerly imprisoned at Ely, Banbury, and Broughton were ordered back to their respective prisons; but an exception was made (17 September, 1592) in favour of John Talbot. However, next year we find him in Ely gaol. Thence he was liberated on bail for a considerable period to act as umpire in a family dispute. Later on he was allowed to take "the Bathes", presumably at Bath, on account of his health. Between Michaelmas, 1593, and 10 March following, he paid £120 in fines for recusancy. Afterwards he was imprisoned in Banbury Castle, whence he was released on bail for two months, 27 Feb., 1596–7, his leave being subsequently extended on 29 April, 1597, and 6 Nov., 1597. In 1601 he was living in Worcestershire and pressure was brought to bear on him to secure his influence to promote the candidature of Sir Thomas Leighton as one of the parliamentary representatives of the shire. In 1604 he was paying £20 a month in fines for his recusancy, the benefit of which was on 26 August granted to Sir William Anstruther, who on 13 October in the same year obtained his pardon. On the following 8 December a warrant was issued for the release to him of £160, due from him to the Crown in fines for recusancy. In 1605 he was suspected of complicity with the conspirators of the Gunpowder Plot, one of whom, Robert Winter, of Haddington, near Droitwich, had married his daughter Gertrude. Robert Winter, however, declared that he had said nothing on the subject to his father-in-law, knowing that he would not join the plot under any circumstances. Indeed he had actually driven the fugitive conspirators from his door. Talbot was, nevertheless, arrested, and on 4 December, 1605, examined. On 26 September, 1606, the value of his recusancy was granted to Lord Hay. His second son, John, father of the tenth Earl of Shrewsbury, died in London in 1607, and he himself probably died about the same year.

Calendars of State Papers Domestic, 1581 to 1610; DASENT, *Acts of the Privy Council* (London, 1890–1907); STRYPE, *Life and Acts of John Whitgift*, I (Oxford, 1822), 529; IDEM, *Annals of the Reform in England*, IV (Oxford, 1824), 276; *Hist. MSS. Commission Cal. of Cecil MSS.*, IV, 268; COKAYNE, *Complete Peerage* (London, 1887–1898); *Rec. of Hon. Soc. of Lincoln's Inn, Admissions*, I (London, 1896), 62.

JOHN B. WAINEWRIGHT.

Talbot, JOHN, VENERABLE. See PALASOR, THOMAS, VENERABLE.

Talbot, PETER, Archbishop of Dublin, 1669–1680; b. at Malahide, Dublin, in 1620. At an early age he entered the Society of Jesus in Portugal, where he pursued his sacred studies with great distinction. He was ordained priest at Rome, and subsequently for some years held the chair of theology at the College of Antwerp. Meantime, through the Cromwellian usurpation, Charles II and the royal family were compelled to seek a refuge first in Paris and then at Cologne. Throughout the whole period of the king's exile, the four brothers of Dr. Talbot were attached to the royal Court. The eldest brother, Sir Robert Talbot, had held a high commission under Lord Ormond in the army in Ireland during the Federation period, and was now reckoned among the king's most confidential advisers. A younger brother, Colonel Richard Talbot, was also remarkable for his devotedness to the cause of the exiled monarch and stood high in royal favour. Under James II he became Duke of Tyrconnell and Lord-Lieutenant of Ireland. Dr. Talbot himself was constantly in attendance on the king and his Court. On account of his knowledge of the continental languages he was repeatedly dispatched on private embassies to Lisbon, Madrid, and Paris, and in all of them gave abundant proof of ability and fidelity to the royal cause. It appears unquestionable that during his exile in Cologne, Charles II received instruction in the Catholic faith, and was privately received into the Church by Dr. Talbot. It used to be said of the king by his friends that whenever he was in a serious mood he was a Catholic, but when he was in a merry mood he bade adieu to all religion. Unfortunately this second mood generally prevailed, especially after the Restoration, and this explains why he needed to be again received into the Church on his death-bed by Father Hudlestone, O.S.B. On the return of the king to London, Dr. Talbot received an appointment as Queen's Almoner, but the Clarendon and Ormond faction, that was then predominant, feared his influence with the king. A plot was devised against him. He was even accused of conspiring with the aid of four Jesuits to assassinate the Duke of Ormond, and so fierce was the persecution stirred up against him that he was forced to seek safety by resigning his position at Court and retiring to the Continent. The king allowed him a pension of three hundred pounds a year. Before his return to England Dr. Talbot had, with the approval of the General of the Jesuits, dissevered his connexion with the Society. He was appointed Archbishop of Dublin on 11 January, 1669, and was consecrated at Antwerp on 9 May the same year, by the Bishop of Antwerp, assisted by the Bishops of Ghent and Ferns. It was a propitious time for appointments to the Irish sees. Lord Ormond was no longer in favour and was soon after removed from the Viceroyalty, and those who succeeded him were supposed not to be so hostile to the religious interests of Ireland; they were even said to have received instructions from the king to be lenient in their dealings with his Irish Catholic subjects, and to show special favour to Dr. Talbot. The archbishop entered with great zeal on the administration of the diocese and was untiring in his efforts to promote the interests of his long persecuted flock. In the month of August, 1670, he held his first diocesan synod in Dublin. It was a memorable event that gave joy to the Catholic body. It was opened with High Mass, which for forty years many of the faithful had not witnessed. To add to the solemnity, rich embroidery and other ornaments were sent from the viceregal castle to adorn the altar. One of the abuses that called for remedy tells of the difficulties that pressed upon the priests of those days in their endeavour to meet the wants of the faithful. On week days they had been accustomed to duplicate, whilst on Sundays they had to celebrate holy Mass three times. In the same year an assembly of the archbishops and bishops and representatives of the clergy was held in Dublin, having for its main purpose the consideration of a form or Declaration of Allegiance which was drawn up by Father Peter Walsh and his associate Remonstrants, and which was urged on the bishops for general acceptance by the Ormondist party, the better to sow dissensions among the Irish Catholics. The assembled bishops and clergy rejected the proposed form of allegiance, but, to prove that this was not done through any lack of loyalty, they drew up another Declaration expressive of their due allegiance, but omitting some phrases offensive to Catholics that had been cunningly inserted in the rejected Declaration. A fierce discussion was in consequence raised by the Remonstrants backed by the Ormondists, that distracted the country for several years. At this assembly the question of precedence and of the primatial authority gave rise to considerable discussion and led to an embittered controversy between the Archbishop of Dublin and Ven. Oliver Plunkett, Archbishop of Armagh. Both prelates considered that they were asserting the rights of their respective sees, and each published a learned treatise on the subject. Whilst this controversy lasted Dr. Talbot wrote some severe censures regarding the Archbishop of Armagh, but when in prison for the Faith in later years, he addressed to the Archbishop of Armagh, then a brother prisoner, an ample apology asking his forgiveness for the harsh things that had been formerly written, and the Ven. Oliver Plunkett, as we will just now see, showed in a most practical manner how sincerely and affectionately he was reconciled to his former opponent. Another meeting of the Catholic gentry, convened by Dr. Talbot, at which it was resolved to send to the Court at London a representative who would seek redress for some of the grievances to which the Catholics of Ireland were subjected, gave great alarm to the Cromwellian settlers and to the Ormondists. It was an attempt, they said, to reverse the Act of Settlement and to foster a fresh rebellion. An address from Parliament was presented to the king praying that by royal edict all the Catholic prelates and clergy, and in particular "Peter Talbot, pretended Archbishop of Dublin", be banished from the kingdom, and further "that all convents, seminaries, and popish public schools be suppressed; that no Irish papist be admitted to inhabit in any corporation of that kingdom; that all the Irish Papists might be disarmed, and no Papist be either continued or admitted to be a commander or soldier in that Kingdom". The king knew full well how groundless and absurd were the pretences for such a royal edict, but he was too weak to offer any resistance, and thus, in 1673, a fierce storm of persecution was let loose against the whole Catholic body in Ireland, and Dr. Talbot was compelled to seek safety in exile. During his banishment he resided generally in Paris; but by pastoral letters and written instructions he continued to do all that was in his power to guide and comfort his flock. In 1675 Dr. Talbot, worn out with infirmities, obtained permission to return to England only, and for two years he resided with a family friend at Poole Hall in Cheshire. Towards the close of 1677, he petitioned the Crown for leave "to come to Ireland to die in his own country", and through the influence of the Duke of York his petition was granted. Just then the "Popish Plot" was being organized by Lord Shaftesbury and Titus Oates, and very soon information was forwarded to the Lord-Lieutenant, the Duke of Ormond, to the effect that a rebellion was being planned in Ireland, that Peter Talbot, Archbishop of Dublin, was one of the accomplices, and that assassins were hired to murder the duke himself. Ormond replied that he had no apprehension whatever on these heads, and that as regards Peter Talbot there could be no foundation for them, as he was in a dying state. Nevertheless as it was necessary to give some colour to the existence of such a plot, on 8 October, 1678, he signed a warrant for the archbishop's arrest, and he writes on the same day to the Council in London: "I have sent a squadron of his Majesty's guard of horse to apprehend Peter Talbot, the Titular Archbishop of Dublin". He was arrested at Cartown near Maynooth at the house of his brother, Colonel Richard Talbot, and, as Carte attests, was removed to Dublin "in a chair, and committed close prisoner to the Castle with a person to attend him in his miserable and helpless condition, the violence of his distemper being scarce supportable and threatening his death at every

XIV.—28

moment." For two years Dr. Talbot endured with heroic constancy all the sufferings of his painful disease and the hardships and filth of his loathsome dungeon. He died in prison in the beginning of November, 1680. Ormond, in a postscript to a letter of 20 Nov., 1680, addressed to Lord Sutherland, writes: "I have for two or three posts forgot to acquaint your Lordship that Peter Talbot, the Titular Archbishop of Dublin, is dead, and that care was taken to have the body looked upon by some that knew him." It is the tradition that he was interred in the churchyard of St. Andeon's, close by Lord Portlester's tomb. From his prison cell Dr. Talbot had written on 12 April, 1679, petitioning that a priest be allowed to visit him, as he was bed-ridden "these six months past" and was now in imminent danger of death. The petition was refused, but the Venerable Oliver Plunkett, Archbishop of Armagh, was a prisoner for the Faith in an adjoining cell, and on hearing of Dr. Talbot's dying condition forced his way through the warders and administered to the dying prelate the last consolations of religion. Dr. Talbot may justly be styled a confessor of the Faith and a true martyr of Christ.

WRITINGS.—Dr. Talbot, whilst living on the Continent, published several works, as well before his appointment to the See of Dublin, as during his years of exile. His principal writings are: "A Treatise on the Nature of Catholic Faith and Heresy with Reflexions upon the Nullity of the English Protestant Church and Clergy" (8 vols., Rouen, 1657); "The Politician's Catechism", by N. N., printed at Antworp (sic) in the year 1658; "The Nullity of the Prelatique Clergy" (Brussels, 1659); "The Duty and Comfort of Suffering Subjects" (a pastoral letter to the Irish Catholics), Paris, 1674; "Blackloanæ Hæresis, Historia et Confutatio, Auctore M. Lomino Theologo, Gandavi anno 1675" (mainly directed against Dr. Sargent; in the appendix is inserted a letter of the nuncio in Paris of 26 July, 1676, congratulating Dr. Talbot on his excellent work and intimating that Sargent had retracted his erroneous propositions); "Primatus Dublinensis, vel summa rationum quibus innititur ecclesia Dublinensis in possessione et prosecutione sui juris ad primatum Hyberniæ. Insulis, Ex Officina Nicolai de Rache, sub Bibliis aureis, 1674" (an exceedingly rare work; there is a copy in the library of the College of Propaganda at Rome, with the inscription, "Ex libris Jacobi Eustachii, Dublinensis, 1683").

PATRICK FRANCIS CARDINAL MORAN.

Talbot, THOMAS JOSEPH, b. 14 February, 1727; d. at Hotwells, near Bristol, 24 April, 1795. Brother of the fourteenth Earl of Shrewsbury, and of Bishop James Talbot (q. v.), he was sent to Twyford School, and thence to Douai (1739). In 1745–46, together with his brother James, he made the grand tour under the tutelage of Alban Butler. He returned to Douai to study theology; and after ordination he spent some time with Alban Butler at Norwich. In 1754 he was placed at Brockhampton. On the expulsion of the Jesuits from France, Talbot was named President of the College of St. Omer's by the committee of the Parliament of Paris (August, 1762), a post which he accepted only after much hesitation and with great reluctance. He was consecrated to the titular See of Acon (March, 1766) as coadjutor to Bishop Hornyold, whom he succeeded in the government of the Midland District (26 December, 1778). His rule fell in a time of transition, when the desire and prospect of relief from the Penal Laws led many prominent Catholics to adopt a policy of excessive compromise, the period of the Catholic Committees and the Cisalpine Club, for the difficulties of which his peaceful character was but ill-adapted. Although he joined the three other vicars Apostolic in condemning the proposed oath in 1789, he hesitated to promulgate the condemnation in his district, and in the second condemnation which the other vicars Apostolic published in 1791 he thought it neither expedient nor justifiable to concur. The explanation of this action is to be found in his conviction that peace and concord could only be restored to the distracted Catholics by means of mutual concession and charity, a sentiment which almost all his letters manifest. Certainly the most memorable, as also the most permanent, act of his administration was his invitation to Dr. John Bew (November, 1793) to take charge of the mission of Oscott and to undertake there the training of students for the priesthood, whereby was made the beginning of Oscott College. Deeply characteristic of the man is his only recorded literary publication, a small treatise on "Almsgiving" which he translated from the French. He was buried in the vault under Trenchard Street church; in 1906 his remains were removed to Downside Abbey.

BRADY, *Episcopal Succession* (London, 1877); KIRK, *Biographies of English Catholics* (London, 1909); WARD, *Dawn of Catholic Revival in England* (2 vols., London, 1909); IDEM, *History of St. Edmunds' College* (London, 1893); BURTON, *Life of Bishop Challoner* (2 vols., London, 1909); AMHERST, *History of Catholic Emancipation* (London, 1886); IDEM, *History of Oscott* in *Oscotian*; KNOX, *Douay Diaries*.

J. L. WHITFIELD.

Talisman. See AMULET.

Talleyrand-Périgord, CHARLES-MAURICE DE, Prince of Benevento, Bishop of Autun, French minister and ambassador, b. in Paris, 13 February, 1754; d. there, May, 1838. The eldest of an ancient French family, he was destined for Holy orders, owing to an accident which had made him lame. After having completed his studies at the Collège d'Harcourt, he went to St-Sulpice and, against his inclination, became an abbé. He then read the "most revolutionary books", and at length, giving up his priestly life, plunged into the licentiousness of the period. Having, nevertheless, been ordained priest (1779) and appointed general agent of the clergy (1780) he rapidly acquired a reputation as a man of ability. The Assembly of the Clergy of France of 1782 appointed him their promoter, and in 1785 he became secretary. Owing to his notorious immorality he obtained an episcopal see only through a promise wrung from the dying king by his father, Comte Daniel de Talleyrand. Consecrated on 16 January, 1789, and promoted to the Bishopric of Autun, he appeared in his diocese only to be elected a member of the "Etats Généraux". He soon became one of the most important personages in Europe, and utilized every opportunity to advance his private interests.

Opposed in his heart to a revolution which he accused of having "dismembered France", he first advised Louis XVI to dissolve the Assembly, but believing the democratic movement irresistible he joined it. As a member of the Constitutional Committee, he took part in the "Declaration of the Rights of Man". He extolled the spoliation of the clergy and took the oath to the Civil Constitution. His chapter, however, having described him as deserving "infamy in this world and damnation in the next", he resigned his see. But he had consecrated several constitutional bishops, given Gobel the Bishopric of Paris, and was excommunicated by pontifical Brief of 13 April, 1791. In 1792 he was sent to London on an unofficial diplomatic mission and endeavoured to organize a Franco-English alliance. He did not, however, obtain more than a promise of neutrality. Finally banished by the Convention, he escaped to the United States. He returned to Paris in March, 1796, and, owing to the influence of Barras, was appointed Minister of Foreign Affairs. He immediately welcomed Bonaparte as the great auxiliary "who would make everything smooth". With Bonaparte and Sieyès he prepared the *coup d'état* of Brumaire, after which he assisted the First Consul in the drafting of the Concordat. The pope meanwhile had released him from the ban of excommunication and restored him to secular life and the lay communion. Napoleon then compelled him (1803) to marry by civil law his mistress, Madame Grand, an English *divorcée*, who had not lived with her former husband. As the principal agent in the treaties concluded by Napoleon, he obtained for his services a fortune of some sixty million francs. He was made grand chamberlain, vice-elector of the Empire, and Sovereign Prince of Benevento. However, he advised against the Franco-Russian Alliance and resigned the ministry in August, 1807. His opposition to the Spanish War in 1809 was the cause of his complete disgrace, and he awaited at Valençay at his hotel in the Rue St. Florentin the fall of Napoleon.

In 1814 the Emperor of Russia, his guest, "committed himself entirely into his hands". Once more leader of the provisional Government, he made the Senate establish a constitution to give power to Louis XVIII. On his appointment as Minister of Foreign Affairs he preserved to France its frontiers of 1792, and at the Congress of Vienna he broke the union of the great powers by secretly concluding a treaty with Austria and England. Again appointed minister of Louis XVIII (1815) he preserved his country from dismemberment, but left the presidency of the Council after the election of 22 August, 1815. As grand chamberlain and peer of France, he henceforward contented himself with watching and sententiously criticizing events. In 1830 Louis Philippe, whose accession he had favoured, appointed him to the embassy of London, where the representatives of all the countries "bent before him". After having established the *entente cordiale* with England, he resigned office in November, 1834. In his magnificent "solitude" of Valençay he wrote his "Mémoires", in which he asserts he "never had betrayed a government which had not betrayed itself first", nor ever put his "own interests in the balance with those of France". Four hours before his death he signed, in the presence of Abbé Dupanloup, a solemn declaration in which he openly disavowed "the great errors which . . . had troubled and afflicted the Catholic, Apostolic and Roman Church, and in which he himself had had the misfortune to fall".

PALLAIN, *Correspondance diplomatique de Talleyrand. La Mission de Talleyrand à Londres en 1792. Les lettres d'Amérique à lord Lansdowne* (Paris, 1887); IDEM, *Correspondance diplomatique de Talleyrand. Le ministère de Talleyrand sous le Directoire* (Paris, 1891–1892); DE BROGLIE, *Mémoires du prince de Talleyrand* (Paris, 1892); FLAMMERMONT, *De l'authenticité des Mémoires de Talleyrand* (Paris, 1892); SOREL, *Talleyrand et ses Mémoires* (Paris, 1894); BERTRAND, *M. de Bacourt et les Mémoires de Talleyrand* (Paris, 1893); BULWER, *Historical Characters, Talleyrand* (London, 1867), tr. PERROT (Paris, 1868); SAINTE-BEUVE, *Monsieur de Talleyrand* (Paris, 1870); PICHOT, *Souvenirs intimes sur Talleyrand* (Paris, 1870); MARCADÉ, *Talleyrand prêtre et évêque* (Paris, 1883); PINGAUD, *Le Congrès de Vienne et la politique de Talleyrand in Revue Historique*, LXX; BLENNERHASSETT, *Talleyrand* (Berlin, 1894); DE NOUVION, *Talleyrand prince de Bénévent in Revue Historique*, LXXIII (Nogent-le-Rotrou, 1900); DE LACOMBE, *Talleyrand, évêque d'Autun* (Paris, 1903); ROSENTHAL, *Fürst Talleyrand u. die auswärtige Politik Napoleons I* (Leipzig, 1905); MACCABE, *Talleyrand, a biographical study* (London, 1906); LEROY, *Talleyrand économiste et financier* (Paris, 1907); DE BARANTE, *La conversion et la mort de M. de Talleyrand, récit de l'un des cinq témoins, le Baron de Barante, publié par son petit-fils le Baron de Nervo* (Paris, 1910); DE LACOMBE, *La vie privée de Talleyrand* (Paris, 1910).

GUSTAVE GAUTHEROT.

Tallis, THOMAS, English composer, b. about 1514; d. 23 Nov., 1585. He was a chorister at Saint Paul's Cathedral, London, becoming organist of Waltham Abbey in 1536. In 1540 his post was forfeited on the dissolution of the abbey, and in 1542 he appears as a gentleman of the Chapel Royal, continuing as such under Henry VIII, Edward VI, Queens Mary and Elizabeth. Owing to his extraordinary eminence as a musician, he retained his Chapel Royal appointment unmolested, although he steadfastly clung to the old Faith amid all the changes from 1545 to 1584. Like Byrd he was an avowed Catholic, and even Elizabeth herself connived at the retention of Tallis in his court appointments. In conjunction with Byrd he obtained the valuable monopoly of printing music and ruled music paper from 1575 till his death, and he was also given lands valued at 30 pounds sterling per year by Elizabeth, as well as various tithes. He was buried in Greenwich parish church. The metrical epitaph which was placed over his tomb was subsequently set to music by De Cooke. His fecundity as a composer was enormous, and he wrote several *tours de force* including a forty-part motet "Spem aliam non habui". Many of his masses are of great merit, especially his "Salve intemerata" and his mass for four voices. Owing to his religious views most of his compositions were not printed during his lifetime, but in recent years his MS. work has received much attention from skilled editors. His Dorian service and five-part Litany are gems of musical art, but are not to be compared to his exquisite Latin motets, and above all his glorious "Lamentations". Some charming motets are included in his printed "Cantiones" (1576), while many of his Latin settings are tinkered to suit Anglican tastes, e. g. his "O Sacrum Convivium" adapted to "I call and cry" by Barnard. He essayed all the existing art-forms, including "Fancies for the Organ" and some virginal pieces. Unfortunately, he has been too frequently judged by his English services, but these were merely written ex officio and do not reveal the genuine Tallis, whose best contrapuntal work may be placed almost on a par with that of Palestrina.

EITNER, *Quellen Lexikon* (Leipzig, 1900–04); GROVE, *Dict. of Music and Musicians*, V (London, 1904–10); TERRY, *Catholic Church Music* (London, 1907); WALKER, *A History of Music in England* (Oxford, 1907).

W. H. GRATTAN-FLOOD.

Talmud.—I. DEFINITION.—תַּלְמוּד, a post-Biblical substantive formation of Pi'el לִמּוּד, "to teach" originally signified "doctrine", "study". In a special sense, however, it meant the justification and explanation of religious and legal norms or *Halakhoth* ("conduct", signifying "the law in accordance with which the conduct of life is to be regulated"). When in the third century the Halakhoth collection of Jehuda I or the recorded Mishna became the chief object of study, the expression "Talmud" was applied chiefly to the discussions and explanations of the Mishna. Finally, it became the general designation for the Mishna itself and the collection of discussions concerned with it. For the latter, the designation Gemara, interpreted as "completion" from גְּמַר, "to complete", Aramaic גְּמָרָא, abbreviated גְּמ׳, subsequently became the accepted term. The word first found entrance into the Talmud editions through Christian censorship; manuscripts and the old printed editions use the expression *Talmud*. We therefore understand by Talmud a compilation consisting of the *Mishna*, i. e. the codification of Jewish religious and legal norms, and of the *Gemara*, or the collection of discussions and explanations concerning the Mishna.

II. ORIGIN OF THE TALMUD.—Since Esdras the foundation of the Jewish religious community was the law. Everything was regulated in accordance with fixed norms; nothing could be added or changed in the law laid down in the Pentateuch. Yet the ever-varying conditions of life called for new ordinances, and these were decreed in accordance with the needs of the time and the special cases to be determined. There were thus formed a traditional law and custom orally transmitted. Every decree of this kind (*halakha*), if it had existed from time immemorial and nothing further could be said in regard to its origin, was called הֲלָכָה לְמֹשֶׁה מִסִּינַי, a law given to Moses on Mount Sinai. Even for orthodox Judaism of to-day it is an article of faith that Moses, at the same time that he received the written law, recorded in the Pentateuch also received detailed explanations of the different laws, which were handed down by tradition as oral law. In addition to this the scribes at an early period attempted, by interpretation of the Torah, to make the law applicable to the changed conditions of life, to base the new precepts at least retrospectively on the Torah, and to draw out of it further religious laws. For this kind of Scriptural learning hermeneutic rules (*Middoth*) were at a later period established, at first seven, which were then divided into fourteen, and finally increased to thirty-two. All the older additions to the Torah as well as the constantly increasing new material were for a long time transmitted orally, and, according to the prevailing view, it was forbidden to record it in writing. But it is at all events wrong to assume that there was a formal prohibition to record Halakhoth in writing. The prohibition probably referred to written records intended for public use; for a fixed record of the traditional law would have acted as a hindrance to its further development in accordance with the existing needs of the day. It is by no means improbable that the final reduction of the Mishna was preceded by previous written records, especially after Rabbi Aqiba, at the beginning of the second century, had divested the study of the law of its previous Midrash character and had undertaken to arrange the materials systematically. Among his pupils it was probably Rabbi Me'ir who continued these systematic labours. But of such collections only one finally attained canonical recognition, and therefore was called Mishna *par excellence*, viz. the one edited about the end of the second century of our era by Rabbi Jehuda I, called *Ha-nashi* (the prince) or *Ha-qadosh* (the saint) or simply the Rabbi. This then is our Mishna, the basis of the Talmud.

Rabbi Jehuda had adopted only a part of the doctrines, which in course of time had been handed down in the different schools. Although he selected what was most important, he sometimes omitted much that seemed important to others; and, on the other hand, it was felt that even the unimportant should not be allowed to sink into oblivion. In consequence, other collections soon originated, which, though not canonical, were nevertheless highly valued. All the Halakhoth which were not included in the Mishna of Jehuda received the name *Baraithoth* (sing. *Baraitha*, "omitted doctrine"). The most important Baraitha collection is the Tosephta.

The precise brevity of expression and the pregnant form in which the Mishna had codified the Halakhoth made an interpretation of them necessary, while the casuistic features of the work were a stimulus to further casuistic development. In the profound study and explanation of its contents much weight was placed upon the Haggada, i. e. the doctrines not included in the law (folk-lore, legends, historic recollections, ethics and didactics, etc.), of which Jehuda, who aimed to draw up a code of laws, had taken little or no account. Everything, in fact, that tradition offered was brought within the range of discussion. In order to give a suitable designation to the new tendency in the teaching of the law, scholars, up to the time of the final transcription of the Mishna, were known as *Tanna'im* (sing. *Tanna*, "teacher"), those who came after them, *Amora'im* (sing. *Amora*, "speaker"). The collection of the Amora'im, as finally recorded, was called, as stated above, Talmud, later Gemara: that of the Palestinian schools, the Palestinian Gemara, that of the Babylonian schools, the Babylonian Gemara. The combined edition of the Mishna and Gemara, or the Talmud in our sense of the word, discriminates, therefore, between Mishna and Palestinian Gemara, or "Palestinian Talmud", and Mishna and Babylonian Gemara or "Babylonian Talmud". The latter is meant when the Talmud without further specification is referred to.

III. THE MISHNA (משנה, "repetition", translated by the Fathers of the Church δευτέρωσις). The word is a substantive formation from the root שנה, "to repeat". From this meaning was developed, in the language of the later schools, the characteristic method of all teaching and learning, particularly of doctrines orally transmitted, which was accomplished by repeated enunciation on the part of the teacher and frequent repetition on the part of the pupil. Both expressions (שנה and משנה) thus became a term for the science of tradition, the former signifying the special study of orally transmitted law, the latter the law itself in contrast to מקרא (from קרא, "to read"), the written law. But the expression is also used for each of the doctrines orally transmitted, and differs from Halakha in that the latter signifies the traditional law so far as it is binding, while the former designates it as an object of study. Furthermore, the word Mishna is applied to the systematic collection of such doctrines, and finally to that collection which alone has attained canonical recognition, i. e. the collection of Jehuda I. This collection represents Jewish law codified in that development which it received in the schools of Palestine up to the end of the second century after Christ. Through it the orally transmitted law was finally established along with the written law or the Torah. The foundation of this collection is formed by the collections which already existed before Jehuda, particularly that of Rabbi Me'ir. The Mishna does not pretend to be a collection of sources of the Halakha, but merely to teach it. Whether its fixation in writing was the work of Jehuda himself or took place after him is a debated point; but the former is the more probable theory. The only question then is how much of it he wrote; in the extended form which it now presents it could not have been written by him alone. It has evidently received additions in course of time, and in other respects also the text has been altered.

As regards the subject matter the Mishna is divided into six institutes or *Sedarim;* for this reason Jews are accustomed to call the Talmud *Shas.* Each Seder has a number (7–12) of treatises; these are divided into chapters or *Peraqim*, and each chapter into precepts. The six institutes and their treatises are as follows:

A. *Seder Zera'im* (harvest), containing in eleven treatises the laws on the cultivation of the soil and its products.

(1) *Berakhoth* (benedictions) blessings and prayers, particularly those in daily use. (2) *Pe'a* (corner), concerning the parts of the fields and their products which are to be left to the poor (cf. Lev., xix, 9 sq.; xxiii, 22; Deut., xxiv, 19 sq.) and in general concerning the poor laws. (3) *Demai*, more properly *Dammai* (doubtful), concerning the fruits of the soil of which it is doubtful whether the tithes have been paid. (4) *Kil'ayim* (heterogenea), concerning the unlawful combinations of plants, animals, and garments (cf. Lev., xix, 19; Deut., xxii, 9 sq.). (5) *Shebi'ith* (seventh), i. e. Sabbatical year (Deut., xv, 1 sq.). (6) *Terumoth* (heave offerings) for the priests (Num., xviii, 8 sq.; Deut., xviii, 4). (7) *Ma'asroth* (tithes) for the Levites (Num., xviii, 21 sq.). (8) *Ma'aser shenî* (second tithe), (Deut., xiv, 22 sq.; xxvi, 12 sq.) which had to be spent at Jerusalem. (9) *Halla* (yeast) (cf. Num., xv, 18 sq.). (10) *'Orla* (foreskin) concerning uncircumcised fruits and trees (Lev., xix, 23). (11) *Bikkurim* (first fruits) brought to the temple (Deut., xxvi, 1 sq; Ex., xxiii, 19).

B. *Seder Mo'ed* (season of feasts), treats in twelve

treatises of the precepts governing rest on the Sabbath, the other feast and holy days, as well as fast days. (1) *Shabbath.* (2) *'Erubin* (combinations), the means by which one could circumvent especially onerous provisions of the Sabbath laws. (3) *Pesaḥim* (Passover). (4) *Sheqalim* (shekels), treats of the tax of half a shekel for the maintenance of Divine service in the temple (cf. Neh., x, 33), based upon Ex., xxx, 12 sq. (5) *Yoma* (day), i. e. day of expiation. (6) *Sukka* (Tabernacle), treats of the feast of Tabernacles. (7) *Beca* (egg), taken from the first word with which the treatise begins or *Yom tob* (feast), is concerned with the kinds of work permitted or prohibited on festivals. (8) *Rosh hashana* (beginning of the year), treats of the civil new year on the first of Tishri (Lev., xxiii, 24 sq.; Num., xxix, 1 sq.). (9) *Ta'anith* (fast). (10) *Megilla* (roll) of Esther, respecting the laws to be observed on the feast of Purim. (11) *Mo'ed qatan* (minor feast), the laws relating to the feasts intervening between the first and last days of the Passover and Sukkoth. (12) *Hagiga* (feast-offering), treats (chaps. i and iii) of the duty of pilgrimage to Jerusalem and the private offerings on such occasions (cf. Deut., xvi, 16 sq.).

C. *Seder Nashim* (women), elucidates in seven treatises the laws of marriage and all pertaining thereto, vows, and the marriage laws of the Nazarites. (1) *Jebamoth*, levirate marriages (Deut., xxv, 5 sq.). (2) *Kethuboth* ("marriage deeds" and marriage settlements). (3) *Nedarim* ("vows") and their annulment. (4) *Nazir* (Nazarite; cf. Num., vi). (5) *Sota* ("suspected woman"; cf. Num., v, 11 sq.). (6) *Gittin* (letters of divorce; cf. Deut., xxiv, 1 sq.). (7) *Giddushin* (betrothals).

D. *Seder Nezigin* ("damages"), explains in eight treatises civil and criminal law. In this institute are included the Eduyyoth, a collection of traditions, and the Haggadic treatise, Aboth.

The treatises 1–3, *Baba Kamma* (the first gate), *Baba meçi'a* (the middle gate), and *Baba bathra* (the last gate), originally formed a single treatise, the subdivision of which was caused by its great length (30 chaps.). They treat of the laws of property, inheritance, and obligation. *Baba Kamma* treats of damages in a narrow sense (along with theft, robbery, and bodily injury) and the right to damages; *Baba meçi'a* is concerned chiefly with legal questions in regard to capital and treats finding, deposits, interest and loans; *Baba Bathra* is concerned with questions of social polity (possessions, limitations, buying and selling, security, inheritance and documents). (4) *Sanhedrin*, i. e. συνέδριον, treats of the law courts, legal processes, and criminal justice. (5) *Makkoth* (stripes), treats of punishment by stripes legally acknowledged (cf. Deut., xxv, 1 sq.). (6) *Shebu'oth* (oaths). (7) *'Eduyyoth* (test), containing a collection of legal decisions gathered from the testimonies of distinguished authorities. (8) *'Aboda Zara* (idolatry). (9) *'Aboth* (fathers) or *Pirqe Aboth* (sections of fathers) contains ethical maxims of the *Tanna'im* (200 B. C.–A. D. 200). (10) *Horayoth* (decisions), concerning legal decisions and religious questions which were erroneously rendered.

E. *Seder Qodashim* (sacred things), treats in twelve treatises of the sacrifices, temple service, and dedicated objects (1) *Zebahim* (animal sacrifices). (2) *Menahoth* (meat offerings). (3) *Hullin* (things profane) of the sacrifice of pure and impure animals and of laws concerning food. (4) *Bekhoroth* (first born) of men and animals (cf. Ex., xiii, 2, 12 sq.; Lev., xxvii, 26 sq.; Num., viii, 16 sq.; xviii, 15 sq.; Deut., xv, 19 sq. (5) *'Arakhin* (valuations), that is equivalents to be given for the redemption of persons and things dedicated to God (Lev., xvii, 2 sq., xxv, 15 sq.). (6) *Temura* (exchange) of a sacred object (Lev., xxvii, 10–33). (7) *Kerithoth* (excisions), concerning the sins punished by this penalty, and what was to be done when anyone intentionally committed such a sin. (8) *Me'ild* (violation) of a sacred object (cf. Num., v, 6 sq.; Lev., v, 15 sq.). (9) *Tamid* (continual sacrifice), concerning the daily morning and evening sacrifice and the temple in general. (10) *Middoth* (measurements), a description of the temple and of the temple service. (11) *Quinnim* ("nests" of birds), of the sacrifices of doves by the poor (Lev., i, 14 sq.; xii, 8).

F. *Seder Teharoth* (purifications), treats in twelve treatises of the ordinances of cleanness and of purifications. (1) *Kelim* (vessels), treats of the conditions under which domestic utensils, garments, etc., become unclean. (2) *Ohaloth* (tents) of the defilement of dwellings by a corpse (Num., xix, 14 sq.). (3) *Nega'im* (leprosy). (4) *Para* (red heifer; cf. Num., xix). (5) *Teharoth* (purifications) (euphemistically), treats of the lesser degrees of defilement lasting only till sunset. (6) *Miqwa'oth* (wells), the conditions under which wells and reservoirs are fit to be used for ritual purification. (7) *Nidda* (menstruation). (8) *Makhshirin* (preparers), the conditions under which certain articles, by coming in contact with liquids, become ritually unclean (Lev., xi, 34, 37, 38). (9) *Zabim* (persons afflicted with running issues; cf. Lev., xv). (10) *Tebul yom* (immersed at day), i. e. the condition of the person who had taken the ritual bath, but who has not been perfectly purified by sunset. (11) *Yadâyim* (hands), treats of the ritual uncleanness of the hands and their purification. (12) *'Uqcin* (stalks) of fruits and shells and their ritual uncleanness.

In our editions the number of treatises is sixty-three; originally there were only sixty, because the four paragraphs of the treatise Baba kamma, Baba bathra, Baba meci'a, likewise Sanhedrin and Makkoth, formed only one treatise. The Mishna exists in three recensions: in the manuscripts of editions of the separate Mishna, in the Palestinian Talmud in which the commentaries of the Amora'im follow short passages of the Mishna, and in the Babylonian Talmud, in which the Gemara is appended to an entire chapter of the Mishna. The contents of the Mishna, aside from the treatises Aboth and Middoth, are with few exceptions Halakhic. The language, the so-called Mishna Hebrew or New Hebrew, is a fairly pure Hebrew, not without proof of a living development—enriched by words borrowed from Greek and Latin and certain newly-created technical expressions, which seem partly developed as imitations of Roman legal formulas. The Mishna is cited by giving the treatise, chapter, and precept, e. g. 'Berakh, i, 1.

Among the commentators of the whole Mishna the following deserve special mention: Maimonides, the Hebrew translation of whose Arabic original is printed in most editions of the Mishna; Obadia di Bertinoro (d. 1510), Jom Tob Lippmann Heller (d. 1654), Jisrael Lipschütz (his Mishna with commentary תפארת ישראל (6 vols., Königsberg, 1830–50).

The first edition of the complete Mishna was at Naples in 1492. Texts with Hebrew commentaries exist in great numbers. Of importance as a confirmation of the Palestinian version is the edition of W. H. Lowe (Cambridge, 1883), after the Cambridge manuscript. Also deserving of mention are: "Misna . . . Latinitate donavit G. Lurenhusius" (text, Latin translation, notes, Latin translation of Maimonides and Obadia, 6 vols., Amsterdam, 1698–1703); "Mishnajoth", with punctuation and German translation in Hebrew letters, begun by Sammter (Berlin, 1887— still incomplete); Ger. tr. of the Mishna by Rabe (6 parts, Onolzbach, 1760–63).

IV. THE PALESTINIAN TALMUD.—On the basis of the Mishna, juridical discussions were continued, at first in the schools of Palestine, particularly at Tiberias, in the third and fourth centuries. Through the final codification of the material thus collected, there arose in the second half of the fourth century the so-called Jerusalem, more properly Palestinian, Talmud. The usual opinion, which originated with Maimonides, that its author was Rabbi Jochanan, who lived in the third century, is untenable because of the names of the later scholars which occur in it. In the Palestinian Talmud the text of the Mishna is taken sentence by sentence, and explained with increasingly casuistic acumen. The Baraithoth, i. e. the maxims of the Torah not found in the Mishna, as well as the legal paragraphs are always given in Hebrew, and so are most of the appended elucidations; the remainder is written in a West Aramaic dialect (G. Dalman, "Grammatik des jüdisch-Palästinischen Aramäisch", Leipzig, 1905). Along with the Halakha it contains rich Haggadic material. Whether the Palestinian Talmud ever included the entire Mishna is a matter of dispute. The only parts preserved are the commentaries on the first four Sedarim (with the exception of several chapters and the treatises Eduyyoth and Aboth) and on the three first divisions of the treatise Nidda in the sixth Seder. The supposed discovery by S. Friedländer of treatises on the fifth Seder is based upon a forgery (cf. "Theologische Literaturzeitung", 1908, col. 513 sq., and "Zeitschr. d. Deutsch. Morgenländisch. Gesellsch.", LXII, 184). The Palestinian Talmud is generally cited by giving the treatise, chapter, page, and column after the Venetian and Cracow editions, mostly also the line, indicated by j (= jerus.) or pal.; e. g. pal. Makkoth, 2 Bl. 31^d 56. Many scholars cite in the same manner as for the Mishna, but this is not to be recommended.

Editions: Venice (Bomberg), 1523–24; Cracow, 1609; Krotoshin, 1866; Zhitomir, 1860–67; Piotrkow, 1900–02. French translation by M. Schwab, 11 vols., Paris, 1879–80; I² 1890.

Several treatises are printed with Latin translations in Ugolini, "Thesaurus antiquitatum sacrarum", vols. XVII–XXX, Venice, 1755–65; Wünsche, "Der palästinische Talmud in seinen haggadischen Bestandteilen ins Deutsche übersetzt" (Zurich, 1880).

V. BABYLONIAN TALMUD.—The Mishna is said to have been brought to Babylon by Aba Areka, generally called Rab (d. 247), a pupil of Rabbi Jehuda. In the schools there it became a norm of legal religious life and a basis of juridical discussion. But while in Palestine there was a greater tendency to preserve and propagate what had been handed down, the Babylonian Amora'im developed their interpretation of the law in all directions, which explains why the Babylonian Talmud acquired a greater significance for Judaism than the Palestinian. Thus the material grew rapidly and gradually led to a codification, which was undertaken by R. Ashi (d. 427), head of the school at Sura, and by R. Abina or Rabbina (d. 499), the last of the Amora im. The scholars who lived after him (at the end of the fifth and in the first half of the sixth centuries), called *Sabora im* ("those who reflect, examine", because they weighed and also completed what had been written by the Amora'im), are to be regarded as those who really completed the Babylonian Talmud.

Like the Palestinian, the Babylonian Talmud does not include the entire Mishna. In the first and sixth divisions only the treatises Berakhoth and Nidda are considered; in the second division Shegalim is omitted, in the fourth Eduyyoth and Aboth, in the fifth Middoth, Ginnim, and half of Tamid. It is indeed questionable if the greater number of these treatises were included in the Babylonian Gemara; Eduyyoth and Aboth are excluded, by reason of the subject matter, while the remainder treat for the most part ordinances which could not be applied outside of Palestine. The Babylonian Talmud therefore includes only 36½ treatises, but is at least four times the extent of the Palestinian, although the latter deals with 39 treatises. The Haggada is even more fully represented than in the Palestinian. The language, excepting the legal paragraphs and the quotations of the older scholars and Palestinian rabbis, is that of the East Aramaic dialect of Babylonia (cf. Levias, "A Grammar of the Aramaic Idiom contained in the Babylonian Talmud", Cincinnati, 1900; M. L. Margolis, "Grammatik des babylonischen Talmuds", Munich, 1910). The Babylonian Talmud is cited according to treatise, folio, and page, as the content in nearly all the editions since that of the third Bomberg one (1548) is the same, e. g. Berakh 22^a. In these editions there are usually appended at the end of the fourth Seder seven small treatises, partly from Talmudic, partly from post-Talmudic times, among which is the post-Talmudic treatise Sopherim (directions for the writer and public reader of the Torah). Among the commentaries the first place belongs to that of Rashi (d. 1105), completed by his grandson Samuel ben Me' ir (d. about 1174). Chiefly of a supplementary character are the works of the Tosaphists or authors of the *Tosaphoth* (additions), who lived in France and Germany during the twelfth and thirteenth centuries. They give amplifications and learned explanations of certain treatises. Other commentaries are enumerated by Strack, op. cit. infra, 149–51.

The Babylonian Talmud has often been printed, but until the present time a critical edition has remained a desideratum. Material for this purpose is furnished by Raphael Rabbinovicz, among others, in his "Variæ lectiones in Mischnam et in Talm. Babyl.", etc. (15 vols., Munich, 1868–86); Vol. XVI was edited by Ehrentreu (Przemysl, 1897). Serious mutilations and bungling changes in the text were caused by the Christian censorship, at first in the Basle edition (1578–81). The numerous bickerings among the Jews had the further consequence that they themselves practised censorship. The excised passages were partly collected in small treatises, published for the most part anonymously.

EDITIONS.—Raphael Rabbinovicz, מאמר על הדפסת התלמוד (*Ma'amar al hadpasath ha-talmud*), (Munich, 1877), a critical review of the editions of the Babylonian Talmud, as a whole or in part since 1484. The first complete edition appeared at Venice (Bomberg), (12 vols., 1520–23). The advantage of this edition consists in its complete character; the text itself is full of errors. A certain reputation is enjoyed by the Amsterdam edition (1644–48), in which the censured passages have been as far as possible restored. The edition of Frankfort (1720–22) served directly or indirectly as a basis for those which followed. Of the later editions may be mentioned those of Berlin (1862–68), Vienna (1864–72), and Vilna (1880–86). A quarto edition, the text after the *editio princeps*, with the variants of the Munich manuscripts and a German translation, was begun by Lazarus Goldschmidt in 1897. Up to date 6 vols., containing the Institutes I, II, IV, V, and the two first treatises of III, have appeared. Unfortunately this publication is by no means faultless. M. L. Rodkinson, "New Edition of the Babylonian Talmud", New York, 1896; M. Mielziner, "Introduction to the Talmud" (Cincinnati, 1894; New York, 1903); M. L. Rodkinson, "The History of the Talmud" (New York, 1903); H. L. Strack, "Einleitung in den Talmud" (Leipzig, 1908), pp. 139–175, containing an extensive bibliography of the Talmud and of the questions concerning it.

F. SCHÜHLEIN.

Talon, JEAN, first intendant in exercise of New France, b. at Châlons-sur-Marne, 1625, of Philippe and Anne Beuvy; d. at Versailles, 23 Nov., 1691. After studying at the Jesuit college of Clermont, in Paris, he embraced the career of military administration, beginning as war commissary in Flanders (1654), where he acted as intendant to Turenne's army. His success won Cardinal Mazarin's favour, and he was promoted (1655) Intendant of the Province of Hainaut Louis XIV and Colbert being determined to save Canada, then in great distress, Talon was appointed intendant the same day (23 March, 1655) that Courcelles became Governor of New France. They, with Tracy, lieutenant-general of all the French possessions in America, formed a powerful triumvirate. Talon's faculties were most ample, comprising justice, police, and finance. Reaching Quebec in 1665, he immediately began colonizing in the neighbourhood. In 1666 he had the first Canadian census taken; it gave only 3215 souls. Had his colonization policy been adopted, New France would have had 500,000 inhabitants in 1760, instead of only 60,000. Talon shared the glory of Tracy and Courcelles's expedition against the Iroquois (1666), by the preparation that had alone rendered it possible. He consented to remain after the two years of his term of office. The annexation of the New Netherlands to the French domain, which he suggested to Colbert, was not favoured by the king. He concurred (1666) in reorganizing the Sovereign Council and in reforming the petty courts. By his plan of grouping settlers round the city, a defence corps of volunteer militia would have dispensed with reinforcements of regular troops. Three years of Talon's administration had renewed the face of the country. Agriculture had progressed, cod and seal fishing were developed, shipbuilding began to thrive, and trade with the Antilles was inaugurated.

After returning to France (1668) he strove to promote Canada's interests. Reappointed in 1670, he brought with him freedom of trade. He sent explorers north, west, and south. St-Lusson took possession of Lake Superior. Forts were built and the Kennebec route opened between Quebec and Acadia, lately restored to France by the treaty of Breda. Father Albanel and his party reached James Bay and planted the cross in the far north. Jolliet, charged by Talon to find the north-west passage, discovered the Mississippi. At Talon's bidding, New France set her seal on the three-fourths of North America. He returned to France in 1672, after having, during his last weeks in office, created many seigniories for officers of the Carignan regiment, thereby contributing to the development of colonization and to the foundation of an aristocracy. During his seven years of office Talon had realized the programme he had traced in 1665. By establishing administrative and judiciary institutions that lasted throughout the entire French regime, by encouraging industry and commerce, fostering charitable works, creating new centres of population, and fortifying the colony's frontiers he prepared the way with remarkable foresight for the future development of the country, and ranks among the foremost makers of Canada. Louis XIV created him Count d'Orsainville (1675), honouring him with several important dignities and ample emoluments. Talon generously aided James II in his efforts to regain his throne, likewise assisting the exiled followers of the Stuarts. Naturally influenced by the Gallican spirit of his age, he was inclined to overmagnify the royal authority in its centralizing and domineering attitude towards the Church. His excessive zeal for the financial prosperity of the State caused him to resent unreasonably the wise restrictions imposed by Bishop Laval on the liquor traffic with the Indians.

FERLAND, *Histoire du Canada* (Quebec, 1892); GARNEAU, *Histoire du Canada* (Montreal, 1882); ROCHEMONTEIX, *Les Jésuites et la Nouvelle-France* (Paris, 1896); CAAPAIS, *Jean Talon* (Quebec, 1904).

LIONEL LINDSAY.

Talon, NICOLAS, French Jesuit, historian, and ascetical writer, b. at Moulins, 31 August, 1605; d. at Paris, 29 March, 1691. Entering the Society in 1621, he taught literature for several years, with remarkable success. After his ordination he gained some reputation as a preacher, was a devoted worker in the prisons and hospitals of Paris, and served as army-chaplain with the French troops in Flanders, winning the admiration and love of the men and the life-long friendship of the Prince de Condé. He assisted the notorious Aimé du Poncet during his painfully protracted execution. Thanks to Talon's gentleness, the terrible outlaw died penitent and resigned. This striking conversion made a profound impression. As a writer, Talon had original, if not always correct, views, a lively imagination, a quaint and comparatively pure and elegant style. Besides his "Oraison funèbre de Louis XIII" (Paris, 1644), a "Description de la pompe funèbre du Prince de Condé" (Paris, 1646), and some books of minor importance, Talon wrote "La vie de St. François de Sales" (Paris, 1640), "La vie de St. François Borgia" (Paris, 1671), "Les peintures chrétiennes" (Paris, 1667 according to Weiss, 1647 according to Sommervogel), and a Bible history, the first part of which, "Histoire sainte", was published at Paris in 1640. The author's purpose was to interest his readers in the Old-Testament story. The book became popular and was several times reprinted, notably in a fine Cramoisy edition (1665). The Marquis of Winchester gave an English translation in 1653. Talon's "Histoire sainte" is deficient in taste and critical judgment; it is a romance, not a reliable exposition of facts. Its methods, if not as objectionable as Berruyer's in his "Histoire du peuple de Dieu", are unsound. The author published a sequel, "L'histoire sainte du Nouveau Testament" (Paris, 1669). It met with little success. Talon's portrait has been engraved by Heer. Sommervogel mentions 300 of his letters in the d'Aumale collection at Chantilly.

SOUTHWELL, *Bibliotheca scriptorum soc. Jesu* (Rome, 1676), 636; D'ARTIGNY, *Nouveaux mémoires*, IV (Paris, 1749), 138–48; CARÉYON, *Une exécution en place de Grève, au XVIIe siècle (pièce inédite)* (Poitiers, 1863); DE BACKER, *Bibl. des écrivains de la C. de J.*, 1st ed., V, 717; DE GUILHERMY, *Ménologe de la C. de J., Assistance de France* (1st ed., Paris, 1892), 429; HURTER, *Nomenclator*, II, 457; SOMMERVOGEL, *Bibl. de la C. de J.*, i, VII, 1821–3; LEMOINE-LICHTENBERGER, *Trois familiers du Grand Condé, l'abbé Bourdelot, le père Talon, le père Tirier* (Paris, 1909).

JOHN C. REVILLE.

Talon, PIERRE, a French-Canadian explorer, b. at Quebec, 1676, of Lucien and Isabelle Planteau; d. in France in the first half of the eighteenth century. His entire family had just emigrated to France, when they were all engaged to follow Cavalier de La Salle in his attempt to colonize Louisiana (1684). Shortly after landing there, Pierre Talon was sent to learn the language of the Cenis Indians, and spent six years in their country about one hundred leagues inland at the limit of La Salle's discoveries. After the murder of the latter by one of his party, and the massacre of many of the colonists, in their first settlement by the Clamcoët Indians, the country was occupied by the Spaniards. Talon's father had perished in the woods, but his brothers and sisters had been saved by Indian women. They all followed the invaders to New Spain, first to San Luis Potosi; and then to Mexico City, where they spent ten years. The viceroy took them all into his palace as servants and treated them well. Talon and his brother Jean-Baptiste enlisted as Spanish marines and embarked at Vera Cruz. When their vessel was captured by Captain Desaugurs, they begged to be sent back to Spain, but were enrolled in the Fouguerolles company of French marines. Talon, in his evidence sworn at Brest (1698), gives abundant details regarding the character, customs, and religious rites of the Indian tribes with whom he had lived, as well as of the fauna and flora of the southern portion of the continent. The tribes he mentions are inscribed under the following names: Clamcoëts, Temerlouans, Tohos, Cenis, Ayennys, Amalchams, Canotinos, Paouitas, and Chomans. There is a great probability, although Talon cannot affirm it as certain, that one of the rivers seen by him during his intercourse with the Indians was the Mississippi which La Salle's premature death prevented the discoverer from seeing again.

TANGUAY, *Dict. généalogique* (Montreal, 1881); *Archives of the Marine* (France, 1698); GARNEAU, *Hist. du Canada* (Montreal, 1883).

LIONEL LINDSAY.

Tamanac Indians, a formerly important tribe of Cariban linguistic stock occupying the territory about the Cuchivero River, a tributary of the lower Orinoco, Venezuela. In 1749 they were in part, together with a part of the Saliva, gathered into the mission of San Luis del Encaramada (briefly Encaramada), established in that year by the celebrated Jesuit missionary and historian, Father S. Gilii, on the east bank of the Orinoco, some distance above the Apure. Father Gilii resided with the tribe for eighteen years until the expulsion of the order, when the Jesuit missions of the Orinoco were turned over to the Franciscans. Change of administration, disorders of the revolutionary period and governmental neglect ruined the missions, while frequent fever epidemics and terrible losses during the War of Independence decimated the Orinoco tribes, and as early as 1840 the Tamanac were virtually extinct with the exception of a few scattered individuals. In culture and mode of living the Tamanac resembled the Maipure. They had a lengthy genesis myth, with a deluge, in which a man and a woman saved themselves by climbing to the top of a high mountain called Tamanaca and miraculously created a new human race from the fruit of the mauritius palm. Hence the name of the tribe. Their great culture hero was Amalivaca, who came to them in a boat from over the eastern ocean and finally returned in the same way, after carving numerous sacred pictographs upon now inaccessible cliffs in the Tamanac country. Hence the missionaries were supposed by some of the Indians to be messengers from their lost culture hero and benefactor. (See also MAIPURE; SALIVA.)

GILII, *Saggio di storia americana* (Rome, 1784); HUMBOLDT, *Travels in the Equinoctial Regions of America* (London, 1818); HERVAS, *Catálogo de las lenguas*, I (Madrid, 1800); CODAZZI, *Geografia de Venezuela* (Paris, 1841); BRINTON, *American Race* (New York, 1891).

JAMES MOONEY.

Tamassus, a titular see in Cyprus, suffragan of Salamis, was situated in the great central plain of the island, south-west of Soli, on the road from Soli to Tremithus. As there were copper mines in the neighbourhood, it is very probably the Temese, mentioned by Homer (Odyssey, I, 184), which was in his time the principal copper market of the island. To-day the three villages of Pera, Episkopio, and Politiko occupy the former site. The coins warrant our use of the spelling, Tamassus. According to the legends of Saints Barnabas and Auxibius, the first consecrated bishop was St. Heraclides, later transferred to Salamis, where he was succeeded by St. Myron, like himself a martyr (27 September). Three other bishops are mentioned: Tychon present at the Council of Constantinople, 381; Epaphroditus at the Council of Chalcedon, 451; Nicetas in 1210. The see was suppressed by the Latins in 1222, and never re-established.

SMITH, *Dict. of Gr. and Rom. Geog.*, s. v.; HACKETT, *A History of the Orthodox Church of Cyprus* (London, 1901), 240 sq., 313; LE QUIEN, *Oriens christ.*, II, 1059; MÜLLER, ed. DIDOT, *Notes on Ptolemy*, I, 959; DELEHAYE in *Analecta Bollandiana*, XXVI (Brussels, 1907), 237.

S. PÉTRIDÈS.

Tamaulipas, DIOCESE OF (CIVITATIS VICTORIÆ SIVE TAMAULIPENSIS), in the Mexican Republic, suffragan of Linares. Its area is that of the state of the same name, 31,758 sq. miles, besides two parishes in the northern part of the State of Vera Cruz; it has a population of 249,253 (Census of 1910). The residence of the bishop and governor is in Ciudad Victoria, 2467 feet above sea level, which has a population of 17,861 inhabitants (1910). Father André Olmos, who was the first to preach the Gospel in the region now known as the above bishopric, came from Burgos, Spain, in 1528, and worked until 1571, when he died at Tampico, beloved by all. In 1530 the Franciscan Fathers founded the Guardianship of San Salvador, which comprised twelve convents, and were almost all situated in the territory now known as the State of Tamaulipas; a few of these convents, however, were situated outside of this territory, for instance, that of Ozuloama, which is now a parish, and which, although situated in the State of Vera Cruz, belongs to the Bishopric of Tamaulipas. In 1748 the Fathers of the Apostolic College of Nuestra Señora de Guadalupe de Zacatecas took charge of the missions; these were placed in the hands of the Fathers of the Province of Santo Evangelio de Mexico in 1768. This see was planned as early as 1722. In 1860 Pius IX made a vicariate Apostolic of the territory, and in 1869 the pope's Bull "Apostolicum in Universas Orbis Ecclesias" raised it to the rank of a bishopric, naming Ciudad Victoria as its episcopal see, and making it suffragan of Mexico. When the new Archbishopric of Linares (or Monterey) was created in 1891 it became part of it, and so remains to this day.

There are no seminaries in this bishopric, priests and rectors being furnished by the Diocese of Zamora and others. It is credited, however, with 3 parochial schools, and 6 Catholic colleges with 700 students; there are 10 Protestant colleges, numbering about 500 students, and 14 Protestant churches. The episcopal city of Ciudad Victoria was founded in 1750 under the name of Santa Maria del Refugio de Aguayo, and has been known by its present name only since 1825.

VERA, *Catecismo geográfico histórico, y estadístico de la Iglesia mexicana* (Amecameca, 1881).

CAMILLUS CRIVELLI.

Tamburini, MICHELANGELO, fourteenth General of the Society of Jesus, b. at Modena, 27 Sept., 1648; d. 28 Feb., 1730. After having taught Scholastic philosophy and theology for twelve years, he was successively made rector of several colleges, was chosen by Cardinal Reynold of Este as his private theologian, held the offices of secretary general and vicar to Thyrsus Gonzalez, and finally, on the latter's death, was elected general on 3 Jan., 1706, a post which he occupied till his death. The reputation for solid virtue, patience, and courage, which he had acquired in the different grades of his order, was by no means dimmed in the long years of his generalate. During Tamburini's superiorship, the apostolic activity of the Society was at its best; but, at the same time, could be seen signs of the storm which was, half a century later, to annihilate it. The Reductions of Paraguay were beginning to bear fruit; missionaries were laying down their lives for the pest-stricken in the Levant or were pushing into the steppes of Tibet amid untold hardships. Peter the Great, desirous of giving his barbarous subjects the benefits of true religion and genuine civilization, admitted the Jesuits into Russia. Jansenism, the Society's bitterest foe, received its death-blow in 1708 by a Bull of Clement XI ordering the suppression of Port-Royal. Three Jesuits, Tolomei, Cienfuegos, and Salerno, were, in short succession, raised to the dignity of the cardinalate. John Francis Regis was beatified, Aloysius of Gonzaga and Stanislaus Kostka were given the honours of the altar. At the same time, future saints (St. Francis de Hieronymo and Bl. Anthony Baldinucci in Italy, Emmanuel Padial in Spain) were labouring with extraordinary success for the salvation of souls. But at this period, too, the debate over the Chinese Rites was at its height.

The Jesuit missionaries in China had been accused of not obeying the orders of the Supreme Pontiff. Tamburini, though naturally of a gentle disposition, could be firm when the honour of the Society was at stake. In the name of all the assistants and procurators gathered at Rome, he protested to Clement XI the fidelity and obedience of the whole Society to the Vicar of Christ. Thus ran the finishing sentence of his declaration: "But if, which God forbid, there be anyone among us who should harbour other thoughts or breathe other sentiments—for, where the number of subjects is so large, human prudence finds it difficult to prevent or hinder all such things—the General, in the name of the Society, declares, assures and protests that we reprove and reject him even now, that he is worthy of chastisement, and that he cannot be regarded as a true and legitimate son of the Society of Jesus".

CRÉTINEAU-JOLY, *Hist. de la Comp. de Jésus*, IV–V; DE GUILHERMY, *Ménologe, Assistance d'Italie*, 266–68; SOMMERVOGEL, *Bibl. de la C. de J.*, VII, 1827–30.

A. C. COTTER.

Tamburini, THOMAS, moral theologian, b. at Caltanisetta in Sicily, 6 March, 1591; d. at Palermo, 10 October, 1675. He entered the Society of Jesus when fifteen years old; there he became distinguished for extraordinary virtue and a rare talent for teaching. After a successful course of studies, he held the professorship of philosophy four years, of dogmatic theology seven years, of moral theology seventeen years, and during thirteen years was rector of various colleges. His writings are: "Methodus expeditæ confessionis" (5 vols., Rome, 1647); "De communione" (Palermo, 1649); "Explicatio decalogi" (Venice, 1654, 1707; Milan, 1655; Munich, 1659); "De sacrificio missæ" (3 vols., Antwerp, 1656); "De bulla cruciata" with other works (Palermo, 1663); "Juris divini, naturalis et eccles. expositio" (3 vols., Palermo, 1659–60). All these works exhibited solidity of doctrine and elegance of style and went through several editions. Though severe towards himself, Tamburini, when deciding cases of conscience for others, was inclined to follow the milder views which he found reputable authors declaring probable. This is the basis of the accusation of laxity frequently brought against him, and led to his controversy with Vincent Baron. Tamburini published a refutation of the attacks of his adversary under the title, "Germana doctrina R. P. Th. Tamburini, S.J." In determining the value of Tamburini's works, it is well to recall the criticism of St. Alphonsus Liguori in his "Theologia Moralis": "Let us add a word about this author [Tamburini], who is not estimated by many at his full value. It cannot be denied that he was apt to consider some opinions probable which do not deserve that note; hence he must be used with caution. But when Tamburini establishes his own opinions, he shows that he is a thorough theologian and solves the questions by reducing them to their last principles. Competent judges will find that the opinions which he then sets down as the more tenable are in the majority of cases the more correct".

DE FELLER, *Dict. Hist.*, VIII, 353; HURTER, *Nomenclator*, II, 270; SOMMERVOGEL, *Bibliothèque*, VII, 1830.

JOHN M. FOX.

THOMAS TAMBURINI
From Desrochers' "Recueil de Portraits", 1773

Tametsi (ALTHOUGH), the first word of ch. i, sess. 24, De Ref. Matr., of the Council of Trent. This chapter contains the legislation of the Church which was in force until Easter, 1908, concerning clandestine marriage. It decrees thus: Those who attempt to contract marriage otherwise than in the presence of the parish priest or of another priest delegated by him or by the ordinary, and before two or three witnesses, the holy synod renders wholly incapable of contracting and declares such contracts null and void. The reader is referred to the article CLANDESTINITY for a complete study of this decree. In a modified form the prescriptions of "Tametsi" were extended to the universal Church by the decree "Ne temere". The chapter "Tametsi" declares that clandestine contracts of marriage freely entered into are valid, unless rendered null by the non-observance of regulations made by the Church, and anathematizes those who hold the contrary, as well as those who falsely assert the invalidity of a marriage contracted without parents' consent, or who affirm that parents by their approval or disapproval may affect the binding force of such contracts. It is declared, however, that the Church has always disapproved of marriages contracted secretly, or without the consent of parents. This same chapter of the Tridentine Council prescribes the promulgation of the banns of marriage, which is a repetition of the Fourth Lateran Council, the form expressing consent to be used and the inscribing of the marriage in the parochial register. It declares also that any priest, secular or regular, other than the pastor, assisting at a marriage or giving the solemn nuptial blessing without proper delegation is suspended at once and remains under suspension till rightly absolved by the ordinary of the parish priest of the contracting parties. This censure, however, is no longer incurred, though punishment may be meted out to those who offend in this matter. Finally, "Tametsi" recommends that those about to marry approach the Sacraments of Penance and the Eucharist, and that local customs and rites connected with marriage be observed. (See also MARRIAGE, MORAL AND CANONICAL ASPECT OF.)

ANDREW B. MEEHAN.

Tamisier, MARIE-MARTHE-BAPTISTINE (called by her intimates EMILIA), initiator of international Eucharistic congresses, b. at Tours, 1 Nov., 1834; d. there 20 June, 1910. From her childhood her devotion to the Blessed Sacrament was extraordinary; she called a day without Holy Communion a veritable Good Friday. In 1847 she became a pupil of the Religious of the Sacred Heart at Marmoutier, remaining there four years. Without any special attraction for the life of a religious she made three unsuccessful attempts to enter it; the third was in the Convent of Perpetual Adoration founded by Ven. Père Eymard, who assured her she still belonged to our Lord in the Blessed Sacrament. A lady of wealth sought her aid in establishing a community of perpetual adoration but this plan also came to naught. She then (1871) went to live near the tomb of Blessed Jean Vianney at Ars. Coming under the direction of Abbè Chevrier of Lyons she found her true vocation, at once contemplative and active, in the Eucharistic cause. She had been prepared for it by many trials and disappointments. Throughout France and beyond, by extensive correspondence and by travel she spread the devotion. With the help of Mgr de Ségur and Mgr

Richard, then Bishop of Belley, pilgrimages were started to sanctuaries where Eucharistic miracles had taken place. Their success led to Eucharistic congresses. At the Lourdes Congress she was called the Jeanne d'Arc of the Blessed Sacrament, but her name was not publicly associated with the congresses until after her death. Canon Vaudon's history of the congresses published just before her death, though giving a detailed account of her apostolic career, calls her only "Mlle . . . ". She lived for some years at Issoudun and ministered there to the Shrine of Our Lady of the Sacred Heart. All her spare means, though often depriving herself, she devoted to the education of poor aspirants to the priesthood.

Mlle Tamisier in *The Sentinel of the Blessed Sacrament* (New York, July, 1911); VAUDON, *L'Œuvre des Congrès Eucharistiques* (Paris and Montreal, 1910); *L'Idéal* (Paris, 1910).

B. RANDOLPH.

Tanagra, a titular see in Hellas, suffragan of Corinth; it was a town of Bœotia, in a fertile plain on the right bank of the Æsopus. It was also called Poemandria and its territory Poemandris. In 457 B. C. the Athenians were defeated near Tanagra by the Lacedæmonians, but early in the following year they in turn defeated the Bœotians, thereby becoming masters of Bœotia. The city walls were destroyed. In 426 the Athenians invaded the territory of Tanagra and defeated the Tanagrians and Bœotians. The people of Tanagra were noted for their frugality, loyalty, and hospitality. Their land yielded little wheat, but the best wine in Bœotia, and the town was also noted for its fighting-cocks. Under Augustus Tanagra and Thespiæ were the chief towns of Bœotia. It had numerous temples, one of Dionysius with a famous statue by Calanus and a remarkable Triton, other temples of Themis, Aphrodite, Apollo, Hermes Criophorus, and Hermes Promaclius. The gymnasium contained a portrait of the poetess, Corinna, who was born at Tanagra and commemorated there by a monument. Pliny calls Tanagra a free state. It was still important in the sixth century, but must soon after have been destroyed by Slavic invasions. A station on the railway between Athens and Thebes is now called Tanagra; it connects with the village of Skimatari (650 inhabitants), about eight miles south of which are the ruins of the ancient town including the acropolis, necropolis etc. Excavations have made the tombs famous for the pretty little terra-cotta figurines which they contain. Duchesne has published ("Bulletin de correspondance hellénique", III, Paris, 1879, 144) a Christian inscription dating from the fifth or sixth century. Only one bishop is known, Hesychius, who in 458 signed the letter from the provincial synod to the Emperor Leo (Le Quien, "Oriens Christ.", II, 212); the other bishop mentioned by him belongs to another see.

SMITH, *Dict. of Greek and Roman Geog.*, s. v.

S. PÉTRIDÈS.

TANAGRA FIGURINE

Tancred, Prince of Antioch, b. about 1072; d. at Antioch, 12 Dec., 1112. He was the son of Marquess Odo and Emma, probably the daughter of Robert Guiscard. He took the Cross in 1096 with the Norman lords of Southern Italy and joined the service of his uncle Bohemund. Having disembarked at Arlona (Epirus), they marched towards Constantinople, and Tancred soon attracted attention by his activity, bravery, and somewhat undisciplined zeal; according to his biographer, Raoul de Caen, he was noted also for his humanity and kindness towards the defenceless. He brilliantly repulsed the Byzantine army which attacked him as he was crossing the Vardar (28 Feb., 1097), from which time Tancred became and remained the bitter enemy of the Greeks. Unlike Bohemund, he was the only one of all the leaders who refused to take the oath of fidelity demanded by Alexis Comnenus. He played an important part in the siege of Nicæa, and later, during the difficult march through Asia Minor, he led the way southwards and captured Tarsus which Baldwin tried in vain to wrest from him (Sept., 1097). While Baldwin advanced towards the Euphrates, Tancred seized the towns of Cilicia. He took an active part also in the siege of Antioch. In the march on Jerusalem he commanded the vanguard, and on 15 July, 1099, he entered the city, after making a breach in the gate of St. Stephen. He vainly endeavoured to save the lives of 300 Mussulmans who had taken refuge in the Mosque of Omar (*Templum Domini*). On the other hand he looted the treasures amassed in that building and distributed them among his knights. He received from Godfrey de Bouillon, who had been selected over him as king, the fiefs of Tiberias and Caïfa. When Bohemund was captured by the Turks in July, 1100, Tancred assumed the government of the Principality of Antioch, and extended its boundaries at the expense of the Turks and the Greeks. During the war between Bohemund and Alexis Comnenus (1104–08), Tancred defended both the Principality of Antioch and the Countship of Edessa; he also strengthened the Christian power in those districts, and refused to recognize the Treaty of Durazzo by which Bohemund had ceded the suzerainty of Antioch to the emperor. A skilled politician, he knew how to placate the Greeks and issued Greek money on which he is represented adorned with gold and jewels, wearing a turban surmounted by a cross.

TANCRED, PRINCE OF ANTIOCH
From an old print

RAOUL DE CAEN, *Gesta Tancredi* (the author went to Palestine in 1107 and was attached to the army of Tancred) in *Hist. Occid. des Croisades*, III, 537–601; SCHLUMBERGER, *Numismatique de l'Orient latin* (Paris, 1878), 45; DE SAULCY, *Tancrède* in *Biblioth. Ecole des Chartes* (1843); O. DE SYDOW, *Tankred* (Leipzig, 1880); REY, *Hist. des princes d'Antioche* in *Revue Orient Latin* (1896), 334; KUGLER, *Boemund u. Tankred* (Tübingen, 1862); CHALANDON, *Essai sur le régne d'Alexis Comnène* (Paris, 1900); STEVENSON, *The Crusaders in the East* (Cambridge, 1907).

LOUIS BRÉHIER.

Taney, ROGER BROOKE (pronounced Tawney), fifth chief justice of the Supreme Court of the United States, b. in Calvert County, Maryland, 17 March, 1777; d. at Washington, 12 October, 1864. His father, Michael Taney, was a gentleman of Catholic ancestry and education, and his mother, Monica Brooke, was also a Catholic. He was educated at private schools and by tutors until 15 years old, when he entered Dickinson College, Carlisle, Pennsylvania. He obtained his B. A. in 1795, and in the spring of 1796 went to Annapolis to read law in the office of Jeremiah Townley Chase, one of the chief justices of the General Court of Maryland. Early in 1799 he was admitted to the bar. Returning to his father's home in Calvert County to practice his profession, he shortly afterwards was elected to the House of Delegates, being then scarcely twenty-three years of age and the youngest member of the Assembly. In March, 1801, he went to Frederick to establish himself better in his legal practice, having been defeated for re-election to the Legislature from Calvert County. He was a candidate for member of the House of Delegates from Frederick county in 1803 on the Federal ticket, but, the county being strongly Republican, he was again defeated. On 7 January, 1806, he married Anne Phoebe Charlton Key, only daughter of John Ross Key, and sister of Francis Scott Key, a law student with Taney, at Annapolis, who afterwards wrote the "Star-spangled Banner".

When General Wilkinson, then Commander-in-Chief of the United States Army, was tried before a court martial, convened at Frederick in 1811, on charges of being an accomplice of Aaron Burr, Taney was one of the counsel in his defence, and, together with John Hanson Thomas, succeeded in winning his acquittal. Both refused any fee for their service because they had shared the suspicion against the accused. Taney was defeated on the Federal ticket for member of the House of Representatives of the United States, but in 1816 was elected to the state Senate. At the March term, 1819, of the Frederick County Court, he successfully defended Jacob Gruber, a Methodist minister, who was indicted for inciting slaves to the disturbance of the peace of the state. In 1823, he moved to Baltimore, and was soon recognized as the leading lawyer of that city, being appointed in 1827 by Governor Kent as Attorney-General of Maryland, upon the unanimous recommendation of the Baltimore bar. President Andrew Jackson, a warm admirer of Taney, appointed him Attorney-General of the United States on 21 June, 1831, and, upon the refusal of William J. Duane, Secretary of the Treasury, to remove the government deposits from the United States Bank, the president removed Duane from office on 23 Sept., 1833, and, on the same day, appointed Taney in his stead. The latter assumed the duties of the secretaryship on the following day, and two days later gave the order for the removal of the deposits to take effect on the first of October following. His appointment to the office of Secretary of the Treasury having been made during a recess of Congress, his nomination was sent to the Senate by the president on 23 June, 1834, and was rejected after a heated debate. This was the first time in the history of the Government that a cabinet officer appointed by a president had been rejected. Taney immediately submitted his resignation to President Jackson, and the latter accepted it with much regret. Judge Gabriel Duvall of Maryland, an associate justice of the Supreme Court of the United States, resigned in 1835, and President Jackson nominated Taney in his stead, but the nomination was not brought up in the Senate until the end of the session, and was then indefinitely postponed, which amounted to a rejection. This was due to the fact that the Senate as then constituted was violently opposed on political grounds to the president. In the same year Jackson again named Taney for a place on the Supreme Bench, this time as Chief Justice Marshall's successor. The nomination was strongly opposed by Senators Webster and Clay, but was finally confirmed on 15 March, 1836, by a majority of fourteen votes.

In the outbreak of yellow fever of 1855, Justice Taney's wife, who never became a Catholic, was stricken and died at Old Point Comfort on 29 September, and their youngest child died the following day. The most famous case decided by the Supreme Court during Chief Justice Taney's incumbency was that of Dred Scott *v.* John F. A. Sanford, the opinion in which, delivered by Taney, has been much misquoted and misunderstood. Chief Justice Taney did much towards the building up of the system of practice in the Supreme Court, framing it after that of the English courts, yet so modified as to be adaptable to the changed conditions existing in the United States. His opinions were arrived at rather by deep reflection and application of established legal principles to the questions presented to him than through exhaustive research of authorities. While giving due respect to former decisions, he did not rely slavishly upon precedents. By his dignified, though kindly, bearing, he always commanded the utmost respect for his Court. He had few, if any, personal enemies, and the purity of his private life was never questioned, even by his political opponents. Early in life he manumitted the slaves inherited from his father, and as long as they lived, he provided for the older ones by monthly pensions. He was buried at Frederick by the side of his mother's grave, in accordance with his own request. There is a handsome statue of him in Mount Vernon Place, Baltimore.

VAN SANDVOORT, *Lives of the Chief Justices*, (2 vols., Albany, 1822); TYLER, *Memoir of Roger Brooke Taney* (Baltimore, 1872); *Southern Library Messenger*, IV (Richmond, 1838), 348; *National Quarterly Review*, X (New York, 1864), 50; *The Catholic World*, LXVIII (New York, 1898), 396; *The Green Bag*, XIV (New York, 1902), 559.

J. P. W. McNEAL.

Tanguay, CYPRIEN, genealogist, b. at Quebec, 1819; d. 1902. After a course of classics and theology at Quebec Seminary, he was ordained in 1843. The first twenty-two years of his priesthood were devoted to parochial work, especially at Rimouski, where he greatly contributed to the foundation of the future diocesan seminary. His early taste for genealogical studies fully manifested itself after his official appointment to the Dominion Statistics Department (1867). His whole time was henceforth spent in consulting and compiling parochial and historical records throughout Quebec, the Maritime Provinces, Ontario, and the old French settlements in the United States. He also twice visited France for the same purpose. As the result of his labours he published (1871–90) his "Dictionnaire généalogique des familles canadiennes françaises depuis les origines de la colonie jusqu'à nos jours", comprising seven large double column volumes of over six hundred pages: a colossal undertaking, fit for a numerous body of collaborators, which he achieved alone. Although he was unable to realize the latter part of his programme entirely and many inaccuracies have crept into his work, yet on the whole it is highly reliable and almost unique. Every French Canadian by completing from contemporary registers the information supplied by this dictionary can proudly trace back his genealogy to his ancestors from old France. It has proved valuable for the discovery of canonical impediments to marriage through relationship, and has given birth to a copious genealogical literature of less comprehensiveness. In recognition of his labours the author received a prelature from Leo XIII (1887). He likewise published "Répertoire du clergé canadien-français" (1868) and "A travers les registres" (1886).

McLEAN-ROSE, *Canadian Biography* (Toronto, 1886); ALLAIRE, *Dict. biog. du clergé canadien-français* (Montreal, 1910).

LIONEL LINDSAY.

Tanis, a titular see, suffragan of Pelusium in Augustamnica Prima, capital of the fourteenth district of Lower Egypt. Tanis (in Egyptian Zani, in Hebrew Zoan) was situated on a branch of the Nile, to which it gave its name. It was one of the oldest cities in the world, as the Bible bears witness (Num., xiii, 23), and hieroglyphic inscriptions attest its existence under Pharao Pepi I Merira of the sixth dynasty. It flourished especially under the pharoas of the twelfth dynasty, under the Hyksos, or shepherd kings (fifteenth to seventeenth dynasties), under the pharoas of the nineteenth, twenty-first, and twenty-third dynasties, who had made Tanis their capital. It was under the shepherd kings that the Jews installed themselves in Egypt in the land of Gessen, near Tanis, and it is in this city, which was the residence of Rameses II, that Moses and Aaron performed many wonders (Ps. lxxvii, 12 and 43). It is a mistake to confound Tanis with the Ramesses built by the Israelites (Ex., i, 10 and 11) and situated very probably at Tell-Rotab. The Prophet Isaias (xix, 11–13; xxx, 4) denounced Tanis and the Jewish politicians who had recourse to its kings; so too Ezechiel (xxx, 14 and 18), who announced its approaching destruction. Jeremias, who also pronounced (ii, 16) anathemas against the city, was forced to follow the Jews thither after the conquest of Palestine by Nabuchodonosor (Jer., xliii, 7–10; xliv, 1; xlvi, 14). In these last passages however the Bible uses Thacphanes or Thaphanhes, in Latin Taphnes, and it is not absolutely certain that this is the same as Tanis, some identifying Taphnes with Tell Dafaneh, about seventeen miles from Ṣan or Tanis. The earliest Bishop of Tanis is Eudæmon, a Melitian bishop at the beginning of the fourth century. Mention may be made also of Hermion, bishop in 362; Apollonius, present at the Robber Synod of Ephesus and Paul in 458. Besides these Le Quien speaks of eight Jacobite bishops (Oriens christ., II, 535–38), the last of whom lived in 1086. About 870 the French monk Bernard visited Tanis, "in qua sunt christiani multum religiosi, nimia hospitalite ferventes" (Tobler and Molinier, "Itinera hierosolymitana", I, 313). At the present time Tanis is a poor village called San el Haggar containing 1570 inhabitants, near Lake Menzaleh. The ruins, situated about twenty minutes distance, consist of a large temple, a small granite temple, and of other monuments not identified.

PETRIE, *Tanis* in *Egypt Exploration Fund* (London, 1885–8); ROUGÉ, *Géog. ancienne de la Basse-Egypte* (Paris, 1891); 90–5; JULLIEN, *L'Egypte* (Lille, 1891), 151–7; AMÉLINEAU, *La géog. de l'Egypte à l'époque copte* (Paris, 1893), 413 sq.

S. VAILHÉ.

Tanner, ADAM, controversialist, b. at Innsbruck in 1571; d. at Unken, 25 May, 1632. He entered the Society of Jesus in 1589, and taught at first Hebrew, apologetics, and moral theology. When in 1601 the religious debate between Catholics and Lutherans was arranged at Ratisbon, Tanner aided his fellow Jesuit Gretser in proving that the dead word of the Bible could not be the supreme arbiter in matters of faith. He himself published an account of the proceedings (Mainz, 1602) and in subsequent apologies hurled back the charges brought against the Catholics by the Reformers. In 1603, the Bavarian duke invited him to occupy the chair of Scholastic theology in the University of Ingolstadt. A stranger in no field of science and gifted with a keen intellect, Tanner now developed an increasing activity both in teaching and writing on theological subjects. In his "Anatomiæ confessionis augustanæ" (Ingolstadt, 1613), he points out the fallacies of the Augsburg Confession, both from Luther's own assertions and from the qualities essential to the true Church. Against the so-called Utraquists, he wrote several works, both in Latin and in German, defending the Church's practice of giving Communion under one species only, and the sacrifice of the Mass. Other pamphlets were issued by him to clear his order from the false accusations of its enemies. When the conflict between the Venetians and Pope Paul V (q. v.) broke out, an able defence from his pen, "Defensionis ecclesiæ libertatis libri duo" (Ingolstadt, 1607), vindicated the Church's freedom against the tyrannical aggressions of the State.

After fifteen years spent at Ingolstadt, he was called by the Emperor Matthias to the University of Vienna. While there he published his greatest work, the "Universa theologia scholastica" (Ingolstadt, 1626–27), which resembles the "Summa" of St. Thomas not only in its arrangement, but also in its solidity of doctrine and conciseness of diction. Ferdinand II, Matthias's successor on the throne of the Habsburgs, appointed him chancellor of the University of Prague. Fleeing from the Swedes, Tanner died at Unken, an insignificant village near Salzburg. There he still rests amid unlettered peasants in an unknown grave. But, as Cordara says, "his virtues, coupled with his eminent erudition, will ever be his most splendid epitaph and mausoleum."

CORDARA, *Hist. Soc. Iesu*, VI, 583; GUILHERMY, *Ménologe*, I, 470; THÖLEN, *Menologium*, 325; HURTER, *Nomenclator*, I, 254; SOMMERVOGEL, *Bibliothèque* VII, 1843, sqq.

A. C. COTTER.

Tanner, CONRAD, Abbot of Einsiedeln, b. at Arth in the Canton of Schwyz, 28 Dec., 1752; d. 7 April, 1825. He studied the classics and theology at Einsiedeln; made vows in the Order of St. Benedict on 8 Sept., 1772, and was ordained in May, 1777. He was engaged as teacher at the *gymnasium* of Einsiedeln and later at Bellinzona. In 1787 he held the position of librarian at his abbey, and in 1789 he was made director of the college at Bellinzona. During the Revolution Tanner fled to the Tyrol, taking with him the miraculous statue, the head of St. Meinrad, and other valuables, and remained there until he could restore the treasures to the abbey. He was appointed pastor of St. Gerold in Vorarlberg in 1802, where he remained for three years, until recalled to act as master of novices. At the death of Abbot Beat in 1808 Tanner was elected abbot. With great prudence he accommodated himself to the political situation and thus secured the existence of the monastery. He encouraged the pursuit of studies, renovated the buildings, and rebuilt the Holy Chapel which had been destroyed 1798 by the French. Although the village of Einsiedeln was no longer under his jurisdiction, he retained for it a fatherly solicitude which he manifested especially in the years of famine (1816 and 1817). It was the intention of Pius VII to create the new Diocese of Waldstätten out of the cantons Uri, Schwyz, and Unterwalden, to make Tanner bishop, and to constitute the monks of Einsiedeln as cathedral chapter. The matter was proposed in 1818, but was declined by the abbot and his capitulars. Tanner's writings are: "Betrachtungen zur sittlichen Aufklärung im neunzehnten Jahrhundert" (5 vols., Augsburg, 1804–1808); "Bildung des Geistlichen durch Geistesübungen" (Augsburg, 1807), of which a fifth edition appeared at Einsiedeln in 1846; his pedagogical works were published by his successor, Abbot Celestine Müller.

RINGHOLZ, *Wallfahrtsgeschichte unserer lieben Frau von Einsiedeln* (Freiburg, 1876), 26; KUHN, *Der jetzige Stiftsbau von M. E.* (Einsiedeln, 1883), 111; RÉGNIER, *Chronique d'Einsiedeln* (Paris, 1837), 222.

FRANCIS MERSHMAN.

Tanner, EDMUND, Bishop of Cork and Cloyne, Ireland, 1574–1579; b. about 1526; d. 1579. The statement in his brief of appointment that he was born in the ecclesiastical province of Dublin is all that is known of his early life. His surname was borne by persons of humble station at Calverstown, Co. Kildare, which, coupled with his familiarity with the Eustaces of Baltinglas, may give colour to a surmise that he was a native of that district. In 1565 he was at Rome, being then probably in Holy orders, and entered the Society of Jesus; after a year in the Roman College he was sent to Dillingen University in 1567, and became doctor of divinity. His health, however, failed and he left the Society. In 1574 he was again at Rome, and the See of Cork and Cloyne being vacant, he was appointed thereto, 5 November, 1574, and was consecrated at Rome. In May, 1575, he set out for Ireland with exceptional faculties for his own diocese and for those of Cashel, Dublin, and its suffragan sees in the absence of their respective prelates. Not long after his reaching Ireland he was captured while exercising his functions at Clonmel, and was thrown into prison; here, as Holing tells, he was visited by a schismatical bishop whom he reconciled to the Church. A few days later he was himself released through the influence of a noble earl. Thereafter he did not venture into his own diocese, but as commissary-Apostolic he traversed the other districts assigned him, administering the sacraments and discharging in secret the other duties of his office. Four years he laboured thus in continual peril and distress, and at length succumbed to his privations and fatigues in the Diocese of Ossory, 4 June, 1579. Bruodin states that he died in Dublin Castle after eighteen months of imprisonment and cruel torture.

HOGAN, *Distinguished Irishmen of the 16th Century* (London, 1894); BRADY, *Episcopal Succession in Great Britain and Ireland* (Rome, 1876–1877); MORAN, *Spicilegium Ossoriense*, I (Dublin, 1874); BRUODIN, *Propugnaculum catholicæ veritatis* (Prague, 1669).

CHARLES MCNEILL.

Tanner, MATTHIAS, b. at Pilsen in Bohemia, 28 Feb., 1630; d. at Prague, 8 Feb., 1692. He entered the Society of Jesus in 1646. The greatest part of his life was spent at Prague, where he taught humanities, philosophy, theology, and Scripture, was made rector of the imperial university, and guided for six years the Bohemian province of his order. Not only did Tanner burn to imitate the apostles and martyrs of the Society, but, to awaken in his brethren a like desire, he employed his leisure hours in recounting to them the lives and deaths of the most prominent sons of St. Ignatius. His two works, "Societas Jesu ad sanguinis et vitæ profusionem militans" (a history of the lives and deaths of those Jesuits who suffered martyrdom for the faith) and "Societas Jesu Apostolorum imitatrix" (describing the heroic deeds and virtues of the Jesuits who laboured in all parts of the world with extraordinary success for the salvation of souls) were written in this spirit. He paid special attention to reverence and devotion during the holy sacrifice of the Mass. According to his biographer, he used to celebrate with such living piety that he was like a lodestone, attracting the faithful to the altar where he offered the sacrifice. To foster this reverence in others, he wrote two other works, "Explanation of the Bloody Sacrifice of Christ in the Unbloody Sacrifice of the Mass", which was re-edited three times, and a pamphlet proclaiming God's wrath against those who should dare to desecrate holy temples by their misbehaviour. His name became more widely known through his work, "Dialogus controversisticus" on the validity of the Holy orders conferred on Andrew Frommens during the lifetime of his wife.

SOMMERVOGEL, *Bibl. de la C. de J.*, VII, 1858–61; DE GUILHERMY, *Ménologe. Assistance de Germanie*, I, 132–34; FELLER, *Dict. hist.*, VIII, 357–58; HURTER, *Nomenclator*, I, 254; II, 561.

A. C. COTTER.

Tantum Ergo, the opening words of the penultimate stanza of the Vesper hymn (see PANGE LINGUA GLORIOSI, II) of Corpus Christi. This stanza and the closing one, or doxology ("Genitori" etc.), form a separate hymn which is prescribed for Benediction of the Blessed Sacrament (q. v.).

In private exposition, where permission has been obtained to give benediction with the pyx, the two stanzas are recited by the priest (or sung by a choir, if this is feasible: "si fieri potest, optandum est", says Van der Stappen). In other expositions they must always be sung. Customs vary in respect of the method of singing. In some places the choir sings the stanzas; in others, the celebrant sings the opening words of each stanza, the choir continuing. The Ritual (Tit. IX, c. 5) speaks of all the clergy present singing the stanzas, and Schober (Cæremoniæ missarum solemnium et pontificalium), commenting on this, suggests that either the celebrant and assisting clergy should intone the first line of the stanza, or the choir alone should sing both stanzas. A profound inclination of the head is made at the words "veneremur cernui" (Wapelhorst). The "American Ecclesiastical Review" (XXI, 1889, 644) points out that the rubrics do not prescribe an inclination of the head at the words "veneremur cernui", although the practice is frequent. "Gardellini, in his "Commentary on the Clementine Instruction" (XXIV, 9–10), cites the custom of the churches of Rome; and the Rituals before his day make mention of the profound inclination at the Tantum ergo down to the word "cernui": "nam in verbo cernui completur dictionis sensus, qui inclinationem postulat". Authorities differ as to the time for incensing. Martinucci directs the placing of incense in the thurible before "Tantum ergo" and the incensing after "veneremur cernui". De Carpo suggests both either before "Tantum ergo" or after "veneremur cernui", according to the custom of the particular church. Wapelhorst, following De Herdt, directs that both take place when "Genitori" is intoned.

The "magnificent doxology" (W. A. Shoults in Julian, "Dict. of Hymnol.") is a fitting climax to the great hymn. It borrows, however, the expressions "Genitori Genitoque"—"Procedenti ab utroque, Compar" from a Pentecost sequence by Adam of St-Victor. Dreves, "Analecta hymnica", IV, 70, gives a sequence in honour of St. Agnes, in which occurs the stanza:—

Genitori Genitoque,
Psallat nostra concio;
Procedenti ab utroque
Compar sit laudatio;
Virginalis ipsum quoque
Laudet benedictio.

Of the musical settings, which are very abundant, the appropriate word must be one of caution in view of the direction of Pius X in his Instruction on Sacred Music (22 Nov., 1903, §IV): "In the hymns of the Church the traditional form of the hymn is to be preserved. It is not lawful, therefore, to compose, for instance, a *Tantum ergo* in such wise that the first strophe presents a *romanza*, a *cavatina*, an *adagio*, and the *Genitori* an *allegro*." Singenberger, "Guide to Catholic Church Music" (St. Francis, Wisconsin, 1905), gives grade, voices, composer, etc., of more than six hundred settings of the "Tantum ergo" and the "Pange lingua", almost wholly of the German Cecilian School. Since 1903 many settings, also liturgically correct, have appeared by composers of other nationalities. The Vatican Graduale (1908) gives two plainchain melodies, or rather two forms of the same melody.

Neale, "Mediæval Hymns and Sequences" (3rd ed., London, 1867, 178–81), discusses translations of the "Pange lingua", and, speaking of the penultimate stanza, remarks that the lines "Præstet fides supplementum Sensuum defectui" are "avoided by all" the four authors he mentions, and notes that "Caswall's translation, unshackled by rhyme, is nearest" to the original Latin: "Faith for all defects supplying, Where the feeble senses fail". Neale's own translation of this stanza is given, with slight alterations, in

"Hymns Ancient and Modern" in the (Baltimore) "Manual of Prayers", and in the "English Hymnal". Some of the earliest translations of the two lines are: "And where our sense is seen to fail, There must faith supply restore" (Primer, 1604); "And faith with all, those wants supply Wherein the senses feel defect" (Primer, 1619); "Let faith in Jesus Christ supply The senses' insufficiency" (Primer, 1685); "And faith for all defects supply, Whilst sense is lost in mystery" (Primer, 1706). One of the most recent translations is that of the revised Husenbeth, "The Missal for the Use of the Laity" (London, 1903, 286): "Let us profoundly bend before This awful mystery, and adore; Let types of former days give way, Like darkness at the blaze of day; And sense's failure be supplied By faith, our firm support and guide."

H. T. HENRY.

Tanucci, BERNARDO, Marchese, Italian statesman, b. at Stia in Tuscany, of poor family, in 1698; d. at Naples, 29 April, 1793. At the University of Pisa, where certain benefactors enabled him to study, he was appointed in 1725 to a chair of law, and attracted attention in the republic of scholars by the vehemence, rather than by the erudition, with which he defended the authenticity of the Codex Pisanus of the Pandects. When Charles, son of Philip V of Spain, passed through Tuscany on his way to conquer the Kingdom of Naples, he took Tanucci with him; he appointed him at first council of state, then superintendent of posts, and finally prime minister. On the last occasion the king ennobled him. As prime minister he was most zealous in establishing the supremacy of the State over the Church, and in abolishing the privileges of the nobility together with feudalism. He restricted the jurisdiction of the bishops, impeded the last increment of the so-called mortmain, and reduced the taxes belonging to the chancery of the Roman Curia. All this was sanctioned in the Concordat of 1741, the application of which, however, went far beyond the intentions of the Holy See. For controversies which might arise in consequence of the Concordat a mixed tribunal, composed of ecclesiastics and laymen, was constituted. But Tanucci went much farther, establishing the principle that not more than ten priests should be ordained for every thousand souls, which number was later reduced to five for each thousand. The *Placet* was rigorously enforced. The censures of bishops against laymen incurred by obedience to the state laws were annulled. Without permission of the king new churches could not be erected.

His hostile policy to the Church led Tanucci to neglect other interests, above all the foreign relations. In 1742 an English fleet seriously threatened the Neapolitan coasts, and the kingdom was saved only by the signature of an act of neutrality in the war between Spain and Austria. For the reformation of the laws he instituted a commission of learned jurists with instructions to compile a new code, which was, however, not put into force. When Charles III of Naples succeeded to the throne of Spain in 1759, Tanucci was made president of the council of regency instituted for the nine-year-old Ferdinand V. The latter, even when he attained his majority, preferred to hold aloof from the government business and plunged into the pleasures of the chase. Furthermore, the former King Charles III, although in Spain, continued by his instructions to Tanucci to govern the kingdom. The latter could now with greater freedom take up his hostile policy to the Church. The revenues of the vacant bishoprics and abbeys—and as time went on their number always increased—were confiscated. Thirty-eight convents were suppressed; tithes were at first restricted, then abolished; the acquisition of new property by mortmain was forbidden, and new restrictions were made against the recruitment of the clergy. The *Placet* was even extended to ancient papal Bulls, and the principle was established that concessions of an ecclesiastical nature, not made or assented to by the king, could be revoked at pleasure by the same king or by his successors. In this manner it was possible to suppress or change testaments in favour of the Church at the pleasure of the king, who, according to Tanucci, possessed this power directly from God. Appeals to Rome were forbidden without the royal permission. Matrimony was declared a civil contract by nature, from which principle the trial of matrimonial cases by civil courts was deduced. By the order of Charles III the Jesuits were suppressed and expelled from the Kingdom of Naples (1767).

This expulsion of the Jesuits was part of the movement of the Bourbon courts throughout Europe to destroy the Society, Pombal in Portugal, Aranda in Spain, Choiseul in France, and Tanucci in Naples acting in concert to this end. Scarcely had Clement XIV been elevated to the pontificate than he was urgently solicited by the Bourbon courts to suppress the Jesuits, and no effort was left untried by the Bourbon ministers to accomplish this purpose. The pope pleaded time and patience in the examination of the charges against the Society, but was overborne by the incessant and menacing attitude of the Bourbon league against the Jesuits. Tanucci laboured with no less energy in the war upon the Society of Jesus than Pombal, Aranda, and Choiseul, with whom he was in close sympathy in their general hostility to the Church as well as in their determination to bring about the complete suppression of an order of men, whose widespread influence was a check upon their own high-handed methods against the freedom of the Church. To excommunication by Clement XIII Tanucci responded with the occupation of Benevento and Pontecorvo, which were not evacuated until after the suppression of the Jesuits in 1773. The protests of the bishops against many of the new teachings in the schools after the expulsion of the Jesuits were dismissed as invalid. One of the last of his acts was the abolition of the *chinea*, that is the annual tribute which the kings of Naples since the time of Charles of Anjou had paid to the pope as sovereign (1776). His unfortunate policy in finance and in regard to the food taxes provoked popular revolutions on several occasions. But when, in 1774, Queen Caroline, an Austrian princess, entered the Council of State, the power of Tanucci began to decline. In vain he endeavoured to neutralize the influence of the queen, and in 1777 he fell into disgrace and was dismissed. Retiring into the country, he died neglected and childless.

Tanucci represents the Italian type of that unfortunate species of statesman of the eighteenth century the most prominent example of which was the notorious Pombal. Sceptics in faith and in morals, they were "anti-clerical" because they aspired to a universal tyranny of the State, in which the king should be a figurehead while the minister himself was the master. They desired to expel the Jesuits, accusing them, as one would say to-day, "of liberalism"; they ably prepared the way for the power of sects and the crash of revolutions.

LASTRE, *Elogio del marchese Tanucci* (*Novelle letterarie fiorentine*) (Florence, 1783); COLLETTA, *Storia del regno di Napoli dal 1735 al 1825*, I (Capolago, 1834). See also the documents and statutes on the suppression of the Jesuits. Among the publications of Tanucci are *Epistola de pandectis pisanis* (2 vols., Florence, 1731).

U. BENIGNI.

Taoism (TAO-KIAO) is the second of the three state religions (*San-kiao*) of China. This religion is derived from the philosophical doctrines of Lao-tze. "Lao-tze's Taoism", says Legge (Religions of China, 229), "is the exhibition of a way or method of living which men should cultivate as the highest and purest development of their nature". According to De Groot (Religious System of China, IV, p. 66): "Taoism, as the word indicates, is the Religion of the Tao, a term meaning Path or Way, but denoting in this peculiar case the way, course or movement of the Universe, her processes and methods. In other words, Taoism is the Religion of Heaven and Earth, of the Cosmos, of the World or Nature in the broadest sense of these words. Hence we may call it Naturism".

Lao-tze, the equivalent to "the Old or Venerable Philosopher" (if taken as a title of respect), or to "Old Boy" (if literally translated), was born in the third year of Ting Wang, Prince of Chou, i. e. in 604, at K'io-jin, in the Kingdom of Ts'u, to-day Ho-nan Province. The legend given by Ko Hung in his "Record of Spirits and Immortals" (written in the fourth century A.D.), says that "he was not born till his mother had carried him in her womb seventy-two years or, according to some accounts, eighty-one years". "No wonder", adds Legge (l. c., pp. 203–4), "that the child should have had white hair,—an 'old boy' of about fourscore years"! This date of 604, in accordance with historical tradition, is not given by Sze-ma Ts'ien in the biography which he devoted to the philosopher in his "She-ki" (Historical Memoirs); if this date be accepted, it is difficult to admit of the authenticity of the meeting between Lao-tze and Confucius, 500 B.C.; if the latter was then fifty-one years old according to Chwang-tze, Lao-tze was then one hundred and four years old. The family name of Lao-tze was Li, his name Eul (meaning "Ear"), his honorary title Pe-yang, and his posthumous name Tan (meaning "Flat-eared"). He was one of the "Sze", recorders, historiographers, keepers of the archives of Lo, the Court of the princes of the Chou dynasty. Foreseeing the decay of this dynasty, he gave up his office, and undertook a journey; at the Han-kou Pass, Ho-nan Province, the watchman, Yin Hi, begged him to write his thoughts for his own instruction before he retired from the world; consequently, Lao-tze wrote his work in two parts in the Tao and the Te, and having entrusted it to Yin Hi, he disappeared; the time of the death of the philosopher is not known. Lao-tze had a son called Tsung who was a general of the Kingdom of Wei and who obtained the grant of land at Twan-kan. His son named Chu had himself a child Kung; Hia, grandson of Kung, was an official under Emperor Hiao-wen-ti, of the Han dynasty. Kiai, son of Hia, became a minister of K'iang, King of Kiao-si, and, owing to this circumstance, settled with his family in the Kingdom of Ts'i.

This story is too matter of fact and lacks the marvellous legend which should surround the person of the chief of a new religion. Legend was provided for. Ko Hung, already mentioned, had placed the legend of Lao-tze at the beginning of the "Shon-sion-ch'-wan" (Records of Spirits and Immortals), and he says: "His mother carried him after the emotion she felt in seeing a large shooting star. He received from Heaven the vital breath; as he was born in a house whose proprietor was called Li (Pear tree), so he was named Li". Some authors say that Lao-tze was born before heaven and earth. According to others, he possessed a pure soul emanated from heaven. He belonged to the class of spirits and gods. The chief work of Lao-tze, in fact the only one which has been ascribed to him with some probability, is the "Tao-teh-king". In the "China Review" (March-April, 1886), Dr. Herbert A Giles wrote a sensational article, "The Remains of Lao Tzu", to show by various arguments that the "Tao-teh-king" is a spurious work and that its now spurious portions have been mostly mistranslated. It was the starting-point of a controversy in which Dr. Chalmers, Dr. Legge, Dr. Edkins, and some other sinologues took part. The authenticity of the work has been admitted by most of them. Wylie says (Notes on Chinese Literature, new ed., p. 216): "The only work which is known to be truly the production of Lao Keun is the 'Taòu tih king', which has maintained its reputation and secured a popularity to a certain extent among reading men generally of every denomination." Legge writes (Religions of China, p. 203): "No other writing has come down to us from the pencil of Lâo-tsze, its author", and (Brit. Quart. Rev., July, 1883, p. 9): "We know that Lao Tzu wrote the 'Tao Tê Ching'", and (p. 11): "The 'Tao Tê Ching' is a genuine relic of one of the most original minds of the Chinese race, putting his thoughts on record 2400 years ago." The German E. Faber (China Rev., XIII, 241) says that "there is little room left for doubts regarding the authenticity of our Canon."

Besides the "Tao-teh-king", a good many works treat of Taoism: the "Yin-fu-king-kiai" which professes to be an exposition of the oldest Taoist record in existence; "Ts'ing-tsing-king" (The Book of Purity and Rest); the "T'ai-hsi-king" (Respiration of the Embryo); the "T'ai-shang-Kan-ying-pien" (Tractate of Actions and their Retributions). The chief Taoist philosophers are: Tsou-yuen (400 B. C.), author of a work on the influences of the five ruling elements, influenced by Buddhist doctrines; Kwei-ku-tze (380 B. C.), a mystic, astrologer, and fortune-teller; Ho-kwan-tze (325–298 B. C.), an orthodox Confucianist when writing on jurisprudence, a Taoist in other writings; Chwang-tze (330 B. C.), the author of the "Nan-hua" classic, the adversary to Mencius, and according to Eitel "the most original thinker China ever produced"; Shi-tze (280 B. C.), a Taoist writer, influenced by the heterodox philosopher, Yang-chu (450 B. C.), the Apostle of Selfishness; the statesman Han-fei-tze (250 B. C.); Liu-ngan or Hwai-nan-tze (d. 112 B. C.), a cosmogonist. But the first disciples of Lao-tze were Kang-sang-tze (570–543 B. C.), the first expositor of Taoism as a distinct system, the sceptic Li-tze (500 B. C.), and Wen-tze (500 B. C.). The historian Sze-ma-ts'ien speaking of Chwang-tze says: "He wrote with a view to asperse the Confucian school and to glorify the mysteries of Lao Tze... His teachings are like an overwhelming flood, which spreads at its own sweet will. Consequently, from rulers and ministers downwards, none could apply them to any definite use." Giles (Chinese Literature, 60) concludes from this passage: "Here we have the key to the triumph of the Tao of Confucius over the Tao of Lao Tze. The latter was idealistic, the former a practical system for every-day use."

As De Groot observes (l. s. c., IV, 67): "Taoism being fundamentally a religion of the Cosmos and its subdivisions, old Chinese Cosmogony is its Theogony. It conceives the Universe as one large organism of powers and influences, a living machine, the core of which is the Great Ultimate Principle or *T'ai-kih*, comprising the two cosmic Breaths or Souls, known as the *Yang* and the *Yin*, of which, respectively, Heaven and Earth are the chief depositories. These two souls produce the four seasons, and the phenomena of Nature represented by the lineal figures called *kwa*". In fact the *Yang* and the *Yin* produce by the power of their co-operation all that exists, man included. Ancient Chinese philosophy attributes to man two souls: (1) the *shen*, or immaterial soul, emanates from the ethereal, celestial part of the Cosmos, and consists of *yang* substance. When operating actively in the living human body, it is called *k'i* or 'breath', and *hwun*; when separated from it after death, it lives as a refulgent spirit, styled *ming*. (2) The *kwei*, the material, substantial soul, emanates from the terrestrial part of the Universe, and is formed of *yin* substance. In living man it operates under the name of *p'oh* and on his death it returns to the Earth" (De Groot, IV, p. 5). Thus the *kwei* is buried with the man and the *shen* lingers about the tomb. Marking the distinction between the two souls, there existed in the legendary period, according to the "Li-ki", a sacrificial worship to each soul separately: the *hwun* or *k'i* returns to heaven, the *p'oh* returns to earth. These two souls are composite; in fact all the viscera have a particular *shen*. "There are medical authors who ascribe to man an indefinite number of souls or soul-parts, or, as they express it, a hundred *shen*. Those souls, they say, shift in the body according to the age of the owner; so, e. g. when he is 25, 31, 68 or 74, and older, they dwell in his forehead, so that it is then very dangerous to have boils or ulcers there, because effusion of the blood would entail death. At other times of life they nestle under the feet or in other parts and limbs, and only in the 21st, 38th, 41st, and 50th years of life they are distributed equally through the body, so that open abscesses, wherever they appear, do not heal then at all. Such pathologic nonsense regulates, of course, medical practice to a high degree" (De Groot, IV, p. 75). The liver, the lungs, and the kidneys correspond to the spring, to the autumn, to the winter, as well as to the east, the west, and the north. The soul may be extracted from a living man; the body may still live when left by the soul, for instance during sleep; the soul of a dead man may be reborn into other bodies. Ghosts may enter into relation with the living, not only in dreams, but they may take revenge on their enemies.

At the head of the Taoist Pantheon is a trinity of persons: (1) *Yuen-shi-t'ien-tsun*, "the honoured one of heaven, first in time", residing in "the jade-stone region", who created the three worlds; (2) *Ling-pan-t'ien-tsun*, "the honored one of heaven who is valued and powerful", residing in the "upper pure region", collector of the sacred books, calculator of the succession of time, and the regulator of the two principles *yin* and *yang*; (3) Lao-tze himself, who exposed to mankind the doctrines uttered by the first person in the trinity and collected in the form of books by the second. Next come: *Yuh-hwang-ta-ti*, "the great jade-stone emperor", who governs the physical universe; *Hen-t'u-hwang-ti-k'i*, "Spirit of imperial earth, ruler of the soil"; the star gods, whose lord (*sing-chu*) resides in a star near the pole; *T'ien-hwang-ta-ti*, who lives in the pole star, etc.; *Liu-tsu*, the "father of thunder". "While he discourses on doctrine, his foot rests on nine beautiful birds. He has under him thirty-six generals, *t'ien tsiang*" (Edkins, "Journ. North China Br. Roy. Asiat. Soc.," III, Dec., 1859, p. 311); the sun and moon; the *San-yuen* or *San-kwan*, "the three rulers" who preside over three departments of physical nature, heaven, earth, and water; *Hiuen-kien-shang-ti*, "high emperor of the dark heaven", who is described as the model of the true ascetic. He has transformed himself eighty-two times to become the instructor of men in the three national religions (Edkins, l. c., p. 312). A number of personages were worshipped under the name of *tsu*, patriarchs. Confucius himself has a place assigned him among the deities of this religion, and he is addressed as "the honoured one of heaven who causes literature to flourish and the world to prosper" (Edkins). Some men have been worshipped as gods after their death: Kwan-ti, the god of war; Hu-tsu, a physician; a medical divinity, Ko-tsu Sa-tsu; etc.

One may well ask how the pure, abstract doctrine of Lao-tze was turned into a medley of alchemical researches, a practice of witchcraft, with the addition of Buddhist superstitions, which constitute to-day what is called *Tao-kiao*, the religion or the teaching of Tao. This was the work of a legendary being, Chang Tao-ling, a descendant of the eighth generation of Chang Leang, a celebrated advisor of Liu-pang, founder of the Han dynasty. He was born in the tenth year of the Emperor Kwang Wu-ti (A. D. 34) in a cottage of a small village of the Che-kiang Province, at the foot of the T'ien-mu-Shan, in the Hang-chou Prefecture. At an early age Chang studied the works of Lao-tze to which he added researches of alchemy, a science aiming at "prolonging life beyond the limits assigned by nature". He found the drug of immortality, and by order of Lao-tze he destroyed the six great demons of the province; Lao-tze gave him also two books, two swords, one male, one female, a seal called *Tu-kung*, etc. Chang gave his swords and books to his son Heng, bidding him to continue his pontificate from generation to generation. At noon on the seventh day of the first moon of the second year Yung-shou of the Han Emperor Heng (A. D. 157), Tao-ling ascended the Cloudy Mountain (*Yun-shan*) with his wife and two disciples, and with them disappeared into heaven. Chang Heng, son of Chang Tao-ling, continued his father's tradition both in spiritual and alchemical researches, and Chang Lu, the grandson, played an important part in the Yellow Cap Rebellion at the beginning of the Han dynasty. During the fifth century A. D., when the Wei dynasty was ruling in Northern China, a certain K'iu Kien-che tried to substitute himself to the Chang family and received in 423 from the emperor the title of *T'ien-shi*, "Preceptor of Heaven", which formerly belonged to Tao-ling. In 748 the T'ang Emperor Hiuen-Tsung conferred this title upon the heirs of the latter, and a grant of a large property near Lung-hu Shan was made to them in 1016 by the Sung Emperor Chen-Tsung. Heredity in the charge of high priest of the cult was secured to the descendants of Chang by the transmigration of the soul of Tao-ling's successor, at the time of his demise, to the body of a junior member of the family, whose selection is indicated by a supernatural phenomenon.

To-day, at the head of the Taoist hierarchy is the *Cheng-i-sze-kiao-chen-jen*, "Heir to the founder of the Taoist sect"; this title was conferred by the Ming dynasty upon Chang Cheng-shang, descendant from Chang Tao-ling of the thirty-ninth generation. This title belongs, by an hereditary privilege, to the first-born descending in a direct line from Chang Tao-ling. He lives upon the Lung-hu Mountain, in the Kiang-si Province. His office consists in using his magical art to frighten demons away, to baffle diabolical influence, and to refrain the evil-doing souls of the dead. He names the new *Ch'eng-hwang*, 'tutelary deities of the cities', and for a fee, he gives to Taoists titles permitting them to celebrate the ceremonies with more solemnity" (P. Hoang, "Mélanges sur l'Administration", 34). In the capital of the empire the Taoist priesthood includes: two *Tao-lu-sze*, superiors, a title corresponding with that of the Buddhists, *Seng-lu-sze*; two *Cheng-i*, Taoists of right simplicity; two *Yen-fa*, ritual Taoists; two *Che-ling*, Taoists of great excellence, thaumaturgus; and two *Che-i*, Taoists of great probity, an inferior class of priests. In the provinces at the head of the priesthood are: *Tao-ki-sze Ton-ki*, superior of the Taoists of a *fu* (prefecture), and *Tao-ki-sze Fou Ton-ki*, vice-superior of the Taoists of a *fu*; *Tao-cheng*, superior of the Taoists of a *chou* or a *t'ing*; *Tao-hwei*, superior of the Taoists of a *hien*. The superiors are appointed by the governors-general (*tsung-tu*), or by the governors (*fu-t'ai*), on the presentation of the prefect of sub-prefect of the *chou*, *t'ing*, or *hien*. HENRI CORDIER.

Taos Pueblo, an important town of the Pueblo group, inhabited by Indians speaking the Tigua language of Shoshonean linguistic stock, and situated on Taos River, Taos County, New Mexico, United States of America, about fifty miles north-east from Santa Fe. From an estimated population of 2500 in 1630, and 2000 just previous to the outbreak of the rebellion in 1680, it had dwindled to 578 in 1788 and

Typogravure Goupil of Paris, France

THE REPOSE IN EGYPT

FLEMISH WOOL AND GOLD TAPESTRY, LATE XV CENTURY, SPITZER COLLECTION

stands now at about 450. It was first visited by Coronado's men in 1540. About the year 1620 a Spanish Franciscan mission was established there under the name of San Gerónimo de Taos. In the great Pueblo revolt of 1680 the people of Taos took a prominent part, their town being the headquarters of Popé, the leader of the rebellion; the two resident missionaries were killed. On the reconquest of the country some fifteen years later, most of the missions were re-established, but under the attacks of the wild Ute and Navaho the prosperity of the Pueblo steadily declined. In 1847 the people of Taos resisted the American occupation, killing the newly-appointed governor, Charles Bent, and a number of others. As a result their town was stormed by the American troops, and some 150 of the Indians were killed in addition to sixteen others afterwards executed for their part in the massacre. In 1910 troops were again called out to quell a threatened rising. In general culture and condition the Taos people resemble the other Pueblos, but are noted for their extreme tenacity of ancient custom, and for a greater boldness of spirit, probably due to the large admixture of Ute blood. The mission of San Gerónimo still exists, served by a secular priest, and the principal festival occasion is the patronal feast of San Gerónimo, 30 Sept., a leading feature being a relay foot-race; but many of the old-time tribal rites are still kept up by a large proportion of the people.

MILLER, *Prelim. Study of the Pueblo of Taos* in University of Chicago publications (Chicago, 1898); see also bibliography under PUEBLO INDIANS.

JAMES MOONEY.

Taparelli (D'AZEGLIO), ALOYSIUS (christened PROSPERO), philosopher and writer on sociological subjects, b. at Turin, 24 Nov., 1793; d. at Rome, 20 Sept., 1862; interred near the altar of St. Aloysius in the Church of St. Ignatius. His father, Cesare, was at one time ambassador of Victor Emmanuel I of Sardinia to the Holy See, and his brother, Massimo, was one of the Italian ministers of State. He was educated under the Calasanctians at Senis and in the Atheneo of Turin. He attended the military school of St-Cyr at Paris for some months, but he was not destined to be a soldier. He entered the Society of Jesus at Rome, 12 Nov., 1814. In his youth he displayed a bent for mechanics, painting, and music, and later invented a musical instrument which he called the *violicembolo* (highly praised by Liszt and afterwards at his suggestion named the *symphonium*), and which was exhibited at the London Exhibition. He was the first rector of the Roman College after its restoration to the Jesuits by Leo XII. He taught philosophy for sixteen years at Palermo, and for many years afterwards was attached to the editorial staff of the "Civiltà Cattolica". His chief work, "Saggio teoretico di diritto naturale appogiato sul fatto", i. e. "A Theoretical Essay on Natural Right from an Historical Standpoint" (2 vols., 7th ed., Rome, 1883), was in a way the beginning of modern sociology. It was translated into German (Ratisbon, 1845) and twice into French (Tournai, 1851; Paris, 1896). Herein was developed the position, at once widely accepted in conservative circles on the Continent, that the normal origin of civil government was by extension of paternal power through the patriarchal head of a group of families. This essay was later abridged into "An Elementary Course in Natural Right" (6th ed., Naples, 1860; also in French, Tournai, 1864; and in Spanish, Paris, 1875), which was in use as a text-book in the University of Modena. Next in importance is his "Esame critico degli ordini rappresentativi nella società moderna", i. e. "Critical Examination of Representative Government in Modern Society" (2 vols., Rome, 1854; in Spanish, Madrid, 1867). Besides his striking monographs on "Nationality" (Rome, 1847), "Sovereignty of the People" (Palermo, 1848; Florence, 1849), and "The Grounds of War" (Genoa, 1847) he left a long list of articles in the "Civiltà Cattolica" chiefly on subjects in political economy and social right, as well as an equally long list of book reviews on kindred topics, which were acute and penetrating essays.

De claris sodalibus provinciæ Taurinensis (Turin, 1906); SOMMERVOGEL, *Bibliothèque de la C. de. J.* (Brussels, 1896); *Civiltà Cattolica*, series V, vol. IV, and series X, vol. XI. The last reference gives a critical estimate of his writings.

CHARLES MACKSEY.

Tapestry.—A word of French origin naming a fabric in which the two processes of weaving and embroidering are combined. The woof is not made in the usual way by throwing the threads with a shuttle, but is added to the warp by the aid of a needle carrying a short thread of the colour called for by the design. The fabric produced by this method of work, in which richness of colour and exquisite gradation of tints are easily obtainable, is a mosaic made up of dyed threads. It is used for wall-hangings, floor and furniture coverings. It was so employed by the ancient Egyptians, passing from them through Western Asia to Europe. Here, during the later Middle Ages and the Renaissance the art of the tapiser reached a high state of perfection, more particularly at Arras in France, so much so that arras-work came to be the common designation for all sorts of tapestry, no matter where made. In England, prior to the Reformation, the making of tapestry was the special handicraft of the monastic houses; and their arras-work was in very great demand for reredoses, altar-frontals, antependiums, hearse-cloths, sanctuary carpets, palace wall and choir hangings. They were not only wrought along purely ornamental lines, but more often represented Biblical subjects, incidents in the lives of the saints, historic scenes, or illustrated by symbols some point of Faith.

Matthew Paris records the fact that, among other ornaments which, in the reign of Henry I, Abbot Geoffrey had made for his Church of St. Albans "were three tapestry reredoses: the first a large one wrought with the finding of the body of St. Alban; the other two figured with the parables of the man who fell among thieves and of the prodigal son". Antedating this gift, the Abbot Egetric gave to the Abbey of Croyland, some time before the year 992, "two large foot-clothes (tapestry-carpets) woven with lions to be laid out before the high altar on great festivals and two shorter ones trailed all over with flowers for the feast days of the Apostles". A number of these early English tapestries, in a good state of preservation, were saved from the vandalism of the first Reformers, but the art of making tapestry declined before their mistaken zeal, so much so that, when tapestries were wanted to decorate the walls of the House of Lords, representing the defeat of the Spanish Armada, the order had to be placed in Flanders. A number of great artists have made designs for tapestry work, notably Raphael, who, with the assistance of Francisco Penni and Giovanni da Udine, executed the coloured cartoons for the tapestries of wool, silk, and gold that now hang in the Vatican at Rome, the most beautiful in existence. Raphael also prepared cartoons for other tapestries; the last he designed, twelve in number, were made for Francis I of France in 1519. He did not, however, live to finish the cartoons; his pupil, Giulio Romano, completed them. The tapestries made from them now hang in the Vatican, in the apartment of Pius V.

DE CHAMPEAUX, *Tapestry* (London, 1878); COLE, *Tapestry and Embroidery* (London, 1888); GUIFFREY, *Histoire de la tapisserie, depuis le moyen âge jusqu'à nos jours* (Tours, 1886); THOMSON, *A History of Tapestry from the Earliest Times until the Present Day* (London, 1906); GENTILI, *Arazzi antichi e moderni* (Rome, 1897); HAUSER Y MENET, *Tapices de la Corona de España* (Madrid, 1903); GETZ, *A Short Historical Sketch on Tapestry and Embroidery* (New York, 1895); RONCHAUD, *La tapisserie dans l'antiquité* (Paris, 1884); MÜNTZ, *La tapisserie* (Paris, 1882), tr. DAVIS, *A Short History of Tapestry* (London, 1886).

CARYL COLEMAN.

Tapis, Esteban, b. at Santa Coloma de Farnes, Catalonia, Spain, 25 Aug., 1754; d. 3 Nov., 1825. He entered the Franciscan Order at Gerona, 27 Jan., 1778, and joined the missionary College of San Fernando, Mexico, in 1786. Reaching California in 1790, he was in succession stationed at the Indian missions of San Luis Obispo till 1793; Santa Barbara till 1806; San Carlos till 1811; Purísima Concepción till 1813; Santa Ines in 1814; San Juan Bautista to the day of his death. He was three times elected *presidente,* or superior, of the California missions, holding the office from 1803 to 1812. During the same period he was also *vicario foraneo* of the Bishop of Sonora for California. Father Tapis was familiar with several Indian languages, and noted for his fondness for teaching Indian boys to read and write. He was a truly evangelical man, and was held in the highest esteem by the missionaries for his learning and piety. Numerous letters from his hand are still extant. His best and longest literary effort was his defence of the missionary fathers and their missionary system against the accusations of Captain Goyoechea of the Santa Barbara *presidio.* The arguments proved so crushing that the Government deemed it advisable to promote the officer to a post in Mexico. Father Tapis strenuously opposed taking the oath of allegiance to the so-called Republic of Mexico, which to him was nothing but an attempt at putting Voltairean principles into practice.

Santa Barbara Mission Archives; Mission Records of various missions, notably *San Juan Bautista;* Engelhardt, *The Missions and Missionaries of California,* II (San Francisco, 1912); *The Franciscans in California* (Harbor Springs, Mich., 1897).

Zephyrin Engelhardt.

Tarabotti, Helena, nun and authoress, b. at Venice, 1605; d. there 1652. Obliged by her father, who was descended from a family of Bergamo, to enter the Convent of Sta. Anna at Venice, at the age of eleven years, she remained there, under the name of Arcangela, without any religious vocation. In earnest study, her keen spirit found its element, and through various works she became an authoress of some repute. Her first books betray an unsettled state of mind, but later she wrote treatises on the spiritual life in which, through the influence of Cardinal Cornaro, Patriarch of Venice, she finally found peace. Her more worldly works, partly pseudonymous, are: "Antisatira d'A[rcangela]T[arabotti] in risposta alla satira Menippea contro il lusso donnesco di Francesco Buoninsegni", Venice, 1644; "Lettere familiari e di complemento", Venice, 1650; "Difesa delle donne contro Orazio Plata", Venice, 1651; "La semplicità ingannata", Leyden, 1654; the last two were written under the name of Galerana Barcitotti. The books referring to spiritual life are: "La luce monacale"; "Via per andare al cielo"; "Paradiso monacale"; "Purgatorio delle mal maritate"; "Contemplazioni dell' anima amante".

Cicogna, *Delle Tuscrizioni Veneziane* (Venice, 1824–65), I, 135–36, 164, 359; II, 430; V, 536–37; VI, 807–08; *Dizionario geografico storico biografico italiano,* part II (Florence, 1848), 1610; Cantù, *Parini e la Lombardia* (Milan, 1854), 119.

Livarius Oliger.

Tarachus, Probus, and Andronicus, Saints, martyrs of the Diocletian persecution (about 304). The "Martyrologium Hieronymian." contains the names of these three martyrs on four different days (the four days 8–11 October evidently signify no more than the date of a single day), with the topographical identification: "In Tarso Cilicie", on 27 Sept. (ed. De Rossi-Duchesne, 126), to which corresponds the expression, "In Cilicia", given on the two days of 5 April, and 8–11 October. The expression, "In Palestina", given under 13 May (ibid., 60), is either an error or refers to a special shrine of the martyrs in Palestine. There are two accounts of the glorious martyrdom of these three witnesses by blood, the first account being held by Ruinart (Acta Martyrum, ed. Ratisbon, 448 sq.) to be entirely authentic. According to these Acts, Tarachus, a native of Claudiopolis in Isauria, Probus of Side in Pamphylia, and Andronicus, who belonged to a prominent family of Ephesus, were tried and horribly tortured three times in various cities, at Tarsus, and at Anazarbus of Cilicia. They were then condemned to death by wild beasts, and when the animals would not touch them in the amphitheatre they were put to death with the sword. Harnack, however, expressed doubts as to the genuineness of the account (Geschichte der altchristlichen Literatur, pt. II: Die Chronologie, I, 479 sq., note 5), and Delehaye (Les légendes hagiographiques, 135 sq.) puts the martyrdom in the class of legends of martyrs that he calls "historical romances". At the same time, however, there can be no doubt as to the actual existence of the three martyrs. Their feast is celebrated in the Latin Church on 11 October, and in the Greek Church on 12 October.

Acta SS., October, V, 566 sq., earliest form of the *Acts, P. G.,* CXV, 1068 sq., second form, *Bibliotheca hagiographica græca,* ed. Bolland. (2nd ed.), 220; Quentin, *Les martyrologes historiques* (Paris, 1908), 279.

J. P. Kirsch.

Taranto, Diocese of (Tarentina), in southern Italy, on a bay in the Gulf of Taranto. The ancient city was situated on an island, joined by two bridges with the mainland, where the new city is built. Two islets, S. Pietro and S. Paolo, protect the bay (*Mar grande*), the commercial port, while the old city forms another bay (*Mar piccolo*), a military port next in strategic importance to Spezzia; the coast and islets are therefore very strongly fortified. The city has a large export trade and extensive works connected with the construction of warships, while the fishing industry, especially in the *Mar piccolo,* is flourishing. The cathedral dates from the eleventh century, but has been partially reconstructed in modern times. The high altar has a silver statue of St. Cathaldus; the saint's chapel, rich in marble and statues, with a cupola decorated with a fresco of Paolo de Matteis, is due to the munificence of Archbishops Lelio Brancaccio, Sarria, and Pignatelli.

Tarentum, called Taras by the Greeks, was founded in 707 B. C. by some Spartans, who, the sons of free women and enslaved fathers, were born during the Messenian War. They succeeded in conquering the Menapii and Lucani. Like Sparta, Tarentum was an aristocratic republic, but became democratic when the ancient nobility dwindled. Its government was praised by Aristotle. The people were industrious and commercial, employing a mercenary army commanded by foreign leaders, like the King of Sparta Archidamus II, Cleonymus, and later Pyrrhus. Alexander, King of Epirus, tried in vain to capture the city; he then became an ally of the Romans, and his death in a new expedition against the Tarentines led to the first dispute between the two republics. War resulted from the violation of a maritime treaty by the Romans (281). Tarentum engaged the services of Pyrrhus, who, victorious at first, was finally conquered at Beneventum (275); in 272 the city was taken by the Romans and included in the federation. Even in those early days it was renowned for its beautiful climate. In 208 it sided with Hannibal, but was retaken in 205, losing its liberty and its art treasures, including the statue of Victory. In ancient times its poets Apollodorus and Clinias, its painter Zeuxis, and its mathematician Archytas were renowned. The Byzantines captured Taranto in 545 during the Gothic wars, but abandoned it in 552. In 668 it belonged to Romuald, Duke of Beneventum. In 882 the Saracens, having been invited by Duke Radelchis to assist him, captured it and held it for some time. It was retaken by the Byzantines, who were forced to cede it to Otto II in 982; in 1080 it fell into the hands of Robert Guiscard, who made it the capital of the Principality of Taranto, and gave it to Boemund, his son. When the House of Anjou was divided, Taranto fell to Durazzo (1394–1463). In 1504 Ferdinand, King of Naples, valiantly defended this extremity of his kingdom, but had to cede it to Gonsalvo di Cordova. In 1801 it was taken by the French, who fortified the port; in 1805 the Russian fleet, allied with the British, remained there for several months. Taranto is the birthplace of the musician Paisiello.

According to the local legend, the Gospel was preached in Taranto by the same St. Peter who had consecrated St. Amasianus bishop. The city venerates also the martyr St. Orontius. The first bishop whose date is known is Innocentius (496). In the time of St. Gregory the Great, three bishops filled the episcopal chair: Andreas (590), Joannes (601), Honorius (603). It is uncertain whether St. Cataldus belongs to the sixth or the seventh century. Joannes (978) is the first who had the title of archbishop. It is well known that Taranto even under the Byzantines never adopted the Greek Rite. Stephanus presided in the battle of Nelfi (1041) fought by the Greeks and the Normans; Draco (1071) erected the cathedral; Filippo (1138) was deposed for supporting the antipope Anacletus II, and died in the monastery of Chiaravalle; Archbishop Angelo was employed in several embassies by Innocent III; Jacopo da Atri was slain (1370); Marino del Giudice (1371) was one of the cardinals condemned by Urban VI (1385). Cardinal Ludovico Bonito (1406) was one of the few who remained faithful to Gregory XII; Cardinal Giovanni d'Aragona (1478), was son of King Ferdinand of Naples; Giovanni Battista Petrucci suffered for the complicity of his father in the conspiracy of the barons; Cardinal Battista Orsini died in 1503 in the Castle of Sant' Angelo; Cardinal Marcantonio Colonna (1560) introduced the Tridentine reforms and established the seminary; Girolamo Gambara (1569) was a distinguished nuncio; Lelio Brancaccio (1574) suffered considerable persecution on account of his efforts at reformation; Tommaso Caracciolo (1630), a Theatine, died in the odour of sanctity. The city of Taranto forms a single parish divided into four *pittagerii*, each of which contains a *sub-pittagerio*. It includes the Basilian Abbey of S. Maria di Talfano, where there are still some Albanians following the Greek Rite. The suffragan sees are Castellaneta and Oria. The archdiocese contains 26 parishes, 214 secular and 47 regular priests; 5 religious houses of men, and 12 of nuns; and 220,300 inhabitants.

CAPPELLETTI, *Le chiese d'Italia*, XXI; DE VICENTINI, *Storia di Taranto* (Taranto, 1865).

U. BENIGNI.

Tarapacá, VICARIATE APOSTOLIC OF (DE TARAPACÁ), situated in Chile, bounded on the north by the cañon of the Camarones and on the south by the Loa River. It comprises the civil province of the same name, has an area of 19,305 square miles, and a population of 106,215 Catholics and 3821 non-Catholics. The diocese is divided into 11 parishes, and has 63 churches and chapels, and 30 secular and 14 regular priests. The male religious orders are represented by the Franciscans, Redemptorists, and Salesians; they have 4 houses and 24 members. The female orders are Sisters of the Good Shepherd of Angers, of St. Joseph of Cluny, and the Salesian Sisters; they have 50 members and 5 houses. In Iquique the Salesian Fathers have a college for boys and the Salesian Sisters one for girls, the latter having more than 200 pupils. The Sisters of St. Joseph of Cluny have a school in Pica, and a hospital and asylum for children in Iquique. The Sisters of the Good Shepherd have a house of correction for women in Iquique. There are many societies and pious associations in the diocese, the principal being that of *Orden Social* for men, the *Centro Cristiano* and the Society of St. Philomena for women in Iquique, and the Society of St. Andrew in Pica. There are 5 primary schools with 481 pupils. The State pays an annuity to the vicar Apostolic, and to the employees of the vicarage, the parish priests, and curates, and also contributes towards the construction of the churches. The vicariate was erected in 1882, when Chile took possession of the Province of Tarapacá, which had formerly belonged to Peru and to the Diocese of Arequipa. Five vicars apostolic have ruled the vicariate since its erection: Camilo Ortúzar; Plácido Labarca; Daniel Fuenzalida; Guillermo Juan Cárter, titular Bishop of Anthedon; and Martín Rücker. The principal cities are: Iquique (45,000 inhabitants) and Pisaqua (5105 inhabitants). The population is composed mainly of miners and workers in the saltpetre beds, who are homeless and little given to the practice of their religion. To provide a remedy and alleviate this condition, missions are preached almost every year in the saltpetre works.

Catálogo de los Eclesiásticos, etc. de Chile (Santiago, 1911); *Anuario Estadístico de Chile* (Santiago, 1910); *Censo de la República de Chile en 1907* (Santiago, 1908).

CARLOS S. COTAPOS.

Tarasius, SAINT, Patriarch of Constantinople, date of birth unknown; d. 25 February, 806. He was the son of the Patrician and Prefect of Constantinople, George, and his wife Eukratia, and entered the service of the State. In 784 when Paul IV Patriarch of Constantinople died Tarasius was an imperial secretary, and a champion of the veneration of images. It may be that before his death the patriarch had recommended Tarasius as his successor in the patriarchate to the Empress Irene who was regent for her son Constantine VI (780–797). After the burial of Paul IV a great popular assembly was held before the Magnaura Palace to discuss the filling of the vacant see. The empress delivered an oration on the new appointment to the patriarchate and the people proclaimed Tarasius as the most worthy candidate. The empress agreed but said that Tarasius refused to accept the position. Tarasius now made a speech himself in which he declared he felt himself unworthy of the office, further that the elevation of a layman was very hazardous, and that the position of the Church of Constantinople had become a very difficult one, as it was separated from the Catholics of Western Europe and isolated from the other Oriental patriarchates; consequently he would only be willing to accept the position of patriarch on condition that Church unity be restored and that, in connexion with the pope, an œcumenical council be called. The majority of the populace approved of these views and the imperial Court agreed to it. So on 25 December, 784, Tarasius was consecrated patriarch. In 785 he sent the priest George as his legate to Hadrian I with a letter in which he announced his appointment. In his reply the pope expressed his disapproval of the elevation of Tarasius directly from the laity to the dignity of a bishop contrary to canonical regulation, but allowed clemency to rule in view of the orthodoxy of the new patriarch's views, and recognized him as patriarch. After this by joint action with the pope and the imperial Court Tarasius called the Second Council of Nicæa, the Seventh Œcumenical Council, which rejected Iconoclasm (q. v.). Union with the Roman Church was restored.

After the synod the patriarch had a number of struggles not only with the Iconoclastic party of the capital but also with a party of Orthodox monks. First, the latter upbraided him for restoring to office the bishops who had formerly maintained Iconoclasm, but who had submitted to the decrees of the Council of 787. As, however, this was in accordance with the decrees of the council the accusation was allowed to drop. Another accusation was much more serious, namely, that Tarasius tolerated and encouraged simony, because those bishops who had given money to obtain their positions were only commanded by him to do a year's penance and were permitted to retain their offices. The patriarch defended himself in writing against this accusation which he denied in toto; moreover, he issued a severe synodal letter against Simonists. The monks, however, were not satisfied; they maintained their accusations and also attacked the Council of 787. At a later date Theodore of Studium, who took part in these disputes, changed his opinion of Tarasius, and also of the Second Council of Nicæa, the œcumenical character of which he acknowledged. Many serious difficulties still existed in regard to Western Europe. There were also fresh disputes in Constantinople when the Emperor Constantine VI put aside his lawful wife and wished to marry Theodata, a relative of Abbot Theodore of Studium. Tarasius positively refused to perform the second marriage and expressed his displeasure at the conduct of the priest Joseph who had married the emperor. The zealous monks, whose leaders were the Abbots Plato of Saccudium and Theodore of Studium, accused the patriarch of weakness, because he took no further steps against the emperor. They refused to have Church fellowship any longer with Tarasius, and were, consequently, violently persecuted by the emperor who, however, also treated the patriarch harshly. After Irene had dethroned Constantine in 797, Tarasius deposed the priest Joseph and peace was once more restored between the patriarch and the monks. (See THEODORE OF STUDIUM). In 802 Tarasius crowned as emperor Nicephorus, who had overthrown Irene, an act that greatly dissatisfied the populace. The patriarch had nothing to do with the intrigues of the Court. His life was ascetic and simple, he checked the luxury of the clergy, preached with great zeal, and was very benevolent to the poor. After his death he was venerated as a saint. His name is also placed in the Roman Martyrology under the date of 25 February.

IGNATIUS DIACONUS, *Vita S. Tarasii*, ed. HEIKEL (Helsingfors, 1891); HERGENRÖTHER, *Photius*, I (Ratisbon, 1867), 264–61; HERGENRÖTHER-KIRSCH, *Kirchengesch.*, II, 25 sq.

J. P. KIRSCH.

Tarazona, DIOCESE OF (TURIASONENSIS), comprises the Spanish provinces of Saragossa, Soria, Navarre, and Logroño. The city of Tarazona has a population of 8650, and is situated on a commanding point, surrounded by a beautiful open plain, through which the River Queiles flows. Turiaso was one of the principal towns of the ancient Celtiberian province, and within the confines of the diocese are found many very ancient cities: Bilbilis (Calatayud); Aquæ Bilbilitanorum (Alhama); Atacum (Ateca); Augustobriga (Muro); Boverca (Buvierca); Bursao (Borja); Cascantum (Cascante); Gracuris (Corella); Monóbriga (Munébrega); and Vergegium (Verdejo). Pliny numbers Tarazona among the principal cities of the Celtiberians, and its inhabitants had the privileges of citizenship. Its coat of arms bore the motto "Tubal-Cain built me and Hercules rebuilt me". Nothing definite is known of the origin of Christianity in Tarazona. Owing to its proximity to Saragossa it is supposed that it was visited at an early date by the disciples of St. James, but until the fifth century there is no reliable mention of a bishop of Tarazona. The chronicler Idatius names Leo and says that he lived in 449; the chronological list of bishops gives St. Prudentius, but the history of this saint is not positively known. The Tarazona Breviary gives 390 as the date, but other sources place him as late as the ninth century. Idatius says that Leo was killed in an uprising led by a certain Basilius where the Bagandæ took refuge in the cathedral, and in which a great number were killed.

St. Gaudiosus, a former monk of the Monastery of Asanense and a disciple of St. Victorian, was bishop in 530. He worked against the Arians, and died in his native city, Escoron. His remains were translated to the Monastery of Asanense, and King Sancho Ramírez had them removed to Montearagón. St. Braulio, in his life of St. Emilianus, speaks of a Didymus, Bishop of Tarazona. A Bishop Stephen assisted at the Third Council of Toledo and at the Council of Saragossa; Floridius, at that of Gundemar (611); Elpisius, at the Fourth and Fifth Council of Toledo; Antherius (683) sent a deacon to represent him at the Thirteenth Council of Toledo; and Nepotianus assisted at the fifteenth and seventeenth. He seems to have been the last bishop of the Visigothic epoch. When the Moors took Tarazona they were able to hold it for a long time on account of its fortified position near the Moncaya, between the Douro and the Ebro. The names of its Mozarabic bishops have not come down to us, although it is very probable there were such; on the other hand we know of the Mozarabic saints, St. Attilanus, Bishop of Zamora and St. Iñigo of Calatayud. Alfonso I the Warrior (*el Batallador*) took possession of Tarazona in 1119, and named Miguel Cornel the bishop. Alfonso VII, in an effort to get possession of Tarazona, intruded a certain de Bujedo into the see; but de Bujedo repented shortly afterwards, restored the see to its rightful owner, Miguel, and retired to the Monastery of Valpuesta. The Council of Burgos, which was convened in 1139, and was presided over by the legate Guido, took from the jurisdiction of Tarazona most of the towns of Soria, but bestowed in its place the Archdeaconry of Calatayud.

Miguel was the real restorer of the see. He governed for thirty-three years, and established the chapters of Tarazona, Calatayud, and Tudela, under the Rule of St. Augustine. In his time also were founded the Monasteries of Fitero and Veruela. Three bishops of the name of Frontin succeeded him: Juan (1173–94); Garcia, who was present at the battle of Las Navas, and Garcia II, the counsellor of Jaime the Conqueror (*el Conquistador*). In a species of national council held at Tarazona, the marriage of Jaime to Leonor of Castile was declared null on account of the relationship existing between them. The Franciscans, Mercedarians, Dominicans, and Trinitarians, and the Cistercian and Poor Clare nuns were established in the diocese at this time. Miguel Jiménez de Urrea, bishop from 1309 to 1316, was protected by Jaime II, and during the time of Pedro Perez Calvillo the war between Pedro IV the Ceremonious (*el Ceremonioso*) and Pedro the Cruel of Castile took place. Tarazona was laid waste and its cathedral desecrated by the Castilians. The episcopal palace was burned, and la Zuda, sometimes also called Alcázar de Hércules, the palace of the Arab governors, was taken to replace it.

The following bishops are also worthy of special mention: Jorje Bardaji (1443–64), son of an Aragonese magistrate; Cardinal Pedro Ferriz, favourite of Paul II and Sixtus IV; Guillén Ramon de Moncada; Pedro Cerbuna, founder of the seminary and of the University of Saragossa (1585–97); Jerónimo Castellon y Salas, last Inquisitor-General of Spain (1815–35). The Church of the Magdalen was the ancient cathedral, but the Moors, objecting to its prominent position, compelled them to use a church on the outskirts of the town. In the records left by Miguel this was variously called Santa Maria de la Hidria, de la Vega, or de la Huerta, on account of its position. It was endowed by Teresa Cajal, mother of Pedro de Atarés and wife of Borja, and had been commenced in 1152. Architecturally it is a combination of Byzantine and Gothic, with a high portico entrance and a high brick-trimmed tower. The centre nave with its pointed arches rises above the side aisles and merges into a spacious transept. In the windows the Gothic gives place to the Plateresque, but in the side chapels dedicated to St. Lawrence, St. Andrew, the Rosary, St. Peter, the Beheading of St. John the Baptist, the Annunciation, St. Elizabeth, the Purification, and St. James, the Gothic prevails in the reredos and mausoleums. Bishop Moncada attempted to rebuild the beautiful cloister which had been destroyed in the war with Castile, but as late as 1529 this had not been completed. Besides the Church of the Magdalen, the Church of St. Michael, with its simple Gothic nave and that of the Conception nuns, are also notable. The Church of St. Francis is said to have been founded by St. Francis himself in 1214, and Cisneros was consecrated Bishop of Toledo in the Chapel of La Piedad in 1495.

The episcopal palace, the ancient Azuda, is built upon a commanding eminence and has a beautiful view. Bishop Calvillo purchased this from the Aragonese governor, Jordán Pérez de Urríes, in 1386, and entailed it to the bishopric. The diocesan seminary, dedicated to St. Gaudiosus, was founded in 1593 by Bishop Cerbuna. It has recently been extensively renovated. Mention should be made of the monastery of Nuestra Señora de Veruela, a Cistercian abbey founded by Pedro de Atarés, and now a Jesuit novitiate; also of the Church of Borja, ranking as a collegiate church since the time of Nicholas V (1449), favoured and protected by Alexander VI; and of the ancient collegiate church of Calatayud, Santa Maria de Mediavilla, whose priors ranked as mitred deans.

DE LA FUENTE, *España Sagrada*, XLIX, L (Madrid, 1865); CUADRADO, *España, Sus monumentos* (Barcelona, 1884); ARGAIZ, *Soledad laureada y teatro monastico de Tarazona*, the most complete history of this diocese.

RAMON RUIZ AMADO.

Tarbes, DIOCESE OF (TARBIA), comprises the Department of the Hautes-Pyrénées (ancient territory of Bigorre), included in 1802 in the Diocese of Bayonne, re-established theoretically by the Concordat of 1817 and actually by the Bull of 6 October, 1822. The new Diocese of Tarbes lost twenty-one parishes which were added to the Diocese of Bayonne, and twenty to the Archdiocese of Auch; but the parishes of the country of the Quatre Vallées and of the Vallée de Louron, formerly part of the archdiocese of Auch and the bishopric of Comminges, were reunited to the Diocese of Tarbes, suffragan of Auch. Tradition has preserved the names of St. Girinus and St. Evex or Erex, as the first martyrs of Bigorre. The district was laid waste by the Vandals, who were afterwards put to flight by St. Missolinus, a priest; it was disturbed by the Priscillianist heresy and finally terrorized by the Arian Visigoths, who, in the reign of Ewarik, waged a bloody persecution against the clergy. Mgr Duchesne considers St. Justin whom the "Gallia Christiana" cites as the first in the list of bishops of Tarbes, to have been only a priest, and excludes from that list St. Faustus, who, in his opinion, is none other than the celebrated Faustus of Riez. He considers Aper, represented at the Council of Agde in 506, as the first historically known bishop of the see. Among the successors are cited: St. Landeolus, bishop in 870;

THE CATHEDRAL, TARBES

William I (1120–41) who helped to draw up the ancient "For de Bigorre," one of the oldest and most curious monuments of the law of the Middle Ages; Pierre de Foix (1462–64), cardinal in 1437; Gabriel de Gramont (1524–34), cardinal in 1531, who attempted to negotiate between Henry VIII and the Holy See to prevent a rupture.

The Benedictine monastery of St. Savin of Lavedan was founded by Charlemagne and shortly took the name of the hermit and miracle worker, St. Savin, who was one of its monks and died before 840; the abbot was lord of the territory and the villages under his obedience were called a republic. The Benedictine Abbeys of St. Orens of Larreule and of St. Orens of Lavedan were founded, one in 970 and the other before the eleventh century in honour of St. Orens, Bishop of Auch, who had first lived as a hermit in the Lavedan. The monastery of St-Pé de Génèrès, was founded about 1032 by Sanche, Duke of Gascony; it was the cradle of the town of Saint-Pé. The priory of Sarrancolin was founded about 1050 in memory of St. Ebbons, who fought against the Moors in Catalonia and died at Sarrancolin. The Abbey of Escale Dieu was founded in 1140; it was the daughter of the Cistercian Abbey of Morimond. St. Bertrand of Comminges was one of its monks; another, St. Raymond, was sent to Spain in 1158, where he founded the Abbey of Fitère, and the celebrated semi-religious, semi-military order of Calatrava. St. Bertrand, Bishop of Comminges (1073–1123), preached the Gospel in the Vallée d'Azun in the Diocese of Tarbes. To make amends for the hostile reception that had been given him, the inhabitants pledged themselves to give the See of Comminges all the butter that should be produced in the territory of Azun during the week preceding Pentecost; this impost was paid down to 1789. As natives of Bigorre may be cited: Cardinal Arnaud d'Ossat (1536–1604), born at Larroque Magnoac, who played an important part in the reign of Henry IV; Bernard Pierre Carasse, born at Tarbes at the opening of the sixteenth century, who, from being a warrior, became general of the Carthusians, revised the constitutions of the order, and was so illustrious in his day, that in 1582 Catherine de Medici visited La Chartreuse to see him.

The fame of the Diocese of Tarbes has been spread throughout the Christian world since 1858 by the pilgrimages and the miracles of Lourdes (q. v.). Mention must also be made of the pilgrimage of Notre Dame de Garraison at Monléon, dating back to the fifteenth century; that of Notre Dame de Poueylahun near Eaux Bonnes, dating back to the sixteenth century; the pilgrimage to Mazères, near the vacant shrine of St. Liberata, perhaps a martyr under Julian the Apostate; the pilgrimage to Arreau, to the chapel of St. Exuperius, friend of St. Jerome, who died Archbishop of Toulouse, about 417, after combating the heresy of Vigilantius. Before the application of the law of 1901 against the congregations there were in the Diocese of Tarbes, the Priests of the Immaculate Conception at Lourdes, Carmelites, and various teaching orders of brothers. Several congregations of nuns were originally founded in the diocese: the Sisters of St. Joseph, hospitallers and teachers, with their mother-house at Cantaous; the Sisters of Notre Dame des Douleurs, hospitallers, with their mother-house at Tarbes, and a branch house in Cairo; the Sisters of the Immaculate Conception of Notre Dame de Lourdes, with their mother-house at Lourdes. At the close of the nineteenth century the religious congregations directed in the diocese: 5 schools, 1 home for sick children, 1 school for the deaf and dumb, 6 girls' orphanages, 6 workshops, 3 homes for the poor, 12 hospitals or hospices, 3 houses of retreat, 6 houses of nuns devoted to nursing the sick in their own homes. At the time of the abrogation of the Concordat (1905) the Diocese of Tarbes contained 215,546 inhabitants, 28 cures, 300 succursal churches, and 135 vicariates towards the support of which the State contributed.

Gallia Christiana (nova) (1715), I, 1223–42, *instrum.*, 191–7; DUCHESNE, *Fastes épiscopaux*, II (Paris, 1894–9), 101–02; COUTURE, *Le diocèse de Tarbes et son dernier historien* in *Revue de Gascogne*, VI (1865), 575–85; DE LAGRÈZE, *Histoire religieuse de la Bigorre* (Paris, 1862); BATSERE, *Esquisses: Tarbes et ses environs, Bagnères, Baudéan, épisodes* (Tarbes, 1856).

GEORGES GOYAU.

Tarentaise, DIOCESE OF (TARANTASIENSIS), comprises the arrondissement of Moutiers in the Department of Savoie; it is also sometimes called the Diocese of Moutiers en Tarentaise, and is suffragan of Chambéry. Legend relates that the "Centrones" were evangelized in the fifth century by James the Assyrian, secretary to St. Honoratus, Archbishop of Arles. He became the first Bishop of Darantasia or Tarentaise, the metropolis of the "Centrones", and named St. Marcellus as his successor. The first document in which the Diocese of Tarentaise is reliably mentioned is a letter of Leo the Great (5 May, 450) which assigns to the Archdiocese of Vienne, among other suffragans, the Bishop of Tarentaise. The first historically known bishop is Sanctius who in 517 assisted at the Council of Epaon. A plea was brought before the Council of Frankfort (794) against the decision of Leo I that had been confirmed by Popes Symmachus and Gregory the Great. Leo III partly acceded to this plea, and made Darantasia a metropolis with three suffragans, Aosta, Sion, and Maurienne, but maintained the primacy of Vienne. For four centuries this primacy was the cause of conflicts between the archbishops of Tarentaise and those of Vienne; subsequently Maurienne was again attached to the metropolis of Vienne.

The city of Darantasia was destroyed by the Saracens in the tenth century, whereupon the archbishops moved their residence to the right bank of the Isère, calling it their *moutier* (monastery), and it was at this place that the town of Moutiers began to be built in the second half of the tenth century. In the twelfth century the archbishops of Tarentaise were powerful sovereigns. In 1186 a bull of Frederick Barbarossa recognized the Archbishop of Tarentaise as immediate vassal of the empire and prince of the Holy Roman Empire in disregard of the pretensions of Humbert III, Count of Savoy; but in 1358 a transaction between Archbishop Jean de Bertrand and the Count of Savoy, Amadeus VI, fixed the respective rights of the archbishops and the counts. Tarentaise belonged to France from 1536 to 1559, and from the sixteenth to the eighteenth century was on four occasions wrested for a time by France from the House of Savoy. In 1792 it formed the Department of Mont Blanc. The Treaty of Paris (30 May, 1814) gave it to the King of Sardinia, while the Plebiscite of 22 and 23 April, 1860, gave it to France. The Archdiocese of Moutiers in Tarentaise was suppressed in 1792 by the French Revolution. In 1825 a diocese was re-established at Moutiers, suffragan of Chambéry, and was maintained in 1860 in virtue of a special clause in the treaty ceding Savoy to France.

Among the archbishops of Moutiers in Tarentaise may be mentioned: St. Peter I (about 1130), the first Cistercian raised to the episcopate, who founded in a defile the Cistercian Abbey of Tamié, to serve as a shelter for pilgrims and travellers; the Cistercian monk St. Peter II (1141–74) founded the charity of the *pain de Mai*, which until the second half of the eighteenth century distributed bread at Moutiers at the expense of the archdiocese during the first twenty-eight days of May; it was he who upheld Alexander III against Frederick Barbarossa and the Antipope Victor IV, and maintained in obedience to Alexander III the seven hundred abbeys of the Cistercian Order. Alexander decided (3 Feb., 1171) that thenceforth the metropolitan See of Tarentaise should depend only on Rome; St. Peter III (1271–83); Cardinal Antoine de Chalant (1402–18), to whom has been ascribed "Le livre du Roi Modus et de la reine Ratio", a much-esteemed treatise on hunting; Cardinal Jean d'Arces' (1438–54), who at the Council of Basle in 1440 supported Duke Amadeus of Savoy, antipope under the name of Felix V, against Eugene IV; Cardinals Christopher and Dominic de la Rovère (1472–78 and 1478–83), whose tomb erected at Rome in the Church of Santa Maria del Popolo is a splendid monument of the Renaissance; Germonio (1607–27), who played an important part in the seventeenth-century reform of the clergy and whose "Commentaries" and "Acta Ecclesiæ Tarentasiensis" are important documents for the history of the time. As natives of the diocese may be mentioned: Pope Nicholas II (1059), b. at Chevron-Villette of the family of the lords of Miolans; Pierre d'Aigueblanche, who in 1240 became Archbishop of Hereford in England, and for twenty-five years was councillor and minister to Henry III of England; Blessed Peter of Tarentaise, who became pope in 1276 under the name of Innocent V.

The chief pilgrimages of the diocese are: Notre Dame de Briançon, which dates from the victory over the Saracens in the tenth century. Francis I and Henry IV visited this shrine; Notre Dame des Vernettes, at Peisey, created in the eighteenth century near a miraculous fountain; Notre Dame de la Vie at St. Martin de Belleville; Notre Dame de Beaufort; St. Anne at Villette dating from 1248. Before the application of the Law of 1901 regarding associations there were in the diocese Augustinians of the Assumption, Capuchins, and two orders of teaching brothers. The Sisters of St. Joseph, nursing and teaching sisters, separated in 1825 from the Congregation of Puy. Several hospitals and schools in Brazil are dependent on their motherhouse at Moutiers. At the end of the nineteenth century religious congregations in the diocese were charged with: 4 infant schools, 2 orphanages for girls, 6 infirmaries or hospitals, 4 houses of retreat. In 1905 (end of the period of the Concordat) the diocese numbered 68,000 inhabitants, 7 parishes, 79 succursal churches, and 21 vicariates remunerated by the Government.

Gallia Christ. (nova) (1779), XII, 700–24; *instrumenta*, 377–420; DUCHESNE, *Fastes épiscopaux*, I (Paris, 1894), 207–41; PASCALEIN, *Hist. de Tarentaise jusqu'en 1792* (Moutiers, 1903); IDEM, *Hist. de la Tarentaise depuis 1792* (Moutiers, 1887); BORREL, *Hist. de la Révolution en Tarentaise et de la réunion de la Savoie à la France en 1792* (Moutiers, 1901).

GEORGES GOYAU.

Targum (TARGUMIM; תרגומים singular, תרגום "translation" (cf. מתרגם, Ezra, iv, 7) is the distinctive designation of the Aramaic translations or paraphrases of the Old Testament. After the return from exile Aramaic gradually won the ascendancy as the colloquial language over the slowly decaying Hebrew until, from probably the last century before the Christian era, Hebrew was hardly more than the language of the schools and of worship. As the majority of the population ceased to be conversant with the sacred language it became necessary to provide translations for the better understanding of the passages of the Bible read in Hebrew at the liturgical services. Thus to meet this need it became customary to add to the portions of the Scriptures read on the Sabbath an explanatory oral translation—a Targum. At first this was probably done only for the more difficult passages, but as time went on, for the entire text. The "Mishna" gives elaborate instructions as to the way in which this translating should be done. According to the "Megillah" (IV, 4), when the lesson to be read aloud was from the "Torah" only one verse was to be read to the translator (*Methurgeman*, מתורגמן). When the lesson was from the "Nebi'im" it was permitted to read three to him, unless each verse formed a special division. The directions also state which portions are to be read aloud but not translated (cf. for instance "Meg.", IV, 10), and a warning is given against translations that are either too free, palliative, allegorical etc.

Another regulation was that the Targum was not to be written down ("Jer. Meg.", IV, i=fol. 74 d). This prohibition, however, probably referred only to the interpretation given in the synagogue and did not apply to private use or to its employment in study. In any case, written Targums must have existed at an early date. Thus, for instance, one on the Book of Job is mentioned in the era of Gamaliel I (middle of the first century A. D.), which he, however, was not willing to recognize ("Sabb.", 115a; cf. "Tos. Sabb.", 13, 2=p. 128, ed. Zuckermandel). If Matt., xxvii, 46, gives the Aramaic form of Ps., xxi, 2, the last utterance of the Saviour upon the Cross, this shows that even then the Psalms were current among the people in the Aramaic language; moreover, Ephes., iv, 8, has a closer connexion with the Targum to Ps., lxvii, 19, than with the Masoretic text. In addition, the "Mishna Yadayim", IV, 5, and "Sabb.", XVI, also indicates the early existence of MSS. of the Targum. These MSS., however, were only owned privately not officially as for a long period the Targums were without authoritative and official importance in Palestine. This authoritative position was first gained among the Babylonian Jews and through their influence the Targums were also more highly esteemed in Palestine, at least the two older ones. In the form in which they exist at present no Targum that has been preserved goes back further than the fifth century. Various indications, however, show the great antiquity of the main contents of many Targums, their theology among other things. That as early as the third century the text, for instance, of the Targum on the Pentateuch was regarded by the synagogue as traditionally settled is evident from the "Mishna Meg.", IV, 10, "Jer. Meg.", 74d, "Hab. Kidd.", 49d, "Tos. Meg.", IV, 41. There are Targums to all the canonical books excepting Daniel, Ezra, and Nehemiah; for some books of the Bible there are several Targums. As regards age and linguistic character they may be divided into three classes: (1) Targum of Onkelos and Targum of Jonathan; (2) Jerusalem Targums; (3) Targum on the Hagiographa.

The form of language used in the Targums is called specifically the "Targum dialect". It belongs to western Aramaic and more particularly to the Aramaic of Palestine. Its home is to be sought in Judea, the ancient seat of the learning of the scribes. It should be borne in mind that this Targumic language does not represent the spoken Aramaic, but is the result of the labours of scholars. Consequently the point under discussion turns on a literary Aramaic originally formed in Judea. This is particularly true of the two earlier Targums; the later ones show generally an artificially mixed type of language. The traditional pointing of the texts is valueless and misleading: a more certain basis was first offered by MSS. from Southern Arabia in which the pointing for the vowels was placed above the line. In Arabia the old synagogal custom of reciting the Targum at the religious services had been retained, and consequently more interest was felt there in the pronunciation. It must be acknowledged, however, that this cannot be regarded as a direct reproduction of the Palestinian pronunciation; it may have sprung from a formal treatment of the Targum of Onkelos customary among the Babylonian scholars. As regards the method of translation all Targums in common strive to avoid as much as possible anthropomorphisms and anthropopathic terms, as well as other apparently undignified expressions concerning, and descriptive of God. The Targums are printed in the Rabbinical and Polyglot Bibles, although the two do not always contain the same Targums or an equal number of them. See below for particulars as to individual editions.

ZUNZ, *Die gottesdienstlichen Vorträge der Juden* (Berlin, 1832), 61–83; HAUSDORFF, *Zur Gesch. der Targumim nach talmudischen Quellen* in *Monatschr. für Gesch. u. Wissensch. des Judentums*, XXXVIII (1894), 203 sqq., 241 sqq., 289 sqq.; MAYBAUM, *Die Anthropomorphien u. Anthropopathien bei Onkelos u. in den späteren Targumim* (Breslau, 1878); GINSBURGER, *Die Anthropomorphismen in den Thargumim* in *Jahrbücher für prot. Theol.* (Brunswick, 1891), 262 sqq., 430 sqq. As regards the language: DALMAN, *Grammatik des jüdisch-palästinischen Aramäisch* (2nd ed., Leipzig, 1905); IDEM, *Aramäisch-neuhebr. Wörterbuch* (Frankfort, 1897–1901).

I. THE TARGUM OF ONKELOS.—The official Targum to the Pentateuch (תרגום של תורה) is designated by the name of Onkelos (אנקלוס). In the Babylonian Talmud and in the Tosephta, Onkelos is the name of a proselyte who is mentioned as a contemporary of the elder Gamaliel ("Aboda zara", 11a; cf. "Tos. sabb.", 8=p. 119, ed. Zuckermandel). The labours of Onkelos are referred to in "Meg.", 3a, in the following words: "Rab Jeremiya, according to others Rab Hiya bar Abba says: 'According to the statement (מפי) of Rab Eliezer and Rab Josua, Onkelos the proselyte has said, אמרו that is, has orally formulated, the Targum of the Torah'". Gaon Sar Shalon (d. 859) was the first who, taking this passage as a basis, called the Pentateuch-Targum the Targum of Onkelos. This he did in an opinion concerning the Targum which he evidently had before him at the time in a written copy. The designation that thus arose became customary through its acceptance by Rashi and others. It is evident, however, that in the passage mentioned ("Meg.", 3a) there has been a confusion with the name of Aquila, the translator of the Bible, for the older parallel passage of the Palestinian Talmud ("Meg.", I, 11 = fol. 71c) says the same of Aquila and his Greek translation of the Bible. Compare also Midrash, Tanchuma, Mishpatim, 91, 92 (ed. Mantua, 1863, fol. 36b). Thus it seems that in Babylonia the old and correct knowledge of the Greek translation of the proselyte Aquila was erroneously transferred to the anonymous Aramaic translation, that consequently Onkelos (instead of Akylas) is a corrupted form or a provincial modification of Aquila (עקילס), as, for instance, the Tosephta has אנקלס always (five times) for עקילס. It is not necessary to discuss here earlier views concerning this point. The effort to prove the existence of an Onkelos distinct from Aquila is still made by Friedmann ("Onkelos und Akylas" in "Jahresber. der Israelit.-theol. Lehranstalt in Wien", 1896), but the proof adduced is not convincing (cf. Blau in "Jewish Quarterly Review," IX, 1897, p. 727 sqq.).

Thus it is not known who wrote the Targum named after Onkelos. In any case the Targum, at least the greater part of it, is old, a fact indicated by the connexion with Rab Eliezer and Rab Josua, and belongs probably to the second, or it may be to the first century of our era. It arose, as the idiom shows, in Judea, but it received official recognition first from the Babylonian Rabbis, and is therefore called by them תרגום דידן (our Targum), or is quoted with the formula כדמתרגמינן (as we translate). Rab Natronay (d. 869) in speaking of this ת׳ דרבנן says, that it is not permitted to replace it in the services of the synagogue by any other translation of the Pentateuch. The high reputation of this authorized translation is shown by the fact that it has a Masorah of its own. The fixing of the written form, and thereby the final settlement of the text as well, should not be assigned to a date before the fifth century. The language is, in general, an artificial form of speech closely connected with the Biblical Aramaic. It is probably not the spoken Aramaic used as a dialect by the Jewish people, but a copy made by scholars of the Hebraic original, of which the Targum claims to give the most faithful reproduction possible. In doing this the Aramaic language is treated similarly to the Greek in the translation of Aquila, consequently the many Hebraic idioms. There is no positive proof (Dalman, "Gramm", 13) of a corrupting influence of the Babylonian dialect as Noldeke held ["Semit. Sprachen" (1887), 32; (2nd ed., 1899), 38].

As regards the character of the translation it is, taken altogether, fairly literal. Anthropomorphic and anthropopathic expressions are avoided by roundabout expressions or in other ways; obscure Hebrew words are often taken without change into the text; proper names are frequently interpreted, as Shinar-Babylon, Ishmaelites-Arabs; for figurative expressions are substituted the corresponding literal ones. Haggadic interpretation is only used at times, for instance in prophetic passages, as Gen., xlix; Num., xxiv; Deut., xxxiii. This Targum was first printed at Bologna (1482) together with the Hebrew text of the Bible and the commentary of Rashi; later, in the Rabbinical Bibles of Bomberg and Buxtorf, and with a Latin translation in the Complutensian Polyglot (1517), and the Polyglots of Antwerp (1569), Paris (1645), and London (1657). Among separate editions of the Targum special mention should be made of that printed in 1557 at Sabbioneta. More modern editions are: Berliner, "Targum Onkelos" (2 vols., Berlin, 1884), in which vol. I contains the text according to the Sabbioneta edition, and vol. II, elucidations; the Yemanites at Jerusalem have printed with an edition of the Pentateuch (sefer Keter tora) from MSS. the Arabic translation by Saadya (Jerusalem, 1894–1901), in which publication the vowel pointing above the line has been changed to sublinear pointing; Barnheim, "The Targum of Onkelos to Genesis" (London, 1896), on the text of the Yemen manuscripts. In addition to the Latin translations in the Polyglot Bibles there is one by Fagius (Strasburg, 1546); there is also an English translation by Etheridge, "The Targum of Onkelos and Jonathan ben Uzziel on the Pent., with the Fragments of the Jerusalem Targum", from the Chaldee (2 vols., London, 1862–65).

KAUTZSCH, *Mitteilung über eine alte Handschr. des Targ. Onk.* in *Cod. Socini, No. 84* (Halle, 1893); BERLINER, *Die Massorah zum Targ. O.* (Leipzig, 1877); LANDAUER, *Die Mâsôrâh zum O.* (Amsterdam, 1896); BREDEREK, *Concordanz zum T. O.* (Giessen, 1906); IDEM, *Uber die Art der Übersetzung im T. Onk.* in *Theol. Studien u. Kritiken* (Gotha, 1901), 351–77.

THE TARGUM OF JONATHAN (YONATHAN).—The Targum to the Prophets (*priores*, historical books; *posteriores*, the actual Prophets) now in existence is ascribed to Jonathan ben Uzziel, who is said on the authority of the Babylonian "Megillah", 3a, to have formulated it orally (אמרו), in accordance with the instructions (מפי) of Haggai, Zachariah, and Malachi. This assertion probably means that in his exposition he gives the traditional interpretation that had been handed down from one generation to another since early times. According to the Babylonian "Sukkah" (28a=baba bathra 134a), he was the most noted pupil of the elder Hillel, and is therefore assigned to the first Christian century. The Babylonian Talmud in quoting passages from this Targum ascribes them to Rab Joseph bar Hiya (d. 333), the head of the school at Pumbaditha. Rab Joseph was regarded as a great authority on the tradition of the Targum and his judgment on the translation of individual passages was eagerly listened to; he may perhaps be considered as the editor of this Targum. For Jonathan as for Onkelos the final settlement of the written form did not occur until the fifth Christian century. Cornill claims to show ("Einleitung", 2nd ed., 1893, p. 308) that the Targum on the Prophets is older than the Torah-Targum, but the reasons produced are not convincing (cf. Dalman, 15, *passim*). Linguistically, this Targum approaches most closely that of Onkelos; in grammatical construction the two are alike but the words used differ, and this Targum is more paraphrastic. In the historical books Jonathan himself is often the expounder, but in the actual prophetic books the exposition is in reality Haggadic. The religious opinions and theological conceptions of the era that are interwoven are very instructive. The text, further, is not free from later additions; from this cause arise the double translations of which the Targum contains several. The "Prophetæ priores" was first printed with the Hebrew text and the commentaries of Gimhi and Levi at Leiria, Portugal, in 1494. At a later date the whole Targum was printed in the Rabbinical Bibles of Bomberg and Buxtorf and in the Polyglot Bibles of Antwerp, Paris, and London. The last edition is that of de Lagarde, "Prophetæ chaldaice e fide codicis Reuchliniani" (Leipzig, 1872). There are supplementary additions to this from an Erfurt MS. in "Symmicta", I, 139. The Targum to the Haphtarah is to be found in what is called the Pentateuch edition of the Yemanites at Jerusalem. English translations are: Pauli, "The Chaldee Paraphrase on the Prophet Isaiah Translated" (London, 1871); Levy, "Targum on Isaiah," I (London, 1889).

PRACTORIUS, *Das Targum zu Josua nach Yemenischer Uberlieferung* (Berlin, 1899); IDEM, *Das Targum zum Buch der Richter nach yemen. Uberlieferung* (Berlin, 1900); WOLFSOHN, *Das Targum zum Propheten Jeremias in yemen. Uberl.* (Halle, 1902), ch. i–xii; SILBERMANN, *Das Targum zu Ezechiel nach einer südarabischen Handschrift* (Strasburg, 1902), ch. i–x; WRIGHT, *Targum zu Jonas* (London, 1857); ADLER, *Targum to Nahum* in *Jew. Quart. Rev.*, VII (1895), 630 sqq.; BACHER, *Kritische Untersuchungen zum Prophetentargum* in *ZDMG*, XXVIII (1874), 1 sqq.; KLEIN in loc. cit., XXIX (1875), 157 sqq.; FRANKEL, *Zu dem Targum der Propheten* (Breslau, 1872).

II. THE JERUSALEM TARGUMS.—This designation is not correct; the older and more correct name is תרגום ארע ישראל, i. e. Palestinian Targum, is found for instance in the writings of Gaon Haï (d. 1038). At a later date this designation was displaced by the term ירושלמי, just as before this the Palestinian Talmud (תלמוד ארץ ישראל) is called in the writings of Gaon Sar Shalon ת׳ ירושלמי. Fundamentally the language of these Targums is Palestinian Aramaic but of a very mixed type. Neither of them is homogeneous grammatically and lexically. Besides expressions that recall the Galilean dialect of the Palestinian Talmud a preference is shown for imitation of the language of the Targum of Onkelos, while there are also various terms belonging to the language of the Babylonian Talmud.

A. *Targum Yerushalmi I on the Pentateuch.*—This is generally called the Targum of Jonathan or of Pseudo-Jonathan, because it is cited in the first printed edition (Venice, 1591) under the name of Jonathan ben Uzziel. This designation, however, rests on a mistaken solution of the abbreviation י ת, that is, ת׳ירושלמי. The Targum could not have appeared in its present form before the second half of the seventh century. For example (Gen., xxi, 21), a wife and daughter of Mohammed are mentioned. Compare also (Gen., xlix, 26) the position of Esau and Ishmael as representatives of the Christian and the Mohammedan world. The Targum covers the entire Pentateuch. The only passages that are lacking are: Gen., vi, 15; x, 23; xviii, 4; xx, 15; xxiv, 28; xli, 49; xliv, 30–31; Exod., iv, 8; Lev., xxiv, 4; Num., xxii, 18; xxx, 20[b], 21[a]; xxxvi, 8–9. As to its form it is a free Haggadic treatment of the text, that is, an exposition rather than a translation. A large part of it is made up of legendary narratives; there are also dialogues, rhetorical and poetical digressions. The paraphrase also discusses religious and metaphysical conceptions, as was the custom of the Jewish mystics of the seventh century. This Targum was first printed: as "תרגום החדוש יונתן בן עוזיאל", at Venice in 1591. It is also to be found in volume IV of the London Polyglot. A separate edition of this Targum was edited from the manuscript in the British Museum (MS. Addit. 27031) by Ginsburger, "Targum Jonathan ben Usiel zum Pentat." (Berlin, 1903). Concerning this codex cf. Barnstein in "Jew. Quart. Rev.", XI (1899), 167 sqq. An English translation has been published by Etheridge (*supra*).

SELIGSOHN AND TRAUB, *Über den Geist der Übersetzung des Jonathan ben Usiel zum Pent. etc.* in *Monatsschrift für Gesch. u. Wissenschaft des Judentums* (1857), 96 sqq., 138 sqq.; MARMORSTEIN, *Studien zum Pseudo-Jonathan Targum* (Presburg, 1905).

B. *Targum Yerushalmi II* on the Pentateuch is also called the Fragmentary Targum, because the Targum on the entire Pentateuch has not been preserved, but only portions of it on numerous longer and shorter passages, frequently only the Targum on individual verses or parts of such. These fragments were first printed in the rabbinical Bible of 1517 as תרגום ירושלמי. In language, method of translation, and exegetical form they are related to the Pseudo-Jonathan. A perspicuously arranged compilation of the fragments that have been preserved is given by Ginsburger in the "ZDMG", LVII (1903), 67 sqq., and in loc. cit., LVIII (1904), 374 sqq., on a page that came from a *geniza* or repository in a synagogue for damaged manuscripts. A Latin translation from the Venice edition of 1517 was published by Taylor (London, 1649); English tr. by Etheridge (*supra*).

GINSBURGER, *Das Fragmententargum* (Berlin, 1899); (1) Targum according to Cod. 110 of the National Library at Paris; (2) variants from Cod. Vat. 440 and Lips. 1; (3) quotations from old writers; matter supplementary to this work is given by MARX in *Zeitschrift für hebr. Bibliographie* (1902), 55–58.

Opinions concerning the connexion between the Targums Jerushalmi I and Jerushalmi II agree in general that both are to be traced back to different recensions of an old Jerusalem Targum. This is the view of Zunz (p. 73, and passim), and also that of Geiger, "Urschrift und Übersetzungen der Bibel" (Berlin, 1857), 454. Bassfreund (*infra*) reaches the conclusion that the basis both of the Fragmentary Targum and that of the Pseudo-Jonathan is a complete Jerusalem Targum of post-Talmudic origin, but that the two Targums, Jerushalmi I and II, presuppose the existence of the Targum of Onkelos. The Fragmentary Targum gives from this ancient Jerusalem Targum, according to Bassfreund, only matter supplementary to Onkelos, while Onkelos and the Jerusalem Targum have been used in preparing the Pseudo-Jonathan. In the preface to his edition of the Pseudo-Jonathan (see below) Ginsburger tries to prove that both the Fragmentary Targum and the Pseudo-Jonathan may be traced back to a very ancient Palestinian Targum, which was not influenced by the Targum of Onkelos until a later date. The Fragmentary Targum, in Ginsburger's opinion, represents a variant collection, not to Onkelos (as Bassfreund thinks), but to another recension of that ancient Jerusalem Targum. Ginsburger's views will have to be accepted as the more probable.

BASSFREUND, *Das Fragmententargum u. sein Verhältnis zu den anderen paläst. Targumim* in *Monatsschrift für Gesch. u. Wissenschaft des Judentums*, XL (1896), 1 sqq., 49 sqq., 97 sqq., 145 sqq., 241 sqq., 352 sqq., 396 sqq.; GINSBURGER, loc. cit., XLI (1897), 289 sqq., 340 sqq.; preface to *Pseudo-Jonathan*, ed. IDEM (Berlin, 1903); NEUMARK, *Lexikalische Untersuchungen zur Sprache der jerusalemischen Pentat. Targume* (Berlin, 1905).

C. *Targum Yerushalmi III* is the name assigned by Dalman (Gramm., 29) to fragments which are given in old editions of the Pentateuch, as Lisbon (1491), Salonica (1520), Constantinople (1546), Venice (1591), and in several MSS. Nearly all have been published by Ginsburger, "Das Fragmententargum" (1899), 71–74.

D. There have also been Jerusalem Targums on the Prophets and on individual books of the Hagiographa. As regards the Targums on the Prophets de Lagarde has given Reuchlin's notes from the "Nebi'im Codex" in the introduction (pp. VI–XLII) to his "Prophetæ chaldaice" (*infra*). There are fragments on Josue, Judges, Samuel, Kings, Isaias, Jeremias, Amos, Jonas, Zacharias. [Cf. Bacher in "ZDMG", XXVIII (1874), 1–72; XXIX (1875), 157 sqq., 319 sq.]

III. TARGUMS ON THE HAGIOGRAPHA.—They are the work of various authors and have the character more or less of private undertakings, with the production of which the schools had nothing to do. Linguistically they are to be regarded as the work artificially produced of a late age. They depend in the main on the Jerusalem Targums and probably belong to the same era; the Targum on Chronicles may be somewhat later. Three groups are to be distinguished as regards linguistic character and relation to the original text: (a) Targums to Proverbs, Psalms, and Job; (b) Targums to the five *Megilloth*, that is Ruth, Esther, Lamentations, Ecclesiastes, Canticles; (c) Targums to the Books of Chronicles. The Targums mentioned under (a) adhere relatively closest to the text of the Bible. The Targum to Proverbs is in language and contents very dependent on the text of the Syriac Peschitto, and is but little more than a Jewish recension of the same. [Cf. Nöldeke in "'Merx' Archiv für wissenschaftl. Erforschung des A. T.", II (1872), 246 sqq.; Baumgartner, "Etude critique sur l'état du texte du livre des Proverbes" (Leipzig, 1890), 267 sqq.] Haggadic additions are found only occasionally in the Targum on the Psalms. In a number of passages a second translation is introduced with the remark ת׳ א׳ (that is, תרגום אחר another Targum). The Targum to Job contains many more additions. There are also variants of the usual formula of citation ת׳ א׳, and much oftener than in the Targum on the Psalms. In style and language this Targum resembles that on the Psalms, consequently both perhaps are the work of the same author.

(b) The Targums on the *Megilloth* are not in reality translations but rather Haggadic commentaries. The Biblical text is most clearly evident in the Targums to Ruth and to Lamentations. The Targum to Ecclesiastes is a tasteless declamation upon the text on which it is based; that on Canticles is an allegorico-mystical Midrash. There are two Targums to Esther, the one closely resembles a paraphrase and has no legends interwoven with it; the other, called Targum *scheni*, has altogether the character of a Midrash. It is only to a small degree a translation; the greater part of it consists of stories, legends, and discourses that have but slight connexion with the contents of the book. (c) A Targum on the Books of Chronicles was edited from a MS. in Erfurt by Matthias Beck (2 pts., Augsburg, 1680–83); a more complete and correct text taken from a MS. at Cambridge was edited by Wilkins, "Paraphrasis Chaldaica in librum priorem et posteriorem Chronicorum" (Amsterdam, 1715).

All the Targums to the Hagiographa (excepting Chronicles) were printed for the first time in the Bomberg Bible in 1517; afterwards in the "Polyglots" of Antwerp, Paris, and London. A modern edition from the Bomberg text, with Chronicles from the Erfurt Codex, was edited by de Lagarde, "Hagiographa chaldaice" (Leipzig, 1873).

LEVY, *Das Targum zu Koheleth nach südarab. Handschriften* (Berlin, 1905); GOLLANCZ, *Targum to the Song of Songs* (London, 1908), translation; POSNER, *Das Targum Rischon zu d. bibl. B. Esther* (Breslau, 1896); DAVID, *Das Targum scheni zum B. Esther* (Berlin, 1898); TAYLOR, *Targ. prius et posterius in Estheram . . . in linguam Latinam translatum* (London, 1655); GELBHAUS, *Das Targum scheni zum B. Esther* (Frankfort, 1893).

FR. SCHÜHLEIN.

Tarisel, PIERRE, master-mason to the king, b. about 1442; d. in August, 1510. (In 1555 the title of architect was used at Amiens for the first time, but it was not until 1609 that a master-mason of the town called himself an architect). We have no details concerning his birthplace, save that he belonged to no family of masons known at Amiens. It is certain that he was the most renowned master-mason at Amiens at the time in which he lived. He was already famous in 1475, when he was summoned to inspect the cathedral of Noyon, which threatened to become ruinous in many places. Although he was not then entitled master-mason of the city, he was so in fact, as nothing of importance was done without him. In 1477 he was at Arras, at work for the King of France. In 1500 the plan of Martin Cambiche for the restoration and decoration of the cathedral of Beauvais was submitted to him. On 4 Nov., 1483, at the death of Guillaume Postel, Pierre Tarisel was appointed master-mason of the city of Amiens. His predecessors had been paid at the rate of 4s. per day; according to the accounts which have been preserved, Tarisel received 5s. The rate was again reduced to 4s. for his successor, which shows with what esteem his talent was regarded.

There is no document to show in what year he became master-mason of the cathedral; but it seems certain beyond doubt that he fulfilled these duties in 1482–83. On 7 March, 1497, Tarisel visited all the cloistered houses subject to the cathedral chapter. Shortly afterwards he undertook the task of restoring the cathedral. The second pillar of the choir, on the left, threatened to fall, but under Tarisel's direction it was restored in 1497. The projecting arch and the arches near it were restored, and the outer wall was propped by an additional flying buttress. In 1503 the same was done for the remaining pillars. Between 1497 and 1503 the pillars of the transept "buckled", owing to the weight of the rear side arches, and cracks formed. The remedy was found in bands of Spanish iron, reaching from the transept to the ends of the choir, the nave, and the cross bars. The great iron chainwork upholding the four large pillars of the transept running the length of the triforium in four directions still exists, and is justly famous. All this was the work of Tarisel, by whom the cathedral of Amiens was saved from ruin in the fifteenth and sixteenth centuries, and which is a sufficient claim to renown.

DURAND, *Maître Pierre Tarisel, maître maçon du roi, de la ville et de la cathédrale d'Amiens*; IDEM, *Monographie de la cathédrale d'Amiens*; DESJARDINS, *Histoire de la cathédrale de Beauvais*; archives of the city of Amiens; archives of the Department of the Somme.

M. VACCON.

Tarkin, SAINT (TALARICAN), Bishop of Sodor (including the western islands of Scotland), was probably of purely Pictish origin, though the Aberdeen Breviary (1509) says he was born in Ireland. The legend in the Breviary states that he was raised to the episcopate by Pope Gregory; and Adam King's Kalendar (1558) styles him "bishop and confess. in Scotland under King Solvathius". The Bollandists, following the chronology of the Dalriadic kings as adopted by Pinkerton and Skene, place the reign of Selvach from 706 to 726; and, as Gregory II was pope from 715 to 731, conclude that Talarican became bishop about 720, a few years after the Columban monks of Iona had been induced by St. Egbert to conform to the Roman Rite. He is said to have offered the Holy Sacrifice every day, to have been noted for his zeal and his mortified life, and to have converted many pagans in the northern coasts of Scotland through his preaching and example. According to Dempster, he died in the Island of Lismore. Many churches subsequently founded in the Dioceses of Moray, Ross, and Aberdeen were dedicated in his honour. His name is perpetuated in the great district of Kiltarlity (Inverness-shire), the church and cemetery of Ceilltarraglan (Skye), and wells still known as "St. Tarkin's" at Fordyce, Kilsyth, and elsewhere.

Acta SS., LXI (Paris, 1883), 447–50; *Kalendars of Scottish Saints*, ed. FORBES (Edinburgh, 1872), 216, 449; *Breviarum Aberdonense* (London, 1854), pars æstiv., fol. cxxxv; *Origin Paroch. Scot.* (Edinburgh, 1850), I, 43; II, 355, 377; KEITH, *Hist. Cat. of Scottish Bishops*, ed. RUSSEL (Edinburgh, 1824), 296; PINKERTON, *Enquiry into the Hist. of Scotland*, II (Edinburgh, 1814), 122; DEMPSTER, *Hist. Eccles. Gent. Scot.*, II (Edinburgh, 1829), 611.

D. O. HUNTER-BLAIR.

Tarnow, DIOCESE OF (TARNOVIENSIS), in western Galicia, Austria. The See of Posen, founded in 968 by Duke Miecyslaw, was the only one in Poland until 1100. In that year Otto III and Duke Boleslaw Chabry founded the Sees of Gnesen and Cracow, to which also belonged what is to-day western Galicia. When in the First Partition of Poland, in 1772, the latter fell to Austria, it was separated from the foreign See of Cracow, and the administration entrusted to the vicar-general, Johann von Duval, who resided at Tarnow. On the erection of the See of Tarnow in 1783, he became its first bishop. By the Third Partition of Poland in 1795, Cracow too fell to Austria, whereupon it was considered advisable after the death of the second bishop (1801) to divide the See of Tarnow between Cracow and Przemysl. By the Peace of Vienna in 1809 Austria was obliged to relinquish western Galicia, and with it Cracow, both assigned to the Duchy of Warsaw. The Diocese of Tarnow thereupon came under Lemberg, whose bishop gave the management of it to the prior of Alt Sandek as his vicar-general. In the Congress of Vienna, Austria once more incorporated the Kingdom of Galicia. The Emperor Francis in 1822 gave Tarnow another bishop, Gregorius Thomas Ziegler. He had been a Benedictine at Wiblingen, but was at that time professor of dogma at Vienna. He established his residence in the former Benedictine monastery of Tyniec. This, however, was too near Cracow, and Ziegler removed thence to Bochnia and finally in 1826 back to Tarnow. There are to-day in this diocese 809,000 Catholics; 379 secular priests; 72 male religious and 340 nuns.

ZACHARIASIEWICZ, *Vitæ episcoporum Premysliensium* (Vienna, 1844), LXVIII–LXXIII.

CÖLESTIN WOLFSGRUBER.

THE CATHEDRAL, TARNOW

Tarquini, CAMILLUS, cardinal, Jesuit canonist and archæologist, b. at Marta in the Diocese of Montefiascone, Italy, 27 Sept., 1810; d. at Rome, 15 Feb., 1874. Tarquini entered the Society of Jesus on 27 Aug., 1837, but before his entrance he had published, as a thesis for his doctorate, a work on canon law: "Institutionum juris canonici tabulæ synopticæ juxta ordinem habitum a Joanne Devoti" (Rome, 1835). As a professor, Tarquini held the chair of canon law at the Roman College, and he attracted notice by his masterly explanations of Sacred Scripture at the Gesù. Besides his published works, he contributed many articles to reviews, notably to the "Civiltà Cattolica". It is principally as a canonist that he achieved fame. His first work on the law of the Church to bring him into international celebrity was that on the *Regium Placet*, or *Exequatur*, for papal Bulls (Rome, 1851), which was translated into German, Spanish, and French. This treatise is generally published as an appendix to his main work on canon law: "Juris ecclesiastici publici institutiones" (Rome, 1862), which has gone through fourteen editions.

The work was translated into French (Brussels, 1868). Other works on canon law are his treatise on the French Concordat of 1801 (Rome, 1871), and a disquisition on the Pauline Privilege (published posthumously in 1888).

Though best known, perhaps, as a canonist, Tarquini was also an archæologist of no mean repute, especially on matters relating to the ancient Etruscans of Italy. His earliest archæological treatise is "Breve commento di antiche iscrizioni appartenenti alla città di Fermo" (1847). He began the Etruscan series of his works specifically with "Dichiarazione dell' epigrafe del lampadario di Cortona" (1862), which was soon followed by a more general treatise: "Dizzertazioni intorno ad alcuni monumenti etruschi" (Rome, 1862). The "Civiltà Cattolica" of 1857 and 1858 contains many of Tarquini's articles on Etruscan antiquities, the most noted being: "Origini italiche e principalmente etruschi rivelate dei nomi geografici" (Ser. 3, Vol. VI); "I misteri della lingua etrusca" (Vol. VIII); "Iscrizioni etrusche in monumenti autofoni" (Vol. IX); "Di vasi etruschi divinatorii" (Vol. X); "Iscrizione etrusca di Perugia" (Vol. XI); and "Sopra il semitismo della lingua etrusca" (Ser. 4, Vol. VII). He also wrote an Etruscan grammar and a dictionary of the Etruscan language. Other archæological treatises are: "Della iscrizione della cattedra Alessandrina di San Marco" (1868), and "De l'origine des phéniciens et leur identité avec les Pasteurs qui envahirent l'Egypte" (1870). Tarquini was a member of the Pontifical Roman Academy of Archæology and of the Imperial and Royal Academy of Science of Lucca. He was also president of the historical and archæological sections of the Accademia de' Quriti. He was raised to the cardinalate by Pius IX with the diaconal title of St. Nicholas at the Tullian Prison on 22 Dec., 1873, only a few months before his death.

SOMMERVOGEL, *Bibli. de le comp. de Jésus*, VIII (Brussels, 1896); DE BACKER, *Bibli. des écrivains de la comp. de Jésus*, II (Louvain, 1876).

WILLIAM H. W. FANNING.

Tarragona ARCHDIOCESE OF (TARRACONENSIS), bounded on the N. by Barcelona and Lérida, on the E. by Barcelona, on the S. by the Mediterranean Sea and Tortosa, and on the W. by Tortosa. It comprises the civil Provinces of Tarragona and Lérida, and its capital city has 24,335 inhabitants. Its suffragans are Barcelona, Lérida, Gerona, Urgel, Vich, Tortosa, and Solsona. Tarragona is one of the most ancient cities of Spain, probably of Iberian origin, as its coins and Cyclopean walls indicate. The Romans selected Tarragona as the centre of their government in Spain. In the division it was the capital first of Hither Spain (*Hispania Citerior*) and then of the Province of Tarraconensis. In the fifth century it was overrun by the Vandals, Suevi, and Alani. The Visigothic king, Euric, took possession of it in 475 and totally demolished it. During the occupation of the Visigoths it flourished once more, but the Arabs again destroyed it in 719.

The Church of Tarragona is undoubtedly one of the most ancient in Spain, holding as it does the tradition of the coming of St. James and St. Paul. The visit of St. Paul to Tarragona is not altogether beyond the range of possibilities, supposing that he came from Rome to Spain, as he promised to do, in the Epistle to the Romans, and as St. Jerome affirms that he did. The first written testimony which we have concerning the bishops of Tarragona dates from the third century. This is in the Acts of the Martyrdom of the bishop St. Fructuosus and his deacons Augurius and Eulogius. The list of the bishops of Tarragona, therefore, begins with St. Fructuosus, but it is supposed that other bishops, whose names have been lost to us, preceded him. The see of Tarragona, which was vacant at that time, was represented at the Council of Arles (314) by two procurators, the priest Probatius and the deacon Castorius. Himerius, who sent the priest Basianus to Pope St. Damasus, and who obtained a letter from Pope St. Siricius, was Archbishop of Tarragona in 384. It is also conjectured that the Hilarius who was the subject of the Decretal issued by Innocent I was also a Bishop of Tarragona. Ascanio was bishop in 465, and previous to 516 we find the name of Archbishop John, who, on 6 November, 516, assembled all the bishops of his province and held the first provincial council of Tarragona, at which ten bishops were present. In 517 he assembled another provincial council in Gerona.

Sergius, who was bishop from 535 to 546, held councils in Barcelona and Lérida. St. Justus, Bishop of

TOWER AND APSE OF THE CATHEDRAL, TARRAGONA

Urgel, dedicated to him his commentary on the Song of Solomon. Tranquillinus was bishop for many years previous to 560. He had been a monk in the Monastery of Asana under the direction of St. Victornus. Artemius, bishop prior to 589, was not able to attend the Third Council of Toledo, but sent a substitute, Stephen. He called provincial councils at Saragossa (599) and Barcelona. Eusebius (610-32) held the council of Egara (Tarrasa) to enforce the canons of the Council of Huesca. Audax (633-38) was present at the Fourth Council of Toledo, and Protasius (637-46) at the Sixth and Seventh. Cyprianus (680-88) sent representatives to the Thirteenth, Fourteenth, and Fifteenth Councils of Toledo, and Vera assisted personally at the Sixteenth and Seventeenth. In his time or in that of his successor, George, the Mohammedan invasion took place. Ludovico Pio appears to have temporarily taken possession of the city. A portion of its territory was bestowed on the Bishop of Barcelona, and the metropolitan rank was given to the Bishop of Narbonne, but was recovered in 759. Cæsarius endeavoured to obtain recognition as titular Archbishop of Tarragona, but was not successful, although he was consecrated by the bishops of Leon and Galicia, and obtained from the pope the abbey of Santa Cecilia, which belonged to the Archbishop of Tarragona. Borrell, Count of Barcelona, induced

Pope John XIII to confer the title of Archbishop of Tarragona on Bishop Attón of Vich, although he never was called Archbishop of Tarragona but of Ausona.

The Bishop of Vich, Berengarius of Rosanes, petitioned Pope Urban II for permission to promote a crusade for the reconquest of Tarragona. Count Berenguer Ramón II (the Fratricide) succeeded in taking the city and made it a fief of the Holy See. The pope, in recognition of the efforts of the Bishop of Vich, conferred on him the pallium as Archbishop of Tarragona, transferring to him all rights to the city and its churches which had previously belonged to the Holy See. The new bishop, however, was to remain in possession of the Church of Vich. A similar concession was granted to St. Olegarius, Bishop of Barcelona, who was permitted to retain possession of his former Church until he had obtained complete and peaceful possession of that of Tarragona, of which he had been named Archbishop. It was not until 1116 that Tarragona was definitively reconquered by Ramón Berenguer III (the Great). Bishop Berenguer had died in 1110, after having assisted, in 1096, at the Council of Nîmes convoked by Urban II. His successor in the See of Tarragona, St. Olegarius, had been a canon regular at St. Rufus in Provence, later an abbot, and then Bishop of Barcelona. To him is due the restoration of the metropolitan authority of Tarragona. In 1117 Count Ramón Berenguer III conferred on him the government of the city that he might endeavour to recolonize it, which work he carried on with great zeal. He assisted at the councils of Toulouse and Reims (1109), of the Lateran (1123), and of Clermont (1130), and accompanied the Count of Barcelona as pontifical legate in the war which terminated in the imposition of a tribute upon Tortosa and Lérida. The Norman Robert Burdet also joined the forces of the Count of Barcelona, established himself in Tarragona and obtained dominion over a great part of the city. The consequent dissensions among his sons led to the murder by them of Archbishop Hugo de Cervellón 22 April, 1171. On the death of St. Olegarius (6 March, 1137), Gregory, Abbot of Cuxana, succeeded him in the vacant See of Tarragona, and was the first incumbent of that see to receive the title of archbishop.

The dissensions between the archbishops and the kings, on account of the jurisdiction over Tarragona granted to the bishops who had begun its resettlement, continued during the time of Alfonso II, who bestowed the city as a dowry on his wife, Doña Sancha, and of Pedro IV (the Ceremonious), who, after forcibly seizing the dominions of the archbishop, repented in his last illness and restored to St. Tecla, patroness of the city, all that he had unjustly acquired. By special privilege of the pope, all the kings of Aragon were crowned at Saragossa by the archbishop of Tarragona, until the metropolitan See of Sargossa was re-established. When Jaime I, a child of six years, took the oath, the Archbishop of Tarragona, Don Aspargo Barca, carried him in his arms. Although he was far advanced in years, he wished to accompany the king in his expedition to conquer Majorca, and when Don Jaime refused his consent, he contributed a thousand marks in gold and twelve hundred armed men. In 1242 a provincial council was convoked at Tarragona to regulate the procedure of the Inquisition and canonical penances. In 1312 a provincial council was assembled in the Corpus Christi Chapel of the cathedral cloister, to pass sentence on the Templars, whom it declared innocent. Don Pedro Zagarriga, Archbishop of Tarragona, was one of the arbitrators at Caspe. One of the most celebrated prelates of Tarragona, Don Antonio Agustin (d. 1586), a native of Saragossa, was an eminent jurisconsult and numismatist. He put an end to the struggles referred to in "Don Quixote", between the Narros and Cadells factions, which had disturbed the peace of Catalonia.

The cathedral, it is believed, was begun by St. Olegarius. The edifice is solid and elegant, combining the Romanesque, Arabic, and Gothic styles of architecture, producing a very original and unique effect. Its façade is composed of three sections, and the ground plan, in the form of a Latin cross, has three naves and a wide transept. In the right nave is the chapel of St. Tecla, patroness of the city, begun in 1760 under the direction of Don José Prats and finished in 1776. The baptismal font is a magnificent marble basin found in the ruins of the palace of Augustus. The chapter house, celebrated for the councils held there, has a Byzantine door and a notable dome. As late as the fifteenth century the cathedral had not yet been completed, as the sculptor, Pedro Juan, did not begin work on the main altar until 1426. The choir was not finished until 1493. The chapel of the Blessed Sacrament, the organ, built by the cura of Tivisa, Don Jaime Amigó, the stained glass, etc. date from the sixteenth century.

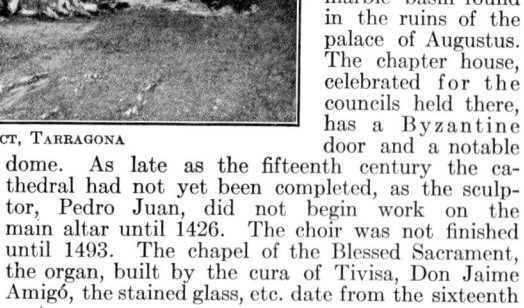

Among the buildings worthy of mention are the Churches of San Pablo and Santa Tecla, the convent of the Poor Clares, near the walls, that of Santa Teresa, and the church of the Capuchins, the parish church of the port. The former Convent of San Francisco has been converted into government offices and a secondary school, the Jesuit college turned into barracks, their church, however, having been restored to them. The convent of the Dominicans is now the town hall, and the convents of the Mercedarians and Carmelites turned over to military uses. The archiepiscopal palace is situated on the site of the ancient capitol, one tower of which still remains. The palace was rebuilt by Don Romualdo Mon y Valarde (1815-19). Near the sea, in the Roman amphitheatre, is the edifice called *el Milagro* (the Miracle), which belonged to the Knights Templar. It was afterwards used by the Trinitarian Fathers, and has since been converted into a penitentiary. The remains of many Roman buildings are to be found at Tarragona; the walls, the capitol, or citadel, the forum, the palace of Augustus, called the house of Pilate, the circus or amphitheatre, the aqueduct, known as the Puente del Diablo, the so-called tower, or sepulchre, of the Scipios, the arch of Sura, or of Bara, and the Aurelian Way. There is also a good archæological museum. The conciliar seminary of San Pablo and Santa Tecla was founded in 1570 by the cardinal archbishop, Gaspar de Cervan-

ROMAN AQUEDUCT, TARRAGONA

tes, and was the first to comply with the decrees of the Council of Trent. In 1858 Archbishop Costa y Borrás built a fourth wing. Benito Villamitjana built a new seminary behind the cathedral in 1886, in the courtyard of which stands the old chapel of San Pablo. Leo XIII raised this to the rank of a pontifical university. In the district of Montblanc, in this archdiocese, is the ancient monastery of Poblet, founded in 1151 by Ramón Berenguer IV, which was the pantheon of the kings of Aragon.

PIFERRER, *España. sus monumentos: Cataluña* (Barcelona, 1884); FLÓREZ, *Esp. Sagrada*, XXIV, XXV (Madrid, 1859); FULGOSIO, *Crónica general de Esp.: Tarragona* (Madrid, 1870); AGUSTÍN, *Catálogo de los prelados tarraconenses* (1586).

RAMÓN RUIZ AMADO.

Tarsicius, SAINT, martyr. The only positive information concerning this Roman martyr is found in the poem composed in his honour by Pope Damasus ("Damasi epigrammata", ed. Ihm, 14). In these lines Damasus compares Tarsicius to the protomartyr Stephen: just as the latter was stoned by the people of Judea so Tarsicius, carrying the Blessed Sacrament, was attacked by a heathen rabble, and he suffered death rather "than surrender the Sacred Body [of Christ] to the raging dogs". This tradition so positively asserted by Damasus is undoubtedly historical. Nothing definite is known concerning the personality of this martyr of the Eucharist. He may have been a deacon, as Damasus compares him to Stephen. An addition to the sixth-century legend of the martyrdom of Pope St. Stephen makes Tarsicius, for some unknown reason, an acolyte; this addition, however, is based on the poem of Damasus. It is evident that the death of this martyr occurred in one of the persecutions that took place between the middle of the third century and the beginning of the fourth. He was buried in the Catacomb of St. Callistus, and the inscription by Damasus was placed later on his tomb. In the seventh century his remains rested in the same grave as those of Pope Zephyrinus; according to Wilpert they lay in the burial vault above ground (*cella trichora*) which was situated towards the west over the Catacomb of St. Callistus. The feast of the saint is observed on 15 August.

WILPERT, *Die Papstgräber u. die Cäciliengruft in der Katakombe des hl. Kallistus* (Freiburg, 1909), 91 sq., there is in the same work a note by FRANCHI DE' CAVALIERI, 96–98; MARUCCHI, *La cella tricora di S. Sotere ed il gruppo topografico di Marco-Marcelliano e Damaso* in *Nuovo Bullettino di arch. crist.* (1908), 157 sq. (1910), 205 sq., opposes Wilpert's opinion concerning the grave of Tarsicius; LAMBERT, *Etude historique et critique sur St. Tarsicius* (Rome, 1890); ALLARD, *Hist. des persécutions*, III, 71 sq.

J. P. KIRSCH.

Tarsus, a metropolitan see of Cilicia Prima. It appears to have been of Semitic origin and is mentioned several times in the campaigns of Salmanasar and Sennacherib. The Greek legend connects it with the memory of Sardanapalus, still preserved in the Dunuk-Tach, called tomb of Sardanapalus, a monument of unknown origin. When in the year 401 B. C., the younger Cyrus marched against Babylon, the city was governed by King Syennesis in the name of the Persian monarch. Tarsus was already Greek and had a tendency to become more and more hellenized. Alexander the Great came near meeting his death there after a bath in the Cydnus, the modern Tarsus-Irmak. By its literary schools, Tarsus rivalled Athens and Alexandria. It was then comprised in the kingdom of the Seleucides, took the name of Antioch, and the Bible (II Mach., iv, 30) records its revolt against Antiochus IV Epiphanes, about 171 B. C. Pompey subjected it to Rome. To flatter Cæsar it took the name of Juliopolis; it was there that Cleopatra and Anthony met, and it was the scene of the celebrated feasts which they gave during the construction of their fleet. Tarsus was already the *caput Ciliciæ*, the metropolis, where the governor resided. When the province was divided it remained the civil and religious metropolis of Cilicia Prima. The greatest glory of Tarsus is that it was the birthplace of St. Paul (Acts, ix, 11; xxi, 39; xxii, 3), who took refuge there after his conversion (Acts, ix, 30), and was joined by Barnabas (Acts, xi, 25). It is probable that at this time a Christian community was established there, although the first bishop, Helenus, dates only from the third century; he went several times to Antioch in connexion with the dispute concerning Paul of Samosata (Eusebius, "Hist. eccl.", VI, xlvi; VII, v).

Le Quien (Oriens christianus, II, 869–76) mentions twenty-two of its bishops, of whom several are legendary. Among them are Lupus, present at the Council of Ancyra in 314; Theodorus, at that of Nicæa in 325; Helladius, condemned at Ephesus, and who appealed to the pope in 433; above all the celebrated exegete Diodorus, teacher of Theodore of Mopsuestia and consequently one of the fathers of Nestorianism. From the sixth century the metropolitan See of Tarsus had seven suffragan bishoprics (Echos d'Orient, X, 145); the Greek archdiocese is again mentioned in the tenth century (op. cit., X, 98), and has existed down to the present day, being comprised in the Patriarchate of Antioch. Owing to the importance of Tarsus many martyrs were put to death there, among them being St. Pelagia, St. Boniface, St. Marinus, St. Diomedus, and Sts. Cerycus and Julitta; several Roman emperors were interred there—namely, Tacitus, Maximinus Daza, and Julian the Apostate. The Arabs took possession of Tarsus from the seventh century and kept it until 965, when Nicephorus Phocas annexed it again to the Byzantine Empire. The union continued for nearly a century. The crusaders captured it again from the Turks in 1097, and then it was disputed between Latins, Greeks, and Armenians of the Kingdom of Lesser Armenia; these last became definitively masters until about 1350, when it was sold to the Egyptians. Since then Tarsus has belonged to the Mussulmans. About the end of the tenth century, the Armenians established a diocese of their rite, which still exists; St. Nerses of Lambroun was its most distinguished representative in the twelfth century. Tarsus, which has preserved its name, is a caza of the vilayet of Adana on the railroad from Adana to Mersina; the city numbers about 18,000 inhabitants, of whom 10,000 are Mussulmans, the remainder are Greek or schismatic Armenian. Only a few Catholics are found there.

SMITH, *Dict. of Greek and Roman Geog.*, s. v.; LANGLOIS, *Voyage dans la Cilicie* (Paris, 1861), 259–331; CUINET, *La Turquie d'Asie*, II, 44–8; ALISHAN, *Sissouan* (Venice, 1899), 305–21.

S. VAILHÉ.

Tartaglia (TARTALEA), NICOLÒ, Italian mathematician, b. at Brescia, c. 1500; d. at Venice, 13 December, 1557. His father, Michele Fontana, died in 1506, leaving his widow, two sons, and two daughters in poverty. As a result of a blow across the mouth inflicted by some French soldiers at the sack of Brescia in 1512, Nicolò stammered in his speech, thus obtaining the nickname of Tartaglia, afterwards assumed by himself. He was self-taught. In 1521, he was teaching mathematics in Verona and in 1534 he went to Venice. By 1541, he had achieved the remarkable triumph of solving the cubic equation. In a mathematical contest with Antonio del Fiore, held in 1535, he had shown the superiority of his methods to the method previously obtained by Scipione del Ferro (d. 1526) and known at that time to del Fiore alone. The glory of giving these results to the world was not for Tartaglia, as Cardan (q. v.) having in 1539 obtained a knowledge of them under the most solemn pledges of secrecy, inserted them, with some additions and with some mention of indebtedness, in his "Ars Magna", published in 1545. A long and bitter controversy ensued in which Cardan was supported by his pupil Ferrari. In 1548 Tartaglia became professor of Euclid at Brescia but returned, after eighteen months, to Venice, where he died. In his will he expressed the request to be buried in the Church of San Silvestro, which wish, according to Dr. Giuseppe Tassin ("Curiosità Veneziane", Venice, 1864), was fulfilled.

The published works of Tartaglia include: "Nuova Scienza", dealing with gunnery (Venice, 1537, French translation by Rieffel, Paris, 1845–6); the first Italian translation of Euclid (Venice, 1543); the earliest Latin version of some of the works of Archimedes (Venice, 1543) "Quesiti ed Invenzioni Diverse", including problems in ballistics and fortification (Venice, 1546, new ed., 1554); "Regola Generale per sollevare ogni affondata Nave, intitolata la Travagliata Invenzione" (Venice, 1551, English version published by Salusbury, London, 1564); "Ragionamenti sopra la Travagliata Invenzione" (Venice 1551); "Trattato Generale di Numeri e Misure" (Venice, 2 pts. in 1556, 4 pts. in 1560); "Trattato di aritmetica" (Venice, 1556, French tr. by Gosselin, Paris, 1578); "Opere del Famosissimo Nicolò Tartaglia" (Venice, 1606); and an English translation, by Lucar in 1588, of his writings on gunnery. A letter of Tartaglia's is in the archives of Urbino and another letter and his will are in the archives of Venice.

TARTAGLIA'S *Quesiti* (Venice, 1554); BITTANTI, *Discorso di Niccolò Tartaglia* (Brescia, 1871); BUONCOMPAGNI, ed. CREMONA AND BELTRAMI, *Intorno ad un Testamento Inedito di Nicolò Tartaglia* in *Collectanea Math.*, *Mem. Dom. Chelini* (Milan, 1881), 363–410; GIORDANI, *I sei cartelli di mat. disfida primamente intorno alla generale risoluzione delle equazioni cubiche i con sei Contro-Cartelli in risposta di N. T.* (Milan, 1876); ROSSI, *Elogi di Bresciani Illustri* (Brescia, 1620), 386; TONNI-BAZZA, *Di una lettera inedita di Nicolò Tartaglia* in *R. Accad. dei Lincei, Rendiconti, Classe d. sci. fis.*, ser. 5, X, pt. II (Rome, 1901), 39–42; TONNI-BAZZA, *Di Nicolò Tartaglia; frammenti di nuove ricerche*, loc. cit., ser. 5, XIII, pt. I (Rome, 1904), 27–30.

PAUL H. LINEHAN.

Tartini, GIUSEPPE, violinist, composer, and theorist, b. at Pirano, Italy, 12 April, 1692; d. at Padua, 16 Feb., 1770. He resisted the earnest desire of his parents that he enter the Franciscan Order, and matriculated at the University of Padua in 1710 as a student in jurisprudence. It was not long before he abandoned this for the study of music, especially the violin, and the art of fencing, in which latter he soon became a master. Having secretly married a relative of Cardinal Cornaro, and being accused of abduction, he fled to Assisi, where he found an asylum and a guide of the first order for his musical studies in the person of Padre Boemo. After two years he emerged from his seclusion—the charge against him having in the meantime been dropped—and returned to Padua, settling later in Ancona for several years. There he developed into one of the greatest violin players of all time, and also continued his theoretical studies. In 1721 he was appointed solo violinist and orchestra conductor at the Cathedral of Padua, a position which he held, with the exception of two years spent in the service of Count Kinsky at Prague, until the end of his life. He refused many flattering invitations to visit other countries. In 1728 Tartini established at Padua a school for violin-playing which has given to the world some of its greatest masters, among them Nardini, Pasqualino, Bini, and many others. The manner of bowing originated by Tartini is still standard. He published an enormous number of compositions for the violin and for several combinations of instruments. Of the former many are the repertoires of present-day violin virtuosi. His single composition for the Church was a "Miserere" for four, five, and eight voices, which was performed by the Sistine choir in 1768. Although not the first to discover the so-called combination tone, or third tone, which results when two tones forming a perfect consonance are sounded, his name has always been associated with this discovery because he made it the basis of a new system of harmony. This system he laid down in his "Trattato di musica" in 1754.

MENDEL, *Musikalisches Conversations-Lexikon*, X (Berlin, 1878); FANGAZO, *Orazione delle lodi di Giuseppe Tartini* (Padua, 1770); UGONI, *Giuseppe Tartini, sua vita* (Brescia, 1802).

JOSEPH OTTEN.

Taschereau, ELZÉAR-ALEXANDRE, Archbishop of Quebec and first Canadian cardinal, b. 17 February, 1820, at La Beauce, Province of Quebec; d. 1898, at Quebec. He entered the Seminary of Quebec in 1828, and graduated after brilliant studies in 1836. While pursuing further studies in Rome he was on the point of joining the Benedictines, owing to his relations with Dom Guéranger. He reconsidered his decision, however, and returned to Quebec, was ordained priest at La Beauce, 10 Sept., 1842, and thenceforth devoted himself to the work of the seminary. He was successively occupied as disciplinarian and professor, and as member of the seminary council was one of the founders of Laval University in 1852. In 1854 he again studied in Rome, residing at the French Seminary, where he took the degree of Doctor of Canon Law in 1856. He was superior, 1860–66. In 1862 and 1864 he returned to Rome in defence of the rights of Laval, and again in 1869, as theologian of Archbishop Baillargeon during the Vatican Council. In the same year he was re-elected superior of the seminary and Rector of Laval University, and in 1871 was made Archbishop of Quebec. In 1886 he was raised to the cardinalate, taking his title from Santa Maria della Vittoria. He was particularly zealous in educational matters; the Seminary of Quebec found him at all times a devoted protector; he saved from extinction the classical college of Ste. Anne de la Pocatière, and aided the growth of new colleges at Lévis and Chicoutimi.

Mgr Taschereau's episcopal administration was very fruitful. He founded at Quebec the Sacred Heart Hospital, canonically erected forty parishes, founded thirty missions, established various devotions, procured the creation of an episcopal see at Chicoutimi, consecrated seven bishops, ordained more than three hundred priests, convened three provincial councils, and introduced the Redemptorist Order into his diocese, giving it charge of the parish of St. Patrick, and of the shrine of Ste. Anne de Beaupré. He organized the memorable celebration of the second centenary of the foundation of the See of Quebec, consecrated the new basilica of Ste. Anne de Beaupré, and performed the solemn translation of the remains of Mgr de Laval. He was much devoted to the Holy See, to which he paid episcopal visits in 1872, 1884, and 1888. He also welcomed at Quebec on three occasions the representatives of the Holy See, Monsignori Conroy, Smeulders, and Merry del Val. In 1871 he was himself charged with the office of papal delegate in a very important matter concerning Montreal. His theological ability and literary gifts were of a high order. Though obliged to give most of his time to administrative matters, he left a manuscript "History of the Seminary of Quebec"; his published discourses, and pastoral and other letters fill six folio volumes of 900 pages each. Cardinal Taschereau was of a silent disposition, but his speech was always pointed and effective. He was venerated by his clergy and people, who admired his Christian piety and dignified bearing.

TÊTU, *Les Evêques de Québec* (Quebec, 1889); IDEM, *Notice biog. S. E. le card. Taschereau* (Quebec, 1891); ANON., *Le premier Cardinal Canadien* (Quebec, 1886); ANON., *Jubilé Sacerdotal de S. E. le cardinal E. A. Taschereau* (Quebec, 1892).

H. TETU.

Tasmania. See HOBART, ARCHDIOCESE OF.

Tassach, SAINT, Irish saint, b. in the first decade of the fifth century; d. about 497. He was one of St. Patrick's artificers. When St. Patrick founded the Church of Raholp he placed St. Tassach over it as first bishop. This ancient monastic see (Rath-colpa), a couple of miles north-east of Saul, County Down, ultimately merged into the Diocese of Down. Tassach's rule is for ever memorable for the fact that he was selected by the national Apostle to be with him in his last moments and to administer the Holy Viaticum to him. This event is thus chronicled in "The Martyrology of Donegall": "Tassach of Raholp gave the Body of Christ to Saint Patrick before his death in the monastery of Saul". His feast is on 14 April.

STOKES, *Tripartite Life of St. Patrick* (London, 1887); O'LAVERTY, *Down and Connor* (Dublin, 1878–95); O'HANLON, *Lives of Irish Saints*, IV (Dublin, s. d.); HEALY, *Life and Writings of St. Patrick* (Dublin, 1905).

W. H. GRATTAN-FLOOD.

Tassé, JOSEPH, writer and journalist, b. at Montreal, 23 Oct., 1848; d. 17 Jan., 1895; son of Joseph, and Adeline Daoust. He received a classical education at Bourget College, Rigaud, Province of Quebec, and began his literary career at nineteen, as chief editor of "Le Canada", a tri-weekly, then daily, newspaper at Ottawa. In 1869 he became editor of "La Minerve", Montreal, the foremost Conservative organ, resigning in 1872. In 1878 he was elected member of the House of Commons for the City of Ottawa, and re-elected in 1882. He was appointed to the Senate in 1891. Besides contributing over a hundred articles to "La Revue canadienne", and presenting several valuable historical articles to the Royal Society of Canada, he wrote the following highly-appreciated works: "Philémon Wright ou colonization et commerce de bois" (1871); "Le chemin de fer canadien du Pacifique" (1873); "La Vallée de l'Outaouais" (1873); "Le 38ᵉ fauteuil" (1891). His most important work is: "Les Canadiens de l'Ouest" (1878). Tassé lectured frequently and effectively in Canada and the United States. His style is characterized by clearness and warmth.

MCLEAN-ROSE, *A cyclopedia of Canadian Biography* (Toronto, 1886); *La Minerve* (Montreal, 17 Jan., 1895); *Le Courrier du Canada* (Quebec, 18 Jan., 1895).

LIONEL LINDSAY.

Tassin, RENÉ-PROSPER, French historian, belonging to the Benedictine Congregation of Saint-Maur, b. at Lonlay, in the Diocese of Le Mans, in 1697; d. at Paris, 1777. He was professed at the Abbey of Jumièges in 1718. United in close friendship with his brother-religious, Dom Toustain, he collaborated with him on a new edition of the works of Theodore the Studite, which task led them to visit Rome together. Their work was interrupted by a dispute between the Benedictine Abbey of St. Ouen and the chapter of Rouen which was supported by the erudite Saas. Tassin and his friend wrote against Saas in defence of their brethren. They then resided at the Abbey of Rouen where they remained till 1747, when they were summoned to the convent of Saint-Germain-des-Prés, at Paris, by their general. To defend the authenticity of the deeds of their abbey they were obliged to make a deep study of diplomacy, a science dealing with diplomas, charters, and other official documents, which Mabillon had already set forth in his celebrated Latin work, "De re diplomatica". As a result of their researches they wrote the "Nouveau traité de diplomatique", six quarto volumes, which appeared between the years 1750 and 1765. Toustain having died before the second volume was entirely printed, Tassin completed the great work alone, but he wished the name of his friend to be associated with all the volumes; these, consequently, are known like the first two as the work of "two Benedictines". Later Tassin wrote his "Histoire littéraire de la Congrégation de Saint-Maur" (Paris and Brussels, 1770, in quarto), a model history containing the lives and list of works, printed or in MS., of all the learned authors of the Congregation, from its formation (1618) till the time when Tassin wrote, together with a list of their works, printed or in MS. Several MS. works of Tassin are in the National Library at Paris.

HAURÉAU, *Hist. littéraire du Maine* (Paris, 1870–77).

GEORGES BERTRIN.

Tasso, TORQUATO, Italian poet, b. at Sorrento near Naples in 1544; d. at Rome, in 1595; son of Bernardo Tasso, who was also an author and of noble family, and of Porzia de Rossi. He enriched the Italian literature of the Renaissance with an epic glorifying the Crusades. The depth of his Catholic feeling accords well with the growing resistance to the Reformation developed at Rome in the latter half of the sixteenth century. Educated at the Court of the Dukes of Urbino and later at Venice and the University of Padua, and soon carried away by the whirl of frivolous society, he manifested great precocity, composing his poem "Rinaldo" before reaching the age of twenty.

TORQUATO TASSO
Portrait by Alessandro Allori in the Uffizi

Already he had determined to celebrate in verse the prowess of Godfrey de Bouillon, and had composed the entire first canto. When he had settled at Ferrara in the suite of Cardinal Louis d'Este, he resumed the work. In 1570 he accompanied the cardinal on a voyage to France, and returned in time to hear at Rome the news of the victory of Lepanto. The atmosphere was suitable for the composition of the "Gerusalemme liberata", on which Tasso continued to work after his return to the Court of Duke Alphonso II at Ferrara. Moreover he composed an excellent pastoral idyl, "Aminta" (1573). The poet had now adopted the practice of consulting some learned friends, among others Mgr. Scipio Gonzaga, on the definitive form of his great work, and was very careful not to violate the rules of good literature then commonly accepted.

After 1575, in addition to his literary anxieties, Tasso suffered from intense religious scruples. His life had not been free from reproach; he had frequently been carried away by the storms of passion, and now he became an almost helpless victim of remorse of conscience. He was tormented by the thought of the liberties he had allowed himself in his poems, and consulted the inquisitors. Months of painful doubt followed, with happily a little respite which allowed him to complete his work, some dangerous passages of which he wished to justify by allegorical interpretation. In 1587 his anxieties returned with increased intensity. Court life became unsuitable for him under the circumstances. He began to travel and left Duke Alphonso, but only temporarily, for he returned a prey to a kind of mania about persecution which induced the duke, who had lost patience, to send him to St. Anne's lunatic asylum. The publication of the "Gerusalemme liberata" was undertaken by his friends Angelo Ingegneri and Febo Bonna, the latter working almost in accordance with the wishes of the poet. When at length Tasso left the asylum and was received by the Gonzaga, he began about 1586 to revise his poem and after six years he transformed it into the "Gerusalemme conquistata", an inferior work. It was, however, more satisfactory to certain critics, who had taken umbrage at the "Gerusalemme liberata". Finally, accepting the invitation of Cardinal Aldobrandini, Tasso went to Rome, where he died in the Convent of Sant' Onofrio, under the protection of the pope, the day before he was to be crowned as poet laureate.

MONUMENT OF TASSO IN THE CONVENT OF S. ONOFRIO, ROME

Gerusalemme liberata (Florence, 1895), critical edition by SOLERTI; translations of the epic by SMITH (London, 1851) and JAMES (London, 1865); *Opere minori di T. Tasso* (Bologna, 1895); *Prose diverse* (Florence, 1875); *Lettere di T. Tasso* (Florence, 1855–8); *Appendice alle opere in prosa* (Florence, 1893); SERASSI, *Vita di Torquato Tasso* (1785); SOLERTI, *Vita di Torquato Tasso* (Turin, 1895); MILMAN, *Life of Torquato Tasso* (London, 1850); D'OVIDIO, *Studi critici* (Naples, 1879); MAZZONI, *Tra Libri e carte;* CANTU, *Storia della letteratura italiana*, XI (Florence, 1865); DE SANCTIS, *Storia della litt. ital.*, II (Naples, 1894), xvi; FERRASSI, *T. Tasso* (Bassano, 1880); *T. Tasso e i benedettini cassinessi* (Rome,1886–7), BOULTING, *Tasso and his Time* (London, 1907).

GIUSEPPE GALLAVRESI.

Tassoni, ALESSANDRO, Italian poet, b. at Modena in 1565; d. there in 1635. He spent his life in the service of prelates and princes in Italy, acting as secretary or in some similar capacity. His fame depends chiefly upon the undoubted success of his mock-heroic poem, the "Secchia rapita" (1614), which deals in a pretendedly serious way with a mighty struggle between the citizens of two adjoining towns in Italy over the purloining of a well-bucket. The comic and the serious are skilfully blended throughout and the methods of the ancient epic description are faithfully copied. While in a measure the poem develops germs of the mock-heroic already perceptible in Italian literature back as far as the fourteenth century, it is more particularly significant as marking a natural outcome of poetizing on chivalrous, romantic subjects, such as Ariosto and Tasso had treated, once these subjects ceased to be regarded with any degree of seriousness as meet for artistic treatment. The "Secchia rapita" belongs to the same category as the ancient "Battle of the Frogs and Mice", Lope de Vega's "Gatomaquia", Boileau's "Lutrin" and Pope's "Rape of the Lock", and ranks worthily with them. The patriotic Italian's dislike of the arrogant invading Spaniard is clear in his "Filippiche contra gli Spagnuoli"; his views on literary criticism and his disapproval of the bad taste of his time may be seen in his "Considerazioni sopra le rime del Petrarca" and his "Pensieri diversi". There are various editions of the "Secchia rapita", e. g., Paris (1622); Modena (1744), with a life by Muratori; Florence (1861), with a study by Carducci; Florence (1887); with the addition of certain minor writings in prose and verse.

RONCA, *La Secchia rapita di Alessandra Tassoni* (Caltanisetta, 1884); CHICCO, *L'umorismo e la Secchia rapita* (Parma, 1894).

J. D. M. FORD.

Tatian, a second-century apologist about whose antecedents and early history nothing can be affirmed with certainty except that he was born in Assyria and that he was trained in Greek philosophy. While a young man he travelled extensively. Disgusted with the greed of the pagan philosophers with whom he came in contact, he conceived a profound contempt for their teachings. Repelled by the grossness and immorality of the pagans and attracted by the holiness of the Christian religion and the sublimity and simplicity of the Scriptures, he became a convert, probably about A. D. 150. He joined the Christian community in Rome, where he was a "hearer" of Justin. There is no reason to think he was converted by the latter. While Justin lived Tatian remained orthodox. Later (c. 172) he apostatized, became a Gnostic of the Encratite sect, and returned to the Orient. The circumstances and date of his death are not known. Tatian wrote many works. Only two have survived. One of these, "Oratio ad Græcos" (Πρὸς Ἕλληνας), is an apology for Christianity, containing in the first part (i–xxxi) an exposition of the Christian Faith with a view to showing its superiority over Greek philosophy, and in the second part a demonstration of the high antiquity of the Christian religion. The tone of this apology is bitter and denunciatory. The author inveighs against Hellenism in all its forms and expresses the deepest contempt for Greek philosophy and Greek manners.

The other extant work is the "Diatesseron", a harmony of the four Gospels containing in continuous narrative the principal events in the life of Our Lord. The question regarding the language in which this work was composed is still in dispute. Lightfoot, Hilgenfeld, Bardenhewer, and others contend that the original language was Syriac. Harnack, Burkitt, and others are equally positive that it was composed in Greek and translated into Syriac during the lifetime of Tatian. There are only a few fragments extant in Syriac but a comparatively full reconstruction of the whole has been effected from St. Ephraem's commentary, the Syriac text of which has been lost, but which exists in an Armenian version. Two revisions of the "Diatesseron" are available: one in Latin preserved in the "Codex Fuldensis" of the Gospels dating from about A. D. 545, the other in an Arabic version found in two manuscripts of a later date. The "Diatesseron" or "Evangelion da Mehallete" (the Gospel of the mixed) was practically the only gospel text used in Syria during the third and fourth centuries. Rabbula, Bishop of Edessa (411–435), ordered the priests and deacons to see that every church should have a copy of the separate Gospels (Evangelion da Mepharreshe), and Theodoret, Bishop of Cyrus (423–457), removed more than two hundred copies of the "Diatesseron" from the churches in his diocese. Several other works written by Tatian have disappeared. In his apology (xv) he mentions a work "on animals" and (xvi) one on the "nature of demons". Another work in refutation of the calumnies against the Christians (xl) was planned but perhaps never written. He also wrote a "Book

TASSO'S CELL IN THE CONVENT OF S. ONOFRIO, ROME

of Problems" (Eus., "Hist. Eccl.", V, 13), dealing with the difficulties in the Scriptures, and one "On Perfection according to the Precepts of Our Saviour" (Clem. Alex., "Strom.", III, 12, 81).

Text of *Oratio* in SCHWARTZ, *Texte u. Untersuchungen*, IV (Leipzig, 1888), tr. in *Ante-Nicene Fathers*, II, 65–83; PUECH, *Recherches sur le discours aux Grecs de Tatian suivies d'une traduction du discours, avec notes* (Paris, 1903); ZAHN, *Tatian's Diatesseron* (1881); CIASCA, *Tatiani Evangeliorum Harmoniæ Arabice* (Rome, 1888), tr. HOGG in *Ante-Nicene Fathers*, IX, 36–138; BURKITT, *Evangelion da Mepharreshe* (Cambridge, 1904).

PATRICK J. HEALY.

Tatti, JACOPO. See SANSOVINO, ANDREA CONTUCCI.

Tatwin (TATUINI), SAINT, Archbishop of Canterbury; d. 30 July, 734. A Mercian by birth, he became a monk at Briudun in Worcestershire. The Venerable Bede describes him as "a man illustrious for religion and prudence and excellently instructed in the sacred letters" (Hist. Eccl., V, xxiii). He was elected to succeed Brihtwald as Archbishop of Canterbury, and was consecrated there on 10 June, 731, afterwards receiving the pallium from the pope. (Symeon Dunelm., "Hist. Reg.", II, 30). During his brief episcopate of three years he blessed Nothbald, the new Abbot of St. Augustine's Abbey, who had succeeded Tatwin's friend, Albinus, and he also consecrated bishops for Lindsey and Selsey. After his death miracles were wrought through his intercession, an account of which was written by Goscelin. Certain rhymed *ænigmata* or riddles (published by Giles in "Anecdota Bedæ", 1851) are ascribed to him, and he is said to have written some poems in Anglo-Saxon which have perished.

VEN. BEDE, *Hist. Ecc.*, V, xxiii–xxiv; WILLIAM OF MALMESBURY, *Gesta pontificum* in R. S. (London, 1870); CHALLONER, *Britannia Sancta* (London, 1745); KEMBLE, *Codex diplomaticus ævi Saxonici* (London, 1839–48); HADDAN AND STUBBS, *Councils and Ecclesiastical Documents* (Oxford, 1869–78); HOOK, *Lives of the Archbishops of Canterbury* (London, 1860); HARDY, *Descriptive Catalogue* (London, 1862); STUBBS in *Dict. Christian Biog.*; HUNT in *Dict. Nat. Biog.*; EBERT, *Ueber die Räthselpoesie der Angelsachsen, insbesondere die Ænigmata des Tatwine u. Eusebius* in *Ber. Sächs. Ges. Wissensch.* (Berlin, 1877); HAHN, *Die Räthseldichter Tatwin u. Eusebius* in *Forsch. deutsch. Gesch.* (Berlin, 1887); SEARLE, *Anglo-Saxon Bishops, Kings and Nobles* (Cambridge, 1899).

EDWIN BURTON.

Taubaté, DIOCESE OF (DE TAUBATÉ), in Brazil, South America, established on 29 April, 1908, as a suffragan of São Paulo. The present incumbent and first bishop, the Right Rev. Epaminondas Nuñes de Avila e Silva (b. 4 July, 1869; consecrated 8 Sept., 1909) entered upon his duties on 21 Nov., 1909. In the town of Taubaté, there are, besides the cathedral, which is one of the finest in Brazil, the churches of Sant' Anna, Nossa Senhora do Pilar, and Santa Clara (built in 1644), and the chapels of the San José school of Santa Isabel Hospital, and of the Mendicant Asylum. The Catholic educational institutions in Taubaté are: the Seminario Menor, under the Capuchin Fathers; the Collegio de Nossa Senhora do Bom Conselho, and the San José School, both under the Sisters of St. Joseph; the Collegio Immaculado Coraçao de Maria, and the Collegio de Santa Veronica, administered by the Third Order of St. Francis. The religious orders in the diocese are: Capuchins; Franciscans; and Sisters of St. Joseph. There are seven religious associations or brotherhoods. The official organ of the diocese is "O Labaro", which was founded by Mgr. Nuñes de Avila.

For bibliography see BRAZIL.

JULIAN MORENO-LACALLE.

Tauler, JOHN, German Dominican, one of the greatest mystics and preachers of the Middle Ages, b. at Strasburg about 1300; d. at the same place, 16 June, 1361. He was the son of a prosperous citizen of that city. Apparently while still a youth he entered the Dominican Order at Strasburg, because according to his own confession the ascetic life of the order attracted him. It is possible that while taking the customary eight-years' course of study at the monastery he heard Eckhart preach. When a student at the university of the order at Cologne, he became more closely acquainted with Eckhart. In the same way he probably came to know Henry Suso at Cologne. Whether he also studied at Paris is uncertain; more probably he returned from Cologne to Strasburg. From about 1339 to 1347 or 1348 he lived at Basle where he and Henry of Nördlingen were the centre of the large society called the Friends of God of Basle; these were persons who favoured the mystical life and who gave themselves this name from St. John, xv, 15. Tauler then returned to Strasburg where he laboured as a preacher. Christina Ebner praises his fiery tongue that kindled the entire world; Rulman Merswin chose him as confessor. Later he lived for some time at Cologne. During the last period of his life he was again at Strasburg.

The "Meisterbuch" of the "Friend of God of the Upland" gives an account of a master of the Scriptures who attracted great attention in 1346 by his preaching. One day a layman accused the master of seemingly seeking his own honour rather than that of God, saying also that probably he had not himself borne the burdens he had laid upon others. Without making any stipulations the master allowed himself to be guided by the layman and learned from him to forget the world and himself, to turn all his thoughts upon God and to lead a life of the Spirit. For two years he lived in seclusion. When after this he preached again for the first time the effect was so great that forty of his hearers went into convulsions and twelve could hardly be revived. After the master had lived and laboured for nine years more he fell dangerously ill, and calling for the layman gave him a written account of his conversion. To this account the layman added five sermons of the master that he had copied. It was customary at an earlier date to regard Tauler as this master, and the "Meisterbuch" was from the year 1498 included in the editions of Tauler's sermons. In more recent times Preger has also supported this opinion. But in the treatise "Taulers Bekehrung" Denifle has produced strong proofs against attributing to Tauler the rôle of this master; this view is now generally maintained. The story told by the later Strasburg chronicler, Speckle (d. 1589) is a tissue of falsehoods; it relates that Tauler opposed the pope and the interdict that the pope had laid upon Strasburg in the struggle between the papacy and the Emperor Louis the Bavarian.

Tauler's writings have not yet been subjected to a thorough critical investigation. Much that is attributed to him is doubtful, much not genuine. He certainly did not write the book of the "Nachahmung des armen Lebens Christi" or "Von der geistlichen Armut". The "Exercitia super vita et passione Jesu Christi" and the spiritual songs attributed to him are also spurious. At the most he only wrote a small part of the "Medulla animæ" or of "Institutiones divinæ". Only the sermons, therefore, remain as the actual works of Tauler. The first edition appeared in 1498 at Leipzig and includes 84 sermons; the second edition (Basle, 1521–22) added 42 more some of which, however, even in the opinion of the editor of the edition, were not Tauler's; in the third edition (Cologne, 1543) 25 new sermons were added, part of which are also spurious. The Cologne edition was translated into or rather paraphrased in, Latin by Laurentius Surius (Cologne, 1548). This Latin edition was the copy used for translations into various foreign languages and for both Catholic and Protestant retranslations into German. The modern editions (Frankfort, 1826, 1864, 1872; Berlin, 1841) are based on the old German editions. Lately, Ferdinand Vetter has prepared an edition (Berlin, 1910) based on the Engelberg manuscript (the only one made at Cologne and the oldest one that may perhaps represent the collection revised by Tauler himself), also on the Freiburg manuscript, and on copies of the three manuscripts burned at Strasburg in 1870. This edition contains 81 sermons. The sermons are among the finest monuments of the German language, of German fervour of belief, and of profound spiritual feeling. The language is quiet and measured, yet warm, animated, and full of imagery. Tauler is not so speculative as his teacher Eckhart, but he is clearer, more practical, and more adapted to the common people; with all this he united Suso's fervour. The expression used by Christina Ebner, that he had set the whole world aflame by his fiery tongue, does not mean that he was a preacher of fiery, entrancing eloquence, but a preacher who warmed and inflamed the hearts of his hearers by the quiet flame of the pure love that burned in his own breast.

The centre of Tauler's mysticism is the doctrine of the *visio essentiæ Dei*, the blessed contemplation or knowledge of the Divine nature. He takes this doctrine from Thomas Aquinas, but goes further than the latter in believing that the Divine knowledge is attainable in this world also by a perfect man, and should be sought by every means. God dwells within each human being. In order, however, that the transcendent God may appear in man as a second subject, the human, sinful activities must cease. Aid is given in this effort by the light of grace which raises nature far above itself. The way to God is through love; God replies to its highest development by His presence. Tauler gives advice of the most varied character for attaining that height of religion in which the Divine enters into the human subject. Something needs to be said as regards Tauler's position towards the Church. Luther praised him greatly and Protestants have always had a very high opinion of him, and have included him among the "reformers before the Reformation". However, it is now conceded by Protestants that he was "in reality entirely mediæval and not Protestant". He was in fact a dutiful son of the Church and never thought of withdrawing his allegiance. He expresses his opinion very plainly in his sermon on St. Matthew. He set his face against all heresy, especially that of the Brethren of the Free Spirit. What attracted Luther was probably not Tauler's doctrine itself, but only here and there some subordinate thought. Perhaps it pleased him that the word indulgence appears only once in Tauler's sermons, or it aroused his sympathy that Tauler laid less stress upon works, or again he was attracted by the tremendous earnestness of this seeker after God.

QUÉTIF-ECHARD, *Scriptores ordinis prædicatorum*, I (Paris, 1719), 677–9; SCHMIDT, *Johannes Tauler von Strassburg* (Hamburg, 1841); PREGER, *Gesch. der deutschen Mystik im Mittelalter*, III (Leipzig, 1893), 1–241; DENIFLE, *Das Buch von der geistlichen Armut* (Munich, 1877); IDEM, *Taulers Bekehrung* (Strasburg, 1879); SIEDEL, *Die Mystik Taulers* (Leipzig, 1911).

KLEMENS LÖFFLER.

Taunton, ETHELRED, writer, b. at Rugeley, Staffordshire, England, 17 Oct., 1857; d. in London, 9 May, 1907. He was educated at Downside, and formed a desire both then and later in life to enter the Benedictine Order, but his weak health was an insuperable obstacle to the realization of his wishes. He succeeded in entering the Institute of St. Andrew, founded by the well-known convert, Rev. George Bampfield, at Barnet; but again his health prevented him from remaining. Finally, he joined the congregation of the Oblates founded by Cardinal Manning at Bayswater, and in 1883 he was ordained priest. Three years later he left the Oblates, and went on the mission at Stoke Newington in North London. Here he built a new church, which was opened in 1888; but shortly afterwards he received serious injury by the accidental fall of some scaffolding, which brought on partial paralysis, and permanently incapacitated him from active work. He continued, however, to be busy with his pen. He was a man of wide reading, and wrote on a large number of subjects. For a while he lived at Bruges, where he founded and edited "St. Luke's Magazine"; but it had only a brief existence, and having partially recovered his health, he returned to England and devoted himself to literature. His two chief works on the Jesuits and Benedictines, respectively, were to have been followed by a similar one on the English secular clergy, had he lived. Though he always professed to aim at setting forth truth unadorned and regardless of consequences, his partisan tone and apparent prejudice gave offence to many. Those who knew him best, however, testified to his singleness of purpose and genuine piety. He was also an authority on Church music and liturgy. His death took place somewhat suddenly, in London, from heart failure, at the age of fifty.

Publications: "History of Church Music" (London, 1817); "Lead Kindly Light" (London, 1893); "English Black Monks of St. Benedict" (London, 1898); "History of the Jesuits in England" (London, 1901); "Thomas Wolsey" (London, 1901); "Little Office B.V.M." (London, 1903); "The Law of the Church" (London, 1906); numerous articles in "Downside Review", "St. Luke's Magazine", "Irish Ecclesiastical Record", etc. He also translated Bacuez, "The Divine Office" (1886); and Bourdaloue, "The Lord's Prayer" (1894).

Dict. Nat. Biog., Supplement 1900–1910, s. v.; obituary notices in *Tablet, Downside Review*, etc.

BERNARD WARD.

Taveggia, SANTINO. See KRISHNAGAR, DIOCESE OF.

Taverner, JOHN, composer, b. in the County of Norfolk, England, about 1475; d. at Boston, England, 1535 or 1536. He was organist of Boston Parish Church from 1500 to 1525, when he was appointed master of the choristers at Cardinal College, Oxford, by Cardinal Wolsey. His fame as organist and choirmaster was fully equalled, if not eclipsed, by his powers as a composer of masses and motets. He continued at Oxford till 1533, and then retired to Boston. On the strength of a statement of Foxe, in his so-called "Book of Martyrs", Taverner has been branded as a heretic, but it is more than probable that Foxe confounded the composer with John Taverner, a correspondent of Cromwell, or else with Richard Taverner, a Canon of Wolsey's College, Oxford, who revised Matthew's Bible. He wrote nothing for the English Service, but he has bequeathed eight masses, as well as fragments of others, and Latin Magnificats, that stamp him as a composer of the first rank. His beautiful four-part "In nomine" has been altered to fit two English anthems, "O give thanks" and "In trouble and adversity", in Day's "Morning and Evening Prayer" (1565). He contributed three songs to Wynkyn de Worde's English song book, printed in 1530; but by far the greater part of his work is sacred. His "Gaude Maria Virgo", for three voices, and his "Mater Christi", for five voices, are good examples of his style, but he is best known by his "Western Wynde" mass. Although obsessed by the conventions of the early sixteenth century, Taverner showed some good pioneer work, which was afterwards successfully developed by Shepherd, Byrd, Tallis, and Whyte. He must not be confounded with a later John Taverner, who was appointed professor of music at Gresham College in 1610.

GROVE'S *Dict. of Music and Musicians*, V (new ed., London, 1904–10); WALKER, *A History of Music in England* (Oxford, 1907); GRATTAN-FLOOD, *Notes on English Church Composers* in MS.

W. H. GRATTAN-FLOOD.

Tavistock Abbey, on the Tavy River in Devonshire, England, founded for Benedictine monks in 961 by Earl Ordgar of Devon, and completed by his son Ordulf in 981, in which year the charter of confirmation was granted by King Ethelred. It was endowed with lands in Devon, Dorset, and Cornwall, and became one of the richest monasteries in the west of England. The church, dedicated to Our Lady and St. Rumon (one of the early Irish saints in Cornwall), was burned by the Danes in 997, but magnificently rebuilt under Livingus, the second abbot. He and his successor Aldred both became bishops of Worcester, and the latter is said to have crowned William the Conqueror. The thirty-sixth abbot, John Dynynton, was granted leave in 1458 to use the mitre and other *pontificalia;* and the thirty-ninth, Richard Banham, was made a lord of Parliament by Henry VIII in 1513. Twenty-five years later the last abbot, John Peryn, with twenty monks, surrendered the monastery to the king, receiving a pension of a hundred pounds. The abbey revenues at the dissolution were estimated at £902. The monastic buildings, with the borough of Tavistock, were granted to John Lord Russell, whose descendant, the Duke of Bedford, still owns them. Nothing is left of the monastery except the refectory, two gateways, and a porch; the splendid abbey church has entirely disappeared.

DUGDALE, *Monast. Anglic.*, II (London, 1817), 489–503; WILLIS, *Hist. of the Mitred Parliamentary Abbies* (London, 1718), 170–176; TANNER, *Notitia Monastica* (Cambridge, 1787), *Devonshire*, xliv; BRAY, *The Borders of the Tamar and the Tavy*, I (London, 1879), I, 356–440, II, 8, 416, 423; OLIVER, *Historic Collections relating to the Monasteries in Devon* (Exeter, 1820); GASQUET, *Henry VIII and the English Monasteries*, I (London, 1888), 29, 295.

D. O. HUNTER-BLAIR.

Tavium, a titular see in Galatia Prima, suffragan of Ancyra. Tavium, or Tavia, was the chief city of the Galatian tribe of Trocmi, and owing to its position on the high roads of commerce was an important trading post. There are still extant some of the coins of Marcus Aurelius and Elagabalus. In the temple at Tavium there was a colossal statue of Jupiter in bronze, greatly venerated by the Galatians. There was some doubt about the exact site of the city, but it is to-day generally believed to be the ruins situated close to the village of Nefez Keui, inhabited during the winter by nomadic Turkish tribes, lying in a very fertile plain east of Halys in the caza of Songourlou and the vilayet of Angora. These ruins were partly used in building the neighbouring village of Yuzgad. We find there the remains of a theatre and possibly of a temple of Jupiter; these have a number of inscriptions, mostly Byzantine. In the "Notitiæ Episcopatuum" this see is mentioned up to the thirteenth century as the first suffragan of Ancyra. We have the names of five bishops: Dicasius, present at the Councils of Neocæsarea and Nice; Julian, at the Robber Synod of Ephesus (449), and at the Council of Chalcedon (451), and a signer of the letter from the Galatian bishops to the Emperor Leo (458); Anastasius, present at the Council of Constantinople (553); Gregory at the Council in Trullo (692); Philaretus at Constantinople (869).

LE QUIEN, *Oriens Christ.*, I, 473; SMITH, *Dict. Greek and Roman Geog.*, s. v.; TEXIER, *Asie mineure*, 497; PERROT, *Exploration archéol. de la Galatie et de la Bithynie* (Paris,1872), 288–93; RAMSAY, *Asia Minor*, 243; MÜLLER, notes to *Ptolemy*, ed. DIDOT, I, 853.

S. PÉTRIDÈS.

Taxa Innocentiana, a Decree issued by Innocent XI, 1 Oct., 1678, regulating the fees that may be demanded or accepted by episcopal chancery offices for various acts, instruments, or writings. According to this Decree bishops or their officials are not allowed to accept anything though freely offered (1) for ordinations or anything connected therewith, such as dimissorial letters, etc.; (2) for institution to benefices; (3) for matrimonial dispensations. In this last case, however, alms to be applied to pious uses may be demanded. A moderate charge, fixed by Innocent, may be exacted by the chancellor for expediting necessary documents, except those granting permission to say Mass, administer the sacraments, preach, etc. The Taxa Innocentiana is silent in regard to contentious matters, e. g. the charge for copies of the acts of ecclesiastical trials. Some maintained that Innocent's legislation was promulgated for Italy only, but it evidenced the mind of the Church, and at least in substance was of universal application. The Sacred Congregation of the Council on 10 June, 1896, modified the prescriptions of Innocent, decreeing that while taxes or fees may be imposed according to justice and prudence in matters pertaining to benefices and sacraments, especially matrimony, yet the sacraments themselves must be conferred without charge and pious customs connected therewith observed. In other matters not directly affecting the administration of the sacraments, e. g. dispensations from the banns, it is decreed that: (1) laudable customs must be observed and allowances made for various circumstances of time, place, and persons; (2) the poor are not to be taxed; (3) in any case the amount demanded must be moderate, so that persons may not be deterred thereby from receiving the sacraments; (4) as regards matrimony the exaction is to be remitted, if otherwise there would be danger of concubinage; (5) in regard to benefices the tax must be in proportion to the fruits or income of the benefice in question; (6) all such fees are to be determined not by individual bishops but in provincial council, or at least in a special meeting of the ordinaries of the province for this purpose. The approval of the Holy See is required for the fees determined upon. Rome's sanction is given tentatively for five years to Italy, for ten years to other countries.

FERRARIS, s. v. *Taxa;* LUCIDI, *De visitat. ss. liminum*, doc. XX, III, 144.

ANDREW B. MEEHAN.

Taxster (TAYSTER), JOHN DE, sometimes erroneously called Taxter or Taxston, was a thirteenth-century chronicler, of whose life nothing is known except that he was professed as a Benedictine at Bury St. Edmund's 20 Nov., 1244. It is probable that he died in or about 1265, when his chronicle ceases. His work, which in the earlier part is compiled from Florence of Worcester, William of Malmesbury, and Ralph de Diceto, begins with the creation of the world. The value of the chronicle arises from Taxster's account of his own times; and his description of contemporary events was subsequently used by Everisden, Oxenedes, and Bartholomew Cotton. This part of his work has accordingly attracted more attention, and his chronicle for the period 1258–1263 has been printed by Luard in his edition of Cotton (Rolls Series). Taxster's chronicle as a whole has never been printed, and exists only in two MSS., one in the British Museum (Cott., Julius, A. 1.), the other in the College of Arms (Arundelian MS., 6). A faulty MS. for the years 1173–1265 was printed in 1849 for the English Historical Society, and passages relating to German affairs have been included by Pertz in "Mon. Germ. Hist.: Script.", XXVIII.

LIEBERMANN in PERTZ, *Mon. Germ. Hist.: Script.*, XXVIII; LUARD, in *R. S.*, loc. cit. (London, 1859); HARDY, *Descriptive Catalogue*, III (London, 1871); TOUT in *Dict. Nat. Biog.*, s. v.

EDWIN BURTON.

Taylor, FRANCES MARGARET (MOTHER M. MAGDALEN TAYLOR), Superior General, and foundress of the Poor Servants of the Mother of God, b. 20 Jan., 1832; d. in London, 9 June, 1900. Her father was a Protestant clergyman, the vicar of a Lincolnshire parish where her early years were spent in works of charity among the poor. She was a very clever woman, full of energy, with a wide sympathetic nature and a remarkably retentive memory. In 1854 her patriotism moved her to join Miss Nightingale's staff of nurses, and to go with them to the Crimean War. This threw her into contact with Catholic priests, Sisters of Mercy, and soldiers, and opened her eyes to the truth of the Catholic religion. After instruction she was received into the Church by Father Woollett, S.J. On her return to England she first worked among the poor of London, and made the acquaintance of Lady Georgiana Fullerton, with whose co-operation she laid the foundation of her institute. In addition to this, and to opening various refuges, convents, schools, etc., she did a great deal of literary work. She wrote a good many stories and always employed her pen for the promotion of the Catholic religion. For some time she edited "The Lamp", and helped to start both "The Month", and "The Messenger of the Sacred Heart", to which, as to other Catholic papers and periodicals of the day, she contributed. She had imbibed from Father Dignam, S.J., a great devotion to the Sacred Heart, and was very active in spreading this devotion and the Apostleship of Prayer, especially in Ireland. In 1892 her health gave way, and the rest of her life was suffering, borne with exemplary patience. She died in a home she had founded for penitents in Soho Square, London. Her works are "Memoir of Father Dignam, S.J."; "Retreats given by Father Dignam, S.J."; "Conferences by Father Dignam, S.J."; "The Inner Life of Lady Georgiana Fullerton"; "Tyborne and Who Went Thither"; "Convent Stories"; "Lost, and Other Tales"; "Dame Dolores"; "Life of Father Curtis, S.J."; "Religious Orders"; "Holywell and Its Pilgrims"; "The Stoneleighs of Stoneleigh"; "Irish Homes and Irish Hearts"; "Eastern Hospitals and English Nurses."

The Messenger of the Sacred Heart (April, 1901); GILLOW, *Bibl. Dict. Eng. Cath.*, s. v. *Taylor, Frances Magdalen*.

FRANCESCA M. STEELE.

Taylor, HUGH, VENERABLE, English martyr, b. at Durham; hanged, drawn, and quartered at York, 25 (not 26) November, 1585. He arrived at Reims on 2 May, 1582, and having been ordained priest was sent thence on the mission on 27 March, 1585. He was the first to suffer under the Statute 27 Eliz. c. 2. lately passed. On 26 November, Marmaduke Bowes, a married gentleman, was hanged for having harboured him. Bowes is described by Challoner as of Angram Grange near Appleton in Cleveland, but is not mentioned in the will of Christopher Bowes of Angram Grange, proved on 30 Sept., 1568, nor in the 1612 pedigree. The sole evidence against him was that of a former tutor to his children, an apostate Catholic. Having been previously imprisoned at York with his wife, he was under bond to appear at the Assizes which began on 23 November at York, and on his arrival found that Taylor was about to be arraigned. Bowes, though always a Catholic at heart, had outwardly conformed to the Established Church. "Before his death he was made a member of the Catholic Church the which he boldly confessed with great alacrity of mind".

MORRIS, *Troubles of our Catholic Forefathers* (London, 1872–7), I, 244; III, passim; CHALLONER, *Missionary Priests*, I (Edinburgh, 1877), no. 29; KNOX, *Douay Diaries* (London, 1878), passim; FOSTER, *Visitation of Yorkshire in 1612* (1875), 497.

JOHN B. WAINEWRIGHT.

Tebaldeo, ANTONIO, Italian poet, b. at Ferrara, in 1463; d. in 1537. His family name (Tebaldi) he changed to Tebaldeo, in consonance with the practice of the Humanists, who sought to Latinize the form of their appellation as much as possible. After serving as tutor to Isabella d'Este and secretary to Lucrezia Borgia, he became an habitué of the court of Leo X at Rome, enjoying the favour of that scholarly pope and the companionship of many of the erudite men and artists then in the Imperial City. He lost all his means in the sack of Rome (1527), and spent the remainder of his life in very narrow circumstances. He wrote verse in both Latin and Italian. His Italian verse is remarkable rather for vices of diction and style than for any poetical excellence. With his artificial manner, his abuse of metaphor, and his studied imagery, he was a forerunner of those extravagant versifiers who, in the seventeenth century, developed the movement called Marinism or *Secentismo*. To Tebaldeo has been ascribed a redaction of Poliziano's play, "Orfeo", which aims to make that piece accord better with the principles of classic composition. He figured among the writers of the time who engaged in the discussion concerning the nature of literary Italian. (See his verse in the edition of Venice, 1530, "Di M. Antonio Tebaldeo ferrarese l'opere d'amore".)

D'ANCONA, *Del secentismo nella poesia cortegiana del sec. XV* in *Nuova Antologia* (1876); CAN, *Un decennio della vita del Bembo* (Turin, 1885), 234; LUZIO, *I precettori di Isabella d'Este* (Ancona, 1887).

J. D. M. FORD.

Te Deum, THE, an abbreviated title commonly given both to the original Latin text and the translations of a hymn in rhythmical prose, of which the opening words, *Te Deum laudamus*, formed its earliest known title (namely in the Rule of St. Cæsarius for monks, written probably when he was Abbot of Lérins, before A. D. 502). This longer title is used in the "Rules for Virgins" composed by St. Cæsarius while Archbishop of Arles, and by his second successor in the same see, St. Aurelian, also in the Rule of St. Benedict; and generally in earlier literature. The hymn is also sometimes styled "Hymnus Ambrosianus", the "Ambrosian Hymn"; and in the Roman Breviary it is still entitled, at the end of Matins for Sunday, "Hymnus SS. Ambrosii et Augustini". It is interesting to note that the title has been changed to "Hymnus Ambrosianus" in the "Psalterium" of the new Roman Breviary of Pius X. This Psalterium has been printed (1912), but became obligatory only from 1 Jan., 1913. The Te Deum is found in the first part of the "Psalterium" ("Ordinarium", etc.) The tradition that it was spontaneously composed and sung alternately by these saints on the night of St. Augustine's baptism (A. D. 387) can be traced back to the end of the eighth century, and is referred to in the middle of the ninth century by Hincmar of Reims (*ut a majoribus nostris audivimus*) in his second work, "De prædestinatione" (P. L., CXXV, 290), and in an elaborated form in a Milanese chronicle attributed to Datius, Bishop of Milan (d. about 552), but really dating only from the eleventh century (thus Mabillon, Muratori, Merati, etc.). This tradition is now generally rejected by scholars.

(a) It should naturally have held, from earliest times, a prominent place in Milan; but of the earlier manuscripts of the Te Deum which refer to the tradition in their titles, none has any connexion with Milan, while the "Milan Cathedral Breviary" text (eleventh century) has no title whatever. (b) The tradition ascribing the authorship to the two saints is not unique. Another tradition is represented by the remark of Abbo of Fleury (A. D. 985) in his "Quæstiones grammaticales" (P. L., CXXXIX, 532, §19) concerning the erroneous substitution of "suscepisti" for "suscepturus" in the verse "Tu ad liberandum suscepturus hominem", etc., in what he styles "Dei palinodia quam composuit Hilarius Pictaviensis episcopus". It may be added that an eighth- or ninth-century MS. of the hymn, now at Munich, refers it to St. Hilary. (c) But neither to Hilary nor to Ambrose may the hymn be prudently ascribed, because although both composed hymns, the Te Deum is in rhythmical prose, and not in the classical metres of the hymns known to have been written by them. While, from the ninth century down to the present day, there is no century and no country of Western Europe that has not given its witness to the traditional ascription, the earliest MS., the "Bangor Antiphonary" (seventh cent.) gives as title merely "Ymnum in die dominica", while other early MSS. make no reference to the authorship, either giving no titles or contenting themselves with such general ones as "Laudatio Dei" (MS. of eighth cent.), "Laus angelica" (twelfth cent.), "Laus angelorum" (twelfth cent.), "Hymnus matutinalis" . . ."Hymnus die dominico", "Hymnum dominicale", etc. Other MSS. ascribe the hymn variously to St. Nicetus, Vicetus (obviously a slip of the pen for Nicetus), Nicetius, Nicetes, Neceta (all of these being thought identical with Niceta or Nicetas, Bishop of Remesiana, q. v.), to St. Hilarius, St. Abundius, St. Sisebutus, St. Ambrose, or St. Augustine. (d) The importance of the occasion to which the legend assigns the composition of the hymn (the baptism of St. Augustine) and the comparatively late appearance of the ascription to the two saints are additional arguments against the tradition. Merati thinks the legend may have been based on the words of a spurious sermon, given as no. 92 in an edition of the works of St. Ambrose (Paris, 1549), "De Augustini Baptismo": "In quo una vobiscum cum divino instinctu Hymnum cantavimus de Christi fide". It may be added that the Maurists omitted the Te Deum from their edition of St. Ambrose; that Batiffol ("Hist. du Brév. romain", Paris, 1893, p. 98; authorized and corrected tr., London, 1898, p. 110) writes: "No one thinks now of attributing this cento either to St. Ambrose or to St. Augustine"; that Father Burton, in his "Life of St. Augustine, . . . An Historical Study" (Dublin, 3rd ed., 1897) does not even mention the legend about the dual authorship and the baptism of St. Augustine; and finally that Portalié (see AUGUSTINE OF HIPPO) remarks: "The tradition maintaining that the Te Deum was sung on that occasion by the bishop and the neophyte alternately is groundless".

The other names mentioned above not being favoured by scholars, the question of authorship remained open. In 1894 Dom Morin put forward Nicetas of Remesiana for the honour of authorship. His suggestion has been adopted by Zahn, Kattenbusch, Kirsch (in Germany); Frere, Burn (in England), while the Anglican Bishop of Salisbury considers Morin's conjecture "very plausible"; and in France, by Batiffol. The reasons for this view are: (1) Ten MSS. (the earliest of the tenth century), mostly of Irish origin, name Nicetas (with variant spellings and identifications, however); and Ireland, remote from the continent of Europe, could easily keep until the tenth century a tradition of the fifth. (2) The probable date of composition of the hymn corresponds with that of the literary activity of Nicetas. (3) St. Paulinus of Nola praises (Carmina, xvii, xxvii) the poetic and hymnodal gifts of his friend Nicetas. (4) Gennadius speaks of the neat and simple style of his prose, and Cassiodorus commends his conciseness. These critical appreciations are thought applicable to the style of the Te Deum, which depends for its effect mostly on the nobility of the theme and the simplicity and directness of the expression. (5) The authorship of the treatises "De psalmodiæ bono" and "De vigiliis servorum Dei" was formerly ascribed to Nicetas of Trier, but is now attributed with greatest probability to Nicetas of Remesiana. Their "internal evidence . . . proves that Nicetas felt the need of such a hymn as the Te Deum, and, so to speak, lived in the same sphere of religious thought" (Burn, cii), while parallel passages from his writings (given by Burn, ciii–civ), although offering no direct quotation, exhibit similarity of thought and diction.

The authorship of St. Nicetas is questioned by some scholars (Cagin, P. Wagner, Agaesse, Koestlin, Blume). Among the passages cited to indicate a much earlier origin perhaps the most notable one is that from the "De mortalitate" (xxvi) of St. Cyprian of Carthage, written during the plague in 252: "Illic apostolorum gloriosus chorus; illic prophetarum exsultantium numerus; illic martyrum innumerabilis populus ob certaminis et passionis gloriam coronatus; triumphantes virgines, quæ concupiscentiam carnis et corporis continentiæ robore subegerunt; remunerati misericordes . . ." There is an obvious similarity between this and the verses of the Te Deum: "Te gloriosus apostolorum chorus; te prophetarum laudabilis numerus; te martyrum candidatus laudat exercitus [verses 7–9] . . . Æterna fac cum sanctis tuis gloria munerari [verse 21]". Perhaps the "remunerati" of St. Cyprian and the "munerari" of the oldest texts of the Te Deum are a mere coincidence; but the rest of the similar passages cannot be an accident. Which was the earlier—the Te Deum or the text of St. Cyprian? It is contended that, however well known and highly esteemed the works of the saint, there is little in this particular passage to strike the fancy of a hymn-writer, while it would be a very natural thing for a prose writer to borrow some expressions from such a widely-sung hymn as the Te Deum may have been. Moreover, if the hymn was borrowed from St. Cyprian, why did it not include the "virgines" instead of stopping with "martyrum"? Additional argument for a very early origin of at least the first ten verses of the hymn is found in comparisons between these and the texts and melody of the Prefaces, in the structure of the Gloria in excelsis, in the rhythmic and melodic character of the Te Deum, in the Greek translations.

This archæological argument cannot be stated intelligibly in a few words, but some of its bases may be mentioned: (a) If the Te Deum were composed in the latter years of the fourth century, it would be a unique exception to the hymnology of that time, which was all fashioned in the regular strophic and metric manner introduced and popularized by St. Ambrose. (b) From the point of view of melody, the hymn has three divisions: verses 1–13, 14–20, 21 to the end. The first melody (1–13) is apparently older than the others. (c) From the point of view of rhythm, there are also three divisions: verses 14–21 exhibit perfect conformity with the laws of the "cursus", or rhythmic closes, which date from the fourth century, verses 1–10, however, have only five (4, 6 and 8–10) verses closed with the rhythmical cursus, and these five are supposed to be the result of accident; verses 22 to the end belong to a wholly different category, being taken mostly from the Psalms (xxvii, 9; cxliv, 2; cxxii, 3; xxxii, 22; xxx, 2). It is argued that, judged by melody and rhythm, the first ten verses form a complete hymn (verses 11–13 having been added subsequently as a doxology) to God the Father, while verses 14–21 form a hymn (added in the fourth century) to Christ. As noted above, the first ten verses offer (vv. 7–9) the parallelism with the words of St. Cyprian, and are, for the various reasons outlined, supposed to antedate the year 252. Speculation ascribes their authorship to Pope St. Anicetus (d. about A. D. 168).

Three textual points may be noted here. "Unigenitum" in v. 12 is considered the original reading ("unicum" having supplanted it perhaps through the influence of the Apostles' Creed, in which "unigenitum" was rare). In v. 21 nearly all MSS. read "munerari" (*gloria munerari*) instead of the present "numerari" (*in gloria numerari*) which Blume has found in a twelfth-century MS., and which perhaps was suggested by the words in the Canon of the Mass: "in electorum tuorum jubeas grege numerari". Verse 16, "Tu ad liberandum suscepturus hominem", etc., offers much opportunity for critical discussion. Most of the old MSS. favour "suscepisti" (with "liberandum", followed sometimes by "mundum"— *Tu ad liberandum mundum suscepisti hominem*): but "suscepturus", contended for by Abbo of Fleury, Hincmar, and others, and quoted in a letter of Cyprian of Toulon (about 530), was probably the original word. The verse does not lend itself readily to translation. A fifteenth-century translation runs: "When thou shouldest take upon Thee mankind for the deliverance of men, thou horydest not the Virgin's womb". With similar accuracy a Sarum "Primer" of 1504 has: "Thou (when thou shouldest take upon our nature to delyver man) dydest not abhorre a virgynes wombe". The last "Primer" of Henry VIII (1546) was probably the first to introduce the ambiguous rendering: "When thou tookest upon thee to deliver man". The (Baltimore) "Manual of Prayers" is not more accurate: "Thou having taken upon Thee to deliver man, didst not abhor the Virgin's womb". The "Roman Missal Adapted to the Use of the Laity" (New York, 1901) is laboriously accurate: "Thou, when about to take upon Thee man to deliver him, didst not fear the Virgin's womb". The "Missal for the Use of the Laity" (London, new ed. 1903, cxxxiv) gives a new version in rhyme:

"Thou, to redeem lost man from hell's dark doom,
Didst not abhor the lowly Virgin's womb".

This is not far removed from Dryden's version:

"Thou, who to save the world's impending doom,
Vouchsaf'dst to dwell within a Virgin's womb".

The general rubrics (titulus XXXI) of the Roman Breviary direct the recitation of the Te Deum at the end of Matins: (a) on all feasts throughout the year, whether of nine or of three lessons, and throughout their octaves. It is said on the octave day of the feast of the Holy Innocents, but not on the feast itself unless this should fall on Sunday; (b) on all Sundays from Easter (inclusively) to Advent (exclusively) and from Christmas (inclusively) to Septuagesima (exclusively); (c) on all ferial days during Eastertide (namely from Low Sunday to Ascension Day) except Rogation Monday. For the sake of greater explicitness, the rubrics add that it is not said on the Sundays of Advent, or from Septuagesima to Palm Sunday inclusively, or on ferial days outside of Eastertide. It is said immediately after the last lesson, and therefore replaces the third or ninth responsory, as the case may be; but on days when it is not said, its place is occupied by the responsory. The Te Deum is followed immediately by Lauds except on Christmas Day (when it is followed by the prayer, and this by Mass). In general, the Te Deum may be said to follow the same rubric as the Gloria in excelsis at Mass.

In addition to its use in the Divine Office, the Te Deum is occasionally sung in thanksgiving to God for some special blessing (e. g. the election of a pope, the consecration of a bishop, the canonization of a saint, the profession of a religious, the publication of a treaty of peace, a royal coronation, etc.), and then usually after Mass or Divine Office, or as a separate religious ceremony. When sung thus immediately before or after Mass, the celebrant, who intones the hymn, may wear the vestments appropriate in colour to the day, unless these should happen to be black. Otherwise, while the rubrics prescribe no special colour, violet is forbidden in processions of thanksgiving (*pro gratiarum actione*), green is inappropriate for such solemn occasions, red (though permissible) would not suggest itself, unless some such feast as Pentecost, for example, should call for it. White, therefore, or gold, which is considered its equivalent, is thus left as the most suitable colour. The choir and congregation sing the hymn standing, even when the Blessed Sacrament is exposed, but kneel during the verse "Te ergo quæsumus . . ." At the end the versicles "Benedicamus Patrem" etc. are added, followed by the single prayer "Deus cujus misericordiæ".

There is practically but one plain-chant melody for the hymn, varying greatly, however, in different MSS. The official and typical melody is now given in the Vatican Gradual (1908) in the Appendix (*pro gratiarum actione*) in two forms, the *tonus solemnis* (in which every verse begins with preparatory or intoning notes) and *juxta morem romanum* (in which the verse begins *ex abrupto*). Pothier notes a strong affinity between the melodies of the Te Deum laudamus, te dominum confitemur and those of the Preface, Per omnia . . . Sursum corda. He also points out (Mélodies grégoriennes, 239) a psalmodic turn in the melody of the Te Deum, strengthened by the introduction of a distinct antiphon-form at the words "Æterna fac", etc., the antiphonal melody being thrice repeated. While the chant melody has been frequently used as a *canto fermo* for polyphonic Masses, the polyphonic settings are few compared with many hymns of less prominence. Palestrina, Jacob Haendl, and Felice Anerio have thus treated the old melody. Italian composers of the seventeenth century made settings for several choirs with organ and orchestra. Cherubini's manuscript setting is lost. Berlioz considered the finale of his own setting (for two choirs, orchestra, and organ) "undoubtedly his finest work". Sometimes the alternate verses only are set to music, so that another choir or the congregation may sing the other verses in plain-chant (as in the Miserere, q. v.). The Latin text has been translated into English and has received many settings in that form. Handel's "Utrecht" and "Dettingen" Te Deums are famous. One interesting feature of the latter is that it borrows inspiration for ten of its numbers from a Te Deum composed by the Minorite Francesco Urio, an able Milanese composer of the seventeenth–eighteenth century. Perhaps the most satisfactory of the recent settings of the Te Deum for use in Church is that of Edgar Tinel, written to celebrate the seventy-fifth anniversary of Belgian independence (1830–1905). It is composed for six-voiced mixed choir, orchestra, and organ.

There are about twenty-five metrical translations into English, including the sonorous version of Dryden, "Thee, Sovereign God, our grateful accents praise", and that of the Rev. Clarence A. Walworth, commonly used in American Catholic hymnals, "Holy God, we praise Thy Name", but written before his conversion, as it appeared with date of 1853 in the "Evangelical Hymnal". There are also six versions into English based on Luther's free rendering into German. There are many German versions, of which the "Grosser Gott, wir loben dich" is commonly used in Catholic churches. Probably the most recent Catholic translation is that found in the new edition (London, 1903) of Provost Husenbeth's "Missal for the Use of the Laity", "We praise thee, God: we glorify thee, Lord."

JULIAN, *Dict. of Hymnology* (2nd ed., London, 1907), s. v., 1119–34, 1547–8, 1709, an extensive and excellent article comprising contributions from JOHN SARUM (i. e. JOHN WORDSWORTH, Anglican Bishop of Salisbury) on the history and texts of the hymn, BIRKBECK on the plain-song melody, JULIAN on the translations with bibliographical references; KAYSER, *Beiträge zur Gesch. und Erklärung der ältesten Kirchenhymnen* (Paderborn, 1881), 435–60.
MORIN, *Nouvelles recherches sur l'auteur du "Te Deum"* in *Revue bénédictine* (Feb., 1894), was the first to ascribe the authorship to Nicetas. The ascription was adopted by BURN, *Niceta of Remesiana, His Life and Works* (London, 1905), mentioning (Introduction, xcvii, footnote) other adherents of this view, among them the Anglican Bishop of Salisbury. BURN gives a bibliography. Reviewing BURN's work, MORIN declares in the *Rassegna gregoriana* (May–June, 1905) that the hymn can almost certainly be attributed to Nicetas. A much earlier origin is sought by CAGIN, *L'Euchologie latine étudiée dans la tradition de ses formules et de ses formulaires. Te Deum ou Illatio?* (Solesmes, 1906), which was reviewed unfavourably by MORIN, *Le 'Te Deum' type anonyme de l'anaphore latine préhistorique* in the *Rev. bénédictine* (1907), 180–223, and defended by AGAESSE, *Que Nicetas de Remesiana n'est pas l'auteur du "Te Deum"* in the *Revue des sciences eccles.* (Lille, Feb., Apr., June, 1910), who emphasizes the negative argument, considering the silence of antiquity as perhaps equal to a formal denial of Nicetas's authorship. BLUME, *Ursprung des ambrosianischen Lobgesanges* in *Stimmen aus Maria-Laach* (1911), nos. 8–10, argues for an origin earlier than A. D. 252. For the first (i. e. Trinitarian) part of the hymn NOLAN, *St. Ambrose and St. Augustine the Authors of the "Te Deum"* in *The Tablet* (London, 22 Oct., 1910), 644–5, should be read in connexion with MERATI in his notes on GAVANTUS, *Thesaurus sac. rit.*, II (Venice, 1769), 109–112. A briefer statement of the question at issue (i. e. the traditional ascription to the two saints) is that of DANIEL, *Thesaur. hymnolog.*, II (Leipzig, 1844), 279–88, who agrees with MERATI in rejecting the ascription.

Daniel gives (*op. cit.*, 283) an imitation of the Te Deum (ascribed to St. Bonaventure) constructed into a Marian canticle: "Te Matrem Dei laudamus, te omnis terra veneratur, æterni patris sponsam", etc., and remarks that, so far as he knew, it had never been used in any public service of the Church. WORDSWORTH (*op. cit.*) refers to this as a "travestying" of the Te Deum, and expresses his gratification that the imitation had never been in public use. He is answered by SHIPLEY, *A Dict. of Hymnology* in *Eccles. Review* (June, 1895, 451–2), who refers to LEGG (Secretary of the "Henry Bradshaw Liturgical Text Society"), *Some Imitations of Te Deum*, showing that in the Middle Ages there was "no such dislike as now prevails, to retouch a masterpiece", and that "every popular hymn had a hundred imitations", etc. DREVES, *Analecta hymn.*, XXXI, 212–4, gives a "Te Deum" Marianum (from a fourteenth century MS.) in thirty stanzas of the type: "Te deam digne laudibus et dominam fatemur. Te in terris virginem æternam veneramur. Te feminam eximiam omnes laude famur". MONE, *Lateinische Hymnen des Mittelalt.*, II (Freiburg, 1854), 229–31, gives interesting notes on some Marian imitations, and remarks that the imitators tried, with more or less success, to avoid any occasion for a misunderstanding of their meaning when adapting the Te Deum to the praise of the Blessed Virgin.

For the liturgical beginnings of the Te Deum, see the *Rules of* STS. BENEDICT (*P. L.*, LXVI, 436), CÆSARIUS (*P.L.*, LXVII, 1102), and AURELIAN (*P. L.*, LXVIII, 396); see also BLUME for the Rules, *Der Cursus S. Benedicti Nursini*, etc. (Leipzig, 1908), 33, 44, 48, 50, 55, 57, 86; and for very significant early paraphrase of Te Deum, "Christi, cœli Domine", 92,—text, 118–9; BATIFFOL, *Hist. of the Roman Breviary*, tr. BAYLAY (London, 1898), 109–10; BAUDOT, *Roman Breviary* (London, 1909), 107, 110, 113. For variants, see BURN, op. cit., 83–91 (the ordinary, the Irish, and the "Milan" texts are given in columns; also the Greek texts). OTT, *L'innodia ambrosiana* in *Rassegna gregoriana* (1907), 491–6, compares, with musical illustrations, the Ambrosian and the Gregorian melody of the hymn; SINGENBERGER, *Guide to Catholic Church Music* (St. Francis, Wisconsin, 1905), 186–7, mentions fifty-three liturgically correct settings for mixed voices and twenty-three for equal voices, with grade, composer, voices, etc. noted; see also *Church Music* (June, 1906, 433–6) for reviews of settings by PONTEN, MITTERER, TINEL. Of TINEL'S setting BONVIN writes: "Of all the settings of the Te Deum that are known to me that can be used for liturgical purposes I do not hesitate to declare TINEL'S the finest and grandest", and reviews it at length. KURTHEN, *Das Te Deum als Formproblem für die musikalische Komposition* in *Gregorius-Blatt* (1911), nos. 1–6; BRUDERS, *Das Te Deum in seinen literarischen Beziehungen* in *Literar. Rundschau* (1 June, 1911).

H. T. HENRY.

Tegakwitha (TEKAKWITHA, TAKWITA), CATHERINE, known as the "Lily of the Mohawks", and the "Genevieve of New France", an Indian virgin of the Mohawk tribe, b. according to some authorities at the Turtle Castle of Ossernenon, according to others at the village of Gandaouge, in 1656; d. at Caughnawaga, Canada, 17 April, 1680. Her mother was a Christian Algonquin who had been captured by the Iroquois and saved from a captive's fate by the father of Tegakwitha, to whom she also bore a son. When Tegakwitha was about four years old, her parents and brother died of small-pox, and the child was adopted by her aunts and an uncle who had become chief of the Turtle clan. Although small-pox had marked her face and seriously impaired her eyesight and her manner was reserved and shrinking, her aunts began when she was as yet very young to form marriage projects for her, from which, as she grew older, she shrank with great aversion. In 1667 the Jesuit missionaries Frémin, Bruyas, and Pierron, accompanying the Mohawk deputies who had been to Quebec to conclude peace with the French, spent three days in the lodge of Tegakwitha's uncle. From them she received her first knowledge of Christianity, but although she forthwith eagerly accepted it in her heart she did not at that time ask to be baptized. Some time later the Turtle clan moved to the north bank of the Mohawk River, the "castle" being built above what is now the town of Fonda. Here in the midst of scenes of carnage, debauchery, and idolatrous frenzy Tegakwitha lived a life of remarkable virtue, at heart not only a Christian but a Christian virgin, for she firmly and often, with great risk to herself, resisted all efforts to induce her to marry. When she was eighteen, Father Jacques de Lamberville arrived to take charge of the mission which included the Turtle clan, and from him, at her earnest request, Tegakwitha received baptism. Thenceforth she practised her religion unflinchingly in the face of almost unbearable opposition, till finally her uncle's lodge ceased to be a place of protection to her and she was assisted by some Christian Indians to escape to Caughnawaga on the St. Lawrence. Here she lived in the cabin of Anastasia Tegonhatsihonga, a Christian squaw, her extraordinary sanctity impressing not only her own people but the French and the missionaries. Her mortifications were extreme, and Chauchtière says that she had attained the most perfect union with God in prayer. Upon her death devotion to her began immediately to be manifested by her people. Many pilgrims visit her grave in Caughnawaga where a monument to her memory was erected by the Rev. Clarence Walworth in 1884; and the Councils of Baltimore and Quebec have petitioned for her canonization.

WALWORTH, *Life and Times of Katerei Tekakwitha* (Buffalo, 1891); BURTIN, *Vie de Catherine Tekakwitha, vièrge iroquoise* (Quebec, 1894); CAMPBELL, *Pioneer Priests of North America*, I (New York, 1908).

BLANCHE M. KELLY.

Tegernsee, called Tegrinseo in 817, Tegernsee in 754, a celebrated Benedictine abbey of Bavaria that was of much importance for the civilization of the early Middle Ages. It was situated on the state road to the Tyrol by Lake Tegern in a south-south-easterly direction from Munich. According to the latest Germanistic researches the word *Tegern* signified in Old High German "large", consequently the name meant "large lake". It was not the Agilolfinger family, as is erroneously supposed, but Counts Adalbert and Otkar (Ottokar) of Warngau and Tegernsee who founded in 746 (not 719) a Benedictine abbey on Lake Tegern near the little Church of Our Saviour that was already in existence; this abbey was consecrated and occupied in 754. Counts Adalbert and Otkar belonged to the family of the Huosi, one of the five old ruling families who had come into the country with the Bavarians. The story of the colonizing of the monastery with monks by St. Othmar of St. Gall is legendary and is based on chronicles of a later era. On account of the disorders caused by the incursions of the Magyars at the beginning of the tenth century the founding of Tegernsee itself and the first decades of its history are hidden in deep obscurity. On the other hand, it is a perfectly well established fact that the founders of the abbey obtained the relics of St. Quirinus, a Roman martyr, from Pope St. Paul I (757–67), not from Pope Zacharias (741–52), and that these relics were translated from Rome to Tegernsee in the second half of the eighth century and were placed in the Church of Our Saviour, the first church of Tegernsee. The first abbot was Adalbert who is mentioned in a charter of 804 as having died recently. As early as the year 770 Abbot Adalbert took part in the Synod of Dingolfing, and just before the close of the eighth century (before 798) Adalbert and his "representative" Zacho were present at a synod at St. Emmeram in Ratisbon. At this synod they were obliged to promise to restore thirteen baptisteries that were in the possession of Tegernsee but which had been claimed by Bishop Atto of Freising. This demand was a result of the efforts of the episcopate of Bavaria of that era to limit as much as possible the parochial labours of the monasteries. The decision, however, was not executed but was adjusted by a settlement made at Tegernsee on 16 June, 804, on the occasion of the dedication of the Church of St. Peter at Tegernsee and the translation to it of the relics of St. Quirinus from the Basilica of St. Saviour (cf. "Historia Frising.", 12, 92).

The abbey soon attained to great distinction and importance, as is evident from a capitulary of the Emperor Louis the Pious of Aachen that was issued in the year 817. This capitulary called upon the monastery of "Tegrinseo" (Tegernsee) among others to furnish military contingents (M.G.L.L.I. sect. 11350, 20).

In the early part of the tenth century the monastery of Tegernsee fell completely into decay on account of the disastrous defeat of the Bavarians by the Magyars in 907, whereby nearly all the religious foundations of Bavaria were entirely destroyed. Laymen with their wives, dogs, and horses settled in the monastery of Tegernsee and finally a fire destroyed the buildings and with them the books and church vestments. When the monastery was restored by Emperor Otto II and Duke Otto of Bavaria in 979 all knowledge of its original foundation had disappeared at Tegernsee. In order to restore and maintain discipline the Emperor Otto called the monk Hartwich (979–982) of St. Maximinus at Trier to be Abbot of Tegernsee. The same charter that contains this appointment of 10 June, 979 (M.G. D.D. II, 1, 219, 199), also contains a grant from the emperor of the right of free election of the abbot, as well as freedom from taxes and the imperial protection, by which the abbey was withdrawn from the suzerainty of the rulers of Bavaria. Consequently the abbey became prosperous once more. Considerable information as to the efforts for reform of this abbot is given by a note in the manuscript of the Gospels, written in uncial characters that belonged to Tegernsee and is now at Munich (Clm. 19101). The note says: "Monastic reform was begun in this monastery by the reverend monk Hartwich of St. Maximinus on 6 May of the year 978. In the year 982 this same Hartwich received staff and benefice from Emperor Otto II and was consecrated by the very venerable Bishop Abraham [of Görz, Bishop of Freising]. The monks made their profession". Abbot Hartwich had an excellent successor (982–1001) in the Benedictine monk Gozbert of St. Emmeram, who had received his religious education at Augsburg. Gozbert introduced the study of the classics at Tegernsee, especially Statius, Persius, the letters of Horace and Cicero, and Boethius; the works of these men were read and copied.

Particularly distinguished among the monks during the administration of this abbot was the poet and prose writer Froumund (d. 20 October, 1012), who in a manuscript still preserved at Munich (Clm. 19412) made a collection of letters and poems of his own and others. He also copied at Cologne the treatise of Boethius "On the Consolation of Philosophy" and brought the copy to Tegernsee. It was this Froumund who brought about the intellectual and literary connexion between his abbey and the monasteries and churches of St. Emmeram at Ratisbon, Feuchtwangen, Augsburg, and Würzburg. It was at this era also that the glass works were established at Tegernsee to make stained-glass windows for Bishop Gottschalk of Freising. The opinion that glass-staining was invented at Tegernsee is erroneous, for before this in the ninth century stained-glass windows can be proved to have existed at St. Gall and in Westphalia. This prosperous period under the immediate successors of Gozbert, namely St. Gotthard (1001–1002), Eberhard I (d. 4 March, 1004), and Beringer (1004–1012), did not last long. As soon after this as the year 1031 Tegernsee was reformed, at the command of the Emperor Henry III, by the monks of Niederaltaich from which place monks, who were accompanied by Abbot Ellinger, were sent to occupy the Abbey of Tegernsee. Abbot Ellinger, however, met with opposition at Tegernsee and was obliged to return to his original monastery, from whence he did not venture to come back to Tegernsee until 1056, dying there in the same year. He was the abbot who began the "Urbar", or book of donations at Tegernsee, and who did so much at Tegernsee to improve and perfect technical skill. In 1015 a colony of monks went from Tegernsee to settle in the monastery of Sts. Ulrich and Afra at Augsburg. The prestige of Tegernsee was still maintained in the twelfth century and continued up to the middle of the thirteenth century. In the imperial documents of the twelfth century the names of the abbots of Tegernsee are often found signed as witnesses, as they were princes of the empire.

During the rule of Abbot Bertold I (1206–1217) the great minnesinger Walther von der Vogelweide stayed at the abbey. Most probably the literary importance of Tegernsee had led him to tie his steed at the monastery gate and to claim its hospitality. However, it is evident from Walther's songs that the singer of the Vogelweide, who rejoiced in the wine-cup, was not greatly delighted by the reception at Tegernsee, for he sang:

People often told me of Tegernsee,
How glorious was that house:
So I went to it more than a mile from the road.
I am a queer fellow,
I cannot even understand myself
And why I think so much of pious folks.
I am not grumbling at it, for may God bless us both,
I took the water:
But henceforth
I shall keep away from the monks' table.

The lines mean that according to the custom of the time Walther expected a good bumper of wine after the meal, but to his great astonishment only water was brought for the washing of the hands. This short poem of Walther von der Vogelweide, however, is not, as some have sought to prove, to be taken as a justification of the Abbey of Tegernsee in a lawsuit that was then being carried on over a vineyard.

In the thirteenth and fourteenth centuries the abbey suffered greatly from the wars carried on by the princes of Southern Germany, as well as by the prodigality of several of its abbots. In the reign of the Emperor Louis, Tegernsee lost its immediacy and became subject to Bavaria. At the time of the visitations in 1426 the Conventual, Caspar Ayndorffer, who was the second founder of Tegernsee and a close friend of the reforming Cardinal Nicholas of Cusa, was made abbot (1426–1460) by papal authority. He completely reformed Tegernsee and thus made the abbey a centre of the reform movement of that era. Ayndorffer was willing to accept as monks men who were not noble, as well as members of aristocratic families, consequently monastic discipline was maintained until the abbey was suppressed. The monk Ulrich Stöckl (in Latin *Trunculus*) was the legate of the Benedictine abbeys of the Diocese of Freising to the Council of Basle during the years 1432–1437; he wrote a valuable account of the council. As the researches of Guido Maria Dreves show, Stöckl was also a good writer of rhyming poetry. The last and sixty-third Abbot of Tegernsee was the excellent Gregory II Rottenkolber (from 1787), who encouraged learning and sent the young clerics to the Universities of Salzburg and Ingolstadt. He also made a collection of coins and engravings at Tegernsee. The abbey still continued to exist, notwithstanding many changes of fortune, until 1803, in which year it was secularized on 17 March. This sealed its fate, and the "Primas Bavariæ", as the Abbot of Tegernsee was called on account of his primacy over all other Bavarian prelates, resigned. The monastery became the property of the State; the abbey lands situated in Austria were confiscated by Austria; and the monastic buildings were bought by Freiherr von Drechsel for 3000 florins. In 1805 Abbot Rottenkolber and twenty monks were able to purchase for 5000 florins the monastery building for a house where they could lead a common life. In 1810 the abbot died there. In 1817 the former monastery became the property of King Maximilian I, who also bought the building owned by the Benedictines. The king had the place altered into a royal summer residence. At present it belongs to the family of the lately deceased Duke Charles Theodore who established in 1884 at Tegernsee an ophthalmic infirmary for the poor. The splendid library, that contained about 60,000 volumes, 6600 incunabulæ, and more than 2000 manuscripts, was incorporated in part in the National Library at Munich.

The intellectual importance of the Abbey of Tegernsee was less in the sphere of history than in the domains of literature and art. As is learned from a monk of Tegernsee of the fifteenth century, the abbey owned six Tegernsee chronicles that agreed in sense but varied in the way the events were related. Only four of them are known, and these are largely interwoven with legendary additions. They are: the "Translatio des hl. Quirinus" (Petz, "Anecdota," III, 3); that is erroneously ascribed to Froumund; the poetic presentation of the same subject by Metellus called the "Quirinalia"; and the two "Passiones S. Quirini", of which the shorter is the more ancient. Especially important was the purely literary work done at Tegernsee. Mention should be made of the "Ruodlieb", the earliest poetic romance, which was written in rhyming hexametres, not by Froumund, but by some Benedictine monk about the year 1030.

Tegernsee also took a very important part in the development of art, especially, as has already been said, in the making of stained glass. Glass works were established and, by order of Count Arnold Welsen-Klammbach, the churches were adorned with stained-glass windows instead of the old cloth hangings with which the window openings had formerly been covered. In 1083 Abbot Gozbert established a bell foundry which, after Freising, was the oldest in Bavaria. He secured the first bell-founder from Freising, a cleric named Adalrich, who, at the instigation of Abbot Gozbert, cast the bell of St. Quirinus, for which both the mould and the metal had been ready for three years. The glass-painter and monk, Werinher, who was also the goldsmith of Tegernsee, made the double doors of the cathedral of Mainz that were cast in 1014. Werinher, who was also nicknamed Wenzel (Petz, "Anecd.", VI), was a skilful sculptor (*artificiosus anaglypha*). In particular he understood how to ornament the covers of books with lettering and enamel. Tegernsee was also a noted monastic school in the medieval period. About 1067 the celebrated monk Otloh of St. Emmeram expressed his thanks for the knowledge he had gained at the abbey ("in loco illo, quo talia didici, id est in Cœnobio Tegernsee"; cf. Mabillon, "Analecta", 1723, 119). It was also Tegernsee that under the rule of Abbot Quirinus (1568–94) established a printing-press in 1573. The importance of printing was probably recognized at the very first on account of the art of wood-engraving which had been practised for a long time at Tegernsee, and of which very beautiful proof-impressions of the years 1472 and 1477 are still extant. The press at Tegernsee issued chiefly religious and popular works, and also scholarly and liturgical books of great typographical beauty. The architectural remains still existing at Tegernsee are the former monastery church of the fifteenth century, which, however, was so altered by rebuilding at the close of the seventeenth century that it can only be reconstructed by analysis. Over the door of the church is a marble relief dating from 1457, representing the founders of the church. Mention should also be made of the Church of St. Quirinus erected on the spot where, according to legend, a spring bubbled up when the coffin of St. Quirinus rested there during the translation to the monastery church. The building was erected by Abbot Ayndorffer in 1450 to replace a wooden church.

BÖTTCHER, *Germania. sacra* (Leipzig, 1875), 852; *Die Kunstdenkmäler des Königreiches Bayern vom XI. bis Ende des XVIII. Jahrh.*, I (Munich, 1901), 1496 sqq.; FUCHS, *Geschichte des Klosters Tegernsee* (Munich, 1876); *Legenda S. Quirini martyris Romæ*, cf. the MSS. referred to as guides to the subject in POTTHAST, *Bibliotheca Historica medii ævi* (Berlin, 1896), 1539; MAYER, *Beschreibung des Erzbistums München-Freising*, II (Ratisbon, 1880–84), 282 sqq.; OBERMAIER, *Geschichte Tegernsees* (Freising, 1888), goes to 1429; OESTERLEY, *Histor.-geograph. Wörterbuch des Deutschen Mittelalters* (Gotha, 1881–83), 677; PETZ, *Thes. anecdot. noviss.*, III (Vienna, 1721), 475–594; RATZINGER, *Forschungen zur Bayerischen Geschichte* (Kempten, 1898), 457–91; SIGHART, *Geschichte der bildenden Künste im Königreich Bayern* (Munich, 1862); WATTENBACH, *Deutschlands Geschichtsquellen im Mittelalter*, I (7th ed., Berlin, 1904).

ULRICH SCHMID.

Te Gestientem Gaudiis. See ROSARY, THE.—*Breviary Hymns of the Rosary.*

Tegianum. See DIANO, DIOCESE OF.

Tehuantepec, DIOCESE OF (TEHUANTEPECENSIS), in the Republic of Mexico, suffragan of Oaxaca. Its area covers the southern part of the States of Oaxaca and Vera Cruz, through the Isthmus of Tehuantepec. Its population is about 202,000; the residence of the bishop, the city of Tehuantepec, has 10,000 inhabitants.

Burgoa relates the following, which he deciphered from ancient Zapotecan pictures: A short time before the Spanish set foot on Mexican soil the subjects of the King of Tehuantepec begged him to make a sacrifice to their gods, and in particular to Guiscipocoché. This the king did and then said: "The great God announces that the time has come when he shall be driven from this earth because his enemies shall soon arrive from the regions of the rising Sun; these men will be white, and none of the Kings of these regions shall be able to resist their strength or their arms. They will subject us to misery and shall bring in their wake men who will be our priests and to whom those of us who shall remain will be forced to disclose our sins on bended knees".

On 24 April, 1522, Fray Bartolomé de Olmedo with Pedro de Alvarado arrived at Tehuantepec. The monarch, Cosijopii, a relative of the Emperor Montezuma, received them with open arms. He embraced the Catholic Faith, and a few years later erected at his expense in his royal city the convent of S. Domingo. The Franciscan Fathers, as well as the famous Dominican Fray Bartolomé de las Casas, Bishop of Chiapas, preached the Gospel in Tehuantepec. The first priests to settle there were Fray Gregorio Beteta and Fray Bernardo de Albuquerque. A few years later an attempt was made by the descendants of the King Cosijopii to return to paganism, but this plot when discovered was quickly suppressed (see MEXICO). When the See of Oaxaca was created in 1535, all the territory on which the city of Tehuantepec is situated belonged to it and remained so until 1891 when Leo XIII made of it a separate see, suffragan of Oaxaca or Antequera. There are 5 parochial schools with about 600 pupils, 4 Protestant colleges with 70 pupils, and 3 Protestant churches. In the capital, Tehuantepec, there are 14 churches, among which that of Santo Domingo is noted for its phenomenal size and splendid construction. Coatzacoalcos (to-day known as Puerto Mexico) is known for the tradition that from this port the celebrated Quetzalcoatl sailed for his native land.

GILLOW, *Apuntes históricos* (Mexico, 1889); DOMENECH, *Giuía general descriptiva de la republica Mexicana* (Mexico, 1889).

CAMILLUS CRIVELLI.

Teilo (ELIUD), SAINT, "Archbishop" of Llandaff, b. at Eccluis Gunniau, near Tenby, Pembrokeshire; d. at Llandilo Vawr, Carmarthenshire, probably in or before 560, an old man, but Ussher puts his death at 604. Sir John Rhys thinks that his true name was Eliau or Eilliau; in Latin it usually appears as Teliarus, in Breton as Teliau, and in French as Télo. He was cousin to St. David and born of a good family settled at Penally, near Tenby. His father, whose name was probably Usyllt, may possibly be identified with St. Issell, the patron of the parish church of Saundersfoot. His sister Anaumed, or Anauved, married King Budic of

Armorica, and became the mother of St. Oudaceus, Teilo's successor. The earliest extant biographies of the saint are late and uncritical. Educated under St. Dyfrig or Dubric (q. v.), at Hentland, Herefordshire, and under St. Paul the Old or Paulinus at Whitland, Carmarthenshire, he subsequently ruled the monastic school at Llandaff, named after him Bangor Deilo. The story of his visit to Palestine with SS. David and Padarn (or Paternus) about 518, and their consecration there as bishops by John III, Patriarch of Jerusalem, is not now generally credited; but it seems that about that date, when St. Dubric withdrew to Bardsey, St. Teilo succeeded him at Llandaff. In 547 the "yellow plague" began to ravage Wales, and shortly afterwards St. Teilo with many of his flock crossed to Armorica, where they were hospitably entertained by his friend St. Sampson, Abbot and Bishop of Dol. After seven years and seven months Teilo returned to Wales, and is said to have been elected to the archiepiscopate vacant by the death of St. David, and to have transferred it from Menevia (q. v.) to Llandaff (q. v.); but the more general modern opinion seems to be that in Wales at that epoch the episcopate was not yet diocesan.

The story of the three bodies of the saint, which were discovered the day after his death, was probably invented to account for the fact that the churches at Llandaff, Llandilo Vawr, and Penally, all claimed to possess his body. Doubtless at his death his relics were widely distributed. To-day they are venerated at Landeleau (Finistère), Plogonnac (Finistère), and Saint Télo (Côtes-du-Nord). Five parish churches in Brittany are dedicated to him (Landeleau, Leuhan, Montertelot, Plédéliac, and Saint Télo) as well as a chapel between Plogonnac and Locronan. The modern Catholic church at Tenby bears the names of "Holyrood and St. Teilo". The dedication of twelve churches in the present Anglican Diocese of St. David's, and of six in that of Llandaff, show they owe their origin to this zeal. Borlase argues his connexion with six dedications in Cornwall and Devon. It is stated that he was formally canonized, but no date is given. He is not infrequently represented in Breton churches as riding on a stag. His festival is, or was, kept in Wales and at Saint Télo on 9 February; at Dol, as a double, on 29 November; and in other places in Brittany on 25 November.

Acta SS., V (Paris, 1864), 303; Le Grand, *Saints de la Brétagne, Armorique* (Quimper, 1901), 331, 610; Lloyd in *Dict. Nat. Biog.*, s. v.; Gammack in *Dict. Christ. Biog.* (London, 1911), s. v.; Guérin, *Les Petits Bollandistes*, XIII (Paris, 1882), 583; Arnold Foster, *Church Dedications*, II (London, 1899), 201; Baring-Gould, *Lives of the Saints*, II (London, 1897), 238; Stanton, *Menology of England and Wales* (London, 1887), 60; Evans, *Liber Landavensis* (London, 1893); Borlase, *Age of the Saints* (Truro, 1893), 134; Loth, in *Annales de Bretagne*, IX, X; Rees, *Welsh Saints* (London, 1836), 253.

JOHN B. WAINEWRIGHT.

Teleology (from Greek τέλος, end, and λόγος, science) is seldom used according to its etymological meaning to denote the branch of philosophy which deals with ends or final causes. It means the doctrine that there is design, purpose, or finality in the world, that effects are in some manner intentional, and that no complete account of the universe is possible without reference to final causes (for the notion of final cause, see CAUSE). With mechanism (q. v.) teleology admits the determinism of physical efficient causes. It also acknowledges that the object of scientific research is to discover the laws of phenomena, and that any fact is scientifically explained when adequate causes are assigned to it, and the conditions of its occurrence are known. But against mechanism, teleology claims that this determinism, these laws, and the mode of activity of efficient causes reveal the existence of a directive principle and of finality in the works of nature. Hence the question is not whether there are efficient or final causes, whether, for instance, man sees because he has eyes or has eyes in order to see. Final causes and efficient causes are not mutually exclusive. It must be admitted that any result in nature is to be ascribed to an unbroken chain of active causes, and the function of the final cause is not to supply any missing link but to explain how the activity of efficient causes is directed toward useful results. Nor can the teleologist be asked to indicate the end of every activity any more than the mechanist can be required to indicate the efficient cause of every phenomenon. Finally the problem does not refer to conscious and intelligent finality such as is manifested in human purposive actions, for it is obvious that in many of his actions man is guided by the idea of a preconceived plan which he endeavours to realize. Human works are for something; the house is built to live in; the clock is made to keep time; the machine is constructed to perform some work; the statue is carved to realize some ideal; etc. Are we justified in speaking of the works of nature in the same way? When we speak of ends and purposes in nature do we not attribute to it that which is distinctly human? Do we not carry too far the process of personification and analogy, and thereby incur the reproach of anthropomorphism? According to mechanists, because we foresee results we falsely conclude that nature strives to realize them. Ends exist in the mind which studies nature, not in nature itself. To admit ends is mentally to reverse the natural process, to look upon the effect as a cause, and from it to ascend the causal series regressively.

I. It is important at first to make a distinction between extrinsic and intrinsic finality. The former consists in realizing an end which is outside of the being that realizes it, and thus in contributing to the utility and welfare of other beings. In this way the mineral is utilized by the plant, and the plant by the animal. Or again the heat of the sun is a condition of growth and development. From this extrinsic finality result the subordination of various beings, and the order and harmony of the universe. But while extrinsic finality seems obvious in several instances many of its details escape us, and it is easy to make a wrong use of it by attributing false or childish ends to every being and event, and by taking a narrow anthropocentric view of finality. This abuse of final causes called for the vigorous protests of Bacon ("De Dignitate et Augmentis Scientiarum," III, iv), Descartes ("Principia Philosophiæ", I, 28; III, 2, 3; "Meditationes", III, IV), Spinoza (Ethica, I, prop. 36, app.). The exclusive consideration of extrinsic ends contributed probably more than any other cause to the discredit into which teleology fell at the time of the Renaissance. Yet, as Voltaire rightly remarks, it is clear that if the nose was not made to wear spectacles, it was made for the sense of smell (Dictionnaire philosophique, s. v. Causes finales). Here Voltaire appeals to the principle of intrinsic finality which, according to Aristotle and St. Thomas, is primary, while extrinsic finality is derived and secondary.

Intrinsic finality consists in the fact that every being has within itself a natural tendency whereby its activity is directed towards the perfection of its own nature. "As the influx of the efficient cause consists in its own action, so the influx of the final cause consists in its being sought after and desired" (St. Thomas, "De veritate", Q. xxii, a. 2). But this desire or *appetitus* (see APPETITE) is not necessarily conscious. St. Thomas does not hesitate to speak of "natural appetite", "natural inclination", and even "intention of nature", to mean that every being has within itself a directive principle of activity. The final cause is a good which satisfies a tendency springing immediately from the nature (q. v.) of every being. "By the form which gives it its specific perfection, everything in nature has an inclination to its own operations and to its own end, which it reaches through these operations. Just as everything is, such also are its operations and its tendency to what is suitable to itself" (St. Thomas, "Contra Gentiles", IV, xix). Accordingly, God does not direct creatures to their ends from outside, but through their own nature. This teleological view does not suppose that every efficient cause in the world is directed immediately by an intelligence, but by its own natural tendency. The Divine plan of creation is carried out by the various beings themselves acting in conformity with their nature. When, however, this finality is called immanent, this expression must not be understood in a pantheistic sense, as if the intelligence which the world manifests were to be identified with the world itself, but in the sense that the immediate principle of finality is immanent in every being.

II. Thus understood the principle of teleology seems almost obvious. Activity is essential to every being, and the same substance, placed in the same conditions, always acts in the same way. Its effect, therefore, does not happen by chance, for chance cannot account for fixity and stability. Within the substance itself must be found a principle of determination. Now what is a determination but an adaptation and an orientation toward an end? The fact that the world is governed by laws, far from giving any support to the mechanistic conception, is rather opposed to it. A law is not a cause, but the expression of the constant manner in which causes produce their effects. To say that there are laws is simply to state the determinism of nature, and it is precisely to this determinism that St. Thomas appeals to establish teleology. "Every active cause acts for an end, otherwise from its activity one effect would not result rather than another, except by chance" (Summa Theol., I, Q. xliv, a. 4). And again: "It is necessary that every active cause should act for an end. For in a series of causes, if the first be removed, the others also are removed [i. e., fail to produce their effects]. But the final cause is the first of all causes. The reason is that matter does not receive a form [i. e., does not change] except through the influence of an active cause. For nothing of itself passes from *potentia* to *actus* [see ACTUS ET POTENTIA], and the active cause does not act except in consequence of the intention of an end. Otherwise, if the active cause were not determined to produce some particular effect, it would not produce this rather than some other. In order to produce a determined effect, it must, therefore, be determined to something in particular which serves as an end. As in rational beings this determination takes place through the rational appetite or will, so in other beings it takes place through a natural inclination which is called natural appetite" (Summa Theol., I–II, Q. i, a. 2).

Efficient causes are not indifferent, and their effects are not fortuitous. As a matter of fact, from the many individual activities of the various beings of the world order and harmony result in the universe. And when different forces converge toward a harmonious result, their convergence cannot be explained except by admitting that they tend to realize a plan. Life is essentially teleological. There is a co-ordination of all the organs, the functions of every one depending on those of the others, and tending to the welfare of the whole organism. Little by little the primitive cell develops according to the general type of the species and evolves into the complete organism. To Aristotle's statement that "nature adapts the organ to the function, and not the function to the organ" (De partib., animal., IV, xii, 694b, 13), Lucretius replied: "Nothing in the body is made in order that we may use it. What happens to exist is the cause of its use" (De nat. rerum, IV, 833; cf. 822–56),—an objection which had been presented more forcibly by Aristotle himself (Phys., II, viii, 198b). The function, it is true, is the result of the organ; the eye sees because it is an eye, and, in general, every function is an effect of active causes. But what is not explained by mechanism is the convergence of many different causes toward a given result. If organs are so many mechanisms, it remains to be indicated how these mechanisms were organized. If appeal is made to evolution, it must be remembered that evolution is not a cause, but a mode of development, and that organic evolution rather accentuates the need of final causes. In the inorganic world, the constancy of the laws of nature and the resulting order of the world manifest the existence in every being of a principle of direction and orientation.

The fundamental defect of mechanism consists in giving exclusive attention to the analyzing of every event into its causes, and in forgetting to look for the reason of their synthesis. If we take a clock to pieces, we discover in it nothing but springs, wheels, pivots, levers etc. When we have explained the mechanism which ultimately causes the revolutions of the hands on the dial, shall we say that the clock was not made to keep time? The intelligence that designed it is not in the clock itself which now obeys its own laws. Yet in reality we have an adaptation of means to an end. Thus the unconscious finality in the world leads to the conclusion that there must be an intelligent cause of the world. The whole preceding doctrine is well summed up in the following passage from St. Thomas (Summa Theol., I, Q. ciii, a., ad 3um): "The natural necessity inherent in things that are determined to one effect is impressed on them by the Divine power which directs them to their end, just as the necessity which directs the arrow to the target is impressed on it by the archer, and does not come from the arrow itself. There is this difference, however, that what creatures receive from God is their nature, whereas the direction imparted by man to natural things beyond what is natural to them is a kind of violence. Hence, as the forced necessity of the arrow shows the direction intended by the archer, so the natural determinism of creatures is a sign of the government of Divine Providence".

FARGES, *Théorie fondamentale de l'acte et de la puissance* (7th ed., Paris, 1909); FLINT, *Theism* (London, 1889); GUTBERLET, *Allgemeine Metaphysik* (Münster, 1906); IDEM, *Der mechanische Monismus* (Paderborn, 1893); JANET, *Les causes finales* (Paris, 1882), tr. by AFFLECK (Edinburgh, 1883); MERCIER, *Métaphysique générale* (Louvain, 1905); PESCH, *Institutiones philosophiæ naturalis* (Freiburg, 1880); SULLY-PRUDHOMME AND RICHET, *Le problème des causes finales* (Paris, 1902); DE VORGES, *Cause efficiente et cause finale* (Paris, 1889); BALDWIN AND MOORE in *Dict. of Philos. and Psychol.* (New York, 1901), s. v.; EISLER, *Wörterbuch der philosophischen Begriffe* (Berlin, 1910), s. v. *Zweck*, etc.

C. A. DUBRAY.

Telepathy (τῆλε, far, and παθεῖν, to experience), a term introduced by F. W. H. Myers in 1882 to denote "the ability of one mind to impress or to be impressed by another mind otherwise than through the recognized channels of sense" (Gurney, "Phantasms of the Living", I, 6); or: "the communication of impressions of any kind from one mind to another, independently of the recognized channels of sense" (Myers, "Human Personality", I, xxi).

I. The term telepathy is sometimes used, in conformity with its derivation, to mean the direct communication between minds at a great distance. Such terms as thought-transference, mind-reading, or mental suggestion would then apply to the direct communication between minds in the same room or at a small distance. Generally, however, at least in English, telepathy connotes only the exclusion of the recognized channels of sensation, irrespective of the distance. It supposes that, in some cases, the usual signs by which ideas are manifested—speech, writing, gestures, muscular contraction, facial expression, etc.—may be dispensed with, and that minds are able to communicate, if not directly and immediately, at any rate through some medium which is distinct from the ordinary medium of sense-perception. Thus understood, telepathy includes two classes of facts.

A. The first class consists of intentional communications, when a person (the agent) by the concentration of his mind on some object makes an effort to transfer an idea to another person (the percipient) who may or may not be aware of the attempt, and who may or may not make an effort to receive the communication. The experiments, made sometimes on normal, more generally and more successfully on hypnotized subjects, include the transference of tastes, sounds, visual images, pain etc.; the guessing of numbers, cards, colours, diagrams etc., thought of by the agent; the execution or inhibition of movements in compliance with the agent's will; the production or cessation of the hypnotic condition at a command mentally given; and other similar transferences of thought. In a few successful instances the agent has been able to produce apparitions of himself or even of a third person to the percipient in another room or house. In these experiments the main difficulty is to make sure that the percipient in no way uses his senses, which are in a state of hyperæsthesia or extraordinary acuteness, and that the correct guesses cannot be accounted for by similar habits, suggestions, and associations in both the agent and the percipient. Exhibitions of so-called mind-reading are generally explainable either by clever collusion, or by muscle-reading when there is contact between the agent and the percipient, or by the interpretation of sensory indications consciously or unconsciously given.

B. The other class of facts consists of spontaneous communications in which, as far as we can know, the agent has no intention of manifesting himself to the percipient. Herein are included especially the intimation of the danger, illness, distress, or death of some person, generally a friend or relative, and the apparition of the phantasm of such a person, especially at the time of his death. The degree of precision and exactness of these monitions varies indefinitely. Sometimes they consist in a merely physical occurrence coincident with the death, such as noise, the fall of some object, of a picture, etc. Sometimes ill-defined and inexplicable feelings of restlessness and uneasiness are experienced, or the sudden idea of what is happening flashes across the mind. Sometimes finally, either in the waking state or in dreams, apparitions are seen, and even entire scenes witnessed in all their details. The main difficulty in these cases is to determine whether they present mere coincidences due to subjective factors, such as habit, association, memory, expectation etc., or a real causality.

II. Two problems are to be solved regarding telepathy: A. Is the existence of telepathy as a fact demonstrated? B. If it is, what is its explanation?

A. Is the fact of telepathy established? In the past thirty or forty years, this subject has been studied critically. A large number of facts have been collected, especially by the Society for Psychical Research, founded in 1882, and have been published in "Phantasms of the Living", the "Proceedings" of the society, and many other works. In France, the "Annales des Sciences Psychiques" also record numerous cases. At present the literature on the subject is very extensive. After considering the cumulative evidence for the existence of telepathy, there cannot fail to remain in the mind at least a general impression that chance does not account for the number of coincidences, which is far greater than could be expected according to chance-probability. In the "Census of Hallucinations", after due allowance for possible causes of error, whereas ordinary chance coincidence would give 1:19,000 as the proportion of the coincidences of apparitions with the fact of death, the actual proportion is 1:43, or 440 times greater than would be expected. In experiments, the proportion of successful attempts varies greatly, yet, in general, it is far above that which chance-coincidence would lead us to expect. Nevertheless, the fact of telepathy is not yet accepted universally as strictly demonstrated. There are so many difficulties to meet, so many causes of error to avoid, and so many obstacles to overcome, that results obtained so far are not looked upon by all as sufficient to give a scientific certitude of the fact.

B. Various theories have been proposed to account for the fact of telepathy. Some, appealing to a preternatural causality, have supposed the intervention of good or evil spirits. But the principle admitted by all scientists, philosophers, and theologians is that a fact must be looked upon as natural until the contrary is proved. The present impossibility of giving a scientific explanation is no proof that there is no scientific explanation. The unexplained is not to be identified with the unexplainable, and the strange and extraordinary nature of a fact is not a justification for attributing it to powers above nature. Another attempt, namely the spiritistic hypothesis, cannot be discussed here (see SPIRITISM). Attempts at a scientific explanation rest either on a psychological basis (Myers, Sir Oliver Lodge) or on a physical and physiological basis (Sir W. Crookes, Flournoy, Ochorowicz). Among psychological attempts is the supposition of the existence of a sub-conscious mind or subliminal self endowed with all the powers required to account for all the facts. While the considerable influence of the subconscious or the subliminal cannot be denied, the theory in its generality has the grave defect of being the fact itself expressed in other terms, and of having for its only proof the fact itself which it seeks to explain. Others simply appeal to supernormal faculties that are purely psychological. Among physiological and physical attempts are the suppositions of some neurotic fluid, brain vibrations, or a special form of energy transmitted from brain to brain through some unknown medium. All these attempts are unsatisfactory, and, according to all, the problem is still unsolved. Further experiments are needed, both to establish the fact itself beyond all doubt, and chiefly to determine its psychological and physical conditions. Until this is done, any theory is premature.

GRASSET, *L'occultisme hier et aujourd'hui* (Montpellier, 1907), tr. TUBEUF, *The Marvels beyond Science* (New York, 1910); GURNEY, MYERS, PODMORE, *Phantasms of the Living* (London, 1886); MYERS, *Human Personality and its Survival of Bodily Death* (London and New York, 1903); GUTBERLET, *Der Kampf um die Seele* (Mainz, 1903); MASON, *Telepathy and the Subliminal Self* (New York, 1899); MAXWELL, *Les Phénomènes psychiques* (Paris, 1903); tr. FINCH, *Metapsychical Phenomena* (New York and London, 1905); MERCIER, *Psychologie* (Louvain, 1903); OCHOROWICZ, *La suggestion mentale* (Paris, 1889), tr. FITZGERALD (New York, 1891); PODMORE, *Apparitions and Thought-Transference* (London and New York, 1894); THOMAS, *Thought-Transference* (New York, 1905); ANON., *Pressentimenti e telepatie*, a series of articles in *Civiltà cattolica* (1899, 1900); *Annales des sciences psychiques*, passim; *Proceedings of the Society for Psychical Research*, passim, especially *Report on the Census of Hallucinations*, X (1894), 25–422; SIDGWICK in BALDWIN, *Dict. of Philos. and Psychol.* (New York, 1902), s. v. *Telepathy, and Psychical Research*.

C. A. DUBRAY.

Telese, DIOCESE OF (TELESINENSIS).—Telese, a small town in the Province of Benevento, Southern Italy, is situated in the valley of the Calore, well known for its hot sulphur springs. The ruins of the ancient Telesia, the Tedis of the Oscan coins, are to be seen yet on Monte Acerro. The city was captured by Hannibal in 207 B. C.; Scipio founded a colony there. Having fallen into decay it was rebuilt in the ninth century. Its first bishop mentioned is Agnellus (487); in the tenth century it was subject to the Archbishop of Benevento. In 1612 Bishop Gian Francesco Leoni (1508) transferred the episcopal residence to Cerreto Sannita. In 1818 the see was united to that of Piedimonte d'Alife, but was re-established in 1852. Among its bishops we may note: Alberico Giacquinto (1540), renowned for his learning and piety; Angelo Massarelli (1567), secretary of the Council of Trent, of which he wrote the acts and a diary; Vincenzo Lupoli (1792), a distinguished jurisconsult. The diocese contains 24 parishes with 60,600 inhabitants, 40 secular and 10 regular priests, 2 convents of men and 5 nunneries, and a school for young girls.

CAPPELLETTI, *Le chiese d'Italia*, XIX; PACELLI, *Memorie storiche di Telese* (1775).

U. BENIGNI.

Telesio, BERNARDINO, Italian humanist and philosopher, b. of a noble family at Cosenza, near Naples, 1508; d. there, 1588. He studied successively at Milan, Rome, and Padua. In Southern Italy the revolt against Aristoteleanism had already begun. At Padua Telesio first came to be recognized as a leader of the anti-Aristoteleans. After residing several years in Rome, where he enjoyed the patronage of Paul IV, Telesio returned to Naples, and later founded an academy at Cosenza. His principal work is entitled "De rerum natura juxta propria principia", the first part of which was published in Rome, 1565, and the second in Naples, 1587. He was a radical opponent both of the method and of the content of Aristotelean philosophy. He considered that the scholastic followers of Aristotle relied too much on reason and too little on the senses. The "reasoners", he believed, were over-confident of their power to reach the secrets of nature by syllogistic methods. With conscious humility, therefore, he determined to trust to his senses alone, and, beginning "in the dust", he strove to reach the highest pinnacle of natural truth. This exclusion of reason from the task and the consequent exaltation of sense above every other faculty of the mind resulted naturally in the sensistic doctrine that all knowledge is feeling (*sensus*) or sensation, and in the materialistic doctrine that the soul itself is material. In the content of his philosophy he opposed the Aristotelian doctrine of matter and form, substituting for it the doctrine that everything is composed of matter and force, the two principal forces being heat and cold. Heat is centralized in the sun, and cold in the earth. As the Platonist Patrizzi pointed out, there is an inherent contradiction in Telesio's system. For, if we are to rely on the senses and not on reason, since the senses do not reveal the existence of matter except as modified by forces, the central doctrinal principle is in contradiction with the most important methodological tenet. This point was brought out in the discussions between the advocates of Aristotle and the followers of Telesio in the sixteenth century. Among the most ardent disciples of Telesio were Campanella and Giordano Bruno.

BERNARDINUS TELESI
Philosoph. Prof. Neapoli.

From Freher's Theatrum Virorum Clarorum, Nuremberg, 1688.

FIORENTINO, *Bernardino Telesio, Studi storici*, etc. (2 vols., Florence, 1872); HÖFFDING, *Hist. of Mod. Phil.*, tr. MEYER, I (London, 1900), 92 sqq.; WINDELBAND, *Hist. of Phil.*, tr. TUFTS (New York, 1901), 356 sqq.

WILLIAM TURNER.

Telesphorus, SAINT, POPE (about 125–136). He was the seventh Roman bishop in succession from the Apostles, and, according to the testimony of St. Irenæus (Adv. hæreses, III, iii, 3), suffered a glorious martyrdom. Eusebius (Hist. eccl., IV, vii, xiv) places the beginning of his pontificate in the twelfth year of Hadrian's reign (128–129), his death in the first year of the reign of Antoninus Pius (138–139). These statements, however, should be compared with Lightfoot, "The Apostolic Fathers", I (London, 1899), 201 sq., section on "Early Roman Successions", and Harnack, "Geschichte der altchristl. Literatur", pt. II, "Die Chronologie", I (Leipzig, 1879), 70 sq. In the fragment of the letter of Irenæus of Lyons to Pope Victor concerning the celebration of Easter (Euseb., "Hist. eccl.," V, xxiv), Telesphorus is mentioned as one of the Roman bishops who always celebrated Easter on Sunday, without, however, abandoning church fellowship with those communities that did not follow this custom. None of the statements in the "Liber pontificalis" and other authorities of a later date as to liturgical and other decisions of this pope are genuine. In the Roman Martyrology his feast is given under 5 January; the Greek Church celebrates it on 22 February.

DUCHESNE, *Liber pontificalis*, I (Paris, 1886), 129 sq.; JAFFÉ, *Regesta rom. pont.*, I (2nd ed.), 6; LANGEN, *Geschichte der römischen Kirche*, I (Bonn, 1881), 103–104.

J. P. KIRSCH.

Telesphorus of Cosenza (THEOPHORUS, THEOLOPHORUS), a name assumed by one of the pseudoprophets during the time of the Great Schism. He gave out that he was born at Cosenza and lived as a hermit near the site of the ancient Thebes. His book of predictions on the schism was the most popular of the numerous prophetic treatises that were spread broadcast by the many self-constituted prophets of that period. More than twenty manuscripts of it are still extant, and it first appeared in print with various interpolations: "Liber de magnis tribulationibus in proximo futuris, etc." (Venice, 1516). The work was originally compiled about 1386 from the writings of Joachim of Flora, John of Roquetaillande, the "Cyrillic Prophecy", and other apocalyptic treatises whose authors are mentioned in the dedicatory preface addressed to Antoniotto Adorno, the Doge of Venice. Its chief prophecies are: the schism will end in 1393 at Perugia, where the antipope and his followers will be punished; a short period of peace will follow, whereupon the Emperor Frederick III with three antipopes will inaugurate a cruel persecution of the clergy, who will be deprived of all their temporalities; King Charles of France will be imprisoned, but miraculously liberated; the "Angelic Pastor" will ascend the papal throne; under his pontificate the clergy will voluntarily renounce their temporal possessions and a general council will legislate that the income of the clergy is limited to what is necessary for a decent livelihood; the "Angelic Pastor" will take from the German electors the right to elect the emperor, he will crown the French King Charles emperor, and restore the Church to its original poverty and service of God; finally, the pope and the emperor will undertake a crusade, regain the Holy Land, and bring the Jews, Greeks, and infidels back to Christ. A refutation of these prophecies, written by the German theologian Henry of Langenstein, is printed in Pez, "Thesaurus Anecdotorum Noviss," I, II (Augsburg, 1721–9), 507–64.

KAMPERS, *Kaiserprophetien u. Kaisersagen* (Munich, 1896), 235 sq.; PASTOR, *Gesch. der Päpste.*, tr. ANTROBUS, I (London, 1891), 152–5.

MICHAEL OTT.

Tell el-Amarna Tablets, THE, are a collection of some 350 clay tablets found in 1887 amid the ruins of the ancient Egyptian city of Akhetaton (modern Tell el-Amarna) about midway between Memphis and Thebes. 200 of them are now in Berlin, 82 in the British Museum, 50 in Cairo, 22 in Oxford; only a few are private property. They are written in the Babylonian language and cuneiform characters and date from the fifteenth century B. C. They consist mostly of letters and State records sent to Kings Amenhotep III and Amenhotep IV of Egypt, by rulers of Western Asia (Babylonia, Assyria, Mittani) and provincial governors of Amurru (Northern Syria) and Canaan (Palestine). All these documents throw considerable light on the conditions of Western Asia from about 1500 to 1300 B. C.; they contain most precious information concerning the history, geography, religion, and language of the predecessors and contemporaries of the Hebrews in Palestine, and, in many cases, illustrate and confirm what we already know from the Old Testament.

The best work on the Tell el-Amarna tablets (transcription, German translation, glossary, and notes) is that of KNUDTZON, *Die El Amarna Tafeln* in *Hinrichs' Vorderasiatische Bibliothek*, II (Leipzig, 1907–9). The Berlin and Cairo tablets were edited by ABEL and WINCKLER, *Der Thontafelfund von El Amarna* (1889–90), and those in the British Museum by BEZOLD, *The Tell el-Amarna Tablets in the B. M.* (London, 1892). For all tablets known in 1896 see also: WINCKLER, *Die Thontafeln von Tell-el-Amarna* (transcription, German translation, and glossary); SCHRADER, *Keilinschriftliche Bibliothek* (Berlin, 1896); English translation by METCALF (Berlin and New York, 1896); CONDER, *The Tell-Amarna Tablets* (2nd ed., London, 1894); NIEBUHR, *The Tell-el-Amarna Period; Relations of Egypt and Western Asia in the 15th century B. C. according to the Tell-el-Amarna tablets* (*The Ancient East*), (London, 1901); FLANDERS PETRIE, *Tell el-Amarna* (London, 1894); IDEM, *Syria and Egypt from the Tell el-Amarna Letters* (London, 1898); IDEM, *A Hist. of Ancient Egypt*, II (4th ed., London, 1904); JEREMIAS, *Das Alte Testament im Lichte des Alten Orients*. (Leipzig, 1906); WEBER, *Die Literatur der Babylonier u. Assyrer* (Leipzig, 1907); DHORME, *Les Pays Bibliques au temps d'el Amarna* in *Revue Biblique* (1908–9).

A. A. VASCHALDE.

Téllez, GABRIEL, Spanish priest and poet, better known by his pseudonym of Tirso de Molina, b. at Madrid, c. 1571; d. at Soria, Aragón, 21 March, 1648. Little is known of his early years except that he studied at Alcalá de Henares. The exact date of his ordination to the priesthood is not known, but the earliest notice of him in that connexion is in 1610 when he is mentioned by Andrés de Claramonte y Corroy in his "Letanía Moral", as Padre Fray Gabriel Téllez of the Order of Nuestra Senora de la Merced. He appears to have devoted the last years of his life to the affairs of his order and occupied responsible offices in it. In 1619 he was superior of a convent at Trujillo in Estremadura; in 1620, and for several years following, he lived in the monastery of the order in Madrid; and in 1645 he became prior of the monastery at Soria where he died three years later. It has been stated that he adopted his *nom de plume* on account of his Holy orders, but this theory is apparently disproved by the fact that both names appeared on the same title-page.

Tirso's first printed volume, "Los Cigarrales de Toledo," appeared in Madrid in 1624 and Barcelona, 1631. The name is taken from *cigarral*, a Toledian word meaning a country house. The work is patterned after Boccaccio's "Decameron" and is a collection of tales and poems and three comedies, supposed to be recited and played by a company of ladies and gentlemen who meet at a *cigarral* for the purpose of diversion. A second collection, entitled "Deleitar aprovechando," appeared in Madrid in 1635, and contains essays, *autos sacramentales*, and three religious tales. As a dramatic writer, Tirso was very prolific. He is credited with having written four hundred plays, but only about eighty are now available. During his life his comedies were published in five parts, the first in Seville, 1627, the third in Tortosa, 1634, the second and fourth in Madrid, 1635, and the last in Madrid, 1636. These contain fifty-nine plays. The play which has given Tirso his fame is his "Burlador de Sevilla y Convidado de Piedra", in which he created the character of Don Juan, afterward immortalized by Mozart in his opera of that name and by Lord Byron in his poem. Hs is at his best in his comedies and his secular *novelas*. He excels in wit, originality of dialogue, and ingenuity of plot.

DE OCHOA, *Tesoro del Teatro Español* (Paris, 1838); HARTZENBUSCHE, *Teatro Escogido de Fr. Gabriel Téllez* (Madrid, 1839–42); MUÑOZ PEÑA, *El Teatro del Maestro Tirso de Molina* (Valladolid, 1889); BLANCA DE LOS RIOS, *Tirso de Molina* (Madrid, 1900).

VENTURA FUENTES.

Tellier, MICHEL LE, b. 19 April, 1603; d. at Paris, 30 Oct., 1685. He was commissioned by Cardinal Mazarin to organize the royal army, and having helped to appease the troubles of the Fronde, he left to his son Louvois in 1666 his duties as secretary of war. After his appointment as chancellor by Louis XIV in 1677 he had a decisive share in the revocation of the Edict of Nantes, which he signed, 2 Oct., 1685, a few days before his death. Before expiring he sang the canticle of Simeon "Nunc dimittis". He shared Louis XIV's illusion that there were almost no Protestants left in France, and that the act suppressing the liberty of Protestant worship was no more than the public recognition of an accomplished fact, the disappearance of Protestantism. His eldest son, Michel Le Tellier, Marquis de Louvois (b. at Paris, 18 Jan., 1641; d. 16 July, 1691), noted for the remarkable expedition with which he organized the armies for the wars of Louis XIV, was partly responsible for this false idea, for he led the king to believe that the dragonades, military expeditions which Louvois sent into Protestant villages, had finally overcome all resistance. The youngest son of Michel Le Tellier was Charles-Maurice Le Tellier. Michel's funeral oration was delivered by Bossuet and Fléchier.

MICHEL LE TELLIER
Engraving by Dequevauviller after a painting by Charles Champagne

ANDRÉ, *Michel Le Tellier et l'organisation de l'armée monarchique* (Paris, 1906); ROUSSET, *Hist. de Louvois* (4 vols., Paris, 1861–1863).

GEORGES GOYAU.

Telmessus, titular see in Lycia, suffragan of Myra. Telmessus (or incorrectly Telmissis) was a flourishing city west of Lycia, on a bay of the same name (also called *Glaucus sinus*). It was famed for its school of diviners, consulted among others by Crœsus, prior to declaring war against Cyrus, and by Alexander, when he came to the town after the siege of Halicarnassus. It must not be confounded with a city of the same name in Caria. Telmessus was also called Anastasiopolis in honour of the emperors of that name. Its ruins are located at Makri (1500 inhabitants, half of them Greek), the capital of a caza in the vilayet of Smyrna, and situated upon a rather important harbour. The acropolis is still in existence surrounded by walls erected by the Knights of Rhodes and the Genoese. The ruins include the remains of a theatre and a curious tomb cut in the rock. Makri derives its name from the Macra of the ancients —the Isla Longa of the medieval Italians, which lay at the entrance to the gulf. Le Quien (Oriens Christ., I, 971) mentions two bishops of Telmessus: Hilary (370) and Zenodotus, at the Council of Chalcedon (451). The latter is called "Bishop of the Metropolis of Telmessæi and the Isle of Macra". The "Notitiæ episcopatuum" mentions Telmessus among the suffragans of Myra until the tenth century, when it is no longer called Macra; in 1316 mention is made of the See of "Macra and Lybysium". Lybysium or Levissi is about four miles south-west of Makri, and has 3000 inhabitants, nearly all Greeks.

SMITH, *Dict. of Greek and Roman Geogr.* s. v.; TEXIER, *Asie mineure* (Paris, 1862), 667-670; CUINET, *La Turquie d'Asie* (Paris, 1891-4), 333, III, 676 seq.; TOMASCHEK, *Zur historischen Topographie von Kleinasien im Mittelalter* (Vienna, 1891), 44.

S. PÉTRIDÈS.

Te Lucis Ante Terminum, the hymn at Compline in the Roman Breviary. The authorship of St. Ambrose, for which Pimont contends, is not admitted by the Benedictine editors or by Biraghi (see AMBROSIAN HYMNOGRAPHY). The hymn is found in a hymnary in Irish script (described by Blume in his "Cursus", etc.) of the eighth or early ninth century; but the classical prosody of its two stanzas (*solita* in the third line of the original text is the only exception) suggests a much earlier origin. In this hymnary it is assigned, together with the hymn "Christe qui lux es et dies", to Compline. An earlier arrangement (as shown by the Rule of St. Cæsarius of Arles, c. 502) coupled with the "Christe qui lux" the hymn "Christe precamur adnue", and assigned both to the "twelfth hour" of the day for alternate recitation throughout the year. The later introduction of the "Te lucis" suggests a later origin, although in its simple dignity the hymn is not unworthy of the muse of St. Ambrose. The two hymns "Te lucis" and "Christe qui lux" did not maintain everywhere the same relative position; the latter was used in winter, the former in summer and on festivals; while many cathedrals and monasteries replaced the "Te lucis" by the "Christe qui lux" from the first Sunday of Lent to Passion Sunday or Holy Thursday—a custom followed by the Dominicans. The old Breviary of the Carthusians used the "Christe qui lux" throughout the year. The Roman Breviary assigns the "Te lucis" daily throughout the year, except from Holy Thursday (Te Lucis Ante Terminum, p. 2) to the Friday after Easter, inclusively. Merati, in his notes on Gavantus's Thesaurus, says that it has always held, without variation, this place in the Roman Church. As it is sung daily, the Vatican Antiphonary (now passing through the press) gives it many plain-song settings for the varieties of season and rite (e. g. the nine melodies, pp. 117-121, 131, 174, 356, 366).

MEARNS AND JULIAN in *Dictionary of Hymnology* (2nd ed., London, 1907), 1135, 1710. To its list of transl. add BAGSHAWE, *Breviary Hymns and Missal Sequences* (London, s. d.), no. 30; DONAHOE, *Early Christian Hymns* (New York, 1908), 41; HENRY, *Hymns of the Little Hours* in *Ecclesiastical Review* (Sept., 1890), 204-09; KENT in SHIPLEY, *Annus Sanctus*, part II, 88; PIMONT, *Les hymnes du bréviaire romain*, I (Paris, 1874), 124-30, defends (128-9) the simple directness of the language of the second stanza. *Hymns Ancient and Modern* (historical edition, London, 1909), no. 34, gives Latin text and tr., harmonized plainsong and a modern setting credited to the *Katholische Geistliche Gesangbuch* (Andernach, 1608), no. 163; DANIEL, *Thesaurus Hymnologicus*, I, 53; BLUME, *Der Cursus S. Benedicti Nursini*, etc. (Leipzig, 1908), 65, 68, 75.

H. T. HENRY.

Temiskaming, VICARIATE APOSTOLIC OF, suffragan of Ottawa, Canada, is bounded on the north by Hudson Bay and the Great Whale River; on the south by the height of land, or watershed, except in the Temiskaming district, where the southern boundary is 47° N. lat.; on the east by 72° W. long.; and on the west by 91° W. long. It was erected on 22 Sept., 1908, by dividing the Diocese of Pembroke. Father de Bellefeuille, S.S., and Father Dupuy, of Montreal, first preached the Gospel here in 1836. Annual visits were made to the Indians of the district, missions being held at the Hudson Bay Company's trading posts. The Oblates of Mary Immaculate were given charge in 1843. Father Laverlochère was the first of these zealous missionaries. They established a residence at Fort Temiskaming in 1863, but removed to Ville Marie in 1886. Lumbering succeeded the fur trade and was followed by agriculture, the fertile shores of Lake Temiskaming rapidly attracting settlers. Railway construction with the discovery of silver and gold (1903), advanced the Ontario section. The Catholic population of the vicariate is about 20,000, including some 5000 Indians. Haileybury, Ontario, is the residence of the first vicar Apostolic, the Right Rev. Elie-Anicet Latulipe. There are 17 parishes, 20 missions, and many stations, served by 21 secular priests, 4 Missionaries of the Sacred Heart (who have a college also), and 9 Oblates of Mary Immaculate. The Marist Brothers, the Sisters of the Assumption (novitiate at Haileybury), the Grey Nuns of the Cross, the Sisters of the Sacred Heart, the Sisters of Providence, and the Sisters of the Holy Family conduct four boarding-convents, two hospitals, and one industrial school and refuge for Indians, besides several parochial schools. The Rt. Rev. Elie-Anicet Latulipe, D.D., was born at St. Anicet, Province of Quebec, 3 Aug., 1859. Ordained on 30 May, 1885, he was successively curate at St. Henri, Montreal, chaplain at the convents of the Good Shepherd, Montreal, and St. Anne's, Lachine, rector of Pembroke Cathedral, and pastor of Haileybury. He was named Bishop of Catenna and first Vicar-Apostolic of Temiskaming on 1 Oct., 1908, and consecrated on 30 Nov., 1908.

JOHN R. O'GORMAN.

Temnus, a titular see in Asia, a suffragan of Ephesus. Temnus was a little town of Æolia, near the River Hermus, which is shown on its coins. Situated on an elevation it commanded the territories of Cyme, Phocæa, and Smyrna. Under Augustus it was already on the decline; under Tiberius it was destroyed by an earthquake; and in the time of Pliny it was no longer inhabited. It was however rebuilt, and became one of the suffragans of Ephesus. Le Quien (Oriens Christ., I, 707), mentions three bishops: Eustathius, who lived in 451; Theophilus, present at the Council of Nice (787); Ignatius, at Constantinople (869). This see is not mentioned in the "Notitiæ Episcopatuum". Ramsay (Asia Minor, 108) thought the Diocese of Temnus identical with that of Archangelus, which from the tenth to the thirteenth century the "Notitiæ Episcopatuum" assigns to Smyrna. In 1413 the Turks seized the fortress of Archangelus, which they called Kaiadjik, i. e., small rock; this fortress was situated on the plains of Mænomenus, now known as Menemen. Doubtless, Temnus and Menemen are the same. The latter is now the chief place in the vilayet of Smyrna, with 9000 inhabitants, of whom 2000 are Greeks, 500 Armenians, the remainder Mussulmans. However, Texier (Asie Mineure, 227) identifies Temnus with the village of Guzel Hissar, to the north of Menemen.

SMITH, *Dict. Greek and Roman Geog.*, s. v.

S. PÉTRIDÈS.

Tempel, WILHELM (ERNEST LEBERECHT), German astronomer, b. 4 December, 1821, at (Nieder-) Cunnersdorf near Löbau, Saxony; d. 16 March, 1889, in Arcetri near Florence. Having lost his mother in early infancy, he was placed under a schoolmaster from his ninth to his fourteenth year, and employed as sexton, beadle, gardener, and collector of fees on occasions of New Year, of baptisms, and marriages. He then learned the art of lithography, and about his twentieth year, went to Copenhagen with letters of recommendation to a distant relative Lehmann, the father of the Danish statesmen and journalist, Orla Lehmann. During a three-years' stay he was a welcome and frequent guest with a number of artists and academicians. The sculptor Reinhold carved his bust, and the painter Bünsen drew his portrait. His German poems to friends and benefactors show a complete mastery of his native tongue. He became enthusiastic over the literature and national songs of the Danes, and translated selections into German, e. g., "King Réné's Daughter". These three years in Denmark were, as he used to say, his academic career. With a desire to know peoples and countries from experience, he went to Christiania, but soon turned his path to the land of the fine arts. About 1850 he settled in Venice as lithographer. The Palace of the Doge seems to have attracted his artistic tastes, for he became intimately acquainted with the family of the Porter Gambin, whose daughter Marianna he married, embracing at the same time the Catholic faith. His wife testified that Tempel had never been satisfied with his former religion and purposely chose a Catholic companion in life. The marriage proved very happy, although not blessed with children. Contact with cultured people in Venice awakened in him a taste for astronomy. From his earnings he bought a 4-inch (Steinheil) comet-seeker, and in 1859 made two discoveries, one of a comet (designated 1859 I), on 2 April, and another of the Merope-Nebula in the Pleiades, on 19 October. The new talent for discoveries matured in him the plan of embracing the astronomical career. In his enthusiasm he moved to Paris, but found that lack of scientific training precluded entrance to the Imperial Observatory. Greatly disappointed by Leverrier, the director, he moved with his wife to Marseilles in 1860, where he was accepted by Benjamin Valz as assistant astronomer.

HEAD OF WILHELM TEMPEL
By Reinhold in the Observatory, Copenhagen

Tempel began his career in Marseilles with the discoveries of a comet (1860 IV) on 22 October, and of two minor planets on 4 and 8 March, 1861, all with his own 4-inch comet-seeker, on the terrace of the observatory. The position however lasted only half a year, owing partly, it would seem, to continued strained relations with Leverrier. He then settled down once more as lithographer without, however, giving rest to his comet-seeker. From window or garden he discovered, during ten years, no less than thirteen comets and four minor planets, more than half of them new. From Marseilles he began publishing his observations in the "Astronomische Nachrichten". In France he missed cordial and intellectual intercourse, and a literary attempt of his in "Les Mondes", in May, 1863, on the question of the variability of nebulæ, was severely criticized by Leverrier. In the same year (1863) he paid a two-months' visit to his native country, spending most of the time at the observatory of Leipzig. Just two years before, in 1861, a former astronomer of Leipzig, d'Arrest, had built a new observatory at Copenhagen. Unfortunately for Tempel, d'Arrest was the very one who criticized his publication on the Merope-Nebula as exaggerated, although the controversy ended in justifying Tempel's assertion, that nebulæ must be observed with low magnifying powers. Tempel's effort, in 1870, to get a position under d'Arrest was fruitless.

In January, 1871, the Provisional Government ordered the Germans out of Marseilles. In spite of his experiences in France, Tempel sympathized with the unfortunate country during the war. Arrived at Milan he found in Schiaparelli the man who appreciated his talents. Though he had no academic degrees, he was offered a position in the Brera Observatory. Two of Tempel's comets had attracted Schiaparelli's attention: that of 1866 (I) which furnished to him the proof of connexion with the November stream of meteors, and that of 1867 (II) which proved to revolve entirely between the orbits of Mars and Jupiter and to run almost parallel with the latter planet in 1869, so as to furnish a type specimen of planetary perturbation. Comet "1869 III" is called Tempel's "third periodic comet", but its periodicity was not recognized until 1880. Four new comets were discovered in Milan. Comet "1873 II", called Tempel's "second periodic", is remarkable for the shortness of its period, being little over five years, and second only to Encke's comet. Tempel's publication in the Milan "Ephemeris" for 1872 shows that he reduced his own observations. His mind was sufficiently mathematical to acquire the use of logarithms and trigonometry and to draw elliptical orbits. Number V of the Brera Publications contains masterly lithographic plates of a lunar eclipse (1 June, 1863), of the Merope-Nebula, of Jupiter's satellites and a series of Coggia's Comet. A more perfect map of the Pleiades appeared in "Monthly Notices" (XL, 1880). Contact with Schiaparelli brought honours to Tempel. The Vienna Academy rewarded him four times for the discovery of comets, the two of 1869 discovered in Marseilles, and the two of 1871. Once in 1872, in the absence of the director, he received the Emperor of Brazil at the observatory, acted as cicerone, and presented some of his drawings. The year after, he received, through the Brazilian Consul, the diploma of "Knight of the Imperial Brazilian Order of Roses".

When, in 1873, the Arcetri Observatory lost its director Donati, by death, Schiaparelli proposed Tempel as successor. The severe winters of Milan and the prospect of an independent position made it easy for Tempel to accept, although the unfinished state of the buildings and instruments, the title and scanty salary of assistant astronomer, the lack of library and assistants, were fraught with disappointments. After four years' work in Milan (1871–74) Tempel moved to his last station, which he was to hold for fourteen years. He found the observatory situated in an earthly paradise. It was designed and commenced in 1869 by Donati, under the University of Florence, but interrupted in 1872 by Donati's sickness. For two years it had been left in this state. The rain poured in on all sides and a wall of the meridian room had to be supported. A description of the observatory is given by Tempel in the "Astr. Nachr.", CII (1882). The predecessor of Donati, Amici, had constructed two object-glasses, one of 9.4 inches and one of 11 inches, large sizes in those times, but their mountings were imperfect and incomplete. The former had a wooden stand and could only be used on the terrace; pointing to objects of over 40° altitude was found dangerous. The mounting of the largest instrument was parallactic, but without divided circles, without clock-work, without clamp and slow motion. The observing chair was a ladder that did not reach to stars within 20° of the horizon. Both instruments had only one eye-piece. The books present contained no star catalogues, and were lying on the floor. Money was still owing on the building, and no resources for the future open. The habitation was so defective that Tempel had to live in a neighbouring villa until his death.

On examination the object-glasses proved a little

defective in colour correction but excellent in definition; hence less adapted for planets, but perfectly suitable for comets, asteroids, and nebulæ, the very programme of Tempel. Nebulæ, however, became now his main field. In Arcetri he picked up only one more comet, "1877 V". The work with the large equatorial proved very slow and laborious. To find and to identify the stars, the observer had to descend from the ladder, use the comet-seeker on the terrace and make triangulations on the small charts at hand, all without electric light. And yet, after four years' work, Tempel presented to the Royal Academy of the Lincei a collection of drawings of the more interesting nebulæ, which secured him the royal prize given every six years for the best astronomical work in Italy. The Academy even offered to publish the drawings, but the proofs of the lithographs did not satisfy the author. The designs are the more valuable as they contain many stars, measured with a double ringmicrometer. Tempel discovered many new nebulæ, observed a number that had been neglected since Herschel's time, wrote a mass of careful notes that are not yet published, occasionally correcting errors. Extracts of his observations are found in the "Astr. Nachr." (vols. 93–113). Drawings of the Orion nebula were published in the "Astr. Nachr.", vol. LVIII (1862), and in the Memoirs of the R. Bohemian Society of 1885 (reviewed in the Vierteljahrsschrift, XXII). Tempel was elected foreign associate of the Royal Astronomical Society of England in 1881, together with Gyldén, Pickering, Tietjen, and Tisserand (Monthly Notices, XLI, 377). In 1886 he was honoured with a letter from King Humbert, handed to him by the Adjutant General, in recognition of his astronomical drawings. In the intercourse with scientific men, the lack of academic training betrayed itself occasionally, and Tempel himself regretted all his life that he had not learnt Latin. Diffusiveness of style and uncritical assertions provoked contradiction. A controversy with Dreyer, the astronomer of Birr Castle, about the reality of spiral forms in many of Lord Rosse's drawings of nebulæ, may be found in "The Observatory" (vols. I–II, 1878). The existence of a faint nebula drawn by Tempel (near H. 1 55 Pegasi) was denied by Keeler (Astroph. J. XI, 1900).

Tempel's intercourse with old friends in Copenhagen remained cordial to his end. He received them or friends recommended by them, like brothers, and always regretted that his means did not allow him to revisit Copenhagen. His letters to them breathe a deeply religious spirit. He glories in his honesty from childhood, regrets complaining about injuries received, speaks of the blessings of Providence, of friendship beyond death, gives thanks and praises to God, promises prayers to friends and benefactors, and looks confidently towards eternity. Expressions like these made his Protestant friend say in the "Dagbladet": "During the many years' sojourn in Italy his mind, which was subject to depressions, had found peace by entering the Catholic Church". The same friend assured the writer of this article that, on a visit to Arcetri, he had found Tempel very happy in his religious convictions. His dearest company was an old priest who visited him regularly. A Franciscan from the Convent of Quaracchi was his confessor, and the Carthusians of the Certosa were his friends. Towards the end of 1886 Tempel was attacked by a liver complaint and, in the beginning of 1887, by partial paralysis. Unable to observe, he put his notes in order for publication. During his illness he received the sacraments repeatedly. The parish priest of S. Leonardo (now Canon Emilio Nunziati) testifies that Tempel was a thoroughly convinced Catholic and died a saintly death, having his mind clear to the last. Tempel was hardly sixty-eight years old. He is buried near the tomb of Donati, in the cemetery of S. Felice a Elma, a suburb of Florence. He left neither debts nor property, and his widow was provided for by what is called in Italy a "spaccio di sali e tabacchi", this again, as it seems, through Schiaparelli. More than 186 drawings of nebulæ and stars, with numerous notes, are now the property of the university and deposited in the Tribune of Galileo (via Romana). A list of them is in the "Astron. Nachr.", CII (1882), and in the "Bohemian Memoirs" (1885).

Dagbladet (Copenhagen, 4 April, 1889); *Monthly Notices R. A. S.*, L (1890), 179; Schiaparelli, *Astron. Nachr.*, CXXI (1890), 95; Abetti, *Publicazioni*, fasc. XXVII (Arcetri, 1909), 163; Idem, *Rivista di Astronomia*, III (Turin, 1909). Private letters from Copenhagen, Armagh, and Florence.

J. G. Hagen.

Temperance (Lat. *temperare*, to mingle in due proportions; to qualify) is here considered as one of the four cardinal virtues. It may be defined as the righteous habit which makes a man govern his natural appetite for pleasures of the senses in accordance with the norm prescribed by reason. In one sense temperance may be regarded as a characteristic of all the moral virtues; the moderation it enjoins is essential to each of them. It is also according to St. Thomas (I–II, Q. cxli, a. 2) a special virtue. Thus, it is the virtue which bridles concupiscence or which controls the yearning for pleasures and delights which most powerfully attract the human heart. These fall mainly into three classes: some are associated with the preservation of the human individual; others with the perpetuation of the race, and others still with the well-being and comfort of human life. Under this aspect temperance has for subordinate virtues, abstinence, chastity, and modesty. Abstinence prescribes the restraint to be employed in partaking of food and drink. Obviously the measure of this self-restraint is not constant and invariable. It is different for different persons as well as for different ends in view. The diet of an anchorite would not do for a farm labourer. Abstinence is opposed to the vices of gluttony and drunkenness. The disorder of these is that food and drink are made use of in such wise as to damage instead of benefit the bodily health. Hence gluttony and drunkenness are said to be intrinsically wrong. That does not mean, however, that they are always grievous sins. Gluttony is seldom such; drunkenness is so when it is complete, that is when it destroys the use of reason for the time being. Chastity as a part of temperance regulates the sensual satisfactions connected with the propagation of the human species. The contrary vice is lust. As these pleasures appeal with special vehemence to human nature, it is the function of chastity to interpose the norm of reason. Thus it will decide that they are altogether to be refrained from in obedience to a higher vocation or at any rate only availed of with reference to the purposes of marriage. Chastity is not fanaticism; much less is it insensibility. It is the carrying out of the mandate of temperance in a particular department where such a steadying power is acutely needed.

The virtue of modesty, as ranged under temperance, has as its task the holding in reasonable leash of the less violent human passions. It brings into service humility to set in order a man's interior. By transfusing his estimates with truth, and increasing his self-knowledge it guards him against the radical malice of pride. It is averse to pusillanimity, the product of low views and a mean-spirited will. In the government of the exterior of a man modesty aims to make it conform to the demands of decency and decorousness (*honestas*). In this way his whole outward tenor of conduct and method of life fall under its sway. Such things as his attire, manner of speech, habitual bearing, style of living, have to be made to square with its injunctions. To be sure they cannot always be settled by hard and fast rules. Convention will often have a good deal to say in the case, but in turn will have its propriety determined by modesty. Other virtues are enumerated by St. Thomas as subordinated to temperance inasmuch as they imply moderation in the management of some passion. It ought to be noted, however, that in its primary and generally understood sense temperance is concerned with what is difficult for a man, not in so far as he is a rational being precisely, but rather in so far as he is an animal. The hardest duties for flesh and blood are self-restraint in the use of food and drink and of the venereal pleasures that go with the propagation of the race. That is why abstinence and chastity may be reckoned the chief and ordinary phases of this virtue. All that has been said receives additional force if we suppose that the self-control commanded by temperance is measured not only by the rule of reason but by the revealed law of God as well. It is called a cardinal virtue because the moderation required for every righteous habit has in the practice of temperance a specially trying arena. The satisfactions upon which it imposes a check are at once supremely natural and necessary in the present order of human existence. It is, not, however, the greatest of moral virtues. That rank is held by prudence; then come justice, fortitude, and finally temperance.

RICKABY, *Ethics and Natural Law* (London, 1908); D'ANNIBALE, *Summula theologiæ moralis* (Rome, 1908); RICKABY, *The Moral Teaching of St. Thomas* (London, 1896); ST. THOMAS, *Summa*.

JOSEPH F. DELANY.

Temperance Movements.—EUROPE.—Reasons for a temperance movement exist to a greater or less degree in all the countries of Europe, although the kind and amount of alcoholic drinks consumed vary greatly in the different lands. In former days the greatest amount of drunkenness was to be found in Russia and Sweden, while now the latter country is the most temperate of all. On the other hand, conditions at present are very bad in France and Belgium, largely because these are almost the only lands where absinthe is habitually drunk. Unfortunately, it is just in these countries that there are but few signs of an energetic temperance movement, for in them wine and beer are still called "hygienic drinks". A strong opposition to the use of alcoholic liquors exists in Great Britain, in the Scandinavian kingdoms, and, for the last ten years, in the Netherlands and Germany. It is only of late that the southern countries of Europe have begun to take part in the temperance movement, and of these Italy is the most active.

A. *Consumption of Alcohol.*—Statistics as to the consumption of intoxicating liquors should be used with great caution, especially when different countries are compared. The amount of alcohol in various liquors, and even in the same liquor in different countries, varies greatly. The most reliable international statistics concerning alcoholic beverages are probably those repeatedly issued since 1897 by the British Board of Trade. These statistics were taken by the Imperial Bureau of Statistics at Berlin in 1906 as the basis for the excellent papers on the alcohol question that appeared in the "Reichsarbeitsblatt". According to them, the average amount of alcohol in distilled liquors may be taken as 50 per cent; in wine in Germany and Switzerland, 10 per cent; in wine in Italy, France, Belgium, and Holland, 12 per cent; in Great Britain, 15 per cent; the average amount of alcohol in beer may be taken as 4 per cent (in Great Britain, 6 per cent). The alcoholic beverages most generally used are distilled spirits, beer, and wine. The drinking of absinthe, since its prohibition by popular vote in Switzerland in 1908, is limited to France and Belgium, where the prohibition is to a large degree evaded. Distilled spirits is the principal alcoholic beverage in the following countries: Russia, where it is 93 per cent of all the alcoholic beverages consumed; the three Scandinavian countries, 65–69 per cent; Austria-Hungary, 59 per cent. The largest proportion of beer is drunk in Great Britain (78 per cent of all alcoholic beverages consumed) and Belgium (64 per cent). Wine is the alcoholic beverage most used in the following countries: Switzerland, 58 per cent of all alcoholic beverages; France, 75 per cent; Italy, 95 per cent. In Germany, besides a small consumption of wine, an almost equal amount of beer and spirits is used (beer, 49 per cent; spirits, 44 per cent). The figures are, of course, quite different if the question is as to the amount of liquor actually drunk. The amount depends in the first place on whether moderate drinking is the daily habit in a country, or whether alcoholic beverages are drunk only occasionally, even though immoderately; and, secondly, whether beverages containing a large amount of alcohol are most used, or the consumption is of weaker ones, but in larger quantities. This is the reason why the beer-drinking countries rank first when the inquiry is how much alcoholic drink is consumed per capita of population, while, on the other hand, the lands where the largest amounts of wine and brandy are consumed take the lead if the question is as to the amount of alcohol consumed. In the former respect, Belgium stands first with a consumption of nearly 54.22 gallons per capita of population, 49.52 gallons being beer; then come Great Britain and Switzerland, each about 33.01 gallons per capita; Germany, 30.66 gallons; Italy and France, each 28.30 to 30.66 gallons; Denmark, 25.94 gallons. In the other countries the consumption is less than 25 gallons per capita, e. g. Norway, 4 gallons; Holland and Russia, each about 2.35 gallons. On the other hand, the countries where the largest quantity of alcohol is drunk are: France, 4 gallons per capita, and Italy, 3.7 gallons. The countries showing the lowest figures are: Holland, .94 gallon; Russia, .61 gallon; Norway, .51 gallon. Germany and Austria are in the middle with about 2.24 gallons. If, finally, the individual beverages are considered, the largest consumption of distilled spirits is in Denmark, 3.3 gallons per capita, and Austria-Hungary, 2.39 gallons; the largest consumption of beer is in Bavaria and Belgium, where it is more than 50 gallons per capita; the consumption of wine is largest in Italy, 27.59 gallons, and France, 36.55 gallons. The absolute figures are as follows: Germany, 58,962,028.3 gallons of distilled spirits, 1,757,675,471.69 gallons of beer, 87,264,150.94 gallons of wine, for which nearly £150,000,000 ($714,500,000) is paid annually, a sum nearly three times as large as the cost of the German army and navy. The annual expenditure in Austria for alcoholic beverages is about £104,166,000 ($500,000,000).

B. *Development of the Temperance Movement.*—Two main periods are to be distinguished. The first, which began about 1830, was fairly general, but substantially affected only the British Isles and the Germanic countries. The second began in 1850 in Great Britain; after a decade it extended to Scandinavia, and after thirty years to Germany. It was, however, only at the close of the century that it attained its great importance, by gradually obtaining a footing in all civilized countries. In both periods the immediate stimulus came from the United States of North America. The chief distinction between the earlier and later movements is generally expressed thus: that the former laid the emphasis on temperance, the latter on total abstinence. But this hardly reaches the root of the matter. Apart from the fact that even in the earlier period teetotal societies existed in England (from 1832), refraining from spirituous beverages was at that time practically equivalent to total abstinence, as other intoxicating drinks were almost unknown, or at least their injurious qualities were much underrated. Beer was then strongly recommended (even in popular songs) as a "most delicious drink"; thus the brewing industry was encouraged. It was thought that poisonous substances existed only in distilled spirits, consequently nothing was said of combating alcohol, but always distilled spirits, and this through abstinence. The earlier movement is better characterized by calling it the era of naïve enthusiasm, supported especially by religious ideas. Drunkenness was regarded chiefly as a vice to be overcome by strong religious sentiments. Clergymen were the principal leaders of the movement, and the pledge was its highest attainment.

The new movement is more dispassionate; its fundamental ideas are largely hygienic and social. The nature of alcoholic beverages has been more thoroughly investigated and the danger of habitual moderate drinking, which merely avoids intoxication, has been recognized. Intemperance is no longer generally regarded as a matter of individual morality, but as a menace to the public health (because of its effects on the offspring) and as a danger to national welfare (inasmuch as it promotes criminality and immorality, while lessening mental and economic productivity). The present movement is promoted by physicians, sociologists, and government officials; its final aim is rather to do away with the drinking of alcohol either by national prohibition or by local option. Still, of late, the religious side of the movement has shown renewed vigour, especially in rescue work for drunkards; and strong religious organizations have sprung up, especially among the Catholics of Germany and Holland. It is entirely in keeping with the social character of the movement that the effort is made to influence children and young people also (as in the "Bands of Hope") and that even the schools are called on to co-operate by means of special instruction.

The first traces of an organized temperance movement in Europe are found in the union formed at Växjö, Sweden, in 1819, by a number of pupils at a gymnasium under the guidance of Per Wieselgren (1800–77), who afterwards became famous as the father of the Swedish temperance agitation. The members of the union pledged themselves to abstain from all harmful spirituous beverages. However, impulses from America ("American Temperance Society", 1826) first led to the foundation of regular societies—almost immediately in Ireland (New Ross, 1829; by 1830, 60 societies); Scotland (Greenock, 1829; the "Scottish Temperance Society", a central organization, founded in 1831, soon had 300 branches); England (Bradford, 1830; by the end of 1830, 30 local societies; the "British and Foreign Temperance Society", 1831); Sweden (Stockholm, 1830; the "Swedish Temperance Society", a central organization, founded in 1837, had 100,000 members by 1845). The movement spread most rapidly in Ireland, where from 1834 Father Mathew (q. v.), probably the greatest preacher of temperance of all times, laboured with extraordinary success; by 1844 he had secured nearly 5,500,000 adherents. In Dublin alone 180,000 took the pledge from him; later he went to England, gaining 60,000 in London, then to Scotland and America. In 1858 the "Irish Temperance League", now the most important abstinence organization in Ireland, was founded. As in Sweden, the first movement in Norway and Germany was also an independent one, but it did not attain in either country much importance until it came into contact with the American and English movements. In Norway, Kjell Andresen established throughout the country numerous societies which, in 1845, he united into a central organization, "Den norske verening modbraendevinsdrikken", an association that received at once considerable financial aid from the State.

The campaign was opened in Germany about 1800 by a number of medical treatises, especially those of Hufeland (Die Branntweinvergiftung), and also the circular addressed by King Frederick William III of Prussia to the Protestant consistories urging them to exhort the people to abstain from spirits. The first societies were established at Hamburg in 1830 and at Dresden in 1832, through English influence. About 1833 Frederick William III asked the American Government for information concerning the temperance movement. In answer to this request Robert Baird, author of the epoch-making "History of the Temperance Societies in the United States", was sent to Europe in 1835. At Berlin Baird gave the French version of his work to the king, who had it translated immediately into German, and 30,000 copies distributed. The movement was now carried on with great zeal, mainly by the different Churches. The chief workers among the Catholics were: Father Seling (1792–1860) in the Diocese of Osnabrück; the Archpriest Fitzek and Father Schaffranek in Silesia; the missioner Hillebrandt in Westphalia; Father Ketterer and other Jesuits in Ermland; much influence was also exerted by the writings of the popular author Alban Stolz. Father Mathew's work was taken as the model of the movement, but an effort was made to secure greater permanence by forming temperance confraternities; these still exist in the east of Germany. The work was carried on among Protestants by Pastor Böttcher of Hanover (also active as a writer) and by Freiherr von Seld, who covered much territory lecturing on temperance. The result of these labours was that when the first temperance congress was held (Hamburg, 1843) there were already over 450 temperance societies in Northern Germany, and 1702 when the second congress was held (Berlin, 1845). At the same date the total number of abstainers in Germany was stated to be 1,650,000, of whom over 500,000 were in Upper Silesia. This was the culminating point of the movement, which rapidly declined after the Revolution of 1848. Besides the countries already mentioned, the early movement attained prominence only in Holland and Denmark, although the American influence was felt in other countries also. In 1842 the "Nederlandsche Vereeniging tot abschaffing van sterken drank" was formed at Leyden; its membership rose to over 20,000 and then declined. Baird spent 1840 in Denmark; 40 societies were quickly formed there, and, in 1845, were united into a national association with its own newspaper, the "Folkevennen". In Denmark also the conflict between the temperance and total abstinence advocates ended the entire movement.

With the exception of England, where the High Church Anglicans founded (1862) the "Church of England Temperance Society", which quickly attained great success, little progress was made in Europe from 1860 to 1870. Pastor Böttcher, it is true, succeeded in organizing another continental congress at Hanover in 1863, but the interest in temperance had died out. Nearly twenty years afterwards begins the later movement, which in most countries was distinctly influenced by the "Order of Good Templars", and in Switzerland and adjacent countries also by the society of the "Blue Cross", founded by Pastor Rochat at Geneva in 1877 as a society for the rescue of drunkards. In 1868 the "Independent Order of Good Templars" extended from America to England, where, at first, internal dissensions occasioned an acute crisis. About ten years later the order was established in Scandinavia (Norway, 1877; Sweden, 1879; Denmark, 1880). In these countries it proved more successful than anywhere else, particularly in Sweden, where, owing to the exertions of Oscar Eklund and Edvard Wavrinsky, its membership in 1887 was over 60,000. It must be acknowledged that here also internal discords had to be overcome. In 1883 the order entered Germany, appearing first at Hadersleben in the Danish-speaking district, and in 1887 the first German lodge was established at Flensburg. The main strength of the order is still in Schleswig-Holstein and Hamburg. In the same year (1887) the first lodge was established in Switzerland. It is only within the last ten years that grand lodges have been established in Holland and Austria.

Organizations of the different social classes and business men have become of great importance in the new movement. The first of these societies was the "British Medical Temperance Association", formed by the English physicians in 1876. Special organizations for clergymen, teachers, railway men, and workmen have been established, and are striving with increasing success to form international associations. Unfortunately, the Social Democrats have in many instances used the movement as a means for carrying on their own agitation, and in this way have gained the sympathy of many who would otherwise hold aloof from them. This statement, however, has little application to Germany. Women take an increasingly great part in the work of temperance. The "Woman's Christian Temperance Union", established in the United States in 1873, became a world-wide association in 1883, and then affiliated many national associations (some very small) in Europe. Owing to these energetic labours the number of total abstainers has increased greatly in most countries; in some they form from 5 to 12 per cent of the entire population, as: United Kingdom, about 5,000,000 (including 3,200,000 children); Sweden, 500,000; Norway, 240,000 (including 65,000 children); Denmark, 170,000; Germany, over 220,000 (including 85,000 children); Switzerland, 75,000 (including 26,000 children); Finland and Holland, each 30,000; and Iceland, 5000. The total number in Europe may be safely estimated at over 6,500,000.

C. *Present Status of the Temperance Movement.*—Under this head will be considered: the international organizations, which, with one exception, are total abstinence societies; the larger associations of the individual countries; the Catholic movement, which is of chief interest here; finally, the most important congresses, in which in a certain manner the associations show their concentrated strength and the success of the movement.

(1) *International Organizations.*—The largest organization is still that of the "Independent Order of Good Templars", which has 18 grand lodges in Europe; of these 6 are in Great Britain, 2 in Germany, 1 each in Ireland, Scotland, Denmark, Norway, Sweden, Holland, Belgium, Switzerland, Roumania, and Hungary. There are also some district lodges in France and Russia. The total number of lodges on the Continent is 4661 with 257,638 members, and 1855 lodges for the young with 123,634 members. In Great Britain there are 2266 lodges with 92,725 members and 1380 lodges for the young with 109,220 members. A strong competitor of this order in Switzerland is the "Neutral Independent Order of Good Templars", established in 1906 by Professor Forel, because he considered the large order laid too much stress on religious elements. The Swiss grand lodge of the new order contains 3500 adults and 3200 young members; the German, 2100 members. A large number of the Dutch, Belgian, French, and Hungarian lodges have also joined the Neutral Order. On account of the law in Austria regarding associations a national association with ten local branches has been formed under the special title "Nephalia". The organization next in size is the "Blue Cross" (headquarters at Geneva), which contains about 1550 branches and 60,000 members, including a large number of reformed drunkards (9000 in Germany). Divided as to the different countries the number of societies is as follows: Switzerland, 468; Germany, 661; Denmark, 364 (the organization is here called "Det blaa Kors"); France, 65; there are also several scattered societies in Belgium, Russia, and Hungary. Affiliated to the "Blue Cross" is an association for youth called the "Band of Hope for German Switzerland" (*Deutsch-schweizerische Hoffnungsbund*). A society small in membership but important on account of the circulation of its publications is the "International Anti-Alcoholic Association" (*Int. Alkoholgegnerbund*) with national organizations in Germany and Switzerland. Affiliated with this since 1907 is the "International Bureau for Combating Alcoholism" (*Int. Bureau zur Bekämpfung des Alkoholismus*), Lausanne, conducted by Dr. Hercod, which possesses a large bureau of information.

Notwithstanding their international organizations, two associations, the "Independent Order of Rechabites" and the "Blue Ribbon", are essentially English societies. The "Rechabites" form a life insurance society with 300,000 members, and have a few branches in Germany and Denmark; the "Blue Ribbon" has about 1,000,000, of whom less than a tenth are in Denmark, Norway, and Sweden. The international organization of women, the "Woman's Christian Temperance Union", is strongest in English-speaking countries. Among its numerous branches on the Continent, those of Germany and Switzerland are prominent for their activity, especially in the establishing of temperance eating-houses. Of all the international associations of different social classes the "International Society of Physicians" is, owing to the view now taken of the alcohol question, the most important. This society includes the German-speaking countries, Scandinavia, Russia, and Belgium. The "International Railway Anti-Alcoholic Association" (founded in 1904 by de Terra) has branches in Germany, Austria, Switzerland, and Denmark. The "International Association against the Abuse of Spirituous Beverages", founded in 1905, includes about 30 organizations in Germany, England, Holland, Belgium, France, and Russia. These are temperance societies, and promote equally total abstinence and temperance. The association aims at establishing an international bureau against alcohol.

(2) *National Associations.*—Most important of those in Germany is the "Association Against the Abuse of Spirituous Beverages" (*Verein gegen Missbrauch geist. Getränke*); this was established in 1883 and has 37,000 members who take no personal pledge. The society carries on its work by periodicals, pamphlets (of which over a million were circulated in 1908), charts, exhibitions etc. Among the total abstinence societies are: the "German Federation of the Blue Cross Societies of the Evangelical Church" (*Deutsche Bund evangelisch-kirchlicher Blaukreuzvereine*), with 8500 members; several societies that have separated from the "Independent Order of Good Templars"; and abstinence societies for various classes of society, as workmen, school-children, teachers, post-office officials, lawyers, philologists etc.; the societies for lawyers and philologists are confined to German territory. In defence of their common interest nearly all the German total abstinence societies have joined the "General German Union for Combating Alcoholism" (*Allgemeiner deutscher Zentralband zur Bekämpfung des Alkoholismus*) of Hamburg, which has a large bureau of information, a section for testing beverages free from alcohol, a bureau for lectures, etc. Germany has altogether sixty large anti-alcoholic organizations.

The movement against alcohol is weak in Austria, probably because the Government puts great difficulties in the way of international organizations. The large associations, about thirty in number, have nearly all sprung up within the last few years. The temperance societies (*Oest. Verein gegen Trunksucht* and similar provincial societies in Vorarlberg, the German Tyrol, and Moravia) have attained considerable importance. The leading abstinence society is undoubtedly the Polish "Eleuterya", with 5300 members in 20 branches. The "Central Union of Austrian Anti-Alcoholic Societies" (*Zentralverband öst. Alkoholgegnervereine*"), in Vienna, serves as a common headquarters for most of these societies. Besides the "Neutral Independent Order of Good Templars", Hungary possesses a fairly important abstinence association for workmen (1100 members) and a central organization. The main organizations in Switzerland are international. Compared with these the national societies are not very important, excepting the "Catholic Abstinence League" (see below). Among the national associations all that call for mention are: the "Alliance Abstinence Union" of Lausanne; the temperance societies, the "Society of St. Gall against the Abuse of Spirituous Liquors" (*St. Gallischerverein gegen den Missbrauch geistiger Getränke*), with 14,000 members, and the "Patriotic League of Switzerland against Alcoholism" (*Ligue patriotique suisse contre l'alcoolisme*). The total abstainers have complete control; the active participation of pupils in schools and children is especially worthy of mention. The "Swiss Abstinence Secretariate" at Lausanne is the headquarters for the society. In Holland there is still considerable rivalry between the total abstinence and the temperance advocates. The organizations of the latter are large, particularly the "People's Union" (*Volksbond*), which has over 20,000 members. Most of the societies are connected with the different Churches; the Protestant ones, five in number, have since 1907 been united in the "People's Union of the Christian Anti-Alcoholic Societies of Holland" (*Niederländischer Volksbund der christlichen Antialkoholvereine*).

Hitherto the associations in Belgium and France have been almost exclusively temperance societies; in both countries temperance societies for school-children play an important part. The "French National League against Alcoholism" (*Ligue nat. française contre l'alcoolisme*) has nearly 100,000 members in 1730 branches, of which many are for children. Belgium has also a similar "Patriotic League" and 120,000 children in more than 5000 temperance societies organized during the last thirty years through the efforts of school inspector Robyn. Only the beginnings of a temperance movement are to be found in Italy. In 1907 various local organizations united in the "Italian Anti-Alcohol Federation" (*Federazione Antialcoolista Italiana*), which allows daily half a litre (about a pint) of wine at meal-times. The members of the federation are mainly Social Democrats. Still less organization is there in Spain, where the first associations are just beginning to be formed. Portugal is without organization. Total abstinence prevails in the Scandinavian kingdoms, Iceland, and Finland, although home-brewed beer appears to be still frequently permitted. The Norwegian society "Det Norske Totalafholdsselskab" has 135,000 members. In Sweden, besides the very strong "Independent Order of Good Templars", there are the Social-Democratic "Verdandiorden" and many total abstinence societies for different classes, as physicians, students, teachers, preachers, soldiers, merchants, nurses etc., as well as a society for giving instruction in abstinence. A central abstinence bureau exists in both countries. The largest abstinence society in Denmark is the "Danmarks Afholdsforening" (about 60,000 members). Many total abstainers also belong to the "Good Templars" and the "Blue Cross".

(3) Catholic Temperance Organizations.—Just as Catholics shared in the earlier movement sixty or seventy years ago they have also of late years taken an active part in the battle against alcohol. At first the entirely Catholic countries, excepting Belgium, had not a very large share in the movement. Generally speaking, Germany, Switzerland, Holland, and England have been the chief champions of the cause. About 1885 the Catholic movement began in Belgium. Under the leadership of Abbé Lemmens there now exists a federation consisting of nine large associations with about 600 local branches and 50,000–60,000 members, who, as a body, represent temperance, not total abstinence. The most important of these associations are the "Sint-Jansgenootschap" in the Province of Limburg (which has a division for young people founded and conducted by Canon Senden), the "Onthoudersbond van West-Flanderen", and the "Société belge de Tempérance". The main organization in Germany is the "Alliance of the Cross" (*Kreuzbündnis*), a society of Catholic abstainers, with headquarters at Heidhausen near Werden. This organization was established in 1899 by Father Neumann as a temperance society; in 1904 a separate section for total abstainers was formed, and since 1909 the entire organization has been a total abstinence society, with sections for women (*Frauenbund*), for young people (*Johannesbund*), and for children (*Schutzengelbund*). Altogether the association has a membership of 12,000 adults and 60,000 children. Unfortunately, the children's society has divided, about half of its members joining the "Catholic Temperance Society" (*Kath. Mässigkeitsbund*), established in 1905 (headquarters at Trier). Recently the relations of this latter society to the "Alliance of the Cross" have constantly grown more strained, and it has even established a total abstinence branch (*Kreuzbund*) of its own. Excellent work is done by the Catholics of Switzerland, where the former Bishop of St-Gall, Augustine Egger (1833–1904), laboured as an apostle of temperance. Good feeling exists there between the different tendencies of the movement, although total abstinence is the most conspicuous. The "Swiss Catholic Abstinence League" (*Schweizerische kath. Abstinentenliga*), founded in 1895 with headquarters at St-Gall, has 90 branches and nearly 4000 members, three-fourths of whom are Germans. Affiliated with this society is the "Young People's Union of German Switzerland" (*Deutsch-Schweizerischer Jugendbund*) which has over 60 branches with 10,500 members; a similar union (*Réveil*) for French Switzerland has 22 branches and 1200 members. Nearly all the members of the society previously mentioned, "St. Galler Bezirksvereins gegen Missbrauch geistiger Getränke", are Catholics. In Holland Dr. Ariens and Dr. Banning established in 1895 the "Kruis verbonden" which has over 30,000 members; both this and the special associations for women (*Mariavereenigingen*), which have about 30,000 members, admit temperance and total abstinence advocates. Instead of children's societies, associations have been formed of parents who promise not to give their children (minors) any alcoholic beverage; these are called the "St. Anna vereenigingen" (membership 25,000). These societies are arranged according to dioceses and since 1907 their central organization has been the "Sobrietas" with headquarters at Maastricht. Since 1901 Austria also has had its "Catholic Alliance of the Cross" and "Schutzengelbund"; so far, however, the membership has not reached 1000. Hungary has a Catholic temperance society with 10,000 members. The French Catholics have the "White Cross" society (*Croix blanche*). Some beginnings of international organizations should, finally, be mentioned: the "Abstinence Society for Priests" (650 members) in Germany, Austria-Hungary, Switzerland, and Holland; the "Catholic Academic Abstinence Union" with about 100 members in Germany, Austria, and Switzerland. The "International Catholic Association", opposed to moderate drinking of spirituous liquors, is, so far, of little importance. Mention should also be made of a branch of the Order of Benedictines founded by Father Hager, the members of which are both total abstainers and vegetarians; the mother-house is at Innsbruck.

(4) Congresses.—The great international congresses

against alcoholism meet regularly every two years; the sessions, excepting that held in 1909 in London, have always been held on the Continent. According to official statistics thirteen congresses have been held (1912). The congress has met twice at The Hague, and once at each of the following cities: Paris, Brussels, Antwerp, Christiania, Stockholm, Bremen, Vienna, Budapest, Zürich, Basle, London. At first the advocates of temperance exercised most influence; in 1887 at Zürich and in 1903 at Bremen sharp disputes arose between this party and the total abstainers, who now control the meetings of the congresses. Since 1899 the Holy See has been repeatedly represented. Full reports of the sessions of the congresses are published. For about ten years a German total abstinence congress has been held on an average every two years, the seventh meeting being at Augsburg in 1910; similar congresses have been held for Scandinavia and Finland for the same length of time at the same intervals. The eighth Swiss abstinence congress was held at Lausanne in 1910; at its sessions local option was urged. In other countries the holding of national conferences began at still later dates: the first Austrian congress against alcohol was held at Vienna in 1908; the first Russian at St. Petersburg in 1910; the first Italian at Milan in 1910; the first French total abstinence congress at Grenoble in 1910. A French congress of the opponents of the use of alcohol (held in 1903) was not of much importance. The Catholics of Holland and Belgium have so far had two national congresses. Among the special congresses held by the members of a single organization, those of the "Good Templars" are noteworthy. In some countries, particularly Germany and Switzerland, there are societies which hold educational courses of a scientific character for the study of alcoholism.

(5) Successes of the Temperance Movement.—The main success is the increased understanding, everywhere apparent, of its claims. Civil rulers repeatedly emphasize in their public utterances the great importance of strict temperance, while churchmen of high rank are either total abstainers or else warm friends of the movement, in whose interest they have issued many pastoral letters. As regards legislative action the advance of the movement is slower. Complete prohibition exists in Iceland. In Finland it has been repeatedly demanded from the provincial diet, and a similar demand has been made once in Sweden. As in these two countries the number of deputies who are total abstainers grows continually larger (in Sweden they form one-half of the house), the Governments cannot permanently withstand the pressure. In Sweden the ministry in 1911 appointed a special commission to take the preparatory steps. Prohibition of spirits for the country districts in general exists in Sweden, Norway, and Finland, and a local option law for the cities, which is to a great extent enforced. An energetic struggle is now being carried on in Holland, Switzerland, and Germany for a local option law. In criminal jurisprudence the Pollard system is slowly winning adherents; of late two small German states have adopted it, and it is elsewhere in use. Russia and Switzerland have introduced a government monopoly of spirits, but this has not been of any particular use to the temperance movement, except that in Switzerland one-tenth of the profits (alcohol tithe) must be applied to the work against alcoholism. Many countries voluntarily give such aid, as: Sweden, about 200,000 kronen ($54,000) in 1910–1911; Norway about 17,000 kronen ($4590); Holland, 20,000 florins ($8000), etc. A number of countries have introduced special instruction in temperance into the primary schools, notably Belgium, Sweden (where there is a special course for male and female teachers), Norway, and France. Especially great has been the effect of the temperance movement on the reform of taverns. The celebrated Gothenburg system is largely used in Scandinavia and Finland. In this system the taverns are entrusted by the Government or commune to special societies (*Samlag*), who only receive a limited gain while the profits go to the State or commune for public purposes. In Sweden these profits have amounted in twenty years to 83,000,000 kronen ($22,410,000). The tavern is carried on by a government official appointed for the purpose. The "Independent Order of Good Templars" opposes the system because it gives the communes too great an interest in the sale of alcohol. The "German Society for the Reform of Taverns" (*Deutsche Verein für Gasthausreform*) employs the following method: the inn or tavern established by the commune or by a society is given a manager with a fixed salary, who has in addition a commission on the sale of food and non-alcoholic beverages. It is always provided that strong alcoholic liquors are never to be in stock. There are many temperance taverns in Switzerland and Sweden, and some in Germany, Hungary, and Holland. Reference should, lastly, be made to the very satisfactory increase of provision for the cure of drunkards. In Germany there are over 40 institutions (six Catholic) where treatment is given, besides numerous homes for drunkards belonging to cities and societies. Several cities have appointed official nurses to take care of drunkards; about half of the patients become permanent abstainers. In Switzerland there are about ten such institutions, one being Catholic. These two countries are far in advance of the others in the effort to cure drunkenness.

The bibliography of the temperance question is enormous. Nearly 15,000 publications in Europe and the United States are listed by ABDERHALDEN, *Bibliographie der gesamten wissenschaftl. Literatur über Alkohol u. Alkoholismus* (1904). The current literature of the subject is given by the bibliographical journal *Blätter für die Gesamten Sozialwissenschaften* (Berlin), and by the two international temperance periodicals (see below). The most important systematic work is, probably, HELENIUS, *Die Alkoholfrage*, which has excellent bibliographies of all countries. The original work was translated from Finnish into German in 1903. The best historical work is BERGMAN, *Nykterhetsrörelsens världhistoria* (1900), well illustrated, also issued in a much altered German translation by KRAUT (1907). The most important statistical work is that issued by the British Board of Trade mentioned at the beginning of this article, in connexion with which see HOPPE, *Die Tatsachen über den Alkohol*. Year-books concerning the movement in various countries are published by WARMING, for Germany and Austria-Hungary; HERCOD, for Switzerland; NIELSEN, for Denmark; DUCKERT, for Norway; etc. Numerous periodicals are published: in Germany, over 70; in Denmark and Sweden, about 25; etc. The most important of these journals are: *Internat. Monatsschrift zur Bekämpfung der Trinksitten* (Basle); *Die Alkoholfrage* (Berlin), issued in German, French, and English; *Mässigkeitsblätter* (Berlin); *Mimer* (Stockholm); *De Wegwijzer* (Amsterdam); *Afholdsbladet* (Christiania); *L'abstinence* (Lausanne); *Folkevennen* (Copenhagen); *Le bien social* (Brussels); *Les annales antialcooliques* (Paris). Catholic periodicals are: *Volksfreund* and *Der Morgen*, for Germany; *Volkswohl* and *La Ligue de la Croix*, for Switzerland; *Kreuzfahrer*, for Austria; *Sobrietas* and *De Drankbestrijding*, for Holland. See also for movement in Belgium: MALHERBE AND LEMMENS, *Les Sociétés de tempérance* (Brussels, 1900); WASLET, *Het Volksgeluk*; BARELLA, *La lutte antialcoolique en Belgique* (Brussels, 1901); VERMEERSCH, *Manuel social* (Louvain, 1904); in France: DENIS, *Manuel de tempérance*; BERGERET, *L'alcoolisme*; BERTILLON, *L'alcoolisme et les moyens de le combattre*; SAVOY, *Les trésors de la sainte abstinence*; in Switzerland: FOREL, *La boisson dans nos mœurs*; BUNGE, *Die Alkoholfrage*; EGGER, numerous writings, including *Alkohol, Alkoholismus u. Abstinenz*; *Alkohol u. Volkswohl*, etc.; in the northern lands: *Erklund, Dryckenskapen* (Stockholm, 1890); PETERSSON, *En studie öfner Göteborgsystemet*; HALVERSEN, *Det norske Totalafholdsselskab*; JÖRGENSON, *Afholdssagens historie in Danmark*.

WILHELM LIESE.

GREAT BRITAIN AND IRELAND.—In Great Britain and Ireland the State regulates the liquor traffic by imposing duties on the manufacture and importation of spirituous drink and by confining its sale to those who pay for the privilege and fulfil other conditions as to place, time etc. Those who drink, therefore, must pay more for their liquor than its intrinsic value and must observe certain legal limits in the circumstances of their drinking. Thus the State aims by the one act at maintaining public order and promoting social welfare and also at raising revenue from the quasi-monopoly it creates. These two purposes are not always in harmony, which explains to some extent why State interference from the beginning to this day has often failed of success. A full history of liquor legislation and its results would occupy volumes; here there is space only for a brief summary of the chief Acts affecting the British Isles as a whole.

It is significant that up to the Reformation there occurs no civil legislation against drunkenness, although it was prevalent enough in Catholic times. The crop of laws against intemperance began to spring up in the reign of Edward VI, but they can no more be attributed to the higher morality of the new religion than can that monarch's grammar schools to his zeal for education, or Queen Elizabeth's workhouses to her compassion for the poor. All these phenomena point to the passing away of an influence hitherto found sufficient to promote social welfare by moral means. Laws concerning liquor were, indeed, enacted from early times, but their main object was to prevent fraud on the part of the sellers. Scotch legislation, for instance, was busy in the reign of David I (1124-53) regulating the brewing and selling of ale. In England, in 1200, prices were fixed by law for the different sorts of wine, and we find many subsequent enactments tending to encourage the wine trade with the English possessions in France. With the overthrow of the ancient Church and the destruction of her restraining influence, the spread of intemperance became very marked, as is attested by contemporary writers, and the State began to interfere in the interests of public welfare. An English Act was passed in 1495, empowering justices of the peace to suppress at discretion "common alehouses", as centres of disorder. The licensing system was introduced in 1551, by an Act which made the consent of the justices necessary for the establishment of ale-houses. The Irish Parliament in 1556 prohibited the manufacture of *aqua vitæ* except by certain specified classes. At the beginning of the seventeenth century laws were passed in England to prevent inns from becoming public-houses in the modern sense. In 1634 the licensing system was extended to Ireland. The close of this century brought a new element into the question. Hitherto only fermented liquors were commonly drunk in England, for, owing to high duties, the price of imported spirits put them beyond the reach of the people, but in 1689 the Government of the Revolution, out of hostility to France, prohibited the importation of foreign spirits and removed the restrictions on home manufacture, with alarming results to public morality. In spite of the retail trade being put under the licensing system in 1700, by 1724 the passion for gin-drinking had spread "with the rapidity and violence of an epidemic" (Lecky, "English History", I, iii), and in vain was the famous "Gin Act" passed in 1736, making the licence practically prohibitive. Illicit distilling and smuggling spread enormously, and high licences had to be repealed in 1742. Although gradually the State resumed control, still "the fatal passion for drink was at once and irrevocably planted in the nation" (Lecky, op. cit.). From 1751 dates a series of laws dealing more stringently with the conduct of the drink traffic, and in 1755 the licensing system was introduced into Scotland.

An attempt was made in 1828, as the result of a Parliamentary inquiry into illicit spirit-dealing, to simplify and consolidate the various licensing laws for England and Scotland, and, in 1833, for Ireland, and these acts form the basis of the existing law. But experimental legislation still continued. In order to cure the nation of spirit-drinking, to encourage a British industry, and to break up the growing system of "tied houses", an Act was passed in 1830 giving practically free trade in beer. A fortnight after the Act was passed, Sydney Smith wrote: "The New Beer Bill has begun its operations. Everybody is drunk. Those who are not singing are sprawling. The Sovereign People is in a beastly state." The Act failed miserably of its purpose. In less than three months 24,000 licenses were taken out. The number of "tied houses" was not ultimately lessened and the consumption of spirits steadily rose. In 1869 the beerhouses were again brought under the licensing system. Another well-meant but unsuccessful effort to alter popular taste was the establishment (1860-1) of "off" grocers' licences, by which measure Gladstone hoped to wean the people from beer-drinking in public-houses to the use of light wines and spirits at home. Much intermediate and subsequent legislation was concerned with the conditions of holding licences, particularly with the hours of closing. The "Forbes-Mackenzie" Act of 1853 closed the public-houses of Scotland on Sundays, except to travellers, and the measure was extended to Ireland (except five chief towns) in 1878, and to Wales in 1881, with very noticeable results in the decrease of drunkenness. In England the hours of Sunday opening have been restricted to seven. In 1873 a licensing Act prohibited the sale of spirits to children under sixteen, required the confirmation of the County Bench for new licences, and deprived that Bench of the power of granting licences in opposition to local refusal. Other measures for the protection of children were passed, culminating in the Act of 1909 which forbids children under fourteen access to public bars. For the last forty years under the influence of State regulations the number of licensed houses has steadily decreased. Shadwell shows that the number of "on" licenses per 10,000 persons in England and Wales was forty-nine in 1871, thirty-one in 1901, twenty-six in 1909. In Scotland there were 17,713 public-houses in 1829; in 1909 with more than double the population there were 6845 only or 14.03 per 10,000. The decrease in numbers has obtained in Ireland also, but a greater decrease in population has counteracted the relative diminution. With a smaller population than Scotland there are in Ireland more than three times as many licensed houses—in 1909, 22,591 in all. The Act of 1904 has tended to accelerate the decrease of licences by admitting the principle of compensation and giving licence holders for the first time a legal claim to renewal unless forfeited by misconduct. In the eyes of those who desire to suppress altogether traffic in drink for private gain this is considered a step backwards, a view which is strengthened by the notable increase of "clubs" since the passing of the Act. Finally, one marked effect of the Finance Act of 1910, so far as it concerns the Temperance Movement, was to reduce the consumption of spirits by ten millions of gallons; against this must be set an increased consumption of fermented liquors and presumably of illicitly distilled spirits. In the history of State activities for the promotion of temperance must be included the action of the various education departments in making temperance teaching an integral part of the elementary code. A temperance syllabus was made compulsory by the Irish Commissioners in 1906. The English department issued its syllabus for England and Wales in 1909, and a similar syllabus was drawn up for Scotland in 1910. If future generations of the populace indulge in drunkenness, it will not be through ignorance of its evil effects on the human frame and the body politic.

This brief sketch of the history of legislation for the control of the liquor traffic is enough to indicate the nature of the problem. The State interferes to secure such observance of temperance as is necessary for social well-being. But reasonable liberty to do what in itself is not unlawful is also a part of social well-being. Were all its citizens sufficiently self-controlled the State would have no claim to interfere, but in its own interests it has to supply by external pressure defects of personal character. The difficulty, then, is so to legislate that the weak may be protected without the freedom of the temperate being unduly infringed. The most obvious thing to do was to lessen temptation by lessening the number of licensed houses. But this policy involves evils of its own. The giving of licences creates a quasi-monopoloy, and monopolies legally secured have a tendency to breed fraud of every sort. The drink-seller tends to become a publican in the old sense. He pays a heavy sum in excise and licence for the privilege of trading in liquor, and he must recoup himself from the purchaser. Hence, on the one hand, the evils of smuggling or illicit production, and, on the other, of adulterated liquor, of inducements to drink to excess, of "tied houses" in the hands of producers. The heavy taxation, induced both by considerations of revenue and of social welfare, crushes out free competition and brings the trade into a few hands, and thus within the state is begotten a powerful trust, the interests of which are purely financial and not necessarily in harmony with those of the commonwealth. If legislation opposed to those interests has not behind it, as a permanent force, the moral sense of the larger and saner part of the community, it becomes inoperative and defeats itself. Hence true reform in the matter of the drink traffic depends ultimately on rightly educated public opinion.

Until the end of the eighteenth century the medical profession did little to dispel the ancient tradition about the health-giving qualities of strong drink, to which the name given to the distilled essence of fermented liquors, *aqua vitæ*, and the word "spirit" itself remain as witnesses. And in default of the Church, persecuted and gagged by the civil law, there was none amongst the sects to preach temperance as a principle of ascetics. Isolated physicians like Dr. George Cheyne (1671–1743) had pointed out the dangers of spirit-drinking; Dr. Trotter of Edinburgh and Dr. Rush of Philadelphia both published papers to the same effect in 1788. But it was in the United States that the first combined efforts were made to educate public opinion in this matter. In tracing the history of these voluntary associations which aimed at temperance reform primarily by persuading the individual, it will be convenient to deal with the non-Catholic bodies separately; historically they were the first in the field, and, arising in communities predominantly non-Catholic, they are naturally much more numerous. As will be pointed out, though alike in aim, they sometimes differ in method from Catholic organizations. We cannot pretend to give more than a few salient features of so enduring and widespread a movement.

Influenced by the formation at Boston in 1826 of the Society for the Promotion of Temperance Dr. John Edgar, of Belfast, a Presbyterian, founded on the same lines the Ulster Temperance Society in 1829, and the Rev. G. W. Kerr, a Quaker, a similar society at New Ross. Later in the same year the Glasgow and West of Scotland Society was started by John Dunlop. The next year an English society was formed by Henry Forbes in Bradford. All these and many others which sprang up throughout the British Isles originated in the desire to suppress the spirit-drinking which had become so prevalent, and hence their pledges allowed the moderate use of fermented liquors. It was not until 1832 that at Preston under the advocacy of Joseph Livesay total abstainers first appeared, and the word "teetotal", applied to abstinence, came into general use. The new pledge caused a sort of schism in many of the earlier societies, but gradually, as the illogicality of taking alcohol in one form and renouncing its use in another became apparent, teetotalism prevailed almost everywhere. Yet the phenomenon observable to-day, that less spirit consumption means more consumption of beer, was evident even then. Another cause of dissension amongst non-Catholic reformers sprang from erroneous views about the moral character of strong drink itself. In their hatred of its abuse, many extremists declaimed against its use as something intrinsically evil and thus were betrayed into irrational attitudes which injured their cause. If alcohol is evil *in se*, no one is justified in offering it to others, or in licensing its sale by others. The publican must be classed with the pandar: the State must put down the drink traffic by force. In addition to these violent views, men who based their religion on the Bible were hard put to it to explain the toleration and even implicit commendation of the use of wine to be found in its pages, and a vast controversy arose over the question whether the "wine" of Scripture was fermented or not. Undoubtedly, these disputes, and the adoption in many cases of a standpoint opposed to common sense, have done much to prevent the cause of real temperance from progressing, as it might have done, outside the Church, and its practical identification with false religious beliefs has operated to create distrust of the movement amongst many Catholics. But, notwithstanding this ethical confusion amongst the sects, the social and physical benefits of temperance are so marked that its advocacy has had a constant and growing influence upon public opinion. By 1842 the chief societies in England were, the National Temperance Society, the British and Foreign Society for the Suppression of Intemperance, and the British Temperance Association: the Scottish Temperance League was founded in 1844, and in Ireland all the Protestant bodies had drawn new vigour from the great campaign of Father Mathew.

But the mid-century ended in universal political and social disturbance, and the original impulse towards temperance lost for a time much of its vitality. Later, in more settled conditions, the campaign against strong drink took on a more scientific character. It aimed, by the organization of women and children, by teaching temperance in the schools, and by setting forth the physical effects of excessive indulgence, at creating such a weight of opinion as to influence the legislature. The juvenile societies, called "Bands of Hope", so marked a feature to-day of Protestant propaganda, were started in 1847. Inspired by the Prohibition Law of Maine (1851) the United Kingdom Alliance, which had for express object "the total and immediate legislative suppression of the traffic in intoxicating liquors as beverages" and which is still the most active of modern organizations, came into being in Manchester in 1853. We need not trace in greater detail the development during the next half-century of these various societies in the British Isles, a development which, as far as numbers are concerned, is of imposing extent. A recent Presbyterian movement, inaugurated in 1909 in the north of Ireland by the Rev. R. J. Patterson and called "Catch-My-Pal", may be mentioned as having met with much success both there and in England. As for other societies, the Alliance Handbook (and as regards Ireland and Scotland its enumeration is by no means exhaustive) reckons 18 temperance bodies which are legislative and general, 17 which are sectional (Army, Navy, etc.), 22 identified with different "Churches", 14 which are sects or orders of themselves, 10 confined to women, 8 juvenile societies, 62 county and 176 town societies—in all 327. These various associations, of course, produce a large amount of Temperance literature, whether in book form or as newspapers and tracts. This vigorous polemic, as is natural, has called forth similar measures of defence on the part of the trade. The Alliance Annual enumerates 10 main associations of those engaged in the drink traffic and estimates the local societies throughout the United Kingdom at about 700. On the grounds that their trade is a lawful one and, under proper conditions (which they profess their readiness to observe), even necessary for social well-being, the sellers of drink are justified in resisting attacks which deny the soundness of those grounds. No Catholic temperance society will base its opposition to the drink traffic on such unsound foundations.

As an organization existing to teach and make feasible man's duty of self-control, the Catholic Church is the first and the greatest of temperance societies. She teaches, and has always taught, that all are bound under sin not to misuse strong drink themselves or co-operate in the abuse of it by others —and this, whatever means they employ, is the ultimate end of all temperance associations. With the social evil of drunkenness (before she was robbed of her due influence and before the common use of spirits intensified the evil), the Church had been able in great measure to cope by her ordinary discipline— her preaching of self-denial, her administration of the Sacrament of Penance, her institution of penitential seasons, and her canonical legislation. All these moral influences were swept away at the Reformation and nothing effective set in their place. Hence the excesses of the seventeenth and eighteenth centuries are largely attributable to the destruction of Catholicism as a social force. Even after Emancipation in 1829, the effects of the Penal Laws still continued, and it is not till 1838 that we find mention in Great Britain of a purely Catholic temperance association. It is true that in 1819 there was founded at Skibbereen in Kerry a temperance organization presumably Catholic, but it seems to have been rather of the nature of a benefit society with a temperance resolution amongst its rules. At Chelsea, in 1838, the Rev. T. Sisk started a Catholic Total Abstinence Society, and in 1840 we find mention of a South London Catholic Temperance Association which was addressed by Daniel O'Connell. Moreover in the same year a Metropolitan Catholic Association was instituted through the exertions of Mr. John Giles, a Quaker. But these little local efforts were thrown completely into the shade by the gigantic work accomplished (at the providential instigation of another Quaker, William Martin) by the greatest temperance apostle the world has ever seen, Father Theobald Mathew. As a result of his advocacy in the years 1838 to 1845 it is computed that Ireland, with a population of over eight million, counted from three to four million total abstainers, and the annual consumption of spirits, which from 1835 to 1839 averaged 11,595,536 gallons, sank in 1842 to 5,290,650 gallons. The want of permanence that marked this great movement was no doubt mainly due to the catastrophe of the famine, but also in no slight degree to the fact that it won scant support amongst the upper and middle classes and even from the clergy themselves. Its inspiration, however, is alive and growing in strength to-day, not only in the land of its origin, but in Great Britain as well. For Great Britain in 1843 came under the spell of Father Mathew's zeal and eloquence, and many Catholic associations were formed in the towns he visited in England and Scotland as parts of the parochial organization.

After the general reaction that preceded and followed the year of Revolution (1848) there is record of further Catholic effort. St. Patrick's Total Abstinence Society, founded in Dundalk in 1850, still flourishes. In 1858 a Catholic Temperance Hall was opened in Spitalfields by the Rev. Dr. Spratt of Dublin, one of Father Mathew's most zealous coadjutors; in 1858, we are told, a new Roman Catholic Total Abstinence Society was founded in London, where also in 1863 there is recorded a meeting of the Roman Catholic Teetotal Union. But not until 1866, when Archbishop Manning began to take practical interest in the temperance question, was anything attempted on a larger scale. The United Kingdom Alliance of Manchester and the late Mgr. Nugent of Liverpool put facts and figures before him with the result that both in Liverpool and in London in 1873 a Catholic organization was formed called the League of the Cross which, under those zealous leaders, accomplished a vast deal for temperance in Great Britain. Branches of this organization were set up in many parishes abroad as well as in England and Scotland, and under the eyes of its founders it became a great social force. In 1869 Dr. Delany of Cork promoted a temperance revival in his diocese, and the bishops, by their joint pastoral in 1875, gave a great stimulus to the movement. In that year was instituted in Dublin the Confraternity of the Sacred Thirst of Jesus and in Salford the Diocesan Crusade by Bishop, afterwards Cardinal, Vaughan. The Crusade, or Catholic Association for the Suppression of Drunkenness, inaugurated by Dr. Richardson of London, and various lesser associations date from the same period. Another remarkable revival in Catholic advocacy of total abstinence in the British Isles began towards the end of last century. Father James Nugent did wonderful work in Liverpool for the cause. As a temperance reformer, Father F. C. Hays, a nephew of Father Nugent, has won a like renown. In 1896 he founded his Catholic Temperance Crusade, which aims to prevent, rather than reclaim from, intemperance, and includes members who are total abstainers, children over ten who take the resolution till the age of twenty-one years, and associates who lead a strictly temperate life. There is no central governing body, but the crusade readily co-operates with all other temperance endeavours, aiming at establishing some sort of organization in every parish and, by means of lectures and literature, at spreading a healthy public opinion on the matter. The promoter of the crusade has travelled and worked extensively in its interests, and the influence of his zeal is felt in the whole English-speaking world. The League of the Cross, under the care of Canon Murnane, one of Cardinal Manning's earliest and most energetic lieutenants, is renewing its youth in England and Scotland.

A Father Mathew Union, the membership of which is confined to the clergy, was founded in London in 1908. But it is in Ireland, where poverty and depopulation make the ravages of strong drink most apparent, that the most strenuous efforts are being made to combat it. In 1898 there was formed in Dublin by Father James Cullen, S.J., the Pioneer Total Abstinence League of the Sacred Heart which numbers to-day 180,000 members and 172 centres. Particularly noticeable is the large accession to its ranks of the younger clergy. It was the first temperance association to insist on a two-years' probation as a test of purpose and a guarantee of stability; it was enriched by Pius X with many indulgences in 1905. In that year, moreover, the Irish Hierarchy called upon the Capuchins, the religious brethren of Father Mathew, to take up again his work. This they have done with much of his success. Recently under their stimulating zeal one-fourth of the whole population of Limerick took the pledge. Still more recent is the formation by the bishops of the western province of St. Patrick's League of the West, an organization planned to cover the whole of Connaught with a network of temperance societies and to stamp out drunkenness by the most carefully devised methods. Other less heroic devices, like the Anti-Treating League, aim at counteracting one of the most frequent sources of demoralization. Such vigorous and sustained efforts have had a marked effect in Ireland. Arrests for drunkenness, which were 98,401 in 1899, have fallen each year to 68,748 in 1909, and the expenditure on drink, though still appallingly large (£13,310,469), considering the needs and poverty of the country, is now more than a million less than it was ten years ago. And though the "Drink Bill" of the United Kingdom, which was £179,499,817 in 1902, has now decreased to £155,162,485, owing to some extent to the growth of a more enlightened public opinion, there is yet abundant need of temperance propaganda before the population of the British Isles learns as a whole to avoid excessive drinking, as a vice that is both degrading to the individual and very injurious to the State.

General works: WOOLLEY AND JOHNSON, *Temperance and Social Progress of the Century* (London); DAWSON AND BURNS, *Temperance History* (1889-91); ROWNTREE AND SHERWELL, *The Temperance Problem and Social Reform* (New York, 1900); SHADWELL, *Drink, Temperance and Legislation* (New York, 1902); PATERSON, *Licensing Acts, 1828-1904*; *The Royal Commission on Liquor Licensing Laws* (1896-99); *The Alliance Year Book* (1911); *Annual Report (Thirty-Second) of the Irish Association for the Prevention of Intemperance* (1910—); *New Encyclopedia of Social Reform*. Catholic works: BRIDGETT, *The Discipline of Drink* (1876); MANNING, *Our National Vice* (1886); CULLEN, *The Pioneer Temperance Catechism* (1911); MORAN, *Early Church Legislation in Ireland*; PURCELL, *Life of Cardinal Manning*, II (London, 1895), xxii; *Handbook of the League of the Cross*.

JOSEPH KEATING.

IN THE UNITED STATES AND CANADA.—*United States*.—The first temperance work in the United States was due to a reaction against intemperance, which threatened to make the Americans a nation of drunkards. The culminating period of intemperance was the seventy-five years between 1750 and 1825. Nearly everyone drank intoxicating liquor. It was the family beverage. It was the prevailing mark of hospitality. It was regarded as a discourtesy, even an insult, to refuse it. At all functions, public and private, social and commercial, sacred and solemn, intoxicating beverages were used. Not only was liquor regarded as indispensable on such occasions, but the erroneous belief prevailed that no hard work could be accomplished without the stimulating glass. Labourers and mechanics were provided with their quota of liquor, twice a day, at the sound of the town bell, that summoned them regularly at eleven and four o'clock. The farmer stipulated with his help when he hired them for harvesting that they were to receive a certain amount of "spirits", which was generally whisky or New England rum. Strong liquor was supposed to make strong men. This supposition was not questioned until the fatal effects of drinking habits were evident in the multitude who went down to drunkards' graves. Intemperance was widespread, increasing day by day, till it reached its climax at the close of the Revolutionary War. Congress furnished the Colonial troops with liquor to strengthen them in the hardships of war. The soldiers returned to their homes and added to the wave of drunkenness that rose high and spread far and wide. It was commonly stated at the end of the Revolution that the United States consumed more liquor *per capita* than any other nation. It was generally admitted that no man could be found who had not been drunk on some occasion. The outcome of this universal intemperance was a reaction in favour of temperance.

The first pronounced effort at reform was inaugurated by Dr. Benjamin Rush of Philadelphia, a member of the Continental Congress in 1776, and one of the signers of the Declaration of Independence. In 1785 he issued a pamphlet entitled "Inquiry into the effects of ardent spirits on the human body and mind", which was widely read in America and England. No organized movement resulted from it, but it affected public opinion strongly and laid the foundation of subsequent temperance work. The reform inaugurated by Dr. Rush did not advocate total abstinence; the public was not prepared for any such remedial measure. The first step toward it was the abolition of the custom of affording liquor to employees. Then moderation in the use of distilled liquors was encouraged; this developed into abstinence from this class of liquors, and the moderate use of wine, beer, and cider. Finally after a half-century of effort in regulating the use of liquor, it was demonstrated that the plan of moderation had proved a failure, and that the only practical remedy was total abstinence.

The first temperance organization was formed by two hundred farmers in Litchfield, Connecticut, in 1789. The members merely pledged themselves not to give liquor to their farm hands. This action met with bitter opposition from the workmen, who persecuted the members of the new society and heaped every indignity upon them. Such was the prejudice in favour of strong drink that this very moderate temperance movement was considered drastic and revolutionary. The first society of pledged abstainers was formed in April, 1808, at Moreau, Saratoga County, New York. Forty-seven members pledged themselves to abstain from distilled spirits and wine except in case of sickness or at public dinners, under penalty of a fine of twenty-five cents, and fifty cents for actual intoxication. Other societies were established which prohibited not the use but the intemperate use of intoxicating liquors. One of these societies was organized in a tavern, at the bar of which the officers treated the others. Members were fined twenty-five and fifty cents for drunkenness, and a by-law of one society required members who had become drunk to treat all the other members.

The vice of drunkenness called for a more adequate effort than the mere advocacy of moderation. On 13 February, 1826, "The American Temperance Society" was established at Boston. This opened a new era, and paved the way to total abstinence. The new society advocated total abstinence, but, from considerations of prudence, it was not enforced. The purpose of the society was to mould public sentiment and to reform the habits and customs of the community. Gradually men began to see that drunkenness was to be combatted by attacking the drink-habit. Ten years later, in 1836, the second national temperance convention held at Saratoga declared for total abstinence from distilled and fermented liquors. Dr. Dorchester in his "Liquor Problem in All Ages", commenting on the work of this period, says: "In the year 1835 more than eight thousand societies had been formed, with more than one million five hundred thousand members, every state except one being organized. More than four thousand distilleries had been stopped, and eight thousand merchants had ceased to sell ardent spirits. More than twelve hundred vessels in which it is not used sail from our ports." The year 1840 gave birth to the Washingtonian Temperance Society, a total abstinence organization, which began at Baltimore with six members, and grew to six hundred thousand. In time, two-thirds of this large society fell away. Other societies lost members and men who regarded teetotalism as the sovereign remedy of intemperance turned their attention from the drinker and the drunkard to the dealer in liquor, whose livelihood depended on the drinker, and inaugurated another phase of temperance reform, which eventually took the shape of prohibition. Neal Dow of Maine became the leader of the new agitation, and after persistent and unwearying effort succeeded in 1851 in securing the passage of an absolute prohibitory law commonly known as the "Maine Law". In subsequent years prohibition of the liquor traffic became a law in Minnesota, Rhode Island, Massachusetts, Vermont, Michigan, Connecticut, New York, New Hampshire, Delaware, Nebraska, Indiana, Iowa, South Dakota, Illinois, Alaska, North Dakota, Oklahoma, Alabama, Georgia, Kansas, Mississippi, North Carolina, Tennessee. In time the law was repealed in all except the eight latter and Maine (1 Jan., 1911).

Among the early prominent advocates of temperance reform who deserve especial mention are Rev. Lyman Beecher and Dr. Nathaniel Hewitt of Connecticut, Edward C. Delevan, Dr. Clark, and Gerrit Smith of New York, Rev. Thomas P. Hunt of Pennsylvania, Bishop Charles P. McIlravie of Ohio, John B. Gough, Rev. Justin Edwards of Massachusetts, and Abraham Lincoln of Illinois. Before the Civil War the principal organizations that advocated temperance were the Washingtonian Movement, 1840, Rechabites, 1841, Sons of Temperance, 1842, Cadets of Temperance, Templars of Honour and Temperance, 1845, Good Templars, 1851. The first national temperance convention was held at Philadelphia in May, 1833. Twenty-one states were represented, with four hundred delegates. By vote of Congress and approval of President Jackson the sale of spirits to the Indians was prohibited in 1834. On 5 Nov., 1832, General Lewis Cass, secretary of war, issued an order prohibiting the introduction of liquors in any garrison, fort, or camp in the United States. The secretary of the navy offered a money substitute for the grog ration.

An era in temperance work was inaugurated in the United States on 2 July, 1849, which marked the advent of Father Theobald Mathew, the Irish apostle of temperance. He was received at New York with tremendous enthusiasm. Mayor Woodhull and the city council gave him a public reception. At Washington he was entertained by President Taylor, and was admitted to a seat within the bar of the Senate and on the floor of the House, a distinction granted only once previously to a foreigner—General Lafayette. On this occasion, Henry Clay said: "It is but a merited tribute of respect to a man who has achieved a great social revolution—a revolution in which no blood has been shed, a revolution which has involved no desolation, which has caused no bitter tears of widows and orphans to flow, a revolution which has been achieved without violence, and a greater one, perhaps, than has ever been accomplished by any benefactor of mankind." Father Mathew spent two years and a half in the United States and, though in feeble health, travelled 37,000 miles, visiting 25 states, administering the pledge in over 300 of the principal cities and towns to more than 500,000 persons.

Several Catholic total abstinence societies were organized during Father Mathew's visit, but their influence was exerted only in the restricted sphere in which they originated. No bond united them till 1871, when the societies of Connecticut formed a state union, out of which a national union grew, at a convention held at Baltimore on 22 February, 1872. One hundred and seventy-seven societies, comprising 26,481 members, represented Connecticut Rhode Island, New York, New Jersey, Pennsylvania, Maryland, Georgia, Illinois, Ohio, Minnesota, and the District of Columbia. A constitution was adopted, an address was issued to the Catholics of America, and the union was named "The Catholic Total Abstinence Union of America". In the address to the Catholic body, the aim of the convention was proclaimed in these terms: "Our motto is moral suasion. With prohibitory laws, restrictive license systems, and special legislation we have nothing whatever to do. There is blended with our proposed plan of organization the attractive feature of mutual relief. Thus Temperance and Benevolence go hand in hand." Moral suasion was favoured by some, legislative action by others, and a combination of both by a third class. It was finally determined to work on the lines of moral suasion as the belief prevailed that neither prohibitory nor restrictive laws availed unless supported by public opinion. The mind of the convention concerning the suppression and restriction of the liquor traffic was expressed in the following resolution: " Resolved, That this convention, though not deeming it expedient to take part in any political or legislative action, in reference to 'Prohibitory Liquor Laws', recognizes, however, the great good that would accrue from the suppression of public drinking places, and from such legislation as would restrain the manufacture of intoxicating liquors within bounds consistent with public morality, and will gladly hail such legislation whenever the proper authorities may grant it." The convention advocated the organization of subordinate unions of the different states or dioceses in affiliation with the national union. State unions were established in Alabama, California, Connecticut, Illinois, Indiana, Louisiana, Missouri, New Jersey, Ohio, Pennsylvania, Wisconsin, also in Canada. Diocesan unions were formed in Albany, Baltimore, Boston, Brooklyn, Buffalo, Dubuque, Duluth, Erie, Louisville, New York, Philadelphia, Pittsburg, Providence, Savannah, Scranton, Springfield, St. Paul, Syracuse, Wheeling, Wilmington, and Winona.

Annual conventions of the national union were held in different cities of the East and Middle West. Archbishops, bishops, and a host of priests attended the conventions, took active interest in the work of the Union, and propagated its principles in their respective dioceses. The Apostolic delegate, the Most Rev. Diomede Falconio, attended the forty-first convention at Scranton, Pennsylvania, in August, 1911, and gave unmistakable evidence of his interest in the work, in his address to the delegates, and in an eloquent discourse at the public meeting, of which the following is an extract: "Ladies and gentlemen, you here find in your presence a great body of men who, with manly courage and the true Christian spirit, have bound themselves together for the great cause of temperance. Follow their example, for the cause of temperance means the cause of Christian perfection and the cause of suffering humanity. Should you, however, not find it convenient to join their ranks, at least help their cause by your prayers and your constant co-operation. Gentlemen of the Total Abstinence Union, we admire your spirit of self-abnegation in professing the great virtue of total abstinence, and we appreciate your efforts in encouraging it both by words and example. Your associations are of paramount importance for the spiritual and temporal welfare of our people, and are, consequently, of great service to religion and to society."

At the convention of the national union held at Indianapolis, 28 August, 1878, a memorial was forwarded to Pope Leo XIII, who in reply addressed a papal Brief to the members of the union, of which the following is an extract: "Especially pleasing to us is that noble determination of yours to oppose and uproot the baneful vice of drunkenness, and keep far from yourselves and those united with you all incentive to it, for, in the words of the wise man, 'It goeth in pleasantly but in the end it will bite like a snake, and will spread abroad poison like a Basilisk'." A papal Brief was addressed by Pope Pius X to the Rt. Rev. J. Francis Regis Canevin, president of the national union, on 10 July, 1906. The pontiff commended the work of the union in these terms: "Following the example of our predecessors, and especially the latest among them, to whom there seemed to be no greater enemy of the teachings and commands of Christ than the abuse of strong drink, we heartily approve the work of the union, and congratulate all in this commendable assemblage, because they are our associates and helpers in persuading men to practise one of the principal Christian virtues—temperance."

The union is composed of men's, women's, and juvenile societies, and the Priests' Total Abstinence League, and numbers in all over 90,000 members.

The women's societies were admitted in 1878 as honorary members, and in 1880 as active members; in 1888 women delegates were first received, the women's societies having previously been represented by men; three years later Miss S. A. Moore of Philadelphia was elected third vice-president.

The union issues a monthly publication "The C. T. A. U. Advocate". In 1911 the union was represented for the first time at the (Thirteenth) International Congress against alcohol, held at The Hague, Holland. It has also joined the Catholic International Society against Alcoholism founded in 1907 by Father Neumann of Mündt, Prussia.

In 1873 "The Women's Crusade" started in Hillsboro, Ohio. The members appealed directly to the saloon-keeper to desist from liquor traffic, visiting all the saloons in the towns in which they were organized. The movement spread from Ohio, through the North Central States, to Iowa, Missouri, Kansas, California, Oregon, and eastward to the Atlantic coast. In Ohio the saloons in two hundred and fifty towns were closed by the crusade. The result of this movement was the organization of a total abstinence society called the Women's Christian Temperance Union, which was established at Cleveland on 18 Nov., 1874, at a national convention of one hundred and thirty-five delegates from about a dozen states. In 1880 six departments were instituted—organization, preventive, educational, evangelistic, social, and legal. At the head of each department was a superintendent. Under each department were sub-departments, in charge of superintendents, the total number of departments and superintendents being thirty-eight. Juvenile societies were formed in the various local unions, and through the efforts of the union scientific temperance instruction was introduced in the schools. In 1910, 22,000,000 children received instruction on the baneful effects of alcohol. In 1883 the union was organized in every state and territory of the United States, and was introduced into Canada. The World's Women's Christian Temperance Union, which has societies in many countries, was a fuller development of the Women's Christian Temperance Union. For nearly twenty years the destinies of the W. C. T. U. were guided by a gifted woman of high character, who had resigned her position as dean of the Woman's College and Professor of Æsthetics in the Northwestern University to devote all her energies to the cause of temperance—Miss Frances E. Willard.

Canada.—In the beginning of the nineteenth century, the sale of intoxicating liquor was scarcely restricted by law in Canada and its use was almost universal. Intemperance developed and spread to such an extent that a reaction set in, and called forth active opposition. A meeting was held at Brockville, Ontario, in the autumn of 1828, and the first pledged Temperance Society in Canada was formed. It was not a total abstinence society. Moderation was inculcated in this and many other societies established throughout the country until 1839, when the total abstinence pledge succeeded the old moderation pledge, as was the case in the United States. Moderation had proved a failure, and total abstinence was adopted as the best remedy against the drink evil. Immediately a noticeable progress was made against intemperance. Societies were organized as "open temperance societies", with no bond of union till 1847, when the Sons of Temperance established a branch in Canada. An executive council governed local societies and systematized their work. An aid to thorough organization was afforded in 1858 by the Independent Order of Good Templars, whose pledge lasted for life, and who admitted women to membership. In 1874 the Women's Christian Temperance Union instituted a union in Canada, and by systematic work gave a strong impulse to temperance reform. The Canada Temperance Union came into existence in 1869, and, after various modifications in name and methods, was replaced in 1877 by the Dominion Alliance for the Total Suppresion of the Liquor Traffic. The Alliance worked with vigour in securing legislation for the restriction of the liquor traffic, and was actively engaged in the enforcement of excise laws, throughout most of the provinces of Canada. Since 1850, nearly every Canadian Parliament has been called upon to enact legislation prohibitive or restrictive of the liquor traffic. Repeated petitions made to Parliament for total prohibition urged the enactment of the Canada Temperance Act of 1878, commonly called the "Scott Act", authorizing counties and cities to prohibit the retail sale of liquor. The popular vote was overwhelming in favour of prohibition, but disputes as to its constitutionality and controversy concerning the responsibility of enforcement by federal or provincial authorities rendered it inoperative.

The Church of England Temperance Society, established in a way in every province, was for a time active in the temperance reform movement. In latter years the success of the Protestant societies has been in the way of local option or "banish the bar" campaign. In the rural districts of Ontario this work is popular, and has been effective. The Catholic Church grappled with the drink evil, from the earliest days of the colony of New France. For many years her adherents have been most active in propagating temperance principles through the League of the Cross, the Catholic Total Abstinence Union, and other societies scattered throughout Canada. Since 1900 the Diocese of Peterborough has taken the lead in temperance work. In the episcopal city there is a society of 1200 men. Archbishop Bruchesi of Montreal has taken active interest in the work, and has developed a strong total abstinence sentiment.

KNIGHTS OF FATHER MATHEW.—The Knights of Father Mathew, a total abstinence and semi-military body, was instituted at St. Louis, Mo., on 26 April, 1872. A life-insurance feature was adopted on 18 July, 1881, having been authorized by a charter empowering the society to include life insurance among its aims and objects, and to form branches of the order, called "councils", throughout the State of Missouri. As the work and benefits of the society became known, invitations to establish councils beyond Missouri were received. At present (1911) it has councils in Missouri, Illinois, Iowa, and Kansas. There are two classes of membership: active and honorary. To be eligible to active membership, it is necessary to be a practical Catholic, to pass a physical examination, and to be not less than sixteen nor more than seventy years of age. For honorary membership, it is sufficient to be a practical Catholic. The Society has been active in promoting temperance and frugality, and has expended over eight hundred thousand dollars in benefits for the families of its deceased members. Councils of the order are permitted to organize branches of Catholic women, to be designated as "Ladies' Auxiliaries of the Knights of Father Mathew," and to be governed by laws in harmony with the laws of the parent organization. The Ladies' Auxiliaries have been instrumental in upbuilding the male organization, in promoting temperance among boys and girls, and have been active in charitable work among the poor. The Knights of Father Mathew and the Ladies' Auxiliaries of the Knights of Father Mathew were affiliated with the Catholic Total Abstinence Union of America in 1895, and have been among its most energetic members in advancing the work of the national union.

One Hundred Years of Temperance (New York, 1886); BLAIR, *The Temp. Movement* (Boston, 1888); STEARNS, *Temp. in all Nations* (New York, 1893); ROUNTREE AND SHERWELL, *Temp. Problem and Social Reform* (New York, 1899); FEHLANDT, *A Century of Drink Reform* (Cincinnati, 1904); GIBBS, *Hist. of Cath. Tot. Abstinence Union of America* (Philadelphia, 1907).

WALTER J. SHANLEY.

Templars, KNIGHTS, THE.—The Knights Templars were the earliest founders of the military orders, and are the type on which the others are modelled. They are marked in history (1) by their humble beginning, (2) by their marvellous growth, and (3) by their tragic end.

(1) Immediately after the deliverance of Jerusalem, the Crusaders, considering their vow fulfilled, returned in a body to their homes. The defence of this precarious conquest, surrounded as it was by Mohammedan neighbours, remained. In 1118, during the reign of Baldwin II, Hugues de Payens, a knight of Champagne, and eight companions bound themselves by a perpetual vow, taken in the presence of the Patriarch of Jerusalem, to defend the Christian kingdom. Baldwin accepted their services and assigned them a portion of his palace, adjoining the temple of the city; hence their title "pauvres chevaliers du temple" (Poor Knights of the Temple). Poor indeed they were, being reduced to living on alms, and, so long as they were only nine, they were hardly prepared to render important services, unless it were as escorts to the pilgrims on their way from Jerusalem to the banks of the Jordan, then frequented as a place of devotion. The Templars had as yet neither distinctive habit nor rule. Hugues de Payens journeyed to the West to seek the approbation of the Church and to obtain recruits. At the Council of Troyes (1128), at which he assisted and at which St. Bernard was the leading spirit, the Knights Templars adopted the Rule of St. Benedict, as recently reformed by the Cistercians. They accepted not only the three perpetual vows, besides the crusader's vow, but also the austere rules concerning the chapel, the refectory, and the dormitory. They also adopted the white habit of the Cistercians, adding to it a red cross. Notwithstanding the austerity of the monastic rule, recruits flocked to the new order, which thenceforth comprised four ranks of brethren: the *knights*, equipped like the heavy cavalry of the Middle Ages; the *serjeants*, who formed the light cavalry; and two ranks of non-fighting men: the *farmers*, entrusted with the administration of temporals; and the *chaplains*, who alone were vested with sacerdotal orders, to minister to the spiritual needs of the order.

(2) The order owed its rapid growth in popularity to the fact that it combined the two great passions of the Middle Ages, religious fervour and martial prowess. Even before the Templars had proved their worth, the ecclesiastical and lay authorities heaped on them favours of every kind, spiritual and temporal. The popes took them under their immediate protection, exempting them from all other jurisdiction, episcopal or secular. Their property was assimilated to the church estates and exempted from all taxation, even from the ecclesiastical tithes, while their churches and cemeteries could not be placed under interdict. This soon brought about conflicts with the clergy of the Holy Land, inasmuch as the increase of the landed property of the order led, owing to its exemption from tithes, to the diminution of the revenue of the churches, and the interdicts, at that time used and abused by the episcopate, became to a certain extent inoperative wherever the order had churches and chapels in which Divine worship was regularly held. As early as 1156 the clergy of the Holy Land tried to restrain the exorbitant privileges of the military orders, but in Rome every objection was set aside, the result being a growing antipathy on the part of the secular clergy against these orders. The temporal benefits which the order received from all the sovereigns of Europe were no less important. The Templars had commanderies in every state. In France they formed no less than eleven bailiwicks, subdivided into more than forty-two commanderies; in Palestine it was for the most part with sword in hand that the Templars extended their possessions at the expense of the Mohammedans. Their castles are still famous owing to the remarkable ruins which remain: Safèd, built in 1140; Karak of the desert (1143); and, most important of all, Castle Pilgrim, built in 1217 to command a strategic defile on the sea-coast.

In these castles, which were both monasteries and cavalry barracks, the life of the Templars was full of contrasts. A contemporary describes the Templars as "in turn lions of war and lambs at the hearth; rough knights on the battlefield, pious monks in the chapel; formidable to the enemies of Christ, gentleness itself towards His friends" (Jacques de Vitry). Having renounced all the pleasures of life, they faced death with a proud indifference; they were the first to attack, the last to retreat, always docile to the voice of their leader, the discipline of the monk being added to the discipline of the soldier. As an army they were never very numerous. A contemporary tells us that there were 400 knights in Jerusalem at the zenith of their prosperity; he does not give the number of serjeants, who were more numerous. But it was a picked body of men who, by their noble example, inspirited the remainder of the Christian forces. They were thus the terror of the Mohammedans. Were they defeated, it was upon them that the victor vented his fury, the more so as they were forbidden to offer a ransom. When taken prisoners, they scornfully refused the freedom offered them on condition of apostasy. At the siege of Safèd (1264), at which ninety Templars met death, eighty others were taken prisoners, and, refusing to deny Christ, died martyrs to the Faith. This fidelity cost them dear. It has been computed that in less than two centuries almost 20,000 Templars, knights and serjeants, perished in war.

These frequent hecatombs rendered it difficult for the order to increase in numbers, and also brought about a decadence of the true crusading spirit. As the order was compelled to make immediate use of the recruits, the article of the original rule in Latin which required a probationary period fell into desuetude. Even excommunicated men, who, as was the case with many crusaders, wished to expiate their sins, were admitted. All that was required of a new member was a blind obedience, as imperative in the soldier as in the monk. He had to declare himself forever "serf et esclave de la maison" (French text of the rule). To prove his sincerity, he was subjected to a secret test concerning the nature of which nothing has ever been discovered, although it gave rise to the most extraordinary accusations. The great wealth of the order may also have contributed to a certain laxity in morals, but the most serious charge against it was its insupportable pride and love of power. At the apogee of its prosperity, it was said to possess 9000 estates. With its accumulated revenues it had amassed great wealth, which was deposited in its temples at Paris and London. Numerous princes and private individuals had banked there their personal property, because of the uprightness and solid credit of such bankers. In Paris the royal treasure was kept in the Temple. Quite independent, except from the distant authority of the pope, and possessing power equal to that of the leading temporal sovereigns, the order soon assumed the right to direct the weak and irresolute government of the

Kingdom of Jerusalem, a feudal kingdom transmissible through women and exposed to all the disadvantages of minorities, regencies, and domestic discord. However, the Templars were soon opposed by the Order of Hospitallers, which had in its turn become military, and was at first the imitator and later the rival of the Templars. This ill-timed interference of the orders in the government of Jerusalem only multiplied the intestine dissensions, and this at a time when the formidable power of Saladin threatened the very existence of the Latin Kingdom. While the Templars sacrificed themselves with their customary bravery in this final struggle, they were, nevertheless, partly responsible for the downfall of Jerusalem.

To put an end to this baneful rivalry between the military orders, there was a very simple remedy at hand, namely their amalgamation. This was officially proposed by St. Louis at the Council of Lyons (1274). It was proposed anew in 1293 by Pope Nicholas IV, who called a general consultation on this point of the Christian states. This idea is canvassed by all the publicists of that time, who demand either a fusion of the existing orders or the creation of a third order to supplant them. Never in fact had the question of the crusaders been more eagerly taken up than after their failure. As the grandson of St. Louis, Philip the Fair could not remain indifferent to these proposals for a crusade. As the most powerful prince of his time, the direction of the movement belonged to him. To assume this direction, all he demanded was the necessary supplies of men and especially of money. Such is the genesis of his campaign for the suppression of the Templars. It has been attributed wholly to his well-known cupidity. Even on this supposition he needed a pretext, for he could not, without sacrilege, lay hands on possessions that formed part of the ecclesiastical domain. To justify such a course the sanction of the Church was necessary, and this the king could obtain only by maintaining the sacred purpose for which the possessions were destined. Admitting that he was sufficiently powerful to encroach upon the property of the Templars in France, he still needed the concurrence of the Church to secure control of their possessions in the other countries of Christendom. Such was the purpose of the wily negotiations of this self-willed and cunning sovereign, and of his still more treacherous counsellors, with Clement V, a French pope of weak character and easily deceived. The rumour that there had been a prearrangement between the king and the pope has been finally disposed of. A doubtful revelation, which allowed Philip to make the prosecution of the Templars as heretics a question of orthodoxy, afforded him the opportunity which he desired to invoke the action of the Holy See.

(3) In the trial of the Templars two phases must be distinguished: the royal commission and the papal commission. Philip the Fair made a preliminary inquiry, and, on the strength of so-called revelations of a few unworthy and degraded members, secret orders were sent throughout France to arrest all the Templars on the same day (13 October, 1307), and to submit them to a most rigorous examination. The king did this, it was made to appear, at the request of the ecclesiastical inquisitors, but in reality without their co-operation. In this inquiry torture, the use of which was authorized by the cruel procedure of the age in the case of crimes committed without witnesses, was pitilessly employed. Owing to the lack of evidence, the accused could be convicted only through their own confession and, to extort this confession, the use of torture was considered necessary and legitimate. There was one feature in the organization of the order which gave rise to suspicion, namely the secrecy with which the rites of initiation were conducted. The secrecy is explained by the fact that the receptions always took place in a chapter, and the chapters, owing to the delicate and grave questions discussed, were, and necessarily had to be, held in secret. An indiscretion in the matter of secrecy entailed exclusion from the order. The secrecy of these initiations, however, had two grave disadvantages. As these receptions could take place wherever there was a commandery, they were carried on without publicity and were free from all surveillance or control from the higher authorities, the tests being entrusted to the discretion of subalterns who were often rough and uncultivated. Under such conditions, it is not to be wondered at that abuses crept in. One need only recall what took place almost daily at the time in the brotherhoods of artisans, the initiation of a new member being too often made the occasion for a parody more or less sacrilegious of baptism or of the Mass. The second disadvantage of this secrecy was, that it gave an opportunity to the enemies of the Templars, and they were numerous, to infer from this mystery every conceivable malicious supposition and base on it the most monstrous imputations. The Templars were accused of spitting upon the Cross, of denying Christ, of permitting sodomy, of worshipping an idol, all in the most impenetrable secrecy. Such were the Middle Ages, when prejudice was so vehement that, to destroy an adversary, men did not recoil from inventing the most criminal charges. It will suffice to recall the similar, but even more ridiculous than ignominious accusations brought against Pope Boniface VIII by the same Philip the Fair. Most of the accused declared themselves guilty of these secret crimes after being subjected to such ferocious torture that many of them succumbed. Some made similar confessions without the use of torture, it is true, but through fear of it; the threat had been sufficient. Such was the case with the grand master himself, Jacques de Molay, who acknowledged later that he had lied to save his life. Carried on without the authorization of the pope, who had the military orders under his immediate jurisdiction, this investigation was radically corrupt both as to its intent and as to its procedure. Not only did Clement V enter an energetic protest, but he annulled the entire trial and suspended the powers of the bishops and their inquisitors. However, the offence had been admitted and remained the irrevocable basis of the entire subsequent proceedings. Philip the Fair took advantage of the discovery to have bestowed upon himself by the University of Paris the title of Champion and Defender of the Faith, and also to stir up public opinion at the States General of Tours against the heinous crimes of the Templars. Moreover, he succeeded in having the confessions of the accused confirmed in presence of the pope by seventy-two Templars, who had been specially chosen and coached beforehand. In view of this investigation at Poitiers (June, 1308), the pope, until then sceptical, at last became concerned and opened a new commission, the procedure of which he himself directed. He reserved the cause of the order to the papal commission, leaving individuals to be tried by the diocesan commissions to whom he restored their powers.

The second phase of the process was the papal inquiry, which was not restricted to France, but extended to all the Christian countries of Europe, and even to the Orient. In most of the other countries —Portugal, Spain, Germany, Cyprus—the Templars were found innocent; in Italy, except in a few districts, the decision was the same. But in France the episcopal inquisitions, resuming their activities, took the facts as established at the trial, and confined themselves to reconciling the repentant guilty members, imposing various canonical penances extending even to perpetual imprisonment. Only those who persisted in heresy were to be turned over to the secular arm, but, by a rigid interpretation of this provision, those who had withdrawn their former confessions were considered relapsed heretics; thus fifty-four Templars who had recanted after having confessed were condemned as relapsed and publicly burned on 12 May, 1310. Subsequently all the other Templars, who had been examined at the trial, with very few exceptions declared themselves guilty. At the same time the papal commission, appointed to examine the cause of the order, had entered upon its duties and gathered together the documents which were to be submitted to the pope, and to the general council called to decide as to the final fate of the order. The culpability of single persons, which was looked upon as established, did not involve the guilt of the order. Although the defence of the order was poorly conducted, it could not be proved that the order as a body professed any heretical doctrine, or that a secret rule, distinct from the official rule, was practised. Consequently, at the General Council of Vienne in Dauphiné on 16 October, 1311, the majority were favourable to the maintenance of the order. The pope, irresolute and harassed, finally adopted a middle course: he decreed the dissolution, not the condemnation of the order, and not by penal sentence, but by an Apostolic Decree (Bull of 22 March, 1312). The order having been suppressed, the pope himself was to decide as to the fate of its members and the disposal of its possessions. As to the property, it was turned over to the rival Order of Hospitallers to be applied to its original use, namely the defence of the Holy Places. In Portugal, however, and in Aragon the possessions were vested in two new orders, the Order of Christ in Portugal and the Order of Montesa in Aragon. As to the members, the Templars recognized guiltless were allowed either to join another military order or to return to the secular state. In the latter case, a pension for life, charged to the possessions of the order, was granted them. On the other hand, the Templars who had pleaded guilty before their bishops were to be treated "according to the rigours of justice, tempered by a generous mercy".

The pope reserved to his own judgment the cause of the grand master and his three first dignitaries. They had confessed their guilt; it remained to reconcile them with the Church, after they had testified to their repentance with the customary solemnity. To give this solemnity more publicity, a platform was erected in front of the Notre-Dame for the reading of the sentence. But at the supreme moment the grand master recovered his courage and proclaimed the innocence of the Templars and the falsity of his own alleged confessions. To atone for this deplorable moment of weakness, he declared himself ready to sacrifice his life. He knew the fate that awaited him. Immediately after this unexpected coup-de-théâtre he was arrested as a relapsed heretic with another dignitary who chose to share his fate, and by order of Philip they were burned at the stake before the gates of the palace. This brave death deeply impressed the people, and, as it happened that the pope and the king died shortly afterwards, the legend spread that the grand master in the midst of the flames had summoned them both to appear in the course of the year before the tribunal of God. Such was the tragic end of the Templars. If we consider that the Order of the Hospitallers finally inherited, although not without difficulties, the property of the Templars and received many of its members, we may say that the result of the trial was practically equivalent to the long-proposed amalgamation of the two rival orders. For the Knights (first of Rhodes, afterwards of Malta) took up and carried on elsewhere the work of the Knights of the Temple.

This formidable trial, the greatest ever brought to light whether we consider the large number of accused, the difficulty of discovering the truth from a mass of suspicious and contradictory evidence, or the many jurisdictions in activity simultaneously in all parts of Christendom from Great Britain to Cyprus, is not yet ended. It is still passionately discussed by historians who have divided into two camps, for and against the order. To mention only the principal ones, the following find the order guilty: Dupuy (1654), Hammer (1820), Wilcke (1826), Michelet (1841), Loiseleur (1872), Prutz (1888), and Rastoul (1905); the following find it innocent: Father Lejeune (1789), Raynouard (1813), Havemann (1846), Ladvocat (1880), Schottmuller (1887), Gmelin (1893), Lea (1888), Fincke (1908). Without taking any side in this discussion, which is not yet exhausted, we may observe that the latest documents brought to light, particularly those which Fincke has recently extracted from the archives of the Kingdom of Aragon, tell more and more strongly in favour of the order.

In chronological order, the most important works are: DUPUIS, *Hist. de l'ordre militaire des templiers* (Paris, 1654); LEJEUNE, *Hist. critique et apologétique de l'ordre des Templiers* (2 vols., Paris, 1789); WILCKE, *Gesch. des Tempelordens* (2 vols., 2nd ed., Halle, 1860); PRUTZ, *Entwickelung und Untergang des Tempelordens* (Berlin, 1888); GMELIN, *Schuld oder Unschuld des Tempelordens* (Stuttgart, 1893); FINCKE, *Papsttum und Untergang des Tempelordens* (2 vols., Münster, 1907). Documents: *La règle du temple* (Paris, 1886); *Die ursprungliche Templeregel* (Freiburg, 1903); VIOLLET, *Les interrogatoires de Jacques de Molay* (Paris, 1910). See also CLEMENT V.

CHARLES MOELLER.

Temple.—The Latin form, *templum*, from which the English *temple* is derived, originally signified an uncovered area marked off by boundaries; especially a space marked off by the augurs to be excepted from all profane uses. Among the Romans the precincts of a temple were always quadrangular in ground plan; hence the so-called temple of Vesta, one of the most famous sanctuaries of Rome, being circular in plan, was not strictly a temple, but only an *ædes sacra*, or sacred building. When the augurs had determined the boundaries of a temple-enclosure, the boundary lines could not lawfully be interrupted except at one point, which was to serve as an entrance. To mark these boundaries no walls were needed; a formula spoken by the augur was sufficient, and from this ceremony, came the phrase *effari locum*, literally, "to proclaim a place", hence, to define and dedicate.

It is certain that the Indo-Germanic peoples originally had no buildings for the worship of their gods, but worshipped the gods upon mountains, as Herodotus expressly says of the Persians, or believed the supernatural beings were present in groves and trees. Consequently among the ancient Germans the conception of a grove was identified with that of a temple. Among the Greeks, also, the worship of trees seems to be indicated by the word for temple, ναός, which, according to some authorities, signified originally "tree" or "tree-trunk". It is certain that the Greeks believed that at Dodona they heard the voice of the gods foretelling the future from the rustling of the sacred oaks. In the Homeric age, the temple as a space set apart and containing an altar, which was perhaps shaded by a group of trees, was more commonly found than the temple built by man. If actual temples are mentioned in Homer, as at Troy and the fabulous city of the Phæacians, the circumstance is probably attributable to Oriental influence. The pagan Germans were never able to bring themselves to give up their original worship of the gods in groves to any such extent as the Greeks and Romans did under the influence of the East. Still the German peoples were hardly entirely without temples, any more than the Scandinavians, although these temples could only have been of wood. The beginnings of stone temples among the Germans probably go back to the first Christian centuries and are attributable to the influence of their neighbours, the Gauls.

When new temples were built precincts already consecrated to the divinity were preferably chosen. It was also customary to select the highest spot in a city, the acropolis, as the general preference at that time was for high, open spaces. Further the kind of divinity had also influence on the choice of the spot: thus Zeus preferred the heights, Mars the market-places, Hercules the gymnasium, others, the fortified castle, the gates of the city, the plain. If the temple could not be erected on an open space dedicated to the divinity, it was customary to surround the temple by an enclosed precinct, whereby it was separated from all that was profane. Still other buildings were frequently inside this enclosure, as the houses of the priests, or the stalls for the sacrificial animals. Vessels containing water were placed at the entrance; from these, those entering sprinkled themselves in order to be purified from all guilt, as nothing impure was permitted to enter the precincts.

As a rule a Greek temple faced the east. The point towards which a Roman temple faced varied, according to the theory of H. Nissen, who investigated a large number of these temples in respect to this matter. He claimed that the position of the front depended upon the altitude of the sun on the feast day of the respective god. Nissen started from the assumption that the Greeks and Romans regarded the gods as the manifestation of the world-pervading spirit, and as such subordinated them to the original symbol of the world-spirit, the sun. Consequently, according to his theory, the temples were so placed that on the day settled by the calendar as the birthday and feast day of the god the rays of the rising sun fell along the axis of the temple and thus also on his statue. This theory suffers, however, from the fatal uncertainty as to the date the day of dedication fell on. Moreover, the instances in which of late it has been possible to determine the formerly unknown god occupying a temple of known position, so as to test the correctness of this hypothesis, have proved unfavourable to it [Nissen, "Templum" (Berlin, 1869)]. At the same time, however, it remains as a fact that the orientation of the temple was universally customary, just as it was later in the case of the Christian church.

Among the Romans when the building of the temple was completed it was dedicated to the divinity by the public authorities or by a person specially delegated for this office, while the priests only pronounced the formulæ without personally completing the sacred act. The dedication adhered permanently to the soil which was released by it from all other religious obligations and was withdrawn from profane use. The anniversary of the dedication was celebrated annually by a sacrifice.

Among the equipments of the temple were a massive altar, sacrificial tables, movable hearths for fire, sacrificial utensils, and other objects, which were dedicated at the same time as the temple. They formed a temple property that could not be sold. However, in times of necessity, especially of war, these treasures were as often melted down as were the costly church utensils of the medieval era and of later periods. The doorkeeper, who permitted visitors to enter the temple at stated times, also guarded the treasures.

The massive altar, mentioned above, did not stand in the temple but before it. Either it was built upon a high stone platform, and thus united architecturally with the temple, or it stood in front of the steps or in the portico. There was, as a rule, only one sacrificial table in the temple and only one altar in front of it.

The cella of the temple contained the most important object, the statue of the divinity, which stood on a pedestal against the rear wall opposite the entrance. In the earliest period it was made of wood or clay, later it was cast from bronze or made of marble. Besides the statue of the god to whom the temple was dedicated, statues of other gods were at times placed in the temple, partly as ornaments, partly because of their connexion with the principal god.

Taking their use as the basis of classification three kinds of temples may be distinguished: temples for worship, for use in connexion with the *agones*, or festival games, and for the Mysteries. The temple for worship was small and its cella contained only the statue of the god that was the object of veneration; it served religious uses exclusively. This temple frequently had connected with it the temple for the festival games which served for the solemn crowning of the victor in the national competitive contests, and as the place for keeping the apparatus for the festivals. The temples of the mysteries were used by the initiated for the celebration of the secret cults, and differed from the others, so far as the scanty remains permit a judgment, both in extent and form. Such temples were to be found, for instance, at Eleusis and at Samothracia. As has just been said, the temple contained only the statue of the god; it existed not so much for men as for the gods. It was exclusively the house of the god to whom it was dedicated. Still the god was pleased when at the national feasts men appeared in his sanctuary with prayers and incense, and thus these days became religious as well as national festivals.

Again, because the objects placed in the temple were more secure, it served as a treasury both for the State and for private persons. From 438 B. C. the public treasure of Athens was kept in the Parthenon. Naturally the temple also contained the votive offerings presented to the gods, as statues, lamps, wreaths, rings, and bracelets. A list of these objects was annually compiled, and once in four years it was engraved in marble; some fragments of such marbles are still in existence. Sometimes, too, the temple contained the mint.

Besides material things men also found security and protection in the temple against threatening danger. Every temple was an ἄσυλον, that is, it was inviolable, and none ventured to drive a malefactor away from the altar unless such a one wished to draw down the wrath of the gods upon himself. All temples did not grant the same protection: only certain temples had the privilege of unconditional security. Still there were ways of making the right of asylum ineffective, as was shown in the case of the Spartan Pausanias. During the reign of Tiberius the great number of asylums in Asia Minor was a subject of complaint.

As to the form and manner of construction of the temple, we must in the first place not imagine that the Greeks and Romans at all times built for their gods those magnificent structures that even to-day all men of taste admire. The earliest sanctuaries of the gods were cave-temples, if grottoes and crypts deserve this name at all. Even in a later age the worship of Mithras was preferably celebrated in grottoes. Related to the natural cave-temples are the artificial rock-temples, of which magnificent examples are still to be found in India. A third form, found especially in Assyria, Mexico, and Peru, may be called tower, or pyramidal temples, because the actual sanctuary is placed on a truncated pyramid. The fourth, finally, is the classical form of the Greeks and Romans. It is a development of the *megaron*, or ruler's house, of primitive times, which consisted only of a large hall with a portico. This portico was formed by the projecting side-walls of the hall and was ornamented in front with two columns.

Having thus briefly considered the subject as a whole, we will now examine somewhat more closely the kinds of temple used by various civilized nations. This is all the more necessary in order to guard against identifying the temple of the Greeks with that of other peoples. The discussion, however, must be brief, because temples, both pagan and Christian, have always been the highest achievements of architecture and have therefore been treated incidentally in other articles. The oldest architectural remains are those of Egypt. The main point of interest here is the structure of the great temples of the eighteenth to the twentieth dynasties (about 1530–1150 B. C.). Of special importance are the ruins of temples at Thebes or the present villages of Luxor and Karnak. The Egyptian temple is not an organic structure complete in itself; instead of unity there are the following distinct parts: *dromos*, enclosing wall, *pylon*, peristyle, hypostyle, and *sekos*. The temple of the Egyptians therefore consisted of a large complex of buildings and the temple precincts, the whole surrounded by a massive wall, and reached by a broad avenue (*dromos*) bordered by figures of sphinxes and rams. Between the temples of Luxor and Karnak this avenue for processions was nearly a mile and a quarter in length and more than 75 feet wide. In the enclosing wall, which at Karnak was about 32 feet wide, there were several gigantic gateways called pylons, flanked by tower-like buildings. These led into the sacred precincts, within which was a lake. On certain days the statue of the god was rowed round this lake in a golden bark. A second pylon led into the peristyle, or *protikos*, a quadrangular open space containing covered halls with columns; a third pylon led into the hypostyle, or large covered colonnade. The hypostyle was called "the hall of manifestation", and only "the enlightened" were permitted to enter it, the lower classes of the population might come only as far as the peristyle. On the farther side of the hypostyle there were still other large halls which led ultimately to the actual sanctuary, or *sekos*, in which the divinity was represented by a statue or some symbol; only the king or his representative, the high priest, could enter the *sekos*. Beyond this sanctuary were other large halls and chambers for keeping the apparatus for the festivals. A peculiarity of this extended series of sacred buildings is that the greater the distance from the entrance the narrower and lower the structure, so that the *sekos* is only a small dark chamber.

The huge size and rich equipment of Egyptian temples is explained by the fact that they were monuments of the piety of the ruler, royal houses of prayer; consequently the king alone had the right to enter the sanctuary. For this reason the paintings and reliefs on a sunken background (cœlanaglyphic), with which the temple walls were richly ornamented, presented in the most varied forms the homage and worship paid to the ruler. The ruler also showed the depth of his piety by the magnificent festivals which were connected with the temple.

The architecture of the temple was in harmony with the obscure, mysterious, and sensual religious conceptions of the Egyptians. The temple was an inorganic conglomeration of structures fitted the one into the other, that only arouse our astonishment by their size and magnificence. It is hardly necessary to say that no rigid system prevailed in the plan of either the Egyptian temples or those to be mentioned further on, and that there were small temples as well as large.

The Chaldean temples differed essentially from those of the Egyptians; if in the latter the chief extent was horizontal, in the former it was vertical. The large temples of the Chaldeans were constructed so as to form a series of terraces or steps or something like a pile of rectangular prisms, decreasing in size from the base up. According to Herodotus, the temple of Bel at Babylon, built in a series of terraces, measured at the base two stadia (1214 feet) each way. On this broad base the tower-like structure rose in seven stories which were topped by the actual sanctuary. The upper stories were reached by means of an exterior stairway or by an inclined roadway. Half-way up the ascent was a chamber where those who were mounting could sit down and rest. This peculiar form of architecture was certainly influenced by astrology which had so authoritative a position in the Chaldæo-Assyrian religion. The temples raised on terraces were constructed in three, or five, or more stories, according to the importance of the divinity. Besides these there must certainly have been smaller houses of one story for the gods, though of this no positive proof has yet been discovered. Temples raised on terraces have also been found in Mexico and Peru, as, for instance, at Tehuacan and Santiago Guatusca.

The Indian temples are principally grottoes or caves. They are generally constructed in one or two forms: either hewn out of the rock and remaining connected with the main mass, or, cut away from the surrounding mass of rock so as to stand alone. To the first class belong largely the Buddhist temples (*chaitya*), while the latter form is preferred by the Brahmins. The more developed ground-plan of the Buddhist *chaitya* resembles in some points the plan of the early Christian basilica. It is a quadrangular space, its length much greater than its width, and has a kind of apse opposite the entrance. The inner space is divided into several naves by pillars which follow the line of the apse. In the apse is the dagoba, a circular mound like a grave, terminating at the top in a hemisphere with a *ti* or *tee* (stone in the form of an altar). The dagoba is used to hold relics of Buddha, and the entire tumulus is covered by a large umbrella. Noted cave-temples are to be found at Karli in the Chatt mountains (second century B. C.), at Agunta, and at Pandu-Lena. The detached temple consists sometimes of several buildings and halls connected by stairs and bridges. These buildings have been cut out of the parent rock so as to stand in a court surrounded by columned cloisters. Such a temple is the wonderful structure of Kailas (Seat of the Blessed) at Ellora, a work of the ninth century. Sometimes the temple is of small dimensions, as that at Mahavelliopore on the Coromandel Coast, which is hewn out of a detached rock; the ground-plan is a quadrangle, and it rises in several stories like a pyramid built in several terraces.

The typical Greek temple stood alone on a broad foundation platform, built on all sides in terraces, which was called the *crepidoma*. The temple consisted, generally, first, of the *naos*, or *cella*, which was a rectangular enclosed space for holding the statue of the god; second, of the *pronaos*, a portico or vestibule in front of the *cella* with which it was connected by a door, while to the front it had rows of columns with open spaces between; third, the *posticum*, a portico behind the cella and corresponding to the *pronaos*. Large buildings contained two further structures, the *opisthodomos*, a chamber between the *cella* and the *osticum*, and fifth, the peristyle, a covered walk with a system of columns surrounding the temple and open on the outer side. These two last-mentioned parts of the temple were probably added in the seventh century B. C.

The name of the Greek temple varied with its ground-plan. The simplest form was called the temple with *antæ* (*templum in antis*), *antæ* signifying pilasters which form the terminations of walls. If the two side-walls of the *cella* extend a little beyond the transverse wall, and these ends of the side-walls are finished with *antæ*, then these give the name to the entire structure. Two columns generally stand in the space between the two *antæ*. The sense of symmetry led to the same construction at the rear without there being any change in the name. If the portico were formed merely by a row of columns without the aid of walls it was called a prostyle temple; if the same construction were also placed at the rear of the building it was amphiprostyle. The actual creation of the Greek mind was the peristyle, in which the entire temple was surrounded by a row of columns which carried the projecting beams of the roof. A second, inner, row of columns was generally arranged at the front and back of the building. If the columns were replaced by engaged columns on the walls of the cella, the temple was a pseudo-peripteral temple. A temple was called a *dipteros* if it were surrounded by a double colonnade, and *pseudodipteros* when the inner row of columns was not used. A circle of columns with a roof over them, but without a cella, formed a monopteral temple. A third method of designating or distinguishing the temples is by the number of columns in front, thus temples are called tetrastyle, hexastyle, octastyle, that is having five, six, or eight columns.

Up to the seventh century B. C. the method of building was very simple: the walls of the cella were made of unburnt brick resting on a stone base, the columns were of wood, for originally the Greek temple in its essential parts was not built of stone. In the buildings of better construction the walls were ornamented with terra-cotta tiles, and the columns were covered with precious metals. The earliest temples were built in the Doric style; this was followed from the sixth century by the Ionic style that came from Asia Minor, and later by the Corinthian style. One style, however, never entirely supplanted another. If in the Doric temple the impression made was that of massiveness, the Ionic temple conveyed a sense of agreeable lightness and grace. The effect produced by the Greek temple was not that of gigantic size, as in the Egyptian, or of colossal mass as in the Assyrian; it arose from the harmonious relation between all its members, by the spiritualizing of the styles of architecture and the ornamentation, as well as by the careful execution of all parts, even those least seen. Thus it became a model for all succeeding centuries, which always return to it after they have tried for a time new architectural designs of their own. The Romans were the first to adopt the plan of the Greek temple, but they impressed their national character upon it in several ways: the foundation platform was frequently omitted or was replaced by a *podium* without any steps except those leading to the entrance; the front was emphasized by prolonging the portico and increasing the number of columns. The finely balanced harmony of the Greeks was sacrificed to ostentatious display of material and the huge size of the structure. The round temple is peculiar to the Romans, who greatly developed it. Among the temples of this style is one of the most important masterpieces of Roman architecture, the Pantheon, as well as several small, graceful structures like that at Tivoli.

However important a Greek or Roman temple may be architecturally, still it is essentially nothing more than a beautiful and stately private house, a dwelling-place of the divinity, not a house of prayer and a place for the people to offer sacrifice. In this is made evident the marked difference between the temple and the Christian church. From the beginning the Christian church was intended to hold all those who believed and its interior was divided into sanctuary and nave for the clergy and the laity. It contained in itself the fruitful seed which enabled it in the course of centuries to develop, even architecturally, far beyond the classical temple. In the latter, excepting in the prostyle temple, the front had hardly any distinctive characteristic, in the peripteral, amphiprostyle, and other temples the back and front were alike. On the other hand, the façades of many Christian churches are works of the finest finish and highest architectural value. Although the temple contained several chambers within, yet this fact exercised no actual influence on its external construction, while in the Christian church, either of the Romanesque or of the Gothic style, the inner arrangement is easily recognized from the external construction. It is a striking fact, and one that is, perhaps, not to be explained entirely by the dislike of the early Christians for the places of heathen worship, that from the beginning the model chosen for the Christian church was not the classic temple, but the basilica, which, as the court and place of exchange, was intended to hold large numbers of people.

BEDA KLEINSCHMIDT.

LITURGY OF THE TEMPLE.—The three great national festivals of the Jews—the Passover, Pentecost, and the Feast of Tabernacles—were the occasion of special liturgical service of the temple (Ex., xxiii, 14, 17; xxxiv, 23; Deut., xvi, 16). Other feasts could be celebrated by local observance. Not so these three national feasts. All males were supposed to appear at Jerusalem on these occasions: "in the place which the Lord thy God shall choose, that his name may dwell there" (Deut., xvi, 6). It was during the Passover, while the lambs for the Pasch were dressed, that the Levites in the Temple chanted the Hallel (Pss. cxiii–cxviii: Vulg., cxii–cxvii). These same Psalms were repeated during the paschal meal,—the first two after the second cup, the remainder after the fourth cup.

The ordinary temple liturgy is not clear to us. Scant and obscure details are preserved in the Sacred Text. The people gathered in the courts of the Temple to receive instruction from the Prophets and to join them in prayer (Is., i, 12–15). The Deuteronomic custom was that the Torah should be read to the people in the Temple at the Feast of the Tabernacles (Deut., xxxi, 10–13). After the Exile, Esdras brought back this custom (II Esd., viii, 5–8). And yet, not even the reading of Torah was the chief purpose of the Temple; it was essentially a "house of prayer for all nations" (Is., lvi, 7); prayer to Jahweh was its chief purpose. It was in the Temple of Silo that Anna prayed for a man child (I Kings, i, 11). In the first Temple of Jerusalem, Solomon said his inspiring prayer for Israel (III Kings, viii, 12–53). Apart from the Psalms, set forms of prayer were rare. In such set forms, the priest offered the first-fruits and tithes before the altar of the Temple (Deut., xxvi, 5–10); and the high-priest laid the sins of Israel upon the head of the scape-goat (Lev., xvi, 21). During the morning and the evening sacrifices, the Levites sang praises to the Lord and gave thanks (I Par., xxiii, 30). These praises would seem to have been the Psalms, since the leader of the Levites in the time of Nehemias was a son of Asaph (II Esd., xi, 17). The titles of many of the Psalms give evidence of their liturgical use in the temple or "the House of Jahweh" that preceded the Temple. The Psalms of Asaph and of the sons of Korah (see PSALMS) at one time made up a liturgical collection for temple service. The sons of Asaph were among the temple levites (I Par., xxv, 1). The sons of Korah were also a levitical family of temple singers (II Par., xx, 19). In fact, there can be no doubt but the Psalms are evidence of a gradual development of a liturgical hymnal for temple service.

Certain elements of synagogal liturgy (see SYNAGOGUE) probably have their origin in temple service. The "Shema" (Deut., vi, 4–9), together with the Ten Commandments and several benedictions, were recited by the priest at the morning sacrifice (Tamid, v). Josephus (Ant. Jud., IV, viii, 13) dates this synagogal practice from the time of Moses.

ZENNER, *Die Chorgesänge im Buche der Psalmen* (Freiburg, 1896); ZENNER-WIESMANN, *Die Psalmen nach dem Urtext* (Münster, 1906). The latter work edits the text over much, and has consequently been put on the *Index* (1911).

WALTER DRUM.

Temple, SISTERS OF THE.—The Sisters of the Temple (whose full title is SISTERS OF THE FINDING OF

Jesus in the Temple) are a pre-Reformation foundation. They were established in London for educational purposes at the time of the Crusades by a dean whose name has not come down to us. They spread widely in England in the following centuries, but were driven into exile at the Reformation. In 1860 Cardinal Wiseman, with the generous help of the Abbé Roullin, re-established them in the Archdiocese of Westminster, whence they moved to Clifton. But it was not until a house was opened at Vernon, Normandy, that they began once more to flourish; from Vernon they have opened six houses in France and Belgium, and now number 170 sisters. They have a home for invalid priests at Clifton, and the chief work of the sisters now is nursing among all classes of society. They are known as the Blue Nuns in England and France, from the blue habit they wear.

Datin, *Discours pour le cinquantenaire des Sœurs de Jésus au Temple* (1910).

Francesca M. Steele.

Temple of Jerusalem.—The word "temple" is derived from the Latin *templum*, signifying an uncovered place affording a view of the surrounding region; in a narrower sense it signifies a place sacred to the Divinity, a sanctuary. In the Bible the sanctuary of Jerusalem bears the Hebrew name of *Bêt Yehôvâh* (house of Jehovah). The sacred edifice consisted of two chief halls, one called *hêkāl* (the house or temple), or *qôdes* (the Holy), and the other *děbîr* (that which is the oracle), or *gôdesh haggodâshim* (the Holy of Holies). The New Testament speaks of it as οἶκος, "the house", ναός, Latin *cella*, "the most holy place of the temple", and ἱερόν, "the whole of the sacred enclosure". The Temple which Solomon erected to the Lord about 966 b. c. was destroyed by Nabuchodonosor in 586 b. c. After the return from captivity Zorobabel raised it again from its ruins (537 b. c.), but in such modest conditions that the ancients who had seen the former Temple wept. In the eighteenth year of his reign, which corresponds to 19 b. c., King Herod destroyed the Temple of Zorobabel to replace it by another which would equal, if not surpass in splendour, that of Solomon.

Many writers admit three temples materially different. Now as the Prophet Aggeus (Vulg., ii, 10) says of that of Zorobabel: "Great shall be the glory of this last house more than of the first", because of the coming of the Messias (v, 8–9), they claim that this prophecy was not fulfilled because Christ never entered the second Temple. Others assert that Zorobabel's work was not completely destroyed but gradually replaced by a larger and much richer temple (Josephus, "Ant. Jud.," ed. Dindorf, XV, xi, 2), and they consequently admit only two materially different temples. The whole difficulty disappears if we choose the Septuagint in preference to the Vulgate. The Prophet has already asked: "Who is left among you, that saw this house in its first glory?" (ii, 4). According to the Septuagint he afterwards says: "The last glory of this house shall be greater than its first glory." To the Prophet, therefore, there was but one and the same house of Jehovah from Solomon to the time of Messias, built always in the same place and according to the same plan, that of the Tabernacle. We may therefore admit three different temples, and this article will describe: I. that of Solomon; II. that of Zorobabel; III. that of Herod.

I. Temple of Solomon. *History.*—Through a motive of pride David had commanded the numbering of his people, in punishment of which God decimated the Israelites by a pestilence. One day the king saw near the threshing-floor of Ornan (Areuna) the Jebusite an angel about to strike the people of the city, whereupon David humbled himself before the Lord, Who forgave him and stayed the plague. The king hastened to purchase the property of the Jebusite for fifty sicles of silver and built an altar on the threshing-floor, upon which he offered holocausts and peace-offerings (II Kings, xxiv). This hill, which is the Mount Moria (II Par., iii, I) of Genesis (xxii, 2), was thenceforth destined to be the site of the Temple of Jehovah, for which David had already amassed great treasures, but the building of which was reserved to Solomon. As hitherto the Hebrews had not cultivated the arts, Solomon addressed himself to Hiram, King of Tyre in Phœnicia, to obtain builders and skilful workers in stone, brass, and the cedar and cypress wood of Lebanon. After seven and a half years of toil the king was able to dedicate solemnly the Temple of the true God. Near the sacred precincts he afterwards built large buildings, among which the Bible makes special mention of the palace of the king, that of the queen, Pharao's daughter, the house of the forest, the porch of the throne, and that of pillars.

Site.—Mount Moria, which stretches from north to south, is a long spur, or promontory, connected at the north with Mount Bezetha and bounded on the east and west by two deep valleys which are joined at their southern extremity (see Jerusalem, VIII, 345 d). Between its two steep declivities the crest of the hill afforded but narrow space for buildings, and to secure an adequate site for the Temple, the courts, and royal palaces a platform was formed by raising sustaining walls of carefully-hewn beautiful stones measuring eight or ten cubits (III Kings, v, 17; vii, 9–10). According to Jewish tradition the Temple stood on the highest point of Mount Moria, while the royal quarters were built south of its enclosure and on a lower level.

It is generally admitted that the "sacred rock" in the centre of the Mosque of Omar (see Jerusalem, VIII, 360 d) formed the foundation of the altar of holocausts in the Temple of Jerusalem. On this hill, according to an ancient tradition, Abraham made ready to sacrifice his son Isaac; here, near the threshing-floor of Ornan, the exterminating angel restored his sword to its scabbard; and on this threshing-floor, which according to custom was situated at the highest point, David erected an altar to the Lord. If this prominent rock was constantly spared at the various rebuildings of the platform it must have been because of its associations. Moreover, it corresponds to all the requirements of Exodus (xx, 24 sq.) for the altar of holocausts. It is a limestone rock, unhewn and irregular, fifty-eight feet long, by forty-five wide, and standing three or four feet above the ground. Furthermore, in its upper almost level surface there is a hole whereby it is believed the blood and the water of the ablutions flowed into the cavity beneath to be carried off by a subterranean conduit to the valley of Cedron. The Mishna (Yoma, II, i) asserts that under the altar of holocausts there was a canal of this kind. This point admitted, the "sacred rock" will serve as a mark to discover the exact site of the house of Jehovah, because the latter opened to the east opposite the altar of holocausts and consequently west of the court of the priests which contained the altar.

Sources.—The chief sources of information concerning the plan, construction, and adornment of the Temple are, first III Kings, vi, vii; then the parallel account in II Par., iii, iv, which tends to magnify the dimensions immeasurably. The Prophet Ezechiel described the Temple in the light of a heavenly vision, and though his description is symbolic it agrees in its essential features with that of the Book of Kings; to all appearances he describes the Lord's house as he saw it while he performed his priestly duties. The information supplied by Josephus and the Middoth treatise of the Mishna inspires less confidence; it seems based rather on the Temple of Herod than on that of Solomon. Indeed we possess but a brief description of the first Temple and the technical terms used by the Bible are not always readily intelligible in modern times; hence there is great diversity of opinion among writers who have attempted to reconstruct the Temple of Solomon in its architectural details.

Architecture and Measurement.—Solomon reproduced in solid materials and double proportions the Tabernacle which Moses had built in the desert (Wisdom, ix, 8), the entire plan of which is therefore outlined (Ex., xxvi, xxxvi). With regard to the style adopted by the Phœnician architects we know simply that at that period the architecture of all Semitic peoples was very similar to that of the Egyptians. In Egypt there were two measures of length; the smaller cubit formed of the breadth of six hands or twenty-four fingers and equal to 1 ft. 5¾ inches, the large or royal cubit, which was a handbreadth (three inches) longer. The lesser cubit of six hands, or twenty-four fingers, existed in the eastern empire, but it was somewhat longer, being equal to 1 ft. 7⅓ inches. The large or royal cubit was likewise longer, being equal to 1 ft. 9⅙ inches. Now judging from the excavations made at Taanath and Megiddo in Palestine the royal Babylonian cubit, introduced by the long Chaldean domination, was the one in use at that time (Benzinger, "Hebr. Archäologie", 190). It is probable that only the small cubit was in use at the time of the Babylonian Captivity, hence the sacred writer (II Par. iii, 3) gives the dimensions of the Temple by the "first measure", or ancient cubit, and Ezechiel (xl, 5; xliii, 13) adds to each cubit a handbreadth (the ancient *palmus minor*, one-sixth of the small cubit) in order to obtain the length given in the Book of Kings. The royal Babylonian cubit therefore was the *mesura verissima* (Ezech., xliii, 13) used in the construction of the Temple of Solomon.

The Holy Place; the Holy of Holies.—The house of God was of rectangular shape, sixty cubits long from east to west by twenty cubits wide and thirty high (III Kings, vi, 2; II Par., iii, 3). These were the interior dimensions which did not include the thickness of the walls, as is shown by numerous texts. This space was divided into two chambers of unequal size. The first, the *hêkāl*, or Holy Place (see plan, fig. I), was forty cubits long by twenty wide. It was entered at the eastern end by a square gate (III Kings, vi, 33), ten cubits in breadth (Ezech., xli, 2). The framework was of wild-olive wood, furnished with two doors of cypress wood. Each door was subdivided vertically into two leaves which folded by means of hinges (III Kings, vi, 33, 34). On the other side of the compartment was a pentagonal-shaped gate (III Kings, vi, 31) with an opening of six cubits through a partition wall two cubits in thickness (Ezech., xli, 3–4). It opened into the *dĕbîr*, or Holy of Holies (2), a chamber measuring twenty cubits every way.

The two doors of wild-olive wood in the gate opened towards the east and stood always open to allow the passage of fresh air and the smoke of incense to enter the interior, but a veil of byssus in violet, purple, and scarlet, embroidered with cherubim, always concealed the Holy of Holies (II Par., iii, 14), which was entered only by the high-priest once a year. On the doors of the two gates Solomon caused figures of cherubim, palm-trees, and blossoming flowers to be carved and overlaid with gold (III Kings, vi, 32, 35). The walls of *dĕbîr* and *hêkāl* were lined with boards of cedar adorned with colocinths and flowers carved in relief and profusely overlaid with gold. Within the *dĕbîr* even the fir-wood floor was covered with plates of fine gold and the front was closed with chains of the same metal (III Kings, vi, 15).

Secondary Chambers.—The whole building, including the Holy of Holies which formed the chief part, was thirty cubits high. Now as the interior of the *dĕbîr* was only twenty cubits high there must have been above it a space of ten cubits. The height of the Holy Place is not indicated in the Bible, but there is mention of "cenacles", or upper chambers (II Par., iii, 9); hence the Holy Place must have been of the same height as the *dĕbîr* and like it have had above it a chamber ten cubits high. The same text informs us that these "upper chambers" were richly adorned like those below and there is little doubt that the Tabernacle was preserved in the large upper chamber (III Kings, viii, 4; Par., v, 5), and in the lower one relics and remembrances of the life in the desert. In front of the *hêkāl* was the vestibule or porch (3) *ûlâm*, Greek πρόναος, of the same length as the Temple but only ten cubits deep (III Kings, vi, 3); it was a kind

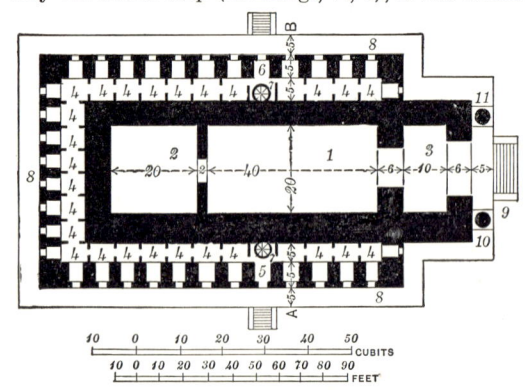

Fig. 1. Plan of the Temple of Solomon
1. The Holy Place. 2. The Holy of Holies. 3. The porch. 4. Side chambers. 5–6. Doors of the side chambers. 7. Winding stairways. 8. Foundations. 9. Grand staircase. 10. Pillar of Jachin. 11. Pillar of Booz.

of stately tower, recalling the pylons of the Egyptian temples and like them having a large gateway without doors. II Paralipomenon (iii, 4) states that its height was one hundred and twenty cubits. But a porch six times higher than it was long would be so out of proportion that many exegetes are inclined to reduce this figure to sixty cubits, the height of the porch of the Temple of Zorobabel. According to Ezechiel the walls were six cubits thick.

Along the three other sides of the sanctuary rose a building divided into three stories (III Kings, vi, 5–6), each story having thirty chambers [Ezech., xli, 6; Ant. Jud., VIII, iii, 2]. (4) The house of Jehovah was so sacred that the beams of cedar which supported the ceilings of the side chambers were not suffered to be fastened to the walls of the Temple; hence in the walls of the Holy Place and the Holy of Holies there were three recesses in which rested the ends of the joists. Thus the under chambers were five cubits in breadth, those of the first floor six cubits, and those of the second seven. Each story was five cubits high. The entrance was by a door (5) which opened to the south (III Kings, vi, 6–8); Ezechiel (xli, II) mentions another (6) on the north, which would be very natural. Ascent from one floor to another was made by means of a winding-stair (7), and it is very probable that the upper chambers, or cenacles, were reached by way of one of the stories of the porch. In these low-ceiled and narrow cells were preserved the archives, the public treasure, the accessories of worship, and the sacred vestments (cf. III, Kings, viii, 4; II Par., v, 5). In this manner the Holy Place and the Holy of Holies were completely surrounded by imposing structures.

Roofs and Windows.—The Temple was covered with a roofing formed of beams and planks of cedar (III Kings, vi, 9). Any broad surface which rests on a framework instead of on arches of mason-work is unstable and cannot prevent the rain leaking through; hence it is our opinion that the roofs of Solomon's temple were sloping, and the planks covered with large slabs. On the other hand several writers consider that they were flat. The upper story of the Holy of Holies, the numerous small chambers of the adjacent building, as also the porch, were furnished with windows having fixed gratings of wood, of which mention is made in the text (III Kings, vi, 4). The walls of the *hêkāl* had similar openings at the north and south, at least in the lower portion; but the position of these windows scarcely allowed the admission of light into the large chamber, which, furthermore, was lighted night and day by numerous lamps. The windows were intended rather to permit the circulation of fresh air and the escape of incense-smoke through the side chambers. The Holy of Holies seems to have had no windows and was always enveloped in darkness (III Kings, viii, 12).

Bronze Pillars.—It should be borne in mind that the entire building was constructed of the beautiful red and white limestone of the country, which could be polished like marble. We cannot believe that such a sumptuous monument was built on the earth without any foundations. Moreover Ezechiel tells us (xli, 8) that it rested on a foundation six cubits high, which formed all about it a border five cubits broad (8). The porch was reached by a stairway of ten steps [Ezech, xl, 49, (9)], which in ancient times were always rather high. At the top of the stairway on the foundation stood two pillars of molten brass each eighteen cubits high and twelve cubits in circumference (III Kings, vii, 15). The pillars were hollow, but the metal was four fingers in thickness (Jer., lii, 21). The capitals which surmounted them were five cubits high, and their tops were fashioned in the shape of lilies. They were richly adorned with network, garlands, pomegranates, foliage, etc., but despite the details furnished by the Bible (III Kings, vii, 16-19; II Par., iii, 13-17), it is very difficult to reconstruct them in their true form. The pillar which stood at the right of the porch door (10) was called Jachin, "He will establish", and that on the left Booz, "in strength". There is no mention in the text of base or pedestal, but some sort of a base would not have been out of place. Despite their squat shape these magnificent pillars recall the obelisks before the pylons of the Egyptian temples.

Furniture.—In the *hêkāl* before the gate of the *děbîr* stood the altar of incense, a rectangular square chest of cedar wood, each side measuring a cubit wide and two cubits high. The wood was completely covered with plates of gold (III Kings, vi, 20, 22; vii, 48; I Par., xviii, 18; II Par., iv, 19). At the north side stood the table of gold on which the loaves of proposition were set every Sabbath. III Kings, vii, 48, speaks of only one golden table for these sacred loaves, while I Par., xxviii, 16, and II Par., iv, 19, mention several, but the text has been mutilated by the copyist, for elsewhere (II Par., xiii, 11, and xxix, 18) there is likewise mention of only one. The ten tables of II Par., iv, 8, were those which held the candlesticks. On each side of the south and north courts stood five candlesticks of pure gold adorned with flowers which held gold oil-lamps, probably seven in number. The snuffers, bowls, knives, mortars, cups, censers, and other vessels were likewise all of pure gold (III Kings, vii, 48-50; II Par., iv, 8-9; 21-22). The Ark of the Covenant made by Moses in the Desert, with its staves, stood in the *děbîr* (III Kings, viii, 6). It contained a golden vessel holding manna, the rod of Aaron, and the two tables of the Law (Heb., ix, 4). At the ends of the Ark with wings outspread stood two cherubim ten cubits high carved from wild-olive wood and covered with gold. The inner wings met above the mercy-seat or cover of the Ark and the outer wings touched the walls (see ARK).

Court of the Priests.—On the north, south, and west sides of the building was a court about twenty cubits wide which extended in front of the house a distance of one hundred cubits each way (Ezech., xl, 47). This was the "inner court" (III Kings, vi, 36), called also the "court of the priests" (II Par., iv, 9), because they alone entered it, laymen being admitted only in exceptional circumstances (cf. IV Kings, xii, 12; Jer., xxxv, 1 sq., and xxxvi) (10). It was surrounded by a wall of three rows of polished stones and one row of beams of cedar (III Kings, vi, 36), probably placed edgewise in the form of a railing. The court was paved with stone slabs (II Par., vii, 3) and was entered by three doorways on the north, south, and east sides (Jer., xxxviii, 14; lii, 24; Ezech., xl, 28, 32, 35), the last-named was called the "king's gate" (I Par., ix, 18). In this court opposite the porch gate and at a distance of twenty-two cubits stood the brazen altar of holocausts (III Kings, viii, 64), which was twenty cubits in length and breadth and ten cubits high (II Par., iv, 1). The ascent to it was made by an incline facing the east. According to Ezech., xlii, 13 sq., the altar consisted of a square base measuring twenty cubits on the sides and one cubit high, with a trench around the border; on the base stood a large section eighteen cubits sideways and two high, above which was a second section sixteen cubits sideways and four high. Lastly came the *harel*, "mountain of God", measuring fourteen cubits on the sides and two high. The top of the altar consisted of the *ariel*, "hearth of God", having at each corner a horn one cubit high, and of a section one cubit high surmounted by a crown.

Between the Temple and the altar, but somewhat towards the south, was the famous "sea of molten brass", a vessel "round all about", the height of it five cubits and the diameter ten cubits. The outer brim which was a handbreadth (four fingers) in thickness was adorned with colocynths. It contained 2000 *bates* (III Kings, vii, 23-26). (The capacity must have been doubled by the copyist, for a *bate* equals 36⅔ litres; but the interior diameter of the vessel instead of allowing a capacity of 72,800 litres allows barely 36,000.) The brazen sea rested upon twelve oxen, likewise of brass, which stood in four groups facing the four cardinal points. This magnificent vessel was used by the priests for washing their hands and feet at the hours of sacrifice. Along each of the right and left wings of the Temple were arranged five movable brazen vessels. On four wheels a cubit and a half in diameter stood a base four cubits in width and length and three high; the ledges were decorated with figures of oxen, lions, and cherubim. On this vehicle was fixed a cylinder a cubit and a half in diameter and a cubit high, on which was placed a laver four cubits in diameter and shaped like an elongated dish. Four shoulders fastened at the four corners of the base supported the laver (III Kings, vii, 27-39). These movable lavers each having a capacity of forty bates, were chiefly used for washing the flesh of the victims. There has recently been discovered at Larnaca in Cyprus a Phœnician vessel in brass which corresponds in the smallest details to that described in the Bible (see Benzinger, op. cit., 218, 221).

Outer Court.—The inner court (III Kings, vi, 36), also called the "upper court" (Jer., xxxvi, 10), implies the existence of an outer and lower court, and the court of the priests (II Par., iv, 49) supposes another for laymen. There is mention of still another in the time of Josaphat (II Par., xx, 5), but we have very little interesting information concerning these courts, which must have been completed and adorned by the successors of Solomon. It is stated, for instance, that Joatham "built the highest gate of the house of the Lord" (IV Kings, xv, 35), which refers to a new gate, probably north of a court. On the other hand Achaz replaced the altar of holocausts by another, the model of which he had seen at Damascus. He also removed the twelve brazen oxen and the graven bases of the ten movable lavers and changed the gate of the Sabbath and the outer entrance for the king (IV Kings, xvi, 10-18). Ezechias emptied the treasury of the

Temple and took away the plates of gold and silver with which he himself had covered the doors and the lintels, and gave them to purchase peace from Sennacherib (IV Kings, xviii, 15-16). Manasses profaned the Temple of Jehovah by the worship of idols (IV Kings, xxi, 4). At last the monument of Solomon, in ancient times more celebrated for its splendour than its size, was reduced to ashes by Nabuchodonosor in 586.

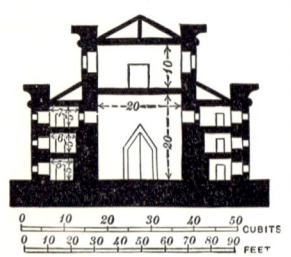

FIG. 2. ELEVATION OF THE TEMPLE OF SOLOMON IN A-B OF PLAN

II. TEMPLE OF ZOROBABEL.—In 537 Sassabasar, appointed Governor of Jerusalem by Cyrus, King of Persia, and Zorobabel, a descendant of King Joachim, returned from captivity with a vast number of Jews and armed with authority to rebuild the Temple of Jerusalem. In the seventh month after their return the altar of holocausts of unhewn stones was set up on the foundations of the former one. In the second month of the second year they laid the first stone of the new Temple. But the work was impeded and even suspended through the hostility and plots of the Samaritans, and the Temple was not finished until 516 (I Esd., iii, 6). The Temple of Zorobabel was sixty cubits broad and the same in height (I Esd., vi, 3), these being the interior dimensions. Josephus tells us (Ant. Jud., XV, xi, 1) that this was really its height, for Herod reminded the people that the height of the second Temple was sixty cubits less than that of the first, making the Temple of Solomon one hundred and twenty cubits high, according to II Par., iii, 1. It is difficult to say whether the breadth of sixty cubits ascribed by the decree of Cyrus to the Temple was in round numbers, or whether the figures indicate the smaller cubit then in use, but it matters little, for if the breadth were really sixty royal cubits it would mean only that the side chambers had been enlarged five cubits on each side. The Holy Place and the Holy of Holies in Zorobabel's Temple retained the dimensions they had in Solomon's, and they remained the same in the third Temple.

We know from Esdras (iii, 12) and from Aggeus (ii, 3) that the Temple of Zorobabel was much inferior to that of Solomon. The poverty of the new Temple consisted chiefly in the scarcity of its furnishing. The Ark of the Covenant had not been recovered and the *debîr* was empty, but as it was the dwelling-place of God on earth the entrance was once more screened with a costly veil. In the Holy Place stood a new altar of incense and a table for the loaves of proposition, but there was only one seven-branch candlestick. Treasures once more accumulated, and the entire furnishing was again in gold or covered with plates of gold, including the walls. In 168 B. C. the precious metals adorning the Temple aroused the covetousness of Antiochus Epiphanes, who "took away the golden altar, and the candlestick of light, and all the vessels thereof, and the table of proposition, and the pouring vessels, and the vials, and the little mortars of gold, and the veil, and the crowns, and the golden ornament that was before the temple, and he broke them all in pieces" (I Mach., i. 23). Judas Machabeus hastened to provide the house of God with new furnishings. The table of proposition escaped the destruction of the Temple by Titus and with other sacred utensils figures in the conqueror's triumphal procession at Rome (Bell. Jud., VII, v, 4–6). The inner court had the same circumference as that in the first Temple (I Esd., vi, 4), and according to Hecatæus, as quoted by Josephus, the altar of holocausts had the same dimensions as that of Solomon.

The Mishna (Middoth, III, vi,) mentions a movable vessel on wheels. Josephus (Ant. Jud., XI, iv, 7) relates that Zorobabel had erected several porches with vestibules within the inner precincts of the temple and in I Mach., iv, 38, 57, there is mention of chambers built in the inner court.

During the heroic wars of the Machabees with the Syrians the Temple had to undergo many vicissitudes. The walls with their large towers built by Judas Machabeus for the protection of the Temple (I Mach., iv, 60) were destroyed by Antiochus Eupator (I Mach., vi, 62), but Jonathan and Simon soon rebuilt them (Ant. Jud., XIII, v, 11). In 63 B. C. Pompey, after taking the city, laid siege to the Temple in order to break the last resistance of the Jews (Ant. Jud., XIV, iv, 4), and nine years later the procurator Crassus despoiled it of its riches (Ant. Jud., XIV, vii, 1). Finally Herod, made King of the Jews by the Senate, was obliged to take the city by storm and to besiege the fortress of the Temple (Ant. Jud., XVI, xvi, 2 sq.).

III. TEMPLE OF HEROD. *History.*—Herod undertook the restoration of the Temple in its original splendour and traditional arrangements. The buildings were demolished one after another according as the materials for the new structures were available. A host of priests became masons and carpenters and themselves took charge of tearing down and rebuilding the sanctuary, which task was accomplished in eighteen months. Nearly 10,000 workmen were employed on the other buildings. After eight years' labour (10 B. C.) the new edifice was opened for service. But this monument, which in its vast proportions and magnificence rivalled the most beautiful buildings of antiquity and far surpassed even that of Solomon, was completed only in A. D. 62 or 64 (Cf. John, ii, 20), at that time 18,000 workmen being still employed (Ant. Jud., XX, ix, 7). For Herod doubled the artificial platform which held the Temple of Zorobabel, enlarging the sacred precincts to the south and especially to the north where the galleries reached as far as the rock of Baris and the Antonia (Ant. Jud., XV, xi, 3; Bell. Jud., I, xxi, 1; V, v, 2). The Temple with its courts, galleries, and porches occupied the whole of the present site of the *haram esh sherif*, which measures 1070 feet on the north, 1540 on the east, 920 on the south, and 1630 on the west. The Temple of Herod consisted of two courts, an inner and an outer one. The former included all the buildings of the Temple properly so called and was divided into: (1) The Court of the Priests, which contained the house of God and the altar of holocausts; (2) the Court of Israel; and (3) the Court of the Women. All the space between the inner court and the outer wall of the platform was called the Court of the Gentiles, because non-Jews were permitted to enter it. The following are the arrangements of the Temple according to Josephus (Ant. Jud., XV, xi; Bell. Jud., V, v), other sources being indicated in the course of the descriptions.

Priests' Court and House of God.—The Court of the Priests formed a rectangle one hundred and eighty-seven cubits from east to west and one hundred and thirty-seven cubits from north to south [(Middoth, II, 6 (fig. 3)]. To the west stood the house of Jehovah and to the east the altar of holocausts. The sanctuary was reached by a stairway of twelve steps (2), which terminated in a majestic porch one hundred cubits high and the same in breadth (3). A door without leaves twenty cubits wide and forty high led into a vestibule eleven cubits wide. According to the Mishna this doorway was flanked by two square-shaped pillars each formed of ten cubes measuring four cubits on the sides. On these two pillars rested a sort of entablature formed of five oaken beams, separated from each other by square stones set on a line with the pillars. It was a reproduction of the triumphal arches then so common in the East. Upon the immense trellis, or grille, stretched a golden vine, of which the grapes, according to Josephus, were of the height of a man. He adds that it extended twenty-five cubits from north to south and that its top was seventy cubits from the ground. Tacitus (Ann., V, v) also speaks of this vine. Above it Herod placed a colossal golden eagle, the Roman eagle, which greatly displeased the Jews (Ant. Jud., XVII, vi, 2-4). The *hêkâl* (4) and the *dĕbîr* retained their ancient dimensions in length and breadth, but their height was increased to sixty cubits. A doorway ten cubits wide and twenty high gave access to the Holy Place. The door leaves were of carved wood covered with leaves of gold, and the door was further embellished with a magnificent curtain of Babylonian-dyed linen. The richly-decorated chamber contained the altar of perfumes before the entrance to the *dĕbîr*, north of the table of proposition and south of the seven-branch candlestick. It was not so well lighted or aired as that of Solomon. The priests alone entered this court to offer incense every night and morning, to trim the lamps, and change the loaves of proposition on the Sabbath-day. It was near the altar of incense that the angel appeared to Zacharias (Luke, i, 11).

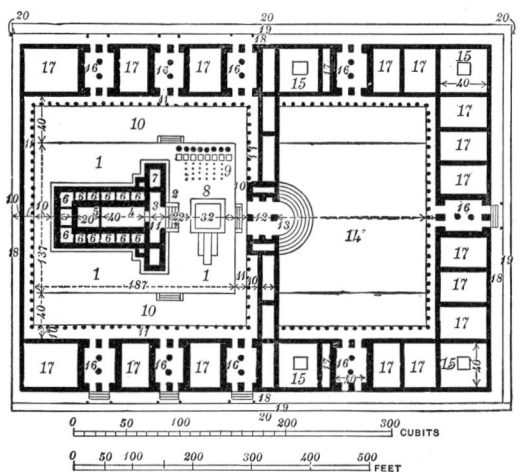

The entrance to the *dĕbîr* had no doors, but, as formerly, was shielded by a costly curtain. According to the Mishna (Yoma, V, i) no partition wall separated the *hêkâl* from the *dĕbîr*, the latter being formed by two veils hung the distance of a cubit from each other; but Josephus distinguished between the two chambers giving the dimensions of each. Furthermore he speaks only of one veil "at the entrance" of the *dĕbîr*, which must signify a doorway. Moreover, the absence of a partition would have necessitated a curtain sixty cubits long by twenty broad, which would never have sealed hermetically the Holy of Holies. The statement of the rabbis on this point is open to suspicion. They could not have been ignorant that according to the Gospel (Matt., xxvii, 51; Mark, xv, 38; Luke, xxiii, 45), when Christ died on the cross the veil of the temple was rent in two from top to bottom. The *dĕbîr* was empty. Only the high-priest entered it once a year. Above the *dĕbîr* and the *hêkâl* was a story forty cubits high, so the entire building was the same height as the porch. On the north, south, and west sides was a building divided into three stories each twenty cubits high. The ground floor and the first floor each had thirteen chambers six cubits wide (6) and the top floor twelve. A doorway (7) opened northward from the vestibule on a winding-stair three cubits in diameter and located in the corner formed by the wall of the house and the projection of the porch. The two walls which formed the cage of the stairway were five cubits thick. In the opposite corner to the south was a similar cage intended to facilitate the outflow of water. The total width of the house, including the side chambers, was fifty-four cubits and near the porch seventy cubits, and its total length, including the porch, was one hundred and six cubits, allowing six cubits thickness for the walls. The base was ten cubits larger than the dimensions given above.

Twenty-two cubits east of the house stood the altar of holocausts, constructed of unhewn stone (8). The rabbis speak of a three-tiered altar, ten cubits high and thirty-two cubits along the sides of the base, and twenty-four in the centre (Maimonides, "Beth Haberasch", II, 16). The figures of Josephus, fifty cubits on the sides by fifteen high, are obviously incorrect. North of the altar (9) four rows of rings were fastened in the ground and were used while slaying the animals. Next came eight marble tables for cutting up and washing the flesh of the victims, and higher up were eight pillars with hooks for suspending and flaying the animals (Middoth III, 5-V, ii; Talmud, Shek, VI, 4). Laymen were admitted to this court only when they offered sacrifice, for they had to place their hands on the head of the victims. The four sides of the court were surrounded by a parapet of stones a foot and a half high.

Court of Israel.—Five steps led down from the court of the priests to the court of Israel, which surrounded the former on three sides (10). At the north and south it was forty cubits wide and on the east only eleven cubits. A gallery ten cubits wide (11), supported by splendid marble columns, went round this court, probably on the west side also, and afforded a shelter from the sun and rain. Men only were admitted here and only the king was permitted to be seated.

East of this court opposite the house of God (12) rose a superb gateway, the most beautiful of all, which according to Josephus and the Mishna (Middoth, I, 4) was the gift of Nicanor, a wealthy Alexandrian Jew. This was the Θύρα ὡραία, the *porta speciosa* (Acts, iii, 2), where St. Peter healed the man crippled from birth. It was fifty cubits high and forty wide, and its gates of Corinthian brass, carved and covered with plates of gold and silver, were so heavy that twenty men were required to move it. Josephus adds that among the signs premonitory of the destruction of the Temple this gate opened of itself at midnight about the year 30 B. C. (Bell. Jud., VI, v, 3).

Court of the Women.—From the Gate of Nicanor a semicircular stairway (13) of fifteen steps led down to the women's court (14), surrounded by a gallery on the north, east, and south. Here the women were admitted and places were reserved for them on the north and south, but the men also frequented this court and usually crossed it when they went to the Temple. There were benches there, for it was permitted to sit (cf. Mark, xii, 41). Along the sides probably near the Gate of Nicanor, were thirteen boxes, an inscription indicating the special purpose of each: oil, wood, priestly vestments, doves, etc. There Christ saw the rich men and the poor widow deposit their offering (Luke, xxi, 1). At the four corners were four hypethral chambers, forty cubits square (15). According to the Talmud the north-west chamber was where the unclean and lepers, who had been healed, bathed and were declared clean by the priests. In the north-east chamber the priests sorted the wood; in the south-

FIG. 3. PLAN OF THE TEMPLE OF HEROD
(1) Court of the priests; (2) Stairway of the Temples; (3) Porch and vestibule; (4) The Holy Place; (5) The Holy of Holies; (6) Side chambers; (7) Entrance to the winding stairway; (8) Altar of holocausts; (9) Abattoir; (10) Court of Israel; (11) Gallery; (12) Beautiful Gate; (13) Stairway of fifteen steps; (14) Court of the women; (15) Hypethral room; (16) Gate; (17) Hall; (18) Hel; (19) Stairway of 14 steps; (20) Court of the gentiles.

west oil and wine were preserved in vaults; in the south-east those who had fulfilled the vow of Nazarites shaved their heads (cf. Num., vi, 13 sqq; Acts, xviii, 18). In these chambers it was also permitted to wash, cook etc. According to Middoth, II, 5, there were also in this court four chambers in which certain women were lodged.

Gates and Chambers.—Three sides of the inner court were surrounded by buildings forty cubits broad, separated by nine gates in the shape of towers (16), four on the north and four on the south, of which only two opened into the women's court, with the eastern gate. These gateways or rather sumptuous porches were 40 cubits in height, breadth, and length. A large bar divided the entrance into two bays each ten cubits broad and twenty high with wooden leaves covered with plates of gold and silver. The vestibule was thirty cubits square and its six arches were supported by two pillars twelve cubits in circumference. At the sides of the court of Israel five steps led to the gateway whose vestibule was likewise provided with ten steps or an incline. There are still three gates within the *haram esh sherif*, the Golden Gate, the double gate, and the triple gate, constructed according to the same plan. Between these gates was a series of chambers devoted to various uses (17). West of the second southern gate was the *lishkat gazit*, hall of the Sanhedrin (Middoth, II, 5), with a chamber, for the instruction of the people, and in the court of the women was the γαζοφυλάκιον, hall of the treasury (Ant. Jud., XIX, vi, 1). This vast edifice rested on a foundation with a projection of ten cubits forming a deambulatory (18), which was reached by a stairway of twelve or fourteen steps. This was the *hel*; it was surrounded by a stone parapet called *sôrêg* and in front of the nine gates stood pillars with inscriptions in Greek and Latin notifying visitors that every non-Jew was forbidden under pain of death to approach nearer the Temple. Some years ago one of the pillars with a Greeek inscription was found in the vicinity of the *haram esh sherif*.

Outer Court.—The remainder of the vast platform formed the outer court of the gentiles. It was paved with large slabs and surrounded on all sides by a double gallery formed of two rows of columns twenty-five cubits high. That overlooking the valley of Cedron was called "Gate of Solomon" (cf. I Par., ix, 18). It was certainly prior to Herod, and Josephus dates its origin from Solomon, himself. He relates that in A. D. 62 or 64 the 18,000 workmen still employed on the adornment of the Temple began to lack work and requested that they might demolish the Gate of Solomon; but this, although ancient, was so beautiful and the cost of replacing it would have been so great that King Agrippa II decided to preserve it and to employ the workmen in paving the city streets (Ant. Jud., XX, ix, 7). Whether it dates from the kings of Juda or only from Zorobabel it is sufficient to afford an idea of the magnificence of the first two temples of Jerusalem. At the corners of these galleries were chambers (*pastophoria*) for the guards. From the side towards the city the entrance to the sanctuary was made through several gates of surpassing beauty, four on the west of the esplanade, two on the south, one on the east, and one on the north. On a lower terrace in the centre Herod erected a royal basilica, a sumptuous building divided into three naves by four rows of forty-one Corinthian columns. Each column was more than five feet in diameter. At the north of the esplanade he built two vast courts surrounded by gates which extended to the scarp of the rock of Baris. These courts communicated with the Antonia only by two stairways (cf. Acts, xxi, 35).

De Vogüe, *Le temple de Jérusalem* (Paris, 1864); Perrot and Chipiez, *Hist. de l'art: Judée*, IV (Paris, 1887); Benzinger, *Hebräische Archäologie* (Tübingen, 1907); Schick, *Die Stiftshutte,* *Der Tempel in Jerusalem;* Robinson, *Biblical Researches in Palestine* (Boston, 1841);

Barnabas Meistermann.

Temporal Power. See Pope, The; States of the Church.

Temptation (Lat. *tentare*, to try or test) is here taken to be an incitement to sin whether by persuasion or by the offer of some good or pleasure. It may be merely external, as was the case of Christ's encounter in the desert after the forty days' fast; or it may be internal as well, inasmuch as there is a real assault upon a person's will power. It arises sometimes from the propensity to evil inherent in us as a result of original sin. Sometimes it is directly chargeable to the intervention of the Devil, who can furnish the imagination with its sinful subject-matter and stir up the lower powers of the soul. Not infrequently both causes are at work. Temptation is not in itself sin. No matter how vivid the unholy image may be, no matter how strong the inclination to transgress the law, no matter how vehement the sensation of unlawful satisfaction, as long as there is no consent of the will, there is no sin. The very essence of sin in any grade is that it should be a deliberate act of the human will. Attack is not synonymous with surrender. This, while obvious enough, is important especially for those who are trying to serve God sedulously and yet find themselves beset on all sides by temptations. They are apt to take the fierceness and repetition of the onset as proof that they have fallen. A wise spiritual guide will point out the error of this conclusion and thus administer comfort and courage to these harassed souls.

Temptations are to be combated by the avoidance, where possible, of the occasions that give rise to them, by recourse to prayer, and by fostering within oneself a spirit of humble distrust of one's own powers and of unbounded confidence in God. The resistance which a Christian is bound to offer need not always be direct. Sometimes, particularly when there is question of reiterated evil interior suggestions, it may be useful to employ an indirect method, that is, to simply ignore them and quietly divert the attention into another channel. Temptations as such can never be intended by God. They are permitted by Him to give us an opportunity of practising virtue and self-mastery and acquiring merit. The fact of temptation, no matter how large it looms in a person's life, is not an indication that such an one is under the ban. Indeed those whom God calls to special heights of sanctity are just those who may expect to have to wrestle bravely with temptations more numerous and fearsome than fall to the lot of the average mortal.

Lehmkuhl, *Theologia moralis* (Freiburg, 1887); Mütz, *Christliche Ascetik* (Paderborn, 1907); Hense, *Die Versuchungen* (Freiburg, 1884); Scaramelli, *Directorium asceticum.*

Joseph F. Delany.

Temptation of Christ.—In the Catholic translation of Holy Writ, the word "temptation" is used in various senses, the principal of which are the following: (1) the act of testing or trying (Deut., iv, 34; Tob., ii, 12; Luke, xxii, 28; etc.); (2) enticement to evil (Matt., xxvi, 41; I Cor., x, 13; etc.); (3) the state of being tempted (Matt., vi, 13; Luke, iv, 13; etc.); (4) that which tempts or entices to evil (James, i, 12; II Pet., ii, 9; etc.); (5) the name of a place (Ex., xvii, 7; Deut., vi, 16; etc.). Taken in an unfavourable sense as denoting enticement to evil, temptation cannot be referred directly to God or to Christ, so that when we read in Gen., xxii, 1, for instance, "God tempted Abraham", and in John, vi, 6, "Hoc autem dicebat tentans eum", literally: "This He [Jesus] said tempting him [Philip]", the expressions must be taken in the sense of testing, trying. According to St. James (i, 12 sqq.), the natural source of man's temptations is concupiscence, or that proneness to evil which is the result of the fall of Adam, and which remains in human nature after baptismal regeneration, and even though the soul is in the state of sanctifying grace (cf. Rom., viii, 1). Concupiscence becomes sinful only when freely yielded to; when resisted with God's help, it is an occasion of merit. Together with inward concupiscence, and outward creatures, which may be the occasion of sin (I John ii, 15 sqq.), the chief cause of temptation is Satan, "the tempter" (Matt., iv, 3), bent on man's eternal ruin (Eph., vi, 10 sqq.). In the Lord's Prayer, the clause "Lead us not into temptation" is an humble and trusting petition for God's help to enable us to overcome temptation when His Fatherly Providence allows us to experience the allurements of evil. Prayer and watchfulness are the chief weapons against temptation (Mark, xiv, 38; etc.). God does not allow man to be tempted beyond his strength (I Cor., x, 13).

Like Adam, Christ, the second Adam, endured temptation only from without, inasmuch as His human nature was free from all concupiscence; but unlike Adam, He withstood the assaults of the Tempter on all points, thereby affording His mystical members a perfect model of resistance to their spiritual enemy, and a permanent source of victorious help (Heb., iv, 15–16). In our first three Gospels (Matt., iv, 1–11; Mark, i, 12–13; Luke, iv, 1–13), the narrative of Christ's temptation is placed in immediate connexion with His baptism on the one hand, and with the beginning of His public ministry on the other. The reason of this is clear. The Synoptists naturally regard the baptism of Christ as the external designation of Jesus from above for His Messianic work to be pursued under the guidance of the Holy Spirit bestowed upon Him on this occasion; and they no less naturally regard Christ's sojourn in the desert where He was tempted, as His own immediate preparation for that great work under the guidance of the same Holy Spirit. As our first three Gospels agree concerning the time to which they assign the temptation of Christ, so they are at one in ascribing the same general place to its occurrence, viz. "the desert", whereby they no doubt mean the Wilderness of Judea, where Jesus would indeed be, as St. Mark says: "with beasts". From St. Mark (i, 13)—with whom compare St. Luke iv, 2—we learn that Jesus Christ was tempted during the forty days which He spent in the desert (cf. St. Augustine, "Harmony of the Evangelists", II, xvi), so that the three onsets given in detail by St. Matthew and St. Luke are apparently the three final assaults of Satan against Christ. The first of these assaults is directly connected in both St. Matthew and St. Luke with the prolonged fast of Jesus in the wilderness. The Tempter suggested to Jesus that He should use His miraculous power to relieve His hunger, by changing into bread the loaf-like flints of the desert. The two other assaults are given in a different order, St. Matthew adhering probably to the order of time, and St. Luke to that of place. The spot pointed out by tradition as the summit from which Satan offered to Jesus dominion over all earthly kingdoms is the "Quarantania", a limestone peak on the road from Jerusalem to Jericho. As regards the Temple's pinnacle from which the Tempter bade Jesus cast Himself down, it was not the top of the House of Yahweh, but probably the roof of Solomon's portico from which, at a later date, St. James was actually hurled to the pavement below (Eusebius, "Hist. eccl.", IV, xiii).

According to St. Luke (iv, 13), after having subjected Christ to all kinds of temptations,—the Messianic import of which is undoubted,—Satan withdrew, awaiting a favourable opportunity like that which followed Christ's prolonged fast in the desert. The later conflict thus alluded to is no other than that of Christ's Passion (cf. Luke, xxii, 53; John, xiv, 30). The ministry of angels to Jesus, in connexion with His temptation, is mentioned in Mark, i, 13. Satan's exact manner of appearance to Jesus is not stated by the Evangelists. Despite the difficulties urged, chiefly by non-Catholic scholars, against the historical character of the three temptations of Jesus, as recorded by St. Matthew and St. Luke, it is plain that these sacred writers intended to describe an actual and visible approach of Satan, to chronicle an actual shifting of places, etc., and that the traditional view, which maintains the objective nature of Christ's temptations, is the only one meeting all the requirements of the Gospel narrative.

(Catholic Authors are marked with an asterisk). *Life of Christ:* * CIGOI (Klagenfurt, 1896–1905); * DIDON (tr. New York, 1891); EDERSHEIM (New York, 1884); FARRAR (London, 1874); * FORNARI (Rome, 1901); * FOUARD (tr. New York, 1891); GEIKIE (New York, 1886); * GRIMM (Ratisbon, 1876); HOLTZMANN (tr. London, 1904); KEIM (tr. London, 1876–83); * LE CAMUS (tr. New York, 1906–08); NEANDER (tr. London, 1871); PRESSENSÉ (Paris, 1884); ROBINSON (London, 1898); * SCHEGG (Freiburg, 1875); * SEPP AND * HANEBERG (Ratisbon, 1898–1902); WEISS (tr. Edinburgh, 1883–4). For *Commentaries* see bibliographies under MATTHEW, GOSPEL OF ST.; MARK, GOSPEL OF ST.; LUKE, GOSPEL OF ST. For the literary analysis of the Synoptical accounts of Christ's temptation, see *New York Review*, Oct.–Nov., 1905.

FRANCIS E. GIGOT.

Tencin, PIERRE-GUÉRIN DE, French statesman and cardinal, b. at Grenoble, 22 August, 1680; d. at Lyons, 2 March, 1758. After studying with the Oratorians at Grenoble he entered the Sorbonne, where he became prior in 1702, and obtained the doctorate in 1705. He was then appointed Vicar-General of Sens and, in 1721, accompanied Cardinal de Rohan to Rome as his conclavist, to support the candidacy of Cardinal Conti (Innocent XIII), from whom he had obtained a promise to bestow the purple on the unworthy French minister Dubois. He remained at Rome as French chargé d'affaires until Benedict XIII, with whom he was very influential, consecrated him Archbishop of Embrun (26 June, 1724). With the selfish motive of paving his way to higher ecclesiastical honours, he was overzealous in the persecution of the Jansenists, and, at the provincial synod which he held at Embrun from 16 August to 28 September, 1727, he suspended Bishop Jean Soanen of Senez, a prelate eighty years of age, who had appealed against the Bull "Unigenitus". On 22 February, 1739, Tencin was created cardinal, of the title of Sts. Nereus and Achilleus. He remained at Rome as French ambassador until 1742, when he took possession of the archiepiscopal See of Lyons, to which he had succeeded on 19 November, 1740. King Louis XV appointed him minister of state in September, 1742. After the death of the Prime Minister Fleury, to whom he owed much of his political advancement, his influence began to decrease. The death of his profligate sister, Madame Tencin, on 4 Dec., 1749, removed the greatest spur of his political ambition, and in 1752 he retired to his See of Lyons.

MASSON, *Madame de Tencin* (Paris, 1909), passim; CARDELLA, *Memorie storiche de' cardinali della santa romana chiesa*, VIII (Rome, 1794), 296–8; M. R., *Merkwürdige Lebensgeschichte aller Cardinäle der röm. kathol. Kirche die in diesem jetztlaufenden Seculo das Zeitliche verlassen haben*, III (Ratisbon, 1772), 282–98. For the complete Acts of the Provincial Synod of Embrun, see MANSI, *Collectio amplissima*, continued by MARTIN and PETIT, XXXVII (Paris, 1905), 693, 888.

MICHAEL OTT.

Tenebræ is the name given to the service of Matins and Lauds belonging to the last three days of Holy Week. This service, as the "Cæremoniale episcoporum" expressly directs, is to be anticipated and it should be sung shortly after Compline "about the twenty-first hour", i. e. about three p. m. on the eve of the day to which it belongs. "On the three days before Easter", says Benedict XIV (Institut., 24), "Lauds follow immediately on Matins, which in this occasion terminate with the close of day, in order to signify the setting of the Sun of Justice and the darkness of the Jewish people who knew not our Lord and condemned Him to the gibbet of the cross." Originally Matins on these days, like Matins at all other seasons of the year, were sung shortly after midnight, and consequently if the lights were extinguished the darkness was complete. That this putting out of lights dates from the fifth century, so far at least as regards the night Office, is highly probable. Both in the first Ordo Romanus and in the Ordo of St. Amand published by Duchesne a great point is made of the gradual extinction of the lights during the Friday Matins; though it would seem that in this earliest period the Matins and Lauds of the Thursday were sung throughout with the church brightly illuminated (*ecclesia omni lumine decoretur*). On Friday the candles and lamps were gradually extinguished during the three Nocturns, while on Saturday the church was in darkness from beginning to end, save that a single candle was kept near the lectern to read by.

All this suggests, as Kutschker has remarked, that the Office of these three days was treated as a sort of funeral service, or dirge, commemorating the death of Jesus Christ. It is natural also that, since Christ by convention was regarded as having lain three days and three nights in the tomb, these obsequies should have come in the end to be celebrated on each of the three separate occasions with the same demonstrations of mourning. There can be no reasonable doubt that it was from the extinguishing of lights that the service came to be known as Tenebræ, though the name itself seems to have arisen somewhat later. The liturgist de Vert has suggested an utilitarian explanation of the putting out of the candles one by one, contending that the gradual approach of the dawn rendered the same number of lights unnecessary, and that the number was consequently diminished as the service drew to a close. This view seems sufficiently refuted by the fact that this method of gradual extinction is mentioned by the first Ordo Romanus on the Friday only. On the Saturday we are explicitly told that the lights were not lit. Moreover, as pointed out under HOLY WEEK (VII, 437), the tone of the whole Office, which seems hardly to have varied in any respect from that now heard in our churches, is most noticeably mournful—the lessons taken from the Lamentations of Jeremias, the omission of the Gloria Patri, of the Te Deum, and of blessings etc., all suggest a service cognate to the Vigiliæ Mortuorum, just as the brilliant illumination of the Easter eve spoke of triumph and of joy, so the darkness of the preceding night's services seems to have been designedly chosen to mark the Church's desolation. In any case it is to be noticed that the Office of these three days has been treated by liturgical reformers throughout the ages with scrupulous respect. The lessons from Jeremias in the first Nocturn, from the Commentaries of St. Augustine upon the Psalms in the second, and from the Epistles of St. Paul in the third remain now as when we first hear of them in the eighth century.

The Benedictine Order, who normally have their own arrangement of psalms and nocturns, differing from the Roman, on these three days conform to the ordinary Roman practice. Even the shifting of the hour from midnight to the previous afternoon, when no real darkness can be secured, seems to have been prompted by the desire to render these sublime Offices more accessible to clergy and laity. Already in the thirteenth century it seems probable that at Rome Tenebræ began at four or five o'clock on the Wednesday (see Ord. Rom., xiv, 82, and Ord. Rom., xv, 62). Despite the general uniformity of this service throughout the Western Church, there was also a certain diversity of usage in some details, more particularly in the number of candles which stood in the Tenebræ hearse, and in some accretions which, especially in the Sarum Use, marked the termination of the service. With regard to the candles Durandus speaks of as many as seventy-two being used in some churches and as few as nine or seven in others. In England the Sarum Ordinal prescribed twenty-four, and this was the general number in this country, variously explained as symbolizing the twenty-four hours of the day, or the twelve Apostles with the twelve Prophets. A twenty-fifth candle was allowed to remain lighted and hidden, as is done at the present day, behind the altar, when all the others had been gradually extinguished. At present, the rubrics of the "Ceremoniale", etc., prescribe the use of fifteen candles. The noise made at the end of Tenebræ undoubtedly had its origin in the signal given by the master of ceremonies for the return of the ministers to the sacristy. A number of the earlier Ceremoniales and Ordines are explicit on the point. But at a later date others lent their aid in making this knocking. For example Patricius Piccolomini says: "The prayer being ended the master of ceremonies begins to beat with his hand upon the altar step or upon some bench, and all to some extent make a noise and clatter". This was afterwards symbolically interpreted to represent the convulsion of nature which followed the death of Jesus Christ.

KUTSCHKER, *Die heiligen Gebräuche* (Vienna, 1843); CATALANI, *Comment. in cæremoniale episcoporum*, II (Rome, 1744), 241–50; MARTÈNE, *De antiquis ecclesiæ ritibus*, III (Venice, 1788), 81–82; and IV, 122–24; THURSTON, *Lent and Holy Week* (London, 1904).

HERBERT THURSTON.

Tenedos, a titular see, suffragan of Rhodes in the Cyclades. The island, called in Turkish Boghaz-Adassi, has an area of 16 square miles and 5000 inhabitants, of whom 3000 are Greek schismatics. It is a caza of the sanjak of Lemnos in the vilayet of Rhodes. It seems to have been called by various names, such as Leucophrys, Calydna, Phœnice, and Lyrnessus. The name Tenedos is derived from Tenes, one of the heroes of the Trojan War. In this connexion Homer and Virgil make frequent mention of the island, which must have been used by the Greeks as a station for their fleet. Captured by the Persians, who used it as a naval station, it afterwards became the ally and tributary of Athens, to which it was faithful during the Peloponnesian War until the peace of Antalcidas in 358 B. C. Subject to Alexander and his successors, though retaining its internal organization, it fell into the power of the Romans in 129 B. C. and was ravaged by Verres. In 73 B. C. Lucullus destroyed a part of the fleet of Mithridates there. Justinian built there large storehouses to contain the grain brought from Alexandria (Procopius, "De ædificiis", V, i). The Venetians captured it in 1377; Mohammed II wrested it from them in the fifteenth century, but they recaptured it in 1656, though but for a short time. Canaris burned the Turkish fleet there in 1822. Le Quien (Oriens christ., I, 947–50) mentions the bishops: Diodorus, at Sardica in 344; Anastasius, a partisan of Nestorius; Florentius in 451; Joseph in 1356. In September, 1369, Harmodius, Bishop of Boreia Potamia, was transferred to the metropolitan See of Tenedos (Miklosich and Müller, "Acta patriarchatus Constantinopolitani", I, 511). At first a suffragan of Cyzicus and then of Mitylene, at least from the tenth century (Gelzer, "Ungedruckte . . . Texte der

Notitiæ episcopatuum", 559; "Georgii Cyprii Descriptio orbis romani", 83), Tenedos was raised to the rank of a metropolitan see shortly after the death of Andronicus III in 1341 (Gelzer, op. cit., 601; 608). In 1342 it had already become such (Miklosich and Müller, op. cit., I, 230). In October, 1368, the metropolitan See of Tenedos was given to the metropolitan of Peritheorium in Thrace (op. cit., I, 501). In a "notitia" of the fifteenth century the see is no longer mentioned.

HEMMER, *Respublica Tenediorum* (Copenhagen, 1735); SMITH, *Dict. of Greek and Roman Geog.*, s. v.; LACROIX, *Iles de la Grèce*, (Paris, 1853), 338–47; CUINET, *La Turquie d'Asie*, I, 490–97.

S. VAILHÉ.

Teneriffe, DIOCESE OF (TENERIFENSIS), suffragan of Seville, formerly called Nivariensis from Nivaria, the ancient name of the island (Pliny, VI, xxxii; Filippo Bergamo, XVI, "sup. chronic."). Teneriffe, which is situated in the centre of the Canary Archipelago, is the principal, most fertile, and most populous of the islands. It contains the famous Pico de Teyde (Peak of Teneriffe), the ancient Mount Atlante, rising 12,200 feet high, a guiding point for sailors since the time of the Phœnician Hercules. This diocese comprises the Islands of Teneriffe, Palma, Gomera, and Ferro (Hierro), is situated between 13° and 16° W. long., and has belonged to Spain since the time of its conquest, 1402–1496. Teneriffe was the last of the Canary Islands to surrender; more Spanish blood was shed in its conquest than in the subjugation of the empires of the Incas and Montezumas. In the battle of Acentejo alone 900 of the 1120 who composed the conquering army were lost. The aborigines, of the Guanche race, were, however, quick to assimiliate the manners and the customs of the conquerors, and if this island were the last to surrender, it was soon the centre of the political and military organizations, although not of the ecclesiastical, because of the unexpected translation of the first see in the Canaries from Rubicón on the Island of Lanzarote to Las Palmas of the Gran Canaria.

The people, however, through their representatives petitioned the Cortes of Cadiz (14 Sept., 1813) for their own ecclesiastical administration. It is interesting to note that it was one of these representatives, who, being at Philadelphia in 1788, urged through the Nuncio Vincenti the establishment of the first Catholic diocese in the United States of America (Diario de las Cortes de Cadiz sesion de 18 de Enero de 1813). As a result of their petition an auxiliary bishop was appointed in 1816, and the Diocese of Teneriffe was erected in 1819 by the Bull of Pius VII dated 1 February, 1818, the Church of Los Remedios at San Cristóbal de la Laguna being designated as the cathedral. In 1823 the Nuncio Mastai Ferreti, during his voyage to Chile, was impressed by the importance and the necessity of this see, and on this account when later as Pius IX he was obliged by the Concordat of 1851 with Spain to suppress it, he did so with regret, and in 1876, when certain concessions and modifications of this concordat were solicited, one of the conditions for granting them was the restoration of this see. This was granted, but, as the Bull of suppression had never been issued, Rome was not obliged to take any steps for the re-establishment. In the ninety-two years of its existence, besides the vicars capitular who have administered the diocese during the time of vacancies, the following bishops have governed the see: Folgueras Sión, first bishop, academician, author of various works, including a translation of Juvenal (1825–48); Lluch and Urquinaona, bishops of Gran Canaria, as administrators Apostolic (1825–48); Infante Macias, author of a volume of sermons (1877–82); Cervera Cervera (1882–4); Torrijos Gómez (1888–94); and since 1894 the present bishop, Mgr. Nicolás Rey Redondo, who was born at Melgar de Fernamental, Burgos, Spain, on 6 Jan., 1834, ordained in 1860, appointed to this see on 21 May, 1894, and consecrated at Burgos, 9 Sept., 1894.

The diocese numbers 208,000 souls, and has a cathedral, fifty-nine parishes, a seminary, 6 religious communities of men: Missionaries of the Immaculate Heart of Mary, 1; Lazarists, 3; Christian Brothers, 2; and 14 houses of women: Dominicanesses, 1; Franciscanesses, 1; Conceptionists, 1; Assumptionists, 1; Teaching Sisters of St. Dominic, 2; Servants of Mary, 3; Franciscan Hospitaller Sisters, 1; Sisters of Charity, 3; Little Sisters of the Poor, 1. A Catholic daily, "Gaceta de Tenerife", and the official bulletin, "Buletín oficial del obispado de Tenerife", are published in the diocese. Among the notable personages who are natives of this island may be mentioned the Ven. José Anchieta, apostle of Brazil, and Ven. Pedro Bethancourt, founder of the Bethlemites, a hospitaller order of Latin America. It has also given two martyrs to the Church, Fray Luis de Aguirre, Augustinian, in Guecija, Granada, and the Jesuit, Pedro Parrado de León, in Japan, three archbishops, and ten bishops, six to America and four to Europe. Among the notable buildings may be mentioned the cathedral rebuilt by the present bishop, the parochial churches of La Concepción of Laguna, and those of Santa Cruz, Orotava, and Realejo-bajo, Garachico and Icod on the Island of Teneriffe, and Salvador on the Island of Palma, all containing art works of merit. The pulpit of the cathedral, carved in marble, and that of La Concepción, a wood carving, bear comparison with those of the churches of Brussels.

VIERA Y CLAVIJO, *Noticias de la hist., gen. de las Islas Canarias* (Madrid, 1772–3), I, iii, 244, 284; II, ix, 208, 255; IV, xviii, 423, 489; NÚÑEZ DE LA PEÑA, VII, 50; XI, 81; MILLARES, *Hist. gen. de las Islas Canarias* (Las Palmas, 1893); *The Canarian, or Book of the Conquest and Conversion of the Canarians in the year 1402, by Messire Jean de Bóthencourt, composed by Pierre Bontier, Monk, and Jean Le Verrier, Priest*, tr. and ed. with notes, MAJOR (London, 1872).

JOSÉ RODRÍGUEZ MOURE.

Teniers, DAVID, the name of two eminent Flemish landscape painters; the elder, b. at Antwerp in 1582; d. there in 1649; the younger, b. at Antwerp in 1610; d. at Brussels in 1694. Of these two men, the younger was by far the greater, eclipsing in skill the work of his father. Teniers the elder was the son of a mercer, Julian Teniers, and was brought up and trained by his elder brother. He entered for a while the school of Rubens, later on visited Italy, and studied under Elsheimer in Rome. He returned to his own country in 1606 and spent the rest of his life at Antwerp, painting landscape pictures, illustrations from rural sports, and some classical and historical scenes. His son, David Teniers the younger, was one of four brothers, David, Julian, Theodore, and Abraham, and he in his turn had a son and a grandson named David. Nothing whatever is known of the persons who taught the younger Teniers; in all probability he was brought up in his father's studio, although it has been stated by some writers that he worked under Rubens, or under Brouwer. He

DAVID TENIERS, THE YOUNGER
Engraved from a self-portrait

certainly was on terms of intimate acquaintance with Rubens, but we hear nothing of this acquaintance until 1637, when he married Anne, the daughter of Brueghel, the pupil of Rubens, and the great painter came to the wedding. The girl was not yet seventeen; she bore Teniers five children and died in 1656. Six months later, Teniers married Isabel, the daughter of an eminent person who was secretary to the Council of Brabant.

Teniers is said to have received a fortune with each wife, and to have made a great deal of money from the sale of his pictures. It is certain that he had ample means, was able to purchase a château, to live in good circumstances, and eventually to obtain admission to the ranks of the nobility after he had ceased to exercise his profession for gain. The statement of his appeal to be received as a member of an old family and the description of his coat of arms are still in existence. He was patronized by the Governor of the Netherlands, the Archduke William, and by his successor Don Juan of Austria. Philip IV and Christina of Sweden were also amongst the eminent persons who gave him commissions for pictures. He was a man of the greatest industry, and his delightful little works, perhaps numbering nearly eight hundred in all, are to be found all over Europe. As a rule, they are scenes from peasant life, painted in beautiful colour schemes and dexterously handled. They can be studied especially in the galleries of Dresden, Glasgow, the National Gallery in London, the Louvre, the Prado, the Imperial Gallery at Vienna, and the Hermitage at St. Petersburg. Of these galleries the Louvre has the greatest number, possessing nearly forty examples of the work of this skilful painter. Alone amongst the members of his family, he appears to have been a practical Catholic.

WAUTERS, *The Flemish School of Painting* (Brussels, 1877).
GEORGE CHARLES WILLIAMSON.

Tennessee.—The State of Tennessee lies between 35° and 36° 30′ N. lat. and 81° 37′ and 90° 28′ W. long. Its greatest length from east to west is 432 miles, and its extreme width 109 miles; its total area is 43,022 square miles. It touches eight states on its borders, a greater number than is touched by the boundaries of any other state in the Union except Missouri. It is unequalled in the number and excellence of its navigable rivers. The Mississippi River washes its western boundary and the placid Tennessee and beautiful Cumberland, with sources in other states, furnish cheap water transportation for the varied products of the soil and of the mines.

I. PHYSICAL CHARACTERISTICS.—The state has eight great natural divisions: the Appalachian chain of mountains, called the Unakas, rises on its eastern borders, the highest peaks of which attain an elevation of more than 6000 feet above the sea. Adjoining these mountains on the west and in between them and the Cumberland table-land is the valley of east Tennessee, a succession of ridges and minor valleys running in almost unbroken lines from north-east to south-west. Next in order comes the Cumberland table-land, an elevated plateau, which rises 2000 feet above the sea. The soil of this division is sandy, thin and unproductive, and of but little agricultural importance. Beneath it, however, are buried vast treasures of coal and iron, and its area is 5100 square miles. Rising against the western edge of the Cumberland table-land and extending to the Tennessee River, with an average elevation of 1000 feet above the sea, are the highlands or terrace lands, diversified in places with rolling hills and wide valleys. The soil in this divison is of varying fertility and of great agricultural importance and wealth. In the centre of these highlands and surrounded by them is the great central basin. The soil of this basin is highly productive of all crops suitable to the altitude, and it has been well named "The Garden of Tennessee". Its area is 5450 square miles and it has an average depression of 300 feet below the highlands. The next natural division is the western valley, or the Valley of the Tennessee. This is a comparatively narrow valley with spurs from the highlands running in towards it and sometimes down to the margin of the Tennessee River. The soil is fertile, but marshy spots covered with cypress occur in places along the river. The average width of this valley is ten or twelve miles and its length the breadth of the state. It has an area of 1200 square miles and an elevation of 350 feet above the sea. The plateau or slope of west Tennessee is the seventh natural division and peculiar in having but few rocks, differing in this particular from all the divisions above mentioned. It is a great plain, sloping gradually towards the Mississippi River and varying widely in the character of its soil and scenery. Furrowed with river valleys, this division extends for a distance of 84 miles, when it abruptly terminates in the greater plain, the bottoms of the Mississippi. The soil of this division is light and very fertile. The bottoms of the Mississippi form the last natural division of the state and constitute a low, fertile, alluvial plain teeming with a luxuriant vegetable life that is almost tropical.

These eight natural divisions have been reduced to three civil divisions: (1) east Tennessee comprises all the territory from the North Carolina line to about the centre of the Cumberland table-land; (2) middle Tennessee extends from the dividing line on the Cumberland table-land to the Tennessee River; (3) west Tennessee extends from the Tennessee River to the Mississippi River. The climate is mild, resulting from latitude and elevation interwoven and modified by varieties of soil, position, exposure, and chains of mountain ranges, so that the characteristic climate of every state in the Union may be found in it. In the spring and autumn the climate is unsurpassed. The summer and winter seasons are short. The mean annual temperature is about 57 in the valley of east Tennessee, 58 in middle Tennessee, and 59 in west Tennessee.

II. HISTORY.—The first expedition of white men into the country included within the limits of the present State of Tennessee was that of Fernando De Soto in the year 1540. Accounts given of De Soto's marches by his followers have led to the belief that he entered Tennessee near its eastern boundary and advanced across almost its entire width, reaching the Mississippi River at a point now occupied by the city of Memphis. At the time of this expedition Tennessee was unoccupied except by the Cherokee Indians, who inhabited that part bordering on the Tennessee River; the Choctaws, the upper Cumberland; Shawnees, the lower Cumberland; and the Chickasaws used and claimed the territory between the Tennessee and Mississippi Rivers, now west Tennessee. The rich section of middle Tennessee was then regarded by the Indians as common hunting-ground and was not used by them for any other purpose. In 1673 Father Marquette and Joliet descended the Mississippi River and made maps of the country, especially noting Chickasaw Bluffs, on which Memphis is now situated. In 1682 La Salle made his famous voyage

Typogravure Goupil of Paris, France

THE KITCHEN
TENIERS THE YOUNGER, THE HERMITAGE, ST. PETERSBURG

down the Mississippi, claiming the territory for France, and named it Louisiana. He stopped at Chickasaw Bluffs and constructed a cabin and fort which he named "Prud 'homme", made a treaty with the Indians, and established trading-posts. Other French trading-posts were soon thereafter established among the Indians. Among these was the post of M. Charleville, the French trader who built the first store at Salt Lick on the Cumberland, where Nashville now stands. The English, in the meantime, were colonizing the country from the Atlantic seaboard westward, and in 1756 completed their first structure in Tennessee, when the first English settlements were made within its limits.

In 1772 the Watauga settlement established a free and independent Government with the first written Constitution adopted in America. This Government continued until the beginning of the Revolution in 1775, preserving its independence of all other Governments, including that of North Carolina, its mother colony, until the beginning of the conflict with Great Britain, when the Watauga and Nollachucky settlements of Tennessee formed themselves into the Washington District. In 1776 these settlements were annexed to the State of North Carolina and became Washington County. In 1779 a band of adventurous spirits from Watauga, led by James Robertson, known as "The Father of Tennessee", reached the present site of Nashville. The settlement was then called Nashboro. Captain Demonbreun, a Frenchman, had, however, established a post at the same place in 1775. In 1780 another band of colonists reached Nashville by way of the Cumberland and Tennessee Rivers, and in the same year a public meeting or convention was held in Nashville, which adopted articles of agreement for the common defense and general welfare, the control of this Government being vested in a court or government of notables, consisting of ten. This settlement was engaged in almost constant warfare with the Indians. In 1780 an army of Tennessee colonists was organized for service against the British. These colonists, having been isolated from the colony of North Carolina by the mountains, were up to this year so constantly engaged in resisting the attacks of the Indians, it was impossible to render much, if any, assistance directly against the British. However, after the defeat of the Revolutionary army by General Clinton in North Carolina, an army of Tennessee colonists, led by Colonel Isaac Shelby and Colonel John Sevier, advanced into North Carolina and after several successful engagements with detachments of the British army met and annihilated on King's Mountain an army of British veterans under command of the distinguished British officer, Colonel Ferguson. The skill and gallantry of the officers and the valour of the men of Tennessee in this battle mark it as one of the glorious events of the state's history.

In 1785 the territory including the State of Tennessee was ceded by North Carolina to the United States. Some dissatisfaction having arisen between the colonists of Tennessee and the Government of North Carolina, in August, 1784, a convention composed of delegates from several of the counties petitioned Congress to accept the cession of North Carolina and permit the inhabitants of the territory to form a government to be admitted into the Union as a state. In September of the same year a convention was held at Jonesboro, but adjourned without taking any decisive action. Another convention was held in the same place in November, 1785, and a provisional Constitution was put into operation. The new state was called "Frankland, the Land of the Free". The name was soon after changed or recognized as "Franklin", when or by whom cannot be accurately determined. North Carolina continued to legislate and execute her laws within the jurisdiction of Franklin, and a compromise was ineffectually attempted. Pending these negotiations and the operations of the contending Governments, control of the State of Franklin was generally recognized, peace was maintained among the colonists under the laws of Franklin, and a continuous Indian warfare carried on. The cession of North Carolina was attempted by Congress, 2 April, 1790, and the country was governed as a territory for six years, during which the Indian wars were constant and bloody. In 1813 news reached Nashville of the outbreak of the Indians in Alabama and several massacres by them of the whites, particularly the settlement at Fort Mimms near Mobile. A public meeting was held, resulting in a request to General Andrew Jackson to take command of an army of volunteers called by the Legislature of the State of Tennessee and enrolled in service after a few days. Although Jackson was then convalescing from wounds he had received in a fray with the Bentons, within nine days he took command of the volunteer army and proceeded against the Indians. After several encounters they were signally defeated and their power utterly and permanently broken at Enotachopco and Tohopeka on 24 and 27 January, 1813. It was the creation of this army under Jackson that gave Tennessee the name of "The Volunteer State".

On 8 Jan., 1815, Jackson with an army consisting largely of Tennesseeans fought the battle of New Orleans. The main attack of the British, who were commanded by Sir Edward Packingham, one of the ablest of Wellington's lieutenants and composed of veterans seasoned by the Napoleonic wars, was defeated by the Tennessee riflemen under Generals Carroll and Coffee. With the adoption of the Constitution of 1834 Tennessee entered upon a new epoch in her history and then became an important factor in national politics. Jackson was elected president in 1828 and re-elected in 1832. James K. Polk was elected president in 1844. Tennesseeans figured prominently in the Mexican War of 1847, 30,000 volunteers tendering their services upon the call of Governor Brown. On 9 Feb., 1861, an election was held upon the question of holding a convention to determine whether or not Tennessee should secede from the Union of States. The State refused to secede by a vote of 24,794 favouring secession to 88,803 in favour of the Union. After the proclamation of President Lincoln on 15 April calling for 75,000 troops, a series of proclamations were issued declaring the ports of the seceded states in a state of blockade and all vessels acting under the seceded states guilty of piracy. This announcement of the purpose of the Federal Government to resort to coercion produced a revolution of sentiment in Tennessee. The Legislature, convened in extra session 25 April, passed an ordinance of secession and submitted it to popular vote in an election to be held 8 June, 1861. The ordinance was ratified by a vote of 104,913 in its favour to 47,238 against it.

Meantime an intense Union sentiment developed extensively in east Tennessee. The leading statesmen of that section, Andrew Johnson, afterwards President of the United States, Wm. G. Brownlow, Thomas A. R. Nelson, and Horace Maynard, espoused the cause of the Union. A convention was held on 17 June, 1861, at Greenville, to consider the formation of a new state composed of east Tennessee and such adjoining counties of middle Tennessee as might vote to be included. The new state was never formed, but many east Tennesseeans joined the Federal army. Many of the bloodiest battles of the Civil War were fought within the borders of Tennessee: Fort Henry, Fort Donelson, Shiloh, Murfreesboro or Stone's River, Nashville, Franklin; the battle of Chickamauga was fought largely on the Georgia border and for the possession of Tennessee. On 15 Feb., 1862, in consequence of the fall of Fort Donelson, the Legislature adjourned to Memphis. On 22 Feb., 1862, Gen. Grant issued an order suspending civil government in Tennessee and declaring martial law. President Lincoln appointed Andrew Johnson, Brigadier-General and Military Governor of Tennessee. In 1865 the Constitution of the state was amended so as to abolish slavery, and also to prohibit the General Assembly from making laws recognizing the right of property in man. On 4 March, 1865, Governor Johnson was inaugurated as Vice-President of the United States, and on 5 April following, Wm. G. Brownlow was inaugurated governor.

Following the return of the Confederate soldiers the Legislature passed a number of enactments which were strongly opposed by the conservative wing of the Union, which led to sentiments of animosity more bitter than the feelings engendered by war. One of these laws practically disfranchised all persons except those who had always been unconditional Union men. Tennessee was readmitted to the Union, 23 July, 1866, Andrew Johnson, then President of the United States, signing the bill. Tennessee was the only one of the seceding states to abolish slavery by its own act. From the beginning of the slavery agitation there was a strong abolition party in Tennessee. In 1820, "The Emancipator", the first abolition journal in the United States, was published by Elihu Embry at Jonesboro. The Ku Klux Klan was organized in Pulaski, middle Tennessee, in the summer of 1866, and was originally intended for the amusement of a band of young men who had returned from the Confederate army. It afterwards spread throughout the South, becoming a strongly partisan organization operated for the protection of Confederate sympathizers against the evils and dangers of the period. In 1869 the Confederate element regained control of the State, and on 10 June, 1870, another constitutional convention was held. The Constitution there adopted was ratified by the people, 26 March, 1871, and is still in force.

III. POPULATION.—The population of the state under the federal census of 1900 was 2,020,616: 1,021,224 males and 999,392 females; of whom 2,002,870 were native born: 1,010,793 males and 992,077 females. The coloured population, including mulattoes, Chinese, and others not of the white race, was 480,430: 238,522 males and 241,908 females. In 1910 the population was 2,184,789, an increase of 8.1 per cent.

IV. RESOURCES.—The resources of Tennessee are abundant, rich, and varied. In the eastern and a large part of the middle divisions minerals abound in practically inexhaustible beds, principally coal, iron, copper, lead, and zinc. Oil and natural gas is found in some sections. There are over 200 varieties of marble found in Tennessee. In middle Tennessee grass and grain are abundant and the stock-breeding interests in this section are famous. Here phosphate rock in great volume and richness is found. In west Tennessee fruits and grain are extensively produced. The principal products of this section are cotton and corn. The timber interests of the state are large and extensive, numerous forests in various sections of the state (poplar, oak, gum, hickory, and other varieties of timber) being untouched. The chief agricultural products are cotton, wheat, hay, corn, forage, and tobacco. The value of these products, according to the census of 1900, was $70,745,242. Animal products such as dairy, poultry, eggs, honey, and wax amount to $35,421,198. The chief manufactories are flour and grist mills, producing annually, according to the census of 1900, products valued at $21,798,929: lumber and timber, $18,127,-784; tobacco, snuff, cigars, etc., $3,010,602. These with other manufactures make an annual production valued at $108,144,565. The productions of the mines were: coal, $5,399,721; phosphate rock, $1,308,872; iron, $1,123,527; marble, $518,256; limestone and dolomites, $482,033; all others, $761,373, aggregating $9,533,782.

V. EDUCATION.—With a scholastic population of 771,-734, of which 587,088 are white and 184,646 coloured, there are enrolled in the public schools of Tennessee, 411,910 white and 100,248 coloured pupils. There are over 200 universities, colleges, and private training schools in the state. Its universities are among those leading in the South, notably: Vanderbilt University, University of Nashville, and Peabody Normal College at Nashville; University of the South at Sewanee; University of Tennessee at Knoxville; Cumberland University at Lebanon; Fisk, Roger Williams, and Walden Universities and Meharry Medical College at Nashville, the last four being devoted to the higher education of negroes. For Catholic education, diocese and population see NASHVILLE, DIOCESE OF.

VI. RELIGION AND RELIGIOUS REGULATIONS.—The present Constitution of the State of Tennessee declares that "all men have a natural and indefeasible right to worship Almighty God according to the dictates of their own conscience; that no man can of right be compelled to attend, erect or support any place of worship or maintain any minister against his consent; that no human authority can, in any case whatever, control or interfere with the rights of conscience; and that no preference shall be given by law to any religious establishment or mode of worship. That no political or religious test, other than an oath to support the Constitution of the United States and of this state, shall ever be required as a qualification to any office or public trust in this state". Christmas Day and Good Friday are legal holidays. Doing or exercising on Sunday any of the common avocations of life, acts of real necessity or charity excepted, is forbidden. The mere violation of this law is not indictable, but a succession of such acts, if done so openly as to attract public observation, is indictable as a nuisance. It is forbidden by law to swear profanely or curse in the hearing of any justice of the peace or to use profane or blasphemous language in public places; any person executing any public duty, convicted of profanely swearing or cursing, must forfeit and pay one dollar for each oath or curse. There is no provision in law for the use of prayer in the Legislature, but the rules of each branch usually provide for the appointment of a chaplain by the respective speakers. There is no statute in this state modifying the rule at common law requiring a clergyman to disclose communications made in confessions. The question has not been decided by its courts, but it is probable that when the question is presented the courts of the state will follow the rule generally adopted by the courts of other states on this subject, which is, that all communications in the nature of confessions or applications for spiritual guidance, made to a priest or clergyman as such, in confidence and in the course of the discipline required by the church of which the clergyman is a member, are privileged.

According to the census bulletin of 1906, the church membership of all denominations was 697,570: total Protestant bodies, 677,947: Baptists, Southern and National conventions, 253,141; Free Baptists, 1,840; Free Will Baptists, 3,093; Duck River, etc. (Baptist Church of Christ), 4,099; Primitive Baptists, 10,204; coloured Primitive Baptists, 3,268; Congregationalists, 2,426; Disciples of Christ, 14,904; Churches of Christ, 41,411; Lutheran, United Synods in the South, 1,678; Methodist Episcopal, 46,180; Methodist Protestant, 2,716; Methodist Episcopal Church South, 140,308; African Methodists, 50,662; Presbyterian Church in U. S. A., 6,786; Cumberland Presbyterians, 42,464; Presbyterian Church in U. S., 21,390; Coloured Cumberland Presbyterians, 6,640; Presbyterian,

Associated Reformed Synod of the South, 1504; Protestant Episcopal Church, 7874; United Brethren in Christ, 2875; other Protestant bodies, 12,484; Roman Catholic Church, 17,252; Jewish congregations (heads of families), 919; all other bodies, 1452.

VII. STATE LAWS.—A. *Oaths* are to be administered upon the New Testament in the usual form, kissing the book as seal of confirmation of the same. Those conscientiously scrupulous about taking the book oath may be sworn by calling on God to witness the truth of the statements to be made. Persons conscientiously scrupulous about taking an oath may make solemn affirmation in the words required. Persons may also be sworn according to the forms of their own country or particular religious creed.

B. *Marriage* cannot be contracted with a lineal ancestor or descendant, nor a lineal ancestor or descendant of either parent, nor the child of a grandparent, nor the lineal descendant of the husband or wife as the case may be, nor the husband or wife of the parent or lineal descendant. The intermarriage of white persons with negroes, mulattoes or persons of mixed blood descended from a negro to the third generation inclusive, or their living together as man and wife in this state is prohibited and punishable by imprisonment in the penitentiary. A second marriage cannot be contracted before a dissolution of the first, but the first shall be regarded as dissolved for this purpose if either party has been absent five years and is not known to the other party to be living. All regular ministers of the Gospel of every denomination, and Jewish rabbis, having the care of souls, all justices of the peace, judges, chancellors, the governor, speaker of the Senate, and speaker of the House of Representatives may solemnize the rite of matrimony. No formula need be observed for such solemnization, except that the parties shall respectively declare in the presence of the minister or officer, that they accept each other as husband or wife.

C. *Divorce.*—The following are causes of divorce from the bonds of matrimony: impotency or incapacity; second marriages in violation of previous marriage still subsisting; adultery; wilful and malicious desertion; absence of either party without reasonable excuse for two years; conviction of crime which, by the laws of the state, renders the party infamous; conviction of any crime which, by the laws of the state, is declared a felony and sentenced to confinement in the penitentiary; if either party has attempted the life of the other by poison or other means showing malice; refusal on the part of the wife to remove with her husband to this state, without reasonable excuse, and wilfully absenting herself from home for two years; that woman was pregnant at time of marriage by another person without knowledge of her husband; habitual drunkenness acquired after marriage. The following are causes of divorce from bed and board and from the bonds of matrimony at the discretion of the court: if the husband is guilty of such cruel and inhuman treatment or conduct towards his wife as renders it unsafe and improper for her to cohabit with him and to be under his domination and control; that he has offered such indignities to her person as to render her condition intolerable and thereby force her to withdraw; that he has abandoned her or turned her out of doors and refuses or neglects to provide for her. The petitioner must reside within the state for two years next preceding the filing of the petition. If upon false rumour, apparently well founded, of the death of one of the parties who has been absent two whole years, the other party marries again, the party remaining single may upon returning obtain a restoration of conjugal rights or a dissolution of the marriage. This dissolution of a marriage shall not in any wise affect the legitimacy of the children of same.

D. *Wills* may be verbal or written, but a verbal will is valid only so far as relates to personal property. A nuncupative or verbal will is a verbal declaration made by one in his last sickness as to the disposition of his property after death, made with the intention and purpose to dispose of such property, and where the estate exceeds $250 it must be made in the hearing and presence of at least two disinterested persons. Lands can be devised only by a written will attested by two witnesses, the subscription of the witnesses being made in the testator's presence; or by holographic will, a paper written entirely by the testator, the handwriting to be proved by at least three credible witnesses, every part of such writing to be in the testator's hand. Personalty may be disposed of by a paper containing a disposition of property to take effect after death, although neither written nor signed by the testator, if such paper can be shown to be the will of the testator and is complete in itself as to its provisions. No particular form is required.

E. *Cemeteries.*—All managers and trustees of any cemetery have full power to adopt and use all rules and regulations necessary for the good government, order, and discipline of the cemetery under their charge and keeping, not in conflict with any law of the state. They may appoint as many day and night watchmen on their grounds as they deem expedient. Such watchmen, and also all of their superintendents, gardeners, agents, and gate-keepers stationed on said grounds, may take the oath required by law of constables, exercise and possess all the powers of police officers within said cemetery and within one hundred yards of said cemetery grounds.

F. *Pensions.*—The State has a pension system under which pensions are allowed to disabled soldiers, Federal and Confederate, that enlisted from the State of Tennessee in Tennessee regiments or were citizens of this state at the time of their enlistment in regiments of other states. They must be residents of Tennessee, or former citizens of other states who enlisted in some regiment and who have been citizens of this state for one year. The character of the applicants as soldiers must have been free from dishonour, and it must appear that they are not already entitled to pension under the laws of the Federal Government or of any other state, and that they are not already in possession of a competency, the object of the law being to provide for the indigent and disabled. A pension is withheld from any pensioner who may habitually waste the state's bounty in dissipation or other dishonourable manner. Pensions are also granted to widows whose husbands were killed or died while in active service in the Civil War, and to the widows of deceased soldiers who were married to such soldiers prior to the year 1870, if such widows are of good moral character and in indigent circumstances. The number on the pension rolls for 1910 was 7899, of which 5367 were veterans and 2530 widows. The annual appropriation for this purpose is $475,000.

G. *Excise.*—By Acts of 1909 the sale of any intoxicating liquor, including wine, ale, and beer, within four miles of any public or private schoolhouse where school is kept, whether the school be then in session or not, is prohibited. At the same session an Act was passed prohibiting the manufacture of such liquors in the state. These measures virtually prohibit the sale or manufacture of liquor anywhere in the state.

VIII. PRISONS.—The state penitentiary is at Nashville. A branch prison is located at Brushy Mountain, east Tennessee, where the State owns extensive coal mines, in which a large number of prisoners are worked. The operation of these mines has been very profitable to the State. At the main prison are a number of manufactories operated by lessees of convict labour. There is also a large farm connected with the penitentiary on which convict labour is employed. The affairs of the penitentiary are administered by a commission of three, appointed by the governor.

IX. CHARITIES.—A. *Associations.*—Any association of individuals for the support of public worship, to build churches, and for the maintenance of all missionary undertakings may be incorporated. All property belonging to any religious, charitable, scientific, literary, or educational institution is exempt from taxation, except such part thereof as is used in secular business to compete with a like business which pays taxes to the State. Where rents and profits are used exclusively for religious or charitable purposes, including church parsonages not exceeding $5000 in value, and in cases where buildings are used partially for the purposes named and other portions rented out or otherwise used, the assessor shall, in making assessment, apportion the same and assess that portion for taxation which is under this section taxable. All property belonging to any of the above-named institutions and not used for any purpose is not exempt. All clergymen are exempt from jury service.

B. *Trusts.*—The general rule is that a trust for a charitable purpose must be of such a tangible nature that a court of equity can deal with it. It must be to some person, body, or association of persons having a legal existence and with capacity to take and administer the trust for some definite and lawful purpose. A devise or bequest made directly to a voluntary or unincorporated association must fail for want of capacity in the devisee to take it as a gift for itself; but if the gift be sufficiently definite and made to competent trustees for the benefit of the unincorporated institution or association it will be good, that is, if the will defines how such bequest is to be applied. The distinction taken in England between superstitious and charitable uses, being inconsistent with the principles of religious freedom that obtain in this state, is not recognized. Gifts for the good of the soul, or for prayers for the soul of the testator, or for the dead whether in or out of the chapel or church, or for the maintenance of Catholic priests are valid. A charitable use, where neither law nor public policy forbids, may be applied to almost anything that tends to promote the well-being and well-doing of social man and in favour of all religions of whatever form and creed.

C. *Institutions.*—There are three hospitals for the insane, one in each of the civil divisions of the state: at Bolivar, Nashville, and Knoxville. A Confederate Soldiers' Home and a home for blind girls is maintained at Nashville; also a school for blind boys and girls and an industrial school for boys and girls, both white and coloured at the same place. A school for the deaf and dumb is maintained at Knoxville.

HAYWOOD, *Civil and Political History of Tennessee* (Knoxville, 1823); RAMSEY, *Annals of Tennessee* (Philadelphia, 1860); PHELAN, *History of Tennessee* (Boston and New York, 1880); GARRETT AND GOODPASTURE, *History of Tennessee* (Nashville, 1903); KILLEBREW, *Resources of Tennessee* (Nashville, 1874); PAINE, *Hand Book of Tennessee* (Nashville, 1903).

THOS. J. TYNE.

Tenney, WILLIAM JEWETT, author, editor, b. at Newport, Rhode Island, 1814; d. at Newark, New Jersey, 20 Sept., 1883. Graduating from Yale in 1832 he studied medicine, but abandoned it for the law and, on being admitted to the bar, opened an office in New York. He then tried journalism on the editorial staff of the "Journal of Commerce," and contributed editorially to the "Evening Post", during 1841–43 and 1847–48. In 1853 he entered the service of D. Appleton and Co., publishers, as editor, and, in addition to a large amount of literary and critical work, began for them, in 1861, the compilation of the "Annual Cyclopædia" which he continued till his death. He indexed T. H. Benton's "Abridgment of the Debates of Congress" and added a sixteenth volume to the series (New York 1857–60). He edited the "Queens of England" (1852); and wrote a "Military and Naval History of the Rebellion in the U. S." (1865), and a "Grammatical Analysis" (1866). During a long residence at Elizabeth, N. J., he held several local public offices including that of collector of the port during President Buchanan's administration. He became a convert to the Catholic Faith and married, as his second wife, Sarah, daughter of Orestes H. Brownson (q. v.).

Appleton's Cyclopædia of American Biog. (New York, 1900), s. v.; LAMB, *Biog. Dict. of U. S.* (Boston, 1903); *Freeman's Journal* (New York), files.

THOMAS F. MEEHAN.

Tentyris (TENTYRA), seat of a titular suffragan see of Ptolemais in Thebaid Secunda. The city was the capital of the nome of that name, according to Amélineau, the real name being Nikentori or Nitentori, which signifies willow wood or willow earth. Others give the derivation from the goddess Hathor, or Aphrodite, who was specially worshiped there. The crocodile is recognized as the deity of the city and was also venerated as such in the other Egyptian cities, which caused many quarrels, notably with Ombos. Little is known of Christianity in that place, as only the names of two ancient bishops are given: Pachymius, companion of Melece at the beginning of the fourth century; and Serapion, or Aprion, contemporary and friend of the monk St. Pachomius, who had in his diocese his celebrated convent of Tabennisi. It is to-day Denderah, a town of 6000 inhabitants in the district of Qeneh. The temple of Hathor is still to be seen, built on the foundation of another, yet more ancient, which was in existence during the reign of Cheops under the fourth dynasty, and in which was found the celebrated zodiac now in Paris; there are also the temples of Mammisi and of Isis, of the Roman or Ptolemaic epoch.

LE QUIEN, *Oriens christ.*, II, 607; SMITH, *Dict. of Gr. and Rom. Geog.*, s. v.; AMÉLINEAU, *La géographie de l'Égypte à l'époque copte* (Paris, 1893), 140–2.

S. VAILHÉ.

Tenure, ECCLESIASTICAL.—I. In the feudal system an ecclesiastical fief followed all the laws laid down for temporal fiefs. The suzerain, e. g. bishop, abbot, or other possessor, granted an estate in perpetuity to a person, who thereby became his vassal. As such, the grantee at his enfeoffment did homage to his overlord, took an oath of fealty, and made offering of the prescribed money or other object, by reason of which he held his fief. These requirements had to be repeated as often as there was a change in the person of the suzerain or vassal. These fiefs were granted by churchmen to princes, barons, knights, and others, who thereupon assumed the obligation of protecting the church and domains of the overlord. This system of feudal tenure was not always restricted to lands, as church revenues and tithes were often farmed out to secular persons as a species of ecclesiastical fief. Strictly speaking, however, a fief was usually defined as immovable property whose usufruct perpetually conceded to another under the obligation of fealty and personal homage. A fief was not ecclesiastical simply because its overlord was a churchman; it was requisite also that the domain granted should be church property. Lands, which belonged to the patrimony of an ecclesiastic, became a secular fief if he bestowed them on a vassal.

All fiefs were personal and hereditary, and many of the latter could be inherited by female descent. Fiefs bestowed by the Church on vassals were called active fiefs; when churchmen themselves undertook obligations to a suzerain, the fiefs were called passive. In the latter case, temporal princes gave certain lands to the Church by enfeoffing a bishop or abbot, and the latter had then to do homage as pro-vassal and undertake all the implied obligations. When these included military service, the ecclesiastic was empowered to fulfil this duty by a substitute. It was as passive fiefs that many bishoprics, abbacies, and prelacies, as to their temporalities, were held of kings in the medieval period, and the power thereby acquired by secular princes over elections to ecclesiastical dignities led to the bitter strife over investitures. These passive fiefs were conferred by the suzerain investing the newly-elected churchman with crozier and ring at the time of his making homage, but the employment of these symbols of spiritual power gradually paved the way to exorbitant claims on the part of the secular overlords (see INVESTITURES, CONFLICT OF). Among papal fiefs were included not merely landed estates, however vast, but also duchies, principalities, and even kingdoms. When the pope enfeoffed a prince, the latter did homage to him as to his liege lord, and acknowledged his vassalage by an annual tribute. Pius V (29 Mar., 1567) decreed that, in future, fiefs belonging strictly to the Patrimony of St. Peter should be incorporated with the Pontifical States whenever the vassalage lapsed, and that no new enfeoffment take place. John, King of England, declared that he held his realm as a fief from the pope in 1213, and James II, King of Aragon, accepted the same relation for Sardinia and Corsica in 1295. The most famous papal fief was the Kingdom of Naples and Sicily, springing from investitures of 1059 and 1269. Modern conditions in Italy have made impossible any continuance of such feudal relations.

II. As to the tenure by which church lands are now held by legal titles before the civil law, see PROPERTY, ECCLESIASTICAL; and TRUSTEE SYSTEM.

III. For the perpetual tenure by incumbents of benefices and ecclesiastical dignities, see BENEFICE.

FERRARIS, *Bibliotheca Canonica*, III (Rome, 1886), s. v. *Feudum;* MASCHAT, *Institutiones Canonicæ*, II (Rome, 1757).

W. H. W. FANNING.

Teos, titular see, suffragan of Ephesus in Asia Minor. A city of Caria, situated on a peninsula opposite Samos, it was an asylum for the Greeks, likewise for the Minyæ of Orchomenos; then came colonies from Ionia, Athens, and Bœotia and gradually the population became Grecian. This very prosperous city was one of the first attacked by the Persians; the inhabitants fled into Thrace and founded Abdera, during the reign of Cyrus. Those who remained in Teos allied themselves with the Athenians. Later they revolted, going over to the Spartan rule, but were afterwards reconquered by the Athenians. The walls, recently discovered, 3¾ miles in circumference, date from this time, as do also the greater part of the monuments which made it one of the most beautiful cities of Ionia. Teos was celebrated for its wine and, therefore, for the worship of Bacchus. Here was born the poet Anacreon. Here too was the home of a body of bacchanalian artists who furnished actors for the theatres of Asia and the Archipelago. It was the beginning of the ancient theatre. In order to further commerce and the pursuit of the fine arts, Teos, after having saved the fleet of the Roman prætor Regulus from Antiochus, King of Syria, secured for its territory in 193 B. C. from Rome and a great number of Grecian cities the right of perpetual asylum, this privilege being largely due to the temple of Bacchus. During the Christian era almost nothing is known of this city. It figures in all the "Notitiæ Episcopatuum" as a suffragan of Ephesus, but in the fifteenth century no mention is made of it. Teos is believed to have been destroyed by an earthquake. Among its bishops Le Quien (Oriens christianus, I, 727) mentions: Maximus at the Council of Nice; Gennadius at Chalcedon, 451; finally St. Sisinnius, who is said to have lived about the eleventh century, and whose feast days are 2 February and 14 July, at Torcelli near Venice. To-day Teos is known as Sighadjik, near Sivri-Hissar; it is a nahié of the sanjak of Smyrna; its ruins have furnished a great many inscriptions.

SMITH, *Dict. of Gr. and Rom. Geog.*, s. v.; TEXIER, *Asie Mineure* (Paris, 1862), 361–6; WADDINGTON, *Explication des inscriptions grecques et latines, Asie Mineure*, 28–55; *Bulletin de correspondance hellénique*, IV, 54–9, 110–21, 164–82; SCHEFFLER, *De rebus Teiorum* (Leipzig, 1882); CUINET, *La Turquie d'Asie*, III, 493–5; CHAPOT, *La province romaine proconsulaire d'Asie* (Paris, 1904), passim.

S. VAILHÉ.

Tepic, DIOCESE OF (TEPICENSIS).—Diocese of the Mexican Republic, suffragan of the Archbishopric of Guadalajara. Its area is that of the federal state of the same name, that is, 10,951 sq. m., besides a few parishes situated in the western part of Jalisco. It has a population of 171,837 inhabitants (Census of 1910). The principal city which is also the residence of the bishop and the political head is Tepic, 3146 feet above sea level and has 16,805 inhabitants. All this territory was discovered and devastated and the natives cruelly treated by the famous Nuno de Guzman in 1530. It is said that during the conquest, many plots and even attempts at insurrection were made, not only by the allied Indians but also by the Spanish themselves. To check this evil, some were hanged and others were put in prison; many were tortured to obtain confessions as to the instigators of these conspiracies, the object of which in most cases was to return to Mexico. These cruelties caused such despair among the Indians who carried the supplies of the expedition that a great many committed sucide by hanging themselves in groups of ten. The Spanish had already established themselves, and cities such as Tepic, Compostela, S. Blas, Acaponetam, etc. had already been founded when religious services were established. These soon developed and thrived after the foundation of the Bishopric of Guadalajara in 1548.

The mountainous region of the wonderful provinces of Nayarit, inhabited by barbarous and ferocious tribes of Indians, were still remaining refractory to civilization and Christianity. In 1668 the Franciscan Fathers J. Caballero and Juan B. Ramirez attempted, but in vain, to penetrate these mountains. The venerable Father Margil of the convent of Zacatecas also tried to reach these regions in 1711, but he was forced to retreat without satisfaction. Nayarit, which belonged to the Bishopric of Durango since its creation in 1620, remained so until the Bishop of Durango gave the mission of civilizing this wild country to Father Tomas de Solchaga, S.J., professor of moral theology at the college at Durango; he was successful in penetrating the country to the heart of the mountains and there began to sow fruitful seeds in 1716. When the Marquis of Valero was Viceroy of New Spain he received through the royal cedula of Philip V an order to subdue the Indians of that territory and make them swear allegiance to the Spanish monarch; after many bloody battles and with many difficulties and hardships, he succeeded, with the help of his brave captains in taking possession of the famous Mesa del Tonatiy. At his request the Father Provincial of the Society of Jesus of New Spain sent several missionaries to convert the newly-conquered Indians. They soon established flourishing missions which, when the Jesuits were expelled by the Decree of Charles III, included the following missions: Santa Rita, Santa Teresa, Iscatán, Jesus María, SSma. Trinidad, Giuanamota, and Rosario. After the expulsion of the Jesuits the parish priest of Bolaños on several occasions visited the reductions. The Franciscan Fathers took charge of the missions until the year 1807, when the Fathers of the College of Nuestra Señora de Zacatecas returned and remained until the mother-house at Zacatecas was abolished.

In 1891 Leo XIII created the Diocese of Tepic which became suffragan of the Archbishopric of Guadalajara; it was completed with several parishes situated in the present State of Jalisco. The bishopric has 1 seminary and 72 alumni; 23 Catholic schools and 6 Catholic colleges with about 3,000 alumni. The present bishop is the Rt. Rev. Andrew Segura, who was consecrated, 16 Sept., 1906. There are 3 Protestant churches.

ORTEGAS, *Hist. del Nayarit* (Mexico, 1887); DAVILA, *Continuacion de la Hist. de la Comp. de Jesus en Nueva España* (Puebla, 1889); *Mexico à través de los siglos*, II, (Barcelona).

CAMILLUS CRIVELLI.

Tepl, a Premonstratensian abbey in the western part of Bohemia, included in the Archdiocese of Prague; it was founded in 1193 by the blessed martyr Hroznata, a Bohemian nobleman (d. 1217). The first monks came from the Abbey of Strahov in Prague. Tepl escaped any damage in the Hussite Wars, probably on account of the military spirit of its Abbot, Račko of Risenberg (1411–44), who was aided by his relatives. It suffered, however, all the more during the era of the Reformation. Luther's doctrine soon found adherents among the subjects of the abbey. In 1525 there was a rebellion against the abbot and peace was not restored until the ringleaders of the revolt were executed. In the following years a number of the monks left the order and married. Monastic discipline was restored by Abbot Johann Kurz (1555–59), who also established a theological school. But his successor, Johann Meyskönig (1559-85), had a struggle with insubordination in the monastery. With the aid of the archbishop he was able to improve the monastery and the school. He brought back most of his subjects to the Catholic Church by compulsion, after gentle treatment had failed. The reform was continued by Mathias Göhl (1585–96). Andreas Ebersbach (1598–1629) was a zealous reformer of the abbey and raised it to such a height that it was called the "nursery of pastoral work". Parochial work and higher education are still important features of the life of the abbey. The abbey has the pastoral care of twenty-four parishes that are all in the western part of Bohemia, a section which is almost entirely German. A twenty-fifth parish is being formed. The abbey has a theological school of the order with a two-years' course and three professors. Since 1809 it has had charge of the German *gymnasium* at Pilsen where there are fourteen canons. It also owns the celebrated cure of Marienbad. It supports hospitals at Tepl and Marienbad. The members of the abbey include 84 priests, 13 clerics, and 2 novices. The present monastery building was erected by Abbot Raimund Wilfert II (1688–1724); the library was built by Abbot Gilbert Helmer (since 1900). The Romanesque church, with additions in the style of the transition to the Gothic, is one of the oldest churches of Bohemia.

KARLIK, *Hroznata u. die Prämonstratenser-Abtei Tepl* (2nd ed., Pilsen, 1883); *Festschrift zum 700-jährigen Jubiläum der Gründung des Prämonstratenserstiftes Tepl* (Tepl, 1893); GRASSL, *Gesch. u. Beschreibung des Stiftes Tepl* (Pilsen, 1910); ŽÁK, *Oesterreiches Klosterbuch* (Vienna, 1911), 54–56.

KLEMENS LÖFFLER.

Teramo, DIOCESE OF, in southern Italy. In the past the city was injured by earthquakes. It is situated at the confluence of the Tordino and the Vessola in a very fertile district, and was formerly noted for its manufacture of delf; ore is found in the vicinity. The cathedral is far from being uniform in style, the façade being like a fortress wall in which a Gothic gate had been constructed; it contains, however, several works of art, among them the tomb of Bishop Nicola Arcioni (1317). The Churches of S. Domenico and of S. Francesco are also worth visiting. In ancient days it was called Interamnia and was the seat of government of the Præcutii, a Samnite people; in 315 B. C. a Roman colony, Interamnia Præcutiana, was settled there; from them is derived the name of the entire region, Abruzzi, a name already adopted in the sixth century. Among the ruins of the Roman period are an amphitheatre, a theatre, and an aqueduct. After the Longobard invasion it became the residence of a *gastaldo*, depending on the Duke of Spoleto; under the Franks it was the seat of a count. In the beginning of 1108 it was annexed by the Normans; in 1155 Count Loretello rebelled against King Roger and destroyed the city, soon rebuilt through the efforts of Bishop Guido (1122), for which he and his successors were granted the investiture of the principality. Probably at this time arose the custom of the bishops of Teramo of pontificating armed and having arms also on the altar. Hardly had the town risen again when it began a series of quarrels with Ascoli, which more than once threatened to become sanguinary. Teramo resisted till the end of 1270 during the Angevin invasion. A little later the bishops abandoned their temporal sovereignty and a royal captain was installed. In the beginning of the fifteenth century the Melatino, di Janni, and Acquaviva began to struggle for possession of the town. In 1416 it was sacked by Lordino, a Frenchman, exasperated by being deprived of the title of high constable of the kingdom; during the pillage the treasures of the cathedral, including a precious silver altar frontal, disappeared.

The city which at that time contained 70,000 inhabitants began to decay. From 1438 till 1443 it belonged to the principality which Francesco Sforza had formed in the Marches. Alfonso made it the capital of the Abruzzi, and in 1459 Giosia Acquaviva was made Duke of Teramo, against the will of the citizens. The following year it was taken by Piccinino for Réné of Anjou; in 1461 it was retaken by Matteo di Capua. In 1519 Andrea Acquaviva assumed anew the lordship of Teramo and besieged the town; but he was forced to resign. About 600 A. D., according to St. Gregory the Great, the Abruzzian church having been long without a bishop, the election of Opportunus was procured; hence the origin of the see dates back to the fifth century at least, and the bishop's title was taken not from the town but from the district. It may be even more ancient. Among its other prelates were: St. Berardus (1115), descended from the family of the Counts dei Marsi; Matteo de Balato (1251), captured during the inroad of the Ascolani and liberated through the intervention of Innocent IV; Blessed Antonio Fatati (1450), counsellor of King Alfonso I; Gian Ant. Campano (1463), a littérateur and poet; Giacomo Silveri-Piccolomini (1553), distinguished at the Council of Trent; Leonardo Cassiani (1693), who improved the state of the clergy; Michele Milella (1859), incarcerated by the new government in 1861. In 1818 the Diocese of Ortona, which is now only an archipresbyteral church, was incorporated with the See of Teramo. The latter is immediately subject to the Holy See and contains 121 parishes, 220 secular and 13 regular priests, 3 houses of religious and 1 of monks, 2 institutes for boys and 4 for girls.

CAPPELLETTI, *Le chiese d'Italia*, XXI; PALMA, *Storia ecclesiastica e civile . . . di Teramo* (Teramo, 1852–6).

U. BENIGNI.

Terce.—The origin of Terce, like that of Sext and None, to which it bears a close relationship, dates back to Apostolic times. As has already been stated (see NONE) according to an ancient custom of the Romans and Greeks, the day and the night respectively were divided into four parts of about three hours each. The second division of the day hours was that of Terce from nine o'clock until midday. These divisions of the day were also in vogue among the Jews at the time of Christ. In the New Testament we find mention of the sixth hour in Matt., xx, 5; xxvii, 45; Mark, xv, 33; John, xix, 14; of the ninth hour, in Matt., xxvii, 46; Mark, xv, 34; Acts, x, 3 and 30. (See NONE.) The hour of Terce is mentioned in the following passages: the householder hires labourers at the third hour, Matt., xx, 3; Jesus is crucified at the third hour, Mark, xv, 25; the Holy Ghost descends upon the Apostles on the day of Pentecost at the third hour, Acts, ii, 15. Some of these texts prove that these three hours were, in preference to others, chosen for prayer by the Christians, and probably also by the Jews, from whom the Christians appear to have borrowed the custom. We find frequent mention in the Fathers of the Church and the ecclesiastical writers of the third century of Terce, Sext, and None as hours for daily prayers. For example, Tertullian, Clement of Alexandria, and the Canons of Hippolytus (see Clement, "Stromat.", VII, vii, in P. G., IX, 455-458). Tertullian says expressly that we should always pray, and that there is no prescribed time for prayer, but adds: "As regards the time, there should be no lax observation of certain hours—I mean, of those common hours which have long marked the divisions of the day, the third, the sixth, and the ninth—and which we may observe in Scripture to be more solemn than the rest" (De Orat., XXXIII, xxv, in P. L., I, 1191–1193).

Clement and Tertullian in these passages refer only to private prayer at these three hours. The Canons of Hippolytus also speak of these three hours as suitable for private prayer. However, on the days called "days of station", that is to say Wednesday and Friday, which were set apart as especially consecrated to prayer, and Sunday, these hours were recited in public (Canon, xx, xxvi). St. Cyprian remarked that these three hours had been observed in the Old Testament, and that Christians should also observe them (De Oratione, XXXIV, in P. L., IV, 541). In the fourth century the custom of praying at these hours became more frequent, and even obligatory, at least for monks (see the texts of the Apostolic Constitutions, of St. Ephrem, of St. Basil, of the author of "De Virginitate" quoted in Bäumer-Biron, "Histoire du bréviaire", 116, 121, 129, 186). Our texts say nothing as to what were the elements of the prayer of Terce, Sext, or None before the fourth century. Doubtless, like all prayers at that time, they were composed of psalms, canticles, hymns, and litanies. It is from the fourth century onwards that we can gather a more precise idea as to the composition of the hour of Terce. In the fourth century, as we have said, the custom of prayer at Terce spread, and tended to become obligatory, at least for monks. There is no mention in the "Peregrinatio ad Loca Sancta" of an office of Terce on ordinary days. Some authors have misunderstood the text here, but there is no mention of a meeting at this hour, except on Sunday and during Lent (see Cabrol, "Etude sur la Peregrinatio Silviæ", Paris, 1895, p. 45, 46). The hour of Terce is also mentioned in St. Jerome, "Ep. ad Lætam." in P. L., XXII, 875; "Ep. ad Eustoch." in P. L., XXII, 420; in the Life of St. Melania the Younger, "Analecta Bollandiana", VIII, 1889, p. 16; in Cassian, "De instit. cœnob.", in P. L., LXIX, 112, 126, etc.

At this period it is composed of the same elements as the hours of Sext and None; the distribution is the same, and it is clear that the three "little hours" were composed at the same time and that they have the same origin. The psalms of Terce are different from those of the other two hours. There were also certain varieties of composition. Thus, in certain countries, three psalms were assigned to Terce, six to Sext, nine to None, in virtue of the symbolism.

The composition varies also in the various liturgies. In the Greek Church Terce is composed of two parts, each made up of psalms (two for the first, three for the second), with invitatory, troparia, and final prayer. (See Neale and Littledale, "Commentary on the Psalms", I, p. 34.) In the Benedictine Rite, Terce comprises, on week days, the Gradual Psalms, 119, 120, and 121, with a capitulum, verse, Kyrie, Pater, and prayer. On Sundays and Mondays the Gradual Psalms are replaced by three octonaries (i. e. three sections of eight verses each) of Psalm cxviii. In the Mozarabic Rite, three octonaries of Ps. cxviii are also recited, the composition otherwise differing very little. In the main, the recitation of three psalms at Terce, as at the other two "little hours" of the day, is founded on a universal and very ancient tradition. Divergencies on this point are only exceptional. The practice of the Roman Liturgy, which at first sight appears to be somewhat different, may be traced to this tradition also. In this rite a part of Ps. cxviii is recited at Terce as well as at the other "little hours", the psalm being divided into three double octonaries. After the new Psalter arranged in 1911-12, the psalms are: on Sunday, Ps. cxviii (three divisions); on Monday, Ps. xxvi (two divisions); on Tuesday, Ps. xxxix (three divisions); on Wednesday, Ps. liii (two divisions); on Thursday, Ps. lxxii (three divisions); on Friday, Ps. xxxix (two divisions); on Saturday, Ps. ci (three divisions). The number three is therefore preserved in each case. The hymn "Nunc Sancte nobis Spiritus" recalls the descent of the Holy Ghost upon the Apostles. The other elements are the same as for Sext and None.

The Fathers of the Church and the liturgists of the Middle Ages considered the hour of Terce as corresponding to the hour of Christ's condemnation to death. They also often point out on this occasion the mysteries of the number three, which in ecclesiastical symbolism is a sacred number (see Bona, loc. cit.). What gives to it its especial dignity, however, is its association with the Descent of the Holy Ghost upon the Apostles on the day of Pentecost at this very hour ("seeing it is but the third hour of the day", Acts, II, 15). In several liturgies, and particularly in the Roman, this connexion is brought to mind by one or other of the formulæ. Again, this is the reason why, from the earliest times, the hour of Terce was chosen as that of the Mass on feast days. Sometimes, also, this hour is called in liturgical language *hora aurea* or *hora sacra* (see Durandus, "De rit. eccles.", c. viii).

FRANCOLINIUS, *De tempore horar. canonic.* (Rome, 1571); BONA, *Opera omnia: De tertia* (Antwerp, 1677), 727 sqq.; the texts from TERTULLIAN, CLEMENT OF ALEXANDRIA, ST. CYPRIAN, etc., quoted in BÄUMER-BIRON, *Histoire du bréviaire*, I. 73, 78, 194-197, etc.; MARTÈNE, *De antiquis ecclesiæ ritibus*, III, 20 sqq.; *De antiquis monachorum ritibus*, IV, 27; LECLERCQ, in CABROL, *Dict. de liturgie et d'archéologie*, s. v. *Bréviaire*; NEALE AND LITTLEDALE, *Commentary on the Psalms*, I, 34; BATIFFOL, *Hist. du bréviaire* (1911—). See also bibliographies under NONE; SEXT.

F. CABROL.

Terenuthis, titular see, suffragan of Antinoë in Thebais Prima. Le Quien (Oriens christ., II, 611) mentions two of its bishops: Arsinthius in 404; Eulogius at the Council of Ephesus in 431. The monks sometimes sought refuge there during incursions of the barbarian Maziks (Cotelier, "Ecclesiæ græcæ monumenta", I, 393). John Moschus went there at the beginning of the seventh century (Pratum spirituale, LIV, CXIV). There is frequent mention of this town in Christian Coptic literature. The present village of Tarraneh in the Province of Beherah replaces Terenuthis, the ruins of which lie about a mile and a quarter to the west. It has 1330 inhabitants. About nine and a quarter miles distant are the Lakes of Nitria and Scetis, near which were the lauras of these names.

Georgii Cyprii Descriptio orb. rom., ed. GELZER, 125; AMÉLINEAU, *La géog. de l'Egypte à l'époque Copte* (Paris, 1893), 493.

S. VAILHÉ.

Teresa of Jesus, SAINT (TERESA SANCHEZ CEPEDA DAVILA Y AHUMADA), b. at Avila, Old Castille, 28 March, 1515; d. at Alba de Tormes, 4 Oct., 1582. The third child of Don Alonso Sanchez de Cepeda by his second wife, Doña Beatriz Davila y Ahumada, who died when the saint was in her fourteenth year, Teresa was brought up by her saintly father, a lover of serious books, and a tender and pious mother. After her death and the marriage of her eldest sister, Teresa was sent for her education to the Augustinian nuns at Avila, but owing to illness she left at the end of eighteen months, and for some years remained with her father and occasionally with other relatives, notably an uncle who made her acquainted with the Letters of St. Jerome, which determined her to adopt the religious life, not so much through any attraction towards it, as through a desire of choosing the safest course. Unable to obtain her father's consent she left his house unknown to him on 2 Nov., 1535, to enter the

Carmelite Convent of the Incarnation at Avila, which then counted 140 nuns. The wrench from her family caused her a pain which she ever afterwards compared to that of death. However, her father at once yielded and Teresa took the habit.

After her profession in the following year she became very seriously ill, and underwent a prolonged cure and such unskilful medical treatment that she was reduced to a most pitiful state, and even after partial recovery through the intercession of St. Joseph, her health remained permanently impaired. During these years of suffering she began the practice of mental prayer, but fearing that her conversations with some worldly-minded relatives, frequent visitors at the convent, rendered her unworthy of the graces God bestowed on her in prayer, discontinued it, until she came under the influence, first of the Dominicans, and afterwards of the Jesuits. Meanwhile God had begun to visit her with "intellectual visions and locutions", that is manifestations in which the exterior senses were in no way affected, the things seen and the words heard being directly impressed upon her mind, and giving her wonderful strength in trials, reprimanding her for unfaithfulness, and consoling her in trouble. Unable to reconcile such graces with her shortcomings, which her delicate conscience represented as grievous faults, she had recourse not only to the most spiritual confessors she could find, but also to some saintly laymen, who, never suspecting that the account she gave them of her sins was greatly exaggerated, believed these manifestations to be the work of the evil spirit. The more she endeavoured to resist them the more powerfully did God work in her soul. The whole city of Avila was troubled by the reports of the visions of this nun. It was reserved to St. Francis Borgia and St. Peter of Alcantára, and afterwards to a number of Dominicans (particularly Pedro Ibañez and Domingo Bañez), Jesuits, and other religious and secular priests, to discern the work of God and to guide her on a safe road.

The account of her spiritual life contained in the "Life written by herself" (completed in 1565, an earlier version being lost), in the "Relations", and in the "Interior Castle", forms one of the most remarkable spiritual biographies with which only the "Confessions of St. Augustine" can bear comparison. To this period belong also such extraordinary manifestations as the piercing or transverberation of her heart, the spiritual espousals, and the mystical marriage. A vision of the place destined for her in hell in case she should have been unfaithful to grace, determined her to seek a more perfect life. After many troubles and much opposition St. Teresa founded the convent of Discalced Carmelite Nuns of the Primitive Rule of St. Joseph at Avila (24 Aug., 1562), and after six months obtained permission to take up her residence there. Four years later she received the visit of the General of the Carmelites, John-Baptist Rubeo (Rossi), who not only approved of what she had done but granted leave for the foundation of other convents of friars as well as nuns. In rapid succession she established her nuns at Medina del Campo (1567), Malagon and Valladolid (1568), Toledo and Pastrana (1569), Salamanca (1570), Alba de Tormes (1571), Segovia (1574), Veas and Seville (1575), and Caravaca (1576). In the "Book of Foundations" she tells the story of these convents, nearly all of which were established in spite of violent opposition but with manifest assistance from above. Everywhere she found souls generous enough to embrace the austerities of the primitive rule of Carmel. Having made the acquaintance of Antonio de Heredia, prior of Medina, and St. John of the Cross (q. v.), she established her reform among the friars (28 Nov., 1568), the first convents being those of Duruelo (1568), Pastrana (1569), Mancera, and Alcalá de Henares (1570).

A new epoch began with the entrance into religion of Jerome Gratian, inasmuch as this remarkable man was almost immediately entrusted by the nuncio with the authority of visitor Apostolic of the Carmelite friars and nuns of the old observance in Andalusia, and as such considered himself entitled to overrule the various restrictions insisted upon by the general and the general chapter. On the death of the nuncio and the arrival of his successor a fearful storm burst over St. Teresa and her work, lasting four years and threatening to annihilate the nascent reform. The incidents of this persecution are best described in her letters. The storm at length passed, and the province of Discalced Carmelites, with the support of Philip II, was approved and canonically established on 22 June, 1580. St. Teresa, old and broken in health, made further foundations at Villanueva de la Jara and Palencia (1580), Soria (1581), Granada (through her assistant the Venerable Anne of Jesus), and at Burgos (1582). She left this latter place at the end of July, and, stopping at Palencia, Valladolid, and Medina del Campo, reached Alba de Tormes in September, suffering intensely. Soon she took to her bed and passed away on 4 Oct., 1582, the following day, owing to the reform of the calendar, being reckoned as 15 Oct. After some years her body was transferred to Avila, but later on reconveyed to Alba, where it is still preserved incorrupt. Her heart, too, showing the marks of the Transverberation, is exposed there to the veneration of the faithful. She was beatified in 1614, and canonized in 1622 by Gregory XV, the feast being fixed on 15 October.

St. Teresa's position among writers on mystical theology is unique. In all her writings on this subject she deals with her personal experiences, which a deep insight and analytical gifts enabled her to explain clearly. The Thomistic substratum may be traced to the influence of her confessors and directors, many of whom belonged to the Dominican Order. She herself had no pretension to found a school in the accepted sense of the term, and there is no vestige in her writings of any influence of the Areopagitic, the Patristic, or the Scholastic Mystical schools, as represented, among others, by the German Dominican Mystics. She is intensely personal, her system going exactly as far as her experiences, but not a step further.

A word must be added on the orthography of her name. It has of late become the fashion to write her name Teresa or Teresia, without "h", not only in Spanish and Italian, where the "h" could have no place, but also in French, German, and Latin, which ought to preserve the etymological spelling. As it is derived from a Greek name, *Tharasia*, the saintly wife of St. Paulinus of Nola, it should be written Theresia in German and Latin, and Thérèse in French.

The bibliography of St. Teresa is exceedingly lengthy. Unfortunately, even DE CURZON'S *Bibliographie Thérèsienne* (Paris, 1902) is far too incomplete and inaccurate to be of much use. Here we can only deal with her own writings. The autographs of the life written by herself, and of the *Book of Foundations* have been published in photo-lithography by DON VICENTE DE LA FUENTE (Madrid, 1873 and 1880 respectively); the *Interior Castle*, under the direction of CARDINAL LLUCH (Seville, 1882); the *Way of Perfection* (MS. of the Escorial) and the *Visitation of Nunneries* by DON FRANCISCO HERRERO BAYONA (Valladolid, 1883), with a transcript of the MS. of the *Way of Perfection* preserved at Valladolid. Of the remaining works, the *Relations*, the *Exclamations*, the *Conceptions*, the *Maxims*, the *Constitutions*, and the poems (about thirty-six of these being considered genuine), no autographs, or only small fragments, are known to exist. The *Seven Meditations on the Lord's Prayer* are not authentic. The most recent English translations are by LEWIS: *Life and Relations*, ed. ZIMMERMAN (4th ed., London, 1911); *Foundations*, with the *Visitation* and *Constitutions* (London, 1871, a new edition being now in the press). The *Interior Castle, Exclamations*, and the *Way of Perfection*, translated by the BENEDICTINES OF STANBROOK, ed. ZIMMERMAN; the two former, London, 1906 (a second edition being now in the press); the third, London, 1911. The *Conceptions of Divine Love*, the *Maxims* and the poems, by the same translators and editor, are also in the press. Pending the publication of a complete English edition of the *Letters* we cannot do better than refer the reader to the *Lettres de Sainte Thérèse, par le R. P. Grégoire de St. Joseph* (3 vols., 2nd ed., 1906). Mention must be made of the new French translation of the works of the saint (with numerous documents and *pièces justifica-*

tives, not previously published): *Œuvres complètes de Sainte Térèse, par les Carmélites du premier monastere de Paris* (6 vols., Paris, 1907–10); *St. Teresa*, ed. BURKE (New York, 1911).

BENEDICT ZIMMERMAN.

Teresian Martyrs of Compiègne, THE SIXTEEN BLESSED, guillotined at the Place du Trône Renversé, now called Place de la Nation, Paris, 17 July, 1794. They are the first sufferers under the French Revolution on whom the Holy See has passed judgment, and were solemnly beatified 27 May, 1906. Before their execution they knelt and chanted the "Veni Creator", as at a profession, after which they all renewed aloud their baptismal and religious vows. The novice was executed first and the prioress last. Absolute silence prevailed the whole time that the executions were proceeding. The heads and bodies of the martyrs were interred in a deep sand-pit about thirty feet square in a cemetery at Picpus. As this sand-pit was the receptacle of the bodies of 1298 victims of the Revolution, there seems to be no hope of their relics being recovered. Their names are as follows: (1) Madeleine-Claudine Ledoine (Mother Teresa of St. Augustine), prioress, b. in Paris, 22 Sept., 1752, professed 16 or 17 May, 1775; (2) Marie-Anne (or Antoinette) Brideau (Mother St. Louis), sub-prioress, b. at Belfort, 7 Dec., 1752, professed 3 Sept., 1771; (3) Marie-Anne Piedcourt (Sister of Jesus Crucified), choir-nun, b. 1715, professed 1737; on mounting the scaffold she said "I forgive you as heartily as I wish God to forgive me"; (4) Anne-Marie-Madeleine Thouret (Sister Charlotte of the Resurrection), sacristan, b. at Mouy, 16 Sept., 1715, professed 19 Aug., 1740, twice sub-prioress in 1764 and 1778. Her portrait is reproduced opposite p. 2 of Miss Willson's work cited below; (5) Marie-Antoinette or Anne Hanisset (Sister Teresa of the Holy Heart of Mary), b. at Rheims in 1740 or 1742, professed in 1764; (6) Marie-Françoise Gabrielle de Croissy (Mother Henriette of Jesus), b. in Paris, 18 June, 1745, professed 22 Feb., 1764, prioress from 1779 to 1785; (7) Marie-Gabrielle Trézel (Sister Teresa of St. Ignatius), choir-nun, b. at Compiègne, 4 April, 1743, professed 12 Dec., 1771; (8) Rose-Chrétien de la Neuville, widow, choir-nun (Sister Julia Louisa of Jesus), b. at Loreau (or Evreux), in 1741, professed probably in 1777; (9) Anne Petras (Sister Mary Henrietta of Providence), choir-nun, b. at Cajarc (Lot), 17 June, 1760, professed 22 Oct., 1786. (10) Concerning Sister Euphrasia of the Immaculate Conception accounts vary. Miss Willson says that her name was Marie Claude Cyprienne Brard, and that she was born 12 May, 1736; Pierre, that her name was Catherine Charlotte Brard, and that she was born 7 Sept., 1736. She was born at Bourth, and professed in 1757; (11) Marie-Geneviève Meunier (Sister Constance), novice, b. 28 May, 1765, or 1766, at St. Denis, received the habit 16 Dec., 1788. She mounted the scaffold singing "Laudate Dominum". In addition to the above, three lay sisters suffered and two *tourières*. The lay sisters are: (12) Angélique Roussel (Sister Mary of the Holy Ghost), lay sister, b. at Fresnes, 4 August, 1742, professed 14 May, 1769; (13) Marie Dufour (Sister St. Martha), lay sister, b. at Beaune, 1 or 2 Oct., 1742, entered the community in 1772; (14) Julie or Juliette Vérolot (Sister St. Francis Xavier), lay sister, b. at Laignes or Lignières, 11 Jan., 1764, professed 12 Jan., 1789. The two *tourières*, who were not Carmelites at all, but merely servants of the nunnery were: (15 and 16) Catherine and Teresa Soiron, b. respectively on 2 Feb., 1742 and 23 Jan., 1748 at Compiègne, both of whom had been in the service of the community since 1772. The miracles proved during the process of beatification were (1) The cure of Sister Clare of St. Joseph, a Carmelite lay sister of New Orleans, when on the point of death from cancer, in June, 1897; (2) The cure of the Abbé Roussarie, of the seminary at Brive, when at the point of death, 7 March, 1897; (3) The cure of Sister St. Martha of St. Joseph, a Carmelite lay sister of Vans, of tuberculosis and an abcess in the right leg, 1 Dec., 1897; (4) The cure of Sister St. Michæl, a Franciscan of Montmorillon, 9 April, 1898. Five secondary relics are in the possession of the Benedictines of Stanbrook, Worcestershire.

PIERRE, *Les Seize Carmélites de Compiègne* (Paris, 1905); WILLSON, *The Martyrs of Compiègne* (Westminster, 1907).

JOHN B. WAINEWRIGHT.

Terill (BONVILLE), ANTHONY, English theologian, b. at Canford, Dorsetshire, in 1623; d. at Liège, 11 Oct., 1676. His mother was a Catholic but his father was estranged from the Faith, and in consequence the young Anthony was reared in heresy until his fifteenth year, when he was converted and left England, taking the alias Terill. He studied for about three years at the English College of St. Omer and then began his studies for the priesthood at the English College, Rome, where he was ordained on 16 March, 1647. Two months later he entered the Jesuit novitiate at San Andrea. After his noviceship he was successively penitentiary at Loreto, professor of philosophy at Florence, professor of philosophy and scholastic theology at Parma, director of theological studies and professor of theology and mathematics at the English College, Liège, and for three years rector of the same college where he died with a reputation for "extraordinary piety, talent, learning, and prudence". He wrote "Conclusiones philosophicæ" (Parma, 1657), "Problema mathematico-philosophicum de termino magnitudinis ac virium in animalibus" (Parma, 1660), "Fundamentum totius theologiæ moralis, seu tractatus de conscientia probabili" (Liège, 1668), and "Regula morum" which was published shortly after his death (Liège, 1677). His reputation as a moral theologian was established by these last two works. In the "Fundamentum" he ably defended the doctrine of probabilism, and in the "Regula morum" refuted the objections brought against his first work by the Dominican Concina, the Jesuit Elizalde, and other exponents of the Rigorist School. Amort speaks of him as "eruditissimum et probabilistarum antesignanum".

FOLEY, *Records of the English Province S.J.*, III (London, 1878), 420; SOMMERVOGEL, *Bib. de la Comp. de Jésus*, VII (Brussels, 1896); HURTER, *Nomenclator*, II (Innsbruck, 1893), 275–276.

EDWARD C. PHILLIPS.

Termessus, a titular see, suffragan of Perge in Pamphylia Secunda. This is one of the most ancient cities of the Pisidians, inhabited by the Solymi, whose name was preserved for several centuries in Mount Solyma, known to-day as Guldéré-Dagh, and was referred to by Homer, II, VI, 184, and Strabo, XIII, 630. A warlike city, Termessus maintained its independence even under the dominion of the Persians, and refused to receive Alexander the Great, who dared not besiege it (Arianus, I, 27). Under the successor of Alexander, Termessus preserved its autonomy and, in 189 B. C., formed an alliance with the Roman consul, Cn. Manlius, who confirmed it; under the Emperor Domitian it still enjoyed this alliance. Subsequently the city was incorporated with the Province of Pisidia and later with that of Pamphylia. From the ruins of the monuments which remain, it is evident that this was one of the richest and the most civilized cities of Asia Minor; as far back at least as the fourth century B. C., it had been colonized by the Hellenic race. Among its bishops we note: Euresius present at the Council of Nicæa in 325; Timothy at Ephesus in 431; Sabinianus in 448; and Auxentius in 458. Timothy and Sabinianus bear the double title of Termessus and Eudocias. Ramsay (Asia Minor, 18) has taken for granted that these two names refer to one and the same city, but in the year 458 we find at the same period Auxentius, Bishop of Termessus, and Innocentius, Bishop of Eudocias; moreover, in the Ecthesis of Pseudo-Epiphanius, towards 640 (Gelzer, "Ungedruckte . . . Texte der Notitiæ episcopatuum", 541), in the Notitiæ of Leon le Sage and of Constantin Porphyrogenetus ("Georgii Cyprii Descriptio Orbis Romani", ed. Gelzer, 74), these two archdioceses are absolutely distinct in the tenth century. It is not known when the Diocese of Termessus or the city disappeared. The ruins of the city situated at Karabounar, Keui in the sanjak of Adalia and the vilayet of Koniah, figure among the richest monuments of antiquity in Asia Minor.

LE QUIEN, *Oriens christianus*, I, 1019; SPATT AND FORBES, *Travels in Lycia*, I (London, 1847), 233; SMITH, *Dict. of Greek and Roman Geography*, s. v.; LEBAS-WADDINGTON, *Asie-Mineure* (Paris, 1847–68), 1202–10; *Journal of Hellenic Studies* (London, 1895), 126–128; LANCKÓRONSKI, *Les villes de la Pamphylie et de la Pisidie* (Paris, 1890), 23–126, 207–35; COUSIN, *Termessos de Pisidie* in *Bull. de corresp. hellénique*, XXIII (Paris, 1893), 165–192, 280–303.

S. VAILHÉ.

Termoli, DIOCESE OF (THERMULARUM), on the Italian coast of the Adriatic, having a small harbour near the mouth of the Petraglione. In ancient days it was called Buca; in 1567 it was put to fire and sword by the Turks. Termoli contains a fine Gothic cathedral. It is first mentioned as a diocese in 946, when Benefetto, an usurper of the episcopal see, was forced to withdraw by order of Agapitus II; the earliest known legitimate bishop was Scio (969). Among his successors were: Jacopo Cini, O.P. (1379), author of a commentary on the "Sentences"; Domencio Girada (1381), a learned Servite theologian; Fedrico Merzio (1602), a collaborator of Baronius. In 1818 this see was united with Guardia Alferia, a small town near Cerrato, which had its first bishop in 1075 and its last in 1775. Termoli is suffragan of Benevento, and contains 19 parishes, 54 secular priests, and 1 convent of nuns.

CAPPELLETTI, *Le chiese d'Italia*, XIX.

U. BENIGNI.

Ternan, SAINT, Bishop of the Picts, flourished in the sixth century. Much obscurity attaches to his history, and it is difficult to reconcile his chronology as given by various writers. Some say that he was consecrated by St. Palladius in 440, others that he was a monk of Culross in Fife, one of the monasteries founded by St. Serf, or Servan, the tutor of St. Kentigern. The Picts were not converted till about 570, by the zeal of St. Columba. St. Kentigern died in 603, and St. Serf of Culross died in 583 (feast 1 July). It is safe to assert that St. Ternan was a contemporary of St. Serf. In the "Aberdeen Martyrology" there is mention of "the Gospel of St. Matthew belonging to St. Ternan", which was "enshrined in a metal case or *cumdach* (book shrine), covered with silver and gold, after the Irish fashion." St. Ternan is commemorated on 12 June. He must not be confounded with St. Trumwine.

SKENE, *Celtic Scotland* (3 vols., Edinburgh, 1876–80); MORAN, *Irish Saints in Great Britain* (Rome, 1903); BEDE, *Eccl. Hist. of England*, tr. SELLAR (London, 1907); STOKES, *Early Christian Art in Ireland* (Dublin, 1911).

W. H. GRATTAN-FLOOD.

Terni. See NARNI AND TERNI, DIOCESE OF.

Terracina, Sezze, and Piperno, DIOCESE OF (TERRACINENSIS, SETINENSIS ET PRIVERNENSIS), in the Province of Rome. The city of Terracina is near the estuary of the Amaseno, on a promontory (the old town), and beside the Via Appia (the new town, founded by Pius VI). The harbour, one of the safest in the Mediterranean, is frequented mostly by coasting-vessels engaged in exporting grain from the Pontine marshes, and wine, oil, and vegetables from the Lepinian hills; hunting in the neighbouring woods and the fishing industry are also carried on with profit by the inhabitants. There are ruins of the temple of Rome and Augustus, at the place now occupied by the cathedral of St. Cæsareus, containing the pillars of the temple and an ambo with mosaics. On one of the promontories are ruins of the great temple of Venus; also traces of the fortifications and of the palace of Theodoric. Terracina, called by the Romans Tarracina, the ancient Auxur, was a Latin city, and was subject to Rome under the kings. Later it was captured by the Volscians, who in 406 B. C. ceded it to the Romans. Hannibal, after capturing Capua, failed to take it. Under Antoninus Pius the harbour was enlarged. It was included in Pepin's donation to the Holy See, but about 780 was captured by the Byzantines, who, however, were expelled by Charlemagne. The Saracens landed there on several occasions during the ninth century. Later it was a fief of the Frangipani, but Gregory IX included it among the places which were always to be immediately subject to the Holy See. In 1798, the French commander having been slain during a revolt, the city was sacked. According to tradition, the first Bishop of Terracina was St. Epaphroditus. The most ancient Christian record of the city is that of the martyrdom of St. Julianus, priest, and St. Cæsareus, deacon, who were cast into the sea under Trajan; in the third century St. Quartus (bishop?) suffered. The first bishop whose date is known with certainty is Sabinus (313). Among his successors were: an African priest, St. Silvianus, a fugitive during the Vandal persecution (about 443); Petrus (590), during whose episcopate the Jews were persecuted so severely in Terracina that St. Gregory the Great had to intervene; under Agnellus, former Bishop of Fundi, which city had been destroyed, the two dioceses were united; the last three letters only of the name of another Bishop of Terracina, . . . vsa, are preserved in an inscription (Corp. Inscr. Lat., X, I, 6419); other bishops were: Joannes (969), who made the vow that the inhabitants of the city should offer each year 6,000 eels to the monastery of Monte Cassino; Ambrosius (1066), a Benedictine and ecclesiastical reformer; Gregorius (1106), a Benedictine, surnamed *Columna Ecclesiæ*. About this time, if not earlier, the sees of Piperno (Privernum) and Sezze (Setia), situated on the side of the Lepinian hills, were united to Terracina. The earliest of the seven known bishops of Piperno is Bonifacius (769). There is moreover an ancient Christian cemetery at Piperno. The first mention of a Bishop of Sezze is a reference to Stephanus (1036); in the time of Pollidius (1046), St. Ligdanus founded the Monastery of St. Cecilia near Sezze: among the others was Lando, who in 1178, under the name of Innocent III, usurped the papal tiara. The union of the three dioceses was confirmed by Honorius III (1217) during the episcopate of Simeone. Among his successors were: the Franciscan Fra Giovanni (1362), who consecrated the cathedral; Zaccaria Mori (1510), present at the Fifth Lateran Council; Ottaviano Rovera (1545), nuncio in Switzerland and Spain; Bernardo M. Conti (1710), brother of Innocent XIII, cardinal. In 1725 Benedict XIII restored the See of Piperno and Sezze, declaring them united *æque principaliter*. Bishop Francesco Antonio Mondelli (1805) was exiled in 1809, for refusing to take the oath of loyalty to Napoleon. The famous Cistercian Abbey of Fossa Nuova is within the territory of this see. The diocese, which is immediately subject to the Holy See, contains 22 parishes, 45,000 inhabitants, 94 secular and 15 regular priests, 3 religious houses for men, 10 for nuns, 1 institute for boys and 3 for girls.

CAPPELLETTI, *Le chiese d'Italia*, VI (Venice, 1847); DE LA BLANCHERE, *Terracina, essai d'hist. locale* (Paris, 1884); GIORGI, *Docum. Terracinesi* in *Bull. Instituto Stor. Ital. XVI* (Rome, 1895); LOMBARDINI, *Della istoria di Sezze* (Velletri, 1876); VALLE, *La citta nuova di Piperno* (Naples, 1646).

U. BENIGNI.

Terrasson, ANDRÉ, French preacher, b. at Lyons in 1669; d. at Paris, 25 April, 1723. He was the eldest son of a councillor of the Lyons presidial (court of justice). Entering the Congregation of the

Oratory he devoted himself to preaching, and winning high reputation was called to fill important pulpits. He preached the Lenten sermons of 1717 before Louis XIV, next at the Court of Lorraine, and later twice in the metropolitan church of Paris with considerable success; the last of these series broke down his health and led to his death. His eloquent diction, which was enhanced by his outward action, was marked by nobility and simplicity of thought, by forcefulness and absence of artificiality. His good judgment led him to avoid mere brilliancy of expression and clever artifices of speech, but he was sometimes cold, perhaps as a result of his Jansenistic proclivities. About fifty of his discourses, mostly delivered as Lenten lectures, are preserved, and were published at Paris (4 vols., 1726, 1736).

GASPARD, brother of the preceding, b. at Lyons, Oct., 1680; d. at Paris, 2 Jan., 1752. He was also a member of the Oratory, teaching humanities and afterwards philosophy. His oratorical gifts were revealed at Troyes, 1711, on delivering the funeral oration of the Dauphin, son of Louis XIV; but he did not devote himself to the pulpit till after his brother's death, when he fulfilled several engagements which the latter had made. Soon his reputation increased beyond that of André. For five years he preached at Paris, and finally delivered a Lenten course in the Church of Notre Dame. More stubborn even than his brother, he appealed time after time against the Bull "Unigenitus"; he even published anonymously twelve "Lettres sur la justice chrétienne" (Paris, 1733), in which, to support the Jansenists whom the bishops deprived of the sacraments, he endeavoured to prove the inutility of sacramental confession. This work was condemned by the faculty of theology at Paris (1 Sept., 1734), and by the Archbishops of Sens and Embrun, as containing erroneous, schismatical and heretical assertions. Terrasson had to leave the Oratory and abandon preaching. He withdrew to the Diocese of Auxerre where the bishop, M. de Caylus, a well-known Jansenist, confided to him the care of Treigni. But he was soon arrested (Oct., 1735) by the order of the king for his Jansenistic activities, and was confined during nine years either at Vincennes or with the Minims of Argenteuil. A belated retractation, the authenticity or sincerity of which has never been well established, was attributed to him. He was living in retirement with his family when he died. As a preacher his chief characteristics are simplicity and clearness, but at times he carries the subdivision of his matter to excess; his style is somewhat dry and lacks vigour. Like his brother he holds a high place among the orators of second rank. A volume of his discourses appeared at Utrecht in 1733, but the first real edition was at Paris in 1744 (4 vols.). The sermons of the two brothers were reprinted by Migne in his "Collection des orateurs sacrés", XXIX (Paris, 1849).

CURSAY, *Mémoires sur les savants de la famille de Terrasson* (Trévoux, 1761); *Nouvelles ecclésiastiques* (1736, 1744); *Supplément au nécrologe des plus célèbres défenseurs de la vérité* (s. l., 1763), 120; CANDEL, *Les prédicateurs français dans la première moitié du XVIIIe siècle* (Paris, 1904); FÉRET, *La Faculté de théologie de Paris, Epoque moderne*, VI (Paris, 1909), 144.

ANTOINE DÉGERT.

Terrestrial Paradise (פרדס, παράδεισος, *Paradisus*). The name popularly given in Christian tradition to the scriptural Garden of Eden, the home of our first parents (Gen., ii). The word paradise is probably of Persian origin and signified originally a royal park or pleasure ground. The term does not occur in the Latin of the Classic period nor in the Greek writers prior to the time of Xenophon. In the Old Testament it is found only in the later Hebrew writings in the form פרדם (*Pardês*), having been borrowed doubtless from the Persian. An instructive illustration of the origin and primary meaning of the term appears in II Esdras (ii, 8) where "Asaph the keeper of the king's forest" (הפרדס, *happerdês*) is the custodian of the royal park of the Persian ruler. The association of the term with the abode of our first parents does not occur in the Old-Testament Hebrew. It originated in the fact that the word παράδεισος was adopted, though not exclusively, by the translators of the Septuagint to render the Hebrew גן־עדן, or Garden of Eden described in the second chapter of Genesis. It is likewise used in divers other passages of the Septuagint where the Hebrew generally has "garden", especially if the idea of wondrous beauty is to be conveyed. Thus in Gen., xiii, 10, the "country about the Jordan" is described as a "paradise of the Lord" (rendering followed by the Vulgate). Cf. Numbers, xxiv, 6 (Greek) where the reference is to the beautiful array of the tents of Israel, also Isaias, i, 30; Ezechiel, xxxi, 8, 9, etc. Those interested in speculation as to the probable location of the Scriptural Garden of Eden, the primeval home of mankind, are referred to the scholarly work of Friedrich Delitsch, "Wo lag das Paradies?" (Berlin, 1881). In the New-Testament period the word paradise appears with a new and more exalted meaning. In the development of Jewish eschatology which marks the post-Exilic epoch the word paradise or "Garden of God", hitherto mainly associated with the original dwelling-place of our first parents, was transferred to signify the future abode of rest and enjoyment which was to be the reward of the righteous after death. The term occurs only three times in the New Testament, though the idea which it represents is frequently expressed in other terms, v. g. "Abraham's bosom" (Luke, xvi, 22). The signification of the word in these remarkably few passages can be determined only from the context and by reference to the eschatological notions current among the Jews of that period. These views are gathered chiefly from the Rabbinical literature, the works of Josephus, and from the apocryphal writings, notably the Book of Enoch, the Book of Jubilees, the Apocalypse of Baruch, etc. An inspection of these sources reveals a great confusion of ideas and many contradictions regarding the future paradise as also concerning the original Garden of Eden and the condition of our first parents. The scanty references to *Sheol* which embody the vague eschatological beliefs of the Hebrews as expressed in the earlier Old Testament writings give place in these later treatises to elaborate theories worked out with detailed descriptions and speculations often of a most fanciful character. As a sample of these may be noted the one found in the Talmudic tract "Jalkut Schim., Bereschith, 20". According to this description the entrance to paradise is made through two gates of rubies beside which stand sixty myriads of holy angels with countenances radiant with heavenly splendour. When a righteous man enters, the vestures of death are removed from him; he is clad in eight robes of the clouds of glory; two crowns are placed upon his head, one of pearls and precious stones, the other of gold; eight myrtles are placed in his hands and he is welcomed with great applause, etc. Some of the Rabbinical authorities appear to identify the paradise of the future with the primeval Garden of Eden which is supposed to be still in existence and located somewhere in the far-distant East. According to some it was an earthly abode, sometimes said to have been created before the rest of the world (IV Esdras iii, 7, cf. viii, 52); others make it an adjunct of the subterranean *Sheol*, while still others place it in or near heaven. It was believed that there are in paradise different degrees of blessedness. Seven ranks or orders of the righteous were said to exist within it, and definitions were given both of those to whom these different positions belong and of the glories pertaining to each ("Baba bathra", 75 *a*, quoted by Salmond, Hastings, "Dict. of the Bible", s. v. "Paradise"). The uncertainty and confusion of the current Jewish ideas concerning paradise may explain the paucity of reference to it in the New Testament. The first mention of the word occurs in Luke, xxiii, 43, where Jesus on the cross says to the penitent thief: "Amen I say to thee, this day thou shalt be with me in paradise". According to the prevailing interpretation of Catholic theologians and commentators, paradise in this instance is used as a synonym for the heaven of the blessed to which the thief would accompany the Saviour, together with the souls of the righteous of the Old Law who were awaiting the coming of the Redeemer. In II Corinthians (xii, 4) St. Paul describing one of his ecstasies tells his readers that he was "caught up into paradise". Here the term seems to indicate plainly the heavenly state or abode of the blessed, implying possibly a glimpse of the beatific vision. The reference cannot be to any form of terrestrial paradise, especially when we consider the parallel expression in verse 2, where relating a similar experience he says he was "caught up to the third heaven". The third and last mention of paradise in the New Testament occurs in the Apocalypse (ii, 7), where St. John, receiving in vision a Divine message for the "angel of the church of Ephesus", hears these words: "To him that overcometh, I will give to eat of the tree of life, which is in the paradise of my God." In this passage the word is plainly used to designate the heavenly kingdom, though the imagery is borrowed from the description of the primeval Garden of Eden in the Book of Genesis. According to Catholic theology based on the Biblical account, the original condition of our first parents was one of perfect innocence and integrity. By the latter is meant that they were endowed with many prerogatives which, while pertaining to the natural order, were not due to human nature as such—hence they are sometimes termed preternatural. Principal among these were a high degree of infused knowledge, bodily immortality and freedom from pain, and immunity from evil impulses or inclinations. In other words, the lower or animal nature in man was perfectly subjected to the control of reason and the will. Besides this, our first parents were also endowed with sanctifying grace by which they were elevated to the supernatural order. But all these gratuitous endowments were forfeited through the disobedience of Adam "in whom all have sinned", and who was "a figure of Him who was to come" (Rom., v) and restore fallen man, not to an earthly, but to a heavenly paradise.

According to Josephus (Ant. Jud., I, i, 3), the Nile is one of the four great rivers of paradise (Gen., ii, 10 sqq.). This view, which has been adopted by many commentators, is based chiefly on the connection described between Gehon, one of the yet unidentified rivers, and the land of Cush, which, at least in later times, was identified with Ethiopia or modern Abyssinia (cf. Vulgate, Gen., ii, 13). Modern scholars, however, are inclined to regard this African Cush as simply a colony settled by tribes migrating from an original Asiatic province of the same name, located by Fried. Delitsch (op. cit., 71) in Babylonia, and by Hommel ("Ancient Hebrew Tradition", 314 sqq.) in Central Arabia.

Hurter, *Theologiæ Dogmaticæ Compendium*, II (Innsbruck, 1893), 264–83; von Hummelauer, *Comment. in Genesim* (Paris, 1895): Comment. in Cap. ii; Vigouroux, *Dict. de la Bible*, s. v.; Gigot, *Special Introduction to the Study of the Old Testament*, Pt. I, 168 sqq. (New York, 1901).

James F. Driscoll.

Terrien, Jean-Baptiste, dogmatic theologian, born at St-Laurent-des-Autels, Maine-et-Loire, 26 Aug., 1832; d. at Bellevue, near Paris, 5 Dec., 1903. He entered the Society of Jesus at Angers, 7 Dec., 1854; taught philosophy for two years and dogmatic theology for twenty-two at the seminaries of Laval (France), 1864–80, and St. Helier (Jersey), 1880–88, then, after being spiritual father at Laval he was appointed professor of dogmatic theology and taught three years, 1891–94, at the Catholic Institute of Paris, remaining afterwards in this city as spiritual father and writer. During his first period of teaching, he did not publish any theological work, except a treatise, "De Verbo incarnato", Jersey, 1882, for private circulation; there are also five or six other treatises in MS. or lithographed, which form a substantial body of Positive rather than Scholastic theology, after the manner and doctrine of Cardinal Franzelin. In a quite different style is framed a neo-Thomistic monograph, published at Paris in 1894: "S. Thomæ Aquinatis, O.P., doctrina sincera de unione hypostatica Verbi Dei cum humanitate amplissime declarata". At this time, Father Terrien began to apply his deep knowledge of theology to popular instruction, and published the following doctrinal treatises in French: "La Dévotion au Sacré-Cœur de Jésus, d'après les documents authentiques et la théologie", 1893; Italian translation by G. M. Rossi (Naples, 1895); "La grâce et la gloire ou la filiation adoptive des enfants de Dieu étudiée dans sa réalité, ses principes, son perfectionnement, et son couronnement final", 2 vols., 1897; new ed., 1908; "La Mère de Dieu et la Mère des hommes d'après les Péres et la théologie", 4 vols., 1900, 1902. These three works form unquestionably the most conspicuous part of Terrien's literary performance, as they are highly valuable on account of precision and richness of doctrine.

Xavier Le Bachelet.

Tertiaries (from the Latin *tertiarius*, the relative adjective of *tertius*, "third"), or what is known as "Third Orders", are those persons who live according to the Third Rule of religious orders, either outside of a monastery in the world, or in a religious community. The idea which forms the basis of this institute is in general this, that persons who on account of certain circumstances cannot enter a religious order, strictly so-called, may, nevertheless, as far as possible enjoy the advantages and privileges of religious orders. This is most clearly expressed in the Rule of the Third Order of St. Francis which, although not the oldest, has, nevertheless, become the model for the rule of almost all other Third Orders. Tertiaries are divided into Regular and Secular (see Third Orders).

Ferdinand Heckmann.

Tertullian (Quintus Septimius Florens Tertullianus), ecclesiastical writer in the second and third centuries, b. probably about 160 at Carthage, being the son of a centurion in the proconsular service. He was evidently by profession an advocate in the law-courts, and he shows a close acquaintance with the procedure and terms of Roman law, though it is doubtful whether he is to be identified with a jurist Tertullian who is cited in the Pandects. He knew Greek as well as Latin, and wrote works in Greek which have not come down to us. A pagan until middle life, he had shared the pagan prejudices against Christianity, and had indulged like others in shameful pleasures. His conversion was not later than the year 197, and may have been earlier. He embraced the Faith with all the ardour of his impetuous nature. He became a priest, no doubt of the Church of Carthage. Monceaux, followed by d'Alès, considers that his earlier writings were composed while he was yet a layman, and if this be so, then his ordination was about 200. His extant writings range in date from the apologetics of 197 to the attack on a bishop who is probably Pope Callistus (after 218). It was after the year 206 that he joined the Montanist sect, and he seems to have definitively separated from the Church about 211 (Harnack) or 213 (Monceaux). After writing more virulently against the Church than even against heathen and persecutors, he separated from the Montanists and founded a sect of his own. The remnant of the Tertullianists was reconciled to the Church by St. Augustine. A number of the works of Tertullian are on special points of belief or discipline. According to St. Jerome he lived to extreme old age.

The year 197 saw the publication of a short address by Tertullian, "To the Martyrs", and of his great apologetic works, the "Ad nationes" and the "Apologeticus". The former has been considered a finished sketch for the latter; but it is more true to say that the second work has a different purpose, though a great deal of the same matter occurs in both, the same arguments being displayed in the same manner, with the same examples and even the same phrases. The appeal to the nations suffers from its transmission in a single codex, in which omissions of a word or several words or whole lines are to be deplored. Tertullian's style is difficult enough without such superadded causes of obscurity. But the text of the "Ad nationes" must have been always rougher than that of the "Apologeticus", which is a more careful as well as a more perfect work, and contains more matter because of its better arrangement; for it is just the same length as the two books "Ad nationes".

The "Ad nationes" has for its entire object the refutation of calumnies against Christians. In the first place they are proved to repose on unreasoning hatred only; the procedure of trial is illogical; the offence is nothing but the name of Christian, which ought rather to be a title of honour; no proof is forthcoming of any crimes, only rumour; the first persecutor was Nero, the worst of emperors. Secondly, the individual charges are met; Tertullian challenges the reader to believe in anything so contrary to nature as the accusations of infanticide and incest. Christians are not the causes of earthquakes and floods and famine, for these happened long before Christianity. The pagans despise their own gods, banish them, forbid their worship, mock them on the stage; the poets tell horrid stories of them; they were in reality only men, and bad men. You say we worship an ass's head, he goes on, but you worship all kinds of animals; your gods are images made on a cross framework, so you worship crosses. You say we worship the sun; so do you. A certain Jew hawked about a caricature of a creature half ass, half goat, as our god; but you actually adore half-animals, As for infanticide, you expose your own children and kill the unborn. Your promiscuous lust causes you to be in danger of the incest of which you accuse us. We do not swear by the genius of Cæsar, but we are loyal, for we pray for him, whereas you revolt. Cæsar does not want to be a god; he prefers to be alive. You say it is through obstinacy that we despise death; but of old such contempt of death was esteemed heroic virtue. Many among you brave death for gain or wagers; but we, because we believe in judgment. Finally, do us justice; examine our case, and change your minds. The second book consists entirely in an attack on the gods of the pagans; they are marshalled in classes after Varro. It was not, urges the apologist, owing to these multitudinous gods that the empire grew.

Out of this fierce appeal and indictment was developed the grander "Apologeticus", addressed to the rulers of the empire and the administrators of justice. The former work attacked popular prejudices; the new one is an imitation of the Greek Apologies, and was intended as an attempt to secure an amelioration in the treatment of Christians by alteration of the law or its administration. Tertullian cannot restrain his invective; yet he wishes to be conciliating, and it breaks out in spite of his argument, instead of being its essence as before. He begins again by an appeal to reason. There are no witnesses, he urges, to prove our crimes; Trajan ordered Pliny not to seek us out, but yet to punish us if we were known;—what a paralogism! The actual procedure is yet more strange. Instead of being tortured until we confess, we are tortured until we deny. So far the "Ad nationes" is merely developed and strengthened. Then, after a condensed summary of the second book as to the heathen gods, Tertullian begins in chapter xvii an exposition of the belief of Christians in one God, the Creator, invisible, infinite, to whom the soul of man, which by its nature is inclined to Christianity, bears witness The floods and the fire have been His messengers. We have testimony, he adds, from our sacred books, which are older than all your gods. Fulfilled prophecy is the proof that they are divine. It is then explained that Christ is God, the Word of God born of a virgin; His two comings, His miracles, passion, resurrection, and forty days with the disciples, are recounted. The disciples spread His doctrine throughout the world; Nero sowed it with blood at Rome. When tortured the Christian cries, "We worship God through Christ". The demons confess Him and they stir men up against us. Next, loyalty to Cæsar is discussed at greater length than before. When the populace rises, how easily the Christians could take vengeance: "We are but of yesterday, yet we fill your cities, islands, forts, towns, councils, even camps, tribes, decuries, the palace, the senate, the forum; we have left you the temples alone". We might migrate, and leave you in shame and in desolation. We ought at least to be tolerated; for what are we?—a body compacted by community of religion, of discipline, and of hope. We meet together to pray, even for the emperors and authorities, to hear readings from the holy books and exhortations. We judge and separate those who fall into crime. We have elders of proved virtue to preside. Our common fund is replenished by voluntary donations each month, and is expended not on gluttony but on the poor and suffering. This charity is quoted against us as a disgrace; see, it is said, how they love one another. We call ourselves brethren; you also are our brethren by nature, but bad brethren. We are accused of every calamity. Yet we live with you; we avoid no profession, but those of assassins, sorcerers, and such like. You spare the philosophers, though their conduct is less admirable than ours. They confess that our teaching is older than theirs, for nothing is older than truth. The resurrection at which you jeer has many parallels in nature. You think us fools; and we rejoice to suffer for this. We conquer by our death. Inquire into the cause of our constancy. We believe this martyrdom to be the remission of all offences, and that he who is condemned before your tribunal is absolved before God.

These points are all urged with infinite wit and pungency. The faults are obvious. The effect on the pagans may have been rather to irritate than to convince. The very brevity results in obscurity. But every lover of eloquence, and there were many in those days, will have relished with the pleasure of an epicure the feast of ingenious pleading and recondite learning. The rapier thrusts are so swift, we can hardly realize their deadliness before they are renewed in showers, with sometimes a blow as of a bludgeon to vary the effect. The style is compressed like that of Tacitus, but the metrical closes are observed with care, against the rule of Tacitus; and that wonderful maker of phrases is outdone by his Christian successor in gemlike sentences which will be quoted while the world lasts. Who does not know the *anima naturaliter Christiana* (soul by nature Christian); the *Vide, inquiunt, ut invicem se diligant* (see, they exclaim, how they love one another), and the *Semen est sanguis Christianorum* (The blood of Christians is seed)? It was probably about the same time that Tertullian developed his thesis of the "Testimony of the soul" to the existence of one God, in his little book with this title. With his usual eloquence he enlarges on the idea that common speech bids us use expressions such as "God grant", or "If God will", "God bless", "God sees", "May God repay". The soul testifies also to devils, to just vengeance, and to its own immortality.

Two or three years later (about 200) Tertullian assaulted heresy in a treatise even more brilliant, which, unlike the "Apologeticus", is not for his own day only but for all time. It is called "Liber de præscriptione hæreticorum". Prescription now means the right obtained to something by long usage. In Roman law the signification was wider; it meant the cutting short of a question by the refusal to hear the adversary's arguments, on the ground of an anterior point which must cut away the ground under his feet. So Tertullian deals with heresies: it is of no use to listen to their arguments or refute them, for we have a number of antecendent proofs that they cannot deserve a hearing. Heresies, he begins, must not astonish us, for they were prophesied. Heretics urge the text, "Seek and ye shall find", but this was not said to Christians; we have a rule of faith to be accepted without question. "Let curiosity give place to faith and vain glory make way for salvation", so Tertullian parodies a line of Cicero's. The heretics argue out of Scripture; but, first, we are forbidden to consort with a heretic after one rebuke has been delivered, and secondly, disputation results only in blasphemy on the one side and indignation on the other, while the listener goes away more puzzled than he came. The real question is, "To whom does the Faith belong? Whose are the Scriptures? By whom, through whom, when and to whom has been handed down the discipline by which we are Christians? The answer is plain: Christ sent His apostles, who founded churches in each city, from which the others have borrowed the tradition of the Faith and the seed of doctrine and daily borrow in order to become churches; so that they also are Apostolic in that they are the offspring of the Apostolic churches. All are that one Church which the Apostles founded, so long as peace and intercommunion are observed [*dum est illis communicatio pacis et appellatio fraternitatis et contesseratio hospitalitatis*]. Therefore the testimony to the truth is this: We communicate with the apostolic Churches". The heretics will reply that the Apostles did not know all the truth. Could anything be unknown to Peter, who was called the rock on which the Church was to be built? or to John, who lay on the Lord's breast? But they will say, the churches have erred. Some indeed went wrong, and were corrected by the Apostle; though for others he had nothing but praise. "But let us admit that all have erred:—is it credible that all these great churches should have strayed into the same faith"? Admitting this absurdity, then all the baptisms, spiritual gifts, miracles, martyrdoms, were in vain until Marcion and Valentinus appeared at last! Truth will be younger than error; for both these heresiarchs are of yesterday, and were still Catholics at Rome in the episcopate of Eleutherius (this name is a slip or a false reading). Anyhow the heresies are at best novelties, and have no continuity with the teaching of Christ. Perhaps some heretics may claim Apostolic antiquity: we reply: Let them publish the origins of their churches and unroll the catalogue of their bishops till now from the Apostles or from some bishop appointed by the Apostles, as the Smyrnæans count from Polycarp and John, and the Romans from Clement and Peter; let heretics invent something to match this. Why, their errors were denounced by the Apostles long ago. Finally (36), he names some Apostolic churches, pointing above all to Rome, whose witness is nearest at hand,—happy Church, in which the Apostles poured out their whole teaching with their blood, where Peter suffered a death like his Master's, where Paul was crowned with an end like the Baptist's, where John was plunged into fiery oil without hurt! The Roman Rule of Faith is summarized, no doubt from the old Roman Creed, the same as our present Apostles' Creed but for a few small additions in the latter; much the same summary was given in chapter xiii, and is found also in "De virginibus velandis" (chapter i). Tertullian evidently avoids giving the exact words, which would be taught only to catechumens shortly before baptism. The whole luminous argument is founded on the first chapters of St. Irenæus's third book, but its forceful exposition is not more Tertullian's own than its exhaustive and compelling logic. Never did he show himself less violent and less obscure. The appeal to the Apostolic churches was unanswerable in his day; the rest of his argument is still valid.

A series of short works addressed to catechumens belong also to Tertullian's Catholic days, and fall between 200 and 206. "De spectaculis" explains and probably exaggerates the impossibility for a Christian to attend any heathen shows, even races or theatrical performances, without either wounding his faith by participation in idolatry or arousing his passions. "De idololatria" is by some placed at a later date, but it is anyhow closely connected with the former work. It explains that the making of idols is forbidden, and similarly astrology, selling of incense, etc. A schoolmaster cannot elude contamination. A Christian cannot be a soldier. To the question, "How am I then to live?", Tertullian replies that faith fears not famine; for the Faith we must give up our life, how much more our living? "De baptismo" is an instruction on the necessity of baptism and on its effects; it is directed against a female teacher of error belonging to the sect of Gaius (perhaps the Anti-Montanist). We learn that baptism was conferred regularly by the bishop, but with his consent could be administered by priests, deacons, or even laymen. The proper times were Easter and Pentecost. Preparation was made by fasting, vigils, and prayers. Confirmation was conferred immediately after by unction and laying on of hands. "De pænitentia" will be mentioned later. "De oratione" contains an exposition of the Lord's Prayer, *totius evangelii breviarium*. "De cultu feminarum" is an instruction on modesty and plainness in dress; Tertullian enjoys detailing the extravagances of female toilet and ridiculing them. Besides these didactic works to catechumens, Tertullian wrote at the same period two books, "Ad uxorem", in the former of which he begs his wife not to marry again after his death, as it is not proper for a Christian, while in the second book he enjoins upon her at least to marry a Christian if she does marry, for pagans must not be consorted with. A little book on patience is touching, for the writer admits that it is an impudence in him to discourse on a virtue in which he is so conspicuously lacking. A book against the Jews contains some curious chronology, used to prove the fulfilment of Daniel's prophecy of the seventy weeks. The latter half of the book is nearly identical with part of the third book against Marcion. It would seem that Tertullian used over again what he had written in the earliest form of that work, which dates from this time. "Adversus Hermogenem" is against a certain Hermogenes, a painter (of idols?) who taught that God created the world out of pre-existing matter. Tertullian reduces his view *ad absurdum*, and establishes the creation out of nothing both from Scripture and reason.

The next period of Tertullian's literary activity shows distinct evidence of Montanist opinions, but he has not yet openly broken with the Church, which had not as yet condemned the new prophecy. Montanus and the prophetesses Priscilla and Maximilla had been long dead when Tertullian was converted to belief in their inspiration. He held the words of Montanus to be really those of the Paraclete, and he characteristically exaggerated their import. We find him henceforth lapsing into rigorism, and condemning absolutely second marriage and forgiveness of certain sins, and insisting on new fasts. His teaching had always been excessive in its severity; now he positively revels in harshness. Harnack and d'Alès look upon "De Virginibus velandis" as the first work of this time, though it has been placed later by Monceaux and others on account of its irritated tone. We learn that Carthage was divided by a dispute whether virgins should be veiled; Tertullian and the pro-Montanist party stood for the affirmative. The book had been preceded by a Greek writing on the same subject. Tertullian declares that the Rule of Faith is unchangeable, but discipline is progressive. He quotes a dream in favour of the veil. The date may be about 206. Shortly afterwards Tertullian published his largest extant work, five books against Marcion. A first draft had been written much earlier; a second recension had been published, when yet unfinished, without the writer's consent; the first book of the final edition was finished in the fifteenth year of Severus, 207. The last book may be a few years later. This controversy is most important for our knowledge of Marcion's doctrine. The refutation of it out of his own New Testament, which consisted of St. Luke's Gospel and St. Paul's Epistles, enables us to reconstitute much of the heretic's Scripture text. The result may be seen in Zahn's, "Geschichte des N. T. Kanons", II, 455–524. A work against the Valentinians followed. It is mainly based on the first book of St. Irenæus.

In 209 the little book "De pallio" appeared. Tertullian had excited remark by adopting the Greek pallium, the recognized dress of philosophers, and he defends his conduct in a witty pamphlet. A long book, "De anima", gives Tertullian's psychology. He well describes the unity of the soul; he teaches that it is spiritual, but immateriality in the fullest sense he admits for nothing that exists,—even God is *corpus*. Two works are against the docetism of the Gnostics, "De carne Christi" and "De resurrectione carnis". Here he emphasizes the reality of Christ's Body and His virgin-birth, and teaches a corporal resurrection. But he seems to deny the virginity of Mary, the Mother of Christ, *in partu*, though he affirms it *ante partum*. He addressed to a convert who was a widower an exhortation to avoid second marriage, which is equivalent to fornication. This work, "De exhortatione castitatis", implies that the writer is not yet separated from the Church. The same excessive rigour appears in the "De corona", in which Tertullian defends a soldier who had refused to wear a chaplet on his head when he received the donative granted to the army on the accession of Caracalla and Geta in 211. The man had been degraded and imprisoned. Many Christians thought his action extravagant, and refused to regard him as a martyr. Tertullian not only declares that to wear the crown would have been idolatry, but argues that no Christian can be a soldier without compromising his faith. Next in order is the "Scorpiace", or antidote to the bite of the Scorpion, directed against the teaching of the Valentinians that God cannot approve of martyrdom, since He does not want man's death; they even permitted the external act of idolatry. Tertullian shows that God desires the courage of the martyrs and their victory over temptation; he proves from Scripture the duty of suffering death for the Faith and the great promises attached to this heroism. To the year 212 belongs the open letter "Ad scapulam", addressed to the proconsul of Africa who was renewing the persecution, which had ceased since 203. He is solemnly warned of the retribution which overtakes persecutors.

The formal secession of Tertullian from the Church of Carthage seems to have taken place either in 211 or at the end of 212 at latest. The earlier date is fixed by Harnack on account of the close connexion between the "De corona" of 211 with the "De fuga", which must, he thinks, have immediately followed the "De corona". It is certain that "De fuga in persecutione" was written after the secession. It condemns flight in time of persecution, for God's providence has intended the suffering. This intolerable doctrine had not been held by Tertullian in his Catholic days. He now terms the Catholics "Psychici", as opposed to the "spiritual" Montanists. The cause of his schism is not mentioned. It is unlikely that he left the Church by his own act. Rather it would seem that when the Montanist prophecies were finally disapproved at Rome, the Church of Carthage excommunicated at least the more violent among their adherents. After "De fuga" come "De monogamia" (in which the wickedness of second marriage is yet more severely censured) and "De jejunio", a defence of the Montanist fasts. A dogmatic work, "Adversus Praxean", is of great importance. Praxeas had prevented, according to Tertullian, the recognition of the Montanist prophecy by the pope; Tertullian attacks him as a Monarchian, and develops his own doctrine of the Holy Trinity (see MONARCHIANS and PRAXEAS). The last remaining work of the passionate schismatic is apparently "De pudicitia", if it is a protest, as is generally held, against a Decree of Pope Callistus, in which the pardon of adulterers and fornicators, after due penance done, was published at the intercession of the martyrs. Monceaux, however, still supports the view which was once commoner than it now is, that the Decree in question was issued by a bishop of Carthage. In any case Tertullian's attribution of it to a would-be *episcopus episcoporum* and *pontifex maximus* merely attests its peremptory character. The identification of this Decree with the far wider relaxation of discipline with which Hippolytus reproaches Callistus is uncertain.

The argument of Tertullian must be considered in some detail, since his witness to the ancient system of penance is of first-rate importance. As a Catholic, he addressed "De pænitentia" to catechumens as an exhortation to repentance previous to baptism. Besides that sacrament he mentions, with an expression of unwillingness, a "last hope", a second plank of salvation, after which there is no other. This is the severe remedy of exomologesis, confession, involving a long penance in sackcloth and ashes for the remission of post-baptismal sin. In the "De pudicitia" the Montanist now declared that there is no forgiveness for the gravest sins, precisely those for which exomologesis is necessary. It is said by some modern critics, such as Funk and Turmel among Catholics, that Tertullian did not really change his view on this point between the writing of the two treatises. It is pointed out that in "De pænitentia" there is no mention of the restoration of the penitent to communion; he is to do penance, but with no hope of pardon in this life; no sacrament is administered, and the satisfaction is lifelong. This view is impossible. Tertullian declares in "De pud." that he has changed his mind and expects to be taunted for his inconsistency. He implies that he used to hold such a relaxation, as the one he is attacking, to be lawful. At any rate in the "De pæn." he parallels baptism with exomologesis, and supposes that the latter has the same effect as the former, obviously the forgiveness of sin in this life. Communion is never mentioned, since catechumens are addressed; but if exomologesis did not eventually restore all Christian privileges, there could be no reason for fearing that the mention of it should act as an encouragement to sin, for a lifelong penance would hardly be a reassuring prospect. No length is mentioned, evidently because the duration depended on the nature of the sin and the judgment of the bishop; had death been the term, this would have been emphatically expressed. Finally, and this is conclusive, it could not be insisted on that no second penance was ever allowed, if all penance was lifelong.

For the full understanding of Tertullian's doctrine we must know his division of sins into three classes. There are first the terrible crimes of idolatry, blasphemy, homicide, adultery, fornication, false witness, fraud (Adv. Marc., IV, ix; in "De pud." he substitutes apostasy for false witness and adds unnatural vice). As a Montanist he calls these irremissible. Between these and mere venial sins there are *modica* or *media* (De pud., i), less grave but yet serious sins, which he enumerates in "De pud.", xix: "Sins of daily committal, to which we are all subject; to whom indeed does it not occur to be angry without cause and after the sun has set, or to give a blow, or easily to curse, or to swear rashly, or break a contract, or lie through shame or necessity? How much we are tempted in business, in duties, in trade, in food, in sight, in hearing! So that, if there were no forgiveness for such things, none could be saved. Therefore there will be forgiveness for these sins by the prayer of Christ to the Father" (De pud., xix).

Another list (De pud., vii) represents the sins which may constitute a lost sheep, as distinguished from one that is dead: "The faithful is lost if he attend the chariot races, or gladiatorial combats, or the unclean theatre, or athletic shows, or playing, or feasts on some secular solemnity, or if he has exercised an art which in any way serves idolatry, or has lapsed without consideration into some denial or blasphemy". For these sins there is forgiveness, though the sinner has strayed from the flock. How is forgiveness obtained? We learn this only incidentally from the words: "That kind of penitence which is subsequent to faith, which can either obtain forgiveness from the bishop for lesser sins, or from God only for those which are irremissible" (ib., xviii). Thus Tertullian admits the power of the bishop for all but "irremissible" sins. The absolution which he still acknowledges for frequent sins was obviously not limited to a single occasion, but must have been frequently repeated. It is not even referred to in "De pæn.", which deals only with baptism and public penance for the gravest sins. Again, in "De pud.", Tertullian repudiates his own earlier teaching that the keys were left by Christ through Peter to His Church (Scorpiace, x); he now declares (De pud., xxi) that the gift was to Peter personally, and cannot be claimed by the Church of the Psychici. The spiritual have the right to forgive, but the Paraclete said: "The Church has the power to forgive sins, but I will not do so, lest they sin afresh."

The system of the Church of Carthage in Tertullian's time was therefore manifestly this: those who committed grievous sins confessed them to the bishop, and he absolved them after due penance enjoined and performed, unless the case was in his judgment so grave that public penance was obligatory. This public penance was only allowed once; it was for protracted periods, even sometimes until the hour of death, but at the end of it forgiveness and restoration were promised. The term was frequently shortened at the prayer of martyrs.

Of the lost works of Tertullian the most important was the defence of the Montanist manner of prophesying, "De ecstasi", in six books, with a seventh book against Apollonius. To the peculiarities of Tertullian's views which have already been explained must be added some further remarks. He did not care for philosophy: the philosophers are the "patriarchs of the heretics". His notion that all things, pure spirits and even God, must be bodies, is accounted for by his ignorance of philosophical terminology. Yet of the human soul he actually says that it was seen in a vision as tender, light, and of the colour of air! All our souls were contained in Adam, and are transmitted to us with the taint of original sin upon them,—an ingenious if gross form of traducianism. His Trinitarian teaching is inconsistent, being an amalgamation of the Roman doctrine with that of St. Justin Martyr. Tertullian has the true formula for the Holy Trinity, *tres Personæ, una Substantia*. The Father, Son, and Holy Ghost are numerically distinct, and each is God; they are of one substance, one state, and one power. So far the doctrine is accurately Nicene. But by the side of this appears the Greek view which was one day to develop into Arianism: that the unity is to be sought not in the Essence but in the origin of the Persons. He says that from all eternity there was reason (*ratio*) in God, and in reason the Word (*Sermo*), not distinct from God, but in *vulva cordis*. For the purpose of creation the Word received a perfect birth as Son. There was a time when there was no Son and no sin, when God was neither Father nor Judge. In his Christology Tertullian has had no Greek influence, and is purely Roman. Like most Latin Fathers he speaks not of two Natures but of two Substances in one Person, united without confusion, and distinct in their operations. Thus he condemns by anticipation the Nestorian, Monophysite, and Monothelite heresies. But he seems to teach that Mary, the Mother of Christ, had other children. Yet he makes her the second Eve, who by her obedience effaced the disobedience of the first Eve.

Tertullian's doctrine of the Holy Eucharist has been much discussed, especially the words: "Acceptum panem et distributum discipulis corpus suum illum fecit, hoc est corpus meum dicendo, id est, figura corporis mei". A consideration of the context shows only one interpretation to be possible. Tertullian is proving that Our Lord Himself explained bread in Jer., xi, 19 (*mittamus lignum in panem ejus*) to refer to His Body, when He said, "This is My Body", that is, that bread was the symbol of His Body. Nothing can be elicited either for or against the Real Presence; for Tertullian does not explain whether the bread is the symbol of the Body present or absent. The context suggests the former meaning. Another passage is: *Panem, quo ipsum corpus suum repræsentat*. This might mean "Bread which stands for His Body", or "Presents, makes present". D'Alès has calculated that the sense of presentation to the imagination occurs seven times in Tertullian, and the similar moral sense (presentation by picture, etc.) occurs twelve times, whereas the sense of physical presentation occurs thirty-three times. In the treatise in question against Marcion the physical sense alone is found, and fourteen times. A more direct assertion of the real presence is *Corpus ejus in pane censetur* (De orat., vi). As to the grace given, he has some beautiful expressions, such as: "Itaque petendo panem quotidianum, perpetuitatem postulamus in Christo et individuitatem a corpore ejus" (In petitioning for daily bread, we ask for perpetuity in Christ, and indivisibility from His body.—Ibid.). A famous passage on the Sacraments of Baptism, Unction, Confirmation, Orders, and Eucharist runs: "Caro abluitur ut anima maculetur; caro ungitur ut anima consecretur; caro signatur ut et anima muniatur; caro manus impositione adumbratur ut et anima spiritu illuminetur; caro corpore et sanguine Christi vescitur ut et anima de Deo saginetur" (The flesh is washed, in order that the soul may be cleansed; the flesh is anointed, that the soul may be consecrated; the flesh is signed [with the cross], that the soul, too, may be fortified; the flesh is shadowed with the imposition of hands, that the soul also may be illuminated by the Spirit; the flesh feeds on the body and blood of Christ, that the soul likewise may have its fill of God—"De res. carnis.", viii). He testifies to the practice of daily communion, and the preserving of the Holy Eucharist by private persons for this purpose. What will a heathen husband think of that which is taken by his Christian wife before all other food? "If he knows that it is Bread, will he not believe that it is simply what it is called?" This implies not merely the Real Presence, but transubstantiation. The station days were Wednesday and Friday; on what other days besides Holy Mass was offered we do not know. Some thought that Holy Communion would break their fast on Station days; Tertullian explains: "When you have received and reserved the Body of the Lord, you will have assisted at the Sacrifice and have accomplished the duty of fasting as well" (De oratione, xix). Tertullian's list of customs observed by Apostolic tradition though not in Scripture (De cor., iii) is famous: the baptismal renunciations and feeding with milk and honey, fasting Communion, offerings for the dead (Masses) on their anniversaries, no fasting or kneeling on the Lord's Day and between Easter and Pentecost, anxiety as to the falling to the ground of any crumb or drop of the Holy Eucharist, the Sign of the Cross made continually during the day.

Tertullian's canon of the Old Testament included the deuterocanonical books, since he quotes most of them. He also cites the Book of Enoch as inspired, and thinks those who rejected it were wrong. He seems also to recognize IV Esdras, and the Sibyl, though he admits that there are many sibylline forgeries. In the New Testament he knows the Four Gospels, Acts, Epistles of St. Paul, I Peter (Ad Ponticos), I John, Jude, Apocalypse. He does not know James and II Peter, but we cannot tell that he did not know II, III John. He attributes Hebrews to St. Barnabas. He rejects the "Pastor" of Hermas and says that many councils of the Psychici had also rejected it. Tertullian was learned, but careless in his historical statements. He quotes Varro and a medical writer, Soranus of Ephesus, and was evidently well read in pagan literature. He cites Irenæus, Justin, Miltiades, and Proclus. He probably knew parts of Clement of Alexandria's writings. He is the first of Latin theological writers. To some extent, how great we cannot tell, he must have invented a theological idiom and have coined new expressions. He is the first witness to the existence of a Latin Bible, though he seems frequently to have translated from the Greek Bible as he wrote. Zahn has denied that he possessed any Latin translation, but this opinion is commonly rejected, and St. Perpetua certainly had one at Carthage in 203.

Besides the general histories and histories of dogma and the patrologies, see HESSELBERG, *Tertullians Lehre* (2 vols., Dorpat, 1848); FREPPEL, *Tertullien* (Paris, 1864); HAUCK, *Tertullians Leben u. Schriften* (Erlangen, 1877); NÖLDECHEN, *Tertullian* (Gotha, 1890); MONCEAUX, *Hist. litt. de l'Afrique chrét.*, I (Paris, 1901), the best general work on Tert.; D'ALÈS, *La théologie de Tertullien* (2nd ed., Paris, 1905), the best account of his theology; TURMEL, *Tertullien* (2nd ed., Paris, 1905); DE LABRIOLLE, *Tert. jurisconsulte* in *Nouvelle revue d'hist. et de droit* (1906); IDEM, *L'argument de préscription* in *Rev. d'hist. et de litt. religieuses* (1906); SCHLOSSMANN, *Tertullian im Licht der Jurisprudenz* in *Z. für Kirchengesch.* (1906). On Tertullian's theology see NEANDER, *Antignosticus* (Berlin, 1825, 1849); CAUCANAS, *Tert. et le montanisme* (Geneva, 1876); COURDAVEAUX, *Tert.* in *Revue de l'hist. des religions* (1891); CABROL, *Tert. selon M. Courdaveaux* in *La science catholique* (1891); ESSER, *Die Seelenlehre Tert.'s* (Paderborn, 1893); RAUCH, *Der Einfluss der stoischen Philosophie auf die Lehrbildung Tert's* (Halle, 1890); BONFIGLIOLI, *Teologia di Tert. nei suoi rapporti con la philos-storica* in *Revista delle scienze teolog.* (1906); also MONCEAUX, TURMEL, and especially D'ALÈS. On penance in Tert., see under PENANCE, also PREUSCHEN, *Die Schriften De Pœn. u. De Pud. mit Rücksicht auf die Bussdisciplin untersucht* (1890); ROLFFS, *Das Indulgenzedikt des röm. Bisch. Kallist* (Leipzig, 1893); FUNK, *Das Indulgenzedikt des P. Kallistus* in *Theol. Quartalschr.* (Oct., 1906). On apologetics see HEFELE, *Beiträge zur Kirchengesch.*, I (Tübingen, 1864); J. E. B. MAYOR, *Tertullian's Apology* in *Journal of Theol.* (1893); GAUCHER, *L'apologétique de Tert.* (Auteuil, 1898); WALTZING, *L'apologétique de Tert., trad. et comm.* (Louvain, 1910). On Tertullian's style see KELLNER, *Uber die sprachlichen Eigentümlichkeiten Tertullian's* in *Theol. quartalschr.* (1876); HOPPE, *De sermone Tertullianeo* (Marburg, 1897); IDEM, *Syntax u. Stil des T.* (Leipzig, 1903); and the general works of KOFMANNE and NORDEN. On the MSS. see WISSOWA, *Tertulliani opera*, I in *Corpus scr. eccl. lat.*, XX (Vienna, 1880); HARTEL, *Patristische Studien in Sitzungsber. der K. Akad. der Wiss.*, CXX (Vienna, 1890); VLIET, *Studia eccl., Tertull. critica et interpr.* (Leyden, 1891); KROYMANN, *Quæstiones Tertullianeæ criticæ* (Innsbruck, 1894); GOMPERTZ, *Tertullianea* (Vienna, 1895); CALLEWAERT, *Le codex Fuldensis, le meilleur MSS. de l'Apologét. de T.* in *Rev. d'hist. et de litt. rel.* (1903), 322. On chronology see UHLHORN, *Fundamenta chronologiæ Tert.* (Göttingen, 1851); BONWETSCH, *Die Schriften Tert.'s nach der Zeit ihrer Abfassung untersucht* (Bonn, 1878); and especially NÖLDECHEN, MONCEAUX, D'ALÈS, and HARNACK; *Chronol.*, II (1904). On Tertullian's Latin Bible see ZAHN, *Gesch. des N. T. Kanons*, I, 51; HARNACK; MONCEAUX, etc. The citations are carefully collected in RÖNSCH, *Das N. T. Tert.'s* (Leipzig, 1871). For details, and for some of the innumerable editions of separate treatises, see BONWETSCH in *Realencycl.*, and especially BARDENHEWER, *Gesch. der altkirchl. Litt.*, II (Freiburg, 1903).

JOHN CHAPMAN.

Teruel, DIOCESE OF (TUROLENSIS), suffragan of Saragossa, comprises the civil province of the same name, excepting the town of Bechi (Castellón). It is believed by some that Teruel and the ancient Turba are the same. Turba was the city whose disputes with the Saguntines gave Hannibal an excuse for attacking Saguntum and beginning the Second Punic War. According to the annals of Teruel it appears that Turba was not situated on the site of the present city of Teruel, but at its boundary line. Teruel was founded in 1176 by Sancho Sánchez Muñoz and Blasco Garcés Marcilla. It formed a separate community and was governed by the *Fuero de Sepúlveda* until 1598, when the inhabitants abjured it before the courts of Aragon, in order to come under the Government of Aragon. Jaime I received its support in the conquest of Valencia, and the standards of Teruel were the first to wave in the gateway of Serranos. In 1271 it joined in the war against Castile, invaded Huete and Cuenca, and sided with Pedro IV in his war against the "Union". In recognition of this the king visited the city in 1348 and conferred upon it the title of *exenta* (exempt). Gregory XIII at the earnest solicitations of Philip II created the diocese in 1577. The first bishop, Juan Pérez de Artieda, was elected but not consecrated; the first bishop installed was Andrés Santos, who was transferred to Saragossa in 1579. All the churches of Teruel are contemporary with its foundation, as the founders built nine churches, one, Santa María de Media Villa, in the centre, and the remaining eight in a circle following the circuit of the walls. The central church was made a collegiate church in 1423 and named the cathedral in 1577. It was originally built of brick and rubble-work, but since the restoration in the seventeenth century it has lost its primitive character. The Doric choir stalls were the gift of Martín Ferrer, Bishop of Teruel, and later of Tarazona.

Ferdinand and Isabella visited Teruel in 1482, took the oath in the cathedral, and received the freedom of the city. The founding of the Inquisition in 1484 produced serious changes because the converts were numerous and powerful. The inquisitor, Juan de Solivellia, was forced to leave. Property to the amount of 133,000 *sueldos* was confiscated and turned over to the city. The Churches of San Martín and El Salvador are remarkable for their Arabic towers. The first, Moorish in style, was built in the twelfth century. Pierre de Bedel, builder of the Arcos de Teruel (Aqueduct) and of the Mina de Daroca, repaired its foundations from 1549 to 1551. The tower of the Church of El Salvador, Moorish style of the thirteenth century, was reinforced in the nineteenth century by brick additions. In the Church of San Pedro rest the bodies of the famous "lovers of Teruel", Diego Martínez de Marcilla and Isabel de Segura. The seminary, dedicated to St. Toribio de Mogrovejo, was founded by the bishop Francisco José Rodríguez Chico, who after the expulsion of the Jesuits in 1769 was granted the use of their magnificent college by Charles III. During the wars of independence and the civil wars that followed, the building was taken over for military quarters and shortly afterwards the seminary was suppressed. It was re-established in 1849 by Don Antonio Lao y Cuevas, who gave his own palace for the purpose. The Jesuit college has since been restored to the order. The episcopal palace is in no way remarkable except perhaps for its courtyard, which has a well-proportioned Ionic colonnade. The *Casa del Capítula*, where the ecclesiastical chapter used to assemble, has an altar dedicated to the Immaculate Conception and to St. Emerentia, patroness of the city.

Among the distinguished citizens of Teruel must be mentioned Jerónimo Ripalda, S.J.; the jurisconsult Gaspar de Castellot; Miguel Jerónimo de Castellot, judge of the courts of Aragon, 1665; Fray Juan Cebrian de Perales, Bishop of Albarracín, and Juan Martínez Salafranca, Viceroy of Aragon, founder of the Academy of History.

CUADRADO, *España, sus monumentos: Aragón* (Barcelona, 1886); PRUNEDO, *Crónica general de España; Crónica de Teruel* (Madrid, 1866).

RAMÓN RUIZ AMADO.

Test Act. See OATHS, ENGLISH POST-REFORMATION.

Testament, THE OLD.—I. NAME.—The word "testament", Hebrew *berîth*, Greek διαθήκη, primarily signifies the covenant which God entered into first with Abraham, then with the people of Israel. The Prophets had knowledge of a new covenant to which the one concluded on Mount Sinai should give way. Accordingly Christ at the Last Supper speaks of the blood of the new testament. The Apostle St. Paul declares himself (II Cor., iii, 6) a minister "of the new testament", and calls (iii, 14) the covenant entered into on Mount Sinai "the old testament". The Greek expression διαθήκη is employed in the Septuagint for the Hebrew "berîth". The later interpreters Aquila and Symmachus substituted for διαθήκη the more common συνθήκη, which probably agreed more with their literary taste. The Latin term is "fœdus" and oftener "testamentum", a word corresponding more exactly to the Greek.

As regards Christian times, the expression at an early period came to signify the whole of God's Revelation as exhibited in the history of the Israelites, and because this old covenant was incorporated into the Canonical Books, it was but an easy step to make the term signify the Canonical Scriptures. Even the text referred to above (II Cor., iii, 14) points to that. So, the Scriptures are called "books of the Old Testament" by Melito of Sardis and Clement of Alexandria (τὰ παλαιὰ βιβλία; τα τῆς παλαιᾶς διαθήκης βιβλία). It is not clear whether with these authors "Old Testament" and "Scriptures of the Old Testament" mean the same. Origen shows that in his time the transition was complete, although in his writings signs of the gradual fixing of the expression may be still traced. For he repeatedly speaks of the "so-called" Old Testament, when meaning the Scriptures. With the Western writers this use of the term in the most ancient period cannot yet be proved. To the lawyer Tertullian the Sacred Books are, above all, documents and sources of argument, and he therefore frequently calls them "vetus and novum instrumentum". Cyprian once mentions the "scripturæ veteres et novæ". Subsequently the Greek use of the term becomes established among the Latins as well, and through them it has been made common property of the Christian world. In this meaning, as signifying the Canonical Scriptures of the Old Testament, the expression "Old Testament" will be used in what follows.

II. HISTORY OF THE TEXT.—The canon of the Old Testament, its manuscripts, editions and ancient versions are treated in the articles BIBLE; CANON OF THE HOLY SCRIPTURES; CODEX ALEXANDRINUS, etc.; HEBREW BIBLE; MASSORAH; MANUSCRIPTS OF THE BIBLE; VERSIONS OF THE BIBLE. Questions concerning the origin and contents of the single books are proposed and answered in articles on the respective books. This article is confined to the general introduction on the text of the parts of the Old Testament written in Hebrew; for the few books originally composed in Greek (Wisdom; II Machabees) and those of which the Semitic original has been lost (Judith; Tobias; Sirach, i. e. Ecclus.; I Machabees) call for no special treatment.

A. *Text of the Manuscripts and Massoretes.*—The sure starting-point for a correct estimation of the text of the Old Testament is the evidence obtained from the MSS. In this connexion, the first thing to observe is that however distant the oldest MSS. are—the earliest are of the ninth century A. D.—from the time when the books were composed, there is a uniform and homogeneous tradition concerning the text. The fact is all the more striking, as the history of the New Testament is quite different. We have New-Testament MSS. written not much more than 300 years after the composition of the books, and in them we find numerous differences, though but few of them are important. The textual variants in the MSS. of the Old Testament are limited to quite insignificant differences of vowels and more rarely of consonants. Even when we take into account the discrepancies between the Eastern, or Babylonian, and Western, or Palestinian schools, no essential differences are found. The proof for the agreement between the MSS. was established by B. Kennicott after comparing more than 600 MSS. ("Vetus Testamentum Hebraicum cum variis lectionibus", Oxford, 1776, 1780). De Rossi has added considerably to this material ("Variæ lectiones veteris Testamenti", Parma, 1784–88). It is obvious that this striking uniformity cannot be due to chance; it is unique in the history of text-tradition, and all the more remarkable as the imperfect Hebrew system of writing could not but occasion many and various errors and slips. Besides many peculiarities in the method of writing show themselves uniformly everywhere. False readings are retained in the same manner, so that the text is clearly the result of artificial equalization.

The question now arises: How far back can we trace this care in handing down the text to posterity? Philo, many authorities on the Talmud, and later Jewish rabbis and savants of the sixteenth and seventeenth century favoured the opinion that the Hebrew text, as it is now read in our MSS., was written down from the outset and bequeathed to us unadulterated. The works of Elias Levita, Morinus, Cappellus have shown this view to be untenable; and later investigations have established the history of the text in its essential features. The uniformity of the MSS. is ultimately the outcome of the labours of the Massoretes, which were not concluded till after the writing of the oldest MSS. The work of the Massoretes chiefly consisted in the faithful preservation of the transmitted text. This they accomplished by maintaining accurate statistics on the entire state of the Sacred Books. Verses, words, letters were counted; lists were compiled of like words and of forms of words with full and defective spelling, and possibilities of easy mistakes were catalogued. The invention of the signs for vowels and accents— about the seventh century—facilitated a faithful preservation of the text. Incorrect separation and connexion of syllables and words was henceforth all but excluded.

Textual criticism was employed by the Massoretes very moderately, and even the little they did, shows that as much as possible they left untouched all that had been handed down. If a reading proved untenable, they did not correct the text itself, but were satisfied with noting the proper reading on the margin as "Qerê" (read), in opposition to "Kethîbh" (written). Such corrections were of various kinds. They were first of all corrections of real mistakes, whether of letters or of entire words. A letter or a word in the text had, according to the note on the margin, either to be changed, or inserted, or omitted by the reader. Such were the so-called "Tiqqunê Sopherîm", corrections of the scribes. The second group of corrections consisted in changing an ambiguous word,—of such eighteen are recorded in the Massorah. In the Talmud no mention has as yet been made of them. But its compilers were aware of the "'Itturê Sopherîm", or erasures of the connecting *Waw*, which had been made in several places in opposition to the Septuagint and the Samaritan Versions. When later the Massoretes speak only of four or five instances, we must say with Ginsburg that these cases are merely recorded as typical. Cases are not rare when consideration for religious or moral feeling has led to the substitution of a more harmless euphemism for an ill-sounding word. The vowels of the expression to be read are attached to the written word of the text, whilst the consonants are noted on the margin. Well known is the ever-recurring "Qerê" Adonai instead of Jahvé; it seems to date back to the time before Christ, and probably even the first Greek interpreters were acquainted with it.

The fact that the Massoretes did not dare insert the changes described in the Sacred Text itself shows that the latter was already fixed. Other peculiarities point to the same reverence for tradition. We repeatedly find in the text a so-called inverted *Nun* (e. g., Num., x, 35–36). In Is., ix, 6, there is a final *Mêm* within the word. A *Waw* is interrupted or letters are made bigger, whilst others are placed higher up—the so-called suspended letters. Not a few of these oddities are already recorded in the Talmud, and therefore must be of great age. Letters with points are mentioned even in the "Mishna". The counting of the letters also probably belongs to the older period. Records serving for textual criticism are extant from the same time. In its essentials the work is completed with the post-Talmudic treatise "Sopherim". This treatise, which gives a careful introduction to the writing of the Sacred Text, is one of the most conclusive proofs of the scrupulosity with which at the time of its origin (not before the seventh century) the text was generally treated.

B. *Older Witnesses*.—The condition of the text previous to the age of the Massoretes is guaranteed by the "Talmud" with its notes on text-criticism and its innumerable quotations, which are, however, frequently drawn only from memory. Another help are the "Targums", or free Aramaic versions of the Sacred Books, composed from the last centuries B. C. to the fifth A. D. But the state of the text is chiefly evidenced by the Vulgate Version made by St. Jerome at the end of the fourth and the beginning of the fifth centuries. He followed the Hebrew original, and his occasional remarks on how a word was spelt or read enable us to arrive at a sure judgment on the text of the fourth century. As was to be expected from the statements of the Talmud, the consonant-text of the MSS. tallies almost in every respect with the original of St. Jerome. There appear greater discrepancies in vocalization, which is not to be wondered at, for at that time the marking of the vowels was not known. Thus the reading is necessarily often ambiguous, as the saint expressly states. His comment on Is., xxxviii, 11, shows that this statement is not only to be taken as a learned note, but that thereby the interpretation might often be influenced practically. When St. Jerome occasionally speaks of vowels, he means the quiescent or vowel letters. Nevertheless, the opinion that in the fourth century the pronunciation was still fluctuating, would be erroneous. For the saint knew how, in a definite case, an ambiguous word was to be vocalized; he appealed to the custom of the Jews standing in opposition to the interpretation of the Septuagint. A fixed pronunciation had already resulted from the practice, in vogue for centuries, of reading the Holy Writ publicly in the synagogue. There might be doubt in particular cases, but, on the whole, even the vowel-text was secured.

The letters in which the MSS. of that time were written are the "square characters", as appears from St. Jerome's remarks. This writing distinguished the final forms of the well-known five letters (Prologus galeatus), and probably supposed the separation of words which, excepting a few places, is the same as in our Massoretic Text. Sometimes the Vulgate alone seems to have preserved the correct separation in opposition to the Massoretes and the Greek Version.

The loss of Origen's hexapla is very much to be regretted. This work in its first two columns would have handed down to us both the consonant-text and the vocalization. But only a few scattered remnants of the second are left. They show that the pronunciation, especially of the proper names, in the third century disagrees not infrequently with the one used later. The alphabet at the time of Origen was the same as that of a century and a half afterwards. As regards the consonants there is little change, and the text shows no essential transformation.

We are led still further back by the Greek versions originating in the second century. The most valuable is Aquila's, as it was based upon the Hebrew text, and rendered it to the letter, with the greatest fidelity, thus enabling us to draw reliable conclusions as to the condition of the original. The work is all the more valuable, as Aquila does not care about the Greek position of words and the peculiar Greek idiom. Moreover, he consciously differs from the Septuagint, taking the then official text for his norm. Being a disciple of Rabbi Aqiba he presumably maintains the views and principles of the Jewish scribes in the beginning of the second century. The two other versions of the same period are of less importance for the critic. Theodotion depends upon the Septuagint, and Symmachus allows himself greater liberty in the treatment of the text. Of the three versions only very small fragments have come down to us. The form of the text which we gather from them is almost the one transmitted by the Massoretes; the differences naturally became more numerous, but it remains the one recension we know of from our MSS. It must, therefore, be ascribed at least to the beginning of the second century, and recent investigations in fact assign it to that period.

But that is not all. The perfect agreement of the MSS., even in their critical remarks and seemingly irrelevant and casual peculiarities, has led to the assumption that the present text not only represents a single recension, but that this recension is even built upon one archetype containing the very peculiarities that now strike us in the MSS. In favour of this hypothesis, which, since the time of Olshausen, has been defended and based upon a deeper argument especially by de Lagarde, evidence has been brought forward which seems overwhelming. Hence it is not surprising that, of late, the assertion was made that this view had long since become an admitted fact in the textual criticism of the Old Testament. Yet, however persuasive the argument appears at first sight its validity has been constantly impugned by authorities such as Kuenen, Strack, Buhl, König, and others distinguished by their knowledge of the subject. The present state of the Hebrew text is doubtless the outcome of systematic labour during the course of several centuries, but the question is whether the supposed archetype ever existed.

At the outset the very assumption that about A. D. 150 only a single copy was available for the preparation of the Bible text is so improbable as scarcely to deserve consideration. For even if during the insurrection of Bar-Cocheba a great number of Scripture rolls perished, there nevertheless existed enough of them in Egypt and Persia, so that there was no need to rely on one damaged copy. And how could this copy, the defective peculiarities of which could not have been overlooked, attain to such undisputed authority? This could have happened only if it had much greater weight than the others, for instance, for its being a temple scroll; this would imply further that there existed official texts and copies, and so the uniformity goes further back. On the supposition that it were but a private scroll, preserved merely by chance, it would be impossible to explain how the obvious mistakes were retained. Why, for instance, should all copies have a closed *Qoph*, or a letter casually made larger, or a final *Mem* within a word? Such improbabilities arise necessarily from the hypothesis of a single archetype. Is it not much more likely that the supposed mistakes are really not erroneous, but have some critical signification? For several of them a satisfactory explanation has already been given. Thus the inverted *Nun* points to the uncertainty of the respective passages: in Prov., xvi, 28, for instance, the small *Nun*, as Blau rightly conjectures, might owe its origin to a textual emendation suggested by the feeling prevalent later on. The larger letters served perhaps to mark the middle of a book. Possibly something similar may have given rise to the other peculiarities for which we cannot at present account. As long as there exists the possibility of a probable explanation, we should not make chance responsible for the condition of our text, though we do not deny that here and there chance has been at play. But the complete agreement was certainly brought about gradually. The older the witnesses, the more they differ, even though the recension remains the same. And yet it might have been expected, the more ancient they were the more uniform they should become.

Besides, if one codex had been the source of all the rest, it cannot be explained why trifling oddities were everywhere taken over faithfully, whilst the consonant-text was less cared for. If, again, in later times the differences were maintained by the Western and the Eastern schools, it is clear that the supposed codex did not possess the necessarily decisive authority.

The present text on the contrary seems to have resulted from the critical labour of the scribes from the first century B. C. to the second century A. D. Considering the reading of the Bible in the synagogue and the statements of Josephus (Contra Apionem, I, viii) and of Philo (Eusebius, "Præp. evang.", VIII, vi) on the treatment of the Scriptures, we may rightly suppose that greater changes of the text did not occur at that time. Even the words of Jesus in Matt., v, 18, about the jot and tittle not passing away, seem to point to a scrupulous care in the preservation of the very letter; and the unconditional authority of the Scripture presupposes a high opinion of the letter of Holy Writ.

How the work of the scribes was carried out in detail, we cannot ascertain. Some statements of Jewish tradition suggest that they were satisfied with superficial investigation and criticism, which, however, is all that could have been expected at a time when serious textual criticism was not even thought of. When difficulties arose, it is said that the witnesses were counted and the question decided according to numerical majority. However simple and imperfect this method was, under the circumstances an objective account of the actual state of the question was much more valuable than a series of hypotheses the claims of which we could not now examine. Nor is there any reason for supposing, with some early Christian writers, conscious changes or falsifications of the text. But we are, perhaps, justified in holding that the disputes between the Jews and Christians about the text of the Scriptures were one of the reasons why the former hastened the work of unifying and fixing the text.

The MSS. of that period probably showed little difference from those of the subsequent epoch. The consonant-text was written in a more ancient form of the square characters; the so-called final letters presumably came into use then. The Nash Papyrus (the Ten Commandments) would give some information if it were only certain that it really belongs to the first century. The question cannot be decided, as our knowledge of Hebrew writing from the first to the third century is quite imperfect. The papyrus is written in well-developed square characters, exhibits division of words throughout, and always uses the "final letters". As in the Talmud, the memory of the relatively late distinction of the double forms of the five letters is still alive, their application in Holy Writ cannot be dated back too far. Even the Massorah contains a number of phrases having final letters which are divided differently in the text and on the margin, and must, therefore, belong to a period when the distinction was not as yet in use. From the Nabatæan and Palmyrian inscriptions we learn that at the time of Christ the distinction already existed, but it does not follow that the same usage prevailed in the land west of the Jordan and, in particular, in the Sacred Books. The Palmyrian inscriptions of the first to the third century apply the final form of only one letter, viz., *Nun*, whilst the Nabatæan go beyond the Hebrew and use, though not consistently, double forms also for *Aleph* and *Hê*. The time when the Jewish copyists began to distinguish the double forms must then remain an open question. Moreover, the term "final letters" does not seem very appropriate, considering the historical development. It is not the final forms then invented, but rather the others, that seem to be the product of a new writing. For, with the single exception of *Mêm*, the so-called final forms are those of the old characters as exhibited partly at least even in the oldest inscriptions, or at any rate in use in the Aramaic papyri of the fifth century B. C.

C. *The Bible Text before Christ.*—As regards the preceding centuries, we are relatively well informed. In place of the missing MSS. we have the ancient Greek Version of the Old Testament, the so-called Septuagint, or Alexandrian, Version. The Pentateuch was translated in the first half of the third century, but it cannot be determined in what order and at what intervals the other books followed. Yet in the case of the majority of the books the work was probably completed about the middle of the second century B. C. Of primary importance for us is the question of the state of the text at the time of the translation. As the version is not the work of one man—not even the Pentateuch had only one translator—nor the work of one period, but is extended over more than a hundred years, it cannot all be judged by the same criterion. The same holds good of its Hebrew original. Some of the Old-Testament Scriptures had, at the time of the translation, existed for about a thousand years, whilst others had just been composed. Considering this historical development, we must, in judging the texts, not simply oppose the whole of the M. T. (Massoretic Text) on the one hand to the whole Septuagint on the other. Results of any practical value can be obtained only by a separate study of the different books of Holy Scripture.

The oldest, the Pentateuch, presents considerable differences from the M. T. only in Ex., xxxvi–xl, and in Num. Greater divergences appear in Sam., Jer., Job, Prov., and Daniel. The M. T. of the Books of Samuel has suffered in many places. The Greek Version often serves to correct it, though not always. In Jeremias text-tradition is very unsettled. In the Greek Version not less than 2700 words of the M. T., about an eighth part of the whole, are missing. Additions to the M. T. are inconsiderable. Some of the parts wanting in Sept. may be later additions, whilst others belong to the original text. The transpositions of the Greek text seem to be secondary. Still the order of the M. T. is not unobjectionable either, and sometimes Sept. is right in opposition to M. T. On the whole, the text of Sept. seems to be preferable to the M. T. In Job the textual problem is quite similar. The Greek text is considerably shorter than the M. T. The Greek rendering of Proverbs diverges still more from the Hebrew. Lastly, the Greek Ecclesiasticus, a translation which we must consider to have been made by the author's grandson, is altogether different from the Hebrew recension lately found. These facts prove that during the third–second century B. C. texts were circulated which manifest traces of careless treatment. But it must be remembered that translators, sometimes, may have treated the text more freely, and that even our Greek Version has not come down to us in its original form. It is hard to determine how far we may recognize the official text of the period in the present form of the Greek text. The legend of the solemn mission to Jerusalem and the deputation of the translators to Egypt cannot be treated as historical. On the other hand it is arbitrary to assume that the original of the Greek Version represents a corrupted text every time it differs from M. T. We have to distinguish various forms of the text, whether we call them recensions or not.

For a judgment on the Sept. and its original, the knowledge of the Hebrew writing then in vogue is indispensable. In the case of the Minor Prophets attempts have been made by Vollers to discover the characters employed. The Books of Samuel have been investigated by Wellhausen and Driver; Jeremias by Köhler; Ezechiel by Cornill; Job by Beer; Ecclesiasticus by Peters. Full certainty as to the characters of the Hebrew scrolls of the third–second century B. C. has not as yet been obtained. According to Jewish tradition, Esdras brought over the new (Assyrian) writing when returning from the Exile, in which script the Sacred Books were thereafter transcribed. A sudden change is improbable. It is not possible that the writing of the fourth century was quite similar to that of the Nash Papyrus or of the first-century inscriptions. The Aramaic writing of the fifth century shows an unmistakable tendency towards the latter forms, yet many letters are still closely related to the ancient alphabet: as *Bêth*, *Caph*, *Mêm*, *Samech*, *Ayin*, *Tsade*. How did this change take place? Did it pass through the Samaritan alphabet, which clearly betrays its connexion with the Phœnician? We know the Samaritan letters only after the time of Christ. The oldest inscription belongs, perhaps, to the fourth century A. D.; another, that of Nablus, to the sixth. But this writing is undoubtedly decorative, displaying care and art, and offers, therefore, no sure basis for a decision. Still there was presumably a time in which the Sacred Scriptures were written in an ancient form of the Samaritan characters which are closely related with those of the Hasmonæan coin inscription.

Others suggest the Palmyrian alphabet. Some letters, indeed, agree with the square characters; but *Ghimel*, *Hê*, *Pê*, *Tsade*, and *Qôph* differ so much that a direct relation is inadmissible. In short, considering the local nature of this artificial writing, it is hardly credible that it exerted a wider influence towards the west. The Hebrew square characters come nearer to the Nabatæan, the sphere of which is more extended and is immediately adjacent to Palestine.

As the change of the alphabet probably took place step by step, we must reckon with transition writings, the form and relation of which can perhaps be approximately determined by comparison. The Greek Version offers excellent material; its very mistakes are an inestimable help to us. For the errors in reading or writing, occasioned, or already supposed, by the original, will often find their reason and explanation in the form of the characters. A group of letters repeatedly read erroneously is a clue as to the form of the alphabet of the original. For the well-known possibilities in the square writing of confounding *Daleth* with *Rêsh*, *Yôdh* with *Waw*, *Bêth* with *Caph* do not exist in the same way in the transition writ-

XIV.—34

ings. The interchanging of *Hê* and *Hêth*, of *Yôdh* and *Waw*, so easy with the new characters, is scarcely conceivable with the old ones; and the mistaking of *Bêth* for *Caph* is altogether excluded. *Aleph* and *Tau* on the other hand can easily be mixed up. Now in Paralipomenon, in itself recent and translated into Greek long after the Pentateuch, *Waw* and *Tau*, *Yôdh* and *Hê*, *Caph* and *Rêsh* have been mistaken for each other. This can be accounted for only if an older form of writing were employed. Hence we are compelled to suppose that the old alphabet, or a transition form like it, was in use up to the second or first century B. C. From Christ's words about the jot (Matt., v, 18) it has been concluded that *Yôdh* must have been regarded as the smallest letter; this holds good with the square characters. We know otherwise that, at the time of Christ, the new writing was all but developed; at least the inscriptions of the Benê Chezîr and of many ossuaries sufficiently testify to this. But in these inscriptions *Zayin* and *Waw* are as small as or even smaller than *Yôdh*.

In addition to the form of the characters, orthography is of importance. The unpointed consonant-text can be made essentially clearer by writing "plene", i. e. by using the so-called quiescent letters (matres lectionis). This means was often absent in the original of the Sept. In the text of the Minor Prophets *Aleph* seems not to have been written as a vowel-letter. Thus it came about that the translators and the M. T. diverge, according as they suppose the *Aleph* or not. If the vowel-letter was written, only one interpretation was possible. The same applies to the use of *Waw* and *Yôdh*. Their omission occasions mistakes on the one or other side. The liberty prevailing in this regard is expressly testified even for a much later period. But it is going too far to consider the omission of the vowel-letters as the rule commonly observed. The oldest inscriptions (Mesha, Siloah) and the whole history of Semitic writing prove that this practical device was known.

In particular cases the possibility of connecting or separating the letters differently must be considered as another source of divers interpretations. Whether the division of the words was expressed in the ancient MSS. or not cannot be shown by direct testimonies. The Mesha and Siloah inscriptions and some of the oldest Aramaic and Phœnician divide the words by a dot. The later monuments do not abide by this usage, but mark the division here and there by a little interval. This custom is universal in the Aramaic papyri from the fifth century downwards. The Hebrew fragments make no exception, and the Syriac writing applies the word-division in the earliest MSS. Therefore the conjecture that word-division was used in the old scrolls is not to be rejected at the outset. Still the intervals must have been so small that wrong connexions easily came about. Instances are not wanting, and both the Massorah and the Greek Version testify to that. Thus Gen., xlix, 19–20, is correctly divided in the Greek and in the Vulgate, whilst the M. T. erroneously carries the *Mêm*, that belongs to the end of verse 19, over to the following word "Asher". The passage, moreover, is poetical and a new stanza begins with verse 20. Hence in the archetype of our M. T. the stichic writing, known perhaps at an earlier period and used in the later MSS., was not applied.

The mistakes occurring in consequence of interchanging of letters, of wrong vocalization or connexion, show how text-corruption originated, and thus suggest ways of repairing the damaged passages. Other slips which always occur in the handing down of MSS., such as haplography, dittography, insertion of glosses, transposition, even of entire columns, must also be taken into consideration whilst estimating the text of the Sacred Books. In books or passages of poetical nature, metre, alphabetical order of verses and stanzas, and their structure, supply a means of textual emendation, which ought nevertheless, to be used with great prudence, especially where the MSS. seem disarranged.

We must, however, beware of comparing the Sept. as a unit with the Massorah. In textual criticism we must distinguish between the questions: What is the relation of the Greek Version of the Scriptures in general to the Hebrew? and, How far in a particular case may one text be corrected by the other? The Sept. may on the whole differ considerably from the M. T., and yet often clear up an obscure passage in the Hebrew, while the reverse happens just as frequently. Apart from the Sept. there is but little to assist us. The Samaritan Text throws light on the Pentateuch, at least up to the fourth century, perhaps up to the time before Esdras. Yet until the critical edition, announced a couple of years ago, appears it must remain an open question whether the Samaritan Text was not influenced by the Sept. at a later period. Regarding shorter passages, the parallel texts allow of comparison. The deviations observed in them show that changes have taken place, which betray carelessness or intentional or accidental variations. Jewish tradition tells of a restoration of the Sacred Scriptures by Esdras. Underlying this narrative may be the recollection of historical events that proved disastrous both to the political and religious life of the people of Israel and to its Sacred Books. The consequences do not everywhere manifest themselves as much as in the books of Samuel and Jeremias, for instance, but often enough are such that the application of all critical means is needed to come to a readable text. Sometimes in spite of all nothing can be done and the passage is irremediably disfigured. It will be impossible to make the M. T. agree entirely with the Sept. until we are favoured by some unexpected discoveries. However, all these discrepancies do not alter the Sacred Texts to such a degree as to affect in any way the religious content of the Old Testament.

MORINUS, *Exercitat. biblicarum de hebræi græcique textus sinceritate lib. duo* (Paris, 1669); CAPPELLUS, *Critica sacra* (Halle, 1775–86); HODY, *De Bibl. textibus original. version græc. et lat. vulgata libri* IV (Oxford, 1705); GEIGER, *Urschrif. und Ubersetzungen der Bibel* (Breslau, 1867); STRACK, *Proleg. crit. in Vet. Test. hebr.* (Leipzig, 1873); BUHL, *Kanon und Text des Alten Test.* (Leipzig, 1891), tr. MACPHERSON (Edinburgh, 1892); GINSBURG, *Introd. to the Massoretico-critical Edit. of the Hebr. Bib.* (London, 1897); KITTEL, *Uber die Notwendigkeit und Möglichkeit einer neuen Ausgabe der hebr. Bibel* (Leipzig, 1902); BLAU, *Masoretische Untersuchungen* (Strasburg, 1891); IDEM, *Zur Einleitung in die hl. Schrift* (Strasburg, 1894); IDEM, *Studien zum althebräischen Buchwesen* (Strasburg, 1902); Bible Dictionaries and Introductions to the Old Testament, as CORNELY, *Historica et critica introductio in utriusque Testamenti libros sacros*, I (Paris, 1894, 2nd ed.); GIGOT, *Gen. Introd. to the Study of the Holy Scripture* (New York, 1905); STRACK, *Einleitung in das A. T.* (Munich, 1906); KÖNIG, *Einleitung in das A. T.* (Bonn, 1893); FELL, *Lehrbuch der allgemeinen Einleitung in das A. T.* (Paderborn, 1906).

AUG. MERK.

Testament, THE NEW.—I. Name; II. Description; III. Origin; IV. Transmission of the Text; V. Contents, History, and Doctrine.

I. NAME.—Testament comes from *testamentum*, the word by which the Latin ecclesiastical writers translated the Greek διαθήκη. With the profane authors this latter term means always, one passage of Aristophanes perhaps excepted, the legal disposition a man makes of his goods for after his death. However, at an early date, the Alexandrian translators of the Scripture, known as the Septuagint, employed the word as the equivalent of the Hebrew *berith*, which means a pact, an alliance, more especially the alliance of Yahweh with Israel. In St. Paul (I Cor., xi, 25) Jesus Christ uses the words "new testament" as meaning the alliance established by Himself between God and the world, and this is called "new" as opposed to that of which Moses was the mediator. Later on, the name of testament was given to the collection of sacred texts containing the history and the doctrine of the two alliances; here again and for the same reason we meet the distinction between the Old and the New Testaments. In this meaning the expression Old Testament (ἡ παλαιὰ διαθήκη) is found for the first time in Melito of Sardis, towards the year 170. There are reasons for thinking that at this date the corresponding word "testamentum" was already in use amongst the Latins. In any case it was common in the time of Tertullian.

II. DESCRIPTION.—The New Testament, as usually received in the Christian Churches, is made up of twenty-seven different books attributed to eight different authors, six of whom are numbered among the Apostles (Matthew, John, Paul, James, Peter, Jude) and two among their immediate disciples (Mark, Luke). If we consider only the contents and the literary form of these writings they may be divided into historical books (Gospels and Acts), didactic books (Epistles), a prophetical book (Apocalypse). Before the name of New Testament had come into use the writers of the latter half of the second century used to say "Gospel and Apostolic writings" or simply "the Gospel and the Apostle", meaning the Apostle St. Paul. The Gospels are subdivided into two groups, those which are commonly called synoptic (Matthew, Mark, Luke), because their narratives are parallel, and the fourth Gospel (that of St. John), which to a certain extent completes the first three. They relate the life and personal teaching of Jesus Christ. The Acts of the Apostles, as is sufficiently indicated by the title, relates the preaching and the labours of the Apostles. It narrates the foundation of the Churches of Palestine and Syria only; in it mention is made of Peter, John, James, Paul, and Barnabas; afterwards, the author devotes sixteen chapters out of the twenty-eight to the missions of St. Paul to the Greco-Romans. There are thirteen Epistles of St. Paul, and perhaps fourteen, if, with the Council of Trent, we consider him the author of the Epistle to the Hebrews. They are, with the exception of this last-mentioned, addressed to particular Churches (Rom.; I, II Cor.; Gal.; Ephes.; Philip.; Colos.; I, II Thess.) or to individuals (I, II Tim.; Tit.; Philem.). The seven Epistles that follow (James; I, II Peter; I, II, III John; Jude) are called "Catholic", because most of them are addressed to the faithful in general. The Apocalypse addressed to the seven Churches of Asia Minor (Ephesus, Smyrna, Pergamus, Thyatira, Sardis, Philadelphia, Laodicea) resembles in some ways a collective letter. It contains a vision which St. John had at Patmos concerning the interior state of the above-mentioned communities, the struggle of the Church with pagan Rome, and the final destiny of the New Jerusalem.

III. ORIGIN.—The New Testament was not written all at once. The books that compose it appeared one after another in the space of fifty years, i. e. in the second half of the first century. Written in different and distant countries and addressed to particular Churches, they took some time to spread throughout the whole of Christendom, and a much longer time to become accepted. The unification of the canon was not accomplished without much controversy (see CANON OF THE HOLY SCRIPTURES). Still it can be said that from the third century, or perhaps earlier, the existence of all the books that to-day form our New Testament was everywhere known, although they were not all universally admitted, at least as certainly canonical. However, uniformity existed in the West from the fourth century. The East had to await the seventh century to see an end to all doubts on the subject. In early times the questions of canonicity and authenticity were not discussed separately and independently of each other, the latter being held brought forward as a reason for the former; but in the fourth century, the canonicity was held, especially by St. Jerome, on account of ecclesiastical prescription and, by the very fact, the authenticity of the contested books became of minor importance. We have to come down to the sixteenth century to hear the question repeated, whether the Epistle to the Hebrews was written by St. Paul, or the Epistles called Catholic were in reality composed by the Apostles whose names they bear. Some Humanists, as Erasmus and Cardinal Cajetan, revived the objections mentioned by St. Jerome, and which are based on the style of these writings. To this Luther added the inadmissibility of the doctrine, as regards the Epistle of St. James. However, it was practically the Lutherans alone who sought to diminish the traditional Canon, which the Council of Trent was to define in 1546.

It was reserved to modern times, especially to our own days, to dispute and deny the truth of the opinion received from the ancients concerning the origin of the books of the New Testament. This doubt and the negation regarding the authors had their primary cause in the religious incredulity of the eighteenth century. These witnesses to the truth of a religion no longer believed were inconvenient, if it was true that they had seen and heard what they related. Little time was needed to find, in analyzing them, indications of a later origin. The conclusions of the Tübingen school, which brought down to the second century the compositions of all the New Testament except four Epistles of St. Paul (Rom.; Gal.; I, II Cor.), was very common thirty or forty years ago, in so-called critical circles (see Dict. apolog. de la foi catholique, I, 771-6). When the crisis of militant incredulity had passed, the problem of the New Testament began to be examined more calmly, and especially more methodically. From the critical studies of the past half century we may draw the following conclusion, which is now in its general outlines admitted by all: It was a mistake to have attributed the origin of Christian literature to a later date; these texts, on the whole, date back to the second half of the first century; consequently they are the work of a generation that counted a good number of direct witnesses of the life of Jesus Christ. From stage to stage, from Strauss to Renan, from Renan to Reuss, Weizsäcker, Holtzmann, Jülicher, Weiss, and from these to Zahn, Harnack, criticism has just retraced its steps over the distance it had so inconsiderately covered under the guidance of Christian Baur. To-day it is admitted that the first Gospels were written about the year 70. The Acts can hardly be said to be later; Harnack even thinks they were composed nearer to the year 60 than to the year 70. The Epistles of St. Paul remain beyond all dispute, except those to the Ephesians and to the Hebrews, and the pastoral Epistles, about which doubts still exist. In like manner there are many who contest the Catholic Epistles; but even if the Second Epistle of Peter is delayed till towards the year 120 or 130, the Epistle of St. James is put by several at the very beginning of Christian literature, between the years 40 and 50, the earliest Epistles of St. Paul about 52 till 58.

At present the brunt of the battle rages around the writings called Johannine (the fourth Gospel, the three Epistles of John, and the Apocalypse). Were these texts written by the Apostle John, son of Zebedee, or by John the presbyter of Ephesus whom Papias mentions? There is nothing to oblige us to endorse the conclusions of radical criticisms on this subject. On the contrary, the strong testimony of tradition attributes these writings to the Apostle St. John, nor is it weakened at all by internal criteria, provided we do not lose sight of the character of the fourth Gospel —called by Clement of Alexandria "a spiritual gospel", as compared with the three others, which he styled "corporal". Theologically, we must take into consideration the recent ecclesiastical documents (Decree "Lamentabili", prop. 17, 18, and the answer of the Roman Commission for Biblical Questions, 29 May, 1907). These decisions uphold the Johannine and Apostolic origin of the fourth Gospel. Whatever may be the issue of these controversies, a Catholic will be, and that in virtue of his principles, in exceptionally favourable conditions for accepting the just exigencies of criticism. If it be ever established that II Peter belongs to a kind of literature then common, namely the pseudepigraph, its canonicity will not on that account be compromised. Inspiration and authenticity are distinct and even separable, when no dogmatic question is involved in their union.

The question of the origin of the New Testament includes yet another literary problem, concerning the Gospels especially. Are these writings independent of one another? If one of the Evangelists did utilize the work of his predecessors how are we to suppose it happened? Was it Matthew who used Mark or vice versa? After thirty years of constant study, the question has been answered only by conjectures. Amongst these must be included the documentary theory itself, even in the form in which it is now commonly admitted, that of the "two sources". The starting-point of this theory, namely the priority of Mark and the use made of him by Matthew and Luke, although it has become a dogma in criticism for many, cannot be said to be more than a hypothesis. However disconcerting this may be, it is none the less true. None of the proposed solutions has been approved of by all scholars who are really competent in the matter, because all these solutions, while answering some of the difficulties, leave almost as many unanswered. If then we must be content with hypothesis, we ought at least to prefer the most satisfactory. The analysis of the text seems to agree fairly well with the hypothesis of two sources—Mark and Q. (i. e. Quelle, the non-Marcan document); but a conservative critic will adopt it only in so far as it is not incompatible with such data of tradition concerning the origin of the Gospels as are certain or worthy of respect.

These data may be resumed as follows. (a) The Gospels are really the work of those to whom they have been always attributed, although this attribution may perhaps be explained by a more or less mediate authorship. Thus, the Apostle St. Matthew, having written in Aramaic, did not himself put into Greek the canonical Gospel which has come down to us under his name. However, the fact of his being considered the author of this Gospel necessarily supposes that between the original Aramaic and the Greek text there is, at least, a substantial conformity. The original text of St. Matthew is certainly prior to the ruin of Jerusalem; there are even reasons for dating it earlier than the Epistles of St. Paul and consequently about the year 50. We know nothing definite of the date of its being rendered into Greek. (b) Everything seems to indicate the date of the composition of St. Mark as about the time of St. Peter's death, consequently between 60 and 70. (c) St. Luke tells us expressly that before him "many took in hand to set forth in order" the Gospel. What then was the date of his own work? About the year 70. It is to be remembered that we must not expect from the ancients the precision of our modern chronology. (d) The Johannine writings belong to the end of the first century, from the year 90 to 100 (approximately); except perhaps the Apocalypse, which some modern critics date from about the end of the reign of Nero, A. D. 68 (see GOSPEL AND GOSPELS).

IV. TRANSMISSION OF THE TEXT.—No book of ancient times has come down to us exactly as it left the hands of its author—all have been in some way altered. The material conditions under which a book was spread before the invention of printing (1440), the little care of the copyists, correctors, and glossators for the text, so different from the desire of accuracy exhibited to-day, explain sufficiently the divergences we find between various MSS. of the same work. To these causes may be added, in regard to the Scriptures, exegetical difficulties and dogmatical controversies. To exempt the sacred writings from ordinary conditions a very special providence would have been necessary, and it has not been the will of God to exercise this providence. More than 150,000 different readings have been found in the older witnesses to the text of the New Testament—which in itself is a proof that Scriptures are not the only, nor the principal, means of revelation. In the concrete order of the present economy God had only to prevent any such alteration of the sacred texts as would put the Church in the moral necessity of announcing with certainty as the word of God what in reality was only a human utterance. Let us say, however, from the start, that the substantial tenor of the sacred text has not been altered, notwithstanding the uncertainty which hangs over some more or less long and more or less important historical or dogmatical passages. Moreover—and this is very important—these alterations are not irremediable; we can at least very often, by studying the variants of the texts, eliminate the defective reading and thus re-establish the primitive text. This is the object of textual criticism.

A. *Brief History of the Textual Criticism.*—The ancients were aware of the variant readings in the text and in the versions of the New Testament; Origen, St. Jerome, and St. Augustine particularly insisted on this state of things. In every age and in diverse places efforts were made to remedy the evil; in Africa, in the time of St. Cyprian (250); in the East by means of the works of Origen (200–54); then by those of Lucian at Antioch and Hesychius at Alexandria, in the beginning of the fourth century. Later on (383) St. Jerome revised the Latin version with the aid of what he considered to be the best copies of the Greek text. Between 400 and 450 Rabbula of Edessa did the same thing for the Syriac version. In the thirteenth century the universities, the Dominicans, and the Franciscans undertook to correct the Latin text. In the fifteenth century printing lessened, although it did not completely suppress, the diversity of readings, because it spread the same type of text, viz., that which the Hellenists of the Renaissance got from the Byzantine scholars, who came in numbers to Italy, Germany, and France, after the capture of Constantinople. This text, after having been revised by Erasmus, Robert Estienne, and Théodore de Bèze, finally, in 1633, became the Elzeverian edition, which was to bear the name of the "received text". It remained the *ne varietur* text of the New Testament for Protestants up to the nineteenth century. The British and Foreign Bible Society continued to spread it until 1904. All the official Protestant versions depended on this test of Byzantine origin up to the revision of the Authorized Version of the Anglican Church, which took place in 1881.

The Catholics on their side followed the official edition of the Latin Vulgate (which is in substance the revised version of St. Jerome), published in 1592 by order of Clement VIII, and called on that account the Clementine Bible. Thus it can be said that, during two centuries at least, the New Testament was read in the West in two different forms. Which of the two was the more exact? According as the ancient MSS. of the text were discovered and edited, the critics remarked and noted the differences these MSS. presented, and also the divergences between them and the commonly received Greek text as well as the Latin Vulgate. The work of comparison and criticism that became urgent was begun, and for almost two centuries has been conducted with diligence and method by many scholars, amongst whom the following deserve a special mention: Mill (1707), Bentley (1720), Bengel (1734), Wetstein (1751), Semler (1765), Griesbach (1774), Hug (1809), Scholz (1830), both Catholics, Lachmann (1842), Tregelles (1857), Tischendorf (1869), Westcott and Hort, Abbé Martin (1883), and at present B. Weiss, H. Von Soden, R. C. Gregory.

B. *Resources of Textual Criticism.*—Never was it as easy as it is in our own days to see, consult, and control the most ancient documents concerning the New Testament. Gathered from almost everywhere they are to be found in the libraries of our big cities (Rome, Paris, London, Saint Petersburg, Cambridge, etc.), where they can be visited and consulted by everyone. These documents are the MSS. of the Greek text, the old versions and the works of ecclesiastical or other writers who have cited the New Testament. This collection of documents, daily increasing in number, has been called the *apparatus criticus*. To facilitate the use of the codices of the text and versions they have been classed and denominated by means of letters of the Hebrew, Greek, and Latin alphabets. Von Soden recently introduced another notation, which essentially consists in the distribution of all the MSS. into three groups designated respectively by the three Greek letters δ (i. e. διαθήκη, the MSS. containing the Gospels and something else as well), ε (i. e. εὐαγγέλια, the MSS. containing the Gospels only), α (i. e. ἀπόστολος, the MSS. containing the Acts and the Epistles. In each series the MSS. are numbered according to their age.

(1) *Manuscripts of the Text.*—More than 4000 have been already catalogued and partly studied, only the minority of which contain the whole New Testament. Twenty of these texts are prior to the eighth century, a dozen are of the sixth century, five of the fifth century, and two of the fourth. On account of the number and antiquity of these documents the text of the New Testament is better established than that of our Greek and Latin classics, except Virgil, which, from a critical point of view, is almost in the same conditions. The most celebrated of these manuscripts are: B *Vaticanus*, δ 1, Rome, fourth cent.; *Sinaiticus*, δ 2, Saint Petersburg, fourth cent.; C *Ephræmus rescriptus*, δ 3, Paris, fifth cent.; A *Alexandrinus*, δ 4, London, fifth cent.; D *Cantabrigiensis* (or Codex Bezæ) δ 5, Cambridge, sixth cent.; D 2 *Claromontanus*, α 1026, Paris, sixth cent.; *Laurensis*, δ 6, Mount Athos, eighth–ninth cent.; E *Basilcensis*, ε 55, Bâle, eighth cent. To these copies of the text on parchment a dozen fragments on papyrus, recently found in Egypt, most of which go back to the fourth century, one even to the third century, must be added.

(2) *Ancient Versions.*—Several are derived from original texts prior to the most ancient Greek MSS. These versions are, following the order of their age, Latin, Syriac, Egyptian, Armenian, Ethiopian, Gothic, and Georgian. The first three, especially the Latin and the Syriac, are of the greatest importance. (1) *Latin version.*—Up to about the end of the fourth century, it was diffused in the West (Proconsular Africa, Rome, Northern Italy, and especially at Milan, in Gaul, and in Spain) in slightly different forms. The best known of these is that of St. Augustine called the "Itala", the sources of which go as far back as the second century. In 383 St. Jerome revised the Italic type after the Greek MSS., the best of which did not differ much from the text represented by the Vaticanus and the Sinaiticus. It was this revision, altered here and there by readings from the primitive Latin version and a few other more recent variants, that prevailed in the west from the sixth century under the name of Vulgate. (2) *Syriac Version.*—Three primitive types are represented by the Diatessaron of Tatian (second cent.), the palimpsest of Sinai, called the Lewis codex from the name of the lady who found it (third cent., perhaps from the end of the second), and the Codex of Cureton (third cent.). The Syriac Version of this primitive epoch that still survives contains only the

Gospels. Later, in the fifth century, it was revised after the Greek text. The most widespread of these revisions, which became almost the official version, is called the *Pesittâ* (Peshitto, simple, vulgate); the others are called Philoxenian (sixth cent.), Heraclean (seventh cent.), and Syro-Palestinian (sixth cent.). (3) Egyptian Version.—The best-known type is that called Bohaïric (used in the Delta from Alexandria to Memphis) and also Coptic from the generic name Copt, which is a corruption of the Greek αἴγυπτος Egyptian. It is the version of Lower Egypt and dates from the fifth century. A greater interest is attached to the version of Upper Egypt, called the Sahidic, or Theban, which is a work of the third century, perhaps even of the second. Unfortunately it is only incompletely known as yet.

These ancient versions will be considered precise and firm witnesses of the Greek text of the first three centuries only when we have critical editions of them; for they themselves are represented by copies that differ from one another. The work has been undertaken and is already fairly advanced. The primitive Latin version had been already reconstituted by the Benedictine D. Sabatier ("Bibliorum Sacrorum latinæ versiones antiquæ seu Vetus Italica", Reims, 1743, 3 vols.); the work has been taken up again and completed in the English collection "Old-Latin Biblical Texts" (1883–1911), still in course of publication. The critical edition of the Latin Vulgate published at Oxford by the Anglicans Wordsworth and White, from 1889 to 1905, gives the Gospels and the Acts. In 1907 the Benedictines received from Pius X the commission to prepare a critical edition of the Latin Bible of St. Jerome (Old and New Testament). The "Diatessaron" of Tatian is known to us by the Arabic version edited in 1888 by Mgr. Ciasca, and by the Armenian version of a commentary of St. Ephraem (which is founded on the Syriac of Tatian) translated into Latin, in 1876, by the Mechitarists Auchar and Moesinger. The recent publications of H. Von Soden have contributed to make the work of Tatian better known. Mrs. A. S. Lewis has just published a comparative edition of the Syriac palimpsest of Sinai (1910); this had been already done by F. C. Burkitt for the Cureton codex, in 1904. There exists also a critical edition of the Peshitto by G. H. Gwilliam (1901). As regards the Egyptian versions of the Gospels, the recent edition of G. Horner (1901–1911, 5 vols.) has put them at the disposition of all those who read Coptic and Sahidic. The English translation, that accompanies them, is meant for a wider circle of readers.

(3) *Citations of Ecclesiastical Authors.*—The text of the whole New Testament could be reconstituted by putting together all the citations found in the Fathers. It would be particularly easy for the Gospels and the important Epistles of St. Paul. From a purely critical point of view, the text of the Fathers of the first three centuries is particularly important, expecially Irenæus, Justin, Origen, Clement of Alexandria, Tertullian, Cyprian, and later on Ephraem, Cyril of Alexandria, Chrysostom, Jerome, and Augustine. Here again a preliminary step must be taken by the critic. Before pronouncing that a Father read and quoted the New Testament in this or that way, we must first be sure that the text as in its present form had not been harmonized with the reading commonly received at the time and in the country where the Father's works were edited (in print or in MSS.). The recent editions of Berlin for the Greek Fathers and of Vienna for the Latin Fathers, and especially the monographs on the citations of the New Testament in the Apostolic Fathers (Oxford Society for Historical Theology, 1905), in St. Justin (Bousset, 1891), in Tertullian (Ronsch, 1871), in Clement of Alexandria (Barnard, 1899), in St. Cyprian (von Sodon, 1909), in Origen (Hautsch, 1909), in St. Ephraem (Burkett, 1901), in Marcion (Zahn, 1890), are a valuable help in this work.

C. *Method followed.*—(1) The different readings attested for the same word were first noted, then they were classed according to their causes; involuntary variants: lapsus, homoioteleuton, itacismus, scriptio continua; voluntary variants, harmonizing of the texts, exegesis, dogmatical controversies, liturgical adaptations. This however was only an accumulation of matter for critical discussion. (2) At first, the process employed was that called individual examination. This consists in examining each case by itself, and it nearly always had as result that the reading found in most documents was considered the right one. In a few cases only the greater antiquity of certain readings prevailed over numerical superiority. Yet one witness might be right rather than a hundred others, who often depend on common sources. Even the oldest text we have, if not itself the original, may be corrupt, or derived from an unfaithful reproduction. To avoid as far as possible these occasions of error, critics were not long before giving preference to the quality rather than to the number of the documents. The guarantees of the fidelity of a copy are known by the history of the intermediate ones connecting it with the original, that is by its genealogy. The genealogical process was brought into vogue especially by two great Cambridge scholars, Westcott and Hort. By dividing the texts, versions, and Patristic citations into families, they arrived at the following conclusions:

(a) The documents of the New Testament are grouped in three families that may be called Alexandrian, Syrian, and Western. None of these is entirely free from alterations. (i) The text called Western, best represented by D, is the most altered although it was widely spread in the second and third centuries, not only in the West (primitive Latin Version, St. Irenæus, St. Hippolitus, Tertullian, St. Cyprian), but also in the East (primitive Syriac Version, Tatian, and even Clement of Alexandria). However, we find in it a certain number of original readings which it alone has preserved. (ii) The Alexandrian text is the best, this was the received text in Egypt and, to a certain extent, in Palestine. It is to be found, but adulterated, in C (at least as regards the Gospels). It is more pure in the Bohaïric Version and in St. Cyril of Alexandria. The current Alexandrian text however is not primitive. It appears to be a sub-type derived from an older and better preserved text which we have almost pure in B and N. It is this text that Westcott and Hort call neutral, because it has been kept, not absolutely, but much more than all the others, free from the deforming influences which have systematically created the different types of text. The neutral text which is superior to all the others, although not perfect, is attested by Origen. Before him we have no positive testimony, but historical analogies and especially the data of internal criticism show that it must be primitive. (iii) Between the Western text and the Alexandrian text is the place of the Syrian, which was that used at Antioch in Cappadocia and at Constantinople in the time of St. John Chrysostom. It is the result of a methodical "confluence" of the Western text with that received in Egypt and Palestine towards the middle of the third century. The Syrian text must have been edited between the years 250 and 350. This type has no value for the reconstruction of the original text, as all the readings which are peculiar to it are simply alterations. As regards the Gospels, the Syrian text is found in A and E, F, G, H, K, and also in most of the Peschitto MSS., Armenian Version, and especially in St. John Chrysostom. The "received text" is the modern descendant of this Syrian text.

(b) The Latin Vulgate cannot be classed in any of these groups. It evidently depends on an eclectic text. St. Jerome revised a western text with a neutral text and another not yet determined. The whole was contaminated, before or after him, by the Syrian text. What is certain is that his revision brought the Latin version perceptibly nearer to the neutral text, that is to say to the best. As to the received text which was compiled without any really scientific method, it should be put completely aside. It differs in nearly 8000 places from the text found in the Vaticanus, which is the best text known.

(c) We must not confound a received text with the traditional text. A received text is a determined type of text used in some particular place, but never current in the whole Church. The traditional text is that which has in its favour the constant testimony of the entire Christian tradition. Considering the substance of the text, it can be said that every Church has the traditional text, for no Church was ever deprived of the substance of the Scripture (in as far as it preserved the integrity of the Canon); but, as regards textual criticism of which the object is to recover the *ipsissima verba* of the original, there is no text now existing which can be rightly called "traditional". The original text is still to be established, and that is what the editions called critical have been trying to effect for the last century.

(d) After more than a century's work are there still many doubtful readings? According to Westcott and Hort seven-eighths of the text, that is 7000 verses out of 8000, are to be considered definitely established. Still more, critical discussions can even now solve most of the contested cases, so that no serious doubts exist except concerning about one-sixtieth of the contents of the New Testament. Perhaps even the number of passages of which the authenticity has not yet had a sufficient critical demonstration does not exceed twelve, at least as regards substantial alterations. We must not forget, however, that the Cambridge critics do not include in this calculation certain longer passages considered by them as not authentic, namely the end of St. Mark (xvi, 9-20) and the episode of the adulteress (John, viii, 1-11).

(3) These conclusions of the editors of the Cambridge text have in general been accepted by the majority of scholars. Those who have written since them, for the past thirty years, B. Weiss, II. Von Soden, R. C. Gregory, have indeed proposed different classifications; but in reality they scarcely differ in their conclusions. Only in two points do they differ from Westcott and Hort. These latter have according to them given too much importance to the text of the Vaticanus and not enough to the text called Western. As regards the last-mentioned, recent discoveries have made it better known and show that it is not to be overmuch depreciated.

D. *Results*.—(1) The critical editions of the New Testament resulting from a personal study of the sources, which have appeared during the past fifty years are those of Const. Tischendorf, "Novum Testamentum græce, editio octava critica major" (1869-1872), with the Prolegomena to Tischendorf's eighth edition of C. R. Gregory, 1894; that of S. P. Tregalles, "The Greek New Testament, with the Latin version of Jerome from the cod. Amiatinus" (1857-1872), and an appendix of Dr. Hort (1879); that of B. F. Westcott and F. J. A. Hort, "The New Testament in the original Greek" (1881), with a volume of introduction edited by Hort; that of B. Weiss, "Das neue Testament" (1892-9), and a more recent edition (1902-5). H. Von Soden has published only the valuable introduction to the edition of the text, which is being prepared for the last twelve years, under the title "Die Schriften des neuen Testaments in ihrer ältesten erreichbaren Textgestalt hergestellt auf Grund ihrer Textgeschichte" (1902-10). C. R. Gregory also has announced that he is preparing a new critical edition (cf. Vorschläge für eine kritische Ausgabe des griechischen neuen Testaments, 1911).

(2) From the materials thus collected manuals have been edited. The best known to students are the following: R. F. Weymouth, whose work aims at being the resultant of the critical editions that appeared before 1886. The author usually sides with the majority. O. de Gebhart (1895) follows Tischendorf; E. Nestle (1898) (Greco-Latin) keeps in his text the reading accepted by both Tischendorf and Westcott-Hort (this ordinarily means the accord of B with N). If they do not agree, the editor generally follows Weymouth and Weiss. Since the year 1904 the British and Foreign Bible Society have substituted the text of Nestle for the received text, which it had used from the time of its establishment. Besides these Protestant texts there are three Greco-Latin editions of manuals of Catholic origin: F. Brandscheid (1893); Hetzenauer (1896); E. Bodin, who published an anonymous edition (Paris, 1911). Between the Protestant and Catholic editions there is a double difference. The latter keep in their text the sections of which the authenticity is contested (Mark xvi, 9-20; Luke xxii, 43-44; John v, 4, viii, 1-11; I John v, 7); and also in their choice of variants they pay more attention to the readings authorized by the Latin Vulgate.

V. CONTENTS OF THE NEW TESTAMENT. *History and Doctrine*.—The New Testament is the principal and almost the only source of the early history of Christianity in the first century. All the "Lives of Jesus Christ" have been composed from the Gospels. The history of the Apostles, as narrated by Renan, Farrar, Fouard, Weizsäcker, and Le Camus, is based on the Acts and the Epistles. The "Theologies of the New Testament", of which so many have been written during the nineteenth century, are a proof that we can with canonical texts build up a compact and fairly complete doctrinal system. But what is the worth of these narrations and syntheses? In what measure do they bring us in contact with the actual facts? It is the question of the historical value of the New Testament which to-day preoccupies higher criticism.

A. *History*.—Everybody agrees that the first three Gospels reflect the beliefs regarding Jesus Christ and his work current among Christians during the last quarter of the first century, that is to say at a distance of forty or fifty years from the events. Few ancient historians were in such favourable conditions. The biographers of the Cæsars (Suetonius and Tacitus) were not in a better position to get exact information. All are forced to admit, moreover, that in the Epistles of St. Paul we come into immediate contact with the mind of the most influential propagator of Christianity, and that a quarter of a century after the Ascension. The faith of the Apostle represents the form of Christian thought most victorious and most widespread in the Greco-Roman world. The writings of St. John introduce us to the troubles of the Churches after the fall of the Synagogue and the first encounter of Christianity with the violence of pagan Rome; his Gospel expresses, to say the least, the Christian attitude of that period towards Christ. The Acts inform us, at all events, what was thought in Syria and Palestine towards the year 65 of the foundation of the Church; they lay before our eyes a traveller's diary which allows us to follow St. Paul from day to day during the ten best years of his missions.

Must our knowledge stop here? Do the earliest monuments of Christian literature belong to the class of writings called "memoirs", and reveal only the impressions and the judgments of their authors? Not a single critic (meaning those who are esteemed as such) has yet ventured to underrate thus the historical worth of the New Testament taken as a whole. The ancients did not even raise the question, so evident did it seem to them that these texts narrated faithfully the history of early Christianity. What aroused the distrust of modern critics was the fancied discovery that these writings although sincere were none the less biased. Composed, as was said, by believers and for believers or, at all events, in favour of the Faith, they aim much more at rendering credible the life and teaching of Jesus than at simply relating what He did and preached. And then they say these texts contain irreconcilable contradictions which testify to uncertainty and variety in the tradition taken up by them at different stages of its development.

(1) It is agreed that the authors of the New Testament were sincere. Were they deceived? If so the writing of truthful history should, apparently, be given up altogether. They were near the events: all eye-witnesses or depending immediately on eye-witnesses. In their view the first condition to be allowed to "testify" on Gospel history was to have seen the Lord, especially the risen Lord (Acts, i, 21–22; I Cor., ix, 11; xi, 23; I John, i, 1–4; Luke, i, 1–4). These witnesses guarantee matters easy to observe and at the same time of supreme importance to their readers. The latter must have controlled assertions claiming to impose an obligation of faith and attended with considerable practical consequences; all the more so as this control was easy, since the matters were in question that had taken place in public and not "in a corner", as St. Paul says (Acts, xxvi, 26; cf. ii, 22; iii, 13–14). Besides, what reasonable hope was there to get books accepted which contained an altered form of the tradition familiar from the teaching of the Churches for more than thirty years, and cherished with all the affection that was borne to Jesus Christ in person? In this sentiment we must seek the final reason for the tenacity of ecclesiastical traditions. Finally, these texts control each other mutually. Written in different circumstances, with varying preoccupations, why do they agree in substance? For history only knows one Christ and one Gospel; and this history is based on the New Testament. Objective reality alone accounts for this agreement.

It is true that these same texts present a multitude of differences in details, but the variety and uncertainty to which that may give rise does not weaken the stability of the whole from a historical point of view. Moreover, that this is compatible with the inspiration and inerrancy of the Holy Scriptures, see INSPIRATION OF THE BIBLE. The causes of these apparent contradictions have been long since pointed out: viz., fragmentary narratives of the same events abruptly put side by side; different perspectives of the same object according as one takes a front or a side view; different expressions to mean the same thing; adaptation, not alteration, of the subject-matter according to the circumstances a feature brought into relief; documents or traditions not agreeing on all points, and which nevertheless the sacred writer has related, without claiming to guarantee them in everything or decide the question of their divergence. These are not subtleties or subterfuges invented to excuse as far as possible our Evangelists. Similar observations would be made about profane authors if there was anything to be gained by doing so. Try for example to harmonize Tacitus with himself in "Historiæ", V, iv, and V, ix. But Herodotus, Polybius, Tacitus, Livy did not narrate the history of a God come on earth to make men submit their whole life to His word. It is under the influence of naturalistic prejudice that some people easily, and as it were a priori, are opposed to the testimony of the Biblical authors. Have not recent discoveries come to show that St. Luke is a more exact historian than Flavius Josephus? It is true that the authors of the New Testament were all Christians, but to be truthful must we be indifferent towards the facts we relate? Love does not necessarily make us blind or untruthful, on the contrary it can allow us to penetrate more deeply into the knowledge of our subjects. In any case, hate exposes the historian to a greater danger of partiality; and is it possible to be without love or hate towards Christianity?

(2) These being the conditions, if the New Testament has handed on to us a counterfeit of history, the falsification must have come about at an early date, and be assignable neither to the insincerity nor the incompetence of its authors. It is the early Christian tradition on which they depend that becomes suspected in its vital sources, as if it had been formed under influences of religious instincts, which irrevocably doomed it to be mythical, legendary, or, again, idealistic, as the symbolists put it. What it transmitted to us was not so much the historical figures of Christ (in the modern acceptation of the term) as His prophetic image. The Jesus of the New Testament had become such as He might or ought to have been imagined to be by one who saw in Him the Messias. It is, doubtless, from the saying of Isaias, "Behold a virgin shall conceive", that the belief in the supernatural conception of Jesus springs—a belief which is definitely formulated in the narratives of St. Matthew and St. Luke. Such is the explanation current amongst unbelievers of to-day, and amongst an ever-increasing number of liberal Protestants. It is notoriously that of Harnack.

Avowedly or no, this way of explaining the formation of Gospel tradition has been put forward principally to account for the supernatural element with which the New Testament is permeated: the objectivity of this element is refused recognition for reasons of a philosophical order, anterior to any criticism of the text. The starting-point of this explanation is a merely speculative prejudice. To the objection that the position of Strauss became untenable the day that critics began to admit that the New Testament was a work of the first century, and therefore a witness closely following on the events, Harnack answers that twenty years or even less suffice for the formation of legends. As regards the abstract possibility of the formation of a legend that may be, but it still remains to be proved that it is possible that a legend should be formed, still more, that it should win acceptance, in the same concrete conditions as the Gospel narrative. How is it that the apocrypha never succeeded in forcing their way into the mighty current that bore the canonical writings to all the Churches, and got them accepted? Why were the oldest known to us not composed till at least a century after the events?

Furthermore, if the Gospel narrative is really an exegetical creation based on the Old Testament prophecies, how are we to explain its being what it is? There is no reference in it to texts of which the Messianic nature is patent and accepted by the Jewish schools. It is strange that the "legend" of the Magi come from the East at the summons of a star to adore the infant Jesus should have left aside completely the star of Jacob (Num., xxiv, 17) and the famous passage in Isaias, lx, 6–8. On the other hand, texts are appealed to of which the Messianism is not obvious, and which do not seem to have been commonly interpreted (then, at least) by the Jews in the same way as by the Christians. This is exactly the case with St. Matthew, ii, 15, 18, 23, and perhaps i, 23. The Evangelists represent Jesus as the popular preacher, *par excellence*, the orator of the crowd in town and country; they show Him to us whip in hand, and they put into His mouth words more stinging still addressed to the Pharisees. According to St. John (vii, 28, 37; xii, 44), He "cries out" even in the Temple. Can that trait in his physiognomy be readily explained by Isaias, xlii, 2, who had foretold of the servant of Yahweh: "He shall not cry nor have respect to person, neither shall his voice be heard abroad"? Again,

"The wolf shall dwell with the lamb . . . .and the sucking child shall play on the hole of the asp" (Isaias, xi, 6-8) would have afforded material for a charming idyl, but the Evangelists have left that realism to the apocrypha and to the Millenarians. What passage of the Prophets, or even of the Jewish apocalypse, inspired the first generation of Christians with the fundamental doctrine of the transitory character of the Law; and, above all, with the prediction of the destruction of Jerusalem and its Temple? Once one admits the initial step in this theory, he is logically led to leave nothing standing in the Gospel narrative, not even the crucifixion of Jesus, nor His existence itself. Solomon Reinach actually pretends that the Passion story is merely a commentary on Psalm xxi, while Arthur Drews denies the very existence of Jesus Christ.

Another factor which contributed to the alleged distortion of the Gospel story was the necessity imposed on primitive Christianity of altering, if it were to last, the conception of the Kingdom of God preached by Jesus in person. On His lips, it is said, the Gospel was merely a cry of "*Sauve qui peut*" addressed to the world which He believed to be about to end. Such was also the persuasion of the first Christian generation. But soon it was perceived that they had to do with a world which was to last, and the teaching of the Master had to be adapted to the new condition of things. This adaptation was not achieved without much violence, done, unconsciously, it is true, to historical reality, for the need was felt of deriving from the Gospel all the ecclesiastical institutions of a more recent date. Such is the eschatological explanation propagated particularly by J. Weiss, Schweitzer, Loisy; and favourably received by Pragmatists.

It is true that it was only later that the disciples understood the significance of certain words and acts of the Master. But to try and explain all the Gospel story as the retrospect of the second Christian generation is like trying to balance a pyramid on its apex. Indeed the hypothesis, in its general application, implies a state of mind hard to reconcile with the calmness and sincerity which is readily admitted in the Evangelists and St. Paul. As for the starting-point of the theory, namely, that Christ was the dupe of an illusion about the imminent destruction of the world, it has no foundation in the text, even for one who regards Christ as a mere man, except by distinguishing two kinds of discourses (and that on the strength of the theory itself), those that are traced back to Jesus, and those that have been attributed to Him afterwards. This is what is called a vicious circle. Finally, it is false that the second Christian generation was prepossessed by the idea of tracing, *per fas et nefas*, everything—institutions and doctrines—back to Jesus in person. The first generation itself decided more than once questions of the highest importance by referring not to Jesus but to the Holy Spirit and to the authority of the Apostles. This was especially the case with the Apostolic conference at Jerusalem (Acts, xv), in which it was to be decided in what concrete observances the Gospel was to take the place of the Law. St. Paul distinguishes expressly the doctrines or the institutions that he promulgates in virtue of his Apostolic authority, from the teachings that tradition traced back to Christ (I Cor., vii, 10, 12, 25).

Again it is to be presumed that if Christian tradition had been formed under the alleged influence, and that, with such historical freedom, there would remain less apparent contradictions. The trouble taken by apologists to harmonize the texts of the New Testament is well known. If the appellation "Son of God" points out a new attitude of the Christian conscience towards Jesus Christ, why has it not simply replaced that of "Son of Man"? The survival in the Gospels of this latter expression, close by in the same texts with its equivalent (which alone showed clearly the actual faith of the Church), could only be an encumbrance; nay more, it remained as a telltale indication of the change that came—afterwards. It will be said perhaps that the evolution of popular beliefs, coming about instinctively and little by little, has nothing to do with the exigencies of a rational logic, and therefore has no coherence. Granted, but it must not be forgotten that, on the whole, the literature of the New Testament is a thoughtful, reasoned, and even apologetic work. Our adversaries can all the less deny it this character, as, according to them, the authors of the New Testament are "tendentious", that is to say, inclined more than is right to give a bias to things so as to make them acceptable.

B. *Doctrines.*—They are: (1) specifically Christian; or (2) not specifically Christian.

(1) Christianity being the normal continuation of Judaism, the New Testament must needs inherit from the Old Testament a certain number of religious doctrines concerning God, His worship the original destinies of the world, and especially of men, the moral law, spirits, etc. Although these beliefs are not specifically Christian, the New Testament develops and perfects them. (a) The attributes of God, particularly His spirituality, His immensity, His goodness, and above all His fatherhood are insisted on more fully. (b) The moral law is restored to its primitive perfection in what regards the unity and perpetuity of marriage, respect for God's name, forgiveness of injuries, and in general the duties towards one's neighbours; the guilt of the simple desire of a thing forbidden by the Law is clearly set forth; external works (prayer, almsgiving, fasting, sacrifice) really derive their worth from the dispositions of the heart that accompany them. The Messianic hope is purified from the temporal and material elements with which it had become enveloped. (d) The retributions of the world to come and the resurrection of the body are specified more clearly.

(2) Other doctrines, specifically Christian, are not added on to Judaism to develop, but rather to supersede it. In reality, between the New and Old Testaments there is a direct but not revolutionary succession as a superficial observer might be inclined to believe; just as in living beings, the imperfect state of yesterday must give way before the perfection of to-day although the one has normally prepared the other. If the mystery of the Trinity and the spiritual character of the Messianic Kingdom are ranked among the peculiarly Christian dogmas, it is because the Old Testament was of itself insufficient to establish the doctrine of the New Testament on this subject; and still more because, at the time of Jesus, the opinions current among the Jews went decidedly in the opposite direction.

(a) The Divine life common to the Three Persons (Father, Son and Holy Ghost) in the Unity of one and the same Nature is the mystery of the Trinity, obscurely typified or outlined in the Old Testament. (b) The Messias promised by the Prophets has come in the person of Jesus of Nazareth, who was not only a man powerful in word and work, but the true God Himself, the Word made man, born of a virgin, crucified under Pontius Pilate, but risen from the dead and now exalted to the right hand of His Father. (c) It was by an ignominious death on the Cross, and not by power and glory, that Jesus Christ redeemed the world from sin, death, and the anger of God; He is the Redeemer of all men (Gentiles as well as Jews) and He unites them to Himself all without distinction. (d) The Mosaic Law (rites and political theocracy) having been given only to the Jewish people, and that for a time, must disappear, as the figure before the reality. To these practices powerless in themselves Christ substitutes rites really sanctifying, especially baptism, eucharist, and penance. However the new economy is to such a degree a religion in spirit and truth, that, absolutely speaking, man can be saved, in the absence of all exterior means, by submitting himself fully to God by the faith and love of the Redeemer.

(e) Before Christ's coming, men had been treated by God as slaves or children under age are treated, but with the Gospel begins a law of love and liberty written first of all in the heart; this law does not consist merely in the letter which forbids, commands, or condemns; it is also, and chiefly, an interior grace which disposes the heart to do the will of God. (f) The Kingdom of God preached and established by Jesus Christ, though it exists already visibly in the Church, will not be perfected until the end of the world (of which no one knows the day or the hour), when He will come Himself in power and majesty to render to each one according to his works. In the meantime, the Church assisted by the Holy Spirit, governed by the Apostles and their successors under the authority of Peter, teaches and propagates the Gospel even to the ends of the earth. (g) Love of our neighbour is raised to the height of the love of God, because the Gospel makes us see God and Christ in all men since they are, or ought to be, His mystical members. When necessary, this love must be carried as far as the sacrifice of self. Such is Christ's commandment. (h) Natural morality in the Gospel is raised to a higher sphere by the counsels of perfection (poverty and chastity), which may be summed up as the positive renouncement of the material goods of this life, in so far as they hinder our being completely given up to the service of God. (i) Eternal life, which shall not be fully realized until after the resurrection of the body, consists in the possession of God, seen face to face, and of Jesus Christ.

Such are the fundamental points of Christian dogma, as expressly taught in the New Testament. They are not found collected together in any of the Canonical books, but were written throughout a period extending from the middle of the first century to the beginning of the second; and, consequently, the history of the way in which they were expressed at different times can be reconstructed. These texts never could, and were never meant to, dispense with the oral tradition which preceded them. Without this perpetual commentary they would not always have been understood and frequently would have been misunderstood.

Catholic Works.—JACQUIER, *Hist. des livres du Nouveau Testament* (4 vols., Paris, 1903–8); IDEM, *Le Nouv. Test. dans l'Eglise chrét.* (Paris, 1911); BACUEZ-BRASSAC, *Man. biblique: Nouv. Test.* (2 vols., Paris, 1910–11); BATIFFOL, *L'enseignement de Jésus* (Paris, 1906); IDEM, *Orpheus et l'évangile* (Paris, 1910); HUBY, *Christus* (Paris, 1912), xv; DURAND, *Le texte du Nouv. Test.* in *Etudes* (Paris, Feb.-May, 1911); CHAPMAN, *Notes on the Early Hist. of the Vulgate Gospels* (Oxford, 1908); GIGOT, *Outlines of N. T. Hist.* (New York, 1898); IDEM, *Gen. Introd. to the Holy Scriptures* (New York, 1903).
Protestant Works.—WESTCOTT-HORT, *The New Testament in the original Greek* (2 vols. Cambridge, 1881); BURKITT, *The Gospel Hist. and its Transmission* (Edinburgh, 1904); SANDAY, *Studies in the Synoptic Problem* (Oxford, 1911); MOFFAT, *Introd. to the N. T.* (Edinburgh, 1911); GARDNER, *A Hist. View of the N. T.* (London, 1901); HARNACK, *What is Christianity?* (tr. London, 1901); IDEM, *Luke the Physician* (tr. London, 1906); IDEM, *Sayings of Jesus* (tr. London, 1907); IDEM, *Acts of the Apostles* (tr. London, 1908); SCHWEITZER, *Quest of the Hist. Jesus* (tr. London, 1906); SANDAY, *Life of Christ in the Light of Recent Research* (Oxford, 1907); STANTON, *The Gospels as Hist. Documents* (Cambridge, 1909); PEAKE, *Crit. Introd. to the N. T.* (New York, 1910); GREGORY, *Canon and Text of the N. T.* (New York, 1907).
Jewish.—MONTEFIORE, *Synoptic Gosp.* (London, 1909).

ALFRED DURAND.

Testaments of the Twelve Patriarchs. See APOCRYPHA, subtitle II.

Testem Benevolentiæ, an Apostolic Letter of Leo XIII addressed to Cardinal Gibbons, 22 January, 1899. It opens by explaining its title, remarking that just as His Holiness had given frequent proof of his affection for the people as well as for the Church in the United States, by praising their spirit and their progress, so now the same affection prompts him to point out certain things which should be avoided or corrected, in order to set at rest controversies that were injurious to peace. Referring to the preface of the French translation of the "Life of Isaac Hecker", as the occasion of these controversies, he proposes to examine certain opinions therein advanced on the manner of leading a Christian life. The basis of these opinions is that, to make converts, the Church should adapt herself to our advanced civilization and relax her ancient rigour as regards not only the rule of life but also the deposit of faith, and should pass over or minimize certain points of doctrine, or even give them a meaning which the Church has never held. On this the Vatican Council is clear; faith is not a doctrine for speculation like a philosophical theory, to be relinquished or in any manner suppressed under any specious pretext whatsoever; such a process would alienate Catholics from the Church, instead of bringing converts. In the words of the council the Church must constantly adhere to the same doctrine in the same sense and in the same way; but the rule of Christian life admits of modifications according to diversity of time, place, or national custom, only such changes are not to depend on the will of private individuals but on the judgment of the Church. What makes the new opinions more dangerous is the pretext of those who follow them that in matters of faith and of Christian life each one should be free to follow his own bent in the spirit of the large measure of civil liberty recognized in these days. The difference between the two spheres had already been indicated in the Encyclical on the Constitution of States. The argument now adduced in favour of this new liberty is a preposterous one. When declaring the infallibility of the pope, the Vatican Council did not have in mind a situation in which, this papal prerogative acknowledged, the faithful might have a wider field of thought and action in religious matters; rather the infallibility was declared in order to provide against the special evils of our times, of license which is confounded with liberty, and the habit of thinking, saying, and printing everything regardless of truth. It was not intended to hamper real serious study or research, or to conflict with any well-ascertained truth, but only to use the authority and wisdom of the Church more effectually in protecting men against error.

Next follows a consideration of the consequences that flow from the principles and opinions just rejected. First, it is declared wrong to say that spiritual direction is less needed in our days, on the score that the Holy Ghost is now more bounteous with His gifts than in times past. The history of the Church does not warrant this view. The Holy Ghost is active in His influences and good impulses; but His promptings are not easily discerned or properly followed without external guidance. Divine Providence has so arranged that men should be saved by men, and that men should be led to loftier holiness by the direction of their fellows as in the case of Saul by the help of Ananias. The more perfect the way of life one may enter the more direction is necessary. This has been the invariable view of the Church and of those who have been remarkable for holiness. Secondly, natural virtues must not be extolled above the supernatural. The former, according to the new opinions, are more in accordance with present ways and requirements, and make men more ready and strenuous; as if nature with grace added to it were weaker than when unaided, or as if the habit of acting always with good natural motives could be sustained without grace. Even were the acts of natural virtue all they seem to be in appearance, how can they without grace become solid and enduring, or avail for the supernatural beatitude to which we are destined? Thirdly, it will not do to establish a division between the virtues and regard some as passive, others as active, and advocate the practice of the latter as more suitable for our day. There can be no really passive virtue. All virtue implies power and action, and every virtue is suitable at all times. Christ, meek and humble of heart or obedient unto death, is a model in every age, and the men who have imitated Him in these virtues have been powerful helps to religion and the State. Fourthly, the vows taken in religious orders must not be considered as narrowing the limits of true liberty, or as of little use for human society or for Christian perfection. This view is not in accord with the usage and doctrine of the Church. To assume the obligations of the counsels, in addition to those of the commandments, is not a sign of weak-mindedness, nor unprofitable, nor hurtful, nor injurious to liberty; rather it is a way to the fuller liberty by which Christ has set us free. The history of the Church, particularly in the United States, is a testimony to the alacrity and success with which the religious orders work everywhere, by preaching, teaching, and by good example. Whether in active ministration, or in contemplative seclusion, they all merit well of human society, and their prayer propitiates the majesty of God. And the congregations that do not take vows are not to magnify their manner of life above that of the religious orders. Finally, as for methods of dealing with those who are not Catholics, it is not prudent to neglect any method which has proved useful in the past. Should the proper authority approve of other methods such as, for instance, preaching, not in the church, but in any private or proper place, or by amicable conferences rather than by disputations, let this be done, provided that the men devoted to this task be men of tried knowledge and virtue.

The Letter concludes with a brief exhortation for unity, as against a spirit that would tend towards developing a national Church. The term Americanism is approved as applying to the characteristic qualities which reflect honour on the American people, or to the conditions of their commonwealths, and to the laws and customs prevailing in them; but as applied to the opinions above enumerated it would be repudiated and condemned by the Bishops of America. "If by that name be designated the characteristic qualities which reflect honour on the people of America, just as other nations have what is special to them; or, if it implies the condition of your commonwealths, or the laws and customs prevailing in them, there is no reason why we should deem that it ought to be discarded. But if it is to be used not only to signify, but even to commend the above doctrines, there can be no doubt that our venerable brethren, the bishops of America, would be the first to repudiate and condemn it, as being especially unjust to them and to the entire nation as well. For it raises the suspicion that there are some among you who conceive and desire a Church in America different from that which is in the rest of the world."

This Letter put an end to a bitter controversy which had been agitated for nearly ten years, particularly in the Catholic press. In expressing their adhesion to the Holy See and their unqualified acceptance of the teachings set forth in the Letter, the bishops of the United States made it clear that whatever departures from the same might have occurred in this country they had not been either widespread or systematic as they had been made to appear by the interpretation put upon the "Life of Father Hecker" in the preface to the French translation. (See HECKER, ISAAC THOMAS.)

ELLIOTT, *The Life of Father Hecker* (New York, 1894), Fr. tr. KLEIN (Paris, 1898); MAIGNEN, *Le Père Hecker, est-il un saint?* (Rome and Paris, 1898); DELATTRE, *Un Catholicisme Americain* (Namur, 1898); KLEIN, *Catholicisme Américain* in *Revue Française d'Edinbourg* (Sept.-Oct., 1897); SCHELL, *Die neue Teit und der alte Glaube;* COPPINGER, *La Polémique Française sur la Vie du père Hecker* (Paris, 1898); BARRY, *The French Life of Father Hecker* in *Catholic Times and Catholic Opinion* (Liverpool, 9 Dec., 1898).

CONDÉ B. PALLEN.

Test-Oath, MISSOURI.—In January, 1865, there assembled in St. Louis, Missouri, a "Constitutional Convention" composed of individuals, most of whom were unknown outside of the localities in which they claimed to reside. They had been chosen by a fraction of the voters, as people of voting age were generally in either the Confederate or Federal army, or in the guerrilla companies then abounding, or were fugitives from their homes, in order to save their lives. The "Constitution" made by this convention was put in force on July, 1865, no one being allowed to vote on it unless he first took the test oath it provided. A reign of terror, accompanied by arson, robbery, and murder, in many parts of the state followed. Certain classes of persons, including bishops, priests, or other clergymen "of any religious persuasion, sect or denomination", and teachers in any educational institution, were by the provisions of this Constitution allowed sixty days, after 4 July, 1865, in which "to take, subscribe and file", the oath prescribed by it. Those who failed to file it, and continued to preach, solemnize marriage, or teach, were subject to fine and imprisonment. The terms of the oath, according to Justice Field of the Supreme Court of the United States, required amongst other things, the affiant to deny, not only that he had ever been in armed hostility to the United States, or to the lawful authorities thereof, but that he had ever "by act or word", manifested his adherence to the cause of the enemies of the United States, foreign or domestic, or his desire for their triumph, over the arms of the United States; or his sympathy with those engaged in rebellion, or had ever harboured, or aided, any person engaged in guerrilla warfare against the loyal inhabitants of the United States. About the last of July, 1865, a pastoral letter, in Latin, of which the following is a translation, was sent by the Most Rev. Peter Richard Kenrick, Archbishop of St. Louis, to every priest in his diocese, which was then coextensive with the state.

St. Louis, July 28th, 1865.

Reverend Sir: Since under the new Constitution, a certain oath is to be exacted of Priests, that they may have leave to announce God's word, and officiate at marriage, which oath, they can in no wise take, without a sacrifice of ecclesiastical liberty, I have judged it expedient, to indicate to you my opinion in the matter, that you may have before your eyes, a rule to be followed, in this extraordinary matter. I hope, that the civil power will abstain from exacting such an oath. But, should it happen otherwise, I wish you to inform me of the particular circumstances of your position, that I may be able to give you counsel and assistance. I am, Reverend Sir,
 Your servant in the Lord,
  Peter Richard,
   Archbishop of St. Louis.

The state officials ignored this letter, but their party newspaper organ in St. Louis referred to it, "as important in view of the large number of persons whom the Archbishop of St. Louis in one sense, may be said to represent; and further because of the fact that at least three-fourths of such persons, have, throughout the war, been disloyal men". The opposition press was almost silent.

At that time, Rev. John A. Cummings, a young priest, was in charge of St. Joseph's Church at Louisiana, Pike County, Missouri. He had not taken the oath, and he said Mass and preached as usual, on Sunday, 3 September, 1865. The court having jurisdiction of crimes committed in this county was held at Bowling Green some twelve miles distant, and convened with its accompanying grand jury on Monday, 4 September. Father Cummings was indicted by a grand jury composed of men who had taken the infamous oath, promptly, on the first day of the court, and the charge was, that he acted as a priest and minister of the Catholic religious persuasion without having first taken, subscribed, and filed the oath of loyalty. He was arrested a few days afterwards, and brought into court in the custody of the sheriff on the 8th. When asked to say whether he was guilty or not guilty, he declined to answer, but recited the Apostles' Creed. Hon. R. A. Campbell, subsequently lieutenant-governor of the state, then took charge of his defence at the instance of some of Father Cummings' parishioners, and made the same defense which was afterwards successful in the Supreme Court of the United States. He was tried on the 9th, found guilty, and in default of payment of a fine of $500, committed to jail, and placed in confinement with three persons of the most degraded type, charged with felonies. On 15 September, he gave bond, being directed to do so by Archbishop Kenrick, who caused an appeal to be taken to the Supreme Court of Missouri. That court had been, a few months before, reorganized by military force, and its bench filled with men committed to upholding the oath. Father Cummings' appeal was promptly denied in the following month of October, and then his case was appealed to the Supreme Court of the United States. Pending his appeal, many priests and religious were indicted and arrested; amongst others, the saintly Bishop Hogan, of the diocese of Kansas City, Missouri, yet living at the age of 82 years, then a priest at Chillicothe in Livingston County. He made the oath as odious as possible by accompanying the arresting officer to the court-house, dressed in soutane, surplice, stole, and biretta, carrying in his right hand a crucifix, and in his left a large Bible. He took a change of venue, gave bond, and was finally discharged by the effect of the decision in the Cummings case. In an address to some of his parishioners, referring to his arrest and the oath, he said: "The civil authority has been, ever from the days of Herod, the enemy of Christ. The question, now pending, is not one merely of loyalty or disloyalty, past, present, or prospective. The issue is, whether the Church shall be free or not to exercise her natural and inherent right of calling into, or rejecting from, her ministry whom she pleases; or whether, yielding to the dictation of the civil power, she shall admit those only, who, according to its judgment, are fit for the office."

In Cape Girardeau County, the fanatics did not stop with priests, but indicted eight Sisters of Loretto for teaching. Sisters Augusta and Margaret were arrested by the sheriff, but the others could not be found, and probably fled from their persecutors.

When the case of Father Cummings was heard in the Supreme Court of the United States in March, 1866, there appeared for him, David Dudley Field, Reverdy Johnson, and Montgomery Blair, all three lawyers of national reputation. Notwithstanding the sanctity of the principles involved, the Supreme Court, on 14 January, 1867, by only one majority declared the oath void, and thus relieved the priests and nuns of Missouri from further persecution. The effect of the decision in Father Cummings' case is best summarized by Justice Miller in his dissenting opinion in *ex parte* A. H. Garland (4 Wall 333) where he says of it: "In this case, the Constitution of the State of Missouri, the fundamental law of the people of that state, adopted by their popular vote, declares that no priest of any church shall exercise his ministerial functions, unless he will show, by his own oath, that he has borne a true allegiance to his government. This court now holds this constitutional provision void on the ground that the Federal Constitution forbids it". Father Cummings' health was seriously injured by his brutal treatment, and a few years afterwards he lost his mind, and died a martyr to the cause of civil and religious liberty.

Constitution of Missouri of 1865, Art. II, Sections 3, 6, 7, 9, 14; *Mo. Sup. Ct. Reports*, XXXVI–XLI, *Cummings vs. Missouri*; Vol. 71 U. S. *Sup. Ct. Reports*, LXXI, 277.

WILLIAM T. JOHNSON.

Tetzel, JOHANN, first public antagonist of Luther, b. at Pirna in Meissen, 1465; d. at Leipzig, 11 Aug., 1519. He began his studies at Leipzig during the semester of 1482–83; was promoted to the baccalaureate in 1487, being the sixth in a class of fifty-six. Not long after he entered the Dominican Order, whether at Pirna or Leipzig, cannot be established. Disaffection and friction having arisen in the Leipzig community, he went to Rome in 1497 to secure permission from Joachim Turrianus, the general of the order, to enter another monastery. In spite of a recall of this permission, he seems to have carried his point. A few years later we find him as prior of the monastery at Glogau, which belonged to the Polish province. At the request of the Polish provincial John Advocati, he was appointed inquisitor for Poland by the master-general, Cajetan. At this time he also received permission to take the necessary steps to have himself promoted to the doctorate of theology. His relations with the Leipzig convent must in the meantime have been friendly again, for not only do we find him preaching a number of times in the Dominican church at Leipzig, but after severing his relations with the Polish province he was appointed inquisitor of the Saxon province. The activity of his life and publicity of his office made him a well-known figure. In 1503 he made his first appearance as a preacher of indulgences, when the Teutonic Order of Knights in Livonia obtained permission from Alexander VI to have a jubilee indulgence for three years preached in the ecclesiastical provinces of Magdeburg, Bremen, and Riga. After the lapse of three years Julius II (22 Nov., 1506) granted a new indulgence for three additional years in the provinces of Cologne, Mainz, and Trier. At the end of 1509 he was indulgence commissary at Strasburg, and from here in 1510 he went to Nuremberg, Würzburg, and Bamberg.

From July, 1510, to April, 1516, all traces of him were lost. It was his appearance as an indulgence preacher in 1516, to aid the construction of St. Peter's at Rome (see LUTHER, vol. IX, 441), that thrust him into an undue prominence, invested him with an exaggerated importance, and branded him with an unmerited odium that only the most painstaking critical research is now slowly lifting. It was while preaching at Jüterbog, a small town outside of Saxony, not far from Wittenberg (where the indulgences were not allowed to be preached), that Luther in one of his most violent philippics in 1541 relates "many people of Wittenberg flocked after indulgences to Jüterbog" (Wider Hans Worst in "Sammtl. W.", XXVI, 50–53), and then after much hesitation nailed the ninety-five theses on indulgences on the castle church door at Wittenberg, 31 Oct., 1517. That this preaching of the indulgences was not the primary and immediate cause that precipitated the promulgation of Luther's ninety-five theses may be inferred not only from his subsequent course but also from the fact that the "Annales" of Jüterbog (Hechtius, "Vita Joannis Tezelii", Wittenberg, 1717, 53 sq.) prove that Tetzel preached there as early as 10 April; that Luther in his letter to Archbishop Albrecht (Oct. 31, 1517) admits that he entertained the thought for a long time to preach against indulgence abuses (Enders, "Dr. Martin Luther's Brief wechsel", I, Frankfort, 1884, 115); that Tetzel for several weeks had already been in the district of Brandenburg (Paulus, "Johann Tetzel", Mainz, 1899, 47).

The theses dispute between Luther and Tetzel, is handled so circumstantially in a preceding volume of THE CATHOLIC ENCYCLOPEDIA (IX, 441–442) that we need not repeat it here. The publication of Luther's "Sermon on Indulgences and Grace" was replied to by Tetzel's "Vorlegung", issued in April, 1518 (Lea, in "A History of Auricular Confession and Indulgences", III, 395, erroneously makes it *Vorlesung*), in which the scholastically-trained theologian, though not profound, scents nevertheless with keen penetration, not a mere academic tournament, but a far-reaching and momentous battle of principles, involving the very fundamentals of the Christian religion and the authority of the Church. He lays bare with extraordinary precision the unfortunate consequences that would arise. At the close of his "Vorlegung", Tetzel announces that he would presently publish "a few other principles and positions". These are the second series of theses, fifty in number, with Tetzel as author, and published in May, 1518. In these, indulgences are but lightly touched upon, the burden of the argumentation being shifted to the authority of the Church. Tetzel as yet was only a bachelor of theology. In the course of 1518 he was promoted to the doctorate, whether by the master-general or the University of Frankfort is not known. Luther's agitation having frustrated further efforts to popularize the granted indulgence of eight years, Tetzel, deserted by the public, broken in spirit, wrecked in health, retired to his monastery at Leipzig in 1518. Here in the middle of January, 1519, he had to face the bitter reproaches and unjust incriminations of Carl von Meltitz. It was at this time that Luther magnanimously penned a letter in which he tries to console him by declaring "that the agitation was not that of his [Tetzel's] creation, but that the child had an entirely different father". Tetzel died soon after, received an honourable burial, and was interred before the high altar of the Dominican church at Leipzig.

History presents few characters that have suffered more senseless misrepresentation, even bald caricature, than Tetzel. "Even while he lived stories which contained an element of legend gathered around his name, until at last, in the minds of the uncritical Protestant historians, he became typical indulgence-monger, upon whom any well-worn anecdote might be fathered" (Beard, "Martin Luther", London, 1889, 210). For a critical scholarly study which shows him in a proper perspective, he had to await the researches of our own time, mainly at the hands of Dr. Nicholas Paulus, who is closely followed in this article. In the first place, his teaching regarding the indulgences for the living was correct. The charge that the forgiveness of sins was sold for money regardless of contrition or that absolution for sins to be committed in the future could be purchased is baseless. An indulgence, he writes, can be applied only "to the pains of sin which are confessed and for which there is contrition". "No one", he furthermore adds, "secures an indulgence unless he have true contrition". The confessional letters (*confessionalia*) could of course be obtained for a mere pecuniary consideration without demanding contrition. But such document did not secure an indulgence. It was simply a permit to select a proper confessor, who only after a contrite confession would absolve from sin and reserved cases, and who possessed at the same time facilities to impart the plenary indulgence (Paulus, "Johann Tetzel", 103).

As much cannot be said about his teaching regarding indulgences for the dead. The couplet attributed to him—

> As soon as the gold in the casket rings
> The rescued soul to heaven springs,

like that attributed to Luther,

> Who loves not wine and wife and song
> Remains a fool his life long;

though verbally spurious, can in both instances be in substance unfailingly traced to the writings of their respective authors. By Tetzel they are substantially acknowledged in his Frankfort theses. Here he accepted the mere school opinion of a few obscure writers, which overstepped the contents of papal indulgence Bulls. This opinion found no recognition but actual condemnation at the hands of authoritative writers, and was rejected in explicit terms by Cardinal Cajetan as late as 1517–19. By the teaching he laid himself open to just censure and reproach. To condition a plenary indulgence for the dead on the mere gift of money, without contrition on the part of the giver, was as repugnant to the teaching of the Church, as it violated every principle of elementary justice. "Preachers act in the name of the Church", writes Cardinal Cajetan, "so long as they teach the doctrines of Christ and the Church; but if they teach, guided by their own minds and arbitrariness of will, things of which they are ignorant, they cannot pass as representatives of the Church; it need not be wondered at that they go astray" (Paulus, "Johann Tetzel", 165). It was this deviation from the correct teaching of the Church and the obtrusive and disgraceful injection of the treasury chest, that led to abuses and scandals reprobated by such contemporaries as Cochlæus, Emser, and Duke George (Paulus, op. cit., 117–18). "Grave abuses arose; the attitude of the preachers, the manner of offering and publishing the indulgences aroused many scandals: above all, Tetzel is in no way to be exonerated" (Janssen-Pastor, "Geschichte des deutsch. Volkes", 18th ed., Freiburg, II, 84).

If Tetzel was guilty of unwarranted theological views, if his advocacy of indulgences was culpably imprudent, his moral character, the butt of every senseless burlesque and foul libel, has been vindicated to the extent of leaving it untainted by any grave moral dereliction. These would hardly be worth alluding to, did not some of them have Miltitz as the source. But Miltitz has been so discredited that he no longer carries historical weight. "All efforts", writes Oscar Michael, a Protestant, "to produce Miltitz as a reliable witness will prove futile" (Münch. Allg. Zeit., 18 April, 1901). "The circulated reports of Miltitz about Tetzel deserve in themselves no credence", writes another Protestant author (ibid., 14 March, 1910). The Ratisbon adultery charge, with its penalty of drowning, detailed by Luther, Mathesius, Sleidan and almost every Protestant Reformation historian, has been proved so preposterous, that Brieger (Theodor) claims "it is high time . . . . . that it vanish from all history" (Theol. Literaturzeit., 1900, 84). Dibelius of Dresden says: "Among the faults and shortcomings ascribed to Tetzel by his enemies, that of immorality cannot stand" (Lecture on "Tetzel's Leben u. Lehre" in "Dresdner Journal", 20 March, 1903). "Paulus", in the words of Berger (A.), "has so effectually refuted the notorious adultery anecdote, that no one will ever revive it" (Histor. Vierteljahrschr. f. Gesch., 1902, p. 256). The charge made by Luther in his seventy-fifth thesis, that Tetzel had preached impiously concerning the Blessed Virgin, and repeated in Luther's letter to Archbishop Albrecht (Enders, I, 115) and in most explicit terms in his pamphlet "Wider Hans Worst", was not only promptly and indignantly denied by Tetzel (13 Dec., 1518), declared false by an official resolution of the entire city magistracy of Halle (12 Dec., 1517), where it was claimed the utterance was made, but has now been successfully proved a clumsy fabrication (Paulus, op. cit., 56–61).

The charge of embezzling the indulgence funds is also legendary. The precautions adopted to safeguard the alms were of a character that precluded all chance of misappropriation. The chest to receive the money always had two or three locks, the keys of which were in the custody of different persons, including a representative of the banking-house of Fugger. It could never be opened save in the presence of a notary. The ecclesiastical injunction was that the faithful had to deposit their contributions in person. To give it to the confessor or indulgence subcommissary invalidated the indulgence (Paulus, op. cit., 76–77). The Tetzel indulgence chests exhibited at Jüterbog and other German towns, are counterfeits, according to the Protestant writer Körner (Tetzel's Leben, 73). The latest Catholic biographer of Luther, Grisar, writes: "To ascribe to the unhappy monk the 'cause' of the entire apostasy that set in since 1517 . . . is an untrue legend" ("Luther", Freiburg, 1911, I, 281).

HECHTIUS, *Vita Joannis Tetzelii* (Wittenberg, 1717); VOGEL, *Leben Johann Tetzels* (Leipzig, 1717); GRÖNE, *Tetzel u. Luther* (2nd ed., Soest, 1860); HOFMANN, *Lebensbeschreibung des Ablasspredigers Johann Tetzel* (Leipzig, 1844); KÖRNER, *Tetzel der Ablassprediger* (Frankenburg, 1880); JANSSEN-PASTOR, *Gesch. des deutschen Volkes*, II (Freiburg, 1897), 81–83; GRISAR, *Luther*, I (Freiburg, 1911), 276–88; PAULUS, *Johann Tetzel der Ablassprediger* (Mainz, 1899); the last-named for thoroughness of research and objective character supersedes all that has ever been written on Tetzel, on both the Catholic and Protestant sides.

H. G. GANSS.

Teuchira, a titular see in Libyan Pentapolis. Teuchira, Τεύχειρα, neuter plural, was a city on the coast of Cyrenaica, 200 stadia west of Ptolemais. It was celebrated for its worship of Cybele, in whose honour annual festivals were held. During the reign of the Ptolemies it was called Arsinoë; at a later period it became a Roman colony, and was garrisoned by Justinian. The ruins are called Tokra (vilayet of Benghasi). Two of its bishops are known, Secundus, at the Council of Nicæa in 325, and Zeno, at that of Ephesus in 431 (Le Quien, "Oriens christ.", II, 623). The see is mentioned in Parthey (Notitia episcopatuum, I) about 840.

SMITH, *Dict. of Gr. and Rom. Geogr.*, s. v. *Teuchira*; MÜLLER, notes to Ptolemy, ed. DIDOT, I, 666.

S. PÉTRIDÈS.

Teutonic Order, a medieval military order modelled on the Hospitallers of St. John, which changed its residence as often as the latter. These residences, marking as many stages in its development, are: (1) Accon (Acre), its cradle in Palestine (1190–1309); (2) Marienburg, Prussia, the centre of its temporal domination as a military principality (1309–1525); (3) Mergentheim in Franconia, which inherited its diminished possessions after the loss of Prussia (1525–1805); (4) finally, Vienna in Austria, where the order has gathered the remains of its revenues and survives as a purely hospital order. A Protestant branch likewise subsists in Holland.

(1) There was already a Teutonic hospital for pilgrims from Germany in the Latin Kingdom of Jerusalem, with a church dedicated to the Blessed Virgin, who is still the patroness of the order and after whom the name Mariani is sometimes given to its members. But this establishment, which was under the jurisdiction of the Grand Master of St. John, was broken up at the conquest of Jerusalem by Saladin (1187). During the Third Crusade German pilgrims from Bremen and Lübeck with the Duke of Holstein established a temporary hospital under the besieged walls of Acre; this was a large tent, constructed from the sails of their ships, in which the sick of their country were received (1190). After the capture of Acre this hospital was permanently established in the city with the co-operation of Frederick of Suabia, leader of the German crusade, and at the same time religious knights were attached to it for the defence of pilgrims. The Order of Teutonic Knights was founded and took its place beside the other two orders of Jerusalem, the Hospitallers and the Templars. As early as 1192 they were endowed by Celestine III with the same privileges as the Order of St. John, whose hospital rule they adopted, and as the Order of the Temple, from which they borrowed their military organization. Innocent III in 1205 granted them the use of the white habit with a black cross. The emperors of the House of Suabia heaped favours upon them. Moreover, they took sides with Frederick II even after he had broken with the papacy and in opposition to the other two military orders. During the Fourth Crusade, when the gates of Jerusalem were for the last time opened to Christians, under the command of this emperor, the Teutonic Knights were able to take possession of their first house, St. Mary of the Germans (1229). But it was not for long and before the end of the century they left Palestine, which had again fallen under the yoke of Islam (1291).

(2) A new career was already open to their warlike and religious zeal, in Eastern Europe, against the pagans of Prussia. This coast of the Baltic, difficult of access, had hitherto resisted the efforts of the missionaries, many of whom had there laid down their lives. To avenge these Christians a crusade had been preached; a military order founded with this object, the Sword-bearers (see MILITARY ORDERS, THE), had not been very successful, when a Polish duke, Conrad of Massovia, determined to ask the assistance of the Teutonic Knights, offering them in return the territory of Culm with whatever they could wrest from the infidels. Hermann of Salza, fourth Grand Master of the order, was authorized to make this change by Honorius III and the Emperor Frederick II, who, moreover, raised him to the rank of prince of the empire (1230). The knight Hermann Balk, appointed Provincial of Prussia, with twenty-eight of his brother knights and a whole army of crusaders from Germany began this struggle which lasted twenty-five years and was followed by colonization. Owing to the privileges assured to German colonists, new towns arose on all sides and eventually Germanized a country of which the natives belonged to the Letto-Slavic race. Thenceforth the history of this military principality is identified with that of Prussia (q. v.). In 1309 the fifteenth Grand Master, Sigfried of Feuchtwangen, transferred his residence from Venice, where at that time the knights had their chief house, to the Castle of Marienburg, which they made a formidable fortress.

FIGURE ON THE TOMB OF CONRAD OF THURINGIA, XIII CENTURY, SHOWING THE HABIT OF THE TEUTONIC KNIGHTS

The number of knights never exceeded a thousand, but the whole country was organized in a military manner, and with the constant arrival of new crusaders the order was able to hold its own among its neighbours, especially the inhabitants of Lithuania, who were of the same race as the natives of Prussia and, like them, pagans. In the battle of Rudau (1307) the Lithuanians were driven back, and they were converted only some years later, with their grand duke, Jagellon, who embraced Christianity when he married the heiress of the Kingdom of Poland (1386). With this event, which put an end to paganism in that section of Europe, the Teutonic Knights lost their *raison d'être*. Thenceforth their history consists of incessant conflicts with the kings of Poland. Jagellon inflicted on them the defeat of Tannenberg (1410), which cost them 600 knights and ruined their finances, in order to repair which the order was obliged to have recourse to exactions, which aroused the native nobility and the towns and provided the Poles with an opportunity to interfere against the order. A fresh war cost the order half its territory and the remaining half was only held under the suzerainty of the King of Poland (Treaty of Thorn, 1466). The loss of Marienburg caused the transfer of the Grand Master's residence to Königsberg, which is still the capital of Prussia properly so-called. To maintain itself against the kings of Poland the order had to rely on Germany and to confide the office of Grand Master to German princes. But the second of these, Albert of Brandenburg (1511), abused his position to secularize Prussia, at the same time embracing Lutheranism (1525). He made Prussia an hereditary fief of his house under the suzerainty of the Crown of Poland.

(3) Nevertheless, the dignitaries of the order in the remainder of Germany faithfully preserved its possessions, and having broken with the apostate chose a new Grand Master, Walter of Cronenberg, who fixed his residence at Mergentheim in Franconia (1526). After the loss of Prussia the order still retained in Germany twelve bailiwicks, which they lost one by one. The secession of Utrecht (1580) meant the loss of the bailiwick of that name in the Low Countries. Louis XIV secularized its possessions in France. The Treaty of Lunéville (1801) took away its possessions on the left bank of the Rhine and in 1809 Napoleon abandoned its possessions on the right bank to his allies of the Confederation of the Rhine. The Teutonics retained only the bailiwick in the Tyrol and that in the Austrian States.

(4) Thus the order became purely Austrian, under the supreme authority of the Emperor of Austria, who reserves the dignity of Grand Master for an archduke of his house. Since 1894 it has been held by Archduke Eugene. There are at present 20 professed knights who are bound to celibacy while they enjoy a benefice of the order, and 30 knights of honour who are not bound to this observance, but who must furnish an entrance fee of 1500 florins and an annual contribution of 100 florins. Moreover, their admission exacts a nobility of sixteen quarterings. The revenues of the order are now devoted to religious works; it has charge of 50 parishes, 17 schools, and 9 hospitals, for which object it supports 2 congregations of priests and 4 of sisters. Moreover, it performs ambulance service in time of war; it pays the cost of the ambulance, while lay Marians are engaged as ambulance bearers. Thus, after various vicissitudes the Teutonic Knights are restored to their original character of hospitallers. Besides this Catholic branch in Austria the order has a Protestant branch in the ancient bailiwick of Utrecht, the possessions of which have been preserved for the benefit of the nobility of the country. The members, who are chosen by the chapter of knights, must give proof of four quarterings of nobility and profess the Calvinistic religion, but are dispensed from celibacy. When Napoleon took possession of Holland in 1811 he suppressed the institution, but as early as 1815 the first King of the Low Countries, William I of Orange, re-established it, declaring himself its protector. The present order comprises 10 commanders, *Jonkheeren*, and aspirants (*expectanten*), who pay an entrance fee of 525 florins and have the right to wear in their buttonhole a small cross of the order.

Histoire de l'ordre teutonique par un chevalier de l'ordre (4 vols., Paris, 1784); VOIGT, *Gesch. des deutschen Ritterordens* (Berlin, 1859); KÖHLER, *Ritterzeit*, II (Breslau, 1886); LAVISSE, *Les chevaliers teutoniques en Preusse* in *Revue des Deux Mondes* (Paris, 1879); *Rangliste u. Personnalstatus des deutschen Ritterordens für das Jahr 1909* (Vienna, 1909); *Staatsalmanach der Nederlanden* (The Hague, 1911).

CH. MOELLER.

Tewdrig (THEODORIC), a Welsh saint, son of King Teithfallt of Morganwg or Southern Wales, flourished probably in the sixth century. He was a liberal benefactor of the church of Llandaff. He resigned the government to his son Meurig and devoted himself to religion and contemplation at Tintern in Monmouthshire. When, however, the Saxons under Ceolwulf crossed the Severn and pressed hard upon Meurig, Tewdrig left his solitude and gained a brilliant victory at the head of his old troops, but was killed in the main battle. A church was erected over the grave of the royal martyr; it was called Marthyr Tewdrig and is now Mathern at the junction of the Rivers Wye and Severn. The day of his death is 3 January; the year is uncertain, the dates 610, 577, 527, or even 470 being given.

GODWIN, *De præsulibus Angliæ* (London, 1616), 619; REES, *An Essay on the Welsh Saints* (London, 1836), 183 sq.

KLEMENS LÖFFLER.

Tewkesbury, JOHN. See TUNSTED, SIMON.

Tewkesbury Abbey, Gloucestershire, England, derives its name from Theoc, a hermit of early times, to whose memory a monastery

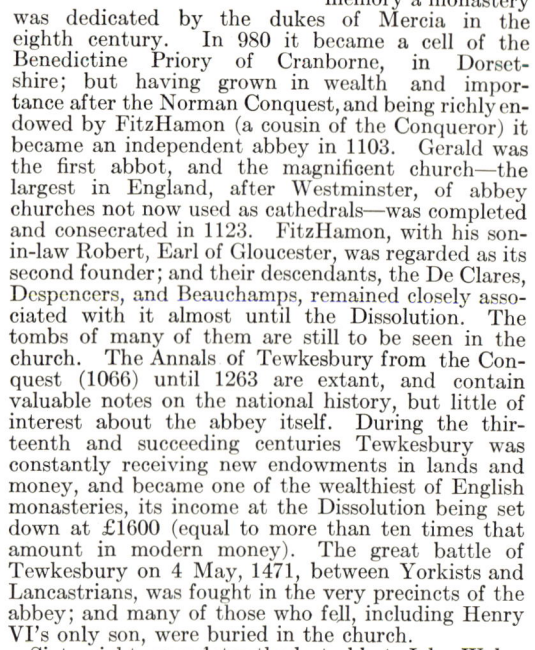

TEWKESBURY ABBEY

was dedicated by the dukes of Mercia in the eighth century. In 980 it became a cell of the Benedictine Priory of Cranborne, in Dorsetshire; but having grown in wealth and importance after the Norman Conquest, and being richly endowed by FitzHamon (a cousin of the Conqueror) it became an independent abbey in 1103. Gerald was the first abbot, and the magnificent church—the largest in England, after Westminster, of abbey churches not now used as cathedrals—was completed and consecrated in 1123. FitzHamon, with his son-in-law Robert, Earl of Gloucester, was regarded as its second founder; and their descendants, the De Clares, Despencers, and Beauchamps, remained closely associated with it almost until the Dissolution. The tombs of many of them are still to be seen in the church. The Annals of Tewkesbury from the Conquest (1066) until 1263 are extant, and contain valuable notes on the national history, but little of interest about the abbey itself. During the thirteenth and succeeding centuries Tewkesbury was constantly receiving new endowments in lands and money, and became one of the wealthiest of English monasteries, its income at the Dissolution being set down at £1600 (equal to more than ten times that amount in modern money). The great battle of Tewkesbury on 4 May, 1471, between Yorkists and Lancastrians, was fought in the very precincts of the abbey; and many of those who fell, including Henry VI's only son, were buried in the church.

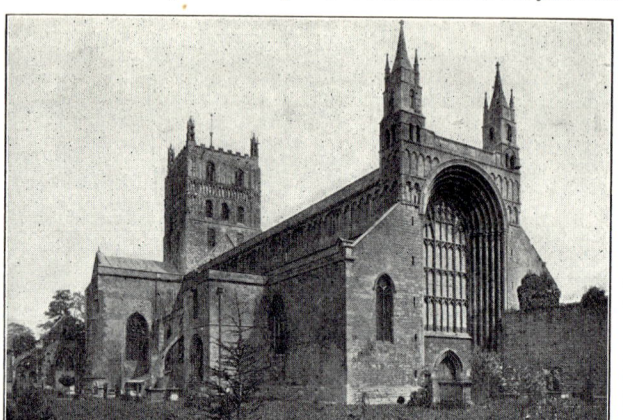

Sixty-eight years later the last abbot, John Wakeman, surrendered the abbey to Henry VIII. Wakeman himself was handsomely pensioned, and in 1541 became first bishop of the newly-erected See of Gloucester. The abbot's house was preserved intact; most of the remaining monastic buildings were destroyed as "superfluous"; but the magnificent church was subsequently sold by the king to the parishioners of Tewkesbury, and was thus saved from destruction. It measures 317 feet long by 122 across the transepts, and the massive central tower is 132 feet high. The pillars and triforium of the nave and the lower part of the choir belong to the original Norman church; the splendid groined roof, replacing the original Norman ceiling, and apsidal choir with chevet of surrounding chapels (closely resembling Westminster Abbey), date from the fourteenth and fifteenth centuries. The choir windows contain some fine old stained glass. The whole church underwent careful restoration under Sir Gilbert Scott (1875–79), and four years later the restoration committee was enabled to repurchase what remained of the monastic buildings.

BENNETT, *Hist. of Tewkesbury* (London, 1830); BLUNT, *Tewkesbury Abbey and its Associations* (London, 1898); *Annales monastici*, ed. LUARD, I (London, 1864), xv–xxvii, 43–180; DUGDALE, *Monast. anglic.*, II (London, 1817), 53–80; TANNER, *Notitia monastica: Glouc.*, (London, 1787), xxxi; GASQUET, *Henry VIII and the English Monasteries* (London, 1889), I, 58, 295, 418; II, 469; *Antiquarian and Topogr. Cabinet*, II (London, 1808), E, E2 (interesting plates).

D. O. HUNTER-BLAIR.

Texas, STATE OF.—The name, Texas, is probably derived from *Tejas*, the name of a friendly tribe of Indians met within the territory by the early Spanish explorers.

GEOGRAPHY AND PHYSICAL CHARACTERISTICS.— The state is bounded on the north by Oklahoma, on the west by New Mexico and Mexico, on the south by Mexico and the Gulf of Mexico, and on the east by the Gulf of Mexico, Louisiana, and Arkansas. It lies between 25° 50' and 36° 45' N. lat. and 93° 30' and 106° 30' W. long. It embraces 265,896 sq. miles, of which 3498 sq. miles are water. Four great natural provinces, running in general direction from south to north, are formed by geological development. The first of these, nearest the coast, is called the Coastal Plain, consisting of Coast Prairies, a Tertiary area, and Black Prairies. Extending back from the Gulf Coast for from thirty to fifty miles, an outcrop of underlying clays gives a flat, almost treeless tract running along the whole length of the coast and known as the Coast Prairie. Different climatic conditions with respect to rainfall vary the products of different parts of this region. The eastern and northern part, where the rainfall reaches from forty to fifty inches annually, are suitable for rice culture, which is localized there; in the central portion along the coast where the rainfall is less, sugar-cane, fruit, and "truck" are extensively cultivated, while in the southwest, with a rainfall of only 20 to 28 inches annually, cotton culture and "cattle raising on the range" are the chief industries. Irrigation, however, in this south-western region makes the cultivation of sugar-cane and sorghum as well as cotton of some profit. Favourable underground conditions make this Coast Prairie the location of important oil-fields. Further to the interior the Coast Prairie is succeeded by Tertiary deposits giving a generally sandy condition to the soil. This Tertiary area also is divided by climatic conditions. The south-western and western part, the "Rio Grande Plain", having a very shallow rainfall, produces only a dwarfed and shrubby natural vegetation and is hence called the "Chaparral Country"; the humid part, however, north and north-east, called the East Texas timber belt, grows both

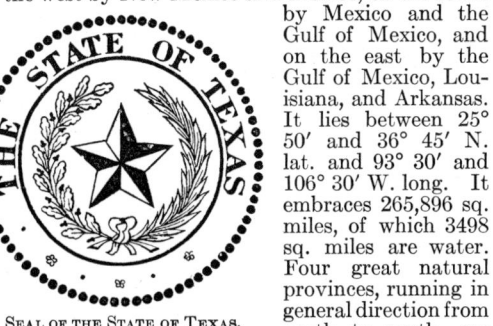

SEAL OF THE STATE OF TEXAS.

the short and long-leaf pine. Lumbering is here the important industry. In the northern part of this region more fertile soil affords the great fruit and "truck" products; cotton and tobacco are also grown. In one part of the west of this Tertiary region cotton is cultivated, and valuable deposits of brick and pottery clays and lignite are extensively worked. Further inland and north of the Colorado River in this Coastal Plain are the Black and Grand Prairies, the most important agricultural region of Texas. Black waxy calcareous clay soil, for the most part underlaid by prolific and widespread water-bearing formations, makes this region the great cotton and corn producing section, while oats, wheat, alfalfa, and sorghum are also extensively grown. Wherever the climate becomes arid cattle raising increases as an industry. The Central Basin is the second great natural province. This region, situated in north-west and central-west Texas, was once covered with cretaceous materials, but now is denuded by the head waters of the Red, Brazos, and Colorado Rivers. Its southern extremity, the "Llano Country", as it is called, has a granite foundation, much quarried, and deposits of hematite and magnetite occur here plentifully. On the eastern side the soils show a carboniferous area, and include sands, loams, black and light-coloured clays, producing, in the heavier soils, cotton, wheat, oats, sorghum, milo-maize, and in the lighter, cotton, maize, fruit, and garden products. The western portion contains notably fertile soils, yielding abundant crops of kafir-corn, milo-maize, cotton, wheat, oats, peaches, and alfalfa. Deposits of salt, clay, and gypsum occur in this area. The third natural province of Texas is the Plateau Province, having three great divisions: the Llano Estacado, Staked or Palisaded Plains, which extend beyond the limits of the state, and the Edward's and Stockton Plateau. The Llano Estacado, a plateau 2500 to 4000 feet in elevation, derives its name from being itself an extensive uplifted *mesa*, surrounded, except on the Edward's Plateau side, by "breaks", cliffs, or walls, which, as palisades, have to be climbed before the plateau is attained. The plateaux are treeless, grass-covered prairies; the soils are fine, sandy loams, and the annual rainfall only from fifteen to twenty inches. Formerly this region was devoted entirely to cattle, but now alfalfa, barley, broom-corn, maize, cotton, wheat, and fruits are being successfully cultivated. The water supply may be made abundant mainly from wells at a depth of 100 to 600 feet. Attempts to utilize these for irrigation on a small scale are now being made. On the Edward's Plateau the upland prairies are mainly given over to cattle, sheep, and goats; in the cañon valleys, however, are alluvial plains in which cotton, corn, milo-maize, wheat, and oats are a success. On the Stockton Plateau the formation resembles that of Edward's, but the rainfall being less, averaging only fifteen inches annually, it is used almost entirely for cattle.

The fourth province is that of the Trans-Pecos Mountains, with elevations ranging from 5000 to 9500 feet. Here the chief wealth is in the minerals, consisting of silver, copper, and lead of good grade and some gold, tin, zinc, and quicksilver. Local conditions have, however, retarded the mining development, and silver and quicksilver are the only ores worked on a commercial basis. The annual rainfall on these mountains is as low as ten to fifteen inches, but irrigation of the valley lands is practised by means of impounded storm-water, and alfalfa and kafir-corn are commonly grown. The chief industry of the section is the care of cattle. Over such an extended area the drainage is naturally diverse. In the east there are numerous small streams flowing south and east into the Gulf of Mexico, in the Trans-Pecos region there are practically no streams at all that reach the sea. In the arid regions the drainage channels flow only for a short time after rainfall. On the west and south-west boundary the Rio Grande runs for 1200 miles. The Pecos River crosses the western portion of the state, from north to south, without a tributary. It has a broad plain where it enters the state, but descends into an inaccessible cañon as it approaches the Rio Grande. The Canadian River crosses the extreme north of the state from west to east merely as a small stream on a wide bed of wet sand. The Red, Brazos, and Colorado rivers and their numerous tributaries rise in the Llano Estacado and flow south and east to the Gulf. Their valleys broaden as they approach the coast and end in very wide alluvial bottoms. Many other rivers originate from artesian springs at the foot of the escarpments, called *Balcones*, at the south of Edward's Plateau. The annual rainfall in Texas varies from 40 to 50 inches in the east—it is 60 at Texarkana—to 10 in the west. Moreover, the evaporation in the west is excessive as compared with that in the east, hence the eastern part of the state is humid, the west arid. The Gulf breezes cool the air in the summer, and bring rains to the north and east in winter and spring. The northern limit of the Mexican rainy season, with its water from the Pacific in summer and autumn, reaches the Trans-Pecos Province and along the Rio Grande. The cold winds called "Northers", blowing from the north-west or from the Rocky Mountains, sweep at times over the whole state. A considerable difference, 20° in average temperature between various places in the state, is observable.

POPULATION AND RESOURCES.—The population of Texas as given by the thirteenth decennial census is 3,896,542. This causes the state to rank fifth in population in the Union. In 1850, when Texas was first enumerated in the United States census, the number of inhabitants was given as 212,592.

Agriculture.—There are in Texas, according to the Federal Census Report (1910), 109,226,000 acres of farm-land, and 27,120,000 acres of this are improved farm-land. It is estimated that the state has 167,865,000 acres of tillable land. At present the number of farms is given by the census (1910) as 416,377, with an average of 262 acres to the farm. Over 1,000,000 acres are now (1911) under irrigation, representing an investment of $17,000,000 for irrigating plants. Several large irrigating enterprises are being inaugurated that will greatly extend the acreage under irrigation in 1912. The total value of farm property in the state (lands, buildings, implements, and machinery) was $1,879,246,000 in 1910. In 1911 the acreage for some staple crops is given officially as follows: cotton, 10,868,000; corn, 9,240,000; wheat, 1,240,957; potatoes 60,000; rice, 275,000; tobacco, 600.

The following figures, culled from the offices of the State and Federal Commissioners of Agriculture, show the values of same Texas crop yields for the year 1910: cotton and cotton seed, $265,955,944; corn, $114,206,000; wheat, $18,404,000; oats, $11,443,000; barley, $135,000; rye, $47,000; rice, $5,942,000; emmet and spelt, $30,000; kafir-corn and milo-maize, $3,900,000; peanuts, $1,430,000; other grasses and seeds, $750,000; potatoes, $3,366,000; sweet-potatoes and yams, $2,600,000; hay and forage, $13,900,000; tobacco, $105,000; sugar-cane, $4,360,000; broom corn, $160,000; truck, $30,000,000: total value, $476,733,944.

The United States Government Bulletin, showing the number of bales of cotton ginned to 20 March, 1912, gives Texas 4,437,876 bales as against 3,172,488 for the entire season in 1910. The table given above names only the principal crops and products. The Texas Haymakers' Association has estimated the value of the Texas hay crop, including local consumption and inter-state shipments—the census does not give such local shipments—at $180,000,000. Altogether, the estimate of Texas farm and garden products, not including livestock, gives a market valuation of $650,000,000 annually. As Texas leads in the production of cotton so also in range cattle, pecans, figs, watermelons, bees, and honey.

Livestock.—The livestock statistics given below are taken from the office of the Commissioner of Agriculture of the State of Texas and from the U. S. Census (1910). The figures give the value of animals in the state:

Milch cows, $33,542,000; other cattle, $109,104,000; horses, $97,199,000; mules, $69,498,000; sheep, $5,154,300; goats, $2,000,000; hogs, $18,702,400; poultry, $4,806,653; total value, $340,006,352; number of colonies of bees 238,107; value, $675,000. The wool product given by the Federal census, 1910, for the then current year is valued at $2,202,342. Conservative estimates of the dairying industry in Texas state 4,000,000 lbs. as the output from the creameries in 1910. Official reports of the Fish and Oyster Commission for the year ending 1 August, 1911, relative to the fish and oyster catch in Texas waters, give: oysters, 110,550 barrels; fish, 3,231,159 lbs. Many thousands of pounds of fish are also taken by fishermen and sportsmen who do not come under the License Act, and whose catch is not recorded. The timber and lumber industry from the last report is valued for its output at $1,150,000.

Minerals.—The following figures are taken from a statement made by the director of the Bureau of Economic Geology and Technology of the University of Texas. They have been compared with figures from the United States Geological Survey for 1909 and show the increase or decrease that may be expected from one year to another though the general sums may differ but comparatively little.

Asphalt, $1,040,845; clay industries, excluding pottery, $2,744,845; coal, $2,397,858; fuller's earth, $8,582; granite, $60,909; iron ore, $34,003; lignite, $763,107; lime, $226,592; limestone, $477,239; mineral waters, $128,549; petroleum, $6,605,755; pottery, $112,604; quicksilver, $151,413; salt, $272,568; sandstone, $40,471; sand and gravel, $517,225; silver, $205,374; stone (crushed), $306,862; tin, $2,586; cement, gypsum, natural gas and sand, lime-brick, estimated $500,000; total, $16,597,367.

Manufactures.—The value of the manufactured products of Texas as shown for 1909 (U. S. Census, 1910) is $227,896,000, the capital invested being $216,876,000 and the raw material used being valued at $178,179,000. The industries given do not include any whose products are less than $500 a year and likewise exclude steam laundries. The total wealth of the state as shown by the report compiled by the State Comptroller's Department for 1911 is valued at $2,515,632,745. The capital and surplus of Texas banks amounts to $113,055,617, while the deposits, 1 June, 1911, amounted to $206,664,471, these figures being taken from the Texas Bank Directory (1911), excluding a number of private banks not rendering a report.

MEANS OF COMMUNICATION.—Texas has 140,000 miles of public highways, 35,000 miles of which are graded and are classed as improved highways. Besides these last many thousand miles are naturally of such good formation as to be passable at all seasons of the year and do not require much expenditure, while many thousand miles more receive attention in places, but are not included in the class "improved highway". The total railroad mileage of the state is 16,192.34 miles. These figures are derived from the report compiled by the comptroller's department of the state. The Port of Galveston is the principal port of Texas and the south-west. The total foreign business of the Galveston customs district for the fiscal year ending 30 June, 1911, was $225,155,912;

of this the exports were in value $220,491,365. The coast-wise commerce of the port is estimated at $200,000,000. Port Arthur, the port next in importance to Galveston, had on 30 June, 1911, foreign exports for the year to the value of $23,981,681; the value of the imports was $173,815. The domestic commerce of this port is said to be in excess of the foreign. The towns of Beaumont and Orange will soon share with Port Arthur in the commercial benefits of deep water, all three being connected by the Sabine Neches Canal, now about to be deepened to 25 feet. Houston also is to share with Galveston by the completion of the ship-channel which connects the city with Galveston Bay. The securing of deep water at Aransas Pass will make Harbor Island another deep-water port. Velasco at the mouth of the Brazos River, and Point Isabel at the mouth of the Rio Grande, will yet be important ports for deep-sea commerce, although only beginnings are now in evidence. The project of the Federal Government to form an inland water-way from the west coast of Florida to the Rio Grande, skirting the Gulf Coast, through the protected bays where possible, has been already begun in one section in Texas, between the Brazos River and Matagorda Bay, through the mainland. Other channels are being maintained in various places while some of the rivers are utilized for navigation and projects for rendering them more navigable are being prosecuted. The value of Texas shipping, steamships, and sailing vessels given by the comptroller's department is $2,299,850.

Educational System.—The public educational system of Texas includes, under State control, the University of Texas at Austin, and its medical department at Galveston; the Agricultural and Mechanical College at College Station; four normal schools situated respectively at Huntsville, San Marcos, Denton, and Canyon; the College of Industrial Arts (for women) at Denton; the normal and industrial school for coloured youths at Prairie View, and the high schools and common schools in the various independent and common school districts of the State. The intention expressed in the Constitution of the Republic of Texas of establishing a university, and the later endowment granted by the Congress to give it effect (1839), never attained fruition. In 1869 the new Constitution of the State again directed the establishment of a university and in accordance with this mandate the Legislature (1871) refunded a prior endowment of $100,000 and added thereto 1,000,000 acres of land. In 1881 the main university was located at Austin and the medical department at Galveston. The main university was opened in 1883 with an enrollment of 221 students. Not until 1891 did the medical department receive its first students. The income of the university from its lands is about $170,000 yearly; the legislative appropriation for 1912 is $268,545, in 1913 it will be $400,000. The institution has 49 professors, 43 instructors, 10 tutors, 10 fellows, 34 student assistants; the present enrolment in the main university at Austin is 1777; in the medical department, Galveston, 285.

The Agricultural and Mechanical College was opened in 1876 with Federal aid. Its present enrolment is 1126. The Legislative appropriation for its maintenance and that of other colleges is shown below.

	1911	1912
Agricultural and Mechanical College	$ 96,750	$368,350
Sam Houston Normal School	33,000	51,000
South-west Texas Normal School	33,000	68,600
North Texas Normal School	33,000	92,000
West Texas Normal School	27,500	59,945
College of Industrial Arts	39,575	121,300
Prairie View Normal and Industrial College	48,600	
	1910–11	1912–13
Institute for the Blind	$161,430	$155,540
Institute for the Deaf and Dumb	106,370	110,520

The school property in independent school districts, including cities and towns, is valued at $16,602,342, and in common school districts at $6,644,998. Enrolled in the scholastic census of the independent districts are 368,303 children, in the common school districts are 623,106; in all 991,409 between the ages of 7 and 17, the scholastic age fixed by law. The total available fund for the current year from all sources for the education of these children is $13,351,121.

MISSION OF SAN FRANCISCO DE ESPADA, EIGHT MILES SOUTH OF SAN ANTONIO, BUILT 1730

Political History.—Early in the sixteenth century Spanish explorers along the Gulf Coast and in the interior of the territory had gained a knowledge of Texas, among the first being Alonzo Alvarez de Pineda. Alvar Nunez, better known as Caveza de Vaco, unmistakably investigated the Gulf shore from Florida to Mexico before 1530, and had even traversed Texas from the coast probably near Galveston to a point in the vicinity of El Paso. There is evidence to show that Coronado, in his memorable northern expedition from Mexico, 1540, travelled near San Elisario and entered the *pueblo* of the Tigvas, afterwards called Ysleta, where a church was built. A church still exists on what is said to be the site of that built under the eye of Coronado. Spain's knowledge of this country, however, had no result towards its occupation before the landing of La Salle in 1685. Robert Cavelier de La Salle, who had sailed down the Mississippi to its mouth in 1682, was returning from France in 1685 prepared to found a colony on the banks of the "Father of Waters" and hold the great river for France; because of an error in his estimate of the latitude of its mouth he passed the mighty stream, and sweeping along the Gulf Coast landed in Matagorda Bay in Texas, which he named the Bay of St. Bernard. In this neighbourhood he attempted to found a colony and called the place Fort St. Louis. From it he made expeditions to discover the position of his confrère de Tonti, who had been left in charge of a colony near the mouth of the Illinois River. On one of these La Salle was slain by one of his own followers, an enemy of his nephew, Duhaut. His faithful friend and companion, Father Anastase Douay, buried in Texas soil the body of this intrepid and enterprising explorer.

The colony was soon scattered and destroyed by sickness and the Indians. When news of the French attempt reached Mexico, Don Alonzo de Leon was sent by the Count of Monclova, Viceroy of Mexico (1686), to scour the country and drive out the French. De Leon visited the ruins of Fort St. Louis and made some little explorations on his way. Later, in 1690 and 1691, some attempts were made to occupy the "New Philippines", as the territory was called. Twenty-three years later (1714), Cadillac, Governor of Louisiana, sent Hucherau St-Denis into Texas territory to establish trade with Mexico. St-Denis, adventurous and enterprising, met with remarkable success and the trail known as the old San Antonio road from Nacogdoches to the Rio Grande was the artery through which commerce flowed between the nations. Other movements of the French evoked counter actions from the Spanish. It may be remarked that the appellation Texas probably arose from La Harpe's dating a letter from the territory of "Las Tekas", although some ascribe the bestowal of the name to de Leon. The French trade enterprises stimulated Spain to inaugurate in 1715 an extended presidio and mission plan to hold the country and to civilize and Christianize the Indians. Many tribes of these inhabited the broad prairies; some, wild and untamable; others, sedentary, gathered in towns or *pueblos*, and possessing a rude kind of civilization. Some of these pueblos are still traceable and the ancient town of the Tejas Indians once occupied the site of the present town of Mound Prairie. The Spanish missionary effort spoken of more particularly in another part of this article covers the period from 1715 to 1794. Other efforts were made by the French to utilize this land, claimed because of La Salle's discovery and settlement, and various struggles between both countries were finally settled by the cession to Spain of Louisiana in 1763. Previous to this in 1728, however, Spanish settlers from the Canary Islands supplemented by others from Mexico were introduced at great expense, and Texas was made a separate province. The civilized population, half or more European, however, grew very slowly (3000 in 1714 and in 1805 only 7000).

From the latter part of the eighteenth century there had been renewed attempts to enter the territory of New Spain from the Louisiana side for the purpose of trade. The policy of Spain had opposed all trade with foreign nations, but some contraband was no doubt connived at or legitimate rights to trade granted from time to time. The expedition of Philip Nolan towards the end of this eighteenth century (1797), to provide horses for the army in Louisiana from the wild herds roaming the prairies of Texas, attracted the attention of United States citizens to Texas. When, after the purchase of Louisiana, the excitement of the consequent dispute between the United States and Spain had been allayed in 1805–06 and Captain Zebulon M. Pike had made his famous expedition and returned his glowing report, and when Burr's attempt at empire came to naught, this interest was still more stimulated. Hence, the efforts of Mexico to gain independence beginning in 1810 gave rise to filibustering movements into Texas, whose eastern boundary was determined on the purchase of Florida in 1819. These were followed by attempts to colonize, so that when in 1821 Mexico had achieved independence Stephen F. Austin and other *empresarios*, as they were named, received grants of lands for colonies and introduced many families from the United States into Texas. Great land privileges were given these early settlers, but some restrictions were also involved in their tenure, one being that they profess the Catholic Faith. In practice, however, this was interpreted in a very nominal way. Real Catholics also entered from the States and from Europe at this period. Catholic colonies even were founded, e. g. Irish settlements near Refugio and San Patricio on the Nueces River (1828 and 1829). President Bustamente's decree of 1830 prohibiting further entry into Texas of colonists from the United States and delay in separating Texas politically from Coahuila—they had been united in 1824—with other sources of discontent, brought about a successful revolution in 1835–36. On 16 March, 1836, a constitution was adopted for the Republic of Texas and signed on the seventeenth. Its independent existence lasted until 1845, when it was annexed to the United States.

The Territory embraced besides its present area what now forms part of New Mexico, of Oklahoma, of Kansas, of Colorado, and even of Wyoming. The portions outside its present borders were sold to the United States in 1850 for $10,000,000. The magnificent public domain possessed by the Texas Government as a republic and retained by her as a State gave ample opportunity for colonizing schemes, and hence grants of land were made to promoters of colonies, some of which were largely Catholic. Henry Castro, consul general for Texas at Paris, obtained large grants from the Republic in 1842, and introduced five hundred families from France a few years later. Castroville on the Medina River was thus founded. Similarly New Braunfels was settled by the Prince de Solms, who brought over German and Alsatian families a year or so earlier. By this liberality in granting lands Texas invited settlers, using also the same means to encourage the building of railroads within her borders. The war with Mexico in 1846 concerning the Texas boundary cemented the union of the young State to her older sister nation, but this union was rudely broken. The Secession movement of 1861 carried Texas away from the Federal Government. Texas furnished not a few distinguished generals and over 90,000 soldiers to the "Lost Cause", and at Brownsville, Brazos Santiago, within its borders was fought the last skirmish of the war between the States, on 13 April, 1865, between a party of Confederates and a detachment from the division of General Banks. After the vicissitudes of Reconstruction the State Constitution at present in force was adopted (1876), and under its provisions and legislation the State has encouraged every form of legitimate enterprise. In population and wealth the State has made rapid strides. The nations of the world have poured, and continue to pour healthy, industrious agriculturists into her territory. Her development has only begun and her untold possibilities promise comfort and wealth to him who fears not toil.

CATHOLIC HISTORY AND PROGRESS.—The history of the Catholic Church in Texas begins practically with the landing of La Salle in February, 1685. With him was a missionary force of seven priests, four Recollects, and three Sulpicians, who ministered to the spiritual wants of the French colony at Fort St. Louis while it lasted. On its destruction by the Indians in 1687 some of these doubtless perished with their flock, the others made their way to the French settlements further north. Don Alonzo de Leon, Governor of Coahuila, was accompanied in his expedition from Monclova to the site of La Salle's settlement in 1689 by Fray Damian Martinez or Marzanet from the Franciscan Apostolic college of Santa Cruz at Queretaro. Two of these colleges were established in Mexico, one at Queretaro in the seventeenth century, the other later (1706), at Zacatecas. From these centres missionary activity, on the representation of Father Damian, began among the Indians of Texas. In 1690 Leon again returned to the ruins of Fort St. Louis. This time Father Damian with four other Franciscans again accompanied him and established the mission of San Francisco de los Tejas in eastern Texas among the Tejas Indians on the Trinity River. On 16 May, 1691, Domingo de Teran, successor of

Leon as Governor of the Province of Coahuila, with the intent of occupying and settling Texas, set out from Monelova with "officers, civil and military", bringing with them soldiers, labourers, and artisans, together with domestic animals and seeds for farming. With this expedition went nine Franciscan fathers, Francisco Hidalgo, Nicolas Recio, Miguel Estelles, Pedro Fortuny, Pedro Garcia, Ildefonso Monge, Jose Saldona, Antonio Miranda, and Juan de Garayuschea. These priests attended the settlements founded during the expedition on the Red River, the Neches, and the Guadalupe, establishing there missions for the Indians and baptizing many thousands of them.

Although, in consequence of the rebellion of the Indians against the military and religious discipline of the presidios and missions (1693), King Philip II of Spain authorized the abandonment of these posts, "until such time as circumstances should offer more hope of success", it is certain that the devoted missionaries did all that was possible to attend to the religious needs of such of their converts as remained faithful. Indeed we know that during the period from 1693 to 1714 the Spanish missionaries, when forced to withdraw, took with them to San Antonio their faithful Indians and were brought back to these missions by Don Domingo Ramon in 1714. In 1703 the Mission San Francisco de Solano was founded on the Rio Grande by Franciscans from Queretaro; afterwards this mission was moved in 1708 or 1709 to the interior of Texas and called San Ildefonso; again in 1710 or later (1713) it was moved back to the Rio Grande and called San José. This mission was moved by Father Antonio Margil de Jesus to San Antonio de Bexar and located at San Pedro Springs under the name of San Antonio de Valero about 1718; in 1732 it was moved to the military plaza in San Antonio, and in 1744 to the site it now occupies, where it was named the "Alamo". About 1783 the mission became a parish church, and on 2 January, 1793, the Bishop of Monterey directed the records to be handed over to the curate of San Antonio de Bexar. The expedition of St. Denis in 1714 led the Duke of Linares, Viceroy of Mexico, to favour a widespread mission movement in Texas, and so from that date the founding of these religious institutions went on with great spirit. Father Margil, referred to above, whose virtues were declared heroic by Pope Gregory XVI, founded the missions of Guadalupe among the Nacogdoches, Dolores among the Aes, and San Miguel among the Adaes Indians, also the mission of Nuestra Senora del Pilar de los Adaes. The founding of other missions in the northern part of the territory is also ascribed to this holy priest. In June, 1719, during the war between Spain and France, the missionaries and their faithful flocks were again forced to retire to San Antonio, but after the cessation of hostilities these missions were re-established and the French settlers in Louisiana, as well as the Indians, profited by them, that of Nuestra Senora del Pilar de los Adaes being only about twenty miles from Natchitoches.

Father Margil was also the founder of other missions; among them one of the most beautiful in the neighbourhood of the city of San Antonio, the Mission San José, founded 1720. Even in decay this mission arouses the most intense interest, its artistic carvings and sculpture exciting wonder. In the same neighbourhood is the mission of La Purissima Concepcion, dating back to 5 March, 1731, when the cornerstone of its church was laid by Father Bargarro and Captain Perez of the San Antonio garrison. At the same time and near the same site were built the missions San Juan Capistrano and San Francisco de la Espada, but the original missions of all these titles were founded in 1716 on the San Marcos River. Other missions were founded in various parts of the territory of Texas up to 1791. Among these may be mentioned Espiritu Santo, founded first in 1722 near Fort St. Louis; La Bahia, also founded in 1722 at Fort St. Louis, and with its neighbour transferred later to Goliad; Rosario (1754), near San Juan, and Refugio, on Mission River, the last foundation of the kind, in 1791. San Saba Mission, on the San Saba River, in what is now Menard County, was founded in 1734 by a company of priests from Santa Fe, among the *Indios Bravos* (Wild Indians) —the Apaches and Comanches, for the humane reason of the priests that it was better to civilize than to kill them. This mission gave great encouragement to the zealous workers until the reopening of the San Saba silver mines, Las Almagras, a project which resulted in the demoralization of the Indians. During a war between the Comanches and Apaches in 1758, the former, seizing the opportunity when the small Spanish garrison was absent, fell upon the mission and destroyed all, both pastors and flock. Even the small guard of soldiers did not escape. Tradition informs us that no one was left to tell the news of the massacre. The remains of the missions still to be seen, in a greater or less degree of preservation or ruin, give ample testimony to the labours of the Franciscans among the Indians, and demonstrate what could have been achieved if the work of God had not been interfered with. Sufficient has been said under CALIFORNIA MISSIONS to indicate the method of the missionaries with the Indians, the nature of their buildings and enclosures, and the routine of their work for the spiritual betterment and civilization of the Indians.

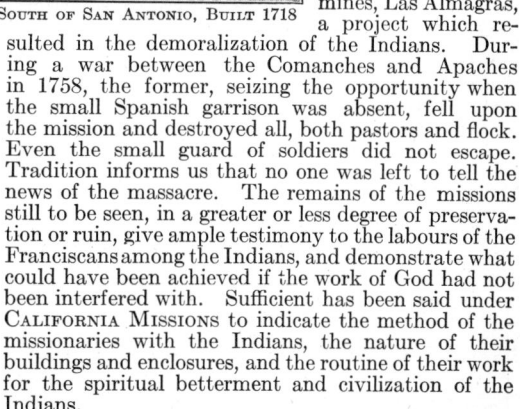

When the movement before referred to, of colonizing the Province of Texas with settlers from Canary Islands and other Spanish dependencies, was put into effect (1728), the first colony was founded in San Antonio and the colonists were fairly well established in 1731. They had built their dwellings around the "Plaza of the Constitution", or present Main Plaza (called by these colonists, however, in memory of the sea-girt home they had left, "Plaza des las Islas"), and given their city the name San Fernando. Content for a short time with a small chapel of their own, which, together with the mission church of San Antonio de Valero in the adjoining and pre-existing settlement, temporarily satisfied their religious needs, they founded in 1744 and dedicated in 1749 the church of San Fernando, part of which is still used as the sanctuary of the cathedral of San Fernando, the cathe-

MISSION OF SAN JOSÉ, FOUR MILES SOUTH OF SAN ANTONIO, BUILT 1718

dral church of the Diocese of San Antonio. The spiritual jurisdiction of the Diocese of Guadalajara extended over Texas until the erection, in Mexico, of the Diocese of Nuevo León, now Monterey, under the title of Linares, in 1777, and Texas formed part of its territory. The Franciscan missions were immediately under a president of missions. One of these at this date (1777), by an Indult of Pope Clement XIV, was empowered to administer confirmation in all parts of Texas. Don Pedro de Nava, commandant-general of Chihuahua, whose jurisdiction included part of Texas, issued a decree in 1794 by which the temporalities of all the missions of his two provinces "were placed in the hands of the civil authorities". It also "directed the division of their lands in severalty among the inhabitants of these establishments". In Texas, however, the process of secularization went on very slowly. In 1813 the missions in some parts of Texas were still flourishing when the Spanish Cortes secularized all the missions in Texas. Not until 1823 did the last of the missions at San Antonio become extinct, when the Government of Mexico put into execution the decree of the Cortes. It was not until 1827 that the last of the mission lands were distributed among the individual *Indios reducidos*, who formerly had possessed them in common. Diocesan priests took the places of the Franciscan friars as they departed, when the population required it. The archives of the missions went with their keepers to Queretaro and Zacatecas. These with the various reports sent from time to time, during the century and a quarter of missionary activity, would be a most interesting field for the historian, while furnishing unbounded pathos for the poet.

The experiment of 1728 proved too expensive to be repeated and so the population of European extraction remained small, as we have seen. Later, however (1805), when the boundary dispute with the United States seemed likely to assume a warlike aspect, besides troops to occupy military posts Spain hurried hundreds of families of settlers to take possession of the country. These were of course provided with priests and in 1805–1806 we find Don Primo Feliciano Marin, Bishop of Nuevo León, making a visitation in the province, setting church affairs in order, and making a circumstantial report of the spiritual condition of the people.

When Capt. Zebulon M. Pike visited Texas on his famous expedition (1805–06), he remarked the holy lives and refinement of the priests he had met, their blessed influence upon their flocks, and the general happiness and morality of the people. The European population of course remained small (7000 in 1806), and the revolutionary period beginning in 1810 and lasting fully a decade lowered the general standard both of morals and religion. After settlements from the United States began to be made (1820), we find in the correspondence of the settlers occasional mention of priests still serving some of the old mission churches and in the towns. In the official documents regulating the laying-out of colonial towns provision is always made for the site of a church and priest's house on one of the public squares, though of course most of these colonists were Protestant. The Irish settlements, largely Catholic, made near Refugio and on the Nueces River, San Patricio, were served by priests, one of whom, Father Henry Doyle (1830), is mentioned by non-Catholic historians. A Father Michael Muldoon was an especial favourite of the old settlers from the United States, non-Catholic as well as Catholic. His visits and those of his colleagues were events in the settlements, his ministrations longed for. He is mentioned as participating in some of the stirring events immediately preceding the Texas Revolution. When not from Mexico these priests were from Kentucky, the Diocese of St. Louis, or that of New Orleans. Even in the accounts of the Texas Revolution there is mention of the intervention of priests between the contending parties, to arrange for the burial of the dead after a battle or otherwise provide for human needs, corporal as well as spiritual. Yet when the Republic of Texas was established (1836) very few priests were in Texas: Father J. M. Odin and Father John Timon, of the Congregation of the Mission, from their seminary at the Barrens, Perry County, Missouri, in the Diocese of St. Louis, had visited in Texas territory previous to its independence, and continued to visit there with other priests of their congregation. In June, 1838, Archbishop Blanc of New Orleans wrote to Bishop Rosati (q. v.) of St. Louis and to Father John Timon, then visitor of the Congregation of the Mission in the United States, declaring that it was the wish of the Holy See that a trustworthy person be sent to examine into the condition of religion in Texas and to report to Rome. The Bishop of New Orleans wished Father Timon to undertake this work. Father Timon accordingly went to Texas, landing at Galveston in December, 1838, accompanied by M. L'Eberia. On the feast of the Holy Innocents the visitor celebrated in Galveston what was probably the first Mass ever said in the city. Many ministrations to Catholics were required of him, both there and in Houston, then the capital of the Republic, whither he went on 31 December, where he preached in the hall of Congress in the presence of many legislators. On his return to Galveston (9 January, 1839) after his tour through the Republic, a committee whom he had appointed to provide ways and means for acquiring a lot whereon to build a church, met him and reported favourably. On his visit through the country he had found the care of religion in anything but a good state, although there were not a few Catholics. He made an official report of his findings to Bishop Blanc, who forwarded it to Rome. Although Father Timon had previously refused to be made Coadjutor Bishop of St. Louis with the right of succession (7 September, 1839), he was prevailed upon to accept the honour of Prefect Apostolic of Texas with power to administer confirmation (12 April, 1840). He immediately dispatched Mgr Odin (q. v.) to Texas as vice-prefect and Father Douterlounge as assistant, and a little later obtained for the vice-prefect the power of conferring the Sacrament of Confirmation. On 5 December, 1840, Father Timon reached Galveston for the second time. He at once urged forward the efforts of the people to build a church there and provide means to support a priest, displaying the same energy at Houston. Pushing on to Austin, now the capital, he presented letters from Cardinal Fransoni of Propaganda, addressed to President Mirabeau G. Lamar, which letters were virtually a recognition by the papal government of the independence of the Republic. The Texas executive, Vice-President David G. Burnet, acting for President Lamar, then absent, was greatly pleased to receive these letters. On 23 December, 1840, the first Mass was celebrated in Austin. Mgr Timon was well received by the legislators as well as by the executive. He preached in the capitol more than once, and in conversation with acting-President Burnet and a few prominent members of Congress created a very favourable estimate of the Catholic Faith. With the diplomatic aid of M. de Saligny, minister from France to the Republic of Texas, Mgr Odin's bill for the restoration of church property was spontaneously endorsed by the legislators to whom it was first read in private, was then introduced to Congress, and passed. Thus by Act of Congress were restored to "the Chief Pastor of the Catholic Church in the Republic of Texas", the churches of San Fernando, the "Alamo" (San Antonio de Valero), La Purissima Concepcion, San José, San Juan Capistrano, San Francisco de la Espada, Goliad, Victoria and Refugio, with their lots, the latter not to exceed fifteen acres. Returning to Galveston Father Timon administered confirmation (18 Jan., 1841), to Margaret De Lacy whom he had converted and baptized on the 15th of the same month. The entry in the "Liber Confirmatorum" of Galveston Diocese certifying to this sacred function may be said, together with the baptismal record beginning 7 December, 1840, to mark the beginning of the history of the Diocese of Galveston (q. v.).

The Prefecture Apostolic of Texas was made a vicariate Apostolic in 1842 by the Bull of Pope Gregory XVI, published 10 July, 1841. Rt. Rev. Jean-Marie Odin, previously vice-prefect Apostolic, was consecrated Bishop of Claudiopolis and made vicar Apostolic. Bishop Odin, too, had previously refused to be made Coadjutor Bishop of Detroit (May, 1841).

In fact Texas was singularly blessed at that time in having labourers who were quickly deemed worthy of important bishoprics. Bishop Timon was visitor of the houses of his order in Texas and throughout the United States until 1847 when he was made Bishop of Buffalo. Rev. John J. Lynch, C.M., one of the companions of Bishop Odin on his coming to Galveston (29 May, 1841), was made president of St. Mary's College, Barrens, Missouri, in 1848; after a service of some years in Texas founded Niagara University (Our Lady of Angels, Niagara Falls, N. Y.) in 1856; and was consecrated Bishop of Æchinas and Coadjutor of Toronto in 1859. In 1860 he succeeded to the See of Toronto and became its first archbishop and Metropolitan of Ontario in 1870. In 1844 the settlement of New Braunfels, Comal County, was founded and in 1845 Castroville. The colonists were mainly Catholic Alsatians. Other Catholic immigrants, Poles, Germans, Bohemians, Italians, and others, have since continually come into the State. The State of Texas, with the exception of El Paso County, which was subject to the Vicariate of Arizona, was erected into a diocese in 1847 with Bishop Odin as bishop. There were then thirteen priests, including the bishop, in this vast territory. Of these at least six were of the Congregation of the Mission. In 1849 three Oblates of Mary Immaculate were brought from Canada by Bishop Odin and two of these were sent to Fort Brown, Brownsville, on the Rio Grande. In spite of the privations and hardships of the Rio Grande Mission, and even their temporary withdrawal, enforced by lack of means, the Oblate Fathers have exercised their zeal in the State of Texas. Schools, colleges, and churches have arisen where they had trodden on the cactus and chaparral, and to-day these devoted missionaries have flourishing institutions in every ecclesiastical division of the great State. The very existence of religion among the Mexicans along the Rio Grande is largely due to the mighty labours of this Congregation.

Religious orders of nuns (1848) and of teaching brothers (1853) began their fruitful labours. All the activities of a fully developed diocese assumed shape under the guiding hand of Bishop Odin and were prosecuted with all possible vigour and success.

On Archbishop Odin's retirement he was succeeded in the See of Galveston in 1862 by Rt. Rev. Claude Marie Dubuis, D.D. In 1872 we find the immense territory of the diocese organized into the four districts of Galveston, San Antonio, Brownsville, and Laredo, a vice-chancellor being provided for each district. This organization prepared the way for the ecclesiastical division (1874) of the State of Texas, El Paso County excepted as before. All east of the Colorado River remained the Diocese of Galveston, while out of the territory west and south of this river and within the limits of the State were erected the Diocese of San Antonio (q. v.), reaching from the Colorado to the Nueces River, and the Vicariate Apostolic of Brownsville (q. v.), now (1912) the Diocese of Corpus Christi, westward to the Rio Grande. A second division of the Diocese of Galveston was made in 1890 at the request of Bishop N. A. Gallagher and the Diocese of Dallas (q. v.) was formed out of its northern and north-western portions. In 1891 El Paso County hitherto belonging to the Vicariate Apostolic of Arizona was attached to the Diocese of Dallas. Thus within the State and embracing all of its territory are the four Dioceses, Galveston, San Antonio, Dallas, and Corpus Christi. The population of the Diocese of Galveston is given (1912) as 70,000: whites, 65,000; blacks, 1200; Mexicans, 3800. St. Mary's University, Galveston, is conducted by the Jesuit fathers. St. Mary's Seminary at La Porte is now being managed by diocesan priests, under the presidency of Very Rev. J. M. Kirwin. The Congregation of the Oblates of Mary Immaculate have taken charge of parish work in Harris County. A Josephite Father also serves a church in the city of Houston, where the Basilians conduct St. Thomas College. Among the Orders of Nuns formerly recorded may be named the Sisters of the Incarnate Word and Blessed Sacrament who have charge of an academy and parochial schools, also in Houston. The Diocese of San Antonio shows no change in the statistics given under the title except that the Redemptorist Order has taken charge of the parish of St. Gerard Majella in the city of San Antonio, where a new church and school are now being erected. Besides the information given under the title, the following facts about the Diocese of Dallas are worthy of record: Rev. Father J. M. Giraud in 1864 erected a church at Jefferson in North Texas. The church at St. Paul's, Collin County, an Irish settlement, was the religious centre of a parish organized in 1870 by Father Thomas Hennessy, the present pastor of the Annunciation, Houston. The population of the Diocese of Dallas (1912) includes about 40,000 Caucasians; 22,000 Mexicans, and 250 negroes. The present bishop of the see is Rt. Rev. Joseph Patrick Lynch, D.D., b. 16 November, 1872, at St. Joseph, Mich. When appointed to the see (after the sudden death of Bishop Dunne at Green Bay, Wis., 5 August, 1910), Bishop Lynch was administrator of the diocese and rector of St. Edward's Church in the city of Dallas. His consecration took place 12 July, 1911. Besides the orders of nuns mentioned in the article on the diocese the following should be noted: the Sisters of the Good Shepherd (Ottawa, Canada), conducting a house in Dallas with

MISSION OF LA PURISIMA CONCEPCION, SAN ANTONIO, BUILT 1731

forty-eight penitents; the Sisters of the Holy Ghost (San Antonio, Texas), devoted to the coloured race. The Josephite Fathers also have charge of the coloured people. The Vincentians conduct the University of Dallas, which has an enrolment of 206 students. The Catholic population shows rapid increase because of the immigration, chiefly from the northern States, of settlers, European in origin, and the work of organizing new parishes goes on quickly here as in the other dioceses. The new Diocese of Corpus Christi is a vacant see at the present writing (1912). It has 15 churches with resident priests and sixty missions with chapels. Thirty-three priests, sixteen secular and seventeen Oblates, serve the Catholic population, which is over 81,917, chiefly Mexicans. Probably between three and four thousand are Caucasians. The Oblates have their novitiate for the province of the south-west, which includes Mexico, in this diocese. A new building for the novitiate is now in course of construction at La Lomita on the Rio Grande near the town of Mission. The Marist Brothers conduct St. Joseph's College for boys at Brownsville. The following orders of nuns are engaged in their various works in the diocese: the Ursuline Sisters, convent and academy and St. Peter's School at Laredo; the Sisters of Mercy, the Mercy Hospital, Laredo, and schools in various towns in the diocese; the Sisters of the Holy Ghost, Academy of Our Lady of Guadalupe, Laredo; the Sisters of Divine Providence, St. Mary's Academy, Beeville; the Sisters of the Incarnate Word, convent and academy, Brownsville; the Sisters of the Incarnate Word and Blessed Sacrament, schools at Corpus Christi, Rio Grande City, and Roma; Sisters of Charity of the Incarnate Word, Spohn Sanitarium, Corpus Christi; the Hermanas del Sagrado Corazón de Jesus conduct an orphanage in Laredo. The number of pupils attending the academies and parochial schools in the diocese is over 1200.

Distinguished Catholics.—In the organization of the Texas revolutionary Government of 1836 the loyalty, patriotism, and talents of Lorenzo de Zavala were deemed of such high order as to qualify him for the office of Vice-President of the Republic. A man of culture, a statesman, and a soldier, de Zavala was above all an ardent Catholic. He was born 3 Oct., 1788, and died 15 Nov., 1836. Colonel Francisco Ruiz, another distinguished Catholic and patriot, exerted himself to achieve Mexican independence, hence endured exile in the United States from 1813 to 1822. After his return to Texas he united with those struggling in their turn for Texan freedom and later independence. He was elected as a delegate to the convention held at Washington on the Brazos, and his name appears among the signers of the Texas Declaration of Independence, 2 March, 1836. As a representative of his native Texas to the Mexican Congress, 1833, as a delegate to the Revolutionary Convention of Texas and signer of the Declaration of Texan Independence, as an upholder of the rights of the Texas Government, member of the Congress of the Republic (1838), and Senator of the first Texas State Legislature (1846), Jose Antonio Navarro commended himself to the gratitude of his fellow-countrymen and edified them by his loyalty to his Catholic Faith. Lieutenant-General Cabell of the Army of the Confederacy, who died in the Diocese of Dallas, 17 February, 1911, was a convert to the Catholic Faith.

Population According to Religious Belief.— In numbers, the Catholic population ranks third of all the religious denominations in the State. The Census Bureau's figures (1906) give Baptist bodies in the State, 401,720 communicants; Disciples of Christ 73,556; Lutherans 27,437; Methodists 317,495; Presbyterians, 62,090; Protestant Episcopalians, 14,346; Catholics, 308,556; Jewish congregation, 11,676. The figures given more recently by Catholic diocesan authorities show 311,667, and doubtless since the increase in the number of children communicants a larger showing may well be claimed. Altogether, of the population of Texas about 25 per cent is Protestant, about 9 per cent Catholic; all other religions, less than 1 per cent, leaving about 65 per cent having no definite religious belief.

Legislation.—The Constitution of Texas in its "Bill of Rights" (Act 1, Sec. 4) prohibits a religious test as a qualification for holding office or a public trust, or the exclusion of any one from office on account of religious sentiments, "provided he acknowledge the existence of a Supreme Being". Sec. 5 prohibits disqualification to give evidence in any court on account of religious opinions or of the want of religious belief, "but all oaths or affirmations shall be administered in the mode most binding upon the conscience". Sec. 6 enunciates the right of freedom of worship, prohibits compulsion to worship or to support or attend places of worship, or preference before the law of any religious society or mode of worship. Sec. 7 prohibits the appropriation of state money or property for the benefit of any sect or religious society, theological or religious seminary. For the proper observance of the Sunday etc. the laws of the State prohibit, under penalty, disturbing public worship also labour on Sunday or compelling to labour thereon. Hunting within one-half mile of a church or schoolhouse, horse-racing, and the sale of goods are also prohibited on Sunday. Cursing, swearing, and indecent language are punishable by statute as breaches of the peace. Under the Constitution each Legislative Chamber determines the rules of its own proceedings. Hence a chaplain for each chamber is usually elected and the sessions are opened with prayer. Christmas Day and all days appointed by the President of the United States or by the governor of the State as fasting or thanksgiving days are the only holidays of a religious nature in addition to Sunday sanctioned by law. Should the occasion ever arise wherein the integrity of the seal of confession should be in question before a Texas court there is little doubt that the constitutional guarantee of religious liberty would protect it, although no statutory provision covers the hypothesis.

The general law of incorporation obtains in the case of churches. Among the first-named purposes enumerated in the statute under which corporations are formed are, the "support of public worship, the support of any benevolent, charitable, educational or missionary undertaking". Any religious society may become a body corporate and any church or association failing to organize under the provisions of the statute cannot sue as a corporation or hold real estate. Schools and churches, cemeteries, public charity, and endowment funds of institutions of learning not used for profit and all buildings used by persons or associations of persons for school purposes are exempt from taxation. Clergymen, all ministers of the Gospel, engaged in the active discharge of their ministerial duties, are exempt from jury service. No compulsory military service is required of any one under Texas law.

Marriage is regarded as a civil contract, a common-law marriage; all licensed or ordained ministers of religion are among the officers in whose presence the marriage ceremony may be legally performed. For a legal marriage there must be in the parties capacity to contract, mutual consent, mutual wills expressed in the prescribed manner. A licence must be obtained from the county clerk of the county. The age at which marriage may be contracted is for males 16, for females 14. The consent of the parents of the parties is necessary for the issuance of a licence by the county clerk until, for males, 21 years of age, for females, 18. Marriage may be annulled because of certain legal impediments. A marriage between one of the Caucasian and one of the negro race is illegal and forbidden under penalty. Marriages are prohibited between persons related in certain degrees of kindred: A man with his mother, his father's sister or half-sister; his mother's sister or half-sister; his daughter, his father's daughter; his mother's daughter; his brother or sister's daughter; the daughter of his half-brother or half-sister; the daughter of his son or daughter; his father's widow; his son's widow; his deceased wife's daughter; or the daughter of his deceased wife's son or daughter. Similarly for a woman with male relatives of equal degree.

The grounds for divorce may practically be classed under four heads: (1) Excesses in, or outrageous treatment from one of the parties, such that living together is insupportable; (2) adultery by one party; (3) Abandonment of one party for three years; (4) conviction of felony and confinement in State prison of one of the parties. The district court has jurisdiction in cases of divorce and petitions are granted only upon full and satisfactory evidence, and upon verdict of a jury, if a jury be demanded; if not, upon judgment of the court, affirming material facts alleged in the petition. Evidence of collusion between the parties being known, or where both parties are equally guilty, no divorce is granted. Divorced persons may legally re-marry. The custody of the children by the marriage is granted by the court to either party as may appear suitable. The court also makes such division of community estate as seems just.

The system of public education is non-sectarian in the meaning of the law. "The reading of the Bible without comment, the recitation of the Lord's Prayer and the singing of songs" of a generally religious character have been judged by the courts as legitimate exercises in the public schools. By a decision, however, of the State department of education the wearing of a distinctively religious garb or religious symbols by the teacher constitutes the school sectarian. No law, however, covers this contingency. No compulsory education law has been passed by the Legislature though some little agitation to that end has been made. The State Constitution and consequent legislation provide for lunatic asylums, an institute for the blind, for the deaf and dumb, for orphans and confederate veterans, and the widows of confederate veterans. For the care of orphans, the aged, and other infirm, private charity also exerts itself, in the lead of which is the Catholic Church.

Besides the regulation of the sale of liquor by licence, penalties more or less severe are attached by statute to selling intoxicating liquor to certain persons: wild Indians, minors, habitual drunkards; to the sale of intoxicants at certain times: Sundays, days of election; or in certain places: places of religious worship, places devoted to educational and literary purposes; to permitting in places, licensed for the sale of liquor, certain stated pastimes and persons: gaming, dancing, minors, etc. Local option may be voted in any county or legal subdivision thereof, and penalties are attached to selling or giving liquor in such prohibited districts. The sale of tobacco to minors is also regulated by law.

The Legislature makes an annual appropriation for a chaplain of the penitentiary, but any clergyman may, with the consent of the superintendent, visit the inmates at seasonable times, and even preach, though then the teaching must be non-sectarian. Any inmate also may have such religious ministrations as he desires. The same rules govern religious ministrations in the house of correction and the reformatory. Bequests for religious purposes are undoubtedly recognized. The provisions of the Constitution with respect to religion would most probably protect bequests for Masses for the repose of the testator's soul especially if the bequests were made to a named person. The law highly favours bequests made for charitable purposes of general philanthropic character. The incorporation of cemetery associations is authorized with but little different conditions from the general law. Severe penalties are attached to the desecration of graves.

YOAKUMS, *History of Texas*, ed. WOOTEN (Dallas, 1898); WINSOR, *Narrative and Critical History of America*, II, IV, VIII; STEVENS, *American Bibliographer;* NAVARRETTE, *Colección*, III; BANCROFT, H. H., *North Mexican States and Texas*, I; IDEM, *Arizona and New Mexico;* WEISE, *Discoveries of America;* CABEZA DE VACA, *Narrative* (Valladolid, 1555), tr. BUCKINGHAM SMITH (Washington, 1851); SHEA, *History of Catholic Missions* (New York, 1855); IDEM, *Hist. Cath. Ch. in U. S.* (New York, 1894); *Records of the Diocese of Galveston* (unpublished); DEUTHER, *Life and Times of the Rt. Rev. John Timon, D. D.* (Buffalo, N. Y., 1870); *Records of the Oblates of Mary Immaculate, Province of The Southwest* (unpublished); *Catholic Directory* (1911); *Bulletins, Thirteenth Census of the United States; Diocesan and other Notes from various authorities in Texas; Texas Almanac* (Galveston - Dallas, 1912); *Southern Messenger* (San Antonio, late files).

JOHN F. O'SHEA.

Thabor, MOUNT.—The name of Mount Thabor, הר תבור, is rendered in the Septuagint as ὄρος Θαβώρ, and in Jeremias and Osee as Ἰταβύριον. It is under this last form (Itabyrion or Atabyrion) that the mount figures in the historical works of the ancients. The Arabs call it Jebel et Tur (mountain of mountains), a name which they give likewise to Mounts Garizim, Sinai, and Olivet. Mount Thabor is distinguished among the mountains of Palestine for its picturesque site, its graceful outline, the remarkable vegetation which covers its sides of calcareous rock, and the splendour of the view from its summit. Nearly isolated on all sides and almost hemispherical in shape it rises in a peak 1650 feet above the Plain of Esdraelon, which it bounds on the north and east, about five miles south-east of Nazareth. It attains a height of 1843 feet above the level of the Mediterranean and of 2540 feet above that of the Lake of Tiberias. Josephus (Bell. Jud., IV, i, 8) gives it a height of thirty stadia, or 18,201 feet, but he doubtless made use of the figure Δ (four stadia or 2427 feet), which the copyist must have replaced by Λ (thirty). The summit forms an oblong plateau about 3000 feet long, from north-west to south-east, by 1000 wide. The eye is immediately attracted to the north-east by the gigantic masses of Great Hermon, then to the Valley of the Jordan, the Lake of Tiberias and the mountain chains of Hauran, Basan, and Galaad. To the south are Naim and Endor at the foot of Jebel Dahy or Mount Moreh (Judges, vii, 1), wrongly identified by Eusebius and St. Jerome with Little Hermon (Ps. xli, 7); somewhat farther off is seen Mount Gelboe. Westward the rich plain of Esdrelon stretches as far as Mount Carmel and innumerable Biblical and historical localities stir thoughts of the past.

THE TOWER, MISSION OF SAN JOSÉ

Mount Thabor is the object of poetical comparisons on the part of the Psalmist (Ps. lxxxviii, 13), the Prophet Jeremias (xlvi, 18), and the Prophet Osee (v, 1). The beautiful mountain also played an important part in history. There the Prophetess Debbora secretly assembled 10,000 Israelites under the command of Barac, who subsequently swept down upon the army of Sisara and put it to flight at the torrent of Cison (Judges, iv, v). Later the Madianites and Amalecites slew there the brothers of Gedeon and other Israelites who had sought refuge there from the enemy (Judges, vi, 2-viii, 18–19). At the division of the Promised Land, Thabor formed the boundary between Issachar and Zabulon (Jos., xix, 22). Within the tribe of Zabulon, but near Dabereth, a city of Issachar, the Book of Josue (xix, 12) mentions the city of Ceseleththabor, in Hebrew Chisloth-Thabor, which means "slope or side of Thabor". I Par. (vi, 77) also speaks of a city of Zabulon called simply Thabor and assigned to the Levites descended from Merari. This is an abbreviated form of the name of the same city, and is probably the same as that which as Dabour figures among the Galilean cities conquered by Rameses II, according to the "Papyrus Anastasii" (I, xxii, 2). Polybius (Hist., V, lxx, 6) relates that in 218 B.C. Antiochus the Great captured by stratagem the city of Atabyrion in Galilee. History makes no further mention of this city, not even in connexion with the bloody battles fought at the foot of Mount Thabor in 53 B. C. between Alexander, the son of Aristobulus, and Gabinius, the lieutenant of Pompey ("Ant. Jud.", XIV, vi, 3; "Bell. Jud.", I, viii, 7). Eusebius alone again refers to it in the words "Dabira . . . a village of the Jews on Mount Thabor" ("Onom.", ed. Klostermann, 78). Dabereth (Jos., xix, 12; xxi, 28) is indisputably the modern village of Dabûriyéh, at the foot of Mount Thabor towards the west.

A ten minutes' ascent northward from Nazareth brings one to the ruins of a Hebrew place called by the natives Khirbet Daboura (ruins of Daboura) and also Abu Amoûd (father of columns). This is the site of the Biblical Ciseleth Thabor, of the Daboura of the Egyptians, and the Atabyrion of the Greeks. It commanded the road of caravans and armies. During the revolt of the Jews against the Romans, Josephus surrounded "the plateau of Thabor" with a wall of circumvallation twenty-six stadia or about two miles in circumference, which task was accomplished in forty days. This formed a kind of entrenched camp where the rebels, pursued from all directions, sought refuge in order to organize their last stand. Vespasian's lieutenant, Placidus, marched against them with a force of 600 horsemen, enticed them into the plain by stratagem, and completely defeated them ("Vita", 37; "Bell. Jud.", II, iv, xx, 6; i, 8). In the fourth century of our era Mount Thabor, which was acknowledged as the scene of Christ's Transfiguration, became a place of pilgrimage and was surmounted by a basilica and several churches and chapels. In 1101 the Benedictine monks rebuilt the sacred edifices and erected a fortified abbey, where they withstood several attacks by the Saracens, but after the battle of Hattin (1187) they had to abandon the mountain. Melek el Adel built there (1210–12) a large and solid fortress which the Crusaders attacked in vain in 1217; in the following year Melek el Adel caused it to be dismantled. The plateau of Mount Thabor is now occupied by Franciscans and Schismatic Greek monks.

ROBINSON, *Biblical Researches in Palestine*, III (Boston, 1841); *Survey of W. Pal. Memoirs*, I (London, 1881); GUÉRIN, *Description de la Palestine: Galilée* (Paris, 1880); MEISTERMANN, *Le mont Thabor* (Paris, 1900).

BARNABAS MEISTERMANN.

Thabraca, a titular see of Numidia near the sea, between the Armua and the Tusca. Thabraca was the last Numidian city in the direction of the Zeugitana and was a Roman colony. It was connected by a road with Simitthu, to which it served as a port for the exportation of its famous marbles. At Thabraca Gildo, the brother of Firmus, committed suicide. Under Genseric it had a monastery for men and one for women. It is now Tabarka, annexed to the civil district of Souk el-Arba, Tunis, and a rather important fishing centre. Confronting it, at a distance of about 365 yards, is the small Island of Tabarca, where the Genoese Lomellini, who had purchased the grant of the coral fishing from the Turks, maintained a garrison from 1540 to 1742. Here may still be seen the ruins of a stronghold, a church, and some Genoese buildings. At Tabarka the ruins consist of a pit used as a church and some fragments of walls which belonged to Christian buildings. There are also two Turkish fortresses, one of which has been repaired. The city contains several Christian cemeteries, many of the tombs having covers adorned with curious mosaics. An inscription (C. I. L., VIII, 173–82) mentions the cult of the martyr Anastasia and her companions. The bishops of Thabraca, who met with those of the proconsulate, were: Victoricus, at the Council of Carthage (256); Rusticianus, at the Conference of Carthage in 411, where his competitor was the Donatist Charentius, and signer in 416 of the letter from the council of Proconsular Africa to Pope Innocent; Clarissimus, who in 646 signed the letter from the same Council to Patriarch Paul of Constantinople against the Monothelites.

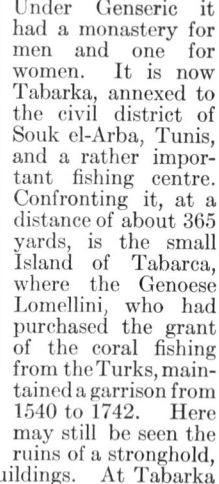

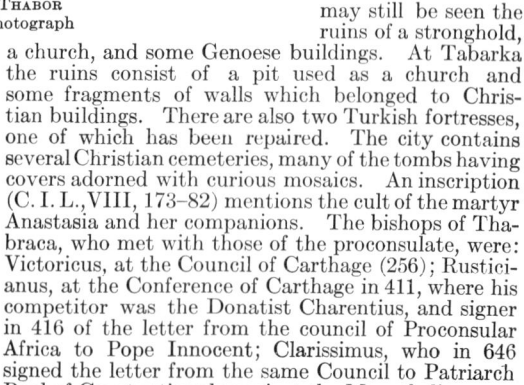

SMITH, *Dict. Greek and Roman Geog.*, s. v.; TOULOTTE, *Géographie de l'Afrique chrétienne: Numidie* (Paris, 1894), 277–80; DIEHL, *L'Afrique byzantine* (Paris, 1896), passim.

S. PÉTRIDÈS.

Thacia Montana, a titular see in Africa Proconsularis, suffragan of Carthage. An inscription discovered in the ruins known as Henshir Bedji, among them a church, near Bordj Messaoudi, seems to indicate that this was the site of the *municipium* of Thacia, to which Wady Tasaa, or Tessa, also owes its name. It was located on the highway between Carthage and Theveste, midway between Musti (Mest) and Drusiliana (Khanguet Kdim), Tunisia. It is mentioned by Ptolemy (IV, 3), the "Tabula Peutinger.", and the "Geogr. Ravennat." (151); it was fortified during the Byzantine period, and at the end of 545 the Byzantine general, John, was defeated and slain there. On the other hand, at the present Eufida, 6¼ miles west of Botria (Henshir Batria), at the ruins called Henshir Zaktoun, an inscription has been found proving the existence at that place of another *municipium* called Thaca, also fortified during the Byzantine period. Mgr Toulotte ("Geog. de l'Afrique Chrétienne Proconsulaire", Paris, 1892, 258–60) assigns to the first locality two bishops, the Donatist Cresconius, present at the Council of Cabarsussi in 393, and Victor, who in 646 signed the letter against the Monothelites from the Council of Proconsular Africa to the Patriarch Paul of Constantinople; to the second locality he assigns Rufinus, present at the Council of Carthage in 525, and Probus who in 646 signed the letter to the Patriarch Paul. The two last-named were entitled bishops of "Tacia Montana". It may be questioned whether there were really bishops of Thaca, or if there was not near Thacia a place of the same name to which was added a distinctive epithet. The official list of titular sees of the Roman Curia mentions only Thacia Montana and identifies it with Bordj Messaoudi.

MÜLLER, Notes à Ptolémée, ed. DIDOT, I, 651; DIEHL, L'Afrique byzantine (Paris, 1896), passim.

S. PÉTRIDÈS.

Thaddeus, SAINT. See JUDE, EPISTLE OF SAINT.

Thænæ, a titular see in Africa Byzacena. It is mentioned in numerous ancient geographical documents and was a maritime city of Byzacium in Africa Propria, situated at the mouth of a river (now Wady Tina) which emptied into the Syrtis Minor. Its ruins (Henshir Tina) are somewhat north of Ounca, formerly Junca, Tunis. The city was crowned by a hill surmounted by an acropolis, its walls attained a length of about two Roman miles and it had a large cemetery. The name Thænæ has numerous variations in Greek and Latin writers, but is borne out by epigraphy. The Punic coins of the city show that its native name was Tainat. Under Hadrian or Antoninus it became a colony which was called "Colonia Ælia Augusta Mercurialis Thænitana". Six of its bishops are known, Eucratius at the Council of Carthage (256); Latonius, at the conference of Carthage (411), where he had as rival the Donatist Securus, and at a Council of Thelepte; Peregrinus, a former deacon of St. Augustine; Paschasius, exiled by Huneric in 484; Pontianus, present at the Council of Junca (525); Felix, who in 641 signed the letter from the provincial council to the emperor against the Monothelites. A council was held at Thænæ at the beginning of the fourth century, three of its canons being extant (Mansi, "Amplissima Coll. conciliorum", IV, 440).

SMITH, Dict. Greek and Rom. Geog., s. v. Thenæ; GUÉRIN, Voyage archéologique dans la régence de Tunis (Paris, 1862), I, 178; MÜLLER, notes to Ptolemy, ed. DIDOT, I, 624; TOULOTTE, Géographie de l'Afrique chrétienne: Byzacène et tripolitaine (Montreuil, 1894), 196–99.

S. PÉTRIDÈS.

Thagaste (TAGASTE), a titular see in Numidia, was a rather important municipality. It is mentioned by Pliny (V, iv, 4) and the "Itinerar. Antonini" (44), but nothing is known of its history. It is famous as having been the birthplace of St. Augustine, who was born there in 354 of the pagan Patricius and St. Monica. St. Augustine speaks of a monastery of Thagaste where he lived with Severus his compatriot and friend, later Bishop of Milevis. Only three bishops of Thagaste are known: St. Firmus (end of third century), mentioned in the Roman Martyrology on 31 July; St. Alypius (q. v.), b. at Thagaste, the friend of Augustine, whose feast is 15 August; and Januarius, sent by Huneric into exile (484), where he died for the Faith. The See of Thagaste still existed about 600. At the time of the French occupation the country was under the dominion of the Arabized Berber tribe of the Hanensha, whose territory bordered on the modern Tunisia. Thagaste is now Souk Ahras, capital of a commune of 7500 inhabitants of whom 4000 are Europeans, and of a mixed community of 42,600 inhabitants, Department of Constantine, Algeria. Souk-Ahras, its modern representative, is built on a small peaked plateau, and is well served by railways. It is a very important agricultural centre, its industries consisting of vineyards, cattle-breeding, vast forests, and mining. Ruins of a basilica and various Christian monuments have been found.

TOULOTTE, Géographie de l'Afrique chrétienne. Numidie (Paris, 1894), 281–85; RENIER in Comptes rendus de l'académie des inscriptiones et belles-lettres (1857–58), 82.

S. PÉTRIDÈS.

Thagora (Tagora), titular see in Numidia, mentioned by the "Tabula Peutingeriana", which calls it Thacora, and by the "Itinerarium Antoninum"; Justinian fortified it. It is now the village of Taoura, near Ain Guettar, about thirteen miles south-east of Souk Ahras (ancient Thagaste), Department of Constantine, Algeria. It has ruins of baths, a church, and the fortress of Justinian, and a number of inscriptions have been discovered. Thagura was the birthplace of St. Crispin, martyred at Theveste (now Tebessa) under Diocletian, and whose feast is observed on 5 December. It was also the scene of the martyrdoms of Sts. Julius and Potamia and ten other martyrs who are likewise commemorated in the Roman Martyrology on the same day. The first two figure in the Hieronymian Martyrology and the Calendar of Carthage. Three bishops of Thagura are known: Xanthippus in 401, mentioned in a letter of St. Augustine's; Restitutus, present in 411 at the conference of Carthage; Timotheus, exiled by Huneric in 484.

TOULOTTE, Géographie de l'Afrique chrétienne: Numidie (Paris, 1894), 285–87; DIEHL, L'Afrique byzantine (Paris, 1896), 605.

S. PÉTRIDÈS.

Thais (THAISIS, OR THAISIA), SAINT, a penitent in Egypt in the fourth century. In the Greek menology her name occurs on 8 Oct., it is found also in the martyrologies of Maurolychus and Greven, but not in the Roman. Two lives are extant, one, originally in Greek, perhaps of the fifth century, the other, in verse, by Marbod, Bishop of Rennes, who died in 1123 ("Acta SS.", IV, Oct., 223; "Bibl. hag. lat.", II, 1161). The saint is represented burning her treasures and ornaments, or praying in a cell and displaying a scroll with the words: "Thou who didst create me have mercy on me". According to the legend Thais was a public sinner in Egypt who was converted by St. Paphnutius, brought to a convent and enclosed in a cell. After three years of penance she was released and placed among the nuns, but lived only fourteen days more. The name of the hermit is given also as Bessarion and Serapion the Sindonite. Delahaye says (Anal. boll., XXIV, 400), "If the legend is historical the hermit must have been Paphnutius".

BUTLER, Lives of the Saints: 8 October; DUNBAR, Dict. of Saintly Women (London, 1904); Anal. boll., XI, 291, 298; NAU, Hist. de Thaïs in Annales du musée Guimet, XXX (1903), 51; BATTIFOL, La légende de Thaïs in Bull. de litt. eccl. (Toulouse, 1903), 207.

FRANCIS MERSHMAN.

Thalberg, SIGISMOND, musical composer and pianist, b. at Geneva, 1812; d. at Posilipo, Italy, 27 April, 1871. The precise date of his birth is a matter of dispute. He was a natural son of Prince Moritz Dietrichstein, and at an early age was brought by him to Vienna. While yet a boy, at the Polytechnic Institute of the Austrian capital, Thalberg formed a friendship with the young Duc de Reichstadt (popularly known as L'Aiglon), who so fired his imagination with the vision of military glory that he was upon the point of entering that career. From this step he was saved by the early discovery of his musical genius through Mittag, the Viennese bassoonist. Devoting himself in good earnest to music, of which he had acquired some knowledge from Mittag, he studied theory under Sechter and pianoforte technic under Hummel. At the age of fourteen he had already made his first public appearance as a pianist in Prince Metternich's salon. Four years later (1830) he began touring Europe, was received with enthusiasm by the virtuosi of the day, and was eventually (1834) appointed court chamber-musician by the emperor. During the next quarter of a century, a period in which the development of the pianoforte made enormous advances, Thalberg's fame was unrivalled save for his great contemporary, Franz Liszt. His concerts and recitals drew crowds, not only in all the capitals of Europe, including London, but also in Brazil and in the United States (1857). The world of musical criticism was for a time divided between the two parties of Thalberg's admirers and those of Liszt. To Liszt, nevertheless, is due perhaps the most decisive encomium of Thalberg as a pianist: "Thalberg is the only artist who can play the violin on the piano". In 1843 he married the widow of Boucher, the painter, a daughter of the famous operatic basso, Lablache.

Thalberg's chief contribution to the advancement of musical art seems to have been as an exponent of possibilities in pianoforte technic which had been unsuspected before his time. He not only possessed the mastery of touch in a transcendent degree and excelled in *sostenuto* playing by the use of the pedal, but actually discovered a method of making two hands produce the triple effect of melody, accompaniment, and bass on one keyboard—a resource exploited by many composers after him. His compositions, some 100 in number, include two operas, "Florinda" and "Christina di Suezia", both important only as demonstrating his unfitness for this field of art. He composed successfully only for the instrument of which he was an unquestioned master, his best-known works being the fantasias on operatic and other popular melodies.

Hume, in *Dict. of Music and Musicians* (London, 1903–11); *Thalberg and Vieux-temps Grand Concert Book* (pamphlet preserved in the British Museum, London).

E. MACPHERSON.

Thalhofer, VALENTIN, German theologian, b. at Unterroth, near Ulm, 21 January, 1825; d. at the same place, 17 September, 1891. He took his gymnasial studies and philosophy at Dillingen, then from 1845 studied theology at the University of Munich. In 1848 he received the degree of Doctor of Theology and was ordained priest. After this he was prefect at the seminary for priests at Dillingen (1850–63), professor of exegesis at the lyceum of Dillingen (1863–1876), director of the seminary for priests, the Georgianum, at Munich, and professor of pastoral theology at the University of Munich. In 1877 he was made cathedral dean and professor of liturgy at Eichstätt, and in 1899 became the cathedral provost there. He was an able and highly respected teacher, a man of noble character, a zealous confessor, pulpit orator, and catechist, and was a fruitful writer, thorough and intellectual in his work. His labours at the Georgianum, for which he was highly praised, greatly benefited the institution. His first publication was a prize essay at Munich on the bloodless sacrifice of the Mosaic worship (1848). In 1855 he wrote in the report of the Dillingen lyceum for that year, a dissertation on the doctrine of sacrifice contained in the Epistle to the Hebrews. In the same year he began a successful opposition to the pseudo-mysticism and Irvingism which were spreading in Swabia at that time. His chief work in this direction was the "Beiträge zur Geschichte des Aftermysticismus und insbesondere des Irvingianismus im Bistum Augsburg" (1857). His excellent commentary on the Psalms was very popular (first published in 1857; 7th ed., 1904). In 1860–63 he edited the official publication of the Augsburg Diocese and brought it to greater prosperity. Among the literary work done during his residence at Munich should be mentioned his editing of a "Library of the Fathers" in eighty volumes (1869–88); a work on the sacrifice of the Old and New Covenants (1870); and the editing of the "Lehrbuch der biblischen Hermeneutik" of his deceased friend Franz Xavier Reithmayr (1874). At Eichstätt he was commissioned by the bishop to revise the "Rituale Romano-Eystettense", and in addition issued a smaller ritual as a manual for the clergy of the diocese (1879–80). He then began his chief work, a large "Handbuch der Liturgik", which rests on a thorough study of the original authorities and is still indispensable. Of the special liturgies, he published himself in 1890 the "Liturgie des heiligen Messopfers", and from the papers of the deceased Andreas Schmid he added to this in 1893 the "Liturgie des kirchlichen Stundengebetes", the "Liturgie der Sakramente und Sakramentalien", and the doctrine of the church year. Adalbert Ebner began a revised edition of this work, but unfortunately no more has been published than the first section of the first volume (1894). Schmid also edited from Thalhofer's literary remains "Die heilige Messe und das Priestertum der katholischen Kirche in 25 Predigten dargestellt" (1893). In addition to these larger works Thalhofer also wrote excellent articles for theological reviews and for the "Kirchenlexikon" of Freiburg.

SCHMID, *Dr. Thalhofer* (Kempten, 1892), compiled from the subject's own papers.

KLEMENS LÖFFLER.

Thangmar (THANKMAR), historian, b. about the middle of the tenth century; d. probably at Hildesheim after 1022. His first appearance in history is as the head of the cathedral school at Hildesheim; at a later date he became dean of the cathedral, and being at the same time notary and librarian his position was a very important one. Thangmar was distinguished both as a scholar and a statesman; he taught Bishops Bernward of Hildesheim, Meinwerk of Paderborn, and Benno of Meissen, as well as the Emperor Henry II. He exercised great influence over Bernward of Hildesheim, and a large part of the affairs under episcopal control were directed by him. In 1000 he accompanied Bernward to Rome, and was sent several times to the imperial court as the representative of the bishop to settle important matters, being highly esteemed by Emperor Otto III. After the death of Bernward in 1022 he wrote an account of the active and varied life of the bishop, a biography for which he had already gathered the material and of which he had probably written the first ten chapters during the years 1008–13. He had been an eye-witness of many of the events he relates and had taken an active part in all important measures. As he says himself, Bernward trusted him as a child does its father. Consequently his "Vita Bernwardi" is one of the finest biographical productions of the Middle Ages, and is also one of the most valuable authorities for an important period of German history. He displays much affection for the dead bishop, and has written a plain and simple narrative, unrhetorical and truthful. It is only in the account of the dispute between the Archbishops of Hildesheim and Mainz as to the right of jurisdiction over Gandesheim that Thangmar appears at times to be a partisan of Bernward. The best edition is that in the "Mon. Germ. Hist.: Scriptores", IV, 757–782; it is also found in Migne, P. L., CXL, 393–436. The life has been edited in German by Hüffer (Berlin, 1857), and by Wattenbach (Leipzig, 1892).

WATTENBACH, *Deutschlands Geschichtsquellen*, I (Berlin, 1893), 346–349; BEELTE, *Thangmar, sein Leben u. Beurteilung seiner Vita Bernwardi* (Hildesheim, 1891).

PATRICIUS SCHLAGER.

Thanksgiving before and after Meals.—The word *grace*, which, as applied to prayer over food, always in pre-Elizabethan English took the plural form *graces*, means nothing but thanksgiving. (Cf. the Latin *gratiarum actio* and the Italian *grazie*, "thanks".) Although the expression of gratitude to God for His bounty when He has supplied the wherewithal to satisfy the most primary of human needs is an idea which is by no means exclusively Christian (see Deut., viii, 10; Ex., xviii, 12; Livy, XXXIX, xliii; Athenæus, iv, 27), still in the Christian dispensation, following the personal example of our Saviour (John, vi, 11 and 23), the obligation of thanksgiving seems to have been emphasized from the very beginning. Thus, under conditions which altogether exclude the idea of a Eucharistic celebration, we are told of St. Paul (Acts, xxvii, 35) that "taking bread he gave thanks to God in the sight of them all and when he had broken it he began to eat" (Cf. I Tim., iv, 3–5; Rom. xiv, 6; I Cor., x, 30). Passing over the "Didache", in which the formulæ of prayer over food may be connected with the Eucharist or the Agape, we find (c. A. D. 123) the apologist Aristides declaring of his fellow Christians that "over their food and over their drink they render God thanks" (Camb. Texts and Studies, I, 49). Similarly Tertullian, "We do not recline at a banquet before prayer be first tasted—in like manner prayer puts an end to the feast" (De orat., xxv). In nearly all the Fathers similar passages may be found. In particular the Christian poet Prudentius, at the beginning of the fifth century, has a set of hymns "Ante cibum" and "Post cibum" in which occur such verses as the following (Cath. Hymn., III, Ante cib., ii, 10 sq.):—

"Without Thy presence, nought, O Lord, is sweet,
No pleasure to our lips can aught supply.
Whether 'tis wine we drink or food we eat,
Till Grace divine and Faith shall sanctify."

Many anecdotes also might be cited from such early writers as Gregory of Tours and Bede, clearly attesting the prevalence of the practice of saying grace. Bede, for example, when he wishes to tell us that Oswald and Bishop Aidan were about to begin dinner, remarks that "they were on the point of stretching out their hands to bless the bread" (Hist. Eccl., III, vi). The Welsh legal codes, ascribed to the ninth and tenth centuries, when speaking of the king's three indispensable attendants, name first "his priest to say Mass and bless his meat and drink", while the function of the queen's priest is also to bless her meat and drink (Haddan and Stubbs, I, 231 and 235). William of Malmesbury (Gest. pont., IV, 140) refers to St. Wulstan's blessings at table as if they perpetuated some custom that was peculiarly English; but that the Normans were no strangers to such a practice is curiously proved by a scene in the Bayeux tapestry, where we look on Bishop Odo at Bayeux as he stands up before the table at the banquet, while the inscription beside him tells us: "Et hic episcopus cibum et potum benedicit."

In the religious orders, naturally the custom of grace was much insisted upon. A special section is assigned to it in c. xliii of the Rule of St. Benedict, and this was much amplified in later expositions. The early monastic rules in fact generally required that each dish brought to table should be separately blessed before it was set before the community. In the "Ancren Riwle" (c. A. D. 1200), which preserves perhaps the earliest instance of the word "graces" in an English treatise, the grace is described as said standing, and, since it included the "Miserere", it must have been pretty long. The souls of the faithful are also prayed for in the thanksgiving after meat. Great importance was attached to the proper learning of the grace by children. It is commonly a prominent feature in the Books of Curtesye and other medieval works for the instruction of the young. Moreover most educational foundations, like the English public schools and the colleges at the universities, had special forms of grace prescribed for them, often metrical in part, some of which are maintained to the present day. The grace officially provided by the Church is contained in the "Breviarium Romanum" under the heading "Benedictio Mensæ". The form for supper, both before and after eating, varies slightly from that assigned for dinner, and during the octaves of certain greater festivals special verses are substituted for those in ordinary use. Grace begins with the acclamation "Benedicite", which is spoken by the officiant and repeated by all present. The "Grace before and after meals" commonly found in the catechisms for children and used by the laity consists substantially of a translation of two items in the longer Latin grace, the blessing spoken before the meal and the thanksgiving afterwards.

As for this longer Latin grace contained in the Breviary, Abbot Cabrol says with reason that the whole series of formulæ with their appropriate citations from the Psalms, particularly Ps. xxxiii, possess a very high antiquity. In point of fact a great part of the existing forms can be traced back to the ninth century. See for example Rhabanus Maurus, "De ins. cleric.", II, x. The benediction, "Bless us, O Lord, and these Thy gifts", etc., which is retained in our short grace, is to be found in the "Gelasian Sacramentary", which is considerably earlier. Moreover, without precise verbal coincidence, it may be said that our existing longer grace echoes the language of the very earliest document of the kind preserved to us. This is contained in a treatise dubiously ascribed to St. Athanasius, but certainly of early date and, probably at least, the work of a contemporary. It is upon this treatise that G. von der Goltz largely bases his theory of the development of grace for meals out of the primitive Eucharist (Goltz, "Tischgebete und Abendmahlsgebete", pp. 33 sq.). This work (De virginitate) is remarkable for the circumstance that the writer recommends as a prayer before an ordinary meal precisely that form of words which we find in the "Didache" in connexion seemingly with a Eucharistic celebration. We also find in this fourth-century document the versicle, "Our merciful and compassionate God has given food to them that fear Him", and in the existing Breviary grace we have:—

"The Lord merciful and compassionate, has perpetuated the memory of His wonders. He has given food to them that fear Him."

Another very early grace may be found in the "Apostolic Constitutions", VII, xliv.

BAUDOT in *Dictionnaire d'archéol. chret. et de liturgie*, s. v. *Bénédiction de la Table*; CABROL, *Le livre de la prière antique* (Paris, 1900), 364–369; GAVANTUS, *Thesaurus sacrorum rituum*, III (Venice, 1823), 233–25; MARTÈNE, *De antiquis ecclesiæ ritibus*, IV (Venice, 1783), 29–32; BRADSHAW in FURNIVALL, *the Babees Book*, Early Eng. Text Soc., Preface (London, 1885).

The fullest details however are given in the excellent little monograph of H. L. Dixon, *Saying Grace* (London, 1903), which contains many documents printed entire. But see also: VON DER GOLTZ, *Tischgebete und Abendmahlsgebete* (Leipzig, 1905), one of the series *Texte u. Untersuchungen*, and KELLER in *Archæological Journal*, XXI, 347–365.

HERBERT THURSTON.

Thanksgiving Day.—A civil holiday observed annually in the United States of America on the last Thursday in November. The president issues a proclamation, calling on the citizens, all Federal officials, and others subject to Federal authority to observe the day as one of national thanksgiving and prayer. The governors of states concur in the president's proclamation and also recommend the citizens to observe the holiday, and all public business is suspended. The custom originated in 1621, when Governor Bradford of the Plymouth colony appointed a day for public praise and prayer after the first harvest, and the practice spread throughout the other New England colonies. The first national observance was when President Washington, at the request of

Congress, recommended Thursday, 26 November, 1789, to the people of the United States "as a day of public thanksgiving and prayer to be observed by acknowledging with grateful hearts the many and signal favours of Almighty God". This proclamation exhorted the people to "beseech Him to pardon our national and other transgressions, to promote the knowledge and practice of true religion and virtue, and to grant unto all mankind such a degree of temporal prosperity as He alone knows to be best". It was the first observation of the day on the date that present custom holds it. In 1817 Thanksgiving Day was first officially noticed in New York State, and by 1859 its observance had spread to twenty-eight states and two territories. In 1863 President Lincoln made his first proclamation, naming the last Thursday of November as a day of national observance, which day President Johnson also selected in 1867 and President Grant in 1870. Since then there has been no change, the last Thursday in November being named in each year's proclamation. Catholic recognition of the day by special religious features has only been of comparatively recent date and not as yet (1911) of official general custom. Historians of the day attempt to trace the origin of Governor Bradford's idea (1621) back to the old Hebrew Feast of the Tabernacles and through the ages to the ancient Greek Harvest Feast, Thesmophoria, the Roman Cerealia, and the English Harvest Home. In the Dominion of Canada the governor-general by proclamation sets aside the last Monday in October as a legal holiday for the purpose of acknowledging God's providence and expressing the nation's dependence on His bounty.

SCHAUFFER, *Thanksgiving* (New York, 1907); HOUGH, *Proclamations for Thanksgiving* (Albany, 1858); LOVE, *The Fasts and Thanksgiving Days of New England* (Boston, 1895); *America* (New York, 19 Nov., 1910), files.

THOMAS F. MEEHAN.

Thapsus, a titular see in Byzacene Africa. It was a Phœnician market on the coast of Byzacium in Africa Propria, established near a salt lake on a point of land eighty stadia from the Island of Lopadussa, confronting it, between Leptis Minor and Sullectum, and had both military and trading ports. In 46 B. C. it was the scene of the defeat by Cæsar of the generals of Pompey and King Juba. He exacted of the vanquished a payment of 50,000 sesterces. Thapsus then became a Roman colony. Vigilius, the only known bishop, assisted at the assembly convoked at Carthage in 484 by King Huneric and was exiled by the latter with his colleagues. He is the author of several controversial works against the Arians and the Eutychians (see VIGILIUS). The ruins of Thapsus are located at Ras Dimas, near Bekalta in Tunisia. They consist of the remains of a mole, a fortress, an amphitheatre, and large cisterns; in the neighbourhood there is a Punic necropolis.

SMITH, *Dictionary of Greek and Roman Geography* (London, 1878), s. v.; MÜLLER, *Notes to Geographi græci minores*, ed. DIDOT, I (Paris, 1882), 88, 469; TOULETTE, *Géographie de l'Afrique chrétienne, Byzacène et Tripolitaine* (Montreuil, 1894), 201.

S. PÉTRIDÈS.

Thasos, a titular see in Macedonia, suffragan of Thessalonica. The island of Thasos was anciently known under many names, such as Æria, Æthra, and, on account of its gold mines, Chrysos. Its first known inhabitants were the Phœnicians, whom the Greeks supplanted. The latter extended the prosperity of the island, which had a powerful navy and founded many colonies—Parium, Datos (afterwards Philippi), and others. After having repulsed, in 494 B.C., an attack by Histiæus of Miletus, Thasos surrendered in 492 B. C. to Xerxes, who took its navy and exhausted the island with the taxes he levied. After the defeat of the Persians, Thasos joined the Confederation of Delos, but, having quarrelled with Athens, was defeated by sea and by land and, completely ruined by its rival, became its tributary in 465 B. C. Polygnotus, the celebrated painter, a native of Thasos, then followed the Athenians. The island passed from the dominion of Athens to that of Sparta, then again to that of Athens, and at last became a Macedonian possession. The Romans gave it back its independence in 197 B. C., until it was annexed to the Roman Empire and included in the Province of the Islands. Le Quien (Oriens christianus, II, 87) mentions only one bishop, Honoratus, who was present at Chalcedon in 451. Alexander, in the eighth century, is known by an inscription (Echos d'Orient, IV, 93). At least as early as the tenth century, Thasos was a suffragan of Mitylene (Gelzer, "Ungedruckte . . . Texte der Notitiæ Episcopatuum", 559); under Manuel Palæologus (1391–1425) it was raised to the rank of an autocephalous archbishopric (Gelzer, op. cit., 613). The relics of the holy martyrs Mark, Sotericus, and Valentina, venerated on 24 October, were brought thither. The Patriarch St. Nicephorus lived as an exile there under Leo the Armenian.

The Venetians took Thasos in 1204, and it was given to the Dandolo family; the Greeks afterwards recaptured it, and it was then occupied by the princes Gateluzi of Lesbos, and finally conquered by Mohammed II, in 1462. In 1841 the Sultan Mahmoud II granted its revenues to Mehemet Ali, Khedive of Egypt, who introduced a garrison of Egyptians into the island; but the Turks reoccupied it in 1908, and Egypt now (1911) receives only the revenues, according to the terms of the treaty of 1841. The island constitutes a caza depending upon the sanjak of Drama and the vilayet of Salonica. It is fertile and well timbered, and has an area of 100 square miles and a population of 18,000, all Greek schismatics.

LACROIX, *Iles de la Grèce* (Paris, 1853), 372–6; HASSELBACH, *De insula Thaso* (Marburg, 1830); PROKESCH D'OSTEN, *Dell' isola di Taso* in *Dissertazioni della pontificia academia romana di archeologia*, VI (Rome, 1835), 181 sq.; MILLER, *Le Mont Athos, Vatopédi, l'île de Thasos* (Paris, 1889); CUINET, *La Turquie d'Asie*, I (Paris, 1892), 524–528.

S. VAILHÉ.

Thaumaci, a titular see in Thessaly, suffragan of Larissa, commanding the defile of Cœle at the entrance to the Thessalonian plain. Vainly besieged in 198 B. C. by Philip, it was taken in 191 by the consul Acilius Glabrio in the war against Antiochus. The Greeks call it to-day Domokos; it is the chief town of the demos of Thaumakoi, and a well-fortified place; it has 1600 inhabitants, and is beautifully situated on a rock crowned by a medieval fortress, west of which are some old walls. During the last Greco-Turkish war, in 1897, it was the final halting-place of the vanquished Greek army. We do not know if Thaumaci was a bishopric whilst Thessaly owned allegiance to the pope; in any case, when Illyricum, in 732, was withdrawn from the pope's jurisdiction by the emperors of Constantinople, this city became a suffragan of Larissa. In 1882, during the annexation of Thessaly to Greece, the diocese became dependent upon the autocephalous Church of the Kingdom of Greece. After a while the diocese was suppressed by the new organization of this Church (1899). Le Quien, "Oriens christianus", II, 127, names only three bishops of Thaumaci from the sixteenth to the eighteenth century; it would be easy to augment this list. After the Frankish conquest in the thirteenth century, Thaumaci became a Latin bishopric, and four of its titularies are mentioned: Gualo, 1208; Marcus Morellus, about 1334; John, d. 1366; and another John, a Franciscan monk, who replaced him.

LE QUIEN, *Oriens christianus*, III, 981, 1123; EUBEL, *Hierarchia catholica medii ævi*, I, 233.

S. PÉTRIDÈS.

Thayer, JOHN, missionary, convert, first native of New England ordained to the priesthood, b. at Boston, Mass., 1755; d. in Limerick, Ireland, 5 February, 1815. His family were among the early Puritan settlers of New England and all during his career he manifested much of their stern unbending character. Educated at Yale, he became a Congregationalist minister and as such served during the Revolutionary War as chaplain of a company organized for the defence of Boston and of which John Hancock was commander. After the war he wandered over Europe and was in Rome when the beggar-saint Benedict Joseph Labre died. An attempt he made to dispute some of the miracles wrought through Blessed Labre's intercession resulted in Thayer's conversion to the Faith, 25 May, 1783. His own account of this conversion, one of the first of prominent New England Protestants, was printed in 1787 and reissued in several editions in the United States, in London, and in Ireland. It was also translated into French and Spanish, and created a great controversial sensation at the time. Ambitious to convert his non-Catholic fellow-countrymen, he then took a theological course under the Sulpicians in Paris where he was ordained priest in 1789. He returned to the United States the following year and was put in charge of the newly organized Catholic congregation in Boston but soon failed as a pastor because of his erratic and contentious temper. He left Boston in 1799, and ministered for a very short time at Alexandria, Virginia, whence he went to Kentucky as a missionary. Here he remained for four years, his zeal, however, not compensating for his lack of policy and his infirmity of temperament. His wandering inclinations carried him across the ocean again in 1803 and he finally settled down in Limerick, Ireland, where he died, locally esteemed as a priest of edifying piety and ascetic life. The remainder of his small private fortune, with some gifts he had collected, he left by will to found a convent in Boston. Inspired by this wish the three daughters of a merchant named James Ryan, with whom he lived in Limerick, emigrated to Boston (1819) and there founded the Ursuline Community, whose convent, Mount Benedict, near Bunker Hill, Charlestown, was burned and sacked by an anti-Catholic mob on the night of 11 August, 1834.

SHEA, *Life and Times of Most Rev. John Carroll* (New York, 1888); FINOTTI, *Bibliographia Cath. Americana* (New York, 1872); SPALDING, *Sketches of Early Catholic Missions in Kentucky* (Louisville, 1857); WEBB, *The Centenary of Catholicity in Kentucky* (Louisville, 1884); *Am. Cath. Hist. Researches* (Philadelphia), passim; *Massachusetts Soldiers and Sailors of the Revolutionary War* (Boston, 1907); *Memorial Hist. of Boston*, III (Boston, 1880); *U. S. Cath. Hist. Magazine*, II (New York, 1888).

THOS. F. MEEHAN.

Theatines (CLERICS REGULAR), a religious order of men, founded by Gaetano dei Conti di Tiene, Paolo Consiglieri, Bonifacio da Colle, and Giovanni Pietro Carafa, afterwards Pope Paul IV. Carafa was Bishop of Chieti (Theate), a city of the Abruzzi in Southern Italy, from which the congregation adopted its specific name to distinguish it from other congregations (Jesuits, Barnabites, Somaschi, Caracciolini, etc.) modelled upon it. Gaetano consecrated his order to the Cross, which he adopted as its emblem, and the foundation took place on the feast of the Finding of the Holy Cross, 3 May, 1524. It was approved on 24 June, 1524, by Clement VII in the Brief "Exponi Nobis". On 14 Sept., feast of the Exaltation of the Holy Cross, St. Gaetano and his companions made solemn profession before the papal altar of St. Peter's, Rome, in the presence of Mgr. Giovanni Battista Bonziano, Bishop of Caserta, special papal delegate. The chief object of the order was to recall the clergy to an edifying life and the laity to the practice of virtue. St. Gaetano and his companions zealously endeavoured to combat the errors of Martin Luther, which, having gained a foothold in Switzerland, Germany, England, and France, then threatened Italy. They founded oratories (among them the celebrated *Divino Amore*) and hospitals, devoted themselves to preaching the Gospel, and reforming lax morals. Through their good example clergy and laity were induced to better living.

Notwithstanding their severe rule of life and strict vow of poverty, the congregation rapidly developed, and soon numbered among its members illustrious names of the Italian aristocracy (Vezzosi, "Illustri scrittori Teatini", Rome, 1780). They founded many beautiful churches, among them that of S. Andrea della Valle in Rome, a gift of Costanza Piccolomini D'Aragona, Duchess of Amalfi. This church is the masterpiece of Carlo Maderno, and contains several paintings by Domenichino. The Theatines were invited to Turin, Genoa, Venice, Milan, Padua, Piacenza, Parma, Modena, Florence, Naples, Palermo, Messina, Lecce, etc., by the authorities of these places. They also attained a great development in foreign countries. In France, through the efforts of Cardinal Mazarin, they built the Church of St. Anne la Royale opposite the Louvre in 1644. In Spain, under Philip II, the Theatine Cardinal Paolo Burali d'Arezzo, afterwards beatified, filled various embassies at the command of the viceroy of Naples. In Portugal John IV, in 1648, gave the Theatines a splendid house and college for the education of noble youth. In England, under Henry VIII, Goldwell, Bishop of St. Asaph, entered the order of Theatines (see GOLDWELL, THOMAS).

The Theatines were the first to found papal missions in foreign lands, as in: Golconda, Ava, Peru, Mingrelia, the Islands of Sunda, Borneo, Sumatra, the history of which was written by the Theatine Bartolomeo Ferro (Missioni Teatine nelle Indie Orientali); Georgia, Arabia, Armenia, in which latter country Father Galano, author of the history of the Armenian Church, negotiated and concluded the reconciliation and union of that Church with the Roman Catholic; Persia and in many other places, as is shown by Theatine manuscripts dating from 1530 till the end of the eighteenth century. In the nineteenth century the order began to decline, and in 1860, through the well-known suppression of religious orders, it was reduced to a shadow of its former greatness. In accordance with the spirit of its rule, it had never acquired possessions and is the only order which feels the consequences of the law of suppression.

Father Francesco di Paola Ragonesi, general of the order and the last surviving representative of its ancient traditions, restored the Church of S. Andrea della Valle to its former splendour, by his care and zeal aided by the munificence of Comm. Filippo Giove Romano. The Theatines maintain a flourishing mission at Durango in Colorado, U. S. A. Pius X, in a Motu Proprio of 15 December, 1909, decreed the union of the ancient Congregation of the Regular Theatine Clergy with the youthful Spanish Congregation of the Holy Family at Barcelona. Besides the two saints, Gaetano, invoked for the interposition of Providence, and Andrea Avellino, against sudden death, the order furnished one pope, Paul IV (Giovanni Pietro Carafa), 250 bishops, archbishops, and papal legates, and the cardinals: Blessed Giovanni Marinoni, Blessed Paolo Burali d'Arezzo, Blessed Giuseppe Maria Tomasi, Giovanni Bernardino Scotti, Francesco and Domenico Pignatelli, Giuseppe Capece-Zurlo, Francesco Maria Banditi, and Ferdinando Pignatelli, the last named created cardinal by Gregory XVI. Father Anton Francesco Vezzosi (whom Clement XIII wished to make cardinal, but chose instead Fr. Ganganelli of the Conventuals who succeeded him in the papacy as Clement XIV) treats of the illustrious men of the order in his work "I scrittori de' chierici regolari detti Teatini", Rome, 1780. The last famous Theatine was the philosopher, *littérateur*, and great sacred orator, Father Gioacchino Ventura dei baroni di Raulica, a Sicilian. He preached and wrote in both Italian and French. His most celebrated work is his funeral oration on the death of Daniel O'Connell. He was the friend of the most illustrious men of his day, among them the Abbé de Lamennais whom he sought to save for the Catholic Church. He died at Versailles in 1860.

THEATINE NUNS, a religious congregation of women—oblates and hermitesses—existing in Naples and Sicily, founded under the name of Sisters of the Immaculate Conception of the Virgin Mary, by Venerable Ursula Benincasa. This illustrious woman, who, according to Padre Silos ("Istorie Theatine", Palermo, 1666, XII, p. 657), united in herself the spirit of Gertrude, of Catherine of Siena, of Brigid, and of Paula, was born at Naples, 7 August, 1547. Her parents were Girolamo Benincasa and Vincenza Genuina. Her family came originally from Siena, in Tuscany, and had given to the arts, to the sciences, and to the Church both men and women of great distinction. Venerable Ursula herself displayed great talent; while still a young girl, she comprehended the most recondite meanings of Latin books and of the Holy Scriptures. Her inclination to the monastic life was strongly pronounced from her earliest years. Many of her biographies (that of Maggio; Flamino da Latera, "Compendio della storia degli ordini regolari" s. v. "Theatine dell'Immacolata Concezione"; Bonanni in "Catalogo delle Vergine dedicate a Dio") state that when ten years old she attempted to enter the monastery of S. Maria di Gerusalemme, which flourished at Naples under the rule of St. Clare, and after various pilgrimages and trials she founded the Congregation of the Theatine Oblate Sisters. Her sisters, among them Christina who became the first superioress, and some of her nieces formed the community. Little by little, other pious women joined them, to the number of sixty.

The date of this formation is fixed by some as 1581, according to others (including so weighty an authority as Padre Bonanni, S. J.) as 1583. The latter date is the better substantiated, for in 1581 Ven. Ursula merely determined the spot on which she intended a church to be erected; it was in fact built near Castel S. Elmo, with the help of the Spanish priest Gregorio Navarro, Abbot of Francavilla, whom she had told of a vision in which the Blessed Virgin had commanded her to build a church in honour of the Most Holy Conception of Mary. At this period, having created much popular excitement by her visions, her ecstasies, and the loftiness of her teaching, and having attracted enthusiastic admiration and envenomed calumny, she was accused of being possessed by a devil and was therefore summoned to Rome. Baronius and Tarugi, Oratorians and illustrious cardinals, received her and took her to have audience of Gregory XIII at Frascati, 3 May, 1582. By the pope's authority she was placed under the spiritual direction of St. Philip Neri, who subjected her to the most severe trials; he was constantly astonished by her piety and humility. In 1583 the foundation proper took place, under the protection of the Blessed Virgin, St. Joseph, St. Michael the Archangel, and St. Peter.

The rules of the Congregation of the Oblates are those of the active life of St. Martha, with simple vows. They include recitation of the Office of the Blessed Virgin and the Divine Office daily; one hour of prayer in common at morning, besides the recitation of the Veni Creator and the De Profundis at None; one hour of adoration before the Blessed Sacrament, exposed in the church every Friday, with singing of appropriate hymns. In addition to the ordinary fasts prescribed by the Church, the Oblates fast on the vigils of the feasts of Corpus Christi, the Purification, and the Immaculate Conception, and they are exhorted to wear the hairshirt on Fridays. The daily recitation of one-third of the Rosary is also prescribed. They are recommended to labour with their hands, to practise the common life, poverty, and the other virtues. The habit is that of the Theatine clerics: a white tunic under a black garment with wide sleeves and girdle of wool; on the head a white veil without wimple, the place of which is supplied by the collar of the outer garment, like that of the Theatine clerics (Baronius and Bonanni).

The Theatine Hermitesses (*Romite Teatine*) were founded in 1617. As Venerable Ursula wished to completely withdraw from the world she took thirty-three companions, in memory of the thirty-three years of Christ upon earth, and retired to a hermitage. The rules of the Hermitesses are much like those of the Oblates as regards works of piety; but the former religious follow the contemplative life of St. Magdalene. In addition to their solemn vows, their constitution imposes on them great austerities. They are bound to perpetual abstinence from flesh meat except in case of illness, to fast on the vigils of feasts of the Blessed Virgin and with still greater rigour on the vigils of the Immaculate Conception, the Ascension, and Corpus Christi. They also fast every Saturday and on the last two days of Carnival, besides the ordinary fasts of the church. They are bound to keep the Blessed Sacrament exposed for five hours every Friday, with continual adoration by five religious, and to practise penance regularly. The age of reception to the hermitage is twenty, and the novitiate lasts two years. On admission to solemn profession, a religious may converse with her nearest relatives for one day, but must not expect to see them again. Their enclosure is of the strictest, and they hold no communication with anyone except those charged with supplying them food, which is given to them through a turnstile. Their habit is of white cloth with a leather girdle, light blue scapular and mantle, black veil and wimple like other nuns (Bonanni, op. cit.). The building of the Hermitage was begun on 10 June, 1633, and completed in 1667. The rules of the Hermitesses and those of the Oblates were approved by Gregory XVI in 1623.

The Theatine Sisters, more particularly the Oblates, were under the government and spiritual direction of the Fathers of the Naples Oratory, by the request of the Abbot Navarro mentioned above, until 1633. In this year the Theatine Order, under the pressing and insistent solicitation of important personages, among them Pope Urban VIII, undertook this charge, under the generalship of Padre Matteo Santomagno, who was the depositary of Ven. Ursula's last wishes and desires. Oblates and Hermitesses practised fervent and incessant prayer to avert from mankind the terrible chastisements which Ven. Ursula by Divine Providence foresaw in her ecstasy. The life of the Oblates is active, that of the Hermitesses contemplative. These institutes—like many others which have not lived in touch with the world through schools, hospitals, and the like—continued to live and prosper while the days were less evil than now, and their members were regarded with wonder as victims expiating with prayer the sins of humanity; but through the spoliation of monasteries they have now almost disappeared and are reduced to a shadow of their former greatness. Venerable Ursula's rule and the pious practice of the Blue Scapular, which she introduced, are still observed.

Constitutiones Clericorum Regularium (Rome, 1604, 1610); *Regole per le vergine Romite Theatine dell' Immacolata Concettione* (Naples, 1680); *Acta SS.*, Aug. II, 282 sqq.; CARACCIOLI, *De vita Pauli IV* (Cologne, 1612); TUFFO, *Storia dei chierici regolari* (Rome, 1610); PEPE, *Vita di S. Gaetano* (Rome, 1657); SILOS, *Historia clericorum regolarium* (Palermo, 1666); MORELLI, *San Gaetano* (Verona, 1843); TRACY, *Saint Cajetan* (Paris, 1774); FIORI, B. *Paolo Giustiniani* (Rome, 1729); CANCELLIERI, *Campane descritte* (Rome, 1806); CURRIER, *Hist. of Religious Orders* (New York, 1896), 357–9; DUMORTIER, *St. Gaëtan de Thienne* (Paris, 1882); FERRO, *Storia delle missioni dei chierici Teatini* (Rome, 1704); HEIMBUCHER, *Die Orden und Kongregationen*, III (Ratisbon, 1908), 258–69; HÉLYOT, *Dict. des ordres religieux*, III

(Paris, 1850), 648-73; LA CLAVIÈRE, *St. Gaëtan* (Paris, 1901), tr. ELY (London, 1902); LÜBEN, *Der hl. Cajetan von Tiene* (Ratisbon, 1893); RASTOUL, *Le R. P. Ventura* (Paris, 1906), *Vita della Ven. Suor Orsola, scritta da un Padre Teatino* (Rome, 1796); BAGOTTA, *Vita della Venerabile Orsola Benincasa;* BONI, *La chiesa di S. Andrea della Valle* (Rome, 1907): RAGONESI, *Della vita di S. Andrea Avellino* (Rome, 1908); DE MAULDE, *San Gaetano e la Riforma Cattolica* (Rome, 1480-1547), tr. SALVADORI (Rome, 1911).

FRANCISCUS RAGONESI.

Theatre, THE.—Considering the tone of what is preserved to us of the works of the Greek tragedians and even of the comedies of Plautus and Terence, it seems at first difficult to understand the uncompromising attitude adopted towards the theatre by Christian writers of the early centuries. But the fact remains that by the Fathers of both East and West all forms of the drama were banned indiscriminately and in terms of the severest reprobation. We can only infer that the plays and mimes most popular under the Empire were as a rule grossly indecent and poisonous to virtue. The surviving plays of Aristophanes would alone suffice to show how inconceivably lax public opinion was, even at the most cultured periods of paganism, while the *infamia* which marked the legal status of an actor at Rome is significant of the degradation involved by such a profession. Under the Empire tragedies and even the better class of comedies were not much represented in public. They were regarded rather as literature, and at best read aloud in a select circle of friends. The most popular form of play was the *mimus*, and, as Diomedes, a rhetorician of the fifth century, implies, the note of indecency might be said to enter into its very definition. (*Mimus est factorum et dictorum turpium cum lascivia imitatio:* cf. Ovid, "Tristia", II, 497, and Valerius Maximus, ii, 6 and 7, etc.) Further, there is a good deal of evidence that in the third and fourth centuries the parody of Christian rites formed a regular feature of the mimes. Probably the Christian (ὁ χριστιανὸς κωμῳδούμενος) was almost as familiar an object of ridicule at these representations as is the pantaloon in a modern pantomine (Greg. Nazianz., "Orat", II, 84; P. G., XXXV, 489). There are Acts of the martyrs, no doubt more or less legendary, in which is recorded the conversion of an actor brought to know the truth by the very rite of baptism, which he simulated on the stage. Porphyrius (4 Nov.) and Genesius (25 Aug.) are thus commemorated, while the story of St. Pelagia (8 Oct.), however apocryphal it may be, presents the actor's profession in even darker colours (see Delehaye, "Légendes hagiographiques"). But even accepting these facts, the violence of the language in which the Fathers condemn all scenic representations is remarkable. Tertullian in his treatise "De Spectaculis" strikes the key-note and, as Chambers observes, "his vivid African rhetoric is no unfair sample of a catena of outspoken comment which extends across the third century from Tatian to Lactantius" ("Mediæv. Stage", I, ii). For Chrysostom and nearly all his contemporaries the theatre is the temple of the Evil One, and all who frequent the theatre thereby acknowledge him as their master (P. G., LVI, 263; LVII, 71, 426; LVIII, 120, 188, etc.). Even Julian the Apostate forbade access to the theatre to the new pagan priesthood he was anxious to create. Almost alone amongst the Fathers, St. Augustine ("De Civ. Dei", ii, 8) seems to make some distinction between the gross indecency of the mimes and the classical drama of an earlier age, approving the study of the latter for educational purposes. It is not entirely clear from the "Confessions" of the same writer (iii, 2) whether the performance of serious tragedies was still maintained in his youth.

Vile and degrading as were the more popular forms of scenic representation under the Empire, the proletariat were so wedded to them that even the Christian emperors dared not altogether suppress such amusements. Still something was done. By the Theodosian Code (XV, 5), *omnis theatorum atque circensium voluptas* (all diversions in the theatre and circus) were prohibited on Sundays, festivals, and seasons of special sanctity. Disabilities of various kinds, including restrictions as to dress, were imposed upon actresses, etc., but on the other hand the laws of caste were set aside and it was now made possible for an actress, upon becoming a Christian and quitting this way of life, to acquire a status of respectability. At an even earlier date some of the Christian councils had dealt with the subject. At Elvira in Spain, about A.D. 302, it was decided that actors might be baptized, but only on condition of their giving up that way of life. At Arles in 314 *theatrici* and *agitatores* (actors and charioteers in the games) were declared excommunicate. Somewhat later the Synod of Laodicea directed that the clergy who were present at wedding festivities or banquets ought not to remain for the plays that might be performed afterwards. At Hippo in 393 it was forbidden that the sons of bishops or of ecclesiastics should be present at plays or give them. With regard to actors it was decided that, if they wished to become Christians, their baptism need not be postponed indefinitely. In 401 a Council of Carthage decided that plays ought not to take place on Sundays and feasts, and fulminated against actors being decoyed back to their old way of life (but cf. Cod. Theod., XV, vii, 13). Finally, the Council in Trullo in 692, for those that recognized it, condemned plays altogether, threatening degradation against all clerics and excommunication against the laity who assisted at the performances (Hefele-Leclercq, "Conciles", I, 256, 283, 1032; II, 87, 89, 126, 471; III, 566, 569). The tone of all this legislation is milder than the language used by individual Fathers, but it is quite clear that the actor's profession was looked upon as that of a public sinner and most of the early bishops would have agreed with St. Cyprian (Ep., ii) that it was preferable to maintain such a man out of the funds of the Church rather than allow him to continue in his calling.

With the debased drama of the Roman Empire the theatre of Shakespeare, Calderon, Molière, and Schiller has no direct connexion. The isolated *mimi*

or *nugatores*, who may for a while have survived the downfall of the Empire and become strollers, tumblers, *joculatores* (jongleurs), and even minstrels, cannot be shown to have inspired any new dramatic developments. Their connexion with the Norman *estrifs*, one of the forms of the old French *débats* or dialogues, is quite problematical. Moreover, the Teutonic races had their *scop* or gleeman, who was just as likely as these strollers to have evolved ultimately a dialogue form for some of his compositions. Again the Christian imitations of Terence by the Abbess Hroswitha of Gandersheim (d. 1002) or "the Suffering Christ" (χριστὸς πάσχων) of Byzantine literature inspired no imitators and apparently were not even intended for representation. Thus there is a consensus of opinion that the modern drama has sprung out of the mystery or miracle plays of the Middle Ages and is ultimately religious in its origin (see MIRACLE PLAYS AND MYSTERIES). We can even put our finger with some confidence upon the primitive germ of the whole subsequent development. It is to be found in a trope which Frere and others have printed from a St. Gall MS. of the ninth century, attached to the Introit of the Easter Mass. In the earliest English tropes written before 1016 it appears thus, the dramatic form being clearly indicated by the headings:

Angelica de Christi Resurrectione.
Quem queritis in sepulchro christiocle?
Sanctarum Mulierum Responsio.
Ihesum Nazarenum crucifixum o celicole.
Angelice vocis consolatio.
Non est hic, surrexit sicut prædixerat;
Ite nuntiate quia surrexit, dicentes;
Sanctarum mulierum ad omnem clerum modulatio.
Alleluia. Resurrexit dominus hodie,
Leo fortis, christus filius dei, deo gratias dicite; eia.
Dicat Angelus.
Venite et videte locum; etc.

This dialogue was transformed at an early date into a separate interlude following the third lesson of the Easter Matins and representing the visit to the Sepulchre. The Sepulchre itself had been previously constituted on Good Friday by curtaining off a vacant altar and depositing there the crucifix and sometimes the Blessed Sacrament. The whole rite is fully described in the "Concordia regularis" of St. Æthelwold (tenth century), where the compiler remarks by way of introduction: "since on this day we celebrate the interment of the body of our Saviour, if it seems good or pleasing to any to follow on similar lines the use of certain of the religious which is worthy of imitation for the strengthening of faith in the unlearned vulgar and in the neophytes, we have ordered it in this wise". These scenes of the deposition on Good Friday and the visit to the Sepulchre on Easter morning became gradually more and more developed and less and less distinctly liturgical, until we reach a stage when we have a dramatic representation performed by lay folk, outside the Church. Great light has recently been thrown on the transition stages in England by the discovery of the Shrewsbury fragments, which show how the matter was brought to the level of the people by the insertion of vernacular verses in Latin songs. Equally "for the strengthening of faith in the unlearned vulgar and in the neophytes" there were kindred dramatic tropes adopted at Christmas time. The form of one of the tenth century Tropes of St. Martial at Limoges seems to show direct imitation of the Paschal interlude: *Quem quæritis in præsepe pastores?* (Whom seek ye, shepherds, in the manger?) So the dialogue began. There were also other influences besides the tropes which led to the same result. For example portions of a sermon, wrongly attributed to St. Augustine, used to be read among the lessons at the Christmas matins. It introduced various Prophets who bore testimony to Christ. A separate voice was assigned to each, much as in the Gospel of the Passion when read in Holy Week, and this at once supplied the elements of a promising Christmas drama (see Sepet, "Prophètes du Christ", 10).

We may probably, with Mr. Chambers, distinguish three stages in the whole evolution: (1) the liturgical stage, i. e. the development of these dramatic dialogues, aided as they were by impersonation and gesture, within the Church ceremonial itself; (2) the transitional stage, i. e. these Latin plays were translated into the vernacular or interpolated with vernacular passages, while different incidents coalesced to form one representation and other new elements were added, until the whole cycle of the matter treated extended from the Creation to the Judgment; (3) the final stage in which the plays were completely secularized. They fell into the hands of the guilds, some plays being assigned to one guild and others to another, while there were constant changes in the dialogue and rearrangement of incidents to suit new conditions; but the cyclic form was firmly adhered to. On the other hand, these stages in the evolution of the drama were not of course sharply defined and they merged into one another. For further details the reader must be referred to the articles MIRACLE PLAYS AND MYSTERIES and MORALITIES, but it should be noted that an important influence in the process of secularization was supplied by the Latin plays, partly scholastic exercises and partly diversions, which the cathedral and monastic schools acquired the habit of performing, more particularly at the Christmas and Easter seasons. It is easy to see how readily such representations addressed to a young or miscellaneous audience might come to be interpolated by passages in the mother tongue, particularly those of a more humorous character. Moreover, it was natural to extend the scope of such diversions and we have evidence that in the twelfth century, in France, England, and Germany, dramatic compositions were represented dealing with such subjects as the life of St. Nicholas, the martyrdom of St. Catherine, the resurrection of Lazarus, the parable of the virgins, or a *ludus prophetarum ornatissimus*, which included Gideon and the Philistines, David and Herod. But the further transference of such representations to the guilds must have taken place early, for it is generally agreed that the play of "Adam", written in Anglo-Norman French of the twelfth century, was probably first represented by a guild and upon English soil (see Grass, "Das Adamsspiel", 1907). In Germany, however, the religious plays seem to have remained almost entirely in the hands of the students, though in Italy the main impulse came from the *laudesi* confraternities, the survivors of the Flagellant movement, who met together in their own chapel to sing *laudi* (canticles) in honour of the Blessed Virgin, which gradually assumed a dramatic form and grew into *rappresentazioni sacre*. A play in the Roman dialect of the fourteenth century, edited by Vattasso (Studi e Testi, no. 4), explicitly bears the title *lauda* (loc. cit., p. 53). But in every country of Europe, Spain and Poland not excepted, a new drama seems to have arisen which sprang into existence in dependence on the Church. Only by slow degrees did the subjects of such plays in the vernacular lose touch with any religious purpose. An entirely new source of inspiration came into play contemporaneously with the humanism of the expiring Middle Ages. In Italy especially it began as early as the fourteenth century, with the revival of the study of the tragedies of Seneca and, what was more important, with the composition of original Latin tragedies upon themes supplied by medieval history. From these it was but a step to the plays called *mescidati*, in which the influence both of the *rappresentazioni sacre*, which were the final development of the religious drama, and also of classical models may be clearly discerned. But it is impossible to pursue the subject here. We have an Italian tragedy, the "Sofonisba", by G. Trissino, acted before Pope Leo X in 1515, while the early comedies (Boiardo's "Timone" was presented before 1494) were introduced gradually in the wake of improvised burlesques to which the *arlecchino* (harlequin) contributed a thread of unity but which still savoured something of the earliest moralities. In any case it is to be noted that no sooner had a popular drama established itself independently of ecclesiastical influence than the licentious excesses of such writers as Ariosto, Macchiavelli, and Aretino (Leonardo Bruni) forced the Church back into much the same attitude of uncompromising hostility to the stage which existed under the Roman Empire. The representation of sacred and moral dramas and sometimes of classical plays was indeed encouraged in colleges and similar institutions. The plays, mostly in Latin, which were written and acted in the Jesuit schools, form quite a literature by themselves (See e. g. Bahlmann, "Jesuiten-Dramen d. niederrhein. Ordensprov.", 1896). But apart from such scholastic exercises the public theatres, on account of the laxity of morals which as a rule prevails at such representations, are nearly everywhere forbidden to the clergy by the decrees of provincial and diocesan synods (see the "Collectio Lacensis", passim). It is maintained by some that these prohibitions have only force to bind the clergy belonging to the diocese or province in which they are issued whilst they remain within the limits of the diocese, but the point is at best doubtful. No authoritative decision has ever been given which would allow clerics who come from a diocese in which attendance at the theatre is forbidden, when passing through another diocese in which it is equally forbidden, to regard themselves as free to visit the theatre at will. To assist at performances which are grossly improper is of course forbidden both to clergy and laity alike, both on account of the proximate danger of sin as also of the scandal which may thereby be given to others. Finally we may note that in the Papal States no permanent public theatre was allowed to be constructed until 1691 and the theatre which was then opened by permission of Alexander VIII at Tor di Nona was subsequently dismantled by his successor Innocent XII. But in the course of the eighteenth century several theatres were built in Rome with papal sanction, though they were subjected to a very strict censorship and were closed at sacred seasons.

THE CHURCH AND THE THEATRE.—STARA, *Zur Wündigung der kirch. Anschauungen über der Theaterwesen* in *Theol. Quartalschrift*, LXIX (1887), 832–666; HEFELE, *Ueber den Rigorismus*, etc. in *Theol. Quartalschrift*, XXIII (1841), 396 seq., afterwards reprinted in his *Beiträge* (1864); MÖHLER, *Symbolik*, 6th ed., 512 ff.; BOSSUET, *Maximes et réflexions sur la comédie* (Paris, 1693); PLUMPTRE, in *Dict. Christ. Ant.*, s. v. *Actors;* MAYOR, *loc. cit.* s. v. *Theatre;* PRYNNE, *Histriomastix* (London, 1672).

MEDIEVAL DRAMA.—A vast literature has grown up about this subject especially of late years. Only a few leading works can be mentioned here. E. K. CHAMBERS, *The Mediæval Stage* (2 vols., Oxford, 1903); CREIZENACH, *Geschichte des neueren Dramas*, I (Halle, 1873); PETIT DE JULLEVILLE, *Les Mystères* (2 vols., Paris, 1880); D'ANCONA, *Origini del Teatro Italiano* (2nd ed., 2 vols., Turin, 1891); A. W. WARD, *History of Eng. Dramatic Literature*, I (2 ed., London, 1899); GAYLEY, *Plays of our Forefathers*, New York, 1908; W. MEYER, *Fragmenta Burana* (Göttingen, 1901); DAVIDSON, *English Mystery Plays* (London, 1892); DU MERIL, *Origines latines du Théâtre moderne* (Caen, 1849); COUSSEMAKER, *Drames liturgiques du moyen âge* (Paris, 1860); with music (Paris, 1896); MILCHSACK, *Die Oster- und Passionsspiele* (Wolfenbüttel, 1880); CASTÉ, *Les drames liturgiques de la cathédrale de Rouen* (Évreux, 1893); R. FRONING, *Das Drama des Mittelalters* (3 vols., Stuttgart, 1891); LANGE, *Die lateinischen Osterfeiern* (Munich, 1887); WECHSSLER, *Die romanischen Marienklagen* (Halle, 1893); SCHÖNBACH, *Die Marienklagen* (Graz, 1875); COHEN, *Histoire de la mise-en-scène dans le théâtre religieux français du moyen âge* (Paris, 1906); SEPET, *Les Prophétes du Christ* in *Bib. de l'Ecole des Chartes*, XXVIII, and published separately (Paris, 1878); IDEM, *Le drame chrétien au moyen âge* (Paris, 1878); IDEM, *Origines catholiques du théâtre moderne* (Paris, 1878); WIRTH, *Die Oster- und Passionsspiele bis zum XVI. jahrhundert;* FRONING, *Das Drama des Reformationszeit* (Stuttgart, 1910); HARTMANN, *Ueber das altspanische Dreikönig-spiel* (Leipzig, 1679); ANZ, *Die lateinischen magier-spiele* (Leipzig, 1905); POLLARD, *English Miracle Plays* (2nd ed., London, 1898); CADY, *Liturgical Basis of Towneley Mysteries* in *Publications of Modern Lang. A'n of America*, XXIV (Baltimore, 1909), 419–69; K. YOUNG, *Some Texts of Liturg. Plays* in *Publications of Modern Lang. A'n*, XXIV (Baltimore, 1909), 294–332 and other papers in the same periodical; K. YOUNG, *The 'Harrowing of Hell' in Liturgical Drama* in *Trans. of Wisconsin Academy*, XVI, pt. 2, 1909; RAND, *Sermo de Confusione Diaboli* in *Modern Philology*, II (1904); FRERE, *The Winchester Troper* (Henry Bradshaw Society, Lond., 1878; WARD and others in *Cambridge History of English Literature*, V, i–iii.

HERBERT THURSTON.

Thebaid.—The valley of the Nile, under Roman domination, was divided into four provinces: Lower and Upper Egypt, Lower and Upper Thebaid. The last two comprised the upper part of the valley. During the fourth and fifth centuries it was the chosen land of the monks, who by their sanctity and by the form they impressed on the monastic system greatly influenced the East and the West. Their monasteries may be divided into several groups. The best known is the Pachomian group, founded and legislated for by St. Pachomius. They formed a real religious order with Tabenna as a mother-house and its superior as their general. Besides Tabenna there were Peboou, Schenesit, Akhmin, Esneh, Monchosis, Thebaid, Tesminé, Hermopolis, and Armoutim. Saint Pachomius governed this group till his death (346), and was succeeded by Abbot Orcisius, and then by Abbot Theodore. There was a community of women, governed by Pachomius's sister, following the same rule as the men. The life of the holy founder and the rule he drew up reveal the interior organization of these monasteries and the congregation. It has all the essential characteristics of cenobitic religious life. Vows of poverty, chastity, and obedience, a dress distinct from that of secular persons, lengthy psalmodies, manual work, and penitential exercises. The monks lived in huts scattered in groups. The groups were enclosed by a wall and formed the monastery. The superior general had absolute authority over each house and over its superior. He held a general assembly of all the religious twice a year. Bgol founded at Atripe a group distinct from that of Tabenna. We know of it from the life of his successor Schnoudi. The monks even increased the austerities prescribed by St. Pachomius and could change from the cenobitic to the eremitical life. Schnoudi died about 452 at the age of 118. His reform had only a mediocre success.

The eremitical life was introduced into the Lower Thebaid by St. Anthony. Born in 251, he embraced the ascetic life at the age of twenty; then impelled by a love of solitude he buried himself in the desert. After twenty years of complete isolation the fame of his sanctity drew around him disciples who imitated his mode of life. Like him they were hermits though remaining under his authority. Their solitude was relative. Those more advanced in years had one or more disciples, whom they instructed in the paths of perfection. Others had companions or neighbours. They visited one another. Grottoes or huts like those of the fellaheen served them as cells. The rules called by St. Anthony's name are not his composition; but his biography, compiled by his admirer and friend St. Athanasius in 365, preserves the memory of his virtues and his teaching. The author wished to illustrate what the life of a monk should be. It influenced the development of eastern and western monachism very considerably. Most of the Egyptian monks of that period were more or less directly connected with the school of St. Anthony, for instance the two Macarii, Isidore, Heraclides, and Pambo, who are looked upon as the founders of the group of Nitria. The group of Scete derives its origin from the same school. They were numerous fervent centres of a partly cenobitical, partly eremitical life. The "Historica Lausiaca" of Palladius gives us the details of the ordinary life of the Nitrian monks; the "Apophthegmata patrum" and the "Vitæ patrum" tell us those of the Scete. In the wilderness along the two banks of the Nile there were many monks, living some alone, some in groups. Others dwelt in populated regions, some even in the towns. The monks disappeared with the fall of the Byzantine domination in these countries and the success of the Saracen invaders. Nothing remains of Tabenna. The two monasteries of St. Anthony and of Nitria by their name and location recall those ancient days. The rules observed there are entirely different from those of the fourth and fifth centuries.

BUTLER, *The ancient Coptic Churches of Egypt* (Oxford, 1884); IDEM, *The Lausiac History of Palladius* (2 vols., Cambridge, 1884, 1904); AMÉLINEAU, *Hist. de Saint Pakhome et de ses communautés* (Paris, 1884); IDEM, *Les moines égyptiens: Vie de Schnoudi* (Paris, 1884); LADEUZE, *Etude sur le cénobitisme pakhomien pendant le IVe siècle et la première moitié du Ve* (Louvain, 1898); BESSE, *Les moines d'Orient antérieurs au concile de Chalcédoine* (Poitiers, 1900); LECLERCQ in *Dict. d'arch. chrét. et de liturgie*, s. v. *Cénobtisme*.

J. M. BESSE.

Theban Legion. See AGAUNUM.

Thébaud, AUGUSTUS, Jesuit educator, and publicist, b. at Nantes, France, 20 Nov., 1807; d. at St. John's College, Fordham, New York, 17 Dec., 1885. Father Thébaud was the son of a worthy but not wealthy merchant who was married to his pious wife in the dark days of the Terror by a loyal priest, a circumstance which eloquently proves their earnest Catholicity. Their children were brought up with great care and given the best religious education which France at that time afforded. Young Thébaud studied at first in the preparatory seminary at Nantes, then entered the *grand séminaire* and was ordained to the secular priesthood at the usual age. After three years of parochial work in his native city, he entered the Society of Jesus in Italy, on 27 Nov., 1835, whence he returned to France in 1837 to pursue a course of scientific studies at the Sorbonne under Ampère and other distinguished professors. He landed in the United States on 18 Dec., 1838, and was called to the chair of chemistry at St. Mary's College, Kentucky, where he became rector in 1846. Before the end of that year however the Jesuits left Kentucky to take charge of St. John's College, Fordham, New York, which had been transferred to them by Archbishop Hughes. Father Thébaud was the first Jesuit President of St. John's, a position which he held from 1846 to 1851 and again from 1860 to 1863. In the interval he taught the sciences for two years, 1851–52, under Father Larkin, and the following eight years he spent as the pastor of St. Joseph's Church at Troy. To this charge he returned after his second rectorship at Fordham and filled the position from 1863–69, and again from 1873–74. The intervening years we find him at first in Montreal and then at St. Joseph's Church, Hudson City, New Jersey. After spending another year at Fordham, he was assigned to St. Francis Xavier's parish, New York, where he passed the rest of his days.

Father Thébaud, who always had a strong literary bent, wrote a series of books on religious and historical subjects and published, besides numerous articles in the "Catholic World" and the "Catholic Quarterly Review", two novels, "Louisa Kirkbridge, A Tale of New York" (1879), and "Twit Twats, An Allegorical Story of Birds" (1881). His more important works are: "The Irish Race in the Past and in the Present" (1873); "The Church and the Gentile World" (2 vols., 1878); "The Church and the Moral World" (1881). From 1875 to his death, he also prepared his reminiscences in three volumes. Of these the United States Catholic Historical Society published volume III (1904), giving an account of his American experiences, and volume I (1911), containing the recollections of his life in France. Father Thébaud was a man full of energy, even in old age, an untiring student, and well-informed scholar. Withal he was a most agreeable companion, witty and full of life, and universally beloved by his friends and his pupils.

HILL, *Some Reminiscences of St. Mary's College, Kentucky* in the *Woodstock Letters*, XX (1891), 25–38; *Letters* in the *Annales de la propagation de la foi*, XIV, 383–401; XVI, 449–76; *Three Quarters of a Century*, I, III, edited by HERBERMANN (1904 and 1911).

CHARLES G. HERBERMANN.

Thebes (THEBÆ), a metropolitan titular see of Achaia Secunda. The city was founded by the Phœnician Cadmus in the sixteenth century B. C., afterwards made illustrious by the legends of Laius, Œdipus, and of Antigone, the rivalry of Eteocles and Polynices, and the unfortunate siege by the seven chiefs of Argos. After the taking of Troy, Thebes became the capital of Bœotia, but did not succeed in imposing its hegemony, for Athens supported certain towns in their opposition. Thebes allied itself to the Persians against the Greeks, but was conquered with them and submitted to Sparta, until its two generals Pelopidas and Epaminondas restored it to the first rank. The death of the latter before Mantinea in 363 B. C., opened a new series of misfortunes for the city. Conquered by Philip of Macedon, in 338 B. C., it revolted two years after and drew on itself the vengeance of Alexander who killed or sold all the inhabitants and destroyed all the houses save that of the poet Pindar. Rebuilt in 316 B. C., by Cassander, it was taken and retaken again. In the second century B. C., the acropolis alone was inhabited. In the Middle Ages the city was repeopled through the silk industry. In 1040 the Bulgarians took possession of it; six years after the Normans sacked it. In 1205 it was taken by Boniface III of Montferrat and assigned with Athens to Othon de la Roche; by marriage it passed later to the lords of Saint-Omer; one of them, Nicholas II, constructed the Frankish château of the Cadmi which was destroyed in 1311 by the Catalans. In 1364 the Turks took it in behalf of Frederick III of Sicily and later on their own account, but its neighbour, Livadia, soon supplanted it.

The first known bishop, Cleonicus, was at Nicæa in 325 (Gelzer, "Patrum nicænorum nomina", LXIV). Le Quien (*Oriens Christ.*, II, 207–11) quotes ten other titulars, among them: Julius at Sardica in 344; Anysius at Ephesus in 431; Architimus in 458; Marcianus in 867. At first a suffragan, Thebes was an autocephalous archbishopric at the beginning of the tenth century and until 970 (Gelzer, "Ungedruckte . . . Texte der Notitiæ episcopatuum", 551, 571); about 1080 it was a metropolitan see (Le Quien, op. cit., II, 210); and about 1170 it numbered five suffragan sees (Gelzer, op. cit., 585). In 1833 Thebes was reduced to the rank of bishopric with the title of Bœotia; since 1882 the diocese has had the title of Thebes and Livadia. The bishop resides at Livadia and exercises his jurisdiction over the entire district of Bœotia. The city numbers 5000 inhabitants including the suburbs. Since 1210 it has had a Latin metropolis which became by degrees a titular. Eubel (*Hierarchia catholica medii ævi*, I, 508; II, 274; III, 331) mentions a number of bishops. During the Frankish occupation, the Franciscans had a custody named Thebæ.

SANKEY, *The Spartan and Theban Supremacies* (London, 1877); MÜLLER, *Gesch. Thebens* (Leipzig, 1879); FABRICIUS, *Theben* (Fribourg, 1890); DURUY, *Histoire des Grecs* (3 vols., Paris, 1886).

S. VAILHÉ.

Thebes (THEBÆ), titular see of Thebais Secunda, suffragan of Ptolemais, and the seat of a Coptic Catholic diocese. Thebes was the No-Amon of the Jews, the Nouit-Amen of the Egyptians (City or Kingdom of Amon), the Nia of the Assyrians, and the Diospolis of the Greeks, which is the exact translation of Nouit-Amen. The Egyptians also called it Per or Pi–Amen, the dwelling of Amon, and also Apet, whence, with the article Ta before the feminine name Apet, is derived Ta-Apet, or Tape, as it is called by the modern Copts, the Θῆβαι of the Greeks. Thebes is mentioned three times in the Bible under the name of No-Amon in the Hebrew text, which the Vulgate each time renders incorrectly by Alexandria. Nahun (iii, 8–10) refers to the victories of Assurbanipal, King of Ninive, over Tanutamon, King of Egypt, as we now know from the cylinders of that sovereign (G. Smith, "History of Assurbanipal", 52–56). It is thought that Jeremias (xlvi, 25) and Ezechiel (xxx, 14–16) allude to the two campaigns of Nabuchodonosor against Thebes, which took place in 583 and 588 B. C.

Originally a mere borough, Thebes grew by degrees, and as early as the twelfth dynasty its sovereigns dominated Egypt. Thenceforth also its god Amon-Ra, to whom the pharaohs had erected numerous monuments, became the foremost of the gods. Halted for a time by the invasion of the Hyksos, the growth of Thebes continued under the pharaohs of the eighteenth and especially those of the nineteenth dynasty, who extended their dominion to the sources of the Euphrates. When the sovereigns of Thebes had become degenerate they were replaced by the priests of the god Amon, who constituted themselves the twenty-first dynasty. They disappeared in turn and the capital of Egypt was then transferred to the Delta. The city began to fall away, especially after the Assyrian armies had captured and devastated it in 668 and 664 B. C. and Nabuchodonosor had twice rifled it of its treasures. However, as long as there were Egyptian sovereigns, even under the Ptolemies, work was done at the temple of Karnak, which was only abandoned under the Roman domination. Thebes then became a place of pilgrimage and sight-seeing. Christians established their churches in the temples, monks and laymen dwelt everywhere, preferably in the ancient tombs. The great earthquake of 27 B. C. caused some damage, but that which ruined the temples of Karnak must have occurred two or three centuries later.

A see was established at Thebes at an early date. Ammonius of Diospolis assisted at the Council of Nicæa in 325, unless he was Bishop of Diospolis Parva (Harnack, "Mission und Ausbreitung des Christentums", II); Maletius was a partisan of Arius, according to Philostorgius and Nicetas Choniates ("Thesaurus orthodoxæ fidei", V, 7); Hero apostatized under Julius the Apostate, according to Philostorgius (Hist. eccl., VII, 13); Stephen was Catholic metropolitan at the time of Photius, and Kalta was Jacobite metropolitan in 1086 (Le Quien, "Oriens christ.", II, 611). The Coptic diocese, created in 1895, has 15,000 Catholics to 300,000 Jacobite Copts and about 3,000,000 Mussulmans. There are 31 Coptic priests, 35 churches, besides 6 which belong to the Franciscans, 18 stations, 26 primary schools with about 500 pupils, 4 convents of Franciscans, 3 of Brothers of the Christian Schools, and 1 of native Sisters. The seminary which is used by the three Coptic Catholic dioceses has 17 students and is situated at Tahtah, the residence of the Bishop of Thebes.

The ruins of Thebes are among the most beautiful in the world. The city was situated on both banks of the Nile, which is more than two miles wide at this point. On the right bank was the temple of Luxor, built by King Amenothes III and Rameses II, the great temple of Amon, and the great hypostylic hall of Karnak, the work of the pharaohs Rameses I, Seti I, and Rameses II, and which is 337 feet broad by 169 feet deep. A veritable forest of 134 colossal columns divides it into three naves, forming a hall which has not its like in the world. The temples of Luxor and Karnak were joined by an alley nearly two miles long by about 3¾ miles wide, bordered by rams or criocephalous sphinxes. On the left side is Quournah, which begins the line of temples of which the Ramesseum is almost in the centre and Medinet-Habou at the southern extremity. A line drawn around all these monuments either from the right or the left bank describes a circuit of nearly 8¾ miles. Now Diodorus Siculus (I, 45) and Strabo (XVII, 46) give almost the same dimensions to the Diospolis of the first century before Christ. But in the time of its real splendour, according to Eustathius and Stephanus Byzantius, confirmed by other geographers and modern discoveries, Thebes was almost 400 stadia in circumference, or nearly 28 miles. It is probable, however, that these figures included not only the extent of the city, but also the entire territory of the commune.

LAGIER in *Dict. de la Bible*, s. v. *No-Amon;* BÉNÉDITE, *Guide Joanne: Egypte* (Paris, 1900). Both these authors give a detailed bibliography.

S. VAILHÉ.

Thecla (TECLA), SAINT, Benedictine Abbess of Kitzingen and Ochsenfurt; date of birth unknown; d. at Kitzingen about 790 or later. St. Boniface, Apostle of Germany, kept up a constant intimate correspondence with the community of Wimborne, Dorset, and from the abbess, Tetta, in 748–49, he obtained monastic colonies for Germany. Among these nuns one of the most illustrious for sanctity and learning was Thecla, a relative of St. Lioba, whom she accompanied from Wimborne and under whose rule she lived for some time at Tauberbischofsheim, until St. Boniface appointed her abbess of the newly founded abbey at Ochsenfurt. Later, on the death of St. Adelheid, or Hadelonga, the foundress and first Abbess of Kitzingen on the Main, she was called to rule that abbey while still retaining the government of Ochsenfurt. The Roman as well as the English and Benedictine Martyrology commemorate her on 15 October; others on 27 or 28 September. The name Thecla does not appear on the list of the abbesses of Kitzingen, but it is generally thought that she is designated as Heilga, or "the saint"; unless we admit this, the list must be considered interpolated. Among Boniface's letters is one addressed to Lioba, Thecla, and Cynehilde, as the heads of separate religious communities. Its tone reveals how far the nuns had entered as intelligent fellow-labourers into his apostolate. St. Boniface seems to have had a threefold purpose in summoning these Anglo-Saxon nuns as his auxiliaries:— to propagate the full observance of the Benedictine Rule by new foundations; to introduce it into already founded monasteries, and to restore its observance in others; and finally to bring their gentle influence to bear on the fierce Teuton women, both by example and by the education imparted to their children. The ruined Chapel of St. Thecla, on an islet in the Severn, may have been dedicated to her, as Walstod, a Saxon bishop, was set over that part at this time. Some have tried to prove St. Thecla one of the nuns of Barking to whom St. Aldhelm dedicated his "Treatise on Virginity", but as this treatise was written before 705, and as St. Lioba went to Germany about 748–49, it is evident that her disciple who survived her was not this nun of Barking.

Ochsenfurt gradually declined, most probably owing to its proximity to Kitzingen. There is no record of its having any other abbess after St. Thecla. Kitzingen was used for secular purposes by the margraves of Brandenburg, to whom it had been mortgaged from 1440 to 1629, when it was redeemed by Philip Adolphus, Bishop of Würzburg, and restored by John Godfrey of Guttenberg as a school for the Ursulines. In 1803 the institute of the Ursulines was secularized, and to-day the abbey church is in the hands of Protestants and serves as their parish church. The tombs of St. Thecla and St. Adelheid in this church were profaned in the Peasants' War, 1525; a fanatic of Kitzingen used the heads to play at skittles; when the church was rebuilt (1695), the venerable bodies were covered with rubbish. The monastery contains a Catholic and a Protestant school for girls, a Protestant school for boys, apartments for some teachers, and the district court. The abbess's castle is private property.

Acta SS., Oct., VIII; KYLIE, *The English Correspondence of St. Boniface* (London, 1911); ANON., *Life of St. Lioba* (London); HOPE, *St. Boniface and the Conversion of Germany* (London, 1877); KURTH, *St. Boniface* (Paris, 1902); SEITERS, *Bonifatius, der Apostel der Deutschen* (Mainz, 1845); SCHNÜRER, *Bonifatius* (Mainz, 1909).

GERTRUDE CASANOVA.

Thecla, SAINTS.—I. Thecla of Iconium, the reputed pupil of the Apostle Paul, who is the heroine of the apocryphal "Acta Pauli et Theclæ" (cf. APOCRYPHA). Our knowledge of her is derived exclusively from these Acts, which appeared about 180. According to this narrative Thecla was a virgin of Iconium who was converted to Christianity and led to dedicate herself to perpetual virginity by the preaching of the Apostle Paul. Miraculously saved from death at the stake to which she had been condemned, she went with St. Paul to Antioch in Pisidia where she was thrown to the wild beasts and was again saved from death by a miracle. After this she went to Myra where the Apostle was, and finally to Seleucia where she died. With the consent of St. Paul she had acted as a "female Apostle" in proclaiming the Gospel. Notwithstanding the purely legendary character of the entire story, it is not impossible that it is connected with an historical person. It is easy to believe that a virgin of this name who was a native of Iconium was actually converted by St. Paul and then, like many other women of the Apostolic and later times, laboured in the work of Christian missions (cf. Harnack, "Die Mission und die Ausbreitung des Christentums in den ersten drei Jahrhunderten", 2nd ed., I, 295; II, 58). In the Eastern Church the wide circulation of the Acts led to a great veneration of Thecla. She was called "Apostle and protomartyr among women". Her veneration was especially great in a number of Oriental cities, as Seleucia where she was buried, Iconium, and Nicomedia. Her cult appeared very early also in Western Europe, particularly in those districts where the Gallican Liturgy prevailed; there is direct proof of this in the fourth century. Her name is given with various topographical comments (Nicomedia, Seleucia, Asia) on several days in the "Martyrologium Hieronymianum". Thus Thecla is mentioned in this martyrology on 22 February, 25 February, 12 September, 23 September, and 17 November ("Mart. Hieron.", ed. de Rossi-Duchesne, 24, 36, 120, 124, 144). It seems certain that on all these dates, and probably also on 20 and 21 December, the same St. Thecla, the pupil of St. Paul, is meant. In Bede's Martyrology (cf. Quentin, "Martyrologes historiques du moyen âge", 93) her name is mentioned with a brief notice taken from the Acts on 23 September, the same date as that on which her feast is given in the present Roman Martyrology. The Greek Church celebrates her feast on 24 September and gives her the title of "Protomartyr among women and equal to the Apostles" (cf. Nilles, "Calendarium utriusque ecclesiæ", I, 283 sq.).

See bibliography of APOCRYPHA; HOLZHEY, *Die Thecla-Akten, ihre Verbreitung u. Beurteilung in der Kirche* (Munich, 1905).

II. We possess historically accurate accounts of the martyrdom of a Christian of Gaza in Palestine named Thecla. According to Eusebius ("De martyribus Palestinen.", 3) she was condemned to death in the second year of the great persecution (304–05) together with a Christian named Agapius and was torn to pieces in a horrible manner by the wild beasts to which she was thrown. The present Roman Martyrology gives the feast of this saint under the date of 19 August. III. The "Martyrologium Hieronymianum" mentions a Thecla in connexion with a Zosimus among the martyrs whose feast was celebrated on 1 June; these two saints were commemorated at Antioch. Whether this Thecla was a local saint of the Oriental metropolis is not known. IV. A catacomb of St. Thecla on the Via Ostiensis, not far from the burial place of St. Paul, is mentioned in the seventh-century itineraries to the graves of the Roman martyrs. A church stood on this spot on a hill over the catacomb where the body of the saint rested. St. Thecla must be regarded as a Roman martyr. Armellini believes that he has found the cemetery of St. Thecla (cf. Marucchi, "Les catacombes romaines", Rome, 1903, p. 91 sqq.). V. The Martyrology of St. Jerome mentions under 31 May (69), in connexion with two martyrs buried on the Via Aurelia, a group of martyrs named Tertulla, Lupus, Justa, and Thecla. It is very possible that besides the St. Thecla buried on the Via Ostiensis another Roman female martyr bearing the same name was buried on the Via Aurelia. Still we have no further account of this group of martyrs, and just as little of a number of Roman martyrs, among whom the name of a Thecla also occurs, that are given under 26 March in the present Roman Martyrology.

VI. In the "Martyrologium Hieronymianum" (58, 78) a long list of the names of African martyrs is given under the dates of 10 May, 13 and 14 June, and each time a Thecla is mentioned. Nothing further is known of this saint. In the legend of the twelve brothers and martyrs, Donatus, etc. (cf. Acta SS., Sept., I, 138–41), the parents of the brothers are called Boniface and Thecla, and these two are also given in the present Roman Martyrology as martyrs under 30 August. Apart from the purely legendary Acts just mentioned nothing is known of them. VII. In the "Acts of St. Hermagoras", which are equally legendary (Baronius, "Martyr. Romanum cum notis Baronii", Venice, 1609, p. 494) a St. Thecla of Aquileia is mentioned together with several other martyrs who are only known through this legend. Their feast is observed on 3 September.

HAUCK, *Kirchengesch. Deutschlands*, I, 476–79.

J. P. KIRSCH.

Theft is the secret taking of another's property against the reasonable will of that other. It is to be noted that the word secret is not employed to exclude the idea of the owner's presence and advertence whilst the theft is being committed. It is used merely to signify that the crime has been perpetrated without violence towards him. Not only the taking, but the keeping or the use unjustly of what belongs to another against his will, is to be considered theft. This would happen, for instance, where one unwarrantably refused to restore what had been entrusted to him as a pledge or loan or only for safe-keeping. Likewise where one would manage to ride on the railway without paying any fare. For the notion of theft, the unwillingness of the owner to part with what is rightfully his, is essential. If he be content, or if under some circumstances he can legitimately be presumed to be satisfied with what is done although perhaps displeased at the manner of its doing, there is no theft properly so called. Moreover his unwillingness must be reasonable not simply insensate close-fistedness. He is not justified in declining always and without regard to conditions to assent to the alienation of what belongs to him merely because it is his. Thus one in danger of death from want of food, or suffering any form of extreme necessity, may lawfully take from another as much as is required to meet his present distress even though the possessor's opposition be entirely clear. Neither, therefore, would he be bound to restitution if his fortunes subsequently were notably bettered, supposing that what he had converted to his own use was perishable. The reason is that individual ownership of the goods of this world, though according to the natural law, yields to the stronger and more sacred right conferred by natural law upon every man to avail himself of such things as are necessary for his own preservation. St. Thomas (II–II, Q. lxvi, a. 7) declares that in such straits what is taken becomes, because of the dire need experienced, one's very own, and so cannot be said to be stolen. This doctrine is sometimes expressed by saying that at such a time all things become common, and thus one reduced to such utter destitution only exercises his right.

The sin of theft is of itself grievous, because it violates the great virtues of justice and charity. St. Paul (I Cor., vi, 10) enumerates it as one of the transgressions which bars the offender from the kingdom of heaven. Still, as happens with regard to other delinquencies, its guilt may often be venial. This is particularly true when the value of what is filched is inconsiderable, or as the theologians say, is not grave matter. The determination of what is grave matter, whose taking, namely, is prohibited under pain of mortal sin, is beset with great difficulties and has offered room for widespread difference of opinion. It is agreed, however, that a distinction is to be drawn between relatively and absolutely grave matter. The grievousness of theft seems to depend on the way in which the purposes which make the respecting of property rights obligatory are set at naught. These ends are, first the preservation of peace and harmony among individuals, and then the guaranteeing of the security of human society, as well as the providing an incentive for each one to pursue an industrious career. A man who steals may bid defiance to either or both of these ends. So far as the first is concerned it is obvious that the unjust appropriation of goods to such a value as to destroy this concord and furnish reasonable ground for great sorrow to the owner must be reputed a mortal sin. That amount is clearly not a constant quantity. It will vary according to the circumstances of the person injured as well as of place and time in which commodities may be more or less valuable. It will even take account of the special relationship which perchance the thief holds to the one he has despoiled, as when children steal from their parents. The sum so ascertained is termed the relatively grave matter. Thus the theft of an amount equal to a day's wages from an ordinary artisan would unquestionably be a mortal sin. The same thing must be said of the taking of an insignificant sum from a beggar. Theologians teach that this method of establishing the grievousness of theft cannot be employed indefinitely and exclusively. There is an absolute sum which it is always a mortal sin to take even from the wealthiest person or corporation. Were this not so the very fabric of human society would be imperilled, the stimulus to labour and enterprise extinguished, and the axe laid to the root of that confidence which must accompany human intercourse.

In the attempt to compute this sum in money theologians are not at one; nor is this surprising. In the settlement of the question we have to reckon with a most important factor, that is with the purchasing power of money which is not the same everywhere nor at all times. Writers on economics tell us that for the last hundred years or so this value has decreased from thirty to forty per cent. Of course, the less the value of money at any given time or in any region the more of it would be required to constitute a mortal sin of theft, always, however, within the limits of the principle already laid down. Comparisons instituted between the United States and Europe in the matter of wages prevailing and cost of living, seem to point unmistakably to the conclusion that money has less purchasing capacity here than abroad. Hence where reputable moralists assign as absolutely grave matter, six dollars for Italy, eight for Belgium, and from seven to ten for England, it will not be deemed excessive to fix the amount for this country as ranging from ten to fifteen dollars. One of the greatest of modern theologians, Palmieri, writing in Europe, professes his willingness to stand sponsor for the opinion which makes the sum twenty dollars. He gives as his reason the greatly lessened value of money in our own time. We may not feel obliged to accept this decision, but it is at any rate an indication of the trend of expert opinion. There is no doubt but that small pilferings perpetrated at different times, whether to the prejudice of one or of many owners, can eventually coalesce and reach a sum forbidden under pain of mortal sin. The contrary doctrine was condemned by Innocent XI. The reason, of course, is that the damage wrought is serious. This coalescence may be brought about by the specific intention of the thief in his petty stealing to ultimately arrive at a conspicuous amount. When several persons join forces to steal from another and the loss incurred is notable, then each one contracts the guilt of grievous sin, even though his own contribution to the wrong-doing has been but small. One who hoards the proceeds of his petty thefts is chargeable with mortal sin when the sum accumulated is grave. Even when he has disposed of his ill-gotten goods as fast as they were acquired, his thievings will still be held to coalesce unless there has been a considerable interval of time between them.

SLATER, *Manual of Moral Theology* (New York, 1908); BALLERINI, *Opus theologicum morale* (Prato, 1899); GENICOT, *Institutiones theologiæ moralis* (Louvain, 1898); BUCCERONI, *Enchiridion morale* (Rome, 1887).

JOSEPH F. DELANY.

Thegan (**Degan**) **of Treves**, chronicler, d. about 850. Very little is known of his life; all that is certain is that he was assistant Bishop of Trier and was a warm friend of Walafrid Strabo. These facts are learned from some letters and verses still in existence. It cannot be positively determined whether he is identical with Theganbert, provost of the Monastery of St. Cassius at Bonn, who placed the relics of Sts. Chrysanthus and Daria in the church at Münstereifel. He wrote a history of Louis the Pious, "Vita Ludovici imperatoris", an unsatisfactory narrative written in the form of scanty annals. It begins with St. Arnulf of Metz, describes the vicissitudes of the brothers of Louis, and gives a more detailed account of Louis's reign during the years 814–835. The later narrative is probably by another author. Strabo wrote an introduction to the chronicle. The narrative is very partisan, as the merits of Louis are exalted while the actions of Lothair and of a number of bishops, especially of Bishop Ebo of Reims, are severely criticised. The best edition of this work is that of Pertz in the "Mon. Germ. Hist.: Scriptores", II, 585–604. It was also published in P. L., CVI, 405–428, and was translated into German by Jasmund (Berlin, 1850) and by Wattenbach (Leipzig, 1889).

SIMSON, *Ueber Thegan, den Geschichtsschreiber Ludwigs des Frommen* (Göttingen, 1870); WATTENBACH, *Geschichtsquellen*, I (Berlin, 1893), 208 sq.; POTTHAST, *Bibliotheca* (Berlin, 1896), 1049.

PATRICIUS SCHLAGER.

Theiner, AUGUSTIN, theologian and historian, b. at Breslau, 11 April, 1804; d. at Civitavecchia, 8 Aug., 1874. He was the son of a shoemaker. As a boy he was a pupil at the gymnasium of St. Mathias at Breslau, and studied theology in the same city. Together with his brother Anthony he wrote, "Einführung der erzwungenen Ehelosigkeit bei den Geistlichen" (1828). At the advice of this brother he abandoned theology and turned his attention to law, which he studied at Breslau and Halle, and in 1829 he obtained a degree in law at the latter university. He then received a scholarship from the Prussian Government, which enabled him to make researches in Belgium, England, and France as to the sources of canon law. He finally went to Rome, where he settled permanently. Here, under the influence of Count Reisach then rector of the Propaganda and later cardinal, the change in his opinions was completed. In 1835 he wrote the "Geschichte der geistlichen Bildungsanstalten", and in 1836 the "Disquisitiones criticæ", on the sources of canon law. Soon after this he became a priest and entered the Oratory of St. Philip Neri. In the succeeding years he wrote the following works: "Die neuesten Zustände der kath. Kirche in Polen und Russland" (1841); "Die Rückkehr der regierenden Häuser Braunschweig und Sachsen zur kath. Kirche" (1843); "Zustände der kath. Kirche in Schlesien 1740–58" (1846); "Kardinal Frankenberg" (1850). He was commissioned by Pius IX, who had given him a position in the Vatican Library in 1850, to write the "Geschichte des Pontifikats Klemens XIV" (1853; Italian translation, 1855). In this work he showed himself an opponent of the Jesuits, with whom he had been on good terms until 1844, so that the work was forbidden in the States of the Church. In 1855 Pius IX appointed Theiner prefect of the Vatican archives. He now published his valuable collections of authorities drawn from these treasures: "Die Fortsetzung der Annalen des Baronius" (3 vols., 1856); "Vetera monumenta Hungariæ" (2 vols., 1859–60); "Poloniæ et Lithuaniæ" (4 vols., 1860–64); "Slavorum meridionalium" (2 vols., 1863); "Hibernorum et Scotorum" (1864); "Codex dominii temporalis apostolicæ sedis" (3 vols., 1861–62); "Monumenta spectantia ad unionem ecclesiarum Græcæ et Romanæ" (1872). Both before and during the Vatican Council he was in close connexion with the opponents of Infallibility. Because he communicated to them the order of business of the Council of Trent that had been kept secret he was deposed from his dignities and offices. Whether he died at peace with the Church is doubtful. His correspondence with the Old Catholic Professor Johann Friedrich during the years 1870–73 shows that he had the same views as the latter; on the other hand Count Hermann Stainlein asserts that he knew Theiner during this period as a loyal Catholic priest. There is no doubt as to his large scholarship and his services to history. After his death appeared the work, "Acta genuina Concilii Tridentini" (1874), very imperfectly edited.

GISIGER, *P. Theiner und die Jesuiten* (Mannheim, 1875); WITMEUR, *Auszüge aus dem Tagebuch des Grafen Hermann Stainlein von Saalenstein* (Leipzig, 1909), 352.

KLEMENS LÖFFLER.

Theism. See GOD.

Thelepte, a titular see in Byzacene. From an inscription we learn that it was a colony. An important network of Roman roads here branches out, joining the city to Cilium and Theveste, on the north; to Gafsa and Gabes, on the south. In the sixth century Thelepte became the residence of the military governor of Byzacene. Procopius (De Ædificiis, VI, 6) says that the city was fortified by Justinian. We have the names of several bishops: Julianus, present at the Council of Carthage in 256; Donatianus, who assisted at the Conference of Carthage in 411; he is said to have held a council in his episcopal city in 418, but this is uncertain (Tillemont, "Mémoires pour servir à l'hist. eccl.", X, 790–3). Thelepte was the native place of St. Fulgentius, Bishop of Ruspe. We have also the names of other bishops: Frumentius, exiled by Huneric, 484, after the Conference of Carthage; Stephen, present at the Council of Byzacene, 641. The ruins of Thelepte may be seen at Medinet el-Kedima, in Tunisia, a little to the north of Gafsa. The Byzantine citadel, in utter ruins, occupies the centre of the city. There are also the remains of baths, a theatre, and of ten churches recently discovered, one of which had five naves.

DIEHL, *Rapport sur deux missions dans l'Afrique du Nord* in *Nouvelles archives des missions scientifiques* (Paris, 1892), IV, 336–343; TOULOTTE, *Géographie de l'Afrique chrétienne, Byzacène et Tripolitaine* (Paris, 1894), 202–206.

S. VAILHÉ.

Themiscyra, a titular see, suffragan of Amasea in the Hellespont. There was a town of this name near the mouth of the Thermodon, the modern Therme-Tchai, mentioned by Herodotus (IV, 86) and by most classical authors. Scylax calls it a Greek town while Diodorus (II, 44) makes it an Amazonian foundation. Mythology made this region the native land of these warrior-women.

After Mithridates withdrew his troops from Cyzicus, Themiscyra was besieged by Lucullus and was courageously defended by the inhabitants. The town must have been destroyed on this occasion, for neither Mela nor Strabo mentions it, while the latter treats extensively the country of Themiscyra, which he makes the subject of great eulogy. It is, however, mentioned by Ptolemy (V, vi, 3). It is not found in the "Notitiæ episcopatuum" nor in the "Oriens christianus" of Le Quien. It was situated near the present Therme on the Black Sea, in the sanjak of Samsoun and the vilayet of Trebizond. The country is one of the richest and most beautiful in the world.

SMITH, *Dict. of Roman Geography,* s. v.; PAPE-BENSELER, *Wörterbuch der Griechischen Eigennamen,* s. v.; TEXIER, *Asie Mineure* (Paris, 1862), 620.

S. VAILHÉ.

Themisonium, a titular see in Phrygia Pacatiana, suffragan of Laodicea. Themisonium was a city of Phrygia, but near the limits of Pisidia, so that at one time it was said to be in that province. The inhabitants relate that during an invasion of the Gauls, warned by a dream which they attributed to the gods, Hercules, Apollo, and Hermes, they took refuge with their wives and children in a grotto or cave thirty stadia from their city, and placed at the entrance for protection the statues of the three divinities. The coins of the city show the god, Lycabas Sozon. It may be identified with the village of Kara Eyuk Bazar, vilayet of Smyrna.

Le Quien (Oriens christianus, I, 813) mentions the name of only one bishop of Themisonium, but he really belongs to Temenothyræ. On the other hand (ibid., 821), there was a see at Thampsiopolis, with two bishops: Zosimus, who lived in 451, and John, present at the Council of Constantinople, 869. These two sees are certainly one and the same: Thampsiopolis, mentioned in the "Notitiæ episcopatuum" from the tenth to the thirteenth century, is no other than Themisonium. If the earlier "Notitiæ episcopatuum" says nothing of this see it is probably because it was united with Agathe Come, of whose bishops there is no notice, and which disappeared from the later "Notitiæ". To the two bishops mentioned above we may add Magnus, present at the Council of Seleucia, 359.

SMITH, *Dict. of Gr. and Rom. Geog.*, s. v.; RAMSAY, *Asia Minor* (London, 1890), 135; IDEM, *The Cities and Bishoprics of Phrygia* (New York, 1895), 260, 274, and passim.

S. PÉTRIDÈS.

Thénard, LOUIS-JACQUES, BARON, chemist, b. at Louptière, near Nogent-sur-Seine, Aube, France, on 4 May, 1777; d. at Paris, 21 June, 1857. In 1865 his native village obtained the right to add his name, so the place is now known as Louptière-Thénard. When quite young he went to Paris, and sought permission to work at chemistry with Vauquelin as his master. It was only by the intercession of the sisters of the great chemist that he was taken into the laboratory, Vauquelin like him being very poor. He was unable to pay the small regular fee of twenty francs a month. After three years' work, when he undertook to lecture, his provincial accent and appearance told against him, and he made the most earnest efforts to overcome these defects. He cut down his meagre expenses in order to save enough to go to the theatre and hear the actors. His first original memoir was published in 1799, and for half a century he continued to pour out a flood of contributions to the science of chemistry. In a single month at the request of the Minister of the Interior he invented Thénard blue, a pigment for the use of the great Sèvres factory. The base of this is cobalt. He was intimately associated in his scientific work with Gay-Lussac for many years. In 1813 he published his "Treatise on Chemistry", which for twenty-five years had a great vogue, so that it was said that nearly all Europe learned chemistry from Thénard. After many honours he was elected to a seat in the Academy of Sciences. He at once set off for his home to receive the congratulations of his aged mother. He had found a copy of "The Imitation of Christ" in large print, that his mother could read without glasses. This he took with him, and he used to say that the finding of this book with its large type was one of his great discoveries. His work covered so great a range that there is not room here to tell of it. Dioxide of hydrogen was one of his best-known discoveries; he worked on the electrolysis of the oxides at the same time as Sir Humphry Davy, discovered boron, and came near antedating Davy in the isolation of chlorine. Most of his family died before him and his last years were filled with sadness. He was made a baron by Charles X in 1825 and served in the legislature.

Louis-Jacques Thénard
From a lithographic Portrait

Funeral eulogiums by SAINT HILAIRE and PELOUZE in *Comptes rendus de l'Académie des sciences* (1857), 1286 sqq.

T. O'CONOR SLOANE.

Thennesus, a titular suffragan see of Pelusium in Augustamnica Prima. Cassian (Collat., XI, 1–3) gives a very exact description of the little island which includes this bishopric. Its inhabitants were given solely to commerce owing to the lack of arable land. The bishop of this locality had just died when Cassian arrived there; and they were about to name a successor. In 451 Heron, another of its bishops, was condemned by the Council of Chalcedon for not having anathematized the Patriarch Dioscorus (Mansi, "Concil. coll.", VI, 572; VII, 52). During the eighth century the Patriarch of Antioch, Dionysius of Tell Mahré, landed there (Bar-Hebræus, "Hist. eccles.", I, 360). About 870 the monk Bernard was well received there by the inhabitants, who were almost all Christians (Tobler and Molinier, "Itinera hierosolymitana", I, 313). Thennesus is also mentioned in a Coptic "Notitia episcopatuum" (Rougé, "Géog. anc. de la Basse Egypte", 156). It is to-day Tell-Tenis, at the extremity of an island in Lake Menzaleh, near the Suez Canal. There still remain there ruins and tombs of the Roman era.

LE QUIEN, *Oriens chris.*, II, 549; GELZER, *Georgii Cyprii Descrip. orb. romani* (Leipzig, 1890), 113; AMÉLINEAU, *La géog. de l'Egypte à l'époque copte* (Paris, 1893), 507.

S. VAILHÉ.

Theobald, SAINT, b. at Provins in the Province of Champagne, France, in 1017; d. at Salanigo in Italy 30 June, 1066. He was a member of a noble family. In 1054 without the knowledge of his parents he and his friend Walter gave themselves to the life of hermits at Sussy in the Ardennes, then at Pittingen (now Pettingen) in the Diocese of Trier, a district that to-day belongs to the Grand Duchy of Luxemburg. From this place the two made a pilgrimage to Compostella in Spain, and afterwards returned into the territory of Trier. They made a second pilgrimage to Rome. As they returned they desired to go to Palestine by way of Venice, but Walter's strength failed near Salanigo in the Diocese of Vicenza. They therefore settled in a solitary place near Salanigo. After two years Walter died. A large number of disciples eager for salvation gathered around Theobald, who severed himself more and more from all earthly things. The bishop ordained him priest. His mother, who came to visit him, did not wish to leave him again, and led thenceforth under his direction a religious life.

Shortly before his death he entered the Camaldolese Order. Numerous miracles, some occurring before and some after his death, are reported of him. Alexander II (1061–1073) permitted the public veneration of St. Theobald. His veneration spread especially in Italy, France, Belgium, and Luxemburg. He is the patron saint of charcoal-burners.

Acta SS., June, V, 588–606; *Bibliotheca hagiogr. lat.* (Brussels, 1898–1900), 1163–4; WEICHERDING, *Der hl. Theobald* (Luxemburg, 1879); ALLOU, *Vie de saint Thibaud* (Meaux, 1873).

KLEMENS LÖFFLER.

Theobald (TEDBALD), Archbishop of Canterbury; d. 18 April, 1161. He was a Norman by descent and became a Benedictine monk at Bec late in the eleventh or early in the twelfth century. In 1127 he was made prior, and abbot in 1137. On 28 Dec., 1138, he was elected archbishop and was consecrated on 8 January following. He went to Rome for his pallium and took part in the second Lateran Council. He proved a wise and capable prelate, devout in his private life, charitable, and a lover of learning. During the civil war he adhered to King Stephen, whom he crowned, though for a time he was at the Empress Maud's court, and always worked for the Angevin succession.

In his household he collected many young men of ability, including his successor St. Thomas of Canterbury, and he encouraged the formation of scholars and statesmen of a new type. He was the first to introduce civil law into England, and founded a law school at Canterbury, inducing the famous jurist Roger Vacarius to come and lecture there. This introduction of Roman law had important effects on the fortunes of the common law of England, and incidentally led to the establishment of the Inns of Court to maintain the national body of law against the newly introduced code. Theobald suffered many difficulties owing to the appointment of his suffragan bishop, Henry of Winchester, as legate. Among these was the appointment of St. William of York as archbishop of that see, which Theobald felt bound to oppose. Celestine II did not reappoint Henry of Blois as legate and finally in 1150, or possibly before, Theobald was named legate by Blessed Eugene III, probably on the recommendation of St. Bernard (Ep. 238).

When the pope summoned the English bishops to a council at Reims the king forbade them to go, whereupon Theobald defied the king and went. Though he saved the king from excommunication, his property was confiscated and he was banished. The pope then put England under interdict, which was disregarded except in Canterbury, and finally the king and archbishop were reconciled in 1148. In 1151 Theobald held a legatine council in London. In the following year, acting on papal authority, he refused to crown Eustace, the king's son, and was again compelled to seek flight. While in Normandy he reconciled Henry of Anjou to Stephen, with the result that in 1153 the Treaty of Wallingford ended the Civil War. On Stephen's death Theobald crowned Henry II, and during the rest of his life, though not without anxiety for the future of the Church, he maintained good relations with the Court, especially with his former disciple Thomas, who had now become chancellor. He expressed to John of Salisbury his hope that Thomas would succeed him. Throughout his pontificate he had continual trouble with the monks of Christchurch, but in every instance his action was justified finally. He was buried in Canterbury Cathedral, where eighteen years afterwards his body was found incorrupt.

The *Chronicles* of Gervase of Canterbury, William of Malmesbury, Ralph de Diceto, Henry of Huntingdon, Giraldus Cambresis in *Rolls Series*, and many other medieval chroniclers including Howlett, *Chronicles of the reigns of Stephen, Henry II*, etc. in *R. S.* (London, 1884–9); *Materials for the History of St. Thomas à Becket* in *R. S.* (London, 1875–85); Milo, *Vita Theobaldi* in P. L., CL., 734; *Theobaldi Cantuariensis Episcopi Epistolæ et Testamentum* in *P. L.*, CXCIX, and CXC; Berington, *History of Henry II* (London, 1790); Lingard, *History of England* (London, 1819–30); Hook, *Lives of the Archbishops of Canterbury* (London, 1860–84); Hardy, *Descriptive Catalogue*, II (London, 1865); Norgate, *England under the Angevin Kings* (London, 1887); Hunt in *Dict. Nat. Biog.*, s. v.

Edwin Burton.

Theocracy, a form of civil government in which God himself is recognized as the head. The laws of the commonwealth are the commandments of God, and they are promulgated and expounded by the accredited representatives of the invisible Deity, real or supposed—generally a priesthood. Thus in a theocracy civic duties and functions form a part of religion, implying the absorption of the State by the Church or at least the supremacy of the latter over the State. The earliest recorded use of the term "theocracy" is found in Josephus, who apparently coins it in explaining to Gentile readers the organization of the Jewish commonwealth of his time. Contrasting this with other forms of government—monarchies, oligarchies, and republics—he adds: "Our legislator [Moses] had no regard to any of these forms, but he ordained our government to be what by a strained expression, may be termed a theocracy [θεοκρατίαν], by ascribing the power and authority to God, and by persuading all the people to have a regard to him as the author of all good things" (Against Apion, book II, 16). In this connexion Josephus enters into a long and rather rambling discussion of the topic, but the entire passage is instructive.

The extent to which the ideals of the Mosaic theocracy were realized in the history of the Chosen People is a matter of controversy. Many eminent scholars are inclined to restrict its sway almost exclusively to the post-exilic period, when unquestionably the hierocratic rule and the ordinances of the Priestly Code were more fully carried into effect than in any of the preceding epochs. Be that as it may, and waiving critical discussion of the Old-Testament writings with which the solution of the question is intimately connected, attention may be called to the fact that a belief in the theocratic rulership of nations and tribes is, in form more or less crude, characteristic of the common fund of Semitic religious ideas. The various deities were considered as having a territorial jurisdiction, fighting for their respective peoples and defending the lands in which they dwelled. This is amply proved by the extant historic and religious records of the Assyrians and Babylonians, and the same idea finds occasional expression in the Old Testament itself (see, for instance, Judges, xi, 23 sq.; I Kings, xxvi, 19; Ruth, i, 15, 16, etc.). In a passage of the Book of Judges, Gideon is represented as refusing to accept the kingship offered to him by the people after his victory over the Madianites, in terms implying that the establishment of a permanent monarchy would involve disloyalty to the rule of Yahweh. "I will not rule over you, neither shall my son rule over you, but the Lord shall rule over you" (Judges, viii, 23).

More explicit and stronger expression is given to the same view in the First Book of Kings in connexion with the appeal of the people to the aged prophet Samuel to constitute a king over them after the manner of the other nations. The request is displeasing to Samuel and to the Lord Himself, who commands the prophet to accede to the wishes of the people that they may be punished for their rejection of His kingship. "And the Lord said to Samuel: Hearken to the voice of the people in all that they say to thee. For they have not rejected thee, but me, that I should not reign over them" (I Kings, viii, 7). Again in chap. xii Samuel, in his final discourse to the people, reproaches them in similar words: "you said to me: Nay, but a king shall reign over us: whereas the Lord your God was your king". And at the call of the prophet the Lord sends thunder and rain as a sign of His displeasure, "and you shall know and see that you yourselves have done a great evil in the sight of the Lord, in desiring a king over you".

The bearing of these passages on the historic institution of the theocracy varies in the estimation of different scholars according to the date assigned by them to the sources to which the passages belong. Wellhausen and his school, chiefly on a priori grounds, consider them as retouches of the post-exilic period, but it is far more probable that they form a part of a much older tradition, and indicate that a belief in the Lord's kingship over the Chosen People existed prior to the establishment of the earthly monarchy. At the same time, there is no sufficient warrant for assuming on the authority of these texts that the theocratic rule in Israel came to an end with the inauguration of the monarchy, as is plain from the narration of the Lord's covenant with King David and his descendants (II Kings, vii, 1–17). According to the terms of this covenant the earthly monarch remains under the control of the heavenly King, and is constituted His vicegerent and representative. And this direct dependence of the king on the Lord for wisdom and guidance is assumed throughout the historical records of the Hebrew monarchy. The supreme test of the worthiness of any king to occupy his exalted position is his fidelity to the Lord and His revealed law. The historical books, and still more the writings of the prophets, voice the constant belief that God exercised a special and efficient rule over Israel by blessings, punishments, and deliverances. In the post-exilic period the hierocratic rule became the dominant feature of the Jewish theocracy, and, in spite of its limitations and perversions, it prepared, according to the designs of a wise Providence, the way for the New Dispensation— the Kingdom of Heaven so often mentioned in the Gospels.

Vigouroux, *Dictionnaire de la Bible*, s. v.

James F. Driscoll.

Theodard, Saint, Archbishop of Narbonne, b. at Montauban about 840; d. at the same place 1 May, 893. He seems to have belonged to a noble and wealthy family and to have studied with great zeal both ecclesiastical and secular learning in his youth. He gave proof of his education and skill when he was a subdeacon at a synod at Toulouse that was called upon to settle a dispute between the Jews of the place and Bishop Bernhard. In this way the presiding officer of the synod, Archbishop Sigebod of Narbonne (873–885), came to have so high an opinion of Theodard that he made him his archdeacon. In this position Theodard distinguished himself by faultless morals, modesty, piety, and charitableness, and was "eyes to the blind, feet to the lame, a father to the poor, and the consoler of all the oppressed". After Sigebod's death (885) Theodard was elected his successor, consecrated on 15 August, 885, and in 886 went to Rome to obtain the pallium from Stephen VI.

Theodard maintained with energy the rights of his see and its suffragans, repaired the damages that these dioceses had suffered from the incursions of the Saracens, restored the cathedral, and gave up his revenues and the treasures of his church for the release of captive Christians. At a later date he was able to replace the treasures he had used. He died where he had lived in the Benedictine Abbey of St. Martin and was buried there. The abbey bore his name from 845. It was later plundered by the Huguenots; since then all the relics of St. Theodard, excepting a small remnant, have disappeared.

Acta SS., May, I, 141–56; *Gallia christiana*, VI (Paris, 1739), 19–22; *Bibliotheca hagiogr. Lat.* (Brussels, 1898–1900), 1165; GUYARD, *Vie de St. Théodard* (Montauban, 1857; 2nd ed., Paris, 1887).

KLEMENS LÖFFLER.

Theodicy.—Etymologically considered theodicy (θεός δίκη) signifies the justification of God. The term was introduced into philosophy by Leibniz (q. v.), who, in 1710, published a work entitled: "Essais de Théodicée sur la bonté de Dieu, la liberté de l'homme et l'origine du mal". The purpose of the essay was to show that the evil in the world does not conflict with the goodness of God, that, indeed, notwithstanding its many evils, the world is the best of all possible worlds (see OPTIMISM). The problem of evil (see EVIL) has from earliest times engrossed the attention of philosophers. The well-known sceptic Pierre Bayle had denied in his "Dictionnaire historique et critique" the goodness and omnipotence of God on account of the sufferings experienced in this earthly life. The "Théodicée" of Leibniz was directed mainly against Bayle. Imitating the example of Leibniz other philosophers now called their treatises on the problem of evil "theodicies". As in a thorough treatment of the question the proofs both of the existence and of the attributes of God cannot be disregarded, our entire knowledge of God was gradually brought within the domain of theodicy. Thus theodicy came to be synonymous with natural theology (*theologia naturalis*), that is, the department of metaphysics which presents the positive proofs for the existence and attributes of God and solves the opposing difficulties. Theodicy, therefore, may be defined as the science which treats of God through the exercise of reason alone. It is a science because it systematically arranges the content of our knowledge about God and demonstrates, in the strict sense of the word, each of its propositions. But it appeals to nature as its only source of proof, whereas theology sets forth our knowledge of God as drawn from the sources of supernatural revelation.

The first and most important task of theodicy is to prove the existence of God. It is of course presupposed that the suprasensible can be known and that the limits of experience pure and immediate can be transcended. The justification of this assumption must be furnished by other branches of philosophy, e. g. criteriology and general metaphysics. The natural demonstrability of God's existence was always accepted by the majority of theists. Hume and Kant were the first to awaken in the minds of would-be theists serious doubt on this point. Not that these philosophers presented any solid reason against the long-tested arguments for the existence of God, but because in their systems a scientific proof of the existence of a supernatural being is impossible. New ways of establishing theism were now sought. The Scotch School led by Thomas Reid taught that the fact of the existence of God is accepted by us without knowledge of reasons but simply by a natural impulse. That God exists, this school said, is one of the chief metaphysical principles that we accept not because they are evident in themselves or because they can be proved, but because common sense obliges us to accept them. In Germany the School of Jacobi taught that our reason is able to perceive the suprasensible. Jacobi distinguished three faculties: sense, reason, and understanding. Just as sense has immediate perception of the material so has reason immediate perception of the immaterial, while the understanding brings these perceptions to our consciousness and unites them to one another (Stöckl, "Geschichte der neueren Philosophie", II, 82 sqq.). God's existence, then, cannot be proved—Jacobi, like Kant, rejected the absolute value of the principle of causality—it must be felt by the mind. In his "Emile", Jean-Jacques Rousseau asserted that when our understanding ponders over the existence of God it encounters nothing but contradictions; the impulses of our hearts, however, are of more value than the understanding, and these proclaim clearly to us the truths of natural religion, e. g., the existence of God, the immortality of the soul, etc. The same theory was advocated in Germany by Friedrich Schleiermacher (d. 1834), who assumed an inner religious sense by means of which we feel religious truths. According to Schleiermacher, religion consists solely in this inner perception, dogmatic doctrines are unessential (Stöckl, loc. cit., 199 sqq.). Nearly all Protestant theologians who have not yet sunken into atheism follow in Schleiermacher's footsteps. They generally teach that the existence of God cannot be demonstrated; certainty as to this truth is only furnished us by inner experience, feeling, and perception.

As is well known the Modernists also deny the demonstrability of the existence of God. According to them we can only know something of God by means of the vital immanence, that is, under favourable circumstances the need of the Divine dormant in our subconsciousness becomes conscious and arouses that religious feeling or experience in which God reveals himself to us (see MODERNISM). In condemnation of this view the oath against Modernism formulated by Pius X says: "Deum . . . naturali rationis lumine per ea quæ facta sunt, hoc est per visibilia creationis opera, tanquam causam per effectus certo cognosci adeoque demonstrari etiam posse, profiteor", i. e., I declare that by the natural light of reason, God can be certainly known and therefore His existence demonstrated through the things that are made, i. e., through the visible works of creation, as the cause is known through its effects.

There is, however, still another class of philosophers who assert that the proofs for the existence of God present indeed a fairly large probability but no absolute certainty. A number of obscure points, they say, always remain. In order to overcome these difficulties there is necessary either an act of the will, a religious experience, or the discernment of the misery of the world without God, so that finally the heart makes the decision. This view is maintained, among others, by the noted English statesman Arthur Balfour in his widely read book "The Foundations of Belief" (1895). The opinions set forth in this work were adopted in France by Brunetière, the editor of the "Revue des deux Mondes". Many orthodox Protestants express themselves in the same manner, as, for instance, Dr. E. Dennert, President of the Kepler Society, in his work "Ist Gott tot?" (Stuttgart, 1908). It must undoubtedly be conceded that for the perception of religious truths the mental attitude and temper are of great importance. As the questions here under consideration are those that penetrate deeply into practical life and their solution is not directly evident, the will is thus able to hold fast to the opposing difficulties and to prevent the understanding from attaining to quiet, objective reflection. But it is false to say that the understanding cannot eliminate every reasonable doubt as to the existence of God, or that a subjective inclination of the heart is a guarantee of the truth, even though there is no evidence that it is based on objective facts. This latter view would open the door wide to religious extravagance. It is not, therefore, an excess of intellectualism to demand that the truths which serve as the rational basis of faith shall be strictly proved.

Even in earlier times there were those who denied that the existence of God could be proved absolutely by the understanding alone, and took refuge in Revelation. In his "Summa contra Gentiles" (I, c. xii) St. Thomas refers to such reasoners. At a later date this opinion was championed by the Nominalists, William of Occam and Gabriel Biel, as well as by the Reformers; the Jansenists demanded the special aid of grace. In the nineteenth century the Traditionalists (see TRADITIONALISM) asserted that only when some vestiges of the original revelation reached man could he deduce with certainty the existence of God. Dr. J. Kuhn, formerly professor at Tübingen, declares that the clear recognition of the existence of God requires a pure soul unstained by sin. Ontologism (q. v.) went to the other extreme and asserted the immediate cognition of God. St. Anselm offered an a priori proof of the existence of God. This, however, has been always and rightly rejected by the majority of Catholic philosophers, notwithstanding the modifications by which Duns Scotus, Leibniz, and Descartes sought to save it (cf. Dr. Otto Paschen, "Der ontologische Gottesbeweis in der Scholastik", Aachen, 1903; M. Esser, "Der ontologische Gottesbeweis und seine Geschichte", Bonn, 1905). In regard to the various a posteriori proofs for the existence of God, see the article GOD. A dispute has arisen of late as to whether there are a number of proofs of the existence of God or whether all are not merely parts of one and the same proof (cf. Dr. C. Braig, "Gottesbeweis oder Gottesbeweise?", Stuttgart, 1888). It is certain that we always reach God as the cause, the last ground of all existence, and thus constantly follow as a guide the principle of sufficient reason. But the starting-point of the individual proofs varies. St. Thomas calls them aptly (Summ. theol., I, Q. ii, a. 3) *viæ*, i. e., roads to the apprehension of God which all open on the same highway.

After demonstrating the existence of God, theodicy investigates the question as to His nature and attributes. The latter are in part absolute (*quiescentia*) in part relative (*operativa*). In the first class belong the infinity, unity, immutability, omnipresence, and eternity; to the second class the knowledge, volition, and action of God. The action of God includes the creation, maintenance, and government of the world, the co-operation of God with the activity of the creature, and the working of miracles. The understanding affords us abundant knowledge concerning God, although it allows us but faint glimpses of His essential greatness and beauty. For one thing should not be forgotten, namely, that all our cognition of God is incomplete and analogous, that is, is formed from notions that we have deduced from created things. Hence it is that much remains obscure to us, as for instance, how God's immutability harmonizes with His freedom, and how He knows the future. But the inadequacy of our knowledge does not justify the assertion of the Agnostic that God is unknowable and that consequently any attempt such as theodicy makes to reason about His attributes and our relations to Him is foredoomed to failure (see AGNOSTICISM).

An historical survey of the development of the proofs from Plato to Leibniz for the existence of God may be found in the work of GRATRY, *De la connaissance de Dieu*, I (Paris, 1853), 72–434, II, 1–98. Of value are also: GRUNWALD, *Gesch. der Gottesbeweise im Mittelalter bis zum Ausgang der Hochscholastik* (Münster, 1907); DANIELS, *Quellenbeiträge u. Untersuchungen zur Gesch. der Gottesbeweise im XIII. Jahrhundert mit besonderer Berücksichtigung des Arguments im Proslogion des hl. Anselm* (Münster, 1909); STAAB, *Die Gottesbeweise in der katholischen deutschen Litteratur von 1850–1900* (Paderborn, 1910).

In addition to the bibliography under the article GOD, the following works may be mentioned: LILLY, *The Great Enigma* (London, 1892); LUCAS, *Agnosticism and Religion* (New York, 1895); MOYES, *The Existence of God* (London, and Edinburgh, 1906); WARD, *Essay on the Philosophy of Theism* (London, 1884); FLINT, *Antitheistic Theories* (2nd ed., London and Edinburgh, 1880); HONTHEIM, *Institutiones Theodiceæ* (Freiburg, 1893); URRÁBURU, *Theodicea* (Vallodolid, 1899); SCHIFFINI, *Disputationes metaphysicæ*, 2 vols. of *Theologia naturalis* (2nd ed., Turin, 1894); BOEDDER, *Theologia naturalis* (3rd ed., Freiburg, 1911); ZIGLIARA, *Theologia naturalis* (Rome, 1886); GEYSER, *Das philosophische Gottesproblem* (Bonn, 1899); GUTBERLET, *Die Theodicee* (4th ed., Münster, 1909); LEHMEN, *Theodicee* (2nd ed., Freiburg, 1906); MAYER, *Der teleologische Gottesbeweis u. der Darwinismus* (Mainz, 1901); ROLFES, *Die Gottesbeweise bei Thomas von Aquin und Aristoteles* (Cologne, 1898); MOISANT, *Dieu, l'expérience en métaphysique* (Paris, 1907); DE BROGLIE, *Preuve psychologique de l'existence de Dieu* (Paris, 1905). See also the bibliographies to AGNOSTICISM, ATHEISM, EVIL, MODERNISM, MONISM, and PANTHEISM.

CONSTANTIN KEMPF.

Theodore I, POPE, from 642 to 649; the date of his birth is unknown. He was a Greek of Jerusalem and the son of a bishop, Theodore. His election as pope was promptly confirmed by the Exarch of Ravenna, perhaps because he was a Greek, and he was consecrated 24 Nov., 642. Engaged throughout all his pontificate in the struggle against Monothelitism, he at once wrote to the Byzantine Emperor Constans II to inform him that he could not recognize Paul as Patriarch of Constantinople, because the deposition of his predecessor (Pyrrhus) had not been canonical. He then urged Constans to withdraw the Ecthesis. He also wrote to Paul and to the bishops who had consecrated him, to impress upon them the importance of securing the legal deposition of Pyrrhus, if the accession of Paul was to be recognized. If Theodore's vigorous action produced no result at Constantinople, it elsewhere excited strong opposition to Monothelitism. The Bishops of Cyprus, Palestine, and Africa expressed their loyal submission to his teaching in very striking language. Even the deposed patriarch Pyrrhus recanted his heresy before Theodore (645), but soon relapsed into his old errors, and was excommunicated by the pope (648). Meanwhile, urged by the bishops of Africa, Theodore made another effort to reclaim Paul, but only succeeded in drawing from him an express declaration of his belief in the doctrine of one Will in our Lord. This brought upon him sentence of excommunication and deposition from Rome (649). To this Paul replied by barbarously ill-treating the papal *apocrisiarii* (or nuncios) at Constantinople. He also prevailed upon Constans to issue a new decree known as the Type (*Typus*). This document ordered the *Ecthesis* to be taken down, and enjoined that in future there was to be no more discussion on the doctrine of one or two Wills or Operations. The Type was promptly condemned "by the whole West" in general, and specifically by Theodore's successor (St. Martin I), but it is not certain whether Theodore lived long enough to anathematize it. This energetic pontiff, who was good to the poor of Rome, and a benefactor of its churches, was buried in St. Peter's, 14 May, 649.

Liber Pontificalis, I, 330 sqq., ed. DUCHESNE (Paris, 1886); JAFFÉ, *Regesta*, I, 228 sqq. (Leipzig, 1888); MAXIMI, *Disputatio, vita*, etc., in LABBE, *Concil.*, V, pp. 1813 sqq.; or *P. L.*, CXXIX; or COMBEFIS (2 vols., Paris, 1675); *Acts of the Lateran Council under Martin I;* MANN, *Lives of the Popes in the early Middle Ages*, I (London, 1902), 369 sqq.

HORACE K. MANN.

Theodore II, POPE, son of Photius. His pontificate lasted only twenty days; neither the date of his birth nor of his accession to the papacy is known; it is probable that he was pope during December 897. He reinstated in synod the clerics who had been degraded by Stephen (VI) VII, ordered the burning of the acts of resignation which they had been forced to tender, and formally recognized the validity of the orders conferred by Pope Formosus. He caused the body of the last-named pope, which had been thrown into the Tiber and cast ashore by a flood, to be reburied in St.

Peter's. By his contemporary Frodoard he is said to have been beloved by the clergy, to have himself loved and promoted peace, and to have been temperate, and chaste, and charitable to the poor.

FRODOARD, *De Christi triumph.* in *P. L.*, CXXXV; AUXILIUS in DÜMMLER, *Auxilius und Vulgarius* (Leipzig, 1866); JAFFÉ, *Regesta*, I (Leipzig, 1888); MANN, *Lives of the Popes in the early Middle Ages* (London, 1910), 88 sqq.

HORACE K. MANN.

Theodore, seventh Archbishop of Canterbury, b. at Tarsus in Cilicia about 602; d. at Canterbury 19 September, 690; was a monk (probably of the Basilian Order), but not yet in Holy orders, living at Rome in 667, when Pope Vitalian chose him for the See of Canterbury in place of Wighard, who had died before consecration. After receiving orders, Theodore was consecrated by the pope himself, on 26 March, 668, and set out for England, but did not reach Canterbury until May, 669. The new primate found the English Church still suffering from the jealousies and bitterness engendered by the long Paschal controversy, only lately settled, and sadly lacking in order and organization. The dioceses, conterminous with the divisions of the various kingdoms, were of unwieldy size, and many of them were vacant. Theodore, says Bede, at once "visited all the island, wherever the tribes of the Angles inhabited", and was everywhere received with respect and welcome. He made appointments to the vacant bishoprics, regularized the position of St. Chad, who had not been duly consecrated, corrected all that was faulty, instituted the teaching of music and of sacred and secular learning throughout the country, and had the distinction of being, as Bede specially mentions, "the first archbishop whom all the English Church obeyed". In 673 he convoked at Hertford the first synod of the whole province, an assembly of great importance as the forerunner and prototype of future English witenagemotes and parliaments. Going later to the court of the King of Northumbria, which country was entirely under the jurisdiction of St. Wilfrid, he divided it into four dioceses against the will of Wilfrid, who appealed to Pope Agatho. The pope's decision did not acquit Theodore of arbitrary and irregular action, although his plan for the subdivision of the Northumbrian diocese was carried out. For the See of Lindisfarne Theodore himself consecrated St. Cuthbert in 685, and in the following year he was fully reconciled to Wilfrid, who was restored to his See of York. Thus, before his death, which occurred five years later, Theodore saw the diocesan system of the English Church fully organized under his primatical and metropolitical authority. Stubbs emphasizes the immensely important work done by Theodore not only in developing a single united ecclesiastical body out of the heterogeneous Churches of the several English kingdoms, but in thus realizing a national unity which was not to be attained in secular matters for nearly three centuries.

Apart from the epoch-making character of his twenty-one years' episcopate, Theodore was a man of commanding personality: inclined to be autocratic, but possessed of great ideas, remarkable powers of administration, and intellectual gifts of a high order, carefully cultivated. Practically his only literary remains are the collected decisions in disciplinary matters, well known as "The Penitential of Theodore". It was first published complete by Wasserschleben in 1851, and several editions of it have been printed during the past sixty years. Theodore was buried in St. Augustine's Monastery, Canterbury, a long poetical epitaph, of which Bede has preserved only eight verses, being inscribed upon his tomb.

BEDE, ed. MOBERLY, *Hist. Ecclesiastica Gent. Angl.* (Oxford, 1879), 212–215, 227, 236–39, etc.; HADDAN AND STUBBS, *Councils and Eccles. Documents*, III (Oxford, 1871), 114–213; STUBBS in *Dict. Christ. Biog.* (London, 1887), s. v. *Theodorus* (7); MANN, *Lives of the Popes*, I (London, 1902), ii, 10, 11, 28–36, bks. WILLELM. MALMESB., ed. HAMILTON, *De Gestis Pontificum Angl.* I-III (London, 1870); EDDIUS, *Vita S. Wilfridi* in RAINE, *Historians of the Ch. of York*, I (London, 1879), 1–103.—For text of Theodore's *Penitential* and other reputed works, see *P. L.*, XCIX, 901–1229.

D. O. HUNTER-BLAIR.

Theodore, Bishop of Mopsuestia in Cilicia and ecclesiastical writer, b. at Antioch about 350 (thus also known as Theodore of Antioch), of wealthy and prominent parents; d. 428.

I.—According to Syrian sources Theodore was the cousin of the somewhat younger Nestorius (Nestle, op. cit. in bibliography); Polychromius, afterwards Bishop of Apamea, was a brother of Theodore. The clever and highly gifted youth received the education in classical literature usual to his station and studied philosophy and rhetoric in the school of the renowned pagan rhetorician Libanius. He here became acquainted with his early friends, St. John Chrysostom and Maximus, later Bishop of Seleucia (perhaps as fellow-student). Following the example of Chrysostom (Socrates, "Hist. eccl.",VI, iii), Theodore renounced a secular career when about eighteen years old, and devoted himself to the ascetic life in the school of Diodorus (later Bishop of Tarsus) and Carterius, situated near Antiochia. His youthful and too tempestuous zeal soon grew cold, and, owing chiefly to the memory of Hermione whom he intended to take as wife, he resolved to return to the world (Sozomen, "Hist. eccl.", VIII, 2; Hesychius Hieros., "Hist. eccl." in Mansi, "Concil.", IX, 248). Chrysostom's grief at this step of his friend was so great that he addressed him two letters or treatises ("Ad Theodorum lapsum" in P. G., XLVII, 277 sqq.) to recall him to his early resolution. A little later Theodore did indeed return to the "divine philosophy" of the ascetic-monastic life. He quickly acquired a great acquaintance with the Holy Scriptures. Impetuous and restless of character, he had already, when scarcely twenty years old (at eighteen according to Leontius, "Adv. Incorrupticolas", viii, in P. G., LXXXVI, 1364), applied himself to theological compositions. His first work was the commentary on the Psalms, in which his extreme exegetical tendencies in the sense of an almost exclusively grammatico-historical and realistic explanation of the text is already manifest (see below Theodore's Hermeneutics). Between 383 and 386 he was ordained priest (perhaps together with Chrysostom) by his early teacher (now bishop) Flavian. Theodore soon displayed a very keen interest in the theologico-polemical discussions of the time, writing and preaching against the Origenists, Arians, Eunomians, Apollinarists, magicians, Julian the Apostate, etc. His keen and versatile literary activity won him the name of "Polyhistor" (Sozomen, op. cit., VIII, ii). Theodore apparently left Antioch before 392 to join his older teacher Diodorus, who was then Bishop of Tarsus (Hesychius Hier., op. cit., in Mansi, IX, 248). Probably through the influence of Diodorus he was named Bishop of Mopsuestia in 392, in which capacity he was to labour thirty-six years. In 394 he attended the Synod of Constantinople, and during its progress preached before the Emperor Theodosius the Great. During the confusion concerning Chrysostom, Theodore remained faithful to his early friend (cf. Chrysostom,"Epp.", cxii, in P. G., LII, 668; Latin translation in Facundus, loc. cit., VII, 7). Later (about 421) he received hospitably Julian of Eclanum and other Pelagians, and doubtless allowed himself to be further influenced by their dogmatic errors. However, he later associated himself with the condemnation of Pelagianism at a synod in Cilicia (Marius Merc. in P. L., XLVIII, 1044). He died in 428, the year in which Nestorius succeeded to the episcopal See of Constantinople. During his lifetime Theodore was always regarded as orthodox and as a prominent ecclesiastical author, and was even consulted by distant bishops on theological questions.

II. WRITINGS.—The most complete list of the writings of Theodore is given by Ebedjesu (d. 1318; see Assemani, "Bibl. orient.", III, 30–36). According to this the following works existed in a Syrian translation. A. *Exegetical Commentaries:* (a) On the Old Testament: (1) on Genesis, 3 books (Greek fragments in the Nicephoruscatene, Leipzig, 1772; Syrian in Sachau, 1–21); (2) on the Psalms, 5 books (Greek fragments in P. G., LXVI, 648; Latin translation discovered by Mercati, see bibliography; Greek text discovered by Lietzmann, but not yet edited, cf. ibid.); (3) on the twelve Minor Prophets (extant in its entirety; edited by Mai in P. G., LXVI, 124–632); (4) on the First and Second Books of Kings, 1 book (lost); (5) on Job, 2 books, dedicated to St. Cyril of Alexandria (only four fragments preserved in P. G., loc. cit., 697 sq.); (6) on Ecclesiastes, 1 book (lost); (7) to the four Great Prophets, 4 books (lost). Assemani adds "Quæstiones et Responsiones in Sacram Scripturam"; the fragments mentioned by the Fifth Œcumenical Council (Mansi, IX, 225) on the Canticle of Canticles are perhaps taken from a letter. (b) On the New Testament: (1) on Matthew, 1 book (fragments in P. G., LXVI, 705 sqq.); (2) on Luke, 1 book (fragments, ibid., 716 sqq.); (3) on John, 1 book (fragments, ibid., 728; Syrian, discovered and edited by Chabot, Paris, 1897); (4) on the Acts, 1 book (fragments in P. G., LXVI, 785 sq.); (5) on all the Epistles of St. Paul (Greek fragments in P. G., LXVI, 188–968; the Epistles to the Galatians, Colossians, Thessalonians, Philemon, Latin edition by H. B. Swete, Cambridge, 1880–82). B. *Opuscula:* (1) "De sacramentis", 1 book (lost); (2) "De fide", 1 book ("Liber ad baptizatos", according to Facundus, op. cit., IX, 3; fragments in Swete, II, 323–27); (3) "De sacerdotio", 1 book (lost); (4) "De Spiritu Sancto", 2 books, against the Macedonians (lost); (5) "De Incarnatione", 15 books (cf. Facundus, IX, 3; Gennadius, 12; written at Antioch about 382–92 against the Apollinarians and Eunomians; Greek fragm. in P. G., LXVI, 969 sqq., and Swete, II, 290–312); (6) "Contra Eunomium", 2 books (one fragment in Facundus, IX, 3); (7) "Contra dicentes: peccatum naturæ inesse", 2 books (cf. Photius, "Bibl.", 177); (8) "Contra magicam artem", 2 books (cf. Photius, 81); (9) "Ad monachos", 1 book (lost); (10) "De obscura locutione", 1 book (lost); (11) "De perfectione operum", 1 book (lost); (12) "Contra allegoristas", 5 books (cf. Facundus, III, 6: "De allegoria et historia"); (13) "De Assumente et Assumpto", 1 book (lost); (14) "De legislatione", 1 book (lost). Many unidentified fragments are perhaps taken from lost works. The fifteen books "De mysteriis" or "Opus mysticum", mentioned by Assemani (III, 1, 563), are probably identical with the "Codex mysticus" cited by Facundus (III, 2). Concerning the "Symbolum fidei" (Facundus, III, 2; Leontius, P. G., LXXXVI, 1367), cf. Fritzsche in P. G., LXVI, 73 sqq. Leontius Byzant. ("Advers. Incorr.", xx, in P. G., LXXXVI, 1368) says, perhaps with reference to the so-called Nestorian Liturgy, that Theodore had also introduced a new Liturgy. C. *Letters:* These were collected in one volume which is now lost.

III. THEODORE'S DOCTRINE.—A. *Hermeneutics and Canon.*—As regards the Old Testament, Theodore seems to have accepted Flavius Josephus's idea of inspiration and his canon. He rejected as uncanonical the Book of Job, the Canticle of Canticles, the Book of Esdras, and the deutero-canonical books. From the New Testament he excised the Catholic Epistles (except I Peter and I John) and the Apocalypse (cf. Leontius, loc. cit., III, 13–17, in P. G., LXXXVI, 1365–68). In his explanation of the Holy Writ Theodore employs primarily the prevailing historical and grammatical method of the Antiochene school. Of all the Psalms he recognized only ii, viii, xlv, and cx as containing direct prophetic reference to the Messias; the Canticle of Canticles was pronounced by him a vulgar nuptial poem. B. *Anthropology and Doctrine of Justification.*—Theodore's doctrine concerning justification gave rise to very grave misgivings, even if we reject the accusations of Leontius (loc. cit., 20–37) as exaggerated. According to Theodore, the sin of Adam rendered himself and mankind subject to death, because he was then mutable. But that which was the consequence of sin in the case of Adam is in his descendants its cause, so that in consequence of mutability all men in some manner or other sin personally. The object of the Redemption was to transfer mankind from this condition of mutability and mortality to the state of immutability and immortality. This happened first in the case of Christ, fundamentally by the union with the Logos, to a greater extent at His baptism, and completely at His Resurrection. In mankind this change is effected by union with Christ. The union begins in baptism, through which (1) all (personal) sins are remitted, (2) the grace of Christ is granted, which leads us to immutability (sinlessness) and immortality. At the baptism of children only this second effect occurs. That these ideas show a certain resemblance to the fundamental thoughts of Pelagianism is not to be denied; whether, however, Theodore influenced Pelagius and Cælestius (according to Marius Mercator, through the medium of the Syrian Rufinus; P. L., XLVIII, 110), or whether these influenced Theodore, is very difficult to determine. C. *Christology.*—Theodore's Christology exercised a more direct and eventful influence on the doctrine of his (mediate) disciple Nestorius (q. v.). The contemporary polemics against Arianism and Apollinarianism led the Antiochenes (Diodorus, Theodore, and Nestorius) to emphasize energetically the perfect Divinity and the unimpaired Humanity of Christ, and to separate as sharply as possible the two natures. Thus, in a sermon which he delivered at Antioch (perhaps the first as bishop), Theodore vehemently attacked the use of the term θεοτόκος, long employed in ecclesiastical terminology, because Mary was strictly speaking ἀνθρωποτόκος, and only indirectly θεοτόκος. It was only by recalling his words and correcting himself that Theodore could appease the excitement resulting from this view (see John of Antioch, "Epist. ad Theodosium imper." in Facundus Herm., "Pro defensione trium capp.", X, 2; P. L., LXXXVII, 771). It cannot indeed be denied that the Antiochene separation of the natures must result in an improper weakening of the union in Christ. Like Nestorius, Theodore expressly declares that he wished to uphold the unity of person in Christ; perhaps they recognized some distinction between nature and person, but did not know exactly what was the distinguishing factor, and therefore used faulty paraphrases and comparisons, and spoke of the two natures in a way which, taken strictly, presupposed two persons. Thus, according to Theodore, the human nature of Christ was not only *passibilis*, but also really *tentabilis*, since otherwise His actual freedom from sin would be the result of His physical union with God, not a merit of His free will. The union of the human and Divine nature happens not κατ' οὐσίαν nor κατ' ἐνέργειαν, but κατ' εὐδοκίαν (at will), and indeed a εὐδοκία ὡς ἐν υἱῷ it is a συνάφεια, which effects a ἕνωσις εἰς ἓν πρόσωπον. The two natures form a unity, "like man and wife" or "body and soul". Consequently, according to Theodore, the *communicatio idiomatum*, fundamentally speaking, is also lawful.

IV. THE CONDEMNATION OF THE DOCTRINE OF THEODORE.—While during his lifetime (apart from the episode at Antioch) Theodore was regarded as orthodox (cf. Theodoret, "Hist. eccl.", V, xxxix; John of Antioch, in Facundus, II, 2), a loud outcry was raised against him when the Pelagians and Nestorians appealed to his writings. The first to represent him as the father of Pelagianism was Marius Mercator in his work "Liber subnotationum in verba Juliani, Præf." (about 431; in P. L., XLVIII, 111). He was accused of Nestorianism by Hesychius of Jerusalem in his Church History (about 435). Rabulas of Edessa went so far as to pronounce anathema on Theodore. Acting under the influence of the latter, St. Cyril of Alexandria expressed himself in fairly sharp terms concerning Theodore, naming him with Diodorus the "patres Nestorii blasphemiæ" ("Ep. lxxi ad Theodosium imp.", in P. G., LXXVII, 341–44); he was, however, unwilling to condemn Theodore, as he had died in peace with the Church. Meanwhile the Nestorian strife passed by without any official action being taken by the Church against Theodore, although his writings stood in higher favour among the Nestorians of Edessa and Nisibis than those of Nestorius himself. The General Council of Chalcedon seemed rather to favour Theodore, when it declared his disciples and admirers, Theodoret and Ibas of Edessa, orthodox, although the latter in his epistle to Maris had referred to Theodore in terms of the highest praise. The Monophysitic reaction under the Council of Chalcedon in the sixth century first succeeded in bringing Theodore's person and writings under the ban of the ecclesiastical anathema through the ill-famed dispute of the Three Chapters. Theodore was for the first time condemned as a heretic by the Emperor Justinian in his edict against the Three Chapters (544). Under the influence of imperial pressure Pope Vigilius composed (553) at Constantinople a document in which sixty propositions taken from Theodore's writings were declared heretical. Finally, at the Fifth General Synod (553), at which, however, Vigilius did not participate, the three Chapters, including Theodore's writings and person, were placed under anathema. It was only on 8 December that Vigilius, broken with exile, gave his approval to the decrees of the synod. Among the most zealous defenders of Theodore and the Three Chapters, besides Pope Vigilius (until 533), were the African Facundus of Hermiana ("Pro defensione trium capitulorum libri XII", in P. L., LXVII, 527 sqq.) and the bishops, Paulinus of Aquileia and Vitalis of Milan.

The most complete edition of Theodore's works is given in P. G., LXVI, 124 sqq.; see also: SWETE, *Theodori Ep. Mopsuesteni in epistolas B. Pauli. The Latin Version with the Greek Fragments* (2 vols., Cambridge, 1880–82); SACHAU, *Theodori Mopsuesteni fragmenta syriaca* (Leipzig, 1869); and some fragments in *S. Innocenti ep. Maroniæ: De his qui unum ex trinitate vel unum Subsistentiam seu personam Dominum nostrum Jesum Christum dubitant confiteri*, ed. AMELLI in *Spicilegium Casinense*, I (1888), 148-54. TILLEMONT, *Mémoires*, XII (1732), 433 sqq.; FRITZSCHE, *De Theodori Mopsuesteni vita et scriptis* (Halle, 1836; reprinted in P. G., LXVI, 9 sqq.; SWETE in *Dict. Christ. Biog.*, s. v.; SPECHT, *Der exeget. Standpunkt des Theodor u. Theodoret in Auslegung der messian. Weissagungen* (Munich, 1871); KIHN, *Theodor von M. u. Junilius Africanus als Exegeten* (Freiburg, 1880); ZAHN, *Das Neue Testament Theodors v. M. u. der ursprüngl. Kanon der Syrer* in *Neue kirchl. Zeitschr.*, XI (1900), 788–806; DENNEFELD, *Der alttestam. Kanon der Antiochen. Schule* (Freiburg, 1909), 44–61 (*Bibl. Studien*, 14, 4); BAETHGEN, *Der Psalmenkommentar des Theodor v. M. in syrischer Bearbeitung* in *Zeitschr. für alttestam. Wissenschaft*, V (1885), 53–101; VI (1886), 261–88; VII (1887), 1–60; LIETZMANN, *Der Psalmenkommentar Theodors v. M.* in *Sitzungsberichte der kgl. preussichen Akademie der Wissenschaften* (1902), 334–46; MERCATI, *Un palimpsesto Ambrosiano dei Salmi Esapli* (Turin, 1896); cf. ASCOLI, *Il codice irlandese dell' Ambrosiana* in *Archivio glottologico italiano*, V, VI; VON DOBSCHÜTZ in *American Journal of Theology*, II (1898), 353–87; FENDT, *Die Christologie des Nestorius* (Kempten, 1910), 9–12: *Theodor v. Mopsuestia*; NESTLE, *Theodor von M. u. Nestorius; Eine Mitteilung aus syrischen Quellen* in *Theolog. Studien aus Württemberg* (1881), 210-11.

CHRYS. BAUR.

Theodore of Amasea, SAINT, surnamed TYRO (TIRO), not because he was a young recruit, but because for a time he belonged to the Cohors Tyronum (Nilles, Kal. man., I, 105), called of Amasea from the place where he suffered martyrdom, and Euchaita from the place, Euchais, to which his body had been carried, and where he was held in such veneration that the city was frequently spoken of as Theodoropolis. His martyrdom seems to have taken place 17 Feb., 306, under the Emperors Galerius Maximian and Maximin, for on this day the Menologies give his feast. The Greeks and Armenians honour him also on the first Saturday of Lent, while the Roman Martyrology records him on 9 Nov. In the twelfth century his body was transferred to Brindisi, and he is there honoured as patron; his head is enshrined at Gaeta. There are churches bearing his name at Constantinople, Jerusalem, Damascus, and other places of the East. An ancient church of Venice, of which he is titular, is said to have been built by Narses. At the foot of the Palatine in Rome is a very old church, circular in shape and dedicated to S. Teodoro, whom the Roman people call S. Toto, which was made a collegiate church by Felix IV. The people showed their confidence in the saint by bringing their sick children to his temple. His martyrdom is represented in the choir of the cathedral of Chartres by thirty-eight glass paintings of the thirteenth century (Migne, "Dict. iconogr.", 599). He is invoked against storms. Emblems: temple, torch, crocodile, pyre, crown of thorns.

St. Gregory of Nyssa delivered a panegyric on his feast and gave several data concerning his life and martyrdom (P. G., XLVI, 741, and Ruinart, 505). The oldest text of the "Martyrium S. Theodori Tironis" was published by Delehaye in "Les légendes grecques des saints militaires", p. 227, but it is considered largely interpolated (Anal. Boll., XXX, 323). St. Theodore is said to have been born in the East (Syria or Armenia are mentioned by some writers). He enlisted in the army and was sent with his cohort to winter quarters in Pontus. When the edict against the Christians was issued by the emperors, he was brought before the Court at Amasea and asked to offer sacrifice to the gods. Theodore, however, denied their existence and made a noble profession of his belief in the Divinity of Jesus Christ. The judges, pretending pity for his youth, gave him time for reflection. This he employed in burning the Temple of Cybele. He was again taken prisoner, and after many cruel torments was burned at the stake.

BUTLER, *Lives of the Saints; Dict. of Christ. Biog.;* STADLER, *Heiligenlexikon;* ARMELLINI, *Le chiese di Roma* (Rome, 1887); ALLARD, *Hist. des persécut.*, V (Paris, 1908), 44; CHEVALIER, *Bio-Bibl.*, II, 4410.

FRANCIS MERSHMAN.

Theodore of Gaza, a fifteenth-century Greek Humanist and translator of Aristotle, b. at Thessalonica early in the fifteenth century; d. in Southern Italy in 1478. In 1429 he went to Italy, where he made his home, like many other learned Greeks who did not wish to submit to the rule of the Turks at Constantinople. He taught Greek at Siena, Ferrara, and Rome. Having learned Latin from Victorino da Feltre, he devoted himself to the translation of Aristotle's works into that language. He was received with favour at the Court of Nicholas V, and, although a pronounced Aristotelean, remained on terms of friendship with Cardinal Bessarion. Through the good offices of the cardinal he obtained a small benefice in the Abruzzi. His chief service to the cause of Peripatetic philosophy consisted in his translations, which were superior both in point of accuracy and in that of style to the versions in use before his time. He devoted particular attention to the translation and exposition of Aristotle's works on natural science. In the campaign waged by Plethon (q. v.) against Aristotelianism he contributed his share to the defence of the Stagyrite. His influence on the humanistic movement was considerable, owing to the success with which he taught Greek language and literature at the various seats of learning in Italy. At Ferrara he founded an academy to offset the influence of the Platonic academy founded by Plethon at Florence.

UEBERWEG, *Hist. of Philosophy*, tr. MORRIS, I (New York, 1892), 10.

WILLIAM TURNER.

Theodore of Studium, SAINT, a zealous champion of the veneration of images and the last great representative of the unity and independence of the Church in the East, b. in 759; d. on the Peninsula of Tryphon, near the promontory Akrita on 11 November, 826. He belonged to a very distinguished family and like his two brothers, one of whom, Joseph, became Archbishop of Thessalonica, was highly educated. In 781 Theodore entered the monastery of Saccudion on the Asiatic side of the Bosphorus near Constantinople, where his uncle Plato was abbot. In 787 or 788 Theodore was ordained priest and in 794 succeeded his uncle. He insisted upon the exact observance of the monastic rules. During the Adulterine heresy dispute (see NICEPHORUS, SAINT), concerning the divorce and remarriage of the Emperor Constantine VI, he was banished by Constantine VI to Thessalonica, but returned in triumph after the emperor's overthrow. In 799 he left Saccudion, which was threatened by the Arabs, and took charge of the monastery of the Studium at Constantinople. He gave the Studium an excellent organization which was taken as a model by the entire Byzantine monastic world, and still exists on Mount Athos and in Russian monasticism. He supplemented the somewhat theoretical rules of St. Basil by specific regulations concerning enclosure, poverty, discipline, study, religious services, fasts, and manual labour. When the Adulterine heresy dispute broke out again in 809 he was exiled a second time as the head of the strictly orthodox church party, but was recalled in 811. The administration of the iconoclastic Emperor Leo V brought new and more severe trials. Theodore courageously denied the emperor's right to interfere in ecclesiastical affairs. He was consequently treated with great cruelty, exiled, and his monastery filled with iconoclastic monks. Theodore lived at Metopa in Bithynia from 814, then at Bonita from 819, and finally at Smyrna. Even in banishment he was the central point of the opposition to Cæsaropapism and Iconoclasm. Michael II (820-9) permitted the exiles to return, but did not annul the laws of his predecessor. Thus Theodore saw himself compelled to continue the struggle. He did not return to the Studium, and died without having attained his ideals. In the Roman Martyrology his feast is placed on 12 November; in the Greek martyrologies on 11 November.

Theodore was a man of practical bent and never wrote any theological works, except a dogmatic treatise on the veneration of images. Many of his works are still unprinted or exist in Old Slavonic and Russian translations. Besides several polemics against the enemies of images, special mention should be made of the "Catechesis magna", and the "Catechesis parva" with their sonorous sermons and orations. His writings on monastic life are: the iambic verses on the monastic offices, his will addressed to the monks, the "Canones", and the "Pœnæ monasteriales", the regulations for the monastery and for the church services. His hymns and epigrams show fiery feeling and a high spirit. He is one of the first of hymn-writers in productiveness, in a peculiarly creative technic, and in elegance of language. 550 letters testify to his ascetical and ecclesiastico-political labours.

Theodorus Studites, Opera varia, ed. SIRMOND (Paris, 1696); *P. G.*, XCIX; *Nova patrum bibl.*, V, VIII, IX, X (Rome, 1849, 1871, 1888, 1905); *Theodorus Studites, Parva Catechesis*, ed. AUVRAY-TOUGARD (Paris, 1891); *Bibl. hagiogr. Græca* (2nd ed., Brussels, 1909), 249; THOMAS, *Theodor von Studion* (Osnabrück, 1892); GARDNER, *Theodore of Studium* (London, 1905).

KLEMENS LÖFFLER.

Theodoret, Bishop of Cyrus and theologian, b. at Antioch in Syria about 393; d. about 457. He says himself that his birth was an answer to the prayers of the monk Macedonius ("Hist. rel.", IX; Epist. lxxxi). On account of a vow made by his mother he was dedicated from birth to the service of God and was brought up and educated by the monks Macedonius and Peter. At a very early age he was ordained lector. In theology he studied chiefly the writings of Diodorus of Tarsus, St. John Chrysostom, and Theodore of Mopsuestia. Theodoret was also well trained in philosophy and literature. He understood Syriac as well as Greek, but was not acquainted with either Hebrew or Latin. When he was twenty-three years old and both parents were dead, he divided his fortune among the poor (Epist. cxiii; P. G., LXXXIII, 1316) and became a monk in the monastery of Nicerte not far from Apamea, where he lived for seven years, devoting himself to prayer and study. Much against his will about 423 he was made Bishop of Cyrus. His diocese included nearly 800 parishes and was suffragan of Hierapolis. A large number of monasteries and hermitages also belonged to it, yet, notwithstanding all this, there were many heathen and heretics within its borders. Theodoret brought many of these into the Church, among others more than a thousand Marcionites. He also destroyed not less than two hundred copies of the "Diatessaron" of Tatian which were in use in that district ("Hæret. fab.", I, xx; P. G., LXXXIII, 372). He often ran great risks in his apostolic journeys and labours; more than once he suffered ill-usage from the heathen and was even in danger of losing his life. His fame as a preacher was widespread and his services as a speaker were much sought for outside of his diocese; he went to Antioch twenty-six times. Theodoret also exerted himself for the material welfare of the inhabitants of his diocese. Without accepting donations (Epist. lxxxi) he was able to build many churches, bridges, porticos, aqueducts, etc. (Epist. lxxxi, lxxviii, cxxxviii).

Towards the end of 430 Theodoret became involved in the Nestorian controversy. In conjunction with John of Antioch he begged Nestorius not to reject the expression Θεοτόκος as heretical (Mansi, IV, 1067). Yet he held firmly with the other Antiochenes to Nestorius and to the last refused to recognize that Nestorius taught the doctrine of two persons in Christ. Until the Council of Chalcedon in 451 he was the literary champion of the Antiochene party. In 436 he published his Ἀνατροπή (Confutation) of the Anathemas of Cyril to which the latter replied with an Apology (P. G., LXXVI, 392 sqq.). At the Council of Ephesus (431) Theodoret sided with John of Antioch and Nestorius, and pronounced with them the deposition of Cyril and the anathema against him. He was also a member of the delegation of "Orientals", which was to lay the cause of Nestorius before the emperor but was not admitted to the imperial presence a second time (Hefele-Leclerq, "Hist. des Conc.", II, i, 362 sqq.). The same year he attended the synods of Tarsus and Antioch, at both of which Cyril was again deposed and anathematized. Theodoret after his return to Cyrus continued to oppose Cyril by speech and writing. The symbol (Creed) that formed the basis of the reconciliation (c. 433) of John of Antioch and others with Cyril was apparently drawn up by Theodoret (P. G., LXXXIV, 209 sqq.), who, however, did not enter into the agreement himself because he was not willing to condemn Nestorius as Cyril demanded. It was not until about 435 that Theodoret seems to have become reconciled with John of Antioch, without, however, being obliged to agree to the condemnation of Nestorius (Synod. cxlviii and cli; Epist. clxxvi). The dispute with Cyril broke out again when in 437 the latter called Diodorus of Tarsus and Theodore of Mopsuestia the real originators of the Nestorian heresy. Theodore entered the lists in their defence. The bitterness with which these polemics were carried on is shown both by the letter and the speech of Theodoret when he learned of the death in 444 of the Patriarch of Alexandria (Epist. clxxx).

The episcopate of Dioscurus, the successor of Cyril, was a period of much trouble for Theodoret. Dioscurus, by the mediation of Eutyches and the influential Chrysaphius, obtained an imperial edict which forbade Theodoret to leave his diocese (Epist. lxxix-lxxxii). In addition Theodoret was accused of Nestorianism (Epist. lxxxiii–lxxxvi); in answer to this attack he wrote his most important polemical work, called "Eranistes". Theodoret was also considered the prime mover of the condemnation of Eutyches by the Patriarch Flavian. In return Dioscurus obtained an imperial decree in 449 whereby Theodoret was forbidden to take any part in the synod of Ephesus (Robber Council of Ephesus). At the third session of this synod Theodoret was deposed by the efforts of Dioscurus and ordered by the emperor to re-enter his former monastery near Apamea. Better times, however, came before long. Theodoret appealed to Pope Leo who declared his deposition invalid, and, as the Emperor Theodosius II died the following year (450), he was allowed to re-enter his diocese. In the next year, notwithstanding the violent opposition of the Alexandrine party, Theodoret was admitted as a regular member to the sessions of the Council of Chalcedon, but refrained from voting. At the eighth session (26 Oct., 451), he was admitted to full membership after he had agreed to the anathema against Nestorius; probably he meant this agreement only in the sense: in case Nestorius had really taught the heresy imputed to him (Mansi, VII, 190). It is not certain whether Theodoret spent the last years of his life in the city of Cyrus, or in the monastery where he had formerly lived. There still exists a letter written by Pope Leo in the period after the Council of Chalcedon in which he encourages Theodoret to co-operate without wavering in the victory of Chalcedon (P. G., LXXXIII, 1319 sqq.). The writings of Theodoret against Cyril of Alexandria were anathematized during the troubles that arose in connexion with the war of the Three Chapters.

WRITINGS.—A. *Exegetical.*—Theodoret wrote brief treatises in the form of questions and answers on special passages of the Octateuch, four Books of Kings, and two Books of Paralipomenon (P. G., LXXX, 75–858). He wrote commentaries covering the whole books on: the Psalms (P.G., LXXX, 857–1998, and LXXXIV, 19–32), written before 436 (Epist. lxxxii); Canticles (P. G., LXXXI, 27–214); the Greater Prophets, Daniel and Ezechiel before 436, Isaias and Jeremias before 448, of which the commentary on Isaias has been lost, excepting some fragments preserved in the "Catenæ" (q. v.); the Minor Prophets before 436 (P. G., LXXXI, 495–1988); and the Epistles of St. Paul, written before 448 (P. G., LXXXII, 35–878). B. *Apologetic.*—"Græcarum affectionum curatio" (Remedy for the diseases of the Greeks), twelve books, written before 437, "the last and probably also the most complete of the numerous apologies which Greek antiquity has produced" (Bardenhewer, "Patrologie", 3rd ed., 1910, p. 327). "De divina Providentia", ten sermons, probably his best work, in which he proves the administration of Divine Providence from the physical, moral, and social systems of the world. C. *Dogmatico-Polemical.*—"Refutatio duodecim Anathematum", against St. Cyril; it has been preserved in Cyril's answer (P. G., LXXVI, 392 sqq.; Latin by Marius Mercator, P. L., XLVIII, 972 sqq.). "De Sancta et vivifica Trinitate" (P. G., LXXV, 1147–90), and "De Incarnatione Domini" (ib., 1419–78); these two last mentioned treatises have been proved by A. Ehrhard to have been written by Theodoret (see bibliography). "Eranistes seu Plymorphos" (P. G., LXXXIII, 27–336), written in 448 in the form of three dialogues between an Orthodox (Theodoret) and a beggar (Eutyches); these dialogues sought to prove that the Divinity of Christ is (a) unchangeable, (b) unmixed with humanity, (c) incapable of suffering. In the fourth book the first three are briefly summed up in syllogisms. "Hæreticarum fabularum compendium" in five books (ib., 336–556); the first four contain a brief summary of heresies up to the time of Theodoret, and the last book contrasts them with Catholic faith and morals. D. *Historical.*—"Historia Ecclesiastica" (P. G., LXXXII, 881–1280) treats in five books the period from Arius up to 429. In this work Theodoret used Eusebius, Rufinus, Socrates, Sozomenus, Philostorgius, as well as documents long since lost. As an ecclesiastical historian, however, he is inferior to his predecessors. "Historia religiosa" (ib., 1283–1522) contains the biographies of thirty celebrated ascetics or hermits; the treatise "De divina charitate" forms the close of the work. E. *Letters.*—Theodoret's letters are of much value, both for his personal history and for that of his era. Cf. P. G., LXXXIII, 1173–1494, and Sakkelion, "Forty-eight Letters of Theodoret of Cyrus" (Athens, 1885). F. *Lost Writings.*—"Opus mysticum", in twelve books; "Responsiones ad quæstiones magorum persarum" (Epist. lxxxii and cxiii), five "Sermones in laudem S. Johannis Chrysostomi", of which the fragments are to be found in Photius, "Bibl.", 273; and other "Sermones". Von Harnack ("Texte und Untersuchungen", N. F. 6, IV, 1901) assigned the "Responsiones ad quæstiones" to Diodorus of Tarsus, but a manuscript of the tenth century, edited by Papadopulos Kerameus (St. Petersburg, 1895), ascribes the work to Theodoret (see A. Ehrhard in "Byzantinische Zeitschrift", VII, 1898, 609 sqq.).

DOCTRINE.—In Hermeneutics Theodoret followed the principles of the Antiochene school, but avoided the bias of Theodore of Mopsuestia. In his Christology also he followed the terminology of Diodorus and Theodore, and saw in the teaching of Cyril a revival of Apollinarianism. He would never acknowledge that the teaching of Nestorius presupposed the acceptance of two persons in Christ or, as Cyril believed, necessarily led to it.

TILLEMONT, *Mémoires*, XV (Paris, 1700–13), 207–340; CAVE, *Hist. litt.*, I (Oxford, 1740–43), 405 sqq.; CEILLIER, *Auteurs sacrés*, X (Paris, 1729–63), 19–142; NEANDER, *Church History*, ed. CLARK, IV (Edinburgh, 1851–58), 141–247; NEWMAN, *Trials of Theodoret* in *Hist. Sketches*, III (2 vols., London, 1890), 307–62; GLUBOKOVSKIJ, *Der seelige Theodoret, Bischof von Cyrus* (2 vols., Moscow, 1890), in Russian; SPECHT, *Der exegetische Standpunkt des Theodor von Mopsuestia u. Theodoret von Cyrus* . . . (Munich, 1871); SALTET, *Les sources de l'Eranistes de Théodoret* in *Revue d'Histoire Ecclés.*, VI (Louvain, 1905), 289–303, 513–536, 741–754; GÜLDENPENNING, *Die Kirchengesch. des Theodoret von Kyrrhos, Eine Untersuchung ihrer Quellen* (Halle, 1889); SCHULTE, *Theodoret von Cyrus als Apologet* (Vienna, 1904); EHRHARD, *Die Cyrill von Alexandrien zugeschriebene Schrift* Περὶ τῆς τοῦ κυρίου ἐνανθρωπήσεως, *ein Werk Theodorets von Cyrus* (Tübingen, 1888); MAHÉ, *Les anathématismes de S. Cyrille d'Alexandrie et les évêques orientaux du patriarchat d'Antioche* in *Revue d'Hist. Eccl.*, VII (Louvain, 1906), 505–542; BERTRAM, *Theodoreti Episcopi Cyrensis Doctrina christologica* (Hildesheim, 1883).

CHRYS. BAUR.

Theodoric, ANTIPOPE. See PASCHAL II, POPE.

Theodoric (Thierry) of Chartres, a Platonist philosopher of the twelfth century, b. in France at the beginning of the twelfth century; d. at Chartres about 1150. It is probable that he studied at Chartres under his brother Bernard, at least, we know that in 1121 he was head of the school of Chartres. Later, he seems to have gone to Paris and to have taught there, among his disciples being John of Salisbury. In 1141 he was teaching once more at Chartres. He wrote a work on the seven liberal arts entitled "Eptateuchon", a treatise "De Sex Dierum Operibus", and a commentary on "De Inventione Rhetorica ad Herennium". The first still exists in MS. at Chartres, the others were published 1884 and 1890. Theodoric was an ardent lover of the Classics, the study of which he defended against the sect of Obscurantists known as "Cornificians". He was also interested in the natural sciences, as is indicated by the fact that he was the recipient of a Latin translation of the "Planisphere" of Ptolemy made by Herman the Dalmatian. In philosophy he adopted the Platonic explanation of reality and the ultra-realistic theory of universals. He was influenced also by neo-Pythagorean principles. Nevertheless, he did not, as was formerly contended, go the length of professing explicit pantheism; he did not identify Divinity with reality. He did, indeed, maintain that Divinity is a form of essence (*forma essendi*) in all things; but, as Bäumker has shown (Archiv f. Gesch. der Phil., X, 138) we are to understand this phrase in a theistic sense. For, while it necessarily implies the existence of a Divine something in all things, it does not imply the identity of the essence of God with the individual essences of things. In his exposition of the first chapters of Genesis (De Sex Dierum Operibus) he attempts to reconcile the Mosaic account of creation with the Platonic explanation of the origin of the universe.

CLERVAL, *Les écoles de Chartres* (Paris, 1895), 169 sqq.; DE WULF, *Hist. of Medieval Phil.*, tr. COFFEY (New York, 1909), 182 sqq.; BÄUMKER in *Archiv f. Gesch. der Phil.*, X; TURNER, *Hist. of Philosophy* (Boston, 1903), 294.

WILLIAM TURNER.

Theodoric the Great, King of the Ostrogoths, b. A. D. 454 (?); d. 26 Aug., 526. He was an illegitimate son of Theodomir, of the royal Ostrogothic family of Amali. When eight years old Theodoric was brought as a hostage to the Court of Constantinople. Here he learned to comprehend the education given by ancient civilization. At eighteen he was allowed to return home and became the leader of a great horde of his countrymen, whose increasing numbers drove them to seek new lands. As King of the Ostrogoths he was sometimes an ally, sometimes an enemy, of the emperors. The inconsistencies of his policy may probably be explained by his having as rival another Theodoric, called Strabo (squint-eyed), who was able to influence the Court of Constantinople against him. When Strabo died in 481, Theodoric the Great received from the Emperor Zeno the titles of *patricius* and *magister militum*, and in 484 was appointed consul.

Theodoric was now compelled to set out with his own people to conquer new territory. The course to be pursued was suggested by the Emperor Zeno. The Ostrogoths were to expel the usurper Odoacer, and thus the emperor thought to be rid of dangerous neighbours. In 488 Theodoric started on the march with his own people and a large number of Rugians. In 489 he defeated Odoacer on the Nonsa, later at Verona, and in 490 on the Adige. He then besieged him in Ravenna and forced him to surrender in 493. Theodoric promised Odoacer both life and freedom, but murdered him at a banquet fearing perhaps that he might revolt again.

Theodoric's mastery of Italy being thus established, he at once showed his appreciation of the ancient culture and political organization of the Empire, claiming to be its vicegerent and restorer in Western Europe. His efforts in this capacity were faithfully seconded by his minister Cassiodorus. Proud of his Gothic nationality, Theodoric, unlike the earlier barbarian emperors, believed it possible to reconcile Roman and Germanic interests. His people seemed to him equal to the Romans in antiquity of descent and military renown, and he realized that his power rested solely on Gothic prowess. Apparently his kingdom was a continuation of the Roman Empire; in reality his policy was in direct and fundamental contradiction to the Roman conception, by which all national individuality was to be lost in the State as a whole. This theory of government which sought to suppress nationalities was opposed by Theodoric: he had a profound respect for national independence, and had repeatedly taken up arms to maintain it.

Among his many schemes was a great project to combine in one harmonious system, around the shores of the Mediterranean, all the conflicting barbarian nations, and for this reason he repeatedly aided the Frankish king Clovis against the Alamanni and Visigoths. He based his authority to carry out this wide policy not on his office as vicegerent of the Eastern Emperor, but, as he said, on the *leges gentium*. The precise degree of his dependence on the Byzantine Empire is not known: he certainly recognized its suzerainty and desired to maintain friendly relations with Constantinople. Still, the "Variæ" of Cassiodorus, a collection of documents of the reign of Theodoric, shows that he firmly believed the Western Empire to be continued in his person. The many intermarriages between his family and the royal families of

STREET IN RAVENNA, SHOWING THE PALACE OF THEODORIC

other Germanic kingdoms were undoubtedly intended to prepare the way for the predominance of his dynasty in the West. Yet his supremacy was a divided one: to the Goths he was the king; to the Romans the patrician. Both nations were ruled by their own laws. The *Edictum Theodorici* of 512 was intended to introduce some degree of uniformity into the criminal law. All Theodoric's decrees, including this code, were in their language very conciliatory towards the Romans: the Roman population was to consider Gothic supremacy the guarantee of its security and prosperity.

In reality Theodoric's reign appeared to bring once more a Golden Age to the sorely-tried peninsula. Experts in well-boring were brought from Africa to help restore the cultivation of the waterless country where the woods had been cut down; and swamps were drained. Books of magic and theatres were forbidden, edicts were issued for the protection of ancient monuments. Roman literature once more flourished in Italy: its most brilliant representative was Boethius, who was able to combine the lofty ideals of Christianity with the dignity of the ancient philosophy. While tolerating the Catholic Church, Theodoric considered himself the protector of Arianism; accordingly he sought to intervene diplomatically in favour of the Arians who were being persecuted by Justinian I. Nevertheless he allowed complete freedom to the Catholic Church, at least so far as dogma was concerned, though he considered himself entitled to appoint a pope, or to act as arbitrator in the schism between Symmachus and Laurentius, and in general to bring any ecclesiastic to judgment. This same king who had come to Italy as the emperor's representative should not, at the end of his reign, have used such barbarous cruelty in suppressing that Roman national revolt againt Gothic rule in which the opposition of the Roman Church to Arianism led the pope, Constantinople, and the educated laity to

THEODORIC'S TOMB, RAVENNA, SIXTH CENTURY

unite. The Senate in its judicial capacity was ordered to try those implicated in this conspiracy, and Boethius and his aged father-in-law, the Senator Symmachus, were condemned to death. Theodoric succumbed to the effects of the bitter conviction that his conciliatory policy had failed, and from that time his health declined. He was buried in the truly regal tomb at Ravenna. At a later date excessive zeal prompted the disinterment of the Arian king, but he continues to live in a wonderful legend, which assumes many forms, as the warrior king of the heroic age of the German people. On stormy nights the peasants still whisper of Dietrich of Berne, as they call Theodoric, riding through the air with his wild followers.

CASSIODORUS, ed. MOMMSEN, *Variæ* (Berlin, 1894); MOMMSEN, *Ostgotische Studien* in *Neues Archiv der Gesellschaft für ältere deutsche Geschichtskunde*, XIV, XV; HODGKIN, *Italy and her Invaders* (London, 1892——); VILLARI, *Le invasione barbariche in Italia* (Milan, 1905); HARTMANN, *Geschichte Italiens im Mittelalter*, I (Leipzig, 1897); PFEILSCHOFTER, *Theodorich der Grosse* (Mainz, 1910).

FRANZ KAMPERS.

Theodorus and Theophanes (called *Grapti*, "written upon", γραπτοί), SAINTS: Theodorus, b. about 775; d. about 842–43; Theophanes, b. about 778; d. 845. These champions of the veneration of images during the second Iconoclastic controversy in the East were brothers and natives of Jerusalem. Both entered the monastery of St. Sabas, near Jerusalem, which, at that time was under the guidance of Michael, later *syncellus* of the Patriarch of Jerusalem. The brothers had an excellent theological training and were zealous, strict ascetics. About 812 they entered a monastery at Constantinople, where in opposition to the Emperor Leo V (813–20) they energetically defended the veneration of images, and consequently were exiled. Under the succeeding emperor, Michael II (820–29), they were brought into the monastery of Sosthenes on the Bosphorus. Michael's successor, the tyrannical and Iconoclastic Theophilos (829–42), exiled them again, but recalled them in 836 to the capital, had them scourged several times, and had twelve lines of verse cut into their skin (hence the nickname "written upon"). They were once more sent into exile, where Theodorus died, while Theophanes lived to see the close of the Iconoclastic controversy in 842 during the reign of the Empress Theodora. In this same year he was raised to the Archdiocese of Nicæa and administered it until his death. Theophanes wrote a large number of religious poems, among them one on his dead brother, but they have not yet been published (cf. Christ and Paranikas, "Anthologia græca carminum christianorum", Leipzig, 1781). The brothers are venerated as saints. In the Greek Church the feast of Theophanes is observed on 11 October, that of Theodorus on 27 December. In the Roman Church the feasts of both are celebrated on 27 December (Cf. Nilles, "Kalendarium manuale utriusque Ecclesiæ", I, 300, 368 sq.).

Vita Theodori Grapti in *P. G.*, CXVI, 653–683; THEODORA CANTACUZENA, *Vita Theodori et Theophanis*, ed. PAPADOPOULOS-KERAMEUS in 'Ἀναλέκτα Ἱεροσολυμιτικῆς σταχυολογίας, IV, 185–223; V, 379–99; VAILHÉ, *St. Michel le Syncelle et les deux frères Grapti, St. Théodore et St. Théophane* in *Revue de l'orient chrétien*, VI (1901), 313 sq., 610 sq.

J. P. KIRSCH.

Theodorus Lector, a lector attached to the Church of St. Sophia of Constantinople in the early part of the sixth century. At the request of a friend he compiled in four books his "Historia Tripartita", an epitome of the historians Socrates, Sozomen, and Theodoret, made up of excerpts from them. An imperfect copy of this work exists in MS. but it has never been published; Valesius used it, attaching perhaps too much importance to the readings he found in it, in his edition of the above-named historians. Theodorus also composed a history in two books which carried the narrative of the "Hist. Trip." from the death of Theodosius II up to the times of Justin I. This work is unfortunately lost, but two long series of excerpts are preserved usually bearing the title Ἀπὸ φωνῆς Νικηφόρου Καλλίστου which, however, is spurious (De Boor, "Zeitschrift f. Kirchengesch.", VI, 489; Preuschen in "Realenencyk. f. Prot. theol.", s. v.); quotations also are found in the writings of St. John of Damascus and the Acts of the Seventh General Council. The history owes its value to the scantiness of our information concerning the period it treats rather than to its merits. It is full of marvellous stories. The only indications of the time when Theodore lived are the date at which his history ended and his speaking of the "holy memory" of Theodoret—he would hardly have done this after the "Three Chapters" controversy.

DE BOOR, *op. cit.*; PREUSCHEN, *op. cit.* (Leipzig, 1907); NOLTE in *Tübingen Theol. Quart.* (1861), 569 sq.; SARRAZIN, *De Theod. Lectore. Theophanis præcipuo fonte* in *Comment. philol. Jenensis*, I, 163 sqq.; BARDENHEWER-SHAHAN, *Patrology* (St. Louis, 1908), 552. The fragments of the *History* were published by VALESIUS and reprinted in *P. G.*, LXXXVI. For additional excerpts to be found in the writings of NICETAS, and CHARTOPHYLAX OF NICÆA, see DIEKAMP in *Hist. Jahrb.*, XXIV, 553 sq.

F. J. BACCHUS.

Theodosiopolis, a titular metropolitan see of Thracia Prima. In the beginning the city was called Apros, or preferably Aproi; later in its history it became known as the Colonia Claudia Aprensis (Ptolemy, "Geographia", vol. III, cap. xi, p. 7). In the fourth century, according to Ammianus Marcellinus (XXVII, iv, 12), it was the principal city of the country south of Heraclea. The official name of Theodosiopolis, which was given to the city by either Theodosius I, or Theodosius II, was rarely used; it was commonly called Apros. At first suffragan episcopal see of Heraclea in the European province, Apros had already in 640 been elevated to an autocephalous archiepiscopal see (Gelzer, "Ungedruckte . . . Texte der Notitiæ episcopatuum", 535), which title it still retained in 1170. However in 1179, Romanus signs himself as Metropolitan of Apros, and the "Notitia episcopatuum" of Manuel I Comnenus, which dates from this same epoch, also refers to Apros as a metropolitan see (Gelzer, op. cit., 587). This see must have disappeared at the end of the fourteenth century, or in the beginning of the fifteenth century, for in the "Notitiæ" subsequent to 1453 no mention of it is to be found. Le Quien, "Oriens christianus", I, 1125–1128, makes special mention of eleven bishops belonging to this see, among whom are Babylas in 458; Andreas in 536; John in 787; Sabbas in 878; and in 1351, Gabriel, the last one known. From 1204, as long as the city remained in the hands of the Crusaders, Apros was a Roman archdiocese; in 1244 it was already a titular archbishopric (Eubel, "Hierarchia catholica medii ævi", I, 94; II, 101). Under the Franks, who called it Naples, Apros belonged to Theodosius Branas, the Greek, who had married Agnes, sister of King Philip Augustus. The Bulgarians took the city and destroyed it in 1205; later it fell anew under the sway of the Franks and the Greeks (Villehardouin, ed. Wailly, 390–91, 403, 413–15, 564). The exact situation of Apros is not known; Tomaschek, "Zur Kunde der Hæmus-Halbinsel", 52, identifies it with Kestridje on the Podja-Dere, south of Haïreboli in the sanjak of Rodosto.

PTOLEMY, *Geographia*, ed. MÜLLER, I, 489; PAULY-WISSOWA, *Real-Encyclopädie der classischen Altertumswissenschaft*, s. v. *Aproi*.

S. VAILHÉ.

Theodosiopolis. See ERZERUM, DIOCESE OF.

Theodosius I (FLAVIUS THEODOSIUS), Roman Emperor, b. in Spain, about 346; d. at Milan, 17 January,

395. Theodosius is one of the sovereigns by universal consent called Great. He stamped out the last vestiges of paganism, put an end to the Arian heresy in the empire, pacified the Goths, left a famous example of penitence for a crime, and reigned as a just and mighty Catholic emperor. His father, the Comes Theodosius, was a distinguished general; both he and the mother Thermantia were Catholics at a time when Arianism was at its strongest. Theodosius the son distinguished himself in the army, was made Dux of Mœsia, defeated the Sarmatians (Ammianus Marcellinus, XXIX, 6); then, when an intrigue brought about the disgrace and execution of his father (376) he retired to his own property in Spain. But his reputation was not forgotten. The Emperor Gratian (375–383) after the death of Valens (378) took Theodosius from private life and made him his fellow-emperor (Augustus) for the East (19 Jan., 379). He was already married to Ælia Flacilla, by whom he had two sons, Arcadius and Honorius (his future successors) and a daughter Pulcheria. As Augustus he carried on the Gothic war vigorously and successfully. During the year 380 he was able to conclude a victorious peace with the Goths; on 24 November he held his triumph at Constantinople. Meanwhile he had also repressed the Vandals and Huns. Early in the same year a severe sickness at Thessalonica made him seek baptism, and he was baptized by the Catholic Bishop of Thessalonica, Ascholios. Socrates (H. E., V, 6) says that since Theodosius "was a Christian from his parents and professed the faith of the Homoousios" he first assured himself that the bishop was not an Arian (cf. Sozomen; "H. E.", VII, 4). A great part of the emperor's activity was now spent in establishing the Catholic faith and repressing Arianism. In February, 380, he and Gratian published the famous edict that all their subjects should profess the faith of the Bishops of Rome and Alexandria (Cod. Theod., XVI, 1, 2; Sozomen, VII, 4). The conventicles of the heretics were not to be called churches.

As soon as he came to Constantinople Theodosius began expelling the Arians, who had hitherto been in possession. The Arian bishop, Demophilus, left the city (Socr., V, 7; Soz., VII, 5), St. Gregory of Nazianzus undertook the administration of the diocese. In January, 381, the prefect had orders to close all Arian chapels in the city and to expel those who served them. The same severe measures were ordered throughout Theodosius's dominion, not only against Arians, but also in the case of Manichæans and all other heretics. However Sozomen says that the emperor "made severe punishments by his laws, but did not carry them out, for he did not wish to punish, but only to frighten his subjects, that they might think as he did about Divine things. And he praised those who were converted of their own accord" (H. E., VII, 12). In 381 the Second General Council was held at Constantinople under his auspices (Socr., V, 8; Soz., VII, 7). In 383 he attempted a conference at his capital between Catholics and Arians, with a view to a reconciliation; but no result was obtained (Socr., V, 10; Soz., VII, 12). In the same year Gratian was murdered at Lyons (25 Aug.) and Clemens Maximus usurped the imperial title in the West (383–388). Theodosius acknowledged the usurper on condition that he would allow Gratian's brother, Valentinian II, to reign in Italy. In 387 Maximus broke the contract and expelled Valentinian, who fled to Theodosius. Theodosius brought him back with an army, and defeated and executed Maximus at Aquileia. Valentinian II now reigned in the West till 392. It was also in 387 that Theodosius showed such tolerance in the affair of the statues at Antioch (see JOHN CHRYSOSTOM).

During all his reign Theodosius took severe measures against the surviving remnants of paganism. In 388 a prefect was sent around Egypt, Syria, and Asia Minor for the purpose of destroying temples and breaking up pagan associations; it was then that the Serapeum at Alexandria was destroyed (Socr., V, 16). Libanius wrote a "Lamentation" about the destruction of the fanes of the gods (περὶ τῶν ἱερῶν, ed. R. Foerster, Bibl. Script. Gr. et Rom. Teubner). In 391 Theodosius refused to allow the Altar of Victory to be restored in the Roman Senate (cf. Gibbon, "Decline and Fall", xxviii). Pagan sacrifices, omens, and witchcraft were to be punished as læsa majestas (Cod. Theod., XVI, X, 10–12). In short his laws put an end finally to the old cult, at any rate as far as open and public use is concerned. One of its last acts was a despairing appeal to the sword, which offers again the dramatic situation of a field of battle on which the religion of Europe seemed to depend. Argobast, the Frankish tutor of Valentinian II, at least indirectly caused his ward's death (Hodgkin, "Italy and her Invaders", I, 590) and set up a rhetorician, Eugenius, in his stead (15 May, 392). Theodosius hastened to Italy to avenge this crime. Eugenius, although nominally a Christian, tried to unite the remains of paganism in his defence. He set up pagan altars again (including that of Victory at Rome), his soldiers marched under the standard of Hercules invictus. But near Aquileia on 6 Sept., 394, once more the Christian Labarum triumphed over the banner of the ancient gods; Theodosius entered Rome sole master of the now finally Christian empire. Further laws enforced the keeping of Sunday and the disabilities of pagans, Jews, and heretics. During the greater part of his reign Theodosius was in intimate relation with St. Ambrose. The story of the emperor's worst crime, the massacre of at least 7000 citizens of Thessalonica in revenge for a tumult (April, 390); of St. Ambrose's refusal to allow him to enter the Church; of his acceptance of eight months of penance, is one of the memorable incidents of Church history.

Theodosius married Galla (daughter of Valentinian I) after the death of his first wife, and by her had a daughter, Galla Placidia, the mother of Valentinian III. St. Ambrose preached his funeral oration ("De obitu Theodosii", P. L., XVI, 1385). His two sons Arcadius and Honorius had already been proclaimed Augustus during his life. Arcadius became emperor of the eastern half of the empire, Honorius of the western. The Roman world was never again united. Theodosius stands out as the destroyer of heresy and paganism, as the last sovereign of the undivided empire. A coin representing him holding the Labarum with the inscription, Restitutor Reipublicæ, expresses perfectly his title to remembrance.

SOCRATES; SOZOMEN; ZOSIMUS; LIBANIUS; AMMIANUS MARCELLINUS, and other Church historians; Codex Theodosianus, ed. MOMMSEN (Berlin, 1905); RAUSCHEN, Jahrbücher der christl. Kirche unter dem Kaiser Theodosius dem Grossen (Freiburg, 1897); GÜLDENPENNING AND ISLAND, Der Kaiser Theodosius der Grosse (Halle, 1878); TILLEMONT, Histoire des Empereurs, V.; SCHILLER, Gesch. der romischen Kaiserzeit, II (Gotha, 1887); SCHULTZE, Gesch. des Untergangs des griech.-röm. Heidentums (Jena, 1887–92); GIBBON, Decline and Fall of the Roman Empire, ed. BURY, III (London, 1897); GRISAR, Gesch. Roms. u. der Päpste, I (Freiburg, 1901).

ADRIAN FORTESCUE.

Theodosius Florentini, b. at Münster, in the Grisons, Switzerland, 23 May, 1808; d. at Heiden, in Appenzell, 15 Feb., 1865. He entered the Capuchin Franciscan Order, 22 Oct., 1825, was ordained priest in 1830, and appointed novice master, and lecturer on philosophy and theology. In 1838 he became guardian at Baden; in 1845 superior and parish priest at Chur; in 1857 definitor, and in 1860 vicar-general of the Diocese of Chur. In the first half of the nineteenth century the Catholics in Switzerland found themselves in a lamentable position. In addition to Protestant ascendency there was the spirit of unbelief and of false mysticism. Even the Governments of Catholic cantons lent themselves to the persecution of the Church and the conventual houses. The unfortunate Sonderbund war had broken the power and confidence of the Catholics, and the victorious Radical party forced upon the country a constitutional league pledged to the destruction of Catholic interests. In consequence of his zealous defence of the Church, Father Theodosius was forced to fly to Alsace in 1841. But in August of the same year he returned, and brought his experience to bear on plans for the welfare of the Church and people. First he founded the Institute of the Franciscan Sisters of the Holy Cross. In the Capuchin church at Altorf on 16 Oct., 1844, the first three sisters received the habit of the Third Order of St. Francis. Their constitutions enjoin upon them to make themselves all to all in order to win souls to Christ and to do nothing which might repel any from their mode of life. From this foundation grew the congregation of teaching sisters, with their motherhouse at Memingen, which has now about 1200 members. Later on Father Theodosius founded the congregation of Sisters of Mercy at Ingenbohl, which numbers 5251 sisters in 878 institutions. These congregations have been approved by the Holy See. Both are actively engaged in educational works; they have foundling asylums, orphanages, kindergartens, poor schools, boarding-schools for girls, and seminaries for teachers. Both have in their homes for girls a *patronage*, as the French call it, for servant girls, factory workers, shop assistants, and others. The Sisters of Mercy have, besides, homes for the poor and sick, and undertake private nursing.

In the meantime Father Theodosius was himself busy as a schoolmaster. He superintended the people's schools (*Volksschülen*), which are attended by others besides the poor. He promoted continuation schools and was in favour of technical instruction for apprentices and workmen. He founded anew the suppressed Jesuit College, Maria-Hilf zu Schwyz, where there are now more than 400 pupils. It comprises a gymnasium, lyceum, and an industrial school with technical and mercantile departments. To stir up anew Catholic life he engaged in popular missions and retreats for priests. To provide for the needs of Catholics in Protestant parts of Switzerland he founded the home missions for which he provided a special fund. The institution of the annual conference of the Swiss bishops was largely due to his efforts. To bring Swiss Catholics together, to strengthen Catholic feeling, and to organize social works, he founded the Pius Society. For this society Father Theodosius worked harder than for all else; it was in connexion with this that he more fully expounded his Christian social ideas. He was very keen upon the care and inspection of the helpless and dependent, such as boarded-out children, apprentices, neglected children, and discharged prisoners. With regard to the labour question Father Theodosius expressed himself very fully in his speech at Frankfort in 1863. In demanding the Christianizing of industry, trade unions, and workmen's credit banks, he said: "Formerly monasteries were turned into factories, now factories must become monasteries, and the profits must be shared with the workers". Factories were established to carry out this idea, but they failed, owing to a lack of business capacity in the founders. At Ingenbohl Father Theodosius founded a printing and book-binding establishment and a society for the distribution of good books. Among his own writings are the "Legends of the Saints" in four volumes. His spirit was well expressed in the saying of St. Augustine which on the eve of his death he wrote in the notebook of a teacher: "In necessariis unitas, in dubiis libertas, in omnibus charitas". A favourite maxim of his was: "Whatever is the need of the time, is God's Will".

KRAUTHAHN, *P. Theodosius* (St. Gall, 1865); ELSENER, *P. Theodosius* (Lucerne, 1865); FUHRER, *Leben u. Wirken des P. Theodosius* (Ingenbohl, 1878); PLANTA, *P. Theodosius* (Bern, 1893); VESCH, *P. Theodosius Florentini* (Ingenbohl, 1897).

FATHER CUTHBERT.

Theodotion Version. See VERSIONS OF THE BIBLE.

Theodotus of Ancyra, SAINT, martyr. On 18 May the Roman Martyrology says: "At Ancyra, in Galatia, the martyr Saint Theodotus and the saintly virgins Thecusa, his aunt, Alexandra, Claudia, Faina, Euphrasia, Matrona, and Julitta", etc. They are mentioned in all the menologies, and Theodotus has a special feast on 7 June (Nilles, "Kal. man.", I, 162, and II, 583). He is patron of innkeepers. Emblems: torches and the sword. According to the Acts (Acta SS., May, IV, 147) Theodotus was a married man who kept an inn at Ancyra, the capital of Galatia. He is described as a man very zealous in the performance of his Christian duties, endowed with many virtues, especially charity towards his neighbour. He brought sinners to repentance and strengthened many in their faith during the persecution which Theoctenus, the governor of the province, was carrying on, about 303, in accordance with the edict of Diocletian. The name of a certain Victor is mentioned as one who grew weak in his profession of Christianity and received much encouragement from Theodotus. The governor ordered that all provisions exposed for sale should first be offered to the idols. Theodotus laid in stores of goods and his house became a refuge for the Christians, a hospital for the sick, and a place for Divine worship. At Malos, about five miles from Ancyra, he sought out the body of the martyr, Valens, and gave it Christian burial. Returning to Ancyra he found the Christians in great trouble. The seven virgins mentioned above had been called before the judges and made a valiant profession of their faith; they were then sent to a house of debauchery, but preserved their purity. Then they were obliged to suffer cruel torments and were cast into the sea with stones attached to their bodies. Theodotus succeeded in rescuing the bodies and honourably burying them. In consequence he was arrested, and after many sufferings was killed by the sword; his body was miraculously brought to Malos and there entombed by the priest Fronto. A chapel was built over the grave, and the saint was held in great veneration. The legend is told by Nilus who claims to have been an eye-witness to a great part of what he describes. Ruinart (page 372) places it among his "Acta sincera et selecta". Pio Franchi produced a critical edition of the Acts in "Studi e Testi" (Rome, 1901). He considered them trustworthy, but later changed his opinion. Delehaye (Anal. Boll., XXII, 320, and XXIII, 478) says: "The kernel of the legend is a tale narrated by Herodotus, while the existence of the hero of the narrative is not vouched for by any historic document."

BUTLER, *Lives of the Saints; Dict. of Christ. Biog.*, IV, 580; *Röm. Quartalschrift*, XVIII, 289; *Der Katholik* (1895), 569; LECLERCQ, *Les Martyrs*, II, VIII (Paris, 1903); CHEVALIER, *Bio-Bibl.*, II, 4429.

FRANCIS MERSHMAN.

Theodulf (THEODULFUS, THEODULFE), Bishop of Orléans, a writer skilled in poetic forms and a learned theologian, b. in Spain about 760; d. at Angers, France, 18 Dec., 821. By descent a Goth, he became before 794 a member of the court of Charlemagne, where he was, next to Alcuin, the most distinguished and learned person. Charlemagne granted him (about 798) the Bishopric of Orléans and several abbeys. He laboured successfully in his diocese as a reformer both of the clergy and people, as is shown by his two Capitularies, one of which has forty-six chapters; he also encouraged schools. In 798 he was sent, with Bishop Leidrad of Lyons, as a royal messenger (*missus dominicus*) to the southern part of France. In his poem, "Versus contra judices", in which he complains of the severity of Frankish law and addresses earnest warnings to the judges, he gives an account of his experiences while on this mission. As a writer on theology he took part in the dispute over the term *Filioque* (the procession of the Holy Ghost from the Son as well as from the Father) and defended this doctrine at the request of Charlemagne in the treatise, "De spiritu sancto". He also wrote at the wish of the emperor, "De ordine baptismi", a description of the ceremonies at baptism. He is further, apparently, the author of an exposition of the Holy Mass and of the Creed. As regards language and metre he occupies the first place among the poets of the Carlovingian era and distinguished himself by spirit and skill; particularly interesting are the letters which he wrote in the form of poems giving an animated picture of the life at court. His hymn for Palm Sunday, "Gloria, laus, et honor" (Analecta hymnica, L, 160 sq.), came into liturgical use. He is also known as a patron and lover of art. He was still in favour at the beginning of the reign of Louis the Pious, but later, being accused of sharing in the conspiracy of King Bernard of Italy, was consequently deposed in 818 and exiled to Angers.

P.L., CV, 187–380; *Mon. Germ. Hist.: Poetæ ævi Carolini*, I, 437–581; BAUNARD, *Théodulfe évêque d'Orléans* (Orléans, 1860); CUISSARD, *Théodulfe* (Orléans, 1892); MANITIUS, *Gesch. der lat. Litteratur des Mittelalters*, I (Munich, 1911), 537–43.

KLEMENS LÖFFLER.

Theological Virtues. See FAITH; HOPE; LOVE; VIRTUE.

Theology.—The subject will be treated under the several heads of: I. Dogmatic (with its parts, Christology and Soteriology); II. Moral; III. Pastoral; IV. Ascetical; V. Mystical.

I. DOGMATIC THEOLOGY.—Dogmatic theology is that part of theology which treats of the theoretical truths of faith concerning God and His works (*dogmata fidei*), whereas moral theology has for its subject-matter the practical truths of morality (*dogmata morum*). At times, apologetics or fundamental theology is called "general dogmatic theology", dogmatic theology proper being distinguished from it as "special dogmatic theology". However, according to present-day usage, apologetics is no longer treated as part of dogmatic theology but has attained the rank of an independent science, being generally regarded as the introduction to and foundation of dogmatic theology. The present article shall deal first with those questions which are *fundamental* to dogmatic theology and then briefly review its historical development due to the acumen and indefatigable industry with which the theologians of every civilized country and of every century have cultivated and promoted this science.

A. *Fundamental Questions.*—(1). Definition and Nature of Dogmatic Theology.—To define dogmatic theology, it will be best to start from the general notion of theology. Considered etymologically, theology (Gr. Θεολογία, i. e. περὶ Θεοῦ λόγος) means objectively the science treating of God, subjectively, the scientific knowledge of God and Divine things. If defined as the science concerning God (*doctrina de Deo*), the name of theology applies as well to the philosophical knowledge of God, which is cast into scientific form in natural theology or theodicy. However, unless theodicy is free from errors, it cannot lay claim to the name of theology. For this reason, pagan mythology and pagan doctrines about the gods, must at once be set aside as false theology. The theology of heretics also, so far as it contains grave errors, must be excluded. In a higher and more perfect sense we call theology that science of God and Divine things which, objectively, is based on supernatural revelation, and subjectively, is viewed in the light of Christian faith. Theology thus broadens out into Christian doctrine (*doctrina fidei*) and embraces not only the particular doctrines of God's existence, essence, and triune personality, but all the truths revealed by God. The Patristic era did not, as a rule, take theology in this wide sense. For the earlier Fathers, strictly limiting the term *theology* to doctrine about God, distinguished it from the doctrine of His external activity, especially from the Incarnation and Redemption, which they included under the name of the "Divine economy". Now, if God is not only the primary object but also the first principle of Christian theology, then its ultimate end likewise must be God; that is to say, it must teach, effect, and promote union with God through religion. Consequently, it lies in the very essence of theology to be the doctrine not only of God and of faith, but also of religion (*doctrina religionis*). It is this triple function which gave rise to the old adage of the School: *Theologia Deum docet, a Deo docetur, ad Deum ducit* (Theology teaches of God, is taught by God, and leads to God).

However, neither supernatural theology in general nor dogmatic theology in particular is sufficiently specified by its material object or its end, since natural theology also treats of God and Divine things and shows that union with God is a religious duty. What essentially distinguishes the two sciences is the so-called formal principle or formal object. Supernatural theology considers God and Divine things solely in the supernatural light of external revelation and internal faith, analyzes them scientifically, proves them and penetrates as far as possible into their meaning. From this it follows that theology comprehends all those and only those doctrines which are to be found in the sources of faith, namely Scripture and Tradition, and which the infallible Church proposes to us. Now, among these revealed truths there are many which reason, by its own natural power, can discover, comprehend, and demonstrate, especially those that pertain to natural theology and ethics. These truths, however accessible to unaided reason, receive a theological colouring only by being at the same time supernaturally revealed and accepted on the ground of God's infallible authority. The act of faith being nothing else than the unconditional surrender of human reason to the sovereign authority of the self-revealing God, it is plain that Catholic theology is not a purely philosophical science like mathematics or metaphysics; it must rather, of its very nature be an authoritative science, basing its teachings, especially of the mysteries of faith, on the authority of Divine revelation and the infallible Church established by Christ; for it is the Divine mission of the Church to preserve intact the entire deposit of faith (*depositum fidei*), to preach and explain it authoritatively. There are, it is true, many non-Catholics and even some Catholics who are irritated at seeing Catholic theology bow before an external authority. They take offence at conciliar decrees, papal decisions *ex cathedra*, the censure of theological opinions, the index of forbidden books, the Syllabus, the oath against Modernism. Yet all these ecclesiastical regulations flow naturally and logically from the formal principle of Christian theology: the existence of Divine revelation and the right of the Church to demand, in the name of Christ, an unwavering belief in certain truths concerning faith and morals. To reject the authority of the Church would be equivalent to abandoning supernatural revelation, and contemning God himself, who can neither deceive nor be deceived, since He is Truth itself, and who speaks through the mouth of the Church. Consequently, theology as a science, if it would avoid the danger of error, must ever remain under the tutelage and guidance of the Church. To a Catholic, theology without the Church is as absurd as theology without God. Dogmatic theology, then, may be defined as the scientific exposition of the entire theoretical doctrine concerning God Himself and His external activity, based on the dogmas of the Church.

(2) **Dogmatic Theology as a Science.**—Considering that theology depends essentially on the Church, a serious difficulty arises at once. How, one may ask, can theology claim to be a science in the genuine sense of the word? If the aim and result of theological investigation is settled in advance by an authority that attributes to itself infallibility and will brook no contradiction, if the line of march is, as it were, clearly mapped out and strictly prescribed, how can there be any question of true science or of scientific freedom? Are not the dogmatic proofs, supposed to demonstrate an infallible dogma, after all mere dialectical play, sham science, reasoning made to order? Prejudice against Catholic theology, prevalent in the world at large, is beginning to bear fruit; in many countries the theological faculties, still existing in the state universities, are looked upon as so much useless ballast, and the demand is being made to relegate them to the episcopal seminaries, where they can no longer injure the intellectual freedom of the people. The downright unfairness of this attitude is obvious when one considers that the universities sprang up and developed in the shadow of the Church and of Catholic theology; and that, moreover, the exaggeration of scientific freedom may prove fatal to the profane sciences as well. Unless it presuppose certain truths, which can no more be demonstrated than many mysteries of faith, science can achieve nothing; and unless it recognize the limits that are set to investigation, the boasted freedom will degenerate into lawless and arbitrary anarchy. As the logician starts from notions, the jurist from legal texts, the historian from facts, the chemist from material substances as things which demand no proof in his case, so the theologian receives his material from the hands of the Church and deals with it according to the rules which the scientist applies in his own branch.

The view, moreover, that scientific research is absolutely free and independent of all authority is fanciful and distorted. To the freedom of science, the authority of the individual conscience, and of human society as well, sets an impassable limit. Even the civil power would have to exercise its authority in the form of punishment if a university professor, presuming on the freedom of scientific thought and research, should teach openly that burglary, murder, adultery, revolution, and anarchy are permissible. We may concede that the Catholic theologian, being subject to ecclesiastical authority, is more closely bound than the professor of the secular sciences. Yet the difference is one of degree only, inasmuch as every science and every investigator is bound by the moral and religious duty of subordination. Some Scholastics, it is true, e. g. Durandus and Vasquez, denied to Christian theology a strictly scientific character, on the ground that the content of faith is obscure and incapable of demonstration. But their argument does not carry conviction. At most it proves that dogmatic science is not of the same kind and order as the profane sciences. What is essential to any science is not internal evidence, but merely certainty of its first principles.

There are many profane sciences which borrow unproved from a superior science their highest principles; these are the so-called *lemmata*, subsidiary propositions, which serve as premises for further conclusions. The theologian does the same. He, too, borrows the first principles of his science from the higher knowledge of God without proving them. Every subaltern science supposes of course in the superior discipline the power to give a strict demonstration of the assumed premises. But all scientific axioms rest ultimately on metaphysics, and metaphysics itself is unable to prove strictly all its principles; all it can do is to defend them against attack. It is plain then that every science without exception rests on axioms and postulates which, though certain, yet admit of no demonstration. The mathematician is aware that the existence of geometry, the surest and most palpable of all sciences, depends entirely on the soundness of the postulate of parallels. Nevertheless, this very postulate is far from being demonstrable. In fact, since no convincing proof of it was forthcoming, there has arisen since the time of Gauss a more general, non-Euclidean geometry, of which the Euclidean is only a special case. Why, then, should Catholic theology, because of its postulates, *lemmata*, and mysteries, be denied the name of a science? Apart from the domain of dogma proper, the theologian may approach the numerous controversial questions and more intricate problems with the same freedom as is enjoyed by any other scientist. One thing, however, must never be lost sight of. No science is at liberty to upset theorems which have been established once and for all; they must be regarded as unshaken dogmas upon which the entire structure is based. Similarly, the articles of faith must not be looked upon by the theologian as troublesome barriers, but as beacon-lights that warn the mariner, show him the true course, and preserve him from shipwreck.

(3) **Methods of Dogmatic Theology.**—Whereas other sciences, as, for instance, theodicy, begin with proving the existence of God, it lies beyond the scope of theology to discover dogmatic truths. The subject-matter with which the student of theology has to deal is offered to him in the deposit of faith and, reduced to its briefest form, is to be found in the Catechism. If the theologian is content with deriving the dogmas from the sources of faith and with explaining them, he is occupied with "positive" theology. Guided by the doctrinal authority of the Church, he calls history and criticism to his aid to find in Scripture and Tradition the genuine, unalloyed truth. If to this positive element is joined a polemic tendency, we have "controversial" theology, which was carried to its highest perfection in the seventeenth century by Cardinal Bellarmine. Positive theology must prove its theses by conclusive arguments drawn from Scripture and Tradition; hence it is closely related to exegesis and history. As exegete, the theologian must first of all accept the inspiration of the Bible as the Word of God. But even when elucidating its meaning, he will always bear in mind the unanimous interpretation of the Fathers, the hermeneutical principles of the Church, and the directions of the Holy See. In his character as historian, the theologian must not lay aside his belief in the supernatural origin of Christianity and in the Divine institution of the Church, if he is to give a true and objective account of tradition, of the history of dogma, and of patrology. For, just as the Bible, being the Word of God, was written under the immediate inspiration of the Holy Ghost, so Tradition was, and is, guided in a special manner by God, Who preserves it from being curtailed, mutilated, or falsified.

Consequently, he who from the outset declares the Bible to be an ordinary book, miracles and prophecies impossible and old-fashioned, the Church a great institution for deadening thought, the Fathers of the Church pious prattlers, is quite incapable, even from a purely scientific standpoint, of understanding God's momentous dispensations to mankind. From this we may conclude how unecclesiastical and at the same time how unscientific are those historians who prefer to explain the works of the Fathers without due regard for ecclesiastical tradition, which was the mental environment in which they lived and breathed. For it is only when we discover the living link which bound them to the Apostolic Tradition of which they are witnesses, that we shall understand their writings and establish the heterodoxy of some passages, as for instance, the Origenistic *apocatastasis* in the writings of Gregory of Nyssa. When Pius X, by his Motu Proprio of 1 Sept., 1910, solemnly obliged all priests to adhere to these principles, he did more than recall to our minds the time-hallowed rules of Christian faith; he freed history and criticism from those baneful excrescences which impeded the growth of true science.

When the dogmatic material with the help of the historical method has been derived from its sources, another momentous task awaits the theologian: the philosophical appreciation, the speculative examination and elucidation of the material brought to light. This is the purpose of the "scholastic" method, from which "scholastic theology" takes its name.

The scope of the scholastic method is fourfold: (a) to open up completely the content of dogma and to analyze it by means of dialectics; (b) to establish a logical connexion between the various dogmas and to unite them in a well-knit system; (c) to derive new truths, called "theological conclusions", from the premises by syllogistic reasoning; (d) to find reasons, analogies, congruous arguments for the dogmas, but above all to show that the mysteries of faith, though beyond the reach of reason, are not contrary to its laws, but can be made acceptable to our intellect. It is evident that the ultimate purpose of these philosophical speculations cannot be to resolve dogma finally into mere natural truths, or to strip the mysteries of their supernatural character, but to explain the truths of faith, to provide for them a philosophical basis, to bring them nearer to the human mind. Faith must ever remain the solid rock-bottom on which reason builds up, and faith in its turn strives after understanding (*fides quærens intellectum*). Hence the famous axiom of St. Anselm of Canterbury: *Credo ut intellegam*. However highly one may esteem the results of positive theology, one thing is certain: the scientific character of dogmatic theology does not rest so much on the exactness of its exegetical and historical proofs as on the philosophical grasp of the content of dogma. But in attempting this task, the theologian cannot look for aid to modern philosophy with its endless confusion, but to the glorious past of his own science. What else are the modern systems of philosophy, sceptical criticism, Positivism, Pantheism, Monism, etc., than ancient errors cast into new moulds? Rightly does Catholic theology cling to the only true and eternal philosophy of common sense, which was established by Divine Providence in the Socratic School, carried to its highest perfection by Plato and Aristotle, purified from the minutest traces of error by the Scholastics of the thirteenth century.

This is the Aristotelo-scholastic philosophy, which has gained an ever stronger foothold in ecclesiastical institutions of learning. Guided by sound pedagogical principles, Popes Leo XIII and Pius X officially prescribed this philosophy as a preparation for the study of theology, and recommended it as a model method for the speculative treatment of dogma. While in his famous Encyclical "Pascendi" of 8 Sept., 1907, Pius X praises positive theology and frankly recognizes its necessity, yet he sounds a note of warning not to become so absorbed in it as to neglect scholastic theology, which alone can impart a scientific grasp of dogma. These papal rescripts were probably inspired by the sad experience that any other than Scholastic philosophy, instead of elucidating and clarifying, only falsifies and destroys dogma, as is clearly shown by the history of Nominalism, the philosophy of the Renaissance, Hermesianism, Güntherianism, and Modernism. The development also of Protestant theology, which, entering into close union with modern philosophy, swayed to and fro between the extremes of faith and unfaith and did not even recoil from Pantheism, is a warning example for the Catholic theologian. This does not mean that Catholic theology has received no stimulus whatever from modern philosophy since the days of Kant (d. 1804). As a matter of fact, the critical tendency has quickened the critico-historical sense of Catholic theologians in regard to method and demonstration, has given more breadth and depth to their statement of problems, and has shown fully the value of the "theoretical doubt" as the starting-point of every scientific investigation. All these advances, as far as they mark real progress, have exerted a salutary influence on theology also. But they can never repair the material damages caused to sacred science, when, abandoning St. Thomas Aquinas, it went hand in hand with Kant and other champions of our age. But since the Aristotelo-scholastic philosophy also is capable of continual development, there is reason to expect for the future a progressive improvement of speculative theology.

Another method of arriving at the truths of faith is mysticism, which appeals rather to the heart and the feelings than to the intellect, and sensibly imparts a knowledge of Divine things through pious meditation. As long as mysticism keeps in touch with scholasticism and does not exclude the intellect completely, it is entitled to existence for the simple reason that faith lays hold on the whole man, and penetrates his thoughts, desires, and sentiments. The greatest mystics, as Hugh of St. Victor, Bernard of Clairvaux, and Bonaventure, were at the same time distinguished Scholastics. A heart that has preserved the faith and simplicity of its childhood, takes delight even now in the writings of Henry Suso (d. 1365). But whenever mysticism emancipates itself from the guidance of reason and makes light of the doctrinal authority of the Church, it readily falls a prey to Pantheism and pseudo-mysticism, which are the bane of all true religion. Meister Eckhart, whose propositions were condemned by Pope John XXII in 1329, is a warning example. There is little in the present trend of thought that would be favourable to mysticism. The scepticism which has poisoned the minds of our generation, the uncontrolled greed for wealth, the feverish haste in commercial enterprises, even the dulling habit of reading the daily papers—all these are only too apt to disturb the serene atmosphere of Divine contemplation, and play havoc with the interior life, the necessary conditions under which alone the tender flower of mystical piety can blossom. Modernism claims to possess in its immediate and immanent sense of God a congenial soil for the growth of mysticism; this soil, however, does not receive its waters from the undefiled fountain-head of Catholic piety, but from the cisterns of Liberal Protestant pseudo-mysticism, which are tainted, either confessedly or secretly, by Pantheism.

(4) Relation of Dogmatic Theology to other Disciplines.—At first, it was a thing altogether unknown to have different theological branches as independent sciences. Dogmatic theology was the only discipline, and comprised apologetics, dogmatic and moral theology, and canon law. This internal unity was also marked externally by the comprehensive name of science of faith (*scientia fidei*), or sacred science (*scientia sacra*). First to assert its independence was canon law, which, together with dogmatic theology, was the chief study in the medieval universities. But since the underlying principles of canon law, as the Divine constitution of the Church, the hierarchy, the power of ordinations, etc., were at the same time doctrines of faith to be proved in dogmatic theology, there was little danger that the internal connexion with and dependence on the principal science would be broken. Far longer did the union between dogmatic and moral theology endure. They were treated in the medieval "Books of Sentences" and theological "Summæ" as one science. It was not until the seventeenth century, and then only for practical reasons, that moral theology was separated

from the main body of Catholic dogma. Nor did this division degenerate into a formal separation of two strictly co-ordinated disciplines. Moral theology has always been conscious that the revealed laws of morality are as much articles of faith as the theoretical dogmas, and that the entire Christian life is based on the three theological virtues, which are part of the dogmatic doctrine on justification. Hence the superior rank of dogmatic theology, which is not only the centre around which the other disciplines are grouped, but also the main stem from which they branch out. But the necessity of a further division of labour as well as the example of non-Catholic methods led to the independent development of other disciplines: apologetics, exegesis, church history.

The relation existing between apologetics, or fundamental theology as it has been called of late, and dogmatic theology is not that of a general to a particular science; it is rather the relation of the vestibule to the temple or of the foundation to its superstructure. For both the method and the purpose of demonstration differ totally in the two branches. Whereas apologetics, intent upon laying the foundation of the Christian or Catholic religion, uses historical and philosophical arguments, dogmatic theology on the other hand makes use of Scripture and Tradition to prove the Divine character of the different dogmas. Doubt could only exist as to whether the discussion of the sources of faith, the rule of faith, the Church, the primacy, faith and reason, belongs to apologetics or to dogmatic theology. While a dogmatic treatment of these important questions has its advantages, yet from the practical standpoint and for reasons peculiar to the subject, they should be separated from dogmatic theology and referred to apologetics. The practical reason is that the existing denominational differences demand a more thorough apologetic treatment of these problems; and again, the subject-matter itself contains nothing else than the preliminary and fundamental questions of dogmatic theology properly so called. A branch of the greatest importance, ever since the Reformation, is exegesis with its allied disciplines, because that science establishes the meaning of the texts necessary for the Scriptural argument. As the Biblical sciences necessarily suppose the dogma of the inspiration of the Bible and the Divine institution of the Church, which alone, through the assistance of the Holy Ghost, is the rightful owner and authoritative interpreter of the Bible, it is manifest that exegesis, though enjoying full liberty in all other respects, must never lose its connexion with dogmatic theology. Not even church history, though using the same critical methods as profane history, is altogether independent of dogmatic theology. As its object is to set forth the history of God's kingdom upon earth, it cannot repudiate or slight either the Divinity of Christ or the Divine foundation of the Church without forfeiting its claim to be regarded as a theological science. The same applies to other historic sciences, as the history of dogma, of councils, of heresies, patrology, symbolics, and Christian archæology. Pastoral theology, which embraces liturgy, homiletics, and catechetics, proceeded from, and bears close relationship to, moral theology; its dependence on dogmatic theology needs, therefore, no further proof.

The relation between dogmatic theology and philosophy deserves special attention. To begin with, even when they treat the same subject, as God and the soul, there is a fundamental difference between the two sciences. For, as was said above, the formal principles of the two are totally different. But, this fundamental difference must not be exaggerated to the point of asserting, with the Renaissance philosophers and the Modernists, that something false in philosophy may be true in theology, and vice versa. The theory of the "twofold truth" in theology and history, which is only a variant of the same false principle, is therefore expressly abjured in the anti-Modernist oath. But no less fatal would be the other extreme of identifying theology with philosophy, as was attempted by the Gnostics, later by Scotus Eriugena (d. about 877), Raymond Lullus (d. 1315), Pico della Mirandola (d. 1463), and by the modern Rationalists. To counteract this bold scheme, the Vatican Council (Sess. III, cap. iv) solemnly declared that the two sciences differ essentially not only in their cognitive principle (faith, reason) and their object (dogma, rational truth), but also in their motive (Divine authority, evidence) and their ultimate end (beatific vision, natural knowledge of God). But what is the precise relation between these sciences? The origin and dignity of revealed theology forbid us to assign to philosophy a superior or even a co-ordinate rank. Already Aristotle and Philo of Alexandria, in determining the relation of philosophy to that part of metaphysics which is directly concerned with God, pronounced philosophy to be the "handmaid" of natural theology. When philosophy came into contact with revelation, this subordination was still more emphasized and was finally crystallized in the principle: *Philosophia est ancilla theologiæ*. But neither the Church nor the theologians who insisted on this axiom, ever intended thereby to encroach on the freedom, independence, and dignity of philosophy, to curtail its rights, or to lower it to the position of a mere slave of theology. Their mutual relations are far more honourable. Theology may be conceived as a queen, philosophy as a noble lady of the court who performs for her mistress the most worthy and valuable services, and without whose assistance the queen would be left in a very helpless and embarrassing position. That the Church, in examining the various systems, should select the philosophy which harmonized with her own revealed doctrine and proved itself to be the only true philosophy by acknowledging a personal God, the immortality of the soul, and the moral law, was so natural and obvious that it required no apology. Such a philosophy, however, existed among the pagans of old, and was carried to an eminent degree of perfection by Aristotle.

(5) *Division and Content of Dogmatic Theology.*—Not only for non-Catholics, but also for Catholic laymen it may be of interest to take a brief survey of the questions and problems generally discussed in dogmatic theology.

(a) *God* (*De Deo uno et trino*).—As God is the central idea around which all theology turns, dogmatic theology must begin with the doctrine of God, essentially one, Whose existence, essence, and attributes are to be investigated. While the arguments, strictly so called, for the existence of God are given in philosophy or in apologetics, dogmatic theology insists upon the revealed doctrine that God may be known from creation by reason alone, that is, without external revelation or internal illumination by grace. From this it follows at once that Atheism must be branded as heresy and that Agnosticism may not plead mitigating circumstances. Nor can Traditionalism and Ontologism be reconciled with the dogma of the natural knowableness of God. For if, as the Traditionalists assert, the consciousness of God's existence, found in all races and ages, is due solely to the oral tradition of our forefathers and ultimately to the revelation granted in Paradise, the knowledge of God derived from the visible creation is at once discounted. The same must be said of the Ontologists, who fancy that our mind enjoys an intuitive vision of God's essence, and is thus made certain of His existence. Likewise, to assume with Descartes an inborn idea of God (*idea Dei innata*) is out of the question; consequently, the knowableness of God by mere reason, means in the last analysis that His existence can be demonstrated, as the anti-Modernist oath prescribed by Pius X expressly affirms. But this method of arriving at a knowledge of God is toilsome; for it must proceed by way of denying imperfection in God and of ascribing to Him in higher excellence (*eminenter*) whatever perfections are found in creatures; nor does the light of revelation and of faith elevate our knowledge to an essentially higher plane. Hence all our knowledge of God on this earth implies painful deficiencies which will not be filled except by the beatific vision.

The metaphysical essence of God is generally said to be self-existence, which means, however, the fulness of being (Gr. αὐτουσία), and not merely the negation of origin (*ens a se—ens non ab alio*). The so-called positive aseity of Prof. Schell, meaning that God realizes and produces himself, must be as uncompromisingly rejected as the Pantheistic confusion of *ens a se* with the impersonal *ens universale*. The relation existing between God's essence and His attributes may not be called a real distinction (theoretical.Realism, Gilbert de La Porrée), nor yet a purely logical distinction of the mind (Nominalism). Intermediary between these two objectionable extremes is the formal distinction of the Scotists. But the virtual distinction of the Thomists deserves preference in every regard, because it alone does not jeopardize the simplicity of the Divine Being. If self-existence is the fundamental attribute of God, both the attributes of being and of operation must proceed from it as from their root. The first class includes infinity, simplicity, substantiality, omnipotence, immutability, eternity, and immensity; to the second category belong omniscience and the Divine will. Besides, many theologians distinguish from both these categories the so-called moral attributes: veracity, fidelity, wisdom, sanctity, bounty, beauty, mercy, and justice. Monotheism is best treated in connexion with God's simplicity and unity. The most difficult problems are those which concern God's knowledge, especially His foreknowledge of free future actions. For it is here that both Thomists and Molinists throw out their anchors to gain a secure hold for their respective systems of grace, the former for their *præmotio physica*, the latter for their *scientia media*. In treating of the Divine will, theologians insist on God's freedom in His external activity, and when discussing the problem of evil, they prove that God can intend sin neither as an end nor as a means to an end, but merely permits it for reasons both holy and wise. While some theologians use this chapter to treat of God's salvific will and the allied questions of predestination and reprobation, others refer these subjects to the chapter on grace.

Being the corner-stone of the Christian religion, the doctrine of the Trinity is thoroughly and extensively discussed, all the more because the Liberal theology of the Protestants has relapsed into the ancient error of the Antitrinitarians. The dogma of God's threefold personality, traces of which may be found in the Old Testament, can be conclusively proved from the New Testament and Tradition. The combat which the Fathers waged against Monarchianism, Sabellianism, and Subordinationism (Arius, Macedonius) aids considerably in shedding light on the mystery. Great importance attaches to the logos-doctrine of St. John; but as to its relation to the logos of the Stoic Neoplatonists, the Jewish Philonians, and the early Fathers, many points are still in an unsettled condition. The reason why there are three Persons is the twofold procession immanent in the Godhead: the procession of the Son from the Father by generation, and the procession of the Holy Ghost from both the Father and the Son by spiration. In view of the Greek schism, the dogmatic justification of the addition of the *Filioque* in the Creed must be scientifically established. A philosophical understanding of the dogma of the Trinity was attempted by the Fathers, especially by St. Augustine. The most important result was the cognition that the Divine generation must be conceived as a spiritual procession from the intellect, and the Divine spiration as a procession from the will or from love. Active and passive generation, together with active and passive spiration, lead to the doctrine of the four relations, of which, however, only three constitute persons, to wit, active and passive generation (Father, Son), and passive spiration (Holy Ghost). The reason why active spiration does not result in a distinct (fourth) person, is because it is one and the same common function of the Father and the Son. The philosophy of this mystery includes also the doctrine of the Divine properties, notions, appropriations, and missions. Finally, with the doctrine of circuminsession, which summarizes the whole theology of the Trinity, the treatment of this dogma is brought to a fitting conclusion.

(b) Creation (*De Deo creante*).—The first act of God's external activity is creation. The theologian investigates both the activity itself and the work produced. With regard to the former, the interest centres in creation out of nothing, around which, as along the circumference of a circle, are grouped a number of secondary truths: God's plan of the universe, the relation between the Trinity and creation, the freedom of the Creator, the creation in time, the impossibility of communicating the creative power to any creature. These momentous truths not only perfect and purify the theistic idea of God, they also give the death-blow to heretical Dualism (God, matter) and to the Protean variations of Pantheism. As the beginning of the world supposes creation out of nothing, so its continuation supposes Divine conservation, which is nothing less than a continued creation. However, God's creative activity is not thereby exhausted. It enters into every action of the creature, whether necessary or free. What is the nature of God's universal co-operation with free, rational beings? On this question Thomists and Molinists differ widely. The former regard the Divine activity as a previous, the latter as a simultaneous, concursus. According to Molinism, it is only by conceiving the concursus as simultaneous that true freedom in the creature can be secured, and that the essential holiness of the Creator can be maintained, the fact of sin notwithstanding. The crowning achievement of God's creative activity is His providence and universal government, which aims at the realization of the ultimate end of the universe, God's glory through His creatures.

The work produced by creation is divided into three kingdoms, rising in tiers one above another: world; man; angel. To this triad correspond dogmatic cosmology, anthropology, angelology. In discussing the first of these, the theologian must be satisfied with general outlines, e. g. of the Creator's activity described in the hexaemeron. Anthropology is more thoroughly treated, because man, the microcosm, is the centre of creation. Revelation tells us many things about man's nature, his origin and the unity of the human race, the spirituality and immortality of the soul, the relation of soul and body, the origin of individual souls. Above all, it tells us of supernatural grace with which man was adorned and which was intended to be a permanent possession of the human race. The discussion of man's original state must be preceded by a theory of the supernatural order without which the nature of original sin could not be understood. But original sin, the wilful repudiation of the supernatural state, is one of the most important chapters. Its existence must be carefully proved from the sources of faith; its nature, the mode of its transmission, its effects, must be subjected to a thorough discussion. The fate of the angels runs in many respects parallel to that of mankind: the angels also were endowed with both sanctifying grace and high natural excellences; some of them rose in rebellion against God, and were thrust into hell as demons. While the devil and his angels are inimical to the human race, the faithful angels have been appointed to exercise the office of guardians over mankind.

(c) Redemption (*De Deo Redemptore*).—As the fall of man was followed by redemption, so the chapter on creation is immediately followed by that on redemption. Its three main divisions: Christology, Soteriology, Mariology, must ever remain in the closest connexion. [For the first of these three (Christology) see I. a. below, immediately following sub-section B. *History*.]

(i) Soteriology.—Soteriology is the doctrine of the work of the Redeemer. As in Christology the leading idea is the Hypostatic Union, so here the main idea is the natural mediatorship of Christ. After having disposed of the preliminary questions concerning the possibility, opportuneness, and necessity of redemption, as well as of those regarding the predestination of Christ, the next subject to occupy our attention is the work of redemption itself. This work reaches its climax in the vicarious satisfaction of Christ on the cross, and is crowned by His descent into limbo and His ascension into heaven. From a speculative standpoint, a thorough and comprehensive theory of satisfaction remains still a pious desideratum, though promising attempts have often been made from the days of Anselm down to the present time. It will be necessary to blend into one noble whole the hidden elements of truth contained in the old patristic theory of ransom, the juridical conception of St. Anselm, and the ethical theory of atonement. The Redeemer's activity as Mediator stands out most prominently in His triple office of high priest, prophet, and king, which is continued, after the ascension of Christ, in the priesthood and the teaching and pastoral office of the Church. The central position is occupied by the high-priesthood of Christ, which manifests the death on the cross as the true sacrifice of propitiation, and proves the Redeemer to be a true priest.

(ii) Mariology, or the doctrine of the Mother of God, cannot be separated either from the person or from the work of the Redeemer and therefore has the deepest connexion with both Christology and Soteriology. Here the central idea is the Divine Maternity, since this is at once the source of Mary's unspeakable dignity and of her surpassing fulness of grace. Just as the Hypostatic Union of the Divinity and humanity of Christ stands or falls with the truth of the Divine Maternity, so too is this same maternity the foundation of all special privileges which were accorded to Mary on account of Christ's dignity. These singular privileges are four: her Immaculate Conception, personal freedom from sin, perpetual virginity, and her bodily Assumption into heaven. For the three former we have doctrinal decisions of the Church, which are final. However, though Mary's bodily Assumption has not yet been solemnly declared an article of faith, nevertheless the Church has practically demonstrated such to be her belief by celebrating from the earliest times the feast of the Assumption of the Mother of God. Two more privileges are connected with Mary's dignity: her special mediatorship between the Redeemer and the redeemed and her exclusive right to hyperdulia. Of course, it is clear that the mediatorship of Mary is entirely subordinate to that of Her Divine Son and derives its whole efficacy and power therefrom. In order the better to understand the value and importance of Mary's peculiar right to such veneration, it will be well to consider, by way of contrast, the dulia paid to the saints and, again, the doctrine concerning the veneration paid to relics and images. For the most part, dogmatic theologians prefer to treat these latter subjects under eschatology, together with the Communion of Saints.

(iii) Grace (*De gratia*).—The Christian idea of grace is based entirely upon the supernatural order. A distinction is made between actual and sanctifying grace, according as there is question of a supernatural activity or merely the state of sanctification. But the crucial point in the whole doctrine of grace lies in the justification of the sinner, because, after all, the aim and object of actual grace is either to lay the foundation for the grace of justification when the latter is absent, or to preserve the grace of justification in the soul that already possesses it. The three qualities of actual grace are of the utmost importance: its necessity, its gratuitousness, and its universality. Although on the one hand we must avoid the exaggeration of the Reformers, and of the followers of Baius and Jansenius, who denied the capability of unaided nature altogether in moral action, yet, on the other hand, theologians agree that fallen man is quite incapable, without the help of God's grace, of either fulfilling the whole natural law or of resisting all strong temptations. But actual grace is absolutely necessary for each and every salutary act, since all such acts bear a causal relation towards the supernatural end of man. The heretical doctrines of Pelagianism and Semipelagianism are refuted by the Church's doctrinal decisions based upon Holy Scripture and Tradition. From the supernatural character of grace flows its second quality: gratuitousness. So entirely gratuitous is grace that no natural merit, no positive capability or preparation for it on the part of nature, nor even any purely natural petition, is able to move God to give us actual grace. The universality of grace rests fundamentally upon the absolute universality of God's salvific will, which, in regard to adults, simply means His antecedent will to distribute sufficient grace to each and every person, whether he be already justified or in the state of sin, whether he be Christian or heathen, believer or infidel. But the salvific will, in as far as it is consequent and deals out just retribution, is no longer universal, but particular, for the reason that only those who persevere in justice, enter heaven, whereas the wicked are condemned to hell. The question of the predestination of the blessed and the reprobation of the damned is admittedly one of the most difficult problems with which theology has to deal, and its solution is wrapped in impenetrable mystery. The same may be said of the relation existing between grace and the liberty of the human will. It would be cutting the Gordian knot rather than loosing it, were one to deny the efficacy of grace, as did Pelagianism, or again, following the error of Jansenism, deny the liberty of the will. The difficulty is rather in determining just how the acknowledged efficacy of grace is to be reconciled with human freedom. For centuries Thomists and Molinists, Augustinians and Congruists have been toiling to clear up the matter. And while the system of grace known as syncretic has endeavoured to harmonize the principles of Thomism and Molinism, it has served but to double the difficulties instead of eliminating them.

The second part of the doctrine on grace has to do with sanctifying grace, which produces the state of habitual holiness and justice. Preparatory to receiving this grace, the soul undergoes a certain preliminary process, which is begun by theological faith, the "beginning, root and foundation of all justification", and is completed and perfected by other supernatural dispositions, such as contrition, hope, love. The Protestant conception of justifying faith as a mere fiducial faith is quite as much at variance with revelation as is the *sola fides* doctrine. Catholics also differ from Protestants in explaining the essence of justification itself. While Catholic dogma declares that justification consists in a true blotting-out of sin and in an interior sanctification of the soul, Protestantism would have it to be merely an external cloaking of sins which still remain, and a mere imputation to the sinner of God's or Christ's justice. According to Catholic teaching, the forgiveness of sin and the sanctification of the soul are but two moments of one and the same act of justification, since the blotting-out of original and mortal sin is accomplished by the very fact of the infusion of sanctifying grace. Although we may, to a certain extent, understand the nature of grace in itself, and may define it philosophically as a permanent quality of the soul, an infused habit, an accidental and analogous participation of the Divine nature, yet its true nature may be more easily understood from a consideration of its so-called formal effects produced in the soul. These are: sanctity, purity, beauty, friendship with God, adopted sonship. Sanctifying grace is accompanied by additional gifts, viz., the three theological virtues, the infused moral virtues, the seven gifts of the Holy Ghost, and the personal indwelling of the Holy Ghost in the soul of the justified. This latter it is that crowns and completes the whole process of justification. We must also mention three qualities special to justification or sanctifying grace: its uncertainty, its inequality, and the possibility of its being lost. All of them are diametrically opposed to the Protestant conception, which asserts the absolute certainty of justification, its complete equality, and the impossibility of its being lost. Finally, the fruits of justification are treated. These ripen under the beneficent influence of sanctifying grace, which enables man to acquire merit through his good works, that is to say, supernatural merit for heaven. The doctrine on grace is concluded with the proof of the existence, the conditions, and the objects of merit.

(iv) Sacraments (*De sacramentis*).—This section is divided into two parts: the treatise on the sacraments in general and that on the sacraments in particular. After having defined exactly what is meant by the Christian sacraments, and what is meant by the sacrament of nature and the Jewish rite of circumcision as it prevailed in pre-Christian times, the next important step is to prove the existence of the seven sacraments as instituted by Christ. The essence of a sacrament requires three things: an outward, visible sign, i. e. the matter and form of the sacrament; interior grace; and institution by Christ. In the difficult problem as to whether Christ himself determined the matter and form of each sacrament specifically or only generically, the solution must be sought through dogmatic and historical investigations. Special importance attaches to the causality of the sacraments, and an efficacy *ex opere operato* is attributed to them. Theologians dispute as to the nature of this causality, i. e. whether it is physical or merely moral. In the case of each sacrament, regard must be had to two persons, the recipient and the minister. The objective efficacy of a sacrament is wholly independent of the personal sanctity or the individual faith of the minister. The only requisite is that he who confers the sacrament intend to do what the Church does. As regards the recipient of a sacrament, a distinction must be made between valid and worthy reception; the conditions differ with the various sacraments. But since the free will is required for validity, it is evident that no one can be forced to receive a sacrament.

Furthermore, as regards the sacraments in particular, the conclusions reached with reference to the sacraments in general of course hold good. Thus, in the case of the first two sacraments, baptism and confirmation, we must prove in detail the existence of the three requisites mentioned above, as well as the disposition of both the minister and the recipient. The question whether their reception is absolutely necessary or only of precept must also be examined. More than ordinary care is called for in the discussion of the Eucharist, which is not only a sacrament, but also the Holy Sacrifice of the Mass. Everything centres of course around the dogma of the Real Presence of Christ under the appearances of bread and wine. His presence there is effected by means of the transubstantiation of the Eucharistic elements and lasts as long as the accidents of bread and wine remain incorrupt. The dogma of the totality of the Real Presence means that in each individual species the whole Christ, flesh and blood, body and soul, Divinity and humanity, is really present. The Holy Eucharist is, of course, a great mystery, one that rivals that of the Holy Trinity and of the Hypostatic Union. It presents to us a truth utterly at variance with the testimony of our senses, asking us, as it does, to assent to the continued existence of the Eucharistic species without their subject, a sort of spiritual existence, unconfined by space, yet of a human body, and, again, the simultaneous presence of Christ in many different places. The sacramental character of the Eucharist is established by the presence of the three essential elements. The outward sign consists in the Eucharistic forms of bread and wine and the words of consecration. Its institution by Christ is guaranteed both by the promise of Christ and by the words of institution at the Last Supper. Finally, the interior effects of grace are produced by the worthy reception of Holy Communion. As Christ is wholly present in each species, the reception of the Eucharist under one species is sufficient to obtain fully all the fruits of the sacrament. Hence the chalice need not be communicated to the laity, though at times the Church has so allowed it to be, but not in any sense as though such were necessary. Not everyone is capable of pronouncing the words of consecration with sacramental effect, but only duly ordained bishops and priests; for to them alone did Christ communicate the power of transubstantiation in the Holy Sacrifice of the Mass. A distinct phase of the Eucharist is its sacrificial character. This is proved not only from the oldest Fathers and the liturgical practice of the early Christian Church, but also from certain prophecies of the Old Testament and from the Gospel narrative of the Last Supper. To find the physical essence of the Sacrifice of the Mass, we must consider its essential dependence on, and relation to, the bloody sacrifice of the Cross; for the Mass is a commemoration of the latter, its representation, its renewal, and its application. This intrinsically relative character of the sacrifice of the Mass does not in the least destroy or lessen the universality and oneness of the sacrifice on the Cross, but rather presupposes it; likewise the intrinsic propriety of the Mass is shown precisely in this, that it neither effects nor claims to effect anything else than the application of the fruits of the sacrifice of the Cross to the individual, and this in a sacrificial manner. The essence of the sacrifice is generally thought to consist neither in the Offertory nor in the Communion of the celebrant, but in the double consecration. Widely divergent are the views of the theologians as to the metaphysical essence of the sacrifice of the Mass, that is to say, as to the question how far the idea of a real sacrifice is verified in the double consecration. A concurrence of opinion on this point is all the more difficult owing to the fact that the very idea of sacrifice is involved in no little obscurity. As regards the causality of the sacrifice of the Mass, it has all the effects of a true sacrifice: adoration, thanksgiving, impetration, atonement. Most of its effects are *ex opere operato*, while some depend on the co-operation of the participants.

The Sacrament of Penance presupposes the Church's

power to forgive sins, a power clearly indicated in the Bible in the words with which Christ instituted this sacrament (John, xx, 23). Moreover, this power is abundantly attested both by the patristic belief in the Church's power of the Keys and by the history of the ancient penitential system. As at the time of Montanism and Novatianism it was a question of vindicating the universality of this power, so nowadays it is a matter of defending its absolute necessity and its judicial form against the attacks of Protestantism. These three qualities manifest at the same time the intrinsic nature and the essence of the Sacrament of Penance. The universality of the power to forgive sins means that all sins without exception, supposing, of course, contrition for the same, can be remitted in this sacrament. Owing to its absolute necessity and its judicial form, however, the sacrament really becomes a tribunal of penance in which the penitent is at once plaintiff, defendant, and witness, while the priest acts as judge. The matter of the sacrament consists in the three acts of the penitent: contrition, confession, and satisfaction, while the priestly absolution is its form. To act as judge in the Sacrament of Penance, the confessor needs more than priestly ordination: he must also have jurisdiction, which may be restricted more or less by the ecclesiastical superiors. As the validity of this sacrament, unlike that of the others, depends essentially on the worthiness of its reception, great attention must be paid to the acts of the penitent. Most important of all is contrition with the purpose of amendment, containing, as it does, the virtue of penance. The opinion, held by many of the early Scholastics, that perfect contrition is required for the validity of the absolution, is quite irreconcilable with the *ex opere operato* efficacy of the sacrament; for sorrow, springing from the motive of perfect love, suffices of itself to free the sinner from all guilt, quite antecedent to, and apart from, the sacrament, though not indeed without a certain relation to it. According to the mind of the Council of Trent, imperfect contrition (attrition), even when actuated by the fear of hell, is sufficient for the validity of the sacrament, though we should, of course, strive to call in nobler motives. Therefore the addition of a formal *caritas initialis* to attrition, as the Contritionists of to-day demand for the validity of absolution, is superfluous, at least so far as validity is concerned. The contrite confession, which is the second act of the penitent, manifests the interior sorrow and the readiness to do penance by a visible, outward sign, the matter of the sacrament. Since the Reformers rejected the Sacrament of Penance, great care must be bestowed upon the Biblical and patristic proof of its existence and its necessity. The required satisfaction, the third act of the penitent, is fulfilled in the penances (prayers, fasting, alms) which, according to the present custom of the Church, are imposed by the confessor immediately before the absolution. The actual fulfilment of such penances is not essential to the validity of the sacrament, but belongs rather to its integrity. The Church's extra-sacramental remission of punishment due to sin is called indulgence. This power of granting indulgences, both for the living and the dead, is included in the power of the Keys committed to the Church by Christ.

Extreme Unction may be considered as the complement of the Sacrament of Penance, inasmuch as it can take the place of the latter in case sacramental confession is impossible to one who is unconscious and dangerously ill.

While the five sacraments of which we have treated so far were instituted for the welfare of the individual, the last two, Holy Orders and Matrimony, aim rather at the well-being of human society in general. The Sacrament of Holy Orders is composed of various grades, of which those of bishop, priest, and deacon are certainly of a sacramental nature, whereas that of subdeacon and the four minor orders are most probably due to ecclesiastical institution. The decision depends on whether or no the presentation of the instruments is essential for the validity of ordination. In the case of the subdiaconate and the minor orders this presentation indeed occurs, but without the simultaneous imposition of hands. The common opinion prevalent to-day holds that the imposition of hands, together with the invocation of the Holy Ghost, is the sole matter and form of this sacrament. And since this latter obtains only in the case of the consecration of a bishop, priest, or deacon, the conclusion is drawn that only the three hierarchical grades or orders confer *ex opere operato* the sacramental grace, the sacramental character, and the corresponding powers. The ordinary minister of all orders, even those of a non-sacramental character, is the bishop. But the pope may delegate an ordinary priest to ordain a subdeacon, lector, exorcist, acolyte, or ostiarius. Beginning with the subdiaconate, which was not raised to the rank of a major order until the Middle Ages, celibacy and the recitation of the Breviary are of obligation.

Three disciplines treat the Sacrament of Matrimony: dogmatic theology, moral theology, and canon law. Dogmatic theology leads the way, and proves from the sources of faith not merely the sacramental nature of Christian marriage, but also its essential unity and indissolubility. In the case of a consummated marriage between Christians the marriage bond is absolutely indissoluble; but where there is question of a consummated marriage between pagans the bond may be dissolved if one of the parties is converted to the Faith, and if the other conditions of what is known as the "Pauline Privilege" are fulfilled. The bond of a non-consummated marriage between Christians may be dissolved in two cases: when one of the parties concerned makes the solemn profession of religious vows, or when the pope, for weighty reasons, dissolves such a marriage. Finally, the grounds of the Church's power to establish diriment impediments are discussed and thoroughly proved.

(v) Eschatology (*De novissimis*).—The final treatise of dogmatic theology has to do with the four last things. According as we consider either the individual or mankind in general, there is seen to be a double consummation of all things. For the individual the last things are death and the particular judgment, to which corresponds, as his final state and condition, either heaven or hell. The consummation of the human race on doomsday will be preceded by certain indications of the impending disaster, right after which will occur the resurrection of the dead and the general judgment. As for the opinion that there will be a glorious reign of Christ upon earth for a thousand years previous to the final end of all things, suffice it to remark that there is not the slightest foundation for it in revelation, and even a moderate form of Chiliasm must be rejected as untenable.

Definition and Nature: KUHN, *Einleitung in die katholische Dogmatik* (2nd ed., Tübingen, 1859); SCHRADER, *De theologia generatim* (Freiburg, 1861); HUNTER, *Outlines of Dogmatic Theology*, I, (London, 1894); 1 sqq.; WILHELM AND SCANNELL, *A Manual of Catholic Theology Based on Scheeben's Dogmatik*, I (London, 1899), 1 sqq.; VAN NOORT, *De fontibus revelationis necnon de fide divina* (2nd ed., Amsterdam, 1911); PICCIRELLI, *De catholico dogmate universim. Disquisitio theologica contra Modernistas* (Rome, 1911); POHLE, *God: His Knowability, Essence and Attributes*, tr. PREUSS, (St. Louis, 1911), pp. 1-14; SCHEEBEN, *Die Mysterien des Christentums* (3rd ed., Freiburg, 1912); SCHANZ in *Kirchenlexikon*, s. v. *Theologie*.—From the Anglican standpoint: HALL, *Introduction to Dogmatic Theology* (New York, 1907).

Dogmatic Theology as a Science: SCHANZ, *Ist die Theologie eine Wissenschaft?* (Tübingen, 1900); BRAIG, *Freiheit der philosophischen Forschung in kritischer u. christlicher Fassung* (Freiburg, 1894); VON HERTLING, *Das Princip des Katholicismus u. die*

Wissenschaft (4th ed., Freiburg, 1899); Pertner, *Voraussetzungslose Forschung, freie Wissenschaft u. Katholicismus* (Vienna, 1902); Donat, *Freiheit der Wissenschaft* (Innsbruck, 1910); Förster, *Autorität u. Freiheit* (Kempten, 1910); Cohauss, *Das moderne Denken oder die moderne Denkfreiheit u. ihre Grenzen* (Cologne, 1911).—About the anti-Modernist oath cf. Reinhold, *Der Antimodernisteneid u. die Freiheit der Wissenschaft* (Vienna, 1911); Baur, *Klarheit u. Wahrheit. Eine Erklärung des Antimodernisteneids* (Freiburg, 1911); Marx, *Der Eid wider den Modernismus u. die Geschichtsforschung* (Trier, 1911); Mausbach, *Der Eid wider den Modernismus* (Cologne, 1911); Verweyen, *Philosophie u. Theologie im Mittelalter. Die historischen Voraussetzungen des Antimodernismus* (Bonn, 1911).

The Methods: de Smedt, *Principes de la critique historique* (Liège, 1883); Langlois et Seignobos, *Introduction aux études historiques* (3rd ed., Paris, 1905); Bernheim, *Lehrbuch der historischen Methode u. Geschichtsphilosophie* (5th ed., Leipzig, 1908).—On the Scholastic method cf. Kleutgen, *Theologie der Vorzeit*, V (2nd ed., Münster, 1874), 1 sq.; Wolff, *Credo ut intelligam: Short Studies in Early Greek Philosophy and its Relation to Christianity* (London, 1891); Rickaby, *Scholasticism* (London, 1909); Grabmann, *Geschichte der scholastischen Methode*, I, II (Freiburg, 1909-11). On Neoscholasticism cf. Talamo, *Il rinnovamento del pensiere tomistico* (Siena, 1878); Berthier, *L'étude de la Somme théologique de St. Thomas* (Fribourg, 1893); De Wulf, *Introduction à la philosophie néo-scolastique* (Louvain, 1904).—Subsidiary to these are: Signoriello, *Lexicon peripateticum philosophico-theologicum* (Naples, 1872); Schütz, *Thomas-Lexikon* (2nd ed., Paderborn, 1895); Garcia, *Lexicon scholasticum, in quo definitiones, distinctiones et effata a Joanne Duns Scoto exponuntur* (Quaracchi, 1910).—Periodicals: *Divus Thomas* (Piacenza, 1879); *Jahrbuch für Philosophie u. spekulative Theologie*, by Commer (Paderborn, 1887—); *Philosophisches Jahrbuch der Görresgesellschaft* (Fulda, 1888—); *Revue thomiste* (Fribourg, 1893—); *Revue néo-scolastique* (Louvain, 1894—); *Rivista di Filosofia neo-scholastica* (Florence, 1908—); *Ciencia tomista* (Madrid, 1909—).—On Mysticism cf. Sandreau, *Les degrés de la vie spirituelle* (2 vols., Angers, 1897); Idem, *La vie d'union à Dieu* (Angers, 1900); Idem, *L'état mystique* (Paris, 1903); Idem, *Les faits extraordinaires de la vie spirituelle* (Angers, 1908); Poulain, *Des Grâces d'oraison* (5th ed., Paris, 1906), tr. Yorke Smith, *the Graces of Interior Prayer* (London, 1910); Zahn, *Einführung in die christliche Mystik* (Paderborn, 1908); Sharpe, *Mysticism: Its True Nature and Value* (London, 1910).

Relation to other Sciences: Staudenmeier, *Encyklopädie der Theologie* (Freiburg, 1834-40); Wirthmüller, *Encyklopädie der katholischen Theologie* (Landshut, 1874); Kihn, *Encyklopädie u. Methodologie der Theologie* (Freiburg, 1892); Krieg, *Encyklopädie der theologischen Wissenschaft nebst Methodenlehre* (2nd ed., Freiburg, 1910); Newman, *Idea of a University* (London, 1893); Clemens, *De Scholasticorum sententia Philosophiam esse Theologiæ ancillam* (Münster, 1857); Kneib, *Wissen u. Glauben* (2nd ed., Mainz, 1902); Cathrein, *Glauben u. Wissen* (5th ed., Freiburg, 1911); Willmann, *Geschichte des Idealismus* (3 vols., Brunswick, 1908); Heitz, *Essai historique sur les rapports entre la Philosophie et la Foi de Bérenger à St. Thomas* (Paris, 1909). Division and Contents: Pohle, *Christlich-katholische Dogmatik* in *Die Kultur der Gegenwart* by Hinneberg (Leipzig, 1909), I, IV, 2, p. 37 sqq.; Hettinger, *Timothy, or Letters to a Young Theologian*, tr. Stepka (St. Louis, 1902); Hogan, *Clerical Studies* (Philadelphia, 1896); Scannell, *The Priest's Studies* (London, 1908).

B. *History of Dogmatic Theology*.—The imposing edifice of Catholic theology has been reared not by individual nations and men, but rather by the combined efforts of all nations and the theologians of every century. Nothing could be more at variance with the essential character of theology than an endeavour to set upon it the stamp of nationalism: like the Catholic Church itself, theology must ever be international. In the history of dogmatic theology, as in the history of the Church, three periods may be distinguished: (1) the patristic; (2) the medieval; (3) the modern.

(1) *The Patristic Period* (about A. D. 100–800).—The Great Fathers of the Church and the ecclesiastical writers of the first 800 years rendered important services by their positive demonstration and their speculative treatment of dogmatic truth. It is the Fathers who are honoured by the Church as her principal theologians, excelling as they did in purity of faith, sanctity of life, and fulness of wisdom, virtues which are not always to be found in those who are known simply as ecclesiastical writers. Tertullian (b. about 160), who died a Montanist, and Origen (d. 254), who showed a marked leaning towards Hellenism, strayed far from the path of truth. But even some of the Fathers, e. g. St. Cyprian (d. 258) and St. Gregory of Nyssa, went astray on individual points; the former in regard to the baptism of heretics, the latter in the matter of apocatastasis. It was not so much in the catechetical schools of Alexandria, Antioch, and Edessa as in the struggle with the great heresies of the age that patristic theology developed. This serves to explain the character of the patristic literature, which is apologetical and polemical, parenetical and ascetic, with a wealth of exegetical wisdom on every page; for the roots of theology are in the Bible, especially in the Gospels and in the Epistles of St. Paul. Although it was not the intention of the Fathers to give a methodical and systematic treatise of theology, nevertheless, so thoroughly did they handle the great dogmas from the positive, speculative, and apologetic standpoint that they laid the permanent foundations for the centuries to follow. Quite justly does Möhler call attention to the fact that all modes of treatment may be found in the writings of the Apostolic Fathers: the apologetic style is represented by the letter of Diognetus and the letters of St. Ignatius; the dogmatic in pseudo-Barnabas; the moral, in the Pastor of Hermas; canon law, in the letter of St. Clement of Rome; church history, in the Acts of the martyrdom of Polycarp and Ignatius. Owing to the unexpected recovery of lost manuscripts we may add: the liturgical style, in the Didache; the catechetical, in the "Proof of the Apostolic Preaching" by St. Irenæus.

Although the different epochs of the patristic age overlap each other, it may be said in general that the apologetic style predominated in the first epoch up to Constantine the Great, while in the second epoch, that is to say up to the time of Charlemagne, dogmatic literature prevailed. We can here only trace in the most general outlines this theological activity, leaving to patrology the discussion of the literary details.

When the Christian writers entered the lists against paganism and Judaism, a double task awaited them: they had to explain the principal truths of natural religion, such as God, the soul, creation, immortality, and freedom of the will; at the same time they had to defend the chief mysteries of the Christian faith, as the Trinity, Incarnation, etc., and had to prove their sublimity, beauty, and conformity to reason. The band of loyal champions who fought against pagan Polytheism and idolatry is very large: Justin, Athenagoras, Tatian, Theophilus of Antioch, Hermias, Tertullian, Clement of Alexandria, Origen, Cyprian, Minucius Felix, Commodianus, Arnobius, Lactantius, Prudentius, Firmicius Maternus, Eusebius of Cæsarea, Athanasius, Gregory of Nazianzus, Cyril of Alexandria, Nilus, Theodoret, Orosius, and Augustine. The most eminent writers in the struggle against Judaism were: Justin, Tertullian, Hippolytus, Cyprian, Athanasius, Gregory of Nyssa, Epiphanius, Chrysostom, Cyril of Alexandria, Isidore of Seville. The attacks of the Fathers were not, of course, aimed at the Israelitic religion of the Old Testament, which was a revealed religion, but at the obstinacy of those Jews who, clinging to the dead letter of the Law, refused to recognize the prophetic spirit of the Old Testament.

But far greater profit resulted from conflict with the heresies of the first eight centuries. As the flint, when it is struck by the steel, gives off luminous sparks, so did dogma, in its clash with heretical teaching, shed a new and wonderfully brilliant light. As the errors were legion, it was natural that in the course of the centuries all the principal dogmas were, one by one, treated in monographs which established their truth and provided them with a philosophical basis. The struggle of the Fathers against Gnosticism, Manichæism, and Priscillianism served not only to bring into clearer light the essence of God, creation, the problem of evil; it moreover secured the true principles of faith and the Church's authority against heretical aberrations. In the mighty struggle against Monarchianism, Sabellianism, and Arianism an opportunity was afforded to the Fathers and the œcumenical councils to establish the true meaning of the dogma of the Trinity, to secure it on all sides and to draw out, by speculation, its genuine import. When the contest with Eunomianism broke out, the fires of theological and philosophical criticism purified the doctrine of God and our knowledge of Him, both earthly and heavenly. Of world-wide interest were the Christological disputes, which, beginning with the rise of Apollinarianism, reached their climax in Nestorianism, Monophysitism, and Monothelitism, and were revived once more in Adoptionism. In this long and bitter strife, the doctrine of Christ's person, of the Incarnation, and Redemption, and in connexion herewith Mariology also, was placed on a sure and permanent foundation, from which the Church has never varied a hair's breadth in later ages. The following may be mentioned as the Eastern Champions in this scientific dispute on the Trinity and Christology: the great Alexandrines, Clement, Origen, and Didymus the Blind; the heroic Athanasius and the three Cappadocians (Basil, Gregory of Nazianzus, and Gregory of Nyssa); Cyril of Alexandria and Leontius of Byzantium; finally, Maximus the Confessor and John Damascene. In the West the leaders were: Tertullian, Cyprian, Hilary of Poitiers, Ambrose, Augustine, Jerome, Fulgentius of Ruspe, and the two popes, Leo I and Gregory I. As the contest with Pelagianism and Semi-pelagianism purified the dogmas of grace and liberty, providence and predestination, original sin and the condition of our first parents in Paradise, so in like manner the contests with the Donatists brought out more clearly and strongly the doctrine of the sacraments (baptism), the hierarchical constitution of the Church, her *magisterium*, or teaching authority, and her infallibility. In all these struggles it was Augustine who ever led with indomitable courage, and next to him came Optatus of Mileve and a long line of devoted disciples. The last contest was decided by the Second Council of Nicæa (787); it was in this struggle that, under the leadership of St. John Damascene, the communion of saints, the invocation of the saints, the veneration of relics and holy images were placed on a scientific basis.

It may be seen from this brief outline that the dogmatic teachings of the Fathers are a collection of monographs rather than a systematic exposition. But the Fathers broke the ground and furnished the material for erecting the system afterwards. In the case of some of them there are evident signs of an attempt to synthesize dogma into a complete and organic whole. Irenæus (Adv. hær., III V) shows traces of this tendency; the well-known trilogy of Clement of Alexandria (d. 217) marks an advance in the same direction; but the most successful effort in Christian antiquity to systematize the principal dogmas of faith was made by Origen in his work "De principiis", which is unfortunately disfigured by serious errors. His work against Celsus, on the other hand, is a classic in apologetics and of lasting value. Gregory of Nyssa (d. 394), skilled in matters philosophical and of much the same bent of mind as Origen, endeavoured in his "Large Catechetical Treatise" (λόγος κατεχητικὸς ὁ μέγας) to correlate in a broad synthetic view the fundamental dogmas of the Trinity, the Incarnation, and the Sacraments. In the same manner, though somewhat fragmentarily, Hilary (d. 366) developed in his valuable work "De Trinitate" the principal truths of Christianity. The catechetical instructions of St. Cyril of Jerusalem (d. 386), especially his five mystagogical treatises, on the Apostles' Creed and the three Sacraments of Baptism, Confirmation, and the Holy Eucharist, contain an almost complete dogmatic treatise. St. Epiphanius (d. 496), in his two works "Ancoratus" and "Panarium", aimed at a complete dogmatic treatise, and St. Ambrose (d. 397) in his chief works: "De fide", "De Spiritu S.", "De incarnatione", "De mysteriis", "De pœnitentia", treated the main points of dogma masterfully and in classic Latinity, though without any attempt at a unifying synthesis. In regard to the Trinity and Christology, St. Cyril of Alexandria (d. 444) is even to-day a model for dogmatic theologians. Though all the writings of St. Augustine (d. 430) are an inexhaustible mine, yet he has written one or two works, as the "De fide et symbolo" and the "Enchiridium", which may justly be called compendia of dogmatic and moral theology. Unsurpassed is his speculative work "De Trinitate". His disciple Fulgentius of Ruspe (d. 533) wrote an extensive and thorough confession of faith under the title, "De fide ad Petrum, seu regula rectæ fidei", a veritable treasure for the theologians of his day.

Towards the end of the Patristic Age Isidore of Seville (d. 636) in the West and John Damascene (b. ab. 700) in the East paved the way for a systematic treatment of dogmatic theology. Following closely the teachings of St. Augustine and St. Gregory the Great, St. Isidore proposed to collect all the writings of the earlier Fathers and to hand them down as a precious inheritance to posterity. The results of this undertaking were the "Libri III sententiarum seu de summo bono". Tajus of Saragossa (650) had the same end in view in his "Libri V sententiarum". The work of St. John Damascene (d. after 754) was crowned with still greater success; for not only did he gather the teachings and views of the Greek Fathers, but by reducing them to a systematic whole he deserves to be called the first and the only scholastic among the Greeks. His main work, which is divided into three parts, is entitled: "Fons scientiæ" (πηγὴ γνώσεως), because it was intended to be the source, not merely of theology, but of philosophy and Church history as well. The third or theological part, known as "Expositio fidei orthodoxæ" (ἔκθεσις τῆς ὀρθοδόξου πίστεως), is an excellent combination of positive and scholastic theology, and aims at thoroughness both in establishing and in elucidating the truth. Greek theology has never gone beyond St. John Damascene, a standstill caused principally by the Photian schism (869). The only Greek prior to him who had produced a complete system of theology was Pseudo-Dionysius the Areopagite, in the fifth century; but he was more popular in the West, at least from the eighth century on, than in the East. Although he openly wove into the genuine Catholic system neo-Platonic thoughts and phrases, nevertheless he enjoyed an unparalleled reputation among the greatest Scholastics of the Middle Ages because he was supposed to have been a disciple of the Apostles. For all that, Scholasticism did not take its guidance from St. John Damascene or Pseudo-Dionysius, but from St. Augustine, the greatest of the Fathers. Augustinian thought runs like a golden thread through the whole progress of Western philosophy and theology. It was Augustine who led everywhere, who always pointed out the right path, and from whom all schools sought direction. Even the heretics tried to bolster up their errors with the strength of his reputation. To-day his greatness is recognized and appreciated more and more, as specialized research goes more deeply into his works and brings to view his genius. As Scheeben remarks, "It would be easy to compile from his writings a rich system of dogmatic theology." We cannot help admiring the skill with which he ever kept God, as the beginning and end of all things, in the central position, even where he was compelled to depart from earlier opinions which he had found to be untenable. The English-speaking world may well be proud of the Venerable Bede (d. 735), a contemporary of St. John Damascene. Owing to his unusually solid education in theology, his extensive knowledge of the Bible and of the Fathers of the Church, he is the link which joins the patristic with the medieval history of theology.

(2) The Middle Ages (800–1500).—The beginnings of Scholasticism may be traced back to the days of Charlemagne (d. 814). Thence it progressed in ever-quickening development to the time of Anselm of Canterbury, Bernard of Clairvaux, and Peter the Lombard, and onward to its full growth in the Middle Ages (first epoch, 800–1200). The most brilliant period of Scholasticism embraces about 100 years (second epoch, 1200–1300), and with it are connected the names of Alexander of Hales, Albertus Magnus, Bonaventure, Thomas Aquinas, and Duns Scotus. From the beginning of the fourteenth century, owing to the predominance of Nominalism and to the sad condition of the Church, Scholasticism began to decline (third epoch, 1300–1500).

(a) First Epoch: Beginning and Progress of Scholasticism (800–1200).—In the first half of this epoch, up to the time of St. Anselm of Canterbury, the theologians were more concerned with preserving than with developing the treasures stored up in the writings of the Fathers. The sacred science was cultivated nowhere with greater industry than in the cathedral and monastic schools, founded and fostered by Charlemagne. The earliest signs of a new thought appeared in the ninth century during the discussions relative to the Last Supper (Paschasius Radbertus, Ratramnus, Rabanus Maurus). These speculations were carried to a greater depth in the second Eucharistic controversy against Berengarius of Tours (d. 1088), (Lanfranc, Guitmund, Alger, Hugh of Langres, etc.). Unfortunately, the only systematic theologian of this time, Scotus Eriugena (d. after 870), was an avowed Pantheist, so that the name of "Father of Scholasticism" which some would give him, is wholly unmerited. But the one who fully deserves this title is St. Anselm of Canterbury (d. 1109). For he was the first to bring a sharp logic to bear upon the principal dogmas of Christianity, the first to unfold and explain their meaning in every detail, and to draw up a scientific plan for the stately edifice of dogmatic theology. Taking the substance of his doctrine from Augustine, St. Anselm, as a philosopher, was not so much a disciple of Aristotle as of Plato, in whose masterly dialogues he had been thoroughly schooled. Another pillar of the Church was St. Bernard of Clairvaux (d. 1153), the "Father of Mysticism". Though for the most part the author of ascetic works with a mystical tendency, he used the weapons of scientific theology against Abelard's Rationalism and the exaggerated Realism of Gilbert de La Porrée. It is upon the doctrine of Anselm and Bernard that the Scholastics of succeeding generations took their stand, and it was their spirit which lived in the theological efforts of the University of Paris. Less prominent, yet noteworthy, are: Ruprecht of Deutz, William of Thierry, Gaufridus, and others.

The first attempts at a theological system may be seen in the so-called "Books of Sentences", collections and interpretations of quotations from the Fathers, more especially of St. Augustine. One of the earliest of these books is the "Summa sententiarum" of Hugh of St. Victor (1141). His works are characterized throughout by a close adherence to St. Augustine and, according to the verdict of Scheeben, may even yet serve as guides for beginners in the theology of St. Augustine. Less praise is due to the similar work of Robert Pulleyn (d. 1146), who is careless in arranging the matter and confuses the various questions of which he treats. Peter the Lombard, called the "Magister Sententiarum" (d. 1164), on the other hand, stands far above them all. What Gratian had done for canon law the Lombard did for dogmatic and moral theology. With untiring industry he sifted and explained and paraphrased the patristic lore in his "Libri IV sententiarum", and the arrangement which he adopted was, in spite of the lacunæ, so excellent that up to the sixteenth century his work was the standard text-book of theology. The work of interpreting this masterpiece began as early as the thirteenth century, and there was no theologian of note in the Middle Ages who did not write a commentary on the Sentences of the Lombard. Hundreds of these commentaries are still resting, unprinted, beneath the dust of the libraries. No other work exerted such a powerful influence on the development of scholastic theology. Neither the analogous work of his disciple, Peter of Poitiers (d. 1205), nor the important "Summa aurea" of William of Auxerre (d. after 1230) superseded the Lombard's "Sentences". Along with Alain of Lille (d. 1203), William of Auvergne (d. 1248), who died as Archbishop of Paris, deserves special mention. Though preferring the free, unscholastic method of an earlier age, he yet shows himself at once an original philosopher and a profound theologian. Inasmuch as in his numerous monographs on the Trinity, the Incarnation, the Sacraments, etc., he took into account the anti-Christian attacks of the Arabian exponents of Aristoteleanism, he is, as it were, the connecting link between this age and the most brilliant epoch of the thirteenth century.

(b) Second Epoch: Scholasticism at its Zenith (1200–1300).—This period of Scholasticism was marked not only by the appearance of the "Theological Summæ", but also by the building of the great Gothic cathedrals, which bear a sort of affinity to the lofty structures of Scholasticism. (Cf. Émil Michael, S. J., "Geschichte des deutschen Volkes vom 13. Jahrh. bis zum Ausgang des Mittelalters", V, Freiburg, 1911, 15 sq.) Another characteristic feature was the fact that in the thirteenth century the champions of Scholasticism were to be found in the great religious orders of the Franciscans and Dominicans, beside whom worked the Augustinians, Carmelites, and Servites. This brilliant period is ushered in by two master-minds: the one a Franciscan, Alexander of Hales (d. about 1245), the other a Dominican, Albert the Great (d. 1280). The "Summa theologiæ" of Alexander of Hales, the largest and most comprehensive work of its kind, is distinguished by its deep and mature speculation, though flavoured with Platonism. The arrangement of the subjects treated reminds one of the method in vogue to-day. An intellectual giant not merely in matters philosophical and theological, but in the natural sciences as well, was Albert the Great. It was he who made the first attempt to present the entire philosophy of Aristotle in its true form and to place it at the service of Catholic theology—an undertaking of far-reaching consequences. The logic of Aristotle had indeed been rendered into Latin by Boethius and had been used in the schools since the end of the sixth century; but the physics and metaphysics of the Stagirite were made known to the Western world only through the Arabian philosophers of the thirteenth century, and then in such a way that Aristotle's doctrine seemed to clash with the Christian religion. This fact explains why his works were prohibited by the Synod of Paris, in 1210, and again by a Bull of Gregory IX in 1231. But after the Scholastics, led by Albert the Great, had gone over the faulty Latin translation once more, had reconstructed the genuine doctrine of Aristotle and recognized the fundamental soundness of his principles, they no longer hesitated to take, with the approval of the Church, the pagan philosopher as their guide in the speculative study of dogma.

Two other representatives of the great orders are the gigantic figures of Bonaventure (d. 1274) and of Thomas Aquinas (d. 1274), who mark the highest development of Scholastic theology. St. Bonaventure, the "Seraphic Doctor", clearly follows in the footsteps of Alexander of Hales, his fellow-religious and predecessor, but surpasses him in depth of mysticism and clearness of diction. Unlike the other Scholastics of this period, he did not write a theological "Summa", but amply made up for it by his "Commentary on the Sentences", as well as by his famous "Breviloquium", a "casket of pearls", which, brief as a compendium, is nothing less than a condensed Summa. Alexander of Hales and Bonaventure are the real representatives of the old Franciscan Schools, from which the later School of Duns Scotus essentially differed. Yet it is not Bonaventure, but Thomas Aquinas, who has ever been honoured as the "Prince of Scholasticism". St. Thomas holds the same rank among the theologians as does St. Augustine among the Fathers of the Church. Possessed of angelic rather than human knowledge, the "Doctor angelicus" is distinguished not only for the wealth, depth, and truth of his ideas and for his systematic exposition of them, but also for the versatility of his genius, which embraced all branches of human knowledge. For dogmatic theology his most important work is the "Summa theologica". Experience has shown that, as faithful adherence to St. Thomas means progress, so a departure from his teachings invariably brings with it a decline of Catholic theology. It seems providential, therefore, that Leo XIII in his Encyclical "Æterni Patris" (1879) restored the study of the Scholastics, especially of St. Thomas, in all higher Catholic schools, a measure which was again emphasized by Pope Pius X. The fears prevalent in some circles that by the restoration of Scholastic studies the results of modern thought would be forced back to the antiquated viewpoint of the thirteenth century are shown to be groundless by the fact that both popes, while insisting on the acquisition of the "wisdom of St. Thomas", yet emphatically disclaim any intention to revive the unscientific notions of the Middle Ages. It would be folly to ignore the progress of seven centuries, and, moreover, the Reformation, Jansenism, and the philosophies since Kant have originated theological problems which St. Thomas in his time could not foresee. Nevertheless, it is a convincing proof of the logical accuracy and comprehensiveness of the Thomistic system that it contains at least the principles necessary for the refutation of modern errors.

Before the brilliancy of the genius of St. Thomas even great theologians of this period wane into stars of the second and third magnitude. Still, Richard of Middleton (d. 1300), whose clearness of thought and lucidity of exposition recall the master mind of Aquinas, is a classical representative of the Franciscan School. Among the Servites, Henry of Ghent (d. 1293), a disciple of Albert the Great, deserves mention; his style is original and rhetorical, his judgments are independent, his treatment of the doctrine on God attests the profound thinker. In the footsteps of St. Thomas followed his pupil Peter of Tarentaise, who later became Pope Innocent V (d. 1276), and Ulric of Strasburg (d. 1277), whose name is little known, though his unprinted "Summa" was held in high esteem in the Middle Ages. The famous General of the Augustinians, Ægidius of Rome (d. 1316), a scion of the noble family of the Colonna, while differing in some details from the teaching of St. Thomas yet in the main adhered to his system. In his own order his writings were considered as classics. But the attempt of the Augustinian Gavardus in the seventeenth century to create a distinctly "Ægidian School" proved a failure. On the other hand, adversaries of St. Thomas sprang up even in his lifetime. The first attack came from England and was led by William de la Mare, of Oxford (d. 1285). Speaking broadly, English scholars, famous for their originality, played no mean part in the intellectual life of the Middle Ages. Being more of an empirical and practical than of an aprioristic and theoretical bent of mind, they enriched science with a new element. Their predilection for the natural sciences is also the outcome of this practical sense. Like the links of an unbroken chain follow the names of Bede, Alcuin, Alfred (Anglicus), Alexander of Neckham, Alexander of Hales, Robert Grosseteste, Adam of Marsh, John Basingstoke, Robert Kilwardby, John Pecham, Roger Bacon, Duns Scotus, Occam. Kuno Fischer is right when he says: "When travelling along the great highway of history, we may traverse the whole of the middle ages down to Bacon of Verulam without leaving England for a moment" ("Francis Bacon", Heidelberg, 1904, p. 4).

This peculiar English spirit was embodied in the famous Duns Scotus (1266–1308). While in point of ability he belongs to the golden age of scholasticism, yet his bold and virulent criticism of the Thomistic system was to a great extent responsible for its decline. Scotus cannot be linked with the old Franciscan school; he is rather the founder of the new Scotistic School, which deviated from the theology of Alexander of Hales and Bonaventure not so much in matters of faith and morals as in the speculative treatment of dogma. Greater still is his opposition to the fundamental standpoint of Thomas Aquinas. St. Thomas likens the system of theology and philosophy to the animal organism, in which the vivifying soul permeates all the members, holds them together, and shapes them into perfect unity. In Scotus's own words, on the other hand, the order of things is rather symbolized by the plant, the root shooting forth branches and twigs which have an innate tendency to grow away from the stem. This fundamental difference also sheds light on the peculiarities of Scotus's system as opposed to Thomism: his formalism in the doctrine of God and the Trinity, his loose conception of the Hypostatic Union, his relaxation of the bonds uniting the sacraments with the humanity of Christ, his explanation of transubstantiation as an adductive substitution, his emphasis on the supremacy of the will, and so on. Though it cannot be denied that Scotism preserved theological studies from a one-sided development and even won a signal victory over Thomism by its doctrine concerning the Immaculate Conception, it is nevertheless evident that the essential service it rendered to Catholic theology in the long run was to bring out, by the clash of arguments, the enduring solidity of the Thomistic structure. No one can fail to admire in St. Thomas the perspicuity of thought and the lucidity of diction, as contrasted with the abstruse and mystifying conceptions of his critic. In later centuries not a few Franciscans of a calmer judgment, among them Constantine Sarnanus (1589) and John of Rada (1599), set about minimizing or even reconciling the doctrinal differences of the two masters.

(c) Third Epoch: Gradual Decline of Scholasticism (1300–1500).—The death of Duns Scotus (d. 1308) marks the close of the golden era of the Scholastic system. What the following period accomplished in constructive work consisted chiefly in preserving, reproducing, and digesting the results of former ages. But simultaneously with this commendable labour we encounter elements of disintegration, due partly to the Fraticelli's wrong conception of mysticism, partly to the aberrations and superficiality of Nominalism, partly to the distressing conflict between Church and State (Philip the Fair, Louis of Bavaria, the Exile at Avignon). Apart from the fanatical enthusiasts who were leaning towards heresy, the development and rapid spread of Nominalism must be ascribed to two pupils of Duns Scotus: the Frenchman Peter

Aureolus (d. 1321) and the Englishman William Occam (d. 1347). In union with Marsilius of Padua and John of Jandun, Occam used Nominalism for the avowed purpose of undermining the unity of the Church. In this atmosphere flourished regalism and opposition to the primacy of the pope, until it reached its climax in the false principle: "Concilium supra Papam", which was preached from the housetops up to the time of the Councils of Constance and Basle. It is only fair to state that it was the pressing needs of the times more than anything else which led some great men, as Pierre d'Ailly (d. 1425) and Gerson (d. 1429), to embrace a doctrine which they abandoned as soon as the papal schism was healed. To understand the origin of the errors of Wyclif, Huss, and Luther, the history of Nominalism must be studied. For what Luther knew as Scholasticism was only the degenerated form which Nominalism presents. Even the more prominent Nominalists of the close of the Middle Ages, as the general of the Augustinians, Gregory of Rimini (d. 1359), and Gabriel Biel (d. 1495), who has been called the "last Scholastic", did not escape the misfortune of falling into grievous errors. Nominalistic subtleties, coupled with an austere pseudo-Augustinism of the ultra-rigoristic type, made Gregory of Rimini the precursor of Bajanism and Jansenism. Gabriel Biel, though ranking among the better Nominalists and combining solidity of doctrine with a spirit of loyalty to the Church, yet exerted a baneful influence on his contemporaries, both by his unduly enthusiastic praise of Occam and by the manner in which he commented on Occam's writings.

The order which suffered least damage from Nominalism was that of St. Dominic. For, with the possible exception of Durand of St. Pouçain (d. 1332) and Holkot (d. 1349), its members were as a rule loyal to their great fellow-religious St. Thomas. Most prominent among them during the first half of the fourteenth century were: Hervæus de Nedellec (d. 1323), a valiant opponent of Scotus; John of Paris (d. 1306); Peter of Palude (d. 1342); and especially Raynerius of Pisa (d. 1348), who wrote an alphabetical summary of the doctrine of St. Thomas which even to-day is useful. A prominent figure in the fifteenth century is St. Antonine of Florence (d. 1459), distinguished by his industry as a compiler and by his versatility as an author; by his "Summa Theologiæ" he did excellent service for positive theology. A powerful champion of Thomism was John Capreolus (d. 1444), the "Prince of Thomists" (*princeps Thomistarum*). Using the very words of St. Thomas, he refuted, in his adamantine "Clypeus Thomistarum", the adversaries of Thomism in a masterly and convincing manner. It was only in the early part of the sixteenth century that commentaries on the "Summa Theologica" of St. Thomas began to appear, among the first to undertake this work being Cardinal Cajetan of Vio (d. 1537) and Konrad Köllin (d. 1536). The philosophical "Summa contra Gentes" found a masterly commentator in Francis of Ferrara (d. 1528).

Far less united than the Dominicans were the Franciscans, who partly favoured Nominalism, partly adhered to pure Scotism. Among the latter the following are worthy of note: Francis Mayronis (d. 1327); John of Colonia; Peter of Aquila (d. about 1370), who as abbreviator of Scotus was called Scotellus (little Scotus); Nicolaus de Orbellis (ca. 1460); and above all Lichetus (d. 1520), the famous commentator of Scotus. William of Vorrilong (about 1400), Stephen Brulefer (d. 1485), and Nicholas of Niise (d. 1509) belong to a third class which is characterized by the tendency to closer contact with St. Bonaventure. A similar want of harmony and unity is discernible in the schools of the other orders. While the Augustinians James of Viterbo (d. 1308) and Thomas of Strasburg (d. 1357) attached themselves to Ægidius of Rome, thereby approaching closer to St. Thomas, Gregory of Rimini, mentioned above, championed an undisguised Nominalism. Alphonsus Vargas of Toledo (d. 1366), on the other hand, was an advocate of Thomism in its strictest form. Among the Carmelites, also, divergencies of doctrine appeared. Gerard of Bologna (d. 1317) was a staunch Thomist, while his brother in religion John Baconthorp (d. 1346) delighted in trifling controversies against the Thomists. Drifting now with Nominalism, now with Scotism, this original genius endeavoured, though without success, to found a new school in his order. Generally speaking, however, the later Carmelites were enthusiastic followers of St. Thomas. The Order of the Carthusians produced in the fifteenth century a prominent and many-sided theologian in the person of Dionysius Ryckel (d. 1471), surnamed "the Carthusian", a descendant of the Leevis family, who set up his chair in Roermond (Holland). From his pen we possess valuable commentaries on Holy Writ, Pseudo-Dionysius, Peter the Lombard, and St. Thomas. He was equally conversant with mysticism and scholasticism. Albert the Great, Henry of Ghent, and Dionysius form a brilliant constellation which shed undying lustre on the German theology of the Middle Ages.

Leaving the monasteries and turning our attention to the secular clergy, we encounter men who, in spite of many defects, are not without merit in dogmatic theology. The first to deserve mention is the Englishman Thomas Bradwardine (d. 1340), the foremost mathematician of his day and Archbishop of Canterbury. His work "De causa Dei contra Pelagianos" evinces a mathematical mind and an unwonted depth of thought. Unfortunately it is marred by an unbending, sombre rigorism, and this to such an extent that the Calvinistic Anglicans of a later century published it in defence of their own teachings. The Irish Bishop Richard Radulphus of Armagh (d. 1360), in his controversy with the Armenians, also fell into dogmatic inaccuracies, which paved the way for the errors of Wyclif. We may note in passing that the learned Carmelite Thomas Netter (d. 1430), surnamed Waldensis, must be regarded as the ablest controversialist against the Wyclifites and Hussites. The great Cardinal Nicholas of Cusa (d. 1404) stands out prominently as the inaugurator of a new speculative system in dogmatic theology; but his doctrine is in many respects open to criticism. A thorough treatise on the Church was written by John Torquemada (d. 1468), and a similar work by St. John Capistran (d. 1456). A marvel of learning, and already acknowledged as such by his contemporaries, was Alphonsus Tostatus (d. 1454), the equal of Nicholas of Lyra (d. 1341) in Scriptural learning. He merits a place in the history of dogmatic theology, inasmuch as he interspersed his excellent commentaries on the Scriptures with dogmatic treatises, and in his work "Quinque paradoxa" gave to the world a fine treatise on Christology and Mariology.

As was to be expected, mysticism went astray in this period and degenerated into sham pietism. A striking example of this is the anonymous "German Theology", edited by Martin Luther. This work must, however, not be confounded with the "German Theology" of the pious bishop Berthold of Chiemsee (d. 1543), which, directed against the Reformers, is imbued with the genuine spirit of the Catholic Church.

(3) Modern Times (1500–1900).—As during the Patristic Period the rise of heresies was the occasion of the development of dogmatic theology in the Church, so the manifold errors of the Renaissance and of the Reformation brought about a more accurate definition of important articles of faith. Along

other lines also both these movements produced good effects. While in the period of the Renaissance the revival of classical studies gave new vigour to exegesis and patrology, the Reformation stimulated the universities which had remained Catholic, especially in Spain (Salamanca, Alcalá, Coimbra) and in the Netherlands (Louvain), to put forth an enthusiastic activity in intellectual research. Spain, which had fallen behind during the Middle Ages, now came boldly to the front. The Sorbonne of Paris regained its lost prestige only towards the end of the sixteenth century. Among the religious orders the newly-founded Society of Jesus probably contributed most to the revival and growth of theology. Scheeben distinguishes five epochs in this period.

(a) First Epoch: Preparation (1500–1570).—It was only by a slow process that Catholic theology rose from the depths into which it had fallen. The rise of the Reformation (1517) had inflicted serious wounds on the Church, and the defection of so many priests deprived her of the natural resources on which the study of theology necessarily depends. Nevertheless the list of the loyal contains many brilliant names, and the controversial works of those times include more than one valuable monograph. It was but natural that the whole literature of this period should bear an apologetical and controversial character and should deal with those subjects which had been attacked most bitterly: the rule and sources of faith, the Church, grace, the sacraments, especially the holy Eucharist. Numerous defenders of the faith arose in the very country which had given birth to the Reformation: John Eck (d. 1543), Cochlæus (d. 1552), Staphylus (d. 1564), James of Hoogstraet (d. 1527), John Gropper (d. 1559), Albert Pighius (d. 1542), Cardinal Hosius (d. 1579), Martin Cromer (d. 1589), and Peter Canisius (d. 1597). The last-named gave to the Catholics not only his world-renowned catechism, but also a most valuable Mariology. With pride and enthusiasm we look upon England, where the two noble martyrs John Fisher, Bishop of Rochester (d. 1535), and Thomas More (d. 1535) championed the cause of the Catholic faith with their pen, where Cardinal Pole (d. 1568), Stephen Gardiner (d. 1555), and Cardinal William Allen (d. 1594), men who combined refinement with a solid education, placed their learning at the service of the persecuted Church, while the Jesuit Nicholas Saunders wrote one of the best treatises on the Church. In Belgium the professors of the University of Louvain opened new paths for the study of theology; foremost among them were: Ruardus Tapper (d. 1559), John Driedo (d. 1535), Jodocus Ravesteyn (d. 1570), John Hessels (d. 1566), John Molanus (d. 1585), and Garetius (d. 1571). To the last-named we owe an excellent treatise on the holy Eucharist. In France James Merlin, Christopher Cheffontaines (d. 1595), and Gilbert Genebrard (d. 1597) rendered great services to dogmatic theology. Sylvester Pierias (d. 1523), Ambrose Catharinus (d. 1553), and Cardinal Seripandus are the boast of Italy. But, above all other countries, Spain is distinguished by a veritable galaxy of brilliant names: Alphonsus of Castro (d. 1558), Michael de Medina (d. 1578), Peter de Soto (d. 1563). Some of their works have remained classics up to our own times, as "De natura et gratia" (Venice, 1547) of Dominic Soto; "De iustificatione libri XV" (Venice, 1546) of Andrew Vega; "De locis theologicis" (Salamanca, 1563) of Melchior Cano.

(b) Second Epoch: Late Scholasticism at its Height (1570–1660).—Even in the preceding epoch the sessions of the Council of Trent (1545–1563) had exerted a beneficial influence on the character and extent of dogmatic literature. After the close of the council there sprang up everywhere a new life and a marvellous activity in theology which recalls the best days of the Patristic Era and of Scholasticism but surpasses both by the wealth and variety of its literary productions. We are not here concerned with the industry displayed in Biblical and exegetical research. But the achievements of controversial, positive, and scholastic theology deserve a passing notice.

(i) Controversial theology was carried to the highest perfection by Cardinal Bellarmine (d. 1621). There is no other theologian who has defended almost the whole of Catholic theology against the attacks of the Reformers with such clearness and convincing force. Other theologians remarkable for their masterly defence of the Catholic Faith were the Spanish Jesuit Gregory of Valencia (d. 1603) and his pupils Adam Tanner (d. 1635) and James Gretser (d. 1625), who taught in the University of Ingolstadt. To the Englishman Thomas Stapleton (d. 1598) we owe a work, unsurpassed even in our days, on the material and formal principle of Protestantism. Cardinal du Perron (d. 1618) of France successfully entered the arena against James I of England and Philip Mornay, and wrote a splendid treatise on the holy Eucharist. The eloquent pupil orator Bossuet (d. 1627) wielded his pen in refuting Protestantism from the standpoint of history. The "Præscriptiones Catholicæ", a voluminous work of the Italian Gravina (7 vols., Naples, 1619–39), possesses enduring value. Martin Becanus (d. 1624), a Belgian Jesuit, published his handy and well-known "Manuale controversiarum". In Holland the defence of religion was carried on by the two learned brothers Adrian (d. 1669) and Peter de Walemburg (d. 1675), both auxiliary bishops of Cologne and both controversialists, who easily ranked among the best. Even the distant East was represented in the two Greek converts, Peter Arcudius (d. 1640) and Leo Allatius (d. 1669).

(ii) The development of positive theology went hand in hand with the progress of research into the Patristic Era and into the history of dogma. These studies were especially cultivated in France and Belgium. A number of scholars, thoroughly versed in history, published in excellent monographs the results of their investigations into the history of particular dogmas. Morinus (d. 1659) made the Sacrament of Penance the subject of special study; Isaac Habert (d. 1668), the doctrine of the Greek Fathers on grace; Hallier (d. 1659), the Sacrament of Holy orders; Garnier (d. 1681), Pelagianism; Dechamps (d. 1701), Jansenism; Tricassinus (d. 1681), St. Augustine's doctrine on grace. Unfortunately, among the highly gifted representatives of this historico-dogmatical school were to be found men who deviated more or less seriously from the unchangeable teachings of the Catholic Church, as Baius, Jansenius the Younger, Launoy, de Marca, Dupin, and others. Though Nicole and Arnauld were Jansenists, yet their monumental work on the Eucharist, "Perpétuité de la foi" (Paris, 1669–74), has not yet lost its value. But there are two men, the Jesuit Petavius (d. 1647) and the Oratorian Louis Thomassin (d. 1695), who by their epoch-making works: "Dogmata theologica", placed positive theology on a new basis without disregarding the speculative element.

(iii) So great was the enthusiasm with which the religious orders fostered scholastic theology and brought it to perfection that the golden era of the thirteenth century seemed to have once more returned. It was no mere chance that St. Thomas and St. Bonaventure were just then proclaimed Doctors of the Church, the first by Pius V, the other by Sixtus V. By these papal acts the two greatest luminaries of the past were proposed to the theologians as models to be zealously imitated. Thomism, guarded and cherished by the Dominicans, proved anew its full vitality. At the head of the Thomistic movement was Bañez (d. 1604), the first and greatest opponent of the Jesuit Molina (d. 1600). He wrote a valuable commentary on the theological "Summa" of St. Thomas, which, combined with a similar work by Bartholomew Medina (d. 1581), forms a harmonious whole. Under the leadership of Bañez a group of scholarly Dominicans took up the defence of the Thomistic doctrine on grace: Alvarez (d. 1635), de Lemos (d. 1629), Ledesma (d. 1616), Massoulié (d. 1706), Reginaldus (d. 1676), Nazarius (d. 1646), John a St. Thoma (d. 1644), Xantes Mariales (d. 1660), Gonet (d. 1681), Goudin (d. 1695), Contenson (d. 1674), and others. However, the most scholarly, profound, and comprehensive work of the Thomistic school did not come from the Dominicans, but from the Carmelites of Salamanca; it is the invaluable "Cursus Salmanticensis" (Salamanca, 1631–1712) in 15 folios, a magnificent commentary on the "Summa" of St. Thomas. The names of the authors of this immortal work have unfortunately not been handed down to posterity. Outside the Dominican Order, also, Thomism had many zealous and learned friends: the Benedictine Alphonsus Curiel (d. 1609), Francis Zumel (d. 1607), John Puteanus (d. 1623), and the Irishman Augustine Gibbon (d. 1676), who laboured in Spain and at Erfurt in Germany. The Catholic universities were active in the interest of Thomism. At Louvain William Estius (d. 1613) wrote an excellent commentary on the "Liber Sententiarum" of Peter the Lombard, which was permeated with the spirit of St. Thomas, while his colleagues Wiggers and Francis Sylvius (d. 1649) explained the theological "Summa" of the master himself. In the Sorbonne Thomism was worthily represented by men like Gammaché (d. 1625), Andrew Duval (d. 1637), and especially by the ingenious Nicholas Ysambert (d. 1624). The University of Salzburg also furnished an able work in the "Theologia scholastica" of Augustine Reding, who held the chair of theology in that university from 1645 to 1658, and died as Abbot of Einsiedeln in 1692.

The Franciscans of this epoch in no wise abandoned their doctrinal opposition to the school of St. Thomas, but steadily continued publishing commentaries on Peter the Lombard, which throughout breathe the genuine spirit of Scotism. It was especially Irish Franciscans who promoted the theological activity of their order, as Mauritius Hibernicus (d. 1603), Anthony Hickay (Hiquæus, d. 1641), Hugh Cavellus, and John Ponce (Pontius, d. 1660). The following Italians and Belgians also deserve to be mentioned: Francis de Herrera (about 1590), Angelus Vulpes (d. 1647), Philip Fabri (d. 1630), Bosco (d. 1684), and Cardinal Brancatus de Laurea (d. 1693). Scotistic manuals for use in schools were published about 1580 by Cardinal Sarnanus and by William Herincx, this latter acting under the direction of the Franciscans. The Capuchins, on the other hand, adhered to St. Bonaventure, as, e. g., Peter Trigos (d. 1593), Joseph Zamora (d. 1649), Gaudentius of Brescia (d. 1672), Marcus a Baudunio (d. 1673), and others.

But there can be no question that Scholastic theology owes most of its classical works to the Society of Jesus, which substantially adhered to the "Summa" of St. Thomas, yet at the same time made use of a certain eclectic freedom which seemed to be warranted by the circumstances of the times. Molina (d. 1600) was the first Jesuit to write a commentary on the theological "Summa" of St. Thomas. He was followed by Cardinal Toletus (d. 1596) and by Gregory of Valencia (d. 1603), mentioned above as a distinguished controversialist. A brilliant group in the Society of Jesus are the Spaniards Francis Suarez, Gabriel Vasquez, and Didacus Ruiz. Suarez (d. 1617), the most prominent among them, is also the foremost theologian that the Society of Jesus has produced. His renown is due not only to the fertility and the wealth of his literary productions, but also to his "clearness, moderation, depth, and circumspection" (Scheeben). He truly deserves the title of "Doctor eximius" which Benedict XIV gave him. In his colleague Gabriel Vasquez (d. 1604) Suarez found a critic both subtle and severe, who combined positive knowledge with depth of speculation. Didacus Ruiz (d. 1632) wrote masterly works on God and the Trinity, subjects which were also thoroughly treated by Christopher Gilles (d. 1608). Harruabal (d. 1608), Ferdinand Bastida (d. about 1609), Valentine Herice, and others are names which will forever be linked with the history of Molinism. During the succeeding period James Granado (d. 1632), John Præpositus (d. 1634), Caspar Hurtado (d. 1646), and Anthony Perez (d. 1694) won fame by their commentaries on St. Thomas. But, while devoting themselves to scientific research, the Jesuits never forgot the need of instruction. Excellent, often voluminous, manuals were written by Arriaga (d. 1667), Martin Esparza (d. 1670), Francis Amicus (d. 1651), Martin Becanus (d. 1625), Adam Tanner (d. 1632), and finally by Sylvester Maurus (d. 1687), who is not only remarkable for clearness, but also distinguished as a philosopher. Hand in hand with this more general and comprehensive literature went important monographs, embodying special studies on certain dogmatic questions. Entering the lists against Baius and his followers, Martinez de Ripalda (d. 1648) wrote the best work on the supernatural order. To Leonard Lessius (d. 1623) we owe some beautiful treatises on God and His attributes. Ægidius Coninck (d. 1633) made the Trinity, the Incarnation, and the sacraments the subject of special studies. Cardinal John de Lugo (d. 1660), noted for his mental acumen and highly esteemed as a moralist, wrote on the virtue of faith and the Sacraments of Penance and the Eucharist. Claude Tiphanus (d. 1641) is the author of a classical monograph on the notions of personality and hypostasis. Cardinal Pallavicini (d. 1667), known as the historiographer of the Council of Trent, won repute as a dogmatic theologian by several of his writings.

(c) Third Epoch: Further Activity and Gradual Decline of Scholasticism (1660–1760).—While the creative and constructive work of the previous epoch still continued, though with languishing vitality, and ushered in a second spring of dogmatic literature, other currents of thought set in which gradually prepared the way for the decline of Catholic theology. Cartesianism in philosophy, Gallicanism, and Jansenism were sapping the strength of the sacred science. There was scarcely a country or nation that was not infected with the false spirit of the age. Italy alone remained immune and preserved its ancient purity and orthodoxy in matters theological.

One might have expected that, if anywhere at all, theology would be securely sheltered within the schools of the old religious orders. Yet even some of these succumbed to the evil influences of the times, losing little by little their pristine firmness and vigour. Nevertheless, it is to them that almost all the theological literature of this period and the revival of Scholasticism are due. A product of the Thomistic school, widely used and well adapted to the needs of the time, was the standard work of the Dominican Billuart (d. 1757), which with exceptional skill and taste explains and defends the Thomistic system in scholastic form. The dogmatic theology of Cardinal Gotti, however, rivals, if it does not surpass, Billuart's work, both as regards the substance and the soundness of its contents. Other Thomists produced valuable monographs: Drouin on the sacraments and Bernard de Rubeis (d. 1775) on original sin. More eclectic in their adherence to

Thomism were the Cardinals Celestine Sfondrato (d. 1696) and Aguirre (d. 1699); the latter's work "Theology of St. Anselm" in three volumes is replete with deep thought. Among the Franciscans Claudius Frassen (d. 1680) issued his elegant "Scotus academicus", a counterpart to the Thomistic theology of Billuart. Of the Scotistic School we also mention Gabriel Boyvin, Krisper (d. 1721), and Kick (d. 1769). Eusebius Amort (d. 1775), the foremost theologian in Germany, also represented a better type, combining sound conservatism with due regard for modern demands. The Society of Jesus still preserved something of its former vigour and activity. Simmonet, Ulloa (d. about 1723), and Marin were the authors of voluminous scholastic works. But now the didactical and pedagogical interests began to assert themselves, and called for numerous text-books of theology. We mention Platel (d. 1681), Antoine (d. 1743), Pichler (d. 1736), Sardagna (d. 1775), Erber, Monschein (d. 1769), and Gener. But both as regards matter and form all these text-books were surpassed by the "Theologia Wirceburgensis", which the Jesuits of Würzburg published in 1766–71. In addition to the old religious orders, we mention during this period the new school of Augustinians, who based their theology on the system of Gregory of Rimini rather than on that of Ægidius of Rome. Because of the stress they laid on the rigoristic element in St. Augustine's doctrine on grace, they were for a time suspected of Baianism and Jansenism, but were cleared of this suspicion by Benedict XIV. To this school belonged the scholarly Lupus (d. 1681) at Louvain and Cardinal Noris (d. 1704), distinguished for his subtle intellect. But its best work on dogmatic theology came from the pen of Lawrence Berti (d. 1766). His fellow-workers in the same field were Bellelli (d. 1742) and Bertieri. The French Oratory, falling from its lofty eminence, was buried in Jansenism, as the names of Quesnel, Lebrun, and Juenin sufficiently indicate.

The Sorbonne of Paris, developing the germs of Jansenism and Gallicanism, ceased to keep abreast of the time. Abstracting, however, from this fact, theology owes works of great merit to men like Louis Habert (d. 1718), du Hamel (d. 1706), L'Herminier, Witasse (d. 1716). Creditable exceptions were Louis Abelly (d. 1691) and Martin Grandin, who distinguished themselves by their loyalty to the Church. The same encomium must be said of Honoratus Tournely (d. 1729), whose "Prælectiones dogmaticæ" are numbered among the best theological text-books. A staunch opponent of Jansenism, he would certainly have challenged Gallicanism, had not the law of the realm prevented him. For the rest, the Church depended almost exclusively on Italy in its scientific combat against the pernicious errors of the time. There had gathered a chosen band of scholars who courageously fought for the purity of the faith and the rights of the papacy. In the front rank against Jansenism stood the Jesuits Dominic Viva (d. 1726), La Fontaine (d. 1728), Alticozzi (d. 1777), and Faure (d. 1779). Gallicanism and Josephinism were hard pressed by the theologians of the Society of Jesus, especially by Zaccaria (d. 1795), Muzzarelli (d. 1749), Bolgeni (d. 1811), Roncaglia, and others. The Jesuits were ably seconded by the Dominicans Orsi (d. 1761) and Mamachi (d. 1792). Another champion in this struggle was Cardinal Gerdil (d. 1802). Partly to this epoch belongs the fruitful activity of St. Alphonsus Liguori (d. 1787), whose popular rather than scientific writings energetically opposed the baneful spirit of the time.

(d) Fourth Epoch: Decay of Catholic Theology (1760–1840).—Many circumstances, both from within and from without, contributed towards the further decadence of theology which had already begun in the preceding epoch. In France it was the still powerful influence of Jansenism and Gallicanism, in the German Empire the spread of Josephinism and Febronianism that sapped the vitality of orthodox theology. The suppression of the Society of Jesus by Clement XIV in 1773 deprived theology of its ablest representatives. To these factors must be added the paralyzing influence of the "Enlightenment" which, rising through English Deism, was swelled by French Encyclopedism and finally deluged all European countries. The French Revolution and the military expeditions of Napoleon all through Europe were not without evil consequences. The false philosophy of the time (Kant, Schelling, Fichte, Hegel, Cousin, Comte, etc.), by which even many theologians were misled, engendered not only an undisguised contempt for Scholasticism and even for St. Thomas, but also fostered a shallow conception of Christianity, the supernatural character of which was obscured by Rationalism. True, the spirit of former centuries was still alive in Italy, but the unfavourable circumstances of the times impeded its growth and development. In France the Revolution and the continual campaigns paralyzed or stifled all productive activity. De Lamennais (d. 1854), the beginning of whose career had held out promises of the highest order, turned from the truth and led others astray. The Catholics of England groaned under political oppression and religious intolerance. Spain had become barren. Germany suffered from the mildew of "Enlightenment". No matter how mildly one may judge the aberrations of Wessenberg (1774–1860), Vicar-General of Constance, who had absorbed the false ideas of his age, it is certain that the movement begun by him marked a decadence in matters both ecclesiastical and scientific. But the poorer the productions of the theologians the greater their pride. They despised the old theologians, whom they could neither read nor understand. Among the few works of a better sort were the manuals of Wiest (1791), Klüpfel (1789), Dobmayer (1807), and Brenner (1826). The ex-Jesuit Benedict Stattler (d. 1797) tried to apply to dogma the philosophy of Christian Wolff, Zimmer (1802), even that of Schelling. The only work which, joining soundness with a loyal Catholic spirit, marked a return to the old traditions of the School was the dogmatic theology of Liebermann (d. 1844), who taught at Strasburg and Mainz; it appeared in the years 1819–26 and went through many editions. But even Liebermann was not able to conceal his dislike for the Scholastics. The renewed attempt of Hermes (d. 1831) of Bonn to treat Catholic theology in a Kantian spirit was no less fatal than that of Günther (d. 1863) in Vienna, who sought to unravel the mysteries of Christianity by means of a modern Gnosis and to resolve them into purely natural truths. If positive and speculative theology were ever to be regenerated, it was by a return to the source of its vitality, the glorious traditions of the past.

(e) Fifth Epoch: Restoration of Dogmatic Theology (1840–1900).—The reawakening of the Catholic life in the forties naturally brought with it a revival of Catholic theology. Germany especially, where the decline had gone farthest, showed signs of a remarkable regeneration and vigorous health. The external impulse was given by Joseph Görres (d. 1848), the "loud shouter in the fray". When the Prussian Government imprisoned Archbishop von Droste-Vischering of Cologne on account of the stand he had taken in the question of mixed marriages, the fiery appeals of Görres began to fill the hearts of the Catholics, even outside of Germany, with unwonted courage. The German theologians heard the call and once more applied themselves to the work which was theirs. Döllinger (d. 1890) developed Church history, and Möhler advanced patrology and symbolism. Both positive and speculative theology received a new lease of life, the former through Klee (d. 1840), the latter through Staudenmeier (d. 1856). At the same time men like Kleutgen (d. 1883), Werner (d. 1888), and Stöckl (d. 1895) earned for the despised Scholasticism a new place of honour by their thorough historical and systematic writings. In France and Belgium the dogmatic theology of Cardinal Gousset (d. 1866) of Reims and the writings of Bishop Malou of Bruges (d. 1865) exerted great influence. In North America the works of Archbishop Kenrick (d. 1863) did untold good. Cardinal Camille Mazzella (d. 1900) is to be ranked among the North American theologians, as he wrote his dogmatic works while occupying the chair of theology at Woodstock College, Maryland. In England the great Cardinals Wiseman (d. 1865), Manning (d. 1892), and Newman (d. 1890) became by their works and deeds powerful agents in the revival of Catholic life and in the advance of Catholic theology.

In Italy, where the better traditions had never been forgotten, far-seeing men like Sanseverino (d. 1865), Liberatore (d. 1892), and Tongiorgi (d. 1865) set to work to restore Scholastic philosophy, because it was found to be the most effective weapon against the errors of the time, i. e. traditionalism and ontologism, which had a numerous following among Catholic scholars in Italy, France, and Belgium. The pioneer work in positive theology fell to the lot of the famous Jesuit Perrone (d. 1876) in Rome. His works on dogmatic theology, scattered throughout the Catholic world, freed theology of the miasmas which had infected it. Under his leadership a brilliant phalanx of theologians, as Passaglia (d. 1887), Schrader (d. 1875), Cardinal Franzelin (d. 1886), Palmieri (d. 1909), and others, continued the work so happily begun and reasserted the right of the speculative element in the domain of theology. Eminent among the Dominicans was Cardinal Zigliara, an inspiring teacher and fertile author. Thus from Rome, the centre of Catholicism, where students from all countries foregathered, new life went forth and permeated all nations. Germany, where Baader (d. 1841), Günther, and Frohschammer (d. 1893) continued to spread their errors, shared in the general uplift and produced a number of prominent theologians, as Kuhn (d. 1887), Berlage (d. 1881), Dieringer (d. 1876), Oswald (d. 1903), Knoll (d. 1863), Denzinger (d. 1883), v. Schäzler (d. 1880), Bernard Jungmann (d. 1895), Heinrich (d. 1891), and others. But Germany's greatest theologian at this time was Joseph Scheeben (d. 1888), a man of remarkable talent for speculation. In the midst of this universal reawakening the Vatican Council was held (1870), and the Encyclical of Pope Leo XIII on the value of Scholastic, especially Thomistic, philosophy and theology was issued (1879). Both these events became landmarks in the history of dogmatic theology. An energetic activity was put forth in every branch of sacred science and is still maintained. Even though, consulting the needs of the time and the hostile situation, theologians cultivate most assiduously historical studies, such as Church history, Christian archæology, history of dogma, and history of religion, yet signs are not wanting that, side by side with positive theology, Scholasticism also will enter upon a new era of progress. History shows that periods of progress in theology always follow in the wake of great œcumenical councils. After the first Council of Nicæa (325) came the great period of the Fathers; after the Fourth Lateran Council (1215) the wonderful age of mature Scholasticism; and after the Council of Trent (1545–63) the activity of later Scholasticism. It is not too much to hope that the Vatican Council, which had to be adjourned indefinitely after a few general sessions, will be followed by a similar period of progress and splendour.

No critical history of Catholic dogma has as yet been written. In general cf. LAFORÊT, *Coup d'œil sur l'histoire de la Théologie dogmatique* (Louvain, 1851). Ample material is given in: POSSEVIN, *Apparatus sacer* (3 vols., Venice, 1603–06); DU PIN, *Nouvelle Bibliothèque des auteurs ecclésiastiques* (11 vols., Paris, 1686–1714); OUDIN, *Commentarius de scriptoribus ecclesiasticis* (3 vols., Leipzig, 1722); CAVE, *Scriptorum ecclesiasticorum historia literaria* (2nd ed., Oxford, 1740–43); FABRICIUS, *Bibliotheca latina mediæ et infimæ ætatis* (5 vols., Hamburg, 1734—); CEILLIER, *Histoire générale des Auteurs sacrés et ecclésiastiques* (2nd ed., 19 vols., Paris, 1858–70); SMITH AND WACE, *Dict. Christ. Biog.*, MICHAUD, *Biographie universelle ancienne et moderne* (2nd ed., 45 vols., Paris, 1842–65); WERNER, *Geschichte der apologetischen und polemischen Literatur der christl. Religion* (5 vols., Schaffhausen, 1861—); CAPOZZA, *Sulla Filosofia dei Padri e Dottori della Chiesa e in ispecialità di San Tommaso* (Naples, 1868); WILLMANN, *Geschichte des Idealismus* (2nd ed., 3 vols., Brunswick, 1908). An invaluable work of reference is HURTER, *Nomenclator*. With regard to the several countries cf. TANNER, *Bibliotheca Brittanico-Hibernica seu de scriptoribus, qui in Anglia, Scotia et Hibernia ad sæc. xviii initium floruerunt* (London, 1748); *Dict. Nat. Biog.* The MAURISTS published: *Histoire littéraire de la France* (12 vols., Paris, 1733–63), which was continued by the INSTITUT DE FRANCE (20 vols., Paris, 1814–1906); MAZZUCHELLI, *Gli scrittori d'Italia* (2 vols., Brescia, 1753–63); TIRABOSCHI, *Storia della Letteratura italiana* (13 vols., Modena, 1771–82); KRUMBACHER, *Geschichte der byzantinischen Literatur* (2nd ed., Munich, 1897); WRIGHT, *A Short History of Syriac Literature* (London, 1894); CHABOT, *Corpus scriptorum Christianorum orientalium* (Paris, 1903—). With regard to various religious orders cf. ZIEGELBAUER, *Historia rei literariæ Ordinis S. Benedicti* (4 vols., Augsburg, 1754); TASSIN, *Histoire littéraire de la Congrégation de Saint-Maure* (Brussels, 1770); WADDING, *Scriptores Ordinis Minorum* (2nd ed., 2 vols., Rome, 1805); DE MARTIGNY, *La Scolastique et les traditions franciscaines* (Paris, 1888); FELDER, *Geschichte der wissenschaftlichen Studien im Franziskanerorden* (Freiburg, 1904); QUÉTIF ECHARD, *Scriptores Ordinis Prædicatorum* (2 vols., Paris, 1719–21); REICHERT, *Monumenta Ordinis Fratrum Prædicatorum historica* (Rome, 1896—); DE VILLIERS, *Bibliotheca, Carmelitana notis criticis et dissertationibus illustrata* (2 vols., Orléans, 1752); DE VISCH, *Bibliotheca scriptorum Ordinis Cisterciensis* (2nd ed., Colm, 1656); GOOVAERTS, *Dictionnaire bio-bibliographique des écrivains, artistes et savants de Ordre de Prémontré* (2 vols., Brussels, 1899–1907); WINTER, *Die Prämonstratenser des 12. Jahrhunderts* (Berlin, 1865); OSSINGER, *Bibliotheca Augustiniana historica, critica et chronologica* (Ingolstadt, 1768); SOUTHWELL, *Bibliotheca scriptorum Societatis Jesu* (Rome, 1676); SOMMERVOGEL, *Bibliothèque de la Compagnie de Jésus* (9 vols., Brussels and Paris, 1890–1900). The histories of dogma by SCHWANE, HARNACK, TIXERONT, etc., may also be consulted with profit.

With regard to the special literature of the Patristic Period, cf. EHRHARD, *Die altchristliche Literatur u. ihre Erforschung seit 1880* (2 vols., 1894–1900); DONALDSON, *A Critical History of Christian Literature and Doctrine from the Death of the Apostles to the Nicene Council* (3 vols., London, 1865–66); RICHARDSON, *The Antenicene Fathers. A Bibliographical Synopsis* (Buffalo, 1887); CRUTTWELL, *A Literary History of Early Christianity* (2 vols., London, 1893); SCHOENEMANN, *Bibliotheca historico-litteraria Patrum latinorum a Tertulliano usque ad Gregorium M. et Isidorum Hispalensem* (2 vols., Leipzig, 1792–94); HARNACK, *Geschichte der altchristlichen Literatur bis Eusebius* (3 vols., Leipzig, 1893–1904); MÖHLER, *Patrologie* (Ratisbon, 1840); MIGNE-SEVESTRE, *Dictionnaire de Patrologie* (4 vols., Paris, 1851–55); NIRSCHL, *Lehrbuch der Patrologie u. Patristik* (3 vols., Mainz, 1881–85); ALZOG, *Grundriss der Patrologie* (4th ed., Freiburg, 1888); FESSLER-JUNGMANN, *Institutiones Patrologiæ* (2 vols., Innsbruck, 1890–1896); BARDENHEWER, *Geschichte der altkirchlichen Literatur*, I–II (Freiburg, 1902–03); IDEM, *Patrologie* (3rd ed., Freiburg, 1910); RAUSCHEN, *Grundriss der Patrologie* (3rd ed., Freiburg, 1910); STÖCKL, *Geschichte der christl. Philosophie zur Zeit der Kirchenväter* (Mainz, 1891). Of great importance are also: A. HARNACK u. C. SCHMIDT, *Texte u. Untersuchungen zur Geschichte der altchristl. Literatur* (Leipzig, 1882—); ROBINSON, *Texts and Studies* (Cambridge, 1891—); HEMMER-LEJAY, *Textes et Documents* (Paris, 1904—).

With regard to the Middle Ages cf. especially SCHEEBEN, *Dogmatik*, I (Freiburg, 1873) 423 sqq.; GRABMANN, *Geschichte der scholastichen Methode*, I, II (Freiburg, 1909–11); IDEM in BUCHBERGER, *Kirchliches Handlexikon*, s. v. *Scholastik*; SIGHARDT, *Albertus Magnus, sein Leben u. seine Werke* (Ratisbon, 1857); WERNER, *Der hl. Thomas von Aquin* (3 vols., Ratisbon, 1858—); BACH, *Die Dogmengeschichte des Mittelalters vom christologischen Standpunkt* (2 vols., Vienna, 1873–75); SIMLER, *Des sommes de théologie* (Paris, 1871). With regard to the universities cf. BULÆUS, *Historia Universitatis Parisiensis* (Paris, 1665–73); DENIFLE, *Die Universitäten des Mittelalters*, I (Berlin, 1885); DENIFLE AND CHATELAIN, *Chartularium Universitatis Parisiensis* (4 vols., Paris, 1889–97); RASHDALL, *The Universities of Europe in the Middle Ages* (Oxford, 1895); FERET, *La Faculté de Théologie de Paris et ses Docteurs les plus célèbres*, I: *Moyen-âge* (4 vols., Paris, 1894–97); ROBERT, *Les écoles et l'enseignement de la Théologie pendant la première moitié du XIIe siècle* (Paris, 1909); MICHAEL, *Geschichte des deutschen Volkes vom 3. Jahrh. bis zum Ausgang des Mittelalters*, II, III (Freiburg, 1899–1903); EBERT, *Allgemeine Geschichte der Literatur des Mittelalters im Abendlande* (3 vols., Leipzig, 1874–87). With regard to Scholastic philosophy, cf. HAURÉAU, *Histoire de la Philosophie scolastique* (3 vols., Paris, 1872); DE WULF, *History of Medieval Philosophy*, tr. COFFEY (London, 1909); STÖCKL, *Geschichte der Philosophie des Mittelalters* (3 vols., Mainz, 1864–66); BÄUMKER in *Die Kultur der Gegenwart* by HINNEBERG, I (Leipzig, 1909), 5; DENIFLE

AND EHRLE, *Archiv für Literatur- u. Kirchengeschichte* (7 vols., Berlin and Freiburg, 1885-1900); BÄUMKER AND VON HERTLING, *Beiträge zur Philosophie des Mittelalters* (Münster, 1891—). On mysticism cf. PREGER, *Geschichte der deutschen Mystik im Mittelalter* (3 vols., Leipzig, 1874-93); LANGENBERG, *Quellen u. Forschungen zur Geschichte der deutschen Mystik* (Leipzig, 1904); RIBET, *La Mystique divine* (4 vols., Paris, 1895—); DELACROIX, *Etudes d'histoire et de psychologie du Mysticisme* (Paris, 1908).

On modern times cf. GILLOW, *Bibl. Dict. Eng. Cath.*; FERET, *La Faculté de Théologie de Paris et ses Docteurs les plus célèbres*: II, *Epoque moderne* (3 vols., Paris, 1900-04); LAEMMER, *Vortridentinische Theologen des Reformationszeitalters* (Berlin, 1858); WERNER, *Franz Suarez u. die Scholastik der letzten Jahrhunderte* (2 vols., Ratisbon, 1860); IDEM, *Geschichte der Theologie in Deutschland seit dem Trienter Konzil bis zur Gegenwart* (2nd ed., Ratisbon, 1889); for the time of "Enlightenment" in particular, cf. RÖSCH, *Das religiöse Leben in Hohenzollern unter dem Einfluss des Wessenbergianismus* (Freiburg, 1908); IDEM, *Ein neuer Historiker der Aufklärung* (Freiburg, 1910); against him, MERKLE, *Die katholische Beurteilung des Aufklärungszeitalters* (Würzburg, 1909); IDEM, *Die kirchliche Aufklärung im katholischen Deutschland* (Würzburg, 1910); SÄGMÜLLER, *Wissenschaft u. Glaube in der kirchlichen Aufklärung* (Tübingen, 1910); IDEM, *Unwissenschaftlichkeit u. Unglaube in der kirchlichen Aufklärung* (Tübingen, 1911); HETTINGER, *Thomas von Aquin u. die europäische Civilisation* (Würzburg, 1880); WEHOFER, *Die geistige Bewegung im Anschluss an die Thomas-Enzyklika Leos XIII* (1897); DE GROOT, *Leo XIII u. der hl. Thomas* (1897); BELLAMY, *La théologie catholique au XIXe siècle* (Paris, 1904).

J. POHLE.

I. a. CHRISTOLOGY.—Christology is that part of theology which deals with Our Lord Jesus Christ. In its full extent it comprises the doctrines concerning both the person of Christ and His works; but in the present article we shall limit ourselves to a consideration of the person of Christ. Here again we shall not infringe on the domain of the historian and Old-Testament theologian, who present their respective contributions under the headings JESUS CHRIST, and MESSIAS; hence the theology of the Person of Jesus Christ, considered in the light of the New Testament or from the Christian point of view, is the proper subject of the present article.

The person of Jesus Christ is the Second Person of the Most Holy Trinity, the Son or the Word of the Father, Who "was incarnate by the Holy Ghost of the Virgin Mary and was made man." These mysteries, though foretold in the Old Testament, were fully revealed in the New, and clearly developed in Christian Tradition and theology. Hence we shall have to study our subject under the triple aspect of the Old Testament, the New Testament, and Christian Tradition.

(A) *Old Testament*.—From what has been said we understand that the Old Testament is not considered here from the viewpoint of the Jewish scribe, but of the Christian theologian. Jesus Christ Himself was the first to use it in this way by His repeated appeal to the Messianic passages of the prophetic writings. The Apostles saw in these prophecies many arguments in favour of the claims and the teachings of Jesus Christ; the Evangelists, too, are familiar with them, though they appeal less frequently to them than the patristic writers do. Even the Fathers either state the prophetic argument only in general terms or they quote single prophecies; but they thus prepare the way for the deeper insight into the historical perspective of the Messianic predictions which began to prevail in the eighteenth and nineteenth centuries. Leaving the statement of the historical development of the Messianic prophecies to the writer of the article MESSIAS, we shall briefly call attention to the prophetic predictions of the genealogy of Christ, of His birth, His infancy, His names, His offices, His public life, His sufferings, and His glory.

(1) References to the human genealogy of the Messias are quite numerous in the Old Testament: He is represented as the seed of the woman, the son of Sem, the son of Abraham, Isaac, and Jacob, the son of David, the prince of pastors, the offspring of the marrow of the high cedar (Gen., iii, 1-19; ix, 18-27; xii, 1-9; xvii, 1-9; xviii, 17-19; xxii, 16-18; xxvi, 1-5; xxvii, 1-15; Num., xxiv, 15-19; II Kings, vii, 1-16; 1 Par., xvii, 1-17; Jer., xxiii, 1-8; xxxiii, 14-26; Ezech., xvii). The Royal Psalmist extols the Divine genealogy of the future Messias in the words: "The Lord hath said to me: Thou art my son, this day have I begotten thee" (Ps. ii, 7).

(2) The Prophets frequently speak of the birth of the expected Christ. They locate its place in Bethlehem of Juda (Mich., V, 2-14), they determine its time by the passing of the sceptre from Juda (Gen., xlix, 8-12), by the seventy weeks of Daniel (ix, 22-27), and by the "little while" mentioned in the Book of Aggeus (ii, 1-10). The Old-Testament seers know also that the Messias will be born of a Virgin Mother (Is., vii, 1-17), and that His appearance, at least His public appearance, will be preceded by a precursor (Is., xl, 1-11; Mal., iv, 5-6).

(3) Certain events connected with the infancy of the Messias have been deemed important enough to be the subject of prophetic prediction. Among these are the adoration of the Magi (Ps. lxxxi, 1-17), the slaughter of the innocents (Jer., xxxi, 15-26), and the flight into Egypt (Osee, xi, 1-7). It is true that in the case of these prophecies, as it happens in the case of many others, their fulfilment is their clearest commentary; but this does not undo the fact that the events were really predicted.

(4) Perhaps there is less need of insisting on the predictions of the better known Messianic names and titles, seeing that they involve less obscurity. Thus in the prophecies of Zacharias the Messias is called the Orient, or, according to the Hebrew text, the "bud" (iii; vi, 9-15), in the Book of Daniel He is the Son of Man (vii), in the Prophecy of Malachias He is the Angel of the Testament (ii, 17; iii, 6), in the writings of Isaias He is the Saviour (li, 1; lii, 12; lxii), the Servant of the Lord (xlix, 1), the Emmanuel (viii, 1-10), the Prince of peace (ix, 1-7).

(5) The Messianic offices are considered in a general way in the latter part of Isaias (lxi); in particular, the Messias is considered as prophet in the Book of Deuteronomy (xviii, 9-22); as king in the Canticle of Anna (I Kings, ii, 1-10) and in the royal song of the Psalmist (xliv); as priest in the sacerdotal type Melchisedech (Gen., xiv, 14-20) and in the Psalmist's words "a priest forever" (cix); as Goel, or Avenger, in the second part of Isaias (lxiii, 1-6); as mediator of the New Testament, under the form of a covenant of the people (Is., xlii, 1; xliii, 13), and of the light of the Gentiles (Is., xlix).

(6) As to the public life of the Messias, Isaias gives us a general idea of the fulness of the Spirit investing the Anointed (xi, 1-16), and of the Messianic work (lv). The Psalmist presents a picture of the Good Shepherd (xxii); Isaias summarizes the Messianic miracles (xxxv); Zacharias exclaims, "Rejoice greatly, O daughter of Sion", thus predicting Christ's solemn entrance into Jerusalem; the Psalmist refers to this same event when he mentions the praise out of the mouth of infants (viii). To return once more to the Book of Isaias, the prophet foretells the rejection of the Messias through a league with death (xxvii); the Psalmist alludes to the same mystery where he speaks of the stone which the builders rejected (cxvii).

(7) Need we say that the sufferings of the Messias were fully predicted by the prophets of the Old Testament? The general idea of the Messianic victim is presented in the context of the words "sacrifice and oblation thou wouldst not" (Ps. xxxix); in the passage beginning with the resolve "Let us put wood on his bread" (Jer., xi), and in the sacrifice described by the prophet Malachias (i). Besides, the series of the particular events which constitute the history of Christ's Passion has been described by the prophets with a remarkable minuteness: the Psalmist refers to His betrayal in the words "the man of my peace . . . supplanted me" (xl), and Zacharias knows of the

"thirty pieces of silver" (xi); the Psalmist praying in the anguish of his soul is a type of Christ in His agony (Ps. liv); His capture is foretold in the words "pursue and take him" and "they will hunt after the soul of the just" (Ps. lxx; xciii); His trial with its false witnesses may be found represented in the words "unjust witnesses have risen up against me, and iniquity hath lied to itself" (Ps. xxvi); His flagellation is portrayed in the description of the man of sorrows (Is., lii, 13; liii, 12) and the words "scourges were gathered together upon me" (Ps. xxxiv); the betrayer's evil lot is pictured in the imprecations of Psalm cviii; the crucifixion is referred to in the passages "What are these wounds in the midst of thy hands?" (Zach., xiii), "Let us condemn him to a most shameful death" (Wisd., ii), and "They have dug my hands and my feet" (Ps. xxi); the miraculous darkness occurs in Amos, viii; the gall and vinegar are spoken of in Ps. lxviii; the pierced heart of Christ is foreshadowed in Zach., xii. The sacrifice of Isaac (Gen., xxi, 1–14), the scapegoat (Lev., xvi, 1–28), the ashes of purification (Num., xix, 1–10), and the brazen serpent (Num., xxi, 4–9) hold a prominent place among the types prefiguring the suffering Messias. The third chapter of Lamentations is justly considered as the dirge of our buried Redeemer.

(8) Finally, the glory of the Messias has been foretold by the Prophets of the Old Testament. The context of such phrases as "I have risen because the Lord hath protected me" (Ps. iii), "My flesh shall rest in hope" (Ps. xv), "On the third day he will raise us up" (Osee, v, 15, vi, 3), "O death, I will be thy death" (Osee, xiii, 6–15a), and "I know that my Redeemer liveth" (Job, xix, 23–27) referred the devout Jewish worshipper to something more than a merely earthly restoration, the fulfilment of which began to be realized in the Resurrection of Christ. This mystery is also implied, at least typically, in the first fruits of the harvest (Lev., xxiii, 9–14) and the delivery of Jonas from the belly of the fish (Jon., ii). Nor is the Resurrection of the Messias the only element of Christ's glory predicted by the Prophets. Ps. lxvii refers to the Ascension; Joel, ii, 28–32, to the coming of the Paraclete; Is., lx, to the call of the Gentiles; Mich., iv, 1–7, to the conversion of the Synagogue; Dan., ii, 27–47, to the kingdom of the Messias as compared with the kingdom of the world. Other characteristics of the Messianic kingdom are typified by the tabernacle (Ex., xxv, 8–9; xxix, 43; xl, 33–36; Num., ix, 15–23), the mercy-seat (Ex., xxv, 17–22; Ps. lxxix, 1), Aaron the high priest (Ex., xxviii, 1; xxx, 1; 10; Num., xvi, 39–40), the manna (Ex., xvi, 1–15; Ps. lxxvii, 24–25), and the rock of Horeb (Ex., xvii, 5–7; Num., xx, 10–11; Ps. civ, 41). A Canticle of thanksgiving for the Messianic benefits is found in Is., xii.

The Books of the Old Testament are not the only source from which the Christian theologian may learn the Messianic ideas of pre-Christian Jewry. The Sibylline oracles, the Book of Enoch, the Book of Jubilees, the Psalms of Solomon, the Ascensio Moysis, the Revelation of Baruch, the Fourth Book of Esdras, and several Talmudic and Rabbinic writings are rich depositories of pre-Christian views concerning the expected Messias. Not that all of these works were written before the coming of Christ; but, though partially post-Christian in their authorship, they preserve a picture of the Jewish world of thought, dating back, at least in its outline, centuries before the coming of Christ.

(B) *New Testament*.—Some modern writers tell us that there are two Christs, as it were, the Messias of faith and the Jesus of history. They regard the Lord and Christ, Whom God exalted by raising Him from the dead, as the subject of Christian faith; and Jesus of Nazareth, the preacher and worker of miracles, as the theme of the historian. They assure us that it is quite impossible to persuade even the least experienced critic that Jesus taught, in formal terms and at one and the same time, the Christology of Paul, that of John, and the doctrines of Nicæa, of Ephesus, and of Chalcedon. Otherwise the history of the first Christian centuries appears to these writers to be quite inconceivable. The Fourth Gospel is said to lack the data which underlie the definitions of the first œcumenical councils and to supply testimony that is not a supplement, but a corrective, of the portrait of Jesus drawn by the Synoptics. These two accounts of the Christ are represented as mutually exclusive: if Jesus spoke and acted as He speaks and acts in the Synoptic Gospels, then He cannot have spoken and acted as He is reported by St. John. We shall here briefly review the Christology of St. Paul, of the Catholic Epistles, of the Fourth Gospel, and the Synoptics. Thus we shall give the reader a complete Christology of the New Testament and at the same time the data necessary to control the contentions of the Modernists. The Christology will not, however, be complete in the sense that it extends to all the details concerning Jesus Christ taught in the New Testament, but in the sense that it gives His essential characteristics taught in the whole of the New Testament.

(1) Pauline Christology.—St. Paul insists on the truth of Christ's real humanity and Divinity, in spite of the fact that at first sight the reader is confronted with three objects in the Apostle's writings: God, the human world, and the Mediator. But then the latter is both Divine and human, both God and man.

(a) Christ's Humanity in the Pauline Epistles.—The expressions "form of a servant", "in habit found as a man", "in the likeness of sinful flesh" (Phil., ii, 7; Rom., viii, 3) may seem to impair the real humanity of Christ in the Pauline teaching. But in reality they only describe a mode of being or hint at the presence of a higher nature in Christ not seen by the senses, or they contrast Christ's human nature with the nature of that sinful race to which it belongs. On the other hand the Apostle plainly speaks of Our Lord manifested in the flesh (I Tim., iii, 16), as possessing a body of flesh (Col., i, 22), as being "made of a woman" (Gal., iv, 4), as being born of the seed of David according to the flesh (Rom., i, 3), as belonging according to the flesh to the race of Israel (Rom., ix, 5). As a Jew, Jesus Christ was born under the Law (Gal., iv, 4). The Apostle dwells with emphasis on Our Lord's real share in our physical human weakness (II Cor., xiii, 4), on His life of suffering (Heb., v, 8) reaching its climax in the Passion (ibid., i, 5; Phil., iii, 10; Col., i, 24). Only in two respects did Our Lord's humanity differ from the rest of men: first in its entire sinlessness (II Cor., v, 21; Gal., ii, 17; Rom., viii, 3); secondly, in the fact that Our Lord was the second Adam, representing the whole human race (Rom., v, 12–21; I Cor., xv, 45–49).

(b) Christ's Divinity in the Pauline Epistles.—According to St. Paul, the superiority of the Christian revelation over all other Divine manifestations, and the perfection of the New Covenant with its sacrifice and priesthood, are derived from the fact that Christ is the Son of God (Heb., i, 1 sq.; v, 5 sq.; ii, 5 sq.; Rom., i, 3; Gal., iv, 4; Eph., iv, 13; Col., i, 12 sq.; ii, 9 sq.; etc.). The Apostle understands by the expression "Son of God" not a merely moral dignity, or a merely external relation to God which began in time, but an eternal and immanent relation of Christ to the Father. He contrasts Christ with, and finds Him superior to, Aaron and his successors, Moses and the Prophets (Heb., v, 4; x, 11; vii, 1–22; iii, 1–6; i, 1). He raises Christ above the choirs of angels, and makes Him their Lord and Master (Heb., i, 3; 14; ii, 2–3), and seats Him as heir of all things at the right hand of the Father (Heb., i, 2–3;

Gal., iv, 14; Eph., i, 20-21). If St. Paul is obliged to use the terms "form of God", "image of God", when he speaks of Christ's Divinity, in order to show the personal distinction between the Eternal Father and the Divine Son (Phil., ii, 6; Col., i, 15), Christ is not merely the image and glory of God (I Cor., xi, 7), but also the first-born before any created beings (Col., i, 15), in Whom, and by Whom, and for Whom all things were made (Col., i, 16), in Whom the fulness of the Godhead resides with that actual reality which we attach to the presence of the material bodies perceptible and measurable through the organs of our senses (Col., ii, 9), in a word, "who is over all things, God blessed for ever" (Rom., ix, 5).

(2) Christology of the Catholic Epistles.—The Epistles of St. John will be considered together with the other writings of the same Apostle in the next paragraph. Under the present heading we shall briefly indicate the views concerning Christ held by the Apostles St. James, St. Peter, and St. Jude.

(a) The Epistle of St. James.—The mainly practical scope of the Epistle of St. James does not lead us to expect that Our Lord's Divinity would be formally expressed in it as a doctrine of faith. This doctrine is, however, implied in the language of the inspired writer. He professes to stand in the same relation to Jesus Christ as to God, being the servant of both (i, 1): he applies the same term to the God of the Old Testament as to Jesus Christ (passim). Jesus Christ is both the sovereign judge and independent lawgiver, who can save and can destroy (iv, 12); the faith in Jesus Christ is faith in the Lord of Glory (ii, 1). The language of St. James would be exaggerated and overstrained on any other supposition than the writer's firm belief in the Divinity of Jesus Christ.

(b) Belief of St. Peter.—St. Peter presents himself as the servant and the apostle of Jesus Christ (I Pet., i, 1; II Pet., i, 1), who was predicted by the Prophets of the Old Testament in such a way that the Prophets themselves were Christ's own servants, heralds, and organs (I Pet., i, 10-11). It is the pre-existent Christ who moulds the utterances of Israel's Prophets to proclaim their anticipations of His advent. St. Peter had witnessed the glory of Jesus in the Transfiguration (II Pet., i, 16); he appears to take pleasure in multiplying His titles: Jesus Our Lord (II Pet., i, 2), our Lord Jesus Christ (ibid., i, 14, 16), the Lord and Saviour (ibid., iii, 2), our Lord and Saviour Jesus Christ (ibid., i, 1), Whose power is Divine (ibid., i, 3), through whose promises Christians are made partakers of the nature of God (ibid., i, 4). Throughout his Epistle, therefore, St. Peter feels, as it were, and implies the Divinity of Jesus Christ.

(c) Epistle of St. Jude.—St. Jude, too, introduces himself as the servant of Jesus Christ, through union with whom Christians are kept in a life of faith and holiness (1); Christ is our only Lord and Saviour (4), Who punished Israel in the wilderness and the rebel angels (5), Who will come to judgment surrounded by myriads of saints (14), and to Whom Christians look for the mercy which He will show them at His coming (21), the issue of which will be life everlasting. Can a merely human Christ be the subject of this language?

(3) Johannean Christology.—If there were nothing else in the New Testament to prove the Divinity of Christ, the first fourteen verses in the Fourth Gospel would suffice to convince a believer in the Bible of that dogma. Now the doctrine of this prologue is the fundamental idea of the whole Johannean theology. The Word made flesh is the same with the Word Who was in the beginning, on the one hand, and with the man Jesus Christ, the subject of the Fourth Gospel, on the other. The whole Gospel is a history of the Eternal Word dwelling in human nature among men.

The teaching of the Fourth Gospel is also found in the Johannean Epistles. In his very opening words the writer tells his readers that the Word of life has become manifest and that the Apostles had seen and heard and handled the Word incarnate. The denial of the Son implies the loss of the Father (I John, ii, 23), and "whosoever shall confess that Jesus is the Son of God, God abideth in him and he in God" (ibid., iv, 15). Towards the end of the Epistle the writer is still more emphatic: "And we know that the Son of God is come: and he hath given us understanding that we may know the true God, and may be in his true Son. This is the true God and life eternal" (ibid., v, 20).

According to the Apocalypse, Christ is the first and the last, the alpha and the omega, the eternal and the almighty (i, 8; xxi, 6; xxii, 13). He is the king of kings and lord of lords (xix, 16), the lord of the unseen world (xii, 10; xiii, 8), the centre of the court of heaven (v, 6); He receives the adoration of the highest angels (v, 8), and, as the object of that uninterrupted worship (v, 12), He is associated with the Father (v, 13; xvii, 14).

(4) Christology of the Synoptists.—There is a real difference between the first three Evangelists and St. John in their respective representations of our Lord. The truth presented by these writers may be the same, but they view it from different standpoints. The three Synoptists set forth the humanity of Christ in its obedience to the law, in its power over nature, and in its tenderness for the weak and afflicted; the fourth Gospel sets forth the life of Christ not in any of the aspects which belong to it as human, but as being the adequate expression of the glory of the Divine Person, manifested to men under a visible form. But in spite of this difference, the Synoptists by their suggestive implication practically anticipate the teaching of the Fourth Gospel. This suggestion is implied, first, in the Synoptic use of the title Son of God as applied to Jesus Christ. Jesus is the Son of God, not merely in an ethical or theocratic sense, not merely as one among many sons, but He is the only, the well-beloved Son of the Father, so that His sonship is unshared by any other, and is absolutely unique (Matt., iii, 17; xvii, 5; xxii, 41; cf. iv, 3, 6; Luke, iv, 3, 9); it is derived from the fact that the Holy Ghost was to come upon Mary, and the power of the Most High was to overshadow her (Luke, i, 35). Again, the Synoptists imply Christ's Divinity in their history of His nativity and its accompanying circumstances; He is conceived of the Holy Ghost (Luke, 1, 35), and His mother knows that all generations shall call her blessed, because the mighty one had done great things unto her (Luke, i, 48). Elizabeth calls Mary blessed among women, blesses the fruit of her womb, and marvels that she herself should be visited by the mother of her Lord (Luke, i, 42-43). Gabriel greets Our Lady as full of grace, and blessed among women; her Son will be great, He will be called the Son of the Most High, and of His kingdom there will be no end (Luke, i, 28, 32). As new-born infant, Christ is adored by the shepherds and the Magi, representatives of the Jewish and the Gentile world. Simeon sees in the child his Lord's salvation, the light of the Gentiles, and the pride and glory of his people Israel (Luke, ii, 30-32). These accounts hardly fit in with the limits of a merely human child, but they become intelligible in the light of the Fourth Gospel.

The Synoptists agree with the teaching of the Fourth Gospel concerning the person of Jesus Christ not merely in their use of the term *Son of God* and in their accounts of Christ's birth with its surrounding details, but also in their narratives of Our Lord's doctrine, life, and work. The very term *Son of Man*, which they often apply to Christ, is used in such a way that it shows in Jesus Christ a self-consciousness for which the human element is not something primary, but something secondary and superinduced. Often Christ is simply called Son (Matt., xi, 27;

xxviii, 20), and correspondingly He never calls the Father "our" Father, but "my" Father (Matt., xviii, 10, 19, 35; xx, 23; xxvi, 53). At His baptism and transfiguration He receives witness from heaven to His Divine Sonship; the Prophets of the Old Testament are not rivals, but servants in comparison with Him (Matt., xxi, 34); hence the title Son of Man implies a nature to which Christ's humanity was an accessory. Again, Christ claims the power to forgive sins and supports His claim by miracles (Matt., ix, 2–6; Luke, v, 20, 24); He insists on faith in Himself (Matt., xvi, 16, 17); He inserts His name in the baptismal formula between that of the Father and the Holy Ghost (Matt., xxviii, 19), He alone knows the Father and is known by the Father alone (Matt., xi, 27), He institutes the sacrament of the Holy Eucharist (Matt., xxvi, 26; Mark, xiv, 22; Luke, xxii, 19), He suffers and dies only to rise again the third day (Matt., xx, 19; Mark, x, 34; Luke, xviii, 33), He ascends into Heaven, but declares that He will be among us till the end of the world (Matt., xxviii, 20).

Need we add that Christ's claims to the most exalted dignity of His person are unmistakably clear in the eschatological discourses of the Synoptists? He is the Lord of the material and moral universe; as supreme lawgiver He revises all other legislation; as final judge He determines the fate of all. Blot the Fourth Gospel out of the Canon of the New Testament, and you still have in the Synoptic Gospels the identical doctrine concerning the person of Jesus Christ which we now draw out of the Four Gospels; some points of the doctrine might be less clearly stated than they are now, but they would remain substantially the same.

(C) *Christian Tradition.*—Biblical Christology shows that one and the same Jesus Christ is both God and man. While Christian tradition has always maintained this triple thesis that Jesus Christ is truly man, that He is truly God, and that the God-man, Jesus Christ, is one and the same person, the heretical or erroneous tenets of various religious leaders have forced the Church to insist more expressly now on the one, now on another element of her Christology. A classified list of the principal errors and of the subsequent ecclesiastical utterances will show the historical development of the Church's doctrine with sufficient clearness. The reader will find a more lengthy account of the principal heresies and councils under their respective headings.

(1) Humanity of Christ.—The true humanity of Jesus Christ was denied even in the earliest ages of the Church. The Docetist Marcion and the Priscillianists grant to Jesus only an apparent body; the Valentinians, a body brought down from Heaven. The followers of Apollinaris deny either that Jesus had any human soul at all, or that He possessed the higher part of the human soul; they maintain that the Word supplies either the whole soul in Christ, or at least its higher faculties. In more recent times it is not so much Christ's true humanity as His *real* manhood that is denied. According to Kant, the Christian creed deals with the ideal, not with the historical Jesus; according to Jacobi, it worships Jesus not as an historical person, but as a religious ideal; according to Fichte there exists an absolute unity between God and man, and Jesus was the first to see and teach it; according to Schelling, the incarnation is an eternal fact, which happened to reach in Jesus its highest point; according to Hegel, Christ is not the actual incarnation of God in Jesus of Nazareth, but the symbol of God's incarnation in humanity at large. Finally, certain recent Catholic writers distinguish between the Christ of history and the Christ of faith, thus destroying in the Christ of faith His historical reality. The New Syllabus (Proposit. 29 sq.) and the Encyclical "Pascendi dominici gregis" may be consulted on these errors.

(2) The Divinity of Christ.—Even in Apostolic times the Church regarded a denial of Christ's Divinity as eminently anti-Christian (I John, ii, 22–23; iv, 3; II John, 7). The early martyrs, the most ancient Fathers, and the first ecclesiastical liturgies agree in their profession of Christ's Divinity. Still, the Ebionites, the Theodotians, the Artemonites, and the Photinians looked upon Christ either as a mere man, though singularly enlightened by Divine wisdom; or as the appearance of an æon emanating from the Divine Being according to the Gnostic theory; or again as a manifestation of the Divine Being such as the Theistic and Pantheistic Sabellians and Patripassians admitted; or, finally, as the incarnate Word indeed, but the Word conceived after the Arian manner as a creature mediating between God and the world, at least not essentially identical with the Father and the Holy Ghost. Though the definitions of Nice and of the subsequent councils, especially of the Fourth Lateran, deal directly with the doctrine concerning the Most Holy Trinity, still they also teach that the Word is consubstantial with the Father and the Holy Ghost, and thus establish the Divinity of Jesus Christ, the Word incarnate. In more recent times, our earliest Rationalists endeavoured to avoid the problem of Jesus Christ; they had little to say of him, while they made St. Paul the founder of the Church. But the historical Christ was too impressive a figure to be long neglected. It is all the more to be regretted that in recent times a practical denial of Christ's Divinity is not confined to the Socinians and such writers as Ewald and Schleiermacher. Others who profess to be believing Christians see in Christ the perfect revelation of God, the true head and lord of the human race, but, after all, they end with Pilate's words, "Behold, the man".

(3) Hypostatic Union.—His human nature and His Divine nature are in Jesus Christ united hypostatically, i. e. united in the hypostasis or the person of the Word. This dogma too has found bitter opponents from the earliest times of the Church. Nestorius and his followers admitted in Christ one moral person, as a human society forms one moral person; but this moral person results from the union of two physical persons, just as there are two natures in Christ. These two persons are united, not physically, but morally, by means of grace. The heresy of Nestorius was condemned by Celestine I in the Roman Synod of A. D. 430 and by the Council of Ephesus, A. D. 431; the Catholic doctrine was again insisted on in the Council of Chalcedon and the second Council of Constantinople. It follows that the Divine and the human nature are physically united in Christ. The Monophysites, therefore, believed that in this physical union either the human nature was absorbed by the Divine, according to the views of Eutyches; or that the Divine nature was absorbed by the human; or, again, that out of the physical union of the two resulted a third nature by a kind of physical mixture, as it were, or at least by means of their physical composition. The true Catholic doctrine was upheld by Pope Leo the Great, the Council of Chalcedon, and the Fifth Œcumenical Council, A. D. 553. The twelfth canon of the last-named council excludes also the view that Christ's moral life developed gradually, attaining its completion only after the Resurrection. The Adoptionists renewed Nestorianism in part because they considered the Word as the natural Son of God, and the man Christ as a servant or an adopted son of God, thus granting its own personality to Christ's human nature. This opinion was rejected by Pope Adrian I, the Synod of Ratisbon, A. D. 782, the Council of Frankfort (794), and by Leo III in the Roman Synod (799). There is no need to point out that the human nature of Christ is not united with the Word, according to the Socinian and rationalistic

views. Dorner shows how widespread among Protestants these views are, since there is hardly a Protestant theologian of note who refuses its own personality to the human nature of Christ. Among Catholics, Berruyer and Günther reintroduced a modified Nestorianism; but they were censured by the Congregation of the Index (17 April, 1755) and by Pope Pius IX (15 Jan., 1857). The Monophysite heresy was renewed by the Monothelites, admitting only one will in Christ and thus contradicting the teaching of Popes Martin I and Agatho and of the Sixth Œcumenical Council. Both the schismatic Greeks and the Reformers of the sixteenth century wished to retain the traditional doctrine concerning the Word Incarnate; but even the earliest followers of the Reformers fell into errors involving both the Nestorian and the Monophysite heresies. The Ubiquitarians, for example, find the essence of the Incarnation not in the assumption of human nature by the Word, but in the divinization of human nature by sharing the properties of the Divine nature. The subsequent Protestant theologians drifted away farther still from the views of Christian tradition; Christ for them was the sage of Nazareth, perhaps even the greatest of the Prophets, whose Biblical record, half myth and half history, is nothing but the expression of a popular idea of human perfection. The Catholic writers whose views were derogatory either to the historical character of the Biblical account of the life of Christ or to his prerogatives as the God-man have been censured in the new Syllabus and the Encyclical "Pascendi dominici gregis".

For Christology consult the following:—

Patristic Works: ATHANASIUS, GREGORY NAZIANZUS, GREGORY OF NYSSA, BASIL, EPIPHANIUS wrote especially against the followers of Arius and Apollinaris; CYRIL OF ALEXANDRIA, PROCLUS, LEONTIUS BYZANTINUS, ANASTASIUS SINAITA, EULOGIUS OF ALEXANDRIA, PETER CHRYSOLOGUS, FULGENTIUS, opposing the Nestorians and Monophysites; SOPHRONIUS, MAXIMUS, JOHN DAMASCENE, the Monothelites; PAULINUS OF AQUILEIA, ETHERIUS, ALCUIN, AGOBARDUS, the Adoptionists. See *P. G.* and *P. L.*

Scholastic Writers: ST. THOMAS, *Summa theol.*, III, QQ. l–lix; IDEM, *Summa contra gentes*, IV, xxvii–lv; *In III Sentent.*; *De veritate*, QQ. xx, xxix; *Compend. theol.*, QQ. cxcix–ccxlii; *Opusc.*, 2; etc.; BONAVENTURA, *Breviloquium*, 1, 4; *In III Sentent.*; BELLARMINE, *De Christo capite totius ecclesiæ controvers.*, I, col. 1619; SUAREZ, *De Incarn.*, opp. XIV, XV; LUGO, *De Incarn.*, op. III.

Positive Theologians: PETAVIUS, *Theol. dogmat.*, IV, 1–2; THOMASSIN, *De Incarn., dogm. theol.*, III, IV.

Recent Writers: FRANZELIN, *De Verbo Incarn.* (Rome, 1874); KLEUTGEN, *Theologie der Vorzeit*, III (Münster, 1873); JUNGMANN, *De Verbo incarnato* (Ratisbon, 1872); HURTER, *Theologia dogmatica*, II, tract. vii (Innsbruck, 1882); STENTRUP, *Prælectiones dogmaticæ de Verbo incarnato* (2 vols., Innsbruck, 1882); LIDDON, *The Divinity of Our Lord* (London, 1885); MAAS, *Christ in Type and Prophecy* (2 vols., New York, 1893–96); LEPIN, *Jésus Messie et Fils de Dieu* (Paris, 1904). See also recent works on the life of Christ, and the principal commentaries on the Biblical passages cited in this article.

For all other parts of dogmatic theology see bibliography at the end of this section (I.).

A. J. MAAS.

II. MORAL THEOLOGY.—Moral theology is a branch of theology, the science of God and Divine things. The distinction between natural and supernatural theology rests on a solid foundation. Natural theology is the science of God Himself, in as far as the human mind can by its own efforts reach a definite conclusion about God and His nature: it is always designated by the adjective natural. Theology, without any further modification, is invariably understood to mean supernatural theology, that is, the science of God and Divine things, in as far as it is based on supernatural Revelation. Its subject-matter embraces not only God and His essence, but also His actions and His works of salvation and the guidance by which we are led to God, our supernatural end. Consequently, it extends much farther than natural theology; for, though the latter informs us of God's essence and attributes, yet it can tell us nothing about His free works of salvation. The knowledge of all these truths is necessary for every man, at least in its broad outlines, and is acquired by Christian faith. But this is not yet a science. The science of theology demands that the knowledge won through faith, be deepened, expanded, and strengthened, so that the articles of faith be understood and defended by their reasons and be, together with their conclusions, arranged systematically.

The entire field of theology proper is divided into dogmatic and moral theology, which differ in subject-matter and in method. Dogmatic theology has as its end the scientific discussion and establishment of the doctrines of faith, moral theology of the moral precepts. The precepts of Christian morals are also part of the doctrines of faith, for they were announced or confirmed by Divine Revelation. The subject-matter of dogmatic theology is those doctrines which serve to enrich the knowledge necessary or convenient for man, whose destination is supernatural. Moral theology, on the other hand, is limited to those doctrines which discuss the relations of man and his free actions to God and his supernatural end, and propose the means instituted by God for the attainment of that end. Consequently, dogmatic and moral theology are two closely related parts of universal theology. Inasmuch as a considerable number of individual doctrines may be claimed by either discipline, no sharp line of demarcation can be drawn between the subject-matter of dogma and morals. In actual practice, however, a division and limitation must be made in accordance with practical needs. Of a similar nature is the relation between moral theology and ethics. The subject-matter of natural morals or ethics, as contained in the Decalogue, has been included in positive, Divine Revelation, and hence has passed into moral theology. Nevertheless, the argumentative processes differ in the two sciences, and for this reason a large portion of the matter is disregarded in moral theology and referred to ethics. For instance, the refutation of the false systems of the modern ethicists is generally treated under ethics, especially because these systems are refuted by arguments drawn not so much from faith, as from reason. Only in as far as moral theology requires a defence of revealed doctrines, does it concern itself with false systems. However, it must discuss the various requirements of the natural law, not only because this law has been confirmed and defined by positive revelation, but also because every violation of it entails a disturbance of the supernatural moral order, the treatment of which is an essential part of moral theology.

The field of moral theology, its contents, and the boundaries which separate it from kindred subjects, may be briefly indicated as follows: moral theology includes everything relating to man's free actions and the last, or supreme, end to be attained through them, as far as we know the same by Divine Revelation; in other words, it includes the supernatural end, the rule, or norm, of the moral order, human actions as such, their harmony or disharmony with the laws of the moral order, their consequences, the Divine aids for their right performance. A detailed treatment of these subjects may be found in the second part of St. Thomas's "Summa theologica", a work still unrivalled as a treatise of moral theology.

The position of moral theology in universal theology is briefly sketched by St. Thomas in the "Summa theol.", I, Q. i, a. 7 and Q. ii in the proemium and in the prologus of I–II; likewise by Fr. Suàrez in the proemium of his commentaries on the I–II of St. Thomas. The subject-matter of the entire second part of the "Summa theol." is, man as a free agent. "Man was made after the image of God, by his intellect, his free will, and a certain power to act of his own accord. Hence, after we have spoken of the pattern, viz. of God, and of those things which proceeded from His Divine power according to His will, we must now turn our attention to His image, that is, man, inasmuch as he also is the principle of his actions in virtue of his free will and his power over his own actions." He includes all this in theology, not only because it is viewed as the object of positive Divine Revelation (I, Q. i, a. 3), but also because God always is the principal object, for "theology treats all things in their relation to God, either in as far as they are God Himself or are directed towards God as their origin or last end" (I, Q. i, a. 7). "Since it is the chief aim of theology to communicate the knowledge of God, not only as He is in Himself but also as the beginning and end of all things and particularly of rational creatures . . . , we shall speak first of God, secondly of the tendency of the rational creature towards God", etc. (I, Q. ii, proem.). These words point out the scope and the subject-matter of the moral part of theology. Suárez, who pregnantly calls this tendency of the creatures towards God "the return of the creatures to God", shows that there is no contradiction in designating man created after the image of God, endowed with reason and free will and exercising these faculties, as the object of moral theology, and God as the object of entire theology. "If we are asked to name the proximate object of moral theology, we shall undoubtedly say that it is man as a free agent, who seeks his happiness by his free actions; but if we are asked in what respect this object must be treated chiefly, we shall answer that this must be done with respect to God as his last end."

A detailed account of the wide range of moral theology may be found in the analytical index of Pars Secunda of St. Thomas's "Summa theologica". We must confine ourselves to a brief summary. The first question treats of man's last end, eternal happiness, its nature and possession. Then follows an examination of human acts in themselves and their various subdivisions, of voluntary and involuntary acts, of the moral uprightness or malice of both interior and exterior acts and their consequences; the passions in general and in particular; the habits or permanent qualities of the human soul, and the general questions about virtues, vices, and sins. Under this last title, while enquiring into the causes of sin, the author embodies the doctrine on original sin and its consequences. This portion might, however, be with equal right assigned to dogmatic theology in the stricter meaning of the word. Although St. Thomas regards sin chiefly as a transgression of the law, and in particular of the "lex æterna" (Q. ii, a. 6), still he places the chapters on the laws after the section on sin; because sin, a free human act like any other human act, is first discussed from the standpoint of its subjective principles, viz. knowledge, will, and the tendency of the will; only after this are the human actions viewed with regard to their objective or exterior principles, and the exterior principle, by which human actions are judged not merely as human, but as moral actions, either morally good or morally bad, is the law. Since morality is conceived by him as supernatural morality, which exceeds the nature and the faculties of man, Divine grace, the other exterior principle of man's morally good actions, is discussed after the law. In the exordium to Q. xc, St. Thomas states his division briefly as follows: "The exterior principle which moves us to good actions is God; He instructs us by His law and aids us with His grace. Hence we shall speak first of the law, secondly of grace."

The following volume is wholly devoted to the special questions, in the order given by St. Thomas in the prologue: "After a cursory glance at the virtues, vices, and the moral principles in general, it is incumbent on us to consider the various points in detail. Moral discussions, if satisfied with generalities, are of little value, because actions touch particular, individual things. When there is question of morals, we may consider individual actions in two ways: one, by examining the matter, i. e., by discussing the different virtues and vices; another, by inquiring into the various avocations of individuals and their states of life." St. Thomas then goes on to discuss the whole range of moral theology from both these standpoints. First, he closely scrutinizes the various virtues, keeping in view the Divine aids, and the sins and vices opposed to the respective virtues. He examines first the three Divine virtues which are wholly supernatural and embrace the vast field of charity and its actual practice; then he passes to the cardinal virtues with their auxiliary and allied virtues. The volume concludes with a discussion of the particular states of life in the Church of God, including those which suppose an extraordinary, Divine guidance. This last part, therefore, discusses subjects which specifically belong to mystical or ascetical theology, such as prophecy and extraordinary modes of prayer, but above all the active and the contemplative life, Christian perfection, and the religious state in the Church. The contents of a modern work on moral theology, as, for instance, that of Slater (London, 1909), are: Human acts, conscience, law, sin, the virtues of faith, hope, charity; the precepts of the Decalogue, including a special treatise on justice; the commandments of the Church; duties attached to particular states or offices; the sacraments, in so far as their administration and reception are a means of moral reform and rectitude; ecclesiastical laws and penalties, only in so far as they affect conscience; these laws forming properly the subject-matter of canon law, in so far as they govern and regulate the Church as an organization, its membership, ministry, the relations between hierarchy, clergy, religious orders, laity, or of spiritual and temporal authority.

One circumstance must not be overlooked. Moral theology considers free human actions only in their relation to the supreme order, and to the last and highest end, not in their relation to the proximate ends which man may and must pursue, as for instance political, social, economical. Economics, politics, social science are separate fields of science, not subdivisions of moral science. Nevertheless, these special sciences must also be guided by morals, and must subordinate their specific principles to those of moral theology, at least so far as not to clash with the latter. Man is one being, and all his actions must finally lead him to his last and highest end. Therefore, various proximate ends must not turn him from this end, but must be made subservient to it and its attainment. Hence moral theology surveys all the individual relations of man and passes judgment on political, economical, social questions, not with regard to their bearings on politics and economy, but with regard to their influence upon a moral life. This is also the reason why there is hardly another science that touches other spheres so closely as does moral theology, and why its sphere is more extensive than that of any other. This is true inasmuch as moral theology has the eminently practical scope of instructing and forming spiritual directors and confessors, who must be familiar with human conditions in their relation to the moral law, and advise persons in every state and situation.

The manner in which moral theology treats its subject-matter, must be, as in theology generally, chiefly positive, that is, drawing from Revelation and theological sources. Starting from this positive foundation, reason also comes into play quite extensively, especially since the whole subject-matter of natural ethics has been raised to the level of supernatural morals. It is true reason must be illumined by supernatural faith, but when illumined its duty is to explain, prove, and defend most of the principles of moral theology.

From what has been said it is manifest that the

chief source of moral theology is Sacred Scripture and Tradition together with the teachings of the Church. However, the following points must be observed regarding the Old Testament. Not all precepts contained in it are universally valid, as many belong to the ritual and special law of the Jews. These statutes never obliged the non-Jewish world and have simply been abrogated by the New Covenant, so that now the ritual observances proper are illicit. The Decalogue, however, with the sole change in the law enjoining the celebration of the Sabbath, has passed into the New Covenant a positive Divine confirmation of the natural law, and now constitutes the principal subject matter of Christian morality. Moreover, we must remember that the Old Covenant did not stand on the high moral level to which Christ elevated the New Covenant. Jesus Himself mentions things which were permitted to the Jews "on account of the hardness of their hearts", but against which He applied again the law at first imposed by God. Hence, not everything that was tolerated in the Old Testament and its writings, is tolerated now; on the contrary, many of the usages approved and established there would be counter to Christian perfection as counselled by Christ. With these limitations the writings of the Old Testament are sources of moral theology, containing examples of and exhortations to heroic virtues, from which the Christian moralist, following in the footsteps of Christ and His Apostles, may well draw superb models of sanctity.

Apart from Sacred Scripture, the Church recognizes also Tradition as a source of revealed truths, and hence of Christian morals. It has assumed a concrete shape chiefly in the writings of the Fathers. Furthermore, the decisions of the Church must be regarded as a source, since they are based on Holy Writ and Tradition; they are the proximate source of moral theology, because they contain the final judgment about the meaning of Sacred Scripture as well as the teachings of the Fathers. These include the long list of condemned propositions, which must be considered as danger signals along the boundary between lawful and illicit, not only when the condemnation has been pronounced by virtue of the highest Apostolic authority, but also when the congregation instituted by the pope has issued a general, doctrinal decision in questions bearing on morals. What Pius IX wrote concerning the meetings of scholars in Munich in the year 1863 may also be applied here: "Since there is question of that subjection which binds all Catholics in conscience who desire to advance the interests of the Church by devoting themselves to the speculative sciences; let the members of this assembly recall that it is not sufficient for Catholic scholars to accept and esteem the above-mentioned dogmas, but that they are also obliged to submit to the decisions of the papal congregations as well as to those teachings which are, by the constant and universal consent of Catholics, so held as theological truths and certain conclusions that the opposite opinion even when not heretical, still deserves some theological censure." If this is true of the dogmatic doctrines in the strict sense of the word, we might say that it is still more true of moral questions, because for them not only absolute and infallibly certain, but also morally certain decisions must be accounted as obligatory norms.

The words of Pius IX just quoted, point to another source of theological doctrines, and hence of morals, viz., the universal teachings of the Catholic schools. For these are the channels by which the Catholic doctrines on faith and morals must be transmitted without error, and which have consequently the nature of a source. From the unanimous doctrine of the Catholic schools follows naturally the conviction of the universal Church. But since it is a dogmatic principle that the whole Church cannot err in matters of faith and morals, the consent of the various Catholic schools must offer the guarantee of infallibility in these questions.

Moral theology, to be complete in every respect, must accomplish in moral questions what dogmatic theology does in questions pertaining to dogma. The latter has to explain clearly the truths of faith and prove them to be such; it must also, as far as possible, show their accordance with reason, defend them against objections, trace their connexion with other truths, and, by means of theological argumentation, deduce further truths. Moral theology must follow the same processive questions of morals.—It is evident that this cannot be done in all branches of moral theology in such a way as to exhaust the subject, except by a series of monographs. It would take volumes to sketch but the beauty and the harmony of God's dispositions, which transcend the natural law, but which God enacted in order to elevate man to a higher plane and to lead him to his supernatural end in a future life—and yet all this is embraced in the subject of supernatural morals. Nor is moral theology confined to the exposition of those duties and virtues which cannot be shirked if man wishes to attain his last end; it includes all virtues, even those which mark the height of Christian perfection, and their practice, not only in the ordinary degree, but also in the asceticism and mystical life. Hence, it is entirely correct to designate asceticism and mysticism as parts of Christian moral theology, though ordinarily they are treated as distinct sciences.

The task of the moral theologian is by no means completed when he has explained the questions indicated. Moral theology, in more than one respect, is essentially a practical science. Its instructions must extend to moral character, moral behaviour, the completion and issue of moral aspirations, so that it can offer a definite norm for the complex situations of human life. For this purpose, it must examine the individual cases which arise and determine the limits and the gravity of the obligation in each. Particularly those whose office and position in the Church demand the cultivation of theological science, and who are called to be the teachers and counsellors, must find in it a practical guide. As jurisprudence must enable the future judge and lawyer to administer justice in individual cases, so must moral theology enable the spiritual director or confessor to decide matters of conscience in varied cases of every-day life; to weigh the violations of the natural law in the balance of Divine justice; it must enable the spiritual guide to distinguish correctly and to advise others as to what is sin and what is not, what is counselled and what not, what is good and what is better; it must provide a scientific training for the shepherd of the flock, so that he can direct all to a life of duty and virtue, warn them against sin and danger, lead from good to better those who are endowed with necessary light and moral power, raise up and strengthen those who have fallen from the moral level. Many of these tasks are assigned to the collateral science of pastoral theology; but this also treats a special part of the duties of moral theology, and falls, therefore, within the scope of moral theology in its widest sense. The purely theoretical and speculative treatment of the moral questions must be supplemented by casuistry. Whether this should be done separately, that is, whether the subject matter should be taken casuistically before or after its theoretical treatment, or whether the method should be at the same time both theoretical and casuistical, is unimportant for the matter itself; the practical feasibility will decide this point, while for written works on moral theology the special aim of the author will determine it. However, he who teaches or writes moral theology for the training of Catholic priests, would not do full justice to the end at which he must aim, if he did not unite the casuistical with the theoretical and speculative element.

What has been said so far, sufficiently outlines the concept of moral theology in its widest sense. Our next task is to follow up its actual formation and development.

Moral theology, correctly understood, means the science of supernaturally revealed morals. Hence, they cannot speak of moral theology who reject supernatural Revelation; the most they can do is to discourse on natural ethics. But to distinguish between moral theology and ethics is sooner or later to admit a science of ethics without God and religion. That this contains an essential contradiction, is plain to everyone who analyzes the ideas of moral rectitude and moral perversion, or the concept of an absolute duty which forces itself with unrelenting persistency on all who have attained the use of reason. Without God, an absolute duty is inconceivable, because there is nobody to impose obligation. I cannot oblige myself, because I cannot be my own superior; still less can I oblige the whole human race, and yet I feel myself obliged to many things, and cannot but feel myself absolutely obliged as man, and hence cannot but regard all those who share human nature with me as obliged likewise. It is plain then that this obligation must proceed from a higher being who is superior to all men, not only to those who live at present, but to all who have been and will be, nay, in a certain sense even to those who are merely possible. This superior being is the Lord of all, God. It is also plain that although this Supreme lawgiver can be known by natural reason, neither He nor His law can be sufficiently known without a revelation on His part. Hence it is that moral theology, the study of this Divine law is actually cultivated only by those who faithfully cling to a Divine Revelation, and by the sects which sever their connexion with the Church, only as long as they retain the belief in a supernatural Revelation through Jesus Christ.

Wherever Protestantism has thrown this belief overboard, there the study of moral theology as a science has suffered shipwreck. To-day it would be merely lost labour to look for an advancement of it on the part of a non-Catholic denomination. In the seventeenth and eighteenth centuries there were still men to be found who made an attempt at it. J. A. Dorner states in Herzog, "Real-Encyklopädie", IV, 364 sqq. (s. v. "Ethik"), that prominent Protestant writers upholding "theological morals" have grown very scarce since the eighteenth century. However, this is not quite correct. Of those who still cling to a positive Protestantism, we may name Martensen, who recently entered the lists with deep conviction for "Christian Ethics"; the same, though in his own peculiar manner, is done by Lemme in his "Christliche Ethik" (1905); both attribute to it a scope wider and objectively other than that of natural ethics. A few names from the seventeenth and eighteenth centuries may here suffice: Hugo Grotius (d. 1645), Pufendorf (d. 1694), and Christian Thomasius (d. 1728), all see the difference between theological and natural morals in that the former is also positive, i. e. Divinely revealed, but with the same subject matter as the latter. This last assertion could spring only from the Protestant view which has staked its all on the "fides fiducialis"; but it can hardly acknowledge a range of duties widened by Christ and Christianity. Other writers of a "theologia moralis" based on this "fides fiducialis", are Buddeus, Chr. A. Crusius, and Jerem. Fr. Reuss. A logical result of Kantianism was the denial of the very possibility of moral theology, since Kant had made autonomous reason the only source of obligation. On this point Dorner says (loc. cit.): "It is true that the autonomy and the autocracy of the moral being separates morals and religion"; he would have been nearer the mark, had he said: "they destroy all morals". Generally speaking the modern Liberal Protestants hardly know any other than autonomous morals; even when they do speak of "religious" morals, they find its last explanation in man, religion, and God or Divine Revelation being taken in their Modernistic sense, that is subjective notions of whose objective value we have no knowledge and no certainty.

This being the case, there remains only one question to be discussed: What has been the actual development and method of moral theology in the Church? and here we must first of all remember that the Church is not an educational institution or a school for the advancement of the sciences. True, she esteems and promotes the sciences, especially theology, and scientific schools are founded by her; but this is not her only, or even her chief task. She is the authoritative institution, founded by Christ for the salvation of mankind; she speaks with power and authority to the whole human race, to all nations, to all classes of society, to every age, communicates to them the doctrine of salvation unadulterated and offers them her aids. It is her mission to urge upon educated and uneducated persons alike the acceptance of truth, without regard to its scientific study and establishment. After this has been accepted on faith, she also promotes and urges, according to times and circumstances, the scientific investigation of the truth, but she retains supervision over it and stands above all scientific aspirations and labours. As a result, we see the subject matter of moral theology, though laid down and positively communicated by the Church, treated differently by ecclesiastical writers according to the requirements of times and circumstances.

In the first years of the early Church, when the Divine seed, nourished by the blood of the martyrs, was seen to sprout in spite of the chilling frosts of persecution, when, to the amazement of the hostile world, it grew into a mighty tree of heavenly plantation, there was hardly leisure for the scientific study of Christian doctrine. Hence morals were at first treated in a popular, parenetic form. Throughout the Patristic period, hardly any other method for moral questions was in vogue, though this method might consist now in a concise exposition, now in a more detailed discussion of individual virtues and duties. One of the earliest works of Christian tradition, if not the earliest after the Sacred Scripture, the "Didache" or "Teaching of the Apostles", is chiefly of a moral-theological nature. It is hardly more than a code of laws, an enlarged decalogue, to which are added the principal duties arising from the Divine institution of the means of salvation and from the Apostolic institutions of a common worship—in this respect valuable for dogmatic theology in its narrow sense. The "Pastor" of Hermas, composed a little later, is of a moral character, that is, it contains an ascetical exhortation to Christian morality and to serious penance if one should have relapsed into sin.

There exists a long series of occasional writings bearing on moral theology, from the first period of the Christian era; their purpose was either to recommend a certain virtue, or to exhort the faithful in general for certain times and circumstances. Thus, from Tertullian (d. about 240) we have: "De spectaculis", "De idololatria", "De corona militis", "De patientia", "De oratione", "De poenitentia", "Ad uxorem", not to take into consideration the works which he wrote after his defection to Montanism and which are indeed of interest for the history of Christian morals, but cannot serve as guides in it. Of Origen (d. 254) we still possess two minor works which bear on our question, viz., "De martyrio", parenetic in character, and "De oratione", moral and dogmatic in content; the latter meets the objections which are advanced or rather reiterated even to-day against the efficacy of prayer. Occasional writings and monographs are offered to us in the precious works of St. Cyprian (d. 258); among the former must be numbered: "De mortalitate" and "De martyrio", in a certain sense also "De lapsis", though it bears rather a disciplinary and judicial character; to the latter class belong: "De habitu virginum", "De oratione", "De opere et eleemosynis", "De bono patientiæ", and "De zelo et livore". A clearer title to be classed among moral-theological books seems to belong to an earlier work, the "Pædagogus" of Clement of Alexandria (d. about 217). It is a detailed account of a genuine Christian's daily life, in which ordinary and every-day actions are measured by the standard of supernatural morality. The same author touches upon Christian morals also in his other works, particularly in the "Stromata"; but this work is principally written from the apologetic standpoint, since it was intended to vindicate the entire Christian doctrine, both faith and morals, against pagan and Jewish philosophies.

In subsequent years, when the persecutions ceased, and patristic literature began to flourish, we find not only exegetical writings and apologies written to defend Christian doctrine against various heresies, but also numerous moral-theological works, principally sermons, homilies, and monographs. First of these are the orations of St. Gregory of Nazianzus (d. 391), of St. Gregory of Nyssa (d. 395), of St. John Chrysostom (d. 406), of St. Augustine (d. 430), and above all the "Catecheses" of St. Cyril of Jerusalem (d. 386). Of St. John Chrysostom we have "De sacerdotio"; of St. Augustine, "Confessiones", "Soliloquia", "De cathechizandis rudibus", "De patientia", "De continentia", "De bono coniugali", "De adulterinis coniugiis", "De sancta virginitate", "De bono viduitatis", "De mendacio", "De cura pro mortuis gerenda", so that the titles alone suffice to give an intimation of the wealth of subjects discussed with no less unction than originality and depth of thought. A separate treatment of the supernatural morality of Christians was attempted by St. Ambrose (d. 397) in his books "De officiis", a work which, imitating Cicero's "De officiis", forms a Christian counterpart of the pagan's purely natural discussions. A work of an entirely different stamp and of larger proportions is the "Expositio in Job, seu moralium lib. XXV", of Gregory the Great (d. 604). It is not a systematic arrangement of the various Christian duties, but a collection of moral instructions and exhortations based on the Book of Job; Alzog (Handbuch der Patrologie, 92) calls it a "fairly complete repertory of morals". More systematic is his work "De cura pastorali", which was intended primarily for the pastor and which is considered even to-day a classical work in pastoral theology.

Having broadly outlined the general progress of moral theology during the Patristic era proper, we must supplement it by detailing the development of a very special branch of moral theology and its practical application. For moral theology must necessarily assume a peculiar form when its purpose is restricted to the administration of the Sacrament of Penance. The chief result to be attained was a clear notion of the various sins and their species, of their relative grievousness and importance, and of the penance to be imposed for them. In order to ensure uniform procedure, it was necessary for ecclesiastical superiors to lay down more detailed directions; this they did either of their own accord or in answer to inquiries. Writings of this kind are the pastoral or canonical letters of St. Cyprian, St. Peter of Alexandria, St. Basil of Cappadocia, and St. Gregory of Nyssa; the decretals and synodal letters of a number of popes, as Siricius, Innocent, Celestine, Leo I, etc.; canons of several œcumenical councils. These decrees were collected at an early date and used by the bishops and priests as a norm in distinguishing sins and in imposing ecclesiastical penance for them.

The ascendancy of the so-called "penitential books" dated from the seventh century, when a change took place in the practice of ecclesiastical penance. Till then it had been a time-honoured law in the Church that the three capital crimes: apostasy, murder, and adultery, were to be atoned for by an accurately determined penance, which was public at least for public sins. This atonement, which consisted chiefly in severe fasts and public, humiliating practices, was accompanied by various religious ceremonies under the strict supervision of the Church; it included four distinct stations or classes of penitents and at times lasted from fifteen to twenty years. At an early period, however, the capital sins mentioned above were divided into sections, according as the circumstances were either aggravating or attenuating, and a correspondingly longer or shorter period of penance was set down for them. When in the course of centuries, entire nations, uncivilized and dominated by fierce passions, were received into the bosom of the Church, and when, as a result, heinous crimes began to multiply, many offences, akin to those mentioned above, were included among sins which were subject to canonical penances, while for others, especially for secret sins, the priest determined the penance, its duration and mode, by the canons. The seventh century brought with it a relaxation, not indeed in canonical penance, but in the ecclesiastical control; on the other hand, there was an increase in the number of crimes which demanded a fixed penance if discipline was to be maintained; besides, many hereditary rights of a particular nature, which had led to a certain mitigation of the universal norm of penance, had to be taken into consideration; substitutes and so-called *redemptiones*, which consisted in pecuniary donations to the poor or to public utilities, gradually gained entrance and vogue; all this necessitated the drawing up of comprehensive lists of the various crimes and of the penances to be imposed for them, so that a certain uniformity among confessors might be reached as to the treatment of penitents and the administration of the sacraments.

There appeared a number of "penitential books". Some of them, bearing the sanction of the Church, closely followed the ancient canonical decrees of the popes and the councils, and the approved statutes of St. Basil, St. Gregory of Nyssa, and others; others were merely private works, which, recommended by the renown of their authors, found a wide circulation, others again went too far in their decisions and hence constrained ecclesiastical superiors either to reprehend or condemn them. A more detailed account of these works will be found in another article.

These books were not written for a scientific, but for a practical, juridical purpose. Nor do they mark an advance in the science of moral theology, but rather a standing-still, nay, even a decadence. Those centuries of migrations, of social and political upheavals, offered a soil little adapted for a successful cultivation of the sciences, and though in the ninth century a fresh attempt was made to raise scientific studies to a higher level, still the work of the subsequent centuries consisted rather in collecting and renewing treasures of former centuries than in adding to them. This is true of moral-theological questions, no less than of other scientific branches. From this stagnation theology in general and moral theology in particular rose again to new life towards the end of the twelfth and the beginning of the thirteenth century. A new current of healthy development was noticeable in moral theology and that in two directions: one in the new strength infused into the practice of the confessors, the other in renewed vigour given to the speculative portion.

With the gradual dying out of the public penances, the "penitential books" lost their importance more and more. The confessors grew less concerned about the exact measure of penances than about the essential object of the sacrament, which is the reconciliation of the sinner with God. Besides, the "penitential books" were by far too defective for teaching confessors how to judge about the various sins, their consequences and remedies. In order to meet this need, St. Raymond of Penafort wrote towards the year 1235 the "Summa de pœnitentia et matrimonio". Like his famous collection of decretals, it is a repertory of canons on various matters, i. e. important passages from the Fathers, councils, and papal decisions. More immediately adapted for actual use was the "Summa de casibus conscientiæ", which was written about 1317 by an unknown member of the Order of St. Francis at Asti in Upper Italy, and which is, therefore, known as "Summa Astensana" or "Summa Astensis". Its eight books cover the whole subject matter of moral theology and the canonical decrees, both indispensable for the pastor and confessor: Book I, the Divine commandments; II, virtues and vices; III, contracts and wills; IV–VI, sacraments, except matrimony; VII, ecclesiastical censures; VIII, matrimony. The fourteenth and fifteenth centuries produced a number of similar *summæ* for confessors; all of them, however, discarded the arrangement in books and chapters, and adopted the alphabetical order. Their value is, of course, widely different. The following are the most important and most popular among them: The "Summa confessorum" of the Dominican Johannes of Freiburg (d. 1314), which was published a few years previous to the "Summa Astensis"; its high reputation and wide circulation was due to its revision by another member of the Dominican Order, Bartholomæus of Pisa (d. 1347), who arranged it alphabetically and supplemented its canonical parts; it is commonly known as the "Summa Pisana". This work served as the foundation for the "Summa angelica", a clear and concise treatise, composed about 1476 by the Franciscan Angelus Cerletus, called "Angelus a Clavasio" after his native city, Chiavasso. Its great popularity is attested by the fact that it went through at least thirty-one editions from 1476 to 1520. A like popularity was enjoyed by the "Summa casuum" of the Franciscan, J. B. Trovamala, which appeared a few years later (1484) and, after being revised by the author himself, in 1495, bore the title of "Summa rosella". One of the last and most renowned of these *summæ* was probably the "Summa Silvestrina" of the Dominican Silvester Prierias (d. 1523), after which moral theology began to be treated in a different manner. The *summæ* here mentioned, being exclusively written for the practical use of confessors, did not spurn the more elementary form; but they represented the results of a thorough, scientific study, which produced not only writings of this kind, but also other systematic works of a profound scholarship.

The twelfth century witnessed a busy activity in speculative theology, which centred about the cathedral and monastic schools. These produced men like Hugh and Richard of St. Victor, and especially Hugh's pupil, Peter the Lombard, called the Master of the Sentences, who flourished in the cathedral school of Paris towards the middle of the century, and whose "Libri sententiarum" served for several centuries as the standard text-book in theological lecture-halls. In those days, however, when dangerous heresies against the fundamental dogmas and mysteries of the Christian faith began to appear, the moral part of the Christian doctrine received scant treatment; Peter the Lombard incidentally discusses a few moral questions, as e. g., about sin, while speaking of creation and the original state of man, or more in particular, while treating of original sin. Other questions, e. g., about the freedom of our actions and the nature of human actions in general, are answered in the doctrine on Christ, where he discusses the knowledge and the will of Christ. Even the renowned commentator of the "Sentences", Alexander of Hales, O. Min., does not yet seriously enter into Christian morals. The work of constructing moral theology as a speculative science was at last undertaken and completed by that great luminary of theology, St. Thomas of Aquin, to whose "Summa theologica" we referred above. Aside from this masterpiece, of which the second part and portions of the third pertain to morals, there are several minor works extant which bear a moral and ascetical character; the last-named branch was cultivated with extraordinary skill by St. Bonaventure of the Franciscan Order, though he did not equal the systematic genius of St. Thomas.

This and the subsequent centuries produced a number of prominent theologians, some of whom contested various doctrines of Aquinas, as Duns Scotus and his adherents, while others followed in his footsteps and wrote commentaries on his works, as Ægidius Romanus and Capreolus. Nevertheless, purely moral-theological questions were rarely made the subject of controversy during this time; a new epoch in the method of moral theology did not dawn until after the Council of Trent. However, there are two extremely fertile writers of the fifteenth century who not only exerted a powerful influence on the advancement of theology but raised the standard of practical life. They are Dionysius the Carthusian and St. Antoninus, Bishop of Florence. The former is well known for his ascetical works, while the latter devoted himself to the practice of the confessional and the ordinary work of the pastor. His "Summa theologica" belongs specially to our subject. It went through several editions, and A. Ballerini's revision of it, which appeared in 1740 at Florence, contains four folios. The third volume treats chiefly of ecclesiastical law; it discusses at great length the legal position of the Church and its penal code. A few chapters of the first volume are devoted to the psychological side of man and his actions. The remainder of the whole work is a commentary, from the purely moral standpoint, on the second part of St. Thomas's "Summa theologica", to which it constantly refers. It is not a mere theoretical explanation, but is so replete with juridical and casuistical details that it may be called an inexhaustible fountain for manuals of casuistry. How highly the practical wisdom of Antoninus was esteemed even during his lifetime, is attested by the surname "Antoninus consiliorum", Antoninus of good counsel, given to him in the Roman Breviary.

A new life was breathed into the Catholic Church by the Council of Trent. Reformation of morals gave a fresh impetus to theological science. These had gradually fallen from the high level to which they had risen at the time of St. Thomas; the desire of solid advancement had frequently given place to seeking after clever argumentations on unimportant questions. The sixteenth century witnessed a complete change. Even before the council convened, there were eminent scholars of a serious turn of mind as Thomas of Vio (usually called Cajetanus), Victoria, and the two Sotos, all men whose solid knowledge of theology proved of immense benefit to the Council itself. Their example was followed by a long series of excellent scholars, especially Dominicans and members of the newly-founded Society of Jesus. It was above all the systematic side of moral theology which was now taken up with renewed zeal. In former centuries, Peter the Lombard's "Sentences" had been the universal text-book, and more prominent theological works of subsequent ages professed to be nothing else than commentaries upon them; henceforth, however, the "Summa theologica" of St. Thomas was followed as guide in theology and a large number of the best theological works, written after the Council of Trent, were entitled "Commentarii in Summam Sti. Thomæ". The natural result was a more extensive treatment of moral questions, since these constituted by far the largest portion of St. Thomas's "Summa". Among the earliest classical works of this kind is the "Commentariorum theologicorum tomi quattuor" of Gregory of Valentia (q. v.). It is well thought out and shows great accuracy; vols. III and IV contain the explanation of the "Prima Secundæ" and the "Secunda Secundæ" of St. Thomas. This work was succeeded, at the end of the sixteenth and the beginning of the seventeenth century, by a number of similar commentaries; among them stand out most prominently those of Gabriel Vásquez, Lessius, Suárez, Becanus, and the works of Thomas Sanchez "In decalogum" as well as "Consilia moralia", which are more casuistical in their method; the commentaries of Dominic Bánez, which had appeared some time before; and those of Medina (see MEDINA, BARTHOLOMEW; PROBABILISM).

Prominent among all those mentioned is Francis Suárez, S.J., in whose voluminous works the principal questions of the "Secunda" of St. Thomas are developed with great accuracy and a wealth of positive knowledge. Almost every question is searchingly examined, and brought nearer its final solution; the most varied opinions of former theologians are extensively discussed, subjected to a close scrutiny, and the final decision is given with great circumspection, moderation, and modesty. A large folio treats the fundamental questions of moral theology in general: (1) De fine et beatitudine; (2) De voluntario et involuntario, et de actibus humanis; (3) De bonitate et malitia humanorum actuum; (4) De passionibus et vitiis. Another volume treats of "Laws"; several folio volumes are devoted to treatises which do indeed belong to morals, but which are inseparably connected with other strictly dogmatic questions about God and His attributes, viz., "De gratia divina"; they are to-day assigned everywhere to dogma proper; a third series gives the entire doctrine of the sacraments (with the exception of matrimony) from their dogmatic and moral side. Not all of the various virtues were examined by Suárez; besides the treatise on the theological virtues, we possess only that on the virtue of religion. But if any of Suárez's works may be called classical it is the last-named, which discusses in four volumes the whole subject "De religione". Within the whole range of "religio", including its notion and relative position, its various acts and practices, as prayers, vows, oaths, etc., the sins against it, there can hardly be found a dogmatic or casuistic question that has not been either solved or whose solution has not at least been attempted. Of the last two volumes one treats of religious orders in general, the other of the "Institute" of the Society of Jesus.

In the course of the seventeenth and eighteenth century, there appeared a number of similar, though conciser, works which treat moral-theological questions as a part of universal theology with the genuine spirit of Scholastic science. There are those of Tanner, Coninck, Platel, Gotti, Billuart, and many others, the mere enumeration of whom would lead us too far afield. We must, however, mention one to whom nobody can deny the honour of having advanced both speculative and practical theology, and especially practical morals, John de Lugo. Endowed with uncommon, speculative genius and clear, practical judgment, he in many instances pointed out entirely new paths towards the solution of moral questions. Speaking of his moral theology, St. Alphonsus styles him "by all odds leader after St. Thomas". The works that have come down to us are: "De fide", "De incarnatione", "De justitia et jure", "De sacramentis", viz., "De sacramentis in genere", "De baptismo et eucharistia", and "De pœnitentia". It is above all the volume "De pœnitentia" which, through its sixteenth disputation, has become the classical handbook for casuistical moral theology and particularly for the specific distinction of sins; to the same subject belong the posthumous "Responsa moralia", a collection of answers given by de Lugo in complicated cases of conscience. This is not the place to point out his eminence as a dogmatist; suffice it to say that many far-reaching questions receive original solutions, which, though not universally accepted, have yet shed considerable light on these subjects.

The method which Lugo applies to moral theological questions, may well be called mixed, that is, it is both speculative and casuistical. Such works of a mixed character now grow common, they treat the whole subject-matter of moral theology, in as far as it is serviceable for the confessor and the pastor, in this mixed manner, though they insist more on casuistry than did Lugo. A type of this kind is the "Theologia moralis" of Paul Laymann (d. 1635); in this category may also be numbered the "Theologia decalogalis" and "Theologia sacramentalis" of Sporer (d. 1683), the "Conferentiæ" of Elbel (d. 1756), and the "Theologia moralis" of Reuter (d. 1762). Almost numberless are the manuals for confessors, written in a simple casuistical form, though even these justify their conclusions by internal reasons after legitimatizing them by an appeal to external authority. They are not unfrequently the fruit of thorough, speculative knowledge and extensive reading. One of the most solid is probably the "Manuale confessariorum et pœnitentium" of Azpilcueta (1494–1586), the great canonist, commonly known as "Doctor Navarrus"; furthermore, the "Instructio sacerdotum" or "Summa casuum conscientiæ" of Cardinal Tolet (d. 1596), which was highly recommended by St. Francis of Sales. One other work must also be mentioned, viz., the so-called "Medulla theologiæ moralis" of Hermann Busenbaum (d. 1688), which has become famous on account of its very extensive use (forty editions in less than twenty years during the lifetime of the author) and the number of its commentators. Among these are included Claude Lacroix, whose moral theology is considered as one of the most valuable of the eighteenth century, and St. Alphonsus Liguori, with whom, however, an entirely new epoch of moral theology commences.

Before entering upon this new phase, let us glance at the development of the so-called systems of morals and the controversies which sprang up among Catholic scholars, as well as at the casuistical method of treating moral theology in general. For it is precisely the casuistry of moral theology around which these controversies centre, and which has experienced severe attacks in our own day. These attacks were for the most part confined to Germany. The champions of the adversaries are J. B. Hirscher (d. 1865), Döllinger, Reusch, and a group of Catholic scholars who, in the years 1901 and 1902, demanded a "reform of Catholic moral theology", though all were not moved by the same spirit. In Hirscher it was the zeal for a supposedly good cause, though he was implicated in theological errors; Döllinger and Reusch attempted to cover their defection from the Church and their refusal to acknowledge the papal infallibility by holding up to the ridicule of the world ecclesiastical conditions and affairs which they thought militated against that infallibility; the latest phase of this opposition is mainly the result of misunderstandings. In order to elucidate the accusations brought against casuistry, we use the wholly unjustifiable criticism which Hirscher launched against Scholastic theology in general in his work of 1832, "On the Relation between the Gospel and Theological Scholasticism"; it is quoted approvingly by Döllinger and Reusch (Moralstreitigkeiten, 13 sqq.):—

(1) "Instead of penetrating into the spirit which makes virtue what it is and underlies everything that is good in this world, in other words, instead of beginning with the one indivisible nature of all goodness, they begin with the material of the various moral precepts and prohibitions without adverting to where these originate, on what foundation they rest, and what is their life-giving principle." This means that Scholastics and casuists know only individual things, see nothing universal and uniform in the virtues and duties.

(2) "Instead of deriving these precepts and prohibitions from the one, individual essence of all goodness and thereby creating certainty in the moral judgments of their audience, they, rejecting principles, string 'shalt' to 'shalt', provide them with innumerable statutes and clauses, confuse and oppress the hearer by the overflowing measure of duties, half-duties, non-duties." In other words, the Scholastics oppress and confuse by an unnecessary multiplication of duties and non-duties.

(3) "It is more in accordance with the spirit of Mosaism than with that of Christianity when Christian morality is treated less as a doctrine of virtues than of laws and duties, and when by adding commandment to commandment, prohibition to prohibition, it gives us a full and shaken measure of moral rules instead of building up on the Christian spirit, deriving everything from it and pointing out all particular virtues in its light." Or briefly, casuistry promotes exterior sanctimoniousness without the interior spirit.

(4) "Those who treat morals from the standpoint of casuistry, assign an important part to the distinction between grave and light laws, grave and light duties, serious and slight transgressions, mortal and venial sins. . . . Now, the distinction between grievous and venial sins is not without a solid foundation, and if it is chiefly based on the different qualities of the will, and if, besides, the various degrees of goodness and malice are measured by the presence, e. g., of a purely good and strong will, of one less pure and less strong, of a weak, inert, impure, malicious, perverted will, then nobody will raise his voice against it. But it is wholly different when the distinction between mortal and venial sins is taken objectively, and based on the gravity and lightness of the commandments. . . . Such a distinction between mortal and venial sins, founded on the material differences of the commandments and the prohibitions, is a source of torment and anxiety for many. . . . True morality cannot be advanced through such an anxiety. . . . The mass of the people will derive only this one profit from such a method: many will refrain from what is forbidden under pain of mortal sin and will do what is commanded under the same penalty, but they will care little for what is commanded or forbidden under pain of venial sin only; on the contrary they will seek a compensation in the latter for what they sacrificed to the grave commandments. But can we call the lives of such men Christian?" In other words, casuistry falsifies the consciences by distinguishing objectively between mortal and venial sins, leads to a contempt of the latter, and renders a genuinely Christian life impossible.

It is not difficult to refute all these accusations. One glance at the "Summa theologica" of St. Thomas will prove how incorrect is the first charge that Scholasticism and casuistry know only individual good acts and individual virtues, without inquiring into the foundation common to all virtues. Before treating the individual virtues and the individual duties, St. Thomas gives us a whole volume of discussions of a general nature, of which we may note the profound speculations on the last end, the goodness and malice of human actions, the eternal law.

The second accusation, that the Scholastic casuistry confuses the mind by its mass of duties and non-duties, can only mean that the Scholastic casuistry sets these up arbitrarily and contrary to truth. The complaint can only refer to those works and lectures which aim at the instruction of the clergy, pastors, and confessors. The reader or hearer who is confused or oppressed by this "mass of duties etc." shows by this very fact that he has not the talent necessary for the office of confessor or spiritual guide, that he should therefore choose another vocation.

The third charge, directed against Judaical hypocrisy which neglects the fostering of the interior life, is refuted by every work on casuistry, however meagre, for every one of them states most emphatically that, without the state of grace and a good intention, all external works, no matter how difficult and heroic, are valueless in the sight of God. Can the necessity of the internal spirit be brought out more clearly? And even if, in some cases, the external fulfilment of a certain work is laid down as the minimum demanded by God or the Church, without which the Christian would incur eternal damnation, yet this is not banishing the internal spirit, but designating the external fulfilment as the low-water mark of morality.

Lastly, the fourth charge springs from a very grave theological error. There can be no doubt that, in judging the heinousness of sin and in distinguishing between mortal and venial sins, the subjective element must be taken into consideration. However, every compendium of moral theology, no matter how casuistical, meets this requirement. Every manual distinguishes sins which arise from ignorance, weakness, malice, without, however, labelling all sins of weakness as venial sins, or all sins of malice as mortal sins; for there are surely minor acts of malice which cannot be said to cause the death of the soul. Every manual also takes cognizance of sins which are committed without sufficient deliberation, knowledge, or freedom: all these, even though the matter be grave, are counted as venial sins. On the other hand, every manual recognizes venial and grievous sins which are such by the gravity of the matter alone. Or who would, abstracting from everything else, put a jocose lie on a par with the denial of faith? But even in these sins, mortal or venial according to their object, the casuists lay stress on the personal dispositions in which the sin was actually committed. Hence, their universal principle: the result of a subjectively erroneous conscience may be that an action which is in itself only venial, becomes a mortal sin, and vice versa, that an action which is in itself mortally sinful, that is, constitutes a grave violation of the moral law, may be only a venial sin. Nevertheless, all theologians, also casuists, consider a correct conscience a great boon and hence endeavour, by their casuistic discussions, to contribute towards the formation of correct consciences, so that the subjective estimate of the morality of certain actions may coincide, as far as possible, with the objective norm of morality.

When, lastly, various opponents of the casuistical method object that the moralist occupies himself exclusively with sins and their analysis, with the "dark side" of human life, let them remember that it is physically impossible to say everything in one breath, that, just as in many other arts and sciences, a division of labour may also be advantageous for the science of moral theology, that the particular purpose of manuals and lectures may be limited to the education of skilled confessors and that this purpose may very well be fulfilled by centring attention on the dark side of human life. Nevertheless, it must be granted that this cannot be the only purpose of moral theology: a thorough discussion of all Christian virtues and the means of acquiring them is indispensable. If at any time this part of moral theology should be pushed to the background, moral theology would become one-sided and would need a revision, not by cutting down casuistry, but by devoting more time and energy to the doctrine of virtues in their scientific, parenetical, and ascetical aspect.

In all these branches of moral theology, a great advance was noticeable at the time of the Council of Trent. That more stress was laid on casuistry in particular, finds its explanation in the growing frequency of sacramental confession. This is freely conceded by our adversaries. Döllinger and Reusch say (op. cit., 19 sqq.): "The fact that casuistry underwent a further development after the sixteenth century, is connected with further changes in the penitential discipline. From that time on the custom prevailed of approaching the confessional more frequently, regularly before Communion, of confessing not only grievous, but also venial sins, and of asking the confessor's advice for all troubles of the spiritual life, so that the confessor became more and more a spiritual father and guide." The confessor needed this schooling and scientific training, which alone could enable him to give correct decisions in complex cases of human life, to form a correct estimate of moral goodness or defect, duty or violation of duty, virtue or vice. Now, it was inevitable that the confessor should meet cases where the existence or exact measure of the obligation remained obscure even after careful examination, where the moralist was therefore confronted by the question what the final decision in these cases should be: whether one was obliged to consider oneself bound when the duty was obscure and doubtful, or how one could remove this doubt and arrive at the definite conclusion that there was no strict obligation. That the former could not be the case, but that an obligation, to exist, must first be proved, had always been known and had been variously expressed in practical rules: "In dubiis benigniora sequenda", "odiosa sunt restringenda", etc. The basic principle, however, for solving such dubious cases and attaining the certitude necessary for the morality of an action was not always kept clearly in view. To establish this universal principle, was equivalent to establishing a moral system; and the various systems were distinguished by the principle to which each adhered.

The history of Probabilism is given under this title, suffice it to say here that from the middle of the seventeenth century when the violent discussion of this question begins, the development of moral theology coincides with that of Probabilism and of other Probabilistic systems; although these systems touch only a small portion of morals and of moral truths and nothing is farther from the truth than the opinion, so wide-spread among the adversaries of Catholic morals, that Probabilism gave a new shape and a new spirit to the whole of moral theology. Probabilism and the other systems of morals are concerned only about cases which are objectively doubtful; hence they abstract entirely from the wide sphere of certain, established truths. Now, the latter class is by far the larger in moral theology also; were it not so, human reason would be in a sorry plight, and Divine providence would have bestowed little care on the noblest of its visible creatures and on their highest goods, even in the supernatural order, in which a full measure of gifts and graces was showered upon those ransomed in Christ. The certain and undoubted portion includes all the fundamental questions of Christian morals; it comprises those principles of the moral order by which the relations of man to himself, to God, to his neighbour, and to the various communities are regulated; it embraces the doctrine of the last end of man and of the supernatural means of attaining this end. There is only a comparatively small number of objectively obscure and doubtful laws or duties that appeal to Probabilism or Antiprobabilism for a decision. However, as has been said, since the middle of the seventeenth century, the interest of moral theologians centred in the question about Probabilism or Antiprobabilism.

Just as far from the truth is the second opinion of the adversaries of Probabilism, viz., that this system induces people to evade the laws and hardens them into callousness. On the contrary, to moot the question of Probabilism at all, was the sign of a severely conscientious soul. He who proposes the question at all knows and confesses by that very fact: first, that it is not lawful to act with a doubtful conscience, that he who performs an action without being firmly convinced of its being allowed, commits sin in the sight of God; secondly, that a law, above all the Divine law, obliges us to take cognizance of it and that, therefore, whenever doubts arise about the probable existence of an obligation we must apply sufficient care in order to arrive at certainty, so that a frivolous disregard of reasonable doubts is in itself a sin against the submission due to God. In spite of all this, it may happen that all our pains and inquiries do not lead us to certainty, that solid reasons are found both for and against the existence of an obligation: under these circumstances, a conscientious man will naturally ask whether he must consider himself bound by the law or whether he can, by further reflections—reflex principles, as they are called—come to the plain conclusion that there is no obligation either to do or to omit the act in question. Were we obliged to consider ourselves bound in every doubt, the result, obviously, would be an intolerable severity. But since before performing an action the final verdict of our conscience must be free from doubt, the necessity of removing in one way or another such doubts as may have arisen, is self-evident.

At first there was a lack of clearness with regard to Probabilism and the questions connected with it. Conflicting definitions of opinion, probability, and certitude, could not but cause confusion. When works on moral theology and practical manuals began to multiply, it was inevitable that some individuals should take the word "probable" in too wide or in too lax a sense, although there can be no doubt that in itself it means "something acceptable to reason", in other words, since reason can accept nothing unless it has the appearance of truth, "something based on reasons which generally lead to the truth". Hence it is that opinions were actually advanced and spread as practicable which were little in accord with the demands of the Christian Faith, and which brought down upon them the censure of the Holy See. We refer particularly to the theses condemned by Alexander VII on 24 Sept., 1665, and on 18 March, 1666, and by Innocent XI on 2 March, 1679. It is not Probabilism that must be made responsible for them, but the vagaries of a few Probabilists.

As a result of these condemnations, some theologians thought themselves obliged to oppose the system itself and to side with Probabiliorism. Previous to this turn of affairs, the Jansenists had been the most pronounced adversaries of Probabilism. But they, too, had received a setback when Innocent X condemned (31 May, 1653) in the "Augustinus" of Jansenius, then recently deceased, the proposition: "Just men, with the strength now at their disposal, cannot keep certain commandments of God, even if they wish and endeavour to do so; besides, they are without the help of grace which might make it possible for them", was taken from the work and rejected as heretical and blasphemous. Now Probabilism was least reconcilable with this Jansenistic thesis, which could be maintained the easier, the stricter the moral obligations laid upon man's conscience were and the severer the system proclaimed as solely justified was. Consequently, the adherents of the Jansenistic doctrine endeavoured to attack Probabilism, to throw suspicion on it as an innovation, to represent it even as leading to sin. The exaggerations of a few Probabilists who went too far in their laxity, gave an opportunity to the Jansenists to attack the system, and soon a number of scholars, notably among the Dominicans, abandoned Probabilism, which they had defended till then, attacked it and stood up for Probabiliorism; some Jesuits also opposed Probabilism. But by far, the majority of the Jesuit writers as well as a vast number of other orders and of the secular clergy, adhered to Probabilism. An entire century was taken up with this controversy, which probably has not its equal in the history of Catholic theology.

Fortunately, the works on either side of this controversy were not popular writings. Nevertheless, exaggerated theories caused a glaring inequality and much confusion in the administration of the Sacrament of Penance and in the guidance of souls. This seems to have been the case particularly in France and Italy; Germany probably suffered less from Rigorism. Hence it was a blessing of Divine Providence that there arose a man in the middle of the eighteenth century, who again insisted on a gentler and milder practice, and who, owing to the eminent sanctity which he combined with solid learning, and which raised him soon after his death to the honour of the altar, received the ecclesiastical approbation of his doctrine, thereby definitively establishing the milder practice in moral theology.

This man is Alphonsus Maria Liguori, who died in 1787 at the age of 91, was beatified in 1816, canonized in 1839, and declared Doctor Ecclesiæ in 1871. In his youth Liguori had been imbued with the stricter principles of moral theology; but, as he himself confesses, the experience which a missionary life extending over fifteen years gave him, and careful study, brought him to a realization of their falseness and evil consequences. Chiefly for the younger members of the religious congregation which owed its existence to his fervent zeal, he worked out a manual of moral theology, basing it on the widely used "Medulla" of the Jesuit Hermann Busenbaum, whose theses he subjected to a thorough examination, confirmed by internal reasons and external authority, illustrated by adverse opinions, and here and there modified. The work, entirely Probabilistic in its principles, was first published in 1748. Received with universal applause and lauded even by popes, it went through its second edition in 1753; edition after edition then followed, nearly every one showing the revising hand of the author; the last, ninth, edition, published during the lifetime of the saint, appeared in 1785. After his beatification and canonization his "Theologia moralis" found an even wider circulation. Not only were various editions arranged, but it almost seemed as though the further growth of moral theology would be restricted to a reiteration and to compendious revisions of the works of St. Alphonsus. An excellent critical edition of the "Theologia moralis Sti. Alphonsi" is that of Léonard Gaudé, C.SS.R. (Rome, 1905), who has verified all the quotations in the work and illustrated it with scholarly annotations.

No future work on practical moral theology can pass without ample references to the writings of St. Alphonsus. Hence it would be impossible to gain a clear insight into the present state of moral theology and its development without being more or less conversant with the system of the saint, as narrated in the article PROBABILISM. The controversy, which is still being waged about Probabilism and Æquiprobabilism, has no significance unless the latter oversteps the limits set to it by St. Alphonsus and merges into Probabiliorism. However, though the controversy has not yet been abandoned theoretically, still in every-day practice it is doubtful if there is any one who follows other rules in deciding doubtful cases than those of Probabilism. This ascendancy of the milder school in moral theology over the more rigorous gained new impetus when Alphonsus was canonized and when the Church pointed out in particular that Divine Providence had raised him up as a bulwark against the errors of Jansenism, and that by his numerous writings he had blazed a more reliable path which the guides of souls might safely follow amid the conflicting opinions either too lax or too strict. During his lifetime the saint was forced to enter several literary disputes on account of his works on moral theology; his chief adversaries were Concina and Patuzzi, both of the Dominican Order, and champions of Probabiliorism.

The last decades of the eighteenth century may well be called a period of general decadence as far as the sacred sciences, moral theology included, are concerned. The frivolous spirit of the French Encyclopedists had infected, as it were, the whole of Europe. The Revolution, which was its offspring, choked all scientific life. A few words about the state of moral theology during this period may suffice. Italy was torn asunder by the dispute about Rigorism and a milder practice; in France, Rigorism had received the full rights of citizenship through the Jansenistic movement and held its own till late in the nineteenth century; Germany was swayed by a spirit of shallowness which threatened to dislodge Christian morals by rationalistic and natural principles. The "general seminaries" which Joseph II established in the Austrian states, engaged professors who did not blush to advance heretical doctrines and to exclude Christian self-restraint from the catalogue of moral obligations. Other German institutions, too, offered their chairs of theology to professors who had imbibed the ideas of "enlightenment", neglected to insist on Catholic doctrines of faith and, putting aside the supernatural life, sought the end and aim of education in a merely natural morality. But in the second decade of the nineteenth century the French Revolution had spent itself, quiet had again followed the turmoil, the political restoration of Europe had been begun. A restoration also of the ecclesiastical spirit and learning was also inaugurated and the gradual rise of moral theology became noticeable. Apart from the purely ascetical side, there are three divisions in which this new life was plainly visible: catechism, popular instruction, pastoral work.

Though it is the purpose of catechetical teaching to instruct the faithful in the entire range of Christian religion, in the doctrines of faith no less than in those of morals, yet the former may also be conceived and discussed with respect to the duties and the way by which man is destined to obtain his last end. Hence, the catechetical treatment of religious questions may be regarded as a portion of moral theology. During the period of "enlightenment", this branch had been degraded to a shallow moralizing along natural lines. But that it rose again in the course of the past century to a lucid explanation of the sum-total of the Christian doctrine, is attested by numerous excellent works, both catechisms and extensive discussions. To these may be added the more thorough manuals of Christian doctrine intended for higher schools, in which the apologetical and moral portions of religious instruction are treated scientifically and adapted to the needs of the time. There is nothing, however, which prevents us from placing these writings in the second of the above-mentioned classes, since their aim is the instruction of the Christian people, though principally the educated laymen. It is true these works belong exclusively, even less than the catechetical, to moral theology, since their subject-matter embraces the whole of the Christian doctrine, yet the morally destructive tendencies of Atheism and the new moral questions brought forward by the conditions of our times, impressed upon writers the importance of moral instruction in manuals of Catholic faith. The last decades in particular prove that this side of theology has been well taken care of. Various questions bearing on Christian morals were extensively treated in monographs, as e. g., the social question, the significance of money, the Church's doctrine on usury, the woman question, etc. To quote single works or to enter on the different subjects in detail would exceed the limits of this article.

The third line along which we noted an advance was called the pastoral, that is, instruction which has as its special aim the education and aid of pastors and confessors. That this instruction is necessarily, though not exclusively, casuistic, was mentioned above. The scarcity of priests, which was keenly felt in many places, occasioned a lack of time necessary for an all-round scientific education of the candidates for the priesthood. This circumstance explains why scientific manuals of moral theology, for decades, were merely casuistic compendia, containing indeed the gist of scientific investigations, but lacking in scientific argumentation. The correctness of ecclesiastical doctrine had been insured and facilitated by the approbation with which the Church distinguished the works of St. Alphonsus. Hence, many of these compendia are nothing else than recapitulations of St. Alphonsus's "Theologia moralis", or, if following a plan of their own, betray on every page that their authors had it always ready at hand. Two works may here find mention which enjoyed a wider circulation than any other book on moral theology and which are frequently used even to-day: the Scavini's "Theologia moralis universa", and the shorter "Compendium theologiæ moralis" by Jean-Pierre Gury, together with the numerous revisions which appeared in France, Germany, Italy, Spain, and North America.

We must not, however, deceive ourselves by concluding that, owing to the ecclesiastical approbation of St. Alphonsus and his moral writings, moral theology is now settled forever and, so to speak, crystallized. Nor does this approbation assure us that all individual questions have been solved correctly, and therefore the discussion of certain moral questions remains still open. The Apostolic See itself, or rather the Sacred Penitentiary, when asked, "Whether a professor of moral theology may quietly follow and teach the opinions which St. Alphonsus Liguori teaches in his Moral Theology", gave indeed an affirmative answer on 5 July, 1831; it added, however, "but those must not be reprehended who defend other opinions supported by the authority of reliable doctors". He who would conclude the guarantee of absolute correctness from the ecclesiastical approbation of the saint's works, would make the Church contradict herself. St. Thomas of Aquin was at least as solemnly approved for the whole field of theology as St. Alphonsus for moral theology. Yet, e. g, on the subject of the efficacy of grace, which enters deeply into morals, St. Thomas and St. Alphonsus defend wholly contradictory opinions; both cannot be right, and so may be freely discussed. The same may be said of other questions. In our own days, Antonio Ballerini above all made a simple use of this freedom of discussion, first in his annotations to Gury's "Compendium", then in his "Opus theologicum morale", which was recast and edited after his death by Dominic Palmieri. It rendered an eminent service to casuistry; for though we cannot approve of everything, yet the authority of various opinions has been carefully sifted and fully discussed.

Lately, attempts have been made to develop moral theology along other lines. The reformers assert that the casuistical method has choked every other and that it must give place to a more scientific, systematic treatment. It is evident that a merely casuistical treatment does not come up to the demands of moral theology, and as a matter of fact, during the last decades, the speculative element was more and more insisted on even in works chiefly casuistic. Whether the one or the other element should prevail, must be determined according to the proximate aim which the work intends to satisfy. If there is question of a purely scientific explanation of moral theology which does not intend to exceed the limits of speculation, then the casuistical element is without doubt speculative, systematic discussion of the questions belonging to moral theology; casuistry then serves only to illustrate the theoretical explanations. But if there is question of a manual which is intended for the practical needs of a pastor and confessor and for their education, then the solid, scientific portion of general moral-theological questions must be supplemented by an extensive casuistry. Nay, when time and leisure are wanting to add ample theoretical explanations to an extensive casuistical drill, we should not criticize him who would under these circumstances insist on the latter at the expense of the former; it is the more necessary in actual practice.

SLATER, *A Short History of Moral Theology* (New York, 1909); BOUQUILLON, *Theologia moralis fundamentalis*, (3rd ed., Bruges, 1903), Introductio; BUCCERONI, *Commentar. de natura theologiæ moralis* (Rome, 1910); SCHMITT, *Zur Gesch. des Probabilismus* (1904); MAUSBACH, *Die kathol. Moral, ihre Methoden, Grundsätze und Aufgaben* (2nd ed. 1902); MEYENBERG, *Die kath. Moral als Angeklagte* (2nd ed. 1902); KRAWUTZKI, *Einleitung in das Studium der kath. Moraltheologie* (2nd. ed. 1898); GERIGK, *Die wissenschaftliche Moral und ihre Lehrweise* (1910).

AUG. LEMKUHL.

III. PASTORAL THEOLOGY, the science of the care of souls. This article will give the definition of pastoral theology, its relations to other theological sciences, its history, sources, and contents.

A. *Definition*.—Pastoral theology is a branch of practical theology; it is essentially a practical science. All branches of theology, whether theoretical or practical, purpose in one way or another to make priests "the ministers of Christ, and the dispensers of the mysteries of God" (I Cor., iv, 1). Pastoral theology presupposes other various branches; accepts the apologetic, dogmatic, exegetic, moral, juridical, ascetical, liturgical, and other conclusions reached by the ecclesiastical student, and scientifically applies these various conclusions to the priestly ministry.

B. *Relation to Other Theological Sciences*.— Dogmatic theology establishes the Church as the depository of revealed truth and systematizes the deposit of faith which Christ entrusted to His Church to hand down to all generations; pastoral theology teaches the priest his part in this work of Catholic and Christian tradition of revealed truth. Moral theology explains the laws of God and of the Church, the means of grace and hindrances thereto; pastoral theology teaches the practical bearing of these laws, means, and hindrances upon the daily life of the priest, alone and in touch with his people. Canon law collects, correlates, and co-ordinates the laws of the Church; pastoral theology applies those laws to the care of souls. In brief, pastoral theology begins where the other theological sciences leave off; takes the results of them all and makes these results effective for the salvation of souls through the ministry of the priesthood established by Christ.

C. *History*.—The name pastoral theology is new;

the science is as old as the Church itself, as appears from the manifold instructions given by Jesus to His Apostles for the care of souls (Matt., x, 6 sqq.; Mark, vi, 8 sqq.; Luke, ix, 3 sqq.; x, 4 sqq.; xxii, 35) and from the pastoral letters of St. Paul and the very detailed instructions they give to Timothy and to Titus in regard to the sacred ministry. The writings of the Fathers, from the Apostolic age onward, are replete with pastoral instruction. St. Ignatius of Antioch [A. D. 110 (Harnack)] scatters such advice throughout his epistles—see, for instance, "Ad Magnesios" (Harnack's ed., "Patres apostolici", II, 29). The letters of St. Cyprian (A. D. 248) are, many of them, either wholly or in part written about the care of souls (cf. P. L., IV, 194 sq.)—"Qui Antistites in ecclesia eligendi?" "Qualis esse debeat vita sacerdotum?" etc. His "De lapsis" (P. L., IV, 477) is a classic among pastoral instructions. St. Gregory Nazianzen (A. D. 389), explaining his flight to Pontus, tells his ideas of the pastor of souls in "Oratio apologetica de fuga sua", a work sometimes called "De sacerdotio" (P. G., XXXV, 408), and sets down pastoral care as a great science and art, "Ars quædam artium et scientia scientiarum mihi esse videtur hominem regere". Other landmarks in the history of pastoral theology are St. Ambrose, "De officiis ministrorum" (P. L., XVI, 25); St. John Chrysostom, "De sacerdotio" (P. G., XLVIII, 623); St. Isidore of Seville, "De institutione clericorum", "De institutionibus monachorum", "De regulis clericorum" (P. L., LXXXIV, 25, 45, 77); St. Bernard's letters and treatises "De consideratione", "De moribus episcoporum", "De conversione ad clericos" (P. L., CLXXXII, 727, 809, 833). The great classic among patristic works on the care of souls is "Regulæ pastoralis liber" (P. L., LXXVII, 13), written by St. Gregory the Great (c. A. D. 590) to John, Bishop of Ravenna.

During the Middle Ages, there was not yet a separated and systematized science of pastoral theology. Scholasticism did not recognize this science apart from other branches of theology. Dogma and moral were so taught as to include the application of their conclusions to the care of souls. Still, even then writings of the great Doctors of the Church were at times purely pastoral; such were the "Opuscula", 17–20, of St. Thomas Aquinas; St. Bonaventure's "De sex alis seraphim", "De regimine animæ", "Confessionale"; the "Summa theologica" (Books II, III), together with the "Summa confessionalis" of St. Antoninus, Bishop of Florence. At the same time, writers on mystical theology (see V. MYSTICAL THEOLOGY) have often entered into the domain of pastoral theology. Not until the period of the Counter-Reformation did the science of pastoral theology take its present systematized form. During the latter half of the fifteenth century, in certain places, pastoral duties were very much neglected. By the dawn of the sixteenth century, the care of souls was to many priests and not a few bishops a lost or a never-acquired art, with the result that the laity were ready to throw off what was deemed to be a useless clerical yoke. In such places, a reform of the clergy was sorely needed. The Council of Trent set itself to bring about a true reformation of the priesthood. Catholic bishops and theologians followed the lead of the council. The result was the treatment of the care of souls as a science by itself. During the following centuries of true reform and of battle with false reform, the most scientific treatises on pastoral duties and rights were written. John of Avila, Louis of Granada, Peter de Soto, Claude le Jay (Institutiones practicæ), Neumayr (Vir apostolicus), Possevin (Praxis curæ pastoralis), Segneri, Olier, Molina, Toledo (De instructione sacerdotum), Cardinal Cajetan, St. Charles Borromeo (Instructio pastorum), the works of St. Francis de Sales, of Rodriguez, of Scaramelli—such are a few of the scientific treatises that did much to illumine and to strengthen the pastors of the Counter-Reformation. In 1759 St. Alphonsus Liguori issued his great pastoral theology, "Homo apostolicus". He epitomized the conclusions reached by him in his "Moral Theology", applied these conclusions practically to the work of hearing confessions, and added four appendices bearing specifically upon such pastoral duties as the direction of souls, the assistance of the dying, the examination of those to be ordained priests, and the duties of confessors and pastors in regard to their own as well as their flock's sanctification. This work, together with the legislation of Benedict XIV in the matter of diocesan synods, gave a great impetus to the science of pastoral theology.

D. *Sources.*—Tradition and Holy Writ, in so far as they portray the ideal Priest, Teacher, and Pastor, and hand down to us His ideas for the care of souls, are the first sources of pastoral theology. As evidence of Tradition the decrees of general councils are of the highest moment. Next come pontifical Constitutions—Bulls, Briefs, and Motu Proprios; decrees of Roman Congregations; the works cited in Sanford-Drum, op. cit. below; the various sources of dogmatic and moral theology and of canon law, in so far as they bear directly or indirectly upon the care of souls. Decrees of various provincial councils and diocesan synods together with pastoral letters of archbishops and bishops are also among the sources whence pastoral theology draws. For ecclesiastical legislation, one must follow the "Acta Apostolicæ Sedis", a monthly official bulletin published in Rome; the promulgation of laws, authentic interpretations, decisions and rescripts of the Roman Curia is now effected *ipso facto* by publication in this periodical. For past decisions, the various *decreta authentica* of different Roman Congregations must be consulted. Such are "Thesaurus resolutionum Sacræ Congregationis Concilii", from 1718 (Rome); "Decreta authentica Congregationis Sacrorum Rituum" (Rome, 1898); "Decreta authentica sacræ Congregationis Indulgentiis Sacrisque Reliquiis Præpositæ", from 1668 to 1882 (Ratisbon); Pallottini, "Collectio omnium decretorum Sacræ Congregationis Concilii" (Rome, 1868); Bizarri, "Collectanea Sacræ Congregationis Episcoporum et Regularium" (Rome, 1863, 1885); "Collectanea Sacræ Congregationis de Propaganda Fide" (Rome, 1893, 1907). A handy reference work in this matter is Ferraris, "Prompta bibliotheca", together with its supplement edited by Bucceroni (Rome, 1885). Ojetti, "Synopsis rerum moralium et juris pontificii" (Prato, 1904), is also useful. For the pastoral care of religious communities, necessary information may be obtained from Vermeersch, "De religiosis et missionariis supplementa et monumenta", together with the periodical supplements thereto (Bruges, 1904——), and Dom Bastien, "Constitution de Léon XIII sur les instituts à vœux simples et leur relations avec les autorités diocésaines" (Bruges), a work which has been translated into English by Lanslots (Pustet, New York). Periodicals giving current direction and information as to the care of souls are: "Acta Sanctæ Sedis" (Rome, from 1865), now discontinued; "Analecta juris pontificii" (Rome, 1833; Paris, 1869), replaced by "Analecta ecclesiastica" (Rome, 1893–1911); "Il Monitore Ecclesiastico" (Rome, 1876); "The American Ecclesiastical Review" (Philadelphia, 1889); "The Irish Ecclesiastical Record" (Dublin, 1865); "Nouvelle Revue Théologique" (Tournai, 1869); "Theologischpraktische Quartalschrift" (Linz); "Zeitschrift für katholische Theologie" (Innsbruck, 1877).

E. *Contents.*—From the days when St. Gregory the Great wrote his classic "Regulæ pastoralis liber", the duties that make for the care of souls have been conveniently divided into those of the teacher, of the minister of the sacred mysteries, and of the shepherd; pastoral theology purposes to impart the knowledge of these duties and of the treatise known as "pastoral medicine", the medical knowledge requisite for the proper care of souls.

Under the head of teacher are treated the duty of teaching, the qualities of the teacher, his training, the models of teaching left us by the Fathers and Doctors of the Church, as well as by distinguished preachers and catechists, and the occasions and forms of instruction suited for the various needs of the faithful, young and old, literate and illiterate. The Council of Trent, in the fifth session, lays down a twofold duty of the teacher, to preach on Sundays and festivals, and to give catechetical instruction to children and to others who have need of such instruction. Benedict XIV, in his Constitution, "Etsi Minime", calls special attention to this latter most important duty. Pius X, in his Encyclical on the teaching of Christian doctrine (15 April, 1905), insists once again on the paramount need of catechetical instruction. All parish priests, and all others to whom the care of souls is committed, must teach the catechism to their young girls and boys for the space of one hour on all Sundays and holy days of the year without exception, and must explain to them what one is bound to believe and practise in order to be saved. These children shall, at stated times during each year, be prepared by more extended instruction for the Sacraments of Penance and Confirmation. Daily instruction during Lent, and even after Easter, will make the young children of both sexes ready for their first Holy Communion. Moreover, an hour every Sunday and holy day shall be devoted to the catechetical instruction of adults. This lesson in catechism, in plain and simple language, is to be given over and above the Sunday homily on the Gospel and the children's instruction in Christian doctrine.

As minister of the sacred mysteries, the priest must not only know the nature of the sacraments, so far as dogmatic theology explains it, besides what is needed for their valid administration, as taught in moral theology, but must also possess such additional knowledge as may serve him in his spiritual ministrations—for instance, in attending the sick, in advising what is lawful or unlawful in critical operations, especially in such as may affect childbirth; in directing others, when necessary, how to baptize the unborn child; in deciding whether to confer extreme unction or other sacraments in cases of apparent death, etc.

Finally, as pastor, a variety of duties have to be mastered, which keep growing and varying in number constantly with the complicated conditions of modern life, especially wherever there is a tendency to mass people together in large cities, or wherever migration to and fro causes frequent change. This, perhaps, is the main part of pastoral theology. The organization of parishes; the maintenance of a church and other institutions that grow up around it; the management of parish schools; the formation of societies for men and women, young and old; the vast number of social works into which a priest in a modern city is almost necessarily drawn—all these points furnish material for instruction, which, as the fruit of experience, can rarely be conveyed through books. Usually the priest acquires sufficient knowledge of all these things from prudent directors as he goes through his seminary course, or from his own experience under a competent pastor; but gradually an extensive literature on these subjects has accumulated during the past half century, and it is the systematization of such writings that constitutes pastoral theology.

The chief authorities down to the time of St. Alphonsus, *Homo apostolicus* (1759), have already been mentioned in the body of the article. Since (1759) have appeared the *Pastoral Theologies* of Gollowitz-Wiedemann (Ratisbon, 1836); Amberger (1850); Stang (New York, 1897); Schulze (Milwaukee, 1906); Alberti (Rome, 1901–1904); Poey (Montrejeau, 1912); Neumayr, ed. De Auer, *Vir Apostolicus* (Schaffhausen, 1853); Reuter, ed. Lehmkuhl, *Neo-confessarius* (Freiburg im Br., 1905); Zenner, *Instructio practica confessarii* (Vienna, 1840); Frassinetti, *Parish Priests' Manual*; Berardi, *Praxis confessarii* (Faenza, 1899); Heuser, *The Parish Priest on Duty* (New York); Krieg, *Wissenschaft der Seelenleitung* (Freiburg im Br.). For questions on pastoral medicine, the following works are of use: Eschbach, *Disputationes physiologico-theologicæ* (Rome, 1901); Antonelli, *De conceptu impotentiæ et sterilitatis relate ad matrimonium* (Rome, 1900); Debreyne-Ferrand, *La théologie morale et les sciences medicales* (Paris, 1884); Surbled, *La morale dans ses rapports avec la médicine et l'hygiène* (Paris, 1897); *Pastoral Medicine* by Stöhr (Freiburg im Br., 1878); von Olfers (Freiburg im Br., 1881); Capellmann (Aachen, 1901); O'Malley and Walsh (New York, 1907); Sanford-Drum (New York, 1905); Antonelli (Rome, 1909).

WALTER DRUM.

Ascetical Theology.—Ascetics, as a branch of theology, may be briefly defined as the scientific exposition of Christian asceticism. Asceticism (ἄσκησις, ἀσκεῖν), taken in its literal signification, means a polishing, a smoothing or refining. The Greeks used the word to designate the exercises of the athletes, whereby the powers dormant in the body were developed and the body itself was trained to its full natural beauty. The end for which these gymnastic exercises were undertaken was the laurel-wreath bestowed on the victor in the public games. Now the life of the Christian is, as Christ assures us, a struggle for the kingdom of heaven (Matt., xi, 12). To give his readers an object-lesson of this spiritual battle and moral endeavour, St. Paul, who had been trained in the Greek fashion, uses the picture of the Greek pentathlon (I Cor., ix, 24). The exercises to be assumed in this combat tend to develop and strengthen the moral stamina, while their aim is Christian perfection leading up to man's ultimate end, union with God. Human nature having been weakened by original sin and ever inclining toward what is evil, this end cannot be reached except at the price of overcoming, with God's grace, many and serious obstacles. The moral struggle then consists first of all in attacking and removing the obstacles, that is the evil concupiscences (concupiscence of the flesh, concupiscence of the eyes, and pride of life), which effects of original sin serve to try and test man (Trid., Sess. V, De peccato originali). This first duty is called by the Apostle Paul the putting off of "the old man" (Eph., iv, 22). The second duty, in the words of the same Apostle, is to "put on the new man" according to the image of God (Eph., iv, 24). The new man is Christ. It is our duty then to strive to become like unto Christ, seeing that He is "the way, and the truth, and the life" (John, xiv, 6), but this endeavour is based on the supernatural order and, therefore, cannot be accomplished without Divine grace. Its foundation is laid in baptism, whereby we are adopted as sons of God through the imparting of sanctifying grace. Thenceforth, it must be perfected by the supernatural virtues, the gifts of the Holy Ghost, and actual grace. Since, then, ascetics is the systematic treatise of the striving after Christian perfection, it may be defined as the scientific guide to the acquisition of Christian perfection, which consists in expressing within ourselves, with the help of Divine grace, the image of Christ, by practising the Christian virtues, and applying the means given for overcoming the obstacles. Let us subject the various elements of this definition to a closer examination.

A. *Nature of Christian Perfection.*—(1) To begin with, we must reject the false conception of the Protestants who fancy that Christian perfection, as understood by Catholics, is essentially negative asceticism (cf. Seberg in Herzog-Hauck, "Realencyklopädie für prot. Theologie", III, 138), and that the correct notion of asceticism was discovered by the Reformers. There can be no doubt as to the Catholic position, if we but hearken to the clear voices of St. Thomas and St. Bonaventure. For these masters of Catholic theology, who never tired of repeating that the ideal of asceticism upheld by them was the ideal of the Catholic past, of the Fathers, of Christ Himself, emphatically state that bodily asceticism has not an absolute, but only a relative, value. St. Thomas calls it a "means to an end", to be used with discretion. St. Bonaventure says that bodily austerities "prepare, foster, and preserve perfection" (ad perfectionem præparans et ipsam promovens et conservans; "Apolog. pauperum", V, c. viii). In proof of his thesis, he shows that to put an absolute value on bodily asceticism would lead to Manichæism. He also points to Christ, the ideal of Christian perfection, who was less austere in fasting than John the Baptist, and to the founders of religious orders, who prescribed fewer ascetic exercises for their communities than they themselves practised (cf. J. Zahn, "Vollkommenheitsideal" in "Moralprobleme", Freiburg, 1911, p. 126 sqq.). On the other hand, Catholics do not deny the importance of ascetic practices for acquiring Christian perfection. Considering the actual condition of human nature, they declare these necessary for the removal of obstacles and for the liberation of man's moral forces, thus claiming for asceticism a positive character. A like value is put upon those exercises which restrain and guide the powers of the soul. Consequently, Catholics actually fulfil and always have fulfilled what Harnack sets down as a demand of the Gospel and what he pretends to have looked for in vain among Catholics; for they do "wage battle against mammon, care, and selfishness, and practise that charity which loves to serve and to sacrifice itself" (Harnack, "Essence of Christianity"). The Catholic ideal, then, is by no means confined to the negative element of asceticism, but is of a positive nature.

(2) The essence of Christian perfection is love. St. Thomas (Opusc. de perfectione christ., c. ii) calls that perfect which is conformable to its end (*quod attingit ad finem ejus*). Now, the end of man is God, and what unites him, even on earth, most closely with God is love (I Cor., vi, 17; I John, iv, 16). All the other virtues are subservient to love or are its natural prerequisites, as faith and hope. Love seizes man's whole soul (intellect, will), sanctifies it, and fuses new life into it. Love lives in all things and all things live in love and through love. Love imparts to all things the right measure and directs them all to the last end. "Love is thus the principle of unity, no matter how diversified are the particular states, vocations, and labours. There are many provinces, but they constitute one realm. The organs are many, but the organism is one" (Zahn, l. c., p. 146). Love has, therefore, rightly been called "the bond of perfection" (Col., iii, 14) and the fulfilment of the law (Rom., xiii, 8). That Christian perfection consists in love has ever been the teaching of Catholic ascetical writers. A few testimonies may suffice. Writing to the Corinthians, Clement of Rome says (Ep. I Cor., xlix, 1): "It was love that made all the elect perfect; without love nothing is acceptable to God" (ἐν τῇ ἀγάπῃ ἐτελειώθησαν πάντες οἱ ἐκλεκτοὶ τοῦ θεοῦ, δίχα ἀγάπης οὐδὲν εὐάρεστόν ἐστιν τῷ θεῷ; Funk, "Patr. apost.", p. 163). The "Epistle of Barnabas" insists that the way of light is "the love of him who created us" (ἀγαπήσεις τὸν σε ποιήσαντα; Funk, l. c., p. 91), "a love of our neighbour that does not even spare our own life" (ἀγαπήσεις τὸν πλησίον σου ὑπὲρ τὴν ψυχήν σου), and it affirms that perfection is nothing else than "love and joy over the good works which testify to justice" (ἀγάπη εὐφροσύνης καὶ ἀγαλλιάσεως ἔργων δικαιοσύνης μαρτυρία). St. Ignatius never wearies in his letters of proposing faith as the light and love as the way, love being the end and aim of faith ("Ad Ephes.", ix, xiv; "Ad Philad.", ix; "Ad Smyrn.", vi). According to the "Didache", love of God and of one's neighbour is the beginning of the "way of life" (c. i), and in the "Epistle to Diognetus" active love is called the fruit of belief in Christ. The "Pastor" of Hermas acknowledges the same ideal when he sets down "a life for God" (ζῆν τῷ θεῷ) as the sum-total of human existence. To these Apostolic Fathers may be added St. Ambrose (De fuga sæculi, c. iv, 17; c. vi, 35–36) and St. Augustine, who regards perfect justice as tantamount to perfect love. Both St. Thomas and St. Bonaventure speak the same language, and their authority is so overpowering that the ascetical writers of all subsequent centuries have faithfully followed in their footsteps (cf. Lutz, "Die kirchl. Lehre von den evang. Räten", Paderborn, 1907, pp. 26–99).

However, though perfection is essentially love, it is not true that any degree of love is sufficient to constitute moral perfection. The ethical perfection of the Christian consists in the perfection of love, which requires such a disposition "that we can act with speed and ease even though many obstacles obstruct our path" (Mutz, "Christl. Ascetik", 2nd ed., Paderborn, 1909). But this disposition of the soul supposes that the passions have been subdued; for it is the result of a laborious struggle, in which the moral virtues, steeled by love, force back and quell the evil inclinations and habits, supplanting them by good inclinations and habits. Only then has it really become "a man's second nature, as it were, to prove his love of God at certain times and under certain circumstances, to practise virtue and, as far as human nature may, to preserve his soul even from the slightest taints" (Mutz, l. c., p. 43). Owing to the weakness of human nature and the presence of the evil concupiscence (*fomes peccati*: Trid., Sess. VI, can. xxiii), a perfection that would exclude every defect cannot be attained in this life without a special privilege (cf. Prov., xx, 9; Eccl., vii, 21; James, iii, 2). Likewise, perfection, on this side of the grave, will never reach such a degree that further growth is impossible, as is clear from the mind of the Church and the nature of our present existence (*status viæ*); in other words, our perfection will always be relative. As St. Bernard says: "An unflagging zeal for advancing and a continual struggle for perfection is itself perfection" (Indefessus proficiendi studium et iugis conatus ad perfectionem, perfectio reputatur; "Ep. ccliv ad Abbatem Guarinum"). Since perfection consists in love, it is not the privilege of one particular state, but may be, and has as a fact been, attained in every state of life (cf. PERFECTION, CHRISTIAN AND RELIGIOUS). Consequently it would be wrong to identify perfection with the so-called state of perfection and the observance of the evangelical counsels. As St. Thomas rightly observes, there are perfect men outside the religious orders and imperfect men within them (Summa theol., II–II, Q. clxxxiv, a. 4). True it is that the conditions for realizing the ideal of a Christian life are, generally speaking, more favourable in the religious state than in the secular avocations. But not all are called to the religious life, nor would all find in it their contentment (cf. COUNSELS, EVANGELICAL). To sum up, the end is the same, the means are different. This sufficiently answers Harnack's objection (Essence of Christianity) that the Church considers the perfect imitation of Christ possible only for the monks, while she accounts the life of a Christian in the world as barely sufficient for the attainment of the last end.

(3) The ideal, to which the Christian should conform and towards which he should strive with all his powers both natural and supernatural, is Jesus Christ. His justice should be our justice. Our whole life should be so penetrated by Christ that we become Christians in the full sense of the word ("until Christ be formed in you"; Gal., iv, 19). That Christ is the supreme model and pattern of the Christian life is proved from Scripture, as e. g. from John, xiii, 15, and I Peter, ii, 21, where imitation of Christ is directly recommended, and from John, viii, 12, where Christ is called "the light of the world". Cf. also Rom., viii, 29, Gal., ii, 20, Phil., iii, 8, and Heb., i, 3, where the

Apostle extols the excellent knowledge of Jesus Christ, for whom he has suffered the loss of all things, counting them but as dung, that he may gain Christ. Of the numerous testimonies of the Fathers we only quote that of St. Augustine, who says: "Finis ergo noster perfectio nostra esse debet; perfectio nostra Christus" (P. L., XXXVI, 628; cf. also "In Psalm.", 26, 2, in P. L., XXXVI, 662). In Christ there is no shadow, nothing one-sided. His Divinity guarantees the purity of the model; His humanity, by which He became similar to us, makes the model attractive. But this picture of Christ, unmarred by addition or omission, is to be found only in the Catholic Church and, owing to her indefectibility, will always continue there in its ideal state. For the same reason, the Church alone can give us the guarantee that the ideal of the Christian life will always remain pure and unadulterated, and will not be identified with one particular state or with a subordinate virtue (cf. Zahn, l. c., p. 124). An unprejudiced examination proves that the ideal of Catholic life has been preserved in all its purity through the centuries and that the Church has never failed to correct the false touches with which individuals might have sought to disfigure its unstained beauty. The individual features and the fresh colours for outlining the living picture of Christ are derived from the sources of Revelation and the doctrinal decisions of the Church. These tell us about the internal sanctity of Christ (John, i, 14; Col., ii, 9; Heb., i, 9; etc.). His life overflowing with grace, of whose fulness we have all received (John, i, 16), His life of prayer (Mark, i, 21, 35; iii, 1; Luke, v, 16; vi, 12; ix, 18; etc.), His devotion to His heavenly Father (Matt., xi, 26; John, iv, 34; v, 30; viii, 26, 29), His intercourse with men (Matt., ix, 10; cf. I Cor., ix, 22), His spirit of unselfishness and sacrifice, His patience and meekness, and, finally, His asceticism as revealed in his fastings (Matt., iv, 2; vi, 18).

B. *Dangers of the Ascetical Life.*—The second task of ascetical theology is to point out the dangers which may frustrate the attainment of Christian perfection and to indicate the means by which they can be avoided successfully. The first danger to be noticed is evil concupiscence. A second danger lies in the allurements of the visible creation, which occupy man's heart to the exclusion of the highest good; to the same class belong the enticements of the sinful, corrupt world (I John, v, 19), that is, those men who promulgate vicious and ungodly doctrines and thereby dim or deny man's sublime destiny, or who by perverting ethical concepts and by setting a bad example give a false tendency to man's sensuality. Thirdly, ascetics acquaints us not only with the malice of the devil, lest we should fall a prey to his cunning wiles, but also with his weakness, lest we should lose heart. Finally, not satisfied with indicating the general means to be used for waging a victorious combat, ascetics offers us particular remedies for special temptations (cf. Mutz, "Ascetik", 2nd ed., p. 107 sqq.).

C. *Means for Realizing the Christian Ideal.*— (1) Prayer, above all, in its stricter meaning, is a means of attaining perfection; special devotions approved by the Church and the sacramental means of sanctification have a special reference to the striving after perfection (frequent confession and communion). Ascetics proves the necessity of prayer (II Cor., iii, 5) and teaches the mode of praying with spiritual profit; it justifies vocal prayers and teaches the art of meditating according to the various methods of St. Peter of Alcantara, of St. Ignatius, and other saints, especially the "tres modi orandi" of St. Ignatius. An important place is assigned to the examination of conscience, and justly so, because ascetical life wanes or waxes with its neglect or careful performance. Without this regular practice, a thorough purification of the soul and progress in spiritual life are out of the question. It centres the searchlight of the interior vision on every single action: all sins, whether committed with full consciousness or only half voluntarily, even the negligences which, though not sinful, lessen the perfection of the act, all are carefully scrutinized (*peccata, offensiones, negligentiæ;* cf. "Exercitia spiritualia" of St. Ignatius, ed. P. Roothaan, p. 3). Ascetics distinguishes a twofold examination of conscience: one general (*examen generale*), the other special (*examen particulare*), giving at the same time directions how both kinds may be made profitable by means of certain practical and psychological aids. In the general examination we recall all the faults of one day; in the particular, on the contrary, we focus our attention on one single defect and mark its frequency, or on one virtue to augment the number of its acts.

Ascetics encourages visits to the Blessed Sacrament (*visitatio sanctissimi*), a practice meant especially to nourish and strengthen the divine virtues of faith, hope, and charity. It also inculcates the veneration of the saints, whose virtuous lives should spur us on to imitation. It is plain that imitation cannot mean an exact copying. What ascetics proposes as the most natural method of imitation is the removal or at least the lessening of the contrast existing between our own lives and the lives of the saints, the perfecting, as far as is possible, of our virtues, with due regard to our personal disposition and the surrounding circumstances of time and place. On the other hand, the observation that some saints are more to be admired than imitated must not lead us into the mistake of letting our works be weighted with the ballast of human comfort and ease, so that we at last look with suspicion on every heroic act, as though it were something that transcended our own energy and could not be reconciled with the present circumstances. Such a suspicion would be justified only if the heroic act could not at all be made to harmonize with the preceding development of our interior life. Christian ascetics must not overlook the Blessed Mother of God; for she is, after Christ, our most sublime ideal. No one has received grace in such fulness, no one has co-operated with grace so faithfully as she. It is for this reason that the Church praises her as the Mirror of Justice (*speculum justitiæ*). The mere thought of her transcendent purity suffices to repel the alluring charms of sin and to inspire pleasure in the wonderful lustre of virtue.

(2) Self-Denial is the second means which ascetics teaches us (cf. Matt., xvi, 24–25). Without it the combat between spirit and flesh, which are contrary to each other (Rom., vii, 23; I Cor., ix, 27; Gal., v, 17), will not lead to the victory of the spirit (Imitatio Christi, I, xxv). How far self-denial should extend is clear from the actual condition of human nature after the fall of Adam. The inclination to sin dominates both the will and the lower appetites; not only the intellect, but also the outer and the inner senses are made subservient to this evil propensity. Hence, self-denial and self-control must extend to all these faculties. Ascetics reduces self-denial to exterior and interior mortification: exterior mortification is the mortification of sensuality and the senses; interior mortification consists in the purification of the faculties of the soul (memory, imagination, intellect, will) and the mastering of the passions. However, the term "mortification" must not be taken to mean the stunting of the "strong, full, healthy" (Schell) life; what it aims at is that the sensual passions do not gain the upper hand over the will. It is precisely through taming the passions by means of mortification and self-denial that life and energy are strengthened and freed from cumbersome shackles. But while the masters of asceticism recognize the necessity of mortification and self-denial and are far from

deeming it "criminal to assume voluntary sufferings" (Seeberg), they are just as far from advocating the so-called "non-sensual" tendency, which, looking upon the body and its life as a necessary evil, proposes to avert its noxious effects by wilful weakening or even mutilation (cf. Schneider, "Göttliche Weltordnung u. religionslose Sittlichkeit", Paderborn, 1900, p. 537). On the other hand, Catholics will never befriend the gospel of "healthy sensuality", which is only a pretty-sounding title, invented to cloak unrestricted concupiscence.

Special attention is devoted to the mastering of the passions, because it is with them above all else that the moral combat must be waged most relentlessly. Scholastic philosophy enumerates the following passions: love, hatred, desire, horror, joy, sadness, hope, despair, boldness, fear, anger. Starting from the Christian idea that the passions (*passiones*, as understood by St. Thomas) are inherent in human nature, ascetics affirms that they are neither sicknesses, as the Stoics, the Reformers, and Kant maintain, nor yet harmless, as was asserted by the Humanists and Rousseau, who denied original sin. On the contrary, it insists that in themselves they are indifferent, that they may be employed for good and for evil, and that they receive a moral character only by the use to which the will puts them. It is the purpose of ascetics to point out the ways and means by which these passions can be tamed and mastered, so that, instead of goading the will to sin, they are rather turned into welcome allies for the accomplishment of good. And since the passions are inordinate in as far as they turn to illicit things or exceed the necessary bounds in those things which are licit, ascetics teaches us how to render them innocuous by averting or restraining them, or by turning them to loftier purposes.

(3) Labour, also, is subservient to the striving after perfection. Untiring labour runs counter to our corrupt nature, which loves ease and comfort. Hence labour, if well-ordered, persistent, and purposeful, implies self-denial. This is the reason why the Catholic Church has always looked upon labour, both manual and mental, as an ascetic means of no small value (cf. Cassian, "De instit. cœnob.", X, 24; St. Benedict, Rule, xlviii, li; Basil, "Reg. fusius tract." c. xxxvii, 1–3; "Reg. brevius tract.", c. lxxii; Origen, "Contra Celsum", I, 28). St. Basil is even of the opinion that piety and avoidance of labour are irreconcilable in the Christian ideal of life (cf. Mausbach, "Die Ethik des hl. Augustinus", 1909, p. 264).

(4) Suffering, too, is an integral constituent of the Christian ideal and pertains consequently to ascetics. But its real value appears only when seen in the light of faith, which teaches us that suffering makes us like unto Christ, we being the members of the mystic body of which He is the head (I Peter, ii, 21), that suffering is the channel of grace which heals (*sanat*), preserves (*conservat*), and tests (*probat*). Finally, ascetics teaches us how to turn sufferings into channels of heavenly grace.

(5) The Virtues are subjected to a thorough discussion. As is proved in dogmatic theology, our soul receives in justification supernatural habits, not only the three Divine, but also the moral virtues (Trid., Sess. VI, De justit., c. vi; Cat. Rom., p. 2, c. 2, n. 51). These supernatural powers (*virtutes infusæ*) are joined to the natural faculties or the acquired virtues (*virtutes acquisitæ*), constituting with them one principle of action. It is the task of ascetics to show how the virtues, taking into account the obstacles and means mentioned, can be reduced to practice in the actual life of the Christian, so that love be perfected and the image of Christ receive perfect shape in us. Conformable to the Brief of Leo XIII, "Testem benevolentiæ" of 22 Jan., 1899, ascetics insists that the so-called "passive" virtues (meekness, humility, obedience, patience) must never be set aside in favour of the "active" virtues (devotion to duty, scientific activity, social and civilizing labour); for this would be tantamount to denying that Christ is the perpetual model. Rather, both kinds must be harmoniously joined in the life of the Christian. True imitation of Christ is never a brake, nor does it blunt the initiative in any field of human endeavour. On the contrary, the practice of the passive virtues is a support and aid to true activity. Besides, it not rarely happens that the passive virtues reveal a higher degree of moral energy than the active. The Brief itself refers us to Matt., xxi, 29; Rom., viii, 29; Gal., v, 24; Phil., ii, 8; Heb., xiii, 8 (cf. also Zahn, l. c., 166 sqq.).

D. *Application of the Means in the Three Degrees of Christian Perfection.*—Imitation of Christ is the duty of all who strive after perfection. It lies in the very nature of this formation after the image of Christ that the process is gradual and must follow the laws of moral energy; for moral perfection is the terminus of a laborious journey, the crown of a hard-fought battle. Ascetics divides those who strive after perfection into three groups: the beginners, the advanced, the perfect; and correspondingly sets down three stages or ways of Christian perfection: the purgative way, the illuminative way, the unitive way. The means stated above are applied with more or less diversity according to the stage which the Christian has reached. In the purgative way, when the appetites and inordinate passions still possess considerable strength, mortification and self-denial are to be practised more extensively. For the seeds of the spiritual life will not sprout unless the tares and thistles have first been weeded out. In the illuminative way, when the mists of passion have been lifted to a great extent, meditation and the practice of virtues in imitation of Christ are to be insisted on. During the last stage, the unitive way, the soul must be confirmed and perfected in conformity with God's will ("And I live, now not I; but Christ liveth in me": Gal., ii, 20). Care must, however, be taken not to mistake these three stages for wholly separate portions of the striving after virtue and perfection. Even in the second and the third stages there occur at times violent struggles, while the joy of being united with God may sometimes be granted in the initial stage as an inducement for further advance (cf. Mutz, "Aszetik," 2nd ed., 94 sq.).

E. *Relation of Ascetics to Moral Theology and Mysticism.*—All these disciplines are concerned with the Christian life and its last end in the next world; but they differ, though not totally, in their mode of treatment. Ascetical theology, which has been separated from moral theology and mysticism, has for its subject-matter the striving after Christian perfection; it shows how Christian perfection may be attained by earnestly exercising and schooling the will, using the specified means both to avoid the dangers and allurements of sin and to practise virtue with greater intensity. Moral theology, on the other hand, is the doctrine of the duties, and in discussing the virtues is satisfied with a scientific exposition. Mysticism treats essentially of "union with God" and of the extraordinary, so-called mystic prayer. Though also those phenomena which are accidental to mysticism, such as ecstasy, vision, revelation, fall within its scope, yet they are by no means essential to the mystic life (cf. Zahn, "Einführung in die christl. Mystik", Paderborn, 1908). It is true that mysticism includes also matter of ascetics, such as the endeavour of purification, vocal prayer, etc.; but this is done because these exercises are looked upon as preparatory to the mystical life and must not be discarded even in its highest stage. Nevertheless, the mystical life is not merely a higher degree of the ascetical life, but differs from it essentially, the mystical life being a special grace granted to the Christian without any immediate merit on his part.

F. *Historical Development of Asceticism.* — (1) Holy Writ abounds in practical instructions for the life of Christian perfection. Christ himself has drawn its outlines both as to its negative and positive requirements. His imitation is the supreme law (John, viii, 12; xii, 26), charity the first commandment (Matt., xxii, 36–38; John, xv, 17); the right intention is that which imparts value to the exterior works (Matt., v–vii), while self-denial and the carrying of the cross are the conditions for His discipleship (Matt., x, 38; xvi, 24; Mark, viii, 34; Luke, ix, 23; xiv, 27). Both by His own example (Matt., iv, 2) and His exhortations (Matt., xvii, 20; Mark, ix, 28) Christ recommended fasting. He inculcated sobriety, watchfulness, and prayer (Matt., xxiv, 42; xxv, 13; xxvi, 41; Mark, xiii, 37; xiv, 37). He pointed to poverty as a means of gaining the kingdom of heaven (Matt., vi, 19; xiii, 22; Luke, vi, 20; viii, 14; xii, 33; etc.) and counselled the rich youth to relinquish everything and to follow Him (Matt., xix, 21). That this was a counsel and not a strict command, given in view of the particular attachment of the youth to the things of this world, is shown by the very fact that the Master had twice said "keep the commandments", and that he recommended the renunciation of all earthly goods only on the renewed inquiry after the means that lead to perfection (cf. Lutz, l. c., against the Protestants Th. Zahn, Bern, Weiss, Lemme, and others). Celibacy for God's sake was praised by Christ as worthy of a special heavenly reward (Matt., xix, 12). Yet marriage is not condemned, but the words, "All men take not this word, but they to whom it is given", imply that it is the ordinary state, celibacy for God's sake being merely a counsel. Indirectly, Christ also commended voluntary obedience as a means for attaining the most intimate union with God (Matt., xviii, 4; xx, 22, 25). What Christ had outlined in his teachings the Apostles continued to develop. It is especially in St. Paul that we find the two elements of Christian asceticism brought out in well-defined terms: mortification of inordinate desires as the negative element (Rom., vi, 8, 13; II Cor., iv, 16; Gal., v, 24; Col., iii, 5), union with God in all our thoughts, words, and deeds (I Cor., x, 31; Gal., vi, 14; Col., iii, 3–17), and active love of God and our neighbour (Rom., viii, 35; I Cor., xiii, 3) as the positive element.

(2) Fathers and Doctors of the Church.—With Holy Writ as a basis, the Fathers and Doctors of the Church explained particular features of the Christian life in a more coherent and detailed manner. The Apostolic Fathers called the love of God and man the sun of Christian life, which, animating all virtues with its vital rays, inspires contempt of the world, beneficence, immaculate purity, and self-sacrifice. The "Didache" (q. v.), which was intended to serve as a manual for catechumens, thus describes the way of life: "First, thou shalt love God, who created thee; secondly, thou shalt love thy neighbour as thyself; whatever thou wishest that it should not be done to thee, do not to others." Following probably the "Didache", the so-called "Epistle of Barnabas", written at the end of the second century, represents the Christian life under the figure of the two ways, that of light and that of darkness. Two Epistles, which purport to come from the pen of St. Clement, but were probably written in the third century, exalt the life of virginity, if grounded on the love of God and accompanied by the corresponding works, as heavenly, divine, and angelic. We also mention St. Ignatius of Antioch, of whose letters St. Polycarp says that they contain "faith and patience and all edification in the Lord", and the "Pastor" of Hermas, who in the twelve commandments inculcates simplicity, truthfulness, chastity, meekness, patience, continence, confidence in God, and perpetual struggle against concupiscence. With the third century the works on Christian asceticism begin to show a more scientific character. In the writings of Clement of Alexandria and Gregory the Great ("Moral.", XXXIII, c. xxvii; cf. also Cassian, "Coll.", IX, XV) there may be observed traces of the threefold degree which was afterwards systematically developed by Dionysius the Areopagite. In his "Stromata" Clement sets forth the full beauty and grandeur of "true philosophy". It is particularly remarkable that this author delineates, even in its details, what is now known as ethical culture, and that he endeavours to harmonize it with the example given by Christ. The life of the Christian is to be ruled in all things by temperance. Following out this idea, he discusses in a casuistic form food and drink, dress and love of finery, bodily exercises and social conduct. Beginning with the fourth century, a twofold line of thought is discernible in the works on Christian life: one speculative, laying stress on the union of the soul with God, the Absolute Truth and Goodness; the other practical, aiming principally at instruction in the practice of the Christian virtues. The speculative element prevailed in the mystical school, which owes its systematic development to Pseudo-Dionysius and which reached its highest perfection in the fourteenth century. The practical element was emphasized in the ascetical school with St. Augustine as its chief representative, in whose footsteps followed Gregory the Great and St. Bernard.

It may suffice to detail the principal points on which the writers prior to the medieval-scholastic period dwelt in their instructions. On prayer we have the works of Macarius the Egyptian (d. 385) and of Tertullian (d. after 220), who supplemented his treatise on prayer in general by an explanation of the Lord's Prayer. To these two must be added Cyprian of Carthage (d. 258), who wrote "De oratione dominica", and St. Chrysostom (d. 407). Penance and the spirit of penance were treated by Tertullian (De pœnitentia), Chrysostom ("De compunctione cordis", "De pœnitentia"), and Cyril of Jerusalem (d. 386) in his second catechetical instruction. That the life of the Christian is a warfare is amply illustrated in St. Augustine's (d. 430) "De agone christiano" and in his "Confessions". Chastity and virginity were treated by Methodius of Olympus (d. 311) in his "Convivium", a work in which ten virgins, discussing virginity, demonstrate the moral superiority of Christianity over the ethical tenets of pagan philosophy. The same subject is discussed by the following Fathers: Cyprian (d. 258); Gregory of Nyssa (d. 394) in his "De virginitate"; Ambrose (d. 397), the indefatigable eulogist and champion of the virginal life; Jerome in his "Adversus Helvidium de virginitate" and "Ad Eustachium"; Chrysostom (d. 407) in his "De virginitate", who, though extolling virginity as a heavenly life, yet recommends it only as a counsel; Augustine in his works "De continentia", "De virginitate", "De bono viduitatis".

On patience we have the works of Cyprian, Augustine, and Tertullian's "De patientia", in which he speaks of this virtue as an invalid might speak of health to console himself. Chrysostom's "De jejunio et eleemosyna" discusses fasting. Almsgiving and good works are encouraged in Cyprian's "De opere et eleemosynis" and in Augustine's "De fide et operibus". The value of labour is explained in "De opere monachorum" by St. Augustine. Nor are treatises on the different states of life wanting. Thus St. Augustine's "De bono conjugali" treats of the married state; his "De bono viduitatis" of widowhood. A frequent subject was the priesthood. Gregory of

Nazianzus, in his "De fuga", treats of the dignity and responsibility of the priesthood; Chrysostom's "De sacerdotio" exalts the sublimity of this state with surpassing excellence; St. Ambrose in his "De officiis", while speaking of the four cardinal virtues, admonishes the clerics that their lives should be an illustrious example; St. Jerome's "Epistola ad Nepotianum" discusses the dangers to which priests are exposed; finally, the "Regula pastoralis" of Gregory the Great inculcates the prudence indispensable to the pastor in his dealings with different classes of men. Of prime importance for the monastic life was the work "De institutis cœnobiorum" of Cassian. But the standard work from the eighth to the thirteenth century was the Rule of St. Benedict, which found numerous commentators. Of the saint or rather his Rule St. Bernard says: "Ipse dux noster, ipse magister et legifer noster est" (Serm. in Nat. S. Bened., n. 2). Illustrations of the practice of Christian virtues in general were the "Expositio in beatum Job" of Gregory the Great and the "Collationes Patrum" of Cassian, in which the various elements of Christian perfection were discussed in the form of dialogues.

(3) The Medieval-Scholastic Period.—The transition period up to the twelfth century exhibits no specially noteworthy advance in ascetical literature. To the endeavour to gather and preserve the teachings of the Fathers we owe Alcuin's "De virtutibus et vitiis". But when in the twelfth century speculative theology was celebrating its triumphs, mystical and ascetical theology, too, showed a healthy activity. The results of the former could not but benefit the latter by placing Christian morality on a scientific basis and throwing ascetical theology itself into a scientific form. The pioneers in this field were St. Bernard (d. 1156) and Hugh and Richard of St. Victor. St. Bernard, the greatest mystical theologian of the twelfth century, also holds a prominent place among ascetical writers, so that Harnack calls him the "religious genius" of the twelfth century. The basic idea of his works, especially prominent in his treatise "De gratia et libero arbitrio", is that the life of the Christian should be a copy of the life of Jesus. Like Clement of Alexandria, he, too, lays down precepts for the regulation of the necessities of life, as food and dress, and for the implanting of God's love in man's heart, which would sanctify all things ("Apologia", "De præcepto et dispensatione"). Many are the steps by which love ascends till it reaches its perfection in the love for God's sake. Among his ascetical writings are: "Liber de diligendo Deo", "Tractatus de gradibus humilitatis et superbiæ", "De moribus et officio episcoporum", "Sermo de conversione ad clericos", "Liber de consideratione".

Frequent allusions to St. Augustine and Gregory the Great are scattered through the pages of Hugh of St. Victor (d. 1141), so much so that he earned the distinction of being called a second Augustine by his contemporaries. He was undoubtedly the first to give to ascetical theology a more or less definite, scientific character. The ever-recurring theme of his works is love. But what he aimed at above all in his writings was to lay bare the psychological bearings of mystical and ascetical theology. Noteworthy are his works: "De vanitate mundi", "De laude caritatis", "De modo orandi", "De meditatione". His pupil, Richard of St. Victor (d. 1173), though more ingenious and systematic, is yet less intent upon practical utility, except in his work "De exterminatione mali et promotione boni". The great theologians of the thirteenth century, who were no less famous for their scholastic "Summæ" than for their ascetical and mystical writings, brought ascetical teaching to its perfection and gave it the definite shape it has retained as a standard for all future times. No other epoch furnishes such convincing proof that true science and true piety are rather a help than a hindrance to each other. Albert the Great, the illustrious teacher of the great Thomas, who was the first to join Aristotelean philosophy with theology and to make philosophy the handmaid of theology, was at the same time the author of excellent works on ascetics and mysticism, as, e. g., "De adhærendo Deo", the ripest fruit of his mystic genius, and "Paradisus animæ", which was conceived along more practical lines. To St. Thomas we owe the ascetic work "De perfectione vitæ spiritualis"; in it he explains the essence of Christian perfection so lucidly that his line of argumentation may even in our days serve as a model. His other works, too, contain ample material of value both for ascetics and for mysticism.

The Seraphic Doctor, St. Bonaventure, "treats of mystic theology", to use the words of Leo XIII, "in a manner so perfect that the unanimous opinion of the most expert theologians regards him as the prince of mystic theologians". Of his authentic works the following deserve to be mentioned: "De perfectione evangelica", "Collationes de septem donis Spiritus sancti", "Incendium amoris", "Soliloquium", "Lignum vitæ", "De præparatione ad Missam", "Apologia pauperum". From the pen of David of Augsburg, a contemporary of these great masters, we have an ascetic instruction for novices in his book entitled "De exterioris et interioris hominis compositione". He leads the reader along the three well-known ways, purgative, illuminative, and unitive, purposing to make the reader a spiritual man. By severely disciplining the faculties of the soul and subordinating the flesh to the spirit, man must restore the original order, so that he may not only do what is good, but likewise do it with ease. There remains to be mentioned the "Summa de vitiis et virtutibus" of Peraldus (d. c. 1270). The fourteenth century is characterized throughout by its mystical tendencies. Among the works which this period produced, Henry Suso's "Booklet of Eternal Wisdom" deserves special mention on account of its highly practical value. Pre-eminent in the fifteenth century were Gerson, Dionysius the Carthusian, and the author of the "Imitation of Christ". Relinquishing the ideals of the mystic writers of the fourteenth century, Gerson attached himself again to the great scholastic writers, thus avoiding the vagaries which had become alarmingly frequent among the mystics. His "Considerationes de theologia mystica" shows that he belongs to the practical school of asceticism. Dionysius the Carthusian is esteemed as a highly gifted teacher of the spiritual life. Both mysticism properly so called and practical asceticism owe valuable works to his pen. To the latter category belong: "De remediis tentationum", "De via purgativa", "De oratione", "De gaudio spirituali et pace interna", "De quatuor novissimis".

The "Imitatio Christi", which appeared in the middle of the fifteenth century, deserves special attention on account of its lasting influence. "It is a classic in its ascetical unction and perfect in its artistic style" (Hamm, "Die Schönheit der kath. Moral", Munich-Gladbach, 1911, p. 74). In four books it treats of the interior spiritual life in imitation of Jesus Christ. It pictures the struggle which man must wage against his inordinate passions and perverse inclinations, the indulgence of which sullies his conscience and robs him of God's grace: "Vanity of vanities and all is vanity, except to love God and serve Him alone" (Vanitas vanitatum et omnia vanitas præter amare Deum et illi soli servire: I, i). It advises mortification and self-denial as the most efficacious weapons in this struggle. It teaches man to establish God's kingdom in his soul by the practice of virtues according to the example of Jesus Christ.

It finally leads him to union with Christ by exciting love for him as well as by pointing out the frailty of all creatures: "It is necessary to leave the beloved thing for the beloved, because Jesus wishes to be loved above all things" (Oportet dilectum propter dilectum relinquere, quia Jesus vult solus super omnia amari: II, xvii). The thoughts of the "Imitation" are thrown into epigrams so simple that they are within the mental grasp of all. Though the book betrays that the author was well versed not only in Scholastic philosophy and theology, but also in the secrets of the mystical life, yet this fact never obtrudes itself on the reader, nor does it obscure the meaning of the contents. There are a number of quotations from the great doctors Augustine, Bernard, Bonaventure, and Thomas, from Aristotle, Ovid, and Seneca; yet these do not mar the impression that the whole work is the spontaneous outburst of an intensely glowing soul. It has often been said that the teachings of the "Imitation" are "unworldly" and show little appreciation for science. But, to judge the work aright, one must take into consideration the peculiar circumstances of the time. Scholasticism had entered on a period of decline and had lost itself in intricate subtleties; mysticism had gone astray; all classes had been more or less infected with the spirit of licentiousness. It is conditions like these that give us the key to interpret phrases such as the following: "I would rather feel compunction than know how to define it" (Opto magis sentire compunctionem quam scire ejus definitionem) or "This is the highest wisdom: through contempt of the world to strive for the kingdom of heaven" (Ista est summa sapientia: per contemptum mundi tendere ad regna cœlestia).

(4) Modern Times.—During the sixteenth century St. Teresa and St. Ignatius of Loyola stand out most prominently owing to the wide-felt influence which they exerted upon the religion of their contemporaries, an influence that is still at work through their writings. The writings of St. Teresa arouse our admiration by the simplicity, clearness, and precision of her judgment. Her letters show her to be an enemy of everything that smacks of eccentricity or singularity, sham piety or indiscreet zeal. One of her principal works, the "Way to Perfection", though written primarily for nuns, also contains apposite instructions for those who live in the world. While teaching the way to contemplation, she yet insists that not all are called to it and that there is greater security in the practice of humility, mortification, and the other virtues. Her masterpiece is the "Castle of the Soul", in which she expounds her theory of mysticism under the metaphor of a "castle" with many chambers. The soul resplendent with the beauty of the diamond or crystal is the castle; the various chambers are the various degrees through which the soul must pass before she can dwell in perfect union with God. Scattered throughout the work are many hints of inestimable value for asceticism as applied in everyday life. This fact is undoubtedly due to the well-founded conviction of the saint that even in extraordinary states the ordinary means must not be set aside altogether, so that illusions may be guarded against (cf. J. Zahn, "Introduction to Mysticism", p. 213).

In his "Exercitia spiritualia" St. Ignatius has left to posterity not only a grand literary monument of the science of the soul, but also a method unparalleled in its practical efficacy of strengthening the willpower. The booklet has appeared in numberless editions and revisions and, "despite its modest guise, is in reality a complete system of asceticism" (Meschler). The four weeks of the Exercises acquaint the exercitant with the three degrees of the spiritual life. The first week is taken up with cleansing the soul from sin and from its inordinate attachment to creatures. The second and third weeks lead the exercitant along the illuminative way. The portrait of Christ, the most lovable of all men, is outlined before his eyes, so that he can contemplate in the humanity the reflex of Divine light and the supreme model of all virtues. The meditations of the fourth week, the subject of which are the resurrection etc., lead to union with God and teach the soul to rejoice in the glory of the Lord. It is true, there are many rules and regulations, the sequence is most logical, the arrangement of the meditations follows the laws of psychology; yet these exercises do no violence to the free will, but are meant to strengthen the faculties of the soul. They do not, as has often been asserted, make the exercitant a powerless instrument in the hands of the confessor, nor are they a mystic flight to heaven, accomplished by means of a compulsion which intends a rapid advance in perfection by a mechanical process (Zöckler, "Die Tugendlehre des Christentums", Gütersloh, 1904, p. 335). Their marked intellectualism, so frequently objected to, in no way constitutes a hindrance to mysticism (Meschler, "Jesuitenaszese u. deutsche Mystik" in "Stimmen aus Maria-Laach", 1912). On the contrary, they make man's moral will truly free by removing the hindrances, while, by cleansing the heart and by accustoming the mind to meditative prayer, they are an excellent preparation for the mystical life. Louis of Granada, O. P. (d. 1588), also belongs to this period. His work "La guia de pecadores" may justly be styled a book full of consolation for the erring. His "El memorial de la vida cristiana" contains instructions which take the soul from the very beginning and lead her to the highest perfection. Louis of Blois (Blosius), O. S. B. (d. 1566), is of a mind kindred to St. Bernard. His "Monile spirituale" is the best known of his numerous works. Thomas of Jesus (d. 1582) wrote the "Passion of Christ" and "De oratione dominica".

A great number of ascetical writers sprang up during the seventeenth century. Among them St. Francis de Sales stands out most prominently. According to Linsemann, the publication of his "Philothea" was an event of historical importance. To make piety attractive and to adapt it to all classes whether living in Court circles, in the world, or in a monastery, this was his aim and in this he succeeded. Of a mild and sweet temperament, he never lost sight of the habits and particular circumstances of the individual. Though unwavering in his ascetical principles, he yet possessed an admirable facility for adapting them without constraint or rigidity. In the practice of mortification he recommends moderation and adaptation to one's state of life and to personal circumstances. Love of God and of man: this he puts down as the motive power of all actions. The spirit of St. Francis pervades the whole of modern asceticism, and even to-day his "Philothea" is one of the most widely read books on asceticism. "Theotimus", another work of his, treats in the first six chapters of the love of God, the rest being devoted to mystical prayer. His letters, too, are very instructive. Attention may be called to the new edition of his works (Œuvres, Annecy, 1891 sqq.). "Il combattimento spirituale" of Scupoli (d. 1610) was spread very widely and earnestly recommended by Francis de Sales.

To the same period belong the following authors and works. Bellarmine, S.J. (d. 1621): "Gemitus columbæ"; "De ascensione mentis in Deum"; "De arte bene moriendi". Alphonsus Rodriguez, S.J. (d. 1616): "Exercicio de perfección y virtudes cristianas" (3 vols., Seville, 1609), which has frequently been re-edited and translated into nearly all languages. John of Jesus-Mary, O.C.D. (d. 1615): "Teologia Mistica" (Naples, 1607), highly esteemed by Bellarmine and Francis de Sales. Alvarez de Paz, S.J. (d. 1620): "De vita spirituali ejusque perfectione" (1608); "De exterminatione mali et promotione boni" (1613); "De inquisitione pacis" (1617), which was frequently re-edited. Gaudier, S.J. (d. 1620): "De perfectione vitæ spiritualis" (1619; new ed., 3 vols., Turin, 1903–4). La Puente, S.J. (d. 1624): "Guia espiritual" (Valladolid, 1609), containing, according to his own statement, a brief epitome of the spiritual life both active and contemplative (prayer, meditation, trials, mortification, practice of virtue); "De la Perfección del Cristiano en todos sus estados" (1612). Both works have ever been highly esteemed by all ascetical men and have been translated into many languages. Lessius, S.J. (d. 1623): "De perfectionibus moribusque divinis", a work distinguished both for its scientific and ascetical spirit. Nicholas Lancicius, S.J. (d. 1638), past-master in the spiritual life, whose saintly personality is reflected in his writings (new ed., Cracow, 1889 sqq.): "De exteriore corporis compositione"; "De quatuor viis perveniendi ad perfectionem"; "De humanarum passionum dominio"; "De mediis ad virtutem"; "De causis et remediis in oratione". Greatly valued is his book of meditations: "De piis erga Deum et cœlites affectibus"; it has been translated into several languages. Schorrer, S.J.: "Synopsis theol. ascet." (Dillingen, 1662; rare edition). Godinez, S.J.: "Práctica de la teologia mystica" (La Puebla de los Angeles, 1681), of which we have a Latin edition together with a commentary by de la Reguera, S.J. (Rome, 1740).

Surin, S.J. (d. 1665), wrote his important "Catéchisme spirituel" at a time when he was subject to interior trials (cf. Zahn, "Mystik", p. 441). The book appeared in many editions and translations, but was placed on the Index. The edition of Fr. Fellon, S.J. (1730), and the latest edition of Fr. Bouix (Paris, 1882) probably do not fall under this prohibition, because in them the errors have been corrected. After Surin's death appeared: "Les fondements de la vie spirituelle" (Paris, 1667); "Lettres spirituelles" (ib., 1695); "Dialogues spirituels" (ib., 1704). Gaspar Druzbicki, S.J. (d. 1662), is the author of a considerable number of ascetical works both in Polish and in Latin, many of which were translated into other languages. There are two complete editions of his works: one published at Ingolstadt (1732) in two folios, the other at Kalisz and Posen (1681–91). Among his numerous works are: "Lapis lydius boni spiritus"; "Considerationes de soliditate veræ virtutis"; "De sublimitate perfectionis"; "De brevissima ad perfectionem via"; "Vota religiosa". The "Mystica theologia Divi Thomæ" of Thomas a Vallgornera, O.P. (d. 1665), published at Barcelona (1662 and 1672) and at Turin (1890), is almost exclusively made up of quotations from St. Thomas and is a rich storehouse of ascetical material. From the pen of Cardinal Bona, O. Cist. (d. 1674), we have: "Principia et documenta vitæ christianæ" (Rome, 1673) and "Manuductio ad cœlum" (Rome, 1672 and 1678), both of which works, remarkable for their simplicity and practical utility, were frequently re-edited; the still valuable "De sacrificio Missæ"; "De discretione spirituum"; "Horologium asceticum". Complete editions of his works appeared at Antwerp, Turin, Venice. Morotius, O. Cist., in his "Cursus vitæ spiritualis" (Rome, 1674; new ed., Ratisbon, 1891), follows closely the lead of St. Thomas. The "Summa theologiæ mysticæ" (new ed., 3 vols., Freiburg, 1874) is the best and most widely read work of Philip of the Blessed Trinity (d. 1671), the philosopher among the mystic writers. He wrote in the spirit of St. Thomas, following definite scientific principles and showing their practical application in the spiritual life. Anthony of the Holy Ghost, O.C.D. (d. 1674), was a disciple of the author just named. His "Directorium mysticum" (new ed., Paris, 1904), dominated by the spirit of his master, was written for the instruction of his pupils. He is also the author of the following works: "Seminarium virtutum" (3rd ed., Augsburg and Würzburg, 1750), "Irriguum virtutum" (Würzburg, 1723), "Tractatus de clericorum ac præcipue sacerdotum et pastorum dignitate", etc. (Würzburg, 1676).

In the course of the eighteenth century a number of valuable works on asceticism and mysticism were published. To Neumeyer, S.J. (d. 1765), we owe the "Idea theol. ascet.", a complete, scientifically arranged epitome. Rogacci, S.J. (d. 1719), wrote "Del uno necessario", an instruction in the love of God, which ranks high in ascetical literature and was translated into several languages. Among the best literary productions, and widely read even to-day, is Scaramelli's (d. 1752) "Direttorio ascetico". The author treats asceticism apart from mysticism. A treatise on the virtues is contained in Dirkink, S.J., "Semita perfectionis" (new ed., Paderborn, 1890). Designed along broad lines is the "Trinum perfectum" (3rd ed., Augsburg, 1728) by Michael of St. Catherine. Katzenberger, O.F.M., wrote "Scientia salutis" (new ed., Paderborn, 1901). Schram's "Institutiones theol. mysticæ" (2 vols.) combines asceticism with mysticism, though the author is at his best in the ascetical parts. St. Alphonsus Liguori (d. 1787), rightly called the "Apostolic Man", published a large number of ascetic works, full of heavenly unction and tender-hearted piety. The best-known and most important of them are: "Pratica di amar Gesù Cristo" (1768), "Visita al SS. Sacramento", perhaps the most widely read of all his ascetical works: "La vera sposa di Gesù Cristo" (1760), a sure guide to perfection for countless souls.

Complete treatises on asceticism, published during the nineteenth and twentieth centuries, are the following: Grundkötter, "Anleitung zur christl. Vollkommenheit" (Ratisbon, 1896). Leick, C.SS.R., "Schule der christl. Vollkommenheit" (Ratisbon, 1886), inspired by the writings of St. Alphonsus Liguori. Weiss, O.P., "Philosophie der christl. Vollkommenheit" (vol. V of his "Apologie"; Freiburg, 1898). The author is extraordinarily well read, and his conception of the spiritual life is unusually deep. Ribet, "L'ascétique chrétienne" (Paris, 1888). Tissot, "La vie intérieure". Saudreau, "Les degrés de la vie spirituelle" (Angers, 1896 and 1897), a work full of unction. His other works, "Les faits extraordinaires de la vie spirituelle" (1908) and "La vie d'union à Dieu" (1909), belong to mysticism properly so called. Poulain, S.J., "La grâce d'oraison", though of a mystic character, yet treats of the ordinary method of prayer. Saudreau and Poulain are reliable throughout and their works are among the best productions in this branch. Rousset, O.P., "Directorium asceticum" (Freiburg, 1893). Meynard, O.P., "Traité de la vie intérieure" (Paris, 1899), based on St. Thomas. Meyer, S.J., "First Lessons in the Science of the Saints" (2nd ed., St. Louis, 1903), translated into several languages. Francis X. Mutz, "Die christliche Aszetik" (2nd ed., Paderborn, 1909). Joseph Zahn, "Einführung in die christliche Mystik" (Paderborn, 1908), important also for asceticism. Berthier, "De la perfection chrétienne et de la perfection religieuse d'après S. Thomas et S. François de Sales" (2 vols., Paris, 1901). A. Devine, "Manual of Ascetical Theology" (London). Ryan, "Groundwork of Christian Perfection" (London). Buchanan, "Perfect Love of God" (London).

An exhaustive list of Catholic ascetical writers is given in Migne, "Encycl. théologique", XXVI; "Dict. d'ascéticisme", II, 1467.

Non-Catholic authors: Otto Zöckler, "Die Tugendlehre des Christentums, geschichtlich dargestellt" (Gütersloh, 1904). W. Hermann, "Der Verkehr des

Christen mit Gott" (6th ed., Stuttgart, 1908), and "Die sittlichen Weisungen Jesu" (Göttingen, 1907). Kähler, "Verkehr mit Christo in seiner Bedeutung für das eigene Leben" (Leipzig, 1904). Peabody, "Jesus Christ and the Christian Character". A. Ritschl, "Christliche Vollkommenheit" (Göttingen, 1902). Sheldon, "In his Steps—What Would Jesus do?", widely read in England.

FRANZ X. MUTZ.

MYSTICAL THEOLOGY.—Mystical theology is the science which treats of acts and experiences or states of the soul which cannot be produced by human effort or industry even with the ordinary aid of Divine grace. It comprises among its subjects all extraordinary forms of prayer, the higher forms of contemplation in all their varieties or gradations, private revelations, visions, and the union growing out of these between God and the soul, known as the mystical union. As the science of all that is extraordinary in the relations between the Divinity and the human spirit, mystical theology is the complement of ascetical, which treats of Christian perfection and of its acquisition by the practice of virtue, particularly by the observance of the counsels. The contents of mystical theology are doctrinal as well as experimental, as it not only records the experiences of souls mystically favoured, but also lays down rules for their guidance, which are based on the authority of the Scriptures, on the teachings of the Fathers of the Church, and on the explanations of theologians, many of them eminent as mystics. Its rules and precepts are usually framed for the special use of those who have occasion to direct souls in the ways of mysticism, so as to preserve them from error while facilitating their advancement. It must therefore take note of the erroneous systems of prayer, like Quietism (q. v.) or Semiquietism, and of the self-illusion or deception of souls that mistake the powers of darkness for those of light or the promptings of their own self-seeking for Divine communications. It is this part of the science that necessitates inquiry into various phases of occultism, diabolism, etc., into which writers like Görres have gone so extensively. Mystical theology has a nomenclature all its own, seeking to express acts or states that are for the most part purely spiritual in terms denoting analogous experiences in the material order. Usually it does not form part of the ordinary class-room studies, but is imparted by spiritual masters in their personal direction of souls, or inculcated, as in seminaries and novitiates, by special conferences and courses of spiritual reading. Preliminary to the study of mystical theology is a knowledge of the four ordinary forms of prayer: vocal, mental, affective, and the prayer of simplicity (see PRAYER). The last two, notably the prayer of simplicity, border on the mystical. Prayer is often called active or acquired contemplation to distinguish it from passive or higher contemplation, in which mystical union really consists.

Mystical theology begins by reviewing the various descriptions of extraordinary contemplation, contained in the works of mystics and of writers on mystical subjects, and the divisions which help to describe its various phases, indicating chiefly whether it consists of an enlargement or elevation of knowledge, or of absorption in the Divine vision, or, again, whether the cherubic, i. e., intellectual, or seraphic, i. e., affective, element predominates. The objects of contemplation are set forth: God, His Attributes, the Incarnation, and all the Sacred Mysteries of the Life of Christ; His presence in the Eucharist; the supernatural order; every creature of God in the natural order, animate or inanimate, particularly the Blessed Virgin, the angels, the saints, Providence, the Church. In analyzing the causes of contemplation, what may be called its psychology next comes up for consideration, in so far as it necessitates the ordinary or exceptional use of any human faculty, of the senses of the body, or of the powers of the soul. On God's part, grace must be considered as a principle, or cause, of contemplation, the special or unusual graces (gratis datæ) as well as ordinary graces, the virtues, theological as well as moral, the gifts of the Holy Spirit. The closing chapter in this part of the science dwells on the fruits of contemplation, especially the elevation of spirit, joy, charity, zeal; on the influences that may contribute to its duration, interruption, or cessation. Here some theologians treat in detail of the preliminary or preparatory dispositions for contemplation, of natural or moral aptitude, solitude, prayer, mortification or self-denial, corporal and spiritual, as a means of soul-purification; these topics, however, belong more properly to the domain of ascetical theology.

What strictly comes within the province of mystical theology is the study of the processes of active and passive purification through which a soul must pass to reach the mystical union. Although the active processes are also treated to some extent in ascetical theology, they require special study inasmuch as they lead to contemplation. They comprise: purity of conscience, or aversion even to the slightest sin; purity of heart, the heart being taken as the symbol of the affections, which to be pure must be free of attachments to anything that does not lead to God; purity of the spirit, i. e. of the imagination and memory; and purity of action. It is to these processes that the well-known term "night" is applied by St. John of the Cross, since they imply three things which are as night to the soul in so far as they are beyond or contrary to its own lights, viz., the privation of pleasure, faith as substituted for human knowledge, and God as incomprehensible, or darkness, to the unaided soul. Passive purifications are the trials encountered by souls in preparation for contemplation, known as desolation, or dryness, and weariness. As they proceed sometimes from God and sometimes may be produced by the Evil Spirit, rules for the discernment of spirits are set down to enable directors to determine their source and to apply proper means of relief, especially should it happen that the action of the Evil One tends to possession or obsession.

These passive purifications affect the soul when every other object of contemplation is withdrawn from it, except its own sins, defects, frailties, which are revealed to it in all their enormity. They put the soul in the "obscure night", as St. John of the Cross calls it, or in the "great desolation", to use the phrase of Father Baker. In this state the soul experiences many trials and temptations, even to infidelity and despair, all of which are expressed in the peculiar terminology of writers on mystical theology, as well as the fruits derived from resisting them. Chief among these fruits is the purification of love, until the soul is so inflamed with love of God, that it feels as if wounded and languishes with the desire to love Him still more intensely. The first difficulty mystical writers encounter in their treatises on contemplation is the proper terminology for its degrees, or the classification of the experiences of the soul as it advances in the mystical union with God effected by this extraordinary form of prayer. Ribet in "La Mystique Divine" has a chapter (x) on this subject, and the present writer treats it in chapter xxix of his "Grace of Interior Prayer" (tr. of the sixth edition). Scaramelli follows this order: the prayer of recollection; the prayer of spiritual silence; the prayer of quiet; the inebriation of love; the spiritual sleep; the anguish of love; the mystical union of love, and its degrees from simple to perfect union and spiritual marriage. In this union the soul experiences various spiritual impressions, which mystical writers try to describe in the terminology used to describe sense impressions, as if the soul could see, hear, touch, or enjoy the savour or odour of the Divinity. Ecstatic union with God is a further degree of prayer. This and the state of rapture require careful observation to be sure that the Evil One has no share in them. Here again mystical writers treat at length the deceits, snares, and other arts practised by the Evil One to lead souls astray in the quest for the mystical union. Finally, contemplation leads to a union so intimate and so strong that it can be expressed only by the terms "spiritual marriage" (see MARRIAGE, MYSTICAL). The article on contemplation (q. v.) describes the characteristics of the mystical union effected by contemplation. No treatise of mystical theology is complete without chapters on miracles, prophecies, revelations, visions, all of which have been treated under their respective headings.

As for the history or development of mysticism, it is as difficult to record as a history of the experiences of the human soul. The most that can be done is to follow its literature, mindful that the most extraordinary mystical experiences defy expression in human speech, and that God, the Author of mystical states, acts upon souls when and as He wills, so that there can be no question of what we could consider a logical or chronological development of mysticism as a science. Still, it is possible to review what mystical writers have said at certain periods, and especially what St. Teresa did to treat for the first time mystical phenomena as a science. Before her, mystics were concerned principally with ecstasies, visions, and revelations; she was the first to attempt a scientific analysis of the process of mystical union brought about by contemplation. As the contribution to the science and history of mystical theology by each of the writers in the following list has been sufficiently noted in the articles on them, it will suffice here to mention the titles of some of their characteristic works.

Famous Mystics Prior to the Nineteenth Century. —St. Gregory I the Great (b. at Rome, c. 540; d. there, 604): "Commentaries on Job"; this book is called the Ethics of St. Gregory. The writings of Dionysius the Pseudo-Areopagite did not reach the West until about 824, when they were sent to Louis the Pious by Michael the Stammerer, Emperor of Constantinople: "Opera". Hugh of St. Victor, canon regular at Paris (b. in Saxony, 1096; d. at Paris, 1141): *passim*. St. Bernard, Abbot of Clairvaux (b. near Dijon, 1090; d. at Clairvaux, 1153): "On the Canticle of Canticles". Richard of St. Victor, canon regular at Paris (d. at Paris, 1173): "De contemplatione". St. Bonaventure, Minister General of the Friars Minor (b. at Bagnorea, 1221; d. at Lyons, 1274): "Journey of the Soul towards God". The "Seven Roads of Eternity", which has sometimes been attributed to him, is the work of a Friar Minor, Rudolph of Bibrach, of the fourteenth century. St. Gertrude, a Benedictine (b. at Eisleben, 1256; d. at Helfta, Saxony, 1302): Revelations. Blessed Angela of Foligno (b. at Foligno, 1248; d. there, 1309): "Life and Revelations" in "Acta SS.", I, January, 186–234; this work is one of the masterpieces of mysticism. Tauler, a Dominican (b. at Strasburg, c. 1300; d. there, 1361): "Sermons" (Leipzig, 1498). Blessed Henry Suso, a Dominican (b. at Constance, c. 1295; d. at Ulm, 1366): "Exemplar" (Augsburg, 1482). "The Book of the Nine Rocks" is not by him but by a merchant of Strasburg, the somewhat unorthodox Rulman Merswin. St. Bridget of Sweden (b. c. 1303; d. at Rome, 1373): "Revelations" (Nuremberg, 1500). Blessed Ruysbroeck, surnamed the Admirable (b. at Ruysbroeck, 1293; d. at Groenendael, 1381): "Opera omnia", Latin tr. by the Carthusian Surius (Cologne, 1692). François-Louis Blosius (de Blois), Benedictine Abbot of Liessies (b. near Liège, 1506; d. at Liessies, 1566): "Opera" (Ingolstadt, 1631).

St. Teresa (b. at Avila, 1515; d. at Aba de Tormes, 1582): "Opera" (Salamanca, 1588). St. John of the Cross, founder of the Discalced Carmelites (b. at Hontiveros, 1542; d. at Ubeda, 1591): "Opera" (Seville, 1702). Venerable Luis de Lapuente (b. at Valladolid, 1554; d. there, 1624): "Life of Father Baltasár Alvarez", confessor of St. Teresa (Madrid, 1615); "Spiritual Guide" (Valladolid, 1609); "Life of Marina de Escobar" (2 vols., Madrid, 1665–73). St. Francis de Sales, Bishop of Geneva (b. at Thorens, near Annecy, 1567; d. at Lyons, 1622): "Treatise on the Love of God" (Lyons, 1616). Alvarez de Paz, S. J. (b. at Toledo, 1560; d. at Potosi, 1620): "De inquisitione pacis" in "Opera", III (Lyons, 1647). Philip of the Blessed Trinity, General of the Discalced Carmelites (b. at Malancène, near Avignon, 1603; d. at Naples, 1671): "Summa theologiæ mysticæ" (Lyons, 1656). Jean-Joseph Surin (q. v.). Venerable Marie de l'Incarnation (b. at Tours, 1599; d. at Quebec, 1672): "Life and Letters", published by her son Dom Claude Martin, O. S. B. (Paris, 1677). Bossuet called her the "Teresa of the New World". Bossuet, Bishop of Meaux (b. at Dijon, 1627; d. at Paris, 1704): "Instruction sur les états d'oraison" (Paris, 1697). Joseph of the Holy Ghost, Definitor General of the Discalced Carmelites (d. 1639): "Cursus theologiæ mystico-scholasticæ" (6 vols., Seville, 1710–40). Emmanuel de la Reguera, S. J. (b. at Aguilàr del Campo, 1668; d. at Rome, 1747): "Praxis theologiæ mysticæ" (2 vols., Rome, 1740–45), a development of the mystical theology of Wading (Father Godinez). Scaramelli, S. J. (b. at Rome, 1687; d. at Macerata, 1752): "Direttorio mistico" (Venice, 1754). As a description, this is the best treatise of the eighteenth century despite its too complicated classification; Voss has published a compendium of it, entitled "Directorium Mysticum" (Louvain, 1857). Schram, O. S. B. (b. at Bamberg, 1722; d. at Bainz, 1797): "Institutiones theologiæ mysticæ" (Augsburg, 1777), chiefly an abridgment of la Reguera. More complete lists (176 names) will be found in Poulain, "Graces d'Oraison" (7th ed., Paris, 1911); tr., "The Graces of Interior Prayer" (London, 1910); and in Underhill, "Mysticism" (New York, 1912).

MARÉCHAUX, *Le merveilleux divin et le merveilleux démoniaque* (Paris, 1901); MIGNE, *Dict. de mystique chrétienne* (Paris, 1858); LEJEUNE, *Manuel de théologie mystique* (Paris, 1897); VALLGORNERA, *Mystica Theologia Divi Thomæ* (Turin, 1891); BAKER, *Holy Wisdom* (London, 1908); CHANDLER, *Ara Cœli Studies in Mystical Religion* (London, 1908); DALGAIRNS, *The German Mystics of the Fourteenth Century* (London, 1858); DELACROIX, *Essai sur le mysticisme spéculatif en Allemagne au XIX siècle* (Paris, 1900); IDEM, *Etudes d'histoire et de psychologie du mysticisme. Les grands mystiques chrétiens* (Paris, 1908); DENIFLE, *Das geistliche Leben: Blumenlese aus der deutschen Mystikern der 14. Jahrhunderts* (Graz, 1895); DEVINE, *A Manual of Mystical Theology* (London, 1903); GARDNER, *The Cell of Self-Knowledge* (London, 1910); GÖRRES, *Die Christliche Mystik* (Ratisbon, 1836–42); POIRET, *Theologiæ Mysticæ idea generalis* (Paris, 1702); RIBET, *La Mystique Divine* (Paris, 1879); IDEM, *L'Ascétique Chrétienne* (Paris, 1888); SAUDREAU, *La vie d'union à Dieu* (Paris, 1900); IDEM, *L'état mystique* (Paris, 1903); IDEM, *Les faits extraordinaires de la vie spirituelle* (Paris, 1908); IDEM, tr. CAMM, *The Degrees of the Spiritual Life* (London, 1907); IDEM, tr. SMITH, *The Way that Leads to God* (London, 1910); THOROLD, *An Essay in Aid of the Better Appreciation of Catholic Mysticism*. (London, 1900); VON HÜGEL, *The Mystical Element of Religion* (London, 1908).

AUG. POULAIN.

Theonas, Bishop of Alexandria from about 283 to 301 (Eusebius, "Chronicle", Ann. Abr. 2299, St. Jerome's version). In his time Achillas, who had been appointed presbyter at Alexandria, at the same time with Pierius, became celebrated (Euseb., "Hist. eccl.", III, xxxii). The celebrated letter of Theonas to Lucianus, chamberlain to Diocletian, which has often been quoted as giving such a lifelike description of the position of a Christian in the imperial Court has been pronounced, first by Batiffol and then by Harnack, to be a forgery. Their verdict is endorsed by Bardenhewer. It was first published from what purported to be a transcript made by Jérôme Vignier, by Dacherius in his "Spicilegium". Theonas is commemorated in the Roman Martyrology on 27 August. St. Athanasius in his apology to Constantinus speaks of a church dedicated by his predecessor, St. Alexander, to Theonas. The same church is alluded to in the "Acts of SS. Pachomius and Theodorus".

For the *Epistle to Lucianus* see: BATIFFOL, *Bulletin Critique* (1886), 155-60; HARNACK, *Der gefälschte Brief des Bischofs Theonas* in *Texte u. Untersuchungen*, IX (Leipzig, 1903), iii, new series, English tr. of epistle in CLARKE, *Ante-Nicene Fathers: The Writings of Methodius etc.* For a number of fabulous stories told by medieval Arabic writers (SEVERUS, EUTYCHIUS, etc.) see RENAUDOT, *Hist. Patriarch: Alexand.*, 50 sq.; *Acta SS.*, IV, August, 579 sq.

F. J. BACCHUS.

Theophanes, SAINT, chronicler, b. at Constantinople, about 758; d. in Samothracia, probably 12 March, 817, on which day he is commemorated in the Greek menologies and in the Roman Martyrology. He was the son of Isaac, imperial governor of the islands of the White Sea, and of Theodora, of whose family nothing is known. After the early death of his parents he came to the Court of Constantine Copronimus. He was married at the age of twelve, but induced his wife to lead a life of virginity, and in 799, after the death of his father-in-law, they separated with mutual consent to embrace the religious state, she choosing a convent on an island near Constantinople, while he entered the monastery called Polychronius in the district of Sigriano near Cyzicus. Later he built a monastery on his own lands on the island Calonymus (now Calomio). After six years he returned to Sigriano, founded an abbey known by the name "of the great acre", and governed it as abbot. As such he was present at the second General Council of Nicæa, 787, and signed its decrees in defence of the sacred images. When the Emperor Leo the Armenian again began his iconoclastic warfare, he ordered Theophanes to be brought to Constantinople and tried in vain to induce him to condemn what had been sanctioned by the council. Theophanes was cast into prison and for two years suffered cruel treatment; he was then banished to Samothracia, where, overwhelmed with afflictions, he lived only seventeen days and wrought many miracles after death.

At the urgent request of his friend George Syncellus (d. 810), Theophanes undertook the continuation of his chronicle, during the years 810-15 (P. G., CVIII, 55). He treated of the time from the year 284-813, and made use of material already prepared by Syncellus, probably also the extracts from the works of Socrates, Sozomenus, and Theodoret, made by Theodore Lector, and the city chronicle of Constantinople. The work consists of two parts, the first giving the history, arranged according to years, the other containing chronological tables, full of inaccuracies and therefore of little value. It seems that Theophanes had only prepared the tables, leaving vacant spaces for the proper dates, but that these had been filled out by some one else (Hurter, "Nomencl.", I, Innsbruck, 1903, 735). The first part, though lacking in historical precision and criticism, which could scarcely be expected from a man of such ascetical disposition, greatly surpasses the majority of Byzantine chronicles (Krumbacher, "Gesch. der byz. Litt.", 1897, 342). The chronicle was edited at Paris in 1655 by Goar; again at Venice in 1729 with annotations and corrections by Combefis. A Latin version was made by Anastasius Bibliothecarius, and both were ably edited by de Boor (Leipzig, 1883).

BROOKS, *The Sources of Theophanes and the Syriac chroniclers* in *Byzant. Zeitschrift*, XV (1906), 578; STADLER, *Heiligenlexicon*, a dithyramb on Theophanes, in *Münchener Sitzungsbericht*, 1896, 583; *Acta SS.*, II, March, 210; CHEVALIER, *Biog-Bibl.*, II, 4437; *Anal. Boll.*, XXXI, 11.

FRANCIS MERSHMAN.

Theophanes Kerameus (Κεραμεύς, potter), Archbishop of Rossano in Calabria (1129-52), a celebrated homiletic writer. His sermons, ninety-one of which are known in manuscript, are mostly exegetical, and written in Greek, which was then still extensively spoken in Sicily and Southern Italy. They are remarkable for their simplicity and naturalness, and are masterpieces of oratorical skill and, for those times, rare examples of lucid and unforced expositions of biblical texts. They were first edited, together with a Latin translation and extensive annotations, by Francesco Scorso, S.J. (Paris, 1644), which edition is reprinted in P. G., CXXXII, 125-1078. A new edition was prepared by Gregory Palamas (Jerusalem, 1860). The fact that various other individuals also bore the surname "Kerameus" has given rise to a controversy concerning the authorship of these homilies. Scorso, their first editor, falsely supposed Theophanes Kerameus to have lived in the ninth century and to have been Bishop of Taormina in Sicily. Batiffol, in his work entitled "L'abbaye de Rossano" (Paris, 1891), XXXI, 36-56, holds that part of the homilies were written by the Calabrian monk John Philagathos, a disciple of Abbot Bartholomæus of Grottaferrata (d. c. 1050).

LANCIA DI BROLO, *Storia della Chiesa in Sicilia* (Palermo, 1884), 459-92; IDEM, *Sopra Teofano Cerameo ricerche e schiarimenti* in *Archivio storico Siciliano B.*, I (Palermo, 1877), 391-421. Concerning a probable interpolation in homily 55, see LANGEN, in *Revue Internationale de Théologie*, III (1895), 122-7.

MICHAEL OTT.

Théophane Vénard, BLESSED (JEAN-THÉOPHANE VÉNARD), French missionary, b. at St-Loup, Diocese of Poitiers, 1829; martyred in Tonkin, 2 Feb., 1861. He studied at the College of Doué-la-Fontaine, Montmorillon, Poitiers, and the Paris Seminary for Foreign Missions which he entered as a sub-deacon. Ordained priest 5 June, 1852, he departed for the Far East, 19 Sept. After fifteen months at Hong Kong he arrived at his mission in West Tonkin, where the Christians had recently been tried by a series of persecutions under Minh-Menh, a monster of cruelty. Shortly after Father Vénard's arrival a new royal edict was issued against Christians, and bishops and priests were obliged to seek refuge in caves, dense woods, and elsewhere. Father Vénard, whose constitution had always been delicate, suffered almost constantly, but continued to exercise his ministry at night, and, more boldly, in broad day. On 30 Nov., 1860, he was betrayed and captured. Tried before a mandarin, he refused to apostatize and was sentenced to be beheaded. He remained a captive until 2 Feb., and during this interval lived in a cage, from which he wrote to his family beautiful and consoling letters, joyful in anticipation of his crown. His bishop, Mgr Retord, wrote of him at this time: "Though in chains, he is as gay as a little bird".

On the way to martyrdom Father Vénard chanted psalms and hymns. To his executioner, who coveted his clothing and asked what he would give to be killed promptly, he answered: "The longer it lasts the better it will be". His head, after exposure at the top of a pole, was secured by the Christians and is now venerated in Tonkin. The body rests in the crypt at the Missions Etrangères, Paris. Other precious relics are in the hands of the martyr's brother, Canon Eusebius Vénard, curé of Assais Deux Sèvres, France, who possesses, also, most of the martyr's letters, including those written from the cage. In a letter addressed to his father, Théophane refers thus to his approaching sacrifice: "A slight sabre-cut will separate my head from my body, like the spring flower which the Master of the garden gathers for His pleasure. We are all flowers planted on this earth, which God plucks in His own good time: some a little sooner, some a little later . . . Father and son may we meet in Paradise. I, poor little moth, go first. Adieu". The cause of his beatification was introduced at Rome in 1879, and he was declared Blessed, 2 May, 1909. The beatification ceremony brought a large delegation from France, including the Bishop of Poitiers and the martyr's only surviving brother. Théophane Vénard was beatified in company with thirty-three other martyrs, most of whom were natives of Tonkin, Cochin-China, or China.

HERBERT, *Théophane Vénard* (London); WALSH, *A Modern Martyr; Thoughts from Modern Martyrs; The Field Afar; Vie et Correspondance de J. Théophane Vénard* (Poitiers, 1865); *Le Bienheureux Théophane Vénard* (Paris, 1911); *Lettres Choisies du Bienheureux Théophane Vénard* (Paris, 1909); CATTANEO, *Un Martire Moderno* (Milan, 1910).

JAMES ANTHONY WALSH.

Theophilanthropists, or "Friends of God and Man", a deistic sect formed in France during the latter part of the French Revolution. The legal substitution of the Constitutional Church, the worship of Reason, and the cult of the Supreme Being in place of the Catholic Religion had practically resulted in atheism and immorality. With a view to offsetting those results, some disciples of Rousseau and Robespierre resorted to a new religion, wherein Rousseau's deism and Robespierre's civic virtue (*règne de la vertu*) would be combined. Chemin wrote the "Manuel des théophilanthropes", and Haüy offered his institute for the blind as a provisional place of meeting. When, later, the Convention turned over to them the little church of Sainte-Catherine, in Paris, the nascent sect won a few followers and protectors; still its progress was slow till La Réveillière-Lépeaux, an influential member of the Directory, took up its cause. But it was only after the Revolution of 18 Fructidor, which left him master of the situation, that his sympathy bore fruit. Then was the apogee of Theophilanthropism. Blended in a way with the *culte décadaire*, it came into possession of some of the great churches of Paris like Notre-Dame, St-Jacques du Haut-Pas, St-Médard etc.; it took a conspicuous part in all the national celebrations, and from the metropolis passed into the provinces, chiefly the Department of Yonne. The movement, in spite of a strong opposition not only on the part of Catholics but also from Constitutionals and Philosophers, was gradually taking hold of the masses when the overthrow of the Directory brought it to an abrupt end. The First Consul set his face against the new religionists and they disbanded. Sporadic attempts at reviving Theophilanthropism were made in the course of the nineteenth century. In 1829, Isambert circulated a manifesto for the purpose of grouping the French deists, but nothing came of it. In 1854 Henri Carle founded "L'alliance religieuse universelle" with "La libre conscience" as its organ, but both society and periodical disappeared during the Franco-Prussian war. In 1882, Décembre and Vallières, through "La fraternité universelle" and many similar publications, sought directly to reorganize the sect, but the attempt failed and, in 1890, Décembre confessed the impossibility of rousing public interest. Camerlynck's voluminous book, "Théisme", published at Paris in 1900, had a similar aim and met a similar fate.

Theophilanthropism is described in the "Manuel du théophilanthropisme", of which there were new editions made as the work progressed. The governing body consisted of two committees, one called "comité de direction morale", in charge of the spiritual, the other styled "comité des administrateurs", in charge of the temporalties. No dogmatic creed was imposed on the adherents of the new religion, the two fundamental tenets, viz. the existence of God and the immortality of the soul, being purely sentimental beliefs (*croyances de sentiment*), deemed necessary for the preservation of society and the welfare of individuals. The moral teaching, considered as by far the principal feature of the movement, held a middle position between the severity of Stoicism and the laxity of Epicureanism. Its basic principle was: good is all that tends to preserve and perfect man; evil is all that tends to destroy or impair him. It is in the light of that axiom and not of the Christian standard—in spite of the phraseology—that we should view the commandments concerning the adoration of God, the love of our neighbour, domestic virtues, and patriotism. Theophilanthropist worship was at first very simple and meant chiefly for the home: it consisted in a short invocation of God in the morning and in a kind of examination of conscience at the end of the day. A plain altar on which were laid some flowers and fruits, a few inscriptions appended to the walls, a platform for the readers or speakers, were the only furnishings allowed. The founders were particularly anxious that this simplicity be strictly adhered to. Nevertheless, the progress of the sect led gradually to a much more elaborate ceremonial. It is a far cry from the early meetings where the minister, or *père de famille*, presided at prayer or mimicked Christian baptism, First Communion, marriages, and funerals, to the gorgeous display of the so-called national festivals. There even was a Theophilanthropist Mass, which, however, came much nearer to a Calvinist service than to the Catholic Liturgy. Of the hymns adopted by the sect, some taken from the writings of J. B. Rousseau, Madame Deshoulières, or even Racine, breathe a noble spirit but, side by side with these, there are bombastic lucubrations like the "Hymne à la fondation de la république" and the "Hymne à la souveraineté du peuple". The same strange combination is found in the feasts where Socrates, Jean-Jacques Rousseau, and St. Vincent de Paul are equally honoured, and in the sermon where political harangues interlard moral exhortations. Quite noteworthy is Dubroca's funeral oration of George Washington, wherein the orator, under cover of the American hero, catered to the rising Bonaparte and laid out for him a whole political programme which, read in the light of subsequent events, sounds like irony. Despite the hint, Bonaparte chose to be the Cromwell rather than the Washington of the new religionists.

Under the appearance of moderation, Theophilanthropism was really an anti-Christian movement. Whenever superstition was mentioned, it meant the Christian religion. There is no doubt that the first Theophilanthropists were Freemasons and that Freemasonry was the leading spirit of the movement throughout. Neither can a secret collusion between Protestantism and Theophilanthropism, at least in the beginning, be denied. The first idea of the sect really belongs to David Williams, an English minister who exercised a considerable influence in Paris during the Revolution. Chemin consulted the French Calvinists before launching his "Manuel". If later a controversy arose between Protestants themselves as to the merits of Theophilanthropism, this was due to the imprudence of the Theophilanthropists, who, elated by apparent success, lifted the mask. The constitutional clergy, in the national council held at Notre-Dame in 1797, protested against the new religion, and Grégoire wrote in his "Annales de la Religion" (VI, no. 5): "Theophilanthropism is one of those derisive institutions which pretend to bring to God those very people whom they drive away from Him by estranging them from Christianity. . . . Abhorred by Christians, it is spurned by philosophers who, though they may not feel the need of a religion for themselves, still want the people to cling to the faith of their fathers." Catholics went further in their denunciations and exposed, beside the anti-Christian and masonic spirit that animated the sect, the political intrigues hiding under the mask of religion. Pope Pius VII, 17 May, 1800, placed an interdict on the churches that had been desecrated by the deistic rites, and Cardinal Consalvi, in the course of the negotiations regarding the Concordat of 1801, demanded that a speedy end be put to the Theophilanthropists' profanation of the Catholic temples.

MATHIEZ, *La Théophilanthropie* (Paris, 1903); IDEM, *Contributions à l'histoire religieuse de la révolution* (Paris, 1907); BRUGERETTE, *Les créations religieuses de la révolution* (Paris, 1904); REID, *The rise and dissolution of the infidel societies in the metropolis* (London, 1800); FERRERO, *Disamina filosofica de'Dommi e della Morale religiosa de'Teofilantropi* (Turin, 1798); for a complete bibliography see TOURNEUX, *Bibliographie de l'histoire de Paris pendant la révolution* (Paris, 1890–1900).

J. F. SOLLIER.

Theophilus, Bishop of Antioch. Eusebius in his "Chronicle" places the name of Theophilus against that of Pope Soter (169–77), and that of Maximinus, Theophilus's successor, against the name of Eleutherus (177–93). This does not mean that Maximinus succeeded Theophilus in 177, but only that Theophilus and Maximinus flourished respectively in the times of Soter and Eleutherus. Lightfoot and Hort showed that Eusebius, having no such precise chronological data for the bishops of Antioch as he had for those of Rome and Alexandria, placed the names of the Antiochene bishops against those of contemporary Roman bishops (Lightfoot, "St. Ignatius", etc., II, 468 sq., and "St. Clement", etc., I, 224 sqq.). When therefore we find in the third book of Theophilus, "Ad Autolycum", that the writer was alive after the death (180) of Marcus Aurelius, it does not follow, as even writers like Harnack and Bardenhewer suppose, that Eusebius made a chronological blunder.

The "Ad Autolycum", the only extant writing of Theophilus, is an apology for Christianity. It consists of three books, really separate works written at different times, and corresponds exactly to the description given of it by Eusebius as "three elementary works" (Hist. eccl., IV, xxiv). The author speaks of himself as a convert from heathenism. He treats of such subjects as the Christian idea of God, the Scripture accounts of the origin of man and the world as compared with pagan myths. On several occasions he refers (in connexion with the early chapters of Genesis) to an historical work composed by himself. Eusebius (op. cit.) speaks of refutations of Marcion and Hermogenes, and "catechetical books". To these St. Jerome (De vir. illust., xxv) adds commentaries on Proverbs and the Gospels. He speaks of the latter in the prologue to his own commentary on the Gospels, and also in his epistle "Ad Algasiam", where we learn that Theophilus commented upon a Diatessaron or Gospel Harmony composed by himself ("Theophilus . . . quattuor Evangelistarum in unum opus compingens"). A long quotation in the same epistle is all that survives of this commentary, for Zahn's attempt to identify it with a Latin commentary ascribed in some MSS. to Theophilus has found no supporters.

BATIFFOL, *Anciennes littératures chrétiennes: Lit. grecque*, 101–2; ZAHN, *Forschung. zur Gesch. des N.T. Kanons*, II; HARNACK, *Altchrist. Lit.*, 496 sq.; IDEM, *Chronologie*, I, 319 sq.; BARDENHEWER-SHAHAN, *Patrology* (St. Louis, 1908), 65–7. For Theophilus's teaching concerning the Eternal Word see NEWMAN, *Causes of Rise and Success of Arianism* in *Tracts Theol. and Eccles.* (London, 1908), 255–57. The *Ad Autolycum* was first published by FRISIUS (Zurich, 1546); the latest ed. by OTTO, *Corp. apologet.*, VIII (Jena, 1861). English tr. by FLOWER (London, 1860), and in CLARKE, *Ante-Nicene Library*. The supposed *Commentary on the Gospels* was first printed by DE LA BIGNE, *Bibl. SS. Patrum*, V (Paris, 1575), then by OTTO (loc. cit.), then by ZAHN (loc. cit., 29–85). For references to literature in this commentary see BARDENHEWER; MORIN in *Revue Bénédictine*, XXII, 12 sq.; and QUENTIN in *Revue Bénédictine*, XXIV, 107 sq. QUENTIN gives reasons for regarding John of Jerusalem as possibly the author. For monographs on Theophilus's doctrine see BARDENHEWER.

F. J. BACCHUS.

Theophilus, Patriarch of Alexandria (385–412). Concerning the extraction and early life of Theophilus we have but scanty information. He had a sister of similar temperament and St. Cyril, his successor, was his nephew. Hydatius ("Chron.", II; P. L., LI, 874) calls him a "most learned man", and dedicates to him an Easter table for 100 years. St. Jerome informs us that he did not come forward as a public teacher before 385 ("Contra Rufin.", III, 18, in P. L., XXIII, 492). After his election to the Patriarchate of Alexandria (385) he showed himself a man of great intellectual gifts and capacity, but also extremely violent and unscrupulous in the choice of his means. His name is connected with three important historical events: the decay of paganism in Egypt, the Origenistic controversy, and the deposition and banishment of St. John Chrysostom. About 390 Theophilus deprived the pagans of Alexandria of a temple, probably with the consent of the Emperor Theodosius I, and apparently destroyed several other temples (Socrates, V, 16; Ammian., XXII, xi, 7). A riot ensued, and a number of Christians were slain. With Theophilus at their head, the Christians retaliated by destroying the celebrated temple of Serapis, on the ruins of which the patriarch erected a church. He also erected a magnificent church at Canope. In 391 or 392 Theophilus was requested by the Synod of Capua to exert his influence to end the schism at Antioch. However, he failed to establish peace, and it was only in 398 that St. John Chrysostom, with the assistance of Theophilus, succeeded in re-establishing ecclesiastical communion between Flavian and Rome.

Until 399 Theophilus was regarded as a friend of Origen and the Origenists. Many of the so-called Origenist monks were among his best friends; some of them he appointed to ecclesiastical offices and dignities: for example, he named Isidore archpresbyter and patriarchal œconomus, and raised others to the episcopate. In the quarrel between Johannes-Rufinus and Epiphanius-Jerome he took the side of the first (Socrates, VI, 10), informed Jerome through Isidore in 396 that he should show more respect for the authority of his bishop, John of Jerusalem (Epp. lxiii and lxxxii; "Contra Rufin.", III, 17; "Contra Johannem Hieros.", 37), and accused St. Epiphanius of anthropomorphism. He also banished the Egyptian bishop Paulus, an opponent of the Origenists, and reproached St. Jerome for the hospitality he showed him (Jerome, "Cont. Rufinum", III, 17 and 78). Between 399 and 400 Theophilus suddenly altered his attitude; the chief motive for the change seems to have been a personal quarrel with the archpresbyter Isidore, well known as a friend of the Origenists. Isidore had taken charge of a sum of money and, in accordance with the express request of the donor, did not inform Theophilus, who suffered from a "mania for building" and avarice (St. Isidore Pelus., Ep. i, 152). The patriarch heard of the matter, however, and did not shrink from the vilest slanders against Isidore and even acts of violence (Pall., VI; Sozomen, VIII, 12). Isidore found protection with his friends, the monks of Nitria, whereupon Theophilus turned against them also. At first he set the anthropomorphic-minded monks, the enemies of the Origenists, against them, although he had condemned their views in his Easter letter of 399 (Sozomen, VIII, 11; Cassian, "Coll.", X, 2), then directed against them his Easter letter of 401 (P. L., XXI, 773), and finally condemned Origenism at the Synod of Alexandria in 401.

Then placing himself at the head of soldiers and armed servants he marched against the monks, burned their dwellings, and ill-treated those whom he captured (Pall., vii; Socrates, VI, 7; for Jerome's congratulations to Theophilus see Jerome, Ep. lxxxvi). The monks, about 300 in number, proceeded first to Palestine, where the majority of them settled near Scythopolis; the four Tall Brethren meanwhile proceeded to Constantinople to ask protection and justice from St. John Chrysostom and the emperor. Theophilus was summoned to Constantinople to answer their charges, and thus begins his connexion with the tragedy of Chrysostom, which soon took the first place in his and the public interest (see JOHN CHRYSOSTOM, SAINT). At the Synod of the Oak in 403 Theophilus concluded an equitable peace with the persecuted monks, and on his return to Alexandria is said to have again received the books of Origen (Socrates, VI, 17). That Theophilus may have been really very "broad-minded", is shown by the fact that he consecrated the philosopher Synesius bishop about 410, although the latter had not yet been baptized, and had stipulated that, as bishop, he might retain his wife and adhere to his Platonic views (pre-existence of soul, allegorical explanation of the Resurrection, etc.). As a writer Theophilus did not attain much prominence. In addition to his Easter letters, of which three are extant in a Latin translation by Jerome (P. L., XXII, and P. G., LXV, 53 sqq.), he wrote "one large volume against Origen" (Gennadius, 33), of which some fragments are preserved (collected in Gallandi, "Bibl. vet. patr.", VII, 801–52; P. G., LXV, 33–68; Zahn, "Forschungen zur Gesch. des neutest. Kanons", II, Erlangen, 1883, p. 234 sqq.). The Canons ascribed to Theophilus are in Pitra, "Juris eccles. Græcor. hist. et monum.", I (Rome, 1864), 546–649. Inauthentic and doubtful writings were also in circulation under Theophilus's name (Gennadius, 33: "Legi et tres libros suo nomine titulatos, sed lingua inconsonans est. Non valde credidi").

In addition to the sources already mentioned, consult: THEODORET, *Hist. eccl.*, V, xxii; SULPICIUS SEVERUS, *Dial.*, I, 6–7, in *P. L.*, XX, 187–8; TILLEMONT, *Mémoires*, XI (Paris, 1698–1712), 441–99, 633–8; CEILLIER, *Hist. générale*, VII (Paris, 1729–63), 438–47; PRAT, *Origène* (Paris, 1907), xlviii sq.; VINCENZI, *Historia critica; quæstiones inter Theophilum Epiphanium, Hieronymum, adversarios Origenis et inter Origenis patronos Joh. Chrysostomum, Rufinum et monachos Nitrienses* (Rome, 1865); CAVALLERA, *Le schisme d'Antioche* (Paris, 1905), 283–4; KOCH, *Synesius von Cyrene bei seiner Wahl u. Weihe zum Bischof* in Histor. Jahrb., XXIII (1902), 751–74.

CHRYS. BAUR.

Theosophy, Θεοσοφία, wisdom concerning God, is a term used in general to designate the knowledge of God supposed to be obtained by the direct intuition of the Divine essence. In method it differs from theology, which is the knowledge of God obtained by revelation, and from philosophy, which is the knowledge of Divine things acquired by human reasoning. It is often incorrectly confounded with mysticism, for the latter is properly the thirst for the Divine, the aspiration for the invisible, and hence a natural manifestation of the religious sentiment. By intuition or illumination the initiated Theosophists are considered to be in harmony with the central principle of the universe. This knowledge of the secret forces of nature, of the true relation between the world and man, frees them from the ordinary limitations of human life, and gives them a peculiar power over the hidden forces of the macrocosm. Their exceptional faculties are alleged as experimental proof of their superior science; they are the only guarantee of the truth of their teaching. They are said to transmit this truth by way of revelation. Thus theosophy appeals to tradition, but not in the Christian sense.

(1) India is the home of all theosophic speculation. Oltramere says that the directive idea of Hindu civilization is theosophic. Its development covers a great many ages, each represented in Indian religious literature. There are formed the basic principles of theosophy. Knowledge of the occult laws in nature and in life, the intuitive method, superhuman powers, hostility to established religion are not all equally apparent in each age, but are present conjunctively or separately through the whole course of its history. The early Brahmanic writings contain the germs, which have gradually developed into a rich vegetation of ideas and beliefs. These ideas are organized into systems, not however homogeneous or autonomous but mixed with other belief. Then they leave the schools to act upon the masses, either in forming a religion, e. g. Buddhism, or in penetrating popular religions already existing, e. g. Hinduism. Thus the Upanishads teach: that the individual soul is identical with the universal soul, hence the doctrine of *advaita*, i. e. non-duality; that the individual existence of the soul is a state of suffering, hence the doctrine of *samsara*, i. e. metempsychosis; that the individual soul is delivered from suffering by its reunion with the universal soul, a reunion realized by seizing the consciousness of identity with it, hence the doctrine of *moksa*, i. e. salvation. The basic doctrines of the Vedanta and Saukhya systems are monistic Pantheism, intuition as the supreme means to reach truth, metempsychosis, the world of sense is only a very little part of the category of things, the theory and method of salvation strictly intellectual. These systems developed from the Upanishads. The final development is the Yoga. Yoga, i. e. "one who fits himself, or exercises", refers to the exercises practised to free the soul from the body, which to it is like a string to a bird. Some of these exercises were: to rid one's self of moral faults (though the masters do not agree as to what these faults are); to sit in certain painful postures, check the breath, and reduce thought to a minimum by staring at the tip of the nose; to place the soul in a particular part of the body, and so gradually acquire mastery over it, or, rather, let the soul, the true self, acquire mastery over the body; to starve and learn to subsist on air, or even without it; to concentrate thought by meditation, i. e. to think of nothing, *Thyana*, the highest state of which is the cataleptic trance *samadhi*, in which mind is suppressed but the soul is in full activity. In this state the person is a *mahatma*, i. e. master-soul and can enjoy a temporary release from the body which it leaves to go roaming about, performing wonderful feats on material nature and controlling other less powerful souls. This latter was the secret of the Yoga's real power and was supposed to be done by a transfer of soul. When the soul re-enters the body, the Yoga wakes and is like other people. By repeated exercises the soul can become so strong that it secures perpetual release from the body, thus, according to the older Yoga teaching, it flies to heaven where it enjoys great happiness, riding in a celestial car attended by lovely women and music; but with the latter Yogas, on breaking all bodily bonds it formed immediate absorption into the Supreme Soul.

(2) Theosophic teaching comes to the front in the third period of Greek philosophy. Hence it is found in the Jewish-Greek philosophy with the neo-Platonists. The theosophic atmosphere due to the influence of the Orient is plainly shown in Plotinus. The Gnostic systems reveal more theosophy than theology, and in the Jewish Kabbala is found a theosophy mixed with various forms of magic and occultism. The Renaissance brought into modern thought neo-Platonism and the Kabbala, e. g. Reuchlin (d. 1492), Agrippa (d. 1535), Cardano (d. 1576), Paracelsus (d. 1540), Weigel (d. 1588). More important is the teaching of Jakob Böhme (d. 1624). He taught that the "eternal dualism" of God is the ultimate cause of all evil; that there is a "dark" negative principle in God, which evil element makes manifest His goodness. Without this there would be no revelation. Further, were it not for this principle God could not know Himself. Böhme's teaching influenced Baader (q. v.), Schelling, and Hegel. Theosophic principles colour the theology of Swedenborg, and are found in the group of modern thinkers, especially neo-Hegelians, who claim that the existence of God is known by direct intuition or by a special faculty of the soul.

A new importance of these teachings in modern thought is due to the school of Modern theosophy dating from the foundation of the Theosophical Society in New York City by Madame Blavatsky in 1875. She is the chief and only authority for the revelation of so-called Tibetan occultism. A. P. Sinnett however uses the term Esoteric Buddhism. They claimed to have the true solution for the problems of the universe and of man from the Upanishads and Buddhist Sutras through Oriental savants, *mahatmas*, the faithful depositories of a profound and superhuman wisdom. In fact, a great part of their nomenclature is derived from India, and they seek there for a justification of teachings drifting about in modern thought and derived to a great extent, if not wholly, from neo-Platonic and Jewish sources through the Renaissance. The objects of the society are: to form the nucleus of a universal brotherhood of humanity without distinction of race, creed, sex, caste, or colour; to encourage the study of comparative religion, philosophy, and science; to investigate the unexplained laws of nature and the powers latent in man. This last clause gives occasion to include magic, the occult, the uncanny, and the marvellous in any and every form. Madame Blavatsky, with Colonel Olcott, went to India in 1878. Shortly afterwards her frauds were exposed through letters written by her and published by Columb and his wife, who had been in her service. This was acknowledged by the London Society of Psychical Research, which in Nov., 1884 sent R. Hodgson, of St. John's College, Cambridge to investigate (Edmund Garrett, "Isis very much Unveiled", London, 1895; Francis Podmore, "Studies in Psychical Research"). In spite of this, however, the teaching was continued and propagated by her disciples Mrs. Besant, Col. Olcott, A. P. Sinnett, and others.

Modern theosophy claims to be a definite science. Its teachings are the product of thought, and its source is consciousness, not any Divine revelation. As a science it is supposed to be based on investigation and experimentation of the occult laws in nature and in human life. Only those qualified for the inquiry can grasp these laws, and they gain from this knowledge certain superhuman powers. Mrs. Besant calls it the great synthesis of life, i. e. of religion, science, and philosophy, as old as thoughtful humanity, proclaimed in a new form suited to the present time. Its aim is that spirit is and can become the master of matter. Hence it is considered as a protest against materialism which teaches that thought and feeling are the results of the aggregations of matter. Theosophy on the contrary sees in matter an instrument of life, and in thought the creative and moulding power of matter.

The basic teaching of theosophy is the universal brotherhood of humanity. Hence springs the preaching of toleration to all persons and to all varieties of belief, e. g. Buddhists, Christians, Atheists. It considers the different religions as methods adopted by man in the search for God. They are of necessity various, because men differ in temperament, type, needs, and stages of evolution. Hence they are different and imperfect expressions of truth. As such it says: "we cannot afford to lose any of the world's religions, for each has its partial truth and its characteristic message which the perfect man must acquire." Hence theosophy appeals to men as the great peacemaker, for it teaches that all religions mean one and the same thing, or rather that they are all branches of a single tree. In this sense it attacks comparative mythology which tries to show that religion was originally the fruit of man's ignorance and will disappear with the increase of knowledge, whereas in fact religion comes from Divine knowledge, i. e. theosophy.

The principle of universal brotherhood rests upon the "solidarity" of all living, of all that is, in the one life and one consciousness. Solidarity springs from the belief in the immanence of God, the only and external life manifested in the multiplicity of creation. All forces are external; there is no supernatural, except the superhuman and supersensuous, i. e. powers greater than those normally exercised by man, which, however, can be developed. Ignorance therefore makes the miracle. Hence there is no personal God, and for this reason Madame Blavatsky and Mrs. Besant say that theosophy is more readily embraced by Atheists and Agnostics. Hence also Colville could teach that the spirit or soul in man is the only real and permanent part of his being; everything else pertaining to him is illusory and transitory. Solidarity, i. e. the common life pervading all things, is thus made the basis of morality. Hence a wrong done to one is done to all, as e. g. an injury inflicted on one part of the human organism results in pain diffused and felt throughout. At the same time we are told that God is good and man immortal, that the "immanence of God justifies religion", i. e. the search after Him, that all things move to good and to man's benefit, that man must understand and co-operate with the scheme of things.

Man has seven aspects, or rather is a being composed of seven principles. These are viewed in two groups: the Quaternary, corresponding to our animal nature, i. e. soul and body, the mortal part of man, the products of evolution; and the Triad, corresponding to our spiritual nature, i. e. spirit, for theosophists say that Christian philosophy holds the threefold division of body, soul, and spirit in man. The Quaternary is made up of *Sthula Sharira*, i. e. physical body; *Linga Sharira*, i. e. astral double; *Prana*, i. e. principle of life; *Kama*, i. e. our passional nature. The Triad is composed of: *Manas*, i. e. mind or the thinker; *Buddhi*, i. e. the dwelling-place of spirit; *Atmir*, i. e. spirit. Hence we find *Atmir-Buddhi* used conjointly. This Triad is called the Immortal Triad. It is united to the Quaternary by *Manas*, in itself viewed as *Higher Manas*, sending out a Ray, which as *Lower Manas* is imbedded in *Kama*. Thus *Kama-Manas* is the link joining our animal to our spiritual nature, and is the battle-ground of life's struggles. Man is primarily divine, a spark of the Divine life; this living flame passing out from the Central Fire, weaves for itself coverings within which it dwells and thus becomes the Triad, the *Atma-Buddhi-Manas*, the Immortal Self. This sends out its Ray, which becomes encased in grosser matter, in the Kamic body, in the Astral Double, and in the physical body. The Astral Double, i. e. rarer matter, the exact double of the physical body, plays a great part in spiritualistic phenomena. The *Manas* is the real I, the reincarnating ego makes the human personality. The Quaternary as a whole is viewed as the Personality, i. e. the shadow of the Self. In fact each principle or aspect may be considered a Personality in so far as it undervalues *Atma*, i. e. throws its shadow over *Atma* and prevents us from seeing in everything *Atma*, i. e. the One Eternal Existence. The seer however knows that *Atma* is the one reality, the essence of all things, that *Atma-Buddhi* is the Universal One Soul, itself an aspect of *Atma*, that *Atma-Buddhi-Manas* is the individual mind or Thinker, that the shadow of *Manas*, our *Atma-Buddhi*, makes men say "my soul" and "thy soul", whereas in reality we are all one with *Atma*, the Unknown Root. After death all of the Manasic Ray that is pure and unsoiled gradually disentangles itself, carrying with it such of life's experiences as are of a nature fit for assimilation with the Higher Ego. The Manasic Ego united to *Atma-Buddhi* passes into the Devachonic state of consciousness, rapt in blissful dreams coloured by the experiences of the earth-life. This state is a continuation of the earth-life shorn of its sorrows, and a completion of its noble and pure wishes.

Theosophy is not only a basis of religion; it is also a philosophy of life. As such, its main teachings are reincarnation and the law of Karma. Karma is the outcome of the collective life, a law of ethical causation. In the past incarnation the ego had acquired certain faculties, set in motion certain causes. The effect of these causes and of causes set in motion in previous incarnations and not yet exhausted are its Karma and determine the conditions into which the ego is reborn. Thus inequalities of natural gifts, e. g. genius, of temperament and of character are explained. The law of progress is the law of involution and evolution, the returning of the Divine Spark into a unity with Spirit through various reincarnations, which are viewed as a process of purification. Sin, poverty, and misery are the fruits of ignorance, and are gradually removed as the spirit in us becomes freed from earthly dross. There is no heaven nor hell. Death is the passage from this state of life to another. There is an evolution behind and before, with absolute certainty of final attainment for every human soul, i. e. to be one with the Absolute. As man advances in this process his spirit becomes stronger, and can develop latent powers, not shown in ordinary mortals.

Criticism.—In spite of a Christian ethical phraseology, theosophy in reality is a form of pantheism, and denies a personal God and personal immortality. Its appeal to the spiritual in man, and its striving after union with the Divine are based upon a contradictory metaphysic, an imaginary psychology, a system of ethics which recognizes no free-will, but only the absolute necessity of Karma. No evidence or proof is given for its teaching except the simple statements of its leaders. The denial of a personal God nullifies its claim to be a spiritualistic philosophy. Judging it as presented by its own exponents, it appears to be a strange mixture of mysticism, charlatanism, and thaumaturgic pretension combined with an eager effort to express its teaching in words which reflect the atmosphere of Christian ethics and modern scientific truths.

WRIGHT, *Modern Theosophy* (Boston and New York, 1894); BESANT, *Theosophical Manuals* (London, New York and Madras, 1892); *Lectures on the History of Religions: Catholic Truth Society:* V, *Theosophy* (London and New York, 1911); HULL, *Theosophy and Christianity* (Catholic Truth Society); DE GRANDMAISON, *Le Lotus Bleu* in series *Science et Religion* (Paris); BUSNELLI, *Manuale di Teosofia* (Rome, 1910); OLTRAMERE, *L'histoire des idées théosophiques dans l'Inde* (Paris); CLARKE in *The Month* (Jan., Feb., March, 1897).

JOHN T. DRISCOLL.

Theotocopuli, DOMENICO (EL GRECO), one of the most remarkable Spanish artists, b. in Crete, between 1545 and 1550; d. at Toledo, 7 April, 1614. On 15 Nov., 1570, the miniature-painter Giulio Clovio wrote to Cardinal N. Farnese, recommending El Greco to his patron, describing him as a Cretan, who was then in Rome and had been a pupil of Titian. El Greco, however, derived very little influence from his master, for his works, beyond a certain influence of Bassano, Baroccio, Veronese, or Tintoretto, are individual and distinct. El Greco came to Spain in 1577. He signed his name in Greek characters, using the Latin form of his Christian name, and repeatedly declaring himself as a native of Crete. He appeared before the tribunal of the Inquisition at Toledo in 1582, as interpreter for one of his compatriots who was accused of being a Moor; he then definitely announced that he had settled in Toledo. Nothing is known of his parentage or early history, nor why he went to Spain; but in time he became typically Spanish, and his paintings exhibit all the characteristics of the people amongst whom he resided. From very early days he struck out a definite line for himself, glorying in cold tones with blue, in the use of grey and many varied tones of white, and in impressionistic work which foreshadowed ideas in art that were introduced one hundred and fifty years later. His first authenticated portrait is that of his patron and fellow-countryman Clovio, now at Naples; his last, that of a cardinal, in the National Gallery. His first important commission in Spain was to paint the reredos of the Church of Santo Domingo el Diego at Toledo. He may have been drawn to Spain in connexion with the work in the Escorial, but he made Toledo his home. The house where he lived is now a museum of his works, saved to Spain by one of her nobles.

His earliest important work is "El Espolio", which adorns the high altar in Toledo, but by far

DETAIL FROM THE BURIAL OF THE CONDE D'ORGAZ, BY THEOTOCOPULI, IN THE CHURCH OF S. TOMÉ, TOLEDO

his greatest painting is the famous "Burial of the Count of Orgaz" in the Church of Santo Tomé. The line of portraits in the rear of the burial scene represents with infinite skill almost every phase of the Spanish character, while one or two of the faces in the immediate background have seldom, if ever, been equalled in beauty. It is one of the masterpieces of the world. The influence of El Greco in the world of art was for a long time lost sight of, but it was very real, and very far-reaching. Velasquez owed much to him, and, in modern days, Sargent attributes his skill as an artist to a profound study of El Greco's works. El Greco's separate portraits are marvels of discernment; few men have exhibited the complexities of mental emotion with equal success. The largest collection of his works outside of Spain belongs to the King of Rumania, some of the paintings being at Sinaia, others in Bukarest. In the National Gallery of London, in the collections of Sir John Stirling-Maxwell, the Countess of Yarborough, and Sir Frederick Cook, in the galleries of Dresden, Parma, and Naples, and in the possession of several eminent French collectors are fine examples of his work. But to study El Greco's work to perfection one must visit Toledo, Illescas, Madrid, the Escorial, and many of the private collections of Spain, and his extraordinary work will be found worthy of the closest study. He was a man of eccentric habits and ideas, of tremendous determination, extraordi-

BURIAL OF THE CONDE D'ORGAZ
THEOTOCOPULI, CHURCH OF S. TOMÉ, TOLEDO

nary reticence, and extreme devoutness. He was a constant attendant at the sacraments, made complete arrangements for his funeral before he died, and was buried in the Church of Santo Tomé.

Cossio, *Memoir of El Greco* (3 vols., Madrid, 1908); Barres and Lafond, *Domenico Theotocopuli* (Paris, 1911).

George Charles Williamson.

Thera (or Santorin), Diocese of (Santorino), in the Cyclades. About the year 2000 B. C., the extinguished volcano of the island renewed its activities, destroyed the population, and a portion of the island which was engulfed in the sea. In 236 B. C. another eruption separated the island of Therasia from Thera; in 196 B. C. the islet of Hiera sprang up (Palæo-Kaïmeni); in A. D. 46 appeared Thia which was afterwards swallowed up by the sea; in 1570 a portion of the island of Thera caved in; in 1573 and 1711 two new islands arose; in 1866 there was a new volcanic eruption which lasted two years. The ancient town of Thera has been discovered at Haghios-Stephanos, near Mesavouno; the Ptolemies established an important garrison there. Some time after the eruption of the year 2000 B. C., the island called Calliste was repeopled by the Phœnicians, then by the Dorians who named it Thera about the year 620 B. C.; it became successively a tributary of Sparta, Athens, the Ptolemies, and finally the Romans. It is believed that Christianity was already introduced there in the second century and that certain tombs belonged to that epoch (Hiller von Gärtringen, "Thera", III, 195); a very old church dedicated to Saint Michael and other very ancient churches have been found there. The See of Thera was a suffragan of Rhodes in the seventh and tenth centuries (Gelzer, "Ungedrucktc . . . Texte der Notitiæ episcopatuum", 542, 558). It became a metropolitan see in the eighteenth century and after the incorporation of the island with the Kingdom of Greece it was reduced in 1833 to a bishopric, which rank it still holds.

Le Quien (Oriens christ., I, 941) and Hiller von Gärtringen (Thera, III, 198) give a list of twenty Greek bishops, of whom the greater part are posterior to the sixteenth century; this list could easily be completed. In 1207 the island fell into the power of a Latin lord, himself subject to the Duke of Naxos; the population decreased continually and in 1457 there were no more than 300 persons. In 1566 Thera fell under the domination of the Turks and took the name of Deir-Menlik. It received the name of Santorin only in the Middle Ages from Saint Irene, to whom the island had a special devotion. A Latin diocese, suffragan of Naxos, was established there; a number of bishops are known, who belonged principally to the fourteenth century (Le Quien, op. cit., III, 1007–12; Eubel, "Hierarchia catholica medii ævi", I, 456; II, 252; III, 309). Thera, in the district of the Cyclades, numbers 15,000 inhabitants, of whom 400 are Catholics; 8 secular priests; 1 parish; 2 churches with a resident priest; and 6 chapels. There is also a house of Lazarists, a convent belonging to the Sisters of Charity and another to the Dominican Sisters. The bishop has jurisdiction also over the islands of Ios, Amorgos, Siphnos, Seriphos, and Melos; the last only has Catholic inhabitants.

Smith, *Dict. of Gr. and Rom. Geog.*, s. v.; Pègues, *Histoire du volcan et des îles volcaniques de Santorin* (Paris, 1842); Cigalla, *General statistics of the Island of Thera* (Hermopolis, 1850), in Greek; Lacroix, *Iles de la Grèce* (Paris, 1853), 484–92; Mamet, *De insula Thera* (Lille, 1874); Fouqué, *Santorin et ses éruptions* (Paris, 1879); von Gärtringen, *Thera* (3 vols., Berlin, 1899–1904); *Missiones catholicæ* (Rome, 1907), 149.

S. Vailhé.

Thermæ Basilicæ, a titular see in Cappadocia Prima, suffragan of Cæsarea. The Greek "Notitiæ episcopatuum" down to the thirteenth century describe the see as the first suffragan of Cæsarea. Perhaps there was a bishop from the time of St. Basil; in any case four others are mentioned: Firminus, present at the Council of Chalcedon, 451; Photinus, at the Council of Constantinople, under the patriarch Gennadius (459); Musonius, exiled by Justin I, about 518; Theodore, present at the Sixth Œcumenical Council of Constantinople, 681, and at the Council in Trullo, 692 (Le Quien, "Oriens christ.", I, 389). This see is evidently the city which Hierocles (Synecdemus, 699, 2) names Therma, and which he places in Cappadocia Prima under the Cæsarean metropolis. It may quite probably be identified with Aquæ Sarvenæ, which the "Tabula" of Peutinger places on the road between Tavium and Cæsarea, the same, doubtless, as Sarvena, a city described on an inscription and by Ptolemy (V, 6, 12). This would be to-day Terzili Hammam, a village about twenty hours north of Cæsarea, a vilayet of Angora, where there are hot mineral sulphur waters, still frequented. A part of the building containing the baths is of Roman construction; a Christian inscription has been found thereon. Therma, which the "Itinerarium Antonini", 204, places also on the road from Tavium to Cæsarea, must be Iamush Pisheren Sou, a mineral spring to the north of Kir Shehir.

Ramsay in *Bulletin de correspondance hellénique*, VII (Paris, 1883), 302 sq.; Idem, *Asia Minor* (London, 1890), passim; Müller, ed. Didot, *Notes on Ptolemy*, I, 854, 876.

S. Pétridès.

Thermopylæ, a titular see and suffragan of Athens in Achaia Prima. It is the name of a defile about 4 miles long, whose principal passage was barred by a wall, which the Phocidians erected against the Thessalians in the sixth century B. C. It receives its name from two hot springs called to-day Loutra (the baths). There in the month of July, 480 B. C., Leonidas, King of Sparta, with 1300 Spartan soldiers and allies fell with his men while bravely opposing the enormous army of Xerxes. In 279 B. C. Brennus with 170,000 Gauls penetrated into Greece by this pass; it was there also that Antiochus III, King of Syria, was defeated by the Romans in 191 B. C., and where in A. D. 395 Alaric, King of the Goths, passed on his way to devastate Greece. In the sixth century Justinian restored the fortifications (Procopius, "De ædificiis", IV, 2). After the Latins in 1204 had overthrown the Byzantine Empire, Thermopylæ was made a Latin diocese. Many letters from Innocent III, written in 1208 and 1210 to Bishop Arnulfus, are extant. The other bishops from the thirteenth to the sixteenth century are mentioned by Le Quien ("Oriens christianus", III, 847–850; Gams, "Series episcoporum", 431; Eubel, "Hierarchia catholica medii ævi", I, 509; II, 275; III, 332); but many of them were only titulars. The see is also referred to shortly after in the "Liber censuum" of the Roman Church (ed. Fabre), II, 8; it was never a Greek diocese. To-day it is known as Lycostomos on the bank of the Maliac Gulf in the district of Phoiotis. The passage is less difficult than formerly because the alluvium deposited by the Sperchios has caused the sea to recede and has facilitated a road between the waters and the mountain.

Smith, *Dict. of Greek and Roman Geog.*, s. v.

S. Vailhé.

Thessalonians, Epistles to the, two of the canonical Epistles of St. Paul. This article will treat the Church of Thessalonica, the authenticity, canonicity, time and place of writing, occasion, and contents of the two Epistles to that Church.

I. The Church of Thessalonica.—After Paul and Silas had, during the Apostle's second missionary journey, left Philippi, they proceeded to Thessalonica (Θεσσαλονίκη, the modern Saloniki), perhaps because there was in the city a synagogue of the Jews (Acts, xvii, 2). Thessalonica was the capital of the Roman Province of Macedonia; it was a free city, ruled by a popular assembly (cf. Acts, xvii, 5, εἰς τὸν δῆμον) and magistrates (cf. verse 6, ἐπὶ τοὺς πολιτάρχας). St. Paul at once began to preach the Gospel to the Jews and proselytes. For three successive sabbaths he explained the Scriptures in the synagogue, opening up the way and gradually leading his hearers to the tremendous truth that there was need the Christ should die and rise again from the dead, and that Jesus whom Paul preached was in very truth this Christ. Some of the Jews believed and took sides with Paul and Silas. It would seem that Paul stayed in the city some time thereafter, for, according to the reading of Codex Bezæ (fifth century), and the Vulgate and Coptic Versions (Acts, xvii, 4), he converted a large number not only of proselytes ($\tau\hat{\omega}\nu$ $\tau\epsilon$ $\sigma\epsilon\beta o\mu\acute{\epsilon}\nu\omega\nu$) but of Gentile Greeks ($\kappa\alpha\grave{\iota}$ $\text{'}E\lambda\lambda\acute{\eta}\nu\omega\nu$). In the first place, it is unlikely that a large number of these latter were won over to the Faith during the three weeks devoted to the synagogues; for Paul did manual labour night and day, so as not to be burdensome to his converts (I Thess., ii, 9). Secondly, these converts from idolatry (I Thess., i, 9) would scarcely have become, after so brief an apostolate, a "pattern to all that believe in Macedonia and in Achaia" (I Thess., i, 7). Thirdly, the Church of Philippi sent alms twice to Paul at Thessalonica (Phil., iv, 16), a fact which seems to indicate that his sojourn there was longer than three weeks. Be this as it may, the signal success of Paul's apostolate among Jews, proselytes, and Hellenes, together with the conversion of "not a few noble ladies" (Acts, xvii, 4), aroused the Jews to a fury of envy; they gathered together a mob of idlers from the agora and set the whole city in tumult; they beset the home of Jason, found the Apostle away, dragged his host to the tribunal of the politarchs and charged him with harbouring traitors, men who set Jesus up as king in place of Cæsar. That night the brethren made good the escape of their teacher to Berea. There the Gospel of Paul met with a much more enthusiastic reception than that accorded to it by the synagogue of Thessalonica. The Jews of that city drove Paul to Berea and there, too, stirred up the mob against him. He left Silas and Timothy to complete his work and went to Athens (Acts, xvii, 1–15).

II. FIRST EPISTLE. A. *Authenticity.* (1) External Evidence. (a) II Thess.—The strongest external evidence in favour of the authenticity of I Thess. is II Thess., which, whatsoever be its date of composition, is the very earliest document that clearly presupposes I Thess. to have been written by Paul.

(b) Manuscripts.—The evidence of MSS. alone is such as to set the authenticity of this letter beyond all doubt; it is in the Greek text of the Codex Sinaiticus (fourth cent.), Cod. Vaticanus (fourth cent.), and Cod. Alexandrinus (fifth cent.); it is in the Old Latin and Syriac Versions, which trace its authenticity down to the middle of the second century.

(c) The Apostolic Fathers give evidence of very early use of the Epistle as Sacred Scripture. St. Ignatius of Antioch (d. A. D. 110–17, according to the chronology of Harnack which we shall follow in this article), in "Eph.", X, i, probably uses the $\dot{\alpha}\delta\iota\alpha\lambda\epsilon\acute{\iota}\pi\tau\omega s$ $\pi\rho o\sigma\epsilon\acute{\upsilon}\chi\epsilon\sigma\theta\alpha\iota$, "pray without ceasing", of I Thess., v, 17; and undoubtedly had in mind I Thess., ii, 4, when writing to the Romans (II, i) the distinctly Pauline thought $o\dot{\upsilon}$ $\theta\acute{\epsilon}\lambda\omega$ $\dot{\upsilon}\mu\hat{\alpha}s$ $\dot{\alpha}\nu\theta\rho\omega\pi\alpha\rho\epsilon\sigma\kappa\epsilon\hat{\iota}\nu$ $\dot{\alpha}\lambda\lambda\grave{\alpha}$ $\theta\epsilon\hat{\omega}$, "I will that ye please not man but God". Because St. Ignatius, as the other Apostolic Fathers, cites from memory, without the exactness of later Fathers and without ever mentioning the name of the sacred writer quoted, Dr. Inge, the Lady Margaret professor of divinity in the University of Cambridge, says: "The evidence that Ignatius knew I Thessalonians is almost nil" (cf. "The New Testament in the Apostolic Fathers", Oxford, 1905, p. 74). Against such scepticism, the clear use of St. Paul by the Apostolic Fathers is of no avail. Harnack, who cannot be accused of overmuch credulity, thinks that St. Ignatius of Antioch possessed a collection of the Pauline Epistles; and that by the year 117, St. Polycarp of Smyrna had a complete collection (*eine ganze Sammlung*) thereof before him and veritably lived therein (cf. Chronologie der altchristlichen Litteratur, I, 249, note 2). In the "Pastor" of Hermas (A. D. 140), we find the phrase of I Thess., v, 13, "Be at peace among yourselves" ($\epsilon\grave{\iota}\rho\eta\nu\epsilon\acute{\upsilon}\epsilon\tau\epsilon$ $\dot{\epsilon}\nu$ $\dot{\epsilon}\alpha\upsilon\tau o\hat{\iota}s$) several times, used almost as it occurs in the Alexandrian and Vatican Codices (cf. Hermas, "Simil.", VIII, vii, 2; "Vis.", III, vi, 3; III, ix, 2, 10; III, xii, 3).

The Apologetic Fathers are clear and to the point. St. Irenæus (A.D. 181–9) cites I Thess., v, 23, expressly attributing the words to the Apostle's First Epistle to the Thessalonians ("Contra hæreses", V, vi, 1 in P. G., VIII, 1138), and I Thess., v, 3, as the saying of the Apostle (ibid., V, xxx, 2 in P. G., VII, 1205). Tertullian quotes at length passages from each of the five chapters of I Thess. to prove his thesis of the resurrection of the body ("Liber de resurrectione carnis", xxiv, in P. L., II, 874); and uses the Epistle against Marcion ("Adv. Marcionem", V, xv in P. L., II, 541). St. Clement of Alexandria (A. D. 190–210) very often cites this brief letter—cf. "Pædagogus", I, v, 19 (Stählin's ed., I, 101) and "Stromata", I, i, 6 (Stählin's ed., II, 5) for I Thess., ii, 5–7; "Stromata", II, xi, 4, IV, xii (Stählin's ed., II, 138 and 286), for an allusion to I Thess., iv, 3, and an accurate citation of six verses (3–8) of the same chapter; "Pædagogus", II, ix, III, xii, IV, xxii (Stählin's ed. I, 206 and 288, and P. G., VIII, 1352) for the appeal to almost every verse of I Thess., v, i. e. verses 5, 8, 13, 15, 19, 22; "Stromata", I, xi (Stählin's ed., II, 34) for a quotation from the same chapter. So strong is the external evidence in favour of the authenticity of I Thess. as to convince all scholars save only those who, on account of internal evidence, deny to Paul the authenticity of all his Epistles.

(2) Internal evidence.—In I Thess. all the main Pauline doctrines are taught,—the Death and Resurrection of Jesus Christ (i, 10; iv, 14; v, 10); His Divinity and Sonship of the living God (i, 9, 10); the resurrection of our bodies (iv, 15–18); the mediatorship of Christ (v, 10); the call of the nations to the Kingdom of Christ, which is the Church (ii, 12), sanctification by the indwelling of the Holy Spirit (iv, 8). The plain and direct style, the writer's affectionate concern for his spiritual children, his impatience of Judaizers, the preponderance of personal over doctrinal statements, the frank and honest self-revelation of the writer—all these distinctly Pauline characteristics argue strongly for the authenticity of this letter.

Baur, the prime mover of neo-Tübingen ideas, was the first to wave aside recklessly all external evidence and seriously to attack the authenticity of I Thess. from internal evidence (cf. "Der Apostel Paulus", ed. 2, II, 94). He was followed by Nowack, "Der Ursprung des Christentums" (Leipzig, 1857), II, 313; Volkmar, "Mose, Prophezie und Himmelfahrt" (Leipzig, 1867), 114; and Van der Vries, "De beiden brieven aan de Thessalonicensen" (Leyden, 1865). The reasons which impel Baur and his followers are trivial. (i) The lack of doctrine makes the letter unworthy of Paul. We have noted that the main heads of Paul's teaching are included in this short letter. Moreover, the letter is a most touching revelation of the great heart of St. Paul and as such alone is befitting the outspoken Apostle. (ii) The Epistle is a clumsy forgery. The author has worked up his story from Acts. Paul could not have written ii, 14–16. It is far-fetched to compare the woes inflicted by the Jews upon the Church of Thessalonica with the ills they wrought upon the Church of Judea. It is un-Pauline to set Jewish Christians up as an example to Gentile converts (Baur, op. cit., 482). These purely subjective objections are worthless. The Apostle was too broad-minded to be tied down to the narrow ideas of Baur. True, in his later letters—to the Romans and Corinthians and Galatians, for instance—we might not look for the juxtaposition of Jewish with Gentile Christians; but the Judaizers were not so troublesome to Paul when he wrote to the Thessalonians as when he wrote to the Romans.

(iii) The expression ἔφθασε δὲ ἐπ' αὐτοὺς ἡ ὀργὴ εἰς τέλος, "the wrath hath come upon them unto the end" (ii, 16), naturally refers to the destruction of Jerusalem (A. D. 70) as an accomplished punishment of the Jews for killing the Lord Jesus. This is an unwarranted assumption. The phrase εἰς τέλος is indefinite; it has no definite article nor any defining qualificative; it modifies ἔφθασε and refers to no definite end either accomplished or to be accomplished. St. Paul indefinitely but surely sees the oncoming end, reads the easily legible writing on the wall, and interprets that writing: "The wrath [of God] hath come upon them even unto making an end of them". (iv) Baur (op. cit., 485) finds the eschatology of the Epistle un-Pauline. In the Epistles to the Corinthians, Romans, and Galatians, for instance, there is no *diving* into the future, nothing said of the Parousia, or second coming of Jesus. But the reason is clear,—those to whom Paul wrote his great and later Epistles had not the eschatological difficulties of the Thessalonians to meet. He adapted his letters to the wants of those to whom he wrote. The very fact that the apprehension of an immediate Parousia is not mentioned in the later letters would have prevented a forger from palming off as Pauline such an unusual topic.

B. *Canonicity.*—The two Epistles to the Thessalonians are included among the canonical books accepted by the Councils of the Vatican, of Trent, and of Florence, and are among the *homologoumena* of all early lists of canonical New-Testament Scriptures; for instance, to mention only such early lists as accord with the received canon of Trent, these two Epistles are listed in the Muratorian Fragment (A. D. 195–205), in the canons of St. Athanasius of Alexandria (A. D. 373), of the Third Council of Carthage (A. D. 397), in which Saint Augustine took part, of St. Epiphanius (A. D. 403), of Innocent I (A. D. 405), and of Gelasius (A. D. 492). In fact there can be no reason whatsoever to doubt the canonicity of either letter.

C. *Time and Place.*—The *textus receptus*, at the end of the two Epistles, gives a subscription stating that they were written from Athens (ἐγράφη ἀπὸ Ἀθηνῶν); and this same subscription is contained in the great uncial codices A, B², K², L²— that is, Alexandrinus (fourth century), Vaticanus (fifth-century corrector), Mosquensis, and Angelicus (both of the ninth century); it is likewise translated in important Latin, Syriac, and Coptic MSS. None the less, there can be no doubt but that the letters were written during Paul's first stay in Corinth. Timothy had been sent to Thessalonica by Paul from Athens (I Thess., iii, 2). Hence some Fathers inferred that, on this mission, Timothy brought along I Thess. The inference is wrong. As Rendel Harris says in "The Expositor" (1898), 174, Paul may have sent another letter from Athens by Timothy to the Thessalonians. He cannot have sent I Thess. from there by him. Paul clearly states that Timothy had returned from Thessalonica before the writing of I Thess. (cf. iii, 6). Whither did he return? I Thess. does not state. Acts, xviii, 5, supplies answer. When Timothy returned from Macedonia with Silas to Paul, the Apostle was at Corinth. The news brought him by Timothy was the occasion of I Thess. Moreover, in the greeting with which each letter begins, the names of Paul, Silvanus (i. e. Silas), and Timothy are grouped together; and we know that the three were together at Corinth (Acts, xviii, 5) during Paul's first visit to that city (cf. also II Cor., i, 19). We have no proof that they were ever elsewhere together. I Thess., then, was written during the eighteen months Paul stayed at Corinth, i. e. in the year 48 or 49, according to the chronology of Harnack, "Chronologie der altchristlichen Litteratur" (Leipzig, 1897), I, 717; in the year 53 or 54 according to the commonly received scheme of Pauline chronology. Both letters are generally considered to be the earliest extant writings of St. Paul. Some few now deem it proved that Paul wrote to the South Galatians even before he wrote to the Thessalonians, cf. Zahn, "Einleitung in das Neue Testament" (Leipzig, 1897), I, 138.

D. *Occasion.*—Having arrived at Athens, Paul at once set himself to convert the Jews, proselytes and Gentiles of that city. Among the latter he met with unusually small success. The Epicureans and Stoics for the most part rated him as a talkative lounger in the agora and either berated him with ridicule upon the Hill of Ares or waved him aside (Acts, xvii, 16–32). Meanwhile he trembled for the Church of Thessalonica. So long as he had been there, only the Jews strove to set his work at naught; now in his absence, the Gentiles joined the Jews (I Thess., ii, 14), and made a vigorous onslaught upon the faith of his children. Paul yearned mightily to see their face once more. In his intense affection and concern, he breaks away from his wonted first plural: "We willed to have come to you, even I, Paul, and that once and again; but Satan hindered us" (ii, 18). The hindrance wrought by Satan was probably a security against his return given by Jason and some friends (Acts, xvii, 9). Being unable to follow the yearnings of his heart, Paul sent Timothy to save the flock from the ravening wolves (I Thess., ii, 2). The Acts make no mention of this legation of Timothy from Athens to Thessalonica. Not long after, Paul left for Corinth (Acts, xviii, I). Thither Timothy, who returned from Thessalonica, brought back an eyewitness's testimony as to the conditions of the faithful of that city. Rendel Harris, in "The Expositor" (1898), 167, thinks that the Thessalonians sent Paul a letter by Timothy and, to make good his theory, appeals to I Thess., i, 2, 5; ii, 1, 5, 9–13; iii, 3–6. There may be some ground for such conjecture in "We also" (καὶ ἡμεῖς) of I, ii, 13; "Also I" (κἀγώ) of I, iii, 5, and in "you have a good remembrance of us always" (ἔχετε μνείαν ἡμῶν ἀγαθήν) of I, iii, 6. Be this as it may, whether by letter or by word of mouth, Timothy fully informed Paul of the needs of the Christian community at Thessalonica; and these needs were the occasion of the first Epistle to that community.

E. *Contents.*—No other letter of Paul to a Church is so free and easy and epistolary as is this letter; it defies strict doctrinal analysis, and is far more personal than doctrinal. Merely for the sake of some division, we may consider chapters i and iii as personal, chapters iv and v as doctrinal. (1) Personal part—a missionary's free outpouring of a noble heart's yearnings.—He is filled with joy at hearing how they stand fast by the faith which he preached to them (i, 2, 8); fondly talks about his labours and about his stay with them (i, 9–ii, 12); thanks God for the way they received from him the word of God (ii, 13–16); delicately hints at his apprehensions for them, by telling how at Athens he yearned to see them, how he sent Timothy in his stead, how relieved he now is as Timothy's message has brought him peace of mind (ii, 17–iii, 10). Then follows a brief and beautiful prayer which sums up the yearnings of the great soul of the Apostle (iii, 11–13).

(2) Doctrinal part.—With this prayer ends what is meant to be free and epistolary. Now follows a little phrase of transition—"For the rest, therefore, brethren"—and a thoroughly Pauline and direct exhortation upon how they "ought to walk and to please God" by purity (iv, 1–8), brotherly love (iv, 9–10), and peaceful toil (verse 11). The peace of everyday toil had been disturbed by a fanatical

lethargy due to the supposed oncoming Parousia. Hence the eschatological passage that follows. The brethren who have died will have part in the Second Coming just as they that are now alive (verses 12–17); the time of the Parousia is uncertain, so that watchfulness and not lethargy are needed (v, 1–11). The letter ends with a series of pithy and pointed exhortations to respect for their religious teachers, and to the other virtues that make up the glory of Christian life (v, 12–22); the Apostolic benediction and salutation, a request for prayers and the charge that the letter be read in public (verses 23–28).

III. SECOND EPISTLE. A. *Authenticity*. (1) External Evidence.—MS. evidence is the same for II Thess. as for I Thess., so, too, the evidence of the ancient versions. The Apostolic and Apologetic Fathers are more clearly in favour of II Thess. than of I Thess. St. Ignatius, in Rom., x, 3, cites a phrase of II Thess., iii, 5, εἰς τὴν ὑπομονὴν τοῦ Χριστοῦ, "in the patience of Christ". St. Polycarp (XI, 3) refers the letter expressly to Paul, although, by a slip of the memory, he takes it that the Apostle glories (II Thess., i, 4) in another Macedonian Church, that of the Philippians; elsewhere (XI, 1) Polycarp uses II Thess., iii, 15. St. Justin (about A. D. 150), in "Dialog.", xxxii (P. G., VI, 544), seems to have in mind the eschatological language of this letter. Besides it is set down as Pauline in the Canon of Marcion (about A. D. 140).

(2) Internal Evidence.—The literary dependence of II Thess. on I Thess. cannot be gainsaid. The writer of the former must have written the latter, and that too not very long thereafter. II Thess., ii, 15, and iii, 6, are to be explained by I Thess., iv, 1–8 and 11. The style of the two letters is admittedly identical; the prayers (I, iii, 11, v, 23; II, ii, 16, iii, 16), greetings (I, i, 1; II, i, 1, 2), thanks (I, i, 2; II, i, 3), and transitions (I, iv, 1; II, iii, 1) are remarkably alike in form. Two-thirds of II Thess. is like to I Thess. in vocabulary and style. Moreover, the structure of the Epistle, its subject-matter, and its affectionate outbursts of prayer for the recipients and of exhortation are all decidedly Pauline characteristics. The argument from internal evidence is so strong as to have won over such critics as Harnack (Chronologie, I, 238) and Jülicher (Einleitung, 40). Schmiedel, Holtzmann, Weizäcker, and others deny the force of this argument from internal evidence. Its very similarity to I Thess. in vocabulary and style is made to militate against the authenticity of II Thess.; the letter is too Pauline; the author was a clever forger, who, some sixty years later, took up I Thess. and worked it over. There has been no motive assigned for such a forgery; no proof given that any post-Apostolic writer was so cunning as to palm off this letter as a Pauline imitation.

Eschatology of Paul.—The chief objection is that the eschatology of II Thess. contradicts that of I Thess.: the letter is in this un-Pauline. In I Thess., iv, 14–v, 3, the writer says the Parousia is imminent; in II Thess., ii, 2–12, iii, 11, the writer sets the Parousia a long time off. Non-Catholics who hold the Pauline authorship of the two letters generally admit that Paul predicted the second coming would be within his own lifetime and deem that the signs narrated in II Thess., ii, as preludes to that coming do not imply a long interval nor that Paul expected to die before these signs occurred. Catholics insist that Paul cannot have said the Parousia would be during his lifetime. Had he said so he would have erred; the inspired word of God would err; the error would be that of the Holy Spirit more than of Paul. True, the Douay Version seems to imply that the Parousia is at hand: "Then we who are alive, who are left, shall be taken up together with them in the clouds to meet Christ, into the air, and so shall we always be with the Lord" (I Thess., iv, 16). The Vulgate is no clearer: "Nos, qui vivimus, qui residui sumus" etc. (iv, 15–17). The original text solves the difficulty: ἡμεῖς οἱ ζῶντες οἱ παραλειπόμενοι, ἅμα σὺν αὐτοῖς ἁρπαγησόμεθα. Here the Hellenistic syntax parallels the Attic. The sentence is conditional. The two participles present stand for two futures preceded by εἰ; the participles have the place of a protasis. The translation is: "We, if we be alive—if we be left—[on earth], shall be taken up" etc. A similar construction is used by Paul in I Cor., xi, 29 (cf. Moulton, "Grammar of New Testament Greek", Edinburgh, 1906, I, 230). St. Paul is here no more definite about the time of the Parousia than he was in I Thess., v, 2, when he wrote "that the day of the Lord shall so come, as a thief in the night." There is in St. Paul's eschatology the very same indefiniteness about the time of the Parousia that there is in the eschatological sayings of Jesus as related in the Synoptics (Matt., xxiv, 5–45; Mark, xiii, 7–37; Luke, xxi, 20–36). "Of that day or hour no man knoweth, neither the angels in heaven, nor the Son, but the Father" (Mark, xiii, 32). In the deposit of faith given by the Father to the Son, to be given by the Son to the Church, the time of the Parousia was not contained. We readily admit that St. Paul did not know the time of the Parousia; we cannot admit that he knew it wrong and wrote it wrong as the inspired Word of God and a part of the deposit of faith.

As for the further objection that the apocalyptic character of ii, 2–12, is post-Pauline and dependent upon so late a composition as the Apocalypse of John (A. D. 93–96) or, worse still, upon the Nero *redivivus* story (Tacitus, "Hist.", II, viii), we answer that this assertion is entirely gratuitous. St. Paul got his apocalyptic ideas from the very same source as John, that is either from revelation to himself or from the Old Testament or from tradition. Most of the details of his apocalyptic description of the Parousia are given in other apocalypses (I John, ii, 18; Matt., xxiv, 24; Luke, xxi, 8; Mark, xiii, 22; Deut., xiii, 1–5; Ezech., xxxviii and xxxix; Dan., vii–ix, xi, xii, etc.). The man of sin, Antichrist, Belial, the well-nigh complete triumph of evil just before the end of time, the almost general apostasy, the portents, and other items are features familiar to Old-Testament and New-Testament apocalyptic writings.

B. *Canonicity*.—The canonicity of II Thess. has been treated together with that of I Thess.

C. *Time and Place*.—II Thess. was written at Corinth not long after I Thess., for both Timothy and Silas are still with Paul (i, 1), and the silence of the Acts shows that, once Paul left Corinth, Silas was not again his companion in the ministry. There seem to be allusions in iii, 2, to the troublous stay of a year and a half at Corinth (Acts, xviii); in ii, 14, to the letter quite recently written to the Thessalonians; and in iii, 7–9, to the ministry of Paul among them as not long passed.

D. *Occasion*.—The eschatology of I Thess. had been misunderstood by the Thessalonians; they took it, the day of the Lord was at hand (ii, 2); they were overwrought by the exaggerations of some meddlers and perhaps by a forged letter which purported to have come from Paul (ii, 2; iii, 17). Moreover the disorderly conduct of some (iii, 6, 11) gave the Apostle no little concern; this concern he showed by the letter.

E. *Contents*.—The three chapters into which the letter is now divided, aptly analyze the thought. In the first chapter are a greeting, thanksgiving for the faith and love of the Thessalonians, and an assurance of Divine recompense to them and to their persecutors. In the second chapter is the main thought of the letter—the eschatology. Certain signs are detailed which must precede the Parousia. Until these signs appear, there is no reason for terror or taking leave of their senses. The third chapter is the usual Pauline request for prayers, a charge to avoid the disorderly, a truly Pauline allusion to the example he set them, and the final identification of the letter by a greeting written with his own hand.

Of the Greek Fathers whose commentaries on I and II Thess. have come down to us, ST. JOHN CHRYSOSTOM is by far the most scholarly; THEODORET is pithy and to the point. THEODORE OF MOPSUESTIA (about A. D. 415) forces the Apostle to his ideas. EUTHALIUS THE DEACON depends on THEODORE; ST. JOHN DAMASCENE on ST. JOHN CHRYSOSTOM. Among the Latin Fathers AMBROSIASTER (about 730) at times errs in matters of faith; PRIMASIUS (about 556) collated the expositions of AMBROSIASTER, PELAGIUS, ST. AUGUSTINE, and ST. JEROME. The great Catholic commentators of more recent time are: JUSTINIANI (Lyons, 1612), A LAPIDE (Antwerp, 1614), CAJETAN (Rome, 1529), SALMERÓN (Madrid, 1602), KISTEMAKER (Münster, 1822), MCEVILLY (Dublin, 1875), BISPING (Münster, 1873), MAUNOURY (Paris, 1878), ROEHM (Passau, 1885), JOHANNES (Dillingen, 1898), PANEK (Ratisbon, 1886), PRAT, *La théologie de Saint Paul* (Paris, 1908), PICONIO (Paris, 1837), PERONNE (Paris, 1881), TOUSSAINT (Paris, 1910). The chief Protestant commentaries are those of LIGHTFOOT (*Notes*, 1895), DRUMMOND (1899), FINDLAY (1904), MILLIGAN (1908), SCHMIEDEL (1892), B. WEISS (1896).

WALTER DRUM.

Thessalonica (SALONIKI), titular metropolis in Macedonia. It was at first a village called Alia, situated not far from Axius, the modern Vardar; it subsequently took the name of Therma, from the thermal springs east and south of it. The gulf on which it was situated was then called the Thermaic Gulf. After having sheltered the fleet of King Xerxes and having belonged to the Athenians during the Peloponnesian War, Therma passed to the kings of Macedonia after the death of Alexander. Cassander, the son of Antipater, having enlarged the village and transported thither the inhabitants of the neighbouring villages, called it Thessalonica, in honour of his wife. Thenceforth the city grew steadily in importance. Unsuccessfully besieged by Æmilius Paulus, it only opened its gates after the victory of Pydna which made the Romans masters of Macedonia (168 B. C.). The kingdom was then divided into four districts, each of which had its capital and its *conventus*. Thessalonica was the capital of the second district. In 146 B. C. Macedonia was made a single province with Thessalonica as capital. This was the arrangement until the third and fourth century of our era, when four provinces were again formed. The proconsul had his residence at Thessalonica, as did later the prefect of Illyricum Orientale, who first resided at Sirmium. During the first civil war Thessalonica was the principal headquarters of Pompey and the Roman senators; during the second it supported Anthony and Octavius against the Triumvirs, receiving from them after the battle of Philippi the title of free city and other advantages, being allowed to administer its own affairs and obeying magistrates called politarchs.

Thessalonica received the title of *colonia* under the Emperor Valerian. Theodosius the Great punished the revolt of its inhabitants (390) by a general massacre in which 7000 were slain. In 479 the Goths attacked the city. Between 675 and 681 the Slavs unsuccessfully besieged Thessalonica four times. On 31 July, 904, a Mussulman corsair, Leo of Tripoli, came unexpectedly with his fleet and attacked the city, then the second in the empire, captured and pillaged it, and took away a great many prisoners. A dramatic account of the affair was written by a priest of Thessalonica, John Cameniates, who was an eyewitness (Schlumberger, "Nicéphore Phocas", Paris, 1890, 35 sqq.). In 1083 Euthymius, Greek Patriarch of Jerusalem, was commissioned by Alexius I Comnenus to negotiate peace at Thessalonica with Tancred of Sicily, who had conquered a portion of Epirus and Macedonia and threatened to take possession of the rest. In August, 1185, Guillaume d'Hauterive, King of Sicily, besieged Thessalonica by sea with a fleet of 200 ships and by land with an army of 80,000 men; the city was captured, and all resistance from the Greeks punished with death. In the following year the city was recaptured by the Byzantines; the metropolitan Eustathius wrote an account of the campaign in a homily, which was read during the Lent of 1186. In 1204, after the Latins had occupied Constantinople and a portion of the Byzantine Empire, Boniface, Marquis of Monferrato, proclaimed himself King of Thessalonica, his Latin Kingdom depending on the Latin Empire of Byzantium. He defended it against the Bulgars, whose tsar, the terrible Calojan, was assassinated under the walls of Thessalonica in 1207, and against the Greeks from Epirus. In 1222 the latter put an end to the Frankish Kingdom and took possession of Thessalonica, setting up an independent empire, the rival of that of Nicæa, with Theodore Comnenus as first sovereign. He was defeated in 1230 at Klokotinitza by the Bulgar Tsar, Assen II, and most of his empire passed into the hands of the Bulgars. Thessalonica with the remaining cities was given to Theodore's brother, the Emperor Manuel.

In 1242 after a successful campaign against the Emperor of Thessalonica, John Vatatzes, Emperor of Nicæa, forced John Angelo to take only the title of despot and to declare himself his vassal. After the expedition of Vatatzes in 1246 Thessalonica lost all independence and was annexed to the Empire of Nicæa which in 1261 was once more removed to Constantinople. Unable to defend it against the Turks, the Greeks in 1423 sold Thessalonica to the Venetians, the city being captured 28 March, 1430, by the Sultan Murad and definitively incorporated in the Ottoman Empire. It was the scene of unheard-of cruelties on the part of the Turks. In order to weaken the Greek element, so powerful in the city and in that part of Macedonia, the Sublime Porte offered a refuge about the end of the sixteenth century to the Jews driven from Spain by Philip II. They now number 80,000 out of 120,000 inhabitants; the remainder of the population consists of Turks, Greeks, Bulgars, Armenians, and nearly 3000 Catholics. The parish is directed by the Lazarists, the schools by the Christian Brothers. Thessalonica, which is the capital of a vilayet, grows constantly in importance, owing to its situation and its commerce, as well as to the part it played in the two military revolutions of 1908 and 1909 which modified the authoritative régime of the Turkish Empire.

The establishment of Christianity in Thessalonica seems to date from St. Paul's first journey to the city (see THESSALONIANS, EPISTLES TO THE). Secundus and Aristarchus, companions of St. Paul, were natives of Thessalonica (Acts, xx, 4); Demas who abandoned the Apostle to go thither, seems likewise to have been born there (II Tim., iv, 9). According to Origen, who repeats an ancient tradition ("Comment. in Ep. ad Rom.", in P. G., XIV, 1289), Gaius was the first Bishop of Thessalonica. Four persons of this name are mentioned in the New Testament, but the Gaius of Origen would be a native of Corinth (I Cor., i, 14). Melito of Sardes relates that Antoninus Pius wrote to the Thessalonians not to tolerate in their city the tumult against the Christians (Eusebius, "Hist. eccl.", IV, 26). Alexander assisted at the Council of Nicæa in 325, at Tyre in 335, and at the consecration of the Holy Sepulchre in the same year. At the end of the same century Acholius baptized Theodosius the Great. Le Quien has compiled a list of 74 Greek titulars of this city, some of whom do not belong to it. Father Petit continued his task and gives a biographical account of more than 130. The most famous were: Rufus, who in the early fifth century a ted constantly as intermediary between the papacy and the Eastern Churches; Eusebius, the correspondent of St. Gregory the Great and author of a work in ten books against the Monophysites; John, who early in the seventh century compiled the first book on the miracles of St. Demetrius; St. Joseph, brother of St. Theodore the Studite, and the victim in 832 of the Iconoclast persecutions; Leo the Philosopher, professor at the Magnaura, the master of Photius and of all the literary celebrities of the period; Michael Chumnos, the author of several canonical treatises in the twelfth century; Basil of Achrida, who took part in the theological discussions with the envoys of the pope or of the Emperor of the West; Eustachius, the celebrated scholiast of Homer; Gregory Palamas, the defender of the Hesychast theories and the bitter enemy of the Catholics in the fourteenth century, who is still regarded as one of the greatest doctors of the Schismatic Church; Isidore Glabas; Simeon, liturgist and canonist, d. in 1429, a year before the capture of the city by the Turks.

When Illyricum Orientale, comprising the two civil Dioceses of Dacia and Macedonia, was ceded by Gratian in 379 to the Empire of the East, Pope St. Damasus in order to retain jurisdiction over these distant provinces appointed the Bishop of Thessalonica his vicar Apostolic. In this capacity the bishop presided at the local councils of the various provinces, judging and solving difficulties, save in more serious matters, wherein the decision was reserved to the pope. He also confirmed the election of metropolitans and simple bishops and granted authorization to proceed to ordination. Finally, he occupied a privileged place at the œcumenical councils and signed their decisions immediately after the patriarchs. He thus enjoyed the prerogatives of a patriarch, even to bearing the title, but was subject to the Patriarch of Rome. The Bishop of Constantinople sought to modify this organization by inducing Theodosius II to pass a law (14 July, 421) which attached all the bishops of Illyria to the Byzantine Church, and by having this law inserted in the Code (439); but the popes protested against this injustice and prevented the application of the law. Until 535 the Vicar Apostolic of Thessalonica exercised jurisdiction over all the provinces of Illyricum Orientale, but subsequent to Novel xi of Justinian the authority was divided between him and the new Archbishop of Justiniana Prima. The latter, likewise appointed vicar Apostolic of the pope, directed the seven provinces of the north while the Bishop of Thessalonica continued to occupy the six others: Macedonia Prima, Thessalia, Achaia, Creta, Nova and Vetus Epirus. Matters remained so until 732 when the Emperor Leo the Isaurian, after his excommunication by the pope, connected all the bishoprics of Illyria with the Patriarchate of Constantinople. Thenceforth, despite the protests of Rome, Thessalonica was dependent on the Church of Byzantium.

After the establishment of the Latin Kingdom of Thessalonica in 1205 Nivelo de Chérisy, Bishop of Soissons, who had taken an active part in the Fourth Crusade, was appointed by Innocent III (10 December, 1206) first Latin archbishop of the city. He died in the following year; his successors were at first residential and afterwards titular (see list in Le Quien, "Oriens Christ.", III, 1089–96; Eubel, "Hierarchia catholica medii ævi", I, 510; II, 275). From a letter of Innocent III written in 1212 we learn that Thessalonica had then eleven suffragans. Apart from the saintly bishops mentioned above Thessalonica had other saints: Agape, Irene, and Chionia, martyred under Diocletian; Agothopodus, deacon, and Theodulus, rector, martyred under Diocletian; Anysia, martyred under Maximian; Demetrius, martyr, the protector of the city, from whose tomb flowed an oil which worked miracles, and whose superb basilica has been converted into a mosque; David, solitary (sixth century); Theodora, d. in 892; etc. The Vicariate Apostolic of Macedonia, for the Bulgars, whose titular resides at Thessalonica, was established in 1883. It has upwards of 6000 Catholics, 26 residential stations, 33 secular priests, most of them married, 10 Lazarist priests, 21 churches and chapels, 27 primary schools for boys and girls with 1110 pupils. The seminary, directed by the Lazarists, is at Zeitenlik, near Thessalonica. The Sisters of Charity and the Bulgarian Eucharistine Sisters also have schools and orphanages.

Le Quien, *Oriens christ.*, II, 27–66; Tafel, *De Thessalonica eiusque agro* (Berlin, 1839); Belley, *Observations sur l'histoire et sur les monuments de la ville de Thessalonique* in *Histoire de l'Académie des Inscriptions*, XXXVIII (Paris), 125 sq.; Vigouroux, *Le Nouveau Testament et les découvertes archéologiques modernes* (Paris, 1890), 215–38; Spata, *I Siciliani in Salonico nell'anno MCLXXXV* (Palermo, 1892); Petit, *Les évêques de Thessalonique* in *Echos d'Orient*, IV, V, VI, and VIII; Duchesne, *L'Illyricum ecclésiastique* in *Byzantinische Zeitschrift*, I, 531–50; Vailhé, *Annexion d'Illyricum au patriarcat œcuménique* in *Echos d'Orient*, XIV, 29–36; *Missiones catholicæ* (Rome, 1907), 798; Cheyne, *Encyclopædia biblica*, s. v.

S. Vailhé.

Theveste, titular see of Numidia. The city seems to have had some importance even prior to Christianity. During the first century of our era the Legio III Augusta resided there before being transferred to Lambæsis. It was made a *colonia* probably under Trajan. There is mention of a council held there by the Donatists. Among its saints were St. Lucius, its bishop, who in 256 assisted at the Council of Carthage and died for the Faith two years later; St. Maximilianus, martyred 12 March, 295; St. Crispina, martyred 5 December, 304. Some of its bishops are known: Romulus in 349; Urbicus in 411; Felix exiled by the Vandals in 484; Palladius mentioned in an inscription. It was rebuilt by the patrician Solomon at the beginning of the reign of Justinian, and he built a tomb there which still exists. Under the Turks Theveste had a garrison of janizaries. Since 1851 it has been occupied by the French. Under the name of Tebessa it is the capital of a canton of the Department of Constantine in Algeria. It has 7000 inhabitants, of whom about 1200 are Europeans. It has a Catholic parish. Tebessa is very rich in ancient monuments, among them being a triumphal arch of Caracalla, a temple, a Christian basilica of the fourth century 216 feet long by 72 feet wide, near which are buried a number of pious persons.

Toulotte, *Géog. de l'Afrique chrét.: Proconsulaire* (Rennes, 1894), 292–99; Diehl in *Nouvelles archives des missions scientif.* (Paris, 1893), 325–32; Ballu, *Le monastère byz. de Tébessa* (Paris, 1897).

S. Vailhé.

Thibaris, titular see in Byzacena (Africa), not mentioned by any ancient author. The official list of the Roman Curia places it in Byzacena, but in reality it belonged to Africa Proconsularis. An inscription fixes the exact site at the ruins now called Henshir Hamamet, in a plain watered by the Wady Tibar which has retained the name of the town. These ruins are situated about five miles north-east of Djebba, near the Djebel Gorra Tunaiai. There are galena and calamine mines at Djebba. The former were worked even in ancient times and are mentioned in a letter from St. Cyprian to the faithful of Thibaris (Ep. lvi). The chief ruins are those of an aqueduct and a Christian church. Nearby is the native orphanage of St. Joseph of Tibar, where the White Fathers receive chiefly Algerian Kabyles. Two bishops of Thibaris are known: Vincent, present at the Council of Carthage in 256, and Victor, at the Conference of Carthage in 411, where his rival was the Donatist, Victorian.

Toulotte, *Géog. de l'Afrique chrét.: Proconsulaire* (Paris, 1892), 266.

S. Pétridès.

Thibaut de Champagne.—Thibaut IV, Count of Champagne and King of Navarre, a French poet, b. 1201, at Troyes; d. 8 July, 1253. He was the posthumous son of Thibaut III, Count of Champagne and Blois, and Blanche, sister of Sancho VII, King of Navarre. He had to defend his rights to his countship first in 1221 against his uncle, Count of Brienne, and later against his aunt, Alice, Queen of Cyprus. During the minority of Louis IX, he first sided with the nobles against Blanche of Castile, but he soon separated from them, and being attacked by them, he was defended by the queen. In 1234, his uncle Sancho VII having died childless, he succeeded him as King of Navarre. He was the leader of the crusade organized in 1239 by Gregory IX, and landed at Acre on the first of September, fought several unsuccessful battles, and after his troops were decisively defeated at Gaza, he left Syria on 1 September, 1240. In order to arouse the zeal of the nobility for the defence of the Holy Land, he composed four songs, known as Crusade songs, which rank among his best; their literary value is equal to their Christian inspiration. Very little is known of his life after he returned from his campaign in Palestine. There is some uncertainty concerning the place where he died, at Provins, Troyes, or in Navarre. He is regarded as one of the greatest lyrical poets of the thirteenth century. His rhythms are most harmonious, his combinations of metres show a real skill, while his expressions are full of refinement and true sentiment. His verses have been published, under the title of "Poésies du Roi de Navarre", by Lévesque de la Ravallière (Paris, 1742). They consist of sixty-six poems, divided as follows: thirty-nine love sings, twelve *jeux-partis*, or debating songs, four Crusade songs, and eight *serventois*. Dante and Petrarch had the greatest regard for this poet and spoke of him in most laudatory terms.

THIBAUT, COMTE DE CHAMPAGNE
After a Painting by Jouannin

D'ARBOIS DE JUBAINVILLE, *Hist. des comtes de Champagne* (Paris, 1866); PETIT DE JULLEVILLE, *Hist. de la langue et de la littérature française*, II (Paris, 1894); BEDIER, *Chansons de croisade* (Paris, 1909).

LOUIS N. DELAMARRE.

Thierry of Freiburg (OR OF SAXONY), a philosopher and physician of the Middle Ages, and a member of the Order of Saint Dominic. We cannot with any degree of certainty identify him with Frater Theodoricus, who in 1283, was named prior of the convent of Würzburg, but there is abundant evidence that at the Chapter General held at Strasburg (1293) he was made superior general of the province of Germany, holding this post until 1296. In 1297 we find him at Paris, teaching the "Sentences" of Peter Lombard; in 1303, at Coblenz; and in 1304, at Toulouse, taking part in the Chapter General of his order. In 1310, the Chapter General of Plaisance appointed him *Vicarius Provinciæ Teutonicæ*, while awaiting the nomination of a new provincial. Nothing is known of his after life.

Thierry was a very active writer. A list of the works of Dominican authors, compiled in 1330, ascribes to him thirty-one different treatises, twenty-one of which are still in existence, on the most diverse subjects of theology, metaphysics, and cosmology. But the one which especially redounds to the glory of Thierry is that composed in 1304 "De Fride" for the Chapter General of Toulouse, at the request of Améric de Plaisance, superior-general of the order. Therein with wonderful clearness Thierry describes the different reflections and refractions of every ray which forms either the first or second rainbow. This experiment was made with a spherical drop of water. Furthermore, with the help of spherical glass vases filled with water, he verified experimentally the phenomena which he planned. This work, which made its author a precursor of Descartes, is a model of the art of logically combining experiments.

VENTURI-REGIANO, *Commentari sopra la storia e le teorie dell' ottica*, I (Bologna, 1814), pt. III: *Dell' Fride*, etc., 149–246. KREBS, *Meister Dietrich (Theodoricus Teutonicus de Vriberg) sein Leben, seine Werke. seine Wissenschaft* in *Beiträge zur Geschichte der Philosophie des Mittelalters Texte u. Untersuchungen*, V (Münster, 1906), 5–6.

PIERRE DUHEM.

Thiers, LOUIS-ADOLPHE, French statesman and historian, first president of the Third French Republic, b. at Marseilles, 16 April, 1797; d. at Paris, 3 Sept., 1877. Established at Paris in 1821 he at once took an important place in the Liberal Opposition Press as editor of the "Constitutionnel", and in the literary world through his "Histoire de la révolution française" (10 vols., 1823–27). The foundation in 1829 of "Le National" by Thiers, Mignet, and Armand Carrel provided the Liberals with a powerful weapon against the Polignac ministry, and furthered the movement which resulted in 1830 in the fall of the Bourbons. A proclamation drawn up by Thiers 29 July, 1830, directed the attention of the people to the Duc d'Orléans who became King Louis-Philippe. Thiers became a member of the French Academy in 1834 and between 1830 and 1840 was several times minister under the July Monarchy. When the long Guizot ministry freed him from political occupations he undertook the "Histoire du consulat et de l'émpire" (20 vols., 1845–62). It was he who caused the adoption by the Chamber of Deputies, 3 May, 1845, of an order of the day aimed at the Jesuits and stipulating that the Chamber should rely on the Government to enforce the laws of the State. The result of this vote was the negotiation undertaken at Rome by the ambassador Rossi in behalf of the Government of Louis-Philippe to secure the suppression of the Jesuits in France. In 1846 Thiers accused the Guizot ministry of making concessions to the Catholic party at the expense of the university. But after the advent of the Second Republic, having taken fright at the rise of certain Revolutionary ideas, he served the interests of the Church, and as early as March, 1848, he acknowledged in a letter to Madier de Montjan that his ideas had changed with regard to liberty of instruction. In the committee which prepared the vote for the *loi Falloux* Thiers was influenced by Dupanloup and declared to Cousin: "The abbé is right. In fighting against the congregations we have fought against justice and virtue and we owe them reparation." He voted also for the Roman expedition.

Under the Second Empire Thiers was elected (1863) deputy of the Opposition, but on several occasions he criticised in the Chamber the Italian revolution and besought the Government of Napoléon not to permit the downfall of the temporal power. After having eloquently opposed the policy of the Second Empire with regard to Prussia he was sent to various European courts by the Bureau of National Defence, which

ADOLPHE THIERS
From the Portrait by Bonnat

was seeking assistance for defeated France. On 8 Feb., 1871, he was elected deputy by twenty-six departments, and nine days later the National Assembly almost unanimously elected him chief executive. He negotiated the Treaty of Frankfort and induced the Assembly of Bordeaux (1 March, 1871) to ratify the peace preliminaries. The rigorous measures by which he overcame the Commune of Paris made many enemies for him. It is still a debated question whether he might have saved the life of Mgr Darboy by consenting to release the revolutionist Blanquil. Several episcopal nominations made under Thiers by the philosopher Jules Simon, minister of public worship, redounded to the glory of the French episcopate. After the treaty with Germany (15 March, 1873) for the evacuation of French territory the National Assembly declared that Thiers deserved well of his country. But the defeat at Paris of his friend Rémusat by the Radical Barodet and the subsequent disturbances among the Monarchists in the Assembly induced Thiers to resign his office 24 May, 1873. He was succeeded by MacMahon. Having thus given up power Thiers took his seat in the Left Centre of the Assembly amid the applause of the Left; and although the advanced members of the Left, because of his severity during the Commune, deliberately treated him as "a sinister old man", he upheld with all his strength and prestige during his last years a policy designed to bring about the defeat of the Right and of MacMahon. His long career sometimes seems inconsistent. After having contributed by his historical works to the prestige of Napoleon I and by his vote to the election of the future Napoleon III to the presidency of the Republic, he became the adversary of the Empire. After having supported anti-religious Liberalism under the Restoration and the monarchy of July, he supported the Catholic claims under the Second Republic, and during his old age under the Third Republic he assisted the anti-clerical parties. But the unity of his life consisted in his always being the defender of a certain category of ideas, aspirations, and interests proper to a social class—the *bourgeoisie*; and his book on the right of ownership (1848), besides being very interesting as a document, is the expression of an individualistic conception, more pagan than Christian, of the right of ownership, one which is the very antithesis of social Christianity. He was buried with the rites of the church.

CALMON, *Discours parlementaires de M. Thiers* (16 vols., Paris, 1878–89); THIERS, *Notes et Souvenirs*, 1870–1873 (Paris, 1893); LEGOFF, *Life of L. Ad Thiers* (New York, 1897); JULES SIMON, *Le Gouvernement de M. Thiers* (Paris, 1876, tr. New York, 1829); HANOTAUX, *Hist. de la France contemporaine: Le Gouvernement de M. Thiers* (Paris, 1903); DE MARCÈRE, *L'Assemblée nationale de 1871, gouvernement de M. Thiers* (Paris, 1904); GAUTHEROT, *L'Exchange des otages. Thiers et Mgr Darboy* (Paris, 1910); PIERRE SIMON, *Thiers chef du pouvoir exécutif* (Paris, 1911).

GEORGES GOYAU.

Thietmar of Merseburg. See DITHMAR.

Thignica, titular see in Numidia. The Roman Curia's official list of titular sees places Thignica in Numidia. It belonged to Proconsular Africa. Its ruins are called Ain Tounga, south-west of Testour, Tunisia. They are very extensive and cover the summit and slopes of a series of hills. One inscription calls it "Civitas Thignicensis" and states that it was divided into three parts, another that it became a *municipium* at the beginning of the third century under the name of "municipium Septimium Aurelium Antoninianum Herculeum Frugiferum Thignica". Towards the centre of the ruins is a Byzantine fortress, trapezoidal in shape, flanked by five square towers. Here an inscription makes mention of the proconsul Domitius Zenophilus (326–32), famous in the annals of Christian Africa. Among the other ruins are a small triumphal arch, a temple, a Christian church, the remains of the enclosure, etc. Despite the splendour and importance of this town we know only one bishop, Aufidius, who assisted in 411 at the Conference of Carthage where he had a Donatist rival.

TOULOTTE, *Géographie de l'Afrique chrétienne. Proconsulaire* (Paris, 1892), 269–271; DIEHL, *L'Afrique byzantine* (Paris, 1896), passim.

S. PÉTRIDÈS.

Thijm, JOSEPH ALBERT ALBERDINGK, b. at Amsterdam, 8 July, 1820; d. there, 17 March, 1889. After finishing his studies in his native city, he took up a commercial career. But this prosaic occupation did not smother his talents. Art and literature had a great attraction for him. He made his entry into the literary world as an art critic in the "Spectator" in 1842, and immediately attracted great attention by his views and his style. The following year he published an essay on the spelling of hybrid words, in which he came out as a philologist. In his poems, which are numerous and take rank with what is best in the Dutch poetry of the nineteenth century, he shows that he is a disciple of Bilderdijk. This he himself declares in his celebrated poem "U min ik, Oude met uw stroefgeplooide trekken" (I love you, old one, with your rugged features). In his triple capacity of art critic, philologist, and poet, Thijm did so much from 1842 to 1889 that he not only led the way for Catholics and laid the foundation of Catholic literature, but became one of the foremost writers of the Netherlands of the nineteenth century.

His whole activity, all his writings, bear the stamp of Catholicity. No one attacked Catholic art or Catholic history without having to reckon with Thijm. "Nil nisi per Christum" was his motto. By his writings and the earnest character of his Catholicism Thijm played one of the most influential rôles in the Catholic revival. To him is due no less than to Dr. W. Cramer and Mgr. J. Smits, first editor-in-chief of "De Tyd," the restoration of the hierarchy in the Netherlands. In 1852 Thijm sent a memorial to Rome setting forth the historic reasons for considering Utrecht to be the traditional archiepiscopal see of Holland, and the anxiety of the Catholics at that time that the historic tradition be not broken. Besides the periodical "Dietsche Warande" which he edited from 1855 to 1886, the people's almanac for the Catholics of the Netherlands (1852–89), and numberless brochures in defence of the Church and church history, his most important works are: "Het Voorgeborchte", "Palet en Harp", "Portretten van Joost van den Vondel", "Verspreide Verhalen", "Kerstliederen", "De la Litérature Néerlandaise", "Karolingische Veihalen", "De Heilige Linie". His last efforts were devoted to the preparation of a complete edition of the works of van den Vondel.

Katholieke Illustratie (1889), 377 sq.; *Dietsche Warande* (1889), p. 239 sq.; VAN DER DUYS (Amsterdam, 1889); *Kath. Alberd. Thijm* (Amsterdam, 1896); *Busken Huet, Litterarische Fantasieen en Kritieken* (Harlem, 1881); *Levensgeschiedenissen van de leden der Maatschappij van Letterkunde van Leiden* (Leyden, 1889).

P. ALBERS.

Thijm, PETER PAUL MARIA ALBERDINGK, brother of the foregoing, b. at Amsterdam, 21 Oct., 1827, d. at Louvain, 1 Feb., 1904. He made his studies in his home city, at first at the Gymnasium and later at the Athenæum, from which he was graduated in letters and history in 1857. For some years he was instructor in history in Maestricht. After being called to a professorship in the University of Louvain in 1870, he succeeded in establishing a chair for the special study of the history of Holland's literature. Although not as gifted as his elder brother, he had a great deal of the latter's enthusiasm for literature and art and was an ever ready champion of the Christian ideal in art. This savant of artistic temperament and zeal contributed not a little to the revival of the Flemish spirit in the University of Louvain. He was President of the Association Tijd en Vlijt and of Constantius Buter. He was also a member of the Flemish Academy, and, for a time, its President. From 1888 on, Paul Thijm edited the periodical "Dietsche Warande", which was in this way transplanted into Belgium. His chief works are: "De H. Willibrord, Apostel der Nederlanden" (1867); "Karel de groote en zijne eeuw" (1866); "Gestichten van liefdadigehied in België, van Karel den Groote tot aan de XVI eeuw", awarded a prize by the Royal Academy of Brussels (1883); "Schets der Algemeene Geschiedenis" (1870); "Vroolijke historie van Ph. van Marnix" (1876); "Spiegel van Nederlandsche letteren" (1877).

Dietsche Warande en Belfort (Antwerp-Ghent, 1904); *Levensgeschiedenissen van de leden der Maatschappij van Letterkunde te Leiden* (Leyden, 1904).

P. ALBERS.

Thimelby, RICHARD (*alias* ASHBY), missionary priest, b. in Lincolnshire, England, 1614; d. at St. Omer's, Belgium, 7 Jan., 1672. He entered the Society of Jesus in 1632. Having taught philosophy and theology at Liège for about sixteen years, he was sent to England where he laboured for the most part in his native county. In 1666 he became Master of Novices at Ghent, and Rector of St. Omer's, Belgium, in 1672, where he remained until his death. His translation of Father Binet's "Treatise on Purgatory" was edited by Father Anderdon in 1874. He also wrote a controversial work entitled "Remarks on Stillingfleet" (London, 1672).

OLIVER, *Collections* (London, 1845); *Menology of the Society of Jesus* (London, 1902); SOMMERVOGEL, *Bibliothèque de la Compagnie de Jésus* (Brussels, 1890).

EDWARD P. SPILLANE.

Third Orders.—I. GENERAL.—Third Orders signify in general lay members of religious orders, i. e. men and women who do not necessarily live in community and yet can claim to wear the habit and participate in the good works of some great order.

A. *Origin*.—The general idea of lay people affiliated to religious orders, as seen in the Benedictine Oblates (q. v.) or *confraters* (Taunton, "Black Monks of St. Benedict", London, 1897, I, 60–63; for Norbertines cf. Hurter, "Papst Innocenz III", Schaffhausen, 1845, IV, 148), is too natural for there to be any need to seek its origin. Founders and benefactors of monasteries were received in life into spiritual fellowship, and were clothed in death in some religious habit. So too the Templars had a whole system whereby layfolk could partake in some sort in their privileges and in the material administration of their affairs (English Hist. Rev., London, April, 1910, 227). But the essential nature of the tertiary is really an innovation of the thirteenth century. At that date many of the laity, impatient of the indolent and sometimes scandalous lives of the clergy in lower Europe, were seized with the idea of reforming Christendom by preaching. This admirable intention caused the rise of the Vaudois under Valdez of Lyons ("Anecdotes Historiques tirés du Recueil inédit d'Etienne de Bourbon, O.P.", ed. by Lecoq de La Manche, Paris, 1878, 290–314), and under somewhat more curious conditions the Fratres Humiliati. The Vaudois were at first welcomed by the pope, Alexander III, who authorized their preaching, but as they were unacquainted with theological teaching and had pursued no clerical studies, their sermons were not seldom dogmatically inaccurate and eventually defiantly heretical. The Humiliati also soon became suspect and were forbidden by Lucius III to preach, till in 1207 Innocent III gave a section of them permission to resume their work, provided that they limited themselves to moral questions and did not venture on doctrinal subjects ("De articulis fidei et sacramentis ecclesiæ", cf. Denifle, O.P., "Archiv für Litteratur und Kirchengeschichte des Mittelalters", I, 419). Moreover some became priests, were gathered into a cloister, and took up religious life. The others remained outside, yet spiritually dependent on the clerical portion, and now for the first time in history called a Third Order, *Tertius Ordo* (Mandonnet, "Les Origines de l'Ordo de Penetentia"; the Bull is to be found in Tiraboschi, "Vetera Humiliatorum monumenta", II, Milan, 1766–68, 139).

B. *Division*.—The Third Orders can each be divided into (a) regulars, i. e. living in convents, and (b) seculars, i. e. living in the world. Of these the first take vows, the latter can only make a solemn promise (except that Carmelite Tertiaries apparently take some sort of vows of obedience and chastity, cf. Angelus a S.S. Corde, O.C.D., "Manuale juris communis Regularium", Ghent, 1899, q. 1067), which, however, distinguishes them from members of mere confraternities and constitutes them legally a religious order (Constitution of Leo XIII, "Misericors Dei Filius").

C. *Members*.—Any Catholic may join a Third Order, but may not at once belong to more than one, nor may he without grave cause leave one for another. The laying aside of the distinctive sign or prayers for any space of time does not in itself put an end to membership with a Third Order, but the deliberate wish to dissociate oneself from it is sufficient to produce that effect (S. Cong. Indulg., 31 Jan., 1893).

D. *Privileges*.—The Regular Third Order participates in all the indulgences granted to the First and Second Orders (S. Cong. Indulg., 28 Aug., 1903), but not in those granted to the Secular Third Order (ibid.). This latter no longer participates in any privileges save those directly granted to itself (S. Cong. Indulg., 31 Jan., 1893; S. Cong. Indulg., 18 July, 1902; S. Cong. Indulg., 28 Aug., 1903).

TIRABOSCHI, *Vetera Humiliatorum Monumenta* (Milan, 1766–68), I, II, III; HÉLYOT, *Dictionnaire des Ordres Religieux* (Paris, 1862), I–IV; MANDONNET, *Les Origines de l'Ordo de Pænitentia* (Fribourg, 1898); SABATIER, *Regula Antiqua Fratrum et Sororum de Pænitentia seu Tertii Ordinis S. Francisci* (Valence, 1901); GOETZ, *Die Regel des Tertiarordens* in *Zeitschrift für Kirchengeschichte* (1902), XXIII; ADDERLY AND MARSON, *Third Orders* (Oxford, 1902); MANDONNET, *Les Règles et le Gouvernement de l'Ordo de Pænitentia au XIII Siècle* (Paris, 1902); MORTIER, *Histoire des Maîtres Géneraux de l'Ordre des Frères Prêcheurs*, II (Paris, 1905), 220–50; HEIMBUCHER, *Die Orden und Kongregationen der katholischen Kirche* (Paderborn, 1907); PRÜMMER, *Manuale Juris Ecclesiastici*, II (Fribourg, 1907), 311–16.

BEDE JARRETT.

II. THIRD ORDER OF OUR LADY OF MOUNT CARMEL.—Soon after the Order of Our Lady of Mount Carmel was established in Europe in the thirteenth century, lay persons, not bound by religious vows, seem to have attached themselves to it more or less closely. There is evidence of the existence of a "Confrairie N.-D. du Mont-Carmel" at Toulouse in 1273, and of a "Compagnia di Santa Maria del Carmino" at Bologna in 1280, but the exact nature of these bodies is uncertain owing to a lack of documents. Somewhat later mention is frequently made of trade-guilds having their seat in churches of the order, members of which acted as their chaplains. Thus the master-bakers, innkeepers and pastry-cooks at Nîmes, the barbers and surgeons of the same town, who were also connected with the Dominicans, the goldsmiths at Avignon. Benefactors of the order received letters of fraternity with the right of participation in the privileges and good works of the friars. Others, under the name of *bizzoche* and *mantellatæ*, wore the habit and observed the rule, e. g. "M. Phicola nostra Pinzochera" at Florence in 1308. Others again became recluses in the anchorages attached to Carmelite churches, and made profession under the form: "Ego frater N. a Spiritu Sancto ad anachoreticam vitam vocatus offero me, coram Deo, Patri et Filio et Spiritui Sancto, et promitto me in servitio Dei secundum Scripturam sacram Novi et Veteris Testamenti more anchoreticæ vitæ usque ad mortem permansurum." Among the tertiaries not living in community must be mentioned Blessed Louis Morbioli of Bologna (d. 1495).

The canonical institution of the third order dates from the middle of the fifteenth century, when a community of Beguines at Guelders sought affiliation to the order, and Blessed John Soreth, General of the Carmelites, obtained a Bull (7 Oct., 1452) granting the superiors of his order the faculties enjoyed by the Hermits of St. Augustine and the Dominicans of canonically establishing convents of "virgins, widows, beguines and mantellatæ". Further legislation took place in 1476 by the Bull "Mare magnum privilegiorum", and under Benedict XIII and his successors. The rule observed by the tertiaries, whether living in the world or gathered into communities, was originally that of the friars with modifications as required by their status. Theodor Stratius, General of the Calced Carmelites, composed in 1635 a new rule, revised in 1678, which is still observed among the tertiaries of the Calced and the Discalced Carmelites. It prescribes the recitation of the canonical office, or else of the Little Office of the Blessed Virgin, or, in its place, of the Pater noster and Ave Maria to be said thirty-five times a day, five times in lieu of each of the canonical hours; also half an hour's meditation every morning and evening; fasting on all Fridays and also on Wednesdays and Saturdays from 14 September till Easter, abstinence during Advent and Lent, and various works of mortification, devotion, and charity. Superiors may in their discretion dispense from some of these obligations.

It is impossible to estimate even approximately the number of tertiaries living in the world. Besides these there are numerous corporations of tertiaries established in different countries, viz. two communities of tertiary brothers in Ireland (Drumcondra and Clondalkin near Dublin) in charge of an asylum for the blind and of a high-school for boys; eighteen communities of native priests in British India belonging partly to the Latin and partly to the Syro-Malabar rites; four houses of Brothers of Christian Education in Spain. Far more numerous are the communities of nuns, namely twenty-three in India (Latin and Syro-Malabar rites) for the education of native girls, and four convents in Syria in connexion with the missions of the Order; two congregations of tertiaries in Spain with nineteen and forty-eight establishments respectively, and one unattached, for educational work. In Spain there are also tertiary nuns called "Carmelitas de la caridad" engaged in works of charity with 150 establishments. The Austrian congregation of nuns numbers twenty-seven houses, while the most recent branch, the Carmelite Tertiaries of the Sacred Heart, founded at Berlin towards the end of the last century for the care and education of orphans and neglected children, have spread rapidly through Germany, Holland, England, Switzerland, Italy, Austria, and Hungary, and have twenty houses. In Italy there are three different congregations with thirty-two convents. There are smaller branches of the tertiaries in South America with two houses at Santiago, Chile, in Switzerland with four convents, and in England with one.

Bullarium Carmelitanum (Rome), 1715 sqq.; *Catalogus conventuum religiosorum et Monialium carmelitarum discalceatorum* (Rome, 1911).

BENEDICT ZIMMERMAN.

III. THE THIRD ORDER SECULAR OF THE ORDER OF OUR LADY OF MOUNT CARMEL has been introduced into the United States. There are at present two congregations, with 125 members.

FERDINAND HECKMANN.

IV. THIRD ORDER OF ST. DOMINIC.—*Origin.*—This was one of the earliest developments of St. Francis's Ordo de Pœnitentia. It was not indeed the primal organism from which the Friars Preachers evolved, but rather represents that portion of the Order of Penance which came under Dominican influence. At first vaguely constituted and living without system or form, its members gradually grew more and more dependent on their spiritual guides. The climax was reached, and the work of St. Francis received its final perfection, when Muñon de Zamora, the seventh master-general of the Friars Preachers, formulated a definite rule in 1285. By this the Ordo de Pœnitentia was to be ruled in each local centre by a Dominican priest (Federici, "Istoria de cavalieri Gaudenti", Venice, 1787, Codex Diplomaticus, II, 35) and was to be subject to the obedience of the Dominican provincials and master-generals. No longer were there to be any of those vague transitions and extravagant vagaries (ibid., 28) which disfigured in history these Orders of Penance. Henceforward this branch was linked to the fortunes of the Friars Preachers, wore their habits of black and white (with few minor differences varying according to time and country), and was to participate in all their good works. They were not called a third order indeed until after the thirteenth century (Mandonnet, "Les règles et le gouvernement de l'ordo de Pœnitentia", Paris, 1902, p. 207) but continued to be known as "Brothers and Sisters of Penance" with the addition "of St. Dominic", that is "The Brothers and Sisters of the Penance of St. Dominic".

Simultaneously with them there came into being another and very different institution which, however, subsequently amalgamated with the Ordo de Pœnitentia to form the Dominican Third Order. This was a military order, called the *Militia Jesu Christi* (soldiery of Jesus Christ) created for the defence of the Church against the Albigenses. It owed its origin to Bishop Foulques of Toulouse, Simon de Montfort (Federici, "Istoria de cavalieri Gaudenti", Codex Diplomaticus, I), and not improbably to St. Dominic, then a canon of St. Augustine. This connexion with the founder of the Friars Preachers is first definitely propounded by Bl. Raymund of Capua, who became a Dominican about 1350. But the truth of this assertion is borne out by several other indications. As early as 1235, Gregory IX confided the Militia to the care of Bl. Jordan of Saxony, second master-general, by a Bull of 18 May (Federici, op. cit., 10); and in the same year he decreed for the knights a habit of black and white (op. cit., 14). Further, when the Militia was brought across the Alps and established in Italy it is found to be always connected with some Dominican church (op. cit., I, 13). Lastly, it was very largely influenced by a famous Dominican, Fra Bartolomeo of Braganza, or of Vicenza, as he is sometimes called (op. cit., I, 12, 42, etc.). Originally working side by side and independent of each other, owing to the fact that both received the same spiritual administration of the Friars Preachers, they appear to have been merged together at the close of the thirteenth century. This is what Raymund of Capua implies as the result of his researches. So too their ultimate coincidence is hinted at by Honorius III in 1221 when he designates the Militia "nomine pœnitentiæ" (Federici, Codex Diplomaticus), and a comparison also of the rules of the two institutions: that of Gregory IX for the Militia in 1235 (op. cit., 12–16) and that of Muñon de Zamora for the Order of Penance of St. Dominic in 1285 (op. cit., 28–36) would lead one to the same conclusion. The only considerable difference that could be cited against this identity is that Muñon de Zamora expressly forbids the carrying of arms. But this is in reality but a further proof of their approximation, for he allows for the one exception which could possibly apply to the Militia, viz. in defence of the Church (ibid., 32). This amalgamation is admitted by the Bollandists to have become general in the fourteenth century (Acta Sanctorum, Aug., I, 418–422). From this double movement therefore, i. e. from the Ordo de Pœnitentia S. Dominici and the Militia Jesu Christi, was born the modern Third Order of St. Dominic. Though its source is therefore anterior to the First Order, its full perfection as an organized society, with a distinctive habit, a definite rule, and a declared *ethos* or spirit, is due to the genius of the children of St. Dominic. They took up the work of St. Francis, and, with their characteristic love of order and systematic arrangement, brought it into something compact and symmetrical. From them this idea of subjection to a First Order was taken up by the Franciscans and has been adopted by all subsequent Third Orders.

Spirit.—Primarily the work of the Third Order and its definite spirit may be summed up by saying that it was established first to help in reform of church discipline. Its initial purpose was the preaching of penance; but under Dominican influences it rather leaned to the intellectual aspect of the Faith and based its message to the world on the exposition of the Creed; it was to reform church discipline by the more widespread knowledge of the mysteries of faith. Secondly, to defend the Church. Originally this was a military necessity, demanding physical force with which to restrain equally material opposition. Thirdly, to develop the communion of prayer. The medieval ideal of Christ's Mystical Body which has captivated all spiritual-minded people implies a harmony of prayer. To achieve this end the contemplative and monastic orders were begun; and the Third Order of St. Dominic endeavours to link pious souls to this great throng of religious (Proctor, "The Dominican Tertiary's Daily Manual", London, 1900, 15–20).

Reformation.—Only for one period in its history was there any real fear of suppression. Many held that the condemnation passed on the Beguines and Beghards at the Council of Vienna in 1312 applied no less to the Orders of Penance. In consequence the master-general petitioned Pope John XXII in 1326 to settle definitely the difficulty. As a result he answered by a Bull of 1 June, 1326 (Cum de Mulieribus), which is a long eulogium on the work of the Dominican Third Order. After the plague of 1348, a great deal of laxity and disorganization crept into the Third Order, but a wonderful throng of saints soon caused its rejuvenation. The influence of St. Catherine of Siena gave a powerful impetus to the movement in Italy and her work was carried on by Bl. Clara Gambacorta (d. 1419) and Bl. Maria Mancini (d. 1431). This new spiritual vigour reached across the Alps to the sisterhoods of Germany, where the effect was almost abnormal (Heimbucher, "Die Orden und Kongregationen der katholischen Kirche", Paderborn, 1907, II, 169–177). But there has never been any reform in the sense of a separate organization with a change of rule or habit. As in the First Order, there has been a peculiar gift of unity which has enabled it to last undivided for seven hundred years.

Divisions.—The Third Order as it exists to-day can be divided into two categories: regular, i. e. comprising Tertiaries, whether men or women, who live in community and wear the habit externally; and secular, i. e. whether married or single, cleric or lay, who live their lives like others of their profession, but who privately take up practices of austerity, recite some liturgical Office, and wear some symbol of the Dominican habit. The origin of the conventual women Tertiaries has never been very clearly worked out. It is usual to trace them back to Bl. Emily Bicchieri, about the year 1255 ("Manual of Third Order of St. Dominic", London, 1871, 9). But if the view taken above of the origin of the Third Order in the Ordo de Pœnitentia be correct, we are forced to the conclusion that the communities of women established by St. Dominic at Prouille, S. Sisto, etc. were really of this Third Order. Their constitutions, approved first for S. Sisto, though previously observed at Prouille, expressly speak of the nuns as "de Pœnitentia S. Mariæ Magdalenæ" ("Analecta Ord. Præd.", Rome, 1898, 628 sqq.). It would seem then that the Ordo de Pœnitentia did not exclude convents of enclosed nuns from its ranks, and this was due probably to St. Dominic himself. Very much later came a conventual order of men, originated by the genius of Père Lacordaire. He considered that the democratic spirit of the Dominican Order fitted it especially for the task of training the youth. But he knew how impossible it was for his preaching associates to tie themselves down to schoolwork among boys; as a consequence, he began, in 1852, a Third Order of men, wearing the habit, living in community yet without the burdens of monastic life. The rule was approved provisionally in 1853 and definitely in 1868 (for the rule cf. "Acta Capituli Generalis Ord. Præd.", Rome, 1904, 106 sqq.). But by far the greatest portion of the Third Order consists of secular Tertiaries. These are of every rank of society, and represent the old Ordo de Pœnitentia and the old Militia. In certain countries they are grouped into chapters, having a lay prior and sub-prior or prioress and sub-prioress, and hold monthly meetings. Since the Rule of Muñon de Zamora (1285), they have always been subject to a Dominican priest appointed by the Dominican provincial. For the actual reception of the habit, the master-general can give faculties to any priest. The full habit is the same as that of the members of the First and Second Orders, but without the scapular (granted, however, to communities since 1667). Though the habit is not worn during life many procure it so that they may be buried in the recognized dress of St. Dominic's children.

Extent.—It is practically impossible to obtain, even in a vague way, the number of the secular Dominican Tertiaries. No general register is kept, and the records of each priory would have to be searched. From the time of St. Louis—who wished to join the Dominican and Franciscan Orders (Acta Sanctorum, August, V, 545), and is represented in old illuminations, sometimes in the habit of one, sometimes in the habit of the other (Chapotin, "Histoire des dominicains de la province de France", Rouen, 1898, p. 497), but probably never joined either—to our own time, it can be stated only that with the rise and fall of the First Order's greatness rose and fell the number of the Tertiaries. In England during the thirteenth century very many are said to have become Tertiaries. But of this nothing for certain can be specified. At the time of St. Catherine of Siena the Mantellate (women secular Tertiaries) made difficulties about receiving her to the habit as they included at the date only widows (Gardner, "St. Catherine of Siena", London, 1907, II), and there were no men at all in the Third Order in Italy at that date (Acta Sanctorum, April, III, 1881). Under Bl. Raymund of Capua, her confessor and, after her death, twenty-third master-general, attempts were made to re-establish the order and no doubt much was done (Mortier, "Maîtres généraux", III, 605–606). But by the time of St. Antoninus (d. 1450) the numbers had again dwindled down to insignificance ("Summa Moralis", Verona, 1750, III, 23, 5, 5, pp. 1291–2). Just previous to the Reformation there are a few isolated notices; thus Bl. Adrian Fortescue, the martyr, notes in his diary: "Given to the Black Friars of Oxford to be in their fraternity 12d" ("Letters and Papers of the Reign of Henry VIII", London, 1883, Rolls Series, VII, 101). But these give us no ground at all for any surmise as to statistics. In America the first canonized saint (St. Rose of Lima, d. 1617) and the first beatified negro (Bl. Martin Porres, d. 1639) were both Dominican Tertiaries, and later in France were men like M. Olier and Bl. Grignion de Montfort.

Then came the influence of Lacordaire, from whose time there dates a new enthusiasm in the Third Order ("Année Dominicaine", Paris, 1910, 149-65). Of the regular Tertiaries it is easier to speak more definitely. The numbers of all the sixteen approved congregations existing in 1902 are given, and they amount to some 7000 nuns ("Analecta Ord. Præd.", Rome, 1902, 389). To these must be added another 7000 of congregations not yet definitively authorized by Rome. But every year fresh convents are opened and the numbers continually increase. In England they began under Mother Margaret Hallahan (d. 1868) in 1842, and now in all the separate groupings there are 22 convents with some 500 sisters; in the United States their success has been remarkable. Founded in 1846 by Mother Amalie Barth (d. 1895), the congregation in 1902 included 34 convents and over 2000 nuns. In 1876 they passed into California, where they are rapidly increasing. In Ireland they have many establishments, especially for educational purposes, for their work is as varied as the needs of humanity require. Some are enclosed, others teach, visit the sick, nurse the lepers, look after old people, take care of penitent girls, work among the poor in the slums, etc. As for the congregation of teaching men, they have been greatly disorganized since their expulsion from France. At present they comprise but a half-dozen colleges in Fribourg, San Sebastian, and South America, and do not amount to more than 100 members in all. Finally, a citation from Faber's "Blessed Sacrament" (2nd ed., p. 565) may be made: "Those who are conversant with, indeed who find the strength and consolation of their lives in, the Acts of the Saints well know that there is not a nook in the mystical Paradise of our heavenly spouse where the flowers grow thicker or smell more fragrantly than this order of multitudinous child-like saints. Nowhere in the Church does the Incarnate Word show His delight at being with the children of men in more touching simplicity, with more unearthly sweetness, or more spouse-like familiarity than in this, the youngest family of S. Dominic."

FEDERICI, *Istoria de' cavalieri Gaudenti* (2 vols., Venice, 1787); MANDONNET, *Les Origines de l'Ordo de Pœnitentia* (Fribourg, 1898); CHAPOTIN, *Hist. des dominicains de la province de France* (Rouen, 1898), 494-505; PROCTOR, *Dominican Tertiary's Daily Manual* (London, 1900); MANDONNET, *Les règles et le gouvernemente de l'Ordo de Pœnitentia au XIIIe siècle* (Paris, 1902); MORTIER, *Hist. des maîtres généraux de l'Ordre des Frères Prêcheurs*, II (1905, Paris), 220-50; III, 605-6 sq.; HEIMBUCHER, *Die Orden u. Kongregationen der katholischen Kirche*, II (Paderborn, 1907); *Catalogus Sacris Ord. Præd.* (Rome, 1910), 277-79.

BEDE JARRETT.

V. THIRD ORDER REGULAR OF ST. DOMINIC, IN THE UNITED STATES.—*Congregations of Women*.—A. Sisters of St. Dominic:—

(1) Congregation of St. Catherine of Siena, with mother-house at St. Catherine of Siena Convent, Springfield, Kentucky. Founded in 1822 by Rev. Thomas Wilson, O.P. Sisters, 300; novices, 30; postulants, 7; academies, 6; schools, 13; pupils, 5000. By this congregation were founded: (a) Congregation of Dominican Tertiaries of the Blessed Virgin, with mother-house at St. Mary's of the Springs, Sheppard, Ohio, in 1830. Sisters, 195; novices, 28; academies, 3; schools, 12; pupils, 4493. From this congregation were founded (i) Congregation with mother-house at Sacred Heart Convent, Galveston, Texas. Sisters and novices, 81; postulants, 3; schools, 6; pupils, 1130. (b) Congregation with mother-house at the Convent of Our Lady of the Sacred Heart, West Springfield, Illinois, in 1873. Sisters, 120; schools, 19; pupils, 4000, academy, I. (2) Congregation with mother-house at St. Cecilia's Convent, Nashville, Tennessee. Founded in 1860 by sisters from St. Mary's, Somerset, Ohio. Sisters, 98; novices, 15; academy, 1; orphan asylum, 1; institute for young ladies, 1; schools, 6; pupils, 1042. (3) Congregation of the Most Holy Name of Jesus, with mother-house at San Rafael, California. Founded in 1850 by Most Rev. Joseph Alemany, O.P., Archbishop of San Francisco, at Benicia, California. Sisters, 135; academies, 3; schools, 6.

(4) Congregation of the Holy Rosary, with mother-house at St. Clara's Convent, Sinsinawa, Wisconsin. Founded in 1847 by Rev. Samuel Ch. Mazzuchelli, O.P. Sisters, 650; college, 1; academies, 9; schools, 46; pupils, 14,800. (5) Congregation of the Holy Cross, with mother-house at Holy Cross Convent, Brooklyn, New York. Founded in 1853 by 4 sisters from Holy Cross Convent, Ratisbon, Bavaria. Sisters, 518; novices, 25; postulants, 17; training school, 1; academies, 3; schools, 33; hospitals, 2; sanatorium, 1; infirmary, 1; orphan asylums, 6. From this congregation were founded: (a) Congregation of the Most Holy Rosary with mother-house at Mission San José, California, in 1876. Sisters, 193; novices, 20; postulants, 16; academy, 1; orphan asylum, 1; schools, 9; pupils, 2926. (b) Congregation of the Immaculate Conception, with mother-house at Great Bend, Kansas, in 1902. Sisters, 17; novice, 1; postulant, 1; hospital, 1; school, 1; pupils, 194. (6) Congregation with mother-house at Holy Rosary Convent, Second Street, New York City. Founded in 1859 by sisters from Holy Cross Convent, Ratisbon, Bavaria. Sisters, 600; academies, 8; hospitals, 2; schools, 60; pupils, 25,000. From this congregation were founded (a) Congregation with mother-house at Grand Rapids, Michigan, in 1877. Sisters, 187; novices, 50; postulants, 15; high school, 1; academies, 2; orphan asylum, 1; schools 32; pupils, 5000. (b) Congregation with mother-house at St. Dominic's Convent, Blauvelt, New York. Sisters, 139; novices, 11; postulants, 3; schools, 8; asylum, 1. (c) Congregation with mother-house at St. Dominic's Academy, Jersey City, New Jersey, in 1882. Sisters, 215; academies, 3; schools, 21; pupils, 4427. From this congregation was founded: (i) Congregation with mother-house at St. Thomas Aquinas Convent, Tacoma, Washington, in 1888. Sisters, 52; schools, 3; pupils, 300.

(7) Congregation with mother-house at St. Joseph's Convent, Adrian, Michigan. Sisters, 180; novices, 28; academies, 3; schools, 29. (8) Congregation with mother-house at St. Catherine of Siena's Convent, Racine, Wisconsin. Founded in 1862 by Mother Benedicta Bauer and Sister Thomasina Gincker from Holy Cross Convent, Ratisbon, Bavaria. Sisters, 286; postulants, 24; academies, 2; home for ladies, 1; schools, 38; pupils, 6307. (9) Congregation with mother-house at St. Mary's Convent, New Orleans, Louisiana. Founded in 1860 by sisters from Cabra, Dublin, Ireland. Sisters, 57; academies, 2; schools, 2; pupils, 565. (10) Congregation with mother-house at Reno, Nevada; founded by sisters from New Orleans, Louisiana. Sisters, 4. (11) Congregation with mother-house at St. Catherine of Siena Convent, Fall River, Massachusetts. Founded in 1891 by sisters from Carrollton, Missouri. Sisters, 52.

B. Dominican Sisters of the Third Order of St. Dominic:—

Congregation with mother-house at the Convent of Our Lady of the Rosary, 63rd Street, New York City. Founded in 1867 by Father Rochford, O.P. Sisters, 160; novices, 10; postulants, 5; academy, 1; orphan asylums, 2; schools, 11; pupils, 4000.

C. Third Order Secular of St. Dominic was introduced into the United States by the early Dominican missionaries. There are at present congregations of Dominican Tertiaries in almost all the churches in charge of Dominican Fathers, numbering from 100-600 members, and many hundred tertiaries throughout the country not belonging to any congregation.

HEIMBUCHER, *Die Orden u. Kongregationen* (2nd ed., Paderborn, 1907); *The Catholic Church in the United States*, I, II (New York, 1909); *Official Catholic Directory* (New York,)

FERDINAND HECKMANN

VI. THIRD ORDER OF ST. FRANCIS (REGULAR AND SECULAR; MALE AND FEMALE), a branch of the great Franciscan family. We deal here: A. with the secular Third Order; B. with the regular.

A. *Origin, Development, and Present State of the Secular Third Order.*—It has been believed for some time that the Third Order of St. Francis was the oldest of all Third Orders, but historical evidence is against such an opinion. For, besides similar institutions in some monastic orders in the twelfth century, we find, before the foundation of St. Francis, a Third Order, properly so called, among the Humiliati, confirmed together with its rule by Innocent III in 1201 (see text in Tiraboschi, "Vetera Humiliatorum monumenta", II, Milan, 1767, 128). But if the Third Order of St. Francis was not the first of its kind, it was, and still is, undoubtedly the best known and most widely distributed and has the greatest influence. About its origin there are two opposite opinions. According to Karl Müller, Mandonnet, and others, the Secular Third Order is a survival of the original ideal of St. Francis, viz. a lay-confraternity of penitents, from which, through the influence of the Church, the First and Second Orders of the Friars Minor and the Poor Clares have been detached. According to others, St. Francis merely lent his name to pre-existing penitential lay-confraternities, without having any special connexion with or influence on them. The two opinions are equally at variance with the best texts we have on the subject, such as Thomas of Celano, "Vita prima", I, 15; Julian of Spires, "Office of St. Francis: Third Antiphon at Lauds"; Gregory IX, Bull of 7 June, 1230 (Bull. Franc., I, 65); St. Bonaventure, "Leg. Maior", IV, 6; Bernard of Besse, in "Anal. Franc.", III, 686. According to these sources, St. Francis really founded a Third Order and gave it a Rule. If we complete these notices with some early papal Bulls bearing on the penitential movement and with the account given by Mariano of Florence (end of the fifteenth and beginning of the sixteenth century) we can state what follows:

The preaching of St. Francis, as well as his own living example and that of his first disciples, exercised such a powerful attraction on the people that many married men and women wanted to join the First or the Second Order. This being incompatible with their state of life, St. Francis found a middle way: he gave them a rule animated by the Franciscan spirit. In the composition of this rule St. Francis was assisted by his friend Cardinal Ugolino, later Gregory IX. As to the place where the Third Order was first introduced nothing certain is known. Of late however the preponderance of opinion is for Florence, chiefly on the authority of Mariano of Florence, or Faenza, for which the first papal Bull (Potthast, "Regesta Pontificum", 6736) known on the subject is given, whilst the "Fioretti" (ch. xvi), though not regarded as an historical authority, assigns Cannara, a small town two hours' walk from Portiuncula, as the birthplace of the Third Order. Mariano and the Bull for Faenza (16 Dec., 1221) point to 1221 as the earliest date of the institution of the Third Order, and in fact, besides these and other sources, the oldest preserved rule bears this date at its head. This Rule was published by P. Sabatier and H. Boehmer (see bibliography), and contained originally twelve chapters, to which at the time of Gregory IX (1227) a thirteenth was added. It prescribes simplicity in dress (1), considerable fasting and abstinence (2–3), the canonical office or other prayers instead (4–5), confession and communion thrice a year, and forbids carrying arms or taking solemn oaths without necessity (6); every month the brothers and sisters have to assemble in a church designated by the ministers, and a religious has to give them an instruction (7); they also exercise the works of charity with their brothers (8); whenever a member dies the whole confraternity has to be present at the funeral and to pray for the departed (9); everyone has to make his last will three months after his reception; dissensions among brothers and sisters or other persons are to be settled peaceably; if any troubles arise with local authorities the ministers ought to act with the counsel of the bishop (10). No heretic or anyone suspected of heresy can be received, and women only with the consent of their husbands (11); the ministers have to denounce shortcomings to the visitor, who will punish the culprits; every year two new ministers and a treasurer are to be elected; no point of the rule obliges under pain of sin (12). On account of the prohibition of arms and unnecessary oaths, the followers of this rule came into conflict with local authorities, a fact of which we have evidence in many papal Bulls all through the thirteenth century, issued to safeguard the privileges of the Tertiaries (see list of these Bulls in Mandonnet, "Les Règles", 146–47).

Wadding ("Annales Min.", ad a. 1321, n. 13) gives another longer redaction of the rule, which is almost identical with the one solemnly confirmed by Nicholas IV through the Bull "Supra montem", 17 Aug., 1289. This last form has for long been considered as the work of St. Francis, whilst Karl Müller denied any connexion of St. Francis with it. If we compare the rule published and approved by Nicholas IV with the oldest text of 1221, we see that they substantially agree, slight modifications and different dispositions of chapters (here 20 in number) excepted. Through a most interesting text published by Golubovich (Arch. Franc. Hist., II, 1909, 20) we know now that this Rule of Nicholas IV was approved on the petition of some Italian Tertiaries. Another recent publication by Guerrini (Arch. Franc. Hist., I, 1908, 544 sq.) proves that there existed in the thirteenth century Third Order Confraternities with quite different rules. On the whole, it can safely be affirmed that until Nicholas IV there was no Rule of the Third Order generally observed, but besides the one quoted above, and probably the most widely spread, there were others of more local character. The same might be said as to the government of the confraternities. Besides their own officials, they had to have a visitor, who seems to have been usually appointed by the bishop. In 1247 Innocent IV ordered that the Friars Minor were to assume the direction of the Tertiaries in Italy and Sicily (Bull. Franc., I, 464), but about twenty years later when St. Bonaventure wrote his question: "Why do not the Friars Minor promote the Order of 'Penitents'?" (Op. om., VIII, 368) the contrary had practically prevailed. Nicholas IV introduced unity of rule and of direction into the Third Order, which henceforward was entrusted to the care of the Friars Minor.

If we except a few points, bearing especially on fasts and abstinence, mitigated by Clement VII in 1526 and Paul III in 1547, the Rule as given by Nicholas IV remained in vigour till 1883, when Leo XIII, himself a tertiary, through the Apostolic Constitution "Misericors Dei Filius", modified the text, adapting it more to the modern state and needs of the society. All substantial points, however, remained; only the daily vocal prayers were reduced, as also the fasts and abstinences, whilst the former statute of confession and communion thrice a year was changed into monthly communion. Other points of the modified Rule of Leo XIII are of great social and religious importance, such as the prohibition of pomp in dressing, of frequenting theatres of doubtful character, and keeping and reading papers and books at variance with faith and morals. The direction is entrusted to

XIV.—41

the three branches of the First Order: Friars Minor, Conventuals, Capuchins, and to the Regular Third Order. By delegation, confraternities can be established and directed by any parish priest. Those who for serious reasons cannot join a confraternity may be received as single tertiaries. Finally, great spiritual privileges are granted to all members of the Third Order.

The beneficent influence of the secular Third Order of St. Francis cannot be highly enough appreciated. Through the prohibition against carrying arms a deadly blow was given to the feudal system and to the ever-fighting factions of Italian municipalities: through the admission of poor and rich, nobles and common people, the social classes were brought nearer each other. How far the religious ideal of St. Francis was carried out by the secular Third Order we may judge from the great number (about 75) of saints and blessed of every condition it produced. It may suffice to mention: St. Elizabeth of Hungary; St. Louis, King of France; St. Ferdinand, King of Castile; St. Elizabeth of Portugal; St. Rosa of Viterbo; St. Margaret of Cortona; Bl. Umiliana Cerchi; Bl. Angela of Foligno; Bl. Raymond Lullus; Bl. Luchesius of Poggibonsi, who passes as the first tertiary received by St. Francis; St. Ivo; and in our times Bl. Jean-Baptiste Vianney, the curé of Ars; of names celebrated in history for literature, arts, politics, inventions, etc., Dante, Giotto, Petrarch, Cola di Rienzo, Columbus, Vasco da Gama, Cervantes, Lope de Vega, Thomas More, Galvani, Volta, Garcia Moreno, Liszt, and, finally, Lady Georgiana Fullerton. Popes Pius IX and Leo XIII were members of the Third Order, as also is Pope Pius X. Since the adaptation of the rule by Leo XIII the Third Order has grown more active than ever. At present the total number of members is esteemed about two and a half millions, spread all over the world. National and local congresses have been held in different countries: seven in the period from 1894 to 1908 in France, others in Belgium, some in Italy, the first general congress in Assisi (1895), many local ones from 1909 to 1911; others have been held in Spain, the last one at Santiago in 1909; in Argentina the last one at Buenos Aires in 1906; in India, Canada, and in Germany and Austria, in the last two instances in connexion with general congresses of Catholics. There exist almost in all civilized languages numerous monthly periodicals which, whilst keeping up the union amongst the different confraternities, serve also for the instruction and edification of its members. The "Acta Ordinis Frat. Min.", XXVI, Quaracchi, 1907, 255–58, gives the names of 122 such periodicals. French periodicals are indicated by P. B. Ginnet, O.F.M., "Le Tiers Ordre et le Prêtre", Vanves, 1911, p. 51 sq.; German periodicals by Moll, O.M. Cap., "Wegweiser in die Literatur des Dritten Ordens", Ratisbon, 1911. In Italy even a regular newspaper was founded, "Rinascita Francescana", Bologna, 1910; another in Germany, "Allgemeine deutsche Tertiaren-Zeitung", Wiesbaden, 1911. —We may mention also the special organs for directors of the Third Order, e. g. "Der Ordensdirektor", published at Innsbruck by the Tyrolese Franciscans, "Revue sacerdotale du Tiers-Ordre de Saint François", published by French Capuchins. Both reviews appear once every two months.

B. Third Order Regular (*Male and Female*). (1) Its origin and general development till Leo X.— The origin of the Regular Third Order, both male and female, can be traced back to the second half of the thirteenth century, but no precise date can be indicated. It was organized, in different forms, in the Netherlands, in the south of France, in Germany, and in Italy. Probably some secular tertiaries, who in many cases had their house of meeting, gradually withdrew entirely from the world and so formed religious communities, but without the three substantial vows of religious orders. Other religious associations such as the Beguines (women) and Beghards (men) in the Netherlands, sometimes passed over to the Third Order, as has been clearly shown from recent study. Towards the end of the thirteenth and the beginning of the fourteenth century some suspicion of heretical opinions fell on some of these free religious unions of the Third Order (*bizocchi*), as we can infer from the Bull of John XXII "Sancta Romana", Dec., 1317 (Bull. Franc., V, 134). More than a century later St. John of Capistran (1456) had to defend the Tertiaries in a special treatise: "Defensorium tertii ordinis d. Francisci", printed with other minor works of the saint at Venice in 1580. Throughout the fourteenth century the regular tertiaries of both sexes had in the most cases no common organization; only in the following century we can observe single well-ordered religious communities with solemn vows and a common head. Martin V submitted in 1428 all tertiaries, regular and secular, to the direction of the Minister-General of the Friars Minor (Bull. Franc., VII, 715), but this disposition was soon revoked by his successor Eugene IV. We meet thus in the same fifteenth century with numerous independent male congregations of regular tertiaries with the three vows in Italy, Sicily, Dalmatia, Spain, Portugal, France, Germany, and in the Netherlands. Contemporaneously there existed sister congregations of the Third Order with solemn vows, for instance, the Grey sisters of the Third Order, serving in hospitals, spread in France and the Netherlands, whose remarkable statutes of 1483 have recently been published by H. Lemartre in "Arch. Franc. Hist.", IV, 1911, 713–31, and the congregation still existing founded at Foligno in 1397 by Blessed Angelina of Marsciano (1435). Leo X, in order to introduce uniformity into the numerous congregations, gave in 1521 a new form to the rule, now in ten chapters, retaining of the rule as published by Nicholas IV all that could serve the purpose, adding new points, especially the three solemn vows, and insisting on subjection to the First Order of St. Francis. For this last disposition the Rule of Leo X met with resistance, and never was accepted by some congregations, whilst it serves till the present day as the basis of the constitutions of many later congregations, especially of numerous communities of sisters.

(2) Single congregations after Leo X, of women.— The two Italian congregations, the Lombardic and Sicilian, which had constituted themselves in the course of the fifteenth century, were united by Paul III, and since Sixtus V enjoyed entire independence from the First Order. It had then already 11 provinces. In the seventeenth century the congregations of Dalmatia and the Netherlands (of Zeppern) were united with the Italian family. In 1734 Clement XIII confirmed their statutes. Whilst the French Revolution swept away all similar congregations, the Italian survived with four provinces, of which one was in Dalmatia. In 1906 a small congregation of Tertiary lay brothers in the Balearic Islands and a little later two convents with colleges in the United States joined the same congregation, which in 1908 numbered about 360 members. The dress is that of the Conventuals, from whom they can hardly be distinguished. The residence of the minister-general is at Rome, near the Church of Sts. Cosmas and Damian. After the time of Leo X the Spanish congregation often had troubles on the question of its submission to the First Order. After Pius V (1568) had put the whole Third Order again under the care of the Minister-General of the Friars Minor, the superiors of the three provinces constituted in Spain could, after 1625, partake at the General Chapters of the Friars Minor and since 1670 they have had even a definitor-general to represent them. The French congregation, named from their house at Paris "of Picpus",

was reformed by V. Mussart (d. 1637), and maintained close ties with the First Order till its extinction in the French Revolution. A well-known member of this congregation is Hyppolit Hélyot, the author of an important history of the religious orders. In 1768 it had four provinces with 61 convents and 494 religious. Other congregations of Tertiaries existed after the fifteenth century in Germany, Bohemia, Hungary, Ireland, and England. They perished either at the time of the Reformation or in the French Revolution. We may mention also the Obregonians, the "Bons-Fils" in northern France founded in 1615, and the "Pénitents gris" at Paris after the sixteenth century, all now extinct. In the nineteenth century some new congregations arose, e. g. the Poor Brothers of St. Francis, the Brothers of St. Francis at Waldbreitbach (Rhine) after 1860, the "Frati bigi", founded in 1884 at Naples by Ludovic of Casoria, O.F.M. The most of these modern tertiary communities consist only of lay brothers and depend on the diocesan bishop.

(3) Congregation of Sisters.—Whilst Leo X in the reform of the rule had left it free to the congregations to adopt papal enclosure or not, Pius V (1568) prescribed it to all convents of tertiary sisters with solemn vows. Still this order was not carried out everywhere. In this regard the custom prevailed that the Friars Minor refused to take the direction of those convents which had only episcopal enclosure. Besides those already mentioned above, we may add the different offshoots of the Sisters of St. Elizabeth in Austria, Germany, the Netherlands, and France (there, under the name of Sœurs du Refuge, some of them still exist). The first Ursulines, also, founded by St. Angela Merici (1540), belonged to the Third Order.

In the nineteenth century many of the new congregations adopted the Rule of the Third Order, but most of them have no further connexion with the First Order. Many of them have widely varying names; a good many are of mere local character, others again are of international importance. As to their activities, almost all dedicate themselves to works of charity, either in hospitals, homes, or ateliers; others work in schools, not a few are in foreign missions. We can give here scarcely more than a list of the names, with the dates of the foundation. In Germany there are the Poor Sisters of St. Francis, founded 1845 (1851) by M. Schervier at Aachen, with some houses in America; the Franciscan Sisters of the Holy Family, founded in 1857 at Eupen, Diocese of Cologne; the Franciscan Sisters, at Münster, Westphalia, founded in 1850; the Poor Franciscan Sisters of the Perpetual Adoration, at Olpe, Diocese of Paderborn (1857); the Poor Franciscan Sisters of the Sacred Hearts of Jesus and Mary, at Salzkotten, near Paderborn (1863); the Sisters of Mercy of the Third Order, at Thuine, Diocese of Osnabrück (1869); the Sisters of Mercy of St. Francis, at Waldbreitbach, Diocese of Trier (1863); the Franciscan Sisters at Nonnenwerth, an island on the Rhine, founded in 1872 at Heythuizen in Holland; Franciscan Sisters of Maria-Stern, at Augsburg, whose first foundation can be followed back to the thirteenth century; Franciscan Sisters at Dillingen, Diocese of Augsburg, founded in the fourteenth century; the Poor Franciscan Sisters, at Mallersdorf, Diocese of Ratisbon (1855); the Congregation of Ursperg (1897); the Franciscan Sisters of Kaufbeuren, Diocese of Augsburg, founded in the fifteenth century, to which had belonged Blessed Crescentia Hess (1744). In the Diocese of Rottenburg, in Würtemberg, we note the communities of Bonlanden near Erolzheim (1855); of Heiligenbronn (1857); of the Sisters of Christian Charity, at Reute, founded 1849 at the same place where in the fifteenth century Blessed Elizabeth of Reute, called also the "good Beta" (d. 1420), had professed the Third Order; the Franciscan Sisters of Süssen (1853). In Baden is noteworthy the Congregation of Gengenbach (1867), since 1876 also in the United States, Joliet, Illinois. At Mainz there is the Convent of Perpetual Adoration (1860).

In Austria-Hungary the School Sisters of the Third Order (1723), with mother-houses at Hallein, Diocese of Salzburg, at Vienna (III), and at Judenau, Diocese of St. Pölten; the Sisters of the Third Order of St. Francis at Vienna (V), (1857); the Poor School Sisters at Voklabruck, Diocese of Linz (1850); the Sisters of Mercy of the Third Order of St. Francis at Troppau, Diocese of Olmütz (1853); Congregation of School Sisters of the Third Order of St. Francis, at Mährisch-Trübau, Diocese of Olmütz (1851); the School Sisters of the Third Order of St. Francis at Marburg on the Drau, Diocese of Lavant (1864); the Grey Sisters of the Third Order of St. Francis, at Prague (I), 1856; and three small communities in Tyrol. In Luxemburg there is the Congregation of Pfaffental; the Sisters of Mercy of St. Francis with the mother-house in the town of Luxemburg, and communities in Sweden and the Carolines. In Holland there are the Congregations of Rosendaal, of Breda, of Heythuizen, all of which have communities in foreign missions; lastly the Congregation of Heerlen. In Belgium there exist, besides the old congregation of the Grey Sisters of Hospitals (see above) at Antwerp, Léau, Tirlemont, Hasselt, and Tongres, the more recent communities of Ghent (founded 1701), of Hérines, Diocese of Malines, of Macon-lez-Chimay, of Opwyk, Diocese of Malines (1845). In Switzerland there once existed many congregations of the Third Order, and even now there are several convents of strict enclosure. Of the active congregations the most noteworthy are the two founded by the Capuchin Theodosius Florentini, viz. the Sisters of the Holy Cross for schools, with mother-house at Menzingen (1844), with numerous convents outside Switzerland, and the Sisters of the Holy Cross for hospital work (1852), with mother-house at Ingenbohl.

In France, before the last suppression of convents, there were about fifty communities of the Third Order; the most important was that of the Missionaries of Mary, founded by Mother de Chapotin de Neuville (d. 1904) in India, with actual mother-house at Rome, with communities spread all over the world. In Italy there are the Stigmatins, founded near Florence by Mother Lapini (d. 1860); the Sisters of Egypt, for missionary work, with mother-house at Rome; the Sisters of Gemona; finally, the Sisters of the Child Jesus, with mother-house at Assisi. On the whole, the sisters professing the Rule of the Third Order amount at least to 50,000.

The Regular Third Order produced one saint, Hyacintha of Mariscotti, and five Blessed: Lucia of Callagirone, Elizabeth of Reute, Angelina of Marsciomo, Jeremias Lambertenghi and Crescentia Höss of Kaufbeuren.

Text of the Rule: RULE of 1221, SABATIER, *Regula antiqua fratrum et sororum de Pœnitentia* (Paris, 1901), in *Opuscules de critique historique*, I (Paris, 1903), 1–30; BOEHMER, *Analekten zur Geschichte des Franciscus von Assisi* (Tübingen and Leipzig, 1904), 73–82; tr. ADDERLEY AND MASON, *Third Orders. A translation of an ancient Rule of the Tertiaries together with an account of some modern Third Orders* (Oxford and London, 1902), 11–23.
Rule of 1289: *Seraphicæ Legislationis textus originales* (Quaracchi, 1897), 77–94; SBARAGLIA, *Bullarium Franciscanum*, IV (Rome, 1768), 94–97; WADDING, *Annales Minorum*, II (2nd ed., Rome, 1732), 9–14; DE GUBERNATIS, *Orbis Seraphicus*, II (Lyons, 1685), 784–87; tr. according to the text of WADDING: *Works of the seraphic Father St. Francis of Assisi* (London, 1882), 80–91.
Rule of Leo X of 1521: *Seraph. Legisl. textus orig.*, 287–97; *Regola del Terz. Ordine di S. Francesco approvata da Leone X* (Quaracchi, 1889), with Latin, Italian, French, and English text in four columns.
Rule of Leo XIII, 1883: FERNANDEZ GARCIA, *SS.D.N. Leonis PP. XIII Acta ad Tertium Franciscalem Ordinem spectantia* (Quaracchi, 1901), 72–87.
On the origin of the Third Order: MÜLLER, *Die Anfänge des Minoritenordens und der Bussbruderschaften* (Freiburg im Br., 1885); IDEM, *Zur Geschichte des Bussbrüderordens* in *Zeitschrift für Kirchengeschichte*, XXIII (Gotha, 1902), 496–524; MANDONNET,

Les origines de l'Ordo de Pœnitentia in *Compte rendu du quatrième Congrès scientifique international des Catholiques*, sect. V (Fribourg, 1898), 183–215; IDEM, *Les Règles et le gouvernement de l'Ordo de Pœnitentia au XIIIe siècle* in *Opuscules de critique*, I (Paris, 1902), 143–250; GOETZ, *Die Regel des Tertiarierordens* in *Zeitschrift für Kirchengeschichte*, XXIII (Gotha, 1902), 97–107; DAVIDSOHN, *Die Entstehung der Franziskaner-Tertiarier-Regel in Florenz* in *Forschungen zur Geschichte von Florenz*, IV (Berlin, 1908), 67–81; cf. BIHL in *Archivum Franciscanum Historicum*, I (Quaracchi, 1908), 642–43; VAN ORTREY in *Analecta Bollandiana*, XXIV (Brussels, 1905), 515–19; MARIANUS FLORENTINUS, *Compendium Chronicarum Ordinis FF. Minorum* (Quaracchi, 1911), 17 [*Arch. Franc. Hist.*, II (Quaracchi, 1909, 98)]; ZANZONI, *Gli Umiliati nei loro rapporti con l'eresia l'industria della lana ed i Comuni nei secoli XIIe XIII* (Milan, 1911), 120–31, and passim; GUERRINI, *Gli statuti di un'antica congregazione francescana di Brescia* in *Archivum Francisc. Hist.*, I (Quaracchi, 1908), 544–68; GOLUBOVICH, *Acta et statuta generalis capituli Tertii Ordinis Pœnitentium D. Francisci Bononiæ celebrati an. 1298* in *Arch. Franc. Hist.*, II (Quaracchi, 1909), 63–71.

General sources and monographs: DE GUBERNATIS, loc. cit., II, 783–921; CARILLO, *Historia de la tercera Orden de San Francisco* (2 vols., Saragossa, 1610–13); BORDONI, *Archivium Bullarum, privilegiorum et decretorum fratrum et sororum tertii Ordinis S. Francisci* (Parma, 1658); IDEM, *Cronologium fratrum et sororum tertii Ordinis S. Francisci tam regularis quam secularis* (Parma, 1658); JOANNES MARIA, *Tertii Ordinis S. Francisci Assisiatis Annales perpetui* (Paris, 1686); JEAN MARIE DE VERNON, *Histoire générale et particulière du Tiers Ordre* (3 vols., Paris, 1667; Lat. version, Paris, 1668); HILARION DE NOLAY, *La gloire du tiers ordre de S. François ou l'histoire de son établissement et de son progrès* (Lyons, 1694); PIETR' ANTONIO DA VENEZIA, *Vite de' Santi, Beati e Venerabili Servi di Dio del Terz' Ordine di S. Francesco* (Venice, 1725); ANGELICO DA VICENZA, *Storia cronologica dei tre Ordini*, III (Vicenza, 1761); RICCARDI, *L'Anno francescano ossia Vite de' Fratelli e Sorelle del Terz' Ordine di S. Francesco d'Assisi* (2 vols., Turin, 1789); HILARIUS PARISIENSIS, *Liber tertii Ordinis S. Francisci Assisiensis* (Geneva, 1888); ANTONIUS DE SILLIS, *Studio originem provectum atque complementum tertii Ordinis de Pœnitentia concernentia* (Naples, 1621), with statistics of the Italian Regular Third Order; *Generalia statuta sive decreta fratrum tertii Ordinis de Pœnitentia nuncupati regularis Observantiæ Congregationis Langobardiæ* (Venice, 1551); NELIS, *Le Manuscrit N° 757e des Archives générales du Royaume* [Belgium] (*Fonds des Cartulaires manuscrits*) in *Revue des Bibliothèques et Archives de Belgique*, II (Brussels, 1904), 364–70; HAUSAY, *Note sur un Manuscrit de Hasselt concernant les Bogards ou Frères du Tiers Ordre de St. François à Zeppern*, ibid., IV (1906), 86–93; VAN DEN GHEYN, *Encore les Statuts des Bogards de Zeppern*, ibid., VII (1908), 176–77; VANNÉRUS, *Documents concernant le tiers-Ordre à Anvers et ses rapports avec l'industrie drapière (1296–1572)* (Brussels, 1910); IDEM, *Documents concernant les Bogards de Malines (1284–1558)* (Brussels, 1911); GOYENS, *Documenta quædam ad historiam Tertii Ordinis Regularis in Belgio spectantia* in *Arch. Franc. Hist.*, IV (Quaracchi, 1911), 537–43; CALLAEY, *Les Beggards des Pays-Bas* in *Université catholique de Louvain, Séminaire Historique, Rapport sur les travaux pendant l'année acc. 1909–10* (Louvain, 1911), 438–51; COFANELLI, *Cannara ed il Terz' Ordine Francescano* (Foligno, 1895); CAMBIASO, *S. Francesco e il Terz' Ordine in Genova* (Genoa, 1909); LECESTRE, *Abbayes Prieures et Couvents d'hommes en France. Liste générale d'après les papiers de la Commission des Réguliers en 1768* (Paris, 1902), 85–87; LANZONI, *I Primordi dell' Ordine Francescano in Faenza* (Faenza, 1910), 30–31; HOLZAPFEL, *Handbuch der Geschichte des Franziskanerordens* (Freiburg im Br., 1909), 660–87; Lat. ed. (Freiburg im Br., 1909), 594–618; HEIMBUCHER, *Die Orden und Kongregationen der katholischen Kirche*, II (2nd ed., Paderborn, 1907), 489–527; NORBERT, *Les Religieuses Franciscaines en France* (Paris, 1897); for statistics: *Acta Ordinis Fratrum Minorum*, XXX (Quaracchi, 1911), 93, 95.

Books for practical use, besides the numerous manuals of the Third Order: GÉRARD DE VAUCOULEURS, *Documents pour expliquer la Règle du Tiers-Ordre de Saint-François d'Assise, au point de vue spirituel, social et économique* (3 vols., Paris, 1899); BRÖLL, *Ruhmesblätter aus der Geschichte des Dritten Ordens des hl. Franziskus* (Ratisbon, 1911); LISMONT, *Godsdienstige en maatschappelijke Invloed der Derde-Orde van St. Franciscus bij haren oorsprong en op onze dagen* (Turnhout, 1908); ANON., *Le Tiers-Ordre Franciscain d'après ses traditions* (Ligugé, 1897); CALISETE ALBERT, *Le Code franciscain entre les mains des hommes du monde, nouveaux aperçus sur le Tiers-Ordre de Saint François d'Assise* (Metz, 1905); LEGUIL, *Le Tiers-Ordre de Saint François d'Assise, pourquoi y entrer, pourquoi n'y entre-t-on pas?* (Metz, 1910); CERRI, *La Regola del Terz' Ordine Francescano spiegato con lezioni popolari* (Turin, 1910).

LIVARIUS OLIGER.

VII. THIRD ORDER OF ST. FRANCIS, IN CANADA.—The Third Order of St. Francis was established by the Friars Minor Recollects at Quebec in 1671, and some years later at Three Rivers and Montreal. Considering the population of the country, it was in a flourishing condition. In 1681 a Recollect notes that "many pious people of Quebec belong to the Third Order". After the cession of Canada to England the Third Order, deprived of its directors, the Recollects, seemed to have disappeared gradually, only to flourish anew thirty years after the death at Montreal, 1813, of the last Recollect priest. The Third Order was re-established about 1840 by Mgr Ignatius Bourget, Bishop of Montreal. Fervent fellow-labourers helped the holy prelate to spread the Third Order in Montreal, notably Canon J. A. Paré and the Sulpicians C. E. Gilbert and A. Giband. Mgr Bourget established a fraternity of women, 6 May, 1863, and one of men, 13 June, 1866; both were directed by the Sulpicians till 1874, by Canon P. E. Dufresne from 1874 till 1881, by the Jesuits from 1881 till 1888, and by the Sulpicians from 1888 till 1890; since then by the Friars Minor. Mgr Fabre, successor to Bishop Bourget, in a letter (3 Sept., 1882) to the priests and faithful of his diocese, says: "We have in our midst the tertiaries of St. Francis, who are known to you all by the edification they give, and by the good odour of all the virtues which they practise in the world." The Third Order was reintroduced at Quebec almost at the same time as at Montreal. On 19 Nov., 1859, Father Flavian Durocher, O. M. I., received the profession of two women, after a year's novitiate. These were joined by others, until in 1876 Quebec possessed over 2000 tertiaries, while in the Province of Quebec several parishes had groups of tertiaries. Among priests zealous for the spread of the Third Order at this epoch we must name, besides the above-mentioned Montreal priests: Father Durocher, St. Sauveur, Quebec; L. N. Bégin, now Archbishop of Quebec; James Sexton, Quebec; Oliver Caron, Vicar-General of Three Rivers; E. H. Guilbert, L. Provancher, and G. Fraser, all three of the Quebec diocese. Father Provancher was one of the most zealous. In 1866, having received faculties from the General of the Friars Minor, he established a very fervent fraternity in his parish of Portneuf. He propagated the Third Order by his writings. For two years he edited a review, in which he published nearly every month an article on the Third Order, or answered questions appertaining thereto. At that epoch (1876) the brothers' fraternity at Montreal counted 137 members; the sisters, a still greater number. At Three Rivers the tertiaries were less numerous—enough, however, to form a fraternity a little later. Quebec with its 200 tertiaries did not have a fraternity till 1882.

In 1881 the arrival in Canada of Father Frederic of Ghyvelde gave new spirit to the Third Order. He spent eight months in Canada, and worked actively for the Third Order. He began at Quebec, where he held the Holy Visit prescribed by the rule and admitted 100 new members. At Three Rivers he found "a numerous and fervent fraternity". His visit to the fraternities of Montreal was followed by a notable increase in membership. Shortly afterwards Leo XIII published his Encyclicals on the Third Order. The Canadian bishops, in obedience to the pope's wishes, recommended the Third Order to their clergy and faithful. But the Friars of the First Order alone could give the Third a fitting development; hence, when Father Frederic returned in 1888, several bishops, among them Bishop Laflêche of Three Rivers and Archbishop Taschereau, welcomed him as its promoter. The foundation of a convent of Friars Minor at Montreal in 1890 inaugurated a new era of prosperity for the Third Order. The Franciscans took over the direction of the Third Order at Montreal. The fraternities of other districts were visited regularly, and new ones were formed. The Third Order has since spread rapidly. To-day the Third Order in Canada numbers nearly 200 fraternities with over 50,000 members, under the jurisdiction of the Friars Minor. The Capuchins have a small number of fraternities. The Friars Minor have also the direction of 20 fraternities with 5000 members in the Franco-Canadian centres of the United States. All these with large numbers of isolated tertiaries give a total of nearly 60,000. These tertiaries are mostly French Canadians. There are very few fraternities for English-speaking tertiaries; of these there are two very flourishing ones at Montreal. It is in the Province of Quebec that the Third Order is most flourishing. Three monthly reviews, treating specially of the Third Order, are published in Canada: (1) "La Revue du Tiers Ordre", founded in 1884 by the tertiaries of Montreal, and directed since 1891 by the Friars Minor of that city; (2) "The Franciscan Review and St. Anthony's Record", founded in 1905 by the Friars Minor of Montreal; (3) "L'Echo de St. François", published since 1911 by the Capuchins of Ottawa. The principal social works of the Third Order in Canada are: three houses of the Third Order in Montreal and one in Quebec, directed by lady tertiaries; a lodging-house and an industrial school at Montreal, directed also by lady tertiaries; several work-rooms for the benefit of the poor; and public libraries, one in Quebec and two in Montreal.

The Third Order Regular is represented in Canada by three flourishing institutions: A. *Little Franciscan Sisters of Mary*, founded at Worcester, Massachusetts, in 1889 and transferred to Baie-St-Paul, Canada, in 1891; their constitutions were approved in 1903. They follow the Rule of the Third Order Regular. Their habit comprises a brown tunic and scapular, a white hood and wimple, and a white woollen cord; they wear a silver crucifix. Work.—Assistance of the sick, the poor, the aged, of orphans and instruction of the young—in a word, all the works of mercy. Development.—This congregation possesses 8 houses, nearly all in the United States. The mother house is at Baie-St-Paul, Province of Quebec, Canada. The institution numbers 150 professed sisters, 7 novices, 30 postulants, and 8 associates.

B. *Franciscan Missionaries of Mary*, founded in India, and following the Rule of the Third Order Regular. They have six houses in Canada: (1) Quebec, founded 1892; novitiate, perpetual adoration, printing, embroidery, workshop, house of probation for aspirants, patronage, visiting the sick. (2) St. Anne of Beaupré (1894); patronage, workshop, hospitality for pilgrims, visiting the sick. (3) St. Lawrence, Manitoba (1897); boarding-school, parochial schools, dispensary, visiting the sick. (4) Pine Creek, Manitoba (1899); school, model farm, dispensary, visiting the sick. (5) St. Malo, Quebec (1902); day nursery, primary schools, school of domestic economy, dispensary, pharmacy, visiting the sick. (6) Winnipeg (1909); day nursery, embroidery, patronage, visiting the poor and the hospitals. These houses possess 150 sisters, novices included. Since its establishment in Canada, the congregation has had 290 Canadian members, many of whom are now engaged in mission work in China, Japan, India, Ceylon, Congo, Zululand, Natal, Mozambique, Madagascar, and South America. The mother-house of Quebec has founded six others in the United States: Woonsocket in 1904; New York and New Bedford in 1906; Boston in 1907; Providence in 1909; Fall River in 1910.

C. *Religious of St. Francis of Assisi*, founded at Lyons, France, in 1838. Their object is the care of the sick and of orphans and the education of the young. They were introduced into Canada in 1904, and have at present 5 houses, comprising a hospital, a boarding-school for girls, and model and elementary schools.

Third Order Secular: LECLERCQ, *Premier Etablissement de la foi* (Paris, 1691); *Eclaircissements sur l'établissement d'un hospice à Québec* (1681), *Archives de Versailles, Fonds Récollets; Gazette des Familles, Bulletin Mensuel* (Quebec, 1869–76); *Revue du Tiers-Ordre; Fr. Bienvenu d'Osimo, tertiaire, Notice historique sur le Tiers-Ordre à Québec* (Quebec, 1903). Third Order Regular: information furnished by the congregations themselves.

ODORIC M. JOUVE.

VIII. THIRD ORDER OF ST. FRANCIS IN GREAT BRITAIN AND IRELAND.—A. *In Great Britain*.—The Third Order Secular comprises ninety-six congregations of which forty are under the jurisdiction of the Friars Minor of the Leonine Union and fifty-four under that of the Friars Minor Capuchin, and about 12,000 members, amongst whom are several diocesan bishops, a number of the clergy, and laity of all ranks. In their organization the British tertiary congregations follow the common rule, but many of them add some corporal works of mercy, reclaiming negligent Catholics, and so forth. All the tertiaries are governed by a commissary-provincial appointed by the minister-provincial of the first order. His duty is to grant the necessary faculties to directors of congregations, to hold visitations, and generally supervise the affairs of the Third Order under his jurisdiction. A national conference of British tertiaries with a view to strengthening and consolidating the order, was held in 1898 at Liverpool in the hall attached to the Jesuit church, and was presided over by the bishop of the diocese. The opening address was delivered by the Archbishop of Paris. A second national conference was held at Leeds. Since the institution of the English national Catholic congress, in 1910, the tertiaries have taken part in these and have had their sectional meeting in the congress.

Of the Third Order in Great Britain in pre-Reformation days little is known. It is, however, certain that there existed in Scotland several houses of Sisters of the Third Order Regular. Blessed Thomas More is frequently spoken of as a tertiary of St. Francis, but there seems to be no historical evidence to support this statement. The Third Order, however, was known in England in the penal days. Fr. William Staney, the first commissary of the order in England after the Dissolution, wrote "A Treatise of the Third Order of St. Francis" (Douai, 1617). An interesting fact in connexion with the Third Order in England is the appointment in 1857, as commissary-general, of Dr. (afterwards Cardinal) Manning, by a letter patent, dated 10 April, 1857, given by the minister-general of the Capuchin Friars Minor, empowering him to act as "Superior, visitor and Our Commissary of each and all the brothers and sisters of the Third Order Secular dwelling in England". Amongst notable English tertiaries of modern times, besides Cardinal Manning, may be mentioned Cardinal Vaughan, Lady Herbert of Lea, the late Earl of Denbigh, and the poet Coventry Patmore. The Third Order Regular is represented in England by nineteen convents of sisters and in Scotland by six convents. There are no communities of brothers. These convents belong to various congregations, most of which are of English institution. They devote themselves either to education or to parochial works of mercy or to the foreign missions. Most notable historically amongst these congregations are the convents at Taunton and Woodchester, which represent the English convent of the Third Order established at Brussels, Belgium, in 1621. Their founder was Father Gennings, the brother of the martyr Edmund Gennings. This was, in fact, the first convent of the Third Order Regular, enclosed, founded for English women. The community later on migrated to Bruges where it remained until 1794, when, owing to the troubles caused by the French Revolution, it crossed over into England and, after eleven years' residence at Winchester, settled finally at Taunton in Somerset. The congregation was under the jurisdiction of the Friars Minor until 1837 when, owing to the dissolution of the Recollect province, it came under the jurisdiction of the diocesan bishop. In 1860 a second foundation was made at Woodchester.

B. *In Ireland*.—The congregations of the Third Order Secular in Ireland are almost exclusively attached to churches of the First Order. Under the jurisdiction of the Friars Minor of the Leonine Union are fourteen congregations with 9741 members, and subject to the Capuchin Friars Minor are four congregations with 5100 members. The Third Order Regular comprises two houses of brothers at Clara and Farragher, and eleven in the Archdiocese of Tuam, all devoted to educational work. At Drumshambo the sisters of the order have a convent where perpetual adoration is maintained day and night. There is also one convent of the Franciscan Missionary Sisters of Mary.

Franciscan Annals (Pantasaph, North Wales), a monthly magazine; *Franciscan Monthly* (Forest Gate, London); various details will be found in THADDEUS, *The Franciscans in England* (London, 1898) and in the statistical tables published yearly in *Acta ord. ff. min.* and *Analecta ord. ff. min. capp.*

FATHER CUTHBERT.

IX. THIRD ORDER REGULAR OF ST. FRANCIS, IN THE UNITED STATES.—A. *Congregations of Men.*— (1) Province of the Sacred Heart of Jesus of the Fathers of the Third Order Regular of St. Francis. In 1847 Bishop O'Connor of Pittsburgh obtained from the Irish congregation six brothers, who founded a monastery and college at Loretto, Pennsylvania. Pius IX, by a Rescript of 12 Nov., 1847, erected this foundation into an independent congregation under the obedience of the Bishop of Pittsburgh. This congregation in 1908 joined the Italian congregation, and together with the community at Spalding, Nebraska, which in 1906 had joined the Italian congregation, was erected into a province, 24 Sept., 1910. Houses, 4; colleges, 2; religious, 62; novices, 5. (See below.)

(2) Congregation of the Franciscan Brothers, of Brooklyn, New York. Founded 31 May, 1858, by 2 brothers from the Irish congregation, Pius IX, by a Rescript of 15 Dec., 1859, erected it into an independent congregation. The ordinary of the Diocese of Brooklyn is the superior-general, and governs the congregation through a provincial superior with an assistant and seven consultors, chosen by the brothers from among themselves for a term of three years. Brothers, 67; novices, 8; academy, 1; college, 1; schools, 14; pupils, 9875. (See below.)

(3) Congregation of the Brothers of the Poor of St. Francis Seraphicus. Founded 25 Dec., 1857, at Aachen by John Hoever for the protection and education of poor, homeless boys, it was introduced into the United States in 1866. Brothers, 43; novices, 5; postulants, 3; candidates, 13; homes for boys, 2.

B. *Congregations of Women.*—(1) Sisters of the Third Order Regular of St. Francis:—(a) Congregation with mother-house at Oldenburg, Indiana. Founded in 1851 by Rev. F. J. Rudolf, its rules and constitutions were approved by the Holy See. Sisters, 536; novices, 41; postulants, 7; schools, 67; pupils, 12,273. (b) Congregation with mother-house at Mt. St. Clare, Clinton, Iowa. Founded in 1867 by Rt. Rev. Bishop Lavialle of Louisville, Kentucky. Sisters, 130; novices and postulants, 40; hospital, 1; schools, 16; pupils, 2590.

(2) Sisters of the Third Order of St. Francis:— (a) Congregation with mother-house at Glen Riddle, Pennsylvania. Founded by the Ven. John Nepomucene Neumann, C.SS.R., Bishop of Philadelphia, who on 9 April, 1855, invested three devout women, Marianne Bachmann (Mother M. Francis), Barbara Boll (Sister M. Margaret), and Anna Dorn (Sister M. Bernardina), with the habit of St. Francis. In 1896 the mother-house was transferred from Philadelphia to Glen Riddle. This congregation is divided into three provinces. Houses, 80; sisters, 818; novices, 48; postulants, 15; academies, 4; seminaries, 2; orphan asylums, 9; hospitals, 12; schools, 42; schools for Indians and negroes, 8. By and from this congregation were established (i) Congregation with mother-house at 337 Pine Street, Buffalo, New York in 1861. Sisters, 277; novices, 30; postulants, 16; asylums for aged, 3; schools, 30; pupils, 6540; orphan asylum, 1; hospitals, 2. From this congregation were founded (a) Congregation with mother-house at Mt. Alvernia, Millvale Station, Pennsylvania, in 1868. Sisters, 210; novices, 17; postulants, 13; schools, 14; pupils, 6429; orphan asylum, 1; hospital, 1; home for ladies, 1. (β) Congregation with mother-house at Mt. Hope, Westchester Co., New York, 1893. Legal title: Sisters of St. Francis, Conventuals of the Third Order of the M.I.V. Sisters, 182; novices, 19; postulants, 9; academy, 1; schools, 6; (ii) Congregation with mother-house at St. Anthony's Convent, Syracuse, New York, 1862. Sisters, 173; novices, 9; candidates, 6; schools, 17; pupils, 4500; hospitals, 3; home for aged, 1; home for children, 1; convents at Hawaiian Islands, 4. (b) Congregation with mother-house at St. Francis's Hospital, Peoria, Illinois; founded in 1867 by Rt. Rev. John L. Spalding, Bishop of Peoria, and sisters from the House of Bethlehem, Herford, Germany. Sisters, 163; novices, 38; postulants, 26; hospitals, 10; patients, 5320. (c) Congregation with mother-house at Tiffin, Ohio. Founded in 1867 by Rev. J. L. Bihn. Sisters, 56; novices, 9; postulants, 4; hospital, 1; orphan asylums, 2; homes for aged, 2; schools, 13. (d) Congregation with provincial house at Peekskill, New York. Founded by Mother M. Gertrude and two sisters from the general mother-house, Gemona, Italy, who, at the request of Rev. Andrew Feifer, O.F.M., came to this country in 1865. Sisters, 284; novices, 18; postulants, 15; academy, 1; schools, 18; day nurseries, 3; institution for destitute children, 1; home for working girls, 1; children in charge of sisters, 7768. (e) Congregation with mother-house at Bay Settlement, Wisconsin, founded 6 Dec., 1867. Sisters, 35.

(3) Sisters of St. Francis:—(a) Congregation with mother-house at St. Elizabeth's Convent, Allegany, New York. Founded in 1857 by Very Rev. Pamfilo di Magliano, O.F.M. [Sisters, 300; novices, 25; postulants, 12; schools, 11; hospitals, 2; homes, 4. (b) Congregation with mother-house at St. Francis's Convent, Dubuque, Iowa. Founded in 1876 by Mother Xaveria Termehr and sisters from the house of Bethlehem, Herford, Germany, who on account of the infamous "May laws", were compelled to leave Germany. Sisters, 399; novices, 34; postulants, 20; orphan asylums, 2; industrial school, 1; academy, 1; home for aged, 1; schools, 43; pupils, 6829. (c) Congregation with mother-house at St. Joseph's Hospital, Maryville, Missouri. Founded with the approbation of Rt. Rev. M. F. Burke, Bishop of St. Joseph, Missouri, in 1894. Sisters, 45; novices, 7; postulants, 1; hospitals, 6. (4) Sisters of St. Francis of Penance and Christian Charity:—Congregation with mother-house at Stella Niagara, near Lewiston, New York. Established in 1874 by Mother M. Aloysia and three sisters from Nonnenwerth, near Rolandseck, Rhenish Prussia, Germany. Sisters, 253; academies, 5; schools, 18; pupils, 6348; orphan asylum, 1; Indian schools, 2; pupils, 577; foundling-house, 1.

(5) Franciscan Sisters:—(a) Congregation with mother-house, Grand Avenue and Chippewa Street, St. Louis, Missouri. Founded in 1872 by sisters from the general mother-house at Salzkotten, Germany. Sisters, 224; hospitals, 6; schools, 1; orphan asylums, 2; house of providence, 1; convent, 1; (b) Congregation with mother-house at Mill Hill, London, England, for coloured missions. Introduced into the United States in 1881. Sisters, 58; industrial school, 1; parochial schools, 4; pupils, 765. (6) Sisters of St. Francis of the Sacred Heart:—Congregation with mother-house at Mercy Hospital, Burlington, Iowa. Sisters, 22; hospital, 1. (7) Franciscan Sisters, Minor Conventuals:—Congregation with mother-house at St. Joseph's Convent, Buffalo, New York. Sisters, 58; novices, 16; postulants, 21. (8) Sisters of the Third Order of St. Francis of Assisi, M.C.:—Congregation with mother-

house at St. Francis, Wisconsin. Founded in 1849 by sisters from Bavaria. Its rules and constitutions were compiled by Rev. M. Heiss in 1852, and approved by Rt. Rev. J. M. Henni, Bishop of Milwaukee. In June, 1873, this congregation was affiliated to the Order of Minor Conventuals, and Pius X on 6 Dec., 1911, gave it its definite approbation. Sisters, 303; novices, 22; postulants, 30; academy, 1; orphanage, 1; institute for deaf mutes, 1; for feeble minded, 1; schools, 36; pupils, 4500. (9) School Sisters of St. Francis:—Congregation with mother-house, Greenfield and Twenty-Second Avenues, Milwaukee, Wisconsin. The sisters conduct schools in Wisconsin, Minnesota, South Dakota, Nebraska, Iowa, Missouri, Illinois, Michigan, and Oregon. There are two branch-houses of this congregation in Europe, one in Luxemburg, the other at Erlenbad, Baden. Sisters, 814.

(10) Franciscan Sisters of the Perpetual Adoration:—Congregation with mother-house at St. Rose Convent, La Crosse, Wisconsin. Founded by six sisters from Bavaria, and rules compiled in 1853 by Most Rev. M. Heiss, Archbishop of Milwaukee. The Perpetual Adoration was introduced in 1878. Sisters, 420; novices, 42; postulants, 40; schools, 63; pupils, 8448; orphan asylums, 2; Indian school, 1; domestic science schools, 2. (11) Franciscan Sisters of Christian Charity:—Congregation with mother-house at Holy Family Convent, Alverno, Wisconsin. Founded in 1869 at Manitowoc, Wisconsin, by Rev. Joseph Fessler, it was affiliated to the Order of Friars Minor Conventual 19 March, 1900. Sisters, 303; novices, 40; postulants, 10; hospitals, 2; home for aged, 1; schools, 53; pupils, 8500. (12) Franciscan Sisters of the Sacred Heart:—Congregation with mother-house at St. Joseph's Hospital, Joliet, Illinois. Founded in 1867 at Avila, Indiana, by sisters from Germany. Sisters, 325; novices, 40; postulants, 12; hospitals, 10; home for aged, 1; orphan asylum, 1; schools, 9. (13) Sisters of the Third Order of St. Francis of Perpetual Adoration:—Congregation with mother-house at St. Francis's Convent, Nevada, Missouri. Established in 1893 by Sister M. John Hau and sisters from the mother-house at Grimmenstein, Switzerland. Sisters, 25; orphan asylum, 1. (14) Hospital Sisters of St. Francis:—Congregation with provincial house at St. John's Hospital, Springfield, Illinois. Founded in 1875 by sisters from the general mother-house, Münster, Germany. Sisters, 299; novices, 29; postulants, 11; hospitals, 12. (15) The Poor Sisters of St. Francis Seraph of the Perpetual Adoration:—Congregation with provincial house at St. Francis Convent, Lafayette, Indiana. Introduced into this country in 1875 by sisters from the general mother-house at Olpe, Germany. Sisters, 613; novices, 35; postulants, 21; academies, 3; orphan asylum, 1; home for aged, 1; schools, 36; hospitals, 18; high schools, 2. (16) Sisters of the Poor of St. Francis. See POOR OF ST. FRANCIS, SISTERS OF THE.

(17) Franciscan Sisters of St. Kunegunda (Polish): —(a) Congregation with mother-house at Chicago, Illinois. Founded in 1896. Sisters, 107; novices, 22; postulants, 18; orphan asylum, 1; home for aged and crippled, 1; day-nursery, 1; schools, 11; pupils, 2070. (b) Congregation with mother-house at Chicago Heights, Illinois. Foundation of English-speaking Franciscan Sisters. Sisters, 17. (18) Sisters of St. Francis of the Immaculate Conception:—Congregation with mother-house at Peoria, Illinois. Founded in 1890. Sisters, 47; novices, 20; postulants, 17; schools, 6; homes, 2; asylum, 1. (19) Missionary Franciscan Sisters of the Immaculate Conception:—Congregation with mother-house, Rome, Italy. The sisters conduct establishments in the Archdioceses of New York and Boston, the Diocese of Newark, Pittsburgh, and Savannah. (20) Franciscan Sisters of the Immaculate Conception:—(a) Congregation with mother-house at Little Falls, Minnesota. Sisters, 60; postulants, 3; orphan asylum, 1; hospitals, 3. (b) Congregation with mother-house at St. Anthony's Hospital, Rock Island, Illinois. Sisters, 18; novices, 6.

(21) Polish Franciscan School Sisters:—Congregation with mother-house, 3419 Gasconde Street, St. Louis, Missouri. Founded 29 May, 1901, by Most Rev. John J. Kain, Archbishop of St. Louis. Sisters 63; schools, 9; pupils, 700. (22) Felician Sisters, O.S.F.:—Congregation with general mother-house, Cracow, Austria. Founded in 1855 by Sophia Truszkowska at Warsaw, Russia. Introduced into the United States in 1874. (a) Western Province of the Presentation B. V. M. Mother-house, Detroit, Michigan. Sisters, 273; novices, 30; postulants, 55; candidates in preparatory course, 65; schools, 33; pupils, 12,500; orphan asylum, 1. (b) Eastern Province. Mother-house at Buffalo, New York, established 20 Aug., 1900. Choir Sisters, 278; novices, 32; postulants, 93; lay sisters, 66; novices, 6; postulants, 21; candidates in preparatory course, 73; schools, 55; pupils, 21,556; orphan asylums, 2; home for aged, 1; emigrant home, 1; working-girls' home, 1; day nursery, 1. (c) North-western Province of the Presentation B. V. M. Mother-house, St. Joseph's Orphanage, Milwaukee, Wisconsin, established 1910. Sisters, 170; novices, 17; postulants, 27; schools, 24; pupils, 6482; orphan asylums, 3. (23) Sisters of the Third Order of St. Francis of the Congregation of Our Lady of Lourdes. Mother-house, Rochester, Minnesota. Established 1877 by sisters of St. Francis, Joliet, Illinois. Sisters, 336; novices, 9; postulants, 16; academies, 5; normal school, 1; schools, 20; pupils, 5767; hospital, 1; nurses' training school, 1.

HEIMBUCHER, *Die Orden und Kongregationen der katholischen Kirche* (2nd ed., Paderborn, 1907); *The Catholic Church in the United States*, I, II (New York, 1909); *Official Catholic Directory* (New York).

FERDINAND HECKMANN.

X. PROVINCE OF THE SACRED HEART OF JESUS.—Prior to 1906 several communities of the Third Order existed in the United States, all lay institutes dedicated to teaching and other works of charity. Amongst these were three branches of Franciscan Brothers: at Brooklyn, New York; at Loretto, Pennsylvania; and at Spalding, Nebraska. The communities at Loretto and Brooklyn were founded more than half a century ago from Mount Bellew Monastery, Archdiocese of Tuam, Ireland; Spalding Institute was a branch of the Brooklyn community. In 1905 Brother Linus Lynch, then superior of the institute, asked the ordinary of the diocese for permission to have some of his subjects ordained priests. This request the bishop refused, as the community had been introduced into the diocese for the care of parish schools, and he feared that in the event of its members becoming priests this work would suffer. A petition was then sent to the minister-general, Rt. Rev. Angelus de Mattia, asking for union with the third Order Regular; as this union could not be effected, some of the community determined to ask for a dispensation from their vows in order to enter the institute. In 1907 fifteen were dispensed; these, together with eleven novices, went to Spalding, Nebraska, where a small community of brothers had been united to the order in 1906. They were received by Very Rev. Dr. Stanislaus Dujmoric, commissary-general, and by dispensation of Pius X from the ordinary year of probation they made the vows of the order. A college was then opened at Spalding, giving the order its first house in the United States.

In 1908 the diocesan community of Franciscan Brothers at Loretto, Pennsylvania, were admitted to the solemn profession, and eight young men were received into the novitiate.

In 1910–11 Rt. Rev. Eugene A. Garvey, D.D.,

Bishop of Altoona, requested the fathers to take charge of the Italian Church of St. Anthony of Padua at Johnstown, Pennsylvania, and the Church of Our Lady of Mount Carmel, Altoona, Pennsylvania. The four houses in the United States were erected into a province, 24 Sept., 1910, Very Rev. Dr. Jerome Zazzara being elected provincial. The Archbishop of Chicago has since given the fathers charge of Sts. Peter and Paul's Slavic Church in that city, and a new college is to be opened at Sioux City, Iowa, in 1912. The provincial mother-house is at St. Francis's College, Loretto, Pennsylvania. The American Province has now five convents, two colleges, sixty-five professed members, and twenty novices and postulants.

BORDONI, *Cronologium Fratrum et Sororum Tertii Ordinis* (Parma, 1658); HÉLYOT, *Histoire des Ordres Monastiques;* ZEC, *Brevis Historia Tertii Ordinis Regularis S. Francisci;* MSS. contained in the archives of Loretto Convent, Loretto, Pennsylvania.

JOHN P. M. DOYLE.

XI. THE THIRD ORDER SECULAR OF ST. FRANCIS was established in the United States by the early Franciscan missionaries for the white settlers and soldiers and Indian converts, especially in the Southern States. A confraternity existed at Santa Fé long before 1680. Another confraternity existed in New Mexico almost from the time of the reconquest (1692–1695). The document stating this fact is a report of the Father custos, José Bernal, dated Santa Fé, 17 Sept., 1794. There is no documentary evidence of the existence of a Third Order for lay people as a regularly organized confraternity anywhere else, though we learn from documents that single individuals were termed tertiaries among the Indians. It is most probable, however, that a confraternity existed at St. Augustine, Florida, before the close of the sixteenth century, and at San Antonio, Texas, before the middle of the eighteenth century. The establishment of provinces of the order of Friars Minor brought about the establishment of many confraternities. There are at present 186 confraternities of Franciscan Tertiaries in this country, with a membership of 35,605. Of these, 142 congregations with 27,805 members are under the direction of the Friars Minor, 32 with 6800 members under the direction of the Friars Minor Capuchin, and 12 congregations with 1000 members under the direction of the Friars Minor Conventual. Besides these, there are many hundreds of tertiaries throughout the country not belonging to any congregation.

XII. THE THIRD ORDER SECULAR OF THE SERVITES was established in the United States in 1893. There are at present 2 congregations, with a membership of 400.

XIII. THE THIRD ORDER REGULAR OF SERVITES. See MARY, SERVANTS OF.

HEIMBUCHER, *Orden u. Kongregationen* (2nd ed., Paderborn, 1907); *The Catholic Church in the U. S.*, I, II (New York, 1909); *Official Catholic Directory* (New York).

FERDINAND HECKMANN.

Thirty Years War, THE.—The Thirty Years War (1618–48), though pre-eminently a German war, was also of great importance for the history of the whole of Europe, not only because nearly all the countries of Western Europe took part in it, but also on account of its connexion with the other great European wars of the same era and on account of its final results.

I. CAUSES OF THE WAR.—The fundamental cause was the internal decay of the empire from 1555, as evidenced by the weakness of the imperial power, by the gross lack of patriotism manifested by the estates of the empire, and by the paralysis of the imperial authority and its agencies among the Protestant estates of South-western Germany, which had been in a state of discontent since 1555. Consequently the whole of Germany was in a continual state of unrest.

The decay of the empire encouraged the other nations of Western Europe to infringe upon its territory. Spain and the Netherlands made use of the period of the twelve-years truce to secure a footing in the neighbouring district of the Lower Rhine so as to increase their strategic base. For nearly a hundred years France had made treaties with many of the estates hostile to the emperor. Henry IV of France was murdered in 1610 at the very moment he was about to interfere in the war over the Jülich-Cleve succession. James I of England was the father-in-law of the head of the Protestant party of action in Germany, Elector Frederick V of the Palatinate, and was inclined to take part in a continental quarrel. Denmark sought obstinately to obtain the power of "administration" over the dioceses of Northern Germany that had become Protestant, and to get control of the mouth of the Elbe. Gustavus Adolphus (1611–32), of Sweden, also showed a strong desire to interfere in German affairs. At the outbreak of the Thirty Years War all these countries, it is true, were prevented from taking part in it by internal difficulties or by wars in other directions. Still the disposition to do so existed everywhere.

Another cause of the war was that the countries forming the Austrian provinces belonged to the empire. For, in the first place, the empire, owing to the geographical position of these countries, became involved in the contemporary affairs in Eastern Europe. The general aristocratic reaction that appeared throughout Europe at the end of the fifteenth and in the sixteenth centuries gradually became so powerful in the eastern and northern countries that a life-and-death struggle between its representatives and the sovereign power broke out at the beginning of the seventeenth century in the more active districts of these sections. These causes gave the first impulse to the Thirty Years War (see section II below). In addition the dynasty ruling the countries forming Austria was a branch of the Habsburg family, whose most distinguished line at that era ruled Spain. From the reign of Philip II (1556–98) the Spanish Habsburgs were the champions of Catholicism in Western Europe and the chief rivals of France in the struggle for supremacy in Europe. From about 1612, especially during the administration of Philip IV (1621–65) and his distinguished minister, Olivarez, they displayed increased energy and tried to induce the German Habsburgs to support their plans. The empire was all the more affected by this Spanish policy as the head of the German Habsburgs was Emperor of Germany.

A further important cause was the religious sectarianism which, after diminishing for a short time, grew more intense early in the seventeenth century. In the Catholic movement (about 1592) which followed the Council of Trent only Catholic theologians and a few princes had taken part; the second movement, on the contrary, carried with it the masses of the clergy and laity, and was marked by an ardent spirit of faith and a passionate demand for the spread of Catholicism. If among Protestants the idealistic enthusiasm was perhaps not so great, still their partisan feeling was equally violent and their combativeness no less ardent. After the war began it soon became manifest that social and economic reasons made Germany a favourable soil for its growth. Economic life, which for a long time had flourished greatly, from the second half of the sixteenth century had grown stagnant. Consequently there existed a large number who were glad to have the opportunity of supporting themselves as paid soldiers and of enriching themselves by plunder. The nobles, also, who were numerous in proportion to the rest of the population, took advantage of the opportunity to indulge their private feuds and robberies. As only a small number of them were attracted by foreign wars, they were ready therefore for internal disorders. Soon there appeared leaders of ability who gathered both nobles and burghers under their banners and retained them in their service by indulging their evil instincts. On the other hand, the people of Germany, who had been long unaccustomed to war and were not trained to bear public burdens, chafed under the hardships now imposed upon them. This discontent, combined with the ease with which troops were equipped, aided in prolonging the war.

II. THE BOHEMIAN REVOLT.—At the beginning of the seventeenth century the regions ruled by the German Habsburgs included Upper and Lower Austria, Bohemia together with Moravia and Silesia, the lesser part of Hungary which had not been conquered by the Turks, Styria, Carinthia, Carniola, the Tyrol, and the provinces bordering on Germany. This territory, however, was divided among three branches of the family, the main line, the Styrian, and that of Tyrol-Vorarlberg. Although the main line of the German Habsburgs held by far the larger part of these landed possessions yet its territories did not form a compact whole, but were only a number of loosely connected countries, each having its own provincial estates, which were largely composed of nobles and which maintained an incessant opposition to the dynasty, and therefore largely desired religious freedom, that is the right to become Protestant and to introduce Protestantism into their domains. The struggle of the nobility against the dynasty reached its height during the last decade of the reign of Rudolph II (1576–1612). Even at that time the nobility maintained relations with the active Protestant party in the empire. In 1604 the Hungarian nobles revolted with the aid of the ruler of Transylvania, and in 1607 they rebelled again and became the allies of the Turks. On 25 June, 1608, Rudolph was obliged to transfer the government of Hungary, Austria, and Moravia to his more compliant brother Matthias; he did not, however, give up his rights as King of Bohemia, and in 1609 was able to pacify an outbreak of the Bohemian nobility only by granting the Imperial Charter (*Majestätsbrief*) which gave religious liberty not only to the nobles and their dependents in Bohemia but also to those living on the crown lands. This concession greatly strengthened the power of the nobles.

After Rudolph's death Cardinal Klesl sought, as the councillor of Matthias (1612–19), to avoid above all any new crisis, so as to gain time to reorganize the resources of the ruling dynasty. Matthias, like Rudolph, had no son and the royal family chose as his successor Ferdinand, the head of the Styrian branch of the Habsburgs, who had restored Catholicism in Styria. In 1617 the dynasty persuaded the Bohemians to accept Ferdinand as their future king, and in 1618 they prevailed upon the Hungarians to elect him king. Before this (May, 1618) the Bohemian nobles had revolted anew under the leadership of Count von Thurn on account of the alleged infringement of the charter granted by Rudolph. The dynasty was not yet ready for war. When Matthias died (March, 1619) the Hungarians and the inhabitants of Moravia joined the revolt, and in June Thurn advanced on Vienna with an army to persuade the Austrians also to join. However, the determined attitude of Ferdinand prevented the insurrection and Thurn withdrew. Ferdinand was now able to go to Frankfort, where his election as emperor (28 August) secured the imperial dignity for his family. Two days before this the Bohemians had elected the leader of the Protestants, Frederick of the Palatinate, as rival King of Bohemia.

The inhabitants of Lower Austria now joined the revolt. Bethlen Gabor, Prince of Transylvania, made an alliance with its leaders, and in conjunction with them once more threatened Vienna at the close of 1619. Thenceforth, however, discipline steadily declined in the Bohemian army, and the leaders disagreed. The expected aid was never received from the Protestant party, excepting that a few of the less important nobles of the empire joined the insurrectionary forces. On the other hand, in October, 1619, Ferdinand obtained the help of Maximilian of Bavaria, who had the largest army in the empire, and of the Protestant Elector of Saxony. Spain and Poland also sent troops. Maximilian so greatly terrified the Protestant party, which since 1608 had formed the Union, that it was broken up. He then advanced into Bohemia supported by Austrian troops and decisively defeated the Bohemians in the battle of the White Mountain, near Prague. The Elector Frederick, called the "Winter King" on account of the brief duration of his rule, fled. Ferdinand took possession of his provinces and restored order there. The war with Transylvania, however, was carried on with interruptions until 1626.

III. THE WAR IN THE PALATINATE AND THE WAR WITH DENMARK.—The emperor placed Frederick, the Elector Palatine, under the ban of the empire on 22 January, 1621; the latter refused to beg for pardon. Reconciliation was made more difficult by the demand of Maximilian of Bavaria that part of the Palatine lands called the Upper Palatinate, as recompense for the expenses of the war; he also desired, in accordance with a traditional claim of the Bavarian ruling family, the electoral dignity belonging to the Palatinate; this the emperor gave him with hesitation and under certain conditions (21–25 February, 1623). Maximilian gained for himself the desired land by transplanting the war to the territory of the Palatinate. Spanish troops had established themselves in these districts as early as 1620, and aimed at retaining possession of the Palatinate for the purpose of establishing communication between the Italian possessions of Spain and its territories in Burgundy and the Netherlands. In carrying out this scheme the Spaniards in the same year (1620) had seized the Valtellina and the territory of the Rhætian League. Before this, in 1617, when Ferdinand became the head of the German-Habsburg dynasty, Spain had expressed its desires for the reversion of the Austrian possessions in Alsace.

MARSHAL TURENNE
Philippe de Champaigne, the Pinakothek, Munich

None of the victors desired to continue the war. The emperor was fully occupied with the restoration of his power in his hereditary possessions and with the war against Transylvania. The Spaniards had only a small military force, as was shown by the spiritless manner in which they recommenced war with the Netherlands in 1621. Maximilian, it is true, desired to obtain possession of his conquests; but he had no confidence in the Spaniards, and found it very difficult to bear the burdens of war, as he received no outside aid of importance. On the other hand, the Count Palatine received no active help either from the Protestant estates of the empire or from abroad, but by the beginning of 1622, several adventurous partisans of his—Ernest of Mansfeld, Christian of Brunswick (called "mad Christian"), and Margrave George

Frederick of Baden—collected 50,000 mercenaries, an army of unusual size for that era. This force was intended to oppose the army of Maximilian and the Spaniards, and as quickly as its numbers decreased they were recruited afresh. The Bavarian commander-in-chief Tilly defeated this force when it attempted to prevent his army and the Spaniards from occupying the fortified towns of the Electoral Palatinate (undecisive engagement at Wiesloch, 27 April, 1622; complete defeat of the army of the margrave at Baden at Wimpfen, 6 May, 1622; severe defeat of Christian at Höchst, 20 June, 1622). After this, however, the Netherlands, the foe of Spain, allowed the still unconquered Mansfeld to enter their territory; from here he advanced in 1623 into East Frisia. The plan was that Christian should come to his support with a new army. Tilly, however, pursued Christian and completely defeated him on 6 August, 1623, at Stadtlohn in Westphalia, but was not able at that moment to attack Mansfeld. Under these circumstances Tilly was obliged to remain in north-western Germany; the estates of this territory had taken no part in the war, and soon the quartering of the soldiers and the forced contributions aroused violent discontent among them.

A denominational movement now also gradually made itself felt. In 1623 for the first time a Catholic was elected bishop in the Diocese of Osnabrück. Hereupon the estates of Lower Saxony demanded the emperor's guarantee for the security of their lands which had formerly belonged to the Church. The emperor, however, was willing only to promise security against force, not against a judgment of dispossession. In 1624 Maximilian began to make the Upper Palatinate once more Catholic. In Swabia the Catholic estates sought to regain the many ecclesiastical foundations that had been acquired by the Protestants. A large number of suits concerning ecclesiastical property were still in litigation before the courts of the empire. There developed on the one side the desire, and on the other the dread, that all the changes in the entire empire made by the Protestants contrary to the Religious Peace of Augsburg might be done away with. Foreign countries began to give increasing attention to the war. France sought especially to separate Maximilian from the emperor; the Netherlands granted subsidies; in 1624 a French embassy intrigued against the Habsburg dynasty at the German and northern Courts; England and Holland negotiated both with King Christian IV of Denmark and with Gustavus Adolphus to induce these rulers to take part in the war. Christian, who belonged to the estates of the empire as Count of Holstein, was elected commander of their forces by the oppressed and aroused estates of the lower Saxon circle, and on 9 December, 1625, he came to an agreement with England and Holland and marched into the empire.

Thus the enemies of the emperor and the Duke of Bavaria became so powerful that the emperor could no longer leave the burdens or the direction of the war to a single prince of the empire, even though this prince were as able as Maximilian. The struggle now threatened to engage all Europe. Wallenstein, a Bohemian noble, and the ablest of all the leaders of mercenaries, offered to collect and maintain in the same way as the enemy a force larger and better equipped than that of the Protestants. Ferdinand accepted Wallenstein's offer, and on 7 April, 1625, appointed him general. For some unknown reason Wallenstein and Tilly did not come to an understanding. In 1626 Wallenstein took up a position on the Elbe. Mansfeld planned to surround him and establish communication with the Prince of Transylvania, but Wallenstein defeated him on 25 April at the bridge over the Elbe at Dessau. However, Mansfeld was able to march to Transylvania, where he found that Bethlen Gabor had decided to make peace. Shortly after his arrival he died of fever. Wallenstein increased his army to 70,000 men and in the summer of 1627 he defeated Mansfeld's troops, now without a leader, at Kosel in Silesia on 9 July. In the meantime Tilly had defeated the Danish King Christian on 27 August, 1626, in a hotly-contested battle at Lutter on the Barenberg. During the winter Christian equipped a new army; nevertheless, Tilly drove him from the lower Weser and Elbe, but did not take Stade.

IV. The Edict of Restitution.—The success of the imperial and Bavarian armies in Northern Germany enabled the Catholics to reclaim the lands of the Church. In 1626 the energetic Francis William of Wartenberg, a relative of Maximilian, became Bishop of Osnabrück. He sought to be made bishop also of the dioceses of Minden and Verden, which had become Protestant. In 1627 the Austrian Archduke Leopold William became Bishop of Halberstadt; in the early part of 1628 he was defeated by a prince of Saxony in his attempt to secure the Archdiocese of Magdeburg, but in the summer of 1628 he obtained the right of succession to the Archdiocese of Bremen. In Southern Germany Maximilian undertook in 1627 to make the Electoral Palatinate Catholic again. Catholic demands were now sent to the emperor from all sides. In accordance with the Habsburg method of administration and with the emperor's own way of thinking, these demands were all turned over in September, 1628, to the Aulic Council for judicial investigation. Following this, Ferdinand issued in March, 1629, the Edict of Restitution. In its first part the edict settled the meaning of the disputed ordinances of the Religious Peace; it then ordered that all legal suits arising from the Religious Peace which were pending before the imperial courts were to be settled summarily in accordance with the edict. It further appointed three commissions which were to determine and correct the infringements of the Religious Peace in all parts of the empire. The Guelphs in Northern Germany were obliged to surrender what they had taken of the Diocese of Hildesheim in 1523 with the exception of a small part; in March, 1630, imperial commissioners took possession of Magdeburg, and in May and July, 1630, Francis William of Wartenberg established himself at Verden and Minden. In Southern Germany Würtemberg, in particular, was forced to make restitution.

In the beginning of the trouble, at the period of the Bohemian revolt the more powerful of the Protestant estates had held to the emperor. The transfer of the electorate to Maximilian, however, had made Saxony and Brandenburg indignant because it put an end to the parity of religions in the Electoral College. To keep Brandenburg from joining the other side Wallenstein devastated it between 1626 and 1627. The Edict of Restitution, however, alienated all the Protestant rulers and nobles from the emperor. From desire of peace and from lack of strength they took no steps against him. It was not until the Catholic estates also became estranged from the emperor that a crisis arose in the internal affairs of the empire which largely influenced the continuance of the war.

Wallenstein's method of recruiting and maintaining his army required the establishment of extremely large divisions of the army. Following a custom introduced by Ferdinand in Austria, he assigned to each of these divisions a definite district for the collection of recruits and supplies. At first these districts were in the domains of the rulers and nobles hostile to the emperor; gradually, however, the territories of the spiritual princes who had been united by Maximilian in the League were thus assigned and finally, in May, 1628, the domains of the Elector of Saxony who had, in other respects, been protected by the Habsburgs. The estates resisted, appealing to the Law of the Imperial Diet of 1570, and complaining that their countries were used as recruiting depots without their consent. They protested against the extraordinary amount of the enforced contributions, their long duration, and against the amount of plunder. They emphasized these complaints by threats to take the law in their own hands. They watched the emperor with suspicion when, after he had placed (1621) the Elector Palatine under the ban of the empire without the consent of the Electors, he revived other imperial privileges that had fallen into disuse. Thus he declared the estates of Lower Saxony, which had taken part in the Danish war against his orders, guilty of treason punishable by the loss of their territories. The estates knew instinctively that their territorial sovereignty, which had existed as a fact from 1555, depended solely on the passivity of the empire in foreign affairs, and that they would have to be more submissive to the emperor's authority should the civil war develop into a European one, as appeared more likely from year to year. This thought troubled them greatly. Their horizon was narrow; they were ignorant of European politics. They said that under Wallenstein's influence Ferdinand would make the imperial power absolute, and that German liberty, that is their freedom as princes, was endangered. The fact that Wallenstein's army was composed of Catholics and Protestants alike, and that he appointed as general so zealous a Lutheran as Hans Georg von Arnim, impressed the Catholic estates with the idea that their community of interests with the emperor had become weaker, and induced them through self-interest to unite with the Protestant estates in opposition to the emperor. Maximilian in particular was anxious and discontented. An Italian Capuchin, Valerio Magni, irritated him by reports about Wallenstein and the intentions of the emperor, while Wallenstein fanned the flame by his harsh treatment of the Bavarian Elector, by his constant demands for greater military authority from the emperor, and by securing his own appointment as prince of the empire (April, 1628).

The first clear symptoms of the tension between the emperor and the estates of the empire were: the meeting of the League at Würzburg in January, 1627; the session of the Electors at Mülhausen in October-November, 1627; and the meeting of the Catholic Electors at Bingen in June, 1628. The assembly at Mülhausen already demanded a change in the military organization and the dismissal of Wallenstein. At first Ferdinand sought to reduce the tension by working upon Maximilian; in the Treaty of Munich, 1628, he guaranteed to him the Electoral dignity and the possession both of the Upper Electoral Palatinate and of that on the right bank of the Rhine for thirty years. In the course of 1628, however, the emperor's markedly advantageous position over the estates was seriously injured by his desire, after completing the reorganization of his Austrian territories, to secure the continuance of the imperial crown in his family by the election of his son as King of the Romans. This desire made him dependent on the good will of the Electors. In the spring of 1628 he forced Wallenstein to reduce the size of his army a little, and in the autumn of the same year to make a much larger reduction. Encouraged thereby the Electors refused to accede to the emperor's wish for the convocation of the Electoral College, and wanted to defer it until the end of the war. The Edict of Restitution also deferred the meeting, but only for a short time. At Ferdinand's demand the Elector of Mainz finally convoked the college for June, 1630. Before it met the emperor again forced Wallenstein to dismiss a large part of his troops. The meeting of the Electors, which was held at Ratisbon from 3 July till 12 November, 1630, the two Protestant Electors not attending, took place under entirely changed political and military conditions.

V. THE WAR BECOMES A EUROPEAN CONFLICT.— About 1625 the Spanish Habsburgs began to develop an energetic policy, as they had done in the sixteenth century. They believed a great opportunity had come to give Protestantism a crushing blow; they even hoped for the aid of France, although this hope proved vain. The Spanish troops were sent first against the Netherlands; in 1626 Spinola took the important fortress of Breda. In the meantime Austria and Bavaria were to aid Spain by cutting off the Netherlands from its main source of commercial revenue, the Baltic. In this way the Spaniards thought to use against the Dutch the same means which the latter had employed against them when they strove to cut off the Spanish fleets carrying to Spain the product of the silver mines of America. At first Ferdinand hesitated and Maximilian still more. However, it was agreed at the Brussels conference of 1626 to blockade the coast of the North Sea and at least one port on the Baltic. Austria soon found that it could further its own interests in this enterprise. Ferdinand planned to gain a free water-route to the sea for his products by treaties with the countries on the banks of the Elbe and Oder, and by treaties with the large Dutch commercial cities to obtain a good outlet for his exports, especially in sending Hungarian copper to Spain. In 1627 the Dukes of Mecklenburg were deprived of their possessions for aiding the King of Denmark, and Wismar was confiscated as a good port on the Baltic. In pursuance of the scheme the Spaniards were now to appear with a fleet in the Baltic so as to enable Wallenstein to gain the supremacy at sea. During this period, however, Spain's performances on sea were a disappointment, and on this occasion, also, no fleet appeared. Upon this the Hanseatic towns, whose aid in carrying out the plan had been counted on from the first, were intimidated by Denmark from sending ships. Wallenstein attempted to build a fleet himself, but only a small flotilla, capable of inflicting occasional surprises under Gabriel Leroy, came into existence. The last hope of aid from Spain vanished when the Spanish fleet carrying silver was destroyed in the autumn of 1628. The defects of Wallenstein's method of carrying on war appeared at the same time in consequence

COUNT VON OXENSTIERN
From a contemporary print

of the peculiar character of the problems he was to solve. He did not dare to use his army for difficult sieges or sudden attacks; where he was forced to do so his projects failed. He left the strongly fortified city of Magdeburg, which controlled the passage over the Elbe, untaken in his rear. He wished to take by storm in May, 1628, the city of Stralsund, which formed the connexion between the German Baltic coast and Sweden, but he gave up this plan, and besieged it from the land side. He could not force the city to surrender, however, as Danish and Swedish troops came to its aid. His victory in August, 1628, over a Danish army of relief at Wolgast did not change the result. Denmark, it is true, signed the Peace of Lubeck, 22 May, 1629, on condition that all conquered territories should be restored. But this brought Gustavus Adolphus on the scene of war.

In the autumn of 1629, Gustavus Adolphus declared before the Swedish Diet that the emperor wanted to conquer Sweden and the Baltic, and that he should be prevented from doing so, but that if Sweden were victorious on German soil the German states would become the booty of Sweden. Up to this time, notwithstanding many offered inducements, the king had limited himself to wars with weaker opponents. He had, however, always carried on war, not only from love of it, but also from the necessity of supporting his army in foreign countries, as Sweden, being a poor country, could not otherwise maintain it. In the meantime the king neglected nothing to increase the prosperity of Sweden. Just then he hoped to secure the wealth of the north German cities and princes. But now, the politico-commercial plans of the emperor threatened to put an end to Sweden's trade in copper, its one valuable natural source of wealth, while Wallenstein's troops threatened to expel the Swedish forces from the country beyond the Baltic, from the revenues of which, especially the customs, it largely drew its pecuniary means. Self-defence as well as the spirit of adventure forced the king to put some check upon the emperor. Nevertheless, he hesitated until the summer of 1630, when on 6 June he landed on the German coast of Pomerania. Except for a few persons of importance Gustavus was not welcomed, even by the Protestants, and was obliged to make his way in Pomerania by force of arms. In a short time his money was entirely gone, and he debated for months whether he might venture inland. Wallenstein could, perhaps, have crushed him, but instead, he left the way open to him, for, through resentment at the emperor's command in the spring of 1630 to reduce the number of his troops, he had disbanded the greater part of the imperial forces in the districts now entered by Gustavus, and had allowed other detachments to be sent to fight in the Netherlands and Italy. The year previous Tilly had vainly begged Maximilian's permission to attack the Netherlanders at the right moment in their own country, giving as his reason that the money of the Dutch was constantly used to renew the opposition to the Bavarian troops. Maximilian, however, had not the courage to enter into open conflict with a foreign foe. Thus the Dutch stadtholder, Frederick Henry, in 1629, after the great Spanish general Spinola had been recalled, was able to besiege Bois-le-Duc, and thus give the first great rebuff to Spain. It was not Tilly who now hastened to the aid of the Spaniards; an imperial force, detached from Wallenstein's army, was sent. But when the Dutch seized the fortification of Wesel and thus endangered the retreat of the imperial troops, a part of the imperial force fell back. Bois-le-Duc surrendered on 14 September, and the Dutch were able to take the offensive.

In France Richelieu had, from 1624 to 1628, re-established the internal authority of the government to such an extent that after twenty years of cautious foreign policy more positive measures could be adopted. This change was first of all made evident to the Habsburgs in Lorraine. Duke Charles of Lorraine (from 1624), a vassal of the emperor, laid claim as heir to the Duchy of Barr in Alsace; but Richelieu disputed his rights and harassed the secular authority of the Bishop of Verdun so that the latter took refuge in the empire. In 1627 the male line of the Dukes of Mantua-Montferrat in upper Italy became extinct. The next heir was the Duke of Nevers, a relative of the Bourbons. He took possession at once of Mantua, and hoped to secure Montferrat also by the marriage of his son with the daughter of his predecessor, for the succession to Montferrat was in the female line. Montferrat, though, lay far below Mantua in the western part of upper Italy. Consequently Spain and Savoy were able to seize the district for themselves before the Duke of Nevers could enter it. Spain wished to maintain controlling influence in upper Italy, which it had acquired during the reign of Charles V. France, on the other hand, now saw Savoy, which had become dependent on it, suddenly taking sides with Spain. Spain asked for the decision of the emperor, who was suzerain of Mantua. Ferdinand interfered in the quarrel, not only because his dynasty had always considered the imperial rights in Italy of much value, but also because he had constantly, from the time he ruled Styria, been opposed to Venice, which he believed might become dangerous. Still, neither he nor Spain carried on the negotiations rapidly nor with insistence, as their attention was claimed in other directions. Thus Richelieu had time to punish Savoy (1628–29). After this Ferdinand's troops besieged Mantua and the Spaniards under Spinola besieged Casale. Richelieu did not yet consider France strong enough to oppose the Habsburgs directly. When Mantua was taken and Casale's position became very precarious, Richelieu proposed a truce; this was signed at Rialto on 4 September, 1630. Then Richelieu sent his most adroit negotiator, Père Joseph, to Ratisbon, where the electors were still in session. He hoped to withdraw France from the struggle but to raise up enemies enough against Austria elsewhere.

On 17 June, 1630, Richelieu made a treaty with the Netherlands by which he gave them a subsidy for the continuance of the war against Spain. By means of the truce, which was brought about by France, between Gustavus Adolphus and Poland at Altmark in September, 1629, Gustavus was at liberty to take part in the war within the empire. Nevertheless, he hesitated to assume responsibilities which would permit France to interfere with his management of the war. From March, 1629, negotiations had been actively carried on by Richelieu with the imperial estates but so far to little purpose. His aim was to separate them from the emperor by bringing them into a neutral confederation under his guidance. By

CHRISTIAN IV, KING OF DENMARK
From a contemporary print

representing that the friendship of France, an essentially peaceful country, would protect them against the pretensions of the warlike emperor, and that their alliance with France would guarantee their "German liberties" against Austria, he hoped to separate them from the emperor in a neutral confederacy. However, Maximilian was not slow to make the counter-proposal that France should form an alliance only with the Catholic estates, abandoning all the agreements made so far with the Protestants. In this way it would be possible to isolate the Habsburgs and yet complete the Catholic restoration in western Europe. The basis of these negotiations from October, 1629, was the draft of a treaty between France and Bavaria. Richelieu transferred the negotiations with the emperor to the place where the College of Electors was in session, because he hoped here to come to a settlement with the estates. Success in these undertakings, however, was made difficult for Richelieu by the landing of Gustavus Adolphus on German soil in June. When the emperor announced (13 August, 1630) Wallenstein's resignation to the Electors, they declared themselves ready to aid him against Gustavus on condition that both the imperial troops and those of the different estates should be united under Maximilian as commander-in-chief. Ferdinand used the friendliness of the Electors to exert pressure upon the French negotiator. Although the latter was only to come to an agreement regarding upper Italy, still Ferdinand made him promise in the Peace of Ratisbon (13 October) that when the Duke of Nevers received Mantua and Montferrat in fief, France would neither attack the empire itself nor aid others in any manner to attack it, and that the Duke of Lorraine should be included in this agreement. This imperial success, however, came to nothing, because the estates and the emperor did not reach an agreement. The Protestant Electors, instead, invited the Protestant estates to meet at Leipzig and form a neutral party (Assembly of the Princes at Leipzig, February-April, 1631). The Catholics came to an agreement with the emperor that the imperial troops should be under the command of Tilly, but Maximilian had made up his mind that Tilly should only be employed to protect Bavaria against a possible attack by Gustavus Adolphus. He insisted, therefore, that the imperial troops and his own should not be united into one army. This enabled Richelieu, whose overthrow seemed certain in November, 1630, to avoid confirming the Peace of Ratisbon, and, contrary to agreement, to make the treaty of Bärwalde (23 January, 1631) with Gustavus Adolphus. In this treaty Gustavus, whom the need of money had finally made compliant, pledged himself to carry on war against the emperor for four years.

VI. THE WAR WITH SWEDEN WITHIN THE EMPIRE. —After Wallenstein's deposition Gustavus was able to clear the entire lower course of the Elbe of the imperial troops, which were disbanding and had no commander. His farther advance would take him through the territories of the Electors of Brandenburg and Saxony, and these princes refused to let him pass. Tilly thus gained time to assume command on the Elbe and Oder, and immediately attempted (February, 1631) to force Gustavus to a battle; but the latter was not to be drawn into one. During this period, in which no decisive action took place, Tilly's position became critical, because, as had happened at Stralsund, a Swedish detachment under Dietrich von Falkenberg had thrown itself into Magdeburg, in September, 1630, and, supported by the citizens, refused to permit the imperial troops to enter. Magdeburg was the city which Wallenstein had so carefully avoided. Tilly determined to take it, and stormed it on 20 May, 1631. But a fire, which the Swedes are accused of starting when they saw that the city was lost, laid it in ashes, and took from Tilly the advantage he had gained. In the meantime Gustavus had taken advantage of the withdrawal of his opponents towards Magdeburg to seize the fortresses of Frankfurt and Landsberg on the middle course of the Oder, and to wring from the Elector of Brandenburg Küstrin and the fortress of Spandau at the junction of the Spree and the Havel Rivers. Fearing that the Elector of Saxony would also yield to Gustavus, Tilly tried to terrify the wavering ruler; this, however, forced the latter under the influence of the Lutheran general, von Arnim, who had formerly been an officer of Wallenstein's, and forming a temporary alliance with Sweden, on 17 September, 1631, the combined troops of Saxony and Sweden destroyed Tilly's army at Breitenfeld, near Leipzig. The victory had a great moral effect, but did not decide the war. In northwestern Germany Pappenheim had an excellent position which enabled him to control the line of the Weser for the emperor, and the emperor and Bavaria had sufficient means to raise new troops. The strength of Gustavus Adolphus was always much below that of his enemies. Conscious of this, he felt the necessity of entering rich districts which he could use for the support and strengthening of his troops; in addition he wished to come into communication with the Protestant estates of south-western Germany that were favourable to him, and perhaps hoped when there to persuade France to undertake a common war against the emperor. These views probably influenced his military decisions after the battle of Breitenfeld. He left the Saxons to occupy the Austrians by an attack on Prague, and without moving against Pappenheim he went straight towards the dioceses on the Main and the middle course of the Rhine in order first to defeat them, and then their chief, Maximilian, before striking a decisive blow against the emperor. While living in the centre of the empire during the winter of 1631-32 he prepared his plans to secure absolute Swedish control over the Protestant estates and to secularize the dioceses that had remained Catholic. He also carried out his schemes for using German money to increase the prosperity of Sweden.

THE EMPEROR FERDINAND II (1578-1637)
From an old print

Maximilian's fear of Sweden constantly increased, and in May, 1631, he made his first treaty with France. It was, however, very hard for him to assume a neutral position towards the Protestant princes who opposed the emperor and the empire. Gustavus Adolphus on his part was not inclined to spare the champion of Catholicism in the empire for the sake of Richelieu. Finally, Maximilian so completely lost courage that negotiations for a truce were begun in December, 1631, and the truce was concluded in January, 1632. For the emperor, this was the most dangerous moment of the war. The Saxons had taken Prague. Richelieu continued to be hostile although the emperor had agreed to the Treaty of Cherasco (April, 1631), in which he waived the recognition by the Duke of Nevers of his suzerainty over Mantua; this treaty replaced that of Ratisbon. Contrary to the agreement made at Cherasco, Richelieu did not withdraw his troops from Piedmont, but, through the treachery of Pignerolo, retained it. He made the flight to Lorraine of Gaston of Orléans, who lived in discord with his brother Louis XIII, a pretext to carry the war into Lorraine and there to seize one fortress after another. In this way his troops were kept near the seat of war, between the Germans and Dutch. In January, 1632, Gustavus Adolphus urged that Richelieu should take Hagenau and Zabern in Alsace from the Habsburgs. Richelieu hesitated, and Père Joseph persuaded him for religious reasons to reject the proposal. During all these months the emperor had had no commander to whom he could entrust the direction of his forces. His son, Ferdinand III, was still too young, so from necessity he turned again to Wallenstein. The latter kept him in suspense and only consented when granted powers so great as to raise suspicion against himself. The contract was made on 13 April, 1632, although Wallenstein actually assumed command several weeks earlier. Gustavus reopened the campaign in February, 1632, and began the siege of Bamberg. But Tilly came with fresh troops and relieved the city. He wished to open communications with Wallenstein at Eger and thus force Gustavus to withdraw from the interior of Germany, but Wallenstein did not stir; consequently Gustavus was free to advance directly towards Bavaria. On 15 April there was an undecided battle at Rain on the Lech; Tilly was mortally wounded and the Bavarians withdrew from the battlefield. This left the road to Munich open to the Swedes and permitted them to plunder the Bavarian lowlands. However, Maximilian retained Ingolstadt and Ratisbon, the two strategically important points of his country. Gustavus Adolphus simply lost time in the Bavarian campaign. In north-western Germany Pappenheim was successful in his undertakings. New imperial forces gathered both in Bohemia and Swabia. In June Wallenstein conquered Bohemia, formed a junction then with Maximilian, and kept Gustavus inactive at Nuremberg for weeks. In vain Gustavus tried to draw Wallenstein into a battle, and when he attempted to storm Wallenstein's position (3 September) he was defeated. For about six weeks he marched aimlessly through Franconia and Swabia pursued by Wallenstein. The latter suddenly drew off towards Saxony in order to unite there with Pappenheim, and cut off Gustavus's road to the Baltic. Gustavus followed and on 16 November, forced a battle at Lützen near Leipzig, just as the forces of Wallenstein and Pappenheim met. The Swedes gained the victory, but they paid for it with the life of Gustavus Adolphus. On the imperial side Pappenheim, the emperor's most daring and capable cavalry general, was killed.

The death of the Swedish king did not make any essential change. His policies were carried on in the same manner and with equal skill by his trusted councillor Axel Oxenstiern. The strength of the Swedish forces had been declining throughout the year 1632. The important questions to be decided were: whether, as the Swedish power declined, the Protestant princes would act independently of it under the leadership of Saxony, taking upon themselves the cause of Protestantism and of the independence of the princely rulers; also whether the emperor could find a commander who would make the unreliable and sluggish Wallenstein unnecessary. On account of these difficulties the next two years were more occupied with negotiations than with battles. Oxenstiern brought Duke Bernhard of Saxe-Weimar, who had been trained under Gustavus Adolphus and who was the ablest of the younger commanders among the German Protestants, and with him Saxony into closer union with Sweden; he also made an agreement with the Protestant rulers of the central German states at the assembly at Heilbron (March, 1633). In November, 1633, Bernhard by a daring advance took Ratisbon; Austria lay open to him, while a revolt of the Bavarian peasants crippled Bavaria's strength. The duke, however, did not venture into Austria and by January Maximilian had subdued the peasants. Sweden rapidly lost its popularity even among the Protestants of central Germany, for it demanded much. In addition, Oxenstiern flooded these states with Swedish copper coin and sent their good silver to Sweden, thus ruining them economically. As early as 1634 the influence of Richelieu over these states was greater than that of Sweden. Wallenstein used his army but little in 1633. He was constantly occupied with negotiations, chiefly with Saxony, but also with Sweden, with a view to imposing a peace on the Habsburgs. The commander of the Saxon forces, von Arnim, persuaded him to agree to one truce after another. In this way Saxony saved its strength and gained time to improve its position in the empire both as regards Sweden and the emperor. Although he afterwards denied it, even Richelieu believed early in 1634 that Wallenstein was ready to enter into relations with France also. Ferdinand and Maximilian, however, had already planned his downfall; he was murdered at Eger on 25 February, 1634.

France was the only country successful in war and politics from 1632 to the middle of 1634. An increasing number of fortresses in Lorraine came under its control. In the spring of 1632, after making a treaty with the Archbishop of Trier to protect him from the Swedes, French troops occupied Coblenz and Ehrenbreitstein on the opposite side of the Rhine. Richelieu also carried on negotiations with the Archbishop of Cologne, who was Bishop of Liège as well, by which he hoped to bring French troops into north-western Germany in the flank of the imperial forces there, and also to garrison Dinan which belonged to the Diocese of Liège. From this latter point France would be able to exercise a strong influence on the war between Spain and the Netherlands. Dinan was not obtained owing to a revolt of the citizens of Cologne. However, from this time on, Richelieu pressed steadily forward towards Alsace. He wished the Protestant princes to request him to garrison the fortified Alsatian towns, and for a time in 1634 he occupied Montbéliard, which belonged to Wurtemberg, and the Diocese of Basle. Spain had already, in 1633, sent troops both from Italy and from the Netherlands to the upper Rhine as protection. Richelieu's plans were held in check by the slow progress of the war in the Netherlands. Notwithstanding the treaty of 1630, by which France granted subsidies, the States General showed but little warlike spirit, while the southern part of the Netherlands was positively averse to war. A Spanish attack by sea on the Netherlands ended in September, 1632, in a complete defeat. On the other hand, an attack by the Stadtholder of the Netherlands on Maastricht in 1633 led to the capture of the fortress, not, as hoped and planned, to a revolt of the southern provinces against Spain. Neither did it force France to openly take part in the war. Nego-

BERNHARD, DUKE OF SAXE-WEIMAR
From an old engraving

tiations for peace were begun and it was only by his greatest efforts, and by his promise that France also should declare war on Spain, that Richelieu was able to frustrate them.

In the autumn of 1634 conclusive action was also taken in the empire. Ferdinand's son assumed command of the imperial troops, and Maximilian drove the Swedes out of Ratisbon. In this year the command of the Bavarian army was assumed by the Duke of Lorraine who had been obliged to fly from his country. Von Arnim's attempt to take Prague a second time failed. In south-western Germany the Swedes had undoubtedly the strongest army. Early in September the imperial and Bavarian armies united at Nördlingen, which the Swedes under Horn had wished to capture, and completely destroyed (6 September, 1634) the remainder of the finely-disciplined troops to which Gustavus Adolphus had owed his successes. After this the men who fought under the Swedish flag were only mercenaries, greedy for plunder, like those of the other armies of the time. To prevent the emperor from becoming absolute master in the empire, Richelieu had to declare war on him. Almost at the time of his declaration, war was also proclaimed by Ferdinand and Philip IV (May, 1635).

VII. WAR OF THE EMPIRE AND SPAIN AGAINST FRANCE AND SWEDEN UP TO ITS TURNING POINT.— The prospect of the interference of France had led Saxony to make friends with the emperor. Both desired by the Treaty of Prague (30 May, 1635) to lay the foundation for a general peace between the estates of the empire and the emperor and for their union against a foreign foe. To this end amnesty was to be granted to all the estates which, within a definite time, agreed to the treaty. The treaty also sought to readjust the constitutional relations between the emperor and the estates suitably to the historical development and yet so as to make the empire an organic whole. From 1555 the estates had almost forgotten the advantages of their union in the empire until the Swedish supremacy had reawakened this consciousness. France's declaration of war also aroused the sense of nationality; most of the German rulers, following the example of Brandenburg, agreed to the treaty between the emperor and Saxony. On 12 May, 1636, it was proclaimed as a peace of the empire. Some, indeed, signed it very unwillingly at Strasburg; the widowed Landgravine of Hesse Cassel put off her agreement without daring openly to reject the treaty. Finally, in December, 1636, Ferdinand's son was elected King of the Romans, and on 15 February, 1637, he succeeded his father as emperor.

The emperor, Bavaria, and Spain, decided to begin energetic offensive operations against France. In 1635 a combined imperial and Bavarian army forced back the French in Alsace and Lorraine, but the commanders of these forces lacked courage and caution. In 1636 the combined troops had to be withdrawn, finally, across the Rhine, after their numbers had been greatly reduced. In 1635 the Spaniards had seized and rendered powerless the Elector of Trier, and, by skilful Fabian movements, had destroyed two armies of French and Dutch which had entered the Spanish Netherlands. In 1636, it is true, the forces of Spain and Holland soon balanced each other. Spain now turned with superior forces against France. The German cavalry general, Jan van Werth, who shared in the direction of the campaign, wished to advance straight towards Paris, but the heads of the expedition allowed themselves to be detained before the small fortress Corbie, until the French had brought together 50,000 men. This army forced the Spaniards to withdraw once more. Saxony made an unfortunate attempt, with the aid of imperial troops, to drive the remains of the Swedish forces completely out of Germany; the campaign ended in the severe defeat of the combined army by the Swedish general, Baner, at Wittstock (4 October, 1636). The fantastic plan of the Spaniards to revenge the defeat, by a combined attack of their fleet and the imperial and Saxon land forces on Livonia so as to strike the Swedes in the rear, failed because the fleet, while on its way, was defeated (1639) by the Dutch in the English Channel. By a desperate defence, Brandenburg sought to save at least its fortresses from the Swedes. In 1639 Baner twice made forced marches as far as Prague, plundering and terrifying as he went. From the close of 1536 the Habsburgs were placed in an unfavourable defensive position in the west. France took into its service the army fighting under Bernhard of Saxe-Weimar, on the upper Rhine, and in December, 1638, Bernhard conquered Briesach on the right bank of the Rhine. In 1637, after a celebrated siege, Holland retook the town of Breda which had been lost in 1626. Neither the Dutch nor the French made any further progress in the Netherlands, nor could they derive the expected advantages from the capture of Arras (August, 1640), by which they had pierced the line of fortresses protecting the southern Netherlands. Even in 1639, the Habsburgs maintained their superiority in numbers, but their enemies conducted the war with greater skill. Consequently the imperialists gained but little when Piedmont in 1639 proclaimed its independence of France.

The union of the German estates consequent upon the French attack did not beget any warlike enthusiasm. They longed for peace and hoped that the peace congress proposed in 1636 would assemble. Soon the prolongation of the war, and its disasters, aroused renewed discontent with the imperial policy. The complaint was everywhere heard that the emperor was continuing the war only for the advantage of Spain. The negotiations between Maximilian and France, which had been carried on almost from the beginning of the war, were renewed in 1637, although, as usual, without result. In 1639 Duke Bernhard died unexpectedly. France enlisted his troops and placed them under the command of the able General Guébriant; and in this way acquired, what it had not had before, an experienced army of its own on German soil. In the winter of 1639–40 Guébriant boldly forced his way into the interior of the empire intending to unite with Baner. As he advanced the Landgravine of Hesse broke off the negotiations with the emperor; thus once more foreigners gained allies in the heart of Germany. In January, 1641, Baner planned to capture Ratisbon again, but the thaw that set in discouraged him. Guébriant also saw that he could not long maintain himself in so advanced a position; as in 1631, the imperial forces controlled the line of the Weser and threatened him on that side. In the spring of 1641 Saxony and the emperor prepared to repeat against Sweden the offensive operations which had failed in 1663. The plan failed, owing to the simultaneous deaths of von Arnim, the Brandenburg statesman, Count Schwarzenberg, and Baner. The young Frederick William became Elector of Brandenburg in December, 1640, and early in the summer of 1641 issued a proclamation of neutrality. This gave the Swedes time to place their troops under the command of Torstenson, who was much superior to Baner in energy. Moreover, the rising of the French nobility was not as successful as the Habsburgs had hoped. Guébriant, indeed, was obliged to withdraw from the empire to aid in its suppression, but on his way to France he defeated at Kempen in January, 1642, the imperial and Spanish troops, who were going to the help of the French nobles. In the meantime the war had taken a decisive turn in favour of the French, in an unexpected place. The inhabitants of Barcelona, oppressed by the Spanish soldiers quartered upon them, revolted and were soon joined by the whole of Catalonia (June, 1640). Richelieu at once sent aid to the rebels. In December, 1640, Portugal also shook off the Spanish yoke. For several years Spain was crippled at the chief seat of war by these conflicts in the Pyrenean peninsula. On the other hand the French, under the leadership of young commanders, Turenne and Condé, became experts in the art of war. By June, 1642, Piedmont was again under control. In 1643 Condé completely destroyed the finest and most celebrated troops of the Spanish army at Rocroi in the Netherlands. The Provinces of Hainault and Luxemburg in the southern Netherlands fell into his hands. In 1644, Holland seized the mouth of the Scheldt and France Grevelingen, and in 1645 France occupied the greater part of Flanders and in 1646 Dunkirk. Henceforth, the Spaniards held only a few of the large cities in the Spanish Netherlands. The people, excepting the nobility, remained loyal to them.

VIII. THE RESULTS OF THE WAR.—The German Habsburgs were forced to take the defensive and their cause was in great danger. Allied with Maximilian they were compelled to use their main force to prevent the occupation of southern Germany by the French. They bravely fought in this part of Germany under Mercy during the years 1643–45, but were continually obliged to fall back. On 5 May, 1645, they gained a famous victory over Turenne at Mergentheim; on 3 August, 1645, the French were victorious at Allersheim and Mercy was killed. Still the imperial and Bavarian troops were always at least strong enough to save Bavaria from the incursions of the French. In the meantime, however, the imperial forces had not been able to bring a sufficiently large army against the Swedes. These, it is true, were obliged to encounter (1642) a new enemy in Denmark. But the Danes accomplished just as little as their imperial allies. The imperial forces were severely defeated by Torstenson at Breitenfeld in November, 1642, and at Jüterbogk and Magdeburg in October, 1644. After these two victories, Torstenson formed an alliance with George Rákóczy, the successor to Bethlen Gabor as Prince of Transylvania. Resolved to carry the war directly into the hereditary lands of the emperor, Torstenson advanced at once as far as Brünn, but there saw that he was too weak for such an undertaking. The result of the Swedish victories in this year was the permanent loss by the imperialists of the control of the Weser, and of their position in north-western Germany. Denmark concluded a treaty of peace in 1645.

During the years 1642–45 the German estates unceasingly demanded peace. As early as 1640, at a session of the Electors at Nuremberg, the opinion was expressed, that a part of Pomerania should be ceded to the Swedes if this would content them. In 1641, at the suggestion of the electors the first Diet held since 1613 met at Ratisbon, and its success proved that the effort made in the Peace of Prague to revive the organization of the empire had borne good fruit. The Diet granted the emperor considerable subsidies. The estates, however, showed very plainly that they believed the emperor was over-considerate of Spain.

France and Sweden encouraged this view by expressing their readiness to open negotiations. The opinion gained ground among the estates that if Austria did not break off its connexion with Spain the estates would once more abandon the emperor, form a union among themselves, and make a treaty of peace for the empire with France and Sweden. The estates hoped that these two countries would consent not to interfere in the internal affairs of the empire, especially as regards religion. The economic suffering and misery of the population of the empire had greatly increased, largely through the marauding expeditions of the Swedes, and final success in the war was clearly out of the question. John Philip von Schönborn, Bishop of Würzburg, was especially active in supporting the proposal that the estates should separate from the emperor and establish peace in the empire without him. Maximilian encouraged the bishop, though reluctantly. One after another, the smaller German estates brought letters of protection from the Swedes in order to escape being plundered by them. In this way these territories became neutral without any further formalities. Of the larger principalities Brandenburg abandoned its neutrality in 1644 without, however, becoming friendly to the emperor on this account. On the other hand, Saxony, which was exhausted and desperate, made a direct treaty of neutrality with Sweden in 1645. Under these circumstances the emperor early in 1643 also declared himself ready to negotiate. He wished, however, that the treaty of peace should be general, not limited in geographical extent as was the case in 1630. The negotiations were to be carried on with France at Münster, with Sweden at Osnabrück, where the Swedish embassy had been since the spring of 1643. About the middle of 1643 the imperial delegates appeared at both designated places, and the French delegates followed in the spring of 1644. At the close of 1644, the imperial delegates presented their first proposition, to which the French did not reply until November, 1645. A last dispute had arisen over the question whether the emperor alone should negotiate for the empire or whether the estates should also be represented. The quarrel was practically settled by the invitation to be present sent to the various estates by France and Sweden. On 26 August, 1645, the emperor also invited them. In the same year representatives of Spain and Holland also appeared at Münster. An ambassador of Venice and a papal nuncio likewise took part as mediators between France and the emperor.

The course of the negotiations was influenced by the results of the last events of the war, and it was decided by the military conditions of 1646. In this year the Swedes under Wrangel united with Turenne and the two armies occupied Bavaria. This led Maximilian to make a treaty of neutrality with Sweden in March, 1647. The entire empire was now occupied by the armies of France and Sweden, but the emperor retained undisputed possession of his hereditary lands. The outbreaks of the years 1647–48 were directed against him. The French, however, could not aid these revolts, as internal troubles in France claimed their attention and made them desirous of coming to a settlement with the emperor and the empire. While Turenne marched back to France (1647) Wrangel seized Prague, but was expelled by the emperor and Maximilian, who broke his agreement with Sweden. In 1648 Turenne appeared again and, allied with the Swedes, defeated the imperial and Bavarian forces at Zusmarhausen and cruelly ravaged Bavaria. The attack on Prague was renewed by the Swedes alone in July, 1648, under Königsmark. They took part of the city, but the Austrians brought together a larger army and forced them to withdraw in November, 1648.

At the opening of the negotiations for peace the

emperor had hoped to be able to indemnify Sweden and to separate it from France, but on Sweden's refusal to accept his proposals he was obliged to give up his intention of making peace only if Spain were included in it. Supported by Maximilian, France induced the emperor and empire to remain neutral during the Franco-Spanish war. This success for France, however, did not prevent Holland from concluding peace with Spain on 5 June, 1648. But France received recompense for this disappointment in a new and great victory of Condé at Lens in the Netherlands, on 20 August, 1648. To secure peace for the empire, Austria consented in 1648 to give up its hereditary lands in Alsace and the city of Breisach to France; it also finally recognized the incorporation of the territories of Metz, Toul, and Verdun into France. It postponed, however, the decision as to the claims of France on the Duchy of Lorraine, and prevented France being made an estate of the empire for its conquests in Alsace. Sweden received the land around the mouth of the Oder with Stettin and Hither Pomerania, the territory near the outlet of the Weser, and the dioceses of Bremen and Verden, as well as Wismar, and was made an estate of the empire, because it, and not the Electorate of Saxony, had been the leader of the Protestant estates in the negotiations for peace. In addition it was to receive money to pay its mercenaries.

Taken in general, all the states and territories of the empire were confirmed in the possessions that they had had in 1618. The exceptions were: Electoral Saxony was confirmed in the possession of Lusatia which had been conceded to it in 1620; Bavaria was left in possession of the Upper Palatinate and of the fourth electorship, while a new, eighth electorate was created for the Palatinate; by the intervention of France, Brandenburg received, besides Further Pomerania, a number of dioceses with the right to secularize them. This and the similar concession to Sweden for Bremen and Verden undermined one of the main foundations of the organization of the empire, which for hundreds of years had rested on the existence and importance of the spiritual domains. In other particulars it was evident that the more important states sought, and probably sincerely, not to damage the efforts made in the Peace of Prague to revive the organization of the empire, yet in various instances they inflicted much injury upon it. It was contrary to the organization of the empire that the negotiations, deviating from the original intention, were not limited to external matters. Sweden and a large number of the Protestant estates were not willing to consent to this. To settle the claims made by the different religious denominations to one and the same territory the year 1624 was taken as the normal year, and the denomination which had prevailed in that year in a territory, was, as a rule, to be the permanent religion of that territory. Calvinism was included in the religious peace. The compulsory force of the principle, *cujus regio, ejus religio*, was restricted by granting private liberty of conscience, but only to a limited extent. The result of these regulations was in the main that the period of the violent religious disputes which had divided the empire was closed. It was also hoped that an effective working of the organic parts of the empire—the imperial and provincial diets, the supreme court, the Aulic Council, and the district constitution—would be secured for the future by an arrangement of their relations with one another and of their authority. The details of this reconstruction were left to the decision of a future Diet. It was settled, however, that grants of supplies were to be made not by majority votes, but by the voluntary agreement of the estates. All the rulers, even the petty ones in southern and western Germany, were declared sovereign in the internal government of their territories with certain exceptions. Moreover, the right to have diplomatic relations with foreign countries and to make treaties with them was granted to every estate. In reality this regulation only gave legal recognition to conditions that actually existed.

Austria was exempt from all these regulations, especially from the changes in the canon law prevailing there. This showed how little injury the war had inflicted upon it, and also the increasing differentiation between its domains and those of the other estates of the empire. The seal was impressed upon this differentiation by the fact that France secured (1647) the appointment of John Philip von Schönborn as Elector of Mainz and consequently Chancellor of the Empire, and especially by the fact that the treaty conceded to France and Sweden lasting diplomatic influence in the empire in return for their evacuation of the imperial territories. To counterbalance the influence which Austria exercised within the empire in virtue of her possession of the imperial crown, France and Sweden received the right to superintend the execution of the treaty in the empire, consequently to continually interfere in imperial affairs. On this basis the Peace of Westphalia with France and Sweden was settled on 24 October, 1648. The chief results of the Thirty Years War were: the foundation and recognition of a unified Austria under the rule of the German Habsburgs; the revival, in a certain doubtful sense though, of the Holy Roman Empire; the establishment of Sweden on German soil; the permanent weakening of Denmark; the renunciation by Holland of all efforts to drive Spain out of southern Netherlands; an enormous increase of the power of France. The question whether Spain would be able to maintain itself as a great power alongside of France led to eleven more years of war between the two states, and was decided, in favour of France, by the Treaty of the Pyrenees. This treaty and that of Westphalia were the basis of the pre-eminent position of France during the second half of the seventeenth century.

Theatrum Europæum (1635—); KHEVENHILLER, *Annales Ferdinandei* (Ratisbon, 1640–46, 2nd ed., 1716–26); WASSENBERG, *Commentariorum de bello inter imperatores Ferdinandos II et III et eorum gesto liber singularis* (many editions since 1639); CARAFA, *Commentaria de Germania sacra restaurata* (1639), supplement (1641); CHEMNITZ, *Kgl. Schwedischen in Teutschland geführten Krieges*, pt. i (1648), pt. ii, (1653); PUFENDORF, *Commentariorum de rebus Suecicis* (1686); AITZEMA, *Saken van Staet en Oorlogh in ende ontrent de Vereenigde Nederlanden* (1621–1669; 1657–71); *Korrespondenz Kaiser Ferdinands II…mit P. Becanus und P. Wilhelm Lamormaini, k. Beichtvätern* in *Archiv für Oesterr. Gesch.*, n. 54; *Nuntiaturberichte aus Deutschland*, division 4 (1628–1635; 2 vols. up to the present); IRMER, *Die Verhandlungen Schwedens und seiner Verbündeten mit Wallenstein und dem Kaiser, 1631–1634* (3 vols., 1888–91); *Negociations sécrites touchant la paix de Münster et d'Osnaburg* (4 vols., 1725–26); *Correspondencia diplomatica de los plenipotenciarios Españoles en el congresso de Münster* (3 vols., 1884–85); GÄRTNER, *Westphälische Friedenskanzley* (9 vols., 1731–38); MEIERN, *Acta pacis Westphalicæ publica* (6 vols., 1735–36); *Politische Korrespondenz des Grafen Franz Wilhelm von Wartenberg, Bischofs von Osnabrück, 1621–31* (1897); GINDELY, *Gesch. des 30 jährigen Krieges* (4 vols., Prague, 1869–80), only covers up to 1623; GARDINER, *The Thirty Years War* (London, 1874), many editions; WINTER, *Gesch. des 30 jährigen Krieges* (1883); RITTER, *Deutsche Gesch. im Zeitalter der Gegenreformation u. des 30 jährigen Krieges*, III (Stuttgart, 1908); HURTER, *Gesch. Kaiser Ferdinand's II.*, VIII–XI (Schaffhausen, 1857–64); KOCH, *Gesch. des deutschen Reichs unter die Regierung Ferdinands III* (2 vols., 1865–66); KLOPP, *Der 30 jährige Krieg bis zum Tode Gustav Adolfs 1632* (3 vols., Paderborn 1891–96); RIEZLER, *Gesch. Baierns*, V; HANOTAUX, *La crise européenne de 1621* in *Revue de deux mondes*, V, 7; STIEVE, *Ernst v. Mansfeld* (1890); OPEL, *Der niedersächsisch-dänische Krieg* (4 vols., 1872–94); SCHMITZ, *Die maritime Politik der Hapsburger 1625–28* (1903); GÜNTHER, *Das Restitutionsedikt v. 1629 u. die kathol. Restauration Altwirtembergs* (1901); TUPETZ, *Der Streit um die geistlich. Güter u. das Restaurationsedikt 1629* (1883); *Uber den Anteil Frankreichs am Kriege namentlich die Untersuchungen v. Fagniez*. Researches concerning the burning of Magdeburg, especially those of WITTICH; CRONHOLM, *Seriges historia under Gustav Adolfs regering* (6 vols., Stockholm, 1857–72); *Trettioariga kriget og underhandlingarna i Tyksland fran Gustav Adolfs död till Westfalisca freddslutet* (1876–80); GFRÖRER, *Gesch. Gustav Adolfs* (4th ed., 1864); EHSES, *Papst Urban VIII u. Gustav Adolfs* in *Hist. Jahrbuch der Görresgesellschaft*, XVI; IRMER, *Arnim* (1894); STRUCK, *Johann Georg u. Oxenstierna* (Stralsund, 1899); SODEN, *Gustav Adolf und sein Heer in Süddeutschland 1631–33* (3 vols., 1865–69); JAKOB, *Von Lützen nach Nördlingen* (Strasburg, 1904);

DROYSEN, *Bernhard von Weimar* (2 vols., 1885); IDEM, *Gustav Adolf* (2 vols., 1859–70). The period 1635–48 has been insufficiently investigated on its diplomatic side; the bibliography on this point is to a large degree of little value. ODHNER, *Die Politik Schwedens im westfäl. Friedenskongress* (1887); STEINBERGER, *Die Jesuiten u. die Friedensfrage 1635–1650* (1906). Of the works on the cession of Alsace cf. JAKOB, *Erwerbung des Elsass durch Frankreich* (1897); OVERMANN, *Die Abtretung des Elsass an Frankreich* (1905).

MARTIN SPAHN.

Thmuis, a titular see in Augustamnica Prima, suffragan of Pelusium; a city of Lower Egypt, on the canal east of the Nile, between its Tanitic and Mendesian branches. Herodotus (II, 166) gives it as the capital of a nome bearing its name, and Ptolemy as that of the Mendesian nome. In the fourth century it was still important, having its own administration and being exempt from the jurisdiction of the Prefect of Alexandria. It was in existence at the time of the Arabian conquest, and was later called Al-Mourad or Al-Mouradeh; it must have disappeared after the Turkish conquest. Its ruins are at Tell el-Meî, about five miles north-west of Senbelâouîn, a station on the railway from Zagazig to Mansoûrah. Le Quien ("Oriens Christ.", II, 537) names nine bishops of Thmuis, the last three being Monophysites of the Middle Ages. The others are St. Phileas, martyr (in the Martyrology, 4 Feb.); St. Donatus, his successor, martyr; Liberius (not Caius), at the Council of Nicæa in 325; St. Serapion, d. shortly before 360, the author of various works, in part preserved; Ptolemæus, at the Council of Seleucia (359); Aristobulus, at the Council of Ephesus (431).

SMITH, *Dict. Greek and Rom. geog.*, s. v.; DE ROUGÉ, *Géog. ancienne de la Basse-Egypte* (Paris, 1891); AMÉLINEAU, *Géog. de l'Egypte à l'époque copte* (Paris, 1893), 286, 500 sq.

S. PÉTRIDÈS.

Thomas, SAINT, the Apostle.—Little is recorded of St. Thomas the Apostle, nevertheless thanks to the fourth Gospel his personality is clearer to us than that of some others of the Twelve. His name occurs in all the lists of the Synoptists (Matt., x, 3; Mark, iii, 18; Luke, vi, 15, cf. Acts. 1, 13), but in St. John he plays a distinctive part. First, when Jesus announced His intention of returning to Judea to visit Lazarus, "Thomas", who is called Didymus [the twin], said to his fellow disciples: "Let us also go, that we may die with him" (John, xi, 16). Again it was St. Thomas who during the discourse before the Last Supper raised an objection: "Thomas saith to him: Lord, we know not whither thou goest; and how can we know the way?" (John, xiv, 5). But more especially St. Thomas is remembered for his incredulity when the other Apostles announced Christ's Resurrection to him: "Except I shall see in his hands the print of the nails, and put my finger into the place of the nails, and put my hand into his side, I will not believe" (John, xx, 25); but eight days later he made his act of faith, drawing down the kindly rebuke of Jesus: "Because thou hast seen me, Thomas, thou hast believed: blessed are they that have not seen, and have believed" (John, xx, 29).

This exhausts all our certain knowledge regarding the Apostle but his name is the starting-point of a considerable apocryphal literature, and there are also certain historical data which suggest that some of this apocryphal material may contain germs of truth. The principal document concerning him is the "Acta Thomæ", preserved to us with some variations both in Greek and in Syriac, and bearing unmistakable signs of its Gnostic origin. It may indeed be the work of Bardesanes himself. The story in many of its particulars is utterly extravagant, but it is of early date, being assigned by Harnack (Chronologie, ii, 172) to the beginning of the third century, before A. D. 220. If the place of its origin is really Edessa, as Harnack and others for sound reasons supposed (ibid., p. 176), this would lend considerable probability to the statement, explicitly made in the "Acta" (Bonnet, cap. 170, p. 286), that the relics of the Apostle Thomas, which we know to have been venerated at Edessa ("Peregrinatio Silviæ", ed. Geyer, p. 60), had really come from the East. The extravagance of the legend may be judged from the fact that in more than one place (cap. 31, p. 148) it represents Thomas (Judas Thomas, as he is called here and elsewhere in Syriac tradition) as the twin brother of Jesus. The word Thomas in Syriac is equivalent to δίδυμος in Greek, and means twin. Rendel Harris who exaggerates very much the cult of the Dioscuri, wishes to regard this as a transformation of a pagan worship of Edessa but the point is at best problematical. The story itself runs briefly as follows: At the division of the Apostles, India fell to the lot of Thomas, but he declared his inability to go, whereupon his Master Jesus appeared in a supernatural way to Abban, the envoy of Gundafor, an Indian king, and sold Thomas to him to be his slave and to serve Gundafor as a carpenter. Then Abban and Thomas sailed away until they came to Andrapolis, where they landed and attended the marriage feast of the ruler's daughter. Strange occurrences followed and Christ under the appearance of Thomas exhorted the bride to remain a virgin. Coming to India Thomas undertook to build a palace for Gundafor, but spent the money entrusted to him on the poor. Gundafor imprisoned him, but the Apostle escaped miraculously and Gundafor was converted. Going about the country to preach, Thomas met with strange adventures from dragons and wild asses. Then he came to the city of King Misdai (Syriac Mazdai), where he converted Tertia the wife of Misdai and Vazan his son. After this he was condemned to death, led out of the city to a hill, and pierced through with spears by four soldiers. He was buried in the tomb of the ancient kings but his remains were afterwards removed to the West.

Now it is certainly a remarkable fact that about the year A. D. 46 a king was reigning over that part of Asia south of the Himalayas now represented by Afghanistan, Baluchistan, the Punjab, and Sind, who bore the name Gondophernes or Guduphara. This we know both from the discovery of coins, some of the Parthian type with Greek legends, others of the Indian type with legends in an Indian dialect in Kharoshthi characters. Despite sundry minor variations the identity of the name with the Gundafor of the "Acta Thomæ" is unmistakable and is hardly disputed. Further we have the evidence of the Takht-i-Bahi inscription, which is dated, and which the best specialists accept as establishing that the King Guduphara probably began to reign about A. D. 20 and was still reigning in 46. Again there are excellent reasons for believing that Misdai or Mazdai may well be a transformation of a Hindu name made on Iranian soil. In this case it will probably represent a certain King Vāsudēva of Mathura, a successor of Kanishka. No doubt it can be urged that the Gnostic romancer who wrote the "Acta Thomæ" may have adopted a few historical Indian names to lend verisimilitude to his fabrication, but as Mr. Fleet urges in his severely critical paper "the names put forward here in connexion with St. Thomas are distinctly not such as have lived in Indian story and tradition" (Jour. of R. Asiatic Soc., 1905, p. 235).

On the other hand, though the tradition that St. Thomas preached in "India" was widely spread in both East and West and is to be found in such writers as Ephraem Syrus, Ambrose, Paulinus, Jerome, and, later, in Gregory of Tours and others, still it is difficult to discover any adequate support for the long-accepted belief that St. Thomas pushed his missionary journeys as far south as Mylapore, not far from Madras, and there suffered martyrdom. In that region is still to be found a granite bas-relief cross with a Pahlavi (ancient Persian) inscription dating from the seventh century, and the tradition that it was here that St. Thomas laid down his life is locally very strong. Certain it is also that on the Malabar or west coast of southern India a body of Christians still exists using a form of Syriac for its liturgical language. Whether this Church dates from the time of St. Thomas the Apostle (there was a Syro-Chaldean bishop John "from India and Persia" who assisted at the Council of Nicea in 325) or whether the Gospel was first preached there in 345 owing to the Persian persecution under Shapur, or Sapor, or whether the Syrian missionaries who accompanied a certain Thomas Cana penetrated to the Malabar coast about the year 745 seems difficult to determine. We know only that in the sixth century Cosmas Indicopleustes speaks of the existence of Christians at Male (?Malabar) under a bishop who had been consecrated in Persia. King Alfred the Great is stated in the "Anglo-Saxon Chronicle" to have sent an expedition to establish relations with these Christians of the Far East. On the other hand the reputed relics of St. Thomas were certainly at Edessa in the fourth century, and there they remained until they were translated to Chios in 1258 and afterwards to Ortona. The improbable suggestion that St. Thomas preached in America (American Eccles. Rev., 1899, pp. 1–18) is based upon a misunderstanding of the text of the Acts of the Apostles (i, 8; cf. Berchet "Fonte italiane per la storia della scoperta del Nuovo Mondo", II, 236, and I, 44).

Besides the "Acta Thomæ" of which a different and notably shorter redaction exists in Ethiopic and Latin, we have an abbreviated form of a so-called "Gospel of Thomas", originally Gnostic, but as we know it now merely a fantastical history of the childhood of Jesus, without any notably heretical colouring. There is also a "Revelatio Thomæ", condemned as apocryphal in the Decree of Pope Gelasius, which has recently been recovered from various sources in a fragmentary condition (see the full text in the Revue bénédictine, 1911, pp. 359–374).

The most recent and thorough work is: DAHLMANN, *Die Thomas-Legende* (Freiburg, 1912). See also: WECKER in *Theol. Quartalschrift* XCII (Tübingen, 1910), 538–565; DAHLMANN, *Indische Fahrten*, II (Freiburg, 1908), 130 sqq.; PICK, *The Apocryphal Acts of Paul, Peter and Thomas* (Chicago, 1909) gives a tr. of the *Acta Thomæ*; WRIGHT, *Apocryphal Acts of the Apostles* (London, 1871), in Syriac, with tr.; LIPSIUS AND BONNET, *Acta apostol. apocr.* (Leipzig, 1891–1903), the third part of this collection gives the full Greek text of the *Acts of Thomas*, critically edited; BURKITT in *Jour. of Theol. Studies* (I, 280 sqq.; III, 94 sqq.) has shown that the Syriac is probably the original language; IDEM, *Texts and Studies* (Cambridge, 1897 and 1903), V; MALAN, *The Conflicts of the Holy Apostles* (London, 1871), 187–220; MEDLYCOTT, *India and the Apostle Thomas* (London, 1905), a work written by a Catholic vicar Apostolic but uncritical in tone; PEETERS in *Analecta bollandiana* (1906), 197, (1908), 207; RICHARDS, *Indian Christians of St. Thomas* (London, 1908); RENDEL HARRIS, *Cult of the Heavenly Twins* (1906), 105–25; FLEET in *Jour. of R. Asiatic Society* (London, 1905), 223–36, (1906), 706–11; BURKITT-PREUSCHEN, *Unchristentum in Orient* (Tübingen, 1907); MILNE RAE, *The Syrian Church in India* (Edinburgh, 1892); WILHELM, *Deutsche Legenden und Legendare* (Leipzig, 1907); MICHEL AND PEETERS, *Évangiles apocryphes; I Évangile de Thomas* (Paris, 1911); TISCHENDORF, *Evangelia apocr.* (Leipzig, 1876); HAULER in *Wiener Studien* (Vienna, 1908), 308–340; BIHLMEYER in *Revue bénédictine*, XXVIII (Maredsous, 1911).

HERBERT THURSTON.

Thomas, CHARLES L. A., French composer, b. at Metz, 5 Aug,. 1811; d. at Paris, 12 Feb., 1896. He gained the Grand Prix at the Paris Conservatoire in 1832, having previously won first prize for piano and for harmony. Continuing his studies with Kalkbrenner, Barbereau, and Lesueur, he composed much during the years 1836–50, including three motets and a requiem mass. Turning his attention to comic opera he produced a number of ballets, of which "Le Caïd" showed great promise. In 1851 he became a member of the Institute, and in the following year was appointed professor of composition at the Conservatoire. At length he captured the opera-going public with "Mignon", produced on 17 Nov., 1866. This success he followed up with "Hamlet", a five-act opera first given on 9 March, 1868. In 1871, on the death of Auber, he was appointed Director of the Conservatoire, a position he held till his death. Among his sacred compositions, his "Messe Solennelle" was given on 22 November, 1857, the feast of St. Cecilia, at the Church of St. Eustache, for the benefit of the Society of Artist Musicians. On the same feast, in 1865, his "Marche Religieuse" was performed. His merit was recognized by several decorations including the Grand Cross of the Legion of Honour in 1894. From a musical standpoint, Thomas holds a high place by reason of his dramatic instinct, admirably shown in "Mignon" and "Hamlet". He just falls short of being in the first rank, but his "Mignon" retains its popularity, after close on half a century.

MATTHEW, *Handbook of Musical History* (London, 1898); GROVE'S *Dict. of Music and Musicians*, ed. MAITLAND (London, 1904–10), s. v.; LEE, *Story of Opera* (London, 1909); DUNSTAN, *A Cyclopedic Dict. of Music* (London, 1909).

W. H. GRATTAN-FLOOD.

Thomas, GOSPEL OF SAINT. See APOCRYPHA, subtitle III.

Thomas Abel, BLESSED (also ABLE, or ABELL), priest and martyr, b. about 1497; d. 30 July, 1540. He was chaplain to Queen Catharine, and defender of the validity of her marriage with Henry VIII, for which reason he was eventually put to death. He was a graduate of Oxford, and appears to have taught the queen modern languages and music. After a journey to Spain in her behalf, he received the parochial benefice of Bradwell in Sussex. He soon published (May, 1532?) in defence of the queen's marriage a work entitled: "Invicta Veritas, an answer to the determination of the most famous Universities, that by no manner of law it may be lawful for King Henry to be divorced from the Queen's grace, his lawful and very wife". For this he was thrown (1532) into Beauchamp Tower, and after a year's liberation again imprisoned, in December, 1533, on the charges of disseminating the prophecies of the Maid of Kent, encouraging the queen "obstinately to persist in her wilful opinion against the same divorce and separation", and maintaining her right to the title of queen. He was kept in close confinement until his execution at Tyburn, two days after the execution of Cromwell himself. There is extant a very pious Latin letter written by him to a fellow-martyr, and another to Cromwell, begging for some slight mitigation of his "close prison"—i. e. "license to go to church and say Mass here within the Tower and for to lie in some house upon the Green". It is signed "by your daily bedeman, Thomas Abell, priest". His act of attainder states that he and three others "have most traitorously adhered themselves unto the bishop of Rome, being a common enemy unto your Majesty and this your Realm, refusing your Highness to be our and their Supreme Head of this your Realm of England". There is in Beauchamp Tower a rebus of the Martyr, probably executed by himself; the figure of a bell carved on the wall, the letter A in front and the word "Thomas" above. He is one of the fifty-four English martyrs beatified by Leo XIII 29 Dec., 1886.

POLLEN, *Lives of the English Martyrs*, I (London, 1904). 462–83.

THOMAS J. SHAHAN.

BLESSED EDWARD POWELL.—With Blessed Thomas Abel there suffered Edward Powell, priest and martyr, b. in Wales about 1478; M. A. Oxon.; Fellow of Oriel, 1495; D.D. 26 June, 1506 and styled *perdoctus vir* by the university. He was rector of Bleadon, Somerset, and prebendary of Centum Solidorum in Lincoln, which he exchanged for Carlton-cum-Thurlby in 1505, and the latter for Sutton-in-Marisco in 1525. He also held the prebends of Lyme Regis, Calstock, Bedminster, and St. Mary Redcliffe, Bristol, and the living of St. Edmond's Salisbury. A court preacher in high favour with Henry VIII, he was ordered to publish a reply to Luther ("Propugnaculum summi Sacerdotii Evangelici, ac septem Sacramentorum, æditum per virum eruditum, sacrarum literarum professorem Edoardum Poelum adversus Martinum Lutherum fratrem famosum et Wiclifistan insignem", London, 1523, three books in the form of a dialogue between Powell and Luther). The University of Oxford commended this work, and styled Powell "the glory of the university" in a letter to the king. Powell was one of the four theologians selected to defend the legality of the marriage of Catharine of Aragon, in connexion with which he wrote the very rare "Tractatus de non dissolvendo Henrici Regis cum Catherina matrimonio" (London).

In March, 1533, Powell was selected to answer Latimer at Bristol, and was alleged to have disparaged his moral character. Latimer complained to Cromwell, and Powell fell into further disfavour by denouncing Henry's marriage with Anne Boleyn. He was discharged from the proctorship of Salisbury in Jan., 1534, and in November he was attainted, together with Blessed John Fisher, for high treason in refusing to take the oath of succession, deprived of his benefices, and imprisoned in the Tower of London. His confinement was very rigorous: the keeper himself was sent to the Marshalsea Prison for allowing Powell and Abel out on bail. The sentence was not carried out until 30 July, 1540. Three Catholics (Powell, Abel, and Richard Featherstone) and three Protestants suffered together. The victims were dragged on hurdles from the Tower to Smithfield, a Catholic and a Protestant on each hurdle. Powell's companion was Robert Barnes, the Protestant divine. A dialogue in verse was published shortly after, "The metynge of Doctor Barnes and Dr. Powell at Paradise Gate and of theyre communicacion bothe drawen to Smithfylde fro the Towar" (London, 1540), in the British Museum. The Catholics were hanged, drawn, and quartered as traitors; the others were burned as heretics.

CHURTON, *Lives of the Founders of Brasenose*, 118, 181, 245, 363.

C. F. WEMYSS BROWN.

Thomas á Jesu (DIAZ SANCHEZ DE AVILA), Discalced Carmelite, writer on mystical theology, b. at Bæza, Andalusia, 1564; d. in Rome, 24 (or 27) May, 1627. Son of Don Baltasar de Avila and Doña Teresa de Herrera, he took degrees in the humanities at an unusually early age, applied himself afterwards to the study of Divinity, and in 1583 to that of law at the university of Salamanca. Having heard one of the professors extol the writings of St. Teresa (as yet unpublished) he procured a copy, the study of which resulted in a determination to embrace her manner of life. He took the habit at Valladolid, April, 1586, and made his profession in the following year. As a novice he was commissioned to write a ceremonial according to the Roman Rite lately introduced into the order, which remained in force until the last century. He filled the posts of reader of Divinity at Seville, prior at Saragossa, and provincial of Old Castile. At the expiration of his term of office he withdrew to the Desert of Las Batuecas situated in a mountain gorge of difficult access near Alberca. Later he became prior of this convent. He himself had been the originator of this peculiar kind of life. The Carmelite Rule was written for hermits, but the strictly eremitical life, at least on a large scale, being incompatible with the exigencies of modern times, he devised a compromise by restricting the number of such convents to one for each province, and limiting that of the religious to four permanent ones, and volunteers from other houses who were to reside there only one year at the time. He established the first Desert at Bolarque (New Castile) in 1592, Las Batuecas (Old Castile) during his provincialship, and later on a similar house in Belgium. He was called to Italy by Paul V who desired to evangelize the Congo States. Unlike the Spanish Congregation of the Order, the Italian had decided on principle to engage in missionary work, and Thomas being noted for his zeal was selected for it. The expedition, however, was frustrated, but he, with a view to furthering missionary enterprise, established with the pope's consent a new branch of the order under the title of Congregation of St. Paul, which was to cultivate exclusively missionary work (22 July, 1608). Both the Spanish and the Italian superiors resented this step on the ground that it might lead to a split in the order; the pope withdrew his approval, and Thomas remained two years under a cloud.

He wrote his large work, "Stimulus missionum" (Rome, 1610), and soon afterwards another, "De procuranda salute omnium gentium" (Antwerp, 1613), in which he outlined the organization and functions of a papal congregation with such wisdom that Gregory XV when instituting Propaganda in 1622 followed the lines suggested by Thomas. The latter had been sent by Paul V to the Low Countries where he was favourably received by the archdukes, and founded convents at Brussels (1610), Louvain (1611), Cologne (1613), Douai (1613), Lille (1616), Liège (1617), Antwerp (1618), Marlagne (Desert, 1619), Louvain (missionary college for the East, and also for England and Holland, 1621), and Namur (1622). From 1617 he filled the post of Provincial of Flanders. While at Brussels he placed the Carmelite Nuns who had come there from Spain and France under the jurisdiction of the Italian superiors, and assisted them in the establishment of numerous convents. In 1621 he was recalled to Rome as definitor general, and died there three years later in the odour of sanctity. By order of Urban VIII his writings were collected in two volumes, and were published at Cologne in 1684, while a third volume was never carried through the press. Besides the works already mentioned there are some on subjects connected with his order (its antiquity, Salamanca, 1599; the privileges of the confraternity, 1599, commentaries on various points of the rule, notices of prominent men, etc.). Other works deal with mystical theology, of which the principal are: "De contemplatione divina", Antwerp, 1620, and "Divinæ orationis methodus", Antwerp, 1623. The small treatise "La meilleure part, ou la Vie contemplative", translated and edited by Berthold-Ignace de Ste Anne (Brussels, 1686), is from an unpublished work. In his mystical writings Thomas á Jesu systematized St. Teresa's teaching on the basis of St. Thomas Aquinas, II–II, QQ. clxxi–clxxv.

Not less active than Thomas á Jesu in helping to establish the Propaganda was Venerable Dominic á Jesu Maria (Ruzzola), b. at Calatajud, 16 May, 1559; d. at Vienna, 16 Feb., 1630. At an early age he entered the convent of Calced Carmelites in his native town where his uncle was prior, and was sent after his profession to Saragossa and Valencia, receiving Holy orders at Tortosa. The desire of a stricter life led him to the Discalced Carmelites at Pastrana (1589), who sent him as master of novices to Madrid, and afterwards to Alcalá for his higher studies. He assisted the plague-stricken at Barcelona, and was five years subprior at Valencia. He resigned the priorship of Toledo at the command of Philip III who desired his presence at Madrid. After a short time he withdrew to the Desert of Bolarque. The papal nuncio sent him to Rome where he filled the posts of master of novices and prior at the convent of La Scala. The pope entrusted him with a mission to the Viceroy of Naples at Palermo, but would not consent to his permanently absenting himself from Rome. In 1614 he became procurator general, and three years later general, in which capacity he undertook the canonical visitation of the northern Italian convents, and founded the Desert of Varazzo near Genoa, having previously established a convent at Loano in Liguria. The struggle between the Catholic and Protestant powers which ultimately developed into the Thirty Years War having broken out, Paul V sent Dominic to Ferdinand II, who was preparing to engage in what was hoped would prove a decisive battle. With a crucifix in his hand and a picture of the Madonna, which had been shamefully mutilated by the heretics, suspended from his neck, he moved among the combatants, animating the Catholics to fight for their Faith and to gain the victory he promised would be theirs. The Battle of Prague proved indeed a signal success (8 Nov., 1620). Dominic continued his journey through Vienna, Lorraine, Cologne, Brussels, (where he assisted Archduke Albert on his deathbed), Paris, and Marseilles, being everywhere hailed as a hero. Back in Rome towards the end of 1621 he assisted the pope in the establishment of Propaganda, towards which end he had collected considerable funds during his apostolic journey; he was nominated a member of the Congregation. Urban VIII sent him to Vienna to bring about a settlement of the differences between the Court of Austria and the House of Mantua, but he was taken ill and died, surrounded by the imperial family. His body, partly incorrupt, now rests in the Carmelite church at Unter Doebling near Vienna. His biographers relate numberless miracles alleged to have been wrought by him during life (for which he was called the Thaumaturgus of his time), and after his death, but until the conclusion of the process of beatification it is impossible to speak of these. He wrote, besides some works which remained in MS.: "Sententiæ spirituales' (on mystical theology), translated into French (Paris, 1623), German, and Flemish; "Argumenta psalmorum" (Rome, 1623); "De protectione B. Virginis" (French translation, Paris, 1645); "Concordia spiritualis" (Spanish translation, Brussels, 1626).

Besides the extensive notices contained in PHILIPPUS A SS. TRINITATE, *Decor. Carmeli*, in the *Reforma de los Descalzos*, and the *Hist. generalis Congregationis S. Eliæ*, see BERTHOLD-IGNACE DE STE ANNE, *Vie de la Mère Anne de Jésus* (Mechlin, 1882), II, 344–386, concerning Thomas à Jesu. PHILIPPUS A SS. TRINITATE, *Vita Ven. P. Dominici* (Lyons, 1659), also in French, and MARIA GABRIELA, *Leben des ehrw. Dominikus* (Innsbruck, 1902).

BENEDICT ZIMMERMAN.

Thomas a Kempis, author of the "Imitation of Christ", b. at Kempen in the Diocese of Cologne, in 1379 or 1380; d. 25 July, 1471. His parents, John and Gertrude Haemerken, were of the artisan class; it is said that Gertrude kept the village school, and most probably the father worked in metals, a common calling in Kempen, whence perhaps the surname Haemerken, or Haemerlein, Latinized *Malleolus* (a little hammer). We have certain information of only two children, John, the senior by about fourteen years, and Thomas. Thomas was only thirteen when he set out for the schools of Deventer, in Holland. His brother had preceded him thither by ten or twelve years, and doubtless Thomas expected to find him still there. On his arrival, however, he learned that he had gone two years since with five other Brothers of the Common Life to lay the foundations of a new congregation of Canons Regular at Windesheim, about twenty miles from Deventer, where he then went and was lovingly received by his brother who provided him with a letter of introduction to the superior of the Brothers of Common Life at Deventer, Florentius Radewyn. Radewyn gave a warm welcome to the young brother of John Haemerken of Kempen, placed him for the time being in the house and under the maternal care of "a certain noble and devout lady", presented him to the rector of the schools, and paid his first fees, though the master returned the money when he learned whence it came. These particulars we have from the pen of Thomas himself in the biographies, written in his old age, of Gerard Groote, Florentius Radewyn, and their followers (see "The Founders of the New Devotion", London, 1905). For seven years he remained at Deventer, numbered from the first among the disciples of Radewyn, and for a good portion of the time living in his house under his immediate care. It is impossible to exaggerate the influence of those years in the formation of his character. The "new devotion", of which Deventer was then the focus and centre, was a revival in the Low Countries in the fourteenth century of the fervour of the primitive Christians at Jerusalem and Antioch in the first. It owed its inception to the fervid preaching of the Deacon Gerard Groote, its further organization to the prudence and generous devotedness of Florentius Radewyn. Its associates were called the "Devout Brothers and Sisters", also the "Brothers and Sisters of the Common Life". They took no vows, but lived a life of poverty, chastity, and obedience, as far as was compatible with their state, some in their own homes and others, especially clerics, in community. They were forbidden to beg, but all were expected to earn their living by the labour of their hands; for the clerics this meant chiefly the transcribing of books and the instruction of the young. All earnings were placed in a common fund at the disposal of the superior; the one ambition of all was to emulate the life and virtues of the first Christians, especially in the love of God and the neighbour, in simplicity, humility, devotion. Furthermore, partly to provide the Devout Brothers and Sisters with effective protectors and experienced guides, partly to afford an easy transit to the religious state proper for those of their number who should desire it, Gerard Groote conceived the idea of establishing a branch of the canonical order, which should always maintain the closest relations with the members of the new devotion. This scheme was carried into effect after his untimely death, at the early age of forty-three, by the foundation of the congregation of Windesheim, as it was afterwards called from the tract of land where the first priory was established (1386). These details are given as helpful to a better understanding of the life and character of a Kempis, a typical and exemplary Brother, and for seventy-two years he was one of the most distinguished of the Canons Regular.

THOMAS A KEMPIS
From the Getruidenberg Portrait

At Deventer Thomas proved an apt pupil, already noted for his neatness and skill in transcribing manuscripts. This was a life-long labour of love with him; in addition to his own compositions he copied numerous treatises from the Fathers, especially St. Bernard, a Missal for the use of his community, and the whole Bible in four large volumes still extant. After completing his humanities at Deventer, in the autumn of 1399, with the commendation of his superior, Florentius Radewyn, Thomas sought admission among the Canons Regular of Windesheim at Mount St. Agnes, near Zwolle, of which monastery his brother John was then prior. The house had been established only the previous year, and as yet there were no claustral buildings, no garden, no benefactors, no funds. During his term of office, which lasted nine years, John a Kempis built the priory and commenced the church. In these circumstances we find the explanation of the fact that Thomas was not clothed as a novice until 1406, at which date the cloister was just completed, nor ordained priest until 1413, the year after the church was consecrated. The point is worth noting, as some writers in their eagerness to discredit the claims of a Kempis to the authorship of the "Imitation" have actually fastened upon the length of this period of probation to insinuate that he was a dullard or worse. Thomas was himself, to within a few months of his death, the chronicler of Agnetenberg. The story which he tells of the early struggles of the priory on the Mount, its steady progress, and eventual prosperity is full of charm and edification ("The Chronicle of the Canons Regular of Mount St. Agnes", London, 1906). These records reveal to us the simplicity and holiness of his religious brethren. He was twice elected subprior, and once he was made procurator. The reason assigned by an ancient biographer for the latter appointment is one that does honour both to Thomas and his brethren, his love for the poor. However, we can scarcely imagine the author of the "Imitation" a good business manager, and after a time his preference for retirement, literary work, and contemplation prevailed with the Canons to relieve him of the burden. The experience thus gained he made use of in a spiritual treatise, "De fideli dispensatore".

His first tenure of office as subprior was interrupted by the exile of the community from Agnetenberg (1429), occasioned by the unpopular observance by the Canons of Windesheim of an interdict laid upon the country by Martin V. A dispute had arisen in connexion with an appointment to the vacant See of Utrecht and an interdict was upon the land. The Canons remained in exile until the question was settled (1432). The community of Mount St. Agnes had dwelt meanwhile in a canonry of Lunenkerk, which they reformed and affiliated to Windesheim. More than a year of this trying period Thomas spent with his brother John in the convent of Bethany, near Arnheim, where he had been sent to assist and comfort his brother, who was ailing. He remained until his death (November, 1432). We find record of his election as subprior again in 1448, and doubtless he remained in office until age and infirmity procured him release. It was part of the subprior's duties to train the young religious, and to this fact no doubt we owe most of his minor treatises, in particular his "Sermons to the Novices Regular" (tr. London, 1907). We also know from early biographers that Thomas frequently preached in the church attached to the priory. Two similar series of these sermons are extant (tr. "Prayers and Meditations on the Life of Christ" and "The Incarnation and Life of Our Lord", London, 1904, 1907). They treat of a Kempis's favourite subjects, the mystery of our Redemption, and the love of Jesus Christ as shown in His words and works, but especially in the sufferings of His Passion. In person Thomas is described as a man of middle height, dark complexion and vivid colouring, with a broad forehead and piercing eyes; kind and affable towards all, especially the sorrowful and afflicted; constantly engaged in his favourite occupations of reading, writing, or prayer; in time of recreation for the most part silent and recollected, finding it difficult even to express an opinion on matters of mundane interest, but pouring out a ready torrent of eloquence when the conversation turned on God or the concerns of the soul. At such times often he would excuse himself, "My brethren," he would say, "I must go: Someone is waiting to converse with me in my cell." A possibly authentic portrait, preserved at Gertruidenberg, bears as his motto the words: "In omnibus requiem quæsivi et nusquam inveni nisi in een Hoecken met een Boecken" (Everywhere I have sought rest and found it nowhere, save in little nooks with little books). He was laid to rest in the eastern cloister in a spot carefully noted by the continuator of his chronicle. Two centuries after the Reformation, during which the priory was destroyed, the holy remains were transferred to Zwolle and enclosed in a handsome reliquary by Maximilian Hendrik, Prince-Bishop of Cologne. At present they are enshrined in St. Michael's Church, Zwolle, in a magnificent monument erected in 1897 by subscriptions from all over the world and inscribed: "Honori, non memoriæ Thomæ Kempensis, cujus nomen perennius quam monumentum" (To the honour not to the memory of Thomas a Kempis, whose name is more enduring than any monument). It is interesting to recall that the same Maximilian Hendrik, who showed such zeal in preserving and honouring the relics of a Kempis, was also eager to see the cause of his beatification introduced, and began to collect the necessary documents; but little more than a beginning was made when he died (1688) and since that date no further steps have been taken.

A few words on Thomas's claim, once disputed but now hardly so, to the authorship of the "Imitation of Christ". The book was first issued anonymously (1418) and was soon accorded a wide welcome, copied by different scribes, and attributed to various spiritual writers, among others St. Bernard, St. Bonaventure, Henry de Kalkar, Innocent III, Jean Charlier de Gerson, and John a Kempis. In 1441 Thomas completed and signed his name to a codex still extant (Royal Library, Brussels, 5855–61), containing the four books of the "Imitation" and nine minor treatises. Then for two hundred years no serious attempt was made to dispossess a Kempis of his title; but early in the seventeenth century a fierce and prolonged controversy was commenced with the object of establishing the claim either of Jean Charlier de Gerson, Chancellor of Paris, or of his Italian variant, Giovanni Gersen, alleged Benedictine Abbot of Vercelli. At one period an Englishman, Walter Hilton, Canon Regular of Thurgarton, the author of the "Scale (Ladder) of Perfection", was brought forward, but his claim was not long maintained. Incredible as it may sound, the very existence of Giovanni Gersen of Vercelli is yet to be proved. Of Jean Charlier de Gerson the following facts have been established and they may be found demonstrated at length in such works as Cruise, "Thomas à Kempis", and Kettlewell, "The Authorship of the De Imitatione Christi". Not a single contemporary witness is found in Gersen's favour; not a single manuscript during his life or for thirty years after his death ascribes the work to him; internal evidence, style, matter, etc. are in every respect unfavourable. On the other hand we find the title of a Kempis proved by the following: several contemporary witnesses of unimpeachable authority, including members of his own order, name Thomas as the author; contemporary MSS., including one autograph codex, bear his name; internal evidence is wholly favourable. Sir Francis Cruise summarizes this last item under three headings: (1) identity of style, including peculiarities common to the "Imitation" and other undisputed works of a Kempis, viz.: barbarisms, Italianized words, Dutch idioms, systematic rhythmical punctuation, and the word *devotus* as used primarily of associates of the new devotion; (2) The "Imitation" breathes the whole spirit of the Windesheim school of mysticism; (3) it is impregnated throughout with the Scriptures and the writings of the Fathers, especially St. Augustine and Bernard, all favourite founts of inspiration for a Kempis and his fellow Canons of Windesheim. The "Imitation" itself, the best known and the first in order of merit of his original writings, comprises in bulk about one-tenth of the works of a Kempis. Many were originally instructions for the novices and junior Canons of whom, as subprior, Thomas had charge; others are spiritual treatises of wider application and some of these indeed, as the "Oratio de elevatione mentis in Deum", rise to sublime heights of mysticism. There are numerous prayers of sweet devotion and quaint Latin hymns of simple rhythm and jingling rhyme. One work, of which Thomas was editor rather than author, is a "Life of (St.) Lydwine, Virgin" (tr. London, 1911). The best complete edition so far of the "Opera omnia" of a Kempis is that of the Jesuit Sommalius, published by Nut of Antwerp, 1607; even this does not contain the "Chronicon Montis Sanctæ Agnetis", which was edited by H. Rosweyd, S.J., and published in one volume with the "Chronicon Windesemense" (Antwerp, 1621). Of the innumerable editions of the "Imitation", doubtless by far the most interesting is a facsimile from the 1441 codex, published in London, 1879. A splendid critical edition of the "Opera omnia" is now being published by Herder under the able editorship of Dr. Pöhl; five of eight projected volumes have appeared (1911). Messrs. Kegan Paul have published in a uniform edition five volumes of translation, already mentioned in the course of this article. Messrs. Burns and Oates have brought out a sixth. It is hoped eventually to offer a complete translation. This series will prove a boon to students of a Kempis, as, although several lesser works, such as "The Soliloquy of the Soul", "The Discipline of the Cloister", the "Manuale Parvulorum", etc., have been rendered into English, the work hitherto accomplished has been of unequal merit. Perhaps in this connexion we may quote the enthusiastic commendation of Prior Pirkhamer addressed to Peter Danhausser, the publisher of the first edition of Thomas a Kempis's works, 1494: "Nothing more holy, nothing more honourable, nothing more religious, nothing in fine more profitable for the Christian commonweal can you ever do than to make known these works of Thomas à Kempis."

CRUISE, *Thomas à Kempis* (London, 1887); IDEM, *Who was the Author of the Imitation?* (London, 1898); GEM, *Hidden Saints* (London, 1907); KETTLEWELL, *The Authorship of the De Imitatione Christi* (London, 1877); IDEM, *Thomas à Kempis and the Brothers of the Common Life* (London, 1882); MONTMORENCY, *Thomas à Kempis, His Age and His Book* (London, 1906); SCULLY, *Life of the Venerable Thomas à Kempis* (London, 1901); WATERTON, *Thomas à Kempis and the Imitation of Christ* (London, 1883); AMORT, *Deductio critica qua juxta leges sanioris criticæ moraliter certum redditur Ven. Thomam Kempensem Librorum de Imitatione Christi Authorem esse, etc.* (Augsburg, 1761); IDEM, *Moralis certitudo pro Ven. Thoma Kempensi* (Augsburg, 1764); IDEM, *Scutum Kempense* (Cologne, 1728); IDEM, *Plena et succincta informatio de statu totius controversiæ, etc.* (Augsburg, 1725); BECKER, *L'Auteur de l'Imitation et les documents Néerlandais* (La Haye, 1882); BUSCH, *Chronicon Windesemense*, and *Liber de reformatione monasteriorum* (Halle, 1887); GREGORY, *Histoire du livre de l'Imitation de Jésus-Christ et de son véritable auteur* (Paris, 1843); HIRSCHE, *Thomæ Kempensis De Imitatione Christi*, (Berlin, 1874); IDEM, *Prolegomena zu Einer Neuen Ausgabe der Imitatio Christi* (Berlin, 1883); ed. SOMMALIUS, *Opera omnia* (Antwerp, 1607); ed. PÖHL, *Opera omnia* (5 vols., Freiburg, 1902–11); *Complete Works*, I–V (London, 1904–7); *Chronicon Montis Sanctæ Agnetis* (Antwerp, 1621); MALOU, *Recherches historiques et critiques sur le véritable auteur du livre de l'Imitation de Jésus-Christ* (Paris, 1858); MELLA, *Della Controversia Gerseniana* (Prato, 1875); PUYOL, *La doctrine du livre De Imitatione Christi* (Paris, 1881); SANTINI, *I diritti de Thommaso da Kempis* (Rome, 1879, 1880); SPITZEN, *Thomas à Kempis*, etc. (Utrecht, 1880); IDEM, *Les Hollandismes de l'Imitation de Jésus-Christ* (Utrecht, 1884); IDEM, *Nouvelle défense* (Utrecht, 1884); WOLFSGRUBER, *Giovanni Gersen, sein Leben und sein Werk de Imitatione Christi* (Augsburg, 1880); IDEM, *Septem Motiva contra Thomam de Kempis* (Vienna, 1882).

VINCENT SCULLY.

Thomas Alfield (AUFIELD, ALPHILDE, HAWFIELD, OFFELDUS), VENERABLE (alias BADGER), priest, b. at Gloucestershire; martyred at Tyburn, 6 July, 1585. He was educated at Eton and Cambridge (1568). He was afterwards converted and came to Douai College in 1576, but the troubles there compelled him to intermit his studies for four years, and he was eventually ordained and sent forth from Reims in 1581. Here he was associated with the celebrated mission of Blessed Edmund Campion and Father Persons, and he persuaded the latter to take as his servant his brother Robert Alfield, then recently converted, but who afterwards became a traitor of note. Thomas seems to have laboured chiefly in the north, where after a time he was arrested and sent to the Tower of London, 2 May, 1582. Here he at first made a "glorious" confession, and even endured torture; but being afterwards sent back to the north, he fell, and went to the Protestant Church. Upon regaining liberty he was deeply penitent for his fall, and returned to Dr. Allen at Reims to gather new resolution. Returning again to England he was induced by the famous seaman John Davis (about March, 1584) to make for him offers—presumably insincere on Davis's part—of services to Spain. In August of the same year Dr. Allen's celebrated "True and modest Defence" appeared in answer to Burghley's "Execution of Justice". To circulate such books as Allen's was of the greatest service to the Faith. Alfield undertook the dangerous task with the help of a dyer by the name of Thomas Webley, and of one Crabbe. After some months he was again arrested, and again sent to the Tower, whence he was removed to Newgate and tried. Crabbe renounced the pope and thereby saved his life; the other two were hanged. A reprieve had, for some unknown reason, been granted for Alfield, but it arrived too late.

CHALLONER, *Missionary Priests* (Edinburgh, 1877); GILLOW, *Bibl. Dict. Eng. Cath.*, s. v. *Alfield, Thomas*; KNOX, *Letters of Cardinal Allen* (London, 1882); there are also several references to Alfield in the Record Office, London, many of which are given by SIMPSON in *The Rambler*, new ser., VII, 420–431.

PATRICK RYAN.

Thomas Anglicus. See THOMAS OF JORZ.

Thomas Aquinas, SAINT, philosopher, theologian, doctor of the Church (*Angelicus Doctor*), patron of Catholic universities, colleges, and schools, b. at Rocca Secca in the Kingdom of Naples, 1225 or 1227; d. at Fossa Nuova, 7 March, 1274.

I. LIFE.—The great outlines and all the important events of his life are known, but biographers differ as to some details and dates. Death prevented Henry Denifle from executing his project of writing a critical life of the saint. Denifle's friend and pupil, Dominic Prümmer, O.P., professor of theology in the University of Fribourg, Switzerland, has taken up the work and is publishing the "Fontes Vitæ S. Thomæ Aquinatis, notis historicis et criticis illustrati"; and the first fascicle (Toulouse, 1911) has appeared, giving the life of St. Thomas by Peter Calo (1300) now published for the first time. From Tolomeo of Lucca (see BARTHOLOMEW OF LUCCA) we learn that at the time of the saint's death there was a doubt about his exact age (Prümmer, op. cit., 45). The end of 1225 is usually assigned as the time of his birth. Father Prümmer, on the authority of Calo, thinks 1227 is the more probable date (op. cit., 28). All agree that he died in 1274.

Landulph, his father, was Count of Aquino, Theodora, his mother, Countess of Teano. His family was related to the Emperors Henry VI and Frederick II, and to the Kings of Aragon, Castile, and France. Calo relates that a holy hermit foretold his career, saying to Theodora before his birth: "He will enter the Order of Friars Preachers, and so great will be his learning and sanctity that in his day no one will be found to equal him" (Prümmer, op. cit., 18). At the age of five, according to the custom of the times, he was sent to receive his first training from the Benedictine monks of Monte Cassino. Diligent in study, he was thus early noted as being meditative and devoted to prayer, and his preceptor was surprised at hearing the child ask frequently: "What is God?" About the year 1236 he was sent to the University of Naples. Calo says that the change was made at the instance of the Abbot of Monte Cassino, who wrote to Thomas's father that a boy of such talents should not be left in obscurity (Prümmer, op. cit., 20). At Naples his preceptors were Pietro Martini and Petrus Hibernus. The chronicler says that he soon surpassed Martini in grammar, and he was then given over to Peter of Ireland, who trained him in logic and the natural sciences. The customs of the times divided the liberal arts into two courses: the Trivium, embracing grammar, logic, and rhetoric; the Quadrivium, comprising music, mathematics, geometry, and astronomy (see ARTS, THE SEVEN LIBERAL). Thomas could repeat the lessons with more depth and lucidity than his masters displayed. The youth's heart had remained pure amidst the corruption with which he was surrounded, and he resolved to embrace the religious life.

Some time between 1240 and August, 1243, he received the habit of the Order of St. Dominic, being attracted and directed by John of St. Julian, a noted preacher of the convent of Naples. The city wondered that such a noble young man should don the garb of a poor friar. His mother, with mingled feelings of joy and sorrow, hastened to Naples to see her son. The Dominicans, fearing she would take him away, sent him to Rome, his ultimate destination being Paris or Cologne. At the instance of Theodora, Thomas's brothers, who were soldiers under the Emperor Frederick, captured the novice near the town of Aquapendente, and confined him in the fortress of San Giovanni at Rocca Secca.

ST. THOMAS AQUINAS
Piero della Francesca, Poldi-Pezzoli Gallery, Milan

Here he was detained nearly two years, his parents, brothers, and sisters endeavouring by various means to destroy his vocation. The brothers even laid snares for his virtue, but the pure-minded novice drove the temptress from his room with a brand which he snatched from the fire. Towards the end of his life, St. Thomas confided to his faithful friend and companion, Reginald of Piperno, the secret of a remarkable favour received at this time. When the temptress had been driven from his chamber, he knelt and most earnestly implored God to grant him integrity of mind and body. He fell into a gentle sleep, and, as he slept, two angels appeared to assure him that his prayer had been heard. They then girded him about with a white girdle, saying: "We gird thee with the girdle of perpetual virginity." And from that day forward he never experienced the slightest motions of concupiscence.

The time spent in captivity was not lost. His mother relented somewhat, after the first burst of anger and grief; the Dominicans were allowed to provide him with new habits, and through the kind offices of his sister he procured some books—the Holy Scriptures, Aristotle's Metaphysics, and the "Sentences" of Peter Lombard. After eighteen months or two years spent in prison, either because his mother saw that the hermit's prophecy would eventually be fulfilled or because his brothers feared the threats of Innocent IV and Frederick II, he was set at liberty, being lowered in a basket into the arms of the Dominicans, who were delighted to find that during his captivity "he had made as much progress as if he had been in a *studium generale*" (Calo, op. cit., 24). Thomas immediately pronounced his vows, and his superiors sent him to Rome. Innocent IV examined closely into his motives in joining the Friars Preachers, dismissed him with a blessing, and forbade any further interference with his vocation. John the Teutonic, fourth master general of the order, took the young student to Paris and, according to the majority of the saint's biographers, to Cologne, where he arrived in 1244 or 1245, and was placed under Albertus Magnus, the most renowned professor of the order (on chronology of this period see Prümmer, op. cit., p. 25). In the schools Thomas's humility and taciturnity were misinterpreted as signs of dulness, but when Albert had heard his brilliant defence of a difficult thesis, he exclaimed: "We call this young man a dumb ox, but his bellowing in doctrine will one day resound throughout the world."

In 1245 Albert was sent to Paris, and Thomas accompanied him as a student. In 1248 both returned to Cologne. Albert had been appointed regent of the new *studium generale*, erected that year by the general chapter of the order, and Thomas was to teach under him as Bachelor. (On the system of graduation in the thirteenth century see PREACHERS, ORDER OF.—II, A, 1, d; Fleury, "Hist. Eccl.", diss. V.; Touron, "Vie de S. Thomas d'Aquin", Paris, 1740, II, v; Drane, "Christian Schools and Scholars", London, 1881, 413; Douais, "L'organisation des études dans l'ordre des FF. Prêcheurs, au 13ème siècle", Paris, 1884.) During his stay in Cologne, probably in 1250, he was raised to the priesthood by Conrad of Hochstaden, archbishop of that city. Throughout his busy life, he frequently preached the Word of God, in Germany, France, and Italy. His sermons were forceful, redolent of piety, full of solid instruction, abounding in apt citations from the Scriptures (see "D. Th. Aquinatis sermones et opuscula concionatoria", 2 vols., Paris, 1881). In the year 1251 or 1252 the master general of the order, by the advice of Albertus Magnus and Hugo a S. Charo (Hugh of St. Cher), sent Thomas to fill the office of Bachelor (sub-regent) in the Dominican *studium* at Paris. This appointment may be regarded as the beginning of his public career, for his teaching soon attracted the attention both of the professors and of the students. His duties consisted principally in explaining the "Sentences" of Peter Lombard, and his commentaries on that text-book of theology furnished the materials and, in great part, the plan for his chief work, the "Summa theologica".

In due time he was ordered to prepare himself to obtain the degree of Doctor in Theology from the University of Paris, but the conferring of the degree was postponed, owing to a dispute between the university and the friars. The conflict, originally a dispute between the university and the civic authorities, arose from the slaying of one of the students and the wounding of three others by the city guard. The university, jealous of its autonomy, demanded satisfaction, which was refused. The doctors closed their schools, solemnly swore that they would not reopen them until their demands were granted, and decreed that in future no one should be admitted to the degree of Doctor unless he would take an oath to follow the same line of conduct under similar circumstances. The Dominicans and Franciscans, who had continued to teach in their schools, refused to take the prescribed oath, and from this there arose a bitter conflict which was at its height when St. Thomas and St. Bonaventure were ready to be presented for their degrees (see Vaughan, "Life and Labours of St. Thomas of Aquin", 2 vols., London, 1871-72, I, xxi). William of St-Amour extended the dispute beyond the original question, violently attacked the Friars, of whom he was evidently jealous, and denied their right to occupy chairs in the university. Against his book, "De periculis novissimorum temporum" (The Perils of the Last Times), St. Thomas wrote a treatise "Contra impugnantes religionem", an apology for the religious orders (Touron, op. cit., II, cc. vii sqq.). The book of William of St-Amour was condemned by Alexander IV at Anagni, 5 October, 1256, and the pope gave orders that the mendicant friars should be admitted to the doctorate.

About this time St. Thomas also combated a dangerous book, "The Eternal Gospel" (Touron, op. cit., II, cxii). The university authorities did not obey immediately; the influence of St. Louis IX and eleven papal Briefs were required before peace was firmly established, and St. Thomas was admitted to the degree of Doctor in Theology. The date of his promotion, as given by many biographers, was 23 October, 1257. His theme was "The Majesty of Christ". His text, "Thou waterest the hills from thy upper rooms: the earth shall be filled with the fruit of thy works" (Ps. ciii, 13), said to have been suggested by a heavenly visitor, seems to have been prophetic of his career. A tradition says that St. Bonaventure and St. Thomas received the doctorate on the same day, and that there was a contest of humility between the two friends as to which should be promoted first. From this time St. Thomas's life may be summed up in a few words: praying, preaching, teaching, writing, journeying. Men were more anxious to hear him than they had been to hear Albert, whom St. Thomas surpassed in accuracy, lucidity, brevity, and power of exposition, if not in universality of knowledge. Paris claimed him as her own; the popes wished to have him near them; the *studia* of the order were eager to enjoy the benefit of his teaching; hence we find him successively at Anagni, Rome, Bologna, Orvieto, Viterbo, Perugia, in Paris again, and finally in Naples, always teaching and writing, living on earth with one passion, an ardent zeal for the explanation and defence of Christian truth. So devoted was he to his sacred task that with tears he begged to be excused from accepting the Archbishopric of Naples, to which he was appointed by Clement IV in 1265. Had this appointment been accepted, most probably the "Summa theologica" would not have been written.

Yielding to the requests of his brethren, he on several occasions took part in the deliberations of the general chapters of the order. One of these chapters was held in London in 1263. In another held at Valenciennes (1259) he collaborated with Albertus Magnus and Peter of Tarentasia (afterwards Pope Innocent V) in formulating a system of studies which is substantially preserved to this day in the *studia generalia* of the Dominican Order (cf. Douais, op. cit.). It is not surprising to read in the biographies of St. Thomas that he was frequently abstracted and in ecstasy. Towards the end of his life the ecstasies became more frequent. On one occasion, at Naples in 1273, after he had completed his treatise on the Eucharist, three of the brethren saw him lifted in ecstasy, and they heard a voice proceeding from the crucifix on the altar, saying "Thou hast written well of me, Thomas; what reward wilt thou have?". Thomas replied, "None other than Thyself, Lord" (Prümmer, op. cit., p. 38). Similar declarations are said to have been made at Orvieto and at Paris. On 6 December, 1273, he laid aside his pen and would write no more. That day he experienced an unusually long ecstasy during Mass; what was revealed to him we can only surmise from his reply to Father Reginald, who urged him to continue his writings: "I can do no more. Such secrets have been revealed to me that all I have written now appears to be of little value" (*modica*, Prümmer, op. cit., p. 43).

The "Summa theologica" had been completed only as far as the ninetieth question of the third part (De partibus pœnitentiæ). Thomas began his immediate preparation for death. Gregory X, having convoked a general council, to open at Lyons on 1 May, 1274, invited St. Thomas and St. Bonaventure to take part in the deliberations, commanding the former to bring to the council his treatise "Contra errores Græcorum" (Against the Errors of the Greeks). He tried to obey, setting out on foot in January, 1274, but strength failed him; he fell to the ground near Terracina, whence he was conducted to the Castle of Maienza, the home of his niece the Countess Francesca Ceccano. The Cistercian monks of Fossa Nuova pressed him to accept their hospitality, and he was conveyed to their monastery, on entering which he whispered to his companion: "This is my rest for ever and ever: here will I dwell, for I have chosen it" (Ps. cxxxi, 14). When Father Reginald urged him to remain at the castle, the saint replied: "If the Lord wishes to take me away, it is better that I be found in a religious house than in the dwelling of a lay person." The Cistercians were so kind and attentive that Thomas's humility was alarmed. "Whence comes this honour", he exclaimed, "that servants of God should carry wood for my fire!" At the urgent request of the monks he dictated a brief commentary on the Canticle of Canticles.

The end was near; extreme unction was administered. When the Sacred Viaticum was brought into the room he pronounced the following act of faith: "If in this world there be any knowledge of this sacrament stronger than that of faith, I wish now to use it in affirming that I firmly believe and know as certain that Jesus Christ, True God and True Man, Son of God and Son of the Virgin Mary, is in this Sacrament." Then he added: "I receive Thee, the price of my redemption, for Whose love I have watched, studied, and laboured. Thee have I preached; Thee have I taught. Never have I said anything against Thee: if anything was not well said, that is to be attributed to my ignorance. Neither do I wish to be obstinate in my opinions, but if I have written anything erroneous concerning this sacrament or other matters, I submit all to the judgment and correction of the Holy Roman Church, in whose obedience I now pass from this life" (Prümmer, op. cit., p. 48). He died on 7 March, 1274. Numerous miracles attested his sanctity, and he was canonized by John XXII, 18 July, 1323. The monks of Fossa Nuova were anxious to keep his sacred remains, but by order of Urban V the body was given to his Dominican brethren, and was solemnly translated to the Dominican church at Toulouse, 28 January, 1369. A magnificent shrine erected in 1628 was destroyed during the French Revolution, and the body was removed to the Church of St. Sernin, where it now reposes in a sarcophagus of gold and silver, which was solemnly blessed by Cardinal Desprez on 24 July, 1878. The chief bone of his left arm is preserved in the cathedral of Naples. The right arm, bestowed on the University of Paris, and originally kept in the St. Thomas's Chapel of the Dominican church, is now preserved in the Dominican Church of S. Maria Sopra Minerva in Rome, whither it was transferred during the French Revolution.

A description of the saint as he appeared in life is given by Calo (Prümmer, op. cit., p. 401), who says that his features corresponded with the greatness of his soul. He was of lofty stature and of heavy build, but straight and well proportioned. His complexion was "like the colour of new wheat":

his head was large and well shaped, and he was slightly bald. All portraits represent him as noble, meditative, gentle yet strong. St. Pius V proclaimed St. Thomas a Doctor of the Universal Church in the year 1567. In the Encyclical "Æterni Patris", of 4 August, 1879, on the restoration of Christian philosophy, Leo XIII declared him "the prince and master of all Scholastic doctors". The same illustrious pontiff, by a Brief dated 4 August, 1880, designated him patron of all Catholic universities, academies, colleges, and schools throughout the world.

II. WRITINGS.—A. *General Remarks.*—Although St. Thomas lived less than fifty years, he composed more than sixty works, some of them brief, some very lengthy. This does not necessarily mean that every word in the authentic works was written by his hand; he was assisted by secretaries, and biographers assure us that he could dictate to several scribes at the same time (Vaughan, op. cit., vol. I, p. 469). Other works, some of which were composed by his disciples, have been falsely attributed to him. The most recent, and probably the most satisfactory, treatise on the authenticity of his works is the series of articles by P. Mandonnet, "Des écrits authentiques de S. Thomas d'Aquin" (Fribourg, 1910), originally written for the "Revue Thomiste" (March-April, 1909). The "Dissertationes in singula opera D. Th. Aquinatis" (Venice, 1750) of Bernard de Rubeis are given in all important editions of the saint's works. A reliable and convenient list is given by Fr. Sertillanges, O. P., in his "S. Thomas d'Aquin" (2 vols., Paris, 1910).

In the "Scriptores Ordinis Prædicatorum" (Paris, 1719) Fr. Echard devotes eighty-six folio pages to St. Thomas's works, the different editions and translations (I, pp. 282–348). Touron (op. cit., pp. 691 sqq.) says that manuscript copies were found in nearly all the libraries of Europe, and that, after the invention of printing, copies were multiplied rapidly in Germany, Italy, and France, portions of the "Summa theologica" being one of the first important works printed. Peter Schoeffer, a printer of Mainz, published the "Secunda Secundæ" in 1467. This is the first known printed copy of any work of St. Thomas. The first complete edition of the "Summa" was printed at Basle, in 1485. Many other editions of this and of other works were published in the sixteenth and seventeenth centuries, especially at Venice and at Lyons. The principal editions of all the works (Opera Omnia) were published as follows: Rome, 1570; Venice, 1594, 1612, 1745; Antwerp, 1612; Paris, 1660, 1871–80 (Vivès); Parma, 1852–73; Rome, 1882 (the Leonine). The Roman edition of 1570, called "the Piana", because edited by order of St. Pius V, was the standard for many years. Besides a carefully revised text it contained the commentaries of Cardinal Cajetan and the valuable "Tabula Aurea" of Peter of Bergamo. The Venetian edition of 1612 was highly prized because the text was accompanied by the Cajetan-Porrecta commentaries (see PORRECTA, SERAFINO). The Leonine edition, begun under the patronage of Leo XIII, now continued under the master general of the Dominicans, undoubtedly will be the most perfect of all. Critical dissertations on each work will be given, the text will be carefully revised, and all references will be verified: By direction of Leo XIII (Motu Proprio, 18 Jan., 1880) the "Summa contra gentiles" will be published with the commentaries of Sylvester Ferrariensis, whilst the commentaries of Cajetan go with the "Summa theologica". The latter has been published, being vols. IV–XII of the edition (last in 1906). St. Thomas's works may be classified as philosophical, theological, scriptural, and apologetic, or controversial. The division, however, cannot always be rigidly maintained. The "Summa theologica", e. g., contains much that is philosophical, whilst the "Summa contra gentiles" is principally, but not exclusively, philosophical and apologetic. His philosophical works are chiefly commentaries on Aristotle, and his first important theological writings were commentaries on Peter Lombard's four books of "Sentences"; but he does not slavishly follow either the Philosopher or the Master of the Sentences (on opinions of the Lombard rejected by theologians, see Migne, 1841, edition of the "Summa" I, p. 451).

B. *His Principal Works in Detail.*—Amongst the works wherein St. Thomas's own mind and method are shown, the following deserve special mention:—

(1) "Quæstiones disputatæ" (Disputed Questions). —These were more complete treatises on subjects that had not been fully elucidated in the lecture halls, or concerning which the professor's opinion had been sought. They are very valuable, because in them the author, free from limitations as to time or space, freely expresses his mind and gives all arguments for or against the opinions adopted. These treatises, containing the questions "De potentia", "De malo", "De spirit. creaturis", "De anima", "De unione Verbi Incarnati", "De virt. in communi", "De caritate", "De corr. fraterna", "De spe", "De virt. cardinal.", "De veritate", were often reprinted, e. g. recently by the Association of St. Paul (2 vols., Paris and Fribourg, Switzerland, 1883). (2) "Quodlibeta" (may be rendered "Various Subjects", or "Free Discussions").—They present questions or arguments proposed and answers given in or outside the lecture halls, chiefly in the more formal scholastic exercises, termed *circuli*, *conclusiones*, or *determinationes*, which were held once or twice a year. (See Mandonnet, "Siger de Brabant", 2nd ed., Louvain, 1911, IV, p. 85; Turner, "Hist. of Philosophy", Boston, 1903, p. 346.) (3) "De unitate intellectus contra Averroistas".—This *opusculum* refuted a very dangerous and widespread error, viz., that there was but one soul for all men, a theory which did away with individual liberty and responsibility. (See AVERROES; Mandonnet, op. cit.) (4) "Commentaria in Libros Sententiarum" (mentioned above).—This with the following work are the immediate forerunners of the "Summa theologica". (5) "Summa de veritate catholicæ fidei contra gentiles" (Treatise on the Truth of the Catholic Faith, against Unbelievers).—This work, written at Rome, 1261–64, was composed at the request of St. Raymond of Pennafort, who desired to have a philosophical exposition and defence of the Christian Faith, to be used against the Jews and Moors in Spain. It is a perfect model of patient and sound apologetics, showing that no demonstrated truth (science) is opposed to revealed truth (faith). The best recent editions are those of Rome, 1878 (by Uccelli), of Paris and Fribourg, Switzerland, 1882, and of Rome, 1894. It has been translated into Greek, Hebrew, and Syriac, and quite recently Father Rickaby, S. J., gave to the world an annotated translation into English (with some abridgment) under the title "Of God and His Creatures" (London and St. Louis, 1905). It is divided into four books: I. Of God as He is in Himself; II. Of God the Origin of Creatures; III. Of God the End of Creatures; IV. Of God in His Revelation. It is worthy of remark that the Fathers of the Vatican Council, treating the necessity of revelation (Const. "Dei Filius", c. 2), employed almost the very words used by St. Thomas in treating that subject in this work (I, cc. iv, v), and in the "Summa theologica" (I, Q. i, a. 1).

(6) Three works written by order of Urban IV (see Mandonnet, "Ecrits authentiques", p. 128).—(a) The "Opusculum contra errores Græcorum" refuted the errors of the Greeks on doctrines in dispute between them and the Roman Church, viz., the procession of the Holy Ghost from the Father and the Son, the primacy of the Roman pontiff, the Holy Eucharist, and purgatory. It was used against the Greeks with telling effect in the Council of Lyons

(1274) and in the Council of Florence (1493). In the range of human reasonings on deep subjects there can be found nothing to surpass the sublimity and depth of the argument adduced by St. Thomas to prove that the Holy Ghost proceeds from the Father and the Son (cf. Summa theol., I, Q. xxxvi, a. 2); but it must be borne in mind that our Faith is not based on that argument alone. (b) "Officium de festo Corporis Christi".—Mandonnet (Ecrits, p. 127) declares that it is now established beyond doubt that St. Thomas is the author of the beautiful Office of Corpus Christi, in which solid doctrine, tender piety, and enlightening Scriptural citations are combined, and expressed in language remarkably accurate, beautiful, chaste, and poetic. Here we find the well-known hymns, "Sacris Solemniis", "Pange Lingua" (concluding in the "Tantum Ergo"), "Verbum Supernum" (concluding with the "O Salutaris Hostia"), and, in the Mass, the beautiful sequence "Lauda Sion". In the responses of the office, St. Thomas places side by side words of the New Testament affirming the real presence of Christ in the Blessed Sacrament and texts from the Old Testament referring to the types and figures of the Eucharist (see Vaughan, op. cit., pp. 810 sqq.; Caswall, "Lyra Catholica", London, 1840; Guéranger, "The Liturgical Year; Feast of Corpus Christi"). Santeuil, a poet of the seventeenth century, said he would give all the verses he had written for the one stanza of the "Verbum Supernum": "Se nascens dedit socium, convescens in edulium: Se moriens in pretium, Se regnans dat in præmium"—"In birth, man's fellow-man was He, His meat, while sitting at the Board: He died his Ransomer to be, He reigns to be his Great Reward" (tr. by Marquis of Bute). Perhaps the gem of the whole office is the antiphon "O Sacrum Convivium" (cf. Conway, "St. Thomas Aquinas", London and New York, 1911, p. 61). (c) The "Catena Aurea", though not as original as his other writings, furnishes a striking proof of St. Thomas's prodigious memory and manifests an intimate acquaintance with the Fathers of the Church. The work contains a series of passages selected from the writings of the various Fathers, arranged in such order that the texts cited form a running commentary on the Gospels. The commentary on St. Matthew was dedicated to Urban IV. An English translation of the "Catena Aurea" was edited by John Henry Newman (4 vols., Oxford, 1841–1845; see Vaughan, op. cit., vol. II, pp. 529 sqq.).

(7) The "Summa theologica".—This work immortalized St. Thomas. The author himself modestly considered it simply a manual of Christian doctrine for the use of students. In reality it is a complete, scientifically arranged exposition of theology and at the same time a summary of Christian philosophy (see SUMMÆ, SUMMULÆ). In the brief prologue St. Thomas first calls attention to the difficulties experienced by students of sacred doctrine in his day, the causes assigned being: the multiplication of useless questions, articles, and arguments; the lack of scientific order; frequent repetitions, "which beget disgust and confusion in the minds of learners". Then he adds: "Wishing to avoid these and similar drawbacks, we shall endeavour, confiding in the Divine assistance, to treat of these things that pertain to sacred doctrine with brevity and clearness, in so far as the subject to be treated will permit." In the introductory question, "On Sacred Doctrine", he proves that, besides the knowledge which reason affords, Revelation also is necessary for salvation, first, because without it men could not know the supernatural end to which they must tend by their voluntary acts; secondly, because, without Revelation, even the truths concerning God which could be proved by reason would be known "only by a few, after a long time, and with the admixture of many errors". When revealed truths have been accepted, the mind of man proceeds to explain them and to draw conclusions from them. Hence results theology, which is a science, because it proceeds from principles that are certain (a. 2). The object, or subject, of this science is God; other things are treated in it only in so far as they relate to God (a. 7). Reason is used in theology not to prove the truths of faith, which are accepted on the authority of God, but to defend, explain, and develop the doctrines revealed (a. 8). He thus announces the division of the "Summa": "Since the chief aim of this sacred science is to give the knowledge of God, not only as He is in Himself, but also as He is the Beginning of all things, and the End of all, especially of rational creatures, we shall treat first of God; secondly, of the rational creature's advance towards God (*de motu creaturæ rationalis in Deum*); thirdly, of Christ, Who, as Man, is the way by which we tend to God." God in Himself, and as He is the Creator; God as the End of all things, especially of man; God as the Redeemer —these are the leading ideas, the great headings, under which all that pertains to theology is contained.

(a) Sub-divisions.—(i) The First Part is divided into three tracts: (α) On those things which pertain to the Essence of God; (β) On the distinction of Persons in God (the mystery of the Trinity); (γ) On the production of creatures by God and on the creatures produced. (ii) The Second Part, On God as He is in the End of man, is sometimes called the Moral Theology of St. Thomas, i. e., his treatise on the end of man and on human acts. It is subdivided into two parts, known as the First Section of the Second (I–II, or 1a 2æ) and the Second of the Second (II–II, or 2a 2æ). (α) The First of the Second.—The first five questions are devoted to proving that man's last end, his beatitude, consists in the possession of God. Man attains to that end or deviates from it by human acts, i. e. by free, deliberate acts. Of human acts he treats, first, in general (in all but the first five questions of the I–II), secondly, in particular (in the whole of the II–II). The treatise on human acts in general is divided into two parts: the first, on human acts in themselves; the other, on the principles or causes, extrinsic or intrinsic, of those acts. In these tracts, and in the Second of the Second, St. Thomas, following Aristotle, gives a perfect description and a wonderfully keen analysis of the movements of man's mind and heart. (β) The Second of the Second considers human acts, i. e., the virtues and vices, in particular. In it St. Thomas treats, first, of those things that pertain to all men, no matter what may be their station in life, and, secondly, of those things that pertain to some men only. Things that pertain to all men are reduced to seven headings: Faith, Hope, and Charity; Prudence, Justice, Fortitude, and Temperance. Under each title, in order to avoid repetitions, St. Thomas treats not only of the virtue itself, but also of the vices opposed to it, of the commandment to practise it, and of the gift of the Holy Ghost which corresponds to it. Things pertaining to some men only are reduced to three headings: the graces freely given (*gratiæ gratis datæ*) to certain individuals for the good of the Church, such as the gifts of tongues, of prophecy, of miracles; the active and the contemplative life; the particular states of life, and duties of those who are in different states, especially bishops and religious. (iii) The Third Part treats of Christ and of the benefits which He has conferred upon man, hence three tracts: On the Incarnation, and on what the Saviour did and suffered; On the Sacraments, which were instituted by Christ, and have their efficacy from His merits and sufferings; On Eternal Life, i. e., on the end of the world, the resurrection of bodies, judgment, the punishment of the wicked, the happiness of the just who, through Christ, attain to eternal life in heaven.

Eight years were given to the composition of this

work, which was begun at Rome, where the First Part and the First of the Second were written (1265–69). The Second of the Second, begun in Rome, was completed in Paris (1271). In 1272 St. Thomas went to Naples, where the Third Part was written, down to the nineteenth question of the tract On Penance (see Leonine edition, I, p. xlii). The work has been completed by the addition of a supplement, drawn from other writings of St. Thomas, attributed by some to Peter of Auvergne, by others to Henry of Gorkum. These attributions are rejected by the editors of the Leonine edition (XI, pp. viii, xiv, xviii). Mandonnet (op. cit., 153) inclines to the very probable opinion that it was compiled by Father Reginald de Piperno, the saint's faithful companion and secretary. The entire "Summa" contains 38 Treatises, 612 Questions, subdivided into 3120 articles, in which about 10,000 objections are proposed and answered. So admirably is the promised order preserved that, by reference to the beginning of the Tracts and Questions, one can see at a glance what place it occupies in the general plan, which embraces all that can be known through theology of God, of man, and of their mutual relations (see accompanying chart, reproduced by permission of "The Rosary Magazine"). "The whole Summa is arranged on a uniform plan. Every subject is introduced as a question, and divided into articles. . . . Each article has also a uniform disposition of parts. The topic is introduced as an inquiry for discussion, under the term *Utrum*, whether—e. g. *Utrum Deus sit?* The objections against the proposed thesis are then stated. These are generally three or four in number, but sometimes extend to seven or more. The conclusion adopted is then introduced by the words, *Respondeo dicendum*. At the end of the thesis expounded the objections are answered, under the forms, *ad primum, ad secundum*, etc." (Eng. tr., see below). The "Summa" is Christian doctrine in scientific form; it is human reason rendering its highest service in defence and explanation of the truths of the Christian religion. It is the answer of the matured and saintly doctor to the question of his youth: What is God? Revelation, made known in the Scriptures and by tradition; reason and its best results; soundness and fulness of doctrine, order, conciseness and clearness of expression, effacement of self, the love of truth alone, hence a remarkable fairness towards adversaries and calmness in combating their errors; soberness and soundness of judgment, together with a charmingly tender and enlightened piety—these are all found in this "Summa" more than in his other writings, more than in the writings of his contemporaries, for "among the scholastic doctors, the chief and master of all, towers Thomas Aquinas, who, as Cajetan observes (In 2am 2æ, Q. 148, a. 4) 'because he most venerated the ancient doctors of the Church in a certain way seems to have inherited the intellect of all'" (Encyclical, "Æterni Patris", of Leo XIII).

(b) *Editions and Translations.*—It is impossible to mention the various editions of the "Summa", which has been in constant use for more than six hundred years. Very few books have been so often republished. The first complete edition, printed at Basle in 1485, was soon followed by others, e. g., at Venice in 1505, 1509, 1588, 1594; at Lyons in 1520, 1541, 1547, 1548, 1581, 1588, 1624, 1655; at Antwerp in 1575. These are enumerated by Touron (op. cit., p. 692), who says that about the same time other editions were published at Rome, Antwerp, Rouen, Paris, Douai, Cologne, Amsterdam, Bologna, etc. The editors of the Leonine edition deem worthy of mention those published at Paris in 1617, 1638, and 1648, at Lyons in 1663, 1677, and 1686, and a Roman edition of 1773 (IV, pp. xi, xii). Of all old editions they consider the most accurate two published at Padua, one in 1698, the other in 1712, and the Venice edition of 1755. Of recent editions the best are the following: the Leonine; the Migne editions (Paris, 1841, 1877); the first volume of the 1841 edition containing the "Libri quatuor sententiarum" of Peter Lombard; the very practical Faucher edition (5 vols. small quarto, Paris, 1887), dedicated to Cardinal Pecci, enriched with valuable notes; a Roman edition of 1894. The "Summa" has been translated into Greek and Armenian, and some parts have been translated into Chinese (see De Rubeis in Leonine ed., I, p. cxcvii; Echard, "Script. Ord. Præd.", I, p. 345; Touron, op. cit., VI, ix; Vaughan, op. cit. II, p. 167). In 1896 Father Joseph Rickaby, S.J., published "Aquinas Ethicus", a translation of the principal portion of the Second Part of the "Summa theologica". At the present time Father Thomas Pègues, O.P., is publishing a French translation of the whole "Summa" with commentaries, under the title "Commentaire français littéral de la Somme Théologique de S. Thomas d'Aquin". The five volumes which have appeared (Paris, 1907–10) bring the work down to the end of the First Part. (For reviews, see "Cath. University Bulletin", Jan., 1908; Jan., 1909; March, 1910; April, 1911.) For the English-speaking world "The Summa Theologica of St. Thomas Aquinas, literally translated by Fathers of the English Dominican Province," is being prepared. The first number (London and New York, 1911) contains the treatise on the Divine Essence (De Deo Uno, QQ. i–xxvi). Interesting introductory chapters treat of "The Scholastic Philosophy", "The Summa theologica", "The Method of St. Thomas", and "The Leonine Edition".

C. *Method and Style of St. Thomas.*—It is not possible to characterize the method of St. Thomas by one word, unless it can be called eclectic. It is Aristotelean, Platonic, and Socratic; it is inductive and deductive; it is analytic and synthetic. He chose the best that could be found in those who preceded him, carefully sifting the chaff from the wheat, approving what was true, rejecting the false. His powers of synthesis were extraordinary. No writer surpassed him in the faculty of expressing in a few well-chosen words the truth gathered from a multitude of varying and conflicting opinions; and in almost every instance the student sees the truth and is perfectly satisfied with St. Thomas's summary and statement. Not that he would have students swear by the words of a master. In philosophy, he says, arguments from authority are of secondary importance; philosophy does not consist in knowing what men have said, but in knowing the truth (In I lib. de Cœlo, lect. xxii; II Sent., D. xiv, a. 2, ad 1um). He assigns its proper place to reason used in theology (see below: Influence of St. Thomas), but he keeps it within its own sphere. Against the Traditionalists the Holy See has declared that the method used by St. Thomas and St. Bonaventure does not lead to Rationalism (Denzinger-Bannwart, n. 1652). Not so bold or original in investigating nature as were Albertus Magnus and Roger Bacon, he was, nevertheless, abreast of his time in science, and many of his opinions are of scientific value in the twentieth century. Take, for instance, the following: "In the same plant there is the twofold virtue, active and passive, though sometimes the active is found in one and the passive in another, so that one plant is said to be masculine and the other feminine" (3 Sent., D. III, Q. ii, a 1.—For other examples see Conway, O.P., op. cit., pp. 73 sqq.; Walsh, "St. Thomas Aquinas", in "Rosary Magazine", May, 1911.).

The style of St. Thomas is a medium between the rough expressiveness of some Scholastics and the fastidious elegance of John of Salisbury; it is remarkable for accuracy, brevity, and completeness. Pope Innocent VI (quoted in the Encyclical, "Æterni Patris", of Leo XIII) declared that, with the excep-

A CHART OF THE SUMMA.

								Ques.
Sacred Doctrine.—What it is and to what it extends.—All things are treated in it under the idea of God, either because they are God Himself or because they have relation to God.							1. Sacred Doctrine	i

Part I

1st.—Concerning those things which pertain to the production of creatures.
2d.—Concerning those things which pertain to the distinction of persons.

1. God. *Threefold Consideration.*
   - 1st. Concerning those things which pertain to the production of creatures.
     - 2. The One God. — ii–xxvi
     - 3. The Most Holy Trinity. — xxvii–xliii
     - 4. The Creation. — xliv–xlix
   - 2d. The Distinction of creatures.
     - 5. The Distinction of Things in General. — xlvii
     - 6. The Distinction of Good and Evil. — xlviii–xlix
     - (a) The distinction of good and evil.
     - (b) The distinction of corporeal and spiritual creatures.
       - 1st. The creature purely spiritual. — 7. The Angels. — l–lxiv
       - 2d. The creature purely corporeal. — 8. The Creature purely corporeal. — lxv–lxxiv
       - 3d. The creature composed of body and spirit, i.e., man. — 9. On Man. — lxxv–cii
   - 3d. The preservation and government of creatures. — 10. The Conservation and Government of Creatures. — ciii–cxix

Part II

2. The Advance of the Rational Creature to God.
Twofold Consideration:
Those things should be considered by means of which man attains to or deviates from his end, i. e., Human Acts. But because singular things are the objects of operations and acts, therefore every operative science is perfected by the consideration of things in particular. Therefore a moral consideration of human acts must be given:—

I–II — In General.
- The end of man.
  - Some acts are peculiar to man; some are common to man and other living creatures; and since beatitude is the peculiar good of man inasmuch as he is rational, the acts which are peculiar to him have a more intimate connection to that good than those that are common to man and living creatures.
    - 1st. The acts themselves.
      - (a) Acts which are peculiar to man. — 11. The End of Man and Beatitude. — i–v
      - (b) Acts which are common to man and other animals. — 12. Human Acts. — vi–xxi
      - — 13. The Passions. — xxii–xlviii
    - 2d. The principles of acts.
      - (a) Intrinsic principles.—The intrinsic principles are powers of the soul and habits; but we have already treated of powers in the 1st part. Therefore we come to the consideration of habits:—
        - 1st. Habits in General. — 14. Habits in General. — xlix–liv
        - 2d. Habits in particular.
          - Good habits, i.e., virtues. — 15. The Virtues. — lv–lxx
          - Evil habits, i.e., vices. — 16. On Vices and Sins. — lxxi–lxxxix
      - (b) Extrinsic principles.—The extrinsic principle of good is God, who instructs us by His law, and helps and moves us by grace. The external principle of evil is the Devil. But we treated of him in the 1st part. There fore it remains to treat of:—
        - 1st. Laws. — 17. On Laws. — xc–cviii
        - 2d. Grace. — 18. On Grace. — cix–cxiv

II–II — In Particular.
- Those acts which pertain to all conditions of life (the virtues and vices affecting all men.)
  - (a) Theological virtues.
    - (a) In the intellect.—Faith. — 19. Faith. — i–xvi
    - (b) In the will
      - Hope. — 20. Hope. — xvii–xxii
      - Charity. — 21. Charity. — xxiii–xlvi
  - (b) Cardinal virtues.
    - Prudence. — 22. Prudence. — xlvii–lvi
    - Justice. — 23. Justice. — lvii–cxxii
    - Fortitude. — 24. Fortitude. — cxxiii–cxl
    - Temperance. — 25. Temperance. — cxli–clxx
- Acts which pertain in a special manner to some men.
  - (a) Graces gratuitously given (gratiæ gratis datæ). — 26. Graces Gratuitously Given. — clxxi–clxxviii
  - (b) Active and contemplative life. — 27. The Active and Contemplative Life. — clxxix–clxxxii
  - (c) The various offices and conditions of men. — 28. The Various Offices and Conditions of Men. — clxxxiii–clxxxix

Part III

3. Christ.
Since our Lord and Saviour Jesus Christ, redeeming His people from their sins, has shown to us in Himself the way of truth, by which we, arising from the dead, are able to arrive at the happiness of immortal life, it is necessary, in order to attain the scope of all theology, after the consideration of the final end of man and of the virtues and vices, that we should consider the Saviour of all and the benefits He has conferred on us. Therefore we should consider:—

- 1st. The Saviour Himself, i. e., the mystery of the Incarnation, what He did and suffered.
  - (a) In General. — 29. The Incarnation. — i–lix
  - (b) In particular.
- 2d. The Sacraments, which have their efficacy from the Incarnate Word.
  - 30. The Sacraments in General. — lx–lxv
  - 31. Baptism. — lxvi–lxxi
  - 32. Confirmation. — lxxii
  - 33. Eucharist. — lxxiii–lxxxiii
  - 34. Penance, Qu. lxxxiv–xc. Supplement. — i–xxviii
  - 35. Extreme Unction. — xxix–xxxiii
  - 36. Orders. — xxxiv–xl
  - 37. Matrimony. — xli–lxvii
- 3d. Immortal Life,—the end to which we attain through Christ, both dying, and rising from the dead.
  - 38. The Resurrection and Four Last Things. — lxviii–cxix

tion of the canonical writings, the works of St. Thomas surpass all others in "accuracy of expression and truth of statement" (habet proprietatem verborum, modum dicendorum, veritatem sententiarum). Great orators, such as Bossuet, Lacordaire, Monsabré, have studied his style, and have been influenced by it, but they could not reproduce it. The same is true of theological writers. Cajetan knew St. Thomas's style better than any of his disciples, but Cajetan is beneath his great master in clearness and accuracy of expression, in soberness and solidity of judgment. St. Thomas did not attain to this perfection without an effort. He was a singularly blessed genius, but he was also an indefatigable worker, and by continued application he reached that stage of perfection in the art of writing where the art disappears. "The author's manuscript of the Summa Contra Gentiles is still in great part extant. It is now in the Vatican Library. The manuscript consists of strips of parchment, of various shades of colour, contained in an old parchment cover to which they were originally stitched. The writing is in double column, and difficult to decipher, abounding in abbreviations, often passing into a kind of shorthand. Throughout many passages a line is drawn in sign of erasure" (Rickaby, op. cit., preface: see Ucelli ed., "Sum. cont. gent.", Rome, 1878).

III. INFLUENCES EXERTED ON ST. THOMAS.—How was this great genius formed? The causes that exerted an influence on St. Thomas were of two kinds, natural and supernatural.

A. *Natural Causes*.—(1) As a foundation, he "was a witty child, and had received a good soul" (Wis., viii, 19). From the beginning he manifested precocious and extraordinary talent and thoughtfulness beyond his years. (2) His education was such that great things might have been expected of him. His training at Monte Cassino, at Naples, Paris, and Cologne was the best that the thirteenth century could give, and that century was the golden age of education. That it afforded excellent opportunities for forming great philosophers and theologians is evident from the character of St. Thomas's contemporaries. Alexander of Hales, Albertus Magnus, St. Bonaventure, St. Raymond of Pennafort, Roger Bacon, Hugo a S. Charo, Vincent of Beauvais, not to mention scores of others, prove beyond all doubt that those were days of really great scholars. (See Walsh, "The Thirteenth Greatest of Centuries", New York, 1907.) The men who trained St. Thomas were his teachers at Monte Cassino and Naples, but above all Albertus Magnus, under whom he studied at Paris and Cologne. (3) The books that exercised the greatest influence on his mind were the Bible, the Decrees of the councils and of the popes, the works of the Fathers, Greek and Latin, especially of St. Augustine, the "Sentences" of Peter Lombard, the writings of the philosophers, especially of Plato, Aristotle, and Boethius. If from these authors any were to be selected for special mention, undoubtedly they would be Aristotle, St. Augustine, and Peter Lombard. In another sense the writings of St. Thomas were influenced by Averroes, the chief opponent whom he had to combat in order to defend and make known the true Aristotle. (4) It must be borne in mind that St. Thomas was blessed with a retentive memory and great powers of penetration. Father Daniel d'Agusta once pressed him to say what he considered the greatest grace he had ever received, sanctifying grace of course excepted. "I think that of having understood whatever I have read", was the reply. St. Antoninus declared that "he remembered everything he had read, so that his mind was like a huge library" (cf. Drane, op. cit., p. 427; Vaughan, op. cit., II, p. 567). The bare enumeration of the texts of Scripture cited in the "Summa theologica" fills eighty small-print columns in the Migne edition, and by many it is not unreasonably supposed that he learned the Sacred Books by heart while he was imprisoned in the Castle of San Giovanni. Like St. Dominic he had a special love for the Epistles of St. Paul, on which he wrote commentaries (recent edition in 2 vols., Turin, 1891). (5) Deep reverence for the Faith, as made known by tradition, characterizes all his writings. The *consuetudo ecclesiæ*—the practice of the Church—should prevail over the authority of any doctor (II–II, Q. x. a. 12). In the "Summa" he quotes from 19 councils, 41 popes, and 52 Fathers of the Church. A slight acquaintance with his writings will show that among the Fathers his favourite was St. Augustine (on the Greek Fathers see Vaughan, op. cit., II, cc. iii sqq.). (6) With St. Augustine (II De doctr. Christ., c. xl), St. Thomas held that whatever there was of truth in the writings of pagan philosophers should be taken from them, as from "unjust possessors", and adapted to the teaching of the true religion (Sum. theol., I, Q. lxxxiv, a. 5). In the "Summa" alone he quotes from the writings of 46 philosophers and poets, his favourite authors being Aristotle, Plato, and, among Christian writers, Boethius. From Aristotle he learned that love of order and accuracy of expression which are characteristic of his own works. From Boethius he learned that Aristotle's works could be used without detriment to Christianity. He did not follow Boethius in his vain attempt to reconcile Plato and Aristotle. In general the Stagirite was his master, but the elevation and grandeur of St. Thomas's conceptions and the majestic dignity of his methods of treatment speak strongly of the sublime Plato (see Vaughan, op. cit., II, pp. 49, 627 sqq.; Huit, "Le Platonisme au treizième siècle" in "Annales de Philos. Chrétienne", Feb., 1890; "Les éléments Platoniciens de la doctrine de St Thomas" in "Revue Thomiste", Nov.–Dec., 1911).

B. *Supernatural Causes*.—Even if we do not accept as literally true the declaration of John XXII, that St. Thomas wrought as many miracles as there are articles in the "Summa", we must, nevertheless, go beyond causes merely natural in attempting to explain his extraordinary career and wonderful writings. (1) Purity of mind and body contributes in no small degree to clearness of vision (see St. Thomas, "Commentaries on I Cor., c. vii", Lesson v). By the gift of purity, miraculously granted at the time of the mystic girdling, God made Thomas's life angelic; the perspicacity and depth of his intellect, Divine grace aiding, made him the "Angelic Doctor". (2) The spirit of prayer, his great piety and devotion, drew down blessings on his studies. Explaining why he read, every day, portions of the "Conferences" of Cassian, he said: "In such reading I find devotion, whence I readily ascend to contemplation" (Prümmer, op. cit., p. 32). In the lessons of the Breviary read on his feast day it is explicitly stated that he never began to study without first invoking the assistance of God in prayer; and when he wrestled with obscure passages of the Scriptures, to prayer he added fasting. (3) Facts narrated by persons who either knew St. Thomas in life or wrote at about the time of his canonization prove that he received assistance from heaven. To Father Reginald he declared that he had learned more in prayer and contemplation than he had acquired from men or books (Prümmer, op. cit., p. 36). These same authors tell of mysterious visitors who came to encourage and enlighten him. The Blessed Virgin appeared, to assure him that his life and his writings were acceptable to God, and that he would persevere in his holy vocation. Sts. Peter and Paul came to aid him in interpreting an obscure passage in Isaias. When humility caused him to consider himself unworthy of the doctorate, a venerable religious of his order (supposed to be St. Dominic) appeared to encourage him and suggested the text for his opening discourse (Prümmer, op. cit., 29, 37; Tocco in "Acta

ST. THOMAS AQUINAS AMONG THE DOCTORS OF THE CHURCH
Francisco Zurbaran, the Museum, Seville.

SS.", VII Mar.; Vaughan, op. cit., II, 91). His ecstasies have been mentioned. His abstractions in presence of King Louis IX (St. Louis) and of distinguished visitors are related by all biographers. Hence, even if allowance be made for great enthusiasm on the part of his admirers, we must conclude that his extraordinary learning cannot be attributed to merely natural causes. Of him it may truly be said that he laboured as if all depended on his own efforts and prayed as if all depended on God.

IV. INFLUENCE OF ST. THOMAS.—A. *Influence on Sanctity*.—The great Scholastics were holy as well as learned men. Alexander of Hales, Blessed Albertus Magnus, St. Thomas, and St. Bonaventure prove that learning does not necessarily dry up devotion. The angelic Thomas and the seraphic Bonaventure represent the highest types of Christian scholarship, combining eminent learning with heroic sanctity. Cardinal Bessarion called St. Thomas "the most saintly of learned men and the most learned of saints". His works breathe the spirit of God, a tender and enlightened piety, built on a solid foundation, viz. the knowledge of God, of Christ, of man. The "Summa theologica" may be made a manual of piety as well as a text-book for the study of theology (cf. Drane, op. cit., p. 446). St. Francis de Sales, St. Philip Neri, St. Charles Borromeo, St. Vincent Ferrer, St. Pius V, St. Antoninus constantly studied St. Thomas. Nothing could be more inspiring than his treatises on Christ, in His sacred Person, in His life and sufferings. His treatise on the sacraments, especially on penance and the Eucharist, would melt even hardened hearts. He takes pains to explain the various ceremonies of the Mass ("De ritu Eucharistiæ" in "Sum. theol.", III, Q. lxxxiii, and no writer has explained more clearly than St. Thomas the effects produced in the souls of men by this heavenly Bread (ibid., Q. lxxix). The principles recently urged, in regard to frequent Communion, by Pius X ("Sacra Trid. Synodus", 1905) are found in St. Thomas (Q. lxxix, a. 8, Q. lxxx, a. 10), although he is not so explicit on this point as he is on the Communion of children. In the Decree "Quam Singulari" (1910) the pope cites St. Thomas, who teaches that, when children begin to have some use of reason, so that they can conceive some devotion to the Blessed Sacrament, they may be allowed to communicate (Q. lxxx, a. 9, ad 3um). The spiritual and devotional aspects of St. Thomas's theology have been pointed out by Father Contenson, O.P., in his "Theologia mentis et cordis". They are more fully explained by Father Vallgornera, O.P., in his "Theologia Mystica D. Thomæ", wherein the author leads the soul to God through the purgative, illuminative, and unitive ways. The Encyclical Letter of Leo XIII on the Holy Spirit is drawn largely from St. Thomas, and those who have studied the "Prima Secundæ" and the "Secunda Secundæ" know how admirably the saint explains the gifts and fruits of the Holy Ghost, as well as the Beatitudes, and their relations to the different virtues (see Froget, O.P. "De L'habitation du Saint Esprit dans les âmes justes, d'après la doctrine de S. Thomas d'Aquin", Paris, 1898). Nearly all good spiritual writers seek in St. Thomas definitions of the virtues which they recommend. Recently his minor works on the religious life have been translated into English ("An Apology for the Religious Orders", by St. Thomas Aquinas, St. Louis, 1902; "The Religious State", "The Episcopate", "The Priestly Office", by St. Thomas, St. Louis, 1902).

B. *Influence on Intellectual Life*.—Since the days of Aristotle, probably no one man has exercised such a powerful influence on the thinking world as did St. Thomas. His authority was very great during his lifetime. The popes, the universities, the *studia* of his order were anxious to profit by his learning and prudence. Several of his important works were written at the request of others, and his opinion was sought by all classes. On several occasions the doctors of Paris referred their disputes to him and gratefully abided by his decision (Vaughan, op. cit., II, p. 544). His principles, made known by his writings, have continued to influence men even to this day. This subject cannot be considered in all its aspects, nor is that necessary. His influence on matters purely philosophical is fully explained in histories of philosophy (see e. g. Gonzalez, O.P., "Hist. de la philosophie", II, Paris, 1890; Turner, op. cit., pp. 343 sqq.; Vallet, C.S.S., "Hist. de la phil.", Paris, 1886; Jourdain, "La Philosophie de S. Thomas d'Aquin", 2 vols., Paris, 1858; Hauréau, "Hist. de la Phil. scolastique", Paris, 1872–80; Ueberweg, "Hist. of Philosophy", 2 vols., New York, 1903, I, pp. 443 sqq.). (Theologians who followed St. Thomas will be mentioned in THOMISM. See also PREACHERS, ORDER OF.—II, A, 2, d.) His paramount importance and influence may be explained by considering him as the Christian Aristotle, combining in his person the best that the world has known in philosophy and theology. It is in this light that he is proposed as a model by Leo XIII in the famous Encyclical "Æterni Patris". The work of his life may be summed up in two propositions: he established the true relations between faith and reason; he systematized theology.

(1) Faith and Reason.—The principles of St. Thomas on the relations between faith and reason were solemnly proclaimed in the Vatican Council. The second, third, and fourth chapters of the Constitution "Dei Filius" read like pages taken from the works of the Angelic Doctor. First, reason alone is not sufficient to guide men: they need Revelation; we must carefully distinguish the truths known by reason from higher truths (mysteries) known by Revelation. Secondly, reason and Revelation, though distinct, are not opposed to each other. Thirdly, faith preserves reason from error; reason should do service in the cause of faith. Fourthly, this service is rendered in three ways: (a) reason should prepare the minds of men to receive the Faith by proving the truths which faith presupposes (*præambula fidei*); (b) reason should explain and develop the truths of Faith and should propose them in scientific form; (c) reason should defend the truths revealed by Almighty God. This is a development of St. Augustine's famous saying (De Trin., XIV, c. i), that the right use of reason is "that by which the most wholesome faith is begotten . . . is nourished, defended, and made strong". These principles are proposed by St. Thomas in many places, especially in the following: "In Boethium, de Trin. Proem.", Q. ii, a. 1; "Sum. cont. gent.", I, cc. iii–ix; "Summa", I, Q. i, aa. 1, 5, 8; Q. xxxii, a. 1; Q. lxxxiv, a. 5 (cf. Vaughan, op. cit., cc. viii, ix, x; Manning, "The Vatican Council and Its Definitions", New York, 1905, pp. 206 sqq.). St. Thomas's services to the Faith are thus summed up by Leo XIII in the Encyclical "Æterni Patris": "He won this title of distinction for himself: that single-handed he victoriously combated the errors of former times, and supplied invincible arms to put to rout those which might in after times spring up. Again, clearly distinguishing, as is fitting, reason and faith, he both preserved and had regard for the rights of each; so much so, indeed, that reason, borne on the wings of Thomas, can scarcely rise higher, while faith could scarcely expect more or stronger aids from reason than those which she has already obtained through Thomas." St. Thomas did not combat imaginary foes; he attacked living adversaries. The works of Aristotle had been introduced into France in faulty translations and with the misleading commentaries of Jewish and Moorish philosophers. This gave rise to a flood of errors which so alarmed the authorities that the reading of Aristotle's Physics and Metaphysics was forbidden by Robert de Courçon in 1210,

the decree being moderated by Gregory IX in 1231. There crept into the University of Paris an insidious spirit of irreverence and Rationalism, represented especially by Abelard and Raymond Lullus, which claimed that reason could know and prove all things, even the mysteries of Faith. Under the authority of Averroes dangerous doctrines were propagated, especially two very pernicious errors: first, that philosophy and religion being in different regions, what is true in religion might be false in philosophy; secondly, that all men have but one soul. Averroes was commonly styled "The Commentator", but St. Thomas says he was "not so much a Peripatetic as a corruptor of Peripatetic philosophy" (Opusc. de unit. intell.). Applying a principle of St. Augustine (see I, Q. lxxxiv, a. 5), following in the footsteps of Alexander of Hales and Albertus Magnus, St. Thomas resolved to take what was true from the "unjust possessors", in order to press it into the service of revealed religion. Objections to Aristotle would cease if the true Aristotle were made known; hence his first care was to obtain a new translation of the works of the great philosopher (see A. Jourdain, "Recherches critiques sur l'âge et l'origine des traductions latines d'Aristote", Paris, 1819, 1843: Ueberweg, op. cit., I, p. 430; Barthélemy Saint-Hilaire). Aristotle was to be purified; false commentators were to be refuted; the most influential of these was Averroes, hence St. Thomas is continually rejecting his false interpretations.

(2) *Theology Systematized.*—The next step was to press reason into the service of the Faith, by putting Christian doctrine into scientific form. Scholasticism does not consist, as some persons imagine, in useless discussions and subtleties, but in this, that it expresses sound doctrine in language which is accurate, clear, and concise. In the Encyclical "Æterni Patris" Leo XIII, citing the words of Sixtus V (Bull "Triumphantis", 1588), declares that to the right use of philosophy we are indebted for "those noble endowments which make Scholastic theology so formidable to the enemies of truth", because "that ready coherence of cause and effect, that order and array of a disciplined army in battle, those clear definitions and distinctions, that strength of argument and those keen discussions by which light is distinguished from darkness, the true from the false, expose and lay bare, as it were, the falsehoods of heretics wrapped around by a cloud of subterfuges and fallacies". When the great Scholastics had written, there was light where there had been darkness, there was order where confusion had prevailed. The work of St. Anselm and of Peter Lombard was perfected by the Scholastic theologians. Since their days no substantial improvements have been made in the plan and system of theology, although the field of apologetics has been widened, and positive theology has become more important.

C. *St. Thomas's Doctrine Followed.*—Within a short time after his death the writings of St. Thomas were universally esteemed. The Dominicans naturally took the lead in following St. Thomas. The general chapter held in Paris in 1279 pronounced severe penalties against all who dared to speak irreverently of him or of his writings. The chapters held in Paris in 1286, at Bordeaux in 1287, and at Lucca in 1288 expressly required the brethren to follow the doctrine of Thomas, who at that time had not been canonized (Const. Ord. Præd., n. 1130). The University of Paris, on the occasion of Thomas's death, sent an official letter of condolence to the general chapter of the Dominicans, declaring that, equally with his brethren, the university experienced sorrow at the loss of one who was their own by many titles (see text of letter in Vaughan, op. cit., II, p. 82). In the Encyclical "Æterni Patris" Leo XIII mentions the Universities of Paris, Salamanca, Alcalá, Douai, Toulouse, Louvain, Padua, Bologna, Naples, and Coimbra as "the homes of human wisdom where Thomas reigned supreme, and the minds of all, of teachers as well as of taught, rested in wonderful harmony under the shield and authority of the Angelic Doctor". To the list may be added Lima and Manila, Fribourg and Washington. Seminaries and colleges followed the lead of the universities. The "Summa" gradually supplanted the "Sentences" as the text-book of theology. Minds were formed in accordance with the principles of St. Thomas; he became the great master, exercising a world-wide influence on the opinions of men and on their writings; for even those who did not adopt all of his conclusions were obliged to give due consideration to his opinions. It has been estimated that 6000 commentaries on St. Thomas's works have been written. Manuals of theology and of philosophy, composed with the intention of imparting his teaching, translations, and studies, or digests (*études*), of portions of his works have been published in profusion during the last six hundred years and to-day his name is in honour all over the world (see THOMISM). In every one of the general councils held since his death St. Thomas has been singularly honoured. At the Council of Lyons his book "Contra errores Græcorum" was used with telling effect against the Greeks. In later disputes, before and during the Council of Florence, John of Montenegro, the champion of Latin orthodoxy, found St. Thomas's works a source of irrefragable arguments. The "Decretum pro Armenis" (Instruction for the Armenians), issued by the authority of that council, is taken almost verbatim from his treatise, "De fidei articulis et septem sacramentis" (see Denzinger-Bannwart, n. 695). "In the Councils of Lyons, Vienne, Florence, and the Vatican", writes Leo XIII (Encyclical "Æterni Patris"), "one might almost say that Thomas took part in and presided over the deliberations and decrees of the Fathers, contending against the errors of the Greeks, of heretics, and Rationalists, with invincible force and with the happiest results. But the chief and special glory of Thomas, one which he has shared with none of the Catholic doctors, is that the Fathers of Trent made it part of the order of the conclave to lay upon the altar, together with the code of Sacred Scripture and the decrees of the Supreme Pontiffs, the Summa of Thomas Aquinas, whence to seek counsel, reason, and inspiration." Greater influence than this no man could have.

Before this section is closed mention should be made of two books widely known and highly esteemed, which were inspired by and drawn from the writings of St. Thomas. The Catechism of the Council of Trent, composed by disciples of the Angelic Doctor, is in reality a compendium of his theology, in convenient form for the use of parish priests. Dante's "Divina Commedia" has been called "the Summa of St. Thomas in verse", and commentators trace the great Florentine poet's divisions and descriptions of the virtues and vices to the "Secunda Secundæ" (see Berthier, O.P., "La divina commedia con commenti secondo la scholastica", Turin, 1893; Ozanam, "Dante et la philosophie au treizième siècle", Paris, 1845, p. 319; Jourdain, op. cit., II, p. 128).

D. *Appreciation of St. Thomas.*—(1) In the Church. —The esteem in which he was held during his life has not been diminished, but rather increased, in the course of the six centuries that have elapsed since his death. The position which he occupies in the Church is well explained by that great scholar Leo XIII, in the Encyclical "Æterni Patris", recommending the study of Scholastic philosophy: "It is known that nearly all the founders and framers of laws of religious orders commanded their societies to study and religiously adhere to the teachings of St. Thomas. . . . To say nothing of the family of St. Dominic, which rightly claims this great teacher for its own glory, the statutes of the Benedictines, the Carmelites, the

Augustinians, the Society of Jesus, and many others, all testify that they are bound by this law." Amongst the "many others" the Servites, the Passionists, the Barnabites, and the Sulpicians have been devoted in an especial manner to the study of St. Thomas. (See Berthier, "L'Etude de la Somme Théologique de S. Thomas d'Aquin", Paris, 1905, pp. 18 sqq.; Goudin, O.P., "Phil. D. Thomæ", Paris, 1886, introd. a 3; Touron, op. cit., V, cc. xi, xii.) The principal ancient universities where St. Thomas ruled as the great master have been enumerated above. The Paris doctors called him the morning star, the luminous sun, the light of the whole Church. Stephen, Bishop of Paris, repressing those who dared to attack the doctrine of "that most excellent Doctor, the blessed Thomas", calls him "the great luminary of the Catholic Church, the precious stone of the priesthood, the flower of doctors, and the bright mirror of the University of Paris" (Drane, op. cit., p. 431). In the old Louvain University the doctors were required to uncover and bow their heads when they pronounced the name of Thomas (Goudin, op. cit., p. 21). (On the universities, see Touron, op. cit., l. V, cc. IX, X; Echard, op. cit., I, 435, pp. 15 sqq.; cf. also Thomism.)

"The œcumenical councils, where blossoms the flower of all earthly wisdom, have always been careful to hold Thomas Aquinas in singular honour" (Leo XIII in "Æt. Patris"). This subject has been sufficiently treated above. The "Bullarium Ordinis Prædicatorum", published in 1729–39, gives thirty-eight Bulls in which eighteen sovereign pontiffs praised and recommended the doctrine of St. Thomas (see also Vaughan, op. cit., II, c. ii; Berthier, op. cit., pp. 7 sqq.). These approbations are recalled and renewed by Leo XIII, who lays special stress on "the crowning testimony of Innocent VI: 'His teaching above that of others, the canons alone excepted, enjoys such an elegance of phraseology, a method of statement, a truth of proposition, that those who hold it are never found swerving from the path of truth, and he who dare assail it will always be suspected of error'" (ibid.). Leo XIII surpassed his predecessors in admiration of St. Thomas, in whose works he declared a remedy can be found for many evils that afflict society (see Berthier, op. cit., introd.). The notable Encyclical Letters with which the name of that illustrious pontiff will always be associated show how he had studied the works of the Angelic Doctor. This is very noticeable in the letters on Christian marriage, the Christian constitution of states, the condition of the working classes, and the study of Holy Scripture. Pope Pius X, in several Letters, e. g. in the "Pascendi Dominici Gregis" (Sept., 1907), has insisted on the observance of the recommendations of Leo XIII concerning the study of St. Thomas. An attempt to give names of Catholic writers who have expressed their appreciation of St. Thomas and of his influence would be an impossible undertaking; for the list would include nearly all who have written on philosophy or theology since the thirteenth century, as well as hundreds of writers on other subjects. Commendations and eulogies are found in the introductory chapters of all good commentaries. An incomplete list of authors who have collected these testimonies is given by Father Berthier (op. cit., p. 22). Other names will be given in bibliography. (See Thomists.)

(2) Outside the Church.—(a) Anti-Scholastics.— Some persons have been and are still opposed to everything that comes under the name of Scholasticism, which they hold to be synonymous with subtleties and useless discussions. From the prologue to the "Summa" it is clear that St. Thomas was opposed to all that was superfluous and confusing in Scholastic studies. When people understand what true Scholasticism means, their objections will cease (see De Wulf, "Scholasticism Old and New", New York, 1907; Perrier, "The Revival of Scholastic Philosophy", New York, 1909; and especially the Encyclical "Æterni Patris"). (b) Heretics and Schismatics.— "A last triumph was reserved for this incomparable man—namely, to compel the homage, praise, and admiration of even the very enemies of the Catholic name" (Leo XIII, ibid.). St. Thomas's orthodoxy drew upon him the hatred of all Greeks who were opposed to union with Rome. The united Greeks, however, admire St. Thomas and study his works (see above, translations of the "Summa"). The leaders of the sixteenth-century revolt honoured St. Thomas by attacking him, Luther being particularly violent in his coarse invectives against the great doctor. Citing Bucer's wild boast, "Take away Thomas and I will destroy the Church", Leo XIII (ibid.) remarks, "The hope was vain, but the testimony has its value". Calo, Tocco, and other biographers relate that St. Thomas, travelling from Rome to Naples, converted two celebrated Jewish rabbis, whom he met at the country house of Cardinal Richard (Prümmer, op. cit., p. 33; Vaughan, op. cit., II, p. 795). Rabbi Paul of Burgos, in the fifteenth century, was converted by reading the works of St. Thomas. Theobald Thamer, a disciple of Melancthon, abjured his heresy after he had read the "Summa", which he intended to refute. The Calvinist Duperron was converted in the same way, subsequently becoming Archbishop of Sens and a cardinal (see Conway, O.P., op. cit., p. 96). After the bitterness of the first period of Protestantism had passed away, Protestants saw the necessity of retaining many parts of Catholic philosophy and theology, and those who came to know St. Thomas were compelled to admire him. Ueberweg says "He brought the Scholastic philosophy to its highest stage of development, by effecting the most perfect accommodation that was possible of the Aristotelian philosophy to ecclesiastical orthodoxy" (op. cit., p. 440). R. Seeberg in the "New Schaff-Herzog Religious Encyclopedia" (New York, 1911) devotes ten columns to St. Thomas, and says that "at all points he succeeded in upholding the church doctrine as credible and reasonable" (XI, p. 427). For many years, especially since the days of Pusey and Newman, St. Thomas has been in high repute at Oxford. Recently the "Summa contra gentiles" was placed on the list of subjects which a candidate may offer in the final honour schools of *Litteræ Humaniores* at that university (cf. Walsh, op. cit., c. xvii). For several years Father De Groot, O.P., has been the professor of Scholastic philosophy in the University of Amsterdam, and courses in Scholastic philosophy have been established in some of the leading non-Catholic universities of the United States. Anglicans have a deep admiration for St. Thomas. Alfred Mortimer, in the chapter "The Study of Theology" of his work entitled "Catholic Faith and Practice" (2 vols., New York, 1909), regretting that "the English priest has ordinarily no scientific acquaintance with the Queen of Sciences", and proposing a remedy, says, "The simplest and most perfect sketch of universal theology is to be found in the Summa of St. Thomas" (vol. II, pp. 454, 465).

V. St. Thomas and Modern Thought.—In the Syllabus of 1864 Pius IX condemned a proposition in which it was stated that the method and principles of the ancient Scholastic doctors were not suited to the needs of our times and the progress of science (Denzinger-Bannwart, n. 1713). In the Encyclical "Æterni Patris" Leo XIII points out the benefits to be derived from "a practical reform of philosophy by restoring the renowned teaching of St. Thomas Aquinas". He exhorts the bishops to "restore the golden wisdom of Thomas and to spread it far and wide for the defence and beauty of the Catholic Faith, for the good of society, and for the advantage of all the sciences". In the pages of the Encyclical immediately preceding these words he explains why the teaching of St. Thomas would produce such most desirable results: St. Thomas is the great master to explain and defend the Faith, for his is "the solid doctrine of the Fathers and the Scholastics, who so clearly and forcibly demonstrate the firm foundations of the Faith, its Divine origin, its certain truth, the arguments that sustain it, the benefits it has conferred on the human race, and its perfect accord with reason, in a manner to satisfy completely minds open to persuasion, however unwilling and repugnant". The career of St. Thomas would in itself have justified Leo XIII in assuring men of the nineteenth century that the Catholic Church was not opposed to the right use of reason. The sociological aspects of St. Thomas are also pointed out: "The teachings of Thomas on the true meaning of liberty, which at this time is running into license, on the Divine origin of all authority, on laws and their force, on the paternal and just rule of princes, on obedience to the highest powers, on mutual charity one towards another—on all of these and kindred subjects, have very great and invincible force to overturn those principles of the new order which are well known to be dangerous to the peaceful order of things and to public safety" (ibid.). The evils affecting modern society had been pointed out by the pope in the Letter "Inscrutabili" of 21 April, 1878, and in the one on Socialism, Communism, and Nihilism ("The Great Encyclicals of Leo XIII", pp. 9 sqq.; 22 sqq.). How the principles of the Angelic Doctor will furnish a remedy for these evils is explained here in a general way, more particularly in the Letters on the Christian constitution of states, human liberty, the chief duties of Christians as citizens, and on the conditions of the working classes (ibid., pp. 107, 135, 180, 208).

It is in relation to the sciences that some persons doubt the availability of St. Thomas's writings; and the doubters are thinking of the physical and experimental sciences, for in metaphysics the scholastics are admitted to be masters. Leo XIII calls attention to the following truths: (a) The Scholastics were not opposed to investigation. Holding as a principle in anthropology "that the human intelligence is only led to the knowledge of things without body and matter by things sensible, they well understood that nothing was of greater use to the philosopher than diligently to search into the mysteries of nature, and to be earnest and constant in the study of physical things" (ibid., p. 55). This principle was reduced to practice: St. Thomas, Blessed Albertus Magnus, Roger Bacon, and others "gave large attention to the knowledge of natural things" (ibid., p. 56). (b) Investigation alone is not sufficient for true science. "When facts have been established, it is necessary to rise and apply ourselves to the study of the nature of corporeal things, to inquire into the laws which govern them and the principles whence their order and varied unity and mutual attraction in diversity arise" (p. 55). Will the scientists of to-day pretend to be better reasoners than St. Thomas, or more powerful in synthesis? It is the method and the principles of St. Thomas that Leo XIII recommends: "If anything is taken up with too great subtlety by the scholastic doctors, or too carelessly stated; if there be anything that ill agrees with the discoveries of a later age or, in a word, is improbable in any way, it does not enter into our mind to propose that for imitation to our age" (p. 56). Just as St. Thomas, in his day, saw a movement towards Aristotle and philosophical studies which could not be checked, but could be guided in the right direction and made to serve the cause of truth, so also, Leo XIII, seeing in the world of his time a spirit of study and investigation which might be productive of evil or of good, had no desire to check it, but resolved to propose a moderator and master who could guide it in the paths of truth.

No better guide could have been chosen than the clear-minded, analytic, synthetic, and sympathetic Thomas Aquinas. His extraordinary patience and fairness in dealing with erring philosophers, his approbation of all that was true in their writings, his gentleness in condemning what was false, his clear-sightedness in pointing out the direction to true knowledge in all its branches, his aptness and accuracy in expressing the truth—these qualities mark him as a great master not only for the thirteenth century, but for all times. If any persons are inclined to consider him too subtle, it is because they do not know how clear, concise, and simple are his definitions and divisions. His two *summæ* are masterpieces of pedagogy, and mark him as the greatest of human teachers. Moreover, he dealt with errors similar to many which go under the name of philosophy or science in our days. The Rationalism of Abelard and others called forth St. Thomas's luminous and everlasting principles on the true relations of faith and reason. Ontologism was solidly refuted by St. Thomas nearly six centuries before the days of Malebranche, Gioberti, and Ubaghs (see "Sum. theol.", I, Q. lxxxiv, a. 5). The true doctrine on first principles and on universals, given by him and by the other great Scholastics, is the best refutation of Kant's criticism of metaphysical ideas (see, e. g., "Post. Analyt.", I, lect. xix; "De ente et essentia", c. iv; "Sum. theol.", I, Q. xvii, a. 3, *corp*. and ad 2um; Q. lxxix, a. 3; Q. lxxxiv, a. 5, a. 6, *corp*. and ad 1um, Q. lxxxv, a. 2, ad 2um, a. 3, ad 1um, ad 4um. Cf. index to "Summa": "Veritas", "Principium", "Universale"). Modern psychological Pantheism does not differ substantially from the theory of one soul for all men asserted by Averroes (see "De unit. intell." and "Sum. theol.", I, Q. lxxvi, a. 2; Q. lxxix, a.5). The Modernistic error, which distinguishes the Christ of faith from the Christ of history, had as its forerunner the Averroistic principle that a thing might be true in philosophy and false in religion.

In the Encyclical "Providentissimus Deus" (18 Nov., 1893) Leo XIII draws from St. Thomas's writings the principles and wise rules which should govern scientific criticism of the Sacred Books. From the same source recent writers have drawn principles which are most helpful in the solution of questions pertaining to Spiritism and Hypnotism (see Coconnier, "L'âme humaine", Paris, 1890; "L'hypnotisme franc", Paris, 1898; Berthier, "Spiritisme et hypnotisme d'après S. Thomas": appendix III to "L'Etude"). Are we to conclude, then, that St. Thomas's works, as he left them, furnish sufficient instruction for scientists, philosophers, and theologians of our times? By no means. *Vetera novis augere et perficere*—"To strengthen and complete the old by aid of the new"—is the motto of the restoration proposed by Leo XIII. Were St. Thomas living to-day he would gladly adopt and use all the facts made known by recent scientific and historical investigations, but he would carefully weigh all evidence offered in favour of the facts (see "L'Avenir du Thomisme" in Sertillanges, op. cit., p. 327). Positive theology is more necessary in our days than it was in the thirteenth century. Leo XIII calls attention to its necessity in his Encyclical, and his admonition is renewed by Pius X in his Letter on Modernism. But both pontiffs declare that positive theology must not be extolled to the detriment of Scholastic theology. In the Encyclical "Pascendi", prescribing remedies against Modernism, Pius X, following in this his illustrious predecessor, gives the first place to "Scholastic philosophy, especially as it was taught by Thomas Aquinas". St. Thomas is still "The Angel of the Schools".

Specimen of Text of the Summa; I, Q. i, a. 1. With translation by English Dominican Fathers.

Utrum sit necessarium præter philosophicas disciplinas aliam doctrinam haberi.	Whether, besides philosophy, any further doctrine is required?

Ad primum sic proceditur.

1. Videtur quod non sit necessarium præter philosophicas disciplinas aliam doctrinam haberi. Ad ea enim quæ supra rationem sunt, homo non debet conari, secundum illud Eccli. 3, 22: Altiora te ne quæsieris. Sed ea quæ rationi subduntur, sufficienter traduntur in philosophicis disciplinis. Superfluum igitur videtur præter philosophicas disciplinas aliam doctrinam haberi.

2. Præterea, doctrina non potest esse nisi de ente; nihil enim scitur nisi verum, quod cum ente convertitur. Sed de omnibus entibus tractatur in disciplinis philosophicis et etiam de Deo; unde quædam pars philosophiæ dicitur theologia, sive scientia divina, ut patet per Philosophum in 6 Metaph. (com. 2). Non fuit igitur necessarium præter philosophicas disciplinas aliam doctrinam haberi.

Sed contra est quod dicitur 2 ad Timoth., 3, 16: Omnis scriptura divinitus inspirata utilis est ad docendum, ad arguendum, ad corripiendum, ad erudiendum, ad justitiam. Scriptura autem divinitus inspirata non pertinet ad philosophicas disciplinas, quæ sunt secundum humanam rationem inventæ. Utile igitur est præter philosophicas disciplinas esse aliam scientiam divinitus inspiratam.

Respondeo dicendum quod, necessarium fuit ad humanam salutem esse doctrinam quamdam secundum revelationem divinam præter philosophicas disciplinas quæ ratione humana investigantur. Primo quidem quia homo ordinatur ad Deum sicut ad quemdam finem, qui comprehensionem rationis excedit, secundum illud Isai. 64, 4: Oculus non vidit, Deus, absque te, quæ præparasti expectantibus te. Finem autem oportet esse præcognitum hominibus, qui suas intentiones et actiones debent ordinare in finem. Unde necessarium fuit homini ad salutem quod ei nota fierent quædam per revelationem divinam quæ rationem humanam excedunt.

Ad ea etiam quæ de Deo ratione humana investigari possunt, necessarium fuit hominem instrui revelatione divina; quia veritas de Deo per rationem investigata, a paucis, et per longum tempus, et cum admixtione multorum errorum homini proveniret; a cujus tamen veritatis cognitione dependet tota hominis salus, quæ in Deo est. Ut igitur salus hominibus et convenientius et certius proveniat, necessarium fuit quod de divinis per divinam revelationem instruerentur. Necessarium igitur fuit, præter philosophicas disciplinas quæ per rationem investigantur, sacram doctrinam per revelationem haberi.

We proceed thus to the first article:

Objection 1.—It seems that, besides philosophical science, we have no need of any further knowledge. Man should not seek to know what is above reason: Seek not the things that are too high for thee (Ecclus., iii, 22). But whatever is not above reason is fully treated of in philosophical science. Therefore any other knowledge besides philosophical science is superfluous.

Objection 2.—Further, knowledge can only be concerned with being, for nothing can be known, save what is true; and all that is, is true. But everything that is, is treated of in philosophical science—even God himself—so that there is a part of philosophy called theology, or the Divine science, as Aristotle has proved. Therefore, besides philosophical science, there is no need of any further knowledge.

On the contrary, it is said: All Scripture inspired of God is profitable to teach, to reprove, to correct, to instruct in justice (II Tim., iii, 16). Scripture, inspired of God, is no part of philosophical science, which has been built up by human reason. Therefore, it is useful that, besides philosophical science, there should be other knowledge, i. e., inspired of God.

I answer that, It was necessary for man's salvation that there should be a knowledge revealed by God, besides philosophical science built up by human reason. First, indeed, because man is ordained to God, as to an end that surpasses the grasp of his reason. The eye hath not seen, besides Thee, O God, what things Thou hast prepared for them that wait for Thee (Isa., lxiv, 4). But the end must first be known by men who are to direct their thoughts and actions to the end. Hence it was necessary for the salvation of man that certain truths which exceed human reason should be made known to him by Divine Revelation.

Even as regards those truths about God which human reason could have discovered, it was necessary that man should be taught by a Divine Revelation; because the truth about God such as reason could discover, would only be known by a few, and that after a long time, and with the admixture of many errors. Whereas man's whole salvation, which is in God, depends upon the knowledge of this truth. Therefore, in order that the salvation of men might be brought about more fitly and more surely, it was necessary that they should be taught Divine Truths by Divine Revelation. It was therefore necessary that, besides philosophical science built up by reason, there should be a sacred science learnt through Revelation.

Ad primum ergo dicendum, quod, licet ea quæ sunt altiora hominis cognitione non sint ab homine per rationem inquirenda, sunt tamen a Deo revelata, suscipienda per fidem; unde et ibidem (Eccli., III, 25), subditur: Plurima supra sensum hominum ostensa sunt tibi. Et in hujusmodi sacra doctrina consistit.

Ad secundum dicendum quod diversa ratio cognoscibilis diversitatem scientiarum inducit. Eamdem enim conclusionem demonstrant astrologus, et naturalis, puta quod terra est rotunda; sed astrologus per medium mathematicum, id est, a materia abstractum; naturalis autem per medium circa materiam consideratum. Unde nihil prohibet de eisdem de quibus philosophicæ disciplinæ tractant, secundum quod sunt cognoscibilia lumine naturalis rationis, etiam aliam scientiam tractare, secundum quod cognoscuntur lumine divinæ revelationis. Unde theologia, quæ ad sacram doctrinam pertinet, differt, secundum genus, ab illa theologia quæ pars philosophiæ ponitur.

Reply Objection 1.—Although those things which are beyond man's knowledge may not be sought for by man through his reason, nevertheless, once they are revealed by God they must be accepted by faith. Hence, the sacred text continues: For many things are shown to thee above the understanding of man (Ecclus., iii, 25). And in this the sacred science consists.

Reply Objection 2.—Sciences are differentiated according to the various means through which knowledge is obtained. The astronomer and the physicist both may prove the same conclusion—that the earth, for instance, is round; the astronomer by means of mathematics (i.e., abstracting from matter), but the physicist by means of matter itself. Hence there is no reason why those things which may be learnt from philosophical science, so far as they can be known by natural reason, may not also be taught us by another science so far as they fall within revelation. Hence theology included in Sacred Doctrine differs in kind from that theology which is part of philosophy.

BOLLANDISTS, *Acta SS.*, VII Mar.; HURTER, *Nomencl.*, II (Innsbruck, 1906), 308; MORTIER, *Histoire des maîtres généraux de l'Ordre des FF. Prêcheurs* (Paris, 1903); CHEVALIER, *Répertoire des sources historiques du moyen âge*, II (2nd ed., Paris, 1907), 447 sqq.; UEBERWEG, tr., *Hist. of Philosophy*, I (New York, 1903), 442; SERTILLANGES, *S. Thomas d'Aquin*, II (Paris, 1910), 337; PERRIER, *The Revival of Scholastic Philosophy* (New York, 1909), 249.

On Life and Works.—The earliest biographers were PETER CALO (d. 1310 or 1348), WILLIAM DE TOCCO (d. about 1324), PTOLOMEO OF LUCCA (d. 1327), and BERNARD GUIDONIS (d. 1331). CALO, *Life*, is printed in PRÜMMER, *Fontes vitæ S. Thomæ* (Toulouse, 1911); Tocco is given in *Acta SS*. In vol. I of the 1588 Venetian edition of the *Summa* is found the same Life, viz., *Authoris vita R. P. Fr. Guil. de Thocco authore, qui eum vidit, et audivit legentem et prædicantem; Nunc primum edita*. GERARDUS DE FRACHETO (d. 1271), *Vitæ Fratrum Ord. Præd.*, ed. REICHERT (Louvain, 1896). Notices of these biographers are given in ECHARD, *Script. Ord. Præd.* (Paris, 1719–21), also an extensive account of St. Thomas and his writings, I, 271 sqq. ST. ANTONINUS and NATALIS ALEXANDER are numbered amongst the biographers. TOURON, *La vie de S. Thomas d'Aquin, avec un exposé de sa doctrine et ses ouvrages* (Paris, 1740) is a mine of valuable information. VIELMUS, *De D. Th. Aquin. doctrina et scriptis* (Padua, 1564; Venice, 1575; Brescia, 1748; Vienna, 1763); DENIFLE, *Die Universitäten des Mittelalters* (Berlin, 1885); *Archiv für Literatur und Kirchengeschichte des Mittelalters*, II (Berlin, 1886); DENIFLE-CHATELAIN, *Chartularium Univ. Parisiensis* (Paris, 1889–91); CHEVALIER, *Catalogue critique des œuvres de S. Th. d'Aquin* (Romans, 1886); MANDONNET, *Siger de Brabant: Ecrits authentiques* (see above) and *Les titres doctoraux de S. Th. d'Aquin* in *Rev. Thomiste* (1909), XVII, 597–608; FRIGERIO, *Vita di S. Tomaso* (Rome, 1615, 1668); WERNER, *Der heil. Thomas von Aquino* (Ratisbon, 1858); DE GROOT, *Het Leven van den H. Thomas van Aquinas* (Amsterdam, 1882; Utrecht, 1907); BAREILLE, *Hist. de S. Th. d'Aquin* (Paris, 1846, 1859, 1862); DIDIOT, *Le Docteur Angélique* (Lille, 1894); VAUGHAN, *Life and Labours of S. Thomas of Aquin* (2 vols., London, 1871–72: abridged, in one vol., London, 1875); KAVANAUGH, *The Life of S. Th. Aquinas* (London, 1890); CONWAY, *St. Thomas Aquinas* (London and New York, 1911).

Commentaries.—The principal commentators on St. Thomas's works are: ST. ANTONINUS, BANNEZ, BILLUART, CAJETAN, CAPREOLUS, CONTENSON, GONET, JOHN OF ST. THOMAS, LUGO, MEDINA, PORRECTA (CAPPONI), SALAMANTICENSES (see SALMANTICENSES AND COMPLUTENSES), SOTO, SUAREZ, SYLVESTER, SYLVIUS, TOLETUS, VALENTIA, VASQUEZ, VICTORIA, FRANCIS. The following have appeared since the publication of the *Æterni Patris* (1879): BUONPENSIERE, *Comment. in I^{am} P. S. Theol. S. Th. Aquin.* (Rome, 1902); BILLOT, JANSSENS, *Sum. Theol. ad modum Comment. in Aquin. Sum.* (Rome, 1899, sqq.); PAQUET, *Disp. Theol., seu Comment. in Sum. Theol. S. Thomæ* (Quebec, 1893–1903); PÈGUES, *Comment. français littéral de la Somme Théol. de S. Th. d'Aquin* (Toulouse, 1906 sqq.); SATOLLI, *In Sum. Theol. D. Th. Aquin. Prælectiones* (Rome, 1884–88).

Digests, Indices, Special Treatises.—PETER OF BERGAMO, *Tabula Aurea in omnia opera S. Th. Aquin.* (late ed., Parma, 1883); MEDICES (DE MEDICIS), *Sum. Theol. S. Th. Aquin. formalis explicatio* (new ed., Vico, 1858–62), gives the whole Summa in syllogistic form. Valuable indices are given in all good editions of *Opera Omnia* and of the *Summa Theologica*. Thus, in Migne editions of the *Summa* the following are found: I. *De præcipuis rebus;* II. *In Script. Sacram* (all texts cited in the *Summa* and *Supplement*); III. *Ad præcipua doctrinæ Christ. capita;* IV. *De Hæresibus* (heresies refuted in the *Summa*); V. *De Antilogiis* (explanations of apparent contradictions); VI. *Aug. Hunnæi Axiomata de sacramentis, Schema de Sacram. Catæchismus Catholicus;* VII. *Catalogus Auctorum a D. Th. Laudatorum* (philosophers, poets, pontiffs, councils, Fathers mentioned in the *Summa*); VIII. *Index in Epist. et Evang. Dominicarum.* BERTHIER, *L'Etude de la Somme Théol. de S. Thomas d'Aquin* (Paris, 1906); *Tabulæ systematicæ et synopticæ totius Sum. Theol.* (Fribourg, 1893); *Tabulæ system. et synopt. totius Sum. Cont. Gent.* (Paris, 1900); LÉPICIER, *Sacr. Doctr. Thomisticæ utilitas demonstrata* (Rome, 1893).

For discussions relating to St. Thomas and the Immaculate Conception: CAJETAN, *In 3 P., Q. 27, a. 2; De Conceptu B. V.;* PORRECTA, *In 3 P. Q. 27, a. 2;* JOANNES A ST. THOMA, *De Approb. Doct. S. Th. disp. 2, a. 2;* ALEXANDER NATALIS, *Hist. Eccl., sæc. XIII et XIV; De Erroribus Joannis de Montesono;* CORNOLDI, *Sent. S. Thomæ de immunitate B. V. a peccati originalis labe* (reprinted in vol. XXV, Parma ed. of St. Thomas's works); ECALLE in *Comp. of* BILLUART, *Sum. Summæ S. Th.,* T. II, pp. 311 sqq. (Paris, 1889); BERTHIER in *Append.* to *L'Etude de la Somme Théol.,* 399 sqq., who cites many authors, not Dominicans, giving interpretations favourable to St. Thomas; SPADA, *Animadversiones in opus Rmi. Malon, de dogmate Imm. Conc.* (Rome, 1862); ROUARD DE CARD, *L'Ordre des Frères Prêcheurs et L'Immaculée Conception* (Brussels, 1864). On the other hand many authors hold either that St. Thomas did not teach the Immaculate Conception or that his opinion is doubtful.

Amongst dogmatico-devotional treatises besides works already cited (above IV) the following may be mentioned: MÉZARD, *Medulla S. Th. Aquin seu meditationes ex operibus S. Th.* (2 vols., Paris, 1907); MONSABRÉ, *Exposition du Dogme Catholique* (Paris, 1873–90); JANVIER, *Exposition de la morale catholique* (8 vols., Paris, 1903–10); SCHWALM, *Le Christ d'après S. Thomas d'Aquin* (Paris, 1910); DE LA BARRE, *La Morale d'après S. Thomas et les théologiens scolastiques* (Paris, 1911); MORGOTT, *Der Spender der. heil. Sacramente nach . . . der heil. Thomas* (Freiburg, 1886); *Mariologie des heil. Thomas v. Aquin* (Freiburg, 1878); ROUSSET-MASSOULIÉ, *Traité de la véritable oraison, d'après les principes de S. Thomas* (Paris, 1911); *D. Th. Aquin. Officium Parvum: Accedunt Ang. Doct. monita et preces* (Paris, 1901) contains St. Thomas's advice to students. On The Angelic Warfare, a confraternity established in honour of St. Thomas's purity and the girdle of purity, see *Acta SS.* VII Mar.; MORTIER, *Hist. des maîtres gén. de l'Ordre des Frères Prêcheurs,* II (Paris, 1905), vi; *The Angelic Guide, by a Dominican Father* (Boston, 1899).

Summaries of St. Thomas's philosophy are given in all *Histories of Philosophy;* also in JOURDAIN, *La Phil. de S. Th. d'Aquin* (2 vols., Paris, 1858); CROLET, *Doct. Philos. de S. Th. d'Aquin, d'après le Dr. Stoeckl* (Paris, 1890); MAUMUS, *St. Thomas et la Philosophie Cartesienne* (2 vols., Paris, 1890); GARDIER, *La Phil. de S. Thomas* (4 vols., Paris, 1892–96); SERTILLANGES, *S. Thomas d'Aquin* (2 vols., Paris, 1910); GONZALEZ, *Phil. elementaria* (3 vols., Madrid, 1868; 7th ed., 1894); *Estudios sobra la Filosofia de S. Tomas* (Manila, 1864; Madrid, 1886); *Estudios religiosos, filosoficos, cientificos y sociales* (Madrid, 1873); ZIGLIARA, *Saggio sui principii del Traditionalismo* (Viterbo, 1865); IDEM, *Propædeutica ad S. Theol.* (Viterbo, 1884); IDEM, *Summa Philosophica* (3 vols., Rome, 1876; 7th ed., Paris, 1889); IDEM, *Osservazioni su alcune interpretazioni di G. C. Ubaghs sull' ideologia di S. Tommaso d'Aquino* (Viterbo, 1870); IDEM, *Della luce intellectuale e dell' Ontologismo secundo la dottrina di S. Bonavent. e Tommaso d'Aquino* (2 vols., Rome, 1874); IDEM, *De ment. Concilii Viennensis in definiendo dogmate unionis animæ humanæ cum corpore* (Rome, 1878); LEPIDI, *Examen phil-theologicum de Ontologismo* (Louvain, 1874); *Opuscules philosophiques,* tr. VIGNON (Paris, 1899); *Elementa philosophiæ christianæ: Logica* (Louvain, 1875); *Ontologia* (Louvain, 1877); *Cosmologia* (Louvain, 1879); FARGES, *Etudes philosophiques pour vulgariser les théories d'Aristote et S. Thomas* (8 vols., Paris, 1887–1902); FEUGERAY, *Essai sur les doctrines politiques de S. Thomas* (Paris, 1857); MURGUE, *Questions d'ontologie: études sur S. Thomas* (Lyons, 1876); ALIBERT, *La psycologie Thomiste et les théories modernes* (Lyons, 1902); O'NEILL, *New Things and Old in S. Thomas Aquinas, Introd.* (London, 1909); WALKER, *Essay on the origin of knowledge According to the Philosophy of St. Thomas* (London, 1858); SCHUMACHER, *The Knowableness of God. Its Relation to the Theory of Knowledge in St. Thomas* (Notre Dame, 1905).

For St. Thomas and Social Doctrines.—SCHWALM, *Leçons de philosophie sociale* (Paris, 1910), gives an excellent bibliography on p. xvii; LEO XIII, *Encyclicals, Æterni Patris; Quod Apostolici muneris; Immortale Dei; Sapientiæ Christianæ; Rerum Novarum; Graves de Communi,* in *The Great Encyclical Letters of Leo XIII* (New York, 1903); SCHAUB, *Die Eigentumslehre nach Thomas von Aquin und den modernen Sozialismus* (Freiburg, 1898); WALTER, *Das Eigenthum nach der Lehre des hl. Thomas von Aquin und des Sozialismus* (Freiburg, 1895); ANTONIADES, *Die Staatslehre des Thomas von Aquin* (Leipzig, 1890); BESONE, *Der Aufsatz, De Regimine Principum, von Thomas von Aquin* (Bonn, 1894); BLISS in *Encyclopedia of Social Reform;* ASHLEY in *Palgrave's Dictionary of Political Economy.*

Periodicals.—Many articles on St. Thomas's doctrine have been published in the following Reviews: *Annales de Philosophie Chrétienne* (Paris, 1831——); *La Civiltà Cattolica* (Florence and Rome, 1850——); *Etudes Religieuses* (Paris, 1856); *Philosophisches Jahrbuch* (Fulda, 1888——); *Sanct Thomas Blätter* (Ratisbon, 1888——); *Revue Thomiste* (Paris, 1893); *Revue Néo-Scolastique* (Louvain, 1894——); *Revue des Sciences Philosophiques et Théologiques* (Kain, 1907——); *Catholic University Bulletin* (Washington, D. C., 1894——); *Cienza Tomista* (Madrid, 1910——).

For additional bibliography see ALBERTUS MAGNUS, BLESSED; PHILOSOPHY; PREACHERS, ORDER OF; NEO-SCHOLASTICISM; THOMISM.

D. J. KENNEDY.

Thomas Becket, SAINT, martyr, Archbishop of Canterbury, b. at London, 21 Dec., 1118(?); d. at Canterbury, 29 Dec., 1170. St. Thomas was born of parents who, coming from Normandy, had settled in England some years previously. No reliance is to be placed upon the legend that his mother was a Saracen. In after life his humble birth was made the subject of spiteful comment, though his parents were not peasants, but people of some mark, and from his earliest years their son had been well taught and had associated with gentlefolk. He learned to read at Merton Abbey and then studied in Paris. On leaving school he employed himself in secretarial work, first with Sir Richer de l'Aigle and then with his kinsman, Osbert Huitdeniers, who was "Justiciar" of London. Somewhere about the year 1141, under circumstances that are variously related, he entered the service of Theobald, Archbishop of Canterbury, and in that household he won his master's favour and eventually became the most trusted of all his clerks. A description embodied in the Icelandic Saga and derived probably from Robert of Cricklade gives a vivid portrait of him at this period. "To look upon he was slim of growth and pale of hue, with dark hair, a long nose, and a straightly featured face. Blithe of countenance was he, winning and loveable in his conversation, frank of speech in his discourses, but slightly stuttering in his talk, so keen of discernment and understanding that he could always make difficult questions plain after a wise manner." Theobald recognized his capacity, made use of him in many delicate negotiations, and, after allowing him to go for a year to study civil and canon law at Bologna and Auxerre, ordained him deacon in 1154, after bestowing upon him several preferments, the most important of which was the Archdeaconry of Canterbury (see Radford, "Thomas of London", p. 53).

It was just at this period that King Stephen died and the young monarch Henry II became unquestioned master of the kingdom. He took "Thomas of London", as Becket was then most commonly called, for his chancellor, and in that office Thomas at the age of thirty-six became, with the possible exception of the justiciar, the most powerful subject in Henry's wide dominions. The chroniclers speak with wonder of the relations which existed between the chancellor and the sovereign, who was twelve years his junior. People declared that "they had but one heart and one mind". Often the king and his minister behaved like two schoolboys at play. But although they hunted or rode at the head of an army together it was no mere comradeship in pastime which united them. Both were hard workers, and both, we may believe, had the prosperity of the kingdom deeply at heart. Whether the chancellor, who was after all the elder man, was the true originator of the administrative reforms which Henry introduced cannot now be clearly determined. In many matters they saw eye to eye. The king's imperial views and love of splendour were quite to the taste of his minister. When Thomas went to France in 1158 to negotiate a marriage treaty, he travelled with such pomp that the people said: "If this be only the chancellor what must be the glory of the king himself?"

In 1153 Thomas acted as justice itinerant in three counties. In 1159 he seems to have been the chief organizer of Henry's expedition to Toulouse, upon which he accompanied him, and though it seems to be untrue that the impost of "scutage" was called into existence for that occasion (Round, "Feudal England", 268–73), still Thomas undoubtedly pressed on the exaction of this money contribution in lieu of military service and enforced it against ecclesiastics in such a way that bitter complaints were made of the disproportionately heavy burden thus imposed upon the Church. In the military operations Thomas took a leading part, and Garnier, a French chronicler, who lived to write of the virtues of St. Thomas and his martyrdom, declares that in these encounters he saw him unhorse many French knights. Deacon though he was, he led the most daring attacks in person, and Edward Grim also gives us to understand that in laying waste the enemy's country with fire and sword the chancellor's principles did not materially differ from those of the other commanders of his time. But although, as men then reported, "he put off the archdeacon", in this and other ways, he was very far from assuming the licentious manners of those around him. No word was ever breathed against his personal purity. Foul conduct or foul speech, lying or unchastity were hateful to him, and on occasion he punished them severely. He seems at all times to have had clear principles with regard to the claims of the Church, and even during this period of his chancellorship he more than once risked Henry's grievous displeasure. For example, he opposed the dispensation which Henry for political reasons extorted from the pope, and strove to prevent the marriage of Mary, Abbess of Romsey, to Matthew of Boulogne. But to the very limits of what his conscience permitted, Thomas identified himself with his master's interests, and Tennyson is true to history when he makes the archbishop say:

I served our Theobald well when I was with him:
I served King Henry well as Chancellor:
I am his no more, and I must serve the Church.

Archbishop Theobald died in 1161, and in the course of the next year Henry seems to have decided that it would be good policy to prepare the way for further schemes of reform by securing the advancement of his chancellor to the primacy. Our authorities are agreed that from the first Thomas drew back in alarm. "I know your plans for the Church", he said, "you will assert claims which I, if I were archbishop, must needs oppose." But Henry would not be gainsaid, and Thomas at the instance of Cardinal Henry of Pisa, who urged it upon him as a service to religion, yielded in spite of his misgivings. He was ordained priest on Saturday in Whitweek and consecrated bishop the next day, Sunday, 3 June, 1162. It seems to have been St. Thomas who obtained for England the privilege of keeping the feast of the Blessed Trinity on that Sunday, the anniversary of his consecration, and more than a century afterwards this custom was adopted by the papal Court itself and eventually imposed upon the whole world.

A great change took place in the saint's way of life after his consecration as archbishop. Even as chancellor he had practised secret austerities, but now in view of the struggle he clearly saw before him he gave himself to fastings and disciplines, hair shirts, protracted vigils, and constant prayers. Before the end of the year 1162 he stripped himself of all signs of the lavish display which he had previously affected. On 10 Aug. he went barefoot to receive the envoy who brought him the pallium from Rome. Contrary to the king's wish he resigned the chancellorship. Whereupon Henry seems to have required him to surrender certain ecclesiastical preferments which he still retained, notably the archdeaconry, and when this was not done at once showed bitter displeasure. Other misunderstandings soon followed. The archbishop, having, as he believed, the king's express permission, set about to reclaim alienated estates belonging to his see, a procedure which again gave offence. Still more serious was the open resistance which he made to the king's proposal that a voluntary offering to the sheriffs should be paid into the royal treasury. As the first recorded instance of any determined opposition to the king's arbitrary will in a matter of taxation, the incident is of much constitutional importance. The saint's protest seems to have been successful, but the relations with the king only grew more strained.

Soon after this the great matter of dispute was reached in the resistance made by Thomas to the king's officials when they attempted to assert jurisdiction over criminous clerks. The question has been dealt with in some detail in the article

ENTRANCE TO THE TRANSEPT OF MARTYRDOM, CANTERBURY

ENGLAND (V, 436). That the saint himself had no wish to be lenient with criminous clerks has been well shown by Norgate (Angevin Kings, ii, 22). It was with him simply a question of principle. St. Thomas seems all along to have suspected Henry of a design to strike at the independence of what the king regarded as a too powerful Church. With this view Henry summoned the bishops at Westminster (1 Oct., 1163) to sanction certain as yet unspecified articles which he called his grandfather's customs (*avitæ consuetudines*), one of the known objects of which was to bring clerics guilty of crimes under the jurisdiction of the secular courts. The other bishops, as the demand was still in the vague, showed a willingness to submit, though with the condition "saving our order", upon which St. Thomas inflexibly insisted. The king's resentment was thereupon manifested by requiring the archbishop to surrender certain castles he had hitherto retained, and by other acts of unfriendliness. In deference to what he believed to be the pope's wish, the archbishop in December consented to make some concessions by giving a personal and private undertaking to the king to obey his customs "loyally and in good faith". But when Henry shortly afterwards at Clarendon (13 Jan., 1164) sought to draw the saint on to a formal and public acceptance of the "Constitutions of Clarendon", under which name the sixteen articles, the *avitæ consuetudines* as finally drafted, have been commonly known, St. Thomas, though at first yielding somewhat to the solicitations of the other bishops, in the end took up an attitude of uncompromising resistance.

Then followed a period of unworthy and vindictive persecution. When opposing a claim made against him by John the Marshal, Thomas upon a frivolous pretext was found guilty of contempt of court. For this he was sentenced to pay £500; other demands for large sums of money followed, and finally, though a complete release of all claims against him as chancellor had been given on his becoming archbishop, he was required to render an account of nearly all the moneys which had passed through his hands in his discharge of the office. Eventually a sum of nearly £30,000 was demanded of him. His fellow bishops, summoned by Henry to a council at Northampton, implored him to throw himself unreservedly upon the king's mercy, but St. Thomas, instead of yielding, solemnly warned them and threatened them. Then, after celebrating Mass, he took his archiepiscopal cross into his own hand and presented himself thus in the royal council chamber. The king demanded that sentence should be passed upon him, but in the confusion and discussion which ensued the saint with uplifted cross made his way out through the mob of angry courtiers. He fled away secretly that night (13 Oct., 1164), sailed in disguise from Sandwich (2 Nov.), and, after being cordially welcomed by Louis VII of France, he threw himself at the feet of Pope Alexander III, then at Sens, on 23 Nov. The pope, who had given a cold reception to certain episcopal envoys sent by Henry, welcomed the saint very kindly, and refused to accept his resignation of his see. On 30 Nov., Thomas went to take up his residence at the Cistercian Abbey of Pontigny in Burgundy, though he was compelled to leave this refuge a year later, as Henry, after confiscating the archbishop's property and banishing all the Becket kinsfolk, threatened to wreak his vengeance on the whole Cistercian Order if they continued to harbour him.

SEAL OF THE SEE OF CANTERBURY
Showing the Martyrdom of St. Thomas

The negotiations between Henry, the pope, and the archbishop dragged on for the next four years without the position being sensibly changed. Although the saint remained firm in his resistance to the principle of the Constitutions of Clarendon, he was willing to make any concessions that could be reasonably asked of him, and on 6 Jan., 1169, when the kings of England and France were in conference at Montmirail, he threw himself at Henry's feet, but as he still refused to accept the obnoxious customs Henry repulsed him. At last in 1170 some sort of reconciliation was patched up. The question of the customs was not mentioned and Henry professed himself willing to be guided by the archbishop's council as to amends due to the See of Canterbury for the recent violation of its rights in the crowning of Henry's son by the Archbishop of York. On 1 Dec., 1170, St. Thomas again landed in England, and was received with every demonstration of popular enthusiasm. But trouble almost immediately occurred in connexion with the absolution of two of the bishops, whose sentence of excommunication St. Thomas had brought with him, as well as over the restoration by the de Broc family of the archbishop's castle at Saltwood. How far Henry was directly responsible for the tragedy which soon after occurred on 29 Dec. is not quite clear. Four knights who came from France demanded the absolution of the bishops. St. Thomas would not comply. They left for a space, but came back at Vesper time with a band of armed men. To their angry question, "Where is the traitor?" the saint boldly replied, "Here I am, no traitor, but archbishop and priest of God." They tried to drag him from the church, but were unable, and in the end they slew him where he stood, scattering his brains on the pavement. His faithful companion, Edward Grim, who bore his cross, was wounded in the struggle.

A tremendous reaction of feeling followed this deed of blood. In an extraordinarily brief space of time devotion to the martyred archbishop had spread all through Europe. The pope promulgated the bull of canonization, little more than two years after the martyrdom, 21 Feb., 1173. On 12 July, 1174, Henry II did public penance, and was scourged at the archbishop's tomb. An immense number of miracles were worked, and for the rest of the Middle Ages the shrine of St. Thomas of Canterbury was one of the wealthiest and most famous in Europe. The martyr's holy remains are believed to have been destroyed in Sept., 1538, when nearly all the other shrines in England were dismantled; but the matter is by no means clear, and, although the weight of learned opinion is adverse, there are still those who believe that a skeleton found in the crypt in January, 1888, is the body of St. Thomas. The story that Henry VIII in 1538 summoned the archbishop to stand his trial for high treason, and that when, in June, 1538, the trial had been held and the accused pronounced contumacious, the body was ordered to be disinterred and burnt, is probably apocryphal.

By far the best English life is MORRIS, *The Life of St. Thomas Becket* (2nd ed., London, 1885); there is a somewhat fuller work of L'HUILLIER, *Saint Thomas de Cantorbéry* (2 vols., Paris, 1891); the volume by DEMIMUID, *St. Thomas Becket* (Paris, 1909), in the series *Les Saints* is not abreast of modern research. There are several excellent lives by Anglicans, of which HUTTON, *Thomas Becket* (London, 1900), and the account by NORGATE in *Dict. Nat. Biog.*, s. v. *Thomas*, known as *Thomas à Becket*, are probably the best. The biography by ROBERTSON, *Becket, Archbishop of Canterbury* (London, 1859), is not sympathetic. Nearly all the sources of the Life, as well as the books of miracles worked at the shrine, have been edited in the *Rolls Series* by ROBERTSON under the title *Materials for the History of Thomas Becket* (7 vols., London, 1875–1883). The valuable Norse saga is edited in the same series by MAGNUSSON, *Thomas Saga Erkibyskups* (2 vols., London, 1884). The chronicle of GARNIER DE PONT S. MAXENCE, *Vie de St. Thomas Martyr*, has been edited by HIPPEAU (Paris, 1859). The miracles have been specially studied from an agnostic standpoint by ABBOT, *Thomas of Canterbury, his death and miracles* (2 vols., London, 1898). Some valuable material has been collected by RADFORD, *Thomas of London before his Consecration* (Cambridge, 1894). On the relics see MORRIS, *Relics of St. Thomas* (London, 1888); THORNTON, *Becket's Bones* (Canterbury, 1900); WARD, *The Canterbury Pilgrimages* (London, 1904); WARNER in *Eng. Hist. Rev.*, VI (1891), 754–56.

HERBERT THURSTON.

Thomas Christians, SAINT, an ancient body of Christians on the east and west coasts of India, claiming spiritual descent from the Apostle St. Thomas. The subject will be treated under the following heads, viz.:—I. Their early traditions and their connexion with the Apostle St. Thomas; II. The Apostle's tomb at Mylapur; III. This upheld by the Edessan Church; IV. For their earliest period they possess no written but a traditional history; V. Record of these traditions embodied in a MS. Statement dated 1604; VI. The Syrian merchant Thomas Cana arrives in Malabar, an important event in their history and the social benefits therefrom; VII. The arrival also of two pious brothers, church-builders; VIII. Ancient stone crosses and their inscriptions; IX. Their early prelates; X. Were these Christians infected with Nestorianism before 1599? XI. Medieval travellers on the Thomas Christians; XII. Their two last Syrian bishops; XIII. Archbishop Menezes and the Synod of Diamper; XIV. Their first three Jesuit bishops; XV. The Carmelite Period; XVI. Two Latin Vicars Apostolic; XVII. Divided into three vicariates with native bishops.

I. Interest in the history of these Christians arises from more than one feature. Their ancient descent at once attracts attention. Theophilus (surnamed the Indian), an Arian, sent by Emperor Constantius (about 354) on a mission to Arabia Felix and Abyssinia, is one of the earliest, if not the first, who draws our attention to them. He had been sent when very young a hostage *a Divæis*, by the inhabitants of the Maldives, to the Romans in the reign of Constantine the Great. His travels are recorded by Philostorgius, an Arian Greek Church historian, who relates that Theophilus, after fulfilling his mission to the Homerites, sailed to his island home. Thence he visited other parts of India, reforming many things—for the Christians of the place heard the reading of the Gospel in a sitting, etc. This reference to a body of Christians with church, priest, and liturgy, in the immediate vicinity of the Maldives, can only apply to a Christian Church and faithful on the adjacent coast of India, and not to Ceylon, which was well known even then under its own designation, Taprobane. The people referred to were then Christians known as a body who had their liturgy in the Syriac language and inhabited the west coast of India, i. e. Malabar. This Church is next mentioned and located by Cosmas Indicopleustes (about 535) "in Male [Malabar] where the pepper grows"; and he adds that the Christians of Ceylon, whom he specifies as Persians, and "those of Malabar" (the latter he leaves unspecified, so they must have been natives of the country) had a bishop residing at Caliana (Kalyan), ordained in Persia, and one likewise on the Island of Socotra.

II. St. Gregory of Tours (Glor. Mart.), before 590, reports that Theodore, a pilgrim who had gone to Gaul, told him that in that part of India where the *corpus* (bones) of Thomas the Apostle had first rested (Mylapur on the east or Coromandel Coast of India) there stood a monastery and a church of striking dimensions and elaborately adorned, adding: "After a long interval of time these remains had been removed thence to the city of Edessa." The location of the first tomb of the Apostle in India is proof both of his martyrdom and of his Apostolate in India. The evidence of Theodore is that of an eye-witness who had visited both tombs—the first in India, while the second was at Edessa. The primitive Christians, therefore, found on both coasts, east and west, witness to and locate the tomb at Mylapur, "St. Thomas", a little to the south of Madras; no other place in India lays any claim to possess the tomb, nor does any other country. On these facts is based their claim to be known as St. Thomas Christians.

III. Further proof may be adduced to justify this claim. A Syrian ecclesiastical calendar of an early date confirms the above. In the quotation given below two points are to be noted which support its antiquity—the fact of the name given to Edessa and the fact that the memory of the translation of the Apostle's relics was so fresh to the writer that the name of the individual who had brought them was yet remembered. The entry reads: "3 July, St. Thomas who was pierced with a lance in India. His body is at Urhai [the ancient name of Edessa] having been brought there by the merchant Khabin. A great festival." It is only natural to expect that we should receive from Edessa first-hand evidence of the removal of the relics to that city; and we are not disappointed, for St. Ephraem, the great doctor of the Syrian Church, has left us ample details in his writings. Ephraem came to Edessa on the surrender of Nisibis to the Persians, and he lived there from 363 to 373, when he died. This proof is found mostly in his rhythmical compositions. In the forty-second of his "Carmina Nisibina" (Leipzig, 1866) he tells us that the Apostle was put to death in India, and that his remains were subsequently buried at Edessa, brought there by a merchant—but his name is never given; apparently at that date the name had dropped out of popular memory. The same is repeated in varying form in several of his hymns edited by Lamy (Ephr. Hymni et Sermones, IV). "It was to a land of dark people he was sent, to clothe them by Baptism in white robes. His grateful dawn dispelled India's painful darkness. It was his mission to espouse India to the One-Begotten. The merchant is blessed for having brought so great a treasure. Edessa thus became the blessed city by possessing the greatest pearl India could yield. Thomas works miracles in India, and at Edessa Thomas is destined to baptize peoples perverse and steeped in darkness, and that in the land of India."

For fuller proof of the Apostleship of St. Thomas the reader is referred to the work of the present writer "India and the Apostle Saint Thomas" (London, 1905). This short excursus was necessary to establish the claim of the Christians on the coast and especially that of the Malabar Syrian Church to be the daughter of the Apostle St. Thomas.

IV. These Christians have no written records of the incidents of their social life from the time of their first conversion down to the arrival of the Portuguese on the coast, just as India had no history until the arrival of the Mohammedans.

V. Fortunately the British Museum has a large collection consisting of several folio volumes containing MSS. letters, reports, etc., of Jesuit missions in India and elsewhere; among these in addl. vol. 9853, beginning with the leaf 86 in pencil and 525 in ink, there is a "Report" on the "Serra" (the name by which the Portuguese designated Malabar), written in Portuguese by a Jesuit missionary, bearing the date 1604 but not signed by the writer; there is evidence that this "Report" was known to F. de Souza, author of the "Oriente Conquistado", and utilized by him. The writer has carefully put together the traditional record of these Christians; the document is yet unpublished, hence its importance. Extracts from the same, covering what can be said of the early part of this history, will offer the best guarantee that can be offered. The writer of the "Report" distinctly informs us that these Christians had no written records of ancient history, but relied entirely on traditions handed down by their elders, and to these they were most tenaciously attached.

Of their earliest period tradition records that after the death of the Apostle his disciples remained faithful for a long time, the Faith was propagated with great zeal, and the Church increased considerably. But later, wars and famine supervening, the St. Thomas Christians of Mylapur got scattered and sought refuge elsewhere, and many of them returned to paganism. The Christians, however, who were on the Cochin side, fared better than the former, spreading from Coulac (Quilon) to Palur (Paleur), a village in the north of Malabar. These had fared better, as they lived under native princes who rarely interfered with their Faith, and they probably never suffered real persecution such as befell their brethren on the other coast; besides, one of the paramount rajahs of Malabar, Cheruman Perumal, had conferred on them a civil status. The common tradition in the country holds that from the time of the Apostle seven churches were erected in different parts of the country, besides the one which the Apostle himself had erected at Mylapur. This tradition is most tenaciously held and is confirmed by the "Report". It further asserts that the Apostle Thomas, after preaching to the inhabitants of the Island of Socotra and establishing there a Christian community, had come over to Malabar and landed at the ancient port of Cranganore. They hold that after preaching in Malabar the Apostle went over to Mylapur on the Coromandel Coast; this is practicable through any of the many paths across the dividing mountain ranges which were well known and much frequented in olden times. The Socotrians had yet retained their Faith when in 1542 St. Francis Xavier visited them on his way to India. In a letter of 18 Sept. of the same year, addressed to the Society at Rome, he has left an interesting account of the degenerate state of the Christians he found there, who were Nestorians. He also tells us they render special honours to the Apostle St. Thomas, claiming to be descendants of the Christians begotten to Jesus Christ by that Apostle. By 1680 when the Carmelite Vincenzo Maria di Santa Catarina landed there he found Christianity quite extinct, only faint traces yet lingering. The extinction of this primitive Christianity is due to the oppression of the Arabs, who now form the main population of the island, and to the scandalous neglect of the Nestorian Patriarchs who in former times were wont to supply the bishop and clergy for the island. When St. Francis visited the island a Nestorian priest was still in charge.

VI. There is one incident of the long period of isolation of the St. Thomas Christians from the rest of the Christian world which they are never tired of relating, and it is one of considerable importance to them for the civil status it conferred and secured to them in the country. This is the narrative of the arrival of a Syrian merchant on their shores, a certain Mar Thoma Cana—the Portuguese have named him Cananeo and styled him an Armenian, which he was not. He arrived by ship on the coast and entered the port of Cranganore. The King of Malabar, Cheruman Perumal, was in the vicinity, and receiving information of his arrival sent for him and admitted him to his presence. Thomas was a wealthy merchant who had probably come to trade; the king took a liking to the man, and when he expressed a wish to acquire land and make a settlement the king readily acceded to his request and let him purchase land, then unoccupied, at Cranganore. Under the king's orders Thomas soon collected a number of Christians from the surrounding country, which enabled him to start a town on the ground marked out for his occupation. He is said to have collected seventy-two Christian families (this is the traditional number always mentioned), and to have installed them in as many separate houses erected for them; attached to each dwelling was a sufficient piece of land for vegetable cultivation for the support of the family as is the custom of the country. He also erected a dwelling for himself and eventually a church. The authorization to possess the land and dwellings erected was granted to Thomas by a deed of the paramount Lord and Rajah of Malabar, Cheruman Perumal, said to have been the last of the line, the country having been subsequently divided among his feudatories. (The details given above as well as what follows of the copper plate grant are taken from the "Report".) The same records also speak of several privileges and honours by the king to Thomas himself, his descendants, and to the Thomas Christians, by which the latter community obtained rank and a social status above the lower classes, and which made them equal to the Nayars, the middle class in the country.

The deed read as follows:—"May Cocurangon [personal name of the king] be prosperous, enjoy a long life and live 100,000 years, divine servant of the gods, strong, true, just, full of good deeds, reasonable, powerful over the whole earth, happy, conquering, glorious, rightly prosperous in the service of the gods, in Malabar, in the city of the Mahadeva [the great idol of the temple in the vicinity of Cranganore] reigning in the year of Mercury on the seventh day [Portuguese text: elle no tepo de Mercurio de feu to no dia, etc.] of the month of March before the full moon the same king Cocurangon being in Carnallur there landed Thomas Cana, a chief man who arrived in a ship wishing to see the farthest parts of the East. And some men seeing how he arrived informed the king. The king himself came and saw and sent for the chief man Thomas, and he disembarked and came before the king, who spoke graciously to him. To honour him he gave him his name, styling him Cocurangon Cana, and he went to rest in his place, and the king gave him the city of Mogoderpatanam (Cranganore) for ever. And the same king being in his great prosperity went one day to hunt in the forest, and he hastily sent for Thomas, who came and stood before the king in a propitious hour, and the king consulted the astrologer. And afterwards the king spoke to Thomas that he should build a town in that forest, and he made reverence and answered the king: 'I require this forest for myself', and the king granted it to him for ever. And forthwith another day he cleared the forest and he cast his eyes upon it in the same year on the eleventh of April, and in a propitious time gave it to Thomas for a heritage in the name of the king, who laid the first stone of the church and of the house of Thomas Cana, and he built there a town for all, and he entered the church and prayed there on the same day. After these things Thomas himself went to the feet of the king and offered his gifts, and after this he asked the king to give that land to him and his descendants: and he measured out two hundred and sixty-four elephant cubits and gave them to Thomas and his descendants for ever, and jointly sixty-two houses which immediately were erected there, and gardens with their enclosures and paths and boundaries and inner yards. And he granted him seven kinds of musical instruments and all honours and the right of travelling in a palanquin, and he conferred on him dignity and the privilege of spreading carpets on the ground and the use of sandals, and to erect a pavilion at his gate and ride on elephants, and also granted five taxes to Thomas and his companions, both men and women, for all his relations and to the followers of his law for ever.

The said king gave his name and these princes witnessed it. . . ."

Then follow the names of eight witnesses, and a note is added by the Portuguese translator that this is the document by which the Emperor of all Malabar gave the land of Cranganore to Thomas Cana and also to the Christians of St. Thomas. This document, transcribed from the MS. "Report", has been carefully translated into English, as it forms the "Great Charter" of the St. Thomas Christians. The "Report" adds: "and because at that time they reckoned the era in cycles of twelve years according to the course, therefore they say in the Olla [Malayalam term for a document written on palm leaf] that the said settlement was founded in the year of Mercury . . . that mode of reckoning is totally forgotten, because for the last seven hundred and seventy-nine years in all this Malabar time has been reckoned by the Quilon era. However, since the said Perumal, as we have said above, died more than a thousand and two hundred years, it follows: that the same number of years have elapsed since the Church and Christians were established at Cranganore." The writer of the "Report" had previously stated "it is one thousand and two hundred and fifty and eight years since Perumal died on the first of March". Deducting the date of the "Report" this would give A. D. 346 for his death. Diego de Couto (Decada XII), quoting the above grant in full, says that the Syrian Christians fix A. D. 811 as corresponding to the date borne on the grant; the first is far too early, and the second is an approximately probable date. The "Report" informs us that the copper plates on which this deed or grant was inscribed were taken away to Portugal by Franciscan Fathers, who left behind a translation of the same. It is known that the Syrian Bishop of Malabar, Mar Jacob, had deposited with the Factor of Cochin all the Syrian copper grants for safe custody; providing however that when necessary access could be had to the same. Gouvea at p. 4 of his "Jornada" says that after having remained there for some long time they could not be found and were lost through some carelessness; de Couto asserts the same in the passage quoted above and also elsewhere. In 1806 at the suggestion of Rev. Claude Buchanan, Colonel Macaulay, the British resident, ordered a careful search for them and they turned up in the record room of Cochin town. The tables then found contained (1) the grant to Irani Corttton of Cranganore, and (2) the set of plates of the grant to Maruvan Sopir Iso of Quilon, but those of the grant to Thomas Cana were not among them; had they not been removed they would have been found with the other plates; this confirms the statement of the writer of the "Report" that they had been taken to Portugal. From what is stated in the royal deed to Thomas Cana it may be taken for granted that the latter brought with him a small colony of Syrians from Mesopotamia, for the privileges conceded include his companions, both men and women, and all his relations.

VII. Besides the arrival of Thomas Cana and his colony, by which the early Christians benefited considerably, the "Report" also records the arrival on this coast of two individuals named Soper Iso and Prodho; they are said to have been brothers and are supposed to have been Syrians. The "Report" gives the following details: they came to possess a promontory opposite Paliport on the north side, which is called Maliankara, and they entered the port with a large load of timber to build a church; and in the Chaldean books of this Serra there is no mention of them, except that they were brothers, came to Quilon, built a church there, and worked some miracles. After death they were buried in the church they had erected; it is said that they built other smaller churches in the country; they were regarded as pious men and were later called saints, their own church was eventually dedicated to them as well as others in the country. Archbishop Alexis Menezes afterwards changed the dedication of these churches to other saints in the Roman Calendar. There is one important item that the "Report" has preserved: "the said brothers built the church of Quilon in the hundredth year after the foundation of Quilon." (This era commences from 25 August, A. D. 825, and the date will thus be A. D. 925). The second of the aforesaid copper-plates mentions Meruvan Sober Iso, one of the above two brothers. The "Report" also makes mention of pilgrims coming from Mesopotamia to visit the shrine of the Apostle at Mylapur; some of these at times would settle there and others in Malabar. It may be stated here that the Syrians of Malabar are as a body natives of the land by descent, and the Syriac trait in them is that of their liturgy, which is in the Syriac language. They call themselves Syrians by way of distinction from the other body of Christians on the coast, who belong to the Latin Rite. The honorific appellation bestowed upon them by the rulers of the country is that of *Mapla*, which signifies great son or child, and they are commonly so called by the people; this appellation had also been given to the descendants of Arabs in the country; the St. Thomas Christians now prefer to be called *Nasrani* (Nazarenes), the designation given by the Mohammedans to all Christians.

VIII. There are certain stone crosses of ancient date in southern India, bearing inscriptions in Pahlavi letters. Extraordinary legends have been spread about them in some parts of Europe; the present writer was shown an engraving purporting to reproduce one of them, with a legend of the Apostolate and martyrdom of St. Thomas, a reproduction of the inscription on his cross. This was attached to the calendar of one of the dioceses of France, and this writer was asked if it were authentic.

To prevent the spreading of such reports it may be useful to state here that of these crosses one is in the Church of Mount St. Thomas, Mylapur, discovered in 1547 after the arrival of the Portuguese in India; the other is in the church of Kottayam, Malabar. Both are of Nestorian origin, are engraved as a bas-relief on a flat stone with ornamental decorations around the cross, and bear an inscription. The inscription has been variously read. Dr. Burnell, an Indian antiquary, says that both crosses bear the same inscription, and offer the following reading: "In punishment by the cross was the suffering of this one. Who is the true Christ, God above and Guide ever pure." These crosses bear some resemblance to the Syro-Chinese Nestorian monument discovered in 1625 at Singan-fu, an ancient capital of China, but erected in 781, and commemorating the arrival in China of Chaldean Nestorian missionaries in 636.

IX. Of the prelates who governed the Church in India after the Apostle's death very little is known; that little is collected and reproduced here. John the Persian, who was present at the Council of Nice (325), is the first known to history claiming the title. In his signature to the decrees of the council he styles himself; John the Persian [presiding] over the churches in all Persia and Great India. The designation implies that he was the [primate] Metropolitan of Persia and also the Bishop of Great India. As metropolitan and chief bishop of the East he may have represented at the council the Catholics of Seleucia. His control of the Church in India could only have been exercised by his sending priests under his jurisdiction to minister to those Christians. It is not known at what date India first commenced to have resident bishops; but between the years 530–35 Cosmas Indicopleustes in his "Topographia" informs us of the presence of a bishop residing at Caliana, the modern Kalyan at a short distance from Bombay. That residence was, in all probability, chosen because it was then the chief port of commerce on the west coast of India, and had easy access and communication with Persia. We know later of a contention which took place between Jesuab of Adiabene the Nestorian Patriarch and Simeon of Ravardshir, the Metropolitan of Persia, who had left India unprovided with bishops for a long period. The patriarch reproached him severely for this gross neglect. We may take it that up to the period 650–60 the bishops sent to India, as Cosmas has said, were consecrated in Persia, but after this gross neglect the patriarch reserved to himself the choice and consecration of the prelates he sent out to India, and this practice was continued till the arrival of the Portuguese on the coast in 1504.

Le Quien places the two brothers Soper Iso and Prodho on the list of bishops of India, but Indian tradition gives it no support, and in this the British Museum MS. Report and Gouvea (Jornada, p. 5) concur. The brothers were known as church-builders, and were reputed to be holy men. Moreover, to include Thomas Cana in the list of bishops is preposterous on the face of the evidence of the copper-plate grant. The "Report" mentions a long period when there was neither bishop nor priest surviving in the land, for they had all died out; the only clerical survival was a deacon far advanced in age. The ignorant Christians, finding themselves without prelates, made him say Mass and even ordain others, but as soon as prelates came from Babylon they put a stop to this disorder. The next authentic information we have on this head comes from the Vatican Library and has been published by Assemani (Bibl. Or., III, 589). It consists of a statement concerning two Nestorian bishops and their companions and a letter from the former written in Syriac to the patriarch announcing their arrival, dated 1504; there is a translation in Latin added to the documents. In 1490 the Christians of Malabar despatched three messengers to ask the Nestorian Patriarch to send out bishops; one died on the journey, the other two presented themselves before the patriarch and delivered their message; two monks were selected and the Patriarch consecrated them bishops, assigning to one the name of Thomas and to the other that of John. The two bishops started on their journey to India accompanied by the two messengers. On arrival they were received with great joy by the people, and the bishops commenced consecrating altars and ordaining a large number of priests "as they had been for a long time deprived of bishops". One of them, John, remained in India, while the other, Thomas, accompanied by Joseph, one of the two messengers, returned to Mesopotamia, taking with them the offerings collected for the patriarch. Joseph returned to India in 1493, but Thomas remained in Mesopotamia.

After about ten years, when the next patriarch ordained three other bishops for India, Thomas went back with them. These new bishops were also chosen from the monks, one was named Jaballa (he was the metropolitan), the second was named Denha, and the third Jacob. These four bishops took ship from Ormus and landed at Kananur; they found there some twenty Portuguese who had recently arrived and presented themselves to them, said they were Christians, explained their condition and rank, and were kindly treated. Of this large number of bishops only one remained to work, and this was Mar Jacob; the other three, including the metropolitan, after a short time returned to their country. Gouvea adds that they were either dissatisfied with their charge or did not like the country. The Portuguese writers mention only two bishops as residents, John who had come before their arrival in India and Mar Jacob. Nothing further is known of John, but Jacob lived in the country till his death. St. Francis Xavier makes a very pretty *elogium* of him in a letter written to King John III of Portugal on 26 Jan., 1549. "Mar Jacob [or Jacome Abuna, as St. Francis styles him] for forty-five years has served God and your Highness in these parts, a very old, a virtuous, and a holy man, and at the same time unnoticed by your Highness and by almost all in India. God rewards him . . . He is noticed only by the Fathers of St. Francis, and they take so good care of him that nothing more is wanted. . . . He has laboured much among the Christians of St. Thomas, and now in his old age he is very obedient to the customs of the Holy Mother Church of Rome." This *elogium* of St. Francis sums up his career for the forty-five years he worked in Malabar (1504–49). He came out as a Nestorian, remained such during his early years, but gradually as he came in touch with the Catholic missionaries he allowed them to preach in his churches and to instruct his people; in his old age he left Cranganore and went to live in the Franciscan convent at Cochin and there he died in 1549. There remain two others—the last of the Mesopotamian prelates who presided over these Christians— Mar Joseph and Mar Abraham; their career will be detailed further on.

X. When Cosmas gave us the information of the existence of a Christian community in "Male (Malabar) where the pepper is grown" he also supplied us with additional details: that they have a bishop residing at Kalyan; that in Taprobane [Ceylon] "an island of interior India where the Indian Ocean is s tuated" there is a "Christian Church with clergy and the faithful; similarly in the island of Dioscordis [Socotra] in the same Indian Ocean". Then he enumerates the churches in Arabia Felix, Bactria, and among the Huns; and all these churches are by him represented to be controlled by the Metropolitan of Persia. Now at that time the holder of this dignity was Patrick, the tutor, as Assemani designates him, of Thomas of Edessa, a prominent Nestorian to which sect Cosmas also belonged; hence his interest in supplying all these details. The bishop and clergy whom the Metropolitan, Patrick, would send out to all the above-mentioned places and churches would and must have been undoubtedly infected with one and the same heresy. Hence it is quite safe to conclude that at the time of the visit of Cosmas to India (A. D. 530–35) all these churches, as also the Church in India, were holding the Nestorian doctrine of their bishops and priests. Nor should this historical fact cause surprise when we take into consideration the opportunities, the bold attitude and violent measures adopted by the promoters of this heresy after expulsion from the Roman Empire. When the Emperor Zeno ordered Cyrus, Bishop of Edessa, to purge his diocese of that heresy (A. D. 489), the Nestorians were forced to seek refuge across the Roman boundary into Persia. Among them were the banished professors and students of the Persian School of Edessa, the centre of the Nestorian error, and they found refuge and protection with Barsumas, Metropolitan of Nisibis, himself a fanatical adherent of Nestorius. Barsumas at this time also held from the Persian king the office of governor of the frontier.

With the influence Barsumas possessed at court it was an easy thing for him to make the king, already so disposed, believe that the actual bishops holding sees in his territory were friendly to his enemies, the Romans, and that it would be better to replace them by men he knew who would owe allegiance only to the Persian monarch. This stratagem rapidly succeeded in capturing most of those sees; and the movement became so strong that although Barsumas predeceased Acka (Acacius), the occupant of the chief see of Seleucia, a Catholic, yet a Nestorian was selected to succeed the latter (A. D. 496). Thus within the short space of seven years the banished heresy sat mistress on the throne of Seleucia, in a position to force every existing see eastward of the Roman Empire to embrace the heresy and to secure its permanence. Thus the Indian Church suffered the same fate which befell the Churches of Persia, and by 530–35 we find that she has a Nestorian prelate consecrated in Persia and presiding at Kalyan over her future destiny. If further proof is wanted to uphold the above finding, we offer the following historical facts of the control exercised by the Nestorian Patriarch. In 650–60, as above stated, Jesuab of Adiabene claimed authority over India and reproached Simeon of Revardshir, the Metropolitan of Persia, for not having sent bishops to India and so deprived that Church of the succession of her ministry. In 714–28 Saliba Zacha, another Nestorian Patriarch, raised the see of India to metropolitan rank. Again in 857 Theodosius, another Nestorian Patriarch, included the See of India among the exempted which, owing to distance from the patriarchal see, should in future send letters of communion but once in six years. This ruling was subsequently incorporated in a synodal canon.

If we look to the general tradition of the St. Thomas Christians it will be found that all their prelates came from Babylon, the ancient residence as they say, of the Patriarch or Catholicos of the East. It is further known and acknowledged by them that whenever they remained deprived of a bishop for a long time they used to send messengers to that Patriarchate asking that bishops be sent out to them. Sufficient proof of this practice has been given above when discussing the arrival of four bishops in 1504. The Holy See was fully aware that the Malabar Christians were under the control of the Nestorian Patriarch. When Julius III gave Sulaka his Bull of nomination as the Catholic Chaldean patriarch, he distinctly laid down the same extent of jurisdiction which had been claimed and controlled by his late Nestorian predecessor; hence in the last clause it is distinctly laid down: "In Sin Massin et Calicuth et tota India." It becomes necessary to fix this historical truth clearly, because during this decade some of the younger generation in Malabar have begun to deny this historical fact. They would wish people to believe that all the Portuguese missionaries, bishops, priests, and writers were completely mistaken when they styled them Nestorians in belief, and because of this false report all subsequent writers continued to call them Nestorians. The reader who has gone through the statement of facts above related must be conscious that such an attempt at distorting or boldly denying public facts is utterly hopeless. They maintain, in support of their false view, that there always had been a small body among the Chaldeans in Mesopotamia who remained attached to the true Faith, and from them they received their bishops. This plea is historically false for the bishops they received all came to them from the Nestorians, and as to the hypothesis of the existence during all these centuries back of a Catholic party among the Nestorian Chaldeans, it is too absurd to be discussed. It was only after the conversion of Sulaka in 1552 that the Chaldeans in part returned to the unity of faith. The truth is that the Malabar Church remained from A. D. 496 up till then in heresy.

XI. During the centuries that these Christians were isolated from the rest of Christendom their sole intercourse was limited to Mesopotamia whence the Nestorian Patriarch would from time to time supply them with prelates. But from the close of the thirteenth century Western travellers, chiefly missionaries sent out by the popes, sent to the West occasional news of their existence. Some of these it will be useful to reproduce here. The first who informed the world of the existence of these St. Thomas Christians was Friar John of Monte Corvino. After he had spent several years as a missionary in Persia and adjoining countries, he proceeded to China, passing through the Indian ports between the years 1292 and 1294. He tells us in a letter written from Cambales (Peking) in 1305 that he had remained thirteen months in that part of India where the Church of St. Thomas the Apostle stood (Mylapore); he also baptized in different places about one hundred persons. In the same letter he says that there were in Malabar a few Christians and Jews, but they were of little worth; he also says that "the inhabitants persecute much the Christians" (Yule, "Cathay and the Way Thither", I).

The next visitor is Marco Polo, who on his return from China (c. 1293) touched the India of St. Thomas. Of his tomb he tells us: "The body of Messer Saint Thomas the Apostle lies in the province of Malabar, at a certain little town having no great population; 'tis a place where few traders go . . . Both Christians and Saracens however greatly frequent it in pilgrimage, for the Saracens also hold the Saint in great reverence. . . . The Christians who go in pilgrimage take of the earth from the place where the Saint was killed and give a portion thereof to any who is sick, and by the power of God and of St. Thomas the sick man is incontinently cured. . . . The Christians", he resumes later, "who have charge of the church have a great number of Indian nut trees [cocoanuts], and thereby get their living" (Marco Polo, Yule's, 2nd edit., II, 338). Friar Jordan, a Dominican, came to India as a missionary in 1321; he then had as companions four Franciscan friars, but on approaching India he had parted from them to make diversion; in the meanwhile the vessel conveying the others was by stress of weather compelled to enter Tana, a port on the west coast, where the Khasi of the place put them to death as they would not embrace Mohammedanism; the feast of Blessed Thomas of Tolentino and his companions is fixed on 6 April in the "Martyrologium Romanum". Later Jordanus, hearing what had happened, rescued their bodies and gave them burial. He must then have gone back to Europe, for he is next heard of in France in 1330, when Pope John XXII consecrated him at Avignon Bishop of Quilon. He left for the East the same year with two letters from the pope, one to the chief of the Christians of Quilon and the other to the Christians at Molephatam, a town on the Gulf of Manaar. In the first the pope beseeches "that divisions cease and clouds of error stain not the brightness of faith of all generated by the waters of baptism . . . and that the phantom of schism and wilful blindness of unsullied faith darken not the vision of those who believe in Christ and adore His name".

Much the same in other words is repeated in the second letter, and they are urged to unity with the Holy Catholic Roman Church. The pope recommends the bishop to the kindness of the people, and thanks them for that shown to the friars who are working among them. All we know is that Bishop Jordanus was sent out with these letters, but nothing further is heard of him. He wrote a small book named "Mirabilia", edited by Col. A. Yule for the Hakluyt Society, published in 1863 (see also "Cathay", I, 184). The next visitor is Blessed Oderic of Pordenone, who about 1324–25 landed at Tana, recovered the bodies of the four friars, Thomas and his companions who had there suffered martyrdom, and conveyed them to China. On his way he halted at Quilon, which he calls *Palumbum;* thence he took passage on a Chinese junk for a certain city called Zayton in China. He mentions the Christians at Quilon, and that at Mylapore there were fourteen houses of Nestorians ("Cathay", I, 57). A few years later Giovanni de Marignolli, the papal delegate to China, arrived at Quilon. He stayed there at a church dedicated to St. George, belonging to the Latin Rite, and he adorned it with fine paintings and taught there the Holy Law. After dwelling there for upwards of a year he sailed to visit the shrine of the Apostle; he calls the town *Mirapolis.* After describing the culture of pepper on the coast he adds: "the pepper does not grow in forests but in gardens prepared for the purpose; nor are the Saracens the proprietors, but the Christians of St. Thomas, and these are the masters of the public weighing-office" [customs' office]. Before quitting Quilon he erected a monument to commemorate his visit, and this was a marble pillar with a stone cross on it, intended to last, as he says, till the world's end. "It had the pope's arms", he says, "and my own engraved on it, with an inscription both in Indian and Latin characters. I consecrated and blessed it in the presence of an infinite multitude of people." The monument stood there till late in the nineteenth century, when by the gradual erosion of the coast it fell into the sea and disappeared. He concludes his narrative by saying that after staying a year and four months he took leave of the brethren, i. e. the missionaries who were working in that field.

XII. The two last Syrian bishops were Mar Joseph Sulaka and Mar Abraham; both arrived in Malabar after the arrival of the Portuguese. Their case presents two questions for discussion; were they canonically appointed, and had they completely rejected Nestorianism? As to the first there is no doubt that his appointment was canonical, for he, the brother of the first Chaldean patriarch, was appointed by his successor Abed Jesu and sent out to Malabar, and both the above patriarchs had their jurisdiction over the Church in Malabar confirmed by the Holy See. Mar Joseph was sent to India with letters of introduction from the pope to the Portuguese authorities; he was besides accompanied by Bishop Ambrose, a Dominican and papal commissary to the first patriarch, by his *socius* Father Anthony, and by Mar Elias Hormaz, Archbishop of Diarbekir. They arrived at Goa about 1563, and were detained at Goa for eighteen months before being allowed to enter the diocese. Proceeding to Cochin they lost Bishop Ambrose; the others travelled through Malabar for two and a half years on foot, visiting every church and detached settlement. By the time they arrived at Angamale war broke out. Then Mar Elias, Anthony the *socius* of the deceased prelate, and one of the two Syrian monks who had accompanied them, left India to return; the other monk remained with Archbishop Joseph Sulaka. For some time the new prelate got on well with the Portuguese and the Jesuit missionaries, in fact, they praised him for having introduced order, decorum, and propriety in the Church services and all went harmoniously for some time. Later, friction arose because of his hindering the locally-ordained Syrians from saying Mass and preaching and instructing his flock. Eventually an incident revealed that Mar Joseph had not dropped his Nestorian errors, for it was reported to the Bishop of Cochin that he had attempted to tamper with the faith of some young boys in his service belonging to the Diocese of Cochin. This came to the knowledge of the bishop, through him to the Metropolitan of Goa, and thence to the viceroy; it was decided to remove and send him to Portugal, to be dealt with by the Holy See.

The following is the nature of the incident. Taking these youths apart, he instructed them that they should venerate the Blessed Virgin as the refuge of sinners, but were not to call her the Mother of God, as that was not true; but she should be styled Mother of Christ (Nestorius, refusing at the Council of Ephesus the term *Theotokos* proposed by the council, substituted that of *Christokos*, which the Fathers refused to accept because under this designation he could cloak his error of two persons in Christ). Mar Joseph was sent to Portugal; arriving there he succeeded in securing the good-will of the queen, then regent for her young son; he abjured his error before Cardinal Henry, expressed repentance, and by order of the queen was sent back to his diocese. Gouvea tells us that as he continued to propagate his errors on his return he was again deported and Cardinal Henry reported his case to St. Pius V. The pope sent a Brief to Jorge, Archbishop of Goa, dated 15 Jan., 1567, ordering him to make enquiries into the conduct and doctrine of the prelate; in consequence of this the first provincial council was held; the charges against Mar Joseph were found to be true and he was sent to Portugal in 1568, thence to Rome, where he died shortly after his arrival.

While the former was leaving India there arrived from Mesopotamia an impostor named Abraham, sent by Simeon the Nestorian Patriarch. He succeeded in entering Malabar undetected. At the appearance of another Chaldean who proclaimed himself a bishop the people were greatly delighted and received him with applause; he set about at once acting as bishop, holding episcopal functions, and conferring Holy orders and quietly established himself in the diocese (Gouvea, p. 7, col. 2). Later the Portuguese captured him and sent him to Portugal, but *en route* he escaped at Mozambique, found his way back to Mesopotamia, and went straight to Mar Abed Jesu, the Chaldean Patriarch, having realized from his Indian experience that unless he secured a nomination from him it would be difficult to establish himself in Malabar. He succeeded admirably in his devices, obtained nomination, consecration, and a letter to the pope from the patriarch. With this he proceeded to Rome, and while there at an audience with the pope he disclosed his true position (Du Jarric, "Rer. Ind. Thesaur.", tom. III, lib. II, p. 69). He avowed to the pope with his own lips that he had received Holy orders invalidly. The pope ordered the Bishop of San Severino to give him orders from tonsure to the priesthood, and a Brief was sent to the Patriarch of Venice to consecrate Abraham a bishop. The facts were attested, both as to the lesser orders and the episcopal consecration, by the original letters which were found in the archives of the Church of Angamale where he resided and where he had died.

Pope Pius IV used great tact in handling this case. Abed Jesu must have taken Abraham to be a priest; he is supposed to have abjured Nestorianism, and professed the Catholic faith, and conferred on him episcopal consecration; the pope had to consider the position in which the patriarch had been placed by his consecration and nomination of the man: the defects were supplied, and Abraham succeeded also in obtaining his nomination and creation as Archbishop Angamale from the pope, with letters to the Archbishop of Goa, and to the Bishop of Cochin dated 27 Feb., 1565. Such was the success of this daring man. On arrival at Goa he was detained in a convent, but again escaped and entered Malabar. His arrival was a surprise and a joy to the people. He kept out of the reach of the Portuguese, living among the churches in the hilly parts of the country. As time passed on he was left in peaceful occupation. As is usual in such cases the old tendencies assumed once more their ascendency, and he returned to his Nestorian teaching and practices. Complaints were made; Rome sent warnings to Abraham to allow Catholic doctrine to be preached and taught to his people. At one time he took the warning seriously to heart. In 1583 Father Valignano, then Superior of the Jesuit Missions, devised a means of forcing a reform. He persuaded Mar Abraham to assemble a synod, and to convene the clergy and the chiefs of the laity. He also prepared a profession of faith which was to be made publicly by the bishop and all present. Moreover, urgent reforms were sanctioned and agreed to. A letter was sent by Pope Gregory XIII, 28 Nov., 1578, laying down what Abraham had to do for the improvement of his diocese; after the above-mentioned synod Abraham sent a long letter to the pope in reply, specifying all that he had been able to do by the aid of the Fathers (see letter, pp. 97–99, in Giamil). This is called the first reconciliation of the Syrians to the Church. It was formal and public, but left no improvement on the general body, the liturgical books were not corrected nor was Catholic teaching introduced in the Church.

In 1595 Mar Abraham fell dangerously ill (Du Jarric, tom. I, lib. II, p. 614). Unfortunately he survived the excellent sentiments he then had and recovered. After about two years, in 1597 (Gouvea, p. ii) he was a second time again dangerously ill; Archbishop Aleixo de Menezes wrote and exhorted him to reform his people, but for answer he had only frivolous excuses. He would not even avail himself of the exhortations of the Fathers who surrounded his bed, nor did he receive the last sacraments. Thus he died. The viceroy made known his death to Archbishop Menezes, then absent on a visitation tour, by letter of 6 Feb., 1597.

XIII. Archbishop Menezes received intelligence of the death of Mar Abraham while on a tour of pastoral visitation at Damão. Fearing the work on hand could not be postponed, he decided to act on the powers delegated to him by the pope in his last Brief, and nominated Father Francisco Roz of the Society of Jesus who undoubtedly fulfilled the requirements demanded by the pope for the appointment. On receipt of the letter and the instructions accompanying it, the superior, knowing that the late Abraham before his death had assigned to his archdeacon the government of the church pending the arrival of another bishop from Babylon, and the same had been accepted by the people, and foreseeing also the insecurity of the position, decided that it would be prudent to await the return of the archbishop before taking any further step. The archbishop on returning to Goa weighed the gravity of the case, and felt bound in conscience to put aside every other duty for the time being, and safeguard the Syrian Christians from falling again into the hands of a new heretical intruder. He decided on visiting the Serra personally. Father Nicholáo Pimenta, then the superior of the Jesuit missions in India, writing to the General of the Society, Father Claudius Acquaviva, takes up the narrative as follows: "It was not small comfort to all that Alexius Menezes, the Lord Archbishop of Goa, moved by his zeal for the salvation of souls and at our persuasion undertook to visit the ancient Christians of St. Thomas, spread through the hilly parts of Malabar. There was great danger that after the death of Archbishop Abraham at Angamale, and the succession of the Archdeacon George to the government of the Church on the demise of the prelate, she would lapse again under the sway of Nestorian prelates; nor were there wanting persons of ecclesiastical rank possessed of means who proposed to proceed to Babylon and bring thence another archbishop. To the Archbishop of Goa not only by metropolitan right, but also in virtue of Apostolic letters appertained the right to assume the administration of that Church *sede vacante;* and he took upon himself the task of retaining the vacillating archdeacon in due submission to the Holy See and avoiding schism."

He therefore issued instructions to the rector of the Vaipicotta College, enclosing a letter of appointment naming the archdeacon administrator of the diocese provided he in the presence of the rector made a solemn profession of faith. The archdeacon expressed his satisfaction on receiving the intimation and promised to make the profession demanded on a feast day. But later on he would neither make the profession, nor would he accept the nomination of administrator as coming from the archbishop of the diocese. Afterwards he caused it to be reported that he had so acted on the advice of others. The Archbishop of Goa, after taking counsel with the Fathers, decided on starting on the visitation of the Archdiocese of Angamale to induce that Church to receive a prelate from the Sovereign Pontiff. On this coming to be known all sorts of difficulties were raised to induce him to abandon his project, even from ecclesiastics, with such pertinacity that the archbishop wrote to Pimenta: "Heaven and earth have conspired against my design." But he manfully faced the work before him, and went through it with singular firmness of character and prudence, and supported by Divine aid he began, continued, and completed the arduous task he had undertaken with complete success.

During the visitation (full details of which are given by Gouvea in the "Jornada", the one source whence all other writers have obtained their information, some even going so far as entirely to distort the facts to satisfy their prejudice) the archbishop underwent all sorts of hardships, visiting the principal parishes, addressing the people, holding services, and everywhere conferring the sacraments, of which these people were deprived. He caused the Nestorian books in the possession of the churches and in the hands of the people to be expurgated of their errors, and they were then restored to their owners. All the books then existing among the Syrians were in MS. form; printed books among them did not exist at this period. Passages that denied the supreme authority of the Apostolic See of Rome were similarly deleted. He also caused capable priests to be sought out, and these he placed in charge of parishes. Eventually he established eighty parishes. Thus he prepared his ground for the reform of this Church which he intended to carry out. The synod was opened with great solemnity and pomp on 20 June, 1599, at the village of Udiamparur, whence it is known as the Synod of Diamper. The Acts were published in Portuguese as an appendix to the "Jornada"; they were also translated into Latin. The opening Act of the synod was the profession of faith. The archbishop was the first to make his profession, then followed the archdeacon who made his in Malayalam, a translation of the former prepared for the purpose. Subsequently the clergy in turn made theirs in the hands of the archbishop as the archdeacon also had done. The Latin text may be found with the Latin text of the synod, and separate in "Juris Pontificii de Propaganda Fide", Pars. I, vol. VI, part II, p. 243. Besides the archbishop and certain Jesuit Fathers who assisted him there were some 153 Syrian priests and about 600 laymen deputed by the congregation to represent them; all these signed the decrees that were passed by the synod and proclaimed the orthodox faith embodied in the act of profession taken by the entire clergy. The archbishop addressed the synod on the falsity of the errors of Nestorius up till then held by that Church, the assembly denounced them, anathematized the Nestorian Patriarch, and promised obedience and submission to the Roman Pontiff.

Among the calumnies spread against Menezes and the synod the most prominent is that all the Syriac books of the community were burnt and destroyed by order of the synod. What was done in this matter under the decree passed in the fifth session is thus described in the "Jornada" (tr. Glen, book I, ch. xxiii, p. 340). After the above condemnation of errors it was decided that certain books which had been named and were current in the Serra and full of errors should be burnt; that others were to be censured only until they were corrected and expurgated. The list of books to be burnt is given in the 14th decree of the third session. The books consist: (1) of those *ex professo* teaching Nestorian errors; (2) containing false legends; (3) books of sorceries and superstitious practices. None of these were capable of correction. In all other books that had any statements containing doctrinal errors, the latter were erased. The "Jornada" (p. 365) gives the system adopted during the visitation of the churches for the correction of books: after Mass was said all books written in Syriac, whether the property of the Church or of private individuals, were handed over to Father Francisco Roz, who with three *Cathanars* (Syrian priests) specially selected for the purpose would retire to the vestry and there correct the books in conformity with the directions given by the synod; those that were condemned and forbidden were handed over to the archbishop, who would order them to be burnt publicly. Under his orders no book capable of being purged from heretical error would be destroyed, but those *ex professo* teaching heresy would be destroyed. After the conclusion of the synod Archbishop Menezes continued his visitation of the churches down to Quilon and then returned to Goa. He did not forget to send from thence a letter of warm thanks to Father Pimenta for the continuous and important aid given him by the Fathers of the Society all through the work he had to perform in Malabar.

XIV. In making provision for the future government of the Syrian Church in Malabar Clement VIII had to adopt such measures as would secure its permanency in the faith and exclude the danger of a relapse. He decided that it would be the safest course to appoint a Latin prelate in sympathy with the people and fully acquainted with their liturgical language. The selection fell on Father Roz, no doubt after hearing the opinion of Archbishop Menezes. Father Roz was consecrated by the Archbishop at Goa under the title of Bishop of Angamale in 1601. Four years later Paul V transferred him (1605) to the new See of Cranganore, which he created an archbishopric in order that the faithful brought to unity should not feel that the honour of their see had suffered any diminution of honour. The new prelate made a visitation tour through the diocese, correcting the liturgical books at every church where this had not been done, and enforcing everywhere the rules sanctioned by the Synod of Diamper. In 1606 he convened and held a diocesan synod; no further details of his administration are handed down to us. After twenty-three years of strenuous episcopate he died at Parur, his ordinary residence, 18 Feb., 1624, and was buried in the church. Besides the Latin Canon of the Mass he had also translated the Latin ritual into Syriac for the administration of the Holy Sacraments by the clergy. Years later, on the occasion of the first pastoral visit of the first Vicar Apostolic of Trichur to the church of Parur in 1888, on enquiring after the tomb of the archbishop, he was told that no tomb of his was known to exist there, but after careful search had been made the tombstone, with its Malayalam inscription in ancient Tamil characters, was found and is now affixed to the inner wall of the church. The loss of all knowledge of the tombstone was caused by the sacking and burning of this church with many others by the soldiers of Tippoo Sultan on his second invasion of the coast. Paulinus a Sancto Bartholomæo, who had visited the church in 1785 and had taken a transcript of the inscription at the time, of which he gives a Latin translation in his "India Christ. Orient.", p. 64, did not read the name Roz on the stone, however the name is there in a flaw of the stone and has been read on rediscovery.

Father Estevão de Brito, also a Jesuit, was designated successor, and was consecrated by the Archbishop of Goa in the Church of Bom Jesus, Goa, on 29 Sept., 1624, and left Goa for his diocese on 4 Nov. He died on 2 Dec., 1641, having governed the see for over seventeen years. The third of the series was Francisco Garcia, of the same society. He was consecrated Bishop of Ascalon on 1 Nov., 1637, with right of succession by the Archbishop of Goa in the Jesuit Church of Bom Jesus, Goa, and succeeded to the See of Cranganore in 1641. Under this prelate a frightful schism broke out (1653) and his entire flock, with all his clergy and churches, withdrew from his allegiance. Out of the entire body of 200,000 Syrian Christians only some 400 individuals remained faithful. This misfortune has by most writers been attributed to Garcia's want of tact, obstinacy, and sarcastic disposition: as to the latter defect there is one instance, and that at the last opportunity for reconciliation, which fell through owing to his harsh treatment of the delegates sent to him by his revolted flock. But he was not responsible for the schism. This had been hatched many years previously during the lifetime of his predecessor de Brito, secretly and unknown to him. Here the dates only of documents can be quoted. On 1 Jan., 1628 (see German, p. 440) the Archdeacon George wrote a letter to the papal nuncio at Lisbon complaining that no answer was given to a letter sent some twenty years earlier regarding the spiritual wants of this Christian people. In 1630 Rome was informed of these complaints the substance of which was that Jesuits only controlled these Christians, that they were unsuited, and had controlled them for over forty years, and they wanted other religious orders to be sent. The Sacred Congregation sent instructions that other orders should be admitted into the diocese.

Paulinus (op. cit., pp. 70 sq.) adduces further evidence of the trickery and treachery of Archdeacon George. In 1632 a meeting was convened by him at Rapolin consisting of clergy and laity, when a letter of complaint was sent to the King of Portugal against the Jesuit Fathers; these very same complaints formed the heads of their grievances in 1653, when open schism was proclaimed to secure independence and oust the Jesuits. The plot had been hatched for a good number of years; it was begun by Archdeacon George (d. 1637) who was succeeded in office by a relative, another Thomas de Campo (Thoma Parambil) who in 1653 headed the revolt. After the schism had broken out the intruder Ahatalla, a Mesopotamian prelate, was deported by the Portuguese, who took him by ship off Cochin and there lay at anchor. The Christians, coming to know of the fact, threatened to storm the fort, which the governor had to man with his soldiers, while the ship sailed away to Goa during the night. The revolted seeing their last attempt to secure a Bagdad prelate frustrated, leaders and people took a solemn vow that they would never again submit to Archbishop Garcia. Finding themselves in this position they thought of calling to their aid the Carmelite Fathers who had visited Malabar but were then at Goa. When Alexander VII came to know the calamity which had befallen the Syrian community, he sent out (1656) the Carmelites, Fathers José de Sebastiani and Vincente of St. Catherine, to work for the return to unity and resubmission to their archbishop of this revolted church. Later other Carmelite Fathers joined in the good work. Within a year of their arrival (1657) the Carmelites had succeeded in reconciling forty-four churches. Although Archdeacon George had remained obdurate, a relative of his, Chandy Perambil (Alexander de Campo), headed the return movement, but they would have nothing to do with Archbishop Garcia.

XV. Under these circumstances Father José de Sebastiani decided to return to Rome and inform the pope of the real difficulty which stood in the way of permanent reconciliation. The pope on learning the state of the case had Father José consecrated and appointed him Commissary Apostolic for Malabar, with power to consecrate two other bishops, naming them vicars Apostolic. Provided with these powers he returned to Malabar in 1661 and took up his work. By this time Archbishop Garcia had been removed from the scene by death. Between 1661 and 1662 the Carmelite Friars under Bishop José had reclaimed the large number of eighty-four churches, leaving to the leader of the revolt, the aforesaid Archdeacon Thomas, only thirty-two churches. Both these figures are of great importance for the subsequent history of the Malabar Syrians. The eighty-four churches and their congregations were the body from which all the Romo-Syrians have descended, while the other thirty-two represent the nucleus whence the Jacobites and their subdivisions, Reformed Syrians, etc., have originated. In January, 1663, the political situation regarding these Christians was entirely changed. The Dutch had arrived on the coast and had captured Cochin. The Portuguese power fell. The new masters expelled not only all the Portuguese clergy but also forced Bishop José and his religious to leave the country. In this predicament the bishop selected and consecrated the native priest Chandy Perambil (Alexander de Campo) and made him a vicar Apostolic over the flock he was forced to leave.

Before departing, however, he handed to the Dutch Government of Cochin a list of the eighty-four churches that were under his control and commended Bishop Chandy and the Christians of these churches to his protection. This the governor undertook to fulfil. Though the Dutch did not trouble themselves about the Syrian Christians, yet they would not permit any Jesuit or Portuguese prelate to reside in Malabar, although simultaneously with Bishop José de Sebastiani the other Carmelite missionaries had also to depart. However, they were not absent long, for eventually they returned by ones and twos and were not molested. Later, in 1673, they established themselves at Verapoly and built a church there, having obtained the land rent-free from the Rajah of Cochin; it is yet the headquarters of the Carmelites in Malabar. One of the Carmelite Fathers named Matthew even came into friendly relations with the Dutch Governor van Rheede, and aided him in compiling his voluminous work on local botany known as "Hortus Malabaricus". The Carmelites working among the Syrians under Bishop Chandy remained on good terms with him; the bishop died in 1676. Raphael, a priest of the Cochin diocese, was selected to succeed the former, but he turned out a failure and died in 1695. The year following, Father Peter-Paul, a Carmelite, was created titular Archbishop of Ancyra, and was appointed vicar Apostolic for Malabar. With his arrival in 1678 there was a considerable improvement in the relations between the Dutch Government and the Carmelite Fathers. The Archbishop Peter-Paul was a prince of the House of Parma, and his mother was the sister of Pope Innocent XII; before coming out to Malabar he had obtained a decree from the Government of Holland authorizing the residence in Malabar of one bishop and twelve Carmelite priests who had to be either Italians, Germans, or Belgians; but they were not admitted into Cochin.

The French traveller Anquetil du Perron, who visited Malabar in 1758, offers the following statistics regarding the number of Christians on the coast which he had obtained from Bishop Florentius, the Carmelite Vicar Apostolic of Malabar. He tells us that the bishop believed the total number of Christians to amount to 200,000; of these 100,000 were Catholic Syrians, another 50,000 were of the Latin Rite; both these were under his jurisdiction, while the revolted Syrians, who may be classed as Jacobites, were under Mar Thomas VI (who on his consecration in 1772 assumed the name and style of Dionysius I), and numbered 50,000. From the death of Archbishop Garcia in 1659 the See of Cranganore had no resident bishop till 1701, when Clement XI appointed João Rebeiro, a Jesuit. When the latter assumed charge the Carmelite Vicar Apostolic, Angelus Francis, told his Syrian flock that his jurisdiction had ceased and they must now pass over to that of the new Archbishop of Cranganore. The Syrians refused to acknowledge the new archbishop and sent a petition to Rome that they preferred to remain under the Carmelites, who had seventy-one churches in complete submission and eighteen in partial union (i. e., the parish was divided and part had submitted to Rome), while only twenty-eight churches remained altogether separate. Pope Clement, after informing the King of Portugal of the state of things, extended in 1709 the jurisdiction of Bishop Angelus over the dioceses of Cranganore and Cochin, and the pope assigned as a reason for doing so that the Dutch would not tolerate any Portuguese prelate in the country, and the Christians threatened rather to return to schism than accept the bishop sent out. For fuller particulars of this period the reader is referred to: G. T. Mackenzie, "History of Christianity in Travancore", in Census Report of 1901, Trevandrum; and Paulinus a Sancto Bartholomæo, "India Orientalis Christ." (Rome, 1794.)

On the arrival of the Dutch and the capture of Cranganore it became impossible for the Jesuits to retain the college at Vipicotta; they abandoned the place and removing to the interior beyond the reach of their open enemies, opened a new college, called St. Paul's College, at Ambalacad, whence they controlled their new missions on the east coast. Bishop Rebeiro returned there and carried on his work; eventually several of the Syrian Catholic parishes went over to the succeeding Archbishop of Cranganore, and these eventually lapsed under the control of the Archbishops of Goa. Bishop Rebeiro died at the college of Ambalacad on 24 Sept., 1716, is buried in the church of Puttencherra and has a tombstone with an inscription in Portuguese. His successors fixed Puttencherra as their residence, and the parish church became a pro-cathedral. The following particulars of their nomination and death are here recorded. Archbishop Rebeiro was succeeded by Antonio Carvallo Pimental also a Jesuit, consecrated as the former had been at the church of Bom Jesus, Goa, by the archbishop on 29 Feb., 1722, d. at Puttencherra on 6 March, 1752. Paulinus says of him: "vir doctus et Malabarensibus gratus, qui eum nomine Budhi Metran, sapientis et eruditi præsulis compellebant." He has a tombstone with inscription. João Luiz Vasconcellos, also a Jesuit, was consecrated at Calicut by Bishop Clemente of Cochin in 1753, and d. at Puttencherra in 1756; the church contains his tomb-stone with inscription. Salvador Reis, the last of the series who resided in India, was also a Jesuit; he was consecrated by the same Bishop Clemente at Angengo on 5 Feb., 1758, d. on 7 April, 1777, at Puttencherra and has his tombstone with inscription in the same church. Paulinus records of him "vir sanctimonia vitæ præclarus"; he survived the suppression of his order. This closes the list of the bishops who have governed the See of Cranganore.

To complete the historical account of the Syrian Malabar Church, brief mention should also be made of the line of prelates who ruled over the schismatics who eventually became Jacobites, embracing that error through their prelates: Thomas I, proclaimed a bishop by those he had led (1653) into the aforesaid schism after the imposition of the hands of twelve priests his followers, and the placing on his head of a mitre and in his hand a pastoral staff. He continued obdurate and died a sudden death in 1673. Thomas II, brother of the former, proclaimed in 1674, died eight days later struck by lightning. Thomas III, nephew of the former, received the mitre in 1676, a Jacobite. Thomas IV of the same family, succeeded in 1676 and d. in 1686, a Jacobite. Thomas V, a nephew of the former, made every effort to obtain consecration but failed, d. in 1717, a Jacobite. Thomas VI received the mitre from his dying uncle and the imposition of hands of twelve priests. He wrote to the Jacobite Patriarch of Antioch to send bishops. Eventually the Dutch authorities helped him and obtained for him three bishops, on condition of his defraying the expenses. Three Jacobite bishops came out to India in 1751, Mar Basil, Mar Gregory, and Mar John. The first named died a year after arrival; the second years later consecrated Mar Thomas VI a bishop in 1772, and he assumed the name of Dionysius I. The Dutch authorities found great difficulty in obtaining payment for the expenses incurred; a suit was instituted against the Jacobites in the Travancore Rajah's court in 1775 and payment of the amount, twelve thousand pounds, was obtained. He died in 1808.

For the long period between 1678 and 1886, the Catholic Syrians remained under the uninterrupted control of about fifteen Carmelite Bishops as vicars Apostolic. During this period there had often arisen severe troubles which cannot here be detailed, quarrels between Syrian and Latin Christians, agitation against the control of some bishops; over and above these the ordinary trials of controlling such a large, factious, and difficult body. There had also been two most serious schismatical intrusions within this Syrian fold by Catholic Chaldean prelates who had come from Mesopotamia with the full connivance of the Chaldean Patriarch and against the express orders of the Roman Pontiff. The Carmelites had to face and surmount all these difficulties and keep the flock in due submission to ecclesiastical regime. Of the two intrusions, the first was that of the Chaldean Bishop Mar Roccos, who entered Malabar in 1861. Pius IX denounced him to the faithful as an intruder, yet he met with a complacent reception in many of the churches, succeeded in stirring up the dormant hydra of schism, and caused a great agitation. Fortunately for the peace of the Church he was persuaded to return to Mesopotamia within the year. The second, who came to Malabar in 1874, caused much greater harm, the evil effects of which seem to be permanent in the principal church of Trichur, though elsewhere in process of time those evil effects have been remedied. This was the Bishop Mellus, whom the patriarch had sent over in spite of the strict prohibition of the same pope. It was only when after repeated admonitions, the pope had fixed a limit of time after which should he continue refractory he would be excommunicated, that he yielded and sent Bishop Mellus instructions to return. When the troublesome character of these people is taken into consideration it reflects great credit on the Carmelite Order that the bishops in charge were successful in retaining them as a body in the unity of Holy Church.

XVI. The Mellusian schism, though broken by the adverse judgments of the Madras High Court, was by no means yet extinct when in the autumn of 1878 the Holy See decided on placing the Syrian Christians under separate administration, appointing two vicars Apostolic of the Latin Rite for the purpose. These were Rev. A. E. Medlycott, Ph.D., Military Chaplain in the Punjab, educated in the Propaganda College, Rome, and consecrated by the Apostolic Delegate Mgr. A. Ajuti on 18 Dec., 1887, at Ootacamund, titular Bishop of Tricomia, appointed to the Vicariate Apostolic of Trichur; and the Rev. Charles Lavigne S.J., former private secretary of the late Father Beckx, General of the Society, consecrated in Belgium before coming out, appointed to the See of Kottayam, later called of Changanacherry. Under the Concordat of Leo XIII with the King of Portugal an important advantage had been gained by the suppression of the Padroado jurisdiction (Cranganore Archbishops) over the Syrian churches. The first task the new bishops had to face was to amalgamate into one harmonious whole the two sections of this Church, that which had been under the Carmelites with that which had belonged to the Goan or Padroado jurisdiction, for the two had been for long years in open antagonism. This union fortunately was successfully effected. The other task was to establish something like a proper administration and control over the churches. This took longer time. The northern churches belonging to Trichur had not seen their prelates for perhaps a century, the two Chaldean Bishops had utilized the fact to their own advantage, and the troubles caused by them in these churches can be easily imagined; but with firmness and patience a fair working administration was introduced.

The result may thus be briefly summed up. The Vicariate of Trichur had a Catholic Syrian population of 108,422 with eighty-three parish churches and twenty-two chapels-of-ease, served by 118 priests of the Syrian Rite, besides 23 Syrian Carmelite Tertiary monks, in two monasteries; there was also a convent of 24 native Tertiary nuns with a middle-class school of 33 girls. The bishop on taking charge found that there were practically no schools, except one provided for clerics; he took early steps to open as many elementary parish schools as possible; within nine years (1888–96) the vicariate was provided with no less than 231 elementary parish schools for both sexes, educating over 12,000 children, besides a high school (St. Thomas's College), with 95 students; there were also 56 boys in St. Aloysius's High School, under the Tertiary monks. A catechumenate was opened, where annually about 150 heathen converts were baptized; a fine building was under construction for a suitable residence, and plans were prepared to house the above college in a handsome structure. This was the condition of things when the bishop went to Europe on sick leave. The Vicariate of Kottayam had a Catholic population of 150,000, with 108 parish churches and 50 dependent chapels, served by a numerous clergy of over 300 priests; it had 35 Tertiary monks, besides novices, in five monasteries; also three convents of native Tertiary Carmelite nuns educating girls, two orphanages under Tertiary Sisters of St. Francis, four catechumenates, two seminaries, with 96 students. The higher class clerical students of both vicariates attended the central Pontifical Seminary at Puttenpally. The parochial schools numbered 200, but the number of pupils was not published. There were three English Schools: Mananam, 60; Campalam, 80; and another with 20 students.

In 1895 both vicars Apostolic happened to be absent on leave. During this period the Holy See decided on a change of régime, yielding to the wishes of the people to grant them native bishops.

XVII. The two vicariates described above were split into three, and they were styled Trichur, Ernakulam, and Changanacherry; the new vicariate was formed of the southern portion of that of Trichur and of the northern portion of Changanacherry. The changes were carried out under Leo XIII by Brief of 28 July, 1896, "Quæ Rei Sacræ". Rev. John Menachery, as Bishop of Paralus, was appointed to Trichur. Rev. Aloysius Pareparambil, titular Bishop of Tio, was appointed to Ernakulam, and Rev. Matthew Makil, Bishop of Tralles, was appointed to Changanacherry; all three received consecration from the Apostolic Delegate Mgr. Zaleski, at Kandy on 15 Oct., 1896.

The latest ecclesiastical returns of these three vicariates (1911) give: *Trichur:* Catholic population, 91,064; children being educated, 19,092; *Ernakulam:* Catholic population, 94,357; children being educated, 9950; *Changanacherry:* Catholic population, 134,791; children being educated, 2844.

The future of this people depends very largely on education for their welfare and technical training for their development.

ASSEMANI, *Bibliotheca Orientalis* (Rome, 1719–28); DE SOUZA, *Oriente Conquistado* (2 vols., Indian reprint, Examiner Press, Bombay); GOUVEA, *Jornada do Arcebispo Aleixo de Menezes quando foy as Serras do Malauvar* (Coimbra, 1606); Fr. tr. DE GLEN, *Histoire Orientale* etc. (Brussels, 1609); DU JARRIC, *Thesaurus rerum mirabilium in India Orient* (3 vols., Cologne, 1615); PAULINUS A SANCTO BARTHOLOMÆO, *India Orientalis Christiana* (Rome, 1794); MACKENZIE, *Christianity in Travancore*, with Census Report of 1901 (Trevandrum); MEDLYCOTT, *India and the Apostle St. Thomas* (London, 1905).

A. E. MEDLYCOTT.

Thomas Cottam, BLESSED, martyr, b. 1549, in Lancashire; executed at Tyburn, 30 May, 1582. His parents, Laurence Cottam of Dilworth and Anne Brewer, were Protestants. Having completed his studies at Brasenose, Oxford (M.A., 14 July, 1572) he became master of a grammar school in London. Converted there to the faith by Thomas Pound he went over to Douai, and was ordained deacon at Cambrai, Dec., 1577. Desirous of the Indian mission, he went to Rome and was received (8 April, 1579) as a Jesuit novice at Sant' Andrea. Attacked by fever about October, he was sent to Lyons to recuperate, and went thence to the College at Reims, considering himself as accepted for India, if his health improved by a visit to England. In May (probably 28th), 1580, he was ordained priest at Soissons, and started (5 June) with four companions for England. Through the treachery of an English spy by the name of Sledd he was immediately arrested at Dover, but by a ruse of Dr. Ely, one of his fellow-travellers, reached London safely. Ely being imperilled through this friendly act, Cottam voluntarily surrendered himself and was committed "close prisoner" to the Marshalsea, where he perhaps said his first Mass. After being tortured, he was removed, 4 December, 1580 (Catholic Record Society, III, 10) to the Tower, where he endured the rack and the "Scavenger's Daughter". He was arraigned with Campion and others and (16 November, 1581) condemned to death. His execution was deferred till 30 May, 1582 (see Munday's "Breefe Reporte"), when with William Filby, Luke Kirby and Laurence Richardson, secular priests (all beatified 29 Dec., 1886), he was drawn to Tyburn and executed. His portrait, with martyrdom misdated, is reproduced in Foley, "Records", VII (1) 174; his relics are the Mass corporal used by him and four other martyrs in the Tower (cf. Camm, English Martyrs, II, 563) and perhaps his autograph in the registers of Sant' Andrea.

CHALLONER, *Memoirs;* FOLEY, *Records*, II, 145 sqq., with ample bibliography and VII (1) 174; GILLOW, *Bibl. Dict. Eng. Cath.*, I; *Dict. Nat. Biog.*, XII; CAMM, *English Martyrs*, II (London, 1905), 536–63.

PATRICK RYAN.

Thomas Ford, BLESSED, b. in Devonshire; d. at Tyburn, 28 May, 1582. He incepted M.A. at Trinity College, Oxford, 14 July, 1567, and was a fellow, Woods says president, of the college. He went to the English College, Douai, in 1570, and was one of the first three of its students to be ordained, receiving all orders in March, 1573, at Brussels. After becoming B.D. at Douai he left for England, 2 May, 1576, and soon became chaplain to Edward Yate and his Bridgettine guests at Lyford, Berkshire. Arrested with Blessed Edmund Campion (q. v.) 17 July, 1581, and committed to the Tower 22 July, he was thrice tortured. He was brought before the Queen's Bench 16 November, with his fellow martyr Blessed John Shert, on an absurd charge of conspiracy at Rome and Reims, where he had never been, on dates when he was in England, and both were condemned 21 November. With him suffered John Shert and Robert Johnson.

JOHN SHERT, BLESSED, a native of Cheshire, took the degree of B. A. at Brasenose College, Oxford, in 1566. Successively schoolmaster in London, and servant to Dr. Thomas Stapleton at Douai, he entered the seminary in 1576, and was ordained subdeacon. He was ordained priest from the English College, Rome, of which he was senior of the first six scholars. He left Reims for England 27 August, 1579, and was sent to the Tower, 14 July, 1581.

ROBERT JOHNSON, BLESSED, b. in Shropshire, entered the German College, Rome, 1 Oct., 1571. Ordained priest at Brussels from the English College Douai, in April, 1576, he started immediately for England. After a pilgrimage to Rome in 1579 he returned to England in 1580, and was committed to the Poultry Counter 12 July, whence he was transferred to the Tower 5 Dec. On 16 December he was terribly racked, and then thrust into an underground dungeon. He was brought before the Queen's Bench 14 Nov., and condemned 20 Nov.

KEOGH AND CAMM, *Lives of the English Martyrs* (London, 1904–5), II, 443–490; HART in Appendix to SANDER, *De Origine, etc. Schismatis Anglicani* (Rome, 1589); ALLEN, *Briefe Historie*, ed. POLLEN (London, 1908), 57–66; CHALLONER, *Missionary Priests*, nos. 9, 10, 11; GILLOW, *Bibl. Dict. Eng. Cath.*, s. v., *Ford, Thomas, Johnson, Robert*; COOPER, in *Dict. Nat. Biog.*, s. v., *Forde, Thomas*; *Cath. Rec. Soc.*, I, II, III, IV, V, IX; SIMPSON, *Edmund Campion* (London, 1896).

JOHN B. WAINEWRIGHT.

Thomas Green, BLESSED. See THOMAS JOHNSON, BLESSED.

Thomas Johnson, BLESSED, Carthusian martyr, d. in Newgate gaol, London, 20 Sept., 1537. On 18 May, 1537, the twenty choir monks and eighteen brothers remaining in the London Charterhouse were required to take the Oath of Supremacy. Of these choir monks Thomas Johnson, Richard Bere, Thomas Green (priests), and John Davy (deacon), refused; and of the brothers Robert Salt, William Greenwood, Thomas Redyng, Thomas Scryven, Walter Pierson, and William Horne. On 29 May all were sent to Newgate, where they were chained standing and with their hands tied behind them to posts in the prison, and so left to die of starvation. However Margaret Clement, who as Margaret Giggs had been brought up in the household of Blessed Thomas More, bribed the gaoler to let her have access to the prisoners, and disguised herself as a milkmaid and carried in a milk-can full of meat, wherewith she fed them. After the king's inquiry as to whether they were not already dead, the gaoler was afraid to let her enter again; but she was allowed to go on the roof, and uncovering the tiles, she let down meat in a basket as near as she could to their mouths. However they could get little or nothing from the basket, and as the gaoler feared discovery even this plan was soon discontinued. Greenwood died first (6 June), then Davy (8 June), Salt (9 June), Pierson and Green (10 June), Scryven (15 June), Redyng (16 June). It is probable that then Cromwell interfered and ordered those still living to be given food in order that they might be preserved for execution; for Bere did not die till 9 August, nor Johnson till 20 September. Horne survived, and, though he could never be induced to quit his religious habit, was not attainted till 1540, when he was hanged, disembowelled, and quartered at Tyburn (4 August) with the five *Prætermissi* Robert Bird (layman), Lawrence Cook (Carmelite Prior of Doncaster), Thomas Empson (Benedictine), Giles Heron (layman), and probably with William Bird (Rector of Fittleton and Vicar of Bradford, Wiltshire). All ten Carthusians were beatified by Leo XIII on 29 Dec., 1886. Blessed Richard Bere was a nephew of Richard Bere (Abbot of Glastonbury 1493–1525), and became a Carthusian on 20 Feb., 1523. Blessed Thomas Green has been identified by Dom Bede Camm with Thomas Greenwood (B. A., Oxon, M.A., Cantab, 1511), who became Fellow of St. John's College Cambridge in 1515 and D.D. in 1532.

KEOGH AND CAMM, in *Lives of the English Martyrs*, ed. CAMM, I (London, 1904), 257–68; HENDRIKS, *The London Charterhouse* (London, 1889), passim.

JOHN B. WAINEWRIGHT.

Thomas Marshall, BLESSED. See BECHE, JOHN, BLESSED.

Thomas More, BLESSED, knight, Lord Chancellor of England, author and martyr, b. in London, 7 February, 1477–78; executed at Tower Hill, 6 July, 1535. He was the sole surviving son of Sir John More, barrister and later judge, by his first wife Agnes, daughter of Thomas Graunger. While still a child Thomas was sent to St. Anthony's School in Threadneedle Street, kept by Nicholas Holt, and when thirteen years old was placed in the household of Cardinal Morton, Archbishop of Canterbury and Lord Chancellor. Here his merry character and brilliant intellect attracted the notice of the archbishop, who sent him to Oxford, where he entered at Canterbury Hall (subsequently absorbed by Christ Church) about 1492. His father made him an allowance barely sufficient to supply the necessaries of life and, in consequence, he had no opportunity to indulge in "vain or hurtful amusements" to the detriment of his studies. At Oxford he made friends with William Grocyn and Thomas Linacre, the latter becoming his first instructor in Greek. Without ever becoming an exact scholar he mastered Greek "by an instinct of genius" as witnessed by Pace (De fructu qui ex doctrina percipitur, 1517), who adds "his eloquence is incomparable and twofold, for he speaks with the same facility in Latin as in his own language". Besides the classics he studied French, history, and mathematics, and also learned to play the flute and the viol. After two years' residence at Oxford, More was recalled to London and entered as a law student at New Inn about 1494. In February, 1496, he was admitted to Lincoln's Inn as a student, and in due course was called to the outer bar and subsequently made a bencher. His great abilities now began to attract attention and the governors of Lincoln's Inn appointed him "reader" or lecturer on law at Furnival's Inn, his lectures being esteemed so highly that the appointment was renewed for three successive years.

It is clear however that law did not absorb all More's energies, for much of his time was given to letters. He wrote poetry, both Latin and English, a considerable amount of which has been preserved and is of good quality, though not particularly striking, and he was especially devoted to the works of Pico della Mirandola, of whose life he published an English translation some years later. He cultivated the acquaintance of scholars and learned men and, through his former tutors, Grocyn and Linacre, who were now living in London, he made friends with Colet, Dean of St. Paul's, and William Lilly, both renowned scholars. Colet became More's confessor, and Lilly vied with him in translating epigrams from the Greek Anthology into Latin, their joint productions being published in 1518 (Progymnasmata T. More et Gul. Lilii sodalium). In 1497 More was introduced to Erasmus, probably at the house of Lord Mountjoy, the great scholar's pupil and patron. The friendship at once became intimate, and later on Erasmus paid several long visits at More's Chelsea house, and the two friends corresponded regularly until death separated them. Besides law and the Classics More read the Fathers with care, and he delivered, in the Church of St. Lawrence Jewry, a series of lectures on St. Augustine's "De civitate Dei" which were attended by many learned men, among whom Grocyn, the rector of the church, is expressly mentioned. For such an audience the lectures must have been prepared with great care, but unhappily not a fragment of them has survived. These lectures were given somewhere between 1499 and 1503, a period during which More's mind was occupied almost wholly with religion and the question of his own vocation for the priesthood.

This portion of his life has caused much misunderstanding among his various biographers. It is certain that he went to live near the London Charterhouse and often joined in the spiritual exercises of the monks there. He wore "a sharp shirt of hair next his skin, which he never left off wholly" (Cresacre More), and gave himself up to a life of prayer and penance. His mind wavered for some time between joining the Carthusians or the Observant Franciscans, both of which orders observed the religious life with extreme strictness and fervour. In the end, apparently with the approval of Colet, he abandoned the hope of becoming a priest or religious, his decision being due to a mistrust of his powers of perseverance. Erasmus, his intimate friend and confidant, writes on this matter as follows (Epp. 447): "Meanwhile he applied his whole mind to exercises of piety, looking to and pondering on the priesthood in vigils, fasts and prayers and similar austerities. In which matter he proved himself far more prudent than most candidates who thrust themselves rashly into that arduous profession without any previous trial of their powers. The one thing that prevented him from giving himself to that kind of life was that he could not shake off the desire of the married state. He chose, therefore, to be a chaste husband rather than an impure priest." The last sentence of this passage has led certain writers, notably Mr. Seebohm and Lord Campbell, to expatiate at great length on the supposed corruption of the religious orders at this date, which, they declare, disgusted More so much that he abandoned his wish to enter religion on that account. Father Bridgett deals with this question at considerable length (Life and Writings of Sir Thomas More, pp. 23–36), but it is enough to say that this view has now been abandoned even by non-Catholic writers, as witness Mr. W. H. Hutton: "It is absurd to assert that More was disgusted with monastic corruption, that he 'loathed monks as a disgrace to the Church'. He was throughout his life a warm friend of the religious orders, and a devoted admirer of the monastic ideal.

BLESSED THOMAS MORE
From an etching by Wickenden of the Dürer portrait preserved in Laval University, Montreal.

He condemned the vices of individuals; he said, as his great-grandson says, 'that at that time religious men in England had somewhat degenerated from their ancient strictness and fervour of spirit'; but there is not the slightest sign that his decision to decline the monastic life was due in the smallest degree to a distrust of the system or a distaste for the theology of the Church."

The question of religious vocation being disposed of, More threw himself into his work at the Bar and scored immediate success. In 1504 he was elected a member of Parliament, but as the returns are missing his constituency is unknown. Here he immediately began to oppose the large and unjust exactions of money which King Henry VII was making from his subjects through the agency of Empson and Dudley, the latter being Speaker of the House of Commons. In this Parliament Henry demanded a grant of three-fifteenths, about £113,000, but thanks to More's protests the Commons reduced the sum to £30,000. Some years later Dudley told More that his boldness would have cost him his head but for the fact that he had not attacked the king in person. Even as it was Henry was so enraged with More that he "devised a causeless quarrel against his father, keeping him in the Tower till he had made him pay a hundred pounds fine" (Roper). Meanwhile More had made friends with one "Maister John Colte, a gentleman" of Newhall, Essex, whose eldest daughter, Jane, he married in 1505. Roper writes of his choice: "albeit his mind most served him to the second daughter, for that he thought her the fairest and best favoured, yet when he considered that it would be great grief and some shame also to the eldest to see her younger sister preferred before her in marriage, he then, of a certain pity, framed his fancy towards" the eldest of the three sisters. The union proved a supremely happy one; of it were born three daughters, Margaret, Elizabeth, and Cecilia, and a son, John; and then, in 1511, Jane More died, still almost a child. In the epitaph which More himself composed twenty years later he calls her "uxorcula Mori", and a few lines in one of Erasmus' letters are almost all we know of her gentle, winning personality.

Of More himself Erasmus has left us a wonderful portrait in his famous letter to Ulrich von Hutten dated 23 July, 1519 (Epp. 447). The description is too long to give in full, but some extracts must be made. "To begin then with what is least known to you, in stature he is not tall, though not remarkably short. His limbs are formed with such perfect symmetry as to leave nothing to be desired. His complexion is white, his face fair rather than pale and though by no means ruddy, a faint flush of pink appears beneath the whiteness of his skin. His hair is dark brown or brownish black. The eyes are greyish blue, with some spots, a kind which betokens singular talent, and among the English is considered attractive, whereas Germans generally prefer black. It is said that none are so free from vice. His countenance is in harmony with his character, being always expressive of an amiable joyousness, and even an incipient laughter and, to speak candidly, it is better framed for gladness than for gravity or dignity, though without any approach to folly or buffoonery. The right shoulder is a little higher than the left, especially when he walks. This is not a defect of birth, but the result of habit such as we often contract. In the rest of his person there is nothing to offend. . . . He seems born and framed for friendship, and is a most faithful and enduring friend. . . . When he finds any sincere and according to his heart, he so delights in their society and conversation as to place in it the principal charm of life. . . . In a word, if you want a perfect model of friendship, you will find it in no one better than in More. . . . In human affairs there is nothing from which he does not extract enjoyment, even from things that are most serious. If he converses with the learned and judicious, he delights in their talent, if with the ignorant and foolish, he enjoys their stupidity. He is not even offended by professional jesters. With a wonderful dexterity he accommodates himself to every disposition. As a rule, in talking with women, even with his own wife, he is full of jokes and banter. No one is less led by the opinions of the crowd, yet no one departs less from common sense. . . ." (see Father Bridgett's Life, p. 56–60, for the entire letter). More married again very soon after his first wife's death, his choice being a widow, Alice Middleton. She was older than he by seven years, a good, somewhat commonplace soul without beauty or education; but she was a capital housewife and was devoted to the care of More's young children. On the whole the marriage seems to have been quite satisfactory, although Mistress More usually failed to see the point of her husband's jokes.

More's fame as a lawyer was now very great. In 1510 he was made Under-Sheriff of London, and four years later was chosen by Cardinal Wolsey as one of an embassy to Flanders to protect the interests of English merchants. He was thus absent from England for more than six months in 1515, during which period he made the first sketch of the "Utopia", his most famous work, which was published the following year. Both Wolsey and the king were anxious to secure More's services at Court. In 1516 he was granted a pension of £100 for life, was made a member of the embassy to Calais in the next year, and became a privy councillor about the same time. In 1519 he resigned his post as Under-Sheriff and became completely attached to the Court. In June, 1520, he was in Henry's suite at the "Field of the Cloth of Gold", in 1521 was knighted and made sub-treasurer to the king. When the Emperor Charles V visited London in the following year, More was chosen to deliver the Latin address of welcome; and grants of land in Oxford and Kent, made then and three years later, gave further proof of Henry's favour. In 1523 he was elected Speaker of the House of Commons on Wolsey's recommendation; became High Steward of Cambridge University in 1525; and in the same year was made Chancellor of the Duchy of Lancaster, to be held in addition to his other offices. In 1523 More had purchased a piece of land in Chelsea, where he built himself a mansion about a hundred yards from the north bank of the Thames, with a large garden stretching along the river. Here at times the king would come as an unbidden guest at dinner time, or would walk in the garden with his arm round More's neck enjoying his brilliant conversation. But More had no illusions about the royal favour he enjoyed. "If my head should win him a castle in France," he said to Roper, his son-in-law, in 1525, "it should not fail to go." The Lutheran controversy had now spread throughout Europe and, with some reluctance, More was drawn into it. His controversial writings are mentioned below in the list of his works, and it is sufficient here to say that, while far more refined than most polemical writers of the period, there is still a certain amount that tastes unpleasant to the modern reader. At first he wrote in Latin but, when the books of Tindal and other English Reformers began to be read by people of all classes, he adopted English as more fitted to his purpose and, by doing so, gave no little aid to the development of English prose.

In October, 1529, More succeeded Wolsey as Chancellor of England, a post never before held by a layman. In matters political, however, he in nowise succeeded to Wolsey's position, and his tenure of the chancellorship is chiefly memorable for his unparalleled success as a judge. His despatch was so great that the supply of causes was actually exhausted, an incident commemorated in the well-known rhyme,

"When More some time had Chancellor been
"No more suits did remain.
"The like will never more be seen,
"Till More be there again."

As chancellor it was his duty to enforce the laws against heretics and, by doing so, he provoked the attacks of Protestant writers both in his own time and since. The subject need not be discussed here, but More's attitude is patent. He agreed with the principle of the anti-heresy laws and had no hesitation in enforcing them. As he himself wrote in his "Apologia" (cap. 49) it was the vices of heretics that he hated, not their persons; and he never proceeded to extremities until he had made every effort to get those brought before him to recant. How successful he was in this is clear from the fact that only four persons suffered the supreme penalty for heresy during his whole term of office. More's first public appearance as chancellor was at the opening of the new Parliament in November, 1529. The accounts of his speech on this occasion vary considerably, but it is quite certain that he had no knowledge of the long series of encroachments on the Church which this very Parliament was to accomplish. A few months later came the royal proclamation ordering the clergy to acknowledge Henry as "Supreme Head" of the Church "as far as the law of God will permit", and we have Chapuy's testimony that More at once proffered his resignation of the chancellorship, which however was not accepted. His firm opposition to Henry's designs in regard to the divorce, the papal supremacy, and the laws against heretics, speedily lost him the royal favour, and in May, 1532, he resigned his post of lord chancellor after holding it less than three years. This meant the loss of all his income except about £100 a year, the rent of some property he had purchased; and, with cheerful indifference, he at once reduced his style of living to match his straitened means. The epitaph which he wrote at this time for the tomb in Chelsea church states that he intended to devote his last years to preparing himself for the life to come.

For the next eighteen months More lived in seclusion and gave much time to controversial writing. Anxious to avoid a public rupture with Henry he stayed away from Anne Boleyn's coronation, and when, in 1533, his nephew William Rastell wrote a pamphlet supporting the pope, which was attributed to More, he wrote a letter to Cromwell disclaiming any share therein and declaring that he knew his duty to his prince too well to criticise his policy. Neutrality, however, did not suit Henry, and More's name was included in the Bill of Attainder introduced into the Lords against the Holy Maid of Kent and her friends. Brought before four members of the Council, More was asked why he did not approve Henry's anti-papal action. He answered that he had several times explained his position to the king in person and without incurring his displeasure. Eventually, in view of his extraordinary popularity, Henry thought it expedient to remove his name from the Bill of Attainder. The incident showed what he might expect, however, and the Duke of Norfolk personally warned him of his grave danger, adding "indignatio principis mors est". "Is that all, my lord," answered More, "then, in good faith, between your grace and me is but this, that I shall die to-day, and you to-morrow." In March, 1534, the Act of Succession was passed which required all who should be called upon to take an oath acknowledging the issue of Henry and Anne as legitimate heirs to the throne, and to this was added a clause repudiating "any foreign authority, prince or potentate". On 14 April, More was summoned to Lambeth to take the oath and, on his refusal, was committed to the custody of the Abbot of Westminster. Four days later he was removed to the Tower, and in the following November was attainted of misprision of treason, the grants of land made to him in 1523 and 1525 being resumed by the Crown. In prison, though suffering greatly from "his old disease of the chest . . . gravel, stone, and the cramp", his habitual gaiety remained and he joked with his family and friends whenever they were permitted to see him as merrily as in the old days at Chelsea. When alone his time was given up to prayer and penitential exercises; and he wrote a "Dialogue of comfort against tribulation", treatise (unfinished) on the Passion of Christ, and many letters to his family and others. In April and May, 1535, Cromwell visited him in person to demand his opinion of the new statutes conferring on Henry the title of Supreme Head of the Church. More refused to give any answer beyond declaring himself a faithful subject of the king. In June, Rich, the solicitor-general, held a conversation with More and, in reporting it, declared that More had denied Parliament's power to confer ecclesiastical supremacy on Henry. It was now discovered that More and Fisher, the Bishop of Rochester, had exchanged letters in prison, and a fresh inquiry was held which resulted in his being deprived of all books and writing materials, but he contrived to write to his wife and favourite daughter, Margaret, on stray scraps of paper with a charred stick or piece of coal.

On 1 July, More was indicted for high treason at Westminster Hall before a special commission of twenty. More denied the chief charges of the indictment, which was enormously long, and denounced Rich, the solicitor-general and chief witness against him, as a perjuror. The jury found him guilty and he was sentenced to be hanged at Tyburn, but some days later this was changed by Henry to beheading on Tower Hill. The story of his last days on earth, as given by Roper and Cresacre More, is of the tenderest beauty and should be read in full; certainly no martyr ever surpassed him in fortitude. As Addison wrote in the Spectator (No. 349) "that innocent mirth which had been so conspicuous in his life, did not forsake him to the last . . . his death was of a piece with his life. There was nothing in it new, forced or affected. He did not look upon the severing of his head from his body as a circumstance that ought to produce any change in the disposition of his mind". The execution took place on Tower Hill "before nine of the clock" on 6 July, the body being buried in the Church of St. Peter *ad vincula*. The head, after being parboiled, was exposed on London Bridge for a month when Margaret Roper bribed the man, whose business it was to throw it into the river, to give it to her instead. The final fate of the relic is somewhat uncertain, but in 1824 a leaden box was found in the Roper vault at St. Dunstan's, Canterbury, which on being opened was found to contain a head presumed to be More's. The Jesuit Fathers at Stonyhurst possess a remarkable collection of secondary relics, most of which came to them from Father Thomas More, S.J. (d. 1795), the last male heir of the martyr. These include his hat, cap, crucifix of gold, a silver seal, "George", and other articles. The hair shirt, worn by him for many years and sent to Margaret Roper the day before his martyrdom, is preserved by the Augustinian canonesses of Abbots Leigh, Devonshire, to whom it was brought by Margaret Clements, the adopted child of Sir Thomas. A number of autograph letters are in the British Museum. Several portraits exist, the best being that by Holbein in the possession of E. Huth, Esq. Holbein also painted a large group of More's household which has disappeared, but the original sketch for it is in the Basle Museum, and a sixteenth-century copy is the property of Lord St. Oswald. Bl. Thomas More was formally beatified by Pope Leo XIII, in the Decree of 29 December, 1886.

WRITINGS.—More was a ready writer and not a few of his works remained in manuscript until some years after his death, while several have been lost altogether. Of all his writings the most famous is unquestionably the "Utopia", first published at Louvain in 1516. The volume recounts the fictitious travels of one Raphael Hythlodaye, a mythical character, who, in the course of a voyage to America, was left behind near Cape Frio and thence wandered on till he chanced upon the Island of Utopia (οὐ, τόπος or "nowhere") in which he found an ideal constitution in operation. The whole work is really an exercise of the imagination with much brilliant satire upon the world of More's own day. Real persons, such as Peter Giles, Cardinal Morton, and More himself, take part in the dialogue with Hythlodaye, so that an air of reality pervades the whole which leaves the reader sadly puzzled to detect where truth ends and fiction begins, and has led not a few to take the book seriously. But this is precisely what More intended, and there can be no doubt that he would have been as delighted at entrapping William Morris, who discovered in it a complete gospel of Socialism; or Cardinal Zigliara, who denounced it as "no less foolish than impious"; as he must have been with his own contemporaries who proposed to hire a ship and send out missionaries to his non-existent island. The book ran through a number of editions in the original Latin version and, within a few years, was translated into German, Italian, French, Dutch, Spanish, and English.

A collected edition of More's English works was published by William Rastell, his nephew, at London in 1557; it has never been reprinted and is now rare and costly. The first collected edition of the Latin Works appeared at Basle in 1563; a more complete collection was published at Louvain in 1565 and again in 1566. In 1689 the most complete edition of all appeared at Frankfort-on-Main, and Leipzig. After the "Utopia" the following are the most important works: "Luciani Dialogi . . . compluria opuscula . . . ab Erasmo Roterodamo et Thoma Moro interpretibus optimis in Latinorum lingua traducta . . ." (Paris, 1506); "Here is conteigned the lyfe of John Picus, Earle of Myrandula . . ." (London, 1510); "Historie of the pitiful life and unfortunate death of Edward the fifth and the then Duke of Yorke his brother . . .", printed incomplete in the "English Works" (1557) and reissued with a completion from Hall's Chronicle by Wm. Sheares (London, 1641); "Thomae Mori v. c. Dissertatio Epistolica de aliquot sui temporis theologastrorum ineptiis . . ." (Leyden, 1625); Epigrammata . . . Thomae Mori Britanni, pleraque e Graecis versa. (Basle, 1518); Eruditissimi viri Gul. Rossi Opus elegans quo pulcherrime retegit ac refellit insanas Lutheri calumnias (London, 1523), written at the request of Henry VIII in answer to Luther's reply to the royal "Defensio Septem Sacramentorum"; "A dyaloge of Syr Thomas More Knt . . . of divers maters, as of the veneration and worshyp of ymages and relyques, praying to sayntys and goyng on pylgrymage . . ." (Lon-

BLESSED THOMAS MORE
RUBENS, THE PRADO, MADRID

don, 1529); "The Supplycacyon of Soulys" (London, 1529[?]), written in answer to Fish's "Supplication of the Beggars"; "Syr Thomas More's answer to the fyrste parte of the poysoned booke . . . named 'The Souper of the Lorde'" (London, 1532); "The Second parte of the Confutacion of Tyndal's Answere . . ." (London, 1533); these two works together form the most lengthy of all More's writings; besides Tindal, Robert Barnes is dealt with in the last book of the whole; "A Letter impugnynge the erronyouse wrytyng of John Fryth against the Blessed Sacrament of the Aultare" (London, 1533); "The Apologye of Syr Thomas More, Knyght, made by him anno 1533, after he had given over the office of Lord Chancellour of Englande" (London, 1533); "The Debellacyon of Salem and Bizance" (London, 1533), an answer to the anonymous work entitled "Salem and Bizance", and vindicating the severe punishment of heresy; "A Dialogue of Comfort against Tribulation . . ." (London, 1553). Among the other writings in the collected volume of "English Works" are the following which had not been previously published: An unfinished treatise "uppon those words of Holy Scripture, 'Memorare novissima et in eternum non peccabis'", dated 1522; "Treatise to receive the blessed Body of our Lorde, sacramentally and virtually both"; "Treatise upon the Passion" unfinished; "Certein devout and vertuouse Instruccions, Meditacions and Prayers"; besides some letters written while in the Tower, including his touching correspondence with his daughter Margaret. A complete bibliography of More's writings will be found in Gillow, "Bibliographical Dictionary of English Catholics" (London, s. d.), V, 99–116.

For fullest list yet published see *Catalogue of books of or on Sir Thomas More, collected by Alfred Cock, Q.C., and now at the Guildhall Library* (London, 1903), also *Transactions of the Bibl. Soc.*, V (1901), 177–180.

Original sources, besides the above: *Letters and Papers of the reign of Henry VIII*, ed. BREWER, GAIRDNER, AND BRODIE, III–VIII (London, 1875–85); *Calendar of State Papers, Venetian*, ed. BROWNE, III, IV (London, 1869, 71); IDEM, *England and Spain*, ed. BERGENROTH AND GAYANGOS, II–V (London, 1866–86); *D. Erasmi Epistolæ*, ed. LE CLERC (Leyden, 1706), contains 19 letters from More to Erasmus and 24 from Erasmus to More; *Baga de Secretis*, pouch 7, bundle 3, contains the records of the trial. Complete lives: ROPER, *The Life, Arraignement and Death of that Mirrour of all true Honour and Vertue, Syr T. More* (Paris, 1626), re-ed. from a better MS. with valuable notes by LEWIS (1729), reprinted in the *King's Classics* (1903); HARPSFIELD, *Life of Sir T. More*, founded on Roper, several copies exist in MS., e. g. British Museum, Harleian MS., 6253; STAPLETON, *Tres Thomae* (Antwerp, 1588); BARNSTAPLE (?), *Life of More*, printed in DR. WORDSWORTH'S *Ecclesiastical Biog.*, II, 181, from a MS. in the Lambeth Library the preface to which is signed Ro. Ba., which GILLOW proposes to read as Robert Barnstaple; CRESACRE MORE, *Life and Death of Sir Thomas More* . . . (Paris, 1626), re-ed. HUNTER with valuable notes (London, 1828); *The Mirrour of Vertue* (London, 1626); HODDESDEN, *The Hist. of the Life and Death of Sir T. More* (London, 1662); WARNER, *Memoirs of the Life of Sir Thomas More* (London, 1758); CAYLEY, *Memoirs of Sir T. More* (London, 1808); VON RUDHART, *T. Morus aus den Quellen bearbeitet* (Nuremberg, 1829); WALTER, *Sir T. More, his Life and Times* (London, 1840); MACKINTOSH, *Life of Sir T. More* (London, 1844); BRIDGETT, *Life and Writings of Sir Thomas More* (London, 1891), quite the most valuable life yet produced; IDEM, *The Wit and Wisdom of Sir Thomas More* (London, 1893); HUTTON, *Life of Sir T. More* (London, 1895); BREMOND, tr. CHILD, *Sir Thomas More* (London, 1904); essays and chapters in larger works, etc.: SANDER (ed. LEWIS), *Rise and Growth of the Anglican Schism* (London, 1877); CAMPBELL, *Lives of the Lord Chancellors*, I (London, 1848), 507–94; NISARD, *Études sur la Renaissance* (Paris, 1877), pt. II; SEEBOHM, *Oxford Reformers of 1498* (London, 1867), fantastic and misleading; DRANE, *The Three Chancellors*, *Wykeham, Waynflete, More* (London, 1890); LILLY, *Renaissance Types* (London, 1901), 309–78; GAIRDNER, *Lollardy and the Reformation*, I (London, 1908); IDEM, *The English Church in the 16th Century* (London, 1902); DIXON, *Hist. of the Church of England*, I (London, 1878); GASQUET, *Henry VIII and the English Monasteries* (London, 1888); IDEM, *The Eve of the Reformation* (London, 1900); IDEM, *The Old English Bible* (London, 1897); BREWER, *The Reign of Henry VIII* (London, 1881); the following are more or less fanciful: HEYWOOD, *Il Moro* (Florence, 1556); MARSDEN, *Philmorus* (London, 1842); MANNING, *The Household of Sir Thomas More* (London, 1851).

G. ROGER HUDLESTON.

Thomas of Beckington (BEKYNTON), Bishop of Bath and Wells, b. at Beckington, Somerset, about 1390; d. at Wells, 14 Jan., 1465. He was educated at Winchester (1404) and New College, Oxford (1406). After his ordination as priest he acquired much ecclesiastical preferment, including the archdeaconry of Buckingham and a canonry at Wells. Being a skilled canon lawyer he was made dean of the Arches in 1423. He was also frequently employed as English ambassador abroad. His influence with the young King Henry VI was so great that he was appointed lord privy seal in 1442; and in the following year the pope nominated him Bishop of Bath and Wells. He was consecrated, 13 Oct., 1442, at the new foundation of Eton College, in which he took great interest. As bishop he rebuilt the episcopal palace at Wells, and greatly improved the city. He was a lover of learning and a munificent patron to houses of education, particularly Winchester School and Lincoln College, Oxford.

BECKINGTON, *Official Correspondence of Beckington, secretary to Henry VI in R. S.* (London, 1872); NICOLAS, *Journal by one of the suite of Beckington during embassy to negotiate marriage between Henry VI and the Count of Armagnac's daughter* (London, 1828); MONRO, *Letters of Margaret of Anjou, Bishop Beckington and others* (Camden Society, London, 1863); GAIRDNER in *Dict. Nat. Biog.*, s. v. *Beckington or Bekynton, Thomas*.

EDWIN BURTON.

Thomas of Bradwardine (BRAGWARDIN, BRANDNARDINUS, BREDWARDYN, BRADWARDYN, DE BREDEWARDINA), b. about 1290; d. in London, 26 August, 1349. His birthplace is variously assigned to Bradwardine, Hertfield, or Cowden; but he himself states that he was born at Chichester. He was educated at Merton College, Oxford, and in 1325 was one of the proctors of the university who took part in the litigation between the university and Cardinal Galhardus de Mora, Archdeacon of Oxford. As a theologian he attained great fame, being known as the *Doctor Profundus*. His theological lectures delivered at Oxford were expanded into the famous treatise on grace known as "Summa Doctoris Profundi" or "De causa Dei contra Pelagium et de virtute causarum ad suos Mertonenses". Chaucer couples him as a theologian with St. Augustine and Boethius,—a testimony to his popular reputation. In 1335 he was called to London by Richard de Bury, Bishop of Durham, who appointed him his chaplain and obtained for him the chancellorship of St. Paul's Cathedral. He also became one of the king's chaplains, and accompanied Edward III on his continental journeys and French wars. To his apostolical labours among the English soldiers many attributed the success achieved. After the victories of Crécy and Neville's Cross, he acted as a commissioner to treat of peace with King Philip. In 1348 the chapter of Canterbury elected Bradwardine to the vacant archbishopric; but the king, offended by their omission to wait for the *congé d'élire*, requested the pope to appoint John Ufford instead. Ufford, however, died of the Black Death before consecration, and Bradwardine was then elected with the king's approval. He was consecrated at the pope's court at Avignon on 19 July, 1349; and then returned to England. But the pestilence was raging there, and immediately on his arrival in London he fell a victim to it. His European reputation as a scholar was based not only on his famous theological treatise but also on his mathematical works: "De proportionibus" (Paris, 1495); "De quadratura circuli" (Paris, 1495); "Arithmetica speculativa" (Paris, 1502); and "Geometria speculativa" (Paris, 1530). Other works of a similar nature exist in MS.

SAVILE, Preface to BRADWARDINE'S *De Causa Dei* (London, 1618); PITTS, *De illustribus Angliæ scriptoribus* (Paris, 1623); HOOK, *Lives of the Archbishops of Canterbury* (London, 1860–84); LECHLER, *De Thoma Bradwardino Commentatio* (Leipzig, 1862); STEPHENS, in *Dict. Nat. Biog.*, s. v., *Bradwardine, Thomas*.

EDWIN BURTON.

Thomas of Cantimpré, medieval writer, preacher, and theologian, b. of noble parentage at Leuw St-Pierre near Brussels, in the Duchy of Brabant, 1201;

d. 15 May, 1272. At the age of five his education began at Liège, where he spent eleven years mastering the difficulties of the *trivium* and *quadrivium*. At the age of sixteen he received the habit of the Canons Regular of St. Augustine in the Abbey of Cantimpré, where he was eventually elevated to the priesthood. In 1232, after fifteen years at Cantimpré, during which he was a constant source of edification to his religious brethren, he entered the Order of St. Dominic at Louvain. Immediately after his profession in the following year, he was sent to Cologne to pursue the higher theological studies of the order, under the tutelage of the illustrious Albert the Great. From Cologne, where he spent four years, he went to Paris, to the Dominican *studium* of St. James, to perfect himself in the sciences and to prepare for the apostolate of preaching. Returning to Louvain in 1240, he was made professor of philosophy and theology—an office he filled with rare distinction. He achieved equal success in the apostolate of preaching, in recognition of which the title of "Preacher General" was conferred upon him. His missionary activities extended throughout Brabant and into Germany, Belgium, and France. To his reputation for missionary zeal and eloquence he added the fame of authorship. In all, seven works, treating of philosophy, theology, and hagiology, are attributed to his pen. His first and most important work is entitled "Opus de natura rerum". In the composition of this great work, which contains twenty books, he spent fifteen years. "Bonum universale de apibus" is an allegory in which, employing the figure of bees, he treats of precepts concerning conduct and of the duties of superiors and subjects. This work, which had a wide vogue among spiritual writers for many centuries, was printed at Deventer (before 1478), at Paris, and three times at Douai (1597, 1605, 1627). His other works treat of hagiology and are as follows: (1) "Vita Christinæ virginis mirabilis dictæ"; (2) "Vita B. Margaritæ Iprensis"; (3) "Vita Piæ Lutgardia"; (4) "Vita Joannis abbatis primi monasterii Cantimpratensis et ejus Ecclesiæ undatoris"; (5) "Supplementum ad vitam B. Mariæ d'Oignies a B.M. Jacobo de Vitriaco".

QUÉTIF-ECHARD, *Scriptores ordinis prædicatorum*, I, 250; *Année Dominic.*, V (1891), 433; AUGER, *Mystiques Pays-Bas moy. âge* (1892), 135; *Hist. litt. France*, XIX (1838), 177; TURON, *Hom. ill. Domin.*, I (1743), 177.

JOHN B. O'CONNOR.

Thomas of Celano, Friar Minor, poet, and hagiographical writer, b. at Celano in the Province of the Abruzzi, about 1200; d. about 1255. He was one of the first disciples of St. Francis of Assisi and joined the order probably in 1215. In 1221 Thomas accompanied Cæsar of Speyer on his mission to Germany. The following year he became *custos* of the convents at Mayence, Worms, Speyer, and Cologne, and soon after Cæsar of Speyer, on his return to Italy, made him his vicar in the government of the German province. Before September, 1223, Thomas returned to Italy, and lived there in familiar intercourse with St. Francis. Soon after the canonization of St. Francis (16 July, 1228) he wrote his "Vita prima", or "First Life" of St. Francis of Assisi, by order of Gregory IX. Between 1244 and 1247, he compiled his "Vita secunda", or "Second Life" of St. Francis, which is in the nature of a supplement to the first one, by commission of Crescentius of Jessi, then minister general of the order. About ten years later Thomas wrote a treatise on the miracles of St. Francis at the bidding of Blessed John of Parma, the successor of Crescentius as minister general. In addition to these works, around which a large controversial literature has grown up in recent years, Thomas of Celano wrote two beautiful sequences in honour of St. Francis: "Fregit victor virtualis" and "Sanctitatis nova signa", and, in all probability, he is also the author of the "Dies Iræ" and of the "Life of St. Clare of Assisi", written between 1255 and 1261 (cf. Robinson, "Life of St. Clare", Introduction, pp. xxii sq.). The best critical edition of the works of Thomas of Celano is that of Père Edouard d'Alençon.

HOWELL, *The Lives of St. Francis of Assisi, by Brother Thomas of Celano*, I (London, 1908), 24; ROBINSON, *Life of St. Clare, ascribed to Thomas of Celano* (Philadelphia, 1910), 22 sq.; IDEM, *A Short Introduction to Franciscan Literature* (New York, 1907), 7–9; DUBOIS, *Thomas of Celano, the Historian of St. Francis*, in *Cath. Univ. Bulletin*, XIII, no. 2 (April, 1907), 250–268; D'ALENÇON, *S. Francisci Assisiensis: vita et miracula, additis opusculis liturgicis, auctore Fr. Thoma de Celano*, IX (Rome, 1906), 22; BARLATI, *Tommaso da Celano e le sue opere* (Casalbordino, 1894); *Analecta Boll.*, XVIII, 81–176; WADDING, *Script. Min.*, 323; SBARALEA, *Supplem. ad script. min.*, 672–74.

FERDINAND HECKMANN.

Thomas of Dover, martyr; d. 2 or 5 Aug., 1295. On the above date the French ravaged Dover with fire and sword, and eventually attacked the Benedictine priory of St. Martin. All the inmates fled, with the exception of one, an old and infirm monk named Thomas Hales or de Halys, whom the sailors found in the dormitory, and slew for refusing to disclose the place where the treasures of the church were hidden. Numerous miracles [for which see Horstmann, "Nova legenda Angliæ" (Oxford, 1901), and Bishop Challoner's work cited below] are recorded by John of Tynemouth as having been wrought through his relics. Friar Simon Simeon, in the narrative of his pilgrimage to the Holy Land about 1322, bears witness to the honour paid to him as a martyr at "the Black Monks under Dover Castle" ("Itin. Sim. Simeon. et Will. de Worc.", ed. Nasmith, Cambridge, 1778, p. 7). Richard II at the instance of his mother requested the pope to canonize Thomas; but though an enquiry was set on foot in 1382 nothing further seems to have been done. He was, however, popularly regarded in the neighbourhood as a saint. In 1500 Thomas Rich, Vicar of Buckland, near Dover, left eightpence for the altar of Blessed Thomas de Halys at Dover Priory. His own church contained a chapel of St. Thomas, which may possibly have been dedicated to Thomas of Dover. He is very generally given the title of saint, and it is remarkable that he is represented (fig. 26) in the copper-plate reproduction of the pictures formerly at the English College, Rome, which resulted in the equivalent beatification of sixty-three martyrs mentioned by name therein (see ENGLISH CONFESSORS AND MARTYRS). On neither day is he mentioned in the "Acta Sanctorum".

Supplement to STANTON, *Menology of England and Wales* (London, 1892), 665; CHALLONER, *Britannia sancta*, II (London, 1745), 72; HUSSEY, *Testamenta Cantiana.: East Kent* (London, 1907), x, 391, 104.

JOHN B. WAINEWRIGHT.

Thomas of Hereford (THOMAS DE CANTELUPE), SAINT, b. at Hambledon, Buckinghamshire, England, about 1218; d. at Orvieto, Italy, 25 August, 1282. He was the son of William de Cantelupe and Millicent de Gournay, and thus a member of an illustrious and influential family. He was educated under the care of his uncle, Walter de Cantelupe, Bishop of Worcester, first at Oxford then at Paris. During his studies he attended the Council of Lyons in 1245, when he became a papal chaplain. Returning to Oxford, he taught canon law, and in 1262 was elected chancellor of the university. In the Barons' Wars he took the popular side and stated the Barons' case before St. Louis at Amiens, 1263. After the defeat of Henry III at the battle of Lewes he was made Chancellor of England (22 Feb., 1265), gaining wide renown for his judicial wisdom and fairness. Deprived of the chancellorship on the death of Simon de Montfort, he went into exile, lecturing at Paris on theology and Scripture (1265–72). He then resumed teaching at Oxford till 1274 when he attended the second Council of Lyons. He held several benefices which he administered most zealously, appointing responsible vicars, visiting them regularly, and showing himself a model pastor by his holiness and wide charity. In June, 1275, he was appointed Bishop of Hereford, and was consecrated by his friend Cardinal Kilwardby (8 Sept., 1275). As bishop he continued his apostolic life, labouring incessantly for the good of his people, maintaining the privileges and property of his diocese against Gilbert of Gloucester, Llewellyn, and others, supporting Edward I in his struggle with Llewellyn, combating the unjust practices of the Jews, and reforming the clergy, secular and regular. He came into conflict with Archbishop Peckham on questions of jurisdiction, and at the Council of Reading (July, 1279) led the resistance of the bishops to the policy of Peckham. (For the articles embodying the points in dispute see Wilkins, "Concilia", II, 75.) His personal differences with Peckham led first to his withdrawal to Normandy that he might avoid an interdict and appeal to Rome, and subsequently in 1282 to his actual excommunication by the archbishop. He then went to Rome to plead his own cause before Pope Martin IV, who received him kindly. But his failing health succumbed to the fatigue of the journey and the summer heat. He was buried at Orvieto, but subsequently his relics were brought back to Hereford, where many miracles were wrought by his intercession and his shrine became second only to that of St. Thomas of Canterbury. He was canonized by John XXII (17 April, 1320), and his festival, formerly observed on 2 October, is now kept in England on 3 October.

STRANGE, *Life and Gests of Thomas of Cantelupe* (Ghent, 1674; London, 1879); BOLLANDISTS, *Acta SS.*, I Oct. (based on the *Processus Canonizationis* (Vatican MS. 4015) also *Bib. Hag. Lat.* (1901); CAPGRAVE, *Nova legenda Angliæ* (Oxford, 1901); SURIUS, *De probatis sanctorum vitis* (Turin, 1875–80); BUTLER, *Lives of the Saints*, Oct. 2; CHALLONER, *Britannia sancta* (London, 1745); TOUT in *Dict. Nat. Biog.*, s. v. *Cantelupe, Thomas de* (giving list of the abundant medieval materials too numerous to be quoted here); HARDY, *Descriptive Catalogue* (for MSS. sources), I and III (London, 1862–71); *Bibl. de l'école de chartes*, IV (Paris, 1893).

EDWIN BURTON.

Thomas of Jesus (THOMAS DE ANDRADA), reformer and preacher, b. at Lisbon, 1529; d. at Sagena, Morocco, 17 April, 1582. He was educated by the Augustinian Hermits from the age of ten, entered the order at Lisbon in 1534, completed his studies at Coimbra, and was appointed novice-master. In his zeal for primitive observance he attempted a thorough reform of the order, but the opposition was such that he was obliged to desist. However, the eventual establishment of the Discalced or Reformed Augustinians is attributed to the initiative of Thomas de Andrada (see HERMITS OF ST. AUGUSTINE). High in favour at Court, Thomas assisted, in 1578, at the death of John III, of which he has left an interesting narrative in a letter still extant.

John's successor, Sebastian, immediately set out on his ill-starred expedition to Africa (see PORTUGAL), and he insisted that Thomas should accompany the forces. The holy Hermit laboured among the soldiery with his accustomed zeal until wounded and taken captive at Alcacer, 1578. A Mohammedan monk became his master and, first by kindness then by torture, strove to secure his perversion. Into the dungeon where he was confined a faint gleam penetrated for a short period at midday, and by that light, day after day, Thomas composed for the comfort of his fellow-prisoners his great work, "Os trabalhos de Jesus", contemplations on the sufferings of Jesus, which have since proved the nourishment and edification of countless souls. The Portuguese ambassador, learning of his pitiable plight, rescued Thomas and placed him under the care of a Christian merchant. But he begged to be sent on at once to Sagena, where some two thousand of the poorest captives were detained. There he commenced an apostolate which was soon blessed with marvellous fruit; the jail seemed transformed into a monastery, numbers were saved from apostasy or reconciled, and several of his penitents suffered a glorious martyrdom. Meanwhile vigorous efforts were being made to procure his complete liberation, but Thomas declared that, captive or free, he would remain to the end in the service of the Christian slaves of the Moors. His enfeebled frame at last succumbed to the combined effects of his sufferings, toils, and austerities. He spent his dying breath in reassuring some poor Christians on the point of apostasy that their ransom would arrive by a certain date if they persevered, as indeed it did.

Since early in the eighteenth century there have been several English editions of Thomas's famous work on the Passion, but the last complete version has long been out of print.

For biography see *Introduction* to *Sufferings of Jesus* (tr., London, 1863). For interesting and complete account of various English versions of *Os trabalhos de Jesus* see PRESTAGE in *Bôletim da segunda classe: Academia das Sciencias de Lisboa*, IV, No. 1 (Lisbon, 1911).

VINCENT SCULLY.

Thomas of Jorz (often but erroneously called JOYCE and frequently referred to as ANGLUS or ANGLICUS), theologian and cardinal, date of birth and circumstances of his education unknown; d. at Grenoble, 13 December, 1310. He entered the Order of Preachers in England, and was remarkable for his piety, erudition, and executive ability. He was master of theology at Oxford, acted as prior of the Dominican convent there, and afterwards served as Provincial of the English Province for seven years (1296–1303). He stood in special favour with Edward, King of England, acting as his confessor and executing several commissions for him. While at Lyons on a commission for the king, 15 Dec., 1305, he was created Cardinal Priest of Santa Sabina by Clement V. This pope also appointed him legate to Henry VII, King of Germany, but in fulfilling the appointment he was taken sick and died. His body was afterwards transferred to Oxford and buried under the choir of the Dominican church. His writings are often confused with those of Thomas of Wales, O.P., also called Anglus or Anglicus. His most important work is "Commentaria in IV libros Sententiarum". The commentary on the first book (Venice, 1523) still enjoys popularity, and offers a concise and complete refutation of the attacks made by Scotus on the teachings of Saint Thomas.

QUÉTIF-ECHARD, *Script. ord. P.*, I (Paris, 1719), 508–10; TOURON, *Hom. ill. Domin.*, I (Paris, 1743), 745–53; BALUZE, *Vitæ pap. Aven.*, I (Paris, 1693), 582–4; KINGSFORD in *Dict. Nat. Biog.*, s. v. *Jorz*, LELONG, *Bibl. sac.*, II (Paris, 1723), 799, 988; TANNER, *Bibl. brit.-hib.* (London, 1748), 749; HURTER, *Nomenclator*.

IGNATIUS SMITH.

Thomas of Strasburg, a fourteenth-century scholastic of the Augustinian Order, b., according to some writers, at Hagenau in Alsace, according to others, at Strasburg; d. 1357. It was probably at Strasburg that he entered the Augustinian Order, and there he began his career as a teacher. About the year 1341 he went to Paris and became famous as a teacher in the university. In 1345 he was elected general of his order, a position which he held until his death. As general, he undertook the revision of the constitution of his order, and published the revised statutes under the title "Constitutiones Ordinis Sui". He interested himself also in the promotion of study among the members of his order, and was instrumental in founding at Verona in 1351 a *studium generale*, or university, for the study of logic, philosophy, and theology. His best known work is a commentary on the "Books of Sentences" of Peter the Lombard, published at Strasburg in 1490 (other editions: Venice, 1564 and 1588; Genoa, 1585; Geneva, 1635). He was also the author of sermons, meditations, and letters, still unpublished.

As a teacher and commentator he adhered closely to the doctrines of Giles of Rome (Ægidius Romanus, or de Columna), who since 1287 had been recognized as the *doctor ordinis* of the Augustinians. He opposed the innovations of Henry of Ghent and the abstruse distinctions of the Scotists. For example, on the question of the distinction between the nature of God and the Divine attributes, he taught that there can be no formal distinction, nor any distinction of any kind except by comparison of the external effects of those attributes. Similarly there is, he maintained, no formal distinction between God and the Divine ideas; whatever distinction exists among the ideas themselves or between the ideas and the Divine essence is the work of the Divine intellect. In regard to the origin of the universe, he maintained that the doctrine of creation can be proved by strict demonstration, the starting-point of the proof being the fact that the power of God, being unlimited, could not postulate a material as a necessary condition of action: just as the existence of God does not postulate any other being, so the Divine action does not postulate a material on which to act. This refers, however, to creation in general. Whether the material universe was created in time or with time, or, on the contrary, was created *ab æterno*, is a question which, he believed, the human mind cannot solve without the aid of revelation.

STÖCKL, *Gesch. der Phil. des Mittelalters*, II (Mainz, 1865), 1045 sqq.; FABRICIUS, *Biblioth. lat. med. et infimae latin.*, V (Florence, 1858), 537 sqq. OSSINGER, *Bibl. augustiniana*, (Ingolstadt, 1768), 71, sqq. DE WULF, tr. COFFEY, *Hist. of Med. Phil.* (New York, 1909), 437, 438, has a paragraph on the Ægidian School.

WILLIAM TURNER.

Thomas of Villanova, SAINT, educator, philanthropist, b. at Fuentellana, Spain, 1488; d. at Valencia, 8 Sept., 1555. Son of Alonzo Tomas García and Lucía Martínez Castellanos, the saint was brought up in the practices of religion and charity. Every Friday his father was wont to give in alms all the meal he earned at his mill, besides his usual daily dole of bread. On great feast-days he added wood, wine, and money; while to poor farmers he loaned money and seed. On the death of her husband, Lucía continued the usual alms, and supplied indigent maidens in the neighbourhood with clothing and money. When sixteen years old, Thomas entered the University of Alcalá, where, after proceeding master of arts and licentiate in theology, he filled the chair (1514) of arts, logic, and philosophy. Among his auditors were the famed scholars Ferdinand de Encina and Dominic Soto. With Alcalá, however, ended his university associations, he having declined the chair of natural philosophy at Salamanca, where he joined the Augustinians in 1516, his vows following a year later, and his ordination to priesthood the year after; his first Mass was celebrated at Christmas, 1518. At Salamanca Convent Thomas was given the class of Scholastic theology because of his attachment for books, chiefly the Lombard and St. Thomas, and his exemplary life. Preaching in the chief pulpits of Spain was soon added to his duties, among other places at Valencia, the field of his later trials, and Valladolid, seat of the imperial Court and residence of the Emperor Charles V when on his visits from the Low Countries. In this last-named city St. Thomas was named by the emperor his court preacher, and one of his councillors of State. Rarely, however, did the saint pay visits of ceremony to the then master of Europe, though his written correspondence with Charles, who held his opinions in high esteem, was voluminous. Towards the close of his life, while at Valencia, he had all the emperor's letters destroyed; his own letters to the emperor, however, are now stored at Simancas.

Apart from these burdens Thomas held many offices of trust in his order, e. g. as convent prior in various cities, among others at Valladolid in 1544, the very year he was called to the See of Valencia. Moreover, he was twice provincial-prior, first of Andalusia and Castile in 1527, then six years later of Castile alone, whence the first mission band of his brethren was sent across the Atlantic in 1533 to establish houses of their order in Mexico. On 5 Aug., 1544, he received his nomination to the Archbishopric of Valencia, a post that for well-nigh a hundred years had witnessed no bishop in residence, an appointment that was confirmed by Paul III. Previously St. Thomas had declined the See of Granada, offered him by the emperor, while that of Valencia he accepted only through obedience to his superiors. He was consecrated in the church of his order at Valladolid by Juan, Cardinal Tavera de Pardo, Archbishop of Toledo. On his entrance to his see on 1 Jan., 1545, of which he was thirty-second bishop and eighth archbishop, St. Thomas opened his career as legislator and philanthropist, which won for him the titles of "Almsgiver", "Father of the Poor", and "Model of Bishops", given him at his beatification in 1618 by Paul V. During his eleven years of episcopal rule his most noteworthy deeds were as follows: a visitation of his diocese, opened a few weeks after entrance into his see. Among other amendments he inhibited his visitators from accepting any gifts whatever. He then held a synod, the first at Valencia for many years, whereby he sought to do away with a number of abuses, as bloodshed, divorce, concubinage, and many excessive privileges or unreasonable exemptions; he abolished the underground prisons; rebuilt the general hospital at Valencia which had just been destroyed by fire; founded two colleges, one for young ecclesiastics, the other for poor students; laboured for the conversion of the *nuevos Cristianos*, whose profession of Christianity was largely mere outward show; established a crèche near his palace for foundlings and the offspring of indigent parents; had Mass said at early hours for the working-classes; and in brief, by statutes, by preaching, and by example, strove to reform the morals of churchman and layman.

Towards the poor especially his heart was ever alive with pity; to them his palace gate was always open; daily he had a repast for every poor person that applied for help, as many even as four to five hundred thus getting their meals at his hands. In every district of the city he had almoners appointed with orders especially to search out the respectable persons who shrank from asking alms; these he had supplied with money, food, clothing, while as to indigent workmen, poor farmers, and mechanics, he replenished their stock and bought them tools, thus putting them in the way of making a living. His whole life was replete with acts of practical kindness. He spent his spare time chiefly in prayer and study; his table was one of simple fare, with no luxuries. His dress was inexpensive; he mended with his own hands whatever needed repairs. Numberless are the instances of St. Thomas's supernatural gifts, of his power of healing the sick, of multiplication of food, of redressing grievances, of his ecstasies, of his conversions of sinners. He was taken ill in August, 1555, of angina pectoris, of which he died at the age of 67, at the termination of Mass in his bedroom. His last words were the versicles: "In manus tuas, Domine", etc.; his remains were entombed at the convent Church of Our Lady of Help of his order outside the city walls, whence later they were brought to the cathedral. The saint was of well-knit frame, of medium height, with dark complexion, brilliant eyes, ruddy cheeks, and Roman nose. He was beatified by Paul V (7 Oct., 1618), who set his feast-day for 18 Sept., and canonized by Alexander VII on 1 Nov., 1658.

Various reasons are given to account for St. Thomas's non-appearance at the Council of Trent, among them that he was ill, unable to stand the fatigue of travel; that his people would not brook his absence; and that the emperor felt unable to do without his aid at home. The writings of St. Thomas, mainly sermons, are replete with practical norms of mystic theology. Some twenty editions have been published, the best and most complete being probably that of Manila, 1882–1884, in 5 tomes.

SALON, *Vita* (Milan, 1880); MAIMBOURG, *Life*, republished in London by the Oratorians, and in Philadelphia in 1874; DABERT, *Histoire* (Paris and Lyons, 1852); *Ciudad de Dios* (Valladolid and Madrid, 1882). EDWARD G. DOHAN.

Thomas Percy, BLESSED, Earl of Northumberland, martyr, b. in 1528; d. at York, 22 August, 1572. He was the eldest son of Sir Thomas Percy, brother of the childless Henry Percy, sixth Earl of Northumberland, and Eleanor, daughter of Sir Guiscard Harbottal. When Thomas was eight years old his father was executed at Tyburn (2 June, 1537) for having taken a leading part in the Pilgrimage of Grace, and he also is considered a martyr by many. Thomas and his brother Henry were then removed from their mother's keeping and entrusted to Sir Thomas Tempest.

In 1549, when Thomas Percy came of age, an Act was passed "for the restitution in blood of Mr. Thomas Percy". Shortly afterwards he was knighted, and, three years later, in Queen Mary's reign, he regained his ancestral honours and lands. Declared governor of Prudhoe Castle he besieged and took Scarborough Castle, which was seized by rebels in 1557. In reward the Earldom of Northumberland together with the Baronies of Percy, Poynings, Lucy, Bryan, and Fitzpane were restored to him. He was installed at Whitehall with great pomp, and soon after was named Warden General of the Marches, in which capacity he fought and defeated the Scots. In 1558 he married Anne Somerset, daughter of the Earl of Worcester, a valiant woman who subsequently suffered much for the Faith.

On Elizabeth's accession the earl, whose steadfast loyalty to the Catholic Church was known, was kept in the North while the anti-Catholic measures of Elizabeth's first Parliament were passed. Elizabeth continued to show him favour, and in 1563 gave him the Order of the Garter. He had then resigned the wardenship and was living in the South. But the systematic persecution of the Catholics rendered their position most difficult, and in the autumn of 1569 the Catholic gentry in the North, stirred up by rumours of the approaching excommunication of Elizabeth, were planning to liberate Mary, Queen of Scots, and obtain liberty of worship. Earl Thomas with the Earl of Westmoreland wrote to the pope asking for advice, but before their letter reached Rome circumstances hurried them into action against their better judgment. After a brief success the rising failed, and Thomas fled to Scotland, where he was captured and, after three years, sold to the English Government. He was conducted to York and beheaded, refusing to save his life by abandoning his religion. He was beatified by Leo XIII on 13 May, 1895, and his festival was appointed to be observed in the Dioceses of Hexham and Newcastle on 14 November. His daughter Mary founded the Benedictine convent at Brussels from which nearly all the existing houses of Benedictine nuns in England are descended.

PHILLIPS in CAMM, *Lives of the English Martyrs*, expanding and correcting the same author's pamphlet *Blessed Thomas Percy* in *Catholic Truth Society*, II (London, 1905), iii, 185; *State Papers of Elizabeth*, especially *Domestic*, Addenda, 1566–79; DE FONBLANQUE, *Annals of the House of Percy* (London, 1887); PERCY in COLLINS, *Peerage of England*, II (London, 1779); *Depositions and Ecclesiastical Proceedings from the Courts of Durham* (London, 1845); BRIDGEWATER, *Concertatio ecclesiæ catholicæ in Anglia* (Trier, 1588); SHARPE, *Memorials of the Rebellion of 1569* (London, 1840). EDWIN BURTON.

Thomas Reddyng, BLESSED. See THOMAS JOHNSON, BLESSED.

Thomas Scryven, BLESSED. See THOMAS JOHNSON, BLESSED.

Thomas Sherwood, BLESSED, martyr, b. in London, 1551; d. at Tyburn, London, 7 February, 1578. His parents also suffered for their conscience, both enduring imprisonment for the Faith. After leaving school in 1566, Thomas assisted his father, a London woollen draper, for about ten years; then, feeling that his vocation was to the priesthood, he made arrangements to go to Douay College and was in London settling his affairs, and obtaining the means for his support and education. While so engaged he was recognized in Chancery Lane and betrayed by George Marten, son of Lady Tregonwell. Being examined before the Recorder as to his opinion of the Bull of Pius V and as to whether an excommunicated queen held lawful sovereignty, he denied all knowledge of both Bull and excommunication, but expressed his opinion that if the queen were indeed excommunicated her rule could not be lawful. He was detained at Westminster, where the attorney-general visited him and found him constant in that opinion. On 17 November, 1577, he was committed to the Tower by the Privy Council to be retained close prisoner, from conference with any person, and if he did not willingly confess such things as were demanded of him, he was to be committed to the dungeon amongst the rats. He was repeatedly examined, and twice racked in order to elicit where he had heard Mass and who had been present thereat, but his constancy was unshaken. After being racked, he was cast into a dark and fetid dungeon, where he was kept absolutely without clothes, without food, and with nothing but the bare earth to lie upon. His friends were not allowed to supply his needs, and the utmost concession that William Romper could obtain was permission to supply him with straw to lie upon. He was brought to trial on 3 February, and pronounced guilty of high treason for denying the queen's supremacy; four days later he was executed. He was a man of good wit and judgment and, being well instructed in religious matters, was very helpful to many poor Catholics. Small in stature, he was of healthy constitution and of a cheerful disposition, which he maintained even amidst his torture.

Vatican Archives; PERSONS, *Memoirs* in *Cath. Rec. Soc.*, II (London, 1906), documents in the Public Record Office; *Tower Bills* in *Cath. Rec. Soc.*, III; POLLEN, *Acts of English Martyrs* (London, 1891); CHALLONER, *Memoirs of the Missionary Priests*.
J. L. WHITFIELD.

Thomassin, LOUIS, theologian and French Oratorian, b. at Aix-en-Provence 28 Aug., 1619; d. in Paris, 24 Dec., 1695. At the age of thirteen he entered the Oratory and for some years was professor of literature in various colleges of the congregation, of theology at Saumur, and finally in the seminary of Saint Magloire, in Paris, where he remained until his death. His chief works are: "Ancienne et nouvelle discipline de l'église touchant les bénéfices et les bénéficiers" (3 vols. in fol., Paris, 1678–79), which passed through several French and Latin editions and several abridgments; "Dogmatum theologicorum....de Incarnatione, de Dei proprietatibus....etc." (3 vols.

in fol., Paris, 1680-89), likewise re-edited several times (the treatise on the Incarnation is regarded as Thomassin's masterpiece); a series of "Traités historiques et dogmatiques" on ecclesiastical fasts, feasts, the Divine Office, the unity of the Church, truth and lying, alms, business and usury (1680-97), a series of methods of studying and teaching the humanities, philosophy, grammar, history (1681-92); the "Glossarium universale hebraicum" (in fol., Paris, 1697); "Traité dogmatique et historique des édits et d'autres moyens.... dont on s'est servi.... pour établir et maintenir l'unité de l'église" (3 vols. in 4°, Paris, 1705). The last-named two posthumous works were published by P. Bordes, who wrote a life of Thomassin at the beginning of the "Glossarium". Thomassin was one of the most learned men of his time, "Vir stupendæ plane eruditionis", as Hurter says, in his "Nomenclator", II (Innsbruck, 1893), 410.

INGOLD, *Essai de bibliographie oratorienne* (Paris, 1880), 170-76; *Mémoires de Batterel*, III, 477-515.

A. INGOLD.

Thomas Woodhouse, BLESSED, martyr, suffered at Tyburn 19 (not 13) June, 1573, being disembowelled alive. Ordained in Mary's reign, he was a Lincolnshire rector for under a year, and in 1560 acted as a private tutor in Wales. On 14 May, 1561, he was committed to the Fleet, London, having been arrested while saying Mass. For the rest of his life he remained in custody, uncompromising in his opposition to heresy, saying Mass in secret daily, reciting his Office regularly, and thirsting for martyrdom; but treated with considerable leniency till on 19 Nov., 1572, he sent the prison washerwoman to Lord Burghley's house with his famous letter. In it he begs him to seek reconciliation with the pope and earnestly to "persuade the Lady Elizabeth, who for her own great disobedience is most justly deposed, to submit herself unto his spiritual prince and father". Some days later in a personal interview he used equally definite language. Confined then by himself he wrote "divers papers, persuading men to the true faith and obedience", which he signed, tied to stones, and flung into the street. He was repeatedly examined both publicly and privately. Once, when he had denied the queen's title, someone said, "If you saw her Majesty, you would not say so, for her Majesty is great". "But the Majesty of God is greater," he answered. After being sentenced at the Guildhall either in April or on 16 June, he was taken to Newgate. He was admitted to the Society of Jesus in prison, though the Decree of the Cong. of Rites, 4 Dec., 1886, describes him as a secular priest. He is not to be confused with Thomas Wood (q. v.).

KEOGH and POLLEN in *Lives of the English Martyrs*, ed. CAMM, II (London, 1905), xx, 186-203; CARLYLE in *Dict. Nat. Biog.*, s. v. *Woodhouse, Thomas*; HUME, *Calendar State Papers: Spanish, 1568-79* (London, 1894), 471; LEWIS, *Sander's Anglican Schism* (London, 1877), 317.

JOHN B. WAINEWRIGHT.

Thomism.—I. THE DOCTRINE IN GENERAL.—In a broad sense, Thomism is the name given to the system which follows the teaching of St. Thomas Aquinas in philosophical and theological questions. In a restricted sense the term is applied to a group of opinions held by a school called Thomistic, composed principally, but not exclusively, of members of the Order of St. Dominic, these same opinions being attacked by other philosophers or theologians, many of whom profess to be followers of St. Thomas. To Thomism in the first sense are opposed, e. g. the Scotists, who deny that satisfaction is a part of the proximate matter (*materia proxima*) of the Sacrament of Penance. Anti-Thomists, in this sense of the word, reject opinions admittedly taught by St. Thomas. To Thomism in the second sense are opposed, e. g. the Molinists, as well as all who defend the moral instrumental causality of the sacraments in producing grace against the system of physical instrumental causality, the latter being a doctrine of the Thomistic School. Anti-Thomism in such cases does not necessarily imply opposition to St. Thomas: It means opposition to tenets of the Thomistic School. Cardinal Billot, for instance, would not admit that he opposed St. Thomas by rejecting the Thomistic theory on the causality of the sacraments. In the Thomistic School, also, we do not always find absolute unanimity. Bañez and Billuart do not always agree with Cajetan, though all belong to the Thomistic School. It does not come within the scope of this article to determine who have the best right to be considered the true exponents of St. Thomas.

The subject may be treated under the following headings: A. Thomism in general, from the thirteenth century down to the nineteenth; B. The Thomistic School; C. Neo-Thomism and the revival of Scholasticism.

A. *Thomism in General.*—(1) Early opposition overcome.—Although St. Thomas (d. 1274) was highly esteemed by all classes, his opinions did not at once gain the ascendancy and influence which they acquired during the first half of the fourteenth century and which they have since maintained. Strange as it may appear, the first serious opposition came from Paris, of which he was such an ornament, and from some of his own monastic brethren. In the year 1277 Stephen Tempier, Bishop of Paris, censured certain philosophical propositions, embodying doctrines taught by St. Thomas, relating especially to the principle of individuation and to the possibility of creating several angels of the same species. In the same year Robert Kilwardby, a Dominican, Archbishop of Canterbury, in conjunction with some doctors of Oxford, condemned those same propositions and moreover attacked St. Thomas's doctrine of the unity of the substantial form in man. Kilwardby and his associates pretended to see in the condemned propositions something of Averroistic Aristoteleanism, whilst the secular doctors of Paris had not fully forgiven one who had triumphed over them in the controversy as to the rights of the mendicant friars. The storm excited by these condemnations was of short duration. Blessed Albertus Magnus, in his old age, hastened to Paris to defend his beloved disciple. The Dominican Order, assembled in general chapter at Milan in 1278 and at Paris in 1279, adopted severe measures against the members who had spoken injuriously of the venerable Brother Thomas. When William de la Mare, O.S.F., wrote a "Correptorium fratris Thomæ", an English Dominican, Richard Clapwell (or Clapole), replied in a treatise "Contra corruptorium fratris Thomæ". About the same time there appeared a work, which was afterwards printed at Venice (1516) under the title, "Correctorium corruptorii S. Thomæ", attributed by some to Ægidius Romanus, by others to Clapwell, by others to Father John of Paris. St. Thomas was solemnly vindicated when the Council of Vienna (1311-12) defined, against Peter John Olivi, that the rational soul is the substantial form of the human body (on this definition see Zigliara, "De mente Conc. Vienn.", Rome, 1878).

The canonization of St. Thomas by John XXII, in 1323, was a death-blow to his detractors. In 1324 Stephen de Bourret, Bishop of Paris, revoked the censure pronounced by his predecessor, declaring that "that blessed confessor and excellent doctor, Thomas Aquinas, had never believed, taught, or written anything contrary to the Faith or good morals". It is doubtful whether Tempier and his associates acted in the name of the University of Paris, which had always been loyal to St. Thomas. When this university, in 1378, wrote a letter condemning the errors of John de Montesono, it was explicitly declared that the condemnation was not aimed at St. Thomas: "We have said a thousand times, and yet, it would seem, not often enough, that we by no means include the doctrine of St. Thomas in our condemnation." An account of these attacks and defences will be found in the following works: Echard, "Script. ord. præd.", I, 279 (Paris, 1719); De Rubeis, "Diss. crit.", Diss. xxv, xxvi, I, p. cclxviii; Leonine edit. Works of St. Thomas; Denifle, "Chart. univ. Paris" (Paris, 1890–91), I, 543, 558, 566; II, 6, 280; Duplessis d'Argentré, "Collectio judiciorum de novis erroribus" (3 vols., Paris, 1733–36), I, 175 sqq.; Du Boulay, "Hist. univ. Par.", IV, 205, 436, 618, 622, 627; Jourdain, "La phil. de s. Thomas d'Aquin" (Paris, 1858), II, i; Douais, "Essai sur l'organization des études dans l'ordre des ff. prêcheurs" (Paris and Toulouse, 1884), 87 sqq.; Mortier, "Hist. des maîtres gén. de l'ordre des ff. prêch.", II, 115–142, 571; "Acta cap. gen. ord. præd.", ed. Reichert (9 vols., Rome, 1893–1904, II; Turner, "Hist. of Phil." (Boston, 1903), xxxix.

B. *Progress of Thomism.*—The general chapter of the Dominican Order, held at Carcassonne in 1342, declared that the doctrine of St. Thomas had been received as sound and solid throughout the world (Douais, op. cit., 106). His works were consulted from the time they became known, and by the middle of the fourteenth century his "Summa theologica" had supplanted the "Libri quatuor sententiarum" of Peter Lombard as the text-book of theology in the Dominican schools. With the growth of the order and the widening of its influence Thomism spread throughout the world; St. Thomas became the great master in the universities and in the *studia* of the religious orders (see Encyc. "Æterni Patris" of Leo XIII). The fifteenth and sixteenth centuries saw Thomism in a triumphal march which led to the crowning of St. Thomas as the Prince of Theologians, when his "Summa" was laid beside the Sacred Scriptures at the Council of Trent, and St. Pius V, in 1567, proclaimed him a Doctor of the Universal Church. The publication of the "Piana" edition of his works, in 1570, and the multiplication of editions of the "Opera omnia" and of the "Summa" during the seventeenth century and part of the eighteenth show that Thomism flourished during that period. In fact it was during that period that some of the great commentators (for example, Suárez, Sylvius, and Billuart) adapted his works to the needs of the times.

C. *Decline of Scholasticism and of Thomism.*—Gradually, however, during the seventeenth and eighteenth centuries, there came a decline in the study of the works of the great Scholastics. Scholars believed that there was need of a new system of studies, and, instead of building upon and around Scholasticism, they drifted away from it. The chief causes which brought about the change were Protestantism, Humanism, the study of nature, and the French Revolution. Positive theology was considered more necessary in discussions with the Protestants than Scholastic definitions and divisions. Elegance of diction was sought by the Humanists in the Greek and Latin Classics, rather than in the works of the Scholastics, many of whom were far from being masters of style. The discoveries of Copernicus (d. 1543), Kepler (d. 1631), Galilei (d. 1642), and Newton (d. 1727) were not favourably received by the Scholastics. The experimental sciences were in honour; the Scholastics, including St. Thomas, were neglected (cf. Turner, op. cit., 433). Finally, the French Revolution disorganized all ecclesiastical studies, dealing to Thomism a blow from which it did not fully recover until the last quarter of the nineteenth century. At the time when Billuart (d. 1757) published his "Summa Sancti Thomæ hodiernis academiarum moribus accomodata" Thomism still held an important place in all theological discussion. The tremendous upheaval which disturbed Europe from 1798 to 1815 affected the Church as well as the State. The University of Louvain, which had been largely Thomistic, was compelled to close its doors, and other important institutions of learning were either closed or seriously hampered in their work. The Dominican Order, which naturally had supplied the most ardent Thomists, was crushed in France, Germany, Switzerland, and Belgium. The province of Holland was almost destroyed, whilst the provinces of Austria and Italy were left to struggle for their very existence. The University of Manila (1645) continued to teach the doctrines of St. Thomas and in due time gave to the world Cardinal Zephyrinus González, O.P., who contributed in no small degree to the revival of Thomism under Leo XIII.

D. *Distinctive Doctrines of Thomism in General.*—(1) In Philosophy. (a) The angels and human souls are without matter, but every material composite being (*compositum*) has two parts, prime matter and substantial form. In a composite being which has substantial unity and is not merely an aggregate of distinct units, there can be but one substantial form. The substantial form of man is his soul (*anima rationalis*) to the exclusion of any other soul and of any other substantial form. The principle of individuation, for material composites, is matter with its dimensions: without this there can be no merely numerical multiplication: distinction in the form makes specific distinction: hence there cannot be two angels of the same species. (b) The essences of things do not depend on the free will of God, but on His intellect, and ultimately on His essence, which is immutable. The natural law, being derived from the eternal law, depends on the mind of God, ultimately on the essence of God; hence it is intrinsically immutable. Some actions are forbidden by God because they are bad: they are not bad simply because He forbids them [see Zigliara, "Sum. phil." (3 vols., Paris, 1889), cxx, xi, 11, M. 23, 24, 25]. (c) The will moves the intellect *quoad exercitium*, i. e. in its actual operation: the intellect moves the will *quoad specificationem*, i. e. by presenting objects to it: *nil volitum nisi præcognitum*. The beginning of all our acts is the apprehension and desire of good in general (*bonum in communi*). We desire happiness (*bonum in communi*) naturally and necessarily, not by a free deliberate act. Particular goods (*bona particularia*) we choose freely; and the will is a blind faculty, always following the last practical judgment of the intellect (Zigliara, 51). (d) The senses and the intellect are passive, i. e. recipient, faculties; they do not create, but receive (i. e. perceive) their objects (St. Thomas, I, Q. lxxviii, a. 3; Q. lxxix, a. 2; Zigliara, 26, 27). If this principle is borne in mind there is no reason for Kant's "Critique of Pure Reason". On the other hand those faculties are not like wax, or the sensitive plate used by photographers, in the sense that they are inert and receive impressions unconsciously. The will controls the exercise of the faculties, and the process of acquiring knowledge is a vital process: the moving cause is always within the living agent. (e) The Peripatetic axiom: "Nihil est in intellectu quod non prius in sensu" (Nothing is in the intellect that was not first in the senses), is admitted; but St. Thomas modifies it by saying: first, that, once the sense objects have been perceived, the intellect ascends to the knowledge of higher things, even of God; and, secondly, that the soul knows its own existence by itself (i. e. by its own act), although it knows its own nature only by reflection on its acts. Knowledge begins by sense perception, but the range of the intellect is far beyond that of the senses. In the soul as soon as it begins to act are found the first principles (*prima principia*) of all knowledge, not in the form of an objective illumination, but in the form of a subjective inclination to admit them on account of their evidence. As soon as they are proposed we see that they are true; there is no more reason for doubting them than there is for denying the existence of the sun when we see it shining (see Zigliara, op. cit., pp. 32–42). (f) The direct and primary object of the intellect is the universal, which is prepared and presented to the passive intellect (*intellectus possibilis*) by the active intellect (*intellectus agens*) which illuminates the phantasmata, or mental images, received through the senses, and divests them of all individuating conditions. This is called abstracting the universal idea from the phantasmata, but the term must not be taken in a materialistic sense. Abstraction is not a transferring of something from one place to another; the illumination causes all material and individuating conditions to disappear, then the universal alone shines out and is perceived by the vital action of the intellect (Q. lxxxiv, a. 4; Q. lxxxv, a. 1, ad 1um, 3um, 4um). The process throughout is so vital, and so far elevated above material conditions and modes of action, that the nature of the acts and of the objects apprehended proves the soul to be immaterial and spiritual. (g) The soul, by its very nature, is immortal. Not only is it true that God will not annihilate the soul, but from its very nature it will always continue to exist, there being in it no principle of disintegration (Zigliara, p. 9). Hence human reason can prove the incorruptibility (i. e. immortality) of the soul. (h) The existence of God is not known by an innate idea, it cannot be proved by arguments *a priori* or *a simultaneo*; but it can be demonstrated by *a posteriori* arguments. Ontologism was never taught by St. Thomas or by Thomists (see Lepidi, "Exam. phil. theol. de ontologismo", Louvain, 1874, c. 19; Zigliara, Theses I, VIII). (i) There are no human (i. e. deliberate) acts indifferent *in individuo*.

(2) In Theology. (a) Faith and science, i. e. knowledge by demonstration, cannot co-exist in the same subject with regard to the same object (Zigliara, O., 32, VII); and the same is true of knowledge and opinion. (b) The metaphysical essence of God consists, according to some Thomists, in the *intelligere actualissimum*, i. e. fulness of pure intellection, according to others in the perfection of *aseitas*, i. e. independent existence (Zigliara, Th. VIII, IX). (c) The happiness of heaven, formally and in the ultimate analysis, consists in the vision, not in the fruition, of God. (d) The Divine attributes are distinguished from the Divine nature and from each other by a virtual distinction, i. e. by a *distinctio rationis cum fundamento a parte rei*. The *distinctio actualis formalis* of Scotus is rejected. (e) In attempting to explain the mystery of the Trinity—in as far as man can conceive it—the relations must be considered *perfectiones simpliciter simplices*, i. e. excluding all imperfection. The Holy Ghost would not be distinct from the Son if He did not proceed from the Son as well as from the Father. (f) The angels, being pure spirits, are not, properly speaking, in any place; they are said to be in the place, or in the places, where they exercise their activity (Summa, I, Q. lii, a. 1). Strictly speaking, there is no such thing as an angel passing from place to place; but if an angel wishes to exercise its activity first in Japan and afterwards in America, it can do so in two instants (of angelic time), and need not pass through the intervening space (Q. liii). St. Thomas does not discuss the question: "How many angels can dance on the point of a needle?" He reminds us that we must not think of angels as if they were corporeal, and that, for an angel, it makes no difference whether the sphere of his activity be the point of a needle or a continent (Q. lii, a. 2). Many angels cannot be said to be in the same place at the same time, for this would mean that whilst one angel is producing an effect others could be producing the same effect at the same time. There can be but one angel in the same place at the same time (Q. lii, a. 3). The knowledge of the angels comes through ideas (*species*) infused by God (QQ. lv, a. 2, lvii, a. 2, lviii, a. 7). They do not naturally know future contingents, the secrets of souls, or the mysteries of grace (Q. lvii, aa. 3, 45). The angels choose either good or evil instantly, and with full knowledge; hence their judgment is naturally final and irrevocable (Q. lxiv, a. 2). (g) Man was created in the state of sanctifying grace. Grace was not due to his nature, but God granted it to him from the beginning (I, Q. xcv, a. 1). So great was the perfection of man in the state of original justice, and so perfect the subjection of his lower faculties to the higher, that his first sin could not have been a venial sin (I–II, Q. lxxxix, a. 3). (h) It is more probable that the Incarnation would not have taken place had man not sinned (III, Q. i, a. 3). In Christ there were three kinds of knowledge: the *scientia beata*, i. e. the knowledge of things in the Divine Essence; the *scientia infusa*, i. e. the knowledge of things through infused ideas (*species*), and the *scientia acquisita*, i. e. acquired or experimental knowledge, which was nothing more than the actual experience of things which he already knew. On this last point St. Thomas, in the "Summa" (Q. ix, a. 4), explicitly retracts an opinion which he had once held (III Sent., d. 14, Q. iii, a. 3). (i) All sacraments of the New Law, including confirmation and extreme unction, were instituted immediately by Christ. Circumcision was a sacrament of the Old Law and conferred grace which removed the stain of original sin. The children of Jews or of other unbelievers may not be baptized without the consent of their parents (III, Q. lxviii, a. 10; II–II, Q. x, a. 12; Denzinger-Bannwart, n. 1481). Contrition, confession, and satisfaction are the proximate matter (*materia proxima*) of the Sacrament of Penance. Thomists hold, against the Scotists, that when Transubstantiation takes place in the Mass the Body of Christ is not made present *per modum adductionis*, i. e. is not brought to the altar, but they do not agree in selecting the term which should be used to express this action (cf. Billuart, "De Euchar.", Diss. i, a. 7). Cardinal Billot holds ("De eccl. sacr.", Rome, 1900, Th. XI, "De euchar.", p. 379) that the best, and the only possible, explanation is the one given by St. Thomas himself: Christ becomes present by transubstantiation, i. e. by the conversion of the substance of bread into the substance of His body (III, Q. lxxv, a. 4; Sent., d. XI, Q. i, a. 1, q. 1). After the consecration the accidents (*accidentia*) of the bread and wine are preserved by Almighty God without a subject (Q. lxxxvii, a. 1). It was on this question that the doctors of Paris sought enlightenment from St. Thomas (see Vaughan, "Life and Labours of St. Thomas", London, 1872, II, p. 544). The earlier Thomists, following St. Thomas (Suppl., Q. xxxvii, a. 2), taught that the sub-diaconate and the four minor orders were partial sacraments. Some recent Thomists—e. g., Billot (op. cit., p. 282)—and Tanquerey (De ordine, n. 16) defend this opinion as more probable and more in conformity with the definitions of the councils. The giving of the chalice with wine and of the paten with bread Thomists generally held to be an essential part of ordination to the priesthood. Some, however, taught that the imposition of hands was at least necessary. On the question of divorce under the Mosaic Law the disciples of St. Thomas, like the saint himself (Suppl., Q. lxvii, a. 3), wavered, some holding that a dispensation was granted, others teaching that divorce was merely tolerated in order to avoid greater evils.

II. THE THOMISTIC SCHOOL.—The chief doctrines distinctive of this school, composed principally of Dominican writers, are the following:—

A. *In Philosophy*.—(1) The unity of substantial form in composite beings, applied to man, requires that the soul be the substantial form of the man, so as to exclude even the *forma corporeitatis*, admitted by Henry of Ghent, Scotus, and others (cf. Zigliara, P. 13; Denzinger-Bannwart, in note to n. 1655). (2) In created beings there is a real distinction between the *essentia* (essence) and the *existentia* (existence); between the *essentia* and the *subsistentia;* between the real relation and its foundation; between the soul and its faculties; between the several faculties. There can be no medium between a *distinctio realis* and a *distinctio rationis*, or conceptual distinction; hence the *distinctio formalis a parte rei* of Scotus cannot be admitted. For Thomistic doctrines on free will, God's knowledge, etc., see below.

B. *In Theology.*—(1) In the beatific vision God's essence takes the place not only of the *species impressa*, but also of the *species expressa*. (2) All moral virtues, the acquired as well as the infused, in their perfect state, are interconnected. (3) According to Billuart (De pecc., diss. vii, a. 6), it has been a matter of controversy between Thomists whether the malice of a mortal sin is absolutely infinite. (4) In choosing a medium between Rigorism and Laxism, the Thomistic school has been Antiprobabilistic and generally has adopted Probabiliorism. Some defended Æquiprobabilism, or Probabilism *cum compensatione*. Medina and St. Antoninus are claimed by the Probabilists. (5) Thomistic theologians generally, whilst they defended the infallibility of the Roman pontiff, denied that the pope had the power to dissolve a *matrimonium ratum* or to dispense from a solemn vow made to God. When it was urged that some popes had granted such favours, they cited other pontiffs who declared that they could not grant them (cf. Billuart, "De matrim.", Diss. v, a. 2), and said, with Dominic Soto, "Factum pontificium non facit articulum fidei" (The action of a pope does not constitute an article of faith, in 4 dist., 27, Q. i, a. 4). Thomists of to-day are of a different mind, owing to the practice of the Church. (6) The hypostatic union, without any additional grace, rendered Christ impeccable. The Word was hypostatically united to the blood of Christ and remained united to it, even during the interval between His death and resurrection (Denzinger-Bannwart, n. 718). During that same interval the Body of Christ had a transitory form, called *forma cadaverica* (Zigliara, P. 16, 17, IV). (7) The sacraments of the New Law cause grace not only as instrumental moral causes, but by a mode of causality which should be called instrumental and physical. In the attrition required in the Sacrament of Penance there should be at least a beginning of the love of God; sorrow for sin springing solely from the fear of hell will not suffice. (8) Many theologians of the Thomistic School, especially before the Council of Trent, opposed the doctrine of Mary's Immaculate Conception, claiming that in this they were following St. Thomas. This, however, has not been the opinion either of the entire school or of the Dominican Order as a body. Father Rouard de Card, in his book "L'ordre des frères prêcheurs et l'Immaculée Conception" (Brussels, 1864), called attention to the fact that ten thousand professors of the order defended Mary's great privilege. At the Council of Trent twenty-five Dominican bishops signed a petition for the definition of the dogma. Thousands of Dominicans, in taking degrees at the University of Paris, solemnly pledged themselves to defend the Immaculate Conception (see bibliog. to THOMAS AQUINAS, SAINT; also Kennedy, "The Imm. Con." in "Cath. Univ. Bulletin", March, 1910). (9) The Thomistic School is distinguished from other schools of theology chiefly by its doctrines on the difficult questions relating to God's action on the free will of man, God's foreknowledge, grace, and predestination. In the articles on these subjects will be found an exposition of the different theories advanced by the different schools in their effort to explain these mysteries, for such they are in reality. As to the value of these theories the following points should be borne in mind: (a) No theory has as yet been proposed which avoids all difficulties and solves all doubts; (b) on the main and most difficult of these questions some who are at times listed as Molinists—notably Bellarmine, Suárez, Francis de Lugo, and, in our own days, Cardinal Billot ("De deo uno et trino", Rome, 1902, Th. XXXII)—agree with the Thomists in defending predestination ante *prævisa merita*. Bossuet, after a long study of the question of physical premotion, adapted the Thomistic opinion ("Du libre arbitre", c. viii). (c) Thomists do not claim to be able to explain, except by a general reference to God's omnipotence, how man remains free under the action of God, which they consider necessary in order to preserve and explain the universality of God's causality and the independent certainty of His foreknowledge. No man can explain, except by a reference to God's infinite power, how the world was created out of nothing, yet we do not on this account deny creation, for we know that it must be admitted. In like manner the main question put to Thomists in this controversy should be not "How will you explain man's liberty?" but "What are your reasons for claiming so much for God's action?" If the reasons assigned are insufficient, then one great difficulty is removed, but there remains to be solved the problem of God's foreknowledge of man's free acts. If they are valid, then we must accept them with their necessary consequences and humbly confess our inability fully to explain how wisdom "reacheth . . . from end to end mightily, and ordereth all things sweetly" (Wis., viii, 1). (d) Most important of all, it must be clearly understood and remembered that the Thomistic system on predestination neither saves fewer nor sends to perdition more souls than any other system held by Catholic theologians. In regard to the number of the elect there is no unanimity on either side; this is not the question in dispute between the Molinists and the Thomists. The discussions, too often animated and needlessly sharp, turned on this point: How does it happen that, although God sincerely desires the salvation of all men, some are to be saved, and must thank God for whatever merits they may have amassed, whilst others will be lost, and will know that they themselves, and not God, are to be blamed?—The facts in the case are admitted by all Catholic theologians. The Thomists, appealing to the authority of St. Augustine and St. Thomas, defend a system which follows the admitted facts to their logical conclusions. The elect are saved by the grace of God, which operates on their wills efficaciously and infallibly without detriment to their liberty; and since God sincerely desires the salvation of all men, He is prepared to grant that same grace to others, if they do not, by a free act, render themselves unworthy of it. The faculty of placing obstacles to Divine grace is the unhappy faculty of sinning; and the existence of moral evil in the world is a problem to be solved by all, not by the Thomists alone. The fundamental difficulties in this mysterious question are the existence of evil and the non-salvation of some, be they few or be they many, under the rule of an omnipotent, all-wise, and all-merciful God, and they miss the point of the controversy who suppose that these difficulties exist only for the Thomists. The truth is known to lie somewhere between Calvinism and Jansenism on the one hand, and Semipelagianism on the other. The efforts made by theologians and the various explanations offered by Augustinians, Thomists, Molinists, and Congruists show how difficult of solution are the questions involved. Perhaps we shall never know, in this world, how a just and merciful God provides in some special manner for the elect and yet sincerely loves all men. The celebrated Congregatio de Auxiliis (q. v.) did not forever put an end to the controversies, and the question is not yet settled.

III. NEO-THOMISM AND THE REVIVAL OF SCHOLASTICISM.—When the world in the first part of the nineteenth century began to enjoy a period of peace and rest after the disturbances caused by the French Revolution and the Napoleonic Wars, closer attention was given to ecclesiastical studies and Scholasticism was revived. This movement eventually caused a revival of Thomism, because the great master and model proposed by Leo XIII in the Encyclical "Æterni Patris" (4 Aug., 1879) was St. Thomas Aquinas. (For information concerning this movement, its leaders, and their work, see NEO-SCHOLASTICISM. The principal works pertaining to this period will be mentioned below in bibliography.) The Thomistic doctrine had received strong support from the older universities. Among these the Encyclical "Æterni Patris" mentions Paris, Salamanca, Alcalá, Douai, Toulouse, Louvain, Padua, Bologna, Naples, and Coimbra as "the homes of human wisdom where Thomas reigned supreme, and the minds of all, teachers as well as taught, rested in wonderful harmony under the shield and authority of the Angelic Doctor". In the universities established by the Dominicans at Lima (1551) and Manila (1645) St. Thomas always held sway. The same is true of the Minerva school at Rome (1255), which ranked as a university from the year 1580, and is now the international Collegio Angelico. Coming down to our own times and the results of the Encyclical, which gave a new impetus to the study of St. Thomas's works, the most important centres of activity are Rome, Louvain, Fribourg (Switzerland), and Washington. At Louvain the chair of Thomistic philosophy, established in 1880, became, in 1889-90, the "Institut supérieur de philosophie" or "Ecole St. Thomas d'Aquin," where Professor Mercier, now Cardinal Archbishop of Mechlin, ably and wisely directed the new Thomistic movement (see De Wulf, "Scholasticism Old and New", tr. Coffey, New York, 1907, append., p. 261; "Irish Eccl. Record", Jan. 1906). The theological department of the University of Fribourg, Switzerland, established in 1889, has been entrusted to the Dominicans. By the publication of the "Revue thomiste" the professors of that university have contributed greatly to a new knowledge and appreciation of St. Thomas. The Constitution of the Catholic University of America at Washington enjoins special veneration for St. Thomas; the School of Sacred Sciences must follow his leadership ("Const. Cath. Univ. Amer.", Rome, 1889, pp. 38, 43). The University of Ottawa and Laval University are the centres of Thomism in Canada. The appreciation of St. Thomas in our days, in Europe and in America, is well set forth in Perrier's excellent "Revival of Scholastic Philosophy in the Nineteenth Century" (New York, 1909).

IV. EMINENT THOMISTS.—After the middle of the fourteenth century the vast majority of philosophical and theological writers either wrote commentaries on the works of St. Thomas or based their teachings on his writings. It is impossible, therefore, to give here a complete list of the Thomists: only the more important names can be given. Unless otherwise noted, the authors belonged to the Order of St. Dominic. Those marked (*) were devoted to Thomism in general, but were not of the Thomistic School. A more complete list will be found in the works cited at the end of this article.

Thirteenth Century.—Thomas de Cantimpré (1270); Hugh of St. Cher (1263); Vincent of Bauvais (1264); St. Raymond de Pennafort (1275); Peter of Tarentaise (Pope Innocent V—1276); Giles de Lassines (1278); Reginald de Piperno (1279); William de Moerbeka (1286); Raymond Marti (1286); Bernard de Trilia (1292); Bernard of Hotun, Bishop of Dublin (1298); Theodoric of Apoldia (1299); Thomas Sutton (1300).

Fourteenth Century.—Peter of Auvergne (1301); Nicholas Boccasini, Benedict XI (1304); Godfrey of Fontaines (1304); Walter of Winterburn (1305); Ægidius Colonna (Ægidius Romanus), O.S.A. (1243-1316); William of Paris (1314); Gerard of Bologna, Carmelite (1317); four biographers, viz. Peter Calo (1310); William de Tocco (1324); Bartolommeo of Lucca (1327); Bernard Guidonis* (1331); Dante (1321); Natalis Hervæus (1323); Petrus de Palude (Paludanusi—1342); Thomas Bradwardin, Archbishop of Canterbury (1349); Robert Holkott (1349); John Tauler (1361); Bl. Henry Suso (1365); Thomas of Strasburg, O.S.A. (1357); Jacobus Passavante (1357); Nicholas Roselli (1362); Durandus of Aurillac (1382), sometimes called Durandulus, because he wrote against Durandus a S. Portiano*, who was first a Thomist, afterwards an independent writer, attacking many of St. Thomas's doctrines; John Bromyard (1390); Nicholas Eymeric (1399).

Fifteenth Century.—Manuel Calecas (1410); St. Vincent Ferrer (1415); Bl. John Dominici (1419); John Gerson*, chancellor of the University of Paris (1429); Luis of Valladolid (1436); Raymond Sabunde (1437); John Nieder (1437); Capreolus (1444), called the "Prince of Thomists"; John de Montenegro (1445); Fra Angelico (1455); St. Antoninus (1459); Nicholas of Cusa*, of the Brothers of the Common Life (1464); John of Torquemada (de Turrecrematai, 1468); Bessarion, Basilian (1472); Alanus de Rupe (1475); John Faber (1477); Petrus Niger (1471); Peter of Bergamo (1482); Jerome Savonarola (1498).

Sixteenth Century.—Felix Faber (1502); Vincent Bandelli (1506); John Tetzel (1519); Diego de Deza (1523); Sylvester Mazzolini (1523); Francesco Silvestro di Ferrara (1528); Thomas de Vio Cajetan (1534); commentaries by these two are published in the Leonine edition of the works of St. Thomas. Conrad Koellin (1536); Chrysostom Javelli (1538); Santes Pagnino (1541); Francisco de Vitoria (1546); Franc. Romæus (1552); Ambrosius Catherinus* (Lancelot Politi, 1553); St. Ignatius of Loyola (1556) enjoined devotion to St. Thomas; Matthew Ory (1557); Dominic Soto (1560); Melchior Cano (1560); Ambrose Pelargus (1561); Peter Soto (1563); Sixtus of Siena (1569); John Faber (1570); St. Pius V (1572); Bartholomew Medina (1581); Vincent Justiniani (1582); Maldonatus* (Juan Maldonado, 1583); St. Charles Borromeo* (1584); Salmerón* (1585); Ven. Louis of Granada (1588); Bartholomew of Braga (1590); Toletus* (1596); Bl. Peter Canisius* (1597); Thomas Stapleton*, Doctor of Louvain (1598); Fonseca (1599); Molina* (1600).

Seventeenth Century.—Valentia * (1603); Domingo Bañez (1604); Vásquez* (1604); Bart. Ledesma (1604); Sánchez * (1610); Baronius * (1607); Capponi a Porrecta (1614); Aur. Menochio * (1615); Petr. Ledesma (1616); Suárez * (1617); Du Perron *, a converted Calvinist, cardinal (1618); Bellarmine * (1621); St. Francis de Sales * (1622); Hieronymus Medices (1622); Lessius * (1623); Becanus * (1624); Malvenda (1628); Thomas de Lemos (1629); Alvarez; Laymann* (1635); Joann. Wiggers *, doctor of Louvain (1639); Gravina (1643); John of St. Thomas (1644); Serra (1647); Ripalda*, S. J. (1648); Sylvius (Du Bois), doctor of Douai (1649); Petavius * (1652); Goar (1625); Steph. Menochio *, S. J. (1655); Franc. Pignatelli * (1656); De Lugo * (1660); Bollandus* (1665); Jammy (1665); Vallgornera (1665); Labbe* (1667); Pallavicini * (1667); Busenbaum * (1668); Nicolai * (1673); Contenson (1674); Jac. Pignatelli * (1675); Passerini * (1677); Gonet (1681); Bancel (1685); Thomassin * (1695); Goudin (1695); Sfrondati * (1696); Quétif (1698); Rocaberti (1699); Casanate (1700). To this period belong the Carmelite Salmanticenses, authors of the "Cursus theologicus" (1631-72).

Eighteenth Century.—Guerinois (1703); Bossuet, Bp. of Meaux; Norisins, O.S.A. (1704); Diana (1705); Thyrsus González * (1705); Massoulié (1706); Duhamel* (1706); Wigandt (1708); Piny (1709); Lacroix*

(1714); Carrières * (1717); Natalis Alexander (1724); Echard (1724); Tourney *, doctor of the Sorbonne (1729); Livarius de Meyer * (1730); Benedict XIII * (1730); Graveson (1733); Th. du Jardin (1733); Hyacintha Serry (1738); Duplessis d'Argentré * (1740); Gotti (1742); Drouin * (1742); Antoine * (1743); Lallemant * (1748); Milante * (1749); Preingue (1752); Concina (1759); Billuart (1757); Benedict XIV * (1758); Cuiliati (1759); Orsi (1761); Charlevoix * (1761); Reuter * (1762); Baumgartner * (1764); Berti * (1766); Patuzzi (1769); De Rubeis (1775); Touron (1775); Thomas de Burgo (1776); Gener * (1781); Roselli (1783); St. Alphonsus Liguori (1787); Mamachi (1792); Richard (1794).

Nineteenth Century.—In this century there are few names to be recorded outside of those who were connected with the Thomistic revival either as the forerunners, the promoters, or the writers of the Neo-Scholastic period.

See also FREE WILL; GRACE; PHILOSOPHY; PREDESTINATION; NEO-SCHOLASTICISM; SCOTISM AND SCOTISTS; THEOLOGY.

For rise and progress of Thomism see works referred to in the first part of this article.

For Thomists, a complete list of theological writers of all schools is found in HURTER, Nomenclator literarius, in Tabulæ chronologicæ at end of each volume. For writers of the Dominican Order, down to the first quarter of the eighteenth century, see QUÉTIF-ECHARD, Script. ord. præd. (2 vols., Paris, 1719–21). Many writers of this school are mentioned in the article PREACHERS, ORDER OF, Academic Organization, Doctrinal activity; also in GARCIA, Tomismo y Neo-Tomismo (San Luis Potosi, 1905).

For Thomistic Philosophers: HAURÉAU, Hist. de la phil. scolastique (Paris, 1872–80); DE WULF, Hist. de la phil. médiévale (Louvain, 1900; 4th ed., 1912); JOURDAIN, La phil. de S. Th. d'Aquin (2 vols., Paris, 1858); GONZÁLEZ, Hist. de la phil. (4 vols., Paris, 1890–91); UEBERWEG-HEINZE, Gesch. der phil. (Berlin, 1902); TURNER, Hist. of Phil. (Boston, 1903).

Neo-Thomism.—Lists of publications pertaining to this period are found in UEBERWEG-HEINZE, II, 297 sqq.; IV, 209 sqq., 561 sqq.; SERTILLANGES, S. Thomas d'Aquin (2 vols., Paris, 1910), bibliography at end of II; PERRIER, Revival of Schol. Philosophy (New York, 1909) (the bibliography, pp. 249 to 337, is excellent and the most available for English readers).

Publications on Thomism in general and on the doctrines of the Thomistic school have been multiplied so rapidly since 1879 that volumes would be required for a complete list. The principal works reviving disputes concerning special doctrines of the Thomistic school are: SCHNEEMAN, Controversiarum de divinæ gratiæ liberique arbitrii concordia initia et progressus (Freiburg, 1881); DUMMERMUTH, Thomas et doctrina præmotionis physicæ (Louvain, 1886); FRINS, Thomas Aquinatis doctrina de cooperatione Dei cum omni creatura præsertim libera (Paris, 1893); DUMMERMUTH, Defensio doctrinæ S. Thomæ Aquin. (Louvain, Paris, 1895); DU PONT, La prédetermination physique et la doctrine de S. Thomas in Rev. Cath. (Louvain, 1882–83); DE REGNON, Bannez et Molina (Paris, 1883); LESSERTUR, S. Thomas et le thomisme; S. Th. et la prédestination (Paris, 1888); GAYRAUD; Le thomisme et le molinisme (Paris, 1889–92); IDEM, St. Thomas et le prédeterminisme (Paris, 1895); GUILLERMIN, St. Thomas et le prédeterminisme (Paris, 1895); DEL PRADO, De gratia et libero arbitrio (3 vols., Fribourg, 1907); De veritate fundamentali philosophiæ christianæ (Fribourg, 1889), 1911, the latter ed. treating the distinction between essence and existence.

See also THOMAS AQUINAS, SAINT, for list of reviews devoted to Thomism. For comparison of St. Thomas and Scotus, see VACANT, Etudes comparées sur la philosophie de S. Thomas d'Aquin et sur celle de Duns Scot (Paris and Lyons, 1891); Etudes franciscaines (Jan., 1912); Revue néo-scolastique, Aug., 1911, 430; Feb., 1912, 136.

D. J. KENNEDY.

Thompson, the name of two English converts: (1) Edward Healy and (2) Harriet Diana.

EDWARD HEALY, b. at Oakham, Rutlandshire, England; d. at Cheltenham, Gloucestershire, on 21 May, 1891. He was educated at Oakham school and Emmanuel College, Cambridge; and having taken Anglican orders, obtained a curacy at Calne, Wiltshire. After some years of the Anglican ministry at Marylebone, Ramsgate, and elsewhere, he became a Catholic in 1846 and published as his defence: "Remarks on certain Anglican Theories of Unity" (1846); "The Unity of the Episcopate considered" (1847); and "A few earnest thoughts on the Duty of Communion with the Catholic Church" (1847). In 1851 jointly with James Spencer Northcote (q. v.) he undertook the editorship of the valuable series of controversial pamphlets known as "The Clifton Tracts". The rest of his life, the latter years of which were spent at Cheltenham, he devoted to religious literature. His chief works were: lives of M. Olier (1861), Marie Harpain (1869), St. Stanislaus Kostka (1869), Baron de Rentz (1873), and Henri-Marie Boudon (1881); "Devotion to the Nine Choirs of Holy Angels" (1869); "The Life and Glories of St. Joseph" (1888); and "Before and After Gunpowder Plot" (1890). Most of this useful work consisted in the skilful adaptations of foreign books which he thought were of value to English-speaking Catholics.

HARRIET DIANA, wife of Edward Healy Thompson, and daughter of Nicholson Calvert of Humsden, b. at Humsden, Hertfordshire, 1811; d. at Cheltenham, Gloucestershire, 21 Aug., 1896. On her husband's conversion she also joined the Catholic Church, and like him devoted herself to literary work. Her chief work is the "Life of Charles Borromeo", but her stories of Catholic life won considerable popularity. These include: "Mary, Star of the Sea" (1848); "The Witch of Malton Hill"; "Mount St. Lawrence" (1850); "Winefride Jones" (1854); "Margaret Danvers" (1857); "The Wyndham Family" (1876); and others, as well as articles in "The Dublin Review".

GILLOW, Bibl. Dict. Eng. Cath., s. v.; GORMAN, Converts to Rome (London, 1910); GONDON, Motifs de conversion de dix ministres anglicanes.

EDWIN BURTON.

Thompson, FRANCIS, poet, b. at Preston, Lancashire, 18 Dec., 1859; d. in London, 13 Nov., 1907. He came from the middle classes, the classes great in imaginative poetry. His father was a provincial doctor; two paternal uncles dabbled in literature; he himself referred his heredity chiefly to his mother, who died in his boyhood. His parents being Catholics, he was educated at Ushaw, the college that had in former years Lingard, Waterton, and Wiseman as pupils. There he was noticeable for love of literature and neglect of games, though as spectator he always cared for cricket, and in later years remembered the players of his day with something like personal love. After seven years he went to Owens College to study medicine. He hated this proposed profession more than he would confess to his father; he evaded rather than rebelled, and finally disappeared. No blame, or attribution of hardships or neglect should attach to his father's memory; every careful father knows his own anxieties. Francis Thompson went to London, and there endured three years of destitution that left him in a state of incipient disease. He was employed as bookselling agent, and at a shoemaker's, but very briefly, and became a wanderer in London streets, earning a few pence by selling matches and calling cabs, often famished, often cold, receiving occasional alms; on one great day finding a sovereign on the footway, he was requested to come no more to a public library because he was too ragged. He was nevertheless able to compose a little—"Dream-Tryst", written in memory of a child, and "Paganism Old and New", with a few other pieces of verse and prose.

Having seen some numbers of a new Catholic magazine, "Merry England", he sent these poems to the editor, Mr. Wilfrid Meynell, in 1888, giving his address at a post-office. The manuscripts were pigeon-holed for a short time, but when Mr. Meynell read them he lost no time in writing to the sender a welcoming letter which was returned from the post-office. The only way then to reach him was to publish the essay and the poem, so that the author might see them and disclose himself. He did see them, and wrote to the editor giving his address at a chemist's shop. Thither Mr. Meynell went, and was told that the poet owed a certain sum for opium, and was to be found hard by, selling matches. Having settled matters between the druggist and his client, Mr. Meynell wrote a pressing invitation to Thompson to call upon him. That day was the last of the poet's destitution. He was never again friendless or without food, clothing, shelter, or fire. The first step was to restore him to better health and to overcome the opium habit. A doctor's care, and some months at Storrington, Sussex, where he lived as a boarder at the Premonstratensian monastery, gave him a new hold upon life. It was there, entirely free temporarily from opium, that he began in earnest to write poetry. "Daisy" and the magnificent "Ode to the Setting Sun" were the first fruits. Mr. Meynell, finding him in better health but suffering from the loneliness of his life, brought him to London and established him near himself. Thenceforward with some changes to country air, he was either an inmate or a constant visitor until his death nineteen years later.

In the years from 1889 to 1896 Thompson wrote the poems contained in the three volumes, "Poems", "Sister Songs", and "New Poems". In "Sister Songs" he celebrated his affection for the two elder of the little daughters of his host and more than brother; "Love in Dian's Lap" was written in honour of Mrs. Meynell, and expressed the great attachment of his life; and in the same book "The Making of Viola" was composed for a younger child. At Mr. Meynell's house Thompson met Mr. Garvin and Coventry Patmore, who soon became his friends, and whose great poetic and spiritual influence was thenceforth preeminent in all his writings, and Mrs. Meynell introduced him at Box Hill to George Meredith. Besides these his friendships were few. In the last weeks of his life he received great kindness from Mr. Wilfrid Blunt, in Sussex. During all these years Mr. Meynell encouraged him to practise journalism and to write essays, chiefly as a remedy for occasional melancholy. The essay on Shelley, published twenty years later and immediately famous, was amongst the earliest of these writings; "The Life of St. Ignatius" and "Health and Holiness" were produced subsequently.

Did Francis Thompson, unanimously hailed on the morrow of his death as a great poet, receive no full recognition during life? It was not altogether absent. Patmore, Traill, Mr. Garvin, and Mr. William Archer wrote, in the leading reviews, profoundly admiring studies of his poems. Public attention was not yet aroused. But that his greatness received no stinted praise, then and since, may be seen in a few citations following. Mr. Meynell, who perceived the quality of his genius when no other was aware of it, has written of him as "a poet of high thinking, of 'celestial vision', and of imaginings that found literary images of answering splendour"; Mr. Chesterton acclaimed him as "a great poet", Mr. Fraill as "a poet of the first order"; Mr. William Archer wrote, "It is no minor Caroline simper that he recalls, but the Jacobean Shakespeare"; Mr. Garvin, "the Hound of Heaven seems to us the most wonderful lyric in our language"; Burne-Jones, "Since Gabriel's [Rossetti's] 'Blessed Damozel' no mystical words have so touched me"; George Meredith, "A true poet, one of a small band"; Coventry Patmore, "the 'Hound of Heaven' is one of the very few great odes of which the language can boast". Of the essay on Shelley (Dublin Review) a journalist wrote truly, "London is ringing with it". Francis Thompson died, after receiving all the sacraments, in the excellent care of the Sisters of St. John and St. Elizabeth, aged forty-eight.

CARROLL B. CHILTON.

Thompson, RIGHT HONOURABLE SIR JOHN SPARROW DAVID, jurist and first Catholic Premier of Canada, b. at Halifax, Nova Scotia, 10 Nov., 1844; d. at Windsor Castle, England, 12 Dec., 1894. He was the son of John Sparrow Thompson, queen's printer in Nova Scotia, superintendent of the money order system, and native of Waterford, and of Catherine Pottinger, who was of Scottish descent. The parents on both sides were rigid Protestants. Young Thompson made a short course in the common schools and in the Free Church Academy in his native city. At the age of fifteen he began the study of law and at the same time of stenography. He was admitted to the bar in 1865 and for a short period he assisted in reporting the debates in the Nova Scotia Legislature. In 1870 he married Miss Annie E. Affleck and shortly afterwards became a Catholic. His progress in public life was rapid and brilliant. Beginning as an alderman in Halifax in 1871, he became a member of the House of Assembly in 1877, attorney-general in 1878, Premier of Nova Scotia in 1882, and a judge of the Supreme Court in the same year. In 1885 he became Minister of Justice of Canada, and from the time of his first great speech on the Riel question in 1886, his position as one of the greatest of Canadian parliamentarians was never disputed. In the federal arena his successes were brilliant and unbroken. In 1887 he went to Washington as legal adviser of the British Government in connexion with the Fisheries Commission, and for this service was knighted by Queen Victoria. In 1892 he became Premier of Canada, and a year later he sat as one of the British arbitrators on the Behring Sea Commission at Paris. In recognition of this service he was appointed a member of the Privy Council of Great Britain. He died suddenly at Windsor Castle whither he was summoned by the queen, and his remains were conveyed to Halifax on H.M.S. Blenheim. A state funeral attended by state and church dignitaries from all parts of Canada, took place on 1 Jan., 1895. His remains were buried in Holy Cross cemetery. "All things considered", says Mr. J. S. Willison, a distinguished Canadian writer, "his is the most remarkable career which Canadian politics have developed."

HOPKINS, *The Life and Work of the Right Hon. Sir John Thompson* (Toronto, 1895); *House of Commons Debates* (Ottawa, 1886–94); MORRIS, *An Elegy* (London, 1894); O'BRIEN, *Funeral Sermon on Sir John Thompson* (Halifax, 1906); BOURINOT, *Builders of Nova Scotia* (Toronto, 1900).

JOSEPH A. CHISHOLM.

Thompson River Indians (THOMPSON INDIANS), an important tribe of British Columbia of Salishan linguistic stock, also known as Knife Indians, occupying the country about the junction of Thompson and Fraser Rivers, Yale district, from about Yale up nearly to Lillooet on the Fraser, and as far as Ashcroft on the Thompson. They surrounded the cognate Lillooet, and Shuswap on the north; the Sechelt, Squamish, Cowichan, and Songish on the west and south-west; and the Okanagan on the south-east. They are now gathered upon a number of small reservations under jurisdiction of the Kamloops-Okanagan agency, of which the principal are Lytton (470), Lower Nicola (355), Cooks Ferry (183), Boothroyd (158), Spuzzum (157), Coldwater (107). Their original population may have been near to 4000 souls, but is now reduced (1910) by smallpox and other causes, consequent upon the advent of the whites, to 1782. The proper name of the tribe is Ntlakyapamuk or Nhlakapmuh, and they recognize five subtribes among themselves. In their primitive condition they subsisted chiefly by hunting and fishing, together with the gathering of wild roots and berries. In arts, organization, religious belief and ceremonial, and general custom they resembled in all essentials their neighbouring kindred, particularly the Lillooet, Shuswap, Sechelt, and Squamish (q. v.), with whose history also their own is closely interwoven. In 1808 Simon Fraser in descending the river which bears his name passed through their territory, and shortly afterward the Hudson's Bay Company established posts throughout the region. In 1845 the Jesuit missionary Father John Nobili visited the Thompson River, Okanagan, Shuswap, and other tribes of the Fraser River country, preaching and baptizing in temporary chapels built by the Indians.

About 1860 the noted missionary Oblate father (afterwards bishop), Paul Durieu, spent a short time with the tribe. In 1861 Rev. John B. Good, acting for the Episcopalians, established a regular mission work among them, continuing for nearly twenty years with the result that most of the tribe are now of that denomination. In 1862 in common with the other Fraser River tribes, they were terribly wasted by smallpox. In 1880 the distinguished Oblate missionary and philologist Father John M. R. Le Jeune, best known for his invention of a Salishan system of shorthand, began work among the Thompson River Indians extended after some years to the Okanagan and Shuswap. The entire tribe is now Christian, about 1500 being Episcopalian, the rest Catholic, including all of the Coldwater band. Valuable ethnologic studies of the Thompson River tribe have been made by Teit and Hill-Tout. Important linguistic contributions are a grammatic sketch and vocabulary and several religious publications by Rev. Mr. Good of the Episcopalian (Anglican) mission, and a number of prayer, hymn, catechism, and primer compilations by Father Le Jeune, all in the Salishan shorthand characters of his own invention. The official report for the Coldwater band (Catholic) will answer for all: "They have a good class of buildings and are steadily improving them. They are industrious, steady and extremely law-abiding. They have made good progress in farming. They class among our most temperate and moral Indians."

TEIT, Thompson Indians of B. C. in Memoir Am. Mus. Nat. Hist. (New York, 1900); IDEM, Traditions of the Thompson River Indians in Memoir Am. Folklore Soc. (Boston, 1898); HILL-TOUT, Thompson River Indians in Rept. Ethnol. Survey Canada, Brit. Assoc. Adv. Science (London, 1889); Annual Rept. Dept. Ind. Affairs (Ottawa); BANCROFT, Hist. Brit. Columbia (San Francisco, 1887); MORICE, Catholic Church in Western Canada (2 vols., Toronto, 1910); PILLING, Bibliography Salishan Languages (Bureau Am. Ethnology, Washington, 1893).

JAMES MOONEY.

Thomson, WILLIAM, VENERABLE. See SERGEANT, RICHARD, VENERABLE.

Thonissen, JEAN-JOSEPH, professor of law at the University of Louvain, minister in the Belgian Government, b. at Hassett, Limbourg, 21 Jan., 1817; d. at Louvain, 17 Aug., 1891. After a brilliant career as a student he first performed duties in the magistracy and the administration of the province, but even then was occupied with juridical works on penal law. When dismissed by the Liberal (anti-clerical) ministry, the University of Louvain appointed him in 1848 to the chair of criminal law. In 1863 he was elected to Parliament. It is difficult to summarize briefly Thonissen's activity. Although he achieved his fame in his chosen field of penal law, his writings covered the most varied points of history and social science, as was evidenced by the fact that in 1886 the national jury of social sciences awarded him the prize. In penal matters he began with commentaries on the penal code and devoted himself especially to the reform of the penal procedure which he advocated while he was minister, and for the history of which he wrote important works. He had conceived the vast plan of a history of criminal law, but realized only a part of it. The first part, which met with considerable success, dealt with Brahminical India, Egypt, and Judea, and contained a "Penal Code of the Pentateuch". He published a work on the penal law of the Athenian Republic. Considering the Roman period as sufficiently well-known, he took up the Frankish period, which he was unable to finish. These works are his chief title to fame from the scientific standpoint as are his reports on penal procedure from the practical standpoint. He aroused lively controversy by advocating the suppression of the death penalty, which his influence brought about in Belgium. While not rejecting it as absolutely unlawful, Thonissen considered it useless in the social condition of the time. In fact, although the death sentence is still legal, capital punishment is no longer inflicted in Belgium.

Detailed lists of Thonissen's numerous publications are given in the Bibliography of the Académie Royale and in that of the Catholic University of Louvain, to which the reader is referred. He showed a marked preference for national political history, his principal work on the subject being the "History of the Reign of Leopold I". He also published biographies of prominent Belgians such as Félix de Mérode. He had been impressed by the events of 1848 which determined his career and he devoted himself to a laborious study of innovating systems, especially of those men who are sometimes called the romanticists of Socialism, St. Simon, Fourier, Cabet, Owen, Louis Blanc, and others, being led eventually to write a history of Socialism from ancient times to 1852. These works and many others secured his admission to the Royal Academy of Belgium and the Institute of France; he was commissioned by the former institution to write the volume devoted to its centenary (1872).

JEAN-JOSEPH THONISSEN

Thonissen's political life began in 1863 and was never interrupted by his constituents. In the Chamber his value as a jurisconsult was much appreciated and he drafted many of the parliamentary reports. He occupied a unique position owing to his characteristic independence which made him disagree with the Right on certain points, for instance, on military matters. He was deeply attached to the Belgian Constitution of 1831, which contained articles proclaiming liberty of worship, of the press, etc. Although profoundly religious he was imbued like many men of his generation with the errors of Liberalism, and he wrongly regarded these liberties as of natural right and defended this opinion in his commentary on the Constitution (1844). After the papal decisions on these matters, he corrected his ideas, but always had a leaning towards solutions favouring broad tolerance. Although tempered by great geniality Thonissen's independence of character was such that even the Right feared him and did not desire his participation in affairs. Thus when the king during a period of stress entrusted him with the formation of a ministry (1872), he was not supported by his party, which dreaded concessions to the Left or to the Crown. When he finally entered the ministry (1884), age had rendered him unfit for laborious work, though he was able to enforce the new school law which the victorious Right had substituted for the lay regime of 1879; this task consumed the last of his strength and left him unable to resume his scientific pursuits in his retirement (1887); his faculties soon became clouded. Thonissen was an intrepid worker, a firm Christian, an upright and simple man, with just a touch of artless vanity, though sometimes brusque in manner and given to occasional outbursts. He was one of the most important members of the faculty of law at Louvain and he will be chiefly remembered in the sphere of penal law, where his name is destined to survive.

Numerous articles have been devoted to Thonissen and to his works. The list of the latter will be found in the bibliography mentioned above. See also LAMY in Annuaire de l'Académie royale de Belgique (1892); NYSSENS in Annuaire de l'université catholique de Louvain (1892).

VICTOR BRANTS.

Thorney Abbey (i. e. "the isle of thorns", anciently called ANCARIG), in Cambridgeshire, England, was for some three centuries the seat of Saxon hermits, or of anchorites living in community, before it was refounded in 972 for Benedictine monks by Ethelwold, Bishop of Winchester, with the aid of King Edgar. The founder brought thither the body of St. Botulph and of other Saxon saints, including, possibly, St. Benet Biscop; and the church, originally dedicated to Jesus Christ and His Blessed Mother, became known thereafter as St. Mary and St. Botulph's. The structure built by Ethelwold stood for a century, and was replaced after the Norman Conquest by a new church 290 feet long, which was finished in 1108. The long series of charters granted to Thorney in the twelfth and thirteenth centuries attests the prosperity of the abbey and the number of its benefactors. In Domesday Book its value is reckoned as equal to that of Peterborough; and William of Malmesbury describes it, in the reign of Henry II, as "an image of Paradise", and flourishing in all respects. Of the thirty-eight abbots whose names are recorded, the first was Godeman, and the last Robert Blyth, who was also Bishop of Down and Connor, in Ireland. Blyth and his community of nineteen monks surrendered the abbey to Henry VIII in 1539, receiving a pension in exchange. The buildings and most of the property were granted by Edward VI to John Earl of Bedford, whose family still owns them. The original Norman nave of five bays, with its perpendicular clerestory, remains, and is used as the parish church. The choir has disappeared, and the nave aisles were demolished in 1636, the material being used to fill up the nave arches. The west front, flanked by square turrets with octagonal terminations 100 feet high, and displaying an elaborate screen, with niches containing nine statues over the west window, is extremely picturesque.

DUGDALE, *Monast. anglican.*, II (London, 1817), 593–613; TANNER, *Notitia monastica: Cambridgeshire* (Cambridge, 1787), xxvi; WILLIS, *Hist. of Mitred Parliamentary Abbies*, I (London, 1718), 187–191; WILLELM. MALMESB., *De gestis pontificum*, ed. HAMILTON (London, 1870), 326–329; GASQUET, *The Greater Abbeys of England* (London, 1908), 205–210.

D. O. HUNTER-BLAIR.

Thorns, FEAST OF THE CROWN OF.—The first feast in honour of the Crown of Thorns (*Festum susceptionis coronæ Domini*) was instituted at Paris in 1239, when St. Louis brought thither the relic of the Crown of Thorns, which was deposited later in the Royal Chapel, erected in 1241–8 to guard this and other relics of the Passion. The feast, observed on 11 August, though at first special to the Royal Chapel, was gradually observed throughout the north of France. In the following century another festival of the Holy Crown on 4 May was instituted and was celebrated along with the feast of the Invention of the Cross in parts of Spain, Germany, and Scandinavia. It is still kept in not a few Spanish dioceses and is observed by the Dominicans on 24 April. A special feast on the Monday after Passion Sunday was granted to the Diocese of Freising in Bavaria by Clement X (1676) and Innocent XI (1689) in honour of the Crown of Christ. It was celebrated at Venice in 1766 on the second Friday of March. In 1831 it was adopted at Rome as a double major and is observed on the Friday following Ash-Wednesday. As it is not kept throughout the universal Church, the Mass and Office are placed in the appendices to the Breviary and the Missal. The hymns of the Office, which is taken from the seventeenth-century Gallican Breviary of Paris, were composed by Habert. The "Analecta hymnica" of Dreves and Blume contains a large number of rythmical offices, hymns, and sequences for this feast.

ROHAULT DE FLEURY, *Instruments de la Passion* (Paris, 1870); NILLES, *Kalendarium manuale* (Innsbruck, 1897); GROTEFEND, *Zeitrechnung*, II, 2, 88.

F. G. HOLWECK.

Thorpe, ROBERT, VENERABLE, priest and martyr, b. in Yorkshire; suffered at York, 15 May, 1591. He reached the English College at Reims 1 March, 1583–4, was ordained deacon in December following, and priest by Cardinal Guise in April, 1585. He was sent on the mission, 9 May, 1585, and laboured in Yorkshire. He was arrested in bed very early on Palm Sunday, 1595, at the house of his fellow-martyr, Thomas Watkinson, at Menthorpe in the East Riding of Yorkshire, someone having seen palms being gathered the night before, and having informed John Gates of Howden, the nearest justice of peace. Watkinson, an old Catholic yeoman who lived a solitary life, is described by the treacherous priest John Cecil as a clerk, so it is possible he was in minor orders. Both, though naturally timorous, met their deaths with great fortitude. Thorpe, condemned as a traitor merely for being a priest, was hanged, drawn, and quartered. Watkinson, condemned as a felon merely for harbouring priests, was only hanged. He was offered his life if he would go to church.

CHALLONER, *Missionary Priests*, I, no. 86; POLLEN, *English Martyrs, 1584–1603* (London, 1908), 200–2; KNOX, *Douay Diaries* (London, 1878), passim.

JOHN B. WAINEWRIGHT.

Thou, JACQUES-AUGUSTE DE, French historian, b. at Paris, 8 October, 1553; d. there, 7 May, 1617. The son of Christophe de Thou, first president of the *Parlement* of Paris, he studied at several French universities, especially at Valence, where he knew Scaliger. Both when he accompanied the ambassador Paul de Foix to Italy (1572–76) and when he went to live in Guienne (1581), it was always his aim to make the acquaintance of the most celebrated men of intellect, such as Muretus, P. Manutius, the Pithous, and Montaigne. During his sojourn in Guienne he knew Henry of Navarre, the future Henry IV. As Master of Petitions of the

JACQUES-AUGUSTE DE THOU
From a contemporary pastel portrait

Parlement of Paris in 1585 and in 1588 as councillor of State, he was the opponent of the League. After the assassination of the Duke of Guise he did much to further the reconciliation between Henry III and Henry of Navarre (April, 1589) and set out for Germany with Gaspard de Schomberg to ask the help of Protestant princes against the League. After the death of Henry III he entered the service of Henry of Navarre, with whom he lived for five years in camp. He had an important share in the conferences of Surênnes, which prepared the entry of Henry IV into Paris (22 May, 1594) and especially in compiling the Edict of Nantes (1598) which established the religious liberty and political influence of the Protestants. During the regency of Maria de' Medici he took part in the negotiation of the Treaties of Sainte Menehould (1614) and Loudun (1616) between the Court and the rebellious Condé. His influence in the royal councils was exercised in behalf of Gallican ideas and he was victorious in his opposition to the reception in France of the Tridentine decrees.

An eminent Latinist, De Thou published several collections of Latin poems, but his fame is chiefly due to his "Historiæ" written in Latin. His father, Christophe de Thou (1508–82), having left numerous materials for a national history, De Thou set to work writing it in 1591. His correspondence with foreign scholars procured for him valuable documents. In 1604 he published the first part, 1546–60; in 1606, the second, to 1572; in 1607, the third, 1572-74; and in 1608, the fourth part, 1574–84. He intended carrying it down to the end of the reign of Henry IV (1610), but his narrative had reached only the year 1607, when he died. The last and unfinished portion of his work was published in 1620 by his friends Dupuy and Rigault. The best edition of the Latin text was prepared in the eighteenth century by the Englishman Thomas Carte, published at London in seven volumes by Samuel Buchley (1733); there are French translations and summaries. At first the influence of Cardinal d'Ossat and of Du Perron put off the condemnation of his work at Rome, but in 1609 to De Thou's great sorrow the Congregation of the Index pronounced against it. The *Parlement* of Paris replied by condemning Cardinal Bellarmine's book on the power of the pope. In his work De Thou commits errors of fact and of appreciation. In his judgment of Mary Stuart, for example, he is too often influenced by Buchanan, an impassioned enemy of the queen's memory. But such as it is his work has a certain value; Bossuet often made use of it in his "Histoire des variations", and he speaks of De Thou as a "great author, a faithful historian".

In 1620 were published his "Memoirs" in Latin: they cover the period between 1553 and 1601 and are an important source for the religious and literary history of the period. Some writers have claimed that his friend, Nicolas Rigault, was their chief author. The eldest son of Jacques-Auguste de Thou, François-Auguste de Thou (1607–42), was beheaded at the command of Richelieu for having kept secret the conspiracy between Cinq-Mars and the Spaniards. The library collected by Jacques-Auguste was famous; it was open to scholars and foreigners. In his will De Thou appointed Pierre Dupuy his children's librarian. The library remained in the family until 1680 when it was bought almost entirely by President de Menars and in the eighteenth century passed to the Rohan Soubise family. It then contained 12,729 works. Successive catologues published during the seventeenth century are very important bibliographical documents.

PATIN, *Eloge de De Thou* (Paris, 1824); DÜNTZER, *De Thou's Leben, Schriften u. historische Kunst* (Darmstadt, 1837); HARRISSE, *Le président de Thou et ses descendants, leur célèbre bibliothèque, leurs armoiries* (Paris, 1905).

GEORGES GOYAU.

Thou, NICOLAS DE, Bishop of Chartres, uncle of the historian Jacques-Auguste de Thou, b. at Paris, 1528; d. at Villebon, 5 Nov., 1598. He became a canon of the cathedral of Paris in 1547, and Bishop of Chartres by a Bull of 8 April, 1573. His antipathy for the League, shared by his brother, President Christophe de Thou (1508–82), made the bishop's position difficult when the people of Chartres, who were devoted to the League, shut their gates (17 Jan., 1589) to the troops of Henry III, subsequently welcomed the Duc de Mayenne, and recognized the aged Cardinal de Bourbon as king. Nicolas de Thou temporized, and on 20 April, 1591, received in his palace Henry of Navarre, the future Henry IV. On 21 Sept., 1591, he attended the assembly of bishops which declared "null, unjust and suggested by the malice of the enemies of France" Gregory XIV's Bull of excommunication against Henry of Navarre, and on 25 July, 1593, he assisted at Henry IV's abjuration in St.-Denis. As Reims was still in the power of the Duc de Mayenne, Chartres was the city chosen for the coronation. To end the dispute with Renaud de Beaune, Archbishop of Bourges, who had just been appointed Archbishop of Sens and who claimed the honour of anointing the king, de Thou by a skilful move had himself appointed by the Archbishop of Reims as his representative and was thus commissioned to proceed with the coronation. Instead of the Sainte Ampoule there was brought from Tours a miraculous oil preserved in the Abbey of Marmoutier. The anointing took place 27 Feb., 1594, and the next day Nicolas de Thou bestowed on the king the Collar of the Order of the Holy Ghost. He left various pastoral writings and a book entitled "Cérémonies observées au sacre et couronnement d'Henri IV, roi de France".

CAYET, *Chronologie novennaire*, bk. VI; FISQUET, *La France pontificale: Chartres* (Paris, 1873).

GEORGES GOYAU.

Three Chapters.—The Three Chapters (τρία κεφάλαια) were propositions anathematizing: (1) the person and writings of Theodore of Mopsuestia; (2) certain writings of Theodoret of Cyrus; (3) the letter of Ibas to Maris. At a very early stage of the controversy the incriminated writings themselves came to be spoken of as the "Three Chapters". In consequence those who refused to anathematize these writings were said to defend the Three Chapters; and, vice versa, those who anathematized them, to condemn the Three Chapters. Thus, that most important work, the "Defensio trium capitulorum" by Facundus, Bishop of Hermiane, was an attack on the anathematization of the writings of Theodore, etc. The history of the controversy may be divided into three periods: the first ending with the arrival of Vigilius at Constantinople; the second with his ratification of the Second Council of Constantinople in which the Three Chapters were condemned; the third with the final healing of the schisms in the West caused by the papal ratification of the aforesaid council. We shall treat very cursorily of the second and third periods, referring the reader for fuller details to the articles on the council, Pelagius I, Pelagius II, and Vigilius.

At the end of 543 or the beginning of 544 an edict was issued in the name of the Emperor Justinian in which the Three Chapters were anathematized. Justinian's purpose was to facilitate the return of the Monophysites to the Church. These heretics accused the Church of Nestorianism, and, when assured that Nestorius was regarded as a heretic, pointed to the writings of his teacher Theodore of Mopsuestia, which were quite as incorrect, and yet had never been condemned. They added that Theodoret, the friend and defender of Nestorius, had been restored to his see by the Council of Chalcedon, and that the epistle of Ibas had even been treated as harmless by the council. It was sincerely hoped by Justinian that when grounds of complaint against the council had been removed, the Monophysites might be induced to accept the decisions of the council and the letters of St. Leo, which they now insisted on misinterpreting in a Nestorian sense. As a temporal ruler he wished to heal religious divisions which threatened the security of the empire, and as a good amateur theologian he was probably rather pleased with himself at being able to lay his finger upon what seemed to him an important omission on the part of the Council of Chalcedon. But upright as he was, he was really being engineered by Origenists who were desirous of escaping his attention. (For Justinian's campaign against the Origenists see XI, 311.) Evagrius(Hist. eccl., IV, xxviii) tells us that Theodorus Ascidas, the leader of the Origenists, came to Justinian who was consulting about further measures against the Origenists, and raised the question of the Three Chapters to divert the attention of the emperor. According to Liberatus (Breviarium, c. 24) Ascidas wished to take his revenge on the memory of Theodore of Mopsuestia, who had written much against Origen; and finding the emperor engaged upon a treatise which was to convert a sect of Monophysites known as the Acephali, suggested a more expeditious plan. If the writings of Theodore and the epistle of Ibas were anathematized, the Council of Chalcedon being thus revised and expurgated (Synodus . . . retractata et expurgata) would no longer be a stumbling block to the Monophysites. The admissions, quoted by Facundus (Def., I, 2; IV, 4), made by Domitian, Bishop of Ancyra, to Vigilius, tell the same story of an Origenist intrigue.

The leading Eastern bishops were coerced, after a short resistance, into subscribing. Mennas, Patriarch of Constantinople, first protested that to sign was to condemn the Council of Chalcedon, and then yielded on the distinct understanding, as he told Stephen the Roman apocrisarius at Constantinople, that his subscription should be returned to him if the Apostolic See disapproved of it. Stephen and Dacius, Bishop of Milan, who was then at Constantinople, broke off communion with him. Mennas had next to coerce his suffragans. They also yielded, but lodged protests with Stephen to be transmitted to the pope, in which they declared that they acted under compulsion. Ephraim, Patriarch of Alexandria, resisted, then yielded and sent a message to Vigilius, who was in Sicily, affirming that he had signed under compulsion. Zoilus, Patriarch of Antioch, and Peter, Bishop of Jerusalem, made a like resistance and then yielded (Facundus, "Def.", IV, 4). Of the other bishops, those who subscribed were rewarded, those who refused were deposed or had to "conceal themselves" (Liberatus, "Brev.", 24; Facundus, "Def.", II, 3 and "Cont. Moc.", in Gallandi, XI, 813). While the resistance of the Greek-speaking bishops collapsed, the Latin, even those like Dacius of Milan and Facundus, who were then at Constantinople, stood firm. Their general attitude is represented in two letters still extant. The first is from an African bishop named Pontianus, in which he entreats the emperor to withdraw the Three Chapters on the ground that their condemnation struck at Chalcedon. The other is that of the Carthaginian deacon, Ferrandus; his opinion as a most learned canonist was asked by the Roman deacons Pelagius (afterwards pope, at this time a strong defender of the Three Chapters) and Anatolius. He fastened on the epistle of Ibas—if this was received at Chalcedon, to anathematize it now was to condemn the council. An even stronger use of the benevolence of the council towards this epistle was made by Facundus at one of the conferences held by Vigilius before he issued his "Judicatum". He wished it to protect the memory of Theodore of Mopsuestia because Ibas had spoken of him in terms of commendation (Cont. Moc., loc. cit.). When in January, 547, Vigilius arrived at Constantinople while Italy, Africa, Sardinia, Sicily, and the countries of Illyricum and Hellas through which he journeyed were up in arms against the condemnation of the Three Chapters, it was clear that the Greek-speaking bishops as a whole were not prepared to withstand the emperor.

With regard to the merits of the controversy, theological errors and, in the case of Theodore, very serious ones, were to be found in the incriminated writings (Theodore was practically a Nestorian before Nestorius); the mistakes of Theodoret and Ibas were chiefly but not wholly due to a misunderstanding of St. Cyril's language. Yet these errors even when admitted did not make the question of their condemnation an easy one. There were no good precedents for thus dealing harshly with the memory of men who had died in the peace of the Church. St. Cyprian, as Facundus argued ("Cont. Moc.", in Gallandi, X, 815), had erred about the rebaptism of heretics, yet no one would dream of anathematizing him. The condemnation was not demanded to crush a heresy, but to conciliate heretics who were implacable enemies of the Council of Chalcedon. Both Ibas and Theodoret had been deprived of their bishoprics by heretics, and had been restored by the Holy See and the Council of Chalcedon on anathematizing Nestorius. Yet the council had their writings before it, and, in the case of the epistle of Ibas, things were said which could easily be construed into an approval of it. All this made the condemnation look like an oblique blow at St. Leo and Chalcedon.

The matter was further complicated by the fact that the Latins, Vigilius among them, were for the most part ignorant of Greek and therefore unable to judge the incriminated writings for themselves. Pelagius II in his third epistle to Elias, probably drawn up by St. Gregory the Great, ascribes all the trouble to this ignorance. All they had to go upon was the general attitude of the Fathers of Chalcedon. These facts should be remembered in judging the conduct of Vigilius. He came to Constantinople in a very resolute frame of mind, and his first step was to excommunicate Mennas. But he must have felt the ground was being cut from under his feet when he was supplied with translations of some of the worst passages in the writings of Theodore. In 548 he issued his "Judicatum" in which the Three Chapters were condemned, and then temporarily withdrew it when the storm it raised showed how ill-prepared the Latins were for it. Next he and Justinian agreed to a general council in which Vigilius pledged himself to bring about the condemnation of the Three Chapters, it being understood that the emperor should take no further steps till the council should be arranged. The emperor broke his pledge by issuing a fresh edict condemning the Chapters. Vigilius had twice to take sanctuary, first in the Basilica of St. Peter, and then in the Church of St. Euphemia at Chalcedon, from which he issued an Encyclical to the whole Church describing the treatment he had received. Then an agreement was patched up and Vigilius agreed to a general council but soon withdrew his assent. Nevertheless, the council was held, and, after refusing to accept the "Consitutum" of Vigilius (see VIGILIUS, POPE), it then condemned the Three Chapters. Finally Vigilius succumbed, confirmed the council, and was set free. But he died before reaching Italy, leaving his successor Pelagius the task of dealing with the schisms in the West. The most enduring of these were those of Aquileia and Milan. The latter came to an end when Fronto, the schismatical bishop, died about 581.

ORIGINAL SOURCES.—The writings of FACUNDUS in P.L., LXVII, 527–878, GALLANDI, XI, 661–821; FULGENTIUS FERRANDUS, Epist. VI in P.L., LXVII, GALLANDI, XI; LIBERATUS, Breviarium in P.L., LXVIII, MANSI, IX (Florence, 1759), 659–700, GALLANDI, XII; PONTIANUS, Epist. in P.L., LXVII, 995; HARDOUIN, Concilia, III. The Chronicon of VICTOR TUNUNENSIS is contained in P.L., LXVIII, 957 sqq., and GALLANDI, XII; this is especially valuable for the history of the suppression of the schism in Africa. For the schism in Italy the most important documents are certain epistles of Pelagius I, Pelagius II, and St. Gregory the Great. For editions see PELAGIUS I, POPE; PELAGIUS II, POPE; GREGORY I (THE GREAT), SAINT, POPE.

GENERAL LITERATURE.—DUCHESNE, Vigile et Pélage in Rev. des quest. hist. (October, 1884); HEFELE, Hist. of the Church Councils, tr. CLARK, IV (Edinburgh, 1895), 229 sqq., where also abundant references to older literature of the subject will be found; CHAPMAN, The first Eight General Councils (London), 48–59; DUDDEN, Gregory the Great; MANN, Lives of the Popes in the early Middle Ages, I, pt. i (London, 1902); HODGKINS, Italy and her Invaders, IV, V, VI; GRISAR, Hist. of Rome and the Popes in the Middle Ages, I (London, 1911).

F. J. BACCHUS.

Three Rivers, DIOCESE OF (TRIFLUVIANENSIS), formed from the Archdiocese of Quebec, to which it is now suffragan, founded on 8 June, 1852. The diocese at first comprised on the northern shore of the St. Lawrence, the Counties of Champlain and of St. Maurice—the County of Maskinongé being at that time a part of the County of St. Maurice; on the southern bank, the Counties of Yamaska, Nicolet, Drummond, and

EPISCOPAL THRONE, CHURCH OF SS. NEREO ED ACHILLEO, ROME
A HOMILY OF ST. GREGORY THE GREAT IS INSCRIBED IN THE NICHE WHICH FORMS THE BACK OF THE SEAT

twenty-four townships in the County of Sherbrooke. Later on, this territory was divided, especially for the erection of the Diocese of Sherbrooke and of the Vicariate-Apostolic of Pontiac. Lastly, in July 1885, all the parishes of the southern shore were erected into the Diocese of Nicolet. It now comprises forty-three parishes and eight missions. The Catholic population is 84,000; non-Catholic 800, of whom 600 are Protestants.

The first bishop, Mgr. Thomas Cooke, died in 1870 and was succeeded by Mgr. Louis-François Laflèche, administrator of the diocese from 1869 to 1898, year of his death. Mgr. F.-X. Cloutier is the present and third Bishop of Three Rivers; born at Ste-Geneviève de Batiscan, Champlain, Quebec, 2 November, 1848, he was ordained priest, 22 September, 1872, appointed Bishop of Three Rivers, 8 May, 1899, and consecrated on 25 July following by Mgr. L.-N. Bégin, Archbishop of Quebec. The diocese contains 100 secular priests; 1 convent of Franciscan Fathers; 1 house of Oblate Fathers; 10 schools of brothers; commercial colleges, academies, etc., 4 under the direction of the Brothers of the Christian Schools, 3 under the direction of the Brothers of Christian Instruction, 2 under the direction of the Brothers of St. Gabriel, 1 under the direction of the Brothers of the Sacred Heart. There is also a juniorate in charge of the Brothers of Christian Instruction.

The institutes of women are: Ursulines, 7 convents; Sisters of the Congregation of Notre-Dame, 2 convents; Sisters of the Assumption, 4 convents; Sisters of the Good Shepherd, 1 convent; Gray Nuns of the Cross, 1 convent; Daughters of Jesus, 2 convents, 1 kindergarten for boys and 13 schools for girls and boys; the Sisters of Charity of Providence, with 4 orphanages, 2 boarding-schools for girls, 4 asylums, and 1 hospital; Dominican Sisters of the Holy Rosary, 1 orphanage, they also have charge of 2 religious institutions; Sisters Adorers of the Precious Blood, 1 monastery.

The churches, mostly all of them remodeled, are remarkable in structure and in size. The cathedral, erected in 1854, and restored in 1904, is a magnificent monument of Gothic architecture. The schools in each parish are numerous and well conducted. The Seminary of Three Rivers, founded in 1860, has a yearly attendance of 300 students. Religious and benevolent societies are numerous and flourishing. The diocese has also literary circles, Young Men's Associations, savings' banks, parochial libraries, and temperance societies.

N. MARCHAND.

Three Witnesses. See JOHN, EPISTLES OF SAINT.

Throndhjem. See TRONDHJEM.

Throne (Lat. *thronus, cathedra, sedes episcopalis*), the seat the bishop uses when not engaged at the altar. If the altar stands near the entrance to the choir, then, according to the "Cæremoniale episcoporum", the throne is to be placed at the apex of the apse in the centre of the stalls of the canons that join it to the right and left. If, however, the altar is placed close to the wall of the apse, or is only a short distance from this wall, the throne must be placed on the Gospel side of the choir. According to the "Cæremoniale episcoporum" the throne is to be made *in modum cathedræ et throni immobilis* (in the fashion of an immovable chair or throne) such as is still to be seen in many old churches. Consequently an ordinary chair, used temporarily or only for the moment, does not suffice as the throne of a bishop. Further directions are *forma præalta et sublimis*, that is, the chair must have a high back and arms, and be raised above the floor so that three steps lead up to it. The steps are to be covered by a carpet, the throne itself is to have spread over it a silk cover of the same colour as the bishop's vestments, but not of cloth of gold, unless the bishop should be a cardinal. The throne can be surmounted by a baldachino only when there is a baldachino above the altar, or when the altar has a ciborium altar over it. When in another diocese, a bishop can only use the throne by virtue of a letter of dispensation from the diocesan bishop. Should a cardinal be present, the bishop must yield the throne to the cardinal and use a *faldistorium* placed on the Gospel side of the altar, that is, a four-legged faldstool with arms. Auxiliary bishops must always use a *faldistorium*. Abbots have the right to a throne in their own churches, but this throne can only have two steps leading to it, and cannot have a baldachino over it.

Time has made no essential changes in the episcopal *cathedra*. At different periods, especially in the twelfth and thirteenth centuries, the throne had the form of a *faldistorium*, but as a rule it always showed the ancient characteristic type of a seat, secured to the spot where it stood, with arms and a back of some height. The modifications that it underwent in the course of time resulted solely from the changes in the style of the art, and were therefore merely conventional. The episcopal throne in the pre-Carlovingian period has been already treated in the article CATHEDRA. Other examples of the same era are the throne at Naples in the Church of St. Januarius, and the one in the Church of Santa Maria della Sanità; at Rome in San Pietro in Vincoli, San Gregorio in Celio, San Alessandro, in the Via Nomentana; at Ravenna, in San Apollinare Nuovo, besides other thrones that are in part ancient stools, especially stools for the bath. Thrones belonging to the Middle Ages and the twelfth century are to be found at Canossa, Bari, in the grotto church of Monte Gargano, in St. Emmeram at Ratisbon, in Santa Maria in Cosmedin and in San Clemente at Rome. Excellent examples of thirteenth-century thrones are those in the Churches of San Cesario, SS. Nereo ed Achilleo, and San Lorenzo fuori le mura, at Rome. There are surprisingly few thrones of the late medieval period still in existence. Episcopal thrones that are or were surmounted by a structure similar to a baldachino are those at Torcello, Grado, and Augsburg. That as early as the eighth or ninth century the throne did not always stand at the apex of the apse, but was also placed to the right of the altar, is evident from the Roman "Ordines" of that era. However, what may have been less usual at that period became from the twelfth century customary, because it became usual to place the altar near the wall of the apse, and also to place a reredos upon the table, at least on feast days.

Cær. episcop., I, xii, 10; xiii, 1 sqq.; THALHOFER, *Liturgik*, I (Freiburg, 1883); LECLERCQ in CABROL, *Dict. d'arch. chrét.*, s.v. *Chaire épiscopale*; see bibli. to CATHEDRA.

JOSEPH BRAUN.

EPISCOPAL THRONE, WITH MOSAIC DECORATION, CHURCH OF S. CESAREO IN PALATIO, ROME

Thuburbo Minus, a titular see in Africa Proconsularis, suffragan of Carthage. Thuburbo Minus is mentioned in the "Itinerar. Antonin.", 44, and the "Tabula

Peutinger. It is to-day Tebourba, a city of 2500 inhabitants, on the left bank of the Medjerda (ancient Bagradas), 21 miles by railway west of Tunis. Situated on a hill, the city proper occupies only a part of the ancient site. It was rebuilt in the fifteenth century by the Andalusian Moors. The Roman amphitheatre was still standing at the end of the seventeenth century, when it was destroyed in order to build a bridge. It was at Thuburbo Minus that the illustrious martyrs St. Perpetua and St. Felicitas with their companions were arrested. The two bishops of this city of whom we know anything are: Victor, present at the Conference of Carthage (411), where he had as his competitor the Donatist Maximinus; and Germanus, who signed (646) the letter of the bishops of the proconsulate to the Patriarch Paul of Constantinople against the Monothelites. Thuburbo Majus, another bishopric of Africa Proconsularis, was a Roman colony the full name of which was Julia Aurelia Commoda Thuburbo Majus. Its many ruins may be seen at Henshir Kasbat, on the banks of the Oued Melian about 34 miles south of Tebourba. It is the country of St. Servus (7 December, Roman Martyrology), who suffered for the Faith under Genseric and Huneric. Four of its bishops are known: Sedatus, present at the Council of Carthage, 256; Faustus, at the Council of Arles, 314; Cyprianus, at the Conference of Carthage, 411, with his competitor, the Donatist, Rufinus; Benenatus, exiled by Huneric, 484. It is impossible to decide to which of these two cities belongs the great number of martyrs, known especially by the "Martyrologium Hieronymianum" as having suffered at Thuburbo.

TOULOTTE, *Géographie de l'Afrique chrétienne. Proconsulaire* (Paris, 1892), 276, 278.

S. PÉTRIDÈS.

Thugga, titular see of Numidia, perhaps the Numidian fortress of Tocai mentioned about 305 B. C. by Diodorus Siculus (XX, v, 4). King Masinissa probably captured Thugga from Carthage in the second century B. C. A pagus under Claudius I, Thugga was dependent on the Roman colony of Carthage. Under Marcus Aurelius it included a pagus and a *civitas;* Septimius Severus erected it into the municipium, Septimianum Aurelium liberum Thugga, which became a colony in 261 under Gallian. Justinian built a fortress there which is still partly preserved (Procopius, "De ædificiis", VI, 5). The existence of a pagus and a *civitas* explains why there were two bishops, Saturninus and Honoratus, who assisted at the Council of Carthage in 256. A Donatist bishop, Paschasius, went to the Council of Carthage in 411. Thugga is now Dougga, a village of Tunis, famous for its ruins, among which are the temple of the Capitol built under Marcus Aurelius, a theatre, three triumphal arches, Roman necropoli, and a Punic mausoleum.

TOULOTTE, *Géog. de l'Afrique chrétienne. Proconsulaire*, 285–88; IDEM, *Byzacène et Tripolitaine*, 208; SALADIN in *Nouvelles archives des missions scientifiques*, II, 448–529; CARTON, *Dougga* (Tunis, 1911).

S. VAILHÉ.

Thugut, JOHANN AMADEUS FRANZ DE PAULA, Austrian statesman, b. at Linz, 31 March, 1736; d. at Vienna, 28 May, 1818. He was the son of a paymaster of the imperial army, Johann Thugut. Until the time of his grandfather the family name was written "Thunichtgut". Although baptized Johann Amadeus, Thugut was called through life Franz. A great many mythical stories are told of his childhood, such as the following. One day Maria Theresa found an abandoned infant on the steps of the Hofburg at Vienna, had compassion on it, and named the infant "Thugut". Another tale relates that the empress while crossing the Danube to Maria-Taferl was attracted by the large eyes of the boy who steered the boat. She was told that he was a foundling, a good-for-nothing (*Thunuchtgut*). The truth is that Maria Theresa, on account of the services of the father, had the boy educated at the academy of Oriental languages that had just been opened. In 1754 Thugut entered the imperial service, first as a translator at Constantinople. Kaunitz praised his linguistic knowledge and abilities and made him secretary of the state chancery. While here he accepted an annual income of 13,000 livres from Louis XV as a secret agent of France. He still received the same pension from France when secretary from 1769 of the Austrian embassy at Constantinople. In 1771, at the request of Kaunitz, he was raised to the ranks of the lower nobility on account of his meritorious services. Joseph II greatly desired to obtain the Province of Bukovina, as this would make a connexion between Galicia and Transylvania. Thugut persuaded the Turkish Government in 1775 to cede the province. To reward him Thugut was made a *Freiherr* or baron. During the war of the Bavarian succession Maria Theresa employed Thugut to negotiate with Frederick the Great, but the negotiations led to nothing. His employments varied greatly during the reign of Joseph II. During the years 1780–85 he was Ambassador at Warsaw, and during 1787–89, Ambassador at Naples; in the intervening years he had an official position at Paris where he was on terms of friendship with Mirabeau and Lafayette.

Emperor Francis II first used Thugut as a military diplomat in Belgium, and finally in 1794, after the death of Prince Kaunitz, appointed him minister of foreign affairs. While holding this office his aim was to check the growth of Prussia's power, and to subdue the wild forces of the French Revolution. Austria was to become a well-rounded, compact whole. Consequently, after the unfortunate occurrences in Belgium, which was too far from Austria to be easily held and ruled, he sought to obtain compensation in the Third Partition of Poland and in Italy. In 1795 he was able to make an offensive and defensive treaty with Russia that opened the way for Austria to gain Bosnia, a part of Servia, and the territories on the Venetian coast. At the same time, during the negotiations concerning the Rhine as a boundary between France and Germany, and on the question of secularization, Thugut spoke emphatically in regard to justice, morality, and the uncompromising duties of the emperor as the head of the empire. It was impossible for him to consent to the robbing of spiritual princes and other estates of the empire of their possessions. After strong opposition he only yielded to necessity when he agreed in the Treaty of Campo Formio to cede the left bank of the Rhine to France and to give compensation in Germany to the princes whose possessions had been encroached upon. He called this peace "an unfortunate peace, the infamy of which would make an era in the annals of Austria, unless, what was much to be feared, the annals of Austria did not soon themselves disappear". Thugut's greatest success, the alliance of Austria, Russia, and England in the second French war, led to his overthrow. In 1801 he resigned his position.

Both in life and in history Thugut seems to have been a kind of Jekyll and Hyde. Baptized Johann and called Franz, in the service of the emperor and sold to France, grasping and yet often rejecting opportunities with indignation, passionately hated and genuinely honoured, it is difficult to consider "Thugut" and "Thunichtgut" as one and the same person. Concerning Thugut, whom he succeeded after eight years as minister of foreign affairs, the courtly Metternich said: "France owed her enormous success above all to the inconsistency of the ministries that had charge of the conduct of affairs. The ideas which underlay the Austrian policy were clearly conceived by them, but probably at no time were they carried out more negligently. The ministry of Baron Thugut shows only an unbroken succession of blunders and false calculations. Sprung from the lower classes Thugut was educated in the Oriental Academy and trained for the subordinate service of the State. Skilful and cunning he owed the good luck of his political life to these qualities, which, aided by great talent for dissimulation and inclination to intrigue, pass current only too easily for real talents" (Aus Metternichs nachgel. Papieren, I, 29 sq.). Count Franz Dietrichstein on the other hand was an enthusiastic admirer of Thugut. He had Thugut buried in the Dietrichstein ancestral vault, and in an obituary expressed the hope that history might finally do honour to Thugut's great qualities. This was the aim of Vivenot's biography of Thugut, on which the author spent many years.

VON VIVENOT, *Thugut, Clerfayt u. Wurmser* (Vienna, 1869); IDEM, *Thugut u. sein politisches System* in *Arch. für österr. Gesch.-Quellen*, XLII, XLIII (Vienna, 1870); IDEM, *Verrtauliche Briefe von Freiherrn von Thugut* (Vienna, 1872); IDEM, *Quellen zur Geschichte der deutschen Kaiserpolitik Oesterreich während der französischen Revolitionskrieg 1790–1801*, I (Vienna, 1873), covering Jan., 1790; April, 1792; II (1874), covering April, 1792, March, 1793; III, ed. VON ZEISSBERG (1882), covering May–Dec., 1793; IV (1885), covering Jan.-Sept., 1794; V (1890), covering Oct., 1794,-Sept., 1795; BAILLEU, *Publikationen aus den kön. preussischen Staatsarchiven*, I (Leipzig, 1881), covering 1795–1800; HARDENBERG, *Denkwürdigkeiten*, ed. VON RANKE (5 vols., Leipzig, 1877).

CÖLESTIN WOLFSGRUBER.

Thulis, JOHN, VENERABLE, English martyr, b. at Up Holland, Lancashire, probably about 1568; suffered at Lancaster, 18 March, 1615 or 1616. He arrived at the English College, Reims, 25 May, 1583, and received tonsure from Cardinal Guise on 23 September following. He left for Rome, 27 March, 1590, where he was ordained priest, and was sent on the mission in April, 1592. He seems to have been a prisoner at Wisbech, Cambridgeshire, when he signed the letter of 8 November, 1598, in favour of the institution of the archpriest, and the letter of 17 November, 1600, against it. Later he laboured in Lancashire, where he was arrested by William, fifteenth earl of Derby, and was committed to Lancaster Castle, where his fellow-martyr Roger Wrenno, a weaver, was confined. They managed to escape one evening just before the Lent assizes, but were recaptured the next day. After that he was imprisoned with thieves, four of whom he converted. These were executed with the martyrs. Thulis suffered after three thieves. His quarters were set up at Lancaster, Preston, Wigan, and Warrington. Wrenno was hanged next, and, the rope breaking, he was once more offered his life for conformity, but ran swiftly to the ladder and climbed it as fast as he could, saying to the sheriff, who remonstrated, "If you had seen that which I have just now seen, you would be as much in haste to die as I am now". A curious metrical account of their martyrdom, as well as portions of a poem composed by Thulis, are printed by Father Pollen in his "Acts of the English Martyrs" (London, 1891), 194–207.

CHALLONER, *Missionary Priests*, II, nos. 155 and 156; KNOX, *Douay Diaries* (London, 1878), 196, 198, 229, 298; POLLEN, *English Martyrs 1584–1603* (London, 1908), 384; LAW, *Jesuits and Seculars* (London, 1859), no. 93.

JOHN B. WAINEWRIGHT.

Thundering Legion (*legio fulminata*, or *fulminea*, not *fulminatrix*).—The story of the Thundering Legion is in substance as follows: When the Emperor Marcus Aurelius led an expedition against the Quadi in 174, his army, exhausted by thirst, was on the point of falling an easy prey to the enemy. It was then that the soldiers of the Twelfth Legion, which was composed of Christians, prayed to their God for help. Forthwith a heavy thunderstorm arose, bringing the desired relief to the Romans, but terrifying and dispersing the barbarians. Hereupon the emperor issued a decree forbidding the persecution of the Christians and to the Twelfth Legion he gave the surname of *fulminata*, or *fulminea*, that is, "thundering". The earliest reference to this occurrence from a Christian source was made by Tertullian ("Apologeticum", v, and "Ad Scapulam", iv). He is quoted by Eusebius (Hist. eccl., V, v), who also cites Apollinaris of Hierapolis, a contemporary of Aurelius, as an authority for the alleged miracle. Later Christian authorities are Orosius (Hist. adv. paganos, VII, xv), Gregory of Nyssa (Oratio II in XL martyres), Jerome (Eusebii Chron., adn. 174), and Xiphilinus (Dionis Nicæi rer. Rom. epitome, LXXI, ix, x). Pagan writers also testify to the miraculous thunderstorm, but they ascribe it either to the prayers of the emperor (Julius Capitolinus, "Vita Marci Antonini philosophi" xxiv; Themistius, "Oratio XV", ed. Harduin, 191; Claudianus, "In VI consulatum Honorii", carmen 28; "Oracula Sibyllina", ed. Alexandre, XII, 194–200) or to the incantations of the Egyptian magician Arnuphis who accompanied the Roman army (Dion Cassius, "Hist. rom.", LXXI, viii-x; Suidas, s. v. Ἰουλιανός). On a coin, struck by the emperor (Eckhel, "Doctrina nummorum vet.", III, 64), and on the Antonine Column in Rome, the "miracle of the thunderstorm" is represented as wrought by Jupiter.

The mass of historical evidence, as seen above, leaves no room for doubting the occurrence of the thunderstorm, but there has been a long controversy concerning various circumstances which early Christian writers mention as connected with it. The researches of Moyle, Mosheim, and especially the more recent ones of Lightfoot, Harnack, and others (see bibliography) have led to the following almost universally accepted results: A detachment of the Twelfth Legion, which was regularly stationed at Melitene in Armenia and comprised many Christians, took part in the expedition against the Quadi, and it is probable, though not certain, that the "miraculous thunderstorm" was an answer to their prayers. The name *fulminatrix* was not given to the legion on this occasion, but there existed since the time of Augustus (Dion Cassius, LV, xxiii) a *legio fulminata* or *fulminea*, probably called thus from the representation of lightning on their armour. The letter (generally appended to the "Apology" of Justin), which Marcus Aurelius is said to have written to the Senate, concerning the miraculous thunderstorm, and in which he is said to have forbidden the further persecution of the Christians, is either a forgery or it was interpolated to suit the Christians. It is an established fact that the persecution of the Christians became even more cruel shortly after this incident.

LIGHTFOOT, *St. Ignatius and St. Polycarp*, I (London, 1889), 487–492; MOYLE, *Works*, II (London, 1726), 79–398; Latin tr. by MOSHEIM (Leipz'g, 1733); HARNACK, *Die Quelle der Berichte über das Regenwunder im Feldzuge Marc Aurels gegen die Quaden* in *Sitzungsberichte der Akad. der Wissensch.* (Berlin, 1894), 835–82; WEIZSÄCKER, *Akademische Rede* (Tübingen, 1894); DOMASZEWSKI in *Rhein. Museum für Philologie* (Frankfort, 1894), 612 sq.; PETERSEN, *ib.* (1895), 453–474; MOMMSEN in *Hermes* (Berlin, 1895), 90–106; GEFFKEN in *Neues Jahrb. für das klass. Altertum*, III (Leipzig, 1899), 253 sq.; ALLARD, *Hist. des persécutions*, I (Paris, 1903), 394–6.

MICHAEL OTT.

Thun-Hohenstein, COUNT LEO, Austrian statesman, b. at the family castle of Tetschen in Bohemia, 7 April, 1811; d. at Vienna, 17 December, 1888. He received his early education under the direction of the distinguished teacher, John Rohrwerk, and later studied law and philosophy at the University of Prague. After graduation he travelled through Germany, France, and England. The bent of his mind was towards politics, and he studied with especial interest the political system of England. In Paris he studied the prison system and the various benevolent institutions for working-men. As soon as he reached home he began to make use of the knowledge he had acquired and issued his first publication: "Die Notwendigkeit der moralischen Reform der Gefängnisse mit Hinweisung auf die zur Einführung derselben in einigen Ländern getroffenen Massregeln beleuchtet".

Shortly afterwards he entered political life and became a member of the Bohemian Diet. He also interested himself in the revival of the Czech language and literature, and in 1842 published a treatise entitled: "Ueber den gegenwärtigen Stand der böhmischen Literatur und ihre Bedeutung". In 1846 a revolt broke out in Galicia, and Thun was appointed a member of the administrative board under Francis Stadion. He took up his residence at Lemberg with his wife, Countess Caroline Clam-Martinitz, whom he had recently married. At the outbreak of the revolution in the spring of 1848, Thun was appointed president of the administrative board and became the actual ruler of Bohemia, for the Archduke Francis Joseph, who had been selected as viceroy, was unable to assume the position. During the outbreak at Prague Thun was captured by the insurgents and imprisoned; they were willing to release him if he would give certain assurances, which he refused to do. When finally set free he supported the commander of the troops in Prague in quelling the revolt by force of arms.

Thun rose rapidly, and in July, 1849, was appointed by the emperor minister of worship and education, the two offices being united for the first time in the person of Thun. He immediately set about reforming the methods of instruction to meet the demands of the times. He improved the primary schools and practically reorganized the administration and courses of study of the gymnasia and the universities. He took a special interest in industrial education and was the first to place trade and technical schools on a firm basis. He also did much to encourage art, especially by making an art university of the Academy of Fine Arts, and by giving employment to artists. Thun's work as minister of worship deserves equal attention. In his memorials to the emperor of 7 and 13 April, 1850, on the religious condition, he made his first attempt to loosen the fetters in which Josephinism had bound the Church. In his first paper he demanded the annulment of the *Placitum regium*, in the second he insisted that no teacher of religion or professor of theology should be appointed without the consent of the bishop. In September, 1852, the emperor appointed Archbishop Rauscher as his plenipotentiary for drawing up a concordat, and Pius IX appointed the nuncio Viale Prelà as his representative. The agreement between the two was laid before the committee of ecclesiastical affairs composed of five members, among which the predominating influence was naturally that of the minister of worship and education. Thun said himself that his share in the drawing up of this agreement was one of the "proudest and happiest recollections" of his life.

Thun acted both in his capacity as minister of education and minister of worship entirely in accordance with a rigid sense of duty, but he kept the two departments during his administration entirely distinct, so that Rauscher, who was associated a great deal with Thun, said of him: "Thun has a Catholic heart and a Protestant head." Grillparzer, who was less in agreement with Thun's policy, said: "I have a suicide to announce. The minister of worship has killed the minister of education." Austria now entered on a new era; it became a constitutional monarchy on 20 October, 1860, and Thun's office was abolished. The next year, however, the emperor appointed him a life member of the Upper House of the Imperial Parliament and he was a member of the Bohemian Diet for several terms. In both bodies he was always the pillar of the conservative Catholic party, was the leader of the Federalist party in Bohemia, and upheld the claims of Bohemia for a full autonomy. He founded the "Vaterland", the organ of the Federalist party, and a powerful influence in the politics of the day.

FRANKFURTER in *Allgemeine deutsche Biographie*, XXXVIII (Leipzig, 1894), 178–212; HELFERT, *Graf Leo Thun* (1891).

CÖLESTIN WOLFSGRUBER.

Thurible. See CENSER.

Thuringia.—The name Thuringia is given to a large part of Central Germany, bounded on the west by the Werra River, on the east by the Saale, on the north by the Harz Mountains, and on the south by the Thuringian Forest. The extent of territory is not exactly defined. Besides the Thuringian states, which include the Grand Duchy of Saxe-Weimar-Eisenach, the Duchies of Saxe-Coburg and Gotha, Saxe-Altenburg, and Saxe-Meiningen, Thuringia comprises some parts of Prussian territory, as the cities of Erfurt, Merseburg, Naumburg, etc.; the two principalities of Schwarzburg and the two principalities of Reuss extend beyond the natural limits of Thuringia, especially in the south and east. The early inhabitants of Thuringia were a German tribe called Hermunduri; about A. D. 420 they became known as Thuringians. The powerful kingdom of the Thuringians, which at the beginning of the sixth century extended to the Danube, was overthrown in 531 by the Franks. Christianity had been introduced in various places through the intermarriage of the royal families of the Thuringians and the Visigoths. The Gospel was preached in Southern Thuringia by the Apostles of the Franks, Kilian and his two companions Coloman and Totnan, and in Northern Thuringia by Willibrord, the Apostle of the Frisians; but these missionaries had little success. The real Apostle of Thuringia is St. Boniface. From the monasteries of Fulda and Hersfeld in Hesse, Christianity spread throughout this region. In 742 St. Boniface established Erfurt as the See of Thuringia, making it an important centre of civilization. After the death of the first Bishop of Erfurt, St. Adelar, the diocese was suppressed and Thuringia was united with the Archdiocese of Mainz. The episcopal assistants of the Archbishop of Mainz, who since the fourteenth century had been auxiliary bishops, resided at Erfurt and in the course of time became almost entirely independent of Mainz. The extreme southern part of Thuringia always belonged to the Diocese of Würzburg, the extreme northern to the Diocese of Halberstadt, and the central or main part to Erfurt-Mainz; in the tenth century Eastern Thuringia was divided between the newly-found Dioceses of Merseburg and Zeitz-Naumburg.

The first monastery established by St. Boniface in Thuringia proper was Ohrdruf, now a city of the Duchy of Saxe-Gotha. Contrary to canon law, no church tithes were paid by the inhabitants of Thuringia up to the time of the Reformation, and they obstinately maintained this right, that had become theirs by custom, against the Archbishop of Mainz. The tribal characteristics of the Thuringians gradually disappeared. The southern Thuringians were absorbed by the Franks, the northern Thuringians adopted the character and racial peculiarities of the Saxons, whose territory closely adjoined theirs. In 804 Charlemagne established the Thuringian mark as a defence against the advance of the Slavs. In the tenth century the country was seized by the Duke of Saxony, and during the reign of Emperor Otto I it came under the suzerainty of the Margraves of Meissen. The Saxon dynasty founded the monasteries of Nordhausen, Memleben, and Wahlbeck. In the eleventh century a family of counts from Franconia arose to great importance in Thuringia. The ancestor of this family was Louis the Bearded (d. 1056). His son Louis the Springer built the Castle of Wartburg near Eisenach. In 1089 he founded the Benedictine Abbey of Reinhardsbrunn near Friedrichroda, which was the burial place of the Thuringian landgraves until 1440. This monastery, which has become known through a series of much controverted historical works called the "Reinhardsbrunner Annalen", was badly damaged in the Peasants War of 1525 and was turned into a hunting castle in 1543; it now belongs to the Duke of Saxe-Coburg and Gotha. Other important Benedictine abbeys founded by the landgraves during the eleventh century were the Abbeys at Heiligenstadt and Saalfeld, and during the twelfth century those at Paulinzella, Gosek, and Bosau. The Cistercian Abbeys of Volkenroda, Pforta, and Georgenthal were of great value in civilizing the country, especially Eastern Thuringia.

In 1130 the Emperor Lothair appointed Louis I (d. 1140), son of Louis the Springer (d. 1123), Landgrave of Thuringia. Landgrave Louis IV of Thuringia (1217–27) married St. Elizabeth of Hungary (q. v.); he was succeeded by his brother Henry (d. 1247), with whom the first dynasty of Thuringian landgraves became extinct. The war of succession which now broke out raged until 1263, when the branch of the Wettin family that ruled Saxe-Meissen assumed control of Thuringia. In 1440 a quarrel arose as to the possession of the country, and by the family compact made at Leipzig in 1485 Thuringia was assigned to the Ernestine branch of the house of Wettin. Thuringia now formed a constituent part of the Electorate of Saxony (q. v.), where the great schism of the sixteenth century had its beginnings. As early as 1520 the Catholic Faith was abolished, priests that remained loyal were driven away and churches and monasteries were largely destroyed, especially during the Peasants War of 1525. The Anabaptists found many adherents in Thuringia, particularly at Mülhausen where the founder of the sect, Thomas Münzer, laboured for it. Within the borders of Thuringia the Catholic Faith was maintained only in the district called Eichsfeld, which was ruled by the Archbishop of Mainz, and to a small degree in the city and vicinity of Erfurt, a result also due to the energetic measures of this archbishop. By the Capitulation of Wittenberg of 1547 that closed the Smalkaldic War, John Frederick the Magnanimous lost both the electoral dignity and the country of Saxe-Wittenberg, retaining only Thuringia, which was partitioned by his sons into numerous duchies (see SAXE-ALTENBURG; SAXE-COBURG AND GOTHA; SAXE-MEININGEN; SAXE WEIMAR-EISENACH). While Thuringia still remained a landgravate, there were a number of independent counts and nobles in the country whose possessions were finally absorbed either by the Saxon-Thuringian duchies or by Prussia. Only the principalities of Schwarzburg and the principalities of Reuss have remained independent.

KNOCHENHAUER, *Geschichte Thüringens in der karolingischen u. sächischen Zeit* (Gotha, 1863); IDEM, *Geschichte Thüringens zur Zeit des ersten Landgrafenhauses* (Gotha, 1871); SCOBEL, *Thüringen* (2nd ed., Bielefeld, 1902); *Thüringen in Wort und Bild*, ed. by the Pestalozzi Society (2 vols., Leipzig, 1900–02); GEBHARDT, *Thüringische Kirchengesch.* (3 vols., Gotha, 1880–82), Protestant.

HERMANN SACHER.

Thurmayr, JOHANNES (called AVENTINUS from the place of his birth), b. at Abensberg, Bavaria, 4 July, 1477; d. at Ratisbon, 9 January, 1534. He studied at the Universities of Ingolstadt, Vienna, Cracow, and Paris. In 1507 he returned to Ingolstadt, and in 1509 was appointed tutor to the younger brothers of Duke William IV of Bavaria. In his zeal for learning he founded the "Sodalitas litteraria Angilostadensis", which, however, soon ceased to exist (1520). In 1512 he wrote the "Rudimenta grammaticæ latinæ". In 1517 he was appointed historiographer of Bavaria and was commissioned to write the history of the country. Many of the important authorities which he collected for this purpose have been preserved only in his copies. He embodied a critical treatment of them in a complete history of Bavaria, "Annales Bojorum", down to the year 1460. His condensed German version of it, the "Bayerische Chronik", is the first important history in the German language. Though he ranked as a Catholic, Thurmayr was in sympathy with the Humanists, inclined to the opinions of the Reformers, rejected auricular confession, objected to pilgrimages and indulgences, and opposed in violent language the claims of the hierarchy as excessive. For this reason his history was not published at Ingolstadt until 1554, and then only with omission of the passages hostile to the Church. The "Bayerische Chronik" was published at Frankfort-on-the-Main, 1566. The Bavarian Academy issued a critical complete edition of his works in five volumes (Munich, 1880–86).

See the biographies by WIEDMANN (Freising, 1858); DITTMAR (Nördlingen, 1862); WEGELE (Bamberg, 1890); DÖLLINGER, *Aventin u. seine Zeit* (Munich, 1877; Nördlingen, 1888).

PATRICIUS SCHLAGER.

Thwing, EDWARD, VENERABLE. See NUTTER, ROBERT, VENERABLE.

Thwing, THOMAS, VENERABLE, martyr, b. at Heworth Hall, near York, in 1635; suffered at York, 23 Oct., 1680. His father was George Thwing, Esq., of Kilton Castle and Heworth, nephew of Venerable Edward Thwing; his mother was Anne, sister of the venerable confessor Sir Thomas Gascoigne, of Barnbrow Hall. Educated at Douai, he was sent to the mission in 1664 and laboured in his native county. Until April, 1668, he was chaplain at Carlton Hall, the seat of his cousins the Stapletons. He next opened a school at Quosque, the dower-house of the Stapletons. When in 1677 the "Institute of Mary" began their foundation in the house given by Sir Thomas Gascoigne at Dolebank, Thwing became their chaplain, three of his sisters being of the community. It was there that he was arrested in the early part of 1679. At the time of the Titus Oates scare, two servants who had been discharged from Sir Thomas Gascoigne's employ for dishonesty, sought vengeance and reward by disclosing a pretended plot on the part of Gascoigne and others to murder the king. In their first allegation no mention was made of Thwing. Gascoigne, Thwing, and others were removed to London for trial at Newgate. All were acquitted except Thwing, who was brought back to York for trial in March, 1680. Owing to his challenging the jurors, his trial was postponed to the summer assizes, and he was brought to the bar on 29 July. He was refused an impartial jury, and was found guilty on the very same evidence upon which his relatives had been acquitted. Upon receiving sentence, which in consideration of his gentle birth was passed on him apart from the felons and murderers found guilty at the same assizes, humbly bowing his head he replied "Innocens ego sum." The king at first reprieved him, but owing to a remonstrance of the Commons the death-warrant was issued on the day after the meeting of Parliament. He was drawn from York Castle, past the convent where his sisters were dwelling, to Tyburn, where the sentence was carried out. He declared his innocence, protested his loyalty to the king and his charity to his neighbour; prayed for the king and royal family, and begged the prayers of all true Catholics. His dying words were "Sweet Jesus, receive my soul". His mangled body was given to his friends, and buried in the churchyard of St. Mary, Castlegate. Relics of the martyr are now preserved at the Bar Convent, York, and at Oscott College.

Knaresborough MSS.; COLERIDGE, *St. Mary's Convent, York*; COBBETT, *State Trials*, VII; FOLEY, *Records S. J.*, V; WAUGH, *Quosque Hall* in *Downside Review* (July, 1909); GILLOW in *Cath. Rec. Soc.*, IV, IX; DODD, *Church History*, III; CHALLONER, *Memoirs of Missionary Priests* (Edinburgh, 1877).

J. L. WHITFIELD.

Thyatira, a titular suffragan see of Sardes in Lydia. According to Stephanus Byzantius, the name was given to the city by Seleucus I Nicator; it is more probable that it is of Lydian origin. A Macedonian colony was established there (Strabo, XIII, 4); several divinities were worshipped there, such as Æsculapius, Bacchus, Artemis, above all Apollo, in whose honour games were instituted. Vespasian began great undertakings at Thyatira; it was visited by Hadrian in the year 123, and by Caracalla in 215. Lydia, the woman converted by St. Paul at Philippi, was from Thyatira (Acts, xvi, 13–15); St. John addressed an epistle to the "angel of the church", to whom he gives great commendation, but after having criticised a false prophetess (Apoc., ii, 18–29). Paprylus, martyred about the year 250 at Pergamus, venerated 13 October, was also from this city; we know from testimony given by St. Epiphanius (Contra hær., LI, 33), that at the beginning of the third century almost all Thyatira was Christian. Among the bishops mentioned by Le Quien (Oriens christianus, I, 875–78), we may note Seras, in 325; Fuscus, at the Council of Ephesus in 431; Diamonius, in 458; Basilius, in 878. The bishopric was suffragan to Sardes as late as the tenth century (Gelzer, "Ungedruckte . . . Texte der notitiæ episcopatuum", 537, 553); it is not known when it disappeared. In the Middle Ages the Turks changed the name of Thyatira to that of Ak-Hissar (the white fortress), which it still bears. It numbers 22,000 inhabitants, 7000 of whom are Greek schismatics, 1000 Armenians and Jews, and 14,000 Mussulmans; it is a caza of the sandjak of Saroukhan and of the vilayet of Smyrna.

SMITH, *Dict. Greek and Roman Geog.*, s. v.; TEXIER, *Asie Mineure* (Paris, 1862), 266–68; *Bulletin de Correspondance hellénique*, X, 398–423; XI, 455–467; CUINET, *La Turquie d'Asie*, III, 548–52; LAMPAKES, *The Seven Stars of the Apocalypse* (Athens, 1909), 301-36, in Greek; RAMSAY, *The Seven Churches of Asia* (London, 1909). S. VAILHÉ.

Thynias, a titular see, suffragan of Nicomedia, in Bithynia Prima. It is an island situated in the Black Sea, mentioned by all ancient geographers, and which was only 1421 yards wide. Its original name was Apollonia, because it had a temple to the god Apollo. It also bore the name of Daphne, whence came the name Daphnusia, almost as ancient as that of Apollonia, and which is the only one met with in the "Notitiæ episcopatuum". Its name of Thynias is derived from the Thynii, a people of Thracian origin, who occupied all the coast of Bithynia. Le Quien (Oriens Christ., I, 629) mentions three bishops of Daphnusia: St. Sabas, venerated on 1 May; Leo, present at the Eighth Œcumenical Council in 869; Anthony, at the Photian Council of 878. One John was exiled to Daphnusia and martyred under Copronymus; his feast is observed on 28 November. In the legendary "Vita" of St. Andrew the Apostle (P. G., CXX, 221) it is said that the relics of Sts. Zoticus, Anicetus, and Photius were preserved in the island. The Diocese of Daphnusia is first mentioned in the "Notitia episcopatuum" of Leo the Wise about 900 (Gelzer, "Ungedruckte . . . Texte der Notitiæ episcopatuum", 553), then in that of Constantine Porphyrogenitus about 940 ("Georgii Cyprii Descriptio orbis romani", ed. Gelzer, 65), and finally in "Notitia 13" of Parthey in the thirteenth century (Hierocles Synecdemus, 247). In 1261 the Latin fleet was engaged in the siege of the island when the Greek Emperor of Nicæa, Michael VIII Palæologus, captured Constantinople and thus put an end to the Latin Empire. The island of Daphnusia is now called Kefken or Kerpe-Adasi, and lies west of the mouth of the Sangarius in the caza of Chile and the vilayet of Constantinople.

MÜLLER, *Geog. Græc. minores*, ed. DIDOT, I, 382, notes; IDEM, *Ptolemæi Geographia*, ed. DIDOT, I, 806, notes; SMITH, *Dict. Greek and Roman Geog.*, s. v.; TOMASCHEK, *Zur historischen Topographie von Kleinasien im Mittelalter* (Vienna, 1891), 75; PAULY-WISSOWA, *Real-Encyclopädie der klassischen Altertumswissenschaft* (3rd ed.), s. v., *Apollonia*, no. 14. S. VAILHÉ.

Thyräus, HERMANN, German Jesuit, b. at Neuss on the Rhine, 1532; d. at Mainz, 26 October, 1591. He studied first at Cologne, and then, after 1522, at the Collegium Germanicum at Rome. On 26 May, 1556, he was received into the Society of Jesus by St. Ignatius Loyola, two months before the latter's death. In the same year, Thyräus was made a professor of theology at Ingolstadt, where he taught for three years the "Magister sententiarum", and in the fourth year controversial theology. In 1560 he became a professor at Trier, and lectured on the Epistles of St. Paul. He was rector of the college at Trier (1565–70), provincial of the Jesuit province of the Rhine (1571–8), and from 1578 until his death rector of the college at Mainz. He did excellent service to the Catholic cause and the Counter-Reformation in Germany. The "Liber de religionis libertate", ascribed to him, was written most probably by his younger brother Peter, also a Jesuit. His "Confessio Augustana", with controversial notes, appeared at Dillingen in 1567. He also left several volumes of sermons. According to the testimony of van Reiffenberg ("Historia Soc. Jesu ad Rhenum infer."), he was skilful, industrious, frank, unaffected, and not lacking in shrewdness; and was in consequence highly esteemed by the archbishops of the Rhine, who often employed him in important matters. He was also a noted preacher, and left several volumes of sermons. When he occupied the pulpit at Trier as many as 4000 people often came together to hear him.

SOMMERVOGEL, *Bibl. de la compagnie de Jésus: Bibliographie*, VIII (Paris, 1898), 10–11; STEINHUBER, *Gesch. des Collegium Germanicum Hungaricum*, I (Freiburg, 1895), 38; DUHR, *Gesch. der Jesuiten in den Ländern deutscher Zunge im XVI. Jahrhundert*, I (Freiburg, 1907), passim. KLEMENS LÖFFLER.

Tiara, the papal crown, a costly covering for the head, ornamented with precious stones and pearls, which is shaped like a bee-hive, has a small cross at its highest point, and is also equipped with three royal diadems. On account of the three diadems it is sometimes called *triregnum*. The tiara is a non-liturgical ornament, which, therefore, is only worn for non-liturgical ceremonies, ceremonial procession to church and back, ceremonial papal processions, such as took place upon stated occasions until Rome was occupied by the Piedmontese, and at solemn acts of jurisdiction, as, for example, solemn dogmatic decisions. The pope, like the bishops, wears a mitre at pontifical liturgical functions. The tiara is first mentioned in the "Vita" of Pope Constantine (708–715) contained in the "Liber Pontificalis". It is here called *camelaucum*; it is then mentioned in what is called the "Constitutum Constantini", the supposed donation of the Emperor Constantine, probably forged in the eighth century. Among the prerogatives assigned to the pope in this document there is especially a white ornament for the head called *phrygium*, which distinguished him; this naturally presupposes that, at the era the document was written, it was customary for the pope to wear such a head-covering. Three periods may be distinguished in the development of the tiara. The first period extends to the time when it was adorned with a royal circlet or diadem; in this period the papal ornament for the head was, as is clear from the "Constitutum Constantini" and from the ninth Ordo of Mabillon (ninth century), merely a helmet-like cap of white material. There may have been a trimming around the lower rim of the cap, but this had still in no way the character of a

ST. GREGORY THE GREAT WEARING THE PAPAL CAP OF WHITE MATERIAL
From an XI-century MS. in the library of the University of Leipzig

royal circlet. It is not positively known at what date the papal head-covering was adorned with such a circlet. At the time the Donation of Constantine appeared, that is in the eighth century, the papal head-covering had still no royal circlet, as is evident from the text of the document. In the ninth century also such circlet does not seem to have existed. It is true that the Ninth Ordo calls the papal cap *regnum*, but in the description that the Ordo gives of this cap we hear nothing at all of a crown, but merely that the *regnum* was a helmet-like cap made of white material. The monumental remains give no clue as to the period at which the papal head-covering became ornamented with a royal circlet. Up into the twelfth century the tiara was not only seldom represented in art, but it is also uncertain whether the ornamental strip on the lower edge is intended to represent merely a trimming or a diadem. This is especially true of the representations of the tiara on the coins of Sergius III (904-911) and Benedict VII (974-983), the only representations of the tenth century and also the earliest ones. Probably the papal head-covering received the circlet at the time when the mitre developed from the tiara, perhaps in the tenth century, in order to distinguish the mitre and tiara from each other. In any case the latter was provided with a circlet by about 1130, as is learned from a statement of Suger of St. Denis. The first proven appearance of the word *tiara* as the designation of the papal head-covering is in the life of Paschal II (1099-1118), in the "Liber Pontificalis".

BONIFACE VIII WITH DOUBLE-CROWNED TIARA
XIV-Century figure in the Lateran Basilica

The second period of the development of the tiara extends to the pontificate of Boniface VIII (1294-1303). There are a large number of representations of the tiara belonging to this period, and of these the Roman ones have naturally the most value. The diadem remained a simple although richly-ornamented ring up into the second half of the thirteenth century; it then became an antique or tooth-edged crown. The two lappets (*caudæ*) at the back of the tiara are first seen in the pictures and sculpture in the thirteenth century, but were undoubtedly customary before this. Strange to say they were black in colour, as is evident both from the monumental remains and from the inventories, and this colour was retained even into the fifteenth century. When the tiara is represented in sculpture and painting as a piece of braiding, this seems to arise from the fact that in the thirteenth century the tiara was made of strips braided together. Of much importance for the tiara was the third period of development that began with the pontificate of Boniface VIII. It is evident from the inventory of the papal treasures of 1295 that the tiara at that era had still only one royal circlet. A change, however, was soon to appear. During the pontificate of Boniface VIII a second crown was added to the former one. Three statues of the pope which were made during his lifetime and under his eyes, and of which two were ordered by Boniface himself, leave no doubt as to this. Two of these statues are in the crypt of St. Peter's, and the third, generally called erroneously a statue of Nicholas IV, is in the Church of the Lateran. In all three the tiara has two crowns. What led Boniface VIII to make this change, whether merely love of pomp, or whether he desired to express by the tiara with two crowns his opinions concerning the double papal authority, cannot be determined. The first notice of three crowns is contained in an inventory of the papal treasure of the year 1315 or 1316. As to the tombs of the popes, the monument of Benedict XI (d. 1304) at Perugia shows a tiara of the early kind; the grave and statue of Clement V at Uzeste in the Gironde were mutilated by the Calvinists, so that nothing can be learned from them regarding the form of the tiara. The statue upon the tomb of John XXII is adorned with a tiara having two crowns. The earliest representation of a tiara with three crowns, therefore, is offered by the effigy of Benedict XII (d. 1342), the remains of which are preserved in the museum at Avignon. The tiara with three crowns is, consequently, the rule upon the monuments from the second half of the fourteenth century, even though, as an anachronism, there are isolated instances of the tiara with one crown up into the fifteenth century. Since the fifteenth century the tiara has received no changes worthy of note. Costly tiaras were made especially in the pontificates of Paul II (d. 1464), Sixtus IV (d. 1484), and above all in the pontificate of Julius II, who had a tiara valued at 200,000 ducats, made by the jeweller Caradosso of Milan.

Various hypotheses, some very singular, have been proposed as to the origin of the papal head-covering, the discussion of which here is unnecessary. The earliest name of the papal cap, *camelaucum*, as well as the Donation of Constantine, clearly point to the Byzantine East; it is hardly to be doubted that the model from which the papal cap was taken is to be found in the *camelaucum* of the Byzantine court dress. The adoption by the popes of the *camelaucum* as an ornament for the head in the seventh or at the latest in the eighth century is sufficiently explained by the important position which they had attained just at this period in Italy and chiefly at Rome; though they could not assume a crown, as they were not sovereign, they could wear a *camelaucum*, which was worn by the dignitaries of the Byzantine Empire.

GARAMPI, *Illustrazione di un antico sigillo della Gavagnana* (Rome, 1759); BOCK, *Gesch. der liturg. Gewänder*, II (Bonn, 1866); ROHAULT DE FLEURY, *La Messe*, VIII (Paris, 1889); MÜNTZ, *La tiare pont.* in *Mémoires de l'Acad. des Inscriptions et Belles-Lettres*, XXXVI (Paris, 1898); BRAUN, *Die liturg. Gewandung im Occident u. Orient* (Freiburg, 1907).

TIARA OF JULIUS II
Made by Caradosso of Milan

JOSEPH BRAUN.

Tibaldi, PELLEGRINO, known also as Pellegrino da Bologna and as Pellegrino Pellegrini, decorator, mural painter, and architect, b. at Bologna, 1527; d. at Milan about 1592. Tibaldi was a pupil of Bagna Cavello, and a profound student of the works of Michelangelo. His early decorative works were executed for Cardinal Poggi, for whom he carried out a large number of commissions, in his palace at Bologna, the chapel he erected in Loretto, his rooms in Rome, and a chapel in the Church of San Giacomo in Bologna. In 1586 he went to Spain on the invitation of Philip II, and painted in the lower cloisters of the Escorial, after first erasing the work of his predecessors, with which he professed to be much dissatisfied. His greatest work was the decoration of the library in that building. He resided for nine years in Spain, returned to Italy, settled at Milan, was appointed architect of the cathedral, and died in that place. His works can be studied in Bologna and Dresden.

LANZI, *Storia Pittorica della Italia* (Bassano, 1809); MALVASIA, *Felsina Pittrice* (Bologna, 1841).

G. C. WILLIAMSON.

Tiberias, titular see, suffragan of Scythopolis, in Palæstina Secunda. The town of Tiberias was founded on the lake in A. D. 17 by Herod Antipas, tetrarch of Galilee, who gave it the name of the reigning emperor, Tiberius. As tombs were discovered there at the time of its foundation the Jews refused to dwell there, and Herod was forced to populate it with foreigners and people of low extraction (Josephus, "Ant. jud.", XVIII, ii, 3). What it was previously called is not known; St. Jerome makes it the site now of Reccath, now of Emath, now of Cenereth or Kinnereth, towns of Nephthali (Jos., XIX, 35). The town seems to have been a little more than three miles in circumference. Although Tiberias gave its name to the neighbouring lake and is mentioned several times in the Gospels, it seems never to have been dwelt in by Christ. At the death of Herod Antipas in 41, Nero gave the town to Herod Agrippa the Younger who made Sephoris or Diocæsarea his capital. At the revolt of the Jews against the Romans the people of Tiberias sided now with one party, now with the other, and the Jewish historian Josephus, who was Governor of Galilee, only took it after several attempts ("Bell. jud.", II, xxi, 6; "Vita Josephi", 18 and 54). At the approach of Vespasian it submitted without resistance and was not disturbed; the Jews secured the privilege of dwelling there alone, to the exclusion of pagans, Christians, and Samaritans. Towards the end of the second century the Sanhedrin was removed thither from Sephoris together with the Talmudic school of Jamnia, whence issued many celebrated Rabbis, among them Juda Hakkodesh, who shortly afterwards codified the vast body of laws and customs known as the Mishna. Between 230 and 270 Rabbi Jochanan composed the Gemara, supplement of the Mishna, and these two codes are called the Jerusalem Talmud. In the sixth century the school of Tiberias produced the celebrated Masorah, or fixed Hebrew text of the Bible. Rabbi Bar Anina of Tiberias gave lessons in Hebrew to St. Jerome.

The introduction of Christianity dates from the time of Constantine the Great. It was Count Joseph, a Jewish convert of this town living at Scythopolis, who built its first church, perhaps on the site of the Hadrianeum (a temple founded by the Emperor Hadrian and never completed). Under Constantine also the Jewish patriarch Hillel was converted and baptized by the missionary bishop who bore the title of Tiberias but resided elsewhere (P. G., XLI, 409–29). Among its bishops were: John, present at the Robber Synod of Ephesus and the Council of Chalcedon in 449 and 451; John II, at the councils of 518 and 536; George, in 553; Basil, in the eighth century (Le Quien, "Oriens christ.", III, 705–10); Theodore, in 808 (Tobler, "Itinerar. hierosolym.", I, 304). Justinian restored the walls of the town (Procopius, "De ædificiis", V, 9). Ancient pilgrims speak of its churches and synagogues. At the Frankish occupation it was given in fief to Tancred who made it his capital. A new town was built, churches restored, and a Latin diocese was instituted, suffragan to Nazareth. Many of its residential or titular bishops are known (Du Cange, "Familles d'outre-mer", 807; Le Quien, op. cit., III, 1301–04; Eubel, "Hierarchia catholica medii ævi", I, 511; II, 275; III, 333). The Greek see never ceased to exist, but has long been titular. In 1187 after the defeat of Hattin, better known as the battle of Tiberias, the town and fortress fell into the power of Saladin. In 1239 it was given to Eudes de Montbéliard, but five years later the Sultan of Egypt recovered it and massacred the garrison and the Christian inhabitants. The last Jew died in 1620 at the passing of Quaresimus, and only Mussulmans remained. The Jews have since returned. Out of 6500 inhabitants, 4500 are Jews, 1600 Mussulmans, 185 Greek Catholics, 35 Latins, 42 Greek Schismatics, and about 20 Protestants dependent on the Scotch mission which has a school and a hospital. The Franciscans have a church and an infirmary. The town, called Tabarieh, besides ramparts has only insignificant ruins and is very dirty.

SMITH, *Dict. of Gr. and Rom. Geog.*, s. v.; NEUBAUER, *La géographie du Talmud* (Paris, 1868), 207–14; GUÉRIN, *Description de la Palestine: Galilée*, I (Paris, 1869–80), 250–63; THOMSEN, *Loca sancta* (Halle, 1907), 111.

S. VAILHÉ.

Tiberias, SEA OF, so called in John, xxi, 1 (cf. vi, 1), otherwise known as "the sea of Galilee" (Matt., iv, 18; Mark, i, 16; John, vi, 1), or as "the lake of Genesareth" (Luke, v, 1, and Rabbinical writings), or as "the sea of Cenereth" (Num., xxxiv, 11; Jos., xiii, 27; cf. Jos., xi, 2), or as "the water of Genesar" (I Mach., xi, 67), or, lastly, as "the Lake of Tarichea" (Pliny, "Hist. Nat.", V, xv). It lies in the Jordan gorge, 682 feet below the level of the Mediterranean. An irregular oval nearly thirteen miles long, its maximum width, near the northern end, is about seven and a half miles. The lake is enclosed on the east and west by mountains; the former, a uniform wall 2000 feet high sloping steeply to within half a mile of the shore; the latter, lower and more broken, gradually approaching the water as they advance northwards till, about half way up the coast, they leave only a narrow strip of littoral. At the north-west corner the mountain inclines somewhat westward and the littoral widens into a triangular plain of marvellous fertility which stretches eastwards for four miles—the Plain of Genesareth. East of this the ground is broken and sterile, overgrown with bush, and strewn with volcanic rock. The lake is fed by several torrents and by copious hot springs on the north and west, but principally by the Jordan, which enters at the north-east corner and rushes out at the south-western extremity. The depth of the lake nowhere exceeds 150 feet. Its water is sweet and good to drink. Fish are so abundant that catches of 600 pounds are not rare, and in one exceptional season (1896) 9200 pounds of fish were hauled ashore in one huge net. Storms are alarmingly sudden and frequent. The hot atmosphere of the gorge (averaging in the shade 93°F. in summer, and 50° in winter) sucks down the cool air of the heights through the narrow wadis to the east and west at the north end, and in half an hour the surface of the lake tosses furiously. Half an hour again suffices to restore the lake to a mirror-like calm.

To-day the shores are barren and desolate, with gloomy patches of volcanic soil to the north and west. There is scarcely a tree to be seen, nor even any verdure except where an overflowing torrent waters the north-western plain, nor any human habitation save the sombre houses of Tiberias to the west and a few straggling villages. But in the days of Christ nature and man united to render these shores singularly attractive. The vine and the fig flourished ten months in the year, and every variety of fruit ripened in the various seasons: thick woods surrounded the lake even down to the eighth century of the present era, and the plains yielded rich harvests twice in the year. Nine, perhaps ten, cities encircled the lake with an almost unbroken front of wharves and har-

Trajan. Its exact site is unknown, but it was situated in the region of Egri Gueuz, caza of Kutahia, vilayet of Brusa. Ancient Greek "Notitiæ episcopatuum" mention it among the suffragans of Laodicea. In the eighth century it was attached to the metropolitan See of Hierapolis and as such appears in the "Notitiæ episcopatuum" until the thirteenth century. Le Quien (Oriens christ., I, 797) mentions five of its bishops known by their presence at councils: Eustathius at Constantinople (536); Silas at Constantinople (553); Anastasius at Constantinople (692); Michael at Nicæa (787); Theoctistus at Constantinople (879).

SMITH, *Dict. of Greek and Roman geog.*, s. v.; RAMSAY, Asia Minor (London, 1890), 147, 458.

S. PÉTRIDÈS.

Tiberius, the second Roman emperor (A. D. 14–37), b. 16 November, 42 B. C.; d. 16 March, A. D. 37. He

THE SEA OF TIBERIAS
From a Watercolour by H. Fenn

bours. Ruins of theatres, hippodromes, temples, synagogues, baths, and villas witness to the presence of all the refinements of Græco-Roman culture. Fishing was an important industry (cf. *Beth Saida*= "Fishing-House", and *Tarichea*="Pickling Factories"), and the fishermen, though reputed generally pious by the Rabbis, were a force to be reckoned with in troubled times. The fish were exported to all parts of the Roman world. The standing population of the towns, of which the smallest had at least 15,000 inhabitants, was largely increased by multitudes of sick who flocked, especially in summer, to the world-renowned springs near Tiberias.

Besides the Bible Dictionaries, consult: SMITH, *Hist. Geography of the Holy Land* (London, 1909), 438–63; MERRILL, *East of Jordan* (London, 1881); GUÉRIN, *Description de la Palestine* (Paris, 1868–80), Pt. III, *Galilée*, 193–263; NEUBAUER, *Géographie du Talmud* (Paris, 1868); BIEVER. *Au bord du Lac de Tibériade* in *Conferences de Saint-Etienne* (Paris, 1910), 109–142; (Paris, 1911), 261–307 (a third lecture before the same audience in January, 1912, has not yet been published); BUHL, *Geographie des alten Palästina* (Freiburg and Leipzig, 1896); *Official Records of the Palestine Exploration Fund and Deutsche Palästina-Verein*.

JEREMIAH HARTIGAN.

Tiberiopolis, titular see in Phrygia Pacatiana. Tiberiopolis is mentioned by Ptolemy (V, 2, 25); Socrates (Hist. eccl., VII, 46); and Herocles (Synec., 668, 9). It struck its own coins at least from the time of

was the son of Tiberius Claudius Nero and Livia. By the marriage of his mother with Emperor Augustus he became the latter's stepson, and was adopted by Augustus in A. D. 4. In the year 10 he was appointed coregent with Augustus. Hard and secretive by nature and embittered by the neglect with which his step-father allowed him to be treated, he did not arouse personal enthusiasm, and until recently was described by historians as a bloody tyrant. It is only during the last sixty years that he has been more fairly judged, and at present the opinion begins to prevail that he was a genuine Roman, a ruler faithful to his duties, just, wise, and self-contained. In his internal policies especially he is one of the most distinguished of all Roman emperors. Like Augustus he reformed and improved every department of the government, and promoted in every direction the prosperity of the empire of which Augustus had laid the foundation. He developed imperial power by declining to have his authority renewed from time to time by the Senate, as Augustus had done. The strong opposition which grew up against him was due to his taciturn and domineering disposition, and to the influence of the prefect of the guard, Ælius Sejanus, who alone possessed his confidence. The persecutions and executions for lese-majesty, which rapidly increased during the second half of his reign, and the gloom which pervaded Rome induced Tiberius to leave the capital altogether in the year 26 and to live partly in Campania and partly on the Island of Capri. Before this date the question as to the succession to the empire had led to a terrible family tragedy. By his first marriage Tiberius had a son called Drusus, while his second marriage with the immoral Julia, daughter of Augustus, was childless. After the death of his nephew Germanicus (A. D. 19), whom he had been obliged to adopt at the command of Augustus to the exclusion of his own son, he hoped to secure the succession for Drusus. A low intrigue was formed against this plan, in which the wife of Drusus, Livilla, who had illicit relations with Sejanus, took part. In the year 23 Drusus was poisoned by Sejanus and Livilla. However, when in 31 Sejanus formed a conspiracy to secure the throne for himself, Tiberius was warned at the last moment and had Sejanus executed. Tiberius spent his last years in constantly increasing seclusion, misanthropy, and cruelty on the Island of Capri, where it is said he abandoned himself to debauchery. However, these reports are at least coloured by prejudice and have not been satisfactorily proved. Neither is it probable that Tiberius was murdered.

TIBERIUS
Antique Fragment in the Lateran Museum

The ministry and death of John the Baptist and of Jesus Christ occurred during the reign of Tiberius. According to St. Luke (iii, 1), St. John the Baptist was called by God, in the fifteenth year of the reign of Tiberius, to prepare the way for Christ as His precursor. Shortly before his death Tiberius recalled the procurator Pontius Pilate from Judea. Tertullian (Apologeticum, v, xxi), from whom Eusebius and Orosius take the story, relates that Tiberius received a report concerning Christ and that he called upon the Senate to place Christ among the gods. The Senate rejected the request; Tiberius then threatened the accusers of the Christians with punishment. The narrative is not worthy of belief, still it is probable that Tertullian knew a document that professed to be a report of Pilate.

STAHR, *Tiberius* (2nd ed., Berlin, 1873); DOMASZEWSKI, *Gesch. der römisch. Kaiser*, I (Leipzig, 1909), 250–319; TARVER, *Tiberius the Tyrant* (London, 1902); SCHILLER, *Gesch. der römisch. Kaiserzeit*, I (Gotha, 1883), 248–304; HARNACK, *Gesch. der altchristl. Litteratur*, II (Leipzig, 1897), pt. I, 604–10; BARDENHEWER, *Gesch. der altkirchl. Litteratur*, I (Freiburg, 1902), 410–11.

KLEMENS LÖFFLER.

Tibet, a vast plateau, about 463,320 square miles, about 1240 miles in its greatest length from east to west, and 740 miles in its greatest breadth from north to south, with an elevation from 13,000 to 16,500 feet, and with a population of some 6,500,-000 inhabitants, according to Chinese estimates; other estimates place it as low as 2 or 3,000,000. It is bounded on the north by Kan-su and Sin-kiang; on the west by India; on the south by India, Nepal, Sikkim, and Bhutan; on the east by Yun-nan, Sze-ch'wan, and Kan-su; or rather the plateau on the north is bounded by the Kwenlun Mountains which limit on the south the Desert of Gobi; and on the south by the Himalaya Mountains with their high peak, Mount Everest, 29,000 feet.

HYDROGRAPHY.—From this plateau flow the following rivers: to the south, the Indus, with its tributary Sutlej, which runs into the Gulf of Oman; to the north of the Himalayas, the Ts'anpo or Brahmaputra River, which falls into the Gulf of Bengal after meeting in an estuary the Ganges, which follows a similar course on the southern side of the Himalayas; to the east, the great Chinese rivers, Hwang-ho or Ma-chu, and Yang-tze; to the south-east, the streams of Indo-China, the Lutze-kiang (Irrawadi), the Lu-kiang (Salwen), and the Lan ts'an kiang (Me-kong). The principal lakes are: on the north-east, the Kuku-nor or Ts'ing hai; on the south, Lake Palti or Yamdok; on the plateau, the Iki-Namur, the Pang-kong, the Tengri-nor, and the famed Mansarovar and Rakas.

GEOGRAPHY.—Many roads lead to Lhasa: (1) by Si-ning in the Kan-su Province and the Kuku-nor; (2) from Sze-ch'wan to Ta-Tsienlu, Ba-tang, Litang and Chamdo; (3) from Yun-nan by Li-kiang (these are the three main routes from China); (4) from Sikkim, in the south, through the Chumbi Valley and Gyan-tze; (5) from the west, by Leh, in Ladakh; (6) from Khotan, through the Aksai Chin, to Rudok. Tibet includes five provinces: (1) Amdo, part of the Chinese province of Kan-su and the Kuku-nor region (Ts'ing-hai), inhabited by Tibetans and administered by a Chinese official at Si-ning; the other four provinces form Tibet proper which is controlled by the viceroy of Sze-Ch'wan; (2) Ts'ien-tang, Eastern or Anterior Tibet (or K'ang, Kham, Khu, Khamdo, Chamdo), which extends between the Chinese Provinces of Sze-Ch'wan and Yun-nan, and the district of Lhorong djong, frontier of Lhasa; (3) Wei, Wu, or Chung-Tsang, Central Tibet, Kingdom of Lhasa; (4) Tsang or Hou Tsang, Ulterior Tibet, i. e. south-west Tibet, extending to Lake Mansarovar, with the town of Shigatze, near which stands the Tashilumbo Monastery at the junction of the Nyang-chu and the Ts'an-po; (5) Ngari (O-li), Western Tibet, which includes the upper courses of the Indus and the Sutlej, and generally north-western Tibet with the towns of Gartok and Rudok, the Kailas Mountain, the Refuge of Siva; it is bounded by the British district of Kumaun.

LAMAIST HIERARCHY AND SECULAR ADMINISTRATION.—At the head of the lamaist hierarchy of Tibet are the dalai lama and the *panch'en erdeni lama;* the word "lama" is derived from a Tibetan word, in Chinese, *wu shang*, meaning "unsurpassed". The dalai lama is a re-embodiment of one of the disciples of the reformer Tsong K'apa, and at the same time an incarnation of the Bodhisattwa Avalokiteçvara; he lives at the monastery Po-ta-la at Lhasa; his title is *Cheptsun Djamts'o Rinpoch'é* (Venerable Ocean Treasure). The *panch'en lama* lives at Tashilumbo. The supporters of the faith may receive the title of *Nomên 'Hân* (regent), or *Dharmâ Râja*. Celibacy would render impossible the re-embodiment if the *'hut'ukht'u* or saints were not chosen to represent the principles of the transmission of authority; these saints are known as the "Living Buddhas". The third lama in the hierarchy is the *Cheptsun Dampa 'Hut'ukht'u*, Patriarch of the Khalkhas, living at Urga; the *Ch'ahan Nomên 'Han* is the descendant of a counsellor sent in the sixteenth century by the dalai lama to the chief of the Ordos; his residence is at Kuku-Khoto; the metropolitan lama, *Ch'ang Kia 'Hut'-ukht'u*, has his see at Dolonnor; the head of lamaist monasteries is called *K'anpu* (abbot). The secular administration of Tibet includes a council (*ka hia*) of four ministers (*kalon* or *kablon*) of the third rank of Chinese officials, elected as a rule by the Peking Government, on presentation by the Chinese *amban;*

the treasury (*shang shang*) presided over by a *kalon* with three first-class councillors (*tsai peng*), and two second-class councillors (*shang chodba*); two controllers of the revenue (*yerts' angba*); two controllers of streets and roads (*hierbang*); two superintendents of police (*shediba*); two controllers of the stud (*tapêng*); there are six military commanders (*taipêng*), with the fourth degree of Chinese rank, with twelve commanders of 200 men (*jupêng*), twenty-four *kiapêng*, and 120 *ting pêng*. Civil and military officials are designed under the general term of *fan muh*.

HISTORY.—Little is known of the ancient history of Tibet, the first dynasty having been founded by the Indian prince Rupati; but the historical period begins at the end of the sixth century A. D. when the first king, Luntsang, made inroads to India. Luntsang's son is the celebrated Srong-tsang Gam-po, one of the great champions of Buddhism; in 639 he married Bribtsun, daughter of Ançuvarman, sovereign of Nepal, and in 641 the princess of Wen ch'eng, daughter of the Chinese emperor T'ai-tsung. Under their influence, the Tibetan prince gave a great extension to Buddhism in his empire; he founded in 639 Lhasa, formerly Lha-ldan, where for centuries his heirs governed the country with the title of *gialbo* in Tibetan, and of *tsanp'o* in Chinese. The Tibetans were the allies of the Khalif of Bagdad and they invaded the Chinese provinces of Yun-nan, Sze-ch'wan and Kan-su, as far as Ch'ang ngan, capital of the T'ang emperors. The two most ancient historical edicts have been found by Dr. L. A. Waddell upon a lofty pillar of victory which stands at the foot of Potala Hill, under the castles of the ancient kings, now incorporated in the palace of the dalai lama; they date between A. D. 730 and 763, are the earliest historical Tibetan documents hitherto discovered, and throw a sidelight on the ancient history and geography of China. The eighth century is the culminating point of Tibetan power, which was destroyed when the Uighurs became the masters of the whole country between Peit'ing and Aksu.

During the eleventh century the priests of the Sakya Monastery began to be predominant in Tibet; they were called *Hung Kiao*, Red Church, on account of the colour of their garments and of their headgear. The laxness of their morals, the marriage of monks, and sorcery were the chief causes of the reform undertaken by Tsong K'apa or Je Rinpoch'e (b. at Amdo near Kuku-nor in 1358), founder of the Gelupa Sect, who adopted a yellow dress (*hwang kiao*), and obliged his followers to return to the primitive religion of Buddha; he founded the Monasteries of Gadan and of Sera, and died in 1418, having established the lamaist hierarchy. His successor, Gedundub, built the Monastery of Tashilumbo, which became in the seventeenth century the residence of the second lama, the *panch'en rinpoch'é*, while the first lama or dalai lama settled in 1641 to the west of Lhasa. The *panch'en lama*, Paldan-yeshes, died at Peking on the 27 Nov., 1780, during a visit to the Emperor of China. During the eighteenth century the Chinese Emperor, K'ien-lung, began to establish his supremacy over Tibet; already in 1725 two high Chinese commissioners had been appointed to control the temporal affairs of the country, and in the first moon of 1793 an imperial edict ordered that future dalai lamas were to be chosen from the names of children drawn from a "golden urn".

CHINESE ADMINISTRATION.—The Chinese administration of Tibet includes an imperial resident (*chu tsang ta ch'ên*) or *amban* (*ngang pai*) with an assistant resident (*pang pan ta ch'ên*); among their duties, they act as intermediary between China and Nepal (Ghorkhas Country); a secretary (*yi ts'ing chang-king*) has to deal with native affairs. Three Chinese commissioners (*liang t'ai*), of the class of sub-prefect, are stationed at Lhasa, Tashilumbo, and Ngari. The imperial resident is Chao Erh-fung (appointed March, 1908), formerly Director-General of the Sze-ch'wan Hu-Pe Railway and acting viceroy of Szech'wan.

TRAVELLERS IN TIBET.—Marco Polo and Rubruk mention Tibet but did not visit it; the first European traveller who appears to have visited Lhasa is the Franciscan Odoric of Pordenone in the first half of the fourteenth century. It was but in 1624 that we have real information on this country in a letter of the Portuguese Jesuit, Antonio de Andrade, dated Agra, 8 Nov., 1624, relating the journey of this father to Lake Mansarovar and to Rudok; Andrade erroneously called the country he visited, Cathay. Two years later, two other Jesuits, Grueber and d'Orville, (1661) left Peking, and by the route of Si-ning reached Lhasa, where they resided two months; they returned to India via Nepal. Two other Jesuits, Desideri and Freyre, went (1715–16) from Leh to Lhasa, where the former lived until 1729, when he was obliged to leave on account of the intrigues of the Capuchins, who had founded a mission which lasted to 1760, when they were expelled by the Tibetans. One of these monks, Francesco Orazio della Penna di Billi, has written an account of Tibet. A most remarkable journey was made by the Dutchman Samuel Van de Putte (d. at Batavia, 27 Sept., 1745), who went from India to Peking via Lhasa, and returned by the same road. In 1774 Warren Hastings, Governor of Bengal, sent George Bogle to the Court of the *panch'an lama;* Captain Samuel Turner went on a visit in 1783 to the Court of the new *panch'en lama;* finally the Englishman Thomas Manning visited Lhasa in 1811. Next we come to the celebrated journey to Lhasa of the Lazarists Huc (q. v.) and Gabet in 1844. For many years afterwards the exploration of Tibet was carried on by "pundits" in the Indian Government service, especially by Naîn Sing and the lama, Ugyen Gyatso. We must mention also among the travellers to Tibet the Russian, Prjevalsky (1880–85); the American, W. W. Rockhill (1888–89, 1891–92), who went to the north-east of Tengri-nor, 110 miles west of Lhasa; the Frenchmen, Gabriel Bonvalot and Prince Henri d'Orléans with the Belgian missionary, De Deken (1889–90); Captain Hamilton Bower (1891 92); Miss A. R. Taylor (1892); the Frenchman, Dutreuil de Rhins (who was murdered, 5 June, 1894, at Tungbumdo by the red lamas), and his companion, Fernand Grenard (who escaped); Sir George K. Littledale (1895); Captain M. S. Wellby and Lieut. Malcolm (1896); Captain H. H. P. Deasy (1896); the celebrated Swedish explorer, Sven Hedin; and finally the Russian captain, P. K. Kozlov.

RELATIONS WITH CHINA, RUSSIA, AND ENGLAND.— By a separate article of the Che-fu Convention (13 Sept., 1876) it had been stipulated that the English Government might in the next year send a mission of exploration by way of Peking through Kan-su and Kuku-nor, or by way of Sze-ch'wan to Tibet, and thence to India. The Tsung-li-Yaman, having due regard to the circumstances, was, when the time arrived, to issue the necessary passports, and address letters to the high provincial authorities, and to the imperial resident in Tibet. The English did not take advantage of this article and countermanded the mission by Article 4 of the Convention signed at Peking, 24 July, 1886, regarding Burmah and Tibet. A convention with China was signed on 17 March, 1890, at Calcutta, settling the boundary frontiers between Sikkim and Tibet, and trade regulations were also signed in December, 1893. But the Tibetans occupied land inside the treaty boundary; on the other hand Russian activity in Tibet was causing great anxiety to the Indian Government; Lord Curzon had attempted to open direct communication with the dalai lama; there were rumours of a Russo-

Tibetan agreement. Notwithstanding Russia's protest, the Indian Government proposed sending a mission to Lhasa. Finally this mission was organized in July, 1903, with Major Francis E. Younghusband at its head; this first mission was turned into a second mission with Younghusband as a commissary and General James R. L. Macdonald as commander of the military escort. The English crossed the Jelep Pass (12 Dec., 1903), occupied Phari (19 Dec.), stormed Gyantse (12 April, 1904), and entered Lhasa on 3 August; the dalai lama was in flight. A treaty was signed on 7 September; the British troops left Lhasa and they were back in India on 25 October. The treaty was ratified by the Viceroy of India on 11 Nov., 1904; it included ten articles: The Government of Tibet engaged to respect the Anglo-Chinese Convention of 1890 and to recognize the frontier between Sikkim and Tibet; undertook to open forthwith trade-marts, to which all British and Tibetan subjects should have free right of access at Gyantse and Gastok as well as at Yatung; the roads to Gyantse and Gastok from the frontier were to be kept clear of all obstructions; an indemnity of £500,000, reduced since to one-third this amount, was to be paid to the British Government for the expense incurred in the despatch of armed troops to Lhasa; all forts and fortifications were to be razed and all armaments removed which might impede the course of free communication between the British frontiers and the towns of Gyantse and Lhasa. These terms were really very moderate. On 27 April, 1906, a convention was signed at Peking by Sir Ernest Mason Satow for Great Britain and by Tang Shao-yi for China, including six articles: the Lhasa Convention was confirmed; Great Britain engaged not to annex Tibetan territory or to interfere in the administration of Tibet; China also undertook not to permit any other foreign state to interfere with the territory or internal administration of Tibet. Finally, in 1907, Russia and Great Britain also signed a convention: both parties engaged to respect the territorial integrity of Tibet and to abstain from all interference in its internal administration, not to send representatives to Lhasa, neither to seek nor to obtain, whether for themselves or for their subjects, any concessions for railways, roads, telegraphs, and mines, or other rights in Tibet. From this time the Tibetan frontier has been closed to all foreigners, though the prohibition has been eluded by the daring Swedish explorer, Sven Hedin. The dalai lama had fled to Urga, in Mongolia, which he left in the summer of 1907 to settle at the Kun Bum Monastery; afterwards, in 1908, he went to the celebrated pilgrimage of Shan-si, Wu tai Shan, whence he repaired to Peking. An audience was granted to him by the emperor and he was allowed to leave the Chinese capital on 21 Dec., 1908, and return to Lhasa, where he was not to stay long; a body of Chinese troops invaded Tibet, the dalai lama fled to Darjeeling, and the result of the policy of both Great Britain and Russia has been the virtual annexation of Tibet by China.

MISSIONS.—Since the Capuchins were expelled in 1760, except the Lazarists Huc and Gabet, who paid a visit to Lhasa in 1844, no missionary entered Tibet proper. The Vicar Apostolic of Hindu Tibet, Giuseppe Antonio Borghi, Bishop of Batsaïda, begged to be relieved of part of his work, and consequently on 21 March, 1846, Gregory XVI created the Vicariate Apostolic of Lhasa. The new vicariate was placed in charge of the Foreign Missions of Paris, and in 1847 Mgr Pérocheau, of Sze-ch'wan, sent Father Charles-René Renou (b. 22 Aug., 1812; d. 18 Oct., 1863) through Bat'ang to Cha-mu-to, some thirty days in the interior of Tibet, but being discovered, he was sent back to Ch'eng-tu. Renou being appointed Prefect Apostolic of Eastern Tibet was to enter his mission via Yun-nan, while Rabin, Prefect Apostolic of Southern Tibet, was to penetrate into the country by the way of Northern India with Fathers Krick and Bernard. Nicholas-Michel Krick (b. 2 March, 1819) and Auguste-Etienne Bourry (b. 26 Dec., 1826) were murdered by the Abors on 1 Sept., 1854. Finally the vicariate was established in the eastern portion of Tibet and the western portion of Sze-ch'wan with Jacques-Léon-Thomine Desmazures (b. 17 Feb., 1804; d. 25 Jan., 1869), Bishop of Sinopolis (1857), who resigned in 1864. His successors have been Joseph-Marie Chauveau (b. 24 Feb., 1816; d. 21 Dec., 1877), Bishop of Sebastopolis (1850) and Vicar Apostolic of Tibet (1864–77); Félix Biet (b. 21 Oct., 1838; d. 9 Sept., 1904), Bishop of Diana. The present vicar Apostolic is Pierre-Philippe Giraudeau (b. 17 March, 1850), since 1901, Bishop of Tiniade (12 Dec., 1897), with his residence at Ta-Tsien-lu. The mission includes (1910) 21 European priests, 2407 Catholics, and 600 catechumens. It has endured cruel persecutions during recent years. Among the missionaries of Tibet must be mentioned the well-known traveller and scholar, Auguste Desgodins (b. 1826), now living at Darjeeling, author of a large "Dictionnaire thibétain-latin-français", and of a Tibetan grammar, printed at Hong-Kong in 1899.

Huc, *Recollections of a journey through Tartary, Thibet, and China* (1844–6), tr. (New York, 1852); DESGODINS, *Le Thibet, d'après la correspondance des missionnaires* (Paris, 1885); KRICK, *Relation d'un voyage au Thibet en 1852* (Paris, 1854); *Narratives of the Missions of George Bogle to Thibet and of the journey of Thomas Manning to Lhasa*, ed. MARKHAM (London, 1877); BONIN, *Les derniers voyages dans le Tibet oriental* (Paris, 1899); HEDIN, *Central Asia and Tibet* (London, 1903); IDEM, *Trans-Himalaya: discoveries and adventures in Tibet* (New York, 1909); ROCKHILL, *The Land of the Lamas* (New York, 1891); IDEM, *The Dalai Lamas of Lhassa* (Leyden, 1910); BONVALOT, *De Paris au Tonkin à travers le Tibet inconnu* (Paris, 1892); CROSBY, *Tibet and Turkestan* (New York, 1903); BLACK, *The Trade and Resources of Tibet* (London, 1908); MACDONALD, *Through the Heart of Tibet* (London, 1910); WADDELL, *Lhasa and its Mysteries* (London, 1905); LANDON, *The Opening of Tibet* (New York, 1905); DEASY, *In Thibet and Chinese Turkestan* (London, 1901); YOUNGHUSBAND, *India and Tibet* (London, 1910).

HENRI CORDIER.

Tiburtius, Valerian, and Maximus, SAINTS. See CECILIA, SAINT.

Tiburtius and Susanna, SAINTS, Roman martyrs, feast 11 August. The story is related in the legend of St. Sebastian that Chromatius, prefect of Rome, condemned several Christians to death. The prefect, however, was converted by St. Tranquillinus and baptized by Polycarp. Tiburtius, the only son of Chromatius, was also baptized through the persuasion of St. Sebastian, who was his godfather in baptism. Tiburtius during the persecution of Diocletian lay hidden in his father's house. Accused by a traitor, he was brought before the prefect Fabianus and tried. He confessed his faith which he confirmed by a miracle, for protecting himself only by the sign of the cross he walked over red-hot coals barefoot without suffering any injury. But the miracle was ascribed to magic and Tiburtius was beheaded at the third mile-stone of the Via Lavicana. This was in the year 286. The spot of execution was called, "at the two laurel trees".

Saint Susanna, virgin and martyr, is said to have been the daughter of St. Gabinius. She was beheaded about the year 295, at the command of Diocletian, in her father's house. This house and the adjoining one belonging to her uncle, the prefect Caius, which were near the two laurel trees, were turned into a church, later the titular church of St. Susanna *ad duas domos* (cf. Kehr, "Italia pontificia", I, 61 sq.). The authenticity of the Acts of Sts. Sebastian and Susanna has been rightly questioned; however, the martyrdoms and the day of death (11 August) are established by the witness of the oldest Martyrologies and the earliest places of worship.

Acta SS., II Feb., 271–7; III April, 14–6; and II August, 613–32.

GABRIEL MEIER.

Ticelia, titular see, suffragan of Cyrene, in the Libya Pentapolis. Under this name it is not found in any "Notitia episcopatuum", nor in any geography sacred or profane. Nevertheless, at the Robber Synod of Ephesus (449), we find a Theodulus, Bishop of Ticelia in Libya (Mansi, "Conciliorum Collectio", VI, 610); the name of the city is much corrupted in the Greek text. It is doubtful if Ticelia is the correct name of this city or see. In a "Notitia episcopatuum", published by Gelzer (Byzantinische Zeitschrift, II, 26), we find the see of Sicelia, evidently the same as ours. Which is the correct name? At the Council of Ephesus (431), among the subscribers is Sosipater, Bishop of Septimiace, a city otherwise unknown, which seems likewise to have been situated in Libya (Mansi, op. cit., IV, 1128, 1221). Just now it is impossible to say if these various names relate to the same city, or what is the correct name of this diocese.

S. VAILHÉ.

Tichborne, NICHOLAS, VENERABLE, martyr, b. at Hartley Mauditt, Hampshire; suffered at Tyburn, London, 24 Aug., 1601. He was a recusant at large in 1592, but by 14 March, 1597, had been imprisoned. On that date he gave evidence against various members of his family. Before 3 Nov., 1598, he had obtained his liberty and had effected the release of his brother, Venerable Thomas Tichborne, a prisoner in the Gatehouse, Westminster, by assaulting his keeper. He is to be distinguished from the Nicholas Tichborne who died in Winchester Gaol in 1587.

With him suffered VENERABLE THOMAS HACKSHOT (b. at Mursley, Buckinghamshire), who was condemned on the same charge, viz. that of effecting the escape of the priest Thomas Tichborne. During his long imprisonment in the Gatehouse he was "afflicted with divers torments, which he endured with great courage and fortitude".

CHALLONER, *Missionary Priests*, I, no. 127; POLLEN, *English Martyrs 1584-1603* (London, privately printed for the Catholic Record Soc., 1908), 361, 395; *Historical MSS. Commission, Cecil MSS.*, IV (London, 1892), 270.

JOHN B. WAINEWRIGHT.

Tichborne, THOMAS, VENERABLE, b. at Hartley, Hampshire, 1567; martyred at Tyburn, London, 20 April, 1602. He was educated at Rheims (1584-87) and Rome, where he was ordained on Ascension Day, 17 May, 1592. Returning to England on 10 March, 1594, he laboured in his native county, where he escaped apprehension till the early part of 1597. He was sent a prisoner to the Gatehouse in London, but in the autumn of 1598 was helped to escape by his brother, Ven. Nicholas Tichborne, and Ven. Thomas Hackshot, who were both martyred shortly afterwards. Betrayed by Atkinson, an apostate priest, he was re-arrested and on 17 April, 1602, was brought to trial with Ven. Robert Watkinson (a young Yorkshire man who had been educated at Rome and ordained priest at Douai a month before) and Ven. James Duckett, a London bookseller. On 20 April he was executed with Ven. Robert Watkinson and Ven. Francis Page, S. J. The last named was a convert, of a Middlesex family though born in Antwerp. He had been ordained at Douai in 1600 and received into the Society of Jesus while a prisoner in Newgate. Ven. Thomas Tichborne was in the last stages of consumption when he was martyred.

CHALLONER, *Memoirs of Missionary Priests* (London, 1741-2); FOLEY, *Records Eng. Prov. S. J.*, I (London, 1877); POLLEN, *Acts of the English Martyrs* (London, 1901); IDEM, *Unpublished documents relating to the English Martyrs* in *Cath. Rec. Soc.*, V (London, 1908); DASENT, *Acts of the Privy Council, 1695-7* (London, 1902); *Douay Diaries*, 1st and 2nd (London, 1878), 3rd (London, 1911).

EDWIN BURTON.

Ticonius (also TYCONIUS, TYCHONIUS, etc.), an African Donatist writer of the fourth century who appears to have had some influence on St. Augustine. He defended a milder form of Donatism than Parmenianus. He admitted a church outside his own sect and rejected the re-baptism of Catholics. Parmenianus wrote a letter against him, quoted by St. Augustine (Contra ep. Parmeniani, I, i; P. L., XVIII, 33). Otherwise almost all we know of him is contained in Gennadius (De vir illustr., XVIII): "Tichonius an African was learned in theology, sufficiently instructed in history, not ignorant of secular knowledge. He wrote books, 'De bello intestino' and 'Expositiones diversarum causarum' [these are both Donatist apologies]: in which, to defend his side, he quotes ancient synods; from which he is seen to have been of the Donatist party. He composed eight [should be seven] rules for discovering the meaning of the Scriptures, which he arranged in one book. He also explained the whole Apocalypse of John, understanding all of it in a spiritual sense, nothing carnally. In this exposition he said that the body [of man] is the dwelling-place of an angel. He denied the idea of a kingdom of the righteous on earth lasting a thousand years after the resurrection. Nor did he admit two future resurrections of the dead in the flesh, one of the good and one of the bad, but only one of all, in which the misbegotten and deformed will rise too, so that no part of the human race ever animated by a soul shall perish. He showed the distinction of the resurrection really to be that we must believe that there is a revelation of the righteous now in this world, when those justified by faith rise by baptism from the death of sin to the reward of the eternal life, and the second [resurrection] to be the general one of all flesh. He flourished at the same time as Rufinus; in the reign of Theodosius and his son" (ed. Bernoulli, Freiburg and Leipzig, 1895, pp. 68–69). This gives us 379-423 as extreme dates. Ticonius's best known work is the "Seven rules of interpretation" (for the Bible). They are quoted and explained by St. Augustine in "De doctrina christiana" (III, 30-37; P. L., XXXIV, 81-90) and his authority gave them great importance for many centuries in the West. St. Bede too quotes them (Explanatio apocalypsis; P. L., XCIII, 130-132). Ticonius's "Commentary on the Apocalypse" (Bede, op. cit., 132-134) is now lost. It was extant in the library of St. Gallen in the ninth century (No. 242; cf. G. Becker, "Catalogi biblioth. antiqui.", Bonn, 1885, p. 48) and is used by Primasius of Hadrumetum (P. L., LXVIII, 793–936), Ambrose Autpert (Bibl. Max., XIII, 403–657), and others. The "Commentary" ascribed to St. Augustine (P. L., XXXV, 2415–52) is believed to be a modified version of Ticonius. St. Augustine reproaches Ticonius with an anticipation of Pelagian ideas (De doctr. Christ., III, 33).

BURKITT, *The Book of Rules of Ticonius* (Cambridge, 1894); *P. L.*, XVIII, 15–66; SCHANZ, *Gesch. der röm. Litt.*, IV (Munich, 1904), 350–53; HAUSLEITER, *Die Kommentare des Victorinus. Ticonius u. Hieronymus zur Apokalypse* in *Ztschr. für kirchl. Wissenschaft u. Leben* (1886), 239–57; HAHN, *Tyconius-Studien* (Leipzig, 1900); TILLEMONT, *Mémoires pour servir, etc.*, VI, 145–50; FESSLER-JUNGMANN, *Institutiones Patrologiæ*, II (Innsbruck, 1892), A, 355.

ADRIAN FORTESCUE.

Ticuna Indians, a tribe of Indians of some importance, constituting a distinct linguistic stock, inhabiting the river settlements or wandering in the forests along the north bank of the upper Amazon (Marañon or Solimoes), about the confluence of the Javari, ranging from about Loreto in Peru to below Tabatinga in Brazil. They number about 2500 souls, nearly equally divided between the two governments. About one-third are more or less Christianized, the others retaining their primitive wild habits. Physically they are one of the finest tribes of the upper Amazon. In character they are frank, honest, and of affectionate disposition. The wandering Ticuna, some of whom at times reside temporarily in the river villages, go naked except for the G-string and a collar of jaguar or monkey teeth, to which is added a painted robe on ceremonial occasions. They wear the hair cut across the forehead and hanging down full length behind. They wear armlets of bright-coloured feathers and paint and tattoo their faces in various patterns. They live by hunting and fishing, and the preparation and sale of the curari poison, here called from them the "Ticuna" poison, for use upon blow-gun arrows. In this manufacture they are recognized experts and hold the process a secret, although it is known that *Strychnos castelneana* and *Cocculus toxicofera* are among the ingredients. The poison is kept in cane tubes or clay pots of their making, and is the chief object of intertribal trade throughout the upper Amazon region. They also gather the forest products, as wax, rubber, gum, and sarsaparilla, for sale to the traders. They believe in a good spirit, Nanuola, and a dreaded evil spirit, Locasi. There is a sort of circumcision and baptismal ceremony in connexion with the naming of children. They are fond of elaborate masked dances. Girls on arriving at puberty are closely secluded for a long period, terminating with a general feast and drinking orgy, the liquor being the masato, or chicha, prepared from chewed and fermented corn or bananas. Wives are obtained by purchase. The dead are buried in great earthen jars, together with food and, in the case of a warrior, broken weapons, the ceremony concluding with a drinking feast.

A TICUNA INDIAN, CARRYING BLOWGUN
From a Narrative of the Explorations of Smyth and Lowe, published in 1836

Some effort at the conversion of the Ticuna was made by the Portuguese Carmelites from Brazil about the middle of the eighteenth century, but without result, owing to the Indian dread of the Portuguese slave-hunters. About 1760 the Jesuit Father Franciscus, of the neighbouring mission of San Ignacio among the Peva, friends and allies of the Ticuna, succeeded in gathering some of the latter into a new mission village which he called Nuestra Señora de Loreto (now Loreto, Peru), one of the "lower missions" of the Jesuit province of Mainas. At the time of the expulsion of the Jesuits in 1768 it was in charge of Father Segundo del Castillo and contained 700 souls, being one of the largest of the province. After the withdrawal of the Jesuits the missions were given over to the Franciscans, under whom the work was continued until interrupted by the long Revolutionary struggle beginning in 1810. Under the new republican government the missions were neglected and rapidly declined, but the Christian Ticuna are still served by resident priests at Loreto and Tabatinga, including the auxiliary villages. Marcoy gives a vocabulary of the language.

From the American officer, Lieut. Herndon, we have the following interesting account (condensed) of the Ticuna mission village of Caballococha near Loreto, as he found it in 1851: "The village is situated on the *caño* (river inlet), about a mile and a half from the entrance and at the same distance from the lake. It contains 275 inhabitants, mostly Ticunas Indians. These are darker than the generality of the Indians of the Marañon, though not so dark as the Marubos, and they are beardless, which frees them from the negro look that these last have. Their houses are generally plastered with mud inside, and are far neater looking and more comfortable than the other Indian residences that I have seen. This is however entirely owing to the activity and energy of the priest, Father Flores, who seems to have them in excellent order. They are now building a church for him, which will be the finest in the Montaña (forest region). The men are all decently clad in frocks and trousers; and the women, besides the usual roll of cotton cloth around the loins, wear a short tunic covering the breast. Father Flores keeps the Indians at work, sees that they keep themselves and houses clean, and the streets of the village in order, and I saw none of the abominable drinking and dancing with which the other Indians invariably wind up the Sunday." Through the kindness of Father Flores he was able to witness a heathen incantation over a sick man. On approaching the house they heard a number of persons singing inside, and, says Herndon, "I was almost enchanted myself. I never heard such tones, and think that even instrumental music could not be made to equal them. I have frequently been astonished at the power of the Indians to mock animals, but I had heard nothing like this before. The tones were so low, so faint, so guttural, and at the same time so sweet and clear, that I could scarcely believe they came from human throats, and they seemed fitting sounds in which to address spirits of another world." When they entered, the singers fled, and they found only two men sitting by a fire of blazing copal gum, filling an earthen pot with the juice of chewed tobacco, and plainly showing by their manner that the ceremony was not intended for strangers.

BRINTON, *American Race* (New York, 1891); CASTELNAU, *Expédition dans ...... l'Amérique du Sud* (6 vols., Paris, 1850–1); CHANTRE Y HERRERA, *Historia de las Misiones de la Compañía de Jesus en el Marañon Español* (written before 1801) (Madrid, 1901); HERNDON, *Exploration of the Valley of the Amazon* (Washington, 1854); MARCOY, *Voyage à travers l'Amérique du Sud* (2 vols., Paris, 1869); VON MARTIUS, *Ethnographie und Sprachenkunde Amerikas*, I (Leipzig, 1867); RAIMONDI, *El Perú*, II (Lima, 1876); IDEM, *Apuntes sobre la provincia litoral de Loreto* (Lima, 1862); MARKHAM, *Tribes in the Valley of the Amazon* in *Jour. Anthrop. Institute*, XXIV (London, 1895).

JAMES MOONEY.

Tieffentaller, JOSEPH, Jesuit missionary and noted geographer in Hindustan, b. at Bozen in the Tyrol, 27 August, 1710; d. at Lucknow, 5 July, 1785. He entered the Society of Jesus 9 October, 1729, and went in 1740 to the East Indian mission where he occupied various positions, chiefly in the empire of the Great Mogul. After the suppression of the Society he remained in India, and on his death was buried in the mission cemetery at Agra, where his tombstone still stands. He was a fine scholar with an unusual talent for languages; besides his native tongue he understood Latin, Italian, Spanish, French, Hindustani, Arabic, Persian, and Sanscrit. He was the first European who wrote an exact description of Hindustan. A brief list of his works is the best proof of his extraordinary power of work and his varied scholarship.

In geography, he wrote a "Descriptio Indiæ", that is a circumstantial description of the twenty-two provinces of India, of its cities, fortresses, and the most important smaller towns, together with an exact statement of geographical positions, calculated by means of a simple quadrant. The work also contains a large number of maps, plans, and sketches drawn by himself, and the list of geographical positions fills twenty-one quarto pages. He also prepared a large book of maps on the basin of the Ganges, entitled: "Cursus Gangæ fluvi Indiæ maximi, inde Priaga seu Elahbado Calcuttam usque ope acus magneticæ exploratus atque litteris mandatus a J. T. S. J." (1765).

The original map of the lower course of the river measures 15', that of the middle course, from Benares to Patna, measures 4' 3" square. In addition there is a map of similar dimensions of the Gagra, the whole accompanied by numerous notes, sketches of particular parts, and maps giving details—an "enormous labour", as Bernoulli calls it. He also wrote a work on the regions containing the sources of the chief rivers of India. In the field of religions he wrote on Brahminism a work directed against the errors of the Englishmen Z. Holwell and Alexander Dow. Others of his writings were on Indian idolatry, Indian asceticism, the religion of the Parsees, Mohammedanism, the relations of these religions to one another, etc. His writings in the department of the natural sciences are: astronomical observations on the sun-spots and the zodiacal light, studies on the astronomy, astrology, and cosmology of the Hindus, descriptions and observations of the flora and fauna of India. The department of history is represented by writings in Latin on the origin of the Hindus and of their religion, an account in German of the expeditions of Nadir Shah to India, the deeds of the Great Mogul Shah Alam in Persian, and in French the incursions of the Afghans and the conquest of Delhi, and the contemporary history of India for the years 1757–64. In linguistics he wrote a Sanscrit-Parsee lexicon, treatises in Latin on the language of the Parsees, on the proper pronunciation of Latin, etc.

Tieffentaller sent these works in manuscript partly to the Danish scholar Dr. Kratzenstein at Copenhagen, partly to the celebrated French Orientalist and geographer A. H. Anquetil-Duperron (1731–1805). The latter gave due credit to the value and importance of the works, especially those on geography, in his addresses before the French Academy of Sciences ("Journal des Scavans", Dec., 1776), and made the writings of Tieffentaller partly accessible to the learned world in his "Recherches hist. et géogr. sur l'Inde" (1786), and also in his "Carte générale du cours du Gange et du Gagra dressée par les cartes particulières du P. Tieffenthaller" (Paris, 1784). A part of the manuscripts at Copenhagen were obtained by the German scholar Johann Bernoulli of Berlin who used them in connexion with the "Recherches" of Anquetil for the great work "Des Pater Joseph Tieffenthalers d. Ges. Jesu und apost. Missionarius in Indien historisch-geographische Beschreibung von Hindustan . . ." (3 volumes, quarto, Berlin-Gotha, 1785–87). The greater part of the first two volumes is devoted to Tieffentaller's writings, his maps, and sketches. The French edition, entitled: "Description hist. et géogr. de l'Inde . . .", appeared at Berlin in three vols., 4to (1786–91). A large part of his manuscripts are probably still extant in Paris and Copenhagen.

HUONDER, *Deutsche Jesuitenmissionäre des 17. und 18. Jahrh.* (Freiburg, 1899), 179; NOTI, Jos. *Tieffentaller, S.J., A Forgotten Geographer of India* (Bombay, 1906); HOSTEN, *Jesuit Missionaries in Northern India* (Calcutta, 1907).

A. HUONDER.

Tiepolo, GIOVANNI BATTISTA (GIAMBATTISTA), b. in Venice in 1696; d. at Madrid, 27 March, 1770.

The son of a sea-captain and marine merchant, who left behind him a considerable fortune, Tiepolo married, in 1721, Cecilia, the sister of the painter Guardi, by whom he had nine children. His earliest master was Lazzerini, but his artistic career was derived from a careful study of the works of Titian, Piazzeta, Ricci, and especially Veronese. Up to 1750 he worked in Venice and various places in the north of Italy, painting some remarkable works at Milan, in Brescia, and in one or two villas near Venice. He then, accompanied by his son, travelled to Würzburg, where he resided for three years, executing some magnificent ceiling paintings in the palace of the archbishop. He was back again in Venice in 1753, full of commissions, elected President of the Academy of Padua, and holding high distinction in his native town. In 1761 he accepted the invitation of Charles III, King of Spain, to come to that country to decorate the royal palace of Madrid. Unfortunately, during his residence there he incurred the jealousy and the bitter opposition of Raphael Mengs. He is the last of the great Venetian painters; his works are magnificent in force, brilliance, and skill. As a draughtsman and colourist, few have approached him; as an etcher, he took a high position.

GIOVANNI DOMENICO, son and pupil of the elder Tiepolo, b. in Venice, 30 August, 1727; d. there, 3 March, 1804. He was his father's assistant but far inferior in every respect in draughtsmanship and colouring. His best work is the ceiling in the Palazzo Ducale at Genoa. In his latter years, having satisfactory means, he retired to a villa near Venice and lived in comfort. His marriage had taken place in 1776, and was a scene of great pomp and magnificence. His widow married again after his decease, and the male line of Tiepolo died out with him.

SACK, *Giambattista und Domenico Tiepolo* (Berlin, 1910); MOLMENTI, *G. B. Tiepolo* (Milan, 1909); LANZI, *Storia Pittorica della Italia* (Bassano, 1809); PITTONI, *Dei Pitoni Artisti Veneti* (Bergamo, 1905).

GEORGE CHARLES WILLIAMSON.

Tierney, MARK ALOYSIUS, b. at Brighton, Sept., 1795; d. at Arundel, 19 Feb., 1862. After his early schooling with the Franciscans at Baddesley Green, Warwickshire, he was educated at St. Edmund's College, Old Hall, which he entered in 1810 and where he was ordained priest, 19 Sept., 1818. He remained at the college as professor and procurator in 1818–19. He then served as assistant priest at Warwick Street, London, and afterwards at Lincoln's-Inn Fields till his ill-health necessitated his removal to the country mission of Slindon in Sussex. In 1824 he was appointed chaplain to the Duke of Norfolk at Arundel, where he spent the rest of his life, devoting himself to historical and antiquarian studies. His chief object was to bring out a new edition of Dodd's "Church History of England", which should incorporate all the documents collected by himself and Kirk. The first volume appeared in 1839, but on the publication of the fifth volume in 1843 the work was unfortunately discontinued, as the revival of the history of the seventeenth-century disputes between seculars and regulars

APOTHEOSIS OF ST. DOMINIC
Giambattista Tiepolo, Church of the Gesuati, Venice

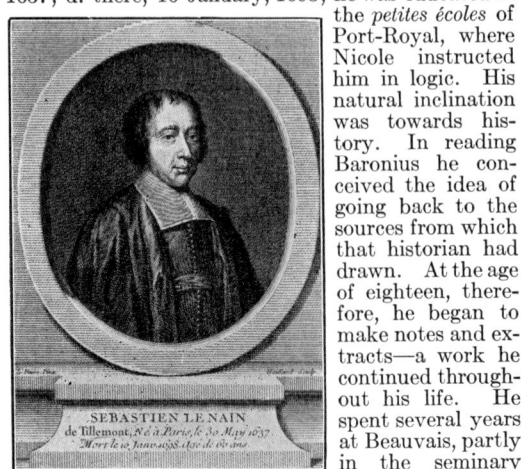

was thought inopportune and gave offence. Meanwhile his position as an antiquarian had received public recognition, for in 1833 he was elected a Fellow of the Society of Antiquaries and in 1841 a Fellow of the Royal Society. He also acted as secretary to the Sussex Archæological Society. After the restoration of the hierarchy he became the first canon penitentiary of the Diocese of Southwark, having long been a member of the old chapter. Shortly afterwards, his relations with Cardinal Wiseman, whose policy he disliked and mistrusted, became very strained. Arising out of Tierney's biographical sketch of Lingard, a controversy began between them on the well-known question whether Lingard had been created a cardinal *in petto*, by Leo XII, and Cardinal Wiseman addressed to his chapter a letter complaining of Tierney's criticism of his "Recollections of the last Four Popes". In answer to this Tierney wrote the "Reply to Cardinal Wiseman's Letter to his Chapter" (1858), which was not published. He also wrote "The History and Antiquities of the Castle of Arundel" (London, 1834) and several controversial pamphlets. For a time he acted as editor of the "Dublin Review", succeeding Quin the first editor.

Lower, *Worthies of Sussex* (Lewes, 1865), 341; B. Ward, *Hist. of St. Edmund's College* (London, 1893); Idem, *The Eve of Catholic Emancipation*, III (London, 1912), appendix; W. Ward, *Life of Cardinal Wiseman* (London, 1897); *Bibl. Dict. Eng. Cath.*, s. v.

Edwin Burton.

Tigris, Saint, Irish saint, sister of St. Patrick. Much obscurity attaches to her life, and she has been frequently confounded with St. Darerca, another of the five sisters, who are treated of at length by Colgan. St. Tigris was the mother of five sons, all of whom became bishops: Sts. Lomam of Trim; Munis of Forgney; Broccaid of Emlagh; Broccen of Breaghwy; and Mugenoc of All Duimi Gluin. Jocelyn credits the saint with seventeen sons and five daughters, but Tirechan and the "Tripartite Life" are preferable authorities. Her husband's name was Gollit. The time and place of her death are uncertain.

Stokes, *Tripartite Life of St. Patrick* (London, 1887); Healy, *Life and Writings of St. Patrick* (Dublin, 1905).

W. H. Grattan-Flood.

Tillemont, Louis-Sébastien Le Nain de, French historian and priest, b. at Paris, 30 November, 1637; d. there, 10 January, 1698; he was educated at the *petites écoles* of Port-Royal, where Nicole instructed him in logic. His natural inclination was towards history. In reading Baronius he conceived the idea of going back to the sources from which that historian had drawn. At the age of eighteen, therefore, he began to make notes and extracts—a work he continued throughout his life. He spent several years at Beauvais, partly in the seminary and partly with Canon Hermant, who was an authority on the early ages of Christianity. He received Holy orders somewhat late in life, becoming a subdeacon in 1672 and a priest four years later, when he was 39. At that time he resided in Port-Royal, but a little later, in 1679, when its community was dispersed, he withdrew to his small estate at Tillemont, between Montreuil and Vincennes, where he remained till his death twenty years later in 1698, devoting his time to exercises of piety and to historical work. He supplied several of his learned friends with much material for their writings. Thus he spent two years collecting notes on St. Louis for Lemaistre de Lacy, who did not live, however, to make use of them. They were published by the Société de l'histoire de France in 1847 (6 vols.). Tillemont wrote in addition: "Histoire des empereurs et autres princes qui ont régné pendant les six premiers siècles de l'Eglise" (6 volumes in 4°), and "Mémoires pour servir à l'histoire ecclésiastique des six premiers siècles" (16 volumes in 4°). Only the first four volumes of each of these works appeared in the lifetime of the author. Tillemont's style is dry, but he is an accurate and learned historian.

Tronchay, *La vie et l'esprit de M. Le Nain de Tillemont* (Nancy, 1706); Sainte-Beuve, *Port Royal*, IV.

Georges Bertrin.

Tilly, Johannes Tserclæs, Count of, b. at Brabant in 1559; d. at Ingolstadt in April, 1632. He was a member of a noble family of Brabant named Tserclæs. His mother was a devoted Catholic; his father took part at first in the revolt of the Netherlands against Spain, but by 1574 became a loyal adherent of Philip II. The son was educated by the Jesuits at Cologne. Like all the great men who fought for the Church and the empire during the era of the Reformation and the Counter-Reformation, Tilly has long been calumniated by Protestant and rationalist historians. In reality he was a man of genuine piety, remarkable self-control, moderation, and disinterestedness, a "monk in the garb of a general". He was honest, even to the enemy, a father to his soldiers, and humane to the common people, whom he protected as far as he could against acts of violence. As a general he was celebrated for his caution, his able grasp of situations, for the excellent preparatory training he gave his troops, and his never-failing readiness to meet the enemy and force him to give battle. He learned the art of war under the celebrated general, Alexander Farnese; at a later date Tilly surpassed his teacher. Up to 1594 he took part in the wars, some political and some religious, which laid waste the country from the mouth of the Rhine to the Seine: the War of Cologne, the revolt in the Netherlands, the War of the Holy League. In 1594 Henry IV would have been glad to have Tilly as one of his generals. During the years 1600–08, Tilly served Emperor Rudolph II and fought in Hungary against the Turks; in 1604 he rescued Gran; in 1605 he was commander-in-chief of the imperial forces; but the quarrels in the House of Austria and Rudolph's mental decay made success impossible. During the period 1610–30 Tilly commanded the army of Maximilian of Bavaria. Maximilian was a man very similar to Tilly; they seemed made to work together. Tilly was to command the army of the newly-founded League of the Catholic States of the empire.

During the era of peace up to 1620, Tilly created the Bavarian army, the flower of the army of the League, and the first standing army in the empire that was paid and fed, not by plundering and enforced contributions, but out of the regular revenues of the State. With these troops as his mainstay he took part in the prolonged war in Bohemia and the empire during the years 1620-30. In 1620 the force of his attack gained the victory at the battle of the White Mountain (8 November) over the Bohemians who had revolted against the emperor. For four years Tilly was engaged in a contest with Ernst of Mansfeld and his confederates. Ernst transferred the war from Bohemia to the lands of the empire, so that Tilly was often hampered by political considerations. In 1622 Tilly forced Mansfeld to give battle at Wiesloch, but the result was indecisive. He then destroyed the army of George Frederick of Baden at Wimpfen, and that of Christian of Halberstadt at Höchst, and took Heidelberg and Mannheim. After this Mansfeld's army dispersed and Tilly had now the strategic control of the whole of southern Germany. But in the next year, Mansfeld and Christian entered north-western Germany with fresh armies. As the estates of Hesse and some of those of Lower Saxony were still adherents of the imperial cause, Tilly was able to make an energetic advance against Mansfeld and to defeat him at Stadtlohn in 1623. Political considerations, however, prevented his pursuit of Mansfeld. The inhabitants of north-western Germany were roused to fanaticism against Tilly by the suggestion that he would force them to become Catholics. The districts on the middle course of the Weser which he garrisoned after his victory at Stadtlohn yielded so little that, in spite of all his efforts to feed his army by orderly methods, the soldiers suffered privations and took to plundering, which increased still more the animosity against them. The danger that the King of Denmark would take part in the war led Tilly in 1625 to beg the emperor to raise an army in the empire and to place it under Wallenstein's command. Wallenstein kept all the prosperous territories for himself and limited Tilly more than ever to the districts poor in revenue of south-western Germany. Tilly now found it increasingly difficult to maintain discipline because Wallenstein collected mercenary soldiers by the promise of rich booty, and raised these troops on a larger scale and more successfully than any previous commander on account of his imposing personality. Moreover, from 1627, and especially after the Edict of Restitution of 1629 Tilly was obliged to carry out numerous orders to restore to the Church lands which had been taken from it contrary to the religious peace; in this way he gained the reputation of being a bitter enemy of Protestantism. By force of character, however, he overcame all difficulties.

In 1626 Tilly prevented the union of the Danes with the Landgrave of Hesse who had revolted, and later, in August, destroyed the Danish army at Lutter on the Barenberg. In 1627 he drove the Danes over the Elbe, but on account of a wound, which prevented him from partaking in the war, Wallenstein gained the honours of the victory in the campaign in Holstein. When he had recovered Tilly took Stade at the mouth of the Elbe, and thus gained control over the whole of north-western Germany excepting Bremen. He was not able to advance against this latter city on account of the effects of Wallenstein's failures about the same time at Stralsund and Magdeburg. The great success he had later led him to hope for a time that peace could be restored in the empire, but in this he was disappointed. Once more for political reasons he could not gain permission to attack the Dutch, who exerted themselves to keep alive the disorders in the empire. On the other hand, the leaders of the League, owing to their hostility to Wallenstein, refused to give Tilly permission to go to Wallenstein's aid at Stralsund, and thus to bar Gustavus Adolphus from entering the empire. They also obliged Tilly and Wallenstein to dismiss a large part of their troops, a course that aroused a bitter and suspicious feeling in the experienced general and politician. Shortly after the arrival of Gustavus Adolphus, Wallenstein was dismissed and Tilly was entrusted by the emperor with the command of the imperial army in addition to his own. It was a difficult task to reorganize the imperial troops which were in process of being disbanded. The last period of Tilly's activities as a general began when he took command of the imperial army. As usual, he took the offensive as soon as he could and began operations near the Baltic coast. Gustavus Adolphus, however, avoided a battle and sought to tire Tilly out by marching about so as to wrest the initiative from him. Tilly put an end to this by marching against Magdeburg in March, 1630; this was the boldest stroke of his entire career as a commander. Gustavus seized the opportunity to advance up the Oder into the territories ruled by the emperor; probably, however, Tilly's bold measures forced Gustavus to follow him, in order to relieve Magdeburg.

When Tilly stormed Magdeburg on 20 May, its Swedish garrison laid the city in ashes, and it lost its strategic importance; he was, therefore, obliged to retreat towards Thuringia. Gustavus Adolphus now showed himself to be superior to Tilly in tactics at the battle of Breitenfeld on 17 September. Tilly followed the methods of Alexander Farnese, but these proved unsuccessful against Gustavus Adolphus's more modern generalship. Tilly's army was nearly destroyed, and he, now seventy-two years old, was for a short time crushed by the blow. However, in the same autumn he advanced from the Weser with new troops to prevent the Swedes from marching into the territories of the chiefs of the League in Franconia. But on account of the insufficient means at his disposal, the fear of the Swedes, and the timidity of the emperor and of the Catholic estates, his army disbanded on the way. Undismayed, Tilly began again on a smaller scale. In March, after carefully making his arrangements, he stormed Bamberg, which had fallen into the hands of the Swedes, and gained here the first victory over them. He now planned to advance towards Eger in order to join Wallenstein, who had again entered the imperial service, but the latter kept him waiting. In the meantime Gustavus Adolphus had advanced from the Main towards Tilly. Abandoning Donauwörth, Tilly took up a position at the Village of Rain on the Lech, being supported by Aldringen, the imperial quartermaster-general. The battle took place 15 April, and at its very beginning Tilly and Aldringen were severely wounded; this gave Gustavus Adolphus the victory. Before his death Tilly provided for the timely garrisoning of Ingolstadt and Ratisbon by the Bavarian troops, a measure which proved of importance for the subsequent course of the war. Tilly was always victorious in every campaign in which he had sufficient resources. He died when the campaign against Gustavus had hardly begun. It is, therefore, unjust to judge of his ability as a commander by his failure at the beginning of this campaign. He was inferior to no commander of his own time.

KLOPP, *Tilly im 30-jährigen Kriege* (Stuttgart, 1861); VILLERMONT, *Tilly ou la guerre de trente ans* (Tournay, 1860).

MARTIN SPAHN.

Timbrias, a titular see in Pisidia, suffragan of Antioch. It is called Thymbrium in the official lists of the Roman Curia, the name being more or less misspelled in documents, but the spelling here adopted is that found on coins where the inhabitants are called, in the genitive plural, τιμβριαδέων. At a late period we find the form *Timbriada*, neuter plural, or perhaps *Thymbriada*. The exact site of the city is unknown. It is mentioned by Strabo (XII, 7, 2); the coins, bearing the figure of the Eurymedon, would indicate a locality near the upper part of that river, the lower part belonging to Byzantine Pamphylia. It was probably situated somewhere in the plain called Yilandi Ovassi, in the vilayet of Koniah. In ecclesiastical writings it is mentioned as late as the thirteenth century. Le Quien (Oriens Christianus, I, 1059) names three of its bishops: Constantine, present at the Councils of Constantinople, 680 and 692; John, at the Council of Nicæa, 787; Theodosius, at the Photian Council of Constantinople (879).

RAMSAY, *Asia Minor*, 406.

S. PÉTRIDÈS.

Time.—The problem of time is one of the most difficult and most keenly debated in the field of natural philosophy. To arrive at a satisfactory orientation in regard to this discussion, it is important to distinguish two questions: (1) What are the notes, or elements, contained in our subjective representation of time? (2) To what external reality does this representation correspond?

(1) As to the first question, philosophers and scientists in general agree in this: that the notion, or concept, of time contains three distinct ideas fused into one indivisible whole. (a) First there is the idea of succession. Every mind distinguishes in time the past, the present, and the future, that is parts which essentially exclude simultaneity and can be realized only one after the other. (b) Again, time implies continuity. Speaking of events here below, in our own life, we cannot conceive the possibility of an interval of duration, however short, in which we should cease to grow older, or in which moment should cease to follow moment. The march of time knows neither pause nor interruption. (c) Lastly, a continuous succession cannot be a continuous succession of nothing. Therefore the concept of time represents to us a reality the parts of which succeed each other in a continuous manner. It matters little here whether this reality is purely ideal, or is realized outside of us, for we are dealing only with the concept of time. Such are the three essential elements of the subjective representation. From these considerations it appears that the question of time belongs to the domain of cosmology. By reason of its character as continuous, successive, divisible, and measurable, time belongs to the category of quantity, which is a general attribute of bodies, and cosmology has for its object the essence and general attributes of matter.

(2) The second question, relating to the objectivity of the concept of time, is one upon which philosophers, as well as scientists, are divided: no fewer than fifteen different opinions may be enumerated; these, however, may be grouped in three classes. One class embraces the subjectivist opinions, of which Kant is the chief representative; these regard time as completely a creation of the knowing subject. To Kant and his followers time is an a priori form, a natural disposition by virtue of which the inner sense clothes the acts of the external senses, and consequently the phenomena which these acts represent, with the distinctive characteristics of time. Through this form internal and external phenomena are apprehended by us as simultaneous or successive, anterior or posterior, to one another, and are submitted to necessary and universal time-judgments. To this class, also, belong a group of opinions which, without being so thoroughly subjective, attribute to time only a conceptual existence. To Leibniz and others time is "the order of successions", or a relation between things that follow one another; but if these things are real, the mind perceives them under the form of instants between which it establishes a relation that is purely mental. According to Balmes, time is a relation between being and non-being; subjective time is the perception of this relation; objective time is the relation itself in things. Though the two ideas of being and non-being are found in every succession, the relation between these two ideas cannot represent to us a real continuousness, and therefore it remains in the ideal order. Locke considers time as a part of infinite duration, expressed by periodic measures such as the revolution of the earth around the sun. According to Spencer, a particular time is the relation between two states in the series of states of consciousness. The abstract notion of a relation of aggregated positions between the states of consciousness constitutes the notion of time in general. To this relation Spencer attaches an essentially relative character, and attributes relative objectivity to psychological time alone. For Bergson homogeneous time is neither a property of things nor an essential condition of our cognitive faculty; it is an abstract schema of succession in general, a pure fiction, which nevertheless makes it possible for us to act upon matter. But besides this homogeneous time, Bergson recognizes a real duration, or, rather, a multiplicity of durations of unequal elasticities which belong to the acts of our consciousness as well as to external things. The systems of Descartes and of Baumann must also be classified as idealistic.

In opposition to this class of opinions which represent the existence of time as purely conceptual, a second class represent it as something which has complete reality outside of our minds. These opinions may fairly be described as ultra-realist. Certain philosophers, notably Gassendi and the ancient Greek Materialists, regard time as a being *sui generis*, independent of all created things and capable of surviving the destruction of them all. Infinite in its extension, it is the receptacle in which all the events of this world are enclosed. Always identical with itself, it permeates all things, regulating their course and preserving in the uninterrupted flow of its parts an absolutely regular mode of succession. Other philosophers, e. g. Clarke and Newton, identify time with the eternity of God or regard it as an immediate and necessary result of God's existence, so that, even were there no created beings, the continuation of the Divine existence would involve as its consequence, duration, or time. These ultra-realist philosophers substantialize time; others again make it a complete being, but of the accidental order. For de San time is an accident *sui generis*, distinct from all ordinary accidents; it is constituted as the local movement of parts which succeed each other in a continuous manner, but with perfect uniformity; by this accident, which is always inherent in substance, being and the accidents of being continue their existence enveloped in a succession which is everywhere and always uniform. Lastly, according to Dr. Hallez, the substantial existence of beings itself increases intrinsically without cessation, and this regular and continuous increase is by no means occasional or transitory, but always remains a veritable acquisition to the being which is its subject. Of this quantitative increment time is the representation. To sum up, all systems of this second class have as their distinctive characteristic the assertion of an external concrete reality—whether substantial or accidental—which adequately corresponds to the abstract concept of time, so that our representation of time is only a copy of that reality.

Between these two extreme classes of opinions is the system proposed by the majority of the Scholastics, ancient and modern. For them the concept of time is partly subjective, partly objective. It becomes concrete in continuous, notably in local, movement; but movement becomes time only with the intervention of our intelligence. Time is defined as the measure of movement according to an order of anteriority and posteriority (*numerus motus secundum prius et posterius*). Once local movement is divided into parts by thought, all the elements of the concept of time are found in it. Motion, being objectively distinct from rest, is something real; it is endowed with true continuity; nevertheless, in so far as it is divided by the intelligence, it contains successive parts actually distinct among themselves—some anterior, some posterior—between which we place a fleeting present. In the elaboration of the idea of time, therefore, movement furnishes the intelligence with a successive, continuous reality which is to be the real object of the concept, while the intelligence conceives it in that which it has in common with all movement—that is without its specific and individual notes—and makes it, formally, time, by dividing the continuity of the movement, making actual that distinction of parts which the movement possesses only potentially. In fact, say the Scholastics, we never perceive time apart from movement, and all our measures of temporal duration are borrowed from local movement, particularly the apparent movement of the heavens.

Whatever be its objectivity, time possesses three inalienable properties. First, it is irreversible; the linking of its parts, or the order of their succession, cannot be changed; past time does not come back. According to Kant, the reason of this property is found in the application to time of the principle of causality. As the parts of time, he says, are to each other in the relation of cause to effect, and as the cause is essentially antecedent to its effect, it is impossible to reverse this relation. According to the Scholastics, this immutability is based upon the very nature of concrete movement, of which one part is essentially anterior to another. Secondly, time is the measure of events in this world. This raises a knotty problem, which has so far not been theoretically solved. Time can be a permanent measure only if it is concretized in a uniform movement. Now, to know the uniformity of a movement, we must know not only the space traversed, but the velocity of the transit, that is the time. Here there is unquestionably a vicious circle. Lastly, for those who concretize time in movement, a much debated question is, whether time or movement can be infinite, that is without beginning. St. Thomas and some of the Scholastics see no absolute impossibility in this, but many modern thinkers take a different view.

St. Thomas, *Opusc. de tempore*; Balmes, tr. Brownson, *Fundamental Philosophy*, III (New York, 1864); Kant, *Kritik der reinen Vernunft*; Spencer, *Principles of Psychology*, II (London, 1881); Baumann, *Die Lehren von Raum, Zeit u. Mathematik*, II (Berlin, 1869); Bergson, *Matière et mémoire* (Paris, 1896); Idem, *Essai sur les données immédiates de la conscience* (Paris, 1895); de San, *Institutiones met. speciales. Cosmologia* (Louvain, 1881); von Olivier, *Was ist Raum, Zeit, Bewegung, Masse?* (2nd ed., Munich, 1902); Isenkrahe, *Der Begriff der Zeit*, in *Philos. Jahrbuch* (1902); Ratzel, *Raum u. Zeit* (Leipzig, 1907); McTaggart, *The Nonentity of Time* in *Mind* (Oct., 1908); Sellars, *Critical Realism and the Time Problem* in *Journ. Phil. Ps. and Sc. Methods* (24 Sept., 1908); Woodbridge, *The Problem of Time in Modern Philosophy*, ibid., VII (1910).

D. Nys.

Timotheus and Symphorian, Saints, martyrs whose feast is observed on 22 August. During the pontificate of Melchiades (311–13), St. Timotheus came from Antioch to Rome, where he preached for fifteen months and lived with Sylvester, who later became pope. The prefect of the city, Tarquinus Perpenna, threw him into prison, tortured, and finally beheaded him in 311. A Christian woman named Theon buried him in her garden. This is related in the legend of Sylvester. The name of Timotheus occurs in the earliest martyrologies.

According to a legend of the early fifth century, St. Symphorian of Autun was beheaded, while still a young man, during the reign of Marcus Aurelius. His mother, the Blessed Augusta (?), encouraged him on his way to execution, 22 August, 178. Bishop Euphronius (d. 490) built a handsome church over his grave, connected with a monastery, which belonged to the Congregation of Sainte-Geneviève from 1656 until its suppression in 1791. Abbot Germanus later became Bishop of Paris, where he dedicated a chapel to the saint. St. Symphorian is the patron saint of Autun. His veneration spread at an early date through the empire of the Franks. His cult was especially popular at Tours; St. Gregory relates a miracle wrought by the saint.

Acta SS., August, IV, 530–35, 491; Ruinart, *Acta Martyrum*; Dinet, *Saint Symphorien et son culte* (2 vols., Autun, 1861); Duchesne, *Fastes épiscopaux*, I, 52.

Gabriel Meier.

Timothy Ælurus. See Eutychianism; Monophysites.

Timothy and Titus, Epistles to (The Pastorals).—Timothy and Titus.—Saints Timothy and Titus were two of the most beloved and trusted disciples of St. Paul, whom they accompanied in many of his journeys. Timothy is mentioned in Acts, xvi, 1; xvii, 14, 15, 1; xviii, 5; xix, 22; xx, 4; Rom., xvi, 21; I Cor., iv, 17; II Cor., i, 1, 19; Phil., i, 1; ii, 19; Col., i, 1; I Thess., i, 1; iii, 2, 6; II Thess., i, 1; I Tim., i, 2, 18; vi, 20; II Tim., i, 2; Philem., i, 1; Heb., xiii, 23; and Titus in II Cor., ii, 13; vii, 6, 13, 14; viii, 6, 16, 23; xii, 18; Gal., ii, 1, 3; II Tim., iv, 10; Tit., i, 4. St. Timothy has been regarded by some as the "angel of the church of Ephesus", Apoc., ii, 1–17. According to the ancient Roman martyrology he died Bishop of Ephesus. The Bollandists (24 Jan.) give two lives of St. Timothy, one ascribed to Polycrates (an early Bishop of Ephesus, and a contemporary of St. Irenæus) and the other by Metaphrastes, which is merely an expansion of the former. The first states that during the Neronian persecution St. John arrived at Ephesus, where he lived with St. Timothy until he was exiled to Patmos under Domitian. Timothy, who was unmarried, continued Bishop of Ephesus until, when he was over eighty years of age, he was mortally beaten by the pagans. According to early tradition Titus continued after St. Paul's death as Archbishop of Crete, and died there when he was over ninety.

Epistles to Timothy and Titus.—Authenticity.—I. *Internal Evidence*.—The remainder of this article will be devoted to the important question of authenticity, which would really require a volume for discussion. Catholics know from the universal tradition and infallible teaching of the Church that these Epistles are inspired, and from this follows their Pauline authorship as they all claim to have been written by the Apostle. There was no real doubt on this question until the beginning of the nineteenth century; but since that time they have been most bitterly attacked by German and other writers. Their objections are principally based on internal evidence and the alleged difficulty of finding a place for them in the lifetime of St. Paul.

A. Objection from the absence of Pauline vocabulary.—Moffatt, a representative writer of this school, writes (Ency. Bib., IV): "Favourite Pauline phrases and words are totally wanting. . . . The extent and significance of this change in vocabulary cannot adequately be explained even when one assigns the fullest possible weight to such factors as change of amanuensis, situation or topic, lapse of time, literary fertility, or senile weakness." Let us examine this writer's list of favourite Pauline words of the absence of which so very much is made:

Ἄδικος (unjust).—This is found in Rom., iii, 5; I Cor., vi, 1, 9, but not in any of the other Pauline epistles, admitted to be genuine by this writer. If its absence be fatal to the Pastorals, why not also to I and II Thess., II Cor., Gal., Philip., Col., and

Philem.? Moreover, the noun ἀδικία is found in the Pastorals, II Tim., ii, 19.

Ἀκαθαρσία (uncleanness) does not occur in I Cor., Phil., II Thess., and Philem. If that does not tell against these Epistles why is it quoted against the Pastorals?

Υἱοθεσία (adoption).—This word is three times in Rom., once in Gal., but it does not occur at all in I and II Cor., I and II Thess., Phil., Col., and Philem. Why its omission should be used against the Pastorals is not easy to understand.

Πατὴρ ἡμῶν (Our Father).—Two expressions, God "our Father" and God "the Father" are found in St. Paul's Epistles. The former is frequent in his earlier Epistles, viz., seven times in Thess., while the latter expression is not used. But in Romans "God our Father" appears but once, and "the Father" once. In I Cor. we read God "our Father" once, and "the Father" twice; and the same has to be said of II Cor. In Gal. we have "our Father" once and "the Father" three times. In Phil. the former occurs twice and the latter once; in Col. the former only once, and the latter three times. "The Father" occurs once in each of the Pastoral Epistles, and from the above it is evident that it is just as characteristic of St. Paul as "our Father", which is found but once in each of the Epistles to the Romans, I and II Cor., Gal., and Col., and it would be absurd to conclude from this that all the remaining chapters were spurious.

Διαθήκη (covenant) occurs twice in Rom., once in I Cor., twice in II Cor., thrice in Gal., and not at all in I and II Thess., Phil., Col., and Philem., admitted to be genuine by Moffatt.

Ἀποκαλύπτειν (reveal), a word not found in II Cor., I Thess., Col., and Philem., and only once in Phil.

Ἐλεύθερος (free), is not in I and II Thess., II Cor., Phil., and Philem., so it is no test of Pauline authorship. Its compounds are not met in I and II Thess., Phil., Col., or Philem., and, with the exception of Gal., in the others sparingly.

Ἐνεργεῖν (to be operative) is seen but once in each of Rom., Phil., Col., I and II Thess.; and no one would conclude from its absence from the remaining portions of these Epistles, which are longer than the Pastorals, that they were not written by St. Paul.

Κατεργάζεσθαι (perform), though several times in Rom. and II Cor., and once in I Cor. and in Phil., is wanting in I and II Thess., Gal., Col., and Philem., which are genuine without it.

Καυχᾶσθαι (boast), only once in Phil., and in II Thess., and not at all in I Thess., Coloss., and Philem.

Μωρία (folly) is five times in I Cor., and nowhere else in St. Paul's Epistles.

But we need not weary the reader by going through the entire list. We have carefully examined every word with the like results. With perhaps a single exception, every word is absent from several of St. Paul's genuine Epistles, and the exceptional word occurs but once in some of them. The examination shows that this list does not afford the slightest argument against the Pastorals, and that St. Paul wrote a great deal without using such words. The compilation of such lists is likely to leave an erroneous impression on the mind of the unguarded reader. By a similar process, with the aid of a concordance, it could be proved that every Epistle of St. Paul has an appearance of spuriousness. It could be shown that Galatians, for instance, does not contain many words that are found in some of the other Epistles. A method of reasoning which leads to such erroneous conclusions should be discredited; and when writers make very positive statements on the strength of such misleading lists in order to get rid of whole books of Scripture, their other assertions should not be readily taken for granted.

B. Objection from the use of particles.—Certain particles and prepositions are wanting. Jülicher in his "Introd. to the New Test.", p. 181, writes: "The fact that brings conviction [against the Pastorals] is that many words which were indispensable to Paul are absent from the Pastoral Epistles, e.g. ἄρα, διό, διότι." But, as Jacquier points out, nothing can be concluded from the absence of particles, because St. Paul's employment of them is not uniform, and several of them are not found in his unquestioned Epistles. Dr. Headlam, an Anglican writer, pointed out in a paper read at the Church Congress, in 1904, that ἄρα occurs twenty-six times in the four Epistles of the second group, only three times in all the others, but not at all in Col., Phil., or Philem. Διό occurs eighteen times in Rom., Gal. and Cor., but not at all in Col. or II Thess. The word διότι does not occur in II Thess., II Cor., Eph., Col., or Philem. We find that ἔπειτα does not appear at all in Rom., II Cor., Phil., Col., II Thess., and Philem., nor ἔτι in I Thess., Col., and Philem. It is unnecessary to go through the entire catalogue usually given by opponents, for the same phenomenon is discovered throughout. Particles were required in the argumentative portions of St. Paul's Epistles, but they are used very sparingly in the practical parts, which resemble the Pastorals. Their employment, too, depended greatly on the character of the amanuensis.

C. Objection from *Hapax Legomena*.—The great objection to the Pastorals is the admittedly large number of *hapax legomena* found in them. Workman (Expository Times, VII, 418) taking the term "hapax legomenon" to mean any word used in a particular Epistle and not again occurring in the New Testament, found from Grimm-Thayer's "Lexicon" the following numbers of *hapax legomena*: Rom. 113, I Cor. 110, II Cor. 99, Gal. 34, Eph. 43, Phil. 41, Col. 38, I Thess. 23, II Thess. 11, Philem. 5, I Tim. 82, II Tim. 53, Titus 33. The numbers have to be somewhat reduced as they contain words from variant readings. These figures would suggest to most people, as they did to Dean Farrar, that the number of peculiar words in the Pastorals does not call for any special explanation. Mr. Workman, however, thinks that for scientific purposes the proportionate length of the Epistles should be taken into account. He calculated the average number of *hapax legomena* occurring on a page of Westcott and Hort's text with the following results: II Thessalonians 3·6, Philemon 4, Galatians 4·1, I Thessalonians 4·2, Romans 4·3, I Corinthians 4·6, Ephesians 4·9, II Corinthians 6·10, Colossians 6·3, Philippians 6·8, II Timothy 11, Titus and I Timothy 13. The proportion of *hapax legomena* in the Pastorals is large, but when compared with Phil., it is not larger than that between II Cor. and II Thess. It has to be noted that these increase in the order of time.

Workman gives a two-fold explanation. First, a writer as he advances in life uses more strange words and involved constructions, as is seen on comparing Carlyle's "Latter-Day Pamphlets" and his "Heroes and Hero-Worship". Secondly, the number of unusual words in any author is a variable quantity. He has found the average number of *hapax legomena* per page of Irving's one-volume edition of Shakespeare's plays to be as follows: "Love's Labour Lost" 7·6, "Comedy of Errors" 4·5, "Two Gentlemen of Verona" 3·4, "Romeo and Juliet" 5·7, "Henry VI, pt. 3" 3·5, "Taming of the Shrew" 5·1, "Midsummer Night's Dream" 6·8, "Richard II" 4·6, "Richard III" 4·4, "King John" 5·4, "Merchant of Venice" 5·6, "Henry IV, pt. I" 9·3, "pt. II" 8, "Henry V" 8·3, "Merry Wives of Windsor" 6·9, "Much Ado About Nothing" 4·7, "As You Like It" 6·4, "Twelfth Night" 7·5, "All's Well" 6·9, "Julius Cæsar" 3·4, "Measure for Measure" 7, "Troilus and Cressida" 10·1, "Macbeth" 9·7, "Othello" 7·3, "Anthony and Cleopatra" 7·4, "Coriolanus" 6·8, "King Lear" 9·7, "Timon" 6·2, "Cymbeline" 6·7, "The Tempest" 9·3, "Titus Andronicus" 4·9, "Winter's Tale" 8,

"Hamlet" 10·4, "Henry VIII" 4·3, "Pericles" 5·2. For a similar argument on Dante see Butler's "Paradise", XI. The totals of *hapax legomena* for some of the plays are: "Julius Cæsar" 93, "Comedy of Errors" 88, "Macbeth" 245, "Othello" 264, "King Lear" 358, "Cymbeline" 252, "Hamlet" 426, "The Merchant of Venice" 148. This scrutiny of the words peculiar to each play throws light on another difficulty in the Pastorals, viz. the recurrence of such expressions as "a faithful saying", "sound words", etc. "Moon-calf" occurs five times in "The Tempest", and nowhere else; "pulpit" six times in one scene of "Julius Cæsar" and never elsewhere; "hovel" five times in "King Lear"; "mountaineer" four times in "Cymbeline", etc. Compare, "God forbid", μὴ γένοιτο of Gal., Rom., once in I Cor.—not in the other Epistles of St. Paul. "Sound words" was used by Philo before St. Paul, in whom it may be due to intercourse with St. Luke. (See Plumptre's list of words common to St. Luke and St. Paul, quoted in Farrar's "St. Paul", I, 481.)

Mr. Workman has overlooked one point in his very useful article. The *hapax legomena* are not evenly distributed over the Epistles; they occur in groups. Thus, more than half of those in Col. are found in the second chapter, where a new subject is dealt with (see Abbott, "Crit. . . . Comment. on Ep. to the Ephes. and to the Coloss." in "Internat. Crit. Comment."). This is as high a proportion as in any chapter of the Pastorals. Something similar is observable in II Cor., Thess., etc. Over sixty out of the seventy-five *hapax legomena* in I Tim. occur in forty-four verses, where the words, for the most part, naturally arise out of the new subjects treated of. The remaining two-thirds of the Epistle have as few *hapax legomena* as any other portion of St. Paul's writings. Compounds of φιλ-, οἰκο-, διδασκ-, often objected to, are also found in his other Epistles.

The "Authorship of the Pastoral Epistles" was discussed in "The Church Quarterly" in October, 1906, and January, 1907. In the first the writer pointed out that the anti-Pauline hypothesis presented more difficulties than the Pauline; and in the second he made a detailed examination of the *hapax legomena*. Seventy-three of these are found in the Septuagint, of which St. Paul was a diligent student, and any of them might just as well have been used by him as by an imitator. Ten of the remainder are suggested by Septuagint words, e. g. ἀνεξίκακος II Tim., ii, 24, ἀνεξικακία Wisd., xii, 20, ἀντίθεσις I Tim., vi, 20, ἀντίθετος Job, xxxii, 3; αὐθεντεῖν I Tim., ii, 12, αὐθέντης Wisd., xii, 6; γενεαλογία I Tim., i, 4, Tit., iii, 9; γενεαλογεῖν I Par., v, 1; πάροινος I Tim., iii, 3, Tit., i, 7, παροινεῖν Is., xli, 12, etc. Twenty-eight of the words now left are found in the classics, and thirteen more in Aristotle and Polybius. Strabo, born in 66 B. C., enables us to eliminate γραώδης. All these words formed part of the Greek language current up to St. Paul's time and as well known to him as to anybody at the end of the first century. Any word used by an author contemporary with St. Paul may reasonably be supposed to have been as well known to himself as to a subsequent imitator. In this way we may deduct eight of the remaining words, which are common to the Pastorals and Philo, an elder contemporary of St. Paul. In dealing with the fifty remaining words we must recall the obvious fact that a new subject requires a new vocabulary. If this be neglected, it would be easy to prove that Plato did not write the Timæus. Organization and the conduct of practical life, etc., cannot be dealt with in the same words in which points of doctrine are discussed. This fairly accounts for eight words, such as ξενοδοχεῖν, οἰκοδεσποτεῖν, τεκνογονεῖν, φίλανδρος, ἑτεροδιδασκαλεῖν, etc., used by the author. His detestation of the errorists doubtless called forth κενοφωνία, λογομαχεῖν, λογομαχία, ματαιολογία, ματαιολόγος, several of which were probably coined for the occasion. The element of pure chance in language accounts for "parchments", "cloak", and "stomach": he had no occasion to speak about such things previously, nor of a pagan "prophet". Seven of the remaining words are dealt with on the modest principle that words formed from composition or derivation from admittedly Pauline words may more reasonably be supposed to come from St. Paul himself than from a purely hypothetical imitator, e. g. αἱρετικός, adj., Tit., iii, 10; αἵρεσις, I Cor., xi, 19; Gal., v, 20; διώκτης, I Tim., i, 13; διώκειν, Rom., xii, 14, etc.; ἐπισωρεύειν, II Tim., iv, 3; σωρεύειν ἐπὶ Rom., xii, 20; LXX, etc. Five other words are derived from Biblical words and would as easily have occurred to St. Paul as to a later writer. The remaining words, about twenty, are disposed of separately.

Ἐπιφάνεια instead of παρουσία, for the second coming of Christ, is not against the Pastorals, because St. Paul's usage in this matter is not uniform. We have ἡ ἡμέρα κυρίου in I Thess., v, 2, I Cor., i, 8, v, 5; ἡ ἀποκάλυψις in II Thess., i, 17; and ἡ ἐπιφάνεια τῆς παρουσίας αὐτοῦ in II Thess., ii, 8. Lilley ("Pastoral Epistles", Edinburgh, 1901, p. 48) states that out of the 897 words contained in the Pastorals 726 are common to them and the other books of the New Testament, and two-thirds of the entire vocabulary are found in the other Epistles of St. Paul; and this is the proportion of common words found in Galatians and Romans. The same writer, in his complete list of 171 *hapax legomena* in the Pastorals, points out that 113 of these are classical words, that is, belonging to the vocabulary of one well acquainted with Greek; and it is not surprising that so many are found in these Epistles which were addressed to two disciples well educated in the Greek language. Another point much insisted upon by objectors is a certain limited literary or verbal affinity connecting the Pastorals with Luke and Acts and therefore, it is asserted, pointing to a late date. But in reality this connexion is in their favour, as there is a strong tendency of modern criticism to acknowledge the Lucan authorship of these two books, and Harnack has written two volumes to prove it (see LUKE, GOSPEL OF SAINT). He has now added a third to show that they were written by St. Luke before A. D. 64. When the Pastorals were written, St. Luke was the constant companion of St. Paul, and may have acted as his amanuensis. This intercourse would doubtless have influenced St. Paul's vocabulary, and would account for such expressions as ἀγαθοεργεῖν of I Tim., vi, 18, ἀγαθοποεῖν of Luke, vi, 9, ἀγαθουργεῖν, contracted from ἀγαθοεργεῖν, Acts, xiv, 17. St. Paul has ἐργαζομένῳ τὸ ἀγαθόν Rom., ii, 10.—From all that has been said, it is not surprising that Thayer, in his translation of Grimm's "Lexicon", wrote: "The monumental misjudgments committed by some who have made questions of authorship turn on vocabulary alone, will deter students, it is to be hoped, from misusing the lists exhibiting the peculiarities of the several books."

D. Objection from style.—"The comparative absence of rugged fervour, the smoother flow, the heaping up of words, all point to another sign-manual than that of Paul" (Ency. Bib.).—Precisely the same thing could be urged against some of St. Paul's other Epistles, and against large sections of the remainder. All critics admit that large portions of the Pastorals are so much like St. Paul's writings that they actually maintain that they are taken from fragments of genuine letters of the Apostle (now lost). Various discordant attempts have been made to separate these portions from the rest, but with so little success that Jülicher confesses that the thing is impossible. On the other hand, it is the general opinion of the best scholars that all three Epistles are from the pen of one and the same writer. That being the case, and it being impossible to deny that portions indistinguishable from the rest are by St. Paul, it follows that the early and universal tradition ascribing the whole of them to the Apostle is correct.

As we pass from one to another of the four groups of St. Paul's Epistles—(1) Thessalonians; (2) Galatians, Corinthians, Romans; (3) Captivity Epistles; (4) Pastorals—we observe considerable differences of style side by side with very marked and characteristic resemblances, and that is precisely what we find in the case of the Pastorals. There are some striking points of connexion between them and Phil., the Epistle probably nearest to them in date; but there are many resemblances in vocabulary, style, and ideas connecting them with portions of all the other Epistles, especially with the practical parts. There are, for instance, forty-two passages connecting I Tim. with the earlier Epistles. The terms are nearly identical, but display an amount of liberty denoting the working of the same independent mind, not a conscious imitation. The Pastorals show throughout the same marks of originality as are found in all the writings of the Apostle. There are similar anacolutha, incomplete sentences, play on words, long drawn periods, like comparisons, etc. The Pastorals are altogether practical, and therefore do not show the rugged fervour of style confined, for the most part, to the controversial and argumentative portions of his large epistles. (See the very valuable book by James, "Genuineness and Authorship of the Pastoral Epistles", London, 1906; also Jacquier, and Lilley.) It may be well to note, in this connexion, that Van Steenkiste, professor at the Catholic Seminary of Bruges, asserted, as long ago as 1876, that the inspiration of the Pastorals and their Pauline authorship would be sufficiently safeguarded if we accepted the view that they were written in the name and with the authority of the Apostle by one of his companions, say St. Luke, to whom he distinctly explained what had to be written, or to whom he gave a written summary of the points to be developed, and that when the letters were finished, St. Paul read them through, approved them, and signed them. This, he thinks, was the way in which "Hebrews", also, was written (S. Pauli Epistolæ, II, 283).

E. Objection from the advanced state of church organization.—This objection is adequately answered in the articles HIERARCHY OF THE EARLY CHURCH, BISHOP, etc. See also "The Establishment of the Episcopate" in Bishop Gore's "Orders and Unity" (London, 1909), 115. The seven, St. Stephen, Philip, etc., were set aside for their ministry by the Apostles by prayer and the laying on of hands. Immediately after this we read that they were filled with the Holy Ghost, and preached with great success (Acts, vi, vii). From St. Luke's usual method we may conclude that a similar ceremony was employed by the Apostles on other occasions when men were set aside to be deacons, presbyters, or bishops. We read of presbyters with the Apostles at an early date in Jerusalem (Acts, xv, 2) and according to the earliest tradition, St. James the Less was appointed bishop there on the dispersion of the Apostles, and succeeded by his cousin Simeon in A. D. 62. Sts. Paul and Barnabas ordained priests in every church at Derbe, Lystra, Antioch of Pisidia, etc. (Acts, xiv, 22). Bishops and priests, or presbyters, are mentioned in St. Paul's speech at Miletus (Acts, xx, 28). In his first Epistle (I Thess., v, 12) St. Paul speaks of rulers who were over them in the Lord,—see also Rom., xii, 8; "governments" are referred to in I Cor., xii, 28, and "Pastors" in Eph., iv, 11. St. Paul wrote "to all the saints in Christ Jesus, who are at Philippi, with the bishops and deacons" (Phil., i, 1).

In Rom., xii, 6–8, 1 Cor., xii, 28, Eph., iv, 11, St. Paul is not giving a list of offices in the Church, but of charismatic gifts (for the meaning of which see HIERARCHY OF THE EARLY CHURCH). Those who were endowed with supernatural and transitory charismata were subject to the Apostles and presumably to their delegates. Side by side with the possessors of such gifts we read of "rulers", "governors", "pastors", and in other places of "bishops", "priests", and "deacons". These, we may lawfully assume, were appointed under the inspiration of the Holy Ghost by the Apostles, by prayer and laying on of hands. Amongst these so appointed before A. D. 64 there were certainly ordained deacons, priests, and possibly bishops also. If so they had bishop's orders, but the limits of their jurisdiction were not as yet, perhaps, very clearly defined, and depended altogether on the will of the Apostles. It is assuredly in the highest degree likely that the Apostles, towards the end of their lives and as the Church extended more and more, ordained and delegated others to appoint such priests and deacons as they had been in the habit of appointing themselves. The earliest tradition shows that such a thing took place in Rome by A. D. 67; and there is nothing more advanced than this in the Pastorals. Timothy and Titus were consecrated delegates to rule with Apostolic authority and appoint deacons, priests, and bishops (probably synonymous in these Epistles).

But a further objection is raised as follows: "The distinctive element, however, i. e. the prominence assigned to Timothy and Titus is intelligible only on the supposition that the author had specially in view the ulterior end of vindicating the evangelic succession of contemporary episcopi and other office bearers where this was liable for various reasons to be challenged. . . . The craving (visible in Clem. Rom.) for continuity of succession as a guarantee of authority in doctrine (and therefore in discipline) underlies the efforts of this Paulinist to show that Timothy and Titus were genuine heirs of Paul" (Ency. Bib., IV).—If this craving is visible in St. Clement of Rome, who was a disciple of the Apostles there and wrote less than thirty years after their death, it is surely more likely that he was maintaining an organization established by them than that he was defending one of which they were ignorant. If these Epistles were written against people who challenged the authority of bishops and priests about A. D. 100, why is it that these opponents did not cry out against forgeries written to confute themselves? But of all this there is not the slightest shred of evidence.

F. Objection. No room for them in the life-time of St. Paul.—The writer in the "Ency. Bib." is never tired of accusing the defenders of the Epistles of making gratuitous assumptions, though he allows himself considerable liberty in that respect throughout his article. It is a gratuitous assertion, for example, to state that St. Paul was put to death at the end of the first Roman captivity, A. D. 63 or 64. Christianity was not yet declared a *religio illicita*, and according to Roman law there was nothing deserving of death against him. He was arrested to save him from the Jewish mob in Jerusalem. The Jews did not appear against him during the two years he was kept in prison. Agrippa said he could have been delivered had he not appealed to Cæsar, so there was no real charge against him when he was brought before the emperor's or his representative's tribunal. The Epistles written during this Roman captivity show that he expected to be soon released (Philem., 22; Phil., ii, 24). Lightfoot, Harnack, and others, from the words of Clem. Rom. and the Muratorian Fragment, think that he was not only released, but that he actually carried out his design of visiting Spain. During the years from 63–67 there was ample time to visit Crete and other places and write I Tim. and Titus. II Tim. was written from his second Roman prison soon before his death.

G. Objection from the errors condemned.—It is said that the errors referred to in the Pastorals did not exist in St. Paul's time, though the most advanced critics (Ency. Bib.) have now abandoned the theory (maintained with great confidence in the nineteenth century) that the Epistles were written against Marcion and other Gnostics about the middle of the second century. It is now conceded that they were known to Sts. Ignatius and Polycarp, and therefore written not later than the end of the first century or early part of the second. It requires a keen critical sense to detect at that time the existence of errors at the time of Ignatius, the seeds of which did not exist thirty or forty years earlier, or of which St. Paul could not have foreseen the development. "The environment is marked by incipient phases of what afterwards blossomed out into the Gnosticism of the second century" (Ency. Bib.):—but the incipient phases of Gnosticism are now placed by competent scholars at a much earlier date than that indicated by this writer. No known system of Gnosticism corresponds with the errors mentioned in the Pastorals; in reply to this, however, it is said that the "errors are not given in detail to avoid undue anachronisms" (ibid.). Sometimes opponents of the authenticity unfairly attack the actual contents, but here the Epistles are condemned for "contents" which they do not contain. An amusing instance of the precariousness of the subjective method is seen in this same article (Ency. Bib.). The writer arguing against the Epistles on the subject of greetings says that "Philemon is the one private note of Paul extant". We are suddenly brought up, however, by a note (editorial?) within square brackets: "compare, however, Philemon." On turning to Philemon we find van Manen asserting, with equal confidence, that the Apostle had nothing whatsoever to do with that Epistle, and he supports his statement by the same kind of subjective arguments and assertions that we find running through the article on Timothy and Titus. He even throws out the absurd suggestion that Philemon was based on the letter of Pliny, which is given in full by Lightfoot in his edition of Philemon.

Hort in his "Judaistic Christianity" (London, 1898), 130-48, does not believe that the errors of the Pastorals had any connexion with Gnosticism, and he gives a very full reply to the objection with which we are dealing. With Weiss he clears the ground by making some important distinctions: (1) We must distinguish prophecies about future false teachers, which imply that germs, to say the least, of the future evils are already perceptible (I Tim., iv, 1-3; II Tim., iii, 1-5, iv, 3) from warnings about the present; (2) The perversities of individuals like Alexander, Hymenæus, and Philetus must not be taken as direct evidence of a general stream of false teaching; (3) Non-Christian teachers, the corrupters of Christian belief, must not be confounded with misguided Christians. The errors which St. Paul easily foresaw would arise amongst false Christians and pagans cannot be urged against the Epistles as if they had already arisen. Hort makes out a good case that there is not the smallest trace of Gnosticism in the existing errors amongst the Ephesian and Cretan Christians, which are treated more as trivialities than serious errors. "The duty laid on Timothy and Titus is not that of refuting deadly errors, but of keeping themselves clear, and warning others to keep clear of mischievous trivialities usurping the office of religion." He shows that all these errors have evident marks of Judaistic origin. The fact that St. Irenæus, Hegesippus, and others used the words of the Pastorals against the Gnostics of the second century is no proof that Gnosticism was in the mind of their author. Words of Scripture have been employed to confute heretics in every age. This, he says, is true of the expressions ψευδώνυμος γνῶσις, ἄφθαρτος, αἰών, ἐπιφάνεια, which have to be taken in their ordinary sense. "There is not the faintest sign that such words have any reference to what we call Gnostic terms."

Hort takes γενεαλογίαι in much the same sense in which it was employed by Polybius, IX, ii, 1, and Diodorus Siculus, IV, i, to mean stories, legends, myths of the founders of states. "Several of these early historians, or 'logographers' are known to have written books of this kind entitled Γενεαλογίαι, Γενεαλογικά (e. g. Hecatæus, Acusilanus, Simonides the Younger, who bore the title ὁ Γενεαλόγος, as did also Pherecydes)" (p. 136). Philo included under τὸ γενεαλογικόν all primitive human history in the Pentateuch. A fortiori this term could be applied by St. Paul to the rank growth of legend respecting the Patriarchs, etc., such as we find in the "Book of Jubilees" and in the "Haggada". This was condemned by him as trashy and unwholesome. The other contemporary errors are of a like Jewish character. Hort takes ἀντίθεσις τῆς ψευδωνύμου γνώσεως to refer to the casuistry of the scribes such as we find in the "Halacha", just as the μῦθοι and γενεαλογίαι designate frivolities such as are contained in the Haggada.

But is it not possible that these (ἀντιθέσεις τῆς ψευδωνύμου γνώσεως) refer to the system of interpretation developed later in the Kabbala, of which a convenient description is given in Gigot's "General Introduction to the Study of the Holy Scriptures", p. 411? (see also "Kabbala" in "Jewish Encyclopedia" and Vigouroux, "Dict. de la Bible"). He who followed only the literal meaning of the text of the Hebrew Bible had no real knowledge, or γνῶσις, of the deep mysteries contained in the letters and words of Scripture. By *notarikon* words were constructed from the initials of several, or sentences formed by using the letters of a word as initials of words. By *ghematria* the numerical values of letters were used, and words of equal numerical value were substituted for each other and new combinations formed. By *themura* the alphabet was divided into two equal parts, and the letters of one half on being substituted for the corresponding letters of the other half, in the text, brought out the hidden sense of the Scripture. These systems date back to time immemorial. They were borrowed from the Jews by the Gnostics of the second century, and were known to some of the early Fathers, and were probably in use before Apostolic times. Now ἀντίθεσις may mean not only opposition or contrast, but also the change or transposition of letters. In this way ἀντίθεσις τῆς ψευδωνύμου γνώσεως would mean the falsely-called knowledge which consists in the interchange of letters just referred to.

Again, we read: "The mischievous feature about them was their presence within the churches and their combination of plausible errors with apparent, even ostentatious, fidelity to principles of the faith—a trouble elsewhere reflected Acts XX. 29f, in connexion with the Ephesian church towards the end of the first century" (Ency. Bib.). We do not admit that Acts, xx, was written towards the end of the first century. The best scholars hold it was written by St. Luke long before; and so the critics of the Epistles, having without proof dated the composition of a genuine early New-Testament book at the end of the first century, on the strength of that performance endeavour to discredit three whole books of Scripture.

I. Miscellaneous objections.—We bring together under this heading a number of objections that are found scattered in the text, foot-notes, sub-foot-notes, of the article in the "Ency. Bib."—(1) "The concern to keep the widow class under the bishop's control is thoroughly sub-apostolic (cp. Ign. ad Polycarp. iv. 5)".—That would not prove that it was not Apostolic as well. On reading the only passage referring to widows (I Tim., v) we get a totally different impression from the one conveyed here. The great aim of the writer of the Epistle appears to be to prevent widows from becoming a burden on the Church, and to point out the duty of their relatives to support them. Thirty years before the death of St. Paul the Seven were appointed to look after the poor widows of Jerusalem; and it is absurd to suppose that during all that time no regulations were made as to who should receive support, and who not. Some few of those who were "widows indeed" probably held offices like deaconesses, of whom we read in Rom., xvi, 1, and who were doubtless under the direction of the Apostles and other ecclesiastical authorities. The supposition that nothing was "done in order", but that everything was allowed to go at random, has no support in St. Paul's earlier Epistles.

(2) "The curious antipathy of the writer to second marriages on the part of the presbyters, episcopi, diaconi, and widows (χῆραι) is quite un-Pauline, but corresponds to the more general feeling prevalent in the second century throughout the churches."—That state of feeling throughout the churches in the second century should make an objector pause. Its Apostolic origin is its best explanation, and there is nothing whatsoever to show that it was un-Pauline. It was St. Paul who wrote as follows at a much earlier date (I Cor., vii): "I would that all men were even as myself: . . . But I say to the unmarried, and to the widows: It is good for them if they so continue, even as I . . . But I would have you to be without solicitude. He that is without a wife, is solicitous for the things of the Lord, how he may please God. But he that is with a wife, is solicitous for the things of the world, how he may please his wife: and he is divided . . . He that giveth his virgin in marriage, doth well; and he that giveth her not, doth better." It would be rash to suppose that St. Paul, who wrote thus to the Corinthians, in general, could not shortly before his death require that those who were to take the place of the Apostles and hold the highest offices in the Church should not have been married more than once.

(3) "The distinctive element, however, i. e. the prominence assigned to Timothy and Titus, is intelligible only on the supposition that the author had specially in view the ulterior end of vindicating the legitimate evangelic succession of contemporary episcopi and other office-bearers in provinces where this was liable for various reasons to be challenged" (in the beginning of the second century).—Thousands have read these Epistles, from their very first appearance until now, without such a conclusion suggesting itself to them. If this objection means anything it means that the Apostles could not assign prominent positions to any of their disciples or delegates; which runs counter to what we read of Timothy and Titus in the earlier Epistles of St. Paul.

(4) "The prominence given to 'teaching' qualities shows that one danger of the contemporary churches lay largely in the vagaries of unauthorized teachers (Did., xvi). The author's cure is simple: Better let the episcopus himself teach! Better let those in authority be responsible for the instruction of the ordinary members! Evidently teaching was not originally or usually (I Tim., v, 17) a function of presbyters, but abuses had led by this time, as the Didache proves, to a need of combining teaching with organised church authority."—What a lot of meaning is read into half a dozen words of these Epistles! In the very first Epistle that St. Paul wrote we read: "And we beseech you, brethren, to know them who labour among you, and are over you in the Lord, and admonish you: That you esteem them more abundantly in charity, for their work's sake" (I Thess., v, 12–13). The capacity for teaching was a gift, probably a natural one working through God's grace for the good of the Church (see HIERARCHY OF THE EARLY CHURCH), and there was no reason why the Apostle, who attached so much importance to teaching when speaking of his own work, should not require that those who were selected to rule the Churches and carry on his work should be endowed with the aptitude for teaching. In Eph., iv, 11, we find that the same persons were "pastors and doctors". The writer who makes this objection does not admit that real bishops and priests existed in Apostolic times; so this is what his assertion implies: When the Apostles died there were no bishops and priests. After some time they originated somewhere and somehow, and spread all over the Church. During a considerable time they did not teach. Then they began to monopolize teaching, and the practice spread everywhere, and finally the Pastorals were written to confirm this state of affairs, which had no sanction from the Apostles, though these bishops thought otherwise. And all this happened before St. Ignatius wrote, in a short period of thirty or forty years, a length of time spanned say from 1870 or 1880 till 1912—a rapid state of development indeed, which has no documentary evidence to support it, and which must have taken place, for the most part, under the very eyes of the Apostles St. John and St. Philip, and of Timothy, Titus, Clement, Ignatius, Polycarp, and other disciples of the Apostles. The early Christians had more respect for Apostolic traditions than that.

(5) "Baptism is almost a sacrament of salvation (Tit., iii, 5)."—It is quite a sacrament of salvation, not only here, but in the teaching of Christ, in the Acts, and in St. Paul's Epistles to the Romans, I Corinthians, Galatians, and Colossians, and in I Pet., iii, 21.

(6) "Faith is tending to become more than ever *fides quæ creditur*."—But it appears as *fides qua creditur* in I Tim., i, 2, 4, 5, 14; ii, 7, 15; iii, 9, 13; iv, 6, 12; vi, 11; II Tim., i, 5, 13; ii, 18, 22; iii, 10, 15; Tit., ii, 2, etc., while it is used in the earlier Epistles not only subjectively but also objectively. See πίστις in Preuschen, "Handwörterbuch zum griech. N. Testament." Faith is *fides quæ creditur* only nine times out of thirty-three passages where πίστις occurs in the Pastorals.

(7) "The church to this unmystical author is no longer *the bride* or *the body* of Christ but God's building or rather *familia dei*, quite in the neo-Catholic style." There are several genuine Epistles of St. Paul in which the Church is neither called the body nor the bride of Christ, and in calling it a building he was only following his Master who said: "On this rock I will build my Church." The idea of a spiritual building is quite Pauline. "For we know, if our earthly house of this habitation be dissolved, that we have a building of God, a house not made with hands, eternal in heaven" (II Cor., v, 1); "And I have so preached this gospel, not where Christ was named, lest I should build upon another man's foundation" (Rom., xv, 20); "For if I build up again the things which I have destroyed, I make myself a prevaricator" (Gal., ii, 18); "Let us work good to all men, but especially to those who are of the household of the faith" (Gal., vi, 10); "You are fellow citizens with the saints, and the domestics of God, built upon the foundation of the apostles and prophets, Jesus Christ himself being the chief corner stone: in whom all the building, being framed together, groweth up into a holy temple in the Lord. In whom you also are built together into an habitation of God in the Spirit" (Eph., ii, 19–22); "You are God's building. According to the grace of God that is given to me as a wise architect, I have laid the foundation. . . . Know you not, that you are the temple of God, and that the Spirit of God dwelleth in you?" (I Cor., iii, 9–17; compare I Pet., ii, 5; "Be you also as living stones built up, a spiritual house"; and I Pet., iv, 17: "For the time is, that judgment should begin at the house of God. And if first at us, what shall

be the end of them that believe not the gospel of God?") There is a development in St. Paul's use of the comparisons body and bride, which is exactly paralleled by his use of the words building and temple. They are applied first to individuals, then to communities and finally to the whole Church (see Gayford in Hast., "Dict. of the Bibl.", s. v. Church).

(8) "Items of the creed, now rapidly crystallizing in Rome and Asia Minor, are conveyed partly in hymnal fragments, which like those in the Apocalypse of John, sprang from the cultus of the churches." There are fragments of the Creed in I Cor. (see CORINTHIANS, EPISTLES TO THE, *The First Epistle—Its teaching*), and there were hymns in use several years before St. Paul's death. He wrote to the Colossians (iii, 16): "Let the word of Christ dwell in you abundantly, in all wisdom: teaching and admonishing one another in psalms, hymns, and spiritual canticles" (cf. Eph., v, 19). The objections from the "Faithful Sayings" are fully answered in James, "The Genuineness of the Pastorals" (London, 1906), 132–6.

(9) "No possible circumstances could make Paul oblivious (through three separate letters) of God's fatherhood, of the believing man's union with Jesus, of the power and witness of the Spirit, or of reconciliation." These doctrines are not quite forgotten: I Tim., i, 15; ii, 6; II Tim., i, 2, 9; ii, 13; Tit., i, 4; iii, 4, 5, 7. There was no necessity to dwell upon them as he was writing to disciples well acquainted with his teaching, and the purpose of the Epistles was to meet new problems. Besides, this objection could be brought against large portions of the genuine Epistles.

There are several other objections but they are so flimsy that they cannot present any difficulty. What Sanday wrote in 1896 in his "Inspiration" (London) is still true: "It may be asserted without fear of contradiction that nothing really un-Pauline has been proved in any of the disputed epistles."

II. *External Evidence.*—The Pauline authorship of the Pastorals was never doubted by Catholics in early times. Eusebius, with his complete knowledge of early Christian literature, states that they were among the books universally recognized in the Church τὰ παρὰ πᾶσιν ʽομολογούμενα ("Hist. eccl.", II, xxii, III, iii; "Præp. evang.", II, xiv, 7; xvi, 3). They are found in the early Latin and Syriac Versions. St. Clement of Alexandria speaks of them (Strom., II, III), and Tertullian expresses his astonishment that they were rejected by Marcion (Adv. Marcion, V, xxi), and says they were written by St. Paul to Timothy and Titus; evidently their rejection was a thing hitherto unheard of. They are ascribed to St. Paul in the Muratorian Fragment, and Theophilus of Antioch (about 181) quotes from them and calls them the "Divine word" (θεῖος λόγος). The Martyrs of Vienne and Lyons (about 180) were acquainted with them; and their bishop, Pothinus, who was born about A. D. 87 and martyred in 177 at the age of ninety, takes us back to a very early date. His successor, St. Irenæus, who was born in Asia Minor and had heard St. Polycarp preach, makes frequent use of the Epistles and quotes them as St. Paul's. He was arguing against heretics, so there could be no doubt on either side. The Epistles were also admitted by Heracleon (about 165), Hegesippus (about 170), St. Justin Martyr, and the writer of the "Second Epistle of Clement" (about 140). In the short letter which St. Polycarp wrote (about 117) he shows that he was thoroughly acquainted with them. Polycarp was born only a few years after the death of Saints Peter and Paul, and as Timothy and Titus, according to the most ancient traditions, lived to be very old, he was their contemporary for many years. He was Bishop of Smyrna, only forty miles from Ephesus, where Timothy resided. St. Ignatius, the second successor of St. Peter at Antioch, was acquainted with Apostles and disciples of the Apostles, and shows his knowledge of the Epistles in the letters which he wrote about A. D. 110. Critics now admit that Ignatius and Polycarp knew the Pastorals (von Soden in Holtzmann's "Hand-Kommentar", III, 155; "Ency. Bib.", IV); and there is a very strong probability that they were known also to Clement of Rome, when he wrote to the Corinthians about A. D. 96.

In judging of the early evidence it should be borne in mind that all three Epistles claim to be by St. Paul. So when an early writer shows his familiarity with them, quotes them as authoritative and as evidently well known to his readers, it may be taken as a proof not only of the existence and widespread knowledge of the Epistles, but that the writer took them for what they claim to be, genuine Epistles of St. Paul; and if the writer lived in the time of Apostles, of Apostolic men, of disciples of Apostles, and of Timothy and Titus (as did Ignatius, Polycarp, and Clement) we may be sure that he was correct in doing so. The evidence of these writers is, however, very unceremoniously brushed aside. The heretic Marcion, about A. D. 150, is held to be of much more weight than all of them put together. "Marcion's omission of the pastorals from his canon tells heavily against their origin as preserved in tradition. Philemon was accepted by him, though far more of a private note than any of the pastorals; and the presence of elements antagonistic to his own views need not have made him exclude them, since he could have easily excised these passages in this as in other cases" (Ency. Bib., IV). Marcion rejected the whole of the Old Testament, all the Gospels except St. Luke's, which he grossly mutilated, and all the rest of the New Testament, except ten Epistles of St. Paul, texts of which he changed to suit his purposes. Philemon escaped on account of its brevity and contents. If he crossed out all that was objectionable to him in the Pastorals there would be little left worth preserving. Again, the testimony of all these early writers is regarded as of no more value than the opinion of Aristotle on the authorship of the Homeric poems (ibid.). But in the one case we have the chain of evidence going back to the times of the writer, of his disciples, and of the persons addressed; while Aristotle lived several hundred years after the time of Homer. "The early Christian attitude towards 'Hebrews' is abundant evidence of how loose that judgment [on authorship] could be" (ibid.). The extreme care and hesitancy, in some quarters, about admitting the Pauline authorship of the Epistle to the Hebrews (q. v.) when contrasted with the universal and undoubting acceptance of the Pastorals tells strongly in favour of the latter.

JAMES, *Genuineness and Authorship of the Pastoral Epistles* (London, 1906); JACQUIER, *Hist. du Nouveau Test.*, I (Paris, 1906; tr. DUGGAN, London); Introductions to N. Test. by CORNELY, SALMON, and other Scriptural scholars; HEADLAM in *Church Congress Reports* (London, 1904); *The Church Quart. Rev.* (October, 1906; January, 1907); BISPING, *Erklärung der drei Past.* (Münster, 1866); WEISS, *Tim. und Tit.* (Göttingen, 1902); BERNARD, *The Pastoral Epistles* (Cambridge, 1899); LILLEY, *The Pastoral Epistles* (Edinburgh, 1901); GORE, *Orders and Unity* (London, 1909); WORKMAN, *The Hapax Legomena of St. Paul* in *Expository Times*, VII (1896), 418; HORT, *Judaistic Christianity* (London, 1898); BELSER, *Die Briefe des Apostels Paulus an Timoth. u. Titus* (Freiburg); KNOWLING has a good defence of the Pastorals in *The Testimony of St. Paul to Christ*; see also his article in the *Critical Review* (July, 1896); RAMSEY, *Expositor* (1910).

C. AHERNE.

Timucua Indians, a principal group or confederacy of ancient Florida, notable for the successful missions established among them by the Spaniards and subsequently utterly destroyed by the English of Carolina and their savage Indian allies. The name—written also *Atimuca*, *Thimapoa*, *Tomoco*, by the Spaniards, French, and English respectively—appears to be derived from a word in their own language, *atimoqua*, "lord, or chief", and was probably a title mistaken by the early Spaniards for the name of the chief or tribe.

Habitat.—The cognate tribes of the Timucuan linguistic stock held all of north Florida from about Cape Canaveral and Tampa Bay on the south to beyond the St. Mary's River on the north and westward to about the Ocilla River, where they bordered upon the celebrated Apalachee, of another (Muskhogean) stock. The tribes forming the Timucua group proper centred chiefly along the St. John's River, the principal being the Timucua along the upper part of the river and about the present St. Augustine, whose chief, known to the French as Outina, had his settlement about the present Welaka, and ruled some forty villages, with perhaps 6000 souls. On the lower course of the river were the Satuniba, the enemies of the Timucua and nearly as numerous, and west of them, toward the Suwanee River, were the Potano, with over a thousand warriors or perhaps four thousand souls. Several other tribes were of minor importance.

Customs.—The Timucua were sedentary and semi-agricultural, but depended largely upon game, fish, wild fruits, and bread prepared from the starchy *koonti* root. Their houses were circular, of upright poles, thatched with palmetto leaves, and with granaries elevated on stakes to keep them out of reach of wild animals. Their villages were strongly stockaded and each important settlement had a large central town-house of logs, for tribal ceremonies and the reception of guests. They had large dug-out canoes. Their pottery, the work of the women, was of the finest type found east of the Mississippi. The principal weapon of the warriors was the bow, and a sort of spade-shaped club of hard wood. The numerous embankments and ancient roadways found in their country may be due in part to Spanish influence. Women wore a short fringed skirt, perhaps of some bark fibre, with their hair flowing loosely. Men went naked, except for the breechcloth, but had the whole body elaborately tattooed. They bunched the hair in a knot on top of the head, and wore inflated fish-bladders through holes in their ears. They were tall and well-made, described as of great strength and agility and remarkable swimmers.

The government by the chiefs was despotic, as was frequently the case among the Gulf State tribes. There were two hereditary classes, nobles, or chiefs, and common people, and each tribe was organized into clans or hereditary family groups, usually bearing animal names. This clan system was so much interwoven with the tribal life that it persisted even under the mission system. Prisoners of war and their descendants constituted a slave class. Their military organization and methods were superior to what was found among the northern tribes. Scalping and mutilation of the slain enemy were universal, and the dismembered limbs were carried from the field as trophies or to serve for cannibal feasts. Polygamy was customary. Gross sensuality was prevalent. The chief gods were the Sun and the Moon, the Deer and other animals. They were extremely ceremonious, celebrating planting and harvest seasons, fishing and hunting expeditions, the going and return of war parties, marriages and funerals, each with special rites of prayer, fasting, feasting, dancing and purification by means of the "black drink" brewed from the leaves of the *Ilex cassine*. On certain great ceremonial occasions the first-born male infants of the tribe were delivered up by their mothers to be sacrificed to the Sun, in whose honour also a sacred fire was kept always burning in their temples. The dead were buried in the ground with protracted mourning rites, which included fasting and cutting off the hair. Over the body of a dead chief was raised a mound of earth upon which was placed his shell drinking cup, surrounded by a circle of arrows stuck in the ground.

From the pictures of the artist Le Moyne we get a vivid idea of the appearance and customs of the Timucua tribes, while the questions in Father Pareja's "Confessionario" throw curious light upon their beliefs, tabus, and ceremonial observance.

History.—The history of the Timucua tribes begins with the landing of the ill-fated Ponce de Leon near the present St. Augustine in 1513. The expeditions of Narvaez in 1528 and de Soto in 1539–41, landing at Tampa Bay, passed through the territory of the cognate tribes, but did not encounter the Timucua proper. In 1562–64 the French Huguenots under Ribault and Laudonnière attempted settlements at the mouth of St. John's River, explored the middle course of the stream, and made acquaintance with the principal tribes. In 1565 the Spaniards under Menendez destroyed the French posts, butchering all the defenders, immediately after which Menendez founded the city of St. Augustine and began the permanent colonization of the country. Jesuit missionaries arrived and began their labours, but seem to have devoted their attention chiefly to the coast tribes of South Carolina, Virginia, and western Florida, probably because of the fact that the Indians of the St. John's region had been won over by the French and for a long time resisted the Spanish occupation. In 1573 a party of Franciscan missionaries arrived at St. Augustine, where some of their order had been from the beginning, and proceeded to organize work among the Indians of the vicinity. The work met a serious check from the recall of Governor Menendez to Spain, where he died in 1574, but in 1594, on request of Father Marron, custos of the Franciscan convent at St. Augustine, twelve other priests of the order were sent out, and the labour of Christianizing the Timucua was taken up with vigour.

Among those who arrived with this party was the noted Father Francisco Pareja, to whom we are indebted for almost all that is known of the language and customs of the tribe. He was stationed at first among the Yamassee on the Georgia coast, in whose language, according to Shea, he composed a summary of Christian doctrine. Later he was in charge at the Timucua mission of San Juan, apparently on Little Talbot Island, north of St. Augustine, and later still was custos of the monastery in that city, until transferred to the Mexican province in 1610, where he died in 1628. His various works in the Timucua language were published in Mexico. Of the priests who arrived from Spain with Father Pareja, several went to the Yamassee, while the others devoted attention to the Timucua, whose principal mission settlements were San Juan, already mentioned; San Pedro, on Cumberland Island; San Mateo, probably about the mouth of the St. John's; and Santa Lucia de Acuera, south of Cape Canaveral; besides the settlement immediately adjoining St. Augustine. The more western cognate Potano tribe, being hostile alike to the Timucua and the Spaniards, were not Christianized until a much later period, but were also brought likewise into the mission fold. In 1597 the mission growth was interrupted by a disastrous revolt of the Yamassee in which several missionaries lost their lives, the Christian Timucua being also attacked. Some years later, however (1612?), following a visit from the Bishop of Havana in 1602, Florida was erected into a Franciscan province, under the name of Santa Elena. From 1612 to 1615 inclusive, 43 Franciscans were added to the workers in addition to those already on the ground.

In 1655 the Christian Indian population of the Florida province, which included north Florida and the coast country of Georgia and South Carolina, was estimated at 26,000 souls, chiefly among the Timucua, Apalachee, and Yamassee. In 1687 a second outbreak of the Yamassee, apparently instigated by the English of Carolina, who claimed northern Florida as within their chartered limits, resulted in the removal of that tribe bodily into (South) Carolina. In 1715 the same restless people headed a war against the English, resulting in their own expulsion and return to Florida. In 1688, following the outbreak of the Yamassee, by which the Timucua missions had also suffered, the chiefs of the latter tribe, as also the Apalachee chiefs, forwarded to the King of Spain an address of loyalty and of commendation for their Spanish governor. These documents, in the Indian and Spanish languages, are still in existence. The Timucua address is signed by the chiefs of five towns, San Mateo, San Pedro, Asile, Machaua, and San Juan de Guacara. In 1699 the Quaker Dickenson, from Philadelphia, shipwrecked on the south coast of Florida and rescued from the savages by the Spanish governor at St. Augustine, was sheltered for a time at the Timucua missions, and has left us a pleasant picture of their prosperous and orderly condition, and the friendly and religious character of their occupants, in striking contrast to that of the unchanged barbarians among whom he had been a prisoner.

It was near the end. The growing hostility of the Carolina colony instigated the Creeks and other heathen tribes to constant inroads upon the Florida missions, furnishing them with arms and ammunition for the purpose, with the further inducement of a profitable sale for all captives to supply the Carolina slave market. Even as early as 1699 Carolina slaves were thus decimating the Indian tribes as far even as the Mississippi. While the wild tribes were thus armed and encouraged in their raids by the English, the Christian mission Indians, on the contrary, in accordance with a fixed, but suicidal, rule of the Spanish colonial government, were refused the use of firearms, even in self-defence and on their most urgent appeal.

In May, 1702, war having again been declared between the two home governments, the Creek allies of the English raided Santa Fe mission of the Timucua and burned the church. Later in the same year a combined English and Indian force from Carolina under Governor Moore, co-operating with a naval force, destroyed three flourishing Timucua missions along the coast—the same where Dickenson had been so hospitably cared for—burned the churches and carried off the missionaries, and then, going farther south, burned St. Augustine, with the church, convent, and library. The fortress held out until relieved by a Spanish fleet. In 1704 Moore invaded the Apalachee country with some fifty Carolina men and a thousand savage Creek, Catawba, and Yamassee, all armed with guns, and completely destroyed ten of the eleven missions towns, with their churches and orange groves, carrying off or destroying the vestments and sacred vessels. Four priests, a Spanish officer, and four soldiers were killed, and their bodies hacked to pieces, two of the missionaries being tortured and burned at the stake. Several hundred Apalachee warriors were killed and 1400 of the tribe carried away as slaves. In 1706 a similar raid into the Timucua country completed the ruin of the missions. The remnant of the Apalachee fled for protection to the French at Mobile. The scattered Timucua were gathered together and formed into small settlements under the walls of St. Augustine. With the English colonization of Georgia and the ensuing war of 1740 all attempt at rehabilitating the Florida missions was abandoned. In 1753 only 136 Indians remained in the vicinity of St. Augustine. On the English occupation in 1763 they were expelled from their two villages and again became refugees. Somewhat later these, or a kindred remnant, were colonized at a new settlement called Pueblo de Atimucas, on Tomoco River, near Mosquito lagoon, in the present Volusia county. A few seem to have resided there as late as the transfer of the territory to the United States in 1821 and it is possible that their descendants may still be found among the Seminole of Florida or Oklahoma.

Language.—With the exception of the Timucua-Spanish document of 1688, already referred to, of which a copy was printed by Buckingham Smith in 1859, and another, with English translation, by Gatschet in 1880 (Am. Philos. Soc. Proc., XVIII), our knowledge of the Timucua language and dialects, as of the tribal customs and beliefs, rests almost entirely upon the works of Father Pareja and of Father Gregorio de Monilla, missionary in the same order and tribe, with the analysis deduced thereupon by Gatschet. A few words, mostly personal or place names, also occur in the early French and Spanish historians. Father Pareja's works include: "Cathecismo en lengua Castellana y Timuquana" (Mexico, 1612); "Catechismo y breve exposicion de la doctrina Cristiana . . . en Lengua Castellana y Timuquana" (Mexico, 1612); "Confessionario en Lengua Timuquana" (Mexico, 1612); "Confessionario en lengua Castellana y Timuquana" (Mexico, 1613); "Gramatica [or Arte?] de la Lengua Timuquana" (Mexico, 1614); "Catecismo de la Doctrina cristiana en dicha [Timuquana] Lengua" (Mexico, 1617); "Catechismo y Examen . . . en Lengua Castellana y Timuquana" (Mexico, 1627). The works of Father Monilla include an "Explicacion de la Doctrina . . . en Lengua Floridiana" (Madrid, 1631?, and Mexico, 1635–36); and a "Forma Breve de administrar los Sacramentos . . . en lengua Floridiana" (Mexico, 1635). Of these works the Pareja "Catechismo" (1612), "Catechismo y breve exposicion" (1612), and "Confessionario" (1613), and the Monilla "Explicacion" (1635–36), and "Forma breve" (1635) form the subject of an extended study of "The Timucua Language" by Dr. Albert S. Gatschet, in the "Proceedings of the American Philosophical Society", vols. XVI–XVIII, Philadelphia, 1877–1880.

BARCIA, *Ensayo* (Madrid, 1723); BRINTON, *Floridian Peninsula* (Philadelphia, 1859); LAUDONNIÈRE, *Histoire notable de la Floride* (Paris, 1586 and 1853), tr. in FRENCH, *Hist. Colls. of Fla.* (New York, 1869); LE MOYNE, *Narrative* (Boston, 1875), an artist with Laudonnière's expedition, pictures with text (from DE BY, Lat. ed., Frankfort, 1591); MOORE, various important papers on archæology of the Gulf States, in *Jour. Academy of Natural Sciences* (Philadelphia, 1894 to 1910); PARKMAN, *Pioneers of France* (Boston, 1865—); PILLING, *Proofsheets of a Bibliography of the Languages of the N. Am. Inds.* (Bur. Am. Ethnology, Washington, 1885); SHEA, *Hist. Catholic Ind. Missions of the United States* (New York, 1855); IDEM, *The Catholic Church in Colonial Days* (1521–1763, vol. I of *History of the Catholic Church in the United States* (New York, 1886).

JAMES MOONEY.

Tincker, MARY AGNES, novelist, b. at Ellsworth, Maine, 18 July, 1833; d. at Boston, Massachusetts, 4 Dec., 1907. At the age of thirteen she began teaching in the public schools. At fifteen her first literary work was printed. At twenty she became a Catholic, and even her Protestant relatives shared in her sufferings from Knownothing bigotry. In 1863 she became a volunteer war nurse, serving in Washington until she grew ill. Boston then became her home. Short stories from her pen appeared in the early numbers of "The Catholic World", where also her first novel "The House of Yorke" was issued as a serial (1871–72). It was followed by "Grapes and Thorns" (1873–74) and "Six Sunny Months" (1876–77). The latter was the first fruit of her sojourn in Italy (1873–87). These three novels sounded a distinctly new note in Catholic literature, and the highest that has been struck by an American Catholic novelist. "Signor Monaldini's Niece" (1879), in "No Name" series; "By the Tiber" (1881); "The Jewel in the Lotus" (1884); "Aurora" (1885); "The Two Coronets" (1887); "San Salvador" (1889); were issued by the most prominent literary publishers and won her great fame as works of real art. They reflected for the most part the beauty of Italy. A lapse from the practice of her religion cast its shadow perhaps over a few of her novels written during that time. She returned to her religious duties many years before her death. Her last book, fittingly called "Autumn Leaves" (1898), was issued by a Catholic firm, and contained matter contributed not long before to "The Catholic World".

TALBOT SMITH in *The Ave Maria* (24 July, 1909); STEDMAN AND HUTCHINSON, *Amer. Lit.*

REGINA RANDOLPH JENKINS.

Tingis, a titular see of Mauretania Tingitana (the official list of the Roman Curia places it in Mauretania Cæsarea). Tingis, now Tangier, is an ancient Phœnician town; Greek legend ascribes its foundation to the giant Antæus, whose tomb and skeleton are pointed out in the vicinity, or to Sophax, son of Hercules and the widow of Antæus. The coins call it Tenga, Tinga, and Titga, the Greek and Latin authors giving numerous variations of the name. Under the Romans this commercial town became, first, a free city and then, under Augustus, a colony (*Colonia Julia*, under Claudius), capital of Mauretania Tingitana. Portuguese in the fifteenth century, Spanish in the sixteenth, it became an English possession by the marriage of Charles II with the Infanta Catharine of Portugual. The English vacated it in 1684. When it was bombarded by the Prince de Joinville in 1844, it belonged to Morocco. The natives call it Tandja. It has about 40,000 inhabitants, of whom half are Mussulmans, 10,000 Jews, 9000 Europeans (7500 Spanish). Towards the end of the third century Tangier was the scene of the martyrdom of St. Marcellus, mentioned in the Roman Martyrology on 30 October, and of St. Cassian, mentioned on 3 December. It is not known whether it was a diocese in ancient times. Under the Portuguese domination it was a suffragan of Lisbon, and in 1570 was united to the Diocese of Ceuta. Six of its bishops are known, the first, who did not reside in his see, in 1468. Tangier is now the residence of the Prefect Apostolic of Morocco, which mission is in charge of the Friars Minor. It has a Catholic church, several chapels, schools, and a hospital.

SMITH, *Dict. of Gr. and Rom. Geogr.*, s. v.; JORDÃO, *Memoria historica sobre os bipados de Ceuta e Tanger* (Lisbon, 1858); TISSOT, *Recherches sur la géographie comparée de la Maurétanie Tingitane* (Paris, 1876), 44 sq.; TOULOTTE, *Géographie de l'Afrique chrétienne. Maurétanies* (Montreuil, 1894), 247; MÜLLER, *Ptolemy*, ed. DIDOT, I, 580.

S. PÉTRIDÈS.

Tinin (KNIN), SEE OF, in Dalmatia, suffragan to Kalocsa-Bacs. Knin is a town on the right bank of the Kerka, twenty-five miles north-east of Sebenico. It was fortified by the Romans, who called it Ardula. At the request of Casimir IV, King of Croatia in 1050, a Bishopric of Knin was created, suffragan to Spalato; the bishop seems to have been attached to the court as preacher. Farlati in his "Illyricum sacrum", IV (Venice, 1775), gives a history of the prelates of Knin, from Mark in 1050 to Joseph in 1755. The residential succession was interrupted by the Saracen invasion in 1622; when Venice captured the district in 1768, the Bishop of Sebenico was appointed to administer the diocese, which was united in 1828 to Sebenico. The ruins of the old Cathedral of St. John the Evangelist are still visible. To-day the see is suffragan to Kalocsa-Bacs, according to the "Schematismus" of Kalocsa (1909); the "Gerarchia cattolica" says the see is merely titular, and this would explain the absence of statistics. The bishop, Monsignor Joseph Lányi, who resides at Nagy-Várad, was born at Német-Prona, Diocese of Neusohl, 29 June, 1868; ordained, 2 July, 1891; Abbot of St. Saviour's and canon of Nagy-Várad; appointed bishop, 7 Nov., 1906, in succession to Monsignor John Maiorosy (b. at Al-Debro, Archdiocese of Eger, 10 July, 1831; appointed, 27 July, 1885).

A. A. MACERLEAN.

Tinos and Mykonos, DIOCESE OF (TINENSIS ET MYCONENSIS), a Latin diocese of the Cyclades, containing over 126 square miles and numbering 13,000 inhabitants. It is called "verdant" though it is so only in comparison with the other Greek islands more arid than itself. In ancient times it was called Hydrussa, i. e. abounding in water, though this is scarcely credible, and Ophiussa because of the number of serpents which inhabited it. Near the river there was a celebrated temple of Poseidon, discovered in 1902. The island subjected itself to Xerxes at the time of his expedition against the Greeks, but afterwards defected to Salamais and Platæa; it became finally subject to Athens, then to Alexander of Pheræ, afterwards to the Rhodians, to whom it was given by Marcus Antonius, later to the Romans. It is not known when Christianity was established there. Le Quien (Oriens Christianus, I, 943) mentions three early bishops; Ecdicius, present in 553 at the Fifth Œcumenical Council; Demetrius, in 681 at the Sixth Council; Eustathius in 787 at the Seventh Council. The bishopric was a suffragan of Rhodes in the seventh and tenth centuries (Gelzer, "Ungedruckte . . . Texte der Notitiæ Episcopatuum", 542, 558); suppressed after the conquest of the island by the Venetians in 1207, it was re-established but as a metropolitan when Tinos passed into the power of the Turks in 1714. The metropolitan see was in its turn suppressed in 1833, "Echos d'Orient", III, 287. Under the Venetian domination, which lasted from 1207 to 1714, Tinos had some Latin bishops; nevertheless the earliest known date only from 1329 (Le Quien, op. cit., III, 1059; Eubel, "Hierarchia catholica medii ævi", I, 512; II, 276; III, 333) Little by little the island became almost completely Catholic. In 1781 it had 7000 Catholics dispersed throughout 32 villages (Hilaire de Barenton, "La France catholique en Orient", 221); some were of the Latin, others of the Greek Rite, and Le Quien (I, 943) affirms that at the same epoch there were more than 120 Greek Catholic priests subject to the Latin bishop. Under the Venetian domination the schismatics were dependent on a *protopapas* who in turn depended on the Patriarchate of Constantinople. The Latin bishopric, at first a suffragan of the Archbishopric of Rhodes, afterwards of Arcadia in Crete, is now a suffragan of Naxos. Since at least the year 1400, the title of Mykonos has been joined to its own; furthermore, the bishop administers the Diocese of Andros. The see numbers 4000 Catholics, 23 secular priests, a chapter-house, 26 parishes, a seminary at Xynara with only seven or eight students; the Franciscans have 2 houses and five religious, the Jesuits one house and ten religious, the Franciscan Tertiaries have about ten, the French Ursulines maintain an orphanage and a large boarding-school at Loutra, and they also direct through the Greek Sisters schools for girls, which number about forty in all. Tinos possesses an image of the Evanghelistria or of the Annunciation discovered in 1823 which attracts each year on 25 March and 15 August from 3000 to 4000 schismatic pilgrims (Echos d'Orient, V, 315).

SMITH, *Dict. Greek and Roman Geog.*, s. v.; ZALLONY, *Voyage à Tine* (Paris, 1809); LACROIX, *Iles de la Grèce* (Paris, 1853), 439–41; MAUROMARAS, *Histoire de Tinos* (Athens, 1888), Greek; GEORGANTOPOULOS, *Tiniaca* (Athens, 1889), Greek.

S. VAILHÉ.

Tintern Abbey, in Monmouthshire, England, was founded in 1131 by Walter de Clare for Cistercian monks, who came from the Abbey of Aumone, in the Diocese of Chartres, itself founded only ten years before. Walter's son Gilbert, first Earl of Pembroke, and probably also his grandson Richard Strongbow, conqueror of Ireland under Henry II, were buried at Tintern, the magnificent church of which dates from the end of the thirteenth century. The abbey received rich benefactions not only from the family of its founder but from other noble houses; and lists of its

TINTERN ABBEY, MONMOUTH

possessions, both from the taxation-roll of 1291, and at the time of the Dissolution under Henry VIII, are given in detail by Dugdale. The accounts submitted by the last abbot, Richard Wych, in 1535, place the net income at under £200 a year; and the abbey, containing at that time thirteen monks, was suppressed under the Act of 1536 which dissolved the smaller monasteries. The king granted it in 1537 to Henry, Earl of Worcester, in whose family (afterwards dukes of Beaufort) it remained until the sale of his Monmouthshire property by the ninth duke, when it was acquired by the Crown.

The ruins of Tintern, which stands on the right bank of the river Wye, backed by a semicircle of wooded hills, rank with Fountains Abbey in Yorkshire as the most beautiful in England. The church, measuring 245 feet in length, with transepts of 110 feet, is almost perfect, though roofless, the architecture being of the transitional style from Early English to Decorated. The window-tracery is especially fine. Hardly anything remains of the domestic buildings of the abbey, the stone having been used for cottages and farm buildings in the neighbourhood.

DUGDALE, *Monasticon Anglicanum* (London, 1825), 265-274; TANNER, *Notitia Monastica* (London, 1788); *Monm. XIV*; WILLIS, *Historie of Abbies*, II (London, 1719), 142, 328; LELAND, *Collectanea*, ed. HEARNE (London, 1770), I, 104; GASQUET, *The Greater Abbeys of England* (London, 1908), 190-197; HEATH, *Tintern Abbey* (London, 1793); COOPER, *Architectural Reliques of Great Britain* (London, 1807); THOMAS, *Tinterne and its vicinity described* (London, 1839).

D. O. HUNTER-BLAIR.

Tintoretto, IL (JACOPO ROBUSTI), Italian painter, b. at Venice, 1518; d. there 1594. His father was a dyer; hence his surname of Tintoretto (the little dyer). In his early youth he displayed an extraordinary taste for the fine arts. He played well on the harp, but his aptitude for painting was still more pronounced. His parents made him an apprentice of the aged Titian, but Jacopo, eager to distinguish himself, soon set up a studio of his own. His ambition was nothing less than to transform Venetian painting by adding to its distinguishing qualities of brilliantly harmonious colouring and pleasant grace of form the merits of the Florentine and Roman Schools, a knowledge of anatomy which excels in the nude, dramatic *mise en scène*, a pose full of movement, a vigorous contrast of light and shade. According to his biographer, C. Ridolfi, he summarized his ideal in the ambitious formula: "The drawing of Michelangelo and the colouring of Titian" (Il disegno di Michelangelo, il colorito del Tiziano). To fit himself for carrying out this magnificent but difficult programme Robusti devoted himself to unremitting labour. He studied the ancient statues; he had sent to him from Florence the reductions which Daniel of Volterra had made in plaster of Michelangelo's masterpieces, "Dawn", "Noonday", "Twilight", and "Night"; he drew incessantly from the living model or the draped lay figure; he dissected dead bodies; he worked not only by sunlight but also by the flicker of torches in order to master the varied play of light. This intense labour was not fruitless. Being gifted with wonderful facility he executed a countless number of works, and even to the end of his life sustained a veritable fever of production.

In order to make himself known he proposed to the clergy of Santa Maria dell' Orto to paint two large pictures for that church (49 feet high, by 19 feet 6 inches wide), asking no payment but what would cover their cost. His offer was eagerly accepted, and Robusti painted the "Adoration of the Golden Calf" and the "Last Judgment". In this rapidly executed and spirited work he displayed a precocious virtuosity, assembling in a tumultuous whole a great number of figures with agitated gestures and attitudes. His aim was to attract public attention and in this he fully succeeded. He painted several other pictures for this church, in which his talent, having grown more confident, shows more poise. These were: "St. Peter venerating the Cross"; "The Martyrdom of St. Paul"; "St. Agnes recalling to life the Prefect's Son"; the "Presentation of the Blessed Virgin". His latest pictures were painted for the Ducal Palace and the Confraternity of San Rocco (*Scuola di San Rocco*). For the Doges' Palace he first painted four scenes from the life of St. Mark (now scattered). The most remarkable is the "Miracle of St. Mark" (the saint releasing a slave about to be tortured), painted in 1548, which is now in the Venetian Academy of Fine Arts. Robusti's eminent qualities as a draughtsman, colourist, and composer are most happily combined and harmonized in this picture. Other pictures painted for the Sala dello Scrutinio perished in the fire of 1577. But the Ducal Palace still preserves many of his works. As examples of plastic beauty so popular at that time may be mentioned: "Pallas in chase of Mars"; "Ariadne crowned by Venus"; "St. George overcoming the Dragon"; "The Marriage of St. Catharine". In this line he succeeded but without excelling, for his manner is not free from heaviness. Among the historic paintings may be mentioned: "The legates of the Pope and the Doge at Pavia before Frederick Barbarossa"; the "Defence of Brescia in 1483"; the "Capture of Gallipoli in 1484"; "Venice, Queen of the Sea".

PORTRAIT OF TINTORETTO, BY HIMSELF
Uffizi Gallery, Florence

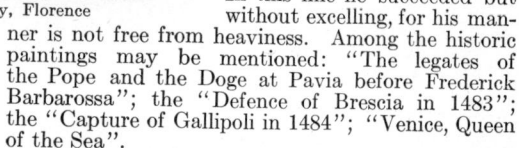

In 1560 the Confraternity of San Rocco near the church of that name opened a contest for the decoration of a central ceiling whereon the "Glorification of St. Rocco" was to be depicted. Tintoretto had formidable competitors: Paolo Veronese, Giuseppe Salviati, Federigo Zuccaro. Instead of submitting the required sketch, Tintoretto, with his feverish ardour, in a short time completed a picture which he quickly put in place. It pleased the Brothers of St. Rocco, who confided to him the entire decoration, to the great displeasure of his rivals, who were offended by the indelicacy of the proceeding. Tintoretto worked on this vast undertaking from 1560 to 1594. It consists of 56 compositions, many of them, such as the "Calvary", of colossal size. "It displays such fulness of light, such a triumphant blossoming of genius and success, that one comes away from it as from too full and loud a concert, half deafened, missing the proportion of things and not knowing whether to believe one's senses" (Taine). Tintoretto also painted pictures for several Venetian churches, the chief of which were the "Crucifixion" and the "Resurrection" at San Cassiano, the "Marriage Feast of Cana" at Santa Maria della Salute, the "Baptism of Christ" at San Silvestro, the "Last Supper" at San Giorgio

Maggiore and San Giovanni, and the "Life of St. Rocco" at San Rocco.

Robusti was not without merit as a portrait painter. At the Ducal Palace there is a series of portraits of the doges; the museum of the Uffizi at Florence has the portrait of Sansovino, the Louvre that of the painter himself. His last religious composition, begun at the age of seventy and finished shortly before his death, is in the Hall of the Grand Council of the Doges' Palace. This gigantic work, measuring 32 feet 10 inches high, by 72 feet 2 inches wide, represents the "Last Judgment". "Although the colouring has grown dark we cannot but admire the broad lines, the close and picturesque grouping, the enormous masses set in motion with extraordinary vigour" (E. Müntz). Also, it may be added, we cannot but admire the spirited strength of the old man who is able to depict about 500 persons. Jacopo Robusti did not fully realize the ambitious programme he outlined for himself. He could not equal the drawing of Michelangelo, whom he took for his model, but he emphasized its defects by exaggerating the anatomical outlines and foreshortenings. These feats of skill are always out of place, but especially so in religious subjects, which Tintoretto too often treated unbecomingly. However, it is to his credit that he infused into some scenes from the Passion a communicative tragic emotion. His colour is inferior to Titian's, whom he hoped to surpass; it is heavier and less brilliant. But he discovered certain sombre tints which are wonderfully adapted to the expression of sad and sorrowful sentiments and which accentuate the bright contrasts. In point of time he is the last of the great Venetian painters, but he belongs already to the period of decadence, because he never succeeded in overcoming his unstudied impetuosity or fusing into a harmonious whole his eminent but warring qualities.

VASARI in *Vita di Battista Franco*; ed. Milanese, VI (Florence, 1881), 587–88; RIDOLFI, *Le Maraviglie dell'Arte, ovvero le Vite degl' illustri pittori Veneti e dello stato* (Venice, 1648); BURCKHARD AND BODE, *Le Cicerone*, Fr. tr. GERARD (Paris, 1892), 759, 61; MÜNTZ, *Hist. de l'Art pendant la Renaissance*, III (Paris, 1895), 660–64; THODE, *Tintoretto* (Bielefeld and Leipzig, 1901).

GASTON SORTAIS.

Tipasa, a titular see of Numidia. The Phœnician word signifies passage. Early in its history we find in Tipasa a Punic counting-house with a port; which passed later under the dominion of the kings of Mauretania, whose kingdom was annexed to the Roman empire in A. D. 39. Claudius I constituted Tipasa a *Colonia juris latini* (Pliny, "Hist. Natur.", V, ii, 20). Later on it became a *civitas* and in the third century an inscription styles it *colonia*. The city, which was very commercial, grew and prospered greatly under the emperors of the second and third centuries. A Jewish colony with its synagogue settled there, early in its history. An inscription belonging to the year 238 is the most ancient trace of Christianity to be found in Tipasa. In the church of Bishop Alexander, built at the end of the fourth century, we find the tombs of nine personages who are called *justi priores* and whom Duchesne considers to have been nine bishops antedating this Alexander. In the beginning of the fourth century, a young girl, Saint Salsa, was martyred by the pagans; later a basilica was erected to her memory. Under Julian the Apostate the inhabitants distinguished themselves by their adherence to Christianity, and this in spite of the violent opposition of two Donatist bishops (Optatus, "De Schismate Donatistarum", II, 18–19). Likewise in 371 or 372, when the Moorish king, Firmus, with the support of the Donatists, tried, but in vain, to take possession of the city. Mention is due to the anonymous author of "The Passion of Saint Salsa" and "The Passion of Saint Fabius of Cartenna" (Anal. bolland., IX, 123–134), who was born at Tipasa and who lived in the beginning of the fifth century.

In 429 the Vandals took possession of the city and the province; ten years later these were restored to the Emperor Valentinian, but came back again into the possession of the Vandals in 455. Bishop Reparatus was exiled in 484, and the secretary of the Arian patriarch was chosen to replace him, a choice which brought about the voluntary exile into Spain of the greater part of the inhabitants; those who remained, having refused to embrace Arianism, had their right hand and tongue cut off, but, nevertheless, continued to talk as before, according to the testimony of Victor de Vita and other contemporaries ("Historia persecutionis Africanæ provinciæ", III, vi, 29–30; Acta SS., October, XI, 847; "Mélanges d'archéologie et d'histoire de l'Ecole française de Rome", XIV, 319). Henceforth Tipasa is not mentioned in history. Today it is a village, called Tipaza by the French, Tefassed by the natives, situated about 44 miles east of Algiers; it numbers 2400 inhabitants, of whom 600 are Europeans, and possesses a Catholic parish. There are ruins of several churches and other monuments.

DUCHESNE, *Sainte Salsa* in *Précis historiques* (Paris, 1890); TOULOTTE, *Géographie de l'Afrique chrétienne. Maurétanies* (Montreuil, 1894), 164–171; GSELL, *De Tipasa Maurétania Cæsariensis urbe* (Algiers, 1894); IDEM, *Tipasa* in *Mélanges d'archéologie et d'histoire de l'Ecole française de Rome*, XIV (Paris, 1894), 291–450.

S. VAILHÉ.

Tiraboschi, GIROLAMO, Italian scholar, b. in the region of Bergamo, 1731; d. 3 June, 1794. At an early age he entered the Society of Jesus. After serving as professor of rhetoric and belles-lettres (*eloquenza*) at the Brera in Milan, he was called by Francesco III, Duke of Modena, to take charge of his library (the Biblioteca Estense); this he directed with patient endeavour and skill, enriching it with many additions of books and manuscripts and providing it with catalogues. His chief work is the monumental "Storia della letteratura italiana", an exhaustive compilation of the materials within his reach. Actuated by the patriotic desire to defend his country's glory in the cultural arts against the attacks of foreign critics, he makes his history extend from Etruscan times down to 1700, and concerns himself with all matters of interest in belles-lettres, philosophy, history, the fine arts, medicine, jurisprudence, etc., accompanying the statement of his views with an abundance of precious documents. Written in a clear and attractive style, the "Storia" appeared in its first edition between 1772 and 1782. With augmentations and connexions, it was published a second time at Modena, between 1787 and 1794. His minor writings include: "Biblioteca Modenese", an account of writers born in Modena; "Memorie storiche modenesi"; "Vita di Fulvio Testi"; and many other historical and critical essays and articles.

Besides the editions of the *Storia* mentioned above, see the reprints of Florence (1805–13), Milan (in the Classici, 1822–26), and Venice (1823–25).

J. D. M. FORD.

Tiraspol (or CHERSONESE), DIOCESE OF (TIRASPOLENSIS; CHERSONENSIS), in Southern Russia, suffragan of Mohilev, covers the governments of Saratov, Samara, Kherson, Ekaterinoslav, Taurida, and Bessarabia. It is one of the largest dioceses in the world, and has an area of 462,504 square miles. There are in the diocese 350,000 Latin Christians, chiefly the descendants of German colonists, in 100 parishes, about 40,000 Armenian Catholics in 50 parishes, and over 300 Chaldean Catholics for whom there is one parish. The priests number about 210, 60 being Armenians. The bishop lives at Saratov, the capital of the government of the same name. The ecclesiastical institutions are, besides the cathedral chapter, the seminary for priests at Saratov, which has a rector, an inspector, a spiritual director, and five professors; there is also a seminary for boys at the same place, with three professors. Religious orders are not permitted. For some years the Armenian Catholics have had an Apostolic administrator of their own (Sarkis Ter Abrahamian) to whom all Armenian Catholics in the whole of Russia are subject. In important decisions he is dependent on the Bishop of Tiraspol.

During the second half of the eighteenth century large numbers of German colonists went to Russia at the urgent request of the Empress Catherine II. These emigrants were chiefly from Bavaria, Würtemberg, Saxony, Alsace-Lorraine, the Tyrol, and Switzerland; they settled in the fruitful but uninhabited lands in the southern part of Russia. The colonies founded by them have retained their German names, as Mannheim, Munich, etc., as well as the German language and character. Among the half-million German settlers there were about 180,000 Catholics, who settled in villages of their own, apart from the members of other confessions. These Catholic villages were generally in the basin of the Volga and of the Caspian Sea. The Catholics were cared for spiritually at first by a few priests who had emigrated with them, but these pastors soon succumbed to privations and the unaccustomed climate. After this the Russian Government sent Catholic priests from the provinces on the Baltic. Alexander I transferred the pastoral care of the Catholic colonies to the Jesuits, who came among them in 1803. Unfortunately, the expulsion of the Jesuits from Russia in 1820 put an end to their fruitful labours. The Jesuits were replaced by priests from various Polish monasteries, chiefly Dominicans, Carmelites, Trinitarians, and Vincentians, many of them old, feeble men, and unacquainted with the German language. The difference in tongues, the racial antipathy between priests and settlers, and the great distance from the residence of the bishop (St. Petersburg) enormously increased the difficulties of spiritual administration. Thus religious conditions grew gradually more and more intolerable. Negotiations between Rome and St. Petersburg led finally, in 1847, to a concordat, by which, in addition to several other dioceses, a German diocese was established for the colonists of Southern Russia, to be suffragan to Mohilev.

Saratov on the right bank of the Volga was settled upon as the see of the bishop, but the diocese received its name from the small town of Tiraspol, which in the fourteenth century had been the capital of the Diocese of Kherson. Besides its vast extent, the new diocese was also singular on account of the varying nationalities of its inhabitants, who included German, French, and Italian colonists, besides Russians, Poles, Armenians, Kirghiz, Circassians, Ossetes, Daghestanians, and other peoples. The Government promised to build a cathedral, an episcopal residence, a building for the episcopal curia, and a seminary, and to provide for the endowment of the cathedral chapter. In 1850 the first bishop, the German Dominican Ferdinand Helanus Kahn, was installed. The auxiliary bishop was a Pole. The promises of the Government were not fulfilled. On account of age and ill-health the bishop was unable to correct the existing grievances, nor was he sufficiently energetic to make the Government fulfil its obligations. In 1857 a seminary was opened, it is true, but in rented and inadequate quarters; the number of German teachers was also insufficient. After Bishop Kahn's death (1864) the see remained vacant for eight years, all communication between Russia and the Holy See being at that time suspended. It was not until 1872 that the rector of the seminary, Franz Xaver Zottmann, was appointed bishop (b. at Ornbau in the Bavarian Diocese of Eichstätt in 1826). In 1864 he had visited Eichstätt and there secured some professors for the seminary.

Bishop Zottmann laboured by speech, writing, and example, and by extraordinary activity in all directions, for the spiritual, moral, and material improvement of his diocese. He collected the money necessary to build a suitable cathedral, obtained a building for the seminaries, and spared no sacrifice to train a capable body of German parish priests. Without abandoning the rights of the Church, he kept on good terms with the Government, and thus could do much that was forbidden to the Polish bishops. He could issue pastoral letters in the diocese, undertake journeys for making confirmations and for visitation, arrange collections of money, and even go to Rome, where, in 1882, he was the first Russian Catholic bishop to pay homage to the pope. On account of illness he resigned in 1888, and died in his native city on 12 December, 1901. He had made his diocese one of the best organized in Russia. His work was worthily carried on, after his resignation, by Anton Zerr, who came from a German colony near Odessa, and had been educated at the Tiraspol seminary. Zerr resigned in 1902 on account of ill-health, and was succeeded by Eduard von der Ropp. Scarcely two years had elapsed before von der Ropp was transferred to the See of Vilna. He was followed by the present bishop, Joseph Kessler, b. at Louis, a village of German colonists in the Government of Samara, in 1862; consecrated 28 October, 1904.

KELLER, *Die deutschen Kolonien in Südrussland* (Odessa, 1905); ZOTTMANN, *Franz X. von Zottmann, Bishof der Diözese Tiraspol* (Munich, 1904); *Katholische Missionen* (1905–06), 125 sq.; *Deutscher Volkskalender für Stadt und Land auf das Jahr 1911* (Odessa, 1911), 177–90.

JOSEPH LINS.

Tirso de Molina. See TELLEZ, GABRIEL.

Tisio da Garofalo, BENVENUTO, an Italian painter of the Ferrarese school; b. in 1481 at Garofalo, whence, as was the custom among artists, he took his name; d. at Ferrara, 6 (or 16) September, 1559. With Mazzolino (1481–1530) and Dosso Dossi (1479–1541), Garofalo makes up the modest triumvirate of the Ferrarese school in the sixteenth century. At an earlier date the school could boast of such men as Cosimo Tura, Francesco Cossa, and Ercole Roberti, and at one time in the sixteenth century was perhaps the foremost school of poetry and painting in Italy. In the wonderful frescoes of the Schifanoja Palace (1470), depicting the life of Prince Borso d'Este, it created an æstheticism all its own, half allegory and half realism, portraying the world of the day in heroic fashion with all the pomp and circumstance of festal parade, and a magnificent display like that described in the "Trionfi" of Petrarch. These frescoes are not only the most precious document we possess of the courtier life and the worldly ideal of the fifteenth century, but they mark in Italy the beginning of what is known as "genre painting", that is, sketches from real life, but characterized by a good taste, a dignity, and a decorative sense so sadly lacking in similar work of the

Dutch school later. This new style forms the artistic glory of the House of Este, which had also the honour of pensioning Ariosto. Its spirit can be still recognized in the famous paintings (now in the Louvre) executed in 1505 for the Duchess Isabella by Mantegna, Perugino, and Lorenzo Costa. It survives in the works of Dosso Dossi—in the charming Judith of the Modena gallery, and in the incomparable Circe of the Casino Borghese.

Garofalo's real vocation lay in such work. His peculiar talent consisted in feeling and giving naïve expression to the joy of life, the charm of the world around him, the beauty of elegant and rural customs, and all that is now called "idyllic", but as it appeared to Italian courtiers of the Renaissance period. His youthful works—the Boar Hunt in the Palazzo Sciarra, the Knight's Procession in the Palazzo Colonna at Rome—gave promise of a Latin Kuyp, less commonplace, more romantic, more artistic, and more refined than the Dutch artist. This was the result of his early study under Panetti and Costa, and of his companionship with his fellow pupil Dossi. In 1495 he had lessons at Cremona from Baccaccino, who initiated him into the secrets of Venetian colouring. But a few years later, when entering on early manhood, he fell unfortunately under an influence quite alien to his own genius. It was at Rome, where he spent three years (1509–1512), that he succumbed to the charm of the new idea. Raphael was painting the "Camera" or hall of the Segnatura, and that of the Heliodorus; Michelangelo was decorating the ceiling of the Sistine Chapel. Garofalo was overcome by these masterpieces; he was unable to refrain from the contemplation of a higher beauty than that which he himself had expressed.

From this moment disappears the charming artist, the delicate painter of contemporary life, into which Garofalo was developing. The majesty of the Roman works imposed on him an ideal beyond his power to realize. The Ferrarese Garofalo might have been a master—of the second class of creative artists, indeed, but of true originality; after his visit to Rome, he was but a "Raphael in miniature". It is not easy to criticise harshly works which are always sincere and whose greatest defect arises from the conscientious pursuit of an ideal. All Garofalo's works bear traces of this extreme conscientiousness of execution—a quality that became ever rarer in the school of Raphael. As a moral force Garofalo has no equal in the group that surrounded the master; in this respect he is vastly superior to such a painter as Giulio Romano. Even his least successful works retain, amid their somewhat frigid and commonplace purity, that transparency, glow, and harmony which are the marks of all Venetian colouring. But though the eye is charmed, all illusion as to the artistic quality of the work soon disappears. The figures have no life, the expression is uncertain, ideal heads betray a lack of intellect. The larger the figure the more emphatic are its defects. No elegance of design or skill in execution can hide the fact that Garofalo's art consists in a clever handling of pure abstractions.

Nevertheless, despite his many ambitious but insignificant (though never vulgar) works, the natural instinct of the Ferrarese school had not quite forsaken him. It asserted itself amid all his idealistic straining, and led him to create a style of "tableaux de piété", little pious scenes as helps to private devotion, to be set up in bed-rooms and oratories. We have here the Bible interpreted in a familiar mode, reduced to the proportions of a "genre" picture and making a popular appeal. The vast number of these little paintings in the Borghese, Doria, and Capitol galleries at Rome is a sufficient indication of their vogue. This was the style so successfully developed by Elsheimer and Rembrandt in the seventeenth century. But, even in this new departure, the false ideal with which Garofalo was smitten at Rome continued to stifle his native genius.

Ever more and more he condemned himself to be but the pale reflection of Raphael. One can follow step by step the progress of his self-imposed decadence. The "Virgin in the Clouds with four Saints" (1518) in the Academy of Fine Arts at Venice is an excellent work; the "Pietà" (1527) in the Brera Gallery at Milan reveals an increasing frigidity of treatment. If one Madonna (1532) in the Modena Gallery is a charming picture, another of slightly later date no longer merits this eulogy. The large "Triumph of Religion" in the Ateneo at Ferrara is a purely "bookish" work, whose ensemble is null and whose stray pleasing episodes are hard to discover. Later even his sense of colour begins to fail; year by year it grows colder and finally deserts him. Henceforth he can produce only such melancholy monochromes as the "Kiss of Judas" in the Church of San Francisco at Ferrara.

Such was the gradual process of distortion under a foreign influence of this charming genius, adapted by nature to feel and proclaim the poetry and homely realities of life, but rendered sterile by an unnatural endeavour to give expression to an ideal which was not its own. In the pursuit of this ideal, we see Garofalo lose his native qualities one by one, his exquisite sensitiveness as painter and colourist being the last to forsake him. From 1550 till his death Garofalo was blind. His history is one of the most eloquent examples of a mistaken vocation. With him the Ferrarese school loses all its originality, and abdicates the place it should have filled in the history of art. Venice soon occupies the vacancy; she is destined to translate to canvas those formulæ for "painting from life", which Ferrara had dimly foreseen; Giorgione, Titian, Palma, Bonifazio are to reap the laurels which Garofalo refused, and to deprive him of the honour of inaugurating a style so fruitful in the subsequent history of painting.

BARUFFALDI, *Vite dei pittori Ferraresi* (Ferrara, 1844); CITTADELLA, *Notizie relative a Ferrara* (Ferrara, 1864); LADERCHI, *Pittura Ferrarese* (Ferrara, 1856); *Documents inédits d'après Campori* in Crowe et Cavalcaselle (German ed.), V, xxi; LERMOLIEFF, *Die Werke italienischer Meister in den Galereien von München, Dresden und Berlin* (Leipzig, 1880); WOERMANN AND WOLTMANN, *Geschichte der Malerei* (Leipzig, 1882), XI; BERENson, *The North Italian Painters of the Renaissance* (New York, 1907).

Louis Gillet.

Tissot, James (Joseph-Jacques), French draughtsman and painter, b. at Nantes, 15 Oct., 1836; d. at Buillon, Department of Doubs, 3 Aug., 1902. He studied at Paris at the Academy of Fine Arts and in the ateliers of Ingres and Flandrin. During this period of his career he became well acquainted with the darker side of the moral and political life of the city. The first paintings that he exhibited at the salon attracted great attention, especially the one picturing the meeting of Faust and Gretchen, now in the Luxemburg Museum. When the Commune came into power Tissot fled to England for fear of coming into conflict with the Government on account of the political intrigues of his brother. In England he gained a reputation as a portrait and genre painter. Tissot, however, was more of an illustrator than a painter, as is shown in the brilliant series of watercolours, "La femme à Paris", in which in careful, correct work done with much dash he lashed the follies of modern Parisian life. Later he issued a similar series of aquarelles on high life in London. The picture of the former of these series entitled "La femme qui chante dans l'église" obliged him to go repeatedly to church during the service, and this suggested to him the conception of the picture, "Christ Appears to Console two Unfortunates in a Ruin". With this last-mentioned work a new epoch began in the life of the painter and, in the course of time, of the man. The figure of Christ had so attracted him that he was never afterwards able to put it out of his mind. He went to Palestine where he spent a year in the most careful geographical and ethnographical studies. After this he spent ten years in preparing the large number of aquarelles that compose his "Life of Christ". The absolutely modern conception of this work shows a complete break with the past. The work was entitled "La vie de notre Seigneur Jésus-Christ, 865 compositions d'après les quatres évangiles, avec des notes et des dessins explicativs, par James Tissot" (Tours, 1896). The price was high, 5000 francs for the edition on Japanese paper, and 1500 francs for that on vellum. A cheaper popular edition in English was issued later. Tissot also designed a series of illustrations for the Old Testament, which, however, are not as fine as the earlier ones. The aquarelles on the New Testament have been called "a revolution in religious art".

Beda Kleinschmidt.

Tithes (Anglo-Saxon, *teotha*, a tenth), generally defined as "the tenth part of the increase arising from the profits of land and stock, allotted to the clergy for their support or devoted to religious or charitable uses". A more radical definition is "the tenth part of all fruits and profits justly acquired, owed to God in recognition of his supreme dominion over man, and to be paid to the ministers of the church". The custom of giving tithes reaches back into unknown antiquity. It is mentioned in Gen., xiv, without anything to indicate that it was something newly instituted. Just as Abraham is there represented as offering tithes of the spoils of the enemy to the royal priest, Melchisedech, so in Gen., xxviii, Jacob is recorded as giving a tithe of all his possessions to the Lord. Under the Mosaic Law the payment of tithes was made obligatory. The Hebrews are commanded to offer to God the tenth part of the produce of the fields, of the fruits of the trees, and of the firstborn of oxen and of sheep (Lev., xxvii, 30; Deut., xiv, 22). In Deuteronomy there is mention not only of an annual tithe, but also of a full tithe to be paid once every three years. While it was to God Himself that the tithes had to be paid, yet we read (Num., xviii, 21) that He transfers them to His sacred ministers: "I have given to the sons of Levi all the tithes of Israel for a possession, for the ministry wherewith they serve me in the tabernacle of the covenant." In paying the tithe, the Hebrews divided the annual harvest into ten parts, one of which was given to the Levites after the firstfruits had been subtracted. This was partitioned by them among the priests. The remainder of the harvest was then divided into ten new parts, and a second tithe was carried by the head of the household to the sanctuary to serve as a sacred feast for his family and the Levites.

If the journey to the temple was unusually long, money could be substituted for the offering in kind. At the triennial tithe, a third decimation was made and a tenth part was consumed at home by the householder with his family, the Levites, strangers, and the poor. This triennial year was called the year of tithes (Deut., xxvi, 12). As the tithes were the main support of the priests, it was later ordained that the offerings should be stored in the temple (II Par., xxxi, 11). It is to be noted that the custom of paying sacred tithes was not peculiar to the Israelites, but common to all ancient peoples. In Lydia a tithe of cattle was offered to the gods; the Arabians paid a tithe of incense to the god Sabis; and the Carthaginians brought tithes to Melkarth, the god of Tyre. The explanation of why the tenth part should have been chosen among so many different peoples is said to be (apart from a common primitive revelation) that mystical signification of the number ten, viz., that it signifies totality, for it contains all the numbers that make up the numerical system, and indeed all imaginable series of numbers, and so it represents all kinds of property, which is a gift of God. All species of property were consequently reckoned in decades, and by consecrating one of these parts to God, the proprietor recognized the Source of his goods. However, the payment of tithes was also a civil custom. They were payable to the Hebrew kings and to the rulers of Babylon, and they are mentioned among the Persians, Greeks, Romans, and later the Mohammedans.

In the Christian Church, as those who serve the altar should live by the altar (I Cor., ix, 13), provision of some kind had necessarily to be made for the sacred ministers. In the beginning this was supplied by the spontaneous offerings of the faithful. In the course of time, however, as the Church expanded and various institutions arose, it became necessary to make laws which would insure the proper and permanent support of the clergy. The payment of tithes was adopted from the Old Law, and early writers speak of it as a divine ordinance and an obligation of conscience. The earliest positive legislation on the subject seems to be contained in the letter of the bishops assembled at Tours in 567 and the canons of the Council of Macon in 585. In course of time, we find the payment of tithes made obligatory by ecclesiastical enactments in all the countries of christendom. The Church looked on this payment as "of divine law, since tithes were instituted not by man but by the Lord Himself" (C. 14, X de decim. III, 30). As regards the civil power, the Christian Roman emperors granted the right to churches of retaining a portion of the produce of certain lands, but the earliest instance of the enforcement of the payment of ecclesiastical tithes by civil law is to be found in the capitularies of Charlemagne, at the end of the eighth century. English law very early recognized the tithe, as in the reigns of Athelstan, Edgar, and Canute before the Norman Conquest. In English statute law proper, however, the first mention of tithes is to be found in the Statute of Westminster of 1285. Tithes are of three kinds: predial, or that derived from the annual crops; mixed, or what arises from things nourished by the land, as cattle, milk, cheese, wool; and personal, or the result of industry or occupation. Predial tithes were generally called great tithes, and mixed and personal tithes, small tithes. Natural substances having no annual increase are not tithable, nor are wild animals. When property is inherited or donated, it is not subject to the law of tithes, but its natural increase is. There are many exempted from the paying of tithes: spiritual corporations, the owners of uncultivated lands, those who have acquired lawful prescription, or have obtained a legal renunciation, or received a privilege from the pope.

At first, the tithe was payable to the bishop, but later the right passed by common law to parish priests. Abuses soon crept in. The right to receive tithes was granted to princes and nobles, even hereditarily, by ecclesiastics in return for protection or eminent services, and this species of impropriation became so intolerable that the Third Council of the Lateran (1179) decreed that no alienation of tithes to laymen was permissible without the consent of the pope. In the time of Gregory VIII, a so-called Saladin tithe was instituted, which was payable by all who did not take part personally in the crusade to recover the Holy Land. At the present time, in most countries where some species of tithes still exist, as in England (for the Established Church), in Austria, and Germany, the payment has been changed into a rent-charge. In English-speaking countries generally, as far as Catholics are concerned, the clergy receive no tithes. As a consequence, other means have had to be adopted to support the clergy and maintain the ecclesiastical institutions (see CHURCH MAINTENANCE), and to substitute other equivalent payments in lieu of tithes. Soglia (Institut. Canon., II, 12) says: "The law of tithes can never be abrogated by prescription or custom, if the ministers of the Church have no suitable and sufficient provision from other sources; because then the natural and divine law, which can neither be abrogated nor antiquated, commands that the tithe be paid." In some parts of Canada, the tithe is still recognized by civil law, and the Fourth Council of Quebec (1868) declared that its payment is binding in conscience on the faithful.

FERRARIS, *Bibliotheca canonica*, III (Rome, 1886), s. v., *Decima*; ADDIS AND ARNOLD, *The Catholic Dictionary* (6th ed., New York, 1889), s. v.; SELDEN, *History of Tithes* (London, 1618); SPELMAN, *Of Tythes* (London, 1723).

WILLIAM H. W. FANNING.

Titian (TIZIANO VECELLI, called TITIAN), the greatest of Venetian painters, b. at Pieve di Cadore (Friuli); d. at Venice, 27 Aug., 1577. It has always been believed that at the time of his death he was a centenarian, and he himself wrote to Philip II in 1571 that he was more than ninety-five, which would make 1477 the year of his birth. But there are good reasons for believing that he made himself out to be older than he was and that he was born about 1487, that is ten years later than the generally accepted date. Vasari makes him seventy-seven in 1566. Titian would therefore have died when he was between 85 and 90 years old, which would render more credible the marvellous freshness of his later works (cf. Herbert Cook, in the "Nineteenth Century", Jan., 1902, and "Repertorium für Kunstwissenschaft", XXV). The vigorous health which the artist inherited from his mountain race together with a habit of order, balance, and labour determined the predominant characteristic of his art. No painter better expressed, if not the highest beauty, at least that kind of beauty which springs from the deep joy of life, adorning it with an impression of calm, harmony, and serenity. The first Venetian School had already proved itself capable of expressing these sentiments. Titian was to give them a still freer and fuller expression with an external charm and a magic of colouring which has sometimes raised the question whether he is not the greatest and most complete of all painters.

At the age of ten Titian was brought to Venice and placed by his brother with the celebrated mosaicist, Sebastian Zuccato, but at the end of four or five years he entered the studio of the aged painter Giovanni Bellini, at that time the most noted artist in the city. There he found a group of young men about his own age, among them Giovanni Palma da Serinalta, Lorenzo Lotto, and Sebastiano Luciani, who were all to become renowned. The foremost of these innovators and their master was Giorgio da Castelfranco, nicknamed Giorgione. With him Titian formed a friendship of which all his early works bore traces, so much so that at this period it is difficult to distinguish the young master of Cadore from him of Castelfranco. The earliest known work of Titian, the little "Ecce Homo" of the Scuola di San Rocco, was long regarded as the work of Giorgione. And the same confusion or uncertainty is connected with more than one of the "Sacred Conversations", in which several holy persons (generally three or four) appear at half length in sweet and familiar association with the Blessed Virgin. The two young masters were likewise recognized as the two leaders of their new school of *Arte moderna*, that is of painting made more flexible, freed from symmetry and the remnants of hieratic conventions still to be found in the works of Giovanni Bellini. Together they executed in 1508 the frescoes of the Fondaco dei Tedeschi, which have unfortunately disappeared and which were to Venice what the cartoons of Leonardo and Michelangelo at the Signiory were to the Florentine School. That of Giorgione and Titian is known to us in part through the engraving of Fontana. An idea of Titian's talent in fresco may be gained from those he painted, in 1511, at Padua in the Carmelite church and in the Scuola del Santo, some of which have been preserved, among them the "Meeting at the Golden Gate", and three scenes from the life of St. Anthony of Padua, the "Murder of a Young Woman by Her Husband", "A Child Testifying to Its Mother's Innocence", and "The Saint Healing the Young Man with a Broken Limb." The arrangement and feeling are not the chief merits of these last-named works, but the beauty of the types, the grace of the female figures, the charm of the landscapes, and particularly the enchantment of the colouring must forever rank these frescoes with the most valuable works of Titian's youth.

Among the religious paintings of this period may be mentioned that of Antwerp, "The Doge Pesaro presented to St. Peter by Alexander VI" (1508), and the beautiful "St. Mark surrounded by Sts. Cosmas and Damian, Sebastian and Rocco" (Venice, S. Maria della Salute, c. 1511). Already the young master was in possession of his type of Virgins with powerful shoulders and somewhat rounded countenances, and in particular he had elaborated an extremely refined type of Christ, the most beautiful example of which is the wonderful Christ of "The Tribute Money", at Dresden, a face whose delicacy, spirituality, and moral charm have never been surpassed by any other School. From the same period seems to date the "Triumph of Faith", a subject borrowed from Savonarola's famous treatise, "The Triumph of the Cross", and treated with a magnificent fire in the spirit of Mantegna's cartoons and Dürer's prints of the "Triumph of Maximilian" (cf. Male, "L'art réligieux en France à la fin du moyen âge", 1908, 296 sqq.). These prints were executed by Andreani. But what may be called the most enduring works of Titian's youth are the profane and indeterminately allegorical ones, whose unmatched poetry of form and colouring breathe so deep a joy of living that it borders on melancholy. Such for example is the charming picture of the "Three Ages", in the Ellesmere Gallery; such especially is the masterpiece in the Cassino Borghese, "Profane and Sacred Love", whose meaning has never been successfully penetrated (cf. Olga von

Gerstfeldt, "Venus und Violante" in "Monatsheft für Kunstwissenschaft", Oct., 1910), but which none the less remains by the contrast of its two figures, the splendour of the motif, the depth of the landscape, the rhythm and mystery of the composition one of the imperishable elegies of all paintings and which even Giorgione does not equal in his "Concert".

Giorgione died in 1511 and the aged Bellini in 1515, leaving Titian after the production of such masterpieces without a rival in the Venetian School. For sixty years he was to be the absolute and undisputed head, the official master, and as it were the painter laureate of the Republic Serenissime. As early as 1516 he succeeded his old master Bellini as the pensioner of the Senate. Fifteen years later began the relations with Charles V, Francis I, Alfonso and Isabella d'Este, the Houses of Ferrara and Urbino, which made him the first of the princely painters of the Renaissance and the one whose position was most international and most glorious of all. However he rarely left Venice. Married to a tenderly loved wife, solidly established in his habits of work, and like all Venetians strongly attached to the life of Venice, he regarded nothing as being worth a separation from his home, his studio, or his country. Except for a visit to Rome in 1545, and two or three visits to Augsburg between 1548 and 1551 to meet the emperor, he never left Venice save to return to Cadore. Even the liveliest curiosity regarding his art, the ardent desire to learn, which to the end of his life impelled him to acquire all that he could concerning art, as he had already devoured all the substance of Bellini and Giorgione, could not induce him to leave his work and his easel. Venice was in this respect a most favourable centre, a meeting-place for artists from all parts of the world, from North and South, Germany and Florence. Leonardo da Vinci passed through the city in 1500, Dürer stayed there in 1506, Fra Bartolommeo in 1508, Michelangelo in 1529; and the commerce of the active city, especially in books and prints, the permanent society of artists and men of letters, could not leave Titian ignorant of what was being done in the world. No invention of art was unfamiliar to him, and all his life he displayed the same eagerness to enrich his style with new elements, the same consuming anxiety for perfection.

During this period (1516–30) which may be called the period of his bloom and maturity, the artist freed himself from the traditions of his youth, undertook a class of more complex subjects and for the first time attempted the monumental style. His most noteworthy work in this style, the "Assumption" of the Church of the Frari (1518), now in the Academy of Venice, is not, despite its celebrity, a very decided work. In more than one sense it is one of his coldest productions. The solution of the problem attempted —that of uniting in the same composition two or three scenes superimposed on different levels, earth and heaven, the temporal and the infinite—was continued in a series of works such as the retable of San Domenico at Ancona (1520), the retable of Brescia (1522), the retable of San Niccolo (1523, at the Vatican), each time attaining to a higher and more perfect conception, finally reaching an unsurpassable formula in the Pesaro retable, (1526), in the Church of the Frari at Venice. This perhaps is his most perfect and most studied work, whose patiently developed plan is set forth with supreme display of order and freedom, of originality and style. Here Titian gave a new conception of the traditional groups of donors and holy persons moving in aerial space, the plans and different degrees set in an architectural framework. To this period belongs a still more extraordinary work, "The Death of St. Peter of Verona" (1530), formerly in the Dominican Church of S. Zanipolo, and destroyed by an Austrian shell in 1867. There now exist only copies of this sublime picture (there is an excellent one at Paris in the Ecole des Beaux Arts). The association of the landscape with a scene of murder—a rapidly brutal scene of slaying, a cry rising above the old oak-trees, a Dominican escaping the ambush, and over all the shudder and stir of the dark branches—this is all, but never perhaps has tragedy more swift, startling, and pathetic been depicted even by Tintoretto or Delacroix.

PORTRAIT OF TITIAN BY HIMSELF
Prado Gallery, Madrid

The artist continued simultaneously his series of small Madonnas which he treated more and more amid beautiful landscapes in the manner of genre pictures or poetic pastorals, the "Virgin with the Rabbit" in the Louvre being the finished type of these pictures. Another marvellous work of the same period, also in the Louvre, is the "Entombment", surpassing all that has been done on the same subject. This was likewise the period of the exquisite mythological scenes, such as the famous "Bacchanals" of Madrid, and the "Bacchus and Ariadne" of London, perhaps the most brilliant productions of the neopagan culture or "Alexandrianism" of the Renaissance, many times imitated but never surpassed even by Rubens himself. Finally this was the period of perfect mastery when the artist composed the half-length figures and busts of young women, such as "Flora" of the Uffizi, or "The Young Woman at Her Toilet" in the Louvre (also called, without reason, "Laura de Dianti" or "The Mistress of Titian"), and which will always remain the ideal image of harmonious beauty and the grace of life at one of the periods which best knew the happiness of existence.

During the subsequent period (1530–50), as was foreshadowed by his "Martyrdom of St. Peter", Titian devoted himself more and more to the dramatic style. From this time date his historical scenes, of which unhappily it is difficult to judge, the most characteristic having been much injured or destroyed; thus the "Battle of Cadore", the artist's greatest effort to master movement and to express even tumult, his most violent attempt to go out of himself and achieve the heroic, wherein he rivals the "War of Pisa", "The Battle of Anghiari", and the "Battle of Constantine", perished in 1577, the year of Titian's death, in the fire which destroyed all the old pictures adorning the Doge's Palace. There is extant only a poor, incomplete copy at the Uffizi, and a mediocre engraving by Fontana. In like manner the "Speech of the Marquis del Vasto" (Madrid, 1541) was partly destroyed by fire. But this portion of the master's work is adequately represented by the "Presentation of the Blessed Virgin" (Venice, 1539), one of his most popular canvases, and by the great "Ecce Homo" (Vienna, 1541), one of the most pathetic and life-like of masterpieces. The School of Bologna and Rubens (Miracles of St. Benedict, St. Francis, etc.) many times borrowed the distinguished and magisterial *mise-en-scène*, the grand and stirring effect, and these horses, soldiers, lictors, these powerful stirrings of crowds at the foot of a stairway, while over all are the light of torches and the flapping of banners against the sky, have been often repeated. Less successful were the pendentives of the cupola at Sta. Maria della Salute ("Death of Abel", "Sacrifice of Abraham", "David and Goliath"). These violent scenes viewed in perspective from below—like the famous pendentives of the Sistine Chapel—were by their very nature in unfavourable situations. They were nevertheless much admired and imitated, Rubens among others applying this system to his forty ceilings (the sketches only remain) of the Jesuit church at Antwerp.

At this time also, the time of his visit to Rome, the artist began his series of reclining Venuses (the

flesh-tints with the gold of the hair, the delicate tone of the linen, countless other beauties of detail merged in the harmony of the whole, nothing obtrudes itself independently." It is impossible to enumerate, even briefly, Titian's splendid gallery of portraits; princes or doges, cardinals or monks, artists or writers, no other painter was so successful in extracting from each physiognomy so many traits at once characteristic and beautiful. Holbein was also individual, but how much less the artist; Van Dyck is perhaps more graceful but how much more monotonous and affected. Among portrait-painters Titian is comparable only to the greatest, a Rembrandt or a Velásquez, with the interior life of the former, and the clearness, certainty, and obviousness of the latter. The last-named qualities are sufficiently manifested in the "Paul III" of Naples, or the sketch of the same pope and his two nephews, the "Aretino" of the Pitti Palace, the "Eleanora of Portugal" (Madrid), and the series of Charles Fifths of the same museum, the "Charles

PRESENTATION OF THE BLESSED VIRGIN, TITIAN, THE ACADEMY, ROME

"Venus" of the Uffizi, "Venus and Love" at the same museum, "Venus and the Organ-Player," Madrid), in which must be recognized the effect or the direct reflection of the impression produced on the master by contact with ancient sculpture. Giorgione had already dealt with the subject in the splendid Dresden picture, but here a purple drapery substituted for its background of verdure was sufficient to change by its harmonious colouring the whole meaning of the scene. Furthermore Titian had from the beginning of his career shown himself to be an incomparable portrait-painter. Portraits like that of Alfonso d'Este (Madrid), of the "Unknown Young Man" (Munich), and the "Man with a Glove" (Louvre) would suffice to place their author in the foremost rank of painters. But a canvas like the "La Bella" (Eleanora de Gonzaga, Duchess of Urbino, at the Pitti Palace) presents something rarer still. The harmony, blue, lilac, white, and gold, is from the standpoint of colour in perfect accord with the lovely and smiling character of the countenance. In charm and magic the execution surpasses even the "Flora" of the Uffizi. "It is such portraits", says Burckhart, "and others of the same order, such as the 'Caterina Cornaro' of the Uffizi, which sometimes mislead modern painting especially the French School." "Why," he continues, "are these eternal forms, while the moderns rarely rise above beautiful sketches or studies? It is because the motif and the moment, the light, the colour, and the form, all were born and grew at the same time in Titian's soul, and whatever is created in such wise is eternal. The voluptuous pose, the harmony of the

V with a Greyhound" (1533), and especially the "Charles V at Mühlenberg" (1548), an equestrian picture which as a symphony of purples is perhaps the *ne plus ultra* of the art of painting.

During the last twenty-five years of his life (1550-76) the artist, more and more absorbed in his work as a portrait-painter and also more self-critical, unable to be satisfied and insatiable of perfection, finished only a few great works. Some of his pictures he kept for ten years in his studio, never wearying of returning to them and retouching them, constantly adding new expressions at once more refined, concise, and subtle. His palette lost the incomparable freshness which characterized the great work of his maturity; the tone became softened, the matter itself grew heavier and more dense, there is less variation, resplendency, and brilliance, but in the gamut selected there were never more powerful notes nor bolder execution. The artist subjects to his ideas and methods the simplification which summed up the experiences of a long life. For each of the problems which he successively undertook he furnished a new and more perfect formula. He never again equalled the emotion and tragedy of the "Crowning with Thorns" (Louvre), in the expression of the mysterious and the divine he never equalled the poetry of the "Pilgrims of Emmaus", while in superb and heroic brilliancy he never again executed anything more grand than "The Doge Grimani adoring Faith" (Venice, Doge's Palace), or the "Trinity", of Madrid. On the other hand from the standpoint of flesh tints, his most moving pictures are those of his old age, the "Danæ" of Naples and of Madrid, the

TITIAN

A KNIGHT OF MALTA, THE PRADO GALLERY
CHARLES V, THE PRADO GALLERY

THE ASSUMPTION, THE ACADEMY, VENICE
CHRIST AND THE PIECE OF SILVER, DRESDEN

"Antiope" of the Louvre, the "Rape of Europa" (Boston, Gardner collection), etc. He even attempted problems of chiaroscuro in fantastic night effects ("Martyrdom of St. Laurence", Church of the Jesuits, Venice; "St. Jerome," Louvre). In the domain of the real he always remained equally strong, sure, and master of himself; his portraits of Philip II (Madrid), those of his daughter, Lavinia, and those of himself are numbered among his masterpieces.

So until the end, until that tragic "Pietà" of the Academy of Venice, which was found incompleted in his studio, the aged master strove indefatigably in pursuit of an ever-changing ideal, or rather one which changed when he believed he had given it full expression. Each time a new impression, the discovery of an artist hitherto unknown to him, revealed to him a new aspect of beauty, the great old man unweariedly recommenced his work and endeavoured to incorporate in it the new elements which he had just perceived. This it is which gives to his work as a whole its great significance and to his very countenance, beneath the health and balance of an iron constitution, an air of sadness and distress the like of which is only found in Rembrandt's last portraits. In fact no one ever expended such obstinate effort in the attempt to realize perfection. It is this which gives to certain parts of his work a tense character, an aspect of deliberateness, which occasionally causes an appearance of coldness. But in the end he is always regarded as the exemplar and the greatest of painters. "Titian is one of those who come closest to the spirit of antiquity", writes Delacroix in his "Journal", and in a note for his "Dictionnaire des beaux arts", defining the antique he cites the work of Titian, and indeed there is no other modern work which shares so fully with the marbles of the Parthenon the privilege of eternally enchanting and moving us.

VASARI, *Lives of Celebrated Painters*, etc., tr. FOSTER, ed. Blashfield and Hopkins (New York, 1896); RIDOLFI, *Meraviglie dell'arte*, I (Venice 1648), 135 sqq.; MAËR, *Dell'imitazione pittorica e dell' eccellenza delle opere di Tiziano* (Venice, 1878); NORTHCOTE, *The Life of Titian*, (London, 1830); CROWE AND CAVALCASELLE, *Titian* (London, 1877); LAFENESTRE, *Titien* (in fol., Paris, 1885); BURCKHARDT, *Cicerone*, II (Paris, 1892), 730 sqq.; DELACROIX, *Journal* (Paris, 1893); KNACKFUSS, *Tiziano* (Bielefeld, 1900); GRONAU, *Tizian* (tr. London, 1904); *Tizian des Meister Gemälde in 230 Abbildungen* (Stuttgart, 1904); WYZEWA, *Maîtres italiens d'autrefois* (Paris, 1907). MORELLI, *Italian Painters* (London, 1892); PHILLIPS, *The Earlier and Later Work of Titian in Portfolio* (1897–8).

LOUIS GILLET.

Title of Ordination. See ALIMENTATION.

Titopolis (TITIOPOLIS), titular see, suffragan of Seleucia Trachæa in Isauria. Le Quien (*Oriens christ.*, II, 1023) mentions three of its bishops: Artemius at the Council of Constantinople in 381; Mompræus at the Council of Chalcedon in 451; Domitius at the Trullan Council in 692. The see is mentioned in the sixth century "Notitia episcopatuum" of Antioch (Echos d'Orient, X, 145). About 732 the ecclesiastical Province of Isauria was annexed to the Patriarchate of Constantinople and henceforth Titiopolis figures in the "Notitia episcopatuum" of that Church, as it does also about 900 in that of Leo the Wise (Gelzer, "Ungedruckte . . . Texte der Notitiæ episcopatuum", 557), and about 940 in that of Constantine Porphyrogenitus ("Georgii Cyprii Descriptio orbis romani", ed. Gelzer, 76). The town is mentioned by "Hieroclis Synecdemus", ed. Burckhardt, 37, by George of Cyprus, 42, and by Constantine Porphyrogenitus "De them.", 36, as one of the cities of the Isaurian Decapolis. Its exact site is unknown.

RAMSAY, *Asia Minor* (London, 1890), 370.

S. VAILHÉ.

Titular Bishop. See BISHOP; IN PARTIBUS INFIDELIUM.

Titulus. In pagan times *titulus* signified an inscription on stone, and later the stone which marked the confines of property. Under Trajan it signified at Rome the limits of the jurisdiction of the priests, which is the germ of the meaning it bears in its ecclesiastico-archeological usage. Baronius explains that a cross sculptured on a church was the *titulus* which designated it as belonging to Christ, just as imperial property was indicated by the *titulus fiscalis*. Nothing remains to establish with certainty where the public Christian edifices of Rome before Constantine were situated. The earliest Christians assembled in the halls of private houses, and these oratories were therefore called *ecclesiæ domesticæ*. St. Paul mentions those at Rome and Corinth; in accordance with the most ancient Roman traditions, they were those of Aquilla and Prisca on the Aventine and the *Ecclesia Pudentianæ* on the Viminal. These *ecclesiæ domesticæ* became the *domus ecclesiæ*, and later *domus Dei*, i. e. the *dominicum;* and in this last period they received the name *tituli*, from the name of the founder or proprietor who held the property in custody for the Church. A populous Christian community, like that of Rome, by the end of the third century must have possessed a *domus Dei*, a social centre which served as church, bishop's residence, refectory, dispensary of charity, hospice, tribunal, and seat of the episcopal government, as was the case at Antioch, Carthage, Cirta, and elsewhere. In the fourth century all this was located at the Lateran, in the palace formerly belonging to Fausta, daughter of Maximinianus. The history of the Lateran begins with A. D. 313 and the most recent excavations there have revealed six Roman public and private edifices, but no Christian building earlier than Constantine. According to de Rossi the centre of episcopal administration before the Lateran was a Christian building at San Lorenzo in Damaso, where in the fourth century the archives of the church were kept, and where now the central chancery (*Cancellaria Apostolica*) of the Papal government is situated.

According to the Liber Pontificalis, Pope Fabian about 250 divided the regions of Rome among the deacons, creating ecclesiastical districts. Probably these districts were provided with an edifice which was the centre of administration and served that purpose for several centuries after Constantine, although no traces of such buildings survive. The *diaconiæ* of the seventh century had nothing to do with these diaconal districts. In the fourth century, although the *domus Lateranensis* was the chief Christian edifice of the city, Rome possessed several places of assembly for the Christian community, which Ammianus Marcellinus calls *conventicula christianorum*. In time the unity of the presbyterium was broken and other ecclesiastical groups were created within the city, similar to the present city parishes independent of one another and dependent on a common centre, under the direction of presbyters permanently appointed. To each one a basilica was assigned, *dominicum domus Dei;* the presbyters resided near this edifice, which in the language of archæology is called *titulus*. The most ancient text which alludes to a titulus is the apology of St. Athanasius against the Arians (xx). The most ancient inscription relating to a titulus goes back to A. D. 377. The Liber Pontificalis attributes the foundation of the tituli to different popes of the first half of the fourth century, and this information, which seems genuine, is in part confirmed by inscriptions and by the names given to the churches. The *tituli presbyterales* therefore go back to the peace of the Church; they were not founded all at one time, but followed the progress of the Christian propaganda among the people of Rome. At the close of the fifth century there were twenty-five tituli; the Liber Pontificalis confirms this number and attributes their foundation to Pope Evaristus at the beginning of the second century. The last titulus recorded in the Liber is that of Vestina under Innocent I. The report of the Council of Rome (1 March, 499), contains the list of the names of the presbyters and their tituli. From this and from the report of a council held by Gregory the Great in 595, we know there were twenty-five tituli, which number, with few fluctuations, remained the same until about 1120 when it is given as twenty-eight. Three or four of the Gregorian tituli do not appear in the list of the council of 499, while the list of Pope Symmachus gives five which are not found in the council of 595. This difference is explained by establishing the location and the surroundings of the disputed tituli and identifying the tituli of Pope Symmachus with those of Pope Gregory. The titular churches are all found at a distance from the classic centre of the City, and correspond to an epoch in which paganism preponderated at Rome. From the studies made and from existing monuments it is safe to attribute the foundation of many tituli to the third century and of most of them to the fourth.

After the presbyteral tituli came the *diaconiæ*; these are not found in Roman documents before the seventh century. The Liber Pontificalis mentions them for the first time in the life of Benedict II (684–85). From the beginning the *diaconiæ* were charitable institutions, and in a measure replaced for the Romans the *frumentatio* of Byzantine times and the doles of bread of the best days of the empire. They were established in the centre of the city, with the materials, or on the site of, public edifices in a period when there was no longer a motive for building Christian churches away from the Forum or the Palatine. Under Pope Adrian (772–95) their number was fixed at eighteen. From the beginning of the twelfth century cardinal deacons adopted the names of their *diaconiæ* and the number of eighteen was maintained until the sixteenth century. By the twelfth century cardinal deacons as well as the presbyters had long been dispensed from personal service at the tituli, since which time titulus of itself acquired a meaning analogous to that of the present time.

DUCHESNE, *Les titres presbytéraux* in *Mélanges d'archéologie et d'histoire*, VII (1887); JORDAN-HÜLSEN, *Topografie der Stadt Rom* (Berlin, 1907); GRISAR, *Rom beim Ausgang der antiken Welt* (Freiburg, 1901); MARUCCHI, *Manuale di archeologia cristiana* (2nd edition, Rome, 1908); ARMELLINI, *Lezioni di archeologia* (Rome, 1898); KRAUS in *Realencyklopädie der christlichen Alterthümer* (Freiburg, 1880–1886), s. v.

ALUIGI COSSIO.

Titus, Bishop of Bostra, b. about 362–371. Sozomen (Hist. eccl., III, xiv) names Titus among the great men of the time of Constantius; he also tells (op. cit., V, xv) of a mean trick played upon Titus by Julian the Apostate. It was expected that the re-establishment of paganism would occasion riots in Bostra as it had elsewhere. Julian wrote to Titus that he would hold him and the clergy responsible for any outbreak. Titus replied that though the Christians were equal in number to the pagans they would obey him and keep quiet. Julian then wrote to the Bostrians urging them to expel Titus because he had calumniated them by attributing their quiet conduct not to their own good dispositions but to his influence. According to Socrates (op. cit., III, xxv) Titus was one of the bishops who signed the Synodal Letter, addressed to Jovian by the Council held at Antioch (363), in which the Nicene Creed was accepted, not, however, without a clause "intended somewhat to weaken and semiarianize the expression ὁμοούσιος" (Hefele, "Councils", II, p. 283; ANTIOCH.—*Synods of Antioch*). St. Jerome (Ep. lxx) names Titus among writers whose secular erudition is as marvellous as their knowledge of Scripture; in his "De vir. ill.", cii, he speaks of his "mighty" (*fortes*) books against the Manichæan and *nonnulla alia*. He places his death under Valens. Of the *nonnulla alia* only fragments of exegetical writings have survived. These show that Titus followed the Antiochene School of Scripture exegesis in keeping to the literal as opposed to the allegorical interpretation. The "Contra Manichæos" is the most important work of the kind that has come down to us, and its historic value is very great because of the number of quotations it contains from Manichæan writers. In one passage Titus seems to favour Origen's view that the pains of the damned are not eternal (on this point see especially Ceillier, "Histoire générale des auteurs sacrés et ecclésiastiques", VI p. 54, who seems disposed to acquit him of this error). The work consists of four books of which the fourth and the greater part of the third are only extant in a Syriac translation.

The Greek and Syriac texts of the *Contra Manich.* were published by LAGARDE (Berlin, 1859). Earlier editions of the Greek text suffer from an insertion from a work of Serapion owing to the misplacement of a leaf in the original codex. For *Contra Manich.* and other writings attributed to TITUS see MIGNE and GALLANDI. The genuine exegetical fragments of this commentary were published by SICKENBERGER in *Texte u. Untersuchen*, VI, i (new series). BARDENHEWER-SHAHAN, *Patrology* (St. Louis, 1908), 270–1.

F. J. BACCHUS.

Titus, EPISTLE TO. See TIMOTHY AND TITUS, EPISTLES TO.

Titus, Roman Emperor 79–81, b. 30 Dec., 41; d. 13 Sept., 81; son of the Emperor Vespasian, and from the year 70 Cæsar and coregent; he was highly educated and a brilliant poet and orator in both Latin and Greek. He won military fame in the war in the years 69–70, against the revolted Jews. In April, 70, he appeared before the walls of Jerusalem, and conquered and destroyed the city after a siege of five months. He wished to preserve the Temple, but in the struggle with the Jews who rushed out of it a soldier threw a brand into the building. The siege and taking of the city were accompanied by barbarous cruelties.

ANTIQUE HEAD OF TITUS
Vatican Museum

The next year Titus celebrated his victory by a triumph; to increase the fame of the Flavian dynasty the inscription on the triumphal arch represented the overthrow of the helpless people as an heroic achievement. The historical significance of the destruction of the Jewish state is that the Jews have since then been scattered among foreign nations. As ruler Titus was by no means popular; he shared in the voluptuousness of the Rome of that era, and was responsible for the acts of violence which occurred during the administration of his father. Consequently an evil reign was expected. However, in the short period of his independent authority, Titus agreeably disappointed these anticipations. His noble benevolence was exhibited in the saying that the day was lost in which he had done no one a kindness; he gained the honourable title of "amor et deliciæ generis humani" (the darling and admiration of the human race). During his reign Italy suffered from two severe calamities. On 24 Aug., 79, the celebrated eruption of Vesuvius buried the cities of Pompeii, Herculaneum, and Stabiæ, and some months later a fearful conflagration did great damage at Rome. On both occasions Titus showed a fine humanitarianism. His actions were not free from ostentation and seeking after effect. He died from the effects of his luxurious life.

SCHILLER, *Geschichte der römischen Kaiserzeit*, I (Gotha, 1883),

TIVOLI

1. MEDIEVAL CASTLE.   2. ARCH OF THE TORRETTA.   3. BASILICA OF THE VILLA ADRIANA.   4. TEMPLES OF VESTA AND THE SIBYL.   5. CATHEDRAL OF S. LORENZO AND MEDIEVAL CAMPANILE

518-20; Domaszewski, *Geschichte der römischen Kaiser*, II (Leipzig, 1909), 128-57; Merivale, *History of the Romans under the Empire* (London, 1850-62), lx.   Klemens Löffler.

Tius (Tium), titular see, suffragan of Claudiopolis in Honorias. According to Strabo (542, 545) the town was not remarkable save as the birthplace of Philetærus, founder of the royal dynasty of Pergamus. The coins give Dionysius as the founder; in fact it was the site of a temple of Dionysius and one of Jupiter. Le Quien (Oriens christ., I, 575) mentions among its bishops: Apragmonius at the Council of Ephesus in 431; Andrew in 518; Eugenius in 536; Longinus at the Sixth General Council in 681; Michael at the Seventh General Council in 787; Constantine at the Eighth General Council in 869 and author of an account of the transfer of the relics of St. Euphemia of Chalcedon (Acta SS., Sept., V, 274-83). This see figures in all the "Notitiæ episcopatuum". Novel xxix of Justinian locates the town in Paphlagonia. George Pachymerus (I, 312) mentions Tium among the Byzantine towns which escaped the ravages of the Seljuks in 1269. The modern village of Filias stands on the ruins of the ancient Tium, which included the remains of ramparts and sculptures. The village is in the caza of Hamidye and the vilayet of Castamouni, not far from the mouth of the Filias-Tchaï, the Billæus.

Smith, *Dict. of Gr. and Rom. Geog.*, s. v.; Boutkowski, *Recherches historiques sur la ville de Tium* (Paris, 1864); Müller, ed. Didot, Notes on *Geographi Græci minores*, I, 385; Cuinet, *La Turquie d'Asie*, IV (Paris, 1894), 537.

S. Vailhé.

Tivoli, Diocese of (Tiburtina), in the Province of Rome. The city is situated where the Anio, issuing from the Sabine hills, leaps down from a height of nearly 300 feet and enters the Roman Campagna. The water power of the beautiful falls, which attract many tourists to the city, is utilized in various industries and supplies the electric current that lights Rome. The slopes of the neighbouring hills are covered with olives, vineyards, and gardens; the most important local industry is the manufacture of paper. The great cascade has existed only since 1835, when the Gregorian tunnel through Monte Catillo was completed, to give an outlet to the waters of the Anio sufficient to preserve the city from inundation. The "Grotto of Neptune" and the "Cascatelle" are ancient. There are ruins of two old temples, one of Hercules Saxanus, commonly called "of the Sybil", the other of Tiburtus, both overlooking the great cascade. Near the Roman gate is the "Tempio della Tosse". Among the more important churches are the cathedral, the Gesù, S. Maria Maggiore, and S. Maria degli Olivi, containing interesting fifteenth-century frescoes; also S. Maria di Quintiliolo, built on the ruins of the villa of Quintilius Varus. In the environs are many ruins of ancient villas, the largest being the famous construction of the Emperor Hadrian, which comprised a villa, portico, theatre, gardens, baths, library, etc., and covered 173 acres of ground. Many of the treasures of the Vatican Museum were discovered here. The most notable of the modern villas are the Villa d'Este, erected by Pirro Ligorio for Cardinal Ippolito d'Este (1549), and decorated with frescoes by Zuccaro; at present it belongs to the Archduke Franz Ferdinand of Austria.

According to some of the ancient writers, Tivoli was founded by the Siculi; according to others, by a colony of Argives. It is first mentioned in Roman history in 493, as included in the alliance against the Volscians, but in 361 it sided with the Gauls against Rome; though twice conquered, it shortly afterwards (339) allied itself with Præneste (Palestrina); for some time it was in the Confederation and in the Social War became a *municipium*. It was strongly fortified by Belisarius in the Gothic War, but almost destroyed by Totila in A. D. 340. After the Lombard invasion it was in the power of the Byzantines and formed part of the Patrimony of St. Peter. It had a count, representing the emperor. In 916 Pope John X won a memorable victory there over the Saracens. In the Middle Ages it rebelled at times against the popes, under Henry IV and V, and against Innocent II; at other times it fought against the Roman rebels, as under Eugene III and Adrian IV. In the thirteenth century the Senate of Rome succeeded (under Innocent IV) in imposing a tribute on the city, and arrogated to itself the right of appointing a count to govern it in conjunction with the local consuls. In the fourteenth century it sided with the Guelphs and strongly supported Urban VI against Clement VII. King Ladislaus was twice, and later Braccio da Montone once, repulsed from the city. But its strength was undermined by internal factions, in consequence of which Pius II constructed the fortress which still exists. Alexander VI withdrew it from the jurisdiction of the Roman Senate. In 1527 it was sacked by bands of the supporters of the emperor and the Colonna, important archives being destroyed during the attack. In 1547 it was again occupied by the Duke of Alba in a war against Paul IV, and in 1744 by the Austrians.

Tivoli is the birthplace of St. Severinus (sixth century), of Popes St. Simplicius and John IX, also of the painter and musician Golia. The Church of Tivoli counts many martyrs, among them St. Getulius, St. Symphorosa with her seven sons, martyred in the days of Hadrian; at a later period a basilica was erected over the place of their martyrdom. Other martyrs were Vincentius, Majorius, and Generosus. The deacon St. Cletus was later confounded with the pope of that name, really St. Anacletus. The first known bishop was Candidus (465); among his successors were: Gualterus (1000), under whom the feast of St. Lawrence, patron of the city, was instituted; Otto (1148), during whose episcopacy Eugene IV died at Tivoli; Giovanni da Gabenna O.P. (1337), who died in the odour of sanctity; Filippo de' Rufini, O.P. (1367), sent by the Romans to Gregory IX to induce him to return to Rome; Fra Lorenzo, O.M. (1450), reformer of the clergy; Cardinal Giulio Roma (1634), restorer of the cathedral and founder of the seminary; Cardinal Marcello di Santacroce (1652), who completed the work of his predecessor; Gregorio Barnaba Chiaramonti (1782), afterwards Pius VII. The diocese is immediately subject to the Holy See. In the process of concentrating the Italian seminaries the course of theology at Tivoli was suppressed. There are: 42 parishes; 40,000 inhabitants; 69 secular and 35 regular priests; 11 convents of male religious and 6 of sisters; 1 college for boys, and 1 for girls.

Cappelletti, *Le chiese d'Italia*; Viola, *Storia di Tivoli* (Rome, 1726); Bruzza, *Regesto della chiesa di Tivoli* (Rome, 1880).

U. Benigni.

Tlaxcala (Tlaxcalensis), a former diocese of the colony of New Spain. It was the fifth diocese established in the Americas by order of seniority; the second established in Mexico (the first in title being Yucatán); and the first diocese of the colony of New Spain with an acting bishop, Fray Julián Garcés, Dominican, nominated by Clement VII, at the request of Charles V. At first Fray Garcés was only presented as Bishop of Yucatán; the royal provision of Charles V reads: "We present you (Rev. Father Julián Garcés) to the Bishopric of Yucatán and Santa María de los Remedios", but, as the territory discovered and conquered by Hernando Cortés became better known, Clement VII in the document sent to Bishop Garcés in 1525 says: "We grant you and the bishops who shall succeed you, that you call yourselves not bishops of Santa María (de los Remedios or of Yucatán) but 'Tenuxtitlán' and of other lands to be mentioned." This document denotes the new title of the bishop but does not determine it. Father Garcés himself in his first declaration enlightens us by saying: "We choose the town of Tlaxcala as the seat of our cathedral church." Bishop Garcés reached New Spain in 1527 and took possession of his see. Subsequently finding that it was impossible to hold the choir office at Tlaxcala because there was no cathedral, but only an altar covered with thatch work, and as a sumptuous church with three naves had been erected in the new city of Puebla de los Angeles, the bishop declared that the chapter should pass to the latter city, and transferred thither the episcopal see on 3 October, 1539. This change was approved by

THE CATHEDRAL, PUEBLA

royal warrant of 6 June, 1543, and since then the bishops of the diocese have resided in Puebla.

Although the official title of the diocese was "of Tlaxcala" or *de Puebla de los Angeles*, it was not until 11 August, 1903, that the ancient See of Tlaxcala (*Angelopolitana*) was made an archbishopric under the name of Puebla de los Angeles, and the name of Tlaxcala was suppressed. The original limits of the Diocese of Puebla (Tlaxcala) comprised the present states of Puebla, Tlaxcala, Vera Cruz, Tabasco, Hidalgo, and Guerrero. As new dioceses were erected (see MEXICO) its territory was gradually reduced to its present limits, the states of Puebla and Tlaxcala, with the exception of a few parishes which belong to the jurisdiction of the dioceses of Huajuápam and Oaxaca. In the first years of its foundation almost all the churches and parishes were under the care of the regulars, the Franciscans having important convents at Tlaxcala, Huexotzingo, and Cholula. In the time of the sixth Bishop of Puebla, Diego Romano (1578–1607), the churches began to pass into the hands of the seculars, and by 1640–49, under Bishop Juan de Palafox y Mendoza, the change was finally accomplished.

The ancient Tlaxcala was a powerful republic which the Aztecs vainly tried to conquer and which waged continuous and ferocious wars against them. The Indian hieroglyphic of its name represents two hands beating a *tortilla*, or corn cake, which is the meaning of the word "tlaxcallan". In former times this republic was thickly populated, but epidemics, emigrations, and the work of constructing the canal of Nochistongo to drain the valley of Mexico brought about the almost entire extinction of the natives, reducing them to an insignificant number. In the archives of Tlaxcala is a royal document, bearing the date of 1539, which orders that the Indians of Tlaxcala be exempted from all works of servitude. This prerogative was conceded in return for their services to Hernán Cortéz during the conquest. It is doubtful whether this order was ever carried out, for a document dated 1625 states that the city of Tlaxcala contained 300,000 inhabitants in the sixteenth century, while only 7000 remained when this document was written. The city of Puebla, which is the residence of the bishop and of the governor of the state, was founded in 1531 by the auditor Juan de Salmerón and Fray Toribio de Motolinía (see MOTOLINIA). The cathedral of Puebla, one of the most beautiful in the whole republic of Mexico, was finished by Bishop Palafox in 1649. There are, counting colleges and parochial schools, about three hundred Catholic schools in the archdiocese. The Protestants have ten colleges. The conciliar seminary was raised to the rank of a Catholic university on 5 August, 1907. It has an attendance of 275 students. Among the notable churches should be mentioned that of Nuestra Señora de los Remedios situated on the top of the Pyramid of Cholula. This pyramid was built by the Indians before the advent of the Spaniards; it measures 177 feet in height and 1444 feet on each side of its base, and is, therefore, larger than, although not as high as, the great pyramid of Egypt. The level space on the top, upon which the church is built, measures 46,444 sq. feet.

Besides the two bishops already mentioned, other notable ones were the successor of Bishop Palafox, Diego Osorio de Escobar y Llamas, who was viceroy of Mexico in 1664, and D. Pelagio Antonio Labastida y Dávalos, who was driven from his see during the reform era and did not return until 1863 as Archbishop of Mexico. The present archbishop, Ramón Ibarra y González, translated from the Diocese of Chilapa, Guerrero, on 6 July, 1902, was preconized first Archbishop of Puebla in 1903, and the Diocese of Huajuápam de León, erected at the same time, was made suffragan to Puebla. Tlaxcala had in 1910 a population of 2812. The town is now silent and desolate. The ancient buildings, preserved for the traditions which cling to them, and the resident Indians transport the visitor to the time of the conquest. The State of Tlaxcala has an area of 1594 sq. m., and a population (1910) of 183,805.

GILLOW, *Apuntes históricos* (Mexico, 1889); RECASENS, *El primer obispo de Tlaxcala* (Mexico, 1884); VERA, *Catecismo geográfico histórico estadístico de la Iglesia Mexicana* (Amecameca, 1881); DOMENECH, *Geografía Gen. Descrip. de la R. M. Mexico*.

CAMILLUS CRIVELLI.

Tlos, titular see in Lycia, suffragan of Myra. Tlos was one of the six cities forming the Lycian confederacy and is said to have been founded by the hero Tlos, son of Tremilus. It is mentioned by Strabo (XIV, 665); Pliny (V, 28); Ptolemy (V, 3, 5); Stephanus Byzant. (s. v.; Hierocles (684, 16). It had its own coinage. It is to-day the village of Douvar in the caza of Macri, vilayet of Smyrna; this village is beautifully situated in the midst of the ancient acropolis, 984 feet above the Xanthus valley, surrounded by precipices, whose sides form inaccessible walls. On the northern side these rocks are broken by hundreds of tombs, some of which bear inscriptions mentioning the people and the "*gerousia*" or municipal council. Among its monuments the principal is the theatre. Until the thirteenth century this see is mentioned by the "Notitiæ episcopatuum" as a suffragan of Myra. Le Quien (Oriens christ., I, 979) gives a list of five known bishops: Andreas, at Chalcedon, 451 (signed in 458 the letter of the Lycian bishops to Emperor Leo); Eustathius at Constantinople, under the patriarch Menas, 536 (also known by Novella 115 of Justinian); John, at the Council of Trullo, 692; Constantine, at Nice, 787; Constantine, at Constantinople, 879.

FELLOWS, *Asia Minor*, 237 sqq.; IDEM, *Lycia*, 132 sqq.; TEXIER, *Asie mineure*, 672; SMITH, *Dict. of Greek and Roman Geogr.* s. v.

S. PÉTRIDÈS.

Toaldo, GIUSEPPE, priest and physicist, b. at Pianezze, 1719; d. at Padua, 1797. In his fourteenth year he entered the seminary of Padua, in which he subsequently taught mathematics and Italian literature. While connected with the seminary he edited the works of Galilei (1744), for which he wrote an appreciative preface and critical notes. In 1754 he was appointed pastor of Montegalda; and, eight years later, was called to the chair of astronomy in the University of Padua. Toaldo, like his contemporaries, Divisch and Beccaria (both priests), gave special attention to the study of atmospheric electricity and to the means of protecting buildings against lightning. He advocated the erection of lightning-rods, adopting the views of Franklin on their preventive and protective action, rather than those of the French school led by Abbé Nollet. His treatise "Della maniera di difendere gli edificii dal fulmine" (1772) and his pamphlet "Dei conduttori metallici a preservazione degli edifici dal fulmine" (1774) contributed largely to remove the popular prejudices of the time against the use of the "Franklinian rod"; and through his exertions lightning-conductors were placed on the Cathedral of Siena, on the tower of St. Mark's, Venice, on powder magazines, and ships of the Venetian navy. Toaldo was a member of many of the learned bodies of Europe, notably of the Royal Society, London.

TIPALDO, *Biografia degli Italiani illustri*.

BROTHER POTAMIAN.

Toba Indians, one of the few still unconquered savage tribes of the great Chaco wilderness of South America, and notable alike for their persistent hostility to the white man and for their close resemblance in language, customs, and manner of living to the celebrated Abipón, among whom the famous Jesuit Dobrizhoffer (q. v.) laboured one hundred and fifty years ago. They are of Guaycuran linguistic stock, which includes also the Abipón, Mocoví, and a number of other tribes of similar predatory habit, and range, in alliance with the Mocoví, through the forests and marshes of the Chaco region on the west bank of the Paraguay River about the lower Pilcomayo and Vermejo, in Paraguay and north-east Argentina, sometimes extending their forays westward to the frontiers of Oran and Tarija. They are known under various names, the most common being from the Guaraní *tobai*, signifying "opposite", i. e. those living on the opposite bank of the Paraguay from the Guaraní. They number now perhaps 2000 souls.

Physically they are tall and well-built, with fierce countenance, and from going constantly barefoot the soles of their feet are toughened to resist thorns and sharp rocks. Both sexes go nearly naked except when in the presence of strangers, and wear their hair long, the men confining it by means of a band or turban. On special occasions they wear shirts or skirts of skins or of woollen stuff, of their own weaving, from the sheep they now possess, together with head-dresses, belts, and wristlets of ostrich feathers. They tattoo their faces and upper bodies with vegetable dye. They live almost entirely by hunting and fishing, but raise a little corn. They have large herds of horses and are fine horsemen. The men are expert in the making of dug-out canoes and fish traps, while the women are expert potters and net weavers. Their huts are simple structures of willow branches covered with grass, sometimes large enough to have several compartments. Their weapons are the bow, lance, and wooden club, besides which they now have some guns. They bury the dead, the aged being sometimes killed by their own children from a feeling of pity for their helplessness. For the same reason, when a mother dies her infant is buried with her. Men have only one wife at a time. There is no head chief, the government resting principally with the old men. Little is known of their religion, which seems to consist chiefly of a special reverence for the sun and the rising moon, and the propitiation of a host of invisible spirits which are held responsible for sickness and other misfortunes. In war they are distinguished for their ferocity and barbarous cruelty, and are dreaded alike by settlers, travellers, and Christianized Indians throughout the whole northern Chaco frontier. In 1882 they massacred an entire exploring expedition of fifteen men under command of the French geographer, Crévaux. In 1854, however, the American expedition up the Paraguay, under Captain Page, held friendly intercourse with them. Some special studies of their language, which is virtually the same as that of the Abipón, have been made by Carranza and Quevedo. An interesting, though strongly anti-religious, account of their latter-day condition and habits is given by the Italian engineer, Pelleschi.

In the early colonization period of the eighteenth century the Toba, with the Abipón and Mocoví, were among the most determined and constant enemies of the Argentine-Paraguayan settlements and missions, and hardly a half year ever passed without a raid or retaliatory punitive expedition. On one occasion six hundred Toba attacked Dobrizhoffer's mission, but were repelled by the missionary himself single-handed with the aid of his firearms, of which the savages were in deadly terror. The missionary received an arrow wound in the encounter. In 1756 a number of Toba and Mataco were gathered into the Mission of San Ignacio de Ledesma, on the Rio Grande tributary of the Vermejo, where they numbered 600 souls at the time of the expulsion of the Jesuits in 1767. Some later attempt was made by the Franciscans to restore the Chaco missions, but with the end of Spanish rule the missions declined and the Indians scattered to the forests. (See MATACO INDIANS; MOCOVÍ INDIANS.)

Consult: BRINTON, *American Race* (New York, 1891); CARRANZA, *Expedición al Chaco Austral* (Buenos Ayres, 1884); CHARLEVOIX, *Hist. du Paraguay* (Paris, 1756; tr. London, 1769); DOBRIZHOFFER, *Account of the Abipones* (London, 1822); HERVÁS, *Catálogo de las Lenguas*, I (Madrid, 1800); LOZANO, *Descripción Chorográphica del Gran Chaco* (Cordova, 1733); D'ORBIGNY, *L'Homme Américain* (Paris, 1839); PAGE, *La Plata, the Argentine Confederation and Paraguay* (New York, 1859); PELLESCHI, *Eight Months on the Gran Chaco* (London, 1886); QUEVEDO, *Lenguas Argentinas, Idioma Abipón* (Buenos Ayres, 1896); RECLUS, *The Earth and its Inhabitants; South America, II, Amazonia and La Plata* (New York, 1895).

JAMES MOONEY.

Tobias.—We shall first enumerate the various Biblical persons and then treat the book of this name.

I. PERSONS. A.—Tobias (II Par., xvii, 8), Heb. *tôbyyāhû* "Yahweh is good"; Sept. Τωβιας, one of the Levites whom Josaphat sent to teach in the cities of Juda. The name is omitted in the Vatican and Alexandrian codices, but given in the other important Greek MSS. and the Vulgate.

B.—Tobias (Zach., vi, 10), Heb. *tôbyyāhû*, *qeri tôbyyâh* which is the reading also of verse 14; Sept. χρησίμων (verse 10), τοῖς χρησίμοις αὐτῆς (verse 14), which infers the reading *tôbêhā*; Vulg. Tobia; one of the party of Jews who came from Babylon to Jerusalem, in the time of Zorobabel, with silver and gold wherewith to make a crown for the head of Jesus, son of Josedec.

C.—Tobia (I Esdr., ii, 60), Heb. *tôbyyâh*, "Jah is

my good"; Sept. Τωβειά (Vat.), Τωβίας (Alex.), the same name occurring in II Esdr., vii, 62, as Τωβιά and in the apocryphal III Esdr., v, 37 as βαενάν (Vat.) or βάν (Alex.), one of the families that, on their return from exile, could show no written proof of their genealogy.

D.—Tobias (II Esdr., ii, 10), an Ammonite who together with Sanaballat the Horonite opposed the fortification of Jerusalem by Nehemias (II Esdr., ii, 19; iv, 3; vi, 17; xiii, 4, 8). He is called "the servant"; we can only conjecture what that means. Cheyne (Encyclopedia Biblica, s. v.) thinks that *há'ebéd*, servant, is a mistake for *há arbî*, the Arab.

(E).—Tobias (II Mach., iii, 11), the father of Hircanus.

(F).—Tobias (Tob., i, 9, and *passim*), the son of the following.

(G).—Tobias the elder, the chief character in the book that bears his name.

II. BOOK OF TOBIAS, a canonical book of the Old Testament.

A. *Name.*—In Cod. Alex., βίβλος λόγων Τωβίτ; in Vat., Τωβείτ; in Sinaitic, Τωβείθ; in Latin MSS. *Liber Tobiæ, Liber Tobit et Tobiæ, Liber utriusque Tobiæ*. In the Vulgate and Hebrew Fagii both father and son have the same name, Tobias, *ţôbyyāh*. In other texts and versions, the name of the father varies: *ţôbî*, "my good" is Jahweh, in Heb. Munster; Τωβίτ or Τωβείτ in the Sept.; *Tobis*, or *Tobit*, standing for *ţôbîth* "goodness" of Jahweh, in the Old Latin.

B. *Text and Versions.*—The original text, supposed to have been Hebrew, is lost; the reasons assigned for an Aramaic original warrant only a probable opinion that an Aramaic translation influenced our present Greek versions.

(1) *Vulgate Versions.*—St. Jerome had not yet learned Aramaic, when, with the aid of a rabbi who knew both Aramaic and Hebrew, he made the Vulgate version. The rabbi expressed in Hebrew the thought of the Aramaic MSS. and St. Jerome straightway put the same into Latin. It was the work of only a day (cf. Præf. in Tobiam). The Old Latin certainly influenced this hurried version. The Vulgate recension of the Aramaic version tells the story in the third person throughout, as do the Aramaic of Neubauer and the two Hebrew texts of Gaster (HL and HG), whereas all the other texts make Tobias speak in the first person up to iii, 15. The following passages occur in the Vulgate alone: the wagging of the dog's tail (xi, 9); the comparison of the coating on Tobias's eye to the membrane of an egg (xi, 14); the wait of half an hour while the gall of the fish effected its cure (xi, 14); Tobias's closing of the eyes of Raguel and Edna in death; also ii, 12, 18; iii, 19, 24; vi, 16–18, 20, 21; viii, 4, 5; ix, 12b. Some parts of the Vulgate, such as the continence of Tobias (vi, 18; viii, 4), were looked upon at times as Christian interpolations of Jerome until they were found in one of Gaster's Hebrew texts (HL). Lastly, the Vulgate and HL omit all mention of Ahikhar; Achior of Vulg., xi, 20, is probably an addition to the text.

(2) *Aramaic Versions.*—Besides the Aramaic version used by Jerome and now lost, there is the extant Aramaic text recently found in an Aramaic commentary on Genesis, "Midrash Bereshit Rabba". The writing of this midrash is fifteenth-century work; it contains the Book of Tobias as a *haggada* on the promise Jacob makes to give tithes to God (Gen., xxviii, 22). Neubauer edited the text, "The Book of Tobit, a Chaldee Text from a unique MS. in the Bodleian Library" (Oxford, 1878). He thinks that it is a briefer form of Jerome's Aramaic text. This is not likely. The language is at times a transliteration of Greek and gives evidence of being a translation of one or other of the Greek texts. It agrees with the Vulgate in that from the outset the tale of Tobias is told in the third person; otherwise it is closer to Codex Vaticanus and closer still to Cod. Sinaiticus.

(3) *Greek Versions.*—There are three Greek recensions of Tobias. We shall refer to them by the numbers given to the Vatican and Sinaitic codices in Vigouroux, "La sainte bible polyglotte", III (Paris, 1902). (a) AB, the text of the Alexandrian (fifth century) and Vatican (fourth century) codices. This recension is found in many other codices of the Greek text, has been used for centuries by the Greek Church, is incorporated into the Sixtine edition of the Septuagint, and has been translated into Armenian as the authentic text of that rite. AB is preferred to the Sinaitic recension by Nöldeke, Grimm, and others, and yet rated by Nestle, Ewald, and Harris as a compendium rather than as a version of the entire original text. It condenses Edna's prayer (x, 13), omits the blessing of Gabael (ix, 6), and has three or four unique readings (iii, 16; xiv, 8, 10; xi, 8). (b) ℵ, the text of the Sinaitic (fourth-century) Codex.— Its style is very much more diffuse than that of AB, which seems to have omitted of set purpose many στίχοι of ℵ—cf. ii, 12, "on the seventh of Dustros she cut the web"; v, 3, the incident of the bond divided into two parts, one for Tobias and the other for Raguel; v, 5, the long conversation between Raphael and young Tobias; vi, 8; x, 10; xii, 8, etc. ℵ omits iv, 7–19, and xiii, 6b–9, of AB. (c) The Text of Codices 44, 106, 107 for vi, 9–xiii, 8.—The first portion (i, 1–vi, 8) and the last (xiii, 9 to end) are identical with AB; the remainder seems to be an attempt at a better version of the original text. Independent work is shown by vi, 9, to vii, 17; viii, 1, to xii, 6, is very close to the Syriac and nearer to ℵ than to AB; xii, 7–xiii, 8 resembles each text in various small details. Distinctive readings of these cursives are Edna's Gnostic prayer, "Let all the Æons praise thee" (viii, 15); and the fact that Anna saw the dog running before Tobias (xi, 5). (d) What seems to be a third recension of the second chapter is presented in Grenfell and Hunt, "Oxyrhyncus Papyri" (Oxford, 1911), part viii. The text differs from both AB and ℵ and consequently the Greek cursives.

(4) *Old Latin Versions.*—Previous to the Latin Vulgate translation of the Aramaic recension (see above) there existed at least three Old Latin versions of a Greek text which was substantially ℵ; (a) The recension of Codex Regius Parisiensis 3654 and Cod. 4 of the Library of St-Germain; (b) the recension of Cod. Vat. 7, containing i–vi, 12; (c) the recension of the "Speculum" of St. Augustine.

(5) *Syriac Version.*—Down to vii, 9, it is a translation of AB; thereafter, it agrees with the Greek cursive text, save that xiii, 9–18, is omitted. This second part is clearly a second recension; its proper names are not spelled as in the first part. Ahikhar (xiv, 10) is Achior (ii, 10); 'Edna (vii, 14) is 'Edna (vii, 2) 'Arag (ix, 2) is Raga (iv, 1, 20).

(6) *Hebrew Versions.*—There are four Hebrew versions of this deuterocanonical story: (a) HL, Hebrew Londinii, a thirteenth-century MS., found by Gaster in the British Museum, and translated by him in the "Proceedings of the Soc. of the Bibl. Archæology" (xviii and xx). Besides a cento of Scriptural exhortations, this MS. contains the narrative portion of Tobias, translated, Gaster thinks, from a text that stood in closest relation to the Aramaic used by St. Jerome. It is just possible, though not in the least probable, that the thirteenth-century Jewish author of HL made use of the Vulgate. (b) HG, Hebrew Gasteri, a text copied by Gaster from a midrash on the Pentateuch and published in the "Proc. of the Soc. of Bib. Arch." (xix). This MS., now lost, agreed with the Aramaic of Neubauer and was in a compact style like that of the Vulgate recension. (c) HF, Hebrew Fagii, a very free translation of AB, done in the twelfth century by a Jewish

scholar; it is found in Walton's "Polyglot". (d) HM, Hebrew Munsteri, published by Münster in Basle A. D. 1542, found in Walton's "Polyglot". This text agrees as a rule with Neubauer's Aramaic, even when the latter is at variance with AB. It is, according to Ginsburg, of fifth-century origin. The Hebrew versions together with the Aramaic omit reference to the dog, which plays a prominent part in the other versions.

The foregoing review of the various and diverse recensions of the Book of Tobias shows how hard it would be to reconstruct the original text and how easily textual errors may have crept into our Vulgate or the Aramaic on which it depends.

C. *Contents.*—Unless otherwise stated, these references are to the Vulgate recension, whereof the Douay is a translation. The story naturally divides itself into two parts: (1) the fidelity of Tobias the elder and of Sara to the Lord (i, 1–iii, 25); (a) the fidelity of Tobias (i, 1–iii, 6),—before the captivity (i, 1–10), during the captivity (i, 11–iii, 6) shown by his acts of mercy to fellow captives (i, 11–17) and especially to the dead (i, 18–25), acts that resulted in his blindness (ii, 1–18), the taunts of his wife (ii, 19–23), and the recourse of Tobias to God in prayer (iii, 1–6). (b) The fidelity of Sara, daughter of Raguel and Edna (iii, 7–23). The very day that Tobias in Ninive was taunted by his wife and turned to God, Sara in Ecbatana was taunted by her maid as the murderess of seven husbands (iii, 7–10), and turned to God in prayer (iii, 11–23). The prayers of both were heard (iii, 24–25).

(2) The fidelity of the Lord to Tobias and to Sara through the ministrations of the angel Raphael (iv, 1–xii, 22).—(a) Raphael cares for the young Tobias on his journey to Gabael in Rages of Media to obtain the ten talents of silver left in bond by his father (iv, 1–ix, 12). The young man set out, after long instruction by his father (iv, 1–23); Raphael joins him as guide (v, 1–28); Tobias while bathing in the Tigris is attacked by a large fish, catches it, and, at the advice of Raphael, keeps its heart, liver, and gall (vi, 1–22); they pass through Ecbatana, stop at Raguel's; Tobias asks Sara for wife and receives her (vii, 1–20); by continence and exorcism and the odour of the burning liver of the fish and the aid of Raphael, he conquers the devil who had slain the seven previous husbands of Sara (viii, 1–24); Raphael gets the money of Gabael in Rages, and brings him to Ecbatana to the marriage celebration of young Tobias (ix, 1–12). (b) Raphael cures the blindness of the elder Tobias, on the return of his son, and manifests the truth that he is an angel (x, 2–xii, 31). Conclusion: The hymn of thanksgiving of Tobias the elder, and the subsequent history of both father and son (xiii, 1–xiv, 7).

D. *Purpose.*—To show that God is faithful to those that are faithful to Him is evidently the chief purpose of the book. Neubauer (op. cit., p. xvi) makes out the burial of the dead to be the chief lesson; but the lesson of almsgiving is more prominent. Ewald, "Gesch. des Volkes Israel", IV, 233, sets fidelity to the Mosaic code as the main drift of the author, who writes for Jews of the Dispersion; but the book is meant for all Jews, and clearly inculcates for them many secondary lessons and one that is fundamental to the rest—God is true to those who are true to Him.

E. *Canonicity.* (1) In Judaism.—The Book of Tobias is deuterocanonical, i. e. contained not in the Canon of Palestine but in that of Alexandria. That the Jews of the Dispersion accepted the book as canonical Scripture is clear from its place in the Septuagint. That the Palestinian Jews reverenced Tobias as a sacred book may be argued from the existence of the Aramaic translation used by St. Jerome and that published by Neubauer, as also from the four extant Hebrew translations. Then, most of these Semitic versions were found as Midrashim, or *haggada*, of the Pentateuch.

(2) Among Christians.—Despite the rejection of Tobias from the Protestant Canon, its place in the Christian Canon of Holy Writ is undoubted. The Catholic Church has ever esteemed it as inspired. St. Polycarp (A. D. 117), "Ad Philippenses", x, urges almsgiving, and cites Tob., iv, 10, and xii, 9, as authority for his urging. Deutero-Clement (A. D. 150), "Ad Corinthios", xvi, has praises of almsgiving that are an echo of Tob., xii, 8, 9. St. Clement of Alexandria (A. D. 190–210), in "Stromata", vi, 12 (P. G., IX, 324), cites as the words of Holy Writ "Fasting is good with prayer" (Tob., xii, 9); and in "Stromata", i, 21; ii, 23 (P. G., VIII, 853, 1089), "What thou hatest, do not unto another" (Tob., iv, 16). Origen (about A. D. 230) cites as Scripture Tob., iii, 24, and xii, 12, 15, in "De oratione", II; Tob., ii, 1, in sec. 14; Tob., xii, 12, in sec. 31 (cf. P. G., XI, 448, 461, 553); and writing to Africanus (P. G., XI, 80) he explains that, although the Hebrews do not use Tobias, yet the Church does. St. Athanasius (A. D. 350) uses Tob., xii, 7, and iv, 19, with the distinctive phrase "as it is written", cf. "Apol. contra arianos", II, and "Apol. ad Imper. Constantium" (P. G., XXV, 268, 616). In the Western Church, St. Cyprian (about A. D. 248) very often refers to Tobias as of Divine authority just as he refers to the other books of Holy Writ; cf. "De mortalitate", x; "De opere et eleemosynis", v, xx; "De patientia", xviii (P. L., IV, 588, 606, 634); "Ad Quirinum", i, 20, for Tob., xii; iii, 1 for Tob., ii, 2; and iv, 5–11; iii, 62, for Tob., iv, 12 (P. G., IV, 689, 728, 729, 767). St. Ambrose (about A. D. 370) wrote a book entitled "De Tobia" against usury (P. L., XIV, 759), and introduced it by referring to the Biblical work of that name as "a prophetic book", "Scripture". In the entire Western Church, however, the canonicity of Tobias is clearest from its presence in the Old Latin Version, the authentic text of Scripture for the Latin Church from about A. D. 150 until St. Jerome's Vulgate replaced it. The canonical use of Tobias in that part of the Byzantine Church whose language was Syriac is seen in the writings of St. Ephraem (about A. D. 362) and of St. Archelaus (about A. D. 278). The earliest canonical lists all contain the Book of Tobias; they are those of the Council of Hippo (A. D. 393), the councils of Carthage (A. D. 397 and 419), St. Innocent I (A. D. 405), St. Augustine (A. D. 397). Moreover, the great fourth- and fifth-century MSS. of the Septuagint are proof that not only the Jews but the Christians used Tobias as canonical. For the Catholic the question of the canonicity of Tobias was infallibly settled by the decisions of the Councils of Trent, Session IV (8 April, 1546) and of the Vatican, Session III, ch. 2 (24 April, 1870).

Against the canonicity of Tobias are urged several rather trivial objections which would at first sight seem to impugn the inspiration of the narrative. (a) Raphael told an untruth when he said he was "Azarias the son of the great Ananias" (v, 18). There is no untruth in this. The angel was in appearance just what he said he was. Besides, he may have meant by 'ăzáryāh, "the healer of Jah"; and by 'ănányāh, "the goodness of Jah". In this event he only told the young Tobias that he was God's helper and the offspring of the great goodness of God; in this there would be no falsehood. (b) A second objection is that the angelology of Tobias is taken over from that of the Avesta either directly by Iranian influence or indirectly by the inroad of Syriac or Grecian folk-lore. For Raphael says: "I am the angel Raphael, one of the seven who stand before the Lord" (xii, 15). These seven are the Amesha Spentas of Zoroastrianism: cf. Fritzsche, "Exegetisches Handbuch zu den Apocr.", II (Leipzig, 1853), 61. The answer is that the reading seven is doubtful; it is in ℵ, AB, Old Latin, and Vulg.; it is wanting in the Greek cursive text, Syriac, and HM. Still, admitting the reading of the Vulgate, the Amesha Spentas have infiltrated into Avestic religion from the seven Angels of Hebraistic Revelation and not vice versa. Moreover, there are not seven Amesha Spentas in the angelology of the Avesta, but only six. They are subordinated to Ahura Mazda, the first principle of good. True, he is, at times, grouped with the six lower spirits as seven Amesha Spentas; but in this grouping we have not by any means seven angels standing before the Deity.

F. *Historical Worth*. (1) *To Protestants*.—The destructive criticism which, among Protestants, has striven to do away with the canonical books of the Old Testament has quite naturally had no respect for those books the critics call apocryphal. The Book of Tobias is to them no more than are the Testament of Job, the Book of Jubilees, and the story of Ahikhar. From the standpoint of historical criticism it is to be grouped with these three apocryphal (J. T. Marshall, Principal of the Baptist College, Manchester, in Hastings's "Dict. of the Bible", s. v.). Simrock in "Der gute Gerhard und die dankbaren Todten" (Bonn, 1858) reduces the story to the folk-lore theme of the gratitude of the departed spirit; the yarn is spun out of this slim thread of fancy that the souls of the dead, whose remains Tobias buried, did not forget his benevolence. Erbt (Encycl. Biblica, s. v.) finds traces of Iranian legend in the name of the demon Asmodeus (Tob., iii, 8) which is the Persian *Aëshma daêva;* as also in the dog,—"with the Persians a certain power over evil spirits was assigned to the dog." And again: "the Jewish nation takes up a foreign legend, goes on repeating it until it has got it into fixed oral form, in order next to pass it on to some story-writer who is able to shape it into an edifying household tale, capable of ministering comfort to many succeeding generations." Moulton, "The Iranian background of Tobit" (Expository Times, 1900, p. 257), considers the book to be Median folk-lore, in which the Semitic and Iranian elements meet. On the Ahikhar story, cf. "The Story of Ahikhar from the Syriac, Arabic, Armenian, Ethiopic, Greek, and Slavonic versions" by Conybeare, Harris, and Mrs. Smith, a work which will be brought back to 407 B. C. in a new edition soon to appear (Expositor, March 1912, p. 212).

(2) *To Catholics*.—Until recently there never was question among Catholics in regard to the historicity of Tobias. It was among the historical books of the Old Testament, the Fathers had always referred to both elder and younger Tobias and to the other personages of the narratives as to facts and not to fancies. The stories of almsgiving, burial of the dead, angelophany, exorcism, marriage of Sara with Tobias the younger, cure of the elder Tobias,—all these incidents were taken for granted as fact-narrative; nor was there ever any question of likening them to the tales of "The Arabian Nights" and the "Fables of Æsop". Jahn, "Introductio in libros sacros", 2nd ed. (Vienna, 1814), 452, gives the stock objections to the historicity of Tobias, and suggests that either the entire composition is a parable to teach that the prayers of the upright are heard or at most only the main outline is fact-narrative. His book was put on the Index (26 Aug., 1822). Anton Scholz, "Die heilige Schrift", II, iii, p. 12, and Movers in "Kirchenlexicon" (first ed., I, p. 481) hold that Tobias is a poetic fiction. Cosquin, in "Revue biblique" (1899, pp. 50–82), tries to show that the sacred writer of Tobias had before his eyes a form of the Ahikhar story and worked it over rather freely as a vehicle to carry the inspired thought of the moral he wished to convey to his readers. Barry, "The Tradition of Scripture" (New York, 1906), p. 128, says: "Its relation to other stories, such as *The Grateful Dead* and the tale of *Ahichar*, has been used in illustration of the romantic nature ascribed to it by modern readers; so, too, the symbolical names of its personages, and the borrowings, as they say, from Persian mythology of Asmodeus, etc." Gigot, "Special introduction to the study of the Old Testament", I (New York, 1901), 343–7, gives at length the arguments in favour of the non-historical character of the book and attempts no refutation of the same.

With these and a few other exceptions, Catholic exegetes are unanimous in clearly defending the historicity of Tobias. Cf. Welte in "Kirchenlexikon" (first ed., s. v. *Tobias*); Reusch, "Das Buch Tobias", p. vi; Vigouroux, "Manuel biblique", II (Paris, 1883), 134; Cornely, "Introd. in utriusque testamenti libros sacros", II (Paris, 1887), i, 378; Danko, "Hist. revelationis v. t.", 369; Haneburg, "Gesch. der bibl. Offenbarung" (3d ed., Ratisbon, 1863), 489; Kaulen, "Einleitung in die heilige Schrift" (Freiburg, 1890), 215; Zschokke, "Hist. sacra A. T.", 245; Kaulen in "Kirchenlexikon" (second ed., s. v. *Tobias*); Seisenberger, "Practical Handbook for the Study of the Bible" (New York, 1911), 343. This almost unanimity among Catholic exegetes is quite in keeping with the decision of the Biblical Commission (23 June, 1905). By this Decree Catholics are forbidden to hold that a book of the Holy Writ, which has generally been looked upon as historical, is either entirely or in part not history properly so called, unless it be proven by solid arguments that the sacred writer did not wish to write history; and the solidity of the arguments against the historicity of an historical book of the Bible we are not to admit either readily or rashly. Now the arguments against the historical worth of Tobias are not at all solid; they are mere conjectures, which it would be most rash to admit. We shall examine some of these conjectures.

(a) The Ahikhar story is not in the Vulgate at all. As it is in AB, ℵ, and the Old Latin, St. Jerome undoubtedly knew it. Why did he follow the Aramaic text to the exclusion of this episode? He may have looked upon it as an interpolation, which was not written by the inspired author. Even though it were not an interpolation, the Ahikhar episode of Tobias has not been proven to be a legend drawn from a non-canonical source. (b) The angelic apparition and all incidents connected therewith are no more difficult to explain than the angelophanies of Gen., xviii, 19, and Acts, xii, 6. (c) The demonology is not unlike to that of the New Testament. The name "Asmodeus" need not be of Iranian origin; but may just as readily be explained as Semitic. The Aramaic word *'áshmeday* is cognate with the Hebrew *háshmed*, "destruction". And even though it be a mutilated form of some Iranian ancestor of the Persian *Aëshma daêva*, what more natural than a Median name for a demon whose obsession was accomplished upon Median soil? The slaying of the seven husbands was allowed by God in punishment of their lust (Vulg., vi, 16); it is the youth Tobias, not the sacred writer, that suggests (according to AB, ℵ, and Old Latin) the demon's lust as the motive of his killing all rivals. The binding of the devil in the desert of Upper Egypt, the farthest end of the then known world (viii, 3), has the same figurative meaning as the binding of Satan for a thousand years (Apoc., xx, 2). (d) The unlikelihood of the many coincidences in the Book of Tobias is mere conjecture (cf. Gigot, op. cit., 345). Divine Providence may have brought about these similarities of incident, with a view to the use of them in an inspired book.

(e) Certain historical difficulties are due to the very imperfect condition in which the text has reached us. (i) It was Theglathphalasar III who led Nephthali (IV Kings, xv, 29) into captivity (734 B. C.), and not, as Tobias says (i, 2), Salmanasar. Yet this reading of the Vulgate, Old Latin, and Aramaic is to be corrected by the name Enemesar of AB and ℵ. This latter reading would be equivalent to the Hebrew ענם סר, a transliteration of the Assyrian *kenum šar*. As the appellative *šar*, "king", may precede or follow a personal name, *kenum šar* is *šar kenum*, that is Sargon (*šarru-kenu* II, B. C. 722). It can readily be that, twelve years after Theglathphalasar III began the deportation of Israel out of Samaria, Sargon's scouts completed the work and routed some of the tribe of Nephthali from their fastnesses. (ii) A like solution is to be given to the difficulty that Sennacherib is said to have been the son of Salmanasar (i, 18), whereas he was the son of the usurper Sargon. The Vulgate reading here, as in i, 2, should be that of AB and ℵ, to wit, Enemesar; and this stands for Sargon. (iii) In B, xiv, 15, Ninive is said to have been captured by Ahasuerus (Ασύηρος) and Nabuchodonosor. This is a mistake of the scribe. ℵ reads that Achiacharos took Ninive and adds that "he praised God for all He had done against the children of Ninive and Assyria". The word for Assyria is Αθουρείας, Hebrew *'asshûr*, Aramaic *'áhûr;* this Greek word misled the scribe to write Ἀσύηρος for the name of the king, Αχιάχαρος, i. e. the Median King Cyaxares. According to Berossus, Cyaxares was, in his campaign against Ninive, allied to the Babylonian King Nabopalassar, the father of Nabuchodonosor; the scribe of B has written the name of the son for that of the father, as Nabopalassar was unknown to him. (iv) Rages is a Seleucid town and hence an anachronism. Not at all; it is an ancient Median town, which the Seleucids restored.

G. *Origin*.—It is likely that the elder Tobias wrote at least that part of the original work in which he uses the first person singular, cf. i, 1–iii, 6, in all texts except the Vulgate and Aramaic. As the entire narrative is historical, this part is probably autobiographical. After revealing his angelic nature, Raphael bade both father and son to tell all the wonders that God had done them (Vulg., xii, 20) and to write in a book all the incidents of his stay with them (cf. same verse in AB, ℵ Old Latin, HF, and HM). If we accept the story as fact-narrative, we naturally conclude that it was written originally during the Babylonian Exile, in the early portion of the seventh century B. C.; and that all save the last chapter was the work of the elder and younger Tobias. Almost all Protestant scholars consider the book post-Exilic. Ewald assigns it to 350 B. C.; Ilgen, the bulk to 280 B. C.; Grätz, to A. D. 130; Kohut, to A. D. 226.

The introductions of CORNELY, KAULEN, DANKO, GIGOT, SEISENBERGER. Although the Fathers use Tobias, only BEDE (*P. L.*, XCI, 923–38) and WALAFRID STRABO (*P. L.*, CXIII, 725) have left us commentaries thereon. During the Middle Ages, HUGH OF ST. VICTOR, *Allegoriarum in Vetus Testamentum*, IX (*P. L.*, CLXXV, 725), and NICHOLAS OF LYRA, DENIS THE CARTHUSIAN, HUGH DE S. CARO, in their commentaries on all Scripture, interpreted the Book of Tobias. Later commentators are SERARI (Monza, 1599); SANCTIUS (Lyons, 1628); MAUSCHBERGER (Olmutz, 1758); JUSTINIANI (Rome, 1620); DE CELADA (Lyons, 1644); DREXEL (Antwerp, 1652); NEUVILLE (Paris, 1723); GUTBERLET (Münster, 1854); REUSCH (Freiburg, 1857); GILLET (Paris, 1879); SCHOLZ (Würzburg, 1889); CURCI (Naples, 1890); DE MOOR, *Tobie et Akhiahar* (Louvain, 1902); VETTER, *Das Buch Tobias und die Achikar-Sage* in *Theol. Quartalschrift* (Tübingen, 1904). The principal Protestant authorities have been cited in the body of the article.

WALTER DRUM.

Tocqueville, CHARLES-ALEXIS-HENRI-MAURICE CLEREL DE, writer and statesman, b. at Verneuil, Department of Seine-et-Oise, 29 July, 1805; d. at Cannes, 16 April, 1859. He was the great-grandson of Malesherbes, the defender of Louis XVI. As a judge at Versailles in 1830 he formed a friendship with Gustave de Beaumont, with whom he travelled to America in 1831. Tocqueville's letters show that he foresaw what strides the Church was destined to make in America and likewise the dogmatic nothingness which would result from Unitarianism and the absurdities of Illuminism. Two publications resulted from this journey: the collective work of the two friends published in 1832 under the title "Du système pénitentiaire aux Etats-Unis et de son application en France"; the second, Tocqueville's personal work, is the celebrated book "La démocratie en Amérique", of which the first volume appeared in 1835 and the second in 1840. The work won for Tocqueville admission to the Académie des sciences morales et politiques (1838) and the French Academy (1841).

The library of the Seminary of St-Sulpice preserves a copy of "La Démocratie" annotated by Mgr Bruté, first Bishop of Vincennes, who registered in the margin a number of exceptions to Tocqueville's assertions. Those notes have been transcribed by Mgr Baunard. Tocqueville held that democracy could exist

CHARLES-ALEXIS DE TOCQUEVILLE
From a lithographic portrait

only by seeking a moral support in religion, and that religion could prosper only by accommodating itself to democracy, but he is inclined to regard as too severe the doctrinal, disciplinary, and liturgical exactions of Catholicism, and in Mgr Baunard's opinion his work leaves the impression that he was only half Catholic.

The work has been charged with several serious defects as regards political observation; he dealt at too great length with the constitution and organism of the central government, paying too little attention to the provincial legislation of the various states of the Union. He relegates to the end of the first part the study of what he calls "the accidental or providential causes" of the maintenance of the democracy, and his work would be clearer if he had treated in the beginning the geographical and economic conditions of America. As his work progresses he loses sight of American democracy and deals in a general way with democratic societies.

As a deputy for Valognes from 1839 Tocqueville sat with the opposition and voted for liberty of instruction. Under the Second Republic he was a member of the Constituent and Legislative Assemblies and vice-president of the latter.

The Roman expedition had been for some weeks under way when Tocqueville assumed the portfolio for foreign affairs in the Odilon Barrot cabinet (2 June–31 October, 1849). He caused it to be proceeded with, at the same time writing to the French ambassador Corcelle: "The Roman question is the mountain which threatens to bury us all." He recommended that Oudinot's army refrain from bombarding the monuments of Rome, which were, he wrote to Corcelle, "the property of the Christian world", and according to his instructions Pius IX's return should have been accompanied by an amnesty and the granting of a Constitution.

Under the Empire he returned to private life and undertook his work "L'ancien régime et la révolution", of which only the first part appeared (1856). In pages of beautiful religious psychology Mgr Baunard has shown how Tocqueville's mind and conscience, chiefly under Madame Swetchine's influence, climbed upwards toward a profoundly Christian death. These pages are an interesting document on the evolution of the Liberal ideas of the middle of the nineteenth century. After Tocqueville's death Gustave de Beaumont collected his works in nine volumes. Tocqueville's memoirs of the Republic of 1848 were published in 1893, his correspondence with Gobineau in 1908.

DE BEAUMONT, *Notice sur Alexis de Tocqueville* (Paris, 1897); D'EICHTHAL, *Tocqueville et la démocratie libérale* (Paris, 1897); FAGUET, *Politiques et moralistes du 19e siècle*, 3rd series (Paris, 1900); MARCEL, *Essai politique sur Alexis de Tocqueville* (Paris, 1910); FALLOUX, *Correspondance d'Alexis de Tocqueville avec Mme Swetchine* in *Correspondant* (25 Feb., 1866); BAUNARD, *La foi et ses victoires*, II (Paris, 1884).

GEORGES GOYAU.

Todeschini, FRANCESCO. See PIUS III, POPE.

Todi, DIOCESE OF (TUDERTINA), in Central Italy, is immediately dependent on the Holy See. The city of Todi stands on a steep hill commanding the valley of the Tiber. Its triple walls may still be seen; the innermost, built of rough grey travertine stone, is of Umbrian or Etruscan origin; the middle wall is Roman, and the outside wall dates from the sixth or seventh century. The cathedral, in Lombard style, contains ten pillars of oriental marble. S. Fortunata is a splendid specimen of Italian Gothic. S. Maria della Consolazione, one of the most harmonious works of the Renaissance, was begun in 1508 by Cola Matteuccio; the cupola was constructed in 1606. The church of the Servites of Mary contains the body of St. Philip Benizi, whose statue is the work of Bernini. Almost all the churches possess pictures by Polinari, a native of Todi. The communal hall (1267) is also worthy of notice. On the pre-Roman coins the city is called Tutere; the Romans called it Tuder, or Tudertum. It was sacked by Crassus in the Civil War (83 B.C.); Augustus established a colony there. During the war of the Goths it withstood Totila during a long and severe siege. The Lombards failed to capture it, and Todi and Perugia remained the two chief fortresses defending the passage through the duchy from Rome to the Exarchate. It was included in Pepin's donation to the Holy See. In the eleventh century Todi was a republic, and in 1340 its municipal statutes were drawn up by the jurisconsult Bartolo. In the factions of the Middle Ages Todi was almost always Ghibelline, and was in constant conflict with Perugia. Boniface IX gave the city to the Malatesta of Rimini, but soon took it back. During the fifteenth century it often changed rulers—Biondo Michelotti, Pandolfo Malatesta, Francesco Sforza (1434), Piccinino, Gabriello Catalani (Guelph), who was treacherously slain (1475). The city fell into the hands of Giordano Orsini, who was expelled by Cardinal Giuliano della Rovere (Julius II). The factions were ended by the agreement of the Chiaravalle and the Atti. In 1503 the Orsini were again expelled, on which occasion the fortress of Gregory IX, reputed impregnable, was destroyed.

Todi is the birthplace of Fra Jacopone, the adversary of Boniface VIII and supposed author of the "Stabat Mater", and of the humanist Antonio Pasini (Antonio da Todi). The city honours several martyrs, its bishops, among whom are St. Terentius, or Terentianus, martyred under Diocletian. Other bishops are: St. Callistus, killed by the Goths, succeeded by Fortunatus, whose body was taken to France; Theophylactus (787), sent by Pope Adrian to England and to the Council of Frankfort (794); Rustico Brancaleone (1179), several times a papal legate; Rainuccio degli Atti (1326), expelled from the city by the partisans of Nicolas V, the antipope; Andrea degli Atti (1356), the restorer of ecclesiastical discipline; Guglielmo Dallavigna (1405), who tried to induce the antipope Benedict XIII to renounce his claim; Bartolomeo Aglioni (1436), imprisoned during the troublesome times; Marcello Sante (1606), who erected the seminary; Carpegno (1638), who promoted study and discipline; Cardinal Ulderico; Cardinal Giambattista Altieri (1643), brother of Clement X, a famous canonist; the brothers Filippo (1709) and Ludovico Gualtieri (1719), who erected a new seminary; Francesco M. Pasini (1760), under whom the restoration of the cathedral was completed. The diocese contains 49,200 inhabitants, 98 parishes, 97 secular and 15 regular priests, 6 religious houses of men and 8 of women, 1 boys' college, and 2 girls' schools.

CAPPELLETTI, *Le chiese d'Italia*, XXII (Venice, 1857); LEONI, *Memorie storiche de Todi* (Todi, 1860).

U. BENIGNI.

Tokio, ARCHDIOCESE OF (TOKIENSIS), comprises 21 provinces or 15 departments with a population of over 16,000,000 inhabitants. From 1866 until 1876 Japan formed only one vicariate Apostolic administered by Mgr Petitjean, the first vicar Apostolic of the country (1866–1884). In 1876 it was divided into two vicariates; that of South Japan, extending from Biwa Lake to the Loochoo Islands, with Mgr Petitjean at Osaka, and that of North Japan, comprising the northern provinces from Biwa Lake to the Kurile Islands, ruled by Mgr Osouf (1876–1906), the new vicar Apostolic, residing at Tokio. In 1891 Leo XIII established the ecclesiastical hierarchy in Japan, and erected the Diocese of Hakodate out of the eight most northern provinces and the Yezo, Sado, and Kurile Islands. The same year Mgr Osouf was created Archbishop of Tokio, with the Bishops of Nagasaki, Osaka, and Hakodate as his suffragans. When, in 1866, Mgr Petitjean visited the territory of the future Archdiocese of Tokio, he found only two missionaries at Yokohama, where they had built a church (1862) especially for the use of foreigners, Japanese converts numbering only a few dozens. The actual expansion took place during the thirty years of Mgr Osouf's administration. It was also Mgr Osouf who erected the cathedral of Tokio (1878), and was the first envoy of the pope to the mikado, to whom Leo XIII, 12 Sept., 1885, had him present an autographic letter. The

THE CATHEDRAL, TODI
Built, XIII Century; restored, XIV and XV

archdiocese numbers (1911) one archbishopric, Mgr Bonne, 27 missionaries, 2 native priests, 23 catechists and 9858 Catholics. Tokio has 4186 Catholics divided into six parishes, while Yokohama, the cradle of the mission, besides the parish for foreigners, who number 492, has another church for the Japanese, who number 1213. In different towns and villages there are 50 stations provided with chapels or oratories. Until lately a great many of these parishes and stations had their parochial schools, which, however, had all to be closed for want of means. Besides their ordinary work the missionaries direct a seminary for native priests, two homes for Catholic students, an industrial school for destitute boys (69), an asylum for the aged and homeless, and a hospital with 74 lepers. They also publish two monthly magazines. Engaged in charitable, educational, and mission work are: 42 Brothers of Mary, of whom 9 are Japanese; six Jesuit Fathers, of whom one is Japanese; four Fathers of the Divine Word; 48 Ladies of St. Maur (12 Japanese); 23 Sisters of St. Paul (4 Japanese); and 21 Ladies of the Sacred Heart. The chronological order of their work is as follows: in 1873 the Ladies of St. Maur founded in Yokohama an asylum for destitute girls (236 inmates); an academy for foreigners (1874); and a high school for Japanese (1899). In Tokio they founded an academy (1887), and a foreign language and music school for girls of the highest nobility (1898), and in Shizuoka another high school (1903). The total number of their pupils is 947. The Sisters of St. Paul established in Tokio (1881) an asylum for destitute girls (108 inmates), an academy for foreign girls, and another one for Japanese. The total number of their pupils is 477. The Brothers of Mary direct in Tokio a college (1888) with 830 pupils belonging to the best families, and in Yokohama a commercial school for foreigners (1899) with 106 pupils. The Ladies of the Sacred Heart in Tokio have charge of an academy for girls of the higher classes, both foreign and Japanese (1908). Already they have 121 pupils. The Jesuit Fathers arrived in Tokio in 1908, with the intention of starting a Catholic university. Finally, in 1909, Mgr Mugabure, coadjutor (1902) and successor of Mgr Osouf (1906–10), entrusted four of the western provinces to the care of the Fathers of the Divine Word, residing at Kanazawa. In 1911 the number of baptisms were 1383; marriages, 83; burials, 1149; confirmations 452; Easter Communions, 3512.

M. STEICHEN.

Toledo, ARCHDIOCESE OF (TOLETANENSIS), primatial see of Spain, whose archbishop, raised almost always to the dignity of cardinal, occupies the first place in the ranks of the higher Spanish clergy. Its suffragan dioceses are Coris, Cuenca, Madrid-Alcalá, Plasencia, and Sigüenza. In the course of its long and varied history this diocese has undergone many changes which have successively extended and contracted its vast territory. Geographically its present position is a very unique one, as it consists of four sections separated one from the other and surrounded by other dioceses. The first or principal section (in which the City of Toledo, the capital of the diocese, is situated) is in the centre of the peninsula in the region which was known as the Kingdom of Toledo or New Castile. This section comprises the greater part of the civil Province of Toledo (the district in the north-west belonging to the Diocese of Avila; the extreme eastern strip forms a part of the Diocese of Cuenca), and on the western side it takes a small strip from the eastern section of the provinces of Cáceres and Badajoz. It is bounded on the north by the dioceses of Madrid-Alcalá and Avila; on the south by the Diocese-Priorate of the Military Orders; on the east by the Diocese of Cuenca; and on the west by the Diocese of Plasencia. The second territorial section is formed by a half, approximately speaking, of the eastern portion of the Province of Guadalajara, surrounded by the dioceses of Madrid-Alcalá, Segovia, Sigüenza, and Cuenca. The third territorial section is formed by a great portion of the Province of Albacete on the western side (the ancient Vicarage of Alcaraz), surrounded by the dioceses of Cuenca, Murcia, and Jaen, and the Diocese-Priorate of the Military Orders. The last and smallest territorial section consists of the eastern portion of the Province of Jaen (rural deanery of Cazorla) and the north-eastern portion of the Province of Granada (rural deanery of Huescar) surrounded by the dioceses of Jaen, Murcia, Almeria, and Guadix.

Christianity was introduced into Carpetania in the first century. According to an ancient and venerable tradition the Roman, St. Eugenius, is named as the first Bishop of Toledo and the founder of the see. Certain chronological lists give a series of bishops of Toledo prior to and following St. Eugenius, but modern historical criticism has rejected them. A fierce persecution raged in Toledo under the emperors Diocletian and Maximus, St. Leocadia being one of the most illustrious of the martyrs (9 Dec., 306). It has been asserted that after the Edict of Milan (313) Emperor Constantine raised Toledo to the rank of a metropolitan, but there is absolutely no foundation for this, as the prelates of Toledo continued to rank simply as bishops. Among the most famous during the Roman occupation were Melantius (286?–306?), who is supposed to have consecrated the church of Toledo and who wrote the life of St. Severus, martyr; Audentius (367?), author of "De fide adversus hæreticos" (which has been lost); and Isichius (Hesychius), writer, orator, and poet, in whose time the Visigoths took possession of Carpetania and its capital Toledo (466 or 7). The diocese attained great importance during this period, as its principal city was the seat of the Visigothic Court. It was raised to the rank of a metropolitan and became the centre of a vast ecclesiastical province. At this time Toledo had as suffragan dioceses: Acci, Arcabrica, Basta, Beartia, Bigastrum, Castulo, Complutum, Dianium, Elotona, Illici, Mentesa, Oretum, Oxoma, Palentia, Setabi, Secobia, Segobriga, Segontia, Valentia, Valeria, and Urci. Under the bishop or archbishop Montanus Toledo commenced to extend its primatical jurisdiction, although it was not until many centuries afterwards that this title was conferred upon it. During the Visigothic period many bishops, illustrious for their faith and holiness, governed the See of Toledo. Among these may be mentioned: Julian I, author of various apologetic and moral treatises; Euphemius or Epiphanius, in whose time the Visigoths were converted to Christianity; and Aurasius (603–15), who successfully defended the claim of Toledo for metropolitan supremacy which was disputed by Cartagena.

The archbishops of the seventh century (615–90) were distinguished for their holiness: St. Eladius (615–33); St. Eugenius III (646–57), poet, theologian, and musician; St. Ildefonsus (659–68), the most notable prelate of Toledo during the Gothic epoch, conqueror of the Jovinian heresy, favoured with celestial manifestations, author of a celebrated book in defence of the virginity of Mary and of other dogmatic, moral, and historical treatises; and St. Julian II (680–90), author of many works, the best known of which is "Historia Rebellionis Pauli adversus Wambam". During the Mussulman occupation (a period of 373 years) the condition of the Christians who continued to live in the territories they had conquered was subject to many vicissitudes, but the See of Toledo did not cease to exist during this long period of captivity. Cixila (774?–783?) wrote the life of his predecessor, St. Ildefonsus; St.

Eulogius, the noble martyr of Córdova (859), to whom are attributed various Latin treatises, was elected to the see but never took possession of it; Bonitus (862 or 66) wrote an apologetic work in defence of the Abbot Samson. Among the archbishops of the Mozarabic period Elipandus (783–808) is a notable exception to the rest, apostatizing, and embracing and propagating Nestorianism.

With the reconquest of Toledo in 1085 by Alfonso VI of Castile, the diocese entered upon a new and more prosperous era, favoured as it was by donations and privileges not only of the Castilian sovereigns, but of other potentates and of all social classes. It was thus that it reached that height of power and splendour which made it the envy of all the churches of the kingdom, and which enabled it to contribute such large sums to all national enterprises, to the erection of notable monuments, to the succour of the needy, and to the general diffusion of learning and culture. The first bishop of this period was the Frenchman, Bernard, a Cluniac monk and Abbot of Sahagún (1086–1124), in whose time the principal church of Toledo was once more restored to Catholic worship, and Urban II by a Bull (1088) expressly conferred on Toledo the dignity of primacy over the churches of Spain, a declaration which, however, did not prevent the other churches from disputing with Toledo this high distinction. It was during the pontificate of Urban II that the Roman Rite was substituted for the ancient Isidorian or Mozarabic Rite (1089). Archbishop Rodrigo Jiménez de Rada (1210–47) is one of the most notable figures of his time; a statesman, counsellor of kings, strenuous warrior, and a learned writer, he conferred innumerable services on the Church and the State. He assisted at the great battle of Las Navas de Tolosa; annexed the village of Quesada and the district of Cazorla to the diocese; commenced the building of the cathedral at Toledo, which is still in existence; defended and consolidated the primacy of his see; and contributed to the foundation of the first general schools (*Estudios generales*). Rodrigo began a great historic work, basing it on Christian and Arabic sources, completing the plan with the section called "De Rebus Hispaniæ", last and best of his historical works. Gil de Albornoz (1339–50), cardinal, was a great statesman and warrior, and founder of a famous college for Spaniards at the University of Bologna, which produced many celebrated men.

Pedro Tenorio (1376–99), an enterprising and energetic man, was very influential during the reigns of Henry II, John I, and Henry III; he restored buildings and works of public utility at his own expense, and founded the Hospital of Villafranca del Puente, which is still in existence and in active use. Pedro González de Mendoza (1483–95), called *el gran cardenal de España*, was of noble lineage and the counsellor of the Catholic sovereigns; he displayed a princely prodigality in the many works which he undertook and completed. Among these may be mentioned the Colegio Mayor of Valladolid and the Hospital of Santa Cruz for foundlings. His successor, Fray Francisco Ximénez de Cisneros (1495–1517), is perhaps the most illustrious of all the prelates of Toledo, and at the same time one of the most prominent figures in the history of Spain. In him were united qualities rarely found combined, for he was a learned and saintly religious, an austere and energetic reformer, a conqueror and statesman, the father of the poor, and the Mæcenas of Spanish arts and letters. Among the titles conferred on him were Cardinal of Sta. Balbina, confessor of Isabella the Catholic, inquisitor-general, and regent of the kingdom. The Church, humanity, and his diocese found in him a protector and benefactor. He extended the limits of the Diocese of Toledo to Africa, adding Oran and its territory, which he personally and at his own expense conquered (1509). Only some of the many works which he accomplished can be mentioned: among these being the foundation of the University of Alcalá de Henares; the printing of the Complutensian Polyglot Bible; the foundation of the library of the cathedral of Toledo; and the restoration of the Mozarabic Rite in a private chapel. Several monasteries owe their foundation to him, as well as the College of San Juan de la Penitencia at Toledo for the education of virtuous orphan girls, and three public wheat granaries for the benefit of poor labourers at Toledo, Alcalá, and Torrelaguna (his native place).

Some of the archbishops who succeeded Cisneros were distinguished for the liberality with which they promoted the arts, filling the cathedral of Toledo with priceless works of art, the glory of the Spanish Renaissance. Alonso de Fonseca (1524–34) gave during his lifetime to the chapter of Toledo an annual income of 400,000 maravedis to be devoted to providing marriage portions for poor girls; Juan Tavera (1534–45), cardinal, distinguished prelate, and statesman, founded the general Hospital of San Juan Bautista, outside the walls of Toledo; Juan Martínez Guijeno, better known under the latinized form of his name, Silicius (1546–57), cardinal, ardent patriot, and generous protector of the needy, founded at Toledo the College of Nuestra Señora de los Remedios (commonly known as the *Colegio de Doncellas nobles*), an important institution which is still in existence; the Colegio de Infantes, where the choir boys of the cathedral are educated and instructed; and the Monasterio de Recogidas, which he endowed and founded in the ancient synagogue of St. María la Blanca. The Dominican archbishop, Bartolomé Carranza de Miranda (1559–1576), learned theologian and canonist, was the author of the "Suma Conciliorum omnium" published at Venice (1573). Notwithstanding his learning and virtue, he was suspected of heresy, examined before the Inquisition, and eventually acquitted. The learned and pious García de Loaysa Girón (1598–99), strenuous upholder of ecclesiastical discipline, collected and published (with annotations and emendations) the "Collectio conciliorum Hispaniæ". Cardinal Bernardo de Sandoval y Rojas (1599–1618) was liberal and charitable, and a great patron of letters. His administration was advantageous to the diocese; he established its rights over the district of Cazorla; secured the ordinary episcopal jurisdiction in the diocesan territory over the Order of St. John of Jerusalem; and restored to the diocese the important town of Brigueja.

According to reliable statistics the Diocese of Toledo comprised at that time 4 cities, 183 towns, 322 villages and hamlets, with 816 parishes and 751,733 souls. The archiepiscopal estate yielded at the time a revenue of 300,000 ducats. The receipts of the chapter were also ample; the manufacturing industries yielded more than 40,000 ducats annually. The revenues of all the churches of Spain combined did not greatly exceed in value the archiepiscopal estate of Toledo. Cardinal Infante D. Fernando de Austria (1618–41), brother of Philip IV, the successor of Sandoval y Rojas, distinguished himself as an able military commander and as Viceroy of the Low Countries, where victory crowned his military efforts. The cardinal-archbishops who succeeded him were Gaspar de Borja (1643–45); Baltazar Moscoso (1646–65); Pasqual de Aragón (1666–77); and Luis Fernández Porto Carrero (1678–1709). All took an active part in the politics of their time as viceroys, counsellors of state, and governors of the realm. Cardinal Francisco Antonio Lorenzana (1772–1800) understood how to wield, at a time when the Church was passing through a crisis, a power which would have done credit to the great prelates instrumental in the restoration of the Spanish Church in the past. Generous and liberal, "Padre de los Pobres" (Father of the Poor) as he is simply styled in his epitaph, *littérateur*, patron of arts and letters, promoter of national industries and all works of public utility, he carried his zeal into all these spheres. He rebuilt many of the city and country churches of his diocese, made large bequests to the Church, improved the archiepiscopal library, defrayed the expenses of the monumental work entitled "P. P. Toletanorum quotquot extant opera", and of the Gothic Missal and Breviary of the Mozarabic Rite. In the city of Toledo the erection of the university building, the foundation of the hospital for the insane, and of the Real Alcazar (which he also restored), and *la Fonda de la Caridad* (a free lodging-house) are a few of the many works that still bear witness to his zeal. His successor, Cardinal Luis María de Borbón, an Infante of Spain, (1800–23), was president of the regency during the absence of Ferdinand VII. Cardinal Pedro de Inguanzo (1824–36) published some works in defence of the rights of the Church and of ecclesiastical discipline, and commenced the great seminary building.

Cardinal Juan Ignacio Moreno (1875–84), in his youth professor in the Notariado, published a work entitled "Tratado sobre el ortorgamiento de poderes públicos", and as the bishop of various Spanish dioceses (lastly that of Toledo) he defended the Church against the aggressions of revolution, taking part also in Roman affairs, as his high position as cardinal demanded. At this time the Archdiocese of Toledo lost much territory by the erection of the Diocese-Priorate of the Military Orders, which takes up the entire civil Province of Ciudad Real, and was erected by Pius IX, 18 Nov., 1875. Cardinal F. Zeferino González was an illustrious Dominican and the restorer of Scholasticism, author among many other well-known works of the "Estudios sobre la Filosofía" and "Estudios Religiosos, Filosóficos, Scientíficos y Sociales". He had on various occasions declined episcopal honours, but at length, after having occupied the sees of Cordova and Seville, he was raised to that of Toledo, governing from 1884 to 1885, when he resigned the dignity. A still greater reduction in the territorial boundaries of the Diocese of Toledo took place at this time, when the Bull of 7 March, 1885, created the Diocese of Madrid-Alcalá, which comprises the entire civil Province of Madrid. Cardinal Miguel Paya y Rico (1886–92) was a conspicuous figure at the Vatican Council when, as Bishop of Cuenca, he pronounced the decisive discourse which determined the proclamation of papal infallibility. He was learned and charitable, and completed and inaugurated in 1889 the seminary commenced by Inguanzo. Cardinal Antolín Moneseillo (1892–97), a prolific and finished writer, orator, and statesman, wrote among other works: "Manuel del Seminarista", a catechism; various articles touching upon ecclesiastical discipline; and many sermons, panegyrics, and pastorals. Cardinal Ciriaco María Sancha (1898–1909) devoted himself mainly to the study of social questions. He wrote "Regimen del terror en Italia Unitaria" and the "Kulturkampf", and numerous discourses and pastoral letters. Cardinal Gregorio María Aguirre, of the Franciscan Order, has, since October, 1909, occupied the primatial see of Spain.

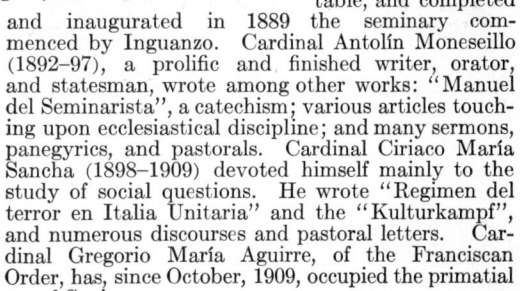

Toledo is one of the greatest art centres not only of Spain but of the civilized world. Of its principal religious edifices, among which are to be found notable works of art in the styles prevailing from the thirteenth to the eighteenth centuries, may be mentioned: the cathedral, a magnificent five-nave Gothic structure, with numerous additional sections commenced in 1227 by King St. Ferdinand and Archbishop Jiménez de Rada; the Franciscan Monastery of San Juan de los Reyes, built in 1476 by Ferdinand and Isabella, to which is attached a church and cloister in ornate Ogival style, and which has recently been richly decorated; the church of the ancient hospital of Santa Cruz founded by Cardinal González de Mendoza, dating from the early part of the sixteenth century, is one of the most beautiful examples of the Plateresque of the early Spanish Renaissance. Of great interest also are a number of the churches of Toledo in which remains of the Visigothic period are preserved, and others built in the Moorish style, called *mudejar* by the Spaniards, which

TOMB OF CARDINAL TAVERA IN THE AFUERA HOSPITAL, TOLEDO
Alonzo Berruguete, 1557

is the Arabic style adopted after the reconquest of the city by Alfonso VI. Mention must also be made of other notable buildings although not of Christian origin—the ancient mosque *del Cristo de la Luz* (reconstructed in the tenth century) and the synagogues of Santa María la Blanca (thirteenth century?) and del Transito (fourteenth century). Many excellent architects, sculptors, and painters worked in Toledo in the numberless monastic and parochial churches of the city, but especially in the construction and embellishment of the cathedral. Among the painters the most important was Dominico Theotocopulis, called "El Greco", native of Crete, who established himself at Toledo and produced numerous works (chiefly of religious character) which are highly prized and studied at the present time, and which represent one of the most curious phases of Spanish art, marking the point of departure of the modern national art. Many important religious buildings are also to be found in various parts of the diocese, among which may be mentioned: the ancient collegiate church (at present a parish church of Talavera de la Reina), a three-naved Ogival building started by Archbishop Jiménez de Rada in 1211 and finished between the thirteenth and fifteenth centuries; the ancient collegiate church of Torrijos (also used at the present time as a parochial church), a three-naved edifice founded and endowed by Doña Teresa Enríquez (built between 1509 and 1518), an interesting example of the florid Ogival style and the Gothic Plateresque of the transition period; the parochial church of Tembleque, also of the early sixteenth century, an example of the transition period from the Gothic to the Renaissance; and the parochial church of Tepes, a magnificent temple of three naves, designed by the celebrated architect Alonzo Covarrubias and built between the years 1533 and 1552 in the style of the transition period Gothic Plateresque and Grecian Romanesque.

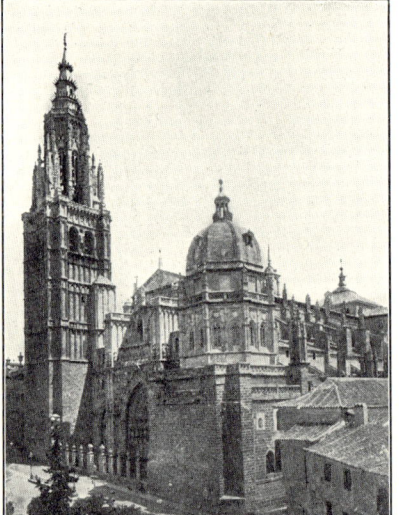

THE CATHEDRAL, TOLEDO

Famous in the history of Toledo are its councils, held in greatest veneration by the sovereign pontiffs, and the source of the purest religious and moral doctrines. They were national and provincial; those held in the years 396 and 400, first of those whose acts have been preserved, opposed the heresy of the Priscillianists and legislated for the reform of the clergy. In 440 or the beginning of 448 a national council seems to have been convoked which once more condemned the doctrines of Priscillian. The second provincial council (527) promulgated five canons in which various points of discipline were established. In the national council held in 540 decisions concerning the reformation of certain disciplinary usages and practices were adopted. The most famous of all the councils of Toledo was the third national council (held in 589), in which King Reccared, the prelates, and grandees, proclaimed their abjuration of the Arian heresy and made a profession of faith according to the doctrine of the Council of Nicæa. In addition, the bishops issued religious decrees against the remaining vestiges of ancient idolatry, restricted the rights of the Jews, commanded that the statutes of previous councils and the decrees of the sovereign pontiffs be observed, and promulgated other canons of great importance for the reformation of accepted usages and the restoration of ecclesiastical discipline. Another national council (597) promulgated two canons relative to the episcopal and priestly state. In the provincial council commonly called the Council of Gundemar (610) the metropolitan jurisdiction of the bishops of Toledo over the entire Province of Cartagena was explicitly stated. In the fourth national council (633), one of the most important held in Spain, presided over by St. Isidore of Seville, very important measures in both canonical and political matters were adopted. The fifth national council (636) was also political in its prescriptions, which were directed towards the defence of the king. The sixth (638) approved constitutions relating to discipline, morals, and political matters. The seventh (646) established certain canons which had been promulgated in previous councils. In the national council which is said to have been held in 650 the heresy of the Monothelites, who denied that Christ had two wills, was condemned. In the reign of the Visigothic king, Recesvindo, besides the councils which are classed as doubtful, were held: the eighth provincial council (653), in which some interesting points relating to discipline and civil law were decided; the ninth provincial (655), in which matters of discipline were discussed; and the tenth national (656) in which certain canons referring to the monastic life were sanctioned. The eleventh provincial council (675), held during the reign of Wamba, formulated certain prescriptions in regard to discipline and the reform of certain usages, concerning the clergy in particular. The twelfth (681) and the thirteenth (683) national, and the fourteenth (684) provincial, councils were held during the reign of Ervigius. The twelfth and thirteenth councils approved certain canons relating to discipline and other usages commonly in practice; and the fathers assembled at the fourteenth professed their adherence to the Sixth Œcumenical Council. The fifteenth national council (688) confirmed the doctrine contained in an apologetic treatise written by St. Julian, Archbishop of Toledo, who presided at the council. The sixteenth and seventeenth (694) councils were also national; the first imposed penance and declared an anathema against Archbishop Sisebert (who had plotted against King Egica), and the second discussed various disciplinary measures. It is believed that still another national council was held during the Visigothic period between 700–712, the acts of which have been lost, but it is said that canons relative to the preservation of the integrity of faith and to the regulation of certain usages were promulgated.

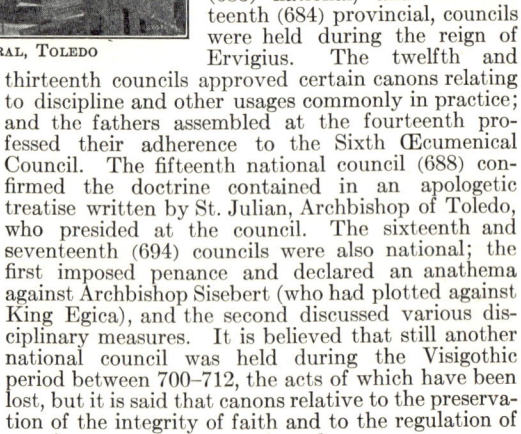

After the reconquest of Toledo by the Christians (1085) at least ten provincial councils were held in the city of Toledo, some of them being of great interest for the canonical history of Spain. Archbishop Raimundo convened that held in 1138, in which certain difficulties existing between the archbishop and the canons with regard to the distribution of the revenues of the Church were adjusted and the number of canonries definitely fixed. The archbishop, Infante Don Juan de Aragón, presided over the council of 1323 which prescribed a formula with regard to articles of faith, the commandments, and the sacraments, and formulated canons relative to points of discipline. The provincial councils of 1324 and

ALCANTARA BRIDGE, TOLEDO

1326 were also called by Don Juan, the first to publish certain papal constitutions and to regulate the life of clerics, and the second to deal with questions of ecclesiastical law and the chastity of the clergy. The council of 1339 convoked by Cardinal Archbishop Albornoz treated points of discipline and ordered all parish priests to take a census of their parishes. Archbishop Don Vasco convoked the council of 1355, the decisions of which were not important. The Western Schism was the occasion of the convoking of another provincial council under Archbishop Tenorio in 1379, in which it was agreed to remain neutral, professing allegiance for the moment neither to the pope at Rome nor the pope at Avignon. The provincial council of 1565–66, held during the time that the trial of Archbishop Carranza de Miranda was pending, was a very notable one giving rise to many incidents; its decrees formed a veritable encyclopedia of ecclesiastical law. The council of 1580 under Cardinal Archbishop Quiroja legislated with regard to converted Moors (Moriscos), and prescribed regulations that were conducive to the preservation of their faith. The council of 1582–83 promulgated very advantageous laws for the propagation of religion and the reform of accepted usages. At that time the suffragan bishops were seven, those of Córdova, Sigüenza, Palencia, Cuenca, Segovia, Jaén, and Osma.

Since the sixteenth century other conciliar reunions have been held, but they do not rank as provincial councils, being simply diocesan synods convoked to arrange diocesan affairs and to compile the constitutions of the archdioceses. The educational and charitable institutions founded in the diocese both in the past and in our own time have been numerous and important; among those still in existence may be mentioned: in Toledo, the Hospital General del Rey, founded in the time of Alfonso VIII of Castile, or St. Ferdinand, for the decrepit, the blind, and the crippled; the Hospital Provincial de la Misericordia, founded in the fifteenth century by Doña Guiomar de Meneses where the sick of both sexes are cared for by the Sisters of Charity; the Hospital de Dementes, commonly called "el nuncio", founded at the end of the fifteenth century by Francisco Ortiz; the Hospital de San Juan Bautista, commonly called "de Afuera", founded about 1539 by Cardinal Archbishop Juan Tavera. Besides these establishments there are in the city of Toledo free public schools for young girls and children and day nurseries, all in charge of the Sisters of Charity. The Colegio de doncellas vírgenes de Na. Sa. de los Remedios, commonly called "Doncellas nobles", was founded in 1551 by Cardinal Archbishop Siliceo for the maintenance, education, and training of respectable young women in reduced circumstances, for whom the college also provides a marriage dower. The Asilio Provincial, supported by the provincial committee, shelters foundlings, orphans, the aged of both sexes, and maintains schools for boys and girls. The Little Sisters of the Poor (established at Toledo in 1879) care for the aged of both sexes; the tertiaries of the Divina Pastora (established in the city in 1885) teach girls and assist the sick in their own homes. The Asylum of the Sacred Heart (founded in 1887 by the priest, Joaquín de la Madrid) supports, educates, and obtains employment for orphan boys. The Marist Brothers (established in 1901) teach boys and young men, and the Hermanas del Servicio Doméstico (established in 1902) prepare girls for domestic service and have some orphans under their care. In various other cities, towns, and villages of the archdiocese there are also asylums, hospitals, and free schools. The recognized and authorized Catholic periodicals published to-day in the archdiocese are printed in Toledo and are as follows: "Boletín oficial del arzobispado" (founded in 1846), official ecclesiastical organ, issued on the 10th, 20th, and 30th of each month; "El Castellano", a purely Catholic publication without political affiliations (founded in January, 1903), issued every Tuesday and Saturday; "El Porvenir" (founded in August, 1903), a politico-Catholic supporter of the Carlist cause, and published weekly.

There is no complete history of the Diocese of Toledo. The bibliography of the city, of its territory, its monuments, and its illustrious men is complete and extensive, and for this reason only some books which principally concern the questions treated in this article are given.
PORREÑO, *Historia episcopal y real de España* (MSS. in the library of the Chapter of the Church of Toledo); CASTEJÓN Y FONSECA, *Primacía de la Santa Iglesia de Toledo* (Madrid, 1645), which account of the early history of the see should be read with caution, owing to the abundant use of the "false chronicles"; SEVILLANO, *Defensa christiana política y verdadera de la primacía de las Españas que goza la Santa Iglesia de Toledo* (Madrid, 1726); *España sagrada*, V, VI, VII, VIII (Madrid, 1750–52). LORENZANA, PP. *Toletanorum quotquot extant opera* (Madrid, 1782–93); TEJADA Y RAMIRO, *Colección de cánones de la Iglesia española* (Madrid, 1849–50); LA FUENTE, *Historia eclesiástica de España* (Barcelona, 1855–59); PARRO, *Toledo en la mano* (Toledo, 1857); MARTÍN GAMERO, *Historia de la ciudad de Toledo* (Toledo, 1862); DE PALAZUELOS, *Los concilios de Toledo* (Barcelona, 1888); DE CEDILLO, *Toledo en al siglo XVI* (Madrid, 1901).

CONDE DE CEDILLO.

Toledo, DIOCESE OF (TOLETANA IN AMERICA), Ohio, U. S. A., formed out of the Diocese of Cleveland and erected into a separate jurisdiction, 15 April, 1910. It includes the Counties of Lucas (Toledo), Allen, Crawford, Defiance, Fulton, Hancock, Henry, Ottawa, Paulding, Putnam, Sandusky, Seneca, Van Wert, Williams, Wood, and Wyandot; an area of 6969 sq. miles. The principal towns are Lima, Tiffin, Fremont, Defiance, and Delphos. Estimated Catholic population, 125,000.

There are 86 parishes with resident priests and 25 missions, 95 diocesan priests and 31 of the regular clergy. The number of parish schools is 65, with an enrolment of 13,500. One college (Jesuit) and three academy-colleges provide the departments for higher education.

The work of charity and reform is supplied by three orphanages, two hospitals, one home for the aged poor, and one house of the Good Shepherd.

History.—The country bordering on Lake Erie was in the path of missioners and trading explorers, who, in the seventeenth century, made their way from Quebec to the upper Great Lakes. French settlers ventured down from Detroit, and a French fort was established on the Maumee in 1680. Traders followed this river to its source in Indiana, whence it was not difficult to reach the more important posts about Vincennes. The lake shore would also have been the natural route for the Jesuit Fathers, who, in the latter half of the eighteenth century, journeyed from Detroit to visit the Hurons, and Father Pierre-Joseph de Bonnécamps, returning to the north with Céloron's company from the expedition to the Ohio, entered Lake Erie on the way to Detroit, at the mouth of the Maumee (Miami of the Lake), 5 Oct., 1749.

Bishop Fenwick, writing to Father Badin in August, 1823 ("Catholic Church in Ohio" in "U. S. Catholic Magazine"), speaks of Catholic Indians along the Seneca River who crossed to Malden and Sandwich in Canada for marriage and baptism. Father Edmund Burke, who signs himself "Vicaire général du Haut Canada", and was stationed near the present Monroe (Frenchtown), Michigan, in 1794, visited, not Fort Meigs, as has been asserted, but Fort Miami, at the rapids of the Maumee; and in 1825 Bishop Fenwick's vicar-general, Father Gabriel Richard, who as early as 1806 had attended Monroe from Detroit, indicates that the district "de la Bai Miamy" was considered as one with that of St-Antoine on the River Raisin. This can be more easily understood, if we remember that the territory of Michigan for a long time laid claim to lands in which Toledo is now located.

Even after Detroit had become a separate diocese, the Rev. P. Carabin, pastor at Monroe, enumerates many on his lists as "inhabitants of Toledo" (1837).

The building of water-ways along the line of the Maumee River from the Ohio and the Wabash to Lake Erie did much to open up the country to German and Irish immigrants invited by Bishops Fenwick and Purcell, of Cincinnati, to avail themselves of the opportunities of labour and farming.

After 1830 organized congregations began to take the place of scattered missions, and a resident pastor was placed at St. Mary's, Tiffin, in 1831.

In 1841 Rev. Amadeus Rappe organized St. Francis de Sales's Parish, Toledo, of which he was pastor until his appointment as first Bishop of Cleveland in 1847. Associated with him and succeeding him in this pastorate was Rev. Louis de Goesbriand, first Bishop of Burlington, Vermont. Among the pioneer priests of this section were Fathers Badin, Ignatius Mullon, Edward T. Collins, Projectus J. Macheboeuf (afterwards Bishop of Denver), E. Thienpont, and Henry Damien Juncker (later Bishop of Alton), men eminent for learning as well as piety; and these had the co-operation of the Redemptorist and Sanguinist Fathers, under the leadership respectively of Father Tschenhens (1832) and Father Francis de Sales Brunnet (1844). Members of the latter congregation (C.PP.S.), which was introduced by Father Brunner, are still (1912) in charge of parishes and missions in the Diocese of Toledo.

The growth of Catholicism was particularly noticeable in the city of Toledo. At the date of its erection into an episcopal see there were within the city twenty parishes. This rapid increase had been greatly promoted by a steady influx after 1870 of Poles and Hungarians, employed largely in factories, quarries, and public works.

Among the priests prominent in Toledo in this period of development were: the Rt. Rev. F. M. Boff (1859), who in 1872 was made Vicar-General of Cleveland and held the unique distinction of having served as administrator of that diocese not less than six times in a period of forty years (d. 22 March, 1912); Father Edward Hannin (1863), who was administrator of the Diocese of Cleveland from the resignation of Bishop Rappe to the appointment of Bishop Gilmour, and who when over seventy years of age undertook the building of one of the finest church edifices in the Middle West; and Rev. Patrick F. Quigley, whose widely-noticed action against state interference in parish schools, in the matter of reports and truancy, gave occasion for much hostile demonstration, especially on the part of members of the A. P. A. This priest's contention before the several courts was ably if not successfully maintained by the Hon. Frank H. Hurd, a convert to Catholicism, and a congressman, celebrated for his convincing advocacy of free trade.

The commercial advantages of the city and the numerical strength of Catholics had long drawn attention to Toledo; and on the death of Bishop Horstmann (1908) the bishops of the Province of Cincinnati recommended to the Holy See the division of the Diocese of Cleveland. The request was favourably considered, and Toledo was named as the seat of the new diocese, with St. Francis de Sales's designated as its cathedral church. Rt. Rev. John P. Farrelly, D.D., who had been consecrated Bishop of Cleveland, 1 May, 1909, was appointed temporary administrator. Rt. Rev. Joseph Schrembs, D.D., first bishop, was born at Wuzelhofen, near Ratisbon, Bavaria, 12 March, 1866. Following his elder brother, Rudesind, who had become a Benedictine monk at St. Vincent's, Pennsylvania, he came to the United States in 1877.

He completed his course of humanities when but 16 years of age at St. Vincent's College, near Pittsburg. After a few years spent in teaching, he was accepted by Bishop Richter as a student for the Diocese of Grand Rapids, and entered the Seminary of Montreal in 1884. On 29 June, 1889, Rev. Mr. Schrembs was ordained priest in the cathedral at Grand Rapids. He was successively assistant and pastor at St. Mary's Church, West Bay City, and was transferred to St. Mary's Church, Grand Rapids, Oct., 1900. In 1903 he was appointed vicar-general of the diocese, and was named domestic prelate, Jan., 1906. Meantime he had brought about the establishment of a high school at Grand Rapids, thus demonstrating the feasibility of intermediate grades for the Catholic common school. On 22 Feb., 1911, he was consecrated titular Bishop of Sophene and auxiliary to the Bishop of Grand Rapids. He at once espoused the cause of workmen in their difficulties with the employers in the furniture factories, skilfully averted a panic, and contributed much to bring about an agreement. On 11 Aug., 1911, he was transferred to the See of Toledo. A notable demonstration marked his entry into the city on Sunday, 1 Oct., and on 4 Oct. he was enthroned in his cathedral church.

PARKMAN, *Lasalle and the Discovery of the Great West* (Boston, 1899), xi, 151; IDEM, *Conspiracy of Pontiac*, I, v, 162; xiii, 281; II, xxxi, 317; SHEA, *Cath. Church in the United States* (New York, 1886), I, 631; II (1888), 387, 474 sqq.; *Jesuit Relations* (Cleveland, 1900), LXIX, 191; SCRIBNER, *Memoirs* (Western Historical Association, Madison, Wisconsin, 1910); HOUCK, *Catholic Church in Northern Ohio*, I (Cleveland, 1903), 1 sqq.; *United States Catholic Historical Magazine*, IV, xiii, 22; *United States Catholic Magazine* (March, 1848), 155; *Diocesan Reports* (Cleveland and Toledo, 1911); parish records: *St. Antoine de la Rivière aux Raisins; St. Francis de Sales, Toledo; St. Mary's, Tiffin, Ohio.*

JOHN T. O'CONNELL.

Toledo, FRANCISCO, philosopher, theologian, and exegete, son of an actuary, b. at Córdova, 4 Oct., 1532; d. at Rome, 14 Sept., 1596. He studied philosophy at Valencia and theology under Domingo Soto at Salamanca. At the age of twenty-three he taught philosophy at Salamanca, and, after his ordination, entered the Society of Jesus there, 3 June, 1558, and made his novitiate at Simanacas. In 1559 he went to Rome and was professed in 1564. He successively filled the posts of master of novices, professor of philosophy for three years,

FRANCISCO CARDINAL TOLEDO

Scholastic and moral theology for six years, and prefect of studies of the Roman College. He was theologian of the Sacred Penitentiary and preacher to the pope and cardinals for twenty-four years, accompanied Monsignor Commendone on his mission to the Emperor Maximilian and King Sigismund of Poland, and was the envoy of various popes to Vienna, Poland, Germany, Bavaria, and Louvain, where he received Baius's abjuration of the propositions which had been condemned by Pius V and Gregory XIII. Clement VIII created him cardinal, 17 September, 1593; this dignity, it seems, he desired to renounce in 1594 so that he would be free to retire and die in one of the Jesuit houses. He was largely instrumental in the reconciliation of Henry IV to the Church and to Spain; at his death Henry had a memorial service for him in Paris. As a religious he is classed by Mariana as of ordinary virtue; he was dispensed from religious obedience by a secret papal Brief, lived in the papal palace, sought the cardinal's hat, and in the latter years of his life intervened in Jesuit affairs with disastrous results. Gregory XIII considered him one of the most learned men of his age, and Soto ranks him as a genius.

His philosophical works, especially "De anima", adopted as a text-book in the University of Salamanca, give indications of a philosophical revival as regards both matter and method. Irrelevant questions are set aside, others are weighed or reduced, and certain problems are stated and discussed in a broader spirit. In his Scriptural commentaries he examines every sentence of the text, points out their relationship, gives Patristic references in the annotations, discusses and judges dogmatic questions learnedly and lucidly. By some he is considered the foremost interpreter of his century, and his exegetical works certainly deserve the first place. In his theological works he is clear, concise, and orderly. He proclaims himself a disciple of St. Augustine and St. Thomas, although on certain questions he is quite at variance with them, as for example the proximate cause of predestination, which for him is *prævisa bona opera*. In regard to the famous Scotist teaching that the Word would have become man even if Adam had not sinned, he says: it is neither true, probable, nor ingenious. His works may be divided into three classes: (1) Philosophical: "Introductio in dialecticam Aristotelis" (Rome, 1561), thirteen editions, apparently the first work of a Jesuit to be printed in Mexico; "Commentaria una cum quæstionibus in universam Aristotelis logicam" (Rome, 1572), seventeen editions; "Commentaria de physica auscultatione" (Venice, 1573), fifteen editions; "De generatione et corruptione" (Venice, 1575), seven editions; "De anima" (Venice, 1574), twenty editions; "Opera omnia. Opera philosophica" (Lyons, 1586–92), only one volume issued. (2) Theological: "In Summam theologiæ S. Thomæ Aquinatis enarratio" (4 vols., Rome, 1869), published by Father José Paría, S.J.; "Summa casuum sive instructio sacerdotum" (Lyons, 1599), forty-six editions (Spanish tr., Juan de Salas; Italian, Andreo Verna; French, Goffar; summaries in Latin, Spanish, French, and Italian). (3) Exegetical: "In sacrosanctum Joannis Evangelium commentarium" (Rome, 1592), nine editions; "In prima XII capita Sacrosancti Jesu Christi D. N. Evangelium secundum Lucam" (Rome, 1600), printing supervised by Father Miguel Vázquez, S. J.; "In Epistolam B. Pauli Apostoli ad Romanos" (Rome, 1602), Chaldean tr., Father Azevedo. Manuscripts: "Emmendationes in Sacra Biblia vulgata", corrected by direction of Clement VIII; "Regulæ hebraicæ pro lingua sancta intelligenda". Sermons: "Motivós y advertencias de cosas dignas de reformación cerca del Breviario".

NIEREMBERG, *Varones ilustres de la compañía de Jesus*, V (Bilbao, 1890); PARIA, *Francisci Toleti e Societate Jesu S. R. E. Præsbyteri Cardinalis*, introduction to *In Summam theologiæ S. Thomæ Aquinatis enarratio* (Rome, 1869); ASTRAIN, *Historia de la compañía de Jesus en la Asistencia de España*, III (Madrid, 1909), 595–604, 630–33; SOMMERVOGEL, *Bibliothèque de la compagnie de Jésus*, VIII, 64; HURTER, *Nomenclator*.

ANTONIO PÉREZ GOYENA.

Tolentino. See MACERATA AND TOLENTINO, UNITED SEES OF.

Toleration, HISTORY OF.—In any attempt to deal historically with the attitude of the Church towards religious toleration two considerations have throughout to be kept in mind. In the first place, nearly all ecclesiastical legislation in regard to the repression of heresy proceeds upon the assumption that heretics are in wilful revolt against lawful authority, that they are, in fact, apostates who by their own culpable act have renounced the true faith into which they were baptized, breaking the engagements made by them, or by sponsors in their name, when they became members of the Church of Christ. It is easy to see that in the Middle Ages this was not an unreasonable assumption. The Church of God was then indeed as a city set upon a hill. No one could be ignorant of her claims, and if certain people repudiated her authority it was by an act of rebellion inevitably carrying with it a menace to the sovereignty which the rest of the world accepted. This at least was the case with the Cathari, the Waldenses, and the Albigenses, with the Lollards and the Hussites, and it was still the case with the immediate followers of Luther, of Calvin, of Knox, and of the other early Reformers. Only by degrees and after a considerable lapse of time did generations come into being who could be regarded as inculpably heretical, for the plea of invincible ignorance implies not only that their education took place entirely under heretical influences, but also that they could attain adult life without being effectively confronted with the claims which the true Church makes upon the loyalty of reasonable men. It might plausibly be maintained, for example, that such conditions were at no time realized among the Huguenots of France, or in the more Catholic districts of Central Europe. Hence we cannot be entirely surprised that there were those who excused such measures as the Revocation of the Edict of Nantes, or who supported the repressive legislation which was inaugurated by the Catholic sovereigns of Poland and Hungary in the sixteenth and seventeenth centuries.

In the second place it is to be remembered that owing to the fact that the canon law deals very largely with the enunciation of principles of right and wrong which are of their own nature irreformable, the direct repeal of its provisions has never or very rarely been resorted to. This course undoubtedly has the great advantage of inspiring respect for the sanctity and stability of the law, but the consequence follows that there remain upon the statute-book a number of enactments which owing to changed conditions are to all practical intents and purposes obsolete. The medieval legislation of the Church with regard to usury, testamentary dispositions, matrimony, and especially heresy, largely falls under this category, while the natural result of the retention of a considerable mass of obsolescent decretals must be the creation of an element of, at least temporary, uncertainty, under which some will favour and others resist the legislation that is passing away. For example there was bound to be a period during which rigourists would still appeal to the very uncompromising measures in dealing with heretics which were contemplated by many texts of the canon law, while on the other hand larger-minded contemporaries, who were themselves perhaps living under political conditions which forced them to appreciate the advantages of toleration, tended to treat these same provisions as a dead letter and to deny them all validity in practical life. The effect of both these considerations has been to make it extremely difficult to draw a hard-and-fast line between the circumstances under which the Church recognized the desirability of a large toleration of dissident opinions on the ground both of justice and expediency, and those under which it seemed a duty to stamp out by a policy of firm repression an evil germ which threatened indefinite mischief to the well-being of Christian society. Every lawfully-constituted society must put down on principle the propagation of such sedition as threatens its own existence, and this is not persecution so long as reason and humanity are respected in the means of suppression employed.

Persecution begins when no reasonable proportion is observed between the force used in compulsion and the importance and power of the interests which it is sought to control. To determine the exact point at which legitimate repression passes into persecution is hence a matter of extreme difficulty. For this reason we should probably obtain a clearer view of the toleration of the Church in past history by studying the relations of the papacy with those bodies which like the Jews and pagans were recognized as lying outside her direct jurisdiction. Regarded as a centre of spiritual authority the Holy See did not claim the unbaptized as subjects, but still the popes as sovereigns of a temporal state had to adopt a definite attitude towards the Jews who lived in their dominions. Tracing these relations as a whole and comparing them with the ideas which prevailed among secular rulers of the time, the principles formulated, and for the most part acted upon, by the popes, set an example of mildness to the rest of Europe. As early as A. D. 598, Gregory the Great clearly laid down that the Jews, while they were to be restrained from presuming upon the toleration accorded to them by the law, had a claim to be treated equitably and justly. They were to be allowed to keep their own festivals and religious practices, and their rights of property, even in the case of their synagogues, were to be respected (Greg. Mag. Regesta, M. G. H., II, 67 and 383). In the later Middle Ages there may be traced through a long series of pontificates the repeated confirmations of the Bull, assignable probably in the first instance to Pope Callixtus II (c. 1120) and known as "Sicut Judæis". It was a sort of papal charter of protection to the Jews and in its first sentence are embodied certain words of one of Gregory the Great's letters just referred to. "As licence", says this document, "ought not to be allowed to the Jews to presume in their synagogues beyond what is permitted by the law so they ought not to be interfered with in such things as are allowed. We therefore, although they prefer to continue in their hardness of heart rather than be guided by the hidden meaning of the prophets to a knowledge of the Christian faith, do nevertheless, since they invoke our protection and aid, following in the footsteps of our predecessors and out of the mildness of Christian piety, extend to them the shield of our protection." The document then lays down (1) that the Jews are not to be compelled by force to embrace Christianity, but are only to be baptized of their own free will; (2) that apart from a judicial sentence in a court of law no one is to injure them in life or limb or to take away their property or to interfere with such customary rights as they may have enjoyed in the places where they live; (3) that they are not to be attacked with sticks and stones on occasion of their festival celebrations, nor are they to be compelled to render any feudal services beyond such as are customary; (4) that their cemeteries in particular are not to be violated. (See M. Stern, "Urkundliche Beiträge", n. 171.) This charter reissued and confirmed as it was by some twenty or thirty pontiffs during a period of 400 years is certainly of much more weight as laying down the Church's view of the duty of toleration, as an abstract principle, than any persecuting edicts evoked by special circumstances or coloured by the prepossessions of the individual legislator.

Looking at the documents of unquestioned authenticity extracted by Stern from the papal Regesta it becomes clear that throughout the later Middle Ages the Jews in almost every emergency turned to the popes as to their natural protectors. Despite such legislation as that of the Fourth Council of Lateran (1215) imposing the wearing of a distinctive badge and excluding Jews from public offices, still even such a summary as that in the Jewish Encyclopedia (s. v. "Popes") distinctly leaves the impression that the Holy See exercised on the whole a markedly restraining influence on the persecuting spirit of the Middle Ages. In particular, more than one of the popes, beginning with Innocent IV, issued Bulls exonerating the Jews from that charge of ritual murder, which, as in the well-known story of little Hugh of Lincoln, prejudiced public opinion so strongly against them (cf. Vacandard, "La question du meurtre rituel chez les Juifs" in "Etudes de critique et d'histoire religieuse", 3d series, Paris, 1912). It was again the popes (e. g., Sixtus IV and Clement VII) who at the time of the worst excesses of the Spanish Inquisition exerted themselves to set some check upon the severities exercised against the Maranos in the Iberian Peninsula. The edicts issued at various times for the destruction of copies of the Talmud, the Bull "Cum nimis absurdum" of Paul IV constraining the Jews of Rome to live segregated in a Ghetto and subject to other harassing disabilities, represent rather the prejudices of individual pontiffs than any consistent principle of persecution. Let it also be noted that the influence of the Church has repeatedly been exerted for the protection of pagan races against forcible conversion, and that it has freely tolerated such religious rites amongst savages as were not openly debasing and immoral. The history of the preaching of Christianity in the New World shows many examples in which the fanatical zeal lay with the profligate Spanish adventurers who conquered the country, while ecclesiastical authority advocated sympathy with the natives and indulgence for their religious observances. On the other hand this indulgence shown to pagan customs, obviously enough, could not be extended without limit. Even British rule in India ultimately considered it desirable to abolish the practice of suttee by which the wives of the upper classes were required to commit suicide upon the death of their husbands. This, however, was not effectively prohibited, even in the British provinces, until 1829.

With regard to the toleration of Christian heretics and schismatics the reader will do well to consult the article INQUISITION. No very systematic measures of repression seem to have come into practice before the twelfth century. The aggressive attitude adopted in the case of the Priscillianists (q. v.) and Donatists (q. v.) was owing less to the action of the bishops than to that of the emperor. On the other hand, it cannot be disputed that after the authority of the popes was firmly established, ecclesiastical campaigns were undertaken against the Cathari, the Waldenses, and Albigenses as well as later on against the followers of Wicklif and Hus. Moreover isolated executions for heresy (burning at the stake being commonly employed for this purpose) were known before the twelfth century both in East and West; though at the same time the actual infliction of the punishment, then as after, must be regarded as an act of the civil power rather than that of any ecclesiastical tribunal. But though an Inquisition of heretical practices may be regarded as having been first formally set up, at any rate in embryo, about the second half of the thirteenth century no measures of extreme severity were in the beginning prescribed or generally adopted. The Fourth Council of Lateran in 1215 imposed as a penalty the deprivation of property and civil stakes. Convicted heretics, even though repentant, were excluded from public offices and were compelled to wear a badge. If their retractation was insincere they were liable to be confined in a public prison. At the same time it must not be forgotten that all these medieval heresies, as such an historian as Gairdner has noticed (Lollardy, I, 46), struck at the foundations of social order. M. Guiraud's account of the extravagant teaching of the Cathari and Albigenses is conclusive upon the point. It cannot be doubted that the severities which then began to be exercised in the name of religion were prompted by no lust for blood. It seemed rather to orthodox churchmen that the Church was so menaced by these subversive doctrines that her very existence was at stake.

Under these circumstances it was not wonderful that the ordinances of the canon law, for the most part formulated at a time when Albigensian teachings were a present danger, should have inclined to the side of severity and that to the lawmakers of that age toleration seemed only a weakness. "The proscription of the Albigenses", says M. Guiraud, "was not the effect of any ferocious hatred of misbelievers too often attributed to the princes of that age. It was inspired by a consideration which has been happily defined by saying that heresy was at that time as much a crime against social order as against religion" (Guiraud, "Chartulaire de Prouille", I, lxxxiv). Even so anti-Roman an historian as Hase sums up the practical effects of the Lollard movement by saying "Wyclif produced no permanent religious impression upon the mass of the people. His teaching was misunderstood and caused a revolt of the peasants which resulted only in disaster" (Kirchengeschichte, 1886, p. 353). Again it was not to be expected that the first fruits of the Reformation would be likely to mitigate the prevalent view of the mischievous nature of heresy. The political and social evils to which the teaching of Luther and Calvin gave rise, as well as the fanatical persecution of the Catholics by so many of their followers, are made clear beyond dispute in such a work as that of Janssen's "History of the German People", to which the reader may be referred. It was only natural that the conception of heresy as an attack upon law and order as well as upon religion should be thereby deepened. Moreover in nearly every case where the reproach of intolerance has been cast against the Church, as for example, the Massacre of Saint Bartholomew (q. v.) or the revocation of the Edict of Nantes (see HUGUENOTS), the persecuting initiative has come far more from temporal rulers than from the Church or her representatives. On the other hand, the ferocity of the leading Reformers more than equalled that of the most fiercely denounced inquisitors. Even the "gentle" Melanchthon wrote to Calvin to congratulate him on the burning of Servetus. "The Church", he said, "both now and in all generations, owes and will owe you a debt of gratitude." "Let there be no pity", Luther exhorted his followers, "it is a time of wrath not of mercy. . . . Therefore, dear Lords, let him who can slay, smite, destroy" (see Beard, "The Reformation and Modern Thought"). "John Knox", said Acton (History of Freedom, p. 44), "thought that every Catholic in Scotland ought to be put to death." Moreover in any case there is more to be urged than a mere "tu quoque" argument. The Church has often given proof of her moderation when brought into relation with those whom she was not logically compelled to treat as rebels. No better examples can perhaps be afforded than the history of the foundation of some of the colonies in the New World, and notably that of the Province of Maryland (q. v.).

HERGENRÖTHER, *Catholic Church and Christian State* (tr. London, 1876); DEVAS, *Key of the World's Progress* (London, 1906), 189–210; ACTON, *Hist. of Freedom* (reprinted London, 1907); CREIGHTON, *Persecution and Tolerance* (London, 1895); DÖLLINGER, *Akademische Vorträge*, III (Leipzig, 1891), 274–301. These last three works can only be recommended with many reserves. See also bibl. of article INQUISITION.

HERBERT THURSTON.

Toleration, RELIGIOUS.—Toleration in general signifies patient forbearance in the presence of an evil which one is unable or unwilling to prevent. By religious toleration is understood the magnanimous indulgence which one shows towards a religion other than his own, accompanied by the moral determination to leave it and its adherents unmolested in private and public, although internally one views it with complete disapproval as a "false faith". Since, in this article, we are to treat toleration only from the standpoint of principle, leaving its historical development to be discussed in a special article, we shall consider: I. The Idea of Toleration; II. The Inadmissibility of Theoretical Dogmatical Toleration; III. The Obligation to Show Practical Civil Toleration; IV. The Necessity of Public Political Toleration.

I. THE IDEA OF TOLERATION.—Considered in the abstract, the general idea of toleration contains two chief moments: (a) the existence of something which is regarded as an evil by the tolerating subject; (b) the magnanimous determination not to interfere with the evil, but to allow it to run its course without molestation. Viewed under the former aspect, toleration is akin to patience which also connotes an attitude of forbearance in the face of an evil. Patience, however, is rather the endurance of physical sufferings (e. g. misfortune, sickness), toleration of ethical evils. When not an evil but some real good (e. g. truth or virtue) is in question, toleration gives way to interior approbation and external promotion of such good. No one will say: "We must show toleration towards science or patriotism", for both these objects are recognized by all as laudable and desirable. A second idea akin to toleration is connivance (*conniventia, dissimulatio*), which means the deliberate closing of one's eyes to evil conditions so as not to be obliged to take measures against them. The distinction between connivance and toleration lies in the fact that the latter not only closes its eyes to the tolerated evil, but also openly concedes it complete liberty of action and freedom to spread. It is indeed in this deliberate granting of liberty that the characteristic quality of toleration lies. For the intolerant person also regards what opposes him as an evil and a source of annoyance; but, it is only by combating it overtly or secretly, that he shows his intolerance. Not all intolerance, however, is a vice, nor is all tolerance a virtue. On the contrary, an exaggerated tolerance may easily amount to a vice, while intolerance keeping within just limits may be a virtue. This statement is substantially in agreement with Aristotle's definition that virtue in general holds the right mean between two extremes, which are as such both vices. Thus the intolerance shown by parents towards grave faults in their children is an obligation imposed by conscience, although, if it be carried to the extreme of cruelty, it degenerates into a vice. On the other hand, excessive toleration towards an evil becomes under certain circumstances a vice, for example, when secular rulers look with folded arms upon public immorality.

The above remarks show that manifold distinctions are necessary before we are in a position to develop the true principles which underlie real toleration. Viewing our subject partly from the ethical and religious, and partly from the political standpoint, we find three distinct kinds of tolerance and intolerance, which refer to entirely different domains and thus rest on different principles. As regards religious tolerance, which alone concerns us here, we must distinguish especially between the thing and the person, the error and the erring. According as we consider the thing or the person, we have theoretical, dogmatic, or practical civic tolerance, or intolerance. Distinct from both is political tolerance, since the distinction between the individual and the State must also be considered. We must inquire somewhat more closely into these three kinds of tolerance and their opposites before considering the principles which underlie each.

(1) By theoretical dogmatic tolerance is meant the tolerating of error as such, in so far as it is an error; or, as Lezius concisely expresses it, "the recognition of the relative and subjective right of error to existence" ("Der Toleranzbegriff Lockes u. Puffendorfs", Leipzig, 1900, p. 2). Such a tolerance can only be the outcome of an attitude which is indifferent to the right of truth, and which places truth and error on the same level. In philosophy this attitude is briefly termed scepticism, in the domain of religion, it develops into religious indifferentism which declares that all religions are equally true and good or equally false and bad. Such an internal and external indifference towards all religions, especially the Christian religion,

is nothing else than the expression of personal unbelief and lack of religious convictions. A person who is tolerant in the domain of dogma resembles the botanist who cultivates in his experimental beds both edible plants and poisonous herbs as alike valuable growths, while a person intolerant of error may be compared to a market-gardener, who allows only edible plants to grow, and eradicates noxious weeds. Just as vice possesses no real right to existence, whatever toleration may be shown to the vicious person, so also religious error can lay no just claim to forbearance and indulgence, even though the erring person may merit the greatest affection and esteem. There is, of course, a psychological freedom both to sin and to err, but this liberty is not equivalent to an inherent right to sin or to err in religion. The "freedom of thought" claimed by free-thinkers is really vitiated by an internal contradiction, since the intellect is bound by the laws of thought and must in many cases yield to the force of evidence. But if by freedom of thought we are to understand the personal right of the individual to form on all questions such internal convictions as he may judge right, this ethical freedom also has its limits, since the inner spiritual life is at all events subject to conscience and to the moral order of the universe, and is, therefore, bound by ethical obligations which no man may disregard. The so-called "freedom of belief", which asserts the right of each person to believe what he pleases, is open to the same criticism. For, if the psychological liberty to accept the wildest phantasies and the most foolish stories is an undeniable prerogative of the human soul, ethical freedom and the ethical right to freedom of belief are nevertheless conditioned by the presumption that a person will spurn all false religions and cling solely to that which he has recognized as alone true and consequently alone legitimate. This obligation was justly emphasized by Leo XIII in his Encyclical "Immortale Dei" of 1 November, 1885: "Officium est maximum amplecti et animo et moribus religionem, nec quam quisque maluerit, sed quam Deus jusserit quamque certis minimeque dubitandis indiciis unam ex omnibus veram esse constiterit" (The gravest obligation requires the acceptance and practice, not of the religion which one may choose, but of that which God prescribes and which is known by certain and indubitable marks to be the only true one). (Cf. Denzinger, "Enchiridion", 9th ed., Freiburg, 1900, n. 1701.) The mere description of this kind of tolerance shows that its opposite, i. e. theoretical dogmatic intolerance, cannot be a vice. For it is essentially nothing else than the expression of the objective intolerance of truth towards error. In the domain of science and of faith alike, truth is the standard, the aim, and the guide of all investigation; but love of truth and truthfulness forbid every honourable investigator to countenance error or falsehood. It, therefore, follows that well-considered opposition to actual or supposed error, in whatever domain, is simply the antagonism between truth and falsehood translated into personal conviction; as impersonal adversaries, truth and error are as bitterly opposed to each other as yes and no, and consequently, in accordance with the law of contradiction, they can tolerate no mean between them. This theoretical dogmatic intolerance—so often misunderstood, so often confounded with other kinds of intolerance, and as a result unjustly combated—is claimed by every scholar, philosopher, theologian, artist, and statesman as an incontestable right, and is unhesitatingly accepted by everyone in daily intercourse.

(2) Practical civic tolerance consists in the personal esteem and love which we are bound to show towards the erring person, even though we condemn or combat his error. The motive for this difference of attitude is to be sought in the ethical commandment of love for all men, which Christianity has raised to the higher ideal of charity or love of neighbour for the sake of God. One of the most beautiful outgrowths of this charity is shown in the correct Christian attitude towards the heterodox. This relation, rooted solely in pure love, is commonly meant when one speaks of "religious tolerance". It springs, not from pharisaic pride or from pity pluming itself on its superiority, but chiefly from respect for another's religious convictions, which out of true charity we do not wish to disturb to no purpose. Since innocent error may attain to the firmest and sincerest conviction, the person's salvation does not seem to be greatly imperilled until good faith turns into bad faith, in which case alone the feeling of pity has no justification. The good faith of the heterodox person must, as a rule, be presumed, until the contrary is clearly established. But even in the extremest cases, Christian charity must never be wounded, since the final judgment on the individual conscience rests with Him who "searches the heart and the reins". The same measure of respect which a Catholic claims for his religion must be shown by him to the religious convictions of non-Catholics. Here obtains the principle which Gregory IX once recommended in a Brief (6 April, 1233), addressed to the French bishops concerning the attitude of Christians towards the Jews: "Est autem Judæis a Christianis exhibenda benignitas, quam Christianis in Paganismo existentibus cupimus exhiberi" (Christians must show towards Jews the same good will which we desire to be shown to Christians in pagan lands). (Cf. Auvray, "Le régistre de Grégoire IX", n. 1216.) Whoever claims tolerance must likewise show tolerance. True tolerance in the right place and under the right conditions is one of the most difficult, and also one of the most beautiful and delicate virtues, and in the possession of it the true greatness of a noble and beautiful soul is reflected. To such a soul has been communicated, as it were, a spark of the burning charity of the God of love, Who with infinite forbearance tolerates the countless evils of the world, and suffers the cockle to grow with the wheat until the harvest.

The precept of fraternal charity is transgressed by practical civic intolerance, which in more or less detestable fashion transfers intolerance of the error to the erring persons. With complete justice did the sarcastic Swift write: "In religion many have just enough to make them hate one another, not enough to make them love one another" (cf. J. S. Mackenzie, "An Introduction to Social Philosophy", Glasgow, 1890, p. 116). The intolerant man is avoided as much as possible by every high-minded person, both in society and in daily intercourse. The man who is tolerant in every emergency is alone lovable and wins the hearts of his fellowmen. Such tolerance is all the more estimable in one whose loyal practice of his own faith wards off all suspicion of unbelief or religious indifference, and whose friendly bearing towards the heterodox emanates from pure neighbourly charity and a strict sense of justice. It is also an indispensable requisite for the maintenance of friendly intercourse and co-operation among a people composed of different religious denominations, and is the root of religious peace in the state. It should, therefore, be prized and promoted by the civil authorities as a safeguard of the public weal, for a warfare of all against all, destructive of the state itself, must again break out (as at the time of the religious wars and of American Knownothingism), if citizens be allowed to assail one another on account of religious differences. A person who by extensive travel or large experience has become acquainted with the world and men, and with the finer forms of life, does not easily develop into a heretic-hunter, a sadly incongruous figure in the modern world.

(3) Public political tolerance is not a duty of the citizens, but is an affair of the State and of legislation. Its essence consists in the fact that the State

grants legal tolerance to all the religious denominations within its boundaries, either through its written constitution, through special charters, or at least through prescriptive right based on long tradition. This tolerance may under certain circumstances amount to the principle of equality of rights or parity, even to the full enjoyment of all civil rights, entirely regardless of one's religious belief. Since the modern State can and must maintain towards the various religions and denominations a more broad-minded attitude than the unyielding character of her doctrine and constitution permit the Church to adopt, it must guarantee to individuals and religious bodies not alone interior freedom of belief, but also, as its logical correlative, to manifest that belief outwardly—that is, the right to profess before the world one's religious convictions without the interference of others, and to give visible expression to these convictions in prayer, sacrifice, and Divine worship. This threefold freedom of faith, profession, and worship is usually included under the general name of religious freedom. Tolerance and religious liberty are not, however, interchangeable terms, since the right implied in state tolerance to grant full or limited religious liberty involves the further right to refuse, to contract, or to withdraw this freedom under certain circumstances, as is clear from the history of toleration laws in every age. Nor is the idea of parity identical with that of religious liberty. For the maintenance of a state Church from public funds (e. g. the Established Church of England) is an offence against parity as regards the dissidents, who must meet their religious needs out of their own means, but it does not affect the general religious liberty, which is enjoyed by the dissidents in the same degree as by the members of the state Church.

Political intolerance finds its harshest expression in the forcible imposition of a religion and its worship, which reached its climax in the drastic political maxim of the Reformation epoch: "Cuius regio, illius et religio". Since external profession and liturgical worship are but the spontaneous expression of faith, it is plain that state compulsion in the matter of worship is a grievous attempt to tyrannize over conscience and tends to breed hypocrisy. Neither political nor ecclesiastical authority can exercise a physical control over interior conviction, since into the secret sanctuary of the mind only the Deity can enter, and He alone can compel the heart. Hence, the principle of Roman law: "De internis non judicat prætor." But, inasmuch as the Church and she alone, with her authority to teach and the power of the keys, may legislate even for conscience, she and only she is justified in making a particular faith obligatory in conscience; consequently she may bring to bear upon interior conviction an *ethical* compulsion, to which corresponds the obligation to believe on the part of the subject. The State on the other hand cannot extend its jurisdiction to religion until this has become visibly embodied in external profession and worship. There are several ways in which the State may interfere. It may either adopt a friendly attitude towards a certain religion and make it the state religion (e. g. the medieval religious States, and certain modern States which have established Churches); or it may adopt a hostile attitude towards a certain religion, which it may eventually endeavour to suppress by the employment of force and the infliction of penalties, as e. g. the pagan Roman Empire tried to suppress Christianity. But the State may also remain neutral, confining itself to simple tolerance, e. g. as did Constantine the Great and Licinius in the Tolerance Edict of Milan, A. D. 313. The modern constitutional State adopts as a basic principle, not mere tolerance towards the various religious bodies, but complete religious freedom; this principle finds its truest and most consistent expression in the United States of America.

II. The Inadmissibility of Theoretical Dogmatic Toleration.—As already said, this kind of tolerance implies indifference towards the truth and in principle, a countenancing of error; hence it is clear that intolerance towards error as such is among the self-evident duties of every man who recognizes ethical obligations. Inasmuch as this dogmatic intolerance is a prominent characteristic of the Catholic Church, and is stigmatized by the modern spirit as obstinacy and even as intolerable arrogance, its objective justification must now be established. We will begin with the incontestable claim of truth to universal recognition and exclusive legitimacy. Just as the knowableness of truth is the fundamental presupposition of every investigator, so also are its final attainment and possession his goal. Error itself, as the opposite of truth, is intelligible only when there is an unchangeable norm of cognition by which the thinking mind is ruled. He who sees in the development of human sciences only one vast graveyard containing thousands of tombstones erected over truth, preaches the death of all science—that is, the scepticism which was avowed in antiquity by the Middle Academy of Arcesilaus and by later Greek Pyrrhonism, and which the sceptics of all the succeeding centuries down to the ingenious Pierre Bayle (d. 1706) have taken for their model. Recent Pragmatism (W. James, Schiller, and others), which denies the eternal, necessary, and unalterable character of truth, is only a dreary relapse into the scepticism of the sophist Protagoras, against which Socrates raised the banner of truth and virtue. The mutability of truth with the passage of time is also a thesis of Modernism. In the Decree "Lamentabili" of 3 July, 1907, Pius X condemned the Modernistic proposition: Veritas non est immutabilis plus quam ipse homo, quippe quæ cum ipso, in ipso et per ipsum evolvitur (Truth is no more unchangeable than man, since with him, in him, and by him it is evolved). (Cf. Denzinger-Bannwart, "Enchiridion", 11th ed., Freiburg, 1911, n. 2058.) The final consequence of this suicidal system led F. Nietzsche to intellectual Nihilism: "Nothing is true, everything is allowed." The transference of this destructive scepticism to the domain of religion breeds religious indifferentism, which is no less unreasonable and immoral, since it also sins against the sacredness of truth.

Nowhere is dogmatic intolerance so necessary a rule of life as in the domain of religious belief, since for each individual his eternal salvation is at stake. Just as there can be no alternative multiplication tables, so there can be but a single true religion, which, by the very fact of its existence, protests against all other religions as false. But the love of truth requires each man to stand forth as the incorruptible advocate of truth and of truth alone. While abstract truth, both profane and religious, asserts itself victoriously through its impersonal evidence against all opposition, its human advocate, engaging in personal contest with adversaries of flesh and blood like himself, must have recourse to words and writing. Hence the sharp, yet almost impersonal clash between opposing views of life, each of which contends for the palm, because each is thoroughly convinced that it alone is right. But the very devotion to truth which supports these convictions determines the kind of polemics which each believes himself called on to conduct. He whose sole concern is for truth itself, will never besmirch his escutcheon by lying or calumny and will refrain from all personal invective. Conscious that the truth for which he fights or in good faith believes he fights, is, by reason of its innate nobility, incompatible with any blemish or stain, he will never claim licence to abuse. Such an ideal champion of truth is fittingly designated by the English word "gentleman". He may, however, by a fair counter-stroke parry an unjust, malicious, and insulting attack, since his adversary has no right to employ invective, to falsify history, to practise sordid proselytism, etc., and may, therefore, be driven without pity from his false position. These principles obtain universally and for all men—for scholars and statesmen, for Catholics and Protestants.

If, therefore, the Catholic Church also claims the right of dogmatic intolerance with regard to her teaching, it is unjust to reproach her for exercising this right. With the imperturbable conviction that she was founded by the God-Man Jesus Christ as the "pillar and ground of the truth" (I Tim., iii, 15) and endowed with full power to teach, to rule, and to sanctify, she regards dogmatic intolerance not alone as her incontestable right, but also as a sacred duty. If Christian truth like every other truth is incapable of double dealing, it must be as intolerant as the multiplication table or geometry. The Church, therefore, demands, in virtue of her Divine commission to teach, the unconditional acceptance of all the truths of salvation which she preaches and proposes for belief, proclaiming to the world with her Divine Founder the stern warning: "He that believeth and is baptized, shall be saved: but he that believeth not shall be condemned" (Mark, xvi, 16). If, by conceding a convenient right of option or a falsely understood freedom of faith, she were to leave everyone at liberty to accept or reject her dogmas, her constitution, and her sacraments, as the existing differences of religions compel the modern State to do, she would not only fail in her Divine mission, but would end her own life in voluntary suicide. As the true God can tolerate no strange gods, the true Church of Christ can tolerate no strange Churches beside herself, or, what amounts to the same, she can recognize none as theoretically justified. And it is just in this exclusiveness that lies her unique strength, the stirring power of her propaganda, the unfailing vigour of her progress. A strictly logical consequence of this incontestable fundamental idea is the ecclesiastical dogma that outside the Church there is no salvation (*extra Ecclesiam nulla salus*). Scarcely any other article of faith gives such offence to non-Catholics and occasions so many misunderstandings as this, owing to its supposed hardness and uncharitableness. And yet this proposition is necessarily and indissolubly connected with the above-mentioned principle of the exclusive legitimacy of truth and with the ethical commandment of love for the truth. Since Christ Himself did not leave men free to choose whether they would belong to the Church or not, it is clear that the idea of the Christian Church includes as an essential element its necessity for salvation. In her doctrine the Church must maintain that intolerance which her Divine Founder Himself proclaimed: "And if he will not hear the church, let him be to thee as the heathen and publican" (Matt., xviii, 17). This explains the intense aversion which the Church has displayed to heresy, the diametrical opposite to revealed truth (cf. I Tim., i, 19; II Tim., ii, 25; Tit., iii, 10 sq.; II Thess., ii, 11). The celebrated church historian Döllinger writes very pertinently: "The Apostles knew no tolerance, no leniency towards heresies Paul inflicted formal excommunication on Hymenæus and Alexander. And such an expulsion from the Church was always to be inflicted. The Apostles considered false doctrine destructive as a wicked example. With weighty emphasis Paul declares (Gal., i, 8): 'But though we, or an angel from heaven, preach a gospel to you besides that which we have preached to you, let him be anathema'. Even the gentle John forbids the community to offer hospitality to heretics coming to it, or even to salute them" ("Christentum und Kirche", Ratisbon, 1860, pp. 236 sq.).

During the Middle Ages the Church guarded the purity and genuineness of her Apostolic doctrine through the institution of the ecclesiastical (and state) Inquisition, which, with many excellent qualities, had unfortunately also its drawbacks. As justly remarked by Cardinal Hergenröther, the Inquisition suffered internally from "serious and lamentable defects", for example, secrecy as to accusers and witnesses, the admission of suspected witnesses, excessive scope for the subjective judgment of the judge, secrecy of the procedure (see INQUISITION). Thus are explained the frightful scenes which Germany witnessed under the grim grand inquisitor, Conrad of Marburg (d. 1233). Following the example of the Apostles, the Church to-day watches zealously over the purity and integrity of her doctrine, since on this rests her whole system of faith and morals, the whole edifice of Catholic thought, ideals, and life. For this purpose the Church instituted the Index of Prohibited Books, which is intended to deter Catholics from the unauthorized reading of books dangerous to faith or morals, for it is notorious that clever sophistry coated with seductive language may render even gross errors of faith palatable to a guileless and innocent heart. The State itself is at times obliged to confiscate books that are dangerous to its existence or to morality in order to protect unsuspecting readers from contagion and to preserve the structure of the social order. But what is right for the State must be also just for the Church. The sharp attack made by Pius X on Modernism, which is undermining the foundations not alone of Christianity, but even of natural religion, is simply an act of necessary self-defence against an assault, not only upon individual dogmas, but likewise upon the whole basis of faith. Again the ancient expression "heretical poison" (*venenum seu virus hæreticum; pravitas hæreticalis*), which has passed from canon law into the set phraseology of the papal chancery and quite naturally sounds hard to Protestants, is to be explained psychologically in view of the above-mentioned fundamental conviction. It is not intended to express any offensive slur on the heterodox, who adhere to their opinions in good faith and in honest conviction. Consequently, the writers who represented Pius X as applying to the present generation of honest Protestants the historical condemnation which he passed on the Reformers of the sixteenth century in his Borromæus Encyclical, and thus ascribed to him a public rebuke which he never in the least intended, were guilty of exaggeration and evident injustice. Besides, Protestant historians have passed much harder judgments on the leaders of the Reformation. No Protestant takes umbrage at the fact established in every manual of church history, that, after long convulsions and spasms, the Lutheran Church, by the Formula of Concord (1577), expelled the "crypto-Calvinist poison" which Philip Melanchthon had instilled into the faith of Orthodox Lutheranism. And did not Crypto-Calvinism really act like blood-poisoning? The canonical expression "heretical poison" is intended to convey no other meaning than that the Catholic faith dreads as blood-poisoning heretical infection of any kind, whatever be its source.

But does the proposition that outside the Church there is no salvation involve the doctrine so often attributed to Catholicism, that the Catholic Church, in virtue of this principle, "condemns and must condemn all non-Catholics"? This is by no means the case. The foolish and unchristian maxim that those who are outside the Church must for that very reason be eternally lost is no legitimate conclusion from Catholic dogma. The infliction of eternal damnation pertains not to the Church, but to God, Who alone can scrutinize the conscience. The task of the Church is confined exclusively to the formulating of the principle, which expresses a condition of salvation imposed by God Himself, and does not extend to the examination of the persons, who may or may not satisfy this condition. Care for one's own salvation is the personal concern of the individual. And in this matter the Church shows the greatest possible consideration for the good faith and the innocence of the erring person. Not that she refers, as is often stated, the eternal salvation of the heterodox solely and exclusively to "invincible ignorance", and thus makes sanctifying ignorance a convenient gate to heaven for the stupid. She places the efficient cause of the eternal salvation of all men objectively in the merits of the Redeemer, and subjectively in justification through baptism or through good faith enlivened by the perfect love of God, both of which may be found outside the Catholic Church. Whoever indeed has recognized the true Church of Christ, but contrary to his better knowledge refuses to enter it, and whoever becomes perplexed as to the truth of his belief, but fails to investigate his doubts seriously, no longer lives in good faith, but exposes himself to the danger of eternal damnation, since he rashly contravenes an important command of God. Otherwise the gentle breathing of grace is not confined within the walls of the Catholic Church, but reaches the hearts of many who stand afar, working in them the marvel of justification and thus ensuring the eternal salvation of numberless men who either, like upright Jews and pagans, do not know the true Church, or, like so many Protestants educated in gross prejudice, cannot appreciate her true nature. To all such, the Church does not close the gate of Heaven, although she insists that there are essential means of grace which are not within the reach of non-Catholics. In his allocution "Singulari quadam" of 9 December, 1854, which emphasized the dogma of the Church as necessary for salvation, Pius IX uttered the consoling principle: "Sed tamen pro certo pariter habendum est, qui veræ religionis ignorantia laborent, si ea est invincibilis, nulla ipsos obstringi hujusce rei culpa ante oculos Domini" (But it is likewise certain that those who are ignorant of the true religion, if their ignorance is invincible, are not, in this matter, guilty of any fault in the sight of God). (Denzinger-Bannwart, 11th ed., Freiburg, 1911, n. 1647.)

As early as 1713 Clement XI condemned in his dogmatic Bull "Unigenitus" the proposition of the Jansenist Quesnel: "Extra ecclesiam nulla conceditur gratia", i. e. no grace is given outside the Church (op. cit., n. 1379), just as Alexander VIII had already condemned in 1690 the Jansenistic proposition of Arnauld: "Pagani, Judæi, hæretici aliique hujus generis nullum omnino accipiunt a Jesu Christo influxum" (Pagans, Jews, heretics, and other people of the sort, receive no influx [of grace] whatsoever from Jesus Christ) (op. cit., n. 1295). In her tolerance toward the erring the Church indeed goes farther than the large catechism of Martin Luther, which on "pagans or Turks or Jews or false Christians" passes the general and stern sentence of condemnation: "wherefore they remain under eternal wrath and in everlasting damnation." Catholics who are conversant with the teachings of their Church know how to draw the proper conclusions. Absolutely unflinching in their fidelity to the Church as the sole means of salvation on earth, they will treat with respect, as ethically due, the religious convictions of others, and will see in non-Catholics, not enemies of Christ, but brethren. Recognizing from the Catholic doctrine of grace that the possibility of justification and of eternal salvation is not withheld even from the heathen, they will show towards all Christians, e. g. the various Protestant bodies, kindly consideration. Concerning these dogmatic questions, cf. Pohle, "Dogmatik", II (5th ed., Paderborn, 1912), 444 sqq., 453 sqq.

III. THE OBLIGATION TO SHOW PRACTICAL CIVIC TOLERATION.—For the practical attitude of Catholics towards the heterodox the Church has inculcated the strict command of neighbourly love, which corresponds to Christian charity: "Thou shalt love thy neighbour as thyself." The sincerest love for the erring is indeed quite compatible with keen repugnance for the error to which they cling. From the very definition of practical civic tolerance (see above, I, 2) springs the maxim which St. Augustine expresses as follows: "Diligite homines, interficite errores; sine superbia de veritate præsumite, sine sævitia pro veritate certate" (Love men, slay error; without pride be bold in the truth, without cruelty fight for the truth) (Contra lit. Petil., I, xxix, n. 31, in P. L., XLIII, 259). God is a God of love, and consequently His children cannot be sons of hate. The gospel of the Divine paternity in heaven is also the joyous tidings of the brotherhood of all men on earth. For all without exception the Saviour prayed in His capacity of high-priest during the night before His Passion, and for all He shed His Blood on the Cross. The sublime example of Christ affords a striking indication of the manner in which we should regulate our conduct towards those who differ from us in faith, for we know that, so to speak, a drop of the redeeming Blood of Christ glistens on every human soul. To penetrate into the inner shrine of another's conscience with feelings of doubt and distrust is forbidden to all in accordance with the principle: "Nemo præsumitur malus, nisi probetur" (No one is presumed to be evil until proved to be so). And St. Paul declares: "Charity is patient, is kind: charity envieth not, dealeth not perversely . . ., is not provoked to anger, thinketh no evil" (I Cor., xiii, 4 sq.). By this Christian love alone is the truly tolerant man, the true disciple of Christ, recognized. But did not the medieval Church by her bloody persecution of heretics trample under foot this commandment of love and thus nullify in practice what in theory indeed she always inculcated with honeyed words? The enemies of the Church search eagerly the musty documents which tell of inquisitional courts, *autos-da-fé*, chambers of horror, instruments of torture, and blazing pyres. Without any palliation of the historical facts, let us examine a little more closely this reproach, and see what importance is to be attached to it.

(1) When the inglorious origin of his forbears is constantly cast in the teeth of an honest nobleman, with the spiteful idea of wounding his feelings, no upright person will regard such conduct as tactful or just. What has the Church of to-day to do with the fact that long-vanished generations inflicted, in the name of religion, cruelties with which the modern man is disgusted? The children's children cannot be held accountable for the misdeeds of their forefathers. Protestants also must take refuge in this principle of justice. However much they endeavour to blink the fact, they have also to regret similar occurrences during the Reformation epoch, when, as everyone knows, the Reformers and their successors made free use of the existing penal ordinances and punished with death many inconvenient and, according to their view, heretical persons (e. g. the anti-Trinitarians Servetus and Sylvanus, the Osiandrist Funk, the Calvinist Nicholas Krell at Dresden). Hundreds of faithful Catholics, who fell victims to the Reformation in England, are venerated to-day as the English martyrs. The greater number of executions occurred, not under Mary the Catholic, but under Queen Elizabeth. It is, however, unjust to hold modern Protestantism, in the one instance, and Catholicism in the other responsible for these atrocities.

(2) In every age the Church has drawn a fundamental distinction (which, on account of its importance, should never be overlooked) between formal and merely material heretics, and her penal legislation was directed solely against the former category. As the open and obstinate rebellion of a Catholic against the Divinely instituted teaching authority of the Church,

formal heresy still remains one of the most grievous sins. Material heresy on the other hand, i. e. an error in faith entertained undesignedly and unconsciously, is in itself neither sinful nor punishable, except where the error is itself inexcusable. In excusable error are all who possess subjectively the firm and honest conviction that they have the true faith of Christ, thus including the vast majority of non-Catholics, who were born and educated in their particular form of belief. Even in the Middle Ages, while using her punitive power only against formal heretics who through baptism had openly belonged to her body from birth, the Church openly proclaimed her incompetency to take action in the case of Jews and pagans, since over these she possessed no jurisdiction. The Church has been always averse to forcible conversions, as was emphasized in modern times by Leo XIII in his Encyclical "Immortale Dei" of 1 November, 1885: "Atque illud quoque magnopere cavere Ecclesia solet, ut ad amplexandam fidem catholicam nemo invitus cogatur, quia quod sapienter Augustinus monet: 'Credere non potest (homo) nisi volens'" (The Church has always taken great care that no one should be compelled against his will to embrace the Catholic Faith, because, as Augustine wisely declares: except he be willing, man cannot believe) (cf. Denzinger, op. cit., n. 1875). Hence the tolerance always displayed by the Church, especially towards the Jews, and also the prohibition in canon law to make war on pagan nations merely on account of their unbelief, except when they put to death Christian missionaries or attacked Christian States, as the Saracens formerly did (cf. Schmalzgrüber, "Jus can. de Judæis", n. 53). A decision of Gregory the Great given in the Decree of Gratian (c. 4 jam vero C. 23, qu. 6) contains no warrant for religious coercion, since the pope simply grants to the Catholic colonists on his domains certain favours which he withholds from settlers obstinately adhering to their paganism.

(3) If in medieval times the Church adopted sterner measures against formal heretics, apostates, and schismatics than she adopts to-day, she did this not as a private individual, who must show only consideration and love, but as the legitimate governing authority within whose sphere also fell the administration of penal justice. The State must also inflict on the thief and revolutionary the legal punishment for theft and revolution, which are not punishable in the abstract. However repulsive, when judged from the more refined standpoint of modern civilization, the barbarous cruelty of medieval penal ordinances may be, as expressed even in the "Cautio criminalis" of the German Emperor, Charles V, against traitors, highway robbers, and notorious debauchees (impaling, breaking on the wheel), we may not for this reason condemn the whole penal system of that age as judicial murder; for the legal punishments, while indeed inhuman, were not unjust. Now, formal heresy was likewise strongly condemned by the Catholic Middle Ages: and so the argument ran: Apostasy and heresy are, as criminal rebellions against God, far more serious crimes than high treason, murder, or adultery. But, according to Rom., xiii, 11 sqq., the secular authorities have the right to punish, especially grave crimes, with death; consequently, "heretics may be not only excommunicated, but also justly (*juste*) put to death" (St. Thomas, II–II, Q. xi, a. 3). But there is no need to go back to the Middle Ages, since the present age likewise furnishes us with examples of extreme severity in the chastisement of certain crimes. With whatever disapproval the philanthropist may view the terrible punishments inflicted on those guilty of rape in parts of the United States, adjudging such penalties as excessive in their severity, the jurist will on the other hand seek their explanation in the special circumstances of time and place. American lynch law will not be unreservedly excused or justified, but, in judging it, allowance will be made for the imperfections of the existing penal procedure. The frequent inefficacy of the ordinary procedure is only too likely to excite the enraged populace to deeds of violence. Keeping these occurrences of modern times before our eyes, we will pass a much juster verdict on the Middle Ages. Catholics have, of course, no desire for the return of an age whose liberal, and in many respects admirable, state institutions were greatly marred by sinister penal ordinances.

(4) A distinction must be drawn between the penal system as such and its external forms. The barbarous penal forms of the Middle Ages are to be credited, not to the Church, but to the State. After the Christianized Roman Empire had developed into a theocratic (religious) State, it was compelled to stamp crimes against faith (apostasy, heresy, schism) as offences against the State (cf. Cod. Justin., I, 5, de hær.: "Quod in religionem divinam committitur, in omnium fertur injuriam"). Catholic and citizen of the State became identical terms. Consequently, crimes against faith were high treason, and as such were punishable with death. This was the universal opinion in the Middle Ages. This idea of the execution of heretics had not the slightest connexion with the essence of the Church or her constitution, and to the primitive Church such a penalty was unknown. St. Cyprian (d. 258) disapproved of all external means of coercion, such as were customary in the Old Testament, and claimed for the New Testament as "spiritual weapon" (*spiritualis gladius*) excommunication, which was worse than death. The earliest example of the execution of a heretic was the beheading of the ringleader of the Priscillianists by the usurper Maximus at Trier (385); this called forth a protest from St. Martin of Tours, St. Ambrose, and Pope Siricius (cf. Histor. polit. Blätter, XC, 1890, pp. 330 sqq.). Even St. Augustine, who towards the end of his life favoured state reprisals against the Donatists, always opposed the execution of heretics (cf. Ep. c [*alias* cxxvii]: "Corrigi eos cupimus, non necari"). During the long dominion of the Merovingians and Carlovingians, heresy was never regarded as a civil crime, and was chastised with no civil penalty. A change came only in the eleventh century, when Manichæism, which had earlier experienced bloody persecution at the hands of the Eastern emperors Theodosius (d. 395) and Justinian (d. 565), revived in the orgies of the Catharists and Albigenses. These disruptive sects attacked marriage, the family, and property, wherefore even Lea has to admit: "Had Catharism become predominant, its influence would infallibly have proved fatal" (History of the Inquisition, I, 117). Influenced by the Roman code, which was rescued from oblivion, the Hohenstaufen emperor, Frederick II, who was anything but a warm supporter of the papacy, introduced the penalty of burning for heretics by imperial law of 1224 (cf. Monum. Germ., IV Leg., II, 326 sqq.). The popes, especially Gregory IX (d. 1241), favoured the execution of this imperial law, in which they saw an effective means not alone for the protection of the State, but also for the preservation of the Faith. And indeed the danger to the common weal seen in Catharism inclined neither the State nor the Church to mildness, just as in the time of St. Augustine the ill-famed Circumcilliones of the Donatists bore every sign of a public rebellion. Would not even a modern state have to proceed against these murderers and incendiaries with weapon in hand? Unfortunately, neither the secular nor the ecclesiastical authorities drew the slightest distinction between dangerous and harmless heretics, seeing forthwith in every (formal) heresy a "contumelia Creatoris", which the theocratic State was called upon to avenge with the pyre. This inability to distinguish may be easily traced even in the writings of

Luther, Calvin, Melanchthon, Butzer, Wenceslaus, Sturm, Strigel, Matthias Coler, and other Protestant leaders. We may, therefore, rightly conclude that the harsh forms of punishment are to be referred partly to the fact that the medieval heretics were a menace to the community, and partly to the excessive strictness of the ancient penal code.

(5) It follows from what has been said that the custom of burning heretics is really not a question of justice, but a question of civilization. History shows that even in an age otherwise highly civilized certain especially detestable criminals are severely dealt with. A regrettable illustration is found in the introduction of torture into the trial of heretics by Innocent IV in 1252. Here again the influence of the ancient Roman code is discernible, since it also was accustomed from the earliest times to employ torture not as a punishment, but simply as a regular means of extracting the truth from the accused. That, despite its promised "evangelical liberty", the Reformation introduced no softening of manners, the continuation of torture and the prevalence of witch-burnings even in the eighteenth century clearly show. Torture was first abolished in Prussia (1745) by Frederick the Great; the last witch was burned in Switzerland in 1783. We cannot read without a shudder how in England high treason, which term included the profession of the Catholic Faith, was punished with hanging and the tearing out of the still throbbing heart from the living body. The law against mendicancy passed in 1572 under Queen Elizabeth ordained that the harmless offence of begging was to be punished with severe scourging, with perforation of the right ear with red hot iron, and, if the offence were repeated, with death (cf. G. Kassel, "Geschichtliche Entwickelung des Deliktes der Bettelei", Breslau, 1898, p. 37). In France no less cruelty was shown. When Henry IV was assassinated by Ravaillac on 14 May, 1610, the unfortunate criminal was mercilessly tortured; he was pierced with red-hot pincers, molten lead was poured over the hand which committed the murder, and finally he was torn to pieces by four horses. Exactly the same punishment, even to the smallest details, was meted out to the half-witted Damiens, although he merely scratched the libertine Louis XV with a pen-knife (cf. Pilatus, "Der Jesuitismus", Ratisbon, 1905, pp. 183 sqq.). After the horrors of the French Revolution the methods of punishment were gradually softened, and during the course of the nineteenth century humanitarian views won the victory everywhere (see PUNISHMENT). It rests with mankind to decide whether the penal systems of the future are to be disgraced by cruelty and barbarism or not. The coming generations must see that the return of inhuman penal ordinances shall be made impossible by the refinement of morals, the deepening of ethical culture, the philanthropic training of the young, and the impression of the mild and gentle characteristics of Christ on civil, national, and religious life. Since the secularized State renounced its union with the Church, and excluded heresy from the category of penal offences, the Church has returned to her original standpoint, and contents herself again with excommunication and other spiritual penalties (irregularity, ineligibility for ecclesiastical prebends, etc.), with which the modern State no longer associates (as in the Middle Ages) any penal or civil actions.

IV. THE NECESSITY FOR PUBLIC POLITICAL TOLERATION.—Since the State may not pose either as the mouthpiece of Divine Revelation or as the teacher of the Christian religion, it is clear that in regard to matters of religion it can adopt a much more broad-minded position than the Church, whose attitude is strictly confined by her teaching. The ethical permissibility, or rather the duty, of political tolerance and freedom of religion is determined by historical presuppositions and concrete relations; these impose an obligation which neither State nor Church can disregard. We will first consider the State in itself, and then the specifically Catholic State.

(1) The State is under obligation to make external conditions subserve the public good, and to protect against arbitrariness or molestation all individuals and corporations within its territory in the enjoyment of their personal, civic, political, and religious rights. This is in an especial manner the function of the constitutional State, which has slowly developed since the end of the eighteenth century. The Church has always combated the idea that the winning of new members and the recovery of the apostate pertain to the State. Christ entrusted, not the State, but the Church with the announcement of His Gospel to the whole world. Not even the medieval "religious State", whose constitution we shall describe in greater detail below, undertook to act as bearer of a supernatural revelation or as preacher and judge of the Catholic Faith. The intimate connexion of both powers during the Middle Ages was only a passing and temporary phenomenon, arising neither from the essential nature of the State nor from that of the Church. The Church is free to enter into a more or less close association with the State, but she can also endure actual separation from the State, and, given favourable circumstances, may even prosper under such conditions, as for example in the United States of North America. For the State also certain conditions may prevail which render a close union with the Church inadvisable or indeed quite impossible. When, for example, several religions have firmly established themselves and taken root in the same territory, nothing else remains for the State than either to exercise tolerance towards them all, or, as conditions exist to-day, to make complete religious liberty for individuals and religious bodies a principle of government.

The final conversion of the old religious State into the modern constitutional State, the lamentable defection of the majority of states from the Catholic Faith, the irrevocable secularization of the idea of the state, and the coexistence of the most varied religious beliefs in every land have imposed the principle of state tolerance and freedom of belief upon rulers and parliaments as a dire necessity and as the starting-point of political wisdom and justice. The mixture of races and peoples, the immigration into all lands, the adoption of international laws concerning colonization and choice of abode, the economic necessity of calling upon the workers of other lands, etc., have so largely changed the religious map of the world during the last fifty years that propositions 77–79 of the Syllabus published by Pius IX in 1864 (cf. Denzinger, op. cit., 1777–79), from which enemies of the Church are so fond of deducing her opposition to the granting of equal political rights to non-Catholics, do not now apply even to Spain or the South American republics, to say nothing of countries which even then possessed a greatly mixed population (e. g. Germany). Since the requisite conditions for the erection of new theocratic states, whether Catholic or Protestant, are lacking to-day and will probably not be realized in the future, it is evident on the basis of hard facts that religious liberty is the only possible, and thus the only reasonable, state principle. If, in those lands where she still enjoys a privileged position as state Church (e. g. Italy and Spain), the Catholic Church would not allow herself to be driven from this position without a protest, she has not only a right, but is even under obligation to offer this protest. For a justly acquired right should not be surrendered in silence. In this matter also the Church does only what is done by Protestant princes, who steadfastly adhere to Protestantism as the state religion (e. g. the King of England). But the priceless asset of religious peace compels the modern State to concede tolerance and religious freedom. Without this peace, the undisturbed continuation of the commonwealth is inconceivable. The history of the world could not easily display before the eyes of a patriot a more revolting picture than the fratricidal struggles which resulted from the Reformation in the religious wars of Europe. Wherever separate religious parties live in the same land, they must work together in harmony for the public weal. But this would be impossible, if the State, instead of remaining above party, were to prefer or oppress one denomination as compared with the others. Consequently, freedom of religion and conscience is an indispensable necessity for the State.

From the standpoint of natural law and Christian public law, however, this political tolerance is subject to a threefold limitation, since neither the completely unreligious character of the State nor the unbridled liberty of all imaginable cults may be set up as a principle of government, nor finally may the separation of State and Church be lauded to the skies as the perfect state ideal. These three limitations can be easily justified.

(a) To propose for the State such downright irreligion as a drastic remedy against intolerance is to advise it to saw through the bough on which it sits. For the "State without God", pledged to the "Principles of 1789", would be an immoral monster, which through lack of internal vitality would as surely encounter decay and destruction as did the atheistic Revolutionary State of France at the opening of the nineteenth century. If it is true that human society as a whole is bound to recognize the supreme dominion of God, then no State can shirk the obligation of confessing this God and of publicly venerating Him. The religionless State would be nothing less than an atheistic State, bearing in its very nature the germ of disintegration; since atheism is in itself and its effects a direct peril to the State. The pantheistic is not a whit better; for Hegel's motto, "the State is God", is pure nonsense, since it makes the absurd claim that the State is the original source of all right, and sets the omnipotent State in the place of God (cf. Syllab. Pii IX, prop. 39). A commonwealth that is to endure can be erected only on a theistic basis, since the fundamental ideas of justice, fidelity, and obedience, indispensable for the preservation of the State, can exercise their full influence only in theism. Furthermore the respect for property, the observance of the laws of chastity, aversion to revolution and high treason are best secured by a lively faith in God. Consequently, not alone Christian statesmen like Montesquieu and Guizot, but also freethinkers like Macchiavelli and Voltaire, strongly defended the religious foundations of the State. Even the pagan Cicero (De nat. deor., I) frankly recognized the impossibility of a State without the fear of God, on which depend in turn fidelity and justice. A State which is not itself permeated with sentiments of religion and idly tolerates the sapping of religion and morality is preparing the way for revolution, that is for its own destruction. The state axiom of religious freedom can therefore mean only freedom for religion, not freedom from religion or irreligion. In his Encyclical "Vehementer nos", of 11 February, 1906, Pope Pius X sharply denounces for its injustice the violent breach of the Concordat by the French Government, instancing as the chief grievance that, by the official recognition of its own irreligion, the French Republic had forsworn God Himself (cf. Denzinger, n. 1995). The historian von Treitschke expressed the conviction that "atheists have strictly speaking no place in the state" ("Politik", I, Leipzig, 1897, p. 326); the philosopher John Locke would hear nothing of state tolerance towards atheists. With a strange perversity of judgment he would indeed extend this intolerance to Catholics also, the firmest believers in God among all classes of mankind and the surest supporters of throne and altar. But, as things are to-day, nothing remains for the State but to tolerate atheists in its midst so long as they do not, by unlawful deeds, render themselves liable to punishment. In its own interest, however, the State must endeavour to protect and promote belief in God among the people by the establishment of good schools, by the training of believing teachers and officials in seminaries, lyceums, secondary schools, and universities, and finally by leaving the Church free to exert her salutary influence.

(b) A well-ordered commonwealth can no more recognize the maxim of unlimited and unbridled religious freedom than it can adopt the suicidal principle of irreligion. For state toleration of all forms of religion without exception, which could be justified only on the basis of disruptive atheism or a deistic indifferentism, is in palpable contradiction to natural law and to every rational system of polity (cf. Encyclical of Pius IX "Quanta cura" of 8 December, 1864). If the State as such is under the same obligation to confess and venerate God as the individual, it must set bounds to religious freedom at least at the point where the unrestricted exercise of this freedom would lead to the subversion of state security and public morality. The history of religion shows that, to deceive unwary authorities, intrigues most immoral and most dangerous to the State have disguised themselves in the mantle of religion: the cults of Moloch and Astarte, religious prostitution and community of women, ritual child-murder and Anabaptist horrors, conventicles for debauchery and anarchistic secret societies, etc. No State with a regard for its own preservation will hesitate to raise a barrier against moral, religious, and political anarchy; and to repel with vigour all such attacks aimed, under the mask of freedom of belief, at the existence of society. Free competition between truth and error, which is sometimes urged in the name of tolerance, promises neither for the State nor the Church an enduring success; the free competition between virtue and vice could be upheld by the same reasoning. There are certain deceits and vices which display their immorality so plainly that the State must mercilessly apply her penal law and, in the interest of the community, prevent their propagation. Thus England, in general so indulgent towards paganism in her colonies, could not tolerate the continuation among the Hindus of the ritual murder of children and the burning of widows (the *Suttee*), prohibiting the former under severe penalties in 1802 and the latter in 1829 (cf. Lecky, "Democracy and Liberty", I, London, 1896, pp. 424 sqq.). Again, although the Constitution of the United States guarantees complete freedom of belief, the American people always found Mormonism unbearable, and never rested until, by forbidding polygamy to the Mormons, the Christian conception of marriage had been recognized (see MORMONS). Not even the atheistic Revolutionary State of France granted an unlimited freedom of religious opinions in its "Déclaration des droits de l'homme" (1791), since it added the clause: "pourvu que leur manifestation ne trouble pas l'ordre public établi par la loi". Almost all modern States have admitted this limitation of religious freedom into their constitutions.

(c) Christian public law erects a third barrier to complete religious freedom in forbidding that the principle of the separation of Church and State be raised to the true ideal of the State and regarded as fundamentally the best form of the State; this does not mean that in certain exceptional cases actual separation may not be more beneficial for both Church and State than their organic union. While this separation may be always viewed as relatively the better condition, it does not thereby become the ideal state. The latter is only then attained when Church and State proceed hand in hand and in perfect harmony to promote by their common efforts the temporal and eternal happiness of their common subjects. As it is unnatural for a married couple to live separated, although separation may be defended in particular instances as the better or less harmful arrangement in view of quarrels which have arisen, so also the ideal relation between Church and State is to be found, not in the separation of the two, but in their harmonious co-operation (cf. Pius IX, Encyclical "Quanta cura" of 8 December, 1864; Syllab. prop. 55). As a practical proof of the internal advantages of a separation in principle, it is usual to point to the example of the United States, which has extended the blessing of its liberal Constitution in recent years to its newly-acquired colonies of Porto Rico and the Philippine Islands. But, while it may be granted without reserve that both Church and State seem to prosper exceedingly well in their friendly juxtaposition, it would be rash to speak of the situation as ideal. It must, however, be acknowledged that no other land in the world has so honourably maintained the amicable separation of Church and State, while in some European countries the law of separation was unfortunately only a pretext for a more violent attack on the rights of the Church. Not without good reason did Leo XIII in his Brief of 1902, addressed to the American hierarchy, express his approval of a wise and patriotic adaptation to the national and legal conditions of the United States. He could do this with a good conscience, although in his Encyclical "Immortale Dei" of 1 November, 1885, he had declared the harmonious union of the two highest powers the ideal situation, and had referred to concordats as the means of arranging questions bordering on both jurisdictions. If the United States forms the sole honourable exception to the rule, this is due partly to the fact that the State neglects neither the religious factor at large nor Christianity, as is shown by the strict laws concerning Sunday observance, Christian monogamy, and the celebration of Thanksgiving Day. What F. Walter wrote fifty years ago is still true to-day: "Even in the United States of North America, to which people so readily appeal, religion is not regarded as a matter of indifference to the State, but is presupposed as the State's complement" ("Naturrecht und Politik im Lichte der Gegenwart", Bonn, 1863, p. 495).

(2) By a Catholic State we understand a community which is composed exclusively of Catholic subjects and which recognizes Catholicism as the only true religion. In this case also the relations between Church and State may be different, according as the two powers are closely united for offence and defence, or, while each maintains its independence, are less compactly joined. The first kind of union finds its truest expression in the "religious state", a distinctive feature of the Middle Ages, while the second or looser union may be realized in a constitutional state that admits various denominations and yet retains its Christian character. In view of the difference of the fundamental ideas on which these two forms of state are based, the principles of political tolerance are subject to important modifications.

(a) Every religious State, Catholic or Protestant, presupposes by its very existence that all or nearly all the citizens have the same faith, otherwise it would be contrary to natural justice and practically impossible. In certain cases such a State must take drastic measures to expel or exclude all elements which do not fit into its framework. Thus a Protestant religious State was forcibly instituted in England under Queen Elizabeth by clearing the country of all Catholics, and the Diet of Upsala in 1593 strove to preserve the strictly Lutheran character of Sweden by making the immigration of Catholics punishable with death. The situation of the Catholic religious State in the Middle Ages was somewhat, though not entirely, similar. The medieval idea required that the State should lend the secular arm to the Church for the maintenance of all her doctrines, laws, and ordinances, and that in return it should receive from the Church spiritual support in all purely secular affairs. Thus State and Church formed the two all-embracing members of the one Christian body, assisting and supporting each other in the broad field of all secular and ecclesiastical interests. Empire and papacy, like body and soul, formed an organic whole. Citizen and Catholic were interchangeable terms. The rebel against the Church was regarded as likewise a rebel against the State, and conversely the political revolutionary was by that very fact an enemy of the Church. Whoever was stricken with excommunication finally incurred also imperial ban, and the imperial ban brought excommunication in its train. It is true that many advantages must be conceded to the religious State. We see an imposing and elevating idea rendered concrete in the supreme dominion of the Christian spirit throughout the civic, national, and religious life, in the organic connexion of the secular and the religious government, and in the strengthening of the state authority by the Church and of ecclesiastical authority by the State. These great advantages, however, must not cause us to overlook the numerous drawbacks which this mystical marriage of Church and State involved. First of all, in consequence of the fusion of the objects of the State and of religion, the Catholic religious State was compelled to adopt an attitude of fundamental intolerance towards all errors of faith, which became so many crimes against the State. Viewed from the historical standpoint one may justly doubt whether the bloody persecutions resulted in greater blessings and advantages or in greater want, hate, and suffering for Christendom (cf. De Laveley, "Le gouvernement dans la démocratie", I, Paris, 1892, pp. 157–62). It is certain that the odium for all those severities and cruelties had to be borne, not by the State which inflicted them, but rather by the Church, since she seemed to stand behind all these measures as the secret motive force, even though she did not know, much less justify many of them. We endeavoured above without partiality to appraise these accusations against the Church at their true value. To refer briefly to another gloomy aspect of this question, the ecclesiastical right to meddle directly in purely secular affairs might easily become a dangerous prerogative, inasmuch as the infliction of excommunication for purely political offences must necessarily have brought ecclesiastical penalties, especially when they were unjustly inflicted, into great discredit among princes and people. On the other hand, the right of protection exercised by the sovereign in ecclesiastical matters, often without or even against the wish of the popes, had for its unavoidable consequence the loss of public respect for both authorities. The proverbial contest between *imperium* and *sacerdotium*, which practically runs through the whole history of the Middle Ages, redounded in fact to the advantage of neither. A third disadvantage, arising essentially from the religious State, may not be passed over in silence; this consists in the danger that the clergy, trusting blindly to the interference of the secular arm in their behalf, may easily sink into dull resignation and spiritual torpor, while the laity, owing to the religious surveillance of the State, may develop rather into a race of hypocrites and pietists than into inwardly convinced Christians. A Catholic clergy which relies on State assistance for its pastoral activity lacks that glowing zeal for souls which springs from heartfelt convictions, and the vitality and sincerity of religion are grievously impaired when practices of piety are made compulsory by the State. The last and most serious disadvantage associated with the religious State lies in the immanent danger that the claim of the Church to supremacy over the State must almost necessarily call forth the opposite extreme of Cæsaropapism. The early protectorate of the State thus develops finally into the complete control and enslavement of the Church. Such in fact has been the historical sequence. Not alone in the Eastern Empire, in which Byzantine Cæsaropapism won its greatest triumphs, but also in the Western Empire these unworthy tendencies were all too clearly revealed, especially under the Hohenstaufens.

(b) When various Christian denominations establish themselves in any country, the Catholic State can no longer maintain its former exclusive attitude, but is compelled for reasons of State to show tolerance towards the heterodox and to grant them religious freedom within the limits described above and determined by natural law. If religious freedom has been accepted and sworn to as a fundamental law in a constitution, the obligation to show this tolerance is binding on conscience. The Catholic Church recognizes unreservedly the inviolability of constitutions confirmed by oath, of traditional laws, and regular religious compacts, because a breach of the constitution, of allegiance, of a treaty, or of an oath is a grievous sin, and because the Christian moral law prescribes fidelity to the State as an obligation strictly binding in conscience. To justify ethically tolerance towards certain religious practices of heathen subjects, medieval theologians appealed to the principle that tolerance might be always exercised wherever either its refusal would cause more harm than good, or, vice versa, whenever the granting of it ensured greater advantage than disadvantage. Thus St. Thomas teaches (Summa theol., II–II, Q. x, a. 11): "Ritus infidelium tolerari possunt vel propter aliquod bonum, quod ex eis provenit, vel propter aliquod maum, quod vitatur" (Heathen worships can be tolerated either because of some good that results from them or because of some evil that is avoided). In all the centuries the Church displayed an admirable tolerance especially towards the Jewish religion, since the survival of Judaism offered a living proof of the truth of Christianity. The medieval principle of tolerance is specially applicable to present conditions, since the historical development of the modern State has created throughout the world so uniform a basis of rights that even Catholic States cannot without violation of oaths and loyalty and without violent internal convulsions disregard it, even if they desired to do so. Besides, there is good reason to doubt if there still exists a purely Catholic State in the world; and it is, of course, just as doubtful whether there is such a thing as a purely Protestant State. Cosmopolites have established colonies and settlements everywhere, and to these international law concedes freedom of belief and worship. Consequently, Leo XIII also supported the principle of tolerance, when he declared (cf. Denzinger, n. 1874): "Revera si divini cultus varia genera eodem jure esse quo veram religionem Ecclesia judicat non licere, non ideo tamen damnat rerum publicarum moderatores, qui magni alicujus adipiscendi boni aut prohibendi causa mali moribus atque usu patienter ferunt, ut ea habeant singula in civitate locum" (If the Church declares that the various kinds of worship should not have the same rights as the true religion, she does not thereby condemn those rulers who, in order to secure some great good or to avert some evil, permit each cult to exist).

There are, however, a number of States, which in virtue of their constitutions are committed not alone to tolerance and religious freedom, but also to parity. By parity is understood the placing of all legalized or recognized religious bodies on the same footing before the law, all show of partiality and disfavour being equally avoided. Such is the basic principle of the constitutional State, which, while ethically Christian, allows various forms of belief. On it devolves especially the duty of placing no obstacle in the way of the public promotion of religion in sermon and writing and of extending to the religious practices of all denominations the same legal protection, to the exclusion of any compulsory system that would bind the citizens to receive certain religious rites (e. g. baptism, burial) from clergymen appointed by the State. With freedom of belief are intimately associated the personal right of changing one's religion and the right of the parties in the case of mixed marriages to decide as to the religious education of the children. The State must likewise recognize and protect the right of the various denominations to hold property and their right of self-government, in so far as these rights are enjoyed by all legally constituted corporations. Wherever such a State makes contributions or grants from the budget of public ownership, all recognized religious associations must receive equal consideration, unless a particular association, in virtue of a special title (e. g. the secularization of religious property), has legal claims to exceptional treatment. Finally, legal equality must be granted to the adherents of all denominations in both their civic and national capacities, especially in the matter of appointment to public office. Concerning Christian States in which various religions exist, F. Walter, the well-known professor of public law, made the wise observation: "The government as such, entirely regardless of the personal belief of the sovereign, must maintain towards every church the same attitude as if it belonged to this Church. In the consistent and upright observance of this standpoint lies the means of being just to each religion and of preserving for the State its Christian character" (loc. cit., p. 491). Such indeed is the admirable theory; wherever deviations from it occur in practice, they are almost without exception to the detriment of Catholics.

I. Concerning the Idea of Toleration: PELISSON-FONTANIER, *De la tolerance des Religions; Lettres de M. Leibniz et Réponses de M. Pelisson* (Paris, 1692); BALMES, *El protestantismo comparado con el catolicismo en sus relaciones con la civilización europea*, I (Barcelona, 1842); LEHMKUHL, *Gewissens-u. Kultusfreiheit* in *Stimmen aus Maria-Laach*, XI (1876), 184 sqq.; REINKENS, *Lessing über Toleranz* (Leipzig, 1884); NILLES, *Tolerari potest* in *Zeitschr. für kath. Theol.*, XVII (1893), 245 sqq.; LEZIUS, *Der Toleranzbegriff Locke's u. Puffendorf's* (Leipzig, 1900); RUFFINI, *La libertà religiosa* (Turin, 1901); SIMAR, *Gewissen u. Gewissensfreiheit* (2nd ed., Freiburg, 1902); CATHREIN, *Gewissen u. Gewissensfreiheit* (Munich, 1906).

II. Concerning Theoretical Dogmatic Toleration: JAMES, *The Meaning of Truth* (New York, 1900); BALDWIN, *Thoughts and Things, or Genetic Logic*, I (New York, 1906); SCHILLER, *Studies in Humanism* (London, 1907); JAMES, *Pragmatism* (New York, 1907). In answer to the theories there advocated: DE TONGEDET, *La notion de la verité dans la philosophie moderne* (Paris, 1909); LECLÈRE, *Pragmatisme, modernisme, protestantisme* (Paris, 1909); SWITALSKI, *Der Wahreitsbegriff des Pragmatismus* (Braunsberg, 1910); SÁNCHEZ, *De tolerantia religiosa* (Madrid, 1785), antiquated; DÖLLINGER, *Kirche u. Kirchen* (Munich, 1861); MERKLE, *Die Toleranz nach kathol. Principien* (Dillingen, 1863); *De intolerantia catholica seu de sententia: Extra Ecclesiam nulla salus* (Turin, 1868); HANSJAKOB, *Die Toleranz u. Intoleranz der kathol. Kirche* (Freiburg, 1899); SEITZ, *Die Heilsnotwendigkeit der Kirche* (Freiburg, 1903); ROMEIS, *Das Heil der Christen ausserhalb der wahren Kirche nach der Lehre des hl. Augustinus* (Paderborn, 1908); MAUSBACH, *Die Ethik des hl. Augustinus*, II (Freiburg, 1909). Concerning the Inquisition: LEA, *A Hist. of the Inquisition in the Middle Ages* (3 vols., New York, 1888); DOUAIS, *L'Inquisition, ses origines, sa procédure* (Paris, 1906); VACANDARD, *L'Inquisition. Etude historique et critique sur le pouvoir coercitif de l'église* (Paris, 1907); DE CAUZONS, *Hist. de l'Inquisition en France*, I (Paris, 1909). Concerning the Tolerance of the Reformers: PAULUS, *Die Strassburger Reformatoren u. die Gewissensfreiheit* (Freiburg, 1895); IDEM, *Protestantismus u. Toleranz im 16. Jahrh.* (Freiburg, 1911); KÖHLER, *Reformation u. Ketzerprozess* (Tübingen, 1901); WAPPLER, *Inquisition u. Ketzerprocesse in Zwickau zur Reformationszeit* (Leipzig, 1908).

III. Concerning Practical Civic Toleration: RICKABY, *Moral Philosophy or Ethics and Natural Law* (London, 1893); DORNER, *Das menschliche Handeln.* (Berlin, 1895); LECKY, *Democracy and Liberty*, I (London, 1896), 424 sqq.; WALDMANN, *Die Feindesliebe in der antiken Welt* (Vienna, 1902); CATHREIN, *Moralphilosophie*, II (Freiburg, 1911); STREHLER, *Das Ideal der kathol. Sittlichkeit* (Breslau, 1912); GRÜNEBAUM, *Sittenlehre des Judentums anderen Bekenntnissen gegenüber* (Strassburg, 1878); MILAS, *Das Kirchenrecht der morgenländ. Kirche* (Zara, 1897), 604 sqq. Concerning the Punishment of Heretics: FICKER, *Die gesetzliche Einführung der Todesstrafe für Ketzer* in *Mitteil. für osterreich. Geschichtsforschung*, I (Vienna, 1880), 177 sqq.; HAVET, *L'hérésie et le bras séculier au moyen-âge jusqu'au XIIIe siècle* (Paris, 1896); HIN-

ALTAR-TOMB OF THE EMPEROR MAXIMILIAN I, HOFKIRCHE, INNSBRUCK

schius, *System des kathol. Kirchenrechts*, V (Berlin, 1895); Pigge, *Die religiöse Toleranz Friedrichs des Grossen* (Mainz, 1899); Timpe, *Die kirchenpolitische Ansichten u. Bestrebungen des Kardinals Bellarmin* (Münster, 1905); Hermelink, *Toleranzgedanken im Reformationszeitalter* (Leipzig, 1908); Beven, *The Birth and Growth of Toleration* (London, 1909); Pohle in *Staatslexikon der Görresgesellschaft*, I (1908), s. v. Bekenntnisfreiheit.

IV. Concerning Political Toleration: von Ketteler, *Freiheit, Autorität u. Kirche* (Mainz, 1862); Montalembert, *L'eglise libre dans l'état libre* (Paris, 1863); Walter, *Naturrecht u. Politik im Lichte der Gegenwart* (Bonn, 1863); Escher, *Handbuch der praktischen Politik* (Leipzig, 1863); Rauscher, *Der Staat ohne Gott* (Vienna, 1865); Trendelenburg, *Naturrecht auf dem Grunde der Ethik* (2nd ed., Leipzig, 1868); Liberatore, *La chiesa e lo stato* (Naples, 1871); Hergenröther, *Kathol. Kirche u. christl. Staat* (Freiburg, 1872); Zeller, *Staat u. Kirche* (Leipzig, 1873); Martens, *Die Beziehungen der Ueberordnung, Nebenordnung u. Unterordnung zwischen Staat u. Kirche* (Stuttgart, 1877); Maassen, *Ueber Kirche u. Gewissensfreiheit* (Graz, 1876); von Scherer, *Handbuch des Kirchenrechts*, I (Graz, 1886); von Treitschke, *Politik*, I (Leipzig, 1897); Haring, *Kirche u. Staat* (Münster, 1907); von Hertling, *Recht, Staat u. Gesellschaft* (Freiburg, 1907); Roscher, *Politik* (3rd ed., Stuttgart, 1908); Kohler, *Katholicismus u. moderner Staat* (1908); Troeltsch, *Politische Ethik u. Christentum* (1909); Niehues, *Gesch. des Verhältnisses zwischen Kaisertum u. Papsttum im Mittelalter* (Münster, 1877–87); Roquain. *La papauté au moyen-âge. Etudes sur le pouvoir pontifical* (Paris, 1881); Bluntschli, *Gesch. der neueren Staatsgemeinschaft* (3rd ed., Munich, 1881); Cathrein, *Die Aufgaben der Staatsgewalt u. ihre Grenzen* (Freiburg, 1882); Chr. Pesch, *Christl. Staatslehre* (Freiburg, 1887); Fürstenau, *Grundrecht der Religionsfreiheit* (Leipzig, 1891); Bas, *Etudes sur les rappogts de l'église et de l'état et sur leur séparation* (St. Quentin, 1882); Schaff, *Church and State in the United States or the American Idea of Religious Liberty and its Practical Effects* (New York, 1888); Jannet and Kämpfe, *Die Vereinigten Staaten von Amerika in der Gegenwart*; Sitten, *Institutionen u. Ideen seit dem Secessionskriege* (Freiburg, 1893); Wappler, *Die Trennung von Staat u. Kirche* (Leipzig, 1907); Rothenbucher, *Die Trennung von Staat u. Kirche* (Leipzig, 1908); Sägmüller, *Die Trennung von Staat u. Kirche* (Tübingen, 1909). Concerning Parity: Drache, *Parität u. Imparität* (Leipzig, 1892); Kahl, *Ueber Parität* (Berlin, 1895); Lilly and Wallis, *A Manual of the Law especially affecting Catholics* (London, 1893); Bachem, *Parität in Preussen* (2nd ed., Cologne, 1899); Erzberger, *Der Toleranzantrag des Zentrums im Deutschen Reichstag* (Berlin, 1906).

J. POHLE.

Toletus, Franciscus. See Toledo, Francisco de.

Tolima. See Garzón, Diocese of.

Tolomei, John Baptist, distinguished Jesuit theologian and cardinal, b. of noble parentage, at Camberaia, between Pistoia and Florence, 3 Dec., 1653; d. at Rome in the Roman College, 19 Jan., 1726, and was buried before the high altar of the Church of Saint Ignatius. At the age of fifteen, after an early schooling at Florence, he studied law at the University of Pisa; on 18 Feb., 1673, he entered the Society of Jesus at Rome. He was master of eleven languages, Latin, Greek, Hebrew, Chaldee, Syriac, Arabic, English, French, Spanish, Illyrian, and Italian. He began his public career at Rome by expounding the Sacred Scriptures on Sunday evenings in the Church of the Gesù. At the age of thirty he was elected in the General Congregation of the Jesuits as the procurator general of the order, which office he held for five years, relinquishing it to take the chair of philosophy at the Roman College. Here his lecture-room was thronged. His lectures were printed at Rome in 1696 under the title of "Philosophia mentis et sensuum", and demonstrated that, while loyal to the principles and method of Aristotle, he welcomed every discovery of his time in the natural sciences and wove these into his course. The lectures were reprinted in 1698 in Germany and evoked the warmest encomiums from the Academy of Leipzig as well as from Leibniz. He later filled the chair of theology at the Roman College (now the Gregorian University) and renewed the courses in controversial dogma begun by Bellarmine a century before. These lectures in MS. filled six volumes in folio but were never printed. Successively Rector of the Roman College and of the German College, he was at the same time Consultor of the Congregations of Rites, of the Index, and of Indulgences, as well as being one of the appointed examiners of bishops. On 17 May, 1712, unexpectedly created cardinal by Clement XI, under the title of Santo Stefano in Monte Coelio, he became chief adviser to the pontiff in matters theological, particularly in the preparation of the condemnation of the errors of Quesnel. As cardinal he assisted at the conclaves which elected Innocent XIII and Benedict XIII. His published works are the "Philosophia mentis et sensuum" (with the addition of natural theology and ethics, Rome, 1702), "De primatu beati Petri" (in the second series of the miscellany printed from the manuscripts in the library of the Roman College, Rome, 1867), and a little pamphlet containing "Daily Prayers for a Happy Death" (in Latin, Vienna, 1742; also in German, Augsburg, 1856).

Hurter, *Nomenclator literarius*, IV (Innsbruck, 1910); Sommervogel, *Bibliothèque de la compagnie de Jésus*, VIII (Brussels, 1898).

CHARLES MACKSEY.

Tomb, a memorial for the dead at the place of burial, customary, especially for distinguished persons, among nearly all peoples. It is of much importance in the history of art because the development of plastic art can be traced almost in its entirety by means of tombs, for the tombs, having, as a rule, been erected in churches, are better preserved. Apart from the sepulchral slabs in the Catacombs, sarcophagi ornamented with portraits, and scattered examples of mausolea, tombs may be divided into four special classes.

The first class consists of tombs with recumbent tombstones; among such are the stone or metal plates inserted in the flooring of churches. These are the oldest Christian monuments. Originally, at least in Germany, they were ornamented with a cross having a long shaft; from the eleventh century they also bore the figure of the deceased. The monumental metal plate of the tomb of King Rudolph of Swabia (d. 1081), in the cathedral of Merseburg, is of this era. During the Gothic period an engraved brass plate was the favourite sepulchral monument, while the Renaissance returned to the plate cast in relief, such as the plates by Peter Vischer of Nuremberg.

The second class consists of detached altar-tombs, that is, a raised tomb containing the body of the deceased. One variety rises like a table above the place of burial. Romanesque art generally left the side walls of the altar-tomb without ornament, while Gothic art adorned them with numerous small figures, as those of relatives, mourners, praying figures, and allegorical forms. On the lid the deceased was represented at full length. Numerous examples are to be found in all the medieval cathedrals and monastic churches. Even England, where there are but scanty plastic remains, has a rich treasure of such monuments. Probably no altar-tomb is more celebrated than that of Emperor Maximilian at Innsbruck. Another worthy of mention is Charles the Bold's tomb at Dijon by Claus Sluter. More elaborate monuments have frequently an additional struc-

Tomb of Can Grande I, Verona
Francesco della Scala, 1329

ture above and around them, as a baldachin, e. g. the tomb of the Della Scala at Verona; chiefly that of Cansignorio (d. 1375). During the Renaissance the baldachin assumed an entirely monumental form, almost that of a triumphal arch; fine examples are the monuments of Galleazzo Visconti in the Certosa at Pavia and of Francis I at Saint-Denis.

The third class may be called mural tombs, that is, altar-tombs set originally in a niche against a wall, and later raised upon pillars, caryatides, or a solid understructure. They were decorated on all sides with rich plastic ornamentation. They were customary as early as the Gothic period and attained their highest development in Italy, where the inordinate craving for fame and the longing to be remembered by posterity led to the production of those magnificent sepulchral monuments for physicians, lawyers, professors, statesmen, and, by no means last, prelates, which fill the churches from Venice to Naples. During the period of the early Renaissance it was a favourite custom to place a recumbent statue of the deceased upon a state bed or a sarcophagus and to set this at a moderate height; this structure is surrounded by standing or kneeling angels who draw back a curtain of the niche in which the Madonna is often visible. A fine example is the tomb of Leonardo Bruni (d. 1444) in Santa Croce at Florence. During the late Renaissance undue consideration was paid to architecture, as in the sepulchral monument of Giovanni Pesaro in the Frari church at Venice. In the seventeenth and eighteenth centuries the art of sculpture obtained again a greater opportunity in the treatment of tombs, but unfortunately only in the monotonous Baroque style. Hardly more than the figure of the deceased was brought into prominence. It was placed within an altar of similar style or upon a broad *podium* and was surrounded by all kinds of symbolical figures in the most daring positions. In a material sense these tombs are often very fine but they frequently lack the desired spiritual earnestness and repose.

TOMB OF THE DOGE GIOVANNI PESARO
Longhena, the Frari, Venice

TOMB OF LEONARDO BRUNI
Rossellino, Church of S. Croce, Florence

The fourth class consists of hanging sepulchral monuments (memorial tablets). These occur as early as Gothic art in the form of funeral escutcheons and coats of arms made of wood or leather; and are especially prominent in the period of the Rococo and Baroque styles. Besides the altar-shaped tablet often constructed in several stories, the cartouche containing a portrait of the deceased was very popular in sepulchral monuments of this class.

Since the modern era put an end nearly everywhere to the burial of the dead within the church building, a new form of sepulchral art has gradually developed; it has produced works of the greatest beauty in all countries, but has also shown great perversions of the artistic sense, especially in Italy where the tendency is more to an excess of technic than to the conception of the eternal. The finest sepulchral monument of modern times is perhaps the one designed by A. Bartholomé and erected at Père Lachaise.

STOTHARD, *Monumental Effigies of Great Britain* (London, 1817); COTMAN, *Engravings of Sepulchral Brasses in Norfolk and Suffolk* (London, 1839); MÂLE, *L'art religieux en France* (Paris, 1908), 423–477; BURGER, *Gesch. des florent. Grabmals* (Strasburg, 1904); SCHUBRING, *Das italien. Grabmal der Frührenaissance* (Berlin, 1904); DAVIES, *The Sculptured Tombs of the Fifteenth Century in Rome, with chapters on the previous centuries* (London, 1910); GERLACH, *Alte Grabmalskunst* (Leipzig, 1909).

BEDA KLEINSCHMIDT.

Tomb of the Blessed Virgin Mary.—The tomb of the Blessed Virgin is venerated in the Valley of the Cedron, near Jerusalem. Modern writers hold, how-

ENTRANCE TO THE CHURCH OF THE ASSUMPTION

ever, that Mary died and was buried at Ephesus. The main points of the question to be taken into consideration are as follows.

I. The apocryphal works of the second to the fourth century are all favourable to the Jerusalem tradition. According to the "Acts of St. John by Prochurus", written (160–70) by Lencius, the Evangelist went to Ephesus accompanied by Prochurus alone and at a very advanced age, i. e. after Mary's death. The two letters "B. Ignatii missa S. Joanni", written about 370, show that the Blessed Virgin passed the remainder of her days at Jerusalem (Funk, "Patres ap.", 1901, II, 214–16). That of Dionysius the Areopagite to the Bishop Titus (363), the "Joannis liber de Dormitione Mariæ" (third to fourth century), and the treatise "De transitu B. M. Virginis" (fourth century) place her tomb at Gethsemane. From an historical standpoint these works, although apocryphal, have a real value, reflecting as they do the tradition of the early centuries. At the beginning of the fifth century a pilgrim from Armenia visited "the tomb of the Virgin in the valley of Josaphat", and about 431 the "Breviarius de Hierusalem" mentions in that valley "the basilica of Holy Mary, which contains her sepulchre". Thenceforth pilgrims of various rites repaired thither to venerate the empty tomb of Mary. St. Gregory of Tours, St. Modestus, St. Sophronius, Patriarch of Jerusalem, St. Germanus, Patriarch of Constantinople, St. Andrew, Bishop of Crete, John of Thessalonica, Hippolytus of Thebes, and Venerable Bede teach this same fact and bear witness that this tradition was accepted by all the Churches of East and West. St. John Damascene, preaching on the feast of the Assumption at Gethsemane, recalls that, according to the "Euthymian History", III, xl (written probably by Cyril of Scythopolis in the fifth century), Juvenal, Bishop of Jerusalem, sent to Constantinople in 452 at the command of the Emperor Marcian and Pulcheria, his wife, the shroud of the Blessed

Plan of the Church of the Assumption and of the Grotto of Gethsemani.
A. Stairs. B. Courtyard. C. The Porch. D. Subterranean Church.
E. Grotto of Gethsemani.

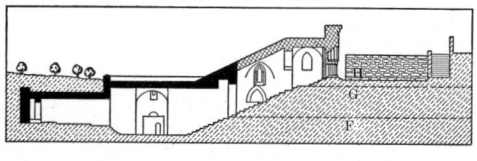

Vertical Section of the Church of the Assumption.
F. Primitive Level of the Courtyard. G. Level in the XII Century.
H. Present Level.

Virgin preserved in the church of Gethsemane (P. G., XCVI, 747-51). The relic has since been venerated in that city at the Church of Our Lady of Blachernæ.

II. There was never any tradition connecting Mary's death and burial with the city of Ephesus. Not a single writer or pilgrim speaks of her tomb as being there; and in the thirteenth century Perdicas, prothonotary of Ephesus, visited "the glorious tomb of the Virgin at Gethsemane", and describes it in his poem (P. G., CXXXIII, 969). In a letter sent in 431 by the members of the Council of Ephesus to the clergy of Constantinople we read that Nestorius "reached the city of Ephesus where John the Theologian and the Mother of God, the Holy Virgin, were separated from the assembly of the holy Fathers", etc. Tillemont has completed the elliptical phrase by adding arbitrarily, "have their tombs". He is followed by a few writers. According to the meditations of Sister Catherine Emmerich (d. 1824), compiled and published in 1852, the Blessed Virgin died and was buried not at Ephesus but three or four leagues south of the city. She is followed by those who accept her visions or meditations as Divine revelations. However, St. Brigid relates that at the time of her visit to the church of Gethsemane the Blessed Virgin appeared to her and spoke to her of her stay of three days in that place and of her Assumption into Heaven. The revelations of Ven. Maria d'Agreda do not contradict those of Catherine Emmerich.

III. As the soil is considerably raised in the Valley of the Cedron, the ancient Church of the Sepulchre of Mary is completely covered and hidden. A score of steps descend from the road into the court (see plan: B), at the back of which is a beautiful twelfth century porch (C). It opens on a monumental stairway of forty-eight steps. The twentieth step leads into the church built in the fifth century, to a great extent cut from the rock. It forms a cross of unequal arms (D). In the centre of the eastern arm, 52 feet long and 20 feet wide, is the glorious tomb of the Mother of Christ. It is a little room with a bench hewn from the rocky mass in imitation of the tomb of Christ. This has given it the shape of a cubical edicule, about ten feet in circumference and eight feet high. Until the fourteenth century the little monument was covered with magnificent marble slabs and the walls of the church were covered with frescoes. Since 1187 the tomb has been the property of the Mussulman Government which nevertheless authorizes the Christians to officiate in it.

ZAHN, *Die Dormitio S. Virginis u. das Haus des Johannes-Markus* (Leipzig, 1899); NIRSCHL, *Das Haus u. das Grab der h. Jungfrau* (Mainz, 1900); MEISTERMANN, *Le tombeau de la Sainte Vièrge à Jérusalem* (Jerusalem, 1903); BARDENHEWER, *Ist Maria zu Jerusalem oder zu Ephesus gestorben?* V (Munich, 1906), 569-77; DE VOGÜÉ, *Les églises de la Terre sainte* (Paris, 1860).

BARNABAS MEISTERMANN.

Tomi, a titular metropolitan see in the Province of Scythia, on the Black Sea. It was a Greek colony from Miletus. In 29 B. C. the Romans captured the country from the Odryses, and annexed it as far as the Danube, under the name of *Limes Scythicus*. The city was afterwards included in the Province of Mœsia, and, from the time of Diocletian, in Scythia Minor, of which it was the metropolis. In A. D. 10 Ovid was exiled thither by Augustus, and died there eight years later, celebrating the town of Tomi in his poems. Few places had so many Christian memories as this town, in the barbarous country of the Getæ; e. g. Sts. Macrobius, Gordianus, and their companions, exiled to Scythia and slain in 319, venerated on 13 Sept.; Sts. Argeus, Narcissus, and Marcellinus, also slain under Licinius and venerated 2 Jan.; a great many others whose names only are known, and who are mentioned in the Roman Martyrology for 3 April, 20 June, 5 July, and 1 October. The first bishop may have been Evangelicus, mentioned in the Acts of Sts. Epictetus and Action (8 July), and who must have lived at the end of the third century. Eusebius (De Vita Constantini, III, 7) mentions a Scythian bishop at Nicæa who may have belonged to Tomi. Mention should be made of St. Bretanion, martyred under Valens, and whose feast is observed 25 Jan.; Gerontius, at the Council of Constantinople, in 381; St. Theotimus, writer and friend of St. John Chrysostom, venerated 20 April; Timotheus, at Ephesus in 431; John, ecclesiastical writer, d. about 448; Alexander, at Chalcedon in 451; Theotimus II, in 458; Paternus, in 519; and Valentinian, in 550. The Province of Scythia formed a single diocese, that of Tomi, an autocephalous archdiocese, subject to the Patriarch of Constantinople. It is mentioned in 640 in the Ecthesis of Pseudo-Epiphanius (Gelzer, "Ungedruckte . . . Texte der Notitiæ episcopatuum", 535). Shortly afterwards the Bulgarians invaded the region and the Archdiocese of Tomi was suppressed. The city subsequently belonged to the Byzantines, again to the Bulgarians, then to the Turks, and finally to the Rumanians since the Treaty of Berlin in 1878. The town of Tomi is near Constantza, the capital of Dobroudja and a port on the Black Sea, which has about 15,000 inhabitants. There is a Catholic parish. A statue of the poet Ovid stands in the chief square.

LE QUIEN, *Oriens christianus*, I, 1211-16; NETZHAMMER, *Das altchristliche Tomi* (Salzburg, 1903); IDEM, *Nach Adam Klissi* (Salzburg, 1906); IDEM, *Die christlichen Altertümer der Dobrogea* (Bukarest, 1906).

S. VAILHÉ.

Tongerloo, ABBEY OF, near Antwerp, Belgium, founded in 1128 in honour of the Blessed Virgin, by de Giselbert, who not only gave the land, but also himself became a lay brother in it. The first religious were sent from St. Michael's Abbey, Antwerp, under Henry, who had come with St. Norbert to Antwerp to extirpate the Tanchelmite heresies. The charter of its foundation was signed, amongst others, by St. Bernard of Clairvaux and by the Blessed Waltman, first Abbot of Antwerp. The Bishop of Cambrai granted synodal rights to the abbots. From very small beginnings the abbey grew to be in time one of the most important in Belgium, making its spiritual and social influence felt in a large district called Campine, now in north-east Belgium and south Holland, then a wild district in which but scanty provision was found for the spiritual and social needs of its scattered inhabitants. Considering the scarcity of priests and the good done by the religious of Tongerloo, the bishops of Cambrai, the chapters of Liège and Maastricht, and several landowners confided the charge of parishes, with the right of patronage, to the abbey; thus it came to pass that in time the abbey had to provide priests for some forty parishes, or small Norbertine residences, in these parts.

With the erection of new dioceses (1559–60) in Belgium and Holland, heavy burdens were cast on the abbey, for not only had it to provide the funds, but the new Bishop of Bois-le-Duc was put at its head as abbot. This state of affairs lasted until 1590, when, to obtain its independence, the abbey had to give up much property in support of the new diocese. Meanwhile the Calvinists had become very powerful in Holland and, in their hatred of the Catholic Church, had put many Catholics to death. Amongst those who received the crown of martyrdom are reckoned three religious of Tongerloo, viz.: Arnold Vessem and Henry Bosch in 1557, and Peter Janssens in 1572. The abbey has always promoted education. Bishop Ophovius says that its religious were educated *in omni pietate et doctrina* and Miræus, that it was *fæcundum pastorum Seminarium*. It possessed one of the largest libraries, and was able to take up the work of the Bollandists. (See BACKX; PREMONSTRATENSIAN CANONS, BOLLANDISTS.)

SPILBEECK, *De Abdy van Tongerloo* (Antwerp, 1888), pp. xii–652

F. M. GEUDENS

TONGERLOO ABBEY, FROM THE SOUTH-WEST

Tongiorgi, SALVATOR, philosopher, b. at Rome, Italy, 25 Dec., 1820; d. there, 12 Nov., 1865. At the age of seventeen he entered the Society of Jesus. After the usual noviceship, literary and philosophical studies, a half-decade was spent in teaching rhetoric at Reggio and humanities at Forlì. Then four years were passed in the study of theology, under the eminent professors Perrone, Passaglia, Ballerini, and Patrizi. Immediately after this, in 1853, the young priest was assigned to the chair of philosophy in the Roman College, and there during twelve years distinguished himself as a teacher and author. Within a few days of his forty-fourth birthday he was appointed assistant to the provincial of the Roman Province; but his health gave way before a year had elapsed. Father Tongiorgi wrote a well-known course of philosophy, "Institutiones philosophicæ", which he published in three volumes at Rome in 1861 and at Brussels in 1862. Nine editions appeared during the next eighteen years, some of them modified by Claude Ramière. A compendium of the same work and a separate volume on ethics also came from his pen. All his works are still used as text-books for college or seminary. On some of the mooted questions in philosophy the author departed from Scholastic traditions, rejecting the Peripatetic theory of matter and form, denying the real distinction between accidents and substance, and claiming that mere resultants of mechanical and chemical forces could produce the life-activity seen in the vegetable world. These doctrines, though not widely accepted, yet stimulated the Scholastics to make better use of the researches carried on in the physical sciences.

SOMMERVOGEL, *Bibl. de la. c. de J.*, VIII, 96; HURTER, *Nomenclator*.

JOHN M. FOX.

Tong-king. See INDO-CHINA.

Tongues, GIFT OF, or GLOSSOLALY ($\gamma\lambda\omega\sigma\sigma o\lambda\alpha\lambda\iota\alpha$), a supernatural gift of the class *gratiæ gratis datæ*, designed to aid in the outer development of the primitive Church. The theological bearing of the subject is treated in the article CHARISMATA (11). The present article deals with its exegetical and historic phases. St. Luke relates (Acts, ii, 1–15) that on the feast of Pentecost following the Ascension of Christ into heaven one hundred and twenty disciples of Galilean origin were heard speaking "with divers tongues, according as the Holy Ghost gave them to speak". Devout Jews then dwelling at Jerusalem, the scene of the incident, were quickly drawn together to the number of approximately three thousand. The multitude embraced two religious classes, Jews and proselytes, from fifteen distinct lands so distributed geographically as to represent "every nation under heaven". All were "confounded in mind" because every man heard the disciples speaking the "wonderful things of God" in his own tongue, namely, that in which he was born. To many the disciples appeared to be in a state of inebriation, wherefore St. Peter undertook to justify the anomaly by explaining it in the light of prophecy as a sign of the last times.

The glossolaly thus described was historic, articulate, and intelligible. Jerusalem was then as now a polyglottal region and could easily have produced one hundred and twenty persons who, in the presence of a cosmopolitan assemblage, might express themselves in fifteen different tongues. Since the variety of tongues is attributed to the group and not to individuals, particular disciples may not have used more than their native Aramaic, though it is difficult to picture any of them historically and socially without at least a smattering of other tongues. The linguistic conditions of the country were far more diverse than those of Switzerland to-day. The number of languages spoken equalled the number of those in which the listeners "were born". But for these Greek and Aramaic would suffice with a possible admixture of Latin. The distinction of "tongues" (v. 6, $\delta\iota\dot{\alpha}\lambda\epsilon\kappa\tau o\varsigma$; v. 11, $\gamma\lambda\hat{\omega}\sigma\sigma\alpha$) was largely one of dialects and the cause of astonishment was that so many of them should be heard simultaneously and from Galileans whose linguistic capacities were presumably underrated. It was the Holy Ghost who impelled the disciples "to speak", without perhaps being obliged to infuse a knowledge of tongues unknown. The physical and psychic condition of the auditors was one of ecstasy and rapture in which "the wonderful things of God" would naturally find utterance in acclamations, prayers or hymns, conned, if not already known, during the preceding week, when they were "always in the temple", side by side with the strangers from afar, "praising and blessing God" (Luke, xxiv, 52, 53).

Subsequent manifestations occurred at Cæsarea, Palæstina, Ephesus, and Corinth, all polyglottal regions. St. Peter identifies that of Cæsarea with what befell the disciples "in the beginning" (Acts, xi, 15). There, as at Ephesus and Jerusalem, the strange incident marked the baptism of several converts, who operated in groups. Corinth, standing apart in this and other respects, is reserved for special study. In post-Biblical times St. Irenæus tells that "many" of his contemporaries were heard "speaking through the Spirit in all kinds ($\pi\alpha\nu\tau\text{o}\delta\alpha\pi\alpha\hat{\iota}\varsigma$) of tongues" ("Contra hær.", V, vii; Eusebius, "Hist. eccl.", V, vii). St. Francis Xavier is said to have preached in tongues unknown to him and St. Vincent Ferrer while using his native tongue was understood in others. From this last phenomenon Biblical glossolaly differs in being what St. Gregory Nazianzen points out as a marvel of speaking and not of hearing. Exegetes observe too that it was never used for preaching, although Sts. Augustine and Thomas seem to have overlooked this detail.

St. Paul's Concept (I Cor., xii–xiv).—For the Biblical data thus far examined we are indebted to the bosom friend and companion of St. Paul—St. Luke. That being true, the views of St. Paul on supernatural glossolaly must have coincided with those of St. Luke. Now St. Paul had seen the gift conferred at Ephesus and St. Luke does not distinguish Ephesian glossolaly from that of Jerusalem. They must therefore have been alike and St. Paul seems to have had both in mind when he commanded the Corinthians (xiv, 37) to employ none but articulate and "plain speech" in their use of the gift (9), and to refrain from such use in church unless even the unlearned could grasp what was said (16). No tongue could be genuine "without voice" and to use such a tongue would be the act of a barbarian (10, 11). For him the impulse to praise God in one or more strange tongues should proceed from the Holy Ghost. It was even then an inferior gift which he ranked next to last in a list of eight charismata. It was a mere "sign" and as such was intended not for believers but for unbelievers (22).

Corinthian Abuses (I Cor., xiv passim).—Medieval and modern writers wrongly take it for granted that the charism existed permanently at Corinth—as it did nowhere else—and that St. Paul, in commending the gift to the Corinthians, therewith gave his guaranty that the characteristics of Corinthian glossolaly were those of the gift itself. Traditional writers in overlooking this point place St. Luke at variance with St. Paul, and attribute to the charism properties so contrary as to make it inexplicable and prohibitively mysterious. There is enough in St. Paul to show us that the Corinthian peculiarities were ignoble accretions and abuses. They made of "tongues" a source of schism in the Church and of scandal without (xiv, 23). The charism had deteriorated into a mixture of meaningless inarticulate gabble (9, 10) with an element of uncertain sounds (7, 8), which sometimes might be construed as little short of blasphemous (xii, 3). The Divine praises were recognized now and then, but the general effect was one of confusion and disedification for the very unbelievers for whom the normal gift was intended (xiv, 22, 23, 26). The Corinthians, misled not by insincerity but by simplicity and ignorance (20), were actuated by an undisciplined religious spirit ($\pi\nu\epsilon\hat{\upsilon}\mu\alpha$), or rather by frenzied emotions and not by the understanding ($\nu\text{o}\hat{\upsilon}\varsigma$) or the Spirit of God (15). What to-day purports to be the "gift of tongues" at certain Protestant revivals is a fair reproduction of Corinthian glossolaly, and shows the need there was in the primitive Church of the Apostle's counsel to do all things "decently, and according to order" (40).

Faithful adherence to the text of Sacred Scripture makes it obligatory to reject those opinions which turn the charism of tongues into little more than infantile babbling (Eichhorn, Schmidt, Neander), incoherent exclamations (Meyer), pythonic utterances (Wiseler), or prophetic demonstrations of the archaic kind (see I Kings, xix, 20, 24). The unalloyed charism was as much an exercise of the intelligence as of the emotions. Languages or dialects, now $\kappa\alpha\iota\nu\alpha\hat{\iota}\varsigma$ (Mark, xvi, 17) for their present purpose, and now spontaneously borrowed by the conservative Hebrew from Gentile foreigners ($\dot{\epsilon}\tau\epsilon\rho\text{o}\gamma\lambda\dot{\omega}\sigma\sigma\text{o}\iota\varsigma$, $\chi\epsilon\dot{\iota}\lambda\epsilon\sigma\iota\nu$ $\dot{\epsilon}\tau\dot{\epsilon}\rho\omega\nu$, I Cor., xiv, 21), were used as never before. But they were understood even by those who used them. Most Latin commentators have believed the contrary, but the ancient Greeks, St. Cyril of Alexandria, Theodoret, and others who were nearer the scene, agree to it and the testimony of the texts as above studied seems to bear them out. (See CHARISMATA.)

CORLUY in JAUGEY, *Dict. apologétique* (Paris, 1889); MELVILLE, *Observationes theologico-exegeticæ de dono linguarum etc.* (Basle, 1816); HILGENFELD, *Die Glossolalie in der alten Kirche* (Leipzig, 1850); FOUARD, *St. Paul, ses missions* (Paris, 1892); BLEEK, *Ueber die Gabe etc.* in *Theologische Studien und Kritiken*, II (1829); REUSS, *La glossolalie* in *Revue de théologie*, III (Strasburg, 1851); SHEPPARD, *The Gift of Tongues in the Early Church* in *Amer. Eccl. Rev.*, XLII (Philadelphia, May, 1910), 513–22; REILLY, *The Gift of Tongues, What was it?* in *Amer. Eccl. Rev* XLIII (Philadelphia, July, 1910), 3–25.

THOS. À K. REILLY.

Tonica Indians (OR TUNICA).—A small tribe constituting a distinct linguistic stock living, when first known to the French, in small villages on the lower Yazoo river, Mississippi, in alliance with the Yazoo and Ofogula, and numbering perhaps 700. Their tribal name signifies "the people". They may be identical with the people of "Tanico", encountered by the De Soto expedition in 1540, apparently about north-eastern Louisiana. Their definite history begins in the summer of 1698 with the visit of the missionary priests of the Quebec Seminary of Foreign Missions, Fathers Montigny, Davion, and La Source. They had been decimated just before by a smallpox epidemic, which had ravaged the whole lower Mississippi country, and numbers were still dying, of whom several, including a chief, received baptism. In the next year Fr. Antoine Davion established a mission among them, studying their language and ministering to the allied tribes. In this year the French commander Iberville visited them, and in 1700 the Jesuit, Father Jacques Gravier, descending the Mississippi, stopped off to wait upon Davion, who was prostrated by fever. The Tonica were noted for their affection and loyalty toward the French. This may have been due in part to their lack of kinship with any of the surrounding tribes. In the fall of 1702 Fr. Nicholas Foucault, of the same order, who had arrived in the previous year to assist Davion, was murdered with three other Frenchmen, while asleep, by treacherous Koroa guides in collusion with the Yazoo. In consequence of these murders Father Davion retired to the French fort at Mobile until, at the urgent request of a delegation of Tonica chiefs, who promised full reparation upon the guilty ones, he returned, probably in 1705. In 1706, in consequence of Chickasaw raids instigated by the Carolina slave-traders, the Tonica fled across the Mississippi and settled near the mouth of Red River, Fr. Davion accompanying them. Their neighbours, the Taensa, were likewise compelled to remove by the same enemy.

In 1719 the historian La Harpe stopped at the Tonica village and found Father Davion still there and "very much revered", although preaching fearlessly against their polygamy and heathen ceremonials. They had given up their worst heathenisms and the head chief, with his family, was a daily attendant at the sermons. Charlevoix visited their principal town in 1721 and describes the chief, Cahura-Joligo, as devoted to the French, wearing civilized dress, wealthy, and having the full confidence of the commandants. The houses were built around an open space used for games. Father Davion had some time before left them for the last time, in despair at their indifference, and notwithstanding their affection for him, which was not disturbed even when in his zeal on one occasion, he had burned their sacred fire temple.

In the various difficulties with the powerful Natchez, beginning in 1716, the Tonica, almost alone of the Indian tribes, rendered efficient service to the French. In the final war, beginning in 1729, they again supported the French. In retaliation a large body of fugitive Natchez, aided by the Chickasaw and Koroa, fell upon the Tonica (1731) and defeated them in a desperate battle, killing their best warriors and their head chief Cahur-Joligo. They never recovered from this blow. In 1758 they still counted about 250 souls in a village above Pointe Coupée but some time between 1784 and 1803 the remnant removed to the neighbourhood of Marksville, Louisiana, on the Red River, where some thirty mixed bloods still remain, besides a few others scattered in the Choctaw Nation, Oklahoma, and elsewhere. In 1886 Dr. Albert Gatschet of the Bureau of American Ethnology collected from the survivors the first recorded vocabulary of the language, by which he was enabled to classify it as constituting a distinct stock. This was supplemented in 1909 by Dr. John R. Swanton, of the same Bureau, who also obtained several interesting myths. The Tonica were an agricultural tribe and in arts, customs and general culture closely resembled their neighbours, the Natchez and Taensa. Both sexes had the head artificially flattened, went nearly naked except on ceremonial occasions, and wore the hair at full length down the back. The men did most of the heavy work, spending most of their time in the corn fields and rarely hunting, so that they ate but little meat. They buried in the ground and kept a light burning, and a watch beside the grave for four nights until the soul was supposed to have reached the spirit world. They had a temple with a sacred fire, and according to Father Gravier, had nine principal gods, viz. the Sun, Thunder, Fire and the gods of the four cardinal points, Sky, and Earth. There is no record of the bloody rites characteristic of the Natchez and Taensa.

French, *Hist. Colls. of Louisiana* (New York, 1851); Le Page du Pratz, *Hist. de la Louisiane* (3 vols., Paris, 1758); Eng. tr. (London, 1763, 1774); *Découvertes et etablissements des français (Penicaut, Iberville, Sauvolle)*, ed. Margry (6 vols., Paris, 1879–86); Shea, *Disc. and Exploration Miss. Valley* (New York, 1852; Albany, 1903); Idem, *Hist. Catholic Indian Missions* (New York, 1855, 1870); Sibley, *Indian Tribes in Louisiana* (Washington, 1806, with Message from President communicating discoveries by Lewis and Clark); Swanton, *Indian Tribes of the Lower Mississippi* (Bull. 43, Bureau Am. Ethnology, Washington, 1911).

James Mooney.

Tonkawa Indians.—A tribal group or confederacy, of low culture status and constituting a distinct linguistic stock, formerly ranging about the middle Trinity and Colorado Rivers, in Eastern Texas, and now represented by a single rapidly dwindling remnant of about forty souls. They may have numbered originally 2000 souls, including the Tonkawa proper, the Yojuane, Mayeye, Ervipiame, and others. The origin and meaning of the name Tonkawa are unknown. They call themselves *Titskan-watich*, "natives". They were inveterate rovers, planting nothing, but subsisting entirely by the buffalo and other game, the fruit of the mesquite and cactus, and wild roots. They dwelt in buffalo skin tipis or brushwood shelters, were notable horsemen, and carried the bow, spear, shield, with the usual head-dress of feathered cap and buffalo horns on ceremonial occasions. They were superior hunters and brave and active warriors, but were hated by all the neighbouring tribes by reason of their cannibal habit, on account of which they were universally known among the other Indians as the "Man Eaters". Of their cannibal practices there is abundant record and it is this propensity which led to their outlawry and final destruction. Almost nothing is known of their myths and ritual, beyond the fact that they had a Wolf Dance and claimed the wolf as an ancestor. They were also leaders in the ritual cult of the peyote, a cactus eaten with ceremonial accompaniment to produce waking visions.

The Tonkawa are first mentioned by name in a Spanish document of 1691. In 1719 they first became known to the French through La Haye's expedition into what is now Eastern Oklahoma. In response to their request, the Franciscan Father Francisco Ano de los Dolores in 1748 established for their benefit the Mission of San Francisco Xavier de Horcasitas on San Xavier (now San Gabriel) River, about nine miles north-west of the present Rockdale Nilamco, Texas. Shortly afterward the Tonkawa together with other tribes of Central Texas, were greatly wasted by a smallpox epidemic. The mission also suffered from the attacks of the Lipan Apache, in consequence of which and another epidemic most of the inmates were removed to a mission on Guadalupe River about 1755. Another band of the same connexion, the Ervipiame, established on request of their chief in the Mission of San Francisco-Xavier de Náxera on San Antonio River in 1722, had later been consolidated with the larger body at the second San Xavier. With the decline and abandonment of the Texas missions, 1790–1800, the mission Indians for the most part rejoined their tribes and relapsed into barbarism. In 1778 the Tonkawa were still estimated at about 1200 souls, but another smallpox epidemic immediately thereafter cut them down one-half. In 1855 the Government settled them, with several other tribes, on a reservation on the Clear Fork of the Brazos River, but in consequence of the opposition of the Texans it was found necessary to remove them in 1857 to a new reservation on Washita River, Oklahoma, the Tonkawa camp being just above the present Anadarko. Taking advantage of the confusion of the Civil War, a combination of the neighbouring tribes—who had a hatred toward the Tonkawa on account of their cannibalism and their activity as scouts for the troops—surprised the Tonkawa camp in a night attack, 25 October, 1862, killing 137 out of a total of 305. They never recovered from this blow. After years as refugees about Fort Griffin, Texas, under military protection, the remnant numbering only 90, were gathered together in 1884 and again removed to a small reservation in Oklahoma, near the present Ponca. They are now citizens, with lands allotted in severalty. Our knowledge of the Tonkawa language is based chiefly on Gatschet's studies of manuscript material with the Bureau of American Ethnology.

Bolten's Zonkawa, San Francisco Xavier de Horcasitas, etc., in *Handbook of Am. Inds.*, ed. Hodge, for *Bull. Bur. Am. Ethnology* (Washington, 1907–10); *Annual Repts. Commissioner of Ind. Affairs* (Washington); Gatschet, *Remarks upon the Tonkawa Language* in *Am. Philos. Soc. Proc.* (Phila., 1877); La Maye, *Journal historique, etc.* (New Orleans, 1831), tr. in *French Hist. Colls. of La.*, III (New York, 1851); Mooney, *Our Last Cannibal Tribe* in *Harper's Mag.* (New York, Sept., 1901); Sibley, *Hist. Sketches of the Ind. Tribes in La., etc., with original Presidential Message conveying report of Lewis and Clark discoveries* (Washington, 1806).

James Mooney.

Tonsure (Lat. *tondere*, "to shear"), a sacred rite instituted by the Church by which a baptized and confirmed Christian is received into the clerical order by the shearing of his hair and the investment with the surplice. The person thus tonsured becomes a partaker of the common privileges and obligations of the clerical state and is prepared for the reception of orders. The tonsure itself is not an ordination properly so called, nor a true order. It is rather a simple ascription of a person to the Divine service in such things as are common to all clerics. Historically, the tonsure was not in use in the primitive Church during the age of persecution. Even later, St. Jerome (in Ezech., xliv) disapproves of clerics shaving their heads. Indeed, among the Greeks and Romans such a custom was a badge of slavery. On this very account, the shaving of the head was adopted by the monks. Towards the end of the fifth, or beginning of the sixth, century, the custom passed over to the secular clergy.

As a sacred rite, the tonsure was originally joined to the first ordination received, as in the Greek Church it still is to the order of lector. In the Latin Church it began as a separate ceremony about the end of the seventh century, when parents offered their young sons to the service of God. Tonsure is to be given by a candidate's ordinary, though mitred abbots can bestow it on their own subjects. No special age for its reception is prescribed, but the recipient must have learnt the rudiments of the Faith and be able to read and write. The ceremony may be performed at any time or place. As to the monastic tonsure, some writers have distinguished three kinds: (1) the Roman, or that of St. Peter, when all the head is shaved except a circle of hair; (2) the Eastern, or St. Paul's, when the entire head is denuded of hair; (3) the Celtic, or St. John's, when only a crescent of hair is shaved from the front of the head. In Britain, the Saxon opponents of the Celtic tonsure called it the tonsure of Simon Magus. According to canon law, all clerics are bound to wear the tonsure under certain penalties. But on this subject, Taunton (loc. cit. inf.) says: "In English-speaking countries, from a custom arising in the days of persecution and having a prescription of over three centuries, the shaving of the head, the priestly crown, seems, with the tacit consent of the Holy See, to have passed out of use. No provincial or national council has ordered it, even when treating of clerical dress; and the Holy See has not inserted the law when correcting the decrees of those councils."

TAUNTON, *The Law of the Church* (London, 1906), s. v.; GASPARRI, *De sacra ordinatione*, I (Paris, 1893); WERNZ, *Jus Decretalium*, II (Rome, 1899).

WILLIAM H. W. FANNING.

Tootell, HUGH, commonly known as Charles Dodd, historian, b. in 1671 or '72, at Durton-in-Broughton, Lancashire; d. at Harvington Hall, Worcestershire, 27 Feb., 1743. He was educated at the English College, Douay (1688–1693), and St. Gregory's Seminary, Paris (1693–1697). After ordination he returned to England in 1698 as chaplain to the Molyneux family at Mosborough Hall, Lancashire. In 1711 he returned to the Continent where he is said to have witnessed the siege of Douay (1712) as chaplain to an English regiment; certainly he wrote in that character a short "History of the English College at Douay" (1713) which purported to be by a Protestant chaplain. As it attacked the Jesuits, Father Thomas Hunter published his "Modest Defence" (1714), to which Dodd replied in "The Secret Policy of the English Society of Jesus" (1715). From 1716 he was again at Mosborough till 1718, when he returned to Douay to collect materials for his great work "The Church History of England from 1500 to 1688", which occupied him for twenty years. The work was written at Harvington Hall, where he resided from 1722 till his death, first as assistant chaplain, then (from 1726) as chaplain. During his sojourn abroad he wrote and published "Pax Vobis: an Epistle to the Three Churches" (London, 1721); and while at Harvington he composed several spiritual, controversial, and historical treatises most of which have never been published. Many of these MSS. (a complete list of which is given by Gillow, Bibl. Dict. Eng. Cath., V, 550–554) are preserved at Oscott. Those certainly published were: "Certamen Utriusque Ecclesiæ" (1724); "An Abridgment of Christian Doctrine" (s. d.); and "Flores Cleri Anglo-Catholici" (s. d.). After many years' labour the Church History was completed in three folio volumes published in 1737, 1739, and 1742 at Wolverhampton, though for prudential reasons Brussels appears on the title-page. Father John Constable, S. J., attacked his work as unfair to the Jesuits, and Dodd replied in "An Apology for the Church History of England", published in 1742. On his death-bed Dodd expressed his desire to die in peace with the Jesuits. Dodd's translation of Panzani's memoirs was subsequently used by Berington (see PANZANI).

KIRK, *Catholicon*, III, IV, V (London, 1816–17); BUTLER, *Hist. Memoirs of Eng. Cath.* (London, 1819); BERINGTON, Preface to *Memoirs of Panzani* (Birmingham, 1793); *Hist. MSS. Comm. Report*, I, III, V; FOLEY, *Records Eng. Prov. S. J.*, II (London, 1884), is inaccurate and corrected by GILLOW, *Bibl. Dict. Eng. Cath.* s. vv. HUNTER and LINGARD; COOPER, in *Dict. Nat. Biog.*, must be used with caution, being very imperfect.

EDWIN BURTON.

Torah. I. *Use of Word.*—Torah, תּוֹרָה (cf. Hiph. of ירה), signifies first "direction, instruction", as, for instance, the instruction of parents (Prov., i, 8), or of the wise (Prov., iii, 1). It is used chiefly in reference to the Divine instruction, especially through the revelation to Moses, the "Law", and to the teaching of the Prophets concerning the will of God. In the sense of law "Torah" refers only to the Divine laws. "Torah" is applied to the books containing the teaching of the Mosaic revelation and the Law, that is, the Pentateuch. In Jewish theology Torah signifies, first, the totality of Jewish doctrine, whether taken as a basis for religious knowledge and conduct, or as a basis for study. The body of Biblical writings, especially the Pentateuch, being the source of religious teaching and law, the term "Torah" is applied also to the entire Scriptures (cf. Blau, "Zur Einleitung in die hl. Schrift", Budapest, 1894, 16 sq.), or to passages from the Prophets and the Hagiographa, for instance, "Ab. zara", 17a, in reference to Prov., v, 8, and "Sanh.", 91b, in connexion with Ps. lxxxiv, 5. The expression, however, generally signifies the Pentateuch. In passages like משולשת תורה נביאים וכתובים התורה ("the Scriptures [Torah] consist of three parts, Torah, Prophets, and Hagiographa" [Midrash Tanchuma to Ex., xix, 1]) "Torah" is used in two senses—one general, meaning the whole Scriptures, the other special, signifying the Pentateuch. Elsewhere (Siphre to 32, 13-135b 24) the Torah is plainly distinguished from the non-Pentateuchal books by the comparison of *miqra* (מקרא) and Torah. Besides the "written" Torah, תורה שבכתב, the Judaism which holds to tradition speaks of an "oral" Torah, תשבעל פה, the commentaries and the ordinances which put into effect the laws contained in the Pentateuch. This oral Torah, it is claimed, was revealed to Moses and has been preserved in Israel by tradition (see TALMUD).

II. *Torah in the restricted sense of Pentateuch.*—The Torah relates the preparatory measures for and the establishment of the Old-Testament theocracy, and contains the institutions and laws in which this theocracy found its visible expression. The Old Testament itself calls the entire work after its main contents (*ha*) *tora* or *sefer* (ספר), *ha-tora*, that is, "the book of the Torah", as in II Esd., viii, 2; to emphasize its Divine origin it is called *torath Yahwe*, *sefer torath*

Yahwe (I Esd., vii, 10; I Par., xvi, 40; II Esd., viii, 8), and *sefer torath Yahwe Elohim* (II Esd., ix, 3); while *sefer torath Moshe* (II Esd., viii, 1), *sefer Moshe* (I Esd., vi, 18; II Esd., xiii, 1; II Par., xxv, 4; xxxv, 12) indicate its author. The Talmud and later Jewish writings call the Pentateuch *sefer (ha) tora*; the name is always used if the whole work were written as a scroll (*megilla*) for use in the Divine service. If the work is written in five scrolls or in book form it is called *hᵃmisha humᵉshe (ha)tora* (חמשה חומשי (ה)תורה), "the five-fifths of the law". This division into five parts is old, and in the time of Nehemias served as a model for the division of the Psalter into five books. The Jews generally named the individual books after the first word: (1) *bᵉreshith*, בראשית; (2) *shᵉmoth* or *wᵉʾelle shᵉmoth*, שמות or ואלא ש׳; (3) *wayyiqra*, ויקרא; (4) *bᵉmidbar* or *wayyᵉdabber*, במדבר, וידבר; (5) *dᵉbarim* or *ʾelle ha-dᵉbarim*, אלא הדברים (cf. as early a writer as Origen on Ps. 1: Βρησιθ, Ουαλεσμωθ, Ουικρα, Ἐλλε αδδεβαριμ). There are also names indicating the main contents of the books given to Leviticus, Numbers, and Deuteronomy: *torath kohᵃnim*, תורת כהנים, "law of the priests", for instance in "Meg.", iii, 6; *ḥomesh ha-piqqudim*, חמש הפקודים, "the fifth of the numberings", as in "Yoma", vii, 1, *mishne tora* (תורה משנה), i. e., Deuteronomy, as in Masorah to Deut., xvii, 18. On the other hand *sefer yeçira*, ספר יצירה, "book of the Creation", in Sanh., 62ᵇ, and *nᵉziqin*, נזיקין, "injuries", Masorah to Gen., xxiv, 8, are not to be applied, as is often done, to Genesis and Exodus; they refer only to the account of the Creation and to Ex., xxi, 22.

Another method of division is that by which the paragraphs, or *parashiyyoth* (פרשיות sing. פרשה), are indicated in the scrolls of the Torah used in the synagogues. In the older Midrashim these divisions are called *parashiyyoth pᵉthuḥoth*, פ׳ פתוחות, "open *parashiyyoth*"; or *parashiyyoth sᵉthumoth*, פ׳ סתומות, "closed *parashiyyoth*". In the former, the portion of the line following the last word is left blank; in the latter the termination of the paragraph is indicated by leaving only part of the line blank. Such paragraphs are called "small *parashiyyoth*" and they are generally indicated in the printed editions of the Bible by פ or ס. The Pentateuch has altogether 290 open and 379 closed parashiyyoth. In quoting they are generally called after the main contents (as *Baba bathra 14a:* פ׳ בלעם that is, Num., xxii, 2–xxiv, 25), but sometimes after the first words (as, *Taʾanith* iv, 3, the first six *parashiyyoth* of Genesis). The *parashiyyoth* are regarded as the arrangement of the divisions of the Pentateuch according to contents; but the basis of the distinction between open and closed *parashiyyoth* is not known with certainty.

Another division of the Torah is connected with the reading of lessons read in the synagogue on the Sabbath, a practice referred to in Acts, xv, 21, ἐκ γενεῶν ἀρχαίων as being ancient (cf. also Josephus, "Contra Apion.", II, xvii). It was customary in Palestine to have a three years' cycle of these lessons (Meg., 29ᵇ); some writers say there was also a cycle of three years and a half. The Pentateuch, therefore, was divided into 154–175 sections or *sᵉdarim* (סדרים, sing. סדר). These *sᵉdarim* though not indicated in our Bibles, are important for understanding the structure of the old Midrashim (cf. Büchler, "The Reading of the Law and Prophets in a Triennial Cycle" in "Jew. Quart. Rev.", V, 420 sqq., VI, 1 sqq., VIII, 528 sq.). In the course of time an annual cycle, which first acquired authority among the Babylonian Jews, and is now accepted by nearly all Jewish communities, was adopted. Maimonides (Hilḥoth Tephilla, XIII, 1) calls it the prevailing custom of his era (twelfth century), but says that some read the Pentateuch in three years, which, according to Benjamin of Tudela, was the practice about 1170 among scattered communities in Egypt (cf. Jew. Quart. Rev., V, 420).

In this one-year cycle the Pentateuch is divided into fifty-four Sabbath lessons generally called large *parashiyyoth*. A Jewish intercalary year consisting of thirteen lunar months contains fifty-three sabbaths, and the final section is always read on the day of the "joy of the Law" (שמחת תורה), that is, the ninth day after the feast of booths (twenty-third day of *Tishri*). In ordinary years, when there are forty-seven sabbaths, two *parashiyyoth* are joined on each of seven sabbaths in order to complete the number. In Genesis there are twelve sabbath *parashiyyoth*, in Exodus eleven, in Leviticus and Numbers ten each, and in Deuteronomy eleven. They are named from and quoted by the first words. In the printed editions of the Bible they are indicated, as they are also the opening words of the open or closed *parashiyyoth*, by פפפ or ססס, with exception of the twelfth lesson, at the beginning of which (Gen., xlvii, 28) only the breadth of a letter should remain blank. Concerning the distribution of the fifty-four *parashiyyoth* for the year, cf. Loeb, "Rev. des études juives", VI, 250 sqq.; Derenbourg, ibid., VII, 146 sqq.; Schmid, "Überverschiedene Einteilungen der hl. Schrift" (Graz, 1892), 4 sqq.

The Old Synagogue and the Talmud firmly maintain the Mosaic authorship of the Torah, but doubts are entertained regarding a number of passages. In "Baba bathra" 15ᵃ only the last eight verses of Deuteronomy, which speak of the death and burial of Moses, are assigned to another author. On the other hand Simon (loc. cit.) teaches, referring to Deut., xxxi, 26, that these verses were also written by Moses under Divine direction (cf. also Josephus, "Antiq. Jud.", IV, viii, 48). During the Middle Ages doubts were expressed as to the possibility of Moses writing certain sentences; for instance, by Rabbi Yishaq (to Gen., xxxvi, 11) who was opposed by Aben Ezra, and as well by Aben Ezra himself (to Gen., xii, 6; Ex., xxv, 4; Deut., i, 1; xxxi, 22). Taken altogether, even in the succeeding period the belief in the Mosaic authorship remained undisputed, at least by the orthodox Jews. They hold, moreover, the Divine origin of the entire Torah, and the eighth of the thirteen articles of faith formulated by Maimonides and incorporated into the prayer-book reads: "I believe with full faith that the entire Torah as it is in our hands is the one which was given to our teacher Moses, to whom be peace." (See PENTATEUCH.)

F. SCHÜHLEIN.

Torbido, FRANCESCO, often called IL MORO (The Moor), Veronese painter and engraver, b. at Verona about 1486; the date of his death is unknown, but in a letter of Aretino he is spoken of as still living in 1546. He studied at Venice under Giorgione, and later returned to his native place, where he married a daughter of Count Zenovello Giusti. He then became a pupil of Liberale, who adopted him as his heir. Torbido seems to have remained at Verona, executing commissions for portraits, and painting frescoes in churches and on the fronts of houses, as was the Veronese fashion of those days. His work shows the varying influences of his Venetian master and of the Veronese artists, which he finally blended into a distinct style of his own, but retained the rich, glowing colour schemes acquired from the great Giorgione. Fine examples of his frescoes may still be seen at Verona, in the cathedral ("Nativity" and "Assumption", signed and dated 1534) and in the Church of St. Fermo ("Virgin and Child in Glory"), whilst others are in St. Eufemia and St. Zeno. His portraiture can be studied at Naples, at Venice, and in the Brera Gallery. Two portraits represent the artist himself, one at Munich, signed and dated 1516, the other, a red chalk drawing, in the Christ Church Collection.

LANZI, *Storia pittorica della Italia* (Bassano, 1509); VASARI, *Le vite de' pittori* (Milan, 1811).

GEORGE CHARLES WILLIAMSON.

Toribio Alfonso Mogrovejo, SAINT, Archbishop of Lima; b. at Mayorga, León, Spain, 1538; d. near Lima, Peru, 23 March, 1606. Of noble family and highly educated, he was professor of laws at the University of Salamanca, where his learning and virtue led to his appointment as Grand Inquisitor of Spain by Philip II and, though not of ecclesiastical rank, to his subsequent selection for the Archbishopric of Peru. He received Holy Orders in 1578 and two years later was consecrated bishop. He arrived at Payta, Peru, 600 miles from Lima, on 24 May, 1581. He began his mission work by travelling to Lima on foot, baptizing and teaching the natives, his favourite topic being: "Time is not our own, and we must give a strict account of it." Three times he traversed the eighteen thousand miles of his diocese, generally on foot, defenceless and often alone; exposed to tempests, torrents, deserts, wild beasts, tropical heat, fevers, and savage tribes; baptizing and confirming nearly one half a million souls, among them St. Rose of Lima, St. Francis Solano, Blessed Martin of Porres, and Blessed Masias. He built roads, school houses, and chapels innumerable, and many hospitals and convents, and founded the first American seminary at Lima in 1591. He assembled thirteen diocesan synods and three provincial councils. Years before he died, he predicted the day and hour of his death. At Pacasmayo he contracted fever, but continued labouring to the last, arriving at Sana in a dying condition. Dragging himself to the sanctuary he received the Viaticum, expiring shortly after. He was beatified by Innocent XI in 1679 and canonized by Benedict XIII in 1726. His feast is celebrated on 27 April.

DE HERRERA, *Life of Toribio*. EDWARD L. AYME.

Tornielli, GIROLAMO FRANCESCO, Italian Jesuit, preacher and writer, b. at Cameri, 1 February, 1693, of a distinguished family from Novara; d. at Bologna, 6 April or 12 May, 1752. He entered the Society in 1710, and manifested oratorical powers; after teaching classics, he entered upon a career of preaching, which lasted for almost twenty years. He first spoke at Venice (1733), and then with increasing popularity at Rome, Milan, Florence, and Bologna. Many hailed him as Segneri's successor. Tornielli, however, did not possess Segneri's vehemence, impassioned logic, and directness. Brilliant rather than solid, he lacked originality and depth; but he had imagination and dramatic feeling. For his pathos and easy, popular style he was surnamed the "Metastasio" of the Italian pulpit. To polished diction he added a refined and affecting delivery. Shocked by the licentious songs then common, Tornielli tried to remedy the evil by adapting sacred hymns to the popular airs. Many criticised him for having thus exposed the mysteries of religion to ridicule and contempt. A Jesuit, Sanchez de Luna, defended him in his "Riposta alla censura fatta alle canzonette marineresche per le festività di Maria Santissima". The Accademia della Crusca requested Tornielli to enter that body and offered to publish his works, but he modestly declined.

Tornielli's principal works are: "Sette canzonette in aria marineresca sopra le sette principale feste di Nostra Signora" (Milan, 1738); "Prediche quaresimali" (Milan, 1753, Bassano, 1820, with a preface by Noghera, Savona, 1889); "Panegirici e discorsi sacri" (Bassano, 1768). Sommervogel and Carrara doubt the authenticity of the "Businate", a burlesque poem, written in Milanese dialect and sometimes attributed to Tornielli. There is a eulogy of the orator in the "Piemontesi illustri", III, p. 305.

CARRARA, *Nuovo dizionario istorico* (Bassano, 1796); BETTINELLI, *Opere edite ed inedite*, XXIII (Venice, 1801); *Prediche scelte di Segneri, Tornielli ed alteri* (Turin, 1824); DE ANGELIS in *Biographie ancienne et moderne*, XLVI (Paris, 1826); *Scelta di prediche dei piu celebri oratori italiani* (Rome, 1837); AUDISIO, *Lezioni di eloquenza sacra*, II (Turin, 1859), 346–49; NAY, *Brevi cenni sulla vita, sull' opere di Tornielli* (Preface to Tornielli's "La felicità del patrocinio del Governo de Gozzano" etc.), (Turin, 1875); DE BACKER, *Bibl. des écrivains de la C. de J.* ser., IV, 699; SOMMERVOGEL, *Bibl. de la C. de J.*, VIII, 101–4.

JOHN C. REVILLE.

Torone, a titular see in Macedonia, suffragan of Thessalonica. Torone was a colony of Chalcideans from Eubœa, on the south-west coast of the peninsula Sithonia, the modern name of which is Longos; this is the middle peninsula of Chalcidice, lying between the Toronaic Gulf, called to-day, Cassandra, and the Gulf of Singitticus (Mt. Athos). Built on a hill, in a fine situation, it had a harbour called *Kophos* (deaf), because the sound of the sea-waves could not be heard there, thus giving rise to the proverb: "Deafer than the port of Torone." Torone had thirty small cities under its government; like the other Grecian cities of the region, it furnished Xerxes with men and ships. After the Persian War it passed under the rule of Athens. In 424 B. C., the Olynthian, Lysistratus, opened its gates to Brasidas; it was shortly afterwards retaken by Cleon. After the peace of Nicias it was ceded to the Athenians; in 379 B. C., it was taken by Agesipolas; in 364–3, by the Athenian, Timotheus; in 349–8, by Philip, who annexed it with the other cities of Chalcidice to his own kingdom. In 169 Torone repelled an attack made by the Roman fleet. Since then history is silent about this city which Pliny calls a free city. Its ruins, in the vilayet of Salonica, still bear the ancient name, pronounced by the Greeks, Toroni. As an episcopal see, Torone does not appear in any of the "Notitiæ episcopatuum", and we know of no bishop of the diocese.

SMITH, *Dict. of Greek and Roman Geogr.*, s. v.; DESDEVISES-DU-DÉSERT, *Géographie ancienne de la Macédoine* (Paris, 1863), 374; LEAKE, *Northern Greece*, III, 119, 155, 455; DEMITSAS, *Ancient Geography of Macedonia: Topography* (Athens, 1874), 426–30 (in Greek).

S. PÉTRIDÈS.

Toronto, ARCHDIOCESE OF (TORONTINA), in the Province of Ontario, Canada. When constituted a diocese, it embraced all Upper Canada west of the Newcastle district, but at present is limited to the counties of York, Simcoe, Ontario, Peel, Dufferin, Lincoln, and Welland. The first missionary in this district was Father Joseph Le Caron, a Recollect, who celebrated Mass on the shore of Georgian Bay in 1615. Thus began the Huron missions, the story of which, replete with heroism of Recollect and Jesuit, is told elsewhere in this work; suffice it to say here that all the missions among that people and some of those attempted among their Neutral kindred lay within the present archdiocesan limits. During the century and a half following the destruction of these nations, a few priests are known to have been in this district; among these were Father Hennepin, in 1678, and Abbé Picquet, who visited Fort Rouillé (Toronto) in 1752. A Catholic chaplain was attached to the troops at Newark (Niagara-on-the-Lake) in 1794, and about the same time missionaries began to visit occasionally the few Catholics of York (Toronto) and the neighbouring territory. Amongst these was Father Burke, afterwards Vicar Apostolic of Nova Scotia, who held the office of Vicar-General of Upper Canada. After 1804 Father Macdonell came as often as his extended field of labour allowed, and, when Bishop of Kingston, resided at York for some years. In 1826 there were two resident priests in this region, one at York, the other at Niagara.

The Diocese of Kingston was divided on 17 Dec., 1841, and Father Power, bishop-elect of the western portion, having permission to name his episcopal city, chose Toronto, the provincial capital. This first bishop, Michael Power, born at Halifax, N. S., 17 Oct., 1804, was Vicar-General of the Diocese of Montreal when raised to the episcopate. Consecrated on 8 May, 1842, he laid the cornerstone of the cathedral, introduced the Jesuits, and made arrangements to bring the Loreto nuns to the diocese. Appointed by the Government to the Council of Public Instruction, he presided over that body. He died on 1 Oct., 1847, of typhus contracted while attending the immigrants at the fever-sheds. His successor, Armand-François-Marie Comte de Charbonnel, a Sulpician, born at Monistrol-sur-Loire, France, 1 Dec., 1802, was consecrated by Pius IX in the Sistine Chapel, 26 May, 1850. He gave his paternal estates to liquidate the debts of his diocese, introduced the Basilians (Annonay), the Brothers of the Christian Schools, and Sisters of St. Joseph, and was present at the First and Second Provincial Councils of Quebec. His diocese was divided in 1856 by the erection of Hamilton and London as sees. With his fellow-bishops of Upper Canada, he engaged in the struggle for separate schools, which had a successful outcome under his successor. In 1860 he resigned to join the Capuchins, being appointed titular Bishop of Sozopolis, and afterwards titular archbishop of the same see. He died on 29 March, 1891. His successor at Toronto was John Joseph Lynch, C. M., who was born at Clones, County Monaghan, Ireland, 6 Feb., 1816. As a Lazarist, he did missionary and professorial work in Ireland and the United States, being rector of a seminary which he founded at Niagara Falls, New York, when appointed (26 Aug., 1859) titular Bishop of Æchinas, and coadjutor with right of succession to Bishop de Charbonnel.

On the resignation of Bishop de Charbonnel on 26 April, 1860, Bishop Lynch became Bishop of Toronto. He brought to the diocese the Redemptorists, Carmelites, Sisters of the Precious Blood, and Sisters of Our Lady of Charity of Refuge; was present at the Third and Fourth Provincial Councils of Quebec; and also at the Council of the Vatican, where he favoured the immediate promulgation of Papal Infallibility, and acted on the commissions on missions and Oriental rites. During the council (18 Mar., 1870) his diocese was raised to metropolitan rank. He died on 12 May, 1888. In 1879 Archbishop Lynch received as auxiliary Timothy O'Mahony, titular Bishop of Eudocia, and former Bishop of Armidale, Australia, who died on 8 Sept., 1892. John Walsh, second archbishop, born at Mooncoin, County Kilkenny, Ireland, 23 May, 1830, was ordained for the Diocese of Toronto, of which he was vicar-general when appointed Bishop of Sandwich in 1867. On 13 August, 1889, he became Archbishop of Toronto, where he renovated the cathedral, and founded St. John's Industrial School. The Irish Race Convention of 1896 was organized at his suggestion. He was noted as a writer and preacher. His death occurred on 31 July, 1898. Denis O'Connor, C.S.B., his successor, was born at Pickering, Ontario, 28 March, 1841. A Basilian, he taught for several years in that community, being superior of the Assumption College, Sandwich, when chosen Bishop of London, Ontario, where he was consecrated on 19 Oct., 1890. On 27 January, 1899, he was created Archbishop of Toronto. Here he established several new parishes, gave special attention to conferences for the clergy and to the study of Christian doctrine by the young. In 1908 he resigned, being appointed titular Archbishop of Laodicea. He died at St. Basil's Novitiate, Toronto, 30 June, 1911. His successor, Fergus Patrick McEvay, was born at Lindsay, Ontario, 8 December, 1856. Ordained for Kingston, he was transferred to the new Diocese of Peterborough, where he was rector of the cathedral, and then went to Hamilton with Bishop Dowling. There he was appointed rector of the cathedral and vicar-general, and received the papal honours of private chamberlain and domestic prelate. Consecrated Bishop of London, Ontario, 6 Aug., 1899, he was promoted to Toronto, 13 April, 1908. He founded new parishes, rebuilt the cathedral palace, erected a new archiepiscopal residence, and began St. Augustine's Seminary, donated by Mr. Eugene O'Keefe (private chamberlain to His Holiness). At the First National Council of Canada, Archbishop McEvay was chairman of the commission *ad novas materias;* he was also instrumental in founding the Catholic Church Extension Society of Canada. He died on 10 May, 1911.

Civil incorporation took place on 25 March, 1845, under the title of "The Roman Catholic Episcopal Corporation for the Diocese of Toronto in Canada". All ecclesiastical property in the archdiocese, except that belonging to religious communities, is vested in this corporation. There have been three synods (1842, 1863, 1882) and one provincial council (1875). Both clergy and people are for the most part of Irish extraction, with a small percentage of English and Scotch. There are however three parishes exclusively French, three mixed (French and English), 1 for Poles, Italians, Ruthenians, and Syrians, respectively, and one Indian mission. In the archdiocese are 58 churches with resident pastors and 37 mission churches, 81 diocesan priests, and 39 of religious orders or communities; 39 separate schools, 2 high schools, 6 academies, 2 industrial schools, 1 domestic science school, 1 college for young men, 2 ladies' colleges, and 1 diocesan seminary (in course of erection). There are 8009 children in the schools and institutions. The Catholic population is about 70,000. The Basilians have St. Michael's College, 1 novitiate and scholasticate, 2 parishes and 2 missions; the Carmelites, a monastery, novitiate, and house of studies, 2 parishes and 1 mission; the Jesuits, 1 parish, 1 Indian mission, 2 other missions and a memorial chapel on the spot where Fathers de Brébeuf and Lalement were killed; the Redemptorists, 1 monastery and 1 parish (they also give missions throughout the province). The Brothers of the Christian Schools have the De La Salle Institute, St. John's Industrial School, a junior novitiate, and 6 separate schools; the Institute of the Blessed Virgin (Sisters of Loreto), the motherhouse for America, a novitiate, a ladies' college, 3 academies, 6 separate schools, and 1 domestic science school; the Sisters of St. Joseph, their mother-house and novitiate, a ladies' college, 3 academies, 1 high school, 21 separate schools, a House of Providence for the aged poor, St. Vincent's Home for Infants, Sacred Heart Orphanage, and St. Michael's Hospital; the Sisters of Our Lady of Charity of Refuge, a convent and novitiate, a girls' industrial school and refuge; the Sisters Adorers of the Precious Blood, a novitiate and convent. The chaplaincies of the central prison, the reformatory for women (each of which has a Catholic chapel), and the hospitals for the insane belong to St. Michael's Cathedral, but are temporarily filled by the Basilians. The jails, hospitals, and military barracks are attended by the parochial clergy of their respective districts.

The city of Toronto has a population of 376,240 (about 45,000 Catholics), and is an educational and commercial centre. There are 22 city parishes, with 40 secular and 12 regular priests. St. Michael's Cathedral, modelled after York Minster, is of the Gothic style of the fourteenth century. It was solemnly dedicated on 29 September, 1848. Toronto University has Catholic representatives on its Board of Governors, Senate, and Staff, and Catholic students under the various faculties. Federated with this institution is St. Michael's College. Catholic pedagogical students attend the provincial normal school and faculty of education. There are sodalities and confraternities in every parish, as well as Catholic fraternal and benefit societies. The Catholic Church Extension Society of Canada aids the Northern and Western missions; St. Vincent de Paul Society relieves the poor; a Children's Aid Society under the same patron protects children of dissolute parents; the St. Elizabeth Nurses' Association cares for the sick in their homes. The Catholic Truth Society and the Holy Name Society are strongly established. The priests have a Eucharistic League and also a society which cares for infirm members of the clergy.

TEFFY (ed.), *Jubilee Volume of the Archdiocese of Toronto* (Toronto, 1892); HARRIS, *The Catholic Church in the Niagara Peninsula* (Toronto, 1895); ROBERTSON, *Landmarks of Toronto*, 4th ser. (Toronto, 1904); MCKEOWN, *Life of Archbishop Lynch* (Montreal, 1886); *The Archives of St. Michael's Cathedral; Acta et decreta primi concilii provincialis Torontini* (Toronto, 1882).

EDW. KELLY.

Torquemada, TOMÁS DE, first Grand Inquisitor of Spain, b. at Valladolid in 1420; d. at Avila, 16 Sept., 1498. He was a nephew of the celebrated theologian and cardinal, Juan de Torquemada. In his early youth he entered the Dominican monastery at Valladolid, and later was appointed prior of the Monastery of Santa Cruz at Segovia, an office which he held for twenty-two years. The Infanta Isabella chose him as her confessor while at Segovia, and when she succeeded to the throne of Castile in 1474 he became one of her most trusted and influential councillors, but refused all high ecclesiastical preferments, choosing to remain a simple friar. At that time the purity of the Catholic Faith in Spain was in great danger from the numerous Marranos and Moriscos, who, for material considerations, became sham converts from Judaism and Mohammedanism to Christianity. The Marranos committed serious outrages against Christianity and endeavoured to judaize the whole of Spain. The Inquisition, which the Catholic sovereigns had been empowered to establish by Sixtus IV in 1478, had, despite unjustifiable cruelties, failed of its purpose, chiefly for want of centralization. In 1483 the pope appointed Torquemada, who had been an assistant inquisitor since 11 February, 1482, Grand Inquisitor of Castile, and on 17 October extended his jurisdiction over Aragon.

As papal representative and the highest official of the inquisitorial court, Torquemada directed the entire business of the Inquisition in Spain, was empowered to delegate his inquisitorial faculties to other inquisitors of his own choosing, who remained accountable to him, and settled the appeals made to the Holy See. He immediately established tribunals at Valladolid, Seville, Jaen, Avila, Cordova, and Villa-real, and, in 1484, at Saragossa for the Kingdom of Aragon. He also instituted a High Council, consisting of five members, whose chief duty was to assist him in the hearing of appeals (see INQUISITION.—*The Inquisition in Spain*). He convened a general assembly of Spanish inquisitors at Seville, 29 November, 1484, and presented an outline of twenty-eight articles for their guidance. To these he added several new statutes in 1485, 1488, and 1498 (Reuss, "Sammlungen der Instructionen des spanischen Inquisitionsgerichts", Hanover, 1788). The Marranos found a powerful means of evading the tribunals in the Jews of Spain, whose riches had made them very influential and over whom the Inquisition had no jurisdiction. On this account Torquemada urged the sovereigns to compel all the Jews either to become Christians or to leave Spain. To frustrate his designs the Jews agreed to pay the Spanish government 30,000 ducats if left unmolested. There is a tradition that when Ferdinand was about to yield to the enticing offer, Torquemada appeared before him, bearing a crucifix aloft, and exclaiming: "Judas Iscariot sold Christ for 30 pieces of silver; Your Highness is about to sell him for 30,000 ducats. Here He is; take Him and sell Him." Leaving the crucifix on the table he left the room. Chiefly through his instrumentality the Jews were expelled from Spain in 1492.

Much has been written of the inhuman cruelty of Torquemada. Llorente computes that during Torquemada's office (1483–98) 8800 suffered death by fire and 96,504 were punished in other ways (Histoire de l'Inquisition, IV, 252). These figures are highly exaggerated, as had been conclusively proved by Hefele (Cardinal Ximenes, ch. xviii), Gams (Kirchengeschichte von Spanien, III, II, 68–76), and many others. Even the Jewish historian Graetz contents himself with stating that "under the first Inquisitor Torquemada, in the course of fourteen years (1485–1498) at least 2000 Jews were burnt as impenitent sinners" ("History of the Jews", Philadelphia, 1897, IV, 356). Most historians hold with the Protestant Peschel (Das Zeitalter der Entdeckungen, Stuttgart, 1877, pp. 119 sq.) that the number of persons burnt from 1481 to 1504, when Isabella died, was about 2000. Whether Torquemada's ways of ferreting out and punishing heretics were justifiable is a matter that has to be decided not only by comparison with the penal standard of the fifteenth century, but also, and chiefly, by an inquiry into their necessity for the preservation of Christian Spain. The contemporary Spanish chronicler, Sebastian de Olmedo (Chronicon magistrorum generalium Ordinis Prædicatorum, fol. 80–81), calls Torquemada "the hammer of heretics, the light of Spain, the saviour of his country, the honour of his order".

MOLÈNES, *Torquemada et l'Inquisition* (Paris, 1877); BARTHÉLEMY, *Erreurs historiques* (Paris, 1875), 170–204; FITA, *La Inquisición de Torquemada* in *Boletín Acad. Hist.*, XXIII (Madrid, 1893), 369–434; TOURON, *Histoire des hommes illustres de l'ordre de Saint Dominique*, III (Paris, 1746), 543–68; TARRIDA DEL MARMOL, *Les Inquisiteurs d'Espagne* (Paris, 1897); RODRIGO, *Historia verdadera de la Inquisición*, II, III (Madrid, 1877); LEA, *History of the Inquisition in Spain* (London and New York, 1906–08).

MICHAEL OTT.

Torres (TURRIANUS), FRANCISCO, Hellenist and polemicist, b. in Herrera, Palencia, about 1509; d. at Rome, 21 November, 1584. He was the nephew of Dr. Torres, Bishop of the Canaries. He studied at Salamanca and lived in Rome with Cardinals Salviati and Seripando. In 1562 Pius IV sent him to the Council of Trent, and on 8 January, 1567, he became a Jesuit. He was professor at the Roman College, took part in the revision of the Sixtine Vulgate, and had Hosius and Baronius for literary associates. His contemporaries called him *helluo librorum* for the rapidity with which he examined the principal libraries. He defended the doctrines of the Immaculate Conception, the authority of the sovereign pontiff over the council, the Divinely appointed authority of bishops, Communion under one kind for the laity, the authenticity of the Apostolic Canons and the Pseudo-Isidorian decretals, and pleading the antiquity of the feast of the Presentation of the Blessed Virgin, which Pius V had suppressed, worked for its reinstatement. Blondel accuses him of want of critical judgment, and Nadal of mordacity against Protestants. He wrote more than seventy books, principally polemical, against Protestants, and translations especially of Greek Fathers, many treatises of whose works he found hidden away in libraries.

SOTUELLUS, *Bibliotheca Scriptorum S. J.* (Rome, 1676), 260; NIEREMBERG, *Varones ilustres*, V (Bilbao, 1890), 57; NICOLAS ANTONIO, *Bibliotheca Hispano Nova*, I (Madrid, 1783), 487; HURTER, *Nomenclator*, I (Innsbruck, 1892), 105; SOMMERVOGEL, *Bibliothèque*, VIII (Brussels, 1898), 113 sqq.

PÉREZ GOYENA.

Torres Naharro, BARTOLEMÉ DE, Spanish poet and dramatist, b. at Torres, near Badajoz, towards the end of the fifteenth century. The date of his death is not known, and little is known of his life. He was a cleric and a man of some learning. About the year 1514 he was living in Rome, where he enjoyed the patronage of Fabricio Colonna, whom he served in the capacity of chaplain. Following the publication of a satire from his pen in which he attacked the vices of the Court, he was banished from Rome and took refuge in Naples, where we lose sight of him. In the latter city was published, in 1517, a collection of his lyric and dramatic works under the title of "propaladia". These consist of satires, epistles, romances, ballads, and some miscellaneous poetry, but chiefly of eight plays which he calls "Comedias". Aside from their literary merit, these latter are of more than passing interest, for their author gives us a theory of his own on the subject of the drama, and with them he set a type or model that was to be followed by later authors. He divides comedies into two classes, namely, "Comedias de Noticia" and "Comedia de Fantasíá". Under the first heading he would include those dealing with real happenings, that have been actually seen; and under the second, things of the fancy, imaginary incidents that seem true though in fact not true. In the development of the plot, he would follow the division of Horace into five acts, though he would change the name of these to "Jornadas", as they seemed to be no more than convenient resting places. He would have not less than six nor more than twelve characters, and in some of his plays there is a tendency to observe the unities of time, place, and action. Among his better known comedies are "Himenea", "Serafina", and "Tinelaria". The authentic editions of the "Propaladia" are: those of Naples (1517), Seville (1520–26), Toledo (1535), and Madrid (1573–90). The "Biblioteca de Autores Españoles" publishes several romances of Torres (vols. X, XVI, and XXXV).

MORATIN, *Orígenes del Teatro Español* in *La Biblioteca de Autores Españoles*, II (Madrid, 1846–80); BOHL DE FABER, *Teatro Español anterior á Lope de Vega* (Hamburg, 1832); TICKNOR, *Hist. of Spanish Lit.* (Boston, 1866).

VENTURA FUENTES.

Torricelli, EVANGELISTA, Italian mathematician and physicist, b. at Faenza, 15 Oct., 1608; d. at Florence, 25 Oct., 1647. Modigliana, in Tuscan Romagna, and Piancaldoli, in the Diocese of Imola, are named as the birthplace by different biographers. Torricelli was educated at the Jesuit college of Faenza, where he showed such great aptitude for the sciences that his uncle, a religious of the order of the Camaldolesi, sent him to Rome in 1626 for the purpose of study. There he fell in with Castelli, the favourite pupil of Galileo, who instructed him in the work of the master on the laws of motion. Torricelli showed his thorough understanding by writing a thesis on the path of projectiles. Castelli sent this essay in manuscript to Galileo with strong recommendations of his young friend. Galileo invited Torricelli to his house, but for personal reasons he was unable to accept until three months before the death of the blind scientist (1641). The grand duke prevailed upon him to remain at Florence and to succeed Galileo at the Academy. He solved some of the great mathematical problems of the day, such as the finding of the area and the centre of gravity of the cycloid. This problem gave rise to disagreeable discussion on the part of Roberval as to priority and originality. Torricelli's honesty, manliness, and modesty are distinctly shown in his reply.

His chief invention was the barometer. Pumpmakers of the Grand Duke of Tuscany attempted to raise water to a height of forty feet or more, but found that thirty-two feet was the limit to which it would rise in the suction pump. Strange enough, Galileo, who knew all about the weight of the air, had recourse to the old theory that "nature abhors a vacuum", modifying the law by stating that the "horror" extended only to about thirty-two feet. Torricelli at once conceived the correct explanation. He tried the experiment with quicksilver, a liquid fourteen times as heavy as water, expecting the column which would counterbalance the air to be proportionally smaller. He filled a tube three feet long, and hermetically closed at one end, with mercury and set it vertically with the open end in a basin of mercury, taking care that no air-bubbles should get into the tube. The column of mercury invariably fell to about twenty-eight inches, leaving an empty space (Torricellian vacuum) above its level (1643). He expressed his sorrow at the fact that Galileo had not made this discovery in connexion with the pressure of air. The barometer is to-day one of the most important instruments in physics and chemistry, while the Torricellian method of getting a very high vacuum is still often employed. Another discovery was the law of efflux of a liquid through a small aperture in the wall of a vessel. He also constructed a number of large objectives and small, short focus, simple microscopes. His literary contributions are noted for their conciseness, clearness, and elegance. His manuscripts have not all been published and are carefully preserved at Florence. The following have appeared in print: "Trattato del moto" (Florence, before 1641); "Opera geometrica" (Florence, 1644); "Lezioni accademichi" (Florence, 1715); "Esperienza dell argento vivo" (reprint, Berlin, 1897).

FABRONI, *Vitæ Italorum*, I (Pisa, 1778), 345–400; TIRABOSCHI, *Storia della litt. it.*, VIII (Florence, 1812), 204–10; POGGENDORFF, *Biographisch-lit. Handwörterbuch*, II (Leipzig, 1863), 1119.

WILLIAM FOX.

Torrubia, JOSÉ, b. towards the end of the seventeenth century at Granada, Spain; d. in 1768 in the monastery of Aracœli. He entered the order of St. Peter of Alcántara at Granada. In the Philippine Islands, whither he had gone as missionary and as secretary to Foguéras, the commissioner-general of Mexico, he was imprisoned for four months, as a result of opposition on the part of the religious orders to reforms attempted by the commissioner. He returned to Cadiz and thence went to Rome, where he withdrew from the order of St. Peter and became a Franciscan. In 1732 he was again in the Philippine Islands as superior of a convent. He travelled in America and Asia, remaining for a time at Canton, China. In 1750 he returned to Spain, whence he made three trips to Rome. A linguist, scientist, collector of fossils and of books, writer on historical, political, and religious subjects, Torrubia was held in high esteem in Spain and at Rome, and by none more so than by Pope Benedict XIV. Among his many works may be mentioned: "Roman Ceremonial of the Discalced Religious of St. Francis in the Province of St. Gregory in the Philippines" (Manila, 1728); "Disertacion histórico-politico-geográfica de las islas Filipinas" (Madrid, 1736, 1753); a poem against Free-masonry (Madrid, 1752); "Introducción a la historia natural de España" (Madrid, 1754; German tr., Halle, 1773; Italian tr. of a part printed under his direction at Rome with the title "La gigantologia española"; second volume, on insects, never printed); "History of the Seraphic Order" (Rome, 1756).

PAUL H. LINEHAN.

Tortona, DIOCESE OF (DERTONENSIS), in Piedmont, Italy. The city is situated on the spurs of the northern Apennines, on the right bank of the Scrivia, in a plain rich in cereals, wine, hemp, rice, and silk. The cathedral is of the sixteenth century, built after

Charles V had destroyed the ancient cathedral situated on a hill which dominated the city, to make room for a fort. In the cathedral, besides pictures of the Lombard School, there is an antique sarcophagus carved with the myths of Phaeton and of Castor and Pollux. Other churches are the very ancient S. Maria Canale, S. Giacomo, and the oratories of Loreto and S. Rocco.

The city of Dertona was founded, or established as a Roman colony, in 147 B. C., at the time of the construction of the Via Posthumiana, which connected Piacenza with Genoa. As two other very important roads for Pisa and Provence began here, Dertona was, under the Empire, an important military station. From the ninth century it was under the rule of its bishop, and in 1090 it became a commune. In the struggles of the Middle Ages Tortona was the faithful ally of the Guelphs, for which reason it was several times destroyed, e. g. in 1155 by Barbarossa and in 1163 by the Pavians. From 1260 to 1347 the city was alternately under the dominion or protectorate of the imperial vicars, the marquesses of Montferrat, the Visconti of Milan, and the kings of Naples. From 1347 it formed a part of the Milanese state, the fate of which it shared until 1735, when by virtue of the Treaty of Vienna it was occupied by the King of Sardinia.

According to the legend, which is, however, a late one, the first Bishop of Tortona was St. Martianus martyred under Hadrian. It is certain that, in the first half of the fourth century, Tortona was subject to the Diocese of Vercelli. The first bishop, according to Savio, was St. Innocent, who he believes was the predecessor of St. Exuperantius (381), the first of whom we have certain historical record, and who was highly praised in a sermon of St. Maximus of Turin. Few other names of bishops of the early period are known; but from the tenth century the list is more complete, comprising: Giseprandus (about 943), who was at the same time Abbot of Bobbio; Ottone (1080), a follower of the schism of Henry IV; Guido (1098), who went to Palestine; Bishop Pietro, one of those who in 1241 were made prisoners by Frederick II, while on their way to attend the Council of Rome. Melchiorre Busetto was killed by the followers of the Marquess Guglielmo of Montferrat, for which the marquess lost all his rights of patronage in the Diocese of Tortona, and was compelled, barefoot and clad in a shirt only, to walk from the scene of the bishop's murder to the cathedral. In the time of Michele Marliano (1461) the body of St. Rochus was found at Vaghera, which was the cause of a lengthy controversy with Arles, which possessed the relics of St. Rochus of Montpellier. Uberto Gambara (1528), afterwards a cardinal, was always absent as papal legate or nuncio in Germany, and renounced the bishopric in favour of his relative Cesare (1548), present at the Council of Trent. Maffeo Gambara (1592) distinguished himself in reforming the church, as did also the Theatine Paolo Aresio (1620). In 1805 the diocese was suppressed by the French Government and united with Casale, and on its re-establishment in 1814 it was taken from the metropolitan See of Turin and made suffragan to Genoa. The diocese has 296 parishes, 317,865 souls, 570 secular and 30 regular priests, five monasteries, five convents for women, three educational institutions for males, and five for females.

CAPPELLETTI, *Le Chiese d' Italia*, XIII; SAVIO, *Gli antichi Vescovi del Piedmonte* (Turin, 1899), 377; CARNEVALE, *Notizie storiche nell' antico e moderno Tortonese* (1845).

U. BENIGNI.

Tortosa, DIOCESE OF (DERTHUSENSIS, DERTUSA), Spain, suffragan of Tarragona, comprises about 6989 square miles, principally in the civil provinces of Tarragona and Castellon. Its principal cities are Tortosa and Castellon. The "Gerarchia Cattolica" (Rome) places the date of creation of the diocese in the fourth century. Local tradition and historians claim St. Paul as founder of the diocese, and St. Rufus, son of Simon of Cyrene, as first bishop. Villanueva (Viaje Literario, vol. V) would explain the origin of the tradition in regard to St. Rufus by the fact that the first bishop after the reconquest of Tortosa from the Moors was Godfrey (Gaufridus), Abbot of the Monastery of St. Rufus, Avignon. Lirioso (364) and Heros (about 400), presented by local historians as the first bishops of whom there is record, are not given by La Fuente or Gams. La Fuente gives Urso (516) as the first known bishop. During Moorish rule in Tortosa (715–1148) the diocese suffered greatly, and little is known of its history. However in 1068 Paternus, "Episcopus Civitatis Tortuensis", is found. After the capture of Tortosa on 31 Dec., 1148, by Raymond Berenger, the diocese was restored to its ancient importance. The cathedral was begun in 1158, and consecrated in 1178 by Berenger, Archbishop of Tarragona; rebuilt from May or June, 1347 until 1597; consecrated 8 June, 1597; again continued from 5 Feb. 1621 to 1725, with latter additions. It is of mixed style, mainly Gothic, and has merit. The cloister is thought to be originally of the twelfth century. A special chapel contains the holy ribbon or sash (La Santa Cinta) which is said to have been left on the main altar of the cathedral by the Blessed Virgin, in an apparition on the night of 24 March, 1178, and which since 1629 is sent to the palace in Madrid before a royal birth. The cathedral archives contain many valuable codices, Bulls, etc.

OBSERVATORY OF THE EBRO, ROQUETAS, DIOCESE OF TORTOSA

The diocese was the scene of a disputation between Christians and Jews in 1413–1414, and figured prominently in the Western Schism, as the antipopes Benedict XIII and Clement VIII resided in Peñiscola, in the diocese. The provincial council of Tortosa (1429) did much to remove the evil effects of the schism. Among distinguished bishops of the diocese were Cardinal Augustin Spinola (1623–26) and Adrian VI, elected pope while holding the Bishopric of Tortosa 1516–22, and to whom the privilege of the red calotte worn by bishops of this diocese is attributed. The present bishop of Tortosa is Dr. D. Pedro Rocamora y Garcia (b. 1832). The diocese is divided into 12 archpriestships and contains: 193 parishes; 540 secular parochial clergy; a diocesan seminary; the Collegium Maximum of the Jesuits of the Aragon Province; a college of ecclesiastical vocations; 31 important convents and houses of sisters; numerous primary and secondary schools; one Catholic daily, "El Restaurador" (Tortosa); 5 Catholic weeklies; one Catholic fortnightly; and two Catholic monthlies.

Observatory of the Ebro, at Roquetas, Catalonia, Spain. The founder and present director is Father Ricardo Cirera, S.J. The construction of the buildings was commenced in March, 1903; they were completed in Sept., 1904, and by 30 Aug., 1905, the date of a total eclipse of the sun, it was possible to make all the observations in the observatory. See "Instrucciones para la observación del eclipse de sol del 30 de Agosto de 1905" and Cirera, "Noticia del Observatorio y de algunas observaciones del eclipse de 30 de Agosto de 1905", issued by the observatory. The observatory comprises branches in astrophysics, meteorology, and geophysics.

With the exception of some of the meteorological apparatus, which is installed in the open air, the apparatus is distributed in six buildings, a seventh being devoted to the library and general offices, and a small building apart for the mechanician. All these buildings are separate, so as to obtain the greatest possible accuracy in the results. In the building for the magnetic observations, all iron or any other substance which could exert a contrary magnetic influence is carefully excluded. The observatory is at some distance from the nearest town, on an elevation which dominates the valley of the Ebro. There is no electric car line or other factor in this valley which could act as a disturbing influence. (See "Boletín Mensual del Observatorio del Ebro", vol. I, no. 1, with introduction, an observatory publication.)

The Government declared this institution a public utility on 18 Oct., 1904.

The observatory publishes a monthly bulletin, in which the observations, reduced to their absolute values, are given in tables. Other scientific treatises published by the observatory are: "Discurso relativo al Establecimiento de la nueva Sección de Astronomía y Física del Globo", by Father Cirera; "La Sección de Astronomía y Física del Globo y la Meteorología española"; "Los Eclipses de 8 de Mayo de 1910 y 26 de Abril de 1911"; and "Recientes progresos de las Ciencias Astronómicas en España".

La Fuente, *Historia Ecclesiástica de España* (Madrid, 1873); Gams, *Series episcoporum Ecclesiæ Catholicæ* (Ratisbon, 1873); Cortes, *Historia manuscrita de la ciudad de Tortosa* (1747, authentic copy, Colegio Del Jesús, Tortosa); Martorell, *Historia de la Hibera* (Tortosa, 1626; reprinted, Tortosa, 1905); O'Callaghan, *Episcopologio de la Santa Iglesia de Tortosa* (Tortosa, 1896); Idem, *La Cathedral de Tortosa* (Tortosa, 1890); Risco, *España Sagrada*, XLII (Madrid, 1801); Villanueva, *Viaje Literario*, V (Madrid, 1806); Fernández, *Historia de Tortosa* (Barcelona, 1867); Miralles Meseguer, *Guía del Obispado de Tortosa* (Tortosa, 1902); *Directorium* (Tortosa, 1911); for observatory of Ebro see *Boletín mensual* (Jano, 1910), Spanish and French; *Nature* (London, 23 March, 1911); *Scientific American* (New York, 15 Oct., 1910); *Physikalische Zeitschrift* (Göttingen, 1 July, 1911); *Le Radium* (Paris, July, 1911); *Ciel et Terre* (Brussels, 1910), 438; *Atti della Pontificia Accademia Romana dei Nuovi Lincei* (Rome, 1910–11), Sess. VIª, 21 May, 1911.

Charles J. Mullaly.

Toscanella. See Viterbo and Toscanella, Diocese of.

Toscanelli, Paolo dal Pozzo, mathematician, astronomer, and cosmographer, b. at Florence in 1397; d. there, 10 May, 1482. Toscanelli, who was one of the most distinguished scientists of the fifteenth century, was the son of the Florentine physician Dominic Toscanelli. He began his mathematical studies at Florence under Giovanni dell'Abacco. At the age of eighteen he entered the University of Padua where he studied mathematics, philosophy, and medicine. In this period he formed his life-long friendship with Nicholas of Cusa who studied law and mathematics at the same university. The two probably met at the college Prosdocimos de'Beldomandi. Both left the university in 1424, Nicholas with the title of *doctor decretorum* and Paolo as a doctor of medicine. In consequence of this Toscanelli afterwards was frequently called Paolo *fisico*. While Nicholas of Cusa went back to Germany Toscanelli returned to Florence, where he spent the remainder of his life with the exception of short journeys in Tuscany and brief sojourns at Todi and Rome. At Florence Toscanelli took up scientific studies in various directions which brought him into connexion not only with distinguished artists, as Brunelleschi, but also with the greatest scholars of Italy and other countries. He may indeed be said to have been the centre of the learned world of that era. His contemporaries pronounced him one of the most distinguished mathematicians of his time. Regiomontanus and Cusa sought his opinion in the most abstruse questions of theoretical mathematics, or supported their assertions by his authority. Thus Nicholas of Cusa, even at the height of his fame, admired in his friend the thorough mathematician, as is shown by his treatise "De transformationibus geometricis" which was dedicated "Ad Paulum magistri dominici Physicum Florentinum". The same admiration is evident when Cusa wrote as a dialogue between himself and Toscanelli the latter's adverse criticism of Cusa's "Mathematica complementa". In this dialogue Toscanelli says that like Regiomontanus he found the "Mathematica complementa", which investigated the squaring of the circle, obscure and lacking in positiveness.

Paolo dal Pozzo Toscanelli
From a painting by Giorgio Vasari in the Signoria, Florence

Toscanelli's services to astronomy are shown by the painstaking and exact observations and calculations, preserved in manuscript, of the orbits of the comets of 1433, 1449–50, of Halley's comet of 1456, of the comets of May, 1457, of June-July-August, 1457, and that of 1472. According to his own testimony these observations cost him immense labours and long vigils. He could not entirely throw off the influence of astrology, although two of his contemporaries, Marsilio Ficino and Giovanni Pico, disbelieved in it. A monument to his astronomical skill still exists at the Cathedral of Santa Maria del Fiore at Florence in the well-known gnomon, which he constructed about 1468 and which was later improved by Cardinal Ximenes. A marble slab having a small opening in it was placed at a height of 277 feet in the dome over the middle of the left transept; by the shadow he could determine midday to a half-second, and could also settle with much precision the altitudes of the solstices. Toscanelli also gave much attention to cosmography. It seems indeed that he was the most distinguished scholar of the fifteenth century in this branch of science, the aim of which was to gain knowledge of the world in its widest extent. The estimation in which he was held as a cosmographer is shown by the generally accepted belief, resting on traditions respecting Columbus, that Columbus before undertaking his dangerous western voyage asked Toscanelli's advice. Toscanelli had a thorough knowledge of the writings of Ptolemy, he had studied the travels of Marco Polo, and had gained personal information from merchants and seamen, above all from the Italian traveller Nicolo Conti. All that he had thus learned had brought him to the conviction that the transverse extent of Europe and Asia covered nearly two-thirds of the earth, that is 230° of latitude, so that the western route across the ocean could only cover 130°. For a half century the Portuguese had sought to sail around Africa towards the east. Toscanelli seems to have made them repeated proposals as to the possibility of a western route, without, however, being able to convince the Portuguese of the feasibility of his theory.

If we may believe the tradition connecting Toscanelli and Columbus, then Toscanelli wrote, in answer to repeated requests of King Alfonso, the celebrated letter dated 25 June, 1474, to the confessor Canon Ferdam Martins of Lisbon whom he knew. In this letter, which was accompanied by a map, he suggested clear directions for the carrying out of his scheme. This letter had no decisive effect upon the king but probably influenced the adventurous Christopher Columbus, then in the full vigour of manhood. Columbus, who had lived in Lisbon from 1476, heard of the correspondence between Toscanelli and the Court. According to the tradition it was only through the intervention of the friend of Columbus, Lorenzo Giraldi, that the former obtained from Toscanelli, in answer to a personal inquiry, an explanation of his scheme of a voyage westwards. Toscanelli is said to have sent Columbus, for this purpose, a copy of his letter and chart. At the beginning and end of the letter Toscanelli added a few words addressed especially to Columbus. The two biographies of Columbus, that of his son Fernando and that of Bishop Las Casas, both include and give the text of another letter from Toscanelli in reply to a second letter sent him by Columbus. Unfortunately Toscanelli's two letters no longer exist in an authentic form. Both apparently have been greatly altered in the Italian translation of Fernando's "Historie", and in the Spanish biography by the Bishop Las Casas of Chiapaz. However, by good fortune, the middle part of Toscanelli's first letter, that is a copy of the letter of 25 June, 1474, has been preserved in its original form. Harrisse discovered in the "Bibliotheca Colombina" at Seville a copy, made by Columbus himself, of the letter to Martins on the cover of an edition of the "Historia rerum ubique gestarum" of Æneas Silvius. This document makes it possible to determine fairly accurately Toscanelli's opinion, which has been so variously interpreted, concerning the western route and the distance apart of the coasts of the two mainlands.

Toscanelli's chart, however, has not been preserved, either in the original or in a copy. A successful reconstruction of this chart was made by Hermann Wagner of Göttingen which shows that Toscanelli covered the customary nautical chart of the fifteenth century with the reticulations of a square flat chart, upon which direction and distance could be correctly measured by means of the spaces. It is not surprising that Columbus was overwhelmed with delight when he saw it, that he took it with him on his first westward voyage, and had absolute confidence in it. Consequently his two biographers are right in laying so much emphasis on the controlling influence of Toscanelli over Columbus. They even praise the Florentine scholar as the actual father of the great idea of sailing to India by the western route. A diametrically opposite opinion has been expressed by the French scholar Henri Vignaud, who since the holding

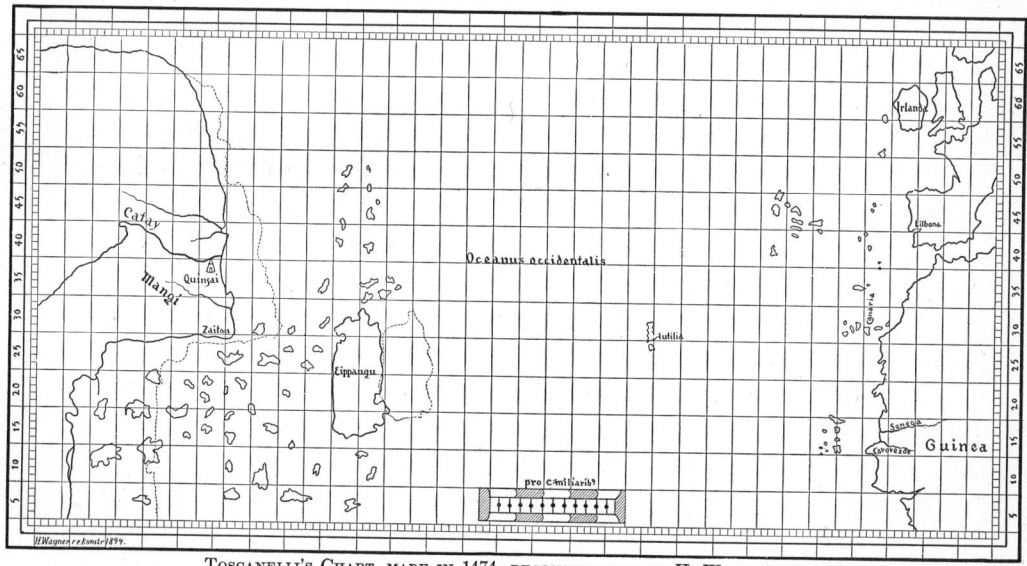

Toscanelli's Chart, made in 1474, reconstructed by H. Wagner, 1894
It is believed that Columbus, on his first voyage to the New World, carried a copy of this chart with him

of the American Congress at Paris in 1900 has attempted to prove that Toscanelli's correspondence with Martins and Columbus, including the accompanying chart, is a forgery. This has led to a violent controversy over the "Toscanelli question", in which Italian, American, English, French, and German scholars have supported the traditional belief of the connexion between Toscanelli and Columbus. Notwithstanding this, Vignaud in 1905 and 1911 published monographs on the life of Columbus for the purpose of maintaining his views. Vignaud's arguments, however, are not decisive. Even though the correspondence between Toscanelli and Columbus be proved to be apocryphal, still Toscanelli's knowledge and ability as a cosmographer does not suffer in the slightest so long as the letter of 1474 is taken as the expression of his cosmographic ideas, and so long as the letter of Duke Ercole of Este, written to his ambassador Manfredo on 26 June, 1494, is regarded as authentic. This letter says that Toscanelli had really occupied himself with the idea of a voyage towards the west. The titles of only three of Toscanelli's works are known, none of them, unfortunately, have been preserved: the "Prospettiva", the "Meteorologia agricola", and also, according to Uzielli, a translation of Ptolemy's geography. A single manuscript is one of the treasures of the Bibliotheca Nazionale centrale of Florence; this was published in 1864 and pertains to astronomy, geodesy, and geography.

UZIELLI, *Paolo dal Pozzo di Toscanelli. Riccordo del solstizio d'estate del 1892* (Florence, 1892); UZIELLI, *La vita e i tempi di Paolo dal Pozzo Toscanelli* (Rome, 1894); WAGNER, *Die Reconstruction der Toscanelli Karte vom Jahre 1474* in *Göttinger Nachrichten* (1894), no. 3; VIGNAUD, *La lettre et la carte de Toscanelli* (Paris, 1901); IDEM, *Etudes sur la vie de Colomb* (Paris, 1905 and 1911). For the controversy over Toscanelli cf. UZIELLI, *Bibliografia della polemica concernente Paolo Toscanelli e Chr. Colombo* (Naples, 1905).

FRIEDRICH STREICHER.

Tosephta (הוספתא, addition, supplement) is the name of a compilation of halakhic-haggadic character, which judged by its contents belongs essentially to the era of the Tanna'im (Teachers), and which is modelled on the plan of the Mishna; all that is lacking are the tractates "Aboth", "Tamid", "Middoth", and "Qinnim". The editors had access to authorities that are older than our Mishna. The individual *Halakhoth* do not show the same subtlety and precision as in the Mishna; often the development of the *Halakha* may be traced from the course of the discussion. The *Haggadah* also is fully represented. The history of the origin of the Tosephta has not yet been satisfactorily cleared up. In any case the work in its present form contains a large number of the doctrines and utterances of later rabbinical teachers (the *Amoraim*), and it was not edited until the late Talmudic period. W. Zuckermandel, "Tosephta, Mishna, und Boraitha in ihrem Verhältnis zu einander" (1 vol., Frankfort, 1908), claims to prove that the Tosephta represents the Palestinian Mishna, and that our Mishna was re-edited in Babylonia.

Edition of the Tosephta by ZUCKERMANDEL (Pasewalk, 1880), supplement to it (Trier, 1882—). Thirty-one tractates, the tractates on the first three orders are to be found translated into Latin in UGOLINO, *Thesaurus*, XVII–XX (Venice, 1755–57).

F. SCHÜHLEIN.

Tostado (TOSTATUS), ALONSO, exegete, b. at Madrigal, Castile, about 1400; d. at Bonilla de la Sierra, near Avila, 3 Sept., 1455. After a course of grammar under the Franciscans he entered the University of Salamanca, where, besides philosophy and theology, he studied civil and canon law, Greek, Hebrew, and the other branches then comprised in the curriculum of a university. By great application joined to an unusually brilliant mind and an extraordinarily retentive memory he accumulated such a vast store of knowledge that his contemporaries styled him the wonder of the world. At twenty-two he began to lecture on a wide variety of subjects to large audiences attracted by his learning. Later he assisted with distinction at the Council of Basle. During a visit to the papal court at Siena in 1443, he was denounced to Eugene IV as having publicly defended an heretical and some rash propositions, but in an explanatory letter he assured the pontiff of his orthodoxy. In his "Defensorium", written on this occasion against Torquemada and other critics, he gave utterance to views derogatory to the authority of the pope. On his return to Spain he was appointed Grand Chancellor of Castile, and in 1449 Bishop of Avila, whence his title Abulensis. Besides a Spanish commentary on the chronicles of Eusebius and other minor works, he wrote commentaries on the historical books of the Old Testament as far as II Par., and on the Gospel of St. Matthew. These are extremely diffuse, containing many digressions on dogmatic and other subjects, which, though often excellent in themselves, are out of place in a commentary. An edition of his works in 13 folio volumes was published at Venice in 1507 and 1547; a more complete edition in 24 folio volumes appeared at the same place in 1615, and another in 27 folio volumes in 1728.

ALONSO TOSTADO
From a print in Thevet's Livre des Vrais Pourtraits, Paris, 1584

HURTER, *Nomenclator*, IV, 762; ANTONIO, *Biblioth. Hisp. Vetus*, II (Madrid, 1788), 255; *Nouv. Biogr. Gén.*, XLV, 518; AMADOR DE LOS RIOS, *Histor. Crit. de la Literat. Españ.*, VI, vii, and xi.

F. BECHTEL.

Tosti, LUIGI, Benedictine historian, b. at Naples, 13 Feb., 1811; d. at Monte Cassino, 24 Sept., 1897. His father, Count Giovanni Tosti, descended from an ancient Calabrian family, having died young, his mother, Vittoria Corigliano, entrusted the child to its uncle, a monk at Monte Cassino. In 1819 Tosti became a pupil at the celebrated abbey, and was drawn early towards the monastic life. He was sent to Rome to complete his studies, was ordained priest in 1833, and soon returned to Monte Cassino, where for twenty years he taught the doctrines of St. Thomas. About 1829 he had begun a deep study of history, and in 1842 he published his "Storia della badia di Monte Cassino", soon followed by the "Storia di Bonifazio VIII". His "Storia della Lega Lombarda", dedicated to Pius IX, appeared in 1848 and was a trumpet-call to the Neo-Guelph party. He laboured so assiduously that in 1851 he published the "Storia di Abelardo e dei suoi tempi", the "Storia del Concilio di Costanza" in 1853, the "Storia dell' origine dello scisma greco" in 1856, "La Contessa Matilde e i Romani pontefici" in 1859, and in 1861 the "Prolegomeni alla storia universale della Chlsa".

Tosti took an energetic and enthusiastic part in the national movement blessed by Pius IX. In 1844, he had planned a review, "L'Ateneo italiano", for the purpose of putting the papacy at the head of the *Risorgimento*. The Neapolitan police authorities opposed it, and forbade Tosti to take part in the projected mediation (between the pope and the triumvirs of the ephemeral Roman Republic), which was advocated by the French envoy, Comte d'Harcourt. Pius IX had to intervene personally to secure the liberation of the learned monk, who had been accused, as Cardinal Capecelatro relates, of belonging to a band of murderous conspirators, and put in prison. Temple, the English ambassador at Naples, also courageously opposed this defenceless persecution. Tosti sought consolation in the study of the Holy Scriptures and his beautiful book, "Ricordi biblici", was the fruit of this mishap. He had the sorrow of seeing his beloved convents threatened by a law of spoliation passed by the Parliament of the new Italian Kingdom, and appealed to distinguished friends, such as W. E. Gladstone, to obtain some exemption for Monte Cassino, which he likewise procured later for the Abbey of Grottaferrata, the Sacro Speco of Subiaco, etc. Pained by these persecutions Tosti refused a chair in the University of Pisa, but became later assistant archivist of the Vatican, under Leo XIII. This great pope's allocution in May, 1887, inviting the Italian Government to make peace, presided over by the former revolutionary, Crispi, rekindled Tosti's patriotism. Deputed by the pope to negotiate the restoration of St. Paul's to the Benedictines, Tosti hoped to effect an official reconciliation of the Vatican and the Quirinal. Crispi's impatience, mutual opposition, the distrusts of French diplomatists, thwarted his noble efforts, and the too hopeful religious had to retract publicly his brochure, "La conciliazione". He withdrew to Monte Cassino and undertook his "Della vita di S. Benedetto". Moved by the pope's generous appeal to the English in 1896, he renewed his efforts with Gladstone, in favour of a reunion of the Churches.

BELLESHEIM in *Katholik*, I (1899), 136 sqq.; CAPECELATRO, *Commemor. di D. Luigi Tosti* (Monte Cassino, 1899); CIPOLLA, *Luigi Tosti e le sue relazioni col Piemonte* in *Atti d. R. acad. delle sc. di Torino*, XXXVI (séance of 25 Nov., 1900); OVIDIO, *Il padre Luigi Tosti* in *Riv. d'Italia*, I (1898), 24 sqq.; GAY, *Le père Tosti* in *Revue de Paris* (Nov., 1904); PISTELLI, *Il padre Tosti in Archivio stor. ital.*, series V, XXI, 241 sqq.; QUINTAVALLE, *La conciliazione fra l'Italia e il papato* (Milan, 1907).

GIUSEPPE GALLAVRESI.

Total Abstinence Union of America, CATHOLIC. See TEMPERANCE MOVEMENTS.

Totemism, from *ote*, root *ot*, possessive form *otem*, in the Ojibway dialect of the Algonquin stock of American Indians; by some authorities spelled *dodeme* (Father de Smet), *todem* (Father Petitot), *Toodaim*, *dodaim*, *totam* (J. Long); the original signification was apparently a person's family or tribe, and in a narrower sense his belongings.

Totemism constitutes the group of superstitions and customs of which the totem is the centre. It is defined as the intimate relation supposed to exist between an individual or a group of individuals and a class of natural objects, i. e. the totem, by which the former regard the latter as identified with them in a mystical manner and in a peculiar sense their own belongings, so that they bear the name of the totem and show this belief in certain customs. The conviction of the intimate union constitutes the religious aspect of Totemism; the customs which result therefrom form its sociological aspect. If the union exists between an individual and a class of natural objects, we have individual Totemism. When it exists between a clan and a natural class we have clan Totemism. Frazer mentions sex Totemism, but that is peculiar to Australia. The totem is most frequently an animal species, more rarely a plant, occasionally an inanimate object, e. g. sun, wind, rock, etc. Totemism is widespread and developed among the American Indians and the aborigines of Australia. Traces of it are found in South Africa, in the Polynesian Islands, and among the Dyaks of India. Mauss says it does not exist in all savage races of our day (Année sociologique, IV, 1899–1900); Reinach maintains that it existed among the Greeks and Celts (Cultes, Mythes et Religions, II, Paris, 1905); Gomme, in the British Isles (Archæological Rev., III, 1889); Thomas, in Wales (Rev. de l'histoire des religions, XXXVIII, 1898); Renel, among the Romans (Cultes militaires de Rome, Lyons, 1903). It is doubtful whether Totemism existed among the Aryan races, and the facts alleged can be explained by idolatry. Loret maintains that Totemism existed among the early Egyptians, but evidently confounds this belief with animal-worship. Robertson Smith holds that Totemism lies at the basis of the Semitic religions. Zapletal has opened up anew this problem, and questions Smith's conclusions. Evidence from animal names is now admitted to be a precarious support for the Totem theory. Frazer clearly shows that there are sacred animals and plants which are not totems; and Levy denies to Totemism any rôle among the early Hebrews. Hence the present writer rejects the opinion of A. Lang that in the education of mankind Totemism has played a part everywhere.

I. HISTORY.—The phenomena of Totemism were first brought to the knowledge of the civilized world by the Jesuit missionaries to North America in the seventeenth century. The earliest accounts in English came from J. Long (Voyages and Travels, London, 1791). Following these are accounts of Major S. H. Long (ed. by Edwin James, London, 1823), James, Warren, Morgan, Schoolcraft, and Catlin. Phenomena of the same kind were observed by travellers and missionaries in Australia. The importance of Totemism in the early history of society was first pointed out by J. F. McLennan, who proposed as a working hypothesis that the ancient nations of the world had passed through a peculiar kind of Fetishism or Animism which finds its typical representation in the totem-tribes of Australia and of North America ("Fortnightly Rev.", Oct.-Nov., 1869; Feb., 1870; "Studies in Ancient History", London, 1896). On these lines Robertson Smith attempted to show that Totemism lay at the root of the Semitic religions and thus was the basis of the faith now embraced by the most civilized nations of the world ("Animal Worship among Arabs" in "Cambridge Jour. of Phil.", 1879; "Kinship and Marriage in early Arabia", 2nd ed., London, 1903; "Religion of the Semitics", Edinburgh, 1889; "Sacrifice" in Encyc. Britannica, 9th ed.); F. B. Jevons went further and affirmed that here are found the germs out of which all religion and all material progress have been evolved (Introd. to the History of Religion, London, 1896); hence Totemism was regarded as an established theory with the foundation laid by McLennan and the superstructure by Frazer, Smith, and Jevons. This theory is now rejected by scholars. Father Brun, writing of French West Africa, says that Totemism does not appear as a precise stage of religious evolution exclusive of all other beliefs; it is simply an element of these beliefs. Murillier criticises Jevons (Revue de l'hist. des religions, XXXVI). The investigation of Franz Boas among the Indians of North-West Canada and of Spencer and Gillen among the Australian aborigines gave the decisive blow to the theory and opened a new phase in the study of Totemism. Hence Hill-Tout says that Totemism is not the ideal and exact social or religious system of savage regimentation which some writers have tried to show. It is found among races varying much in modes of living, e. g. hunting, pastoral, agricultural, and industrial, and, becoming part of their varied beliefs and customs, has appeared to assume differing forms.

II. ORIGIN.—Totemism must be simple to the savage mind, yet it is a puzzle to anthropologists. A great mass of facts different and at times in seeming contradiction have been gathered in America and Australia, yet the resemblances are so many and so close as to justify the classification under one common name. Different explanations have been proposed, and these have varied as new data were added. There is scarcely any other class of social phenomena more difficult to explain. Frazer says a definition is only provisional and A. Lang resorts to "conjectures" and "guesses" (Secret of the Totem, p. 28). The discussion has produced a wealth of literature which has served to exaggerate the real position and influence of Totemism. The difficulty is to define the nature of the relation between the individual or clan and their totem. Hence:—

(a) *The Name-Theory*.—Herbert Spencer classes Totemism under animal-worship and says its explanation is found in the primitive custom of naming children after natural objects from some accidental circumstances or fanciful resemblance, and then in confounding these metaphorical names or nicknames with the real objects, i. e. ancestors, and consequently paying to the animals the same reverence they paid their ancestors. Hence a phase of ancestor-worship founded on mistaking metaphors for facts (Prin. of Sociol., I, xxii). Akin to the "nickname" theory of Spencer is the explanation of Lord Avebury. He views Totemism as nature-worship and says it arose from the practice of naming individuals and then their families after particular animals; the individuals would look upon the animals at first with interest, then with respect, and at length with a sort of awe (Marriage, Totemism, and Religion, London, 1911). A. Lang proposes the "sobriquet" theory. He adopts the opinion of de la Vega that totems were names imposed by outsiders to distinguish the individuals or families from one another (Secret of the

Totem, pref.). Hence he agrees with J. F. McLennan, Loret, and Wake that totems were merely ethnic attributes, symbols, or ensigns of clans. A. K. Keane also holds that Totemism arose in "heraldic badges" (Ethnology, 9). Max Müller writes, "A totem is a clan mark, then a clan name, then the name of the ancestor of the clan, and lastly the name of something worshipped by the clan" (Contributions to the Science of Mythology, I, 201). Lang, however, holds that the name came into use before, not after, its pictorial representation, i. e., the clan mark. Pikler says the germ of Totemism is in the naming and has "its original germ not in religion but in the practical every-day needs of man". Risley also says that the totem is an ancient nickname, usually derived from some animal, of the supposed founder of the exogamous sept, now stripped of its personal association and remembered solely in virtue of the part it plays in giving effect to the rule of exogamy. In criticism it can be said that the name-theory fails to explain the intimate relation of the individual or clan to the totem. Hence Durkheim writes "a totem is not only a name; it is first and above all a religious principle" ("Année sociologique", 1902, 119).

Lang admits that his "theory is not in accordance with any savage explanations of the origin of the totem" (Social Origins, 188). Howlett writes: "It seems most improbable that any such nicknames would have been adopted and have given rise to Totemism, nor do I know of a single instance in which such nicknames have been adopted." Reinach holds that animal names are an effect, not a cause of Totemism (Cultes, Mythes, et Religions, I, 22). Tyler says the theory is not vouched for by sufficient evidence (Primitive Marriage, II, 214). Boas distinguishes three classes of tribal and of clan names, e. g. collective forms of the name of the ancestor, names of region inhabited and names of honour. Miss Fletcher says that with the Wezhishta gens of the Amaha names are classified as *nikie*, i. e. pertaining to the gens, "dream", "fanciful" and "borrowed" names, and nicknames, and women never had more than one name which was of *nikie* class. Hill-Tout declares that the commonest of Indian names in British Columbia are not nicknames, but true *prænomina*, mostly given to infants shortly after birth before any resemblance is apparent or possible.

(b) *The Transmigration Theory*, advocated by G. A. Wilkin, and also by Tylor (Jour. Anth. Inst., XXVIII, 1899), regards the totem as the bridge over the gap between a clan of men and a species of animals, so that they "become united in kinship and mutual alliance". In criticism it may be said that the notion of transmigration is not primitive, for with Tylor Totemism is regarded as primitive. Again the belief in transmigration is found among peoples who show no trace of Totemism, while it is unknown to the African Baganda and to most if not all of the North American Indians whose Totemism is clearly marked. Hence Frazer holds that Totemism and transmigration are distinct and independent. Finally, transmigration may enter into phases of Totemism under the form of the reincarnation of ancestors; this, however, is not the original element but a corrupted phase found only occasionally and hence a later development.

(c) *The Economic Theory*, proposed in accord with those anthropologists who hold that the starting-point of social organization was the necessity of procuring food, appears in two forms. Dr. A. C. Haddon maintains that totems originally were the animals or plants on which the local groups of people chiefly subsisted and after which they were named by the neighbouring groups ("Rep. of the British Assoc.", Belfast, 1902; "Folk Lore", XIII, 393). But this theory fails to explain the existence of inanimate objects as totems. Again, Baldwin Spencer denies such specialization of diet between the local groups (Northern Tribes of Central Australia, p. 767). The second form was advocated by Prof. Frazer, who, following Spencer and Gillen (Jour. Anth. Inst., XXVIII, 1899, 273), taught that Totemism is not so much a religious as an economic system, and held that it originated as a system of magic designed to supply a community with the necessities of life, especially food and drink. Thus each totem group performs magic ceremonies called *intichiuma* for the multiplication of the totem-plant or animal. Hence the prime duty of a totem clan was to provide a supply of its totem-animal or plant for consumption by the rest of the tribe, and thus ensure a plentiful supply of food ("Fort. Rev.", April and May, 1899). Frazer afterwards rejected this theory as too complex, and says that probably the co-operative communities of totemic magicians in Australia are developments of Totemism rather than its germ (Totemism and Exogamy, IV, p. 57). In fact the economic theory does not account for the sense of kinship between man and animal, and the belief prevailing in places that the clan is descended from the animal.

(d) *The External Soul Theory*, earlier propounded by Prof. Frazer, i. e., the possibility of depositing the souls of living people for safety in external objects such as animals or plants, but not knowing which individual of the species is the receptacle of his soul, the savage spares the whole species from a fear of injuring unwittingly the particular individual with which his fate is bound up ("Golden Bough", II, London, 1890). Frazer rejected this theory on the ground that it was not confirmed by subsequent research.

(e) *The Conception Theory* is the third and last explanation of Frazer. He says Totemism has its source in the savage ignorance of paternity, and is a primitive explanation of conception and childbirth, viz. that conception is due to a spirit of an ancestor entering the body of a woman, that she associates it with the object which was nearest her when the child was first felt in the womb, and that this object is regarded as the deserted receptacle of the spirit. And since the spirits of people of one particular totem are believed to congregate in one spot, and the natives know these spots, the totem of the child can easily be determined ("Totemism and Exogamy", IV, 57). In criticism we may say that the theory is based on the beliefs of the Arunta tribe in Australia, that, while van Gennep holds to Arunta primitiveness, A. Lang considers it a decadent sport (Secret of the Totem, appendix), that Spencer and Gillen testify to changes in Arunta Totemism, that it does not explain Totemism in its wide extent, and finally that these beliefs find another and a much better explanation.

(f) *The Manitou, or Guardian Spirit, Theory*, first proposed by the Jesuit missionaries to North America in the seventeenth century and revived in our day by Dr. Franz Boas, Miss Alice Fletcher, Father Morice, Mr. Hill-Tout, and J. Owen Dorsay, teaches that the manitou of the individual has developed into the totem of the clan. This can be explained in two ways. First by real inheritance, e. g. the guardian spirit of an ancestor is transmitted to his descendants. Hence the clan totem is the hereditary manitou of a family. Dr. Boas states that the guardian spirit of the North Pacific Coast becomes hereditary. Father Brun says that the Totemism of French West Africa is essentially familial in the sense of the Roman *gens*. A. Lang objects to the inheritance of the personal totem by the clan on the ground that mother descent is more primitive than paternal descent. But the objection assumes that Totemism is primitive: a contention by no means established. Frazer says the clans would be stable and permanent even with mother descent, if the husband took up his abode with the wife's people or the wife remained at home

(Totemism and Exogamy, II, 103, n). Morgan states that this condition is true of the Iroquois, whose clans are permanent even with mother descent. Hill-Tout writes that in North-West Canada the totem is hereditary either from father to son in the paternal right, or from the man to his sister's children in the maternal right. For even under maternal right the head of the clan is invariably a man—the elder male relative on the maternal side. Thus the founders of families and of totem-crests are as invariably men under matriarchy as under patriarchy; in the former, indirectly through the man's sister, in the latter, directly to his children (Trans. Roy. Soc. Canada, IX, XI; B.A.A.S., London, 1889). Frazer points out that among the Melanesians, where mother-kin prevails, the nearest male relative of the children is the mother's brother (loc. cit., II, 74). And Swanton says of the Tlingit shamans that spirits descended from uncle to nephew. The great difficulty with the real inheritance theory is that it does not explain enough. It may account in places for the change of the personal totem of an ancestor into the clan totem, but it fails to tell how or why the same totem is held by different clans or tribes or stocks not connected by ties of blood-relationship. The natural explanation is that the fauna and flora of a country are substantially the same, and individuals in different parts belonging to different tribes could in the usual way acquire a totem which they would transmit to their descendants. Thus with members of the same clan there would be the same totem with consanguinity. With members of different clans having the same totem there would not be consanguinity but a kind of relationship based in the possession of the same. Hence Dr. Fison writes of the Australians: "All men of the same generation who bear the same totem are tribally brothers, though they may belong to different and widely separated tribes" (quoted by Lang, "Secret of the Totem", 45). If therefore real inheritance be supplemented by supposed inheritance, it can be safely maintained that the clan totem, taken in its widest extent, is a development or extension of the individual totem or manitou through real or supposed inheritance. The nature of the supposed inheritance becomes clear from the following.

III. NATURE.—The basis of Totemism is the animistic conception of nature. The life revealed in living things, the forces manifested by physical objects are ascribed to spirits animating them or dwelling therein. "There is indeed nothing in nature", writes Charlevoix, "if we can believe the savages, which has not its spirit" ("Histoire de la Nouv. France", Paris, 1744, VI, 67). The feeling of weakness in the midst of powers and forces greater than his own leads him to seek union with one or more of these powers. It becomes his guide and support; its power is added to his; its life or "essence" or "mystery" becomes part of his very own, he is called by its name, and some part of its physical embodiment is viewed as his most valued possession, as the mark of his spirit protector and the sign of his strengthened life, i. e. his "medicine" or "mystery". Thus savages believe themselves endowed with the qualities of their totems. Thus we can understand the birth and death ceremonies of the totem tribes, the facts that in the tribal dances and ceremonies the individuals imitate in action or costume the appearance and habits of their totems. So also we can understand the respect or reverence which the individual has for his totem, the intimate relation existing between them, the fact that he regards them as his kin and calls them brothers, and as far as possible identifies himself with them. Thus the savage with a totem has his own human life and strength plus the spirit-life and strength of the animal or object whose totem he possesses. For, as with the natives of British Columbia, the *inua* or *uya*, i. e. the "essence" or "mystery", becomes the totem, not the mere outward form of the animal or object. He either has this spirit-life actually and habitually compenetrating and augmenting his own natural powers or at least possesses the right to invoke the spirit-life to the augmentation of his natural powers in time of need, e. g. an Indian in a canoe, seeing the enemy gaining upon him, reverently calls upon his totem, e. g. sawbill duck, and receives such additional strength that he soon escapes his pursuers (Frazer, "Totemism and Exogamy", III, p. 385). In the former case the possession of the spirit-life is habitual and can be conceived as passing to his descendants; in the latter case it is occasionally present and therefore need not be hereditary. To possess intact this spirit-life, or at least to keep the claim to its assistance clear and unhampered, seems to be the reason for the regular religious ceremonies practised in regard to the totem.

Furthermore, in studying the relation of the spirit-life of the totem to the natural life of the individual, we can conceive that the latter is at times more prominent and at times the spirit-life is principally considered. In the former case the members of the totemic clan are united, not only in the possession of the same common spirit-life, but through ties of consanguinity, by participation in a common human life. In the latter case the members of the totem clan would not of necessity be related to one another by blood, but would consider themselves relatives by a common participation in the spirit-life of the same totem. Thus we can understand why some tribes have both clan and individual totems, and again why some clans have two or more totems. Finally, in the theory that the clan totem is the natural development of the individual totem, the contention of some scholars that the term *totem* should be reserved to the clan totem is of little moment. Thus van Gennep, E. B. Tylor, and Lang hold that the clan totem alone deserves the name; and Frazer now advocates the opinion of van Gennep (Totemism and Exogamy, III, 456).

Hence Totemism, like Fetishism and Shamanism, is based on Animism, but differs from them in the way the spirits are conceived to enter into the lives of men and manifest their power. Miss Kingsley, however, maintains that Totemism is based on the pantheistic conception of the universe, which she says was held by the American Indians. But this is not correct. The Indians always made a distinction between the spirit-life of the totem and the ordinary human life or strength of men. The former was considered sacred, mysterious, mystic, supernatural. This is shown by the terms used to designate the spirit-life, e. g. *wakan* of the Dakotas, *orenda* of the Iroquois, *tlokoala* of the Kwatiutl Indians. Dorsay says that an Indian's *wakaned* is considered inspired and as possessing supernatural power. Thus the Indian's "medicine bag" is his "mystery bag", writes Catlin, and Dr. Hoffman tells us that the young Algonquin receives from the Great Mystery the particular animal form he might adopt as his guardian mystery, and this becomes his advisor, monitor, and intercessor with the superior *manidos*.

The real nature of Totemism, therefore, is the savage conception of a twofold power or life or strength in the individual, i. e. his human life plus the spirit-life of the totem. But the measure in which the spirit-life enters into the human life of the totemic individual varies in different tribes and races, giving rise to the difficulties experienced by students of this subject. Thus we have the spirit-life holding a subordinate position in relation to the human life; or the spirit-life so prominent that the human life is absorbed by it and consequently ignored and forgotten; or we find both the spirit life and the human life equally recognized but at times in a confused manner. In the first case the human element predominates and descent is reckoned by human generation. Miss Fletcher assures us that the Omahas do not hold descent from the totem animals; and Father Brun says the same is true of the natives in West Sudan. Boas writes that the Kwatiutl Indians do not consider themselves to be descendants of the totem; they believe the totem came from an ancestor who had an adventure with an animal which he took as his totem and transmitted to his clan; and that the connexion between the totem and the clan has become so slight that it has degenerated into a crest. The Tlingit do not believe in descent from the totem, yet count the totem as their relative or protector, as e. g. Indians of the Wolf totem implore the wolves: "we are your relations, pray do not hurt us." Hence Powell's statement, that the totem of the clan is considered to be the progenitor or prototype of the clan, is not universally true. This also solves the difficulty experienced by Hill-Tout, who says that the Totemism of British Columbia appears to differ in important and characteristic features from the Totemism of peoples elsewhere.

In the second case, where the spirit-life is considered as absorbing the human life, the fact of human generation is ignored and forgotten. Thus, e. g. among the Aruntes human paternity is unknown. They believe that conception is the entrance of the spirit of an ancestor into the body of a woman, and thus every child born is the reincarnation of an animal or plant ancestor. In the olden times the totemic ancestors were families or groups of families who lived in some definite part of the tribal territory. Some would be swans, others dogs, kangaroos, snakes, etc. They carried with them sacred stones called *churinga*, i. e. soul or spirit-life. Upon death the spirit-life would remain in the *churinga* and would haunt the place where these were. In the course of time all the camping-places, water-holes, large rocks, springs, hills, trees, etc., would be thronged with spirits of all kinds. The exact locality of these ancestral spots, with the specific kind of spirits dwelling there, was known from oral tradition. In virtue of the spirit-life, these spots were considered as related to one another in the same way that human beings are related, e. g. a soakage may be the mother's brother of a certain hill, a rock may be the father of a particular sand-hill, a tree may be the brother of a sand-hole, etc. If in passing a particular spot a woman feels the quickening of the child, she ascribes it to the fact that an ancestral spirit of that spot has at that moment entered her body. The object, e. g. stone, piece of wood, etc., that met her eye at that moment is carefully taken as the *churinga* of the child and placed in the secret store-house of the tribe kept for that purpose. Thus the totem of the child will be the totem of the spot whence the *churinga* was taken. Hence there could be children of the same parents all possessing different totems.

In the third case, where both the spirit-life of the totem and the human life of the individual are recognized but in a confused manner, we find the explanation of another class of beliefs and myths which have gathered around Totemism. Thus we can understand how the North American Indians, in explanation of their origin, can neglect the human so that in the remote past it is lost in the animal. Thus Indians of the Wolf totem say they are descended from wolves, of the Crane totem from cranes, of the Turtle totem from turtles, etc. So too we can see how they were led to believe that their ancestors were monstrosities endowed with superhuman powers, e. g. Salish tribes, or were transformed human or semi-human, e. g. Urabunna or creatures partaking of both human and animal natures with power of transforming themselves into animal or human shapes at will, e. g. Northern Australian tribes, or of retransforming themselves, e. g. Iroquois (Hesitt, "Iroquois Cosmology" in "21st Am. Rep. of Bur. of Ethnol.", Washington, 1904, p. 219). On this hypothesis we can grasp the myths of mixed generation so universal among totemic peoples and see also why the Haides, in venerating the killer-whale, blend in their belief the actual animal and the demon Skana supposed to be embodied in it.

IV. Personal Totem, i. e. *manitou* of Algonquins, *tu kinajek* of Tlingit, *augud* of Torres Straits, *sulia* of British Columbia, *bunjan* of south-east Australia, *ari* of north-east Australia, *oubarre* of West Australia, *atai* and *tamaniu* of Melanesia, *nyarong* of Borneo, *nagual* of South America, *tamanous* of Twana Indians, is not hereditary; it is acquired by the individual and it is his own personal property, whereas the clan totem is considered the possession of the clan. It is obtained either accidentally, as when a savage believes that he owes his life to an animal which he immediately takes as his totem; or bestowed at birth, e. g. in Central America by the parents casting a horoscope; or bestowed on the youth by old wise men, e. g. Sioux; or regularly at the puberty ceremonies. On reaching this age the young Indian goes off alone to the forest and wanders for days without food except roots, etc. After a time when asleep he sees in a dream the animal which is to be his guardian. It or its spirit comes to him. Ever after he wears on his person the object seen, or some portion of it, which is known as his medicine. Catlin describes this in detail. The Salish word *sulia*, from *ulia*, i. e. to dream, indicates the ordinary method by which it is obtained. Boas says that with the Kwatiutl Indians the personal totem must be selected from the totems of the clan, hence the number is limited.

V. Religious Aspect.—Totemism has both a religious and a social aspect. These aspects vary; thus with the interior Australian tribes the religious aspect is predominant; with the coastal tribes the social aspect prevails. Lord Avebury and Spencer hold that Totemism began as a social system only, and that the superstitious regard for the totem is an aftergrowth. A. Lang, failing to grasp the religious meaning of the totem, has helped to popularize this view. McLennan and Robertson Smith teach that the religious reverence for the totem was original. Father Morice says that Totemism among the Dénés is essentially and exclusively connected with their religious system. Investigation into the nature of Totemism shows this to be the true opinion. Durkheim holds the totem to be a god. This is a mistake. The respect paid to the totem is like that given to relatives or brothers; it is his friend and helper, not his superior. Frazer says Totemism has done little to foster the higher forms of religion, and Murillier does not admit the possibility of any transition from Totemism to any other stage of religious evolution. McGee quotes Darsey, that among the Sioux totems were reverenced rather than worshipped. Frazer at first maintained the religious aspect of Totemism ("Totemism", Edinburgh, 1887); now he denies this (Totemism and Exogamy, 1911, IV, 6). He says the key to the Totemism of Australian natives is furnished by the Intichiuma ceremonies; and as these ceremonies, peculiar to each totem group, are performed with spells and enchantments for the multiplication of the totem animal, therefore in its origin Totemism is simply an organized and co-operative system of magic devised for economic purposes. The criticism is that this view is superficial and unsatisfactory, that investigations show the Australian savage life to be saturated with the belief in spirits, e. g. the explanation of conception and birth, and that whereas the Intichiuma ceremonies on the surface may appear to be for the multiplication of the totem animal and thus secure a food supply, yet if we study them in the background of the belief in spirits, their purposes more probably are the multiplication of the reincarnated forms of the spirits. When, e. g. the members of the Kangaroo clan perform magic ceremonies for the multiplication of Kangaroos, we are not warranted in stating that kangaroo animals are in question, for members of this clan are also called Kangaroos. Hence the multiplication of the human species may be intended, so that the Kangaroo spirits may be reincarnated. This seems to be confirmed by the rites having a reference to human generation performed at the puberty or Engwura ceremonies.

The main features in the religious aspect of Totemism are shown in the rites and ceremonies performed with a view to show or to attain identity with the totem. (a) Thus at solemn totemic festivals the totem animal is sacrified and eaten even by its own clan. In Australia the eating of the totem animal was considered essential to the rites for the multiplication of the totem. Hill-Tout says that in British Columbia these ceremonies would last through the winter and the people would be grouped according to their totems, thus changing the usual form of tribal organization. (b) By adoption of personal names referring to the appearance or habits of the totem animal. (c) By dressing in the skin or other parts of the totem animal, wearing badges, masks, crest-hats of the totem, arranging hair, painting face or body, tattooing and mutilating the body so as to resemble the totem; so also totems are painted or carved on weapons, canoes, huts, etc. From this custom we have the totem poles decorated with crests of clan and personal totems, and with red crosses representing the ghosts of their vanquished foes, who are to be their slaves in the other world. (d) By dances and songs as dramatic performances of the myth relating to the acquisition of the spirit protector. (e) By consulting totems as auguries, e. g. the Algonquins and natives of Torres Straits.

VI. SOCIAL ASPECT.—In its social aspect (a) the totem is generally taboo to the members of the clan. They could not kill it or eat its flesh. An exception is in the solemn totemic ceremonies. According to traditions the Australians in earlier times regularly killed and ate their totem. This is not now the custom. The American Indian will address an apology to his totem before killing it. The Melanesian is supposed to have peculiar success in hunting his totem animal. Hill-Tout says the Salish tribes considered the real *sulia* to be a spirit or mystery-being, though it might take the form of an animal and it could not be killed or hurt if the animal were slain, hence the hunter did not respect the life of the totem; in fact he was considered more successful in hunting his *sulia* animals than other men. Again, on the African Gold Coast a hunter of the Leopard family would not hesitate to kill a troublesome leopard, but he would put oil in the wounds (Harper in "Jour. Anth. Inst.", XXXVI).

(b) Among the Iroquois and the Southern Mewuks of California the totem governs the choice of partners in games, the placing and treatment of visitors.

(c) The main social feature of Totemism is shown in binding together the members of the totem clan. All members of the totem clan regard one another as kinsmen and brothers, and are bound to mutual help and protection. Tylor says every Indian looked for and found hospitality in a hut where he saw his own totem figured and, if he was taken captive in war, his clansmen would ransom him (Jour. Anth. Inst., XXVIII). Morgan shows the superiority of the totem bond over the tribal bond among the Iroquois. In the Torres Straits warfare could not affect the friendship of the totem-brethren. Yet Harper says that on the Gulf Coast a man cannot safely visit a person of the same totem belonging to an unfriendly tribe, nor does he hesitate to kill another having the same totem as himself.

(d) In the social phase must be viewed the secret societies so widely prevalent among the American Indians.

(e) Ford holds that in totemic obligations we are confronted with the beginnings of authority ("Annals of American Academy of Political and Social Science", XXIII, Philadelphia, 1904). Jevons and Reinach teach that the totem clan is the earliest social organization known in the evolution of society (Folk Lore, X). Loret sees in Totemism the explanation of the early Egyptian hieroglyphics, and says it is the parent of writing (Musée Guimet, XIX, 1904–05). Frazer says that it had an indirect influence on agriculture, the domestication of animals and the use of metals, that its influence on economic progress appears to be little more than a shadowy conjecture, but it has done something for pictorial and plastic art, e. g. in totemic representations (Totemism and Exogamy, IV, 19–25). Father Brun, however, warns us that although certain social institutions are placed under the protection of totemic beliefs, the social institutions as a whole are not based upon Totemism. The truth is that Totemism, like any other belief which enters into the life of a people, has an influence on their culture.

(f) The influence of Totemism is shown also in the birth, marriage, and death ceremonies. Thus, e. g. a child of the Ottawa deer clan on the fifth day after birth was painted with red spots or stripes in imitation of a fawn; the bride and groom in the Kolong red-dog clan of Java were rubbed before marriage with the ashes of a red-dog's bones; a member of the Amaha buffalo clan was on dying wrapped in a buffalo robe, etc.

VII. EXOGAMY.—The relation of exogamy to Totemism is a problem of great difficulty, and will not be completely solved until the origin of exogamy is definitely established. It is a fact that the custom prevails in many tribes that a man cannot marry a woman of his own totem, but must seek a wife from another totem clan. Hence many writers inferred that Totemism and exogamy existed together as different sides of the same institution. Thus A. Lang regards exogamy as the essential feature of Totemism. Hill-Tout takes issue with him maintaining that it is accidental or secondary, that the possession of the same totem becomes a bar to marriage only because it marks kinship by blood, which is the real bar. Lang by totem means "the hereditary totem of the exogamous clan" and admits that if we take totem in its wider extent as comprehending the "personal" totem, the "secret society" totem and the "tribal" totem, then members of these totem groups can intermarry (ibid., p. 204). McLennan and Robertson Smith held that Totemism is found generally in connexion with exogamy, but must be older than exogamy. This view has been confirmed by the investigations of Spencer and Gillen among the Australian savages. They teach that Totemism is a primary and exogamy a secondary feature, and give traditions proving the existence of totems long before that of exogamous groups, and that when the latter did arise, the totems were not affected by them. Hence the exogamous class is a social organization totally different in origin and nature from the totemic clan, and not a mere extension of it, although they have crossed and blended in many places. Again Totemism and exogamy are found existing separately. Father Brun says the totemic clans of the Sudan are not exogamous. Dr. Rivers points out that the natives of Banks Islands have pure Totemism and pure exogamy existing side by side without influencing each other.

Different theories have been proposed to account for the origin of exogamy. Westermark says it arose in the aversion to marriage between blood relatives or near kin, i. e. in horror of incest. This is very probably the true solution. McLennan holds that exogamy was due originally to scarcity of women, which obliged men to seek wives from other groups, i. e. marriage by capture, and this in time grew into a custom. Durkheim derives exogamy from Totemism, and says it arose from a religious respect for the blood of a totemic clan, for the clan totem is a god and is especially in the blood. Morgan and Howitt maintain that exogamy was introduced to prevent marriage between blood relations: especially between brother and sister, which had been common in a previous state of promiscuity. Frazer says this is the true solution, that it really introduced group marriage, which is an advance to monogamy, and that the most complete record of this is the classificatory system of relationship. Lang, however, denies there is any group marriage, and says the so-called group marriage is only tribe-regulated licence. Hill-Tout writes that exogamous rules arose for political reasons by marriage treaties between the groups. Darwin denies primitive promiscuous intercourse, and says exogamy arose from the strongest male driving the other males out of the group. This is also the opinion of Lang, Atkinson, and Letourneau.

Jesuit Relations, ed. THWAITES (73 vols., Cleveland, 1896–1901); SPENCER AND GILLEN, *Native Tribes of Cent. Australia* (London, 1899); IDEM, *Northern Tribes of Cent. Australia* (London, 1904); BOAS, *Social Organization and Secret Societies of the Kwatiutl Indians* in *Rept. of the U. S. National Museum for 1895* (Washington, 1897); FRAZER, *Totemism and Exogamy* (London, 1910); LANG, *Secret of the Totem* (London, 1905); IDEM, *Totemism* in *Encycl. Britannica* (11th edition); IDEM in *Folk Lore*, XIII (1902); McGEE, *Sioux Indians* in *15th Ann. Report of the Bur. of Ethnology* (Washington, 1897); MATTHEWS in *American Antiquarian*, XXVIII, 81, 140; FRIEND-PEREIRA in *Jour. of Asiatic Soc. of Bengal*, LXXIII, p. 3, n. 3, p. 39; COOK in *Jewish Quart. Rev.* (April, 1902); HILL-TOUT in *Royal Soc. of Canada*, 1901, vol. VII; MERRIAM in *Amer. Anthropologist*, new ser., X (1908); DE MARZAN in *Anthropos*, II (1907); BRUN, *ibid.*, V (1910); LEVY in *Rev. des études juives*, XLV (1902); TONTAIN in *Rev. de l'hist. des religions* (Paris, 1908); HARTLAND in *Folk Lore*, XI (1900); JEVONS, *ibid.*, X (1899); CUOQ, *Lex. de la langue algonquine* (Montreal, 1885); HOWITT, *Native Tribes of South-East Australia* (London, 1904); FLETCHER AND LA FLESCHE in *27th Ann. Report of the Bur. of Ethnology* (Washington, 1911); DORSAY in *15th Ann. Report of Bur. of Eth.* (Washington, 1897); IDEM in *3rd Ann. Report of Bur. of Eth.* (Washington, 1884); IDEM in *11th Ann. Report of Bur. of Eth.* (Washington, 1894); SWANTON in *26th Ann. Report of the Bur. of Eth.* (Washington, 1908); MORICE in *Trans. of the Canadian Inst.*, IV (1892–93); IDEM in *Ann. Archeol. Report 1905* (Toronto); RIGGS, *Dakota-English Dictionary* (Washington, 1900); CATLIN, *Letters and Notes on the Manners, Customs and Condition of the N. Amer. Indians* (London, 1844); HOFFMAN in *14th Ann. Report of the Bur. of Eth.* (Washington, 1896); MORICE, *Hist. of the Northern Interior of Brit. Columbia* (London, 1907); HILL-TOUT, *Brit. North America* (London, 1907).

JOHN T. DRISCOLL.

Totonac Indians, one of the smaller cultured nations of ancient Mexico, occupying at the time of the Spanish conquest the coast province of Totonicapan, comprehending all except the northern border of the present State of Vera Cruz, together with the Zacatlan district in Puebla. Within this territory they had some fifty towns, with a total population of perhaps a quarter of a million. Their capital, Cempoala, about five miles inland from the present city of Vera Cruz, had a population of about 25,000. In spite of wars, epidemics, and oppressions they still number about 100,000.

The Totonac were the first natives whom Cortés met on landing in Mexico in 1519. According to their own traditions, they had come from the northwest nearly eight centuries earlier, and had maintained an independent kingdom—of which the names of the successive kings are on record—until subjugated by the Aztec only about twenty-five years before the arrival of the Spaniards. Being compelled by their conquerors to the payment of a heavy tribute and to other exactions, including the frequent seizure of their people for slaves or for sacrifice in the bloody Aztec rites, they were ripe for revolt, and their king, Chicomacatt, eagerly welcomed Cortés and promised the support of his fifty thousand warriors against Montezuma.

Encouraged by Cortés, King Chicomacatt asserted his independence by seizing the Mexican tax-gatherers then in his country, but was restrained by the Spanish commander from sacrificing them to the idols. They gave willing help in laying the foundations of the city of (Villa Rica de la) Vera Cruz, which Cortés made his starting point for the advance upon the Mexican capital. As a final test of their friendship and obedience, Cortés commanded the destruction of the wooden images of the gods in the great pyramid temple of Cempoala, where every day human victims were sacrificed, their hearts being torn out and placed upon the altars of the gods, the blood sprinkled upon the idols and the walls of the temple, and the dismembered limbs borne away to be served up in a cannibal feast. Notwithstanding the protest of the king and the fierce opposition of the priests and their retainers, the order was carried out by a detachment of Spanish soldiers. The idols were thrown down to the foot of the temple and burned. According to Bancroft (see bibl.), when their pagan temple was cleansed Olmedo preached the Christian Faith and celebrated Mass before the assembled natives. The contrast between the simple beauty of this impressive ceremony and their own bloody worship made a deep impression on the minds of the natives, and at the conclusion those who desired were baptized. So Christianity achieved its first victory in Mexico.

In the subsequent events, culminating in the taking of the city of Mexico and the downfall of the Aztec empire, the Totonac took active part with the Tlascalans as allies of the Spaniards, giving ready allegiance alike to the new rulers and the new religion. In 1526 their territory of Vera Cruz was combined with Tlascala, Tabasco, and Yucatan into a bishopric with seat at Tlascala under Bishop Juliano Garcés, Dominican (d. 1542). The work of Christianizing was given over chiefly to the Dominicans, who had convents at Vera Cruz, Puebla, and Goazacoalco, and who led the fight against Indian slavery (see CASAS, BARTOLOMÉ DE LAS). Franciscans, Augustinians, and other orders were also represented in the Indian work. The Jesuits in the diocese confined their attention to whites and negroes. In 1575–77 the Totonac, in common with all the other tribes of Southern Mexico, were ravaged by the mysterious *matlalzahuatl* epidemic, estimated to have destroyed two millions of the native race. About the year 1600, in accordance with a viceregal scheme of concentration, the entire population of Cempoala was removed to a new site, and the ancient capital thenceforth sank to the level of a village.

The modern Totonac of Puebla and Vera Cruz are industrious farmers, their chief crop being sugar cane, from which they manufacture sugar in their own mills. They are also expert fishermen. Their houses are of pole framework plastered with clay on the outside and thatched with grass. They wear cotton garments of native pattern and weaving. They are much given to dances and festivals, both church festivals and their own, particularly the Costumbre, an interesting survival of an old sacrifical rite in which seeds and portions of earth sprinkled with the blood of fowls killed for the occasion are distributed to the various fields. Aside from this and some other folklore customs, they are all Catholics, and strongly attached to their religious teachers.

The Totonac language, although considered by Sahagun and Orozco y Berra to be connected with that of their next neighbours, the Huastec, of Mayan stock, is held by Brinton to be of independent stock, but with considerable borrowings from Huastec and Aztec. It is spoken in four principal dialects and lacks the sound of r. Of the published works in the language the most important are the "Arte y Vocabulario de la lengua totonaca" and the "Gramatica et Lexicon Linguæ Mexicanæ, Totonaquæ et Huastecæ" (the latter printed in Mexico, 1560) by the Franciscan missionary, Fr. Andres de Olmos (d. 1571), noted for his mastery of several of the native languages. An "Arte" or manual by Fr. Francisco Dominguez was published in Puebla, 1752, and a catechism and extended vocabularies in two dialects by the same author shortly afterward, with a reprint in Puebla, 1837. Pimentel gives a sketch of the language in his "Cuadro Descriptivo", I (Mexico, 1862–65; 1874–75). Much manuscript material, linguistic and religious, remains unpublished.

BANCROFT, *Native Races of the Pacific States* (San Francisco, 1882); IDEM, *Hist. of Mexico* (San Francisco, 1886–88); BRINTON, *American Race* (New York, 1891); PILLING, *Proofsheets of a Bibl. of the Langs. of the North. Am. Inds.* (Bur. Am. Ethnology, Washington, 1885); PRESCOTT, *Hist. Conquest of Mexico* (New York and London, 1843); SAHAGUN, *Historia General de Nueva España* (Mexico, 1829); STARR, *Ethnography of Southern Mexico* in *Proceedings of the Davenport Academy of Sciences*, VIII (Davenport, 1901).

JAMES MOONEY.

Touchet, GEORGE ANSELM, b. at Stalbridge, Dorset; d. about 1689. He was second son of Mervyn, twelfth Lord Audley, second Earl of Castlehaven, and a man of profligate life; his first wife was Elizabeth Barnham. He was professed as a Benedictine at St. Gregory's, Douai, 22 Nov., 1643, taking the name Anselm in religion. Being sent on the mission in the south of England, he was finally appointed chaplain to Queen Catherine of Braganza in 1671. In that capacity he lived at Somerset House till 1675, when he was banished. Dodd states that he was expressly excluded from the succession to the Earldom of Castlehaven by the Act of Parliament which in 1678 confirmed the earldom to his elder brother James. While living in London he published a book called "Historical Collections out of several grave Protestant Historians concerning the Changes in religion, and the strange confusions following, etc." (1674; 2nd ed., 1686), and in 1680 he issued "The Secret Paths of Divine Love", translated by him from the French of Constantine Barbason.

DODD, *Church History*, III (Brussels *vere* Wolverhampton, 1737–1742); KIRK, *Biographies of English Catholics* (London, 1909); OLIVER, *Collections* (London, 1857); WELDON, *Chronological Notes* (London, 1881); SNOW, *Necrology of the English Benedictines* (London, 1883); COOPER in *Dict. Nat. Biog.*; GILLOW, *Bibl. Dict. Eng. Cath.*

EDWIN BURTON.

Toul. See NANCY, DIOCESE OF.

Toulon. See FRÉJUS, DIOCESE OF.

Toulouse, ARCHDIOCESE OF (TOLOSENSIS), includes the Department of Haute-Garonne. As re-established by the Concordat of 1802 it included the Departments of Haute-Garonne and Ariège, at which time the archbishop joined to his own the title of Auch, jurisdiction over Auch being given to the Diocese of Agen, also the title of Narbonne, an archdiocese over which jurisdiction went by the Concordat to the Diocese of Carcassonne, and the title of Albi, over which, though formerly an archdiocese, jurisdiction went by the Concordat to the See of Montpellier. In consequence of the creation of the Archdioceses of Auch and Albi under the Restoration, the Archbishop of Toulouse only styled himself Archbishop of Toulouse and Narbonne, and when the Diocese of Pamiers was created the limits of the Archdiocese were restricted to the Department of Haute-Garonne. As thus marked off by the Bull "Paternæ Caritatis", July, 1822, the Archdiocese of Toulouse includes almost the whole of the ancient Dioceses of Toulouse, Rieux, and Comminges, and a few small portions of the ancient Dioceses of Montauban, Lavaur, St-Papoul, Mirepoix, and Lombez.

I. DIOCESE OF TOULOUSE.—Toulouse, chief town of the Tectosagi, at the end of the second century B. C. tried to shake off the yoke of Rome during the invasion of the Cimbri, but at the beginning of the empire it was a prosperous Roman *civitas* with famous schools in which the three brothers of the Emperor Constantine were pupils. In the fourth century it was reckoned the fifteenth town in importance in the empire. In 413 it was taken by Astulph, the Goth, and in 419 under Wallia it became the capital of the Visigothic Kingdom. In 508 after conquest by Clovis it became Frankish. Legends of more or less recent

THE CATHEDRAL, TOULOUSE

date claim that it was evangelized by St. Martial (see LIMOGES, DIOCESE OF), but as far as historical evidence goes the see seems to have been founded by St. Saturninus (Sernin) in the middle of the third century. The "Passio Sancti Saturnini" corroborates this date as that of his incumbency and martyrdom. Subsequent tradition claims that he was a disciple of St. Peter. St. Papoul (see CARCASSONNE, DIOCESE OF) was his companion and like him a martyr. The name of St. Honoratus, given in some lists as St. Saturninus's successor, seems to have crept in through error from the fabulous legend of St. Firminus of Amiens and, according to Mgr Duchesne, ought to be omitted. Among the bishops of Toulouse may be mentioned: Rhodanius (350–58), exiled by Constantius to Phrygia because of his efforts against Arianism at the Council of Béziers in 356; St. Hilary, whom some historians place before Rhodanius, but who is placed after him by Mgr Duchesne; St. Sylvius (360–400); St. Exuperius (c. 400), who drove from his diocese in 405 the heretic Vigilantius, saved Toulouse from the ravages of the Vandals, and was the friend of St. Jerome; St. Germerius (Germier), whose episcopate (c. 541) is questioned by Mgr Duchesne; Magnulphus (c. 585), exiled by King Gondebaud; St. Erembert (657), a monk of Fontenelle who returned to his monastery to die.

From being the capital of the Duchy of Aquitaine, from 631, Toulouse became in 778 the capital of the County of Toulouse created by Charlemagne, and which in the tenth century was one of the main fiefs of the crown. Raymond IV, Count of Toulouse, known as Raymond de Saint Gilles (1042–1105), was one of the leaders of the First Crusade. Concerning the leanings of Raymond VI and Raymond VII, Counts of Toulouse, towards the Albigensian heresy, and concerning the death of Simon de Montfort in 1218 under the walls of Toulouse, see ALBIGENSES. At this time Toulouse had as bishop Fulk of Marseilles (1206–31), who fought against Raymond VI and protected the Friars-Preachers in their early days. The marriage (1249) of Jeanne, daughter of Raymond VII, with Alphonse de Poitiers, brother of King Louis IX, led to the uniting in 1271 of the County of Toulouse to the Crown of France, and Toulouse became the capital of the Province of Languedoc. The See of Toulouse was for a time made illustrious by St. Louis (1296–97), son of Charles II, King of Naples and the Two Sicilies, and of Mary, daughter of the King of Hungary: he was nephew of St. Elizabeth of Hungary and grand-nephew of St. Louis King of France. Louis had resigned to his brother Robert all rights over the Kingdom of Naples, and had accepted from Boniface VIII the See of Toulouse after donning the habit of St. Francis. His successor was Peter de la Chapelle Taillefer (1298–1312) who was created cardinal in 1305. To this epoch belongs a very important change that took place in the history of the Diocese of Toulouse. It decreased in size but increased in dignity. Before 1295 the Diocese of Toulouse was very extensive. At the beginning of the thirteenth century Bishop Fulk had wished for the sake of religion to divide it into several dioceses. In 1295 a portion of territory was cut off by Boniface VIII to form the Diocese of Pamiers. Then in 1319 John XXII cut off the Diocese of Toulouse from the metropolitan church of Narbonne and made it a metropolitan with the Sees of Montauban, Saint-Papoul, Rieux, and Lombez as suffragans; a little later Lavaur and Mirepoix also became suffragans of Toulouse. The majority of these sees were composed of territory cut off from the ancient See of Toulouse itself.

John XXII offered the See of Riez in Provence to Gaillard de Preyssac, Bishop of Toulouse since 1305, whom he suspected of having conspired against him with Hugues Giraud, Bishop of Cahors. Gaillard refused the offer, and retired to Avignon where he died in 1327. The first archbishop was Raymond de Comminges, Bishop of Maguelonne from 1309, who, when created cardinal in 1327, abandoned the See of Toulouse and went to Avignon where he died in 1348. He left a book on the "Passion of the Saviour", and some "Sermons for Festival Days". Among his successors were: the Dominican William de Laudun (1327–45), previously Bishop of Vienne; Raymond de Canilhac (1345–50), cardinal in 1350; Francis de Gozié (1391–92); Bernard du Rosier (1451–74), author of two treatises on the temporal power of the pope and on the liberty of the Church, and who founded at Toulouse the "Collège de Foix" for the support of twenty-five poor scholars, where he collected one of the first libraries of the period; John of Orleans (1503–33), cardinal in 1533. Protestantism entered Toulouse in 1532 through foreign students. As early as 1563 the Catholics of Toulouse founded a league to uphold the prerogatives of Catholicism, protected by the Parlement but jeopardized by certain Protestant town-councillors. From 1586 to 1595 the League party under Montmorency, Governor of Languedoc, and the Duke de Joyeuse held control in Toulouse. The rule of Henry IV was definitively recognized there in 1596. During this period of religious unrest Toulouse had many notable archbishops: Gabriel de Gramont (1533–34), cardinal in 1530; Odet de Chatillon, Cardinal de Coligny (1534–50), who became a Calvinist, married in 1564, and died in 1571; Anthony Sanguin (1550–59), Cardinal de Meudon in 1539; Georges d'Armagnac (1562–77), cardinal in 1544; François de Joyeuse (1584–1605), cardinal in 1583 and who conducted the negotiations between Henry IV and the Holy See.

Among subsequent archbishops we may mention: Louis de Nogaret (1614–27), Cardinal de Lavalette in 1621, but who never received orders and from 1635 to 1637 led part of the French troops in the Thirty Years War; Charles de Montchal (1628–51), who in 1635 upheld the decision of the Holy See, against the opinion of the majority of the Assembly of Clergy, that the marriages of princes of the blood contracted without royal consent were not null; Pierre de Marca (1652–62), who under Louis XIII aided largely in the re-establishment of Catholicism in Béarn, in 1621 became president of the Parlement of Béarn, was afterwards made Councillor of State by Louis XIII, and wrote a work of Gallican tendency "De concordia Sacerdotii et Imperii", a voluminous work on Spain and especially on the Province of Tarragona, and a commentary on the Psalms; he was secretary to the Assembly of the Clergy of France of April, 1656, which drew up a formula condemning the Five Propositions drawn from the "Augustinus", and he died in 1662 just as he was about to take possession of the See of Paris; Pierre de Bonzy (1672–73), cardinal in 1672; Charles Antoine de Laroche Aymon (1740–52), cardinal in 1771; Etienne Charles de Lomenie (1763–89), Cardinal de Brienne in 1788; Anne de Clermont Tonnerre (1820–30), cardinal in 1822; Paul d'Astros (q. v.) (1830–51), cardinal in 1850; Julien Desprez (1859–95), cardinal in 1879; François Désiré Mathieu (1896–99), cardinal in 1899, was a member of the French Academy, wrote the history of Lorraine under the *ancien régime*, of the Concordat of 1801–2, and of the Conclave of 1903; he died in 1908.

II. DIOCESE OF COMMINGES.—The earliest Bishop of Comminges we know of is Suavis, who assisted at the Council of Agde in 506; but Sidonius Apollinaris speaks of the persecutions suffered at the hands of the Arian Goths in the fifth century by the bishops of Comminges. St. Affricus (c. 540), who died in the Rouergue, is wrongly included among the bishops of Comminges. Among the bishops of Comminges were: St. Bertrand of Comminges (1073–1123), grandson of Raymond Taillefer, Count of Toulouse, previously archdeacon of Toulouse, and who built the cathedral of Comminges and restored the town; Bertrand de Goth (1295–99), who became pope under the name of Clement V; Bertrand de Cosnac (1352–72), cardinal in 1372; Amelius de Lautrec (1384–90), cardinal in 1385; Pierre de Foix (1422–64), cardinal in 1437; John Cibò, who became pope in 1484 under the name of Innocent VIII, for a short time in 1467 held the title of Comminges; Cardinal Amanieu d'Albret, who was Bishop of Comminges in 1504 and 1507; Cardinal Carlo Caraffa, strangled in the pontificate of Pius IV, was probably Bishop of Comminges about the middle of the sixteenth century; Urban de Saint-Gelais, who in 1586, without outside assistance and with the help of a cannon which he caused to be brought from Toulouse, captured the town from the Huguenots. In the church of St. Bertrand of Comminges baptism was administered with peculiar ceremonies: the baptismal water was kept in a large silver dove with wings displayed, and enclosed in a cupola surmounting the font; at the moment of baptizing the dove was lowered, by a pulley, over the head of the child and through its open beak the baptismal water was poured.

III. DIOCESE OF RIEUX.—The See of Rieux was founded in 1317, by cutting off a portion of the Diocese of Toulouse. The cathedral of Toulouse, dedicated to St. Stephen, is remarkable for the contrast between its choir and nave: the nave is Romanesque and was begun in 1211 at the instigation of Count Raymond VI; the choir is Gothic, and was begun between 1273 and 1286 by Bishop Bertrand de l'Isle, and completed in the fifteenth century. The church of St. Sernin of Toulouse was begun by St. Sylvius at the end of the fourth century, and completed by St. Exuperius, who transferred to it the remains of St. Sernin, and later those of St. Papoul and St. Honesta, disciples of St. Sernin, and of the bishops, Saints Honoratus, Hilary, and Sylvius. St. Exuperius himself was buried there. Charlemagne gave to St. Sernin's the bodies of St. Suzanna of Babylon, of St. Ascicla and her sister St. Victoria, martyrs of Cordova. Under Charles the Bald the relics of the *Quattuor Sancti Coronati*, Claudius, Nicostratus, Symphorianus, Castor, and their pupil St. Simplicius, were brought from Rome. The crusaders who in 1096 accompanied Raymond de Saint Gilles to the East brought back the body of St. Barnabas, the head of St. Bartholomew, and perhaps some wood from the Crib or Manger, a stone from the Holy Sepulchre, and a Crucifix known as the Crusaders' Crucifix. In 1187 Guillaume Taillefer deposited there other relics acquired in the East, especially the greater portion of the body of St. George. Louis VIII brought thither the bodies of St. Edmund, King of England, and St. Gilbert, founder of the Gilbertines. The people themselves brought the body of Saint Gilles to save it from the Albigensians. Alphonse, brother of Louis IX, last Count of Toulouse, on his entry to the town in 1251 deposited in the church a thorn from the Crown of Thorns, which Baldwin II, Emperor of Constantinople, had given to St. Louis, and a portion of the True Cross. About 1366 the body of St. Thomas Aquinas, given by Urban V to the Dominicans, was brought to Toulouse, and preserved in their church until the Revolution, when it was transferred to St. Sernin's.

As early as 1100 a confraternity was formed with twelve superintendents and seventy-two *bayles-regents* (guardians), in memory of the number of the Apostles and Disciples; they took oath to watch in turn over the relics. Urban II consecrated St. Sernin's on 8 July, 1097, after it had been restored by the canon, St. Raymond; Callistus II dedicated an altar there and placed in it relics of SS. Peter and Paul, SS. Simon and Jude; Urban VIII granted the same indulgences to those who visited the seven altars of St. Sernin's as could be gained by visiting the seven altars of St. Peter's in Rome. The University of Toulouse was founded in 1229, in consequence of a treaty between Raymond VII, Count of Toulouse, and Blanche of Castile, regent of France; its object was to prevent by higher theological studies a recrudescence of Albigensianism. Raymond VIII had to undertake to maintain in Toulouse at his own expense for ten years a certain number of masters of theology, law, and grammar. In the beginning the university was looked at askance by the people of the South, who considered it an instrument of repression. The teaching of theology was given over to the Mendicant Friars, but the students who wished to take degrees had to pass some time at the University of Paris. John XXII and Innocent VI were students there. In 1329 John XXII reformed its statutes. In 1359 Innocent VI founded the College of St. Martial for the support of twenty poor students at the university; in 1360 he definitively organized a faculty of theology with masters drawn exclusively from among its former pupils, and granted the chancellor authority to confer degrees. This was the university's period of prosperity. The new revision of the statutes after 1394 by a committee nominated by the antipope Clement VII was fatal to it; from the fifteenth century to the end of the *ancien régime* the University of Toulouse merely existed.

In 1751 the University of Cahors was merged into that of Toulouse. It was founded in 1332 by John XXII, a native of Cahors, at the instance of the municipal authorities. The pope granted the new university the rights enjoyed by that of Toulouse, and in fact commanded the latter to communicate its privileges to Cahors. The Bull of erection for Cahors was almost identical with the "Parens Scientiarum" for Paris. The privileges of Cahors were confirmed in 1368 by Edward, Prince of Wales, the "Black Prince", and in 1370 by Louis, Duke of Anjou. The university also enjoyed the favour of Benedict XII, Clement VI, Urban V, Clement VII, and Benedict XIII. In 1460 Pius II ordered a revision of its statutes. The main strength of the university lay in its faculty of law which had as members such noted jurists as Petrus Gregorius (1570), Cujas (1554), and de Lacoste (1594). Of the colleges at Cahors the first was founded by Raymond de Pélegry, canon of London, who provided in his will (1365) for the maintenance of thirteen poor scholars. The College of Rodez was founded in 1371 by Bernard of Rodez, Archbishop of Naples, whose birth-place was Cahors. The College of St. Michel was established (1467) by Jean Rubey, archdeacon of Tormes. Among the students of Cahors the most illustrious was Fénelon, who entered upon his classical course there in 1663. During the eighteenth century the university declined, abuses crept in, especially in the matter of granting degrees. The Irish Seminary at Toulouse was founded in 1659 by Anne of Austria to receive twelve Irish clerical students. The Catholic Institute of Toulouse was founded in 1877 by Archbishop Desprez and completed in 1879 by the addition of a faculty of theology. Cardinal Mathieu suppressed the chair of law, and only retained about a dozen chairs of literary and scientific studies; but under the rectorship of Mgr Batiffol the Institute became, in the early part of the twentieth century, an important centre of sacred studies, and has remained so to this day. Its "Bulletin de littérature ecclésiastique" is highly appreciated in the scientific circles of France.

Toulouse is famous for its *jeux floraux* (floral games). The first meeting dates from early in May, 1324, and was organized by some troubadours. The contest was to laud the Blessed Virgin in a poem. Arnaud Vidal of Castelnaudary was the first to gain a prize. In the fifteenth century the "Clemency" of the Blessed Virgin was the theme of the rival poets; she was styled "Confort del monte Clemensa" (support of the world and clemency). This word "Clemensa" gave rise to a legend which ran that a certain woman named Clémence Isaure had instituted the floral games. Guillaume Benoit, councillor of the Parlement of Toulouse (d. 1520), was the first to put faith in this legend. In 1527 Etienne Dolet wrote a poem on Clémence Isaure; and the municipal magistrates of Toulouse, in order to save some property from taxation, declared it had been given to the city by Clémence Isaure; they even went so far as to erect a statue to her in the capitol of the town in 1557. Castel in 1633 assailed the legend in a very decisive manner, but it died hard: an alleged poem was quoted on the Duguesclin campaign in Spain, in which during the fourteenth century reference is made to a Lady Clémence who was no other than Clémence Isaure; then an ode appeared, said to have been recited in 1499; it has recently been proved that the poem is a seventeenth-century production, and the ode a nineteenth-century forgery. Among the saints specially honoured in or connected with the diocese are: St. Orentius (Orens), Bishop of Auch (fourth century), to whom the inhabitants of Toulouse attribute an important victory they gained in 422; St. Gaudentius (Gaudens) (sixth century), a shepherd lad, beheaded by the Arian Visigoths, who gave his name to the town of Montetavezan, now known as Saint-Gaudens; Saint Vidianus (Vezian), martyred by the Arians in the middle of the sixth century; St. William of Lodève, or Gellon, Count of Toulouse, who died in 812; Blessed Raymond, archdeacon of Toulouse, Blessed Stephen of Narbonne, inquisitor, Blessed Bernard of

Rochefort, and Blessed William Arnauld, all of the Order of Saint Dominic; Blessed Bernard, Bl. Fontanerius, and Bl. Admarus, ecclesiastics, Blessed Garcias and Bl. Peter, laymen, massacred by the Albigensians at Avignon in 1242; the shepherdess St. Germaine Cousin of Pibrac (1579–1601); St. John Francis Regis, who joined the Jesuits at Toulouse at the age of nineteen (1597–1640).

Among natives of the diocese are: William de Nogaret, the famous legist of Philip the Fair (1260–1313), born at St. Felix de Caraman; the Jurisconsult Cujas, born at Toulouse (1522–92); Abbé Sicard (1742–1822), founder of deaf-mute instruction, born at Fousseret. The principal places of pilgrimage are: Notre Dame d'Alet at Montaigut, a shrine dating from the eleventh century; Notre Dame d'Avignonet, which dates from the wonders brought by the statue of the B. Virgin of Avignonet when the church which had been closed for forty years in consequence of the massacres committed by the Albigensians, was once more opened in the thirteenth century; Notre Dame du Bont du Puy at Valentines, a shrine dating from the sixteenth century; Notre Dame de Clary at Cessales, dating from the tenth or eleventh century; Notre Dame de Roqueville at Montgiscard. Prior to the application of the Associations Law of 1901 there were in the Diocese of Toulouse: Augustinians of the Assumption, Olivetans, Capuchins, Jesuits, Dominicans, Lazarists, Trappists, Missionaries of Our Lady of the Sacred Heart, Sulpicians, priests of the Sacred Heart, and various teaching congregations of Brothers. At the close of the nineteenth century, the congregations of nuns had charge of 49 nurseries, 1 school for the blind, 1 school for deaf and dumb, 2 orphanages for boys, 12 orphanages for girls, 4 detention homes, 9 houses of charity, 15 hospitals, 8 district nursing homes, 4 houses of retreat, 2 lunatic asylums. In 1905 at the breach of the Concordat, there were in the Archdiocese of Toulouse 448,481 inhabitants, 44 parishes, 508 auxiliary parishes, and 61 curacies assisted by the State.

Gallia Christiana, nova, I (1715), 1089–1114, *et instr.* 176–181; *nova*, XIII (1785), 1–87, 146–47, 186–99, *et instr.* 1–86, 149–80; DUCHESNE, *Fastes épiscopaux*, II (Paris, 1894–9); DEVIC AND VAISSETE, ed. MOLINIER AND ROSCHACH, *Histoire du Languedoc* (15 vols., Toulouse, 1872–92); SALVAN, *Histoire générale de l'église de Toulouse* (4 vols., Toulouse, 1856–61); CAYRE, *Histoire des évêques et archevêques de Toulouse* (Paris, 1873); VIDAL, *Les origines de la province ecclésiastique de Toulouse* in *Annales du Midi* (Toulouse, 1903); LAHONDÈS, *Toulouse chrétienne, l'église St. Etienne cathédrale de Toulouse* (Toulouse, 1890); DOUAI, *Cartulaire de St. Sernin de Toulouse* (Paris, 1887); BRÉMOND, *Histoire de toutes les saintes reliques conservées dans l'insigne basilique de St. Saturnin* (Toulouse, 1862); GATIEN-ARNOULT, *Histoire de l'université de Toulouse* (Toulouse, 1877–82); MOLINIER, *Etudes sur l'organisation de l'université de Toulouse au XIVe et XVe siècle* in DEVIC AND VAISSETE, *Histoire du Languedoc*, VII (Toulouse, 1879), 570–608; MOREL, *Essai historique et pittoresque sur St. Bertrand de Comminges* (Toulouse, 1852); HAROT, *Armorial des évêques de Comminges* (Toulouse, 1909); IDEM, *Armorial des évêques de Rieux* (Toulouse, 1908).

GEORGES GOYAU.

Tournai (Lat. TURNACUM, TORNACUM; Flemish, DOORNIJK), DIOCESE OF (TORNACENSIS), in Belgium. As early as the second half of the third century St. Piat evangelized Tournai; some writers represent him as the first bishop, but this cannot be proved. Towards the end of the third century the Emperor Maximian rekindled the persecutions, and St. Piat suffered martyrdom. The great barbarian invasions began shortly afterwards, and a wave of Germanic paganism mingled with the Roman paganism, to the destruction of all Christian life. This lasted from the end of the third century till the end of the fifth. But with the progress of the Frankish race Clodion established himself at Tournai; Childeric, his successor, died there in 481. St. Remigius profited by the good will of the Frankish monarchy to organize the Catholic hierarchy in the north of Gaul. He confided the Diocese of Arras and Cambrai to St. Vaast (Vedastus), and erected the See of Tournai (c. 500), appointing as its titular Eleutherius. It was probably its character of royal city which secured for Tournai this premature creation, but it soon lost its rank of capital by the departure of the Merovingian court. Nevertheless it kept its own bishops for nearly a century; then about 626 or 627, under the episcopate of St. Achar, the sees of Tournai and Noyon were united, retaining their separate organizations. Tournai then lost the benefit of a privileged situation, and shared the condition of the neighbouring dioceses, such as Boulogne and Thérouanne, Arras and Cambrai,

THE CATHEDRAL OF NOTRE-DAME, TOURNAI

where the same titular held both sees for five hundred years. It was only in 1146 that Tournai received its own bishop.

Among its bishops may be mentioned: St. Eleutherius (beginning of sixth century); St. Achar (626–27—1 March, 637–38); St. Eloi (641–60); Simon de Vermandois (1121–46); Walter de Marvis (1219–51), the great founder of schools and hospitals; Etienne (1192–1203), godfather of Louis VII and minister of the queen; Andrea Chini Malpiglia (1334–42), cardinal and papal legate; Guillaume Filastre (1460–73), chancellor of the Golden Fleece; Michel de Warenghien (1283–91), a very learned doctor; Michel d'Esne (1597–1614), the author of several works. During the Spanish domination (1521–1667) the see continued to be occupied by natives of the country, but the capture of Tournai by Louis XIV in 1667 caused it to have as bishops a series of Frenchmen: Gilbert de Choiseul du Plessis-Praslain (1670–89); François de La Salle de Caillebot (1692–1705); Louis Marcel de Coëtlogon (1705–07); François de Beauveau (1708–13). After the Treaty of Utrecht (1713) the French were replaced by Germans: Johann Ernst, Count of Löwenstein-Wertheim (1713–31); Franz Ernst, Count of Salm-Reifferscheid (1731–1770); Wilhelm Florentine, Prince of Salm-Salm (1776–94).

It will be readily understood that the union of the see with Noyon and the removal thither of the seat of the bishopric had favoured the growth of the power of the chapter. The privilege possessed by the chapter under the old régime of being composed only of nobles and scholars necessarily attracted to it those most distinguished for birth and learning. Illustrious names of France and Belgium are inscribed in the registers of the archives or on the tombstones of the cathedral. The cathedral, 439 feet long by 216 feet wide, is surmounted by 5 towers 273 feet high. The nave and transept are Romanesque (twelfth century), and the choir is primary Gothic, begun in 1242 and finished in 1325. Originally the boundaries of the diocese must have been those of the *Civitas Turnacensium* mentioned in the "Notice des Gaules". The prescriptions of councils and the interest of the Church both favoured these boundaries, and they were retained throughout the Middle Ages. The diocese then extended along the left bank of the Schelde from the Scarpe to the North Sea, with the exception of the *Vier-Ambachten* (Hulst, Axel, Bouchaute, and Assenede), which seem to have always belonged to the Diocese of Utrecht. The Schelde thus formed the boundary between the Dioceses of Tournai and Cambrai, cutting in two the towns of Termonde, Ghent, Oudenarde, and Tournai itself. The shore of the North Sea between the Schelde and the Yser was wholly included within the perimeter. On the other side of the Yser was the Diocese of Thérouanne, which bordered Tournai as far as Ypres. There began the Diocese of Arras, which bordered Tournai as far as the confluence of the Scarpe and the Schelde at Mortagne, France. This vast diocese was long divided into three archdeaneries and twelve deaneries. The archdeanery of Bruges comprised the deaneries of Bruges, Ardenbourg, and Oudenbourg; the archdeanery of Ghent, the deaneries of Ghent, Roulers, Oudenarde, and Waes; the archdeanery of Tournai, the deaneries of Tournai, Seclin, Helchin, Lille, and Courtrai.

In 1559 in order to wage more successful war against Protestantism, King Philip II of Spain obtained from Paul IV the erection of a series of new dioceses. The ancient Diocese of Tournai was divided, nearly two-thirds of its territory being taken away. The outlines of the archdeaneries of Bruges and Ghent formed the new dioceses of Bruges and Ghent, and six parishes passed to the new Diocese of Ypres. These conditions lasted until the beginning of the nineteenth century. The French Revolution created the Department of Jemappes, which in 1815 became the Province of Hainault, whose boundaries followed those of the Diocese of Tournai, after a concordat between the plenipotentiaries of Pius VII and the consular government of the republic. The Bishop of Tournai retained only two score of the parishes formerly under his jurisdiction, but he governed on the right bank of the Schelde a number of parishes which, prior to the Revolution, belonged to the Dioceses of Cambrai (302), Namur (50), and Liège (50).

The Diocese of Tournai, with 1,240,525 inhabitants, has 537 parishes, divided into 33 deaneries: Antoing (21 parishes), Ath (12), Beaumont (17), Beloeil (15), Binche (18), Boussu (18), Celles (14), Charleroi (18), Châtelet (27), Chièvres (23), Chimay (22), Dour (18), Ellezelles (6), Enghien (12), Fontaine-L'Evêque (20), Frasnes-lez-Buissenal (14), Gosselies (20), La Louvière (15), Lens (23), Lessines (12), Leuze (17), Merbes-le-Château (17), Mons (Ste-Elisabeth, 9), Mons (Ste-Waudru, 10), Pâturages (17), Péruvelz (12), Roeulx (16), Seneffe (21), Soignies (11), Templeuve (13), Thuin (16), Tournai (Notre-Dame, 14), Tournai (St-Brice, 13).

Eight diocesan colleges prepare young men for theological studies in a seminary, or for a liberal course in a university.

Herimanni liber de restauratione monasterii Sancti Martini Tornacensis, ed. WAITZ, in *Mon. Germ. hist.: Script.*, XIV (Hanover, 1883); CATULLE, *Turnacum civitas metropolis et cathedra episcopalis Nerviorum* (Brussels, 1652); CHIFFLET, *Anastasis Childerici I, Francorum regis, sive thesaurus sepulchralis Tornaci effossus et commentariis illustratus* (Antwerp, 1655); COUSIN, *Histoire de Tournay* (2 vols., Douai, 1619-20; 2nd ed., with notes, Tournai 1868); LE MAISTRE D'ANSTAING, *Recherches sur l'histoire et l'architecture de l'église cathédrale de Tournai* (2 vols., Tournai, 1842-43); VOS, *Les dignités et les fonctions de l'ancien chapitre de Notre-Dame de Tournai* (2 vols., Bruges, 1898); WARICHEZ, *Les origines de l'Eglise de Tournai* (Louvain, 1902); IDEM, *Etat bénéficial de la Flandre et du Tournaisis au temps de Philippe le Bon* (1455) in *Analectes pour servir à l'histoire ecclésiastique de la Belgique*, XXXV, XXXVI, XXXVII (Louvain, 1909, 1910, 1911); *Bulletins et Mémoires de la société historique et littéraire de Tournai* (51 vols., Tournai, 1845-95).

J. WARICHEZ.

Tournefort, JOSEPH PITTON DE, French botanist, b. at Aix in Provence, 5 June, 1656; d. at Paris, 28 Dec., 1708. After his school-days at a Jesuit college he studied theology at Aix, but in 1677 he turned his attention entirely to botany. He studied medicine at Montpellier and Barcelona. In 1683 he was made a professor and director at the Jardin des Plantes, Paris; he became later a member of the Academy (1692), a doctor of medicine (1698), and professor of medicine at the Collège de France (1702). Tournefort is recognized as a botanical explorer, and as the author of the artificial system of plants named after him. As a youth he travelled repeatedly through western Europe, exploring particularly the region of the Pyrenees. In 1700-2 he visited the Orient, passing through Greece. The account of this journey, "Relation d'un voyage du Levant" (Paris, 1717), appeared after his death; his work is a classic and was translated into English (1741) and German (1776). He collected 1356 species of plants during this one journey.

FROM AN ENGRAVING DATED LONDON, 1802

Tournefort's system of classifying plants is based on the form of the corolla. Up to about 1750 the system was in high repute, being accepted even by Linnæus, but as research advanced it lost its importance. Of permanent importance are the clear distinction Tournefort makes between genus and species, and the exhaustive analyses of genera which he was the first to draw up and illustrate. Linnæus says of him: "Primus characteres genericos condidit." He expounded his system in his "Eléments de botanique" (3 vols. in 8°, Paris, 1694), containing 451 plates; rewritten in Latin as "Institutiones rei herbariæ" (3 vols., Paris, 1700), with 476 plates (in 1703 a supplement was issued containing thirteen plates; a new edition by Adrien de Jussieu in 1719; English tr., London, 1735, French tr., Lyons, 1797). The "Institutiones" was preceded by a defence of his system which was entitled, "De optima methode instituenda in re herbaria" (Paris, 1697), and by a "Histoire des plantes qui naissent aux environs de Paris" (Paris, 1698), an English translation of which appeared in 1732. A genus with about 120 species, belonging to the family of the Borraginaceæ, was named by Linnæus *Tournefortia*, and still retains this designation.

SPRENGEL, *Gesch. der Botanik*, II (Leipzig, 1818); SACHS, *Gesch. der Botanik* (Munich, 1875).

J. H. ROMPEL.

Tournély, HONORÉ, theologian, b. at Antibes, Provence, 28 August, 1658; d. at Paris, 26 Dec., 1729. His parents were poor and obscure, but an uncle, a priest, at Paris invited him to that city and gave him a good education. On completing his philosophical and theological studies, he became a doctor of the Sorbonne in 1686, and two years later was sent by the king to the University of Douai to teach theology. Here he distinguished himself by the brilliance of his lectures and by his zeal in opposing the Jansenists. He was even accused of literary forgeries in order to compromise them, but the proofs of this accusation have never been forthcoming. Four years later he was recalled to Paris, appointed professor of theology at the Sorbonne, made a canon of the Sainte-Chapelle, and given the Abbey of Plainpied (Diocese of Bourges). He taught with unvarying success for twenty-four years and, as at Douai, showed himself the determined opponent of the Jansenists. In return they published pamphlets and multiplied attacks and calumnies to discredit him and his teaching, especially after the publication of the Constitution "Unigenitus", in which Clement XI condemned (8 Sept., 1713) their error as manifested in the "Reflexions morales" of Quesnel (q. v.). Tournély was actively engaged in furthering the acceptance of this Constitution by the assembly of the French clergy, of which he was consultor, and by the faculty of theology, of which he was an influential member. When, after the death of Louis XIV (1 Sept., 1715) and with the connivance of Cardinal Noailles, the Jansenists became masters of the faculty of theology, they expunged from its registers the Bull "Unigenitus" and expelled from its meetings Tournély and a score of his friends among the doctors (Jan., 1716). It was only at the earnest intervention of the regent, the Duke of Orléans, that they were reinstated five years later (Feb., 1721).

Tournély had so far published nothing, at least in his own name, but he is regarded as the author or inspirer of several anonymous works against the Jansenists which appeared at that time. On his retirement he immediately began to revise his lectures and, at the request of Cardinal de Fleury and others, to publish them in 1725. With the common title "Prælectiones theologicæ", he issued in Latin the following treatises in octavo: "On God and His Attributes" (1725); "On grace" (1726); "On the Trinity" (1726); "On the Church" (1726); "On the Sacraments in general" (1726); "On the Incarnation" (1727); "On the Sacraments of Baptism and Confirmation" (1727); "On Penance and Extreme Unction" (1728); "On the Eucharist" (1729); "On Holy Orders" (1729); "On Marriage" (1730). The work passed through several editions, among others those of Paris (16 vols., in 8vo, 1738–40), Venice (16 vols., 8vo, 1731–46), Cologne (10 vols., in fol., 1752–65). Several of these treatises have been abridged for use in seminaries, and they still appear in Tournély's name, but they are in reality the work of Montagne, Robinet, and Collet. Tournély's own work is still so important in extent and value that he may be regarded as one of the most notable theologians of his age. The learned Lafiteau, Bishop of Sisteron, even then declared him "one of the greatest men who has ever been in the Sorbonne", and his works were highly esteemed by St. Alphonsus Liguori. His chief merits are clearness of explanation, elegance of style, deep learning, and orthodoxy; his one defect was Gallicanism, for, like all French theologians of that time, he was a Gallican.

Journal des savants (Feb., 1731); FÉRET, *La faculté de théologie de Paris, Époque moderne*, VII (Paris, 1910); HILD, *Honoré Tournély u. seine Stellung zum Jansenismus* (Freiburg, 1911).

ANTOINE DEGERT.